The Bill James Handbook 2015

Baseball Info Solutions

www.baseballinfosolutions.com

Published by ACTA Sports

A Division of ACTA Publications

Cover Design by Tom A. Wright
Front Cover Photo by Charles LeClaire, USA TODAY Sports
Back cover Photo by Rick Osentoski, USA TODAY Sports

First Edition: November 2014

Published by:
ACTA Sports, a division of ACTA Publications
4848 North Clark Street
Chicago, IL 60640
(800) 397-2282
www.actasports.com www.actapublications.com

ISBN: 978-0-87946-526-1
ISSN: 1940-8668

Printed in the United States of America by McNaughton & Gunn

Dedication

This book is dedicated to my sister Emily. Thanks for encouraging me to pursue the career I wanted and for making me feel close to home now that I'm here. And thank you to all of my friends and coworkers at Baseball Info Solutions. You guys make work feel less like work, at least for the other 50 weeks of the year.

Scott Spratt

Table of Contents

Introduction

It's virtually impossible for one person to watch every minute of an entire baseball season. With the average time of game over three hours, a 2,430-game season encompasses something like 7,370 hours or 307 days. So, if you started on Opening Day and watched all of the games in sequence, without sleeping, you'd finish in time to get a solid week to catch up on world events before pitchers and catchers report for Spring Training. As appealing as that sounds, most of us haven't been able to pull it off since college.

Instead, we share the enjoyment of the baseball season. No one person can follow every interesting thing that occurs, as the six months of the regular season fly by in seemingly minutes. However, every October we go through the end-of-season stats and double and triple check every number in the entire Handbook before it goes to print. Through this tedious review process, we absorb far more about the season after the fact than we did during the preceding six months. Even though we watch baseball day-in and day-out, we miss many of the idiosyncrasies that make baseball the greatest game in the world. Each oddity occurs so infrequently, yet each game seemingly contains something—if you watch closely enough—that we've never seen before.

With that in mind, we've picked five of our favorite idiosyncrasies from the 2014 MLB season to share with you here:

> • On August 5th, Adam Dunn started as the White Sox designated hitter, the same way he's done numerous times over the past few years. With the opposing Rangers ahead 15-0 at the start of the ninth, Dunn took the mound and pitched an inning, allowing a run. (See the "Pitchers Hitting, Fielding, & Holding Runners, and Hitters Pitching" section of this book on page 367.) He then led off the ninth inning, no longer as the DH but as the pitcher. It's just the second time in the BIS database (back to 2002) that a DH has taken the mound and later came up to bat as the pitcher. (Chris Davis performed a similar feat in 2012, actually earning the win after going 0-for-8 at the plate.)

> • Jason Lane, the outfielder who was a major piece in the 2005 Astros lineup that won the National League pennant, had fallen off the map by 2007. Seven years later, he resurfaced in the majors as a Padres pitcher,

and he put forth a pretty good showing. In three games (including one start), he tossed 10 1/3 innings, allowing 7 hits, 0 walks, 1 run, and threw in 6 strikeouts for good measure. (See his Register entry on page 197.)

• On September 10, pitcher John Lackey was ejected from a game in the middle of an at-bat, with a 3-1 count to be exact. Though this seems harmless enough, he was facing a switch hitter, Brayan Pena, who began the plate appearance from the left side of the plate but completed a walk against lefty relief pitcher Tyler Lyons from the right side. In case you are curious, this counts as a left-handed plate appearance for Pena. (See the "2014 Lefty/Right Statistics" section on page 453.)

• Miguel Cabrera hit a sacrifice fly on May 29 in which he reached base on a fielder's choice. With runners on first and third, Cabrera's flyball to right field was dropped but converted for a force out at second base. Based on the official scorer's judgment, this was considered a "Sacrifice Fly", even though there wasn't an error on the play thanks to the force out at second. As it turns out, this play happens occasionally, and it also happened to Jed Lowrie this year. But, after winning the Triple Crown in 2012 and leading in batting average, on base percentage, and slugging last year, Miguel Cabrera led MLB in just one category this year: sacrifice flies (thanks to this play). (See the American League leaders on page 472.)

• On August 12, Arizona manager Kirk Gibson challenged a call in Cleveland in the top of the first inning. The original call, that Aaron Hill was out at first, was upheld. The game was rained out a couple of innings later and restarted the next day as part of a doubleheader. The replay review, along with Hill's groundout and every other event that happened before the downpour, was purged from the official record. Gibson's unsuccessful challenge was removed from his record in the expanded replay section of this book. (See page 513.)

These aren't the moments that we'll remember ten years from now, even one year from now, but they helped to make the 2014 Major League season unlike any other. As we always do, we'll endure the offseason by reflecting on the season that was and hoping that next year has as much to offer. Thanks for joining us.

Starting Pitcher Rankings

Bill James

Three years ago I developed a way to rank starting pitchers so as to determine who is the World's #1 Starting Pitcher. That may be poorly stated; a blind Yugoslavian rugby fan with no computer could determine who is the World's #1 Starting Pitcher at this moment. What's fun about it is not Who's #1; it's the list. Tennis has a great list; Golf has a great list. I don't care who is the world's #47 ranked golfer at this moment, or any moment, but if I cared, I could go check.

I care about baseball players. I care about Zack Greinke, and David Price, and Matt Cain, and Cole Hamels, and Stephen Strasburg, and Yu Darvish You, and Gio Gonzalez and Bud Norris and Brandon McCarthy. I always wonder how one guy stacks up against the next. The structure of the baseball schedule invites us to wonder. Let's say there is a game tomorrow, and Sonny Gray is matched up against Garrett Richards. Who's got the edge? How big is the edge? Who do you like? Rick Porcello or Francisco Liriano, who's got the edge?

The system is based on Game Scores. An average Game Score is 50; a really, really bad game is zero, and a fantastically good game is 100. 30% of the Game Score is added to the player's score every time he pitches, so that a pitcher picks up 15 points if he has just a decent, ordinary type game—a borderline Quality Start, let's say. Each starting pitcher starts at 300 when he makes his first major league start (300.000), and a player can't go below 300, but with each start he also loses 3% of his previous score—so, for example, if a pitcher racks up a "50" in his first major league start, his score goes from 300 to 306: 300, times .97, plus 50 times .30.

As long as a pitcher pitches well, his score moves upward from 300. When he pitches poorly, his score moves down. There is more to the system than that, of course; this isn't the place to get into every detail. There are park adjustments, and a pitcher's score goes down if he doesn't start on schedule, and goes down more rapidly if he doesn't make a start for several weeks. The won-lost record doesn't play into it; pitching 7 innings with 2 runs in a win is the same as pitching 7 innings with 2 runs in a loss.

The system is set up so that a pitcher cannot (realistically) vault from the bottom of the list to the top in just one season. We're not rating pitchers based on how good a season they have had; there are a lot of systems that do that. In 2013 Jeff Locke had a better season than Cole Hamels; that doesn't make Jeff Locke a better pitcher than Cole Hamels. In 2012 Jon Niese had a better year than Anibal Sanchez.

Corey Kluber began the 2014 season ranked as the 107th best starting pitcher in baseball, between Chris Capuano and Hector Santiago. He had a better year than Capuano or Santiago, though—just my opinion—so Kluber wound up rated the 11th best pitcher in baseball, whereas Santiago wound up the season ranked 107th, and Capuano 163rd. That's what the chart that follows this article shows: it shows that Kluber ranked 107th at the start of the season with a score of 363.0, that he had moved up to 100th by May 1 with a score of 383.7, that he had moved up to 63rd by June 1, with a score of 432.2, that he had moved up to 53rd by July 1, with a score of 451.8, that he had moved up to 22nd by August 1, with a score of 492.8, that he had moved up to 19th by September 1, with a score of 502.9, and that he had climbed to 11th by season's end. He moved up all year because he pitched well all year—unlike Dan Haren, let's say, who moved up 10 spots in April, 12 spots in August and 17 spots in September, but dropped by 8 spots in May, 4 spots in June, and 28 spots in July, when he was 0-4 with a 9.47 ERA. To move from 107th to 11th in one season is a phenomenal campaign—but it does not draw Kluber up to the level of Max Scherzer, David Price, Jon Lester and Adam Wainwright; in other words, up to the level of the guys who have been doing it for years. If he can have *another* season like the one he just had, then he'll be ranked right in the middle of those guys. One season. . .we're impressed, but we're not 100% convinced.

Pitchers who made huge steps forward in 2014: Kluber, 107th to 11th; Johnny Cueto, 43rd to 6th; Phil Hughes, 82nd to 28th; Tyson Ross, 118th to 47th;

Sonny Gray, 129th to 50th; Garrett Richards, 145th to 53rd; Jake Arrieta, 153rd to 61st. Among those going the other direction: Derek Holland, 32nd to 170th; Ivan Nova, 74th to 164th; Jhoulys Chacin, 41st to 121st; CC Sabathia, 36th to 112th; Justin Masterson, 33rd to 105th; Mat Latos, 16th to 73rd; Ubaldo Jimenez, 28th to 69th; Cliff Lee, 3rd to 31st.

Most of the pitchers who are dropping fastest are hurt, of course; it is very difficult to drop as fast by pitching poorly as you can by not pitching. It's possible, but it is not easy. There is "gravity" in the system that drags pitchers constantly backward as they are struggling to move forward.

Of course the number one pitcher in baseball is Kershaw, who scored a 626 at the end of the regular season (the number will change after this is printed, since 2014 post-season performance is not included in this book.) "600" is a historic level in these rankings. Justin Verlander reached the 600 level in 2011, although he didn't go as high as Kershaw in 2014. I have re-constructed the rankings back to 1990. The pitchers who have been ranked #1 since 1990 are, in order: Roger Clemens, Dave Stewart, Roger Clemens again, Greg Maddux, Roger Clemens, Jose Rijo, Greg Maddux.

Maddux held the #1 spot for four years, 1993 to 1997, by far the longest anyone has held that position in the last quarter-century, so I'll break into the list to make that note. Then it went back to Clemens, to Pedro Martinez, back to Maddux, Clemens, Randy Johnson, Pedro, Randy Johnson, Pedro for the third time, then Randy, Pedro, Randy, Pedro, Randy, Pedro, Jason Schmidt, Randy, Jason Schmidt, Randy, Pedro (now for the 7th time), Randy, and Pedro. By now we're up to 2005. Roger Clemens returned to the #1 spot briefly after an eight-year absence, then Pedro again, then Clemens, and then Johan Santana.

After Santana, the #1 pitcher was Pedro again, for the 10th and final time, and then Santana took over for several years. Santana controlled the list for more than two solid years, which is a long time to stay on top. Then the top spot went to CC Sabathia, then Santana, then back to Sabathia. Dan Haren took a three-week turn as the #1 guy, then Lincecum, Sabathia, Lincecum, Sabathia, Lincecum, Sabathia, Roy Halladay, Lincecum, Halladay, Felix Hernandez, Halladay, and Justin Verlander.

Verlander took over as the #1 pitcher in the baseball universe in mid-season, 2011, and by August, 2012 was 42 points ahead of the second-place pitcher, who was Clayton Kershaw. Kershaw had reached the #2 spot in early season 2012, and started to gain on Verlander in August, 2012. He finally caught him on May 16, 2013. It was a clean transition; Verlander and Kershaw did not jockey back and forth a few times before one took over, as often happens. Verlander had a couple of rough outings, and Kershaw pulled quickly away from him. Kershaw has held the top spot now for almost two years, which is a long run.

Some people might think that the #1 spot changes hands too often, but actually, the #1 spot on the pitcher's list changes hands about half as often as the #1 spot in the Golf Rankings or the Tennis Player rankings. The lead changes hands quickly sometimes because two great pitchers will get into a "duel" for the number one spot. The system would not be better without these duels. There are periods where there are some people who think that the best pitcher in baseball is Roy Halladay, while other people think it is CC Sabathia; an argument can be made for either man. One or two good games, and the lead changes hands. Then there are other periods, like now, when it's obvious who is #1, and he's way ahead.

The highest ranked pitcher ever was Pedro Martinez, who reached a peak of 682. 682 is just a stupid level; Kershaw would reach 682 if he pitched at the level he did in 2014 for maybe two more seasons. Only the very greatest pitchers ever reach the 600 level, only the Koufaxes and Bob Gibsons and Big Units and Pedros reach that level. Verlander did reach 600. Roy Halladay—certainly a great pitcher—never did.

It's just intended to add a little bit of fun to the game. If you're a fan of the Seattle Mariners, it is fun to watch Hisashi Iwakuma and Roenis Elias plow through the list, fun to see if the King can make a run at Kershaw. It is fun to see those games when the #172 pitcher goes up against #2, and #172 wins. It is fun to compare starting rotations, 1 through 5.

Part of what is fun about the rankings is that they change every day during the season. When a pitcher pitches really well, most of the time he is going to move up a few spots in the rankings; when he pitches poorly, most often he will fall. People have suggested doing rankings of second basemen, for example, but that doesn't really work because the rankings don't change very often; a hitter can go 4-for-4 with two Falcon Shots, and he won't move up in the rankings because he's 20 points behind the guy ahead of him.

Since I introduced this system in 2011, I've done a poor job of making the rankings available on a constantly updated basis. This is a common failing for me; I like ideas better than I like to work. But we'll do better in 2015; we've got it programmed now so that we can keep the list up to date. We'll put it on line at Bill James Online, and we'll put it outside the paywall so that anybody who is interested can check out the rankings every day, and then if anybody else wants to publish it, like ESPN or USA Today or Fangraphs or Baseball Reference, we'll make it available to them at a reasonable cost so that we can spread the concept. I hope you like it.

Starting Pitcher Rankings

Player	April 1 Score	Rank	May 1 Score	Rank	June 1 Score	Rank	July 1 Score	Rank	Aug 1 Score	Rank	Sept 1 Score	Rank	Sept 28 Score	Rank
Kershaw,Clayton	564.8	1	557.3	1	553.0	1	585.9	1	610.6	1	622.3	1	626.0	1
Hernandez,Felix	495.1	9	513.0	6	524.9	5	558.1	2	577.9	2	574.3	2	578.4	2
Scherzer,Max	524.2	2	543.4	2	538.9	3	537.3	4	554.3	3	562.6	3	564.4	3
Sale,Chris	485.1	13	498.7	11	517.0	7	522.3	7	544.3	5	556.8	4	562.5	4
Price,David	499.4	6	498.7	10	508.2	11	537.2	6	553.5	4	554.4	5	560.8	5
Cueto,Johnny	434.5	43	476.8	21	504.1	14	515.2	12	527.4	11	536.5	9	550.8	6
Hamels,Cole	498.3	8	479.2	20	495.3	19	520.2	9	538.7	7	543.2	7	550.7	7
Lester,Jon	473.8	18	482.7	17	503.0	16	511.3	14	531.1	9	539.5	8	550.5	8
Wainwright,Adam	480.3	15	511.1	8	519.5	6	537.2	5	531.3	8	525.6	12	546.9	9
Bumgarner,Madison	485.9	12	483.5	15	510.0	10	520.1	10	509.5	13	544.3	6	545.3	10
Kluber,Corey	363.0	107	383.7	100	432.2	63	451.8	53	492.8	22	502.9	19	535.9	11
Greinke,Zack	491.3	10	507.3	9	513.6	8	514.7	13	530.7	10	531.8	10	533.3	12
Shields,James	498.9	7	518.4	5	510.3	9	493.0	18	507.3	14	517.5	13	532.8	13
Zimmermann,Jordan	456.1	31	466.5	27	457.7	37	493.1	17	494.3	21	511.4	15	531.8	14
Strasburg,Stephen	458.5	25	465.9	28	483.2	21	487.1	23	496.7	19	509.7	16	531.0	15
Darvish,Yu	502.8	5	512.0	7	539.5	2	545.5	3	540.0	6	531.5	11	524.8	16
Dickey,R.A.	473.3	19	480.5	19	488.7	20	490.5	21	507.1	15	502.1	20	520.6	17
Samardzija,Jeff	426.6	54	445.7	41	463.1	33	470.4	34	489.0	27	497.2	24	518.3	18
Weaver,Jered	480.9	14	487.1	14	504.6	12	509.4	15	513.4	12	511.5	14	516.8	19
Kuroda,Hiroki	469.7	20	465.3	29	468.0	29	481.5	26	486.8	31	495.1	25	509.1	20
Gonzalez,Gio	474.2	17	488.4	13	475.4	24	483.9	25	487.8	30	492.0	28	507.6	21
Lynn,Lance	425.0	56	442.3	42	450.3	40	466.1	37	481.8	32	492.2	27	507.2	22
Tillman,Chris	441.3	48	453.0	35	451.6	39	460.8	44	470.0	41	501.3	21	506.1	23
Sanchez,Anibal	486.2	11	493.2	12	503.6	15	516.8	11	505.2	17	506.1	18	499.4	24
Verlander,Justin	510.8	4	519.1	4	504.4	13	491.6	19	495.6	20	491.7	30	498.4	25
Quintana,Jose	427.2	53	440.7	44	456.2	38	470.8	33	490.7	25	486.0	33	497.0	26
Teheran,Julio	404.4	76	439.4	45	468.8	27	485.8	24	491.1	24	490.8	31	496.6	27
Hughes,Phil	393.8	82	404.5	80	441.2	55	451.4	55	450.7	57	483.2	34	496.5	28
Lohse,Kyle	464.9	23	482.1	18	499.2	18	496.7	16	503.4	18	478.9	37	494.7	29
Fister,Doug	449.5	34	427.8	55	435.1	61	453.0	51	469.4	42	478.7	38	494.3	30
Lee,Cliff	516.5	3	529.9	3	529.6	4	522.1	8	506.6	16	500.1	22	493.3	31
Iwakuma,Hisashi	456.2	30	435.2	48	459.2	35	468.2	36	491.8	23	508.1	17	492.7	32
Peavy,Jake	433.7	46	456.7	33	448.8	42	450.0	56	455.4	52	475.7	43	492.6	33
Cobb,Alex	411.1	66	426.4	59	426.7	67	430.4	72	457.0	50	478.6	40	492.5	34
Bailey,Homer	465.2	22	458.9	30	463.2	32	480.1	28	490.6	26	498.1	23	491.4	35
Liriano,Francisco	434.8	42	441.2	43	439.6	57	438.9	62	454.7	54	468.9	46	490.6	36
Santana,Ervin	458.1	26	476.6	22	466.6	31	472.7	32	488.8	28	494.7	26	480.8	37
Kennedy,Ian	426.1	55	450.4	36	462.8	34	461.1	42	476.1	34	479.2	36	480.8	38
Gallardo,Yovani	457.8	27	473.1	26	467.6	30	477.4	29	488.3	29	489.1	32	479.0	39
Norris,Bud	409.0	68	423.5	62	438.1	60	453.7	48	453.7	55	457.7	56	478.5	40
Buehrle,Mark	438.8	39	457.5	31	481.9	22	490.4	22	475.3	35	463.7	53	478.0	41
Porcello,Rick	412.5	65	423.5	63	439.3	59	468.4	35	474.7	36	491.7	29	477.5	42
De La Rosa,Jorge	380.3	93	396.6	87	427.4	66	423.0	81	449.0	59	464.1	52	475.7	43
Volquez,Edinson	369.0	103	387.9	94	398.9	93	412.4	91	422.5	91	445.3	73	473.9	44
Archer,Chris	376.1	96	392.6	90	413.5	81	440.7	60	446.9	63	457.3	58	473.5	45
Leake,Mike	418.4	61	433.1	49	458.3	36	460.8	43	464.9	45	480.5	35	472.9	46
Ross,Tyson	347.5	118	370.0	111	405.1	87	420.8	84	462.2	48	478.7	39	472.3	47
Burnett,A.J.	459.1	24	474.6	24	471.0	25	480.9	27	480.0	33	477.6	41	470.8	48
Haren,Dan	430.3	48	447.3	38	446.9	46	453.1	50	432.5	78	449.5	66	470.8	49
Gray,Sonny	336.6	129	376.1	109	405.1	86	410.8	94	452.0	56	450.6	64	470.5	50
Miley,Wade	434.1	44	436.6	47	450.2	41	462.8	40	473.6	38	473.5	44	470.5	51
Chen,Wei-Yin	391.2	86	402.4	82	417.3	76	429.1	75	449.0	60	456.4	59	470.4	52
Richards,Garrett	318.2	145	361.2	122	384.3	110	436.0	67	463.5	47	476.9	42	470.2	53
Gonzalez,Miguel	401.4	80	410.3	76	428.5	65	418.5	85	439.6	68	450.3	65	470.1	54
Lackey,John	405.0	75	429.2	53	448.5	43	459.6	45	466.9	43	467.0	48	468.6	55
Keuchel,Dallas	332.3	133	361.8	119	412.3	84	426.4	77	432.3	79	454.0	60	468.4	56
Wilson,C.J.	456.5	29	483.0	16	501.1	17	491.6	20	474.3	37	467.4	47	468.2	57
Miller,Shelby	393.2	84	413.0	72	416.9	77	429.8	73	432.6	77	442.7	77	466.1	58
Feldman,Scott	407.8	70	420.7	68	408.5	85	425.1	79	423.8	87	445.1	75	464.4	59
Colon,Bartolo	428.1	51	429.2	52	441.0	56	463.4	39	470.2	40	469.6	45	463.2	60
Arrieta,Jake	310.0	153	300.0	195	327.0	166	390.5	112	421.7	92	430.8	86	463.1	61
Guthrie,Jeremy	416.4	62	426.0	60	442.6	52	457.3	46	443.3	66	452.0	62	462.9	62
Hammel,Jason	369.4	102	409.9	77	433.9	62	447.7	57	434.1	74	452.7	61	461.7	63
Garza,Matt	390.9	87	404.4	81	415.4	80	433.3	69	457.4	49	459.4	55	460.8	64
Peralta,Wily	376.0	97	400.4	84	420.4	74	431.6	71	440.7	67	435.6	83	460.5	65
Niese,Jon	402.5	78	427.8	56	441.9	54	452.0	52	446.6	64	447.4	70	459.2	66
McCarthy,Brandon	370.8	99	383.2	102	399.2	92	408.3	95	422.8	89	446.7	72	458.8	67
Ryu,Hyun-Jin	414.8	64	419.5	69	425.4	69	440.3	61	450.2	58	465.0	50	458.7	68
Jimenez,Ubaldo	457.2	28	449.6	37	468.4	28	476.2	30	466.3	44	457.5	57	458.6	69
Cain,Matt	469.4	21	473.4	25	478.7	23	474.7	31	472.4	39	464.7	51	457.9	70
Vargas,Jason	410.1	67	436.9	46	447.8	45	453.3	49	456.9	51	465.4	49	457.7	71

Starting Pitcher Rankings

Player	April 1 Score	April 1 Rank	May 1 Score	May 1 Rank	June 1 Score	June 1 Rank	July 1 Score	July 1 Rank	Aug 1 Score	Aug 1 Rank	Sept 1 Score	Sept 1 Rank	Sept 28 Score	Sept 28 Rank
McHugh,Collin	300.0	167	329.2	149	360.0	131	391.4	110	400.3	112	424.9	94	453.9	72
Latos,Mat	477.5	16	456.5	34	425.5	68	432.9	70	447.8	62	459.7	54	452.2	73
Buchholz,Clay	429.7	50	423.6	61	412.6	83	414.9	89	425.9	84	448.0	68	452.2	74
Roark,Tanner	300.0	167	335.9	142	367.5	124	391.6	109	425.7	85	438.6	78	451.7	75
Alvarez,Henderson	343.6	122	365.7	115	388.2	105	421.3	83	437.3	70	436.8	81	450.8	76
Harang,Aaron	383.2	92	412.2	73	424.8	71	424.6	80	436.5	72	435.6	82	449.5	77
Wheeler,Zack	338.7	126	361.4	120	380.6	112	401.6	102	425.4	86	443.3	76	447.6	78
Cashner,Andrew	402.8	77	426.5	58	428.5	64	435.2	68	427.5	83	427.9	89	446.3	79
Minor,Mike	447.0	35	428.3	54	442.8	51	436.7	65	422.9	88	445.3	74	442.2	80
Koehler,Tom	337.1	128	364.1	117	390.9	100	406.7	96	422.8	90	433.8	84	442.0	81
Lincecum,Tim	430.8	47	427.2	57	443.9	49	463.4	38	464.0	46	447.7	69	441.0	82
Fernandez,Jose	443.3	37	475.2	23	470.3	26	462.8	41	455.1	53	447.3	71	440.6	83
Ventura,Yordano	300.0	167	345.0	132	359.3	132	381.4	120	393.8	116	417.5	101	439.0	84
Wood,Travis	433.8	45	445.7	40	442.0	53	451.7	54	436.9	71	449.1	67	439.0	85
Vogelsong,Ryan	343.6	123	358.0	123	394.4	97	403.4	101	420.2	94	438.1	80	438.0	86
Kazmir,Scott	304.7	161	356.0	125	387.8	106	415.9	88	438.8	69	426.5	92	437.7	87
Wood,Alex	310.3	152	344.3	133	342.7	145	353.7	140	375.7	132	416.4	103	437.6	88
Collmenter,Josh	300.0	167	323.6	156	354.9	137	368.0	131	378.4	130	402.9	120	436.2	89
Hutchison,Drew	309.3	154	339.8	136	366.8	125	397.2	105	392.2	118	419.7	100	435.9	90
Hudson,Tim	378.3	94	420.8	67	445.8	47	441.2	59	448.9	61	450.8	63	435.8	91
Cole,Gerrit	359.9	110	384.5	99	402.4	88	398.8	103	401.4	110	408.7	115	435.4	92
Happ,J.A.	357.2	113	338.4	138	365.3	127	381.1	121	400.3	111	414.9	105	434.4	93
Nolasco,Ricky	423.0	58	416.6	70	424.4	72	429.6	74	416.7	96	414.3	107	433.8	94
deGrom,Jacob					333.6	157	347.7	148	387.1	121	403.9	118	433.7	95
Duffy,Danny	300.0	167	300.0	195	325.1	168	375.3	127	402.9	108	432.2	85	432.5	96
Stults,Eric	377.2	95	378.2	106	390.1	102	390.6	111	408.5	101	420.4	99	432.1	97
Arroyo,Bronson	436.2	40	422.7	64	448.1	44	454.1	47	446.3	65	438.6	79	431.8	98
Smyly,Drew	300.0	167	308.4	184	335.8	152	363.7	133	380.0	127	428.3	88	430.3	99
Morton,Charlie	351.5	116	369.6	113	393.3	98	417.1	87	432.9	76	427.3	90	428.0	100
Gee,Dillon	393.3	83	421.0	66	425.1	70	417.6	86	418.1	95	429.5	87	427.7	101
Cosart,Jarred	314.9	146	343.8	134	367.7	123	392.5	108	387.1	122	413.6	110	427.6	102
Kendrick,Kyle	368.7	104	385.6	98	399.6	90	412.6	90	408.9	100	410.1	113	426.8	103
Odorizzi,Jake	300.0	167	313.1	170	349.4	139	385.3	116	408.3	102	423.1	96	425.4	104
Masterson,Justin	449.8	33	445.9	39	443.2	50	447.6	58	435.7	73	426.6	91	420.9	105
Nuno,Vidal	300.0	167	313.4	169	338.2	149	354.3	139	382.4	125	412.6	111	419.9	106
Santiago,Hector	360.7	108	378.0	107	372.0	119	385.4	115	402.1	109	424.8	95	419.6	107
Shoemaker,Matt	300.0	167	300.0	195	328.5	163	341.5	155	362.8	146	408.7	114	419.4	108
Estrada,Marco	407.5	71	432.7	50	439.4	58	438.0	64	433.3	75	425.6	93	418.8	109
Danks,John	337.2	127	361.3	121	378.4	115	398.1	104	405.4	103	403.3	119	418.0	110
Young,Chris	300.0	167	322.2	161	360.5	129	384.2	117	413.7	98	417.4	102	417.4	111
Sabathia,CC	445.5	36	457.2	32	445.6	48	438.1	63	430.3	80	422.6	97	415.8	112
Eovaldi,Nathan	349.2	117	380.6	105	397.5	94	403.5	100	403.1	106	415.9	104	415.2	113
Elias,Roenis			337.0	140	371.7	120	389.3	113	396.6	114	410.7	112	415.0	114
Stroman,Marcus					310.8	187	351.3	145	391.5	120	396.4	125	414.9	115
Tanaka,Masahiro			351.9	127	399.5	91	436.1	66	430.2	81	422.4	98	414.3	116
Gibson,Kyle	300.0	167	322.9	159	348.6	140	385.6	114	393.8	117	404.0	117	413.2	117
Milone,Tommy	383.4	91	389.6	92	416.0	78	425.8	78	427.6	82	413.7	109	407.7	118
Correia,Kevin	388.7	88	383.4	101	396.0	96	410.9	93	415.6	97	414.5	106	407.7	119
Noesi,Hector	300.0	167	301.5	192	332.2	159	353.3	141	369.3	139	395.4	128	407.3	120
Chacin,Jhoulys	436.0	41	415.0	71	419.4	75	428.6	76	421.6	93	413.9	108	407.1	121
Bauer,Trevor	300.0	167	306.0	189	319.5	177	337.6	160	364.5	144	393.8	129	406.0	122
Locke,Jeff	360.1	109	336.9	141	327.5	165	363.6	134	377.4	131	399.2	123	405.7	123
Hernandez,Roberto	314.0	147	331.5	147	352.3	138	371.6	129	395.0	115	405.3	116	405.2	124
Doubront,Felix	408.0	69	411.5	74	415.7	79	411.4	92	403.7	105	402.8	121	403.4	125
Matzek,Tyler							321.1	181	350.5	152	370.3	143	400.4	126
Carrasco,Carlos	300.0	167	312.6	172	304.8	204	300.0	222	300.0	222	344.7	165	399.9	127
Cahill,Trevor	405.8	73	398.9	85	391.2	99	383.7	118	382.1	126	395.8	126	399.6	128
Lyles,Jordan	326.8	140	365.5	116	384.8	108	380.4	122	372.6	134	387.2	132	396.8	129
Oberholtzer,Brett	328.0	139	345.1	131	360.0	130	362.0	136	371.2	136	389.1	131	395.7	130
Gausman,Kevin	300.0	167	300.0	195	300.0	214	327.3	174	351.8	149	373.4	138	394.9	131
Anderson,Chase					313.4	186	345.0	151	366.5	141	385.6	133	393.3	132
Worley,Vance	300.0	167	300.0	195	300.0	214	326.4	175	350.5	151	373.1	139	392.4	133
Lewis,Colby	300.0	167	314.5	168	327.6	164	339.4	159	346.2	155	375.5	137	391.7	134
Beckett,Josh	300.0	167	331.6	146	371.4	121	406.4	97	404.0	104	397.4	124	390.6	135
Salazar,Danny	318.5	144	334.7	144	343.1	143	335.6	162	352.0	148	370.6	142	390.0	136
Jackson,Edwin	401.8	79	407.7	78	422.3	73	421.7	82	409.7	99	400.4	122	389.8	137
Chavez,Jesse	300.0	167	354.8	126	372.6	118	394.1	107	402.9	107	395.6	127	388.9	138
Fiers,Mike	300.0	167	300.0	195	300.0	214	300.0	222	300.0	222	355.1	161	385.7	139
House,T.J.					310.2	190	323.9	179	330.0	173	357.6	159	385.7	140
Peacock,Brad	313.3	148	311.1	177	343.8	142	362.6	135	363.2	145	372.4	141	384.9	141
Moore,Matt	421.8	59	421.1	65	413.3	82	405.8	99	398.1	113	390.3	130	383.6	142
Wacha,Michael	303.4	162	348.4	128	388.6	104	394.3	106	386.6	123	378.8	136	382.0	143
Buchanan,David					310.1	191	334.7	164	345.0	157	364.3	149	382.0	144
Tepesch,Nick	305.8	159	300.0	195	320.7	176	343.2	154	349.5	154	370.2	144	381.0	145

Starting Pitcher Rankings

Player	April 1 Score	April 1 Rank	May 1 Score	May 1 Rank	June 1 Score	June 1 Rank	July 1 Score	July 1 Rank	Aug 1 Score	Aug 1 Rank	Sept 1 Score	Sept 1 Rank	Sept 28 Score	Sept 28 Rank
Kelly,Joe	330.9	134	346.2	130	338.5	148	331.0	169	334.1	170	359.4	156	380.4	146
Hendricks,Kyle									330.8	171	367.3	148	380.3	147
Bedard,Erik	370.1	101	369.8	112	390.6	101	405.6	99	391.9	119	384.2	134	377.4	148
Pineda,Michael			300.0	195	300.0	214	300.0	222	300.0	222	332.4	184	376.8	149
Martinez,Nick			305.4	190	316.1	182	317.6	187	323.5	179	344.1	166	376.2	150
Despaigne,Odrisamer							317.7	186	338.4	166	359.4	155	373.5	151
McAllister,Zach	370.3	100	393.1	89	384.3	109	376.8	125	378.9	128	372.4	140	372.9	152
Skaggs,Tyler	300.0	167	338.7	137	364.6	128	360.1	137	385.5	124	379.0	135	372.3	153
Greene,Shane									327.1	175	358.7	157	370.3	154
Hand,Brad	300.0	167	300.0	195	300.0	214	300.0	222	338.5	165	346.5	164	365.7	155
Wada,Tsuyoshi									315.9	188	357.7	158	364.8	156
Morales,Franklin	300.0	167	325.8	152	332.5	158	326.2	176	350.6	150	353.4	162	361.8	157
Hahn,Jesse							339.8	157	366.5	142	368.1	145	361.4	158
Phelps,David	300.0	167	300.0	195	329.4	161	352.5	143	378.8	129	367.8	146	361.1	159
Straily,Dan	371.2	98	388.7	93	390.0	103	382.5	119	374.7	133	367.6	147	360.9	160
Paxton,James	300.0	167	316.1	164	308.4	198	300.9	218	300.0	222	333.4	181	359.7	161
Williams,Jerome	335.7	130	315.4	166	300.0	214	300.0	222	298.6	387	334.0	179	358.4	162
Capuano,Chris	364.9	106	334.9	143	303.9	205	300.0	222	311.1	197	340.0	170	358.2	163
Nova,Ivan	405.2	74	395.0	88	387.3	107	379.8	123	372.0	135	364.3	150	357.5	164
Maholm,Paul	384.5	90	385.6	97	374.4	117	366.9	132	370.5	137	362.7	151	356.0	165
Cingrani,Tony	354.5	115	381.7	104	383.4	111	377.8	124	370.0	138	362.3	152	355.5	166
Tomlin,Josh	300.0	167	300.0	195	333.8	156	355.3	138	360.5	147	361.9	153	355.2	167
Simon,Alfredo			85.7	379	151.7	384	214.0	387	312.6	193	336.7	174	355.1	168
Hellickson,Jeremy	396.7	81	377.2	108	346.2	141	316.2	191	319.3	182	352.6	163	353.6	169
Holland,Derek	450.4	32	431.6	51	400.6	89	370.6	130	339.6	163	308.6	206	353.4	170
Nicasio,Juan	357.2	112	382.9	103	396.8	95	375.5	126	367.8	140	360.0	154	353.3	171
Perez,Martin	358.5	111	390.4	91	379.8	113	372.3	128	364.5	143	356.8	160	350.0	172
Pomeranz,Drew	300.0	167	300.0	195	334.8	155	345.2	150	337.4	167	340.9	168	346.2	173
Workman,Brandon	300.0	167	300.0	195	310.7	188	339.5	158	340.1	162	341.0	167	344.4	174
Carroll,Scott			309.0	182	303.6	206	300.7	219	330.0	174	329.5	186	344.4	175
Webster,Allen	300.0	167	300.0	195	300.0	214	300.0	222	305.9	209	318.6	190	343.1	176
Petit,Yusmeiro	300.2	166	311.1	176	319.1	179	312.8	195	307.9	203	312.0	199	342.7	177
Rasmus,Cory											309.5	204	339.3	178
Nelson,Jimmy	300.0	167	300.0	195	308.7	195	301.2	216	316.5	186	340.0	169	338.6	179
Turner,Jacob	329.7	137	323.3	158	337.3	150	333.0	166	339.4	164	335.5	175	337.6	180
Flande,Yohan							308.8	200	319.2	183	330.7	185	335.9	181
De La Rosa,Rubby					23.1	385	300.0	222	311.2	196	334.6	177	333.7	182
Ramirez,Erasmo	318.6	143	324.2	155	324.4	171	346.7	149	349.9	153	339.7	171	333.2	183
Lobstein,Kyle											308.1	209	333.0	184
Saunders,Joe	365.5	105	357.8	124	358.9	133	352.2	144	345.7	156	338.0	172	331.2	185
Floyd,Gavin	300.0	167	300.0	195	330.4	160	352.7	142	344.9	158	337.2	173	330.4	186
Whitley,Chase					323.9	173	335.1	163	342.6	159	334.9	176	328.1	187
Chatwood,Tyler	345.8	119	364.0	118	357.3	134	349.8	146	342.0	160	334.3	178	327.5	188
Bergman,Christian							307.3	204	300.0	222	312.7	197	327.5	189
Anderson,Brett	304.7	160	310.9	178	303.2	207	300.0	222	330.2	172	333.8	180	327.1	190
Matsuzaka,Daisuke	300.0	167	300.0	195	308.5	197	330.4	170	340.7	161	333.0	182	326.2	191
Bassitt,Chris											302.6	217	325.9	192
Mikolas,Miles									305.5	210	332.5	183	325.8	193
Ranaudo,Anthony									306.8	207	310.4	202	325.6	194
Bonilla,Lisalverto													325.6	195
Axelrod,Dylan	300.0	167	300.0	195	300.0	214	300.0	222	300.0	222	318.3	191	324.3	196
Holmberg,David	300.0	167	300.0	195	300.0	214	300.0	222	300.0	222	300.0	224	323.6	197
May,Trevor											299.9	385	323.3	198
Walker,Taijuan	300.0	167	300.0	195	300.0	214	307.0	205	316.2	187	308.5	208	322.7	199
Garcia,Jaime	300.0	167	300.0	195	322.0	174	344.1	153	336.4	168	328.6	187	321.9	200
Chen,Bruce	344.3	120	346.2	129	338.5	147	331.0	168	334.2	169	326.7	188	319.9	201
Colome,Alex	300.0	167	300.0	195	300.0	214	308.6	201	301.3	220	300.0	224	319.4	202
Corcino,Daniel													319.4	203
Montero,Rafael					314.3	185	307.8	202	300.1	221	308.5	207	319.2	204
Tropeano,Nicholas													318.8	205
Baker,Scott	300.0	167	300.0	195	309.9	193	302.6	213	300.0	222	314.0	195	317.8	206
LeBlanc,Wade	300.0	167	300.0	195	300.0	214	300.0	222	300.0	222	300.0	224	317.7	207
Erlin,Robbie	300.0	167	316.3	163	335.2	153	327.7	173	320.0	181	312.2	198	316.1	208
Gonzales,Marco							300.4	221	300.0	222	309.9	203	314.7	209
Karns,Nate	300.0	167	300.0	195	300.0	214	300.0	222	300.0	222	300.0	224	314.3	210
Martinez,Carlos	300.0	167	300.0	195	300.0	214	317.1	189	327.0	176	319.3	189	312.5	211
Cumpton,Brandon	300.0	167	312.9	171	302.4	209	334.5	165	325.9	177	318.2	192	311.4	212
Chafin,Andrew											306.0	211	310.6	213
Rienzo,Andre	300.0	167	311.9	175	338.7	146	332.2	167	324.4	178	316.7	194	309.9	214
Treinen,Blake					307.3	199	319.9	183	312.9	192	305.1	212	309.2	215
Delgado,Randall	342.2	125	333.4	145	325.6	167	318.1	185	310.4	198	302.6	218	309.0	216
Ross,Robbie			325.7	153	328.6	162	321.1	180	313.4	191	317.4	193	308.8	217
Hendriks,Liam	300.0	167	300.0	195	319.3	178	309.2	199	301.4	218	311.4	200	308.8	218
Deduno,Samuel	324.2	142	300.0	195	324.9	169	319.9	182	312.2	195	304.4	215	308.7	219

Starting Pitcher Rankings

Player	April 1 Score	Rank	May 1 Score	Rank	June 1 Score	Rank	July 1 Score	Rank	Aug 1 Score	Rank	Sept 1 Score	Rank	Sept 28 Score	Rank
Greenwood,Nick													308.4	220
Wright,Steven	300.0	167	300.0	195	300.0	214	300.0	222	300.0	222	300.0	224	307.9	221
Butler,Eddie							300.0	222	300.0	222	300.0	224	307.4	222
Pelfrey,Mike	343.8	121	342.2	135	335.9	151	328.4	171	320.7	180	312.9	196	306.2	223
Norris,Daniel													305.5	224
Jokisch,Eric													305.0	225
Wieland,Joe	300.0	167	300.0	195									304.9	226
Wright,Jamey	300.0	167	300.0	195	300.0	214	300.0	222	300.0	222	300.0	224	304.3	227
Bolsinger,Mike			310.8	179	306.9	200	327.8	172	318.8	184	311.0	201	304.3	228
Hale,David	300.0	167	326.2	151	318.7	180	319.4	184	312.4	194	304.7	214	303.5	229
Ryan,Kyle											309.2	205	303.5	230
Wilhelmsen,Tom									301.3	219	300.0	224	303.1	231
Penny,Brad											300.0	224	302.8	232
Mitchell,Bryan													302.1	233
Darnell,Logan									299.8	386	300.0	224	302.1	234
Heston,Chris													301.6	235
Heaney,Andrew							315.3	192	306.9	206	300.0	224	301.2	236
Torres,Carlos	300.0	167	300.0	195	300.0	214	300.0	222	300.0	222	307.4	210	300.6	237
All Others													300.0	238

Pitcher Velocity By Season

Bill James

Are you aware that Francisco Rodriguez has 105 more career saves than Mariano Rivera had at the same age? You can pooh-pooh the importance of this on your own time; I'm just sayin'.

In 2007 an average fastball thrown by Francisco Rodriguez was 94 MPH. In 2008 this was 92, in 2009 93, and in 2010, 91. In 2011 he was down to 90, but in 2012 he came back to 92, in 2013 91, and in 2014, 91 again. This is a basic summary of what the chart below is telling us; K-Rod's Velo since 2007 is 94-92-93-91-90-92-91-91.

The best new charts are those which enable us to build understanding in areas in which we have limited understanding. I'm optimistic that we're on to something here. Suppose that there is a 25-year-old pitcher who throws a 95-MPH fastball. How likely is it that he will still be throwing 95 in five years? Should we *expect* that he will still be throwing 95 in five years, or is that a one-in-five shot, or is it a one-in-50 shot? Let's take. . . Bob Gibson, whose best years were in his thirties. Is it reasonably likely that he was throwing as hard when he was 34 (and won the NL Cy Young Award) as he had ten years earlier? If so, how improbable is that?

What is the normal aging curve for a fastball? Do pitchers lose velocity at a mile a year, or a mile every three years?

If a pitcher has an off year, is it *probably* because his velocity is down, or is it more likely something else? If a pitcher's velocity ticks down this year, is it realistic to hope that it will recover next year?

How critical is fastball velocity to a pitcher's success? We know that it is not true that all of the best pitchers have the best fastballs, but how much connection is there?

Let's talk about Yordano Ventura of the Royals, who is probably the hardest-throwing *starting* pitcher in baseball right now. First of all, the announcer will always say that "he throws 100", and will often talk about that one pitch he threw one time that was clocked at 102.9. OK, but that's a mistake a scout would never make. Ventura throws 98. When you throw 98 you'll throw 20 pitches at 97, 40 at 98, 20 at 99, 8 at 96, 8 at 100, a handful below 96 and a handful at 101. A casual fan or an announcer will focus on the atypical fastball, and describe Ventura as a guy who throws 100, but a scout will never do that; a scout will always say that he "sits at 98, touches 100".

What we're dealing with, really, is a pitcher who throws 98—but what will he throw in five years? Will he still be throwing 98, or is 92 more likely? If he is successful at 98, will he be successful at 92?

If a young pitcher's fastball is a little bit short of what it needs to be, how realistic is it to hope for improvement? And. . .this is really a critical question, although not so easy to put in one sentence. Suppose that you look at pitchers having "down" seasons. Some of those pitchers having down seasons are having poor seasons because their velocity is down. Others would be having poor seasons for reasons having nothing to do with velocity. It's a different problem. Which one is in a better position? Justin Verlander in 2014 had a "down" year, and also his velocity was down. But is that a good thing, from his standpoint, that we should expect his performance to recover when his velocity recovers, or is it a bad thing, that we should think that he's lost that extra jolt to his velocity that made him special?

We don't really know how all of this works. The chart that follows is intended to set us up for growth in understanding in these areas. It presents average fastball velocities for pitchers who have been in the majors at least five years and have thrown at least some minimum number of fastballs each year. I'll do a little bit of analysis to start the ball rolling.

If you compare 2010 and 2014 velocities for the pitchers in this chart, you will find that 57% of pitchers threw at least one mile an hour faster in 2010 than they did in 2014. By my count there are 159 pitchers on the charts below. 90 of those 159 (57%) threw harder in 2010 than in 2014, 39 threw the same, and 30 threw harder in 2014 than they had in 2010. That's 57-25-18, the percentages. The average declines are a little bit larger than the average increases, but not a lot.

The average pitcher on these charts lost about 7/10ths of a mile on his fastball between 2010 and 2014. That is not a lot. But this calculation quite certainly understates the normal loss of velocity, because of a selection mechanism as to who is on the chart and who is not. Suppose that there are two pitchers who are both 27 years old and both throw 92. Suppose that one of them loses a mile a year off his fastball, but the other guy keeps his heat. Which one is still going to be in the majors in five years?

Of course, the pitcher who loses his fastball disappears from the majors, thus disappears from this chart. The percentage of pitchers who lose velocity over a four-year-period isn't 57%; it is more probably over 80%. At this point we don't know what percentage of pitchers lose velocity in a year—but in ten years, we should know.

Older pitchers are more certain to lose velocity (over a four-year period) than younger pitchers. In this chart, if you focus on the youngest pitchers, 45% have lost velocity over the five-year period (inclusive); the percentages are 45% (have lost a mile), 31% (same), and 24% (increased). For the oldest pitchers, 76% have lost velocity. For the middle-range age group, 59% lost velocity. The pitchers on this chart are arranged in order of their birthdays, because we can assume that there is some connection between fastball velocity and age. Arranging pitchers by age might help us to see patterns more easily.

Most pitchers do lose velocity over time, but as to why a pitcher would not lose velo, there can be at least six explanations:

1) Most or all pitchers throw harder working in relief than they do as starters. Glen Perkins threw 90, as a starting pitcher; as a reliever, he throws 95. Tommy Hunter as a starter in 2009 was throwing an average of 89; in 2014 he was throwing 96—the largest increase in velocity in the majors. Wade Davis threw 91 as a starter; he was throwing 95 last year out of the bullpen.

2) If you get into better shape, you can run faster. If a pitcher gets into better shape, sometimes he can throw harder.

3) If a pitcher has a knee injury or a back injury, it will interfere with his ability to throw hard. If he has surgery and corrects the problem, his velocity should improve.

4) Sometimes pitchers increase their velocity by changing their mechanics.

5) Sometimes it's just a data glitch. A pitcher throws an average of 90.48 one year, 90.53 the next, nothing really has happened.

Editors Note: Pitchers age as of June 30, 2015

Average Fastball Velocity by Age

Player	Age	07	08	09	10	11	12	13	14
Bumgarner,Madison	25			89	91	92	91	91	92
Sale,Chris	26				96	95	92	93	94
Porcello,Rick	26			91	91	90	92	91	90
Strasburg,Stephen	26				97	96	96	95	95
Kimbrel,Craig	27				95	96	97	97	97
Tillman,Chris	27			92	90	89	91	91	90
Kershaw,Clayton	27		94	94	93	93	93	93	93
Cahill,Trevor	27			90	90	89	89	89	90
Chapman,Aroldis	27				100	98	98	98	100
Gomez,Jeanmar	27				91	90	90	91	91
Chacin,Jhoulys	27			91	91	91	90	90	88
Minor,Mike	27				91	91	90	90	90
Latos,Mat	27			94	94	93	93	93	91
Leake,Mike	27				89	89	89	90	90
Doubront,Felix	27				91	93	92	90	89
Jansen,Kenley	27				94	93	92	92	94
Worley,Vance	27				91	90	89	88	88
Storen,Drew	27				94	95	95	94	93
Ross,Tyson	28				93	92	92	94	93
Hellickson,Jeremy	28				91	91	91	90	90
Matusz,Brian	28			92	90	88	91	91	91
Wood,Travis	28				89	89	88	88	87
Nova,Ivan	28				93	93	93	93	92
Niese,Jon	28		89	89	88	90	89	89	88
Holland,Derek	28			93	92	94	93	94	92
McGee,Jake	28				94	95	96	96	96
Garcia,Jaime	28		89		89	89	88	87	89
Hunter,Tommy	28		91	89	90	90	91	95	96
Cecil,Brett	28			91	90	88	89	91	92
Hughes,Phil	29	91	91	93	92	91	92	92	91
Cishek,Steve	29				93	93	92	92	92
Zimmermann,Jordan	29			93	92	93	94	94	94
Bailey,Homer	29	92	91	94	93	92	92	94	94
Gee,Dillon	29				89	89	90	89	89
Hernandez,Felix	29	96	95	94	94	93	92	92	92
Arrieta,Jake	29				93	92	93	94	92
Detwiler,Ross	29	93		91	90	92	93	92	93
Gallardo,Yovani	29	91	90	92	93	93	92	91	91
Cueto,Johnny	29		93	93	93	93	92	91	92
Webb,Ryan	29			95	95	94	94	92	92
Russell,James	29				89	88	89	89	89
Holland,Greg	29				96	95	96	96	96
Bastardo,Antonio	29			92	94	93	92	92	92
Gonzalez,Gio	29		90	92	92	92	93	93	92
Davis,Wade	29			92	92	91	94	91	95
Price,David	29		94	93	95	95	94	92	92
Rogers,Esmil	29			94	94	94	96	93	93
Frieri,Ernesto	29			95	93	92	94	94	94
Perez,Chris	29		95	94	95	93	94	93	94
Strop,Pedro	30				95	94	97	96	95
Salas,Fernando	30				91	91	92	90	91
Dunn,Mike	30			93	95	94	94	94	95
Danks,John	30	90	90	89	90	90	89	88	87
Robertson,David	30		91	92	92	93	92	92	92
Melancon,Mark	30			93	93	93	93	92	92
Masterson,Justin	30		89	92	91	93	92	92	89
Norris,Bud	30			94	94	93	92	92	93
Clippard,Tyler	30	88	89	90	92	93	92	91	92
Ondrusek,Logan	30				92	92	93	93	93
Samardzija,Jeff	30		95	94	93	94	95	94	94
Kennedy,Ian	30	89	89	92	89	90	89	90	91
Tomlin,Josh	30				88	87	88	89	88

Player	Age	07	08	09	10	11	12	13	14
Cain,Matt	30	93	92	93	92	91	91	91	92
Parnell,Bobby	30		94	95	97	97	96	95	92
Kendrick,Kyle	30	90	90	91	89	89	89	89	89
Buchholz,Clay	30	91	93	94	94	92	91	90	90
LeBlanc,Wade	30		86	84	86	86	86	85	87
Scherzer,Max	30		94	94	93	93	94	93	93
Morrow,Brandon	30	95	95	95	93	94	93	93	94
Lincecum,Tim	31	94	94	92	91	92	90	90	90
Gregerson,Luke	31			91	91	90	89	88	88
Mujica,Edward	31	90	92	93	92	92	92	92	91
LeCure,Sam	31				89	90	90	89	87
Smith,Joe	31	86	89	90	91	90	89	90	89
Stammen,Craig	31			89	90	91	92	92	92
Sanchez,Anibal	31	90	90	91	91	92	92	93	92
Fister,Doug	31			88	88	90	89	89	88
Jimenez,Ubaldo	31	96	95	96	96	93	92	92	91
Lester,Jon	31	88	91	92	92	91	92	92	90
Hamels,Cole	31	90	90	90	91	91	90	91	91
Villanueva,Carlos	31	89	89	89	90	89	88	88	89
Garza,Matt	31	94	93	93	93	94	94	93	93
Morton,Charlie	31		91	91	93	91	90	93	91
Liriano,Francisco	31		91	92	94	92	93	93	93
Greinke,Zack	31	94	93	94	93	93	92	90	92
Ogando,Alexi	31				96	95	97	93	94
Jackson,Edwin	31	94	94	95	94	94	93	93	93
Blevins,Jerry	31	91	91	90	89	88	87	88	90
Street,Huston	31	90	90	92	91	90	89	89	89
Lopez,Wilton	31			92	92	92	92	92	90
Sipp,Tony	31			92	92	91	91	90	92
Estrada,Marco	31		90	90	91	91	90	89	89
Volquez,Edinson	31	94	94	94	94	94	94	92	93
Deduno,Samuel	31				90	89	91	90	89
Johnson,Jim	32	93	94	94	94	95	94	94	94
Axford,John	32			94	95	96	96	95	95
League,Brandon	32	94	97	95	95	96	95	94	94
Romo,Sergio	32		89	90	89	89	88	87	88
Perkins,Glen	32	92	91	90	92	94	95	95	93
Duensing,Brian	32			91	91	91	92	92	91
Verlander,Justin	32	95	94	96	95	95	94	93	92
Badenhop,Burke	32		89	88	89	89	89	89	89
Feldman,Scott	32	91	90	91	90	91	91	89	88
Vargas,Jason	32	86		87	86	87	88	87	87
Floyd,Gavin	32	91	91	92	92	89	89	90	91
Albers,Matt	32	93	91	93	93	94	94	93	93
Nolasco,Ricky	32	89	91	91	91	91	90	90	90
Santana,Ervin	32	92	94	92	92	93	92	92	92
O'Day,Darren	32		87	85	86	84	85	86	87
Happ,J.A.	32	88	87	88	90	90	90	91	93
Weaver,Jered	32	89	90	89	90	89	88	86	86
Hammel,Jason	32	92	92	92	93	93	94	93	92
Coke,Phil	32		93	92	94	92	93	93	94
Gorzelanny,Tom	32	90	89	91	90	90	91	91	89
Maholm,Paul	33	89	90	89	88	87	87	87	87
Stauffer,Tim	33	90		90	91	89	89	90	89
Rodriguez,Francisco	33	94	92	93	91	90	92	91	91
Shields,James	33	90	89	89	90	90	91	90	90
Janssen,Casey	33	90		89	91	91	91	90	89
Saunders,Joe	34	91	91	91	91	90	89	90	91
Burton,Jared	34	92	92	91	89	91	93	92	91
Peavy,Jake	34	92	91	91	90	90	90	89	
Simon,Alfredo	34			93	92	95	94	94	93
De La Rosa,Jorge	34	91	93	93	93	93	90	91	91

Player	Age	Average FB Velocity							
		07	08	09	10	11	12	13	14
Francis,Jeff	34	87	87		87	85	85	86	87
Thayer,Dale	34			93	93	93	94	93	92
Papelbon,Jonathan	34	94	95	95	95	95	94	92	91
Wilson,C.J.	34	92	93	93	90	90	91	91	90
Veras,Jose	34	95	95	94	94	94	94	93	93
Haren,Dan	34	92	91	89	89	87	87	87	86
Hernandez,Roberto	34	93	93	93	93	93	91	92	90
Correia,Kevin	34	90	89	91	90	90	90	89	89
Breslow,Craig	34		89	90	89	90	89	89	88
Casilla,Santiago	34	93	94	95	97	94	94	93	94
Sabathia,CC	34	93	94	94	93	94	92	91	89
Belisle,Matt	35	91	91	92	92	92	91	91	91
Beckett,Josh	35	95	94	94	93	92	91	91	91
Soriano,Rafael	35	95	93	93	92	92	92	91	91
Ziegler,Brad	35		85	85	84	85	86	86	85
Lewis,Colby	35	91			90	89	88		89
Affeldt,Jeremy	36	92	95	94	93	93	91	91	92
Guthrie,Jeremy	36	93	93	92	93	93	93	92	92
Buehrle,Mark	36	85	85	85	85	85	85	83	83
Rodriguez,Wandy	36	89	89	90	90	89	89	89	88
Lackey,John	36	91	91	92	91	92		92	92
Lohse,Kyle	36	91	91	90	90	89	90	90	89
Lee,Cliff	36	89	90	90	90	90	90	90	89
Capuano,Chris	36	87			87	88	88	89	89
Qualls,Chad	36	93	93	93	92	93	93	94	93
Harang,Aaron	37	90	90	90	90	90	90	90	89
Balfour,Grant	37	93	95	93	93	93	93	93	92
Bell,Heath	37	95	93	94	94	94	94	93	91
Benoit,Joaquin	37	93	92		94	94	94	94	95
Chen,Bruce	38	90		87	86	86	86	85	84
Rodney,Fernando	38	93	95	96	96	96	96	96	95
Arroyo,Bronson	38	88	88	88	88	87	87	87	85
Burnett,A.J.	38	95	94	94	93	93	92	93	92
Peralta,Joel	39	90	91	92	91	91	90	90	90
Hudson,Tim	39	91	90	89	91	90	89	90	89
Uehara,Koji	40			86	88	89	88	89	88
Kuroda,Hiroki	40		92	93	92	92	92	91	91
Wright,Jamey	40	89	91	91	90	91	91	88	89
Dickey,R.A.	40		85	85	84	84	83	82	82

Runs Saved Multi-Year Summary

Bill James

We have all known the basic batting and pitching statistics all of our lives. When we were in the third grade and Mrs. Grundy was explaining long division to us, batting averages were one of the first story problems. "If Mike Trout has 7 hits in 20 at bats, what is his batting average?" Of course, in my day it wasn't Mike Trout; in my day it was Honus Wagner or Nap Lajoie, but the principle was the same. RBI were explained to us the first time we went to a ballgame. Errors came into focus the first time we saw Lonnie Smith play; sorry, Lonnie. We know what's normal. A player hits .270 one year, .245 the next. . .that's normal. A player hits 12 homers one year, 22 the next, that's normal. A player strikes out 35 times in 400 at bats one year, 160 times in 600 at bats the next year, that's not normal. That doesn't happen. A pitcher strikes out 120 batters one year, 170 the next; that's normal. If he strikes out 120 one year and 220 the next in the same number of innings, that's not normal.

These are like our oldest friends; we have always known them. We know how they travel. A pitcher goes 11-14 for San Diego and gets traded to St. Louis; we know that he's probably going to be better than 11-14. A player drives in 80 runs batting second; we figure he can drive in 100 batting cleanup. Even the "new" statistics now are like people we met in college. OPS. . .oh, yeah; he was my roommate my sophomore year. He introduced me to WAR. Won-Lost records are like the grouchy old uncle who shows up every time the family gets together, complaining about rap music and liberal college professors; we still love him, but we're ready for him to go.

Fielding Runs Saved may be a very good statistic. . .well, it is a very good statistic, but I'm pretending to present this argument in a neutral way. Runs Saved may be a very good statistic, but we don't have the same level of familiarity with the data. We don't have the same sense of what is normal. A player is +10 one year, -8 the next, I dunno, is that normal or not?

This is not a theoretical concern. Suppose that a baseball team is considering signing Josh Reddick as a free agent; he shows as +19, +13 and +13 the last three years. Really good, but how does that travel? If he moves to New York, what's his number going to be? If he moves to center field, what's it going to be?

We really have no idea, no intuitive or semi-intuitive sense of it. Because this is true, teams are reluctant to rely on this information when they make decisions. Could Reddick be showing up as +13 every year in part because he plays in Oakland, the same way Dexter Fowler hits 10 to 15 triples every year in part because he plays (played) in Colorado? We don't know; we don't have any sense of how these things travel. We don't have any sense of how reliable they are from year to year.

The purpose of this chart, the multi-year summary of Fielding Runs Saved, is not to show who is a good fielder and not such a good fielder as much as it is to create some familiarity with the multi-year patterns of the data. We are proselytizing for the method; yes, that is true. We are trying to make the baseball community a little bit more comfortable with the data, by demonstrating that it does have obvious year to year consistency. Jason Heyward has been in the majors for five years, and has been +15 or better five times. He was +32 last year, but then, he was playing right field next to B. J. Upton; *somebody's* got to make the play.

Ryan Zimmerman was +22 in 2009 and +11 in 2010, but has been -5, -1, -1 and -4 the last four years, but that's not a problem for the data because everybody knows that Zimmerman was a good third baseman when he came up, but lost confidence in his arm. His numbers merely confirm that the system is seeing what everybody else is seeing.

Before sabermetrics, baseball people believed that a player's prime years were ages 28 to 32; in reality, they are 27 to 29 much more often. But what is a player's *defensive* prime? We don't know; we will know, in fifteen years or less, but we don't know now. I *suspect* that a player's defensive prime tends to be ages 22 to 25, and I suspect that many, many players leave their best defense in the minor leagues, but we don't really know yet. This article is a step toward building that understanding.

If a player is a "negative" fielder one year and positive the next, that doesn't present a problem. Many, many hitters are below-average in one season, above average the next. Many pitchers have poor ERAs one season, very good

ERAs the next. Data is not invalid because it is not perfectly consistent or perfectly predictable. It *is* meaningless if it has no consistency or very little consistency, and if it has no predictability.

Gerardo Parra shows in the charts below as +41 in 2013, but -1 in 2014. That's massive inconsistency. Carlos Gomez was +38 in 2013, but +2 in 2014. If that sort of thing was commonplace in this data, the data would be suspect, if not useless—but in fact this is quite uncommon. By my count, 81% of players who were +10 or higher in 2013 were at least in positive territory in 2014 (30 of 37). That's consistency. Of nine players who were negative 10 or more in 2013, six were negative again in 2014 (one was +/- zero.)

Well, we can't convince you that the data is reliable, and that isn't my job. Our job is to present the data and allow you to take from it what you will. Thanks for reading.

Defensive Runs Saved By Season

Player	YOB	Position 1	Position 2	09	10	11	12	13	14
Ackley,Dustin	1988	LF				10	11	-5	7
Adams,Matt	1988	1B					1	-2	8
Alonso,Yonder	1987	1B			2	-6	2	6	9
Altuve,Jose	1990	2B					3	-18	-3	-7
Alvarez,Pedro	1987	3B			-10	-11	-5	3	-5
Andrus,Elvis	1988	SS		15	-7	7	8	11	-13
Aoki,Nori	1982	RF					5	13	-8
Arcia,Oswaldo	1991	RF						-15	-10
Arenado,Nolan	1991	3B						30	16
Arencibia,J.P.	1986	C			0	-5	3	2	-6
Asche,Cody	1990	3B						-7	-3
Avila,Alex	1987	C		-2	-7	-3	6	-4	5
Aybar,Erick	1984	SS		1	4	-1	3	-7	-3
Barmes,Clint	1979	SS		17	13	14	13	12	3
Barney,Darwin	1985	2B			5	2	29	11	10
Bartlett,Jason	1979	SS		5	-1	-9	-3		-2
Barton,Daric	1985	1B		3	18	4	2	-1	4
Bautista,Jose	1980	RF		15	-3	-2	3	4	-7
Beckham,Gordon	1986	2B		-1	-7	3	-6	-3	0
Belt,Brandon	1988	1B				3	4	4	3
Beltran,Carlos	1977	RF		2	-5	-3	4	-6	-6
Beltre,Adrian	1979	3B		20	19	13	13	-5	9
Bogaerts,Xander	1992	SS						-1	-17
Bourjos,Peter	1987	CF			13	12	9	-1	7
Bourn,Michael	1982	CF		11	30	-3	24	3	-6
Bradley Jr.,Jackie	1990	CF						-3	14
Brantley,Michael	1987	LF	CF	-1	-15	6	-1	2	-3
Braun,Ryan	1983	LF	RF	-4	9	3	7	4	-7
Brown,Domonic	1987	LF			-2	-9	-6	-6	-8
Bruce,Jay	1987	RF		5	17	-2	-4	18	-8
Buck,John	1980	C		-3	-11	-5	2	-10	-2
Butler,Billy	1986	1B		-8	-4	-2	-3	0	-3
Byrd,Marlon	1977	CF	RF	-7	4	0	3	12	6
Cabrera,Asdrubal	1985	SS		-4	-1	3	-5	-16	-17
Cabrera,Everth	1986	SS		-8	4	-2	-4	-3	3
Cabrera,Melky	1984	LF		-4	-3	-5	0	-5	-7
Cabrera,Miguel	1983	1B	3B	-1	-5	-3	-4	-18	-2
Cain,Lorenzo	1986	CF			10	1	8	24	24
Calhoun,Kole	1987	RF					1	-6	2
Callaspo,Alberto	1983	3B		-14	1	4	7	-14	-2
Cano,Robinson	1982	2B		0	16	1	15	6	0
Carpenter,Matt	1985	3B			-1	-5	0		-2
Castellanos,Nick	1992	3B						-1	-30
Castillo,Welington	1987	C			0	0	2	19	5
Castro,Jason	1987	C			0		0	2	2
Castro,Starlin	1990	SS			-4	-10	3	-8	-7
Cedeno,Ronny	1983	SS		-6	-9	5	-4	-6	0
Cespedes,Yoenis	1985	LF					-7	0	11
Chirinos,Robinson	1984	C				1		0	4
Chisenhall,Lonnie	1988	3B				3	-4	1	-16
Choo,Shin-Soo	1982	RF		2	5	3	-12	-17	-13
Coghlan,Chris	1985	LF		-19	2	-13	-2	-6	-15
Cozart,Zack	1985	SS				4	12	4	19
Crawford,Brandon	1987	SS				3	12	2	8
Crawford,Carl	1981	LF		12	8	-2	0	1	1
Crisp,Coco	1979	CF		5	7	1	1	6	-17
Cruz,Nelson	1980	RF		0	3	-5	-13	-3	3
Cuddyer,Michael	1979	RF		-7	-20	-16	-7	-16	-5
d'Arnaud,Travis	1989	C						-2	-15
Davis,Chris	1986	1B		-6	2	-5	-5	-7	8
Davis,Ike	1987	1B			12	1	-3	1	-4
Davis,Khris	1987	LF						-2	5
Davis,Rajai	1980	CF		7	-6	-8	3	6	-11
De Aza,Alejandro	1984	LF		2	0	5	-5	-20	-2
Desmond,Ian	1985	SS		-6	-7	-3	-6	-3	1
Dickerson,Corey	1989	LF						0	-2
Dominguez,Matt	1989	3B			-3		0	8	-4
Donaldson,Josh	1985	3B			-1		4	12	20
Doumit,Ryan	1981	C		6	-11	-6	-9	-10	0
Dozier,Brian	1987	2B					1	9	0
Drew,Stephen	1983	SS		9	0	3	-7	-2	4
Duda,Lucas	1986	1B			-1	-12	-16	-12	5
Dunn,Adam	1979	1B		-43	-11	-3	-4	-13	-8
Eaton,Adam	1988	CF					2	-2	12
Ellis,A.J.	1981	C		0	-2	-3	2	0	1
Ellis,Mark	1977	2B		2	8	18	10	12	6
Ellsbury,Jacoby	1983	CF		-5	2	7	3	13	-5
Escobar,Alcides	1986	SS		-2	7	10	-2	4	5
Escobar,Eduardo	1989	SS				0	5	-2	-10
Escobar,Yunel	1982	SS		7	9	7	14	4	-24
Espinosa,Danny	1987	2B			5	5	7	3	0
Ethier,Andre	1982	RF		-8	-14	4	3	1	-7
Fielder,Prince	1984	1B		0	-17	-9	-4	-13	-2
Flowers,Tyler	1986	C		0	0	4	4	2	3
Fowler,Dexter	1986	CF		-11	2	-3	-10	-3	-20
Francoeur,Jeff	1984	RF		11	17	1	-14	-1	1
Frazier,Todd	1986	3B				2	-1	5	8
Freeman,Freddie	1989	1B			0	-2	3	7	-7
Freese,David	1983	3B		-1	-5	-1	2	-14	-9
Furcal,Rafael	1977	SS		7	4	-5	-4		
Gardner,Brett	1983	LF		7	35	23	1	6	5
Gattis,Evan	1986	C						-7	-4
Gennett,Scooter	1990	2B						2	-5
Getz,Chris	1983	2B		-11	-2	-1	-2	5	1
Gillaspie,Conor	1987	3B				-1	-3	-5	-12
Goldschmidt,Paul	1987	1B				-3	1	13	1
Gomes,Jonny	1980	LF		-5	-21	0	-2	0	-9
Gomes,Yan	1987	C					0	11	2
Gomez,Carlos	1985	CF		5	5	15	3	38	2
Gonzalez,Adrian	1982	1B		15	-3	12	14	11	11
Gonzalez,Alex	1977	SS		-5	27	9	-2	0	-4
Gonzalez,Carlos	1985	LF		2	2	8	-13	10	-5
Gordon,Alex	1984	LF		-3	-4	19	24	16	27
Gordon,Dee	1988	2B				-3	-14	-3	-5
Granderson,Curtis	1981	CF	RF	11	12	-6	-10	3	-3
Gyorko,Jedd	1988	2B						-4	-9
Hamilton,Billy	1990	CF						1	14
Hamilton,Josh	1981	LF		-1	11	2	-9	-5	-1
Hanigan,Ryan	1980	C		1	4	0	7	-1	2
Hardy,J.J.	1982	SS		2	-5	8	18	8	10
Harper,Bryce	1992	LF					14	5	-1
Hart,Corey	1982	RF		-2	3	-1	-4		-1
Headley,Chase	1984	3B		-12	14	1	-3	5	13
Hechavarria,Adeiny	1989	SS					-1	-3	-3
Heyward,Jason	1989	RF			15	15	20	16	32
Hill,Aaron	1982	2B		13	-2	2	-2	-9	-10
Holliday,Matt	1980	LF		3	7	-1	-6	-13	0
Hosmer,Eric	1989	1B				-9	-6	3	3
Howard,Ryan	1979	1B		-4	-13	-13	-6	-1	-10
Hundley,Nick	1983	C		-1	-8	5	6	1	-4
Hunter,Torii	1975	RF		12	-11	9	15	-10	-18
Iannetta,Chris	1983	C		3	-4	8	0	-7	-10
Ibanez,Raul	1972	LF		-2	-12	-23	-5	-19	-3
Infante,Omar	1981	2B		-2	7	4	7	-5	1
Jackson,Austin	1987	CF			13	29	5	3	0
Jay,Jon	1985	CF			-6	9	2	-10	6
Jennings,Desmond	1986	CF			1	2	9	-6	4
Jeter,Derek	1974	SS		3	-9	-15	-18	-5	-12
Johnson,Chris	1984	3B		-2	-16	-12	-10	-7	-13
Johnson,Kelly	1982	2B		-4	0	1	5	2	2
Jones,Adam	1985	CF		2	-8	-4	-16	-2	2
Jones,Garrett	1981	1B		4	-7	-7	-8	-4	-7
Joyce,Matt	1984	RF		-4	5	-4	3	-5	0
Kemp,Matt	1984	CF		-3	-37	-5	-13	-6	-23
Kendrick,Howie	1983	2B		5	-5	6	2	-3	7
Kinsler,Ian	1982	2B		22	7	18	1	11	20
Kipnis,Jason	1987	2B				2	3	-1	-11
Konerko,Paul	1976	1B		1	-13	-4	-11	-3	0
Kouzmanoff,Kevin	1981	3B		2	11	-7			0
Lagares,Juan	1989	CF						28	28

Player	YOB	Position 1	Position 2	DRS By Season 09	10	11	12	13	14
Laird,Gerald	1979	C		6	-3	-2	-5	-2	1
LaRoche,Adam	1979	1B		-2	6	5	8	1	0
Lawrie,Brett	1990	3B				14	20	3	1
LeMahieu,DJ	1988	2B				0	8	11	17
Lind,Adam	1983	1B		-6	-4	-4	1	-7	-3
Loney,James	1984	1B		5	4	11	6	4	-1
Longoria,Evan	1985	3B		19	20	22	1	12	-5
Lowrie,Jed	1984	SS		-1	-3	-2	-3	-21	-10
Lucroy,Jonathan	1986	C			4	-5	4	-1	11
Ludwick,Ryan	1978	LF		-4	8	-8	-5	-3	-6
Machado,Manny	1992	3B					7	35	6
Markakis,Nick	1983	RF		-3	-11	3	-7	-7	0
Marte,Starling	1988	LF					6	22	9
Martin,Leonys	1988	CF				-1	0	13	15
Martin,Russell	1983	C		7	5	7	-6	16	12
Mathis,Jeff	1983	C		10	4	8	5	5	5
Mauer,Joe	1983	C	1B	2	3	1	-7	6	4
Maybin,Cameron	1987	CF		-6	6	15	9	-5	4
McCann,Brian	1984	C		-5	-1	-4	-1	-2	0
McCutchen,Andrew	1986	CF		-10	-8	5	-5	7	-11
McGehee,Casey	1982	3B		-10	-14	3	-1		-2
Mercer,Jordy	1986	SS					3	-2	9
Mesoraco,Devin	1988	C				-2	-4	-1	2
Miller,Brad	1989	SS						-3	-5
Molina,Jose	1975	C		2	4	-2	-1	-2	-8
Molina,Yadier	1982	C		10	20	-4	16	12	8
Montero,Miguel	1983	C		2	1	5	-1	-6	-7
Moreland,Mitch	1985	1B			1	-4	0	1	1
Morgan,Nyjer	1980	CF		10	-8	7	7		-5
Morneau,Justin	1981	1B		2	8	-3	0	5	8
Moustakas,Mike	1988	3B				2	14	-3	-2
Murphy,Daniel	1985	2B		10		8	-10	-15	-11
Murphy,David	1981	LF	RF	-3	0	4	6	7	-17
Napoli,Mike	1981	1B		-5	-6	0	-4	10	7
Navarro,Dioner	1984	C		-2	3	1	0	1	1
Norris,Derek	1989	C					0	-5	-3
Olivo,Miguel	1978	C		-6	11	-9	0	0	-1
Overbay,Lyle	1977	1B		6	7	-4	1	3	-1
Ozuna,Marcell	1990	CF						2	11
Pagan,Angel	1981	CF		16	21	-8	-6	-9	-5
Parra,Gerardo	1987	LF	RF	0	13	14	8	41	-1
Pedroia,Dustin	1983	2B		14	5	18	11	15	17
Pena,Carlos	1978	1B		-3	0	-1	0	-5	0
Pence,Hunter	1983	RF		17	2	1	-9	-7	-2
Pennington,Cliff	1984	SS		-9	13	-9	12	13	4
Peralta,Jhonny	1982	SS		-5	3	2	-1	0	17
Perez,Salvador	1990	C				1	9	11	8
Phillips,Brandon	1981	2B		2	10	6	11	1	6
Pierzynski,A.J.	1976	C		-5	0	-9	-5	-2	-11
Plouffe,Trevor	1986	3B			-2	-22	-8	0	6
Posey,Buster	1987	C		0	4	3	-1	4	-2
Prado,Martin	1983	3B		5	10	13	19	4	9
Puig,Yasiel	1990	RF						10	2
Pujols,Albert	1980	1B		17	8	9	9	1	6
Ramirez,Alexei	1981	SS		2	20	7	14	1	-4
Ramirez,Aramis	1978	3B		-5	-15	-18	4	-12	-5
Ramirez,Hanley	1983	SS		2	-19	-13	-18	3	-9
Ramos,Wilson	1987	C			1	-5	-1	5	0
Rasmus,Colby	1986	CF		7	-6	-4	7	11	-7
Reddick,Josh	1987	RF		0	1	10	19	13	13
Rendon,Anthony	1990	3B						-11	16
Revere,Ben	1988	CF			0	-3	8	-5	-18
Reyes,Jose	1983	SS		-1	-4	-13	-16	-4	-16
Reynolds,Mark	1983	3B	1B	-11	-7	-23	-9	-11	6
Rios,Alex	1981	RF	CF	6	-1	-9	7	-5	-3
Rivera,Rene	1983	C				3		5	9
Rizzo,Anthony	1989	1B				2	4	16	6
Roberts,Brian	1977	2B		-8	-1	1	-6	0	3
Rollins,Jimmy	1978	SS		-2	3	-7	-8	-15	4
Rosario,Wilin	1989	C				-1	-1	-3	-9

Player	YOB	Position 1	Position 2	DRS By Season 09	10	11	12	13	14
Ruiz,Carlos	1979	C		10	7	0	3	3	8
Ryan,Brendan	1982	SS		25	22	18	27	6	2
Saltalamacchia,J	1985	C		3	-1	-4	-5	-6	-8
Sanchez,Gaby	1983	1B		0	-10	5	6	-3	-3
Sandoval,Pablo	1986	3B		-12	0	15	-4	-5	4
Santana,Carlos	1986	C	1B		-1	-6	3	-12	-8
Schierholtz,Nate	1984	RF		6	5	-6	2	0	8
Schoop,Jonathan	1991	2B						-1	11
Schumaker,Skip	1980	2B		-12	-13	-1	0	-18	-7
Scutaro,Marco	1975	SS		12	0	1	-10	-7	-1
Seager,Kyle	1987	3B				-1	-4	-8	10
Segura,Jean	1990	SS					0	3	2
Simmons,Andrelton	1989	SS					19	41	28
Smith,Seth	1982	LF		3	-3	-8	2	-1	6
Smoak,Justin	1986	1B			-3	-1	0	-8	-4
Sogard,Eric	1986	2B			0	4	3	4	3
Soriano,Alfonso	1976	LF		-14	-14	-9	-5	1	-7
Soto,Geovany	1983	C		-1	-3	-1	-8	2	0
Span,Denard	1984	CF		1	-5	9	20	3	-3
Stanton,Giancarlo	1989	RF			13	3	10	-7	7
Stewart,Ian	1985	3B		-5	5	3	3		-6
Stubbs,Drew	1984	CF		4	-1	-4	2	-9	0
Suzuki,Ichiro	1973	RF		3	-1	-3	6	9	1
Suzuki,Kurt	1983	C		6	8	-1	2	-2	-5
Swisher,Nick	1980	RF		-8	-1	-6	5	7	-6
Teixeira,Mark	1980	1B		2	6	3	17	0	2
Tejada,Ruben	1989	SS			-2	0	0	-6	3
Thole,Josh	1986	C		-1	-3	-4	4	-3	-5
Trout,Mike	1991	CF				2	21	-9	-9
Trumbo,Mark	1986	1B			2	8	-1	1	-9
Tulowitzki,Troy	1984	SS		13	19	11	-6	6	7
Uggla,Dan	1980	2B		-12	-9	-13	4	-19	-2
Upton,B.J.	1984	CF		0	-19	-7	-4	2	-7
Upton,Justin	1987	RF	LF	4	2	8	2	-6	0
Uribe,Juan	1979	3B		8	-4	5	4	15	17
Utley,Chase	1978	2B		12	17	7	8	-4	3
Valbuena,Luis	1985	3B		-3	5	-1	4	6	-11
Valencia,Danny	1984	3B			3	-13	-1	0	-2
Venable,Will	1982	RF		2	15	6	1	0	8
Victorino,Shane	1980	CF		-1	1	2	4	23	1
Votto,Joey	1983	1B		-2	3	4	9	6	5
Walker,Neil	1985	2B		-3	-6	-3	-4	9	-2
Weeks,Rickie	1982	2B		7	-16	-5	-30	-15	-17
Werth,Jayson	1979	RF		2	-5	-3	-12	1	-4
Wieters,Matt	1986	C		2	7	17	5	-13	-2
Willingham,Josh	1979	LF		-4	1	0	-13	-8	-3
Wong,Kolten	1990	2B						0	9
Wright,David	1982	3B		-14	-14	-6	16	5	13
Yelich,Christian	1991	LF						-1	10
Young,Chris	1983	CF		-6	18	20	7	-6	-1
Young,Delmon	1985	LF		-8	-13	-3	-3	-10	-4
Zimmerman,Ryan	1984	3B		22	11	-5	-1	-1	-4
Zobrist,Ben	1981	2B		25	16	29	4	8	6
Zunino,Mike	1991	C						-5	-7

2014 Team Statistics

The Team Statistics section starts with traditional Won-Lost standings, and then it delves much deeper into team performances. That includes splits of various types, the number of days each team spent in first place in their division, and team-by-team breakdowns with head-to-head win totals.

It was a tough year for some of the early-season division leaders. Milwaukee led the NL Central this season for 150 days, more than three times as long as St. Louis (36 days) and Pittsburgh (9 days) combined, and yet the Brewers fell to third place by the season's end and missed the playoffs. Atlanta led the NL East for 74 days but ended the season 17.0 games back in the standings. Oakland still made the playoffs, but a Wild Card play-in loss to the Royals is likely little consolation for the team that led the AL West for 129 days, nearly three times as long as the eventual division champion Angels.

You will also find batting, pitching, and fielding stats for each team in these pages. This includes a Pitching Staff Summary for each team, as well as a breakdown of the Defensive Runs Saved for each team at each position. New in this year's handbook, we've added Batting and Fielding By Position splits.

The Houston Astros were a fascinating team in 2014 because of their adherence to sabermetric principles. That was never more apparent than in their commitment to defensive shifting. The Rays held the previous record for most Shift Runs Saved in a season with 16 in 2013. The Astros shattered that record in saving 27 runs with their shifts in 2014.

2014 American League Standings

Overall

EAST	W-L	Pct	GB	D1	LD1	LLd
Baltimore Orioles	96-66	.593	0.0	105	9/28	14.5
New York Yankees	84-78	.519	12.0	26	5/21	2.5
Toronto Blue Jays	83-79	.512	13.0	50	7/2	6.0
Tampa Bay Rays	77-85	.475	19.0	9	4/13	1.0
Boston Red Sox	71-91	.438	25.0	1	4/3	0.5

CENTRAL	W-L	Pct	GB	D1	LD1	LLd
Detroit Tigers	90-72	.556	0.0	153	9/28	7.5
Kansas City Royals	89-73	.549	1.0	34	9/11	3.0
Cleveland Indians	85-77	.525	5.0	2	4/1	0.0
Chicago White Sox	73-89	.451	17.0	3	4/2	0.0
Minnesota Twins	70-92	.432	20.0	0	-	0.0

WEST	W-L	Pct	GB	D1	LD1	LLd
Los Angeles Angels	98-64	.605	0.0	44	9/28	12.0
Oakland Athletics	88-74	.543	10.0	129	8/25	6.0
Seattle Mariners	87-75	.537	11.0	11	4/11	2.0
Houston Astros	70-92	.432	28.0	0	-	0.0
Texas Rangers	67-95	.414	31.0	4	4/27	0.5

Wild Card Clinch Dates: Kansas City 9/26, Oakland 9/28. Division Clinch Dates: Baltimore 9/16, Los Angeles 9/17, Detroit 9/28.
D1 = Number of days a team had at least a share of first place of their division; LD1 = Last date the team had at least a share of first place; LLd = The largest number of games that a team led their division by.

East Division

Tm	AT Home	Road	VERSUS East	Cent	West	NL	LHS	RHS	CONDITIONS Day	Night	Grass	Turf	GAME 1-Rn	5+Rn	XInn	MONTHLY April	May	June	July	Aug	Sept	ALL-STAR Pre	Post
Bal	50-31	46-35	47-29	16-17	21-12	12-8	22-19	74-47	24-30	72-36	85-59	11-7	32-23	24-15	14-6	12-12	15-15	16-12	17-8	19-9	17-10	52-42	44-24
NYY	43-38	41-40	37-39	19-16	15-16	13-7	24-20	60-58	32-24	52-54	75-68	9-10	28-24	12-22	7-7	15-11	14-14	12-15	14-12	15-13	14-13	47-47	37-31
Tor	46-35	37-44	39-37	16-16	15-19	13-7	20-19	63-60	29-28	54-51	31-40	52-39	15-20	24-23	5-8	12-15	21-9	12-15	15-11	9-17	14-12	49-47	34-32
TB	36-45	41-40	36-40	14-18	17-17	10-10	20-24	57-61	28-29	49-56	37-35	40-50	25-23	21-22	8-10	11-16	12-17	13-16	17-6	13-16	11-14	44-53	33-32
Bos	34-47	37-44	31-45	17-16	14-19	9-11	22-27	49-64	20-26	51-65	63-79	8-12	28-28	15-21	10-11	13-14	13-15	12-16	10-15	12-16	11-15	43-52	28-39

Central Division

Tm	AT Home	Road	VERSUS East	Cent	West	NL	LHS	RHS	CONDITIONS Day	Night	Grass	Turf	GAME 1-Rn	5+Rn	XInn	MONTHLY April	May	June	July	Aug	Sept	ALL-STAR Pre	Post
Det	45-36	45-36	17-15	43-33	18-16	12-8	28-22	62-50	32-29	58-43	87-69	3-3	23-20	27-21	6-6	14-9	17-12	14-13	13-13	16-15	16-10	53-38	37-34
KC	42-39	47-34	17-17	39-37	18-14	15-5	24-21	65-52	26-25	63-48	85-70	4-3	22-25	21-20	5-7	14-12	12-17	17-10	12-13	19-10	15-11	48-46	41-27
Cle	48-33	37-44	19-14	39-37	17-16	10-10	25-25	60-52	30-25	55-52	82-74	3-3	25-21	24-18	13-8	11-17	15-13	13-13	14-12	18-9	14-13	47-47	38-30
CWS	40-41	33-48	16-18	33-43	13-19	11-9	22-23	51-66	22-34	51-55	68-87	5-2	28-24	14-23	6-8	14-15	14-14	11-15	14-12	9-19	11-14	45-51	28-38
Min	35-46	35-46	14-18	36-40	11-23	9-11	24-32	46-60	32-35	38-57	66-90	4-2	21-24	21-26	6-7	12-12	13-16	12-16	11-15	11-18	11-15	44-50	26-42

West Division

Tm	AT Home	Road	VERSUS East	Cent	West	NL	LHS	RHS	CONDITIONS Day	Night	Grass	Turf	GAME 1-Rn	5+Rn	XInn	MONTHLY April	May	June	July	Aug	Sept	ALL-STAR Pre	Post
LAA	52-29	46-35	19-14	24-9	43-33	12-8	28-20	70-44	21-15	77-49	93-62	5-2	27-22	30-15	10-7	14-13	16-12	15-10	19-8	19-10	15-11	57-37	41-27
Oak	48-33	40-41	20-12	17-17	38-38	13-7	24-25	64-49	32-26	56-48	86-70	2-4	21-28	30-13	13-8	18-10	16-12	17-9	15-10	12-17	10-16	59-36	29-38
Sea	41-40	46-35	18-15	19-14	41-35	9-11	32-23	55-52	30-22	57-53	83-71	4-4	18-27	22-17	4-7	11-14	16-14	13-10	11-14	17-10	14-13	51-44	36-31
Hou	38-43	32-49	16-18	14-18	35-41	5-15	21-26	49-66	21-26	49-66	68-87	2-5	17-28	21-29	6-5	9-19	15-14	12-15	8-17	15-14	11-13	40-56	30-36
Tex	33-48	34-47	10-23	14-19	33-43	10-10	22-29	45-66	25-19	42-76	65-91	2-4	25-22	19-32	2-5	15-13	13-15	9-17	6-20	10-18	14-12	38-57	29-38

Team vs. Team Breakdown

	EAST Bal	NYY	Tor	TB	Bos	CENTRAL Det	KC	Cle	CWS	Min	WEST LAA	Oak	Sea	Hou	Tex
Baltimore Orioles	-	13	11	12	11	1	3	3	5	4	4	2	5	4	6
New York Yankees	6	-	11	8	12	4	3	3	5	4	4	2	3	2	4
Toronto Blue Jays	8	8	-	11	12	5	3	4	2	2	2	3	3	3	4
Tampa Bay Rays	7	11	8	-	10	4	2	2	2	4	2	2	3	5	5
Boston Red Sox	8	7	7	9	-	1	6	2	4	4	2	3	1	4	4
Detroit Tigers	5	3	1	3	5	-	13	11	10	9	3	5	2	4	4
Kansas City Royals	4	4	4	4	1	6	-	9	13	11	3	5	2	3	5
Cleveland Indians	4	4	2	4	5	8	10	-	10	11	2	2	2	5	6
Chicago White Sox	1	2	5	5	3	9	6	9	-	9	1	4	3	3	2
Minnesota Twins	3	3	4	2	2	10	8	8	10	-	0	1	5	3	2
Los Angeles Angels	2	2	5	5	5	4	3	5	5	7	-	10	7	12	14
Oakland Athletics	4	4	4	4	4	2	2	4	3	6	9	-	9	11	9
Seattle Mariners	2	3	4	4	5	4	5	4	4	2	12	10	-	10	9
Houston Astros	3	4	4	2	3	3	3	2	3	3	7	8	9	-	11
Texas Rangers	1	3	2	2	2	3	1	1	4	5	5	10	10	8	-

2014 National League Standings

Overall

EAST

Team	W-L	Pct	GB	D1	LD1	LLd
Washington Nationals	96-66	.593	0.0	110	9/28	17.0
New York Mets	79-83	.488	17.0	0	-	0.0
Atlanta Braves	79-83	.488	17.0	74	7/18	3.5
Miami Marlins	77-85	.475	19.0	9	5/29	0.5
Philadelphia Phillies	73-89	.451	23.0	1	3/31	0.0

CENTRAL

Team	W-L	Pct	GB	D1	LD1	LLd
St Louis Cardinals	90-72	.556	0.0	36	9/28	4.5
Pittsburgh Pirates	88-74	.543	2.0	9	4/8	1.0
Milwaukee Brewers	82-80	.506	8.0	150	8/31	6.5
Cincinnati Reds	76-86	.469	14.0	0	-	0.0
Chicago Cubs	73-89	.451	17.0	0	-	0.0

WEST

Team	W-L	Pct	GB	D1	LD1	LLd
Los Angeles Dodgers	94-68	.580	0.0	100	9/28	6.0
San Francisco Giants	88-74	.543	6.0	96	7/26	10.0
San Diego Padres	77-85	.475	17.0	2	3/31	0.0
Colorado Rockies	66-96	.407	28.0	0	-	0.0
Arizona Diamondbacks	64-98	.395	30.0	0	-	0.0

Wild Card Clinch Dates: Pittsburgh 9/23, San Francisco 9/25. Division Clinch Dates: Washington 9/16, Los Angeles 9/24, St Louis 9/28.
D1 = Number of days a team had at least a share of first place of their division; LD1 = Last date the team had at least a share of first place; LLd = The largest number of games that a team led their division

East Division

Tm	AT Home	AT Road	East	Cent	West	AL	LHS	RHS	Day	Night	Grass	Turf	1-Rn	5+Rn	XInn	April	May	June	July	Aug	Sept	Pre	Post
Was	51-30	45-36	45-31	17-16	24-9	10-10	28-17	68-49	33-21	63-45	96-66	0-0	26-22	26-17	8-9	16-12	11-15	17-11	14-10	19-10	19-8	51-42	45-24
NYM	40-41	39-42	38-38	16-18	14-18	11-9	17-16	62-67	31-22	48-61	79-83	0-0	26-29	19-15	7-8	15-11	11-18	11-17	15-10	12-17	15-10	45-50	34-33
Atl	42-39	37-44	40-36	20-13	12-21	7-13	19-15	60-68	19-26	60-57	79-83	0-0	25-28	16-19	7-10	17-9	13-16	15-13	13-13	14-14	7-18	52-43	27-40
Mia	42-39	35-46	33-43	14-18	17-17	13-7	20-16	57-69	19-30	58-55	75-85	2-0	35-29	17-20	9-12	13-14	15-13	11-16	14-12	13-14	11-16	44-50	33-35
Phi	37-44	36-45	34-42	15-18	17-16	7-13	23-22	50-67	22-32	51-57	73-87	0-2	28-27	16-20	10-11	13-13	11-16	12-17	12-15	14-13	11-15	42-53	31-36

Central Division

Tm	AT Home	AT Road	East	Cent	West	AL	LHS	RHS	Day	Night	Grass	Turf	1-Rn	5+Rn	XInn	April	May	June	July	Aug	Sept	Pre	Post
StL	51-30	39-42	17-16	45-31	20-13	8-12	21-18	69-54	32-23	58-49	87-70	3-2	32-23	19-19	7-6	15-14	15-12	14-13	13-11	16-13	17-9	52-44	38-28
Pit	51-30	37-44	21-13	36-40	20-12	11-9	20-13	68-61	22-31	66-43	86-73	2-1	31-29	21-14	8-7	10-16	15-14	17-10	15-11	14-14	17-9	49-46	39-28
Mil	42-39	40-41	15-19	36-40	20-12	11-9	22-18	60-62	28-28	54-52	81-76	1-4	23-19	21-19	7-6	20-8	13-15	18-10	9-16	13-14	9-17	53-43	29-37
Cin	44-37	32-49	14-18	40-36	16-18	6-14	17-17	59-69	33-23	43-63	76-86	0-0	22-38	17-21	4-9	12-15	13-14	18-10	11-15	12-17	10-15	51-44	25-42
ChC	41-40	32-49	16-16	33-43	15-19	9-11	16-18	57-71	33-41	40-48	73-86	0-3	19-21	17-27	8-10	9-17	11-16	15-13	10-16	16-14	12-13	40-54	33-35

West Division

Tm	AT Home	AT Road	East	Cent	West	AL	LHS	RHS	Day	Night	Grass	Turf	1-Rn	5+Rn	XInn	April	May	June	July	Aug	Sept	Pre	Post
LAD	49-32	45-36	18-14	15-19	50-26	11-9	26-16	68-52	23-21	71-47	94-68	0-0	25-20	28-18	6-12	15-12	15-15	18-10	14-10	15-13	17-8	54-43	40-25
SF	45-36	43-38	22-12	16-16	40-36	10-10	30-30	58-44	38-24	50-50	88-74	0-0	18-22	23-23	9-4	17-11	20-9	10-16	12-14	16-12	13-12	53-43	35-31
SD	48-33	29-52	17-17	18-14	33-43	9-11	19-21	58-64	22-27	55-58	77-85	0-0	33-21	18-20	10-5	13-16	13-14	10-17	12-13	16-11	13-14	41-54	36-31
Col	45-36	21-60	13-20	10-23	36-40	7-13	23-23	43-73	24-29	42-67	66-96	0-0	20-24	26-26	7-7	16-13	12-15	8-20	8-17	10-18	12-13	40-56	26-40
Ari	33-48	31-50	11-21	15-19	31-45	7-13	15-25	49-73	19-31	45-67	64-98	0-0	23-30	10-24	10-6	9-22	14-13	12-14	13-12	9-18	7-19	40-56	24-42

Team vs. Team Breakdown

	Was	NYM	Atl	Mia	Phi	StL	Pit	Mil	Cin	ChC	LAD	SF	SD	Col	Ari
Washington Nationals	-	15	8	13	9	2	4	4	3	4	4	5	4	5	6
New York Mets	4	-	10	11	13	4	3	3	4	2	2	1	3	4	4
Atlanta Braves	11	9	-	9	11	2	3	5	5	5	1	1	3	4	3
Miami Marlins	6	8	10	-	9	4	2	3	3	2	3	3	3	4	4
Philadelphia Phillies	10	6	8	10	-	4	1	4	3	3	4	2	4	3	4
St Louis Cardinals	5	3	4	2	3	-	11	12	12	10	3	3	4	5	5
Pittsburgh Pirates	3	4	4	4	6	8	-	7	7	14	5	4	3	4	4
Milwaukee Brewers	2	4	2	4	3	7	12	-	9	8	5	2	3	6	4
Cincinnati Reds	3	2	2	4	3	7	12	10	-	11	3	5	1	3	4
Chicago Cubs	3	5	1	4	3	9	5	11	8	-	3	2	3	5	2
Los Angeles Dodgers	2	4	6	3	3	4	2	1	4	4	-	10	12	13	15
San Francisco Giants	2	6	5	4	5	4	2	4	2	4	9	-	9	9	13
San Diego Padres	3	3	4	4	3	3	3	3	5	4	7	10	-	9	7
Colorado Rockies	1	3	3	3	3	1	2	1	4	2	6	10	10	-	10
Arizona Diamondbacks	1	2	3	3	2	1	3	3	3	5	4	6	12	9	-

American League Batting

	BATTING																			BASERUNNING					PERCENTAGES		
Tm	G	AB	H	2B	3B	HR	(Hm	Rd)	TB	R	RBI	TBB	IBB	SO	HBP	SH	SF	ShO	SB	CS	SB%	GDP	LOB	Avg	OBP	Slg
LAA	162	5652	1464	304	31	155	(73	82)	2295	773	729	492	42	1266	60	26	54	3	81	39	.68	112	1673	.259	.322	.406
Det	162	5630	1557	325	26	155	(76	79)	2399	757	731	443	51	1144	44	24	61	10	106	41	.72	137	1700	.277	.331	.426
Oak	162	5545	1354	253	33	146	(74	72)	2111	729	686	586	34	1104	49	19	43	11	83	20	.81	118	1755	.244	.320	.381
Tor	162	5549	1435	282	24	177	(98	79)	2296	723	690	502	27	1151	41	35	40	11	78	21	.79	128	1696	.259	.323	.414
Min	162	5567	1412	316	27	128	(67	61)	2166	715	675	544	29	1329	53	25	44	12	99	36	.73	97	1748	.254	.324	.389
Bal	162	5596	1434	264	16	211	(107	104)	2363	705	681	401	29	1285	62	35	36	11	44	20	.69	112	1620	.256	.311	.422
Cle	162	5575	1411	284	23	142	(72	70)	2167	669	644	504	24	1189	42	51	49	8	104	27	.79	126	1783	.253	.317	.389
CWS	162	5543	1400	279	32	155	(74	81)	2208	660	625	417	33	1362	60	19	38	8	85	36	.70	127	1601	.253	.310	.398
KC	162	5545	1456	286	29	95	(43	52)	2085	651	604	380	22	985	53	33	47	7	153	36	.81	131	1704	.263	.314	.376
Tex	162	5460	1400	260	28	111	(51	60)	2049	637	597	417	37	1162	61	41	45	10	105	59	.64	148	1672	.256	.314	.375
Sea	162	5450	1328	247	32	136	(73	63)	2047	634	600	396	33	1232	60	35	34	19	96	42	.70	113	1569	.244	.300	.376
Bos	162	5551	1355	282	20	123	(49	74)	2046	634	601	535	36	1337	68	20	52	15	63	25	.72	138	1722	.244	.316	.369
NYY	162	5597	1349	247	16	147	(88	59)	2089	633	591	452	16	1133	56	29	47	10	112	26	.81	114	1664	.245	.307	.380
Hou	162	5447	1317	240	19	163	(90	73)	2084	629	596	495	27	1442	55	22	36	14	122	37	.77	122	1626	.242	.309	.383
TB	162	5516	1361	263	24	117	(51	66)	2023	612	586	527	31	1124	66	43	53	18	63	27	.70	135	1810	.247	.317	.367
AL	1215	83123	21033	4132	390	2161	(1086	1075)	32428	10161	9636	7091	471	18245	830	457	679	167	1394	492	.74	1855	25343	.253	.316	.390

American League Pitching

	HOW MUCH THEY PITCHED					WHAT THEY GAVE UP												THE RESULTS									
Tm	G	CG	Rel	IP	BFP	H	R	ER	HR	SH	SF	HB	TBB	IBB	SO	WP	Bk	W	L	Pct.	ShO	Sv-Op	Hld	OAvg	OOBP	OSlg	ERA
Sea	162	2	497	1452.0	5974	1240	554	512	137	30	40	52	463	36	1317	80	8	87	75	.537	9	51-62	86	.230	.295	.356	3.17
Oak	162	7	441	1463.1	5972	1269	572	524	147	34	32	48	406	28	1244	59	1	88	74	.543	13	31-52	61	.233	.290	.356	3.22
Bal	162	3	479	1461.1	6104	1342	593	557	151	30	35	59	472	25	1174	42	2	96	66	.593	13	53-72	97	.244	.308	.382	3.43
KC	162	3	451	1450.2	6101	1386	624	565	128	26	45	56	440	14	1168	58	6	89	73	.549	14	53-65	75	.250	.310	.377	3.51
TB	162	3	494	1463.2	6131	1292	625	579	145	27	45	58	482	27	1437	65	3	77	85	.475	22	37-56	75	.234	.300	.362	3.56
LAA	162	3	543	1482.2	6179	1307	630	590	126	29	49	63	504	41	1342	74	4	98	64	.605	13	46-62	81	.236	.305	.351	3.58
Cle	162	6	573	1468.1	6193	1398	653	581	135	33	40	58	464	51	1450	56	2	85	77	.525	15	40-62	76	.250	.312	.385	3.56
NYY	162	5	475	1453.0	6114	1392	664	605	164	38	45	65	398	23	1370	49	6	84	78	.519	10	48-69	85	.250	.305	.395	3.75
Tor	162	3	449	1443.0	6150	1400	686	642	151	25	48	57	490	23	1199	43	5	83	79	.512	16	45-63	78	.253	.318	.407	4.00
Det	162	5	473	1454.0	6191	1475	705	648	127	26	41	42	462	34	1244	43	9	90	72	.556	8	41-57	72	.263	.321	.401	4.01
Bos	162	3	493	1465.2	6231	1458	715	653	154	36	48	47	482	19	1213	51	5	71	91	.438	7	36-54	63	.260	.321	.409	4.01
Hou	162	7	438	1438.2	6154	1437	723	657	139	36	59	52	484	32	1137	57	7	70	92	.432	3	31-56	65	.260	.323	.396	4.11
CWS	162	3	453	1441.0	6255	1468	758	687	140	37	48	69	557	42	1152	75	3	73	89	.451	6	36-57	68	.265	.337	.401	4.29
Tex	162	6	476	1426.1	6195	1510	773	711	160	24	49	61	505	43	1110	61	7	67	95	.414	17	33-47	68	.272	.336	.428	4.49
Min	162	2	491	1435.0	6212	1588	777	728	147	30	63	45	408	24	1031	50	6	70	92	.432	7	38-58	68	.280	.330	.428	4.57
AL	1215	61	7226	21798.2	92156	20962	10052	9239	2151	461	687	832	7017	462	18588	863	74	1228	1202	.505	173	619-892	1118	.252	.314	.389	3.81

American League Fielding

		Fielding																		
Team	G	Inn	PO	Ast	OFAst	E	(Throw	Field)	TC	DP	GDP	SB	CS	SB%	CPkof	PPkof	PB	UER	UERA	FPct
Seattle	162	1452.0	4356	1609	14	82	34	37	6047	139	116	92	35	.72	1	4	11	42	0.26	.986
Los Angeles	162	1482.2	4448	1483	24	83	46	37	6014	128	113	106	39	.73	3	8	5	40	0.24	.986
Baltimore	162	1461.1	4384	1603	34	87	45	42	6074	156	127	84	32	.72	2	3	9	36	0.22	.986
Toronto	162	1443.0	4329	1528	34	87	45	42	5944	130	113	94	24	.80	0	4	18	44	0.27	.905
Boston	162	1465.2	4397	1610	37	92	44	48	6099	155	132	87	33	.73	3	3	18	62	0.38	.985
Tampa Bay	162	1463.2	4391	1309	19	88	44	44	5788	96	79	82	26	.76	1	8	9	46	0.28	.985
New York	162	1453.0	4359	1474	20	92	44	48	5925	107	87	77	38	.67	1	3	15	59	0.37	.984
Minnesota	162	1435.0	4305	1579	36	97	49	48	5981	136	120	100	22	.82	1	5	8	49	0.31	.984
Detroit	162	1454.0	4362	1539	15	101	44	57	6002	153	131	111	51	.69	1	2	8	57	0.35	.983
Houston	162	1438.2	4316	1704	31	106	36	70	6126	151	133	109	32	.77	0	3	14	66	0.41	.983
Kansas City	162	1450.2	4352	1512	26	104	55	49	5968	122	107	69	29	.70	5	13	6	59	0.37	.983
Chicago	162	1441.0	4323	1682	31	107	38	69	6112	170	145	93	32	.74	0	1	17	71	0.44	.982
Oakland	162	1463.1	4390	1634	35	111	56	55	6135	150	131	100	28	.78	0	3	10	48	0.30	.982
Texas	162	1426.1	4279	1413	34	106	51	55	5798	155	129	85	36	.70	4	3	9	62	0.39	.982
Cleveland	162	1468.1	4405	1599	30	116	57	59	6120	139	116	95	44	.68	2	3	9	72	0.44	.981
American League	1215	21798.2	65396	23278	420	1459	688	771	90133	2087	1783	1384	501	.73	24	66	166	813	0.34	.984

National League Batting

Tm	G	AB	H	2B	3B	HR	(Hm	Rd)	TB	R	RBI	TBB	IBB	SO	HBP	SH	SF	ShO	SB	CS	SB%	GDP	LOB	Avg	OBP	Slg
Col	162	5612	1551	307	41	186	(119	67)	2498	755	721	397	39	1281	48	59	48	11	85	48	.64	121	1636	.276	.327	.445
LAD	162	5560	1476	302	38	134	(71	63)	2256	718	686	519	30	1246	61	47	43	5	138	50	.73	119	1741	.265	.333	.406
Was	162	5542	1403	265	27	152	(63	89)	2178	686	635	517	29	1304	56	60	41	8	101	23	.81	115	1730	.253	.321	.393
Pit	162	5536	1436	275	30	156	(62	94)	2239	682	659	520	46	1244	78	54	35	8	104	47	.69	127	1773	.259	.330	.404
SF	162	5523	1407	257	42	132	(53	79)	2144	665	636	427	37	1245	43	45	49	15	56	27	.67	113	1658	.255	.311	.388
Mil	162	5462	1366	297	28	150	(77	73)	2169	650	617	423	32	1197	73	70	37	11	102	43	.70	137	1617	.250	.311	.397
Mia	162	5538	1399	254	36	122	(59	63)	2091	645	614	501	49	1419	35	71	39	8	58	21	.73	143	1683	.253	.317	.378
NYM	162	5472	1306	275	19	125	(59	66)	1994	629	602	516	42	1264	54	59	44	12	101	34	.75	112	1662	.239	.308	.364
Phi	162	5603	1356	251	27	125	(64	61)	2036	619	584	443	42	1306	55	59	37	15	109	26	.81	95	1699	.242	.302	.363
StL	162	5426	1371	275	21	105	(57	48)	2003	619	585	471	28	1133	86	64	39	12	57	32	.64	140	1732	.253	.320	.369
Ari	162	5552	1379	259	47	118	(62	56)	2086	615	573	398	31	1165	43	56	36	13	86	33	.72	115	1692	.248	.302	.376
ChC	162	5508	1315	270	31	157	(69	88)	2118	614	590	442	29	1477	54	57	41	16	65	40	.62	94	1593	.239	.300	.385
Cin	162	5395	1282	254	20	131	(77	54)	1969	595	562	415	22	1252	52	76	37	17	122	52	.70	88	1581	.238	.296	.365
Atl	162	5468	1316	240	22	123	(62	61)	1969	573	545	472	31	1369	43	53	27	16	95	33	.74	121	1666	.241	.305	.360
SD	162	5294	1199	224	30	109	(54	55)	1810	535	500	468	27	1294	41	56	45	19	91	34	.73	118	1576	.226	.292	.342
NL	1215	82491	20562	4005	459	2025	(1008	1017)	31560	9600	9109	6929	514	19196	822	886	598	186	1370	543	.72	1758	25039	.249	.312	.383

National League Pitching

Tm	G	CG	Rel	IP	BFP	H	R	ER	HR	SH	SF	HB	TBB	IBB	SO	WP	Bk	W	L	Pct.	ShO	Sv-Op	Hld	OAvg	OOBP	OSlg	ERA
Was	162	5	458	1470.2	6020	1351	555	495	110	51	32	51	352	26	1288	37	2	96	66	.593	19	45-62	93	.244	.294	.358	3.03
SD	162	4	481	1438.2	6006	1300	577	523	117	65	40	46	462	32	1284	57	4	77	85	.475	10	41-49	75	.241	.304	.362	3.27
Atl	162	5	472	1455.0	6087	1369	597	547	121	70	43	37	472	36	1301	75	1	79	83	.488	13	54-67	81	.251	.312	.370	3.38
StL	162	8	485	1448.2	6069	1321	603	564	123	51	34	61	470	35	1221	44	5	90	72	.556	23	55-72	95	.242	.308	.366	3.50
Cin	162	5	428	1446.0	6067	1282	612	576	163	51	38	69	507	33	1290	45	5	76	86	.469	13	44-63	69	.237	.309	.383	3.59
SF	162	8	475	1449.0	5947	1305	614	564	133	51	38	57	389	35	1211	49	6	88	74	.543	12	46-64	81	.241	.297	.382	3.50
LAD	162	7	496	1464.2	6075	1338	617	554	142	49	34	41	429	35	1373	64	4	94	68	.580	16	47-61	89	.242	.300	.376	3.40
NYM	162	1	489	1463.2	6170	1370	618	568	141	52	25	50	509	38	1303	56	1	79	83	.488	11	42-64	73	.248	.315	.382	3.49
Pit	162	2	452	1456.1	6130	1341	631	562	128	72	42	88	499	43	1228	71	3	88	74	.543	7	48-72	90	.247	.318	.371	3.47
Mil	162	3	478	1457.2	6106	1386	657	594	167	54	30	42	431	20	1246	44	2	82	80	.506	9	45-65	76	.250	.307	.393	3.67
Mia	162	3	487	1457.2	6217	1481	674	613	114	66	39	49	458	35	1190	56	4	77	85	.475	16	42-64	70	.264	.323	.390	3.78
Phi	162	2	461	1468.1	6261	1396	687	619	134	77	48	69	521	43	1255	49	1	73	89	.451	12	40-56	57	.252	.321	.387	3.79
ChC	162	1	537	1463.1	6208	1398	707	686	115	58	36	55	504	37	1311	64	3	73	89	.451	11	37-58	81	.252	.318	.376	3.91
Ari	162	2	488	1444.1	6162	1467	742	683	154	59	49	51	469	43	1278	50	5	64	98	.395	4	35-55	75	.265	.326	.414	4.26
Col	162	1	547	1431.0	6248	1528	818	770	173	59	62	54	531	32	1074	72	8	66	96	.407	4	24-50	74	.276	.342	.443	4.84
NL	1215	57	7234	21815.0	91773	20633	9709	8868	2035	882	590	820	7003	523	18853	833	54	1202	1228	.495	180	645-922	1179	.250	.313	.383	3.66

National League Fielding

Team	G	Inn	PO	Ast	OFAst	E	(Throw	Field)	TC	DP	GDP	SB	CS	SB%	CPkof	PPkof	PB	UER	UERA	FPct
Cincinnati	162	1446.0	4338	1588	24	72	36	36	5998	120	99	71	38	.65	0	7	13	36	0.22	.988
Philadelphia	162	1468.1	4405	1674	15	83	28	55	6162	133	110	115	46	.71	0	4	8	68	0.42	.987
Atlanta	162	1455.0	4365	1527	24	85	36	49	5977	143	128	100	29	.78	0	14	18	50	0.31	.986
St Louis	162	1448.2	4346	1617	16	88	34	54	6051	145	130	54	29	.65	3	1	7	39	0.24	.985
Miami	162	1457.2	4373	1699	30	97	50	47	6169	154	130	109	34	.76	2	1	9	61	0.38	.984
San Francisco	162	1449.0	4347	1699	24	100	52	48	6146	155	132	107	47	.69	1	3	11	50	0.31	.984
Washington	162	1470.2	4412	1624	28	100	51	49	6136	139	117	60	36	.63	3	1	6	60	0.37	.984
Milwaukee	162	1457.2	4373	1602	19	99	50	49	6074	130	110	96	35	.73	4	5	7	63	0.39	.984
Arizona	162	1444.1	4333	1645	43	101	49	52	6079	147	121	75	34	.69	1	4	6	59	0.37	.983
Chicago	162	1463.1	4390	1668	32	103	46	57	6161	137	114	114	38	.75	4	7	13	71	0.44	.983
San Diego	162	1438.2	4316	1560	19	101	53	48	5977	124	100	116	40	.74	2	3	21	54	0.34	.983
New York	162	1463.2	4391	1617	36	104	46	58	6112	158	139	85	25	.77	0	2	16	50	0.31	.983
Colorado	162	1431.0	4293	1809	28	106	58	48	6208	166	143	85	16	.84	2	2	20	48	0.30	.983
Los Angeles	162	1464.2	4394	1706	25	107	46	61	6207	145	126	86	38	.69	3	5	12	63	0.39	.983
Pittsburgh	162	1456.1	4369	1839	24	109	66	43	6317	148	131	107	49	.69	3	7	9	69	0.43	.983
National League	1215	21815.0	65445	24874	387	1455	701	754	91774	2144	1830	1380	534	.72	28	66	176	841	0.35	.984

Team Pitching Staff Summary

Team	Starters				Bullpen					
	IP	ERA	ERA Rank	W-L	IP	ERA	ERA Rank	W-L	Sv-Opp	Sv Pct
Arizona Diamondbacks	937.1	4.44	27	41-69	507.0	3.92	23	23-29	35-55	64%
Atlanta Braves	1014.1	3.42	5	58-60	440.2	3.31	11	21-23	54-67	81%
Baltimore Orioles	953.2	3.61	12	68-45	507.2	3.10	6	28-21	53-72	74%
Boston Red Sox	970.1	4.36	26	50-64	495.1	3.33	12	21-27	36-54	67%
Chicago Cubs	927.0	4.11	24	50-63	536.1	3.61	15	23-26	37-58	64%
Chicago White Sox	970.0	4.26	25	50-57	471.0	4.38	28	23-32	36-57	63%
Cincinnati Reds	1023.2	3.37	3	65-55	422.1	4.11	26	11-31	44-63	70%
Cleveland Indians	955.0	3.82	18	50-55	513.1	3.12	7	35-22	40-62	65%
Colorado Rockies	905.1	4.89	29	44-65	525.2	4.79	29	22-31	24-50	48%
Detroit Tigers	1007.0	3.89	21	68-55	447.0	4.29	27	22-17	41-57	72%
Houston Astros	970.0	3.82	18	50-66	468.2	4.80	30	20-26	31-56	55%
Kansas City Royals	986.2	3.60	10	61-55	464.0	3.30	10	28-18	53-65	82%
Los Angeles Angels	942.2	3.62	13	68-42	540.0	3.52	14	30-22	46-62	74%
Los Angeles Dodgers	975.0	3.20	2	76-44	489.2	3.80	22	18-24	47-61	77%
Miami Marlins	947.1	4.04	23	47-60	510.1	3.33	12	30-25	42-64	66%
Milwaukee Brewers	992.1	3.69	15	61-57	465.1	3.62	16	21-23	45-65	69%
Minnesota Twins	913.1	5.06	30	48-70	521.2	3.73	21	22-22	38-58	66%
New York Mets	985.0	3.66	14	57-55	478.2	3.14	8	22-28	42-64	66%
New York Yankees	951.2	3.77	17	59-51	501.1	3.70	19	25-27	48-69	70%
Oakland Athletics	996.0	3.37	3	62-51	467.1	2.91	3	26-23	31-52	60%
Philadelphia Phillies	1013.1	3.88	20	47-65	455.0	3.64	18	26-24	40-56	71%
Pittsburgh Pirates	971.0	3.60	10	55-49	485.1	3.28	9	33-25	48-72	67%
San Diego Padres	951.1	3.55	9	56-70	487.1	2.73	2	21-15	41-49	84%
San Francisco Giants	977.0	3.74	16	56-60	472.0	3.01	5	32-14	46-64	72%
Seattle Mariners	952.0	3.48	7	62-55	500.0	2.59	1	25-20	51-62	82%
St Louis Cardinals	969.1	3.44	6	64-49	479.1	3.62	16	26-23	55-72	76%
Tampa Bay Rays	954.2	3.48	7	54-57	509.0	3.71	20	23-28	37-56	66%
Texas Rangers	918.2	4.75	28	46-69	507.2	4.02	24	21-26	33-47	70%
Toronto Blue Jays	958.2	3.96	22	63-57	484.1	4.09	25	20-22	45-63	71%
Washington Nationals	1002.1	3.04	1	70-49	468.1	3.00	4	26-17	45-62	73%

Team Defense
Defensive Runs Saved by Position and Team

Team	P	C	1B	2B	3B	SS	LF	CF	RF	Shifts	Total
St Louis Cardinals	20	-2	7	16	-4	13	4	14	-4	12	76
Cincinnati Reds	15	5	4	6	9	18	2	15	-7	4	71
Baltimore Orioles	-2	-1	15	8	6	5	7	6	5	7	56
San Diego Padres	-2	5	9	-10	11	9	-6	7	14	6	43
Oakland Athletics	0	-5	1	4	20	-9	11	-8	18	10	42
Pittsburgh Pirates	11	12	-8	0	4	12	21	-12	-4	5	41
Kansas City Royals	1	6	-1	-2	-6	-4	25	23	-2	0	40
Boston Red Sox	-7	-5	6	15	-18	-9	-1	13	32	13	39
Los Angeles Dodgers	10	4	12	-3	29	0	-3	-18	-4	2	29
Arizona Diamondbacks	-2	-7	-2	-3	2	6	-6	25	8	4	25
Atlanta Braves	-2	-4	-7	-12	-12	32	0	-10	34	3	22
New York Mets	-6	-13	7	-11	12	0	7	28	-7	5	22
Colorado Rockies	-7	-6	8	10	9	2	-5	1	4	1	17
Houston Astros	-3	2	-3	-8	-8	6	5	-15	9	27	12
Washington Nationals	4	6	0	-4	10	3	-4	-3	-4	1	9
San Francisco Giants	2	-2	6	1	5	6	-4	-15	-2	12	9
Milwaukee Brewers	2	14	0	-22	2	1	8	-5	-4	4	0
Seattle Mariners	-10	-6	-6	-2	11	2	4	-6	2	9	-2
New York Yankees	1	1	-1	10	9	-12	0	-1	-10	0	-3
Miami Marlins	-9	-3	-8	-13	-2	-1	13	12	7	-7	-11
Los Angeles Angels	3	-9	1	8	-21	-4	6	-11	11	2	-14
Toronto Blue Jays	5	-2	-8	4	-2	-14	-5	-6	-5	16	-17
Chicago Cubs	7	3	6	4	-9	-9	-19	-2	-4	3	-20
Philadelphia Phillies	-10	14	-10	3	-8	-1	-9	-22	4	10	-29
Texas Rangers	-16	-8	-1	-9	10	-11	-8	7	-7	12	-31
Tampa Bay Rays	-13	-6	0	1	-4	-24	7	-1	6	2	-32
Chicago White Sox	-3	0	-16	2	-12	-5	-10	9	-21	11	-45
Detroit Tigers	-7	2	-6	21	-32	-9	-4	-7	-22	8	-56
Minnesota Twins	-13	-10	2	-3	3	-2	-25	-3	-23	7	-67
Cleveland Indians	-5	8	-10	-7	-19	-5	-10	-11	-16	7	-68

Batting By Position

Pos	AB	H	2B	3B	HR	(Hm	Rd)	TB	R	RBI	TBB	IBB	SO	HBP	SH	SF	SB	CS	SB%	GDP	LOB	Avg	OBP	Slg
P	4746	579	93	3	15	(6	9)	723	234	186	159	0	2011	19	558	10	2	1	.67	59	2014	.122	.153	.152
C	17454	4281	877	30	469	(232	237)	6625	1752	2118	1481	92	4074	210	90	155	44	54	.45	460	5751	.245	.309	.380
1B	18212	4649	1014	45	666	(334	332)	7751	2300	2550	1982	192	4181	165	12	173	105	58	.64	431	5707	.255	.331	.426
2B	18613	4774	913	119	340	(169	171)	6945	2263	1878	1393	103	3429	190	133	140	390	139	.74	406	5540	.256	.313	.373
3B	18433	4775	944	65	491	(225	266)	7322	2134	2222	1483	103	3934	172	57	156	175	80	.69	470	5695	.259	.318	.397
SS	18172	4635	860	110	322	(169	153)	6681	2085	1750	1362	102	3473	156	159	130	389	131	.75	411	5438	.255	.310	.368
LF	18424	4737	958	120	491	(242	249)	7408	2304	2148	1624	81	4226	209	92	137	388	137	.74	362	5271	.257	.322	.402
CF	18959	5020	906	185	393	(202	191)	7475	2507	1794	1577	69	4244	175	122	125	745	221	.77	280	4981	.265	.325	.394
RF	18668	4866	939	129	538	(281	257)	7677	2390	2225	1632	104	4178	177	58	129	340	143	.70	371	5222	.261	.324	.411
DH	9093	2248	432	27	363	(189	174)	3823	1075	1271	844	94	2207	113	7	74	53	24	.69	258	2758	.247	.317	.420
PH	4831	1030	201	16	98	(43	55)	1557	463	603	483	45	1480	66	55	48	46	24	.66	105	1993	.213	.291	.322
PR	6	1	0	0	0	(0	0)	1	254	0	0	0	0	0	0	0	87	23	.79	0	12	.167	.167	.167

Fielding By Position

Pos	Inn	PO	Ast	E	(Throw	Field)	TC	DP	GDP	FPct
P	14538.0	2626	5086	384	302	82	8096	382	264	.953
C	14538.0	37643	2697	295	231	50	40635	257	15	.993
1B	14538.0	41047	3212	321	68	240	44580	3853	231	.993
2B	14538.0	8736	13745	383	143	238	22864	3068	1045	.983
3B	14538.0	3270	9034	528	266	259	12832	885	709	.959
SS	14538.0	6500	13571	539	258	280	20610	2881	1348	.974
LF	14538.0	9020	250	151	41	109	9421	45	1	.984
CF	14538.0	12306	240	157	37	120	12703	58		.988
RF	14538.0	9693	317	156	43	111	10166	63		.985

Team Efficiency Summary

The Kansas City Royals had an exultant season in 2014. They ended what was the longest active postseason drought in baseball, qualifying to play October baseball for the first time since 1985. That drought came to an end with the Royals winning 89 games and capturing one of the two Wild Card spots in the American League. A big reason the Royals were able to pull off 89 wins was that they were the most efficient team in baseball. Based on their actual runs scored and runs allowed, they would have been expected to win 84 games. If, instead, one were to use their component stats to calculate their Runs Created and Expected Runs Allowed, then the Royals would only have been expected to win 82 games. Either way, they would have missed the playoffs, and the drought would have tortuously dragged on. But the Royals found a way to put things together to win ballgames better than any other team, and it made all the difference in the world.

In the tables that follow we lay out how efficient each team in baseball was during the 2014 season. Several standards of efficiency are measured. On offense, we use various components of production (singles, doubles, triples, etc.) to calculate the expected number of runs that the team would score and compare that to how many runs they actually scored. The difference in runs scored from expected is their Hitting Efficiency. Similarly, with pitching, we use components such as walks and hits allowed to calculate a team's expected runs allowed, compare that to their actual runs allowed, and call that Pitching Efficiency. Then there is Run Efficiency. That is the difference between the actual number of games a team won and the number of games they would have been expected to win given the team's actual runs scored and runs allowed totals. And finally there is Overall Efficiency. There, we take a team's expected runs scored and expected runs allowed to calculate their Efficiency Wins total and compare that to their actual number of games won.

2014 American League Team Efficiency Summary

	RC	Runs	Hit Eff	Exp RA	RA	Pit Eff	Exp Wins	Wins	Runs Eff	Eff Wins	Wins	Overall Eff
Kansas City Royals	653	651	100	642	624	103	84	89	105	82	89	108
New York Yankees	645	633	98	660	664	99	77	84	109	79	84	106
Baltimore Orioles	712	705	99	623	593	105	95	96	101	92	96	105
Texas Rangers	621	637	103	768	773	99	66	67	102	64	67	105
Chicago White Sox	660	660	100	739	758	98	70	73	105	72	73	102
Seattle Mariners	601	634	106	563	554	102	92	87	95	86	87	101
Los Angeles Angels	729	773	106	600	630	95	97	98	101	97	98	101
Cleveland Indians	686	669	98	655	653	100	83	85	103	85	85	100
Detroit Tigers	771	757	98	679	705	96	87	90	104	91	90	99
Boston Red Sox	640	634	99	697	715	98	71	71	100	74	71	96
Toronto Blue Jays	729	723	99	677	686	99	85	83	97	87	83	95
Houston Astros	638	629	99	690	723	95	70	70	100	75	70	94
Minnesota Twins	706	715	101	755	777	97	74	70	94	76	70	93
Oakland Athletics	685	729	106	570	572	100	100	88	88	96	88	92
Tampa Bay Rays	643	612	95	613	625	98	79	77	97	85	77	91

2014 National League Team Efficiency Summary

	RC	Runs	Hit Eff	Exp RA	RA	Pit Eff	Exp Wins	Wins	Runs Eff	Eff Wins	Wins	Overall Eff
San Diego Padres	527	535	102	591	577	102	75	77	103	72	77	107
St Louis Cardinals	634	619	98	593	603	98	83	90	108	86	90	104
New York Mets	616	629	102	650	618	105	82	79	96	77	79	103
Milwaukee Brewers	648	650	100	656	657	100	80	82	102	80	82	102
Atlanta Braves	595	573	96	617	597	103	78	79	102	78	79	101
Cincinnati Reds	582	595	102	624	612	102	79	76	97	75	76	101
Miami Marlins	650	645	99	668	674	99	77	77	99	79	77	98
Washington Nationals	704	686	98	558	555	101	98	96	98	99	96	97
Pittsburgh Pirates	729	682	94	643	631	102	87	88	101	91	88	97
San Francisco Giants	657	665	101	572	614	93	87	88	101	92	88	96
Philadelphia Phillies	622	619	100	659	687	96	73	73	101	76	73	96
Los Angeles Dodgers	749	718	96	608	617	99	93	94	101	98	94	96
Chicago Cubs	620	614	99	650	707	92	70	73	105	77	73	95
Arizona Diamondbacks	619	615	99	710	742	96	66	64	97	70	64	91
Colorado Rockies	783	755	96	799	818	98	75	66	89	79	66	83

Adrian Gonzalez   Alex Gordon
Dustin Pedroia   Juan Lagares
Josh Donaldson   Jason Heyward
Andrelton Simmons Jonathan Lucroy
Lorenzo Cain   Dallas Keuchel

THE FIELDING BIBLE AWARDS 2014

The Fielding Bible Awards 2014

John Dewan

The final four teams competing to win their respective league championships this year were the St. Louis Cardinals against the San Francisco Giants in the National League and the Kansas City Royals and the Baltimore Orioles in the AL. What is the most common element that sets these teams apart compared to the other 26 teams in baseball? It's defense. The Orioles and Cardinals had the best defense in each of their leagues (based on Defensive Runs Saved). The Royals were third best in the AL while the Giants were above average in the NL. Looking at batting and pitching, only one team ranked as high as third in any major category (Baltimore, third in the AL in pitching). Defense matters.

The importance of defense and using analytics to measure it has become part of baseball's culture. Baseball highlights involving defense are a mainstay of baseball recap shows. Using defensive metrics such as Defensive Runs Saved and Ultimate Zone Rating has become well accepted. Even the Gold Glove voting has come around to using analytics as a component for determining the Gold Glove Awards.

In 2014, eight of the ten winners of The Fielding Bible Award were also the MLB leader in Defensive Runs Saved. The other two came in second. It is clear that today's baseball experts trust and rely on the fact that the new defensive metrics can truly measure defense.

We've added a 10th Fielding Bible Award this year: the Multi-Position award. Defensive excellence at multiple positions and the value of versatility to play multiple positions is now being recognized. The inaugural winner of this award is Kansas City's Lorenzo Cain.

In this, the ninth year of The Fielding Bible Awards, five other players join Cain as first time winners: Adrian Gonzalez (Dodgers) at first base, Josh Donaldson (A's) at third, Juan Lagares (Mets) in center field, and a pitcher-catcher battery combination of Dallas Keuchel of the Astros and Brewer Jonathan Lucroy. Atlanta teammates Andrelton Simmons (shortstop) and Jason Heyward (right field) win their second awards. Third time winners are Dustin Pedroia at second base and Alex Gordon with his third consecutive award in left field.

Here's a short refresher course on how the awards are determined: We asked our panel of twelve experts to rank 10 players at each position on a scale from one to ten. We then use the same voting technique as the Major League Baseball MVP voting. A first place vote gets 10 points, second place 9 points, third place 8 points, etc. Total up the points for each player and the player with the most points wins the award. A perfect score is 120.

One important distinction that differentiates our award from most other baseball awards, including the Gold Gloves, is that we only have one winner for all of Major League Baseball, instead of separate winners for each league. Our intention is to continue to stand up and say, "This is the best fielder at this position in the major leagues last season."

Here are the Fielding Bible Awards for the 2014 season:

First Base – Adrian Gonzalez, Los Angeles Dodgers

 Adrian Gonzalez has been the best defensive first baseman in baseball over the last six seasons but somehow he has never won a Fielding Bible Award. Until now. Gonzalez wins his first Fielding Bible Award, leading all of baseball's first basemen by saving 11 runs defensively for the Dodgers in 2014. That brings his six-year total to 62 runs saved, 12 more than Albert Pujols' second-place total of 50. Every aspect of Gonzalez's defensive game is superb. He fields his position well, does a great job with difficult throws, and handles bunts and double plays with the best of them. But he's not flashy. Just consistently excellent.

Previous Winners:

2013	Paul Goldschmidt	2009	Albert Pujols
2012	Mark Teixeira	2008	Albert Pujols
2011	Albert Pujols	2007	Albert Pujols
2010	Daric Barton	2006	Albert Pujols

Second Base – Dustin Pedroia, Boston Red Sox

 This is classic Dustin Pedroia: in a game early in the season J.J. Hardy hits a ball sharply up the middle that literally goes through the legs of the pitcher. Pedroia ranges a long way from the normal second base position and dives to field the ball as it enters the grass in short center field. He gets up in less than the blink of an eye while his momentum carries him to the shortstop side of second base. He makes an incredibly difficult and accurate off-balance throw from the outfield grass that would be a huge challenge for a strong-armed shortstop, let alone a second baseman. And the throw has enough velocity to nab Hardy at first base by an eyelash. That one play shows so many of Pedroia's skills: excellent speed, great range, willingness to lay out for anything within reach, incredible quickness getting back up to his feet, quick reactions and a strong arm. This is Pedroia's second consecutive Fielding Bible Award and third overall.

Previous Winners:

2013	Dustin Pedroia	2009	Aaron Hill
2012	Darwin Barney	2008	Brandon Phillips
2011	Dustin Pedroia	2007	Aaron Hill
2010	Chase Utley	2006	Orlando Hudson

Third Base – Josh Donaldson, Oakland Athletics

Josh Donaldson led all MLB third basemen with 20 Defensive Runs Saved. Here's another way to measure Donaldson's excellence. Baseball Info Solutions tracks a stat invented by Bill James called Good Fielding Plays (GFP). It's not as easy as it sounds to define a Good Fielding Play—there are 28 different categories of GFPs. Donaldson's total of 77 GFPs is 13 more than the 64 good plays handled by Colorado's Nolan Arenado. Donaldson is especially good making plays to his right where his excellent reaction time and strong arm really stand out. Nolan Arenado was second in the voting: Donaldson 114 points, Arenado 104.

Previous Winners:

2013	Manny Machado	2009	Ryan Zimmerman
2012	Adrian Beltre	2008	Adrian Beltre
2011	Adrian Beltre	2007	Pedro Feliz
2010	Evan Longoria	2006	Adrian Beltre

Shortstop – Andrelton Simmons, Atlanta Braves

For the second consecutive year Andrelton Simmons wins the Fielding Bible Award with a unanimous vote, first on all 12 ballots for a perfect score of 120 points each year. That expression of how good Simmons is, as rated by the expert Fielding Bible Award panel, might actually fall short of how good he really is. His range is incredible. His reaction time is incredible. His hands are incredible, on backhand plays and on transfers from his glove hand to his throwing hand. And he has the strongest, most accurate throwing arm in the game. Simmons' three-year total of 88 runs saved are the most in baseball by 19 runs (Alex Gordon and Jason Heyward have 67), and blows away the second-best shortstop total of 36 runs saved by J.J. Hardy by a huge margin.

Previous Winners:

2013	Andrelton Simmons	2009	Jack Wilson
2012	Brendan Ryan	2008	Jimmy Rollins
2011	Troy Tulowitzki	2007	Troy Tulowitzki
2010	Troy Tulowitzki	2006	Adam Everett

Left Field – Alex Gordon, Kansas City Royals

It's a three-peat for Alex Gordon. Three Fielding Bible Awards in three years.

And it was unanimous. Every voter had Alex Gordon ranked first. Gordon saved 27 runs for the Royals on the year. This is the highest total ever recorded for a left fielder since the tracking of Defensive Runs Saved began in 2003. Christian Yelich of Miami was a distant second with 13. Gordon's converted third-baseman arm has always set him apart. It counted toward nine of his runs saved in 2014, but his excellent range also makes a huge difference. His range in left field has been above average every year since he started playing there in 2010, but this year he had his career high with 16 Plus/Minus Runs Saved.

Previous Winners:

2013	Alex Gordon	2009	Carl Crawford
2012	Alex Gordon	2008	Carl Crawford
2011	Brett Gardner	2007	Eric Byrnes
2010	Brett Gardner	2006	Carl Crawford

Center Field – Juan Lagares, New York Mets

In 2013, Juan Lagares started only 88 games in center field, yet he saved 26 runs there defensively for the Mets. He finished second in the 2013 Fielding Bible Award voting. This year he started 105 games, blew away the field with another 28 runs saved, and won his first Fielding Bible Award. His throwing arm in center field is superb and deeply respected by baserunners; he had six Outfield Arm Runs Saved in 2014. But it's his ability to cover ground that sets him above the rest. He saved 20 more bases on deep balls than an average center fielder (+20 Plus/Minus), the highest total among all center fielders. This is true despite the fact that, generally speaking, he plays on the shallow side. He had a +11 total on shallow balls, second best among center fielders. His +9 on medium hit balls was fourth best. Lagares finished first on every ballot except one.

Previous Winners:

2013	Carlos Gomez	2009	Franklin Gutierrez
2012	Mike Trout	2008	Carlos Beltran
2011	Austin Jackson	2007	Andruw Jones
2010	Michael Bourn	2006	Carlos Beltran

Right Field – Jason Heyward, Atlanta Braves

The Fielding Bible Award voters were unanimous about Jason Heyward as well. Heyward is the best defensive right fielder in baseball, bar none. He has had double-digit runs saved totals in every season of his five-year career. What makes him so consistently good? He refuses to allow an extra-base hit. Over his career he has been a bit above average on shallow hit balls (+18 plays in the Plus/Minus System) and on medium hit balls (+31). On deeply hit balls he is phenomenal. +140! That means he has saved 140 more bases making catches on deeply hit balls than an average right fielder. He was +40 on deeply hit balls in 2014 alone. Think of it like this: he saved 20 doubles last year! He excels at picking the ball up quickly off the bat and he always takes a good route to the ball. Overall, he had 32 Runs Saved for the Braves defensively in 2014, the highest total at any position in 2014 and a career high for Heyward.

Previous Winners:

2013	Gerardo Parra	2009	Ichiro Suzuki
2012	Jason Heyward	2008	Franklin Gutierrez
2011	Justin Upton	2007	Alex Rios
2010	Ichiro Suzuki	2006	Ichiro Suzuki

Catcher – Jonathan Lucroy, Milwaukee Brewers

It is high time that catchers become recognized defensively for more than just their throwing arm. Jonathan Lucroy is another first-time winner of a Fielding Bible Award and the first of a new breed. Lucroy has an average throwing arm, but his other skills are so much better than everyone else, the expert panel rated him the best overall defensive catcher in baseball in 2014. One area that he excels is in handling pitches thrown in the dirt and other potential wild pitches. Baseball Info Solutions calculates a stat called Catcher Block Rate. It's based on how often a catcher successfully handles difficult pitches. Lucroy's 96% rate in 2014 was the best in baseball. The panel also received a preview version of the new Strike Zone Plus/Minus system from Baseball Info Solutions, previously available only to major league teams, but now to be unveiled in *The Fielding Bible—Volume IV* coming out in the spring. The system measures the ability of a catcher to frame pitches, to get strike calls on borderline pitches. Since 2010 Lucroy has gotten the most extra strikes called of any catcher in the game: 715 extra strikes, saving an estimated 85 runs. The next best total is a distant second: Miguel Montero with 407 extra strikes and 48 runs saved. The voting for the award was close. Lucroy garnered 105 voting points to 102 for Russell Martin of the Pittsburgh Pirates.

Previous Winners:

2013	Yadier Molina	2009	Yadier Molina
2012	Yadier Molina	2008	Yadier Molina
2011	Matt Wieters	2007	Yadier Molina
2010	Yadier Molina	2006	Ivan Rodriguez

Pitcher – Dallas Keuchel, Houston Astros

Dallas Keuchel out-Buehrle'd Mark Buehrle. He one-upped the World's Best Pitcher, Clayton Kershaw. And he duked it out with last year's Fielding Bible Award winner, R.A. Dickey, and won his first Fielding Bible Award for defensive excellence at the pitcher position. Keuchel led all major league pitchers with ten Defensive Runs Saved, better than the second-best total of seven runs saved by Kershaw. The dynamic defensive duo of R.A. Dickey and Mark Buehrle, who've won the last five Fielding Bible Awards at pitcher, saved five runs and two runs, respectively, for the Toronto Blue Jays. Keuchel is channeling Mark Buehrle as he allowed only one runner to steal a base all season, but his ability to cover his position (seven runs saved based on the Plus/Minus System measuring range) is where he excels. Keuchel received 109 voting points. Kershaw was second with 95.

Previous Winners:

2013	R.A. Dickey	2009	Mark Buehrle
2012	Mark Buehrle	2008	Kenny Rodgers
2011	Mark Buehrle	2007	Johan Santana
2010	Mark Buehrle	2006	Greg Maddux

Multi-Position – Lorenzo Cain, Kansas City Royals

This is the first year of the Multi-Position Fielding Bible Award. The goal of this new award is to recognize players who bring versatility to their teams with their ability to play multiple positions, and who play those positions well defensively. Lorenzo Cain was so good in 2014 that if he played full-time in either center field or right field, he might have won the Fielding Bible Award at either position. He saved 14 runs in center field in 93 games he started there for the Royals on the season, and another 10 runs in right despite only 29 games started there. Cain's ability to play right field gives the Royals the best outfield defense in baseball by a wide margin with fellow FBA winner Alex Gordon in left field and baseball's fastest player, Jarrod Dyson, in center. In the closest of margins in this year's balloting, Cain edged out Mr. Versatility, Ben Zobrist of the Tampa Bay Rays, by three points, 92 to 89.

Background of the Fielding Bible Awards

While *The Fielding Bible*, *The Fielding Bible—Volume II*, and *The Fielding Bible—Volume III* put a lot of emphasis on the numbers, especially Defensive Runs Saved and the Plus-Minus system, we feel that visual observation and subjective judgment are still very important parts of determining the best defensive players. Also, we believe people have a right to know who is voting and all the players they are voting for. Therefore, in setting up the Fielding Bible Awards, we took the following steps:

1. *We appointed a panel of experts to vote.* We have a panel of twelve experts plus three "tie-breaker" ballots. (See below.)

2. *We rate everybody in one group.* The Gold Glove vote is divided into National League and American League. We make ours different by putting everybody together. Besides, is playing shortstop in the American League one thing and playing shortstop in the National League a different thing, or are they really very much the same thing? A few years back we had a great example of this decision. Without the Fielding Bible Award, Jack Wilson wins *nada*, because he switched leagues in mid-year. According to our panelists (and unlike the Gold Glove voters), Jack was the best fielding shortstop in baseball in 2009. Period. He deserved to be recognized for that.

3. *We use a ten-man ballot and a ten-point scale.* We use a ten-man ballot. We give ten points for first place, nine points for second place, etc, down to one point for tenth place. We feel strongly that a ten-man ballot with weighted positions leads to more accurate outcomes.

4. *We defined the list of candidates.* Only players who actually were regulars at the position are candidates. This eliminates the possibility of a vote going to somebody who wasn't really playing the position.

5. *We are publishing the balloting.* We summarize the voting at each position, clearly identifying whom everybody voted for. Publishing the actual vote totals encourages the voters to take their votes more seriously. Also, we feel the public will have more respect for the voting if they have more insight into the process.

A perfect score is 120 points. If all 12 voters place one player first on their ballot, he scores 120. Three players had perfect scores of 120 this year: Andrelton Simmons, Alex Gordon, and Jason Heyward.

Here are the tie-breaker rules (which came into play in our very first year, and did so again last year, as well as in 2010). They are applied one at a time until we have a winner:

1. Most first-place votes wins.
2. Count the tie-breaker ballots, highest point tally wins.
3. Award goes to player with the higher plus/minus rating.

Ballots were due four days after the end of the regular season. Here is this year's panel:

Since you have this book, you probably know **Bill James**, a baseball writer and analyst published for more than thirty years. Bill is the Senior Baseball Operations Advisor for the Boston Red Sox.

The **BIS Video Scouts** at Baseball Info Solutions (BIS) study every game of the season, multiple times, charting a huge list of valuable game details.

As the MLB Network on-air host of *Clubhouse Confidential* and *MLB Now*, **Brian Kenny** brings an analytical perspective on the game of baseball to a national television audience. He also won a 2003 Sports Emmy Award as host of ESPN's *Baseball Tonight*.

Dave Cameron is the Managing Editor of FanGraphs. He resides in Winston-Salem, North Carolina, where the local minor league team once forced him to watch Michael Morse play shortstop for an entire season. He has appreciated defensive value ever since.

Doug Glanville played nine seasons in Major League Baseball and was well known for his excellent outfield defense. Currently, he is a baseball analyst at ESPN on *Baseball Tonight* and ESPN.com, as well as a regular contributor to *The New York Times*.

The man who created Strat-O-Matic Baseball, **Hal Richman**, continues to lead his company's annual in-depth analysis of each player's season. Hal cautions SOM players that his voting on this ballot may or may not reflect the eventual fielding ratings for players in his game. Ballots were due prior to the completion of his annual research effort to evaluate player defense.

Named the best sports columnist in America in 2012 by the National Sportswriters and Sportscasters Hall of Fame, **Joe Posnanski** is the National Columnist at NBC Sports.

For over twenty-five years, BIS owner **John Dewan** has collected, analyzed, and published in-depth baseball statistics and analysis. He has authored or co-authored three volumes of *The Fielding Bible*, with *Volume IV* expected in March of 2015.

Mark Simon has been a researcher for ESPN Stats & Information since 2002 and currently helps oversee the Stats & Information blog and Twitter (@espnstatsinfo). He is a regular contributor on baseball (often writing on defense) for ESPNNY.com and ESPN.com.

Peter Gammons serves as on-air and online analyst for MLB Network, MLB.com and NESN (New England Sports Network). He is the 56th recipient of the J. G. Taylor Spink Award for outstanding baseball writing given by the BBWAA (Baseball Writers Association of America).

Rob Neyer has been a working writer for 25 years, and currently is best-known as FOXSports.com's Senior Baseball Editor. His seventh book, *Untitled*, will be published after he writes it.

The **Tom Tango Fan Poll** represents the results of a poll taken at the website, Tango on Baseball (www.tangotiger.net). Besides hosting the website, Tom writes research articles devoted to sabermetrics and is the co-author of *The Book: Playing the Percentages in Baseball*.

Our three tie-breakers are **Ben Jedlovec**, president of Baseball Info Solutions and co-author of *The Fielding Bible—Volume III*, **Dan Casey**, veteran Video Scout and Operations Analyst at BIS, and **Sean Forman**, the founder of Baseball-Reference.com.

The Fielding Bible Awards

Below we show the final point tally for The Fielding Bible Awards in the 2014 season. We asked a panel of experts to complete a 10-man ballot ranking players from 1 to 10 based on their defensive abilities. We show the ranks in the tables below. We then awarded points in the same way as Major League Baseball's MVP voting: 10 points for a first place vote, 9 for second, etc., down to 1 point for 10th place. We cover all nine positions, looking at only their fielding work for the 2014 season. Position players are eligible if they played at least 600 innings while catchers require a minimum of 500 innings. Either can qualify with 10 Runs Saved, as well. Pitchers require a minimum of 120 innings pitched or 5 Runs Saved.

For the first time in 2014, we are also introducing a Multi-Position Award for fielders who are excellent defensive players but do not call any one position their home. For a player to qualify for the Multi-Position Award, he must have played at least 600 innings across all positions and played no more than 70 percent of those innings at any one position.

First Basemen

First Basemen	Bill	BIS Video Scouts	Brian	Dave	Doug	Hal	Joe	John	Mark	Peter	Rob	Tango Fan Poll	Total Points
Adrian Gonzalez	2	1	1	2	1	2	1	1	2	1	1	7	110
Anthony Rizzo	4	4	2	1	8	3		3	9	2	2	4	79
Justin Morneau	1	2	10	4	3		4	6	1	3	5	9	73
Albert Pujols	8	7	9	6	6	7	2	4	5	6	3	8	61
Yonder Alonso		5	3	3			3	2	4		4		53
Matt Adams	5	3		8	2	10	5	7	7	7	8		48
Mike Napoli		6		9	5		6	5	3	5	7	10	43
Paul Goldschmidt	6		6			1	8	10		9		1	36
Chris Davis	3	9		5		9			6	4			30
Mark Teixeira			4	10		8	10	9			6	3	27

Others receiving points: James Loney 18, Lucas Duda 16, Eric Hosmer 16, Steve Pearce 16, Freddie Freeman 14, Ike Davis 7, Adam LaRoche 6, Mark Reynolds 4, Joe Mauer 2, Miguel Cabrera 1

Second Basemen

Second Basemen	Bill	BIS Video Scouts	Brian	Dave	Doug	Hal	Joe	John	Mark	Peter	Rob	Tango Fan Poll	Total Points
Dustin Pedroia	3	1	2	1	1	1	2	1	1	1	3	1	114
Ian Kinsler	4	2	1	3	3	6	1	2	2	2	2	6	98
D.J. LeMahieu	2	3	3	2	2	5	3	3	3	3	1		91
Darwin Barney	1	6	7	6	4	3	5	4	6		4	3	72
Brandon Phillips	7	5	9	5	6	4	8	5	4	6	7	2	64
Jonathan Schoop	5	4	5	7	5	7	6	6	5	7	6		58
Chase Utley		7	4	4		10	4	10		4	8		37
Howie Kendrick		8	6	8	8		7	8	8	5	5		36
Robinson Cano	8			2			10					4	20
Eric Sogard			8	10	7	8		7	7		10		20

Others receiving points: Kolten Wong 10, Gordon Beckham 9, Ben Zobrist 9, Brian Dozier 7, Danny Espinosa 6, Dee Gordon 5, Omar Infante 3, Jose Altuve 1

Third Basemen

Third Basemen	Bill	BIS Video Scouts	Brian	Dave	Doug	Hal	Joe	John	Mark	Peter	Rob	Tango Fan Poll	Total Points
Josh Donaldson	1	1	1	2	1	2	1	2	1	1	1	4	114
Nolan Arenado	4	2	2	4	2	1	2	1	2	2	4	2	104
Juan Uribe	8	4	3	3	3	7	4	3	4	10	2	5	76
Chase Headley	9	5	7	1	7	6	5	6	3	3	3		66
Adrian Beltre	3	3	5	5	6	4	6	7	8	7	10	3	65
David Wright	5	8	4		5		3	4	5	4			50
Manny Machado	6	10	10	7	9	3	7	5	9		5	1	49
Anthony Rendon	2	7		9	4	10	8	9	6	5	6	7	48
Kyle Seager	7	6	8	6	8		9			6	8	8	33
Josh Harrison	10	9		8		9		8	7		9	10	18

Others receiving points: Todd Frazier 15, Evan Longoria 11, Pablo Sandoval 7, Martin Prado 2, Matt Carpenter 1, Trevor Plouffe 1

Shortstops

Shortstops	Bill	BIS Video Scouts	Brian	Dave	Doug	Hal	Joe	John	Mark	Peter	Rob	Tango Fan Poll	Total Points
Andrelton Simmons	1	1	1	1	1	1	1	1	1	1	1	1	120
Zack Cozart	2	2	2	2	2	2	3	2	2	2	2	4	105
J.J. Hardy	4	4	4	3	6	5	4	3	5	3	3	7	81
Jhonny Peralta		3	3	4	3		2	6	4	4	4		66
Troy Tulowitzki	3	6	5	8	7	3	5	5	6		6	2	65
Jordy Mercer	6	5	8	6	4		6	7	3	5	7		53
Brandon Crawford		8	6	7	5			4	8	6	5	3	47
Alcides Escobar	5	9	10			6				9		8	19
Jimmy Rollins			9	9	9		8			8		5	18
Erick Aybar	9		7	10		7	7					10	16

Others receiving points: Alexi Amarista 12, Ian Desmond 10, Elvis Andrus 7, Didi Gregorius 7, Chris Owings 7, Ruben Tejada 6, Adeiny Hechavarria 5, Marwin Gonzalez 4, Miguel Rojas 4, Jean Segura 3, Alexei Ramirez 2, Everth Cabrera 1, Yunel Escobar 1, Brad Miller 1

Left Fielders

Left Fielders	Bill	BIS Video Scouts	Brian	Dave	Doug	Hal	Joe	John	Mark	Peter	Rob	Tango Fan Poll	Total Points
Alex Gordon	1	1	1	1	1	1	1	1	1	1	1	1	120
Christian Yelich	3	2	2	2	2	4	2	4	3	2	2	5	99
Yoenis Cespedes	7	3	4	3	7	5	3	3	2	3	3	7	82
Starling Marte	6	4	3		3	2	5	2	4	5	4	2	81
Brett Gardner	8	5	5	4	4	3	7	5	6	6	5	3	71
Dustin Ackley	2	6	6	5	6	9	4	6	5	4	9		59
Michael Brantley	9	8	7		8	6		10		7	8	4	32
Khris Davis		7	9	10	5		9	9	8	8	6		28
Bryce Harper		8	8	9	8	8					10	6	20
Chris Young	4	10	10					7	10	10			15

Others receiving points: Matt Joyce 13, Rajai Davis 7, Melky Cabrera 6, Shin-Soo Choo 5, Ryan Ludwick 5, Chris Coghlan 4, Carl Crawford 4, Alejandro De Aza 3, Justin Upton 3, Matt Holliday 2, Corey Dickerson 1

Center Fielders

Center Fielders	Bill	BIS Video Scouts	Brian	Dave	Doug	Hal	Joe	John	Mark	Peter	Rob	Tango Fan Poll	Total Points
Juan Lagares	2	1	1	1	1	1	1	1	1	1	1	1	119
Jackie Bradley, Jr.	1	3	3	3	2	5	3	8	3	4	2	2	93
Billy Hamilton	8	2	5	2	6		2	5	2	3	4	7	75
Jarrod Dyson	4	5	4	4	3	7	4	4	5		7		63
Leonys Martin	5	8	2	8	7	10	6	3	7	2	3		60
Lorenzo Cain	10	6	6	10	4	6	5	2	6		6	6	54
Adam Eaton	3	7	8		5			6	4	5			39
Peter Bourjos	7	10		5		2		10		8	8	5	33
Ender Inciarte	9	4	9	6	8			9	8		5		30
Carlos Gomez						4	7	7		9		3	25

Others receiving points: Marcell Ozuna 20, Mike Trout 16, Adam Jones 9, Denard Span 7, Jacoby Ellsbury 4, Sam Fuld 4, Desmond Jennings 4, Andrew McCutchen 3, Dexter Fowler 1, Austin Jackson 1

Right Fielders

Right Fielders	Bill	BIS Video Scouts	Brian	Dave	Doug	Hal	Joe	John	Mark	Peter	Rob	Tango Fan Poll	Total Points
Jason Heyward	1	1	1	1	1	1	1	1	1	1	1	1	120
Kevin Kiermaier	4	2	2	2	2	2	2	4	8	2	7	2	93
Josh Reddick	5	3	5	3	3	3	5	2	2	7	2	3	89
Giancarlo Stanton	3	4	4	8	4	9	7	8	4	4	5	9	63
Nate Schierholtz	2	9	8	6	10	4		5	6		3		46
Marlon Byrd	10	10	3		5		4	3	5		4		44
Daniel Nava	8	5	7	4			3	6	7		8		40
Gerardo Parra			10	5	6			7		5	6	4	34
Nick Markakis	6	6				7			3	6		8	30
Kole Calhoun		7			7		7	6		9	3		27

Others receiving points: Yasiel Puig 17, Ichiro Suzuki 14, Hunter Pence 13, Jay Bruce 8, Jose Bautista 7, Curtis Granderson 5, Chris Denorfia 4, Nori Aoki 3, David Peralta 2, Collin Cowgill 1

Catchers

Catchers	Bill	BIS Video Scouts	Brian	Dave	Doug	Hal	Joe	John	Mark	Peter	Rob	Tango Fan Poll	Total Points
Jonathan Lucroy	5	2	1	1	2	2	1	1	1	2	1	8	105
Russell Martin	4	1	2	2	1	4	4	2	3	3	2	2	102
Yadier Molina	3	4	3	5	4	1	2	3	2	1		1	92
Salvador Perez	1	3	4	9	6	3	3	6	4	6	3	4	80
Yan Gomes	10	7		8	9	5	6	4	10	4	6	3	49
Rene Rivera		5	8	3	5		9	9	6		5		38
Hank Conger	6		7		3		5	7	5		10		34
Buster Posey	8		5	10	10		10	5	8	7	8	6	33
Christian Vazquez	2	6		7					9	5			26
Caleb Joseph	9	8	9			7	9	7		7			21

Others receiving points: Jose Molina 17, Mike Zunino 16, Ryan Hanigan 8, Miguel Montero 8, Welington Castillo 7, Tyler Flowers 6, Brian McCann 5, Alex Avila 4, Dioner Navarro 3, Carlos Ruiz 3, A.J. Ellis 2, Devin Mesoraco 1

Pitchers

Pitchers	Bill	BIS Video Scouts	Brian	Dave	Doug	Hal	Joe	John	Mark	Peter	Rob	Ben	Total Points
Dallas Keuchel	5	1	1	2	1	3	5	1	1	1	1	1	109
Clayton Kershaw	4	3	6	3	3	2	2	4	2	2	2	3	96
Henderson Alvarez	7	2	5	7	2	4	7	2	3	3	7	2	81
R.A. Dickey	8	5	3	4	6	5	6	6	5	6	3	7	68
Zack Greinke	1	4	10		5	9	3	5	4	4	5	5	66
Johnny Cueto	10	6	2	1	4	1	9	3		5	9	6	65
Mark Buehrle	2	10	4	5		6	4	8	9	9	10	8	46
Adam Wainwright	6	7	7			8	1	10	6	7	4	9	45
Julio Teheran		9	8	8	7	7		7			6	4	32
Madison Bumgarner				6					8				8

Others receiving points: David Price 8, J.A. Happ 5, Mike Leake 5, Sonny Gray 4, Masahiro Tanaka 4, Edwin Jackson 3, Garrett Richards 3, James Shields 3, Stephen Strasburg 3, Kyle Kendrick 2, Seth Maness 2, Andrew Cashner 1, Tanner Roark 1

Multi-Position

Pitchers	Bill	BIS Video Scouts	Brian	Dave	Doug	Hal	Joe	John	Mark	Peter	Rob	Tango Fan Poll	Total Points
Lorenzo Cain	3	3	2	3	1	1	2	1	1	8	9	6	92
Ben Zobrist	1	5	6	1	3	5	1	7	7	4	1	2	89
Josh Harrison	8	2	1	5	7	4	9	2	2	3	3	3	83
Kevin Kiermaier	4	1	4	4	2	2		8		1		4	69
Sam Fuld	10	8	7	2	6	3	4		4	2	8	1	66
Brock Holt	2	4	3	6	4					10	2	9	48
Steave Pearce	9	6	5		5		3	6	5		7		42
Daniel Nava	6	7		7				3	8				24
Alexi Amarista					9			4	3				17
Will Venable	5	10				10		5					14

Others receiving points: Yasiel Puig 13, Gregor Blanco 11, Asdrubal Cabrera 11, Stephen Drew 11, Arismendy Alcantara 10, Mike Aviles 10, Rajai Davis 9, Emilio Bonifacio 7, Collin Cowgill 6, Ryan Flaherty 5, Danny Santana 5, Justin Turner 5, Chris Young 5, Mark Reynolds 3, Charlie Blackmon 2, Yasmani Grandal 1, Brayan Pena 1, David Peralta 1

Who Gives A Shift?

John Dewan

Or, maybe the better title to this article would be "If you throw enough shifts against the wall, some of them have gotta stick."

Let's address the main title first. Who does give a shift? Answer: the Houston Astros. Prior to this season, the highest single-season total of shifts deployed by a team was 599 by the Baltimore Orioles in 2013. Six teams exceeded that total in 2014, but the Astros crushed it. The lowly Houston Astros, losers of 92 games, more than doubled the Orioles total with 1,341 shifts this past year.

Over the past four seasons the number of shifts in Major League Baseball, as measured by a ball hit into play when a shift is in effect, has nearly doubled every year. Here are the totals by year:

MLB Shifts by Season

Year	Number of Shifts
2010	2,464
2011	2,357
2012	4,577
2013	8,280
2014	13,296

It is clear that Major League teams have embraced this new defensive strategy. Some more than others. But is it effective? Are the shifts sticking against the wall?

The simplest way to look at this is to see if batting averages go down when the shift is employed. Batting average is not ordinarily the best statistic to use when doing baseball analytics, but in this case it is excellent, because what the shift defense does is prevent singles. This section shows the top 30 most commonly shifted players in 2014. We look at grounders and short liners and see how they performed with and without a defensive shift. Out of these 30 batters, 21 saw a decrease in their batting average on grounders and short liners when they were shifted. If you look at the league as a whole, the average decrease in batting average when players are shifted is about 30 points.

There is another way to look at how effective shifts are. It's more complicated but it's more accurate. We have developed a metric called Shift Runs Saved. It is an estimate of the number of runs saved by a team when employing The Shift Defense. It is a technique similar to other elements of Defensive Runs Saved in that it utilizes info down to the play-by-play level, including direction and velocity of every batted ball. Let's repeat that chart above, but add Shift Runs Saved:

MLB Shifts by Season

Year	Number of Shifts	Shift Runs Saved
2010	2,464	36
2011	2,357	42
2012	4,577	76
2013	8,280	135
2014	13,296	195

As you can see, the more shifts deployed in Major League Baseball, the more runs are saved. And the lowly Astros with their 92 losses? They had the highest total of Shift Runs Saved by a wide margin. They saved 27 runs on their 1,341 shifts. The next best team was the Toronto Blue Jays with 16 runs saved on 686 shifts.

So the answer to all of this is: Shift or get off the pot! Maybe that should have been the title of this article. If you want to save runs, shift. Simple as that. And the more you shift, the more you save. Despite all the shifting that is already done in baseball, many teams are still leaving runs on the table by not committing even more to this strategy.

In *The Fielding Bible—Volume IV*, coming out in the spring, we will provide a more thorough analysis of The Shift Defense.

Shifts by Team

American League

Team	2013	2014	Change
Astros	497	1341	844
Rays	561	824	263
Yankees	476	780	304
Orioles	599	705	106
Blue Jays	250	686	436
Royals	388	543	155
White Sox	72	534	462
Indians	314	516	202
Red Sox	479	498	19
Rangers	357	490	133
Athletics	312	488	176
Twins	85	478	393
Mariners	263	411	148
Angels	250	357	107
Tigers	139	205	66
Total	5042	8856	3814
Average	336	590	254

National League

Team	2013	2014	Change
Pirates	500	659	159
Brewers	544	576	32
Cardinals	107	367	260
Giants	149	361	212
Cubs	508	316	-192
Phillies	45	291	246
Diamondbacks	196	252	56
Padres	88	241	153
Mets	177	221	44
Braves	160	213	53
Reds	298	212	-86
Dodgers	51	208	157
Marlins	181	208	27
Nationals	39	201	162
Rockies	95	114	19
Total	3138	4440	1302
Average	209	296	86

Top 30 Shifted Batters

Batter	Shifted PA	Shift Percent	Grounders and Short Liners Shifted BA	No Shift BA
David Ortiz	505	94.9	.201	.250
Ryan Howard	453	93.6	.167	.333
Chris Davis	400	95.2	.121	.333
Brandon Moss	398	88.1	.236	.091
Brian McCann	394	87.2	.154	.176
Adam Dunn	371	94.6	.223	.200
Lucas Duda	354	77.0	.202	.313
Mark Teixeira	315	82.2	.144	.138
Adam LaRoche	308	71.3	.233	.298
Mike Moustakas	290	70.7	.179	.135
Albert Pujols	279	48.4	.256	.191
Carlos Santana	270	60.0	.144	.321
Anthony Rizzo	269	63.6	.180	.196
Matt Adams	267	59.6	.303	.305
Pedro Alvarez	251	75.1	.263	.167
Kyle Seager	250	52.0	.266	.264
Victor Martinez	242	47.0	.306	.320
Garrett Jones	226	53.3	.253	.303
Jay Bruce	226	59.6	.289	.317
Chris Carter	224	54.9	.250	.327
Jose Bautista	220	45.4	.210	.308
Alex Avila	219	68.4	.177	.325
Curtis Granderson	215	45.8	.290	.262
Edwin Encarnacion	204	51.9	.257	.235
Freddie Freeman	192	38.0	.243	.248
Colby Rasmus	185	68.5	.150	.280
Raul Ibanez	180	79.6	.091	.333
Seth Smith	180	48.0	.173	.253
Josh Hamilton	177	64.1	.219	.300
Alex Gordon	175	36.5	.208	.277

Runs Saved and Plus/Minus Leaders

This section provides the fielding leaders and trailers both for 2014 and over the last three seasons, split by position. Plus/Minus measures range, evaluating fielders based on their ability to turn balls in play into outs. For instance, Andrelton Simmons had a Plus/Minus of +28 in 2014, which means that he converted 28 plays more than an average shortstop given a similar set of balls in play. That was the highest total among all shortstops this season. In contrast, Yunel Escobar made 22 fewer plays (-22 Plus/Minus) than an average shortstop, and that was the worst total by a player at the position.

Plus/Minus provides the foundational component of Defensive Runs Saved, which is the first of the two sets of leaderboards on the following pages. But Runs Saved measures more than just range. Depending on a player's position, Runs Saved also has components that measure his ability to field bunts, to turn double plays, to prevent baserunners from advancing both on balls in play and on stolen base attempts, to limit earned runs, and to make good plays and avoid misplays.

Please see the glossary for a more complete description of Runs Saved and Plus/Minus.

Infield Runs Saved Leaders

First Basemen 3-Year Leaders		Second Basemen 3-Year Leaders		Third Basemen 3-Year Leaders		Shortstops 3-Year Leaders	
Gonzalez,Adrian	38	Barney,Darwin	49	Machado,Manny	48	Simmons,Andrelton	88
Rizzo,Anthony	26	Pedroia,Dustin	43	Arenado,Nolan	46	Hardy,J.J.	36
Votto,Joey	20	LeMahieu,DJ	34	Donaldson,Josh	36	Cozart,Zack	35
Teixeira,Mark	19	Kinsler,Ian	32	Uribe,Juan	36	Ryan,Brendan	31
Alonso,Yonder	18	Ellis,Mark	29	Wright,David	34	Barmes,Clint	28
Napoli,Mike	17	Cano,Robinson	21	Lawrie,Brett	24	Crawford,Brandon	22
Goldschmidt,Paul	15	Casilla,Alexi	19	Beltre,Adrian	17	Florimon,Pedro	22
Pujols,Albert	15	Phillips,Brandon	18	Headley,Chase	15	Peralta,Jhonny	16
Morneau,Justin	13	Goins,Ryan	15	Frazier,Todd	15	Pennington,Cliff	14
Belt,Brandon	12	Pennington,Cliff	13	Prado,Martin	10	Aviles,Mike	13

First Basemen 3-Year Trailers		Second Basemen 3-Year Trailers		Third Basemen 3-Year Trailers		Shortstops 3-Year Trailers	
Moss,Brandon	-20	Weeks,Rickie	-62	Johnson,Chris	-31	Reyes,Jose	-36
Fielder,Prince	-19	Murphy,Daniel	-34	Castellanos,Nick	-30	Jeter,Derek	-35
Dunn,Adam	-18	Altuve,Jose	-28	Cabrera,Miguel	-23	Lowrie,Jed	-31
Howard,Ryan	-17	Hill,Aaron	-18	Freese,David	-21	Nunez,Eduardo	-28
Konerko,Paul	-14	Schumaker,Skip	-17	Nelson,Chris	-19	Cabrera,Asdrubal	-28
Encarnacion,Edwin	-14	Uggla,Dan	-17	Gillaspie,Conor	-19	Rutledge,Josh	-20

First Basemen 2014 Leaders		Second Basemen 2014 Leaders		Third Basemen 2014 Leaders		Shortstops 2014 Leaders	
Gonzalez,Adrian	11	Kinsler,Ian	20	Donaldson,Josh	20	Simmons,Andrelton	28
Alonso,Yonder	9	Pedroia,Dustin	17	Uribe,Juan	17	Cozart,Zack	19
Pearce,Steve	9	LeMahieu,DJ	16	Arenado,Nolan	16	Peralta,Jhonny	17
Morneau,Justin	8	Schoop,Jonathan	10	Wright,David	13	Hardy,J.J.	10
Adams,Matt	8	Barney,Darwin	10	Headley,Chase	13	Mercer,Jordy	9
Davis,Chris	8	Wong,Kolten	9	Rendon,Anthony	12	Crawford,Brandon	8
Napoli,Mike	7	Kendrick,Howie	7	Seager,Kyle	10	Tulowitzki,Troy	7
Rizzo,Anthony	6	Phillips,Brandon	6	Beltre,Adrian	9	Amarista,Alexi	7
Pujols,Albert	6	Sogard,Eric	5	Prado,Martin	8	Owings,Chris	5
Duda,Lucas	5	Hicks,Brandon	5	Harrison,Josh	8	Rollins,Jimmy	4

First Basemen 2014 Trailers		Second Basemen 2014 Trailers		Third Basemen 2014 Trailers		Shortstops 2014 Trailers	
Abreu,Jose	-10	Weeks,Rickie	-17	Castellanos,Nick	-30	Escobar,Yunel	-24
Howard,Ryan	-10	Odor,Rougned	-11	Chisenhall,Lonnie	-14	Reyes,Jose	-16
Freeman,Freddie	-7	Kipnis,Jason	-11	Johnson,Chris	-13	Andrus,Elvis	-13
Encarnacion,Edwin	-5	Cabrera,Asdrubal	-10	Gillaspie,Conor	-12	Jeter,Derek	-12
Singleton,Jon	-5	Murphy,Daniel	-10	Valbuena,Luis	-10	Bogaerts,Xander	-10
Jones,Garrett	-5	Gyorko,Jedd	-9	Freese,David	-9	Lowrie,Jed	-10

Outfield Runs Saved Leaders

Left Fielders 3-Year Leaders		Center Fielders 3-Year Leaders		Right Fielders 3-Year Leaders	
Gordon,Alex	67	Lagares,Juan	54	Heyward,Jason	67
Marte,Starling	36	Gomez,Carlos	43	Reddick,Josh	48
Cespedes,Yoenis	17	Cain,Lorenzo	37	Parra,Gerardo	43
Murphy,David	14	Gentry,Craig	29	Victorino,Shane	25
Lough,David	13	Martin,Leonys	28	Suzuki,Ichiro	19
Prado,Martin	12	Dyson,Jarrod	25	Cain,Lorenzo	19
Blanco,Gregor	12	Pollock,A.J.	25	Byrd,Marlon	18
Yelich,Christian	11	Bourn,Michael	21	Cowgill,Collin	15
Pearce,Steve	10	Span,Denard	20	Ross,Cody	14
Young,Eric	8	Marisnick,Jake	16	Kiermaier,Kevin	14

Left Fielders 3-Year Trailers		Center Fielders 3-Year Trailers		Right Fielders 3-Year Trailers	
Willingham,Josh	-24	Fowler,Dexter	-33	Cuddyer,Michael	-26
Ibanez,Raul	-21	Kemp,Matt	-31	Murphy,David	-18
Holliday,Matt	-19	Saunders,Michael	-29	Pence,Hunter	-18
Quentin,Carlos	-18	Revere,Ben	-26	Arcia,Oswaldo	-16
Coghlan,Chris	-16	De Aza,Alejandro	-24	Choo,Shin-Soo	-16
Brown,Domonic	-15	Pagan,Angel	-20	Cruz,Nelson	-13

Left Fielders 2014 Leaders		Center Fielders 2014 Leaders		Right Fielders 2014 Leaders	
Gordon,Alex	27	Lagares,Juan	28	Heyward,Jason	32
Yelich,Christian	13	Martin,Leonys	15	Kiermaier,Kevin	14
Cespedes,Yoenis	12	Inciarte,Ender	15	Nava,Daniel	14
Marte,Starling	10	Hamilton,Billy	14	Reddick,Josh	13
Ackley,Dustin	7	Bradley Jr.,Jackie	14	Schierholtz,Nate	8
Lough,David	7	Cain,Lorenzo	14	Venable,Will	8
Davis,Khris	5	Dyson,Jarrod	14	Stanton,Giancarlo	7
Young,Eric	5	Eaton,Adam	12	Saunders,Michael	7
Young,Chris	5	Ozuna,Marcell	10	Byrd,Marlon	6
Guyer,Brandon	4	Pollock,A.J.	10	Craig,Allen	3

Left Fielders 2014 Trailers		Center Fielders 2014 Trailers		Right Fielders 2014 Trailers	
Coghlan,Chris	-14	Fowler,Dexter	-20	Hunter,Torii	-18
Gomes,Jonny	-10	Revere,Ben	-18	Murphy,David	-16
Choo,Shin-Soo	-9	Crisp,Coco	-17	Garcia,Avisail	-10
Morse,Michael	-9	McCutchen,Andrew	-11	Arcia,Oswaldo	-10
Viciedo,Dayan	-8	Jones,James	-9	Viciedo,Dayan	-9
Davis,Rajai	-8	Trout,Mike	-9	Aoki,Nori	-8

Pitcher/Catcher Runs Saved Leaders

Pitchers 3-Year Leaders		Catchers 3-Year Leaders	
Dickey,R.A.	18	Molina,Yadier	36
Greinke,Zack	18	Perez,Salvador	28
Buehrle,Mark	18	Castillo,Welington	26
Kershaw,Clayton	17	Martin,Russell	22
Cueto,Johnny	16	Mathis,Jeff	15
Leake,Mike	15	Rivera,Rene	14
Keuchel,Dallas	13	Ruiz,Carlos	14
Alvarez,Henderson	11	Maldonado,Martin	13
Kendrick,Kyle	11	Lucroy,Jonathan	13
Teheran,Julio	11	Gomes,Yan	12

Pitchers 3-Year Trailers		Catchers 3-Year Trailers	
McAllister,Zach	-13	Saltalamacchia,J	-19
Hughes,Phil	-12	Pierzynski,A.J.	-18
Lincecum,Tim	-12	Iannetta,Chris	-17
Feldman,Scott	-12	d'Arnaud,Travis	-17
Burnett,A.J.	-12	Montero,Miguel	-14
Volquez,Edinson	-11		

Pitchers 2014 Leaders		Catchers 2014 Leaders	
Keuchel,Dallas	10	Martin,Russell	12
Kershaw,Clayton	7	Lucroy,Jonathan	11
Alvarez,Henderson	6	Rivera,Rene	9
Cueto,Johnny	6	Ruiz,Carlos	8
Greinke,Zack	5	Joseph,Caleb	8
Wainwright,Adam	5	Perez,Salvador	8
Kendrick,Kyle	5	Molina,Yadier	8
Maness,Seth	5	Avila,Alex	5
Teheran,Julio	5	Castillo,Welington	5
Dickey,R.A.	5	2 tied with	4

Pitchers 2014 Trailers		Catchers 2014 Trailers	
Hughes,Phil	-8	d'Arnaud,Travis	-15
Feldman,Scott	-7	Pierzynski,A.J.	-11
Petit,Yusmeiro	-5	Iannetta,Chris	-10
Lackey,John	-5	Saltalamacchia,J	-8
Burnett,A.J.	-5	Rosario,Wilin	-8
McAllister,Zach	-4	Molina,Jose	-8

Infield Plus/Minus Leaders

First Basemen 3-Year Leaders		Second Basemen 3-Year Leaders		Third Basemen 3-Year Leaders		Shortstops 3-Year Leaders	
Gonzalez,Adrian	+38	Barney,Darwin	+56	Machado,Manny	+61	Simmons,Andrelton	+97
Rizzo,Anthony	+32	Pedroia,Dustin	+47	Arenado,Nolan	+54	Cozart,Zack	+49
Votto,Joey	+24	Kinsler,Ian	+41	Uribe,Juan	+52	Barmes,Clint	+35
Napoli,Mike	+21	LeMahieu,DJ	+40	Wright,David	+45	Ryan,Brendan	+29
Goldschmidt,Paul	+20	Ellis,Mark	+31	Donaldson,Josh	+39	Florimon,Pedro	+29
Teixeira,Mark	+18	Cano,Robinson	+26	Lawrie,Brett	+34	Hardy,J.J.	+27
Belt,Brandon	+17	Phillips,Brandon	+26	Headley,Chase	+29	Crawford,Brandon	+25
Pujols,Albert	+15	Utley,Chase	+18	Frazier,Todd	+22	Peralta,Jhonny	+17
Alonso,Yonder	+13	Casilla,Alexi	+18	Moustakas,Mike	+20	Aviles,Mike	+17
Adams,Matt	+12	Sogard,Eric	+14	Prado,Martin	+18	Pennington,Cliff	+16

First Basemen 3-Year Trailers		Second Basemen 3-Year Trailers		Third Basemen 3-Year Trailers		Shortstops 3-Year Trailers	
Moss,Brandon	-27	Weeks,Rickie	-71	Castellanos,Nick	-39	Reyes,Jose	-48
Fielder,Prince	-20	Altuve,Jose	-41	Cabrera,Miguel	-37	Jeter,Derek	-45
Konerko,Paul	-18	Murphy,Daniel	-31	Johnson,Chris	-33	Cabrera,Asdrubal	-34
Encarnacion,Edwin	-16	Hill,Aaron	-24	Freese,David	-32	Nunez,Eduardo	-33
Dunn,Adam	-15	Schumaker,Skip	-20	Gillaspie,Conor	-31	Rollins,Jimmy	-32
Lind,Adam	-14	Weeks,Jemile	-18	Chisenhall,Lonnie	-26	Lowrie,Jed	-31

First Basemen 2014 Leaders		Second Basemen 2014 Leaders		Third Basemen 2014 Leaders		Shortstops 2014 Leaders	
Adams,Matt	+10	Kinsler,Ian	+30	Uribe,Juan	+22	Simmons,Andrelton	+28
Napoli,Mike	+10	Pedroia,Dustin	+24	Donaldson,Josh	+20	Cozart,Zack	+27
Davis,Chris	+9	LeMahieu,DJ	+20	Headley,Chase	+19	Peralta,Jhonny	+17
Pearce,Steve	+9	Barney,Darwin	+12	Arenado,Nolan	+18	Mercer,Jordy	+13
Gonzalez,Adrian	+8	Wong,Kolten	+9	Wright,David	+17	Cabrera,Everth	+10
Rizzo,Anthony	+7	Sogard,Eric	+9	Prado,Martin	+14	Amarista,Alexi	+10
Pujols,Albert	+7	Roberts,Brian	+9	Seager,Kyle	+13	Segura,Jean	+9
Votto,Joey	+6	Utley,Chase	+8	Harrison,Josh	+9	Owings,Chris	+8
Alonso,Yonder	+6	Phillips,Brandon	+7	Beltre,Adrian	+8	Crawford,Brandon	+7
Morneau,Justin	+5	Zobrist,Ben	+7	Frazier,Todd	+8	Tejada,Ruben	+7

First Basemen 2014 Trailers		Second Basemen 2014 Trailers		Third Basemen 2014 Trailers		Shortstops 2014 Trailers	
Freeman,Freddie	-13	Weeks,Rickie	-19	Castellanos,Nick	-39	Escobar,Yunel	-22
Abreu,Jose	-9	Odor,Rougned	-16	Gillaspie,Conor	-20	Reyes,Jose	-21
Singleton,Jon	-8	Cabrera,Asdrubal	-15	Chisenhall,Lonnie	-16	Andrus,Elvis	-16
Moss,Brandon	-7	Altuve,Jose	-13	Johnson,Chris	-13	Ramirez,Alexei	-14
Santana,Carlos	-7	Hill,Aaron	-12	Freese,David	-11	Ramirez,Hanley	-13
Howard,Ryan	-7	La Stella,Tommy	-8	Valbuena,Luis	-11	Jeter,Derek	-12

Outfield Plus/Minus Leaders

Left Fielders 3-Year Leaders		Center Fielders 3-Year Leaders		Right Fielders 3-Year Leaders	
Marte,Starling	+55	Lagares,Juan	+59	Heyward,Jason	+122
Gordon,Alex	+51	Cain,Lorenzo	+58	Reddick,Josh	+53
Yelich,Christian	+40	Gomez,Carlos	+53	Parra,Gerardo	+49
Heisey,Chris	+23	Dyson,Jarrod	+43	Victorino,Shane	+35
Lough,David	+23	Pollock,A.J.	+37	Cain,Lorenzo	+32
Murphy,David	+22	Gentry,Craig	+36	Stanton,Giancarlo	+31
Blanco,Gregor	+21	Span,Denard	+35	Suzuki,Ichiro	+28
Presley,Alex	+19	Bourjos,Peter	+29	Venable,Will	+28
Crawford,Carl	+18	Bourn,Michael	+28	Kiermaier,Kevin	+26
Davis,Khris	+17	Ellsbury,Jacoby	+25	Ross,Cody	+24

Left Fielders 3-Year Trailers		Center Fielders 3-Year Trailers		Right Fielders 3-Year Trailers	
Cabrera,Melky	-42	Kemp,Matt	-68	Markakis,Nick	-45
Brown,Domonic	-41	Saunders,Michael	-50	Cuddyer,Michael	-42
Kubel,Jason	-38	Jones,Adam	-47	Francoeur,Jeff	-41
Willingham,Josh	-32	Fowler,Dexter	-35	Hunter,Torii	-38
Viciedo,Dayan	-31	Revere,Ben	-31	Bautista,Jose	-37
Duda,Lucas	-26	Cespedes,Yoenis	-25	Arcia,Oswaldo	-31

Left Fielders 2014 Leaders		Center Fielders 2014 Leaders		Right Fielders 2014 Leaders	
Yelich,Christian	+34	Lagares,Juan	+40	Heyward,Jason	+50
Gordon,Alex	+29	Cain,Lorenzo	+26	Kiermaier,Kevin	+26
Davis,Khris	+16	Inciarte,Ender	+24	Reddick,Josh	+19
Marte,Starling	+13	Dyson,Jarrod	+23	Nava,Daniel	+17
Upton,Justin	+12	Eaton,Adam	+20	Venable,Will	+17
Lough,David	+12	Bradley Jr.,Jackie	+18	Granderson,Curtis	+14
Holliday,Matt	+9	Bourjos,Peter	+16	Stanton,Giancarlo	+13
Smith,Seth	+9	Hamilton,Billy	+15	Schierholtz,Nate	+12
Young,Chris	+9	Ozuna,Marcell	+14	Saunders,Michael	+9
Ackley,Dustin	+6	Maybin,Cameron	+14	Suzuki,Ichiro	+7

Left Fielders 2014 Trailers		Center Fielders 2014 Trailers		Right Fielders 2014 Trailers	
Cabrera,Melky	-23	Fowler,Dexter	-29	Hunter,Torii	-28
Coghlan,Chris	-21	Crisp,Coco	-20	Arcia,Oswaldo	-20
Gomes,Jonny	-15	Revere,Ben	-19	Bautista,Jose	-20
Brown,Domonic	-15	Blanco,Gregor	-17	Murphy,David	-17
Morse,Michael	-14	Bourn,Michael	-14	Bruce,Jay	-16
Ludwick,Ryan	-12	Upton,B.J.	-14	Garcia,Avisail	-15

Pitcher Plus/Minus Leaders

Pitchers
3-Year Leaders

Keuchel,Dallas	+17
Dickey,R.A.	+15
Leake,Mike	+15
Greinke,Zack	+13
Alvarez,Henderson	+12
Liriano,Francisco	+12
Cobb,Alex	+11
Stults,Eric	+11
Chen,Wei-Yin	+11
Ziegler,Brad	+11

Pitchers
3-Year Trailers

Hughes,Phil	-14
Scherzer,Max	-12
Mejia,Jenrry	-11
Volquez,Edinson	-10
Gutierrez,Juan	-9
Anderson,Brett	-8

Pitchers
2014 Leaders

Keuchel,Dallas	+10
Alvarez,Henderson	+8
Kershaw,Clayton	+8
Maness,Seth	+6
Vargas,Jason	+6
Happ,J.A.	+6
Cueto,Johnny	+5
Greinke,Zack	+5
Wilson,C.J.	+5
Simon,Alfredo	+5

Pitchers
2014 Trailers

Hughes,Phil	-8
Torres,Carlos	-5
Mejia,Jenrry	-5
Turner,Jacob	-5
Scherzer,Max	-5

2014 Career Register

This section contains the complete career statistics of every active major league player up to date through the end of the 2014 season. There is a major addition this year: on-base plus slugging percentage (OPS), which approximates a player's overall value as a hitter by capturing both his power and his ability to reach base.

We have also included the last five years of minor league statistics for players who have appeared in fewer than three major league seasons, whether or not those players spent any time in the minors in 2014. For players who exceed that three-year cutoff but who also spent time in the minors in 2014—likely because of a rehab assignment—they will show only their 2014 minor league statistics, which will be called out by an asterisk.

If a player led either the AL or NL in a category, that number will appear in **boldface**.

Age is seasonal age as of June 30, 2015.

For pitchers, BFP is Batters Facing Pitcher; TBB is Total Bases on Balls (or Total Walks, intentional and unintentional); Op is Save Opportunities; Hld is Holds.

For the various levels of Class-A ball, we have used "A+" to indicate High-A and "A-" to indicate Low-A. To help readers decode our minor league abbreviations, there is a legend in the back of the book.

A pronunciation guide is provided underneath the name of select players.

In addition to a variety of traditional statistics, the Register also shows Runs Created (RC) for hitters and Component ERA (ERC) for pitchers. Runs created is a comprehensive measurement of a player's offensive production distilled into a single number. It was originally developed by Bill James. Component ERA estimates what a pitcher's ERA should have been based only on his raw pitching statistics and acts as a good indicator of whether a pitcher deserved the ERA he ended the season with. The details of the current formulas for both RC and ERC are in the Baseball Glossary at the back of the Handbook.

A player's total career numbers in the postseason appear on one line above his total regular season career numbers. Since we work hard to bring you this publication by November 1, postseason data from 2014 is not included. In addition, the Japanese baseball season extends a bit beyond our deadline, so the Japanese statistics for posted players will not include a complete record of their most recent games. Those numbers will be updated in the following year's Handbook.

Fernando Abad

Pitches: L **Bats:** L **Pos:** RP-69   ah-BAHD   **Ht:** 6'1" **Wt:** 220 **Born:** 12/17/1985 **Age:** 29

			HOW MUCH HE PITCHED						WHAT HE GAVE UP										THE RESULTS						
Year	Team	Lg	G	GS	CG	GF	IP	BFP	H	R	ER	HR	SH	SF	HB	TBB	IBB	SO	WP	Bk	W	L	Pct	Sh	Sv-Op	Hld	ERC	ERA
2010	Hou	NL	22	0	0	6	19.0	76	14	6	6	3	0	1	0	5	0	12	0	0	0	1	.000	0	0-0	6	2.49	2.84
2011	Hou	NL	29	0	0	1	19.2	99	28	18	16	5	1	2	1	9	0	15	0	0	1	4	.200	0	0-2	7	8.06	7.32
2012	Hou	NL	37	6	0	8	46.0	208	57	27	26	6	2	1	3	19	1	38	4	0	0	6	.000	0	0-0	3	6.13	5.09
2013	Was	NL	39	0	0	17	37.2	166	42	14	14	3	0	0	1	10	0	32	0	0	0	3	.000	0	0-1	2	4.05	3.35
2014	Oak	AL	69	0	0	17	57.1	216	34	11	10	4	1	2	4	15	3	51	0	0	2	4	.333	0	0-2	9	1.64	1.57
	5 ML YEARS		196	6	0	49	179.2	765	175	76	72	21	4	6	9	58	4	148	4	0	3	18	.143	0	0-5	27	3.91	3.61

Bobby Abreu

Bats: L **Throws:** R **Pos:** PH-46;RF-26;LF-5;DH-3   uh-BRAY-you   **Ht:** 6'0" **Wt:** 220 **Born:** 3/11/1974 **Age:** 41

						BATTING														RUNNING			AVERAGES			
Year	Team	Lg	G	AB	H	2B	3B	HR	(Hm	Rd)	TB	R	RBI	RC	TBB	IBB	SO	HBP	SH	SF	SB	CS	GDP	Avg	OBP	Slg	OPS
2014	LsVgs*	AAA	26	75	27	8	0	1	(-	-)	38	11	18	18	16	1	14	0	0	0	0	0	6	.360	.473	.507	.979
1996	Hou	NL	15	22	5	1	0	0	(0	0)	6	1	1	1	2	0	3	0	0	0	0	0	1	.227	.292	.273	.564
1997	Hou	NL	59	188	47	10	2	3	(3	0)	70	22	26	25	21	0	48	1	0	0	7	2	0	.250	.329	.372	.701
1998	Phi	NL	151	497	155	29	6	17	(10	7)	247	68	74	101	84	14	133	0	4	4	19	10	6	.312	.409	.497	.906
1999	Phi	NL	152	546	183	35	11	20	(13	7)	300	118	93	131	109	8	113	3	0	4	27	9	13	.335	.446	.549	.995
2000	Phi	NL	154	576	182	42	10	25	(14	11)	319	103	79	130	100	9	116	1	0	3	28	8	12	.316	.416	.554	.970
2001	Phi	NL	162	588	170	48	4	31	(13	18)	319	118	110	125	106	11	137	1	0	9	36	14	13	.289	.393	.543	.936
2002	Phi	NL	157	572	176	50	6	20	(8	12)	298	102	85	112	104	9	117	3	0	6	31	12	11	.308	.413	.521	.934
2003	Phi	NL	158	577	173	35	1	20	(11	9)	270	99	101	120	109	13	126	2	0	7	22	9	13	.300	.409	.468	.877
2004	Phi	NL	159	574	173	47	1	30	(13	17)	312	118	105	139	127	10	116	5	0	7	40	5	5	.301	.428	.544	.971
2005	Phi	NL	162	588	168	37	1	24	(15	9)	279	104	102	116	117	15	134	6	0	8	31	9	7	.286	.405	.474	.879
2006	2 Tms		156	548	163	41	2	15	(8	7)	253	98	107	123	124	6	138	3	2	9	30	6	13	.297	.424	.462	.886
2007	NYY	AL	158	605	171	40	5	16	(10	6)	269	123	101	101	84	0	115	3	0	7	25	8	11	.283	.369	.445	.814
2008	NYY	AL	156	609	180	39	4	20	(14	6)	287	100	100	100	73	2	109	1	0	1	22	11	14	.296	.371	.471	.843
2009	LAA	AL	152	563	165	29	3	15	(7	8)	245	96	103	109	94	7	113	1	0	9	30	8	15	.293	.390	.435	.825
2010	LAA	AL	154	573	146	41	1	20	(11	9)	249	88	78	91	87	3	132	2	0	5	24	10	13	.255	.352	.435	.787
2011	LAA	AL	142	502	127	30	1	8	(3	5)	183	54	60	74	78	5	113	1	1	3	21	5	8	.253	.353	.365	.717
2012	2 Tms		100	219	53	11	1	3	(1	2)	75	29	24	29	37	3	56	0	0	1	6	2	7	.242	.350	.342	.693
2014	NYM		78	133	33	9	0	1	(1	0)	45	12	14	16	20	0	21	0	0	2	1	0	3	.248	.342	.338	.680
06	Phi	NL	98	339	94	25	2	8	(5	3)	147	61	65	76	91	5	86	2	0	6	20	4	8	.277	.427	.434	.861
06	NYY	AL	58	209	69	16	0	7	(3	4)	106	37	42	47	33	1	52	1	2	3	10	2	5	.330	.419	.507	.926
12	LAA	AL	8	24	5	3	0	0	(0	0)	8	1	5	4	2	0	5	0	0	0	0	0	1	.208	.259	.333	.593
12	LAD	NL	92	195	48	8	1	3	(1	2)	67	28	19	25	35	3	51	0	0	0	6	2	6	.246	.361	.344	.704
	Postseason		20	67	19	6	0	1	(1	0)	28	9	9	11	12	3	15	0	0	0	2	1	0	.284	.392	.418	.810
	18 ML YEARS		2425	8480	2470	574	59	288	(155	133)	4026	1453	1363	1651	1476	115	1840	33	7	85	400	128	165	.291	.395	.475	.870

Jose Abreu

Bats: R **Throws:** R **Pos:** 1B-109;DH-35;PH-1   uh-BRAY-you   **Ht:** 6'3" **Wt:** 255 **Born:** 1/29/1987 **Age:** 28

						BATTING														RUNNING			AVERAGES			
Year	Team	Lg	G	AB	H	2B	3B	HR	(Hm	Rd)	TB	R	RBI	RC	TBB	IBB	SO	HBP	SH	SF	SB	CS	GDP	Avg	OBP	Slg	OPS
2014	CWS	AL	145	556	176	35	2	36	(15	21)	323	80	107	113	51	15	131	11	0	4	3	1	14	.317	.383	.581	.964

Tony Abreu

Bats: B **Throws:** R **Pos:** 2B-1;3B-1;PH-1   uh-BRAY-you   **Ht:** 5'10" **Wt:** 200 **Born:** 11/13/1984 **Age:** 30

						BATTING														RUNNING			AVERAGES			
Year	Team	Lg	G	AB	H	2B	3B	HR	(Hm	Rd)	TB	R	RBI	RC	TBB	IBB	SO	HBP	SH	SF	SB	CS	GDP	Avg	OBP	Slg	OPS
2014	Fresno*	AAA	80	282	80	16	1	7	(-	-)	119	37	33	41	14	1	33	8	1	3	3	0	4	.284	.332	.422	.754
2014	Giants*	R	1	2	0	0	0	0	(-	-)	0	0	0	1	0	0	0	0	0	1	0	1	0	.000	.000	.000	.000
2007	LAD	NL	59	166	45	14	1	2	(0	2)	67	19	17	18	7	1	21	3	0	2	0	0	5	.271	.309	.404	.713
2009	LAD	NL	6	8	2	0	0	0	(0	0)	2	0	1	2	3	0	2	0	0	0	0	1	0	.250	.455	.250	.705
2010	Ari	NL	81	193	45	11	1	1	(1	0)	61	16	13	12	4	0	47	0	0	4	2	1	8	.233	.244	.316	.560
2012	KC	AL	22	70	18	2	1	1	(1	0)	25	5	15	13	2	0	13	1	0	1	0	0	1	.257	.284	.357	.641
2013	SF	NL	53	138	37	12	3	2	(1	1)	61	21	14	14	6	1	33	1	1	1	0	2	5	.268	.301	.442	.743
2014	SF	NL	3	4	0	0	0	0	(0	0)	0	0	0	0	0	0	0	0	0	0	0	0	1	.000	.000	.000	.000
	6 ML YEARS		224	579	147	39	6	6	(3	3)	216	61	60	59	22	2	116	5	1	8	2	4	20	.254	.283	.373	.656

Alfredo Aceves

Pitches: R **Bats:** R **Pos:** RP-10   ah-SEVV-us   **Ht:** 6'2" **Wt:** 205 **Born:** 12/8/1982 **Age:** 32

						HOW MUCH HE PITCHED			WHAT HE GAVE UP											THE RESULTS						
Year	Team	Lg	G	GS	CG	GF	IP	BFP	H	R	ER	HR	SH	SF	HB	TBB	IBB	SO	WP	Bk	W	L	Pct	Sh	Sv-Op	Hld	ERC	ERA
2014	S-WB*	AAA	7	5	0	1	28.1	123	30	13	11	1	1	3	1	9	0	24	1	1	0	1	.000	0	1- -	-	3.73	3.49
2008	NYY	AL	6	4	0	1	30.0	120	25	8	8	4	0	0	0	4	0	16	1	0	1	0	1.000	0	0-0	0	3.23	2.40
2009	NYY	AL	43	1	0	10	84.0	337	69	36	33	10	1	2	5	16	2	69	0	0	10	1	.909	0	1-2	5	2.65	3.54
2010	NYY	AL	10	0	0	2	12.0	53	10	5	4	1	0	0	1	4	1	2	0	0	3	0	1.000	0	1-1	1	2.80	3.00
2011	Bos	AL	55	4	0	15	114.0	474	84	37	33	8	3	3	15	42	1	80	1	2	10	2	.833	0	2-5	11	2.84	2.61
2012	Bos	AL	69	0	0	55	84.0	361	80	51	50	11	2	7	6	31	2	75	3	1	2	10	.167	0	25-33	0	4.16	5.36
2013	Bos	AL	11	6	0	3	37.0	169	42	21	20	8	0	1	0	22	0	24	0	2	4	1	.800	0	0-0	0	6.70	4.86
2014	NYY	AL	10	0	0	5	19.1	85	23	14	14	6	0	0	1	10	4	16	0	1	1	2	.333	0	0-0	1	6.06	6.52
	Postseason		4	0	0	1	4.1	20	5	2	2	0	1	0	0	3	1	2	1	0	1	0	1.000	0	0-0	0	5.01	4.15
	7 ML YEARS		204	15	0	91	380.1	1599	333	172	162	48	6	13	28	129	6	282	5	6	31	16	.660	0	29-41	18	3.60	3.83

A.J. Achter

Pitches: R Bats: R Pos: RP-7   AHK-ter   Ht: 6'5" Wt: 205 Born: 8/27/1988 Age: 26

Year	Team	Lg	G	GS	CG	GF	IP	BFP	H	R	ER	HR	SH	SF	HB	TBB	IBB	SO	WP	Bk	W	L	Pct	Sh	Sv-Op	Hld	ERC	ERA
2010	Elizab	R+	4	0	0	1	7.1	32	7	4	4	0	0	0	1	3	0	8	2	1	1	0	1.000	0	0- -	-	3.68	4.91
2011	Beloit	A	19	19	0	0	99.2	427	97	59	50	13	7	2	4	35	0	108	6	1	5	8	.385	0	0- -	-	4.10	4.52
2012	Beloit	A	18	1	0	2	40.0	161	33	17	11	5	0	2	1	12	1	49	5	0	3	1	.750	0	0- -	-	3.03	2.48
2012	FtMyrs	A+	19	0	0	12	34.1	129	21	8	3	0	1	0	0	3	0	37	5	1	2	1	.667	0	6- -	-	0.92	0.79
2013	NwBrit	AA	25	0	0	9	36.2	157	28	10	9	3	0	2	1	19	0	36	3	1	2	0	1.000	0	3- -	-	3.18	2.21
2013	Roch	AAA	16	0	0	6	23.2	100	17	9	8	4	0	0	0	14	0	20	0	0	1	2	.333	0	1- -	-	3.75	3.04
2014	NwBrit	AA	3	0	0	1	6.2	23	3	0	0	0	0	0	0	1	0	11	0	0	0	0	-	0	1- -	-	0.69	0.00
2014	Roch	AAA	40	0	0	18	72.0	281	44	20	19	4	4	1	2	24	0	69	3	1	4	4	.500	0	6- -	-	1.73	2.38
2014	Min	AL	7	0	0	1	11.0	49	14	7	4	2	0	0	0	3	0	5	0	0	1	0	1.000	0	0-0	0	5.74	3.27

Dustin Ackley

Bats: L Throws: R Pos: LF-133;DH-8;PH-7;PR-4   Ht: 6'1" Wt: 195 Born: 2/26/1988 Age: 27

Year	Team	Lg	G	AB	H	2B	3B	HR	(Hm	Rd)	TB	R	RBI	RC	TBB	IBB	SO	HBP	SH	SF	SB	CS	GDP	Avg	OBP	Slg	OPS
2011	Sea	AL	90	333	91	16	7	6	(3	3)	139	39	36	53	40	1	79	0	0	3	6	0	3	.273	.348	.417	.766
2012	Sea	AL	153	607	137	22	2	12	(2	10)	199	84	50	62	59	7	124	0	1	1	13	3	3	.226	.294	.328	.622
2013	Sea	AL	113	384	97	18	2	4	(2	2)	131	40	31	45	37	1	72	1	4	1	2	3	6	.253	.319	.341	.660
2014	Sea	AL	143	502	123	27	4	14	(8	6)	200	64	65	54	32	1	90	3	3	2	8	4	10	.245	.293	.398	.692
	4 ML YEARS		499	1826	448	83	15	36	(15	21)	669	227	182	214	168	10	365	4	8	7	29	10	22	.245	.309	.366	.676

Cristhian Adames

Bats: B Throws: R Pos: SS-5;2B-2;PH-2   kris-tee-YAHN ah-dah-MAZE   Ht: 6'0" Wt: 180 Born: 7/26/1991 Age: 23

Year	Team	Lg	G	AB	H	2B	3B	HR	(Hm	Rd)	TB	R	RBI	RC	TBB	IBB	SO	HBP	SH	SF	SB	CS	GDP	Avg	OBP	Slg	OPS
2010	Casper	R+	37	145	42	9	0	1	(-	-)	54	30	15	19	14	0	24	1	5	0	4	5	0	.290	.356	.372	.729
2011	Ashvll	A	108	399	109	17	2	8	(-	-)	154	63	44	58	42	0	74	7	7	4	2	0	11	.273	.350	.386	.736
2012	Mdest	A+	115	418	117	21	7	2	(-	-)	158	59	54	60	47	1	82	3	11	6	4	2	8	.280	.352	.378	.730
2013	Tulsa	AA	107	389	104	19	2	3	(-	-)	136	45	36	48	34	0	78	4	17	2	13	7	11	.267	.331	.350	.681
2014	Tulsa	AA	88	330	88	9	4	2	(-	-)	111	42	38	37	29	1	58	2	13	6	7	9	9	.267	.324	.336	.661
2014	ColSpr	AAA	38	145	49	12	0	1	(-	-)	64	19	14	26	13	0	25	0	5	0	5	1	3	.338	.392	.441	.834
2014	Col	NL	7	15	1	0	0	0	(0	0)	1	1	0	0	0	0	5	0	0	0	0	0	1	.067	.067	.067	.133

Austin Adams

Pitches: R Bats: R Pos: RP-6   Ht: 5'11" Wt: 190 Born: 8/19/1986 Age: 28

Year	Team	Lg	G	GS	CG	GF	IP	BFP	H	R	ER	HR	SH	SF	HB	TBB	IBB	SO	WP	Bk	W	L	Pct	Sh	Sv-Op	Hld	ERC	ERA
2010	Lk Cty	A	13	8	0	4	53.1	226	40	22	21	7	2	3	6	21	0	61	1	0	2	4	.333	0	1- -	-	3.29	3.54
2010	Knstn	A+	13	12	0	1	58.2	239	50	14	10	5	0	1	4	15	0	51	3	0	6	1	.857	0	0- -	-	2.93	1.53
2011	Akron	AA	26	26	0	0	136.0	599	147	68	57	6	5	1	5	63	0	131	11	1	11	10	.524	0	0- -	-	4.59	3.77
2013	Akron	AA	45	0	0	13	55.0	237	44	19	16	3	0	1	2	29	1	76	7	0	3	2	.600	0	4- -	-	3.23	2.62
2014	Clmbs	AAA	42	0	0	18	54.0	214	44	16	15	4	2	0	0	16	0	52	5	0	3	2	.600	0	5- -	-	2.61	2.50
2014	Cle	AL	6	0	0	1	7.0	30	9	7	7	1	0	0	1	0	4	0	0	0	0	-	0	0-0	0	5.04	9.00

Lane Adams

Bats: R Throws: R Pos: PR-4;LF-2;CF-2;DH-2   Ht: 6'2" Wt: 198 Born: 11/13/1989 Age: 25

Year	Team	Lg	G	AB	H	2B	3B	HR	(Hm	Rd)	TB	R	RBI	RC	TBB	IBB	SO	HBP	SH	SF	SB	CS	GDP	Avg	OBP	Slg	OPS
2010	Idaho	R+	41	170	48	8	3	2	(-	-)	68	31	18	26	18	1	38	0	3	2	8	0	2	.282	.347	.400	.747
2011	Kane	A	43	152	35	7	2	1	(-	-)	49	22	11	16	14	0	44	2	1	2	7	2	4	.230	.300	.322	.622
2011	Royals	R	4	14	5	3	0	0	(-	-)	8	5	1	3	3	0	4	1	0	0	0	1	0	.357	.500	.571	1.071
2011	Burlgtn	R+	43	167	47	9	3	5	(-	-)	77	31	20	30	17	0	45	3	2	3	9	1	1	.281	.353	.461	.814
2012	Kane	A	67	262	78	13	4	5	(-	-)	114	40	44	43	21	0	48	2	2	4	11	1	4	.298	.349	.435	.785
2012	Wilmg	A+	68	262	63	10	1	6	(-	-)	93	37	25	29	21	0	64	2	0	0	8	4	8	.240	.302	.355	.657
2013	Wilmg	A+	87	323	89	23	2	7	(-	-)	137	56	39	54	43	2	66	2	0	2	23	6	2	.276	.362	.424	.786
2013	NWArk	AA	44	156	38	7	1	5	(-	-)	62	30	26	24	18	0	45	3	0	0	15	0	2	.244	.333	.397	.731
2014	NWArk	AA	105	405	109	25	3	11	(-	-)	173	65	36	68	45	2	86	9	2	4	38	9	5	.269	.352	.427	.779
2014	Burlgtn	R+	3	10	5	2	2	0	(-	-)	11	3	4	5	4	0	1	0	0	0	0	0	0	.500	.643	1.100	1.743
2014	KC	AL	6	3	0	0	0	0	(0	0)	0	1	0	0	0	0	2	0	0	0	0	0	0	.000	.000	.000	.000

Matt Adams

Bats: L Throws: R Pos: 1B-133;PH-10   Ht: 6'3" Wt: 260 Born: 8/31/1988 Age: 26

Year	Team	Lg	G	AB	H	2B	3B	HR	(Hm	Rd)	TB	R	RBI	RC	TBB	IBB	SO	HBP	SH	SF	SB	CS	GDP	Avg	OBP	Slg	OPS
2014	Memp*	AAA	4	15	3	1	0	0	(-	-)	4	1	2	0	0	0	2	0	0	0	0	0	1	.200	.200	.267	.467
2012	StL	NL	27	86	21	6	0	2	(1	1)	33	8	13	9	5	0	24	0	0	0	0	0	3	.244	.286	.384	.669
2013	StL	NL	108	296	84	14	0	17	(10	7)	149	46	51	49	23	0	80	0	0	1	0	0	9	.284	.335	.503	.839
2014	StL	NL	142	527	152	34	5	15	(8	7)	241	55	68	65	26	5	114	3	0	7	3	2	6	.288	.321	.457	.779
	Postseason		17	63	14	3	0	1	(1	0)	20	5	4	7	3	0	19	1	0	0	0	0	0	.222	.269	.317	.586
	3 ML YEARS		277	909	257	54	5	34	(19	15)	423	109	132	123	54	5	218	3	0	7	3	2	21	.283	.323	.465	.788

Mike Adams

Pitches: R **Bats:** R **Pos:** RP-22 **Ht:** 6'5" **Wt:** 210 **Born:** 7/29/1978 **Age:** 36

			HOW MUCH HE PITCHED						WHAT HE GAVE UP										THE RESULTS							
Year	Team	Lg	G	GS	CG	GF	IP	BFP	H	R	ER	HR	SH	SF	HB	TBB	IBB	SO	WP	Bk	W	L	Pct	Sh	Sv-Op	Hld	ERC	ERA
2014	Clrwtr*	A+	3	0	0	0	2.2	12	3	1	1	0	0	0	0	1	0	5	0	0	0	0	-	0	0--	-	3.84	3.38
2014	LV*	AAA	4	1	0	1	4.0	13	3	1	1	0	0	0	0	0	0	2	0	0	0	1	.000	0	0--	-	1.30	2.25
2004	Mil	NL	46	0	0	13	53.0	225	50	21	20	5	5	2	2	14	2	39	2	0	2	3	.400	0	0-5	12	3.22	3.40
2005	Mil	NL	13	0	0	7	13.1	61	12	4	4	2	0	0	0	10	1	14	1	0	0	1	.000	0	1-2	2	5.12	2.70
2006	Mil	NL	2	0	0	0	2.1	13	4	3	3	1	0	0	0	2	0	1	0	0	0	0	-	0	0-0	0	13.74	11.57
2008	SD	NL	54	0	0	11	65.1	259	49	18	18	7	2	3	0	19	2	74	0	0	2	3	.400	0	0-2	10	2.38	2.48
2009	SD	NL	37	0	0	5	37.0	136	14	9	3	1	2	0	0	8	1	45	1	0	0	0	-	0	0-1	15	0.65	0.73
2010	SD	NL	70	0	0	3	66.2	268	48	14	13	2	0	0	0	23	2	73	0	0	4	1	.800	0	0-4	38	1.95	1.76
2011	2 Tms		75	0	0	10	73.2	277	44	13	12	5	2	1	0	14	2	74	0	0	5	4	.556	0	2-5	32	1.31	1.47
2012	Tex	AL	61	0	0	7	52.1	228	56	21	19	4	0	0	3	17	1	45	2	0	5	3	.625	0	1-2	27	4.20	3.27
2013	Phi	NL	28	0	0	4	25.0	107	23	11	11	5	0	0	1	11	0	23	1	0	1	4	.200	0	0-1	8	4.69	3.96
2014	Phi	NL	22	0	0	0	18.2	79	16	8	6	1	2	0	0	8	1	21	0	0	2	1	.667	0	0-2	6	2.99	2.89
11	SD	NL	48	0	0	5	48.0	179	26	7	6	2	1	1	0	9	1	49	0	0	3	1	.750	0	1-3	23	1.06	1.13
11	Tex	AL	27	0	0	5	25.2	98	18	6	6	3	1	0	0	5	1	25	0	0	2	3	.400	0	1-2	9	1.88	2.10
	Postseason		11	0	0	2	8.1	39	11	3	3	2	0	0	0	6	1	6	0	0	2	0	1.000	0	0-0	5	8.84	3.24
	10 ML YEARS		408	0	0	60	407.1	1653	316	122	109	33	13	6	6	126	12	409	7	0	21	20	.512	0	4-24	150	2.44	2.41

Nate Adcock

Pitches: R **Bats:** R **Pos:** RP-7 **Ht:** 6'4" **Wt:** 235 **Born:** 2/25/1988 **Age:** 27

			HOW MUCH HE PITCHED						WHAT HE GAVE UP										THE RESULTS							
Year	Team	Lg	G	GS	CG	GF	IP	BFP	H	R	ER	HR	SH	SF	HB	TBB	IBB	SO	WP	Bk	W	L	Pct	Sh	Sv-Op	Hld	ERC	ERA
2014	RdRck*	AAA	18	0	0	5	21.1	88	14	7	7	1	0	1	2	11	0	22	3	0	1	0	1.000	0	2--	-	2.72	2.95
2011	KC	AL	24	3	0	5	60.1	265	63	34	31	5	3	1	3	26	3	36	4	1	1	1	.500	0	1-1	0	4.47	4.62
2012	KC	AL	12	2	0	3	34.2	148	37	13	9	4	1	2	1	13	2	22	0	0	0	3	.000	0	0-0	1	4.61	2.34
2014	Tex	AL	7	0	0	1	10.0	45	11	5	5	2	0	0	2	5	0	9	1	0	0	0	-	0	0-0	0	7.03	4.50
	3 ML YEARS		43	5	0	9	105.0	458	111	52	45	11	4	3	6	44	5	67	5	1	1	4	.200	0	1-1	1	4.74	3.86

Jim Adduci

ah-DOO-see

Bats: L **Throws:** L **Pos:** LF-20;PH-13;RF-8;DH-4;1B-3;PR-2 **Ht:** 6'2" **Wt:** 210 **Born:** 5/15/1985 **Age:** 30

			BATTING																	RUNNING			AVERAGES			
Year	Team	Lg	G	AB	H	2B	3B	HR	(Hm	Rd)	TB	R	RBI	RC	TBB	IBB	SO	HBP	SH	SF	SB	CS	GDP	Avg	OBP	Slg	OPS
2010	Iowa	AAA	114	367	91	9	1	3	(-	-)	111	60	33	36	27	2	80	3	6	4	23	9	5	.248	.302	.302	.604
2011	Tenn	AA	71	237	73	13	2	4	(-	-)	102	44	20	42	26	1	33	1	3	0	21	4	3	.308	.379	.430	.809
2011	Cubs	R	4	17	3	0	0	0	(-	-)	3	0	0	0	0	0	2	0	0	0	2	0	0	.176	.176	.176	.353
2012	Tenn	AA	84	252	74	12	1	5	(-	-)	103	40	27	41	31	3	47	0	7	3	11	3	2	.294	.367	.409	.776
2012	Iowa	AAA	42	147	45	9	2	2	(-	-)	64	27	17	25	17	2	40	1	3	2	7	4	2	.306	.377	.435	.813
2013	RdRck	AAA	127	473	141	24	3	16	(-	-)	219	75	65	90	65	3	107	2	5	6	32	9	4	.298	.381	.463	.844
2014	Frisco	AA	6	22	7	1	1	1	(-	-)	13	3	6	4	0	0	5	0	0	1	1	0	0	.318	.304	.591	.895
2014	RdRck	AAA	7	27	8	1	0	0	(-	-)	9	3	3	3	2	0	8	0	0	0	2	1	0	.296	.345	.333	.678
2013	Tex	AL	17	31	8	1	0	0	(0	0)	9	2	0	3	3	0	9	0	0	0	2	0	0	.258	.324	.290	.614
2014	Tex	AL	44	101	17	3	0	1	(0	1)	23	13	8	6	10	0	27	0	1	2	3	1	2	.168	.239	.228	.467
	2 ML YEARS		61	132	25	4	0	1	(0	1)	32	15	8	9	13	0	36	0	1	2	5	1	2	.189	.259	.242	.501

Ehire Adrianza

A-ee-ray A-dree-ahn-zuh

Bats: B **Throws:** R **Pos:** 2B-25;PH-20;SS-7;PR-4;3B-3 **Ht:** 6'1" **Wt:** 170 **Born:** 8/21/1989 **Age:** 25

			BATTING																	RUNNING			AVERAGES			
Year	Team	Lg	G	AB	H	2B	3B	HR	(Hm	Rd)	TB	R	RBI	RC	TBB	IBB	SO	HBP	SH	SF	SB	CS	GDP	Avg	OBP	Slg	OPS
2010	SnJos	A+	124	445	114	22	5	3	(-	-)	155	70	35	56	47	0	87	5	10	1	33	15	7	.256	.333	.348	.682
2011	Augsta	A	38	143	33	10	1	3	(-	-)	54	18	17	18	18	0	32	0	6	1	3	2	4	.231	.315	.378	.692
2011	SnJos	A+	56	230	69	24	3	3	(-	-)	108	34	27	42	23	0	46	6	1	2	5	1	3	.300	.375	.470	.845
2012	Rchmd	AA	127	451	99	22	5	3	(-	-)	140	52	32	44	41	2	90	4	13	3	16	4	10	.220	.289	.310	.599
2013	Rchmd	AA	73	250	60	12	0	2	(-	-)	78	31	23	29	31	0	45	4	4	2	11	6	5	.240	.331	.312	.643
2013	Fresno	AAA	45	145	45	7	6	0	(-	-)	64	23	12	28	23	1	31	2	6	1	6	2	1	.310	.409	.441	.851
2014	Fresno	AAA	6	19	6	0	0	1	(-	-)	9	6	1	3	2	0	4	0	1	0	0	0	0	.316	.381	.474	.855
2013	SF	NL	9	18	4	1	0	1	(0	1)	8	3	3	1	1	0	5	0	1	0	0	0	1	.222	.263	.444	.708
2014	SF	NL	53	97	23	6	0	0	(0	0)	29	10	5	6	5	1	22	1	2	1	1	1	2	.237	.279	.299	.578
	2 ML YEARS		62	115	27	7	0	1	(0	1)	37	13	8	7	6	1	27	1	3	1	1	1	3	.235	.276	.322	.598

Jeremy Affeldt

AFF-felt

Pitches: L **Bats:** L **Pos:** RP-62 **Ht:** 6'4" **Wt:** 225 **Born:** 6/6/1979 **Age:** 36

			HOW MUCH HE PITCHED						WHAT HE GAVE UP										THE RESULTS							
Year	Team	Lg	G	GS	CG	GF	IP	BFP	H	R	ER	HR	SH	SF	HB	TBB	IBB	SO	WP	Bk	W	L	Pct	Sh	Sv-Op	Hld	ERC	ERA
2014	Fresno*	AAA	2	1	0	0	1.1	10	3	4	4	0	0	0	1	2	0	2	0	0	0	1	.000	0	0--	-	19.81	27.00
2014	SnJos*	A+	2	0	0	0	3.0	10	2	0	0	0	0	0	0	0	0	3	0	0	0	0	-	0	0--	-	1.01	0.00
2002	KC	AL	34	7	0	4	77.2	353	85	41	40	8	2	1	3	37	4	67	5	2	3	4	.429	0	0-1	1	4.97	4.64
2003	KC	AL	36	18	0	5	126.0	533	126	58	55	12	2	5	5	38	1	98	2	2	7	6	.538	0	4-4	3	3.82	3.93
2004	KC	AL	38	8	0	26	76.1	344	91	49	42	6	4	4	3	32	2	49	4	3	3	4	.429	0	13-17	6	5.26	4.95
2005	KC	AL	49	0	0	13	49.2	232	56	35	29	3	0	1	0	29	2	39	5	0	0	2	.000	0	0-0	12	5.08	5.26
2006	2 Tms		54	9	0	12	97.1	448	102	74	67	13	4	4	2	55	3	48	2	0	4	8	.500	0	1-3	5	5.21	6.20
2007	Col	NL	75	0	0	11	59.0	253	47	26	23	3	6	3	3	33	9	46	6	1	4	3	.571	0	0-4	9	3.19	3.51
2008	Cin	NL	74	0	0	20	78.1	335	78	36	29	9	7	0	3	25	0	80	6	0	1	1	.500	0	0-1	5	3.98	3.33

			HOW MUCH HE PITCHED						WHAT HE GAVE UP												WHAT HE GAVE UP	THE RESULTS							
Year	Team	Lg	G	GS	CG	GF	IP	BFP	H	R	ER	HR	SH	SF	HB	TBB	IBB	SO	WP	Bk	W	L	Pct	Sh	Sv-Op	Hld	ERC	ERA
2009	SF	NL	74	0	0	8	62.1	248	42	14	12	3	0	1	3	31	3	55	5	0	2	2	.500	0	0-0	33	2.61	1.73
2010	SF	NL	53	0	0	14	50.0	228	56	25	23	4	7	1	3	24	5	44	4	0	4	3	.571	0	4-7	7	4.99	4.14
2011	SF	NL	67	0	0	12	61.2	259	47	22	18	5	4	0	4	24	3	54	4	0	3	2	.600	0	3-6	13	2.77	2.63
2012	SF	NL	67	0	0	10	63.1	267	57	23	19	1	4	0	3	23	1	57	5	0	1	2	.333	0	3-4	16	2.98	2.70
2013	SF	NL	39	0	0	11	33.2	146	27	14	14	2	4	1	4	17	5	21	2	0	1	5	.167	0	0-4	11	3.31	3.74
2014	SF	NL	62	0	0	9	55.1	225	47	14	14	1	1	1	4	14	1	41	4	1	4	2	.667	0	0-3	18	2.47	2.28
06	KC	AL	27	9	0	3	70.0	320	71	51	46	9	3	3	1	42	0	28	2	0	4	6	.400	0	0-0	2	5.18	5.91
06	Col	NL	27	0	0	9	27.1	128	31	23	21	4	1	1	0	13	3	20	0	0	2	2	.667	0	1-3	3	6.29	6.91
	Postseason		22	0	0	2	19.2	73	9	3	3	1	0	0	1	6	2	18	2	0	0	0	-	0	0-0	3	1.15	1.37
	13 ML YEARS		722	42	0	155	890.2	3871	861	431	385	70	42	25	40	382	39	699	54	9	41	44	.482	0	28-54	133	3.95	3.89

Jesus Aguilar

Bats: R Throws: R Pos: 1B-12;DH-5;PH-4;3B-1   AGG-you-lahr   Ht: 6'3" Wt: 250 Born: 6/30/1990 Age: 25

			BATTING																	RUNNING			AVERAGES			
Year	Team	Lg	G	AB	H	2B	3B	HR	(Hm	Rd)	TB	R	RBI	RC	TBB	IBB	SO	HBP	SH	SF	SB	CS	GDP	Avg	OBP	Slg	OPS
2010	Indns	R	29	112	29	2	1	7	(-	-)	54	15	22	16	5	0	33	2	0	4	1	1	4	.259	.293	.482	.775
2010	MhVlly	A-	32	123	30	9	0	2	(-	-)	45	8	17	14	11	0	28	0	0	2	2	0	3	.244	.301	.366	.667
2011	Lk Cty	A	95	349	102	27	2	19	(-	-)	190	58	69	70	35	1	98	10	0	3	1	0	7	.292	.370	.544	.915
2011	Knstn	A+	31	113	29	3	0	4	(-	-)	44	12	13	14	11	0	28	0	0	0	1	0	1	.257	.323	.389	.712
2012	Carlina	A+	107	368	102	25	2	12	(-	-)	167	63	58	64	45	2	91	9	0	5	0	1	7	.277	.365	.454	.819
2012	Akron	AA	20	72	21	6	0	3	(-	-)	36	12	13	15	13	0	24	1	0	1	0	0	3	.292	.402	.500	.902
2013	Akron	AA	130	499	137	28	0	16	(-	-)	213	66	105	78	56	1	107	5	0	7	0	1	20	.275	.349	.427	.776
2014	Clmbs	AAA	118	427	130	31	0	19	(-	-)	218	69	77	88	64	5	96	3	0	5	0	0	11	.304	.395	.511	.905
2014	Cle	AL	19	33	4	0	0	0	(0	0)	4	2	3	0	4	0	13	0	0	1	0	0	1	.121	.211	.121	.332

Nick Ahmed

Bats: R Throws: R Pos: SS-18;PR-4;2B-2;PH-1   Ht: 6'3" Wt: 205 Born: 3/15/1990 Age: 25

			BATTING																	RUNNING			AVERAGES			
Year	Team	Lg	G	AB	H	2B	3B	HR	(Hm	Rd)	TB	R	RBI	RC	TBB	IBB	SO	HBP	SH	SF	SB	CS	GDP	Avg	OBP	Slg	OPS
2011	Danvle	R+	59	248	65	13	2	4	(-	-)	94	46	24	36	30	1	46	3	1	2	18	6	2	.262	.346	.379	.725
2012	Lynbrg	A+	130	506	136	36	4	6	(-	-)	198	84	49	74	49	0	102	4	10	2	40	10	10	.269	.337	.391	.728
2013	Mobile	AA	136	487	115	21	5	4	(-	-)	158	58	46	50	33	0	72	5	7	6	26	7	10	.236	.288	.324	.613
2014	Reno	AAA	104	407	127	26	4	4	(-	-)	173	57	47	67	37	2	55	3	4	1	14	6	9	.312	.373	.425	.798
2014	Ari	NL	25	70	14	2	0	1	(1	0)	19	9	4	3	3	0	10	0	2	0	0	1	2	.200	.233	.271	.504

Matt Albers

Pitches: R Bats: L Pos: RP-8   Ht: 6'1" Wt: 225 Born: 1/20/1983 Age: 32

			HOW MUCH HE PITCHED						WHAT HE GAVE UP												THE RESULTS							
Year	Team	Lg	G	GS	CG	GF	IP	BFP	H	R	ER	HR	SH	SF	HB	TBB	IBB	SO	WP	Bk	W	L	Pct	Sh	Sv-Op	Hld	ERC	ERA
2006	Hou	NL	4	2	0	0	15.0	66	17	10	10	1	2	0	0	7	0	11	0	0	0	2	.000	0	0-0	0	4.97	6.00
2007	Hou	NL	31	18	0	2	110.2	508	127	77	72	18	6	8	7	50	6	71	7	0	4	11	.267	0	0-0	0	5.76	5.86
2008	Bal	AL	28	3	0	5	49.0	208	43	21	19	4	1	3	2	22	1	26	1	0	3	3	.500	0	0-2	6	3.62	3.49
2009	Bal	AL	56	0	0	13	67.0	309	80	43	41	3	5	2	2	36	3	49	3	0	3	6	.333	0	0-4	10	5.41	5.51
2010	Bal	AL	62	0	0	19	75.2	329	78	41	38	5	3	0	2	34	5	49	2	0	5	3	.625	0	0-2	7	4.35	4.52
2011	Bos	AL	56	0	0	10	64.2	289	62	35	34	7	4	2	5	31	1	68	2	0	4	4	.500	0	0-3	10	4.44	4.73
2012	2 Tms		63	0	0	12	60.1	241	46	21	16	9	1	2	2	22	3	44	1	0	3	1	.750	0	0-6	9	3.13	2.39
2013	Cle	AL	56	0	0	21	63.0	262	57	25	22	2	2	0	1	23	3	35	6	0	3	1	.750	0	0-0	1	2.99	3.14
2014	Hou	AL	8	0	0	1	10.0	42	10	1	1	0	0	0	1	3	0	8	0	0	0	0	-	0	0-1	3	3.46	0.90
12	Bos	AL	40	0	0	8	39.1	157	30	14	10	6	0	2	1	15	3	25	0	0	2	0	1.000	0	0-4	7	3.16	2.29
12	Ari	NL	23	0	0	4	21.0	84	16	7	6	3	1	0	1	7	0	19	1	0	1	1	.500	0	0-2	2	3.07	2.57
	9 ML YEARS		364	23	0	83	515.1	2254	520	274	253	50	24	17	22	228	22	361	22	0	25	31	.446	0	0-18	46	4.40	4.42

Al Alburquerque

Pitches: R Bats: R Pos: RP-72   AL-buh-kur-kee   Ht: 6'0" Wt: 195 Born: 6/10/1986 Age: 29

			HOW MUCH HE PITCHED						WHAT HE GAVE UP												THE RESULTS							
Year	Team	Lg	G	GS	CG	GF	IP	BFP	H	R	ER	HR	SH	SF	HB	TBB	IBB	SO	WP	Bk	W	L	Pct	Sh	Sv-Op	Hld	ERC	ERA
2011	Det	AL	41	0	0	11	43.1	182	21	9	9	0	2	1	2	29	4	67	4	0	6	1	.857	0	0-0	6	1.73	1.87
2012	Det	AL	8	0	0	3	13.1	53	6	1	1	0	0	0	0	8	0	18	0	1	0	0	-	0	0-0	1	1.50	0.68
2013	Det	AL	53	0	0	12	49.0	220	39	25	25	5	0	1	2	34	5	70	9	1	4	3	.571	0	0-0	10	4.02	4.59
2014	Det	AL	72	0	0	15	57.1	236	46	16	16	7	0	2	3	21	1	63	2	2	3	1	.750	0	1-1	17	3.23	2.51
	Postseason		14	0	0	5	10.0	43	7	6	6	2	1	0	0	6	2	14	1	1	1	1	.500	0	0-0	3	3.51	5.40
	4 ML YEARS		174	0	0	38	163.0	691	112	51	51	12	2	4	7	92	10	218	15	4	13	5	.722	0	1-1	34	2.88	2.82

Arismendy Alcantara

Bats: B Throws: R Pos: CF-48;2B-25;PH-1   air-es-MEN-dee al-CAHN-truh   Ht: 5'10" Wt: 170 Born: 10/29/1991 Age: 23

			BATTING																	RUNNING			AVERAGES			
Year	Team	Lg	G	AB	H	2B	3B	HR	(Hm	Rd)	TB	R	RBI	RC	TBB	IBB	SO	HBP	SH	SF	SB	CS	GDP	Avg	OBP	Slg	OPS
2010	Boise	A-	59	219	62	5	6	3	(-	-)	88	29	24	28	10	0	53	1	3	2	7	3	1	.283	.315	.402	.716
2011	Peoria	A	99	369	100	14	5	2	(-	-)	130	45	37	38	16	1	76	1	4	0	8	8	3	.271	.303	.352	.655
2012	Dytona	A+	85	331	100	13	7	7	(-	-)	148	47	51	54	19	0	61	2	2	5	25	4	5	.302	.339	.447	.786
2013	Tenn	AA	133	494	134	36	4	15	(-	-)	223	69	69	86	62	6	125	2	9	4	31	6	4	.271	.352	.451	.804
2014	Iowa	AAA	89	335	103	25	11	10	(-	-)	180	62	41	65	25	0	83	0	3	3	21	3	2	.307	.353	.537	.890
2014	ChC	NL	70	278	57	11	2	10	(5	5)	102	31	29	23	17	0	93	2	1	2	8	5	3	.205	.254	.367	.621

Cody Allen

Pitches: R Bats: R Pos: RP-76   Ht: 6'1" Wt: 210 Born: 11/20/1988 Age: 26

Year	Team	Lg	HOW MUCH HE PITCHED						WHAT HE GAVE UP												THE RESULTS							
			G	GS	CG	GF	IP	BFP	H	R	ER	HR	SH	SF	HB	TBB	IBB	SO	WP	Bk	W	L	Pct	Sh	Sv-Op	Hld	ERC	ERA
2012	Cle	AL	27	0	0	9	29.0	126	29	12	12	2	1	1	0	15	0	27	0	0	0	1	.000	0	0-1	0	4.39	3.72
2013	Cle	AL	77	0	0	12	70.1	301	62	22	19	7	4	4	1	26	2	88	9	0	6	1	.857	0	2-4	11	3.24	2.43
2014	Cle	AL	76	0	0	44	69.2	279	48	21	16	7	2	2	1	26	5	91	4	0	6	4	.600	0	24-28	9	2.32	2.07
	Postseason		1	0	0	0	0.1	2	1	1	0	0	0	0	0	0	0	1	0	0	0	0	-	0	0-0	0	14.52	0.00
	3 ML YEARS		180	0	0	65	169.0	706	139	55	47	16	7	7	2	67	7	206	13	0	12	6	.667	0	26-33	21	3.03	2.50

Abraham Almonte

Bats: B Throws: R Pos: CF-41;LF-16;PH-6;PR-2;DH-1   Ht: 5'9" Wt: 205 Born: 6/27/1989 Age: 26

Year	Team	Lg	BATTING																RUNNING			AVERAGES			
			G	AB	H	2B	3B	HR	(Hm | Rd)	TB	R	RBI	RC	TBB	IBB	SO	HBP	SH	SF	SB	CS	GDP	Avg	OBP	Slg	OPS
2010	Tampa	A+	15	57	15	3	1	0	(- | -)	20	9	3	6	6	0	16	0	0	0	5	3	0	.263	.333	.351	.684
2011	Tampa	A+	131	537	144	27	11	4	(- | -)	205	92	52	73	52	2	100	2	3	4	30	11	9	.268	.333	.382	.715
2012	Trntn	AA	78	319	88	17	4	4	(- | -)	125	47	25	50	37	2	59	0	2	1	30	5	1	.276	.350	.392	.742
2012	Yanks1	R	7	18	4	2	0	0	(- | -)	6	2	0	2	2	0	4	0	0	0	2	0	0	.222	.300	.333	.633
2013	Jacksn	AA	29	102	26	6	1	4	(- | -)	46	18	18	18	18	2	28	0	0	0	6	1	3	.255	.367	.451	.818
2013	Tacom	AAA	94	338	106	17	5	11	(- | -)	166	63	50	69	49	3	66	2	6	1	20	7	2	.314	.403	.491	.894
2014	Tacom	AAA	72	277	74	10	3	6	(- | -)	108	42	31	37	28	0	66	0	6	1	7	4	6	.267	.333	.390	.723
2013	Sea	AL	25	72	19	4	0	2	(1 | 1)	29	10	9	9	6	0	21	0	2	2	1	0	2	.264	.313	.403	.715
2014	2 Tms		59	204	47	10	1	3	(2 | 1)	68	19	15	18	12	0	60	1	2	1	4	3	5	.230	.275	.333	.609
14	Sea	AL	27	106	21	5	1	1	(0 | 1)	31	10	8	10	6	0	40	1	0	0	3	1	1	.198	.248	.292	.540
14	SD	NL	32	98	26	5	0	2	(2 | 0)	37	9	7	8	6	0	20	0	2	1	1	2	4	.265	.305	.378	.682
	2 ML YEARS		84	276	66	14	1	5	(3 | 2)	97	29	24	27	18	0	81	1	4	3	5	3	7	.239	.285	.351	.637

Zoilo Almonte

Bats: B Throws: R Pos: LF-6;RF-4;PH-2;DH-1   ZOY-low   Ht: 6'0" Wt: 205 Born: 6/10/1989 Age: 26

Year	Team	Lg	BATTING																RUNNING			AVERAGES			
			G	AB	H	2B	3B	HR	(Hm | Rd)	TB	R	RBI	RC	TBB	IBB	SO	HBP	SH	SF	SB	CS	GDP	Avg	OBP	Slg	OPS
2010	CtnSC	A	58	227	63	13	2	10	(- | -)	110	33	35	37	21	1	65	2	3	2	7	6	3	.278	.341	.485	.826
2010	Tampa	A+	63	238	62	10	3	3	(- | -)	87	26	26	31	23	3	65	0	0	3	8	1	9	.261	.322	.366	.688
2011	Tampa	A+	70	259	76	15	3	12	(- | -)	133	38	54	51	31	2	60	2	0	4	14	4	3	.293	.368	.514	.882
2011	Trntn	AA	46	175	44	11	1	3	(- | -)	66	23	23	21	14	0	45	1	0	1	4	1	1	.251	.309	.377	.686
2012	Trntn	AA	106	419	116	23	1	21	(- | -)	204	64	70	67	25	2	103	4	0	3	15	4	11	.277	.322	.487	.808
2013	S-WB	AAA	68	259	77	12	1	6	(- | -)	109	30	36	42	30	0	47	1	0	3	4	1	12	.297	.369	.421	.789
2014	S-WB	AAA	105	421	110	18	1	18	(- | -)	184	50	69	58	29	2	105	2	0	2	6	4	15	.261	.311	.437	.748
2013	NYY	AL	34	106	25	4	0	1	(1 | 0)	32	9	9	9	6	0	19	0	0	1	3	1	2	.236	.274	.302	.576
2014	NYY	AL	13	36	5	0	0	1	(1 | 0)	8	2	3	0	0	0	14	0	0	0	1	0	1	.139	.139	.222	.361
	2 ML YEARS		47	142	30	4	0	2	(2 | 0)	40	11	12	9	6	0	33	0	0	1	4	1	3	.211	.242	.282	.523

Yonder Alonso

Bats: L Throws: R Pos: 1B-77;PH-6;3B-3   YONN-dur ah-LONN-zo   Ht: 6'1" Wt: 230 Born: 4/8/1987 Age: 28

Year	Team	Lg	BATTING																RUNNING			AVERAGES			
			G	AB	H	2B	3B	HR	(Hm | Rd)	TB	R	RBI	RC	TBB	IBB	SO	HBP	SH	SF	SB	CS	GDP	Avg	OBP	Slg	OPS
2014	Padres*	R	2	8	3	0	0	1	(- | -)	6	1	4	2	0	0	1	0	0	0	0	0	0	.375	.375	.750	1.125
2014	ElPaso*	AAA	5	17	4	0	0	0	(- | -)	4	0	1	0	0	0	2	0	0	0	0	0	1	.235	.235	.235	.471
2010	Cin	NL	22	29	6	2	0	0	(0 | 0)	8	2	3	0	0	0	10	0	0	0	0	0	1	.207	.207	.276	.483
2011	Cin	NL	47	88	29	4	0	5	(2 | 3)	48	9	15	16	10	0	21	0	0	0	0	0	2	.330	.398	.545	.943
2012	SD	NL	155	549	150	39	0	9	(3 | 6)	216	47	62	71	62	9	101	3	1	4	3	0	14	.273	.348	.393	.741
2013	SD	NL	97	334	94	11	0	6	(4 | 2)	123	34	45	46	32	5	47	2	0	7	6	0	9	.281	.341	.368	.710
2014	SD	NL	84	267	64	19	1	7	(3 | 4)	106	27	27	26	17	1	36	1	0	3	6	1	8	.240	.285	.397	.682
	5 ML YEARS		405	1267	343	75	1	27	(12 | 15)	501	119	152	159	121	15	215	6	1	14	15	1	34	.271	.334	.395	.729

Aaron Altherr

Bats: R Throws: R Pos: LF-1;PH-1   ALL-tair   Ht: 6'5" Wt: 220 Born: 1/14/1991 Age: 24

Year	Team	Lg	BATTING																RUNNING			AVERAGES			
			G	AB	H	2B	3B	HR	(Hm | Rd)	TB	R	RBI	RC	TBB	IBB	SO	HBP	SH	SF	SB	CS	GDP	Avg	OBP	Slg	OPS
2010	Phillies	R	27	115	35	6	1	1	(- | -)	46	12	15	16	3	0	22	2	0	1	10	3	2	.304	.331	.400	.731
2010	Wmspt	A-	28	94	27	7	3	0	(- | -)	40	11	10	13	8	1	13	1	1	0	2	3	1	.287	.350	.426	.775
2011	Lakwd	A	41	147	31	6	0	1	(- | -)	40	20	15	13	11	0	47	2	1	2	12	0	3	.211	.272	.272	.544
2011	Wmspt	A-	71	269	70	12	2	5	(- | -)	101	41	31	35	13	0	52	5	4	4	25	4	4	.260	.302	.375	.678
2012	Lakwd	A	110	420	106	27	6	8	(- | -)	169	65	50	58	38	1	102	6	1	6	25	8	4	.252	.319	.402	.722
2013	Clrwtr	A+	123	466	128	36	6	12	(- | -)	212	57	69	76	45	0	140	3	5	8	23	5	7	.275	.337	.455	.792
2014	Clrwtr	A+	7	28	7	1	0	2	(- | -)	12	6	2	4	5	0	8	0	0	0	1	0	0	.250	.364	.429	.792
2014	Rdng	AA	120	449	106	27	2	14	(- | -)	179	54	57	53	26	1	110	8	4	5	12	6	16	.236	.287	.399	.686
2014	Phi	NL	2	5	0	0	0	0	(0 | 0)	0	0	0	0	0	0	2	0	0	0	0	0	0	.000	.000	.000	.000

Jose Altuve

Bats: R Throws: R Pos: 2B-156;DH-1;PH-1   al-TOO-vay   Ht: 5'6" Wt: 175 Born: 5/6/1990 Age: 25

									BATTING											RUNNING			AVERAGES			
Year	Team	Lg	G	AB	H	2B	3B	HR	(Hm	Rd)	TB	R	RBI	RC	TBB	IBB	SO	HBP	SH	SF	SB	CS	GDP	Avg	OBP	Slg	OPS
2011	Hou	NL	57	221	61	10	1	2	(2	0)	79	26	12	18	5	0	29	2	5	1	7	3	5	.276	.297	.357	.654
2012	Hou	NL	147	576	167	34	4	7	(4	3)	230	80	37	76	40	0	74	6	4	4	33	11	8	.290	.340	.399	.740
2013	Hou	AL	152	626	177	31	2	5	(4	1)	227	64	52	67	32	5	85	2	4	8	35	13	24	.283	.316	.363	.678
2014	Hou	AL	158	660	225	47	3	7	(4	3)	299	85	59	106	36	7	53	5	1	5	56	9	20	.341	.377	.453	.830
	4 ML YEARS		514	2083	630	122	10	21	(14	7)	835	255	160	267	113	12	241	15	14	18	131	36	57	.302	.340	.401	.741

Dario Alvarez

Pitches: L Bats: L Pos: RP-4   Ht: 6'1" Wt: 170 Born: 1/17/1989 Age: 26

				HOW MUCH HE PITCHED						WHAT HE GAVE UP									THE RESULTS						
Year	Team	Lg	G	GS	CG	GF	IP	BFP	H	R	ER	HR	SH	SF	HB	TBB	IBB	SO	WP	Bk	W	L	Pct	Sh	Sv-Op	Hld	ERC	ERA
2013	Bklyn	A-	12	12	0	0	58.0	254	48	27	20	1	0	4	7	26	1	57	9	0	2	4	.333	0	0--	-	3.10	3.10
2014	Savann	A	20	6	0	5	61.1	243	43	12	9	2	3	0	2	14	0	95	6	2	7	1	.875	0	1--	-	1.65	1.32
2014	StLuci	A+	4	0	0	1	6.1	20	1	0	0	0	0	0	0	3	0	10	2	0	2	0	1.000	0	0--	-	0.60	0.00
2014	Bnghtn	AA	5	0	0	2	5.2	21	4	0	0	0	0	0	1	0	0	9	1	0	1	0	1.000	0	1--	-	1.43	0.00
2014	NYM	NL	4	0	0	0	1.1	8	4	2	2	1	0	0	0	0	0	1	0	0	0	0	-	0	0-1	1	22.76	13.50

Henderson Alvarez

Pitches: R Bats: R Pos: SP-30   Ht: 6'0" Wt: 205 Born: 4/18/1990 Age: 25

				HOW MUCH HE PITCHED						WHAT HE GAVE UP									THE RESULTS						
Year	Team	Lg	G	GS	CG	GF	IP	BFP	H	R	ER	HR	SH	SF	HB	TBB	IBB	SO	WP	Bk	W	L	Pct	Sh	Sv-Op	Hld	ERC	ERA
2011	Tor	AL	10	10	0	0	63.2	259	64	26	25	8	1	2	4	8	0	40	2	0	1	3	.250	1	0-0	0	3.49	3.53
2012	Tor	AL	31	31	1	0	187.1	807	216	110	101	29	2	4	3	54	2	79	3	1	9	14	.391	1	0-0	0	5.01	4.85
2013	Mia	NL	17	17	1	0	102.2	418	90	42	41	2	0	4	7	27	1	57	4	1	5	6	.455	1	0-0	0	2.66	3.59
2014	Mia	NL	30	30	3	0	187.0	772	198	65	55	14	7	4	8	33	3	111	4	0	12	7	.632	3	0-0	0	3.56	2.65
	4 ML YEARS		88	88	5	0	540.2	2256	568	243	222	53	10	14	22	122	6	287	13	2	27	30	.474	5	0-0	0	3.86	3.70

Jose Alvarez

Pitches: L Bats: L Pos: RP-2   Ht: 5'11" Wt: 180 Born: 5/6/1989 Age: 26

				HOW MUCH HE PITCHED						WHAT HE GAVE UP									THE RESULTS						
Year	Team	Lg	G	GS	CG	GF	IP	BFP	H	R	ER	HR	SH	SF	HB	TBB	IBB	SO	WP	Bk	W	L	Pct	Sh	Sv-Op	Hld	ERC	ERA
2010	Grnsbr	A	26	13	0	3	108.0	457	114	52	43	9	1	3	3	32	0	113	6	0	10	3	.769	0	0--	-	4.03	3.58
2011	Jupiter	A+	15	14	0	1	82.0	330	79	32	27	2	0	4	1	19	3	73	2	1	6	5	.545	0	0--	-	2.82	2.96
2011	Jaxnvl	AA	12	12	0	0	65.2	290	80	47	39	9	3	4	1	22	0	45	4	2	2	6	.250	0	0--	-	5.49	5.35
2012	Jaxnvl	AA	25	24	3	0	136.1	560	140	66	64	8	8	6	6	26	1	70	2	0	6	9	.400	1	0--	-	3.36	4.22
2013	Toledo	AAA	21	20	1	1	128.2	518	114	46	40	11	0	4	3	25	0	115	4	0	8	6	.571	0	1--	-	2.70	2.80
2014	Salt Lk	AAA	6	6	0	0	30.2	143	35	25	23	8	0	0	4	15	0	17	0	0	0	2	.000	0	0--	-	7.12	6.75
2014	Angels	R	1	1	0	0	1.0	3	0	0	0	0	0	0	0	1	0	0	0	0	0	0	-	0	0--	-	1.26	0.00
2013	Det	AL	14	6	0	0	38.2	172	42	26	25	7	2	2	2	16	1	31	0	1	1	5	.167	0	0-0	2	5.41	5.82
2014	LAA	AL	2	0	0	1	0.2	3	1	0	0	0	0	0	0	0	0	1	0	0	0	0	-	0	0-0	0	4.47	0.00
	Postseason		1	0	0	0	3.0	10	0	0	0	0	0	0	0	1	0	3	0	0	0	0	-	0	0-0	0	0.13	0.00
	2 ML YEARS		16	6	0	1	39.1	175	43	26	25	7	2	2	2	16	1	32	0	1	1	5	.167	0	0-0	2	5.39	5.72

Pedro Alvarez

Bats: L Throws: R Pos: 3B-99;PH-16;1B-5;DH-3   Ht: 6'3" Wt: 235 Born: 2/6/1987 Age: 28

									BATTING											RUNNING			AVERAGES			
Year	Team	Lg	G	AB	H	2B	3B	HR	(Hm	Rd)	TB	R	RBI	RC	TBB	IBB	SO	HBP	SH	SF	SB	CS	GDP	Avg	OBP	Slg	OPS
2010	Pit	NL	95	347	89	21	1	16	(12	4)	160	42	64	50	37	1	119	0	0	2	0	0	8	.256	.326	.461	.788
2011	Pit	NL	74	235	45	9	1	4	(0	4)	68	18	19	14	24	1	80	2	1	0	1	0	11	.191	.272	.289	.561
2012	Pit	NL	149	525	128	25	1	30	(12	18)	245	64	85	77	57	6	180	1	0	3	1	0	10	.244	.317	.467	.784
2013	Pit	NL	152	558	130	22	2	36	(16	20)	264	70	100	66	48	7	186	4	0	4	2	0	16	.233	.296	.473	.770
2014	Pit	NL	122	398	92	13	1	18	(8	10)	161	46	56	42	45	6	113	2	0	0	8	3	12	.231	.312	.405	.717
	Postseason		6	20	6	1	0	3	(1	2)	16	4	7	5	2	1	7	0	0	1	0	0	0	.300	.348	.800	1.148
	5 ML YEARS		592	2063	484	90	6	104	(48	56)	898	240	324	249	211	21	678	9	1	9	12	3	57	.235	.307	.435	.742

R.J. Alvarez

Pitches: R Bats: R Pos: RP-10   Ht: 6'1" Wt: 200 Born: 6/8/1991 Age: 24

				HOW MUCH HE PITCHED						WHAT HE GAVE UP									THE RESULTS						
Year	Team	Lg	G	GS	CG	GF	IP	BFP	H	R	ER	HR	SH	SF	HB	TBB	IBB	SO	WP	Bk	W	L	Pct	Sh	Sv-Op	Hld	ERC	ERA
2012	CRpds	A	23	0	0	9	27.1	122	22	16	10	2	3	1	5	11	0	38	3	0	3	2	.600	0	0--	-	3.38	3.29
2013	InldEm	A+	37	2	0	12	48.2	208	34	16	16	2	0	1	2	27	0	79	5	1	4	2	.667	0	4--	-	2.75	2.96
2014	Ark	AA	21	0	0	2	27.0	100	13	2	1	0	0	0	3	10	2	38	0	0	0	0	-	0	1--	-	1.34	0.33
2014	SnAnt	AA	17	0	0	12	16.1	69	16	5	5	0	1	0	1	3	0	23	2	0	0	1	.000	0	6--	-	2.65	2.76
2014	SD	NL	10	0	0	4	8.0	33	3	1	1	0	0	1	1	5	1	9	1	0	0	0	-	0	0-0	1	1.42	1.13

Alexi Amarista

ah-mah-REE-stah

Bats: L **Throws:** R **Pos:** SS-73;3B-22;2B-21;CF-21;PH-12;LF-6;PR-3   **Ht:** 5'6" **Wt:** 150 **Born:** 4/6/1989 **Age:** 26

Year Team	Lg	G	AB	H	2B	3B	HR	(Hm	Rd)	TB	R	RBI	RC	TBB	IBB	SO	HBP	SH	SF	SB	CS	GDP	Avg	OBP	Slg	OPS
2011 LAA	AL	23	52	8	3	1	0	(0	0)	13	2	5	1	2	0	8	0	1	1	0	0	1	.154	.182	.250	.432
2012 2 Tms		106	275	66	15	5	5	(0	5)	106	36	32	31	17	1	42	0	6	2	8	4	2	.240	.282	.385	.668
2013 SD	NL	146	368	87	14	4	5	(1	4)	124	35	32	40	22	1	57	2	3	1	4	2	7	.236	.282	.337	.619
2014 SD	NL	148	423	101	13	2	5	(3	2)	133	39	40	43	29	5	69	1	8	5	12	1	6	.239	.286	.314	.600
12 LAA	AL	1	0	0	0	0	0	(0	0)	0	1	0	0	0	0	0	0	0	0	0	0	0	-	-	-	-
12 SD	NL	105	275	66	15	5	5	(0	5)	106	35	32	31	17	1	42	0	6	2	8	4	2	.240	.282	.385	.668
4 ML YEARS		423	1118	262	45	12	15	(4	11)	376	112	109	115	70	7	176	3	18	9	24	7	16	.234	.279	.336	.615

Hector Ambriz

AMM-brizz

Pitches: R **Bats:** L **Pos:** RP-1   **Ht:** 6'2" **Wt:** 235 **Born:** 5/24/1984 **Age:** 31

Year Team	Lg	G	GS	CG	GF	IP	BFP	H	R	ER	HR	SH	SF	HB	TBB	IBB	SO	WP	Bk	W	L	Pct	Sh	Sv-Op	Hld	ERC	ERA
2014 ElPaso*	AAA	51	0	0	28	55.0	246	60	27	24	5	4	4	4	18	3	43	5	0	2	4	.333	0	11--	-	4.34	3.93
2010 Cle	AL	34	0	0	20	48.1	224	68	31	30	10	2	3	1	17	1	37	4	0	0	2	.000	0	0-0	0	7.30	5.59
2012 Hou	NL	18	0	0	2	19.1	83	14	9	9	0	2	0	2	11	2	22	4	0	1	1	.500	0	0-0	3	2.74	4.19
2013 Hou	AL	43	0	0	10	36.1	171	50	28	23	8	0	2	1	14	1	27	4	0	2	4	.333	0	2-5	13	7.28	5.70
2014 SD	NL	1	0	0	0	2.0	9	2	2	1	0	0	0	0	2	0	1	0	0	0	0	-	0	0-0	0	6.15	4.50
4 ML YEARS		96	0	0	32	106.0	487	134	70	63	18	4	5	4	44	4	87	12	0	3	7	.300	0	2-5	16	6.37	5.35

Brett Anderson

Pitches: L **Bats:** L **Pos:** SP-8   **Ht:** 6'4" **Wt:** 225 **Born:** 2/1/1988 **Age:** 27

Year Team	Lg	G	GS	CG	GF	IP	BFP	H	R	ER	HR	SH	SF	HB	TBB	IBB	SO	WP	Bk	W	L	Pct	Sh	Sv-Op	Hld	ERC	ERA
2014 ColSpr*	AAA	2	2	0	0	9.1	37	8	1	1	0	0	0	0	2	0	8	0	0	1	0	1.000	0	0--	-	2.06	0.96
2009 Oak	AL	30	30	1	0	175.1	735	180	94	79	20	4	4	3	45	1	150	0	1	11	11	.500	1	0-0	0	3.84	4.06
2010 Oak	AL	19	19	0	0	112.1	470	112	41	35	6	3	2	7	22	2	75	4	2	7	6	.538	0	0-0	0	3.16	2.80
2011 Oak	AL	13	13	1	0	83.1	356	86	40	37	8	4	1	7	25	1	61	0	1	3	6	.333	0	0-0	0	4.20	4.00
2012 Oak	AL	6	6	0	0	35.0	137	29	11	10	1	0	0	1	7	1	25	1	0	4	2	.667	0	0-0	0	2.13	2.57
2013 Oak	AL	16	5	0	4	44.2	200	51	32	30	5	1	0	0	21	1	46	0	0	1	4	.200	0	3-3	1	5.27	6.04
2014 Col	NL	8	8	0	0	43.1	180	44	18	14	1	1	1	0	13	3	29	0	0	1	3	.250	0	0-0	0	3.20	2.91
Postseason		2	1	0	1	6.1	24	3	1	1	0	0	0	0	3	0	7	1	0	1	0	1.000	0	0-0	0	1.34	1.42
6 ML YEARS		92	81	2	4	494.0	2078	502	236	205	41	13	8	18	133	9	386	5	4	27	32	.458	1	3-3	1	3.68	3.73

Bryan Anderson

Bats: L **Throws:** R **Pos:** PH-1   **Ht:** 6'1" **Wt:** 200 **Born:** 12/16/1986 **Age:** 28

Year Team	Lg	G	AB	H	2B	3B	HR	(Hm	Rd)	TB	R	RBI	RC	TBB	IBB	SO	HBP	SH	SF	SB	CS	GDP	Avg	OBP	Slg	OPS
2014 Pnscla*	AA	21	70	24	2	2	5	(-	-)	45	11	19	18	11	0	14	0	0	1	0	1	1	.343	.427	.643	1.070
2014 Lsvlle*	AAA	52	162	49	12	1	5	(-	-)	78	20	24	30	19	0	29	2	3	1	0	1	4	.302	.380	.481	.862
2014 Scrmto*	AAA	5	21	8	3	1	0	(-	-)	13	4	4	5	1	0	7	1	0	1	0	0	0	.381	.417	.619	1.036
2010 StL	NL	15	32	9	2	0	0	(0	0)	11	1	4	5	1	0	7	1	0	1	0	0	0	.281	.314	.344	.658
2012 StL	NL	10	12	3	1	0	0	(0	0)	4	2	0	2	1	0	6	1	0	0	1	0	0	.250	.357	.333	.690
2013 CWS	AL	10	18	1	1	0	0	(0	0)	2	1	2	0	1	0	5	0	0	0	0	0	0	.056	.105	.111	.216
2014 Oak	AL	1	1	0	0	0	0	(0	0)	0	0	0	0	0	0	0	0	0	0	0	0	1	.000	.000	.000	.000
4 ML YEARS		36	63	13	4	0	0	(0	0)	17	4	6	7	3	0	18	2	0	1	1	0	1	.206	.261	.270	.531

Chase Anderson

Pitches: R **Bats:** R **Pos:** SP-21   **Ht:** 6'0" **Wt:** 190 **Born:** 11/30/1987 **Age:** 27

Year Team	Lg	G	GS	CG	GF	IP	BFP	H	R	ER	HR	SH	SF	HB	TBB	IBB	SO	WP	Bk	W	L	Pct	Sh	Sv-Op	Hld	ERC	ERA
2010 Sbend	A	7	7	1	0	38.1	163	36	16	12	1	1	1	1	9	0	31	1	0	2	4	.333	1	0--	-	2.64	2.82
2010 Visalia	A+	19	4	0	8	70.0	285	58	33	28	7	4	4	5	16	0	83	2	0	5	3	.625	0	3--	-	2.78	3.60
2011 Visalia	A+	3	3	0	0	13.1	57	14	10	8	1	0	0	1	1	0	20	1	0	1	1	.500	0	0--	-	3.08	5.40
2012 Mobile	AA	21	21	0	0	104.0	422	91	35	33	9	5	1	8	25	0	97	7	0	5	4	.556	0	0--	-	3.05	2.86
2013 Reno	AAA	26	13	0	2	88.0	399	107	67	56	11	3	6	1	33	0	80	2	1	4	7	.364	0	0--	-	5.42	5.73
2014 Mobile	AA	6	6	0	0	39.0	146	22	4	3	1	0	2	0	6	0	38	0	0	4	2	.667	0	0--	-	1.12	0.69
2014 Ari	NL	21	21	0	0	114.1	486	117	56	51	16	4	4	2	40	2	105	4	0	9	7	.563	0	0-0	0	4.39	4.01

Elvis Andrus

AHN-drews

Bats: R **Throws:** R **Pos:** SS-153;DH-4;PH-1   **Ht:** 6'0" **Wt:** 200 **Born:** 8/26/1988 **Age:** 26

Year Team	Lg	G	AB	H	2B	3B	HR	(Hm	Rd)	TB	R	RBI	RC	TBB	IBB	SO	HBP	SH	SF	SB	CS	GDP	Avg	OBP	Slg	OPS
2009 Tex	AL	145	480	128	17	8	6	(3	3)	179	72	40	65	40	0	77	6	12	3	33	6	4	.267	.329	.373	.702
2010 Tex	AL	148	588	156	15	3	0	(0	0)	177	88	35	79	64	0	96	5	17	17	32	15	6	.265	.342	.301	.643
2011 Tex	AL	150	587	164	27	3	5	(2	3)	212	96	60	76	56	0	74	5	16	1	37	12	17	.279	.347	.361	.708
2012 Tex	AL	158	629	180	31	9	3	(1	2)	238	85	62	92	57	0	96	5	17	3	21	10	15	.286	.349	.378	.727
2013 Tex	AL	156	620	168	17	4	4	(0	4)	205	91	67	72	52	1	97	4	16	6	42	8	19	.271	.328	.331	.659
2014 Tex	AL	157	619	163	35	1	2	(1	1)	206	72	41	59	46	0	96	3	9	7	27	15	21	.263	.314	.333	.647
Postseason		34	140	38	4	0	0	(0	0)	42	18	5	13	12	0	20	1	4	1	9	3	6	.271	.331	.300	.631
6 ML YEARS		914	3523	959	142	28	20	(7	13)	1217	504	305	443	315	1	536	28	87	20	192	66	82	.272	.335	.345	.680

Dean Anna

Bats: L Throws: R Pos: SS-9;2B-3   Ht: 5'11" Wt: 180 Born: 11/24/1986 Age: 28

									BATTING												RUNNING			AVERAGES			
Year	Team	Lg	G	AB	H	2B	3B	HR	(Hm	Rd)	TB	R	RBI	RC	TBB	IBB	SO	HBP	SH	SF	SB	CS	GDP	Avg	OBP	Slg	OPS
2010	FtWyn	A	80	225	61	14	2	6	(-	-)	97	42	32	41	39	0	40	3	2	3	5	1	3	.271	.381	.431	.813
2011	Lk Els	A+	44	148	46	10	2	3	(-	-)	69	25	18	29	19	1	22	5	2	3	2	0	4	.311	.400	.466	.866
2011	SnAnt	AA	71	198	50	18	1	2	(-	-)	76	45	23	34	41	2	19	3	2	2	3	0	2	.253	.385	.384	.769
2012	SnAnt	AA	129	425	115	16	3	10	(-	-)	167	75	46	70	66	1	76	11	1	7	6	4	8	.271	.377	.393	.770
2013	Tucsn	AAA	132	498	165	38	5	9	(-	-)	240	90	73	100	61	0	65	11	4	8	3	7	6	.331	.410	.482	.892
2014	S-WB	AAA	36	130	25	4	3	1	(-	-)	38	13	14	11	14	0	20	4	0	4	0	1	0	.192	.283	.292	.575
2014	Indy	AAA	29	68	16	4	0	1	(-	-)	23	13	7	11	19	0	5	0	1	1	1	0	2	.235	.398	.338	.736
2014	NYY	AL	12	22	3	1	0	1	(1	0)	7	3	3	1	2	0	6	0	0	1	0	0	0	.136	.200	.318	.518

Nori Aoki

Bats: L Throws: R Pos: RF-119;DH-8;LF-5;PH-3;PR-3   AH-oh-kee   Ht: 5'9" Wt: 180 Born: 1/5/1982 Age: 33

									BATTING												RUNNING			AVERAGES			
Year	Team	Lg	G	AB	H	2B	3B	HR	(Hm	Rd)	TB	R	RBI	RC	TBB	IBB	SO	HBP	SH	SF	SB	CS	GDP	Avg	OBP	Slg	OPS
2014	NWArk*	AA	3	10	1	0	0	0	(-	-)	1	1	0	0	0	0	1	1	0	0	0	0	0	.100	.182	.100	.282
2012	Mil	NL	151	520	150	37	4	10	(4	6)	225	81	50	80	43	1	55	13	7	5	30	8	6	.288	.355	.433	.787
2013	Mil	NL	155	597	171	20	3	8	(5	3)	221	80	37	80	55	1	40	11	8	3	20	12	9	.286	.356	.370	.726
2014	KC	AL	132	491	140	22	6	1	(0	1)	177	63	43	69	43	0	49	6	8	1	17	8	5	.285	.349	.360	.710
	3 ML YEARS		438	1608	461	79	13	19	(9	10)	623	224	130	229	141	2	144	30	23	9	67	28	20	.287	.353	.387	.741

Chris Archer

Pitches: R Bats: R Pos: SP-32   Ht: 6'3" Wt: 190 Born: 9/26/1988 Age: 26

			HOW MUCH HE PITCHED					WHAT HE GAVE UP												THE RESULTS						
Year	Team	Lg	G	GS	CG	GF	IP	BFP	H	R	ER	HR	SH	SF	HB	TBB	IBB	SO	WP	Bk	W	L	Pct	Sh	Sv-Op	Hld	ERC	ERA
2012	TB	AL	6	4	0	1	29.1	122	23	17	15	3	1	0	1	13	0	36	2	0	1	3	.250	0	0-0	0	3.24	4.60
2013	TB	AL	23	23	2	0	128.2	525	107	49	46	15	1	5	8	38	2	101	7	0	9	7	.563	2	0-0	0	3.13	3.22
2014	TB	AL	32	32	0	0	194.2	822	177	85	72	12	4	9	8	72	1	173	8	0	10	9	.526	0	0-0	0	3.36	3.33
	Postseason		2	0	0	0	1.2	6	1	0	0	0	0	1	0	0	0	2	0	0	0	0	-	0	0-0	0	0.75	0.00
	3 ML YEARS		61	59	2	1	352.2	1469	307	151	133	30	6	14	17	123	3	310	17	0	20	19	.513	2	0-0	0	3.27	3.39

Oswaldo Arcia

Bats: L Throws: R Pos: RF-100;PH-5;DH-2   ARR-see-ya   Ht: 6'0" Wt: 220 Born: 5/9/1991 Age: 24

									BATTING												RUNNING			AVERAGES			
Year	Team	Lg	G	AB	H	2B	3B	HR	(Hm	Rd)	TB	R	RBI	RC	TBB	IBB	SO	HBP	SH	SF	SB	CS	GDP	Avg	OBP	Slg	OPS
2010	Elizab	R+	64	259	97	21	7	14	(-	-)	174	47	51	66	19	3	67	4	0	1	4	4	5	.375	.424	.672	1.096
2011	Beloit	A	20	71	25	8	1	5	(-	-)	50	18	18	19	9	0	16	0	0	1	2	2	1	.352	.420	.704	1.124
2011	Twins	R	2	8	4	1	1	0	(-	-)	7	1	1	2	0	0	1	0	0	0	0	0	0	.500	.500	.875	1.375
2011	FtMyrs	A+	59	213	56	14	2	8	(-	-)	98	27	32	29	9	0	53	3	0	2	1	1	3	.263	.300	.460	.760
2012	FtMyrs	A+	55	207	64	16	3	7	(-	-)	107	22	33	39	23	2	45	1	1	3	1	3	3	.309	.376	.517	.893
2012	NwBrit	AA	69	262	86	20	5	10	(-	-)	146	54	67	57	28	1	62	5	0	4	3	2	4	.328	.398	.557	.955
2013	Roch	AAA	38	128	40	6	0	10	(-	-)	76	25	30	30	22	0	37	4	0	1	2	1	1	.313	.426	.594	1.020
2014	Roch	AAA	22	77	24	7	0	5	(-	-)	46	16	18	16	5	0	17	2	0	1	0	3	3	.312	.365	.597	.962
2013	Min	AL	97	351	88	17	2	14	(6	8)	151	34	43	37	23	0	117	4	0	1	1	2	4	.251	.304	.430	.734
2014	Min	AL	103	372	86	16	3	20	(12	8)	168	46	57	51	31	4	127	6	0	1	1	2	6	.231	.300	.452	.752
	2 ML YEARS		200	723	174	33	5	34	(18	16)	319	80	100	88	54	4	244	10	0	1	2	4	10	.241	.302	.441	.743

Nolan Arenado

Bats: R Throws: R Pos: 3B-111   ahr-eh-NOD-oh   Ht: 6'2" Wt: 205 Born: 4/16/1991 Age: 24

									BATTING												RUNNING			AVERAGES			
Year	Team	Lg	G	AB	H	2B	3B	HR	(Hm	Rd)	TB	R	RBI	RC	TBB	IBB	SO	HBP	SH	SF	SB	CS	GDP	Avg	OBP	Slg	OPS
2010	Ashvll	A	92	373	115	41	1	12	(-	-)	194	45	65	65	19	0	52	1	0	7	1	3	8	.308	.338	.520	.858
2011	Mdest	A+	134	517	154	32	3	20	(-	-)	252	82	122	91	47	3	53	1	4	14	2	1	21	.298	.349	.487	.836
2012	Tulsa	AA	134	516	147	36	1	12	(-	-)	221	55	56	77	39	5	58	7	1	10	0	2	18	.285	.337	.428	.766
2013	ColSpr	AAA	18	66	24	11	0	3	(-	-)	44	14	21	15	5	1	9	0	1	3	0	2	0	.364	.392	.667	1.059
2014	ColSpr	AAA	5	20	7	2	0	0	(-	-)	9	2	3	3	0	0	3	0	0	0	0	0	1	.350	.350	.450	.800
2013	Col	NL	133	486	130	29	4	10	(5	5)	197	49	52	48	23	1	72	1	2	2	2	0	16	.267	.301	.405	.706
2014	Col	NL	111	432	124	34	2	18	(16	2)	216	58	61	60	25	1	58	4	1	5	2	1	13	.287	.328	.500	.828
	2 ML YEARS		244	918	254	63	6	28	(21	7)	413	107	113	108	48	2	130	5	3	7	4	1	29	.277	.314	.450	.764

J.P. Arencibia

Bats: R Throws: R Pos: C-22;1B-22;DH-16;PH-2   air-en-SEE-bee-uh   Ht: 6'0" Wt: 205 Born: 1/5/1986 Age: 29

									BATTING												RUNNING			AVERAGES			
Year	Team	Lg	G	AB	H	2B	3B	HR	(Hm	Rd)	TB	R	RBI	RC	TBB	IBB	SO	HBP	SH	SF	SB	CS	GDP	Avg	OBP	Slg	OPS
2014	RdRck*	AAA	48	190	53	8	0	14	(-	-)	103	31	41	33	10	3	53	2	0	1	1	0	0	.279	.320	.542	.862
2010	Tor	AL	11	35	5	1	0	2	(2	0)	12	3	4	4	2	0	11	0	0	0	0	0	0	.143	.189	.343	.532
2011	Tor	AL	129	443	97	20	4	23	(13	10)	194	47	78	58	36	3	133	4	0	3	1	1	6	.219	.282	.438	.720
2012	Tor	AL	102	347	81	16	0	18	(9	9)	151	45	56	47	18	1	108	3	1	3	1	0	4	.233	.275	.435	.710
2013	Tor	AL	138	474	92	18	0	21	(13	8)	173	45	55	30	18	0	148	3	0	2	0	2	8	.194	.227	.365	.592
2014	Tex	AL	63	203	36	9	0	10	(3	7)	75	20	35	19	10	0	62	7	0	2	0	0	6	.177	.239	.369	.608
	5 ML YEARS		443	1502	311	64	4	74	(40	34)	605	160	228	158	84	4	462	17	1	10	2	3	24	.207	.255	.403	.658

Joaquin Arias

wah-KEEN AH-ree-us

Bats: R **Throws:** R **Pos:** 3B-44;PH-37;1B-16;2B-15;SS-11;PR-2   **Ht:** 6'1" **Wt:** 165 **Born:** 9/21/1984 **Age:** 30

							BATTING													RUNNING			AVERAGES			
Year	Team	Lg	G	AB	H	2B	3B	HR	(Hm | Rd)	TB	R	RBI	RC	TBB	IBB	SO	HBP	SH	SF	SB	CS	GDP	Avg	OBP	Slg	OPS
2006	Tex	AL	6	11	6	1	0	0	(0 | 0)	7	4	1	3	1	0	0	0	0	0	0	1	0	.545	.583	.636	1.220
2008	Tex	AL	32	110	32	7	3	0	(0 | 0)	45	15	9	15	7	0	12	2	1	0	4	1	4	.291	.345	.409	.754
2009	Tex	AL	3	8	0	0	0	0	(0 | 0)	0	0	0	0	0	0	3	0	1	0	0	0	0	.000	.000	.000	.000
2010	2 Tms		72	128	33	6	1	0	(0 | 0)	41	23	13	10	4	0	23	0	2	0	1	0	2	.258	.280	.320	.601
2012	SF	NL	112	319	86	13	5	5	(0 | 5)	124	30	34	32	13	4	44	5	2	5	5	1	12	.270	.304	.389	.693
2013	SF	NL	102	225	61	9	2	1	(1 | 0)	77	17	19	18	4	1	33	1	4	2	1	0	4	.271	.284	.342	.627
2014	SF	NL	107	193	49	9	0	0	(0 | 0)	58	18	15	14	8	2	23	0	1	2	1	0	1	.254	.281	.301	.581
10	Tex	AL	50	98	27	5	1	0	(0 | 0)	34	18	9	8	2	0	17	0	1	0	1	0	2	.276	.290	.347	.637
10	NYM	NL	22	30	6	1	0	0	(0 | 0)	7	5	4	2	2	0	6	0	1	0	0	0	0	.200	.250	.233	.483
	Postseason		12	8	3	2	0	0	(0 | 0)	5	3	0	1	0	0	1	0	0	0	0	0	0	.375	.375	.625	1.000
7 ML YEARS			434	994	267	45	11	6	(1 | 5)	352	107	91	92	37	7	138	8	11	9	12	3	23	.269	.298	.354	.652

Jake Arrieta

air-ee-ETT-uh

Pitches: R **Bats:** R **Pos:** SP-25   **Ht:** 6'4" **Wt:** 225 **Born:** 3/6/1986 **Age:** 29

			HOW MUCH HE PITCHED						WHAT HE GAVE UP											THE RESULTS						
Year	Team	Lg	G	GS	CG	GF	IP	BFP	H	R	ER	HR	SH	SF	HB	TBB	IBB	SO	WP	Bk	W	L	Pct	Sh	Sv-Op	Hld	ERC	ERA
2014	Tenn*	AA	4	4	0	0	14.1	56	8	4	2	0	0	0	0	5	0	11	2	0	1	1	.500	0	0--	-	1.28	1.26
2014	Dytona*	A+	1	1	0	0	5.2	24	5	5	3	0	0	0	0	2	0	7	1	0	0	0	-	0	0--	-	5.94	4.76
2010	Bal	AL	18	18	0	0	100.1	449	106	57	52	9	4	2	4	48	3	52	5	0	6	6	.500	0	0-0	0	4.74	4.66
2011	Bal	AL	22	22	0	0	119.1	523	115	70	67	21	3	2	4	59	2	93	0	0	10	8	.556	0	0-0	0	4.93	5.05
2012	Bal	AL	24	18	0	1	114.2	496	122	82	79	16	3	4	5	35	3	109	4	0	3	9	.250	0	0-0	1	4.47	6.20
2013	2 Tms		14	14	0	0	75.1	324	59	41	40	9	2	3	5	41	1	60	1	0	5	4	.556	0	0-0	0	3.82	4.78
2014	ChC	NL	25	25	1	0	156.2	614	114	46	44	5	5	3	3	41	2	167	8	0	10	5	.667	1	0-0	0	1.85	2.53
13	Bal	AL	5	5	0	0	23.2	111	25	19	19	2	0	3	2	17	1	23	1	0	1	2	.333	0	0-0	0	5.91	7.23
13	ChC	NL	9	9	0	0	51.2	213	34	22	21	7	2	0	3	24	0	37	0	0	4	2	.667	0	0-0	0	2.94	3.66
5 ML YEARS			103	97	1	1	566.1	2406	516	296	282	60	17	14	21	224	11	481	18	0	34	32	.515	1	0-0	1	3.73	4.48

Bronson Arroyo

uh-ROY-oh

Pitches: R **Bats:** R **Pos:** SP-14   **Ht:** 6'3" **Wt:** 195 **Born:** 2/24/1977 **Age:** 38

			HOW MUCH HE PITCHED						WHAT HE GAVE UP											THE RESULTS						
Year	Team	Lg	G	GS	CG	GF	IP	BFP	H	R	ER	HR	SH	SF	HB	TBB	IBB	SO	WP	Bk	W	L	Pct	Sh	Sv-Op	Hld	ERC	ERA
2000	Pit	NL	20	12	0	1	71.2	338	88	61	51	10	5	2	4	36	6	50	3	1	2	6	.250	0	0-0	0	6.18	6.40
2001	Pit	NL	24	13	1	1	88.1	390	99	54	50	12	4	6	4	34	6	39	4	1	5	7	.417	0	0-0	2	5.09	5.09
2002	Pit	NL	9	4	0	1	27.0	123	30	14	12	1	1	1	0	15	3	22	0	0	2	1	.667	0	0-0	1	4.64	4.00
2003	Bos	AL	6	0	0	2	17.1	66	10	5	4	0	0	0	1	4	2	14	0	0	0	0	-	0	1-1	0	1.14	2.08
2004	Bos	AL	32	29	0	1	178.2	764	171	99	80	17	5	4	20	47	3	142	5	0	10	9	.526	0	0-0	0	3.65	4.03
2005	Bos	AL	35	32	0	1	205.1	878	213	116	103	22	4	4	14	54	3	100	5	1	14	10	.583	0	0-0	0	4.04	4.51
2006	Cin	NL	35	35	3	0	240.2	992	222	98	88	31	9	2	5	64	7	184	6	0	14	11	.560	1	0-0	0	3.37	3.29
2007	Cin	NL	34	34	1	0	210.2	921	232	109	99	28	10	7	13	63	6	156	4	0	9	15	.375	0	0-0	0	4.68	4.23
2008	Cin	NL	34	34	1	0	200.0	871	219	116	106	29	13	6	6	68	2	163	6	0	15	11	.577	0	0-0	0	4.83	4.77
2009	Cin	NL	33	33	0	0	220.1	923	214	101	94	31	9	5	9	65	6	127	1	0	15	13	.536	2	0-0	0	3.94	3.84
2010	Cin	NL	33	33	2	0	215.2	880	188	99	93	29	6	5	6	59	5	121	1	1	17	10	.630	0	0-0	0	3.21	3.88
2011	Cin	NL	32	32	1	0	199.0	855	227	119	112	46	6	5	6	45	5	108	0	0	9	12	.429	1	0-0	0	5.20	5.07
2012	Cin	NL	32	32	1	0	202.0	835	209	86	84	26	7	6	5	35	1	129	3	0	12	10	.545	1	0-0	0	3.68	3.74
2013	Cin	NL	32	32	2	0	202.0	823	199	88	85	32	4	7	7	34	2	124	1	2	14	12	.538	1	0-0	0	3.63	3.79
2014	Ari	NL	14	14	0	0	86.0	357	92	40	39	10	3	2	3	19	1	47	2	0	7	4	.636	0	0-0	0	4.08	4.08
	Postseason		12	4	0	3	29.1	127	24	17	15	5	0	0	2	13	0	26	0	0	1	0	1.000	0	0-0	2	3.91	4.60
15 ML YEARS			405	369	16	6	2364.2	10016	2413	1201	1100	324	86	62	103	642	58	1526	41	6	145	131	.525	6	1-1	3	4.09	4.19

Erisbel Arruebarrena

ehr-ees-BELL arr-ROO-buh-ray-nuh

Bats: R **Throws:** R **Pos:** SS-21;PR-1   **Ht:** 6'0" **Wt:** 200 **Born:** 3/25/1990 **Age:** 25

							BATTING													RUNNING			AVERAGES			
Year	Team	Lg	G	AB	H	2B	3B	HR	(Hm	Rd)	TB	R	RBI	RC	TBB	IBB	SO	HBP	SH	SF	SB	CS	GDP	Avg	OBP	Slg	OPS
2014	Chatt	AA	25	96	20	4	1	1	(-	-)	29	10	6	7	4	0	31	2	2	1	0	0	0	.208	.252	.302	.555
2014	Albq	AAA	26	84	28	3	2	1	(-	-)	38	7	11	15	10	1	26	0	0	1	1	1	1	.333	.400	.452	.852
2014	Ddgrs	R	5	18	4	2	0	2	(-	-)	12	3	4	2	0	0	10	0	0	0	0	0	0	.222	.222	.667	.889
2014	RCuca	A+	12	49	12	4	1	2	(-	-)	24	8	11	6	2	0	24	0	0	3	1	0	0	.245	.259	.490	.749
2014	LAD	NL	22	41	8	1	0	0	(0	0)	9	4	4	2	3	0	17	0	0	1	0	0	1	.195	.244	.220	.464

Cody Asche

ASH-ee

Bats: L **Throws:** R **Pos:** 3B-112;PH-11;PR-1   **Ht:** 6'1" **Wt:** 200 **Born:** 6/30/1990 **Age:** 25

							BATTING													RUNNING			AVERAGES			
Year	Team	Lg	G	AB	H	2B	3B	HR	(Hm	Rd)	TB	R	RBI	RC	TBB	IBB	SO	HBP	SH	SF	SB	CS	GDP	Avg	OBP	Slg	OPS
2011	Wmspt	A-	68	239	46	11	0	2	(-	-)	63	14	19	16	24	1	50	3	1	1	0	3	2	.192	.273	.264	.537
2012	Clrwtr	A+	62	255	89	13	3	2	(-	-)	114	31	25	44	12	1	37	1	0	2	10	2	4	.349	.384	.447	.825
2012	Rdng	AA	68	263	79	20	3	10	(-	-)	135	42	47	48	22	0	56	3	0	1	1	1	3	.300	.360	.513	.873
2013	LV	AAA	104	404	119	24	4	15	(-	-)	196	52	68	71	35	1	95	3	0	4	11	3	7	.295	.352	.485	.837
2014	Lakwd	A	3	7	3	1	0	2	(-	-)	10	3	5	4	3	0	2	0	0	0	1	0	0	.429	1.429	2.029	
2014	LV	AAA	2	6	5	1	0	1	(-	-)	9	3	4	4	1	0	1	0	0	0	0	0	0	.833	.875	1.500	2.375
2013	Phi	NL	50	162	38	8	1	5	(4	1)	63	18	22	18	15	3	43	1	0	1	1	0	1	.235	.302	.389	.691
2014	Phi	NL	121	397	100	25	0	10	(6	4)	155	43	46	44	33	4	102	0	3	1	0	1	7	.252	.309	.390	.699
2 ML YEARS			171	559	138	33	1	15	(10	5)	218	61	68	62	48	7	145	1	3	2	1	1	8	.247	.307	.390	.697

Scott Atchison

Pitches: R Bats: R Pos: RP-70   Ht: 6'2" Wt: 200 Born: 3/29/1976 Age: 39

Year	Team	Lg	G	GS	CG	GF	IP	BFP	H	R	ER	HR	SH	SF	HB	TBB	IBB	SO	WP	Bk	W	L	Pct	Sh	Sv-Op	Hld	ERC	ERA
2004	Sea	AL	25	0	0	8	30.2	133	29	12	12	4	2	1	0	14	2	36	2	0	2	3	.400	0	0-0	2	4.08	3.52
2005	Sea	AL	6	0	0	2	6.2	27	7	5	5	1	0	0	0	1	0	9	0	0	0	0	--	0	0-0	0	3.77	6.75
2007	SF	NL	22	0	0	4	30.2	131	32	14	14	5	1	2	1	10	0	25	2	0	0	0	--	0	0-1	5	4.65	4.11
2010	Bos	AL	43	1	0	8	60.0	253	58	37	30	9	1	2	1	19	2	41	4	0	2	3	.400	0	0-0	7	3.92	4.50
2011	Bos	AL	17	0	0	4	30.1	122	31	11	11	0	1	2	2	6	0	17	2	0	1	0	1.000	0	1-1	0	3.15	3.26
2012	Bos	AL	42	0	0	7	51.1	200	42	10	9	2	1	2	0	9	3	36	2	0	2	1	.667	0	0-1	5	1.91	1.58
2013	NYM	NL	51	0	0	10	45.1	194	45	27	22	4	3	3	0	12	0	28	5	0	3	3	.500	0	0-0	10	3.33	4.37
2014	Cle	AL	70	0	0	11	72.0	280	60	24	22	4	1	1	0	14	4	49	1	0	6	0	1.000	0	2-7	14	2.16	2.75
	8 ML YEARS		276	1	0	54	327.0	1340	304	140	125	29	9	13	4	85	11	241	18	0	16	10	.615	0	3-10	43	3.11	3.44

Phillippe Aumont

Pitches: R Bats: L Pos: RP-5   fih-LEEP ah-MOHNT   Ht: 6'7" Wt: 260 Born: 1/7/1989 Age: 26

Year	Team	Lg	G	GS	CG	GF	IP	BFP	H	R	ER	HR	SH	SF	HB	TBB	IBB	SO	WP	Bk	W	L	Pct	Sh	Sv-Op	Hld	ERC	ERA
2014	LV*	AAA	35	0	0	8	55.0	244	48	25	24	2	3	2	0	39	1	65	9	0	3	3	.500	0	0- --	-	4.09	3.93
2012	Phi	NL	18	0	0	3	14.2	65	10	6	6	0	2	0	1	9	1	14	2	0	0	1	.000	0	2-3	5	2.50	3.68
2013	Phi	NL	22	0	0	8	19.1	95	24	11	9	0	0	1	3	13	1	19	2	1	1	3	.250	0	0-0	1	6.34	4.19
2014	Phi	NL	5	0	0	4	5.2	35	14	12	12	3	0	1	0	5	0	6	0	0	0	1	.000	0	0-0	0	21.66	19.06
	3 ML YEARS		45	0	0	15	39.2	195	48	29	27	3	2	2	4	27	2	39	4	1	1	5	.167	0	2-3	6	6.53	6.13

Alex Avila

Bats: L Throws: R Pos: C-122;PH-5;1B-1   ah-VEE-lah   Ht: 5'11" Wt: 210 Born: 1/29/1987 Age: 28

Year	Team	Lg	G	AB	H	2B	3B	HR	(Hm	Rd)	TB	R	RBI	RC	TBB	IBB	SO	HBP	SH	SF	SB	CS	GDP	Avg	OBP	Slg	OPS
2009	Det	AL	29	61	17	4	0	5	(4	1)	36	9	14	12	10	0	18	0	0	1	0	0	0	.279	.375	.590	.965
2010	Det	AL	104	294	67	12	0	7	(4	3)	100	28	31	26	36	0	71	2	1	0	2	2	12	.228	.316	.340	.656
2011	Det	AL	141	464	137	33	4	19	(10	9)	235	63	82	86	73	9	131	3	3	8	3	1	8	.295	.389	.506	.895
2012	Det	AL	116	367	89	21	2	9	(7	2)	141	42	48	53	61	2	104	2	2	2	2	0	12	.243	.352	.384	.736
2013	Det	AL	102	330	75	14	1	11	(7	4)	124	39	47	37	44	0	112	1	1	3	0	0	10	.227	.317	.376	.693
2014	Det	AL	124	390	85	22	0	11	(3	8)	140	44	47	48	61	1	151	3	1	0	3	0	6	.218	.327	.359	.686
	Postseason		31	101	14	1	0	3	(2	1)	24	6	7	4	11	0	39	1	1	0	0	0	1	.139	.230	.238	.468
	6 ML YEARS		616	1906	470	106	7	62	(35	27)	776	225	269	262	285	12	587	11	8	16	7	6	48	.247	.345	.407	.752

Luis Avilan

Pitches: L Bats: L Pos: RP-62   ah-VEE-lan   Ht: 6'2" Wt: 220 Born: 7/19/1989 Age: 25

Year	Team	Lg	G	GS	CG	GF	IP	BFP	H	R	ER	HR	SH	SF	HB	TBB	IBB	SO	WP	Bk	W	L	Pct	Sh	Sv-Op	Hld	ERC	ERA
2014	Gwnntt*	AAA	9	0	0	1	11.2	55	13	8	7	0	1	1	0	11	0	6	0	0	0	1	.000	0	0- --	-	6.40	5.40
2012	Atl	NL	31	0	0	2	36.0	142	27	9	8	1	3	0	1	10	1	33	3	1	1	0	1.000	0	0-0	5	2.00	2.00
2013	Atl	NL	75	0	0	7	65.0	256	40	12	11	1	1	1	4	22	2	38	3	1	5	0	1.000	0	0-2	27	1.62	1.52
2014	Atl	NL	62	0	0	14	43.1	193	47	22	22	2	3	2	3	21	7	25	5	0	4	1	.800	0	0-2	8	4.55	4.57
	Postseason		4	0	0	1	2.2	11	3	0	0	0	0	0	0	1	1	1	0	0	0	0	--	0	0-0	2	3.55	0.00
	3 ML YEARS		168	0	0	23	144.1	591	114	43	41	4	7	3	8	53	10	96	11	2	10	1	.909	0	0-4	40	2.50	2.56

Mike Aviles

uh-VEE-less

Bats: R Throws: R Pos: 3B-36;2B-33;LF-27;SS-15;PH-12;CF-3;RF-3;PR-2   Ht: 5'10" Wt: 205 Born: 3/13/1981 Age: 34

Year	Team	Lg	G	AB	H	2B	3B	HR	(Hm	Rd)	TB	R	RBI	RC	TBB	IBB	SO	HBP	SH	SF	SB	CS	GDP	Avg	OBP	Slg	OPS
2008	KC	AL	102	419	136	27	4	10	(4	6)	201	68	51	62	18	4	58	2	0	2	8	3	12	.325	.354	.480	.833
2009	KC	AL	36	120	22	3	1	1	(1	0)	30	10	8	4	4	0	26	0	2	1	1	0	3	.183	.208	.250	.458
2010	KC	AL	110	424	129	16	3	8	(4	4)	175	63	32	47	20	0	49	1	0	3	14	5	13	.304	.335	.413	.748
2011	2 Tms		91	286	73	17	3	7	(4	3)	117	31	39	31	13	0	44	2	4	4	14	4	8	.255	.289	.409	.698
2012	Bos	AL	136	512	128	28	0	13	(7	6)	195	57	60	57	23	0	77	2	3	6	14	6	6	.250	.282	.381	.663
2013	Cle	AL	124	361	91	16	0	9	(3	6)	133	54	46	35	15	0	41	3	7	8	8	5	11	.252	.282	.368	.650
2014	Cle	AL	113	344	85	16	1	5	(2	3)	118	38	39	27	13	0	49	1	11	5	14	5	10	.247	.273	.343	.616
	11 KC	AL	53	185	41	11	3	5	(2	3)	73	14	31	18	9	0	27	2	3	3	10	2	5	.222	.261	.395	.656
	11 Bos	AL	38	101	32	6	0	2	(2	0)	44	17	8	13	4	0	17	0	1	1	4	2	3	.317	.340	.436	.775
	7 ML YEARS		712	2466	664	122	12	53	(25	28)	969	321	275	263	106	4	344	11	27	29	73	28	63	.269	.299	.393	.692

Dylan Axelrod

Pitches: R Bats: R Pos: SP-4; RP-1   Ht: 6'0" Wt: 195 Born: 7/30/1985 Age: 29

Year	Team	Lg	G	GS	CG	GF	IP	BFP	H	R	ER	HR	SH	SF	HB	TBB	IBB	SO	WP	Bk	W	L	Pct	Sh	Sv-Op	Hld	ERC	ERA
2014	Charltt*	AAA	18	16	0	1	88.0	381	96	47	44	9	1	4	5	36	0	76	5	0	6	7	.462	0	0- --	-	5.04	4.50
2014	Lsvlle*	AAA	6	6	1	0	42.1	163	31	14	14	3	0	3	0	7	0	32	2	0	2	2	.500	1	0- --	-	1.71	2.98
2011	CWS	AL	4	3	0	1	18.2	82	18	6	6	1	0	2	1	9	2	19	0	0	1	0	1.000	0	0-0	0	3.89	2.89
2012	CWS	AL	14	7	0	4	51.0	231	56	32	31	8	0	2	1	21	0	40	1	0	2	2	.500	0	0-0	0	5.39	5.47
2013	CWS	AL	30	20	0	8	128.1	586	170	89	81	24	2	3	4	43	2	73	5	0	4	11	.267	0	0-0	0	6.55	5.68
2014	Cin	NL	5	4	0	1	18.1	72	14	6	6	5	0	0	0	4	1	20	0	0	2	1	.667	0	0-0	0	3.06	2.95
	4 ML YEARS		53	34	0	14	216.1	971	258	133	124	38	2	7	9	77	5	152	6	0	9	14	.391	0	0-0	0	5.72	5.16

John Axford

Pitches: R Bats: R Pos: RP-62

Ht: 6'5" Wt: 220 Born: 4/1/1983 Age: 32

			HOW MUCH HE PITCHED						WHAT HE GAVE UP													THE RESULTS							
Year	Team	Lg	G	GS	CG	GF	IP	BFP	H	R	ER	HR	SH	SF	HB	TBB	IBB	SO	WP	Bk	W	L	Pct	Sh	Sv-Op	Hld	ERC	ERA
2009	Mil	NL	7	0	0	6	7.2	34	5	3	3	0	0	0	0	6	1	9	1	0	0	0	-	0	1-1	0	2.62	3.52
2010	Mil	NL	50	0	0	43	58.0	238	42	17	16	1	2	2	1	27	3	76	4	0	8	2	.800	0	24-27	3	2.33	2.48
2011	Mil	NL	74	0	0	63	73.2	305	59	19	16	4	1	1	0	25	1	86	8	0	2	2	.500	0	**46**-48	0	2.44	1.95
2012	Mil	NL	75	0	0	54	69.1	310	61	42	36	10	1	2	2	39	2	93	10	0	5	8	.385	0	35-44	3	4.33	4.67
2013	2 Tms	NL	75	0	0	16	65.0	289	73	32	29	10	4	1	2	26	3	65	5	0	7	7	.500	0	0-7	19	5.25	4.02
2014	2 Tms		62	0	0	28	54.2	243	43	26	24	6	3	4	2	36	3	63	5	0	2	4	.333	0	10-13	2	3.96	3.95
13	Mil	NL	62	0	0	13	54.2	245	62	29	27	10	3	1	1	23	3	54	5	0	6	7	.462	0	0-6	19	5.53	4.45
13	StL	NL	13	0	0	3	10.1	44	11	3	2	0	1	0	1	3	0	11	0	0	1	0	1.000	0	0-1	0	3.75	1.74
14	Cle	AL	49	0	0	24	43.2	196	34	21	19	6	3	3	1	30	3	51	4	0	2	3	.400	0	10-13	2	4.11	3.92
14	Pit	NL	13	0	0	4	11.0	47	9	5	5	0	0	1	1	6	0	12	1	0	0	1	.000	0	0-0	0	3.33	4.09
Postseason			12	0	0	8	12.2	51	7	2	2	1	0	0	0	6	0	18	0	0	1	0	1.000	0	3-4	0	1.91	1.42
6 ML YEARS			343	0	0	210	328.1	1419	283	139	124	31	11	10	7	159	13	392	33	0	24	23	.511	0	116-140	27	3.58	3.40

Erick Aybar

Bats: B Throws: R Pos: SS-155;PH-2

EYE-barr

Ht: 5'10" Wt: 180 Born: 1/14/1984 Age: 31

			BATTING																		RUNNING			AVERAGES			
Year	Team	Lg	G	AB	H	2B	3B	HR	(Hm	Rd)	TB	R	RBI	RC	TBB	IBB	SO	HBP	SH	SF	SB	CS	GDP	Avg	OBP	Slg	OPS
2006	LAA	AL	34	40	10	1	1	0	(0	0)	13	5	2	4	0	0	8	0	0	0	1	0	1	.250	.250	.325	.575
2007	LAA	AL	79	194	46	5	1	1	(0	1)	56	18	19	16	10	0	32	2	3	2	4	4	8	.237	.279	.289	.568
2008	LAA	AL	98	346	96	18	5	3	(2	1)	133	53	39	49	14	0	45	5	9	1	7	2	2	.277	.314	.384	.699
2009	LAA	AL	137	504	157	23	9	5	(2	3)	213	70	58	73	30	1	54	5	12	5	14	7	9	.312	.353	.423	.776
2010	LAA	AL	138	534	135	18	4	5	(3	2)	176	69	29	51	35	1	81	7	11	2	22	8	7	.253	.306	.330	.636
2011	LAA	AL	143	556	155	33	8	10	(8	2)	234	71	59	72	31	1	68	6	9	3	30	6	13	.279	.322	.421	.743
2012	LAA	AL	141	517	150	31	5	8	(4	4)	215	67	45	63	22	1	61	5	7	2	20	4	11	.290	.324	.416	.740
2013	LAA	AL	138	550	149	33	5	6	(4	2)	210	68	54	61	23	1	59	3	8	5	12	7	14	.271	.301	.382	.683
2014	LAA	AL	156	589	164	30	4	7	(2	5)	223	77	68	74	36	4	62	5	3	8	16	9	10	.278	.321	.379	.700
Postseason			14	50	11	2	1	0	(0	0)	15	4	4	4	1	0	4	0	2	0	3	0	2	.220	.235	.300	.535
9 ML YEARS			1064	3830	1062	192	42	45	(19	26)	1473	498	373	463	201	9	470	38	62	28	126	47	75	.277	.318	.385	.702

Burke Badenhop

Pitches: R Bats: R Pos: RP-70

BADE-en-hopp

Ht: 6'5" Wt: 220 Born: 2/8/1983 Age: 32

			HOW MUCH HE PITCHED						WHAT HE GAVE UP													THE RESULTS							
Year	Team	Lg	G	GS	CG	GF	IP	BFP	H	R	ER	HR	SH	SF	HB	TBB	IBB	SO	WP	Bk	W	L	Pct	Sh	Sv-Op	Hld	ERC	ERA
2008	Fla	NL	13	8	0	2	47.1	218	55	34	32	7	2	2	3	21	1	35	2	0	2	3	.400	0	0-0	0	5.74	6.08
2009	Fla	NL	35	2	0	7	72.0	303	71	32	30	5	3	2	1	24	4	57	1	0	7	4	.636	0	0-1	2	3.53	3.75
2010	Fla	NL	53	0	0	16	67.2	281	62	33	30	5	5	1	2	21	5	47	1	0	2	5	.286	0	1-3	5	3.12	3.99
2011	Fla	NL	50	0	0	15	63.2	276	65	29	29	1	1	2	4	24	4	51	4	0	2	3	.400	0	1-1	5	3.65	4.10
2012	TB	AL	66	0	0	14	62.1	262	63	24	21	6	2	4	1	12	5	42	1	0	3	2	.600	0	0-0	5	3.19	3.03
2013	Mil	NL	63	0	0	23	62.1	254	62	32	24	6	7	2	0	12	4	42	2	0	2	3	.400	0	1-4	5	3.16	3.47
2014	Bos	AL	70	0	0	11	70.2	289	70	20	18	1	4	3	2	19	5	40	2	0	0	3	.000	0	1-4	13	3.03	2.29
7 ML YEARS			350	10	0	88	446.0	1883	448	204	184	31	24	16	13	133	28	314	13	0	18	23	.439	0	4-13	38	3.53	3.71

Javier Baez

Bats: R Throws: R Pos: SS-30;2B-25

BYE-ezz

Ht: 6'0" Wt: 190 Born: 12/1/1992 Age: 22

			BATTING																		RUNNING			AVERAGES			
Year	Team	Lg	G	AB	H	2B	3B	HR	(Hm	Rd)	TB	R	RBI	RC	TBB	IBB	SO	HBP	SH	SF	SB	CS	GDP	Avg	OBP	Slg	OPS
2011	Cubs	R	13	12	4	2	0	0	(-	-)	6	2	0	2	0	0	2	0	0	0	2	0	0	.333	.333	.500	.833
2011	Boise	A-	2	6	1	0	0	0	(-	-)	1	0	1	0	0	0	2	0	0	0	0	0	0	.167	.167	.167	.333
2012	Peoria	A	57	213	71	10	5	12	(-	-)	127	41	33	49	9	0	48	10	0	3	20	3	3	.333	.383	.596	.979
2012	Dytona	A+	23	80	15	3	1	4	(-	-)	32	9	13	8	5	1	21	1	0	0	4	2	1	.188	.244	.400	.644
2013	Dytona	A+	76	299	82	19	4	17	(-	-)	160	59	57	56	21	0	78	11	0	6	12	2	8	.274	.338	.535	.873
2013	Tenn	AA	54	218	64	15	0	20	(-	-)	139	39	54	48	19	2	69	0	0	3	8	2	3	.294	.346	.638	.983
2014	Iowa	AAA	104	388	101	24	2	23	(-	-)	198	64	80	65	34	3	130	5	0	7	16	8	14	.260	.323	.510	.833
2014	ChC	NL	52	213	36	6	0	9	(3	6)	69	25	20	12	15	0	95	1	0	0	5	1	5	.169	.227	.324	.551

Pedro Baez

Pitches: R Bats: R Pos: RP-20

BYE-ezz

Ht: 6'2" Wt: 230 Born: 3/11/1988 Age: 27

			HOW MUCH HE PITCHED						WHAT HE GAVE UP													THE RESULTS							
Year	Team	Lg	G	GS	CG	GF	IP	BFP	H	R	ER	HR	SH	SF	HB	TBB	IBB	SO	WP	Bk	W	L	Pct	Sh	Sv-Op	Hld	ERC	ERA
2013	RCuca	A+	32	0	0	13	34.2	163	41	17	14	3	0	5	4	15	1	32	1	0	2	2	.500	0	2- -	-	5.48	3.63
2013	Chatt	AA	16	0	0	3	23.1	102	26	13	11	3	1	1	0	8	0	23	2	1	1	1	.500	0	0- -	-	4.69	4.24
2014	Chatt	AA	17	0	0	13	19.1	82	15	7	6	0	0	0	1	9	1	18	2	0	2	1	.667	0	6- -	-	2.53	2.79
2014	Albq	AAA	23	0	0	15	22.2	97	27	12	12	4	0	2	2	4	0	20	2	1	0	0	-	0	6- -	-	5.29	4.78
2014	LAD	NL	20	0	0	8	24.0	92	16	7	7	3	1	1	0	5	1	18	0	0	0	0	-	0	0-0	5	1.79	2.63

Andrew Bailey

Pitches: R Bats: R Pos: P   Ht: 6'3" Wt: 240 Born: 5/31/1984 Age: 31

					HOW MUCH HE PITCHED					WHAT HE GAVE UP									THE RESULTS							
Year	Team	Lg	G	GS	CG	GF	IP	BFP	H	R	ER	HR	SH	SF	HB	TBB	IBB	SO	WP	Bk	W	L	Pct	Sh	Sv-Op	Hld	ERC	ERA
2009	Oak	AL	68	0	0	54	83.1	323	49	17	17	5	3	2	0	24	3	91	6	0	6	3	.667	0	26-30	2	1.44	1.84
2010	Oak	AL	47	0	0	42	49.0	189	34	8	8	3	2	3	0	13	1	42	0	0	1	3	.250	0	25-28	5	1.82	1.47
2011	Oak	AL	42	0	0	37	41.2	170	34	18	15	3	1	1	0	12	2	41	0	0	0	4	.000	0	24-26	1	2.42	3.24
2012	Bos	AL	19	0	0	13	15.1	74	21	12	12	2	0	0	0	8	2	14	0	1	1	1	.500	0	6-9	1	6.73	7.04
2013	Bos	AL	30	0	0	17	28.2	116	23	12	12	7	1	0	0	12	0	39	0	0	3	1	.750	0	8-13	8	4.13	3.77
5 ML YEARS			206	0	0	163	218.0	872	161	67	64	20	7	6	0	69	8	227	6	1	11	12	.478	0	89-106	12	2.30	2.64

Homer Bailey

Pitches: R Bats: R Pos: SP-23   Ht: 6'4" Wt: 230 Born: 5/3/1986 Age: 29

					HOW MUCH HE PITCHED					WHAT HE GAVE UP									THE RESULTS							
Year	Team	Lg	G	GS	CG	GF	IP	BFP	H	R	ER	HR	SH	SF	HB	TBB	IBB	SO	WP	Bk	W	L	Pct	Sh	Sv-Op	Hld	ERC	ERA
2007	Cin	NL	9	9	0	0	45.1	205	43	32	29	3	1	6	3	28	1	28	1	1	4	2	.667	0	0-0	0	4.61	5.76
2008	Cin	NL	8	8	0	0	36.1	180	59	36	32	8	5	2	0	17	1	18	4	1	0	6	.000	0	0-0	0	9.31	7.93
2009	Cin	NL	20	20	0	0	113.1	496	115	61	57	12	4	4	3	52	1	86	6	0	8	5	.615	0	0-0	0	4.56	4.53
2010	Cin	NL	19	19	1	0	109.0	465	109	55	54	11	2	1	3	40	6	100	3	1	4	3	.571	1	0-0	0	4.01	4.46
2011	Cin	NL	22	22	0	0	132.0	561	136	68	65	18	4	4	5	33	2	106	4	0	9	7	.563	0	0-0	0	4.01	4.43
2012	Cin	NL	33	33	2	0	208.0	874	206	97	85	26	5	5	8	52	3	168	3	0	13	10	.565	1	0-0	0	3.73	3.68
2013	Cin	NL	32	32	2	0	209.0	849	181	85	81	20	8	4	10	54	2	199	5	2	11	12	.478	1	0-0	0	2.99	3.49
2014	Cin	NL	23	23	1	0	145.2	604	134	60	60	16	5	4	7	45	1	124	5	1	9	5	.643	1	0-0	0	3.57	3.71
Postseason			2	1	0	0	9.0	32	3	1	1	0	1	1	1	1	0	12	0	0	0	0	-	0	0-0	0	0.52	1.00
8 ML YEARS			166	166	6	0	998.2	4234	983	494	463	114	34	30	39	321	17	829	31	6	58	50	.537	4	0-0	0	3.92	4.17

Jeff Baker

Bats: R Throws: R Pos: 1B-43;PH-40;2B-21;3B-2   Ht: 6'2" Wt: 220 Born: 6/21/1981 Age: 34

										BATTING												RUNNING			AVERAGES			
Year	Team	Lg	G	AB	H	2B	3B	HR	(Hm	Rd)	TB	R	RBI	RC	TBB	IBB	SO	HBP	SH	SF	SB	CS	GDP	Avg	OBP	Slg	OPS
2005	Col	NL	12	38	8	4	0	1	(1	0)	15	6	4	4	5	0	12	0	0	0	0	0	1	.211	.302	.395	.697
2006	Col	NL	18	57	21	7	2	5	(4	1)	47	13	21	17	1	0	14	0	0	0	2	0	0	.368	.379	.825	1.204
2007	Col	NL	85	144	32	2	2	4	(4	0)	50	17	12	8	13	1	40	2	0	0	0	0	5	.222	.296	.347	.643
2008	Col	NL	104	299	80	22	1	12	(8	4)	140	55	48	40	26	2	85	1	1	6	4	0	5	.268	.322	.468	.791
2009	2 Tms	NL	81	226	65	15	2	4	(3	1)	96	27	24	28	18	0	53	2	0	2	1	0	8	.288	.343	.425	.768
2010	ChC	NL	79	206	56	13	2	4	(3	1)	85	29	21	21	16	0	50	1	0	1	1	0	6	.272	.326	.413	.739
2011	ChC	NL	81	201	54	12	1	3	(1	2)	77	20	23	20	10	0	46	0	0	1	0	0	5	.269	.302	.383	.685
2012	3 Tms	NL	83	188	45	12	1	4	(1	3)	71	18	25	18	11	1	48	0	0	2	4	1	7	.239	.279	.378	.656
2013	Tex	AL	74	154	43	8	0	11	(4	7)	84	21	21	26	18	1	48	2	0	1	1	0	5	.279	.360	.545	.905
2014	Mia	NL	90	208	55	10	4	3	(3	0)	82	27	28	27	13	1	51	1	0	3	1	0	8	.264	.307	.394	.701
09	Col	NL	12	23	3	0	1	0	(0	0)	5	0	3	0	1	0	7	0	0	0	1	0	3	.130	.167	.217	.384
09	ChC	NL	69	203	62	15	1	4	(3	1)	91	27	21	28	17	0	46	2	0	2	0	0	5	.305	.362	.448	.810
12	ChC	NL	54	134	36	10	1	4	(1	3)	60	16	20	17	8	0	28	0	0	2	4	1	4	.269	.306	.448	.753
12	Det	AL	15	35	7	2	0	0	(0	0)	9	1	4	1	2	0	10	0	0	0	0	0	3	.200	.243	.257	.500
12	Atl	NL	14	19	2	0	0	0	(0	0)	2	1	1	0	1	1	10	0	0	0	0	0	0	.105	.150	.105	.255
Postseason			4	4	2	0	0	0	(0	0)	2	0	1	1	0	0	1	0	0	0	0	0	0	.500	.500	.500	1.000
10 ML YEARS			707	1721	459	105	15	51	(32	19)	747	233	227	209	131	6	447	9	1	16	14	1	55	.267	.319	.434	.753

John Baker

Bats: L Throws: R Pos: C-55;PH-12;PR-1   Ht: 6'1" Wt: 215 Born: 1/20/1981 Age: 34

										BATTING												RUNNING			AVERAGES			
Year	Team	Lg	G	AB	H	2B	3B	HR	(Hm	Rd)	TB	R	RBI	RC	TBB	IBB	SO	HBP	SH	SF	SB	CS	GDP	Avg	OBP	Slg	OPS
2008	Fla	NL	61	197	59	14	0	5	(3	2)	88	32	32	36	30	4	48	2	1	3	0	0	6	.299	.392	.447	.839
2009	Fla	NL	112	373	101	25	0	9	(3	6)	153	59	50	54	41	5	89	5	2	2	0	0	10	.271	.349	.410	.759
2010	Fla	NL	23	78	17	3	1	0	(0	0)	22	7	6	4	9	1	18	1	0	0	0	0	5	.218	.307	.282	.589
2011	Fla	NL	16	13	2	0	0	0	(0	0)	2	0	1	0	2	0	3	0	1	0	0	0	0	.154	.267	.154	.421
2012	SD	NL	63	193	46	8	0	0	(0	0)	54	17	14	19	20	2	41	0	1	0	2	1	4	.238	.310	.280	.590
2013	SD	NL	16	40	6	0	0	0	(0	0)	6	0	2	0	6	0	12	0	0	0	0	0	4	.150	.261	.150	.411
2014	ChC	NL	68	182	35	7	0	0	(0	0)	42	9	15	12	19	3	58	2	3	2	0	0	3	.192	.273	.231	.504
7 ML YEARS			359	1076	266	57	1	14	(6	8)	367	124	120	125	127	15	269	10	8	7	2	1	32	.247	.330	.341	.671

Scott Baker

Pitches: R Bats: R Pos: RP-17; SP-8   Ht: 6'4" Wt: 215 Born: 9/19/1981 Age: 33

					HOW MUCH HE PITCHED					WHAT HE GAVE UP									THE RESULTS							
Year	Team	Lg	G	GS	CG	GF	IP	BFP	H	R	ER	HR	SH	SF	HB	TBB	IBB	SO	WP	Bk	W	L	Pct	Sh	Sv-Op	Hld	ERC	ERA
2014	RdRck*	AAA	6	6	0	0	38.0	155	35	16	14	5	0	3	2	11	0	30	1	0	4	1	.800	0	0--	-	3.74	3.32
2005	Min	AL	10	9	0	0	53.2	217	48	21	20	5	2	2	0	14	0	32	0	0	3	3	.500	0	0-0	0	2.97	3.35
2006	Min	AL	16	16	0	0	83.1	377	114	63	59	17	2	4	3	16	1	62	0	0	5	8	.385	0	0-0	0	6.26	6.37
2007	Min	AL	24	23	2	0	143.2	606	162	70	68	15	6	2	5	29	4	102	0	0	9	9	.500	1	0-0	1	4.19	4.26
2008	Min	AL	28	28	0	0	172.1	703	161	66	66	20	2	3	3	42	2	141	6	0	11	4	.733	0	0-0	0	3.31	3.45
2009	Min	AL	33	33	1	0	200.0	828	190	99	97	28	1	6	4	48	1	162	4	0	15	9	.625	1	0-0	0	3.51	4.37
2010	Min	AL	29	29	0	0	170.1	725	186	87	85	23	1	4	6	43	0	148	7	0	12	9	.571	0	0-0	0	4.43	4.49
2011	Min	AL	23	21	1	2	134.2	548	126	50	47	15	1	2	4	32	2	123	4	0	8	6	.571	0	0-0	0	3.32	3.14
2013	ChC	NL	3	3	0	0	15.0	57	9	6	6	3	1	0	0	4	0	6	0	0	0	0	-	0	0-0	0	2.13	3.60
2014	Tex	AL	25	8	0	13	80.2	332	82	49	49	15	0	3	2	14	3	55	0	0	3	4	.429	0	0-0	0	3.90	5.47
Postseason			1	0	0	0	2.1	10	3	1	1	1	0	0	0	0	0	2	0	0	0	0	-	0	0-0	0	6.14	3.86
9 ML YEARS			191	170	4	15	1053.2	4393	1078	511	497	141	16	26	27	242	13	831	21	0	66	52	.559	2	0-0	2	3.87	4.25

73

Grant Balfour

Pitches: R Bats: R Pos: RP-65   BAL-fore   Ht: 6'2" Wt: 200 Born: 12/30/1977 Age: 37

Year Team	Lg	HOW MUCH HE PITCHED						WHAT HE GAVE UP													THE RESULTS							
		G	GS	CG	GF	IP	BFP	H	R	ER	HR	SH	SF	HB	TBB	IBB	SO	WP	Bk	W	L	Pct	Sh	Sv-Op	Hld	ERC	ERA
2001 Min	AL	2	0	0	1	2.2	14	3	4	4	2	1	1	0	3	0	2	0	0	0	0	-	0	0-0	0	13.78	13.50
2003 Min	AL	17	1	0	6	26.0	115	23	12	12	4	2	1	0	14	2	30	0	0	1	0	1.000	0	0-1	1	4.14	4.15
2004 Min	AL	36	0	0	14	39.1	172	35	19	19	4	2	0	2	21	1	42	3	0	4	1	.800	0	0-1	4	4.16	4.35
2007 2 Tms		25	0	0	8	24.2	121	30	21	21	2	2	3	1	20	0	30	0	0	1	2	.333	0	0-0	1	7.15	7.66
2008 TB	AL	51	0	0	12	58.1	224	28	10	10	3	1	3	0	24	1	82	2	0	6	2	.750	0	4-5	14	1.38	1.54
2009 TB	AL	73	0	0	15	67.1	289	59	38	36	6	1	2	2	33	0	69	1	0	5	4	.556	0	4-9	18	3.79	4.81
2010 TB	AL	57	0	0	8	55.1	222	43	16	14	3	2	4	0	17	2	56	4	1	2	1	.667	0	0-1	16	2.24	2.28
2011 Oak	AL	62	0	0	15	62.0	242	44	17	17	8	1	0	0	20	1	59	0	0	5	2	.714	0	2-7	26	2.49	2.47
2012 Oak	AL	75	0	0	34	74.2	289	41	21	21	4	0	3	1	28	2	72	2	0	3	2	.600	0	24-26	15	1.55	2.53
2013 Oak	AL	65	0	0	55	62.2	262	48	20	18	7	2	0	0	27	2	72	9	0	1	3	.250	0	38-41	0	2.92	2.59
2014 TB	AL	65	0	0	34	62.1	270	49	34	34	3	1	1	1	41	3	57	4	0	2	6	.250	0	12-15	11	3.52	4.91
07 Mil	NL	3	0	0	2	2.2	18	4	6	6	1	1	0	1	4	0	3	0	0	0	2	.000	0	0-0	0	15.83	20.25
07 TB	AL	22	0	0	6	22.0	103	26	15	15	1	1	3	0	16	0	27	0	0	1	0	1.000	0	0-0	1	6.19	6.14
Postseason		20	0	0	8	19.2	83	16	7	7	2	1	1	1	10	4	15	1	0	1	1	.500	0	2-2	2	3.41	3.20
11 ML YEARS		528	1	0	202	535.1	2220	403	212	206	46	15	18	7	248	14	571	25	1	30	23	.566	0	84-106	106	2.92	3.46

Clint Barnes

Bats: R Throws: R Pos: SS-27;2B-14;PH-4;PR-4;1B-2;3B-2   BAR-mess   Ht: 6'1" Wt: 200 Born: 3/6/1979 Age: 36

Year Team	Lg	BATTING																			RUNNING			AVERAGES			
		G	AB	H	2B	3B	HR	(Hm	Rd)	TB	R	RBI	RC	TBB	IBB	SO	HBP	SH	SF	SB	CS	GDP	Avg	OBP	Slg	OPS
2014 Altna*	AA	2	6	2	0	0	0	(-	-)	2	0	0	0	0	0	0	0	0	0	0	0	1	.333	.333	.333	.667
2014 Indy*	AAA	5	19	3	0	0	1	(-	-)	6	3	2	1	1	0	1	0	0	1	0	0	0	.158	.190	.316	.506
2003 Col	NL	12	25	8	2	0	0	(0	0)	10	2	2	3	0	0	10	2	0	1	0	0	0	.320	.357	.400	.757
2004 Col	NL	20	71	20	3	1	2	(0	2)	31	14	10	12	3	0	10	1	2	0	0	1	2	.282	.320	.437	.757
2005 Col	NL	81	350	101	19	1	10	(7	3)	152	55	46	49	16	1	36	6	4	1	6	4	4	.289	.330	.434	.764
2006 Col	NL	131	478	105	26	4	7	(3	4)	160	57	56	47	22	6	72	9	19	7	5	4	2	.220	.264	.335	.598
2007 Col	NL	27	37	8	3	0	0	(0	0)	11	5	1	1	1	1	13	0	1	0	0	0	1	.216	.237	.297	.534
2008 Col	NL	107	393	114	25	6	11	(8	3)	184	47	44	54	17	0	69	2	4	1	13	4	9	.290	.322	.468	.790
2009 Col	NL	154	550	135	32	3	23	(13	10)	242	69	76	63	31	2	121	10	6	7	12	10	6	.245	.294	.440	.734
2010 Col	NL	133	387	91	21	0	8	(4	4)	136	43	50	43	35	10	66	5	2	3	3	2	5	.235	.305	.351	.656
2011 Hou	NL	123	446	109	27	0	12	(5	7)	172	47	39	46	38	2	88	7	2	2	3	1	9	.244	.312	.386	.698
2012 Pit	NL	144	455	104	16	1	8	(3	5)	146	34	45	38	20	3	106	8	8	2	0	2	9	.229	.272	.321	.593
2013 Pit	NL	108	304	64	15	0	5	(1	4)	94	22	23	20	14	3	70	2	9	1	0	0	5	.211	.249	.309	.558
2014 Pit	NL	48	102	25	5	0	0	(0	0)	30	15	7	7	9	2	18	4	1	1	1	1	2	.245	.328	.294	.622
Postseason		10	25	3	0	0	0	(0	0)	3	0	0	1	0	0	3	0	1	0	0	0	0	.120	.120	.120	.240
12 ML YEARS		1088	3598	884	194	16	86	(44	42)	1368	410	399	383	206	30	679	56	57	26	43	29	54	.246	.295	.380	.675

Brandon Barnes

Bats: R Throws: R Pos: PH-67;RF-55;LF-18;CF-5;PR-1   Ht: 6'2" Wt: 210 Born: 5/15/1986 Age: 29

Year Team	Lg	BATTING																			RUNNING			AVERAGES			
		G	AB	H	2B	3B	HR	(Hm	Rd)	TB	R	RBI	RC	TBB	IBB	SO	HBP	SH	SF	SB	CS	GDP	Avg	OBP	Slg	OPS
2012 Hou	NL	43	98	20	3	0	1	(0	1)	26	8	7	4	5	0	29	1	1	0	1	1	1	.204	.250	.265	.515
2013 Hou	AL	136	408	98	17	1	8	(7	1)	141	46	41	47	21	0	127	8	6	2	11	11	5	.240	.289	.346	.635
2014 Col	NL	132	292	75	17	4	8	(7	1)	124	37	27	26	15	0	100	0	6	0	5	4	11	.257	.293	.425	.718
3 ML YEARS		311	798	193	37	5	17	(14	3)	291	91	75	77	41	0	256	9	13	2	17	16	17	.242	.286	.365	.651

Matt Barnes

Pitches: R Bats: R Pos: RP-5   Ht: 6'4" Wt: 205 Born: 6/17/1990 Age: 25

Year Team	Lg	HOW MUCH HE PITCHED						WHAT HE GAVE UP													THE RESULTS							
		G	GS	CG	GF	IP	BFP	H	R	ER	HR	SH	SF	HB	TBB	IBB	SO	WP	Bk	W	L	Pct	Sh	Sv-Op	Hld	ERC	ERA
2012 Grnville	A	5	5	0	0	26.2	97	12	1	1	0	0	0	1	4	0	42	0	1	2	0	1.000	0	0--	-	0.72	0.34
2012 Salem	A+	20	20	1	0	93.0	383	85	42	37	6	2	8	8	25	0	91	6	1	5	5	.500	1	0--	-	3.26	3.58
2013 Portlnd	AA	24	24	0	0	108.0	480	112	62	52	11	4	2	4	46	0	135	7	0	5	10	.333	0	0--	-	4.50	4.33
2013 Pwtckt	AAA	1	1	0	0	5.1	20	3	0	0	0	0	0	0	2	0	7	0	0	1	0	1.000	0	0--	-	1.41	0.00
2014 Pwtckt	AAA	23	22	0	0	127.2	500	119	00	50	0	4	3	0	40	0	100	0	0	0	9	.471	0	0--	-	0.40	0.05
2014 Bos	AL	5	0	0	3	9.0	39	11	4	4	1	0	1	0	2	0	8	0	0	0	0	-	0	0-0	0	4.72	4.00

Darwin Barney

Bats: R Throws: R Pos: 2B-79;PH-18;SS-2   Ht: 5'10" Wt: 185 Born: 11/8/1985 Age: 29

Year Team	Lg	BATTING																			RUNNING			AVERAGES			
		G	AB	H	2B	3B	HR	(Hm	Rd)	TB	R	RBI	RC	TBB	IBB	SO	HBP	SH	SF	SB	CS	GDP	Avg	OBP	Slg	OPS
2014 Albq*	AAA	9	35	9	1	0	0	(-	-)	10	5	1	3	3	0	5	0	0	0	0	0	0	.257	.316	.286	.602
2010 ChC	NL	30	79	19	4	0	0	(0	0)	23	12	2	6	6	0	12	0	0	0	0	0	0	.241	.294	.291	.585
2011 ChC	NL	143	529	146	23	6	2	(2	0)	187	66	43	60	22	2	67	8	7	4	9	2	14	.276	.313	.353	.666
2012 ChC	NL	156	548	139	26	4	7	(2	5)	194	73	44	60	33	1	58	3	3	1	6	1	11	.254	.299	.354	.653
2013 ChC	NL	141	501	104	25	1	7	(4	3)	152	49	41	30	36	5	64	6	4	6	4	2	22	.208	.266	.303	.569
2014 2 Tms	NL	94	237	57	11	2	3	(2	1)	81	24	23	27	17	2	34	4	2	2	1	0	1	.241	.300	.342	.642
14 ChC	NL	72	204	47	10	2	2	(2	0)	67	18	16	19	9	2	31	1	2	1	1	0	1	.230	.265	.328	.594
14 LAD	NL	22	33	10	1	0	1	(0	1)	14	6	7	8	8	0	3	3	0	1	0	0	0	.303	.467	.424	.891
5 ML YEARS		564	1894	465	89	13	19	(15	4)	637	224	153	183	114	10	235	21	16	13	20	5	48	.246	.294	.336	.630

Tucker Barnhart

Bats: B **Throws:** R **Pos:** C-20;PH-1   **Ht:** 5'11" **Wt:** 195 **Born:** 1/7/1991 **Age:** 24

							BATTING														RUNNING			AVERAGES			
Year	Team	Lg	G	AB	H	2B	3B	HR	(Hm	Rd)	TB	R	RBI	RC	TBB	IBB	SO	HBP	SH	SF	SB	CS	GDP	Avg	OBP	Slg	OPS
2010	Billings	R+	35	111	34	9	0	0	(-	-)	43	17	12	20	18	0	25	2	0	0	4	1	2	.306	.412	.387	.800
2011	Dayton	A	97	326	89	24	2	3	(-	-)	126	47	43	46	37	0	59	1	3	5	2	1	9	.273	.344	.387	.731
2012	Bkrsfld	A+	59	198	55	12	1	4	(-	-)	81	26	22	31	29	0	45	1	2	1	0	2	4	.278	.371	.409	.780
2012	Pnscla	AA	41	130	26	4	1	2	(-	-)	38	10	12	9	11	0	22	0	1	0	1	1	5	.200	.262	.292	.555
2013	Pnscla	AA	98	339	88	19	1	3	(-	-)	118	31	44	46	45	2	57	3	4	4	1	0	5	.260	.348	.348	.696
2014	Lsvlle	AAA	78	256	63	9	3	1	(-	-)	81	18	29	28	28	1	34	1	4	3	0	1	6	.246	.319	.316	.636
2014	Cin	NL	21	54	10	0	0	1	(1	0)	13	3	1	2	4	1	10	0	2	0	0	0	0	.185	.241	.241	.482

Aaron Barrett

Pitches: R **Bats:** R **Pos:** RP-50   **Ht:** 6'3" **Wt:** 225 **Born:** 1/2/1988 **Age:** 27

			HOW MUCH HE PITCHED						WHAT HE GAVE UP											THE RESULTS							
Year	Team	Lg	G	GS	CG	GF	IP	BFP	H	R	ER	HR	SH	SF	HB	TBB	IBB	SO	WP	Bk	W	L	Pct	Sh	Sv-Op	Hld	ERC	ERA
2010	Vrmnt	A-	10	4	0	2	21.0	111	26	25	22	3	1	0	1	22	0	25	9	0	0	5	.000	0	0- -	-	8.76	9.43
2011	Auburn	A-	19	0	0	15	26.2	114	16	12	12	2	0	0	0	20	0	32	5	0	1	2	.333	0	9- -	-	3.06	4.05
2012	Hgrstn	A	31	0	0	28	34.2	139	25	12	10	2	0	1	0	11	0	52	6	1	3	2	.600	0	16- -	-	2.06	2.60
2012	Ptomc	A+	11	0	0	5	17.0	64	9	2	2	0	0	0	2	3	0	21	2	0	0	0	-	0	1- -	-	1.12	1.06
2013	Hrsbrg	AA	51	0	0	42	50.1	203	40	14	12	2	2	0	0	15	0	69	3	0	1	1	.500	0	26- -	-	2.25	2.15
2014	Syrcse	AAA	10	0	0	5	10.1	37	5	0	0	0	0	0	0	1	0	8	0	0	1	0	1.000	0	2- -	-	0.65	0.00
2014	Was	NL	50	0	0	12	40.2	174	33	17	12	1	1	2	1	20	2	49	6	1	3	0	1.000	0	0-0	8	2.87	2.66

Jason Bartlett

Bats: R **Throws:** R **Pos:** LF-2;PR-2;DH-1   **Ht:** 6'0" **Wt:** 190 **Born:** 10/30/1979 **Age:** 35

							BATTING														RUNNING			AVERAGES			
Year	Team	Lg	G	AB	H	2B	3B	HR	(Hm	Rd)	TB	R	RBI	RC	TBB	IBB	SO	HBP	SH	SF	SB	CS	GDP	Avg	OBP	Slg	OPS
2004	Min	AL	8	12	1	0	0	0	(0	0)	1	2	1	1	1	0	1	0	1	0	2	0	0	.083	.154	.083	.237
2005	Min	AL	74	224	54	10	1	3	(2	1)	75	33	16	22	21	0	37	4	2	1	4	0	6	.241	.316	.335	.651
2006	Min	AL	99	333	103	18	2	2	(0	2)	131	44	32	50	22	1	46	11	1	5	10	5	8	.309	.367	.393	.760
2007	Min	AL	140	510	135	20	7	5	(2	3)	184	75	43	65	50	3	73	8	0	2	23	3	8	.265	.339	.361	.699
2008	TB	AL	128	454	130	25	3	1	(1	0)	164	48	37	56	22	1	69	9	5	4	20	6	9	.286	.329	.361	.690
2009	TB	AL	137	500	160	29	7	14	(3	11)	245	90	66	97	54	2	89	5	4	4	30	7	5	.320	.389	.490	.879
2010	TB	AL	135	468	119	27	3	4	(1	3)	164	71	47	62	45	1	83	5	11	3	11	6	6	.254	.324	.350	.675
2011	SD	NL	139	554	136	22	3	2	(1	1)	170	61	40	50	48	0	98	5	5	6	23	10	13	.245	.308	.307	.615
2012	SD	NL	29	83	11	5	0	0	(0	0)	16	8	4	1	12	0	27	0	2	1	0	0	6	.133	.240	.193	.432
2014	Min	AL	3	3	0	0	0	0	(0	0)	0	3	0	0	0	0	3	1	0	0	0	0	0	.000	.250	.000	.250
	Postseason		24	77	21	3	1	1	(1	0)	29	8	3	6	5	0	13	3	1	0	2	0	0	.273	.341	.377	.718
	10 ML YEARS		892	3141	849	156	26	31	(10	21)	1150	435	286	404	275	8	526	48	31	26	123	37	61	.270	.336	.366	.702

Daric Barton

Bats: L **Throws:** R **Pos:** 1B-30;PR-2   DARE-ick   **Ht:** 6'0" **Wt:** 205 **Born:** 8/16/1985 **Age:** 29

							BATTING														RUNNING			AVERAGES			
Year	Team	Lg	G	AB	H	2B	3B	HR	(Hm	Rd)	TB	R	RBI	RC	TBB	IBB	SO	HBP	SH	SF	SB	CS	GDP	Avg	OBP	Slg	OPS
2014	Scrmto*	AAA	85	313	82	18	1	9	(-	-)	129	46	56	52	51	2	40	6	0	4	0	1	10	.262	.372	.412	.784
2007	Oak	AL	18	72	25	9	0	4	(2	2)	46	16	8	14	10	0	11	1	0	1	1	0	2	.347	.429	.639	1.067
2008	Oak	AL	140	446	101	17	5	9	(1	8)	155	59	47	56	65	5	99	3	6	3	2	1	6	.226	.327	.348	.674
2009	Oak	AL	54	160	43	12	1	3	(2	1)	66	31	24	28	26	0	25	2	1	3	0	2	1	.269	.372	.413	.784
2010	Oak	AL	159	556	152	33	5	10	(1	9)	225	79	57	92	110	2	102	3	12	5	7	3	8	.273	.393	.405	.798
2011	Oak	AL	67	236	50	13	0	0	(0	0)	63	27	21	24	39	3	47	2	0	3	2	1	6	.212	.325	.267	.592
2012	Oak	AL	46	113	23	7	0	1	(0	1)	33	8	6	14	22	0	32	1	0	0	1	0	1	.204	.338	.292	.630
2013	Oak	AL	37	104	28	2	0	3	(2	1)	39	15	16	19	13	0	18	1	0	2	0	0	1	.269	.350	.375	.725
2014	Oak	AL	30	57	9	1	0	0	(0	0)	10	7	5	2	5	0	14	1	0	1	0	0	0	.158	.234	.175	.410
	Postseason		2	3	0	0	0	0	(0	0)	0	0	0	0	0	0	3	0	0	0	0	0	0	.000	.000	.000	.000
	8 ML YEARS		551	1744	431	94	11	30	(8	22)	637	242	184	249	290	10	348	14	19	18	13	7	25	.247	.356	.365	.721

Anthony Bass

Pitches: R **Bats:** R **Pos:** RP-21   **Ht:** 6'2" **Wt:** 200 **Born:** 11/1/1987 **Age:** 27

			HOW MUCH HE PITCHED						WHAT HE GAVE UP											THE RESULTS							
Year	Team	Lg	G	GS	CG	GF	IP	BFP	H	R	ER	HR	SH	SF	HB	TBB	IBB	SO	WP	Bk	W	L	Pct	Sh	Sv-Op	Hld	ERC	ERA
2014	QuadC*	A	3	1	0	1	4.0	16	2	2	0	0	0	0	0	0	0	6	0	0	0	0	-	0	0- -	-	0.47	0.00
2014	OKCity*	AAA	14	0	0	4	16.1	68	15	9	6	3	0	1	0	6	1	14	1	0	0	2	.000	0	1- -	-	4.01	3.31
2011	SD	NL	27	3	0	6	48.1	198	41	9	9	3	2	0	1	21	1	24	1	0	2	0	1.000	0	0-0	3	3.28	1.68
2012	SD	NL	24	15	1	3	97.0	411	89	59	51	10	2	2	1	39	3	80	5	1	2	8	.200	0	1-1	1	3.65	4.73
2013	SD	NL	24	0	0	8	42.0	193	51	26	25	4	1	0	0	20	4	31	5	0	0	0	-	0	0-0	5	5.41	5.36
2014	Hou	AL	21	0	0	8	27.0	119	32	20	19	6	0	1	2	7	1	7	2	0	1	1	.500	0	2-4	-	5.74	6.33
	4 ML YEARS		96	18	1	26	214.1	921	213	114	104	23	5	3	4	87	9	142	13	1	5	9	.357	0	3-5	9	4.15	4.37

Chris Bassitt

Pitches: R Bats: R Pos: SP-5; RP-1   Ht: 6'5" Wt: 210 Born: 2/22/1989 Age: 26

			HOW MUCH HE PITCHED						WHAT HE GAVE UP												THE RESULTS							
Year	Team	Lg	G	GS	CG	GF	IP	BFP	H	R	ER	HR	SH	SF	HB	TBB	IBB	SO	WP	Bk	W	L	Pct	Sh	Sv-Op	Hld	ERC	ERA
2011	Brs	R+	6	0	0	2	8.1	35	9	1	1	0	0	0	0	2	0	11	0	0	0	0	-	0	0--	-	3.23	1.08
2011	WinSa	A+	1	0	0	1	1.2	8	2	1	1	0	0	0	1	0	0	1	0	0	0	0	-	0	0--	-	5.10	5.40
2011	Knapol	A	16	0	0	6	24.2	98	18	6	5	1	2	0	2	6	0	29	4	0	3	1	.750	0	1--	-	2.06	1.82
2012	WinSa	A+	38	10	0	17	91.0	403	74	45	37	6	6	0	4	54	1	75	3	0	5	4	.556	0	4--	-	3.63	3.66
2013	WinSa	A+	18	18	0	0	101.1	443	90	50	39	9	5	2	5	42	0	101	7	0	7	2	.778	0	0--	-	3.53	3.46
2013	Brham	AA	8	8	0	0	47.2	191	35	16	12	2	3	2	4	17	0	37	1	0	4	2	.667	0	0--	-	2.53	2.27
2014	WSX	R	3	2	0	0	8.2	39	9	4	4	0	0	0	1	3	0	13	1	0	0	0	-	0	0--	-	3.70	4.15
2014	Brham	AA	6	6	0	0	34.2	145	26	10	6	2	2	1	2	14	0	36	0	0	3	1	.750	0	0--	-	2.67	1.56
2014	CWS	AL	6	5	0	1	29.2	137	34	13	13	0	1	1	3	13	1	21	0	0	1	1	.500	0	0-0	0	4.57	3.94

Antonio Bastardo

Pitches: L Bats: R Pos: RP-67   bah-STAHR-doh   Ht: 5'11" Wt: 200 Born: 9/21/1985 Age: 29

			HOW MUCH HE PITCHED						WHAT HE GAVE UP												THE RESULTS							
Year	Team	Lg	G	GS	CG	GF	IP	BFP	H	R	ER	HR	SH	SF	HB	TBB	IBB	SO	WP	Bk	W	L	Pct	Sh	Sv-Op	Hld	ERC	ERA
2009	Phi	NL	6	5	0	0	23.2	106	26	18	17	4	0	0	2	9	0	19	0	0	2	3	.400	0	0-0	0	5.41	6.46
2010	Phi	NL	25	0	0	2	18.2	86	19	9	9	1	0	0	2	9	0	26	0	0	2	0	1.000	0	0-1	2	4.46	4.34
2011	Phi	NL	64	0	0	15	58.0	225	28	17	17	6	2	2	0	26	0	70	4	0	6	1	.857	0	8-9	17	1.69	2.64
2012	Phi	NL	65	0	0	10	52.0	224	40	26	25	7	1	2	2	26	3	81	5	0	2	5	.286	0	1-5	26	3.42	4.33
2013	Phi	NL	48	0	0	15	42.2	179	33	12	11	2	4	1	1	21	1	42	4	0	3	2	.600	0	2-5	14	2.91	2.32
2014	Phi	NL	67	0	0	17	64.0	271	43	31	28	4	3	3	2	34	4	81	5	0	5	7	.417	0	0-2	12	2.54	3.94
	Postseason		5	0	0	0	1.2	8	2	0	0	0	1	0	0	1	0	2	0	0	0	0	-	0	0-0	1	5.10	0.00
	6 ML YEARS		275	5	0	59	259.0	1091	189	113	107	24	10	8	9	125	8	324	18	0	20	18	.526	0	11-22	71	2.94	3.72

Trevor Bauer

Pitches: R Bats: R Pos: SP-26   Ht: 6'1" Wt: 190 Born: 1/17/1991 Age: 24

			HOW MUCH HE PITCHED						WHAT HE GAVE UP												THE RESULTS							
Year	Team	Lg	G	GS	CG	GF	IP	BFP	H	R	ER	HR	SH	SF	HB	TBB	IBB	SO	WP	Bk	W	L	Pct	Sh	Sv-Op	Hld	ERC	ERA
2014	Clmbs*	AAA	7	7	1	0	46.0	182	36	11	11	5	0	0	1	14	0	44	1	0	4	1	.800	0	0--	-	2.77	2.15
2012	Ari	NL	4	4	0	0	16.1	77	14	13	11	2	1	1	1	13	0	17	2	0	1	2	.333	0	0-0	0	5.12	6.06
2013	Cle	AL	4	4	0	0	17.0	81	15	11	10	3	0	1	1	16	0	11	1	0	1	2	.333	0	0-0	0	6.47	5.29
2014	Cle	AL	26	26	0	0	153.0	663	151	76	71	16	1	8	11	60	4	143	6	0	5	8	.385	0	0-0	0	4.27	4.18
	3 ML YEARS		34	34	0	0	186.1	821	180	100	92	21	2	10	13	89	4	171	9	0	7	12	.368	0	0-0	0	4.54	4.44

Jose Bautista

Bats: R Throws: R Pos: RF-131;DH-13;1B-12;CF-12;PH-1   bah-TEE-stah   Ht: 6'0" Wt: 205 Born: 10/19/1980 Age: 34

			BATTING																		RUNNING			AVERAGES			
Year	Team	Lg	G	AB	H	2B	3B	HR	(Hm	Rd)	TB	R	RBI	RC	TBB	IBB	SO	HBP	SH	SF	SB	CS	GDP	Avg	OBP	Slg	OPS
2004	4 Tms		64	88	18	3	0	0	(0	0)	21	6	2	2	7	0	40	0	1	0	0	1	1	.205	.263	.239	.502
2005	Pit	NL	11	28	4	1	0	0	(0	0)	5	3	1	0	3	0	7	0	0	0	1	0	2	.143	.226	.179	.404
2006	Pit	NL	117	400	94	20	3	16	(11	5)	168	58	51	55	46	2	110	16	3	4	2	4	12	.235	.335	.420	.755
2007	Pit	NL	142	532	135	36	2	15	(8	7)	220	75	63	71	68	1	101	4	4	6	3	16	12	.254	.339	.414	.753
2008	2 Tms		128	370	88	17	0	15	(5	10)	150	45	54	43	40	5	91	2	8	4	1	1	12	.238	.313	.405	.718
2009	Tor	AL	113	336	79	13	3	13	(5	8)	137	54	40	42	56	1	85	4	6	2	4	0	9	.235	.349	.408	.757
2010	Tor	AL	161	569	148	35	3	54	(33	21)	351	109	124	132	100	2	116	10	0	2	9	2	10	.260	.378	.617	.995
2011	Tor	AL	149	513	155	24	2	43	(20	23)	312	105	103	133	132	24	111	6	0	4	9	5	8	.302	.447	.608	1.056
2012	Tor	AL	92	332	80	14	0	27	(11	16)	175	64	65	58	59	2	63	4	0	4	5	2	11	.241	.358	.527	.886
2013	Tor	AL	118	452	117	24	0	28	(14	14)	225	82	73	81	69	2	84	3	0	4	7	2	13	.259	.358	.498	.856
2014	Tor	AL	155	553	158	27	0	35	(18	17)	290	101	103	112	104	11	96	9	1	6	6	2	18	.286	.403	.524	.928
04	Bal	AL	16	11	3	0	0	0	(0	0)	3	3	0	1	1	0	3	0	0	0	0	0	0	.273	.333	.273	.606
04	TB	AL	12	12	2	0	0	0	(0	0)	2	1	1	0	3	0	7	0	0	0	0	1	0	.167	.333	.167	.500
04	KC	AL	13	25	5	1	0	0	(0	0)	6	1	1	0	1	0	12	0	0	0	0	0	0	.200	.231	.240	.471
04	Pit	NL	23	40	8	2	0	0	(0	0)	10	1	0	1	2	0	18	0	1	0	0	0	1	.200	.238	.250	.488
08	Pit	NL	107	314	76	15	0	12	(3	9)	127	38	44	39	38	4	77	2	6	3	1	1	10	.242	.325	.404	.729
08	Tor	AL	21	56	12	2	0	3	(2	1)	23	7	10	4	2	1	14	0	2	1	0	0	2	.214	.237	.411	.648
	11 ML YEARS		1250	4173	1070	214	13	246	(125	121)	2054	702	679	729	684	50	904	58	23	38	50	22	112	.258	.367	.492	.859

Mike Baxter

Bats: L Throws: R Pos: PH-3;LF-1   Ht: 6'0" Wt: 205 Born: 12/7/1984 Age: 30

			BATTING																		RUNNING			AVERAGES			
Year	Team	Lg	G	AB	H	2B	3B	HR	(Hm	Rd)	TB	R	RBI	RC	TBB	IBB	SO	HBP	SH	SF	SB	CS	GDP	Avg	OBP	Slg	OPS
2014	Alba*	AAA	119	412	119	25	8	7	(-	-)	181	72	36	69	45	1	87	6	2	3	12	5	10	.289	.365	.439	.804
2010	SD	NL	9	8	1	0	0	0	(0	0)	1	0	1	0	0	0	2	0	0	1	0	0	1	.125	.111	.125	.236
2011	NYM	NL	22	34	8	2	1	1	(1	0)	15	6	4	5	5	0	9	1	0	0	0	0	0	.235	.350	.441	.791
2012	NYM	NL	89	179	47	14	2	3	(1	2)	74	26	17	30	25	4	45	5	0	2	5	3	0	.263	.365	.413	.778
2013	NYM	NL	74	132	25	6	1	0	(0	0)	33	14	4	11	17	0	28	5	0	1	5	2	1	.189	.303	.250	.553
2014	LAD	NL	4	7	0	0	0	0	(0	0)	0	0	0	0	1	0	2	0	0	0	0	0	1	.000	.125	.000	.125
	5 ML YEARS		198	360	81	22	4	4	(2	2)	123	46	26	46	48	4	86	11	0	4	10	5	4	.225	.331	.342	.673

Pedro Beato

Pitches: R Bats: R Pos: RP-3   bay-AHH-toe   Ht: 6'6" Wt: 230 Born: 10/27/1986 Age: 28

Year	Team	Lg	G	GS	CG	GF	IP	BFP	H	R	ER	HR	SH	SF	HB	TBB	IBB	SO	WP	Bk	W	L	Pct	Sh	Sv-Op	Hld	ERC	ERA
2014	Gwnntt*	AAA	42	2	0	21	48.1	198	43	23	22	7	0	2	0	17	0	45	1	0	2	0	1.000	0	6- -	-	3.65	4.10
2011	NYM	NL	60	0	0	7	67.0	283	59	41	32	5	2	4	4	27	3	39	1	0	2	1	.667	0	0-1	11	3.45	4.30
2012	2 Tms		11	0	0	2	12.0	51	11	9	9	1	0	0	1	5	0	12	1	0	1	0	1.000	0	0-0	1	3.96	6.75
2013	Bos	AL	10	0	0	5	10.0	46	12	5	4	1	0	0	1	2	0	5	0	0	1	1	.500	0	0-0	0	4.58	3.60
2014	Atl	NL	3	0	0	1	4.1	19	3	0	0	0	0	0	0	3	0	3	0	0	0	0	-	0	0-0	0	2.74	0.00
12	NYM	NL	7	0	0	2	4.1	20	5	5	5	1	0	0	0	2	0	5	1	0	0	0	-	0	0-0	1	6.09	10.38
12	Bos	AL	4	0	0	0	7.2	31	6	4	4	0	0	0	1	3	0	7	0	0	1	0	1.000	0	0-0	0	2.83	4.70
	4 ML YEARS		84	0	0	15	93.1	399	85	55	45	7	2	4	6	37	3	59	2	0	4	2	.667	0	0-1	12	3.60	4.34

Blake Beavan

Pitches: R Bats: R Pos: SP-1   BEV-uhn   Ht: 6'7" Wt: 245 Born: 1/17/1989 Age: 26

Year	Team	Lg	G	GS	CG	GF	IP	BFP	H	R	ER	HR	SH	SF	HB	TBB	IBB	SO	WP	Bk	W	L	Pct	Sh	Sv-Op	Hld	ERC	ERA
2014	Tacom*	AAA	19	2	1	2	39.0	167	38	18	16	7	1	2	1	14	0	31	2	0	4	1	.800	0	0- -	-	4.42	3.69
2014	Hi Dsrt*	A+	1	0	0	1	2.0	10	3	2	2	1	0	0	1	1	0	0	0	0	0	0	-	0	0- -	-	15.00	9.00
2011	Sea	AL	15	15	0	0	97.0	405	106	46	46	13	1	5	3	15	0	42	4	0	5	6	.455	0	0-0	0	3.99	4.27
2012	Sea	AL	26	26	0	0	152.1	638	168	76	75	23	1	5	10	24	0	67	3	0	11	11	.500	0	0-0	0	4.36	4.43
2013	Sea	AL	12	2	0	4	39.2	174	46	27	27	8	1	2	1	8	0	27	0	0	0	2	.000	0	0-0	0	4.89	6.13
2014	Sea	AL	1	1	0	0	4.0	16	6	2	2	2	0	0	0	0	0	1	0	0	0	1	.000	0	0-0	0	9.22	4.50
	4 ML YEARS		54	44	0	4	293.0	1233	326	151	150	46	3	12	14	47	0	137	7	0	16	20	.444	0	0-0	0	4.36	4.61

Josh Beckett

Pitches: R Bats: R Pos: SP-20   Ht: 6'5" Wt: 230 Born: 5/15/1980 Age: 35

Year	Team	Lg	G	GS	CG	GF	IP	BFP	H	R	ER	HR	SH	SF	HB	TBB	IBB	SO	WP	Bk	W	L	Pct	Sh	Sv-Op	Hld	ERC	ERA
2014	RCuca*	A+	1	1	0	0	4.0	19	5	3	3	2	0	0	0	3	0	5	0	0	0	1	.000	0	0- -	-	10.95	6.75
2001	Fla	NL	4	4	0	0	24.0	99	14	9	4	3	0	0	1	11	0	24	1	0	2	2	.500	0	0-0	0	2.36	1.50
2002	Fla	NL	23	21	0	0	107.2	454	93	56	49	13	5	3	1	44	2	113	5	0	6	7	.462	0	0-0	0	3.50	4.10
2003	Fla	NL	24	23	0	1	142.0	601	132	54	48	9	5	1	2	56	4	152	6	1	9	8	.529	0	0-0	0	3.44	3.04
2004	Fla	NL	26	26	1	0	156.2	654	137	72	66	16	9	3	6	54	3	152	5	0	9	9	.500	0	0-0	0	3.32	3.79
2005	Fla	NL	29	29	2	0	178.2	728	153	75	67	14	8	2	7	58	2	166	5	0	15	8	.652	1	0-0	0	3.07	3.38
2006	Bos	AL	33	33	0	0	204.2	869	191	120	114	36	2	3	10	74	1	158	11	1	16	11	.593	0	0-0	0	4.28	5.01
2007	Bos	AL	30	30	1	0	200.2	822	189	76	73	17	3	2	5	40	0	194	3	0	20	7	.741	0	0-0	0	2.99	3.27
2008	Bos	AL	27	27	1	0	174.1	725	173	80	78	18	4	3	9	34	1	172	5	0	12	10	.545	0	0-0	0	3.45	4.03
2009	Bos	AL	32	32	4	0	212.1	883	198	99	91	25	5	5	7	55	1	199	3	1	17	6	.739	2	0-0	0	3.39	3.86
2010	Bos	AL	21	21	0	0	127.2	577	151	89	82	20	4	2	8	45	3	116	3	0	6	6	.500	0	0-0	0	5.56	5.78
2011	Bos	AL	30	30	1	0	193.0	767	146	65	62	21	8	5	9	52	1	175	6	0	13	7	.650	1	0-0	0	2.56	2.89
2012	2 Tms		28	28	0	0	170.1	730	174	91	88	21	5	8	5	52	6	132	5	0	7	14	.333	0	0-0	0	4.02	4.65
2013	LAD	NL	8	8	1	0	43.1	195	50	30	25	8	5	1	1	15	2	41	0	0	0	5	.000	0	0-0	0	5.29	5.19
2014	LAD	NL	20	20	1	0	115.2	475	96	41	37	17	3	3	5	39	2	107	1	0	6	6	.500	1	0-0	0	3.39	2.88
12	Bos	AL	21	21	0	0	127.1	547	131	75	74	16	3	8	5	38	2	94	4	0	5	11	.313	0	0-0	0	4.12	5.23
12	LAD	NL	7	7	0	0	43.0	183	43	16	14	5	2	0	0	14	4	38	1	0	2	3	.400	0	0-0	0	3.73	2.93
	Postseason		14	13	3	0	93.2	366	67	32	32	11	2	1	4	21	1	99	3	0	7	3	.700	3	0-0	0	2.22	3.07
	14 ML YEARS		335	332	12	1	2051.0	8579	1897	957	884	238	66	41	76	629	28	1901	59	3	138	106	.566	6	0-0	0	3.54	3.88

Gordon Beckham

Bats: R Throws: R Pos: 2B-105;3B-13;PH-7;SS-6;DH-1;PR-1   Ht: 6'0" Wt: 185 Born: 9/16/1986 Age: 28

Year	Team	Lg	G	AB	H	2B	3B	HR	(Hm	Rd)	TB	R	RBI	RC	TBB	IBB	SO	HBP	SH	SF	SB	CS	GDP	Avg	OBP	Slg	OPS
2014	Brham*	AA	12	43	7	2	0	1	(-	-)	12	5	6	2	4	0	6	0	0	0	1	0	1	.163	.234	.279	.513
2009	CWS	AL	103	378	102	28	1	14	(4	10)	174	58	63	61	41	0	65	6	1	4	7	4	10	.270	.347	.460	.808
2010	CWS	AL	131	444	112	25	2	9	(7	2)	168	58	49	52	37	0	92	7	6	4	4	6	9	.252	.317	.378	.695
2011	CWS	AL	150	499	115	23	0	10	(7	3)	168	60	44	48	35	0	111	13	7	3	5	3	6	.230	.296	.337	.633
2012	CWS	AL	151	525	123	24	0	16	(12	4)	195	62	60	58	40	0	89	7	8	2	5	4	10	.234	.296	.371	.668
2013	CWS	AL	103	371	99	22	1	5	(3	2)	138	46	24	36	28	2	56	4	1	4	5	1	10	.267	.322	.372	.694
2014	2 Tms		127	446	101	27	0	9	(4	5)	155	53	44	32	22	2	81	7	3	5	3	0	17	.226	.271	.348	.618
14	CWS	AL	101	390	86	24	0	7	(3	4)	131	43	36	28	19	1	70	5	3	5	3	0	12	.221	.263	.336	.598
14	LAA	AL	26	56	15	3	0	2	(1	1)	24	10	8	4	3	1	11	2	0	0	0	0	5	.268	.328	.429	.756
	6 ML YEARS		765	2663	652	149	4	63	(37	26)	998	337	284	287	203	4	494	44	26	22	29	18	62	.245	.307	.375	.681

Erik Bedard

Pitches: L Bats: L Pos: SP-15; RP-2   buh-DARD   Ht: 6'1" Wt: 200 Born: 3/5/1979 Age: 36

Year	Team	Lg	G	GS	CG	GF	IP	BFP	H	R	ER	HR	SH	SF	HB	TBB	IBB	SO	WP	Bk	W	L	Pct	Sh	Sv-Op	Hld	ERC	ERA
2014	Drham*	AAA	1	1	0	0	4.0	15	2	1	1	0	0	1	1	1	0	5	0	0	0	0	-	0	0- -	-	1.51	2.25
2002	Bal	AL	2	0	0	0	0.2	4	2	1	1	0	0	0	0	0	0	1	0	0	0	0	-	0	0-0	0	14.52	13.50
2004	Bal	AL	27	26	0	0	137.1	633	149	83	70	13	0	4	7	71	1	121	7	2	6	10	.375	0	0-0	0	5.11	4.59
2005	Bal	AL	24	24	0	0	141.2	606	139	66	63	10	3	6	5	57	1	125	4	1	6	8	.429	0	0-0	0	3.95	4.00
2006	Bal	AL	33	33	0	0	196.1	844	196	92	82	16	6	4	5	69	0	171	6	0	15	11	.577	0	0-0	0	3.83	3.76
2007	Bal	AL	28	28	1	0	182.0	733	141	66	64	19	2	4	5	57	0	221	3	0	13	5	.722	1	0-0	0	2.71	3.16
2008	Sea	AL	15	15	0	0	81.0	347	70	38	33	9	1	2	4	37	0	72	3	0	6	4	.600	0	0-0	0	3.82	3.67
2009	Sea	AL	15	15	0	0	83.0	348	65	29	26	8	2	1	4	34	0	90	2	0	5	3	.625	0	0-0	0	3.08	2.82
2011	2 Tms	AL	24	24	0	0	129.1	541	118	63	52	14	1	1	1	48	0	125	5	0	5	9	.357	0	0-0	0	3.60	3.62
2012	Pit	NL	24	24	0	0	125.2	557	129	76	70	14	5	2	3	56	2	118	1	1	7	14	.333	0	0-0	0	4.52	5.01

Year	Team	Lg	HOW MUCH HE PITCHED							WHAT HE GAVE UP												THE RESULTS							
			G	GS	CG	GF	IP	BFP	H	R	ER	HR	SH	SF	HB	TBB	IBB	SO	WP	Bk	W	L	Pct	Sh	Sv-Op	Hld	ERC	ERA
2013	Hou	AL	32	26	0	3	151.0	663	149	83	77	18	2	6	6	75	0	138	1	0	4	12	.250	0	1-3	0	4.73	4.59
2014	TB	AL	17	15	0	1	75.2	342	84	44	40	10	1	4	2	29	0	64	3	0	4	6	.400	0	0-0	0	4.86	4.76
11	Sea	AL	16	16	0	0	91.1	373	77	41	35	11	1	0	1	30	0	87	5	0	4	7	.364	0	0-0	0	3.16	3.45
11	Bos	AL	8	8	0	0	38.0	168	41	22	17	3	0	1	0	18	0	38	0	0	1	2	.333	0	0-0	0	4.70	4.03
11 ML YEARS			241	230	1	4	1303.2	5618	1242	643	578	131	23	34	42	533	4	1246	35	4	71	82	.464	1	1-3	0	3.97	3.99

Cam Bedrosian

Pitches: R Bats: R Pos: RP-17 **Ht: 6'0" Wt: 205 Born: 10/2/1991 Age: 23**

Year	Team	Lg	HOW MUCH HE PITCHED							WHAT HE GAVE UP												THE RESULTS							
			G	GS	CG	GF	IP	BFP	H	R	ER	HR	SH	SF	HB	TBB	IBB	SO	WP	Bk	W	L	Pct	Sh	Sv-Op	Hld	ERC	ERA
2010	Angels	R	5	4	0	0	12.0	55	13	11	6	0	0	1	0	7	0	10	6	1	0	2	.000	0	0--	-	4.47	4.50
2012	CRpds	A	21	21	0	0	82.2	385	91	61	58	5	2	5	8	52	0	48	15	1	3	11	.214	0	0--	-	5.74	6.31
2013	Burlgtn	A	37	2	0	20	54.1	241	55	38	32	4	1	0	5	22	1	69	9	0	1	5	.167	0	7--	-	4.27	5.30
2013	InldEm	A+	7	0	0	3	8.2	37	4	0	0	0	1	0	1	7	0	9	0	0	0	0	-	0	0--	-	2.45	0.00
2014	InldEm	A+	5	0	0	4	5.2	20	1	0	0	0	0	0	0	2	0	15	0	0	0	0	-	0	1--	-	0.40	0.00
2014	Ark	AA	30	0	0	25	32.1	114	10	5	4	1	1	0	0	10	0	57	2	0	1	0	1.000	0	15--	-	0.70	1.11
2014	Salt Lk	AAA	8	0	0	6	7.0	35	5	6	6	0	0	0	3	6	1	10	0	0	1	1	.500	0	2--	-	4.62	7.71
2014	LAA	AL	17	0	0	4	19.1	93	23	17	14	2	0	1	0	12	1	20	1	1	0	1	.000	0	0-1	1	5.88	6.52

Dallas Beeler

Pitches: R Bats: R Pos: SP-2 **Ht: 6'5" Wt: 210 Born: 6/12/1989 Age: 26**

Year	Team	Lg	HOW MUCH HE PITCHED							WHAT HE GAVE UP												THE RESULTS							
			G	GS	CG	GF	IP	BFP	H	R	ER	HR	SH	SF	HB	TBB	IBB	SO	WP	Bk	W	L	Pct	Sh	Sv-Op	Hld	ERC	ERA
2010	Cubs	R	8	2	0	0	16.1	69	20	9	6	0	1	0	0	2	0	16	0	0	0	3	.000	0	0--	-	3.56	3.31
2010	Boise	A-	1	0	0	0	2.0	8	2	0	0	0	0	0	0	0	0	2	0	0	0	0	-	0	0--	-	1.95	0.00
2011	Peoria	A	12	11	0	0	43.1	169	35	13	8	1	3	0	2	6	0	35	0	0	1	1	.500	0	0--	-	1.87	1.66
2011	Tenn	AA	9	9	0	0	51.2	228	68	31	26	7	3	0	2	7	0	33	0	0	1	5	.167	0	0--	-	5.21	4.53
2012	Tenn	AA	27	27	1	0	136.0	603	166	74	64	11	5	2	4	48	1	70	3	1	6	7	.462	0	0--	-	5.20	4.24
2013	Tenn	AA	9	9	0	0	54.2	227	43	26	19	3	2	1	6	17	0	35	1	0	4	2	.667	0	0--	-	2.71	3.13
2014	Iowa	AAA	20	20	1	0	124.1	499	112	48	47	8	4	1	4	32	0	83	6	1	9	6	.600	0	0--	-	2.98	3.40
2014	ChC	NL	2	2	0	0	11.0	46	10	5	4	0	1	0	0	7	1	6	1	0	0	2	.000	0	0-0	0	3.83	3.27

Joe Beimel

Pitches: L Bats: L Pos: RP-55 BYE-mull **Ht: 6'3" Wt: 205 Born: 4/19/1977 Age: 38**

Year	Team	Lg	HOW MUCH HE PITCHED							WHAT HE GAVE UP												THE RESULTS							
			G	GS	CG	GF	IP	BFP	H	R	ER	HR	SH	SF	HB	TBB	IBB	SO	WP	Bk	W	L	Pct	Sh	Sv-Op	Hld	ERC	ERA
2001	Pit	NL	42	15	0	9	115.1	511	131	72	67	12	3	1	6	49	4	58	3	0	7	11	.389	0	0-0	0	5.24	5.23
2002	Pit	NL	53	8	0	8	85.1	389	88	49	44	9	7	3	4	45	12	53	2	0	2	5	.286	0	0-1	5	4.68	4.64
2003	Pit	NL	69	0	0	11	62.1	276	69	35	35	7	3	5	4	33	6	42	0	1	1	3	.250	0	0-5	12	5.62	5.05
2004	Min	AL	3	0	0	1	1.2	15	8	8	8	1	0	0	0	2	0	2	0	0	0	0	-	0	0-0	0	44.44	43.20
2005	TB	AL	7	0	0	3	11.0	51	15	4	4	1	0	0	0	4	1	3	1	0	0	0	-	0	0-0	0	5.80	3.27
2006	LAD	NL	62	0	0	10	70.0	295	70	26	23	7	4	3	0	23	3	30	6	1	2	1	.667	0	2-2	10	3.62	2.96
2007	LAD	NL	83	0	0	10	67.1	281	63	30	29	1	5	2	1	24	6	39	3	2	4	2	.667	0	1-1	16	2.93	3.88
2008	LAD	NL	71	0	0	10	49.0	214	50	11	11	0	1	4	3	21	4	32	1	1	5	1	.833	0	0-0	12	3.70	2.02
2009	2 Tms	NL	71	0	0	26	55.1	240	57	24	22	5	4	6	1	19	5	35	4	1	1	6	.143	0	1-6	13	3.84	3.58
2010	Col	NL	71	0	0	11	45.0	188	46	18	17	5	1	1	0	15	3	21	2	1	1	2	.333	0	0-1	20	4.00	3.40
2011	Pit	NL	35	0	0	9	25.1	117	34	17	15	6	1	0	1	9	1	17	0	0	1	1	.500	0	0-2	7	7.15	5.33
2014	Sea	AL	56	0	0	8	45.0	184	39	12	11	4	3	1	1	14	4	25	3	0	3	1	.750	0	0-0	0	2.93	2.20
09	Was	NL	45	0	0	19	39.2	172	38	17	15	3	2	4	1	15	4	24	2	1	1	5	.167	0	1-5	10	3.46	3.40
09	Col	NL	26	0	0	7	15.2	68	19	7	7	2	2	2	0	4	1	11	2	0	0	1	.000	0	0-1	3	4.84	4.02
Postseason			6	0	0	1	1.1	7	1	0	0	0	0	0	0	2	0	0	0	0	0	0	-	0	0-0	0	5.91	0.00
12 ML YEARS			623	23	0	115	632.2	2761	670	306	286	58	32	26	21	256	49	357	25	7	27	33	.450	0	4-18	104	4.41	4.07

Ronald Belisario

Pitches: R Bats: R Pos: RP-62 bell-ih-SAR-ee-oh **Ht: 6'3" Wt: 240 Born: 12/31/1982 Age: 32**

Year	Team	Lg	HOW MUCH HE PITCHED							WHAT HE GAVE UP												THE RESULTS							
			G	GS	CG	GF	IP	BFP	H	R	ER	HR	SH	SF	HB	TBB	IBB	SO	WP	Bk	W	L	Pct	Sh	Sv-Op	Hld	ERC	ERA
2009	LAD	NL	69	0	0	13	70.2	299	52	21	16	4	3	2	6	29	7	64	4	0	4	3	.571	0	0-7	12	2.54	2.04
2010	LAD	NL	59	0	0	13	55.1	233	52	31	31	6	3	0	3	19	4	38	4	1	3	1	.750	0	2-4	16	3.72	5.04
2012	LAD	NL	68	0	0	13	71.0	286	47	22	20	3	1	0	4	29	4	60	1	0	8	1	.889	0	1-5	23	2.14	2.54
2013	LAD	NL	77	0	0	12	68.0	300	72	34	30	3	2	2	5	28	10	49	3	0	5	7	.417	0	1-5	21	4.10	3.97
2014	CWS	AL	62	0	0	19	66.1	292	78	46	41	4	3	2	5	18	7	47	2	0	4	8	.333	0	8-12	12	4.41	5.56
Postseason			13	0	0	2	8.1	38	8	7	7	1	0	0	1	3	1	2	1	0	0	0	-	0	0-0	2	3.89	7.56
5 ML YEARS			335	0	0	70	331.1	1410	301	154	138	20	12	6	23	123	32	267	14	1	24	20	.545	0	12-33	84	3.31	3.75

Matt Belisle

Pitches: R Bats: R Pos: RP-65; SP-1 bell-EYE-el **Ht: 6'4" Wt: 225 Born: 6/6/1980 Age: 35**

Year	Team	Lg	HOW MUCH HE PITCHED							WHAT HE GAVE UP												THE RESULTS							
			G	GS	CG	GF	IP	BFP	H	R	ER	HR	SH	SF	HB	TBB	IBB	SO	WP	Bk	W	L	Pct	Sh	Sv-Op	Hld	ERC	ERA
2003	Cin	NL	6	0	0	2	8.2	39	10	5	5	1	2	1	1	2	0	6	0	0	1	1	.500	0	0-1	0	4.73	5.19
2005	Cin	NL	60	5	0	17	85.2	382	101	49	42	11	4	2	6	26	6	59	3	0	4	8	.333	0	1-4	8	5.08	4.41
2006	Cin	NL	30	2	0	5	40.0	180	43	18	16	5	1	2	3	19	1	26	3	0	2	0	1.000	0	0-1	5	5.29	3.60
2007	Cin	NL	30	30	1	0	177.2	771	212	111	105	26	7	9	7	43	4	125	6	1	8	9	.471	0	0-0	0	5.05	5.32
2008	Cin	NL	6	6	0	0	29.2	142	47	27	24	4	1	2	0	6	0	14	2	0	1	4	.200	0	0-0	0	6.87	7.28
2009	Col	NL	24	0	0	6	31.0	133	35	21	19	6	0	2	1	5	1	22	1	0	3	1	.750	0	0-0	1	4.50	5.52

Year	Team	Lg	G	GS	CG	GF	IP	BFP	H	R	ER	HR	SH	SF	HB	TBB	IBB	SO	WP	Bk	W	L	Pct	Sh	Sv-Op	Hld	ERC	ERA
2010	Col	NL	76	0	0	11	92.0	365	84	34	30	7	4	2	2	16	5	91	3	1	7	5	.583	0	1-2	21	2.67	2.93
2011	Col	NL	74	0	0	10	72.0	301	77	33	26	5	4	0	4	14	3	58	2	0	10	4	.714	0	0-7	14	3.65	3.25
2012	Col	NL	80	0	0	14	80.0	348	91	36	33	5	4	0	3	18	6	69	1	1	3	8	.273	0	3-10	26	3.87	3.71
2013	Col	NL	72	0	0	16	73.0	301	76	37	35	6	2	1	0	15	2	62	3	0	5	7	.417	0	0-5	24	3.42	4.32
2014	Col	NL	66	0	0	13	64.2	282	74	35	35	5	4	5	1	19	2	43	3	0	4	7	.364	0	0-2	6	4.31	4.87
	Postseason		2	0	0	0	2.0	7	0	0	0	0	0	0	0	1	0	2	0	0	0	0	-	0	0-0	1	0.27	0.00
	11 ML YEARS		524	44	1	94	754.1	3244	850	406	370	81	33	26	28	183	30	575	27	3	48	54	.471	0	5-32	100	4.31	4.41

Jeff Beliveau

Pitches: L Bats: L Pos: RP-30

BELL-iv-oh

Ht: 6'1" Wt: 195 Born: 1/17/1987 Age: 28

Year	Team	Lg	G	GS	CG	GF	IP	BFP	H	R	ER	HR	SH	SF	HB	TBB	IBB	SO	WP	Bk	W	L	Pct	Sh	Sv-Op	Hld	ERC	ERA
2014	Drhm*	AAA	30	0	0	17	36.0	140	19	7	6	0	0	0	0	14	0	51	2	0	0	0	-	0	11--	-	1.28	1.50
2012	ChC	NL	22	0	0	4	17.2	86	21	9	9	5	1	0	1	12	1	17	1	1	1	0	1.000	0	0-0	1	7.98	4.58
2013	TB	AL	1	0	0	0	0.2	4	1	0	0	0	0	0	0	1	0	0	0	0	0	0	-	0	0-0	0	10.76	0.00
2014	TB	AL	30	0	0	6	24.0	100	19	7	7	1	1	1	2	7	1	28	1	1	0	0	-	0	1-1	6	2.40	2.63
	3 ML YEARS		53	0	0	10	42.1	190	41	16	16	6	2	1	3	20	2	45	2	2	1	0	1.000	0	1-1	7	4.61	3.40

Heath Bell

Pitches: R Bats: R Pos: RP-13

Ht: 6'3" Wt: 250 Born: 9/29/1977 Age: 37

Year	Team	Lg	G	GS	CG	GF	IP	BFP	H	R	ER	HR	SH	SF	HB	TBB	IBB	SO	WP	Bk	W	L	Pct	Sh	Sv-Op	Hld	ERC	ERA
2014	Norfolk*	AAA	10	0	0	5	10.2	52	15	6	5	0	0	1	1	6	0	11	2	0	2	0	1.000	0	1--	-	6.82	4.22
2014	S-WB*	AAA	5	0	0	5	6.0	30	7	5	5	1	0	0	0	6	0	8	0	0	0	1	.000	0	1--	-	8.29	7.50
2004	NYM	NL	17	0	0	2	24.1	94	22	9	9	5	1	0	0	6	0	27	0	0	0	2	.000	0	0-1	1	3.86	3.33
2005	NYM	NL	42	0	0	12	46.2	206	56	30	29	3	4	0	1	13	3	43	0	1	1	3	.250	0	0-0	4	4.42	5.59
2006	NYM	NL	22	0	0	8	37.0	166	51	25	21	6	1	0	0	11	2	35	1	0	0	0	-	0	0-0	0	6.40	5.11
2007	SD	NL	81	0	0	16	93.2	363	60	21	21	3	4	1	2	30	1	102	4	0	6	4	.600	0	2-6	34	1.67	2.02
2008	SD	NL	74	0	0	8	78.0	324	66	31	31	5	3	2	3	28	4	71	2	0	6	6	.500	0	0-7	23	2.93	3.58
2009	SD	NL	68	0	0	59	69.2	278	54	21	21	3	0	0	0	24	1	79	4	0	6	4	.600	0	42-48	0	2.36	2.71
2010	SD	NL	67	0	0	57	70.0	287	56	17	15	1	4	1	1	28	3	86	1	0	6	1	.857	0	47-50	2	2.47	1.93
2011	SD	NL	64	0	0	54	62.2	256	51	20	17	4	5	1	0	21	2	51	8	0	3	4	.429	0	43-48	0	2.57	2.44
2012	Mia	NL	73	0	0	41	63.2	286	70	38	36	5	2	4	2	29	3	59	2	0	4	5	.444	0	19-27	13	4.74	5.09
2013	Ari	NL	69	0	0	32	65.2	287	74	30	30	12	2	1	3	16	1	72	4	0	5	2	.714	0	15-22	8	4.86	4.11
2014	TB	AL	13	0	0	5	17.1	88	24	16	14	1	1	1	4	8	1	12	1	0	1	1	.500	0	0-0	0	6.96	7.27
	11 ML YEARS		590	0	0	292	628.2	2635	584	258	244	48	27	11	16	214	21	637	27	1	38	32	.543	0	168-209	83	3.36	3.49

Trevor Bell

Pitches: R Bats: L Pos: RP-2

Ht: 6'2" Wt: 205 Born: 10/12/1986 Age: 28

Year	Team	Lg	G	GS	CG	GF	IP	BFP	H	R	ER	HR	SH	SF	HB	TBB	IBB	SO	WP	Bk	W	L	Pct	Sh	Sv-Op	Hld	ERC	ERA
2014	Lsvlle*	AAA	1	0	0	1	1.0	4	0	0	0	0	0	0	0	1	0	1	0	0	0	0	-	0	0--	-	0.95	0.00
2009	LAA	AL	8	4	0	1	20.1	110	40	25	22	3	0	2	0	11	2	14	1	0	1	2	.333	0	0-0	0	11.15	9.74
2010	LAA	AL	25	7	0	8	61.0	273	77	35	32	2	3	1	1	21	2	45	5	0	2	5	.286	0	0-0	1	4.90	4.72
2011	LAA	AL	19	0	0	14	34.1	146	39	14	13	2	0	1	1	10	1	17	2	0	1	1	.500	0	0-1	4	3.29	3.41
2014	Cin	NL	2	0	0	0	0.2	9	5	5	5	0	0	0	0	2	0	0	0	0	0	0	-	0	0-0	0	69.84	67.50
	4 ML YEARS		54	11	0	23	116.1	538	161	79	72	7	3	4	2	44	5	76	8	0	4	8	.333	0	0-1	5	5.99	5.57

Vince Belnome

Bats: L Throws: R Pos: DH-4

bell-NO-may

Ht: 5'11" Wt: 205 Born: 3/11/1988 Age: 27

Year	Team	Lg	G	AB	H	2B	3B	HR	(Hm	Rd)	TB	R	RBI	RC	TBB	IBB	SO	HBP	SH	SF	SB	CS	GDP	Avg	OBP	Slg	OPS
2010	Lk Els	A+	135	498	136	31	1	16	(-	-)	217	81	84	94	102	2	136	2	1	3	4	1	14	.273	.397	.436	.832
2011	SnAnt	AA	75	267	89	19	1	17	(-	-)	161	56	62	66	47	1	59	1	1	2	0	5	13	.333	.432	.603	1.035
2012	Tucsn	AAA	80	258	71	11	1	5	(-	-)	99	28	33	41	43	0	72	1	0	1	5	1	9	.275	.380	.384	.763
2012	Padres	R	3	10	4	1	1	1	(-	-)	10	1	5	4	2	0	0	0	0	0	0	0	0	.400	.500	1.000	1.500
2012	Lk Els	A+	4	14	8	3	0	1	(-	-)	14	2	7	6	3	0	2	0	0	0	0	0	0	.571	.647	1.000	1.647
2013	Drhm	AAA	127	444	133	35	3	8	(-	-)	198	77	67	86	84	4	109	0	1	4	0	2	7	.300	.408	.446	.854
2014	Drhm	AAA	118	413	101	25	1	10	(-	-)	158	59	49	63	72	2	128	3	0	4	2	0	10	.245	.358	.383	.740
2014	TB	AL	4	10	1	1	0	0	(0	0)	2	1	1	1	3	1	3	0	0	0	0	0	0	.100	.286	.200	.486

Brandon Belt

Bats: L Throws: L Pos: 1B-59;PH-4;RF-1

Ht: 6'5" Wt: 220 Born: 4/20/1988 Age: 27

Year	Team	Lg	G	AB	H	2B	3B	HR	(Hm	Rd)	TB	R	RBI	RC	TBB	IBB	SO	HBP	SH	SF	SB	CS	GDP	Avg	OBP	Slg	OPS
2014	SnJos*	A+	2	6	3	0	0	1	(-	-)	6	2	1	3	0	0	1	2	0	0	0	0	0	.500	.625	1.000	1.625
2014	Fresno*	AAA	5	19	10	3	0	2	(-	-)	19	2	5	7	1	1	5	0	0	0	0	1	0	.526	.550	1.000	1.550
2011	SF	NL	63	187	42	6	1	9	(2	7)	77	21	18	20	20	1	57	2	0	0	3	2	3	.225	.306	.412	.718
2012	SF	NL	145	411	113	27	6	7	(5	2)	173	47	56	63	54	5	106	3	0	4	12	2	3	.275	.360	.421	.781
2013	SF	NL	150	509	147	39	4	17	(6	11)	245	76	67	82	52	4	125	6	1	3	5	2	4	.289	.360	.481	.841
2014	SF	NL	61	214	52	8	0	12	(2	10)	96	30	27	24	18	2	64	2	0	1	3	1	4	.243	.306	.449	.755
	Postseason		15	49	9	1	2	1	(1	0)	17	7	3	6	7	0	19	0	0	0	1	1	0	.184	.286	.347	.633
	4 ML YEARS		419	1321	354	80	11	45	(15	30)	591	174	168	189	144	12	352	13	1	8	23	7	14	.268	.344	.447	.791

Carlos Beltran

Bats: B Throws: R Pos: DH-76;RF-32;PH-2;1B-1   BELL-trahn   Ht: 6'1" Wt: 210 Born: 4/24/1977 Age: 38

																				RUNNING			AVERAGES			
Year	Team	Lg	G	AB	H	2B	3B	HR	(Hm | Rd)	TB	R	RBI	RC	TBB	IBB	SO	HBP	SH	SF	SB	CS	GDP	Avg	OBP	Slg	OPS
1998	KC	AL	14	58	16	5	3	0	(0 | 0)	27	12	7	9	3	0	12	1	0	1	3	0	2	.276	.317	.466	.783
1999	KC	AL	156	663	194	27	7	22	(12 | 10)	301	112	108	100	46	2	123	4	0	10	27	8	17	.293	.337	.454	.791
2000	KC	AL	98	372	92	15	4	7	(4 | 3)	136	49	44	43	35	2	69	0	2	4	13	0	12	.247	.309	.366	.675
2001	KC	AL	155	617	189	32	12	24	(7 | 17)	317	106	101	118	52	2	120	5	1	5	31	1	7	.306	.362	.514	.876
2002	KC	AL	162	637	174	44	7	29	(19 | 10)	319	114	105	117	71	1	135	4	3	7	35	7	12	.273	.346	.501	.847
2003	KC	AL	141	521	160	14	10	26	(10 | 16)	272	102	100	117	72	4	81	2	0	7	41	4	8	.307	.389	.522	.911
2004	2 Tms		159	599	160	36	9	38	(15 | 23)	328	121	104	124	92	10	101	7	3	7	42	3	8	.267	.367	.548	.915
2005	NYM	NL	151	582	155	34	2	16	(6 | 10)	241	83	78	88	56	5	96	2	4	6	17	6	9	.266	.330	.414	.744
2006	NYM	NL	140	510	140	38	1	41	(15 | 26)	303	127	116	121	95	6	99	4	1	7	18	3	6	.275	.388	.594	.982
2007	NYM	NL	144	554	153	33	3	33	(11 | 22)	291	93	112	97	69	10	111	2	1	10	23	2	8	.276	.353	.525	.878
2008	NYM	NL	161	606	172	40	5	27	(14 | 13)	303	116	112	116	92	13	96	1	1	6	25	3	11	.284	.376	.500	.876
2009	NYM	NL	81	308	100	22	1	10	(3 | 7)	154	50	48	54	47	10	43	1	0	1	11	1	9	.325	.415	.500	.915
2010	NYM	NL	64	220	56	11	3	7	(3 | 4)	94	21	27	31	30	5	39	1	0	4	3	1	4	.255	.341	.427	.768
2011	2 Tms	NL	142	520	156	39	6	22	(14 | 8)	273	78	84	96	71	7	88	3	0	4	4	2	18	.300	.385	.525	.910
2012	StL	NL	151	547	147	26	1	32	(20 | 12)	271	83	97	87	65	15	124	2	1	4	13	6	9	.269	.346	.495	.842
2013	StL	NL	145	554	164	30	3	24	(12 | 12)	272	79	84	91	38	1	90	1	1	6	2	1	12	.296	.339	.491	.830
2014	NYY	AL	109	403	94	23	0	15	(11 | 4)	162	46	49	44	37	2	80	4	0	5	3	1	11	.233	.301	.402	.703
04	KC	AL	69	266	74	19	2	15	(8 | 7)	142	51	51	57	37	7	44	2	1	3	14	3	4	.278	.367	.534	.901
04	Hou	NL	90	333	86	17	7	23	(7 | 16)	186	70	53	67	55	3	57	5	2	4	28	0	4	.258	.368	.559	.926
11	NYM	NL	98	353	102	30	2	15	(9 | 6)	181	61	66	72	60	6	61	2	0	4	3	0	9	.289	.391	.513	.904
11	SF	NL	44	167	54	9	4	7	(5 | 2)	92	17	18	24	11	1	27	1	0	0	1	2	9	.323	.369	.551	.920
	Postseason		51	180	60	13	1	16	(7 | 9)	123	45	40	53	35	2	24	2	1	1	11	0	3	.333	.445	.683	1.128
	17 ML YEARS		2173	8271	2322	469	77	373	(176 | 197)	4064	1392	1376	1453	971	95	1507	44	18	94	311	49	163	.281	.356	.491	.847

Adrian Beltre

Bats: R Throws: R Pos: 3B-136;DH-12   Ht: 5'11" Wt: 220 Born: 4/7/1979 Age: 36

																				RUNNING			AVERAGES			
Year	Team	Lg	G	AB	H	2B	3B	HR	(Hm	Rd)	TB	R	RBI	RC	TBB	IBB	SO	HBP	SH	SF	SB	CS	GDP	Avg	OBP	Slg	OPS
1998	LAD	NL	77	195	42	9	0	7	(5	2)	72	18	22	20	14	0	37	3	2	0	3	1	4	.215	.278	.369	.648
1999	LAD	NL	152	538	148	27	5	15	(6	9)	230	84	67	84	61	12	105	6	4	5	18	7	4	.275	.352	.428	.780
2000	LAD	NL	138	510	148	30	2	20	(7	13)	242	71	85	85	56	2	80	2	3	4	12	5	13	.290	.360	.475	.835
2001	LAD	NL	126	475	126	22	4	13	(4	9)	195	59	60	60	28	1	82	5	2	5	13	4	9	.265	.310	.411	.720
2002	LAD	NL	159	587	151	26	5	21	(7	14)	250	70	75	74	37	4	96	4	1	6	7	5	17	.257	.303	.426	.729
2003	LAD	NL	158	559	134	30	2	23	(13	10)	237	50	80	66	37	4	103	5	1	6	2	2	13	.240	.290	.424	.714
2004	LAD	NL	156	598	200	32	0	48	(23	25)	376	104	121	120	53	9	87	2	0	4	7	2	15	.334	.388	.629	1.017
2005	Sea	AL	156	603	154	36	1	19	(7	12)	249	69	87	75	38	6	108	5	0	4	3	1	15	.255	.303	.413	.716
2006	Sea	AL	156	620	166	39	4	25	(16	9)	288	88	89	85	47	4	118	10	1	3	11	5	15	.268	.328	.465	.792
2007	Sea	AL	149	595	164	41	2	26	(11	15)	287	87	99	79	38	2	104	2	0	4	14	2	18	.276	.319	.482	.802
2008	Sea	AL	143	556	148	29	1	25	(10	15)	254	74	77	71	50	10	90	2	0	4	8	2	11	.266	.327	.457	.784
2009	Sea	AL	111	449	119	27	0	8	(4	4)	170	54	44	47	19	1	74	7	0	2	13	2	19	.265	.304	.379	.683
2010	Bos	AL	154	589	189	49	2	28	(13	15)	326	84	102	103	40	10	82	5	0	7	2	1	25	.321	.365	.553	.919
2011	Tex	AL	124	487	144	33	0	32	(23	9)	273	82	105	80	25	0	53	5	0	8	1	1	13	.296	.331	.561	.892
2012	Tex	AL	156	604	194	33	2	36	(20	16)	339	95	102	109	36	8	82	5	0	9	1	0	8	.321	.359	.561	.921
2013	Tex	AL	161	631	199	32	0	30	(15	15)	321	88	92	97	50	12	78	7	0	2	1	0	17	.315	.371	.509	.880
2014	Tex	AL	148	549	178	33	1	19	(11	8)	270	79	77	99	57	13	74	3	0	5	1	1	15	.324	.388	.492	.879
	Postseason		22	91	23	5	0	5	(1	4)	43	15	10	8	2	1	22	2	0	1	0	0	1	.253	.281	.473	.754
	17 ML YEARS		2424	9145	2604	528	31	395	(195	200)	4379	1256	1384	1354	686	98	1453	78	14	78	117	41	231	.285	.337	.479	.816

Joaquin Benoit

Pitches: R Bats: R Pos: RP-53   ben-WAH   Ht: 6'3" Wt: 220 Born: 7/26/1977 Age: 37

		HOW MUCH HE PITCHED					WHAT HE GAVE UP										THE RESULTS						
Year	Team	Lg	G	GS	CG	GF	IP	BFP	H	R	ER	HR	SH	SF	HB	TBB	IBB	SO	WP	Bk	W	L	Pct	Sh	Sv-Op	Hld	ERC	ERA
2001	Tex	AL	1	1	0	0	5.0	26	8	6	6	3	0	1	0	3	0	4	0	0	0	0	-	0	0-0	0	13.11	10.80
2002	Tex	AL	17	13	0	2	84.2	405	91	51	50	6	4	3	5	58	2	59	7	0	4	5	.444	0	1-1	0	5.52	5.31
2003	Tex	AL	25	17	0	1	105.0	462	99	67	64	23	1	4	3	51	0	87	3	1	8	5	.615	0	0-0	0	5.03	5.49
2004	Tex	AL	28	15	0	4	103.0	456	113	67	65	19	2	10	8	31	0	95	3	0	3	5	.375	0	0-0	0	5.10	5.68
2005	Tex	AL	32	9	0	6	87.0	369	69	39	36	9	2	1	2	38	0	78	1	0	4	4	.500	0	0-0	5	3.15	3.72
2006	Tex	AL	56	0	0	7	79.2	347	68	49	43	5	0	3	3	38	4	85	3	0	1	1	.500	0	0-2	7	3.30	4.86
2007	Tex	AL	70	0	0	22	82.0	337	68	28	26	8	3	2	2	28	2	87	3	0	7	4	.636	0	6-13	19	2.83	2.85
2008	Tex	AL	44	0	0	8	45.0	209	40	28	25	6	2	0	0	35	2	43	3	0	3	2	.600	0	1-4	13	5.02	5.00
2010	TB	AL	63	0	0	16	60.1	217	30	10	9	6	0	2	0	11	1	75	1	0	1	2	.333	0	1-4	25	1.14	1.34
2011	Det	AL	66	0	0	13	61.0	241	47	22	20	5	1	5	2	17	1	63	0	0	4	3	.571	0	2-7	29	2.46	2.95
2012	Det	AL	73	0	0	18	71.0	288	59	31	29	14	3	3	1	22	2	84	2	0	5	3	.625	0	2-6	30	3.48	3.68
2013	Det	AL	66	0	0	43	67.0	265	47	15	15	5	4	0	1	22	2	73	2	0	4	1	.800	0	24-26	9	2.15	2.01
2014	SD	NL	53	0	0	17	54.1	205	28	10	9	3	2	2	1	14	2	64	3	1	4	2	.667	0	11-12	16	1.20	1.49
	Postseason		20	0	0	5	22.1	88	17	7	7	3	0	0	1	5	0	27	2	0	1	0	1.000	0	3-5	5	2.57	2.82
	13 ML YEARS		594	55	0	155	905.0	3827	767	423	397	110	24	36	28	368	18	897	34	2	48	37	.565	0	48-75	153	3.48	3.95

Christian Bergman

Pitches: R Bats: R Pos: SP-10   Ht: 6'1" Wt: 180 Born: 5/4/1988 Age: 27

		HOW MUCH HE PITCHED					WHAT HE GAVE UP										THE RESULTS						
Year	Team	Lg	G	GS	CG	GF	IP	BFP	H	R	ER	HR	SH	SF	HB	TBB	IBB	SO	WP	Bk	W	L	Pct	Sh	Sv-Op	Hld	ERC	ERA
2010	Casper	R+	14	5	0	0	48.1	228	62	39	32	5	5	5	1	11	0	37	4	0	1	4	.200	0	0- -	-	4.77	5.96
2011	TriCity	A-	15	15	2	0	97.1	383	83	31	28	4	0	0	4	11	0	68	2	0	7	5	.583	2	0- -	-	2.06	2.59
2012	Mdest	A+	27	27	0	0	162.2	668	161	73	66	16	4	3	3	37	0	121	4	0	16	5	.762	0	0- -	-	3.46	3.65

Year	Team	Lg	G	GS	CG	GF	IP	BFP	H	R	ER	HR	SH	SF	HB	TBB	IBB	SO	WP	Bk	W	L	Pct	Sh	Sv-Op	Hld	ERC	ERA
							HOW MUCH HE PITCHED						**WHAT HE GAVE UP**												**THE RESULTS**			
2013	Tulsa	AA	27	27	1	0	171.0	682	162	76	64	25	8	4	5	23	1	111	0	0	8	7	.533	1	0- -	-	3.21	3.37
2014	ColSpr	AAA	15	15	0	0	92.1	387	96	48	43	11	7	3	2	18	0	60	1	0	5	5	.500	0	0- -	-	3.69	4.19
2014	Tulsa	AA	2	2	0	0	9.0	36	8	3	3	1	0	0	0	5	0	5	2	0	0	1	.000	0	0- -	-	4.56	3.00
2014	Col	NL	10	10	0	0	54.2	249	75	37	36	9	1	1	1	10	2	31	0	0	3	5	.375	0	0-0	0	5.74	5.93

Roger Bernadina

burn-ah-DEEN-ah

Bats: L **Throws:** L **Pos:** PH-25;LF-17;RF-10;CF-7;PR-4;1B-1   **Ht:** 6'2" **Wt:** 200 **Born:** 6/12/1984 **Age:** 31

Year	Team	Lg	G	AB	H	2B	3B	HR	(Hm	Rd)	TB	R	RBI	RC	TBB	IBB	SO	HBP	SH	SF	SB	CS	GDP	Avg	OBP	Slg	OPS
									BATTING												**RUNNING**			**AVERAGES**			
2014	Albq*	AAA	23	57	15	2	2	0	(-	-)	21	8	2	10	12	0	23	1	0	1	2	0	1	.263	.394	.368	.763
2008	Was	NL	26	76	16	1	1	0	(0	0)	19	10	2	4	9	0	21	0	1	0	4	3	3	.211	.294	.250	.544
2009	Was	NL	3	4	1	0	0	0	(0	0)	2	1	0	1	1	0	1	0	0	0	1	0	0	.250	.400	.500	.900
2010	Was	NL	134	414	102	18	3	11	(3	8)	159	52	47	53	35	1	93	4	2	6	16	2	3	.246	.307	.384	.691
2011	Was	NL	91	309	75	12	2	7	(5	2)	112	40	27	34	22	1	63	4	2	0	17	3	7	.243	.301	.362	.664
2012	Was	NL	129	227	66	11	0	5	(1	4)	92	25	25	40	28	3	53	2	3	1	15	3	2	.291	.372	.405	.777
2013	2 Tms	NL	112	227	41	10	2	4	(2	2)	67	26	11	15	16	1	65	5	2	0	4	0	4	.181	.250	.295	.545
2014	2 Tms	NL	53	66	11	3	0	1	(1	0)	17	5	9	10	10	0	19	3	1	0	2	1	2	.167	.304	.258	.561
13	Was	NL	85	152	27	6	1	2	(1	1)	41	18	6	8	12	1	44	2	1	0	3	0	4	.178	.247	.270	.517
13	Phi	NL	27	75	14	4	1	2	(1	1)	26	8	5	7	4	0	21	3	1	0	1	0	0	.187	.256	.347	.603
14	Cin	NL	44	59	9	3	0	0	(0	0)	12	3	5	6	10	0	16	1	1	0	2	1	2	.153	.286	.203	.489
14	LAD	NL	9	7	2	0	0	1	(1	0)	5	2	4	4	0	0	3	2	0	0	0	0	0	.286	.444	.714	1.159
	Postseason		4	2	0	0	0	0	(0	0)	0	0	0	0	2	0	1	0	0	0	0	0	0	.000	.500	.000	.500
	7 ML YEARS		548	1323	312	56	8	28	(12	16)	468	159	121	157	121	6	315	18	11	7	59	12	21	.236	.307	.354	.661

Doug Bernier

burr-NEER

Bats: R **Throws:** R **Pos:** SS-3;2B-2;PH-2;PR-2;DH-1   **Ht:** 6'1" **Wt:** 185 **Born:** 6/24/1980 **Age:** 35

Year	Team	Lg	G	AB	H	2B	3B	HR	(Hm	Rd)	TB	R	RBI	RC	TBB	IBB	SO	HBP	SH	SF	SB	CS	GDP	Avg	OBP	Slg	OPS
									BATTING												**RUNNING**			**AVERAGES**			
2014	Roch*	AAA	124	404	113	25	2	6	(-	-)	160	53	54	59	40	0	78	5	12	5	5	4	3	.280	.348	.396	.744
2008	Col	NL	2	4	0	0	0	0	(0	0)	0	0	0	0	0	0	1	0	0	0	0	0	0	.000	.000	.000	.000
2013	Min	AL	33	53	12	3	0	0	(0	0)	15	9	5	7	8	1	15	1	2	0	2	1	1	.226	.339	.283	.622
2014	Min	AL	7	7	2	0	0	0	(0	0)	2	2	0	1	1	0	2	1	0	0	0	0	0	.286	.444	.286	.730
	3 ML YEARS		42	64	14	3	0	0	(0	0)	17	11	5	8	9	1	18	2	2	0	2	1	1	.219	.333	.266	.599

Quintin Berry

Bats: L **Throws:** L **Pos:** PR-8;LF-3;CF-1;RF-1;DH-1   **Ht:** 6'0" **Wt:** 175 **Born:** 11/21/1984 **Age:** 30

Year	Team	Lg	G	AB	H	2B	3B	HR	(Hm	Rd)	TB	R	RBI	RC	TBB	IBB	SO	HBP	SH	SF	SB	CS	GDP	Avg	OBP	Slg	OPS
									BATTING												**RUNNING**			**AVERAGES**			
2014	Norfolk*	AAA	112	365	104	19	1	3	(-	-)	134	53	35	59	56	0	84	3	5	3	25	6	7	.285	.382	.367	.749
2012	Det	AL	94	291	75	10	6	2	(1	1)	103	44	29	44	25	0	80	7	6	1	21	0	4	.258	.330	.354	.684
2013	Bos	AL	13	8	5	0	0	0	(0	0)	8	5	4	5	1	0	2	0	0	0	3	0	0	.625	.667	1.000	1.667
2014	Bal	AL	10	2	0	0	0	0	(0	0)	0	3	0	0	0	0	1	0	0	0	1	0	0	.000	.000	.000	.000
	Postseason		14	26	5	2	0	0	(0	0)	7	3	0	3	2	0	6	0	1	0	5	0	1	.192	.250	.269	.519
	3 ML YEARS		117	301	80	10	6	3	(1	2)	111	52	33	49	26	0	83	7	6	1	25	0	4	.266	.337	.369	.706

Dellin Betances

Pitches: R **Bats:** R **Pos:** RP-70   DELL-inn buh-TAN-siss   **Ht:** 6'8" **Wt:** 260 **Born:** 3/23/1988 **Age:** 27

Year	Team	Lg	G	GS	CG	GF	IP	BFP	H	R	ER	HR	SH	SF	HB	TBB	IBB	SO	WP	Bk	W	L	Pct	Sh	Sv-Op	Hld	ERC	ERA
							HOW MUCH HE PITCHED						**WHAT HE GAVE UP**												**THE RESULTS**			
2011	NYY	AL	2	1	0	0	2.2	16	1	2	2	0	0	1	1	6	0	2	0	0	0	0	-	0	0-0	0	7.94	6.75
2013	NYY	AL	6	0	0	3	5.0	26	9	6	6	1	0	0	0	2	0	10	0	0	0	0	-	0	0-0	0	9.81	10.80
2014	NYY	AL	70	0	0	8	90.0	341	46	15	14	4	2	3	4	24	1	135	2	1	5	0	1.000	0	1-5	22	1.24	1.40
	3 ML YEARS		78	1	0	11	97.2	383	56	23	22	5	2	4	5	32	1	147	2	1	5	0	1.000	0	1-5	22	1.59	2.03

Rafael Betancourt

Pitches: R **Bats:** R **Pos:** P   BETT-an-court   **Ht:** 6'2" **Wt:** 220 **Born:** 4/29/1975 **Age:** 40

Year	Team	Lg	G	GS	CG	GF	IP	BFP	H	R	ER	HR	SH	SF	HB	TBB	IBB	SO	WP	Bk	W	L	Pct	Sh	Sv-Op	Hld	ERC	ERA
							HOW MUCH HE PITCHED						**WHAT HE GAVE UP**												**THE RESULTS**			
2014	ColSpr*	AAA	7	0	0	4	6.0	30	10	7	7	2	0	0	0	3	0	4	0	0	1	0	1.000	0	0- -	-	10.97	10.50
2014	GdJunc*	R+	14	0	0	0	13.1	65	18	7	3	0	0	2	0	5	0	11	1	0	1	0	1.000	0	0- -	-	4.91	2.03
2003	Cle	AL	33	0	0	13	38.0	154	27	11	9	5	1	1	1	13	2	36	1	0	2	2	.500	0	1-3	4	2.54	2.13
2004	Cle	AL	68	0	0	21	66.2	286	71	32	29	7	1	2	0	18	6	76	5	1	5	6	.455	0	4-11	12	3.77	3.92
2005	Cle	AL	54	0	0	12	67.2	272	57	23	21	5	1	0	0	17	2	73	0	0	4	3	.571	0	1-3	10	2.49	2.79
2006	Cle	AL	50	0	0	17	56.2	231	52	25	24	7	2	2	0	11	5	48	0	0	3	4	.429	0	3-6	7	2.84	3.81
2007	Cle	AL	68	0	0	15	79.1	289	51	13	13	4	0	2	0	9	3	80	0	0	5	1	.833	0	3-6	31	1.24	1.47
2008	Cle	AL	69	0	0	20	71.0	309	76	41	40	11	4	5	2	25	5	64	2	0	3	4	.429	0	4-8	12	4.53	5.07
2009	2 Tms		61	0	0	10	56.0	227	42	20	17	4	2	4	0	20	5	61	0	0	4	3	.571	0	2-6	20	2.30	2.73
2010	Col	NL	72	0	0	18	62.1	248	52	25	25	9	3	1	0	8	2	89	7	0	5	1	.833	0	1-5	23	2.35	3.61
2011	Col	NL	68	0	0	24	62.1	237	46	21	20	7	0	2	0	8	0	73	1	2	2	0	1.000	0	8-12	22	1.84	2.89
2012	Col	NL	60	0	0	53	57.2	236	53	19	18	6	2	2	0	12	4	57	0	1	1	4	.200	0	31-38	1	2.81	2.81
2013	Col	NL	32	0	0	29	28.2	123	26	15	13	4	0	1	0	12	1	27	1	0	2	5	.286	0	16-19	0	3.12	4.08

Year	Team	Lg	G	GS	CG	GF	IP	BFP	H	R	ER	HR	SH	SF	HB	TBB	IBB	SO	WP	Bk	W	L	Pct	Sh	Sv-Op	Hld	ERC	ERA
09	Cle	AL	29	0	0	7	30.2	129	25	15	12	3	1	2	0	15	4	32	0	0	1	2	.333	0	1-3	8	3.21	3.52
09	Col	NL	32	0	0	3	25.1	98	17	5	5	1	1	2	0	5	1	29	0	0	3	1	.750	0	1-3	12	1.42	1.78
	Postseason		10	0	0	2	12.1	49	9	8	7	2	1	1	0	2	1	12	0	0	0	0	-	0	0-0	3	1.98	5.11
11 ML YEARS			635	0	0	232	646.1	2612	553	245	229	67	19	22	1	152	36	684	17	4	36	33	.522	0	74-117	142	2.63	3.19

Christian Bethancourt

Bats: R **Throws:** R **Pos:** C-31   BETH-an-court   **Ht:** 6'2" **Wt:** 205 **Born:** 9/2/1991 **Age:** 23

									BATTING												RUNNING			AVERAGES			
Year	Team	Lg	G	AB	H	2B	3B	HR	(Hm	Rd)	TB	R	RBI	RC	TBB	IBB	SO	HBP	SH	SF	SB	CS	GDP	Avg	OBP	Slg	OPS
2010	Rome	A	108	399	100	19	2	3	(-	-)	132	31	34	38	14	1	62	2	0	5	11	3	6	.251	.276	.331	.607
2011	Rome	A	54	221	67	10	3	4	(-	-)	95	25	33	31	8	0	27	1	0	5	6	3	4	.303	.323	.430	.753
2011	Lynbrg	A+	45	166	45	6	0	1	(-	-)	54	11	20	15	3	0	35	0	2	4	3	2	5	.271	.277	.325	.603
2012	Missi	AA	71	268	65	5	1	2	(-	-)	78	30	26	21	11	0	45	2	4	3	8	6	3	.243	.275	.291	.566
2013	Missi	AA	90	358	99	21	0	12	(-	-)	156	42	45	48	16	1	57	2	5	7	11	7	8	.277	.305	.436	.741
2014	Gwnntt	AAA	91	343	97	17	1	8	(-	-)	140	33	48	45	13	0	61	2	1	6	7	1	10	.283	.308	.408	.716
2013	Atl	NL	1	1	0	0	0	0	(0	0)	0	0	0	0	0	0	1	0	0	0	0	0	0	.000	.000	.000	.000
2014	Atl	NL	31	113	28	3	0	0	(0	0)	31	7	9	8	3	0	26	1	0	0	1	1	3	.248	.274	.274	.548
2 ML YEARS			32	114	28	3	0	0	(0	0)	31	7	9	8	3	0	27	1	0	0	1	1	3	.246	.271	.272	.543

Chad Bettis

Pitches: R **Bats:** R **Pos:** RP-21   **Ht:** 6'1" **Wt:** 200 **Born:** 4/26/1989 **Age:** 26

				HOW MUCH HE PITCHED						WHAT HE GAVE UP										THE RESULTS						
Year	Team	Lg	G	GS	CG	GF	IP	BFP	H	R	ER	HR	SH	SF	HB	TBB	IBB	SO	WP	Bk	W	L	Pct	Sh	Sv-Op	Hld	ERC	ERA
2010	TriCity	A-	10	9	0	0	48.1	205	44	11	6	0	1	0	0	10	0	39	4	0	4	1	.800	0	0- -	-	2.13	1.12
2010	Ashvll	A	3	3	0	0	18.2	71	14	2	2	1	0	1	0	3	0	17	0	0	2	0	1.000	0	0- -	-	1.72	0.96
2011	Mdest	A+	27	27	0	0	169.2	690	142	72	63	10	3	4	8	45	0	184	10	1	12	5	.706	0	0- -	-	2.63	3.34
2013	Tulsa	AA	12	12	0	0	63.0	259	60	28	26	9	6	2	3	13	0	68	1	0	3	4	.429	0	0- -	-	3.55	3.71
2014	ColSpr	AAA	20	5	0	7	55.1	225	45	22	19	1	1	0	3	21	0	55	2	0	3	4	.429	0	3- -	-	2.74	3.09
2013	Col	NL	16	8	0	0	44.2	208	55	34	28	6	3	1	2	20	2	30	2	1	1	3	.250	0	0-1	3	5.95	5.64
2014	Col	NL	21	0	0	9	24.2	127	42	26	25	4	5	0	1	10	2	13	5	0	0	2	.000	0	0-1	1	8.84	9.12
2 ML YEARS			37	8	0	9	69.1	335	97	60	53	10	8	1	3	30	4	43	7	1	1	5	.167	0	0-2	4	6.95	6.88

Mookie Betts

Bats: R **Throws:** R **Pos:** CF-28;2B-14;RF-12;PR-1   **Ht:** 5'9" **Wt:** 155 **Born:** 10/7/1992 **Age:** 22

									BATTING												RUNNING			AVERAGES			
Year	Team	Lg	G	AB	H	2B	3B	HR	(Hm	Rd)	TB	R	RBI	RC	TBB	IBB	SO	HBP	SH	SF	SB	CS	GDP	Avg	OBP	Slg	OPS
2011	RedSx	R	1	4	2	0	0	0	(-	-)	2	0	2	1	0	0	0	0	0	0	1	0	0	.500	.500	.500	1.000
2012	Lowell	A-	71	251	67	8	1	0	(-	-)	77	34	31	33	32	0	30	3	2	4	20	4	3	.267	.352	.307	.658
2013	Grnvlle	A	76	277	82	24	1	8	(-	-)	132	63	26	61	58	0	40	1	3	1	18	2	5	.296	.418	.477	.895
2013	Salem	A+	51	185	63	12	3	7	(-	-)	102	30	39	44	23	2	17	1	1	1	20	2	2	.341	.414	.551	.966
2014	Portlnd	AA	54	214	76	18	3	6	(-	-)	118	56	34	55	35	0	20	1	0	3	22	3	6	.355	.443	.551	.994
2014	Pwtckt	AAA	45	185	62	12	2	5	(-	-)	93	31	31	39	26	0	30	0	0	0	11	4	2	.335	.417	.503	.920
2014	Bos	AL	52	189	55	12	1	5	(1	4)	84	34	18	30	21	0	31	2	1	0	7	3	2	.291	.368	.444	.812

Jeff Bianchi

Bats: R **Throws:** R **Pos:** SS-10;3B-9;PH-9;2B-4;PR-1   bee-YANK-ee   **Ht:** 5'11" **Wt:** 185 **Born:** 10/5/1986 **Age:** 28

									BATTING												RUNNING			AVERAGES			
Year	Team	Lg	G	AB	H	2B	3B	HR	(Hm	Rd)	TB	R	RBI	RC	TBB	IBB	SO	HBP	SH	SF	SB	CS	GDP	Avg	OBP	Slg	OPS
2014	Nashv*	AAA	24	98	27	5	0	3	(-	-)	41	11	12	13	6	0	19	0	0	1	2	0	3	.276	.314	.418	.733
2012	Mil	NL	33	69	13	2	0	3	(1	2)	24	8	9	6	4	0	13	0	2	1	0	0	1	.188	.230	.348	.578
2013	Mil	NL	100	236	56	8	1	1	(0	1)	69	22	25	19	11	0	46	1	2	2	4	4	4	.237	.272	.292	.564
2014	Mil	NL	29	70	12	1	0	0	(0	0)	13	4	6	1	3	0	17	0	0	1	0	0	1	.171	.203	.186	.388
3 ML YEARS			162	375	81	11	1	4	(1	3)	106	34	40	26	18	0	76	1	4	4	4	4	6	.216	.251	.283	.534

Bruce Billings

Pitches: R **Bats:** R **Pos:** RP-1   **Ht:** 6'0" **Wt:** 210 **Born:** 11/18/1985 **Age:** 29

				HOW MUCH HE PITCHED						WHAT HE GAVE UP										THE RESULTS						
Year	Team	Lg	G	GS	CG	GF	IP	BFP	H	R	ER	HR	SH	SF	HB	TBB	IBB	SO	WP	Bk	W	L	Pct	Sh	Sv-Op	Hld	ERC	ERA
2010	Tulsa	AA	34	14	0	5	109.2	453	86	40	40	6	4	2	6	44	0	101	3	0	11	6	.647	0	1- -	-	2.86	3.28
2011	ColSpr	AAA	29	0	0	3	50.1	225	58	29	25	4	0	1	2	21	0	47	2	0	6	2	.750	0	1- -	-	5.07	4.47
2011	Scrmto	AAA	15	2	0	0	26.1	114	22	15	13	1	3	2	1	13	0	25	1	0	1	0	1.000	0	0- -	-	3.20	4.44
2012	Mdlnd	AA	2	0	0	0	5.2	25	4	2	2	0	0	0	0	4	0	3	0	0	2	0	1.000	0	0- -	-	2.85	3.18
2012	Scrmto	AAA	25	25	0	0	133.1	546	126	63	59	15	1	0	2	39	0	117	2	0	7	6	.538	0	0- -	-	3.58	3.98
2013	Scrmto	AAA	28	26	0	0	148.1	630	140	78	71	17	2	10	3	51	0	135	4	0	13	8	.619	0	0- -	-	3.70	4.31
2014	S-WB	AAA	15	15	1	0	80.0	349	88	49	45	9	1	3	0	27	0	54	7	1	5	5	.500	0	0- -	-	4.46	5.06
2014	Trntn	AA	1	1	0	0	1.0	4	2	0	0	0	0	0	0	0	0	0	0	0	0	0	-	0	0- -	-	9.49	0.00
2014	Albq	AAA	5	0	0	0	14.2	75	26	13	11	2	0	1	0	8	0	16	0	0	1	1	.500	0	0- -	-	10.12	6.75
2011	2 Tms		4	0	0	1	7.0	38	13	10	8	1	0	0	0	6	0	7	1	0	0	0	-	0	0-0	0	12.51	10.29
2014	NYY	AL	1	0	0	0	4.0	17	4	4	4	2	0	0	0	1	0	7	0	0	0	0	-	0	0-0	0	6.84	9.00
11	Col	NL	1	0	0	1	2.0	9	5	1	1	0	0	0	0	0	0	0	0	0	0	0	-	0	0-0	0	13.40	4.50
11	Oak	AL	3	0	0	0	5.0	29	8	9	7	1	0	0	0	6	0	7	1	0	0	0	-	0	0-0	0	12.25	12.60
2 ML YEARS			5	0	0	1	11.0	55	17	14	12	3	0	0	0	7	0	14	1	0	0	0	-	0	0-0	0	10.24	9.82

Chad Billingsley

Pitches: R **Bats:** R **Pos:** P   **Ht:** 6'1" **Wt:** 240 **Born:** 7/29/1984 **Age:** 30

Year	Team	Lg	G	GS	CG	GF	IP	BFP	H	R	ER	HR	SH	SF	HB	TBB	IBB	SO	WP	Bk	W	L	Pct	Sh	Sv-Op	Hld	ERC	ERA
2014	RCuca*	A+	2	2	0	0	3.0	16	3	3	2	0	0	0	1	3	0	3	0	0	0	1	.000	0	0--	-	6.78	6.00
2006	LAD	NL	18	16	0	0	90.0	403	92	43	38	7	4	0	3	58	3	59	5	0	7	4	.636	0	0--	0	5.22	3.80
2007	LAD	NL	43	20	1	6	147.0	623	131	56	54	15	9	3	3	64	3	141	5	0	12	5	.706	0	0-1	3	3.70	3.31
2008	LAD	NL	35	32	1	1	200.2	859	188	76	70	14	8	5	8	80	6	201	10	0	16	10	.615	1	0-0	1	3.62	3.14
2009	LAD	NL	33	32	0	0	196.1	823	173	94	88	17	9	11	7	86	7	179	14	0	12	11	.522	0	0-0	0	3.63	4.03
2010	LAD	NL	31	31	1	0	191.2	817	176	82	76	8	7	11	10	69	7	171	4	0	12	11	.522	1	0-0	0	3.20	3.57
2011	LAD	NL	32	32	1	0	188.0	829	189	88	88	14	13	8	7	84	4	152	5	0	11	11	.500	0	0-0	0	4.19	4.21
2012	LAD	NL	25	25	0	0	149.2	634	148	66	59	11	6	3	5	45	2	128	5	0	10	9	.526	0	0-0	0	3.55	3.55
2013	LAD	NL	2	2	0	0	12.0	49	12	4	4	1	2	0	0	5	0	6	0	0	1	0	1.000	0	0-0	0	4.29	3.00
	Postseason		6	3	0	0	17.0	78	20	14	13	1	0	0	0	10	2	22	2	0	1	2	.333	0	0-0	0	5.40	6.88
	8 ML YEARS		219	190	4	7	1175.1	5037	1109	519	477	87	58	41	43	491	32	1037	48	0	81	61	.570	2	0-1	4	3.77	3.65

Vic Black

Pitches: R **Bats:** R **Pos:** RP-41   **Ht:** 6'4" **Wt:** 210 **Born:** 5/23/1988 **Age:** 27

Year	Team	Lg	G	GS	CG	GF	IP	BFP	H	R	ER	HR	SH	SF	HB	TBB	IBB	SO	WP	Bk	W	L	Pct	Sh	Sv-Op	Hld	ERC	ERA
2010	WV	A	2	2	0	0	4.2	23	3	5	5	1	0	0	1	5	0	8	2	0	0	0	-	0	0--	-	6.35	9.64
2011	WV	A	22	0	0	5	29.0	131	30	21	17	0	0	1	2	16	0	23	5	0	2	1	.667	0	1--	-	4.40	5.28
2011	Bradtn	A+	5	0	0	1	6.2	31	8	4	3	1	2	0	1	4	0	5	0	0	1	0	1.000	0	0--	-	7.47	4.05
2012	Altna	AA	51	0	0	38	60.0	249	40	14	11	2	2	2	4	29	0	85	12	1	2	3	.400	0	13--	-	2.43	1.65
2013	Indy	AAA	38	0	0	30	46.2	190	28	15	13	2	2	0	1	21	3	63	3	0	5	3	.625	0	17--	-	1.82	2.51
2014	LsVgs	AAA	17	0	0	10	18.2	82	12	5	3	0	1	1	1	17	1	18	4	0	0	1	.000	0	7--	-	3.48	1.45
2013	2 Tms	NL	18	0	0	6	17.0	76	17	7	7	1	0	1	2	6	0	15	4	0	3	0	1.000	0	1-2	4	3.95	3.71
2014	NYM	NL	41	0	0	9	34.2	148	26	12	10	2	2	0	1	19	0	32	1	0	2	3	.400	0	0-0	12	3.08	2.60
13	Pit	NL	3	0	0	2	4.0	21	6	2	2	0	0	0	1	2	0	3	1	0	0	0	-	0	0-0	0	7.52	4.50
13	NYM	NL	15	0	0	4	13.0	55	11	5	5	1	0	1	1	4	0	12	3	0	3	0	1.000	0	1-2	4	2.97	3.46
	2 ML YEARS		59	0	0	15	51.2	224	43	19	17	3	2	1	3	25	0	47	5	0	5	3	.625	0	1-2	16	3.36	2.96

Charlie Blackmon

Bats: L **Throws:** L **Pos:** RF-73;CF-69;LF-22;PH-17   **Ht:** 6'3" **Wt:** 210 **Born:** 7/1/1986 **Age:** 28

Year	Team	Lg	G	AB	H	2B	3B	HR	(Hm	Rd)	TB	R	RBI	RC	TBB	IBB	SO	HBP	SH	SF	SB	CS	GDP	Avg	OBP	Slg	OPS
2011	Col	NL	27	98	25	1	0	1	(1	0)	29	9	8	10	3	1	8	0	1		5	1	2	.255	.277	.296	.573
2012	Col	NL	42	113	32	8	0	2	(1	1)	46	15	9	11	4	0	17	3	1	0	1	2	4	.283	.325	.407	.732
2013	Col	NL	82	264	76	17	2	6	(3	3)	115	35	22	35	7	0	49	3	2	0	7	0	1	.309	.336	.407	.803
2014	Col	NL	154	593	171	27	3	19	(13	6)	261	82	72	87	31	5	96	13	6	5	28	10	3	.288	.335	.440	.775
	4 ML YEARS		305	1050	304	53	5	28	(18	10)	451	141	111	143	45	6	170	19	10	5	41	13	10	.290	.329	.430	.758

Andres Blanco

Bats: B **Throws:** R **Pos:** 3B-10;SS-6;2B-5;PH-5;PR-2   **Ht:** 5'10" **Wt:** 190 **Born:** 4/11/1984 **Age:** 31

Year	Team	Lg	G	AB	H	2B	3B	HR	(Hm	Rd)	TB	R	RBI	RC	TBB	IBB	SO	HBP	SH	SF	SB	CS	GDP	Avg	OBP	Slg	OPS
2014	LV*	AAA	45	137	33	6	0	0	(-	-)	39	16	11	12	13	0	25	2	2	1	3	5	4	.241	.314	.285	.598
2004	KC	AL	19	60	19	2	2	0	(0	0)	25	9	5	12	5	0	6	1	1	0	1	2	0	.317	.379	.417	.795
2005	KC	AL	26	79	17	0	1	0	(0	0)	19	6	5	3	0	0	5	1	4	2	0	1	3	.215	.220	.241	.460
2006	KC	AL	33	87	21	4	1	0	(0	0)	27	9	9	9	5	0	14	1	3	0	0	1	2	.241	.290	.310	.601
2009	ChC	NL	53	123	31	8	0	1	(1	0)	42	15	12	9	8	3	14	1	6	0	0	2	4	.252	.303	.341	.644
2010	Tex	AL	68	166	46	10	1	0	(0	0)	58	17	13	19	11	1	24	3	3	2	0	2	0	.277	.330	.349	.679
2011	Tex	AL	36	76	17	3	0	2	(2	0)	26	9	3	4	4	0	14	0	2	0	0	1	1	.224	.263	.342	.605
2014	Phi	NL	25	47	13	5	0	1	(1	0)	21	4	3	6	2	1	6	0	4	0	0	0	4	.277	.306	.447	.753
	7 ML YEARS		260	638	164	32	5	4	(4	0)	218	69	50	62	35	5	83	7	23	4	1	9	14	.257	.301	.342	.643

Gregor Blanco

GREH-gore BLAHN-koh

Bats: L **Throws:** L **Pos:** CF-72;LF-64;PH-28;PR-7;RF-1   **Ht:** 5'11" **Wt:** 175 **Born:** 12/24/1983 **Age:** 31

Year	Team	Lg	G	AB	H	2B	3B	HR	(Hm	Rd)	TB	R	RBI	RC	TBB	IBB	SO	HBP	SH	SF	SB	CS	GDP	Avg	OBP	Slg	OPS
2008	Atl	NL	144	430	108	14	4	1	(0	1)	133	52	38	60	74	2	99	6	6	3	13	5	3	.251	.366	.309	.676
2009	Atl	NL	24	43	8	0	1	0	(0	0)	10	5	1	2	4	0	9	0	1	0	2	0	1	.186	.255	.233	.488
2010	2 Tms		85	237	67	9	4	1	(1	0)	87	31	14	30	29	1	50	0	2	1	11	4	5	.283	.360	.367	.727
2012	SF	NL	141	393	96	14	5	5	(2	3)	135	56	34	50	51	2	104	2	5	2	26	6	0	.244	.333	.344	.676
2013	SF	NL	141	452	120	17	6	3	(0	3)	158	50	41	54	52	4	95	1	3	3	14	9	10	.265	.341	.350	.690
2014	SF	NL	146	393	102	18	6	5	(2	3)	147	51	38	53	41	1	77	3	6	1	16	5	4	.260	.333	.374	.707
10	Atl	NL	36	58	18	1	1	0	(0	0)	21	9	3	8	8	1	15	0	0	0	1	2	2	.310	.394	.362	.756
10	KC	AL	49	179	49	8	3	1	(1	0)	66	22	11	22	21	0	35	0	2	1	10	2	3	.274	.348	.369	.717
	Postseason		16	51	12	2	2	1	(0	1)	21	10	5	10	7	0	14	1	0	0	0	0	0	.235	.339	.412	.751
	6 ML YEARS		681	1948	501	72	26	15	(5	10)	670	245	166	249	251	10	434	12	23	10	82	29	23	.257	.344	.344	.688

Kyle Blanks

Bats: R Throws: R Pos: 1B-20;PH-6;DH-3;LF-1;RF-1   Ht: 6'6" Wt: 265 Born: 9/11/1986 Age: 28

								BATTING												RUNNING			AVERAGES			
Year	Team	Lg	G	AB	H	2B	3B	HR	(Hm | Rd)	TB	R	RBI	RC	TBB	IBB	SO	HBP	SH	SF	SB	CS	GDP	Avg	OBP	Slg	OPS
2014	ElPaso*	AAA	27	83	22	6	0	9	(- | -)	55	15	20	20	10	0	24	4	0	2	0	0	2	.265	.364	.663	1.026
2014	Scrmto*	AAA	7	21	9	0	0	1	(- | -)	12	4	3	6	6	0	3	0	0	1	0	0	1	.429	.536	.571	1.107
2009	SD	NL	54	148	37	9	0	10	(6 | 4)	76	24	22	21	18	1	55	6	0	0	1	1	4	.250	.355	.514	.868
2010	SD	NL	33	102	16	6	1	3	(2 | 1)	33	14	15	10	15	0	46	3	0	0	1	0	1	.157	.283	.324	.607
2011	SD	NL	55	170	39	7	1	7	(2 | 5)	69	21	26	16	16	0	51	2	0	2	2	0	3	.229	.300	.406	.706
2012	SD	NL	4	5	1	0	0	0	(0 | 0)	1	0	0	0	1	0	2	0	0	0	0	0	0	.200	.333	.200	.533
2013	SD	NL	88	280	68	14	0	8	(3 | 5)	106	31	35	39	21	1	85	5	0	2	1	1	2	.243	.305	.379	.684
2014	2 Tms		26	55	17	1	0	2	(2 | 0)	24	10	7	9	8	0	16	2	0	1	0	0	3	.309	.409	.436	.845
14	SD	NL	5	10	2	0	0	0	(0 | 0)	2	1	0	0	0	0	3	0	0	0	0	0	0	.200	.200	.200	.400
14	Oak	AL	21	45	15	1	0	2	(2 | 0)	22	9	7	9	8	0	13	2	0	1	0	0	3	.333	.446	.489	.935
	6 ML YEARS		260	760	178	37	2	30	(15 | 15)	309	100	105	95	79	2	255	18	0	5	5	2	13	.234	.319	.407	.726

Jerry Blevins

Pitches: L Bats: L Pos: RP-64   Ht: 6'6" Wt: 185 Born: 9/6/1983 Age: 31

			HOW MUCH HE PITCHED					WHAT HE GAVE UP										THE RESULTS						
Year	Team	Lg	G	GS	CG	GF	IP	BFP	H	R	ER	HR	SH	SF	HB	TBB	IBB	SO	WP	Bk	W	L	Pct	Sh	Sv-Op	Hld	ERC	ERA
2007	Oak	AL	6	0	0	1	4.2	25	8	6	5	1	0	0	0	2	0	3	0	0	0	1	.000	0	0-0	0	9.08	9.64
2008	Oak	AL	36	0	0	8	37.2	156	32	14	13	2	0	1	3	13	2	35	0	0	1	3	.250	0	0-1	5	3.00	3.11
2009	Oak	AL	20	0	0	5	22.1	90	19	12	12	2	0	1	0	6	1	23	0	0	0	0	-	0	0-0	0	2.68	4.84
2010	Oak	AL	63	0	0	9	48.2	220	54	20	20	7	3	1	1	18	1	46	0	0	2	1	.667	0	1-2	11	4.81	3.70
2011	Oak	AL	26	0	0	11	28.1	122	24	14	9	2	2	3	1	14	1	26	0	0	0	0	-	0	0-0	3	3.45	2.86
2012	Oak	AL	63	0	0	17	65.1	261	45	20	18	7	5	2	5	25	5	54	2	0	5	1	.833	0	1-1	14	2.66	2.48
2013	Oak	AL	67	0	0	14	60.0	245	47	23	21	7	3	5	4	17	2	52	2	0	5	0	1.000	0	0-4	4	2.78	3.15
2014	Was	NL	64	0	0	25	57.1	240	48	31	31	3	3	3	1	23	6	66	2	0	2	3	.400	0	0-0	9	2.78	4.87
	Postseason		3	0	0	1	3.2	12	1	0	0	0	0	0	0	0	0	5	0	0	0	0	-	0	0-0	0	0.17	0.00
	8 ML YEARS		345	0	0	90	324.1	1359	277	140	129	31	16	16	15	118	18	305	6	0	15	9	.625	0	2-8	43	3.20	3.58

Willie Bloomquist

Bats: R Throws: R Pos: SS-16;2B-10;PH-8;1B-7;3B-5;LF-3;DH-2;PR-2;RF-1   Ht: 5'11" Wt: 190 Born: 11/27/1977 Age: 37

								BATTING												RUNNING			AVERAGES			
Year	Team	Lg	G	AB	H	2B	3B	HR	(Hm	Rd)	TB	R	RBI	RC	TBB	IBB	SO	HBP	SH	SF	SB	CS	GDP	Avg	OBP	Slg	OPS
2002	Sea	AL	12	33	15	4	0	0	(0	0)	19	11	7	10	5	0	2	0	0	0	3	1	0	.455	.526	.576	1.102
2003	Sea	AL	89	196	49	7	2	1	(1	0)	63	30	14	18	19	1	39	1	2	2	4	1	6	.250	.317	.321	.638
2004	Sea	AL	93	188	46	10	0	2	(0	2)	62	27	18	18	10	0	48	0	3	0	13	2	2	.245	.283	.330	.613
2005	Sea	AL	82	249	64	15	2	0	(0	0)	83	27	22	26	11	0	38	1	4	2	14	1	5	.257	.289	.333	.622
2006	Sea	AL	102	251	62	6	2	1	(0	1)	75	36	15	27	24	0	40	4	2	2	16	3	3	.247	.320	.299	.619
2007	Sea	AL	91	173	48	3	0	2	(1	1)	57	28	13	16	10	0	35	1	4	0	7	5	7	.277	.321	.329	.650
2008	Sea	AL	71	165	46	1	0	0	(0	0)	47	32	9	24	25	1	29	1	1	0	14	3	1	.279	.377	.285	.662
2009	KC	AL	125	434	115	11	8	4	(0	4)	154	52	29	45	27	1	73	1	4	2	25	6	7	.265	.308	.355	.663
2010	2 Tms		83	187	50	10	1	3	(2	1)	71	31	17	19	9	0	28	0	2	1	8	5	4	.267	.299	.380	.679
2011	Ari	NL	97	350	93	10	2	4	(2	2)	119	44	26	37	23	3	51	4	2	2	20	10	3	.266	.317	.340	.657
2012	Ari	NL	80	324	98	21	5	0	(0	0)	129	47	23	46	12	0	55	0	0	2	7	10	5	.302	.325	.398	.724
2013	Ari	NL	48	139	44	5	1	0	(0	0)	51	16	14	20	8	0	11	2	0	1	0	2	3	.317	.360	.367	.727
2014	Sea	AL	47	133	37	6	0	1	(1	0)	46	15	14	18	4	1	32	0	1	1	1	1	1	.278	.297	.346	.643
10	KC	AL	72	170	45	10	1	3	(2	1)	66	31	17	18	8	0	25	0	2	1	8	5	4	.265	.296	.388	.684
10	Cin	NL	11	17	5	0	0	0	(0	0)	5	0	0	1	1	0	3	0	0	0	0	0	0	.294	.333	.294	.627
	Postseason		5	22	7	0	0	0	(0	0)	7	3	1	3	1	0	3	0	0	0	3	0	2	.318	.348	.318	.666
	13 ML YEARS		1020	2822	767	109	23	18	(7	11)	976	396	221	324	187	7	481	15	25	15	132	50	47	.272	.319	.346	.665

Brett Bochy

Pitches: R Bats: R Pos: RP-3   Ht: 6'2" Wt: 200 Born: 8/27/1987 Age: 27

			HOW MUCH HE PITCHED					WHAT HE GAVE UP										THE RESULTS						
Year	Team	Lg	G	GS	CG	GF	IP	BFP	H	R	ER	HR	SH	SF	HB	TBB	IBB	SO	WP	Bk	W	L	Pct	Sh	Sv-Op	Hld	ERC	ERA
2011	Augsta	A	35	0	0	13	39.0	147	22	6	6	1	1	0	1	8	0	53	2	0	1	0	1.000	0	10- -	-	1.17	1.38
2012	Rchmd	AA	41	0	0	24	53.1	205	29	15	15	3	2	2	3	18	4	69	1	0	7	3	.700	0	14- -	-	1.52	2.53
2013	Fresno	AAA	45	0	0	13	56.1	239	51	27	25	2	3	3	3	16	0	57	2	1	1	1	.500	0	2- -	-	2.83	3.99
2014	Fresno	AAA	35	2	0	13	54.0	233	53	25	23	8	3	2	0	27	2	47	1	0	4	4	.500	0	0- -	-	4.75	3.83
2014	Giants	R	2	0	0	0	2.0	6	0	0	0	0	0	0	0	0	0	1	0	0	1	0	1.000	0	0- -	-	0.00	0.00
2014	SF	NL	3	0	0	2	3.1	14	1	2	2	1	0	0	1	2	0	3	0	0	0	0	-	0	0-0	0	3.48	5.40

Brennan Boesch

Bats: L Throws: L Pos: DH-14;RF-9;LF-3;PH-3;CF-1;PR-1   BOSH   Ht: 6'4" Wt: 235 Born: 4/12/1985 Age: 30

								BATTING												RUNNING			AVERAGES			
Year	Team	Lg	G	AB	H	2B	3B	HR	(Hm	Rd)	TB	R	RBI	RC	TBB	IBB	SO	HBP	SH	SF	SB	CS	GDP	Avg	OBP	Slg	OPS
2014	Salt Lk*	AAA	95	374	124	25	7	25	(-	-)	238	80	85	86	29	2	86	2	0	2	10	4	8	.332	.381	.636	1.017
2010	Det	AL	133	464	119	26	3	14	(7	7)	193	49	67	61	40	5	99	5	0	5	1	1	5	.256	.320	.416	.736
2011	Det	AL	115	428	121	25	1	16	(9	7)	196	75	54	56	35	2	83	5	0	4	5	3	7	.283	.341	.458	.799
2012	Det	AL	132	470	113	22	2	12	(9	3)	175	52	54	47	26	1	104	5	0	2	6	3	11	.240	.286	.372	.659
2013	NYY	AL	23	51	14	2	1	3	(2	1)	27	6	8	8	2	0	9	0	0	0	0	0	2	.275	.302	.529	.831
2014	LAA	AL	27	75	14	2	0	2	(2	0)	22	6	7	3	2	1	19	0	0	2	3	0	0	.187	.203	.293	.496
	5 ML YEARS		430	1488	381	77	7	47	(29	18)	613	188	190	175	105	9	314	15	0	11	21	7	25	.256	.309	.412	.721

Xander Bogaerts

Bats: R **Throws:** R **Pos:** SS-99;3B-44;PR-1   ZAN-derr BO-garts   **Ht:** 6'1" **Wt:** 210 **Born:** 10/1/1992 **Age:** 22

Year	Team	Lg	G	AB	H	2B	3B	HR	(Hm	Rd)	TB	R	RBI	RC	TBB	IBB	SO	HBP	SH	SF	SB	CS	GDP	Avg	OBP	Slg	OPS
2011	Grnvlle	A	72	265	69	14	2	16	(-	-)	135	38	45	44	25	0	71	2	0	4	1	3	4	.260	.324	.509	.834
2012	Salem	A+	104	384	116	27	3	15	(-	-)	194	59	64	73	43	1	85	5	1	2	4	4	8	.302	.378	.505	.883
2012	Portlnd	AA	23	92	30	10	0	5	(-	-)	55	12	17	18	1	0	21	3	0	1	1	1	1	.326	.351	.598	.948
2013	Portlnd	AA	56	219	68	12	6	6	(-	-)	110	40	35	46	35	0	51	2	1	2	5	1	4	.311	.407	.502	.909
2013	Pwtckt	AAA	60	225	64	11	0	9	(-	-)	102	32	32	38	28	1	44	2	1	0	2	2	8	.284	.369	.453	.822
2013	Bos	AL	18	44	11	2	0	1	(0	1)	16	7	5	4	5	0	13	0	0	1	1	0	1	.250	.320	.364	.684
2014	Bos	AL	144	538	129	28	1	12	(7	5)	195	60	46	43	39	1	138	8	2	7	2	3	11	.240	.297	.362	.660
	Postseason		12	27	8	3	0	0	(0	0)	13	9	2	5	6	0	9	0	0	1	0	0	1	.296	.412	.481	.893
	2 ML YEARS		162	582	140	30	1	13	(7	6)	211	67	51	47	44	1	151	8	2	8	3	3	12	.241	.299	.363	.662

Mike Bolsinger

Pitches: R **Bats:** R **Pos:** SP-9; RP-1   BOWL-sing-er   **Ht:** 6'2" **Wt:** 210 **Born:** 1/29/1988 **Age:** 27

Year	Team	Lg	G	GS	CG	GF	IP	BFP	H	R	ER	HR	SH	SF	HB	TBB	IBB	SO	WP	Bk	W	L	Pct	Sh	Sv-Op	Hld	ERC	ERA
2010	Yakima	A-	6	0	0	0	10.2	39	6	2	2	0	1	0	1	3	0	6	1	0	1	0	1.000	0	0- -	-	1.45	1.69
2011	Sbend	A	32	13	0	7	101.2	398	84	35	30	6	1	3	1	25	0	91	6	0	6	6	.500	0	0- -	-	2.45	2.66
2011	Reno	AAA	1	0	0	0	1.0	4	1	0	0	0	0	1	0	0	0	0	0	0	0	0	-	0	0- -	-	1.95	0.00
2012	Visalia	A+	7	7	0	0	38.0	160	31	15	10	1	0	2	1	13	0	49	2	1	3	2	.600	0	0- -	-	2.43	2.37
2012	Mobile	AA	15	15	0	0	77.2	335	82	40	33	5	2	3	2	38	0	64	8	1	4	3	.571	0	0- -	-	4.77	3.82
2013	Mobile	AA	9	6	1	0	43.0	176	35	14	12	0	3	1	1	15	0	31	5	0	4	0	1.000	1	0- -	-	2.35	2.51
2013	Reno	AAA	17	17	1	0	101.0	451	116	60	53	12	7	3	4	39	1	97	5	1	7	7	.500	0	0- -	-	5.17	4.72
2014	Reno	AAA	17	16	0	0	91.2	390	92	40	40	6	3	0	3	32	1	88	1	0	8	3	.727	0	0- -	-	3.80	3.93
2014	Ari	NL	10	9	0	0	52.1	238	66	36	32	7	3	4	0	17	1	48	0	1	1	6	.143	0	0-0	0	5.42	5.50

Emilio Bonifacio

bo-knee-FAH-see-oh

Bats: B **Throws:** R **Pos:** CF-65;2B-31;PH-13;3B-7;RF-6;SS-4;LF-4;PR-3;DH-1   **Ht:** 5'11" **Wt:** 205 **Born:** 4/23/1985 **Age:** 30

Year	Team	Lg	G	AB	H	2B	3B	HR	(Hm	Rd)	TB	R	RBI	RC	TBB	IBB	SO	HBP	SH	SF	SB	CS	GDP	Avg	OBP	Slg	OPS
2014	Cubs*	R	3	10	3	0	0	0	(-	-)	3	1	0	1	1	0	2	0	0	0	1	0	0	.300	.364	.300	.664
2014	Tenn*	AA	4	16	4	0	0	0	(-	-)	4	1	0	0	0	0	2	0	0	0	0	1	0	.250	.250	.250	.500
2007	Ari	NL	11	23	5	1	0	0	(0	0)	6	2	2	4	4	0	3	0	0	0	0	1	0	.217	.333	.261	.594
2008	2 Tms	NL	49	169	41	6	5	0	(0	0)	57	29	14	16	14	0	46	0	0	3	7	4	2	.243	.296	.337	.633
2009	Fla	NL	127	461	116	11	6	1	(1	0)	142	72	27	41	34	0	95	2	8	4	21	9	5	.252	.303	.308	.611
2010	Fla	NL	73	180	47	6	3	0	(0	0)	59	30	10	24	17	0	42	0	1	3	12	0	1	.261	.320	.328	.648
2011	Fla	NL	152	565	167	26	7	5	(1	4)	222	78	36	83	59	1	129	1	11	5	40	11	4	.296	.360	.393	.753
2012	Mia	NL	64	244	63	3	4	1	(1	0)	77	30	11	30	25	1	52	1	4	0	30	3	3	.258	.330	.316	.645
2013	2 Tms	AL	136	420	102	23	3	3	(1	2)	139	54	31	39	30	0	103	2	6	3	28	8	4	.243	.295	.331	.625
2014	2 Tms	NL	110	394	102	17	4	3	(2	1)	136	47	24	46	26	2	85	0	6	0	26	8	2	.259	.305	.345	.650
08	Ari	NL	8	12	2	1	0	0	(0	0)	3	3	2	1	0	0	5	0	0	0	1	0	0	.167	.167	.250	.417
08	Was	NL	41	157	39	5	5	0	(0	0)	54	26	12	15	14	0	41	0	0	3	6	4	2	.248	.305	.344	.649
13	Tor	AL	94	262	57	16	1	3	(1	2)	84	33	20	19	13	0	66	2	3	2	12	6	3	.218	.258	.321	.579
13	KC	AL	42	158	45	6	2	0	(0	0)	55	21	11	20	17	0	37	0	3	1	16	2	1	.285	.352	.348	.700
14	ChC	NL	69	276	77	14	3	2	(2	0)	103	35	18	37	16	2	49	0	6	0	14	6	1	.279	.318	.373	.692
14	Atl	NL	41	118	25	3	1	1	(0	1)	33	12	6	9	10	0	36	0	0	0	12	2	1	.212	.273	.280	.553
	8 ML YEARS		722	2456	643	92	32	13	(6	7)	838	342	155	283	209	4	555	6	36	18	164	44	21	.262	.319	.341	.660

Lisalverto Bonilla

Pitches: R **Bats:** B **Pos:** SP-3; RP-2   leez-al-VEHR-toe boh-NEE-ya   **Ht:** 6'0" **Wt:** 175 **Born:** 6/18/1990 **Age:** 25

Year	Team	Lg	G	GS	CG	GF	IP	BFP	H	R	ER	HR	SH	SF	HB	TBB	IBB	SO	WP	Bk	W	L	Pct	Sh	Sv-Op	Hld	ERC	ERA
2010	Phillies	R	6	6	0	0	32.1	136	32	15	7	3	0	0	1	5	0	38	0	2	2	1	.667	0	0- -	-	3.05	1.95
2010	Wmspt	A-	10	3	0	2	26.1	122	33	22	19	5	0	2	1	12	0	18	3	1	1	3	.250	0	0- -	-	6.70	6.49
2011	Lakwd	A	26	15	1	8	106.0	438	91	38	33	8	7	3	2	29	3	95	2	0	4	5	.444	0	4- -	-	2.68	2.80
2012	Clrwtr	A+	10	0	0	7	13.1	53	9	4	2	0	1	0	0	4	0	18	1	0	1	1	.500	0	1- -	-	1.53	1.35
2012	Rdng	AA	21	0	0	11	33.0	133	22	6	6	1	0	1	1	17	1	46	1	0	2	1	.667	0	3- -	-	2.44	1.64
2013	RdRck	AAA	26	2	0	8	43.0	206	52	42	38	8	6	1	1	24	3	56	2	0	5	5	.500	0	0- -	-	6.48	7.95
2013	Frisco	AA	21	0	0	16	30.1	117	16	1	1	0	1	0	2	9	0	50	2	0	2	0	1.000	0	6- -	-	1.23	0.30
2014	RdRck	AAA	39	6	0	15	74.2	317	73	36	34	9	0	2	1	25	1	92	7	1	4	2	.667	0	1- -	-	3.86	4.10
2014	Tex	AL	5	3	0	0	20.2	83	13	8	7	2	0	0	1	12	1	17	1	0	3	0	1.000	0	0-0	0	3.00	3.05

Julio Borbon

bore-BONE

Bats: L **Throws:** L **Pos:** CF   **Ht:** 6'0" **Wt:** 195 **Born:** 2/20/1986 **Age:** 29

Year	Team	Lg	G	AB	H	2B	3B	HR	(Hm	Rd)	TB	R	RBI	RC	TBB	IBB	SO	HBP	SH	SF	SB	CS	GDP	Avg	OBP	Slg	OPS
2014	Norfolk*	AAA	124	466	134	9	4	5	(-	-)	166	68	44	62	38	0	73	1	6	1	34	10	10	.288	.342	.356	.698
2009	Tex	AL	46	157	49	4	0	4	(2	2)	65	30	20	27	15	0	28	1	6	0	19	4	3	.312	.376	.414	.790
2010	Tex	AL	137	438	121	11	4	3	(2	1)	149	60	42	48	19	0	59	2	8	1	15	7	5	.276	.309	.340	.649
2011	Tex	AL	32	89	24	1	3	0	(0	0)	31	10	11	14	3	0	9	2	3	1	6	2	2	.270	.305	.348	.654
2013	2 Tms		73	105	21	3	1	1	(0	1)	29	11	3	9	12	0	22	0	1	0	7	1	0	.200	.282	.276	.558

Year	Team	Lg	BATTING G	AB	H	2B	3B	HR	(Hm	Rd)	TB	R	RBI	RC	TBB	IBB	SO	HBP	SH	SF	RUNNING SB	CS	GDP	AVERAGES Avg	OBP	Slg	OPS
13	Tex	AL	1	1	0	0	0	0	(0	0)	0	1	0	0	0	0	0	0	0	0	0	0	0	.000	.000	.000	.000
13	ChC	NL	72	104	21	3	1	1	(0	1)	29	10	3	9	12	0	22	0	1	0	7	1	0	.202	.284	.279	.563
	Postseason		8	9	1	0	0	0	(0	0)	1	4	0	0	1	0	3	0	0	0	0	0	0	.111	.111	.111	.222
	4 ML YEARS		288	789	215	19	8	8	(4	4)	274	111	76	98	49	0	118	5	18	2	47	14	10	.272	.318	.347	.666

Justin Bour

Bats: L **Throws:** R **Pos:** PH-22;1B-15;DH-3   BOOR   **Ht:** 6'4" **Wt:** 250 **Born:** 5/28/1988 **Age:** 27

Year	Team	Lg	BATTING G	AB	H	2B	3B	HR	(Hm	Rd)	TB	R	RBI	RC	TBB	IBB	SO	HBP	SH	SF	RUNNING SB	CS	GDP	AVERAGES Avg	OBP	Slg	OPS
2010	Peoria	A	127	475	138	31	1	12	(-	-)	207	59	87	82	58	7	100	9	0	5	1	0	15	.291	.375	.436	.811
2011	Dytona	A+	133	502	139	30	1	23	(-	-)	240	65	85	83	46	5	105	2	0	8	3	2	15	.277	.335	.478	.813
2012	Tenn	AA	138	506	143	36	0	17	(-	-)	230	64	110	87	62	10	115	3	0	6	4	1	12	.283	.360	.455	.815
2013	Tenn	AA	83	317	75	17	0	18	(-	-)	146	48	64	47	36	8	63	2	0	6	0	2	3	.237	.313	.461	.774
2014	NewOr	AAA	103	385	119	27	0	18	(-	-)	200	59	72	75	39	11	57	3	0	3	3	1	7	.309	.374	.519	.894
2014	Mia	NL	39	74	21	3	0	1	(1	0)	27	10	11	13	9	1	19	0	0	0	0	0	0	.284	.361	.365	.726

Jason Bourgeois

Bats: R **Throws:** R **Pos:** LF-8;PH-7;PR-3;CF-2;RF-1   boosh-WAH   **Ht:** 5'9" **Wt:** 190 **Born:** 1/4/1982 **Age:** 33

Year	Team	Lg	BATTING G	AB	H	2B	3B	HR	(Hm	Rd)	TB	R	RBI	RC	TBB	IBB	SO	HBP	SH	SF	RUNNING SB	CS	GDP	AVERAGES Avg	OBP	Slg	OPS
2014	Lsvlle*	AAA	136	550	153	29	3	4	(-	-)	200	76	43	70	40	0	51	3	3	3	24	9	12	.278	.329	.364	.692
2008	CWS	AL	6	3	1	1	0	0	(0	0)	2	0	0	.0	0	0	0	0	0	0	0	0	0	.333	.333	.667	1.000
2009	Mil	NL	24	37	7	0	0	1	(1	0)	10	6	3	1	3	0	7	0	0	0	3	0	2	.189	.250	.270	.520
2010	Hou	NL	69	123	27	4	1	0	(0	0)	33	16	3	8	13	0	16	0	0	0	12	4	5	.220	.294	.268	.562
2011	Hou	NL	93	238	70	8	2	1	(0	1)	85	30	16	31	10	0	24	0	4	0	31	6	5	.294	.323	.357	.680
2012	KC	AL	30	62	16	2	1	0	(0	0)	20	10	5	5	4	0	4	0	0	0	5	4	1	.258	.303	.323	.626
2013	TB	AL	9	16	3	0	0	1	(0	1)	6	2	2	1	2	0	4	0	0	0	0	0	0	.188	.278	.375	.653
2014	Cin	NL	18	33	8	0	1	0	(0	0)	10	5	1	4	1	0	6	0	0	0	0	0	1	.242	.265	.303	.568
	7 ML YEARS		249	512	132	15	5	3	(1	2)	166	69	30	50	33	0	61	0	4	0	51	14	14	.258	.303	.324	.627

Peter Bourjos

Bats: R **Throws:** R **Pos:** CF-104;PH-16;PR-9   BORE-juss   **Ht:** 6'1" **Wt:** 185 **Born:** 3/31/1987 **Age:** 28

Year	Team	Lg	BATTING G	AB	H	2B	3B	HR	(Hm	Rd)	TB	R	RBI	RC	TBB	IBB	SO	HBP	SH	SF	RUNNING SB	CS	GDP	AVERAGES Avg	OBP	Slg	OPS
2010	LAA	AL	51	181	37	6	4	6	(1	5)	69	19	15	13	6	0	40	2	3	1	10	3	2	.204	.237	.381	.618
2011	LAA	AL	147	502	136	26	11	12	(7	5)	220	72	43	66	32	0	124	10	7	1	22	9	7	.271	.327	.438	.765
2012	LAA	AL	101	168	37	7	0	3	(1	2)	53	27	19	18	15	0	44	3	6	3	3	1	2	.220	.291	.315	.606
2013	LAA	AL	55	175	48	3	3	3	(1	2)	66	26	12	19	10	0	43	6	4	1	6	0	8	.274	.333	.377	.710
2014	StL	NL	119	264	61	9	5	4	(2	2)	92	32	24	27	20	1	78	4	5	1	9	3	5	.231	.294	.348	.643
	5 ML YEARS		473	1290	319	51	23	28	(12	16)	500	176	113	143	83	1	329	25	25	7	50	16	24	.247	.304	.388	.692

Michael Bourn

Bats: L **Throws:** R **Pos:** CF-105;PH-2   BORN   **Ht:** 5'10" **Wt:** 180 **Born:** 12/27/1982 **Age:** 32

Year	Team	Lg	BATTING G	AB	H	2B	3B	HR	(Hm	Rd)	TB	R	RBI	RC	TBB	IBB	SO	HBP	SH	SF	RUNNING SB	CS	GDP	AVERAGES Avg	OBP	Slg	OPS
2014	Clmbs*	AAA	5	20	3	1	0	0	(-	-)	4	1	2	0	0	0	3	0	0	0	1	0	1	.150	.150	.200	.350
2014	Akron*	AA	6	23	2	0	0	0	(-	-)	2	0	0	0	2	0	10	0	0	0	1	0	1	.087	.160	.087	.247
2006	Phi	NL	17	8	1	0	0	0	(0	0)	1	2	0	0	1	0	3	0	2	0	1	2	1	.125	.222	.125	.347
2007	Phi	NL	105	119	33	3	3	1	(1	0)	45	29	6	19	13	2	21	0	1	0	18	1	1	.277	.348	.378	.727
2008	Hou	NL	138	467	107	10	4	5	(3	2)	140	57	29	43	37	0	111	2	7	1	41	10	3	.229	.288	.300	.588
2009	Hou	NL	157	606	173	27	12	3	(2	1)	233	97	35	94	63	1	140	2	5	2	61	12	1	.285	.354	.384	.738
2010	Hou	NL	141	535	142	25	6	2	(0	2)	185	84	38	74	59	5	109	3	6	2	52	12	6	.265	.341	.346	.686
2011	2 Tms	NL	158	656	193	34	10	2	(2	0)	253	94	50	92	53	3	140	4	5	4	61	14	6	.294	.349	.386	.734
2012	Atl	NL	155	624	171	26	10	9	(2	7)	244	96	57	102	70	1	155	3	2	4	42	13	2	.274	.348	.391	.739
2013	Cle	AL	130	525	138	21	6	6	(4	2)	189	75	50	65	40	0	132	2	5	3	23	12	2	.263	.316	.360	.676
2014	Cle	AL	106	444	114	17	10	3	(3	0)	160	57	28	51	35	1	114	3	3	2	10	6	5	.257	.314	.360	.674
	11	Hou	105	429	130	26	7	1	(0	1)	173	64	32	66	38	2	90	3	2	1	39	7	5	.303	.363	.403	.766
	11	Atl	53	227	63	8	3	1	(1	0)	80	30	18	26	15	1	50	1	3	3	22	7	1	.278	.321	.352	.674
	Postseason		4	10	1	0	0	0	(0	0)	1	0	1	0	0	0	4	0	0	0	0	0	0	.100	.100	.100	.200
	9 ML YEARS		1107	3984	1072	163	61	31	(15	16)	1450	591	293	540	371	13	925	19	36	18	309	82	26	.269	.333	.364	.697

Brad Boxberger

Pitches: R **Bats:** R **Pos:** RP-63   **Ht:** 6'2" **Wt:** 220 **Born:** 5/27/1988 **Age:** 27

Year	Team	Lg	HOW MUCH HE PITCHED G	GS	CG	GF	IP	BFP	WHAT HE GAVE UP H	R	ER	HR	SH	SF	HB	TBB	IBB	SO	WP	Bk	THE RESULTS W	L	Pct	Sh	Sv-Op	Hld	ERC	ERA
2014	Drham*	AAA	6	0	0	3	9.1	37	4	2	2	1	0	0	1	4	0	18	0	0	1	0	1.000	0	2- -	-	1.72	1.93
2012	SD	NL	24	0	0	4	27.2	120	22	12	8	3	0	1	2	18	1	33	0	0	0	0	-	0	0-0	1	4.28	2.60
2013	SD	NL	18	0	0	6	22.0	94	19	9	7	3	3	2	0	13	0	24	0	0	0	1	.000	0	1-1	0	4.43	2.86
2014	TB	AL	63	0	0	10	64.2	247	34	17	17	9	2	2	4	20	0	104	3	2	5	2	.714	0	2-5	18	1.84	2.37
	3 ML YEARS		105	0	0	20	114.1	461	75	38	32	15	5	5	6	51	1	161	3	2	5	3	.625	0	3-6	19	2.86	2.52

Blaine Boyer

Pitches: R Bats: R Pos: RP-32   Ht: 6'3" Wt: 225 Born: 7/11/1981 Age: 33

Year	Team	Lg	G	GS	CG	GF	IP	BFP	H	R	ER	HR	SH	SF	HB	TBB	IBB	SO	WP	Bk	W	L	Pct	Sh	Sv-Op	Hld	ERC	ERA
2014	ElPaso*	AAA	25	0	0	10	29.0	118	26	10	10	2	0	0	1	6	0	28	0	0	1	2	.333	0	7- -	-	2.72	3.10
2005	Atl	NL	43	0	0	5	37.2	158	32	13	13	1	1	1	2	17	0	33	2	0	4	2	.667	0	0-2	9	3.21	3.11
2006	Atl	NL	2	0	0	0	0.2	7	4	3	3	0	0	0	0	1	0	0	0	0	0	0	-	0	0-0	1	47.92	40.50
2007	Atl	NL	5	0	0	2	5.1	26	10	3	2	0	1	0	0	1	1	3	2	0	0	0	-	0	0-0	1	7.41	3.38
2008	Atl	NL	76	0	0	18	72.0	313	73	51	47	10	3	4	2	25	4	67	2	0	2	6	.250	0	1-5	14	4.19	5.88
2009	3 Tms	NL	48	0	0	21	54.2	241	56	36	25	1	4	1	5	20	0	29	2	0	0	2	.000	0	0-0	4	3.81	4.12
2010	Ari	NL	54	0	0	11	57.0	251	59	32	27	3	3	2	1	29	1	29	2	0	3	2	.600	0	0-4	5	4.45	4.26
2011	NYM	NL	5	0	0	3	6.2	33	13	8	8	2	1	0	1	1	0	1	0	0	0	2	.000	0	1-1	0	12.04	10.80
2014	SD	NL	32	0	0	11	40.1	160	34	16	16	2	2	1	0	8	0	29	1	0	0	1	.000	0	0-0	5	2.21	3.57
09	Atl	NL	3	0	0	1	1.1	11	3	6	6	0	0	0	1	3	0	2	0	0	0	1	.000	0	0-0	0	23.46	40.50
09	StL	NL	15	0	0	4	16.1	70	14	10	8	1	3	0	1	5	0	9	0	0	0	0	-	0	0-0	2	2.82	4.41
09	Ari	NL	30	0	0	16	37.0	160	39	20	11	0	1	1	3	12	0	18	2	0	0	1	.000	0	0-0	2	3.71	2.68
	8 ML YEARS		265	0	0	71	274.1	1189	281	162	141	19	15	9	11	102	6	191	11	0	9	15	.375	0	2-12	39	4.01	4.63

Brad Brach

Pitches: R Bats: R Pos: RP-46   BROCK   Ht: 6'6" Wt: 215 Born: 4/12/1986 Age: 29

Year	Team	Lg	G	GS	CG	GF	IP	BFP	H	R	ER	HR	SH	SF	HB	TBB	IBB	SO	WP	Bk	W	L	Pct	Sh	Sv-Op	Hld	ERC	ERA
2014	Norfolk*	AAA	17	0	0	5	23.1	101	26	10	9	1	1	3	0	6	2	43	2	0	3	1	.750	0	1- -	-	3.56	3.47
2011	SD	NL	9	0	0	4	7.0	38	9	5	4	0	0	0	1	7	4	11	1	0	0	2	.000	0	0-0	0	6.51	5.14
2012	SD	NL	67	0	0	13	66.2	280	50	28	28	11	1	3	2	33	7	75	4	0	2	4	.333	0	0-1	15	3.47	3.78
2013	SD	NL	33	0	0	6	31.0	141	36	15	11	3	0	3	0	19	0	31	4	0	1	0	1.000	0	0-0	2	6.03	3.19
2014	Bal	AL	46	0	0	8	62.1	254	48	24	22	6	2	4	1	25	1	54	2	0	7	1	.875	0	0-0	8	2.90	3.18
	4 ML YEARS		155	0	0	31	167.0	713	143	72	65	20	3	10	4	84	12	171	11	0	10	7	.588	0	0-1	25	3.83	3.50

Jackie Bradley Jr.

Bats: L Throws: R Pos: CF-113;RF-12;PR-5;PH-2;LF-1   Ht: 5'10" Wt: 195 Born: 4/19/1990 Age: 25

Year	Team	Lg	G	AB	H	2B	3B	HR	(Hm	Rd)	TB	R	RBI	RC	TBB	IBB	SO	HBP	SH	SF	SB	CS	GDP	Avg	OBP	Slg	OPS
2011	Lowell	A-	6	21	4	0	0	0	(-	-)	4	5	0	0	4	0	5	0	0	0	0	2	0	.190	.320	.190	.510
2011	Grnvlle	A	4	15	5	1	0	1	(-	-)	9	2	3	2	0	0	3	0	0	0	0	0	0	.333	.333	.600	.933
2012	Salem	A+	67	234	84	26	2	3	(-	-)	123	53	34	64	52	1	40	10	0	8	16	6	5	.359	.480	.526	1.006
2012	Portlnd	AA	61	229	62	16	2	6	(-	-)	100	37	29	40	35	0	49	4	0	3	8	3	3	.271	.373	.437	.809
2013	Pwtckt	AAA	80	320	88	26	3	10	(-	-)	150	57	35	57	41	2	75	10	2	1	7	7	3	.275	.374	.469	.842
2014	Pwtckt	AAA	14	66	14	1	0	1	(-	-)	18	6	5	3	3	0	18	0	0	0	0	1	0	.212	.246	.273	.519
2013	Bos	AL	37	95	18	5	0	3	(2	1)	32	18	10	8	10	0	31	2	0	0	2	0	1	.189	.280	.337	.617
2014	Bos	AL	127	384	76	19	2	1	(1	0)	102	45	30	27	31	1	121	5	1	2	8	0	10	.198	.265	.266	.531
	2 ML YEARS		164	479	94	24	2	4	(3	1)	134	63	40	35	41	1	152	7	1	2	10	0	11	.196	.268	.280	.548

Michael Brantley

Bats: L Throws: L Pos: LF-107;CF-46;DH-8;PH-2   Ht: 6'2" Wt: 200 Born: 5/15/1987 Age: 28

Year	Team	Lg	G	AB	H	2B	3B	HR	(Hm	Rd)	TB	R	RBI	RC	TBB	IBB	SO	HBP	SH	SF	SB	CS	GDP	Avg	OBP	Slg	OPS
2009	Cle	AL	28	112	35	4	0	0	(0	0)	39	10	11	16	8	0	19	0	1	0	4	4	3	.313	.358	.348	.707
2010	Cle	AL	72	297	73	9	3	3	(2	1)	97	38	22	32	22	0	38	0	4	2	10	2	6	.246	.296	.327	.623
2011	Cle	AL	114	451	120	24	4	7	(4	3)	173	63	46	56	34	2	76	3	3	5	13	5	11	.266	.318	.384	.702
2012	Cle	AL	149	552	159	37	4	6	(3	3)	222	63	60	76	53	12	56	0	4	4	12	9	7	.288	.348	.402	.750
2013	Cle	AL	151	556	158	26	3	10	(9	1)	220	66	73	86	40	1	67	4	3	8	17	4	11	.284	.332	.396	.728
2014	Cle	AL	156	611	200	45	2	20	(11	9)	309	94	97	114	52	4	56	8	0	5	23	1	16	.327	.385	.506	.890
	Postseason		1	4	1	0	0	0	(0	0)	1	0	0	0	0	0	0	0	0	0	0	0	0	.250	.250	.250	.500
	6 ML YEARS		670	2579	745	145	16	46	(29	17)	1060	334	309	380	209	19	312	15	11	24	79	25	54	.289	.343	.411	.754

Rob Brantly

Bats: L Throws: R Pos: C   Ht: 6'1" Wt: 195 Born: 7/14/1989 Age: 25

Year	Team	Lg	G	AB	H	2B	3B	HR	(Hm	Rd)	TB	R	RBI	RC	TBB	IBB	SO	HBP	SH	SF	SB	CS	GDP	Avg	OBP	Slg	OPS
2010	WMich	A	52	188	48	10	1	0	(-	-)	63	26	21	24	23	0	22	1	0	2	0	2	9	.255	.352	.335	.687
2011	WMich	A	75	284	86	16	1	7	(-	-)	125	42	44	47	24	3	39	5	3	1	2	2	12	.303	.366	.440	.806
2011	Lkland	A+	39	146	32	6	0	3	(-	-)	47	16	18	11	5	0	17	0	0	4	0	0	4	.219	.239	.322	.561
2012	Erie	AA	46	180	56	16	1	3	(-	-)	83	16	24	29	12	0	17	2	0	3	0	1	4	.311	.359	.461	.820
2012	Toledo	AAA	36	130	33	4	0	0	(-	-)	37	11	6	11	7	0	25	1	0	1	0	0	5	.254	.295	.285	.580
2012	NewOr	AAA	14	52	19	4	0	2	(-	-)	29	7	11	10	1	0	9	1	0	0	0	0	0	.365	.389	.558	.947
2013	NewOr	AAA	20	70	13	3	0	1	(-	-)	19	9	3	3	3	0	8	0	1	0	0	0	1	.186	.219	.271	.491
2014	NewOr	AAA	101	364	93	15	2	4	(-	-)	124	38	37	37	20	1	61	1	0	7	0	0	6	.255	.291	.341	.631
2012	Mia	NL	31	100	29	8	0	3	(1	2)	46	14	8	14	13	2	16	0	0	0	1	1	1	.290	.372	.460	.832
2013	Mia	NL	67	223	47	9	0	1	(1	0)	59	11	18	14	15	1	53	2	0	3	0	0	8	.211	.263	.265	.528
	2 ML YEARS		98	323	76	17	0	4	(2	2)	105	25	26	28	28	3	69	2	0	3	1	1	9	.235	.298	.325	.623

Ryan Braun

Bats: R **Throws:** R **Pos:** RF-134;CF-1;DH-1;PH-1　　　**Ht:** 6'2" **Wt:** 200 **Born:** 11/17/1983 **Age:** 31

									BATTING													RUNNING			AVERAGES			
Year	Team	Lg	G	AB	H	2B	3B	HR	(Hm	Rd)	TB	R	RBI	RC	TBB	IBB	SO	HBP	SH	SF		SB	CS	GDP		Avg	OBP	Slg	OPS
2007	Mil	NL	113	451	146	26	6	34	(17	17)	286	91	97	94	29	1	112	7	0	5		15	5	13		.324	.370	**.634**	1.004
2008	Mil	NL	151	611	174	39	7	37	(23	14)	338	92	106	100	42	4	129	6	0	4		14	4	13		.285	.335	.553	.888
2009	Mil	NL	158	635	203	39	6	32	(15	17)	350	113	114	133	57	1	121	13	0	3		20	6	7		.320	.386	.551	.937
2010	Mil	NL	157	619	188	45	1	25	(13	12)	310	101	103	104	56	1	105	6	0	3		14	3	17		.304	.365	.501	.866
2011	Mil	NL	150	563	187	38	6	33	(16	17)	336	109	111	124	58	2	93	5	0	3		33	6	9		.332	.397	**.597**	**.994**
2012	Mil	NL	154	598	191	36	3	**41**	(24	17)	**356**	108	112	**125**	63	15	128	11	0	5		30	7	12		.319	.391	.595	**.987**
2013	Mil	NL	61	225	67	14	2	9	(5	4)	112	30	38	39	27	7	56	0	0	1		4	5	8		.298	.372	.498	.869
2014	Mil	NL	135	530	141	30	6	19	(8	11)	240	68	81	74	41	3	113	6	0	3		11	5	17		.266	.324	.453	.777
	Postseason		15	58	22	9	0	2	(2	0)	37	7	12	13	4	0	13	1	0	1		1	0	0		.379	.422	.638	1.060
	8 ML YEARS		1079	4232	1297	267	37	230	(121	109)	2328	712	762	793	373	34	857	54	0	27		141	41	96		.306	.368	.550	.918

Bryce Brentz

Bats: R **Throws:** R **Pos:** LF-6;RF-2;PH-2　　　**Ht:** 6'0" **Wt:** 210 **Born:** 12/30/1988 **Age:** 26

									BATTING													RUNNING			AVERAGES			
Year	Team	Lg	G	AB	H	2B	3B	HR	(Hm	Rd)	TB	R	RBI	RC	TBB	IBB	SO	HBP	SH	SF		SB	CS	GDP		Avg	OBP	Slg	OPS
2010	Lowell	A-	69	262	52	14	4	5	(-	-)	89	28	39	22	21	0	76	1	0	2		5	4	7		.198	.259	.340	.598
2011	Grnvlle	A	40	170	61	10	3	11	(-	-)	110	43	36	41	14	0	35	2	0	2		2	2	5		.359	.414	.647	1.061
2011	Salem	A+	75	288	79	15	1	19	(-	-)	153	48	58	52	26	2	80	3	0	4		1	1	8		.274	.336	.531	.868
2012	Portlnd	AA	122	456	135	30	1	17	(-	-)	218	62	76	78	40	3	130	4	0	4		7	5	9		.296	.355	.478	.833
2012	Pwtckt	AAA	5	17	2	0	0	0	(-	-)	2	0	0	0	1	0	6	0	0	0		0	0	0		.118	.118	.118	.284
2013	Pwtckt	AAA	82	326	86	16	1	17	(-	-)	155	36	56	49	20	1	86	3	0	0		1	0	11		.264	.312	.475	.788
2013	RedSx	R	6	17	4	2	0	2	(-	-)	12	3	8	3	1	0	4	1	0	0		0	0	0		.235	.316	.706	1.022
2014	Pwtckt	AAA	63	230	56	11	2	12	(-	-)	107	42	53	38	32	0	58	3	0	2		1	1	9		.243	.341	.465	.806
2014	RedSx	R	7	18	1	1	0	0	(-	-)	2	1	0	0	3	1	5	0	0	0		0	0	0		.056	.190	.111	.302
2014	Lowell	A-	2	8	1	0	0	0	(-	-)	1	2	1	0	1	1	2	0	0	1		0	0	0		.125	.200	.125	.325
2014	Bos	AL	9	26	8	2	0	0	(0	0)	10	5	2	3	0	0	9	0	0	0		0	0	0		.308	.308	.385	.692

Craig Breslow

Pitches: L **Bats:** L **Pos:** RP-60　　　BREHZ-loh　　　**Ht:** 6'1" **Wt:** 190 **Born:** 8/8/1980 **Age:** 34

			HOW MUCH HE PITCHED						WHAT HE GAVE UP													THE RESULTS							
Year	Team	Lg	G	GS	CG	GF	IP	BFP	H	R	ER	HR	SH	SF	HB	TBB	IBB	SO	WP	Bk	W	L	Pct	Sh	Sv-Op	Hld	ERC	ERA
2014	Pwtckt*	AAA	3	1	0	0	2.2	11	1	0	0	0	0	0	0	2	0	1	0	1	1	0	1.000	0	0- -	0	1.54	0.00
2005	SD	NL	14	0	0	3	16.1	78	15	6	4	1	0	1	1	13	0	14	1	0	0	0	-	0	0 - -	1	4.98	2.20
2006	Bos	AL	13	0	0	3	12.0	55	12	5	5	0	0	2	1	6	1	12	2	1	0	2	.000	0	0-0	3	3.78	3.75
2008	2 Tms	AL	49	0	0	13	47.0	189	34	12	10	1	2	0	1	19	2	39	4	1	0	2	.000	0	1-2	5	2.12	1.91
2009	2 Tms	AL	77	0	0	9	69.2	281	48	31	26	8	4	1	3	29	0	55	3	1	8	7	.533	0	0-2	15	2.79	3.36
2010	Oak	AL	75	0	0	23	74.2	304	53	26	25	9	2	0	0	29	4	71	0	1	4	4	.500	0	5-7	16	2.53	3.01
2011	Oak	AL	67	0	0	10	59.1	261	69	29	25	4	3	2	2	21	1	44	3	0	0	2	.000	0	0-3	8	4.74	3.79
2012	2 Tms	AL	63	0	0	16	63.1	261	52	22	19	5	3	3	2	22	2	61	2	0	3	0	1.000	0	0-1	9	2.86	2.70
2013	Bos	AL	61	0	0	13	59.2	237	49	16	12	3	0	2	2	18	0	33	2	0	5	2	.714	0	0-1	13	2.66	1.81
2014	Bos	AL	60	0	0	16	54.1	260	73	40	36	8	1	0	2	28	1	37	3	1	2	4	.333	0	1-2	2	7.14	5.96
08	Cle	AL	7	0	0	3	8.1	40	10	3	3	1	0	0	0	5	0	7	0	0	0	0	-	0	0-0	0	6.09	3.24
08	Min	AL	42	0	0	10	38.2	149	24	9	7	0	2	0	0	14	2	32	4	1	0	2	.000	0	1-2	5	1.49	1.63
09	Min	AL	17	0	0	5	14.1	64	11	11	10	3	2	1	2	11	0	11	3	0	1	2	.333	0	0-0	2	5.38	6.28
09	Oak	AL	60	0	0	4	55.1	217	37	20	16	5	2	1	2	18	0	44	0	1	7	5	.583	0	0-2	13	2.21	2.60
12	Ari	NL	40	0	0	12	43.1	180	38	15	13	5	2	1	1	13	0	42	1	0	2	0	1.000	0	0-0	4	3.19	2.70
12	Bos	AL	23	0	0	4	20.0	81	14	7	6	0	1	2	1	9	2	19	1	0	1	0	1.000	0	0-1	5	2.12	2.70
	Postseason		10	0	0	0	7.1	36	6	3	2	0	0	1	2	7	1	6	0	0	1	0	1.000	0	0-1	4	5.16	2.45
	9 ML YEARS		479	0	0	106	456.1	1926	405	187	162	39	15	11	13	185	11	366	20	5	22	23	.489	0	7-18	72	3.47	3.20

Reid Brignac

Bats: L **Throws:** R **Pos:** 3B-20;PH-15;2B-3;SS-3　　　BRINN-yak　　　**Ht:** 6'3" **Wt:** 215 **Born:** 1/16/1986 **Age:** 29

									BATTING													RUNNING			AVERAGES			
Year	Team	Lg	G	AB	H	2B	3B	HR	(Hm	Rd)	TB	R	RBI	RC	TBB	IBB	SO	HBP	SH	SF		SB	CS	GDP		Avg	OBP	Slg	OPS
2014	LV*	AAA	36	128	34	8	1	5	(-	-)	59	23	21	21	16	1	31	0	2	3		3	0	1		.266	.340	.461	.801
2014	Clrwtr*	A+	3	8	4	1	0	0	(-	-)	5	0	1	2	2	0	1	0	0	0		0	0	0		.500	.600	.625	1.225
2008	TB	AL	4	10	0	0	0	0	(0	0)	0	1	0	0	1	0	5	0	0	0		0	0	0		.000	.091	.000	.091
2009	TB	AL	31	90	25	8	2	1	(0	1)	40	10	6	10	3	0	20	0	0	0		2	2	1		.278	.301	.444	.746
2010	TB	AL	113	301	77	13	1	8	(3	5)	116	39	45	38	20	3	77	3	0	2		3	3	6		.256	.307	.385	.692
2011	TB	AL	92	249	48	4	0	1	(0	1)	55	18	15	8	10	1	63	1	4	0		3	1	2		.193	.227	.221	.448
2012	TB	AL	16	21	2	0	0	0	(0	0)	2	1	1	0	1	0	5	0	0	0		0	0	0		.095	.136	.095	.232
2013	2 Tms	AL	46	92	17	4	0	1	(0	1)	24	5	6	7	4	1	30	0	2	0		0	0	6		.185	.219	.261	.480
2014	Phi	NL	37	81	18	5	1	1	(1	0)	28	4	10	8	9	1	33	0	1	0		1	1	2		.222	.300	.346	.646
13	Col	NL	29	48	12	3	0	1	(0	1)	18	4	6	7	3	1	13	0	2	0		0	0	3		.250	.294	.375	.669
13	NYY	AL	17	44	5	1	0	0	(0	0)	6	1	0	0	1	0	17	0	0	0		0	0	3		.114	.133	.136	.270
	Postseason		5	4	0	0	0	0	(0	0)	0	0	0	0	0	0	3	0	0	0		0	0	0		.000	.200	.000	.200
	7 ML YEARS		339	844	187	34	4	12	(4	8)	265	78	83	71	48	6	233	4	7	2		9	7	17		.222	.266	.314	.580

Drake Britton

Pitches: L **Bats:** L **Pos:** RP-7   **Ht:** 6'2" **Wt:** 215 **Born:** 5/22/1989 **Age:** 26

			HOW MUCH HE PITCHED					WHAT HE GAVE UP												THE RESULTS							
Year	Team	Lg	G	GS	CG	GF	IP	BFP	H	R	ER	HR	SH	SF	HB	TBB	IBB	SO	WP	Bk	W	L	Pct	Sh	Sv-Op	Hld	ERC	ERA
2010	Grnvlle	A	21	21	0	0	75.2	318	69	32	25	5	3	2	2	23	0	78	7	0	2	3	.400	0	0- --	-	3.07	2.97
2011	Salem	A+	26	26	0	0	97.2	458	111	81	75	12	3	5	6	55	0	89	16	0	1	13	.071	0	0- --	-	5.93	6.91
2012	Salem	A+	10	8	0	0	45.0	201	42	35	29	5	5	2	4	19	0	42	2	0	3	5	.375	0	0- --	-	4.10	5.80
2012	Portlnd	AA	16	16	0	0	84.2	369	86	41	35	3	5	2	1	38	0	76	2	0	4	7	.364	0	0- --	-	3.95	3.72
2013	Portlnd	AA	17	16	1	0	97.1	410	94	52	38	5	1	1	2	36	0	80	6	0	7	6	.538	1	0- --	-	3.56	3.51
2013	Pwtckt	AAA	1	1	0	0	5.1	28	10	5	5	0	1	0	0	1	0	5	0	0	0	1	.000	0	0- --	-	7.22	8.44
2014	Pwtckt	AAA	45	0	0	22	58.1	278	77	41	38	8	1	3	0	38	4	37	5	0	2	3	.400	0	5- --	-	7.39	5.86
2013	Bos	AL	18	0	0	7	21.0	84	21	9	9	1	0	2	0	7	1	17	0	0	1	1	.500	0	0-2	1	3.62	3.86
2014	Bos	AL	7	0	0	0	6.2	27	5	0	0	0	0	0	0	2	0	4	0	0	0	0	-	0	0-0	1	1.79	0.00
	2 ML YEARS		25	0	0	7	27.2	111	26	9	9	1	0	2	0	9	1	21	0	0	1	1	.500	0	0-2	2	3.13	2.93

Zach Britton

Pitches: L **Bats:** L **Pos:** RP-71   **Ht:** 6'3" **Wt:** 195 **Born:** 12/22/1987 **Age:** 27

			HOW MUCH HE PITCHED					WHAT HE GAVE UP												THE RESULTS							
Year	Team	Lg	G	GS	CG	GF	IP	BFP	H	R	ER	HR	SH	SF	HB	TBB	IBB	SO	WP	Bk	W	L	Pct	Sh	Sv-Op	Hld	ERC	ERA
2011	Bal	AL	28	28	0	0	154.1	666	162	93	79	12	8	7	1	62	3	97	7	0	11	11	.500	0	0-0	0	4.24	4.61
2012	Bal	AL	12	11	0	0	60.1	270	61	37	34	6	0	1	2	32	3	53	4	0	5	3	.625	0	0-0	0	4.70	5.07
2013	Bal	AL	8	7	0	0	40.0	182	52	23	22	4	1	1	1	17	1	18	1	0	2	3	.400	0	0-0	0	6.14	4.95
2014	Bal	AL	71	0	0	49	76.1	285	46	17	14	4	3	0	1	23	0	62	0	0	3	2	.600	0	37-41	7	1.62	1.65
	4 ML YEARS		119	46	0	49	331.0	1403	321	170	149	26	12	9	5	134	7	230	12	0	21	19	.525	0	37-41	7	3.86	4.05

Aaron Brooks

Pitches: R **Bats:** R **Pos:** SP-1; RP-1   **Ht:** 6'4" **Wt:** 220 **Born:** 4/27/1990 **Age:** 25

			HOW MUCH HE PITCHED					WHAT HE GAVE UP												THE RESULTS							
Year	Team	Lg	G	GS	CG	GF	IP	BFP	H	R	ER	HR	SH	SF	HB	TBB	IBB	SO	WP	Bk	W	L	Pct	Sh	Sv-Op	Hld	ERC	ERA
2011	Idaho	R+	15	13	0	1	79.2	330	89	42	34	7	6	1	3	8	0	73	5	0	6	2	.750	0	0- --	-	3.64	3.84
2012	Kane	A	27	27	1	0	153.2	670	191	99	85	18	3	9	4	26	0	120	9	0	9	12	.429	0	0- --	-	4.74	4.98
2013	Wilmg	A+	10	10	0	0	56.1	233	60	28	28	4	0	1	0	11	0	43	3	0	2	3	.400	0	0- --	-	3.48	4.47
2013	NWArk	AA	16	16	1	0	103.2	427	113	51	48	13	4	6	3	11	0	67	2	0	7	7	.500	1	0- --	-	3.72	4.17
2014	Omha	AAA	25	23	1	1	139.0	578	151	67	60	14	4	5	1	25	2	97	4	1	12	3	.800	0	1- --	-	3.73	3.88
2014	KC	AL	2	1	0	1	2.2	24	12	13	13	1	0	1	2	3	0	2	0	0	0	1	.000	0	0-0	0	44.02	43.88

Rex Brothers

Pitches: L **Bats:** L **Pos:** RP-74   **Ht:** 6'0" **Wt:** 210 **Born:** 12/18/1987 **Age:** 27

			HOW MUCH HE PITCHED					WHAT HE GAVE UP												THE RESULTS							
Year	Team	Lg	G	GS	CG	GF	IP	BFP	H	R	ER	HR	SH	SF	HB	TBB	IBB	SO	WP	Bk	W	L	Pct	Sh	Sv-Op	Hld	ERC	ERA
2011	Col	NL	48	0	0	6	40.2	172	33	14	13	4	0	0	0	20	2	59	2	0	1	2	.333	0	1-3	16	3.31	2.88
2012	Col	NL	75	0	0	10	67.2	295	63	33	29	5	3	3	1	37	7	83	5	1	8	2	.800	0	0-5	18	3.99	3.86
2013	Col	NL	72	0	0	40	67.1	281	51	16	13	5	1	0	0	36	2	76	3	3	2	1	.667	0	19-21	12	3.09	1.74
2014	Col	NL	74	0	0	15	56.1	273	65	38	35	7	1	4	2	39	0	55	5	1	4	6	.400	0	0-6	15	6.43	5.59
	4 ML YEARS		269	0	0	71	232.0	1021	212	101	90	21	5	7	3	132	11	273	15	5	15	11	.577	0	20-35	61	4.15	3.49

Andrew Brown

Bats: R **Throws:** R **Pos:** LF-8;PH-8;RF-4;DH-2   **Ht:** 6'0" **Wt:** 200 **Born:** 9/10/1984 **Age:** 30

			BATTING																	RUNNING			AVERAGES			
Year	Team	Lg	G	AB	H	2B	3B	HR	(Hm	Rd)	TB	R	RBI	RC	TBB	IBB	SO	HBP	SH	SF	SB	CS	GDP	Avg	OBP	Slg	OPS
2014	LsVgs*	AAA	104	386	109	26	1	21	(-	-)	200	65	69	76	52	1	87	5	0	4	2	0	12	.282	.371	.518	.889
2011	StL	NL	11	22	4	1	0	0	(0	0)	5	1	3	1	0	0	8	0	0	0	0	0	1	.182	.182	.227	.409
2012	Col	NL	46	112	26	7	0	5	(3	2)	48	14	11	7	12	0	34	0	0	2	2	2	3	.232	.302	.429	.730
2013	NYM	NL	68	150	34	5	0	7	(3	4)	60	16	24	19	13	0	44	0	2	0	1	0	3	.227	.288	.400	.688
2014	NYM	NL	19	44	8	1	0	2	(1	1)	15	6	7	4	3	0	15	1	0	1	0	0	2	.182	.245	.341	.586
	4 ML YEARS		144	328	72	14	0	14	(7	7)	128	37	45	31	28	0	101	1	2	3	3	2	9	.220	.281	.390	.671

Brooks Brown

Pitches: R **Bats:** L **Pos:** RP-28   **Ht:** 6'3" **Wt:** 205 **Born:** 6/20/1985 **Age:** 30

			HOW MUCH HE PITCHED					WHAT HE GAVE UP												THE RESULTS							
Year	Team	Lg	G	GS	CG	GF	IP	BFP	H	R	ER	HR	SH	SF	HB	TBB	IBB	SO	WP	Bk	W	L	Pct	Sh	Sv-Op	Hld	ERC	ERA
2010	Erie	AA	28	18	4	6	128.0	534	120	61	59	8	3	1	5	39	3	85	2	0	12	9	.571	2	2- --	-	3.25	4.15
2011	Erie	AA	17	17	0	0	93.2	412	111	68	59	10	6	3	4	27	0	65	6	0	3	9	.250	0	0- --	-	4.93	5.67
2012	Toledo	AAA	29	19	0	4	112.0	502	125	67	61	11	4	5	5	58	0	81	12	0	4	4	.500	0	0- --	-	5.51	4.90
2013	Indy	AAA	37	8	0	8	91.0	379	95	53	48	11	4	0	2	24	1	69	3	0	6	5	.545	0	0- --	-	4.08	4.75
2014	ColSpr	AAA	37	0	0	20	47.1	209	50	29	22	4	2	3	5	17	0	46	2	0	1	1	.500	0	7- --	-	4.55	4.18
2014	Col	NL	28	0	0	9	26.0	104	20	9	8	3	0	2	1	5	1	21	1	0	0	1	.000	0	0-0	5	2.25	2.77

Corey Brown

Bats: L **Throws:** L **Pos:** RF-1;DH-1;PH-1;PR-1 **Ht:** 6'1" **Wt:** 210 **Born:** 11/26/1985 **Age:** 29

								BATTING												RUNNING			AVERAGES			
Year Team	Lg	G	AB	H	2B	3B	HR	(Hm	Rd)	TB	R	RBI	RC	TBB	IBB	SO	HBP	SH	SF	SB	CS	GDP	Avg	OBP	Slg	OPS
2014 Pwtckt*	AAA	91	325	75	15	2	17	(-	-)	145	35	42	44	28	2	106	2	0	2	6	2	1	.231	.294	.446	.740
2011 Was	NL	3	3	0	0	0	0	(0	0)	0	0	0	0	0	0	2	0	0	0	0	0	0	.000	.000	.000	.000
2012 Was	NL	19	25	5	2	0	1	(0	1)	10	4	3	2	1	0	9	0	1	0	0	0	0	.200	.231	.400	.631
2013 Was	NL	14	12	2	1	0	1	(0	1)	6	2	1	2	3	0	4	0	0	0	1	0	1	.167	.333	.500	.833
2014 Bos	AL	3	1	0	0	0	0	(0	0)	0	0	0	0	0	0	1	0	0	0	0	0	0	.000	.000	.000	.000
4 ML YEARS		39	41	7	3	0	2	(0	2)	16	6	4	4	4	0	16	0	1	0	1	0	1	.171	.244	.390	.635

Domonic Brown

Bats: L **Throws:** L **Pos:** LF-127;PH-24;DH-1 **Ht:** 6'5" **Wt:** 230 **Born:** 9/3/1987 **Age:** 27

								BATTING												RUNNING			AVERAGES			
Year Team	Lg	G	AB	H	2B	3B	HR	(Hm	Rd)	TB	R	RBI	RC	TBB	IBB	SO	HBP	SH	SF	SB	CS	GDP	Avg	OBP	Slg	OPS
2010 Phi	NL	35	62	13	3	0	2	(2	0)	22	8	13	5	5	1	24	0	0	3	2	1	1	.210	.257	.355	.612
2011 Phi	NL	56	184	45	10	1	5	(4	1)	72	28	19	21	25	1	35	0	0	1	3	1	2	.245	.333	.391	.725
2012 Phi	NL	56	187	44	11	2	5	(3	2)	74	21	26	25	21	2	34	2	0	2	0	0	6	.235	.316	.396	.712
2013 Phi	NL	139	496	135	21	4	27	(14	13)	245	65	83	76	39	5	97	1	0	4	8	3	5	.272	.324	.494	.818
2014 Phi	NL	144	473	111	22	1	10	(5	5)	165	47	63	54	34	4	91	1	0	4	7	1	9	.235	.285	.349	.634
Postseason		3	3	0	0	0	0	(0	0)	0	1	0	0	0	0	0	0	0	0	0	0	0	.000	.000	.000	.000
5 ML YEARS		430	1402	348	67	8	49	(28	21)	578	169	204	181	124	13	281	4	0	14	20	6	23	.248	.308	.412	.721

Gary Brown

Bats: R **Throws:** R **Pos:** CF-6;PH-1 **Ht:** 6'1" **Wt:** 190 **Born:** 9/28/1988 **Age:** 26

								BATTING												RUNNING			AVERAGES			
Year Team	Lg	G	AB	H	2B	3B	HR	(Hm	Rd)	TB	R	RBI	RC	TBB	IBB	SO	HBP	SH	SF	SB	CS	GDP	Avg	OBP	Slg	OPS
2010 Giants	R	6	22	4	1	0	0	(-	-)	5	6	0	2	4	0	5	1	0	0	2	0	0	.182	.333	.227	.561
2010 SlmKzr	A-	6	22	3	0	1	0	(-	-)	5	2	2	1	2	0	7	2	0	1	0	1	0	.136	.259	.227	.487
2011 SnJos	A+	131	559	188	34	13	14	(-	-)	290	115	80	120	46	1	77	23	6	4	53	19	6	.336	.407	.519	.925
2012 Rchmd	AA	134	538	149	33	2	7	(-	-)	207	73	42	76	40	1	87	19	7	6	33	18	6	.277	.345	.385	.730
2013 Fresno	AAA	137	558	129	29	6	13	(-	-)	209	79	50	60	33	0	135	10	6	1	17	11	6	.231	.286	.375	.660
2014 Fresno	AAA	136	536	145	24	6	10	(-	-)	211	89	54	72	36	0	119	13	6	5	37	20	3	.271	.329	.394	.722
2014 SF	NL	7	7	3	0	0	0	(0	0)	3	1	1	2	0	0	0	0	0	0	0	0	0	.429	.429	.429	.857

Jonathan Broxton

Pitches: R **Bats:** R **Pos:** RP-62 **Ht:** 6'4" **Wt:** 295 **Born:** 6/16/1984 **Age:** 31

		HOW MUCH HE PITCHED						WHAT HE GAVE UP											THE RESULTS						
Year Team	Lg	G	GS	CG	GF	IP	BFP	H	R	ER	HR	SH	SF	HB	TBB	IBB	SO	WP	Bk	W	L	Pct	Sh	Sv-Op	Hld	ERC	ERA
2014 Pnscla*	AA	2	2	0	0	2.0	8	1	0	0	0	0	0	1	0	0	2	0	0	0	0	-	0	0- -	0	1.41	0.00
2005 LAD	NL	14	0	0	5	13.2	68	13	11	9	0	0	2	1	12	2	22	2	0	1	0	1.000	0	0-1	1	4.65	5.93
2006 LAD	NL	68	0	0	20	76.1	320	61	25	22	7	3	1	1	33	6	97	7	0	4	1	.800	0	3-7	12	2.97	2.59
2007 LAD	NL	83	0	0	18	82.0	334	69	30	26	6	0	1	1	25	3	99	4	0	4	4	.500	0	2-8	32	2.71	2.85
2008 LAD	NL	70	0	0	32	69.0	285	54	29	24	2	3	3	3	27	5	88	3	0	3	5	.375	0	14-22	13	2.48	3.13
2009 LAD	NL	73	0	0	58	76.0	300	44	24	22	4	0	3	1	29	1	114	2	0	7	2	.778	0	36-42	1	1.65	2.61
2010 LAD	NL	64	0	0	46	62.1	271	64	30	28	4	3	1	2	28	5	73	1	0	5	6	.455	0	22-29	3	4.21	4.04
2011 LAD	NL	14	0	0	12	12.2	62	15	10	8	2	0	0	0	9	2	10	0	0	1	2	.333	0	7-8	0	6.47	5.68
2012 2 Tms		60	0	0	39	58.0	238	56	18	16	2	2	1	3	17	0	45	0	0	4	5	.444	0	27-33	10	3.34	2.48
2013 Cin	NL	34	0	0	8	30.2	133	27	17	14	4	1	2	4	12	2	25	0	0	2	2	.500	0	0-3	12	3.97	4.11
2014 2 Tms	NL	62	0	0	18	58.2	231	41	15	15	4	2	1	1	19	0	49	0	0	4	3	.571	0	7-15	23	2.14	2.30
12 KC	AL	35	0	0	32	35.2	151	36	11	9	1	2	1	2	14	0	25	0	0	1	2	.333	0	23-27	4	3.93	2.27
12 Cin	NL	25	0	0	7	22.1	87	20	7	7	1	0	0	1	3	0	20	0	0	3	3	.500	0	4-6	6	2.44	2.82
14 Cin	NL	51	0	0	16	48.1	189	32	10	10	3	2	1	1	17	0	37	0	0	4	2	.667	0	7-13	21	2.06	1.86
14 Mil	NL	11	0	0	2	10.1	42	9	5	5	1	0	0	0	2	0	12	0	0	0	1	.000	0	0-2	2	2.55	4.35
Postseason		16	0	0	11	17.1	79	18	8	7	1	0	0	1	7	0	19	0	0	0	3	.000	0	3-5	1	4.06	3.63
10 ML YEARS		542	0	0	256	539.1	2242	444	209	184	35	14	15	17	211	26	622	19	0	35	30	.538	0	118-168	107	2.91	3.07

Jay Bruce

Bats: L **Throws:** L **Pos:** RF-131;PH-4;1B-3 **Ht:** 6'3" **Wt:** 215 **Born:** 4/3/1987 **Age:** 28

								BATTING												RUNNING			AVERAGES			
Year Team	Lg	G	AB	H	2B	3B	HR	(Hm	Rd)	TB	R	RBI	RC	TBB	IBB	SO	HBP	SH	SF	SB	CS	GDP	Avg	OBP	Slg	OPS
2008 Cin	NL	108	413	105	17	1	21	(13	8)	187	63	52	49	33	1	110	4	0	2	4	6	8	.254	.314	.453	.767
2009 Cin	NL	101	345	77	15	2	22	(13	9)	162	47	58	47	38	2	75	2	1	1	3	3	5	.223	.303	.470	.773
2010 Cin	NL	148	509	143	23	5	25	(19	6)	251	80	70	71	58	5	136	1	0	6	5	4	12	.281	.353	.493	.846
2011 Cin	NL	157	585	150	27	2	32	(16	16)	277	84	97	96	71	14	158	5	1	2	8	7	8	.256	.341	.474	.814
2012 Cin	NL	155	560	141	35	5	34	(21	13)	288	89	99	85	62	11	155	4	0	7	9	3	5	.252	.327	.514	.841
2013 Cin	NL	160	626	164	43	1	30	(16	14)	299	89	109	88	63	13	185	2	0	5	7	3	9	.262	.329	.478	.807
2014 Cin	NL	137	493	107	21	1	18	(10	8)	184	71	66	54	44	5	149	2	1	5	12	3	8	.217	.281	.373	.654
Postseason		9	31	8	2	0	2	(0	2)	16	3	6	4	4	0	4	1	0	0	0	1	0	.258	.361	.516	.877
7 ML YEARS		966	3531	887	181	17	182	(108	74)	1648	523	551	490	369	51	968	20	3	27	48	29	55	.251	.323	.467	.790

David Buchanan

Pitches: R **Bats:** R **Pos:** SP-20   **Ht:** 6'3" **Wt:** 200 **Born:** 5/11/1989 **Age:** 26

Year	Team	Lg	G	GS	CG	GF	IP	BFP	H	R	ER	HR	SH	SF	HB	TBB	IBB	SO	WP	Bk	W	L	Pct	Sh	Sv-Op	Hld	ERC	ERA
2010	Wmspt	A-	13	13	0	0	62.0	268	61	32	29	1	0	1	4	23	1	30	2	0	3	1	.750	0	0--	-	3.50	4.21
2011	Lakwd	A	20	20	1	0	125.0	510	115	60	47	6	1	5	4	32	0	86	12	0	11	5	.688	0	0--	-	2.92	3.38
2011	Clrwtr	A+	6	6	0	0	32.1	141	37	15	14	4	0	1	1	11	0	24	0	0	3	2	.600	0	0--	-	5.03	3.90
2012	Rdng	AA	12	12	1	0	72.1	305	73	36	31	7	4	5	6	23	1	40	1	0	3	5	.375	1	0--	-	4.20	3.86
2013	Rdng	AA	22	22	0	0	130.2	567	142	78	70	15	7	7	6	41	0	86	5	1	6	11	.353	0	0--	-	4.53	4.82
2013	LV	AAA	6	6	0	0	39.0	164	36	14	13	2	3	1	3	12	1	22	0	0	4	2	.667	0	0--	-	3.24	3.00
2014	LV	AAA	12	12	0	0	57.0	254	67	26	25	3	2	4	3	21	0	46	3	0	6	2	.750	0	0--	-	4.85	3.95
2014	Phi	NL	20	20	0	0	117.2	503	120	55	49	12	6	3	8	32	2	71	0	0	6	8	.429	0	0-0	0	3.93	3.75

Jake Buchanan

Pitches: R **Bats:** R **Pos:** RP-15; SP-2   **Ht:** 6'0" **Wt:** 235 **Born:** 9/24/1989 **Age:** 25

Year	Team	Lg	G	GS	CG	GF	IP	BFP	H	R	ER	HR	SH	SF	HB	TBB	IBB	SO	WP	Bk	W	L	Pct	Sh	Sv-Op	Hld	ERC	ERA
2010	TriCity	A-	14	14	0	0	61.0	260	69	32	29	3	1		6	11	0	42	6	0	4	5	.444	0	0--	-	4.02	4.28
2011	Lancst	A+	25	25	1	0	158.2	667	157	92	69	10	7	5	6	35	3	102	7	0	5	10	.333	1	0--	-	3.16	3.91
2011	CpChr	AA	1	1	0	0	7.0	27	6	1	1	0	0	0	0	1	0	2	0	0	0	0	-	0	0--	-	1.86	1.29
2012	CpChr	AA	27	19	0	4	134.1	595	142	85	79	11	2	3	6	33	4	83	4	0	5	9	.357	0	0--	-	5.06	5.29
2012	OKCity	AAA	3	1	0	0	8.0	43	17	10	9	1	0	1	0	5	0	5	1	0	0	1	.000	0	0--	-	13.39	10.13
2013	CpChr	AA	18	13	0	2	82.0	311	67	22	19	4	2	1	2	9	1	44	2	0	7	2	.778	0	1--	-	1.92	2.09
2013	OKCity	AAA	12	12	0	0	76.1	316	85	33	33	6	4	1	0	13	1	55	6	0	5	5	.500	0	0--	-	3.69	3.89
2014	OKCity	AAA	16	15	1	0	88.1	369	95	44	38	7	2	2	3	16	1	46	3	0	7	5	.583	1	0--	-	3.64	3.87
2014	Hou	AL	17	2	0	9	35.1	154	41	19	18	4	3	0	1	12	1	20	2	0	1	3	.250	0	0-0	0	5.00	4.58

Clay Buchholz

Pitches: R **Bats:** L **Pos:** SP-28   BUCK-holtz   **Ht:** 6'3" **Wt:** 190 **Born:** 8/14/1984 **Age:** 30

Year	Team	Lg	G	GS	CG	GF	IP	BFP	H	R	ER	HR	SH	SF	HB	TBB	IBB	SO	WP	Bk	W	L	Pct	Sh	Sv-Op	Hld	ERC	ERA
2014	Pwtckt*	AAA	2	2	0	0	10.2	39	6	3	3	2	0	0	1	2	0	10	0	0	0	1	.000	0	0--	-	2.02	2.53
2007	Bos	AL	4	3	1	0	22.2	88	14	6	4	0	0	1	1	10	0	22	0	0	3	1	.750	1	0-0	0	1.90	1.59
2008	Bos	AL	16	15	1	0	76.0	357	93	63	57	11	0	3	2	41	1	72	2	1	2	9	.182	0	0-0	0	6.40	6.75
2009	Bos	AL	16	16	0	0	92.0	399	91	44	43	13	2	3	2	36	1	68	1	0	7	4	.636	0	0-0	0	4.31	4.21
2010	Bos	AL	28	28	1	0	173.2	711	142	55	45	9	5	5	5	67	1	120	7	1	17	7	.708	1	0-0	0	2.88	2.33
2011	Bos	AL	14	14	0	0	82.2	353	76	34	32	10	1	4	2	31	1	60	3	0	6	3	.667	0	0-0	0	3.72	3.48
2012	Bos	AL	29	29	2	0	189.1	802	187	104	96	25	5	9	12	64	2	129	2	2	11	8	.579	1	0-0	0	4.29	4.56
2013	Bos	AL	16	16	1	0	108.1	416	75	23	21	4	1	2	1	36	0	96	1	0	12	1	.923	1	0-0	0	2.00	1.74
2014	Bos	AL	28	28	0	0	170.1	737	182	108	101	17	3	4	10	54	2	132	8	0	8	11	.421	2	0-0	0	4.37	5.34
	Postseason		5	5	0	0	25.2	114	28	13	12	4	0	0	2	9	1	20	2	1	0	0	-	0	0-0	0	5.04	4.21
	8 ML YEARS		151	149	8	0	915.0	3863	860	437	399	89	17	31	35	339	8	699	24	4	66	44	.600	6	0-0	0	3.79	3.92

Ryan Buchter

Pitches: L **Bats:** L **Pos:** RP-1   BOOK-ter   **Ht:** 6'3" **Wt:** 240 **Born:** 2/13/1987 **Age:** 28

Year	Team	Lg	G	GS	CG	GF	IP	BFP	H	R	ER	HR	SH	SF	HB	TBB	IBB	SO	WP	Bk	W	L	Pct	Sh	Sv-Op	Hld	ERC	ERA
2010	Tenn	AA	47	1	0	11	60.0	292	61	37	31	6	3	3	11	47	1	71	7	0	7	2	.778	0	0--	-	6.45	4.65
2011	Tenn	AA	10	0	0	0	11.0	57	13	11	8	1	2	1	0	11	3	13	2	0	3	0	1.000	0	0--	-	6.83	6.55
2011	Dytona	A+	6	0	0	1	10.1	36	2	0	0	0	0	0	0	3	0	17	2	0	1	0	1.000	0	1--	-	0.36	0.00
2011	Lynbrg	A+	34	0	0	32	42.2	189	36	18	17	3	5	4	6	22	0	49	5	0	2	5	.286	0	15--	-	3.96	3.59
2012	Missi	AA	35	0	0	13	41.1	165	24	7	6	1	1	0	2	19	1	50	3	0	3	1	.750	0	4--	-	1.84	1.31
2012	Gwnntt	AAA	9	0	0	4	8.0	53	10	13	9	1	2	1	0	17	0	5	2	0	0	2	.000	0	0--	-	12.70	10.13
2013	Gwnntt	AAA	51	0	0	13	62.0	274	36	23	19	5	3	2	4	51	2	103	5	0	4	0	1.000	0	5--	-	3.40	2.76
2014	Gwnntt	AAA	49	0	0	13	63.0	271	51	23	23	5	2	4	2	40	0	63	2	0	3	3	.500	0	1--	-	3.98	3.29
2014	Atl	NL	1	0	0	0	1.0	3	0	0	0	0	0	0	0	1	0	1	0	0	1	0	1.000	0	0-0	0	1.26	0.00

John Buck

Bats: R **Throws:** R **Pos:** C-24;DH-5;PH-4;1B-1   **Ht:** 6'3" **Wt:** 245 **Born:** 7/7/1980 **Age:** 34

Year	Team	Lg	G	AB	H	2B	3B	HR	(Hm	Rd)	TB	R	RBI	RC	TBB	IBB	SO	HBP	SH	SF	SB	CS	GDP	Avg	OBP	Slg	OPS
2014	Salt Lk*	AAA	33	119	35	8	0	2	(-	-)	49	13	15	19	13	0	22	2	0	1	0	0	0	.294	.370	.412	.782
2004	KC	AL	71	238	56	9	0	12	(6	6)	101	36	30	26	15	0	79	0	4	1	1	1	6	.235	.280	.424	.704
2005	KC	AL	118	401	97	21	1	12	(3	9)	156	40	47	43	23	2	94	3	1	2	2	2	9	.242	.287	.389	.676
2006	KC	AL	114	371	91	21	1	11	(6	5)	147	37	50	43	26	2	84	7	4	1	0	2	7	.245	.306	.396	.702
2007	KC	AL	113	347	77	18	0	18	(6	12)	149	41	48	37	36	0	92	10	0	6	0	1	11	.222	.308	.429	.738
2008	KC	AL	109	370	83	23	1	9	(4	5)	135	48	48	42	34	2	96	6	0	4	0	3	12	.224	.304	.365	.669
2009	KC	AL	59	186	46	12	4	8	(3	5)	90	16	36	31	13	0	55	1	1	1	1	1	2	.247	.299	.484	.782
2010	Tor	AL	118	409	115	25	0	20	(9	11)	200	53	66	61	16	1	111	6	0	6	0	0	6	.281	.314	.489	.802
2011	Fla	NL	140	466	106	15	1	16	(7	9)	171	41	57	55	54	7	115	7	2	1	0	1	11	.227	.316	.367	.683
2012	Mia	NL	106	343	66	15	1	12	(4	8)	119	29	41	40	49	3	103	3	1	2	0	0	9	.192	.297	.347	.644
2013	2 Tms	NL	110	392	87	11	0	15	(6	9)	143	39	62	45	29	4	104	8	0	2	2	1	13	.222	.288	.365	.652
2014	2 Tms	AL	32	89	20	2	0	1	(0	1)	25	9	6	9	8	0	26	0	0	0	0	0	1	.225	.284	.281	.570
13	NYM	NL	101	368	79	11	0	15	(6	9)	135	38	60	43	29	4	99	8	0	2	2	1	12	.215	.285	.367	.652
13	Pit	NL	9	24	8	0	0	0	(0	0)	8	1	2	2	0	0	5	0	0	0	0	0	1	.333	.333	.333	.667

BATTING / RUNNING / AVERAGES

Year Team	Lg	G	AB	H	2B	3B	HR	(Hm	Rd)	TB	R	RBI	RC	TBB	IBB	SO	HBP	SH	SF	SB	CS	GDP	Avg	OBP	Slg	OPS
14 Sea	AL	27	84	19	2	0	1	(0	1)	24	9	6	9	8	0	24	0	0	1	0	0	1	.226	.293	.286	.579
14 LAA	AL	5	5	1	0	0	0	(0	0)	1	0	0	0	0	0	2	0	0	0	0	0	0	.200	.200	.200	.400
Postseason		1	0	0	0	0	0	(0	0)	0	0	0	0	0	0	0	0	0	0	0	0	0	-	-	-	-
11 ML YEARS		1090	3612	844	172	9	134	(54	80)	1436	389	491	432	307	23	959	51	13	26	6	12	86	.234	.301	.398	.698

Billy Buckner

Pitches: R **Bats:** R **Pos:** SP-1   **Ht:** 6'2" **Wt:** 205 **Born:** 8/27/1983 **Age:** 31

Year Team	Lg	G	GS	CG	GF	IP	BFP	H	R	ER	HR	SH	SF	HB	TBB	IBB	SO	WP	Bk	W	L	Pct	Sh	Sv-Op	Hld	ERC	ERA
2014 ElPaso*	AAA	15	14	0	0	63.2	304	85	52	41	10	2	3	3	33	0	44	5	0	4	5	.444	0	0--	-	7.29	5.80
2014 Nashv*	AAA	4	2	0	1	12.0	47	9	8	8	1	0	0	0	3	0	15	3	0	1	1	.500	0	0--	-	2.15	6.00
2007 KC	AL	7	5	0	1	34.0	143	37	20	20	5	0	1	0	16	0	17	0	0	1	2	.333	0	0-0	0	5.57	5.29
2008 Ari	NL	10	0	0	5	14.0	59	16	5	5	3	0	0	1	4	1	11	2	0	1	0	1.000	0	0-0	0	5.72	3.21
2009 Ari	NL	16	13	0	0	77.1	342	94	57	55	12	2	1	3	29	0	64	6	0	4	6	.400	0	0-0	0	5.97	6.40
2010 Ari	NL	3	3	0	0	13.0	72	26	17	16	4	0	1	2	5	0	11	1	0	0	3	.000	0	0-0	0	13.00	11.08
2013 LAA	AL	7	2	0	4	17.1	73	17	9	9	5	1	1	1	7	0	7	2	0	1	0	1.000	0	0-0	0	5.79	4.67
2014 SD	NL	1	1	0	0	5.2	27	6	3	3	1	1	0	0	4	1	4	0	0	0	1	.000	0	0-0	0	5.81	4.76
6 ML YEARS		44	24	0	10	161.1	716	196	111	108	30	4	4	7	65	2	114	11	0	7	12	.368	0	0	0	6.36	6.02

Mark Buehrle

Pitches: L **Bats:** L **Pos:** SP-32   BURR-lee   **Ht:** 6'2" **Wt:** 240 **Born:** 3/23/1979 **Age:** 36

Year Team	Lg	G	GS	CG	GF	IP	BFP	H	R	ER	HR	SH	SF	HB	TBB	IBB	SO	WP	Bk	W	L	Pct	Sh	Sv-Op	Hld	ERC	ERA
2000 CWS	AL	28	3	0	6	51.1	225	55	27	24	5	1	0	3	19	1	37	0	0	4	1	.800	0	0-2	3	4.56	4.21
2001 CWS	AL	32	32	4	0	221.1	885	188	89	81	24	9	4	8	48	2	126	1	5	16	8	.667	2	0-0	0	2.79	3.29
2002 CWS	AL	34	34	5	0	239.0	984	236	102	95	25	9	3	3	61	7	134	6	1	19	12	.613	2	0-0	0	3.53	3.58
2003 CWS	AL	35	35	2	0	230.1	978	250	124	106	22	7	7	5	61	2	119	1	0	14	14	.500	0	0-0	0	4.10	4.14
2004 CWS	AL	35	35	4	0	245.1	1016	257	106	106	33	4	6	8	51	2	165	0	0	16	10	.615	1	0-0	0	4.00	3.89
2005 CWS	AL	33	33	3	0	236.2	971	240	99	82	20	7	4	4	40	4	149	2	2	16	8	.667	1	0-0	0	3.21	3.12
2006 CWS	AL	32	32	1	0	204.0	876	247	124	113	36	6	7	6	48	5	98	0	1	12	13	.480	2	0-0	0	5.37	4.99
2007 CWS	AL	30	30	3	0	201.0	835	208	86	81	22	7	5	5	45	5	115	1	0	10	9	.526	1	0-0	0	3.75	3.63
2008 CWS	AL	34	34	1	0	218.2	918	240	106	92	22	2	6	5	52	4	140	4	0	15	12	.556	0	0-0	0	4.12	3.79
2009 CWS	AL	33	33	1	0	213.1	874	222	97	91	27	11	7	5	43	3	105	2	1	13	10	.565	1	0-0	0	3.91	3.84
2010 CWS	AL	33	33	3	0	210.1	897	246	105	100	17	6	7	1	49	1	99	3	5	13	13	.500	2	0-0	0	4.29	4.28
2011 CWS	AL	31	31	0	0	205.1	858	221	93	82	21	6	7	2	45	3	109	1	0	13	9	.591	0	0-0	0	3.86	3.59
2012 Mia	NL	31	31	1	0	202.1	844	197	88	84	26	14	7	4	40	3	125	2	0	13	13	.500	0	0-0	0	3.41	3.74
2013 Tor	AL	33	33	1	0	203.2	876	223	100	94	24	3	6	9	51	3	139	2	0	12	10	.545	1	0-0	0	4.29	4.15
2014 Tor	AL	32	32	0	0	202.0	857	228	83	76	15	6	6	4	46	0	119	2	1	13	10	.565	0	0-0	0	4.05	3.39
Postseason		6	4	1	2	30.2	124	32	14	14	3	2	1	1	1	1	16	0	0	2	1	.667	0	1-1	0	2.95	4.11
15 ML YEARS		486	461	29	6	3084.2	12878	3258	1442	1307	339	98	82	72	701	45	1779	27	16	199	152	.567	9	0-2	3	3.89	3.81

Francisley Bueno

Pitches: L **Bats:** L **Pos:** RP-30   fran-SISS-lee BWAY-no   **Ht:** 5'11" **Wt:** 205 **Born:** 3/5/1981 **Age:** 34

Year Team	Lg	G	GS	CG	GF	IP	BFP	H	R	ER	HR	SH	SF	HB	TBB	IBB	SO	WP	Bk	W	L	Pct	Sh	Sv-Op	Hld	ERC	ERA
2014 Omha*	AAA	9	3	0	2	14.2	64	14	10	9	1	1	1	2	4	0	17	0	0	0	2	.000	0	0--	-	3.55	5.52
2008 Atl	NL	1	0	0	0	2.1	13	5	2	2	1	0	0	0	1	0	1	0	0	0	0	-	0	0-0	0	14.73	7.71
2012 KC	AL	18	0	0	6	17.1	69	16	4	3	0	0	1	1	2	1	7	0	0	1	1	.500	0	0-0	4	2.16	1.56
2013 KC	AL	7	0	0	0	8.1	31	4	0	0	0	1	0	0	2	1	5	0	0	1	0	1.000	0	0-0	0	0.79	0.00
2014 KC	AL	30	0	0	8	32.1	142	36	16	15	3	0	4	1	7	2	20	1	1	0	0	-	0	0-1	5	3.83	4.18
4 ML YEARS		56	0	0	14	60.1	255	61	22	20	4	1	5	2	12	4	33	1	1	2	1	.667	0	0-1	10	3.10	2.98

Madison Bumgarner

Pitches: L **Bats:** R **Pos:** SP-33   **Ht:** 6'5" **Wt:** 235 **Born:** 8/1/1989 **Age:** 25

Year Team	Lg	G	GS	CG	GF	IP	BFP	H	R	ER	HR	SH	SF	HB	TBB	IBB	SO	WP	Bk	W	L	Pct	Sh	Sv-Op	Hld	ERC	ERA
2009 SF	NL	4	1	0	1	10.0	40	8	2	2	2	1	0	3	3	1	10	0	0	0	0	-	0	0-0	0	3.14	1.80
2010 SF	NL	18	18	0	0	111.0	472	119	40	37	11	0	4	5	26	2	86	1	1	7	6	.538	0	0-0	0	3.98	3.00
2011 SF	NL	33	33	0	0	204.2	844	202	82	73	12	12	4	5	46	5	191	0	1	13	13	.500	0	0-0	0	3.14	3.21
2012 SF	NL	32	32	2	0	208.1	849	183	87	78	23	7	4	7	49	6	191	3	2	16	11	.593	1	0-0	0	2.95	3.37
2013 SF	NL	31	31	0	0	201.1	803	146	68	62	15	10	4	6	62	6	199	6	0	13	9	.591	0	0-0	0	2.23	2.77
2014 SF	NL	33	33	4	0	217.1	873	194	81	72	21	9	5	6	43	3	219	4	1	18	10	.643	2	0-0	0	2.83	2.98
Postseason		7	6	0	0	35.2	147	35	15	15	4	2	1	2	9	1	32	0	0	3	2	.600	0	0-0	0	3.74	3.79
6 ML YEARS		151	148	6	1	952.2	3881	852	360	324	84	39	22	29	229	23	896	14	5	67	49	.578	3	0-0	0	2.92	3.06

A.J. Burnett

Pitches: R **Bats:** R **Pos:** SP-34   **Ht:** 6'4" **Wt:** 225 **Born:** 1/3/1977 **Age:** 38

Year Team	Lg	G	GS	CG	GF	IP	BFP	H	R	ER	HR	SH	SF	HB	TBB	IBB	SO	WP	Bk	W	L	Pct	Sh	Sv-Op	Hld	ERC	ERA
1999 Fla	NL	7	7	0	0	41.1	182	37	23	16	3	1	3	0	25	2	33	0	0	4	2	.667	0	0-0	0	4.00	3.48
2000 Fla	NL	13	13	0	0	82.2	364	80	46	44	8	6	3	2	44	3	57	2	0	3	7	.300	0	0-0	0	4.45	4.79
2001 Fla	NL	27	27	2	0	173.1	733	145	82	78	20	6	8	7	83	3	128	7	1	11	12	.478	1	0-0	0	3.76	4.05
2002 Fla	NL	31	31	7	0	204.1	844	153	84	75	12	4	9	9	90	5	203	14	0	12	9	.571	5	0-1	0	2.77	3.30
2003 Fla	NL	4	4	0	0	23.0	106	18	13	12	2	2	1	2	18	2	21	0	0	2	0	.000	0	0-0	0	4.36	4.70
2004 Fla	NL	20	19	1	0	120.0	490	102	50	49	9	3	3	4	38	0	113	7	0	7	6	.538	0	0-0	0	2.95	3.68

Year Team	Lg	G	GS	CG	GF	IP	BFP	H	R	ER	HR	SH	SF	HB	TBB	IBB	SO	WP	Bk	W	L	Pct	Sh	Sv-Op	Hld	ERC	ERA
		HOW MUCH HE PITCHED						**WHAT HE GAVE UP**												**THE RESULTS**							
2005 Fla	NL	32	32	4	0	209.0	873	184	97	80	12	7	5	7	79	1	198	12	0	12	12	.500	2	0-0	0	3.20	3.44
2006 Tor	AL	21	21	2	0	135.2	577	138	67	60	14	4	3	8	39	3	118	6	1	10	8	.556	1	0-0	0	3.97	3.98
2007 Tor	AL	25	25	2	0	165.2	691	131	74	69	23	0	2	12	66	2	176	5	0	10	8	.556	0	0-0	0	3.47	3.75
2008 Tor	AL	35	**34**	1	1	221.1	957	211	109	100	19	**8**	5	9	86	2	**231**	11	2	18	10	.643	0	0-0	0	3.78	4.07
2009 NYY	AL	33	33	1	0	207.0	896	193	99	93	25	2	5	10	**97**	0	195	**17**	1	13	9	.591	0	0-0	0	4.34	4.04
2010 NYY	AL	33	33	1	0	186.2	829	204	118	109	25	7	10	**19**	78	2	145	16	0	10	15	.400	0	0-0	0	5.43	5.26
2011 NYY	AL	33	32	0	0	190.1	837	190	115	109	31	4	**10**	9	83	2	173	**25**	0	11	11	.500	0	0-0	0	4.83	5.15
2012 Pit	NL	31	31	1	0	202.1	851	189	86	79	18	5	8	9	62	1	180	10	0	16	10	.615	1	0-0	0	3.44	3.51
2013 Pit	NL	30	30	1	0	191.0	801	165	79	70	11	8	3	9	67	3	209	12	0	10	11	.476	0	0-0	0	3.01	3.30
2014 Phi	NL	34	**34**	1	0	213.2	935	205	**122**	**109**	20	11	11	16	**96**	2	190	9	0	8	**18**	.308	0	0-0	0	4.29	4.59
Postseason		8	8	0	0	41.0	189	38	29	29	4	1	0	7	27	3	31	4	0	2	3	.400	0	0-0	0	5.26	6.37
16 ML YEARS		409	404	24	1	2567.1	10966	2345	1264	1152	252	83	84	132	1051	33	2370	155	5	155	150	.508	10	0-1	0	3.81	4.04

Sean Burnett

Pitches: L **Bats:** L **Pos:** RP-3 **Ht:** 6'1" **Wt:** 180 **Born:** 9/17/1982 **Age:** 32

Year Team	Lg	G	GS	CG	GF	IP	BFP	H	R	ER	HR	SH	SF	HB	TBB	IBB	SO	WP	Bk	W	L	Pct	Sh	Sv-Op	Hld	ERC	ERA
		HOW MUCH HE PITCHED						**WHAT HE GAVE UP**												**THE RESULTS**							
2014 Ark*	AA	6	0	0	0	5.1	25	6	3	3	0	1	0	0	3	0	7	0	0	0	0	-	0	0--	-	4.53	5.06
2004 Pit	NL	13	13	1	0	71.2	318	86	41	40	9	2	1	1	28	2	30	2	0	5	5	.500	1	0-0	0	5.49	5.02
2008 Pit	NL	58	0	0	16	56.2	253	57	31	30	7	4	3	2	34	3	42	4	0	1	1	.500	0	0-0	8	5.23	4.76
2009 2 Tms	NL	71	0	0	8	57.2	237	36	21	20	6	6	1	3	28	8	43	4	0	2	3	.400	0	1-3	11	2.43	3.12
2010 Was	NL	73	0	0	10	63.0	261	52	17	15	3	4	0	1	20	4	62	2	0	1	7	.125	0	3-4	20	2.43	2.14
2011 Was	NL	69	0	0	17	56.2	242	54	24	24	6	3	2	3	21	4	33	2	0	5	5	.500	0	4-11	15	3.85	3.81
2012 Was	NL	70	0	0	16	56.2	239	58	16	15	4	1	2	3	12	3	57	2	0	1	2	.333	0	2-5	31	3.38	2.38
2013 LAA	AL	13	0	0	1	9.2	40	9	1	1	1	2	0	0	4	0	7	1	0	0	0	-	0	0-0	5	3.90	0.93
2014 LAA	AL	3	0	0	0	0.2	3	1	1	1	0	0	0	0	0	0	0	0	0	0	0	-	0	0-0	1	4.47	13.50
09 Pit	NL	38	0	0	7	32.1	133	22	12	11	3	4	1	3	15	4	23	2	0	1	2	.333	0	1-2	6	2.77	3.06
09 Was	NL	33	0	0	1	25.1	104	14	9	9	3	2	0	0	13	4	20	2	0	1	1	.500	0	0-1	5	2.02	3.20
Postseason		2	0	0	0	1.0	7	3	4	3	1	0	0	0	1	0	1	0	0	0	0	-	0	0-0	1	32.12	27.00
8 ML YEARS		370	13	1	68	372.2	1593	353	152	146	36	22	9	13	147	24	274	17	0	15	23	.395	1	10-23	91	3.78	3.53

Billy Burns

Bats: B **Throws:** R **Pos:** PR-10;DH-2;PH-2;CF-1 **Ht:** 5'9" **Wt:** 180 **Born:** 8/30/1989 **Age:** 25

Year Team	Lg	G	AB	H	2B	3B	HR	(Hm	Rd)	TB	R	RBI	RC	TBB	IBB	SO	HBP	SH	SF	SB	CS	GDP	Avg	OBP	Slg	OPS
		BATTING																		**RUNNING**			**AVERAGES**			
2011 Auburn	A-	32	107	28	3	2	1	(-	-)	38	21	18	18	12	0	22	7	2	2	13	1	0	.262	.367	.355	.722
2012 Hgrstn	A	113	398	128	14	5	0	(-	-)	152	83	41	78	65	2	68	13	8	1	38	9	2	.322	.432	.382	.814
2013 Ptomc	A+	91	330	103	8	9	0	(-	-)	129	70	29	68	52	2	37	12	6	2	54	5	5	.312	.422	.391	.813
2013 Hrsbrg	AA	30	114	37	4	0	0	(-	-)	41	26	8	23	20	0	17	2	2	0	20	2	0	.325	.434	.360	.793
2014 Mdlnd	AA	91	364	90	20	3	1	(-	-)	119	57	23	51	44	0	65	3	6	4	51	5	6	.247	.330	.327	.657
2014 Scrmto	AAA	28	109	21	2	0	0	(-	-)	23	17	5	5	9	0	19	0	3	0	3	1	2	.193	.254	.211	.465
2014 Oak	AL	13	6	1	0	0	0	(0	0)	1	4	0	0	0	0	0	0	0	0	3	1	0	.167	.167	.167	.333

Jared Burton

Pitches: R **Bats:** R **Pos:** RP-68 **Ht:** 6'5" **Wt:** 225 **Born:** 6/2/1981 **Age:** 34

Year Team	Lg	G	GS	CG	GF	IP	BFP	H	R	ER	HR	SH	SF	HB	TBB	IBB	SO	WP	Bk	W	L	Pct	Sh	Sv-Op	Hld	ERC	ERA
		HOW MUCH HE PITCHED						**WHAT HE GAVE UP**												**THE RESULTS**							
2007 Cin	NL	47	0	0	12	43.0	176	28	15	12	2	1	1	2	22	4	36	3	1	4	2	.667	0	0-3	11	2.37	2.51
2008 Cin	NL	54	0	0	12	58.2	257	56	24	21	6	2	3	2	25	3	58	2	1	5	1	.833	0	0-2	11	3.93	3.22
2009 Cin	NL	53	0	0	13	59.1	265	61	30	29	5	3	1	4	23	6	45	2	0	1	0	1.000	0	0-0	7	4.08	4.40
2010 Cin	NL	4	0	0	2	3.1	10	0	0	0	0	0	0	0	0	0	1	0	0	0	0	-	0	0-0	1	0.00	0.00
2011 Cin	NL	6	0	0	1	4.2	23	6	2	2	1	1	0	0	3	0	3	0	0	0	0	-	0	0-0	1	7.61	3.86
2012 Min	AL	64	0	0	12	62.0	245	41	21	15	5	2	1	5	16	1	55	0	0	3	2	.600	0	5-9	18	1.98	2.18
2013 Min	AL	71	0	0	14	66.0	281	61	29	28	6	2	0	5	22	5	61	2	0	2	9	.182	0	2-7	27	3.50	3.82
2014 Min	AL	68	0	0	21	64.0	272	58	34	31	6	0	3	3	25	3	46	1	0	3	5	.375	0	3-4	14	3.59	4.36
8 ML YEARS		367	0	0	87	361.0	1529	311	155	138	31	11	9	21	136	22	305	10	2	18	19	.486	0	10-25	90	3.25	3.44

Drew Butera

Bats: R **Throws:** R **Pos:** C-57;PH-3;PR-2;1B-1 bue-TARE-ah **Ht:** 6'1" **Wt:** 200 **Born:** 8/9/1983 **Age:** 31

Year Team	Lg	G	AB	H	2B	3B	HR	(Hm	Rd)	TB	R	RBI	RC	TBB	IBB	SO	HBP	SH	SF	SB	CS	GDP	Avg	OBP	Slg	OPS
		BATTING																		**RUNNING**			**AVERAGES**			
2010 Min	AL	49	142	28	6	1	2	(0	2)	42	12	13	7	4	0	25	4	3	2	0	0	5	.197	.237	.296	.533
2011 Min	AL	93	234	39	9	1	2	(1	1)	56	19	23	11	11	0	42	2	6	1	0	0	7	.167	.210	.239	.449
2012 Min	AL	42	111	22	6	0	1	(1	0)	31	7	5	6	9	0	26	2	0	0	0	0	3	.198	.270	.279	.550
2013 2 Tms		6	10	1	0	0	0	(0	0)	1	0	0	0	0	0	5	0	0	0	0	0	0	.100	.100	.100	.200
2014 LAD	NL	61	170	32	6	1	3	(0	3)	49	16	14	10	17	1	41	2	1	2	0	0	1	.188	.267	.288	.555
13 Min	AL	2	3	0	0	0	0	(0	0)	0	0	0	0	0	0	1	0	0	0	0	0	0	.000	.000	.000	.000
13 LAD	NL	4	7	1	0	0	0	(0	0)	1	0	0	0	0	0	4	0	0	0	0	0	0	.143	.143	.143	.286
5 ML YEARS		251	667	122	27	3	8	(2	6)	179	54	55	34	41	1	139	10	10	5	0	0	16	.183	.239	.268	.508

Billy Butler

Bats: R **Throws:** R **Pos:** DH-108;1B-37;PH-8   **Ht:** 6'1" **Wt:** 240 **Born:** 4/18/1986 **Age:** 29

Year	Team	Lg	G	AB	H	2B	3B	HR	(Hm	Rd)	TB	R	RBI	RC	TBB	IBB	SO	HBP	SH	SF	SB	CS	GDP	Avg	OBP	Slg	OPS
2007	KC	AL	92	329	96	23	2	8	(5	3)	147	38	52	50	27	5	55	2	0	2	0	0	8	.292	.347	.447	.794
2008	KC	AL	124	443	122	22	0	11	(4	7)	177	44	55	57	33	0	57	0	0	2	0	1	23	.275	.324	.400	.724
2009	KC	AL	159	608	183	51	1	21	(16	5)	299	78	93	99	58	3	103	2	0	4	1	0	20	.301	.362	.492	.853
2010	KC	AL	158	595	189	45	0	15	(9	6)	279	77	78	91	69	8	78	5	0	9	0	0	**32**	.318	.388	.469	.857
2011	KC	AL	159	597	174	44	0	19	(9	10)	275	74	95	94	66	15	95	3	0	7	2	1	16	.291	.361	.461	.822
2012	KC	AL	161	614	192	32	1	29	(11	18)	313	72	107	102	54	9	111	7	0	4	2	1	20	.313	.373	.510	.882
2013	KC	AL	**162**	582	168	27	0	15	(6	9)	240	62	82	87	79	11	102	3	0	4	0	0	28	.289	.374	.412	.787
2014	KC	AL	151	549	149	32	0	9	(5	4)	208	57	66	65	41	3	96	5	0	8	0	0	21	.271	.323	.379	.702
8 ML YEARS			1166	4317	1273	276	4	127	(65	62)	1938	502	628	645	427	54	697	27	0	40	5	3	168	.295	.359	.449	.808

Daniel Butler

Bats: R **Throws:** R **Pos:** C-7   **Ht:** 5'10" **Wt:** 210 **Born:** 10/17/1986 **Age:** 28

Year	Team	Lg	G	AB	H	2B	3B	HR	(Hm	Rd)	TB	R	RBI	RC	TBB	IBB	SO	HBP	SH	SF	SB	CS	GDP	Avg	OBP	Slg	OPS
2010	Grnvlle	A	61	214	70	18	3	6	(-	-)	112	37	31	45	20	1	44	9	0	1	0	0	7	.327	.406	.523	.929
2010	Pwtckt	AAA	2	5	0	0	0	0	(-	-)	0	0	0	0	0	0	1	0	0	0	0	0	0	.000	.000	.000	.000
2010	Salem	A+	35	113	33	12	0	1	(-	-)	48	16	17	23	23	1	21	6	0	1	1	0	5	.292	.434	.425	.858
2011	Salem	A+	91	312	77	20	0	11	(-	-)	130	39	66	50	45	0	56	7	0	5	4	1	5	.247	.350	.417	.766
2011	Portlnd	AA	21	66	14	5	0	0	(-	-)	19	4	2	6	9	1	11	1	0	0	0	0	1	.212	.316	.288	.604
2011	Pwtckt	AAA	1	3	1	0	0	1	(-	-)	4	1	3	1	0	0	2	0	0	0	0	0	0	.333	.333	1.333	1.667
2012	Portlnd	AA	73	247	62	14	2	6	(-	-)	98	29	26	37	31	0	42	7	0	0	0	0	10	.251	.351	.397	.748
2012	Pwtckt	AAA	22	73	17	5	0	3	(-	-)	31	8	11	10	9	1	20	0	0	1	0	0	1	.233	.313	.425	.738
2013	Pwtckt	AAA	84	282	74	19	0	14	(-	-)	135	32	45	49	34	1	59	5	0	2	1	1	3	.262	.350	.479	.829
2014	Pwtckt	AAA	83	286	69	19	0	4	(-	-)	100	35	30	34	29	0	71	5	0	5	0	0	5	.241	.317	.350	.667
2014	Bos	AL	7	19	4	3	0	0	(0	0)	7	1	2	1	1	0	5	0	0	0	0	0	1	.211	.250	.368	.618

Eddie Butler

Pitches: R **Bats:** R **Pos:** SP-3   **Ht:** 6'2" **Wt:** 180 **Born:** 3/13/1991 **Age:** 24

Year	Team	Lg	G	GS	CG	GF	IP	BFP	H	R	ER	HR	SH	SF	HB	TBB	IBB	SO	WP	Bk	W	L	Pct	Sh	Sv-Op	Hld	ERC	ERA
2012	GdJunc	R+	13	12	0	0	67.2	272	59	18	16	1	1	1	0	13	0	55	7	0	7	1	.875	0	0--	-	2.10	2.13
2013	Ashvll	A	9	9	0	0	54.1	215	25	16	10	2	3	1	3	25	0	51	5	0	5	1	.833	0	0--	-	1.48	1.66
2013	Mdest	A+	13	13	0	0	67.2	279	58	29	18	7	0	0	2	21	0	67	4	0	3	4	.429	0	0--	-	3.10	2.39
2013	Tulsa	AA	6	6	0	0	27.2	101	13	2	2	0	0	0	0	6	0	25	1	0	1	0	1.000	0	0--	-	0.89	0.65
2014	Tulsa	AA	18	18	0	0	108.0	450	103	46	42	10	3	3	2	32	0	63	6	0	6	9	.400	0	0--	-	3.46	3.50
2014	Mdest	A+	1	1	0	0	4.0	18	2	3	3	0	0	0	0	2	0	2	1	0	0	0	-	0	0--	-	1.26	6.75
2014	ColSpr	AAA	1	1	0	0	5.1	26	8	7	6	0	0	0	0	3	0	4	1	0	0	1	.000	0	0--	-	7.02	10.13
2014	Col	NL	3	3	0	0	16.0	76	23	12	12	2	2	0	0	7	1	3	0	0	1	1	.500	0	0-0	0	6.98	6.75

Joey Butler

Bats: R **Throws:** R **Pos:** PH-5;RF-1   **Ht:** 6'2" **Wt:** 220 **Born:** 3/12/1986 **Age:** 29

Year	Team	Lg	G	AB	H	2B	3B	HR	(Hm	Rd)	TB	R	RBI	RC	TBB	IBB	SO	HBP	SH	SF	SB	CS	GDP	Avg	OBP	Slg	OPS
2010	Frisco	AA	132	516	143	26	6	10	(-	-)	211	67	58	74	47	3	120	5	0	5	8	6	21	.277	.340	.409	.749
2011	Frisco	AA	13	44	10	1	0	2	(-	-)	17	11	4	7	7	0	16	4	0	0	2	1	1	.227	.382	.386	.768
2011	RdRck	AAA	113	426	137	27	5	12	(-	-)	210	73	57	82	43	2	138	4	0	1	13	4	9	.322	.388	.493	.881
2012	RdRck	AAA	137	493	143	28	1	20	(-	-)	233	93	78	95	79	3	128	7	0	5	6	4	16	.290	.392	.473	.865
2013	RdRck	AAA	119	426	124	26	0	12	(-	-)	186	71	51	78	69	0	119	6	1	3	1	2	10	.291	.395	.437	.831
2014	Memp	AAA	31	86	31	4	0	4	(-	-)	47	16	20	22	19	1	16	1	0	0	0	0	2	.360	.481	.547	1.028
2014	Orix	Jap	21	52	12	2	0	2	(-	-)	20	5	6	8	9	0	19	4	0	1	0	0	1	.231	.379	.385	.763
2013	Tex	AL	8	12	4	2	0	0	(0	0)	6	3	1	2	3	0	6	0	0	0	0	0	0	.333	.467	.500	.967
2014	StL	NL	6	5	0	0	0	0	(0	0)	0	0	0	0	1	0	3	0	0	0	0	0	0	.000	.167	.000	.167
2 ML YEARS			14	17	4	2	0	0	(0	0)	6	3	1	2	4	0	9	0	0	0	0	0	0	.235	.381	.353	.734

Keith Butler

Pitches: R **Bats:** R **Pos:** RP-2   **Ht:** 6'0" **Wt:** 170 **Born:** 1/30/1989 **Age:** 26

Year	Team	Lg	G	GS	CG	GF	IP	BFP	H	R	ER	HR	SH	SF	HB	TBB	IBB	SO	WP	Bk	W	L	Pct	Sh	Sv-Op	Hld	ERC	ERA
2010	Batvia	A-	27	0	0	16	30.2	139	29	15	10	1	2	1	1	15	3	50	8	0	0	3	.000	0	5--	-	3.44	2.93
2011	QuadC	A	12	0	0	12	15.1	57	7	2	2	0	0	0	0	5	1	16	1	0	0	0	1.000	0	5--	-	0.93	1.17
2011	PlmBh	A+	34	0	0	27	36.0	147	19	6	5	1	0	2	2	18	0	52	0	0	1	0	1.000	0	12--	-	1.75	1.25
2012	Sprgfld	AA	54	0	0	43	59.1	250	53	22	18	5	3	1	2	23	1	59	2	1	5	1	.833	0	25--	-	3.46	2.73
2013	Sprgfld	AA	13	0	0	13	13.2	51	8	1	1	1	0	0	0	2	0	21	0	1	0	0	-	0	7--	-	1.21	0.66
2013	Memp	AAA	20	1	0	7	27.1	111	21	12	11	3	1	1	0	9	2	29	0	1	3	2	.600	0	2--	-	2.53	3.62
2014	Memp	AAA	9	0	0	4	10.2	38	8	1	1	0	0	0	0	2	0	13	0	1	1	0	1.000	0	0--	-	1.67	0.84
2013	StL	NL	16	0	0	8	20.0	85	13	9	9	0	0	1	1	11	0	16	0	0	0	0	-	0	0-0	-	2.25	4.05
2014	StL	NL	2	0	0	1	2.0	14	6	6	6	0	0	0	1	1	0	2	0	0	0	0	-	0	0-0	0	19.55	27.00
2 ML YEARS			18	0	0	9	22.0	99	19	15	15	0	0	1	2	12	0	18	0	0	0	0	-	0	0-0	0	3.40	6.14

Marlon Byrd

Bats: R **Throws:** R **Pos:** RF-149;PH-5;DH-1   **Ht:** 6'0" **Wt:** 245 **Born:** 8/30/1977 **Age:** 37

Year	Team	Lg	G	AB	H	2B	3B	HR	(Hm	Rd)	TB	R	RBI	RC	TBB	IBB	SO	HBP	SH	SF	SB	CS	GDP	Avg	OBP	Slg	OPS
2002	Phi	NL	10	35	8	2	0	1	(1	0)	13	2	1	0	1	0	8	0	0	0	0	2	0	.229	.250	.371	.621
2003	Phi	NL	135	495	150	28	4	7	(3	4)	207	86	45	72	44	3	94	7	4	3	11	1	8	.303	.366	.418	.784
2004	Phi	NL	106	346	79	13	2	5	(3	2)	111	48	33	35	22	1	68	7	2	1	2	2	10	.228	.287	.321	.608
2005	2 Tms	NL	79	229	61	15	2	2	(0	2)	86	20	26	30	19	1	50	2	5	4	5	1	5	.266	.323	.376	.698
2006	Was	NL	78	197	44	8	1	5	(1	4)	69	28	18	18	22	1	47	6	1	2	3	3	6	.223	.317	.350	.667
2007	Tex	AL	109	414	127	17	8	10	(4	6)	190	60	70	68	29	3	88	5	0	6	5	3	9	.307	.355	.459	.814
2008	Tex	AL	122	403	120	28	4	10	(7	3)	186	70	53	63	46	3	62	9	2	2	7	2	10	.298	.380	.462	.842
2009	Tex	AL	146	547	155	43	2	20	(14	6)	262	66	89	91	32	2	98	10	0	10	8	4	11	.283	.329	.479	.808
2010	ChC	NL	152	580	170	39	2	12	(6	6)	249	84	66	80	31	1	98	17	0	2	5	1	12	.293	.346	.429	.775
2011	ChC	NL	119	446	123	22	2	9	(4	5)	176	51	35	43	25	2	78	8	1	2	3	2	13	.276	.324	.395	.719
2012	2 Tms		48	143	30	2	0	1	(0	1)	35	10	9	8	5	1	31	2	1	2	0	3	3	.210	.243	.245	.488
2013	2 Tms	NL	147	532	155	35	5	24	(9	15)	272	75	88	85	31	2	144	8	1	7	2	4	11	.291	.336	.511	.847
2014	Phi	NL	154	591	156	28	2	25	(13	12)	263	71	85	74	35	7	185	8	0	3	3	2	6	.264	.312	.445	.757
05	Phi	NL	5	13	4	0	0	0	(0	0)	4	0	0	2	1	0	3	1	0	0	0	0	0	.308	.400	.308	.708
05	Was	NL	74	216	57	15	2	2	(0	2)	82	20	26	28	18	1	47	1	5	4	5	1	5	.264	.318	.380	.698
12	ChC	NL	13	43	3	0	0	0	(0	0)	3	1	2	0	3	1	10	1	0	0	0	1	2	.070	.149	.070	.219
12	Bos	AL	35	100	27	2	0	1	(0	1)	32	9	7	8	2	0	21	1	1	2	0	2	1	.270	.286	.320	.606
13	NYM	NL	117	425	121	26	5	21	(7	14)	220	61	71	68	25	2	124	7	1	6	2	4	6	.285	.330	.518	.848
13	Pit	NL	30	107	34	9	0	3	(2	1)	52	14	17	17	6	0	20	1	0	1	0	0	5	.318	.357	.486	.843
	Postseason		6	22	8	2	0	1	(1	0)	13	4	5	3	1	0	6	0	0	0	0	0	0	.364	.391	.591	.982
13 ML YEARS			1405	4958	1378	280	34	131	(65	66)	2119	671	618	667	342	27	1051	89	17	44	54	30	104	.278	.333	.427	.760

Cesar Cabral

Pitches: L **Bats:** L **Pos:** RP-4   kuh-BRAWL   **Ht:** 6'3" **Wt:** 250 **Born:** 2/11/1989 **Age:** 26

Year	Team	Lg	G	GS	CG	GF	IP	BFP	H	R	ER	HR	SH	SF	HB	TBB	IBB	SO	WP	Bk	W	L	Pct	Sh	Sv-Op	Hld	ERC	ERA
2010	Grnvlle	A	17	0	0	13	31.1	114	16	1	1	0	3	0	3	7	0	35	0	0	2	0	1.000	0	5--	-	1.15	0.29
2010	Salem	A+	28	0	0	11	48.0	211	60	31	31	1	1	3	2	14	0	45	6	1	2	0	1.000	0	4--	-	4.74	5.81
2011	Salem	A+	12	0	0	11	16.2	71	15	5	3	0	3	0	0	5	0	24	2	0	1	0	1.000	0	8--	-	2.41	1.62
2011	Portlnd	AA	24	0	0	11	38.1	169	41	17	15	3	2	1	1	16	0	46	2	2	2	4	.333	0	1--	-	4.49	3.52
2013	Tampa	A+	5	0	0	0	7.0	35	6	2	2	0	1	1	1	8	0	5	2	0	0	0	-	0	0--	-	5.91	2.57
2013	Trntn	AA	15	0	0	6	19.2	89	22	12	12	2	1	0	2	9	1	22	2	0	1	0	1.000	0	0--	-	5.39	5.49
2013	S-WB	AAA	10	0	0	2	10.0	47	12	8	8	0	0	0	1	5	0	16	3	1	0	1	.000	0	0--	-	5.22	7.20
2014	S-WB	AAA	7	0	0	1	6.2	37	6	7	7	1	1	0	0	11	0	7	1	0	0	0	-	0	0--	-	8.93	9.45
2014	Trntn	AA	25	0	0	4	32.0	152	30	25	20	2	2	3	3	23	1	37	7	0	1	3	.250	0	0--	-	4.87	5.63
2013	NYY	AL	8	0	0	0	3.2	15	3	1	1	0	0	0	1	1	0	6	2	0	0	0	-	0	0-0	1	3.10	2.45
2014	NYY	AL	4	0	0	0	1.0	12	4	3	3	0	0	0	3	2	0	2	1	1	0	0	-	0	0-0	1	48.50	27.00
2 ML YEARS			12	0	0	0	4.2	27	7	4	4	0	0	0	4	3	0	8	3	1	0	0	-	0	0-0	2	11.18	7.71

Asdrubal Cabrera

Bats: B **Throws:** R **Pos:** SS-93;2B-48;DH-3;PH-3;PR-1   azz-DRUE-bull   **Ht:** 6'0" **Wt:** 205 **Born:** 11/13/1985 **Age:** 29

Year	Team	Lg	G	AB	H	2B	3B	HR	(Hm	Rd)	TB	R	RBI	RC	TBB	IBB	SO	HBP	SH	SF	SB	CS	GDP	Avg	OBP	Slg	OPS
2007	Cle	AL	45	159	45	9	2	3	(1	2)	67	30	22	27	17	0	29	2	5	3	0	0	7	.283	.354	.421	.775
2008	Cle	AL	114	352	91	20	0	6	(5	1)	129	48	47	48	46	2	77	4	11	5	4	4	8	.259	.346	.366	.713
2009	Cle	AL	131	523	161	42	4	6	(4	2)	229	81	68	81	44	1	89	1	10	3	17	4	13	.308	.361	.438	.799
2010	Cle	AL	97	381	105	16	1	3	(2	1)	132	39	29	46	25	0	60	5	11	3	6	4	10	.276	.326	.346	.673
2011	Cle	AL	151	604	165	32	3	25	(13	12)	278	87	92	100	44	5	119	11	4	4	17	5	10	.273	.332	.460	.792
2012	Cle	AL	143	555	150	35	1	16	(10	6)	235	70	68	74	52	3	99	6	1	2	9	4	18	.270	.338	.423	.762
2013	Cle	AL	136	508	123	35	2	14	(8	6)	204	66	64	51	35	1	114	8	6	5	9	3	10	.242	.299	.402	.700
2014	2 Tms		146	553	133	31	4	14	(6	8)	214	74	61	57	49	2	108	7	1	6	10	2	15	.241	.307	.387	.694
14	Cle	AL	97	378	93	22	2	9	(5	4)	146	54	40	36	27	1	79	7	0	4	7	2	11	.246	.305	.386	.692
14	Was	NL	49	175	40	9	2	5	(1	4)	68	20	21	21	22	1	29	0	1	2	3	0	4	.229	.312	.389	.700
	Postseason		12	50	10	0	0	1	(1	0)	13	5	6	5	2	0	13	0	3	1	0	0	3	.200	.226	.260	.486
8 ML YEARS			963	3635	973	220	17	87	(49	38)	1488	495	451	484	312	14	695	44	49	31	72	26	91	.268	.330	.409	.740

Everth Cabrera

Bats: B **Throws:** R **Pos:** SS-90   EVV-urth   **Ht:** 5'10" **Wt:** 190 **Born:** 11/17/1986 **Age:** 28

Year	Team	Lg	G	AB	H	2B	3B	HR	(Hm	Rd)	TB	R	RBI	RC	TBB	IBB	SO	HBP	SH	SF	SB	CS	GDP	Avg	OBP	Slg	OPS
2014	ElPaso*	AAA	7	20	7	1	0	0	(-	-)	8	4	1	4	4	0	3	0	0	0	1	0	0	.350	.458	.400	.858
2009	SD	NL	103	377	96	18	8	2	(1	1)	136	59	31	48	46	5	88	5	8	2	25	8	3	.255	.342	.361	.703
2010	SD	NL	76	212	44	6	3	1	(0	1)	59	22	22	15	19	3	54	2	8	0	10	6	8	.208	.279	.278	.557
2011	SD	NL	2	8	1	0	0	0	(0	0)	1	1	0	1	1	0	3	0	0	0	2	0	0	.125	.222	.125	.347
2012	SD	NL	115	398	98	19	3	2	(0	2)	129	49	24	43	43	2	110	3	5	0	44	4	3	.246	.324	.324	.648
2013	SD	NL	95	381	108	15	5	4	(1	3)	145	54	31	59	41	0	69	2	10	1	37	12	1	.283	.355	.381	.736
2014	SD	NL	90	357	83	13	1	3	(0	3)	107	36	20	20	20	0	86	1	9	4	18	8	5	.232	.272	.300	.572
6 ML YEARS			481	1733	430	71	20	12	(2	10)	577	221	128	197	170	10	410	13	40	7	136	38	20	.248	.319	.333	.652

Melky Cabrera

Bats: B Throws: L Pos: LF-133;RF-4;DH-3;CF-1;PH-1   Ht: 5'10" Wt: 210 Born: 8/11/1984 Age: 30

Year	Team	Lg	G	AB	H	2B	3B	HR	(Hm	Rd)	TB	R	RBI	RC	TBB	IBB	SO	HBP	SH	SF	SB	CS	GDP	Avg	OBP	Slg	OPS
2005	NYY	AL	6	19	4	0	0	0	(0	0)	4	1	0	0	0	0	2	0	0	0	0	0	0	.211	.211	.211	.421
2006	NYY	AL	130	460	129	26	2	7	(3	4)	180	75	50	68	56	3	59	2	5	1	12	5	9	.280	.360	.391	.752
2007	NYY	AL	150	545	149	24	8	8	(4	4)	213	66	73	70	43	0	68	5	10	9	13	5	14	.273	.327	.391	.718
2008	NYY	AL	129	414	103	12	1	8	(4	4)	141	42	37	37	29	5	58	3	4	3	9	2	11	.249	.301	.341	.641
2009	NYY	AL	154	485	133	28	1	13	(9	4)	202	66	68	69	43	4	59	4	4	4	10	2	15	.274	.336	.416	.752
2010	Atl	NL	147	458	117	27	3	4	(1	3)	162	50	42	45	42	11	64	1	5	3	7	1	8	.255	.317	.354	.671
2011	KC	AL	155	658	201	44	5	18	(6	12)	309	102	87	92	35	3	94	1	7	5	20	10	13	.305	.339	.470	.809
2012	SF	NL	113	459	159	25	10	11	(2	9)	237	84	60	83	36	4	63	0	1	5	13	5	8	.346	.390	.516	.906
2013	Tor	AL	88	344	96	15	2	3	(3	0)	124	39	30	39	23	0	47	0	2	3	2	2	7	.279	.322	.360	.682
2014	Tor	AL	139	568	171	35	3	16	(7	9)	260	81	73	84	43	3	67	3	2	5	6	2	19	.301	.351	.458	.808
	Postseason		22	75	16	2	0	1	(0	1)	21	8	7	5	3	0	16	0	2	0	0	0	0	.213	.244	.280	.524
	10 ML YEARS		1211	4410	1262	236	35	88	(39	49)	1832	606	520	587	350	33	581	19	40	38	92	34	104	.286	.339	.415	.754

Miguel Cabrera

Bats: R Throws: R Pos: 1B-126;DH-25;3B-10;PH-1   Ht: 6'4" Wt: 240 Born: 4/18/1983 Age: 32

Year	Team	Lg	G	AB	H	2B	3B	HR	(Hm	Rd)	TB	R	RBI	RC	TBB	IBB	SO	HBP	SH	SF	SB	CS	GDP	Avg	OBP	Slg	OPS
2003	Fla	NL	87	314	84	21	3	12	(7	5)	147	39	62	51	25	3	84	2	4	1	0	2	12	.268	.325	.468	.793
2004	Fla	NL	160	603	177	31	1	33	(14	19)	309	101	112	92	68	5	148	6	0	8	5	2	20	.294	.366	.512	.879
2005	Fla	NL	158	613	198	43	2	33	(11	22)	344	106	116	108	64	12	125	2	0	6	1	0	20	.323	.385	.561	.947
2006	Fla	NL	158	576	195	50	2	26	(15	11)	327	112	114	132	86	27	108	10	0	4	9	6	18	.339	.430	.568	.998
2007	Fla	NL	157	588	188	38	2	34	(19	15)	332	91	119	122	79	23	127	5	1	7	2	1	17	.320	.401	.565	.965
2008	Det	AL	160	616	180	36	2	37	(19	18)	331	85	127	109	56	6	126	3	0	9	1	0	16	.292	.349	.537	.887
2009	Det	AL	160	611	198	34	0	34	(19	15)	334	96	103	114	68	14	107	5	0	1	6	2	22	.324	.396	.547	.942
2010	Det	AL	150	548	180	45	1	38	(17	21)	341	111	126	122	89	32	95	3	0	8	3	3	17	.328	.420	.622	1.042
2011	Det	AL	161	572	197	48	0	30	(15	15)	335	111	105	141	108	22	89	3	0	5	2	1	24	.344	.448	.586	1.033
2012	Det	AL	161	622	205	40	0	44	(28	16)	377	109	139	122	66	17	98	3	0	6	4	1	28	.330	.393	.606	.999
2013	Det	AL	148	555	193	26	1	44	(17	27)	353	103	137	146	90	19	94	5	0	2	3	0	19	.348	.442	.636	1.078
2014	Det	AL	159	611	191	52	1	25	(13	12)	320	101	109	110	60	10	117	3	0	11	1	1	21	.313	.371	.524	.895
	Postseason		52	194	53	9	0	12	(4	8)	98	27	37	32	26	7	46	2	1	0	3	0	6	.273	.365	.505	.870
	12 ML YEARS		1819	6829	2186	464	15	390	(194	196)	3850	1165	1369	1370	859	190	1318	50	5	68	37	19	234	.320	.396	.564	.960

Trevor Cahill

Pitches: R Bats: R Pos: SP-17; RP-15   KAY-hill   Ht: 6'4" Wt: 220 Born: 3/1/1988 Age: 27

Year	Team	Lg	G	GS	CG	GF	IP	BFP	H	R	ER	HR	SH	SF	HB	TBB	IBB	SO	WP	Bk	W	L	Pct	Sh	Sv-Op	Hld	ERC	ERA
2014 Visalia*	A+	1	1	0	0	2.0	10	2	4	4	1	0	0	2	0	0	4	0	0	0	1	.000	0	0- -	-	9.87	18.00
2014 Reno*	AAA	6	6	0	0	28.1	118	21	12	11	4	0	0	0	20	0	27	3	0	2	2	.500	0	0- -	-	4.34	3.49
2009 Oak	AL	32	32	0	0	178.2	773	185	99	92	27	4	7	4	72	1	90	5	0	10	13	.435	0	0-0	0	4.79	4.63
2010 Oak	AL	30	30	1	0	196.2	783	155	73	65	19	3	6	6	63	1	118	2	2	18	8	.692	1	0-0	0	2.81	2.97
2011 Oak	AL	34	34	0	0	207.2	901	214	102	96	19	8	6	8	82	1	147	15	0	12	14	.462	0	0-0	0	4.34	4.16
2012 Ari	NL	32	32	2	0	200.0	839	184	93	84	16	12	6	11	74	0	156	10	2	13	12	.520	1	0-0	0	3.66	3.78
2013 Ari	NL	26	25	0	1	146.2	636	143	70	65	13	9	9	9	65	2	102	17	0	8	10	.444	0	0-0	0	4.19	3.99
2014 Ari	NL	32	17	0	8	110.2	499	123	76	69	9	6	3	4	55	2	105	5	0	3	12	.200	0	1-2	0	5.11	5.61
	6 ML YEARS		186	170	3	9	1040.1	4431	1004	513	471	103	42	37	39	411	7	718	54	4	64	69	.481	2	1-2	0	4.04	4.07

Lorenzo Cain

Bats: R Throws: R Pos: CF-93;RF-77;PR-3   Ht: 6'2" Wt: 205 Born: 4/13/1986 Age: 29

Year	Team	Lg	G	AB	H	2B	3B	HR	(Hm	Rd)	TB	R	RBI	RC	TBB	IBB	SO	HBP	SH	SF	SB	CS	GDP	Avg	OBP	Slg	OPS
2014 Omha*	AAA	2	7	0	0	0	0	(-	-)	0	0	0	0	0	0	0	0	0	0	0	0	0	.000	.000	.000	.000
2010 Mil	NL	43	147	45	11	1	1	(1	0)	61	17	13	23	9	0	28	1	0	1	7	1	1	.306	.348	.415	.763
2011 KC	AL	6	22	6	1	0	0	(0	0)	7	4	1	2	1	0	4	0	0	0	0	0	0	.273	.304	.318	.623
2012 KC	AL	61	222	59	9	2	7	(3	4)	93	27	31	32	15	0	56	3	0	4	10	0	4	.266	.316	.419	.734
2013 KC	AL	115	399	100	21	3	4	(3	1)	139	54	46	46	33	2	90	4	0	6	14	6	10	.251	.310	.348	.658
2014 KC	AL	133	471	142	29	4	5	(3	2)	194	55	53	67	24	2	108	4	0	3	28	5	9	.301	.339	.412	.751
	5 ML YEARS		358	1261	352	71	10	17	(10	7)	494	157	144	170	82	4	286	12	0	14	59	12	24	.279	.326	.392	.718

Matt Cain

Pitches: R Bats: R Pos: SP-15   Ht: 6'3" Wt: 230 Born: 10/1/1984 Age: 30

Year	Team	Lg	G	GS	CG	GF	IP	BFP	H	R	ER	HR	SH	SF	HB	TBB	IBB	SO	WP	Bk	W	L	Pct	Sh	Sv-Op	Hld	ERC	ERA
2005 SF	NL	7	7	1	0	46.1	181	24	12	12	4	2	1	0	19	1	30	1	0	2	1	.667	0	0-0	0	1.61	2.33
2006 SF	NL	32	31	1	1	190.2	818	157	93	88	18	11	6	6	87	1	179	9	2	13	12	.520	1	0-0	0	3.35	4.15
2007 SF	NL	32	32	1	0	200.0	832	173	84	81	14	8	5	5	79	3	163	12	0	7	16	.304	1	0-0	0	3.23	3.65
2008 SF	NL	34	34	1	0	217.2	933	206	95	91	19	7	7	7	91	9	186	7	2	8	14	.364	1	0-0	0	3.84	3.76
2009 SF	NL	33	33	4	0	217.2	886	184	73	70	22	10	6	3	73	6	171	9	0	14	8	.636	0	0-0	0	3.06	2.89
2010 SF	NL	33	33	4	0	223.1	896	181	84	79	22	6	7	4	61	4	177	8	0	13	11	.542	2	0-0	0	2.65	3.14
2011 SF	NL	33	33	1	0	221.2	907	177	82	71	9	11	6	9	63	5	179	4	0	12	11	.522	0	0-0	0	2.31	2.88
2012 SF	NL	32	32	2	0	219.1	876	177	73	68	21	11	9	9	51	1	193	8	0	16	5	.762	2	0-0	0	2.57	2.79
2013 SF	NL	30	30	0	0	184.1	760	158	85	82	23	6	2	5	55	3	158	1	0	8	10	.444	0	0-0	0	3.15	4.00
2014 SF	NL	15	15	0	0	90.1	374	81	47	42	13	3	2	2	32	2	70	2	0	2	7	.222	0	0-0	0	3.73	4.18
	Postseason		8	8	0	0	51.1	210	40	13	12	6	1	0	6	14	2	33	1	0	4	2	.667	0	0-0	0	2.92	2.10
	10 ML YEARS		281	280	15	1	1811.1	7463	1518	728	683	165	75	51	50	611	35	1506	61	4	95	95	.500	6	0-0	0	2.99	3.39

Kole Calhoun

Bats: L **Throws:** L **Pos:** RF-123;PH-10;1B-2;PR-1   **Ht:** 5'10" **Wt:** 200 **Born:** 10/14/1987 **Age:** 27

Year	Team	Lg	G	AB	H	2B	3B	HR	(Hm	Rd)	TB	R	RBI	RC	TBB	IBB	SO	HBP	SH	SF	SB	CS	GDP	Avg	OBP	Slg	OPS
2014	Salt Lk*	AAA	5	22	11	2	1	1	(-	-)	18	7	5	6	0	0	3	0	0	0	0	1	0	.500	.500	.818	1.318
2012	LAA	AL	21	23	4	1	0	0	(0	0)	5	2	1	0	2	1	6	0	0	0	1	0	0	.174	.240	.217	.457
2013	LAA	AL	58	195	55	7	2	8	(5	3)	90	29	32	33	21	0	41	1	0	5	2	2	6	.282	.347	.462	.808
2014	LAA	AL	127	493	134	31	3	17	(7	10)	222	90	58	75	38	0	104	2	2	2	5	3	5	.272	.325	.450	.776
	3 ML YEARS		206	711	193	39	5	25	(12	13)	317	121	91	108	61	1	151	3	2	7	8	5	11	.271	.329	.446	.774

Alberto Callaspo

Bats: B **Throws:** R **Pos:** 2B-46;DH-38;1B-23;3B-19;PH-17   ky-AHS-po   **Ht:** 5'9" **Wt:** 225 **Born:** 4/19/1983 **Age:** 32

Year	Team	Lg	G	AB	H	2B	3B	HR	(Hm	Rd)	TB	R	RBI	RC	TBB	IBB	SO	HBP	SH	SF	SB	CS	GDP	Avg	OBP	Slg	OPS
2014	Stcktn*	A+	1	5	1	0	0	0	(-	-)	1	2	0	0	0	0	0	0	0	1	0	0	1	.200	.200	.200	.400
2006	Ari	NL	23	42	10	1	1	0	(0	0)	13	2	6	5	4	0	6	0	0	1	0	1	0	.238	.298	.310	.607
2007	Ari	NL	56	144	31	8	0	0	(0	0)	39	10	7	7	9	0	14	1	1	1	1	1	8	.215	.265	.271	.535
2008	KC	AL	74	213	65	8	3	0	(0	0)	79	21	16	25	19	0	14	0	1	1	2	1	6	.305	.361	.371	.731
2009	KC	AL	155	576	173	41	8	11	(6	5)	263	79	73	90	52	4	51	1	0	5	2	1	15	.300	.356	.457	.813
2010	2 Tms	AL	146	562	149	27	2	10	(2	8)	210	61	56	54	31	3	42	1	1	6	5	3	22	.265	.302	.374	.675
2011	LAA	AL	141	475	137	23	0	6	(1	5)	178	54	46	66	58	8	48	1	0	2	8	1	11	.288	.366	.375	.740
2012	LAA	AL	138	457	115	20	0	10	(3	7)	165	55	53	60	56	1	59	0	3	4	4	3	12	.252	.331	.361	.692
2013	2 Tms	AL	136	453	117	20	0	10	(5	5)	167	52	58	60	53	2	47	1	3	6	0	2	12	.258	.333	.369	.702
2014	Oak	AL	127	404	90	15	0	4	(3	1)	117	37	39	36	40	1	50	1	0	6	0	1	18	.223	.290	.290	.580
10	KC	AL	88	349	96	19	2	8	(2	6)	143	40	43	38	19	2	29	0	0	5	3	1	14	.275	.308	.410	.718
10	LAA	AL	58	213	53	8	0	2	(0	2)	67	21	13	16	12	1	13	1	1	1	2	2	8	.249	.291	.315	.605
13	LAA	AL	86	294	74	13	0	5	(2	3)	102	32	36	37	34	2	22	0	3	5	0	2	8	.252	.324	.347	.671
13	Oak	AL	50	159	43	7	0	5	(3	2)	65	20	22	23	19	0	25	1	0	1	0	0	4	.270	.350	.409	.759
	Postseason		6	8	1	1	0	0	(0	0)	2	0	0	0	0	0	1	0	0	0	0	0	0	.125	.125	.250	.375
	9 ML YEARS		996	3326	887	163	14	51	(20	31)	1231	371	354	403	322	19	331	6	9	32	22	14	98	.267	.330	.370	.700

Arquimedes Caminero

Pitches: R **Bats:** R **Pos:** RP-6   ahr-keh-MEE-deez   **Ht:** 6'4" **Wt:** 250 **Born:** 6/16/1987 **Age:** 28

			HOW MUCH HE PITCHED						WHAT HE GAVE UP										THE RESULTS							
Year	Team	Lg	G	GS	CG	GF	IP	BFP	H	R	ER	HR	SH	SF	HB	TBB	IBB	SO	WP	Bk	W	L	Pct	Sh	Sv-Op	Hld	ERC	ERA
2010	Grnsbr	A	48	0	0	22	74.2	322	55	34	25	4	3	3	7	34	2	97	14	1	5	2	.714	0	3--	-	2.78	3.01
2011	Mrlns	R	1	0	0	0	1.0	6	2	1	1	0	0	0	0	1	0	2	0	0	0	0	-	0	0--	-	12.01	9.00
2012	Jupiter	A+	19	0	0	5	20.2	87	12	2	1	0	0	0	3	9	0	27	1	0	1	0	1.000	0	1--	-	1.86	0.44
2012	Jaxnvl	AA	12	0	0	5	17.2	77	16	6	6	0	1	0	0	10	0	17	3	0	0	0	-	0	2--	-	3.48	3.06
2013	Jaxnvl	AA	42	0	0	11	52.1	211	34	23	21	4	1	0	3	21	0	68	1	0	5	2	.714	0	5--	-	2.33	3.61
2013	NewOr	AAA	1	0	0	0	2.0	6	0	0	0	0	0	0	0	0	0	1	0	0	1	0	1.000	0	0--	-	0.00	0.00
2014	NewOr	AAA	42	0	0	19	63.0	297	70	36	34	7	3	3	7	30	4	79	12	0	4	1	.800	0	10--	-	5.30	4.86
2013	Mia	NL	13	0	0	6	13.0	52	10	4	4	2	0	1	0	3	0	12	1	0	0	0	-	0	0-1	1	2.85	2.77
2014	Mia	NL	6	0	0	1	6.2	31	8	8	8	2	0	0	0	4	0	8	0	0	0	1	.000	0	0-0	0	7.83	10.80
	2 ML YEARS		19	0	0	7	19.2	83	18	12	12	4	0	1	0	7	0	20	1	0	0	1	.000	0	0-1	1	4.37	5.49

Shawn Camp

Pitches: R **Bats:** R **Pos:** RP-3   **Ht:** 6'1" **Wt:** 205 **Born:** 11/18/1975 **Age:** 39

			HOW MUCH HE PITCHED						WHAT HE GAVE UP										THE RESULTS							
Year	Team	Lg	G	GS	CG	GF	IP	BFP	H	R	ER	HR	SH	SF	HB	TBB	IBB	SO	WP	Bk	W	L	Pct	Sh	Sv-Op	Hld	ERC	ERA
2014	LV*	AAA	13	0	0	6	15.0	68	20	7	7	1	2	0	0	5	2	10	1	1	0	1	.000	0	0--	-	5.28	4.20
2014	Clrwtr*	A+	3	0	0	0	4.0	13	2	1	1	0	0	0	0	0	0	6	0	0	0	0	-	0	0--	-	1.21	2.25
2004	KC	AL	42	0	0	12	66.2	286	74	37	29	10	2	3	5	16	1	51	2	1	2	2	.500	0	2-3	5	4.74	3.92
2005	KC	AL	29	0	0	7	49.0	228	69	40	35	4	0	3	4	13	3	28	3	0	1	4	.200	0	0-2	6	6.00	6.43
2006	TB	AL	75	0	0	15	75.0	328	93	43	39	9	2	3	7	19	3	53	4	0	7	4	.636	0	4-6	12	5.48	4.68
2007	TB	AL	50	0	0	8	40.0	198	63	33	32	7	5	1	9	18	6	36	2	0	0	3	.000	0	0-2	11	8.59	7.20
2008	Tor	AL	40	0	0	16	39.1	166	40	18	18	2	0	1	2	11	3	31	0	0	3	1	.750	0	0-0	7	3.47	4.12
2009	Tor	AL	59	0	0	17	79.2	333	73	36	31	7	1	1	4	29	4	58	0	0	2	6	.250	0	1-1	6	3.57	3.50
2010	Tor	AL	70	0	0	13	72.1	298	71	26	24	8	0	2	4	18	5	46	2	0	4	3	.571	0	2-4	13	3.65	2.99
2011	Tor	AL	67	0	0	23	66.1	292	79	36	31	3	2	1	6	22	9	32	0	0	6	3	.667	0	1-4	5	4.72	4.21
2012	ChC	NL	80	0	0	21	77.2	327	79	32	31	7	1	2	0	21	4	54	1	0	3	6	.333	0	2-6	18	3.51	3.59
2013	ChC	NL	26	0	0	8	23.0	108	34	18	18	7	2	3	0	9	2	13	0	2	1	1	.500	0	0-3	4	8.63	7.04
2014	Phi	NL	3	0	0	3	3.1	15	7	2	2	1	0	0	0	0	0	1	0	0	0	0	-	0	0-0	0	12.37	5.40
	11 ML YEARS		541	0	0	143	592.1	2579	682	321	290	65	15	20	35	176	40	403	14	3	29	33	.468	0	12-31	81	4.79	4.41

Tony Campana

Bats: L **Throws:** L **Pos:** CF-23;PH-11;PR-9;LF-6;DH-2   camm-PAH-nah   **Ht:** 5'8" **Wt:** 165 **Born:** 5/30/1986 **Age:** 29

Year	Team	Lg	G	AB	H	2B	3B	HR	(Hm	Rd)	TB	R	RBI	RC	TBB	IBB	SO	HBP	SH	SF	SB	CS	GDP	Avg	OBP	Slg	OPS
2014	Reno*	AAA	47	163	47	5	4	0	(-	-)	60	31	17	22	12	0	28	2	3	1	8	2	0	.288	.343	.368	.711
2014	Salt Lk*	AAA	53	202	54	6	2	0	(-	-)	64	31	17	21	18	0	39	1	6	0	9	9	0	.267	.330	.317	.647
2011	ChC	NL	95	143	37	3	0	1	(1	0)	43	24	6	17	8	1	30	1	3	0	24	2	1	.259	.303	.301	.603
2012	ChC	NL	89	174	46	6	0	0	(0	0)	52	26	5	20	11	0	43	0	7	0	30	3	0	.264	.308	.299	.607
2013	Ari	NL	29	46	12	0	1	0	(0	0)	14	10	0	6	8	0	14	0	0	0	8	2	0	.261	.370	.304	.675
2014	2 Tms		44	75	14	1	1	0	(0	0)	17	10	5	3	0	0	16	1	0	0	4	2	0	.187	.197	.227	.424
14	Ari	NL	26	60	9	1	1	0	(0	0)	12	4	3	2	0	0	10	1	0	0	4	1	0	.150	.164	.200	.364
14	LAA	AL	18	15	5	0	0	0	(0	0)	5	6	2	1	0	0	6	0	0	0	0	1	0	.333	.333	.333	.667
	4 ML YEARS		257	438	109	10	2	1	(1	0)	126	70	16	46	27	1	103	2	10	0	66	9	1	.249	.296	.288	.583

97

Eric Campbell

Bats: R Throws: R Pos: PH-38;LF-20;3B-19;1B-18;RF-3;SS-2;DH-2;2B-1;PR-1   Ht: 6'3" Wt: 205 Born: 4/9/1987 Age: 28

Year	Team	Lg	G	AB	H	2B	3B	HR	(Hm	Rd)	TB	R	RBI	RC	TBB	IBB	SO	HBP	SH	SF	SB	CS	GDP	Avg	OBP	Slg	OPS
2010	StLuci	A+	46	170	57	14	1	4	(-	-)	85	37	20	34	21	1	22	3	1	1	2	5	6	.335	.415	.500	.915
2010	Bnghtn	AA	50	179	50	11	0	6	(-	-)	79	26	30	27	12	0	32	2	4	2	1	0	5	.279	.328	.441	.770
2010	Mets	R	3	11	3	1	0	0	(-	-)	4	1	1	1	0	0	1	0	0	0	1	0	1	.273	.273	.364	.636
2011	Bnghtn	AA	126	405	99	23	2	4	(-	-)	138	46	46	53	54	0	75	8	2	3	6	2	13	.244	.343	.341	.683
2012	Bnghtn	AA	115	394	117	25	2	9	(-	-)	173	53	50	72	58	0	76	6	2	5	10	5	12	.297	.391	.439	.830
2013	LsVgs	AAA	120	341	107	25	3	8	(-	-)	162	61	66	76	66	0	60	10	4	4	12	4	8	.314	.435	.475	.910
2014	LsVgs	AAA	33	141	50	15	0	3	(-	-)	74	39	24	32	20	0	20	2	0	0	3	1	8	.355	.442	.525	.967
2014	NYM	NL	85	190	50	9	0	3	(2	1)	68	16	16	19	17	0	55	1	0	3	3	0	5	.263	.322	.358	.680

Leonel Campos

Pitches: R Bats: R Pos: RP-6   LEE-oh-nel KAM-pohs   Ht: 6'3" Wt: 185 Born: 7/17/1987 Age: 27

Year	Team	Lg	G	GS	CG	GF	IP	BFP	H	R	ER	HR	SH	SF	HB	TBB	IBB	SO	WP	Bk	W	L	Pct	Sh	Sv-Op	Hld	ERC	ERA
2011	Eugene	A-	1	1	0	0	2.0	11	5	4	4	1	0	0	0	4	0	0	0	0	0	0	-	0	0--	-	15.86	18.00
2013	FtWyn	A	28	0	0	8	36.1	150	19	9	9	2	0	0	1	22	0	63	7	0	2	1	.667	0	5--	-	2.14	2.23
2013	SnAnt	AA	26	0	0	3	30.2	122	14	5	3	0	3	1	0	16	0	43	3	0	1	0	1.000	0	2--	-	1.33	0.88
2014	ElPaso	AAA	11	0	0	1	10.0	63	20	15	13	2	0	1	0	13	0	13	4	0	0	0	-	0	0--	-	15.71	11.70
2014	SnAnt	AA	31	14	0	8	72.1	321	69	46	45	6	2	1	3	38	0	95	9	2	2	7	.222	0	1--	-	4.33	5.60
2014	SD	NL	6	0	0	1	7.0	33	9	5	4	0	0	0	0	4	0	9	2	0	0	0	-	0	0-0	0	5.67	5.14

Robinson Cano

Bats: L Throws: R Pos: 2B-150;DH-8   kuh-NOE   Ht: 6'0" Wt: 210 Born: 10/22/1982 Age: 32

Year	Team	Lg	G	AB	H	2B	3B	HR	(Hm	Rd)	TB	R	RBI	RC	TBB	IBB	SO	HBP	SH	SF	SB	CS	GDP	Avg	OBP	Slg	OPS
2005	NYY	AL	132	522	155	34	4	14	(5	9)	239	78	62	59	16	1	68	3	7	3	1	3	16	.297	.320	.458	.778
2006	NYY	AL	122	482	165	41	1	15	(9	6)	253	62	78	74	18	3	54	2	1	5	5	2	19	.342	.365	.525	.890
2007	NYY	AL	160	617	189	41	7	19	(10	9)	301	93	97	94	39	5	85	8	1	4	4	5	19	.306	.353	.488	.841
2008	NYY	AL	159	597	162	35	3	14	(7	7)	245	70	72	64	26	3	65	5	1	5	2	4	18	.271	.305	.410	.715
2009	NYY	AL	161	637	204	48	2	25	(14	11)	331	103	85	79	30	2	63	3	0	4	5	7	22	.320	.352	.520	.871
2010	NYY	AL	160	626	200	41	3	29	(16	13)	334	103	109	118	57	14	77	8	0	5	3	2	19	.319	.381	.534	.914
2011	NYY	AL	159	623	188	46	7	28	(16	12)	332	104	118	111	38	11	96	12	0	8	3	2	18	.302	.349	.533	.882
2012	NYY	AL	161	627	196	48	1	33	(22	11)	345	105	94	110	61	10	96	7	0	2	3	2	22	.313	.379	.550	.929
2013	NYY	AL	160	605	190	41	0	27	(11	16)	312	81	107	120	65	16	85	6	0	5	7	1	18	.314	.383	.516	.899
2014	Sea	AL	157	595	187	37	2	14	(9	5)	270	77	82	106	61	20	68	6	0	3	10	3	19	.314	.382	.454	.836
	Postseason		51	203	45	10	3	8	(5	3)	85	22	33	23	11	3	28	2	0	1	0	2	7	.222	.267	.419	.686
	10 ML YEARS		1531	5931	1836	412	30	218	(119	99)	2962	876	904	935	411	85	757	60	10	44	48	31	190	.310	.358	.499	.857

Carter Capps

Pitches: R Bats: R Pos: RP-17   Ht: 6'4" Wt: 230 Born: 8/7/1990 Age: 24

Year	Team	Lg	G	GS	CG	GF	IP	BFP	H	R	ER	HR	SH	SF	HB	TBB	IBB	SO	WP	Bk	W	L	Pct	Sh	Sv-Op	Hld	ERC	ERA
2014	NewOr*	AAA	7	0	0	2	11.0	46	8	3	2	0	1	1	0	6	0	17	2	0	0	1	.000	0	0--	-	2.50	1.64
2014	Mrlns*	R	2	2	0	0	1.1	7	0	1	0	0	0	0	0	2	0	2	0	0	0	0	-	0	0--	-	1.62	0.00
2014	Jupiter*	A+	1	1	0	0	2.0	6	0	0	0	0	0	0	0	0	0	2	0	0	0	0	-	0	0--	-	0.00	0.00
2012	Sea	AL	18	0	0	2	25.0	109	25	11	11	0	1	1	0	11	0	28	1	0	0	0	-	0	0-0	2	3.49	3.96
2013	Sea	AL	53	0	0	11	59.0	270	73	37	36	12	2	1	2	23	4	66	5	0	3	3	.500	0	0-2	9	6.23	5.49
2014	Mia	NL	17	0	0	5	20.1	86	19	9	9	1	0	1	2	5	0	25	2	0	0	0	-	0	0-0	1	3.13	3.98
	3 ML YEARS		88	0	0	18	104.1	465	117	57	56	13	3	3	4	39	4	119	8	0	3	3	.500	0	0-2	12	4.91	4.83

Chris Capuano

Pitches: L Bats: L Pos: RP-28; SP-12   capp-ue-AHH-noe   Ht: 6'3" Wt: 215 Born: 8/19/1978 Age: 36

Year	Team	Lg	G	GS	CG	GF	IP	BFP	H	R	ER	HR	SH	SF	HB	TBB	IBB	SO	WP	Bk	W	L	Pct	Sh	Sv-Op	Hld	ERC	ERA
2014	ColSpr*	AAA	3	3	0	0	14.2	58	12	5	5	2	2	0	0	3	0	14	0	0	0	0	1.000	0	0--	-	2.61	3.07
2014	Tulsa*	AA	1	1	0	0	4.2	20	4	1	1	0	1	0	0	2	0	7	0	0	0	0	-	0	0--	-	2.67	1.93
2003	Ari	NL	9	5	0	2	33.0	139	27	19	17	3	4	1	6	11	1	23	3	0	2	4	.333	0	0-0	1	3.45	4.64
2004	Mil	NL	17	17	0	0	88.1	385	91	55	49	18	4	1	5	37	1	80	3	1	6	8	.429	0	0-0	0	5.37	4.99
2005	Mil	NL	35	35	0	0	219.0	949	212	105	97	31	14	5	12	91	6	176	3	4	18	12	.600	0	0-0	0	4.44	3.99
2006	Mil	NL	34	34	3	0	221.1	936	229	108	99	29	9	8	9	47	4	174	7	0	11	12	.478	2	0-0	0	3.84	4.03
2007	Mil	NL	29	25	0	0	150.0	669	170	93	85	20	10	3	8	54	2	132	10	0	5	12	.294	0	0-0	0	5.11	5.10
2010	Mil	NL	24	9	0	5	66.0	278	65	29	29	9	3	2	1	21	1	54	5	0	4	4	.500	0	0-0	1	3.98	3.95
2011	NYM	NL	33	31	1	0	186.0	802	198	99	94	27	9	1	5	53	5	168	4	0	11	12	.478	1	0-0	1	4.33	4.55
2012	LAD	NL	33	33	0	0	198.1	817	188	91	82	25	16	4	2	54	4	162	6	0	12	12	.500	0	0-0	0	3.51	3.72
2013	LAD	NL	24	20	0	0	105.2	457	125	57	50	11	6	3	0	24	5	81	5	0	4	7	.364	0	0-1	0	4.36	4.26
2014	2 Tms	NL	40	12	0	0	97.1	429	101	51	47	10	5	3	4	34	3	84	8	1	3	4	.429	0	0-1	0	4.14	4.35
14	Bos	AL	28	0	0	0	31.2	143	34	17	16	3	0	1	1	15	2	29	4	1	1	1	.500	0	0-1	0	4.72	4.55
14	NYY	AL	12	12	0	0	65.2	286	67	34	31	7	3	4	3	19	1	55	4	0	2	3	.400	0	0-1	0	3.86	4.25
	Postseason		1	0	0	0	3.0	11	0	0	0	0	1	0	0	3	0	3	0	0	1	0	1.000	0	0-0	0	1.03	0.00
	10 ML YEARS		278	221	4	11	1365.0	5861	1406	707	649	183	78	33	52	426	32	1134	54	6	76	87	.466	3	0-2	7	4.25	4.28

Buddy Carlyle

Pitches: R Bats: L Pos: RP-27   Ht: 6'3" Wt: 210 Born: 12/21/1977 Age: 37

			HOW MUCH HE PITCHED					WHAT HE GAVE UP											THE RESULTS						
Year Team	Lg	G	GS	CG	GF	IP	BFP	H	R	ER	HR	SH	SF	HB	TBB	IBB	SO	WP	Bk	W	L	Pct	Sh	Sv-Op	Hld	ERC	ERA
2014 LsVgs*	AAA	30	0	0	15	33.1	140	27	11	9	6	5	0	2	12	1	36	1	0	4	2	.667	0	3--	-	3.56	2.43
1999 SD	NL	7	7	0	0	37.2	162	36	28	25	7	1	2	2	17	0	29	1	0	1	3	.250	0	0-0	0	4.95	5.97
2000 SD	NL	4	0	0	2	3.0	18	6	7	7	0	0	0	0	3	0	2	0	0	0	0	-	0	0-0	0	12.01	21.00
2005 LAD	NL	10	0	0	2	14.0	62	16	13	13	4	2	0	1	4	0	13	0	0	0	0	-	0	0-1	0	6.07	8.36
2007 Atl	NL	22	20	0	1	107.0	462	117	67	62	19	11	5	2	32	8	74	3	0	8	7	.533	0	0-0	0	4.71	5.21
2008 Atl	NL	45	0	0	5	62.2	259	52	26	25	5	4	0	1	26	6	59	4	1	2	0	1.000	0	0-0	0	3.03	3.59
2009 Atl	NL	16	0	0	7	21.1	107	35	23	21	5	2	1	0	12	4	12	2	0	0	1	.000	0	0-0	2	9.78	8.86
2011 NYY	AL	8	0	0	6	7.2	34	5	4	4	1	0	0	0	7	1	9	2	0	0	1	.000	0	0-0	0	4.16	4.70
2014 NYM	NL	27	0	0	4	31.0	119	23	6	5	2	1	0	0	5	0	28	0	0	1	1	.500	0	0-0	2	1.72	1.45
8 ML YEARS		139	27	0	27	284.1	1223	290	174	162	43	21	8	6	106	19	226	12	1	12	13	.480	0	0-1	4	4.44	5.13

Mike Carp

Bats: L Throws: R Pos: 1B-32;PH-22;LF-13;3B-1;RF-1;PR-1   Ht: 6'2" Wt: 210 Born: 6/30/1986 Age: 29

							BATTING														RUNNING			AVERAGES			
Year Team	Lg	G	AB	H	2B	3B	HR	(Hm	Rd)	TB	R	RBI	RC	TBB	IBB	SO	HBP	SH	SF	SB	CS	GDP	Avg	OBP	Slg	OPS
2014 Pwtckt*	AAA	7	21	5	1	0	1	(-	-)	9	2	3	2	1	0	7	0	0	0	0	0	0	.238	.273	.429	.701
2009 Sea	AL	54	54	17	3	1	1	(1	0)	25	7	5	8	8	0	10	2	0	1	0	0	1	.315	.415	.463	.878
2010 Sea	AL	14	37	7	2	0	0	(0	0)	9	1	0	2	4	0	8	0	0	0	0	0	0	.189	.268	.243	.512
2011 Sea	AL	79	290	80	17	1	12	(5	7)	135	27	46	39	19	0	81	3	0	1	0	0	2	.276	.326	.466	.791
2012 Sea	AL	59	164	35	6	0	5	(2	3)	56	17	20	15	21	1	46	3	0	1	1	0	7	.213	.312	.341	.654
2013 Bos	AL	86	216	64	18	2	9	(4	5)	113	34	43	40	22	0	67	2	0	3	1	0	3	.296	.362	.523	.885
2014 2 Tms	AL	59	126	22	5	1	0	(0	0)	29	11	13	9	16	0	31	5	0	2	0	1	6	.175	.289	.230	.519
14 Bos	AL	42	86	17	5	1	0	(0	0)	24	9	9	7	11	0	17	5	0	1	0	1	5	.198	.320	.279	.599
14 Tex	AL	17	40	5	0	0	0	(0	0)	5	2	4	2	5	0	14	0	0	1	0	0	1	.125	.217	.125	.342
Postseason		6	8	0	0	0	0	(0	0)	0	0	1	0	0	0	3	0	0	0	0	0	1	.000	.000	.000	.000
6 ML YEARS		318	887	225	51	5	27	(12	15)	367	97	127	113	90	1	243	15	0	8	2	3	27	.254	.330	.414	.744

David Carpenter

Pitches: R Bats: R Pos: RP-65   Ht: 6'2" Wt: 230 Born: 7/15/1985 Age: 29

				HOW MUCH HE PITCHED					WHAT HE GAVE UP											THE RESULTS						
Year Team	Lg	G	GS	CG	GF	IP	BFP	H	R	ER	HR	SH	SF	HB	TBB	IBB	SO	WP	Bk	W	L	Pct	Sh	Sv-Op	Hld	ERC	ERA
2014 Gwnntt*	AAA	2	2	0	0	2.0	7	0	0	0	0	0	0	0	4	0	4	0	0	0	0	-	0	0--	-	0.00	0.00
2011 Hou	NL	34	0	0	12	27.2	125	28	9	9	3	4	1	4	13	7	29	2	1	1	3	.250	0	1-2	3	4.62	2.93
2012 2 Tms		33	0	0	9	32.1	163	51	31	29	5	2	0	2	16	4	31	2	0	0	2	.000	0	0-1	2	8.52	8.07
2013 Atl	NL	56	0	0	14	65.2	256	45	13	13	5	2	4	3	20	3	74	4	0	4	1	.800	0	0-0	12	2.12	1.78
2014 Atl	NL	65	0	0	14	61.0	259	61	27	24	5	1	1	3	16	0	67	1	0	6	4	.600	0	3-6	19	3.59	3.54
12 Hou	NL	30	0	0	8	29.2	143	43	21	20	4	2	0	1	14	3	27	2	0	0	2	.000	0	0-1	2	7.38	6.07
12 Tor	AL	3	0	0	1	2.2	20	8	10	9	1	0	0	1	2	1	4	0	0	0	0	-	0	0-0	0	22.64	30.38
Postseason		3	0	0	1	2.2	12	3	4	4	2	0	0	1	0	3	0	0	0	1	.000	0	0-1	1	9.34	13.50
4 ML YEARS		188	0	0	49	186.2	803	185	80	75	18	9	6	12	65	14	201	9	1	11	10	.524	0	4-9	36	3.94	3.62

David Carpenter

Pitches: R Bats: R Pos: RP-1   Ht: 6'3" Wt: 180 Born: 9/1/1987 Age: 27

				HOW MUCH HE PITCHED					WHAT HE GAVE UP											THE RESULTS						
Year Team	Lg	G	GS	CG	GF	IP	BFP	H	R	ER	HR	SH	SF	HB	TBB	IBB	SO	WP	Bk	W	L	Pct	Sh	Sv-Op	Hld	ERC	ERA
2014 Salt Lk*	AAA	21	1	0	7	29.2	126	30	11	11	0	0	0	0	12	0	22	1	0	2	1	.667	0	3--	-	3.51	3.34
2014 Ark*	AA	24	0	0	15	32.2	132	24	4	4	1	2	0	2	13	1	36	3	1	2	1	.667	0	6--	-	2.46	1.10
2012 LAA	AL	28	0	0	12	39.2	172	42	21	21	6	1	1	0	17	0	28	2	0	1	2	.333	0	0-0	2	4.97	4.76
2013 LAA	AL	1	0	0	0	0.1	5	2	4	4	1	0	0	0	2	0	1	1	0	0	0	-	0	0-0	0	124.7	108.0
2014 LAA	AL	1	0	0	0	3.0	12	1	0	0	0	0	0	2	0	0	0	0	0	0	0	-	0	0-0	0	1.26	0.00
3 ML YEARS		30	0	0	12	43.0	189	45	25	25	7	1	1	2	19	0	29	3	0	1	2	.333	0	0-0	2	5.22	5.23

Matt Carpenter

Bats: L Throws: R Pos: 3B-156;RF-2;PH-2;DH-1   Ht: 6'3" Wt: 215 Born: 11/26/1985 Age: 29

							BATTING														RUNNING			AVERAGES			
Year Team	Lg	G	AB	H	2B	3B	HR	(Hm	Rd)	TB	R	RBI	RC	TBB	IBB	SO	HBP	SH	SF	SB	CS	GDP	Avg	OBP	Slg	OPS
2011 StL	NL	7	15	1	1	0	0	(0	0)	2	0	0	0	4	0	4	0	0	0	0	0	0	.067	.263	.133	.396
2012 StL	NL	114	296	87	22	5	6	(3	3)	137	44	46	46	34	2	63	3	0	7	1	1	10	.294	.365	.463	.828
2013 StL	NL	157	626	199	55	7	11	(6	5)	301	126	78	119	72	1	98	9	3	7	3	3	4	.318	.392	.481	.873
2014 StL	NL	158	595	162	33	2	8	(4	4)	223	99	59	93	95	2	111	8	2	9	5	3	3	.272	.375	.375	.750
Postseason		26	83	19	4	1	1	(1	0)	28	11	7	10	7	0	22	1	0	2	1	0	0	.229	.290	.337	.628
4 ML YEARS		436	1532	449	111	14	25	(13	12)	663	269	183	258	205	5	276	20	5	23	9	7	17	.293	.379	.433	.811

Carlos Carrasco

Pitches: R Bats: R Pos: RP-26; SP-14   Ht: 6'3" Wt: 210 Born: 3/21/1987 Age: 28

				HOW MUCH HE PITCHED					WHAT HE GAVE UP											THE RESULTS						
Year Team	Lg	G	GS	CG	GF	IP	BFP	H	R	ER	HR	SH	SF	HB	TBB	IBB	SO	WP	Bk	W	L	Pct	Sh	Sv-Op	Hld	ERC	ERA
2009 Cle	AL	5	5	0	0	22.1	112	40	23	22	6	0	1	0	11	1	11	0	1	0	4	.000	0	0-0	0	11.36	8.87
2010 Cle	AL	7	7	1	0	44.2	188	47	20	19	6	2	1	1	14	1	38	1	0	2	2	.500	0	0-0	0	4.42	3.83

											WHAT HE GAVE UP												THE RESULTS							
Year	Team	Lg	G	GS	CG	GF	IP	BFP	H	R	ER	HR	SH	SF	HB	TBB	IBB	SO	WP	Bk	W	L	Pct	Sh	Sv-Op	Hld	ERC	ERA
2011	Cle	AL	21	21	1	0	124.2	536	130	68	64	15	3	7	4	40	3	85	3	0	8	9	.471	0	0-0	0	4.24	4.62
2013	Cle	AL	15	7	0	5	46.2	218	64	36	35	4	2	3	1	18	2	30	2	0	1	4	.200	0	0-0	0	6.11	6.75
2014	Cle	AL	40	14	1	12	134.0	529	103	40	38	7	2	3	3	29	1	140	4	0	8	7	.533	1	1-1	0	2.00	2.55
	5 ML YEARS		88	54	3	17	372.1	1583	384	187	178	38	9	15	9	112	8	304	10	1	19	26	.422	1	1-1	0	3.95	4.30

Ezequiel Carrera

Bats: L **Throws:** L **Pos:** CF-38;PR-9;PH-6;LF-1   ee-ZEEK-ee-ull   **Ht:** 5'10" **Wt:** 185 **Born:** 6/11/1987 **Age:** 28

								BATTING												RUNNING			AVERAGES			
Year	Team	Lg	G	AB	H	2B	3B	HR	(Hm | Rd)	TB	R	RBI	RC	TBB	IBB	SO	HBP	SH	SF	SB	CS	GDP	Avg	OBP	Slg	OPS
2014	Toledo*	AAA	97	374	115	15	5	6	(- | -)	158	68	41	68	48	0	65	3	5	4	43	13	4	.307	.387	.422	.809
2011	Cle	AL	68	202	49	8	3	0	(0 | 0)	63	27	14	25	16	0	35	1	7	0	10	5	4	.243	.301	.312	.613
2012	Cle	AL	48	147	40	6	3	2	(0 | 2)	58	20	11	17	8	1	35	1	1	3	8	1	3	.272	.312	.395	.707
2013	2 Tms		15	17	3	0	0	0	(0 | 0)	3	3	1	1	1	0	5	2	1	0	0	0	1	.176	.300	.176	.476
2014	Det	AL	45	69	18	4	1	0	(0 | 0)	24	12	2	6	3	1	14	1	0	0	7	1	2	.261	.301	.348	.649
13	Phi	NL	13	13	1	0	0	0	(0 | 0)	1	2	0	1	0	0	4	2	0	0	0	0	0	.077	.250	.077	.327
13	Cle	AL	2	4	2	0	0	0	(0 | 0)	2	1	1	1	0	0	1	0	1	0	0	0	1	.500	.500	.500	1.000
	4 ML YEARS		176	435	110	18	7	2	(0 | 2)	148	62	28	49	28	2	89	5	9	1	25	7	10	.253	.305	.340	.645

Scott Carroll

Pitches: R **Bats:** R **Pos:** SP-19; RP-7   **Ht:** 6'4" **Wt:** 215 **Born:** 9/24/1984 **Age:** 30

				HOW MUCH HE PITCHED						WHAT HE GAVE UP												THE RESULTS							
Year	Team	Lg	G	GS	CG	GF	IP	BFP	H	R	ER	HR	SH	SF	HB	TBB	IBB	SO	WP	Bk	W	L	Pct	Sh	Sv-Op	Hld	ERC	ERA
2010	Lynbrg	A+	5	4	0	1	30.0	118	24	8	7	4	1	0	1	7	1	13	1	0	1	2	.333	0	0- -	-	2.73	2.10
2010	Carlina	AA	20	20	2	0	117.1	494	120	58	48	6	5	3	9	30	0	66	4	0	3	9	.250	0	0- -	-	3.65	3.68
2011	Lsvlle	AAA	25	25	0	0	145.1	652	186	92	87	12	3	3	3	47	0	85	2	3	7	8	.467	0	0- -	-	5.38	5.39
2012	Lsvlle	AAA	25	0	0	7	39.2	180	51	26	26	4	1	2	1	16	1	27	1	0	2	3	.400	0	0- -	-	5.93	5.90
2012	Charltt	AAA	9	8	0	0	47.2	194	39	21	20	6	0	1	1	18	0	36	1	1	2	3	.400	0	0- -	-	3.33	3.78
2012	Brham	AA	1	1	0	0	5.0	17	1	0	0	0	0	0	0	2	0	2	0	0	0	0	-	0	0- -	-	0.53	0.00
2013	Brs	R+	5	5	0	0	16.0	69	17	4	3	0	0	0	0	4	0	15	0	0	0	0	-	0	0- -	-	3.07	1.69
2013	Brham	AA	6	6	0	0	25.0	103	25	15	12	2	0	0	1	2	0	14	0	0	0	2	.000	0	0- -	-	2.82	4.32
2014	Charltt	AAA	4	4	0	0	23.0	88	18	8	4	0	0	0	0	9	0	13	0	0	3	1	.750	0	0- -	-	2.46	1.57
2014	CWS	AL	26	19	0	5	129.1	573	147	81	69	13	3	4	12	45	1	64	5	1	5	10	.333	0	0-0	0	5.07	4.80

Chris Carter

Bats: R **Throws:** R **Pos:** DH-118;1B-14;PH-7;LF-6   **Ht:** 6'4" **Wt:** 250 **Born:** 12/18/1986 **Age:** 28

								BATTING												RUNNING			AVERAGES			
Year	Team	Lg	G	AB	H	2B	3B	HR	(Hm | Rd)	TB	R	RBI	RC	TBB	IBB	SO	HBP	SH	SF	SB	CS	GDP	Avg	OBP	Slg	OPS
2010	Oak	AL	24	70	13	1	0	3	(1 | 2)	23	8	7	5	7	0	21	0	0	1	1	0	3	.186	.256	.329	.585
2011	Oak	AL	15	44	6	0	0	0	(0 | 0)	6	2	0	0	2	0	20	0	0	0	0	0	1	.136	.174	.136	.310
2012	Oak	AL	67	218	52	12	0	16	(5 | 11)	112	38	39	36	39	1	83	0	0	3	0	0	4	.239	.350	.514	.864
2013	Hou	AL	148	506	113	24	2	29	(10 | 19)	228	64	82	74	70	1	212	4	0	5	2	0	8	.223	.320	.451	.770
2014	Hou	AL	145	507	115	21	1	37	(21 | 16)	249	68	88	74	56	6	182	5	0	4	5	2	12	.227	.308	.491	.799
	5 ML YEARS		399	1345	299	58	3	85	(37 | 48)	618	180	216	189	174	8	518	9	0	13	8	2	28	.222	.313	.459	.772

Curt Casali

Bats: R **Throws:** R **Pos:** C-29;DH-1;PH-1   cuh-SAL-ee   **Ht:** 6'2" **Wt:** 225 **Born:** 11/9/1988 **Age:** 26

								BATTING												RUNNING			AVERAGES			
Year	Team	Lg	G	AB	H	2B	3B	HR	(Hm | Rd)	TB	R	RBI	RC	TBB	IBB	SO	HBP	SH	SF	SB	CS	GDP	Avg	OBP	Slg	OPS
2011	Conn	A-	10	36	10	2	0	1	(- | -)	15	7	2	6	6	0	5	2	0	0	0	0	0	.278	.409	.417	.826
2011	WMich	A	25	75	17	7	0	2	(- | -)	30	10	14	11	13	0	9	1	2	1	0	0	5	.227	.344	.400	.744
2012	WMich	A	48	170	49	12	0	8	(- | -)	85	25	25	35	27	1	18	6	2	1	2	1	6	.288	.402	.500	.902
2012	Lkland	A+	46	160	40	13	0	1	(- | -)	56	18	18	19	11	1	28	6	2	0	0	0	5	.250	.322	.350	.672
2013	Charltt	A+	46	164	44	6	1	5	(- | -)	67	15	19	24	18	0	31	1	0	0	1	0	8	.268	.344	.409	.753
2013	Mont	AA	35	120	46	11	0	5	(- | -)	72	25	31	33	21	1	18	3	0	1	0	0	2	.383	.483	.600	1.083
2014	Mont	AA	22	70	22	5	0	1	(- | -)	30	7	13	17	23	0	16	3	0	0	0	0	1	.314	.500	.429	.929
2014	Drham	AAA	46	156	37	10	0	3	(- | -)	56	11	15	20	22	0	50	2	1	2	0	0	8	.237	.335	.359	.694
2014	Charltt	A+	2	7	0	0	0	0	(- | -)	0	0	0	0	0	0	3	0	0	0	0	0	0	.000	.000	.000	.000
2014	TB	AL	30	72	12	3	0	3	(0 | 0)	15	10	3	3	8	0	23	2	2	0	0	0	2	.167	.268	.208	.477

Andrew Cashner

Pitches: R **Bats:** R **Pos:** SP-19   **Ht:** 6'6" **Wt:** 220 **Born:** 9/11/1986 **Age:** 28

				HOW MUCH HE PITCHED						WHAT HE GAVE UP												THE RESULTS							
Year	Team	Lg	G	GS	CG	GF	IP	BFP	H	R	ER	HR	SH	SF	HB	TBB	IBB	SO	WP	Bk	W	L	Pct	Sh	Sv-Op	Hld	ERC	ERA
2014	Lk Els*	A+	1	1	0	0	2.0	7	1	0	0	0	0	0	0	0	0	3	0	0	0	0	-	0	0- -	-	0.54	0.00
2014	ElPaso*	AAA	2	2	0	0	7.2	33	7	6	6	3	0	0	0	2	0	7	0	0	0	2	.000	0	0- -	-	4.65	7.04
2010	ChC	NL	53	0	0	9	54.1	248	55	31	29	8	6	2	4	30	5	50	4	1	2	6	.250	0	0-1	16	5.22	4.80
2011	ChC	NL	7	1	0	0	10.2	39	3	2	2	1	0	0	0	4	0	8	0	0	0	0	-	0	0-0	1	0.91	1.69
2012	SD	NL	33	5	0	5	46.1	196	42	23	22	5	3	1	1	19	1	52	2	0	3	4	.429	0	0-4	6	3.73	4.27
2013	SD	NL	31	26	1	2	175.0	707	151	68	60	12	6	3	4	47	3	128	5	0	10	9	.526	1	0-0	1	2.74	3.09
2014	SD	NL	19	19	2	0	123.1	506	110	42	35	7	3	4	1	29	3	93	2	0	5	7	.417	2	0-0	0	2.57	2.55
	5 ML YEARS		143	51	3	16	409.2	1696	361	166	148	33	18	10	10	129	12	331	13	1	20	26	.435	3	0-5	24	3.03	3.25

Alexi Casilla

Bats: B Throws: R Pos: 2B-1;3B-1   cuh-SEE-ya   Ht: 5'9" Wt: 170 Born: 7/20/1984 Age: 30

Year	Team	Lg	G	AB	H	2B	3B	HR	(Hm	Rd)	TB	R	RBI	RC	TBB	IBB	SO	HBP	SH	SF	SB	CS	GDP	Avg	OBP	Slg	OPS
2014	Norfolk*	AAA	56	197	52	8	0	1	(-	-)	63	25	19	21	14	0	28	1	0	1	9	2	7	.264	.315	.320	.634
2014	Abrdn*	A-	4	15	7	2	0	0	(-	-)	9	4	1	3	1	0	2	0	0	0	0	1	0	.467	.500	.600	1.100
2006	Min	AL	9	4	1	0	0	0	(0	0)	1	1	0	1	2	0	1	0	0	0	0	0	0	.250	.500	.250	.750
2007	Min	AL	56	189	42	5	1	0	(0	0)	49	15	9	11	9	0	29	0	5	1	11	1	5	.222	.256	.259	.516
2008	Min	AL	98	385	108	15	0	7	(2	5)	144	58	50	50	31	0	45	2	13	6	7	2	8	.281	.333	.374	.707
2009	Min	AL	80	228	46	7	3	0	(0	0)	59	25	17	20	22	0	36	3	2	1	11	0	6	.202	.280	.259	.538
2010	Min	AL	69	152	42	7	4	1	(1	0)	60	26	20	23	13	0	17	0	4	1	6	1	5	.276	.331	.395	.726
2011	Min	AL	97	323	84	21	4	2	(1	1)	119	52	21	33	28	0	45	3	8	3	15	4	4	.260	.322	.368	.691
2012	Min	AL	106	299	72	17	2	1	(0	1)	96	33	30	29	16	0	52	3	3	5	21	1	6	.241	.282	.321	.603
2013	Bal	AL	62	112	24	4	1	1	(1	0)	33	15	10	10	9	0	20	0	2	2	9	2	1	.214	.268	.295	.563
2014	Bal	AL	1	4	0	0	0	0	(0	0)	0	0	0	0	0	0	1	0	0	0	0	0	0	.000	.000	.000	.000
9 ML YEARS			578	1696	419	76	15	12	(5	7)	561	225	157	177	130	0	246	11	37	19	80	11	35	.247	.302	.331	.633

Santiago Casilla

Pitches: R Bats: R Pos: RP-54   cuh-SEE-ya   Ht: 6'0" Wt: 210 Born: 7/25/1980 Age: 34

Year	Team	Lg	G	GS	CG	GF	IP	BFP	H	R	ER	HR	SH	SF	HB	TBB	IBB	SO	WP	Bk	W	L	Pct	Sh	Sv-Op	Hld	ERC	ERA
2014	SnJos*	A+	2	2	0	0	3.0	10	0	0	0	0	0	0	0	1	0	3	0	0	0	0	-	0	0- -	-	0.13	0.00
2004	Oak	AL	4	0	0	2	5.2	32	5	8	8	3	0	0	1	9	0	5	0	0	0	0	-	0	0-0	0	13.22	12.71
2005	Oak	AL	3	0	0	3	3.0	12	2	1	1	0	0	0	0	1	0	1	1	0	0	0	-	0	0-0	0	1.57	3.00
2006	Oak	AL	2	0	0	1	2.1	10	2	3	3	0	0	0	0	2	0	2	0	0	0	0	-	0	0-0	0	4.61	11.57
2007	Oak	AL	46	0	0	10	50.2	219	43	25	25	6	0	3	1	23	6	52	5	0	3	1	.750	0	2-5	12	3.39	4.44
2008	Oak	AL	51	0	0	9	50.1	229	60	22	22	5	3	2	3	20	2	43	6	0	2	1	.667	0	2-3	7	5.34	3.93
2009	Oak	AL	46	0	0	15	48.1	233	61	36	32	6	1	3	3	25	3	35	5	0	1	2	.333	0	0-0	5	6.32	5.96
2010	SF	NL	52	0	0	13	55.1	225	40	14	12	2	2	1	4	26	4	56	10	0	7	2	.778	0	2-3	11	2.68	1.95
2011	SF	NL	49	0	0	20	51.2	211	33	11	10	1	4	0	2	25	1	45	5	0	2	2	.500	0	6-7	6	2.11	1.74
2012	SF	NL	73	0	0	37	63.1	272	55	24	20	8	2	1	2	22	4	55	1	0	7	6	.538	0	25-31	12	3.24	2.84
2013	SF	NL	57	0	0	12	50.0	208	39	14	12	2	2	3	2	25	6	38	8	0	7	2	.778	0	2-3	22	2.88	2.16
2014	SF	NL	54	0	0	31	58.1	218	35	13	11	3	2	0	3	15	2	45	3	1	3	3	.500	0	19-23	10	1.56	1.70
Postseason			15	0	0	2	11.2	52	11	3	2	0	0	0	2	2	1	13	3	0	1	0	1.000	0	0-0	4	2.55	1.54
11 ML YEARS			437	0	0	153	439.0	1869	375	171	156	36	16	13	21	193	28	377	44	1	32	19	.627	0	58-75	85	3.39	3.20

Nick Castellanos

Bats: R Throws: R Pos: 3B-145;PH-6   CAHS-tell-ah-noase   Ht: 6'4" Wt: 210 Born: 3/4/1992 Age: 23

Year	Team	Lg	G	AB	H	2B	3B	HR	(Hm	Rd)	TB	R	RBI	RC	TBB	IBB	SO	HBP	SH	SF	SB	CS	GDP	Avg	OBP	Slg	OPS
2010	Tigers	R	7	24	8	2	0	0	(-	-)	10	5	3	4	4	0	5	0	0	1	0	1	1	.333	.414	.417	.830
2011	WMich	A	135	507	158	36	3	7	(-	-)	221	65	76	83	45	2	130	3	1	6	3	2	5	.312	.367	.436	.803
2012	Lkland	A+	55	215	87	17	3	3	(-	-)	119	37	32	52	22	1	42	3	0	3	3	2	5	.405	.461	.553	1.014
2012	Erie	AA	79	322	84	14	1	7	(-	-)	121	35	25	35	14	1	76	2	0	3	5	4	12	.261	.293	.376	.669
2013	Toledo	AAA	134	533	147	37	1	18	(-	-)	240	81	76	86	54	2	100	3	0	5	4	1	12	.276	.343	.450	.793
2013	Det	AL	11	18	5	0	0	0	(0	0)	5	1	0	1	0	0	1	0	0	0	0	0	0	.278	.278	.278	.556
2014	Det	AL	148	533	138	31	4	11	(6	5)	210	50	66	63	36	3	140	3	0	7	2	2	7	.259	.306	.394	.700
2 ML YEARS			159	551	143	31	4	11	(6	5)	215	51	66	64	36	3	141	3	0	7	2	2	7	.260	.305	.390	.695

Rusney Castillo

Bats: R Throws: R Pos: CF-10   Ht: 5'8" Wt: 186 Born: 9/7/1987 Age: 27

Year	Team	Lg	G	AB	H	2B	3B	HR	(Hm	Rd)	TB	R	RBI	RC	TBB	IBB	SO	HBP	SH	SF	SB	CS	GDP	Avg	OBP	Slg	OPS
2014	Bos	AL	10	36	12	1	0	2	(2	0)	19	6	6	9	3	0	6	1	0	0	3	0	0	.333	.400	.528	.928

Welington Castillo

Bats: R Throws: R Pos: C-106;PH-5   WELL-ing-tunn   Ht: 5'10" Wt: 210 Born: 4/24/1987 Age: 28

Year	Team	Lg	G	AB	H	2B	3B	HR	(Hm	Rd)	TB	R	RBI	RC	TBB	IBB	SO	HBP	SH	SF	SB	CS	GDP	Avg	OBP	Slg	OPS
2014	Iowa	AAA	2	8	3	0	0	0	(-	-)	3	0	1	1	2	0	0	0	0	0	1	0	0	.375	.500	.375	.875
2010	ChC	NL	7	20	6	4	0	1	(0	1)	13	3	5	3	1	0	7	0	0	0	0	0	0	.300	.333	.650	.983
2011	ChC	NL	4	13	2	0	0	0	(0	0)	2	0	0	0	0	0	4	0	0	1	0	0	0	.154	.154	.154	.308
2012	ChC	NL	52	170	45	11	0	5	(4	1)	71	16	22	22	17	2	51	2	0	1	0	0	0	.265	.337	.418	.754
2013	ChC	NL	113	380	104	23	0	8	(1	7)	151	41	32	44	34	3	97	11	1	2	2	0	13	.274	.349	.397	.746
2014	ChC	NL	110	380	90	19	0	13	(7	6)	148	28	46	44	26	0	102	7	2	2	0	0	7	.237	.296	.389	.686
5 ML YEARS			286	963	247	57	0	27	(12	15)	385	88	105	113	78	5	261	20	3	5	2	0	25	.256	.324	.400	.723

Jason Castro

Bats: L Throws: R Pos: C-114;DH-11;PH-3   Ht: 6'3" Wt: 215 Born: 6/18/1987 Age: 28

Year	Team	Lg	G	AB	H	2B	3B	HR	(Hm	Rd)	TB	R	RBI	RC	TBB	IBB	SO	HBP	SH	SF	SB	CS	GDP	Avg	OBP	Slg	OPS
2010	Hou	NL	67	195	40	8	1	2	(1	1)	56	26	8	12	22	2	41	0	0	4	0	0	4	.205	.286	.287	.573
2012	Hou	NL	87	257	66	15	2	6	(3	3)	103	29	29	33	31	2	61	1	2	4	0	0	8	.257	.334	.401	.735
2013	Hou	AL	120	435	120	35	1	18	(13	5)	211	63	56	76	50	2	130	2	0	4	2	1	6	.276	.350	.485	.835
2014	Hou	AL	126	465	103	21	2	14	(10	4)	170	43	56	45	34	1	151	9	1	3	1	0	11	.222	.286	.366	.651
4 ML YEARS			400	1352	329	79	6	40	(27	13)	540	161	149	166	137	8	383	12	3	11	3	1	27	.243	.316	.399	.716

Starlin Castro

Bats: R **Throws:** R **Pos:** SS-133;PH-1   STARR-linn   **Ht:** 6'0" **Wt:** 190 **Born:** 3/24/1990 **Age:** 25

Year Team	Lg	G	AB	H	2B	3B	HR	(Hm Rd)	TB	R	RBI	RC	TBB	IBB	SO	HBP	SH	SF	SB	CS	GDP	Avg	OBP	Slg	OPS
2010 ChC	NL	125	463	139	31	5	3	(1 2)	189	53	41	56	29	7	71	6	4	4	10	8	14	.300	.347	.408	.755
2011 ChC	NL	158	674	207	36	9	10	(4 6)	291	91	66	93	35	2	96	2	0	4	22	9	20	.307	.341	.432	.773
2012 ChC	NL	162	646	183	29	12	14	(7 7)	278	78	78	91	36	5	100	4	0	5	25	13	15	.283	.323	.430	.753
2013 ChC	NL	161	666	163	34	2	10	(9 1)	231	59	44	55	30	0	129	7	1	1	9	6	21	.245	.284	.347	.631
2014 ChC	NL	134	528	154	33	1	14	(3 11)	231	58	65	72	35	4	100	4	0	2	4	4	18	.292	.339	.438	.777
5 ML YEARS		740	2977	846	163	29	51	(24 27)	1220	339	294	367	165	18	496	23	5	16	70	40	88	.284	.325	.410	.735

Garin Cecchini

Bats: L **Throws:** R **Pos:** 3B-9;DH-1;PH-1   chick-KEE-nee   **Ht:** 6'3" **Wt:** 220 **Born:** 4/20/1991 **Age:** 24

Year Team	Lg	G	AB	H	2B	3B	HR	(Hm Rd)	TB	R	RBI	RC	TBB	IBB	SO	HBP	SH	SF	SB	CS	GDP	Avg	OBP	Slg	OPS
2011 Lowell	A-	32	114	34	12	1	3	(- -)	57	21	23	24	17	0	19	2	0	0	12	2	3	.298	.398	.500	.898
2012 Grnvlle	A	118	455	139	38	4	4	(- -)	197	84	62	89	61	5	90	7	0	3	51	6	13	.305	.394	.433	.827
2013 Salem	A+	63	214	75	19	4	5	(- -)	117	44	33	55	43	0	34	5	0	0	15	7	3	.350	.469	.547	1.016
2013 Portlnd	AA	66	240	71	14	3	2	(- -)	97	36	28	46	51	2	52	2	0	2	8	2	7	.296	.420	.404	.825
2014 Pwtckt	AAA	114	407	107	21	1	7	(- -)	151	52	57	56	44	2	99	5	1	1	11	1	17	.263	.341	.371	.712
2014 Bos	AL	11	31	8	3	0	1	(1 0)	14	6	4	5	3	0	11	2	0	0	0	0	0	.258	.361	.452	.813

Brett Cecil

Pitches: L **Bats:** R **Pos:** RP-66   SEE-sill   **Ht:** 6'3" **Wt:** 220 **Born:** 7/2/1986 **Age:** 28

Year Team	Lg	G	GS	CG	GF	IP	BFP	H	R	ER	HR	SH	SF	HB	TBB	IBB	SO	WP	Bk	W	L	Pct	Sh	Sv-Op	Hld	ERC	ERA
2014 Buffalo*	AAA	2	0	0	0	2.0	7	2	1	1	0	0	0	0	0	1	0	0	0	1	0	1.000	0	0--	-	5.45	4.50
2009 Tor	AL	18	17	0	1	93.1	422	116	59	55	17	0	2	5	38	0	69	0	0	7	4	.636	0	0-0	0	6.53	5.30
2010 Tor	AL	28	28	0	0	172.2	726	175	87	81	18	1	6	1	54	2	117	7	1	15	7	.682	0	0-0	0	3.88	4.22
2011 Tor	AL	20	20	2	0	123.2	532	122	68	65	22	3	5	6	42	1	87	1	0	4	11	.267	1	0-0	0	4.47	4.73
2012 Tor	AL	21	9	0	2	61.1	270	70	40	39	11	3	3	3	23	0	51	0	0	2	4	.333	0	0-0	1	5.68	5.72
2013 Tor	AL	60	0	0	12	60.2	250	44	20	19	4	3	2	3	23	3	70	5	1	5	1	.833	0	1-3	11	2.42	2.82
2014 Tor	AL	66	0	0	17	53.1	234	46	16	16	2	0	3	1	27	4	76	1	0	2	3	.400	0	5-7	24	3.16	2.70
6 ML YEARS		213	74	2	32	565.0	2434	573	290	275	74	10	21	19	207	10	470	14	2	35	30	.538	1	6-10	36	4.36	4.38

Ronny Cedeno

Bats: R **Throws:** R **Pos:** PH-4;SS-2;3B-1   seh-DAYN-yo   **Ht:** 6'0" **Wt:** 195 **Born:** 2/2/1983 **Age:** 32

Year Team	Lg	G	AB	H	2B	3B	HR	(Hm Rd)	TB	R	RBI	RC	TBB	IBB	SO	HBP	SH	SF	SB	CS	GDP	Avg	OBP	Slg	OPS
2014 LV*	AAA	42	147	42	9	0	1	(- -)	54	10	20	16	9	1	23	0	4	0	0	4	2	.286	.327	.367	.694
2014 Reno*	AAA	41	134	46	8	2	3	(- -)	67	29	23	28	14	0	25	2	1	1	6	0	2	.343	.411	.500	.911
2005 ChC	NL	41	80	24	3	0	1	(- -)	30	13	6	11	5	1	11	2	2	0	1	0	4	.300	.356	.375	.731
2006 ChC	NL	151	534	131	18	7	6	(4 2)	181	51	41	41	17	4	109	3	15	3	8	8	10	.245	.271	.339	.610
2007 ChC	NL	38	74	15	2	0	4	(2 2)	29	6	13	8	3	0	18	0	2	1	2	1	0	.203	.231	.392	.623
2008 ChC	NL	99	216	58	12	0	2	(2 0)	76	36	28	23	18	2	41	1	1	0	4	1	6	.269	.328	.352	.680
2009 2 Tms		105	341	71	8	3	10	(7 3)	115	32	38	29	19	3	79	3	13	0	5	2	9	.208	.256	.337	.593
2010 Pit	NL	139	468	120	29	3	8	(4 4)	179	42	38	46	23	4	106	2	7	2	12	3	10	.256	.293	.382	.675
2011 Pit	NL	128	413	103	25	3	2	(2 0)	140	43	32	36	30	7	93	0	6	5	2	5	11	.249	.297	.339	.636
2012 NYM	NL	78	166	43	11	1	4	(3 1)	68	18	22	19	17	0	35	1	2	0	1	0	10	.259	.332	.410	.741
2013 2 Tms		89	264	64	8	3	3	(2 1)	87	24	21	23	14	1	73	3	6	1	5	4	6	.242	.287	.330	.617
2014 Phi	NL	7	9	0	0	0	0	(- -)	0	0	0	0	0	0	2	0	0	0	0	0	0	.000	.000	.000	.000
09 Sea	AL	59	186	31	4	2	5	(2 3)	54	15	17	7	10	1	50	1	9	0	3	2	6	.167	.213	.290	.504
09 Pit	NL	46	155	40	4	1	5	(5 0)	61	17	21	22	9	2	29	2	4	0	2	0	3	.258	.307	.394	.701
13 Hou	AL	51	141	31	6	1	1	(1 1)	42	12	12	10	6	0	42	2	5	1	2	1	4	.220	.260	.298	.558
13 SD	NL	38	123	33	2	2	2	(1 1)	45	12	9	13	8	1	31	1	1	0	3	3	2	.268	.318	.366	.684
Postseason		3	0	0	0	0	0	(0 0)	0	0	0	0	0	0	0	0	0	0	1	0	0	-	-	-	-
10 ML YEARS		875	2565	629	116	20	40	(24 16)	905	265	294	236	146	22	567	15	54	12	39	25	66	.245	.289	.353	.641

Xavier Cedeno

Pitches: L **Bats:** L **Pos:** RP-9   seh-DAYN-yo   **Ht:** 6'0" **Wt:** 205 **Born:** 8/26/1986 **Age:** 28

Year Team	Lg	G	GS	CG	GF	IP	BFP	H	R	ER	HR	SH	SF	HB	TBB	IBB	SO	WP	Bk	W	L	Pct	Sh	Sv-Op	Hld	ERC	ERA
2014 Syrcse*	AAA	35	0	0	12	39.1	149	22	10	10	3	2	0	0	12	1	57	3	0	5	1	.833	0	4--	-	1.49	2.29
2011 Hou	NL	3	0	0	0	1.2	11	7	5	5	2	0	0	0	0	0	0	0	0	0	0	-	0	0-0	0	43.10	27.00
2012 Hou	NL	44	0	0	12	31.0	138	30	15	13	3	2	3	1	14	1	36	3	0	0	1	.000	0	1-3	6	4.05	3.77
2013 2 Tms		16	0	0	3	12.1	60	15	12	9	0	1	0	2	8	0	9	0	0	0	0	-	0	0-0	2	6.24	6.57
2014 Was	NL	9	0	0	4	7.0	30	10	4	3	1	0	0	0	0	0	5	0	0	0	0	-	0	0-0	2	5.27	3.86
13 Hou	AL	5	0	0	0	6.1	37	10	11	8	0	1	0	2	7	0	3	0	0	0	0	-	0	0-0	0	11.27	11.37
13 Was	NL	11	0	0	3	6.0	23	5	1	1	0	0	0	0	1	0	6	0	0	0	0	-	0	0-0	2	1.84	1.50
4 ML YEARS		72	0	0	19	52.0	239	62	36	30	6	3	3	3	22	1	50	3	0	0	1	.000	0	1-3	8	5.57	5.19

Juan Centeno

Bats: L Throws: R Pos: C-9;PH-2 sen-TAIN-no Ht: 5'9" Wt: 195 Born: 11/16/1989 Age: 25

Year	Team	Lg	G	AB	H	2B	3B	HR	(Hm	Rd)	TB	R	RBI	RC	TBB	IBB	SO	HBP	SH	SF	SB	CS	GDP	Avg	OBP	Slg	OPS
2010	StLuci	A+	11	35	7	0	0	0	(-	-)	7	1	1	2	3	1	7	0	2	1	1	0	4	.200	.256	.200	.456
2010	Bnghtn	AA	1	1	0	0	0	0	(-	-)	0	0	0	0	0	0	0	0	0	0	0	0	0	.000	.000	.000	.000
2010	Bklyn	A-	32	89	33	8	1	1	(-	-)	46	17	10	19	6	1	8	1	8	0	1	0	1	.371	.417	.517	.934
2011	StLuci	A+	52	157	50	5	1	1	(-	-)	60	22	11	23	12	0	22	1	7	1	3	1	4	.318	.368	.382	.751
2012	Bnghtn	AA	79	281	80	12	2	0	(-	-)	96	29	35	34	23	0	43	1	4	4	1	1	21	.285	.337	.342	.678
2013	Bnghtn	AA	6	23	6	1	1	0	(-	-)	9	4	3	2	0	0	5	0	1	0	0	0	3	.261	.261	.391	.652
2013	LsVgs	AAA	67	213	65	10	2	0	(-	-)	79	25	28	29	12	0	24	3	6	3	1	1	7	.305	.346	.371	.717
2014	LsVgs	AAA	53	179	52	5	0	1	(-	-)	60	19	17	23	15	3	26	1	4	3	2	0	2	.291	.343	.335	.679
2014	Bnghtn	AA	21	77	22	5	0	0	(-	-)	27	8	8	9	6	0	11	0	0	0	0	1	5	.286	.337	.351	.688
2013	NYM	NL	4	10	3	0	0	0	(0	0)	3	0	1	1	0	0	1	0	0	0	0	0	0	.300	.300	.300	.600
2014	NYM	NL	10	30	6	0	0	0	(0	0)	6	1	2	2	3	0	5	0	0	0	0	0	2	.200	.273	.200	.473
	2 ML YEARS		14	40	9	0	0	0	(0	0)	9	1	3	3	3	0	6	0	0	0	0	0	2	.225	.279	.225	.504

Francisco Cervelli

Bats: R Throws: R Pos: C-42;1B-5;PH-2;PR-2;DH-1 serr-VELL-ee Ht: 6'1" Wt: 205 Born: 3/6/1986 Age: 29

Year	Team	Lg	G	AB	H	2B	3B	HR	(Hm	Rd)	TB	R	RBI	RC	TBB	IBB	SO	HBP	SH	SF	SB	CS	GDP	Avg	OBP	Slg	OPS
2014	Tampa*	A+	2	6	0	0	0	0	(-	-)	0	0	0	0	1	0	1	0	0	0	0	0	1	.000	.143	.000	.143
2014	S-WB*	AAA	3	11	2	0	0	0	(-	-)	2	0	0	0	0	0	0	0	0	0	0	0	1	.182	.182	.182	.364
2014	Trntn*	AA	5	15	2	0	0	0	(-	-)	2	2	0	1	4	0	4	1	0	0	0	0	1	.133	.350	.133	.483
2008	NYY	AL	3	5	0	0	0	0	(0	0)	0	0	0	0	0	0	3	0	0	0	0	0	1	.000	.000	.000	.000
2009	NYY	AL	42	94	28	4	0	1	(0	1)	35	13	11	11	2	0	11	0	4	1	0	3	1	.298	.309	.372	.682
2010	NYY	AL	93	266	72	11	3	0	(0	0)	89	27	38	40	33	1	42	6	8	4	1	1	7	.271	.359	.335	.694
2011	NYY	AL	43	124	33	4	0	4	(2	2)	49	17	22	17	9	0	29	2	1	1	4	1	4	.266	.324	.395	.719
2012	NYY	AL	3	1	0	0	0	0	(0	0)	0	1	0	0	1	0	0	0	0	0	0	0	0	.000	.500	.000	.500
2013	NYY	AL	17	52	14	3	0	3	(3	0)	26	12	8	9	8	0	9	1	0	0	0	0	1	.269	.377	.500	.877
2014	NYY	AL	49	146	44	11	1	2	(1	1)	63	18	13	19	11	0	41	5	0	0	1	0	5	.301	.370	.432	.802
	Postseason		3	3	0	0	0	0	(0	0)	0	0	0	0	0	0	2	0	0	0	0	0	0	.000	.000	.000	.000
	7 ML YEARS		250	688	191	33	4	10	(6	4)	262	88	92	96	64	1	135	14	13	6	6	5	19	.278	.348	.381	.729

Yoenis Cespedes

Bats: R Throws: R Pos: LF-125;DH-22;CF-9;PH-5 yo-EHN-ess SESS-peh-des Ht: 5'10" Wt: 210 Born: 10/18/1985 Age: 29

Year	Team	Lg	G	AB	H	2B	3B	HR	(Hm	Rd)	TB	R	RBI	RC	TBB	IBB	SO	HBP	SH	SF	SB	CS	GDP	Avg	OBP	Slg	OPS
2012	Oak	AL	129	487	142	25	5	23	(11	12)	246	70	82	90	43	5	102	7	0	3	16	4	9	.292	.356	.505	.861
2013	Oak	AL	135	529	127	21	4	26	(14	12)	234	74	80	65	37	5	137	5	0	3	7	7	8	.240	.294	.442	.737
2014	2 Tms	AL	152	600	156	36	6	22	(13	9)	270	89	100	85	35	3	128	3	0	7	7	2	13	.260	.301	.450	.751
14	Oak	AL	101	399	102	26	3	17	(11	6)	185	62	67	55	28	3	80	1	0	4	3	2	8	.256	.303	.464	.767
14	Bos	AL	51	201	54	10	3	5	(2	3)	85	27	33	30	7	0	48	2	0	3	4	0	5	.269	.296	.423	.719
	Postseason		10	40	14	2	1	1	(1	0)	21	4	6	8	2	0	6	1	0	0	2	0	0	.350	.395	.525	.920
	3 ML YEARS		416	1616	425	82	15	71	(38	33)	750	233	262	240	115	13	367	15	0	13	30	13	30	.263	.316	.464	.780

Jhoulys Chacin

Pitches: R Bats: R Pos: SP-11 joo-LEEZ cha-SEEN Ht: 6'3" Wt: 215 Born: 1/7/1988 Age: 27

Year	Team	Lg	G	GS	CG	GF	IP	BFP	H	R	ER	HR	SH	SF	HB	TBB	IBB	SO	WP	Bk	W	L	Pct	Sh	Sv-Op	Hld	ERC	ERA
2014	Mdest*	A+	2	2	0	0	7.1	32	8	7	7	1	0	0	0	3	0	4	0	0	0	2	.000	0	0- -	-	4.95	8.59
2014	ColSpr*	AAA	2	2	0	0	10.2	47	9	5	3	0	0	0	1	5	0	8	0	0	1	1	.500	0	0- -	-	3.05	2.53
2009	Col	NL	9	1	0	3	11.0	48	6	6	6	1	1	0	0	11	0	13	2	0	0	1	.000	0	0-0	0	3.87	4.91
2010	Col	NL	28	21	0	2	137.1	583	114	64	50	10	6	5	9	61	5	138	4	0	9	11	.450	0	0-0	0	3.33	3.28
2011	Col	NL	31	31	2	0	194.0	827	168	87	78	20	5	3	4	87	1	150	7	0	11	14	.440	1	0-0	0	3.61	3.62
2012	Col	NL	14	14	0	0	69.0	314	80	35	34	10	1	1	2	32	0	45	3	0	3	5	.375	0	0-0	0	5.73	4.43
2013	Col	NL	31	31	0	0	197.1	816	188	82	76	11	3	7	3	62	3	126	5	1	14	10	.583	0	0-0	0	3.26	3.47
2014	Col	NL	11	11	0	0	63.1	272	63	38	38	8	2	3	1	28	1	42	4	0	1	7	.125	0	0-0	0	4.52	5.40
	6 ML YEARS		124	109	2	5	672.0	2860	619	312	282	60	18	19	19	280	10	514	25	1	38	48	.442	1	0-0	0	3.74	3.78

Andrew Chafin

Pitches: L Bats: R Pos: SP-3 Ht: 6'2" Wt: 220 Born: 6/17/1990 Age: 25

Year	Team	Lg	G	GS	CG	GF	IP	BFP	H	R	ER	HR	SH	SF	HB	TBB	IBB	SO	WP	Bk	W	L	Pct	Sh	Sv-Op	Hld	ERC	ERA
2011	DBcks	R	1	1	0	0	1.0	5	1	0	0	0	0	0	1	0	0	2	0	0	0	0	-	0	0- -	-	5.48	0.00
2012	Visalia	A+	30	22	0	3	122.1	542	112	74	67	12	4	2	2	69	0	150	10	1	6	6	.500	0	0- -	-	4.26	4.93
2013	Visalia	A+	6	6	0	0	31.0	138	32	16	16	1	0	2	0	14	1	32	4	1	3	1	.750	0	0- -	-	3.84	4.65
2013	Mobile	AA	21	21	2	0	126.1	523	118	46	40	5	5	5	3	41	0	87	13	1	10	7	.588	0	0- -	-	3.16	2.85
2014	Mobile	AA	9	9	0	0	55.0	226	49	14	12	4	3	1	1	19	0	41	3	2	4	1	.800	0	0- -	-	3.22	1.96
2014	Reno	AAA	17	16	0	0	92.2	419	111	62	55	11	4	1	2	39	3	73	3	1	5	6	.455	0	0- -	-	5.50	5.34
2014	Ari	NL	3	3	0	0	14.0	60	13	6	6	0	2	0	1	8	1	10	2	0	0	1	.000	0	0-0	0	3.92	3.86

Joba Chamberlain

Pitches: R Bats: R Pos: RP-69
JOBB-ah CHAME-berr-linn
Ht: 6'2" Wt: 250 Born: 9/23/1985 Age: 29

Year	Team	Lg	G	GS	CG	GF	IP	BFP	H	R	ER	HR	SH	SF	HB	TBB	IBB	SO	WP	Bk	W	L	Pct	Sh	Sv-Op	Hld	ERC	ERA
2007	NYY	AL	19	0	0	3	24.0	91	12	2	1	1	1	0	1	6	0	34	1	0	2	0	1.000	0	1-1	8	1.16	0.38
2008	NYY	AL	42	12	0	5	100.1	417	87	32	29	5	2	1	2	39	3	118	4	2	4	3	.571	0	0-1	19	3.04	2.60
2009	NYY	AL	32	31	0	0	157.1	709	167	94	83	21	6	5	12	76	2	133	5	2	9	6	.600	0	0-0	0	5.32	4.75
2010	NYY	AL	73	0	0	18	71.2	305	71	37	35	6	0	1	1	22	2	77	5	1	3	4	.429	0	3-7	26	3.53	4.40
2011	NYY	AL	27	0	0	3	28.2	110	23	10	9	3	0	1	1	7	0	24	1	0	2	0	1.000	0	0-1	12	2.76	2.83
2012	NYY	AL	22	0	0	5	20.2	95	26	11	10	3	0	1	2	6	2	22	0	0	1	0	1.000	0	0-0	4	5.63	4.35
2013	NYY	AL	45	0	0	14	42.0	198	47	23	23	8	0	1	1	26	1	38	3	0	2	1	.667	0	1-1	5	6.38	4.93
2014	Det	AL	69	0	0	10	63.0	263	57	26	25	3	1	2	3	24	3	59	3	0	2	5	.286	0	2-6	29	3.29	3.57
	Postseason		19	0	0	1	15.2	73	20	5	5	1	1	1	1	6	0	15	2	0	1	0	1.000	0	0-2	3	5.54	2.87
	8 ML YEARS		329	43	0	58	507.2	2188	490	235	215	50	10	12	23	206	13	505	22	5	25	19	.568	0	7-17	103	4.04	3.81

Aroldis Chapman

Pitches: L Bats: L Pos: RP-54
ah-ROLL-diss
Ht: 6'4" Wt: 205 Born: 2/28/1988 Age: 27

Year	Team	Lg	G	GS	CG	GF	IP	BFP	H	R	ER	HR	SH	SF	HB	TBB	IBB	SO	WP	Bk	W	L	Pct	Sh	Sv-Op	Hld	ERC	ERA
2014	Dayton*	A	2	2	0	0	2.0	6	0	0	0	0	0	0	0	1	0	3	0	0	0	0	-	0	0--	-	0.32	0.00
2014	Lsvlle*	AAA	2	1	0	0	1.0	13	7	8	8	0	0	0	1	2	0	2	1	0	0	1	.000	0	0--	-	65.20	72.00
2010	Cin	NL	15	0	0	3	13.1	51	9	4	3	0	0	0	0	5	0	19	2	0	2	2	.500	0	0-1	4	1.82	2.03
2011	Cin	NL	54	0	0	13	50.0	207	24	21	20	2	1	0	2	41	0	71	4	0	4	1	.800	0	1-3	13	2.69	3.60
2012	Cin	NL	68	0	0	52	71.2	276	35	13	12	4	0	1	4	23	0	122	4	0	5	5	.500	0	38-43	6	1.35	1.51
2013	Cin	NL	68	0	0	55	63.2	258	37	18	18	7	1	0	3	29	0	112	6	0	4	5	.444	0	38-43	6	2.33	2.54
2014	Cin	NL	54	0	0	44	54.0	202	21	12	12	1	1	1	2	24	0	106	4	0	0	3	.000	0	36-38	0	1.18	2.00
	Postseason		5	0	0	3	4.2	24	5	4	1	0	0	0	1	2	0	4	2	0	1	0	1.000	0	0-1	0	4.11	1.93
	5 ML YEARS		259	0	0	167	252.2	994	126	68	65	14	3	2	11	122	0	430	20	0	15	16	.484	0	113-128	23	1.75	2.32

Kevin Chapman

Pitches: L Bats: L Pos: RP-21
Ht: 6'3" Wt: 225 Born: 2/19/1988 Age: 27

Year	Team	Lg	G	GS	CG	GF	IP	BFP	H	R	ER	HR	SH	SF	HB	TBB	IBB	SO	WP	Bk	W	L	Pct	Sh	Sv-Op	Hld	ERC	ERA
2010	Wilmg	A+	14	0	0	8	18.0	86	20	13	11	1	2	0	1	8	0	20	1	0	1	1	.500	0	1--	-	4.47	5.50
2011	Wilmg	A+	15	0	0	12	22.1	99	24	14	12	1	1	0	0	7	0	40	2	0	0	2	.000	0	7--	-	3.63	4.84
2011	NWArk	AA	25	0	0	8	39.2	173	37	25	22	5	3	2	2	21	0	50	1	0	1	2	.333	0	3--	-	4.67	4.99
2012	CpChr	AA	49	0	0	11	58.0	256	49	19	17	2	3	3	1	32	3	59	2	0	6	3	.667	0	2--	-	3.24	2.64
2013	OKCity	AAA	45	0	0	7	50.2	229	42	23	18	2	3	1	1	36	0	61	2	0	1	2	.333	0	2--	-	3.88	3.20
2014	OKCity	AAA	43	0	0	31	44.0	192	38	11	6	0	0	1	1	25	3	64	3	0	2	1	.667	0	9--	-	1.23	1.23
2013	Hou	AL	25	0	0	2	20.1	87	13	6	4	1	2	0	1	13	2	15	3	0	1	1	.500	0	1-4	4	2.69	1.77
2014	Hou	AL	21	0	0	1	21.1	97	22	11	11	3	3	1	0	11	0	19	0	0	2	0	1.000	0	0-1	5	4.90	4.64
	2 ML YEARS		46	0	0	3	41.2	184	35	17	15	4	5	1	1	24	2	34	3	0	3	1	.750	0	1-5	9	3.79	3.24

Tyler Chatwood

Pitches: R Bats: R Pos: SP-4
Ht: 6'0" Wt: 185 Born: 12/16/1989 Age: 25

Year	Team	Lg	G	GS	CG	GF	IP	BFP	H	R	ER	HR	SH	SF	HB	TBB	IBB	SO	WP	Bk	W	L	Pct	Sh	Sv-Op	Hld	ERC	ERA
2014	ColSpr*	AAA	1	1	0	0	6.1	24	5	1	1	1	0	0	1	0	0	8	0	0	1	0	1.000	0	0--	-	2.49	1.42
2011	LAA	AL	27	25	0	0	142.0	633	166	81	75	14	6	3	6	71	4	74	3	1	6	11	.353	0	0-0	0	5.78	4.75
2012	Col	NL	19	12	0	3	64.2	294	74	43	39	9	4	2	0	33	2	41	4	0	5	6	.455	0	1-1	0	5.62	5.43
2013	Col	NL	20	20	1	0	111.1	476	118	44	39	5	2	4	4	41	5	66	10	0	8	5	.615	0	0-0	0	4.05	3.15
2014	Col	NL	4	4	0	0	24.0	101	21	13	12	4	0	2	2	8	0	20	2	0	1	0	1.000	0	0-0	0	3.91	4.50
	4 ML YEARS		70	61	1	3	342.0	1504	379	181	165	32	12	11	12	153	11	201	19	1	20	22	.476	0	1-1	0	5.03	4.34

Endy Chavez

EN-dee SHAH-vezz

Bats: L Throws: L Pos: RF-46;PH-15;DH-13;LF-11;CF-9;PR-2
Ht: 5'11" Wt: 170 Born: 2/7/1978 Age: 37

Year	Team	Lg	G	AB	H	2B	3B	HR	(Hm	Rd)	TB	R	RBI	RC	TBB	IBB	SO	HBP	SH	SF	SB	CS	GDP	Avg	OBP	Slg	OPS
2014	Tacom*	AAA	37	114	31	2	0	0	(-	-)	33	16	6	11	13	2	17	1	4	2	0	4	6	.272	.346	.289	.636
2001	KC	AL	29	77	16	2	0	0	(0	0)	18	4	5	2	3	0	8	0	0	0	0	2	3	.208	.238	.234	.471
2002	Mon	NL	36	125	37	8	5	1	(0	1)	58	20	9	14	5	0	16	0	7	1	5	5	0	.296	.321	.464	.785
2003	Mon	NL	141	483	121	25	5	5	(4	1)	171	66	47	56	31	3	59	0	9	3	18	7	7	.251	.294	.354	.648
2004	Mon	NL	132	502	139	20	6	5	(4	1)	186	65	34	56	30	0	40	1	12	2	32	7	6	.277	.318	.371	.688
2005	2 Tms		98	116	25	4	3	0	(0	0)	35	19	11	8	7	0	14	0	7	0	2	2	3	.216	.260	.302	.562
2006	NYM	NL	133	353	108	22	5	4	(2	2)	152	48	42	54	24	0	44	0	11	2	12	3	7	.306	.348	.431	.779
2007	NYM	NL	71	150	43	7	2	1	(1	0)	57	20	17	20	9	0	16	0	5	1	5	2	5	.287	.325	.380	.705
2008	NYM	NL	133	270	72	16	2	1	(1	0)	89	30	12	21	17	3	22	0	9	2	6	1	6	.267	.308	.330	.638
2009	Sea	AL	54	161	44	3	1	2	(1	1)	55	17	13	15	14	1	22	0	5	0	9	1	4	.273	.328	.342	.669
2011	Tex	AL	83	256	77	11	3	5	(3	2)	109	37	27	32	10	0	30	0	5	3	10	5	7	.301	.323	.426	.749
2012	Bal	AL	64	158	32	6	0	2	(0	2)	44	15	12	10	6	1	24	1	4	0	3	2	2	.203	.236	.278	.515
2013	Sea	AL	97	266	71	10	0	2	(0	2)	87	22	14	17	9	1	31	0	3	1	1	3	9	.267	.290	.327	.617
2014	Sea	AL	80	232	64	12	2	2	(2	0)	86	22	23	30	15	0	30	0	4	2	5	2	5	.276	.317	.371	.688
05	Was	NL	7	9	2	1	0	0	(0	0)	3	2	1	1	3	0	1	0	0	0	0	1	1	.222	.417	.333	.750
05	Phi	NL	91	107	23	3	3	0	(0	0)	32	17	10	7	4	0	13	0	7	0	2	1	2	.215	.243	.299	.542
	Postseason		19	41	8	2	0	0	(0	0)	10	2	0	0	0	0	2	0	0	0	0	0	1	.195	.195	.244	.439
	13 ML YEARS		1151	3149	849	140	34	30	(18	12)	1147	385	266	335	180	12	356	2	86	19	106	42	61	.270	.308	.364	.672

Eric Chavez

Bats: L **Throws:** R **Pos:** PH-31;3B-11;DH-3   shah-VEZZ   **Ht:** 6'1" **Wt:** 215 **Born:** 12/7/1977 **Age:** 37

								BATTING												RUNNING			AVERAGES			
Year Team	Lg	G	AB	H	2B	3B	HR	(Hm Rd)	TB	R	RBI	RC	TBB	IBB	SO	HBP	SH	SF	SB	CS	GDP	Avg	OBP	Slg	OPS
1998 Oak	AL	16	45	14	4	1	0	(0 0)	20	6	6	7	3	1	5	0	0	0	1	1	1	.311	.354	.444	.799
1999 Oak	AL	115	356	88	21	2	13	(8 5)	152	47	50	50	46	4	56	0	0	0	1	1	7	.247	.333	.427	.760
2000 Oak	AL	153	501	139	23	4	26	(15 11)	248	89	86	86	62	8	94	1	0	5	2	2	9	.277	.355	.495	.850
2001 Oak	AL	151	552	159	43	0	32	(14 18)	298	91	114	99	41	9	99	4	0	7	8	2	7	.288	.338	.540	.878
2002 Oak	AL	153	585	161	31	3	34	(17 17)	300	87	109	103	65	13	119	1	0	2	8	3	8	.275	.348	.513	.860
2003 Oak	AL	156	588	166	39	5	29	(12 17)	302	94	101	97	62	10	89	1	0	3	8	3	14	.282	.350	.514	.864
2004 Oak	AL	125	475	131	20	0	29	(15 14)	238	87	77	84	95	10	99	3	0	4	6	3	21	.276	.397	.501	.898
2005 Oak	AL	160	625	168	40	1	27	(15 12)	291	92	101	95	58	4	129	2	0	9	6	0	9	.269	.329	.466	.794
2006 Oak	AL	137	485	117	24	2	22	(8 14)	211	74	72	70	84	6	100	1	0	6	3	0	19	.241	.351	.435	.786
2007 Oak	AL	90	341	82	21	2	15	(10 5)	152	43	46	38	34	2	76	0	0	4	4	2	9	.240	.306	.446	.752
2008 Oak	AL	23	89	22	7	0	2	(1 1)	35	10	14	14	6	0	18	0	0	0	0	0	2	.247	.295	.393	.688
2009 Oak	AL	8	30	3	1	0	0	(0 0)	4	0	1	0	1	0	7	0	0	0	0	0	0	.100	.129	.133	.262
2010 Oak	AL	33	111	26	8	0	1	(0 1)	37	10	10	7	8	0	31	0	0	4	0	0	3	.234	.276	.333	.610
2011 NYY	AL	58	160	42	7	1	2	(0 2)	57	16	26	26	14	3	34	0	0	1	0	0	4	.263	.320	.356	.676
2012 NYY	AL	113	278	78	12	0	16	(7 9)	138	36	37	39	30	3	59	1	0	4	0	0	10	.281	.348	.496	.845
2013 Ari	NL	80	228	64	14	2	9	(4 5)	109	28	44	35	19	4	45	1	0	5	1	0	7	.281	.332	.478	.810
2014 Ari	NL	44	69	17	3	1	3	(3 0)	31	6	8	10	11	0	19	0	0	1	2	0	2	.246	.346	.449	.795
Postseason		34	125	24	7	0	3	(3 0)	40	11	12	12	7	2	31	0	0	0	1	0	2	.192	.235	.320	.555
17 ML YEARS		1615	5518	1477	318	24	260	(129 131)	2623	816	902	860	639	77	1079	15	0	55	50	17	132	.268	.342	.475	.818

Jesse Chavez

Pitches: R **Bats:** R **Pos:** SP-21; RP-11   CHAH-vezz   **Ht:** 6'2" **Wt:** 160 **Born:** 8/21/1983 **Age:** 31

		HOW MUCH HE PITCHED						WHAT HE GAVE UP											THE RESULTS							
Year Team	Lg	G	GS	CG	GF	IP	BFP	H	R	ER	HR	SH	SF	HB	TBB	IBB	SO	WP	Bk	W	L	Pct	Sh	Sv-Op	Hld	ERC	ERA
2008 Pit	NL	15	0	0	6	15.0	74	20	11	11	2	3	1	0	9	2	16	2	0	0	1	.000	0	0-2	0	6.76	6.60
2009 Pit	NL	73	0	0	24	67.1	286	69	33	30	11	1	1	1	22	3	47	5	0	1	4	.200	0	0-4	15	4.39	4.01
2010 2 Tms		51	0	0	26	62.2	280	69	44	41	11	5	3	1	23	7	45	2	0	5	5	.500	0	0-1	6	4.85	5.89
2011 KC	AL	4	0	0	3	7.2	39	12	9	9	3	0	0	0	5	0	8	0	0	0	0	-	0	0-0	0	11.48	10.57
2012 2 Tms	AL	13	2	0	3	24.2	123	34	29	27	7	0	1	3	11	1	30	1	0	1	1	.500	0	0-0	0	8.32	9.85
2013 Oak	AL	35	0	0	16	57.1	248	50	27	25	3	6	2	3	20	4	55	5	0	2	4	.333	0	1-2	1	2.85	3.92
2014 Oak	AL	32	21	0	5	146.0	621	142	64	56	17	1	4	5	49	3	136	7	0	8	8	.500	0	0-0	0	3.89	3.45
10 Atl	NL	28	0	0	16	36.2	162	40	24	24	6	3	2	1	12	3	29	0	0	3	2	.600	0	0-0	0	4.65	5.89
10 KC	AL	23	0	0	10	26.0	118	29	20	17	5	2	1	0	11	4	16	2	0	2	3	.400	0	0-1	6	5.13	5.88
12 Tor	AL	9	2	0	2	21.1	102	25	22	20	6	0	1	2	10	1	27	0	0	1	1	.500	0	0-0	0	6.90	8.44
12 Oak	AL	4	0	0	1	3.1	21	9	7	7	1	0	0	1	1	0	3	1	0	0	0	-	0	0-0	0	18.70	18.90
7 ML YEARS		223	23	0	83	380.2	1671	396	217	199	54	16	12	13	139	20	337	22	0	17	23	.425	0	1-9	22	4.47	4.70

Bruce Chen

Pitches: L **Bats:** L **Pos:** SP-7; RP-6   **Ht:** 6'2" **Wt:** 215 **Born:** 6/19/1977 **Age:** 38

		HOW MUCH HE PITCHED						WHAT HE GAVE UP											THE RESULTS							
Year Team	Lg	G	GS	CG	GF	IP	BFP	H	R	ER	HR	SH	SF	HB	TBB	IBB	SO	WP	Bk	W	L	Pct	Sh	Sv-Op	Hld	ERC	ERA
2014 NWArk*	AA	1	1	0	0	3.0	16	8	2	2	2	1	0	0	0	0	3	0	0	0	0	-	0	0- -	-	20.17	6.00
2014 Omha*	AAA	3	3	0	0	12.1	57	21	12	12	1	1	0	0	3	0	13	0	0	0	1	.000	0	0- -	-	7.91	8.76
1998 Atl	NL	4	4	0	0	20.1	91	23	9	9	1	1	0	0	9	1	17	0	0	2	0	1.000	0	0-0	0	5.55	3.98
1999 Atl	NL	16	7	0	3	51.0	214	38	32	31	11	1	1	2	27	3	45	0	0	2	2	.500	0	0-0	0	4.07	5.47
2000 2 Tms	NL	37	15	0	4	134.0	559	116	54	49	18	8	3	2	46	4	112	4	1	7	4	.636	0	0-0	0	3.35	3.29
2001 2 Tms	NL	27	27	0	0	146.0	634	146	90	79	29	4	7	1	59	4	126	5	0	7	7	.500	0	0-0	0	4.75	4.87
2002 3 Tms	NL	55	6	0	9	77.2	360	85	53	48	16	2	3	2	43	5	80	4	0	2	5	.286	0	0-0	1	5.99	5.56
2003 2 Tms		16	2	0	4	24.1	110	26	16	15	6	3	3	2	10	1	20	0	0	0	1	.000	0	0-0	1	5.81	5.55
2004 Bal	AL	8	7	1	0	47.2	196	39	19	16	7	2	1	0	16	0	32	0	0	2	1	.667	0	0-0	0	3.13	3.02
2005 Bal	AL	34	32	1	0	197.1	832	187	94	84	33	3	3	9	63	0	133	2	1	13	10	.565	0	0-0	0	4.12	3.83
2006 Bal	AL	40	12	0	16	98.2	453	137	81	76	28	3	5	0	35	3	70	1	0	0	7	.000	0	0-0	0	7.73	6.93
2007 Tex	AL	5	0	0	3	10.0	46	11	11	8	3	0	0	0	6	1	7	0	0	0	0	-	0	0-0	0	6.90	7.20
2009 KC	AL	17	9	0	4	62.1	279	74	42	40	12	2	2	4	25	3	45	4	0	1	6	.143	0	0-0	0	6.18	5.78
2010 KC	AL	33	23	1	4	140.1	608	136	68	65	17	6	7	3	57	4	98	3	0	12	7	.632	1	1-1	0	4.09	4.17
2011 KC	AL	25	25	1	0	155.0	654	152	71	65	18	3	5	7	50	2	97	2	0	12	8	.600	0	0-0	0	3.98	3.77
2012 KC	AL	34	34	0	0	191.2	827	215	114	108	33	3	6	5	47	3	140	5	0	11	14	.440	0	0-0	0	4.80	5.07
2013 KC	AL	34	15	0	3	121.0	498	107	46	44	13	2	5	3	36	4	78	0	1	9	4	.692	0	0-2	0	3.17	3.27
2014 KC	AL	13	7	0	6	48.1	223	69	40	40	7	2	3	3	16	1	36	0	0	2	4	.333	0	0-0	0	6.85	7.45
00 Atl	NL	22	0	0	4	39.2	176	35	15	11	4	3	2	1	19	2	32	0	1	4	0	1.000	0	0-0	0	3.62	2.50
00 Phi	NL	15	15	0	0	94.1	383	81	39	38	14	5	1	1	27	2	80	4	0	3	4	.429	0	0-0	0	3.22	3.63
01 Phi	NL	16	16	0	0	86.1	381	90	53	48	19	2	4	1	31	4	79	2	0	4	5	.444	0	0-0	0	4.87	5.00
01 NYM	NL	11	11	0	0	59.2	253	56	37	31	10	2	3	0	28	0	47	3	0	3	2	.600	0	0-0	0	4.58	4.68
02 NYM	NL	1	0	0	0	0.2	3	1	0	0	0	0	0	0	0	0	0	0	0	0	0	-	0	0-0	0	4.47	0.00
02 Mon	NL	15	5	0	4	37.1	179	47	29	29	9	0	1	1	23	3	43	3	0	2	3	.400	0	0-0	0	7.69	6.99
02 Cin	NL	39	1	0	5	39.2	178	37	24	19	7	2	3	1	20	2	37	1	0	0	2	.000	0	0-0	0	4.55	4.31
03 Hou	NL	11	0	0	2	12.0	60	14	8	8	2	3	2	2	8	1	8	0	0	0	0	-	0	0-0	1	7.11	6.00
03 Bos	AL	5	2	0	2	12.1	50	12	8	7	4	0	1	0	2	0	12	0	0	0	1	.000	0	0-0	0	4.40	5.11
16 ML YEARS		398	225	4	56	1525.2	6584	1561	840	777	254	45	53	45	545	39	1136	30	3	82	80	.506	1	1-3	8	4.59	4.58

Wei-Yin Chen

Pitches: L Bats: L Pos: SP-31   way-ying   Ht: 6'0" Wt: 195 Born: 7/21/1985 Age: 29

Year	Team	Lg	G	GS	CG	GF	IP	BFP	H	R	ER	HR	SH	SF	HB	TBB	IBB	SO	WP	Bk	W	L	Pct	Sh	Sv-Op	Hld	ERC	ERA
2012	Bal	AL	32	32	0	0	192.2	818	186	97	86	29	5	8	5	57	0	154	2	1	12	11	.522	0	0-0	0	3.88	4.02
2013	Bal	AL	23	23	0	0	137.0	572	142	62	62	17	2	6	2	39	2	104	3	0	7	7	.500	0	0-0	0	4.11	4.07
2014	Bal	AL	31	31	0	0	185.2	772	193	77	73	23	5	4	3	35	2	136	2	0	16	6	.727	0	0-0	0	3.67	3.54
	Postseason		1	1	0	0	6.1	29	8	2	1	0	0	0	0	1	0	3	0	0	1	0	1.000	0	0-0	0	3.63	1.42
	3 ML YEARS		86	86	0	0	515.1	2162	521	236	221	69	12	18	10	131	4	394	7	1	35	24	.593	0	0-0	0	3.86	3.86

Robinson Chirinos

Bats: R Throws: R Pos: C-91;PH-2   chee-REE-nos   Ht: 6'1" Wt: 205 Born: 6/5/1984 Age: 31

Year	Team	Lg	G	AB	H	2B	3B	HR	(Hm	Rd)	TB	R	RBI	RC	TBB	IBB	SO	HBP	SH	SF	SB	CS	GDP	Avg	OBP	Slg	OPS
2011	TB	AL	20	55	12	2	0	1	(1	0)	17	4	7	5	5	0	13	0	0	0	0	0	0	.218	.283	.309	.592
2013	Tex	AL	13	28	5	3	0	0	(0	0)	8	3	0	0	2	0	6	0	0	0	0	0	1	.179	.233	.286	.519
2014	Tex	AL	93	306	73	15	0	13	(6	7)	127	36	40	38	17	1	71	7	4	4	0	1	4	.239	.290	.415	.705
	3 ML YEARS		126	389	90	20	0	14	(7	7)	152	43	47	43	24	1	90	7	4	4	0	1	5	.231	.285	.391	.676

Lonnie Chisenhall

Bats: L Throws: R Pos: 3B-114;DH-16;PH-14;1B-11   CHIZZ-en-hall   Ht: 6'2" Wt: 190 Born: 10/4/1988 Age: 26

Year	Team	Lg	G	AB	H	2B	3B	HR	(Hm	Rd)	TB	R	RBI	RC	TBB	IBB	SO	HBP	SH	SF	SB	CS	GDP	Avg	OBP	Slg	OPS
2011	Cle	AL	66	212	54	13	0	7	(2	5)	88	27	22	24	8	1	49	1	1	1	0	0	3	.255	.284	.415	.699
2012	Cle	AL	43	142	38	6	1	5	(4	1)	61	16	16	18	8	0	27	1	0	0	2	1	2	.268	.311	.430	.741
2013	Cle	AL	94	289	65	17	0	11	(4	7)	115	30	36	31	16	0	56	2	1	0	1	0	8	.225	.270	.398	.668
2014	Cle	AL	142	478	134	29	1	13	(6	7)	204	62	59	69	39	3	99	8	4	3	3	1	8	.280	.343	.427	.770
	Postseason		1	4	3	0	0	0	(0	0)	3	0	0	0	0	0	0	0	0	0	0	0	0	.750	.750	.750	1.500
	4 ML YEARS		345	1121	291	65	2	36	(16	20)	468	135	133	142	71	4	231	12	6	4	7	2	21	.260	.310	.417	.727

Randy Choate

Pitches: L Bats: L Pos: RP-61   CHOTE   Ht: 6'1" Wt: 210 Born: 9/5/1975 Age: 39

Year	Team	Lg	G	GS	CG	GF	IP	BFP	H	R	ER	HR	SH	SF	HB	TBB	IBB	SO	WP	Bk	W	L	Pct	Sh	Sv-Op	Hld	ERC	ERA
2000	NYY	AL	22	0	0	6	17.0	75	14	10	9	3	0	1	1	8	0	12	1	0	0	1	.000	0	0-0	2	3.99	4.76
2001	NYY	AL	37	0	0	13	48.1	207	34	21	18	0	2	1	9	27	2	35	3	0	3	1	.750	0	0-0	3	3.03	3.35
2002	NYY	AL	18	0	0	11	22.1	101	18	18	15	1	0	0	3	15	0	17	3	0	0	0	-	0	0-0	0	4.13	6.04
2003	NYY	AL	5	0	0	2	3.2	16	7	3	3	0	0	0	0	1	0	0	0	0	0	0	-	0	0-0	0	9.72	7.36
2004	Ari	NL	74	0	0	17	50.2	232	52	26	26	1	0	4	5	28	11	49	1	1	2	4	.333	0	0-2	11	4.18	4.62
2005	Ari	NL	8	0	0	1	7.0	35	8	7	7	0	0	0	1	5	1	4	1	0	0	0	-	0	0-0	2	5.48	9.00
2006	Ari	NL	30	0	0	3	16.0	75	21	9	7	0	0	0	3	4	0	12	0	0	0	1	.000	0	0-0	5	4.87	3.94
2007	Ari	NL	2	0	0	0	0.0	3	3	0	0	0	0	0	0	0	0	0	0	0	0	0	-	0	0-0	0		
2009	TB	AL	61	0	0	13	36.1	142	28	15	14	4	0	0	0	11	3	28	0	0	1	0	1.000	0	5-5	9	2.54	3.47
2010	TB	AL	85	0	0	8	44.2	187	41	23	21	3	2	2	3	17	5	40	4	0	4	3	.571	0	0-2	18	3.48	4.23
2011	Fla	NL	54	0	0	6	24.2	103	13	7	5	3	1	0	2	13	5	31	0	0	1	1	.500	0	0-0	14	2.16	1.82
2012	2 Tms	NL	80	0	0	4	38.2	168	29	18	13	1	2	2	5	18	3	38	2	0	0	0	-	0	1-1	20	2.76	3.03
2013	StL	NL	64	0	0	9	35.1	141	26	9	9	0	2	1	2	11	0	28	0	0	2	1	.667	0	0-1	15	2.00	2.29
2014	StL	NL	61	0	0	6	36.0	148	27	18	18	2	1	2	5	13	2	32	0	0	2	2	.500	0	0-0	10	2.78	4.50
12	Mia	NL	44	0	0	4	25.1	104	16	11	7	0	1	1	3	9	0	27	2	0	0	0	-	0	1-1	15	1.79	2.49
12	LAD	NL	36	0	0	0	13.1	64	13	7	6	1	1	1	2	9	3	11	0	0	0	0	-	0	0-0	5	4.87	4.05
	Postseason		16	0	0	1	9.2	41	8	5	2	0	0	0	0	3	1	5	0	0	0	0	-	0	0-0	1	1.95	1.86
	14 ML YEARS		601	0	0	98	380.2	1633	321	184	165	18	10	13	39	170	32	326	15	1	15	14	.517	0	6-11	109	3.29	3.90

Michael Choice

Bats: R Throws: R Pos: LF-41;RF-17;DH-16;PH-13;CF-7   Ht: 6'0" Wt: 215 Born: 11/10/1989 Age: 25

Year	Team	Lg	G	AB	H	2B	3B	HR	(Hm	Rd)	TB	R	RBI	RC	TBB	IBB	SO	HBP	SH	SF	SB	CS	GDP	Avg	OBP	Slg	OPS
2010	As	R	3	7	0	0	0	0	(-	-)	0	1	0	0	2	0	2	0	0	0	0	0	0	.000	.222	.000	.222
2010	Vancvr	A-	27	102	29	10	2	7	(-	-)	64	20	26	25	15	1	43	3	0	1	6	1	0	.284	.388	.627	1.016
2011	Stcktn	A+	118	467	133	28	1	30	(-	-)	253	79	82	96	61	2	134	10	0	4	9	5	9	.285	.376	.542	.918
2012	Mdlnd	AA	91	359	102	15	2	10	(-	-)	151	59	57	56	33	4	88	7	0	3	1	1	6	.284	.353	.421	.774
2013	Scrmto	AAA	132	510	154	29	1	14	(-	-)	227	90	89	94	69	0	115	11	0	10	1	2	15	.302	.390	.445	.835
2014	RdRck	AAA	43	150	40	8	0	7	(-	-)	69	25	31	28	23	1	47	6	0	3	2	1	2	.267	.379	.460	.839
2013	Oak	AL	9	18	5	1	0	0	(0	0)	6	2	0	2	1	0	6	0	0	0	0	0	0	.278	.316	.333	.649
2014	Tex	AL	86	253	46	6	1	9	(4	5)	81	20	36	24	21	0	69	3	0	3	1	0	11	.182	.250	.320	.570
	2 ML YEARS		95	271	51	7	1	9	(4	5)	87	22	36	26	22	0	75	3	0	3	1	0	11	.188	.254	.321	.575

Shin-Soo Choo

Bats: L Throws: L Pos: LF-64;DH-45;RF-12;PH-4   SHIN-sue CHEW   Ht: 5'11" Wt: 205 Born: 7/13/1982 Age: 32

Year	Team	Lg	G	AB	H	2B	3B	HR	(Hm	Rd)	TB	R	RBI	RC	TBB	IBB	SO	HBP	SH	SF	SB	CS	GDP	Avg	OBP	Slg	OPS
2005	Sea	AL	10	18	1	0	0	0	(0	0)	1	1	0	0	3	0	4	0	0	0	0	0	0	.056	.190	.056	.246
2006	2 Tms	AL	49	157	44	12	3	3	(2	1)	71	23	22	24	18	2	50	2	1	1	5	3	3	.280	.360	.452	.812
2007	Cle	AL	6	17	5	0	0	0	(0	0)	5	5	5	3	2	1	5	0	0	1	0	1	0	.294	.350	.294	.644
2008	Cle	AL	94	317	98	28	3	14	(10	4)	174	68	66	72	44	4	78	5	0	4	4	3	5	.309	.397	.549	.946
2009	Cle	AL	156	583	175	38	6	20	(11	9)	285	87	86	111	78	5	151	17	0	7	21	2	9	.300	.394	.489	.883

Year	Team	Lg	G	AB	H	2B	3B	HR	(Hm	Rd)	TB	R	RBI	RC	TBB	IBB	SO	HBP	SH	SF	SB	CS	GDP	Avg	OBP	Slg	OPS
																								BATTING	RUNNING	AVERAGES	
2010	Cle	AL	144	550	165	31	2	22	(8	14)	266	81	90	106	83	11	118	11	0	2	22	7	11	.300	.401	.484	.885
2011	Cle	AL	85	313	81	11	3	8	(7	1)	122	37	36	38	36	3	78	6	0	3	12	5	7	.259	.344	.390	.733
2012	Cle	AL	155	598	169	43	2	16	(8	8)	264	88	67	96	73	0	150	14	0	1	21	7	11	.283	.373	.441	.815
2013	Cin	NL	154	569	162	34	2	21	(10	11)	263	107	54	111	112	5	133	26	3	2	20	11	3	.285	.423	.462	.885
2014	Tex	AL	123	455	110	19	1	13	(5	8)	170	58	40	54	58	3	131	12	0	4	3	4	9	.242	.340	.374	.714
06	Sea	AL	4	11	1	1	0	0	(0	0)	2	0	0	0	0	0	4	1	0	0	0	0	1	.091	.167	.182	.348
06	Cle	AL	45	146	43	11	3	3	(2	1)	69	23	22	24	18	2	46	1	1	1	5	3	2	.295	.373	.473	.846
Postseason			1	3	1	0	0	1	(0	1)	4	2	1	1	0	0	1	0	0	0	0	0	0	.333	.500	1.333	1.833
10 ML YEARS			976	3577	1010	216	22	117	(61	56)	1621	555	467	615	507	34	898	93	4	25	108	43	58	.282	.383	.453	.836

Nick Christiani

Pitches: R **Bats:** R **Pos:** RP-10   **Ht:** 6'0" **Wt:** 190 **Born:** 7/17/1987 **Age:** 27

Year	Team	Lg	G	GS	CG	GF	IP	BFP	H	R	ER	HR	SH	SF	HB	TBB	IBB	SO	WP	Bk	W	L	Pct	Sh	Sv-Op	Hld	ERC	ERA
			HOW MUCH HE PITCHED						WHAT HE GAVE UP												THE RESULTS							
2010	Dayton	A	7	0	0	2	14.0	55	12	6	6	1	1	1	0	2	0	12	0	1	1	0	1.000	0	1--	-	2.22	3.86
2010	Lynbrg	A+	38	0	0	17	52.1	219	56	25	20	6	1	0	4	11	1	37	1	0	1	3	.250	0	4--	-	4.18	3.44
2010	Carlina	AA	2	0	0	2	2.0	10	4	1	1	0	1	1	0	0	0	1	0	0	0	0	-	0	0--	-	7.48	4.50
2011	Carlina	AA	20	0	0	6	25.2	96	16	5	5	0	0	2	0	5	0	22	1	0	2	0	1.000	0	3--	-	1.19	1.75
2011	Lsvlle	AAA	33	0	0	17	35.2	170	46	23	21	2	4	0	2	15	2	19	2	0	2	3	.400	0	7--	-	5.49	5.30
2012	Lsvlle	AAA	54	0	0	11	72.2	318	84	34	27	4	4	2	2	29	3	35	1	0	2	5	.286	0	1--	-	4.63	3.34
2013	Lsvlle	AAA	49	0	0	22	56.0	235	49	26	24	6	3	4	3	17	3	49	3	0	6	5	.545	0	3--	-	3.16	3.86
2014	Lsvlle	AAA	24	0	0	3	28.0	145	45	23	21	2	1	0	5	18	0	14	6	0	3	0	1.000	0	0--	-	9.69	6.75
2013	Cin	NL	3	0	0	1	4.0	16	2	1	1	1	0	1	1	2	0	1	0	0	0	0	-	0	0-0	0	3.91	2.25
2014	Cin	NL	10	0	0	4	13.0	57	12	8	8	2	0	1	0	6	3	8	0	0	0	1	.000	0	0-0	0	3.81	5.54
2 ML YEARS			13	0	0	5	17.0	73	14	9	9	3	0	2	1	8	3	9	0	0	0	1	.000	0	0-0	0	3.83	4.76

Tony Cingrani

Pitches: L **Bats:** L **Pos:** SP-11; RP-2
sin-GRAHN-ee   **Ht:** 6'4" **Wt:** 215 **Born:** 7/5/1989 **Age:** 25

Year	Team	Lg	G	GS	CG	GF	IP	BFP	H	R	ER	HR	SH	SF	HB	TBB	IBB	SO	WP	Bk	W	L	Pct	Sh	Sv-Op	Hld	ERC	ERA
			HOW MUCH HE PITCHED						WHAT HE GAVE UP												THE RESULTS							
2012	Cin	NL	3	0	0	1	5.0	22	4	1	1	1	0	0	0	2	0	9	0	0	0	0	-	0	0-0	0	3.38	1.80
2013	Cin	NL	23	18	0	0	104.2	420	72	37	34	14	4	4	2	43	1	120	4	0	7	4	.636	0	0-0	1	2.78	2.92
2014	Cin	NL	13	11	0	2	63.1	280	62	33	32	12	2	1	1	35	2	61	1	2	2	8	.200	0	0-0	0	5.29	4.55
3 ML YEARS			39	29	0	3	173.0	722	138	71	67	27	6	6	3	80	3	190	5	2	9	12	.429	0	0-0	1	3.66	3.49

Pedro Ciriaco

see-ree-AH-koe

Bats: R **Throws:** R **Pos:** 2B-13;PR-9;3B-3;DH-3;SS-2;PH-1   **Ht:** 6'0" **Wt:** 180 **Born:** 9/27/1985 **Age:** 29

Year	Team	Lg	G	AB	H	2B	3B	HR	(Hm	Rd)	TB	R	RBI	RC	TBB	IBB	SO	HBP	SH	SF	SB	CS	GDP	Avg	OBP	Slg	OPS
																					BATTING			RUNNING	AVERAGES		
2014	Omha*	AAA	62	205	62	17	3	2	(-	-)	91	27	24	30	6	0	35	1	1	2	6	0	1	.302	.322	.444	.766
2010	Pit	NL	8	6	3	1	1	0	(0	0)	6	3	1	3	0	0	3	0	0	0	0	0	0	.500	.500	1.000	1.500
2011	Pit	NL	23	33	10	2	1	0	(0	0)	14	4	6	5	1	0	6	0	0	0	2	1	1	.303	.324	.424	.748
2012	Bos	AL	76	259	76	15	2	2	(2	0)	101	33	19	32	8	2	47	0	5	0	16	3	2	.293	.315	.390	.705
2013	3 Tms		56	125	28	4	2	2	(2	0)	42	9	8	11	9	2	23	1	1	1	9	1	2	.224	.279	.336	.615
2014	KC	AL	25	47	10	2	0	0	(0	0)	12	7	2	3	0	0	9	1	1	0	4	0	2	.213	.229	.255	.484
13	Bos	AL	28	51	11	2	1	1	(1	0)	18	4	4	5	6	0	12	0	0	1	2	1	0	.216	.293	.353	.646
13	SD	NL	23	63	15	1	1	1	(1	0)	21	5	4	6	3	2	10	1	1	0	6	0	2	.238	.284	.333	.617
13	KC	AL	5	11	2	1	0	0	(0	0)	3	0	0	0	0	0	1	0	0	0	1	0	0	.182	.182	.273	.455
5 ML YEARS			188	470	127	24	6	4	(4	0)	175	56	36	54	18	4	88	2	7	1	31	5	7	.270	.299	.372	.672

Steve Cishek

Pitches: R **Bats:** R **Pos:** RP-67
SEE-sheck   **Ht:** 6'6" **Wt:** 215 **Born:** 6/18/1986 **Age:** 29

Year	Team	Lg	G	GS	CG	GF	IP	BFP	H	R	ER	HR	SH	SF	HB	TBB	IBB	SO	WP	Bk	W	L	Pct	Sh	Sv-Op	Hld	ERC	ERA
			HOW MUCH HE PITCHED						WHAT HE GAVE UP												THE RESULTS							
2010	Fla	NL	3	0	0	2	4.1	15	1	0	0	0	0	0	0	1	0	3	0	0	0	0	-	0	0-0	0	0.35	0.00
2011	Fla	NL	45	0	0	21	54.2	229	45	18	16	1	3	0	3	19	7	55	5	0	2	1	.667	0	3-3	2	2.38	2.63
2012	Mia	NL	68	0	0	36	63.2	275	54	26	19	3	3	2	6	29	6	68	1	1	5	2	.714	0	15-19	13	3.28	2.69
2013	Mia	NL	69	0	0	62	69.2	281	53	19	18	3	3	3	2	22	6	74	1	0	4	6	.400	0	34-36	1	2.15	2.33
2014	Mia	NL	67	0	0	55	65.1	275	58	26	23	3	5	3	1	21	2	84	1	0	4	5	.444	0	39-43	0	2.78	3.17
5 ML YEARS			252	0	0	176	257.2	1075	211	89	76	10	14	8	12	92	21	284	8	1	15	14	.517	0	91-101	16	2.58	2.65

Jose Cisnero

Pitches: R **Bats:** R **Pos:** RP-5
siss-NEHR-oh   **Ht:** 6'3" **Wt:** 245 **Born:** 4/11/1989 **Age:** 26

Year	Team	Lg	G	GS	CG	GF	IP	BFP	H	R	ER	HR	SH	SF	HB	TBB	IBB	SO	WP	Bk	W	L	Pct	Sh	Sv-Op	Hld	ERC	ERA
			HOW MUCH HE PITCHED						WHAT HE GAVE UP												THE RESULTS							
2010	Lxngtn	A	26	26	0	0	133.0	572	106	69	54	11	4	7	15	65	0	126	16	2	8	6	.571	0	0--	-	3.62	3.65
2011	Lancst	A+	27	27	0	0	123.1	559	115	88	83	13	4	4	8	75	0	152	16	3	8	11	.421	0	0--	-	4.78	6.06
2012	CpChr	AA	20	20	2	0	108.2	464	93	44	41	7	4	4	8	46	2	116	5	1	9	6	.600	1	0--	-	3.17	3.40
2012	OKCity	AAA	8	8	0	0	39.2	182	52	23	20	1	1	2	3	18	0	32	1	0	4	1	.800	0	0--	-	6.02	4.54
2013	OKCity	AAA	12	1	0	2	17.2	90	25	18	17	2	0	0	2	13	0	24	3	0	1	1	.500	0	0--	-	8.77	8.66

Year Team	Lg	G	GS	CG	GF	IP	BFP	H	R	ER	HR	SH	SF	HB	TBB	IBB	SO	WP	Bk	W	L	Pct	Sh	Sv-Op	Hld	ERC	ERA
		HOW MUCH HE PITCHED						**WHAT HE GAVE UP**												**THE RESULTS**							
2014 OKCity	AAA	6	0	0	0	11.0	44	5	3	3	1	0	0	0	4	0	18	0	0	0	0	-	0	0- -	-	1.29	2.45
2013 Hou	AL	28	0	0	11	43.2	198	49	23	20	5	0	2	1	22	5	41	1	2	2	2	.500	0	0-2	5	5.21	4.12
2014 Hou	AL	5	0	0	1	4.2	25	8	5	5	0	0	1	0	4	0	5	0	0	0	0	-	0	0-1	0	9.79	9.64
2 ML YEARS		33	0	0	12	48.1	223	57	28	25	5	0	3	1	26	5	46	1	2	2	2	.500	0	0-3	5	5.63	4.66

Preston Claiborne

Pitches: R Bats: R Pos: RP-18   Ht: 6'2" Wt: 225 Born: 1/21/1988 Age: 27

Year Team	Lg	G	GS	CG	GF	IP	BFP	H	R	ER	HR	SH	SF	HB	TBB	IBB	SO	WP	Bk	W	L	Pct	Sh	Sv-Op	Hld	ERC	ERA
		HOW MUCH HE PITCHED						**WHAT HE GAVE UP**												**THE RESULTS**							
2010 StIsInd	A-	19	0	0	7	23.2	94	20	9	6	0	3	0	0	8	0	30	2	0	1	2	.333	0	2- -	-	2.48	2.28
2010 Tampa	A+	5	0	0	0	7.1	32	7	3	3	1	0	1	1	4	0	6	1	0	0	1	.000	0	0- -	-	5.45	3.68
2011 Tampa	A+	38	0	0	19	81.0	347	73	33	28	8	5	4	7	30	4	75	3	0	3	7	.300	0	5- -	-	3.65	3.11
2012 Trntn	AA	30	0	0	10	48.2	199	33	17	12	1	3	2	1	24	3	49	1	2	2	2	.500	0	5- -	-	2.22	2.22
2012 S-WB	AAA	20	0	0	7	33.1	138	31	17	15	2	2	2	0	12	1	29	1	0	4	0	1.000	0	1- -	-	3.28	4.05
2013 S-WB	AAA	8	0	0	7	10.1	43	14	5	4	0	0	0	0	1	0	11	0	0	0	0	-	0	3- -	-	4.36	3.48
2013 Tampa	A+	1	1	0	0	1.0	4	0	0	0	0	0	0	0	1	0	1	0	0	0	0	-	0	0- -	-	0.95	0.00
2014 S-WB	AAA	15	0	0	5	20.1	93	20	10	8	0	3	1	0	11	2	20	0	0	0	1	.000	0	2- -	-	3.48	3.54
2014 Yanks1	R	2	2	0	0	3.0	14	5	5	5	1	0	0	0	0	0	1	0	0	0	1	.000	0	0- -	-	10.48	15.00
2014 Yanks2	R	2	1	0	0	2.2	13	3	1	1	0	0	0	1	1	0	2	0	0	0	0	-	0	0- -	-	5.24	3.38
2013 NYY	AL	44	0	0	12	51.0	214	51	23	23	7	2	0	2	14	4	42	2	0	0	2	.000	0	0-0	4	3.96	4.11
2014 NYY	AL	18	0	0	9	21.0	96	24	9	7	1	0	2	0	10	3	16	0	0	3	0	1.000	0	0-1	0	4.47	3.00
2 ML YEARS		62	0	0	21	71.1	310	75	32	30	8	2	2	2	24	7	58	2	0	3	2	.600	0	0-1	4	4.12	3.79

Matt Clark

Bats: L Throws: R Pos: 1B-9;PH-7   Ht: 6'5" Wt: 230 Born: 12/10/1986 Age: 28

Year Team	Lg	G	AB	H	2B	3B	HR	(Hm	Rd)	TB	R	RBI	RC	TBB	IBB	SO	HBP	SH	SF	SB	CS	GDP	Avg	OBP	Slg	OPS
		BATTING																		**RUNNING**			**AVERAGES**			
2010 SnAnt	AA	129	498	134	22	1	28	(-	-)	242	61	97	83	46	2	146	8	0	4	0	0	14	.269	.338	.486	.824
2011 Tucsn	AAA	129	462	135	24	1	23	(-	-)	230	71	83	86	58	0	116	1	1	13	0	2	7	.292	.363	.498	.861
2012 Tucsn	AAA	121	445	129	26	2	22	(-	-)	225	75	77	84	57	2	113	1	0	7	0	0	11	.290	.367	.506	.872
2013 Chnchi	Jap	132	407	97	14	0	25	(-	-)	186	56	70	64	49	1	130	1	1	4	0	0	7	.238	.328	.457	.785
2014 Bnghtn	AA	67	219	65	14	0	10	(-	-)	109	32	46	43	25	0	45	7	0	4	0	0	2	.297	.380	.498	.878
2014 Nashv	AAA	53	195	61	9	0	16	(-	-)	118	35	37	42	15	1	52	3	0	5	0	0	5	.313	.371	.605	.976
2014 Mil	NL	16	27	5	0	0	3	(3	0)	14	4	7	2	2	2	8	0	0	2	0	0	1	.185	.226	.519	.744

Alex Claudio

Pitches: L Bats: L Pos: RP-15   Ht: 6'3" Wt: 160 Born: 1/31/1992 Age: 23

Year Team	Lg	G	GS	CG	GF	IP	BFP	H	R	ER	HR	SH	SF	HB	TBB	IBB	SO	WP	Bk	W	L	Pct	Sh	Sv-Op	Hld	ERC	ERA
		HOW MUCH HE PITCHED						**WHAT HE GAVE UP**												**THE RESULTS**							
2010 Rngrs	R	12	1	0	5	15.0	69	19	11	11	1	0	1	1	6	2	13	0	1	0	1	.000	0	0- -	-	5.42	6.60
2011 Rngrs	R	15	0	0	4	25.1	104	20	8	6	1	1	1	3	9	1	29	0	1	4	0	1.000	0	1- -	-	2.82	2.13
2011 Spkane	A-	1	0	0	0	3.0	11	2	0	0	0	0	0	0	1	0	2	0	0	1	0	1.000	0	0- -	-	1.73	0.00
2012 Rngrs	R	14	3	0	4	45.1	169	36	11	9	1	0	1	1	5	0	54	2	2	4	0	1.000	0	1- -	-	1.71	1.79
2013 Hkry	AA	24	0	0	18	47.0	167	22	7	6	2	2	0	0	7	0	62	0	2	3	1	.750	0	11- -	-	0.83	1.15
2013 Frisco	AA	21	0	0	3	31.2	129	28	16	10	2	2	0	1	11	1	29	1	0	1	5	.167	0	0- -	-	3.17	2.84
2014 MrtlBh	A+	17	2	0	8	49.1	190	38	9	6	2	3	0	2	9	0	56	2	2	4	0	1.000	0	4- -	-	1.96	1.09
2014 Frisco	AA	8	6	0	0	37.1	148	31	17	9	1	5	1	1	2	0	22	1	1	2	2	.500	0	0- -	-	1.61	2.17
2014 RdRck	AAA	2	1	0	0	5.1	22	6	2	2	0	0	0	0	2	0	6	0	0	0	1	.000	0	0- -	-	4.24	3.38
2014 Tex	AL	15	0	0	5	12.1	54	14	4	4	0	0	0	0	4	0	14	0	1	0	0	-	0	0-0	0	3.79	2.92

Paul Clemens

Pitches: R Bats: R Pos: RP-13   Ht: 6'4" Wt: 200 Born: 2/14/1988 Age: 27

Year Team	Lg	G	GS	CG	GF	IP	BFP	H	R	ER	HR	SH	SF	HB	TBB	IBB	SO	WP	Bk	W	L	Pct	Sh	Sv-Op	Hld	ERC	ERA
		HOW MUCH HE PITCHED						**WHAT HE GAVE UP**												**THE RESULTS**							
2010 Rome	A	8	0	0	2	19.0	76	11	5	3	1	0	1	0	8	0	16	1	0	2	0	1.000	0	1- -	-	1.71	1.42
2010 MrtlBh	A+	27	8	0	9	75.2	334	83	46	31	5	1	1	2	28	4	65	10	0	0	4	.000	0	2- -	-	4.25	3.69
2011 Missi	AA	20	20	0	0	108.2	468	103	57	45	8	2	3	5	44	0	93	7	1	6	5	.545	0	0- -	-	3.80	3.73
2011 CpChr	AA	5	5	0	0	30.2	127	23	9	8	3	0	0	0	12	1	26	0	1	2	1	.667	0	0- -	-	2.61	2.35
2011 OKCity	AAA	1	1	0	0	4.2	24	4	8	8	1	1	1	0	6	0	6	1	1	0	1	.000	0	0- -	-	7.69	15.43
2012 OKCity	AAA	20	20	0	0	101.2	470	145	82	76	16	7	4	2	32	2	68	4	2	8	8	.500	0	0- -	-	6.82	6.73
2012 CpChr	AA	7	7	0	0	41.2	175	41	18	16	7	0	1	2	11	0	37	5	2	3	2	.600	0	0- -	-	4.12	3.46
2013 OKCity	AAA	6	6	0	0	30.0	131	27	19	15	1	1	2	0	11	1	16	2	0	3	2	.600	0	0- -	-	3.04	4.50
2014 OKCity	AAA	15	5	0	0	46.1	199	37	21	21	4	2	0	3	23	1	41	3	2	6	3	.667	0	1- -	-	3.44	4.08
2013 Hou	AL	35	5	0	8	73.1	323	82	48	44	16	0	5	2	26	1	49	2	0	4	7	.364	0	0-2	7	5.53	5.40
2014 Hou	AL	13	0	0	4	24.2	118	28	20	16	5	1	0	1	13	1	16	0	0	0	1	.000	0	0-0	1	6.03	5.84
2 ML YEARS		48	5	0	12	98.0	441	110	68	60	21	1	5	3	39	2	65	2	0	4	8	.333	0	0-2	8	5.66	5.51

Maikel Cleto

Pitches: R Bats: R Pos: RP-28   MY-kel CLAY-toe   Ht: 6'3" Wt: 250 Born: 5/1/1989 Age: 26

Year Team	Lg	G	GS	CG	GF	IP	BFP	H	R	ER	HR	SH	SF	HB	TBB	IBB	SO	WP	Bk	W	L	Pct	Sh	Sv-Op	Hld	ERC	ERA
		HOW MUCH HE PITCHED						**WHAT HE GAVE UP**												**THE RESULTS**							
2014 Charltt*	AAA	22	0	0	12	35.0	152	37	23	23	7	0	1	0	15	0	50	7	0	3	0	1.000	0	3- -	-	5.32	5.91
2011 StL	NL	3	0	0	2	4.1	25	7	6	6	2	0	0	0	4	0	6	0	0	0	0	-	0	0-0	0	13.10	12.46

Year Team	Lg	G	GS	CG	GF	IP	BFP	H	R	ER	HR	SH	SF	HB	TBB	IBB	SO	WP	Bk	W	L	Pct	Sh	Sv-Op	Hld	ERC	ERA
		HOW MUCH HE PITCHED						WHAT HE GAVE UP												THE RESULTS							
2012 StL	NL	9	0	0	2	9.0	41	13	7	7	4	0	0	1	2	0	15	0	0	0	0	-	0	0-0	1	9.58	7.00
2013 StL	NL	1	0	0	1	2.1	15	5	5	5	1	0	0	2	1	0	5	0	0	0	0	-	0	0-0	0	19.41	19.29
2014 CWS	AL	28	0	0	9	29.1	138	24	18	15	3	0	0	3	23	2	32	4	0	0	1	.000	0	0-0	4	4.73	4.60
4 ML YEARS		41	0	0	14	45.0	219	49	36	33	10	0	0	6	30	2	58	4	0	0	1	.000	0	0-0	5	7.06	6.60

Steve Clevenger

Bats: L **Throws:** R **Pos:** C-25;PH-11;1B-3;DH-1   CLEV-en-jer   **Ht:** 6'0" **Wt:** 195 **Born:** 4/5/1986 **Age:** 29

Year Team	Lg	G	AB	H	2B	3B	HR	(Hm	Rd)	TB	R	RBI	RC	TBB	IBB	SO	HBP	SH	SF	SB	CS	GDP	Avg	OBP	Slg	OPS
							BATTING													RUNNING			AVERAGES			
2014 Norfolk*	AAA	64	226	69	13	0	2	(-	-)	88	28	30	34	23	0	30	1	0	4	1	0	9	.305	.366	.389	.756
2014 Abrdn*	A-	2	6	4	2	0	1	(-	-)	9	2	5	4	1	0	0	0	0	0	0	0	0	.667	.714	1.500	2.214
2011 ChC	NL	2	4	1	1	0	0	(0	0)	2	1	0	0	0	0	1	0	0	0	0	0	0	.250	.400	.500	.900
2012 ChC	NL	69	199	40	12	0	1	(1	0)	55	16	16	12	16	0	39	0	0	0	0	1	10	.201	.260	.276	.537
2013 2 Tms		12	23	5	1	0	0	(0	0)	6	2	2	1	1	0	5	0	0	0	0	0	1	.217	.250	.261	.511
2014 Bal	AL	35	89	20	8	1	0	(0	0)	30	8	8	3	8	1	19	0	0	0	0	0	5	.225	.289	.337	.626
13 ChC	NL	8	8	1	0	0	0	(0	0)	1	1	0	0	1	0	3	0	0	0	0	0	0	.125	.222	.125	.347
13 Bal	AL	4	15	4	1	0	0	(0	0)	5	1	2	1	0	0	2	0	0	0	0	0	1	.267	.267	.333	.600
4 ML YEARS		118	315	66	22	1	1	(1	0)	93	27	26	16	25	1	63	1	0	0	0	1	16	.210	.270	.295	.565

Tyler Clippard

Pitches: R **Bats:** R **Pos:** RP-75   **Ht:** 6'3" **Wt:** 200 **Born:** 2/14/1985 **Age:** 30

Year Team	Lg	G	GS	CG	GF	IP	BFP	H	R	ER	HR	SH	SF	HB	TBB	IBB	SO	WP	Bk	W	L	Pct	Sh	Sv-Op	Hld	ERC	ERA
		HOW MUCH HE PITCHED						WHAT HE GAVE UP												THE RESULTS							
2007 NYY	AL	6	6	0	0	27.0	124	29	19	19	6	0	0	0	17	1	18	2	1	1	1	.750	0	0-0	0	6.37	6.33
2008 Was	NL	2	2	0	0	10.1	48	12	5	5	2	0	0	0	7	1	8	1	0	1	1	.500	0	0-0	0	6.90	4.35
2009 Was	NL	41	0	0	8	60.1	246	36	20	18	9	3	1	1	32	1	67	1	1	4	2	.667	0	0-1	3	2.79	2.69
2010 Was	NL	78	0	0	18	91.0	378	69	33	31	8	3	7	2	41	4	112	1	1	11	8	.579	0	1-11	23	2.91	3.07
2011 Was	NL	72	0	0	8	88.1	329	48	18	18	11	4	3	0	26	2	104	1	0	3	0	1.000	0	0-7	38	1.61	1.83
2012 Was	NL	74	0	0	42	72.2	307	55	32	30	7	3	4	2	29	2	84	5	0	2	6	.250	0	32-37	13	2.73	3.72
2013 Was	NL	72	0	0	6	71.0	275	37	19	19	9	2	1	4	24	1	73	2	0	6	3	.667	0	0-3	33	1.79	2.41
2014 Was	NL	75	0	0	6	70.1	278	47	22	17	5	2	2	1	23	1	82	0	0	7	4	.636	0	1-7	40	1.98	2.18
Postseason		3	0	0	0	3.0	12	1	1	1	1	0	0	0	1	0	5	0	0	0	0	-	0	0-0	2	1.55	3.00
8 ML YEARS		420	8	0	88	491.0	1985	333	168	157	57	17	18	10	199	13	548	13	3	37	25	.597	0	34-66	150	2.55	2.88

Alex Cobb

Pitches: R **Bats:** R **Pos:** SP-27   **Ht:** 6'3" **Wt:** 200 **Born:** 10/7/1987 **Age:** 27

Year Team	Lg	G	GS	CG	GF	IP	BFP	H	R	ER	HR	SH	SF	HB	TBB	IBB	SO	WP	Bk	W	L	Pct	Sh	Sv-Op	Hld	ERC	ERA
		HOW MUCH HE PITCHED						WHAT HE GAVE UP												THE RESULTS							
2014 Charltt*	A+	1	1	0	0	5.0	17	3	0	0	0	0	0	0	0	0	9	2	0	1	0	1.000	0	0--	0	0.80	0.00
2011 TB	AL	9	9	0	0	52.2	224	49	21	20	3	0	1	1	21	1	37	2	0	3	2	.600	0	0-0	0	3.44	3.42
2012 TB	AL	23	23	2	0	136.1	569	130	67	61	11	3	6	9	40	2	106	8	1	11	9	.550	1	0-0	0	3.56	4.03
2013 TB	AL	22	22	1	0	143.1	578	120	46	44	13	1	2	3	45	4	134	5	1	11	3	.786	0	0-0	0	2.92	2.76
2014 TB	AL	27	27	0	0	166.1	681	142	56	53	11	4	4	10	47	1	149	8	0	10	9	.526	0	0-0	0	2.87	2.87
Postseason		2	2	0	0	11.2	51	13	3	2	0	0	0	1	3	0	10	1	0	1	0	1.000	0	0-0	0	3.75	1.54
4 ML YEARS		81	81	3	0	498.2	2052	441	190	178	38	8	13	23	153	8	426	23	2	35	23	.603	1	0-0	0	3.13	3.21

Chris Coghlan

Bats: L **Throws:** R **Pos:** LF-101;PH-25;RF-4;DH-1   COGG-lan   **Ht:** 6'0" **Wt:** 195 **Born:** 6/18/1985 **Age:** 30

Year Team	Lg	G	AB	H	2B	3B	HR	(Hm	Rd)	TB	R	RBI	RC	TBB	IBB	SO	HBP	SH	SF	SB	CS	GDP	Avg	OBP	Slg	OPS
							BATTING													RUNNING			AVERAGES			
2014 Iowa*	AAA	24	70	17	5	0	0	(-	-)	22	9	6	11	13	0	18	3	1	1	6	1	0	.243	.379	.314	.694
2009 Fla	NL	128	504	162	31	6	9	(5	4)	232	84	47	91	53	2	77	4	3	1	8	5	3	.321	.390	.460	.850
2010 Fla	NL	91	358	96	20	3	5	(5	0)	137	60	28	43	33	1	84	4	3	2	10	3	3	.268	.335	.383	.718
2011 Fla	NL	65	269	62	20	1	5	(4	1)	99	33	22	23	22	3	49	4	1	2	7	6	3	.230	.296	.368	.664
2012 Mia	NL	39	93	13	1	0	1	(1	0)	17	10	10	2	9	1	12	0	1	2	0	2	4	.140	.212	.183	.394
2013 Mia	NL	70	195	50	10	3	1	(0	1)	69	10	10	20	17	1	43	1	0	1	2	0	2	.256	.318	.354	.672
2014 ChC	NL	125	385	109	28	5	9	(5	4)	174	50	41	59	39	2	81	3	3	2	7	4	5	.283	.352	.452	.804
6 ML YEARS		518	1804	492	110	18	30	(20	10)	728	247	158	238	173	10	346	16	11	10	34	20	20	.273	.340	.404	.744

Phil Coke

Pitches: L **Bats:** L **Pos:** RP-62   **Ht:** 6'1" **Wt:** 210 **Born:** 7/19/1982 **Age:** 32

Year Team	Lg	G	GS	CG	GF	IP	BFP	H	R	ER	HR	SH	SF	HB	TBB	IBB	SO	WP	Bk	W	L	Pct	Sh	Sv-Op	Hld	ERC	ERA
		HOW MUCH HE PITCHED						WHAT HE GAVE UP												THE RESULTS							
2008 NYY	AL	12	0	0	0	14.2	52	8	1	1	0	0	0	0	2	0	14	1	0	1	0	1.000	0	0-0	5	0.89	0.61
2009 NYY	AL	72	0	0	13	60.0	238	44	34	30	10	1	5	1	20	4	49	7	0	4	3	.571	0	2-7	21	2.84	4.50
2010 Det	AL	74	1	0	18	64.2	279	67	29	27	2	2	3	4	26	4	53	3	0	7	5	.583	0	2-4	17	4.00	3.76
2011 Det	AL	48	14	0	6	108.2	474	118	64	64	5	4	3	4	40	5	69	4	0	3	9	.250	0	1-2	8	4.13	4.47
2012 Det	AL	66	0	0	11	54.0	245	71	28	24	5	5	2	1	18	4	51	3	0	2	3	.400	0	1-3	20	5.56	4.00
2013 Det	AL	49	0	0	14	38.1	177	43	24	23	3	4	4	0	21	7	30	1	0	0	5	.000	0	1-3	4	4.81	5.40
2014 Det	AL	62	0	0	24	58.0	257	69	28	25	5	1	2	2	20	2	41	1	0	5	2	.714	0	1-2	5	4.96	3.88
Postseason		25	0	0	9	18.2	76	17	8	8	2	1	0	0	5	0	19	0	0	0	1	.000	0	3-3	2	3.16	3.86
7 ML YEARS		383	15	0	86	398.1	1722	420	208	184	30	17	19	12	147	26	307	20	0	22	27	.449	0	8-21	80	4.13	4.16

Chris Colabello

Bats: R **Throws:** R **Pos:** 1B-23;RF-19;DH-13;PH-8   CAHL-uh-bell-oh   **Ht:** 6'4" **Wt:** 220 **Born:** 10/24/1983 **Age:** 31

								BATTING												RUNNING			AVERAGES			
Year	Team	Lg	G	AB	H	2B	3B	HR	(Hm | Rd)	TB	R	RBI	RC	TBB	IBB	SO	HBP	SH	SF	SB	CS	GDP	Avg	OBP	Slg	OPS
2010	Wrcstr	IND	82	316	95	16	1	13	(- | -)	152	53	59	57	29	1	53	6	1	4	3	2	-	.301	.366	.481	.847
2011	Wrcstr	IND	92	365	127	32	0	20	(- | -)	219	75	79	86	39	2	39	3	0	5	1	3	-	.348	.410	.600	1.010
2012	NwBrit	AA	134	496	141	37	1	19	(- | -)	237	78	98	87	47	2	94	13	0	5	0	0	19	.284	.358	.478	.836
2013	Roch	AAA	89	338	119	25	0	24	(- | -)	216	58	76	87	43	3	89	5	0	5	2	1	11	.352	.427	.639	1.066
2014	Roch	AAA	61	213	57	13	0	10	(- | -)	100	28	38	34	21	2	55	2	0	2	0	0	8	.268	.336	.469	.806
2013	Min	AL	55	160	31	3	0	7	(1 | 6)	55	14	17	13	20	0	58	1	0	0	0	1	5	.194	.287	.344	.631
2014	Min	AL	59	205	47	13	0	6	(2 | 4)	78	17	39	21	14	1	66	1	0	0	0	2	2	.229	.282	.380	.662
	2 ML YEARS		114	365	78	16	0	13	(3 | 10)	133	31	56	34	34	1	124	2	0	0	0	3	7	.214	.284	.364	.649

Gerrit Cole

Pitches: R **Bats:** R **Pos:** SP-22   **Ht:** 6'4" **Wt:** 240 **Born:** 9/8/1990 **Age:** 24

					HOW MUCH HE PITCHED				WHAT HE GAVE UP											THE RESULTS						
Year	Team	Lg	G	GS	CG	GF	IP	BFP	H	R	ER	HR	SH	SF	HB	TBB	IBB	SO	WP	Bk	W	L	Pct	Sh	Sv-Op	Hld	ERC	ERA
2012	Bradtn	A+	13	13	0	0	67.0	273	53	24	19	5	0	4	3	21	0	69	3	1	5	1	.833	0	0- -	-	2.65	2.55
2012	Altna	AA	12	12	0	0	59.0	252	54	28	19	2	1	0	2	23	0	60	3	1	3	6	.333	0	0- -	-	3.23	2.90
2012	Indy	AAA	1	1	0	0	6.0	24	6	3	3	0	0	1	0	1	0	7	0	0	1	0	1.000	0	0- -	-	2.62	4.50
2013	Indy	AAA	12	12	0	0	68.0	268	44	23	22	4	1	3	4	28	0	47	4	1	5	3	.625	0	0- -	-	2.32	2.91
2014	Indy	AAA	4	4	0	0	22.1	91	21	5	5	1	0	0	1	5	0	16	0	0	3	1	.750	0	0- -	-	2.94	2.01
2013	Pit	NL	19	19	0	0	117.1	469	109	43	42	7	5	2	3	28	0	100	4	0	10	7	.588	0	0-0	0	3.02	3.22
2014	Pit	NL	22	22	0	0	138.0	571	127	58	56	11	10	0	9	40	1	138	9	1	11	5	.688	0	0-0	0	3.37	3.65
	Postseason		2	2	0	0	11.0	40	5	3	3	2	0	0	0	2	0	10	0	0	1	1	.500	0	0-0	0	1.24	2.45
	2 ML YEARS		41	41	0	0	255.1	1040	236	101	98	18	15	2	12	68	1	238	13	1	21	12	.636	0	0-0	0	3.21	3.45

Casey Coleman

Pitches: R **Bats:** L **Pos:** RP-10   **Ht:** 6'0" **Wt:** 185 **Born:** 7/3/1987 **Age:** 27

					HOW MUCH HE PITCHED				WHAT HE GAVE UP											THE RESULTS						
Year	Team	Lg	G	GS	CG	GF	IP	BFP	H	R	ER	HR	SH	SF	HB	TBB	IBB	SO	WP	Bk	W	L	Pct	Sh	Sv-Op	Hld	ERC	ERA
2014	Iowa*	AAA	1	0	0	0	1.0	9	4	5	4	0	0	0	0	2	0	1	0	0	0	0	-	0	0- -	-	32.97	36.00
2014	Omha*	AAA	34	0	0	13	67.0	269	51	19	16	4	2	0	1	26	2	53	10	0	5	1	.833	0	3- -	-	2.58	2.15
2010	ChC	NL	12	8	0	0	57.0	248	56	27	26	3	2	4	2	25	2	27	3	0	4	2	.667	0	0-0	0	3.87	4.11
2011	ChC	NL	19	17	0	1	84.1	398	102	62	60	10	6	2	4	46	3	75	3	1	3	9	.250	0	0-0	0	6.15	6.40
2012	ChC	NL	17	1	0	5	24.1	119	37	20	20	5	1	0	0	12	0	16	1	0	0	2	.000	0	0-1	0	8.62	7.40
2014	KC	AL	10	0	0	4	12.0	55	16	8	7	0	0	0	0	6	0	5	0	0	1	0	1.000	0	0-0	0	5.81	5.25
	4 ML YEARS		58	26	0	10	177.2	820	211	117	113	18	9	6	6	89	5	123	7	1	8	13	.381	0	0-1	0	5.68	5.72

Louis Coleman

Pitches: R **Bats:** R **Pos:** RP-31   **Ht:** 6'4" **Wt:** 205 **Born:** 4/4/1986 **Age:** 29

					HOW MUCH HE PITCHED				WHAT HE GAVE UP											THE RESULTS						
Year	Team	Lg	G	GS	CG	GF	IP	BFP	H	R	ER	HR	SH	SF	HB	TBB	IBB	SO	WP	Bk	W	L	Pct	Sh	Sv-Op	Hld	ERC	ERA
2014	Omha*	AAA	28	1	0	20	39.2	168	32	20	17	6	1	1	2	15	1	53	3	0	2	1	.667	0	7- -	-	3.37	3.86
2011	KC	AL	48	0	0	11	59.2	244	44	20	19	9	1	1	3	26	6	64	4	0	1	4	.200	0	1-2	11	3.23	2.87
2012	KC	AL	42	0	0	18	51.0	217	41	23	21	10	3	0	1	26	3	65	1	0	0	0	-	0	0-0	2	4.07	3.71
2013	KC	AL	27	0	0	8	29.2	110	19	2	2	1	1	0	1	6	1	32	1	0	3	0	1.000	0	0-0	4	1.45	0.61
2014	KC	AL	31	0	0	10	34.0	154	39	21	21	6	0	1	1	18	1	24	3	0	1	0	1.000	0	1-1	1	6.25	5.56
	4 ML YEARS		148	0	0	47	174.1	725	143	66	63	26	5	2	6	76	11	185	9	0	5	4	.556	0	2-3	18	3.65	3.25

Tim Collins

Pitches: L **Bats:** L **Pos:** RP-22   **Ht:** 5'7" **Wt:** 170 **Born:** 8/21/1989 **Age:** 25

					HOW MUCH HE PITCHED				WHAT HE GAVE UP											THE RESULTS						
Year	Team	Lg	G	GS	CG	GF	IP	BFP	H	R	ER	HR	SH	SF	HB	TBB	IBB	SO	WP	Bk	W	L	Pct	Sh	Sv-Op	Hld	ERC	ERA
2014	Omha*	AAA	23	0	0	12	42.1	166	26	13	13	6	0	1	2	16	1	56	3	0	2	1	.667	0	3- -	-	2.44	2.76
2011	KC	AL	68	0	0	18	67.0	295	52	28	27	5	3	1	2	48	2	60	3	0	4	4	.500	0	0-1	11	3.95	3.63
2012	KC	AL	72	0	0	9	69.2	295	55	29	26	8	3	1	2	34	8	93	3	0	5	4	.556	0	0-4	11	3.29	3.36
2013	KC	AL	66	0	0	8	53.1	233	49	26	21	3	2	2	0	28	1	52	0	0	3	6	.333	0	0-5	21	3.74	3.54
2014	KC	AL	22	0	0	9	21.0	90	18	9	9	2	3	1	2	11	0	15	1	0	0	3	.000	0	0-1	1	4.20	3.86
	4 ML YEARS		228	0	0	44	211.0	913	174	92	83	18	11	5	6	121	11	220	7	0	12	17	.414	0	0-11	44	3.70	3.54

Tyler Collins

Bats: L **Throws:** L **Pos:** PH-8;LF-5;RF-5;CF-1;DH-1;PR-1   **Ht:** 5'11" **Wt:** 215 **Born:** 6/6/1990 **Age:** 25

								BATTING												RUNNING			AVERAGES			
Year	Team	Lg	G	AB	H	2B	3B	HR	(Hm	Rd)	TB	R	RBI	RC	TBB	IBB	SO	HBP	SH	SF	SB	CS	GDP	Avg	OBP	Slg	OPS
2011	Tigers	R	1	3	1	1	0	0	(-	-)	2	2	1	1	2	0	0	0	0	0	0	0	0	.333	.600	.667	1.267
2011	Conn	A-	42	163	51	10	1	8	(-	-)	87	28	31	32	10	1	17	3	0	2	6	1	5	.313	.360	.534	.893
2012	Lkland	A+	126	473	137	35	5	7	(-	-)	203	68	66	82	58	2	64	6	0	5	20	3	6	.290	.371	.429	.800
2013	Erie	AA	129	466	112	29	0	21	(-	-)	204	67	79	66	51	1	122	8	0	5	4	5	3	.240	.323	.438	.760
2014	Toledo	AAA	121	468	123	17	2	18	(-	-)	198	63	62	70	49	2	116	4	0	5	12	4	6	.263	.335	.423	.758
2014	Det	AL	18	24	6	0	0	1	(0	1)	9	3	4	3	1	0	4	0	0	0	0	0	1	.250	.280	.375	.655

Josh Collmenter

Pitches: R **Bats:** R **Pos:** SP-28; RP-5 — COLE-men-ter — **Ht:** 6'4" **Wt:** 235 **Born:** 2/7/1986 **Age:** 29

			HOW MUCH HE PITCHED						WHAT HE GAVE UP										THE RESULTS							
Year Team	Lg	G	GS	CG	GF	IP	BFP	H	R	ER	HR	SH	SF	HB	TBB	IBB	SO	WP	Bk	W	L	Pct	Sh	Sv-Op	Hld	ERC	ERA
2011 Ari	NL	31	24	0	3	154.1	621	137	61	58	17	9	2	5	28	2	100	1	1	10	10	.500	0	0-0	0	2.82	3.38
2012 Ari	NL	28	11	0	7	90.1	375	92	39	37	13	5	0	0	22	2	80	1	0	5	3	.625	0	0-0	0	3.85	3.69
2013 Ari	NL	49	0	0	10	92.0	384	79	34	32	8	8	0	2	33	8	85	3	0	5	5	.500	0	0-1	5	3.01	3.13
2014 Ari	NL	33	28	1	2	179.1	719	163	75	69	18	8	5	4	39	2	115	2	0	11	9	.550	1	1-1	0	3.02	3.46
Postseason		1	1	0	0	7.0	26	2	1	1	1	0	0	1	2	0	6	0	0	1	0	1.000	0	0-0	0	1.18	1.29
4 ML YEARS		141	63	1	22	516.0	2099	471	209	196	56	30	7	11	122	14	380	7	1	31	27	.534	1	1-2	5	3.10	3.42

Alex Colome

Pitches: R **Bats:** R **Pos:** SP-3; RP-2 — CAHL-ah-may — **Ht:** 6'2" **Wt:** 210 **Born:** 12/31/1988 **Age:** 26

			HOW MUCH HE PITCHED						WHAT HE GAVE UP										THE RESULTS							
Year Team	Lg	G	GS	CG	GF	IP	BFP	H	R	ER	HR	SH	SF	HB	TBB	IBB	SO	WP	Bk	W	L	Pct	Sh	Sv-Op	Hld	ERC	ERA
2010 BG	A	22	22	1	0	114.0	475	98	59	50	14	3	3	4	45	0	118	4	2	6	6	.500	0	0--	-	3.62	3.95
2010 Charltt	A+	1	1	0	0	4.0	17	5	1	1	0	1	0	1	0	0	8	0	0	0	0	-	0	0--	-	4.32	2.25
2011 Charltt	A+	19	19	1	0	105.2	427	78	45	43	8	8	4	6	44	0	92	9	2	9	5	.643	0	0--	-	2.88	3.66
2011 Mont	AA	9	9	1	0	52.0	222	41	25	24	5	0	1	6	28	1	31	8	0	3	4	.429	1	0--	-	3.91	4.15
2012 Mont	AA	14	14	1	0	75.0	313	69	30	29	2	2	3	0	34	0	75	6	3	8	3	.727	0	0--	-	3.43	3.48
2012 Drham	AAA	3	3	0	0	16.2	68	12	6	6	1	0	0	1	9	0	15	2	0	1	0	1.000	0	0--	-	3.19	3.24
2013 Drham	AAA	14	14	0	0	70.1	303	63	30	24	5	0	3	4	29	0	72	5	0	4	6	.400	0	0--	-	3.54	3.07
2014 Charltt	A+	3	3	0	0	11.0	44	7	2	2	0	0	0	0	5	0	10	2	0	1	0	1.000	0	0--	-	1.81	1.64
2014 Drham	AAA	15	15	0	0	86.0	369	84	40	36	2	4	6	7	30	0	73	5	1	7	6	.538	0	0--	-	3.54	3.77
2013 TB	AL	3	3	0	0	16.0	71	14	8	4	2	0	0	1	9	0	12	1	0	1	1	.500	0	0-0	0	4.41	2.25
2014 TB	AL	5	3	0	1	23.2	97	19	7	7	1	0	1	0	10	0	13	3	0	2	0	1.000	0	0-0	0	2.77	2.66
2 ML YEARS		8	6	0	1	39.2	168	33	15	11	3	0	1	1	19	0	25	4	0	3	1	.750	0	0-0	0	3.40	2.50

Bartolo Colon

Pitches: R **Bats:** R **Pos:** SP-31 — co-LONE — **Ht:** 5'11" **Wt:** 285 **Born:** 5/24/1973 **Age:** 42

			HOW MUCH HE PITCHED						WHAT HE GAVE UP										THE RESULTS							
Year Team	Lg	G	GS	CG	GF	IP	BFP	H	R	ER	HR	SH	SF	HB	TBB	IBB	SO	WP	Bk	W	L	Pct	Sh	Sv-Op	Hld	ERC	ERA
1997 Cle	AL	19	17	1	0	94.0	427	107	66	59	12	4	1	3	45	1	66	5	0	4	7	.364	0	0-0	0	5.53	5.65
1998 Cle	AL	31	31	6	0	204.0	883	205	91	84	15	10	2	3	79	5	158	4	0	14	9	.609	2	0-0	0	3.87	3.71
1999 Cle	AL	32	32	1	0	205.0	858	185	97	90	24	5	4	7	76	5	161	4	0	18	5	.783	1	0-0	0	3.68	3.95
2000 Cle	AL	30	30	2	0	188.0	807	163	86	81	21	2	3	4	98	4	212	4	0	15	8	.652	1	0-0	0	3.97	3.88
2001 Cle	AL	34	34	1	0	222.1	947	220	106	101	26	8	4	2	90	2	201	4	1	14	12	.538	0	0-0	0	4.24	4.09
2002 2 Tms		33	33	8	0	233.1	966	219	85	76	20	19	6	2	70	5	149	4	0	20	8	.714	3	0-0	0	3.29	2.93
2003 CWS	AL	34	34	9	0	242.0	984	223	107	104	30	5	8	5	67	3	173	8	3	15	13	.536	0	0-0	0	3.47	3.87
2004 LAA	AL	34	34	0	0	208.1	897	215	122	116	38	5	8	3	71	1	158	1	0	18	12	.600	0	0-0	0	4.64	5.01
2005 LAA	AL	33	33	2	0	222.2	906	215	93	86	26	9	4	3	43	0	157	2	1	21	8	.724	0	0-0	0	3.28	3.48
2006 LAA	AL	10	10	1	0	56.1	251	71	39	32	11	4	1	3	11	0	31	1	0	5	1	.167	0	0-0	0	5.61	5.11
2007 LAA	AL	19	18	0	0	99.1	453	132	74	70	15	4	3	5	29	1	76	1	0	6	8	.429	0	0-0	1	6.17	6.34
2008 Bos	AL	7	7	0	0	39.0	173	44	23	17	5	3	2	2	10	0	27	0	0	4	2	.667	0	0-0	0	4.53	3.92
2009 CWS	AL	12	12	0	0	62.1	276	69	42	29	13	4	3	2	21	3	38	1	0	3	6	.333	0	0-0	0	5.22	4.19
2011 NYY	AL	29	26	1	0	164.1	694	172	85	73	21	2	6	3	40	3	135	0	0	8	10	.444	1	0-0	0	3.95	4.00
2012 Oak	AL	24	24	0	0	152.1	636	161	62	58	17	3	4	1	23	3	91	0	0	10	9	.526	0	0-0	0	3.45	3.43
2013 Oak	AL	30	30	3	0	190.1	769	193	60	56	14	3	6	0	29	0	117	1	0	18	6	.750	3	0-0	0	3.07	2.65
2014 NYM	NL	31	31	0	0	202.1	846	218	97	92	22	8	4	5	30	3	151	2	0	15	13	.536	0	0-0	0	3.63	4.09
02 Cle	AL	16	16	4	0	116.1	467	104	37	33	11	6	3	2	31	1	75	3	0	10	4	.714	2	0-0	0	3.09	2.55
02 Mon	NL	17	17	4	0	117.0	499	115	48	43	9	13	3	0	39	4	74	1	0	10	4	.714	1	0-0	0	3.48	3.31
Postseason		10	10	1	0	58.1	241	59	24	24	5	1	1	2	22	1	45	0	0	2	4	.333	0	0-0	0	4.28	3.70
17 ML YEARS		442	436	35	0	2786.0	11773	2812	1335	1224	330	98	69	53	832	39	2101	42	5	204	141	.591	12	0-0	1	3.92	3.95

Christian Colon

Bats: R **Throws:** R **Pos:** 2B-11;3B-5;PH-4;PR-3;SS-2;DH-1 — co-LONE — **Ht:** 5'10" **Wt:** 190 **Born:** 5/14/1989 **Age:** 26

			BATTING																RUNNING			AVERAGES			
Year Team	Lg	G	AB	H	2B	3B	HR	(Hm Rd)	TB	R	RBI	RC	TBB	IBB	SO	HBP	SH	SF	SB	CS	GDP	Avg	OBP	Slg	OPS
2010 Wilmg	A+	60	245	68	12	2	3	(- -)	93	38	30	31	13	1	33	6	4	3	2	4	7	.278	.326	.380	.705
2011 NWArk	AA	127	491	126	14	2	8	(- -)	168	69	61	60	46	5	51	6	21	4	17	7	17	.257	.325	.342	.668
2012 NWArk	AA	73	273	79	9	2	5	(- -)	107	33	27	42	31	0	27	2	7	2	12	6	5	.289	.364	.392	.756
2012 Royals	R	7	22	8	3	0	0	(- -)	11	6	4	5	4	0	0	1	0	0	1	1	0	.364	.481	.500	.981
2012 Omha	AAA	5	17	7	1	0	1	(- -)	11	4	5	4	2	0	1	0	0	2	0	0	0	.412	.429	.647	1.076
2013 Omha	AAA	131	512	140	12	3	12	(- -)	194	72	58	70	41	1	57	7	15	2	15	4	16	.273	.335	.379	.713
2014 Omha	AAA	86	344	107	18	0	8	(- -)	149	55	47	58	30	0	29	3	6	5	15	4	9	.311	.366	.433	.800
2014 NWArk	AA	2	8	2	1	0	0	(- -)	3	1	0	1	1	0	2	0	0	0	1	0	0	.250	.333	.375	.708
2014 KC	AL	21	45	15	5	1	0	(0 0)	22	8	6	9	3	0	4	0	1	0	2	0	1	.333	.375	.489	.864

Tyler Colvin

Bats: L **Throws:** L **Pos:** LF-43;PH-15;CF-3 — **Ht:** 6'3" **Wt:** 210 **Born:** 9/5/1985 **Age:** 29

			BATTING																RUNNING			AVERAGES			
Year Team	Lg	G	AB	H	2B	3B	HR	(Hm Rd)	TB	R	RBI	RC	TBB	IBB	SO	HBP	SH	SF	SB	CS	GDP	Avg	OBP	Slg	OPS
2014 Fresno*	AAA	50	163	37	9	2	2	(- -)	56	21	18	16	11	1	43	1	0	1	5	0	6	.227	.278	.344	.622
2009 ChC	NL	6	17	3	0	0	0	(0 0)	3	1	2	1	2	0	5	0	0	1	0	0	0	.176	.250	.176	.426
2010 ChC	NL	135	358	91	18	5	20	(9 11)	179	60	56	46	30	2	100	3	1	2	6	1	6	.254	.316	.500	.816
2011 ChC	NL	80	206	31	8	3	6	(2 4)	63	17	20	9	14	3	58	0	1	1	0	0	2	.150	.204	.306	.509

Year Team	Lg	G	AB	H	2B	3B	HR	(Hm	Rd)	TB	R	RBI	RC	TBB	IBB	SO	HBP	SH	SF	SB	CS	GDP	Avg	OBP	Slg	OPS
2012 Col	NL	136	420	122	27	10	18	(11	7)	223	62	72	73	21	0	117	2	2	1	7	3	6	.290	.327	.531	.858
2013 Col	NL	27	75	12	0	0	3	(3	0)	21	8	10	5	3	1	27	0	0	0	0	0	2	.160	.192	.280	.472
2014 SF	NL	57	139	31	10	3	2	(1	1)	53	16	18	10	8	0	45	1	0	1	1	0	3	.223	.268	.381	.650
6 ML YEARS		441	1215	290	63	21	49	(26	23)	542	164	178	144	78	6	352	6	4	6	14	4	19	.239	.287	.446	.733

Hank Conger

Bats: B **Throws:** R **Pos:** C-79;PH-2   KONG-gerr   **Ht:** 6'2" **Wt:** 220 **Born:** 1/29/1988 **Age:** 27

Year Team	Lg	G	AB	H	2B	3B	HR	(Hm	Rd)	TB	R	RBI	RC	TBB	IBB	SO	HBP	SH	SF	SB	CS	GDP	Avg	OBP	Slg	OPS
2010 LAA	AL	13	29	5	1	1	0	(0	0)	8	2	5	3	5	0	9	0	0	0	0	0	1	.172	.294	.276	.570
2011 LAA	AL	59	177	37	8	0	6	(2	4)	63	14	19	18	17	2	37	1	2	0	0	0	2	.209	.282	.356	.638
2012 LAA	AL	7	18	3	0	0	0	(0	0)	3	0	1	1	1	0	1	1	1	1	0	0	1	.167	.238	.167	.405
2013 LAA	AL	92	233	58	13	1	7	(3	4)	94	23	21	24	17	2	61	4	0	1	0	1	6	.249	.310	.403	.713
2014 LAA	AL	80	231	51	12	0	4	(3	1)	75	24	25	25	22	0	57	2	4	1	0	2	6	.221	.293	.325	.618
5 ML YEARS		251	688	154	34	2	17	(8	9)	243	63	71	71	62	4	164	8	7	3	0	3	16	.224	.294	.353	.648

Brooks Conrad

Bats: B **Throws:** R **Pos:** 2B-10;PH-3   **Ht:** 5'10" **Wt:** 190 **Born:** 1/16/1980 **Age:** 35

Year Team	Lg	G	AB	H	2B	3B	HR	(Hm	Rd)	TB	R	RBI	RC	TBB	IBB	SO	HBP	SH	SF	SB	CS	GDP	Avg	OBP	Slg	OPS
2014 ElPaso*	AAA	78	295	82	18	1	18	(-	-)	156	52	57	55	33	4	79	2	2	5	0	2	6	.278	.349	.529	.878
2008 Oak	AL	6	19	3	1	0	0	(0	0)	4	0	2	1	0	0	9	0	0	0	0	0	1	.158	.158	.211	.368
2009 Atl	NL	30	54	11	1	2	2	(0	2)	22	7	8	6	3	1	14	1	0	0	0	0	1	.204	.259	.407	.666
2010 Atl	NL	103	156	39	11	1	8	(4	4)	76	31	33	32	16	0	45	1	4	0	5	1	0	.250	.324	.487	.811
2011 Atl	NL	92	103	23	5	0	4	(2	2)	40	11	13	12	15	2	41	1	2	1	2	0	0	.223	.325	.388	.713
2012 2 Tms		49	98	13	5	0	4	(2	2)	30	6	15	5	6	0	43	0	0	1	0	0	2	.133	.181	.306	.487
2014 SD	NL	13	30	3	1	0	1	(1	0)	7	2	2	2	3	0	14	0	0	1	0	0	0	.100	.176	.233	.410
12 Mil	NL	25	40	3	0	0	2	(2	0)	9	2	6	0	3	0	16	0	0	1	0	0	0	.075	.136	.225	.361
12 TB	AL	24	58	10	5	0	2	(0	2)	21	4	9	5	3	0	27	0	0	0	0	0	2	.172	.213	.362	.575
Postseason		4	11	1	0	0	0	(0	0)	1	0	0	0	0	0	4	0	1	0	0	0	0	.091	.091	.091	.182
6 ML YEARS		293	460	92	24	3	19	(9	10)	179	57	73	56	43	3	166	3	6	3	7	1	4	.200	.271	.389	.660

Jose Constanza

Bats: L **Throws:** L **Pos:** PR-6;PH-3;LF-2;RF-1   cohn-STAHN-zah   **Ht:** 5'9" **Wt:** 185 **Born:** 9/1/1983 **Age:** 31

Year Team	Lg	G	AB	H	2B	3B	HR	(Hm	Rd)	TB	R	RBI	RC	TBB	IBB	SO	HBP	SH	SF	SB	CS	GDP	Avg	OBP	Slg	OPS
2014 Gwnntt*	AAA	111	447	131	10	2	0	(-	-)	145	65	36	56	37	0	49	0	9	4	30	10	5	.293	.344	.324	.669
2011 Atl	NL	42	109	33	1	1	2	(1	1)	42	21	10	12	6	0	14	0	4	0	7	4	1	.303	.339	.385	.724
2012 Atl	NL	37	76	19	2	0	0	(0	0)	21	8	4	9	8	2	21	0	2	0	5	2	0	.250	.321	.276	.598
2013 Atl	NL	21	31	8	0	0	0	(0	0)	8	2	3	3	0	0	5	0	0	0	0	3	1	.258	.258	.258	.516
2014 Atl	NL	12	4	0	0	0	0	(0	0)	0	1	0	0	0	0	1	0	0	0	0	0	0	.000	.000	.000	.000
Postseason		3	2	2	0	1	0	(0	0)	4	1	1	2	0	0	0	0	0	0	0	0	0	1.000	1.000	2.000	3.000
4 ML YEARS		112	220	60	3	1	2	(1	1)	71	32	17	24	14	2	41	0	6	0	12	9	2	.273	.316	.323	.639

Carlos Contreras

Pitches: R **Bats:** R **Pos:** RP-17   conn-TRAIR-us   **Ht:** 5'11" **Wt:** 205 **Born:** 1/8/1991 **Age:** 24

Year Team	Lg	G	GS	CG	GF	IP	BFP	H	R	ER	HR	SH	SF	HB	TBB	IBB	SO	WP	Bk	W	L	Pct	Sh	Sv-Op	Hld	ERC	ERA
2010 Reds	R	10	6	0	3	37.2	173	44	29	27	8	2	1	1	16	0	30	5	0	2	4	.333	0	2- -	-	6.03	6.45
2011 Billings	R+	18	0	0	2	36.0	165	35	20	20	5	1	1	5	23	1	38	5	0	2	1	.667	0	0- -	-	5.78	5.00
2012 Dayton	A	40	0	0	26	50.2	205	29	22	18	6	0	0	3	19	1	51	3	0	0	1	.000	0	16- -	-	2.04	3.20
2012 Bkrsfld	A+	9	0	0	7	10.0	47	9	5	3	1	1	1	0	5	0	12	1	0	1	0	1.000	0	4- -	-	3.54	2.70
2013 Bkrsfld	A+	18	18	0	0	90.0	377	70	43	38	9	3	3	4	41	1	96	7	3	5	7	.417	0	0- -	-	3.25	3.80
2013 Pnscla	AA	8	8	0	0	42.1	183	36	13	13	2	5	2	4	21	2	26	2	0	3	2	.600	0	0- -	-	3.55	2.76
2014 Pnscla	AA	9	3	0	3	20.0	89	15	7	6	0	0	0	1	11	0	27	3	0	2	1	.667	0	0- -	-	2.64	2.70
2014 Cin	NL	17	0	0	8	19.1	94	19	16	14	2	0	1	0	17	0	19	3	1	0	1	.000	0	0-1	0	5.79	6.52

Ryan Cook

Pitches: R **Bats:** R **Pos:** RP-54   **Ht:** 6'2" **Wt:** 215 **Born:** 6/30/1987 **Age:** 28

Year Team	Lg	G	GS	CG	GF	IP	BFP	H	R	ER	HR	SH	SF	HB	TBB	IBB	SO	WP	Bk	W	L	Pct	Sh	Sv-Op	Hld	ERC	ERA
2014 Stcktn*	A+	3	0	0	0	2.2	12	2	2	2	1	0	0	0	2	0	2	0	0	0	0	-	0	0- -	-	5.96	6.75
2011 Ari	NL	12	0	0	5	7.2	41	11	6	6	0	0	0	0	8	0	7	1	1	0	1	.000	0	0-0	1	8.56	7.04
2012 Oak	AL	71	0	0	23	73.1	288	42	18	17	4	3	1	4	27	4	80	4	0	6	2	.750	0	14-21	21	1.68	2.09
2013 Oak	AL	71	0	0	13	67.1	294	62	22	19	2	0	4	4	25	1	67	7	0	6	4	.600	0	2-9	23	3.16	2.54
2014 Oak	AL	54	0	0	15	50.0	202	32	19	19	3	2	2	2	22	1	50	3	0	1	3	.250	0	1-3	7	2.23	3.42
Postseason		5	0	0	4	4.0	20	5	5	5	0	1	0	1	2	0	5	1	0	1	0	1.000	0	0-1	1	5.98	11.25
4 ML YEARS		208	0	0	56	198.1	825	147	65	61	9	5	7	10	82	6	204	15	1	13	10	.565	0	17-33	52	2.52	2.77

Patrick Corbin

Pitches: L Bats: L Pos: P   Ht: 6'2" Wt: 185 Born: 7/19/1989 Age: 25

Year	Team	Lg	G	GS	CG	GF	IP	BFP	H	R	ER	HR	SH	SF	HB	TBB	IBB	SO	WP	Bk	W	L	Pct	Sh	Sv-Op	Hld	ERC	ERA
2010	CRpds	A	9	9	0	0	58.1	230	52	28	25	2	2	3	3	10	0	42	4	1	8	0	1.000	0	0- -	-	2.50	3.86
2010	RCuca	A+	11	11	0	0	60.1	253	57	29	26	7	1	2	1	18	0	64	6	0	5	3	.625	0	0- -	-	3.54	3.88
2010	Visalia	A+	8	8	0	0	26.0	99	17	4	4	1	0	0	0	9	0	30	0	0	0	1	.000	0	0- -	-	1.85	1.38
2011	Mobile	AA	26	26	1	0	160.1	688	172	78	75	15	7	3	12	40	0	142	16	1	9	8	.529	1	0- -	-	4.15	4.21
2012	Mobile	AA	4	4	0	0	27.0	106	22	5	5	0	3	0	1	8	0	25	2	0	2	0	1.000	0	0- -	-	2.33	1.67
2012	Reno	AAA	9	9	0	0	52.1	227	57	24	20	4	1	2	1	15	1	55	1	0	3	2	.600	0	0- -	-	3.97	3.44
2012	Ari	NL	22	17	0	3	107.0	454	141	56	54	14	2	5	4	25	2	86	1	0	6	8	.429	0	1-1	0	4.31	4.54
2013	Ari	NL	32	32	3	0	208.1	860	189	81	79	19	8	1	9	54	1	178	13	0	14	8	.636	0	0-0	0	3.14	3.41
	2 ML YEARS		54	49	3	3	315.1	1314	306	137	133	33	10	6	13	79	3	264	14	0	20	16	.556	0	1-1	0	3.52	3.80

Daniel Corcino

Pitches: R Bats: R Pos: SP-3; RP-2   cor-SEE-no   Ht: 5'11" Wt: 210 Born: 8/26/1990 Age: 24

Year	Team	Lg	G	GS	CG	GF	IP	BFP	H	R	ER	HR	SH	SF	HB	TBB	IBB	SO	WP	Bk	W	L	Pct	Sh	Sv-Op	Hld	ERC	ERA
2010	Billings	R+	9	9	0	0	39.2	172	38	18	15	2	2	1	3	17	0	31	3	0	1	3	.250	0	0- -	-	3.92	3.40
2010	Dayton	A	6	6	0	0	31.1	142	31	16	15	1	0	2	3	15	0	29	4	0	1	1	.500	0	0- -	-	4.11	4.31
2011	Dayton	A	26	26	1	0	139.1	584	128	61	53	10	3	1	8	34	0	156	5	1	11	7	.611	0	0- -	-	3.03	3.42
2012	Pnscla	AA	26	26	0	0	143.1	592	111	61	48	9	3	3	6	65	0	126	11	1	8	8	.500	0	0- -	-	3.03	3.01
2013	Lsvlle	AAA	28	23	0	1	129.0	594	141	95	84	17	1	4	11	73	0	90	7	0	7	14	.333	0	0- -	-	5.94	5.86
2014	Pnscla	AA	26	25	0	0	143.2	629	123	73	66	16	6	3	16	70	1	113	3	0	10	11	.476	0	0- -	-	4.10	4.13
2014	Lsvlle	AAA	1	1	0	0	5.0	21	3	4	4	3	0	0	0	4	0	6	0	0	0	1	.000	0	0- -	-	7.19	7.20
2014	Cin	NL	5	3	0	1	18.2	80	13	9	9	2	0	0	1	10	0	15	6	0	0	2	.000	0	0-0	0	3.14	4.34

Erik Cordier

Pitches: R Bats: R Pos: RP-7   cor-dee-YAY   Ht: 6'4" Wt: 250 Born: 2/25/1986 Age: 29

Year	Team	Lg	G	GS	CG	GF	IP	BFP	H	R	ER	HR	SH	SF	HB	TBB	IBB	SO	WP	Bk	W	L	Pct	Sh	Sv-Op	Hld	ERC	ERA
2010	Missi	AA	25	21	0	1	135.2	578	116	61	56	3	7	5	5	69	3	113	10	0	11	7	.611	0	0- -	-	3.29	3.71
2010	Gwnntt	AAA	2	2	0	0	8.0	37	7	5	5	0	0	0	0	7	0	4	0	0	1	1	.500	0	0- -	-	4.44	5.63
2011	Missi	AA	1	1	0	0	5.0	22	6	3	3	1	0	0	1	0	0	4	1	0	1	0	1.000	0	0- -	-	5.00	5.40
2011	Gwnntt	AAA	19	19	0	0	86.0	392	88	55	49	9	2	3	7	51	1	61	10	0	5	8	.385	0	0- -	-	5.37	5.13
2012	Gwnntt	AAA	8	4	0	0	24.2	113	27	15	12	1	0	0	1	21	0	15	4	0	1	1	.500	0	0- -	-	6.55	4.38
2012	Braves	R	4	1	0	0	3.2	16	0	0	0	0	0	0	0	6	0	6	1	0	0	0	-	0	0- -	-	3.65	0.00
2012	Missi	AA	5	0	0	1	4.0	26	8	9	9	0	0	1	1	5	0	6	3	0	0	2	.000	0	0- -	-	14.34	20.25
2013	Indy	AAA	44	0	0	11	53.0	232	51	29	27	3	0	3	2	28	1	65	4	0	4	2	.667	0	4- -	-	4.21	4.58
2014	Fresno	AAA	47	0	0	23	52.2	229	40	22	21	4	4	0	3	31	1	68	11	0	4	3	.571	0	3- -	-	3.47	3.59
2014	SF	NL	7	0	0	2	6.0	28	5	4	1	0	0	0	3	2	0	9	1	0	0	0	-	0	0-0	0	3.93	1.50

Carlos Corporan

Bats: B Throws: R Pos: C-54;DH-1;PH-1   CORE-poor-run   Ht: 6'2" Wt: 245 Born: 1/7/1984 Age: 31

			BATTING												RUNNING			AVERAGES			
Year	Team	Lg	G	AB	H	2B	3B	HR	(Hm Rd)	TB	R	RBI	RC	TBB	IBB	SO	HBP	SH	SF	SB	CS	GDP	Avg	OBP	Slg	OPS
2009	Mil	NL	1	1	1	0	0	0	(0 0)	1	1	0	1	0	0	0	0	0	0	0	0	0	1.000	1.000	1.000	2.000
2011	Hou	NL	52	154	29	8	1	0	(0 0)	39	9	11	11	10	4	49	4	3	2	0	0	5	.188	.253	.253	.506
2012	Hou	NL	27	78	21	2	0	4	(3 1)	35	5	13	7	4	0	19	1	1	1	0	1	2	.269	.310	.449	.758
2013	Hou	AL	64	191	43	5	0	7	(4 3)	69	16	20	15	10	1	60	7	1	1	0	0	3	.225	.287	.361	.648
2014	Hou	AL	55	170	40	6	0	6	(5 1)	64	22	19	19	14	0	37	3	1	2	0	0	3	.235	.302	.376	.678
	5 ML YEARS		199	594	134	21	1	17	(12 5)	208	53	63	53	38	5	165	15	6	6	0	1	13	.226	.286	.350	.637

Kevin Correia

Pitches: R Bats: R Pos: SP-26; RP-6   kore-AY-ah   Ht: 6'3" Wt: 200 Born: 8/24/1980 Age: 34

Year	Team	Lg	G	GS	CG	GF	IP	BFP	H	R	ER	HR	SH	SF	HB	TBB	IBB	SO	WP	Bk	W	L	Pct	Sh	Sv-Op	Hld	ERC	ERA
2003	SF	NL	10	7	0	1	39.1	173	41	16	16	6	1	1	4	18	1	28	2	0	3	1	.750	0	0-0	0	5.46	3.66
2004	SF	NL	12	1	0	5	19.0	92	25	20	17	3	3	3	1	10	0	14	0	0	0	1	.000	0	0-0	0	7.12	8.05
2005	SF	NL	16	11	0	1	58.1	264	61	31	30	12	5	1	4	31	2	44	2	0	2	5	.286	0	0-0	0	5.94	4.63
2006	SF	NL	48	0	0	9	69.2	295	64	27	27	5	1	4	3	22	0	57	0	0	2	0	1.000	0	0-1	10	3.25	3.49
2007	SF	NL	59	8	0	9	101.2	437	94	39	39	9	4	3	2	40	7	80	1	1	4	7	.364	0	0-3	12	3.48	3.45
2008	SF	NL	25	19	0	2	110.0	514	141	80	74	15	3	5	4	47	3	66	5	0	3	8	.273	0	0-0	0	6.19	6.05
2009	SD	NL	33	33	1	0	198.0	830	194	92	86	17	9	3	4	64	0	142	5	1	12	11	.522	1	0-0	0	3.64	3.91
2010	SD	NL	28	26	0	0	145.0	641	152	89	87	20	6	5	5	64	6	115	3	0	10	10	.500	0	0-0	0	4.87	5.40
2011	Pit	NL	27	26	1	1	154.0	660	175	90	82	24	7	2	4	39	0	77	3	1	12	11	.522	0	0-0	0	4.74	4.79
2012	Pit	NL	32	28	0	0	171.0	728	176	89	80	20	14	7	3	46	2	89	2	0	12	11	.522	0	0-0	0	3.86	4.21
2013	Min	AL	31	31	0	0	185.1	792	218	89	86	24	6	5	2	45	1	101	2	0	9	13	.409	0	0-0	0	4.77	4.18
2014	2 Tms		32	26	0	3	154.0	687	191	104	93	20	2	6	3	40	2	79	7	1	7	17	.292	0	0-0	0	5.19	5.44
14	Min	AL	23	23	0	0	129.1	572	157	76	71	13	1	5	3	32	1	61	3	1	5	13	.278	0	0-0	0	4.80	4.94
14	LAD	NL	9	3	0	3	24.2	115	34	28	22	7	1	1	0	8	1	18	4	0	2	4	.333	0	0-0	0	7.30	8.03
	12 ML YEARS		353	216	2	31	1405.1	6113	1532	766	717	175	61	45	39	466	30	892	32	4	76	95	.444	1	0-4	22	4.57	4.59

Jarred Cosart

Pitches: R **Bats:** R **Pos:** SP-30 KOZE-art **Ht:** 6'3" **Wt:** 195 **Born:** 5/25/1990 **Age:** 25

Year	Team	Lg	G	GS	CG	GF	IP	BFP	H	R	ER	HR	SH	SF	HB	TBB	IBB	SO	WP	Bk	W	L	Pct	Sh	Sv-Op	Hld	ERC	ERA
2010	Lakwd	A	14	14	1	0	71.1	293	60	34	30	3	2	1	5	16	0	77	7	0	7	3	.700	1	0- -	-	2.44	3.79
2011	Clrwtr	A+	20	19	0	0	108.0	461	98	55	47	7	5	2	8	43	1	79	12	1	9	8	.529	0	0- -	-	3.60	3.92
2011	CpChr	AA	7	7	0	0	36.1	157	33	20	19	4	2	1	0	13	0	22	2	0	1	2	.333	0	0- -	-	3.35	4.71
2012	CpChr	AA	15	15	0	0	87.0	383	83	37	34	3	3	3	7	38	0	68	6	3	5	5	.500	0	0- -	-	3.77	3.52
2012	OKCity	AAA	6	5	0	0	27.2	118	26	10	8	0	0	0	1	13	0	24	3	1	1	2	.333	0	0- -	-	3.51	2.60
2013	OKCity	AAA	18	17	1	0	93.0	401	74	37	34	5	0	1	3	50	1	93	6	0	7	4	.636	0	0- -	-	3.24	3.29
2013	Hou	AL	10	10	0	0	60.0	246	46	15	13	3	0	2	0	35	0	33	3	0	1	1	.500	0	0-0	0	3.31	1.95
2014	2 Tms		30	30	0	0	180.1	766	173	80	74	9	3	8	3	73	1	115	7	0	13	11	.542	0	0-0	0	3.61	3.69
14	Hou	AL	20	20	0	0	116.1	507	119	61	57	7	2	6	3	51	1	75	7	0	9	7	.563	0	0-0	0	4.18	4.41
14	Mia	NL	10	10	0	0	64.0	259	54	19	17	2	1	2	0	22	0	40	0	0	4	4	.500	0	0-0	0	2.64	2.39
2 ML YEARS			40	40	0	0	240.1	1012	219	95	87	12	3	10	3	108	1	148	10	0	14	12	.538	0	0-0	0	3.54	3.26

Neal Cotts

Pitches: L **Bats:** L **Pos:** RP-73 **Ht:** 6'1" **Wt:** 200 **Born:** 3/25/1980 **Age:** 35

Year	Team	Lg	G	GS	CG	GF	IP	BFP	H	R	ER	HR	SH	SF	HB	TBB	IBB	SO	WP	Bk	W	L	Pct	Sh	Sv-Op	Hld	ERC	ERA
2003	CWS	AL	4	4	0	0	13.1	69	15	12	12	1	1	0	0	17	0	10	0	0	1	1	.500	0	0-0	-	8.43	8.10
2004	CWS	AL	56	1	0	12	65.1	281	61	45	41	13	0	1	3	30	2	58	8	0	4	4	.500	0	0-2	4	4.84	5.65
2005	CWS	AL	69	0	0	10	60.1	248	38	15	13	1	0	3	4	29	5	58	3	0	4	0	1.000	0	0-2	13	2.03	1.94
2006	CWS	AL	70	0	0	14	54.0	251	64	33	31	12	3	1	3	24	6	43	3	0	1	2	.333	0	1-4	16	6.24	5.17
2007	ChC	NL	16	0	0	4	16.2	76	15	9	9	1	1	2	3	9	0	14	0	0	0	1	.000	0	0-0	2	4.41	4.86
2008	ChC	NL	50	0	0	7	35.2	160	38	18	17	7	3	0	1	13	2	43	3	0	0	0	.000	0	0-2	9	4.87	4.29
2009	ChC	NL	19	0	0	3	11.0	55	14	9	9	3	0	0	1	9	0	9	0	0	0	0	.000	0	0-1	2	9.64	7.36
2013	Tex	AL	58	0	0	6	57.0	223	36	8	7	2	2	3	0	18	1	65	3	0	8	3	.727	0	1-4	11	1.57	1.11
2014	Tex	AL	73	0	0	18	66.2	286	66	33	32	6	2	1	3	23	3	63	4	2	2	9	.182	0	2-9	19	3.84	4.32
Postseason			8	0	0	3	4.0	16	2	0	0	0	0	0	0	2	0	5	0	0	1	0	1.000	0	0-0	2	1.41	0.00
9 ML YEARS			415	5	0	74	380.0	1649	347	182	171	46	12	11	18	172	19	363	24	2	20	24	.455	0	4-24	74	4.03	4.05

Daniel Coulombe

Pitches: L **Bats:** L **Pos:** RP-5 **Ht:** 5'10" **Wt:** 185 **Born:** 10/26/1989 **Age:** 25

Year	Team	Lg	G	GS	CG	GF	IP	BFP	H	R	ER	HR	SH	SF	HB	TBB	IBB	SO	WP	Bk	W	L	Pct	Sh	Sv-Op	Hld	ERC	ERA
2012	Ogden	R+	3	0	0	1	6.0	25	3	2	1	0	0	0	0	1	0	8	1	0	0	0	-	0	0- -	-	0.70	1.50
2012	Gt Lks	A	20	0	0	4	19.1	95	15	8	8	0	4	1	3	17	4	29	6	0	0	1	.000	0	1- -	-	3.85	3.72
2013	RCuca	A+	54	0	0	16	66.2	301	46	37	30	7	5	2	2	48	3	85	17	0	4	2	.667	0	1- -	-	3.52	4.05
2014	RCuca	A+	31	0	0	13	44.1	181	33	16	15	3	0	1	0	17	0	61	8	0	3	0	1.000	0	5- -	-	2.54	3.05
2014	Chatt	AA	18	0	0	3	21.0	92	18	9	6	1	1	1	2	10	1	31	0	0	0	0	-	0	1- -	-	3.45	2.57
2014	LAD	NL	5	0	0	0	4.1	22	5	3	2	1	0	0	0	2	0	4	2	0	0	0	-	0	0-0	0	5.49	4.15

Collin Cowgill

Bats: R **Throws:** L **Pos:** RF-49;LF-44;CF-11;PR-11;PH-6;DH-3 **Ht:** 5'9" **Wt:** 185 **Born:** 5/22/1986 **Age:** 29

Year	Team	Lg	G	AB	H	2B	3B	HR	(Hm	Rd)	TB	R	RBI	RC	TBB	IBB	SO	HBP	SH	SF	SB	CS	GDP	Avg	OBP	Slg	OPS
2014	Salt Lk*	AAA	3	12	4	2	0	0	(-	-)	6	4	0	2	2	0	2	0	0	0	0	0	0	.333	.429	.500	.929
2011	Ari	NL	37	92	22	3	0	1	(1	0)	28	8	9	8	8	1	28	0	0	0	4	2	0	.239	.300	.304	.604
2012	Oak	AL	38	104	28	2	0	1	(1	0)	33	10	9	14	11	0	27	0	0	1	3	4	3	.269	.336	.317	.654
2013	2 Tms		73	152	32	5	2	4	(3	1)	53	18	16	12	7	0	42	0	3	0	1	0	1	.211	.245	.349	.594
2014	LAA	AL	106	260	65	10	1	5	(2	3)	92	37	21	31	26	0	74	5	2	0	4	0	4	.250	.330	.354	.684
13	NYM	NL	23	61	11	2	0	2	(2	0)	19	7	8	5	2	0	15	0	0	0	0	0	0	.180	.206	.311	.518
13	LAA	AL	50	91	21	3	2	2	(1	1)	34	11	8	7	5	0	27	0	3	0	1	0	1	.231	.271	.374	.644
Postseason			2	1	1	0	0	0	(0	0)	1	0	2	1	0	0	0	0	0	0	0	0	0	1.000	1.000	1.000	2.000
4 ML YEARS			254	608	147	20	3	11	(7	4)	206	73	55	65	52	1	171	5	5	1	12	6	8	.242	.306	.339	.645

Zack Cozart

Bats: R **Throws:** R **Pos:** SS-147;PH-1 COE-zart **Ht:** 6'0" **Wt:** 195 **Born:** 8/12/1985 **Age:** 29

Year	Team	Lg	G	AB	H	2B	3B	HR	(Hm	Rd)	TB	R	RBI	RC	TBB	IBB	SO	HBP	SH	SF	SB	CS	GDP	Avg	OBP	Slg	OPS
2011	Cin	NL	11	37	12	0	0	2	(2	0)	18	6	3	3	0	0	6	0	1	0	0	0	2	.324	.324	.486	.811
2012	Cin	NL	138	561	138	33	4	15	(6	9)	224	72	35	51	31	0	113	3	2	3	4	0	11	.246	.288	.399	.687
2013	Cin	NL	151	567	144	30	3	12	(7	5)	216	74	63	56	26	2	102	2	13	10	0	0	18	.254	.284	.381	.665
2014	Cin	NL	147	506	112	18	5	4	(1	3)	152	48	38	36	25	3	79	7	5	0	7	0	13	.221	.268	.300	.568
Postseason			6	24	5	0	0	0	(0	0)	5	2	0	1	3	0	5	1	0	0	0	0	0	.208	.321	.208	.530
4 ML YEARS			447	1671	406	81	12	33	(16	17)	610	200	139	146	82	5	300	12	21	13	11	0	44	.243	.281	.365	.646

Allen Craig

Bats: R **Throws:** R **Pos:** RF-82;1B-41;LF-11;PH-7;DH-1 **Ht:** 6'2" **Wt:** 215 **Born:** 7/18/1984 **Age:** 30

Year	Team	Lg	G	AB	H	2B	3B	HR	(Hm	Rd)	TB	R	RBI	RC	TBB	IBB	SO	HBP	SH	SF	SB	CS	GDP	Avg	OBP	Slg	OPS
2014	Pwtckt*	AAA	2	5	1	0	0	0	(-	-)	1	1	2	0	1	0	1	0	0	0	0	0	0	.200	.333	.200	.533
2010	StL	NL	44	114	28	7	0	4	(3	1)	47	12	18	14	9	1	26	0	0	1	0	1	1	.246	.298	.412	.711
2011	StL	NL	75	200	63	15	0	11	(3	8)	111	33	40	37	15	0	40	1	1	2	5	0	7	.315	.362	.555	.917
2012	StL	NL	119	469	144	35	0	22	(11	11)	245	76	92	89	37	1	89	1	0	7	2	1	15	.307	.354	.522	.876

Year Team	Lg	G	AB	H	2B	3B	HR	(Hm	Rd)	TB	R	RBI	RC	TBB	IBB	SO	HBP	SH	SF	SB	CS	GDP	Avg	OBP	Slg	OPS
2013 StL	NL	134	508	160	29	2	13	(2	11)	232	71	97	98	40	2	100	10	0	5	2	0	12	.315	.373	.457	.830
2014 2 Tms		126	461	99	20	1	8	(5	3)	145	41	46	35	35	0	113	7	0	2	2	1	14	.215	.279	.315	.594
14 StL	NL	97	367	87	17	1	7	(5	2)	127	34	44	33	26	0	77	3	0	2	1	1	11	.237	.291	.346	.638
14 Bos	AL	29	94	12	3	0	1	(0	1)	18	7	2	2	9	0	36	4	0	0	1	0	3	.128	.234	.191	.425
Postseason		34	100	26	5	1	5	(4	1)	48	14	14	14	14	1	27	2	1	1	0	2	2	.260	.359	.480	.839
5 ML YEARS		498	1752	494	106	3	58	(24	34)	780	233	293	273	136	4	368	19	1	17	11	3	49	.282	.337	.445	.783

Jesse Crain

Pitches: R **Bats:** R **Pos:** P **Ht:** 6'1" **Wt:** 215 **Born:** 7/5/1981 **Age:** 33

		HOW MUCH HE PITCHED						WHAT HE GAVE UP											THE RESULTS						
Year Team	Lg	G	GS	CG	GF	IP	BFP	H	R	ER	HR	SH	SF	HB	TBB	IBB	SO	WP	Bk	W	L	Pct	Sh	Sv-Op	Hld	ERC	ERA
2004 Min	AL	22	0	0	3	27.0	109	17	6	6	2	1	0	1	12	1	14	1	0	3	0	1.000	0	0-1	2	2.25	2.00
2005 Min	AL	75	0	0	17	79.2	326	61	28	24	6	9	3	5	29	7	25	2	0	12	5	.706	0	1-4	11	2.66	2.71
2006 Min	AL	68	0	0	24	76.2	325	79	31	30	6	1	2	2	18	2	60	1	0	4	5	.444	0	1-4	10	3.48	3.52
2007 Min	AL	18	0	0	5	16.1	71	19	16	10	4	0	1	1	4	0	10	0	1	1	2	.333	0	0-0	6	5.73	5.51
2008 Min	AL	66	0	0	14	62.2	268	62	29	25	6	0	2	1	24	3	50	2	0	5	4	.556	0	0-3	17	3.93	3.59
2009 Min	AL	56	0	0	15	51.2	230	48	28	27	3	3	3	5	27	3	43	1	1	7	4	.636	0	0-0	4	4.12	4.70
2010 Min	AL	71	0	0	16	68.0	278	53	27	23	5	3	0	1	27	4	62	3	0	1	1	.500	0	1-4	21	2.71	3.04
2011 CWS	AL	67	0	0	11	65.1	268	50	20	19	7	1	3	0	31	5	70	0	1	8	3	.727	0	1-7	24	3.08	2.62
2012 CWS	AL	51	0	0	6	48.0	194	29	14	13	5	0	0	1	23	1	60	4	0	2	3	.400	0	0-4	10	2.38	2.44
2013 CWS	AL	38	0	0	5	36.2	152	31	6	3	0	2	0	1	11	1	46	0	0	2	3	.400	0	0-1	19	2.27	0.74
Postseason		4	0	0	0	1.2	14	7	5	3	2	0	0	0	1	0	1	0	0	0	1	.000	0	0-0	0	40.37	16.20
10 ML YEARS		532	0	0	116	532.0	2221	449	205	180	44	20	14	18	206	27	440	14	3	45	30	.600	0	4-28	124	3.13	3.05

Brandon Crawford

Bats: L **Throws:** R **Pos:** SS-149;PH-6 **Ht:** 6'2" **Wt:** 215 **Born:** 1/21/1987 **Age:** 28

		BATTING																		RUNNING			AVERAGES			
Year Team	Lg	G	AB	H	2B	3B	HR	(Hm	Rd)	TB	R	RBI	RC	TBB	IBB	SO	HBP	SH	SF	SB	CS	GDP	Avg	OBP	Slg	OPS
2011 SF	NL	66	196	40	5	2	3	(0	3)	58	22	21	20	23	1	31	0	1	0	1	3	4	.204	.288	.296	.584
2012 SF	NL	143	435	108	26	3	4	(1	3)	152	44	45	40	33	6	95	3	2	3	1	4	9	.248	.304	.349	.653
2013 SF	NL	149	499	124	24	3	9	(2	7)	181	52	43	42	42	6	96	5	1	3	1	2	10	.248	.311	.363	.674
2014 SF	NL	153	491	121	20	10	10	(4	6)	191	54	69	72	59	10	129	2	2	10	5	3	4	.246	.324	.389	.713
Postseason		16	46	10	1	1	0	(0	0)	13	3	7	6	7	2	12	0	1	0	1	0	1	.217	.321	.283	.603
4 ML YEARS		511	1621	393	75	18	26	(7	19)	582	172	178	174	157	23	351	10	6	16	8	12	22	.242	.310	.359	.669

Carl Crawford

Bats: L **Throws:** L **Pos:** LF-94;PH-17 **Ht:** 6'2" **Wt:** 225 **Born:** 8/5/1981 **Age:** 33

		BATTING																		RUNNING			AVERAGES			
Year Team	Lg	G	AB	H	2B	3B	HR	(Hm	Rd)	TB	R	RBI	RC	TBB	IBB	SO	HBP	SH	SF	SB	CS	GDP	Avg	OBP	Slg	OPS
2014 Albq*	AAA	4	11	5	0	2	0	(-	-)	9	4	1	3	0	0	2	0	0	0	1	1	0	.455	.455	.818	1.273
2002 TB	AL	63	259	67	11	6	2	(1	1)	96	23	30	34	9	0	41	3	6	1	9	5	0	.259	.290	.371	.661
2003 TB	AL	151	630	177	18	9	5	(5	0)	228	80	54	80	26	4	102	1	1	3	55	10	5	.281	.309	.362	.671
2004 TB	AL	152	626	185	26	19	11	(6	5)	282	104	55	96	35	2	81	1	4	6	59	15	5	.296	.331	.450	.781
2005 TB	AL	156	644	194	33	15	15	(5	10)	302	101	81	102	27	1	84	5	5	6	46	8	11	.301	.331	.469	.800
2006 TB	AL	151	600	183	20	16	18	(7	11)	289	89	77	113	37	3	85	4	9	2	58	9	8	.305	.348	.482	.830
2007 TB	AL	143	584	184	37	9	11	(6	5)	272	93	80	97	32	5	112	5	1	2	50	10	11	.315	.355	.466	.820
2008 TB	AL	109	443	121	12	10	8	(3	5)	177	69	57	57	30	1	60	2	0	5	25	7	10	.273	.319	.400	.718
2009 TB	AL	156	606	185	28	8	15	(9	6)	274	96	68	91	51	1	99	8	2	5	60	16	7	.305	.364	.452	.816
2010 TB	AL	154	600	184	30	13	19	(11	8)	297	110	90	120	46	3	104	3	3	5	47	10	2	.307	.356	.495	.851
2011 Bos	AL	130	506	129	29	7	11	(4	7)	205	65	56	54	23	1	104	3	2	4	18	6	7	.255	.289	.405	.694
2012 Bos	AL	31	117	33	10	2	3	(2	1)	56	23	19	17	3	0	22	2	1	2	5	0	1	.282	.306	.479	.785
2013 LAD	NL	116	435	123	30	3	6	(5	1)	177	62	31	55	28	2	66	3	0	2	15	4	4	.283	.329	.407	.736
2014 LAD	NL	105	343	103	14	3	8	(5	3)	147	56	46	49	16	0	55	6	0	4	23	6	5	.300	.339	.429	.767
Postseason		31	125	34	4	1	7	(5	2)	61	18	15	18	6	0	23	1	0	0	9	0	2	.272	.311	.488	.799
13 ML YEARS		1617	6393	1868	298	120	132	(69	63)	2802	971	744	965	363	23	1015	46	34	47	470	106	73	.292	.332	.438	.771

Coco Crisp

Bats: B **Throws:** R **Pos:** CF-111;DH-12;PH-11 **Ht:** 5'10" **Wt:** 185 **Born:** 11/1/1979 **Age:** 35

		BATTING																		RUNNING			AVERAGES			
Year Team	Lg	G	AB	H	2B	3B	HR	(Hm	Rd)	TB	R	RBI	RC	TBB	IBB	SO	HBP	SH	SF	SB	CS	GDP	Avg	OBP	Slg	OPS
2002 Cle	AL	32	127	33	9	2	1	(1	0)	49	16	9	19	11	0	19	0	1	0	4	1	0	.260	.314	.386	.700
2003 Cle	AL	99	414	110	15	6	3	(3	0)	146	55	27	48	23	1	51	0	7	3	15	9	4	.266	.302	.353	.655
2004 Cle	AL	139	492	146	24	2	15	(8	7)	219	78	71	72	36	4	69	0	9	2	20	13	8	.297	.344	.446	.790
2005 Cle	AL	145	594	178	42	4	16	(4	12)	276	86	69	92	44	1	81	0	13	5	15	6	7	.300	.345	.465	.810
2006 Bos	AL	105	413	109	22	2	8	(4	4)	159	58	36	51	31	1	67	1	7	0	22	4	5	.264	.317	.385	.702
2007 Bos	AL	145	526	141	28	7	6	(1	5)	201	85	60	68	50	1	84	1	9	5	28	6	12	.268	.330	.382	.712
2008 Bos	AL	118	361	102	18	3	7	(1	6)	147	55	41	49	35	0	59	1	8	4	20	7	6	.283	.344	.407	.751
2009 KC	AL	49	180	41	8	5	3	(0	3)	68	30	14	25	29	1	23	1	4	1	13	2	4	.228	.336	.378	.714
2010 Oak	AL	75	290	81	14	4	8	(6	2)	127	51	38	49	30	0	49	0	3	5	32	3	6	.279	.342	.438	.779
2011 Oak	AL	136	531	140	27	5	8	(4	4)	201	69	54	69	41	2	65	1	4	6	49	9	11	.264	.314	.379	.693
2012 Oak	AL	120	455	118	25	7	11	(6	5)	190	68	46	71	45	0	64	0	6	2	39	4	9	.259	.325	.418	.742
2013 Oak	AL	131	513	134	22	3	22	(9	13)	228	93	66	78	61	3	65	0	2	8	21	5	7	.261	.335	.444	.779
2014 Oak	AL	126	463	114	21	3	9	(4	5)	168	68	47	67	66	2	66	0	1	6	19	5	3	.246	.336	.363	.699
Postseason		30	97	27	5	1	1	(0	1)	37	14	7	11	9	0	16	0	0	1	4	0	3	.278	.336	.381	.718
13 ML YEARS		1420	5358	1447	275	53	117	(51	66)	2179	812	578	758	502	16	762	5	76	49	297	74	82	.270	.330	.407	.737

Kyle Crockett

Pitches: L **Bats:** L **Pos:** RP-43　　　　　　　　　　**Ht:** 6'2" **Wt:** 170 **Born:** 12/15/1991 **Age:** 23

Year	Team	Lg	G	GS	CG	GF	IP	BFP	H	R	ER	HR	SH	SF	HB	TBB	IBB	SO	WP	Bk	W	L	Pct	Sh	Sv-Op	Hld	ERC	ERA
2013	MhVlly	A-	8	0	0	2	9.1	36	5	1	0	0	0	0	1	2	0	16	0	0	0	0	-	0	0- -	-	1.17	0.00
2013	Lk Cty	A	4	0	0	0	5.0	20	4	1	1	1	0	0	0	1	0	7	0	0	0	0	-	0	0- -	-	2.80	1.80
2013	Akron	AA	9	0	0	1	10.1	38	7	0	0	0	1	0	0	2	0	9	0	0	1	0	1.000	0	0- -	-	1.38	0.00
2014	Akron	AA	15	0	0	11	15.2	59	8	1	1	0	0	0	1	3	0	17	0	0	0	0	-	0	6- -	-	0.98	0.57
2014	Clmbs	AAA	6	0	0	2	8.2	33	7	4	1	0	1	0	0	0	0	6	0	0	0	0	-	0	0- -	-	1.29	1.04
2014	Cle	AL	43	0	0	7	30.0	122	26	6	6	2	2	0	3	8	2	28	0	1	4	1	.800	0	0-0	5	2.99	1.80

C.J. Cron

Bats: R **Throws:** R **Pos:** 1B-36;DH-36;PH-12　　　　CROHN　　　　　**Ht:** 6'4" **Wt:** 235 **Born:** 1/5/1990 **Age:** 25

Year	Team	Lg	G	AB	H	2B	3B	HR	(Hm	Rd)	TB	R	RBI	RC	TBB	IBB	SO	HBP	SH	SF	SB	CS	GDP	Avg	OBP	Slg	OPS
2011	Orem	R+	34	143	44	5	1	13	(-	-)	90	30	41	32	10	1	34	5	0	1	0	0	2	.308	.371	.629	1.000
2012	InldEm	A+	129	525	154	32	2	27	(-	-)	271	73	123	88	17	1	72	11	0	4	3	4	18	.293	.327	.516	.843
2013	Ark	AA	134	519	142	36	1	14	(-	-)	222	56	83	73	23	5	83	15	0	8	8	4	11	.274	.319	.428	.746
2014	Salt Lk	AAA	49	190	60	14	1	7	(-	-)	97	30	33	37	18	1	40	4	0	1	2	1	3	.316	.385	.511	.896
2014	LAA	AL	79	242	62	12	1	11	(5	6)	109	28	37	35	10	0	61	1	0	0	0	0	10	.256	.289	.450	.739

Aaron Crow

Pitches: R **Bats:** R **Pos:** RP-67　　　　　　　　　　**Ht:** 6'3" **Wt:** 195 **Born:** 11/10/1986 **Age:** 28

Year	Team	Lg	G	GS	CG	GF	IP	BFP	H	R	ER	HR	SH	SF	HB	TBB	IBB	SO	WP	Bk	W	L	Pct	Sh	Sv-Op	Hld	ERC	ERA
2014	NWArk*	AA	2	0	0	0	3.0	11	3	1	1	1	0	0	0	1	0	1	0	0	1	0	1.000	0	0- -	-	6.37	3.00
2011	KC	AL	57	0	0	19	62.0	266	55	20	19	8	3	0	0	31	2	65	9	1	4	4	.500	0	0-7	8	4.00	2.76
2012	KC	AL	73	0	0	20	64.2	260	54	27	25	4	1	2	1	22	2	65	4	0	3	1	.750	0	2-8	19	2.81	3.48
2013	KC	AL	57	0	0	14	48.0	210	49	19	18	6	2	3	2	22	3	44	5	0	7	5	.583	0	1-4	19	4.73	3.38
2014	KC	AL	67	0	0	20	59.0	244	52	32	27	10	2	1	0	24	1	34	2	0	6	1	.857	0	3-6	11	3.97	4.12
4 ML YEARS			254	0	0	73	233.2	980	210	98	89	28	8	6	3	99	8	208	20	1	20	11	.645	0	6-25	57	3.80	3.43

Nelson Cruz

Bats: R **Throws:** R **Pos:** DH-89;LF-60;RF-11　　　　　　　　　**Ht:** 6'2" **Wt:** 230 **Born:** 7/1/1980 **Age:** 34

Year	Team	Lg	G	AB	H	2B	3B	HR	(Hm	Rd)	TB	R	RBI	RC	TBB	IBB	SO	HBP	SH	SF	SB	CS	GDP	Avg	OBP	Slg	OPS
2005	Mil	NL	8	5	1	1	0	0	(0	0)	2	1	0	1	2	0	0	0	0	0	0	0	0	.200	.429	.400	.829
2006	Tex	AL	41	130	29	3	0	6	(3	3)	50	15	22	18	7	0	32	0	0	1	1	0	1	.223	.261	.385	.645
2007	Tex	AL	96	307	72	15	2	9	(4	5)	118	35	34	32	21	1	87	2	1	1	2	4	5	.235	.287	.384	.671
2008	Tex	AL	31	115	38	9	1	7	(4	3)	70	19	26	30	17	2	28	1	0	0	3	1	1	.330	.421	.609	1.030
2009	Tex	AL	128	462	120	21	1	33	(18	15)	242	75	76	72	49	6	118	2	0	2	20	4	9	.260	.332	.524	.856
2010	Tex	AL	108	399	127	31	3	22	(13	9)	230	60	78	77	38	5	81	1	1	6	17	4	12	.318	.374	.576	.950
2011	Tex	AL	124	475	125	28	1	29	(19	10)	242	64	87	79	33	1	116	2	0	3	9	5	8	.263	.312	.509	.821
2012	Tex	AL	159	585	152	45	0	24	(18	6)	269	86	90	80	48	2	140	5	0	4	8	4	7	.260	.319	.460	.779
2013	Tex	AL	109	413	110	18	0	27	(13	14)	209	49	76	69	35	2	109	4	0	4	5	1	14	.266	.327	.506	.833
2014	Bal	AL	159	613	166	32	2	40	(15	25)	322	87	108	93	55	8	140	5	0	5	4	5	17	.271	.333	.525	.859
Postseason			34	126	35	9	0	14	(9	5)	86	26	27	27	10	2	31	1	0	0	1	1	3	.278	.336	.683	1.018
10 ML YEARS			963	3504	940	203	10	197	(107	90)	1754	491	597	551	305	27	851	22	2	26	69	28	74	.268	.328	.501	.829

Tony Cruz

Bats: R **Throws:** R **Pos:** C-47;PH-7;1B-2;3B-1　　　　　　　**Ht:** 5'11" **Wt:** 215 **Born:** 8/18/1986 **Age:** 28

Year	Team	Lg	G	AB	H	2B	3B	HR	(Hm	Rd)	TB	R	RBI	RC	TBB	IBB	SO	HBP	SH	SF	SB	CS	GDP	Avg	OBP	Slg	OPS
2014	Sprgfld*	AA	2	5	1	0	0	0	(-	-)	1	0	0	0	0	0	2	0	0	0	0	0	0	.200	.200	.200	.400
2011	StL	NL	38	65	17	5	0	0	(0	0)	22	8	6	7	6	1	13	1	0	0	0	1	1	.262	.333	.338	.672
2012	StL	NL	51	126	32	9	1	1	(0	1)	46	11	11	9	3	0	19	0	0	2	0	1	4	.254	.267	.365	.632
2013	StL	NL	51	123	25	0	1	1	(0	1)	30	13	13	0	4	1	26	2	0	0	0	0	7	.203	.240	.203	.533
2014	StL	NL	50	135	27	5	0	1	(1	0)	35	11	17	9	13	1	28	0	2	0	0	3	6	.200	.270	.259	.530
Postseason			2	1	0	0	0	0	(0	0)	0	0	0	0	0	0	1	0	0	0	0	0	0	.000	.000	.000	.000
4 ML YEARS			190	449	101	25	2	3	(1	2)	139	43	47	34	26	3	85	3	2	2	0	5	18	.225	.271	.310	.580

Michael Cuddyer

Bats: R **Throws:** R **Pos:** RF-35;1B-14;3B-3;PH-1　　　　cuh-DYE-err　　　　**Ht:** 6'2" **Wt:** 220 **Born:** 3/27/1979 **Age:** 36

Year	Team	Lg	G	AB	H	2B	3B	HR	(Hm	Rd)	TB	R	RBI	RC	TBB	IBB	SO	HBP	SH	SF	SB	CS	GDP	Avg	OBP	Slg	OPS
2014	ColSpr*	AAA	1	1	0	0	0	0	(-	-)	0	0	0	0	1	0	0	0	0	0	0	0	0	.000	.500	.000	.500
2014	GdJunc*	R+	5	19	11	6	0	0	(-	-)	17	5	9	8	1	0	1	0	1	0	0	0	0	.579	.591	.895	1.486
2014	Tulsa*	AA	3	11	2	0	0	0	(-	-)	2	2	0	0	2	0	0	0	0	0	0	0	0	.182	.308	.182	.490
2001	Min	AL	8	18	4	2	0	0	(0	0)	6	1	1	2	2	0	6	0	0	0	1	0	1	.222	.300	.333	.633
2002	Min	AL	41	112	29	7	0	4	(2	2)	48	12	13	14	8	0	30	1	1	1	2	0	3	.259	.311	.429	.740
2003	Min	AL	35	102	25	1	3	4	(1	3)	44	14	8	10	12	0	19	0	0	0	1	1	6	.245	.325	.431	.756
2004	Min	AL	115	339	89	22	1	12	(8	4)	149	49	45	51	37	2	74	3	2	1	5	5	8	.263	.339	.440	.779
2005	Min	AL	126	422	111	25	3	12	(8	4)	178	55	42	43	41	5	93	3	1	3	3	4	19	.263	.330	.422	.752
2006	Min	AL	150	557	158	41	5	24	(15	9)	281	102	109	101	62	5	130	10	0	6	6	0	11	.284	.362	.504	.867
2007	Min	AL	144	547	151	28	5	16	(8	8)	237	87	81	82	64	1	107	7	0	5	5	0	19	.276	.356	.433	.790
2008	Min	AL	71	249	62	13	4	3	(1	2)	92	30	36	37	25	4	40	5	0	0	5	1	7	.249	.330	.369	.699

Year	Team	Lg	G	AB	H	2B	3B	HR	(Hm	Rd)	TB	R	RBI	RC	TBB	IBB	SO	HBP	SH	SF	SB	CS	GDP	Avg	OBP	Slg	OPS
									BATTING												RUNNING			AVERAGES			
2009	Min	AL	153	588	162	34	7	32	(18	14)	306	93	94	89	54	3	118	6	0	2	6	1	22	.276	.342	.520	.862
2010	Min	AL	157	609	165	37	5	14	(7	7)	254	93	81	77	58	7	93	4	0	4	7	3	26	.271	.336	.417	.753
2011	Min	AL	139	529	150	29	2	20	(10	10)	243	70	70	75	48	3	95	4	0	3	11	1	18	.284	.346	.459	.805
2012	Col	NL	101	358	93	30	2	16	(9	7)	175	53	58	46	32	1	78	0	0	4	8	3	12	.260	.317	.489	.806
2013	Col	NL	93	489	162	31	3	20	(11	9)	259	74	84	87	46	5	100	2	0	3	10	3	13	**.331**	.389	.530	.919
2014	Col	NL	49	190	63	15	1	10	(6	4)	110	32	31	33	14	0	30	0	0	1	3	0	5	.332	.376	.579	.955
	Postseason		22	74	25	2	1	2	(2	0)	35	5	8	4	4	1	18	0	0	0	0	2	1	.338	.372	.473	.845
	14 ML YEARS		1419	5109	1424	315	41	187	(104	83)	2382	765	753	747	503	36	1013	45	4	33	73	22	170	.279	.347	.466	.813

Johnny Cueto

KWAY-toe

Pitches: R **Bats:** R **Pos:** SP-34   **Ht:** 5'11" **Wt:** 215 **Born:** 2/15/1986 **Age:** 29

Year	Team	Lg	G	GS	CG	GF	IP	BFP	H	R	ER	HR	SH	SF	HB	TBB	IBB	SO	WP	Bk	W	L	Pct	Sh	Sv-Op	Hld	ERC	ERA
			HOW MUCH HE PITCHED						WHAT HE GAVE UP												THE RESULTS						
2008	Cin	NL	31	31	0	0	174.0	769	178	101	93	29	5	5	14	68	1	158	6	1	9	14	.391	0	0-0	0	4.95	4.81
2009	Cin	NL	30	30	0	0	171.1	740	172	90	84	24	5	3	14	61	0	132	4	0	11	11	.500	0	0-0	0	4.57	4.41
2010	Cin	NL	31	31	1	0	185.2	780	181	79	75	19	9	3	9	56	5	138	5	2	12	7	.632	1	0-0	0	3.75	3.64
2011	Cin	NL	24	24	3	0	156.0	631	123	51	40	8	10	4	10	47	0	104	5	1	9	5	.643	1	0-0	0	2.55	2.31
2012	Cin	NL	33	**33**	2	0	217.0	888	205	73	67	15	6	6	12	49	5	170	1	3	19	9	.679	0	0-0	0	3.13	2.78
2013	Cin	NL	11	11	0	0	60.2	242	46	20	19	7	2	1	1	18	1	51	1	0	5	2	.714	0	0-0	0	2.57	2.82
2014	Cin	NL	34	**34**	4	0	**243.2**	**961**	169	69	61	22	7	1	15	65	2	**242**	1	1	20	9	.690	2	0-0	0	2.18	2.25
	Postseason		3	3	0	0	8.2	42	13	6	5	3	1	1	0	2	0	3	0	0	0	2	.000	0	0-0	0	7.96	5.19
	7 ML YEARS		194	194	10	0	1208.1	5011	1074	483	439	124	48	23	75	364	14	995	23	8	85	57	.599	4	0-0	0	3.35	3.27

Charlie Culberson

Bats: R **Throws:** R **Pos:** 3B-32;SS-23;PH-22;2B-20;PR-6;1B-4   **Ht:** 6'0" **Wt:** 200 **Born:** 4/10/1989 **Age:** 26

Year	Team	Lg	G	AB	H	2B	3B	HR	(Hm	Rd)	TB	R	RBI	RC	TBB	IBB	SO	HBP	SH	SF	SB	CS	GDP	Avg	OBP	Slg	OPS
									BATTING												RUNNING			AVERAGES			
2014	ColSpr*	AAA	2	7	3	2	0	0	(-	-)	5	1	0	2	1	0	2	0	0	0	0	0	0	.429	.500	.714	1.214
2012	SF	NL	6	22	3	0	0	0	(0	0)	3	0	1	0	0	0	7	0	1	0	0	0	0	.136	.136	.136	.273
2013	Col	NL	47	99	29	5	0	2	(0	2)	40	12	12	13	4	1	23	0	0	1	5	1	5	.293	.317	.404	.721
2014	Col	NL	95	210	41	7	2	3	(2	1)	61	17	24	14	12	2	62	5	4	2	2	2	6	.195	.253	.290	.544
	3 ML YEARS		148	331	73	12	2	5	(2	3)	104	29	37	27	16	3	92	5	5	3	7	3	11	.221	.265	.314	.579

Brandon Cumpton

Pitches: R **Bats:** R **Pos:** SP-10; RP-6   **Ht:** 6'2" **Wt:** 220 **Born:** 11/16/1988 **Age:** 26

Year	Team	Lg	G	GS	CG	GF	IP	BFP	H	R	ER	HR	SH	SF	HB	TBB	IBB	SO	WP	Bk	W	L	Pct	Sh	Sv-Op	Hld	ERC	ERA
			HOW MUCH HE PITCHED						WHAT HE GAVE UP												THE RESULTS						
2010	StCol	A-	4	3	0	0	10.2	45	8	3	3	0	0	0	0	5	0	6	0	0	0	1	.000	0	0- -	-	2.30	2.53
2011	WV	A	13	12	0	0	67.0	280	60	34	32	6	2	1	9	18	0	48	3	0	7	4	.636	0	0- -	-	3.48	4.30
2011	Bradtn	A+	13	12	0	0	66.1	284	73	29	27	6	2	3	6	12	1	42	2	0	3	3	.500	0	0- -	-	4.04	3.66
2012	Altna	AA	27	27	0	0	152.1	642	149	72	65	9	6	3	15	46	0	88	7	2	12	11	.522	0	0- -	-	3.74	3.84
2013	Altna	AA	2	2	0	0	9.2	46	11	9	8	0	0	0	2	5	0	7	0	0	1	0	1.000	0	0- -	-	5.34	7.45
2013	Indy	AAA	21	19	1	0	122.0	514	115	52	45	6	6	1	8	44	1	90	6	0	6	7	.462	0	0- -	-	3.55	3.32
2014	Indy	AAA	12	11	1	1	71.1	291	69	27	24	7	2	3	4	20	0	37	0	0	5	4	.556	0	0- -	-	3.78	3.03
2013	Pit	NL	6	5	0	0	30.2	124	26	8	7	1	2	1	1	5	0	22	1	0	2	1	.667	0	0-0	0	2.08	2.05
2014	Pit	NL	16	10	0	4	70.0	309	82	41	38	2	3	4	6	18	2	46	2	0	3	4	.429	0	0-0	0	4.24	4.89
	2 ML YEARS		22	15	0	4	100.2	433	108	49	45	3	5	5	7	23	2	68	3	0	5	5	.500	0	0-0	0	3.53	4.02

Matt Daley

Pitches: R **Bats:** R **Pos:** RP-13   **Ht:** 6'2" **Wt:** 180 **Born:** 6/23/1982 **Age:** 33

Year	Team	Lg	G	GS	CG	GF	IP	BFP	H	R	ER	HR	SH	SF	HB	TBB	IBB	SO	WP	Bk	W	L	Pct	Sh	Sv-Op	Hld	ERC	ERA
			HOW MUCH HE PITCHED						WHAT HE GAVE UP												THE RESULTS						
2014	S-WB*	AAA	28	0	0	21	35.2	160	43	18	18	6	3	2	4	8	1	48	2	0	1	2	.333	0	9- -	-	5.41	4.54
2009	Col	NL	57	0	0	15	51.0	211	43	24	24	6	2	3	2	18	2	55	0	0	1	1	.500	0	0-3	12	3.27	4.24
2010	Col	NL	28	0	0	4	23.1	108	27	11	11	2	2	1	3	10	1	18	1	0	1	1	.000	0	0-0	6	5.41	4.24
2011	Col	NL	7	0	0	0	6.0	27	8	7	7	1	0	1	0	2	0	7	0	0	0	0	-	0	0-0	0	6.38	10.50
2013	NYY	AL	7	0	0	4	6.0	21	2	0	0	0	0	0	1	0	0	8	0	0	1	0	1.000	0	0-0	0	0.45	0.00
2014	NYY	AL	13	0	0	5	14.1	63	12	11	8	4	1	1	1	6	1	10	0	0	0	1	.000	0	0-0	1	4.47	5.02
	Postseason		1	0	0	0	1.0	5	1	0	0	0	1	0	0	1	0	0	1	0	0	0	-	0	0-0	0	5.48	0.00
	5 ML YEARS		112	0	0	28	100.2	430	92	53	50	13	5	6	7	36	4	98	1	0	2	3	.400	0	0-3	19	3.83	4.47

John Danks

Pitches: L **Bats:** L **Pos:** SP-32   **Ht:** 6'1" **Wt:** 210 **Born:** 4/15/1985 **Age:** 30

Year	Team	Lg	G	GS	CG	GF	IP	BFP	H	R	ER	HR	SH	SF	HB	TBB	IBB	SO	WP	Bk	W	L	Pct	Sh	Sv-Op	Hld	ERC	ERA
			HOW MUCH HE PITCHED						WHAT HE GAVE UP												THE RESULTS						
2007	CWS	AL	26	26	0	0	139.0	622	160	92	85	28	7	4	4	54	4	109	3	0	6	13	.316	0	0-0	0	5.73	5.50
2008	CWS	AL	33	33	0	0	195.0	804	182	74	72	15	2	2	4	57	1	159	7	0	12	9	.571	0	0-0	0	3.26	3.32
2009	CWS	AL	32	32	1	0	200.1	839	184	89	84	28	5	6	5	73	1	149	1	0	13	11	.542	0	0-0	0	3.89	3.77
2010	CWS	AL	32	32	1	0	213.0	878	189	93	88	18	5	0	4	70	2	162	2	1	15	11	.577	1	0-0	0	3.18	3.72
2011	CWS	AL	27	27	2	0	170.1	728	182	89	82	19	4	6	7	46	5	135	6	0	8	12	.400	1	0-0	0	4.16	4.33
2012	CWS	AL	9	9	0	0	53.2	238	57	35	34	7	3	2	1	23	0	30	5	0	3	4	.429	0	0-0	0	4.82	5.70
2013	CWS	AL	22	22	0	0	138.1	583	151	81	73	28	1	5	4	27	0	89	3	0	4	14	.222	0	0-0	0	4.61	4.75
2014	CWS	AL	32	32	0	0	193.2	855	205	106	102	25	4	7	9	74	1	129	7	0	11	11	.500	0	0-0	0	4.70	4.74
	Postseason		1	1	0	0	6.2	30	7	3	3	1	0	0	0	3	0	7	0	0	1	0	1.000	0	0-0	0	4.81	4.05
	8 ML YEARS		213	213	4	0	1303.1	5547	1310	659	620	168	31	32	38	424	14	962	34	1	72	85	.459	2	0-0	0	4.13	4.28

Jordan Danks

Bats: L **Throws:** R **Pos:** CF-28;LF-12;RF-8;PH-3;PR-3;DH-1 **Ht:** 6'4" **Wt:** 215 **Born:** 8/7/1986 **Age:** 28

Year	Team	Lg	G	AB	H	2B	3B	HR	(Hm	Rd)	TB	R	RBI	RC	TBB	IBB	SO	HBP	SH	SF	SB	CS	GDP	Avg	OBP	Slg	OPS
2014	Charltt*	AAA	93	348	94	18	0	16	(-	-)	160	51	57	60	47	3	103	3	0	8	2	0	9	.270	.355	.460	.814
2012	CWS	AL	50	67	15	1	0	1	(1	0)	19	12	4	3	6	0	16	0	0	2	3	1	1	.224	.280	.284	.564
2013	CWS	AL	79	160	37	7	0	5	(4	1)	59	15	12	12	18	0	57	1	0	0	7	2	5	.231	.313	.369	.682
2014	CWS	AL	51	117	26	2	0	2	(1	1)	34	14	10	9	14	1	46	0	0	1	5	3	1	.222	.303	.291	.594
	3 ML YEARS		180	344	78	10	0	8	(6	2)	112	41	26	24	38	1	119	1	0	3	15	6	7	.227	.303	.326	.629

Chase d'Arnaud

Bats: R **Throws:** R **Pos:** PR-7;SS-1   dar-NO   **Ht:** 6'1" **Wt:** 205 **Born:** 1/21/1987 **Age:** 28

Year	Team	Lg	G	AB	H	2B	3B	HR	(Hm	Rd)	TB	R	RBI	RC	TBB	IBB	SO	HBP	SH	SF	SB	CS	GDP	Avg	OBP	Slg	OPS
2014	Indy*	AAA	118	376	94	16	9	2	(0	0)	134	59	23	45	29	1	82	7	1	3	30	13	2	.250	.313	.356	.670
2011	Pit	NL	48	143	31	6	2	0	(0	0)	41	17	6	8	4	0	36	1	2	1	12	2	3	.217	.242	.287	.528
2012	Pit	NL	8	6	0	0	0	0	(0	0)	0	2	1	0	0	0	2	0	0	0	1	0	0	.000	.000	.000	.000
2014	Pit	NL	8	0	0	0	0	0	(0	0)	0	2	0	0	0	0	0	0	0	0	0	2	0	-	-	-	-
	3 ML YEARS		64	149	31	6	2	0	(0	0)	41	21	7	8	4	0	38	1	2	1	13	4	3	.208	.232	.275	.507

Travis d'Arnaud

Bats: R **Throws:** R **Pos:** C-105;PH-3;DH-1   dar-NO   **Ht:** 6'2" **Wt:** 210 **Born:** 2/10/1989 **Age:** 26

Year	Team	Lg	G	AB	H	2B	3B	HR	(Hm	Rd)	TB	R	RBI	RC	TBB	IBB	SO	HBP	SH	SF	SB	CS	GDP	Avg	OBP	Slg	OPS
2010	Dnedin	A+	71	263	68	20	1	6	(-	-)	108	36	38	36	20	1	63	4	0	5	3	1	6	.259	.315	.411	.726
2011	NHam	AA	114	424	132	33	1	21	(-	-)	230	72	78	84	33	1	100	8	0	1	4	2	5	.311	.371	.542	.914
2012	LsVgs	AAA	67	279	93	21	2	16	(-	-)	166	45	52	60	19	1	59	3	0	2	1	1	11	.333	.380	.595	.975
2013	LsVgs	AAA	19	56	17	8	0	2	(-	-)	31	19	12	16	21	2	12	0	0	1	0	0	2	.304	.487	.554	1.041
2013	Mets	R	6	22	7	3	0	0	(-	-)	10	4	5	3	1	0	2	0	0	0	0	0	0	.318	.348	.455	.802
2013	Bnghtn	AA	7	27	6	2	1	1	(-	-)	13	2	3	4	3	0	9	0	0	0	0	0	1	.222	.300	.481	.781
2014	Bnghtn	AA	3	8	1	0	0	1	(-	-)	4	2	2	1	1	0	0	0	0	0	0	0	0	.125	.222	.500	.722
2014	LsVgs	AAA	15	55	24	8	0	6	(-	-)	50	13	16	19	3	0	5	1	0	0	0	0	3	.436	.475	.909	1.384
2013	NYM	NL	31	99	20	3	0	1	(-	-)	26	4	5	6	12	0	21	0	0	0	0	0	3	.202	.286	.263	.548
2014	NYM	NL	108	385	93	22	3	13	(5	8)	160	48	41	39	32	5	64	2	1	1	1	0	15	.242	.302	.416	.718
	2 ML YEARS		139	484	113	25	3	14	(6	8)	186	52	46	45	44	5	85	2	1	2	1	0	18	.233	.299	.384	.683

Logan Darnell

Pitches: L **Bats:** L **Pos:** SP-4; RP-3   **Ht:** 6'2" **Wt:** 210 **Born:** 2/2/1989 **Age:** 26

Year	Team	Lg	G	GS	CG	GF	IP	BFP	H	R	ER	HR	SH	SF	HB	TBB	IBB	SO	WP	Bk	W	L	Pct	Sh	Sv-Op	Hld	ERC	ERA
2010	Elizab	R+	11	5	0	3	34.2	139	28	16	8	2	3	1	2	6	0	32	4	0	2	3	.400	0	0- -	-	2.17	2.08
2011	Beloit	A	6	6	0	0	33.1	136	24	17	14	1	0	0	3	8	0	24	1	0	2	2	.500	0	0- -	-	1.90	3.78
2011	FtMyrs	A+	15	15	0	0	86.1	363	95	45	40	6	2	1	3	25	0	46	9	2	8	3	.727	0	0- -	-	4.26	4.17
2011	NwBrit	AA	5	5	0	0	30.2	133	38	26	19	3	1	3	5	4	0	20	2	0	1	1	.500	0	0- -	-	5.12	5.58
2012	NwBrit	AA	28	28	0	0	156.0	687	193	91	88	22	3	7	4	47	1	98	11	3	11	12	.478	0	0- -	-	5.53	5.08
2013	NwBrit	AA	15	15	1	0	96.2	399	96	34	28	4	2	1	8	23	0	77	7	0	6	6	.500	1	0- -	-	3.42	2.61
2013	Roch	AAA	12	11	0	0	57.0	245	63	33	27	5	2	1	4	22	0	43	4	0	4	4	.500	0	0- -	-	5.01	4.26
2014	Roch	AAA	23	19	1	1	115.0	497	108	63	46	16	5	3	1	49	2	90	8	4	7	6	.538	0	0- -	-	4.08	3.60
2014	Min	AL	7	4	0	2	24.0	112	31	20	19	5	0	2	1	8	0	22	0	0	0	2	.000	0	0-0	0	6.39	7.13

Yu Darvish

Pitches: R **Bats:** R **Pos:** SP-22   YOO DARR-vish   **Ht:** 6'5" **Wt:** 215 **Born:** 8/16/1986 **Age:** 28

Year	Team	Lg	G	GS	CG	GF	IP	BFP	H	R	ER	HR	SH	SF	HB	TBB	IBB	SO	WP	Bk	W	L	Pct	Sh	Sv-Op	Hld	ERC	ERA
2012	Tex	AL	29	29	0	0	191.1	816	156	89	83	14	2	7	10	89	1	221	8	0	16	9	.640	0	0-0	0	3.31	3.90
2013	Tex	AL	32	32	0	0	209.2	841	145	68	66	26	0	5	8	80	1	277	7	1	13	9	.591	0	0-0	0	2.70	2.83
2014	Tex	AL	22	22	2	0	144.1	005	133	54	49	13	1	2	2	49	1	102	14	1	10	7	.500	1	0-0	0	3.00	3.06
	Postseason		1	1	0	0	6.2	27	5	3	2	0	1	1	1	0	0	7	0	0	1	0	1.000	0	0-0	0	1.38	2.70
	3 ML YEARS		83	83	2	0	545.1	2262	434	211	198	53	3	14	20	218	3	680	29	2	39	25	.609	1	0-0	0	3.10	3.27

Matt Davidson

Bats: R **Throws:** R **Pos:** 3B   **Ht:** 6'2" **Wt:** 225 **Born:** 3/26/1991 **Age:** 24

Year	Team	Lg	G	AB	H	2B	3B	HR	(Hm	Rd)	TB	R	RBI	RC	TBB	IBB	SO	HBP	SH	SF	SB	CS	GDP	Avg	OBP	Slg	OPS
2010	Sbend	A	113	415	120	35	3	16	(-	-)	209	58	79	78	43	2	109	13	0	4	0	2	8	.289	.371	.504	.874
2010	Visalia	A+	21	71	12	1	0	2	(-	-)	19	6	11	6	12	1	25	1	0	0	0	0	2	.169	.298	.268	.565
2011	Visalia	A+	135	535	148	39	1	20	(-	-)	249	93	106	89	52	1	147	11	0	8	0	1	7	.277	.348	.465	.814
2012	Mobile	AA	135	486	127	28	2	23	(-	-)	228	81	77	87	69	5	126	15	0	5	3	4	12	.261	.367	.469	.836
2013	Reno	AAA	115	443	124	32	3	17	(-	-)	213	55	74	77	46	1	134	5	0	6	1	0	16	.280	.350	.481	.831
2014	Charltt	AAA	130	478	95	18	0	20	(-	-)	173	59	55	51	49	1	164	8	1	3	0	0	5	.199	.283	.362	.644
2013	Ari	NL	31	76	18	6	0	3	(1	2)	33	8	12	12	10	1	24	1	0	0	0	1	1	.237	.333	.434	.768

Chris Davis

Bats: L **Throws:** R **Pos:** 1B-115;3B-21;PH-3;DH-1   **Ht:** 6'3" **Wt:** 230 **Born:** 3/17/1986 **Age:** 29

Year	Team	Lg	G	AB	H	2B	3B	HR	(Hm	Rd)	TB	R	RBI	RC	TBB	IBB	SO	HBP	SH	SF	SB	CS	GDP	Avg	OBP	Slg	OPS
2014	Bowie*	AA	1	4	1	0	0	0	(-	-)	1	1	0	0	0	0	2	0	0	0	0	0	0	.250	.250	.250	.500
2008	Tex	AL	80	295	84	23	2	17	(8	9)	162	51	55	44	20	1	88	1	0	1	1	2	5	.285	.331	.549	.880
2009	Tex	AL	113	391	93	15	1	21	(11	10)	173	48	59	50	24	2	150	2	0	2	0	0	6	.238	.284	.442	.726
2010	Tex	AL	45	120	23	9	0	1	(0	1)	35	7	4	5	15	3	40	0	0	1	3	0	3	.192	.279	.292	.571
2011	2 Tms	AL	59	199	53	12	0	5	(2	3)	80	25	19	23	11	1	63	0	0	0	1	0	4	.266	.305	.402	.707
2012	Bal	AL	139	515	139	20	0	33	(22	11)	258	75	85	85	37	6	169	7	0	3	2	3	8	.270	.326	.501	.827
2013	Bal	AL	160	584	167	42	1	53	(28	25)	370	103	138	134	72	12	199	10	0	7	4	1	4	.286	.370	.634	1.004
2014	Bal	AL	127	450	88	16	0	26	(13	13)	182	65	72	58	60	9	173	9	1	5	2	1	2	.196	.300	.404	.704
11	Tex	AL	28	76	19	3	0	3	(1	2)	31	9	6	7	5	0	24	0	0	0	0	0	2	.250	.296	.408	.704
11	Bal	AL	31	123	34	9	0	2	(1	1)	49	16	13	16	6	1	39	0	0	0	1	0	2	.276	.310	.398	.708
	Postseason		6	24	5	0	0	0	(0	0)	5	1	2	1	1	0	9	1	0	0	0	0	0	.208	.269	.208	.478
	7 ML YEARS		723	2554	647	137	4	156	(84	72)	1260	374	432	399	239	34	882	29	1	19	13	7	32	.253	.322	.493	.815

Ike Davis

Bats: L **Throws:** L **Pos:** 1B-124;PH-37;DH-2;PR-1   **Ht:** 6'4" **Wt:** 220 **Born:** 3/22/1987 **Age:** 28

Year	Team	Lg	G	AB	H	2B	3B	HR	(Hm	Rd)	TB	R	RBI	RC	TBB	IBB	SO	HBP	SH	SF	SB	CS	GDP	Avg	OBP	Slg	OPS
2010	NYM	NL	147	523	138	33	1	19	(8	11)	230	73	71	75	72	6	138	1	0	5	3	2	13	.264	.351	.440	.791
2011	NYM	NL	36	129	39	8	1	7	(5	2)	70	20	25	22	17	3	31	1	0	2	0	0	5	.302	.383	.543	.925
2012	NYM	NL	156	519	118	26	0	32	(11	21)	240	66	90	68	61	3	141	1	0	3	0	2	10	.227	.308	.462	.771
2013	NYM	NL	103	317	65	14	0	9	(5	4)	106	37	33	36	57	5	101	1	0	2	4	0	9	.205	.326	.334	.661
2014	2 Tms	NL	143	360	84	19	0	11	(9	2)	136	43	51	45	63	3	78	0	0	4	0	4	8	.233	.344	.378	.722
14	NYM	NL	12	24	5	1	0	1	(1	0)	9	4	5	4	6	0	4	0	0	0	0	0	0	.208	.367	.375	.742
14	Pit	NL	131	336	79	18	0	10	(8	2)	127	39	46	41	57	3	74	0	0	4	0	4	8	.235	.343	.378	.721
	5 ML YEARS		585	1848	444	100	2	78	(38	40)	782	239	270	246	270	20	489	4	0	16	7	8	45	.240	.336	.423	.759

Khris Davis

Bats: R **Throws:** R **Pos:** LF-134;PH-11   **Ht:** 5'11" **Wt:** 190 **Born:** 12/21/1987 **Age:** 27

Year	Team	Lg	G	AB	H	2B	3B	HR	(Hm	Rd)	TB	R	RBI	RC	TBB	IBB	SO	HBP	SH	SF	SB	CS	GDP	Avg	OBP	Slg	OPS
2010	Wisc	A	128	457	128	26	4	22	(-	-)	228	86	72	94	77	2	120	15	2	4	17	10	11	.280	.398	.499	.897
2011	BrvdCt	A+	90	304	94	21	1	15	(-	-)	162	50	68	69	51	1	70	9	0	7	10	5	11	.309	.415	.533	.948
2011	Hntsvl	AA	35	124	26	7	1	2	(-	-)	41	10	16	11	10	0	23	1	0	1	0	0	6	.210	.272	.331	.603
2012	Hntsvl	AA	44	128	49	9	0	8	(-	-)	82	23	23	36	20	0	33	5	1	0	2	2	3	.383	.484	.641	1.124
2012	Brewrs	R	6	19	7	0	0	3	(-	-)	16	7	5	6	2	0	7	1	0	0	1	1	0	.368	.455	.842	1.297
2012	Nashv	AAA	32	113	35	12	0	4	(-	-)	59	23	24	26	20	1	27	3	0	4	1	0	4	.310	.414	.522	.936
2013	Nashv	AAA	69	243	62	12	1	13	(-	-)	115	35	37	41	31	2	59	5	0	2	6	4	10	.255	.349	.473	.822
2013	Mil	NL	56	136	38	10	0	11	(5	6)	81	27	27	25	11	0	34	5	0	1	3	0	4	.279	.353	.596	.949
2014	Mil	NL	144	501	122	37	2	22	(12	10)	229	70	69	58	32	0	122	10	0	6	4	1	13	.244	.299	.457	.756
	2 ML YEARS		200	637	160	47	2	33	(17	16)	310	97	96	83	43	0	156	15	0	7	7	1	17	.251	.311	.487	.797

Rajai Davis

Bats: R **Throws:** R **Pos:** LF-99;CF-48;PH-6;PR-6;DH-1   RAHJ-ay   **Ht:** 5'9" **Wt:** 195 **Born:** 10/19/1980 **Age:** 34

Year	Team	Lg	G	AB	H	2B	3B	HR	(Hm	Rd)	TB	R	RBI	RC	TBB	IBB	SO	HBP	SH	SF	SB	CS	GDP	Avg	OBP	Slg	OPS
2006	Pit	NL	20	14	2	1	0	0	(0	0)	3	1	0	0	2	0	3	0	1	0	1	3	0	.143	.250	.214	.464
2007	2 Tms	NL	75	190	53	11	2	1	(0	1)	71	32	9	26	21	1	28	4	3	1	22	6	1	.279	.361	.374	.735
2008	2 Tms		113	214	52	5	4	3	(0	3)	74	30	19	24	8	0	40	1	2	0	29	6	1	.243	.272	.346	.618
2009	Oak	AL	125	390	119	27	5	3	(1	2)	165	65	48	63	29	0	70	7	2	4	41	12	12	.305	.360	.423	.784
2010	Oak	AL	143	525	149	28	3	5	(5	0)	198	66	52	62	26	0	78	4	1	5	50	11	10	.284	.320	.377	.697
2011	Tor	AL	95	320	76	21	6	1	(1	0)	112	44	29	32	15	0	63	1	1	1	34	11	4	.238	.273	.350	.623
2012	Tor	AL	142	447	115	24	3	8	(5	3)	169	64	43	59	29	3	102	6	1	4	46	13	8	.257	.309	.378	.687
2013	Tor	AL	108	331	86	16	2	6	(3	3)	124	49	24	36	21	0	67	5	1	2	45	6	8	.260	.312	.375	.687
2014	Det	AL	134	461	130	27	2	8	(4	4)	185	64	51	62	22	0	75	5	3	3	36	11	7	.282	.320	.401	.721
07	Pit	NL	24	48	13	2	1	0	(0	0)	17	6	2	6	7	0	3	0	1	1	5	2	1	.271	.357	.354	.711
07	SF	NL	51	142	40	9	1	1	(0	1)	54	26	7	20	14	1	25	4	2	0	17	4	0	.282	.363	.380	.743
08	SF	NL	12	18	1	0	0	0	(0	0)	1	2	0	0	1	0	6	0	0	0	4	0	0	.056	.105	.056	.161
08	Oak	AL	101	196	51	5	4	3	(0	3)	73	28	19	24	7	0	34	1	2	1	25	6	1	.260	.288	.372	.660
	9 ML YEARS		955	2892	782	160	27	35	(19	16)	1101	415	275	364	173	4	526	33	15	21	304	79	51	.270	.317	.381	.697

Wade Davis

Pitches: R **Bats:** R **Pos:** RP-71   **Ht:** 6'5" **Wt:** 220 **Born:** 9/7/1985 **Age:** 29

Year	Team	Lg	HOW MUCH HE PITCHED						WHAT HE GAVE UP										THE RESULTS						
			G	GS	CG	GF	IP	BFP	H	R	ER	HR	SH	SF	HB	TBB	IBB	SO	WP	Bk	W	L	Pct	Sh	Sv-Op	Hld	ERC	ERA
2009	TB	AL	6	6	1	0	36.1	150	33	19	15	2	0	0	0	13	1	36	1	0	2	2	.500	1	0-0	0	3.12	3.72
2010	TB	AL	29	29	0	0	168.0	722	165	77	76	24	3	6	5	62	2	113	4	0	12	10	.545	0	0-0	0	4.25	4.07
2011	TB	AL	29	29	1	0	184.0	795	190	96	91	23	5	7	8	63	1	105	6	0	11	10	.524	0	0-0	0	4.38	4.45
2012	TB	AL	54	0	0	15	70.1	284	48	20	19	5	0	1	0	29	2	87	2	0	3	0	1.000	0	0-1	6	2.25	2.43
2013	KC	AL	31	24	0	2	135.1	618	169	89	80	15	1	5	4	58	2	114	7	0	8	11	.421	0	0-0	0	5.88	5.32
2014	KC	AL	71	0	0	11	72.0	279	38	8	8	0	0	1	3	23	0	109	1	0	9	2	.818	0	3-6	33	1.23	1.00
	Postseason		3	1	0	2	7.1	33	8	2	2	1	0	0	0	4	0	8	0	0	1	0	1.000	0	0-0	0	5.52	2.45
	6 ML YEARS		220	88	2	28	666.0	2848	643	309	289	69	9	20	20	248	8	564	21	0	45	35	.563	1	3-7	39	3.90	3.91

Alejandro De Aza

day-AH-zah

Bats: L **Throws:** L **Pos:** LF-132;CF-16;PH-3;PR-3;RF-1;DH-1   **Ht:** 6'0" **Wt:** 195 **Born:** 4/11/1984 **Age:** 31

Year	Team	Lg	G	AB	H	2B	3B	HR	(Hm	Rd)	TB	R	RBI	RC	TBB	IBB	SO	HBP	SH	SF	SB	CS	GDP	Avg	OBP	Slg	OPS
2007	Fla	NL	45	144	33	8	2	0	(0	0)	45	14	8	11	6	1	37	1	5	2	2	0	2	.229	.261	.313	.574
2009	Fla	NL	22	20	5	1	0	0	(0	0)	6	6	3	4	5	0	5	0	1	1	0	0	0	.250	.385	.300	.685
2010	CWS	AL	19	30	9	3	0	0	(0	0)	12	7	2	4	1	0	4	0	1	0	2	1	0	.300	.323	.400	.723
2011	CWS	AL	54	152	50	11	3	4	(2	2)	79	29	23	34	17	1	34	1	1	0	12	5	2	.329	.400	.520	.920
2012	CWS	AL	131	524	147	29	6	9	(2	7)	215	81	50	79	47	3	109	9	4	1	26	12	1	.281	.349	.410	.760
2013	CWS	AL	153	607	160	27	4	17	(4	13)	246	84	62	82	50	1	147	6	6	6	20	8	8	.264	.323	.405	.728
2014	2 Tms	AL	142	477	120	24	8	8	(4	4)	184	56	41	58	39	2	119	6	3	3	17	10	7	.252	.314	.386	.700
14	CWS	AL	122	395	96	19	5	5	(4	1)	140	45	31	45	33	2	100	6	2	3	15	7	6	.243	.309	.354	.663
14	Bal	AL	20	82	24	5	3	3	(0	3)	44	11	10	13	6	0	19	0	1	0	2	3	1	.293	.341	.537	.877
	7 ML YEARS		566	1954	524	103	23	38	(12	26)	787	277	189	272	165	8	455	23	21	13	79	36	20	.268	.330	.403	.733

Justin De Fratus

duh-FRAY-tiss

Pitches: R **Bats:** B **Pos:** RP-54   **Ht:** 6'4" **Wt:** 225 **Born:** 10/21/1987 **Age:** 27

Year	Team	Lg	G	GS	CG	GF	IP	BFP	H	R	ER	HR	SH	SF	HB	TBB	IBB	SO	WP	Bk	W	L	Pct	Sh	Sv-Op	Hld	ERC	ERA
2014	LV*	AAA	15	0	0	5	16.0	67	20	8	8	1	2	1	1	4	0	13	1	0	0	0	-	0	3- -	-	5.23	4.50
2011	Phi	NL	5	0	0	2	4.0	17	1	2	1	0	1	0	1	3	1	3	1	0	1	0	1.000	0	0-0	0	1.39	2.25
2012	Phi	NL	13	0	0	2	10.2	44	7	5	4	0	0	0	0	5	1	8	1	0	0	0	-	0	0-0	5	1.75	3.38
2013	Phi	NL	58	0	0	12	46.2	208	45	21	20	3	2	2	5	25	3	42	6	0	3	3	.500	0	0-1	9	4.50	3.86
2014	Phi	NL	54	0	0	17	52.2	219	45	19	14	4	1	1	3	12	4	49	2	0	3	1	.750	0	0-2	5	2.54	2.39
	4 ML YEARS		130	0	0	33	114.0	488	98	47	39	7	4	3	9	45	9	102	10	0	7	4	.636	0	0-3	19	3.17	3.08

Dane De La Rosa

Pitches: R **Bats:** R **Pos:** RP-3   **Ht:** 6'7" **Wt:** 245 **Born:** 2/1/1983 **Age:** 32

Year	Team	Lg	G	GS	CG	GF	IP	BFP	H	R	ER	HR	SH	SF	HB	TBB	IBB	SO	WP	Bk	W	L	Pct	Sh	Sv-Op	Hld	ERC	ERA
2014	Ark*	AA	2	0	0	1	2.0	6	1	0	0	0	0	0	0	0	0	2	0	0	0	0	-	0	0- -	-	0.63	0.00
2014	InldEm*	A+	1	0	0	0	1.0	3	0	0	0	0	0	0	0	0	0	1	0	0	0	0	-	0	0- -	-	0.00	0.00
2014	Salt Lk*	AAA	27	0	0	8	25.1	113	21	16	15	2	0	2	0	18	0	21	3	0	3	2	.600	0	3- -	-	4.15	5.33
2014	Angels*	R	2	1	0	0	2.0	9	2	3	3	1	0	0	1	0	0	2	0	0	0	0	-	0	0- -	-	7.30	13.50
2011	TB	AL	7	0	0	2	7.1	34	10	8	8	1	0	0	0	3	0	8	1	0	0	0	-	0	0-0	0	6.62	9.82
2012	TB	AL	5	0	0	5	5.0	22	7	7	7	2	0	0	0	2	0	5	0	0	0	0	-	0	0-0	0	9.62	12.60
2013	LAA	AL	75	0	0	20	72.1	291	56	25	23	3	2	4	1	28	2	65	6	0	6	1	.857	0	2-5	20	2.53	2.86
2014	LAA	AL	3	0	0	2	2.1	13	3	3	3	0	1	1	0	3	1	0	1	0	0	0	-	0	0-0	0	7.40	11.57
	4 ML YEARS		90	0	0	29	87.0	360	76	43	41	6	3	5	1	36	3	78	8	0	6	1	.857	0	2-5	20	3.29	4.24

Eury De La Rosa

YURR-ee

Pitches: L **Bats:** L **Pos:** RP-25   **Ht:** 5'9" **Wt:** 165 **Born:** 2/24/1990 **Age:** 25

Year	Team	Lg	G	GS	CG	GF	IP	BFP	H	R	ER	HR	SH	SF	HB	TBB	IBB	SO	WP	Bk	W	L	Pct	Sh	Sv-Op	Hld	ERC	ERA
2010	Yakima	A-	27	0	0	12	45.0	180	23	10	5	0	2	1	8	14	0	56	1	0	1	1	.500	0	9- -	-	1.43	1.00
2011	Sbend	A	39	0	0	23	53.0	206	36	11	8	3	2	3	5	13	1	51	5	1	0	1	1.000	0	10- -	-	1.98	1.36
2011	Visalia	A+	1	0	0	0	1.0	5	1	0	0	0	0	0	0	1	0	1	0	0	0	0	-	0	0- -	-	5.48	0.00
2011	Reno	AAA	1	0	0	0	1.0	6	3	2	2	0	0	0	0	1	0	1	1	0	0	0	-	0	0- -	-	22.91	18.00
2012	Mobile	AA	53	0	0	13	63.1	249	47	20	20	3	1	1	2	17	1	68	5	0	4	4	.500	0	8- -	-	2.07	2.84
2013	Reno	AAA	44	0	0	13	49.2	225	52	33	29	6	3	2	2	27	2	49	2	1	3	5	.375	0	0- -	-	5.17	5.26
2014	Reno	AAA	36	0	0	5	39.1	174	33	18	11	3	2	0	5	20	1	36	1	0	2	4	.333	0	2- -	-	3.84	2.52
2013	Ari	NL	19	0	0	6	14.2	62	13	13	12	5	1	0	0	5	0	16	1	0	0	0	-	0	0-0	2	4.70	7.36
2014	Ari	NL	25	0	0	12	36.2	158	37	12	12	2	0	0	3	14	4	32	1	1	2	0	1.000	0	0-1	0	3.93	2.95
	2 ML YEARS		44	0	0	18	51.1	220	50	25	24	7	1	0	3	19	4	48	2	1	2	1	.667	0	0-1	2	4.20	4.21

Jorge De La Rosa

Pitches: L **Bats:** L **Pos:** SP-32   **Ht:** 6'1" **Wt:** 215 **Born:** 4/5/1981 **Age:** 34

Year	Team	Lg	G	GS	CG	GF	IP	BFP	H	R	ER	HR	SH	SF	HB	TBB	IBB	SO	WP	Bk	W	L	Pct	Sh	Sv-Op	Hld	ERC	ERA
2004	Mil	NL	5	5	0	0	22.2	113	29	20	16	1	1	3	1	14	0	5	3	0	0	3	.000	0	0-0	0	6.12	6.35
2005	Mil	NL	38	0	0	13	42.1	208	48	23	21	1	2	2	0	38	4	42	6	0	2	2	.500	0	0-2	5	6.04	4.46
2006	2 Tms		28	13	0	4	79.0	367	81	59	57	14	2	4	2	54	1	67	6	1	5	6	.455	0	0-0	1	6.05	6.49
2007	KC	AL	26	23	0	1	130.0	589	160	88	84	20	2	4	3	53	6	82	4	1	8	12	.400	0	0-0	0	5.93	5.82
2008	Col	NL	28	23	0	0	130.0	571	128	77	71	13	6	7	7	62	3	128	14	1	10	8	.556	0	0-0	0	4.50	4.92
2009	Col	NL	33	32	0	0	185.0	799	172	95	90	20	11	6	9	83	3	193	12	1	16	9	.640	0	0-0	0	4.11	4.38
2010	Col	NL	20	20	0	0	121.2	512	105	62	57	15	3	3	5	55	4	113	9	1	8	7	.533	0	0-0	0	3.86	4.22
2011	Col	NL	10	10	1	0	59.0	245	48	25	23	4	4	1	2	22	0	52	6	1	5	2	.714	0	0-0	0	2.88	3.51
2012	Col	NL	3	3	0	0	10.2	53	17	14	11	5	1	0	0	2	0	6	2	0	0	2	.000	0	0-0	0	9.22	9.28
2013	Col	NL	30	30	0	0	167.2	714	170	70	65	11	11	5	5	62	5	112	5	0	16	6	.727	0	0-0	0	3.92	3.49
2014	Col	NL	32	32	0	0	184.1	768	161	90	84	21	9	5	9	67	2	139	9	0	14	11	.560	0	0-0	0	3.55	4.10
06	Mil	NL	18	3	0	4	30.1	146	32	30	29	4	1	3	1	22	1	31	4	0	2	1	.500	0	0-1	0	5.90	8.60
06	KC	AL	10	10	0	0	48.2	221	49	29	28	10	1	1	1	32	0	36	2	1	3	4	.429	0	0-0	0	6.14	5.18
	11 ML YEARS		253	191	1	18	1132.1	4939	1119	623	579	125	52	40	43	512	28	939	76	6	84	68	.553	0	0-2	6	4.42	4.60

Rubby De La Rosa

Pitches: R Bats: R Pos: SP-18; RP-1 — ROO-bee — Ht: 6'1" Wt: 205 Born: 3/4/1989 Age: 26

Year	Team	Lg	G	GS	CG	GF	IP	BFP	H	R	ER	HR	SH	SF	HB	TBB	IBB	SO	WP	Bk	W	L	Pct	Sh	Sv-Op	Hld	ERC	ERA
2014	Pwtckt*	AAA	12	12	0	0	60.0	248	50	27	23	1	1	3	1	25	0	57	4	1	2	4	.333	0	0- -	-	2.79	3.45
2011	LAD	NL	13	10	0	2	60.2	254	54	26	25	6	2	0	0	31	3	60	3	0	4	5	.444	0	0-1	1	3.94	3.71
2012	LAD	NL	1	0	0	0	0.2	4	0	2	2	0	0	0	0	2	0	0	0	0	0	0	-	0	0-0	0	7.00	27.00
2013	Bos	AL	11	0	0	7	11.1	53	15	7	7	2	0	0	3	2	0	6	1	0	0	2	.000	0	0-0	0	6.76	5.56
2014	Bos	AL	19	18	0	1	101.2	441	116	51	50	12	3	5	2	35	0	74	3	1	4	8	.333	0	0-0	0	4.96	4.43
	4 ML YEARS		44	28	0	10	174.1	752	185	86	84	20	5	5	5	70	3	140	7	1	8	15	.348	0	0-1	1	4.72	4.34

Jorge De Leon

Pitches: R Bats: R Pos: RP-8 — day-lee-OWN — Ht: 6'0" Wt: 185 Born: 8/15/1987 Age: 27

Year	Team	Lg	G	GS	CG	GF	IP	BFP	H	R	ER	HR	SH	SF	HB	TBB	IBB	SO	WP	Bk	W	L	Pct	Sh	Sv-Op	Hld	ERC	ERA
2010	TriCity	A-	23	0	0	20	28.0	121	26	5	2	0	3	0	1	12	2	29	2	0	2	1	.667	0	6- -	-	3.09	0.64
2011	Lxngtn	A	43	0	0	35	55.1	229	48	29	21	5	1	1	1	13	1	51	5	2	6	4	.600	0	16- -	-	2.66	3.42
2012	Lancst	A+	40	14	0	16	87.2	418	116	88	75	11	3	5	4	44	1	60	9	0	2	9	.182	0	6- -	-	6.80	7.70
2013	CpChr	AA	29	3	0	13	52.2	206	42	26	25	7	1	2	2	15	1	36	3	0	0	3	.000	0	6- -	-	3.01	4.27
2013	OKCity	AAA	12	0	0	8	15.0	55	8	1	1	0	0	0	1	2	0	12	0	0	0	0	-	0	6- -	-	0.82	0.60
2014	CpChr	AA	15	0	0	8	20.2	89	18	10	9	5	2	1	1	7	2	18	2	0	1	2	.333	0	2- -	-	3.98	3.92
2014	OKCity	AAA	31	0	0	13	48.0	198	46	16	14	0	1	1	1	16	1	43	1	0	3	3	.500	0	3- -	-	3.04	2.63
2013	Hou	AL	11	0	0	7	10.0	50	12	7	6	1	0	1	1	7	1	6	2	0	0	1	.000	0	0-0	1	6.56	5.40
2014	Hou	AL	8	0	0	3	7.1	33	9	4	4	2	0	1	0	3	0	4	1	0	0	0	-	0	0-0	1	6.86	4.91
	2 ML YEARS		19	0	0	10	17.1	83	21	11	10	3	0	2	1	10	1	10	3	0	0	1	.000	0	0-0	2	6.72	5.19

Jaff Decker

Bats: L Throws: L Pos: PH-4;LF-2 — JEFF — Ht: 5'9" Wt: 190 Born: 2/23/1990 Age: 25

Year	Team	Lg	G	AB	H	2B	3B	HR	(Hm	Rd)	TB	R	RBI	RC	TBB	IBB	SO	HBP	SH	SF	SB	CS	GDP	Avg	OBP	Slg	OPS
2010	Lk Els	A+	79	290	76	14	2	17	(-	-)	145	53	58	56	47	3	80	7	0	4	5	4	3	.262	.374	.500	.874
2011	SnAnt	AA	133	496	117	29	2	19	(-	-)	207	90	92	87	103	7	145	8	1	5	15	5	11	.236	.373	.417	.790
2012	SnAnt	AA	47	147	27	3	2	3	(-	-)	43	30	9	20	40	2	37	2	1	0	6	2	2	.184	.365	.293	.658
2012	Padres	R	9	27	8	1	2	1	(-	-)	16	5	7	6	4	0	3	1	0	1	0	0	1	.296	.394	.593	.987
2013	Tucsn	AAA	105	350	100	23	1	10	(-	-)	155	63	40	61	55	1	94	1	6	3	4	6	8	.286	.381	.443	.824
2014	Indy	AAA	104	350	90	27	1	6	(-	-)	137	41	39	52	51	2	73	3	3	2	7	6	10	.257	.355	.391	.746
2013	SD	NL	13	26	4	0	0	1	(0	1)	7	3	2	0	3	0	4	0	1	0	0	1	0	.154	.233	.269	.503
2014	Pit	NL	5	5	0	0	0	0	(0	0)	0	0	0	0	0	0	3	0	0	0	0	0	0	.000	.000	.000	.000
	2 ML YEARS		18	31	4	0	0	1	(0	1)	7	3	2	0	3	0	7	0	1	0	0	1	0	.129	.200	.226	.426

Samuel Deduno

Pitches: R Bats: R Pos: RP-26; SP-9 — deh-DUE-noh — Ht: 6'3" Wt: 190 Born: 7/2/1983 Age: 31

Year	Team	Lg	G	GS	CG	GF	IP	BFP	H	R	ER	HR	SH	SF	HB	TBB	IBB	SO	WP	Bk	W	L	Pct	Sh	Sv-Op	Hld	ERC	ERA
2010	Col	NL	4	0	0	3	2.2	12	3	1	1	1	0	0	0	1	0	3	0	0	0	0	-	0	0-0	1	6.59	3.38
2011	SD	NL	2	0	0	0	3.0	17	5	1	1	0	0	0	0	3	1	4	1	0	0	0	-	0	0-0	0	8.91	3.00
2012	Min	AL	15	15	0	0	79.0	347	69	40	39	10	1	2	5	53	0	57	5	0	6	5	.545	0	0-0	0	5.03	4.44
2013	Min	AL	18	18	0	0	108.0	461	105	48	46	7	3	3	9	41	0	67	8	2	8	8	.500	0	0-0	0	3.99	3.83
2014	2 Tms	AL	35	9	0	10	100.2	443	97	53	50	9	1	5	10	46	2	83	8	4	2	6	.250	0	0-0	2	4.40	4.47
14	Min	AL	30	8	0	8	92.0	408	92	49	47	9	1	4	10	41	1	74	8	3	2	5	.286	0	0-0	1	4.68	4.60
14	Hou	AL	5	1	0	2	8.2	35	5	4	3	0	0	1	0	5	1	9	0	1	0	1	.000	0	0-0	1	1.76	3.12
	5 ML YEARS		74	42	0	13	293.1	1280	279	143	137	27	5	10	24	144	3	214	22	6	16	19	.457	0	0-0	3	4.48	4.20

Jacob deGrom

Pitches: R Bats: L Pos: SP-22 — day-GRAHM — Ht: 6'4" Wt: 180 Born: 6/19/1988 Age: 27

Year	Team	Lg	G	GS	CG	GF	IP	BFP	H	R	ER	HR	SH	SF	HB	TBB	IBB	SO	WP	Bk	W	L	Pct	Sh	Sv-Op	Hld	ERC	ERA
2010	Kngspt	R+	6	6	0	0	26.0	115	35	15	15	2	1	0	0	6	1	22	1	0	1	1	.500	0	0- -	-	5.21	5.19
2012	Savann	A	15	15	0	0	89.2	363	77	33	25	3	2	4	1	14	0	78	2	1	6	3	.667	0	0- -	-	2.03	2.51
2012	StLuci	A+	4	4	0	0	21.2	87	14	5	5	1	1	0	1	6	0	18	3	0	3	0	1.000	0	0- -	-	1.65	2.08
2013	StLuci	A+	2	2	0	0	12.0	50	12	4	4	1	0	1	1	2	0	13	1	0	1	0	1.000	0	0- -	-	3.38	3.00
2013	Bnghtn	AA	10	10	0	0	60.0	261	69	38	32	4	2	2	2	20	3	44	3	1	2	5	.286	0	0- -	-	4.54	4.80
2013	LsVgs	AAA	14	14	0	0	75.2	331	87	41	38	6	1	3	1	24	0	63	3	0	4	2	.667	0	0- -	-	4.50	4.52
2014	LsVgs	AAA	7	7	0	0	38.1	161	39	13	11	2	1	3	1	10	0	29	2	0	4	0	1.000	0	0- -	-	3.42	2.58
2014	NYM	NL	22	22	0	0	140.1	565	117	44	42	7	5	3	1	43	2	144	1	0	9	6	.600	0	0-0	0	2.57	2.69

David DeJesus

Bats: L Throws: L Pos: DH-58;PH-18;LF-13;CF-3 — da-HAY-soos — Ht: 5'11" Wt: 190 Born: 12/20/1979 Age: 35

Year	Team	Lg	G	AB	H	2B	3B	HR	(Hm	Rd)	TB	R	RBI	RC	TBB	IBB	SO	HBP	SH	SF	SB	CS	GDP	Avg	OBP	Slg	OPS
2014	Rays*	R	1	1	0	0	0	0	(-	-)	0	1	0	0	1	0	0	0	0	0	0	0	0	.000	.500	.000	.500
2014	Charltt*	A+	7	22	5	0	0	0	(-	-)	5	1	2	2	4	0	4	1	0	1	1	1	0	.227	.357	.227	.584
2003	KC	AL	12	7	2	0	0	0	(0	0)	4	0	0	2	1	0	2	1	1	0	0	0	0	.286	.444	.571	1.016
2004	KC	AL	96	363	104	15	3	7	(2	5)	146	58	39	53	33	0	53	9	8	6	8	11	6	.287	.360	.402	.763
2005	KC	AL	122	461	135	31	6	9	(6	3)	205	69	56	77	42	1	76	9	5	6	5	5	6	.293	.359	.445	.804
2006	KC	AL	119	491	145	36	7	8	(4	4)	219	83	56	76	43	4	70	12	2	4	6	3	10	.295	.364	.446	.810

(Batting — continued)

Year	Team	Lg	G	AB	H	2B	3B	HR	(Hm	Rd)	TB	R	RBI	RC	TBB	IBB	SO	HBP	SH	SF	SB	CS	GDP	Avg	OBP	Slg	OPS
2007	KC	AL	157	605	157	29	9	7	(3	4)	225	101	58	87	64	7	83	23	7	4	10	4	10	.260	.351	.372	.722
2008	KC	AL	135	518	159	25	7	12	(6	6)	234	70	73	93	46	3	71	5	4	4	11	8	10	.307	.366	.452	.818
2009	KC	AL	144	558	157	28	9	13	(4	9)	242	74	71	83	51	0	87	8	5	5	4	9	10	.281	.347	.434	.781
2010	KC	AL	91	352	112	23	3	5	(2	3)	156	46	37	50	34	2	47	4	3	1	3	3	10	.318	.384	.443	.827
2011	Oak	AL	131	442	106	20	5	10	(4	6)	166	60	46	49	45	1	86	11	4	4	4	3	14	.240	.323	.376	.698
2012	ChC	NL	148	506	133	28	8	9	(4	5)	204	76	50	73	61	1	89	9	2	4	7	8	9	.263	.350	.403	.753
2013	3 Tms		122	391	98	29	3	8	(5	3)	157	52	38	51	39	0	79	6	2	1	5	3	6	.251	.327	.402	.729
2014	TB	AL	83	238	59	15	2	6	(3	3)	96	24	19	25	30	1	43	5	0	0	0	3	7	.248	.344	.403	.748
13	ChC	NL	84	284	71	19	3	6	(4	2)	114	39	27	40	29	0	55	5	0	0	3	0	3	.250	.330	.401	.732
13	Was	NL	3	3	0	0	0	0	(0	0)	0	0	0	0	0	0	1	0	1	0	0	0	0	.000	.000	.000	.000
13	TB	AL	35	104	27	10	0	2	(1	1)	43	13	11	11	10	0	23	1	1	1	2	3	3	.260	.328	.413	.741
Postseason			5	13	3	1	0	0	(0	0)	4	2	1	2	1	0	6	2	0	0	0	0	1	.231	.375	.308	.683
12 ML YEARS			1360	4932	1367	279	63	94	(43	51)	2054	713	543	719	489	20	786	102	43	33	63	60	98	.277	.352	.416	.769

Steve Delabar

Pitches: R Bats: R Pos: RP-30   DELL-uh-bar   **Ht: 6'5" Wt: 220 Born: 7/17/1983 Age: 31**

Year	Team	Lg	G	GS	CG	GF	IP	BFP	H	R	ER	HR	SH	SF	HB	TBB	IBB	SO	WP	Bk	W	L	Pct	Sh	Sv-Op	Hld	ERC	ERA
2014	Buffalo*	AAA	24	0	0	10	28.0	123	21	9	9	3	1	0	3	18	0	38	4	0	2	2	.500	0	1--	-	4.11	2.89
2011	Sea	AL	6	0	0	4	7.0	28	5	2	2	1	0	0	1	4	1	7	0	0	1	1	.500	0	0-0	0	4.15	2.57
2012	2 Tms	AL	61	0	0	12	66.0	274	46	29	28	12	3	2	5	26	1	92	6	0	4	3	.571	0	0-2	12	3.18	3.82
2013	Tor	AL	55	0	0	14	58.2	253	50	25	21	4	3	3	2	29	5	82	4	1	5	5	.500	0	1-6	6	3.38	3.22
2014	Tor	AL	30	0	0	0	25.2	114	19	14	14	3	1	1	3	19	0	21	2	0	3	0	1.000	0	0-0	12	4.59	4.91
12	Sea	AL	34	0	0	11	36.2	148	23	17	17	9	2	0	5	11	1	46	3	0	2	1	.667	0	0-2	3	3.07	4.17
12	Tor	AL	27	0	0	1	29.1	126	23	12	11	3	1	2	0	15	0	46	3	0	2	2	.500	0	0-0	9	3.27	3.38
4 ML YEARS			152	0	0	30	157.1	669	120	70	65	20	7	6	11	78	7	202	12	1	13	9	.591	0	1-8	30	3.53	3.72

Randall Delgado

Pitches: R Bats: R Pos: RP-43; SP-4   **Ht: 6'3" Wt: 200 Born: 2/9/1990 Age: 25**

Year	Team	Lg	G	GS	CG	GF	IP	BFP	H	R	ER	HR	SH	SF	HB	TBB	IBB	SO	WP	Bk	W	L	Pct	Sh	Sv-Op	Hld	ERC	ERA
2011	Atl	NL	7	7	0	0	35.0	147	29	12	11	5	0	0	1	14	1	18	2	0	1	1	.500	0	0-0	0	3.48	2.83
2012	Atl	NL	18	17	0	0	92.2	401	89	48	45	8	5	3	4	42	4	76	5	1	4	9	.308	0	0-0	0	4.10	4.37
2013	Ari	NL	20	19	1	0	116.1	473	116	59	55	24	5	5	1	23	2	79	3	1	5	7	.417	1	0-0	0	4.03	4.26
2014	Ari	NL	47	4	0	6	77.2	339	71	44	42	6	2	2	3	35	2	86	5	0	4	4	.500	0	0-0	2	3.69	4.87
4 ML YEARS			92	47	1	6	321.2	1360	305	163	153	43	12	10	9	114	9	259	15	2	14	21	.400	1	0-0	2	3.93	4.28

Ryan Dempster

Pitches: R Bats: R Pos: P   **Ht: 6'2" Wt: 215 Born: 5/3/1977 Age: 38**

Year	Team	Lg	G	GS	CG	GF	IP	BFP	H	R	ER	HR	SH	SF	HB	TBB	IBB	SO	WP	Bk	W	L	Pct	Sh	Sv-Op	Hld	ERC	ERA
1998	Fla	NL	14	11	0	1	54.2	243	72	47	43	6	5	6	9	38	1	35	5	0	1	5	.167	0	0-1	0	8.14	7.08
1999	Fla	NL	25	25	0	0	147.0	666	146	77	77	21	3	6	6	93	2	126	8	0	7	8	.467	0	0-0	0	5.49	4.71
2000	Fla	NL	33	33	2	0	226.1	974	210	102	92	30	4	5	5	97	7	209	4	0	14	10	.583	1	0-0	0	4.04	3.66
2001	Fla	NL	34	34	2	0	211.1	918	218	123	116	21	15	7	10	112	5	171	5	0	15	12	.556	1	0-0	0	4.91	4.94
2002	2 Tms	NL	33	33	4	0	209.0	915	228	127	125	28	9	6	10	93	2	153	2	0	10	13	.435	0	0-0	0	5.35	5.38
2003	Cin	NL	22	20	0	1	115.2	545	134	89	84	14	9	4	5	70	4	84	3	0	3	7	.300	0	0-0	0	6.11	6.54
2004	ChC	NL	23	0	0	8	20.2	93	16	9	9	1	1	0	2	13	0	18	1	0	1	1	.500	0	2-2	3	3.61	3.92
2005	ChC	NL	63	6	0	53	92.0	401	83	35	32	4	5	4	4	49	7	89	4	0	5	3	.625	0	33-35	0	3.69	3.13
2006	ChC	NL	74	0	0	64	75.0	342	77	47	40	5	5	4	3	36	3	67	6	0	1	9	.100	0	24-33	2	4.26	4.80
2007	ChC	NL	66	0	0	58	66.2	282	59	36	35	8	3	2	1	30	4	55	2	1	2	7	.222	0	28-31	0	3.77	4.73
2008	ChC	NL	33	33	1	0	206.2	856	174	79	68	14	4	3	7	76	1	187	5	0	17	6	.739	0	0-0	0	3.03	2.96
2009	ChC	NL	31	31	1	0	200.0	842	196	94	81	22	10	8	6	65	4	172	11	0	11	9	.550	1	0-0	0	3.87	3.65
2010	ChC	NL	34	34	1	0	215.1	918	198	110	92	25	9	2	10	86	4	208	9	0	15	12	.556	0	0-0	0	3.91	3.85
2011	ChC	NL	34	34	0	0	202.1	881	211	111	108	23	12	3	5	82	2	191	7	0	10	14	.417	0	0-0	0	4.55	4.80
2012	2 Tms	NL	28	28	0	0	173.0	717	155	71	65	19	5	4	2	52	0	153	2	1	12	8	.600	0	0-0	0	3.23	3.38
2013	Bos	AL	32	29	0	0	171.1	754	170	97	87	20	1	4	0	79	1	157	9	1	8	9	.471	0	0-0	0	4.78	4.57
02	Fla	NL	18	18	3	0	120.1	521	126	66	64	12	7	3	7	55	1	87	0	0	5	8	.385	0	0-0	0	4.95	4.79
02	Cin	NL	15	15	1	0	88.2	394	102	61	61	16	2	3	3	38	1	66	2	0	5	5	.500	0	0-0	0	5.90	6.19
12	ChC	NL	16	16	0	0	104.0	417	81	28	26	9	2	1	1	27	0	83	0	1	5	5	.500	0	0-0	0	2.34	2.25
12	Tex	AL	12	12	0	0	69.0	300	74	43	39	10	3	3	1	25	0	70	2	0	7	3	.700	0	0-0	0	4.73	5.09
Postseason			5	1	0	3	8.2	39	8	5	5	2	0	0	0	7	0	7	0	0	0	1	.000	0	0-0	0	6.53	5.19
16 ML YEARS			579	351	11	186	2387.0	10412	2347	1250	1154	267	100	64	91	1071	47	2075	80	3	132	133	.498	3	87-102	5	4.39	4.35

Matt den Dekker

Bats: L Throws: L Pos: LF-28;CF-18;PH-8;RF-1;PR-1   **Ht: 6'1" Wt: 210 Born: 8/10/1987 Age: 27**

Year	Team	Lg	G	AB	H	2B	3B	HR	(Hm	Rd)	TB	R	RBI	RC	TBB	IBB	SO	HBP	SH	SF	SB	CS	GDP	Avg	OBP	Slg	OPS
2010	Mets	R	5	18	5	2	0	0	(-	-)	7	2	5	2	2	0	5	0	1	0	0	0	1	.278	.350	.389	.739
2010	Savann	A	27	104	36	13	0	0	(-	-)	49	21	15	20	9	0	28	1	0	0	3	0	0	.346	.404	.471	.875
2011	StLuci	A+	67	267	79	19	8	6	(-	-)	132	54	36	49	24	0	65	5	4	2	12	5	3	.296	.362	.494	.857
2011	Bnghtn	AA	72	272	64	13	3	11	(-	-)	116	49	32	38	27	0	91	5	6	4	12	5	3	.235	.312	.426	.738
2012	Bnghtn	AA	58	238	81	21	4	8	(-	-)	134	47	29	51	20	0	64	5	1	4	10	7	3	.340	.397	.563	.960
2012	Buffalo	AAA	77	295	65	10	4	9	(-	-)	110	37	47	30	14	1	90	2	1	5	11	2	2	.220	.256	.373	.629
2013	StLuci	A+	14	58	16	2	0	0	(-	-)	18	8	4	6	3	0	6	0	0	1	1	0	1	.276	.306	.310	.617
2013	LsVgs	AAA	53	179	53	8	4	6	(-	-)	87	34	38	33	20	3	46	1	0	2	8	1	2	.296	.366	.486	.852

Year Team	Lg	G	AB	H	2B	3B	HR	(Hm	Rd)	TB	R	RBI	RC	TBB	IBB	SO	HBP	SH	SF	SB	CS	GDP	Avg	OBP	Slg	OPS
2014 LsVgs	AAA	93	335	112	31	7	8	(-	-)	181	70	46	72	40	2	65	3	3	3	9	5	2	.334	.407	.540	.947
2013 NYM	NL	27	58	12	1	0	1	(0	1)	16	7	6	5	4	0	23	1	0	0	4	1	0	.207	.270	.276	.546
2014 NYM	NL	53	152	38	11	0	0	(0	0)	49	23	7	17	21	0	34	1	0	0	7	4	1	.250	.345	.322	.667
2 ML YEARS		80	210	50	12	0	1	(0	1)	65	30	13	22	25	0	57	2	0	0	11	5	1	.238	.325	.310	.634

Ryan Dennick

Pitches: L **Bats:** L **Pos:** RP-8   **Ht:** 6'0" **Wt:** 185 **Born:** 1/10/1987 **Age:** 28

Year Team	Lg	G	GS	CG	GF	IP	BFP	H	R	ER	HR	SH	SF	HB	TBB	IBB	SO	WP	Bk	W	L	Pct	Sh	Sv-Op	Hld	ERC	ERA
2010 Burlgtn	A	27	0	0	21	43.2	188	44	22	21	2	2	1	0	15	0	41	4	0	3	4	.429	0	6- -	-	3.48	4.33
2010 Wilmg	A+	8	0	0	3	12.2	57	17	8	7	0	0	0	3	7	0	8	1	0	2	0	1.000	0	0- -	-	6.93	4.97
2011 Wilmg	A+	35	0	0	25	53.2	228	55	30	26	4	4	2	2	14	1	51	2	0	3	7	.300	0	4- -	-	3.60	4.36
2012 Wilmg	A+	6	1	0	1	21.2	91	26	11	11	2	0	1	1	6	1	17	0	0	2	1	.667	0	0- -	-	5.06	4.57
2012 NWArk	AA	30	3	0	12	74.0	322	65	45	38	9	5	0	5	30	0	72	8	0	6	5	.545	0	4- -	-	3.75	4.62
2013 Pnscla	AA	19	18	1	0	104.0	429	101	46	41	8	4	1	1	26	0	66	3	0	5	10	.333	0	0- -	-	3.25	3.55
2013 Lsvlle	AAA	8	3	0	0	18.2	85	21	11	11	2	1	0	0	9	0	12	0	0	0	1	.000	0	0- -	-	5.12	5.30
2014 Pnscla	AA	1	0	0	0	0.1	3	2	0	0	0	0	0	0	0	0	1	0	0	0	0	-	0	0- -	-	39.65	0.00
2014 Lsvlle	AAA	57	0	0	8	49.2	204	42	15	13	0	2	1	1	18	1	39	4	1	4	0	1.000	0	3- -	-	2.53	2.36
2014 Cin	NL	8	0	0	2	4.2	25	7	7	6	2	0	1	0	4	0	3	2	0	0	0	-	0	0-0	1	12.12	11.57

Chris Denorfia

denn-ORE-fee-ah

Bats: R **Throws:** R **Pos:** RF-76;PH-37;LF-33;CF-14;PR-3;DH-1   **Ht:** 6'0" **Wt:** 195 **Born:** 7/15/1980 **Age:** 34

Year Team	Lg	G	AB	H	2B	3B	HR	(Hm	Rd)	TB	R	RBI	RC	TBB	IBB	SO	HBP	SH	SF	SB	CS	GDP	Avg	OBP	Slg	OPS
2005 Cin	NL	18	38	10	3	0	1	(1	0)	16	8	2	3	6	0	9	0	0	0	1	0	1	.263	.364	.421	.785
2006 Cin	NL	49	106	30	6	0	1	(0	1)	39	14	7	13	11	1	21	1	2	0	1	1	1	.283	.356	.368	.724
2008 Oak	AL	29	62	18	3	0	1	(0	1)	24	10	9	9	6	0	16	1	2	0	2	0	3	.290	.362	.387	.749
2009 Oak	AL	4	2	0	0	0	0	(0	0)	0	1	1	0	0	0	0	0	0	0	0	0	0	.000	.000	.000	.000
2010 SD	NL	99	284	77	15	2	9	(3	6)	123	41	36	37	27	3	51	2	1	3	8	4	5	.271	.335	.433	.769
2011 SD	NL	111	307	85	13	2	5	(1	4)	117	38	19	34	28	1	49	1	2	2	11	6	10	.277	.337	.381	.718
2012 SD	NL	130	348	102	19	6	8	(3	5)	157	56	36	49	27	0	52	2	2	3	13	5	9	.293	.345	.451	.796
2013 SD	NL	144	473	132	21	2	10	(6	4)	187	67	47	63	42	2	84	1	0	4	11	0	14	.279	.337	.395	.732
2014 2 Tms		121	330	76	12	4	3	(0	3)	105	36	21	31	25	0	70	0	2	1	9	3	6	.230	.284	.318	.602
14 SD	NL	89	248	60	10	3	1	(0	1)	79	25	16	27	18	0	51	0	2	0	8	1	4	.242	.293	.319	.612
14 Sea	AL	32	82	16	2	1	2	(0	2)	26	11	5	4	7	0	19	0	0	1	1	2	2	.195	.256	.317	.573
9 ML YEARS		705	1950	530	92	16	38	(14	24)	768	271	178	239	172	7	352	8	11	13	56	19	49	.272	.331	.394	.725

Daniel Descalso

dess-CAL-so

Bats: L **Throws:** R **Pos:** PH-57;2B-21;SS-19;3B-14;1B-4;PR-2   **Ht:** 5'10" **Wt:** 190 **Born:** 10/19/1986 **Age:** 28

Year Team	Lg	G	AB	H	2B	3B	HR	(Hm	Rd)	TB	R	RBI	RC	TBB	IBB	SO	HBP	SH	SF	SB	CS	GDP	Avg	OBP	Slg	OPS
2010 StL	NL	11	34	9	2	0	0	(0	0)	11	6	4	5	2	0	6	1	0	0	1	0	0	.265	.324	.324	.648
2011 StL	NL	148	326	86	20	3	1	(1	0)	115	35	28	40	33	9	65	3	10	3	2	2	3	.264	.334	.353	.687
2012 StL	NL	143	374	85	10	7	4	(0	4)	121	41	26	29	37	3	83	5	7	1	6	3	6	.227	.303	.324	.627
2013 StL	NL	123	328	78	25	1	5	(1	4)	120	43	43	40	22	5	56	3	3	2	6	3	7	.238	.290	.366	.656
2014 StL	NL	104	161	39	11	0	0	(0	0)	50	20	10	15	20	0	33	2	1	0	1	3	2	.242	.333	.311	.644
Postseason		40	82	18	2	0	2	(1	1)	26	16	6	5	4	2	19	0	4	1	2	0	2	.220	.253	.317	.570
5 ML YEARS		529	1223	297	68	11	10	(2	8)	417	145	111	129	114	17	243	14	21	8	16	11	17	.243	.313	.341	.654

Anthony DeSclafani

DEE-skla-fa-nee

Pitches: R **Bats:** R **Pos:** RP-8; SP-5   **Ht:** 6'1" **Wt:** 190 **Born:** 4/18/1990 **Age:** 25

Year Team	Lg	G	GS	CG	GF	IP	BFP	H	R	ER	HR	SH	SF	HB	TBB	IBB	SO	WP	Bk	W	L	Pct	Sh	Sv-Op	Hld	ERC	ERA
2012 Lnsng	A	28	21	0	0	123.0	510	145	55	46	3	3	7	3	25	0	92	6	2	11	3	.786	0	0- -	-	4.03	3.37
2013 Jupiter	A+	12	12	0	0	54.0	214	48	18	10	3	0	1	1	9	0	53	3	0	4	2	.667	0	0- -	-	2.45	1.67
2013 Jaxnvl	AA	13	13	0	0	75.0	304	74	31	28	7	4	1	4	14	0	62	4	1	5	4	.556	0	0- -	-	3.43	3.36
2014 Jaxnvl	AA	8	8	0	0	43.0	175	45	20	20	4	3	0	0	10	0	38	2	0	3	4	.429	0	0- -	-	3.76	4.19
2014 NewOr	AAA	12	11	0	1	59.1	249	48	23	23	2	3	1	4	21	0	58	4	0	3	3	.500	0	0- -	-	2.66	3.49
2014 Mia	NL	13	5	0	4	33.0	146	40	23	23	4	2	1	0	5	0	26	2	0	2	2	.500	0	0-0	-	4.56	6.27

Ian Desmond

Bats: R **Throws:** R **Pos:** SS-154   **Ht:** 6'3" **Wt:** 215 **Born:** 9/20/1985 **Age:** 29

Year Team	Lg	G	AB	H	2B	3B	HR	(Hm	Rd)	TB	R	RBI	RC	TBB	IBB	SO	HBP	SH	SF	SB	CS	GDP	Avg	OBP	Slg	OPS
2009 Was	NL	21	82	23	7	2	4	(2	2)	46	9	12	10	5	0	14	0	1	1	1	0	2	.280	.318	.561	.879
2010 Was	NL	154	525	141	27	4	10	(8	2)	206	59	65	58	28	3	109	5	9	7	17	5	9	.269	.308	.392	.700
2011 Was	NL	154	584	148	27	5	8	(7	1)	209	65	49	65	35	2	139	4	11	5	25	10	9	.253	.298	.358	.656
2012 Was	NL	130	513	150	33	2	25	(16	9)	262	72	73	73	30	1	113	3	0	1	21	6	17	.292	.335	.511	.845
2013 Was	NL	158	600	168	38	3	20	(10	10)	272	77	80	81	43	3	145	4	2	5	21	6	16	.280	.331	.453	.784
2014 Was	NL	154	593	151	26	3	24	(12	12)	255	73	91	78	46	0	183	6	0	3	24	5	17	.255	.313	.430	.743
Postseason		5	19	7	1	0	0	(0	0)	8	2	0	2	0	0	3	0	0	0	0	0	0	.368	.368	.421	.789
6 ML YEARS		771	2897	781	158	19	91	(55	36)	1250	355	370	365	187	9	703	23	23	22	109	32	70	.270	.317	.431	.748

Odrisamer Despaigne

Pitches: R **Bats:** R **Pos:** SP-16   oh-DREE-sa-mehr des-PAHN-yay   **Ht:** 6'0" **Wt:** 195 **Born:** 4/4/1987 **Age:** 28

			HOW MUCH HE PITCHED						WHAT HE GAVE UP											THE RESULTS							
Year	Team	Lg	G	GS	CG	GF	IP	BFP	H	R	ER	HR	SH	SF	HB	TBB	IBB	SO	WP	Bk	W	L	Pct	Sh	Sv-Op	Hld	ERC	ERA
2014	SnAnt	AA	2	2	0	0	7.2	32	4	1	1	0	0	0	1	5	0	12	0	0		0	-	0	0- -	-	2.31	1.17
2014	ElPaso	AAA	5	5	0	0	23.2	121	36	20	20	3	2	4	1	13	0	29	1	0	1	3	.250	0	0- -	-	8.14	7.61
2014	SD	NL	16	16	0	0	96.1	404	85	44	36	6	8	1	5	32	0	65	1	0	4	7	.364	0	0-0	0	3.12	3.36

Ross Detwiler

Pitches: L **Bats:** R **Pos:** RP-47   DETT-why-lerr   **Ht:** 6'5" **Wt:** 210 **Born:** 3/6/1986 **Age:** 29

			HOW MUCH HE PITCHED						WHAT HE GAVE UP											THE RESULTS							
Year	Team	Lg	G	GS	CG	GF	IP	BFP	H	R	ER	HR	SH	SF	HB	TBB	IBB	SO	WP	Bk	W	L	Pct	Sh	Sv-Op	Hld	ERC	ERA
2007	Was	NL	1	0	0	1	1.0	4	0	0	0	0	0	0	0	0	0	1	0	0	0	0	-	0	0-0	0	0.00	0.00
2009	Was	NL	15	14	1	0	75.2	341	87	43	42	3	4	1	2	33	3	43	4	0	1	6	.143	0	0-0	0	4.65	5.00
2010	Was	NL	8	5	0	1	29.2	135	34	22	14	5	2	0	1	14	1	17	1	0	1	3	.250	0	0-0	0	5.83	4.25
2011	Was	NL	15	10	0	0	66.0	277	63	26	22	7	7	3	3	20	2	41	2	0	4	5	.444	0	0-0	1	3.64	3.00
2012	Was	NL	33	27	0	1	164.1	686	149	75	62	15	8	3	5	52	0	105	4	1	10	8	.556	0	0-0	1	3.30	3.40
2013	Was	NL	13	13	0	0	71.1	316	92	37	32	5	4	1	5	14	2	39	0	0	2	7	.222	0	0-0	0	4.96	4.04
2014	Was	NL	47	0	0	15	63.0	274	68	34	28	5	4	3	5	21	4	39	3	0	2	3	.400	0	1-2	3	4.36	4.00
	Postseason		1	1	0	0	6.0	25	3	1	0	0	1	1	0	3	1	2	0	0	0	0	-	0	0-0	0	1.21	0.00
	7 ML YEARS		132	69	1	18	471.0	2033	493	237	200	40	29	11	21	154	12	285	14	1	20	32	.385	0	1-2	5	4.08	3.82

Jairo Diaz

Pitches: R **Bats:** R **Pos:** RP-5   HIGH-row   **Ht:** 6'0" **Wt:** 195 **Born:** 5/27/1991 **Age:** 24

			HOW MUCH HE PITCHED						WHAT HE GAVE UP											THE RESULTS							
Year	Team	Lg	G	GS	CG	GF	IP	BFP	H	R	ER	HR	SH	SF	HB	TBB	IBB	SO	WP	Bk	W	L	Pct	Sh	Sv-Op	Hld	ERC	ERA
2011	Angels	R	11	10	0	0	57.1	241	59	33	26	3	2	1	3	18	0	44	7	0	4	1	.800	0	0- -	-	3.87	4.08
2011	CRpds	A	4	4	0	0	18.2	90	24	18	17	1	0	0	3	12	1	10	1	0	0	3	.000	0	0- -	-	7.19	8.20
2012	CRpds	A	13	13	0	0	69.0	332	99	63	59	8	2	6	6	29	0	45	7	0	2	7	.222	0	0- -	-	7.32	7.70
2012	Orem	R+	14	14	0	0	74.2	335	93	57	44	5	0	2	4	23	1	61	17	1	5	6	.455	0	0- -	-	5.08	5.30
2013	Burlgtn	A	32	0	0	22	34.0	141	27	16	15	3	1	2	4	11	1	28	2	0	0	3	.000	0	8- -	-	3.01	3.97
2013	InldEm	A+	13	0	0	4	22.1	118	38	27	22	3	2	0	0	14	1	21	6	1	0	2	.000	0	0- -	-	9.57	8.87
2014	InldEm	A+	29	0	0	16	32.0	140	31	18	17	2	2	0	1	10	1	37	8	0	2	3	.400	0	4- -	-	3.25	4.78
2014	Ark	AA	27	0	0	18	32.2	134	30	8	8	2	3	1	1	10	1	48	4	0	2	1	.667	0	11- -	-	3.15	2.20
2014	LAA	AL	5	0	0	2	5.2	24	4	2	2	0	0	1	0	3	0	8	0	0	0	0	-	0	0-0	0	2.29	3.18

Jonathan Diaz

Bats: R **Throws:** R **Pos:** SS-14;2B-5;PH-3;PR-3;LF-1;CF-1;RF-1   **Ht:** 5'9" **Wt:** 155 **Born:** 4/10/1985 **Age:** 30

			BATTING																		RUNNING			AVERAGES			
Year	Team	Lg	G	AB	H	2B	3B	HR	(Hm	Rd)	TB	R	RBI	RC	TBB	IBB	SO	HBP	SH	SF	SB	CS	GDP	Avg	OBP	Slg	OPS
2010	NHam	AA	99	312	72	20	1	0	(-	-)	94	48	33	40	53	0	48	9	8	3	5	2	7	.231	.355	.301	.657
2010	LsVgs	AAA	28	94	25	3	0	2	(-	-)	34	20	10	12	8	0	18	0	10	1	1	0	0	.266	.320	.362	.682
2011	NHam	AA	70	218	55	11	0	1	(-	-)	69	29	19	28	28	0	48	9	6	1	7	5	8	.252	.359	.317	.676
2011	LsVgs	AAA	19	64	19	3	0	1	(-	-)	25	9	10	12	15	0	15	0	0	1	2	1	1	.297	.425	.391	.816
2011	Dnedin	A+	3	10	4	1	0	0	(-	-)	5	3	1	2	3	0	3	0	0	0	0	0	0	.400	.538	.500	1.038
2012	NHam	AA	39	145	26	2	0	1	(-	-)	31	18	9	8	13	0	28	2	2	1	6	2	4	.179	.255	.214	.468
2012	LsVgs	AAA	95	312	75	11	2	3	(-	-)	99	58	31	46	62	0	56	8	15	4	12	4	7	.240	.374	.317	.691
2013	Pwtckt	AAA	103	332	84	11	2	2	(-	-)	105	45	31	44	47	0	67	8	11	1	10	3	6	.253	.358	.316	.675
2014	Buffalo	AAA	92	244	50	13	3	1	(-	-)	72	37	23	26	37	0	43	5	15	2	4	4	5	.205	.319	.295	.615
2013	Bos	AL	5	4	0	0	0	0	(0	0)	0	2	0	0	0	0	0	0	0	0	0	0	0	.000	.000	.000	.000
2014	Tor	AL	23	38	6	1	0	0	(0	0)	7	3	4	2	3	0	14	2	2	0	1	0	1	.158	.256	.184	.440
	2 ML YEARS		28	42	6	1	0	0	(0	0)	7	5	4	2	3	0	14	2	2	0	1	0	1	.143	.234	.167	.401

Jumbo Diaz

Pitches: R **Bats:** R **Pos:** RP-36   **Ht:** 6'4" **Wt:** 315 **Born:** 2/27/1984 **Age:** 31

			HOW MUCH HE PITCHED						WHAT HE GAVE UP											THE RESULTS							
Year	Team	Lg	G	GS	CG	GF	IP	BFP	H	R	ER	HR	SH	SF	HB	TBB	IBB	SO	WP	Bk	W	L	Pct	Sh	Sv-Op	Hld	ERC	ERA
2010	Frdrck	A+	26	0	0	23	26.2	107	21	5	5	1	0	1	0	9	0	33	1	0	3	0	1.000	0	12- -	-	2.37	1.69
2010	Bowie	AA	19	0	0	11	25.0	102	19	7	6	1	0	0	2	11	0	25	1	0	1	0	1.000	0	4- -	-	2.93	2.16
2011	Bowie	AA	34	0	0	30	32.0	132	21	9	5	2	4	1	1	13	0	38	3	0	0	0	.000	0	22- -	-	2.14	1.41
2011	Norfolk	AAA	14	0	0	6	12.2	67	21	10	8	1	0	0	2	8	0	10	1	0	1	0	1.000	0	1- -	-	9.80	5.68
2012	Indy	AAA	41	0	0	16	45.0	197	43	19	18	3	2	2	4	19	4	37	3	0	1	2	.333	0	3- -	-	3.86	3.60
2013	Lsvlle	AAA	44	0	0	27	54.1	217	35	11	10	5	1	1	1	21	3	60	1	0	3	4	.429	0	13- -	-	2.14	1.66
2014	Lsvlle	AAA	30	0	0	28	33.1	134	25	6	4	1	1	2	0	10	1	31	1	0	2	2	.500	0	18- -	-	2.16	1.08
2014	Cin	NL	36	0	0	12	34.2	142	29	13	13	3	0	2	0	14	4	37	1	0	0	1	.000	0	0-1	8	3.00	3.38

Chris Dickerson

Bats: L **Throws:** L **Pos:** LF-19;RF-11;PH-9;CF-5;DH-4;PR-1   **Ht:** 6'4" **Wt:** 230 **Born:** 4/10/1982 **Age:** 33

			BATTING																		RUNNING			AVERAGES			
Year	Team	Lg	G	AB	H	2B	3B	HR	(Hm	Rd)	TB	R	RBI	RC	TBB	IBB	SO	HBP	SH	SF	SB	CS	GDP	Avg	OBP	Slg	OPS
2014	Indy*	AAA	65	236	73	15	2	7	(-	-)	113	44	30	48	33	1	65	8	0	3	12	5	0	.309	.407	.479	.886
2008	Cin	NL	31	102	31	9	2	6	(4	2)	62	20	15	22	17	0	35	2	1	0	5	3	0	.304	.413	.608	1.021
2009	Cin	NL	97	255	70	13	3	2	(0	2)	95	31	15	34	39	1	66	1	2	2	11	3	3	.275	.370	.373	.743
2010	2 Tms	NL	45	97	20	2	0	0	(0	0)	26	11	5	6	6	0	34	0	2	1	4	0	1	.206	.250	.268	.518
2011	NYY	AL	60	50	13	2	0	1	(0	1)	18	9	7	6	2	0	17	1	1	1	4	0	1	.260	.296	.360	.656
2012	NYY	AL	25	14	4	0	0	2	(1	1)	10	5	3	5	3	0	5	0	0	0	3	0	1	.286	.412	.714	1.126

Year	Team	Lg	G	AB	H	2B	3B	HR	(Hm	Rd)	TB	R	RBI	RC	TBB	IBB	SO	HBP	SH	SF	SB	CS	GDP	Avg	OBP	Slg	OPS
2013	Bal	AL	56	105	25	5	0	4	(4	0)	42	17	13	12	4	0	36	0	0	0	5	1	0	.238	.266	.400	.666
2014	Cle	AL	41	98	22	4	0	2	(0	2)	32	12	6	8	12	0	38	0	2	0	3	0	2	.224	.309	.327	.636
10	Cin	NL	20	44	9	1	1	0	(0	0)	12	9	0	3	1	0	19	0	0	0	3	0	1	.205	.222	.273	.495
10	Mil	NL	25	53	11	1	1	0	(0	0)	14	2	5	3	5	0	15	0	2	1	1	0	0	.208	.271	.264	.535
	Postseason		1	1	0	0	0	0	(0	0)	0	1	0	0	0	0	0	0	0	0	0	0	0	.000	.000	.000	.000
	7 ML YEARS		355	721	185	35	7	17	(9	8)	285	105	66	92	83	1	231	4	8	4	35	7	8	.257	.335	.395	.730

Corey Dickerson

Bats: L **Throws:** R **Pos:** LF-99;PH-21;CF-9;DH-7   **Ht:** 6'1" **Wt:** 205 **Born:** 5/22/1989 **Age:** 26

Year	Team	Lg	G	AB	H	2B	3B	HR	(Hm	Rd)	TB	R	RBI	RC	TBB	IBB	SO	HBP	SH	SF	SB	CS	GDP	Avg	OBP	Slg	OPS
2010	Casper	R+	69	276	96	22	9	13	(-	-)	175	54	61	68	28	5	51	3	0	1	12	6	4	.348	.412	.634	1.046
2011	Ashvll	A	106	383	108	27	5	32	(-	-)	241	78	87	84	39	0	99	8	0	5	9	6	5	.282	.356	.629	.986
2012	Mdest	A+	60	240	81	24	4	9	(-	-)	140	43	43	54	25	5	42	1	0	4	9	5	3	.338	.396	.583	.980
2012	Tulsa	AA	67	266	73	16	3	13	(-	-)	134	40	38	44	18	1	51	2	0	3	7	3	2	.274	.322	.504	.826
2013	ColSpr	AAA	75	315	117	21	14	11	(-	-)	199	61	50	74	26	2	49	0	0	4	6	10	2	.371	.414	.632	1.046
2014	ColSpr	AAA	3	13	5	1	1	0	(-	-)	8	2	1	3	1	0	4	0	0	0	0	0	0	.385	.429	.615	1.044
2013	Col	NL	69	194	51	13	5	5	(4	1)	89	32	17	23	16	0	41	0	1	2	2	2	1	.263	.316	.459	.775
2014	Col	NL	131	436	136	27	6	24	(15	9)	247	74	76	79	37	6	101	1	0	4	8	7	6	.312	.364	.567	.931
	2 ML YEARS		200	630	187	40	11	29	(19	10)	336	106	93	102	53	6	142	1	1	6	10	9	7	.297	.349	.533	.883

R.A. Dickey

Pitches: R **Bats:** R **Pos:** SP-34   **Ht:** 6'3" **Wt:** 215 **Born:** 10/29/1974 **Age:** 40

| | | | HOW MUCH HE PITCHED | | | | | | WHAT HE GAVE UP | | | | | | | | | | | THE RESULTS | | | | | | |
Year	Team	Lg	G	GS	CG	GF	IP	BFP	H	R	ER	HR	SH	SF	HB	TBB	IBB	SO	WP	Bk	W	L	Pct	Sh	Sv-Op	Hld	ERC	ERA
2001	Tex	AL	4	0	0	1	12.0	53	13	9	9	3	0	0	0	7	1	4	1	0	0	1	.000	0	0-0	0	6.57	6.75
2003	Tex	AL	38	13	1	6	116.2	513	135	68	66	16	4	3	5	38	5	94	5	2	9	8	.529	1	1-1	3	5.09	5.09
2004	Tex	AL	25	15	0	2	104.1	480	136	77	65	17	3	3	4	33	1	57	5	1	6	7	.462	0	1-1	0	6.08	5.61
2005	Tex	AL	9	4	0	2	29.2	134	29	23	22	4	0	1	2	17	0	15	2	0	1	2	.333	0	0-0	0	5.18	6.67
2006	Tex	AL	1	1	0	0	3.1	18	8	7	7	6	0	0	0	1	0	1	0	0	0	1	.000	0	0-0	0	32.05	18.90
2008	Sea	AL	32	14	0	5	112.1	500	124	65	65	15	4	6	2	51	4	58	11	1	5	8	.385	0	0-0	0	5.19	5.21
2009	Min	AL	35	1	0	13	64.1	293	74	34	33	8	2	2	4	30	1	42	4	0	1	1	.500	0	0-0	1	5.66	4.62
2010	NYM	NL	27	26	2	0	174.1	713	165	62	55	13	7	3	4	42	3	104	11	0	11	9	.550	1	0-0	1	3.11	2.84
2011	NYM	NL	33	32	1	0	208.2	876	202	85	76	18	16	7	9	54	2	134	9	1	8	13	.381	1	0-0	1	3.40	3.28
2012	NYM	NL	34	33	5	1	233.2	927	192	78	71	24	9	7	9	54	2	230	4	1	20	6	.769	3	0-0	0	2.70	2.73
2013	Tor	AL	34	34	3	0	224.2	943	207	113	105	35	2	6	10	71	0	177	1	1	14	13	.519	1	0-0	0	3.87	4.21
2014	Tor	AL	34	34	1	0	215.2	914	191	101	89	26	2	4	14	74	2	173	5	0	14	13	.519	0	0-0	0	3.58	3.71
	12 ML YEARS		306	207	13	34	1499.2	6364	1476	722	663	185	49	42	63	472	21	1089	64	7	89	82	.520	6	2-2	6	3.97	3.98

Jake Diekman

Pitches: L **Bats:** L **Pos:** RP-73   DEEK-man   **Ht:** 6'4" **Wt:** 200 **Born:** 1/21/1987 **Age:** 28

| | | | HOW MUCH HE PITCHED | | | | | | WHAT HE GAVE UP | | | | | | | | | | | THE RESULTS | | | | | | |
Year	Team	Lg	G	GS	CG	GF	IP	BFP	H	R	ER	HR	SH	SF	HB	TBB	IBB	SO	WP	Bk	W	L	Pct	Sh	Sv-Op	Hld	ERC	ERA
2012	Phi	NL	32	0	0	7	27.1	131	25	17	12	1	1	0	3	20	3	35	1	0	1	1	.500	0	0-1	4	4.45	3.95
2013	Phi	NL	45	0	0	11	38.1	164	34	15	11	1	2	1	0	16	2	41	2	1	1	4	.200	0	0-1	11	2.89	2.58
2014	Phi	NL	73	0	0	19	71.0	313	66	36	30	4	2	7	3	35	5	100	7	0	5	5	.500	0	0-4	18	3.73	3.80
	3 ML YEARS		150	0	0	37	136.2	608	125	68	53	6	5	8	6	71	10	176	10	1	7	10	.412	0	0-6	33	3.64	3.49

Derek Dietrich

Bats: L **Throws:** R **Pos:** 2B-44;PH-5;3B-1   DEE-trick   **Ht:** 6'0" **Wt:** 205 **Born:** 7/18/1989 **Age:** 25

Year	Team	Lg	G	AB	H	2B	3B	HR	(Hm	Rd)	TB	R	RBI	RC	TBB	IBB	SO	HBP	SH	SF	SB	CS	GDP	Avg	OBP	Slg	OPS
2010	HudVal	A-	45	179	50	12	2	3	(-	-)	75	33	20	26	11	2	42	6	1	1	2	2	2	.279	.340	.419	.759
2011	BG	A	127	480	133	34	4	22	(-	-)	241	73	81	83	38	2	128	15	0	5	5	7	14	.277	.346	.502	.848
2012	Charltt	A+	98	372	105	21	9	10	(-	-)	174	49	58	61	25	1	78	12	3	5	4	2	6	.282	.343	.468	.811
2012	Mont	AA	34	133	36	7	1	4	(-	-)	57	22	17	18	7	0	36	4	1	1	0	1	2	.271	.324	.429	.753
2013	Jaxnvl	AA	63	218	59	13	3	11	(-	-)	111	35	38	44	29	2	60	10	0	0	3	0	1	.271	.381	.509	.890
2014	NewOr	AAA	21	82	26	3	0	7	(-	-)	50	15	16	19	4	0	18	6	0	0	1	0	1	.317	.391	.610	1.001
2014	Jupiter	A+	5	16	5	1	1	1	(-	-)	11	4	2	4	2	0	5	1	0	0	0	0	0	.313	.421	.688	1.109
2013	Mia	NL	57	215	46	10	2	9	(3	6)	87	32	23	24	11	1	56	7	0	1	1	0	1	.214	.275	.405	.679
2014	Mia	NL	49	158	36	6	2	5	(1	4)	61	31	17	22	13	0	38	10	2	0	1	0	1	.228	.326	.386	.712
	2 ML YEARS		106	373	82	16	4	14	(4	10)	148	63	40	46	24	1	94	17	2	0	2	0	2	.220	.297	.397	.694

Andy Dirks

Bats: L **Throws:** L **Pos:** LF   **Ht:** 6'0" **Wt:** 195 **Born:** 1/24/1986 **Age:** 29

Year	Team	Lg	G	AB	H	2B	3B	HR	(Hm	Rd)	TB	R	RBI	RC	TBB	IBB	SO	HBP	SH	SF	SB	CS	GDP	Avg	OBP	Slg	OPS
2014	Lkland*	A+	2	5	2	1	0	0	(-	-)	3	1	1	1	0	0	2	0	0	0	0	0	0	.400	.400	.600	1.000
2014	WMich*	A	5	14	3	1	0	0	(-	-)	4	2	0	1	3	0	1	0	0	0	1	0	1	.214	.353	.286	.639
2014	Toledo*	AAA	2	5	2	1	0	0	(-	-)	3	1	1	1	0	0	2	0	0	0	0	0	0	.400	.400	.600	1.000
2011	Det	AL	78	219	55	13	0	7	(6	1)	89	34	28	27	11	1	36	3	2	0	5	2	3	.251	.296	.406	.703
2012	Det	AL	88	314	101	18	5	8	(3	5)	153	56	35	50	23	2	53	2	3	2	1	1	4	.322	.370	.487	.857
2013	Det	AL	131	438	112	16	2	9	(5	4)	159	60	37	48	42	2	84	2	1	1	7	1	6	.256	.323	.363	.686
	Postseason		18	54	11	2	0	0	(0	0)	13	3	1	3	3	0	10	0	1	0	2	0	0	.204	.246	.241	.486
	3 ML YEARS		297	971	268	47	7	24	(14	10)	401	150	100	125	76	5	173	7	6	3	13	4	13	.276	.332	.413	.745

Greg Dobbs

Bats: L Throws: R Pos: PH-33;1B-3   Ht: 6'1" Wt: 205 Born: 7/2/1978 Age: 36

Year	Team	Lg	G	AB	H	2B	3B	HR	(Hm	Rd)	TB	R	RBI	RC	TBB	IBB	SO	HBP	SH	SF	SB	CS	GDP	Avg	OBP	Slg	OPS
2014	Syrcse*	AAA	35	97	24	4	0	2	(-	-)	34	12	11	9	5	0	23	0	0	0	0	0	1	.247	.284	.351	.635
2004	Sea	AL	18	53	12	1	0	1	(1	0)	16	4	9	5	1	0	14	1	0	1	0	0	0	.226	.250	.302	.552
2005	Sea	AL	59	142	35	7	1	1	(0	1)	47	8	20	16	9	3	25	0	1	2	1	0	4	.246	.288	.331	.619
2006	Sea	AL	23	27	10	3	1	0	(0	0)	15	4	3	5	0	0	4	1	0	0	0	1	0	.370	.393	.556	.948
2007	Phi	NL	142	324	88	20	4	10	(5	5)	146	45	55	42	29	4	67	1	0	4	3	0	7	.272	.330	.451	.780
2008	Phi	NL	128	226	68	14	1	9	(3	6)	111	30	40	38	11	1	40	1	0	2	3	1	4	.301	.333	.491	.824
2009	Phi	NL	97	154	38	6	0	5	(3	2)	59	15	20	15	11	1	29	1	0	3	1	0	2	.247	.296	.383	.679
2010	Phi	NL	88	163	32	7	0	5	(2	3)	54	13	15	14	12	1	39	0	1	0	1	1	2	.196	.251	.331	.583
2011	Fla	NL	134	411	113	23	0	8	(2	6)	160	38	49	40	22	3	83	1	2	3	0	0	12	.275	.311	.389	.701
2012	Mia	NL	120	319	91	13	2	5	(3	2)	123	26	39	38	14	5	53	2	0	7	4	2	8	.285	.313	.386	.698
2013	Mia	NL	114	237	54	11	0	2	(1	1)	71	21	22	21	22	6	40	5	0	3	1	1	5	.228	.303	.300	.603
2014	2 Tms	NL	36	41	7	1	0	0	(0	0)	8	0	2	1	1	0	8	0	0	1	0	0	0	.171	.186	.195	.381
14	Mia	NL	15	13	1	0	0	0	(0	0)	1	0	0	0	0	0	4	0	0	0	0	0	0	.077	.077	.077	.154
14	Was	NL	21	28	6	1	0	0	(0	0)	7	0	2	1	1	0	4	0	0	1	0	0	0	.214	.233	.250	.483
Postseason			16	21	7	1	0	0	(0	0)	8	2	0	2	3	2	6	0	0	0	0	0	0	.333	.417	.381	.798
11 ML YEARS			959	2097	548	106	9	46	(20	26)	810	204	274	235	132	24	402	13	4	26	14	6	44	.261	.306	.386	.692

Chris Dominguez

Bats: R Throws: R Pos: LF-5;PH-2;3B-1;PR-1   Ht: 6'4" Wt: 235 Born: 11/22/1986 Age: 28

Year	Team	Lg	G	AB	H	2B	3B	HR	(Hm	Rd)	TB	R	RBI	RC	TBB	IBB	SO	HBP	SH	SF	SB	CS	GDP	Avg	OBP	Slg	OPS
2010	Augsta	A	137	559	152	32	4	21	(-	-)	255	85	101	84	35	3	133	11	0	3	14	7	14	.272	.326	.456	.782
2011	SnJos	A+	63	258	75	10	1	11	(-	-)	120	40	40	41	18	0	73	1	0	2	8	2	7	.291	.337	.465	.802
2011	Rchmd	AA	78	295	72	22	2	7	(-	-)	119	35	45	31	9	0	78	4	0	5	1	5	5	.244	.272	.403	.675
2012	Rchmd	AA	49	188	42	9	0	2	(-	-)	57	17	19	14	7	0	50	1	0	1	3	0	4	.223	.254	.303	.557
2012	Fresno	AAA	43	174	43	11	0	3	(-	-)	63	15	25	15	2	0	47	2	0	0	1	2	6	.247	.264	.362	.626
2013	Fresno	AAA	132	466	137	24	5	15	(-	-)	216	60	65	71	23	3	112	6	0	2	4	5	23	.294	.334	.464	.798
2014	Fresno	AAA	131	496	136	23	3	21	(-	-)	228	66	85	71	22	0	143	4	0	6	21	10	10	.274	.307	.460	.766
2014	SF	NL	8	17	1	0	0	1	(0	1)	4	1	2	0	1	1	4	0	0	0	0	0	2	.059	.111	.235	.346

Jose Dominguez

Pitches: R Bats: R Pos: RP-5   Ht: 6'0" Wt: 200 Born: 8/7/1990 Age: 24

	HOW MUCH HE PITCHED							WHAT HE GAVE UP										THE RESULTS							
Year	Team	Lg	G	GS	CG	GF	IP	BFP	H	R	ER	HR	SH	SF	HB	TBB	IBB	SO	WP	Bk	W	L	Pct	Sh	Sv-Op	Hld	ERC	ERA
2011	Ddgrs	R	10	10	0	0	43.2	182	38	20	17	3	0	0	8	13	0	43	3	0	4	1	.800	0	0--	-	3.55	3.50
2011	Ogden	R+	3	3	0	0	10.0	60	26	22	20	2	0	0	1	3	0	9	3	1	0	3	.000	0	0--	-	15.72	18.00
2012	Gt Lks	A	33	5	0	7	72.0	343	77	51	42	4	2	2	5	47	0	78	5	3	4	3	.571	0	4--	-	5.31	5.25
2012	Chatt	AA	5	0	0	5	7.0	23	2	1	1	0	2	0	0	0	0	9	0	0	1	0	1.000	0	1--	-	0.19	1.29
2013	Chatt	AA	14	0	0	6	17.1	68	8	5	5	0	1	0	1	8	1	28	2	0	1	0	1.000	0	5--	-	1.31	2.60
2013	Albq	AAA	8	0	0	2	8.0	30	1	0	0	0	0	0	0	5	0	12	2	0	1	0	1.000	0	0--	-	0.66	0.00
2014	Albq	AAA	31	0	0	22	33.1	151	31	15	12	1	1	1	4	18	0	39	4	1	1	2	.333	0	10--	-	4.12	3.24
2014	Ogden	R+	2	0	0	0	1.1	7	1	2	2	0	0	0	1	1	0	2	2	0	0	0	-	0	0--	-	5.91	13.50
2013	LAD	NL	9	0	0	2	8.1	39	11	3	2	0	0	0	1	3	0	4	1	0	0	0	-	0	0-0	1	5.47	2.16
2014	LAD	NL	5	0	0	2	6.1	30	7	8	8	2	0	0	1	3	0	8	0	0	0	0	-	0	0-0	0	7.23	11.37
2 ML YEARS			14	0	0	4	14.2	69	18	11	10	2	0	0	2	6	0	12	1	0	0	0	-	0	0-0	1	6.25	6.14

Matt Dominguez

Bats: R Throws: R Pos: 3B-153;DH-4   Ht: 6'1" Wt: 215 Born: 8/28/1989 Age: 25

Year	Team	Lg	G	AB	H	2B	3B	HR	(Hm	Rd)	TB	R	RBI	RC	TBB	IBB	SO	HBP	SH	SF	SB	CS	GDP	Avg	OBP	Slg	OPS
2011	Fla	NL	17	45	11	4	0	0	(0	0)	15	2	2	3	2	0	8	1	0	0	0	0	2	.244	.292	.333	.625
2012	Hou	NL	31	109	31	2	2	5	(2	3)	52	14	16	13	4	1	17	0	0	0	0	0	4	.284	.310	.477	.787
2013	Hou	AL	152	543	131	25	0	21	(12	9)	219	56	77	59	30	1	96	7	2	7	0	1	17	.241	.286	.403	.690
2014	Hou	AL	157	564	121	17	0	16	(10	6)	186	51	57	42	29	2	125	5	2	7	0	1	23	.215	.256	.330	.586
4 ML YEARS			357	1261	294	48	2	42	(24	18)	472	123	152	117	65	4	246	13	4	14	0	2	46	.233	.275	.374	.649

Josh Donaldson

Bats: R Throws: R Pos: 3B-150;DH-9;PH-3   Ht: 6'0" Wt: 220 Born: 12/8/1985 Age: 29

Year	Team	Lg	G	AB	H	2B	3B	HR	(Hm	Rd)	TB	R	RBI	RC	TBB	IBB	SO	HBP	SH	SF	SB	CS	GDP	Avg	OBP	Slg	OPS
2010	Oak	AL	14	32	5	1	0	1	(0	1)	9	1	4	3	2	0	12	0	0	0	0	0	0	.156	.206	.281	.487
2012	Oak	AL	75	274	66	16	0	9	(3	6)	109	34	33	33	14	0	61	5	0	1	4	1	6	.241	.289	.398	.687
2013	Oak	AL	158	579	174	37	3	24	(13	11)	289	89	93	112	76	2	110	6	1	6	5	2	15	.301	.384	.499	.883
2014	Oak	AL	158	608	155	31	2	29	(11	18)	277	93	98	105	76	5	130	7	0	4	8	0	16	.255	.342	.456	.798
Postseason			10	38	8	1	0	0	(0	0)	9	1	0	1	2	0	12	0	0	0	0	0	1	.211	.250	.237	.487
4 ML YEARS			405	1493	400	85	5	63	(27	36)	684	217	228	253	168	7	313	18	1	11	17	3	37	.268	.347	.458	.805

Sean Doolittle

Pitches: L **Bats:** L **Pos:** RP-61 **Ht:** 6'3" **Wt:** 210 **Born:** 9/26/1986 **Age:** 28

				HOW MUCH HE PITCHED					WHAT HE GAVE UP										THE RESULTS						
Year	Team	Lg	G	GS	CG	GF	IP	BFP	H	R	ER	HR	SH	SF	HB	TBB	IBB	SO	WP	Bk	W	L	Pct	Sh	Sv-Op	Hld	ERC	ERA
2012	Oak	AL	44	0	0	7	47.1	191	40	18	16	3	2	2	0	11	1	60	0	0	2	1	.667	0	1-2	18	2.36	3.04
2013	Oak	AL	70	0	0	11	69.0	266	53	24	24	4	3	0	2	13	1	60	2	0	5	5	.500	0	2-7	26	2.00	3.13
2014	Oak	AL	61	0	0	40	62.2	236	38	19	19	5	2	1	0	8	1	89	0	0	2	4	.333	0	22-26	5	1.23	2.73
	Postseason		7	0	0	1	7.0	33	8	5	3	1	1	0	0	2	0	11	0	0	0	1	.000	0	0-2	2	4.31	3.86
	3 ML YEARS		175	0	0	58	179.0	693	131	61	59	12	7	3	2	32	3	209	2	0	9	10	.474	0	25-35	49	1.75	2.97

Felix Doubront

Pitches: L **Bats:** L **Pos:** SP-14; RP-7   due-BRAWNDT   **Ht:** 6'2" **Wt:** 225 **Born:** 10/23/1987 **Age:** 27

				HOW MUCH HE PITCHED					WHAT HE GAVE UP										THE RESULTS						
Year	Team	Lg	G	GS	CG	GF	IP	BFP	H	R	ER	HR	SH	SF	HB	TBB	IBB	SO	WP	Bk	W	L	Pct	Sh	Sv-Op	Hld	ERC	ERA
2014	Portlnd*	AA	1	1	0	0	4.0	15	4	2	2	0	0	0	0	1	0	2	0	0	0	0	-	0	0- -	-	2.12	4.50
2014	Pwtckt*	AAA	2	2	0	0	9.2	39	6	2	2	0	1	0	0	5	0	13	1	0	0	0	-	0	0- -	-	1.94	1.86
2014	Iowa*	AAA	2	2	0	0	10.0	44	12	6	6	0	0	0	1	3	0	11	0	0	0	1	.000	0	0- -	-	4.56	5.40
2014	Tenn*	AA	1	1	0	0	4.1	22	5	4	3	0	1	1	0	3	0	5	1	0	0	1	.000	0	0- -	-	4.93	6.23
2010	Bos	AL	12	3	0	5	25.0	113	27	16	12	3	1	1	1	10	0	23	3	0	2	2	.500	0	2-3	1	4.72	4.32
2011	Bos	AL	11	0	0	1	10.1	47	12	7	7	1	0	1	0	8	0	6	0	0	0	0	-	0	1-1	6	6.97	6.10
2012	Bos	AL	29	29	0	0	161.0	709	162	95	87	24	1	6	5	71	0	167	5	0	11	10	.524	0	0-0	0	4.73	4.86
2013	Bos	AL	29	27	0	0	162.1	705	161	84	78	13	3	10	5	71	0	139	8	0	11	6	.647	0	0-0	0	4.18	4.32
2014	2 Tms		21	14	0	2	79.2	364	91	54	49	12	3	2	2	33	0	51	5	1	4	5	.444	0	0-0	0	5.33	5.54
14	Bos	AL	17	10	0	2	59.1	277	69	45	40	10	2	2	2	26	0	43	4	0	2	4	.333	0	0-0	0	5.66	6.07
14	ChC	NL	4	4	0	0	20.1	87	22	9	9	2	1	0	0	7	0	8	1	1	2	1	.667	0	0-0	0	4.36	3.98
	Postseason		4	0	0	1	7.0	27	3	1	1	0	0	0	1	3	1	4	0	0	1	0	1.000	0	0-0	0	1.26	1.29
	5 ML YEARS		102	73	0	8	438.1	1938	453	256	233	53	8	20	13	193	0	386	21	1	28	23	.549	0	3-4	1	4.68	4.78

Ryan Doumit

Bats: B **Throws:** R **Pos:** PH-76;LF-9;RF-9;DH-5;C-2   DOE-mitt   **Ht:** 6'1" **Wt:** 220 **Born:** 4/3/1981 **Age:** 34

								BATTING												RUNNING			AVERAGES			
Year	Team	Lg	G	AB	H	2B	3B	HR	(Hm	Rd)	TB	R	RBI	RC	TBB	IBB	SO	HBP	SH	SF	SB	CS	GDP	Avg	OBP	Slg	OPS
2005	Pit	NL	75	231	59	13	1	6	(4	2)	92	25	35	32	11	1	48	13	1	1	2	1	5	.255	.324	.398	.722
2006	Pit	NL	61	149	31	9	0	6	(3	3)	58	15	17	17	15	1	42	11	1	2	0	0	3	.208	.322	.389	.711
2007	Pit	NL	83	252	69	19	2	9	(7	2)	119	33	32	34	22	2	59	4	0	1	1	2	5	.274	.341	.472	.813
2008	Pit	NL	116	431	137	34	0	15	(8	7)	216	71	69	79	23	4	55	6	0	5	2	2	10	.318	.357	.501	.858
2009	Pit	NL	75	280	70	16	0	10	(6	4)	116	31	38	26	20	6	49	1	0	3	4	0	12	.250	.299	.414	.714
2010	Pit	NL	124	406	102	22	1	13	(7	6)	165	42	45	47	41	4	87	8	0	1	1	0	18	.251	.331	.406	.738
2011	Pit	NL	77	218	66	12	1	8	(6	2)	104	17	30	36	16	0	35	1	1	0	0	1	5	.303	.353	.477	.830
2012	Min	AL	134	484	133	34	1	18	(8	10)	223	56	75	61	29	5	98	7	0	8	0	0	17	.275	.320	.461	.781
2013	Min	AL	135	485	120	28	1	14	(6	8)	192	49	55	51	48	4	99	1	0	4	1	0	13	.247	.314	.396	.710
2014	Atl	NL	100	157	31	4	0	5	(2	3)	50	11	17	9	7	1	49	1	0	1	1	0	1	.197	.235	.318	.553
	10 ML YEARS		980	3093	818	191	7	104	(57	47)	1335	350	413	392	232	28	621	53	3	26	12	6	89	.264	.324	.432	.756

Darin Downs

Pitches: L **Bats:** R **Pos:** RP-45 **Ht:** 6'3" **Wt:** 210 **Born:** 12/26/1984 **Age:** 30

				HOW MUCH HE PITCHED					WHAT HE GAVE UP										THE RESULTS						
Year	Team	Lg	G	GS	CG	GF	IP	BFP	H	R	ER	HR	SH	SF	HB	TBB	IBB	SO	WP	Bk	W	L	Pct	Sh	Sv-Op	Hld	ERC	ERA
2014	OKCity*	AAA	9	0	0	3	13.0	59	17	8	8	0	1	2	0	4	0	15	1	0	1	2	.333	0	0- -	-	4.67	5.54
2014	CpChr*	AA	2	2	0	0	1.2	10	3	1	1	0	0	0	1	2	0	3	0	0	0	1	.000	0	0- -	-	15.74	5.40
2012	Det	AL	18	0	0	5	20.2	86	18	8	8	1	0	0	1	9	2	20	1	0	2	1	.667	0	0-0	4	3.27	3.48
2013	Det	AL	29	0	0	8	35.1	151	36	20	19	4	1	1	2	11	2	37	2	0	0	2	.000	0	0-0	4	4.08	4.84
2014	Hou	AL	45	0	0	7	34.2	148	28	22	21	2	1	1	3	19	2	27	2	2	2	1	.667	0	0-0	10	3.59	5.45
	3 ML YEARS		92	0	0	20	90.2	385	82	50	48	7	2	2	6	39	6	84	5	2	4	4	.500	0	0-0	15	3.71	4.76

Scott Downs

Pitches: L **Bats:** L **Pos:** RP-55 **Ht:** 6'2" **Wt:** 220 **Born:** 3/17/1976 **Age:** 39

				HOW MUCH HE PITCHED					WHAT HE GAVE UP										THE RESULTS						
Year	Team	Lg	G	GS	CG	GF	IP	BFP	H	R	ER	HR	SH	SF	HB	TBB	IBB	SO	WP	Bk	W	L	Pct	Sh	Sv-Op	Hld	ERC	ERA
2000	2 Tms	NL	19	19	0	0	97.0	442	122	62	57	13	2	4	5	40	1	63	1	0	4	3	.571	0	0-0	0	6.19	5.29
2003	Mon	NL	1	1	0	0	3.0	17	5	5	5	2	0	0	0	3	2	4	0	1	0	0	1.000	0	0-0	0	15.01	15.00
2004	Mon	NL	12	12	1	0	63.0	284	79	47	36	9	2	1	3	23	2	38	2	0	3	6	.333	1	0-0	0	5.97	5.14
2005	Tor	AL	26	13	0	0	94.0	407	93	49	45	12	0	1	5	34	0	75	3	0	4	5	.571	0	0-0	0	4.25	4.31
2006	Tor	AL	59	5	0	13	77.0	327	73	38	35	9	1	1	2	30	6	61	7	0	6	2	.750	0	1-4	6	3.87	4.09
2007	Tor	AL	81	0	0	13	58.0	239	47	15	14	3	1	2	1	24	3	57	2	1	4	2	.667	0	1-4	24	2.81	2.17
2008	Tor	AL	66	0	0	14	70.2	290	54	15	14	3	5	0	4	27	7	57	3	0	0	3	.000	0	2-4	24	2.47	1.78
2009	Tor	AL	48	0	0	24	46.2	200	46	18	16	4	0	2	4	23	1	43	1	0	1	3	.250	0	9-13	10	3.50	3.09
2010	Tor	AL	67	0	0	14	61.1	241	47	19	18	3	0	2	0	14	3	48	1	0	5	5	.500	0	0-0	26	2.14	2.64
2011	LAA	AL	60	0	0	10	53.2	218	39	11	8	3	5	2	0	15	3	35	2	0	6	1	.667	0	1-4	26	1.83	1.34
2012	LAA	AL	57	0	0	11	45.2	194	43	17	16	3	0	0	0	17	2	32	1	0	1	1	.500	0	9-12	25	3.33	3.15
2013	2 Tms	AL	68	0	0	5	43.1	189	45	13	12	1	4	1	2	19	2	37	2	0	4	4	.500	0	0-4	26	4.03	2.49
2014	2 Tms	AL	55	0	0	9	38.0	165	36	24	21	2	0	0	0	20	2	25	1	0	4	0	.000	0	1-2	7	3.88	4.97
00	ChC	NL	18	18	0	0	94.0	426	117	59	54	13	2	4	5	37	1	63	1	0	4	3	.571	0	0-0	0	6.07	5.17
00	Mon	NL	1	1	0	0	3.0	16	5	3	3	0	0	0	0	3	0	0	0	0	0	0	-	0	0-0	0	10.34	9.00
13	LAA	AL	43	0	0	3	29.1	122	26	7	6	1	2	0	2	11	2	22	1	0	2	3	.400	0	0-3	18	3.13	1.84

Year	Team	Lg	G	GS	CG	GF	IP	BFP	H	R	ER	HR	SH	SF	HB	TBB	IBB	SO	WP	Bk	W	L	Pct	Sh	Sv-Op	Hld	ERC	ERA
13	Atl	NL	25	0	0	2	14.0	67	19	6	6	0	2	1	0	8	0	15	1	0	2	1	.667	0	0-1	8	6.10	3.86
14	CWS	AL	38	0	0	7	23.2	108	24	17	16	1	0	0	0	15	2	22	0	0	0	2	.000	0	1-1	6	4.46	6.08
14	KC	AL	17	0	0	2	14.1	57	12	7	5	1	0	0	0	5	0	3	1	0	0	2	.000	0	0-1	1	2.93	3.14
13 ML YEARS			619	50	1	113	751.1	3213	729	333	297	67	20	16	28	279	34	575	26	2	38	40	.487	1	27-54	174	3.81	3.56

Brian Dozier

DOUGH-zher

Bats: R **Throws:** R **Pos:** 2B-156   **Ht:** 5'11" **Wt:** 190 **Born:** 5/15/1987 **Age:** 28

									BATTING														RUNNING			AVERAGES			
Year	Team	Lg	G	AB	H	2B	3B	HR	(Hm	Rd)	TB	R	RBI	RC	TBB	IBB	SO	HBP	SH	SF	SB	CS	GDP	Avg	OBP	Slg	OPS
2012	Min	AL	84	316	74	11	1	6	(4	2)	105	33	33	24	16	0	58	1	4	3	9	2	10	.234	.271	.332	.603
2013	Min	AL	147	558	136	33	4	18	(8	10)	231	72	66	74	51	0	120	6	3	4	14	7	14	.244	.312	.414	.726
2014	Min	AL	156	598	145	33	1	23	(11	12)	249	112	71	87	89	1	129	9	3	8	21	7	8	.242	.345	.416	.762
3 ML YEARS			387	1472	355	77	6	47	(23	24)	585	217	170	185	156	1	307	16	10	15	44	16	32	.241	.318	.397	.715

Kyle Drabek

Pitches: R **Bats:** R **Pos:** RP-2   **Ht:** 6'2" **Wt:** 205 **Born:** 12/8/1987 **Age:** 27

Year	Team	Lg	G	GS	CG	GF	IP	BFP	H	R	ER	HR	SH	SF	HB	TBB	IBB	SO	WP	Bk	W	L	Pct	Sh	Sv-Op	Hld	ERC	ERA
2014	Buffalo*	AAA	32	13	0	3	99.0	430	116	57	46	12	1	2	1	30	0	68	10	0	7	7	.500	0	0- -	-	4.92	4.18
2010	Tor	AL	3	3	0	0	17.0	69	18	9	9	2	1	2	0	5	0	12	2	0	0	3	.000	0	0-0	0	4.34	4.76
2011	Tor	AL	18	14	0	0	78.2	365	87	54	53	10	3	5	1	55	0	51	11	0	4	5	.444	0	0-0	0	6.30	6.06
2012	Tor	AL	13	13	0	0	71.1	317	67	41	37	10	0	1	1	47	0	47	7	0	4	7	.364	0	0-0	0	5.21	4.67
2013	Tor	AL	3	0	0	1	2.1	14	4	2	2	1	0	0	1	2	0	3	0	0	0	0	-	0	0-0	0	16.01	7.71
2014	Tor	AL	2	0	0	1	3.0	13	2	0	0	0	0	0	0	2	0	5	0	0	0	0	-	0	0-0	0	2.54	0.00
5 ML YEARS			39	30	0	4	172.1	778	178	106	101	23	4	8	3	111	0	118	20	0	8	15	.348	0	0-0	0	5.69	5.27

Stephen Drew

Bats: L **Throws:** R **Pos:** SS-51;2B-34;PH-4;DH-1   **Ht:** 6'0" **Wt:** 190 **Born:** 3/16/1983 **Age:** 32

									BATTING														RUNNING			AVERAGES			
Year	Team	Lg	G	AB	H	2B	3B	HR	(Hm	Rd)	TB	R	RBI	RC	TBB	IBB	SO	HBP	SH	SF	SB	CS	GDP	Avg	OBP	Slg	OPS
2014	Grnvlle*	A	3	8	3	2	0	0	(-	-)	5	1	2	2	1	0	4	0	0	0	0	0	0	.375	.444	.625	1.069
2014	Pwtckt*	AAA	4	13	2	1	0	0	(-	-)	3	0	0	0	1	0	5	0	0	0	0	0	0	.154	.214	.231	.445
2006	Ari	NL	59	209	66	13	7	5	(3	2)	108	27	23	31	14	4	50	0	0	2	2	0	1	.316	.357	.517	.874
2007	Ari	NL	150	543	129	28	4	12	(6	6)	201	60	60	71	60	5	100	3	5	8	9	0	4	.238	.313	.370	.683
2008	Ari	NL	152	611	178	44	11	21	(9	12)	307	91	67	97	41	6	109	1	3	7	3	3	5	.291	.333	.502	.836
2009	Ari	NL	135	533	139	29	12	12	(4	8)	228	71	65	76	49	7	87	1	5	7	5	1	5	.261	.320	.428	.748
2010	Ari	NL	151	565	157	33	12	15	(5	10)	259	83	61	84	62	2	108	3	2	1	10	5	8	.278	.352	.458	.810
2011	Ari	NL	86	321	81	21	5	5	(3	2)	127	44	45	41	30	0	74	1	1	1	4	4	3	.252	.317	.396	.713
2012	2 Tms		79	287	64	13	1	7	(4	3)	100	38	28	30	37	2	76	0	0	3	1	2	2	.223	.309	.348	.657
2013	Bos	AL	124	442	112	29	8	13	(6	7)	196	57	67	63	54	3	124	1	0	4	6	0	9	.253	.333	.443	.777
2014	2 Tms		85	271	44	14	1	7	(4	3)	81	18	26	19	27	3	75	0	0	2	1	1	1	.162	.237	.299	.536
12	Ari	NL	40	135	26	8	1	2	(0	2)	42	17	12	12	19	1	35	0	0	1	0	1	1	.193	.290	.311	.601
12	Oak	AL	39	152	38	5	0	5	(4	1)	58	21	16	18	18	1	41	0	0	2	1	1	1	.250	.326	.382	.707
14	Bos	AL	39	131	23	6	1	4	(2	2)	43	11	11	12	14	2	39	0	0	0	1	1	1	.176	.255	.328	.583
14	NYY	AL	46	140	21	8	0	3	(2	1)	38	7	15	7	13	1	36	0	0	2	0	0	0	.150	.219	.271	.490
Postseason			28	104	22	3	2	3	(2	1)	38	10	9	8	5	0	33	0	0	1	1	0	1	.212	.245	.365	.611
9 ML YEARS			1021	3782	970	224	61	97	(44	53)	1607	489	442	512	374	32	803	10	18	34	41	16	38	.256	.322	.425	.747

Lucas Duda

DOO-duh

Bats: L **Throws:** R **Pos:** 1B-146;PH-10;DH-3;LF-1   **Ht:** 6'4" **Wt:** 255 **Born:** 2/3/1986 **Age:** 29

									BATTING														RUNNING			AVERAGES			
Year	Team	Lg	G	AB	H	2B	3B	HR	(Hm	Rd)	TB	R	RBI	RC	TBB	IBB	SO	HBP	SH	SF	SB	CS	GDP	Avg	OBP	Slg	OPS
2010	NYM	NL	29	84	17	6	0	4	(3	1)	35	11	13	5	6	0	22	1	0	1	0	0	2	.202	.261	.417	.678
2011	NYM	NL	100	301	88	21	3	10	(2	8)	145	38	50	44	33	3	57	7	1	5	1	0	5	.292	.370	.482	.852
2012	NYM	NL	121	401	96	15	0	15	(9	6)	156	43	57	58	51	0	120	4	0	3	1	0	5	.239	.329	.389	.718
2013	NYM	NL	100	318	71	16	0	15	(9	6)	132	42	33	38	55	4	102	0	0	2	0	3	1	.223	.352	.415	.767
2014	NYM	NL	153	514	130	27	0	30	(14	16)	247	74	92	91	69	8	135	9	0	4	3	2	9	.253	.349	.481	.830
5 ML YEARS			503	1618	402	85	3	74	(37	37)	715	208	245	236	214	15	436	30	1	15	5	5	22	.248	.344	.442	.786

Brian Duensing

DUNN-sing

Pitches: L **Bats:** L **Pos:** RP-62   **Ht:** 6'0" **Wt:** 205 **Born:** 2/22/1983 **Age:** 32

Year	Team	Lg	G	GS	CG	GF	IP	BFP	H	R	ER	HR	SH	SF	HB	TBB	IBB	SO	WP	Bk	W	L	Pct	Sh	Sv-Op	Hld	ERC	ERA
2009	Min	AL	24	9	0	3	84.0	359	84	37	34	7	3	2	3	31	1	53	1	0	5	2	.714	0	0-0	1	4.00	3.64
2010	Min	AL	53	13	1	11	130.2	535	122	42	38	11	4	0	3	35	5	78	1	0	10	3	.769	1	0-0	9	3.18	2.62
2011	Min	AL	32	28	1	0	161.2	711	193	102	94	21	7	6	1	52	3	115	3	0	9	14	.391	1	0-0	0	5.12	5.23
2012	Min	AL	55	11	0	8	109.0	472	126	71	62	10	2	3	2	27	3	69	5	0	4	12	.250	0	0-1	7	4.31	5.12
2013	Min	AL	73	0	0	9	61.0	268	68	28	27	4	2	2	2	22	4	56	6	0	6	2	.750	0	1-4	15	4.35	3.98
2014	Min	AL	62	0	0	10	54.1	229	52	20	20	6	1	2	1	20	2	33	2	0	3	3	.500	0	0-4	7	3.84	3.31
Postseason			2	2	0	0	8.0	39	14	10	10	2	0	0	0	2	0	4	1	0	0	2	.000	0	0-0	0	9.43	11.25
6 ML YEARS			299	61	2	41	600.2	2574	645	300	275	59	19	15	12	187	18	404	18	0	37	36	.507	2	1-9	39	4.19	4.12

Danny Duffy

Pitches: L Bats: L Pos: SP-25; RP-6
Ht: 6'3" Wt: 205 Born: 12/21/1988 Age: 26

Year	Team	Lg	G	GS	CG	GF	IP	BFP	H	R	ER	HR	SH	SF	HB	TBB	IBB	SO	WP	Bk	W	L	Pct	Sh	Sv-Op	Hld	ERC	ERA
2014	Omha*	AAA	1	1	0	0	6.0	22	5	2	2	1	0	0	0	1	0	4	1	0	0	1	.000	0	0--	-	2.95	3.00
2011	KC	AL	20	20	0	0	105.1	474	119	66	66	15	2	2	5	51	1	87	4	1	4	8	.333	0	0-0	0	5.76	5.64
2012	KC	AL	6	6	0	0	27.2	121	26	13	12	2	0	0	0	18	1	28	0	1	2	2	.500	0	0-0	0	4.58	3.90
2013	KC	AL	5	5	0	0	24.1	104	19	5	5	0	0	1	0	14	0	22	2	0	2	0	1.000	0	0-0	0	3.02	1.85
2014	KC	AL	31	25	0	1	149.1	606	113	52	42	12	3	4	5	53	2	113	5	0	9	12	.429	0	0-0	1	2.62	2.53
	4 ML YEARS		62	56	0	1	306.2	1305	277	136	125	29	5	6	11	136	4	250	11	2	17	22	.436	0	0-0	1	3.83	3.67

Matt Duffy

Bats: R Throws: R Pos: PH-16;2B-9;SS-7;3B-2;PR-2
Ht: 6'2" Wt: 170 Born: 1/15/1991 Age: 24

Year	Team	Lg	G	AB	H	2B	3B	HR	(Hm	Rd)	TB	R	RBI	RC	TBB	IBB	SO	HBP	SH	SF	SB	CS	GDP	Avg	OBP	Slg	OPS
2012	SlmKzr	A-	47	182	45	4	0	1	(-	-)	52	31	16	24	26	0	22	7	0	1	10	1	7	.247	.361	.286	.647
2013	Augsta	A	78	287	88	14	3	4	(-	-)	120	48	43	54	45	1	41	3	3	1	22	6	7	.307	.405	.418	.823
2013	SnJos	A+	26	106	31	6	1	5	(-	-)	54	17	14	18	7	0	16	1	1	0	3	1	2	.292	.342	.509	.852
2014	Rchmd	AA	97	367	122	24	4	3	(-	-)	163	53	62	70	42	2	66	2	0	6	20	4	8	.332	.398	.444	.842
2014	SF	NL	34	60	16	2	0	0	(0	0)	18	5	8	8	1	0	14	2	1	0	0	1	1	.267	.302	.300	.602

Zach Duke

Pitches: L Bats: L Pos: RP-74
Ht: 6'2" Wt: 210 Born: 4/19/1983 Age: 32

Year	Team	Lg	G	GS	CG	GF	IP	BFP	H	R	ER	HR	SH	SF	HB	TBB	IBB	SO	WP	Bk	W	L	Pct	Sh	Sv-Op	Hld	ERC	ERA
2005	Pit	NL	14	14	0	0	84.2	341	79	20	17	3	3	1	2	23	2	58	1	0	8	2	.800	0	0-0	0	2.96	1.81
2006	Pit	NL	34	34	2	0	215.1	935	255	116	107	17	13	4	7	68	6	117	8	1	10	15	.400	1	0-0	0	4.82	4.47
2007	Pit	NL	20	19	0	0	107.1	482	161	74	66	14	2	4	3	25	2	41	0	1	3	8	.273	0	0-0	0	6.96	5.53
2008	Pit	NL	31	31	1	0	185.0	829	230	111	99	19	14	4	7	47	1	87	2	2	5	14	.263	1	0-0	0	4.99	4.82
2009	Pit	NL	32	32	3	0	213.0	891	231	101	96	23	18	10	3	49	0	106	2	1	11	16	.407	1	0-0	0	4.05	4.06
2010	Pit	NL	29	29	0	0	159.0	730	212	115	101	25	9	6	4	51	2	96	4	3	8	15	.348	0	0-0	0	6.22	5.72
2011	Ari	NL	21	9	0	5	76.2	338	101	42	42	6	3	3	1	19	0	32	1	0	3	4	.429	0	1-1	0	5.27	4.93
2012	Was	NL	8	0	0	3	13.2	56	11	2	2	0	0	4	0	4	0	10	0	0	1	0	1.000	0	0-0	0	2.00	1.32
2013	2 Tms	NL	26	1	0	3	31.1	142	39	23	21	3	2	2	1	10	3	18	2	0	1	2	.333	0	0-0	1	5.04	6.03
2014	Mil	NL	74	0	0	13	58.2	238	49	19	16	8	3	0	0	17	1	74	3	0	5	1	.833	0	0-4	12	2.46	2.45
13	Was	NL	12	1	0	1	20.2	101	31	22	20	2	2	1	1	8	3	11	1	0	1	1	.500	0	0-0	0	6.83	8.71
13	Cin	NL	14	0	0	2	10.2	41	8	1	1	1	0	0	0	2	0	7	1	0	0	1	.000	0	0-0	1	2.01	0.84
	10 ML YEARS		289	169	6	24	1144.2	4982	1368	623	567	113	64	34	28	313	17	639	23	8	55	77	.417	3	1-5	13	4.80	4.46

Adam Dunn

Bats: L Throws: R Pos: DH-95;1B-23;PH-12;LF-4;RF-2
Ht: 6'6" Wt: 285 Born: 11/9/1979 Age: 35

Year	Team	Lg	G	AB	H	2B	3B	HR	(Hm	Rd)	TB	R	RBI	RC	TBB	IBB	SO	HBP	SH	SF	SB	CS	GDP	Avg	OBP	Slg	OPS
2001	Cin	NL	66	244	64	18	1	19	(8	11)	141	54	43	51	38	2	74	4	0	0	4	2	4	.262	.371	.578	.948
2002	Cin	NL	158	535	133	28	2	26	(13	13)	243	84	71	96	128	13	170	9	1	3	19	9	8	.249	.400	.454	.854
2003	Cin	NL	116	381	82	12	1	27	(16	11)	177	70	57	61	74	8	126	10	0	4	8	2	9	.215	.354	.465	.819
2004	Cin	NL	161	568	151	34	0	46	(25	21)	323	105	102	108	108	11	195	5	0	0	6	1	8	.266	.388	.569	.956
2005	Cin	NL	160	543	134	35	2	40	(26	14)	293	107	101	112	114	10	168	12	0	2	4	2	6	.247	.387	.540	.927
2006	Cin	NL	160	561	131	24	0	40	(22	18)	275	99	92	96	112	12	194	6	1	3	7	0	8	.234	.365	.490	.855
2007	Cin	NL	152	522	138	27	2	40	(19	21)	289	101	106	103	101	8	165	5	0	4	9	2	12	.264	.386	.554	.940
2008	2 Tms	NL	158	517	122	23	0	40	(19	21)	265	79	100	101	122	13	164	7	0	5	2	1	7	.236	.386	.513	.898
2009	Was	NL	159	546	146	29	0	38	(19	19)	289	81	105	109	116	16	177	4	0	2	0	1	10	.267	.398	.529	.928
2010	Was	NL	158	558	145	36	2	38	(20	18)	299	85	103	88	77	10	199	9	0	4	0	1	10	.260	.356	.536	.892
2011	CWS	AL	122	415	66	16	0	11	(8	3)	115	36	42	34	75	0	177	4	0	2	0	1	6	.159	.292	.277	.569
2012	CWS	AL	151	539	110	19	0	41	(18	23)	252	87	96	85	105	3	222	1	0	4	2	1	8	.204	.333	.468	.800
2013	CWS	AL	149	525	115	15	0	34	(21	13)	232	60	86	75	76	7	189	3	0	1	1	1	5	.219	.320	.442	.762
2014	2 Tms	AL	131	429	94	18	0	22	(7	15)	178	49	64	65	71	5	159	7	0	4	1	1	5	.219	.337	.415	.752
08	Cin	NL	114	373	87	14	0	32	(16	16)	197	58	74	74	80	6	120	6	0	5	1	1	4	.233	.373	.528	.901
08	Ari	NL	44	144	35	9	0	8	(5	3)	68	21	26	27	42	7	44	1	0	0	1	0	3	.243	.477	.472	.889
14	CWS	AL	106	363	80	17	0	20	(7	13)	157	43	54	54	65	5	132	3	0	4	1	1	5	.220	.340	.433	.773
14	Oak	AL	25	66	14	1	0	2	(0	2)	21	6	10	11	6	0	27	4	0	0	0	0	0	.212	.316	.318	.634
	14 ML YEARS		2001	6883	1631	334	10	462	(245	217)	3371	1097	1168	1184	1317	122	2379	86	2	40	63	25	100	.237	.364	.490	.854

Mike Dunn

Pitches: L Bats: L Pos: RP-75
Ht: 6'0" Wt: 210 Born: 5/23/1985 Age: 30

Year	Team	Lg	G	GS	CG	GF	IP	BFP	H	R	ER	HR	SH	SF	HB	TBB	IBB	SO	WP	Bk	W	L	Pct	Sh	Sv-Op	Hld	ERC	ERA
2009	NYY	AL	4	0	0	3	4.0	20	3	3	3	1	0	0	0	5	0	5	1	0	0	0	-	0	0-0	0	7.17	6.75
2010	Atl	NL	25	0	0	5	19.0	88	15	4	4	1	0	0	0	17	2	27	2	0	2	0	1.000	0	0-0	1	4.19	1.89
2011	Fla	NL	72	0	0	11	63.0	267	51	28	24	9	4	2	2	31	2	68	3	0	5	6	.455	0	0-4	15	3.77	3.43
2012	Mia	NL	60	0	0	8	44.0	208	49	31	24	3	2	4	0	29	8	47	2	0	0	3	.000	0	1-6	18	5.10	4.91
2013	Mia	NL	75	0	0	15	67.2	282	53	21	20	5	1	3	0	28	4	72	2	0	3	4	.429	0	2-5	18	2.68	2.66
2014	Mia	NL	75	0	0	15	57.0	245	47	25	20	4	4	1	4	22	1	67	2	0	10	6	.625	0	1-4	22	3.03	3.16
	Postseason		3	0	0	0	1.1	6	2	0	0	0	0	0	0	0	0	2	0	0	0	0	-	0	0-1	0	4.47	0.00
	6 ML YEARS		311	0	0	57	254.2	1110	218	112	95	23	11	10	6	132	17	286	12	0	20	19	.513	0	4-19	74	3.60	3.36

Jake Dunning

Pitches: R **Bats:** R **Pos:** RP-1   **Ht:** 6'4" **Wt:** 190 **Born:** 8/12/1988 **Age:** 26

Year	Team	Lg	G	GS	CG	GF	IP	BFP	H	R	ER	HR	SH	SF	HB	TBB	IBB	SO	WP	Bk	W	L	Pct	Sh	Sv-Op	Hld	ERC	ERA
2010	SlmKzr	A-	18	0	0	8	36.2	148	30	15	12	2	1	1	2	8	0	46	4	0	1	0	1.000	0	2--	-	2.36	2.95
2011	SnJos	A+	41	7	0	19	76.0	328	86	42	40	7	2	3	6	24	0	71	5	0	6	3	.667	0	10--	-	4.88	4.74
2012	Rchmd	AA	44	0	0	14	68.0	296	74	36	31	2	6	4	4	22	2	53	6	0	5	2	.714	0	0--	-	3.96	4.10
2013	Fresno	AAA	34	0	0	5	48.1	203	47	14	8	3	2	1	5	14	1	44	4	0	2	2	.500	0	1--	-	3.67	1.49
2014	Fresno	AAA	38	4	0	7	65.0	283	65	35	33	5	4	4	3	26	2	51	7	0	0	3	.000	0	1--	-	4.04	4.57
2013	SF	NL	29	0	0	9	25.1	104	20	8	8	2	0	1	3	11	1	16	1	0	0	2	.000	0	0-0	2	3.45	2.84
2014	SF	NL	1	0	0	0	0.2	2	0	0	0	0	0	1	0	1	0	0	2	0	0	0	-	0	0-0	0	3.22	0.00
	2 ML YEARS		30	0	0	9	26.0	106	20	8	8	2	0	2	3	12	1	16	3	0	0	2	.000	0	0-0	2	3.45	2.77

Adam Duvall

Bats: R **Throws:** R **Pos:** 1B-21;PH-8;3B-1;DH-1   **Ht:** 6'1" **Wt:** 205 **Born:** 9/4/1988 **Age:** 26

Year	Team	Lg	G	AB	H	2B	3B	HR	(Hm	Rd)	TB	R	RBI	RC	TBB	IBB	SO	HBP	SH	SF	SB	CS	GDP	Avg	OBP	Slg	OPS
2010	SlmKzr	A-	54	192	47	10	1	4	(-	-)	71	30	18	23	14	0	45	7	3	1	2	3	6	.245	.318	.370	.688
2011	Augsta	A	116	431	123	30	4	22	(-	-)	227	69	87	89	59	4	98	14	1	5	4	4	9	.285	.385	.527	.912
2012	SnJos	A+	134	534	138	24	4	30	(-	-)	260	101	100	89	47	0	116	10	1	6	8	2	18	.258	.327	.487	.814
2013	Rchmd	AA	105	385	97	23	4	17	(-	-)	179	61	58	59	35	2	72	5	2	3	2	1	5	.252	.320	.465	.785
2014	Fresno	AAA	91	359	107	22	3	27	(-	-)	216	67	90	76	30	0	82	5	0	0	2	0	7	.298	.360	.602	.962
2014	SF	NL	28	73	14	2	0	3	(2	1)	25	8	5	4	3	0	20	1	0	0	0	0	0	.192	.234	.342	.576

Jarrod Dyson

Bats: L **Throws:** R **Pos:** CF-106;PR-18;LF-3;PH-3;DH-2   juh-ROD   **Ht:** 5'10" **Wt:** 160 **Born:** 8/15/1984 **Age:** 30

Year	Team	Lg	G	AB	H	2B	3B	HR	(Hm	Rd)	TB	R	RBI	RC	TBB	IBB	SO	HBP	SH	SF	SB	CS	GDP	Avg	OBP	Slg	OPS
2010	KC	AL	18	57	12	4	2	1	(1	0)	23	11	5	9	6	0	16	0	2	0	9	1	2	.211	.286	.404	.689
2011	KC	AL	26	44	9	1	0	0	(0	0)	10	8	3	7	7	0	14	0	1	1	11	1	0	.205	.308	.227	.535
2012	KC	AL	102	292	76	8	5	0	(0	0)	94	52	9	36	30	1	56	1	4	3	30	5	5	.260	.328	.322	.650
2013	KC	AL	87	213	55	9	4	2	(2	0)	78	30	17	28	21	1	45	1	3	1	34	6	4	.258	.326	.366	.692
2014	KC	AL	120	260	70	4	4	1	(1	0)	85	33	24	32	22	0	52	0	6	2	36	7	5	.269	.324	.327	.651
	5 ML YEARS		353	866	222	26	15	4	(4	0)	290	134	58	112	86	2	183	2	16	7	120	20	16	.256	.323	.335	.657

Sam Dyson

Pitches: R **Bats:** R **Pos:** RP-31   **Ht:** 6'1" **Wt:** 205 **Born:** 5/7/1988 **Age:** 27

Year	Team	Lg	G	GS	CG	GF	IP	BFP	H	R	ER	HR	SH	SF	HB	TBB	IBB	SO	WP	Bk	W	L	Pct	Sh	Sv-Op	Hld	ERC	ERA
2014	NewOr*	AAA	13	0	0	4	25.1	103	21	8	7	0	0	0	2	10	0	20	0	0	2	1	.667	0	1--	-	2.87	2.49
2012	Tor	AL	2	0	0	0	0.2	8	4	3	3	0	0	0	0	2	1	0	0	0	0	0	-	0	0-0	0	56.02	40.50
2013	Mia	NL	5	1	0	1	11.0	54	16	12	11	2	1	1	1	5	1	5	0	0	0	2	.000	0	0-0	0	7.96	9.00
2014	Mia	NL	31	0	0	12	42.0	181	41	14	10	1	2	0	3	15	4	33	1	0	3	1	.750	0	0-1	1	3.36	2.14
	3 ML YEARS		38	1	0	13	53.2	243	61	29	24	3	3	1	4	22	5	39	1	0	3	3	.500	0	0-1	0	4.68	4.02

Adam Eaton

Bats: L **Throws:** L **Pos:** CF-121   **Ht:** 5'8" **Wt:** 185 **Born:** 12/6/1988 **Age:** 26

Year	Team	Lg	G	AB	H	2B	3B	HR	(Hm	Rd)	TB	R	RBI	RC	TBB	IBB	SO	HBP	SH	SF	SB	CS	GDP	Avg	OBP	Slg	OPS
2014	Charltt*	AAA	4	16	5	1	0	0	(-	-)	6	2	2	2	0	0	4	0	0	0	2	0	0	.313	.313	.375	.688
2012	Ari	NL	22	85	22	3	2	2	(1	1)	35	19	5	13	14	0	15	3	1	0	2	3	0	.259	.382	.412	.794
2013	Ari	NL	66	250	63	10	4	3	(2	1)	90	40	22	27	17	0	44	6	3	1	5	2	4	.252	.314	.360	.674
2014	CWS	AL	123	486	146	26	**10**	1	(1	0)	195	76	35	77	43	0	83	5	2	2	15	9	4	.300	.362	.401	.763
	3 ML YEARS		211	821	231	39	16	6	(4	2)	320	135	62	117	74	0	142	14	6	3	22	14	8	.281	.350	.390	.740

Josh Edgin

Pitches: L **Bats:** R **Pos:** RP-47   EDGE-inn   **Ht:** 6'1" **Wt:** 245 **Born:** 12/17/1986 **Age:** 28

Year	Team	Lg	G	GS	CG	GF	IP	BFP	H	R	ER	HR	SH	SF	HB	TBB	IBB	SO	WP	Bk	W	L	Pct	Sh	Sv-Op	Hld	ERC	ERA
2014	LsVgs*	AAA	17	0	0	5	12.2	62	16	7	7	1	1	0	1	11	0	12	1	0	3	0	1.000	0	2--	-	8.11	4.97
2012	NYM	NL	34	0	0	6	25.2	107	19	14	13	5	2	0	2	10	0	30	0	0	1	2	.333	0	0-2	5	3.52	4.56
2013	NYM	NL	34	0	0	5	28.2	122	26	12	12	2	1	0	2	12	3	20	0	0	1	1	.500	0	1-2	3	3.57	3.77
2014	NYM	NL	47	0	0	5	27.1	104	19	6	4	2	0	1	0	6	0	28	2	0	1	0	1.000	0	0-1	5	1.77	1.32
	3 ML YEARS		115	0	0	16	81.2	333	64	32	29	9	3	1	4	28	3	78	2	0	3	3	.500	0	1-5	13	2.93	3.20

Jon Edwards

Pitches: R **Bats:** R **Pos:** RP-9   **Ht:** 6'5" **Wt:** 230 **Born:** 1/8/1988 **Age:** 27

Year	Team	Lg	G	GS	CG	GF	IP	BFP	H	R	ER	HR	SH	SF	HB	TBB	IBB	SO	WP	Bk	W	L	Pct	Sh	Sv-Op	Hld	ERC	ERA
2012	Rngrs	R	3	0	0	3	4.2	19	3	0	0	0	0	0	0	2	1	5	0	0	1	0	1.000	0	1--	-	1.49	0.00
2012	Spkane	A-	11	0	0	0	18.1	86	7	8	3	1	0	0	1	24	0	22	6	1	0	0	-	0	0--	-	3.87	1.47
2012	MrtlBh	A+	4	0	0	3	5.0	21	4	2	2	0	0	1	0	3	0	7	1	0	0	0	-	0	0--	-	3.13	3.60
2012	Frisco	AA	1	0	0	0	2.0	11	2	1	1	0	0	0	1	3	0	3	0	0	0	0	-	0	0--	-	7.45	4.50
2013	MrtlBh	A+	26	0	0	14	40.1	179	28	19	16	0	2	1	2	31	0	51	5	0	3	1	.750	0	4--	-	3.22	3.57

Year	Team	Lg	G	GS	CG	GF	IP	BFP	H	R	ER	HR	SH	SF	HB	TBB	IBB	SO	WP	Bk	W	L	Pct	Sh	Sv-Op	Hld	ERC	ERA
2013	Frisco	AA	9	0	0	0	15.1	68	15	10	9	3	1	1	0	8	0	16	2	0	0	1	.000	0	0--	-	5.11	5.28
2014	Frisco	AA	22	0	0	6	33.1	148	27	26	19	4	2	1	0	23	1	36	5	0	1	2	.333	0	0--	-	4.21	5.13
2014	RdRck	AAA	12	0	0	5	15.2	71	15	6	5	0	0	1	1	9	0	26	0	0	1	1	.500	0	0--	-	3.96	2.87
2014	Tex	AL	9	0	0	3	8.1	43	13	5	4	0	0	0	1	5	0	9	2	0	0	0	-	0	0-0	1	7.97	4.32

Scott Elbert

Pitches: L **Bats:** L **Pos:** RP-7   **Ht:** 6'2" **Wt:** 225 **Born:** 8/13/1985 **Age:** 29

Year	Team	Lg	G	GS	CG	GF	IP	BFP	H	R	ER	HR	SH	SF	HB	TBB	IBB	SO	WP	Bk	W	L	Pct	Sh	Sv-Op	Hld	ERC	ERA
2014	Ogden*	R+	1	1	0	0	0.2	5	2	3	3	1	0	0	0	1	0	1	0	0	0	1	.000	0	0--	-	41.86	40.50
2014	RCuca*	A+	5	1	0	0	4.2	20	4	2	2	1	0	0	0	2	0	3	0	0	0	0	-	0	0--	-	4.09	3.86
2014	Albq*	AAA	18	0	0	1	14.2	66	17	10	8	2	1	1	1	7	0	15	1	0	0	2	.000	0	0--	-	6.03	4.91
2008	LAD	NL	10	0	0	1	6.0	31	9	8	8	2	0	0	1	4	0	8	0	0	0	1	.000	0	0-0	2	11.46	12.00
2009	LAD	NL	19	0	0	3	19.2	83	19	11	11	4	1	0	0	7	0	21	1	0	2	0	1.000	0	0-0	3	4.45	5.03
2010	LAD	NL	1	0	0	0	0.2	6	1	1	1	0	0	0	0	3	0	0	0	0	0	0	-	0	0-0	0	24.61	13.50
2011	LAD	NL	47	0	0	11	33.1	139	27	9	9	1	0	1	1	14	4	34	2	0	0	1	.000	0	2-2	7	2.60	2.43
2012	LAD	NL	43	0	0	12	32.2	133	27	8	8	3	0	2	1	13	1	29	3	0	1	1	.500	0	0-0	9	3.24	2.20
2014	LAD	NL	7	0	0	0	4.1	18	4	1	1	0	0	0	0	1	0	2	0	0	1	0	1.000	0	0-0	1	2.34	2.08
	Postseason		1	0	0	0	0.1	3	0	0	0	0	0	0	0	2	0	1	0	0	0	0	-	0	0-0	0	19.60	0.00
	6 ML YEARS		127	0	0	27	96.2	410	87	38	38	10	1	3	3	42	5	94	6	0	4	3	.571	0	2-2	22	3.76	3.54

Roenis Elias

Pitches: L **Bats:** L **Pos:** SP-29   roh-EN-ees ehl-LEE-us   **Ht:** 6'1" **Wt:** 190 **Born:** 8/1/1988 **Age:** 26

Year	Team	Lg	G	GS	CG	GF	IP	BFP	H	R	ER	HR	SH	SF	HB	TBB	IBB	SO	WP	Bk	W	L	Pct	Sh	Sv-Op	Hld	ERC	ERA
2011	Ms	R	1	0	0	0	1.0	3	1	0	0	0	0	0	0	0	0	0	0	0	0	0	-	0	0--	-	2.79	0.00
2011	Pulaski	R+	3	1	0	0	11.0	47	11	4	1	0	0	0	2	3	0	8	0	0	1	0	1.000	0	0--	-	3.64	0.82
2011	Clinton	A	7	7	0	0	36.1	162	41	24	22	7	0	1	1	18	0	33	4	0	4	2	.667	0	0--	-	6.19	5.45
2012	Hi Dsrt	A+	26	26	0	0	148.1	613	136	80	62	19	3	7	8	41	0	128	2	8	11	6	.647	0	0--	-	3.57	3.76
2013	Jacksn	AA	22	22	0	0	130.0	544	112	57	46	9	6	2	4	50	1	121	2	3	6	11	.353	0	0--	-	3.17	3.18
2014	Tacom	AAA	1	1	0	0	5.0	16	0	0	0	0	0	0	0	1	0	6	0	0	1	0	1.000	0	0--	-	0.05	0.00
2014	Sea	AL	29	29	1	0	163.2	693	151	77	70	16	4	4	11	64	3	143	6	4	10	12	.455	1	0-0	0	3.89	3.85

A.J. Ellis

Bats: R **Throws:** R **Pos:** C-92;PH-2   **Ht:** 6'3" **Wt:** 220 **Born:** 4/9/1981 **Age:** 34

Year	Team	Lg	G	AB	H	2B	3B	HR	(Hm	Rd)	TB	R	RBI	RC	TBB	IBB	SO	HBP	SH	SF	SB	CS	GDP	Avg	OBP	Slg	OPS
2014	Albq*	AAA	2	5	2	0	0	1	(-	-)	5	1	2	1	1	0	1	0	0	0	0	1	1	.400	.500	1.000	1.500
2008	LAD	NL	4	3	0	0	0	0	(0	0)	0	1	0	0	0	0	2	0	0	0	0	0	0	.000	.000	.000	.000
2009	LAD	NL	8	10	1	0	0	0	(0	0)	1	0	1	0	0	0	1	0	0	0	0	0	0	.100	.100	.100	.200
2010	LAD	NL	44	108	30	5	0	0	(0	0)	35	6	16	16	14	1	18	1	4	1	0	0	5	.278	.363	.324	.687
2011	LAD	NL	31	85	23	1	1	2	(0	2)	32	8	11	11	14	0	16	3	1	0	0	1	2	.271	.392	.376	.769
2012	LAD	NL	133	423	114	20	1	13	(6	7)	175	44	52	61	65	11	107	7	6	4	0	0	17	.270	.373	.414	.786
2013	LAD	NL	115	390	93	17	1	10	(2	8)	142	43	52	43	45	1	78	3	4	6	0	2	11	.238	.318	.364	.682
2014	LAD	NL	93	283	54	9	0	3	(0	3)	72	21	25	22	53	5	57	4	3	4	0	0	15	.191	.323	.254	.577
	Postseason		10	31	10	4	1	1	(1	0)	19	3	3	6	3	0	6	1	1	0	0	0	0	.323	.400	.613	1.013
	7 ML YEARS		428	1302	315	52	3	28	(8	20)	457	123	157	153	191	18	279	18	18	15	0	3	50	.242	.343	.351	.694

Mark Ellis

Bats: R **Throws:** R **Pos:** 2B-50;PH-22;1B-3;3B-3   **Ht:** 5'10" **Wt:** 190 **Born:** 6/6/1977 **Age:** 38

Year	Team	Lg	G	AB	H	2B	3B	HR	(Hm	Rd)	TB	R	RBI	RC	TBB	IBB	SO	HBP	SH	SF	SB	CS	GDP	Avg	OBP	Slg	OPS
2014	Memp*	AAA	1	3	1	0	0	0	(-	-)	1	0	0	0	0	1	0	0	0	0	0	0	0	.333	.333	.333	.667
2002	Oak	AL	98	345	94	16	4	6	(6	0)	136	58	35	55	44	1	54	4	8	3	4	2	3	.272	.359	.394	.753
2003	Oak	AL	154	553	137	31	5	9	(7	2)	205	78	52	69	48	4	94	7	9	5	6	2	7	.248	.313	.371	.684
2005	Oak	AL	122	434	137	21	5	13	(5	8)	207	76	52	78	44	1	51	4	4	0	1	3	10	.316	.384	.477	.861
2006	Oak	AL	124	441	110	25	1	11	(7	4)	170	64	52	52	40	3	53	8	4	7	4	0	13	.249	.319	.385	.704
2007	Oak	AL	150	583	161	33	3	19	(10	9)	257	84	76	76	44	1	94	10	2	3	9	4	10	.276	.336	.441	.777
2008	Oak	AL	117	442	103	20	3	12	(7	5)	165	55	41	54	53	2	65	5	5	2	14	2	11	.233	.321	.373	.694
2009	Oak	AL	105	377	99	23	0	10	(4	6)	152	52	61	54	23	1	54	2	3	5	10	3	10	.263	.305	.403	.708
2010	Oak	AL	124	436	127	24	0	5	(0	5)	166	45	49	66	40	4	56	8	3	5	7	6	7	.291	.358	.381	.739
2011	2 Tms		132	480	119	24	1	7	(6	1)	166	55	41	44	22	0	75	6	9	2	14	5	8	.248	.288	.346	.634
2012	LAD	NL	110	415	107	21	1	7	(6	1)	151	62	31	44	40	0	70	7	2	0	5	0	5	.258	.333	.364	.697
2013	LAD	NL	126	433	117	13	2	6	(3	3)	152	46	48	52	26	2	74	10	6	5	4	1	5	.270	.323	.351	.674
2014	StL	NL	73	178	32	6	0	0	(0	0)	38	15	12	10	14	3	38	4	4	2	1	0	4	.180	.253	.213	.466
	11 Oak	AL	62	217	47	11	1	1	(1	0)	63	21	16	10	8	0	32	3	4	1	7	2	3	.217	.253	.290	.544
	11 Col	NL	70	263	72	13	0	6	(5	1)	103	34	25	30	14	0	43	3	5	1	7	3	5	.274	.317	.392	.708
	Postseason		22	83	21	5	1	1	(1	0)	31	8	5	9	8	0	20	1	1	0	1	0	2	.253	.326	.373	.700
	12 ML YEARS		1435	5117	1343	257	25	105	(61	44)	1965	690	550	651	438	20	801	75	59	39	82	29	89	.262	.327	.384	.711

Jacoby Ellsbury

Bats: L Throws: L Pos: CF-141;DH-5;PH-4   Ht: 6'1" Wt: 195 Born: 9/11/1983 Age: 31

Year	Team	Lg	G	AB	H	2B	3B	HR	(Hm	Rd)	TB	R	RBI	RC	TBB	IBB	SO	HBP	SH	SF	SB	CS	GDP	Avg	OBP	Slg	OPS
2007	Bos	AL	33	116	41	7	1	3	(3	0)	59	20	18	26	8	0	15	1	0	2	9	0	2	.353	.394	.509	.902
2008	Bos	AL	145	554	155	22	7	9	(4	5)	218	98	47	71	41	2	80	7	4	3	50	11	10	.280	.336	.394	.729
2009	Bos	AL	153	624	188	27	10	8	(4	4)	259	94	60	97	49	3	74	6	6	6	70	12	13	.301	.355	.415	.770
2010	Bos	AL	18	78	15	4	0	0	(0	0)	19	10	5	4	4	0	9	1	0	0	7	1	0	.192	.241	.244	.485
2011	Bos	AL	158	660	212	46	5	32	(15	17)	364	119	105	134	52	1	98	9	3	5	39	15	8	.321	.376	.552	.928
2012	Bos	AL	74	303	82	18	0	4	(3	1)	112	43	26	37	19	0	43	0	0	1	14	3	5	.271	.313	.370	.682
2013	Bos	AL	134	577	172	31	8	9	(4	5)	246	92	53	90	47	3	92	5	1	2	52	4	12	.298	.355	.426	.781
2014	NYY	AL	149	575	156	27	5	16	(7	9)	241	71	70	84	49	5	93	3	0	7	39	5	9	.271	.328	.419	.747
	Postseason		38	133	40	11	2	0	(0	0)	55	26	17	25	13	2	24	0	0	1	11	2	4	.301	.361	.414	.774
	8 ML YEARS		864	3487	1021	182	36	81	(40	41)	1518	547	384	543	269	14	504	32	14	26	280	51	59	.293	.347	.435	.782

Jake Elmore

Bats: R Throws: R Pos: SS-3;2B-2;PH-1   Ht: 5'9" Wt: 185 Born: 6/15/1987 Age: 28

Year	Team	Lg	G	AB	H	2B	3B	HR	(Hm	Rd)	TB	R	RBI	RC	TBB	IBB	SO	HBP	SH	SF	SB	CS	GDP	Avg	OBP	Slg	OPS
2014	Scrmto*	AAA	47	181	51	15	0	0	(-	-)	66	30	18	27	27	1	26	1	0	2	9	4	9	.282	.374	.365	.739
2014	Lsvlle*	AAA	25	86	24	2	0	0	(-	-)	26	14	6	12	15	0	15	0	1	2	3	0	3	.279	.379	.302	.681
2012	Ari	NL	30	68	13	4	0	0	(0	0)	17	1	7	3	5	0	6	0	0	0	0	0	1	.191	.247	.250	.497
2013	Hou	NL	52	120	29	4	0	2	(1	1)	39	16	6	13	13	0	20	0	2	1	1	6	1	.242	.313	.325	.638
2014	Cin	NL	5	11	2	0	0	0	(0	0)	2	0	0	0	1	0	4	0	0	0	0	0	0	.182	.250	.182	.432
	3 ML YEARS		87	199	44	8	0	2	(1	1)	58	17	13	16	19	0	30	0	2	1	1	6	2	.221	.288	.291	.579

Edwin Encarnacion

Bats: R Throws: R Pos: 1B-80;DH-46;LF-2;PH-1   Ht: 6'1" Wt: 230 Born: 1/7/1983 Age: 32

Year	Team	Lg	G	AB	H	2B	3B	HR	(Hm	Rd)	TB	R	RBI	RC	TBB	IBB	SO	HBP	SH	SF	SB	CS	GDP	Avg	OBP	Slg	OPS
2014	Dnedin*	A+	2	4	1	0	0	0	(-	-)	1	0	0	0	0	0	1	0	0	0	0	0	0	.250	.250	.250	.500
2014	Buffalo*	AAA	2	8	2	0	0	1	(-	-)	5	1	4	1	0	0	0	0	0	0	0	0	0	.250	.250	.625	.875
2005	Cin	NL	69	211	49	16	0	9	(3	6)	92	25	31	24	20	2	60	3	0	0	3	0	8	.232	.308	.436	.744
2006	Cin	NL	117	406	112	33	1	15	(7	8)	192	60	72	66	41	3	78	13	0	3	6	3	9	.276	.359	.473	.831
2007	Cin	NL	139	502	145	25	1	16	(10	6)	220	66	76	86	39	4	86	14	0	1	8	1	5	.289	.356	.438	.794
2008	Cin	NL	146	506	127	29	1	26	(15	11)	236	75	68	72	61	1	102	10	0	5	1	0	13	.251	.340	.466	.807
2009	2 Tms		85	293	66	11	2	13	(5	8)	120	35	39	37	37	0	67	5	0	3	2	1	5	.225	.320	.410	.729
2010	Tor	AL	96	332	81	16	0	21	(7	14)	160	47	51	41	29	1	60	2	0	4	1	0	9	.244	.305	.482	.787
2011	Tor	AL	134	481	131	36	0	17	(14	3)	218	70	55	67	43	2	77	3	0	3	8	2	17	.272	.334	.453	.787
2012	Tor	AL	151	542	152	24	0	42	(23	19)	302	93	110	124	84	12	94	11	0	7	13	3	6	.280	.384	.557	.941
2013	Tor	AL	142	530	144	29	1	36	(12	24)	283	90	104	102	82	7	62	4	0	5	7	1	20	.272	.370	.534	.904
2014	Tor	AL	128	477	128	27	2	34	(19	15)	261	75	98	86	62	6	82	2	0	1	2	0	18	.268	.354	.547	.901
09	Cin	NL	43	139	29	6	1	5	(3	2)	52	10	16	19	24	0	38	2	0	1	1	1	3	.209	.333	.374	.707
09	Tor	AL	42	154	37	5	1	8	(2	6)	68	25	23	18	13	0	29	3	0	3	1	0	2	.240	.306	.442	.748
	10 ML YEARS		1207	4280	1135	246	8	229	(115	114)	2084	636	704	705	498	38	768	67	0	32	51	11	110	.265	.349	.487	.835

Nathan Eovaldi

Pitches: R Bats: R Pos: SP-33   eh-VOLL-dee   Ht: 6'2" Wt: 215 Born: 2/13/1990 Age: 25

			HOW MUCH HE PITCHED					WHAT HE GAVE UP								THE RESULTS						
Year	Team	Lg	G	GS	CG	GF	IP	BFP	H	R	ER	HR	SH	SF	HB	TBB	IBB	SO	WP	Bk	W	L	Pct	Sh	Sv-Op	Hld	ERC	ERA
2011	LAD	NL	10	6	0	1	34.2	146	28	14	14	2	2	0	2	20	0	23	0	0	1	2	.333	0	0-0	1	3.75	3.63
2012	2 Tms	NL	22	22	0	0	119.1	526	133	59	57	10	1	6	3	47	3	78	1	0	4	13	.235	0	0-0	0	4.67	4.30
2013	Mia	NL	18	18	0	0	106.1	451	100	44	40	7	6	1	1	40	3	78	3	0	4	6	.400	0	0-0	0	3.41	3.39
2014	Mia	NL	33	33	0	0	199.2	854	223	107	97	14	9	5	7	43	5	142	6	0	6	14	.300	0	0-0	0	3.89	4.37
12	LAD	NL	10	10	0	0	56.1	241	63	27	26	5	0	3	0	20	2	34	1	0	1	6	.143	0	0-0	0	4.54	4.15
12	Mia	NL	12	12	0	0	63.0	285	70	32	31	5	1	3	3	27	1	44	0	0	3	7	.300	0	0-0	0	4.79	4.43
	4 ML YEARS		83	79	0	1	460.0	1977	484	224	208	33	18	12	13	150	11	321	10	0	15	35	.300	0	0-0	1	3.96	4.07

Robbie Erlin

Pitches: L Bats: R Pos: SP-11; RP-2   Ht: 6'0" Wt: 190 Born: 10/8/1990 Age: 24

			HOW MUCH HE PITCHED					WHAT HE GAVE UP								THE RESULTS						
Year	Team	Lg	G	GS	CG	GF	IP	BFP	H	R	ER	HR	SH	SF	HB	TBB	IBB	SO	WP	Bk	W	L	Pct	Sh	Sv-Op	Hld	ERC	ERA
2010	Hkry	A	28	17	0	2	114.2	447	89	37	27	9	6	2	4	17	0	125	4	0	6	3	.667	0	1--	1	2.01	2.12
2011	MrtlBh	A+	9	9	0	0	54.2	198	25	15	13	7	0	1	3	5	0	62	1	0	3	2	.600	0	0--	0	1.02	2.14
2011	Frisco	AA	11	10	0	0	66.2	274	73	34	32	9	2	3	2	7	0	61	1	2	5	2	.714	0	0--	0	3.83	4.32
2011	SnAnt	AA	6	6	0	0	26.0	103	26	4	4	2	0	1	0	4	0	31	0	0	1	0	1.000	0	0--	0	3.09	1.38
2012	SnAnt	AA	11	11	0	0	52.1	228	53	21	17	6	2	1	3	14	1	72	1	0	3	1	.750	0	0--	0	3.81	2.92
2012	Padres	R	3	3	0	0	8.1	37	7	7	2	0	0	1	0	2	0	8	1	0	0	2	.000	0	0--	0	1.79	2.16
2013	Tucsn	AAA	20	20	0	0	99.1	454	125	65	56	11	5	7	1	34	0	84	4	1	8	3	.727	0	0--	0	5.38	5.07
2014	Padres	R	1	1	0	0	2.0	9	1	0	0	0	0	0	0	0	0	5	0	0	0	0	-	0	0--	0	0.42	0.00
2014	SnAnt	AA	2	2	0	0	10.1	45	12	4	4	1	0	0	0	4	0	10	0	0	0	1	.000	0	0--	0	5.04	3.48
2014	ElPaso	AAA	2	2	0	0	10.2	52	21	12	11	2	2	0	0	2	0	8	1	0	0	1	.000	0	0--	0	10.44	9.28
2013	SD	NL	11	9	0	2	54.2	227	53	26	25	6	3	1	0	15	0	40	3	0	3	3	.500	0	0-0	0	3.50	4.12
2014	SD	NL	13	11	0	1	61.1	264	71	34	34	6	2	4	1	15	1	46	4	0	4	5	.444	0	0-0	0	4.39	4.99
	2 ML YEARS		24	20	0	3	116.0	491	124	60	59	12	5	5	1	30	1	86	7	0	7	8	.467	0	0-0	0	3.96	4.58

Alcides Escobar

Bats: R **Throws:** R **Pos:** SS-162   al-SEE-dess   **Ht:** 6'1" **Wt:** 185 **Born:** 12/16/1986 **Age:** 28

							BATTING													RUNNING			AVERAGES			
Year	Team	Lg	G	AB	H	2B	3B	HR	(Hm | Rd)	TB	R	RBI	RC	TBB	IBB	SO	HBP	SH	SF	SB	CS	GDP	Avg	OBP	Slg	OPS
2008	Mil	NL	9	4	2	0	0	0	(0 | 0)	2	2	0	0	0	0	1	0	0	0	0	0	0	.500	.500	.500	1.000
2009	Mil	NL	38	125	38	3	1	1	(0 | 1)	46	20	11	16	4	0	18	2	2	1	4	2	0	.304	.333	.368	.701
2010	Mil	NL	145	506	119	14	10	4	(3 | 1)	165	57	41	51	36	7	70	3	4	3	10	4	8	.235	.288	.326	.614
2011	KC	AL	158	548	139	21	8	4	(0 | 4)	188	69	46	46	25	1	73	4	18	3	26	9	10	.254	.290	.343	.633
2012	KC	AL	155	605	177	30	7	5	(5 | 0)	236	68	52	72	27	2	100	8	8	0	35	5	14	.293	.331	.390	.721
2013	KC	AL	158	607	142	20	4	4	(1 | 3)	182	57	52	51	19	1	84	3	9	4	22	0	12	.234	.259	.300	.559
2014	KC	AL	162	579	165	34	5	3	(2 | 1)	218	74	50	68	23	1	83	6	8	4	31	6	12	.285	.317	.377	.694
	7 ML YEARS		825	2974	782	122	35	21	(11 | 10)	1037	347	252	304	134	12	429	26	49	15	128	26	56	.263	.299	.349	.648

Eduardo Escobar

Bats: B **Throws:** R **Pos:** SS-98;3B-25;2B-9;PH-5;PR-4;LF-2;CF-1   **Ht:** 5'10" **Wt:** 175 **Born:** 1/5/1989 **Age:** 26

							BATTING													RUNNING			AVERAGES			
Year	Team	Lg	G	AB	H	2B	3B	HR	(Hm	Rd)	TB	R	RBI	RC	TBB	IBB	SO	HBP	SH	SF	SB	CS	GDP	Avg	OBP	Slg	OPS
2011	CWS	AL	9	7	2	0	0	0	(0	0)	2	0	0	1	0	0	1	0	0	0	0	0	0	.286	.286	.286	.571
2012	2 Tms	AL	50	131	28	4	1	0	(0	0)	34	18	9	12	11	0	31	1	2	1	3	0	0	.214	.288	.260	.537
2013	Min	AL	66	165	39	5	2	3	(2	1)	57	23	10	14	11	0	34	0	2	1	0	2	0	.236	.282	.345	.628
2014	Min	AL	133	433	119	35	4	6	(2	4)	176	52	37	53	24	1	93	2	4	2	1	1	6	.275	.315	.406	.721
	12 CWS		36	87	18	4	1	0	(0	0)	24	14	3	7	9	0	23	0	1	0	2	0	0	.207	.281	.276	.557
	12 Min		14	44	10	0	0	0	(0	0)	10	4	6	5	2	0	8	1	1	1	1	0	0	.227	.271	.227	.498
	4 ML YEARS		258	736	188	44	5	9	(4	5)	269	93	56	80	46	1	159	3	8	4	4	3	6	.255	.300	.365	.666

Edwin Escobar

Pitches: L **Bats:** L **Pos:** RP-2   **Ht:** 6'1" **Wt:** 185 **Born:** 4/22/1992 **Age:** 23

			HOW MUCH HE PITCHED						WHAT HE GAVE UP										THE RESULTS						
Year	Team	Lg	G	GS	CG	GF	IP	BFP	H	R	ER	HR	SH	SF	HB	TBB	IBB	SO	WP	Bk	W	L	Pct	Sh	Sv-Op	Hld	ERC	ERA
2010	SlmKzr	A-	14	14	0	0	63.0	289	64	40	34	6	5	4	3	40	0	69	7	4	2	4	.333	0	0- -	-	5.27	4.86
2011	Augsta	A	4	2	0	1	6.0	41	15	15	12	0	0	2	1	5	0	5	1	0	1	3	.250	0	0- -	-	14.89	18.00
2011	Giants	R	15	12	0	0	46.0	201	51	30	26	2	1	3	5	17	0	42	3	2	2	4	.333	0	0- -	-	4.71	5.09
2012	Augsta	A	22	22	0	0	130.2	547	121	57	43	7	3	2	7	32	0	122	10	2	7	8	.467	0	0- -	-	2.95	2.96
2013	SnJos	A+	16	14	0	0	74.2	314	68	33	24	3	2	4	1	17	0	92	0	1	3	4	.429	0	0- -	-	2.52	2.89
2013	Rchmd	AA	10	10	0	0	54.0	218	44	18	16	2	2	0	2	13	0	53	1	0	5	4	.556	0	0- -	-	2.26	2.67
2014	Fresno	AAA	20	20	0	0	111.0	499	128	69	63	16	5	5	6	37	2	96	4	2	3	8	.273	0	0- -	-	5.14	5.11
2014	Pwtckt	AAA	5	5	0	0	27.1	120	33	15	13	3	0	1	0	8	0	20	0	0	0	2	.000	0	0- -	-	4.92	4.28
2014	Bos	AL	2	0	0	2	2.0	8	1	1	1	0	0	0	1	0	0	2	0	0	0	0	-	0	0-0	0	1.41	4.50

Yunel Escobar

Bats: R **Throws:** R **Pos:** SS-136;PH-2;LF-1   you-NELL   **Ht:** 6'2" **Wt:** 215 **Born:** 11/2/1982 **Age:** 32

							BATTING													RUNNING			AVERAGES			
Year	Team	Lg	G	AB	H	2B	3B	HR	(Hm	Rd)	TB	R	RBI	RC	TBB	IBB	SO	HBP	SH	SF	SB	CS	GDP	Avg	OBP	Slg	OPS
2014	Charltt*	A+	2	7	1	0	0	0	(-	-)	1	2	1	0	0	0	1	0	0	0	0	0	0	.143	.143	.143	.286
2007	Atl	NL	94	319	104	25	0	5	(3	2)	144	54	28	52	27	1	44	5	2	2	5	3	6	.326	.385	.451	.837
2008	Atl	NL	136	514	148	24	2	10	(5	5)	206	71	60	70	59	4	62	5	7	2	2	5	24	.288	.366	.401	.766
2009	Atl	NL	141	528	158	26	2	14	(7	7)	230	89	76	90	57	3	62	10	7	2	5	4	21	.299	.377	.436	.812
2010	2 Tms		135	497	127	19	0	4	(2	2)	158	60	35	53	56	1	57	5	9	0	6	2	18	.256	.337	.318	.655
2011	Tor	AL	133	513	149	24	3	11	(8	3)	212	77	48	84	61	1	70	6	5	5	3	3	14	.290	.369	.413	.782
2012	Tor	AL	145	558	141	22	1	9	(6	3)	192	58	51	51	35	1	70	4	7	4	5	1	21	.253	.300	.344	.644
2013	TB	AL	153	508	130	27	1	9	(5	4)	186	61	56	60	57	2	73	3	6	4	4	4	19	.256	.332	.366	.698
2014	TB	AL	137	476	123	18	0	7	(2	5)	162	33	39	49	43	3	60	4	4	2	1	1	15	.258	.324	.340	.664
	10 Atl	NL	75	261	62	12	0	0	(0	0)	74	28	19	25	37	1	31	1	2	0	5	1	9	.238	.334	.284	.618
	10 Tor	AL	60	236	65	7	0	4	(2	2)	84	32	16	28	19	0	26	4	7	0	1	1	9	.275	.340	.356	.696
	Postseason		5	19	8	2	0	0	(0	0)	10	3	2	4	0	0	1	0	0	0	0	0	1	.421	.421	.526	.947
	8 ML YEARS		1074	3913	1080	185	9	69	(38	31)	1490	503	393	509	395	16	498	42	47	21	31	23	138	.276	.347	.381	.728

Danny Espinosa

Bats: B **Throws:** R **Pos:** 2B-89;PH-14;SS-12;PR-4   **Ht:** 6'0" **Wt:** 205 **Born:** 4/25/1987 **Age:** 28

							BATTING													RUNNING			AVERAGES			
Year	Team	Lg	G	AB	H	2B	3B	HR	(Hm	Rd)	TB	R	RBI	RC	TBB	IBB	SO	HBP	SH	SF	SB	CS	GDP	Avg	OBP	Slg	OPS
2010	Was	NL	28	103	22	4	1	6	(4	2)	46	16	15	15	9	1	30	0	0	0	2	0	0	.214	.277	.447	.723
2011	Was	NL	158	573	135	29	5	21	(11	10)	237	72	66	83	57	4	166	19	5	4	17	6	6	.236	.323	.414	.737
2012	Was	NL	160	594	147	37	2	17	(7	10)	239	82	56	69	46	4	189	13	3	2	20	6	11	.247	.315	.402	.717
2013	Was	NL	44	158	25	9	0	3	(2	1)	43	11	12	8	4	0	47	3	1	1	1	0	1	.158	.193	.272	.465
2014	Was	NL	114	333	73	14	3	8	(5	3)	117	31	27	26	18	5	122	12	0	1	8	1	5	.219	.283	.351	.634
	Postseason		5	15	1	0	0	0	(0	0)	1	0	0	0	2	0	7	0	2	0	0	0	0	.067	.176	.067	.243
	5 ML YEARS		504	1761	402	93	11	55	(29	26)	682	212	176	201	134	14	554	47	9	8	46	15	23	.228	.299	.387	.686

Marco Estrada

Pitches: R **Bats:** R **Pos:** RP-21; SP-18

Ht: 6'0" **Wt:** 200 **Born:** 7/5/1983 **Age:** 31

Year	Team	Lg	G	GS	CG	GF	IP	BFP	H	R	ER	HR	SH	SF	HB	TBB	IBB	SO	WP	Bk	W	L	Pct	Sh	Sv-Op	Hld	ERC	ERA
2008	Was	NL	11	0	0	3	12.2	63	17	13	11	4	0	0	2	5	1	10	0	0	0	0	-	0	0-1	3	8.13	7.82
2009	Was	NL	4	1	0	1	7.1	33	6	6	5	1	1	0	0	4	0	9	1	0	0	1	.000	0	0-0	0	3.67	6.14
2010	Mil	NL	7	1	0	0	11.1	58	14	13	12	3	1	0	1	6	0	13	2	0	0	0	-	0	0-0	0	7.17	9.53
2011	Mil	NL	43	7	0	12	92.2	381	83	45	42	11	7	1	2	29	2	88	4	2	4	8	.333	0	0-3	4	3.39	4.08
2012	Mil	NL	29	23	0	0	138.1	562	129	62	56	18	7	3	0	29	0	143	4	1	5	7	.417	0	0-0	1	3.18	3.64
2013	Mil	NL	21	21	0	0	128.0	512	109	56	55	19	3	2	2	29	0	118	3	0	7	4	.636	0	0-0	0	3.01	3.87
2014	Mil	NL	39	18	0	3	150.2	624	137	77	73	29	4	4	3	44	0	127	2	1	7	6	.538	0	0-0	0	3.85	4.36
	Postseason		4	0	0	2	6.0	27	7	4	4	0	0	0	0	2	0	9	1	0	0	0	-	0	0-0	0	3.91	6.00
	7 ML YEARS		154	71	0	19	541.0	2233	495	272	254	85	23	10	10	146	3	508	16	4	23	26	.469	0	0-4	8	3.54	4.23

Andre Ethier

EE-thee-er

Bats: L **Throws:** L **Pos:** CF-68;PH-41;LF-16;RF-15;1B-1;DH-1

Ht: 6'2" **Wt:** 200 **Born:** 4/10/1982 **Age:** 33

Year	Team	Lg	G	AB	H	2B	3B	HR	(Hm	Rd)	TB	R	RBI	RC	TBB	IBB	SO	HBP	SH	SF	SB	CS	GDP	Avg	OBP	Slg	OPS
2006	LAD	NL	126	396	122	20	7	11	(9	2)	189	50	55	62	34	2	77	5	0	6	5	5	11	.308	.365	.477	.842
2007	LAD	NL	153	447	127	32	2	13	(8	5)	202	50	64	65	46	12	68	4	0	8	0	4	10	.284	.350	.452	.802
2008	LAD	NL	141	525	160	38	5	20	(10	10)	268	90	77	99	59	0	88	4	1	7	6	3	6	.305	.375	.510	.885
2009	LAD	NL	160	596	162	42	3	31	(22	9)	303	92	106	94	72	10	116	13	0	4	6	4	19	.272	.361	.508	.869
2010	LAD	NL	139	517	151	33	1	23	(14	9)	255	71	82	89	59	11	102	3	0	6	2	1	11	.292	.364	.493	.857
2011	LAD	NL	135	487	142	30	0	11	(8	3)	205	67	62	73	58	9	103	3	0	3	0	1	8	.292	.368	.421	.789
2012	LAD	NL	149	556	158	36	1	20	(14	6)	256	79	89	89	50	6	124	9	0	3	2	2	13	.284	.351	.460	.812
2013	LAD	NL	142	482	131	33	2	12	(6	6)	204	54	52	62	61	11	95	7	0	3	4	3	9	.272	.360	.423	.783
2014	LAD	NL	130	341	85	17	6	4	(4	0)	126	29	42	42	31	3	74	6	1	1	2	2	5	.249	.322	.370	.691
	Postseason		28	87	20	4	1	3	(1	2)	35	14	6	8	11	0	24	1	0	0	0	1	1	.230	.323	.402	.726
	9 ML YEARS		1275	4347	1238	281	27	145	(95	50)	2008	582	629	675	470	64	847	54	2	41	27	25	92	.285	.359	.462	.821

Nick Evans

Bats: R **Throws:** R **Pos:** PH-13;1B-3;3B-1;LF-1;DH-1;PR-1

Ht: 6'2" **Wt:** 220 **Born:** 1/30/1986 **Age:** 29

Year	Team	Lg	G	AB	H	2B	3B	HR	(Hm	Rd)	TB	R	RBI	RC	TBB	IBB	SO	HBP	SH	SF	SB	CS	GDP	Avg	OBP	Slg	OPS
2014	Reno*	AAA	51	198	70	18	2	11	(-	-)	125	42	47	50	23	2	28	3	0	3	0	0	12	.354	.423	.631	1.054
2014	Tohoku*	Jap	5	18	2	0	0	0	(-	-)	2	0	1	0	0	0	7	0	0	0	0	0	0	.111	.111	.111	.222
2008	NYM	NL	50	109	28	10	0	2	(0	2)	44	18	9	10	7	2	24	1	0	2	0	0	1	.257	.303	.404	.706
2009	NYM	NL	30	65	15	5	1	1	(1	0)	25	5	7	8	4	0	20	0	0	0	0	0	4	.231	.275	.385	.660
2010	NYM	NL	20	36	11	3	0	1	(1	0)	17	5	5	5	1	0	10	0	0	0	0	0	1	.306	.324	.472	.797
2011	NYM	NL	59	176	45	10	2	4	(0	4)	71	26	25	21	15	0	48	1	0	2	0	1	6	.256	.314	.403	.718
2014	Ari	NL	18	22	6	2	0	2	(0	2)	14	2	7	5	1	0	10	0	0	0	0	0	0	.273	.304	.636	.941
	5 ML YEARS		177	408	105	30	3	10	(2	8)	171	56	53	49	28	2	112	2	0	4	0	1	12	.257	.305	.419	.725

Dana Eveland

EVE-land

Pitches: L **Bats:** L **Pos:** RP-30

Ht: 6'1" **Wt:** 235 **Born:** 10/29/1983 **Age:** 31

Year	Team	Lg	G	GS	CG	GF	IP	BFP	H	R	ER	HR	SH	SF	HB	TBB	IBB	SO	WP	Bk	W	L	Pct	Sh	Sv-Op	Hld	ERC	ERA
2014	LsVgs*	AAA	12	8	0	1	46.0	206	55	22	20	5	0	2	3	12	1	58	1	0	4	1	.800	0	0--	-	4.86	3.91
2005	Mil	NL	27	0	0	3	31.2	146	40	21	21	2	0	1	1	18	3	23	1	0	1	1	.500	0	1-2	7	6.16	5.97
2006	Mil	NL	9	5	0	1	27.2	141	39	25	25	4	1	1	5	16	2	32	2	0	0	3	.000	0	0-1	0	8.30	8.13
2007	Ari	NL	5	1	0	0	5.0	28	8	8	8	0	0	1	0	5	0	3	1	0	1	0	1.000	0	0-0	0	9.25	14.40
2008	Oak	AL	29	29	1	0	168.0	737	172	82	81	10	2	5	12	77	2	118	6	1	9	9	.500	0	0-0	0	4.47	4.34
2009	Oak	AL	13	9	0	2	44.0	221	70	39	35	4	1	2	0	26	1	22	2	0	2	4	.333	0	0-0	0	8.50	7.16
2010	2 Tms		12	10	0	1	54.1	262	72	44	41	4	0	4	4	32	2	24	4	0	3	5	.375	0	0-0	0	6.90	6.79
2011	LAD	NL	5	5	0	0	29.2	118	28	10	10	1	1	0	2	6	0	16	0	0	3	2	.600	0	0-0	0	2.98	3.03
2012	Bal	AL	14	2	0	6	32.1	145	32	18	17	3	0	2	5	13	3	18	0	0	0	1	.000	0	0-0	0	4.38	4.73
2014	NYM	NL	30	0	0	10	27.1	115	24	8	8	2	0	4	4	6	1	27	0	0	1	1	.500	0	1-2	2	3.02	2.63
10	Tor	AL	9	9	0	0	44.2	213	57	35	32	4	0	2	2	27	1	21	3	0	3	4	.429	0	0-0	0	6.69	6.45
10	Pit	NL	3	1	0	1	9.2	49	15	9	9	0	0	2	2	5	1	3	1	0	0	1	.000	0	0-0	0	7.85	8.38
	9 ML YEARS		144	61	1	23	420.0	1913	485	255	246	30	5	16	33	199	14	283	16	1	20	26	.435	0	2-5	9	5.36	5.27

Irving Falu

fuh-LOO

Bats: B **Throws:** R **Pos:** 2B-11;PH-7;3B-3;SS-2

Ht: 5'10" **Wt:** 180 **Born:** 6/6/1983 **Age:** 32

Year	Team	Lg	G	AB	H	2B	3B	HR	(Hm	Rd)	TB	R	RBI	RC	TBB	IBB	SO	HBP	SH	SF	SB	CS	GDP	Avg	OBP	Slg	OPS
2014	Nashv*	AAA	76	247	72	8	1	2	(-	-)	88	28	18	31	21	1	22	0	11	3	9	9	6	.291	.343	.356	.699
2012	KC	AL	24	85	29	6	1	0	(0	0)	37	14	7	12	4	0	9	0	2	0	0	2	2	.341	.371	.435	.806
2013	KC	AL	1	4	1	0	0	0	(0	0)	1	0	0	0	0	0	0	0	0	0	0	0	0	.250	.250	.250	.500
2014	2 Tms		22	30	3	0	0	0	(0	0)	3	0	1	0	4	1	5	0	0	1	1	0	2	.100	.200	.100	.300
14	Mil	NL	11	10	0	0	0	0	(0	0)	0	0	1	0	1	0	1	0	0	0	0	0	1	.000	.083	.000	.083
14	SD	NL	11	20	3	0	0	0	(0	0)	3	0	0	0	3	1	4	0	0	1	1	0	1	.150	.261	.150	.411
	3 ML YEARS		47	119	33	6	1	0	(0	0)	41	14	8	12	8	1	14	0	2	1	1	2	4	.277	.320	.345	.665

Jeurys Familia

Pitches: R Bats: R Pos: RP-76 JAY-your-ees fuh-MEAL-yuh Ht: 6'3" Wt: 240 Born: 10/10/1989 Age: 25

Year	Team	Lg	G	GS	CG	GF	IP	BFP	H	R	ER	HR	SH	SF	HB	TBB	IBB	SO	WP	Bk	W	L	Pct	Sh	Sv-Op	Hld	ERC	ERA
2012	NYM	NL	8	1	0	4	12.1	52	10	8	8	0	0	0	0	9	0	10	0	0	0	0	-	0	0-0	0	3.76	5.84
2013	NYM	NL	9	0	0	3	10.2	52	12	5	5	2	2	0	0	9	1	8	3	0	0	0	-	0	1-1	0	7.20	4.22
2014	NYM	NL	76	0	0	16	77.1	322	59	26	19	3	4	2	2	32	5	73	9	0	2	5	.286	0	5-10	23	2.45	2.21
	3 ML YEARS		93	1	0	23	100.1	426	81	39	32	5	6	2	2	50	6	91	12	0	2	5	.286	0	6-11	23	3.04	2.87

Buck Farmer

Pitches: R Bats: L Pos: SP-2; RP-2 BUCK FARMER Ht: 6'4" Wt: 225 Born: 2/20/1991 Age: 24

Year	Team	Lg	G	GS	CG	GF	IP	BFP	H	R	ER	HR	SH	SF	HB	TBB	IBB	SO	WP	Bk	W	L	Pct	Sh	Sv-Op	Hld	ERC	ERA
2013	Conn	A-	12	11	0	0	32.0	134	32	13	11	1	2	0	7	0	33	1	0	0	3	.000	0	0- -	-	2.89	3.09
2014	WMich	A	18	18	0	0	103.2	420	91	37	30	6	2	1	3	24	0	116	7	1	10	5	.667	0	0- -	-	2.65	2.60
2014	Erie	AA	2	2	0	0	12.0	49	10	4	4	1	0	0	0	4	0	11	0	0	1	0	1.000	0	0- -	-	2.84	3.00
2014	Toledo	AAA	2	2	0	0	7.1	36	11	9	8	1	1	0	0	4	0	2	1	0	1	1	.500	0	0- -	-	8.12	9.82
2014	Det	AL	4	2	0	1	9.1	46	12	12	12	2	0	0	2	5	0	11	0	0	0	1	.000	0	0-0	0	8.29	11.57

Kyle Farnsworth

Pitches: R Bats: R Pos: RP-35 Ht: 6'4" Wt: 230 Born: 4/14/1976 Age: 39

Year	Team	Lg	G	GS	CG	GF	IP	BFP	H	R	ER	HR	SH	SF	HB	TBB	IBB	SO	WP	Bk	W	L	Pct	Sh	Sv-Op	Hld	ERC	ERA
1999	ChC	NL	27	21	1	1	130.0	579	140	80	73	28	6	2	3	52	1	70	7	1	5	9	.357	1	0-0	-	5.39	5.05
2000	ChC	NL	46	5	0	8	77.0	371	90	58	55	14	4	4	4	50	8	74	3	0	2	9	.182	0	1-6	6	6.72	6.43
2001	ChC	NL	76	0	0	24	82.0	339	65	26	25	8	2	2	1	29	2	107	2	2	4	6	.400	0	2-3	24	2.76	2.74
2002	ChC	NL	45	0	0	17	46.2	213	53	47	38	9	2	5	1	24	7	46	1	0	4	6	.400	0	1-7	6	5.89	7.33
2003	ChC	NL	77	0	0	13	76.1	312	53	31	28	6	4	1	0	36	1	92	6	0	3	2	.600	0	0-3	19	2.58	3.30
2004	ChC	NL	72	0	0	25	66.2	298	67	39	35	10	5	0	2	33	1	78	1	0	4	5	.444	0	0-4	18	4.91	4.73
2005	2 Tms		72	0	0	34	70.0	277	44	18	17	5	2	1	3	27	0	87	3	1	1	1	.500	0	16-18	19	2.12	2.19
2006	NYY	AL	72	0	0	24	66.0	289	62	34	32	8	3	2	1	28	3	75	5	1	3	6	.333	0	6-10	19	3.88	4.36
2007	NYY	AL	64	0	0	11	60.0	266	60	35	32	9	1	2	2	27	2	48	4	2	2	1	.667	0	0-3	15	4.67	4.80
2008	2 Tms		61	0	0	11	60.1	261	70	32	30	15	3	1	1	22	4	61	1	1	2	3	.400	0	1-4	14	6.11	4.48
2009	KC	AL	41	0	0	18	37.1	168	43	22	19	3	1	2	1	14	2	42	2	1	1	5	.167	0	0-2	5	4.65	4.58
2010	2 Tms		60	0	0	15	64.2	267	55	25	24	4	3	2	4	19	1	61	3	0	3	2	.600	0	0-3	9	2.84	3.34
2011	TB	AL	63	0	0	51	57.2	231	45	15	14	5	1	2	3	12	1	51	2	0	5	1	.833	0	25-31	5	2.29	2.18
2012	TB	AL	34	0	0	8	27.0	120	22	13	12	1	2	1	1	14	2	25	2	0	1	6	.143	0	0-0	7	2.96	4.00
2013	2 Tms		48	0	0	17	38.1	162	43	20	20	5	0	0	1	10	0	28	0	1	3	1	.750	0	2-3	2	4.64	4.70
2014	2 Tms		35	0	0	16	28.2	128	32	14	14	2	0	4	0	15	2	18	1	0	0	3	.000	0	3-5	6	4.96	4.40
05	Det	AL	46	0	0	16	42.2	174	29	12	11	1	1	1	1	20	0	55	2	0	1	1	.500	0	6-8	15	2.26	2.32
05	Atl	NL	26	0	0	18	27.1	103	15	6	6	4	1	0	2	7	0	32	1	1	0	0	-	0	10-10	4	1.86	1.98
08	NYY	AL	45	0	0	6	44.1	185	43	18	18	11	3	1	1	17	3	43	1	1	1	2	.333	0	1-1	11	5.02	3.65
08	Det	AL	16	0	0	5	16.0	76	27	14	12	4	0	0	0	5	1	18	0	0	1	1	.500	0	0-3	3	9.43	6.75
10	KC	AL	37	0	0	9	44.2	185	40	13	12	2	1	1	4	12	0	36	2	0	3	0	1.000	0	0-2	7	3.01	2.42
10	Atl	NL	23	0	0	6	20.0	82	15	12	12	2	2	1	0	7	1	25	1	0	0	2	.000	0	0-1	2	2.46	5.40
13	TB	AL	39	0	0	10	29.2	129	37	19	19	4	0	0	1	7	0	19	0	1	2	0	1.000	0	0-1	2	5.32	5.76
13	Pit	NL	9	0	0	7	8.2	33	6	1	1	1	0	0	0	3	0	9	0	0	1	1	.500	0	2-2	0	2.51	1.04
14	NYM	NL	19	0	0	10	17.0	71	18	6	6	2	0	1	0	6	1	10	0	0	0	3	.000	0	3-4	1	4.41	3.18
14	Hou	AL	16	0	0	6	11.2	57	14	8	8	0	0	3	0	9	1	8	1	0	0	0	-	0	0-1	5	5.70	6.17
	Postseason		15	0	0	5	16.0	66	12	9	9	2	1	1	1	6	2	17	0	0	1	0	1.000	0	0-0	2	2.86	5.06
	16 ML YEARS		893	26	1	293	988.2	4281	944	509	468	132	39	31	28	412	37	963	43	10	43	66	.394	1	57-102	171	4.16	4.26

Danny Farquhar

Pitches: R Bats: R Pos: RP-66 FARK-war Ht: 5'9" Wt: 185 Born: 2/17/1987 Age: 28

Year	Team	Lg	G	GS	CG	GF	IP	BFP	H	R	ER	HR	SH	SF	HB	TBB	IBB	SO	WP	Bk	W	L	Pct	Sh	Sv-Op	Hld	ERC	ERA
2011	Tor	AL	3	0	0	2	2.0	11	4	4	3	0	1	0	1	2	0	1	0	0	0	0	-	0	0-0	0	13.16	13.50
2013	Sea	AL	46	0	0	27	55.2	228	44	29	26	2	1	2	0	22	4	79	2	1	0	3	.000	0	16-20	2	2.44	4.20
2014	Sea	AL	66	0	0	22	71.0	290	58	23	21	5	1	1	4	22	1	81	6	2	3	1	.750	0	1-3	13	2.78	2.66
	3 ML YEARS		115	0	0	51	128.2	529	106	56	50	7	2	4	4	46	5	161	8	3	3	4	.429	0	17-23	15	2.75	3.50

Tim Federowicz

Bats: R Throws: R Pos: C-22;PH-1 fed-ur-OWE-vitch Ht: 5'10" Wt: 215 Born: 8/5/1987 Age: 27

Year	Team	Lg	G	AB	H	2B	3B	HR	(Hm	Rd)	TB	R	RBI	RC	TBB	IBB	SO	HBP	SH	SF	SB	CS	GDP	Avg	OBP	Slg	OPS
2014	Albq*	AAA	78	299	98	26	0	14	(-	-)	166	51	48	62	26	0	66	2	0	2	1	0	5	.328	.383	.555	.938
2011	LAD	NL	7	13	2	0	0	0	(0	0)	2	0	1	1	2	0	4	1	0	0	0	0	0	.154	.313	.154	.466
2012	LAD	NL	3	3	1	0	0	0	(0	0)	1	0	0	1	1	0	2	0	0	0	0	0	0	.333	.500	.333	.833
2013	LAD	NL	56	160	37	8	0	4	(1	3)	57	12	16	9	10	5	56	0	2	1	0	0	5	.231	.275	.356	.631
2014	LAD	NL	23	71	8	3	0	1	(0	1)	14	2	5	0	3	0	18	1	2	1	0	0	0	.113	.158	.197	.355
	4 ML YEARS		89	247	48	11	0	5	(1	4)	74	14	22	11	16	5	80	2	4	2	0	0	8	.194	.247	.300	.547

Ryan Feierabend

Pitches: L Bats: L Pos: RP-6
FEAR-ahh-bend   Ht: 6'3" Wt: 225 Born: 8/22/1985 Age: 29

Year	Team	Lg	G	GS	CG	GF	IP	BFP	H	R	ER	HR	SH	SF	HB	TBB	IBB	SO	WP	Bk	W	L	Pct	Sh	Sv-Op	Hld	ERC	ERA
2014	RdRck*	AAA	25	20	0	0	125.0	546	148	82	71	18	5	6	7	29	1	81	1	1	8	6	.571	0	0- -	-	4.99	5.11
2006	Sea	AL	4	2	0	2	17.0	73	15	7	7	3	1	0	0	7	0	11	1	2	0	1	.000	0	0-0	0	3.91	3.71
2007	Sea	AL	13	9	0	0	49.1	236	73	44	44	10	0	2	4	23	2	27	3	0	1	6	.143	0	0-0	0	8.71	8.03
2008	Sea	AL	8	8	0	0	39.2	183	59	34	34	7	1	1	1	14	0	26	1	0	1	4	.200	0	0-0	0	7.83	7.71
2014	Tex	AL	6	0	0	0	7.1	36	12	5	5	0	1	1	0	2	1	4	1	0	0	0	-	0	0-0	1	6.10	6.14
4 ML YEARS			31	19	0	2	113.1	528	159	90	90	20	3	4	5	46	3	68	6	2	2	11	.154	0	0-0	1	7.44	7.15

Scott Feldman

Pitches: R Bats: L Pos: SP-29
                                  Ht: 6'7" Wt: 230 Born: 2/7/1983 Age: 32

Year	Team	Lg	G	GS	CG	GF	IP	BFP	H	R	ER	HR	SH	SF	HB	TBB	IBB	SO	WP	Bk	W	L	Pct	Sh	Sv-Op	Hld	ERC	ERA
2005	Tex	AL	8	0	0	3	9.1	37	9	1	1	0	0	0	0	2	1	4	0	0	0	1	.000	0	0-0	1	2.48	0.96
2006	Tex	AL	36	0	0	5	41.1	175	42	19	18	4	2	1	4	10	0	30	0	0	0	2	.000	0	0-1	7	3.94	3.92
2007	Tex	AL	29	0	0	10	39.0	192	44	26	25	3	0	2	3	32	5	19	2	2	1	2	.333	0	0-0	0	6.40	5.77
2008	Tex	AL	28	25	0	2	151.1	651	161	103	89	22	1	9	10	56	2	74	4	2	6	8	.429	0	0-0	0	5.03	5.29
2009	Tex	AL	34	31	0	0	189.2	791	178	87	86	18	1	3	9	65	0	113	5	2	17	8	.680	0	0-0	0	3.74	4.08
2010	Tex	AL	29	22	0	2	141.1	641	181	98	86	18	5	8	5	45	2	75	11	0	7	11	.389	0	0-0	0	5.71	5.48
2011	Tex	AL	11	2	0	5	32.0	129	25	14	14	3	0	1	2	10	0	22	2	0	2	1	.667	0	0-0	0	2.83	3.94
2012	Tex	AL	29	21	0	5	123.2	536	139	79	70	14	0	5	1	32	2	96	2	1	6	11	.353	0	0-0	0	4.27	5.09
2013	2 Tms		30	30	2	0	181.2	758	159	87	78	19	7	7	9	56	1	132	7	1	12	12	.500	1	0-0	0	3.24	3.86
2014	Hou	AL	29	29	2	0	180.1	765	185	86	75	16	2	7	11	50	5	107	6	1	8	12	.400	1	0-0	0	3.89	3.74
13	ChC	NL	15	15	0	0	91.0	376	79	42	35	10	6	4	3	25	0	67	4	0	7	6	.538	0	0-0	0	3.05	3.46
13	Bal		15	15	1	0	90.2	382	80	45	43	9	1	3	6	31	1	65	3	1	5	6	.455	1	0-0	0	3.44	4.27
Postseason			9	0	0	1	13.2	56	8	5	5	0	2	0	2	6	2	11	0	0	1	0	1.000	0	0-1	0	1.75	3.29
10 ML YEARS			263	160	4	32	1089.2	4675	1123	600	542	117	18	43	54	358	18	672	39	9	59	68	.465	2	0-1	8	4.22	4.48

Neftali Feliz

Pitches: R Bats: R Pos: RP-30
neff-TAH-lee   Ht: 6'3" Wt: 225 Born: 5/2/1988 Age: 27

Year	Team	Lg	G	GS	CG	GF	IP	BFP	H	R	ER	HR	SH	SF	HB	TBB	IBB	SO	WP	Bk	W	L	Pct	Sh	Sv-Op	Hld	ERC	ERA
2014	RdRck*	AAA	24	0	0	14	28.2	110	19	10	10	6	0	0	1	8	0	31	1	0	1	1	.500	0	7- -	-	2.71	3.14
2009	Tex	AL	20	0	0	3	31.0	117	13	6	6	2	1	0	3	8	0	39	0	0	1	0	1.000	0	2-3	9	1.14	1.74
2010	Tex	AL	70	0	0	59	69.1	269	43	21	21	5	1	0	5	18	1	71	5	0	4	3	.571	0	40-43	3	1.75	2.73
2011	Tex	AL	64	0	0	56	62.1	252	42	22	19	4	3	2	0	30	1	54	2	1	2	3	.400	0	32-38	0	2.45	2.74
2012	Tex	AL	8	7	1	0	42.2	175	28	15	15	5	0	0	2	23	0	37	0	0	3	1	.750	0	0-0	0	3.11	3.16
2013	Tex	AL	6	0	0	2	4.2	21	5	0	0	0	0	0	1	2	0	4	0	0	0	0	-	0	0-0	0	4.78	0.00
2014	Tex	AL	30	0	0	22	31.2	122	20	7	7	5	1	0	1	11	0	21	1	0	2	1	.667	0	13-14	0	2.38	1.99
Postseason			18	0	0	15	18.2	76	8	4	4	1	1	0	1	13	1	23	1	0	0	0	-	0	7-8	0	2.04	1.93
6 ML YEARS			198	7	1	142	241.2	956	151	71	68	21	6	3	11	92	2	226	8	1	12	8	.600	0	87-98	12	2.18	2.53

Jose Fernandez

Pitches: R Bats: R Pos: SP-8
                                  Ht: 6'2" Wt: 225 Born: 7/31/1992 Age: 22

Year	Team	Lg	G	GS	CG	GF	IP	BFP	H	R	ER	HR	SH	SF	HB	TBB	IBB	SO	WP	Bk	W	L	Pct	Sh	Sv-Op	Hld	ERC	ERA
2011	Mrlns	R	1	1	0	0	2.0	9	1	1	0	0	0	0	0	1	0	3	1	0	0	0	-	0	0- -	-	1.26	0.00
2011	Jmstwn	A-	1	1	0	0	2.1	14	4	5	5	0	0	0	1	3	0	4	0	0	0	1	.000	0	0- -	-	14.22	19.29
2012	Grnsbr	A	14	14	0	0	79.0	295	51	16	14	2	2	3	2	18	0	99	1	3	7	0	1.000	0	0- -	-	1.50	1.59
2012	Jupiter	A+	11	11	0	0	55.0	218	38	12	12	0	0	1	3	17	0	59	4	1	7	1	.875	0	0- -	-	1.78	1.96
2013	Mia	NL	28	28	0	0	172.2	681	111	47	42	10	3	4	5	58	5	187	3	1	12	6	.667	0	0-0	0	1.85	2.19
2014	Mia	NL	8	8	0	0	51.2	205	36	19	14	4	0	0	0	13	1	70	2	1	4	2	.667	0	0-0	0	1.80	2.44
2 ML YEARS			36	36	0	0	224.1	886	147	66	56	14	3	4	5	71	6	257	5	2	16	8	.667	0	0-0	0	1.84	2.25

Prince Fielder

Bats: L Throws: R Pos: 1B-39,DH-3
                                  Ht: 5'11" Wt: 275 Born: 5/9/1984 Age: 31

Year	Team	Lg	G	AB	H	2B	3B	HR	(Hm	Rd)	TB	R	RBI	RC	TBB	IBB	SO	HBP	SH	SF	SB	CS	GDP	Avg	OBP	Slg	OPS
2005	Mil	NL	39	59	17	4	0	2	(2	0)	27	2	10	10	2	0	17	0	0	0	0	0	0	.288	.306	.458	.764
2006	Mil	NL	157	569	154	35	1	28	(11	17)	275	82	81	84	59	5	125	12	0	8	7	2	17	.271	.347	.483	.831
2007	Mil	NL	158	573	165	35	2	50	(27	23)	354	109	119	125	90	21	121	14	0	4	2	2	9	.288	.395	.618	1.013
2008	Mil	NL	159	588	162	30	2	34	(18	16)	298	86	102	105	84	19	134	12	0	10	3	2	12	.276	.372	.507	.879
2009	Mil	NL	162	591	177	35	3	46	(23	23)	356	103	141	134	110	21	138	9	0	9	2	3	14	.299	.412	.602	1.014
2010	Mil	NL	161	578	151	25	0	32	(18	14)	272	94	83	94	114	17	138	21	0	1	1	0	12	.261	.401	.471	.871
2011	Mil	NL	162	569	170	36	1	38	(24	14)	322	95	120	120	107	32	106	10	0	6	1	1	17	.299	.415	.566	.981
2012	Det	AL	162	581	182	33	1	30	(18	12)	307	83	108	116	85	18	84	17	0	7	1	0	19	.313	.412	.528	.940
2013	Det	AL	162	624	174	36	0	25	(13	12)	285	82	106	94	75	13	117	9	0	4	1	1	20	.279	.362	.457	.819
2014	Tex	AL	42	150	37	8	0	3	(3	0)	54	19	16	18	25	11	24	2	0	1	0	0	5	.247	.360	.360	.720
Postseason			39	144	28	5	0	5	(4	1)	48	12	11	11	14	5	32	5	0	1	0	1	7	.194	.287	.333	.620
10 ML YEARS			1364	4882	1389	277	10	288	(157	131)	2550	755	886	900	751	149	1004	106	0	51	18	11	125	.285	.388	.522	.910

Josh Fields

Pitches: R Bats: R Pos: RP-54   Ht: 6'0" Wt: 190 Born: 8/19/1985 Age: 29

		HOW MUCH HE PITCHED						WHAT HE GAVE UP												THE RESULTS						
Year	Team	Lg	G	GS	CG	GF	IP	BFP	H	R	ER	HR	SH	SF	HB	TBB	IBB	SO	WP	Bk	W	L	Pct	Sh	Sv-Op	Hld	ERC	ERA
2010	WTenn	AA	21	0	0	14	28.2	121	19	12	10	0	1	2	0	18	2	28	2	0	1	1	.500	0	6--	-	2.34	3.14
2011	Jacksn	AA	20	0	0	11	26.0	115	17	11	8	0	0	0	4	19	0	26	2	0	1	2	.333	0	3--	-	3.28	2.77
2011	Tacom	AAA	9	0	0	4	13.0	63	11	10	9	2	0	2	0	13	0	13	0	1	0	0	-	0	0--	-	5.89	6.23
2011	Portlnd	AA	9	0	0	5	17.1	69	10	6	6	2	0	2	1	10	0	25	3	1	3	0	1.000	0	1--	-	2.95	3.12
2012	Portlnd	AA	32	0	0	28	44.2	182	30	14	13	4	1	2	1	16	1	59	2	0	3	3	.500	0	8--	-	2.16	2.62
2012	Pwtckt	AAA	10	0	0	5	13.2	49	8	0	0	1	0	0	0	2	0	19	0	0	1	0	1.000	0	4--	-	1.01	0.00
2013	QuadC	A	2	1	0	0	4.0	14	2	0	0	0	0	0	0	0	0	4	0	0	0	0	-	0	0--	-	0.54	0.00
2013	CpChr	AA	5	0	0	0	6.0	24	7	2	2	0	0	0	0	0	0	4	0	0	0	0	-	0	0--	-	2.86	3.00
2014	OKCity	AAA	3	0	0	2	3.0	10	0	0	0	0	0	0	0	1	0	4	0	0	0	0	-	0	1--	-	0.13	0.00
2013	Hou	AL	41	0	0	16	38.0	160	31	21	21	8	1	0	0	18	4	40	0	0	1	3	.250	0	5-6	6	3.94	4.97
2014	Hou	AL	54	0	0	16	54.2	231	50	29	27	2	0	5	2	17	3	70	0	0	4	6	.400	0	4-8	8	2.87	4.45
	2 ML YEARS		95	0	0	32	92.2	391	81	50	48	10	1	5	2	35	7	110	0	0	5	9	.357	0	9-14	14	3.30	4.66

Casey Fien

Pitches: R Bats: R Pos: RP-73   FEEN   Ht: 6'2" Wt: 205 Born: 10/21/1983 Age: 31

		HOW MUCH HE PITCHED						WHAT HE GAVE UP												THE RESULTS						
Year	Team	Lg	G	GS	CG	GF	IP	BFP	H	R	ER	HR	SH	SF	HB	TBB	IBB	SO	WP	Bk	W	L	Pct	Sh	Sv-Op	Hld	ERC	ERA
2009	Det	AL	9	0	0	5	11.1	53	13	11	10	2	0	2	0	6	0	9	0	0	0	1	.000	0	0-0	0	5.92	7.94
2010	Det	AL	2	0	0	2	2.2	12	4	3	3	2	1	0	0	0	0	0	0	0	0	0	-	0	0-0	0	9.96	10.13
2012	Min	AL	35	0	0	7	35.0	141	25	9	8	3	1	2	1	9	4	32	0	0	2	1	.667	0	0-0	6	1.90	2.06
2013	Min	AL	73	0	0	20	62.0	244	51	28	27	9	3	2	0	12	3	73	2	0	5	2	.714	0	0-2	17	2.59	3.92
2014	Min	AL	73	0	0	15	63.1	260	64	29	28	7	2	4	0	10	0	51	2	0	5	6	.455	0	1-5	26	3.25	3.98
	5 ML YEARS		192	0	0	49	174.1	710	157	80	76	23	7	10	1	37	7	165	4	0	12	10	.545	0	1-7	49	2.97	3.92

Mike Fiers

Pitches: R Bats: R Pos: SP-10; RP-4   FIRES   Ht: 6'2" Wt: 190 Born: 6/15/1985 Age: 30

		HOW MUCH HE PITCHED						WHAT HE GAVE UP												THE RESULTS						
Year	Team	Lg	G	GS	CG	GF	IP	BFP	H	R	ER	HR	SH	SF	HB	TBB	IBB	SO	WP	Bk	W	L	Pct	Sh	Sv-Op	Hld	ERC	ERA
2014	Nashv*	AAA	17	17	1	0	102.1	410	80	34	29	8	6	2	7	17	0	129	5	0	8	5	.615	1	0--	-	2.17	2.55
2011	Mil	NL	2	0	0	2	2.0	10	2	0	0	0	0	0	0	3	0	2	0	0	0	0	-	0	0-0	0	8.25	0.00
2012	Mil	NL	23	22	0	1	127.2	539	125	56	53	12	4	4	2	36	0	135	4	0	9	10	.474	0	0-0	0	3.50	3.74
2013	Mil	NL	11	3	0	4	22.1	103	28	20	18	8	1	2	0	6	0	15	1	0	1	4	.200	0	0-0	0	6.65	7.25
2014	Mil	NL	14	10	0	1	71.2	274	46	19	17	7	2	1	0	17	1	76	1	0	6	5	.545	0	0-0	0	1.68	2.13
	4 ML YEARS		50	35	0	8	223.2	926	201	95	88	27	7	7	2	62	1	228	6	0	16	19	.457	0	0-0	0	3.19	3.54

Stephen Fife

Pitches: R Bats: R Pos: SP-1   Ht: 6'3" Wt: 220 Born: 10/4/1986 Age: 28

		HOW MUCH HE PITCHED						WHAT HE GAVE UP												THE RESULTS						
Year	Team	Lg	G	GS	CG	GF	IP	BFP	H	R	ER	HR	SH	SF	HB	TBB	IBB	SO	WP	Bk	W	L	Pct	Sh	Sv-Op	Hld	ERC	ERA
2014	Albq*	AAA	11	9	0	1	43.2	207	65	35	34	2	3	2	2	15	0	27	3	0	2	2	.500	0	0--	-	6.54	7.01
2014	Ddgrs*	R	1	1	0	0	6.0	22	3	1	1	1	0	0	0	0	0	5	0	0	0	0	-	0	0--	-	0.89	1.50
2012	LAD	NL	5	5	0	0	26.2	115	25	8	8	2	3	0	2	12	0	20	4	0	0	2	.000	0	0-0	0	4.09	2.70
2013	LAD	NL	12	10	0	0	58.1	258	69	28	24	7	4	2	5	20	2	45	6	0	4	4	.500	0	0-0	0	5.46	3.70
2014	LAD	NL	1	1	0	0	6.0	27	7	4	4	3	0	0	1	1	0	5	0	0	0	0	-	0	0-0	0	7.57	6.00
	3 ML YEARS		18	16	0	0	91.0	400	101	40	36	12	7	2	8	33	2	70	10	0	4	6	.400	0	0-0	0	5.20	3.56

Alfredo Figaro

Pitches: R Bats: R Pos: RP-6   FIGG-uh-roe   Ht: 6'0" Wt: 190 Born: 7/7/1984 Age: 30

		HOW MUCH HE PITCHED						WHAT HE GAVE UP												THE RESULTS						
Year	Team	Lg	G	GS	CG	GF	IP	BFP	H	R	ER	HR	SH	SF	HB	TBB	IBB	SO	WP	Bk	W	L	Pct	Sh	Sv-Op	Hld	ERC	ERA
2014	Nashv*	AAA	42	2	0	13	70.1	304	80	31	29	5	2	1	1	22	1	55	0	1	5	2	.714	0	2--	-	4.38	3.71
2009	Det	AL	5	3	0	0	17.0	83	23	13	12	3	1	0	1	10	0	16	0	0	2	2	.500	0	0-0	0	7.94	6.35
2010	Det	AL	8	1	0	5	14.2	69	18	12	11	1	2	1	0	8	2	5	2	0	2	2	.000	0	0-0	0	5.43	6.75
2013	Mil	NL	33	5	0	8	74.0	316	77	41	34	15	3	4	1	15	2	54	4	1	3	3	.500	0	1-1	0	4.11	4.14
2014	Mil	NL	6	0	0	4	8.2	38	11	7	7	2	0	0	0	1	0	8	1	0	0	1	.000	0	0-0	0	5.26	7.27
	4 ML YEARS		52	9	0	17	114.1	506	129	73	64	21	6	5	2	34	4	83	7	1	5	8	.385	0	1-1	0	4.92	5.04

Chone Figgins

Bats: B Throws: R Pos: PH-23;3B-10;2B-5;SS-2;LF-1   SHAWN   Ht: 5'8" Wt: 180 Born: 1/22/1978 Age: 37

		BATTING																		RUNNING			AVERAGES			
Year	Team	Lg	G	AB	H	2B	3B	HR	(Hm	Rd)	TB	R	RBI	RC	TBB	IBB	SO	HBP	SH	SF	SB	CS	GDP	Avg	OBP	Slg	OPS
2014	Albq*	AAA	19	63	18	3	0	0	(-	-)	21	12	3	9	11	1	14	0	0	0	2	1	1	.286	.392	.333	.725
2002	LAA	AL	15	12	2	1	0	0	(0	0)	3	6	1	0	0	0	5	0	0	0	2	1	0	.167	.167	.250	.417
2003	LAA	AL	71	240	71	9	4	0	(0	0)	88	34	27	39	20	0	38	0	6	4	13	7	1	.296	.345	.367	.711
2004	LAA	AL	148	577	171	22	17	5	(3	2)	242	83	60	93	49	0	94	0	10	2	34	13	6	.296	.350	.419	.770
2005	LAA	AL	158	642	186	25	10	8	(2	6)	255	113	57	94	64	1	101	0	9	5	62	17	9	.290	.352	.397	.749
2006	LAA	AL	155	604	161	23	8	9	(2	7)	227	93	62	84	65	1	100	2	5	7	52	16	6	.267	.336	.376	.712
2007	LAA	AL	115	442	146	24	6	3	(1	2)	191	81	58	88	51	0	81	0	2	8	41	12	7	.330	.393	.432	.825
2008	LAA	AL	116	453	125	14	1	1	(0	1)	144	72	22	59	62	3	80	3	2	0	34	13	6	.276	.367	.318	.685
2009	LAA	AL	158	615	183	30	7	5	(2	3)	242	114	54	110	101	0	114	1	8	4	42	17	8	.298	.395	.393	.789
2010	Sea	AL	161	602	156	21	2	1	(0	1)	184	62	35	66	74	0	114	3	17	6	42	15	20	.259	.340	.306	.646
2011	Sea	AL	81	288	54	11	1	1	(0	1)	70	24	15	10	21	1	42	0	2	2	11	6	6	.188	.241	.243	.484

137

Year Team	Lg	G	AB	H	2B	3B	HR	(Hm Rd)	TB	R	RBI	RC	TBB	IBB	SO	HBP	SH	SF	SB	CS	GDP	Avg	OBP	Slg	OPS
2012 Sea	AL	66	166	30	5	2	2	(1 1)	45	18	11	11	19	0	48	0	7	2	4	1	3	.181	.262	.271	.533
2014 LAD	NL	38	60	13	3	0	0	(0 0)	16	8	1	7	14	0	15	1	1	0	4	1	0	.217	.373	.267	.640
Postseason		35	122	21	5	2	0	(0 0)	30	13	6	6	6	0	35	2	5	0	4	1	1	.172	.223	.246	.469
12 ML YEARS		1282	4701	1298	188	58	35	(11 24)	1707	708	403	661	540	6	832	10	69	40	341	119	74	.276	.349	.363	.712

Cole Figueroa

Bats: L Throws: R Pos: 2B-16;PH-7;PR-4;DH-1   figg-uh-ROE-ah   Ht: 5'10" Wt: 175 Born: 6/30/1987 Age: 28

Year Team	Lg	G	AB	H	2B	3B	HR	(Hm Rd)	TB	R	RBI	RC	TBB	IBB	SO	HBP	SH	SF	SB	CS	GDP	Avg	OBP	Slg	OPS
2010 Lk Els	A+	124	482	146	25	3	4	(- -)	189	88	66	87	81	0	54	6	7	2	26	9	12	.303	.408	.392	.800
2011 Mont	AA	114	410	116	20	6	5	(- -)	163	71	51	67	55	0	41	8	11	4	9	5	6	.283	.375	.398	.773
2012 Mont	AA	25	86	27	6	1	3	(- -)	44	17	12	18	17	2	9	0	0	2	1	2	1	.314	.419	.512	.931
2012 Drhm	AAA	88	311	89	17	4	2	(- -)	120	32	42	43	26	1	22	3	4	3	3	2	6	.286	.344	.386	.730
2013 Drhm	AAA	129	461	132	20	4	3	(- -)	169	65	62	69	54	0	30	4	6	8	10	2	10	.286	.361	.367	.727
2014 Drhm	AAA	71	262	74	13	3	3	(- -)	102	33	33	42	39	0	29	1	5	5	4	1	5	.282	.371	.389	.761
2014 TB	AL	23	43	10	2	1	0	(0 0)	14	6	6	4	4	0	4	0	0	2	0	0	0	.233	.286	.326	.611

Pedro Figueroa

Pitches: L Bats: L Pos: RP-10   figg-uh-ROE-ah   Ht: 6'0" Wt: 215 Born: 11/23/1985 Age: 29

Year Team	Lg	G	GS	CG	GF	IP	BFP	H	R	ER	HR	SH	SF	HB	TBB	IBB	SO	WP	Bk	W	L	Pct	Sh	Sv-Op	Hld	ERC	ERA
2012 Oak	AL	19	0	0	6	21.2	89	16	9	8	2	0	0	0	15	1	14	2	0	0	0	-	0	0-0	0	3.87	3.32
2013 Oak	AL	5	0	0	1	3.0	18	6	4	4	2	0	0	0	3	0	3	0	0	0	0	-	0	0-0	0	19.34	12.00
2014 Tex	AL	10	0	0	1	9.0	42	10	7	4	1	0	1	2	3	0	3	0	0	2	1	.667	0	0-0	0	5.30	4.00
3 ML YEARS		34	0	0	8	33.2	149	32	20	16	5	0	1	2	21	1	20	2	0	2	1	.667	0	0-0	0	5.39	4.28

Brandon Finnegan

Pitches: L Bats: L Pos: RP-7   Ht: 5'11" Wt: 185 Born: 4/14/1993 Age: 22

Year Team	Lg	G	GS	CG	GF	IP	BFP	H	R	ER	HR	SH	SF	HB	TBB	IBB	SO	WP	Bk	W	L	Pct	Sh	Sv-Op	Hld	ERC	ERA
2014 Wilmg	A+	5	5	0	0	15.0	49	5	1	1	1	0	0	0	2	0	13	1	0	0	1	.000	0	0--	-	0.59	0.60
2014 NWArk	AA	8	0	0	3	12.0	56	15	9	3	2	0	0	1	2	0	13	1	0	0	3	.000	0	0--	-	5.06	2.25
2014 KC	AL	7	0	0	1	7.0	28	6	1	1	0	0	0	0	1	0	10	0	0	1	0	1.000	0	0-0	1	1.77	1.29

Doug Fister

Pitches: R Bats: L Pos: SP-25   Ht: 6'8" Wt: 210 Born: 2/4/1984 Age: 31

Year Team	Lg	G	GS	CG	GF	IP	BFP	H	R	ER	HR	SH	SF	HB	TBB	IBB	SO	WP	Bk	W	L	Pct	Sh	Sv-Op	Hld	ERC	ERA
2014 Ptomc*	A+	1	1	0	0	4.0	17	6	3	0	0	0	0	0	0	0	3	0	0	0	0	-	0	0--	-	4.76	0.00
2014 Hrsbrg*	AA	1	1	0	0	3.2	16	2	2	2	0	0	0	0	3	0	5	0	0	0	0	-	0	0--	-	2.44	4.91
2009 Sea	AL	11	10	0	1	61.0	256	63	29	28	11	0	0	2	15	0	36	1	0	3	4	.429	0	0-0	0	4.36	4.13
2010 Sea	AL	28	28	0	0	171.0	720	187	85	78	13	2	4	6	32	2	93	8	3	6	14	.300	0	0-0	0	3.73	4.11
2011 2 Tms	AL	32	31	3	0	216.1	875	193	76	68	11	4	9	12	37	2	146	3	1	11	13	.458	0	0-0	0	2.53	2.83
2012 Det	AL	26	26	2	0	161.2	673	156	73	62	15	3	0	7	37	1	137	1	0	10	10	.500	1	0-0	0	3.33	3.45
2013 Det	AL	33	32	1	0	208.2	881	229	91	85	14	2	5	16	44	2	159	7	0	14	9	.609	0	0-0	0	4.00	3.67
2014 Was	NL	25	25	1	0	164.0	662	153	52	44	18	6	2	7	24	0	98	5	0	16	6	.727	1	0-0	0	2.98	2.41
11 Sea	AL	21	21	3	0	146.0	602	139	57	54	7	3	7	9	32	2	89	3	1	3	12	.200	0	0-0	0	3.02	3.33
11 Det	AL	11	10	0	0	70.1	273	54	19	14	4	1	2	3	5	0	57	0	0	8	1	.889	0	0-0	0	1.63	1.79
Postseason		8	7	0	0	48.1	205	50	16	16	2	2	0	3	13	0	37	1	1	3	2	.600	0	0-0	0	3.62	2.98
6 ML YEARS		155	152	7	1	982.2	4067	981	406	365	82	17	20	50	189	7	669	25	4	60	56	.517	2	0-0	0	3.36	3.34

Ryan Flaherty

Bats: L Throws: R Pos: 3B-43;2B-30;SS-29;1B-3;PH-3;LF-1;RF-1;PR-1   Ht: 6'3" Wt: 210 Born: 7/27/1986 Age: 28

Year Team	Lg	G	AB	H	2B	3B	HR	(Hm Rd)	TB	R	RBI	RC	TBB	IBB	SO	HBP	SH	SF	SB	CS	GDP	Avg	OBP	Slg	OPS
2012 Bal	AL	77	153	33	2	1	6	(3 3)	55	15	19	15	6	0	43	3	3	1	1	0	3	.216	.258	.359	.617
2013 Bal	AL	85	246	55	11	0	10	(6 4)	96	28	27	27	19	3	62	5	1	0	2	0	2	.224	.293	.390	.683
2014 Bal	AL	102	281	62	15	1	7	(7 0)	100	33	32	34	22	2	68	5	3	1	1	0	3	.221	.288	.356	.644
Postseason		4	11	3	0	0	1	(0 1)	6	1	1	0	0	0	2	0	0	0	0	0	0	.273	.273	.545	.818
3 ML YEARS		264	680	150	28	2	23	(16 7)	251	76	78	76	47	5	173	13	7	2	4	0	8	.221	.283	.369	.652

Yohan Flande

Pitches: L Bats: L Pos: SP-10; RP-6   YO-hahn FLAHN-day   Ht: 6'2" Wt: 180 Born: 1/27/1986 Age: 29

Year Team	Lg	G	GS	CG	GF	IP	BFP	H	R	ER	HR	SH	SF	HB	TBB	IBB	SO	WP	Bk	W	L	Pct	Sh	Sv-Op	Hld	ERC	ERA
2010 Rdng	AA	27	27	1	0	158.1	690	178	84	77	10	8	5	10	44	1	84	7	4	10	8	.556	0	0--	-	4.27	4.38
2011 Gwnntt	AAA	33	19	0	3	137.0	596	155	70	61	9	5	9	4	38	2	104	4	1	8	8	.500	0	1--	-	4.16	4.01
2012 Gwnntt	AAA	29	27	0	0	147.2	638	153	75	69	11	6	5	5	55	1	106	12	1	6	11	.353	0	0--	-	4.14	4.21
2013 Gwnntt	AAA	31	19	1	3	131.1	575	142	70	61	9	5	3	4	46	1	92	2	1	9	7	.563	0	1--	-	4.20	4.18
2013 Missi	AA	1	1	0	0	4.2	24	9	6	5	0	1	0	0	2	0	3	1	0	0	1	.000	0	0--	-	9.32	9.64
2014 ColSpr	AAA	18	16	0	0	88.1	396	112	58	55	9	1	4	2	33	1	67	3	1	3	11	.214	0	0--	-	5.72	5.60
2014 Col	NL	16	10	0	2	59.0	241	55	34	34	5	5	4	2	16	2	34	0	0	0	6	.000	0	0-0	1	3.26	5.19

Wilmer Flores

Bats: R **Throws:** R **Pos:** SS-51;2B-19;PH-8;3B-1   **Ht:** 6'3" **Wt:** 205 **Born:** 8/6/1991 **Age:** 23

									BATTING												RUNNING			AVERAGES			
Year	Team	Lg	G	AB	H	2B	3B	HR	(Hm	Rd)	TB	R	RBI	RC	TBB	IBB	SO	HBP	SH	SF	SB	CS	GDP	Avg	OBP	Slg	OPS
2010	Savann	A	66	277	77	18	2	7	(-	-)	120	30	44	42	23	6	37	5	0	2	2	1	8	.278	.342	.433	.775
2010	StLuci	A+	67	277	83	18	1	4	(-	-)	115	32	40	36	9	0	40	2	0	2	2	4	10	.300	.324	.415	.739
2011	StLuci	A+	133	516	139	26	2	9	(-	-)	196	52	81	63	27	3	68	6	2	8	2	2	11	.269	.309	.380	.689
2012	StLuci	A+	64	242	70	12	0	10	(-	-)	112	31	42	39	18	2	30	3	1	8	3	2	6	.289	.336	.463	.799
2012	Bnghtn	AA	66	251	78	18	2	8	(-	-)	124	37	33	45	20	0	30	1	1	2	0	0	9	.311	.361	.494	.855
2013	LsVgs	AAA	107	424	136	36	4	15	(-	-)	225	69	86	79	25	2	63	3	3	8	1	3	13	.321	.357	.531	.887
2014	LsVgs	AAA	55	220	71	11	2	13	(-	-)	125	43	57	44	16	1	39	1	1	3	0	2	5	.323	.367	.568	.935
2013	NYM	NL	27	95	20	5	0	1	(0	1)	28	8	13	7	5	0	23	0	0	1	0	0	1	.211	.248	.295	.542
2014	NYM	NL	78	259	65	13	1	6	(4	2)	98	28	29	25	12	2	31	1	1	1	1	0	6	.251	.286	.378	.664
2 ML YEARS			105	354	85	18	1	7	(4	3)	126	36	42	32	17	2	54	1	1	2	1	0	7	.240	.275	.356	.631

Pedro Florimon

Bats: B **Throws:** R **Pos:** SS-31;PR-4;DH-2   FLOOR-ih-moan   **Ht:** 6'2" **Wt:** 180 **Born:** 12/10/1986 **Age:** 28

									BATTING												RUNNING			AVERAGES			
Year	Team	Lg	G	AB	H	2B	3B	HR	(Hm	Rd)	TB	R	RBI	RC	TBB	IBB	SO	HBP	SH	SF	SB	CS	GDP	Avg	OBP	Slg	OPS
2014	Roch*	AAA	85	280	72	17	4	4	(-	-)	109	38	29	39	30	1	82	1	0	3	12	2	5	.257	.328	.389	.717
2011	Bal	AL	4	8	1	1	0	0	(0	0)	2	1	2	1	1	0	6	0	1	0	0	0	0	.125	.222	.250	.472
2012	Min	AL	43	137	30	5	2	1	(1	0)	42	16	10	8	10	0	30	0	3	0	3	1	3	.219	.272	.307	.579
2013	Min	AL	134	403	89	17	0	9	(3	6)	133	44	44	38	33	1	115	2	5	3	15	6	7	.221	.281	.330	.611
2014	Min	AL	33	76	7	1	1	0	(0	0)	10	7	1	0	8	0	22	0	2	0	6	0	2	.092	.179	.132	.310
4 ML YEARS			214	624	127	24	3	10	(4	6)	187	68	57	47	52	1	173	2	11	3	24	7	12	.204	.266	.300	.565

Tyler Flowers

Bats: R **Throws:** R **Pos:** C-124;PH-2;PR-1   **Ht:** 6'4" **Wt:** 245 **Born:** 1/24/1986 **Age:** 29

									BATTING												RUNNING			AVERAGES			
Year	Team	Lg	G	AB	H	2B	3B	HR	(Hm	Rd)	TB	R	RBI	RC	TBB	IBB	SO	HBP	SH	SF	SB	CS	GDP	Avg	OBP	Slg	OPS
2009	CWS	AL	10	16	3	1	0	0	(0	0)	4	3	0	2	3	0	8	1	0	0	0	0	1	.188	.350	.250	.600
2010	CWS	AL	8	11	1	0	0	0	(0	0)	1	2	0	1	4	0	5	0	0	0	0	0	0	.091	.333	.091	.424
2011	CWS	AL	38	110	23	5	1	5	(3	2)	45	13	16	13	14	0	38	3	0	2	0	1	2	.209	.310	.409	.719
2012	CWS	AL	52	136	29	6	0	7	(5	2)	56	19	13	13	12	0	56	4	1	0	2	1	2	.213	.296	.412	.708
2013	CWS	AL	84	256	50	11	0	10	(7	3)	91	24	24	14	14	1	94	4	0	1	0	1	9	.195	.247	.355	.603
2014	CWS	AL	127	407	98	16	1	15	(7	8)	161	42	50	43	25	0	159	8	1	1	0	1	10	.241	.297	.396	.693
6 ML YEARS			319	936	204	39	2	37	(22	15)	358	103	103	86	72	1	360	20	2	4	2	4	24	.218	.287	.382	.669

Gavin Floyd

Pitches: R **Bats:** R **Pos:** SP-9   **Ht:** 6'4" **Wt:** 235 **Born:** 1/27/1983 **Age:** 32

				HOW MUCH HE PITCHED						WHAT HE GAVE UP											THE RESULTS					
Year	Team	Lg	G	GS	CG	GF	IP	BFP	H	R	ER	HR	SH	SF	HB	TBB	IBB	SO	WP	Bk	W	L	Pct	Sh	Sv-Op	Hld	ERC	ERA
2014	Gwnntt*	AAA	5	5	0	0	19.1	82	17	8	7	3	1	0	1	9	0	11	1	1	1	1	.500	0	0- -	-	4.33	3.26
2014	Missi*	AA	1	1	0	0	4.2	20	4	5	4	0	0	0	1	1	0	6	1	0	0	1	.000	0	0- -	-	2.67	7.71
2004	Phi	NL	6	4	0	0	28.1	126	25	11	11	1	1	0	5	16	0	24	1	1	2	0	1.000	0	0-0	-	4.33	3.49
2005	Phi	NL	7	4	0	0	26.0	127	30	31	29	5	1	1	3	16	2	17	2	0	1	2	.333	0	0-0	-	6.82	10.04
2006	Phi	NL	11	11	1	0	54.1	264	70	48	44	14	2	5	3	32	3	34	2	0	4	3	.571	1	0-0	-	8.02	7.29
2007	CWS	AL	16	10	0	4	70.0	314	85	45	41	17	3	2	6	19	0	49	1	0	1	5	.167	0	0-0	-	6.22	5.27
2008	CWS	AL	33	33	1	0	206.1	878	190	107	88	30	7	5	9	70	6	145	9	0	17	8	.680	0	0-0	-	3.80	3.84
2009	CWS	AL	30	30	1	0	193.0	797	178	99	87	21	2	3	2	59	4	163	8	0	11	11	.500	0	0-0	-	3.38	4.06
2010	CWS	AL	31	31	1	0	187.1	798	199	92	85	14	3	4	6	58	4	151	9	1	10	13	.435	0	0-0	-	4.03	4.06
2011	CWS	AL	31	30	1	1	193.2	798	180	97	94	22	4	8	11	45	2	151	12	1	12	13	.480	0	0-0	-	3.36	4.37
2012	CWS	AL	29	29	0	0	168.0	724	166	84	80	22	3	3	14	63	2	144	8	0	12	11	.522	0	0-0	-	4.50	4.29
2013	CWS	AL	5	5	0	0	24.1	110	27	15	14	4	2	2	0	12	1	25	1	0	0	4	.000	0	0-0	-	5.48	5.18
2014	Atl	NL	9	9	0	0	54.1	229	55	23	16	6	4	2	3	13	0	45	6	0	2	2	.500	0	0-0	-	3.81	2.65
Postseason			1	1	0	0	3.0	16	5	4	4	2	0	0	0	2	0	4	0	0	0	1	.000	0	0-0	-	14.65	12.00
11 ML YEARS			208	196	5	5	1205.2	5165	1205	646	589	156	32	35	62	403	24	948	59	3	72	72	.500	1	0-0	-	4.20	4.40

Brian Flynn

Pitches: L **Bats:** L **Pos:** SP-1; RP-1   **Ht:** 6'7" **Wt:** 250 **Born:** 4/19/1990 **Age:** 25

				HOW MUCH HE PITCHED						WHAT HE GAVE UP											THE RESULTS					
Year	Team	Lg	G	GS	CG	GF	IP	BFP	H	R	ER	HR	SH	SF	HB	TBB	IBB	SO	WP	Bk	W	L	Pct	Sh	Sv-Op	Hld	ERC	ERA
2011	WMich	A	13	13	0	0	67.2	280	58	28	26	3	2	4	4	23	0	57	2	0	7	2	.778	0	0- -	-	2.96	3.46
2012	Lkland	A+	18	18	0	0	102.0	441	113	47	42	5	0	3	3	32	0	84	4	0	8	4	.667	0	0- -	-	4.12	3.71
2012	Erie	AA	1	1	0	0	5.0	24	8	5	5	1	0	1	0	2	0	3	0	0	0	1	.000	0	0- -	-	8.81	9.00
2012	Jaxnvl	AA	8	8	0	0	45.0	195	48	22	19	3	2	4	1	13	0	32	1	0	3	0	1.000	0	0- -	-	4.14	3.80
2013	Jaxnvl	AA	4	4	0	0	23.0	87	18	4	4	2	2	0	1	3	0	26	0	0	1	1	.500	0	0- -	-	2.13	1.57
2013	NewOr	AAA	23	23	0	0	138.0	570	127	52	43	7	8	1	4	40	1	122	7	2	6	11	.353	0	0- -	-	3.02	2.80
2014	NewOr	AAA	25	25	1	0	139.2	625	169	83	63	13	4	5	6	50	2	104	10	1	8	10	.444	0	0- -	-	5.26	4.06
2013	Mia	NL	4	4	0	0	18.0	88	27	17	17	4	2	0	0	13	0	15	3	0	0	2	.000	0	0-0	-	10.71	8.50
2014	Mia	NL	2	1	0	0	7.0	35	12	7	7	0	2	0	0	3	0	6	1	0	0	1	.000	0	0-0	-	7.75	9.00
2 ML YEARS			6	5	0	0	25.0	123	39	24	24	4	2	0	0	16	0	21	4	0	0	3	.000	0	0-0	-	9.47	8.64

Mike Foltynewicz

Pitches: R Bats: R Pos: RP-16   fohl-tuh-NEH-vich   Ht: 6'4" Wt: 220 Born: 10/7/1991 Age: 23

			HOW MUCH HE PITCHED						WHAT HE GAVE UP											THE RESULTS						
Year	Team	Lg	G	GS	CG	GF	IP	BFP	H	R	ER	HR	SH	SF	HB	TBB	IBB	SO	WP	Bk	W	L	Pct	Sh	Sv-Op	Hld	ERC	ERA
2010	Grnvlle	R+	12	12	0	0	44.2	194	46	24	20	3	3	1	6	15	1	39	8	0	0	3	.000	0	0- -	-	4.30	4.03
2011	Lxngtn	A	26	26	0	0	134.0	581	149	84	74	10	3	4	7	51	0	88	8	1	5	11	.313	0	0- -	-	4.78	4.97
2012	Lxngtn	A	27	27	0	0	152.0	653	145	65	53	11	4	2	5	62	0	125	6	0	14	4	.778	0	0- -	-	3.79	3.14
2013	Lancst	A+	7	5	0	1	26.0	122	31	16	11	4	0	1	0	14	0	29	5	1	1	0	1.000	0	0- -	-	6.11	3.81
2013	CpChr	AA	23	16	0	4	103.1	424	75	39	33	8	3	2	5	52	0	95	9	2	5	3	.625	0	3- -	-	3.11	2.87
2014	OKCity	AAA	21	18	0	0	102.2	448	98	63	58	10	1	7	10	52	2	102	9	4	7	7	.500	0	0- -	-	4.68	5.08
2014	Hou	AL	16	0	0	9	18.2	84	23	11	11	3	0	0	0	7	0	14	3	0	0	1	.000	0	0-0	1	5.80	5.30

Eric Fornataro

Pitches: R Bats: R Pos: RP-8   forn-uh-TEAR-oh   Ht: 6'1" Wt: 225 Born: 1/2/1988 Age: 27

			HOW MUCH HE PITCHED						WHAT HE GAVE UP											THE RESULTS						
Year	Team	Lg	G	GS	CG	GF	IP	BFP	H	R	ER	HR	SH	SF	HB	TBB	IBB	SO	WP	Bk	W	L	Pct	Sh	Sv-Op	Hld	ERC	ERA
2010	QuadC	A	28	28	0	0	140.1	630	161	104	82	13	4	6	5	59	0	100	7	1	7	15	.318	0	0- -	-	5.11	5.26
2011	PlmBh	A+	24	24	1	0	144.2	635	150	68	59	7	3	5	12	50	0	116	16	0	7	13	.350	0	0- -	-	4.00	3.67
2012	Sprgfld	AA	57	0	0	17	67.2	271	55	21	18	1	5	2	4	17	1	41	5	0	3	3	.500	0	5- -	-	2.24	2.39
2013	Memp	AAA	37	4	0	13	55.1	256	65	42	37	5	5	3	8	23	2	39	7	1	1	4	.200	0	1- -	-	5.60	6.02
2013	Cards	R	3	0	0	0	3.0	13	3	2	1	0	0	0	0	1	0	3	0	0	0	0	-	0	0- -	-	3.05	3.00
2014	Memp	AAA	44	0	0	28	56.0	228	46	23	16	3	1	2	1	20	1	35	4	0	4	5	.444	0	15- -	-	2.74	2.57
2014	StL	NL	8	0	0	6	9.2	42	11	6	5	0	0	1	1	1	0	3	0	0	0	0	-	0	0-0	0	3.30	4.66

Logan Forsythe

Bats: R Throws: R Pos: 2B-74;PH-26;DH-20;3B-6;PR-4;LF-3;SS-2;1B-1   Ht: 6'1" Wt: 195 Born: 1/14/1987 Age: 28

			BATTING																			RUNNING			AVERAGES			
Year	Team	Lg	G	AB	H	2B	3B	HR	(Hm	Rd)	TB	R	RBI	RC	TBB	IBB	SO	HBP	SH	SF		SB	CS	GDP	Avg	OBP	Slg	OPS
2011	SD	NL	62	150	32	9	1	0	(0	0)	43	12	12	15	12	3	33	3	2	2		3	1	3	.213	.281	.287	.568
2012	SD	NL	91	315	86	13	3	6	(5	1)	123	45	26	37	28	0	57	6	0	1		8	2	6	.273	.343	.390	.733
2013	SD	NL	75	220	47	6	1	6	(2	4)	73	22	19	16	19	2	54	2	1	1		6	1	6	.214	.281	.332	.613
2014	TB	AL	110	301	67	12	1	6	(2	4)	99	32	26	26	25	0	71	4	2	4		2	0	9	.223	.287	.329	.616
	4 ML YEARS		338	986	232	40	6	18	(9	9)	338	111	83	94	84	5	215	15	5	8		19	4	23	.235	.303	.343	.646

Dexter Fowler

Bats: B Throws: R Pos: CF-111;DH-4;PH-2   Ht: 6'4" Wt: 190 Born: 3/22/1986 Age: 29

			BATTING																			RUNNING			AVERAGES			
Year	Team	Lg	G	AB	H	2B	3B	HR	(Hm	Rd)	TB	R	RBI	RC	TBB	IBB	SO	HBP	SH	SF		SB	CS	GDP	Avg	OBP	Slg	OPS
2014	OKCity*	AAA	4	10	3	0	0	0	(-	-)	3	1	1	1	2	0	0	0	0	0		0	0	1	.300	.417	.300	.717
2008	Col	NL	13	26	4	0	0	0	(0	0)	4	3	0	0	0	0	5	1	0	0		0	1	0	.154	.185	.154	.339
2009	Col	NL	135	433	115	29	10	4	(2	2)	176	73	34	68	67	1	116	1	14	3		27	10	4	.266	.363	.406	.770
2010	Col	NL	132	439	114	20	14	6	(5	1)	180	73	36	68	57	0	104	2	7	0		13	8	5	.260	.347	.410	.757
2011	Col	NL	125	481	128	35	15	5	(3	2)	208	84	45	79	68	3	130	6	7	1		12	9	5	.266	.363	.432	.796
2012	Col	NL	143	454	136	18	11	13	(10	3)	215	72	53	81	68	1	128	0	6	2		12	5	5	.300	.389	.474	.863
2013	Col	NL	119	415	109	18	3	12	(7	5)	169	71	42	62	65	1	105	6	4	2		19	9	5	.263	.369	.407	.776
2014	Hou	AL	116	434	120	21	4	8	(5	3)	173	61	35	65	66	2	108	3	1	1		11	4	5	.276	.375	.399	.774
	Postseason		4	14	3	0	0	0	(0	0)	3	1	2	1	1	0	3	0	1	2		0	0	1	.214	.235	.214	.450
	7 ML YEARS		783	2682	726	141	57	48	(32	16)	1125	437	245	423	391	8	696	19	39	9		94	46	31	.271	.366	.419	.786

Jeff Francis

Pitches: L Bats: L Pos: RP-11; SP-1   Ht: 6'5" Wt: 220 Born: 1/8/1981 Age: 34

			HOW MUCH HE PITCHED						WHAT HE GAVE UP											THE RESULTS						
Year	Team	Lg	G	GS	CG	GF	IP	BFP	H	R	ER	HR	SH	SF	HB	TBB	IBB	SO	WP	Bk	W	L	Pct	Sh	Sv-Op	Hld	ERC	ERA
2014	Lsvlle*	AAA	8	8	0	0	48.2	206	52	25	18	3	2	0	1	12	0	45	3	0	4	3	.571	0	0- -	-	3.68	3.33
2004	Col	NL	7	7	0	0	36.2	164	42	22	21	8	2	1	1	13	1	32	2	0	3	2	.600	0	0-0	0	5.62	5.15
2005	Col	NL	33	33	0	0	183.2	828	228	119	116	26	6	10	8	70	5	128	2	0	14	12	.538	0	0-0	0	5.94	5.68
2006	Col	NL	32	32	1	0	199.0	843	187	101	92	18	7	7	16	69	15	117	0	0	13	11	.542	1	0-0	0	3.63	4.16
2007	Col	NL	34	34	1	0	215.1	922	234	103	101	25	7	4	7	63	7	165	1	1	17	9	.654	1	0-0	0	4.37	4.22
2008	Col	NL	24	24	0	0	143.2	636	164	84	80	21	6	4	3	49	4	94	0	0	4	10	.286	0	0-0	0	5.00	5.01
2010	Col	NL	20	19	0	0	104.1	441	119	61	58	11	6	4	2	23	3	67	1	0	4	6	.400	0	0-0	0	4.29	5.00
2011	KC	AL	31	31	1	0	183.0	803	224	102	98	19	7	8	5	39	5	91	5	1	6	16	.273	0	0-0	0	4.67	4.82
2012	Col	NL	24	24	0	0	113.0	502	145	71	70	15	10	3	8	22	5	76	2	0	6	7	.462	0	0-0	0	5.34	5.58
2013	Col	NL	23	12	0	4	70.1	324	89	54	49	12	4	4	1	24	2	63	5	0	3	5	.375	0	0-0	0	5.82	6.27
2014	3 Tms		12	1	0	9	20.0	82	18	13	13	3	1	1	1	3	1	15	1	0	1	2	.333	0	1-1	0	2.96	5.85
14	Cin	NL	1	1	0	0	5.0	20	5	3	3	1	0	0	0	0	0	4	0	0	0	1	.000	0	0-0	0	3.05	5.40
14	Oak	AL	9	0	0	7	13.1	55	11	9	9	1	1	1	1	3	1	10	1	0	0	1	.000	0	1-1	0	2.46	6.08
14	NYY	AL	2	0	0	2	1.2	7	2	1	1	1	0	0	0	0	1	1	0	0	1	0	1.000	0	0-0	0	6.66	5.40
	Postseason		3	3	0	0	16.2	75	21	9	9	3	0	0	0	6	2	15	0	0	2	1	.667	0	0-0	0	6.57	4.86
	10 ML YEARS		240	217	3	13	1269.0	5545	1450	730	698	158	56	46	49	375	48	848	19	2	71	80	.470	2	1-1	0	4.75	4.95

Frank Francisco

Pitches: R **Bats:** R **Pos:** RP-4   **Ht:** 6'2" **Wt:** 250 **Born:** 9/11/1979 **Age:** 35

		HOW MUCH HE PITCHED						WHAT HE GAVE UP											THE RESULTS						
Year	Team	Lg	G	GS	CG	GF	IP	BFP	H	R	ER	HR	SH	SF	HB	TBB	IBB	SO	WP	Bk	W	L	Pct	Sh	Sv-Op	Hld	ERC	ERA
2014	Charltt*	AAA	6	0	0	2	8.0	27	4	1	0	0	0	0	0	1	0	12	1	0	0	0	-	0	1- -	-	0.79	0.00
2004	Tex	AL	45	0	0	7	51.1	216	36	19	19	4	2	1	3	28	2	60	4	1	5	1	.833	0	0-3	10	3.04	3.33
2006	Tex	AL	8	0	0	2	7.1	32	8	4	4	2	0	0	0	2	0	6	1	0	0	1	.000	0	0-0	2	5.17	4.91
2007	Tex	AL	59	0	0	16	59.1	268	57	33	30	3	6	1	2	38	4	49	8	0	1	1	.500	0	0-0	21	4.44	4.55
2008	Tex	AL	58	0	0	18	63.1	264	47	24	22	7	0	3	0	26	2	83	5	0	3	5	.375	0	5-11	12	2.70	3.13
2009	Tex	AL	51	0	0	42	49.1	203	40	21	21	6	0	0	1	15	1	57	3	0	2	3	.400	0	25-29	4	2.85	3.83
2010	Tex	AL	56	0	0	20	52.2	221	49	23	22	5	3	1	1	18	2	60	2	1	6	4	.600	0	2-6	15	3.46	3.76
2011	Tor	AL	54	0	0	38	50.2	218	49	21	20	7	1	0	0	18	2	53	2	0	1	4	.200	0	17-21	2	3.85	3.55
2012	NYM	NL	48	0	0	38	42.1	197	47	27	26	5	0	1	0	21	1	47	2	1	1	3	.250	0	23-26	1	5.01	5.53
2013	NYM	NL	8	0	0	3	6.1	26	4	3	3	0	0	0	1	3	0	6	0	0	1	0	1.000	0	1-1	0	2.37	4.26
2014	CWS	AL	4	0	0	1	3.2	22	7	6	5	2	0	0	0	3	0	5	1	0	0	0	-	0	0-0	0	15.49	12.27
	10 ML YEARS		391	0	0	185	386.1	1667	344	181	172	41	12	7	8	172	14	426	28	3	20	22	.476	0	73-97	67	3.67	4.01

Juan Francisco

Bats: L **Throws:** R **Pos:** 3B-74;1B-20;PH-16;DH-12;PR-1   **Ht:** 6'2" **Wt:** 245 **Born:** 6/24/1987 **Age:** 28

								BATTING												RUNNING			AVERAGES			
Year	Team	Lg	G	AB	H	2B	3B	HR	(Hm	Rd)	TB	R	RBI	RC	TBB	IBB	SO	HBP	SH	SF	SB	CS	GDP	Avg	OBP	Slg	OPS
2014	Buffalo*	AAA	12	44	15	2	1	2	(-	-)	25	9	11	10	6	1	9	0	0	0	0	0	0	.341	.420	.568	.988
2009	Cin	NL	14	21	9	1	0	1	(1	0)	13	4	7	6	3	0	7	1	0	0	0	0	0	.429	.520	.619	1.139
2010	Cin	NL	36	55	15	3	0	1	(1	0)	21	3	7	3	4	0	20	0	0	0	0	1	2	.273	.322	.382	.704
2011	Cin	NL	31	93	24	7	1	3	(1	2)	42	10	15	12	4	1	24	0	0	0	1	0	1	.258	.289	.452	.740
2012	Atl	NL	93	192	45	11	0	9	(4	5)	83	17	32	20	11	2	70	1	0	1	1	1	5	.234	.278	.432	.710
2013	2 Tms	NL	124	348	79	12	1	18	(8	10)	147	36	48	39	32	3	138	3	0	2	0	2	3	.227	.296	.422	.719
2014	Tor	AL	106	287	63	16	2	16	(9	7)	131	40	43	32	27	0	116	3	0	3	0	2	6	.220	.291	.456	.747
	13 Atl	NL	35	108	26	2	0	5	(2	3)	43	10	16	14	7	0	43	0	0	0	0	1	0	.241	.287	.398	.685
	13 Mil	NL	89	240	53	10	1	13	(6	7)	104	26	32	25	25	3	95	3	0	2	0	1	3	.221	.300	.433	.733
	Postseason		1	1	0	0	0	0	(0	0)	0	0	0	0	0	0	0	0	0	0	0	0	0	.000	.000	.000	.000
	6 ML YEARS		404	996	235	50	4	48	(24	24)	437	110	152	112	81	6	375	8	0	6	2	6	17	.236	.297	.439	.736

Maikel Franco

Bats: R **Throws:** R **Pos:** 3B-12;1B-5   MY-kell FRONK-oh   **Ht:** 6'1" **Wt:** 180 **Born:** 8/26/1992 **Age:** 22

								BATTING												RUNNING			AVERAGES			
Year	Team	Lg	G	AB	H	2B	3B	HR	(Hm	Rd)	TB	R	RBI	RC	TBB	IBB	SO	HBP	SH	SF	SB	CS	GDP	Avg	OBP	Slg	OPS
2010	Phillies	R	51	194	43	11	2	2	(-	-)	64	23	29	19	16	0	46	4	1	2	0	0	2	.222	.292	.330	.622
2011	Wmspt	A-	54	202	58	17	1	2	(-	-)	83	19	38	32	25	2	30	1	0	1	0	0	0	.287	.367	.411	.778
2011	Lakwd	A	17	65	8	2	0	1	(-	-)	13	6	6	0	1	0	15	1	0	0	0	0	4	.123	.149	.200	.349
2012	Lakwd	A	132	503	141	32	3	14	(-	-)	221	70	84	77	38	0	80	7	0	6	3	1	24	.280	.336	.439	.775
2013	Clrwtr	A+	65	264	79	23	1	16	(-	-)	152	42	52	52	20	1	39	2	0	3	0	0	14	.299	.349	.576	.925
2013	Rdng	AA	69	277	94	13	2	15	(-	-)	156	47	51	54	10	1	31	2	0	3	1	2	5	.339	.363	.563	.926
2014	LV	AAA	133	521	134	33	4	16	(-	-)	223	64	78	68	30	0	81	2	0	3	3	1	16	.257	.299	.428	.727
2014	Phi	NL	16	56	10	2	0	0	(0	0)	12	5	5	1	1	0	13	0	0	1	0	0	1	.179	.190	.214	.404

Jeff Francoeur

Bats: R **Throws:** R **Pos:** RF-7;PH-4   frann-COOR   **Ht:** 6'4" **Wt:** 220 **Born:** 1/8/1984 **Age:** 31

								BATTING												RUNNING			AVERAGES			
Year	Team	Lg	G	AB	H	2B	3B	HR	(Hm	Rd)	TB	R	RBI	RC	TBB	IBB	SO	HBP	SH	SF	SB	CS	GDP	Avg	OBP	Slg	OPS
2014	ElPaso*	AAA	115	456	132	22	3	15	(-	-)	205	55	69	68	21	1	95	3	0	7	11	2	14	.289	.320	.450	.770
2005	Atl	NL	70	257	77	20	1	14	(11	3)	141	41	45	50	11	3	58	4	0	2	3	2	4	.300	.336	.549	.884
2006	Atl	NL	162	651	169	24	6	29	(19	10)	292	83	103	91	23	6	132	9	0	3	1	6	15	.260	.293	.449	.742
2007	Atl	NL	162	642	188	40	0	19	(7	12)	285	84	105	97	42	5	129	5	0	7	5	2	14	.293	.338	.444	.782
2008	Atl	NL	155	599	143	33	3	11	(5	6)	215	70	71	49	39	5	111	10	0	4	0	1	18	.239	.294	.359	.653
2009	2 Tms	NL	157	593	166	32	4	15	(7	8)	251	72	76	59	23	5	92	6	1	9	6	4	13	.280	.309	.423	.732
2010	2 Tms		139	454	113	18	2	13	(5	8)	174	52	65	46	30	8	81	8	0	11	8	3	9	.249	.300	.383	.683
2011	KC	AL	153	601	171	47	4	20	(10	10)	286	77	87	83	37	3	123	8	0	10	22	10	17	.285	.329	.476	.805
2012	KC	AL	148	561	132	26	3	16	(7	9)	212	58	49	50	34	9	119	7	0	1	4	7	14	.235	.287	.378	.665
2013	2 Tms		81	245	50	10	2	3	(1	2)	73	20	17	11	9	2	61	2	0	0	3	0	7	.204	.238	.298	.536
2014	SD	NL	10	24	2	0	0	0	(0	0)	2	2	1	0	3	0	7	0	0	1	0	0	0	.083	.179	.083	.262
	09 Atl	NL	82	304	76	12	2	5	(3	2)	107	32	35	25	12	2	46	3	1	4	5	1	10	.250	.282	.352	.634
	09 NYM	NL	75	289	90	20	2	10	(4	6)	144	40	41	34	11	3	46	3	0	5	1	3	3	.311	.338	.498	.836
	10 NYM	NL	124	401	95	16	2	11	(5	6)	148	43	54	39	29	8	76	7	0	10	8	2	7	.237	.293	.369	.662
	10 Tex	AL	15	53	18	2	0	2	(0	2)	26	9	11	7	1	0	5	1	0	1	0	1	2	.340	.357	.491	.848
	13 KC	AL	59	183	38	8	2	3	(1	2)	59	19	13	10	8	2	49	2	0	0	2	0	5	.208	.249	.322	.571
	13 SF	NL	22	62	12	2	0	0	(0	0)	14	1	4	1	1	0	12	0	0	0	1	0	2	.194	.206	.226	.432
	Postseason		13	41	7	2	1	0	(0	0)	11	3	2	3	3	1	7	1	1	0	0	0	2	.171	.244	.268	.513
	10 ML YEARS		1237	4627	1211	250	25	140	(72	68)	1931	559	619	536	251	46	913	59	1	48	52	35	111	.262	.305	.417	.722

Kevin Frandsen

FRAND-zen

Bats: R **Throws:** R **Pos:** PH-52;LF-21;3B-16;2B-13;1B-9;PR-2   **Ht:** 6'0" **Wt:** 190 **Born:** 5/24/1982 **Age:** 33

Year Team	Lg	G	AB	H	2B	3B	HR	(Hm	Rd)	TB	R	RBI	RC	TBB	IBB	SO	HBP	SH	SF	SB	CS	GDP	Avg	OBP	Slg	OPS
2006 SF	NL	41	93	20	4	0	2	(0	2)	30	12	7	7	3	0	14	6	0	0	0	1	3	.215	.284	.323	.607
2007 SF	NL	109	264	71	12	1	5	(1	4)	100	26	31	29	21	3	24	5	3	3	4	3	17	.269	.331	.379	.710
2008 SF	NL	1	1	0	0	0	0	(0	0)	0	0	0	0	0	0	0	0	0	0	0	0	0	.000	.000	.000	.000
2009 SF	NL	23	50	7	2	0	0	(0	0)	9	3	1	0	3	0	4	1	0	0	0	0	2	.140	.204	.180	.384
2010 LAA	AL	54	160	40	11	0	0	(0	0)	51	24	14	16	9	0	10	1	3	0	2	0	5	.250	.294	.319	.613
2012 Phi	NL	55	195	66	10	3	2	(1	1)	88	24	14	30	9	2	18	5	1	0	0	1	4	.338	.383	.451	.834
2013 Phi	NL	119	252	59	10	1	5	(2	3)	86	27	26	21	12	0	29	11	1	2	1	0	10	.234	.296	.341	.637
2014 Was	NL	105	220	57	8	0	1	(0	1)	68	17	17	21	6	0	26	7	2	1	0	0	7	.259	.299	.309	.608
8 ML YEARS		507	1235	320	57	5	15	(4	11)	432	133	110	124	63	5	125	36	10	6	7	5	48	.259	.313	.350	.662

Nick Franklin

Bats: B **Throws:** R **Pos:** 2B-12;SS-10;PH-3;RF-2;DH-2;3B-1;PR-1   **Ht:** 6'1" **Wt:** 195 **Born:** 3/2/1991 **Age:** 24

Year Team	Lg	G	AB	H	2B	3B	HR	(Hm	Rd)	TB	R	RBI	RC	TBB	IBB	SO	HBP	SH	SF	SB	CS	GDP	Avg	OBP	Slg	OPS
2010 Clinton	A	129	513	144	22	7	23	(-	-)	249	89	65	90	50	4	123	7	2	2	25	10	4	.281	.351	.485	.837
2010 WTenn	AA	1	3	2	0	0	0	(-	-)	2	3	0	1	1	0	1	0	0	0	0	0	0	.667	.750	.667	1.417
2011 Hi Dsrt	A+	64	258	71	10	5	5	(-	-)	106	50	20	42	31	0	56	2	5	1	13	1	3	.275	.356	.411	.767
2011 Jacksn	AA	21	83	27	3	2	2	(-	-)	40	13	6	14	6	0	18	0	3	0	5	3	1	.325	.371	.482	.853
2011 Ms	R	3	11	1	0	0	0	(-	-)	1	1	0	0	0	0	6	0	1	0	0	0	0	.091	.091	.091	.182
2012 Jacksn	AA	57	205	66	17	4	4	(-	-)	103	25	26	42	24	1	38	1	8	1	9	2	5	.322	.394	.502	.896
2012 Tacom	AAA	64	267	65	15	5	7	(-	-)	111	39	29	35	24	0	68	2	2	1	3	2	6	.243	.310	.416	.725
2013 Tacom	AAA	39	142	46	9	0	4	(-	-)	67	28	20	33	30	2	20	1	2	2	7	0	1	.324	.440	.472	.912
2014 Tacom	AAA	75	279	82	16	1	9	(-	-)	127	45	47	53	47	3	60	1	1	5	9	5	4	.294	.392	.455	.847
2014 Drham	AAA	27	100	21	2	0	2	(-	-)	29	8	9	9	10	0	34	1	2	0	2	0	0	.210	.288	.290	.578
2013 Sea	AL	102	369	83	20	1	12	(4	8)	141	38	45	48	42	1	113	0	0	1	6	1	2	.225	.303	.382	.686
2014 2 Tms	AL	28	81	13	2	1	1	(1	0)	20	7	6	6	6	0	32	1	0	2	2	0	2	.160	.222	.247	.469
14 Sea	AL	17	47	6	0	1	0	(0	0)	8	3	2	1	3	0	21	1	0	1	1	0	0	.128	.192	.170	.363
14 TB	AL	11	34	7	2	0	1	(1	0)	12	4	4	5	3	0	11	0	0	1	1	0	2	.206	.263	.353	.616
2 ML YEARS		130	450	96	22	2	13	(5	8)	161	45	51	54	48	1	145	1	0	3	8	1	4	.213	.289	.358	.647

Jason Frasor

FRAY-zer

Pitches: R **Bats:** R **Pos:** RP-61   **Ht:** 5'9" **Wt:** 180 **Born:** 8/9/1977 **Age:** 37

Year Team	Lg	G	GS	CG	GF	IP	BFP	H	R	ER	HR	SH	SF	HB	TBB	IBB	SO	WP	Bk	W	L	Pct	Sh	Sv-Op	Hld	ERC	ERA
2004 Tor	AL	63	0	0	37	68.1	299	64	31	31	4	3	2	2	36	3	54	4	2	4	6	.400	0	17-19	8	3.97	4.08
2005 Tor	AL	67	0	0	12	74.2	305	67	31	27	8	2	1	3	28	2	62	1	0	3	5	.375	0	1-3	15	3.72	3.25
2006 Tor	AL	51	0	0	12	50.0	215	47	24	24	8	0	3	2	17	1	51	3	0	3	2	.600	0	0-1	12	3.98	4.32
2007 Tor	AL	51	0	0	18	57.0	242	47	29	29	3	1	2	2	23	1	59	2	1	1	5	.167	0	3-6	4	2.88	4.58
2008 Tor	AL	49	0	0	21	47.1	208	36	23	22	4	0	2	1	32	4	42	6	0	1	2	.333	0	0-1	4	3.62	4.18
2009 Tor	AL	61	0	0	36	57.2	227	43	17	16	4	1	2	2	16	3	56	2	0	7	3	.700	0	11-14	4	2.22	2.50
2010 Tor	AL	69	0	0	18	63.2	279	61	30	26	4	1	0	4	27	6	65	5	0	3	4	.429	0	4-8	14	3.72	3.68
2011 2 Tms	AL	64	0	0	10	60.0	261	58	25	24	7	2	4	3	26	3	57	3	0	3	3	.500	0	0-2	14	4.26	3.60
2012 Tor	AL	50	0	0	9	43.2	191	42	20	20	6	1	2	2	22	1	53	5	1	1	1	.500	0	0-3	12	4.74	4.12
2013 Tex	AL	61	0	0	11	49.0	200	36	15	14	4	1	2	0	20	3	48	2	0	4	3	.571	0	0-1	10	2.50	2.57
2014 2 Tms	AL	61	0	0	11	47.1	196	40	17	14	3	0	5	2	18	2	46	3	0	4	1	.800	0	0-2	10	3.05	2.66
11 Tor	AL	44	0	0	6	42.1	178	38	15	14	4	2	3	2	15	1	37	2	0	2	1	.667	0	0-2	10	3.46	2.98
11 CWS	AL	20	0	0	4	17.2	83	20	10	10	3	0	1	1	11	2	20	1	0	1	2	.333	0	0-0	4	6.37	5.09
14 Tex	AL	38	0	0	6	29.2	129	27	14	11	2	0	3	1	14	1	30	2	0	1	1	.500	0	0-2	10	3.68	3.34
14 KC	AL	23	0	0	5	17.2	67	13	3	3	1	0	2	1	4	1	16	1	0	3	0	1.000	0	0-0	0	2.07	1.53
11 ML YEARS		647	0	0	195	618.2	2623	541	262	247	55	12	26	23	265	29	593	36	4	34	35	.493	0	36-60	107	3.50	3.59

Todd Frazier

Bats: R **Throws:** R **Pos:** 3B-124;1B-43;PH-1   **Ht:** 6'3" **Wt:** 220 **Born:** 2/12/1986 **Age:** 29

Year Team	Lg	G	AB	H	2B	3B	HR	(Hm	Rd)	TB	R	RBI	RC	TBB	IBB	SO	HBP	SH	SF	SB	CS	GDP	Avg	OBP	Slg	OPS
2011 Cin	NL	41	112	26	5	0	6	(2	4)	49	17	15	13	7	0	27	2	0	0	1	0	2	.232	.289	.438	.727
2012 Cin	NL	128	422	115	26	6	19	(10	9)	210	55	67	59	36	1	103	3	0	4	3	2	9	.273	.331	.498	.829
2013 Cin	NL	150	531	124	29	3	19	(12	7)	216	63	73	67	50	1	125	14	2	3	6	5	14	.234	.314	.407	.721
2014 Cin	NL	157	597	163	22	1	29	(20	9)	274	88	80	84	52	2	139	7	0	4	20	8	9	.273	.336	.459	.795
Postseason		5	10	2	1	0	0	(0	0)	3	0	1	0	1	0	3	0	0	0	0	0	0	.200	.273	.300	.573
4 ML YEARS		476	1662	428	82	10	73	(44	29)	749	223	235	223	145	4	394	26	2	11	30	15	34	.258	.325	.451	.775

Freddie Freeman

Bats: L **Throws:** R **Pos:** 1B-162   **Ht:** 6'5" **Wt:** 225 **Born:** 9/12/1989 **Age:** 25

Year Team	Lg	G	AB	H	2B	3B	HR	(Hm	Rd)	TB	R	RBI	RC	TBB	IBB	SO	HBP	SH	SF	SB	CS	GDP	Avg	OBP	Slg	OPS
2010 Atl	NL	20	24	4	1	0	1	(0	1)	8	3	1	0	0	0	8	0	0	0	0	0	1	.167	.167	.333	.500
2011 Atl	NL	157	571	161	32	0	21	(9	12)	256	67	76	79	53	3	142	6	0	5	4	4	15	.282	.346	.448	.795
2012 Atl	NL	147	540	140	33	2	23	(12	11)	246	91	94	82	64	4	129	7	0	**9**	2	0	10	.259	.340	.456	.796

				BATTING																	RUNNING			AVERAGES			
Year Team	Lg	G	AB	H	2B	3B	HR	(Hm Rd)	TB	R	RBI	RC	TBB	IBB	SO	HBP	SH	SF	SB	CS	GDP	Avg	OBP	Slg	OPS
2013 Atl	NL	147	551	176	27	2	23	(16 7)	276	89	109	124	66	10	121	7	0	5	1	0	11	.319	.396	.501	.897
2014 Atl	NL	**162**	607	175	43	4	18	(7 11)	280	93	78	101	90	4	145	8	0	3	3	4	18	.288	.386	.461	.847
Postseason		5	20	8	2	0	0	(0 0)	10	4	0	2	2	0	5	0	0	0	0	0	0	.400	.455	.500	.955
5 ML YEARS		633	2293	656	136	8	86	(44 42)	1066	343	358	386	273	21	545	28	0	22	10	8	55	.286	.366	.465	.831

Sam Freeman

Pitches: L **Bats:** R **Pos:** RP-44

Ht: 5'11" **Wt:** 165 **Born:** 6/24/1987 **Age:** 28

			HOW MUCH HE PITCHED					WHAT HE GAVE UP										THE RESULTS						
Year Team	Lg	G	GS	CG	GF	IP	BFP	H	R	ER	HR	SH	SF	HB	TBB	IBB	SO	WP	Bk	W	L	Pct	Sh	Sv-Op	Hld	ERC	ERA
2014 Memp*	AAA	16	0	0	8	20.1	96	25	12	8	1	1	1	1	7	0	26	4	0	0	1	.000	0	0- -	-	4.74	3.54
2012 StL	NL	24	0	0	7	20.0	86	17	13	12	2	1	0	1	10	0	18	0	0	0	2	.000	0	0-0	2	3.84	5.40
2013 StL	NL	13	0	0	2	12.1	50	8	3	3	0	1	0	0	5	0	8	2	0	1	0	1.000	0	0-0	1	1.67	2.19
2014 StL	NL	44	0	0	9	38.0	169	34	13	11	2	1	1	4	19	0	35	3	0	2	0	1.000	0	0-0	11	3.89	2.61
3 ML YEARS		81	0	0	18	70.1	305	59	29	26	4	3	1	5	34	0	61	5	0	3	2	.600	0	0-0	14	3.45	3.33

David Freese

Bats: R **Throws:** R **Pos:** 3B-122;DH-10;PH-6 · FREEZE

Ht: 6'2" **Wt:** 225 **Born:** 4/28/1983 **Age:** 32

				BATTING																	RUNNING			AVERAGES			
Year Team	Lg	G	AB	H	2B	3B	HR	(Hm Rd)	TB	R	RBI	RC	TBB	IBB	SO	HBP	SH	SF	SB	CS	GDP	Avg	OBP	Slg	OPS
2014 Salt Lk*	AAA	3	10	2	0	0	2	(- -)	8	4	4	3	4	0	1	0	0	0	0	0	0	.200	.429	.800	1.229
2009 StL	NL	17	31	10	2	0	1	(0 1)	15	3	7	4	2	0	7	0	0	1	0	0	1	.323	.353	.484	.837
2010 StL	NL	70	240	71	12	1	4	(3 1)	97	28	36	36	21	0	59	4	4	1	1	1	7	.296	.361	.404	.765
2011 StL	NL	97	333	99	16	1	10	(6 4)	147	41	55	50	24	0	75	4	0	2	1	0	18	.297	.350	.441	.791
2012 StL	NL	144	501	147	25	1	20	(8 12)	234	70	79	79	57	2	122	7	0	2	3	3	19	.293	.372	.467	.839
2013 StL	NL	138	462	121	26	1	9	(4 5)	176	53	60	48	47	1	106	9	0	3	1	2	26	.262	.340	.381	.721
2014 LAA	AL	134	462	120	25	1	10	(6 4)	177	53	55	55	38	0	124	6	0	5	1	3	10	.260	.321	.383	.704
Postseason		48	166	48	15	1	7	(3 4)	86	20	29	31	17	2	43	1	0	1	0	1	7	.289	.357	.518	.875
6 ML YEARS		600	2029	568	106	5	54	(27 27)	846	248	292	272	189	3	493	30	4	14	7	9	81	.280	.348	.417	.765

Nate Freiman

Bats: R **Throws:** R **Pos:** 1B-33;PH-7;DH-2;PR-1 · FRY-men

Ht: 6'8" **Wt:** 250 **Born:** 12/31/1986 **Age:** 28

				BATTING																	RUNNING			AVERAGES			
Year Team	Lg	G	AB	H	2B	3B	HR	(Hm Rd)	TB	R	RBI	RC	TBB	IBB	SO	HBP	SH	SF	SB	CS	GDP	Avg	OBP	Slg	OPS
2010 FtWyn	A	136	523	154	43	0	14	(- -)	239	83	84	91	58	5	117	7	0	6	0	0	21	.294	.369	.457	.826
2011 Lk Els	A+	138	548	158	35	4	22	(- -)	267	81	111	98	50	4	93	11	0	9	6	1	15	.288	.354	.487	.842
2012 SnAnt	AA	137	516	154	31	1	24	(- -)	259	80	105	96	49	1	95	12	0	4	0	2	11	.298	.370	.502	.872
2014 Scrmto	AAA	80	310	88	22	1	15	(- -)	157	48	74	60	40	1	73	7	0	7	0	0	10	.284	.371	.506	.877
2014 Beloit	A	2	9	4	2	0	1	(- -)	9	2	2	3	0	0	4	0	0	0	0	0	0	.444	.444	1.000	1.444
2013 Oak	AL	80	190	52	8	1	4	(3 1)	74	10	24	23	14	0	31	2	0	2	0	0	8	.274	.327	.389	.716
2014 Oak	AL	36	87	19	5	0	5	(1 4)	39	12	15	9	5	1	23	1	0	0	0	0	6	.218	.269	.448	.717
2 ML YEARS		116	277	71	13	1	9	(4 5)	113	22	39	32	19	1	54	3	0	2	0	0	14	.256	.309	.408	.717

Carlos Frias

Pitches: R **Bats:** R **Pos:** RP-13; SP-2 · FREE-us

Ht: 6'4" **Wt:** 170 **Born:** 11/13/1989 **Age:** 25

			HOW MUCH HE PITCHED					WHAT HE GAVE UP										THE RESULTS						
Year Team	Lg	G	GS	CG	GF	IP	BFP	H	R	ER	HR	SH	SF	HB	TBB	IBB	SO	WP	Bk	W	L	Pct	Sh	Sv-Op	Hld	ERC	ERA
2010 Ogden	R+	13	8	0	2	39.1	189	45	38	34	7	0	0	6	21	0	43	7	1	2	6	.250	0	0- -	-	6.63	7.78
2011 RCuca	A+	12	0	0	6	16.0	76	17	13	11	3	1	2	0	17	0	11	4	0	1	1	.500	0	0- -	-	8.46	6.19
2012 RCuca	A+	3	1	0	0	5.2	35	9	8	8	0	0	1	2	8	0	5	1	0	0	1	.000	0	0- -	-	12.94	12.71
2012 Ogden	R+	15	15	0	0	78.0	337	83	44	36	5	4	2	2	21	0	67	12	0	7	4	.636	0	0- -	-	3.72	4.15
2013 Gt Lks	A	12	12	0	0	68.1	286	66	26	20	3	0	3	4	23	0	49	6	1	5	3	.625	0	0- -	-	3.56	2.63
2013 RCuca	A+	8	8	0	0	46.0	200	52	22	21	4	0	2	1	11	0	48	2	1	2	3	.400	0	0- -	-	4.11	4.11
2013 Chatt	AA	8	2	0	4	16.0	68	15	7	7	2	0	0	2	7	1	8	0	0	1	1	.500	0	0- -	-	4.63	3.94
2014 Chatt	AA	5	5	0	0	32.0	136	34	16	12	2	1	0	2	9	0	14	1	0	2	1	.667	0	0- -	-	4.00	3.38
2014 Albq	AAA	16	15	2	0	91.2	399	114	57	51	4	3	2	2	21	0	65	7	3	8	4	.667	0	0- -	-	4.50	5.01
2014 LAD	NL	15	2	0	7	32.1	137	33	22	22	4	0	0	0	7	1	29	2	0	1	1	.500	0	0-0	1	3.50	6.12

Christian Friedrich

Pitches: L **Bats:** R **Pos:** RP-13; SP-3 · FREE-drick

Ht: 6'4" **Wt:** 215 **Born:** 7/8/1987 **Age:** 27

			HOW MUCH HE PITCHED					WHAT HE GAVE UP										THE RESULTS						
Year Team	Lg	G	GS	CG	GF	IP	BFP	H	R	ER	HR	SH	SF	HB	TBB	IBB	SO	WP	Bk	W	L	Pct	Sh	Sv-Op	Hld	ERC	ERA
2010 Tulsa	AA	18	18	0	0	87.1	389	100	54	49	10	5	5	3	35	0	78	1	0	3	6	.333	0	0- -	-	5.19	5.05
2011 Tulsa	AA	25	25	0	0	133.1	600	156	88	74	20	6	3	3	43	0	103	17	1	6	10	.375	0	0- -	-	5.10	5.00
2012 ColSpr	AAA	5	5	1	0	30.0	118	23	12	10	1	3	2	1	4	0	27	0	0	2	1	.667	0	0- -	-	1.65	3.00
2013 ColSpr	AAA	4	4	0	0	14.2	66	13	12	7	1	1	2	0	8	0	8	0	0	0	1	.000	0	0- -	-	3.63	4.30
2014 ColSpr	AAA	27	13	0	3	91.1	418	114	76	71	16	2	3	1	39	2	83	3	1	2	9	.182	0	1- - -	-	6.38	7.00
2012 Col	NL	16	16	0	0	84.2	377	102	61	58	14	6	2	2	30	0	74	6	0	5	8	.385	0	0-0	-	5.71	6.17
2014 Col	NL	16	3	0	3	24.1	110	25	21	16	3	1	2	2	10	1	27	5	0	0	4	.000	0	0-0	3	4.59	5.92
2 ML YEARS		32	19	0	3	109.0	487	127	82	74	17	7	4	4	40	1	101	13	0	5	12	.294	0	0-0	3	5.45	6.11

Ernesto Frieri

Pitches: R Bats: R Pos: RP-48 free-AIR-ee **Ht: 6'2" Wt: 205 Born: 7/19/1985 Age: 29**

Year	Team	Lg	G	GS	CG	GF	IP	BFP	H	R	ER	HR	SH	SF	HB	TBB	IBB	SO	WP	Bk	W	L	Pct	Sh	Sv-Op	Hld	ERC	ERA
2014	Indy*	AAA	7	0	0	3	7.0	30	5	3	3	2	1	0	0	4	1	6	0	0	0	0	-	0	1--	-	4.13	3.86
2009	SD	NL	2	0	0	2	2.0	7	0	0	0	0	0	0	0	1	0	2	0	0	0	0	-	0	0-0	0	0.27	0.00
2010	SD	NL	33	0	0	12	31.2	128	18	7	6	2	0	0	0	17	3	41	2	0	1	1	.500	0	0-0	7	1.99	1.71
2011	SD	NL	60	0	0	20	63.0	276	51	21	19	3	1	1	9	34	5	76	1	1	1	2	.333	0	0-0	4	3.60	2.71
2012	2 Tms	AL	67	0	0	51	66.0	269	35	20	17	9	1	1	7	30	0	98	1	0	5	2	.714	0	23-26	7	2.43	2.32
2013	LAA	AL	67	0	0	51	68.2	292	55	29	29	11	2	2	3	30	1	98	1	0	2	4	.333	0	37-41	2	3.64	3.80
2014	2 Tms	AL	48	0	0	30	41.2	184	47	34	34	11	0	0	2	14	2	48	0	0	1	4	.200	0	11-14	3	5.89	7.34
12	SD	NL	11	0	0	5	11.2	50	9	5	3	2	0	0	2	4	0	18	0	0	1	0	1.000	0	0-0	1	3.67	2.31
12	LAA	AL	56	0	0	46	54.1	219	26	15	14	7	1	1	5	26	0	80	1	0	4	2	.667	0	23-26	6	2.18	2.32
14	LAA	AL	34	0	0	22	31.0	133	33	22	22	8	0	0	1	9	1	38	0	0	0	3	.000	0	11-14	3	5.21	6.39
14	Pit	NL	14	0	0	8	10.2	51	14	12	12	3	0	0	1	5	1	10	0	0	1	1	.500	0	0-0	0	7.97	10.13
	6 ML YEARS		277	0	0	166	273.0	1156	206	111	105	36	4	4	21	126	11	363	5	1	10	13	.435	0	71-81	23	3.41	3.46

Eric Fryer

Bats: R Throws: R Pos: C-24;DH-2;PH-2;PR-2 **Ht: 6'2" Wt: 215 Born: 8/26/1985 Age: 29**

Year	Team	Lg	G	AB	H	2B	3B	HR	(Hm	Rd)	TB	R	RBI	RC	TBB	IBB	SO	HBP	SH	SF	SB	CS	GDP	Avg	OBP	Slg	OPS
2014	Roch*	AAA	36	111	28	7	1	0	(-	-)	37	12	11	13	12	0	29	0	1	1	5	0	2	.252	.323	.333	.656
2011	Pit	NL	10	26	7	0	0	0	(0	0)	7	5	0	2	3	1	7	0	0	0	1	1	0	.269	.345	.269	.614
2012	Pit	NL	6	4	1	0	0	0	(0	0)	1	0	0	1	1	0	1	0	0	0	0	0	0	.250	.400	.250	.650
2013	Min	AL	6	13	5	1	0	1	(1	0)	9	2	4	5	3	0	3	0	0	0	0	0	1	.385	.500	.692	1.192
2014	Min	AL	28	75	16	4	0	1	(0	1)	23	11	5	6	5	0	15	1	0	0	1	0	0	.213	.272	.307	.578
	4 ML YEARS		50	118	29	5	0	2	(1	1)	40	18	9	14	12	1	26	1	0	0	2	1	1	.246	.321	.339	.660

Kyuji Fujikawa

Pitches: R Bats: L Pos: RP-15 CUE-jee foo-jee-KOW-uh **Ht: 6'0" Wt: 190 Born: 7/21/1980 Age: 34**

Year	Team	Lg	G	GS	CG	GF	IP	BFP	H	R	ER	HR	SH	SF	HB	TBB	IBB	SO	WP	Bk	W	L	Pct	Sh	Sv-Op	Hld	ERC	ERA
2010	Hnshn	Jap	58	0	0	49	62.2	257	47	14	14	7	-	-	5	20	2	81	1	0	3	4	.429	0	28--	-	2.76	2.01
2011	Hnshn	Jap	56	0	0	49	51.0	193	25	9	7	2	-	-	1	13	1	80	3	0	3	3	.500	0	41--	-	1.07	1.24
2012	Hnshn	Jap	48	0	0	45	47.2	189	34	7	7	1	-	-	1	15	2	58	2	0	2	2	.500	0	24--	-	1.85	1.32
2013	Iowa	AAA	1	0	0	0	1.0	4	0	0	0	0	0	0	0	1	0	2	0	0	0	0	-	0	0--	-	0.95	0.00
2013	Tenn	AA	1	0	0	0	2.0	6	1	0	0	0	0	0	0	0	0	0	0	0	0	0	-	0	0--	-	0.63	0.00
2014	Cubs	R	4	2	0	0	4.0	15	1	0	0	0	0	0	0	1	0	5	0	0	0	0	-	0	0--	-	0.38	0.00
2014	Kane	A	2	0	0	0	1.2	8	1	1	0	0	0	0	0	1	0	4	0	0	0	0	-	0	0--	-	1.70	0.00
2014	Iowa	AAA	6	0	0	0	6.0	22	5	1	1	0	1	0	0	1	1	4	0	0	0	0	-	0	0--	-	1.72	1.50
2013	ChC	NL	12	0	0	5	12.0	50	11	7	7	1	0	0	2	2	0	14	2	0	1	1	.500	0	2-3	5	3.26	5.25
2014	ChC	NL	15	0	0	6	13.0	64	18	8	7	2	0	1	2	6	2	17	2	0	0	0	-	0	0-0	1	7.41	4.85
	2 ML YEARS		27	0	0	11	25.0	114	29	15	14	3	0	1	4	8	2	31	4	0	1	1	.500	0	2-3	1	5.31	5.04

Sam Fuld

Bats: L Throws: L Pos: CF-62;LF-36;RF-17;PH-9;PR-4 **Ht: 5'10" Wt: 175 Born: 11/20/1981 Age: 33**

Year	Team	Lg	G	AB	H	2B	3B	HR	(Hm	Rd)	TB	R	RBI	RC	TBB	IBB	SO	HBP	SH	SF	SB	CS	GDP	Avg	OBP	Slg	OPS
2014	NwBrit*	AA	4	14	6	2	0	1	(-	-)	11	4	2	4	2	0	1	0	0	0	0	0	0	.429	.500	.786	1.286
2007	ChC	NL	14	6	0	0	0	0	(0	0)	0	3	0	0	3	0	3	0	0	0	0	0	0	.000	.333	.000	.333
2009	ChC	NL	65	97	29	6	1	1	(1	0)	40	17	2	15	17	1	10	1	0	0	2	1	1	.299	.409	.412	.821
2010	ChC	NL	19	28	4	1	0	0	(0	0)	5	3	3	1	3	0	5	0	0	0	0	0	2	.143	.226	.179	.404
2011	TB	AL	105	308	74	18	5	3	(2	1)	111	41	27	37	32	0	49	1	4	1	20	8	3	.240	.313	.360	.673
2012	TB	AL	44	98	25	3	2	0	(0	0)	32	14	5	13	8	0	14	1	0	0	7	2	0	.255	.318	.327	.644
2013	TB	AL	119	176	35	0	3	2	(2	0)	47	25	17	14	17	0	28	1	4	2	8	2	6	.199	.270	.267	.537
2014	2 Tms	AL	113	351	84	16	4	4	(0	4)	120	40	36	47	43	2	63	0	6	2	21	4	2	.239	.321	.342	.663
14	Oak	AL	60	187	39	6	4	3	(0	3)	62	25	19	22	17	1	34	0	3	0	9	1	2	.209	.275	.332	.606
14	Min	AL	53	164	45	10	0	1	(0	1)	58	15	17	25	26	1	29	0	3	2	12	3	0	.274	.370	.354	.723
Postseason			5	4	0	0	0	0	(0	0)	0	1	0	0	0	0	2	0	0	0	0	0	0	.000	.000	.000	.000
	7 ML YEARS		479	1064	251	44	15	10	(5	5)	355	143	90	127	123	3	172	4	14	5	58	17	14	.236	.316	.334	.650

Charlie Furbush

Pitches: L Bats: L Pos: RP-67 FUR-bush **Ht: 6'5" Wt: 215 Born: 4/11/1986 Age: 29**

Year	Team	Lg	G	GS	CG	GF	IP	BFP	H	R	ER	HR	SH	SF	HB	TBB	IBB	SO	WP	Bk	W	L	Pct	Sh	Sv-Op	Hld	ERC	ERA
2011	2 Tms	AL	28	12	0	1	85.1	372	97	59	52	16	2	4	6	30	2	67	2	1	4	10	.286	0	0-0	1	5.72	5.48
2012	Sea	AL	48	0	0	8	46.1	182	28	15	14	3	2	1	2	16	4	53	5	0	5	2	.714	0	0-0	6	1.72	2.72
2013	Sea	AL	71	0	0	5	65.0	280	48	33	27	5	2	5	3	29	2	80	3	0	2	6	.250	0	0-6	20	2.71	3.74
2014	Sea	AL	67	0	0	13	42.1	177	40	17	17	4	2	1	3	9	0	51	2	0	1	5	.167	0	1-1	20	3.26	3.61
11	Det	AL	17	2	0	1	32.1	139	36	18	13	5	2	1	3	14	1	26	0	1	1	3	.250	0	0-0	1	5.96	3.62
11	Sea	AL	11	10	0	0	53.0	233	61	41	39	11	0	3	3	16	1	41	2	0	3	7	.300	0	0-0	0	5.57	6.62
	4 ML YEARS		214	12	0	27	239.0	1011	213	124	110	28	8	11	14	84	8	251	12	1	12	23	.343	0	1-7	47	3.57	4.14

Rafael Furcal

Bats: B **Throws:** R **Pos:** 2B-8;PH-1   furr-CALL   **Ht:** 5'8" **Wt:** 195 **Born:** 10/24/1977 **Age:** 37

Year	Team	Lg	G	AB	H	2B	3B	HR	(Hm	Rd)	TB	R	RBI	RC	TBB	IBB	SO	HBP	SH	SF	SB	CS	GDP	Avg	OBP	Slg	OPS
2014	Jupiter*	A+	11	38	12	0	0	0	(-	-)	12	6	1	5	5	0	5	1	0	0	1	0	0	.316	.409	.316	.725
2014	Jaxnvl*	AA	10	37	11	2	0	0	(-	-)	13	5	0	5	3	0	2	0	0	0	4	0	2	.297	.350	.351	.701
2000	Atl	NL	131	455	134	20	4	4	(1	3)	174	87	37	78	73	0	80	3	9	2	40	14	2	.295	.394	.382	.776
2001	Atl	NL	79	324	89	19	0	4	(3	1)	120	39	30	41	24	1	56	1	4	6	22	6	5	.275	.321	.370	.691
2002	Atl	NL	154	636	175	31	8	8	(4	4)	246	95	47	80	43	0	114	3	9	2	27	15	8	.275	.323	.387	.710
2003	Atl	NL	156	664	194	35	10	15	(4	11)	294	130	61	107	60	2	76	3	3	4	25	2	1	.292	.352	.443	.794
2004	Atl	NL	143	563	157	24	5	14	(5	9)	233	103	59	82	58	4	71	1	5	5	29	6	9	.279	.344	.414	.758
2005	Atl	NL	154	616	175	31	11	12	(9	3)	264	100	58	98	62	3	78	1	5	3	46	10	11	.284	.348	.429	.777
2006	LAD	NL	159	654	196	32	9	15	(12	3)	291	113	63	110	73	3	98	1	5	3	37	13	7	.300	.369	.445	.814
2007	LAD	NL	138	581	157	23	4	6	(4	2)	206	87	47	65	55	3	68	1	2	3	25	6	11	.270	.333	.355	.687
2008	LAD	NL	36	143	51	12	2	5	(3	2)	82	34	16	33	20	0	17	1	0	0	8	3	3	.357	.439	.573	1.012
2009	LAD	NL	150	613	165	28	5	9	(5	4)	230	92	47	73	61	2	89	1	3	2	12	6	11	.269	.335	.375	.711
2010	LAD	NL	97	383	115	23	7	8	(5	3)	176	66	43	66	40	5	60	1	2	2	22	4	5	.300	.366	.460	.826
2011	2 Tms	NL	87	333	77	15	0	8	(5	3)	116	44	28	31	28	0	39	4	3	1	9	5	3	.231	.298	.348	.646
2012	StL	NL	121	477	126	18	3	5	(2	3)	165	69	49	57	44	1	57	1	5	4	12	4	7	.264	.325	.346	.671
2014	Mia	NL	9	35	6	0	1	0	(0	0)	8	4	2	1	2	0	7	0	0	0	0	0	1	.171	.216	.229	.445
11	LAD	NL	37	137	27	4	0	1	(1	0)	34	15	12	12	11	0	21	3	1	0	5	3	0	.197	.272	.248	.520
11	StL	NL	50	196	50	11	0	7	(4	3)	82	29	16	19	17	0	18	1	2	1	4	2	3	.255	.316	.418	.735
Postseason			59	247	56	5	5	4	(3	1)	83	33	16	25	27	1	34	2	7	2	13	2	2	.227	.306	.336	.642
14 ML YEARS			1614	6477	1817	311	69	113	(62	51)	2605	1063	587	922	643	24	910	22	55	39	314	94	84	.281	.346	.402	.748

Yovani Gallardo

Pitches: R **Bats:** R **Pos:** SP-32   guy-YARR-doe   **Ht:** 6'2" **Wt:** 210 **Born:** 2/27/1986 **Age:** 29

Year	Team	Lg	G	GS	CG	GF	IP	BFP	H	R	ER	HR	SH	SF	HB	TBB	IBB	SO	WP	Bk	W	L	Pct	Sh	Sv-Op	Hld	ERC	ERA
2007	Mil	NL	20	17	0	1	110.1	466	103	48	45	8	4	3	2	37	2	101	3	0	9	5	.643	0	0-0	0	3.30	3.67
2008	Mil	NL	4	4	0	0	24.0	97	22	5	5	3	2	1	0	8	0	20	0	0	0	0	-	0	0-0	0	3.66	1.88
2009	Mil	NL	30	30	1	0	185.2	793	150	78	77	21	5	5	3	94	5	204	9	0	13	12	.520	0	0-0	0	3.57	3.73
2010	Mil	NL	31	31	2	0	185.0	803	178	89	79	12	11	4	3	75	5	200	7	1	14	7	.667	2	0-0	0	3.61	3.84
2011	Mil	NL	33	33	1	0	207.1	865	193	92	81	27	10	7	1	59	1	207	12	0	17	10	.630	1	0-0	0	3.43	3.52
2012	Mil	NL	33	33	0	0	204.0	860	185	86	83	26	11	6	0	81	3	204	5	0	16	9	.640	0	0-0	0	3.72	3.66
2013	Mil	NL	31	31	0	0	180.2	773	180	92	84	18	8	7	3	66	1	144	5	0	12	10	.545	0	0-0	0	3.98	4.18
2014	Mil	NL	32	32	0	0	192.1	817	195	86	75	21	8	3	4	54	2	146	8	0	8	11	.421	0	0-0	0	3.79	3.51
Postseason			5	4	0	0	26.0	109	22	9	6	2	1	0	0	13	3	20	4	0	1	2	.333	0	0-0	0	3.34	2.08
8 ML YEARS			214	211	4	1	1289.1	5474	1206	576	529	136	59	34	18	474	19	1226	49	1	89	64	.582	3	0-0	0	3.65	3.69

Freddy Galvis

Bats: B **Throws:** R **Pos:** SS-25;3B-11;2B-7;PH-4;PR-1   GAL-viss   **Ht:** 5'10" **Wt:** 185 **Born:** 11/14/1989 **Age:** 25

Year	Team	Lg	G	AB	H	2B	3B	HR	(Hm	Rd)	TB	R	RBI	RC	TBB	IBB	SO	HBP	SH	SF	SB	CS	GDP	Avg	OBP	Slg	OPS
2014	Clrwtr*	A+	5	20	4	0	2	1	(-	-)	11	4	3	2	0	0	2	0	0	0	0	0	0	.200	.200	.550	.750
2014	LV*	AAA	35	135	36	14	1	3	(-	-)	61	22	15	19	11	0	25	0	3	0	1	1	1	.267	.322	.452	.774
2014	Phillies*	R	5	16	4	1	0	0	(-	-)	5	2	3	1	1	0	2	0	0	0	1	0	1	.250	.294	.313	.607
2012	Phi	NL	58	190	43	15	1	3	(3	0)	69	14	24	14	7	0	29	0	3	0	0	0	6	.226	.254	.363	.617
2013	Phi	NL	70	205	48	5	4	6	(4	2)	79	13	19	20	13	2	45	1	3	0	1	0	5	.234	.283	.385	.668
2014	Phi	NL	43	119	21	3	1	4	(2	2)	38	14	12	9	8	0	30	0	0	1	1	0	0	.176	.227	.319	.546
3 ML YEARS			171	514	112	23	6	13	(9	4)	186	41	55	43	28	2	104	1	6	1	2	0	11	.218	.259	.362	.621

Frank Garces

Pitches: L **Bats:** L **Pos:** RP-15   GAR-sehs   **Ht:** 5'11" **Wt:** 175 **Born:** 1/17/1990 **Age:** 25

Year	Team	Lg	G	GS	CG	GF	IP	BFP	H	R	ER	HR	SH	SF	HB	TBB	IBB	SO	WP	Bk	W	L	Pct	Sh	Sv-Op	Hld	ERC	ERA
2012	FtWyn	A	25	25	0	0	121.2	508	102	51	38	3	10	4	1	55	1	112	4	2	9	6	.600	0	0--	-	2.94	2.81
2013	Lk Els	A+	26	26	0	0	120.2	556	131	86	76	15	4	5	13	57	0	126	4	3	7	9	.438	0	0--	-	5.43	5.67
2014	SnAnt	AA	51	0	0	15	65.1	268	46	17	14	3	5	1	3	24	3	74	1	0	2	5	.286	0	8--	-	2.15	1.93
2014	SD	NL	15	0	0	1	9.0	37	8	2	2	1	0	0	1	1	0	10	0	0	0	0	-	0	0-1	3	2.82	2.00

Avisail Garcia

Bats: R **Throws:** R **Pos:** RF-46   ah-vee-sigh-EEL   **Ht:** 6'4" **Wt:** 240 **Born:** 6/12/1991 **Age:** 24

Year	Team	Lg	G	AB	H	2B	3B	HR	(Hm	Rd)	TB	R	RBI	RC	TBB	IBB	SO	HBP	SH	SF	SB	CS	GDP	Avg	OBP	Slg	OPS
2014	Charltt*	AAA	13	50	17	3	0	1	(-	-)	23	9	3	8	1	0	16	2	0	0	0	0	0	.340	.377	.460	.837
2012	Det	AL	23	47	15	0	0	0	(0	0)	15	7	3	5	3	1	10	1	0	0	0	2	1	.319	.373	.319	.692
2013	2 Tms	AL	72	244	69	7	3	7	(3	4)	103	31	31	30	9	0	59	1	0	2	3	3	8	.283	.309	.422	.731
2014	CWS	AL	46	172	42	8	0	7	(2	5)	71	19	29	20	14	1	44	2	0	2	4	1	5	.244	.305	.413	.718
13	Det	AL	30	83	20	3	1	2	(1	1)	31	12	10	7	4	0	21	0	0	0	0	1	3	.241	.273	.373	.646
13	CWS	AL	42	161	49	4	2	5	(2	3)	72	19	21	23	5	0	38	1	0	1	3	2	5	.304	.327	.447	.775
Postseason			12	23	6	1	0	0	(0	0)	7	0	4	4	2	0	5	0	0	0	1	0	0	.261	.320	.304	.624
3 ML YEARS			141	463	126	15	3	14	(5	9)	189	57	63	55	26	2	113	4	0	4	7	6	14	.272	.314	.408	.722

Greg Garcia

Bats: L **Throws:** R **Pos:** PH-7;2B-4;PR-3;SS-1   **Ht:** 6'0" **Wt:** 190 **Born:** 8/8/1989 **Age:** 25

Year	Team	Lg	G	AB	H	2B	3B	HR	(Hm	Rd)	TB	R	RBI	RC	TBB	IBB	SO	HBP	SH	SF	SB	CS	GDP	Avg	OBP	Slg	OPS
2010	JhsCty	R+	58	220	63	15	1	4	(-	-)	92	49	24	34	18	0	36	9	3	1	7	5	3	.286	.363	.418	.781
2011	QuadC	A	46	150	41	10	1	0	(-	-)	53	20	10	21	17	0	24	4	2	1	4	2	3	.273	.360	.353	.714
2011	PlmBh	A+	59	210	61	11	5	2	(-	-)	88	36	16	37	31	1	42	8	7	1	4	4	3	.290	.400	.419	.819
2012	Sprgfld	AA	124	412	117	20	3	10	(-	-)	173	81	51	78	80	4	83	7	4	1	10	5	4	.284	.408	.420	.828
2013	Memp	AAA	116	354	96	23	4	3	(-	-)	136	50	35	58	49	1	70	11	10	0	14	2	10	.271	.377	.384	.761
2014	Memp	AAA	106	382	103	12	3	8	(-	-)	145	60	40	55	41	2	95	11	5	2	7	5	4	.270	.356	.380	.735
2014	Sprgfld	AA	4	15	5	2	0	0	(-	-)	7	2	1	2	1	0	4	0	0	1	1	0	0	.333	.353	.467	.820
2014	StL	NL	14	14	2	1	0	0	(0	0)	3	2	1	1	1	0	6	3	0	0	0	0	0	.143	.333	.214	.548

Jaime Garcia

Pitches: L **Bats:** L **Pos:** SP-7   HY-may   **Ht:** 6'2" **Wt:** 215 **Born:** 7/8/1986 **Age:** 28

Year	Team	Lg	G	GS	CG	GF	IP	BFP	H	R	ER	HR	SH	SF	HB	TBB	IBB	SO	WP	Bk	W	L	Pct	Sh	Sv-Op	Hld	ERC	ERA
2014	Sprgfld*	AA	1	1	0	0	2.0	8	3	2	2	1	0	0	0	1	0	2	0	0	0	0	-	0	0- -	-	13.74	9.00
2014	Memp*	AAA	1	1	0	0	5.0	20	3	2	2	1	0	0	0	2	0	5	1	0	0	0	-	0	0- -	-	2.55	3.60
2008	StL	NL	10	1	0	4	16.0	69	14	10	10	4	0	0	1	8	0	8	3	0	1	1	.500	0	0-0	3	5.15	5.63
2010	StL	NL	28	28	1	0	163.1	695	151	64	49	9	3	3	3	64	4	132	4	1	13	8	.619	1	0-0	0	3.34	2.70
2011	StL	NL	32	32	2	0	194.2	826	207	100	77	15	10	5	2	50	2	156	12	1	13	7	.650	2	0-0	0	3.73	3.56
2012	StL	NL	20	20	0	0	121.2	515	136	58	53	7	8	7	0	30	1	98	12	1	7	7	.500	0	0-0	0	3.86	3.92
2013	StL	NL	9	9	0	0	55.1	234	57	26	22	6	2	0	0	15	0	43	3	0	5	2	.714	0	0-0	0	3.78	3.58
2014	StL	NL	7	7	0	0	43.2	177	39	20	20	6	0	0	3	7	0	39	1	0	3	1	.750	0	0-0	0	3.08	4.12
	Postseason		6	6	0	0	27.2	120	29	13	13	3	1	0	1	11	2	24	1	0	0	2	.000	0	0-0	0	4.48	4.23
	6 ML YEARS		106	97	3	4	594.2	2516	604	278	231	47	23	15	9	174	7	476	35	3	42	26	.618	3	0-0	3	3.64	3.50

Leury Garcia

lay-OOH-ree

Bats: B **Throws:** R **Pos:** PR-18;3B-15;2B-14;CF-14;SS-9;PH-9;RF-3;DH-3;LF-2   **Ht:** 5'8" **Wt:** 170 **Born:** 3/18/1991 **Age:** 24

Year	Team	Lg	G	AB	H	2B	3B	HR	(Hm	Rd)	TB	R	RBI	RC	TBB	IBB	SO	HBP	SH	SF	SB	CS	GDP	Avg	OBP	Slg	OPS
2010	Hkry	A	89	359	94	5	4	3	(-	-)	116	57	22	42	23	0	57	1	8	1	47	9	4	.262	.307	.323	.630
2010	Rngrs	R	6	18	9	2	0	0	(-	-)	11	5	2	6	4	0	4	0	0	0	4	2	0	.500	.591	.611	1.202
2011	MrtlBh	A+	109	442	113	19	5	3	(-	-)	151	65	38	49	28	1	100	4	8	0	30	12	7	.256	.306	.342	.648
2012	Frisco	AA	100	377	110	12	11	2	(-	-)	150	55	30	55	22	2	79	5	9	3	31	7	3	.292	.337	.398	.734
2013	RdRck	AAA	47	193	51	8	4	4	(-	-)	79	31	19	26	14	0	53	0	1	0	12	4	5	.264	.314	.409	.723
2013	Charltt	AAA	8	30	8	1	0	0	(-	-)	9	3	1	3	1	0	8	1	0	0	3	0	0	.267	.313	.300	.613
2013	2 Tms	AL	45	101	20	1	1	0	(0	0)	23	10	2	4	7	0	34	0	2	1	7	2	0	.198	.248	.228	.475
2014	CWS	AL	74	145	24	3	0	1	(0	1)	30	13	6	0	5	1	48	0	4	1	11	1	6	.166	.192	.207	.399
13	Tex	AL	25	52	10	0	1	0	(0	0)	12	8	1	2	3	0	16	0	2	0	1	0	0	.192	.236	.231	.467
13	CWS	AL	20	49	10	1	0	0	(0	0)	11	2	1	2	4	0	18	0	0	1	6	2	0	.204	.259	.224	.484
	2 ML YEARS		119	246	44	4	1	1	(0	1)	53	23	8	4	12	1	82	0	6	2	18	3	6	.179	.215	.215	.431

Luis Garcia

Pitches: R **Bats:** R **Pos:** RP-13   **Ht:** 6'2" **Wt:** 210 **Born:** 1/30/1987 **Age:** 28

Year	Team	Lg	G	GS	CG	GF	IP	BFP	H	R	ER	HR	SH	SF	HB	TBB	IBB	SO	WP	Bk	W	L	Pct	Sh	Sv-Op	Hld	ERC	ERA
2010	Ptomc	A+	6	0	0	1	8.2	57	21	17	10	0	3	1	0	10	0	3	2	0	0	0	-	0	0- -	-	15.85	10.38
2010	Hgrstn	A	26	0	0	5	51.0	221	48	25	22	3	6	0	5	17	1	43	10	0	4	4	.500	0	0- -	-	3.50	3.88
2013	LV	AAA	8	0	0	6	11.0	42	5	1	1	0	0	0	0	4	0	8	2	0	0	0	-	0	3- -	-	1.03	0.82
2013	Clrwtr	A+	14	0	0	10	19.2	78	15	3	3	2	0	0	1	5	0	20	0	0	0	1	.000	0	7- -	-	2.52	1.37
2013	Rdng	AA	11	0	0	8	11.0	43	10	3	3	1	0	0	0	3	0	13	2	0	2	1	.667	0	1- -	-	3.22	2.45
2014	LV	AAA	39	0	0	35	46.2	189	35	8	5	0	1	0	1	16	1	52	6	0	2	1	.667	0	22- -	-	1.99	0.96
2013	Phi	NL	24	0	0	6	31.1	138	27	15	13	3	0	1	0	23	0	23	3	0	1	1	.500	0	0-0	1	4.85	3.73
2014	Phi	NL	13	0	0	5	14.0	69	14	12	10	2	1	0	0	13	0	12	4	0	1	0	1.000	0	0-0	0	6.43	6.43
	2 ML YEARS		37	0	0	11	45.1	207	41	27	23	5	1	1	0	36	0	35	7	0	2	1	.667	0	0-0	1	5.33	4.57

Yimi Garcia

Pitches: R **Bats:** R **Pos:** RP-8   YIM-ee   **Ht:** 6'1" **Wt:** 175 **Born:** 8/18/1990 **Age:** 24

Year	Team	Lg	G	GS	CG	GF	IP	BFP	H	R	ER	HR	SH	SF	HB	TBB	IBB	SO	WP	Bk	W	L	Pct	Sh	Sv-Op	Hld	ERC	ERA
2010	Ddgrs	R	13	4	0	3	30.2	146	47	26	24	1	1	3	2	8	0	22	3	0	1	2	.333	0	1- -	-	6.38	7.04
2011	Ogden	R+	20	1	0	10	52.1	223	46	23	18	4	3	2	4	19	2	71	2	2	4	2	.667	0	4- -	-	3.32	3.10
2012	Gt Lks	A	40	0	0	33	41.2	187	42	19	14	0	2	1	1	17	3	60	4	1	4	4	.500	0	14- -	-	3.27	3.02
2012	RCuca	A+	9	0	0	7	10.2	46	7	5	3	0	0	0	0	5	0	22	0	0	2	1	.667	0	2- -	-	1.78	2.53
2013	Chatt	AA	49	0	0	44	60.1	230	35	17	17	9	1	0	2	14	1	85	1	0	4	6	.400	0	19- -	-	1.74	2.54
2014	Albq	AAA	47	0	0	20	61.0	259	58	23	21	5	0	3	5	18	0	69	0	0	4	2	.667	0	5- -	-	3.59	3.10
2014	LAD	NL	8	0	0	5	10.0	36	6	2	2	2	0	0	0	1	0	9	0	0	0	0	-	0	0-0	1	1.59	1.80

Brett Gardner

Bats: L Throws: L Pos: LF-126;CF-25;PH-3;RF-1;DH-1   Ht: 5'10" Wt: 185 Born: 8/24/1983 Age: 31

Year	Team	Lg	G	AB	H	2B	3B	HR	(Hm	Rd)	TB	R	RBI	RC	TBB	IBB	SO	HBP	SH	SF	SB	CS	GDP	Avg	OBP	Slg	OPS
2008	NYY	AL	42	127	29	5	2	0	(0	0)	38	18	16	17	8	0	30	2	3	1	13	1	0	.228	.283	.299	.582
2009	NYY	AL	108	248	67	6	6	3	(1	2)	94	48	23	38	26	0	40	3	6	1	26	5	3	.270	.345	.379	.724
2010	NYY	AL	150	477	132	20	7	5	(5	0)	181	97	47	77	79	1	101	5	5	3	47	9	6	.277	.383	.379	.762
2011	NYY	AL	159	510	132	19	8	7	(4	3)	188	87	36	77	60	1	93	8	8	2	49	13	5	.259	.345	.369	.713
2012	NYY	AL	16	31	10	2	0	0	(0	0)	12	7	3	7	5	0	7	0	1	0	2	2	0	.323	.417	.387	.804
2013	NYY	AL	145	539	147	33	**10**	8	(6	2)	224	81	52	88	52	1	127	8	7	3	24	8	8	.273	.344	.416	.759
2014	NYY	AL	148	555	142	25	8	17	(8	9)	234	87	58	81	56	0	134	6	**13**	6	21	5	3	.256	.327	.422	.749
	Postseason		33	65	14	1	0	0	(0	0)	15	8	7	5	4	0	17	0	2	1	5	2	0	.215	.257	.231	.488
	7 ML YEARS		768	2487	659	110	41	40	(24	16)	971	425	235	385	286	3	532	32	43	16	182	43	25	.265	.346	.390	.737

Matt Garza

Pitches: R Bats: R Pos: SP-27   Ht: 6'4" Wt: 215 Born: 11/26/1983 Age: 31

Year	Team	Lg	G	GS	CG	GF	IP	BFP	H	R	ER	HR	SH	SF	HB	TBB	IBB	SO	WP	Bk	W	L	Pct	Sh	Sv-Op	Hld	ERC	ERA
2006	Min	AL	10	9	0	0	50.0	232	62	33	32	6	0	3	0	23	0	38	1	0	3	6	.333	0	0-0	0	5.82	5.76
2007	Min	AL	16	15	0	1	83.0	367	96	44	34	8	1	4	4	32	4	67	4	0	5	7	.417	0	0-0	0	5.08	3.69
2008	TB	AL	30	30	3	0	184.2	772	170	83	76	19	3	9	6	59	2	128	3	2	11	9	.550	**2**	0-0	0	3.47	3.70
2009	TB	AL	32	32	0	0	203.0	861	177	93	89	25	2	8	11	79	0	189	3	0	8	12	.400	0	0-0	0	3.69	3.95
2010	TB	AL	33	32	3	1	204.2	855	193	94	89	28	1	6	7	63	2	150	12	2	15	10	.600	1	1-1	0	3.80	3.91
2011	ChC	NL	31	31	2	0	198.0	839	186	90	73	14	11	2	3	63	5	197	6	0	10	10	.500	0	0-0	0	3.21	3.32
2012	ChC	NL	18	18	0	0	103.2	424	90	48	45	15	5	1	4	32	0	96	1	0	5	7	.417	0	0-0	0	3.50	3.91
2013	2 Tms		24	24	1	0	155.1	652	150	73	66	20	8	3	5	42	3	136	6	0	10	6	.625	0	0-0	0	3.66	3.82
2014	Mil	NL	27	27	1	0	163.1	680	143	77	66	12	9	4	4	50	2	126	3	1	8	8	.500	1	0-0	0	2.92	3.64
13	ChC	NL	11	11	0	0	71.0	293	61	26	25	8	2	1	4	20	2	62	2	0	6	1	.857	0	0-0	0	3.12	3.17
13	Tex	AL	13	13	1	0	84.1	359	89	47	41	12	6	2	1	22	1	74	4	0	4	5	.444	0	0-0	0	4.14	4.38
	Postseason		5	5	0	0	31.0	131	26	13	12	5	0	1	1	14	0	29	2	0	2	1	.667	0	0-0	0	3.95	3.48
	9 ML YEARS		221	218	10	2	1345.2	5682	1267	635	570	147	40	40	44	443	18	1127	39	5	75	75	.500	4	1-1	0	3.65	3.81

Evan Gattis

Bats: R Throws: R Pos: C-93;PH-14;DH-3   GAT-iss   Ht: 6'4" Wt: 260 Born: 8/18/1986 Age: 28

Year	Team	Lg	G	AB	H	2B	3B	HR	(Hm	Rd)	TB	R	RBI	RC	TBB	IBB	SO	HBP	SH	SF	SB	CS	GDP	Avg	OBP	Slg	OPS
2010	Danvle	R+	60	222	64	10	0	4	(-	-)	86	33	29	30	6	0	44	12	0	2	0	0	4	.288	.339	.387	.726
2011	Rome	A	88	338	109	24	2	22	(-	-)	203	58	71	74	25	1	53	11	1	2	2	4	9	.322	.386	.601	.986
2012	Lynbrg	A+	21	78	30	7	0	9	(-	-)	64	14	29	26	10	2	12	4	0	2	1	1	0	.385	.468	.821	1.289
2012	Missi	AA	49	182	47	13	4	9	(-	-)	95	24	37	33	20	1	29	4	0	1	1	1	14	.258	.343	.522	.865
2012	Braves	R	4	12	6	0	0	0	(-	-)	6	2	1	3	1	0	2	0	0	0	0	0	0	.500	.538	.500	1.038
2013	Gwnntt	AAA	5	21	7	4	0	1	(-	-)	14	1	1	4	0	0	4	1	0	0	0	0	1	.333	.364	.667	1.030
2014	Gwnntt	AAA	4	16	3	0	0	0	(-	-)	3	2	2	0	0	0	7	0	0	0	0	0	1	.188	.188	.188	.375
2013	Atl	NL	105	354	85	21	0	21	(8	13)	170	44	65	43	21	4	81	4	0	3	0	0	10	.243	.291	.480	.771
2014	Atl	NL	108	369	97	17	1	22	(12	10)	182	41	52	45	22	3	97	8	0	2	0	0	9	.263	.317	.493	.810
	Postseason		4	14	5	0	0	0	(0	0)	5	3	1	3	2	0	3	0	0	0	0	0	0	.357	.438	.357	.795
	2 ML YEARS		213	723	183	38	1	43	(20	23)	352	85	117	88	43	7	178	12	0	5	0	0	19	.253	.304	.487	.791

Kevin Gausman

Pitches: R Bats: L Pos: SP-20   GAHZ-man   Ht: 6'3" Wt: 190 Born: 1/6/1991 Age: 24

Year	Team	Lg	G	GS	CG	GF	IP	BFP	H	R	ER	HR	SH	SF	HB	TBB	IBB	SO	WP	Bk	W	L	Pct	Sh	Sv-Op	Hld	ERC	ERA
2012	Abrdn	A-	2	2	0	0	6.0	19	1	0	0	0	0	0	0	0	0	5	0	0	0	0	-	0	0--	0	0.07	0.00
2012	Frdrck	A+	3	3	0	0	9.0	38	10	6	6	3	1	0	0	1	0	8	0	1	0	1	.000	0	0--	0	4.96	6.00
2013	Bowie	AA	8	8	0	0	46.1	191	44	21	16	3	2	2	3	5	0	49	7	0	2	4	.333	0	0--	0	2.66	3.11
2013	Norfolk	AAA	8	7	0	1	35.2	143	36	16	16	1	0	0	1	9	0	33	2	0	1	2	.333	0	0--	0	3.36	4.04
2014	Norfolk	AAA	11	11	0	0	43.1	188	41	18	16	5	1	2	0	18	0	44	1	0	1	3	.250	0	0--	0	3.88	3.32
2014	Abrdn	A-	1	1	0	0	2.0	8	1	1	0	0	0	0	0	1	0	1	0	0	0	0	-	0	0--	0	1.41	0.00
2013	Bal	AL	20	5	0	3	47.2	201	51	30	30	8	2	1	0	13	2	49	4	0	3	5	.375	0	0-2	0	4.41	5.66
2014	Bal	AL	20	20	0	0	113.1	476	111	48	45	7	3	7	1	38	0	88	9	0	7	7	.500	0	0-0	0	3.52	3.57
	2 ML YEARS		40	25	0	3	161.0	677	162	78	75	15	5	8	1	51	2	137	13	0	10	12	.455	0	0-2	2	3.78	4.19

Dillon Gee

Pitches: R Bats: R Pos: SP-22   JEE   Ht: 6'1" Wt: 205 Born: 4/28/1986 Age: 29

Year	Team	Lg	G	GS	CG	GF	IP	BFP	H	R	ER	HR	SH	SF	HB	TBB	IBB	SO	WP	Bk	W	L	Pct	Sh	Sv-Op	Hld	ERC	ERA
2014	Mets*	R	1	1	0	0	2.0	8	1	0	0	0	0	0	0	0	0	2	0	0	0	0	-	0	0--	-	0.47	0.00
2014	Bklyn*	A-	2	2	0	0	8.2	36	7	2	2	0	0	0	1	2	0	16	0	0	0	1	.000	0	0--	-	2.18	2.08
2010	NYM	NL	5	5	0	0	33.0	136	25	10	8	2	3	0	0	15	2	17	0	0	2	2	.500	0	0-0	0	2.66	2.18
2011	NYM	NL	30	27	1	1	160.2	706	150	85	79	18	10	5	14	71	4	114	6	1	13	6	.684	0	0-0	0	4.23	4.43
2012	NYM	NL	17	17	0	0	109.2	463	108	56	50	12	2	3	6	29	0	97	0	1	6	7	.462	0	0-0	0	3.74	4.10
2013	NYM	NL	32	32	2	0	199.0	841	208	84	80	24	9	7	3	47	0	142	4	0	12	11	.522	0	0-0	0	3.97	3.62
2014	NYM	NL	22	22	0	0	137.1	570	128	61	61	18	7	3	5	43	0	94	3	1	7	8	.467	0	0-0	0	3.77	4.00
	5 ML YEARS		106	103	3	1	639.2	2716	619	296	278	74	31	14	32	205	6	464	13	3	40	34	.541	0	0-0	0	3.88	3.91

Steve Geltz

Pitches: R **Bats:** R **Pos:** RP-11   **Ht:** 5'10" **Wt:** 170 **Born:** 11/1/1987 **Age:** 27

		HOW MUCH HE PITCHED						WHAT HE GAVE UP											THE RESULTS						
Year Team	Lg	G	GS	CG	GF	IP	BFP	H	R	ER	HR	SH	SF	HB	TBB	IBB	SO	WP	Bk	W	L	Pct	Sh	Sv-Op	Hld	ERC	ERA
2010 RCuca	A+	22	0	0	9	34.0	134	20	14	13	4	1	0	3	10	0	51	1	1	3	1	.750	0	2- -		2.01	3.44
2010 Ark	AA	16	0	0	7	18.2	79	9	5	5	0	0	0	1	16	1	36	2	0	1	0	1.000	0	0- -		2.46	2.41
2011 Salt Lk	AAA	2	0	0	1	1.2	11	4	4	4	0	0	0	0	2	0	1	0	0	0	0	-	0	0- -		15.90	21.60
2011 Ark	AA	32	0	0	18	46.2	181	31	16	16	5	1	2	1	14	3	67	1	0	3	3	.500	0	0- -		2.07	3.09
2012 Ark	AA	21	0	0	13	25.1	95	13	1	1	0	0	0	1	6	2	37	1	0	3	0	1.000	0	6- -		0.97	0.36
2012 Salt Lk	AAA	25	0	0	11	33.2	141	29	19	19	4	0	2	2	14	0	33	2	0	0	1	.000	0	5- -		3.80	5.08
2013 Drham	AAA	41	0	0	12	67.0	256	35	21	21	8	2	4	1	24	0	80	1	2	5	3	.625	0	3- -		1.73	2.82
2014 Drham	AAA	29	0	0	6	41.2	168	27	11	11	3	1	2	1	17	0	60	5	0	2	3	.400	0	1- -		2.19	2.38
2012 LAA	AL	2	0	0	2	2.0	11	2	1	1	0	0	1	0	3	0	1	0	0	0	0	-	0	0-0	0	7.45	4.50
2014 TB	AL	11	0	0	1	8.1	37	6	3	3	3	0	0	2	5	0	14	0	0	0	1	.000	0	0-1	0	6.25	3.24
2 ML YEARS		13	0	0	3	10.1	48	8	4	4	3	0	1	2	8	0	15	0	0	0	1	.000	0	0-1	0	6.58	3.48

Scooter Gennett

Bats: L **Throws:** R **Pos:** 2B-119;PH-23;RF-1   jen-ETT   **Ht:** 5'10" **Wt:** 170 **Born:** 5/1/1990 **Age:** 25

							BATTING												RUNNING			AVERAGES			
Year Team	Lg	G	AB	H	2B	3B	HR	(Hm	Rd)	TB	R	RBI	RC	TBB	IBB	SO	HBP	SH	SF	SB	CS	GDP	Avg	OBP	Slg	OPS
2010 Wisc	A	118	482	149	39	4	9	(-	-)	223	87	55	81	31	2	91	5	3	4	14	4	6	.309	.354	.463	.817
2011 BrvdCt	A+	134	556	167	20	6	9	(-	-)	226	74	51	76	27	0	69	4	8	6	11	10	9	.300	.334	.406	.740
2012 Hntsvl	AA	133	533	156	30	2	5	(-	-)	205	66	44	70	28	2	71	3	6	3	11	5	15	.293	.330	.385	.714
2013 Nashv	AAA	79	321	90	10	5	3	(-	-)	119	44	22	40	21	1	59	2	3	2	10	5	4	.280	.327	.371	.697
2013 Mil	NL	69	213	69	11	2	6	(0	6)	102	29	21	35	10	0	42	1	5	1	2	1	0	.324	.356	.479	.834
2014 Mil	NL	137	440	127	31	3	9	(6	3)	191	55	54	59	22	5	67	0	8	4	6	3	11	.289	.320	.434	.754
2 ML YEARS		206	653	196	42	5	15	(6	9)	293	84	75	94	32	5	109	1	13	5	8	4	11	.300	.331	.449	.780

Craig Gentry

Bats: R **Throws:** R **Pos:** CF-50;RF-29;LF-17;PH-16;PR-7   JEN-tree   **Ht:** 6'2" **Wt:** 190 **Born:** 11/29/1983 **Age:** 31

							BATTING												RUNNING			AVERAGES			
Year Team	Lg	G	AB	H	2B	3B	HR	(Hm	Rd)	TB	R	RBI	RC	TBB	IBB	SO	HBP	SH	SF	SB	CS	GDP	Avg	OBP	Slg	OPS
2014 Stcktn*	A+	1	4	2	1	0	0	(-	-)	3	0	0	0	0	1	0	0	0	0	0	1	0	.500	.500	.750	1.250
2014 Scrmto*	AAA	4	15	4	0	0	0	(-	-)	4	2	5	1	1	0	4	0	0	2	0	0	0	.267	.278	.267	.544
2009 Tex	AL	11	17	2	1	0	0	(0	0)	3	4	1	1	2	0	5	0	0	0	1	0	1	.118	.211	.176	.387
2010 Tex	AL	20	33	7	0	0	0	(0	0)	7	4	3	1	1	0	11	0	0	1	1	0	1	.212	.229	.212	.441
2011 Tex	AL	64	133	36	5	1	1	(1	0)	46	26	13	21	10	1	27	6	3	1	18	0	2	.271	.347	.346	.693
2012 Tex	AL	122	240	73	12	3	1	(0	1)	94	31	26	33	14	1	41	10	5	0	13	7	4	.304	.367	.392	.759
2013 Tex	AL	106	246	69	12	4	2	(2	0)	95	39	22	42	29	2	46	8	3	1	24	3	5	.280	.373	.386	.759
2014 Oak	AL	94	232	59	6	1	0	(0	0)	67	38	12	27	17	2	44	5	2	0	20	2	2	.254	.319	.289	.608
Postseason		14	17	5	0	0	0	(0	0)	5	2	1	3	1	0	4	1	1	0	2	1	0	.294	.368	.294	.663
6 ML YEARS		417	901	246	36	9	4	(3	1)	312	142	77	125	73	6	174	29	13	3	76	12	14	.273	.346	.346	.692

Justin Germano

Pitches: R **Bats:** R **Pos:** RP-2   jerr-MAHN-oh   **Ht:** 6'2" **Wt:** 210 **Born:** 8/6/1982 **Age:** 32

			HOW MUCH HE PITCHED					WHAT HE GAVE UP												THE RESULTS						
Year Team	Lg	G	GS	CG	GF	IP	BFP	H	R	ER	HR	SH	SF	HB	TBB	IBB	SO	WP	Bk	W	L	Pct	Sh	Sv-Op	Hld	ERC	ERA
2014 RdRck*	AAA	21	21	3	0	131.2	554	145	72	66	22	2	2	8	22	0	82	2	0	4	13	.235	0	0- -		4.46	4.51
2014 Albq*	AAA	3	2	0	0	13.2	62	20	15	15	4	1	0	0	2	0	14	0	0	1	1	.500	0	0- -		7.21	9.88
2004 SD	NL	7	5	0	0	21.1	109	31	24	21	2	3	1	0	14	0	16	0	0	1	2	.333	0	0-0	0	7.69	8.86
2006 Cin	NL	2	1	0	0	6.2	31	8	4	4	1	0	0	1	3	1	8	0	0	0	1	.000	0	0-0	0	6.26	5.40
2007 SD	NL	26	23	0	3	133.1	566	133	72	66	14	4	0	8	40	3	78	1	0	7	10	.412	0	0-0	0	3.93	4.46
2008 SD	NL	12	6	0	4	43.2	194	54	31	29	8	2	1	1	13	2	17	4	0	0	3	.000	0	0-0	0	5.69	5.98
2010 Cle	AL	23	1	0	4	35.1	146	27	15	13	6	1	0	6	8	1	29	0	0	0	3	.000	0	0-1	2	3.17	3.31
2011 Cle	AL	9	0	0	5	12.2	60	15	8	8	1	1	0	2	5	0	5	0	0	0	1	.000	0	0-0	2	5.46	5.68
2012 2 Tms		14	12	0	1	69.2	320	86	52	48	7	5	3	7	21	2	52	5	0	2	10	.167	0	0-0	0	5.32	6.20
2013 Tor	AL	1	0	0	1	2.0	12	6	2	2	1	0	0	0	0	1	0	0	0	0	0	-	0	0-0	0	20.02	9.00
2014 Tex	AL	2	0	0	1	5.1	28	8	7	7	1	0	1	1	3	1	3	0	0	0	0	-	0	0-0	0	8.88	11.81
12 Bos	AL	1	0	0	1	5.2	24	5	0	0	0	0	0	0	2	0	7	1	0	0	0	-	0	0-0	0	2.55	0.00
12 ChC	NL	13	12	0	0	64.0	296	81	52	48	7	5	3	7	19	2	45	4	0	2	10	.167	0	0-0	0	5.59	6.75
9 ML YEARS		96	48	0	19	330.0	1466	368	215	198	41	16	6	26	107	10	209	10	0	10	30	.250	0	0-1	6	4.85	5.40

Gonzalez Germen

Pitches: R **Bats:** R **Pos:** RP-25   hare-MEN   **Ht:** 6'1" **Wt:** 200 **Born:** 9/23/1987 **Age:** 27

			HOW MUCH HE PITCHED					WHAT HE GAVE UP												THE RESULTS						
Year Team	Lg	G	GS	CG	GF	IP	BFP	H	R	ER	HR	SH	SF	HB	TBB	IBB	SO	WP	Bk	W	L	Pct	Sh	Sv-Op	Hld	ERC	ERA
2010 Kngspt	R+	10	10	0	0	61.0	256	64	33	25	3	4	3	4	11	0	54	2	1	2	5	.286	0	0- -		3.41	3.69
2010 Savann	A	2	2	1	0	13.0	51	11	4	4	1	0	0	0	1	0	10	0	0	1	0	1.000	0	0- -		1.93	2.77
2011 Savann	A	26	21	0	3	119.0	511	126	56	52	9	2	2	7	35	0	111	5	2	7	7	.500	0	0- -		4.07	3.93
2012 StLuci	A+	5	4	0	0	26.2	108	25	10	9	3	0	2	0	8	0	21	1	0	3	0	1.000	0	0- -		3.54	3.04
2012 Bnghtn	AA	20	19	0	1	119.2	514	127	72	61	11	5	5	4	33	0	97	9	0	8	12	.400	0	0- -		3.99	4.59
2012 Buffalo	AAA	1	1	0	0	7.0	30	7	4	4	0	0	0	1	2	0	3	1	0	1	0	1.000	0	0- -		3.51	5.14
2013 LsVgs	AAA	35	0	0	8	44.0	188	47	29	27	7	2	1	0	11	0	51	1	0	3	3	.500	0	4- -		4.22	5.52
2014 StLuci	A+	6	0	0	2	5.1	25	5	0	0	0	0	0	0	3	0	8	0	0	0	0	-	0	0- -		3.36	0.00
2014 LsVgs	AAA	18	0	0	13	22.2	98	20	6	6	2	1	0	0	10	1	21	2	0	3	1	.750	0	6- -		3.36	2.38
2013 NYM	NL	29	0	0	9	34.1	149	32	15	15	1	0	0	0	16	1	33	2	0	1	2	.333	0	1-3	1	3.37	3.93
2014 NYM	NL	25	0	0	9	30.1	133	30	16	16	7	1	0	1	14	1	31	1	0	0	0	-	0	0-1	4	5.31	4.75
2 ML YEARS		54	0	0	17	64.2	282	62	31	31	8	1	0	1	30	2	64	3	0	1	2	.333	0	1-4	5	4.26	4.31

Chris Getz

Bats: L **Throws:** R **Pos:** 2B-10;PH-1   GETS   **Ht:** 6'0" **Wt:** 185 **Born:** 8/30/1983 **Age:** 31

Year	Team	Lg	G	AB	H	2B	3B	HR	(Hm	Rd)	TB	R	RBI	RC	TBB	IBB	SO	HBP	SH	SF	SB	CS	GDP	Avg	OBP	Slg	OPS
2014	Buffalo*	AAA	18	68	21	2	0	0	(-	-)	23	8	9	10	8	1	11	0	0	0	6	1	0	.309	.382	.338	.720
2008	CWS	AL	10	7	2	0	0	0	(0	0)	2	2	1	1	0	0	1	0	0	0	1	1	0	.286	.286	.286	.571
2009	CWS	AL	107	375	98	18	4	2	(1	1)	130	49	31	47	30	1	54	6	1	3	25	2	4	.261	.324	.347	.670
2010	KC	AL	72	224	53	9	0	0	(0	0)	62	23	18	21	19	1	28	2	3	0	15	2	3	.237	.302	.277	.579
2011	KC	AL	118	380	97	6	3	0	(0	0)	109	50	26	43	30	0	45	3	14	2	21	7	5	.255	.313	.287	.600
2012	KC	AL	64	189	52	10	3	0	(0	0)	68	22	17	23	11	0	17	0	8	2	9	3	3	.275	.312	.360	.672
2013	KC	AL	78	209	46	6	1	1	(0	1)	57	29	18	16	20	3	24	0	8	0	16	3	9	.220	.288	.273	.561
2014	Tor	AL	10	25	4	1	0	0	(0	0)	5	1	0	0	1	0	4	1	1	0	2	0	1	.160	.222	.200	.422
	7 ML YEARS		459	1409	352	50	11	3	(1	2)	433	176	111	151	111	5	173	12	35	7	89	18	25	.250	.309	.307	.616

Jason Giambi

Bats: L **Throws:** R **Pos:** DH-18;PH-8   jee-AHM-bee   **Ht:** 6'3" **Wt:** 240 **Born:** 1/8/1971 **Age:** 44

Year	Team	Lg	G	AB	H	2B	3B	HR	(Hm	Rd)	TB	R	RBI	RC	TBB	IBB	SO	HBP	SH	SF	SB	CS	GDP	Avg	OBP	Slg	OPS
2014	Akron*	AA	6	17	2	2	0	0	(-	-)	4	1	1	0	2	0	9	0	0	1	0	0	1	.118	.211	.235	.446
1995	Oak	AL	54	176	45	7	0	6	(3	3)	70	27	25	27	28	0	31	3	1	2	2	1	4	.256	.364	.398	.761
1996	Oak	AL	140	536	156	40	1	20	(6	14)	258	84	79	88	51	3	95	5	1	5	0	1	15	.291	.355	.481	.836
1997	Oak	AL	142	519	152	41	2	20	(14	6)	257	66	81	91	55	3	89	6	0	8	0	1	11	.293	.362	.495	.857
1998	Oak	AL	153	562	166	28	0	27	(12	15)	275	92	110	103	81	7	102	5	0	9	2	2	16	.295	.384	.489	.873
1999	Oak	AL	158	575	181	36	1	33	(17	16)	318	115	123	132	105	6	106	7	0	8	1	1	11	.315	.422	.553	.975
2000	Oak	AL	152	510	170	29	1	43	(23	20)	330	108	137	152	137	6	96	9	0	8	2	0	9	.333	.476	.647	1.123
2001	Oak	AL	154	520	178	47	2	38	(27	11)	343	109	120	153	129	24	83	13	0	9	2	0	17	.342	.477	.660	1.137
2002	NYY	AL	155	560	176	34	1	41	(19	22)	335	120	122	139	109	4	112	15	0	5	2	2	18	.314	.435	.598	1.034
2003	NYY	AL	156	535	134	25	0	41	(12	29)	282	97	107	120	129	9	140	21	0	5	2	1	9	.250	.412	.527	.939
2004	NYY	AL	80	264	55	9	0	12	(5	7)	100	33	40	42	47	1	62	8	0	3	0	1	5	.208	.342	.379	.720
2005	NYY	AL	139	417	113	14	0	32	(16	16)	223	74	87	102	108	5	109	19	0	1	0	0	7	.271	.440	.535	.975
2006	NYY	AL	139	446	113	25	0	37	(20	17)	249	92	113	110	110	12	106	16	0	7	2	0	10	.253	.413	.558	.971
2007	NYY	AL	83	254	60	8	0	14	(6	8)	110	31	39	41	40	2	66	8	0	1	1	0	1	.236	.356	.433	.790
2008	NYY	AL	145	458	113	19	1	32	(16	16)	230	68	96	79	76	5	111	22	0	9	2	1	6	.247	.373	.502	.876
2009	2 Tms		102	293	59	14	0	13	(7	6)	112	43	51	44	57	1	80	7	0	2	0	0	6	.201	.343	.382	.725
2010	Col	NL	87	176	43	9	0	6	(4	2)	70	17	35	35	35	5	47	6	0	5	2	0	5	.244	.378	.398	.776
2011	Col	NL	64	131	34	6	0	13	(6	7)	79	20	32	26	17	0	45	3	0	1	0	0	1	.260	.355	.603	.958
2012	Col	NL	60	89	20	4	0	1	(1	0)	27	7	8	14	20	2	24	2	0	0	0	0	4	.225	.372	.303	.675
2013	Cle	AL	71	186	34	8	0	9	(5	4)	69	21	31	22	23	0	56	4	0	3	0	1	8	.183	.282	.371	.653
2014	Cle	AL	26	60	8	2	0	2	(0	2)	16	3	5	2	9	2	12	1	0	0	0	0	3	.133	.257	.267	.524
09	Oak	AL	83	269	52	13	0	11	(7	4)	98	39	40	36	50	1	72	7	0	2	0	0	6	.193	.332	.364	.697
09	Col	NL	19	24	7	1	0	2	(0	2)	14	4	11	8	7	0	8	0	0	0	0	0	0	.292	.452	.583	1.035
	Postseason		45	138	40	6	0	7	(5	2)	67	19	19	25	30	2	30	4	0	2	2	0	3	.290	.425	.486	.911
	20 ML YEARS		2260	7267	2010	405	9	440	(219	221)	3753	1227	1441	1518	1366	97	1572	180	2	93	20	12	166	.277	.399	.516	.916

Johnny Giavotella

Bats: R **Throws:** R **Pos:** 2B-12   gee-uh-vo-TELL-uh   **Ht:** 5'8" **Wt:** 185 **Born:** 7/10/1987 **Age:** 27

Year	Team	Lg	G	AB	H	2B	3B	HR	(Hm	Rd)	TB	R	RBI	RC	TBB	IBB	SO	HBP	SH	SF	SB	CS	GDP	Avg	OBP	Slg	OPS
2014	Omha*	AAA	114	441	136	33	2	7	(-	-)	194	66	61	77	47	4	36	1	0	4	20	4	7	.308	.373	.440	.813
2011	KC	AL	46	178	44	9	4	2	(2	0)	67	20	21	15	6	0	32	1	0	2	5	2	4	.247	.273	.376	.649
2012	KC	AL	53	181	43	7	1	1	(1	0)	55	21	15	14	8	0	35	0	0	0	3	0	0	.238	.270	.304	.574
2013	KC	AL	14	41	9	3	0	0	(0	0)	12	4	4	5	5	0	4	2	0	0	0	0	0	.220	.333	.293	.626
2014	KC	AL	12	37	8	1	0	1	(0	1)	12	8	5	2	1	0	5	2	0	1	0	1	1	.216	.268	.324	.593
	4 ML YEARS		125	437	104	20	5	4	(3	1)	146	53	45	36	20	0	76	5	0	3	8	3	9	.238	.277	.334	.612

Kyle Gibson

Pitches: R **Bats:** R **Pos:** SP-31   **Ht:** 6'6" **Wt:** 210 **Born:** 10/23/1987 **Age:** 27

Year	Team	Lg	G	GS	CG	GF	IP	BFP	H	R	ER	HR	SH	SF	HB	TBB	IBB	SO	WP	Bk	W	L	Pct	Sh	Sv-Op	Hld	ERC	ERA
2010	FtMyrs	A+	7	7	1	0	43.1	169	33	11	9	2	0	0	2	12	0	40	2	0	4	1	.800	1	0- -	-	2.30	1.87
2010	NwBrit	AA	16	16	1	0	93.0	388	91	39	38	5	3	6	4	22	0	77	3	0	7	5	.583	0	0- -	-	3.19	3.68
2010	Roch	AAA	3	3	0	0	15.2	64	12	5	3	0	0	2	1	5	0	9	1	0	0	0	-	0	0- -	-	2.15	1.72
2011	Roch	AAA	18	18	0	0	95.1	419	109	57	51	11	2	3	1	27	1	91	5	0	3	8	.273	0	0- -	-	4.49	4.81
2012	Twins	R	9	7	0	0	14.2	55	9	4	4	1	0	0	0	4	0	16	1	0	0	0	-	0	0- -	-	1.60	2.45
2012	FtMyrs	A+	2	2	0	0	7.0	29	6	2	2	1	1	0	1	1	0	7	0	0	0	0	-	0	0- -	-	3.08	2.57
2012	Roch	AAA	2	2	0	0	6.2	31	11	7	7	1	0	0	0	1	0	10	0	0	0	2	.000	0	0- -	-	7.43	9.45
2013	Roch	AAA	17	17	2	0	101.2	412	85	36	33	5	4	0	0	33	0	87	3	0	7	5	.583	2	0- -	-	2.63	2.92
2013	Min	AL	10	10	0	0	51.0	238	69	38	37	7	0	2	5	20	0	29	4	0	2	4	.333	0	0-0	0	6.98	6.53
2014	Min	AL	31	31	0	0	179.1	757	178	91	89	12	4	3	2	57	0	107	11	0	13	12	.520	0	0-0	0	3.54	4.47
	2 ML YEARS		41	41	0	0	230.1	995	247	129	126	19	4	5	7	77	0	136	15	0	15	16	.484	0	0-0	0	4.24	4.92

Ken Giles

Ht: 6'2" Wt: 205 Born: 9/20/1990 Age: 24

			HOW MUCH HE PITCHED						WHAT HE GAVE UP										THE RESULTS							
Year	Team	Lg	G	GS	CG	GF	IP	BFP	H	R	ER	HR	SH	SF	HB	TBB	IBB	SO	WP	Bk	W	L	Pct	Sh	Sv-Op	Hld	ERC	ERA
2011	Phillies	R	3	0	0	0	4.2	22	6	4	3	1	0	0	1	3	0	7	1	0	1	1	.500	0	0- -	-	9.42	5.79
2012	Lakwd	A	29	6	0	14	67.1	305	54	30	27	5	1	3	6	44	0	86	8	0	3	3	.500	0	5- -	-	4.02	3.61
2012	Clrwtr	A+	10	0	0	4	14.2	62	10	5	5	1	0	1	0	6	0	25	1	0	1	0	1.000	0	3- -	-	2.13	3.07
2013	Clrwtr	A+	24	0	0	12	25.2	120	23	19	18	4	0	3	1	19	0	34	1	0	2	2	.500	0	6- -	-	5.30	6.31
2014	Rdng	AA	13	0	0	12	15.0	57	8	3	2	0	0	0	0	5	0	29	0	0	0	0	-	0	7- -	-	1.20	1.20
2014	LV	AAA	11	0	0	7	13.2	57	10	4	4	0	1	1	1	8	0	9	1	0	2	0	1.000	0	5- -	-	3.00	2.63
2014	Phi	NL	44	0	0	11	45.2	166	25	7	6	1	2	1	0	11	1	64	1	0	3	1	.750	0	1-1	13	1.15	1.18

Conor Gillaspie

gah-LESS-pee Ht: 6'1" Wt: 195 Born: 7/18/1987 Age: 27

			BATTING																		RUNNING			AVERAGES			
Year	Team	Lg	G	AB	H	2B	3B	HR	(Hm	Rd)	TB	R	RBI	RC	TBB	IBB	SO	HBP	SH	SF	SB	CS	GDP	Avg	OBP	Slg	OPS
2014	Charltt*	AAA	3	12	2	0	0	0	(-	-)	5	1	1	0	0	0	2	0	0	0	0	0	1	.167	.167	.417	.583
2008	SF	NL	8	5	1	0	0	0	(0	0)	1	1	0	1	2	0	0	0	0	0	0	0	0	.200	.429	.200	.629
2011	SF	NL	15	19	5	0	0	1	(1	0)	8	2	2	4	2	0	1	0	0	0	0	0	0	.263	.333	.421	.754
2012	SF	NL	6	20	3	1	0	0	(0	0)	4	2	2	0	0	0	2	0	0	0	0	0	0	.150	.150	.200	.350
2013	CWS	AL	134	408	100	14	3	13	(8	5)	159	46	40	46	37	4	79	1	0	6	0	1	7	.245	.305	.390	.695
2014	CWS	AL	130	464	131	31	5	7	(3	4)	193	50	57	68	36	4	78	3	0	3	0	4	5	.282	.336	.416	.752
	5 ML YEARS		293	916	240	46	8	21	(12	9)	365	101	101	119	77	8	160	4	0	9	0	5	12	.262	.319	.398	.718

Cole Gillespie

gil-EH-spee

Ht: 6'1" Wt: 215 Born: 6/20/1984 Age: 31

			BATTING																		RUNNING			AVERAGES			
Year	Team	Lg	G	AB	H	2B	3B	HR	(Hm	Rd)	TB	R	RBI	RC	TBB	IBB	SO	HBP	SH	SF	SB	CS	GDP	Avg	OBP	Slg	OPS
2014	Tacom*	AAA	16	58	21	5	1	5	(-	-)	43	14	14	18	9	0	9	1	0	0	2	0	0	.362	.456	.741	1.197
2014	B Jays*	R	2	6	2	0	0	0	(-	-)	2	0	0	0	1	0	1	0	0	0	0	1	0	.333	.429	.333	.762
2014	Dnedin*	A+	2	8	3	1	0	0	(-	-)	4	1	3	1	1	0	2	0	0	0	0	0	0	.375	.444	.500	.944
2014	Buffalo*	AAA	26	82	29	4	1	2	(-	-)	41	15	16	19	14	0	14	1	0	7	3	0	0	.354	.423	.500	.923
2010	Ari	NL	45	104	24	8	0	2	(2	0)	38	11	12	10	7	1	29	1	0	1	1	1	2	.231	.283	.365	.649
2011	Ari	NL	5	6	2	0	0	1	(1	0)	5	2	4	3	1	0	1	0	0	0	0	0	0	.333	.429	.833	1.262
2013	2 Tms	NL	28	59	12	2	0	0	(0	0)	14	6	4	5	7	1	13	1	1	1	0	0	2	.203	.294	.237	.531
2014	2 Tms	AL	35	74	18	2	0	1	(0	1)	23	9	5	7	6	0	13	0	1	0	2	2	3	.243	.300	.311	.611
13	SF	NL	3	9	0	0	0	0	(0	0)	0	0	0	0	1	1	0	0	0	0	0	0	0	.000	.100	.000	.100
13	ChC	NL	25	50	12	2	0	0	(0	0)	14	6	4	5	6	0	13	1	1	1	0	0	2	.240	.328	.280	.608
14	SF	AL	34	71	18	2	0	1	(0	1)	23	9	5	7	6	0	13	0	1	0	2	2	3	.254	.312	.324	.636
14	Tor	AL	1	3	0	0	0	0	(0	0)	0	0	0	0	0	0	0	0	0	0	0	0	0	.000	.000	.000	.000
	4 ML YEARS		113	243	56	12	0	4	(3	1)	80	28	25	25	21	2	56	2	2	2	3	3	7	.230	.295	.329	.624

Chris Gimenez

JIMM-inn-ezz Ht: 6'2" Wt: 220 Born: 12/27/1982 Age: 32

			BATTING																		RUNNING			AVERAGES			
Year	Team	Lg	G	AB	H	2B	3B	HR	(Hm	Rd)	TB	R	RBI	RC	TBB	IBB	SO	HBP	SH	SF	SB	CS	GDP	Avg	OBP	Slg	OPS
2014	RdRck*	AAA	39	134	38	4	2	6	(-	-)	64	18	22	24	19	1	30	0	0	3	0	1	2	.284	.365	.478	.843
2009	Cle	AL	45	111	16	2	0	3	(0	3)	27	12	7	3	17	0	36	0	1	1	1	1	3	.144	.256	.243	.499
2010	Cle	AL	28	58	11	5	0	1	(1	0)	19	6	8	5	8	0	22	0	1	0	0	0	1	.190	.288	.328	.615
2011	Sea	AL	24	59	12	1	0	1	(0	1)	16	6	6	5	10	0	13	0	0	1	0	1	1	.203	.314	.271	.585
2012	TB	AL	42	100	26	4	0	1	(0	1)	33	10	9	10	8	0	24	0	1	0	0	0	4	.260	.315	.330	.645
2013	TB	AL	4	3	1	1	0	0	(0	0)	2	0	0	0	1	0	1	0	0	0	0	0	1	.333	.500	.667	1.167
2014	2 Tms	AL	42	116	28	10	0	0	(0	0)	38	13	11	12	12	1	29	0	0	0	0	1	3	.241	.313	.328	.640
14	Tex	AL	34	107	28	10	0	0	(0	0)	38	13	11	12	11	1	26	0	0	0	0	1	3	.262	.331	.355	.686
14	Cle	AL	8	9	0	0	0	0	(0	0)	0	0	0	0	1	0	3	0	0	0	0	0	0	.000	.100	.000	.100
	6 ML YEARS		185	447	94	23	0	6	(1	5)	135	47	41	35	56	1	125	0	3	2	1	3	13	.210	.297	.302	.599

Caleb Gindl

GINN-dul Ht: 5'9" Wt: 210 Born: 8/31/1988 Age: 26

			BATTING																		RUNNING			AVERAGES			
Year	Team	Lg	G	AB	H	2B	3B	HR	(Hm	Rd)	TB	R	RBI	RC	TBB	IBB	SO	HBP	SH	SF	SB	CS	GDP	Avg	OBP	Slg	OPS
2010	Hntsvl	AA	128	463	126	33	1	9	(-	-)	188	61	60	71	55	0	78	5	6	5	10	5	3	.272	.352	.406	.758
2011	Nashv	AAA	125	468	145	23	5	15	(-	-)	223	84	60	88	62	2	93	1	2	0	6	5	10	.310	.392	.476	.868
2012	Nashv	AAA	127	452	118	27	5	12	(-	-)	191	54	50	63	37	1	98	2	2	4	4	1	9	.261	.317	.423	.740
2013	Nashv	AAA	83	312	92	21	3	11	(-	-)	152	33	51	54	30	1	72	1	1	2	1	2	10	.295	.358	.487	.846
2014	Nashv	AAA	110	362	82	20	1	8	(-	-)	128	40	32	42	43	3	88	2	1	1	2	2	9	.227	.310	.354	.663
2013	Mil	NL	57	132	32	7	2	5	(3	2)	58	17	14	20	20	1	25	0	2	1	2	1	0	.242	.340	.439	.779
2014	Mil	NL	8	19	3	0	0	0	(0	0)	3	0	0	2	4	0	5	0	0	0	0	0	0	.158	.304	.158	.462
	2 ML YEARS		65	151	35	7	2	5	(3	2)	61	17	14	22	24	1	30	0	2	1	2	1	0	.232	.335	.404	.739

Brad Glenn

Bats: R **Throws:** R **Pos:** RF-4;DH-1;PH-1 **Ht:** 6'2" **Wt:** 220 **Born:** 4/2/1987 **Age:** 28

Year	Team	Lg	G	AB	H	2B	3B	HR	(Hm	Rd)	TB	R	RBI	RC	TBB	IBB	SO	HBP	SH	SF	SB	CS	GDP	Avg	OBP	Slg	OPS
2010	Lnsng	A	109	398	108	21	5	17	(-	-)	190	63	69	67	41	0	100	4	0	4	14	5	3	.271	.342	.477	.820
2011	Dnedin	A+	111	418	110	25	1	26	(-	-)	215	59	80	69	30	1	123	6	0	4	0	0	8	.263	.319	.514	.833
2012	NHam	AA	112	423	101	28	0	19	(-	-)	186	50	63	56	29	0	122	4	0	5	8	4	6	.239	.291	.440	.730
2013	NHam	AA	111	424	112	28	2	17	(-	-)	195	61	69	67	44	1	104	3	1	4	2	2	11	.264	.335	.460	.795
2013	Buffalo	AAA	18	61	15	1	0	5	(-	-)	31	8	10	10	7	0	13	1	0	1	0	0	0	.246	.329	.508	.837
2014	NHam	AA	48	182	42	10	1	9	(-	-)	81	31	23	26	20	0	53	2	0	2	0	0	3	.231	.311	.445	.756
2014	Buffalo	AAA	61	221	67	13	1	6	(-	-)	100	26	37	36	19	0	54	1	1	1	2	1	4	.303	.360	.452	.812
2014	Tor	AL	6	15	1	0	0	0	(0	0)	1	0	0	0	1	0	5	0	0	0	0	0	0	.067	.125	.067	.192

Jake Goebbert

Bats: L **Throws:** L **Pos:** PH-26;1B-25;LF-8 GO-burt **Ht:** 6'0" **Wt:** 205 **Born:** 9/24/1987 **Age:** 27

Year	Team	Lg	G	AB	H	2B	3B	HR	(Hm	Rd)	TB	R	RBI	RC	TBB	IBB	SO	HBP	SH	SF	SB	CS	GDP	Avg	OBP	Slg	OPS
2010	Lxngtn	A	135	519	151	48	1	10	(-	-)	231	91	98	89	52	0	78	11	2	7	14	4	10	.291	.363	.445	.808
2011	Lancst	A+	26	104	27	1	0	5	(-	-)	43	16	18	15	10	0	16	0	1	2	3	0	3	.260	.319	.413	.732
2011	CpChr	AA	75	272	83	18	4	5	(-	-)	124	32	34	45	22	0	47	6	2	2	2	4	6	.305	.368	.456	.823
2011	OKCity	AAA	30	103	30	8	0	2	(-	-)	44	14	15	15	10	0	18	0	1	0	0	1	1	.291	.354	.427	.781
2012	CpChr	AA	114	368	112	23	6	9	(-	-)	174	71	53	72	55	3	57	5	2	3	5	3	6	.304	.399	.473	.872
2012	OKCity	AAA	16	30	4	1	0	0	(-	-)	5	2	1	1	5	0	7	0	0	0	0	0	1	.133	.257	.167	.424
2013	Mdlnd	AA	105	396	106	20	5	18	(-	-)	190	57	75	70	47	5	83	8	1	7	6	3	8	.268	.352	.480	.831
2013	Scrmto	AAA	21	70	16	3	0	4	(-	-)	31	13	6	12	15	1	16	0	0	0	0	0	2	.229	.365	.443	.808
2014	Scrmto	AAA	31	109	28	6	2	6	(-	-)	56	21	25	22	19	1	20	2	0	2	1	0	4	.257	.371	.514	.885
2014	ElPaso	AAA	48	171	55	13	2	8	(-	-)	96	37	35	42	33	0	33	2	0	1	0	0	5	.322	.435	.561	.996
2014	SD	NL	51	101	22	1	3	1	(0	1)	32	12	10	13	12	3	32	2	0	0	2	1	0	.218	.313	.317	.630

Erik Goeddel

Pitches: R **Bats:** R **Pos:** RP-6 gah-DELL **Ht:** 6'3" **Wt:** 190 **Born:** 12/20/1988 **Age:** 26

Year	Team	Lg	G	GS	CG	GF	IP	BFP	H	R	ER	HR	SH	SF	HB	TBB	IBB	SO	WP	Bk	W	L	Pct	Sh	Sv-Op	Hld	ERC	ERA
2010	Mets	R	1	0	0	0	1.0	4	1	0	0	0	0	0	0	0	0	1	1	0	0	0	-	0	0- -	-	1.95	0.00
2011	Savann	A	15	13	0	0	71.2	292	58	29	27	5	2	1	1	24	2	67	5	0	3	5	.375	0	0- -	-	2.65	3.39
2011	Mets	R	3	3	0	0	6.0	23	5	1	1	0	0	0	0	0	0	2	0	0	0	0	-	0	0- -	-	1.37	1.50
2012	StLuci	A+	22	20	0	1	108.1	467	110	51	41	4	4	1	1	43	0	98	13	0	5	6	.455	0	0- -	-	3.75	3.41
2013	Bnghtn	AA	25	25	0	0	134.0	585	135	72	65	14	5	5	7	58	1	125	10	1	9	7	.563	0	0- -	-	4.51	4.37
2014	LsVgs	AAA	49	0	0	17	63.2	296	77	41	38	6	1	4	1	30	0	64	6	0	3	2	.600	0	0- -	-	5.53	5.37
2014	NYM	NL	6	0	0	5	6.2	26	3	2	2	0	0	0	0	4	1	6	1	0	0	0	-	0	0-0	0	1.37	2.70

Ryan Goins

Bats: L **Throws:** R **Pos:** 2B-57;SS-15;PR-2;PH-1 GO-inns **Ht:** 5'10" **Wt:** 185 **Born:** 2/13/1988 **Age:** 27

Year	Team	Lg	G	AB	H	2B	3B	HR	(Hm	Rd)	TB	R	RBI	RC	TBB	IBB	SO	HBP	SH	SF	SB	CS	GDP	Avg	OBP	Slg	OPS
2010	Lnsng	A	77	295	91	19	2	3	(-	-)	123	49	35	48	35	0	60	1	4	3	6	7	4	.308	.380	.417	.797
2010	Dnedin	A+	47	166	34	9	0	0	(-	-)	43	8	18	10	11	0	33	0	3	2	1	1	1	.205	.251	.259	.510
2011	Dnedin	A+	101	353	101	24	5	3	(-	-)	144	50	52	51	32	0	67	0	10	3	2	2	4	.286	.343	.408	.751
2011	B Jays	R	1	3	0	0	0	0	(-	-)	0	0	0	0	0	0	1	0	0	0	0	0	1	.000	.000	.000	.000
2012	NHam	AA	136	546	158	33	4	7	(-	-)	220	66	61	79	47	3	78	0	19	6	15	9	8	.289	.342	.403	.745
2013	Buffalo	AAA	111	377	97	22	1	6	(-	-)	139	42	46	44	29	0	85	1	9	2	3	5	9	.257	.311	.369	.679
2014	Buffalo	AAA	97	363	103	21	2	0	(-	-)	128	36	30	45	28	0	64	2	7	2	4	4	11	.284	.337	.353	.689
2013	Tor	AL	34	119	30	5	0	2	(2	0)	41	11	8	11	2	0	28	0	0	0	0	0	1	.252	.264	.345	.609
2014	Tor	AL	67	181	34	6	3	1	(1	0)	49	14	15	7	5	0	42	0	6	1	0	1	4	.188	.209	.271	.479
	2 ML YEARS		101	300	64	11	3	3	(3	0)	90	25	23	18	7	0	70	0	6	1	0	1	5	.213	.231	.300	.531

Paul Goldschmidt

Bats: R **Throws:** R **Pos:** 1B-109 **Ht:** 6'3" **Wt:** 245 **Born:** 9/10/1987 **Age:** 27

Year	Team	Lg	G	AB	H	2B	3B	HR	(Hm	Rd)	TB	R	RBI	RC	TBB	IBB	SO	HBP	SH	SF	SB	CS	GDP	Avg	OBP	Slg	OPS
2011	Ari	NL	48	156	39	9	1	8	(2	6)	74	28	26	26	20	0	53	0	0	1	4	0	4	.250	.333	.474	.808
2012	Ari	NL	145	514	147	43	1	20	(10	10)	252	82	82	86	60	4	130	4	0	9	18	3	9	.286	.359	.490	.850
2013	Ari	NL	160	602	182	36	3	36	(17	19)	332	103	125	131	99	19	145	3	0	5	15	7	25	.302	.401	.551	.952
2014	Ari	NL	109	406	122	39	1	19	(10	9)	220	75	69	83	64	10	110	2	0	3	9	3	10	.300	.396	.542	.938
	Postseason		4	16	7	0	0	2	(1	1)	13	4	6	5	2	0	5	1	0	1	0	0	0	.438	.526	.813	1.339
	4 ML YEARS		462	1678	490	127	6	83	(39	44)	878	288	302	326	243	33	438	9	0	18	46	13	48	.292	.381	.523	.904

Brandon Gomes

Pitches: R **Bats:** R **Pos:** RP-29 GOHMS **Ht:** 5'11" **Wt:** 195 **Born:** 7/15/1984 **Age:** 30

Year	Team	Lg	G	GS	CG	GF	IP	BFP	H	R	ER	HR	SH	SF	HB	TBB	IBB	SO	WP	Bk	W	L	Pct	Sh	Sv-Op	Hld	ERC	ERA
2014	Drham*	AAA	27	0	0	3	37.1	160	36	18	15	4	1	1	2	12	0	42	1	1	0	2	.000	0	0- -	-	3.80	3.62
2011	TB	AL	40	0	0	17	37.0	160	34	15	12	3	1	3	1	16	0	32	1	0	2	1	.667	0	0-0	5	3.69	2.92
2012	TB	AL	15	0	0	4	17.2	83	16	12	10	2	0	1	2	12	3	15	1	0	2	2	.500	0	0-0	0	4.76	5.09

	HOW MUCH HE PITCHED						WHAT HE GAVE UP												THE RESULTS							
Year Team	Lg	G	GS	CG	GF	IP	BFP	H	R	ER	HR	SH	SF	HB	TBB	IBB	SO	WP	Bk	W	L	Pct	Sh	Sv-Op	Hld	ERC	ERA
2013 TB	AL	26	0	0	9	19.1	83	18	15	14	4	1	2	0	7	3	29	1	0	3	1	.750	0	0-0	0	3.94	6.52
2014 TB	AL	29	0	0	5	34.0	138	28	14	14	5	0	1	0	11	2	24	3	0	2	2	.500	0	0-0	4	3.07	3.71
Postseason		3	0	0	0	2.1	10	1	2	2	1	0	0	0	2	0	3	0	0	0	0	-	0	0-0	0	4.86	7.71
4 ML YEARS		110	0	0	35	108.0	464	96	56	50	14	2	7	3	46	8	100	6	0	9	6	.600	0	0-0	9	3.72	4.17

Jonny Gomes

Bats: R **Throws:** R **Pos:** LF-84;PH-36;RF-11;DH-10;PR-1 GOHMS **Ht:** 6'1" **Wt:** 230 **Born:** 11/22/1980 **Age:** 34

		BATTING																	RUNNING			AVERAGES			
Year Team	Lg	G	AB	H	2B	3B	HR	(Hm	Rd)	TB	R	RBI	RC	TBB	IBB	SO	HBP	SH	SF	SB	CS	GDP	Avg	OBP	Slg	OPS
2003 TB	AL	8	15	2	1	0	0	(0	0)	3	1	0	0	0	0	6	1	0	0	0	0	0	.133	.188	.200	.388
2004 TB	AL	5	14	1	0	0	0	(0	0)	1	0	1	0	1	0	6	0	0	0	0	0	0	.071	.133	.071	.205
2005 TB	AL	101	348	98	13	6	21	(11	10)	186	61	54	62	39	1	113	14	1	5	9	5	6	.282	.372	.534	.906
2006 TB	AL	117	385	83	21	1	20	(7	13)	166	53	59	53	61	2	116	6	0	9	1	5	10	.216	.325	.431	.757
2007 TB	AL	107	348	85	20	2	17	(10	7)	160	48	49	47	35	1	126	7	0	4	12	4	1	.244	.322	.460	.782
2008 TB	AL	77	154	28	5	1	8	(2	6)	59	23	21	18	15	1	46	7	0	1	8	1	1	.182	.282	.383	.666
2009 Cin	NL	98	281	75	17	0	20	(11	9)	152	39	51	47	26	2	85	5	0	2	3	1	3	.267	.338	.541	.879
2010 Cin	NL	148	511	136	24	3	18	(11	7)	220	77	86	83	39	3	123	12	0	9	5	3	4	.266	.327	.431	.758
2011 2 Tms	NL	120	311	65	12	1	14	(6	8)	121	41	43	36	48	1	105	8	0	5	7	3	2	.209	.325	.389	.714
2012 Oak	AL	99	279	73	10	0	18	(7	11)	137	46	47	54	44	2	104	8	1	1	3	1	2	.262	.377	.491	.868
2013 Bos	AL	116	312	77	17	0	13	(5	8)	133	49	52	54	43	3	89	6	0	5	1	0	6	.247	.344	.426	.771
2014 2 Tms	AL	112	273	64	8	0	6	(4	2)	90	28	37	36	35	2	88	6	0	7	0	0	6	.234	.327	.330	.657
11 Cin	NL	77	218	46	8	0	11	(7	4)	87	30	31	28	38	1	74	5	0	4	5	3	1	.211	.336	.399	.735
11 Was	NL	43	93	19	4	1	3	(1	2)	34	11	12	8	10	0	31	3	0	1	2	0	1	.204	.299	.366	.665
14 Bos	AL	78	209	49	7	0	6	(4	2)	74	22	32	30	26	0	70	6	0	5	0	0	5	.234	.329	.354	.683
14 Oak	AL	34	64	15	1	0	0	(0	0)	16	6	5	6	9	2	18	0	0	2	0	0	1	.234	.330	.250	.570
Postseason		18	49	7	2	0	1	(0	1)	12	8	5	3	5	2	15	1	0	0	0	0	2	.143	.236	.245	.481
12 ML YEARS		1108	3231	787	148	14	155	(76	79)	1428	466	500	490	386	18	1007	80	2	48	49	23	46	.244	.335	.442	.777

Yan Gomes

Bats: R **Throws:** R **Pos:** C-126;DH-8;PH-4 YAHN GOHMS **Ht:** 6'2" **Wt:** 215 **Born:** 7/19/1987 **Age:** 27

		BATTING																	RUNNING			AVERAGES			
Year Team	Lg	G	AB	H	2B	3B	HR	(Hm	Rd)	TB	R	RBI	RC	TBB	IBB	SO	HBP	SH	SF	SB	CS	GDP	Avg	OBP	Slg	OPS
2012 Tor	AL	43	98	20	4	0	4	(3	1)	36	9	13	11	6	0	32	3	1	3	0	0	3	.204	.264	.367	.631
2013 Cle	AL	88	293	86	18	2	11	(6	5)	141	45	38	42	18	0	67	7	0	4	2	0	12	.294	.345	.481	.826
2014 Cle	AL	135	485	135	25	3	21	(9	12)	229	61	74	65	24	3	120	3	0	6	0	0	13	.278	.313	.472	.785
Postseason		1	4	2	1	0	0	(0	0)	3	0	0	0	0	0	0	0	0	0	0	0	0	.500	.500	.750	1.250
3 ML YEARS		266	876	241	47	5	36	(18	18)	406	115	125	118	48	3	219	13	1	13	2	0	28	.275	.318	.463	.781

Carlos Gomez

Bats: R **Throws:** R **Pos:** CF-145;DH-1;PH-1;PR-1 **Ht:** 6'3" **Wt:** 220 **Born:** 12/4/1985 **Age:** 29

		BATTING																	RUNNING			AVERAGES			
Year Team	Lg	G	AB	H	2B	3B	HR	(Hm	Rd)	TB	R	RBI	RC	TBB	IBB	SO	HBP	SH	SF	SB	CS	GDP	Avg	OBP	Slg	OPS
2007 NYM	NL	58	125	29	3	0	2	(1	1)	38	14	12	11	8	2	27	3	0	3	12	3	0	.232	.288	.304	.592
2008 Min	AL	153	577	149	24	7	7	(3	4)	208	79	59	66	25	0	142	7	3	2	33	11	7	.258	.296	.360	.657
2009 Min	AL	137	315	72	15	5	3	(1	2)	106	51	28	33	22	0	72	4	7	1	14	7	1	.229	.287	.337	.623
2010 Mil	NL	97	291	72	11	3	5	(3	2)	104	38	24	28	17	1	72	4	6	0	18	3	10	.247	.298	.357	.655
2011 Mil	NL	94	231	52	11	3	8	(4	4)	93	37	24	25	15	0	64	2	8	2	16	2	2	.225	.276	.403	.679
2012 Mil	NL	137	415	108	19	4	19	(11	8)	192	72	51	59	20	1	98	8	6	3	37	6	6	.260	.305	.463	.768
2013 Mil	NL	147	536	152	27	10	24	(15	9)	271	80	73	81	37	2	146	10	1	6	40	7	11	.284	.338	.506	.843
2014 Mil	NL	148	574	163	34	4	23	(13	10)	274	95	73	98	47	0	141	19	1	3	34	12	11	.284	.356	.477	.833
Postseason		9	18	5	0	0	1	(0	1)	8	4	2	2	1	0	4	2	2	0	2	1	0	.278	.381	.444	.825
8 ML YEARS		971	3064	797	144	36	91	(51	40)	1286	466	344	401	191	6	762	57	32	20	204	51	48	.260	.314	.420	.733

Hector Gomez

Bats: R **Throws:** R **Pos:** SS-7;3B-6;PR-3;PH-2;2B-1 **Ht:** 6'3" **Wt:** 200 **Born:** 3/5/1988 **Age:** 27

		BATTING																	RUNNING			AVERAGES			
Year Team	Lg	G	AB	H	2B	3B	HR	(Hm	Rd)	TB	R	RBI	RC	TBB	IBB	SO	HBP	SH	SF	SB	CS	GDP	Avg	OBP	Slg	OPS
2010 Tulsa	AA	9	35	11	4	0	0	(-	-)	15	6	3	4	0	0	8	0	0	0	0	0	0	.314	.314	.429	.743
2010 TriCity	A-	18	69	17	2	1	2	(-	-)	27	8	7	7	5	0	15	0	0	1	0	3	2	.246	.293	.391	.685
2011 Tulsa	AA	102	425	100	23	6	14	(-	-)	177	46	50	50	19	1	94	3	5	1	16	4	9	.235	.272	.416	.689
2012 Mdest	A+	3	8	3	0	1	0	(-	-)	5	2	3	2	2	0	4	0	0	0	1	0	0	.375	.500	.625	1.125
2012 BrvdCt	A+	23	76	8	3	1	1	(-	-)	16	9	8	1	4	0	19	3	1	1	0	0	4	.105	.179	.211	.389
2013 Hntsvl	AA	113	368	72	12	2	2	(-	-)	94	23	25	18	18	0	77	3	16	1	6	9	7	.196	.238	.255	.494
2014 Nashv	AAA	121	408	115	26	6	15	(-	-)	197	59	49	65	21	1	80	7	2	4	5	3	13	.282	.325	.483	.808
2011 Col	NL	2	6	2	0	0	0	(0	0)	2	1	0	0	1	1	2	0	0	0	0	0	0	.333	.429	.333	.762
2014 Mil	NL	15	20	3	1	0	0	(0	0)	4	2	1	1	1	0	9	0	0	0	0	0	0	.150	.190	.200	.390
2 ML YEARS		17	26	5	1	0	0	(0	0)	6	3	1	1	2	1	11	0	0	0	0	0	0	.192	.250	.231	.481

Jeanmar Gomez

Pitches: R **Bats:** R **Pos:** RP-44   JENN-marr   **Ht:** 6'3" **Wt:** 220 **Born:** 2/10/1988 **Age:** 27

			HOW MUCH HE PITCHED					WHAT HE GAVE UP										THE RESULTS						
Year	Team	Lg	G	GS	CG	GF	IP	BFP	H	R	ER	HR	SH	SF	HB	TBB	IBB	SO	WP	Bk	W	L	Pct	Sh	Sv-Op	Hld	ERC	ERA
2010	Cle	AL	11	11	0	0	57.2	265	73	36	30	7	0	3	2	22	3	34	1	0	4	5	.444	0	0-0	0	5.75	4.68
2011	Cle	AL	11	10	0	0	58.1	259	73	31	29	6	0	2	1	15	1	31	2	0	5	3	.625	0	0-0	0	4.99	4.47
2012	Cle	AL	20	17	0	1	90.2	395	95	66	60	15	2	7	4	34	5	47	2	0	5	8	.385	0	0-0	0	4.83	5.96
2013	Pit	NL	34	8	0	6	80.2	333	65	35	30	6	4	6	3	28	3	53	6	0	3	0	1.000	0	0-0	3	2.75	3.35
2014	Pit	NL	44	0	0	20	62.0	270	70	24	22	6	3	2	2	23	7	38	2	0	2	2	.500	0	1-1	2	4.70	3.19
Postseason			1	0	0	0	4.0	17	3	2	0	0	1	0	0	2	0	0	0	0	0	0	-	0	0-0	0	2.40	0.00
5 ML YEARS			120	46	0	27	349.1	1522	376	192	171	40	9	20	12	122	19	203	13	0	19	18	.514	0	1-1	5	4.47	4.41

Marco Gonzales

Pitches: L **Bats:** L **Pos:** SP-5; RP-5   **Ht:** 6'1" **Wt:** 195 **Born:** 2/16/1992 **Age:** 23

			HOW MUCH HE PITCHED					WHAT HE GAVE UP										THE RESULTS						
Year	Team	Lg	G	GS	CG	GF	IP	BFP	H	R	ER	HR	SH	SF	HB	TBB	IBB	SO	WP	Bk	W	L	Pct	Sh	Sv-Op	Hld	ERC	ERA
2013	Cards	R	4	2	0	0	6.2	32	8	5	4	0	0	0	0	3	0	10	2	0	0	0	-	0	0--	-	4.37	5.40
2013	PlmBh	A+	4	4	0	0	16.2	61	10	3	3	1	0	0	0	5	0	13	0	0	0	0	-	0	0--	-	1.63	1.62
2014	PlmBh	A+	6	6	0	0	37.2	150	34	8	6	1	0	0	0	8	0	32	0	0	2	2	.500	0	0--	-	2.44	1.43
2014	Sprgfld	AA	7	7	0	0	38.2	160	33	14	10	2	0	0	0	10	1	46	2	0	3	2	.600	0	0--	-	2.37	2.33
2014	Memp	AA	8	8	0	0	45.2	188	43	18	17	7	4	1	3	9	0	39	2	0	4	1	.800	0	0--	-	3.58	3.35
2014	StL	NL	10	5	0	0	34.2	156	32	16	16	4	0	1	1	21	1	31	0	0	4	2	.667	0	0-0	1	4.59	4.15

Adrian Gonzalez

Bats: L **Throws:** L **Pos:** 1B-157;PH-4;DH-1   **Ht:** 6'2" **Wt:** 225 **Born:** 5/8/1982 **Age:** 33

			BATTING																	RUNNING			AVERAGES			
Year	Team	Lg	G	AB	H	2B	3B	HR	(Hm	Rd)	TB	R	RBI	RC	TBB	IBB	SO	HBP	SH	SF	SB	CS	GDP	Avg	OBP	Slg	OPS
2004	Tex	AL	16	42	10	3	0	1	(1	0)	16	7	7	7	2	0	6	0	0	0	0	0	0	.238	.273	.381	.654
2005	Tex	AL	43	150	34	7	1	6	(3	3)	61	17	17	13	10	2	37	0	0	2	0	0	3	.227	.272	.407	.678
2006	SD	NL	156	570	173	38	1	24	(10	14)	285	83	82	82	52	9	113	3	1	5	0	1	24	.304	.362	.500	.862
2007	SD	NL	161	646	182	46	3	30	(10	20)	324	101	100	108	65	9	140	3	0	6	0	0	24	.282	.347	.502	.849
2008	SD	NL	162	616	172	32	1	36	(14	22)	314	103	119	107	74	18	142	7	0	3	0	0	24	.279	.361	.510	.871
2009	SD	NL	160	552	153	27	2	40	(12	28)	304	90	99	109	119	22	109	5	1	4	1	1	33	.277	.407	.551	.958
2010	SD	NL	160	591	176	33	0	31	(11	20)	302	87	101	122	93	35	114	2	2	4	0	0	15	.298	.393	.511	.904
2011	Bos	AL	159	630	213	45	3	27	(10	17)	345	108	117	121	74	20	119	6	0	5	1	0	28	.338	.410	.548	.957
2012	2 Tms		159	629	188	47	1	18	(9	9)	291	75	108	113	42	5	110	5	0	8	2	0	10	.299	.344	.463	.806
2013	LAD	NL	157	583	171	32	0	22	(11	11)	269	69	100	89	47	6	98	1	0	10	0	0	12	.293	.342	.461	.803
2014	LAD	NL	159	591	163	41	0	27	(13	14)	285	83	116	95	56	9	112	2	0	11	1	1	13	.276	.335	.482	.817
12	Bos	AL	123	484	145	37	0	15	(8	7)	227	63	86	89	31	4	81	5	0	7	0	0	9	.300	.343	.469	.812
12	LAD	NL	36	145	43	10	1	3	(1	2)	64	12	22	24	11	1	29	0	0	1	2	0	1	.297	.344	.441	.785
Postseason			14	52	17	2	0	3	(2	1)	28	9	7	6	6	1	10	0	0	0	0	0	1	.327	.397	.538	.935
11 ML YEARS			1492	5600	1635	351	12	262	(104	158)	2796	823	966	966	634	135	1100	34	4	58	6	3	158	.292	.364	.499	.863

Alex Gonzalez

Bats: R **Throws:** R **Pos:** SS-9;3B-1   **Ht:** 6'1" **Wt:** 210 **Born:** 2/15/1977 **Age:** 38

			BATTING																	RUNNING			AVERAGES			
Year	Team	Lg	G	AB	H	2B	3B	HR	(Hm	Rd)	TB	R	RBI	RC	TBB	IBB	SO	HBP	SH	SF	SB	CS	GDP	Avg	OBP	Slg	OPS
1998	Fla	NL	25	86	13	2	0	3	(1	2)	24	11	7	5	9	0	30	1	2	0	0	0	0	.151	.240	.279	.519
1999	Fla	NL	136	560	155	28	8	14	(7	7)	241	81	59	69	15	0	113	12	1	3	3	5	13	.277	.308	.430	.739
2000	Fla	NL	109	385	77	17	4	7	(5	2)	123	35	42	26	13	0	77	2	5	2	7	1	7	.200	.229	.319	.548
2001	Fla	NL	145	515	129	36	1	9	(5	4)	194	57	48	56	30	6	107	10	3	3	2	2	13	.250	.303	.377	.680
2002	Fla	NL	42	151	34	7	1	2	(1	1)	49	15	18	14	12	1	32	4	3	2	3	1	2	.225	.296	.325	.620
2003	Fla	NL	150	528	135	33	6	18	(7	11)	234	52	77	67	33	13	106	13	3	5	0	4	8	.256	.313	.443	.756
2004	Fla	NL	159	561	130	30	3	23	(13	10)	235	67	79	58	27	9	126	4	3	4	3	1	17	.232	.270	.419	.689
2005	Fla	NL	130	435	115	30	0	5	(2	3)	160	45	45	47	31	10	81	5	4	3	5	3	16	.264	.319	.368	.686
2006	Bos	AL	111	388	99	24	2	9	(4	5)	154	48	50	40	22	1	67	5	7	7	1	0	6	.255	.299	.397	.695
2007	Cin	NL	110	393	107	27	1	16	(8	8)	184	55	55	51	24	1	75	8	2	3	0	1	13	.272	.325	.468	.793
2009	2 Tms		112	391	93	22	0	8	(7	1)	139	42	41	40	20	4	65	4	10	4	2	1	7	.238	.279	.355	.635
2010	2 Tms		157	595	149	42	3	23	(11	12)	266	74	88	75	31	2	118	7	3	4	1	2	16	.250	.294	.447	.741
2011	Atl	NL	149	564	136	27	1	15	(7	8)	210	59	56	50	22	1	126	1	4	2	0	0	19	.241	.270	.372	.642
2012	Mil	NL	24	81	21	4	0	4	(1	3)	37	8	15	12	6	0	15	2	0	0	1	1	1	.259	.326	.457	.783
2013	Mil	NL	41	113	20	3	0	1	(1	0)	26	14	8	2	3	0	26	1	0	1	0	0	1	.177	.203	.230	.433
2014	Det	AL	9	30	5	0	1	0	(0	0)	7	4	2	2	2	0	4	0	0	0	0	0	2	.167	.219	.233	.452
09	Cin	NL	68	243	51	12	0	3	(2	1)	72	16	26	25	15	4	36	2	6	4	0	1	3	.210	.258	.296	.554
09	Bos	AL	44	148	42	10	0	5	(5	0)	67	26	15	15	5	0	29	2	4	0	2	0	4	.284	.316	.453	.769
10	Tor	AL	85	328	85	25	1	17	(8	9)	163	47	50	47	17	0	65	1	0	2	1	0	9	.259	.296	.497	.793
10	Atl	NL	72	267	64	17	2	6	(3	3)	103	27	38	28	14	2	53	6	3	2	0	2	7	.240	.291	.386	.676
Postseason			24	83	14	5	0	1	(1	0)	22	8	8	3	2	0	22	0	1	0	0	1	2	.169	.188	.265	.453
16 ML YEARS			1609	5776	1418	332	31	157	(80	77)	2283	667	690	614	300	48	1168	79	50	43	30	22	138	.245	.290	.395	.685

Carlos Gonzalez

Bats: L **Throws:** L **Pos:** LF-48;RF-17;PH-3;DH-2   **Ht:** 6'1" **Wt:** 220 **Born:** 10/17/1985 **Age:** 29

			BATTING																	RUNNING			AVERAGES			
Year	Team	Lg	G	AB	H	2B	3B	HR	(Hm	Rd)	TB	R	RBI	RC	TBB	IBB	SO	HBP	SH	SF	SB	CS	GDP	Avg	OBP	Slg	OPS
2014	ColSpr*	AAA	4	13	5	1	1	2	(-	-)	14	4	6	5	1	0	3	1	0	0	0	0	0	.385	.467	1.077	1.544
2008	Oak	AL	85	302	73	22	1	4	(3	1)	109	31	26	30	13	1	81	0	1	4	1	7	.242	.273	.361	.634
2009	Col	NL	89	278	79	14	7	13	(7	6)	146	53	29	42	28	5	70	3	5	3	16	4	3	.284	.353	.525	.878
2010	Col	NL	145	587	197	34	9	34	(26	8)	351	111	117	118	40	8	135	2	0	7	26	8	9	.336	.376	.598	.974

Year	Team	Lg	G	AB	H	2B	3B	HR	(Hm	Rd)	TB	R	RBI	RC	TBB	IBB	SO	HBP	SH	SF	SB	CS	GDP	Avg	OBP	Slg	OPS
2011	Col	NL	127	481	142	27	3	26	(16	10)	253	92	92	95	48	8	105	7	0	6	20	5	11	.295	.363	.526	.889
2012	Col	NL	135	518	157	31	5	22	(13	9)	264	89	85	88	56	11	115	2	0	3	20	5	11	.303	.371	.510	.881
2013	Col	NL	110	391	118	23	6	26	(12	14)	231	72	70	69	41	2	118	1	0	3	21	3	7	.302	.367	.591	.958
2014	Col	NL	70	260	62	15	1	11	(5	6)	112	35	38	32	19	2	70	1	0	1	3	0	7	.238	.292	.431	.723
Postseason			4	17	10	2	0	1	(1	0)	15	5	1	5	2	0	1	0	0	0	2	1	0	.588	.632	.882	1.514
7 ML YEARS			761	2817	828	166	32	136	(82	54)	1466	483	457	474	245	35	694	16	6	23	110	26	55	.294	.351	.520	.872

Gio Gonzalez

Pitches: L Bats: R Pos: SP-27   JEE-oh   Ht: 6'0" Wt: 205 Born: 9/19/1985 Age: 29

			HOW MUCH HE PITCHED							WHAT HE GAVE UP										THE RESULTS						
Year	Team	Lg	G	GS	CG	GF	IP	BFP	H	R	ER	HR	SH	SF	HB	TBB	IBB	SO	WP	Bk	W	L	Pct	Sh	Sv-Op	Hld	ERC	ERA
2014	Ptomc*	A+	2	2	0	0	7.2	41	9	9	9	1	0	0	1	8	0	9	0	0	0	0	0--	0	0--	-	8.48	10.57
2008	Oak	AL	10	7	0	3	34.0	163	32	34	29	9	2	1	3	25	1	34	1	0	1	4	.200	0	0-0	0	6.54	7.68
2009	Oak	AL	20	17	0	0	98.2	455	113	68	63	14	2	3	1	56	2	109	2	0	6	7	.462	0	0-0	0	5.96	5.75
2010	Oak	AL	33	33	1	0	200.2	851	171	75	72	15	5	2	4	92	1	171	4	1	15	9	.625	0	0-0	0	3.39	3.23
2011	Oak	AL	32	32	0	0	202.0	864	175	81	70	17	3	2	8	91	1	197	6	1	16	12	.571	0	0-0	0	3.56	3.12
2012	Was	NL	32	32	2	0	199.1	822	149	69	64	9	9	7	5	76	3	207	10	1	21	8	.724	1	0-0	0	2.37	2.89
2013	Was	NL	32	32	1	0	195.2	819	169	79	73	17	7	1	2	76	1	192	4	1	11	8	.579	1	0-0	0	3.23	3.36
2014	Was	NL	27	27	0	0	158.2	653	134	66	63	10	7	4	3	56	0	162	2	0	10	10	.500	0	0-0	0	2.91	3.57
Postseason			2	2	0	0	10.0	45	6	5	5	0	0	1	0	11	0	10	2	0	0	0	-	0	0-0	0	3.81	4.50
7 ML YEARS			186	180	4	3	1089.0	4627	943	472	434	91	35	20	26	472	9	1072	29	4	80	58	.580	2	0-0	0	3.43	3.59

Marwin Gonzalez

MARR-win

Bats: B Throws: R Pos: SS-71;2B-11;PR-11;3B-10;PH-9;LF-4;DH-3;1B-1;RF-1   Ht: 6'1" Wt: 205 Born: 3/14/1989 Age: 26

			BATTING																	RUNNING			AVERAGES			
Year	Team	Lg	G	AB	H	2B	3B	HR	(Hm	Rd)	TB	R	RBI	RC	TBB	IBB	SO	HBP	SH	SF	SB	CS	GDP	Avg	OBP	Slg	OPS
2012	Hou	NL	80	205	48	13	0	1	(1	1)	67	21	12	12	13	0	29	0	1	0	3	3	9	.234	.280	.327	.607
2013	Hou	AL	72	204	45	8	0	4	(2	2)	65	22	14	10	9	0	37	0	8	1	6	2	5	.221	.252	.319	.571
2014	Hou	AL	103	285	79	15	1	6	(3	3)	114	33	23	26	17	0	58	4	4	0	2	4	6	.277	.327	.400	.727
3 ML YEARS			255	694	172	36	1	12	(6	6)	246	76	49	48	39	0	124	4	13	1	11	9	20	.248	.291	.354	.646

Miguel Gonzalez

Pitches: R Bats: R Pos: SP-26; RP-1   Ht: 6'1" Wt: 170 Born: 5/27/1984 Age: 31

			HOW MUCH HE PITCHED							WHAT HE GAVE UP										THE RESULTS						
Year	Team	Lg	G	GS	CG	GF	IP	BFP	H	R	ER	HR	SH	SF	HB	TBB	IBB	SO	WP	Bk	W	L	Pct	Sh	Sv-Op	Hld	ERC	ERA
2014	Bowie*	AA	1	1	0	0	4.1	21	4	0	0	0	0	0	0	1	0	5	1	0	0	0	-	0	0--	-	2.51	0.00
2014	Norfolk*	AAA	2	2	0	0	9.0	35	6	3	3	1	0	0	0	2	0	1	2	0	1	0	1.000	0	0--	-	1.79	3.00
2012	Bal	AL	18	15	0	0	105.1	434	92	38	38	13	1	2	5	35	2	77	3	2	9	4	.692	0	0-0	0	3.49	3.25
2013	Bal	AL	30	28	0	0	171.1	712	157	81	72	24	3	6	3	53	3	120	4	0	11	8	.579	0	0-0	0	3.58	3.78
2014	Bal	AL	27	26	1	0	159.0	671	155	61	57	25	0	3	8	51	1	111	4	1	10	9	.526	1	0-0	0	4.25	3.23
Postseason			1	1	0	0	7.0	25	5	1	1	0	0	0	0	0	0	8	0	0	0	0	-	0	0-0	0	1.08	1.29
3 ML YEARS			75	69	1	1	435.2	1817	404	180	167	62	4	11	16	139	6	308	11	3	30	21	.588	1	0-0	0	3.80	3.45

Miguel Gonzalez

Pitches: R Bats: R Pos: RP-6   Ht: 6'3" Wt: 200 Born: 9/23/1986 Age: 28

			HOW MUCH HE PITCHED							WHAT HE GAVE UP										THE RESULTS						
Year	Team	Lg	G	GS	CG	GF	IP	BFP	H	R	ER	HR	SH	SF	HB	TBB	IBB	SO	WP	Bk	W	L	Pct	Sh	Sv-Op	Hld	ERC	ERA
2014	Clrwtr	A+	8	3	0	0	15.1	73	20	11	8	0	0	1	0	9	0	11	2	1	0	2	.000	0	0--	-	5.82	4.70
2014	Rdng	AA	11	0	0	9	14.1	59	10	5	5	2	0	0	0	7	0	24	0	0	0	2	.000	0	5--	-	3.05	3.14
2014	LV	AAA	12	0	0	7	16.2	69	10	4	3	0	0	0	1	10	1	19	1	0	0	0	-	0	2--	-	2.20	1.62
2014	Phi	NL	6	0	0	4	5.1	29	9	4	4	1	0	0	0	3	0	5	0	0	0	1	.000	0	0-0	0	9.34	6.75

Alex Gordon

Bats: L Throws: R Pos: LF-156   Ht: 6'1" Wt: 220 Born: 2/10/1984 Age: 31

			BATTING																	RUNNING			AVERAGES			
Year	Team	Lg	G	AB	H	2B	3B	HR	(Hm	Rd)	TB	R	RBI	RC	TBB	IBB	SO	HBP	SH	SF	SB	CS	GDP	Avg	OBP	Slg	OPS
2007	KC	AL	151	543	134	36	4	15	(8	7)	223	60	60	69	41	4	137	13	1	2	14	4	12	.247	.314	.411	.725
2008	KC	AL	134	493	128	35	1	16	(9	7)	213	72	59	71	66	5	120	6	1	5	9	2	8	.260	.351	.432	.783
2009	KC	AL	49	164	38	6	0	6	(2	4)	62	28	22	16	21	0	43	2	1	1	5	0	5	.232	.324	.378	.703
2010	KC	AL	74	242	52	10	0	8	(5	3)	86	34	20	23	34	1	62	2	2	1	1	5	9	.215	.315	.355	.671
2011	KC	AL	151	611	185	45	4	23	(12	11)	307	101	87	103	67	7	139	7	0	3	17	8	9	.303	.376	.502	.879
2012	KC	AL	161	642	189	51	5	14	(6	8)	292	93	72	94	73	3	140	3	0	3	10	5	14	.294	.368	.455	.822
2013	KC	AL	156	633	168	27	6	20	(10	10)	267	90	81	90	52	7	141	9	0	6	11	3	4	.265	.327	.422	.749
2014	KC	AL	156	563	150	34	1	19	(11	8)	243	87	74	95	65	5	126	11	0	4	12	3	11	.266	.351	.432	.783
8 ML YEARS			1032	3891	1044	244	21	121	(63	58)	1693	565	475	561	419	27	908	53	5	25	79	30	72	.268	.345	.435	.781

Dee Gordon

Bats: L **Throws:** R **Pos:** 2B-144;PH-8   **Ht:** 5'11" **Wt:** 170 **Born:** 4/22/1988 **Age:** 27

Year	Team	Lg	G	AB	H	2B	3B	HR	(Hm	Rd)	TB	R	RBI	RC	TBB	IBB	SO	HBP	SH	SF	SB	CS	GDP	Avg	OBP	Slg	OPS
2011	LAD	NL	56	224	68	9	2	0	(0	0)	81	34	11	25	7	0	27	0	2	0	24	7	1	.304	.325	.362	.686
2012	LAD	NL	87	303	69	9	2	1	(0	1)	85	38	17	22	20	0	62	3	2	2	32	10	5	.228	.280	.281	.561
2013	LAD	NL	38	94	22	1	1	1	(1	0)	28	9	6	9	10	2	21	1	1	0	10	2	0	.234	.314	.298	.612
2014	LAD	NL	148	609	176	24	12	2	(2	0)	230	92	34	76	31	0	107	4	3	3	64	19	3	.289	.326	.378	.704
Postseason			2	0	0	0	0	0	(0	0)	0	0	0	0	0	0	0	0	0	0	0	1	0	-	-	-	-
4 ML YEARS			329	1230	335	43	17	4	(3	1)	424	173	68	132	68	2	217	8	8	5	130	38	9	.272	.314	.345	.658

Terrance Gore

Bats: R **Throws:** R **Pos:** PR-9;DH-4;LF-2   **Ht:** 5'7" **Wt:** 165 **Born:** 6/8/1991 **Age:** 24

Year	Team	Lg	G	AB	H	2B	3B	HR	(Hm	Rd)	TB	R	RBI	RC	TBB	IBB	SO	HBP	SH	SF	SB	CS	GDP	Avg	OBP	Slg	OPS
2011	Royals	R	35	94	32	2	2	0	(-	-)	38	22	16	22	15	0	21	4	1	1	17	0	0	.340	.447	.404	.852
2012	Burlgtn	R+	61	227	58	4	2	0	(-	-)	66	50	13	36	36	0	52	9	4	0	36	2	2	.256	.379	.291	.669
2013	Lxngtn	A	128	455	98	6	3	0	(-	-)	110	76	24	54	62	0	120	19	5	0	68	8	3	.215	.334	.242	.576
2014	Wilmg	A+	89	252	55	8	1	0	(-	-)	65	34	15	24	20	0	66	4	9	2	36	4	4	.218	.284	.258	.542
2014	Omha	AAA	17	20	5	0	0	0	(-	-)	5	8	0	3	2	0	4	1	3	0	11	3	0	.250	.348	.250	.598
2014	KC	AL	11	1	0	0	0	0	(0	0)	0	5	0	1	0	0	0	1	0	0	5	0	0	.000	.500	.000	.500

Tom Gorzelanny

Pitches: L **Bats:** R **Pos:** RP-23   gore-zah-LAWN-ee   **Ht:** 6'3" **Wt:** 210 **Born:** 7/12/1982 **Age:** 32

			HOW MUCH HE PITCHED						WHAT HE GAVE UP											THE RESULTS						
Year	Team	Lg	G	GS	CG	GF	IP	BFP	H	R	ER	HR	SH	SF	HB	TBB	IBB	SO	WP	Bk	W	L	Pct	Sh	Sv-Op	Hld	ERC	ERA
2014	BrvdCt*	A+	3	0	0	0	6.0	21	3	1	1	1	1	0	0	1	0	5	0	0	0	1	.000	0	0- -	-	1.36	1.50
2014	Nashv*	AAA	7	2	0	0	9.2	37	8	1	1	0	0	0	0	1	0	7	0	0	0	0	-	0	0- -	-	1.61	0.93
2005	Pit	NL	3	1	0	0	6.0	32	10	8	8	1	1	0	0	3	0	3	0	0	1	0	1.000	0	0-0	0	8.76	12.00
2006	Pit	NL	11	11	0	0	61.2	267	50	29	26	3	7	4	4	31	2	40	3	0	2	5	.286	0	0-0	0	3.23	3.79
2007	Pit	NL	32	32	1	0	201.2	874	214	90	87	18	3	9	11	68	3	135	5	1	14	10	.583	1	0-0	0	4.31	3.88
2008	Pit	NL	21	21	0	0	105.1	490	120	79	78	20	3	6	1	70	0	67	5	1	6	9	.400	0	0-0	0	6.86	6.66
2009	2 Tms	NL	22	7	0	2	47.0	204	45	30	29	6	3	3	1	17	0	47	1	0	7	3	.700	0	0-1	2	3.88	5.55
2010	ChC	NL	29	23	0	3	136.1	604	136	70	62	11	4	6	2	68	4	119	0	0	7	9	.438	1	1-1	1	4.30	4.09
2011	Was	NL	30	15	0	1	105.0	447	102	50	47	15	8	4	6	33	5	95	5	1	4	6	.400	0	0-1	4	4.03	4.03
2012	Was	NL	45	1	0	11	72.0	306	65	27	23	7	3	2	2	30	1	62	4	0	4	2	.667	0	1-1	9	3.68	2.88
2013	Mil	NL	43	10	0	4	85.1	356	77	41	37	11	1	2	2	31	1	83	2	0	3	6	.333	0	0-1	6	3.70	3.90
2014	Mil	NL	23	0	0	7	21.0	95	22	3	2	1	0	0	2	8	0	23	0	0	0	0	-	0	0-0	5	4.15	0.86
09	Pit	NL	9	0	0	2	8.2	36	6	5	5	0	1	0	0	4	0	7	0	0	3	1	.750	0	0-1	1	2.02	5.19
09	ChC	NL	13	7	0	0	38.1	168	39	25	24	6	2	3	1	13	0	40	1	0	4	2	.667	0	0-0	1	4.33	5.63
Postseason			1	0	0	1	0.1	2	1	0	0	0	0	0	0	0	0	0	0	0	0	0	-	0	0-0	0	14.52	0.00
10 ML YEARS			259	121	1	28	841.1	3675	841	427	399	93	33	36	31	359	16	674	25	3	47	51	.480	1	2-5	22	4.37	4.27

Anthony Gose

GOASE

Bats: L **Throws:** L **Pos:** CF-65;RF-14;LF-11;PH-10;DH-1;PR-1   **Ht:** 6'1" **Wt:** 190 **Born:** 8/10/1990 **Age:** 24

Year	Team	Lg	G	AB	H	2B	3B	HR	(Hm	Rd)	TB	R	RBI	RC	TBB	IBB	SO	HBP	SH	SF	SB	CS	GDP	Avg	OBP	Slg	OPS
2014	Buffalo*	AAA	51	205	50	5	2	4	(-	-)	71	29	25	23	17	1	65	1	1	0	21	8	4	.244	.305	.346	.651
2012	Tor	AL	56	166	37	7	3	1	(0	1)	53	25	11	21	17	0	59	2	4	0	15	3	1	.223	.303	.319	.622
2013	Tor	AL	52	147	38	6	5	2	(2	0)	60	15	12	13	5	0	37	0	1	0	4	3	5	.259	.283	.408	.691
2014	Tor	AL	94	239	54	8	1	2	(2	0)	70	31	13	19	25	0	74	5	4	1	15	5	9	.226	.311	.293	.604
3 ML YEARS			202	552	129	21	9	5	(4	1)	183	71	36	53	47	0	170	7	9	1	34	11	15	.234	.301	.332	.633

Tuffy Gosewisch

GOES-uh-wish

Bats: R **Throws:** R **Pos:** C-35;PH-7   **Ht:** 5'11" **Wt:** 200 **Born:** 8/17/1983 **Age:** 31

Year	Team	Lg	G	AB	H	2B	3B	HR	(Hm	Rd)	TB	R	RBI	RC	TBB	IBB	SO	HBP	SH	SF	SB	CS	GDP	Avg	OBP	Slg	OPS
2010	Rdng	AA	98	312	75	22	1	9	(-	-)	126	46	32	48	49	0	67	5	5	0	0	0	2	.240	.352	.404	.756
2011	Rdng	AA	109	369	91	19	0	13	(-	-)	149	41	66	44	20	2	61	8	3	6	4	6	11	.247	.295	.404	.699
2012	LV	AAA	65	213	41	13	0	4	(-	-)	66	22	20	15	9	0	42	5	0	1	0	0	4	.192	.241	.310	.551
2012	LsVgs	AAA	24	83	23	8	1	1	(-	-)	36	9	8	13	9	0	17	3	1	1	0	1	0	.277	.365	.434	.798
2013	Reno	AAA	72	250	71	20	1	7	(-	-)	114	30	33	38	17	0	40	1	0	4	1	1	5	.284	.327	.456	.783
2013	Ari	NL	14	45	8	2	0	0	(0	0)	10	1	3	0	0	0	8	0	1	0	0	0	3	.178	.174	.222	.396
2014	Ari	NL	41	129	29	8	0	1	(0	1)	40	6	7	5	3	0	24	0	0	1	0	1	6	.225	.242	.310	.553
2 ML YEARS			55	174	37	10	0	1	(0	1)	50	7	10	5	3	0	32	0	1	1	0	1	9	.213	.225	.287	.512

Phil Gosselin

Bats: R **Throws:** R **Pos:** 2B-26;3B-9;SS-8;PH-8;PR-4;LF-1   GAHSS-eh-lin   **Ht:** 6'1" **Wt:** 200 **Born:** 10/3/1988 **Age:** 26

Year	Team	Lg	G	AB	H	2B	3B	HR	(Hm	Rd)	TB	R	RBI	RC	TBB	IBB	SO	HBP	SH	SF	SB	CS	GDP	Avg	OBP	Slg	OPS
2010	Rome	A	57	214	63	9	3	2	(-	-)	84	26	24	33	25	0	51	3	1	1	7	3	2	.294	.374	.393	.767
2010	MrtlBh	A+	6	26	4	1	1	0	(-	-)	7	2	0	0	0	0	7	0	0	0	0	0	0	.154	.154	.269	.423
2011	Lynbg	A+	115	424	112	24	6	0	(-	-)	166	60	63	58	37	1	76	5	9	9	6	2	6	.264	.324	.392	.716
2012	Missi	AA	128	484	117	23	3	3	(-	-)	155	55	46	54	46	1	90	9	4	4	12	4	9	.242	.317	.320	.637
2013	Missi	AA	59	218	53	10	1	1	(-	-)	68	27	23	21	12	0	31	4	4	3	5	1	3	.243	.291	.312	.603

155

Year	Team	Lg	G	AB	H	2B	3B	HR	(Hm	Rd)	TB	R	RBI	RC	TBB	IBB	SO	HBP	SH	SF	SB	CS	GDP	Avg	OBP	Slg	OPS
2013	Gwnntt	AAA	58	207	55	4	1	2	(-	-)	67	17	15	21	12	0	38	1	7	1	1	0	1	.266	.308	.324	.631
2014	Gwnntt	AAA	96	378	130	29	5	5	(-	-)	184	58	31	69	19	1	62	3	6	1	6	1	10	.344	.379	.487	.866
2013	Atl	NL	4	6	2	0	0	0	(0	0)	2	2	0	1	1	1	2	0	0	0	0	0	0	.333	.429	.333	.762
2014	Atl	NL	46	128	34	4	0	1	(1	0)	41	17	3	10	5	0	27	2	1	0	2	2	1	.266	.304	.320	.624
2 ML YEARS			50	134	36	4	0	1	(1	0)	43	19	3	11	6	1	29	2	1	0	2	2	1	.269	.310	.321	.631

Yasmani Grandal

Bats: B **Throws:** R **Pos:** C-76;1B-37;PH-24;DH-1   yaz-MON-ee gran-DAHL   **Ht:** 6'2" **Wt:** 225 **Born:** 11/8/1988 **Age:** 26

Year	Team	Lg	G	AB	H	2B	3B	HR	(Hm	Rd)	TB	R	RBI	RC	TBB	IBB	SO	HBP	SH	SF	SB	CS	GDP	Avg	OBP	Slg	OPS
2012	SD	NL	60	192	57	7	1	8	(3	5)	90	28	36	37	31	1	39	1	0	2	0	0	8	.297	.394	.469	.863
2013	SD	NL	28	88	19	8	0	1	(1	0)	30	13	9	12	18	2	18	1	0	1	0	0	1	.216	.352	.341	.693
2014	SD	NL	128	377	85	19	1	15	(7	8)	151	47	49	45	58	1	115	2	0	6	3	0	7	.225	.327	.401	.728
3 ML YEARS			216	657	161	34	2	24	(11	13)	271	88	94	94	107	4	172	4	0	9	3	0	16	.245	.350	.412	.763

Curtis Granderson

Bats: L **Throws:** R **Pos:** RF-142;CF-15;LF-10;PH-6   **Ht:** 6'1" **Wt:** 200 **Born:** 3/16/1981 **Age:** 34

Year	Team	Lg	G	AB	H	2B	3B	HR	(Hm	Rd)	TB	R	RBI	RC	TBB	IBB	SO	HBP	SH	SF	SB	CS	GDP	Avg	OBP	Slg	OPS
2004	Det	AL	9	25	6	1	1	0	(0	0)	9	2	0	2	3	0	8	0	0	0	0	0	1	.240	.321	.360	.681
2005	Det	AL	47	162	44	6	3	8	(5	3)	80	18	20	26	10	0	43	0	2	0	1	1	2	.272	.314	.494	.808
2006	Det	AL	159	596	155	31	9	19	(7	12)	261	90	68	89	66	0	174	4	7	6	8	5	4	.260	.335	.438	.773
2007	Det	AL	158	612	185	38	23	23	(10	13)	338	122	74	106	52	3	141	5	5	2	26	1	3	.302	.361	.552	.913
2008	Det	AL	141	553	155	26	13	22	(11	11)	273	112	66	100	71	1	111	3	1	1	12	4	7	.280	.365	.494	.858
2009	Det	AL	160	631	157	23	8	30	(10	20)	286	91	71	92	72	4	141	2	3	2	20	6	1	.249	.327	.453	.780
2010	NYY	AL	136	466	115	17	7	24	(14	10)	218	76	67	71	53	3	116	2	4	3	12	2	3	.247	.324	.468	.792
2011	NYY	AL	156	583	153	26	10	41	(21	20)	322	136	119	113	85	0	169	12	4	7	25	10	12	.262	.364	.552	.916
2012	NYY	AL	160	596	138	18	4	43	(26	17)	293	102	106	92	75	4	195	5	1	7	10	3	5	.232	.319	.492	.811
2013	NYY	AL	61	214	49	13	2	7	(2	5)	87	31	15	23	27	1	69	1	2	1	8	2	1	.229	.317	.407	.723
2014	NYM	NL	155	564	128	27	2	20	(7	13)	219	73	66	70	79	1	141	6	0	5	8	2	1	.227	.326	.388	.714
Postseason			36	131	30	6	3	6	(4	2)	60	16	17	22	20	1	38	1	1	1	5	1	2	.229	.333	.458	.791
11 ML YEARS			1342	5002	1285	226	82	237	(113	124)	2386	853	672	784	593	17	1308	40	29	34	130	36	40	.257	.338	.477	.815

Kendall Graveman

Pitches: R **Bats:** R **Pos:** RP-5   **Ht:** 6'2" **Wt:** 195 **Born:** 12/21/1990 **Age:** 24

			HOW MUCH HE PITCHED					WHAT HE GAVE UP										THE RESULTS						
Year	Team	Lg	G	GS	CG	GF	IP	BFP	H	R	ER	HR	SH	SF	HB	TBB	IBB	SO	WP	Bk	W	L	Pct	Sh	Sv-Op	Hld	ERC	ERA
2013	Lnsng	A	10	10	0	0	39.2	171	41	23	19	3	1	2	1	13	0	25	0	1	1	3	.250	0	0- -	-	3.89	4.31
2014	Lnsng	A	4	4	0	0	26.1	94	11	2	1	0	0	1	0	6	0	25	0	0	2	0	1.000	0	0- -	-	0.73	0.34
2014	Dnedin	A+	16	16	0	0	96.2	394	89	29	24	1	4	2	4	18	0	64	2	0	8	4	.667	0	0- -	-	2.43	2.23
2014	NHam	AA	1	1	0	0	6.0	25	8	1	1	0	0	1	0	2	0	4	0	0	1	0	1.000	0	0- -	-	5.47	1.50
2014	Buffalo	AAA	6	6	0	0	38.1	145	34	8	8	1	1	0	0	5	0	22	0	0	3	2	.600	0	0- -	-	2.17	1.88
2014	Tor	AL	5	0	0	1	4.2	18	4	2	2	0	0	0	0	0	0	4	1	0	0	0	-	0	0-0	0	1.44	3.86

Sonny Gray

Pitches: R **Bats:** R **Pos:** SP-33   **Ht:** 5'11" **Wt:** 195 **Born:** 11/7/1989 **Age:** 25

			HOW MUCH HE PITCHED					WHAT HE GAVE UP										THE RESULTS						
Year	Team	Lg	G	GS	CG	GF	IP	BFP	H	R	ER	HR	SH	SF	HB	TBB	IBB	SO	WP	Bk	W	L	Pct	Sh	Sv-Op	Hld	ERC	ERA
2011	As	R	1	1	0	0	2.0	9	4	1	1	0	0	0	0	2	0	2	0	0	0	1	.000	0	0- -	-	8.38	4.50
2011	Mdlnd	AA	5	5	0	0	20.0	78	15	1	1	0	2	0	0	6	0	18	2	0	1	0	1.000	0	0- -	-	1.88	0.45
2012	Mdlnd	AA	26	26	1	0	148.0	629	148	73	68	8	0	6	4	57	0	97	16	1	6	9	.400	1	0- -	-	3.87	4.14
2012	Scrmto	AAA	1	1	0	0	4.0	24	10	4	4	0	0	2	1	1	0	2	1	0	0	0	-	0	0- -	-	13.27	9.00
2013	Scrmto	AAA	20	20	1	0	118.1	494	117	51	45	5	1	3	0	39	0	118	10	0	10	7	.588	0	0- -	-	3.40	3.42
2013	Oak	AL	12	10	0	0	64.0	261	51	22	19	4	0	3	0	20	0	67	2	1	5	3	.625	0	0-0	0	2.42	2.67
2014	Oak	AL	33	33	2	0	219.0	899	187	84	75	15	8	5	7	74	2	183	15	0	14	10	.583	2	0-0	0	2.99	3.08
Postseason			2	2	0	0	13.0	53	10	3	3	1	1	0	0	6	1	12	0	0	0	1	.000	0	0-0	0	2.87	2.08
2 ML YEARS			45	43	2	0	283.0	1160	238	106	94	19	8	8	7	94	2	250	17	1	19	13	.594	2	0-0	0	2.86	2.99

Grant Green

Bats: R **Throws:** R **Pos:** LF-17;PH-11;2B-10;3B-5;PR-4;DH-3;1B-1;SS-1   **Ht:** 6'3" **Wt:** 180 **Born:** 9/27/1987 **Age:** 27

Year	Team	Lg	G	AB	H	2B	3B	HR	(Hm	Rd)	TB	R	RBI	RC	TBB	IBB	SO	HBP	SH	SF	SB	CS	GDP	Avg	OBP	Slg	OPS
2010	Stcktn	A+	131	548	174	39	6	20	(-	-)	285	107	87	103	38	2	117	7	3	10	9	5	14	.318	.363	.520	.883
2011	Mdlnd	AA	127	530	154	33	1	9	(-	-)	216	76	62	75	39	2	119	6	6	6	6	8	14	.291	.343	.408	.750
2012	Scrmto	AAA	125	524	155	28	6	15	(-	-)	240	73	75	81	33	1	75	2	0	3	13	9	13	.296	.338	.458	.796
2013	Scrmto	AAA	87	378	123	27	3	11	(-	-)	189	66	50	71	27	1	70	6	3	1	4	1	11	.325	.379	.500	.879
2013	Salt Lk	AAA	6	24	8	1	0	0	(-	-)	9	2	3	3	3	1	7	0	0	1	0	1	0	.333	.393	.375	.768
2014	Salt Lk	AAA	48	198	66	17	3	5	(-	-)	104	38	42	38	13	0	31	2	0	1	4	2	7	.333	.379	.525	.904
2013	2 Tms	AL	45	140	35	8	1	1	(1	0)	48	16	17	16	10	0	44	1	0	2	0	0	3	.250	.301	.343	.644
2014	LAA	AL	43	99	27	5	0	1	(1	0)	35	7	11	8	2	0	20	0	0	2	1	4	3	.273	.282	.354	.635
13	Oak	AL	5	15	0	0	0	0	(0	0)	0	0	1	0	0	0	6	0	0	0	0	0	0	.000	.000	.000	.000
13	LAA	AL	40	125	35	8	1	1	(1	0)	48	16	16	16	10	0	38	1	0	1	0	0	3	.280	.336	.384	.720
2 ML YEARS			88	239	62	13	1	2	(2	0)	83	23	28	24	12	0	64	1	0	4	1	4	6	.259	.293	.347	.640

Shane Greene

Pitches: R **Bats:** R **Pos:** SP-14; RP-1   **Ht:** 6'4" **Wt:** 210 **Born:** 11/17/1988 **Age:** 26

			HOW MUCH HE PITCHED						WHAT HE GAVE UP										THE RESULTS							
Year	Team	Lg	G	GS	CG	GF	IP	BFP	H	R	ER	HR	SH	SF	HB	TBB	IBB	SO	WP	Bk	W	L	Pct	Sh	Sv-Op	Hld	ERC	ERA
2010	StIsInd	A-	10	10	0	0	49.0	228	57	28	25	1	3	0	7	21	0	44	3	0	2	6	.250	0	0- -	-	5.04	4.59
2010	CtnSC	A	4	4	0	0	19.2	82	14	10	10	1	1	0	5	8	0	22	1	0	0	2	.000	0	0- -	-	3.26	4.58
2011	CtnSC	A	27	27	0	0	138.0	615	141	88	67	9	2	2	10	68	0	128	14	0	5	14	.263	0	0- -	-	4.62	4.37
2012	Tampa	A+	24	23	0	0	112.0	505	113	80	65	5	2	4	10	63	0	101	9	1	4	7	.364	0	0- -	-	4.75	5.22
2013	Tampa	A+	13	13	0	0	75.0	313	83	36	30	4	2	1	3	10	0	69	2	0	4	6	.400	0	0- -	-	3.48	3.60
2013	Trntn	AA	14	13	1	1	79.1	349	92	35	28	6	2	2	7	20	0	68	1	2	8	4	.667	1	0- -	-	4.57	3.18
2014	S-WB	AAA	15	13	0	0	66.1	297	79	39	34	3	1	2	0	26	1	57	3	1	5	2	.714	0	0- -	-	4.70	4.61
2014	NYY	AL	15	14	0	0	78.2	345	81	38	33	8	0	1	6	29	0	81	1	0	5	4	.556	0	0-0	0	4.43	3.78

Nick Greenwood

Pitches: L **Bats:** R **Pos:** RP-18; SP-1   **Ht:** 6'1" **Wt:** 180 **Born:** 9/28/1987 **Age:** 27

			HOW MUCH HE PITCHED						WHAT HE GAVE UP										THE RESULTS							
Year	Team	Lg	G	GS	CG	GF	IP	BFP	H	R	ER	HR	SH	SF	HB	TBB	IBB	SO	WP	Bk	W	L	Pct	Sh	Sv-Op	Hld	ERC	ERA
2010	FtWyn	A	21	17	0	2	95.1	404	109	48	44	4	0	0	7	19	0	65	6	2	4	4	.500	0	1- -	-	4.05	4.15
2010	QuadC	A	11	0	0	2	23.1	95	20	5	3	0	0	0	0	9	0	16	3	0	1	0	1.000	0	0- -	-	2.66	1.16
2011	PlmBh	A+	2	0	0	1	3.0	13	3	3	3	1	0	0	1	0	0	3	0	0	0	0	-	0	0- -	-	5.31	9.00
2011	Sprgfld	AA	59	0	0	15	77.1	330	79	42	37	9	6	1	5	21	0	52	5	0	2	4	.333	0	2- -	-	4.06	4.31
2011	Memp	AAA	1	0	0	0	2.0	10	4	2	2	0	0	0	0	0	0	2	0	0	0	0	-	0	0- -	-	7.48	9.00
2012	Memp	AAA	49	4	0	12	59.2	336	87	43	38	6	2	4	5	23	2	47	5	0	4	3	.571	0	0- -	-	4.45	4.40
2013	Memp	AAA	22	7	0	4	54.1	242	65	39	34	9	6	3	1	19	4	24	2	0	2	8	.200	0	0- -	-	5.46	5.63
2013	Sprgfld	AA	11	7	1	1	40.2	182	50	25	18	3	2	1	2	11	1	22	2	0	3	4	.429	0	0- -	-	4.79	3.98
2014	Memp	AAA	27	5	0	5	50.2	201	42	18	17	4	5	1	2	10	0	37	5	0	4	4	.500	0	0- -	-	2.47	3.02
2014	StL	NL	19	1	0	8	36.0	145	36	19	19	5	0	0	1	5	1	17	0	0	2	1	.667	0	0-0	1	3.44	4.75

Luke Gregerson

Pitches: R **Bats:** L **Pos:** RP-72   **Ht:** 6'3" **Wt:** 200 **Born:** 5/14/1984 **Age:** 31

			HOW MUCH HE PITCHED						WHAT HE GAVE UP										THE RESULTS							
Year	Team	Lg	G	GS	CG	GF	IP	BFP	H	R	ER	HR	SH	SF	HB	TBB	IBB	SO	WP	Bk	W	L	Pct	Sh	Sv-Op	Hld	ERC	ERA
2009	SD	NL	72	0	0	7	75.0	318	62	29	27	3	3	1	3	31	9	93	4	0	2	4	.333	0	1-7	27	2.72	3.24
2010	SD	NL	80	0	0	9	78.1	297	47	30	28	8	1	1	1	18	2	89	0	0	4	7	.364	0	2-7	40	1.56	3.22
2011	SD	NL	61	0	0	11	55.2	241	57	23	17	2	5	1	2	19	3	34	2	0	3	3	.500	0	0-4	16	3.55	2.75
2012	SD	NL	77	0	0	15	71.2	294	57	19	19	7	5	0	3	21	3	72	3	0	2	0	1.000	0	9-13	24	2.64	2.39
2013	SD	NL	73	0	0	17	66.1	268	49	24	20	3	4	1	4	18	2	64	1	0	6	8	.429	0	4-9	25	2.07	2.71
2014	Oak	AL	72	0	0	17	72.1	284	58	20	17	6	3	1	1	15	3	59	6	0	5	5	.500	0	3-11	22	2.25	2.12
	6 ML YEARS		435	0	0	76	419.1	1702	330	145	128	29	21	5	14	122	22	411	16	0	22	27	.449	0	19-51	154	2.40	2.75

Kevin Gregg

Pitches: R **Bats:** R **Pos:** RP-12   **Ht:** 6'6" **Wt:** 245 **Born:** 6/20/1978 **Age:** 37

			HOW MUCH HE PITCHED						WHAT HE GAVE UP										THE RESULTS							
Year	Team	Lg	G	GS	CG	GF	IP	BFP	H	R	ER	HR	SH	SF	HB	TBB	IBB	SO	WP	Bk	W	L	Pct	Sh	Sv-Op	Hld	ERC	ERA
2014	Jupiter*	A+	2	0	0	0	1.0	7	3	4	1	1	0	0	0	0	0	2	0	0	0	0	-	0	0- -	-	21.79	9.00
2014	NewOr*	AAA	5	0	0	2	6.0	26	6	2	2	0	0	0	0	2	0	3	0	0	1	0	1.000	0	0- -	-	3.05	3.00
2003	LAA	AL	5	3	0	0	24.2	97	18	9	9	3	0	0	1	8	0	14	0	0	2	0	1.000	0	0-0	0	2.74	3.28
2004	LAA	AL	55	0	0	23	87.2	377	86	43	41	6	4	5	3	28	3	84	13	1	5	2	.714	0	1-2	3	3.47	4.21
2005	LAA	AL	33	2	0	9	64.1	290	70	37	36	8	1	1	3	29	2	52	5	0	1	2	.333	0	0-1	1	5.08	5.04
2006	LAA	AL	32	3	0	12	78.1	341	88	41	36	10	0	3	2	21	0	71	6	0	3	4	.429	0	0-0	0	4.51	4.14
2007	Fla	NL	74	0	0	55	84.0	355	63	34	33	7	3	0	6	40	1	87	6	0	0	5	.000	0	32-36	6	3.15	3.54
2008	Fla	NL	72	0	0	59	68.2	296	51	30	26	3	3	1	4	37	4	58	7	0	7	8	.467	0	29-38	4	2.90	3.41
2009	ChC	NL	72	0	0	51	68.2	298	60	38	36	13	0	3	3	30	2	71	7	0	5	6	.455	0	23-30	1	4.19	4.72
2010	Tor	AL	63	0	0	56	59.0	254	52	24	23	4	1	3	1	30	1	58	3	0	2	6	.250	0	37-43	3	3.66	3.51
2011	Bal	AL	63	0	0	48	59.2	275	58	35	29	7	4	1	2	40	4	53	2	0	0	3	.000	0	22-29	0	5.10	4.37
2012	Bal	AL	40	0	0	13	43.2	200	50	26	24	6	0	1	3	24	2	37	0	0	3	2	.600	0	0-0	0	6.15	4.95
2013	ChC	NL	62	0	0	52	62.0	269	53	26	24	6	4	1	1	32	2	56	1	0	2	6	.250	0	33-38	0	3.67	3.48
2014	Mia	NL	12	0	0	2	9.0	41	11	10	10	2	0	0	0	5	0	6	1	0	0	0	-	0	0-2	4	7.23	10.00
	Postseason		2	0	0	0	4.0	18	4	0	0	0	0	0	0	2	0	3	1	0	0	0	-	0	0-0	0	3.63	0.00
	12 ML YEARS		583	8	0	380	709.2	3093	660	353	327	75	20	19	29	324	21	647	51	1	30	44	.405	0	177-219	22	4.04	4.15

Didi Gregorius

Bats: L **Throws:** R **Pos:** SS-67;2B-11;PH-4;3B-2   dee-dee greh-GORE-ee-us   **Ht:** 6'2" **Wt:** 205 **Born:** 2/18/1990 **Age:** 25

			BATTING																	RUNNING			AVERAGES			
Year	Team	Lg	G	AB	H	2B	3B	HR	(Hm	Rd)	TB	R	RBI	RC	TBB	IBB	SO	HBP	SH	SF	SB	CS	GDP	Avg	OBP	Slg	OPS
2014	Reno*	AAA	57	226	70	14	4	3	(-	-)	101	42	25	41	24	0	26	6	3	1	3	0	6	.310	.389	.447	.836
2012	Cin	NL	8	20	6	0	0	0	(0	0)	6	1	2	2	0	0	5	0	1	0	0	0	0	.300	.300	.300	.600
2013	Ari	NL	103	357	90	16	3	7	(3	4)	133	47	28	42	37	5	65	6	2	1	0	2	4	.252	.332	.373	.704
2014	Ari	NL	80	270	61	9	5	6	(3	3)	98	35	27	37	22	3	52	3	2	2	3	0	1	.226	.290	.363	.653
	3 ML YEARS		191	647	157	25	8	13	(6	7)	237	83	57	81	59	8	122	9	5	3	3	2	5	.243	.313	.366	.680

Zack Greinke

Pitches: R Bats: R Pos: SP-32 GRAIN-key Ht: 6'2" Wt: 195 Born: 10/21/1983 Age: 31

				HOW MUCH HE PITCHED				WHAT HE GAVE UP											THE RESULTS						
Year	Team	Lg	G	GS	CG	GF	IP	BFP	H	R	ER	HR	SH	SF	HB	TBB	IBB	SO	WP	Bk	W	L	Pct	Sh	Sv-Op	Hld	ERC	ERA
2004	KC	AL	24	24	0	0	145.0	599	143	64	64	26	3	2	8	26	3	100	1	1	8	11	.421	0	0-0	0	3.85	3.97
2005	KC	AL	33	33	2	0	183.0	829	233	125	118	23	4	4	13	53	0	114	4	2	5	17	.227	0	0-0	0	5.71	5.80
2006	KC	AL	3	0	0	1	6.1	28	7	3	3	1	0	0	0	3	2	5	0	0	1	0	1.000	0	0-0	0	4.93	4.26
2007	KC	AL	52	14	0	7	122.0	507	122	52	50	12	3	4	3	36	5	106	3	1	7	7	.500	0	1-1	12	3.77	3.69
2008	KC	AL	32	32	1	0	202.1	851	202	87	78	21	2	4	4	56	1	183	8	1	13	10	.565	0	0-0	0	3.68	3.47
2009	KC	AL	33	33	6	0	229.1	915	195	64	55	11	8	3	4	51	0	242	5	0	16	8	.667	3	0-0	0	2.39	2.16
2010	KC	AL	33	33	3	0	220.0	919	219	114	102	18	6	7	7	55	1	181	4	0	10	14	.417	0	0-0	0	3.48	4.17
2011	Mil	NL	28	28	0	0	171.2	715	161	82	73	19	6	1	4	45	0	201	10	0	16	6	.727	0	0-0	0	3.35	3.83
2012	2 Tms		34	34	0	0	212.1	868	200	84	82	18	7	2	2	54	0	200	8	0	15	5	.750	0	0-0	0	3.17	3.48
2013	LAD	NL	28	28	1	0	177.2	717	152	54	52	13	13	1	7	46	1	148	5	0	15	4	.789	1	0-0	0	2.78	2.63
2014	LAD	NL	32	32	0	0	202.1	821	190	69	61	19	2	4	2	43	3	207	12	0	17	8	.680	0	0-0	0	3.03	2.71
12	Mil	NL	21	21	0	0	123.0	504	120	49	47	7	3	0	0	28	0	122	4	0	9	3	.750	0	0-0	0	3.02	3.44
12	LAA		13	13	0	0	89.1	364	80	35	35	11	4	2	2	26	0	78	4	0	6	2	.750	0	0-0	0	3.38	3.53
	Postseason		6	6	0	0	37.2	156	37	21	18	4	1	0	1	6	0	30	0	0	2	2	.500	0	0-0	0	3.15	4.30
	11 ML YEARS		332	291	13	8	1872.0	7769	1824	798	738	181	54	32	54	468	16	1687	60	5	123	90	.577	4	1-1	12	3.45	3.55

Randal Grichuk

Bats: R Throws: R Pos: RF-28;PH-18;LF-5;CF-5;PR-1 GRICH-ick Ht: 6'1" Wt: 195 Born: 8/13/1991 Age: 23

						BATTING															RUNNING			AVERAGES			
Year	Team	Lg	G	AB	H	2B	3B	HR	(Hm	Rd)	TB	R	RBI	RC	TBB	IBB	SO	HBP	SH	SF	SB	CS	GDP	Avg	OBP	Slg	OPS
2010	CRpds	A	52	202	59	19	4	7	(-	-)	107	41	36	35	9	0	50	2	0	1	4	0	2	.292	.327	.530	.857
2010	Angels	R	12	49	16	3	2	4	(-	-)	35	7	10	12	3	0	9	0	0	0	0	0	1	.327	.365	.714	1.080
2011	Angels	R	7	24	8	1	1	0	(-	-)	11	2	6	4	2	0	4	0	0	2	0	0	0	.333	.357	.458	.815
2011	CRpds	A	32	122	28	7	4	2	(-	-)	49	12	13	13	6	0	29	1	0	2	0	1	1	.230	.267	.402	.669
2011	InldEm	A+	14	53	15	4	2	1	(-	-)	26	13	6	8	0	0	13	3	0	1	0	0	1	.283	.316	.491	.806
2012	InldEm	A+	135	537	160	30	9	18	(-	-)	262	79	71	89	23	3	92	9	2	4	16	6	10	.298	.335	.488	.823
2013	Ark	AA	128	500	128	27	8	22	(-	-)	237	85	64	74	28	2	91	9	2	3	9	5	10	.256	.306	.474	.780
2014	Memp	AAA	108	436	113	23	2	25	(-	-)	215	73	71	67	28	2	108	6	0	2	8	5	13	.259	.311	.493	.805
2014	StL	NL	47	110	27	6	1	3	(2	1)	44	11	8	7	5	0	31	0	1	0	0	2	4	.245	.278	.400	.678

A.J. Griffin

Pitches: R Bats: R Pos: P Ht: 6'5" Wt: 230 Born: 1/28/1988 Age: 27

						HOW MUCH HE PITCHED				WHAT HE GAVE UP										THE RESULTS						
Year	Team	Lg	G	GS	CG	GF	IP	BFP	H	R	ER	HR	SH	SF	HB	TBB	IBB	SO	WP	Bk	W	L	Pct	Sh	Sv-Op	Hld	ERC	ERA
2010	As	R	4	0	0	1	5.0	16	1	0	0	0	0	0	0	0	0	6	0	0	0	0	-	0	0- -	-	0.09	0.00
2010	Vancvr	A-	20	0	0	18	21.1	86	14	9	7	0	0	0	3	7	1	27	2	0	1	1	.500	0	15- -	-	1.87	2.95
2011	Burlgtn	A	8	8	0	0	52.0	202	36	10	9	2	1	1	2	5	0	46	0	0	4	0	1.000	0	0- -	-	1.35	1.56
2011	Stckton	A+	12	12	0	0	70.2	283	64	31	28	8	4	3	2	14	0	82	3	1	5	3	.625	0	0- -	-	3.04	3.57
2011	Scrmto	AAA	1	1	0	0	6.0	24	6	3	2	1	0	0	0	2	0	8	0	0	1	0	1.000	0	0- -	-	4.57	3.00
2011	Mdlnd	AA	6	6	0	0	32.0	146	39	24	23	6	0	0	2	11	0	20	0	0	2	3	.400	0	0- -	-	6.00	6.47
2012	Mdlnd	AA	7	7	0	0	43.1	164	31	12	12	4	1	1	1	7	0	44	1	0	3	1	.750	0	0- -	-	1.85	2.49
2012	Scrmto	AAA	10	10	2	0	58.2	238	48	27	20	3	0	2	4	11	1	47	2	0	4	2	.667	0	0- -	-	2.23	3.07
2012	Oak	AL	15	15	0	0	82.1	336	74	29	28	10	0	2	1	19	0	64	0	0	7	1	.875	0	0-0	0	3.06	3.06
2013	Oak	AL	32	32	1	0	200.0	823	171	91	85	36	4	4	4	54	2	171	7	0	14	10	.583	1	0-0	0	3.33	3.83
	Postseason		1	1	0	0	5.0	21	7	2	2	1	1	0	0	0	0	1	0	0	0	0	-	0	0-0	0	5.60	3.60
	2 ML YEARS		47	47	1	0	282.1	1159	245	120	113	46	4	6	5	73	2	235	7	0	21	11	.656	1	0-0	0	3.25	3.60

Jason Grilli

Pitches: R Bats: R Pos: RP-62 GRILL-ee Ht: 6'4" Wt: 235 Born: 11/11/1976 Age: 38

						HOW MUCH HE PITCHED				WHAT HE GAVE UP										THE RESULTS						
Year	Team	Lg	G	GS	CG	GF	IP	BFP	H	R	ER	HR	SH	SF	HB	TBB	IBB	SO	WP	Bk	W	L	Pct	Sh	Sv-Op	Hld	ERC	ERA
2000	Fla	NL	1	1	0	0	6.2	35	11	4	4	0	2	0	2	2	0	3	0	0	1	0	1.000	0	0-0	0	7.84	5.40
2001	Fla	NL	6	5	0	1	26.2	115	30	18	18	6	1	0	2	11	0	17	0	0	2	2	.500	0	0-0	0	6.44	6.08
2004	CWS	AL	8	8	1	0	45.0	203	52	38	37	11	2	1	3	20	0	26	2	0	2	3	.400	0	0-0	0	6.67	7.40
2005	Det	AL	3	2	0	0	16.0	63	14	6	6	1	1	1	0	6	0	5	0	0	1	1	.500	0	0-0	0	3.27	3.38
2006	Det	AL	51	0	0	18	60.0	270	61	31	29	6	2	4	5	25	3	31	5	0	2	3	.400	0	0-0	9	4.23	4.21
2007	Det	AL	57	0	0	13	79.2	352	81	46	42	5	1	5	5	32	1	62	5	0	5	3	.625	0	0-2	11	4.09	4.74
2008	2 Tms		60	0	0	16	75.0	323	67	27	25	2	1	3	2	38	7	69	4	0	3	3	.500	0	1-2	4	3.34	3.00
2009	2 Tms		52	0	0	11	45.2	212	50	27	27	4	2	1	1	27	2	49	2	0	2	3	.400	0	1-1	7	5.25	5.32
2011	Pit	NL	28	0	0	4	32.2	140	24	10	9	2	1	0	4	15	5	37	3	0	2	1	.667	0	1-1	3	2.79	2.48
2012	Pit	NL	64	0	0	11	58.2	244	45	20	19	7	2	1	2	22	4	90	2	0	1	6	.143	0	2-5	32	2.85	2.91
2013	Pit	NL	54	0	0	41	50.0	202	40	15	15	4	1	0	1	13	0	74	1	0	0	2	.000	0	33-35	2	2.44	2.70
2014	2 Tms		62	0	0	22	54.0	235	51	26	24	4	5	3	4	21	2	57	1	0	1	5	.167	0	12-17	12	3.73	4.00
08	Det	AL	9	0	0	4	13.2	59	12	5	5	1	0	0	1	7	1	10	1	0	0	1	.000	0	0-1	0	3.85	3.29
08	Det	AL	51	0	0	12	61.1	264	55	22	20	1	1	3	1	31	6	59	3	0	3	2	.600	0	1-1	4	3.23	2.93
09	Col	NL	22	0	0	6	19.1	99	29	13	13	2	1	1	0	13	2	22	2	0	0	1	.000	0	1-1	3	8.02	6.05
09	Tex	AL	30	0	0	5	26.1	113	21	14	14	2	1	0	1	14	0	27	0	0	2	2	.500	0	0-0	4	3.44	4.78
14	Pit	NL	22	0	0	16	20.1	93	22	11	11	4	1	0	1	11	1	21	0	0	0	2	.000	0	11-15	0	5.99	4.87
14	LAA	AL	40	0	0	6	33.2	142	29	15	13	0	4	3	3	10	1	36	1	0	1	3	.250	0	1-2	11	2.53	3.48
	Postseason		9	0	0	4	6.1	27	4	0	0	0	0	0	0	4	1	5	0	0	0	0	-	0	1-1	1	2.03	0.00
	12 ML YEARS		446	16	1	137	552.0	2394	526	268	255	52	21	19	31	232	24	520	23	0	22	32	.407	0	50-63	86	4.00	4.16

Justin Grimm

Pitches: R **Bats:** R **Pos:** RP-73   **Ht:** 6'3" **Wt:** 210 **Born:** 8/16/1988 **Age:** 26

		HOW MUCH HE PITCHED						WHAT HE GAVE UP												THE RESULTS							
Year Team	Lg	G	GS	CG	GF	IP	BFP	H	R	ER	HR	SH	SF	HB	TBB	IBB	SO	WP	Bk	W	L	Pct	Sh	Sv-Op	Hld	ERC	ERA
2012 Tex	AL	5	2	0	3	14.0	65	22	14	14	1	0	2	0	3	0	13	3	0	1	1	.500	0	0-0	-	6.54	9.00
2013 2 Tms		27	17	0	3	98.0	442	120	70	65	15	4	2	2	34	1	76	4	0	7	9	.438	0	0-0	3	5.61	5.97
2014 ChC	NL	73	0	0	19	69.0	292	59	32	29	4	1	3	4	27	2	70	8	0	5	2	.714	0	0-1	11	3.14	3.78
13 Tex	AL	17	17	0	0	89.0	406	116	67	63	15	2	2	1	31	1	68	4	0	7	7	.500	0	0-0	-	6.21	6.37
13 ChC	NL	10	0	0	3	9.0	36	4	3	2	0	2	0	1	3	0	8	0	0	0	2	.000	0	0-0	3	1.12	2.00
3 ML YEARS		105	19	0	25	181.0	799	201	116	108	20	5	7	6	64	3	159	15	0	13	12	.520	0	0-1	14	4.68	5.37

Robbie Grossman

Bats: B **Throws:** L **Pos:** LF-67;RF-32;CF-6;DH-1;PH-1   **Ht:** 6'0" **Wt:** 195 **Born:** 9/16/1989 **Age:** 25

		BATTING																			RUNNING			AVERAGES			
Year Team	Lg	G	AB	H	2B	3B	HR	(Hm	Rd)	TB	R	RBI	RC	TBB	IBB	SO	HBP	SH	SF		SB	CS	GDP		Avg	OBP	Slg	OPS
2010 Bradtn	A+	125	470	115	29	3	4	(-	-)	162	84	50	62	66	1	118	8	12	6		15	8	8		.245	.344	.345	.688
2011 Bradtn	A+	134	490	144	34	2	13	(-	-)	221	127	56	102	104	0	111	6	9	7		24	10	8		.294	.418	.451	.869
2012 Altna	AA	95	350	93	20	4	7	(-	-)	142	59	36	56	59	1	78	4	4	0		9	10	3		.266	.378	.406	.783
2012 CpChr	AA	36	135	36	8	2	3	(-	-)	57	22	11	23	18	0	43	5	1	1		4	1	0		.267	.371	.422	.793
2013 OKCity	AAA	70	253	71	11	2	2	(-	-)	92	42	20	41	48	2	66	1	7	1		15	8	6		.281	.396	.364	.760
2014 OKCity	AAA	44	175	59	16	0	4	(-	-)	87	30	15	35	22	1	38	2	0	0		10	8	4		.337	.417	.497	.914
2013 Hou	AL	63	257	69	14	0	4	(3	1)	95	29	21	37	23	0	70	2	5	1		6	7	2		.268	.332	.370	.702
2014 Hou	AL	103	360	84	14	2	6	(2	4)	120	42	37	48	55	1	105	2	3	2		9	3	7		.233	.337	.333	.670
2 ML YEARS		166	617	153	28	2	10	(5	5)	215	71	58	85	78	1	175	4	8	3		15	10	9		.248	.335	.348	.683

Jarrett Grube

Pitches: R **Bats:** R **Pos:** RP-1   GROOB   **Ht:** 6'4" **Wt:** 220 **Born:** 11/5/1981 **Age:** 33

		HOW MUCH HE PITCHED						WHAT HE GAVE UP												THE RESULTS							
Year Team	Lg	G	GS	CG	GF	IP	BFP	H	R	ER	HR	SH	SF	HB	TBB	IBB	SO	WP	Bk	W	L	Pct	Sh	Sv-Op	Hld	ERC	ERA
2010 Tacom	AAA	2	1	0	0	8.2	37	10	6	6	2	0	0	1	4	0	4	0	0	0	0	-	0	0- -	-	4.57	6.23
2010 WTenn	AA	15	15	0	0	94.2	387	85	37	34	5	1	2	2	26	0	75	6	0	5	5	.500	0	0- -	-	2.85	3.23
2011 Jacksn	AA	14	14	0	0	84.0	340	79	35	29	4	2	1	2	20	0	69	6	1	5	2	.714	0	0- -	-	2.95	3.11
2011 Tacom	AAA	14	7	0	3	60.0	246	51	34	33	10	0	0	2	18	0	51	3	0	4	4	.500	0	1- -	-	3.45	4.95
2012 Tacom	AAA	16	8	0	1	46.2	244	86	53	48	8	3	1	0	20	1	43	3	0	0	5	.000	0	0- -	-	10.02	9.26
2012 Ark	AA	8	7	0	0	45.1	181	42	16	15	2	2	1	4	5	0	40	0	0	3	3	.500	0	0- -	-	2.62	2.98
2013 Ark	AA	7	7	0	0	40.1	165	32	15	14	4	2	1	2	10	0	49	2	0	4	1	.800	0	0- -	-	2.55	3.12
2013 Salt Lk	AAA	22	21	0	0	108.2	483	113	62	54	12	0	6	9	48	0	104	10	0	7	5	.583	0	0- -	-	4.90	4.47
2014 Salt Lk	AAA	27	27	1	0	147.1	640	164	99	91	26	0	4	7	41	0	121	4	0	8	9	.471	0	0- -	-	4.98	5.56
2014 LAA	AL	1	0	0	0	0.2	3	1	1	1	1	0	0	0	0	0	0	0	0	0	0	-	0	0-0	0	15.46	13.50

Javy Guerra

Pitches: R **Bats:** R **Pos:** RP-42   GEHR-uh   **Ht:** 6'1" **Wt:** 190 **Born:** 10/31/1985 **Age:** 29

		HOW MUCH HE PITCHED						WHAT HE GAVE UP												THE RESULTS							
Year Team	Lg	G	GS	CG	GF	IP	BFP	H	R	ER	HR	SH	SF	HB	TBB	IBB	SO	WP	Bk	W	L	Pct	Sh	Sv-Op	Hld	ERC	ERA
2014 Charltt*	AAA	14	0	0	10	19.1	80	19	8	5	1	0	0	2	8	0	11	4	0	1	1	.500	0	0- -	-	4.38	2.33
2011 LAD	NL	47	0	0	38	46.2	195	37	12	12	2	3	1	3	18	1	38	2	0	2	2	.500	0	21-23	3	2.73	2.31
2012 LAD	NL	45	0	0	17	45.0	196	44	13	13	1	4	2	1	23	5	37	1	0	2	3	.400	0	8-13	4	3.76	2.60
2013 LAD	NL	9	0	0	5	10.2	55	15	9	8	1	0	1	1	6	0	12	0	0	0	0	-	0	0-0	0	7.24	6.75
2014 CWS	AL	42	0	0	10	46.1	198	41	15	15	3	2	4	5	20	5	38	2	0	2	4	.333	0	1-6	7	3.60	2.91
4 ML YEARS		143	0	0	70	148.2	644	137	49	48	7	9	8	10	67	11	125	5	0	6	9	.400	0	30-42	11	3.61	2.91

Alex Guerrero

Bats: R **Throws:** R **Pos:** PH-8;LF-3   guh-RAIR-oh   **Ht:** 5'10" **Wt:** 205 **Born:** 11/20/1986 **Age:** 28

		BATTING																			RUNNING			AVERAGES			
Year Team	Lg	G	AB	H	2B	3B	HR	(Hm	Rd)	TB	R	RBI	RC	TBB	IBB	SO	HBP	SH	SF		SB	CS	GDP		Avg	OBP	Slg	OPS
2014 Albq	AAA	65	243	80	14	5	15	(-	-)	149	38	49	52	10	0	44	4	0	1		4	0	2		.329	.364	.613	.978
2014 Ddgrs	R	7	23	8	1	0	2	(-	-)	15	6	6	6	3	0	5	1	0	2		0	0	0		.348	.414	.652	1.066
2014 RCuca	A+	5	19	7	4	1	0	(-	-)	13	3	2	5	2	0	2	0	0	0		0	0	0		.368	.429	.684	1.113
2014 LAD	NL	11	13	1	0	0	0	(0	0)	1	0	0	0	0	0	6	0	0	0		0	0	0		.077	.077	.077	.154

Matt Guerrier

Pitches: R **Bats:** R **Pos:** RP-27   gurr-REAR   **Ht:** 6'3" **Wt:** 195 **Born:** 8/2/1978 **Age:** 36

		HOW MUCH HE PITCHED						WHAT HE GAVE UP												THE RESULTS							
Year Team	Lg	G	GS	CG	GF	IP	BFP	H	R	ER	HR	SH	SF	HB	TBB	IBB	SO	WP	Bk	W	L	Pct	Sh	Sv-Op	Hld	ERC	ERA
2014 NwBrit*	AA	3	0	0	1	4.0	17	4	1	0	0	0	0	1	2	0	5	0	0	0	0	-	0	0- -	-	5.14	0.00
2014 Roch*	AAA	4	0	0	3	5.0	25	7	4	4	2	0	0	0	3	0	3	1	0	0	1	.000	0	1- -	-	9.80	7.20
2004 Min	AL	9	2	0	5	19.0	84	22	13	12	5	2	0	1	6	0	11	0	0	0	1	.000	0	0-0	-	6.10	5.68
2005 Min	AL	43	0	0	14	71.2	306	71	29	27	6	4	1	3	24	5	46	3	0	0	3	.000	0	0-0	1	3.71	3.39
2006 Min	AL	39	1	0	13	69.2	300	78	29	26	9	3	4	0	21	0	37	6	0	1	0	1.000	0	1-1	2	4.59	3.36
2007 Min	AL	73	0	0	16	88.0	351	71	23	23	9	0	3	5	21	1	68	6	0	2	4	.333	0	1-4	14	2.70	2.35
2008 Min	AL	76	0	0	15	76.1	344	84	47	44	12	1	1	0	37	9	59	2	0	6	9	.400	0	1-5	20	5.20	5.19
2009 Min	AL	79	0	0	15	76.1	304	58	23	20	10	3	1	4	26	2	47	6	0	5	1	.833	0	1-4	33	2.44	2.36
2010 Min	AL	74	0	0	13	71.0	286	56	28	25	7	2	3	3	22	1	42	2	0	5	7	.417	0	1-7	23	2.78	3.17
2011 LAD	NL	70	0	0	12	66.1	282	59	31	30	4	3	1	0	25	5	50	2	0	4	3	.571	0	1-4	13	2.95	4.07
2012 LAD	NL	16	0	0	2	14.0	56	8	6	6	3	1	1	1	7	1	9	0	0	0	2	.000	0	0-1	3	3.15	3.86
2013 2 Tms	NL	49	0	0	7	42.2	181	43	22	19	2	4	0	2	17	2	30	0	0	4	4	.500	0	0-3	8	4.01	4.01

Year Team	Lg	G	GS	CG	GF	IP	BFP	H	R	ER	HR	SH	SF	HB	TBB	IBB	SO	WP	Bk	W	L	Pct	Sh	Sv-Op	Hld	ERC	ERA
2014 Min	AL	27	0	0	11	28.0	124	30	12	12	1	1	2	1	10	3	12	3	0	0	1	.000	0	0-1	3	3.74	3.86
13 LAD	NL	34	0	0	5	30.0	130	32	18	16	3	2	2	1	12	2	21	0	0	2	3	.400	0	0-1	3	4.55	4.80
13 ChC	NL	15	0	0	2	12.2	51	11	4	3	0	0	0	0	5	0	9	0	0	2	1	.667	0	0-2	5	2.80	2.13
Postseason		5	0	0	1	4.2	16	1	0	0	0	0	1	0	1	0	4	0	0	0	0	-	0	0-0	1	0.30	0.00
11 ML YEARS		555	3	0	123	623.0	2618	580	263	244	69	22	19	19	206	29	411	30	0	27	35	.435	0	6-30	120	3.55	3.52

Preston Guilmet

Pitches: R Bats: R Pos: RP-10   GILL-met   **Ht: 6'2" Wt: 200 Born: 7/27/1987 Age: 27**

Year Team	Lg	G	GS	CG	GF	IP	BFP	H	R	ER	HR	SH	SF	HB	TBB	IBB	SO	WP	Bk	W	L	Pct	Sh	Sv-Op	Hld	ERC	ERA
2010 Lk Cty	A	30	0	0	21	52.0	200	35	13	13	3	2	0	2	10	1	79	3	0	4	1	.800	0	11--	-	1.60	2.25
2011 Knstn	A+	52	0	0	48	58.1	226	43	14	14	4	2	0	0	11	1	60	3	0	1	1	.500	0	35--	-	1.78	2.16
2012 Akron	AA	50	0	0	39	52.2	209	41	14	14	4	1	1	0	13	0	51	4	0	2	2	.500	0	24--	-	2.21	2.39
2013 Clmbs	AAA	49	0	0	34	64.1	251	43	19	12	4	0	1	0	14	2	72	2	0	5	4	.556	0	20--	-	1.54	1.68
2014 Norfolk	AAA	40	0	0	26	48.1	197	42	25	21	6	1	1	0	10	3	54	4	0	4	2	.667	0	10--	-	2.66	3.91
2013 Cle	AL	4	0	0	1	5.1	28	8	6	6	0	0	0	0	3	0	1	0	0	0	0	-	0	0-0	0	6.48	10.13
2014 Bal	AL	10	0	0	4	10.1	43	8	6	6	2	0	1	0	2	0	12	1	0	0	1	.000	0	0-0	1	2.47	5.23
2 ML YEARS		14	0	0	5	15.2	71	16	12	12	2	0	1	0	5	0	13	1	0	0	1	.000	0	0-0	1	3.78	6.89

Jeremy Guthrie

Pitches: R Bats: R Pos: SP-32   **Ht: 6'1" Wt: 205 Born: 4/8/1979 Age: 36**

Year Team	Lg	G	GS	CG	GF	IP	BFP	H	R	ER	HR	SH	SF	HB	TBB	IBB	SO	WP	Bk	W	L	Pct	Sh	Sv-Op	Hld	ERC	ERA
2004 Cle	AL	6	0	0	2	11.2	49	9	6	6	1	0	0	1	6	0	7	1	0	0	0	-	0	0-0	0	3.58	4.63
2005 Cle	AL	1	0	0	1	6.0	29	9	4	4	2	1	1	0	2	0	3	0	0	0	0	-	0	0-0	0	8.58	6.00
2006 Cle	AL	9	1	0	1	19.1	93	24	15	15	2	0	0	2	15	1	14	3	0	0	0	-	0	0-0	0	7.78	6.98
2007 Bal	AL	32	26	0	3	175.1	723	165	78	72	23	4	6	4	47	2	123	8	1	7	5	.583	0	0-1	0	3.55	3.70
2008 Bal	AL	30	30	1	0	190.2	796	176	82	77	24	2	2	7	58	2	120	3	0	10	12	.455	0	0-0	0	3.59	3.63
2009 Bal	AL	33	33	1	0	200.0	874	224	120	112	35	1	8	9	60	1	110	1	1	10	17	.370	0	0-0	0	5.08	5.04
2010 Bal	AL	32	32	0	0	209.1	872	193	93	89	25	3	9	16	50	1	119	1	1	11	14	.440	0	0-0	0	3.44	3.83
2011 Bal	AL	34	32	2	1	208.0	889	213	113	100	26	5	10	9	66	5	130	0	0	9	17	.346	0	0-0	0	4.21	4.33
2012 2 Tms		33	29	0	0	181.2	788	206	109	96	30	8	6	9	50	2	101	2	2	8	12	.400	0	0-1	0	5.03	4.76
2013 KC	AL	33	33	3	0	211.2	905	236	99	95	30	2	8	8	59	1	111	7	0	15	12	.556	2	0-0	0	4.76	4.04
2014 KC	AL	32	32	1	0	202.2	864	215	100	93	23	2	10	14	49	0	124	3	0	13	11	.542	0	0-0	0	4.18	4.13
12 Col	NL	19	15	0	0	90.2	422	122	72	64	21	5	3	7	31	2	45	1	1	3	9	.250	0	0-1	0	7.26	6.35
12 KC	AL	14	14	0	0	91.0	366	84	37	32	9	3	3	2	19	0	56	1	1	5	3	.625	0	0-0	0	3.06	3.16
11 ML YEARS		275	248	8	8	1616.1	6882	1670	819	759	221	28	60	79	462	15	962	29	5	83	100	.454	2	0-2	0	4.27	4.23

Franklin Gutierrez

Bats: R Throws: R Pos: CF   **Ht: 6'2" Wt: 195 Born: 2/21/1983 Age: 32**

Year Team	Lg	G	AB	H	2B	3B	HR	(Hm	Rd)	TB	R	RBI	RC	TBB	IBB	SO	HBP	SH	SF	SB	CS	GDP	Avg	OBP	Slg	OPS
2005 Cle	AL	7	1	0	0	0	0	(0	0)	0	2	0	0	1	0	0	0	0	0	0	0	0	.000	.500	.000	.500
2006 Cle	AL	43	136	37	9	0	1	(1	0)	49	21	8	12	3	0	28	0	2	0	0	0	4	.272	.288	.360	.648
2007 Cle	AL	100	271	72	13	2	13	(10	3)	128	41	36	36	21	1	77	1	5	3	8	3	7	.266	.318	.472	.790
2008 Cle	AL	134	399	99	26	2	8	(6	2)	153	54	41	37	27	1	87	8	4	2	9	3	10	.248	.307	.383	.691
2009 Sea	AL	153	565	160	24	1	18	(7	11)	240	85	70	80	46	3	122	4	3	2	16	5	14	.283	.339	.425	.764
2010 Sea	AL	152	568	139	25	3	12	(6	6)	206	61	64	61	50	5	137	1	2	8	25	3	16	.245	.303	.363	.666
2011 Sea	AL	92	322	72	13	0	1	(1	0)	88	26	19	25	16	1	56	1	3	2	13	2	6	.224	.261	.273	.534
2012 Sea	AL	40	150	39	10	1	4	(2	2)	63	18	17	19	9	0	31	2	1	1	3	1	5	.260	.309	.420	.729
2013 Sea	AL	41	145	36	7	0	10	(6	4)	73	18	24	16	5	0	43	0	1	0	3	1	2	.248	.273	.503	.777
Postseason		10	29	6	0	0	1	(0	1)	9	5	4	3	5	0	11	0	0	1	0	0	1	.207	.324	.310	.634
9 ML YEARS		762	2557	654	127	9	67	(38	29)	1000	326	279	286	178	11	581	16	31	18	77	18	58	.256	.306	.391	.697

Juan Gutierrez

Pitches: R Bats: R Pos: RP-61   **Ht: 6'3" Wt: 245 Born: 7/14/1983 Age: 31**

Year Team	Lg	G	GS	CG	GF	IP	BFP	H	R	ER	HR	SH	SF	HB	TBB	IBB	SO	WP	Bk	W	L	Pct	Sh	Sv-Op	Hld	ERC	ERA
2007 Hou	NL	7	3	0	0	21.1	93	25	14	14	3	0	3	0	6	2	16	1	0	1	1	.500	0	0-0	0	4.71	5.91
2009 Ari	NL	65	0	0	21	71.0	307	67	33	32	2	2	4	3	30	5	66	5	0	4	3	.571	0	9-10	7	3.38	4.06
2010 Ari	NL	58	0	0	35	56.2	247	55	33	32	13	1	1	4	23	5	47	1	0	0	6	.000	0	15-17	8	5.00	5.08
2011 Ari	NL	20	0	0	3	18.1	90	22	16	11	3	0	0	1	9	0	23	0	0	0	0	-	0	0-1	2	5.99	5.40
2013 2 Tms	NL	53	0	0	17	55.1	236	56	29	26	5	1	3	1	20	2	45	3	0	1	5	.167	0	0-1	4	3.97	4.23
2014 SF	NL	61	0	0	14	63.2	268	60	30	28	7	3	4	2	16	2	44	1	0	1	2	.333	0	0-1	10	3.27	3.96
13 KC	AL	25	0	0	13	29.1	120	30	13	11	2	0	2	1	8	1	17	1	0	0	1	.000	0	0-0	2	3.72	3.38
13 LAA	AL	28	0	0	4	26.0	116	26	16	15	3	1	1	0	12	1	28	2	0	1	4	.200	0	0-1	2	4.26	5.19
6 ML YEARS		264	3	0	91	286.1	1241	285	155	143	33	7	15	11	104	16	241	11	0	7	17	.292	0	24-30	31	4.04	4.49

Brandon Guyer

Bats: R Throws: R Pos: LF-62;PH-27;CF-11;DH-6;PR-5;RF-1   GUY-er   Ht: 6'2" Wt: 195 Born: 1/28/1986 Age: 29

							BATTING													RUNNING			AVERAGES			
Year	Team	Lg	G	AB	H	2B	3B	HR	(Hm | Rd)	TB	R	RBI	RC	TBB	IBB	SO	HBP	SH	SF	SB	CS	GDP	Avg	OBP	Slg	OPS
2014	Drhm*	AAA	5	20	8	2	2	0	(- | -)	14	8	1	7	6	0	4	0	0	0	0	0	0	.400	.538	.700	1.238
2011	TB	AL	15	41	8	1	0	2	(1 | 1)	15	7	3	2	1	0	9	0	1	0	0	0	1	.195	.214	.366	.580
2012	TB	AL	3	7	1	0	0	1	(0 | 1)	4	2	1	0	0	0	1	0	0	0	0	0	0	.143	.143	.571	.714
2014	TB	AL	97	259	69	15	1	3	(1 | 2)	95	37	26	37	16	0	52	11	7	1	6	1	3	.266	.334	.367	.701
	3 ML YEARS		115	307	78	16	1	6	(2 | 4)	114	46	30	39	17	0	62	11	8	1	6	1	4	.254	.315	.371	.687

Jesus Guzman

Bats: R Throws: R Pos: 1B-52;PH-20;LF-8;DH-4;3B-1   Ht: 6'1" Wt: 200 Born: 6/14/1984 Age: 31

							BATTING													RUNNING			AVERAGES			
Year	Team	Lg	G	AB	H	2B	3B	HR	(Hm	Rd)	TB	R	RBI	RC	TBB	IBB	SO	HBP	SH	SF	SB	CS	GDP	Avg	OBP	Slg	OPS
2014	OKCity*	AAA	4	13	8	3	0	0	(-	-)	11	3	5	6	3	0	2	0	0	1	0	0	0	.615	.647	.846	1.493
2009	SF	NL	12	20	5	0	0	0	(0	0)	5	0	0	0	0	0	3	0	0	0	0	0	2	.250	.250	.250	.500
2011	SD	NL	76	247	77	22	2	5	(4	1)	118	33	44	49	22	2	43	1	0	1	9	2	6	.312	.369	.478	.847
2012	SD	NL	120	287	71	18	2	9	(4	5)	120	32	48	40	29	3	71	2	1	2	3	3	2	.247	.319	.418	.737
2013	SD	NL	126	288	65	17	0	9	(0	9)	109	33	35	35	27	1	79	2	1	0	3	0	4	.226	.297	.378	.675
2014	Hou	AL	69	165	31	4	0	2	(2	0)	41	10	9	8	19	0	52	0	0	0	3	0	4	.188	.272	.248	.520
	5 ML YEARS		403	1007	249	61	4	25	(10	15)	393	108	136	132	97	6	248	5	2	3	18	5	18	.247	.316	.390	.706

Tony Gwynn

Bats: L Throws: R Pos: PH-42;CF-25;LF-16;PR-7;RF-3   Ht: 6'0" Wt: 193 Born: 10/4/1982 Age: 32

							BATTING													RUNNING			AVERAGES			
Year	Team	Lg	G	AB	H	2B	3B	HR	(Hm	Rd)	TB	R	RBI	RC	TBB	IBB	SO	HBP	SH	SF	SB	CS	GDP	Avg	OBP	Slg	OPS
2014	LV*	AAA	20	69	20	2	0	1	(-	-)	25	7	7	9	11	0	12	0	0	1	2	4	1	.290	.383	.362	.745
2006	Mil	NL	32	77	20	2	1	0	(0	0)	24	5	4	5	2	0	15	0	0	1	3	1	2	.260	.275	.312	.587
2007	Mil	NL	69	123	32	3	2	0	(0	0)	39	13	10	16	12	1	24	0	0	0	8	1	0	.260	.326	.317	.643
2008	Mil	NL	29	42	8	1	0	0	(0	0)	9	5	1	2	4	0	7	1	1	1	3	1	1	.190	.271	.214	.485
2009	SD	NL	119	393	106	11	6	2	(1	1)	135	59	21	48	48	2	65	2	5	3	11	7	2	.270	.350	.344	.693
2010	SD	NL	117	289	59	9	3	3	(2	1)	83	30	20	31	41	4	50	1	7	1	17	4	3	.204	.304	.287	.591
2011	LAD	NL	136	312	80	12	6	2	(0	2)	110	37	22	35	23	1	61	1	2	2	22	6	2	.256	.308	.353	.660
2012	LAD	NL	103	259	60	8	4	0	(0	0)	76	29	17	22	16	2	52	0	2	0	13	6	6	.232	.276	.293	.570
2014	Phi	NL	80	105	16	2	1	0	(0	0)	20	14	3	8	15	1	23	1	6	0	3	0	0	.152	.264	.190	.455
	Postseason		3	3	1	0	0	0	(0	0)	1	0	0	0	0	0	1	0	0	0	0	0	0	.333	.333	.333	.667
	8 ML YEARS		685	1600	381	48	23	7	(3	4)	496	192	98	167	161	11	297	6	23	8	80	26	16	.238	.309	.310	.619

Jedd Gyorko

Bats: R Throws: R Pos: 2B-109;PH-5   JERK-oh   Ht: 5'10" Wt: 210 Born: 9/23/1988 Age: 26

							BATTING													RUNNING			AVERAGES			
Year	Team	Lg	G	AB	H	2B	3B	HR	(Hm	Rd)	TB	R	RBI	RC	TBB	IBB	SO	HBP	SH	SF	SB	CS	GDP	Avg	OBP	Slg	OPS
2010	Eugene	A-	26	106	35	6	0	5	(-	-)	56	16	18	20	9	0	26	0	0	0	1	1	3	.330	.383	.528	.911
2010	FtWyn	A	42	162	46	11	0	2	(-	-)	63	19	23	24	19	0	31	2	0	0	1	0	3	.284	.366	.389	.755
2011	Lk Els	A+	81	340	124	35	2	18	(-	-)	217	78	74	88	38	4	64	2	0	2	11	3	6	.365	.429	.638	1.068
2011	SnAnt	AA	59	236	68	12	0	7	(-	-)	101	41	40	38	26	1	50	1	0	2	1	0	5	.288	.358	.428	.786
2012	SnAnt	AA	34	130	34	4	0	6	(-	-)	56	18	17	20	17	2	27	2	0	0	1	1	3	.262	.356	.431	.786
2012	Tucsn	AAA	92	369	121	24	0	24	(-	-)	217	62	83	80	34	0	68	0	0	5	4	3	10	.328	.380	.588	.968
2013	SnAnt	AA	1	1	1	0	0	0	(-	-)	1	0	0	0	0	0	0	0	0	0	0	0	0	1.000	1.000	1.000	2.000
2013	Lk Els	A+	2	7	4	1	0	0	(-	-)	5	2	1	2	0	0	1	0	0	0	0	0	0	.571	.571	.714	1.286
2014	ElPaso	AAA	6	24	7	2	0	1	(-	-)	12	7	5	4	4	0	4	0	0	0	0	0	0	.292	.393	.500	.893
2013	SD	NL	125	486	121	26	0	23	(13	10)	216	62	63	48	33	1	123	4	0	2	1	1	14	.249	.301	.444	.745
2014	SD	NL	111	400	84	17	1	10	(7	3)	133	37	51	42	36	1	100	4	0	3	3	2	8	.210	.280	.333	.612
	2 ML YEARS		236	886	205	43	1	33	(20	13)	349	99	114	90	69	2	223	8	0	5	4	3	22	.231	.291	.394	.685

Nick Hagadone

Pitches: L Bats: L Pos: RP-35   HAGG-uh-donn   Ht: 6'5" Wt: 230 Born: 1/1/1986 Age: 29

			HOW MUCH HE PITCHED					WHAT HE GAVE UP											THE RESULTS						
Year	Team	Lg	G	GS	CG	GF	IP	BFP	H	R	ER	HR	SH	SF	HB	TBB	IBB	SO	WP	Bk	W	L	Pct	Sh	Sv-Op	Hld	ERC	ERA
2014	Clmbs*	AAA	23	0	0	7	28.2	122	26	16	12	5	4	1	1	12	1	41	1	0	3	4	.429	0	1--	-	4.25	3.77
2011	Cle	AL	9	0	0	3	11.0	42	4	6	5	0	0	1	0	6	0	11	2	0	1	0	1.000	0	0-0	1	1.35	4.09
2012	Cle	AL	27	0	0	10	25.1	116	26	18	18	4	0	2	0	15	0	26	2	0	1	0	1.000	0	1-2	2	5.37	6.39
2013	Cle	AL	36	0	0	1	31.1	133	24	21	19	4	2	1	0	21	1	30	3	0	1	0	1.000	0	0-1	4	4.08	5.46
2014	Cle	AL	35	0	0	4	23.1	91	18	7	7	3	1	0	0	6	2	27	0	0	1	0	1.000	0	0-0	3	2.46	2.70
	4 ML YEARS		107	0	0	18	91.0	382	72	52	49	11	3	4	1	48	3	94	7	0	3	1	.750	0	1-3	7	3.61	4.85

Bradin Hagens

Pitches: R Bats: R Pos: RP-2   Ht: 6'3" Wt: 210 Born: 5/12/1989 Age: 26

			HOW MUCH HE PITCHED					WHAT HE GAVE UP											THE RESULTS						
Year	Team	Lg	G	GS	CG	GF	IP	BFP	H	R	ER	HR	SH	SF	HB	TBB	IBB	SO	WP	Bk	W	L	Pct	Sh	Sv-Op	Hld	ERC	ERA
2010	Sbend	A	39	0	0	17	60.1	297	90	50	44	2	5	3	2	25	3	55	7	0	3	6	.333	0	4--	-	6.42	6.56
2011	Sbend	A	24	24	0	0	124.2	547	128	67	57	11	4	4	3	53	0	79	11	0	8	7	.533	0	0--	-	4.33	4.11
2012	Visalia	A+	35	11	0	7	95.0	407	83	48	41	4	1	4	7	49	0	82	9	0	3	4	.429	0	0--	-	3.77	3.88
2012	Mobile	AA	2	2	0	0	11.1	45	9	5	5	2	0	0	1	2	0	5	0	0	0	0	-	0	0--	-	2.96	3.97

Year	Team	Lg	G	GS	CG	GF	IP	BFP	H	R	ER	HR	SH	SF	HB	TBB	IBB	SO	WP	Bk	W	L	Pct	Sh	Sv-Op	Hld	ERC	ERA
2013	Mobile	AA	26	26	0	0	148.0	639	147	63	57	10	5	2	7	66	0	93	12	0	11	8	.579	0	0--	-	4.24	3.47
2014	Mobile	AA	24	18	0	3	110.2	482	108	65	51	7	7	4	4	49	1	60	5	0	8	6	.571	0	0--	-	3.97	4.15
2014	Reno	AAA	4	4	1	0	24.2	103	21	11	7	1	0	0	1	9	0	9	2	0	1	1	.500	0	0--	-	2.90	2.55
2014	Ari	NL	2	0	0	2	2.2	14	4	1	1	0	1	0	0	3	1	2	0	0	0	1	.000	0	0-0	0	8.87	3.38

Matt Hague

Bats: R **Throws:** R **Pos:** PH-3 HAIG **Ht:** 6'3" **Wt:** 220 **Born:** 8/20/1985 **Age:** 29

Year	Team	Lg	G	AB	H	2B	3B	HR	(Hm	Rd)	TB	R	RBI	RC	TBB	IBB	SO	HBP	SH	SF	SB	CS	GDP	Avg	OBP	Slg	OPS
2010	Altna	AA	135	509	150	29	0	15	(-	-)	224	90	86	87	61	5	62	7	0	4	3	6	11	.295	.375	.440	.815
2011	Indy	AAA	141	534	165	37	3	12	(-	-)	244	70	75	93	47	4	68	9	0	4	4	3	12	.309	.372	.457	.829
2012	Indy	AAA	91	367	104	13	0	4	(-	-)	129	41	54	45	26	1	50	2	1	3	3	1	11	.283	.332	.351	.683
2013	Indy	AAA	142	536	153	37	2	8	(-	-)	218	67	69	88	71	3	96	11	1	3	4	3	12	.285	.378	.407	.785
2014	Indy	AAA	93	330	88	16	1	14	(-	-)	148	52	66	57	46	1	66	7	0	3	1	2	5	.267	.365	.448	.814
2014	Buffalo	AAA	13	53	20	7	0	1	(-	-)	30	8	10	11	3	0	10	0	0	0	0	1	1	.377	.411	.566	.977
2012	Pit	NL	30	70	16	2	0	0	(0	0)	18	5	7	4	3	0	14	1	0	0	1	0	1	.229	.270	.257	.527
2014	Pit	NL	3	2	0	0	0	0	(0	0)	0	0	0	0	0	0	1	0	0	0	0	0	1	.000	.000	.000	.000
	2 ML YEARS		33	72	16	2	0	0	(0	0)	18	5	7	4	3	0	15	1	0	0	1	0	2	.222	.263	.250	.513

Jesse Hahn

Pitches: R **Bats:** R **Pos:** SP-12; RP-2 **Ht:** 6'5" **Wt:** 190 **Born:** 7/30/1989 **Age:** 25

Year	Team	Lg	G	GS	CG	GF	IP	BFP	H	R	ER	HR	SH	SF	HB	TBB	IBB	SO	WP	Bk	W	L	Pct	Sh	Sv-Op	Hld	ERC	ERA
2012	HudVal	A-	14	14	0	0	52.0	211	38	18	16	0	1	2	2	15	0	55	2	0	2	2	.500	0	0--	-	1.78	2.77
2013	Charltt	A+	19	19	0	0	67.0	275	55	20	16	1	1	1	3	18	0	63	8	0	2	1	.667	0	0--	-	2.25	2.15
2013	Rays	R	1	1	0	0	2.0	11	4	1	0	0	0	0	0	0	0	4	0	0	0	0	-	0	0--	-	6.75	0.00
2014	SnAnt	AA	13	10	0	0	42.1	172	34	13	9	1	1	1	1	15	0	38	0	1	2	1	.667	0	0--	-	2.49	1.91
2014	SD	NL	14	12	0	2	73.1	306	57	26	25	4	3	1	4	32	1	70	4	0	7	4	.636	0	0-0	0	2.91	3.07

Scott Hairston

Bats: R **Throws:** R **Pos:** PH-47;LF-15;RF-1;DH-1;PR-1 **Ht:** 6'0" **Wt:** 200 **Born:** 5/25/1980 **Age:** 35

Year	Team	Lg	G	AB	H	2B	3B	HR	(Hm	Rd)	TB	R	RBI	RC	TBB	IBB	SO	HBP	SH	SF	SB	CS	GDP	Avg	OBP	Slg	OPS
2014	Syrcse*	AAA	3	10	1	1	0	0	(-	-)	2	0	1	0	2	0	4	0	0	1	0	0	1	.100	.250	.200	.450
2004	Ari	NL	101	339	84	15	6	13	(6	7)	150	39	29	32	21	0	88	1	2	1	3	3	4	.248	.293	.442	.735
2005	Ari	NL	15	20	2	1	0	0	(0	0)	3	0	0	0	0	0	6	0	0	0	0	0	1	.100	.100	.150	.250
2006	Ari	NL	9	15	6	2	0	0	(0	0)	8	2	2	2	1	0	5	0	0	0	0	0	1	.400	.438	.533	.971
2007	2 Tms	NL	107	263	64	18	2	11	(6	5)	119	37	36	36	26	0	55	1	3	1	2	0	4	.243	.313	.452	.765
2008	SD	NL	112	326	81	18	3	17	(9	8)	156	42	31	43	28	2	84	3	3	2	3	1	2	.248	.312	.479	.791
2009	2 Tms	NL	116	430	114	27	2	17	(9	8)	196	50	64	60	25	0	83	3	1	5	11	3	9	.265	.307	.456	.763
2010	SD	NL	104	295	62	10	0	10	(5	5)	102	34	36	28	31	1	69	6	0	4	6	1	3	.210	.295	.346	.640
2011	NYM	NL	79	132	31	8	1	7	(2	5)	62	20	24	16	11	2	34	2	0	0	1	1	2	.235	.303	.470	.773
2012	NYM	NL	134	377	99	25	3	20	(11	9)	190	52	57	53	19	0	83	1	0	1	8	2	10	.263	.299	.504	.803
2013	2 Tms	NL	85	157	30	5	0	10	(7	3)	65	18	26	14	9	0	44	2	1	5	2	0	3	.191	.237	.414	.651
2014	Was	NL	61	77	16	4	0	1	(1	0)	23	6	8	4	4	0	26	2	0	4	0	0	2	.208	.253	.299	.552
07	Ari	NL	76	176	39	13	1	3	(1	2)	63	21	16	19	19	0	37	1	3	0	2	0	4	.222	.301	.358	.659
07	SD	NL	31	87	25	5	1	8	(5	3)	56	16	20	17	7	0	18	0	0	1	0	0	0	.287	.337	.644	.981
09	SD	NL	56	197	59	14	1	10	(5	5)	105	26	29	35	17	0	45	1	1	0	8	1	4	.299	.358	.533	.891
09	Oak	AL	60	233	55	13	1	7	(4	3)	91	24	35	25	8	0	38	2	0	5	3	2	5	.236	.262	.391	.653
13	ChC	NL	40	99	17	2	0	8	(7	1)	43	13	19	9	7	0	25	2	0	4	2	0	3	.172	.232	.434	.666
13	Was	NL	33	58	13	3	0	2	(0	2)	22	5	7	5	2	0	19	0	1	1	0	0	0	.224	.246	.379	.625
	11 ML YEARS		923	2431	589	133	17	106	(56	50)	1074	300	313	288	175	5	577	21	10	23	36	11	41	.242	.296	.442	.738

David Hale

Pitches: R **Bats:** R **Pos:** RP-39; SP-6 **Ht:** 6'2" **Wt:** 210 **Born:** 9/27/1987 **Age:** 27

Year	Team	Lg	G	GS	CG	GF	IP	BFP	H	R	ER	HR	SH	SF	HB	TBB	IBB	SO	WP	Bk	W	L	Pct	Sh	Sv-Op	Hld	ERC	ERA
2010	Rome	A	28	7	0	12	93.2	420	97	52	43	1	6	3	4	44	0	69	11	0	5	8	.385	0	5--	-	4.01	4.13
2011	Lynbrg	A+	28	13	1	3	101.0	432	106	52	46	9	3	4	10	30	1	86	7	0	4	6	.400	0	0--	-	4.33	4.10
2012	Missi	AA	27	27	0	0	145.2	608	121	66	60	11	7	3	10	67	2	124	9	0	8	4	.667	0	0--	-	3.48	3.77
2013	Gwnntt	AAA	22	20	0	1	114.2	495	123	50	41	8	5	6	7	36	3	77	2	1	6	9	.400	0	0--	-	4.16	3.22
2013	Atl	NL	2	2	0	0	11.0	46	11	1	1	0	0	0	0	1	0	14	0	0	1	0	1.000	0	0-0	0	2.18	0.82
2014	Atl	NL	45	6	0	13	87.1	383	89	38	32	5	1	3	3	39	8	44	5	0	4	5	.444	0	0-0	0	4.05	3.30
	Postseason		1	0	0	1	0.1	0	0	0	0	0	0	0	0	0	0	0	0	0	0	0	-	0	0-0	0	0.00	0.00
	2 ML YEARS		47	8	0	13	98.1	429	100	39	33	5	1	3	3	40	8	58	5	0	5	5	.500	0	0-0	4	3.82	3.02

Cole Hamels

Pitches: L **Bats:** L **Pos:** SP-30 **Ht:** 6'3" **Wt:** 195 **Born:** 12/27/1983 **Age:** 31

Year	Team	Lg	G	GS	CG	GF	IP	BFP	H	R	ER	HR	SH	SF	HB	TBB	IBB	SO	WP	Bk	W	L	Pct	Sh	Sv-Op	Hld	ERC	ERA
2014	Clrwtr*	A+	3	3	0	0	17.0	59	12	4	4	3	0	0	1	1	0	12	1	0	0	1	.000	0	0--	-	2.19	2.12
2006	Phi	NL	23	23	0	0	132.1	558	117	66	60	19	6	8	3	48	4	145	16	0	9	8	.529	0	0-0	0	3.61	4.08
2007	Phi	NL	28	28	2	0	183.1	743	163	72	69	25	5	5	3	43	4	177	5	0	15	5	.750	2	0-0	0	3.12	3.39
2008	Phi	NL	33	33	2	0	227.1	914	193	89	78	28	6	2	1	53	7	196	0	0	14	10	.583	2	0-0	0	2.76	3.09
2009	Phi	NL	32	32	1	0	193.2	814	206	95	93	24	7	5	0	43	4	168	1	0	10	11	.476	2	0-0	0	3.98	4.32

162

Year	Team	Lg	G	GS	CG	GF	IP	BFP	H	R	ER	HR	SH	SF	HB	TBB	IBB	SO	WP	Bk	W	L	Pct	Sh	Sv-Op	Hld	ERC	ERA
2010	Phi	NL	33	33	1	0	208.2	856	185	74	71	26	7	0	8	61	5	211	3	0	12	11	.522	0	0-0	0	3.36	3.06
2011	Phi	NL	32	31	3	0	216.0	850	169	68	67	19	9	3	5	44	2	194	3	3	14	9	.609	0	0-0	0	2.23	2.79
2012	Phi	NL	31	31	2	0	215.1	867	190	80	73	24	6	4	3	52	3	216	3	2	17	6	.739	2	0-0	0	2.98	3.05
2013	Phi	NL	33	33	1	0	220.0	905	205	94	88	21	11	3	9	50	5	202	4	0	8	14	.364	0	0-0	0	3.15	3.60
2014	Phi	NL	30	30	0	0	204.2	829	176	60	56	14	7	7	8	59	3	198	6	1	9	9	.500	0	0-0	0	2.88	2.46
	Postseason		13	13	1	0	81.2	326	65	29	28	9	3	2	2	21	1	77	0	0	7	4	.636	1	0-0	0	2.62	3.09
	9 ML YEARS		275	274	13	0	1801.1	7336	1604	698	655	200	64	37	45	453	37	1707	30	6	108	83	.565	6	0-0	0	3.07	3.27

Billy Hamilton

Bats: B **Throws:** R **Pos:** CF-144;PH-9;PR-3;DH-1 **Ht:** 6'0" **Wt:** 160 **Born:** 9/9/1990 **Age:** 24

Year	Team	Lg	G	AB	H	2B	3B	HR	(Hm	Rd)	TB	R	RBI	RC	TBB	IBB	SO	HBP	SH	SF	SB	CS	GDP	Avg	OBP	Slg	OPS
2010	Billings	R+	69	283	90	13	10	2	(-	-)	129	61	24	56	28	0	56	3	0	2	48	9	2	.318	.383	.456	.839
2011	Dayton	A	135	550	153	18	9	3	(-	-)	198	99	50	83	52	0	133	1	4	3	103	20	5	.278	.340	.360	.700
2012	Bkrsfld	A+	82	337	109	18	9	1	(-	-)	148	79	30	76	50	1	70	2	2	1	104	21	2	.323	.413	.439	.852
2012	Pnscla	AA	50	175	50	4	5	1	(-	-)	67	33	15	34	36	1	43	0	1	1	51	16	0	.286	.406	.383	.789
2013	Lsvlle	AAA	123	504	129	18	4	6	(-	-)	173	75	41	63	38	0	102	0	4	1	75	15	4	.256	.308	.343	.651
2013	Cin	NL	13	19	7	2	0	0	(0	0)	9	9	1	5	2	0	4	0	1	0	13	1	0	.368	.429	.474	.902
2014	Cin	NL	152	563	141	25	8	6	(3	3)	200	72	48	64	34	0	117	1	9	4	56	23	1	.250	.292	.355	.648
	2 ML YEARS		165	582	148	27	8	6	(3	3)	209	81	49	69	36	0	121	1	10	4	69	24	1	.254	.297	.359	.656

Josh Hamilton

Bats: L **Throws:** L **Pos:** LF-68;DH-14;CF-7;PH-1 **Ht:** 6'4" **Wt:** 240 **Born:** 5/21/1981 **Age:** 34

Year	Team	Lg	G	AB	H	2B	3B	HR	(Hm	Rd)	TB	R	RBI	RC	TBB	IBB	SO	HBP	SH	SF	SB	CS	GDP	Avg	OBP	Slg	OPS
2014	Salt Lk*	AAA	3	13	6	2	0	0	(-	-)	8	2	0	3	0	0	2	0	0	0	0	0	1	.462	.462	.615	1.077
2007	Cin	NL	90	298	87	17	2	19	(11	8)	165	52	47	58	33	4	65	4	0	2	3	3	6	.292	.368	.554	.922
2008	Tex	AL	156	624	190	35	5	32	(19	13)	331	98	130	119	64	9	126	7	0	9	9	1	8	.304	.371	.530	.901
2009	Tex	AL	89	336	90	19	2	10	(6	4)	143	43	54	51	24	2	79	1	0	4	8	3	5	.268	.315	.426	.741
2010	Tex	AL	133	518	186	40	3	32	(22	10)	328	95	100	121	43	5	95	5	1	4	8	1	11	.359	.411	.633	1.044
2011	Tex	AL	121	487	145	31	5	25	(14	11)	261	80	94	78	39	13	93	2	0	10	8	1	8	.298	.346	.536	.882
2012	Tex	AL	148	562	160	31	2	43	(22	21)	324	103	128	108	60	13	162	5	0	9	7	4	9	.285	.354	.577	.930
2013	LAA	AL	151	576	144	32	5	21	(9	12)	249	73	79	67	47	4	158	4	0	16	4	0	16	.250	.307	.432	.739
2014	LAA	AL	89	338	89	21	0	10	(0	10)	140	43	44	49	32	5	108	5	0	6	3	3	2	.263	.331	.414	.745
	Postseason		34	132	30	8	0	6	(2	4)	56	18	22	17	14	7	23	0	0	3	4	1	4	.227	.295	.424	.720
	8 ML YEARS		977	3739	1091	226	24	192	(103	89)	1941	587	676	651	342	55	886	33	1	53	50	16	65	.292	.352	.519	.871

Jason Hammel

Pitches: R **Bats:** R **Pos:** SP-29; RP-1 **Ht:** 6'6" **Wt:** 225 **Born:** 9/2/1982 **Age:** 32

Year	Team	Lg	G	GS	CG	GF	IP	BFP	H	R	ER	HR	SH	SF	HB	TBB	IBB	SO	WP	Bk	W	L	Pct	Sh	Sv-Op	Hld	ERC	ERA
2006	TB	AL	9	9	0	0	44.0	208	61	38	38	7	0	3	1	21	0	32	3	2	0	6	.000	0	0-0	0	7.40	7.77
2007	TB	AL	24	14	0	2	85.0	384	100	58	58	12	2	0	2	40	1	64	3	0	3	5	.375	0	0-0	0	5.86	6.14
2008	TB	AL	40	5	0	21	78.1	346	83	45	40	11	2	2	2	35	4	44	7	0	4	4	.500	0	2-2	1	4.94	4.60
2009	Col	NL	34	30	1	0	176.2	771	203	94	85	17	10	9	9	42	6	133	4	0	10	8	.556	0	0-0	0	4.37	4.33
2010	Col	NL	30	30	0	0	177.2	770	201	97	95	18	11	6	6	47	1	141	13	2	10	9	.526	0	0-0	0	4.41	4.81
2011	Col	NL	32	27	0	2	170.1	739	175	100	90	21	11	6	6	68	3	94	8	1	7	13	.350	0	1-1	0	4.54	4.76
2012	Bal	AL	20	20	1	0	118.0	493	104	48	45	9	3	1	2	42	2	113	3	0	8	6	.571	1	0-0	0	3.14	3.43
2013	Bal	AL	26	23	0	1	139.1	611	155	81	77	22	2	8	8	48	1	96	1	0	7	8	.467	0	1-1	1	5.19	4.97
2014	2 Tms		30	29	0	1	176.1	715	154	70	68	23	3	4	8	44	2	158	6	0	10	11	.476	0	0-0	0	3.21	3.47
14	ChC	NL	17	17	0	0	108.2	429	88	36	36	10	2	3	5	23	2	104	4	0	8	5	.615	0	0-0	0	2.51	2.98
14	Oak	AL	13	12	0	1	67.2	286	66	34	32	13	1	1	3	21	0	54	2	0	2	6	.250	0	0-0	0	4.42	4.26
	Postseason		3	3	0	0	15.0	62	12	8	8	1	0	0	0	9	2	16	0	0	0	1	.000	0	0-0	0	3.46	4.80
	9 ML YEARS		245	187	2	27	1165.2	5037	1236	631	596	140	44	39	44	387	20	875	48	5	59	70	.457	1	4-4	2	4.43	4.60

Brad Hand

Pitches: L **Bats:** L **Pos:** SP-16; RP-16 **Ht:** 6'3" **Wt:** 220 **Born:** 3/20/1990 **Age:** 25

Year	Team	Lg	G	GS	CG	GF	IP	BFP	H	R	ER	HR	SH	SF	HB	TBB	IBB	SO	WP	Bk	W	L	Pct	Sh	Sv-Op	Hld	ERC	ERA
2014	Jupiter*	A+	2	2	0	0	12.0	41	4	1	1	0	0	0	0	2	0	14	0	0	-	-		0	0--	-	0.46	0.75
2014	NewOr*	AAA	4	4	0	0	22.0	90	18	8	8	3	3	1	0	9	1	22	0	0	2	0	1.000	0	0--	-	3.36	3.27
2011	Fla	NL	12	12	0	0	60.0	263	53	32	28	10	4	3	1	35	1	38	0	1	1	8	.111	0	0-0	0	4.68	4.20
2012	Mia	NL	1	1	0	0	3.2	23	6	7	7	1	0	0	0	6	1	3	0	0	0	1	.000	0	0-0	0	14.74	17.18
2013	Mia	NL	7	2	0	2	20.2	82	13	7	7	2	0	0	0	8	0	15	1	0	1	1	.500	0	0-0	0	2.10	3.05
2014	Mia	NL	32	16	0	5	111.0	474	112	56	54	10	6	2	2	39	3	67	5	0	3	8	.273	0	1-1	0	3.91	4.38
	4 ML YEARS		52	31	0	7	195.1	842	184	102	96	23	10	5	3	88	5	123	6	1	5	18	.217	0	1-1	0	4.10	4.42

Ryan Hanigan

Bats: R **Throws:** R **Pos:** C-79;PH-8;DH-1 HANN-eh-gann **Ht:** 6'0" **Wt:** 210 **Born:** 8/16/1980 **Age:** 34

Year	Team	Lg	G	AB	H	2B	3B	HR	(Hm	Rd)	TB	R	RBI	RC	TBB	IBB	SO	HBP	SH	SF	SB	CS	GDP	Avg	OBP	Slg	OPS
2014	Charltt*	A+	6	20	5	0	0	1	(-	-)	8	4	2	3	2	0	3	2	0	0	0	0	1	.250	.375	.400	.775
2007	Cin	NL	5	10	3	1	0	0	(0	0)	4	3	2	2	1	1	2	0	0	0	0	0	0	.300	.364	.400	.764
2008	Cin	NL	31	85	23	2	0	2	(1	1)	31	9	9	12	10	1	9	3	0	0	0	0	2	.271	.367	.365	.732
2009	Cin	NL	90	251	66	6	1	3	(3	0)	83	22	11	25	37	7	31	2	2	1	0	0	9	.263	.361	.331	.692

163

Year	Team	Lg	G	AB	H	2B	3B	HR	(Hm	Rd)	TB	R	RBI	RC	TBB	IBB	SO	HBP	SH	SF	SB	CS	GDP	Avg	OBP	Slg	OPS
2010	Cin	NL	70	203	61	11	0	5	(2	3)	87	25	40	41	33	4	21	4	1	2	0	0	6	.300	.405	.429	.834
2011	Cin	NL	91	266	71	6	0	6	(4	2)	95	27	31	38	35	3	32	2	1	0	0	0	3	.267	.356	.357	.714
2012	Cin	NL	112	317	87	14	0	2	(0	2)	107	25	24	40	44	13	37	3	4	3	0	0	6	.274	.365	.338	.703
2013	Cin	NL	75	222	44	8	0	2	(1	1)	58	17	21	18	29	9	27	6	2	1	0	1	7	.198	.306	.261	.567
2014	TB	AL	84	225	49	9	0	5	(4	1)	73	18	34	27	31	0	39	3	2	2	1	0	6	.218	.318	.324	.642
Postseason			7	22	3	0	0	0	(0	0)	3	3	3	1	0	0	3	1	0	0	0	0	1	.136	.174	.136	.310
8 ML YEARS			558	1579	404	57	1	25	(15	10)	538	146	172	203	220	38	198	23	12	9	1	1	39	.256	.353	.341	.694

Jack Hannahan

Bats: L Throws: R Pos: PH-14;1B-13;DH-1   Ht: 6'2" Wt: 210 Born: 3/4/1980 Age: 35

Year	Team	Lg	G	AB	H	2B	3B	HR	(Hm	Rd)	TB	R	RBI	RC	TBB	IBB	SO	HBP	SH	SF	SB	CS	GDP	Avg	OBP	Slg	OPS
2014	Dayton*	A	4	12	4	1	0	0	(-	-)	5	0	1	1	1	1	5	0	0	0	0	0	0	.333	.385	.417	.801
2014	Lsvlle*	AAA	8	28	8	2	0	0	(-	-)	10	1	5	3	2	0	4	0	0	1	0	0	2	.286	.323	.357	.680
2006	Det	AL	3	9	0	0	0	0	(0	0)	0	0	0	0	1	0	1	0	0	0	0	0	0	.000	.100	.000	.100
2007	Oak	AL	41	144	40	12	0	3	(1	2)	61	16	24	23	21	0	39	1	1	2	1	0	6	.278	.369	.424	.793
2008	Oak	AL	143	436	95	27	0	9	(4	5)	149	48	47	38	55	4	131	2	3	5	2	0	5	.218	.305	.342	.647
2009	2 Tms	AL	103	267	57	14	2	4	(2	2)	87	27	19	20	30	0	71	2	1	1	1	1	4	.213	.297	.326	.623
2011	Cle	AL	110	320	80	16	2	8	(7	1)	124	38	40	47	38	0	80	2	4	2	2	1	7	.250	.331	.388	.719
2012	Cle	AL	105	287	70	16	0	4	(3	1)	98	23	29	31	27	0	63	2	1	1	0	2	9	.244	.312	.341	.654
2013	Cin	NL	83	139	30	5	1	1	(1	0)	40	12	14	15	19	1	38	2	0	1	0	0	6	.216	.317	.288	.605
2014	Cin	NL	26	48	9	3	0	0	(0	0)	12	3	2	0	2	0	17	0	0	0	0	0	2	.188	.220	.250	.470
09	Oak	AL	52	119	23	6	2	1	(1	0)	36	12	8	7	13	0	36	1	1	0	0	0	2	.193	.278	.303	.581
09	Sea	AL	51	148	34	8	0	3	(1	2)	51	15	11	13	17	0	35	1	0	1	1	1	2	.230	.311	.345	.656
8 ML YEARS			614	1650	381	93	5	29	(18	11)	571	167	175	174	193	5	440	11	10	12	6	4	39	.231	.314	.346	.660

Joel Hanrahan

Pitches: R Bats: R Pos: P   Ht: 6'4" Wt: 250 Born: 10/6/1981 Age: 33

Year	Team	Lg	G	GS	CG	GF	IP	BFP	H	R	ER	HR	SH	SF	HB	TBB	IBB	SO	WP	Bk	W	L	Pct	Sh	Sv-Op	Hld	ERC	ERA
2007	Was	NL	12	11	0	0	51.0	247	59	35	34	9	2	1	0	38	0	43	3	0	5	3	.625	0	0-0	0	7.01	6.00
2008	Was	NL	69	0	0	34	84.1	364	73	40	37	9	2	6	1	42	7	93	6	0	6	3	.667	0	9-13	3	3.65	3.95
2009	2 Tms	NL	67	0	0	30	64.0	297	73	40	34	3	0	1	3	34	1	72	11	1	1	4	.200	0	5-10	9	5.12	4.78
2010	Pit	NL	72	0	0	27	69.2	294	58	28	28	6	0	1	4	26	0	100	5	0	4	1	.800	0	6-10	18	3.16	3.62
2011	Pit	NL	70	0	0	59	68.2	274	56	17	14	1	1	2	1	16	2	61	6	0	1	4	.200	0	40-44	0	2.00	1.83
2012	Pit	NL	63	0	0	57	59.2	254	40	18	18	8	3	0	1	36	0	67	6	0	5	2	.714	0	36-40	0	3.32	2.72
2013	Bos	AL	9	0	0	6	7.1	37	10	8	8	4	1	0	0	6	0	5	1	0	0	1	.000	0	4-6	0	12.34	9.82
09	Was	NL	34	0	0	23	32.2	163	50	28	28	3	0	1	2	14	0	35	6	1	1	3	.250	0	5-10	2	7.49	7.71
09	Pit	NL	33	0	0	7	31.1	134	23	12	6	0	0	0	1	20	1	37	5	0	0	1	.000	0	0-0	7	2.92	1.72
7 ML YEARS			362	11	0	213	404.2	1767	369	186	173	40	9	11	10	198	10	441	38	1	22	18	.550	0	100-123	30	3.95	3.85

Tommy Hanson

Pitches: R Bats: R Pos: P   Ht: 6'6" Wt: 220 Born: 8/28/1986 Age: 28

Year	Team	Lg	G	GS	CG	GF	IP	BFP	H	R	ER	HR	SH	SF	HB	TBB	IBB	SO	WP	Bk	W	L	Pct	Sh	Sv-Op	Hld	ERC	ERA
2014	Charltt*	AAA	10	10	0	0	49.2	224	49	36	34	9	0	1	2	28	0	32	2	0	3	5	.375	0	0- -	-	5.42	6.16
2009	Atl	NL	21	21	0	0	127.2	522	105	42	41	10	4	1	5	46	1	116	2	0	11	4	.733	0	0-0	0	3.02	2.89
2010	Atl	NL	34	34	1	0	202.2	845	182	86	75	14	9	5	14	56	3	173	3	0	10	11	.476	0	0-0	0	3.08	3.33
2011	Atl	NL	22	22	0	0	130.0	540	106	55	52	17	4	3	3	46	3	142	5	0	11	7	.611	0	0-0	0	3.13	3.60
2012	Atl	NL	31	31	0	0	174.2	761	183	95	87	27	8	2	5	71	5	161	6	0	13	10	.565	0	0-0	0	4.88	4.48
2013	LAA	AL	15	13	0	1	73.0	327	83	47	44	10	4	3	3	30	3	56	6	0	4	3	.571	0	0-0	0	5.30	5.42
Postseason			1	1	0	0	4.0	17	5	4	4	1	0	0	0	1	0	5	0	0	0	0	-	0	0-0	0	6.26	9.00
5 ML YEARS			123	121	1	1	708.0	2995	659	325	299	78	25	15	30	249	15	648	22	0	49	35	.583	0	0-0	0	3.72	3.80

J.A. Happ

Pitches: L Bats: L Pos: SP-26; RP-4   JAY   Ht: 6'5" Wt: 205 Born: 10/19/1982 Age: 32

Year	Team	Lg	G	GS	CG	GF	IP	BFP	H	R	ER	HR	SH	SF	HB	TBB	IBB	SO	WP	Bk	W	L	Pct	Sh	Sv-Op	Hld	ERC	ERA
2014	Dnedin*	A+	1	1	0	0	5.0	18	3	2	2	0	0	0	0	1	0	5	0	0	1	0	1.000	0	0- -	-	1.17	3.60
2014	Buffalo*	AAA	1	1	0	0	4.2	20	5	1	1	1	0	0	0	2	0	6	0	0	0	0	-	0	0- -	-	5.61	1.93
2007	Phi	NL	1	1	0	0	4.0	21	7	5	5	3	0	0	0	2	0	5	0	0	0	1	.000	0	0-0	0	15.13	11.25
2008	Phi	NL	8	4	0	1	31.2	138	28	13	13	3	2	1	1	14	1	26	1	0	1	0	1.000	0	0-0	1	3.55	3.69
2009	Phi	NL	35	23	3	4	166.0	685	149	55	54	20	7	6	5	56	2	119	2	0	12	4	.750	2	0-0	0	3.57	2.93
2010	2 Tms	NL	16	16	1	0	87.1	374	73	37	33	8	5	4	1	47	1	70	4	0	6	4	.600	1	0-0	0	3.69	3.40
2011	Hou	NL	28	28	0	0	156.1	698	157	103	93	21	12	8	2	83	5	134	3	2	6	15	.286	0	0-0	0	4.86	5.35
2012	2 Tms	NL	28	24	0	3	144.2	627	147	79	77	19	9	4	2	56	1	144	7	0	10	11	.476	0	0-0	4	4.37	4.79
2013	Tor	AL	18	18	0	0	92.2	415	91	53	47	10	1	3	2	45	0	77	5	0	5	7	.417	0	0-0	1	4.36	4.56
2014	Tor	AL	30	26	0	2	158.0	673	160	79	74	22	1	5	2	51	0	133	1	0	11	11	.500	0	0-0	0	4.17	4.22
10	Phi	NL	3	3	0	0	15.1	70	13	4	3	1	1	0	0	12	0	9	1	0	1	0	1.000	0	0-0	0	4.40	1.76
10	Hou	NL	13	13	1	0	72.0	304	60	33	30	7	4	3	1	35	1	61	3	0	5	4	.556	1	0-0	0	3.53	3.75
12	Phi	NL	18	18	0	0	104.1	457	112	58	56	17	7	2	1	39	0	98	5	0	7	9	.438	0	0-0	0	4.86	4.83
12	Tor	AL	10	6	0	3	40.1	170	35	21	21	2	2	2	1	17	1	46	2	0	3	2	.600	0	0-0	1	3.16	4.69
Postseason			8	1	0	0	9.1	46	12	5	5	1	0	0	0	8	0	10	0	0	0	0	-	0	0-0	1	7.96	4.82
8 ML YEARS			164	140	4	10	840.2	3631	812	424	396	106	37	31	15	354	10	708	23	2	51	53	.490	3	0-0	2	4.20	4.24

Aaron Harang

Pitches: R Bats: R Pos: SP-33 — huh-RANG — Ht: 6'7" Wt: 260 Born: 5/9/1978 Age: 37

Year	Team	Lg	G	GS	CG	GF	IP	BFP	H	R	ER	HR	SH	SF	HB	TBB	IBB	SO	WP	Bk	W	L	Pct	Sh	Sv-Op	Hld	ERC	ERA
2002	Oak	AL	16	15	0	0	78.1	354	78	44	42	7	3	4	3	45	2	64	1	0	5	4	.556	0	0-0	0	4.76	4.83
2003	2 Tms		16	15	0	1	76.1	327	89	47	45	11	5	1	1	19	0	42	3	1	5	6	.455	0	0-0	0	4.84	5.31
2004	Cin	NL	28	28	1	0	161.0	711	177	90	87	26	13	6	5	53	5	125	7	0	10	9	.526	1	0-0	0	4.81	4.86
2005	Cin	NL	32	32	1	0	211.2	887	217	93	90	22	11	5	8	51	3	163	6	0	11	13	.458	0	0-0	0	3.77	3.83
2006	Cin	NL	36	35	6	0	234.1	993	242	109	98	28	21	8	8	56	8	216	6	1	16	11	.593	2	0-0	0	3.82	3.76
2007	Cin	NL	34	34	2	0	231.2	948	213	100	96	28	4	5	8	52	3	218	12	1	16	6	.727	1	0-0	0	3.22	3.73
2008	Cin	NL	30	29	1	0	184.1	793	205	104	98	35	11	7	2	50	5	153	2	0	6	17	.261	1	0-0	0	4.83	4.78
2009	Cin	NL	26	26	2	0	162.1	703	186	82	76	24	6	2	4	43	6	142	6	0	6	14	.300	1	0-0	0	4.76	4.21
2010	Cin	NL	22	20	0	1	111.2	504	139	71	66	16	4	3	4	38	0	82	9	0	6	7	.462	0	0-0	0	5.75	5.32
2011	SD	NL	28	28	0	0	170.2	719	175	73	69	20	5	2	3	58	4	124	3	0	14	7	.667	0	0-0	0	4.22	3.64
2012	LAD	NL	31	31	0	0	179.2	786	167	85	72	14	9	10	4	85	10	131	4	0	10	10	.500	0	0-0	0	3.76	3.61
2013	2 Tms		26	26	2	0	143.1	626	153	91	86	26	1	6	6	40	1	113	4	0	5	12	.294	2	0-0	0	4.62	5.40
2014	Atl	NL	33	33	0	0	204.1	876	215	88	81	15	11	6	1	71	4	161	9	0	12	12	.500	0	0-0	0	3.98	3.57
03	Oak	AL	7	6	0	0	30.1	136	41	19	18	5	2	1	0	9	0	16	0	1	1	3	.250	0	0-0	0	6.32	5.34
03	Cin	NL	9	9	0	0	46.0	191	48	28	27	6	3	0	1	10	0	26	3	0	4	3	.571	0	0-0	0	3.94	5.28
13	Sea	AL	22	22	2	0	120.1	526	133	81	77	21	1	6	5	28	1	87	3	0	5	11	.313	2	0-0	0	4.58	5.76
13	NYM	NL	4	4	0	0	23.0	100	20	10	9	5	0	0	1	12	0	26	1	0	0	1	.000	0	0-0	0	4.84	3.52
13 ML YEARS			358	352	15	2	2149.2	9227	2256	1077	1006	272	104	65	57	661	51	1734	72	3	122	128	.488	8	0-0	0	4.24	4.21

Blaine Hardy

Pitches: L Bats: L Pos: RP-38 — Ht: 6'2" Wt: 230 Born: 3/14/1987 Age: 28

Year	Team	Lg	G	GS	CG	GF	IP	BFP	H	R	ER	HR	SH	SF	HB	TBB	IBB	SO	WP	Bk	W	L	Pct	Sh	Sv-Op	Hld	ERC	ERA
2010	NWArk	AA	12	0	0	7	26.0	96	11	2	2	0	0	0	1	8	0	16	0	0	1	0	1.000	0	4--	-	0.94	0.69
2010	Omha	AAA	28	8	0	8	67.0	281	65	30	26	9	3	1	1	21	2	48	2	0	3	4	.429	0	3--	-	3.84	3.49
2011	Omha	AAA	23	0	0	11	29.0	146	38	25	23	7	1	0	1	19	1	23	0	0	2	3	.400	0	0--	-	8.09	7.14
2011	NWArk	AA	19	0	0	13	39.2	163	28	11	7	2	1	0	2	16	1	41	0	0	2	1	.667	0	8--	-	2.36	1.59
2012	NWArk	AA	10	0	0	6	20.2	86	17	8	6	3	0	1	2	9	0	13	4	0	1	1	.500	0	3--	-	4.04	2.61
2012	Omha	AAA	30	0	0	11	54.2	244	69	24	23	6	5	3	0	22	2	45	1	0	3	2	.600	0	1--	-	5.76	3.79
2013	Erie	AA	16	0	0	2	27.2	108	16	8	5	1	2	0	0	12	0	26	1	0	2	2	.500	0	1--	-	1.72	1.63
2013	Toledo	AAA	14	9	1	1	64.0	253	46	12	12	7	0	0	2	19	0	53	0	0	6	1	.857	1	0--	-	2.43	1.69
2014	Toledo	AAA	20	6	0	5	47.0	185	35	14	14	2	3	0	1	13	1	53	1	0	3	2	.600	0	0--	-	2.04	2.68
2014	Det	AL	38	0	0	7	39.0	167	34	12	11	1	1	2	1	20	3	31	1	0	2	1	.667	0	0-1	4	3.28	2.54

J.J. Hardy

Bats: R Throws: R Pos: SS-141 — Ht: 6'1" Wt: 190 Born: 8/19/1982 Age: 32

Year	Team	Lg	G	AB	H	2B	3B	HR	(Hm	Rd)	TB	R	RBI	RC	TBB	IBB	SO	HBP	SH	SF	SB	CS	GDP	Avg	OBP	Slg	OPS
2005	Mil	NL	124	372	92	22	1	9	(6	3)	143	46	50	49	44	7	48	1	8	2	0	0	10	.247	.327	.384	.711
2006	Mil	NL	35	128	31	5	0	5	(4	1)	51	13	14	13	10	0	23	0	0	1	1	1	4	.242	.295	.398	.693
2007	Mil	NL	151	592	164	30	1	26	(15	11)	274	89	80	84	40	1	73	1	4	1	2	3	13	.277	.323	.463	.786
2008	Mil	NL	146	569	161	31	4	24	(14	10)	272	78	74	78	52	3	98	1	5	2	2	1	18	.283	.343	.478	.821
2009	Mil	NL	115	414	95	16	2	11	(6	5)	148	53	47	32	43	0	85	2	1	5	0	1	14	.229	.302	.357	.659
2010	Min	AL	101	340	91	19	3	6	(1	5)	134	44	38	41	28	1	54	0	3	4	1	1	8	.268	.320	.394	.714
2011	Bal	AL	129	527	142	27	0	30	(15	15)	259	76	80	78	31	3	92	2	2	5	0	0	10	.269	.310	.491	.801
2012	Bal	AL	158	663	158	30	2	22	(15	7)	258	85	68	71	38	4	106	3	7	2	0	0	21	.238	.282	.389	.671
2013	Bal	AL	159	601	158	27	0	25	(11	14)	260	66	76	71	38	3	73	0	3	2	2	1	14	.263	.306	.433	.738
2014	Bal	AL	141	529	142	28	0	9	(5	4)	197	56	52	60	29	1	104	4	3	4	0	0	12	.268	.309	.372	.682
Postseason			13	51	12	4	0	0	(0	0)	16	3	4	4	3	0	7	0	0	0	0	0	1	.235	.278	.314	.592
10 ML YEARS			1259	4735	1234	235	13	167	(92	75)	1996	606	579	577	353	23	756	14	36	28	8	8	124	.261	.312	.422	.734

Dan Haren

Pitches: R Bats: R Pos: SP-32 — Ht: 6'5" Wt: 215 Born: 9/17/1980 Age: 34

Year	Team	Lg	G	GS	CG	GF	IP	BFP	H	R	ER	HR	SH	SF	HB	TBB	IBB	SO	WP	Bk	W	L	Pct	Sh	Sv-Op	Hld	ERC	ERA
2003	StL	NL	14	14	0	0	72.2	320	84	44	41	9	4	2	5	22	0	43	3	0	3	7	.300	0	0-0	0	5.07	5.08
2004	StL	NL	14	5	0	2	46.0	195	45	23	23	4	4	2	2	17	2	32	1	0	3	3	.500	0	0-0	0	3.91	4.50
2005	Oak	AL	34	34	3	0	217.0	897	212	101	90	26	3	5	6	53	5	163	6	0	14	12	.538	0	0-0	0	3.58	3.73
2006	Oak	AL	34	34	0	0	223.0	930	224	109	102	31	3	3	10	45	6	176	10	0	14	13	.519	0	0-0	0	3.72	4.12
2007	Oak	AL	34	34	0	0	222.2	935	214	91	76	24	2	8	3	55	1	192	10	0	15	9	.625	0	0-0	0	3.32	3.07
2008	Ari	NL	33	33	1	0	216.0	881	204	86	80	19	7	3	6	40	4	206	11	0	16	8	.667	1	0-0	0	2.96	3.33
2009	Ari	NL	33	33	3	0	229.1	909	192	83	80	27	8	3	4	38	2	223	13	0	14	10	.583	1	0-0	0	2.50	3.14
2010	2 Tms		35	35	2	0	235.0	994	245	110	102	31	6	10	5	54	6	216	12	2	12	12	.500	0	0-0	0	3.88	3.91
2011	LAA	AL	35	34	4	1	238.1	953	211	91	84	20	12	5	5	33	1	192	6	0	16	10	.615	3	0-0	0	2.45	3.17
2012	LAA	AL	30	30	1	0	176.2	747	190	95	85	28	7	8	3	38	3	142	5	1	12	13	.480	1	0-0	0	4.20	4.33
2013	Was	NL	31	30	0	1	169.2	717	179	92	88	28	4	7	4	31	0	151	8	1	10	14	.417	0	1-1	0	4.09	4.67
2014	LAD	NL	32	32	0	0	186.0	776	183	101	83	27	6	5	3	36	7	145	8	1	13	11	.542	0	0-0	0	3.43	4.02
10	Ari	NL	21	21	1	0	141.0	607	161	79	72	23	4	4	3	29	4	141	8	1	7	8	.467	0	0-0	0	4.55	4.60
10	LAA	AL	14	14	1	0	94.0	387	84	31	30	8	0	6	2	25	2	75	4	1	5	4	.556	0	0-0	0	2.94	2.87
Postseason			7	2	0	0	19.1	86	24	7	7	3	1	0	0	7	0	16	2	0	2	0	1.000	0	0-0	0	5.83	3.26
12 ML YEARS			359	348	16	4	2232.1	9254	2183	1026	934	274	70	58	59	462	37	1881	93	5	142	122	.538	6	1-1	0	3.42	3.77

Bryce Harper

Bats: L Throws: R Pos: LF-90;RF-10;CF-7;PH-2   Ht: 6'3" Wt: 225 Born: 10/16/1992 Age: 22

Year Team	Lg	G	AB	H	2B	3B	HR	(Hm	Rd)	TB	R	RBI	RC	TBB	IBB	SO	HBP	SH	SF	SB	CS	GDP	Avg	OBP	Slg	OPS
2014 Ptomc*	A+	2	4	3	0	0	1	(-	-)	6	3	4	3	2	0	0	0	0	0	0	0	0	.750	.833	1.500	2.333
2014 Hrsbrg*	AA	3	10	6	1	0	3	(-	-)	16	4	7	6	3	0	1	0	0	0	2	2	1	.600	.692	1.600	2.292
2012 Was	NL	139	533	144	26	9	22	(10	12)	254	98	59	82	56	0	120	2	3	3	18	6	8	.270	.340	.477	.817
2013 Was	NL	118	424	116	24	3	20	(13	7)	206	71	58	73	61	4	94	5	3	4	11	4	4	.274	.368	.486	.854
2014 Was	NL	100	352	96	10	2	13	(5	8)	149	41	32	43	38	4	104	1	3	1	2	2	6	.273	.344	.423	.768
Postseason		5	23	3	1	1	1	(1	0)	9	2	2	1	0	0	8	0	0	0	0	0	0	.130	.130	.391	.522
3 ML YEARS		357	1309	356	60	14	55	(28	27)	609	210	149	198	155	8	318	8	9	8	31	12	18	.272	.351	.465	.816

Lucas Harrell

Pitches: R Bats: B Pos: SP-3   HAH-rell   Ht: 6'2" Wt: 205 Born: 6/3/1985 Age: 30

Year Team	Lg	G	GS	CG	GF	IP	BFP	H	R	ER	HR	SH	SF	HB	TBB	IBB	SO	WP	Bk	W	L	Pct	Sh	Sv-Op	Hld	ERC	ERA
2014 Reno*	AAA	22	20	0	0	106.2	492	115	64	61	12	4	2	5	77	0	67	8	0	6	4	.600	0	0--	-	6.32	5.15
2010 CWS	AL	8	3	0	3	24.0	119	34	18	13	2	1	0	1	17	1	15	1	0	1	0	1.000	0	0-0	0	7.77	4.88
2011 2 Tms		9	2	0	2	18.0	86	23	12	9	0	1	1	1	8	0	15	1	1	0	2	.000	0	0-0	0	5.16	4.50
2012 Hou	NL	32	32	1	0	193.2	827	185	90	81	13	8	10	1	78	5	140	10	3	11	11	.500	1	0-0	0	3.59	3.76
2013 Hou	AL	36	22	0	0	153.2	707	174	111	100	20	6	5	6	88	5	89	8	0	6	17	.261	0	0-1	0	5.95	5.86
2014 Hou	AL	3	3	0	0	12.1	66	19	14	13	2	0	2	0	9	1	9	1	0	0	3	.000	0	0-0	0	8.91	9.49
11 CWS	AL	3	0	0	2	5.0	26	11	4	4	0	0	0	0	1	0	5	0	0	0	0	-	0	0-0	0	10.11	7.20
11 Hou	NL	6	2	0	0	13.0	60	12	8	5	0	1	1	1	7	0	10	1	1	0	2	.000	0	0-0	0	3.57	3.46
5 ML YEARS		88	62	1	13	401.2	1805	435	245	216	37	16	18	8	200	12	268	21	4	18	33	.353	1	0-1	0	4.92	4.84

Will Harris

Pitches: R Bats: R Pos: RP-29   Ht: 6'4" Wt: 225 Born: 8/28/1984 Age: 30

Year Team	Lg	G	GS	CG	GF	IP	BFP	H	R	ER	HR	SH	SF	HB	TBB	IBB	SO	WP	Bk	W	L	Pct	Sh	Sv-Op	Hld	ERC	ERA
2014 Reno*	AAA	43	0	0	19	45.2	191	34	10	5	3	2	0	5	20	0	44	3	0	3	2	.600	0	1--	-	3.05	0.99
2012 Col	NL	20	0	0	10	17.2	89	27	18	16	3	2	1	1	6	1	19	4	0	1	1	.500	0	0-0	3	7.39	8.15
2013 Ari	NL	61	0	0	11	52.2	217	50	17	17	3	0	4	2	15	1	53	4	0	4	1	.800	0	0-1	4	3.25	2.91
2014 Ari	NL	29	0	0	8	29.0	120	27	14	14	3	1	1	2	9	2	35	1	0	0	3	.000	0	0-1	3	3.62	4.34
3 ML YEARS		110	0	0	29	99.1	426	104	49	47	9	3	6	5	30	4	107	9	0	5	5	.500	0	0-2	10	4.04	4.26

Josh Harrison

Bats: R Throws: R Pos: 3B-72;LF-26;RF-26;PH-21;2B-17;SS-8;PR-3   Ht: 5'8" Wt: 200 Born: 7/8/1987 Age: 27

Year Team	Lg	G	AB	H	2B	3B	HR	(Hm	Rd)	TB	R	RBI	RC	TBB	IBB	SO	HBP	SH	SF	SB	CS	GDP	Avg	OBP	Slg	OPS
2011 Pit	NL	65	195	53	13	2	1	(1	0)	73	21	16	19	3	0	24	0	5	1	4	1	6	.272	.281	.374	.656
2012 Pit	NL	104	249	58	9	5	3	(1	2)	86	34	16	22	10	0	37	7	7	3	7	3	3	.233	.279	.345	.624
2013 Pit	NL	60	88	22	1	2	3	(1	2)	36	10	14	11	2	0	10	3	2	0	2	0	4	.250	.290	.409	.699
2014 Pit	NL	143	520	164	38	7	13	(4	9)	255	77	52	84	22	1	81	4	2	2	18	7	6	.315	.347	.490	.837
Postseason		2	0	0	0	0	0	(0	0)	0	1	0	0	0	0	0	0	0	0	0	1	0	-	-	-	-
4 ML YEARS		372	1052	297	61	16	20	(7	13)	450	142	98	136	37	1	152	14	16	6	31	11	19	.282	.314	.428	.742

Matt Harrison

Pitches: L Bats: L Pos: SP-4   Ht: 6'4" Wt: 240 Born: 9/16/1985 Age: 29

Year Team	Lg	G	GS	CG	GF	IP	BFP	H	R	ER	HR	SH	SF	HB	TBB	IBB	SO	WP	Bk	W	L	Pct	Sh	Sv-Op	Hld	ERC	ERA
2014 Frisco*	AA	3	3	0	0	16.0	63	12	4	3	0	1	0	0	4	0	10	1	0	1	0	1.000	0	0--	-	1.68	1.69
2008 Tex	AL	15	15	1	0	83.2	372	100	57	51	12	1	5	2	31	2	42	2	2	9	3	.750	1	0-0	0	5.53	5.49
2009 Tex	AL	11	11	2	0	63.1	283	81	43	43	9	1	2	2	23	0	34	0	0	4	5	.444	1	0-0	0	6.17	6.11
2010 Tex	AL	37	6	0	9	78.1	356	80	45	41	10	2	8	2	39	3	46	4	0	3	2	.600	0	2-3	3	4.71	4.71
2011 Tex	AL	31	30	0	0	185.2	772	180	79	70	13	8	5	1	57	1	126	6	1	14	9	.609	0	0-0	0	3.40	3.39
2012 Tex	AL	32	32	4	0	213.1	876	210	82	78	22	1	2	1	59	0	133	2	0	18	11	.621	2	0-0	0	3.63	3.29
2013 Tex	AL	2	2	0	0	10.2	51	14	11	10	2	0	1	0	7	2	12	0	0	0	2	.000	0	0-0	0	7.54	8.44
2014 Tex	AL	4	4	0	0	17.1	84	20	8	8	1	1	0	1	12	0	10	1	0	1	1	.500	0	0-0	0	5.98	4.15
Postseason		5	4	0	0	18.1	83	20	13	11	2	0	0	0	9	1	16	1	0	1	2	.333	0	0-0	0	4.88	5.40
7 ML YEARS		132	100	7	9	652.1	2794	685	325	301	69	14	22	9	228	8	403	15	3	49	33	.598	4	2-3	3	4.27	4.15

Corey Hart

Bats: R Throws: R Pos: DH-55;RF-7;PH-6;1B-2;LF-1   Ht: 6'6" Wt: 230 Born: 3/24/1982 Age: 33

Year Team	Lg	G	AB	H	2B	3B	HR	(Hm	Rd)	TB	R	RBI	RC	TBB	IBB	SO	HBP	SH	SF	SB	CS	GDP	Avg	OBP	Slg	OPS
2014 Tacom*	AAA	19	70	20	4	2	4	(-	-)	40	8	9	13	7	0	13	0	0	0	0	0	0	.286	.351	.571	.922
2004 Mil	NL	1	1	0	0	0	0	(0	0)	0	0	0	0	0	0	1	0	0	0	0	0	0	.000	.000	.000	.000
2005 Mil	NL	21	57	11	2	1	2	(2	0)	21	9	7	4	6	0	11	0	0	0	2	0	6	.193	.270	.368	.638
2006 Mil	NL	87	237	67	13	2	9	(6	3)	111	32	33	30	17	1	58	0	0	2	5	8	7	.283	.328	.468	.796
2007 Mil	NL	140	505	149	33	9	24	(15	9)	272	86	81	94	36	3	99	13	5	7	23	7	6	.295	.353	.539	.892
2008 Mil	NL	157	612	164	45	6	20	(7	13)	281	76	91	81	27	2	109	5	4	9	23	7	17	.268	.300	.459	.759
2009 Mil	NL	115	419	109	24	3	12	(9	3)	175	64	48	51	43	0	92	6	1	3	11	6	9	.260	.335	.418	.753
2010 Mil	NL	145	558	158	34	4	31	(16	15)	293	91	102	83	45	2	140	6	0	5	7	6	14	.283	.340	.525	.865
2011 Mil	NL	130	492	140	25	4	26	(17	9)	251	80	63	79	51	1	114	4	3	1	7	6	12	.285	.356	.510	.866

Year	Team	Lg	G	AB	H	2B	3B	HR	(Hm	Rd)	TB	R	RBI	RC	TBB	IBB	SO	HBP	SH	SF	SB	CS	GDP	Avg	OBP	Slg	OPS
2012	Mil	NL	149	562	152	35	4	30	(22	8)	285	91	83	87	44	5	151	11	2	3	5	0	13	.270	.334	.507	.841
2014	Sea	AL	68	232	47	9	0	6	(2	4)	74	17	21	21	16	1	59	6	0	1	2	0	1	.203	.271	.319	.590
Postseason			14	54	13	0	0	2	(1	1)	19	6	5	4	3	0	11	1	1	1	0	0	1	.241	.288	.352	.640
10 ML YEARS			1013	3675	997	220	33	160	(96	64)	1763	546	529	530	285	15	834	51	15	31	85	40	85	.271	.330	.480	.810

Matt Harvey

Pitches: R Bats: R Pos: P   Ht: 6'4" Wt: 215 Born: 3/27/1989 Age: 26

			HOW MUCH HE PITCHED						WHAT HE GAVE UP													THE RESULTS						
Year	Team	Lg	G	GS	CG	GF	IP	BFP	H	R	ER	HR	SH	SF	HB	TBB	IBB	SO	WP	Bk	W	L	Pct	Sh	Sv-Op	Hld	ERC	ERA
2011	StLuci	A+	14	14	0	0	76.0	308	67	24	20	5	1	0	2	24	0	92	1	0	8	2	.800	0	0--	-	3.07	2.37
2011	Bnghtn	AA	12	12	0	0	59.2	259	59	32	31	4	3	2	3	23	0	64	5	0	5	3	.625	0	0--	-	3.91	4.68
2012	Buffalo	AAA	20	20	0	0	110.0	473	97	46	45	9	2	1	6	48	1	112	9	0	5	5	.583	0	0--	-	3.62	3.68
2012	NYM	NL	10	10	0	0	59.1	245	42	19	18	5	3	3	3	26	0	70	3	0	3	5	.375	0	0-0	-	2.75	2.73
2013	NYM	NL	26	26	1	0	178.1	690	135	46	45	7	5	4	4	31	1	191	2	0	9	5	.643	1	0-0	0	1.76	2.27
2 ML YEARS			36	36	1	0	237.2	935	177	65	63	12	8	7	7	57	1	261	5	0	12	10	.545	1	0-0	0	2.00	2.39

Alex Hassan

Bats: R Throws: R Pos: RF-2;PH-1   HASS-in   Ht: 6'3" Wt: 220 Born: 4/1/1988 Age: 27

			BATTING															RUNNING				AVERAGES				
Year	Team	Lg	G	AB	H	2B	3B	HR	(Hm	Rd)	TB	R	RBI	RC	TBB	IBB	SO	HBP	SH	SF	SB	CS	GDP	Avg	OBP	Slg	OPS
2010	Salem	A+	104	342	98	28	3	8	(-	-)	156	46	48	-	57	1	69	8	-	4	6	1	13	.287	.397	.456	.853
2010	Pwtckt	AAA	3	3	0	0	0	0	(-	-)	0	0	1	0	0	0	0	0	0	1	0	0	0	.000	.000	.000	.000
2011	Portlnd	AA	126	454	132	34	1	13	(-	-)	207	75	64	90	76	4	79	12	0	3	8	2	13	.291	.404	.456	.860
2012	Pwtckt	AAA	94	312	80	13	0	7	(-	-)	114	39	46	49	55	0	70	8	0	4	1	1	7	.256	.377	.365	.743
2013	Pwtckt	AAA	55	187	60	14	0	4	(-	-)	86	26	28	38	36	2	50	1	0	1	0	1	7	.321	.431	.460	.891
2013	Grnvlle	A	8	23	11	2	0	0	(-	-)	13	4	7	8	10	0	2	0	0	0	0	0	0	.478	.636	.565	1.202
2014	Pwtckt	AAA	114	408	117	31	1	8	(-	-)	174	66	55	69	60	1	109	2	0	4	2	2	5	.287	.378	.426	.804
2014	Bos	AL	3	8	1	0	0	0	(0	0)	1	1	0	0	1	0	5	0	0	0	0	0	0	.125	.222	.125	.347

Chris Hatcher

Pitches: R Bats: B Pos: RP-52   Ht: 6'1" Wt: 205 Born: 1/12/1985 Age: 30

			HOW MUCH HE PITCHED						WHAT HE GAVE UP													THE RESULTS						
Year	Team	Lg	G	GS	CG	GF	IP	BFP	H	R	ER	HR	SH	SF	HB	TBB	IBB	SO	WP	Bk	W	L	Pct	Sh	Sv-Op	Hld	ERC	ERA
2014	NewOr*	AAA	15	0	0	14	22.1	87	16	5	5	2	1	0	0	6	1	25	0	0	1	2	.333	0	5--	-	2.04	2.01
2011	Fla	NL	11	0	0	4	10.1	48	14	8	8	2	0	3	0	4	1	8	2	0	0	0	-	0	0-0	0	6.69	6.97
2012	Mia	NL	11	0	0	7	14.2	66	17	9	7	3	0	0	1	6	0	10	1	0	0	0	-	0	0-0	0	6.19	4.30
2013	Mia	NL	7	0	0	2	8.2	44	13	13	12	1	0	0	0	4	1	7	0	0	0	1	.000	0	0-0	0	6.92	12.46
2014	Mia	NL	52	0	0	15	56.0	232	55	22	21	4	1	1	0	12	1	60	1	2	0	3	.000	0	0-2	6	3.03	3.38
4 ML YEARS			81	0	0	28	89.2	390	99	52	48	10	1	4	1	26	3	85	4	2	0	4	.000	0	0-2	6	4.25	4.82

LaTroy Hawkins

Pitches: R Bats: R Pos: RP-57   Ht: 6'5" Wt: 220 Born: 12/21/1972 Age: 42

			HOW MUCH HE PITCHED						WHAT HE GAVE UP													THE RESULTS						
Year	Team	Lg	G	GS	CG	GF	IP	BFP	H	R	ER	HR	SH	SF	HB	TBB	IBB	SO	WP	Bk	W	L	Pct	Sh	Sv-Op	Hld	ERC	ERA
1995	Min	AL	6	6	1	0	27.0	131	39	29	26	3	0	3	1	12	0	9	1	1	2	3	.400	0	0-0	-	7.14	8.67
1996	Min	AL	7	6	0	0	26.1	124	42	24	24	8	1	1	0	9	0	24	1	1	1	1	.500	0	0-0	-	9.49	8.20
1997	Min	AL	20	20	0	0	103.1	478	134	71	67	19	2	2	4	47	0	58	6	3	6	12	.333	0	0-0	-	7.01	5.84
1998	Min	AL	33	33	0	0	190.1	840	227	126	111	27	4	10	5	61	1	105	10	2	7	14	.333	0	0-0	-	5.31	5.25
1999	Min	AL	33	33	1	0	174.1	803	238	136	129	29	1	5	1	60	2	103	9	0	10	14	.417	0	0-0	-	6.55	6.66
2000	Min	AL	66	0	0	38	87.2	370	85	34	33	7	4	1	1	32	1	59	6	0	2	5	.286	0	14-14	7	3.70	3.39
2001	Min	AL	62	0	0	51	51.1	248	59	34	34	3	1	4	1	39	3	36	7	0	1	5	.167	0	28-37	1	6.02	5.96
2002	Min	AL	65	0	0	15	80.1	310	63	23	19	5	2	3	0	15	1	63	5	0	6	0	1.000	0	0-3	13	1.99	2.13
2003	Min	AL	74	0	0	12	77.1	310	69	20	16	4	4	1	1	15	1	75	5	0	9	3	.750	0	2-8	28	2.48	1.86
2004	ChC	NL	77	0	0	82	82.0	333	72	27	24	10	6	2	2	14	5	69	2	0	5	4	.556	0	25-34	4	2.66	2.63
2005	2 Tms	NL	66	0	0	21	56.1	247	58	27	24	7	3	1	0	24	3	43	1	0	2	8	.200	0	6-15	15	4.41	3.83
2006	Bal	NL	60	0	0	12	60.1	261	73	30	30	4	1	2	0	15	3	27	2	0	3	2	.600	0	0-4	16	4.37	4.48
2007	Col	NL	62	0	0	10	55.1	225	52	21	21	6	2	1	0	16	1	29	2	0	2	5	.286	0	0-5	18	3.43	3.42
2008	2 Tms	NL	57	0	0	15	62.0	252	53	29	27	3	1	3	0	22	4	48	3	0	3	1	.750	0	1-2	13	2.75	3.92
2009	Hou	NL	65	0	0	34	63.1	259	60	16	15	7	2	2	2	16	2	45	2	0	1	4	.200	0	11-15	19	3.42	2.13
2010	Mil	NL	18	0	0	5	16.0	74	21	15	15	2	4	0	2	6	1	18	1	0	0	3	.000	0	0-2	6	6.55	8.44
2011	Mil	NL	52	0	0	10	48.1	204	50	15	13	1	1	1	0	10	1	28	2	0	3	1	.750	0	0-0	20	2.91	2.42
2012	LAA	NL	48	0	0	7	42.0	178	45	20	17	5	3	1	0	13	1	23	0	0	2	3	.400	0	1-4	6	4.27	3.64
2013	NYM	NL	72	0	0	28	70.2	288	71	23	23	6	3	5	1	10	2	55	1	0	3	2	.600	0	13-16	12	3.03	2.93
2014	Col	NL	57	0	0	48	54.1	226	52	23	20	3	0	2	0	13	2	32	3	0	4	3	.571	0	23-26	1	2.85	3.31
05	ChC	NL	21	0	0	12	19.0	80	18	9	7	4	1	0	0	7	0	13	0	0	1	4	.200	0	4-8	0	4.44	3.42
05	SF	NL	45	0	0	9	37.1	167	40	18	17	3	2	1	0	17	3	30	1	0	1	4	.200	0	2-7	15	4.36	4.10
08	NYY	AL	33	0	0	11	41.0	173	42	26	26	3	1	2	0	17	3	23	2	0	1	1	.500	0	0-1	1	4.09	5.71
08	Hou	NL	24	0	0	4	21.0	79	11	3	1	0	0	1	0	5	1	25	1	0	2	0	1.000	0	1-1	12	0.95	0.43
Postseason			19	0	0	4	15.2	65	13	7	6	3	1	0		6	1	17	0	0	1	0	1.000	0	0-0	4	2.35	3.45
20 ML YEARS			1000	98	2	357	1428.2	6161	1563	747	688	159	42	50	21	449	34	949	69	7	72	93	.436	0	124-185	179	4.38	4.33

Brett Hayes

Bats: R Throws: R Pos: C-27;PR-2   Ht: 6'0" Wt: 215 Born: 2/13/1984 Age: 31

Year	Team	Lg	G	AB	H	2B	3B	HR	(Hm	Rd)	TB	R	RBI	RC	TBB	IBB	SO	HBP	SH	SF	SB	CS	GDP	Avg	OBP	Slg	OPS
2014	Omha*	AAA	10	42	13	3	0	3			25	8	8	8	2	0	14	0	0	0	1	0	0	.310	.341	.595	.936
2009	Fla	NL	14	11	3	1	0	1	(0	1)	7	5	2	1	0	0	4	1	0	0	0	0	1	.273	.333	.636	.970
2010	Fla	NL	26	77	16	6	1	2	(1	1)	30	6	6	7	6	1	26	0	0	0	0	0	1	.208	.265	.390	.655
2011	Fla	NL	64	130	30	9	0	5	(3	2)	54	19	16	13	11	2	39	0	3	0	0	0	2	.231	.291	.415	.706
2012	Mia	NL	39	114	23	6	0	0	(0	0)	29	7	3	2	4	3	49	0	0	0	1	0	1	.202	.229	.254	.483
2013	KC	AL	5	18	5	3	0	1	(0	1)	11	2	2	3	0	0	3	0	0	0	0	0	0	.278	.278	.611	.889
2014	KC	AL	27	52	7	1	0	1	(1	0)	11	3	2	0	1	0	12	0	0	0	1	0	1	.135	.151	.212	.362
6 ML YEARS			175	402	84	26	1	10	(5	5)	142	42	31	26	22	6	133	1	3	0	1	0	6	.209	.252	.353	.605

Chase Headley

Bats: B Throws: R Pos: 3B-127;1B-7;PH-4;DH-1   HEDD-lee   Ht: 6'2" Wt: 220 Born: 5/9/1984 Age: 31

Year	Team	Lg	G	AB	H	2B	3B	HR	(Hm	Rd)	TB	R	RBI	RC	TBB	IBB	SO	HBP	SH	SF	SB	CS	GDP	Avg	OBP	Slg	OPS
2014	Lk Els*	A+	4	12	4	1	0	0	(-	-)	5	1	2	2	2	1	4	0	0	0	0	0	2	.333	.429	.417	.845
2007	SD	NL	8	18	4	1	0	0	(0	0)	5	1	0	1	2	0	4	1	0	0	0	0	0	.222	.333	.278	.611
2008	SD	NL	91	331	89	19	2	9	(4	5)	139	34	38	42	30	1	104	5	0	2	4	1	5	.269	.337	.420	.757
2009	SD	NL	156	543	142	31	2	12	(7	5)	213	62	64	68	62	3	133	5	0	2	10	2	19	.262	.342	.392	.734
2010	SD	NL	161	610	161	29	3	11	(3	8)	229	77	58	70	56	3	139	3	1	4	17	5	11	.264	.327	.375	.702
2011	SD	NL	113	381	110	28	1	4	(1	3)	152	43	44	61	52	8	92	2	1	3	13	2	6	.289	.374	.399	.773
2012	SD	NL	161	604	173	31	2	31	(13	18)	301	95	**115**	112	86	2	157	4	0	5	17	6	7	.286	.376	.498	.875
2013	SD	NL	141	520	130	35	2	13	(5	8)	208	59	50	64	67	7	142	11	0	2	8	4	9	.250	.347	.400	.747
2014	2 Tms		135	470	114	20	1	13	(6	7)	175	55	49	54	51	1	122	9	0	1	7	3	17	.243	.328	.372	.700
14	SD	NL	77	279	64	12	1	7	(2	5)	99	27	32	29	22	0	73	5	0	1	4	1	12	.229	.296	.355	.651
14	NYY	AL	58	191	50	8	0	6	(5	1)	76	28	17	25	29	1	49	4	0	0	3	2	5	.262	.371	.398	.768
8 ML YEARS			966	3477	923	194	13	93	(40	53)	1422	426	418	472	406	25	893	40	2	19	76	23	76	.265	.347	.409	.756

Andrew Heaney

Pitches: L Bats: L Pos: SP-5; RP-2   HEE-nee   Ht: 6'2" Wt: 185 Born: 6/5/1991 Age: 24

Year	Team	Lg	G	GS	CG	GF	IP	BFP	H	R	ER	HR	SH	SF	HB	TBB	IBB	SO	WP	Bk	W	L	Pct	Sh	Sv-Op	Hld	ERC	ERA
2012	Mrlns	R	2	2	0	0	7.0	31	7	2	2	0	0	1	1	2	0	9	0	0	0	0	-	0	0--	-	3.38	2.57
2012	Grnsbr	A	4	4	0	0	20.0	93	25	15	11	0	1	0	1	4	0	21	0	0	1	2	.333	0	0--	-	3.90	4.95
2013	Jupiter	A+	13	12	0	1	61.2	258	45	11	6	2	2	0	6	17	0	66	3	0	5	2	.714	0	0--	-	2.06	0.88
2013	Jaxnvl	AA	6	6	1	0	33.2	138	31	11	11	2	1	0	0	9	0	23	0	0	4	1	.800	0	0--	-	2.89	2.94
2014	Jaxnvl	AA	9	8	0	0	53.2	218	45	16	14	2	2	1	0	13	0	52	5	0	4	2	.667	0	0--	-	2.23	2.35
2014	NewOr	AAA	15	15	1	0	83.2	350	75	45	36	9	0	2	4	23	0	91	3	0	5	4	.556	1	0--	-	3.23	3.87
2014	Mia	NL	7	5	0	2	29.1	126	32	19	19	6	2	0	3	7	0	20	2	0	0	3	.000	0	0-0	0	5.17	5.83

Adeiny Hechavarria

Bats: R Throws: R Pos: SS-146   a-DAY-nee hetch-a-VA-ree-a   Ht: 5'11" Wt: 185 Born: 4/15/1989 Age: 26

Year	Team	Lg	G	AB	H	2B	3B	HR	(Hm	Rd)	TB	R	RBI	RC	TBB	IBB	SO	HBP	SH	SF	SB	CS	GDP	Avg	OBP	Slg	OPS
2014	Jupiter*	A+	2	8	1	1	0	0	(-	-)	2	0	0	0	0	0	1	0	0	0	0	0	0	.125	.125	.250	.375
2012	Tor	AL	41	126	32	8	0	2	(1	1)	46	10	15	15	4	0	32	1	5	1	0	0	2	.254	.280	.365	.645
2013	Mia	NL	148	543	123	14	8	3	(1	2)	162	30	42	37	30	1	96	0	4	1	11	10	19	.227	.267	.298	.565
2014	Mia	NL	146	536	148	20	10	1	(0	1)	191	53	34	49	26	5	86	1	4	6	7	5	21	.276	.308	.356	.664
3 ML YEARS			335	1205	303	42	18	6	(2	4)	399	93	91	101	60	6	214	2	13	8	18	15	42	.251	.286	.331	.617

Chris Heisey

Bats: R Throws: R Pos: LF-53;PH-47;CF-16;RF-14;PR-1   HY-zee   Ht: 6'1" Wt: 210 Born: 12/14/1984 Age: 30

Year	Team	Lg	G	AB	H	2B	3B	HR	(Hm	Rd)	TB	R	RBI	RC	TBB	IBB	SO	HBP	SH	SF	SB	CS	GDP	Avg	OBP	Slg	OPS
2010	Cin	NL	97	201	51	10	1	8	(2	6)	87	33	21	22	16	1	57	6	1	2	1	2	3	.254	.324	.433	.757
2011	Cin	NL	120	279	71	9	1	18	(11	7)	136	44	50	40	19	3	78	5	1	4	6	1	1	.254	.309	.487	.797
2012	Cin	NL	120	347	92	16	5	7	(4	3)	139	44	31	42	18	0	81	7	3	0	6	3	8	.265	.315	.401	.715
2013	Cin	NL	87	224	53	11	1	9	(6	3)	93	29	23	26	9	0	51	5	4	2	3	0	4	.237	.279	.415	.694
2014	Cin	NL	119	275	61	15	2	8	(4	4)	104	34	22	22	15	0	64	2	5	2	9	2	3	.222	.265	.378	.643
Postseason			6	6	0	0	0	0	(0	0)	0	1	0	0	0	0	2	0	0	0	0	0	0	.000	.000	.000	.000
5 ML YEARS			543	1326	328	61	10	50	(27	23)	559	184	147	152	77	4	331	25	14	10	25	8	19	.247	.299	.422	.721

Jeremy Hellickson

Pitches: R Bats: R Pos: SP-13   Ht: 6'1" Wt: 190 Born: 4/8/1987 Age: 28

Year	Team	Lg	G	GS	CG	GF	IP	BFP	H	R	ER	HR	SH	SF	HB	TBB	IBB	SO	WP	Bk	W	L	Pct	Sh	Sv-Op	Hld	ERC	ERA
2014	Charltt*	A+	2	2	0	0	8.0	34	9	4	2	0	0	0	0	2	0	6	0	0	0	1	.000	0	0--	-	3.51	2.25
2014	Drham*	AAA	5	5	0	0	18.2	99	38	20	15	1	0	2	5	5	0	16	3	0	1	4	.200	0	0--	-	10.14	7.23
2014	Mont*	AA	1	1	0	0	6.0	22	5	1	1	0	0	0	0	0	0	11	0	0	0	0	-	0	0--	-	1.43	1.50
2010	TB	AL	10	4	0	0	36.1	149	32	14	14	5	0	1	2	8	2	33	2	0	4	0	1.000	0	0-1	0	3.10	3.47
2011	TB	AL	29	29	2	0	189.0	774	146	64	62	21	1	2	4	72	8	117	8	1	13	10	.565	1	0-0	0	2.89	2.95
2012	TB	AL	31	31	0	0	177.0	741	163	68	61	25	4	3	4	59	3	124	5	0	10	11	.476	0	0-0	0	3.73	3.10

			HOW MUCH HE PITCHED						WHAT HE GAVE UP										THE RESULTS						
Year	Team	Lg	G	GS	CG	GF	IP	BFP	H	R	ER	HR	SH	SF	HB	TBB	IBB	SO	WP	Bk	W	L	Pct	Sh	Sv-Op	Hld	ERC	ERA
2013	TB	AL	32	31	0	1	174.0	737	185	103	100	24	2	5	4	50	0	135	7	2	12	10	.545	0	0-0	0	4.40	5.17
2014	TB	AL	13	13	0	0	63.2	281	71	35	32	8	0	1	2	21	1	54	8	0	1	5	.167	0	0-0	0	4.70	4.52
	Postseason		2	2	0	0	5.0	22	5	3	3	3	0	0	0	3	0	1	0	0	0	1	.000	0	0-0	0	8.99	5.40
	5 ML YEARS		115	108	2	1	640.0	2682	597	284	269	83	7	12	16	210	14	463	30	3	40	36	.526	1	0-1	0	3.70	3.78

Heath Hembree

Pitches: R **Bats:** R **Pos:** RP-6   HEHM-bree   **Ht:** 6'4" **Wt:** 210 **Born:** 1/13/1989 **Age:** 26

			HOW MUCH HE PITCHED						WHAT HE GAVE UP										THE RESULTS						
Year	Team	Lg	G	GS	CG	GF	IP	BFP	H	R	ER	HR	SH	SF	HB	TBB	IBB	SO	WP	Bk	W	L	Pct	Sh	Sv-Op	Hld	ERC	ERA
2010	Giants	R	12	0	0	10	11.0	41	9	1	1	0	0	0	0	0	0	22	0	0	0	0	-	0	3- -	-	1.35	0.82
2011	SnJos	A+	26	0	0	24	24.2	101	16	2	2	1	0	0	1	12	0	44	2	0	0	0	-	0	21- -	-	2.33	0.73
2011	Rchmd	AA	28	0	0	25	28.2	118	20	11	9	1	0	2	0	13	1	34	1	0	1	1	.500	0	17- -	-	2.21	2.83
2012	Fresno	AAA	39	0	0	31	38.0	167	29	24	20	2	1	2	4	20	0	36	2	0	1	1	.500	0	15- -	-	3.25	4.74
2012	SnJos	A+	5	0	0	3	5.0	17	0	0	0	0	0	0	0	1	0	7	0	0	0	0	-	0	0- -	-	0.04	0.00
2013	Fresno	AAA	54	0	0	48	55.1	236	54	26	25	7	0	1	1	16	0	63	3	1	1	4	.200	0	31- -	-	3.69	4.07
2014	Fresno	AAA	41	0	0	35	39.1	170	40	18	17	5	0	3	2	13	0	46	2	0	1	3	.250	0	18- -	-	4.27	3.89
2014	Pwtckt	AAA	7	0	0	6	6.2	31	5	2	2	0	0	0	0	5	0	9	0	0	0	1	.000	0	2- -	-	3.09	2.70
2013	SF	NL	9	0	0	2	7.2	29	4	0	0	0	0	0	0	2	0	12	0	0	0	0	-	0	0-0	0	1.02	0.00
2014	Bos	AL	6	0	0	3	10.0	43	11	5	5	1	0	0	0	5	2	6	1	0	0	0	-	0	0-0	0	4.94	4.50
	2 ML YEARS		15	0	0	5	17.2	72	15	5	5	1	0	0	0	7	2	18	1	0	0	0	-	0	0-0	0	2.86	2.55

Jim Henderson

Pitches: R **Bats:** L **Pos:** RP-14   **Ht:** 6'5" **Wt:** 220 **Born:** 10/21/1982 **Age:** 32

			HOW MUCH HE PITCHED						WHAT HE GAVE UP										THE RESULTS						
Year	Team	Lg	G	GS	CG	GF	IP	BFP	H	R	ER	HR	SH	SF	HB	TBB	IBB	SO	WP	Bk	W	L	Pct	Sh	Sv-Op	Hld	ERC	ERA
2014	Hntsvl*	A-	3	0	0	0	4.0	14	1	1	0	0	0	0	0	1	0	4	1	0	0	0	-	0	0- -	-	0.40	0.00
2014	Brewrs*	R	3	2	0	0	3.2	14	3	0	0	0	0	0	0	0	0	5	1	0	0	0	-	0	0- -	-	1.32	0.00
2014	Nashv*	AAA	3	0	0	0	2.2	12	2	2	2	1	0	0	1	2	0	4	0	0	0	1	.000	0	3-7	-	8.38	6.75
2012	Mil	NL	36	0	0	6	30.2	131	26	12	12	1	1	3	1	13	0	45	1	0	1	3	.250	0	3-7	14	2.96	3.52
2013	Mil	NL	61	0	0	45	60.0	247	44	18	18	8	1	0	2	24	2	75	0	0	5	5	.500	0	28-32	5	2.93	2.70
2014	Mil	NL	14	0	0	3	11.1	50	14	10	9	3	1	0	0	4	1	17	0	0	2	1	.667	0	0-0	2	6.49	7.15
	3 ML YEARS		111	0	0	54	102.0	428	84	40	39	12	3	3	3	41	3	137	1	0	8	9	.471	0	31-39	21	3.30	3.44

Kyle Hendricks

Pitches: R **Bats:** R **Pos:** SP-13   **Ht:** 6'3" **Wt:** 190 **Born:** 12/7/1989 **Age:** 25

			HOW MUCH HE PITCHED						WHAT HE GAVE UP										THE RESULTS						
Year	Team	Lg	G	GS	CG	GF	IP	BFP	H	R	ER	HR	SH	SF	HB	TBB	IBB	SO	WP	Bk	W	L	Pct	Sh	Sv-Op	Hld	ERC	ERA
2011	Spkane	A-	20	0	0	8	32.2	122	20	7	7	0	0	0	0	4	0	36	2	0	2	2	.500	0	3- -	-	1.00	1.93
2011	Frisco	AA	1	1	0	0	3.0	15	4	1	1	0	0	0	0	2	0	2	0	0	0	0	-	0	0- -	-	6.15	3.00
2012	MrtlBh	A+	20	20	2	0	130.2	519	123	49	41	8	7	4	6	15	0	112	4	1	5	8	.385	0	0- -	-	2.66	2.82
2012	Dytona	A+	5	4	0	0	17.0	71	17	8	8	3	0	0	1	3	0	11	0	0	1	0	1.000	0	0- -	-	3.91	4.24
2013	Tenn	AA	21	21	1	0	126.1	508	107	34	26	3	3	2	5	26	0	101	1	0	10	3	.769	1	0- -	-	2.23	1.85
2013	Iowa	AAA	6	6	0	0	40.0	159	35	12	11	2	0	1	1	8	0	27	1	0	3	1	.750	0	0- -	-	2.49	2.48
2014	Iowa	AAA	17	17	0	0	102.2	416	98	46	41	5	8	0	2	23	4	97	1	0	10	5	.667	0	0- -	-	2.90	3.59
2014	ChC	NL	13	13	0	0	80.1	321	72	24	22	4	4	1	4	15	2	47	0	0	7	2	.778	0	0-0	0	2.61	2.46

Liam Hendriks

Pitches: R **Bats:** R **Pos:** SP-6; RP-3   **Ht:** 6'1" **Wt:** 205 **Born:** 2/10/1989 **Age:** 26

			HOW MUCH HE PITCHED						WHAT HE GAVE UP										THE RESULTS						
Year	Team	Lg	G	GS	CG	GF	IP	BFP	H	R	ER	HR	SH	SF	HB	TBB	IBB	SO	WP	Bk	W	L	Pct	Sh	Sv-Op	Hld	ERC	ERA
2014	Buffalo*	AAA	18	16	1	0	108.1	415	92	32	28	6	3	4	3	7	0	91	4	0	8	1	.889	0	0- -	-	1.95	2.33
2014	Omha*	AAA	5	5	0	0	35.0	137	33	13	11	1	0	1	0	6	0	35	0	0	4	1	.800	0	0- -	-	2.56	2.83
2011	Min	AL	4	4	0	0	23.1	100	29	16	16	3	0	1	0	6	0	16	1	0	0	2	.000	0	0-0	0	5.26	6.17
2012	Min	AL	16	16	1	0	85.1	381	106	61	53	17	3	1	4	26	3	50	4	0	1	8	.111	0	0-0	0	6.03	5.59
2013	Min	AL	10	8	0	1	47.1	224	67	39	36	10	0	2	3	14	1	34	1	0	1	3	.250	0	0-0	0	7.16	6.85
2014	2 Tms	AL	9	6	0	0	32.2	143	38	21	19	3	0	2	3	7	0	23	1	0	1	2	.333	0	0-0	1	4.56	5.23
14	Tor	AL	3	3	0	0	13.1	57	12	9	9	3	0	0	2	4	0	8	0	0	1	0	1.000	0	0-0	1	4.58	6.08
14	KC	AL	6	3	0	0	19.1	86	26	12	10	0	0	2	1	3	0	15	1	0	0	2	.000	0	0-0	1	4.52	4.66
	4 ML YEARS		39	34	1	1	188.2	848	240	137	124	33	3	6	10	53	4	123	7	0	3	15	.167	0	0-0	1	5.95	5.92

Cesar Hernandez

Bats: B **Throws:** R **Pos:** PH-38;3B-14;2B-11;SS-4;PR-2   **Ht:** 5'10" **Wt:** 166 **Born:** 5/23/1990 **Age:** 25

			BATTING																RUNNING			AVERAGES			
Year	Team	Lg	G	AB	H	2B	3B	HR	(Hm | Rd)	TB	R	RBI	RC	TBB	IBB	SO	HBP	SH	SF	SB	CS	GDP	Avg	OBP	Slg	OPS
2010	Wmspt	A-	65	255	83	13	2	0	(- | -)	100	36	23	45	26	1	27	3	0	3	32	6	0	.325	.390	.392	.782
2011	Clrwtr	A+	119	421	113	7	4	4	(- | -)	140	47	37	45	23	1	80	1	5	2	23	10	12	.268	.306	.333	.639
2012	Rdng	AA	103	411	125	26	11	2	(- | -)	179	50	51	61	27	0	67	0	10	2	17	11	11	.304	.345	.436	.781
2012	LV	AAA	30	121	30	4	1	0	(- | -)	36	13	6	9	4	0	11	0	3	1	5	3	1	.248	.270	.298	.567
2013	LV	AAA	104	391	121	12	9	2	(- | -)	157	59	34	65	41	0	81	1	5	2	32	8	4	.309	.375	.402	.776
2013	Rdng	AA	3	10	5	1	0	0	(- | -)	6	2	3	3	1	0	1	0	0	0	1	0	0	.500	.500	.600	1.100
2014	Rdng	AA	26	103	35	4	1	3	(- | -)	50	13	14	19	13	0	13	0	0	1	9	1	3	.340	.410	.485	.896
2014	LV	AAA	40	156	40	6	3	0	(- | -)	52	23	10	17	15	0	34	0	0	0	7	4	4	.256	.322	.333	.655
2013	Phi	NL	34	121	35	5	0	0	(0 | 0)	40	17	10	13	9	0	26	1	0	0	0	3	2	.289	.344	.331	.674
2014	Phi	NL	66	114	27	2	0	1	(1 | 0)	32	13	4	7	9	1	33	0	1	1	1	1	1	.237	.290	.281	.571
	2 ML YEARS		100	235	62	7	0	1	(1 | 0)	72	30	14	20	18	1	59	1	1	1	1	4	3	.264	.318	.306	.624

David Hernandez

Pitches: R **Bats:** R **Pos:** P

Ht: 6'3" **Wt:** 230 **Born:** 5/13/1985 **Age:** 30

Year Team	Lg	G	GS	CG	GF	IP	BFP	H	R	ER	HR	SH	SF	HB	TBB	IBB	SO	WP	Bk	W	L	Pct	Sh	Sv-Op	Hld	ERC	ERA
2009 Bal	AL	20	19	0	0	101.1	462	118	62	61	27	2	3	1	46	0	68	3	0	4	10	.286	0	0-0	0	6.55	5.42
2010 Bal	AL	41	8	0	16	79.1	348	72	40	38	9	1	3	4	42	4	72	9	0	8	8	.500	0	2-6	2	4.28	4.31
2011 Ari	NL	74	0	0	28	69.1	291	49	27	26	4	3	2	2	30	1	77	7	1	5	3	.625	0	11-14	23	2.40	3.38
2012 Ari	NL	72	0	0	21	68.1	278	48	21	19	4	0	1	3	22	1	98	4	1	2	3	.400	0	4-10	25	2.10	2.50
2013 Ari	NL	62	0	0	12	62.1	263	50	33	31	10	2	0	4	24	4	66	6	0	5	6	.455	0	2-8	15	3.45	4.48
Postseason		4	0	0	1	5.0	17	2	2	2	1	0	0	0	0	0	5	0	0	0	0	-	0	0-0	0	0.74	3.60
5 ML YEARS		269	27	0	77	380.2	1642	337	183	175	54	8	9	14	164	10	381	29	2	24	30	.444	0	19-38	65	3.91	4.14

Enrique Hernandez

Bats: R **Throws:** R **Pos:** CF-18;LF-8;SS-5;PH-5;2B-4;3B-3;RF-3;DH-1;PR-1

Ht: 5'11" **Wt:** 170 **Born:** 8/24/1991 **Age:** 23

Year Team	Lg	G	AB	H	2B	3B	HR	(Hm	Rd)	TB	R	RBI	RC	TBB	IBB	SO	HBP	SH	SF	SB	CS	GDP	Avg	OBP	Slg	OPS
2010 TriCity	A-	60	246	69	18	1	3	(-	-)	98	31	33	33	14	0	35	2	1	2	3	0	5	.280	.322	.398	.720
2011 Lxngtn	A	62	215	53	11	0	2	(-	-)	70	30	17	26	31	0	33	0	3	0	0	2	8	.247	.341	.326	.667
2012 Lancst	A+	100	378	104	25	7	5	(-	-)	158	52	49	52	22	0	43	3	5	3	4	2	9	.275	.318	.418	.736
2012 CpChr	AA	23	81	20	2	0	1	(-	-)	25	7	3	7	4	0	9	2	1	0	2	2	4	.247	.299	.309	.607
2013 CpChr	AA	116	437	103	18	2	13	(-	-)	164	53	46	51	34	2	70	5	5	2	5	3	13	.236	.297	.375	.672
2014 CpChr	AA	10	40	13	3	0	1	(-	-)	19	9	5	7	3	0	3	0	0	0	0	0	0	.325	.372	.475	.847
2014 OKCity	AAA	67	264	89	17	2	8	(-	-)	134	41	31	50	18	1	25	2	2	3	6	5	10	.337	.380	.508	.887
2014 NewOr	AAA	21	72	18	5	0	2	(-	-)	29	8	6	14	10	0	13	1	0	1	0	1	1	.250	.345	.403	.748
2014 2 Tms		42	121	30	6	3	3	(1	2)	51	13	14	18	12	0	21	1	0	0	0	0	1	.248	.321	.421	.742
14 Hou	AL	24	81	23	4	2	1	(1	0)	34	10	8	14	8	0	11	0	0	0	0	0	0	.284	.348	.420	.768
14 Mia	NL	18	40	7	2	1	2	(0	2)	17	3	6	4	4	0	10	1	0	0	0	0	1	.175	.267	.425	.692

Felix Hernandez

Pitches: R **Bats:** R **Pos:** SP-34

Ht: 6'3" **Wt:** 225 **Born:** 4/8/1986 **Age:** 29

Year Team	Lg	G	GS	CG	GF	IP	BFP	H	R	ER	HR	SH	SF	HB	TBB	IBB	SO	WP	Bk	W	L	Pct	Sh	Sv-Op	Hld	ERC	ERA
2005 Sea	AL	12	12	0	0	84.1	328	61	26	25	5	1	2	2	23	0	77	3	0	4	4	.500	0	0-0	0	2.08	2.67
2006 Sea	AL	31	31	2	0	191.0	816	195	105	96	23	2	3	6	60	2	176	11	0	12	14	.462	1	0-0	0	4.11	4.52
2007 Sea	AL	30	30	1	0	190.1	808	209	88	83	20	6	1	3	53	4	165	7	1	14	7	.667	1	0-0	0	4.27	3.92
2008 Sea	AL	31	31	2	0	200.2	857	198	85	77	17	4	6	8	80	7	175	8	1	9	11	.450	1	0-0	0	4.05	3.45
2009 Sea	AL	34	34	2	0	238.2	977	200	81	66	15	6	11	8	71	0	217	17	1	19	5	.792	1	0-0	0	2.72	2.49
2010 Sea	AL	34	34	6	0	249.2	1001	194	80	63	17	6	3	8	70	1	232	14	1	13	12	.520	1	0-0	0	2.39	2.27
2011 Sea	AL	33	33	5	0	233.2	964	218	99	90	19	3	7	7	67	0	222	12	1	14	14	.500	0	0-0	0	3.31	3.47
2012 Sea	AL	33	33	5	0	232.0	939	209	84	79	14	2	2	12	56	0	223	13	2	13	9	.591	5	0-0	0	2.94	3.06
2013 Sea	AL	31	31	0	0	204.1	822	185	74	69	15	4	6	3	46	1	216	13	0	12	10	.545	0	0-0	0	2.83	3.04
2014 Sea	AL	34	34	0	0	236.0	912	170	68	56	16	4	5	5	46	1	248	18	0	15	6	.714	0	0-0	0	1.81	2.14
10 ML YEARS		303	303	23	0	2060.2	8424	1839	790	704	161	38	46	62	572	16	1951	116	7	125	92	.576	9	0-0	0	3.02	3.07

Pedro Hernandez

Pitches: L **Bats:** L **Pos:** SP-1

Ht: 5'10" **Wt:** 210 **Born:** 4/12/1989 **Age:** 26

Year Team	Lg	G	GS	CG	GF	IP	BFP	H	R	ER	HR	SH	SF	HB	TBB	IBB	SO	WP	Bk	W	L	Pct	Sh	Sv-Op	Hld	ERC	ERA
2014 ColSpr*	AAA	19	17	1	0	88.1	411	125	66	63	10	3	3	3	30	0	53	2	0	6	7	.462	0	0--	-	6.59	6.42
2012 CWS	AL	1	1	0	0	4.0	25	12	8	8	3	0	0	0	1	0	2	0	0	0	1	.000	0	0-0	0	24.35	18.00
2013 Min	AL	14	12	0	0	56.2	263	80	43	43	10	0	3	0	23	1	29	1	1	3	3	.500	0	0-0	0	7.28	6.83
2014 Col	NL	1	1	0	0	5.2	24	6	3	3	0	1	1	1	2	0	2	0	0	0	1	.000	0	0-0	0	4.43	4.76
3 ML YEARS		16	14	0	1	66.1	312	98	54	54	13	1	4	1	26	1	33	1	1	3	5	.375	0	0-0	0	7.91	7.33

Roberto Hernandez

Pitches: R **Bats:** R **Pos:** SP-29; RP-3

Ht: 6'4" **Wt:** 230 **Born:** 8/30/1980 **Age:** 34

Year Team	Lg	G	GS	CG	GF	IP	BFP	H	R	ER	HR	SH	SF	HB	TBB	IBB	SO	WP	Bk	W	L	Pct	Sh	Sv-Op	Hld	ERC	ERA
2006 Cle	AL	38	7	0	12	74.2	340	88	46	45	9	2	4	7	31	3	58	3	1	1	10	.091	0	0-3	10	5.69	5.42
2007 Cle	AL	32	32	2	0	215.0	879	199	78	73	16	2	4	7	61	2	137	5	1	19	8	.704	1	0-0	0	3.32	3.06
2008 Cle	AL	22	22	1	0	120.2	549	126	80	73	7	1	4	9	70	0	58	8	1	8	7	.533	1	0-0	0	5.07	5.44
2009 Cle	AL	24	24	0	0	125.1	596	151	97	88	16	4	2	8	70	0	79	5	1	5	12	.294	0	0-0	0	6.38	6.32
2010 Cle	AL	33	33	4	0	210.1	880	203	98	88	16	4	2	8	72	0	124	3	0	13	14	.481	1	0-0	0	3.77	3.77
2011 Cle	AL	32	32	0	0	188.2	833	205	125	110	22	9	7	14	60	3	109	3	1	7	15	.318	0	0-0	0	4.59	5.25
2012 Cle	AL	3	3	0	0	14.1	62	17	15	12	4	0	2	1	3	0	2	1	0	0	3	.000	0	0-0	0	6.03	7.53
2013 TB	AL	32	24	1	3	151.0	643	164	87	82	24	3	5	13	38	8	113	3	0	6	13	.316	0	1-1	0	4.74	4.89
2014 2 Tms	NL	32	29	0	1	164.2	722	156	84	75	19	10	5	9	73	7	105	5	0	8	11	.421	0	0-1	0	4.17	4.10
14 Phi	NL	23	20	0	1	121.0	527	108	57	52	11	7	3	7	55	7	75	4	0	6	8	.429	0	0-1	0	3.72	3.87
14 LAD	NL	9	9	0	0	43.2	195	48	27	23	8	3	2	2	18	0	30	1	0	2	3	.400	0	0-0	0	5.50	4.74
Postseason		3	3	0	0	15.0	66	13	12	12	2	0	0	0	11	0	12	0	0	0	1	.000	0	0-0	0	5.02	7.20
9 ML YEARS		248	206	8	16	1264.2	5504	1309	710	646	134	33	43	81	478	23	785	36	5	67	93	.419	3	1-5	10	4.49	4.60

Dilson Herrera

Bats: R Throws: R Pos: 2B-17;PR-1   DILL-sun   Ht: 5'10" Wt: 150 Born: 3/3/1994 Age: 21

Year	Team	Lg	G	AB	H	2B	3B	HR	(Hm	Rd)	TB	R	RBI	RC	TBB	IBB	SO	HBP	SH	SF	SB	CS	GDP	Avg	OBP	Slg	OPS
2012	Pirates	R	53	199	56	11	4	7	(-	-)	96	41	27	34	18	0	41	0	10	0	11	4	2	.281	.341	.482	.823
2012	StCol	A-	7	28	9	1	1	1	(-	-)	15	7	2	5	1	0	6	0	0	0	1	0	1	.321	.345	.536	.881
2013	WV	A	109	423	112	27	3	11	(-	-)	178	69	56	61	37	0	110	7	6	6	11	6	6	.265	.330	.421	.751
2013	Savann	A	7	19	6	0	0	0	(-	-)	6	6	4	3	3	1	6	1	0	1	3	0	0	.316	.417	.316	.732
2014	StLuci	A+	67	283	87	16	2	3	(-	-)	116	48	23	44	18	0	44	4	2	2	14	3	4	.307	.355	.410	.765
2014	Bnghtn	AA	61	241	82	17	3	10	(-	-)	135	50	48	54	29	0	52	2	0	6	9	4	5	.340	.406	.560	.967
2014	NYM	NL	18	59	13	0	1	3	(0	3)	24	6	11	7	7	0	17	0	0	0	0	0	3	.220	.303	.407	.710

Elian Herrera

EH-lee-ahn

Bats: B Throws: R Pos: RF-15;PH-15;SS-14;3B-11;PR-8;2B-7;LF-7;CF-7   Ht: 5'10" Wt: 195 Born: 2/1/1985 Age: 30

Year	Team	Lg	G	AB	H	2B	3B	HR	(Hm	Rd)	TB	R	RBI	RC	TBB	IBB	SO	HBP	SH	SF	SB	CS	GDP	Avg	OBP	Slg	OPS
2014	Nashv*	AAA	33	115	35	9	2	0	(-	-)	48	21	9	17	8	0	19	0	1	0	5	1	2	.304	.350	.417	.767
2012	LAD	NL	67	187	47	10	1	1	(0	1)	62	26	17	20	23	0	50	2	2	0	4	2	5	.251	.340	.332	.671
2013	LAD	NL	4	8	2	0	0	0	(0	0)	2	0	0	0	0	0	2	0	0	0	0	0	0	.250	.250	.250	.500
2014	Mil	NL	69	135	37	7	1	0	(0	0)	46	14	5	9	3	1	36	0	1	1	4	1	2	.274	.288	.341	.629
	3 ML YEARS		140	330	86	17	2	1	(0	1)	110	40	22	29	26	1	88	2	3	1	8	3	7	.261	.318	.333	.651

Jonathan Herrera

Bats: B Throws: R Pos: SS-16;3B-14;2B-9;PH-6;PR-4;DH-2;1B-1   Ht: 5'9" Wt: 180 Born: 11/3/1984 Age: 30

Year	Team	Lg	G	AB	H	2B	3B	HR	(Hm	Rd)	TB	R	RBI	RC	TBB	IBB	SO	HBP	SH	SF	SB	CS	GDP	Avg	OBP	Slg	OPS
2014	Pwtckt*	AAA	13	55	17	2	1	0	(0	0)	21	11	4	7	4	0	11	0	1	1	1	1	2	.309	.350	.382	.732
2008	Col	NL	28	61	14	1	1	0	(0	0)	17	5	3	6	4	0	10	0	1	0	1	1	0	.230	.277	.279	.556
2010	Col	NL	76	222	63	6	2	1	(0	1)	76	34	21	29	25	1	36	0	7	3	2	2	2	.284	.352	.342	.694
2011	Col	NL	104	281	68	5	1	3	(2	1)	84	28	14	24	28	0	40	1	10	0	4	4	7	.242	.313	.299	.612
2012	Col	NL	86	225	59	9	1	3	(3	0)	79	29	12	22	16	3	39	2	7	0	4	1	5	.262	.317	.351	.668
2013	Col	NL	81	195	57	7	2	1	(0	1)	71	16	16	22	14	3	24	0	4	2	3	2	6	.292	.336	.364	.701
2014	Bos	AL	42	90	21	1	2	0	(0	0)	26	10	9	9	7	0	24	3	3	1	1	3	3	.233	.307	.289	.596
	6 ML YEARS		417	1074	282	29	9	8	(5	3)	353	122	75	112	94	7	173	6	32	6	15	13	23	.263	.324	.329	.652

Kelvin Herrera

Pitches: R Bats: R Pos: RP-70   Ht: 5'10" Wt: 200 Born: 12/31/1989 Age: 25

Year	Team	Lg	G	GS	CG	GF	IP	BFP	H	R	ER	HR	SH	SF	HB	TBB	IBB	SO	WP	Bk	W	L	Pct	Sh	Sv-Op	Hld	ERC	ERA
2011	KC	AL	2	0	0	2	2.0	9	2	3	3	1	1	0	1	0	0	0	0	0	0	1	.000	0	0-0	1	7.30	13.50
2012	KC	AL	76	0	0	10	84.1	344	79	24	22	4	5	0	2	21	6	77	3	1	4	3	.571	0	3-4	19	2.84	2.35
2013	KC	AL	59	0	0	16	58.1	245	48	27	25	9	0	3	2	21	2	74	5	0	5	7	.417	0	2-4	20	3.35	3.86
2014	KC	AL	70	0	0	12	70.0	285	54	12	11	0	4	0	3	26	0	59	1	0	4	3	.571	0	0-1	20	2.31	1.41
	4 ML YEARS		207	0	0	38	214.2	883	183	66	61	14	10	3	8	68	8	210	9	1	13	14	.481	0	5-9	60	2.84	2.56

Yoslan Herrera

YOH-slahn

Pitches: R Bats: R Pos: RP-20   Ht: 6'2" Wt: 200 Born: 4/28/1981 Age: 34

Year	Team	Lg	G	GS	CG	GF	IP	BFP	H	R	ER	HR	SH	SF	HB	TBB	IBB	SO	WP	Bk	W	L	Pct	Sh	Sv-Op	Hld	ERC	ERA
2010	Roch	AAA	6	6	0	0	26.2	125	33	19	18	3	0	0	2	15	0	14	2	1	0	3	.000	0	0- -	-	6.69	6.08
2013	Lncstr	IND	59	0	0	25	53.0	214	46	24	22	2	-	-	0	17	0	54	3	1	2	1	.667	0	11- -	-	2.73	3.74
2014	Salt Lk	AAA	41	0	0	21	50.0	218	51	16	14	3	4	3	3	16	2	47	2	0	4	4	.500	0	5- -	-	3.71	2.52
2008	Pit	NL	5	5	0	0	18.1	100	35	20	20	1	3	2	1	12	0	10	1	0	1	1	.500	0	0-0	0	10.94	9.82
2014	LAA	AL	20	0	0	8	16.2	77	22	5	5	0	0	0	0	9	3	13	0	0	1	1	.500	0	0-0	0	5.51	2.70
	2 ML YEARS		25	5	0	8	35.0	177	57	25	25	1	3	2	1	21	3	23	1	0	2	2	.500	0	0-0	0	8.25	6.43

Chris Herrmann

Bats: L Throws: R Pos: RF-13;LF-12;PH-9;PR-4;C-1   HERR-men   Ht: 6'0" Wt: 200 Born: 11/24/1987 Age: 27

Year	Team	Lg	G	AB	H	2B	3B	HR	(Hm	Rd)	TB	R	RBI	RC	TBB	IBB	SO	HBP	SH	SF	SB	CS	GDP	Avg	OBP	Slg	OPS
2014	Roch*	AAA	60	204	62	18	4	5	(-	-)	103	31	26	39	21	4	45	2	0	1	4	1	2	.304	.373	.505	.878
2012	Min	AL	7	18	1	0	0	0	(0	0)	1	0	1	0	1	0	5	0	0	0	0	0	0	.056	.105	.056	.161
2013	Min	AL	57	157	32	7	0	4	(1	3)	51	16	18	15	18	0	49	0	3	0	0	1	3	.204	.286	.325	.611
2014	Min	AL	33	75	16	3	0	0	(0	0)	19	8	4	5	4	0	17	0	0	0	1	0	2	.213	.253	.253	.506
	3 ML YEARS		97	250	49	10	0	4	(1	3)	71	24	23	20	23	0	71	0	3	0	1	1	5	.196	.264	.284	.548

Chris Heston

Pitches: R **Bats:** R **Pos:** RP-2; SP-1   **Ht:** 6'4" **Wt:** 185 **Born:** 4/10/1988 **Age:** 27

			HOW MUCH HE PITCHED						WHAT HE GAVE UP													THE RESULTS							
Year	Team	Lg	G	GS	CG	GF	IP	BFP	H	R	ER	HR	SH	SF	HB	TBB	IBB	SO	WP	Bk	W	L	Pct	Sh	Sv-Op	Hld	ERC	ERA
2010	Augsta	A	26	26	1	0	148.2	642	161	83	62	6	3	5	9	33	0	124	12	1	5	13	.278	0	0- -	-	3.61	3.75
2011	SnJos	A+	24	24	1	0	151.0	614	144	64	53	10	5	4	8	40	1	131	7	0	12	4	.750	0	0- -	-	3.38	3.16
2012	Rchmd	AA	25	25	1	0	148.2	595	124	43	37	2	10	3	4	40	1	135	12	0	9	8	.529	0	0- -	-	2.30	2.24
2013	Fresno	AAA	19	19	1	0	108.2	495	129	75	70	14	6	5	9	46	2	97	8	1	7	6	.538	1	0- -	-	5.84	5.80
2014	Fresno	AAA	28	28	1	0	173.0	716	152	76	65	16	4	1	9	51	1	125	11	0	12	9	.571	1	0- -	-	3.17	3.38
2014	SF	NL	3	1	0	2	5.1	24	6	3	3	0	0	1	0	3	0	4	1	0	0	0	-	0	0-0	0	4.74	5.06

Jason Heyward

Bats: L **Throws:** L **Pos:** RF-149;PH-1   **Ht:** 6'5" **Wt:** 245 **Born:** 8/9/1989 **Age:** 25

						BATTING													RUNNING			AVERAGES			
Year	Team	Lg	G	AB	H	2B	3B	HR	(Hm | Rd)	TB	R	RBI	RC	TBB	IBB	SO	HBP	SH	SF	SB	CS	GDP	Avg	OBP	Slg	OPS
2010	Atl	NL	142	520	144	29	5	18	(9 | 9)	237	83	72	96	91	2	128	10	0	2	11	6	13	.277	.393	.456	.849
2011	Atl	NL	128	396	90	18	2	14	(5 | 9)	154	50	42	49	51	4	93	4	0	3	9	2	7	.227	.319	.389	.708
2012	Atl	NL	158	587	158	30	6	27	(9 | 18)	281	93	82	87	58	1	152	2	0	3	21	8	5	.269	.335	.479	.814
2013	Atl	NL	104	382	97	22	1	14	(10 | 4)	163	67	38	55	48	1	73	8	1	0	2	4	7	.254	.349	.427	.776
2014	Atl	NL	149	573	155	26	3	11	(5 | 6)	220	74	58	84	67	3	98	6	0	3	20	4	2	.271	.351	.384	.735
	Postseason		9	39	6	1	0	1	(0 | 1)	10	1	4	2	1	0	16	0	0	0	0	0	1	.154	.175	.256	.431
	5 ML YEARS		681	2458	644	125	17	84	(38 | 46)	1055	367	292	371	315	11	544	30	1	11	63	24	34	.262	.351	.429	.781

Aaron Hicks

Bats: B **Throws:** R **Pos:** CF-57;PR-7;LF-6;RF-5;DH-2   **Ht:** 6'2" **Wt:** 190 **Born:** 10/2/1989 **Age:** 25

						BATTING													RUNNING			AVERAGES			
Year	Team	Lg	G	AB	H	2B	3B	HR	(Hm | Rd)	TB	R	RBI	RC	TBB	IBB	SO	HBP	SH	SF	SB	CS	GDP	Avg	OBP	Slg	OPS
2010	Beloit	A	115	423	118	27	6	8	(- | -)	181	86	49	79	88	2	112	0	4	3	21	11	4	.279	.401	.428	.829
2011	FtMyrs	A+	122	443	107	31	5	5	(- | -)	163	79	38	64	78	5	110	1	3	3	17	9	6	.242	.354	.368	.722
2012	NwBrit	AA	129	472	135	21	11	13	(- | -)	217	100	61	90	79	2	116	1	3	3	32	11	8	.286	.384	.460	.844
2013	Roch	AAA	22	72	16	4	2	0	(- | -)	24	7	5	8	10	1	21	0	0	0	1	0	2	.222	.317	.333	.650
2014	NwBrit	AA	43	148	44	11	1	4	(- | -)	69	30	21	29	28	1	27	0	0	2	3	3	4	.297	.404	.466	.871
2014	Roch	AAA	24	72	20	5	0	1	(- | -)	28	9	8	10	9	0	13	0	0	1	1	1	3	.278	.349	.389	.738
2013	Min	AL	81	281	54	11	3	8	(3 | 5)	95	37	27	25	24	0	84	2	4	2	9	3	0	.192	.259	.338	.597
2014	Min	AL	69	186	40	8	0	1	(0 | 1)	51	22	18	22	36	0	56	0	2	1	4	3	2	.215	.341	.274	.615
	2 ML YEARS		150	467	94	19	3	9	(3 | 6)	146	59	45	47	60	0	140	2	6	3	13	6	2	.201	.293	.313	.606

Brandon Hicks

Bats: R **Throws:** R **Pos:** 2B-61;PH-9;1B-1;LF-1   **Ht:** 6'2" **Wt:** 215 **Born:** 9/14/1985 **Age:** 29

						BATTING													RUNNING			AVERAGES			
Year	Team	Lg	G	AB	H	2B	3B	HR	(Hm | Rd)	TB	R	RBI	RC	TBB	IBB	SO	HBP	SH	SF	SB	CS	GDP	Avg	OBP	Slg	OPS
2014	Fresno*	AAA	41	133	29	11	0	6	(- | -)	58	18	17	18	14	0	49	4	1	0	0	0	6	.218	.311	.436	.747
2010	Atl	NL	16	5	0	0	0	0	(0 | 0)	0	7	0	0	1	0	2	0	0	0	0	0	0	.000	.167	.000	.167
2011	Atl	NL	17	21	1	0	0	0	(0 | 0)	1	1	1	0	1	0	9	0	0	0	0	0	0	.048	.091	.048	.139
2012	Oak	AL	22	64	11	5	0	3	(2 | 1)	25	8	7	5	6	0	31	0	0	0	1	0	1	.172	.243	.391	.633
2014	SF	NL	71	204	33	6	1	8	(4 | 4)	65	27	22	17	32	3	77	2	3	1	0	1	5	.162	.280	.319	.599
	4 ML YEARS		126	294	45	11	1	11	(6 | 5)	91	43	30	22	40	3	119	2	3	1	1	1	6	.153	.258	.310	.568

Aaron Hill

Bats: R **Throws:** R **Pos:** 2B-116;PH-8;3B-7;DH-2   **Ht:** 5'11" **Wt:** 205 **Born:** 3/21/1982 **Age:** 33

						BATTING													RUNNING			AVERAGES			
Year	Team	Lg	G	AB	H	2B	3B	HR	(Hm | Rd)	TB	R	RBI	RC	TBB	IBB	SO	HBP	SH	SF	SB	CS	GDP	Avg	OBP	Slg	OPS
2005	Tor	AL	105	361	99	25	3	3	(3 | 0)	139	49	40	50	34	0	41	5	3	4	2	1	5	.274	.342	.385	.727
2006	Tor	AL	155	546	159	28	3	6	(4 | 2)	211	70	50	68	42	5	66	9	4	5	2	2	15	.291	.349	.386	.735
2007	Tor	AL	160	608	177	47	2	17	(8 | 9)	279	87	78	88	41	1	102	0	3	5	4	3	21	.291	.333	.459	.792
2008	Tor	AL	55	205	54	14	0	2	(1 | 1)	74	19	20	24	16	0	31	3	4	1	4	2	4	.263	.324	.361	.685
2009	Tor	AL	158	682	195	37	0	36	(21 | 15)	340	103	108	110	42	1	98	5	1	4	6	2	17	.286	.330	.499	.829
2010	Tor	AL	138	528	108	22	0	26	(15 | 11)	208	70	68	57	41	2	85	8	1	2	2	2	8	.205	.271	.394	.665
2011	2 Tms		137	520	128	27	3	8	(4 | 4)	185	61	61	61	35	1	72	7	2	7	21	7	10	.246	.299	.356	.655
2012	Ari	NL	156	609	184	44	6	26	(14 | 12)	318	93	85	101	52	7	86	4	1	2	14	5	15	.302	.360	.522	.882
2013	Ari	NL	87	327	95	21	1	11	(7 | 4)	151	45	41	45	29	2	48	5	0	1	1	4	6	.291	.356	.462	.818
2014	Ari	NL	133	501	122	26	3	10	(6 | 4)	184	52	60	48	28	0	92	5	0	7	4	3	16	.244	.287	.367	.654
11	Tor	AL	104	396	89	15	1	6	(3 | 3)	124	38	45	38	23	1	53	4	0	6	16	3	8	.225	.270	.313	.584
11	Ari	NL	33	124	39	12	2	2	(1 | 1)	61	23	16	23	12	0	19	3	2	1	5	4	2	.315	.386	.492	.878
	Postseason		5	18	5	0	0	1	(1 | 0)	8	3	1	2	5	0	3	0	0	0	0	0	1	.278	.435	.444	.879
	10 ML YEARS		1284	4887	1321	291	21	145	(83 | 62)	2089	649	611	652	360	19	721	51	19	38	63	31	117	.270	.325	.427	.752

Koyie Hill

Bats: B **Throws:** R **Pos:** C-10   COY   **Ht:** 6'1" **Wt:** 205 **Born:** 3/9/1979 **Age:** 36

						BATTING													RUNNING			AVERAGES			
Year	Team	Lg	G	AB	H	2B	3B	HR	(Hm | Rd)	TB	R	RBI	RC	TBB	IBB	SO	HBP	SH	SF	SB	CS	GDP	Avg	OBP	Slg	OPS
2014	LV*	AAA	53	176	40	11	1	3	(- | -)	62	18	17	21	28	1	45	0	2	0	0	3	6	.227	.333	.352	.686
2003	LAD	NL	3	3	1	1	0	0	(0 | 0)	2	0	0	0	0	0	2	0	0	0	0	0	0	.333	.333	.667	1.000
2004	Ari	NL	13	36	9	1	0	1	(1 | 0)	13	3	6	5	2	1	6	0	0	0	1	0	1	.250	.289	.361	.651
2005	Ari	NL	34	78	17	5	0	0	(0 | 0)	22	6	6	6	11	0	27	0	0	2	0	1	0	.218	.308	.282	.590
2007	ChC	NL	36	93	15	4	0	2	(1 | 1)	25	7	12	3	8	0	18	1	1	2	0	0	4	.161	.231	.269	.500

Year	Team	Lg	G	AB	H	2B	3B	HR	(Hm	Rd)	TB	R	RBI	RC	TBB	IBB	SO	HBP	SH	SF	SB	CS	GDP	Avg	OBP	Slg	OPS
									BATTING												RUNNING			AVERAGES			
2008 ChC		NL	10	21	2	1	0	0	(0	0)	3	0	1	0	0	0	12	0	1	0	0	0	0	.095	.095	.143	.238
2009 ChC		NL	83	253	60	12	2	2	(1	1)	82	26	24	23	27	6	78	1	2	1	0	0	9	.237	.312	.324	.636
2010 ChC		NL	77	215	46	13	1	1	(1	0)	64	18	17	17	12	3	61	0	3	1	1	0	5	.214	.254	.298	.552
2011 ChC		NL	46	134	26	3	1	2	(1	1)	37	15	9	2	14	3	40	0	4	1	1	0	3	.194	.268	.276	.545
2012 ChC		NL	11	39	7	1	0	0	(0	0)	8	3	1	1	0	0	7	0	0	0	0	0	0	.179	.179	.205	.385
2013 Mia		NL	18	58	9	2	0	0	(0	0)	11	3	0	0	2	0	18	0	1	0	0	0	1	.155	.183	.190	.373
2014 Phi		NL	10	21	5	1	0	0	(0	0)	6	2	1	2	1	0	5	0	0	0	0	0	0	.238	.273	.286	.558
11 ML YEARS			341	951	197	44	4	8	(5	3)	273	83	77	59	77	13	274	2	12	7	3	1	23	.207	.266	.287	.553

Rich Hill

Pitches: L **Bats:** L **Pos:** RP-16   **Ht:** 6'5" **Wt:** 220 **Born:** 3/11/1980 **Age:** 35

Year	Team	Lg	G	GS	CG	GF	IP	BFP	H	R	ER	HR	SH	SF	HB	TBB	IBB	SO	WP	Bk	W	L	Pct	Sh	Sv-Op	Hld	ERC	ERA
			HOW MUCH HE PITCHED						WHAT HE GAVE UP												THE RESULTS							
2014 Pwtckt*		AAA	25	0	0	4	39.0	161	29	15	14	0	0	1	2	17	1	45	2	0	3	3	.500	0	2- -	-	2.36	3.23
2014 S-WB*		AAA	4	0	0	0	4.0	16	2	0	0	0	0	0	0	1	0	10	2	0	0	0	-	0	0- -	-	0.88	0.00
2005 ChC		NL	10	4	0	1	23.2	115	25	24	24	3	1	0	1	17	1	21	0	0	0	2	.000	0	0-0	0	5.81	9.13
2006 ChC		NL	17	16	2	1	99.1	417	83	51	46	16	8	3	2	39	1	90	3	0	6	7	.462	1	0-0	0	3.59	4.17
2007 ChC		NL	32	32	0	0	195.0	812	170	89	85	27	9	4	12	63	3	183	1	1	11	8	.579	0	0-0	0	3.56	3.92
2008 ChC		NL	5	5	0	0	19.2	89	13	9	9	2	0	2	1	18	0	15	1	0	1	0	1.000	0	0-0	0	4.38	4.12
2009 Bal		AL	14	13	0	0	57.2	275	68	53	50	7	2	2	1	40	2	46	1	1	3	3	.500	0	0-0	0	6.55	7.80
2010 Bos		AL	6	0	0	0	4.0	18	5	0	0	0	0	0	0	1	0	3	0	0	1	0	1.000	0	0-0	1	4.05	0.00
2011 Bos		AL	9	0	0	3	8.0	30	3	0	0	0	0	0	1	3	0	12	1	0	0	0	-	0	0-0	3	1.10	0.00
2012 Bos		AL	25	0	0	3	19.2	83	17	4	4	0	0	0	1	11	1	21	0	0	1	0	1.000	0	0-0	6	3.24	1.83
2013 Cle		AL	63	0	0	3	38.2	182	38	30	27	3	1	2	2	29	6	51	6	1	1	2	.333	0	0-2	13	5.07	6.28
2014 2 Tms		AL	16	0	0	2	5.1	29	7	2	2	0	0	0	1	6	1	9	1	0	0	0	-	0	0-0	1	8.55	3.38
14 LAA		AL	2	0	0	0	0.0	4	1	1	1	0	0	0	0	3	0	0	1	0	0	0	-	0	0-0	0	-	-
14 NYY		AL	14	0	0	2	5.1	25	6	1	1	0	0	0	1	3	1	9	0	0	0	0	-	0	0-0	1	5.10	1.69
Postseason			1	1	0	0	3.0	18	6	3	3	1	0	0	1	2	0	3	0	0	0	1	.000	0	0-0	0	15.68	9.00
10 ML YEARS			197	70	2	13	471.0	2050	429	262	247	58	21	13	21	227	15	451	14	3	24	22	.522	1	0-2	24	4.18	4.72

Taylor Hill

Pitches: R **Bats:** R **Pos:** RP-2; SP-1   **Ht:** 6'3" **Wt:** 235 **Born:** 3/12/1989 **Age:** 26

Year	Team	Lg	G	GS	CG	GF	IP	BFP	H	R	ER	HR	SH	SF	HB	TBB	IBB	SO	WP	Bk	W	L	Pct	Sh	Sv-Op	Hld	ERC	ERA
			HOW MUCH HE PITCHED						WHAT HE GAVE UP												THE RESULTS							
2011 Auburn		A-	9	5	0	0	31.1	128	32	12	11	1	1	0	3	3	0	27	2	0	0	2	.000	0	0- -	-	2.98	3.16
2012 Hgrstn		A	24	20	0	2	124.1	550	144	80	68	12	3	2	6	31	0	60	4	1	10	6	.625	0	0- -	-	4.46	4.92
2012 Ptomc		A+	3	3	1	0	15.0	65	17	11	8	2	1	0	1	3	0	11	3	0	1	1	.500	1	0- -	-	4.50	4.80
2013 Ptomc		A+	15	14	2	0	84.1	333	73	31	28	6	3	2	4	11	0	54	4	0	6	2	.750	2	0- -	-	2.39	2.99
2013 Hrsbrg		AA	11	11	0	0	69.2	284	67	25	21	7	1	4	1	16	0	41	1	0	2	7	.222	0	0- -	-	3.32	2.71
2013 Syrcse		AAA	2	2	0	0	10.2	52	18	6	5	0	1	1	1	2	0	9	0	0	1	0	1.000	0	0- -	-	6.86	4.22
2014 Syrcse		AAA	25	24	4	1	144.0	587	136	48	45	15	2	4	9	25	0	86	3	0	11	7	.611	2	1- -	-	3.20	2.81
2014 Was		NL	3	1	0	2	9.0	45	16	9	9	0	1	0	2	3	1	5	0	0	0	1	.000	0	0-0	0	8.83	9.00

Luke Hochevar

Pitches: R **Bats:** R **Pos:** P   HOE-chay-vur   **Ht:** 6'5" **Wt:** 225 **Born:** 9/15/1983 **Age:** 31

Year	Team	Lg	G	GS	CG	GF	IP	BFP	H	R	ER	HR	SH	SF	HB	TBB	IBB	SO	WP	Bk	W	L	Pct	Sh	Sv-Op	Hld	ERC	ERA
			HOW MUCH HE PITCHED						WHAT HE GAVE UP												THE RESULTS							
2007 KC		AL	4	1	0	0	12.2	54	11	4	3	1	1	0	3	4	0	5	1	0	0	1	.000	0	0-0	0	3.86	2.13
2008 KC		AL	22	22	0	0	129.0	566	143	84	79	12	1	2	5	47	1	72	7	0	6	12	.333	0	0-0	0	4.67	5.51
2009 KC		AL	25	25	2	0	143.0	631	167	109	104	23	2	0	8	46	0	106	9	0	7	13	.350	1	0-0	0	5.46	6.55
2010 KC		AL	18	17	1	0	103.0	450	110	61	55	9	2	2	4	37	1	76	2	1	6	6	.500	0	0-0	0	4.34	4.81
2011 KC		AL	31	31	0	0	198.0	835	192	110	103	23	2	2	7	62	4	128	7	2	11	11	.500	0	0-0	0	3.80	4.68
2012 KC		AL	32	32	2	0	185.1	800	202	127	118	27	4	3	13	61	3	144	8	0	8	16	.333	1	0-0	0	4.99	5.73
2013 KC		AL	58	0	0	22	70.1	262	41	15	15	8	2	0	1	17	1	82	2	0	5	2	.714	0	2-5	9	1.62	1.92
7 ML YEARS			190	128	5	23	841.1	3598	866	510	477	103	14	9	41	274	10	613	36	3	43	61	.413	2	2-5	9	4.32	5.10

L.J. Hoes

Bats: R **Throws:** R **Pos:** LF-36;RF-12;PH-9;PR-4   HOSE   **Ht:** 6'0" **Wt:** 200 **Born:** 3/5/1990 **Age:** 25

Year	Team	Lg	G	AB	H	2B	3B	HR	(Hm	Rd)	TB	R	RBI	RC	TBB	IBB	SO	HBP	SH	SF	SB	CS	GDP	Avg	OBP	Slg	OPS
									BATTING												RUNNING			AVERAGES			
2014 OKCity*		AAA	35	128	38	6	0	2	(-	-)	50	21	15	20	16	0	30	2	1	1	5	4	4	.297	.381	.391	.772
2012 Bal		AL	2	1	0	0	0	0	(0	0)	0	0	0	0	0	0	0	0	0	0	0	0	0	.000	.000	.000	.000
2013 2 Tms		AL	47	170	48	7	2	1	(0	1)	62	24	10	21	12	0	35	1	0	1	7	1	4	.282	.332	.365	.696
2014 Hou		AL	55	122	21	5	0	3	(2	1)	35	12	11	5	10	0	31	0	1	3	0	0	5	.172	.230	.287	.517
13 Bal		AL	1	3	0	0	0	0	(0	0)	0	0	0	0	0	0	1	0	0	0	0	0	0	.000	.000	.000	.000
13 Hou		AL	46	167	48	7	2	1	(0	1)	62	24	10	21	12	0	34	1	0	1	7	1	4	.287	.337	.371	.708
3 ML YEARS			104	293	69	12	2	4	(2	2)	97	36	21	26	22	0	66	1	1	4	7	1	9	.235	.288	.331	.619

Bryan Holaday

Bats: R **Throws:** R **Pos:** C-58;PH-3;PR-3;DH-1   HAHL-ih-daye   **Ht:** 6'0" **Wt:** 205 **Born:** 11/19/1987 **Age:** 27

							BATTING														RUNNING			AVERAGES			
Year	Team	Lg	G	AB	H	2B	3B	HR	(Hm	Rd)	TB	R	RBI	RC	TBB	IBB	SO	HBP	SH	SF	SB	CS	GDP	Avg	OBP	Slg	OPS
2012	Det	AL	6	12	3	1	0	0	(0	0)	4	3	0	1	0	0	2	0	1	0	0	0	0	.250	.250	.333	.583
2013	Det	AL	16	27	8	1	0	1	(1	0)	12	8	2	3	2	0	3	1	3	0	0	0	0	.296	.367	.444	.811
2014	Det	AL	62	156	36	5	1	0	(0	0)	43	14	15	11	8	0	37	1	2	4	1	1	4	.231	.266	.276	.542
	3 ML YEARS		84	195	47	7	1	1	(1	0)	59	25	17	15	10	0	42	2	6	4	1	1	4	.241	.280	.303	.582

John Holdzkom

Pitches: R **Bats:** R **Pos:** RP-9   HOLDS-come   **Ht:** 6'7" **Wt:** 225 **Born:** 10/19/1987 **Age:** 27

			HOW MUCH HE PITCHED					WHAT HE GAVE UP												THE RESULTS						
Year	Team	Lg	G	GS	CG	GF	IP	BFP	H	R	ER	HR	SH	SF	HB	TBB	IBB	SO	WP	Bk	W	L	Pct	Sh	Sv-Op	Hld	ERC	ERA
2010	Mets	R	1	0	0	0	1.0	5	0	0	0	0	0	0	0	2	0	2	1	0	0	0	-	0	0- -	-	3.47	0.00
2010	Kngspt	R+	5	0	0	1	4.0	27	4	7	5	0	0	0	2	8	0	8	3	2	0	0	-	0	0- -	-	11.19	11.25
2012	Bkrsfld	A+	6	1	0	2	8.2	45	6	9	5	0	0	0	1	13	0	10	5	0	0	1	.000	0	0- -	-	6.15	5.19
2014	Altna	AA	4	0	0	2	6.0	21	1	0	0	0	0	0	1	2	0	10	0	0	1	0	1.000	0	0- -	-	0.60	0.00
2014	Indy	AAA	18	0	0	8	21.2	89	14	6	6	1	0	0	1	10	0	27	0	0	2	0	1.000	0	2- -	-	2.27	2.49
2014	Pit	NL	9	0	0	3	9.0	32	4	2	2	1	0	0	0	2	0	14	1	0	1	0	1.000	0	1-2	4	1.13	2.00

Derek Holland

Pitches: L **Bats:** B **Pos:** SP-5; RP-1   **Ht:** 6'2" **Wt:** 210 **Born:** 10/9/1986 **Age:** 28

			HOW MUCH HE PITCHED					WHAT HE GAVE UP												THE RESULTS						
Year	Team	Lg	G	GS	CG	GF	IP	BFP	H	R	ER	HR	SH	SF	HB	TBB	IBB	SO	WP	Bk	W	L	Pct	Sh	Sv-Op	Hld	ERC	ERA
2014	Frisco*	AA	2	2	0	0	5.0	19	3	0	0	0	0	0	0	2	0	8	0	0	0	0	-	0	0- -	-	1.59	0.00
2014	RdRck*	AAA	4	4	0	0	15.1	75	20	15	10	5	1	1	0	8	0	19	0	0	2	1	.667	0	0- -	-	7.99	5.87
2009	Tex	AL	33	21	1	0	138.1	611	160	98	94	26	2	3	4	47	0	107	3	3	8	13	.381	1	0-1	2	5.52	6.12
2010	Tex	AL	14	10	0	2	57.1	253	55	30	26	6	0	2	4	24	0	54	0	1	3	4	.429	0	0-0	1	4.17	4.08
2011	Tex	AL	32	32	4	0	198.0	843	201	97	87	22	1	3	6	67	1	162	2	1	16	5	.762	4	0-0	0	4.15	3.95
2012	Tex	AL	29	27	0	1	175.1	730	162	100	91	32	5	4	3	52	0	145	1	0	12	7	.632	0	0-0	0	3.86	4.67
2013	Tex	AL	33	33	2	0	213.0	894	210	90	81	20	8	9	3	64	0	189	9	1	10	9	.526	2	0-0	0	3.64	3.42
2014	Tex	AL	6	5	0	0	37.0	145	34	8	6	0	2	1	0	5	1	25	1	0	2	0	1.000	0	0-0	0	2.07	1.46
	Postseason		13	4	0	2	35.2	149	32	17	15	7	0	0	1	15	0	24	2	0	3	0	1.000	0	0-0	2	4.46	3.79
	6 ML YEARS		147	128	7	3	819.0	3476	822	423	385	106	18	22	20	259	2	682	16	6	51	38	.573	7	0-1	3	4.08	4.23

Greg Holland

Pitches: R **Bats:** R **Pos:** RP-65   **Ht:** 5'10" **Wt:** 205 **Born:** 11/20/1985 **Age:** 29

			HOW MUCH HE PITCHED					WHAT HE GAVE UP												THE RESULTS						
Year	Team	Lg	G	GS	CG	GF	IP	BFP	H	R	ER	HR	SH	SF	HB	TBB	IBB	SO	WP	Bk	W	L	Pct	Sh	Sv-Op	Hld	ERC	ERA
2010	KC	AL	15	0	0	10	18.2	87	23	15	14	3	1	0	0	8	0	23	2	0	0	1	.000	0	0-0	0	5.88	6.75
2011	KC	AL	46	0	0	15	60.0	233	37	13	12	3	1	1	1	19	3	74	7	0	5	1	.833	0	4-6	18	1.60	1.80
2012	KC	AL	67	0	0	36	67.0	289	58	22	22	2	4	3	0	34	7	91	3	1	7	4	.636	0	16-20	9	3.07	2.96
2013	KC	AL	68	0	0	61	67.0	255	40	11	9	3	1	1	0	18	1	103	2	0	2	1	.667	0	47-50	1	1.41	1.21
2014	KC	AL	65	0	0	60	62.1	240	37	13	10	3	1	1	0	20	0	90	9	0	1	3	.250	0	46-48	0	1.54	1.44
	5 ML YEARS		261	0	0	182	275.0	1104	195	74	67	14	8	6	1	99	11	381	23	1	15	10	.600	0	113-124	28	2.08	2.19

Mario Hollands

Pitches: L **Bats:** L **Pos:** RP-50   **Ht:** 6'5" **Wt:** 220 **Born:** 8/26/1988 **Age:** 26

			HOW MUCH HE PITCHED					WHAT HE GAVE UP												THE RESULTS						
Year	Team	Lg	G	GS	CG	GF	IP	BFP	H	R	ER	HR	SH	SF	HB	TBB	IBB	SO	WP	Bk	W	L	Pct	Sh	Sv-Op	Hld	ERC	ERA
2010	Wmspt	A-	14	14	0	0	65.0	272	63	35	33	6	2	3	1	16	0	63	1	1	4	4	.500	0	0- -	-	3.29	4.57
2011	Lakwd	A	28	15	0	4	97.2	429	109	53	46	5	3	3	2	36	2	73	4	0	6	6	.500	0	0- -	-	4.31	4.24
2012	Lakwd	A	9	2	0	4	21.2	92	25	11	11	1	1	0	0	7	1	21	3	0	0	1	.000	0	0- -	-	4.31	4.57
2012	Clrwtr	A+	6	5	0	1	29.0	114	22	9	7	2	1	1	0	5	0	25	0	0	4	1	.800	0	0- -	-	1.94	2.17
2012	Rdng	AA	9	8	0	0	47.1	211	54	27	25	4	2	1	1	23	0	28	0	0	3	5	.375	0	0- -	-	5.31	4.75
2012	LV	AAA	3	3	0	0	12.2	63	21	13	13	4	0	1	0	4	0	10	1	0	0	2	.000	0	0- -	-	9.44	9.24
2013	Rdng	AA	13	10	0	2	62.2	277	70	32	30	6	1	3	2	20	0	53	1	1	3	2	.600	0	0- -	-	4.46	4.31
2013	Clrwtr	A+	14	10	1	1	69.1	273	60	15	12	2	4	0	1	12	0	61	4	0	4	1	.800	1	0- -	-	2.19	1.56
2014	Phi	NL	50	0	0	2	47.0	204	45	25	23	3	3	1	1	21	2	35	4	0	2	2	.500	0	0-1	3	3.77	4.40

Matt Holliday

Bats: R **Throws:** R **Pos:** LF-150;DH-6   **Ht:** 6'4" **Wt:** 250 **Born:** 1/15/1980 **Age:** 35

								BATTING														RUNNING			AVERAGES			
Year	Team	Lg	G	AB	H	2B	3B	HR	(Hm	Rd)	TB	R	RBI	RC	TBB	IBB	SO	HBP	SH	SF	SB	CS	GDP	Avg	OBP	Slg	OPS
2004	Col	NL	121	400	116	31	3	14	(10	4)	195	65	57	61	31	0	86	6	1	1	3	3	9	.290	.349	.488	.837
2005	Col	NL	125	479	147	24	7	19	(12	7)	242	68	87	88	36	1	79	7	0	4	14	3	11	.307	.361	.505	.866
2006	Col	NL	155	602	196	45	5	34	(22	12)	353	119	114	112	47	3	110	15	0	3	10	5	22	.326	.387	.586	.973
2007	Col	NL	158	636	216	50	6	36	(25	11)	386	120	137	134	63	7	126	10	0	4	11	4	23	.340	.405	.607	1.012
2008	Col	NL	139	539	173	38	2	25	(15	10)	290	107	88	100	74	6	104	8	0	2	28	2	9	.321	.409	.538	.947
2009	2 Tms		156	581	182	39	3	24	(16	8)	299	94	109	112	72	8	101	10	0	7	14	5	13	.313	.394	.515	.909
2010	StL	NL	158	596	186	45	1	28	(13	15)	317	95	103	107	69	10	93	8	0	2	9	5	13	.312	.390	.532	.922
2011	StL	NL	124	446	132	36	0	22	(13	9)	234	83	75	81	60	4	93	8	0	2	2	1	21	.296	.388	.525	.912
2012	StL	NL	157	599	177	36	2	27	(13	14)	298	95	102	99	75	3	132	9	0	5	4	4	16	.295	.379	.497	.877
2013	StL	NL	141	520	156	31	1	22	(14	8)	255	103	94	99	69	5	86	9	0	4	6	1	31	.300	.389	.490	.879
2014	StL	NL	156	574	156	37	0	20	(13	7)	253	83	90	97	74	4	100	17	0	2	4	1	20	.272	.370	.441	.811

174

							BATTING														RUNNING			AVERAGES			
Year	Team	Lg	G	AB	H	2B	3B	HR	(Hm Rd)	TB	R	RBI	RC	TBB	IBB	SO	HBP	SH	SF	SB	CS	GDP	Avg	OBP	Slg	OPS
09	Oak	AL	93	346	99	23	1	11	(7 4)	157	52	54	62	46	3	58	6	0	2	12	3	8	.286	.378	.454	.831
09	StL	NL	63	235	83	16	2	13	(9 4)	142	42	55	50	26	5	43	4	0	5	2	4	5	.353	.419	.604	1.023
	Postseason		59	226	58	8	1	12	(5 7)	104	35	33	27	15	0	49	6	0	0	1	1	5	.257	.320	.460	.780
	11 ML YEARS		1590	5972	1837	412	30	271	(165 106)	3122	1032	1056	1094	670	51	1110	107	1	36	105	36	188	.308	.385	.523	.908

David Holmberg

Pitches: L **Bats:** R **Pos:** SP-5; RP-2   **Ht:** 6'3" **Wt:** 225 **Born:** 7/19/1991 **Age:** 23

			HOW MUCH HE PITCHED					WHAT HE GAVE UP										THE RESULTS							
Year	Team	Lg	G	GS	CG	GF	IP	BFP	H	R	ER	HR	SH	SF	HB	TBB	IBB	SO	WP	Bk	W	L	Pct	Sh	Sv-Op	Hld	ERC	ERA
2010	Gr Falls	R+	8	8	0	0	40.1	178	52	23	20	2	2	0	2	9	0	29	0	0	1	1	.500	0	0- -	-	4.90	4.46
2010	Msoula	R+	7	7	0	0	37.1	173	47	26	16	2	0	2	4	7	0	47	3	1	1	4	.200	0	0- -	-	4.58	3.86
2011	Sbend	A	14	14	1	0	83.0	327	65	27	22	3	0	1	7	13	0	81	3	0	8	3	.727	1	0- -	-	2.01	2.39
2011	Visalia	A+	13	13	0	0	71.1	321	73	44	37	5	3	2	3	35	0	76	3	0	4	6	.400	0	0- -	-	4.46	4.67
2012	Visalia	A+	12	12	0	0	78.1	305	62	31	26	6	0	1	0	14	0	86	0	0	6	3	.667	0	0- -	-	2.07	2.99
2012	Mobile	AA	15	15	0	0	95.0	401	104	45	38	8	5	1	2	23	0	67	4	1	5	5	.500	0	0- -	-	4.00	3.60
2013	Mobile	AA	26	26	1	0	157.1	651	138	59	48	12	9	7	7	50	2	116	3	0	5	8	.385	0	0- -	-	3.11	2.75
2014	Lsvlle	AAA	18	18	0	0	92.2	420	119	53	48	4	3	6	1	33	3	56	3	0	2	6	.250	0	0- -	-	5.10	4.66
2013	Ari	NL	1	1	0	0	3.2	20	6	3	3	0	0	1	0	3	0	0	0	0	0	0	-	0	0-0	-	8.70	7.36
2014	Cin	NL	7	5	0	1	30.0	137	27	16	16	8	2	2	6	16	1	18	2	0	2	2	.500	0	0-0	0	6.03	4.80
	2 ML YEARS		8	6	0	1	33.2	157	33	19	19	8	2	3	6	19	1	18	2	0	2	2	.500	0	0-0	0	6.34	5.08

Brock Holt

Bats: L **Throws:** R **Pos:** 3B-39;RF-35;SS-12;2B-11;CF-10;1B-8;LF-8;PH-1   **Ht:** 5'10" **Wt:** 185 **Born:** 6/11/1988 **Age:** 27

							BATTING														RUNNING			AVERAGES			
Year	Team	Lg	G	AB	H	2B	3B	HR	(Hm Rd)	TB	R	RBI	RC	TBB	IBB	SO	HBP	SH	SF	SB	CS	GDP	Avg	OBP	Slg	OPS
2014	Pwtckt*		27	108	34	8	2	1	(- -)	49	21	7	20	8	0	12	4	0	1	7	1	1	.315	.380	.454	.834
2012	Pit	NL	24	65	19	2	1	0	(0 0)	23	6	3	10	4	0	14	0	2	1	0	0	1	.292	.329	.354	.682
2013	Bos	AL	26	59	12	2	0	0	(0 0)	14	9	11	7	7	0	4	0	3	3	1	0	0	.203	.275	.237	.513
2014	Bos	AL	106	449	126	23	5	4	(1 3)	171	68	29	56	33	0	98	2	5	3	12	2	7	.281	.331	.381	.711
	3 ML YEARS		156	573	157	27	6	4	(1 3)	208	83	43	73	44	0	116	2	10	7	13	2	8	.274	.324	.363	.687

Tyler Holt

Bats: R **Throws:** R **Pos:** RF-28;CF-9;PH-8;LF-1;PR-1   **Ht:** 5'10" **Wt:** 190 **Born:** 3/10/1989 **Age:** 26

							BATTING														RUNNING			AVERAGES			
Year	Team	Lg	G	AB	H	2B	3B	HR	(Hm Rd)	TB	R	RBI	RC	TBB	IBB	SO	HBP	SH	SF	SB	CS	GDP	Avg	OBP	Slg	OPS
2010	Lk Cty	A	22	70	20	8	2	0	(- -)	32	12	8	14	15	0	12	1	1	2	5	3	3	.286	.409	.457	.866
2011	Knstn	A+	123	449	114	18	4	2	(- -)	146	66	26	66	78	0	106	2	5	2	34	6	5	.254	.365	.325	.691
2012	Carlina	A+	81	316	83	10	7	0	(- -)	107	48	22	41	38	0	62	4	4	0	16	8	4	.263	.349	.339	.688
2012	Akron	AA	55	216	54	5	2	0	(- -)	63	29	12	24	24	0	41	1	6	1	13	4	9	.250	.326	.292	.618
2013	Akron	AA	133	521	139	24	9	2	(- -)	187	83	42	71	55	0	90	3	7	3	28	7	16	.267	.338	.359	.697
2014	Akron	AA	39	124	37	4	1	0	(- -)	43	13	14	23	27	0	26	0	2	3	11	2	0	.298	.416	.347	.762
2014	Clmbs	AAA	59	227	70	15	0	2	(- -)	91	61	16	44	39	0	45	3	3	0	20	4	5	.308	.416	.401	.817
2014	Cle	AL	36	71	19	2	0	0	(0 0)	21	4	2	6	3	0	25	1	1	0	2	2	1	.268	.307	.296	.602

J.J. Hoover

Pitches: R **Bats:** R **Pos:** RP-54   **Ht:** 6'3" **Wt:** 230 **Born:** 8/13/1987 **Age:** 27

			HOW MUCH HE PITCHED					WHAT HE GAVE UP										THE RESULTS							
Year	Team	Lg	G	GS	CG	GF	IP	BFP	H	R	ER	HR	SH	SF	HB	TBB	IBB	SO	WP	Bk	W	L	Pct	Sh	Sv-Op	Hld	ERC	ERA
2014	Lsvlle*	AAA	4	0	0	3	5.0	22	3	1	0	0	0	0	0	2	0	7	0	0	0	0	-	0	0- -	-	1.37	0.00
2012	Cin	NL	28	0	0	6	30.2	123	17	7	7	2	2	2	0	13	1	31	0	0	1	0	1.000	0	1-2	1	1.64	2.05
2013	Cin	NL	69	0	0	21	66.0	269	47	21	21	6	3	3	2	26	6	67	1	0	5	5	.500	0	3-5	13	2.46	2.86
2014	Cin	NL	54	0	0	22	62.2	275	56	36	34	13	1	5	1	31	3	75	0	0	1	10	.091	0	0-4	1	4.52	4.88
	Postseason		3	0	0	0	3.1	10	0	0	0	0	0	0	0	2	0	2	0	0	0	0	-	0	0-0	0	0.45	0.00
	3 ML YEARS		151	0	0	51	159.1	667	120	64	62	21	6	10	3	70	10	173	1	0	7	15	.318	0	4-11	15	3.05	3.50

Eric Hosmer

Bats: L **Throws:** L **Pos:** 1B-130;PH-1;PR-1   HOZZ-mer   **Ht:** 6'4" **Wt:** 225 **Born:** 10/24/1989 **Age:** 25

							BATTING														RUNNING			AVERAGES			
Year	Team	Lg	G	AB	H	2B	3B	HR	(Hm Rd)	TB	R	RBI	RC	TBB	IBB	SO	HBP	SH	SF	SB	CS	GDP	Avg	OBP	Slg	OPS
2014	Omha*	AAA	2	10	3	0	0	1	(- -)	6	2	3	2	1	0	3	0	0	0	0	0	0	.300	.364	.600	.964
2011	KC	AL	128	523	153	27	3	19	(3 16)	243	66	78	71	34	7	82	1	0	5	11	5	13	.293	.334	.465	.799
2012	KC	AL	152	535	124	22	2	14	(8 6)	192	65	60	61	56	4	95	2	0	5	16	1	10	.232	.304	.359	.663
2013	KC	AL	159	623	188	34	3	17	(10 7)	279	86	79	88	51	4	100	1	1	4	11	4	15	.302	.353	.448	.801
2014	KC	AL	131	503	136	35	4	9	(5 4)	200	54	58	62	35	4	93	3	0	6	4	2	12	.270	.318	.398	.716
	4 ML YEARS		570	2184	601	118	9	59	(26 33)	914	271	275	282	176	19	370	7	1	20	42	12	50	.275	.328	.418	.747

T.J. House

Pitches: L Bats: R Pos: SP-18; RP-1   Ht: 6'1" Wt: 205 Born: 9/29/1989 Age: 25

		HOW MUCH HE PITCHED						WHAT HE GAVE UP								THE RESULTS						
Year Team	Lg	G	GS	CG	GF	IP	BFP	H	R	ER	HR	SH	SF	HB	TBB	IBB	SO	WP	Bk	W	L	Pct	Sh	Sv-Op	Hld	ERC	ERA
2010 Knstn	A+	27	26	0	0	135.2	593	135	74	59	7	8	7	6	61	0	106	10	1	6	10	.375	0	0--		4.08	3.91
2011 Knstn	A+	25	24	1	1	130.0	581	133	85	75	12	6	8	6	66	0	89	8	0	6	12	.333	0	0--		4.77	5.19
2012 Carlina	A+	4	4	0	0	25.0	101	17	9	4	1	2	0	3	6	0	26	2	0	2	0	1.000	0	0--		1.89	1.44
2012 Akron	AA	23	23	1	0	124.1	524	114	59	55	7	6	3	7	44	0	90	2	1	8	5	.615	1	0--		3.38	3.98
2013 Akron	AA	4	4	0	0	22.1	88	20	8	8	1	0	0	0	3	0	27	0	0	2	1	.667	0	0--		2.23	3.22
2013 Clmbs	AAA	24	24	2	0	141.2	629	163	76	68	11	5	5	4	54	0	110	4	0	7	10	.412	0	0--		4.83	4.32
2014 Clmbs	AAA	10	10	0	0	57.0	233	56	25	24	3	2	1	2	16	0	42	1	0	1	4	.200	0	0--		3.45	3.79
2014 MhVlly	A-	1	1	0	0	5.0	16	2	0	0	0	1	0	0	0	0	4	0	0	0	0	-	0	0--		0.38	0.00
2014 Cle	AL	19	18	0	1	102.0	429	113	41	38	10	1	1	7	22	1	80	1	0	5	3	.625	0	0-0	0	4.30	3.35

Ryan Howard

Bats: L Throws: L Pos: 1B-141;PH-7;DH-5   Ht: 6'4" Wt: 250 Born: 11/19/1979 Age: 35

		BATTING																		RUNNING			AVERAGES			
Year Team	Lg	G	AB	H	2B	3B	HR	(Hm	Rd)	TB	R	RBI	RC	TBB	IBB	SO	HBP	SH	SF	SB	CS	GDP	Avg	OBP	Slg	OPS
2004 Phi	NL	19	39	11	5	0	2	(1	1)	22	5	5	7	2	0	13	1	0	0	0	0	2	.282	.333	.564	.897
2005 Phi	NL	88	312	90	17	2	22	(11	11)	177	52	63	50	33	8	100	1	0	2	0	1	6	.288	.356	.567	.924
2006 Phi	NL	159	581	182	25	1	58	(29	29)	383	104	149	138	108	37	181	9	0	6	0	0	7	.313	.425	.659	1.084
2007 Phi	NL	144	529	142	26	0	47	(23	24)	309	94	136	119	107	35	199	5	0	7	1	0	13	.268	.392	.584	.976
2008 Phi	NL	162	610	153	26	4	48	(26	22)	331	105	146	117	81	17	199	3	0	6	1	1	11	.251	.339	.543	.881
2009 Phi	NL	160	616	172	37	4	45	(18	27)	352	105	141	117	75	8	186	6	0	6	8	1	11	.279	.360	.571	.931
2010 Phi	NL	143	550	152	23	5	31	(16	15)	278	87	108	94	59	11	157	8	0	3	1	1	14	.276	.353	.505	.859
2011 Phi	NL	152	557	141	30	1	33	(17	16)	272	81	116	91	75	16	172	7	0	5	1	0	10	.253	.346	.488	.835
2012 Phi	NL	71	260	57	11	0	14	(10	4)	110	28	56	35	25	7	99	4	0	3	0	0	3	.219	.295	.423	.718
2013 Phi	NL	80	286	76	20	2	11	(9	2)	133	34	43	36	23	4	95	2	0	6	0	0	6	.266	.319	.465	.784
2014 Phi	NL	153	569	127	18	1	23	(12	11)	216	65	95	71	67	7	190	7	0	5	0	0	10	.223	.310	.380	.690
Postseason		46	170	44	13	1	8	(6	2)	83	22	33	28	26	7	67	1	0	2	1	1	1	.259	.357	.488	.845
11 ML YEARS		1331	4909	1303	238	20	334	(172	162)	2583	760	1058	875	655	150	1591	53	0	49	12	4	98	.265	.355	.526	.881

J.P. Howell

Pitches: L Bats: L Pos: RP-68   Ht: 6'0" Wt: 185 Born: 4/25/1983 Age: 32

		HOW MUCH HE PITCHED						WHAT HE GAVE UP								THE RESULTS						
Year Team	Lg	G	GS	CG	GF	IP	BFP	H	R	ER	HR	SH	SF	HB	TBB	IBB	SO	WP	Bk	W	L	Pct	Sh	Sv-Op	Hld	ERC	ERA
2005 KC	AL	15	15	0	0	72.2	328	73	55	50	9	3	3	6	39	0	54	7	0	3	5	.375	0	0-0	0	5.18	6.19
2006 TB	AL	8	8	0	0	42.1	187	52	25	24	4	0	2	3	14	0	33	1	0	1	3	.250	0	0-0	0	5.51	5.10
2007 TB	AL	10	10	0	0	51.0	244	69	45	43	8	2	1	3	21	0	49	3	0	1	6	.143	0	0-0	0	6.84	7.59
2008 TB	AL	64	0	0	9	89.1	370	62	29	22	6	6	1	4	39	1	92	5	0	6	1	.857	0	3-5	14	2.51	2.22
2009 TB	AL	69	0	0	41	66.2	278	47	22	21	7	2	1	3	33	3	79	3	1	7	5	.583	0	17-25	4	2.99	2.84
2011 TB	AL	46	0	0	5	30.2	138	30	24	21	5	1	1	2	18	1	26	2	2	2	3	.400	0	1-2	10	5.43	6.16
2012 TB	AL	55	0	0	10	50.1	203	39	17	17	7	2	0	4	22	2	42	1	0	1	0	1.000	0	0-0	3	3.68	3.04
2013 LAD	NL	67	0	0	6	62.0	246	42	15	15	2	1	3	1	23	3	54	3	0	4	1	.800	0	0-0	11	1.92	2.18
2014 LAD	NL	68	0	0	8	49.0	199	31	14	13	2	4	0	1	25	1	48	3	0	3	3	.500	0	0-0	27	2.26	2.39
Postseason		20	0	0	2	18.0	77	15	5	5	1	0	2	2	7	1	23	2	0	0	3	.000	0	0-0	4	3.13	2.50
9 ML YEARS		402	33	0	79	514.0	2193	445	246	226	50	21	12	27	234	11	477	28	3	28	27	.509	0	21-32	69	3.72	3.96

Daniel Hudson

Pitches: R Bats: R Pos: RP-3   Ht: 6'3" Wt: 225 Born: 3/9/1987 Age: 28

		HOW MUCH HE PITCHED						WHAT HE GAVE UP								THE RESULTS						
Year Team	Lg	G	GS	CG	GF	IP	BFP	H	R	ER	HR	SH	SF	HB	TBB	IBB	SO	WP	Bk	W	L	Pct	Sh	Sv-Op	Hld	ERC	ERA
2014 DBcks*	R	4	4	0	0	4.0	16	4	1	1	0	0	0	0	0	0	5	0	0	0	0	-	0	0--	-	1.95	2.25
2014 Reno*	AAA	2	2	0	0	2.0	7	1	0	0	0	0	0	0	1	0	2	0	0	0	0	-	0	0--	-	1.62	0.00
2009 CWS	AL	6	2	0	1	18.2	82	16	9	7	3	0	1	1	9	0	14	1	0	1	1	.500	0	0-0	0	4.15	3.38
2010 2 Tms		14	14	0	0	95.1	372	68	26	26	8	2	2	4	27	1	84	5	0	8	2	.800	0	0-0	0	2.26	2.45
2011 Ari	NL	33	33	3	0	222.0	921	217	98	86	17	6	6	8	50	1	169	4	1	16	12	.571	0	0-0	0	3.26	3.49
2012 Ari	NL	9	9	0	0	45.1	202	62	37	37	9	2	1	0	12	0	37	2	0	3	2	.600	0	0-0	0	6.56	7.35
2014 Ari	NL	3	0	0	0	2.2	13	4	4	4	0	0	0	0	0	0	2	0	0	0	1	.000	0	0 0	0	4.08	13.60
10 CWS	AL	3	3	0	0	15.2	71	17	11	11	1	1	1	0	11	0	14	2	0	1	1	.500	0	0-0	0	5.69	6.32
10 Ari	NL	11	11	0	0	79.2	301	51	15	15	7	1	1	4	16	1	70	3	0	7	1	.875	0	0-0	0	1.70	1.69
Postseason		1	1	0	0	5.1	24	9	5	5	1	0	0	0	0	0	6	0	0	0	1	.000	0	0-0	0	7.35	8.44
5 ML YEARS		65	58	3	1	384.0	1590	367	174	160	37	10	10	13	98	2	306	12	1	28	18	.609	0	0-0	0	3.40	3.75

Tim Hudson

Pitches: R Bats: R Pos: SP-31   Ht: 6'1" Wt: 175 Born: 7/14/1975 Age: 39

		HOW MUCH HE PITCHED						WHAT HE GAVE UP								THE RESULTS						
Year Team	Lg	G	GS	CG	GF	IP	BFP	H	R	ER	HR	SH	SF	HB	TBB	IBB	SO	WP	Bk	W	L	Pct	Sh	Sv-Op	Hld	ERC	ERA
1999 Oak	AL	21	21	1	0	136.1	580	121	56	49	8	1	2	7	62	2	132	6	0	11	2	.846	0	0-0	0	3.50	3.23
2000 Oak	AL	32	32	2	0	202.1	847	169	100	93	24	5	7	7	82	5	169	7	0	20	6	.769	2	0-0	0	3.43	4.14
2001 Oak	AL	35	35	3	0	235.0	980	216	100	88	20	12	8	6	71	5	181	9	1	18	9	.667	0	0-0	0	3.22	3.37
2002 Oak	AL	34	34	4	0	238.1	983	217	87	79	19	6	5	8	62	9	152	7	1	15	9	.625	2	0-0	0	3.51	2.98
2003 Oak	AL	34	34	2	0	240.0	967	197	84	72	15	11	2	10	61	9	162	6	0	16	7	.696	2	0-0	0	2.47	2.70
2004 Oak	AL	27	27	3	0	188.2	793	194	82	74	8	7	4	12	44	3	103	4	1	12	6	.667	2	0-0	0	3.44	3.53
2005 Atl	NL	29	29	2	0	192.0	817	194	79	75	20	9	1	9	65	5	115	4	0	14	9	.609	0	0-0	0	4.12	3.52
2006 Atl	NL	35	35	2	0	218.1	959	235	129	118	25	8	3	9	79	10	141	7	0	13	12	.520	0	0-0	0	4.54	4.86
2007 Atl	NL	34	34	1	0	224.1	925	221	87	83	10	11	6	8	53	8	132	5	2	16	10	.615	1	0-0	0	3.12	3.33
2008 Atl	NL	23	22	1	0	142.0	573	125	53	50	11	5	4	2	40	5	85	3	1	11	7	.611	1	0-0	0	2.90	3.17

Year	Team	Lg	G	GS	CG	GF	IP	BFP	H	R	ER	HR	SH	SF	HB	TBB	IBB	SO	WP	Bk	W	L	Pct	Sh	Sv-Op	Hld	ERC	ERA
2009	Atl	NL	7	7	0	0	42.1	180	49	17	17	4	1	0	0	13	0	30	0	0	2	1	.667	0	0-0	0	4.70	3.61
2010	Atl	NL	34	34	1	0	228.2	920	189	74	72	20	9	2	9	74	8	139	5	0	17	9	.654	0	0-0	0	2.95	2.83
2011	Atl	NL	33	33	1	0	215.0	884	189	86	77	14	6	7	**15**	56	6	158	10	0	16	10	.615	1	0-0	0	2.91	3.22
2012	Atl	NL	28	28	1	0	179.0	749	168	77	72	12	10	4	9	48	2	102	3	0	16	7	.696	1	0-0	0	3.18	3.62
2013	Atl	NL	21	21	0	0	131.1	534	120	60	58	10	5	1	2	36	3	95	2	0	8	7	.533	0	0-0	0	3.05	3.97
2014	SF	NL	31	31	1	0	189.1	789	199	86	75	15	5	5	7	34	3	120	2	0	9	13	.409	0	0-0	0	3.49	3.57
	Postseason		10	9	1	0	54.2	236	54	28	21	5	4	2	2	20	1	37	1	0	1	3	.250	0	0-0	0	3.91	3.46
16 ML YEARS			458	457	26	0	3003.0	12480	2823	1257	1152	235	111	61	117	880	83	2016	80	6	214	124	.633	13	0-0	0	3.33	3.45

David Huff

Pitches: L **Bats:** B **Pos:** RP-46   **Ht:** 6'2" **Wt:** 215 **Born:** 8/22/1984 **Age:** 30

Year	Team	Lg	G	GS	CG	GF	IP	BFP	H	R	ER	HR	SH	SF	HB	TBB	IBB	SO	WP	Bk	W	L	Pct	Sh	Sv-Op	Hld	ERC	ERA
2014	Fresno*	AAA	1	1	0	0	3.0	12	3	0	0	0	0	0	0	1	0	0	0	0	0	0	-	0	0- --	-	1.95	0.00
2009	Cle	AL	23	23	0	0	128.1	574	159	82	80	16	2	2	1	41	1	65	1	0	11	8	.579	0	0-0	0	5.33	5.61
2010	Cle	AL	15	15	1	0	79.2	369	101	61	55	14	3	3	3	34	1	37	2	0	2	11	.154	0	0-0	0	6.50	6.21
2011	Cle	AL	11	10	0	1	50.2	227	55	35	23	6	0	3	0	17	1	36	4	0	2	6	.250	0	0-0	0	4.23	4.09
2012	Cle	AL	6	4	0	0	26.2	114	30	14	10	5	0	1	1	5	0	19	0	0	3	1	.750	0	0-0	0	4.67	3.38
2013	2 Tms	AL	14	2	0	4	37.2	151	33	23	23	7	1	1	1	9	1	31	1	0	3	1	.750	0	0-0	0	3.45	5.50
2014	2 Tms	AL	46	0	0	16	59.0	258	61	25	22	5	2	0	1	23	2	39	1	0	4	1	.800	0	0-0	4	4.10	3.36
13	Cle	AL	3	0	0	1	3.0	15	7	5	5	0	0	0	0	1	0	5	0	0	0	0	-	0	0-0	0	12.85	15.00
13	NYY	AL	11	2	0	3	34.2	136	26	18	18	7	1	1	1	8	1	26	1	0	3	1	.750	0	0-0	0	2.82	4.67
14	SF	NL	16	0	0	3	20.0	92	27	15	14	2	0	0	1	6	0	11	0	0	1	0	1.000	0	0-0	1	5.92	6.30
14	NYY	AL	30	0	0	13	39.0	166	34	10	8	3	2	0	0	17	2	28	1	0	3	1	.750	0	0-0	3	3.25	1.85
6 ML YEARS			115	54	1	21	382.0	1693	439	240	213	53	8	10	7	129	6	227	9	0	25	28	.472	0	0-0	4	4.98	5.02

Jared Hughes

Pitches: R **Bats:** R **Pos:** RP-63   **Ht:** 6'7" **Wt:** 245 **Born:** 7/4/1985 **Age:** 29

Year	Team	Lg	G	GS	CG	GF	IP	BFP	H	R	ER	HR	SH	SF	HB	TBB	IBB	SO	WP	Bk	W	L	Pct	Sh	Sv-Op	Hld	ERC	ERA
2014	Indy*	AAA	7	0	0	7	7.2	29	5	1	1	0	0	1	1	2	0	7	3	0	1	1	.500	0	4- --	-	1.79	1.17
2011	Pit	NL	12	0	0	1	11.0	46	9	5	5	1	1	0	0	4	0	10	0	0	1	0	1.000	0	0-0	2	2.85	4.09
2012	Pit	NL	66	0	0	20	75.2	316	65	30	24	7	1	0	5	22	4	50	5	0	2	2	.500	0	2-4	11	2.99	2.85
2013	Pit	NL	29	0	0	8	32.0	148	37	17	17	2	2	1	2	16	1	23	2	0	2	3	.400	0	0-0	3	5.27	4.78
2014	Pit	NL	63	0	0	16	64.1	256	51	21	14	4	6	2	6	19	5	36	2	0	7	5	.583	0	0-2	13	2.68	1.96
4 ML YEARS			170	0	0	45	183.0	766	162	73	60	14	10	3	13	61	10	119	9	0	11	11	.500	0	2-6	29	3.24	2.95

Phil Hughes

Pitches: R **Bats:** R **Pos:** SP-32   **Ht:** 6'5" **Wt:** 240 **Born:** 6/24/1986 **Age:** 29

Year	Team	Lg	G	GS	CG	GF	IP	BFP	H	R	ER	HR	SH	SF	HB	TBB	IBB	SO	WP	Bk	W	L	Pct	Sh	Sv-Op	Hld	ERC	ERA
2007	NYY	AL	13	13	0	0	72.2	306	64	39	36	8	2	1	2	29	0	58	4	0	5	3	.625	0	0-0	0	3.61	4.46
2008	NYY	AL	8	8	0	0	34.0	157	43	26	25	3	1	3	1	15	0	23	2	0	0	4	.000	0	0-0	0	5.84	6.62
2009	NYY	AL	51	7	0	6	86.0	351	68	31	29	8	0	4	5	28	1	96	4	2	8	3	.727	0	3-6	18	2.86	3.03
2010	NYY	AL	31	29	0	0	176.1	730	162	83	82	25	2	5	0	58	1	146	9	1	18	8	.692	0	0-0	0	3.65	4.19
2011	NYY	AL	17	14	1	1	74.2	334	84	48	48	9	3	3	4	27	2	47	3	0	5	5	.500	1	0-0	0	4.92	5.79
2012	NYY	AL	32	32	1	0	191.1	815	196	101	90	35	1	4	4	46	0	165	3	0	16	13	.552	0	0-0	0	4.21	4.23
2013	NYY	AL	30	29	0	0	145.2	642	170	91	84	24	3	**11**	5	42	4	121	6	0	4	14	.222	0	0-0	0	5.13	5.19
2014	Min	AL	32	32	1	0	209.2	855	221	88	82	16	3	7	5	16	1	186	1	0	16	10	.615	0	0-0	0	3.05	3.52
	Postseason		18	5	0	2	39.2	176	41	20	20	5	1	0	0	18	3	38	3	0	2	4	.333	0	0-1	2	4.49	4.54
8 ML YEARS			214	164	3	7	990.1	4190	1008	507	476	128	15	38	28	261	9	842	32	3	72	60	.545	1	3-6	18	3.93	4.33

Philip Humber

Pitches: R **Bats:** R **Pos:** P   UMM-burr   **Ht:** 6'3" **Wt:** 210 **Born:** 12/21/1982 **Age:** 32

Year	Team	Lg	G	GS	CG	GF	IP	BFP	H	R	ER	HR	SH	SF	HB	TBB	IBB	SO	WP	Bk	W	L	Pct	Sh	Sv-Op	Hld	ERC	ERA
2014	Scrmto*	AAA	44	3	0	14	69.0	301	67	33	28	8	1	1	3	26	3	68	2	1	6	4	.600	0	1- --	-	3.97	3.65
2006	NYM	NL	2	0	0	0	2.0	7	0	0	0	0	0	0	0	1	0	2	0	0	0	0	-	0	0-0	0	0.27	0.00
2007	NYM	NL	3	1	0	2	7.0	32	9	6	6	1	0	0	0	2	0	2	0	0	0	0	-	0	0-0	0	5.46	7.71
2008	Min	AL	5	0	0	2	11.2	50	11	6	6	4	0	0	1	5	0	6	0	0	0	0	-	0	0-0	0	6.11	4.63
2009	Min	AL	8	0	0	3	9.0	50	17	8	8	1	0	0	0	9	2	9	1	0	0	0	-	0	0-0	0	12.62	8.00
2010	KC	AL	8	1	0	1	21.2	94	22	10	10	1	0	1	1	7	2	16	2	0	2	1	.667	0	0-0	1	3.47	4.15
2011	CWS	AL	28	26	0	0	163.0	676	151	71	68	14	2	5	6	41	2	116	9	1	9	9	.500	1	0-0	0	3.13	3.75
2012	CWS	AL	26	16	1	6	102.0	462	113	74	73	23	1	4	4	44	1	85	9	0	5	5	.500	1	0-0	0	5.86	6.44
2013	Hou	AL	17	7	0	2	54.2	259	75	48	48	9	3	2	1	20	1	36	5	1	0	8	.000	0	0-2	0	6.58	7.90
8 ML YEARS			97	51	1	17	371.0	1630	398	223	219	53	6	12	13	129	8	272	26	2	16	23	.410	1	0-2	1	4.66	5.31

Nick Hundley

Bats: R **Throws:** R **Pos:** C-63;PH-24   **Ht:** 6'1" **Wt:** 200 **Born:** 9/8/1983 **Age:** 31

							BATTING												RUNNING			AVERAGES			
Year	Team	Lg	G	AB	H	2B	3B	HR	(Hm | Rd)	TB	R	RBI	RC	TBB	IBB	SO	HBP	SH	SF	SB	CS	GDP	Avg	OBP	Slg	OPS
2008	SD	NL	60	198	47	7	1	5	(4 | 1)	71	21	24	17	11	0	52	2	0	5	0	0	1	.237	.278	.359	.636
2009	SD	NL	78	256	61	15	2	8	(4 | 4)	104	23	30	33	28	1	76	1	1	3	5	1	2	.238	.313	.406	.719
2010	SD	NL	85	273	68	18	2	8	(7 | 1)	114	33	43	37	25	0	66	1	2	6	0	5	8	.249	.308	.418	.726
2011	SD	NL	82	281	81	16	5	9	(6 | 3)	134	34	29	40	22	3	74	4	0	1	1	1	3	.288	.347	.477	.824

Year Team	Lg	G	AB	H	2B	3B	HR	(Hm Rd)	TB	R	RBI	RC	TBB	IBB	SO	HBP	SH	SF	SB	CS	GDP	Avg	OBP	Slg	OPS
2012 SD	NL	58	204	32	7	1	3	(1 2)	50	14	22	6	15	2	56	2	1	3	0	3	4	.157	.219	.245	.464
2013 SD	NL	114	373	87	19	0	13	(6 7)	145	35	44	36	26	5	98	5	1	3	1	0	7	.233	.290	.389	.679
2014 2 Tms		83	218	53	7	0	6	(4 2)	78	18	22	21	10	0	63	0	2	3	1	0	3	.243	.273	.358	.631
14 SD	NL	33	59	16	3	0	1	(1 0)	22	1	3	5	0	0	13	0	0	0	0	0	1	.271	.271	.373	.644
14 Bal	AL	50	159	37	4	0	5	(3 2)	56	17	19	16	10	0	50	0	2	3	1	0	2	.233	.273	.352	.625
7 ML YEARS		560	1803	429	89	11	52	(32 20)	696	178	214	190	137	11	485	15	7	24	8	10	28	.238	.294	.386	.680

Tommy Hunter

Pitches: R Bats: R Pos: RP-60 **Ht: 6'3" Wt: 260 Born: 7/3/1986 Age: 28**

	HOW MUCH HE PITCHED						WHAT HE GAVE UP											THE RESULTS						
Year Team	Lg	G	GS	CG	GF	IP	BFP	H	R	ER	HR	SH	SF	HB	TBB	IBB	SO	WP	Bk	W	L	Pct	Sh	Sv-Op	Hld	ERC	ERA
2014 Dlmrva*	A	1	0	0	0	1.0	3	0	0	0	0	0	0	1	0	0	2	0	0	0	0	-	0	0--	-	1.26	0.00
2008 Tex	AL	3	3	0	0	11.0	63	23	20	20	4	0	0	1	3	0	9	0	0	0	2	.000	0	0-0	0	12.66	16.36
2009 Tex	AL	19	19	1	0	112.0	475	113	55	51	13	2	1	2	33	2	64	6	1	9	6	.600	0	0-0	0	3.86	4.10
2010 Tex	AL	23	22	1	0	128.0	536	126	55	53	21	3	2	3	33	0	68	1	0	13	4	**.765**	0	0-0	0	3.95	3.73
2011 2 Tms	AL	20	11	0	2	84.2	367	100	50	44	12	2	2	4	15	1	45	0	0	4	4	.500	0	0-1	1	4.65	4.68
2012 Bal	AL	33	20	0	5	133.2	573	161	85	81	32	3	6	4	27	2	77	0	1	7	8	.467	0	0-1	0	5.63	5.45
2013 Bal	AL	68	0	0	20	86.1	336	71	28	27	11	1	0	2	14	1	68	0	0	6	5	.545	0	4-6	21	2.53	2.81
2014 Bal	AL	60	0	0	24	60.2	241	55	22	20	4	1	2	1	12	3	45	2	0	3	2	.600	0	11-17	12	2.65	2.97
11 Tex	AL	8	0	0	2	15.1	62	12	6	5	1	1	1	0	5	0	10	0	0	1	1	.500	0	0-1	0	2.44	2.93
11 Bal	AL	12	11	0	0	69.1	305	88	44	39	11	1	1	4	10	1	35	0	0	3	3	.500	0	0-0	1	5.19	5.06
Postseason		5	3	0	1	12.2	57	16	8	7	2	0	1	1	1	0	14	0	1	0	2	.000	0	0-0	0	4.80	4.97
7 ML YEARS		226	75	2	51	616.1	2591	649	315	296	97	12	13	17	137	9	376	9	2	42	31	.575	0	15-25	34	4.16	4.32

Torii Hunter

Bats: R Throws: R Pos: RF-128;DH-7;PH-7 **Ht: 6'2" Wt: 225 Born: 7/18/1975 Age: 39**

	BATTING																RUNNING			AVERAGES			
Year Team	Lg	G	AB	H	2B	3B	HR	(Hm Rd)	TB	R	RBI	RC	TBB	IBB	SO	HBP	SH	SF	SB	CS	GDP	Avg	OBP	Slg	OPS
1997 Min	AL	1	0	0	0	0	0	(0 0)	0	0	0	0	0	0	0	0	0	0	0	0	0	-	-	-	-
1998 Min	AL	6	17	4	1	0	0	(0 0)	5	0	2	1	2	0	6	0	0	0	0	1	1	.235	.316	.294	.610
1999 Min	AL	135	384	98	17	2	9	(2 7)	146	52	35	44	26	1	72	6	1	5	10	6	9	.255	.309	.380	.689
2000 Min	AL	99	336	94	14	7	5	(4 1)	137	44	44	39	18	2	68	2	0	2	4	3	13	.280	.318	.408	.726
2001 Min	AL	148	564	147	32	5	27	(13 14)	270	82	92	79	29	0	125	8	1	1	9	6	12	.261	.306	.479	.784
2002 Min	AL	148	561	162	37	4	29	(13 16)	294	89	94	85	35	3	118	5	0	3	23	8	17	.289	.334	.524	.859
2003 Min	AL	154	581	145	31	4	26	(12 14)	262	83	102	76	50	7	106	5	0	6	6	7	15	.250	.312	.451	.762
2004 Min	AL	138	520	141	37	0	23	(9 14)	247	79	81	69	40	4	101	7	0	2	21	7	23	.271	.330	.475	.805
2005 Min	AL	98	372	100	24	1	14	(6 8)	168	63	56	53	34	3	65	6	0	4	23	7	8	.269	.337	.452	.788
2006 Min	AL	147	557	155	21	2	31	(15 16)	273	86	98	81	45	2	108	5	0	4	12	6	19	.278	.336	.490	.826
2007 Min	AL	160	600	172	45	1	28	(11 17)	303	94	107	99	40	10	101	5	0	5	18	9	17	.287	.334	.505	.839
2008 LAA	AL	146	551	153	37	2	21	(10 11)	257	85	78	80	50	6	108	6	0	1	19	5	15	.278	.344	.466	.810
2009 LAA	AL	119	451	135	26	1	22	(15 7)	229	74	90	84	47	4	92	3	0	5	18	4	9	.299	.366	.508	.873
2010 LAA	AL	152	573	161	36	0	23	(8 15)	266	76	90	93	61	6	106	7	0	5	9	12	22	.281	.354	.464	.819
2011 LAA	AL	156	580	152	24	2	23	(15 8)	249	80	82	79	62	2	125	4	0	3	5	7	24	.262	.336	.429	.765
2012 LAA	AL	140	534	167	24	1	16	(7 9)	241	81	92	89	38	1	133	8	1	3	9	1	15	.313	.365	.451	.817
2013 Det	AL	144	606	184	37	5	17	(8 9)	282	90	84	81	26	0	113	7	3	10	3	2	11	.304	.334	.465	.800
2014 Det	AL	142	549	157	33	2	17	(8 9)	245	71	83	66	23	0	89	7	0	7	4	3	18	.286	.319	.446	.765
Postseason		45	176	49	12	1	4	(1 3)	75	24	20	19	15	2	30	2	2	1	3	2	7	.278	.340	.426	.766
18 ML YEARS		2233	8336	2327	476	39	331	(156 175)	3874	1229	1310	1198	626	51	1636	91	6	66	193	94	248	.279	.334	.465	.799

Drew Hutchison

Pitches: R Bats: L Pos: SP-32 **Ht: 6'3" Wt: 195 Born: 8/22/1990 Age: 24**

	HOW MUCH HE PITCHED						WHAT HE GAVE UP											THE RESULTS						
Year Team	Lg	G	GS	CG	GF	IP	BFP	H	R	ER	HR	SH	SF	HB	TBB	IBB	SO	WP	Bk	W	L	Pct	Sh	Sv-Op	Hld	ERC	ERA
2010 Auburn	A-	10	10	0	0	45.0	185	34	18	15	1	0	0	4	12	0	44	3	0	1	1	.500	0	0--	-	2.11	3.00
2010 Lnsng	A	5	5	0	0	23.2	99	17	7	4	1	0	1	2	7	0	19	0	1	1	2	.333	0	0--	-	2.08	1.52
2011 Lnsng	A	14	14	0	0	72.0	303	68	29	21	1	2	2	3	19	0	84	2	0	6	2	.750	0	0--	-	2.81	2.63
2011 Dnedin	A+	11	10	0	0	62.1	239	42	20	19	3	2	3	4	14	1	66	1	0	5	3	.625	0	0--	-	1.75	2.74
2011 NHam	AA	3	3	0	0	15.0	56	10	2	2	0	0	0	2	2	0	21	3	0	3	0	1.000	0	0--	-	1.51	1.20
2012 NHam	AA	3	3	0	0	16.2	64	16	4	4	1	0	0	0	3	0	12	0	0	2	1	.667	0	0--	-	2.97	2.16
2013 Dnedin	A+	3	2	0	0	8.2	32	2	1	1	0	0	1	0	6	0	12	1	0	0	0	-	0	0--	-	1.09	1.04
2013 NHam	AA	2	2	0	0	7.2	32	6	5	4	0	0	1	0	2	0	10	0	0	0	1	.000	0	0--	-	1.74	4.70
2013 Buffalo	AAA	4	4	0	0	19.0	92	28	16	14	2	0	0	4	6	0	20	0	0	0	3	.000	0	0--	-	7.61	6.63
2012 Tor	AL	11	11	0	0	58.2	257	59	31	30	8	1	1	5	20	0	49	1	0	5	3	.625	0	0-0	0	4.43	4.60
2014 Tor	AL	32	32	1	0	184.2	786	173	92	92	23	4	**10**	7	60	1	184	4	2	11	13	.458	1	0-0	0	3.70	4.48
2 ML YEARS		43	43	1	0	243.1	1043	232	123	122	31	5	11	12	80	1	233	5	2	16	16	.500	1	0-0	0	3.87	4.51

Chris Iannetta

Bats: R Throws: R Pos: C-104;PH-13 eye-ah-NETT-ah **Ht: 6'0" Wt: 230 Born: 4/8/1983 Age: 32**

	BATTING																RUNNING			AVERAGES			
Year Team	Lg	G	AB	H	2B	3B	HR	(Hm Rd)	TB	R	RBI	RC	TBB	IBB	SO	HBP	SH	SF	SB	CS	GDP	Avg	OBP	Slg	OPS
2006 Col	NL	21	77	20	4	0	2	(0 2)	30	12	10	9	13	2	17	1	1	1	0	1	1	.260	.370	.390	.759
2007 Col	NL	67	197	43	8	3	4	(1 3)	69	22	27	27	29	3	58	5	1	2	0	0	3	.218	.330	.350	.681
2008 Col	NL	104	333	88	22	2	18	(11 7)	168	50	65	65	56	0	92	14	2	2	0	0	6	.264	.390	.505	.895
2009 Col	NL	93	289	66	15	2	16	(8 8)	133	41	52	47	43	3	75	11	1	6	0	1	4	.228	.344	.460	.804
2010 Col	NL	61	188	37	6	1	9	(7 2)	72	20	27	21	30	2	48	4	0	1	1	0	4	.197	.318	.383	.701
2011 Col	NL	112	345	82	17	1	14	(10 4)	143	51	55	62	70	5	89	5	2	4	6	3	10	.238	.370	.414	.785

Year	Team	Lg	G	AB	H	2B	3B	HR	(Hm	Rd)	TB	R	RBI	RC	TBB	IBB	SO	HBP	SH	SF	SB	CS	GDP	Avg	OBP	Slg	OPS
																					RUNNING			**AVERAGES**			
2012	LAA	AL	79	221	53	6	1	9	(3	6)	88	27	26	27	29	0	60	2	0	1	1	3	4	.240	.332	.398	.730
2013	LAA	AL	115	325	73	15	0	11	(1	10)	121	40	39	44	68	2	100	2	0	4	0	1	8	.225	.358	.372	.731
2014	LAA	AL	108	306	77	22	0	7	(6	1)	120	41	43	56	54	3	91	8	0	5	3	0	3	.252	.373	.392	.765
9 ML YEARS			760	2281	539	115	10	90	(47	43)	944	304	344	358	392	20	630	52	7	26	11	9	43	.236	.357	.414	.771

Raul Ibanez

Bats: L **Throws:** R **Pos:** DH-40;PH-26;LF-22;1B-8;RF-5   ee-BAHN-yezz   **Ht:** 6'2" **Wt:** 225 **Born:** 6/2/1972 **Age:** 43

Year	Team	Lg	G	AB	H	2B	3B	HR	(Hm	Rd)	TB	R	RBI	RC	TBB	IBB	SO	HBP	SH	SF	SB	CS	GDP	Avg	OBP	Slg	OPS
1996	Sea	AL	4	5	0	0	0	0	(0	0)	0	0	0	0	0	0	1	1	0	0	0	0	0	.000	.167	.000	.167
1997	Sea	AL	11	26	4	0	1	1	(1	0)	9	3	4	1	0	0	6	0	0	0	0	0	0	.154	.154	.346	.500
1998	Sea	AL	37	98	25	7	1	2	(1	1)	40	12	12	10	5	0	22	0	0	0	0	0	4	.255	.291	.408	.699
1999	Sea	AL	87	209	54	7	0	9	(3	6)	88	23	27	28	17	1	32	0	0	1	5	1	4	.258	.313	.421	.734
2000	Sea	AL	92	140	32	8	0	2	(2	0)	46	21	15	15	14	1	25	1	0	1	2	0	1	.229	.301	.329	.630
2001	KC	AL	104	279	78	11	5	13	(5	8)	138	44	54	46	32	2	51	0	0	1	0	2	6	.280	.353	.495	.847
2002	KC	AL	137	497	146	37	6	24	(14	10)	267	70	103	89	40	5	76	2	1	4	5	3	11	.294	.346	.537	.883
2003	KC	AL	157	608	179	33	5	18	(8	10)	276	95	90	91	49	5	81	3	1	10	8	4	10	.294	.345	.454	.799
2004	Sea	AL	123	481	146	31	1	16	(9	7)	227	67	62	67	36	5	72	3	0	4	1	2	10	.304	.353	.472	.825
2005	Sea	AL	**162**	614	172	32	2	20	(9	11)	268	92	89	99	71	6	99	2	0	3	9	4	12	.280	.355	.436	.792
2006	Sea	AL	159	626	181	33	5	33	(17	16)	323	103	123	114	65	15	115	1	0	7	2	4	13	.289	.353	.516	.869
2007	Sea	AL	149	573	167	35	5	21	(7	14)	275	80	105	101	53	4	97	3	0	7	0	0	14	.291	.351	.480	.831
2008	Sea	AL	162	635	186	43	3	23	(14	9)	304	85	110	107	64	11	110	3	0	5	2	4	13	.293	.358	.479	.837
2009	Phi	NL	134	500	136	32	3	34	(13	21)	276	93	93	80	56	8	119	4	0	5	4	0	16	.272	.347	.552	.899
2010	Phi	NL	155	561	154	37	5	16	(9	7)	249	75	83	86	68	11	108	0	0	7	4	3	15	.275	.349	.444	.793
2011	Phi	NL	144	535	131	31	1	20	(15	5)	224	65	84	64	33	3	106	2	0	5	2	0	13	.245	.289	.419	.707
2012	NYY	AL	130	384	92	19	3	19	(14	5)	174	50	62	50	35	5	67	4	0	2	3	0	14	.240	.308	.453	.761
2013	Sea	AL	124	454	110	20	2	29	(17	12)	221	54	65	65	42	1	128	0	0	0	0	0	8	.242	.306	.487	.793
2014	2 Tms	AL	90	246	41	8	3	5	(3	2)	70	23	26	21	33	0	59	0	0	1	3	2	2	.167	.264	.285	.549
14	LAA	AL	57	166	26	5	2	3	(3	0)	44	16	21	16	23	0	43	0	0	1	3	2	1	.157	.258	.265	.523
14	KC	AL	33	80	15	3	1	2	(0	2)	26	7	5	5	10	0	16	0	0	0	0	0	1	.188	.278	.325	.603
Postseason			44	139	34	9	0	6	(5	1)	61	15	22	18	12	2	38	0	0	0	0	1	2	.245	.305	.439	.743
19 ML YEARS			2161	7471	2034	424	51	305	(161	144)	3475	1055	1207	1134	713	83	1374	29	2	63	50	29	166	.272	.335	.465	.801

Jose Iglesias

Bats: R **Throws:** R **Pos:** SS   ee-GLAY-see-us   **Ht:** 5'11" **Wt:** 185 **Born:** 1/5/1990 **Age:** 25

Year	Team	Lg	G	AB	H	2B	3B	HR	(Hm	Rd)	TB	R	RBI	RC	TBB	IBB	SO	HBP	SH	SF	SB	CS	GDP	Avg	OBP	Slg	OPS
2011	Bos	AL	10	6	2	0	0	0	(0	0)	2	3	0	0	0	0	2	0	0	0	0	0	0	.333	.333	.333	.667
2012	Bos	AL	25	68	8	2	0	1	(0	1)	13	5	2	0	4	0	16	3	2	0	1	0	2	.118	.200	.191	.391
2013	2 Tms	AL	109	350	106	16	2	3	(1	2)	135	39	29	45	15	0	60	11	4	2	5	2	7	.303	.349	.386	.735
13	Bos	AL	63	215	71	10	2	1	(0	1)	88	27	19	34	11	0	30	6	0	2	3	1	4	.330	.376	.409	.785
13	Det	AL	46	135	35	6	0	2	(1	1)	47	12	10	11	4	0	30	5	4	0	2	1	3	.259	.306	.348	.654
Postseason			11	26	6	0	0	0	(0	0)	6	2	1	0	1	0	5	1	3	0	0	1	1	.231	.286	.231	.516
3 ML YEARS			144	424	116	18	2	4	(1	3)	150	47	31	45	19	0	78	14	6	2	6	2	9	.274	.325	.354	.678

Ender Inciarte

END-er in-see-ARR-tay

Bats: L **Throws:** L **Pos:** CF-76;LF-37;PH-6;PR-4;RF-1   **Ht:** 5'10" **Wt:** 165 **Born:** 10/29/1990 **Age:** 24

Year	Team	Lg	G	AB	H	2B	3B	HR	(Hm	Rd)	TB	R	RBI	RC	TBB	IBB	SO	HBP	SH	SF	SB	CS	GDP	Avg	OBP	Slg	OPS
2010	Sbend	A	66	227	51	9	7	1	(-	-)	77	26	20	21	14	0	35	3	7	2	5	4	4	.225	.276	.339	.616
2010	Yakima	A-	19	66	16	4	0	0	(-	-)	20	10	3	6	7	0	17	0	4	1	2	1	1	.242	.311	.303	.614
2011	Sbend	A	116	450	118	19	5	1	(-	-)	150	73	25	54	47	1	59	2	12	3	26	15	8	.262	.333	.333	.666
2012	Sbend	A	65	225	66	16	5	1	(-	-)	95	36	30	40	31	2	31	0	5	3	18	4	4	.293	.375	.422	.797
2012	Visalia	A+	62	248	79	12	5	1	(-	-)	104	46	17	43	22	0	32	2	6	1	28	8	4	.319	.377	.419	.797
2013	Mobile	AA	128	473	133	17	3	5	(-	-)	171	69	25	63	27	1	47	6	8	2	43	8	3	.281	.327	.362	.688
2014	Reno	AAA	26	109	34	4	2	2	(-	-)	48	22	12	18	10	1	21	0	0	1	7	2	1	.312	.367	.440	.807
2014	Ari	NL	118	418	116	18	2	4	(1	3)	150	54	27	49	25	0	53	0	4	0	19	3	3	.278	.318	.359	.677

Omar Infante

Bats: R **Throws:** R **Pos:** 2B-134;PH-1   in-FAHN-tay   **Ht:** 5'11" **Wt:** 195 **Born:** 12/26/1981 **Age:** 33

Year	Team	Lg	G	AB	H	2B	3B	HR	(Hm	Rd)	TB	R	RBI	RC	TBB	IBB	SO	HBP	SH	SF	SB	CS	GDP	Avg	OBP	Slg	OPS
2014	Omha*	AAA	3	11	4	1	0	0	(-	-)	5	1	1	1	0	0	4	0	0	0	0	0	0	.364	.364	.455	.818
2002	Det	AL	18	72	24	3	0	1	(0	1)	30	4	6	12	3	0	10	0	0	0	0	1	0	.333	.360	.417	.777
2003	Det	AL	69	221	49	6	1	0	(0	0)	57	24	8	16	18	0	37	0	3	2	6	3	1	.222	.278	.258	.536
2004	Det	AL	142	503	133	27	9	16	(7	9)	226	69	55	69	40	3	112	1	7	5	13	7	4	.264	.317	.449	.766
2005	Det	AL	121	406	90	28	2	9	(3	6)	149	36	43	38	16	0	73	2	8	2	8	0	5	.222	.254	.367	.621
2006	Det	AL	78	224	62	11	4	4	(0	4)	93	35	25	26	14	0	45	3	2	2	3	2	5	.277	.325	.415	.740
2007	Det	AL	66	166	45	6	1	2	(0	2)	59	24	17	23	9	0	29	0	2	1	4	1	4	.271	.307	.355	.662
2008	Atl	NL	96	317	93	24	3	3	(1	2)	132	45	40	45	22	2	44	2	2	5	0	1	4	.293	.338	.416	.755
2009	Atl	NL	70	203	62	9	1	2	(1	1)	79	24	27	29	19	0	28	1	2	4	2	0	5	.305	.361	.389	.750
2010	Atl	NL	134	471	151	15	3	8	(1	7)	196	65	47	70	29	1	62	0	4	2	7	6	14	.321	.359	.416	.775
2011	Fla	NL	148	579	160	24	8	7	(2	5)	221	55	49	66	34	1	67	2	**17**	8	4	2	12	.276	.315	.382	.696
2012	2 Tms		149	554	152	30	7	12	(5	7)	232	69	53	58	21	0	65	1	8	4	17	3	9	.274	.300	.419	.719
2013	Det	AL	118	453	144	24	3	10	(7	3)	204	54	51	64	20	1	44	0	0	3	5	2	11	.318	.345	.450	.795

Year Team	Lg	G	AB	H	2B	3B	HR	(Hm	Rd)	TB	R	RBI	RC	TBB	IBB	SO	HBP	SH	SF	SB	CS	GDP	Avg	OBP	Slg	OPS
2014 KC	AL	135	528	133	21	3	6	(2	4)	178	50	66	55	33	3	68	2	5	7	9	3	7	.252	.295	.337	.632
12 Mia	NL	85	328	94	23	2	8	(2	6)	145	42	33	36	12	0	42	1	4	2	10	1	7	.287	.312	.442	.754
12 Det	AL	64	226	58	7	5	4	(3	1)	87	27	20	22	9	0	23	0	4	2	7	2	2	.257	.283	.385	.668
Postseason		30	110	28	4	0	0	(0	0)	32	11	3	8	7	1	25	1	1	0	3	1	3	.255	.305	.291	.596
13 ML YEARS		1344	4697	1298	228	45	80	(29	51)	1856	554	487	571	278	11	684	14	60	45	78	31	81	.276	.316	.395	.711

Phil Irwin

Pitches: R Bats: R Pos: SP-1 Ht: 6'3" Wt: 210 Born: 2/25/1987 Age: 28

Year Team	Lg	G	GS	CG	GF	IP	BFP	H	R	ER	HR	SH	SF	HB	TBB	IBB	SO	WP	Bk	W	L	Pct	Sh	Sv-Op	Hld	ERC	ERA
2010 WV	A	23	20	0	0	113.0	455	99	46	42	9	0	6	7	20	0	111	6	1	6	3	.667	0	0--	-	2.70	3.35
2011 Bradtn	A+	10	10	0	0	53.1	217	47	15	12	3	1	0	3	12	0	40	0	0	5	0	1.000	0	0--	-	2.73	2.03
2011 Altna	AA	15	14	0	0	87.1	366	91	42	37	9	2	1	8	10	0	69	6	0	8	4	.667	0	0--	-	3.54	3.81
2012 Bradtn	A+	1	1	0	0	5.0	17	2	1	1	0	0	0	0	0	0	6	0	0	1	0	1.000	0	0--	-	0.35	1.80
2012 Altna	AA	18	16	3	1	104.1	426	97	39	34	7	4	6	15	17	0	83	4	0	4	7	.364	1	0--	-	3.18	2.93
2012 Indy	AAA	4	4	0	0	21.0	89	20	8	6	1	2	2	1	7	0	28	1	0	3	0	1.000	0	0--	-	3.39	2.57
2013 Indy	AAA	2	2	0	0	10.0	40	5	1	1	0	0	1	2	3	0	8	1	0	1	0	1.000	0	0--	-	1.41	0.90
2014 Indy	AAA	10	2	0	3	21.2	103	27	21	21	4	2	0	5	10	2	18	1	0	1	2	.333	0	1--	-	7.44	8.72
2014 RdRck	AAA	11	10	0	0	51.1	224	51	21	20	0	2	2	5	25	0	56	2	0	5	2	.714	0	0--	-	4.12	3.51
2013 Pit	NL	1	1	0	0	4.2	23	6	5	4	0	0	0	4	4	0	2	0	0	0	0	-	0	0-0	-	6.94	7.71
2014 Tex	AL	1	1	0	0	4.0	20	6	3	3	1	0	0	1	2	0	2	1	0	0	1	.000	0	0-0	-	10.40	6.75
2 ML YEARS		2	2	0	0	8.2	43	12	8	7	1	0	0	1	6	0	6	1	0	0	1	.000	0	0-0	0	8.51	7.27

Travis Ishikawa

Bats: L Throws: L Pos: 1B-42;PH-27;LF-8;PR-1 ee-shee-KAU-wuh Ht: 6'3" Wt: 220 Born: 9/24/1983 Age: 31

Year Team	Lg	G	AB	H	2B	3B	HR	(Hm	Rd)	TB	R	RBI	RC	TBB	IBB	SO	HBP	SH	SF	SB	CS	GDP	Avg	OBP	Slg	OPS
2014 Fresno*	AAA	71	240	65	9	0	11	(-	-)	107	34	45	39	24	1	62	6	0	2	0	0	8	.271	.349	.446	.795
2006 SF	NL	12	24	7	3	1	0	(1	0)	12	1	4	4	1	0	6	0	0	0	0	1	0	.292	.320	.500	.820
2008 SF	NL	33	95	26	6	0	3	(1	2)	41	12	15	17	9	1	27	0	0	0	1	0	1	.274	.337	.432	.768
2009 SF	NL	120	326	85	10	2	9	(7	2)	126	49	39	44	30	3	89	4	1	2	2	2	7	.261	.329	.387	.715
2010 SF	NL	116	158	42	11	0	3	(0	3)	62	18	22	19	13	2	29	0	1	1	0	0	3	.266	.320	.392	.712
2012 Mil	NL	94	152	39	12	1	4	(2	2)	65	19	30	24	13	3	42	4	4	1	0	0	4	.257	.329	.428	.757
2013 2 Tms	AL	7	19	2	0	0	0	(0	0)	2	0	1	0	1	0	10	0	0	0	0	0	0	.105	.150	.105	.255
2014 2 Tms	AL	62	107	27	4	1	3	(2	1)	42	9	18	13	9	1	34	1	0	2	0	0	3	.252	.311	.393	.703
13 Bal	AL	6	17	2	0	0	0	(0	0)	2	0	1	0	1	0	8	0	0	0	0	0	0	.118	.167	.118	.284
13 NYY	AL	1	2	0	0	0	0	(0	0)	0	0	0	0	0	0	2	0	0	0	0	0	0	.000	.000	.000	.000
14 Pit	NL	15	34	7	1	1	1	(1	0)	13	2	3	3	3	0	11	0	0	1	0	0	2	.206	.263	.382	.646
14 SF	NL	47	73	20	3	0	2	(1	1)	29	7	15	10	6	1	23	1	0	1	0	0	1	.274	.333	.397	.731
Postseason		10	10	2	1	0	0	(0	0)	3	2	1	1	2	0	4	1	0	0	0	0	1	.200	.385	.300	.685
7 ML YEARS		444	881	228	46	5	22	(12	10)	350	108	129	121	76	10	237	9	6	6	3	2	19	.259	.322	.397	.719

Hisashi Iwakuma

Pitches: R Bats: R Pos: SP-28 he-SAH-shee ee-wuh-KOO-muh Ht: 6'3" Wt: 210 Born: 4/12/1981 Age: 34

Year Team	Lg	G	GS	CG	GF	IP	BFP	H	R	ER	HR	SH	SF	HB	TBB	IBB	SO	WP	Bk	W	L	Pct	Sh	Sv-Op	Hld	ERC	ERA
2014 Tacom*	AAA	1	1	0	0	4.0	18	6	3	2	0	0	1	0	0	0	2	0	0	0	0	-	0	0--	-	4.47	4.50
2012 Sea	AL	30	16	0	6	125.1	519	117	49	44	17	1	1	3	43	3	101	5	0	9	5	.643	0	2-2	0	3.87	3.16
2013 Sea	AL	33	33	0	0	219.2	866	179	69	65	25	3	6	2	42	4	185	10	0	14	6	.700	0	0-0	0	2.43	2.66
2014 Sea	AL	28	28	0	0	179.0	709	167	70	70	20	0	1	2	21	2	154	2	0	15	9	.625	0	0-0	0	2.77	3.52
3 ML YEARS		91	77	0	6	524.0	2094	463	188	179	62	4	8	7	106	9	440	17	0	38	20	.655	0	2-2	0	2.87	3.07

Maicer Izturis

Bats: B Throws: R Pos: 2B-10;PH-1 MY-sare izz-TOUR-iss Ht: 5'8" Wt: 155 Born: 9/12/1980 Age: 34

Year Team	Lg	G	AB	H	2B	3B	HR	(Hm	Rd)	TB	R	RBI	RC	TBB	IBB	SO	HBP	SH	SF	SB	CS	GDP	Avg	OBP	Slg	OPS
2004 Mon	NL	32	107	22	5	2	1	(1	0)	34	10	4	8	10	1	20	2	2	0	2	0	1	.206	.286	.318	.603
2005 LAA	AL	77	191	47	8	4	1	(0	1)	66	18	15	25	17	2	21	0	1		9	3	5	.246	.306	.346	.652
2006 LAA	AL	104	352	103	21	3	5	(1	4)	145	64	44	56	38	1	35	3	5	1	14	6	7	.293	.365	.412	.777
2007 LAA	AL	102	336	97	17	2	6	(4	2)	136	47	51	65	33	2	39	0	1	4	7	1	4	.289	.349	.405	.753
2008 LAA	AL	79	290	78	14	2	3	(1	2)	105	44	37	39	26	0	27	1	2	2	11	2	9	.269	.329	.362	.691
2009 LAA	AL	114	387	116	22	3	8	(3	5)	168	74	65	66	35	2	41	5	3	7	13	5	7	.300	.359	.434	.794
2010 LAA	AL	61	212	53	13	1	3	(0	3)	77	27	27	30	21	0	27	2	1	2	7	3	1	.250	.321	.363	.684
2011 LAA	AL	122	449	124	35	0	5	(1	4)	174	51	38	53	33	3	65	8	0	4	9	6	6	.276	.334	.388	.722
2012 LAA	AL	100	289	74	11	0	2	(0	2)	91	35	20	28	25	0	38	2	3	0	17	2	10	.256	.320	.315	.634
2013 Tor	AL	107	365	86	12	0	5	(4	1)	113	33	32	26	27	0	38	1	3	3	1	5	11	.236	.288	.310	.597
2014 Tor	AL	11	35	10	1	0	0	(0	0)	11	3	1	4	2	0	4	0	1	0	1	0	0	.286	.324	.314	.639
Postseason		10	29	6	3	0	0	(0	0)	9	3	2	2	1	1	5	0	0	1	3	0	0	.207	.226	.310	.536
11 ML YEARS		909	3013	810	159	17	39	(15	24)	1120	406	334	400	267	11	355	24	22	24	93	33	61	.269	.331	.372	.703

Austin Jackson

Bats: R **Throws:** R **Pos:** CF-154;PR-1 **Ht:** 6'1" **Wt:** 185 **Born:** 2/1/1987 **Age:** 28

								BATTING													RUNNING			AVERAGES			
Year	Team	Lg	G	AB	H	2B	3B	HR	(Hm	Rd)	TB	R	RBI	RC	TBB	IBB	SO	HBP	SH	SF	SB	CS	GDP	Avg	OBP	Slg	OPS
2010	Det	AL	151	618	181	34	10	4	(0	4)	247	103	41	84	47	4	170	4	3	3	27	6	5	.293	.345	.400	.745
2011	Det	AL	153	591	147	22	11	10	(5	5)	221	90	45	67	56	3	181	4	14	3	22	5	11	.249	.317	.374	.690
2012	Det	AL	137	543	163	29	10	16	(6	10)	260	103	66	90	67	0	134	2	2	3	12	9	9	.300	.377	.479	.856
2013	Det	AL	129	552	150	30	7	12	(3	9)	230	99	49	73	52	0	129	4	3	3	8	4	12	.272	.337	.417	.754
2014	2 Tms	AL	154	597	153	30	6	4	(2	2)	207	71	47	58	47	0	144	2	1	9	20	6	15	.256	.308	.347	.655
14	Det	AL	100	374	102	25	5	4	(2	2)	149	52	33	42	35	0	85	2	1	8	9	4	9	.273	.332	.398	.730
14	Sea	AL	54	223	51	5	1	0	(0	0)	58	19	14	16	12	0	59	0	0	1	11	2	6	.229	.267	.260	.527
	Postseason		35	133	31	7	1	2	(1	1)	46	18	11	15	19	0	53	1	2	0	2	1	2	.233	.333	.346	.679
	5 ML YEARS		724	2901	794	145	44	46	(16	30)	1165	466	248	372	269	7	758	16	23	21	89	30	52	.274	.336	.402	.738

Brett Jackson

Bats: L **Throws:** R **Pos:** RF-4;PR-4;CF-1;PH-1 **Ht:** 6'2" **Wt:** 210 **Born:** 8/2/1988 **Age:** 26

								BATTING													RUNNING			AVERAGES			
Year	Team	Lg	G	AB	H	2B	3B	HR	(Hm	Rd)	TB	R	RBI	RC	TBB	IBB	SO	HBP	SH	SF	SB	CS	GDP	Avg	OBP	Slg	OPS
2010	Dytona	A+	67	263	83	19	8	6	(-	-)	136	56	38	57	43	2	63	5	0	1	12	7	0	.316	.420	.517	.937
2010	Tenn	AA	61	228	63	13	6	6	(-	-)	106	47	28	42	30	1	63	4	3	3	18	4	2	.276	.366	.465	.831
2011	Tenn	AA	67	246	63	10	3	10	(-	-)	109	45	32	44	45	1	74	2	2	2	15	6	1	.256	.373	.443	.816
2011	Iowa	AAA	48	185	55	13	2	10	(-	-)	102	39	26	40	28	3	64	0	1	1	6	1	0	.297	.388	.551	.939
2012	Iowa	AAA	106	407	104	22	12	15	(-	-)	195	66	47	71	47	1	158	6	2	5	27	5	1	.256	.338	.479	.817
2013	Iowa	AAA	61	215	48	7	3	6	(-	-)	79	24	23	24	21	0	77	3	2	1	7	5	2	.223	.300	.367	.667
2013	Cubs	R	4	14	1	0	0	0	(-	-)	1	1	0	0	1	0	7	0	0	0	0	0	1	.071	.133	.071	.205
2013	Tenn	AA	30	95	19	4	2	0	(-	-)	27	10	4	8	13	0	37	2	0	0	2	2	1	.200	.309	.284	.593
2014	Iowa	AAA	82	224	47	8	4	5	(-	-)	78	23	20	22	24	0	94	0	0	3	4	6	3	.210	.298	.348	.646
2014	Reno	AAA	11	16	3	0	0	1	(-	-)	6	2	3	2	3	0	9	0	0	0	1	0	0	.188	.316	.375	.691
2012	ChC	NL	44	120	21	6	1	4	(3	1)	41	14	9	11	22	0	59	0	0	0	0	3	1	.175	.303	.342	.644
2014	Ari	NL	7	4	0	0	0	0	(0	0)	0	0	0	0	1	0	1	0	0	0	0	0	0	.000	.200	.000	.200
	2 ML YEARS		51	124	21	6	1	4	(3	1)	41	14	9	11	23	0	60	0	0	0	0	3	1	.169	.299	.331	.630

Edwin Jackson

Pitches: R **Bats:** R **Pos:** SP-27; RP-1 **Ht:** 6'3" **Wt:** 210 **Born:** 9/9/1983 **Age:** 31

			HOW MUCH HE PITCHED						WHAT HE GAVE UP											THE RESULTS							
Year	Team	Lg	G	GS	CG	GF	IP	BFP	H	R	ER	HR	SH	SF	HB	TBB	IBB	SO	WP	Bk	W	L	Pct	Sh	Sv-Op	Hld	ERC	ERA
2003	LAD	NL	4	3	0	0	22.0	91	17	6	6	2	1	1	1	11	1	19	3	0	2	1	.667	0	0-0	0	3.36	2.45
2004	LAD	NL	8	5	0	1	24.2	113	31	20	20	7	1	0	0	11	1	16	0	0	2	1	.667	0	0-0	0	7.21	7.30
2005	LAD	NL	7	6	0	0	28.2	134	31	22	20	2	0	2	1	17	0	13	2	1	2	2	.500	0	0-0	0	5.13	6.28
2006	TB	AL	23	1	0	7	36.1	174	42	27	22	2	2	2	1	25	0	27	3	1	0	0	-	0	0-0	0	5.86	5.45
2007	TB	AL	32	31	1	0	161.0	755	195	116	103	19	5	6	4	88	3	128	7	1	5	15	.250	1	0-0	0	6.11	5.76
2008	TB	AL	32	31	0	0	183.1	792	199	91	90	23	3	3	2	77	1	108	7	1	14	11	.560	0	0-1	0	4.99	4.42
2009	Det	AL	33	33	1	0	214.0	890	200	93	86	27	4	2	5	70	3	161	6	0	13	9	.591	0	0-0	0	3.72	3.62
2010	2 Tms		32	32	1	0	209.1	902	214	111	104	21	6	4	6	78	4	181	20	0	10	12	.455	1	0-0	0	4.20	4.47
2011	2 Tms		32	31	1	1	199.2	861	225	92	84	16	15	6	2	62	4	148	9	2	12	9	.571	1	0-0	0	4.34	3.79
2012	Was	NL	31	31	1	0	189.2	790	173	90	85	23	9	8	2	58	5	168	3	0	10	11	.476	0	0-0	0	3.36	4.03
2013	ChC	NL	31	31	0	0	175.1	777	197	110	97	16	8	3	5	59	7	135	14	0	8	18	.308	0	0-0	0	4.46	4.98
2014	ChC	NL	28	27	0	0	140.2	633	168	105	99	18	6	4	3	63	3	123	9	0	6	15	.286	0	0-0	0	5.75	6.33
10	Ari	NL	21	21	1	0	134.1	587	141	80	77	13	6	2	5	60	2	104	13	0	6	10	.375	1	0-0	0	4.72	5.16
10	CWS	AL	11	11	0	0	75.0	315	73	31	27	8	0	2	1	18	2	77	7	0	4	2	.667	0	0-0	0	3.32	3.24
11	CWS	AL	19	19	1	0	121.2	522	134	55	53	8	6	4	0	39	2	97	7	1	7	7	.500	1	0-0	0	4.10	3.92
11	StL	NL	13	12	0	1	78.0	339	91	37	31	8	9	2	2	23	2	51	2	1	5	2	.714	0	0-0	0	4.73	3.58
	Postseason		9	5	0	2	28.0	124	30	17	17	6	2	0	0	15	1	23	0	0	1	2	.333	0	0-0	1	5.97	5.46
	12 ML YEARS		293	262	5	9	1584.2	6912	1692	883	816	176	60	41	32	619	32	1227	83	6	84	104	.447	3	0-1	0	4.57	4.63

Juan Jaime

Pitches: R **Bats:** R **Pos:** RP-16 HIGH-may **Ht:** 6'2" **Wt:** 250 **Born:** 8/2/1987 **Age:** 27

			HOW MUCH HE PITCHED						WHAT HE GAVE UP											THE RESULTS							
Year	Team	Lg	G	GS	CG	GF	IP	BFP	H	R	ER	HR	SH	SF	HB	TBB	IBB	SO	WP	Bk	W	L	Pct	Sh	Sv-Op	Hld	ERC	ERA
2012	Lynbrg	A+	42	0	0	37	51.1	219	31	19	18	4	1	2	4	33	4	73	7	0	1	3	.250	0	18--	-	2.86	3.16
2013	Missi	AA	35	0	0	2	42.0	188	30	19	19	1	4	2	5	28	1	70	7	0	2	5	.286	0	0--	-	3.31	4.07
2014	Gwnntt	AAA	43	0	0	37	41.0	185	27	18	16	1	0	0	6	36	0	63	5	0	1	0	1.000	0	18--	-	3.38	3.51
2014	Atl	NL	16	0	0	4	12.1	62	14	8	8	1	2	0	1	9	0	18	3	0	0	0	-	0	0-0	0	6.13	5.84

Kenley Jansen

Pitches: R **Bats:** B **Pos:** RP-68 KEN-lee JANN-sen **Ht:** 6'5" **Wt:** 265 **Born:** 9/30/1987 **Age:** 27

			HOW MUCH HE PITCHED						WHAT HE GAVE UP											THE RESULTS							
Year	Team	Lg	G	GS	CG	GF	IP	BFP	H	R	ER	HR	SH	SF	HB	TBB	IBB	SO	WP	Bk	W	L	Pct	Sh	Sv-Op	Hld	ERC	ERA
2010	LAD	NL	25	0	0	8	27.0	109	12	2	2	1	0	1	0	15	1	41	1	0	1	0	1.000	0	4-4	4	1.40	0.67
2011	LAD	NL	51	0	0	13	53.2	218	30	17	17	3	0	1	2	26	0	96	0	2	2	1	.667	0	5-6	9	1.96	2.85
2012	LAD	NL	65	0	0	40	65.0	252	33	18	17	6	0	1	3	22	1	99	3	0	5	3	.625	0	25-32	8	1.55	2.35
2013	LAD	NL	75	0	0	45	76.2	292	48	16	16	6	0	3	0	18	1	111	2	0	4	3	.571	0	28-32	16	1.65	1.88
2014	LAD	NL	68	0	0	57	65.1	268	55	20	20	5	1	2	0	19	2	101	2	0	2	3	.400	0	44-49	0	2.60	2.76
	Postseason		6	0	0	6	4.1	20	6	2	2	0	0	0	0	1	0	10	0	0	0	0	-	0	2-2	0	4.72	4.15
	5 ML YEARS		284	0	0	163	287.2	1139	178	73	72	20	2	4	9	100	5	448	8	2	14	10	.583	0	106-123	37	1.85	2.25

Casey Janssen

Pitches: R **Bats:** R **Pos:** RP-50   JANN-sen   **Ht:** 6'4" **Wt:** 205 **Born:** 9/17/1981 **Age:** 33

Year Team	Lg	G	GS	CG	GF	IP	BFP	H	R	ER	HR	SH	SF	HB	TBB	IBB	SO	WP	Bk	W	L	Pct	Sh	Sv-Op	Hld	ERC	ERA
2014 Dnedin*	A+	1	1	0	0	1.0	4	1	0	0	0	0	0	0	0	0	1	0	0	0	0	-	0	0- -	-	1.95	0.00
2014 NHam*	AA	3	2	0	1	3.0	12	3	0	0	0	0	0	0	0	0	2	0	0	0	0	-	0	0- -	-	1.95	0.00
2006 Tor	AL	19	17	0	1	94.0	407	103	58	53	12	2	2	7	21	3	44	3	2	6	10	.375	0	0-0	0	4.32	5.07
2007 Tor	AL	70	0	0	21	72.2	297	67	22	19	4	0	3	3	20	2	39	4	0	2	3	.400	0	6-11	24	3.06	2.35
2009 Tor	AL	21	5	0	5	40.0	192	59	29	26	5	1	2	2	14	1	24	1	0	2	4	.333	0	1-1	2	7.04	5.85
2010 Tor	AL	56	0	0	16	68.2	298	74	29	28	8	0	1	4	21	1	63	3	0	5	2	.714	0	0-0	2	4.48	3.67
2011 Tor	AL	55	0	0	11	55.2	223	47	14	14	2	1	0	2	14	1	53	2	0	6	0	1.000	0	2-4	7	2.44	2.26
2012 Tor	AL	62	0	0	47	63.2	242	44	18	18	7	1	1	3	11	1	67	2	1	1	1	.500	0	22-25	1	1.93	2.54
2013 Tor	AL	56	0	0	44	52.2	210	39	17	15	3	0	2	3	13	1	50	0	0	4	1	.800	0	34-36	1	2.02	2.56
2014 Tor	AL	50	0	0	42	45.2	192	47	22	20	6	3	1	1	7	0	28	0	0	3	3	.500	0	25-30	0	3.48	3.94
8 ML YEARS		389	22	0	187	493.0	2061	480	209	193	47	8	12	24	121	10	368	15	3	29	24	.547	0	90-107	37	3.46	3.52

John Jaso

Bats: L **Throws:** R **Pos:** C-54;DH-35;PH-19   JAY-soe   **Ht:** 6'2" **Wt:** 205 **Born:** 9/19/1983 **Age:** 31

| | | | | | | | BATTING | | | | | | | | | | | | RUNNING | | | AVERAGES | | | |
Year Team	Lg	G	AB	H	2B	3B	HR	(Hm	Rd)	TB	R	RBI	RC	TBB	IBB	SO	HBP	SH	SF	SB	CS	GDP	Avg	OBP	Slg	OPS
2008 TB	AL	5	10	2	0	0	0	(0	0)	2	2	0	0	0	0	2	0	0	0	0	0	1	.200	.200	.200	.400
2010 TB	AL	109	339	89	18	3	5	(1	4)	128	57	44	57	59	1	39	2	1	3	4	0	8	.263	.372	.378	.750
2011 TB	AL	89	246	55	15	1	5	(3	2)	87	26	27	20	25	0	36	1	1	0	1	2	9	.224	.298	.354	.651
2012 Sea	AL	108	294	81	19	2	10	(6	4)	134	41	50	68	56	1	51	5	1	5	5	0	6	.276	.394	.456	.850
2013 Oak	AL	70	207	56	12	0	3	(0	3)	77	31	21	36	38	0	45	2	1	1	2	1	5	.271	.387	.372	.759
2014 Oak	AL	99	307	81	18	3	9	(5	4)	132	42	40	44	28	1	60	7	0	2	2	0	5	.264	.337	.430	.767
Postseason		5	14	3	0	0	0	(0	0)	3	0	1	1	1	0	3	0	0	0	0	0	0	.214	.267	.214	.481
6 ML YEARS		480	1403	364	82	9	32	(15	17)	560	199	182	225	206	3	233	17	4	11	14	3	34	.259	.359	.399	.758

Jon Jay

Bats: L **Throws:** L **Pos:** CF-98;RF-33;LF-27;PH-23;PR-1   **Ht:** 5'11" **Wt:** 195 **Born:** 3/15/1985 **Age:** 30

| | | | | | | | BATTING | | | | | | | | | | | | RUNNING | | | AVERAGES | | | |
Year Team	Lg	G	AB	H	2B	3B	HR	(Hm	Rd)	TB	R	RBI	RC	TBB	IBB	SO	HBP	SH	SF	SB	CS	GDP	Avg	OBP	Slg	OPS
2010 StL	NL	105	287	86	19	2	4	(2	2)	121	47	27	40	24	0	50	3	8	1	2	4	5	.300	.359	.422	.780
2011 StL	NL	159	455	135	24	2	10	(5	5)	193	56	37	56	28	1	81	7	9	4	6	7	11	.297	.344	.424	.768
2012 StL	NL	117	443	135	22	4	4	(1	3)	177	70	40	65	34	3	71	15	9	1	19	7	9	.305	.373	.400	.773
2013 StL	NL	157	548	151	27	2	7	(2	5)	203	75	67	74	52	7	103	14	9	5	10	5	13	.276	.351	.370	.721
2014 StL	NL	140	413	125	16	3	3	(0	3)	156	52	46	57	28	3	78	20	3	4	6	3	17	.303	.372	.378	.750
Postseason		48	160	30	3	1	0	(0	0)	35	21	13	12	16	1	26	1	3	2	5	1	4	.188	.263	.219	.481
5 ML YEARS		678	2146	632	108	13	28	(12	16)	850	300	217	292	166	14	383	59	38	15	43	26	55	.295	.359	.396	.755

Jeremy Jeffress

Pitches: R **Bats:** R **Pos:** RP-32   JEFF-ress   **Ht:** 6'1" **Wt:** 205 **Born:** 9/21/1987 **Age:** 27

Year Team	Lg	G	GS	CG	GF	IP	BFP	H	R	ER	HR	SH	SF	HB	TBB	IBB	SO	WP	Bk	W	L	Pct	Sh	Sv-Op	Hld	ERC	ERA
2014 Nashv*	AAA	30	0	0	15	41.2	167	33	8	7	0	2	0	0	18	2	45	3	0	4	1	.800	0	5- -	-	2.46	1.51
2010 Mil	NL	10	0	0	5	10.0	42	8	4	3	0	0	1	0	6	1	8	1	0	1	0	1.000	0	0-0	0	2.96	2.70
2011 KC	AL	14	0	0	6	15.1	67	12	8	8	1	2	0	0	11	0	13	1	0	1	1	.500	0	1-2	0	3.87	4.70
2012 KC	AL	13	0	0	6	13.1	73	19	14	10	1	0	0	0	13	0	13	1	0	0	0	-	0	0-0	0	7.87	6.75
2013 Tor	AL	10	0	0	3	10.1	43	8	1	1	1	0	0	0	5	0	12	0	0	1	0	1.000	0	0-0	0	3.17	0.87
2014 2 Tms		32	0	0	12	32.0	135	35	10	10	1	3	1	2	10	2	29	1	0	1	1	.500	0	0-1	6	4.06	2.81
14 Tor	AL	3	0	0	3	3.1	21	8	4	4	0	0	1	2	3	0	4	0	0	0	0	-	0	0-0	0	19.06	10.80
14 Mil	NL	29	0	0	9	28.2	114	27	6	6	1	3	0	0	7	2	25	1	0	1	1	.500	0	0-1	6	2.75	1.88
5 ML YEARS		79	0	0	32	81.0	360	82	37	32	3	5	2	2	45	3	75	4	0	4	2	.667	0	1-3	6	4.36	3.56

Chad Jenkins

Pitches: R **Bats:** R **Pos:** RP-21   **Ht:** 6'4" **Wt:** 235 **Born:** 12/22/1987 **Age:** 27

Year Team	Lg	G	GS	CG	GF	IP	BFP	H	R	ER	HR	SH	SF	HB	TBB	IBB	SO	WP	Bk	W	L	Pct	Sh	Sv-Op	Hld	ERC	ERA
2014 Buffalo*	AAA	21	4	0	6	44.0	184	45	26	23	5	1	2	1	9	0	27	2	0	1	3	.250	0	2- -	-	3.60	4.70
2012 Tor	AL	13	3	0	0	32.0	136	32	16	16	5	1	0	1	11	1	16	0	0	1	3	.250	0	0-0	0	4.36	4.50
2013 Tor	AL	10	3	0	0	33.1	132	31	13	10	3	1	0	1	6	2	15	0	0	1	0	1.000	0	0-0	0	2.92	2.70
2014 Tor	AL	21	0	0	12	31.2	136	34	10	9	2	0	0	1	6	1	18	0	0	1	1	.500	0	0-0	2	3.40	2.56
3 ML YEARS		44	6	0	18	97.0	404	97	39	35	10	2	0	3	23	4	49	0	0	3	4	.429	0	0-0	2	3.54	3.25

Dan Jennings

Pitches: L **Bats:** L **Pos:** RP-47   **Ht:** 6'3" **Wt:** 210 **Born:** 4/17/1987 **Age:** 28

Year Team	Lg	G	GS	CG	GF	IP	BFP	H	R	ER	HR	SH	SF	HB	TBB	IBB	SO	WP	Bk	W	L	Pct	Sh	Sv-Op	Hld	ERC	ERA
2014 NewOr*	AAA	6	0	0	1	8.0	37	6	4	3	1	0	0	0	7	0	9	0	0	0	0	-	0	0- -	-	3.64	3.38
2014 Mrlns*	R	1	1	0	0	1.0	5	0	0	0	0	0	0	0	1	0	1	0	0	0	0	-	0	0- -	-	0.76	0.00
2014 Jupiter*	A+	3	3	0	0	6.0	22	3	0	0	0	0	0	0	0	0	8	1	0	0	0	-	0	0- -	-	0.51	0.00
2012 Mia	NL	22	0	0	6	19.0	86	18	5	4	2	0	0	2	11	1	8	0	0	1	0	1.000	0	0-0	2	4.85	1.89
2013 Mia	NL	47	0	0	6	40.2	171	39	17	17	1	0	2	0	16	2	38	3	0	2	4	.333	0	0-2	1	3.27	3.76
2014 Mia	NL	47	0	0	12	40.1	182	45	11	6	3	2	3	0	17	1	38	2	0	0	2	.000	0	0-2	3	4.50	1.34
3 ML YEARS		116	0	0	22	100.0	439	102	33	27	6	2	5	2	44	4	84	5	0	3	6	.333	0	0-4	6	4.06	2.43

Desmond Jennings

Bats: R **Throws:** R **Pos:** CF-118;DH-3;PH-3   **Ht:** 6'2" **Wt:** 200 **Born:** 10/30/1986 **Age:** 28

Year	Team	Lg	G	AB	H	2B	3B	HR	(Hm	Rd)	TB	R	RBI	RC	TBB	IBB	SO	HBP	SH	SF	SB	CS	GDP	Avg	OBP	Slg	OPS
2010	TB	AL	17	21	4	1	1	0	(0	0)	7	5	2	2	2	0	4	1	0	0	2	2	0	.190	.292	.333	.625
2011	TB	AL	63	247	64	9	4	10	(3	7)	111	44	25	45	31	1	59	6	3	0	20	6	1	.259	.356	.449	.805
2012	TB	AL	132	505	124	19	7	13	(9	4)	196	85	47	62	46	1	120	5	6	1	31	2	7	.246	.314	.388	.702
2013	TB	AL	139	527	133	31	6	14	(6	8)	218	82	54	74	64	0	115	3	3	5	20	8	6	.252	.334	.414	.748
2014	TB	AL	123	479	117	30	2	10	(2	8)	181	64	36	55	47	0	108	6	9	1	15	6	10	.244	.319	.378	.697
Postseason			11	33	10	2	0	2	(2	0)	18	5	4	6	5	0	5	0	0	0	1	0	0	.303	.395	.545	.940
5 ML YEARS			474	1779	442	90	20	47	(20	27)	713	280	164	238	190	2	406	21	21	7	88	24	24	.248	.327	.401	.728

Kevin Jepsen

Pitches: R **Bats:** R **Pos:** RP-74   **Ht:** 6'3" **Wt:** 235 **Born:** 7/26/1984 **Age:** 30

Year	Team	Lg	G	GS	CG	GF	IP	BFP	H	R	ER	HR	SH	SF	HB	TBB	IBB	SO	WP	Bk	W	L	Pct	Sh	Sv-Op	Hld	ERC	ERA
2008	LAA	AL	9	0	0	0	8.1	36	8	5	4	0	0	0	0	4	0	7	1	0	0	1	.000	0	0-0	3	3.46	4.32
2009	LAA	AL	54	0	0	13	54.2	237	63	33	30	2	0	2	0	19	2	48	6	0	0	4	.600	0	1-2	17	4.27	4.94
2010	LAA	AL	68	0	0	4	59.0	253	54	26	26	2	4	2	2	29	5	61	8	0	2	4	.333	0	0-4	27	3.53	3.97
2011	LAA	AL	16	0	0	5	13.0	68	21	11	11	2	1	1	1	9	4	6	5	0	1	2	.333	0	0-1	2	9.45	7.62
2012	LAA	AL	49	0	0	11	44.2	178	39	17	15	3	3	1	2	12	1	38	1	0	3	2	.600	0	2-4	18	2.93	3.02
2013	LAA	AL	45	0	0	7	36.0	164	41	21	18	3	3	1	1	14	4	36	2	0	1	3	.250	0	0-2	8	4.50	4.50
2014	LAA	AL	74	0	0	10	65.0	260	45	19	19	4	0	1	2	23	2	75	5	0	2	2	.000	0	2-4	22	2.16	2.63
Postseason			5	0	0	5	5.0	24	8	2	2	1	0	0	0	2	0	3	0	0	1	0	1.000	0	0-0	1	8.81	3.60
7 ML YEARS			315	0	0	50	280.2	1196	271	132	123	16	11	8	8	110	18	271	28	0	13	18	.419	0	5-17	97	3.59	3.94

Derek Jeter

Bats: R **Throws:** R **Pos:** SS-130;DH-15;PH-1   **Ht:** 6'3" **Wt:** 195 **Born:** 6/26/1974 **Age:** 41

Year	Team	Lg	G	AB	H	2B	3B	HR	(Hm	Rd)	TB	R	RBI	RC	TBB	IBB	SO	HBP	SH	SF	SB	CS	GDP	Avg	OBP	Slg	OPS
1995	NYY	AL	15	48	12	4	1	0	(0	0)	18	5	7	5	3	0	11	0	0	0	0	0	0	.250	.294	.375	.669
1996	NYY	AL	157	582	183	25	6	10	(3	7)	250	104	78	92	48	1	102	9	6	9	14	7	13	.314	.370	.430	.800
1997	NYY	AL	159	654	190	31	7	10	(5	5)	265	116	70	99	74	0	125	10	8	2	23	12	14	.291	.370	.405	.775
1998	NYY	AL	149	626	203	25	8	19	(9	10)	301	127	84	115	57	1	119	5	3	3	30	6	13	.324	.384	.481	.864
1999	NYY	AL	158	627	219	37	9	24	(15	9)	346	134	102	146	91	5	116	12	3	6	19	8	12	.349	.438	.552	.989
2000	NYY	AL	148	593	201	31	4	15	(8	7)	285	119	73	118	68	4	99	12	3	3	22	4	14	.339	.416	.481	.896
2001	NYY	AL	150	614	191	35	3	21	(13	8)	295	110	74	112	56	0	99	10	5	1	27	3	13	.311	.377	.480	.858
2002	NYY	AL	157	644	191	26	0	18	(8	10)	271	124	75	108	73	2	114	7	3	3	32	3	14	.297	.373	.421	.794
2003	NYY	AL	119	482	156	25	3	10	(7	3)	217	87	52	86	43	2	88	13	3	1	11	5	10	.324	.393	.450	.844
2004	NYY	AL	154	643	188	44	1	23	(11	12)	303	111	78	100	46	1	99	14	16	2	23	4	19	.292	.352	.471	.823
2005	NYY	AL	159	654	202	25	5	19	(12	7)	294	122	70	105	77	3	117	11	7	3	14	5	15	.309	.389	.450	.839
2006	NYY	AL	154	623	214	39	3	14	(8	6)	301	118	97	132	69	4	102	12	7	4	34	5	13	.343	.417	.483	.900
2007	NYY	AL	156	639	206	39	4	12	(4	8)	289	102	73	112	56	3	100	14	3	2	15	8	21	.322	.388	.452	.840
2008	NYY	AL	150	596	179	25	3	11	(3	8)	243	88	69	88	52	0	85	9	7	4	11	5	24	.300	.363	.408	.771
2009	NYY	AL	153	634	212	27	1	18	(13	5)	295	107	66	109	72	4	90	5	4	1	30	5	18	.334	.406	.465	.871
2010	NYY	AL	157	663	179	30	3	10	(7	3)	245	111	67	86	63	4	106	9	1	3	18	5	22	.270	.340	.370	.710
2011	NYY	AL	131	546	162	24	4	6	(4	2)	212	84	61	75	46	0	81	6	4	5	16	6	10	.297	.355	.388	.743
2012	NYY	AL	159	683	216	32	0	15	(6	9)	293	99	58	98	45	1	90	5	6	1	9	4	24	.316	.362	.429	.791
2013	NYY	AL	17	63	12	1	0	1	(1	0)	16	8	7	4	8	1	10	1	0	1	0	0	3	.190	.288	.254	.542
2014	NYY	AL	145	581	149	19	1	4	(1	3)	182	47	50	59	35	0	87	6	8	4	10	2	15	.256	.304	.313	.617
Postseason			158	650	200	32	5	20	(12	8)	302	111	61	99	66	3	135	5	9	4	18	5	14	.308	.374	.465	.838
20 ML YEARS			2747	11195	3465	544	66	260	(138	122)	4921	1923	1311	1849	1082	39	1840	170	97	58	358	97	287	.310	.377	.440	.817

Cesar Jimenez

Pitches: L **Bats:** L **Pos:** RP-16   hee-MEN-ehs   **Ht:** 5'11" **Wt:** 210 **Born:** 11/12/1984 **Age:** 30

Year	Team	Lg	G	GS	CG	GF	IP	BFP	H	R	ER	HR	SH	SF	HB	TBB	IBB	SO	WP	Bk	W	L	Pct	Sh	Sv-Op	Hld	ERC	ERA
2014	LV*	AAA	38	2	0	16	49.2	194	34	9	8	0	1	2	0	15	0	46	2	0	3	2	.600	0	3- -	-	1.59	1.45
2006	Sea	AL	4	1	0	1	7.1	38	13	12	12	4	0	0	0	4	0	3	2	0	0	0	-	0	0-0	0	14.01	14.73
2008	Sea	AL	31	2	0	8	34.1	141	32	13	13	2	2	1	1	13	0	26	2	0	0	2	.000	0	0-4	4	3.59	3.41
2011	Sea	AL	8	0	0	1	6.2	30	6	4	4	0	0	0	0	3	0	7	2	0	1	0	1.000	0	0-0	0	2.83	5.40
2013	Phi	NL	19	0	0	5	17.0	76	14	7	7	1	1	2	1	10	0	11	2	1	1	1	.500	0	0-0	5	3.66	3.71
2014	Phi	NL	16	0	0	8	16.0	65	14	3	3	1	0	1	0	7	0	8	0	0	0	0	-	0	0-0	0	3.44	1.69
5 ML YEARS			78	3	0	23	81.1	350	79	39	39	8	3	4	2	37	0	55	8	1	2	3	.400	0	0-4	4	4.28	4.32

Luis Jimenez

Bats: R **Throws:** R **Pos:** 3B-16;DH-2;PH-2;PR-2   **Ht:** 6'1" **Wt:** 205 **Born:** 1/18/1988 **Age:** 27

Year	Team	Lg	G	AB	H	2B	3B	HR	(Hm	Rd)	TB	R	RBI	RC	TBB	IBB	SO	HBP	SH	SF	SB	CS	GDP	Avg	OBP	Slg	OPS
2010	CRpds	A	43	168	49	15	5	2	(-	-)	80	32	38	27	11	0	27	1	0	4	6	2	3	.292	.332	.476	.808
2010	RCuca	A+	81	318	91	31	4	12	(-	-)	166	52	43	54	13	0	43	6	4	3	15	8	8	.286	.324	.522	.846
2011	Ark	AA	125	490	142	40	1	18	(-	-)	238	62	94	82	27	2	72	11	4	6	14	6	13	.290	.335	.486	.821
2012	Salt Lk	AAA	122	485	150	38	2	16	(-	-)	240	78	86	81	19	1	70	2	5	6	17	7	10	.309	.334	.495	.829
2013	Salt Lk	AAA	48	197	56	9	2	4	(-	-)	81	28	42	29	12	2	26	3	0	6	11	3	1	.284	.326	.411	.737
2013	Angels	R	3	13	6	0	0	1	(-	-)	9	3	4	3	0	0	2	0	0	0	0	0	0	.462	.462	.692	1.154

Year	Team	Lg	G	AB	H	2B	3B	HR	(Hm	Rd)	TB	R	RBI	RC	TBB	IBB	SO	HBP	SH	SF	SB	CS	GDP	Avg	OBP	Slg	OPS
												BATTING										**RUNNING**			**AVERAGES**		
2014	Salt Lk	AAA	117	469	134	34	3	21	(-	-)	237	67	76	77	24	1	75	2	2	4	12	4	9	.286	.321	.505	.826
2013	LAA	AL	34	104	27	6	0	0	(0	0)	33	15	5	9	2	0	28	3	0	1	0	2	2	.260	.291	.317	.608
2014	LAA	AL	18	37	6	2	0	0	(0	0)	8	3	2	2	0	0	13	2	2	0	0	0	1	.162	.205	.216	.421
	2 ML YEARS		52	141	33	8	0	0	(0	0)	41	18	7	11	2	0	41	5	2	1	0	2	3	.234	.268	.291	.559

Ubaldo Jimenez

Pitches: R **Bats:** R **Pos:** SP-22; RP-3 ooh-BALL-doh **Ht:** 6'5" **Wt:** 210 **Born:** 1/22/1984 **Age:** 31

Year	Team	Lg	G	GS	CG	GF	IP	BFP	H	R	ER	HR	SH	SF	HB	TBB	IBB	SO	WP	Bk	W	L	Pct	Sh	Sv-Op	Hld	ERC	ERA
				HOW MUCH HE PITCHED							**WHAT HE GAVE UP**										**THE RESULTS**							
2014	Abrdn*	A-	1	1	0	0	4.2	20	5	1	0	0	0	0	0	3	0	3	1	0	0	0	-	0	0- -	-	5.04	0.00
2014	Norfolk*	AAA	1	1	0	0	6.0	26	5	1	1	0	0	0	0	2	0	3	0	0	0	0	-	0	0- -	-	2.15	1.50
2006	Col	NL	2	1	0	0	7.2	30	5	4	3	1	0	0	0	3	0	3	0	0	0	0	-	0	0-0	-	2.48	3.52
2007	Col	NL	15	15	0	0	82.0	354	70	46	39	10	3	1	6	37	4	68	3	0	4	4	.500	0	0-0	0	3.80	4.28
2008	Col	NL	34	34	1	0	198.2	868	182	97	88	11	7	4	10	103	4	172	16	0	12	12	.500	0	0-0	0	3.92	3.99
2009	Col	NL	33	33	1	0	218.0	914	183	87	84	13	15	6	10	85	6	198	8	3	15	12	.556	0	0-0	0	3.03	3.47
2010	Col	NL	33	33	4	0	221.2	894	164	73	71	10	7	1	9	92	7	214	16	1	19	8	**.704**	2	0-0	0	2.57	2.88
2011	2 Tms		32	32	2	0	188.1	822	186	111	98	17	2	2	9	78	5	180	8	0	10	13	.435	1	0-0	0	4.13	4.68
2012	Cle	AL	31	31	0	0	176.2	805	190	116	106	25	2	3	8	95	3	143	16	1	9	17	.346	0	0-0	0	5.55	5.40
2013	Cle	AL	32	32	0	0	182.2	777	163	75	67	16	1	11	3	80	0	194	8	0	13	9	.591	0	0-0	0	3.61	3.30
2014	Bal	AL	25	22	0	0	125.1	553	113	68	67	14	3	1	4	77	0	116	4	0	6	9	.400	0	0-0	1	4.62	4.81
11	Col	NL	21	21	2	0	123.0	532	118	68	61	10	2	2	7	51	5	118	6	0	6	9	.400	1	0-0	0	3.94	4.46
11	Cle	AL	11	11	0	0	65.1	290	68	43	37	7	0	0	2	27	0	62	2	0	4	4	.500	0	0-0	0	4.48	5.10
	Postseason		5	5	0	0	28.0	123	26	11	11	3	0	1	1	16	2	24	1	0	0	2	.000	0	0-0	0	4.47	3.54
	9 ML YEARS		237	233	8	0	1401.0	6017	1256	677	623	117	40	29	59	650	29	1288	79	5	88	84	.512	3	0-0	1	3.78	4.00

Chris Johnson

Bats: R **Throws:** R **Pos:** 3B-150; PH-3; 1B-1 **Ht:** 6'3" **Wt:** 225 **Born:** 10/1/1984 **Age:** 30

Year	Team	Lg	G	AB	H	2B	3B	HR	(Hm	Rd)	TB	R	RBI	RC	TBB	IBB	SO	HBP	SH	SF	SB	CS	GDP	Avg	OBP	Slg	OPS
												BATTING										**RUNNING**			**AVERAGES**		
2009	Hou	NL	11	22	2	0	0	0	(0	0)	2	1	1	0	1	0	6	0	0	0	0	0	0	.091	.130	.091	.221
2010	Hou	NL	94	341	105	22	2	11	(6	5)	164	40	52	55	15	2	91	2	0	4	3	0	0	.308	.337	.481	.818
2011	Hou	NL	107	378	95	21	3	7	(2	5)	143	32	42	42	16	3	97	7	0	4	2	2	2	.251	.291	.378	.670
2012	2 Tms	NL	136	488	137	28	5	15	(8	7)	220	48	76	75	31	2	132	4	1	4	5	1	18	.281	.326	.451	.777
2013	Atl	NL	142	514	165	34	0	12	(4	8)	235	54	68	77	29	5	116	2	0	2	0	0	20	.321	.358	.457	.816
2014	Atl	NL	153	582	153	27	0	10	(5	5)	210	43	58	59	23	2	159	2	2	2	6	0	23	.263	.292	.361	.653
12	Hou	NL	92	341	95	21	3	8	(8	0)	146	36	41	47	23	1	92	3	0	1	4	1	12	.279	.329	.428	.757
12	Ari	NL	44	147	42	7	2	7	(0	7)	74	12	35	28	8	1	40	1	1	3	1	0	6	.286	.321	.503	.824
	Postseason		4	16	7	0	0	0	(0	0)	7	1	5	4	0	0	5	0	0	0	0	0	0	.438	.438	.438	.875
	6 ML YEARS		643	2325	657	132	10	55	(25	30)	974	218	297	308	115	14	601	17	3	16	16	3	71	.283	.319	.419	.738

Dan Johnson

Bats: L **Throws:** R **Pos:** 1B-8; DH-6; PH-3 **Ht:** 6'2" **Wt:** 210 **Born:** 8/10/1979 **Age:** 35

Year	Team	Lg	G	AB	H	2B	3B	HR	(Hm	Rd)	TB	R	RBI	RC	TBB	IBB	SO	HBP	SH	SF	SB	CS	GDP	Avg	OBP	Slg	OPS
												BATTING										**RUNNING**			**AVERAGES**		
2014	Buffalo*	AAA	107	362	84	19	0	18	(-	-)	157	62	56	67	86	4	81	5	0	6	0	0	5	.232	.381	.434	.815
2005	Oak	AL	109	375	103	21	0	15	(2	13)	169	54	58	56	50	1	52	1	0	8	0	1	11	.275	.355	.451	.806
2006	Oak	AL	91	286	67	13	1	9	(4	5)	109	30	37	33	40	2	45	0	0	5	0	0	6	.234	.323	.381	.704
2007	Oak	AL	117	416	98	20	1	18	(9	9)	174	53	62	58	72	4	77	3	0	4	0	0	12	.236	.349	.418	.768
2008	2 Tms	AL	11	26	5	0	0	2	(1	1)	11	3	4	3	3	0	7	0	0	0	0	0	0	.192	.276	.423	.699
2010	TB	AL	40	111	22	3	0	7	(4	3)	46	15	23	20	25	0	27	1	0	3	1	0	1	.198	.343	.414	.757
2011	TB	AL	31	84	10	1	0	2	(1	1)	17	7	4	0	6	0	18	1	0	0	0	0	3	.119	.187	.202	.389
2012	CWS	AL	14	22	8	1	0	3	(0	3)	18	8	6	9	9	1	3	0	0	0	0	0	0	.364	.548	.818	1.367
2013	Bal	AL	3	5	0	0	0	0	(0	0)	0	0	0	0	0	0	1	0	0	0	0	0	0	.000	.000	.000	.000
2014	Tor	AL	15	38	8	2	0	1	(0	1)	13	8	7	7	7	0	10	1	0	2	0	0	1	.211	.333	.342	.675
08	Oak	AL	1	1	0	0	0	0	(0	0)	0	0	0	0	0	0	0	0	0	0	0	0	0	.000	.000	.000	.000
08	TB	AL	10	25	5	0	0	2	(1	1)	11	3	4	3	3	0	7	0	0	0	0	0	0	.200	.286	.440	.726
	Postseason		5	9	2	1	0	0	(0	0)	3	1	0	0	3	0	4	0	0	0	0	0	1	.222	.417	.333	.750
	9 ML YEARS		431	1363	321	61	2	57	(21	36)	557	178	201	186	212	8	240	7	0	22	1	1	34	.236	.337	.409	.745

Elliot Johnson

Bats: B **Throws:** R **Pos:** RF-3; 2B-2; PH-2; 3B-1 **Ht:** 6'1" **Wt:** 190 **Born:** 3/9/1984 **Age:** 31

Year	Team	Lg	G	AB	H	2B	3B	HR	(Hm	Rd)	TB	R	RBI	RC	TBB	IBB	SO	HBP	SH	SF	SB	CS	GDP	Avg	OBP	Slg	OPS
												BATTING										**RUNNING**			**AVERAGES**		
2014	Clmbs*	AAA	87	314	74	14	6	5	(-	-)	115	43	37	42	43	0	82	1	3	4	10	1	4	.236	.326	.366	.692
2008	TB	AL	7	19	3	0	0	0	(0	0)	3	0	0	0	0	0	7	0	0	0	0	1	0	.158	.158	.158	.316
2011	TB	AL	70	160	31	7	2	4	(2	2)	54	20	17	10	14	0	53	0	6	1	7	3	3	.194	.257	.338	.595
2012	TB	AL	123	297	72	10	2	6	(1	5)	104	32	33	39	24	0	84	3	5	2	18	6	3	.242	.304	.350	.654
2013	2 Tms		111	254	53	7	3	2	(1	1)	72	27	19	19	16	1	67	0	4	1	22	2	4	.209	.255	.283	.538
2014	Cle	AL	7	19	2	2	0	0	(0	0)	4	1	0	0	0	0	7	0	1	0	0	0	0	.105	.105	.211	.316
13	KC	AL	79	162	29	2	1	2	(1	1)	39	19	9	8	8	1	49	0	3	0	14	0	2	.179	.218	.241	.458
13	Atl	NL	32	92	24	5	2	0	(0	0)	33	8	10	11	8	0	18	0	1	1	8	2	2	.261	.317	.359	.676
	Postseason		5	14	1	0	1	0	(0	0)	3	1	0	0	1	0	4	0	0	0	0	0	1	.071	.133	.214	.348
	5 ML YEARS		318	749	161	26	7	12	(4	8)	237	80	69	68	54	1	218	3	16	4	46	16	10	.215	.269	.316	.586

Erik Johnson

Pitches: R **Bats:** R **Pos:** SP-5 **Ht:** 6'3" **Wt:** 230 **Born:** 12/30/1989 **Age:** 25

			HOW MUCH HE PITCHED						WHAT HE GAVE UP										THE RESULTS					
Year Team	Lg	G GS CG GF	IP	BFP	H	R	ER	HR	SH	SF	HB	TBB	IBB	SO	WP	Bk	W	L	Pct	Sh	Sv-Op	Hld	ERC	ERA
2011 Gr Falls	R+	2 0 0 1	2.0	11	4	1	1	0	0	0	1	1	0	2	0	0	0	0	-	0	0--	-	13.16	4.50
2012 Knapol	A	9 9 0 0	43.0	187	39	15	11	3	0	0	2	19	0	39	1	0	2	2	.500	0	0--	-	3.65	2.30
2012 WinSa	A+	8 8 0 0	49.1	200	43	19	15	0	1	1	1	10	0	48	2	0	4	3	.571	0	0--	-	2.11	2.74
2013 Brham	AA	14 14 3 0	84.2	327	57	22	21	6	2	1	2	21	0	74	1	0	8	2	.800	1	0--	-	1.81	2.23
2013 Charltt	AAA	10 10 0 0	57.1	228	43	13	10	1	0	0	3	19	0	57	0	0	1	0	.800	0	0--	-	2.25	1.57
2014 Charltt	AAA	20 20 1 0	105.2	494	136	82	79	11	4	5	5	54	0	63	4	0	5	7	.417	0	0--	-	6.56	6.73
2013 CWS	AL	5 5 0 0	27.2	128	32	16	10	5	0	2	1	11	0	18	2	0	3	2	.600	0	0-0	0	5.55	3.25
2014 CWS	AL	5 5 0 0	23.2	109	27	18	17	1	0	1	2	15	1	18	3	0	1	1	.500	0	0-0	0	5.82	6.46
2 ML YEARS		10 10 0 0	51.1	237	59	34	27	6	0	3	3	26	1	36	5	0	4	3	.571	0	0-0	0	5.71	4.73

Jim Johnson

Pitches: R **Bats:** R **Pos:** RP-54 **Ht:** 6'6" **Wt:** 240 **Born:** 6/27/1983 **Age:** 32

			HOW MUCH HE PITCHED						WHAT HE GAVE UP										THE RESULTS					
Year Team	Lg	G GS CG GF	IP	BFP	H	R	ER	HR	SH	SF	HB	TBB	IBB	SO	WP	Bk	W	L	Pct	Sh	Sv-Op	Hld	ERC	ERA
2014 Toledo*	AAA	4 0 0 1	4.2	20	4	3	2	0	0	0	0	1	0	2	1	0	0	1	.000	0	0--	-	1.86	3.86
2006 Bal	AL	1 1 0 0	3.0	21	9	8	8	1	0	1	1	3	0	0	0	0	0	1	.000	0	0-0	0	26.81	24.00
2007 Bal	AL	1 0 0 1	2.0	11	3	2	2	0	0	0	0	2	0	1	0	0	0	0	-	0	0-0	0	8.58	9.00
2008 Bal	AL	54 0 0 18	68.2	281	54	18	17	0	2	1	3	28	3	38	1	1	2	4	.333	0	1-1	19	2.45	2.23
2009 Bal	AL	64 0 0 29	70.0	300	73	32	32	8	2	2	3	23	3	49	2	1	4	6	.400	0	10-16	14	4.28	4.11
2010 Bal	AL	26 0 0 6	26.1	117	32	11	10	2	3	0	1	5	1	22	4	0	1	1	.500	0	1-6	11	4.26	3.42
2011 Bal	AL	69 0 0 20	91.0	366	80	30	27	5	4	2	2	21	3	58	2	1	6	5	.545	0	9-14	18	2.58	2.67
2012 Bal	AL	71 0 0 63	68.2	269	55	21	19	3	1	0	3	15	1	41	1	0	2	1	.667	0	51-54	0	2.22	2.49
2013 Bal	AL	74 0 0 63	70.1	291	72	26	23	5	2	0	7	18	4	56	2	0	3	8	.273	0	50-59	0	3.89	2.94
2014 2 Tms	AL	54 0 0 21	53.1	263	69	46	42	5	3	2	6	35	6	42	4	0	5	2	.714	0	2-3	2	7.13	7.09
14 Oak	AL	38 0 0 18	40.1	200	60	33	32	5	2	2	3	23	3	28	4	0	4	2	.667	0	2-3	2	8.28	7.14
14 Det	AL	16 0 0 3	13.0	63	9	13	10	0	1	0	3	12	3	14	0	0	1	0	1.000	0	0-0	0	3.86	6.92
Postseason		5 0 0 3	5.1	25	8	6	5	2	0	0	0	1	0	4	0	0	0	1	.000	0	2-3	0	8.18	8.44
9 ML YEARS		414 1 0 221	453.1	1919	447	194	180	29	17	9	26	150	21	307	16	3	23	28	.451	0	124-153	64	3.67	3.57

Josh Johnson

Pitches: R **Bats:** L **Pos:** P **Ht:** 6'7" **Wt:** 245 **Born:** 1/31/1984 **Age:** 31

			HOW MUCH HE PITCHED						WHAT HE GAVE UP										THE RESULTS					
Year Team	Lg	G GS CG GF	IP	BFP	H	R	ER	HR	SH	SF	HB	TBB	IBB	SO	WP	Bk	W	L	Pct	Sh	Sv-Op	Hld	ERC	ERA
2005 Fla	NL	4 1 0 0	12.1	55	11	5	5	0	1	0	1	10	0	10	0	0	0	0	-	0	0-0	0	4.82	3.65
2006 Fla	NL	31 24 0 1	157.0	659	136	63	54	14	11	0	4	68	6	133	3	1	12	7	.632	0	0-1	0	3.48	3.10
2007 Fla	NL	4 4 0 0	15.2	82	26	17	13	1	2	1	0	12	3	14	1	0	3	0	.000	0	0-0	0	9.16	7.47
2008 Fla	NL	14 14 1 0	87.1	365	91	36	35	7	5	1	1	27	1	77	4	0	7	1	.875	0	0-0	0	3.94	3.61
2009 Fla	NL	33 33 2 0	209.0	855	184	77	75	14	11	6	4	58	6	191	10	0	15	5	.750	0	0-0	0	2.84	3.23
2010 Fla	NL	28 28 1 0	183.2	744	155	51	47	7	5	8	5	48	2	186	4	0	11	6	.647	0	0-0	0	2.44	2.30
2011 Fla	NL	9 9 0 0	60.1	234	39	13	11	2	1	1	1	20	2	56	2	1	3	1	.750	0	0-0	0	1.70	1.64
2012 Mia	NL	31 31 0 0	191.1	798	180	84	81	14	8	8	4	65	7	165	5	0	8	14	.364	0	0-0	0	3.40	3.81
2013 Tor	AL	16 16 0 0	81.1	384	105	64	56	15	3	3	3	30	3	83	4	0	2	8	.200	0	0-0	0	6.23	6.20
9 ML YEARS		170 160 4 1	998.0	4176	927	410	377	74	47	26	25	338	30	915	33	2	58	45	.563	0	0-1	0	3.35	3.40

Kelly Johnson

Bats: L **Throws:** R **Pos:** 3B-60;1B-32;PH-14;2B-5;PR-5;LF-4;DH-3;RF-1 **Ht:** 6'1" **Wt:** 200 **Born:** 2/22/1982 **Age:** 33

								BATTING												RUNNING			AVERAGES			
Year Team	Lg	G	AB	H	2B	3B	HR	(Hm Rd)	TB	R	RBI	RC	TBB	IBB	SO	HBP	SH	SF	SB	CS	GDP	Avg	OBP	Slg	OPS
2014 Portlnd*	AA	2	6	0	0	0	0	(- -)	0	1	0	0	2	0	3	0	0	0	0	0	0	.000	.250	.000	.250
2005 Atl	NL	87	290	70	12	3	9	(2 7)	115	46	40	41	40	1	75	1	2	1	2	1	11	.241	.334	.397	.731
2007 Atl	NL	147	521	144	26	10	16	(5 11)	238	91	68	87	79	3	117	4	2	2	9	5	8	.276	.375	.457	.831
2008 Atl	NL	150	547	157	39	6	12	(5 7)	244	86	69	87	52	2	113	2	9	4	11	6	3	.287	.349	.446	.795
2009 Atl	NL	106	303	68	20	3	8	(4 4)	118	47	29	31	32	1	54	3	6	2	7	2	4	.224	.303	.389	.692
2010 Ari	NL	154	585	166	36	5	26	(16 10)	290	93	71	92	79	1	148	2	1	3	13	7	12	.284	.370	.496	.865
2011 2 Tms		147	545	121	27	7	21	(10 11)	225	75	58	70	60	2	163	4	4	0	16	6	3	.222	.304	.413	.717
2012 Tor	AL	142	507	114	19	2	16	(10 6)	185	61	55	63	62	4	159	5	2	4	14	2	8	.225	.313	.365	.678
2013 TB	AL	118	366	86	12	2	16	(6 10)	150	41	52	49	35	1	99	3	7	4	7	4	8	.235	.305	.410	.715
2014 3 Tms	AL	106	265	57	14	2	7	(5 2)	96	29	27	30	29	0	71	2	0	3	2	2	3	.215	.296	.362	.659
11 Ari	NL	114	430	90	23	5	18	(10 8)	177	59	49	53	44	2	132	3	4	0	13	3	3	.209	.287	.412	.699
11 Tor	AL	33	115	31	4	2	3	(0 3)	48	16	9	17	16	0	31	1	0	0	3	3	0	.270	.364	.417	.781
14 NYY	AL	77	201	44	9	2	6	(5 1)	75	21	22	25	23	0	50	2	0	1	2	1	2	.219	.304	.373	.677
14 Bos	AL	10	25	4	1	0	0	(0 0)	5	1	1	0	0	0	10	0	0	0	0	0	1	.160	.160	.200	.360
14 Bal	AL	19	39	9	4	0	1	(0 1)	16	7	4	5	6	0	11	0	0	1	0	1	0	.231	.333	.410	.744
Postseason		6	5	1	0	1	0	(0 0)	3	0	0	1	1	0	2	0	0	0	0	0	0	.200	.333	.600	.933
9 ML YEARS		1157	3929	983	205	40	131	(63 68)	1661	569	469	550	468	15	999	26	28	19	81	35	56	.250	.333	.423	.755

Kris Johnson

Pitches: L **Bats:** L **Pos:** SP-3 **Ht:** 6'4" **Wt:** 205 **Born:** 10/14/1984 **Age:** 30

			HOW MUCH HE PITCHED						WHAT HE GAVE UP										THE RESULTS					
Year Team	Lg	G GS CG GF	IP	BFP	H	R	ER	HR	SH	SF	HB	TBB	IBB	SO	WP	Bk	W	L	Pct	Sh	Sv-Op	Hld	ERC	ERA
2010 Pwtckt	AAA	28 24 0 2	132.2	594	152	81	72	15	3	9	5	52	1	79	9	0	6	13	.316	0	0--	-	5.12	4.88
2011 Pwtckt	AAA	8 3 0 0	20.2	109	41	31	29	7	0	2	1	6	0	12	1	0	2	2	.500	0	0--	-	12.25	12.63
2012 Altna	AA	15 9 0 3	56.0	242	50	19	13	3	0	1	3	24	0	42	4	0	3	2	.600	0	1--	-	3.44	2.09
2012 Indy	AAA	20 4 0 5	45.2	194	42	25	23	7	1	0	1	18	3	33	2	0	5	2	.714	0	0--	-	3.96	4.53

				HOW MUCH HE PITCHED						WHAT HE GAVE UP													THE RESULTS							
Year	Team	Lg	G	GS	CG	GF	IP	BFP	H	R	ER	HR	SH	SF	HB	TBB	IBB	SO	WP	Bk	W	L	Pct	Sh	Sv-Op	Hld	ERC	ERA
2013	Indy	AAA	26	21	1	2	135.2	550	116	37	36	6	7	1	4	43	0	94	8	0	10	4	.714	0	2--	-	2.79	2.39
2014	Roch	AAA	23	23	2	0	132.0	556	115	58	51	8	3	0	2	55	1	102	7	0	10	7	.588	0	0--	-	3.22	3.48
2013	Pit	NL	4	1	0	2	10.1	46	12	7	7	0	0	1	1	4	1	9	2	0	0	2	.000	0	0-0	0	4.48	6.10
2014	Min	AL	3	3	0	0	13.1	64	17	7	7	2	1	0	0	9	0	12	1	0	0	1	.000	0	0-0	0	7.37	4.73
	2 ML YEARS		7	4	0	2	23.2	110	29	14	14	2	1	1	1	13	1	21	3	0	0	3	.000	0	0-0	0	6.06	5.32

Reed Johnson

Bats: R **Throws:** R **Pos:** PH-77;LF-23;RF-11;DH-2;CF-1;PR-1   **Ht:** 5'10" **Wt:** 190 **Born:** 12/8/1976 **Age:** 38

									BATTING											RUNNING			AVERAGES			
Year	Team	Lg	G	AB	H	2B	3B	HR	(Hm	Rd)	TB	R	RBI	RC	TBB	IBB	SO	HBP	SH	SF	SB	CS	GDP	Avg	OBP	Slg	OPS
2003	Tor	AL	114	412	121	21	2	10	(6	4)	176	79	52	64	20	1	67	20	1	4	5	3	10	.294	.353	.427	.780
2004	Tor	AL	141	537	145	25	2	10	(8	2)	204	68	61	65	28	2	98	12	3	2	6	3	17	.270	.320	.380	.699
2005	Tor	AL	142	398	107	21	6	8	(4	4)	164	55	58	57	22	1	82	16	2	1	5	6	8	.269	.332	.412	.744
2006	Tor	AL	134	461	147	34	2	12	(4	8)	221	86	49	76	33	4	81	21	1	1	8	2	9	.319	.390	.479	.869
2007	Tor	AL	79	275	65	13	2	2	(1	1)	88	31	14	24	16	0	56	11	5	0	4	2	7	.236	.305	.320	.625
2008	ChC	NL	109	333	101	21	0	6	(3	3)	140	52	50	57	19	1	66	12	5	5	5	6	3	.303	.358	.420	.778
2009	ChC	NL	65	165	42	10	2	4	(3	1)	68	23	22	19	13	0	27	6	1	1	2	1	5	.255	.330	.412	.742
2010	LAD	NL	102	202	53	11	2	2	(1	1)	74	24	15	18	5	0	50	4	2	2	2	2	3	.262	.291	.366	.657
2011	ChC	NL	111	246	76	22	1	5	(4	1)	115	33	28	35	5	1	63	11	2	2	2	1	4	.309	.348	.467	.816
2012	2 Tms	NL	119	269	78	14	3	3	(0	3)	107	30	20	37	13	1	61	6	0	0	2	2	4	.290	.337	.398	.735
2013	Atl	NL	74	123	30	7	1	1	(1	0)	42	13	11	11	6	0	32	6	1	0	0	0	3	.244	.311	.341	.653
2014	Mia	NL	113	187	44	15	0	2	(0	2)	65	24	25	19	1	0	37	8	2	3	0	1	4	.235	.266	.348	.614
12	ChC	NL	76	169	51	9	3	3	(0	3)	75	23	16	26	10	1	43	4	0	0	2	1	3	.302	.355	.444	.799
12	Atl	NL	43	100	27	5	0	0	(0	0)	32	7	4	11	3	0	18	2	0	0	0	1	1	.270	.305	.320	.625
	Postseason		3	2	1	0	0	0	(0	0)	1	1	0	1	1	1	0	0	0	0	0	0	0	.500	.667	.500	1.167
	12 ML YEARS		1303	3608	1009	214	23	65	(35	30)	1464	518	405	486	181	11	722	133	25	21	41	29	77	.280	.336	.406	.741

Eric Jokisch

Pitches: L **Bats:** R **Pos:** RP-3; SP-1   YO-kish   **Ht:** 6'2" **Wt:** 185 **Born:** 7/29/1989 **Age:** 25

				HOW MUCH HE PITCHED						WHAT HE GAVE UP													THE RESULTS							
Year	Team	Lg	G	GS	CG	GF	IP	BFP	H	R	ER	HR	SH	SF	HB	TBB	IBB	SO	WP	Bk	W	L	Pct	Sh	Sv-Op	Hld	ERC	ERA
2010	Cubs	R	1	0	0	0	1.0	3	0	0	0	0	0	0	0	0	0	3	0	0	0	0	-	0	0--	-	0.00	0.00
2010	Boise	A-	14	7	0	0	34.1	165	46	29	27	6	0	1	1	23	0	28	4	0	2	3	.400	0	0--	-	8.28	7.08
2011	Peoria	A	25	11	0	7	118.2	483	106	41	39	13	5	0	3	32	0	103	2	4	9	3	.750	0	1--	-	3.20	2.96
2011	Tenn	AA	3	3	0	0	15.1	71	16	8	7	0	1	1	1	9	0	15	1	0	1	0	1.000	0	0--	-	4.48	4.11
2012	Dytona	A+	9	9	0	0	54.1	228	55	24	21	4	2	1	3	16	0	52	0	0	3	4	.429	0	0--	-	3.84	3.48
2012	Tenn	AA	18	17	1	0	105.0	423	86	35	34	7	5	0	4	33	0	63	0	0	7	2	.778	0	0--	-	2.78	2.91
2013	Tenn	AA	27	26	0	0	160.2	666	144	71	61	14	3	6	3	54	1	137	3	0	11	13	.458	1	0--	-	3.27	3.42
2014	Iowa	AAA	26	26	1	0	158.1	651	155	76	63	12	4	4	4	31	0	143	4	1	9	10	.474	1	0--	-	3.12	3.58
2014	ChC	NL	4	1	0	0	14.1	66	18	6	3	3	0	0	0	4	0	10	0	0	0	0	-	0	0-0	0	5.65	1.88

Adam Jones

Bats: R **Throws:** R **Pos:** CF-155;DH-4;PH-2   **Ht:** 6'3" **Wt:** 225 **Born:** 8/1/1985 **Age:** 29

									BATTING											RUNNING			AVERAGES			
Year	Team	Lg	G	AB	H	2B	3B	HR	(Hm	Rd)	TB	R	RBI	RC	TBB	IBB	SO	HBP	SH	SF	SB	CS	GDP	Avg	OBP	Slg	OPS
2006	Sea	AL	32	74	16	4	0	1	(0	1)	23	6	8	4	2	0	22	0	0	0	3	1	3	.216	.237	.311	.548
2007	Sea	AL	41	65	16	2	1	2	(1	1)	26	16	4	5	4	0	21	1	1	0	2	1	0	.246	.300	.400	.700
2008	Bal	AL	132	477	129	21	7	9	(4	5)	191	61	57	56	23	0	108	7	2	5	10	3	12	.270	.311	.400	.711
2009	Bal	AL	119	473	131	22	3	19	(11	8)	216	83	70	71	36	3	93	7	0	3	10	4	13	.277	.335	.457	.792
2010	Bal	AL	149	581	165	25	5	19	(9	10)	257	76	69	72	23	1	119	13	2	2	7	7	17	.284	.325	.442	.767
2011	Bal	AL	151	567	159	26	2	25	(19	6)	264	68	83	77	29	2	113	9	1	12	12	4	16	.280	.319	.466	.785
2012	Bal	AL	162	648	186	39	3	32	(15	17)	327	103	82	101	34	0	126	13	0	2	16	7	15	.287	.334	.505	.839
2013	Bal	AL	160	653	186	35	1	33	(17	16)	322	100	108	101	25	4	136	8	0	3	14	3	15	.285	.318	.493	.811
2014	Bal	AL	159	644	181	30	2	29	(14	15)	302	88	96	92	19	1	133	12	0	7	7	1	11	.281	.311	.469	.780
	Postseason		6	26	2	0	0	0	(0	0)	2	0	1	0	0	0	7	0	0	1	0	0	0	.077	.074	.077	.151
	9 ML YEARS		1105	4182	1169	204	24	169	(90	79)	1928	601	577	579	195	11	871	70	6	34	81	31	102	.280	.320	.461	.781

Garrett Jones

Bats: L **Throws:** L **Pos:** 1B-129;PH-13;RF-9   **Ht:** 6'5" **Wt:** 235 **Born:** 6/21/1981 **Age:** 34

									BATTING											RUNNING			AVERAGES			
Year	Team	Lg	G	AB	H	2B	3B	HR	(Hm	Rd)	TB	R	RBI	RC	TBB	IBB	SO	HBP	SH	SF	SB	CS	GDP	Avg	OBP	Slg	OPS
2007	Min	AL	31	77	16	2	1	2	(1	1)	26	7	5	3	6	0	20	0	0	1	1	1	2	.208	.262	.338	.600
2009	Pit	NL	82	314	92	21	1	21	(13	8)	178	45	44	47	40	8	76	1	0	3	10	2	6	.293	.372	.567	.938
2010	Pit	NL	158	592	146	34	1	21	(11	10)	245	64	86	69	53	2	123	1	0	8	7	3	18	.247	.306	.414	.720
2011	Pit	NL	148	423	103	30	1	16	(8	8)	183	51	58	57	48	2	104	2	0	4	6	3	7	.243	.321	.433	.753
2012	Pit	NL	145	475	130	28	3	27	(13	14)	245	68	86	84	33	2	103	0	0	7	2	0	3	.274	.317	.516	.832
2013	Pit	NL	144	403	94	26	2	15	(6	9)	169	41	51	39	31	0	101	2	0	4	2	0	10	.233	.289	.419	.708
2014	Mia	NL	146	496	122	33	2	15	(7	8)	204	59	53	52	46	4	116	1	0	4	0	1	10	.246	.309	.411	.720
	Postseason		2	2	0	0	0	0	(0	0)	0	0	0	0	0	0	1	0	0	0	0	0	0	.000	.000	.000	.000
	7 ML YEARS		854	2780	703	174	11	117	(59	58)	1250	335	383	351	257	18	643	7	0	31	28	10	56	.253	.314	.450	.764

James Jones

Bats: L **Throws:** L **Pos:** CF-85;PR-17;RF-9;PH-6;DH-5;LF-4　　　　**Ht:** 6'4" **Wt:** 200 **Born:** 9/24/1988 **Age:** 26

									BATTING												RUNNING			AVERAGES			
Year	Team	Lg	G	AB	H	2B	3B	HR	(Hm	Rd)	TB	R	RBI	RC	TBB	IBB	SO	HBP	SH	SF	SB	CS	GDP	Avg	OBP	Slg	OPS
2010	Clinton	A	132	491	132	24	10	12	(-	-)	212	87	65	80	62	0	122	5	1	1	24	10	6	.269	.356	.432	.788
2011	Hi Dsrt	A+	83	296	73	16	4	5	(-	-)	112	42	29	44	42	4	92	4	1	1	16	3	5	.247	.347	.378	.725
2012	Hi Dsrt	A+	126	493	151	28	12	14	(-	-)	245	109	76	92	54	1	124	5	3	4	26	17	6	.306	.378	.497	.875
2013	Jacksn	AA	101	363	100	14	10	6	(-	-)	152	44	45	56	40	2	72	0	2	0	28	9	7	.275	.347	.419	.766
2013	Tacom	AAA	4	15	5	2	0	0	(-	-)	7	2	1	2	2	0	2	0	0	0	0	0	2	.333	.412	.467	.878
2014	Tacom	AAA	37	156	44	6	3	2	(-	-)	62	24	15	22	13	0	31	1	3	0	7	3	4	.282	.341	.397	.739
2014	Sea	AL	108	312	78	9	5	0	(0	0)	97	46	9	26	12	0	67	0	4	0	27	1	4	.250	.278	.311	.589

Nate Jones

Pitches: R **Bats:** R **Pos:** RP-2　　　　**Ht:** 6'5" **Wt:** 220 **Born:** 1/28/1986 **Age:** 29

			HOW MUCH HE PITCHED					WHAT HE GAVE UP											THE RESULTS							
Year	Team	Lg	G	GS	CG	GF	IP	BFP	H	R	ER	HR	SH	SF	HB	TBB	IBB	SO	WP	Bk	W	L	Pct	Sh	Sv-Op	Hld	ERC	ERA
2012	CWS	AL	65	0	0	11	71.2	301	67	19	19	4	2	4	1	32	3	65	5	0	8	0	1.000	0	0-3	7	3.67	2.39
2013	CWS	AL	70	0	0	17	78.0	315	69	40	36	5	3	6	1	26	1	89	8	1	4	5	.444	0	0-4	16	3.09	4.15
2014	CWS	AL	2	0	0	0	0.0	5	2	4	4	0	0	0	0	3	0	0	0	0	0	0	-	0	0-1	0	-	-
	3 ML YEARS		137	0	0	28	149.2	621	138	63	59	9	5	10	2	61	4	154	13	1	12	5	.706	0	0-8	23	3.51	3.55

Taylor Jordan

Pitches: R **Bats:** R **Pos:** SP-5　　　　**Ht:** 6'5" **Wt:** 200 **Born:** 1/17/1989 **Age:** 26

			HOW MUCH HE PITCHED					WHAT HE GAVE UP											THE RESULTS							
Year	Team	Lg	G	GS	CG	GF	IP	BFP	H	R	ER	HR	SH	SF	HB	TBB	IBB	SO	WP	Bk	W	L	Pct	Sh	Sv-Op	Hld	ERC	ERA
2010	Hgrstn	A	1	0	0	0	3.1	18	4	5	5	0	0	1	1	3	0	5	0	0	0	1	.000	0	0--	-	7.49	13.50
2010	Vrmnt	A-	13	13	0	0	62.0	275	73	40	34	6	4	2	5	17	0	54	3	1	2	3	.400	0	0--	-	4.88	4.94
2011	Hgrstn	A	18	17	1	0	94.1	399	90	38	26	1	1	5	6	23	0	63	4	0	9	4	.692	1	0--	-	2.83	2.48
2012	Auburn	A-	6	6	0	0	14.1	70	19	15	13	0	1	0	4	2	0	17	0	0	0	3	.000	0	0--	-	4.95	8.16
2012	Hgrstn	A	9	9	0	0	40.0	178	52	22	18	2	0	0	6	9	0	28	0	3	3	4	.429	0	0--	-	5.48	4.05
2013	Ptomc	A+	6	6	0	0	36.1	143	31	9	5	1	1	0	0	6	0	29	1	0	2	1	.667	0	0--	-	2.03	1.24
2013	Hrsbrg	AA	9	8	2	0	54.0	209	37	6	5	0	3	1	5	9	0	43	0	0	7	0	1.000	2	0--	-	1.50	0.83
2014	Syrcse	AA	6	6	0	0	31.0	131	31	15	14	3	0	0	2	8	1	28	0	1	0	2	.000	0	0--	-	3.71	4.06
2013	Was	NL	9	9	0	0	51.2	220	59	27	21	3	2	1	3	11	0	29	1	0	1	3	.250	0	0-0	0	4.13	3.66
2014	Was	NL	5	5	0	0	25.2	124	34	20	16	3	2	2	2	8	1	17	0	0	0	3	.000	0	0-0	0	5.70	5.61
	2 ML YEARS		14	14	0	0	77.1	344	93	47	37	6	4	3	5	19	1	46	1	0	1	6	.143	0	0-0	0	4.64	4.31

Caleb Joseph

Bats: R **Throws:** R **Pos:** C-78;1B-4;PH-2　　　　**Ht:** 6'3" **Wt:** 180 **Born:** 6/18/1986 **Age:** 29

									BATTING												RUNNING			AVERAGES			
Year	Team	Lg	G	AB	H	2B	3B	HR	(Hm	Rd)	TB	R	RBI	RC	TBB	IBB	SO	HBP	SH	SF	SB	CS	GDP	Avg	OBP	Slg	OPS
2010	Bowie	AA	106	378	89	15	1	11	(-	-)	139	43	51	42	33	0	63	4	2	3	1	6	8	.235	.301	.368	.669
2011	Bowie	AA	108	375	96	15	1	7	(-	-)	134	42	41	49	40	1	60	6	4	5	5	2	9	.256	.333	.357	.691
2012	Bowie	AA	80	279	76	17	1	12	(-	-)	131	38	48	47	29	1	60	3	2	4	2	0	6	.272	.343	.470	.812
2012	Norfolk	AAA	22	68	14	4	1	0	(-	-)	20	6	7	6	8	0	10	0	0	0	0	0	2	.206	.289	.294	.584
2013	Bowie	AA	135	518	155	31	2	22	(-	-)	256	74	97	90	39	2	92	3	0	10	4	2	11	.299	.346	.494	.840
2014	Norfolk	AAA	22	92	24	7	0	2	(-	-)	37	8	11	10	3	0	22	0	0	0	0	0	2	.261	.284	.402	.686
2014	Bal	AL	82	246	51	9	0	9	(4	5)	87	22	28	22	17	0	69	3	6	3	0	1	6	.207	.264	.354	.618

Donnie Joseph

Pitches: L **Bats:** L **Pos:** RP-1　　　　**Ht:** 6'3" **Wt:** 190 **Born:** 11/1/1987 **Age:** 27

			HOW MUCH HE PITCHED					WHAT HE GAVE UP											THE RESULTS							
Year	Team	Lg	G	GS	CG	GF	IP	BFP	H	R	ER	HR	SH	SF	HB	TBB	IBB	SO	WP	Bk	W	L	Pct	Sh	Sv-Op	Hld	ERC	ERA
2010	Dayton	A	19	0	0	16	23.0	88	13	3	2	0	0	0	0	7	0	40	3	0	2	1	.667	0	6--	-	1.23	0.78
2010	Lynbrg	A+	31	0	0	27	35.0	146	23	11	9	2	1	1	1	16	1	56	2	0	4	4	.000	0	17--	-	2.23	2.31
2010	Carlina	AA	7	0	0	4	7.0	30	7	6	4	0	0	0	0	2	0	7	0	1	1	0	1.000	0	1--	-	2.89	5.14
2011	Carlina	AA	57	0	0	32	58.1	272	67	45	45	8	2	1	5	30	3	66	4	0	1	3	.250	0	8--	-	5.94	6.94
2012	Pnscla	AA	26	0	0	20	30.1	112	13	4	3	1	1	1	1	8	2	46	2	0	4	2	.667	0	13--	-	0.91	0.89
2012	Lsvlle	AAA	18	0	0	10	22.0	95	22	8	7	0	1	0	0	9	1	22	0	0	4	1	.800	0	5--	-	3.32	2.86
2012	Omha	AAA	11	0	0	7	17.1	86	21	9	8	1	2	0	0	13	2	19	5	0	1	0	1.000	0	2--	-	6.02	4.15
2013	Omha	AAA	47	0	0	21	54.2	241	39	25	24	5	2	0	3	40	1	84	6	0	4	3	.571	0	6--	-	3.88	3.95
2014	Omha	AAA	19	0	0	7	25.2	124	26	15	11	3	0	0	2	20	0	30	4	0	1	1	.500	0	1--	-	6.05	3.86
2014	NewOr	AAA	9	0	0	3	10.1	63	18	14	11	4	0	0	2	12	1	5	3	0	1	0	1.000	0	0--	-	15.88	9.58
2013	KC	AL	6	0	0	2	5.2	25	4	0	0	0	1	0	0	4	0	7	0	0	0	0	-	0	0-0	-	2.85	0.00
2014	KC	AL	1	0	0	0	0.2	8	5	6	6	1	0	0	0	1	0	2	0	0	0	0	-	0	0-0	0	86.39	81.00
	2 ML YEARS		7	0	0	2	6.1	33	9	6	6	1	1	0	0	5	0	9	0	0	0	0	-	0	0-0	0	8.66	8.53

Matt Joyce

Bats: L **Throws:** R **Pos:** LF-81;DH-34;PH-24;RF-15　　　　**Ht:** 6'2" **Wt:** 200 **Born:** 8/3/1984 **Age:** 30

									BATTING												RUNNING			AVERAGES			
Year	Team	Lg	G	AB	H	2B	3B	HR	(Hm	Rd)	TB	R	RBI	RC	TBB	IBB	SO	HBP	SH	SF	SB	CS	GDP	Avg	OBP	Slg	OPS
2008	Det	AL	92	242	61	16	3	12	(6	6)	119	40	33	36	31	0	65	2	0	2	0	2	3	.252	.339	.492	.831
2009	TB	AL	11	32	6	1	0	3	(2	1)	16	3	7	5	3	0	7	1	0	1	1	0	0	.188	.270	.500	.770
2010	TB	AL	77	216	52	15	4	10	(4	6)	103	30	40	41	40	2	55	2	0	3	2	2	2	.241	.360	.477	.837
2011	TB	AL	141	462	128	32	2	19	(11	8)	221	69	75	77	49	9	106	4	0	7	13	1	7	.277	.347	.478	.825
2012	TB	AL	124	399	96	18	3	17	(4	13)	171	55	59	59	55	4	102	6	1	1	4	3	10	.241	.341	.429	.769

			BATTING																RUNNING			AVERAGES			
Year Team	Lg	G	AB	H	2B	3B	HR	(Hm Rd)	TB	R	RBI	RC	TBB	IBB	SO	HBP	SH	SF	SB	CS	GDP	Avg	OBP	Slg	OPS
2013 TB	AL	140	413	97	22	0	18	(8 10)	173	61	47	51	59	0	87	2	0	7	7	3	8	.235	.328	.419	.747
2014 TB	AL	140	418	106	23	2	9	(2 7)	160	51	52	52	62	4	111	4	0	9	2	5	11	.254	.349	.383	.732
Postseason		12	32	5	1	0	1	(0 1)	9	1	4	3	1	0	13	0	0	0	1	0	0	.156	.182	.281	.463
7 ML YEARS		725	2182	546	127	13	88	(37 51)	963	309	313	321	299	19	533	21	1	30	29	16	41	.250	.342	.441	.783

Jair Jurrjens

Pitches: R **Bats:** R **Pos:** SP-2   jye-AIR JURR-jens   **Ht:** 6'1" **Wt:** 200 **Born:** 1/29/1986 **Age:** 29

		HOW MUCH HE PITCHED						WHAT HE GAVE UP											THE RESULTS						
Year Team	Lg	G	GS	CG	GF	IP	BFP	H	R	ER	HR	SH	SF	HB	TBB	IBB	SO	WP	Bk	W	L	Pct	Sh	Sv-Op	Hld	ERC	ERA
2014 Lsvlle*	AAA	6	6	0	0	34.1	154	42	19	17	1	5	1	0	13	1	27	0	0	2	3	.400	0	0- -	-	4.69	4.46
2014 ColSpr*	AAA	8	8	2	0	47.0	208	52	29	24	6	2	2	2	16	3	24	5	3	0	5	.000	0	0- -	-	4.67	4.60
2007 Det	AL	7	7	0	0	30.2	122	24	16	16	4	0	1	1	11	0	13	2	0	3	1	.750	0	0-0	0	3.19	4.70
2008 Atl	NL	31	31	0	0	188.1	813	188	87	77	11	12	5	4	70	9	139	3	0	13	10	.565	0	0-0	0	3.65	3.68
2009 Atl	NL	34	34	0	0	215.0	884	186	71	62	15	16	4	3	75	1	152	3	2	14	10	.583	0	0-0	0	3.03	2.60
2010 Atl	NL	20	20	0	0	116.1	500	120	63	60	13	7	4	2	42	5	86	2	0	7	6	.538	0	0-0	0	4.20	4.64
2011 Atl	NL	23	23	2	0	152.0	627	142	52	50	14	6	3	4	44	5	90	4	2	13	6	.684	1	0-0	0	3.33	2.96
2012 Atl	NL	11	10	0	1	48.1	227	72	40	37	8	2	0	1	18	0	19	1	0	3	4	.429	0	0-0	0	7.70	6.89
2013 Bal	AL	2	1	0	0	7.1	31	9	4	4	1	0	0	0	1	0	6	1	0	0	0	-	0	0-0	0	4.61	4.91
2014 Col	NL	2	2	0	0	9.1	50	20	11	11	4	0	0	1	3	0	9	1	0	0	1	.000	0	0-0	0	15.34	10.61
8 ML YEARS		130	128	2	1	767.1	3254	761	344	317	70	43	17	16	264	20	514	17	4	53	38	.582	1	0-0	0	3.82	3.72

Tommy Kahnle

Pitches: R **Bats:** R **Pos:** RP-54   KAIN-lee   **Ht:** 6'1" **Wt:** 230 **Born:** 8/7/1989 **Age:** 25

		HOW MUCH HE PITCHED						WHAT HE GAVE UP											THE RESULTS						
Year Team	Lg	G	GS	CG	GF	IP	BFP	H	R	ER	HR	SH	SF	HB	TBB	IBB	SO	WP	Bk	W	L	Pct	Sh	Sv-Op	Hld	ERC	ERA
2010 StsIsnd	A-	11	0	0	6	16.0	59	3	1	1	0	1	1	3	5	0	25	2	0	0	0	-	0	3- -	-	0.62	0.56
2011 CtnSC	A	40	0	0	12	81.0	363	69	50	38	1	1	2	1	49	0	112	11	1	3	5	.375	0	2- -	-	3.36	4.22
2012 Tampa	A+	30	0	0	18	55.0	222	30	16	15	3	5	1	2	24	1	72	4	1	2	1	.667	0	6- -	-	1.70	2.45
2012 Trntn	AA	1	0	0	0	2.0	8	2	0	0	0	0	0	0	0	0	2	0	0	0	0	-	0	0- -	-	1.95	0.00
2013 Trntn	AA	46	0	0	35	60.0	257	38	20	19	4	3	0	0	45	0	74	7	0	1	3	.250	0	15- -	-	3.19	2.85
2014 Col	NL	54	0	0	7	68.2	285	51	39	32	7	2	3	1	31	2	63	7	0	2	1	.667	0	0-2	8	2.91	4.19

Ryan Kalish

Bats: L **Throws:** L **Pos:** PH-24;LF-18;CF-11;RF-11   KAY-lish   **Ht:** 6'0" **Wt:** 215 **Born:** 3/28/1988 **Age:** 27

				BATTING															RUNNING			AVERAGES			
Year Team	Lg	G	AB	H	2B	3B	HR	(Hm Rd)	TB	R	RBI	RC	TBB	IBB	SO	HBP	SH	SF	SB	CS	GDP	Avg	OBP	Slg	OPS
2014 Iowa*	AAA	87	287	72	14	3	8	(- -)	116	34	37	39	28	1	74	2	2	0	12	4	2	.251	.322	.404	.726
2010 Bos	AL	53	163	41	11	1	4	(2 2)	66	26	24	23	12	0	38	1	2	1	10	1	5	.252	.305	.405	.710
2012 Bos	AL	36	96	22	3	0	0	(0 0)	25	12	5	3	6	0	26	0	0	1	3	2	4	.229	.272	.260	.532
2014 ChC	NL	57	121	30	4	4	0	(0 0)	42	13	5	9	8	1	28	0	1	0	3	2	3	.248	.295	.347	.642
3 ML YEARS		146	380	93	18	5	4	(2 2)	133	51	34	35	26	1	92	1	3	2	16	5	12	.245	.293	.350	.643

Nate Karns

Pitches: R **Bats:** R **Pos:** SP-2   **Ht:** 6'3" **Wt:** 230 **Born:** 11/25/1987 **Age:** 27

		HOW MUCH HE PITCHED						WHAT HE GAVE UP											THE RESULTS						
Year Team	Lg	G	GS	CG	GF	IP	BFP	H	R	ER	HR	SH	SF	HB	TBB	IBB	SO	WP	Bk	W	L	Pct	Sh	Sv-Op	Hld	ERC	ERA
2011 Nats	R	5	5	0	0	18.2	65	2	0	0	0	0	0	2	6	0	26	3	0	0	0	-	0	0- -	-	0.37	0.00
2011 Auburn	A-	8	8	0	0	36.2	159	27	14	14	1	0	0	4	27	0	33	7	0	3	2	.600	0	0- -	-	3.91	3.44
2012 Hgrstn	A	11	5	1	5	44.1	179	23	11	10	1	0	0	3	21	0	61	5	0	3	0	1.000	0	2- -	-	1.66	2.03
2012 Ptomc	A+	13	13	1	0	71.2	278	47	23	18	1	0	0	4	26	0	87	4	0	8	4	.667	0	0- -	-	1.94	2.26
2013 Hrsbrg	AA	23	23	3	0	132.2	553	109	54	48	14	7	5	7	48	1	155	13	1	10	6	.625	0	0- -	-	3.19	3.26
2014 Drham	AAA	27	27	0	0	145.1	624	142	89	82	16	1	5	3	62	0	153	7	0	9	9	.500	0	0- -	-	4.25	5.08
2013 Was	NL	3	3	0	0	12.0	61	17	11	10	5	1	0	1	6	0	11	0	0	0	1	.000	0	0-0	0	9.80	7.50
2014 TB	AL	2	2	0	0	12.0	49	7	6	6	3	0	0	2	4	0	13	0	0	1	1	.500	0	0-0	0	3.12	4.50
2 ML YEARS		5	5	0	0	24.0	110	24	17	16	8	1	0	3	10	0	24	0	0	1	2	.333	0	0-0	0	6.20	6.00

Munenori Kawasaki

moo-neh-NO-ree kah-wah-SAH-kee

Bats: L **Throws:** R **Pos:** 2B-64;3B-19;PH-11;SS-4   **Ht:** 5'11" **Wt:** 175 **Born:** 6/3/1981 **Age:** 34

				BATTING															RUNNING			AVERAGES			
Year Team	Lg	G	AB	H	2B	3B	HR	(Hm Rd)	TB	R	RBI	RC	TBB	IBB	SO	HBP	SH	SF	SB	CS	GDP	Avg	OBP	Slg	OPS
2014 Buffalo*	AAA	44	116	32	11	1	0	(- -)	45	12	9	14	8	0	17	0	4	1	1	1	4	.276	.320	.388	.708
2012 Sea	AL	61	104	20	1	0	0	(0 0)	21	13	7	7	8	0	18	1	2	0	2	2	2	.192	.257	.202	.459
2013 Tor	AL	96	240	55	6	5	1	(1 0)	74	27	24	28	32	0	41	4	10	3	7	1	5	.229	.326	.308	.634
2014 Tor	AL	82	240	62	7	1	0	(0 0)	71	31	17	27	22	0	49	3	8	1	1	0	3	.258	.327	.296	.623
3 ML YEARS		239	584	137	14	6	1	(1 0)	166	71	48	62	62	0	108	8	20	4	10	3	10	.235	.315	.284	.599

Scott Kazmir

Pitches: L **Bats:** L **Pos:** SP-32   KAZ-meer   **Ht:** 6'0" **Wt:** 185 **Born:** 1/24/1984 **Age:** 31

			HOW MUCH HE PITCHED						WHAT HE GAVE UP												THE RESULTS							
Year	Team	Lg	G	GS	CG	GF	IP	BFP	H	R	ER	HR	SH	SF	HB	TBB	IBB	SO	WP	Bk	W	L	Pct	Sh	Sv-Op	Hld	ERC	ERA
2004	TB	AL	8	7	0	0	33.1	152	33	22	21	4	0	0	2	21	0	41	3	0	2	3	.400	0	0-0	0	5.36	5.67
2005	TB	AL	32	32	0	0	186.0	818	172	90	78	12	6	9	10	100	3	174	7	1	10	9	.526	0	0-0	0	4.13	3.77
2006	TB	AL	24	24	1	0	144.2	610	132	59	52	15	0	5	2	52	3	163	6	0	10	8	.556	1	0-0	0	3.47	3.24
2007	TB	AL	34	34	0	0	206.2	887	196	91	80	18	6	3	7	89	1	239	10	0	13	9	.591	0	0-0	0	3.97	3.48
2008	TB	AL	27	27	0	0	152.1	641	123	61	59	23	4	5	4	70	2	166	5	0	12	8	.600	0	0-0	0	3.69	3.49
2009	2 Tms	AL	26	26	0	0	147.1	647	149	85	80	16	1	4	6	60	0	117	13	0	10	9	.526	0	0-0	0	4.36	4.89
2010	LAA	AL	28	28	0	0	150.0	682	158	103	99	25	3	6	12	79	2	93	6	0	9	15	.375	0	0-0	0	5.74	5.94
2011	LAA	AL	1	1	0	0	1.2	14	5	5	5	1	0	0	2	2	0	0	0	1	0	0	-	0	0-0	0	35.08	27.00
2013	Cle	AL	29	29	0	0	158.0	672	162	76	71	19	2	1	3	47	1	162	5	1	10	9	.526	0	0-0	0	4.02	4.04
2014	Oak	AL	32	32	2	0	190.1	777	171	81	75	16	5	1	4	50	1	164	9	1	15	9	.625	0	0-0	0	3.00	3.55
09	TB	AL	20	20	0	0	111.0	504	121	77	73	15	1	4	5	50	0	91	10	0	8	7	.533	0	0-0	0	5.18	5.92
09	LAA	AL	6	6	0	0	36.1	143	28	8	7	1	0	0	1	10	0	26	3	0	2	2	.500	0	0-0	0	2.13	1.73
Postseason			8	7	0	0	36.1	176	37	22	21	5	3	2	3	26	0	26	2	0	1	2	.333	0	0-0	0	5.92	5.20
10 ML YEARS			241	240	3	0	1370.1	5900	1301	673	620	149	27	34	52	570	13	1319	64	4	91	79	.535	1	0-0	0	4.06	4.07

Shawn Kelley

Pitches: R **Bats:** R **Pos:** RP-59   **Ht:** 6'2" **Wt:** 220 **Born:** 4/26/1984 **Age:** 31

			HOW MUCH HE PITCHED						WHAT HE GAVE UP												THE RESULTS							
Year	Team	Lg	G	GS	CG	GF	IP	BFP	H	R	ER	HR	SH	SF	HB	TBB	IBB	SO	WP	Bk	W	L	Pct	Sh	Sv-Op	Hld	ERC	ERA
2014	Trntn*	AA	1	1	0	0	0.2	3	0	0	0	0	0	0	0	1	0	2	0	0	0	0	-	0	0- -	-	1.96	0.00
2014	S-WB*	AAA	1	1	0	0	1.0	4	1	0	0	0	0	0	0	0	0	0	0	0	0	0	-	0	0- -	-	1.95	0.00
2009	Sea	AL	41	0	0	12	46.0	191	45	23	23	9	2	2	3	9	1	41	2	1	5	4	.556	0	0-4	9	4.02	4.50
2010	Sea	AL	22	0	0	7	25.0	112	26	11	11	5	0	0	1	12	2	26	0	0	3	1	.750	0	0-0	3	5.38	3.96
2011	Sea	AL	10	0	0	2	12.2	47	7	0	0	0	0	0	0	3	1	10	0	0	0	0	-	0	0-0	1	1.01	0.00
2012	Sea	AL	47	0	0	10	44.1	190	43	20	16	5	4	3	0	15	6	45	2	1	2	4	.333	0	0-2	6	3.49	3.25
2013	NYY	AL	57	0	0	13	53.1	227	47	28	26	8	0	2	0	23	2	71	8	0	4	2	.667	0	0-1	11	3.80	4.39
2014	NYY	AL	59	0	0	15	51.2	220	45	26	26	5	3	1	1	20	4	67	3	0	3	6	.333	0	4-7	12	3.20	4.53
6 ML YEARS			236	0	0	59	233.0	987	213	108	102	32	9	8	5	82	16	260	15	2	17	17	.500	0	4-14	42	3.62	3.94

Don Kelly

Bats: L **Throws:** R **Pos:** 3B-41;1B-30;RF-11;PH-11;PR-11;LF-8;CF-6;2B-1;DH-1   **Ht:** 6'4" **Wt:** 190 **Born:** 2/15/1980 **Age:** 35

			BATTING																		RUNNING			AVERAGES			
Year	Team	Lg	G	AB	H	2B	3B	HR	(Hm	Rd)	TB	R	RBI	RC	TBB	IBB	SO	HBP	SH	SF	SB	CS	GDP	Avg	OBP	Slg	OPS
2007	Pit	NL	25	27	4	0	0	0	(0	0)	4	2	0	1	3	0	3	2	0	0	0	0	1	.148	.281	.148	.429
2009	Det	AL	31	56	14	3	1	0	(0	0)	19	8	3	7	4	0	10	1	0	0	1	0	0	.250	.311	.339	.651
2010	Det	AL	119	238	58	4	0	9	(4	5)	89	30	27	26	8	0	42	2	1	2	3	0	1	.244	.272	.374	.646
2011	Det	AL	113	257	63	8	3	7	(1	6)	98	35	28	27	14	0	32	3	6	1	2	1	8	.245	.291	.381	.672
2012	Det	AL	75	113	21	2	1	1	(1	0)	28	14	7	6	14	0	22	0	0	0	2	0	2	.186	.276	.248	.523
2013	Det	AL	112	216	48	6	1	6	(4	2)	74	33	23	27	27	1	28	2	2	4	2	0	4	.222	.309	.343	.652
2014	Det	AL	95	163	40	5	1	0	(0	0)	47	24	7	14	20	1	29	1	1	0	6	1	6	.245	.332	.288	.620
Postseason			22	32	8	1	0	1	(0	1)	12	5	3	2	3	0	8	0	0	1	0	0	0	.250	.306	.375	.681
7 ML YEARS			570	1070	248	28	7	23	(10	13)	359	146	95	108	90	2	166	11	11	7	16	2	22	.232	.296	.336	.632

Joe Kelly

Pitches: R **Bats:** R **Pos:** SP-17   **Ht:** 6'1" **Wt:** 175 **Born:** 6/9/1988 **Age:** 27

			HOW MUCH HE PITCHED						WHAT HE GAVE UP												THE RESULTS							
Year	Team	Lg	G	GS	CG	GF	IP	BFP	H	R	ER	HR	SH	SF	HB	TBB	IBB	SO	WP	Bk	W	L	Pct	Sh	Sv-Op	Hld	ERC	ERA
2014	Memp*	AAA	3	3	0	0	10.1	42	8	3	3	1	0	0	0	6	0	4	0	1	0	0	-	0	0- -	0	3.72	2.61
2012	StL	NL	24	16	0	4	107.0	457	112	50	42	10	4	1	3	36	2	75	4	0	5	7	.417	0	0-0	0	4.17	3.53
2013	StL	NL	37	15	0	8	124.0	532	124	42	37	10	2	2	5	44	4	79	3	0	10	5	.667	0	0-1	2	3.88	2.69
2014	2 Tms	NL	17	17	0	0	96.1	415	88	48	45	8	2	4	7	42	0	66	3	0	6	4	.600	0	0-0	0	3.92	4.20
14	StL	NL	7	7	0	0	35.0	156	41	19	17	3	1	1	3	10	0	25	3	0	2	2	.500	0	0-0	0	4.82	4.37
14	Bos	AL	10	10	0	0	61.1	259	47	29	28	5	1	3	4	32	0	41	0	0	4	2	.667	0	0-0	0	3.43	4.11
Postseason			11	4	0	0	29.1	127	26	13	12	2	1	0	1	13	1	24	1	0	0	1	.000	0	0-0	0	3.42	3.68
3 ML YEARS			78	48	0	12	327.1	1404	324	140	124	28	8	7	15	122	6	220	10	0	21	16	.568	0	0-1	2	3.99	3.41

Matt Kemp

Bats: R **Throws:** R **Pos:** RF-59;LF-44;CF-41;PH-10;DH-2   **Ht:** 6'4" **Wt:** 215 **Born:** 9/23/1984 **Age:** 30

			BATTING																		RUNNING			AVERAGES			
Year	Team	Lg	G	AB	H	2B	3B	HR	(Hm	Rd)	TB	R	RBI	RC	TBB	IBB	SO	HBP	SH	SF	SB	CS	GDP	Avg	OBP	Slg	OPS
2006	LAD	NL	52	154	39	7	1	7	(4	3)	69	30	23	20	9	1	53	0	0	3	6	0	1	.253	.289	.448	.737
2007	LAD	NL	98	292	100	12	5	10	(9	1)	152	47	42	49	16	0	66	0	0	3	10	5	6	.342	.373	.521	.894
2008	LAD	NL	155	606	176	38	5	18	(14	4)	278	93	76	86	46	6	153	1	1	3	35	11	11	.290	.340	.459	.799
2009	LAD	NL	159	606	180	25	7	26	(13	13)	297	97	101	100	52	6	139	3	0	6	34	8	14	.297	.352	.490	.842
2010	LAD	NL	162	602	150	25	6	28	(15	13)	271	82	89	74	53	4	170	4	0	7	19	15	14	.249	.310	.450	.760
2011	LAD	NL	161	602	195	33	4	39	(19	20)	353	115	126	129	74	24	159	6	0	7	40	11	16	.324	.399	.586	.986
2012	LAD	NL	106	403	122	22	2	23	(13	10)	217	74	69	75	40	8	103	3	0	3	9	4	10	.303	.367	.538	.906
2013	LAD	NL	73	263	71	15	0	6	(0	6)	104	35	33	27	22	3	76	2	0	3	9	0	11	.270	.328	.395	.723
2014	LAD	NL	150	541	155	38	3	25	(17	8)	274	77	89	79	52	3	145	0	0	6	8	5	21	.287	.346	.506	.852
Postseason			16	62	14	3	0	2	(1	1)	23	5	5	1	5	0	25	0	0	0	0	2	2	.226	.284	.371	.655
9 ML YEARS			1116	4069	1188	215	33	182	(104	78)	2015	650	648	639	364	55	1064	19	1	43	170	59	104	.292	.349	.495	.845

Howie Kendrick

Bats: R Throws: R Pos: 2B-154;DH-3   Ht: 5'10" Wt: 210 Born: 7/12/1983 Age: 31

Year	Team	Lg	G	AB	H	2B	3B	HR	(Hm	Rd)	TB	R	RBI	RC	TBB	IBB	SO	HBP	SH	SF	SB	CS	GDP	Avg	OBP	Slg	OPS
2006	LAA	AL	72	267	76	21	1	4	(2	2)	111	25	30	32	9	2	44	4	0	3	6	0	5	.285	.314	.416	.730
2007	LAA	AL	88	338	109	24	2	5	(3	2)	152	55	39	41	9	2	61	4	1	1	5	4	15	.322	.347	.450	.796
2008	LAA	AL	92	340	104	26	2	3	(1	2)	143	43	37	50	12	3	58	4	1	4	11	4	8	.306	.333	.421	.754
2009	LAA	AL	105	374	109	21	3	10	(5	5)	166	61	61	58	20	1	71	4	2	0	11	4	8	.291	.334	.444	.778
2010	LAA	AL	158	616	172	41	4	10	(4	6)	251	67	75	81	28	2	94	5	4	5	14	4	16	.279	.313	.407	.721
2011	LAA	AL	140	537	153	30	6	18	(5	13)	249	86	63	69	33	3	119	10	3	0	14	6	18	.285	.338	.464	.802
2012	LAA	AL	147	550	158	32	3	8	(4	4)	220	57	67	65	29	1	115	4	6	5	14	6	26	.287	.325	.400	.725
2013	LAA	AL	122	478	142	21	4	13	(9	4)	210	55	54	57	23	5	89	6	3	3	6	3	15	.297	.335	.439	.775
2014	LAA	AL	157	617	181	33	5	7	(0	7)	245	85	75	94	48	8	110	4	3	2	14	5	15	.293	.347	.397	.744
Postseason			13	46	9	0	1	1	(1	0)	14	4	2	3	1	0	11	0	2	1	3	0	1	.196	.208	.304	.513
9 ML YEARS			1081	4117	1204	249	30	78	(33	45)	1747	534	501	547	211	27	761	45	23	23	95	36	127	.292	.332	.424	.756

Kyle Kendrick

Pitches: R Bats: R Pos: SP-32   Ht: 6'3" Wt: 210 Born: 8/26/1984 Age: 30

Year	Team	Lg	G	GS	CG	GF	IP	BFP	H	R	ER	HR	SH	SF	HB	TBB	IBB	SO	WP	Bk	W	L	Pct	Sh	Sv-Op	Hld	ERC	ERA
2007	Phi	NL	20	20	0	0	121.0	499	129	53	52	16	4	2	7	25	3	49	0	0	10	4	.714	0	0-0	0	4.23	3.87
2008	Phi	NL	31	30	0	1	155.2	722	194	103	95	23	8	4	14	57	2	68	4	1	11	9	.550	0	0-0	0	6.05	5.49
2009	Phi	NL	9	2	0	2	26.1	112	27	11	10	1	1	2	1	9	0	15	0	1	3	1	.750	0	0-0	0	3.75	3.42
2010	Phi	NL	33	31	1	1	180.2	771	199	103	95	26	9	6	3	49	4	84	1	2	11	10	.524	0	0-0	0	4.51	4.73
2011	Phi	NL	34	15	0	5	114.2	478	110	50	41	14	6	3	7	30	5	59	1	1	8	6	.571	0	0-1	0	3.66	3.22
2012	Phi	NL	37	25	1	2	159.1	674	154	76	69	20	8	4	7	49	4	116	1	0	11	12	.478	1	0-1	2	3.84	3.90
2013	Phi	NL	30	30	2	0	182.0	800	207	104	95	18	11	7	7	47	4	110	3	1	10	13	.435	1	0-0	0	4.33	4.70
2014	Phi	NL	32	32	0	0	199.0	865	214	108	102	25	17	5	11	57	4	121	5	0	10	13	.435	0	0-0	0	4.39	4.61
Postseason			1	1	0	0	3.2	18	5	5	5	2	0	0	0	2	1	2	0	0	0	1	.000	0	0-0	0	9.97	12.27
8 ML YEARS			226	185	4	11	1138.2	4921	1234	608	559	143	64	33	57	323	26	622	15	6	74	68	.521	2	0-2	2	4.43	4.42

Ian Kennedy

Pitches: R Bats: R Pos: SP-33   Ht: 6'0" Wt: 190 Born: 12/19/1984 Age: 30

Year	Team	Lg	G	GS	CG	GF	IP	BFP	H	R	ER	HR	SH	SF	HB	TBB	IBB	SO	WP	Bk	W	L	Pct	Sh	Sv-Op	Hld	ERC	ERA
2007	NYY	AL	3	3	0	0	19.0	77	13	6	4	1	0	0	0	9	0	15	0	0	1	0	1.000	0	0-0	0	2.42	1.89
2008	NYY	AL	10	9	0	1	39.2	194	50	37	36	5	1	4	1	26	0	27	3	0	0	4	.000	0	0-0	0	6.93	8.17
2009	NYY	AL	1	0	0	0	1.0	6	0	0	0	0	0	0	0	2	0	1	0	0	0	0	-	0	0-0	1	7.00	0.00
2010	Ari	NL	32	32	0	0	194.0	810	163	87	82	26	11	5	10	70	2	168	16	0	9	10	.474	0	0-0	0	3.47	3.80
2011	Ari	NL	33	33	1	0	222.0	900	186	73	71	19	9	9	9	55	0	198	11	1	21	4	.840	1	0-0	0	2.71	2.88
2012	Ari	NL	33	33	1	0	208.1	899	216	101	93	28	13	5	14	55	4	187	5	4	15	12	.556	0	0-0	0	4.18	4.02
2013	2 Tms	NL	31	31	0	0	181.1	794	180	108	99	27	8	5	12	73	1	163	10	1	7	10	.412	0	0-0	0	4.64	4.91
2014	SD	NL	33	33	0	0	201.0	846	189	85	81	16	9	8	4	70	4	207	11	0	13	13	.500	0	0-0	0	3.47	3.63
13	Ari	NL	21	21	0	0	124.0	549	128	79	72	18	8	5	10	48	1	108	9	0	3	8	.273	0	0-0	0	4.82	5.23
13	SD	NL	10	10	0	0	57.1	245	52	29	27	9	0	0	2	25	0	55	1	1	4	2	.667	0	0-0	0	4.26	4.24
Postseason			2	2	0	0	12.2	57	13	6	6	1	0	2	3	3	0	8	1	0	0	1	.000	0	0-0	0	4.25	4.26
8 ML YEARS			176	174	2	1	1066.1	4526	997	497	466	122	51	36	51	360	11	966	56	6	66	53	.555	1	0-0	1	3.73	3.93

Clayton Kershaw

Pitches: L Bats: L Pos: SP-27   Ht: 6'3" Wt: 225 Born: 3/19/1988 Age: 27

Year	Team	Lg	G	GS	CG	GF	IP	BFP	H	R	ER	HR	SH	SF	HB	TBB	IBB	SO	WP	Bk	W	L	Pct	Sh	Sv-Op	Hld	ERC	ERA
2014	RCuca*	A+	1	1	0	0	5.0	18	2	1	1	1	0	0	1	0	1	6	0	0	0	0	-	0	0--	-	1.18	1.80
2014	Chatt*	AA	1	1	0	0	5.0	24	6	2	1	0	1	0	1	2	0	9	0	0	0	0	-	0	0--	-	4.13	1.80
2008	LAD	NL	22	21	0	0	107.2	470	109	51	51	11	3	3	1	52	3	100	7	0	5	5	.500	0	0-0	0	4.53	4.26
2009	LAD	NL	31	30	0	1	171.0	701	119	55	53	7	11	2	1	91	4	185	11	2	8	8	.500	0	0-0	0	2.60	2.79
2010	LAD	NL	32	32	1	0	204.1	848	160	73	66	13	8	4	7	81	9	212	5	2	13	10	.565	1	0-0	0	2.72	2.91
2011	LAD	NL	33	33	5	0	233.1	912	174	66	59	15	11	2	3	54	2	248	5	1	21	5	.808	2	0-0	0	2.00	2.28
2012	LAD	NL	33	33	2	0	227.2	901	170	70	64	16	18	4	5	63	5	229	6	2	14	9	.609	2	0-0	0	2.20	2.53
2013	LAD	NL	33	33	3	0	236.0	908	164	55	48	11	8	3	3	52	2	232	12	2	16	9	.640	2	0-0	0	1.65	1.83
2014	LAD	NL	27	27	6	0	198.1	749	139	42	39	9	6	1	2	31	0	239	7	2	21	3	.875	2	0-0	0	1.53	1.77
Postseason			9	6	0	0	38.1	162	33	21	18	3	3	1	1	16	2	39	8	0	1	3	.250	0	0-0	1	3.25	4.23
7 ML YEARS			211	209	17	1	1378.1	5489	1035	412	380	82	65	19	22	424	25	1445	53	11	98	49	.667	9	0-0	1	2.24	2.48

Dallas Keuchel

Pitches: L Bats: L Pos: SP-29   KYE-kull   Ht: 6'3" Wt: 210 Born: 1/1/1988 Age: 27

Year	Team	Lg	G	GS	CG	GF	IP	BFP	H	R	ER	HR	SH	SF	HB	TBB	IBB	SO	WP	Bk	W	L	Pct	Sh	Sv-Op	Hld	ERC	ERA
2012	Hou	NL	16	16	0	0	85.1	377	93	56	50	14	9	3	1	39	1	38	2	0	3	8	.273	0	0-0	0	5.39	5.27
2013	Hou	AL	31	22	0	2	153.2	682	184	96	88	20	2	3	5	52	3	123	7	0	6	10	.375	0	0-0	0	5.33	5.15
2014	Hou	AL	29	29	5	0	200.0	808	187	71	65	11	4	5	7	48	2	146	7	0	12	9	.571	1	0-0	0	3.02	2.93
3 ML YEARS			76	67	6	2	439.0	1867	464	223	203	45	15	11	13	139	6	307	16	0	21	27	.438	1	0-0	2	4.24	4.16

Mike Kickham

Pitches: L **Bats:** L **Pos:** RP-2
KICK-em
Ht: 6'4" **Wt:** 220 **Born:** 12/12/1988 **Age:** 26

			HOW MUCH HE PITCHED							WHAT HE GAVE UP											THE RESULTS							
Year	Team	Lg	G	GS	CG	GF	IP	BFP	H	R	ER	HR	SH	SF	HB	TBB	IBB	SO	WP	Bk	W	L	Pct	Sh	Sv-Op	Hld	ERC	ERA
2010	Giants	R	3	0	0	0	2.1	12	4	3	3	0	0	0	0	2	0	3	0	0	0	0	-	0	0- -	-	10.22	11.57
2011	Augsta	A	21	21	0	0	111.2	476	112	58	51	9	3	4	3	37	0	103	8	1	5	10	.333	0	0- -	-	3.80	4.11
2012	Rchmd	AA	28	27	1	0	150.2	630	119	57	51	8	8	2	2	75	0	137	9	3	11	10	.524	1	0- -	-	3.07	3.05
2013	Fresno	AAA	20	20	0	0	110.2	476	105	60	53	9	5	2	0	49	0	90	1	0	7	7	.500	0	0- -	-	3.83	4.31
2014	Fresno	AAA	27	27	0	0	148.1	667	171	92	73	8	8	1	5	64	0	131	10	0	8	8	.500	0	0- -	-	4.88	4.43
2013	SF	NL	12	3	0	5	28.1	144	46	34	32	8	2	1	0	10	2	29	2	0	0	3	.000	0	0-0	0	8.75	10.16
2014	SF	NL	2	0	0	0	2.0	16	8	5	5	1	0	0	0	1	0	1	0	0	0	0	-	0	0-0	0	29.66	22.50
	2 ML YEARS		14	3	0	5	30.1	160	54	39	37	9	2	1	0	11	2	30	2	0	0	3	.000	0	0-0	0	9.97	10.98

Kevin Kiermaier

Bats: L **Throws:** R **Pos:** RF-68;CF-42;PH-10;LF-1;PR-1
KEER-my-urr
Ht: 6'1" **Wt:** 195 **Born:** 4/22/1990 **Age:** 25

			BATTING																		RUNNING			AVERAGES			
Year	Team	Lg	G	AB	H	2B	3B	HR	(Hm	Rd)	TB	R	RBI	RC	TBB	IBB	SO	HBP	SH	SF	SB	CS	GDP	Avg	OBP	Slg	OPS
2010	Princtn	R+	57	218	66	8	7	2	(-	-)	94	44	16	38	24	2	54	3	1	0	17	5	4	.303	.380	.431	.811
2011	BG	A	120	402	97	11	8	4	(-	-)	136	54	39	47	37	0	99	8	9	3	27	10	3	.241	.316	.338	.654
2012	Charltt	A+	57	177	46	7	6	0	(-	-)	65	16	12	26	26	0	38	2	7	0	10	4	1	.260	.361	.367	.728
2012	Rays	R	2	6	1	0	0	0	(-	-)	1	0	0	0	0	0	2	0	0	0	0	0	0	.167	.167	.167	.333
2012	Drham	AAA	4	9	3	0	0	0	(-	-)	3	2	1	1	3	0	1	0	0	0	0	0	0	.333	.500	.333	.833
2013	Mont	AA	97	371	114	14	9	5	(-	-)	161	65	28	60	31	3	61	8	4	3	14	11	3	.307	.370	.434	.804
2013	Drham	AAA	39	137	36	7	6	1	(-	-)	58	24	13	21	14	0	26	2	0	1	7	1	0	.263	.338	.423	.761
2014	Drham	AAA	34	128	39	7	2	3	(-	-)	59	28	13	23	12	0	23	0	2	1	11	1	1	.305	.362	.461	.823
2013	TB	AL	1	0	0	0	0	0	(0	0)	0	0	0	0	0	0	0	0	0	0	0	0	0	-	-	-	-
2014	TB	AL	108	331	87	16	8	10	(4	6)	149	35	35	37	23	2	71	3	5	2	5	4	3	.263	.315	.450	.765
	Postseason		1	0	0	0	0	0	(0	0)	0	0	0	0	0	0	0	0	0	0	0	0	0	-	-	-	-
	2 ML YEARS		109	331	87	16	8	10	(4	6)	149	35	35	37	23	2	71	3	5	2	5	4	3	.263	.315	.450	.765

Roger Kieschnick

Bats: L **Throws:** R **Pos:** PH-17;LF-5;RF-3
KEESH-nick
Ht: 6'3" **Wt:** 220 **Born:** 1/21/1987 **Age:** 28

			BATTING																		RUNNING			AVERAGES			
Year	Team	Lg	G	AB	H	2B	3B	HR	(Hm	Rd)	TB	R	RBI	RC	TBB	IBB	SO	HBP	SH	SF	SB	CS	GDP	Avg	OBP	Slg	OPS
2010	Rchmd	AA	60	223	56	8	3	4	(-	-)	82	21	23	25	18	1	55	1	0	4	2	3	3	.251	.305	.368	.673
2011	Rchmd	AA	126	459	117	22	5	16	(-	-)	197	71	65	62	34	1	121	3	0	5	13	7	6	.255	.307	.429	.737
2012	Fresno	AAA	55	222	68	13	4	15	(-	-)	134	49	40	48	24	1	68	2	0	2	0	2	4	.306	.376	.604	.980
2012	Giants	R	3	12	1	1	0	0	(-	-)	2	0	4	0	0	0	5	0	0	1	0	0	0	.083	.077	.167	.244
2013	Fresno	AAA	101	374	102	27	9	13	(-	-)	186	50	56	65	40	2	102	1	0	7	4	1	4	.273	.339	.497	.836
2014	Reno	AAA	95	369	96	25	2	15	(-	-)	170	57	49	55	28	0	88	3	0	1	5	1	5	.260	.317	.461	.777
2013	SF	NL	38	84	17	0	1	0	(0	0)	19	6	5	6	11	2	29	0	0	0	0	0	3	.202	.295	.226	.521
2014	Ari	NL	25	41	8	1	0	1	(1	0)	12	2	2	0	0	0	16	0	0	0	0	0	0	.195	.195	.293	.488
	2 ML YEARS		63	125	25	1	1	1	(1	0)	31	8	7	6	11	2	45	0	0	0	0	0	3	.200	.265	.248	.513

Craig Kimbrel

Pitches: R **Bats:** R **Pos:** RP-63
KIM-brull
Ht: 5'11" **Wt:** 220 **Born:** 5/28/1988 **Age:** 27

			HOW MUCH HE PITCHED							WHAT HE GAVE UP											THE RESULTS							
Year	Team	Lg	G	GS	CG	GF	IP	BFP	H	R	ER	HR	SH	SF	HB	TBB	IBB	SO	WP	Bk	W	L	Pct	Sh	Sv-Op	Hld	ERC	ERA
2010	Atl	NL	21	0	0	7	20.2	88	9	2	1	0	0	0	0	16	1	40	4	0	4	0	1.000	0	1-1	2	1.72	0.44
2011	Atl	NL	79	0	0	64	77.0	306	48	19	18	3	1	2	1	32	1	127	4	0	4	3	.571	0	46-54	0	1.88	2.10
2012	Atl	NL	63	0	0	56	62.2	231	27	7	7	3	0	0	2	14	0	116	5	0	3	1	.750	0	42-45	0	0.93	1.01
2013	Atl	NL	68	0	0	60	67.0	258	39	10	9	4	0	0	3	20	2	98	3	0	4	3	.571	0	50-54	0	1.58	1.21
2014	Atl	NL	63	0	0	54	61.2	244	30	13	11	2	3	0	2	26	0	95	6	0	0	3	.000	0	47-51	0	1.41	1.61
	Postseason		6	0	0	4	6.2	21	1	2	1	0	0	0	0	3	0	10	0	0	1	0	1.000	0	1-1	1	0.54	1.35
	5 ML YEARS		294	0	0	241	289.0	1127	153	51	46	12	4	2	8	108	4	476	22	0	15	10	.600	0	186-205	2	1.47	1.43

Ian Kinsler

Bats: R **Throws:** R **Pos:** 2B-160;PH-1
Ht: 6'0" **Wt:** 200 **Born:** 6/22/1982 **Age:** 33

			BATTING																		RUNNING			AVERAGES			
Year	Team	Lg	G	AB	H	2B	3B	HR	(Hm	Rd)	TB	R	RBI	RC	TBB	IBB	SO	HBP	SH	SF	SB	CS	GDP	Avg	OBP	Slg	OPS
2006	Tex	AL	120	423	121	27	1	14	(10	4)	192	65	55	65	40	1	64	3	1	7	11	4	12	.286	.347	.454	.801
2007	Tex	AL	130	483	127	22	2	20	(12	8)	213	96	61	79	62	2	83	9	8	4	23	2	14	.263	.355	.441	.796
2008	Tex	AL	121	518	165	41	4	18	(4	14)	268	102	71	106	45	1	67	6	7	7	26	2	12	.319	.375	.517	.892
2009	Tex	AL	144	566	143	32	4	31	(20	11)	276	101	86	99	59	0	77	6	3	6	31	5	9	.253	.327	.488	.814
2010	Tex	AL	103	391	112	20	1	9	(4	5)	161	73	45	59	56	2	57	7	2	4	15	5	11	.286	.382	.412	.794
2011	Tex	AL	155	620	158	34	4	32	(16	16)	296	121	77	100	89	2	71	8	4	2	30	4	17	.255	.355	.477	.832
2012	Tex	AL	157	655	168	42	5	19	(14	5)	277	105	72	83	60	0	90	10	1	5	21	9	14	.256	.326	.423	.749
2013	Tex	AL	136	545	151	31	2	13	(5	8)	225	85	72	84	51	0	59	8	3	7	15	11	5	.277	.344	.413	.757
2014	Det	AL	161	684	188	40	4	17	(9	8)	287	100	92	89	29	1	79	5	3	5	15	4	20	.275	.307	.420	.727
	Postseason		34	122	38	7	1	4	(1	3)	59	18	20	24	23	1	16	1	1	1	6	5	3	.311	.422	.484	.905
	9 ML YEARS		1227	4885	1333	289	27	173	(94	79)	2195	848	631	764	491	9	647	62	32	47	187	46	114	.273	.344	.449	.793

Brandon Kintzler

Pitches: R Bats: R Pos: RP-64   **Ht:** 5'10" **Wt:** 190 **Born:** 8/1/1984 **Age:** 30

			HOW MUCH HE PITCHED							WHAT HE GAVE UP										THE RESULTS							
Year	Team	Lg	G	GS	CG	GF	IP	BFP	H	R	ER	HR	SH	SF	HB	TBB	IBB	SO	WP	Bk	W	L	Pct	Sh	Sv-Op	Hld	ERC	ERA
2010	Mil	NL	7	0	0	2	7.1	33	10	6	6	2	1	0	0	4	1	9	1	0	0	1	.000	0	0-0	0	8.67	7.36
2011	Mil	NL	9	0	0	3	14.2	61	14	9	6	3	0	2	0	3	0	15	0	1	1	1	.500	0	0-0	0	3.65	3.68
2012	Mil	NL	14	0	0	1	16.2	72	18	7	7	1	0	0	0	7	1	14	1	0	3	0	1.000	0	0-0	2	4.30	3.78
2013	Mil	NL	71	0	0	11	77.0	305	66	26	23	2	4	2	1	16	2	58	1	0	3	3	.500	0	0-4	26	2.21	2.69
2014	Mil	NL	64	0	0	13	58.1	239	62	22	21	8	4	1	0	16	3	31	1	0	3	3	.500	0	0-3	8	4.28	3.24
	5 ML YEARS		165	0	0	30	174.0	710	170	70	63	16	9	5	1	46	7	127	4	1	10	8	.556	0	0-7	36	3.41	3.26

Jason Kipnis

Bats: L Throws: R Pos: 2B-123;DH-5;PH-3   KIP-niss   **Ht:** 5'11" **Wt:** 190 **Born:** 4/3/1987 **Age:** 28

						BATTING																RUNNING			AVERAGES			
Year	Team	Lg	G	AB	H	2B	3B	HR	(Hm	Rd)	TB	R	RBI	RC	TBB	IBB	SO	HBP	SH	SF	SB	CS	GDP	Avg	OBP	Slg	OPS
2014	Clmbs*	AAA	3	9	1	0	0	1	(-	-)	4	1	3	0	0	0	2	0	0	0	0	0	0	.111	.111	.444	.556
2011	Cle	AL	36	136	37	9	1	7	(3	4)	69	24	19	22	11	0	34	2	0	1	5	0	0	.272	.333	.507	.841
2012	Cle	AL	152	591	152	22	4	14	(5	9)	224	86	76	88	67	2	109	5	3	6	31	7	12	.257	.335	.379	.714
2013	Cle	AL	149	564	160	36	4	17	(7	10)	255	86	84	99	76	3	143	3	5	10	30	7	10	.284	.366	.452	.818
2014	Cle	AL	129	500	120	25	1	6	(3	3)	165	61	41	44	50	2	100	2	1	2	22	3	15	.240	.310	.330	.640
	Postseason		1	4	0	0	0	0	(0	0)	0	0	0	0	0	0	0	0	0	0	0	0	0	.000	.000	.000	.000
	4 ML YEARS		466	1791	469	92	10	44	(18	26)	713	257	220	253	204	7	386	12	9	19	88	17	37	.262	.338	.398	.736

Michael Kirkman

Pitches: L Bats: L Pos: RP-12   **Ht:** 6'4" **Wt:** 220 **Born:** 9/18/1986 **Age:** 28

					HOW MUCH HE PITCHED						WHAT HE GAVE UP										THE RESULTS							
Year	Team	Lg	G	GS	CG	GF	IP	BFP	H	R	ER	HR	SH	SF	HB	TBB	IBB	SO	WP	Bk	W	L	Pct	Sh	Sv-Op	Hld	ERC	ERA
2014	RdRck*	AAA	36	4	0	9	54.1	240	50	34	27	6	1	0	2	29	2	62	2	0	5	5	.500	0	1--	-	4.29	4.47
2010	Tex	AL	14	0	0	2	16.1	68	9	3	3	0	0	2	0	10	1	16	0	0	0	0	-	0	0-1	2	1.76	1.65
2011	Tex	AL	15	0	0	7	27.1	122	26	22	20	5	1	2	3	12	2	21	2	0	1	1	.500	0	0-0	1	4.81	6.59
2012	Tex	AL	28	0	0	9	35.1	151	24	16	15	5	0	1	1	17	1	38	2	0	1	2	.333	0	0-2	1	2.88	3.82
2013	Tex	AL	25	0	0	7	22.0	115	36	20	20	2	0	1	0	15	4	25	2	0	0	2	.000	0	1-2	0	8.74	8.18
2014	Tex	AL	12	0	0	1	5.2	22	5	1	1	0	0	0	2	1	0	3	0	0	0	1	.000	0	0-0	2	3.64	1.59
	Postseason		3	0	0	2	2.2	13	4	1	1	0	1	0	0	2	0	2	0	0	0	0	-	0	0-0	0	8.14	3.38
	5 ML YEARS		94	0	0	26	106.2	478	100	62	59	12	1	6	6	55	8	103	6	0	2	6	.250	0	1-5	6	4.29	4.98

Phil Klein

Pitches: R Bats: R Pos: RP-17   **Ht:** 6'7" **Wt:** 260 **Born:** 4/30/1989 **Age:** 26

					HOW MUCH HE PITCHED						WHAT HE GAVE UP										THE RESULTS							
Year	Team	Lg	G	GS	CG	GF	IP	BFP	H	R	ER	HR	SH	SF	HB	TBB	IBB	SO	WP	Bk	W	L	Pct	Sh	Sv-Op	Hld	ERC	ERA
2011	Rngrs	R	3	0	0	0	2.2	12	2	0	0	0	0	0	0	1	0	7	0	0	0	0	-	0	0--	-	1.80	0.00
2011	Spkane	A-	9	0	0	2	17.2	86	18	13	9	1	1	0	1	15	0	24	4	0	1	2	.333	0	0--	-	5.79	4.58
2012	Hkry	A	33	0	0	21	52.0	209	37	12	11	2	2	0	4	21	0	53	3	1	6	0	1.000	0	8--	-	2.53	1.90
2012	MrtlBh	A+	7	0	0	3	10.1	34	2	1	1	1	0	0	0	2	0	14	0	0	0	0	-	0	0--	-	0.45	0.87
2013	MrtlBh	A+	7	0	0	4	13.2	52	6	4	3	0	0	0	2	3	0	12	0	0	1	0	1.000	0	0--	-	0.99	1.98
2013	Frisco	AA	29	2	0	2	53.2	244	45	23	15	3	2	0	2	44	1	74	7	0	5	1	.833	0	0--	-	4.62	2.52
2014	Frisco	AA	24	0	0	14	33.1	129	15	3	3	0	5	1	1	14	0	42	4	0	3	0	1.000	0	10--	-	1.18	0.81
2014	RdRck	AAA	9	0	0	0	18.1	67	7	0	0	0	0	0	2	6	1	28	1	0	0	0	-	0	0--	-	0.97	0.00
2014	Tex	AL	17	0	0	3	19.0	79	11	6	6	3	0	0	2	10	5	23	1	1	1	2	.333	0	0-0	0	2.69	2.84

Corey Kluber

Pitches: R Bats: R Pos: SP-34   CLUE-burr   **Ht:** 6'4" **Wt:** 215 **Born:** 4/10/1986 **Age:** 29

					HOW MUCH HE PITCHED						WHAT HE GAVE UP										THE RESULTS							
Year	Team	Lg	G	GS	CG	GF	IP	BFP	H	R	ER	HR	SH	SF	HB	TBB	IBB	SO	WP	Bk	W	L	Pct	Sh	Sv-Op	Hld	ERC	ERA
2011	Cle	AL	3	0	0	2	4.1	25	6	4	4	0	0	0	2	3	0	5	1	0	0	0	-	0	0-0	0	8.12	8.31
2012	Cle	AL	12	12	0	0	63.0	281	76	44	36	9	1	0	4	18	0	54	2	0	2	5	.286	0	0-0	0	5.38	5.14
2013	Cle	AL	26	24	0	1	147.1	608	163	67	63	16	4	2	6	33	0	136	1	0	11	5	.000	0	0-0	0	3.00	3.05
2013	Cle	AL	34	34	3	0	235.2	951	207	72	64	14	5	2	6	51	3	269	3	0	18	9	.667	1	0-0	0	2.57	2.44
	4 ML YEARS		75	70	3	3	450.1	1865	442	187	167	38	10	4	17	105	3	464	7	0	31	19	.620	1	0-0	0	3.39	3.34

Corey Knebel

Pitches: R Bats: R Pos: RP-8   kuh-NAY-bull   **Ht:** 6'3" **Wt:** 195 **Born:** 11/26/1991 **Age:** 23

					HOW MUCH HE PITCHED						WHAT HE GAVE UP										THE RESULTS							
Year	Team	Lg	G	GS	CG	GF	IP	BFP	H	R	ER	HR	SH	SF	HB	TBB	IBB	SO	WP	Bk	W	L	Pct	Sh	Sv-Op	Hld	ERC	ERA
2013	WMich	A	31	0	0	30	31.0	117	14	4	3	0	2	0	0	10	0	41	4	0	2	1	.667	0	15--	-	0.95	0.87
2014	Erie	AA	11	0	0	8	15.0	61	8	4	2	1	0	1	0	8	0	23	1	0	3	0	1.000	0	1--	-	1.94	1.20
2014	Toledo	AAA	14	0	0	3	18.1	69	6	4	4	0	2	1	2	9	0	20	1	0	1	1	.500	0	2--	-	1.17	1.96
2014	RdRck	AAA	9	0	0	1	12.0	50	9	5	5	2	0	0	1	5	0	20	0	0	1	0	1.000	0	0--	-	3.56	3.75
2014	Det	AL	8	0	0	4	8.2	39	11	7	6	0	0	0	0	3	0	11	1	0	0	0	-	0	0-0	0	4.65	6.23

Jeff Kobernus

Bats: R **Throws:** R **Pos:** 2B-3;PR-1 | CO-burr-ness | **Ht:** 6'2" **Wt:** 195 **Born:** 6/30/1988 **Age:** 27

								BATTING												RUNNING			AVERAGES			
Year	Team	Lg	G	AB	H	2B	3B	HR	(Hm | Rd)	TB	R	RBI	RC	TBB	IBB	SO	HBP	SH	SF	SB	CS	GDP	Avg	OBP	Slg	OPS
2010	Hgrstn	A	74	312	87	18	0	1	(- | -)	108	40	42	36	17	1	58	3	4	7	21	10	2	.279	.316	.346	.662
2011	Ptomc	A+	124	489	138	22	4	7	(- | -)	189	67	52	67	21	0	87	2	8	2	53	8	10	.282	.313	.387	.700
2012	Hrsbrg	AA	82	330	93	10	2	1	(- | -)	110	41	19	41	19	0	57	4	9	4	41	11	1	.282	.325	.333	.658
2013	Syrcse	AAA	95	371	118	19	2	1	(- | -)	144	59	36	60	28	2	59	2	8	3	42	9	1	.318	.366	.388	.754
2014	Syrcse	AAA	59	206	53	13	1	2	(- | -)	74	28	23	28	23	2	44	3	1	2	15	3	5	.257	.338	.359	.697
2014	Hgrstn	A	4	13	3	0	0	1	(- | -)	6	6	2	2	3	0	3	0	0	0	2	1	0	.231	.375	.462	.837
2014	Ptomc	A+	4	15	5	0	0	0	(- | -)	5	5	3	3	3	0	2	0	0	0	5	0	0	.333	.444	.333	.778
2014	Hrsbrg	AA	6	24	7	1	0	0	(- | -)	8	2	3	3	2	0	4	0	0	0	2	0	0	.292	.346	.333	.679
2013	Was	NL	24	30	5	0	0	1	(0 | 1)	8	8	1	2	5	0	6	1	0	0	3	2	0	.167	.306	.267	.572
2014	Was	NL	4	6	0	0	0	0	(0 | 0)	0	2	0	0	1	0	1	1	0	0	0	0	0	.000	.250	.000	.250
	2 ML YEARS		28	36	5	0	0	1	(0 | 1)	8	10	1	2	6	0	7	2	0	0	3	2	0	.139	.295	.222	.518

Tom Koehler

Pitches: R **Bats:** R **Pos:** SP-32 | COLE-err | **Ht:** 6'2" **Wt:** 235 **Born:** 6/29/1986 **Age:** 29

			HOW MUCH HE PITCHED					WHAT HE GAVE UP											THE RESULTS						
Year	Team	Lg	G	GS	CG	GF	IP	BFP	H	R	ER	HR	SH	SF	HB	TBB	IBB	SO	WP	Bk	W	L	Pct	Sh	Sv-Op	Hld	ERC	ERA
2012	Mia	NL	8	1	0	0	13.1	56	15	8	8	4	0	0	2	1	13	0	0	0	1	.000	0	0-0	0	4.99	5.40
2013	Mia	NL	29	23	0	2	143.0	601	140	72	70	14	3	2	5	54	2	92	7	0	5	10	.333	0	0-0	0	4.08	4.41
2014	Mia	NL	32	32	0	0	191.1	803	177	84	81	16	6	5	7	71	0	153	4	0	10	10	.500	0	0-0	0	3.63	3.81
	3 ML YEARS		69	56	0	2	347.2	1460	332	164	159	34	9	7	12	127	3	258	11	0	15	21	.417	0	0-0	0	3.87	4.12

Michael Kohn

Pitches: R **Bats:** R **Pos:** RP-25 | KAHN | **Ht:** 6'2" **Wt:** 200 **Born:** 6/26/1986 **Age:** 29

			HOW MUCH HE PITCHED					WHAT HE GAVE UP											THE RESULTS						
Year	Team	Lg	G	GS	CG	GF	IP	BFP	H	R	ER	HR	SH	SF	HB	TBB	IBB	SO	WP	Bk	W	L	Pct	Sh	Sv-Op	Hld	ERC	ERA
2014	Salt Lk*	AAA	33	0	0	19	34.0	154	28	24	18	6	1	2	1	27	0	33	3	0	1	1	.500	0	8- -	-	5.37	4.76
2010	LAA	AL	24	0	0	8	21.1	95	17	5	5	0	4	0	0	16	1	20	0	0	2	0	1.000	0	1-1	1	3.45	2.11
2011	LAA	AL	14	0	0	7	12.1	60	14	10	10	6	0	0	1	9	0	9	1	0	1	0	1.000	0	1-2	1	9.92	7.30
2013	LAA	AL	63	0	0	13	53.0	231	42	22	22	7	1	1	3	28	3	52	4	0	1	4	.200	0	0-2	8	3.72	3.74
2014	LAA	AL	25	0	0	4	23.2	101	11	9	8	1	0	1	2	20	1	26	3	0	2	1	.667	0	0-0	3	2.73	3.04
	4 ML YEARS		126	0	0	32	110.1	487	84	46	45	14	5	2	6	73	5	107	8	0	5	6	.455	0	2-5	13	4.07	3.67

Paul Konerko

Bats: R **Throws:** R **Pos:** DH-33;PH-31;1B-23 | kun-ER-ko | **Ht:** 6'2" **Wt:** 220 **Born:** 3/5/1976 **Age:** 39

								BATTING												RUNNING			AVERAGES			
Year	Team	Lg	G	AB	H	2B	3B	HR	(Hm	Rd)	TB	R	RBI	RC	TBB	IBB	SO	HBP	SH	SF	SB	CS	GDP	Avg	OBP	Slg	OPS
1997	LAD	NL	6	7	1	0	0	0	(0	0)	1	0	0	0	1	0	2	0	0	0	0	0	1	.143	.250	.143	.393
1998	2 Tms	NL	75	217	47	4	0	7	(5	2)	72	21	29	17	16	0	40	3	0	3	0	1	10	.217	.276	.332	.608
1999	CWS	AL	142	513	151	31	4	24	(16	8)	262	71	81	86	45	0	68	2	1	3	1	0	19	.294	.352	.511	.862
2000	CWS	AL	143	524	156	31	1	21	(10	11)	252	84	97	86	47	0	72	10	0	5	1	0	22	.298	.363	.481	.844
2001	CWS	AL	156	582	166	35	0	32	(19	13)	295	92	99	99	46	6	89	9	0	5	1	0	17	.282	.349	.507	.856
2002	CWS	AL	151	570	173	30	0	27	(13	14)	284	81	104	96	44	2	72	9	0	7	0	0	17	.304	.359	.498	.857
2003	CWS	AL	137	444	104	19	0	18	(9	9)	177	49	65	42	43	7	50	4	0	4	0	0	28	.234	.305	.399	.704
2004	CWS	AL	155	563	156	22	0	41	(29	12)	301	84	117	106	69	6	105	6	0	5	1	0	23	.277	.359	.535	.894
2005	CWS	AL	158	575	163	24	0	40	(23	17)	307	98	100	100	81	10	109	5	0	3	0	0	9	.283	.375	.534	.909
2006	CWS	AL	152	566	177	30	0	35	(21	14)	312	97	113	110	60	3	104	8	0	9	1	0	25	.313	.381	.551	.932
2007	CWS	AL	151	549	142	34	0	31	(17	14)	269	71	90	88	78	9	102	3	0	6	0	1	21	.259	.351	.490	.841
2008	CWS	AL	122	438	105	19	1	22	(15	7)	192	59	62	60	65	4	80	7	0	4	2	0	17	.240	.344	.438	.783
2009	CWS	AL	152	546	151	30	1	28	(18	10)	267	75	88	91	58	4	89	10	0	7	1	0	15	.277	.353	.489	.842
2010	CWS	AL	149	548	171	30	1	39	(26	13)	320	89	111	118	72	7	110	5	0	6	0	1	9	.312	.393	.584	.977
2011	CWS	AL	149	543	163	25	0	31	(19	12)	281	69	105	100	77	17	89	8	0	11	1	1	14	.300	.388	.517	.906
2012	CWS	AL	144	533	159	22	0	26	(14	12)	259	66	75	76	56	4	83	7	0	2	0	0	16	.298	.371	.486	.857
2013	CWS	AL	126	467	114	16	0	12	(6	6)	166	41	54	58	45	2	74	4	0	4	0	0	12	.244	.313	.355	.669
2014	CWS	AL	81	208	43	8	0	5	(4	1)	66	15	22	14	10	0	51	4	0	2	0	0	7	.207	.254	.317	.572
98	LAD	NL	49	144	31	1	0	4	(2	2)	44	14	16	10	10	0	30	2	0	2	0	1	5	.215	.272	.306	.578
98	Cin	NL	26	73	16	3	0	3	(3	0)	28	7	13	7	6	0	10	1	0	1	0	0	5	.219	.284	.384	.668
	Postseason		19	74	18	2	0	7	(3	4)	41	10	17	12	5	2	10	1	0	0	0	0	4	.243	.300	.554	.854
	18 ML YEARS		2349	8393	2340	410	8	439	(261	178)	4083	1162	1412	1363	921	80	1391	104	1	86	9	4	282	.279	.354	.486	.841

George Kontos

Pitches: R **Bats:** R **Pos:** RP-24 | CON-toes | **Ht:** 6'3" **Wt:** 215 **Born:** 6/12/1985 **Age:** 30

			HOW MUCH HE PITCHED					WHAT HE GAVE UP											THE RESULTS						
Year	Team	Lg	G	GS	CG	GF	IP	BFP	H	R	ER	HR	SH	SF	HB	TBB	IBB	SO	WP	Bk	W	L	Pct	Sh	Sv-Op	Hld	ERC	ERA
2014	Fresno*	AAA	30	0	0	14	47.2	195	41	17	15	4	3	1	0	11	0	58	3	0	3	3	.500	0	4- -	-	2.55	2.83
2011	NYY	AL	7	0	0	4	6.0	24	4	2	2	1	0	0	0	3	0	6	0	0	0	0	-	0	0-0	0	3.20	3.00
2012	SF	NL	44	0	0	9	43.2	177	34	15	12	3	0	2	0	12	0	44	1	0	2	1	.667	0	0-1	5	2.23	2.47
2013	SF	NL	52	0	0	9	55.1	238	60	30	27	7	1	4	2	18	2	47	1	0	2	2	.500	0	0-1	5	4.59	4.39
2014	SF	NL	24	0	0	7	32.1	125	24	10	10	1	0	0	0	11	3	27	1	0	4	0	1.000	0	0-0	1	2.07	2.78
	Postseason		8	0	0	1	5.1	22	6	4	4	1	1	0	0	1	0	2	0	0	0	0	-	0	0-0	1	4.65	6.75
	4 ML YEARS		127	0	0	29	137.1	564	122	57	51	12	1	6	2	44	5	124	3	0	8	3	.727	0	0-2	11	3.12	3.34

Bobby Korecky

Pitches: R **Bats:** R **Pos:** RP-2   core-ECK-ee   **Ht:** 5'11" **Wt:** 185 **Born:** 9/16/1979 **Age:** 35

				HOW MUCH HE PITCHED						WHAT HE GAVE UP														THE RESULTS							
Year	Team	Lg	G	GS	CG	GF	IP	BFP	H	R	ER	HR	SH	SF	HB	TBB	IBB	SO	WP	Bk	W	L	Pct	Sh	Sv-Op	Hld	ERC	ERA
2014	Buffalo*	AAA	55	0	0	41	64.0	257	47	14	14	3	1	0	2	18	1	60	1	0	5	3	.625	0	22- -	-	2.02	1.97
2008	Min	AL	16	0	0	9	17.2	74	19	9	9	2	0	0	0	8	0	6	0	0	2	0	1.000	0	0-0	0	5.13	4.58
2009	Ari	NL	5	0	0	0	6.0	32	11	9	9	0	1	1	0	4	0	3	3	0	0	0	-	0	0-0	1	9.65	13.50
2012	Tor	AL	1	0	0	1	1.0	5	1	2	2	1	0	0	0	1	0	0	0	0	0	0	-	0	0-0	0	14.27	18.00
2014	Tor	AL	2	0	0	1	3.1	14	4	3	3	0	0	0	0	1	0	2	0	0	0	0	-	0	0-0	0	4.29	8.10
	4 ML YEARS		24	0	0	11	28.0	125	35	23	23	3	1	1	0	14	0	11	3	0	2	0	1.000	0	0-0	1	6.28	7.39

George Kottaras

Bats: L **Throws:** R **Pos:** C-15;PH-5   kah-TARR-iss   **Ht:** 6'0" **Wt:** 200 **Born:** 5/10/1983 **Age:** 32

									BATTING												RUNNING			AVERAGES			
Year	Team	Lg	G	AB	H	2B	3B	HR	(Hm	Rd)	TB	R	RBI	RC	TBB	IBB	SO	HBP	SH	SF	SB	CS	GDP	Avg	OBP	Slg	OPS
2014	Clmbs*	AAA	14	42	5	0	0	1	(-	-)	8	4	5	0	4	0	18	0	1	0	0	0	0	.119	.196	.190	.386
2014	Buffalo*	AAA	13	42	11	1	0	3	(-	-)	21	6	8	7	7	1	14	0	0	0	0	0	1	.262	.367	.500	.867
2008	Bos	AL	3	5	1	1	0	0	(0	0)	2	1	0	0	0	0	2	0	0	0	0	0	0	.200	.200	.400	.600
2009	Bos	AL	45	93	22	11	0	1	(1	0)	36	15	10	10	11	0	25	0	0	3	0	0	1	.237	.308	.387	.696
2010	Mil	NL	67	212	43	12	1	9	(5	4)	84	24	26	22	33	1	44	0	1	4	2	0	5	.203	.305	.396	.701
2011	Mil	NL	49	111	28	6	1	5	(1	4)	51	15	17	15	10	0	26	0	1	1	0	1	2	.252	.311	.459	.771
2012	2 Tms		85	171	36	6	1	9	(4	5)	71	20	31	30	37	1	48	0	1	0	0	0	4	.211	.351	.415	.766
2013	KC	AL	46	100	18	4	0	5	(3	2)	37	13	12	11	24	2	42	2	0	1	1	0	2	.180	.349	.370	.719
2014	3 Tms		18	30	7	0	0	3	(2	1)	16	4	5	4	6	0	16	0	1	1	0	0	0	.233	.351	.533	.885
12	Mil	NL	58	86	18	4	0	3	(1	2)	31	10	12	15	29	1	24	0	1	0	0	0	2	.209	.409	.360	.769
12	Oak	AL	27	85	18	2	1	6	(3	3)	40	10	19	15	8	0	24	0	0	0	0	0	2	.212	.280	.471	.750
14	Cle	AL	10	21	6	0	0	3	(2	1)	15	4	4	4	4	0	11	0	1	1	0	0	0	.286	.385	.714	1.099
14	StL	NL	4	5	1	0	0	0	(0	0)	1	0	1	0	1	0	2	0	0	0	0	0	0	.200	.333	.200	.533
14	Tor	AL	4	4	0	0	0	0	(0	0)	0	0	0	0	1	0	3	0	0	0	0	0	0	.000	.200	.000	.200
	Postseason		7	12	0	0	0	0	(0	0)	0	0	0	2	1	0	4	0	1	0	0	0	0	.000	.077	.000	.077
	7 ML YEARS		313	722	155	40	3	32	(16	16)	297	92	101	92	121	4	203	2	4	9	3	1	14	.215	.326	.411	.737

Kevin Kouzmanoff

Bats: R **Throws:** R **Pos:** 3B-13;PH-1   KOOZ-ma-noff   **Ht:** 6'1" **Wt:** 210 **Born:** 7/25/1981 **Age:** 33

									BATTING												RUNNING			AVERAGES			
Year	Team	Lg	G	AB	H	2B	3B	HR	(Hm	Rd)	TB	R	RBI	RC	TBB	IBB	SO	HBP	SH	SF	SB	CS	GDP	Avg	OBP	Slg	OPS
2014	RdRck*	AAA	4	16	5	1	0	0	(-	-)	6	1	1	1	0	0	3	0	0	1	0	0	0	.313	.294	.375	.669
2006	Cle	AL	16	56	12	2	0	3	(0	3)	23	4	11	7	5	0	12	0	0	0	0	0	3	.214	.279	.411	.689
2007	SD	NL	145	484	133	30	2	18	(5	13)	221	57	74	69	32	2	94	10	2	6	1	0	9	.275	.329	.457	.786
2008	SD	NL	154	624	162	31	4	23	(11	12)	270	71	84	70	23	3	139	15	0	6	0	0	14	.260	.299	.433	.732
2009	SD	NL	141	529	135	31	1	18	(9	9)	222	50	88	64	27	3	106	11	0	6	1	0	25	.255	.302	.420	.722
2010	Oak	AL	143	551	136	32	1	16	(5	11)	218	59	71	49	24	2	96	6	0	5	2	1	20	.247	.283	.396	.679
2011	2 Tms		73	234	55	11	0	7	(0	7)	87	24	33	26	12	1	46	6	0	5	2	0	4	.235	.284	.372	.656
2014	Tex	AL	13	47	17	6	0	2	(2	0)	29	8	10	10	2	1	7	2	0	0	0	0	2	.362	.412	.617	1.029
11	Oak	AL	46	136	30	6	0	4	(0	4)	48	13	17	13	8	0	27	1	0	4	2	0	2	.221	.262	.353	.615
11	Col	NL	27	98	25	5	0	3	(0	3)	39	11	16	13	4	1	19	5	0	1	0	0	2	.255	.315	.398	.713
	7 ML YEARS		685	2525	650	143	8	87	(32	55)	1070	273	371	295	125	12	500	50	2	28	6	1	77	.257	.302	.424	.726

Pete Kozma

Bats: R **Throws:** R **Pos:** SS-8;2B-6;PH-3   KAHZ-muh   **Ht:** 6'0" **Wt:** 190 **Born:** 4/11/1988 **Age:** 27

									BATTING												RUNNING			AVERAGES			
Year	Team	Lg	G	AB	H	2B	3B	HR	(Hm	Rd)	TB	R	RBI	RC	TBB	IBB	SO	HBP	SH	SF	SB	CS	GDP	Avg	OBP	Slg	OPS
2014	Memp*	AAA	117	379	94	23	0	8	(-	-)	141	59	54	50	41	0	61	7	7	3	10	7	10	.248	.330	.372	.702
2011	StL	NL	16	17	3	1	0	0	(0	0)	4	2	1	2	4	0	4	0	1	0	0	0	0	.176	.333	.235	.569
2012	StL	NL	26	72	24	5	3	2	(0	2)	41	11	14	13	7	1	19	0	1	2	2	0	4	.333	.383	.569	.952
2013	StL	NL	143	410	89	20	0	1	(0	1)	112	44	35	39	34	8	91	0	1	3	3	1	6	.217	.275	.273	.548
2014	StL	NL	14	23	7	3	0	0	(0	0)	10	4	0	3	3	0	4	0	0	0	0	0	0	.304	.385	.435	.819
	Postseason		27	77	14	3	0	1	(0	1)	20	11	9	13	12	3	21	2	1	0	3	1	1	.182	.308	.260	.567
	4 ML YEARS		199	522	123	29	3	3	(0	3)	167	61	50	57	48	9	118	0	3	5	5	1	10	.236	.297	.320	.617

Erik Kratz

Bats: R **Throws:** R **Pos:** C-36;PH-12;DH-5;PR-2   **Ht:** 6'4" **Wt:** 240 **Born:** 6/15/1980 **Age:** 35

									BATTING												RUNNING			AVERAGES			
Year	Team	Lg	G	AB	H	2B	3B	HR	(Hm	Rd)	TB	R	RBI	RC	TBB	IBB	SO	HBP	SH	SF	SB	CS	GDP	Avg	OBP	Slg	OPS
2014	Buffalo*	AAA	27	87	26	10	0	3	(-	-)	45	13	17	16	9	0	18	0	1	3	0	1	2	.299	.354	.517	.871
2010	Pit	NL	9	34	4	0	0	0	(0	0)	4	2	1	0	2	0	9	0	0	0	0	0	0	.118	.167	.118	.284
2011	Phi	NL	2	6	2	1	0	0	(0	0)	3	0	0	1	0	0	1	0	0	0	0	0	0	.333	.333	.500	.833
2012	Phi	NL	50	141	35	9	0	9	(6	3)	71	14	26	26	11	2	34	2	0	3	0	0	2	.248	.306	.504	.809
2013	Phi	NL	68	197	42	7	0	9	(5	4)	76	21	26	15	18	4	45	1	0	2	0	0	11	.213	.280	.386	.666
2014	2 Tms		47	110	24	4	0	5	(1	4)	43	12	13	7	4	1	22	0	0	1	0	0	4	.218	.243	.391	.634
14	Tor	AL	34	81	16	3	0	3	(1	2)	28	8	10	5	3	0	12	0	0	1	0	0	3	.198	.226	.346	.572
14	KC	AL	13	29	8	1	0	2	(0	2)	15	4	3	2	1	1	10	0	0	0	0	0	1	.276	.290	.517	.808
	5 ML YEARS		176	488	107	21	0	23	(12	11)	197	49	66	43	35	7	111	3	0	6	0	0	17	.219	.273	.404	.676

Marc Krauss

Bats: L **Throws:** R **Pos:** 1B-33;LF-19;PH-13;RF-5;DH-4   **Ht:** 6'2" **Wt:** 245 **Born:** 10/5/1987 **Age:** 27

Year	Team	Lg	G	AB	H	2B	3B	HR	(Hm	Rd)	TB	R	RBI	RC	TBB	IBB	SO	HBP	SH	SF	SB	CS	GDP	Avg	OBP	Slg	OPS
2010	Visalia	A+	138	530	160	27	4	25	(-	-)	270	107	87	100	57	0	141	4	0	5	1	3	11	.302	.371	.509	.880
2011	Mobile	AA	125	433	105	25	6	16	(-	-)	190	69	65	68	64	1	123	2	1	4	2	3	9	.242	.340	.439	.779
2012	Mobile	AA	104	346	97	29	2	15	(-	-)	175	75	61	76	73	1	91	9	0	5	6	4	4	.280	.413	.506	.919
2012	CpChr	AA	7	29	12	2	0	5	(-	-)	29	11	16	12	6	0	5	0	0	0	1	0	0	.414	.514	1.000	1.514
2012	OKCity	AAA	22	57	7	0	0	0	(-	-)	7	3	2	0	6	0	20	0	2	1	1	1	2	.123	.203	.123	.326
2013	OKCity	AAA	78	253	71	16	2	10	(-	-)	121	38	39	52	53	6	52	2	0	6	3	3	4	.281	.401	.478	.880
2014	OKCity	AAA	42	159	46	12	0	5	(-	-)	73	22	38	28	22	3	43	1	0	2	1	0	7	.289	.375	.459	.834
2013	Hou	AL	52	134	28	9	0	4	(1	3)	49	11	13	12	10	0	45	1	0	1	2	0	2	.209	.267	.366	.633
2014	Hou	AL	67	186	36	6	0	6	(2	4)	60	16	21	15	21	0	54	1	0	0	0	0	7	.194	.279	.323	.601
	2 ML YEARS		119	320	64	15	0	10	(3	7)	109	27	34	27	31	0	99	2	0	1	2	0	9	.200	.274	.341	.615

Ian Krol

Pitches: L **Bats:** L **Pos:** RP-45   KROHL   **Ht:** 6'1" **Wt:** 210 **Born:** 5/9/1991 **Age:** 24

			HOW MUCH HE PITCHED					WHAT HE GAVE UP										THE RESULTS							
Year	Team	Lg	G	GS	CG	GF	IP	BFP	H	R	ER	HR	SH	SF	HB	TBB	IBB	SO	WP	Bk	W	L	Pct	Sh	Sv-Op	Hld	ERC	ERA
2010	Kane	A	24	23	0	1	118.2	476	98	42	35	5	5	5	7	19	1	91	2	3	9	4	.692	0	0- -	-	2.12	2.65
2010	Stcktn	A+	4	4	0	0	19.2	84	18	9	8	3	1	0	1	9	0	20	0	0	1	0	1.000	0	0- -	-	4.48	3.66
2011	As	R	3	3	0	0	5.0	15	0	0	0	0	0	0	0	0	0	6	0	0	0	0	-	0	0- -	-	0.00	0.00
2012	Stcktn	A+	21	15	0	2	86.1	379	95	64	50	13	1	6	3	24	0	79	1	1	1	7	.125	0	0- -	-	4.57	5.21
2012	Mdlnd	AA	8	0	0	3	10.2	41	11	6	6	0	1	0	0	2	1	10	2	0	1	2	.333	0	0- -	-	2.88	5.06
2013	Hrsbrg	AA	21	0	0	6	26.0	101	14	4	2	1	2	1	2	7	0	29	0	0	0	0	-	0	1- -	-	1.37	0.69
2013	Syrcse	AA	5	0	0	1	3.2	14	2	2	2	0	0	0	0	1	0	7	0	0	1	1	.500	0	0- -	-	1.10	4.91
2014	WMich	A	1	0	0	0	1.0	3	0	0	0	0	0	0	0	0	0	1	0	0	0	0	-	0	0- -	-	0.00	0.00
2014	Toledo	AAA	8	0	0	3	7.0	33	11	3	3	1	0	0	0	1	0	12	0	0	0	0	-	0	0- -	-	6.59	3.86
2013	Was	NL	32	0	0	10	27.1	117	28	12	12	5	2	1	0	8	1	22	2	0	2	1	.667	0	0-1	2	4.24	3.95
2014	Det	AL	45	0	0	5	32.2	154	42	23	18	6	0	1	2	13	4	28	1	1	0	0	-	0	1-4	10	6.35	4.96
	2 ML YEARS		77	0	0	15	60.0	271	70	35	30	11	2	2	2	21	5	50	3	1	2	1	.667	0	1-5	12	5.37	4.50

Jason Kubel

Bats: L **Throws:** R **Pos:** LF-36;PH-5;RF-4;DH-1   KOO-bull   **Ht:** 6'0" **Wt:** 220 **Born:** 5/25/1982 **Age:** 33

Year	Team	Lg	G	AB	H	2B	3B	HR	(Hm	Rd)	TB	R	RBI	RC	TBB	IBB	SO	HBP	SH	SF	SB	CS	GDP	Avg	OBP	Slg	OPS
2004	Min	AL	23	60	18	2	0	2	(0	2)	26	10	7	13	6	0	9	0	0	1	1	1	0	.300	.358	.433	.792
2006	Min	AL	73	220	53	8	0	8	(3	5)	85	23	26	20	12	0	45	0	2	1	2	0	13	.241	.279	.386	.665
2007	Min	AL	128	418	114	31	2	13	(6	7)	188	49	65	64	41	2	79	1	1	5	5	0	9	.273	.335	.450	.785
2008	Min	AL	141	463	126	22	5	20	(9	11)	218	74	78	66	47	2	91	0	0	7	0	1	12	.272	.335	.471	.805
2009	Min	AL	146	514	154	35	2	28	(15	13)	277	73	103	95	56	9	106	3	0	5	1	1	13	.300	.369	.539	.907
2010	Min	AL	143	518	129	23	3	21	(8	13)	221	68	92	65	56	5	116	3	0	1	0	0	16	.249	.323	.427	.750
2011	Min	AL	99	366	100	21	1	12	(4	8)	159	37	58	59	32	2	86	1	0	2	1	1	8	.273	.332	.434	.766
2012	Ari	NL	141	506	128	30	4	30	(18	12)	256	75	90	71	57	7	151	2	0	6	1	1	11	.253	.327	.506	.833
2013	2 Tms		97	259	56	9	1	5	(3	2)	82	21	32	29	29	6	92	0	0	2	0	1	6	.216	.293	.317	.610
2014	Min	AL	45	156	35	6	1	1	(1	0)	46	12	13	18	19	1	59	1	0	0	1	0	1	.224	.313	.295	.607
13	Ari	NL	89	241	53	8	1	5	(3	2)	78	21	32	27	24	3	82	0	0	2	0	1	6	.220	.288	.324	.612
13	Cle	AL	8	18	3	1	0	0	(0	0)	4	0	0	2	5	3	10	0	0	0	0	0	0	.167	.348	.222	.570
	Postseason		8	29	2	1	0	0	(0	0)	3	0	0	0	3	0	13	0	0	0	0	0	0	.069	.156	.103	.260
	10 ML YEARS		1036	3480	913	187	19	140	(67	73)	1558	442	564	500	355	34	834	11	3	34	12	7	89	.262	.330	.448	.777

Hiroki Kuroda

Pitches: R **Bats:** R **Pos:** SP-32   hih-ROE-kee kuh-ROE-duh   **Ht:** 6'1" **Wt:** 205 **Born:** 2/10/1975 **Age:** 40

			HOW MUCH HE PITCHED					WHAT HE GAVE UP										THE RESULTS							
Year	Team	Lg	G	GS	CG	GF	IP	BFP	H	R	ER	HR	SH	SF	HB	TBB	IBB	SO	WP	Bk	W	L	Pct	Sh	Sv-Op	Hld	ERC	ERA
2008	LAD	NL	31	31	2	0	183.1	776	181	85	76	13	7	5	7	42	8	116	5	0	9	10	.474	2	0-0	0	3.18	3.73
2009	LAD	NL	21	20	0	0	117.1	485	110	59	49	12	7	1	1	24	1	87	5	0	8	7	.533	0	0-0	0	2.98	3.76
2010	LAD	NL	31	31	0	0	196.1	810	180	87	74	15	9	7	5	48	13	159	12	0	11	13	.458	0	0-0	0	2.87	3.39
2011	LAD	NL	32	32	0	0	202.0	838	196	77	69	24	6	3	6	49	6	161	12	1	13	16	.448	0	0-0	0	3.49	3.07
2012	NYY	AL	33	33	3	0	219.2	891	205	86	81	25	7	3	8	51	2	167	13	0	16	11	.593	2	0-0	0	3.35	3.32
2013	NYY	AL	32	32	1	0	201.1	824	191	79	74	20	2	7	5	43	2	150	6	0	11	13	.458	1	0-0	0	3.17	3.31
2014	NYY	AL	32	32	0	0	199.0	820	191	91	82	20	5	6	7	35	0	146	13	0	11	9	.550	0	0-0	0	3.11	3.71
	Postseason		5	5	0	0	29.2	120	27	13	13	3	1	0	2	4	1	22	0	0	2	2	.500	0	0-0	0	2.80	3.94
	7 ML YEARS		212	211	6	0	1319.0	5444	1254	564	505	129	43	34	38	292	32	986	66	1	79	79	.500	5	0-0	0	3.18	3.45

Tommy La Stella

Bats: L **Throws:** R **Pos:** 2B-88;PH-5;DH-1   **Ht:** 5'11" **Wt:** 185 **Born:** 1/31/1989 **Age:** 26

Year	Team	Lg	G	AB	H	2B	3B	HR	(Hm	Rd)	TB	R	RBI	RC	TBB	IBB	SO	HBP	SH	SF	SB	CS	GDP	Avg	OBP	Slg	OPS
2011	Rome	A	63	232	76	13	5	9	(-	-)	126	46	40	50	26	0	28	5	3	4	2	2	5	.328	.401	.543	.944
2012	Lynbrg	A+	85	298	90	22	5	5	(-	-)	137	43	56	59	36	2	24	11	3	10	13	2	2	.302	.386	.460	.846
2012	Braves	R	5	13	3	0	1	1	(-	-)	8	4	3	3	4	0	1	0	0	0	0	0	0	.231	.444	.615	1.060
2013	Lynbrg	A+	7	20	11	1	0	1	(-	-)	15	7	4	9	8	0	1	1	0	0	1	1	0	.550	.690	.750	1.440
2013	Missi	AA	81	283	97	21	2	4	(-	-)	134	32	41	58	37	3	34	2	1	0	7	1	6	.343	.422	.473	.896
2014	Gwnntt	AAA	47	167	49	6	1	1	(-	-)	60	18	23	26	25	0	14	2	0	4	1	1	4	.293	.384	.359	.743
2014	Atl	NL	93	319	80	16	1	1	(1	0)	101	22	31	36	36	2	40	1	3	1	2	1	8	.251	.328	.317	.644

John Lackey

Pitches: R Bats: R Pos: SP-31   Ht: 6'6" Wt: 235 Born: 10/23/1978 Age: 36

Year	Team	Lg	G	GS	CG	GF	IP	BFP	H	R	ER	HR	SH	SF	HB	TBB	IBB	SO	WP	Bk	W	L	Pct	Sh	Sv-Op	Hld	ERC	ERA
2002	LAA	AL	18	18	1	0	108.1	465	113	52	44	10	0	4	4	33	0	69	7	2	9	4	.692	0	0-0	0	4.03	3.66
2003	LAA	AL	33	33	2	0	204.0	885	223	117	105	31	2	6	10	66	4	151	11	1	10	16	.385	2	0-0	0	4.88	4.63
2004	LAA	AL	33	32	1	0	198.1	855	215	108	103	22	9	4	8	60	4	144	11	1	14	13	.519	1	0-0	0	4.39	4.67
2005	LAA	AL	33	33	1	0	209.0	892	208	85	80	13	1	2	11	71	3	199	18	0	14	5	.737	0	0-0	0	3.76	3.44
2006	LAA	AL	33	33	3	0	217.2	922	203	98	86	14	8	6	9	72	4	190	16	0	13	11	.542	2	0-0	0	3.31	3.56
2007	LAA	AL	33	33	2	0	224.0	929	219	87	75	18	1	1	12	52	2	179	9	1	19	9	.679	2	0-0	0	3.40	**3.01**
2008	LAA	AL	24	24	3	0	163.1	675	161	71	68	26	5	1	10	40	1	130	5	0	12	5	.706	0	0-0	0	4.10	3.75
2009	LAA	AL	27	27	1	0	176.1	748	177	84	75	17	9	10	9	47	1	139	6	0	11	8	.579	1	0-0	0	3.73	3.83
2010	Bos	AL	33	33	0	0	215.0	930	233	114	105	18	4	5	9	72	2	156	3	0	14	11	.560	0	0-0	0	4.37	4.40
2011	Bos	AL	28	28	0	0	160.0	743	203	119	**114**	20	2	6	**19**	56	1	108	11	0	12	12	.500	0	0-0	0	6.11	6.41
2013	Bos	AL	29	29	2	0	189.1	778	179	80	74	26	3	3	6	40	0	161	4	0	10	13	.435	0	0-0	0	3.42	3.52
2014	2 Tms		31	31	1	0	198.0	833	206	94	84	24	6	3	1	47	1	164	4	2	14	10	.583	0	0-0	0	3.81	3.82
14	Bos	AL	21	21	1	0	137.1	572	137	60	55	15	2	3	0	32	0	116	3	1	11	7	.611	0	0-0	0	3.46	3.60
14	StL	NL	10	10	0	0	60.2	261	69	34	29	9	4	0	1	15	1	48	1	1	3	3	.500	0	0-0	0	4.63	4.30
	Postseason		19	16	0	0	104.0	438	100	37	35	4	2	4	2	35	4	78	7	0	6	5	.545	0	0-0	1	3.23	3.03
	12 ML YEARS		355	354	17	0	2263.1	9655	2340	1109	1013	239	50	51	108	656	23	1790	105	7	152	117	.565	8	0-0	0	4.06	4.03

Bobby LaFromboise

Pitches: L Bats: L Pos: RP-6   lah-frahm-BOYCE   Ht: 6'4" Wt: 215 Born: 6/25/1986 Age: 29

Year	Team	Lg	G	GS	CG	GF	IP	BFP	H	R	ER	HR	SH	SF	HB	TBB	IBB	SO	WP	Bk	W	L	Pct	Sh	Sv-Op	Hld	ERC	ERA
2010	Hi Dsrt	A+	33	14	0	9	113.2	506	138	63	57	15	5	4	1	38	0	92	6	1	10	5	.667	0	1--	-	5.33	4.51
2011	Jacksn	AA	49	0	0	16	61.0	261	62	23	21	6	2	1	3	24	4	53	1	0	3	4	.429	0	0--	-	4.31	3.10
2012	Jacksn	AA	20	0	0	7	26.2	102	15	4	3	0	2	0	0	5	0	32	1	0	1	0	1.000	0	2--	-	0.97	1.01
2012	Tacom	AAA	27	0	0	12	39.2	158	30	7	7	1	2	0	0	16	3	38	1	0	5	2	.714	0	4--	-	2.30	1.59
2013	Tacom	AAA	45	0	0	14	61.0	262	66	29	23	5	1	4	1	18	3	63	6	0	6	0	1.000	0	5--	-	3.98	3.39
2014	ElPaso	AAA	58	0	0	16	53.0	247	68	37	28	4	2	4	0	21	2	45	2	0	1	2	.333	0	3--	-	5.34	4.75
2014	Indy		5	0	0	0	4.0	14	2	0	0	0	0	0	0	0	0	4	0	0	0	0	-	0	0--	-	0.54	0.00
2013	Sea	AL	10	0	0	4	10.2	47	12	8	7	0	1	0	0	4	1	11	0	0	0	1	.000	0	0-0	1	3.77	5.91
2014	Pit	NL	6	0	0	1	3.2	14	3	1	1	1	0	0	0	0	0	4	1	0	0	0	-	0	0-0	2	2.49	2.45
	2 ML YEARS		16	0	0	5	14.1	61	15	9	8	1	1	0	0	4	1	15	1	0	0	1	.000	0	0-0	3	3.52	5.02

Juan Lagares

Bats: R Throws: R Pos: CF-112;PH-4;PR-2   luh-GAR-ess   Ht: 6'1" Wt: 215 Born: 3/17/1989 Age: 26

Year	Team	Lg	G	AB	H	2B	3B	HR	(Hm	Rd)	TB	R	RBI	RC	TBB	IBB	SO	HBP	SH	SF	SB	CS	GDP	Avg	OBP	Slg	OPS
2010	Savann	A	67	290	87	13	9	5	(-	-)	133	42	39	45	7	0	44	3	2	5	18	2	5	.300	.318	.459	.777
2010	StLuci	A+	33	133	31	5	0	2	(-	-)	42	16	16	10	2	0	18	1	0	1	7	3	2	.233	.248	.316	.564
2011	StLuci	A+	82	308	104	15	6	7	(-	-)	152	51	49	55	21	1	47	1	3	2	5	6	5	.338	.380	.494	.873
2011	Bnghtn	AA	38	162	60	11	3	2	(-	-)	83	21	22	32	5	0	29	1	1	1	2	2	0	.370	.391	.512	.903
2012	Bnghtn	AA	130	499	141	29	6	4	(-	-)	194	69	48	68	37	4	93	4	2	5	21	10	12	.283	.334	.389	.723
2013	LsVgs	AAA	17	78	27	3	2	3	(-	-)	43	13	9	14	4	0	14	0	0	0	2	3	0	.346	.378	.551	.929
2014	StLuci	A+	1	4	1	0	0	0	(-	-)	1	0	0	0	0	0	1	0	0	0	0	0	0	.250	.250	.250	.500
2014	LsVgs	AAA	3	9	4	1	0	0	(-	-)	5	2	0	2	0	0	1	1	0	0	0	0	1	.444	.500	.556	1.056
2014	Mets	R	2	8	0	0	0	0	(-	-)	0	0	0	0	0	0	0	0	0	0	0	0	0	.000	.000	.000	.000
2014	Bnghtn	AA	2	8	2	0	0	0	(-	-)	2	2	1	0	1	0	3	0	0	0	0	0	0	.250	.333	.250	.583
2013	NYM	NL	121	392	95	21	5	4	(1	3)	138	35	34	36	20	4	96	2	5	2	6	3	6	.242	.281	.352	.633
2014	NYM	NL	116	416	117	24	3	4	(2	2)	159	46	47	53	20	1	87	7	3	6	13	4	6	.281	.321	.382	.703
	2 ML YEARS		237	808	212	45	8	8	(3	5)	297	81	81	89	40	5	183	9	8	8	19	7	12	.262	.302	.368	.669

Gerald Laird

Bats: R Throws: R Pos: C-48;PH-7   Ht: 6'1" Wt: 230 Born: 11/13/1979 Age: 35

Year	Team	Lg	G	AB	H	2B	3B	HR	(Hm	Rd)	TB	R	RBI	RC	TBB	IBB	SO	HBP	SH	SF	SB	CS	GDP	Avg	OBP	Slg	OPS
2003	Tex	AL	19	44	12	2	1	1	(0	1)	19	9	4	5	5	0	11	1	0	0	0	0	2	.270	.300	.402	.702
2004	Tex	AL	49	147	33	6	0	1	(0	1)	42	20	16	11	12	0	35	2	4	3	0	1	5	.224	.287	.286	.572
2005	Tex	AL	13	40	9	2	0	1	(0	1)	14	7	4	4	2	0	7	0	0	0	0	0	1	.225	.262	.350	.612
2006	Tex	AL	78	243	72	20	1	7	(3	4)	115	46	22	24	12	0	54	2	1	2	3	1	7	.296	.332	.473	.805
2007	Tex	AL	120	407	91	18	3	9	(6	3)	142	48	47	45	30	1	103	2	5	4	6	2	3	.224	.278	.349	.627
2008	Tex	AL	95	344	95	24	0	6	(3	3)	137	54	41	46	23	2	63	6	4	4	2	4	5	.276	.329	.398	.727
2009	Det	AL	135	413	93	23	2	4	(1	3)	132	49	33	41	40	0	68	10	10	4	5	0	11	.225	.306	.320	.626
2010	Det	AL	89	270	56	11	0	5	(2	3)	82	22	25	22	18	0	57	3	6	2	3	1	7	.207	.263	.304	.567
2011	StL	NL	37	95	22	7	1	1	(1	0)	34	11	12	10	9	3	19	1	2	1	1	1	3	.232	.302	.358	.660
2012	Det	AL	63	174	49	8	1	2	(0	2)	65	24	11	19	14	0	21	1	1	1	0	0	4	.282	.337	.374	.710
2013	Atl	NL	47	121	34	8	0	1	(1	0)	45	12	13	18	14	0	23	2	1	1	1	1	4	.281	.367	.372	.739
2014	Atl	NL	53	152	31	8	0	0	(0	0)	39	12	10	9	14	2	33	1	0	0	0	0	6	.204	.275	.257	.532
	Postseason		11	22	1	0	0	0	(0	0)	1	0	0	0	0	0	6	1	0	0	0	0	0	.045	.087	.045	.132
	12 ML YEARS		798	2450	597	137	9	38	(18	20)	866	314	238	254	193	8	494	32	35	22	21	11	58	.244	.305	.353	.658

196

Junior Lake

Bats: R Throws: R Pos: LF-53;CF-36;PH-31;RF-1;PR-1   Ht: 6'3" Wt: 215 Born: 3/27/1990 Age: 25

Year Team	Lg	G	AB	H	2B	3B	HR	(Hm	Rd)	TB	R	RBI	RC	TBB	IBB	SO	HBP	SH	SF	SB	CS	GDP	Avg	OBP	Slg	OPS
2010 Dytona	A+	120	394	104	18	4	9	(-	-)	157	56	46	54	35	0	99	7	8	3	13	9	6	.264	.333	.398	.731
2011 Dytona	A+	49	203	64	11	4	6	(-	-)	101	39	34	35	6	0	49	2	2	3	19	4	3	.315	.336	.498	.834
2011 Tenn	AA	67	242	60	10	2	6	(-	-)	92	41	17	31	13	0	60	5	2	0	19	2	3	.248	.300	.380	.680
2012 Tenn	AA	103	405	113	26	3	10	(-	-)	175	56	50	61	35	0	105	4	2	2	21	12	5	.279	.341	.432	.773
2013 Iowa	AAA	40	156	46	10	2	4	(-	-)	72	30	18	25	10	0	33	2	0	2	14	5	0	.295	.341	.462	.803
2014 Iowa	AAA	14	65	17	3	0	2	(-	-)	26	11	7	8	6	0	15	0	0	0	2	1	2	.262	.324	.400	.724
2013 ChC	NL	64	236	67	16	0	6	(4	2)	101	26	16	26	13	0	68	4	1	0	4	4	2	.284	.332	.428	.760
2014 ChC	NL	108	308	65	10	3	9	(5	4)	108	30	25	18	14	0	110	1	1	2	7	3	3	.211	.246	.351	.597
2 ML YEARS		172	544	132	26	3	15	(9	6)	209	56	41	44	27	0	178	5	2	2	11	7	5	.243	.284	.384	.668

Jake Lamb

Bats: L Throws: R Pos: 3B-34;PH-4   Ht: 6'3" Wt: 220 Born: 10/9/1990 Age: 24

Year Team	Lg	G	AB	H	2B	3B	HR	(Hm	Rd)	TB	R	RBI	RC	TBB	IBB	SO	HBP	SH	SF	SB	CS	GDP	Avg	OBP	Slg	OPS
2012 Msoula	R+	67	280	92	22	5	9	(-	-)	151	47	57	59	24	1	51	7	0	4	8	2	8	.329	.390	.539	.930
2013 Visalia	A+	64	231	70	20	0	13	(-	-)	129	44	47	55	48	2	70	2	0	2	0	0	10	.303	.424	.558	.982
2013 DBcks	R	5	17	5	2	0	0	(-	-)	7	4	5	3	2	0	5	1	0	1	0	0	0	.294	.381	.412	.793
2014 Mobile	AA	103	374	119	35	5	14	(-	-)	206	60	79	83	50	3	99	6	0	9	0	0	7	.318	.399	.551	.949
2014 Reno	AAA	5	18	9	4	0	1	(-	-)	16	3	5	7	3	0	4	0	0	0	2	0	1	.500	.571	.889	1.460
2014 Ari	NL	37	126	29	4	1	4	(2	2)	47	15	11	7	6	0	37	0	0	1	1	1	4	.230	.263	.373	.636

Andrew Lambo

Bats: L Throws: L Pos: PH-15;RF-6;1B-1   Ht: 6'3" Wt: 225 Born: 8/11/1988 Age: 26

Year Team	Lg	G	AB	H	2B	3B	HR	(Hm	Rd)	TB	R	RBI	RC	TBB	IBB	SO	HBP	SH	SF	SB	CS	GDP	Avg	OBP	Slg	OPS
2010 Chatt	AA	47	181	49	11	2	4	(-	-)	76	26	25	25	15	1	39	0	1	1	1	1	6	.271	.325	.420	.745
2010 Altna	AA	26	91	25	1	0	2	(-	-)	32	12	10	12	9	1	30	2	0	0	0	0	0	.275	.353	.352	.705
2011 Indy	AAA	60	185	34	11	0	3	(-	-)	54	19	17	14	17	2	48	2	1	2	1	0	2	.184	.257	.292	.549
2011 Altna	AA	69	252	69	17	0	8	(-	-)	110	35	41	39	26	3	59	3	2	3	4	3	2	.274	.345	.437	.782
2012 Altna	AA	26	92	23	3	1	4	(-	-)	40	13	16	14	14	0	19	0	1	1	0	1	0	.250	.346	.435	.781
2012 Pirates	R	9	33	16	4	0	1	(-	-)	23	10	6	11	5	0	5	1	0	1	1	0	0	.485	.564	.697	1.247
2013 Altna	AA	58	220	64	9	4	14	(-	-)	123	35	46	44	19	1	60	3	2	3	6	1	4	.291	.351	.559	.910
2013 Indy	AAA	62	224	61	15	1	18	(-	-)	132	32	53	45	24	4	67	2	1	3	1	0	4	.272	.344	.589	.933
2014 Indy	AAA	61	238	78	19	2	11	(-	-)	134	44	42	50	22	4	47	2	0	3	3	2	7	.328	.389	.563	.952
2014 Pirates	R	4	13	2	0	0	1	(-	-)	5	3	1	2	4	0	3	0	0	0	0	0	0	.154	.353	.385	.738
2014 Jmstwn	A-	4	12	2	0	0	0	(-	-)	2	2	1	1	4	0	2	0	1	0	0	0	0	.167	.375	.167	.542
2013 Pit	NL	18	30	7	2	0	1	(0	1)	12	4	2	1	3	0	11	0	0	0	0	0	1	.233	.303	.400	.703
2014 Pit	NL	21	39	10	4	0	0	(0	0)	14	3	1	1	0	0	8	0	0	0	0	0	2	.256	.256	.359	.615
2 ML YEARS		39	69	17	6	0	1	(0	1)	26	7	3	2	3	0	19	0	0	0	0	1	2	.246	.278	.377	.655

Jason Lane

Pitches: L Bats: R Pos: RP-2; SP-1   Ht: 6'2" Wt: 225 Born: 12/22/1976 Age: 38

Year Team	Lg	G	GS	CG	GF	IP	BFP	H	R	ER	HR	SH	SF	HB	TBB	IBB	SO	WP	Bk	W	L	Pct	Sh	Sv-Op	Hld	ERC	ERA
2010 LsVgs	AAA	4	0	0	4	4.2	20	5	2	2	1	0	0	0	3	0	3	0	0	0	0	-	0	0- -	-	6.93	3.86
2011 LsVgs	AAA	6	0	0	4	13.0	58	18	7	7	0	0	0	0	2	0	12	1	0	0	0	-	0	0- -	-	4.51	4.85
2012 Reno	AAA	15	0	0	5	21.1	104	33	19	18	2	1	2	0	6	0	18	2	0	2	0	1.000	0	0- -	-	6.58	7.59
2013 Tucsn	AAA	11	6	0	0	46.1	199	55	31	27	7	2	3	0	6	0	33	0	0	2	2	.500	0	0- -	-	4.32	5.24
2014 ElPaso	AAA	24	24	0	0	149.2	644	183	88	75	16	12	5	3	26	2	77	4	0	9	9	.500	0	0- -	-	4.56	4.51
2014 SD	NL	3	1	0	0	10.1	39	7	1	1	1	0	0	0	0	0	6	0	0	0	1	.000	0	0-0	0	1.20	0.87

John Lannan

Pitches: L Bats: L Pos: RP-5   Ht: 6'4" Wt: 235 Born: 9/27/1984 Age: 30

Year Team	Lg	G	GS	CG	GF	IP	BFP	H	R	ER	HR	SH	SF	HB	TBB	IBB	SO	WP	Bk	W	L	Pct	Sh	Sv-Op	Hld	ERC	ERA
2014 StLuci*	A+	6	6	0	0	21.1	103	30	17	16	2	3	1	0	7	0	11	2	0	0	3	.000	0	0- -	-	5.85	6.75
2014 LsVgs*	AAA	8	6	0	0	34.2	166	51	30	26	6	0	1	1	14	0	19	5	0	3	2	.600	0	0- -	-	7.70	6.75
2007 Was	NL	6	6	0	0	34.2	153	36	17	16	3	2	0	2	17	1	10	1	0	2	2	.500	0	0-0	0	4.82	4.15
2008 Was	NL	31	31	0	0	182.0	779	172	89	79	23	13	5	7	72	1	117	6	2	9	15	.375	0	0-0	0	4.09	3.91
2009 Was	NL	33	33	2	0	206.1	875	210	100	89	22	12	1	6	68	5	89	3	0	9	13	.409	1	0-0	0	4.07	3.88
2010 Was	NL	25	25	0	0	143.1	643	175	82	74	14	5	5	4	49	3	71	1	0	8	8	.500	0	0-0	0	5.18	4.65
2011 Was	NL	33	33	0	0	184.2	808	194	90	76	15	10	1	7	76	3	106	4	0	10	13	.435	0	0-0	0	4.42	3.70
2012 Was	NL	6	6	0	0	32.2	144	33	15	15	0	4	0	4	14	1	17	1	0	4	1	.800	0	0-0	0	3.97	4.13
2013 Phi	NL	14	14	0	0	74.1	332	86	48	44	6	5	4	5	27	1	38	2	0	3	6	.333	0	0-0	0	4.95	5.33
2014 NYM	NL	5	0	0	3	4.0	21	7	7	7	3	0	0	0	2	0	2	1	0	0	1	.000	0	0-0	1	15.13	15.75
8 ML YEARS		153	148	2	3	862.0	3755	913	448	400	86	51	16	35	325	15	450	19	2	46	58	.442	1	0-0	1	4.48	4.18

Adam LaRoche

Bats: L Throws: L Pos: 1B-136;PH-4;DH-1   luh-ROASH   Ht: 6'3" Wt: 205 Born: 11/6/1979 Age: 35

								BATTING													RUNNING			AVERAGES			
Year	Team	Lg	G	AB	H	2B	3B	HR	(Hm	Rd)	TB	R	RBI	RC	TBB	IBB	SO	HBP	SH	SF	SB	CS	GDP	Avg	OBP	Slg	OPS
2014 Ptomc*		A+	1	2	0	0	0	0	(-	-)	0	0	0	0	0	0	0	0	0	0	0	0	0	.000	.000	.000	.000
2014 Hrsbrg*		AA	1	3	1	0	0	0	(-	-)	1	0	0	0	1	1	1	0	0	0	0	0	1	.333	.500	.333	.833
2004 Atl		NL	110	324	90	27	1	13	(7	6)	158	45	45	43	27	1	78	1	2	2	0	0	10	.278	.333	.488	.821
2005 Atl		NL	141	451	117	28	0	20	(11	9)	205	53	78	63	39	7	87	4	2	6	0	2	15	.259	.320	.455	.775
2006 Atl		NL	149	492	140	38	1	32	(11	21)	276	89	90	83	55	5	128	2	1	7	0	2	9	.285	.354	.561	.915
2007 Pit		NL	152	563	153	42	0	21	(10	11)	258	71	88	84	62	5	131	3	0	4	1	1	18	.272	.345	.458	.803
2008 Pit		NL	136	492	133	32	3	25	(14	11)	246	66	85	76	54	7	122	2	0	6	1	1	9	.270	.341	.500	.841
2009 3 Tms			150	555	154	38	2	25	(15	10)	271	78	83	84	69	12	142	0	0	5	2	2	11	.277	.355	.488	.843
2010 Ari		NL	151	560	146	37	2	25	(13	12)	262	75	100	84	48	4	172	3	0	4	0	1	8	.261	.320	.468	.788
2011 Was		NL	43	151	26	4	0	3	(1	2)	39	15	15	11	25	0	37	0	0	1	1	0	2	.172	.288	.258	.546
2012 Was		NL	154	571	155	35	1	33	(17	16)	291	76	100	92	67	7	138	1	0	9	1	1	10	.271	.343	.510	.853
2013 Was		NL	152	511	121	19	3	20	(9	11)	206	70	62	68	72	10	131	3	0	4	4	1	13	.237	.332	.403	.735
2014 Was		NL	140	494	128	19	0	26	(14	12)	225	73	92	83	82	9	108	2	0	8	3	0	11	.259	.362	.455	.817
09 Pit		NL	87	324	80	25	1	12	(7	5)	143	46	40	38	41	6	81	0	0	3	2	2	9	.247	.329	.441	.770
09 Bos		AL	6	19	5	2	0	1	(1	0)	10	2	3	3	0	0	2	0	0	0	0	0	1	.263	.263	.526	.789
09 Atl		NL	57	212	69	11	1	12	(7	5)	118	30	40	43	28	6	59	0	0	2	0	0	1	.325	.401	.557	.957
Postseason			13	42	11	2	0	4	(1	3)	25	7	12	7	9	1	9	0	1	0	0	0	1	.262	.392	.595	.987
11 ML YEARS			1478	5164	1363	319	13	243	(122	121)	2437	711	838	771	600	67	1274	20	5	56	13	11	118	.264	.340	.472	.811

Mat Latos

Pitches: R Bats: R Pos: SP-16   LAY-tos   Ht: 6'6" Wt: 245 Born: 12/9/1987 Age: 27

				HOW MUCH HE PITCHED				WHAT HE GAVE UP											THE RESULTS						
Year	Team	Lg	G	GS	CG	GF	IP	BFP	H	R	ER	HR	SH	SF	HB	TBB	IBB	SO	WP	Bk	W	L	Pct	Sh	Sv-Op	Hld	ERC	ERA
2014 Pnscla*		AA	1	1	0	0	4.0	23	7	5	3	1	0	0	1	2	1	3	0	0	0	0	-	0	0- -	-	10.57	6.75
2014 Lsvlle*		AAA	4	4	1	0	19.1	78	17	5	5	1	1	0	0	7	0	13	0	0	2	0	1.000	0	0- -	-	3.07	2.33
2009 SD		NL	10	10	0	0	50.2	212	43	29	26	7	3	1	0	23	1	39	0	2	4	5	.444	0	0-0	0	3.72	4.62
2010 SD		NL	31	31	1	0	184.2	748	150	63	60	16	4	1	2	50	3	189	5	1	14	10	.583	1	0-0	0	2.52	2.92
2011 SD		NL	31	31	0	0	194.1	799	168	82	75	16	8	7	1	62	3	185	5	0	9	14	.391	0	0-0	0	2.93	3.47
2012 Cin		NL	33	33	2	0	209.1	858	179	87	81	25	9	3	4	64	9	185	3	1	14	4	.778	0	0-0	0	3.08	3.48
2013 Cin		NL	32	32	1	0	210.2	881	197	82	74	14	12	3	10	58	5	187	8	0	14	7	.667	0	0-0	0	3.16	3.16
2014 Cin		NL	16	16	0	0	102.1	420	92	42	37	9	8	1	2	26	2	74	1	0	5	5	.500	0	0-0	0	2.94	3.25
Postseason			2	1	0	0	8.1	39	11	7	6	2	0	0	0	2	0	5	0	0	0	1	.000	0	0-0	0	6.03	6.48
6 ML YEARS			153	153	4	0	952.0	3918	829	385	353	87	44	16	19	283	23	859	22	4	60	45	.571	1	0-0	0	2.97	3.34

Ryan Lavarnway

Bats: R Throws: R Pos: 1B-6;PH-5   luh-VARN-way   Ht: 6'4" Wt: 240 Born: 8/7/1987 Age: 27

								BATTING													RUNNING			AVERAGES			
Year	Team	Lg	G	AB	H	2B	3B	HR	(Hm	Rd)	TB	R	RBI	RC	TBB	IBB	SO	HBP	SH	SF	SB	CS	GDP	Avg	OBP	Slg	OPS
2014 Pwtckt*		AAA	62	219	62	10	0	3	(-	-)	81	22	20	35	33	1	45	5	0	0	0	0	6	.283	.389	.370	.759
2014 RedSx*		R	2	5	2	1	0	0	(-	-)	3	1	2	1	1	0	1	0	0	0	0	0	0	.400	.500	.600	1.100
2014 Portlnd*		AA	3	11	3	0	0	1	(-	-)	6	2	2	2	1	0	1	0	0	0	0	0	1	.273	.333	.545	.879
2011 Bos		AL	17	39	9	2	0	2	(0	2)	17	5	8	4	4	0	10	0	0	0	0	0	1	.231	.302	.436	.738
2012 Bos		AL	46	153	24	8	0	2	(0	2)	38	11	12	4	11	0	41	0	0	2	0	0	4	.157	.211	.248	.459
2013 Bos		AL	25	77	23	7	0	1	(1	0)	33	8	14	11	2	0	17	2	0	1	0	0	3	.299	.329	.429	.758
2014 Bos		AL	9	10	0	0	0	0	(0	0)	0	0	0	0	0	0	3	0	0	0	0	0	1	.000	.000	.000	.000
4 ML YEARS			97	279	56	17	0	5	(1	4)	88	24	34	19	17	0	71	2	0	3	0	0	9	.201	.249	.315	.565

Brett Lawrie

Bats: R Throws: R Pos: 3B-63;2B-32   LORI   Ht: 6'0" Wt: 210 Born: 1/18/1990 Age: 25

								BATTING													RUNNING			AVERAGES			
Year	Team	Lg	G	AB	H	2B	3B	HR	(Hm	Rd)	TB	R	RBI	RC	TBB	IBB	SO	HBP	SH	SF	SB	CS	GDP	Avg	OBP	Slg	OPS
2014 Dnedin*		A+	3	10	4	1	0	0	(-	-)	5	3	0	2	2	0	2	0	0	0	0	0	0	.400	.500	.500	1.000
2011 Tor		AL	43	150	44	8	4	9	(5	4)	87	26	25	33	16	1	31	3	2	0	7	1	0	.293	.373	.580	.953
2012 Tor		AL	125	494	135	26	3	11	(7	4)	200	73	48	65	33	0	86	5	2	2	13	8	9	.273	.324	.405	.729
2013 Tor		AL	107	401	102	10	3	11	(4	7)	159	41	46	45	30	1	68	7	1	3	9	5	8	.254	.315	.397	.712
2014 Tor		AL	70	259	64	9	0	12	(5	7)	109	27	38	39	16	0	49	5	0	2	0	0	0	.247	.301	.421	.722
4 ML YEARS			345	1304	345	61	10	43	(23	20)	555	167	157	182	95	2	234	20	5	7	29	14	17	.265	.323	.426	.748

Tom Layne

Pitches: L Bats: L Pos: RP-30   Ht: 6'2" Wt: 190 Born: 11/2/1984 Age: 30

				HOW MUCH HE PITCHED				WHAT HE GAVE UP											THE RESULTS						
Year	Team	Lg	G	GS	CG	GF	IP	BFP	H	R	ER	HR	SH	SF	HB	TBB	IBB	SO	WP	Bk	W	L	Pct	Sh	Sv-Op	Hld	ERC	ERA
2014 Pwtckt*		AAA	37	0	0	24	48.0	190	29	8	8	1	1	0	1	20	0	53	7	0	5	1	.833	0	11- -	-	1.74	1.50
2012 SD		NL	26	0	0	5	16.2	68	9	6	6	0	1	0	3	3	0	25	0	0	2	0	1.000	0	2-3	7	1.20	3.24
2013 SD		NL	14	0	0	2	8.2	39	10	4	2	1	0	1	2	5	0	6	1	0	0	2	.000	0	0-0	0	7.38	2.08
2014 Bos		AL	30	0	0	3	19.0	76	14	4	2	0	0	1	1	8	1	14	2	0	2	1	.667	0	0-1	9	2.32	0.95
3 ML YEARS			70	0	0	10	44.1	183	33	14	10	1	2	1	6	16	1	45	3	0	4	3	.571	0	2-4	16	2.56	2.03

Brandon League

Pitches: R **Bats:** R **Pos:** RP-63 **Ht:** 6'2" **Wt:** 215 **Born:** 3/16/1983 **Age:** 32

			HOW MUCH HE PITCHED						WHAT HE GAVE UP												THE RESULTS							
Year	Team	Lg	G	GS	CG	GF	IP	BFP	H	R	ER	HR	SH	SF	HB	TBB	IBB	SO	WP	Bk	W	L	Pct	Sh	Sv-Op	Hld	ERC	ERA
2004	Tor	AL	3	0	0	0	4.2	18	3	0	0	0	0	0	0	1	0	2	0	0	1	0	1.000	0	0-0	1	1.26	0.00
2005	Tor	AL	20	0	0	4	35.2	162	42	27	26	8	0	1	2	20	1	17	5	0	1	0	1.000	0	0-0	1	7.24	6.56
2006	Tor	AL	33	0	0	8	42.2	173	34	17	12	3	2	0	3	9	2	29	0	0	1	2	.333	0	1-4	12	2.30	2.53
2007	Tor	AL	14	0	0	2	11.2	58	19	8	8	1	0	1	0	7	0	7	3	0	0	0	-	0	0-1	0	8.98	6.17
2008	Tor	AL	31	0	0	8	33.0	141	28	9	8	2	1	0	3	15	2	23	2	0	1	2	.333	0	1-1	5	3.45	2.18
2009	Tor	AL	67	0	0	18	74.2	313	72	40	38	8	5	0	7	21	2	76	9	0	3	6	.333	0	0-3	9	3.85	4.58
2010	Sea	AL	70	0	0	30	79.0	326	67	38	30	7	4	1	2	27	6	56	7	0	9	7	.563	0	6-12	13	2.96	3.42
2011	Sea	AL	65	0	0	60	61.1	250	56	25	19	3	4	0	2	10	2	45	4	0	1	5	.167	0	37-42	8	2.45	2.79
2012	2 Tms		74	0	0	39	72.0	301	65	27	25	1	3	0	1	33	7	54	4	0	2	6	.250	0	15-21	8	3.15	3.13
2013	LAD	NL	58	0	0	35	54.1	249	69	37	32	8	3	2	3	15	1	28	9	0	6	4	.600	0	14-19	2	5.58	5.30
2014	LAD	NL	63	0	0	12	63.0	273	65	23	18	0	4	3	4	27	5	38	4	0	2	3	.400	0	0-1	11	3.82	2.57
12	Sea	AL	46	0	0	24	44.2	193	48	20	18	1	3	0	1	19	3	27	3	0	0	5	.000	0	9-15	6	3.99	3.63
12	LAD	NL	28	0	0	15	27.1	108	17	7	7	0	0	0	1	14	4	27	1	0	2	1	.667	0	6-6	2	1.89	2.30
11 ML YEARS			498	0	0	216	532.0	2264	520	251	216	41	26	8	27	185	28	375	47	0	27	35	.435	0	74-104	62	3.73	3.65

Mike Leake

Pitches: R **Bats:** R **Pos:** SP-33 LEEK **Ht:** 5'10" **Wt:** 190 **Born:** 11/12/1987 **Age:** 27

			HOW MUCH HE PITCHED						WHAT HE GAVE UP												THE RESULTS							
Year	Team	Lg	G	GS	CG	GF	IP	BFP	H	R	ER	HR	SH	SF	HB	TBB	IBB	SO	WP	Bk	W	L	Pct	Sh	Sv-Op	Hld	ERC	ERA
2010	Cin	NL	24	22	0	0	138.1	604	158	77	65	19	7	3	3	49	2	91	2	0	8	4	.667	0	0-0	0	5.12	4.23
2011	Cin	NL	29	26	0	2	167.2	693	159	74	72	23	3	6	8	38	3	118	2	1	12	9	.571	0	0-0	0	3.53	3.86
2012	Cin	NL	30	30	2	0	179.0	757	201	97	91	26	6	7	3	41	3	116	3	0	8	9	.471	0	0-0	0	4.50	4.58
2013	Cin	NL	31	31	0	0	192.1	801	193	78	72	21	8	5	6	48	4	122	2	0	14	7	.667	0	0-0	0	3.69	3.37
2014	Cin	NL	33	33	0	0	214.1	902	217	93	88	23	7	7	13	50	3	164	4	0	11	13	.458	0	0-0	0	3.77	3.70
Postseason			1	1	0	0	4.1	20	6	5	5	2	1	0	0	2	0	1	0	0	0	1	.000	0	0-0	0	10.00	10.38
5 ML YEARS			147	142	2	2	891.2	3757	928	419	388	112	31	28	33	226	15	611	13	1	53	42	.558	0	0-0	0	4.05	3.92

Wade LeBlanc

Pitches: L **Bats:** L **Pos:** RP-8; SP-3 Iah-BLAHNK **Ht:** 6'3" **Wt:** 215 **Born:** 8/7/1984 **Age:** 30

			HOW MUCH HE PITCHED						WHAT HE GAVE UP												THE RESULTS							
Year	Team	Lg	G	GS	CG	GF	IP	BFP	H	R	ER	HR	SH	SF	HB	TBB	IBB	SO	WP	Bk	W	L	Pct	Sh	Sv-Op	Hld	ERC	ERA
2014	Salt Lk*	AAA	22	22	1	0	128.0	551	143	68	63	11	5	4	4	42	0	119	1	0	10	4	.714	0	0--	-	4.56	4.43
2008	SD	NL	5	4	0	0	21.1	104	29	19	19	7	1	0	0	15	2	14	0	0	1	3	.250	0	0-0	0	9.57	8.02
2009	SD	NL	9	9	0	0	46.1	194	35	19	19	6	3	1	4	19	1	30	0	0	3	1	.750	0	0-0	0	3.28	3.69
2010	SD	NL	26	25	0	0	146.0	625	157	69	69	24	7	2	2	51	5	110	2	0	8	12	.400	0	0-0	0	4.84	4.25
2011	SD	NL	14	14	0	0	79.2	339	84	42	41	7	3	3	1	28	1	51	1	1	5	6	.455	0	0-0	0	4.21	4.63
2012	Mia	NL	25	9	0	1	68.2	284	71	30	28	7	5	1	1	19	1	43	1	0	2	5	.286	0	0-0	1	3.94	3.67
2013	2 Tms		17	7	0	1	55.0	259	72	40	33	7	2	1	3	20	3	33	0	0	1	5	.167	0	0-0	0	5.97	5.40
2014	2 Tms	AL	11	3	0	3	29.2	121	27	13	13	2	0	2	2	7	2	21	1	0	1	1	.500	0	0-0	0	2.96	3.94
13	Mia	NL	13	7	0	0	48.2	222	63	30	28	6	2	1	2	15	2	31	0	0	1	5	.167	0	0-0	0	5.67	5.18
13	Hou	AL	4	0	0	1	6.1	37	9	10	5	1	0	0	1	5	1	2	0	0	0	0	-	0	0-0	0	8.25	7.11
14	LAA	AL	10	3	0	2	28.2	114	25	11	11	2	0	1	1	6	1	21	1	0	1	1	.500	0	0-0	0	2.63	3.45
14	NYY	AL	1	0	0	1	1.0	7	2	2	2	0	0	1	1	1	1	0	0	0	0	0	-	0	0-0	0	13.81	18.00
7 ML YEARS			107	71	0	5	446.2	1926	475	232	222	60	21	10	13	159	15	302	5	1	21	33	.389	0	0-0	1	4.62	4.47

Sam LeCure

Pitches: R **Bats:** R **Pos:** RP-62 leh-CURE **Ht:** 6'0" **Wt:** 205 **Born:** 5/4/1984 **Age:** 31

			HOW MUCH HE PITCHED						WHAT HE GAVE UP												THE RESULTS							
Year	Team	Lg	G	GS	CG	GF	IP	BFP	H	R	ER	HR	SH	SF	HB	TBB	IBB	SO	WP	Bk	W	L	Pct	Sh	Sv-Op	Hld	ERC	ERA
2010	Cin	NL	15	6	0	4	48.0	217	50	24	24	6	1	2	5	25	3	37	1	0	2	5	.286	0	0-0	0	5.36	4.50
2011	Cin	NL	43	4	0	7	77.2	307	57	33	32	10	4	0	4	21	3	73	0	0	2	1	.667	0	0-0	5	2.55	3.71
2012	Cin	NL	48	0	0	12	57.1	237	46	22	20	3	4	1	1	23	2	61	2	0	3	3	.500	0	0-1	7	2.73	3.14
2013	Cin	NL	63	0	0	15	61.0	251	50	18	18	4	1	0	1	24	0	66	0	0	1	1	.667	0	1-3	17	2.95	2.66
2014	Cin	NL	62	0	0	16	56.2	251	62	27	24	6	2	3	3	24	1	48	5	0	1	4	.200	0	0-1	17	4.99	3.81
Postseason			4	0	0	1	5.0	19	3	0	0	0	0	1	0	2	1	5	0	0	1	0	1.000	0	0-0	0	1.39	0.00
5 ML YEARS			231	10	0	54	300.2	1263	265	124	118	29	12	6	14	117	9	285	8	0	10	14	.417	0	1-5	46	3.52	3.53

C.C. Lee

Pitches: R **Bats:** R **Pos:** RP-37 **Ht:** 5'11" **Wt:** 190 **Born:** 10/21/1986 **Age:** 28

			HOW MUCH HE PITCHED						WHAT HE GAVE UP												THE RESULTS							
Year	Team	Lg	G	GS	CG	GF	IP	BFP	H	R	ER	HR	SH	SF	HB	TBB	IBB	SO	WP	Bk	W	L	Pct	Sh	Sv-Op	Hld	ERC	ERA
2010	Akron	AA	44	0	0	12	72.2	300	59	30	26	6	1	3	4	22	0	82	6	0	5	4	.556	0	0--	-	2.78	3.22
2011	Akron	AA	23	0	0	9	39.2	162	27	16	11	1	4	3	6	11	1	56	3	0	2	1	.667	0	0--	-	2.00	2.50
2011	Clmbs	AAA	21	0	0	9	31.2	128	26	9	8	2	0	1	1	12	1	43	3	0	4	0	1.000	0	1--	-	2.96	2.27
2012	Clmbs	AAA	5	0	0	1	7.0	27	5	2	2	1	2	0	0	1	0	8	1	0	2	0	1.000	0	0--	-	1.89	2.57
2013	Lk Cty	A	2	0	0	2	2.0	7	1	0	0	0	0	0	0	1	0	4	0	0	0	0	-	0	0--	-	1.62	0.00
2013	Akron	AA	8	0	0	0	8.0	33	3	3	3	0	0	1	1	4	0	9	0	0	0	0	-	0	0--	-	1.26	3.38
2013	Clmbs	AAA	19	0	0	4	19.0	73	14	5	1	0	1	0	1	5	0	24	0	1	1	0	1.000	0	0--	-	2.22	2.37
2014	Clmbs	AAA	25	0	0	7	30.0	127	29	12	11	1	0	0	2	9	0	37	2	0	1	1	.000	0	3--	-	3.31	3.30
2013	Cle	AL	8	0	0	1	4.1	22	4	3	2	1	0	0	1	3	0	4	0	0	0	0	-	0	0-0	1	4.51	4.15
2014	Cle	AL	37	0	0	6	28.0	127	30	15	14	3	2	1	3	12	1	26	3	0	1	1	.500	0	0-1	4	4.98	4.50
2 ML YEARS			45	0	0	7	32.1	149	34	18	16	3	2	3	4	15	1	30	3	0	1	1	.500	0	0-1	5	4.92	4.45

Cliff Lee

Pitches: L Bats: L Pos: SP-13   Ht: 6'3" Wt: 205 Born: 8/30/1978 Age: 36

Year	Team	Lg	G	GS	CG	GF	IP	BFP	H	R	ER	HR	SH	SF	HB	TBB	IBB	SO	WP	Bk	W	L	Pct	Sh	Sv-Op	Hld	ERC	ERA
2014	Clrwtr*	A+	3	3	0	0	10.2	49	13	11	6	1	1	1	1	2	0	8	1	0	0	1	.000	0	0--	-	4.58	5.06
2002	Cle	AL	2	2	0	0	10.1	44	6	2	2	0	1	0	0	8	1	6	0	1	0	1	.000	0	0-0	0	2.38	1.74
2003	Cle	AL	9	9	0	0	52.1	210	41	28	21	7	1	1	2	20	1	44	3	0	3	3	.500	0	0-0	0	3.29	3.61
2004	Cle	AL	33	33	0	0	179.0	802	188	113	108	30	2	6	11	81	1	161	6	0	14	8	.636	0	0-0	0	5.31	5.43
2005	Cle	AL	32	32	1	0	202.0	838	194	91	85	22	5	7	0	52	1	143	4	0	18	5	.783	0	0-0	0	3.35	3.79
2006	Cle	AL	33	33	1	0	200.2	882	224	114	98	29	3	6	8	58	3	129	3	0	14	11	.560	0	0-0	0	4.69	4.40
2007	Cle	AL	20	16	1	1	97.1	443	112	73	68	17	3	2	7	36	1	66	5	0	5	8	.385	0	0-0	0	5.59	6.29
2008	Cle	AL	31	31	4	0	223.1	891	214	68	63	12	2	3	5	34	1	170	4	0	22	3	.880	2	0-0	0	2.75	2.54
2009	2 Tms		34	34	6	0	231.2	969	245	84	83	17	11	9	5	43	1	181	7	0	14	13	.519	2	0-0	0	3.45	3.22
2010	2 Tms		28	28	7	0	212.1	843	195	84	75	16	4	6	1	18	2	185	3	1	12	9	.571	1	0-0	0	2.31	3.18
2011	Phi	NL	32	32	6	0	232.2	920	197	66	62	18	6	4	6	42	0	238	0	0	17	8	.680	6	0-0	0	2.44	2.40
2012	Phi	NL	30	30	0	0	211.0	847	207	79	74	26	3	4	0	28	0	207	4	0	6	9	.400	0	0-0	0	3.11	3.16
2013	Phi	NL	31	31	2	0	222.2	876	193	77	71	22	5	3	4	32	0	222	1	0	14	8	.636	1	0-0	0	2.50	2.87
2014	Phi	NL	13	13	1	0	81.1	352	100	40	33	7	7	3	1	12	0	72	1	0	4	5	.444	0	0-0	0	4.27	3.65
09	Cle	AL	22	22	3	0	152.0	641	165	53	53	10	6	5	3	33	1	107	6	0	7	9	.438	1	0-0	0	3.68	3.14
09	Phi	NL	12	12	3	0	79.2	328	80	35	30	7	5	4	2	10	0	74	1	0	7	4	.636	1	0-0	0	3.03	3.39
10	Sea	AL	13	13	5	0	103.2	408	92	31	27	5	0	3	0	6	0	89	2	1	8	3	.727	1	0-0	0	1.91	2.34
10	Tex	AL	15	15	2	0	108.2	435	103	53	48	11	4	3	1	12	2	96	1	0	4	6	.400	0	0-0	0	2.71	3.98
	Postseason		11	11	3	0	82.0	320	66	27	23	2	1	0	1	10	0	89	2	0	7	3	.700	0			1.68	2.52
	13 ML YEARS		328	324	29	1	2156.2	8917	2116	923	843	223	53	54	50	464	12	1824	41	2	143	91	.611	12	0-0	0	3.37	3.52

Charlie Leesman

Pitches: L Bats: L Pos: SP-1   LEES-min   Ht: 6'4" Wt: 215 Born: 3/10/1987 Age: 28

Year	Team	Lg	G	GS	CG	GF	IP	BFP	H	R	ER	HR	SH	SF	HB	TBB	IBB	SO	WP	Bk	W	L	Pct	Sh	Sv-Op	Hld	ERC	ERA
2010	WinSa	A+	17	17	0	0	84.2	393	98	51	48	6	2	3	11	44	0	39	5	0	9	4	.692	0	0--	-	5.85	5.10
2010	Brham	AA	11	11	0	0	63.2	251	47	20	19	1	2	2	3	20	0	51	1	0	5	2	.714	0	0--	-	2.11	2.69
2011	Brham	AA	27	27	0	0	152.0	678	150	79	68	4	3	9	13	83	0	113	16	2	10	7	.588	0	0--	-	4.40	4.03
2012	Charltt	AAA	26	26	0	0	135.0	570	129	54	37	8	5	3	5	52	0	103	5	0	12	10	.545	0	0--	-	3.69	2.47
2013	Charltt	AAA	16	16	0	0	88.1	394	90	50	38	11	4	3	4	41	0	78	5	0	4	3	.571	0	0--	-	4.77	3.87
2014	Charltt	AAA	14	12	0	0	68.0	295	69	36	31	7	3	2	2	32	0	66	3	0	2	6	.250	0	0--	-	4.67	4.10
2014	WSX	R	2	2	0	0	3.2	15	5	2	2	0	0	0	0	2	0	4	1	0	0	0	-	0	0--	-	7.12	4.91
2013	CWS	AL	8	1	0	1	15.1	77	16	14	12	2	0	0	1	16	0	13	2	0	0	0	-	0	0-0	1	7.56	7.04
2014	CWS	AL	1	1	0	0	2.2	17	9	6	6	1	0	1	0	1	0	0	0	0	0	1	.000	0	0-0	0	25.36	20.25
	2 ML YEARS		9	2	0	1	18.0	94	25	20	18	3	0	1	1	17	0	13	2	0	0	1	.000	0	0-0	1	9.81	9.00

DJ LeMahieu

Bats: R Throws: R Pos: 2B-144;3B-7;1B-1;SS-1;PH-1   la-MAY-hugh   Ht: 6'4" Wt: 205 Born: 7/13/1988 Age: 26

Year	Team	Lg	G	AB	H	2B	3B	HR	(Hm	Rd)	TB	R	RBI	RC	TBB	IBB	SO	HBP	SH	SF	SB	CS	GDP	Avg	OBP	Slg	OPS
2011	ChC	NL	37	60	15	2	0	0	(0	0)	17	3	4	3	1	0	12	0	1	0	0	0	2	.250	.262	.283	.546
2012	Col	NL	81	229	68	12	4	2	(1	1)	94	26	22	28	13	4	42	0	3	2	1	2	8	.297	.332	.410	.742
2013	Col	NL	109	404	113	21	3	2	(1	1)	146	39	28	42	19	2	67	1	7	3	18	7	13	.280	.311	.361	.673
2014	Col	NL	149	494	132	15	5	5	(2	3)	172	59	42	47	33	7	97	2	7	2	10	10	13	.267	.315	.348	.663
	4 ML YEARS		376	1187	328	50	12	9	(4	5)	429	127	96	120	66	13	218	3	18	7	29	19	36	.276	.314	.361	.676

Sandy Leon

Bats: B Throws: R Pos: C-20;PH-1   lay-OHN   Ht: 5'10" Wt: 220 Born: 3/13/1989 Age: 26

Year	Team	Lg	G	AB	H	2B	3B	HR	(Hm	Rd)	TB	R	RBI	RC	TBB	IBB	SO	HBP	SH	SF	SB	CS	GDP	Avg	OBP	Slg	OPS
2014	Syrcse*	AAA	51	170	39	9	0	5	(-	-)	63	26	25	21	23	2	36	0	0	0	1	0	3	.229	.321	.371	.692
2012	Was	NL	12	30	8	2	0	0	(0	0)	10	2	2	2	4	0	11	2	0	0	0	0	1	.267	.389	.333	.722
2013	Was	NL	2	1	0	0	0	0	(0	0)	0	0	0	0	0	0	1	0	0	0	0	0	0	.000	.000	.000	.000
2014	Was	NL	20	64	10	1	0	1	(0	1)	14	7	3	2	6	0	20	0	0	0	0	0	1	.156	.229	.219	.447
	3 ML YEARS		34	95	18	3	0	1	(0	1)	24	9	5	4	10	0	32	2	0	0	0	0	2	.189	.280	.253	.533

Dominic Leone

Pitches: R Bats: R Pos: RP-57   LEE-own   Ht: 5'11" Wt: 210 Born: 10/26/1991 Age: 23

Year	Team	Lg	G	GS	CG	GF	IP	BFP	H	R	ER	HR	SH	SF	HB	TBB	IBB	SO	WP	Bk	W	L	Pct	Sh	Sv-Op	Hld	ERC	ERA
2012	Everett	A-	19	0	0	14	33.0	136	20	6	5	0	3	0	1	19	1	39	1	0	3	0	1.000	0	5--	-	2.09	1.36
2013	Clinton	A	3	0	0	0	6.1	28	6	1	0	0	0	0	0	4	0	10	2	0	0	0	-	0	0--	-	3.98	0.00
2013	Hi Dsrt	A+	29	0	0	21	39.2	155	31	11	11	2	2	2	1	9	0	37	2	1	0	1	.000	0	12--	-	2.15	2.50
2013	Jacksn	AA	16	0	0	13	18.0	71	12	6	5	2	0	0	0	5	1	17	2	2	1	2	.333	0	4--	-	1.90	2.50
2014	Sea	AL	57	0	0	3	66.1	272	52	18	16	4	1	3	3	25	3	70	4	0	8	2	.800	0	0-2	7	2.71	2.17

Chris Leroux

Pitches: R **Bats:** L **Pos:** RP-2
leh-RUE
Ht: 6'6" **Wt:** 225 **Born:** 4/14/1984 **Age:** 31

Year	Team	Lg	G	GS	CG	GF	IP	BFP	H	R	ER	HR	SH	SF	HB	TBB	IBB	SO	WP	Bk	W	L	Pct	Sh	Sv-Op	Hld	ERC	ERA
2014	S-WB*	AAA	12	11	1	0	58.1	250	58	35	32	6	0	2	3	21	0	49	3	1	6	4	.600	0	0- -	-	4.14	4.94
2014	Yanks2*	R	1	1	0	0	4.0	13	1	0	0	0	0	0	0	0	0	5	0	0	0	0	-	0	0- -	0	0.14	0.00
2009	Fla	NL	5	0	0	3	6.2	35	11	8	8	0	0	0	0	4	0	2	0	0	0	0	-	0	0-0	0	7.84	10.80
2010	2 Tms	NL	23	0	0	7	22.2	105	28	18	17	1	0	3	0	14	2	22	1	0	0	1	.000	0	0-2	5	5.86	6.75
2011	Pit	NL	23	0	0	5	25.0	110	26	9	8	0	1	0	1	7	2	24	2	0	1	1	.500	0	0-1	2	3.05	2.88
2012	Pit	NL	10	0	0	3	11.1	48	11	9	7	1	1	0	1	2	0	12	1	0	0	0	-	0	0-0	0	3.24	5.56
2013	Pit	NL	2	0	0	0	4.0	21	4	3	3	1	0	0	0	6	0	3	0	0	0	0	-	0	0-0	0	10.44	6.75
2014	NYY	AL	2	0	0	2	2.0	15	7	5	5	0	0	0	0	2	1	3	0	0	0	1	.000	0	0-0	0	22.06	22.50
	10 Fla	NL	17	0	0	5	18.0	84	24	15	14	1	0	3	0	11	2	18	0	0	0	0	-	0	0-1	3	6.58	7.00
	10 Pit	NL	6	0	0	2	4.2	21	4	3	3	0	0	0	0	3	0	4	1	0	0	1	.000	0	0-1	0	3.39	5.79
	6 ML YEARS		65	0	0	20	71.2	334	87	52	48	3	2	3	2	35	5	66	4	0	1	3	.250	0	0-3	5	5.15	6.03

Jon Lester

Pitches: L **Bats:** L **Pos:** SP-32
Ht: 6'4" **Wt:** 240 **Born:** 1/7/1984 **Age:** 31

Year	Team	Lg	G	GS	CG	GF	IP	BFP	H	R	ER	HR	SH	SF	HB	TBB	IBB	SO	WP	Bk	W	L	Pct	Sh	Sv-Op	Hld	ERC	ERA
2006	Bos	AL	15	15	0	0	81.1	367	91	43	43	7	2	8	5	43	1	60	5	0	7	2	.778	0	0-0	0	5.52	4.76
2007	Bos	AL	12	11	0	0	63.0	275	61	33	32	10	1	5	1	31	0	50	1	0	4	0	1.000	0	0-0	0	4.78	4.57
2008	Bos	AL	33	33	2	0	210.1	874	202	78	75	14	6	3	10	66	1	152	3	1	16	6	.727	2	0-0	0	3.55	3.21
2009	Bos	AL	32	32	2	0	203.1	843	186	80	77	20	2	6	3	64	0	225	6	0	15	8	.652	0	0-0	0	3.35	3.41
2010	Bos	AL	32	32	2	0	208.0	861	167	81	75	14	4	6	10	83	0	225	6	0	19	9	.679	0	0-0	0	3.00	3.25
2011	Bos	AL	31	31	0	0	191.2	799	166	77	74	20	2	2	11	75	0	182	4	0	15	9	.625	0	0-0	0	3.62	3.47
2012	Bos	AL	33	33	3	0	205.1	876	216	117	110	25	5	7	4	68	2	166	6	0	9	14	.391	0	0-0	0	4.36	4.82
2013	Bos	AL	33	33	1	0	213.1	903	209	94	89	19	1	1	7	67	0	177	5	0	15	8	.652	1	0-0	0	3.69	3.75
2014	2 Tms	AL	32	32	1	0	219.2	885	194	76	60	16	6	5	5	48	0	220	3	0	16	11	.593	1	0-0	0	2.70	2.46
	14 Bos	AL	21	21	0	0	143.0	580	128	52	40	9	5	2	4	32	0	149	2	0	10	7	.588	0	0-0	0	2.73	2.52
	14 Oak	AL	11	11	1	0	76.2	305	66	24	20	7	1	3	1	16	0	71	1	0	6	4	.600	1	0-0	0	2.65	2.35
	Postseason		13	11	0	2	76.2	309	59	20	18	8	4	0	2	21	0	68	0	0	6	4	.600	0	0-0	0	2.50	2.11
	9 ML YEARS		253	252	11	0	1596.0	6683	1492	679	635	145	29	43	56	545	4	1457	39	1	116	67	.634	4	0-0	0	3.60	3.58

Colby Lewis

Pitches: R **Bats:** R **Pos:** SP-29
Ht: 6'4" **Wt:** 240 **Born:** 8/2/1979 **Age:** 35

Year	Team	Lg	G	GS	CG	GF	IP	BFP	H	R	ER	HR	SH	SF	HB	TBB	IBB	SO	WP	Bk	W	L	Pct	Sh	Sv-Op	Hld	ERC	ERA
2014	RdRck*	AAA	1	1	0	0	5.0	23	4	4	2	0	0	0	1	3	0	2	0	0	0	1	.000	0	0- -	-	3.64	3.60
2002	Tex	AL	15	4	0	4	34.1	168	42	26	24	4	2	0	2	26	2	28	3	1	1	3	.250	0	0-2	1	7.22	6.29
2003	Tex	AL	26	26	0	0	127.0	594	163	104	103	23	2	2	5	70	1	88	5	0	10	9	.526	0	0-0	0	7.38	7.30
2004	Tex	AL	3	3	0	0	15.1	71	13	7	7	1	0	0	1	13	0	11	0	0	1	1	.500	0	0-0	0	4.98	4.11
2006	Det	AL	2	0	0	1	3.0	18	8	1	1	1	0	0	0	1	0	5	0	0	0	0	-	0	0-0	0	17.35	3.00
2007	Oak	AL	26	1	0	8	37.2	170	44	28	27	7	1	2	3	14	3	23	1	1	0	2	.000	0	0-1	3	5.79	6.45
2010	Tex	AL	32	32	1	0	201.0	844	174	90	83	21	4	4	6	65	0	196	9	0	12	13	.480	0	0-0	0	3.15	3.72
2011	Tex	AL	32	32	2	0	200.1	839	187	103	98	35	4	5	6	56	1	169	4	0	14	10	.583	1	0-0	0	3.82	4.40
2012	Tex	AL	16	16	2	0	105.0	427	99	48	40	16	1	2	6	14	0	93	2	0	6	6	.500	0	0-0	0	3.28	3.43
2014	Tex	AL	29	29	2	0	170.1	762	211	107	98	25	3	9	8	48	5	133	3	1	10	14	.417	1	0-0	0	5.46	5.18
	Postseason		8	8	0	0	50.0	204	32	15	13	7	0	0	2	22	0	44	3	0	4	1	.800	0	0-0	0	2.72	2.34
	9 ML YEARS		181	143	7	13	894.0	3893	941	514	481	133	17	24	37	307	12	746	27	3	54	58	.482	2	0-3	4	4.63	4.84

Tim Lincecum

Pitches: R **Bats:** L **Pos:** SP-26; RP-7
LIN-suh-come
Ht: 5'11" **Wt:** 170 **Born:** 6/15/1984 **Age:** 31

Year	Team	Lg	G	GS	CG	GF	IP	BFP	H	R	ER	HR	SH	SF	HB	TBB	IBB	SO	WP	Bk	W	L	Pct	Sh	Sv-Op	Hld	ERC	ERA
2007	SF	NL	24	24	0	0	146.1	618	122	70	65	12	5	7	2	65	5	150	10	0	7	5	.583	0	0-0	0	3.21	4.00
2008	SF	NL	34	33	2	0	227.0	928	182	72	66	11	11	3	6	84	1	265	17	2	18	5	.783	1	0-0	0	2.69	2.62
2009	SF	NL	32	32	4	0	225.1	905	168	69	62	10	12	5	6	68	2	261	11	0	15	7	.682	2	0-0	0	2.14	2.48
2010	SF	NL	33	33	1	0	212.1	897	194	84	81	18	9	5	5	76	7	231	9	0	16	10	.615	1	0-0	0	3.37	3.43
2011	SF	NL	33	33	1	0	217.0	900	176	74	66	15	13	1	6	86	5	220	9	0	13	14	.481	1	0-0	0	2.92	2.74
2012	SF	NL	33	33	0	0	186.0	825	183	111	107	23	11	6	4	90	3	190	17	2	10	15	.400	0	0-0	0	4.50	5.18
2013	SF	NL	32	32	1	0	197.2	841	184	102	96	21	10	4	7	76	8	193	11	2	10	14	.417	1	0-0	0	3.76	4.37
2014	SF	NL	33	26	1	3	155.2	673	154	86	82	19	4	4	5	63	0	134	15	1	12	9	.571	1	1-1	0	4.33	4.74
	Postseason		12	6	1	0	54.2	212	34	16	15	3	1	3	1	14	0	63	0	0	5	2	.714	1	0-0	2	1.53	2.47
	8 ML YEARS		254	246	10	3	1567.1	6587	1363	668	625	129	75	35	41	608	31	1644	99	7	101	79	.561	7	1-1	0	3.27	3.59

Brad Lincoln

Pitches: R **Bats:** L **Pos:** RP-2
Ht: 6'0" **Wt:** 225 **Born:** 5/25/1985 **Age:** 30

Year	Team	Lg	G	GS	CG	GF	IP	BFP	H	R	ER	HR	SH	SF	HB	TBB	IBB	SO	WP	Bk	W	L	Pct	Sh	Sv-Op	Hld	ERC	ERA
2014	LV*	AAA	27	22	1	0	123.1	548	123	75	70	13	2	4	11	58	1	112	4	0	6	11	.353	0	0- -	-	4.74	5.11
2010	Pit	NL	11	9	0	0	52.2	240	66	42	39	9	3	4	5	15	0	25	1	0	1	4	.200	0	0-0	0	5.99	6.66
2011	Pit	NL	12	8	0	0	47.2	211	54	27	25	4	2	2	2	16	4	29	0	0	2	3	.400	0	0-0	0	4.46	4.72
2012	2 Tms		52	5	0	10	88.0	362	80	37	36	14	4	1	1	24	2	88	1	0	5	2	.714	0	1-2	9	3.49	3.68
2013	Tor	AL	22	0	0	7	31.2	148	28	17	14	4	2	0	3	22	0	25	2	0	1	2	.333	0	0-0	0	5.04	3.98

Year	Team	Lg	G	GS	CG	GF	IP	BFP	H	R	ER	HR	SH	SF	HB	TBB	IBB	SO	WP	Bk	W	L	Pct	Sh	Sv-Op	Hld	ERC	ERA
2014	Phi	NL	2	0	0	1	2.1	13	5	3	3	1	0	0	1	0	0	2	0	0	0	0	-	0	0-0	0	14.73	11.57
12	Pit	NL	28	5	0	6	59.1	239	51	19	18	8	2	0	1	14	1	60	0	0	4	2	.667	0	1-2	5	2.97	2.73
12	Tor	AL	24	0	0	4	28.2	123	29	18	18	6	2	1	0	10	1	28	1	0	1	0	1.000	0	0-0	4	4.63	5.65
5 ML YEARS			99	22	0	18	222.1	974	233	126	117	32	11	7	12	77	6	169	4	0	9	11	.450	0	1-2	9	4.59	4.74

Adam Lind

Bats: L **Throws:** L **Pos:** 1B-47;DH-37;PH-16;PR-1　　　　**Ht:** 6'2" **Wt:** 195 **Born:** 7/17/1983 **Age:** 31

Year	Team	Lg	G	AB	H	2B	3B	HR	(Hm	Rd)	TB	R	RBI	RC	TBB	IBB	SO	HBP	SH	SF	SB	CS	GDP	Avg	OBP	Slg	OPS
2014	Dnedin*	A+	4	14	4	2	0	0	(-	-)	6	5	1	2	2	0	3	0	0	0	0	0	0	.286	.375	.429	.804
2014	B Jays*	R	1	2	2	2	0	0	(-	-)	4	1	0	1	0	0	0	0	0	0	0	0	0	1.000	1.000	2.000	3.000
2006	Tor	AL	18	60	22	8	0	2	(0	2)	36	8	8	13	5	0	12	0	0	0	0	0	0	.367	.415	.600	1.015
2007	Tor	AL	89	290	69	14	0	11	(10	1)	116	34	46	38	16	0	65	1	2	2	1	2	7	.238	.278	.400	.678
2008	Tor	AL	88	326	92	16	4	9	(2	7)	143	48	40	39	16	3	59	2	1	4	2	0	8	.282	.316	.439	.755
2009	Tor	AL	151	587	179	46	0	35	(14	21)	330	93	114	114	58	7	110	5	0	4	1	1	15	.305	.370	.562	.932
2010	Tor	AL	150	569	135	32	3	23	(15	8)	242	57	72	65	38	3	144	3	0	3	0	0	10	.237	.287	.425	.712
2011	Tor	AL	125	499	125	16	0	26	(12	14)	219	56	87	67	32	4	107	3	0	8	1	1	12	.251	.295	.439	.734
2012	Tor	AL	93	321	82	14	2	11	(6	5)	133	28	45	47	29	1	61	0	0	3	0	0	10	.255	.314	.414	.729
2013	Tor	AL	143	465	134	26	1	23	(9	14)	231	67	67	76	51	5	103	1	0	4	1	0	20	.288	.357	.497	.854
2014	Tor	AL	96	290	93	24	2	6	(5	1)	139	38	40	54	28	3	48	0	0	8	0	0	8	.321	.381	.479	.860
9 ML YEARS			953	3407	931	196	12	146	(73	73)	1589	429	519	513	273	26	709	15	3	28	6	4	90	.273	.327	.466	.794

Josh Lindblom

Pitches: R **Bats:** R **Pos:** SP-1　　　　LIN-bloom　　　　**Ht:** 6'4" **Wt:** 240 **Born:** 6/15/1987 **Age:** 28

Year	Team	Lg	G	GS	CG	GF	IP	BFP	H	R	ER	HR	SH	SF	HB	TBB	IBB	SO	WP	Bk	W	L	Pct	Sh	Sv-Op	Hld	ERC	ERA
2014	Scrmto*	AAA	17	16	0	0	84.0	366	92	60	54	10	4	4	3	26	0	60	1	0	4	3	.571	0	0- -	-	4.52	5.79
2011	LAD	NL	27	0	0	8	29.2	116	21	9	9	0	2	3	2	10	3	28	3	0	1	0	1.000	0	0-1	3	1.90	2.73
2012	2 Tms	NL	74	0	0	18	71.0	304	61	31	28	13	2	0	4	35	2	70	2	0	3	5	.375	0	1-4	22	4.47	3.55
2013	Tex	AL	8	5	0	2	31.1	137	35	19	19	4	0	0	1	11	2	21	2	0	1	3	.250	0	0-0	4	4.64	5.46
2014	Oak	AL	1	1	0	0	4.2	22	5	2	2	1	0	0	1	2	0	2	0	0	0	0	-	0	0-0	0	6.25	3.86
12	LAD	NL	48	0	0	12	47.2	197	42	16	16	9	2	0	3	18	0	43	1	0	2	2	.500	0	0-2	15	4.31	3.02
12	Phi	NL	26	0	0	6	23.1	107	19	15	12	4	0	0	1	17	2	27	1	0	1	3	.250	0	1-2	7	4.77	4.63
4 ML YEARS			110	6	0	28	136.2	579	122	61	58	18	4	3	7	58	7	121	7	0	5	8	.385	0	1-5	25	3.96	3.82

Matt Lindstrom

Pitches: R **Bats:** R **Pos:** RP-35　　　　**Ht:** 6'3" **Wt:** 215 **Born:** 2/11/1980 **Age:** 35

Year	Team	Lg	G	GS	CG	GF	IP	BFP	H	R	ER	HR	SH	SF	HB	TBB	IBB	SO	WP	Bk	W	L	Pct	Sh	Sv-Op	Hld	ERC	ERA
2014	Charltt*	AAA	5	0	0	1	4.2	26	9	7	7	0	2	1	1	3	0	3	0	0	0	1	.000	0	0- -	-	11.29	13.50
2007	Fla	NL	71	0	0	11	67.0	284	66	27	23	2	3	1	3	21	4	62	5	0	3	4	.429	0	0-2	19	3.26	3.09
2008	Fla	NL	66	0	0	27	57.1	245	57	21	20	1	6	1	1	26	4	43	4	0	3	3	.500	0	5-6	14	3.69	3.14
2009	Hou	NL	54	0	0	32	47.1	219	54	35	31	5	1	0	2	24	2	39	0	1	2	1	.667	0	15-17	8	5.41	5.89
2010	Hou	NL	58	0	0	41	53.1	244	68	26	26	5	2	0	0	20	1	43	8	0	2	5	.286	0	23-29	4	5.45	4.39
2011	Col	NL	63	0	0	16	54.0	226	52	21	18	3	3	3	2	14	4	36	2	0	2	2	.500	0	2-5	15	3.06	3.00
2012	2 Tms	NL	46	0	0	6	47.0	200	45	17	14	2	0	1	5	14	2	40	1	1	1	0	1.000	0	0-1	5	3.40	2.68
2013	CWS	AL	76	0	0	12	60.2	260	64	23	21	2	2	3	1	23	1	46	6	0	2	4	.333	0	0-4	20	3.92	3.12
2014	CWS	AL	35	0	0	23	34.0	158	47	23	19	3	4	2	1	12	0	18	3	0	2	2	.500	0	6-10	6	6.19	5.03
12	Bal	AL	34	0	0	3	36.1	155	35	14	11	2	0	1	4	12	2	30	1	1	1	0	1.000	0	0-1	2	3.66	2.72
12	Ari	NL	12	0	0	3	10.2	45	10	3	3	0	0	0	1	2	0	10	0	0	0	0	-	0	0-0	3	2.57	2.53
8 ML YEARS			469	0	0	168	420.2	1836	453	193	172	23	21	11	15	154	18	327	29	2	17	21	.447	0	51-74	85	4.13	3.68

Francisco Liriano

Pitches: L **Bats:** L **Pos:** SP-29　　　　**Ht:** 6'2" **Wt:** 215 **Born:** 10/26/1983 **Age:** 31

Year	Team	Lg	G	GS	CG	GF	IP	BFP	H	R	ER	HR	SH	SF	HB	TBB	IBB	SO	WP	Bk	W	L	Pct	Sh	Sv-Op	Hld	ERC	ERA
2014	Indy*	AAA	1	1	0	0	6.0	22	3	0	0	0	0	0	0	0	0	8	0	0	0	0	-	0	0- -	-	0.57	0.00
2005	Min	AL	6	4	0	2	23.2	93	19	15	15	4	0	0	0	7	0	33	0	0	1	2	.333	0	0-0	0	3.15	5.70
2006	Min	AL	28	16	0	2	121.0	473	89	31	29	9	4	2	1	32	0	144	9	1	12	3	.800	0	1-1	1	2.12	2.16
2008	Min	AL	14	14	0	0	76.0	329	74	40	33	7	2	3	1	32	1	67	3	0	6	4	.600	0	0-0	0	3.97	3.91
2009	Min	AL	29	24	0	0	136.2	609	147	93	88	21	5	6	6	65	0	122	5	1	5	13	.278	0	0-0	0	5.46	5.80
2010	Min	AL	31	31	0	0	191.2	806	184	77	77	9	6	2	10	58	0	201	10	1	14	10	.583	0	0-0	0	3.34	3.62
2011	Min	AL	26	24	1	0	134.1	591	125	81	76	14	0	6	7	75	1	112	9	0	9	10	.474	1	0-0	0	4.58	5.09
2012	2 Tms	AL	34	28	0	2	156.2	693	143	97	93	19	4	8	7	87	5	167	11	1	6	12	.333	0	0-0	1	4.47	5.34
2013	Pit	NL	26	26	2	0	161.0	666	134	54	54	9	3	1	6	63	0	163	7	2	16	8	.667	0	0-0	0	2.86	3.02
2014	Pit	NL	29	29	0	0	162.1	691	130	68	61	13	6	5	4	81	3	175	12	0	7	10	.412	0	0-0	0	3.28	3.38
12	Min	AL	22	17	0	2	100.0	440	89	63	59	12	2	7	4	55	4	109	6	1	3	10	.231	0	0-0	1	4.27	5.31
12	CWS	AL	12	11	0	0	56.2	253	54	34	34	7	2	1	3	32	1	58	5	0	3	2	.600	0	0-0	0	4.83	5.40
Postseason			4	3	0	0	20.2	84	14	9	8	1	0	0	2	7	0	18	2	0	1	0	1.000	0	0-0	0	2.20	3.48
9 ML YEARS			223	196	3	8	1163.1	4951	1045	556	526	105	30	33	36	500	10	1184	66	6	76	72	.514	1	1-1	2	3.68	4.07

Rymer Liriano

Bats: R **Throws:** R **Pos:** RF-34;PH-7   RYE-mur   **Ht:** 6'0" **Wt:** 230 **Born:** 6/20/1991 **Age:** 24

								BATTING											RUNNING			AVERAGES			
Year Team	Lg	G	AB	H	2B	3B	HR	(Hm Rd)	TB	R	RBI	RC	TBB	IBB	SO	HBP	SH	SF	SB	CS	GDP	Avg	OBP	Slg	OPS
2010 FtWyn	A	50	188	36	11	1	2	(- -)	55	21	20	12	10	0	54	1	0	2	11	6	3	.191	.234	.293	.526
2010 Eugene	A-	53	203	55	13	6	0	(- -)	80	35	12	28	17	1	53	3	1	1	17	7	10	.271	.335	.394	.729
2010 Lk Els	A+	14	50	11	2	0	1	(- -)	16	3	6	5	5	0	12	0	0	0	3	0	0	.220	.291	.320	.611
2011 Lk Els	A+	15	55	7	1	1	0	(- -)	10	8	6	1	6	0	13	0	0	1	1	1	3	.127	.213	.182	.395
2011 FtWyn	A	116	455	145	30	8	12	(- -)	227	81	62	93	47	1	95	6	2	9	65	20	13	.319	.383	.499	.882
2012 Lk Els	A+	74	282	84	22	2	5	(- -)	125	41	41	48	21	2	69	8	0	3	22	7	9	.298	.360	.443	.803
2012 SnAnt	AA	53	183	46	10	2	3	(- -)	69	24	20	26	20	4	50	3	0	0	10	1	6	.251	.335	.377	.712
2014 SnAnt	AA	99	371	98	20	2	14	(- -)	164	55	53	57	35	1	102	6	0	3	17	7	16	.264	.335	.442	.777
2014 ElPaso	AAA	16	62	28	11	1	0	(- -)	41	14	13	19	8	0	14	1	0	0	3	1	2	.452	.521	.661	1.182
2014 SD	NL	38	109	24	2	0	1	(1 0)	29	13	6	5	9	1	39	2	0	1	4	1	6	.220	.289	.266	.555

Jose Lobaton

Bats: B **Throws:** R **Pos:** C-64;PH-2   LOE-bah-tone   **Ht:** 6'0" **Wt:** 215 **Born:** 10/21/1984 **Age:** 30

								BATTING											RUNNING			AVERAGES			
Year Team	Lg	G	AB	H	2B	3B	HR	(Hm Rd)	TB	R	RBI	RC	TBB	IBB	SO	HBP	SH	SF	SB	CS	GDP	Avg	OBP	Slg	OPS
2009 SD	NL	7	17	3	0	0	0	(0 0)	3	0	0	0	0	0	5	0	0	0	0	0	1	.176	.176	.176	.353
2011 TB	AL	15	34	4	1	0	0	(0 0)	5	2	0	0	4	0	8	1	0	0	0	0	2	.118	.231	.147	.378
2012 TB	AL	69	167	37	10	0	2	(1 1)	53	16	20	19	24	1	46	2	2	2	0	1	6	.222	.323	.317	.640
2013 TB	AL	100	277	69	15	2	7	(5 2)	109	38	32	32	30	0	65	2	2	2	0	1	5	.249	.320	.394	.714
2014 Was	NL	66	214	50	9	0	2	(2 0)	65	18	12	13	15	1	61	1	0	0	0	0	5	.234	.287	.304	.591
Postseason		4	7	2	0	0	1	(1 0)	5	1	1	1	0	0	2	0	0	0	0	0	0	.286	.286	.714	1.000
5 ML YEARS		257	709	163	35	2	11	(8 3)	235	74	64	64	73	2	185	4	4	4	0	2	19	.230	.304	.331	.635

Kyle Lobstein

Pitches: L **Bats:** L **Pos:** SP-6; RP-1   LOB-steen   **Ht:** 6'3" **Wt:** 200 **Born:** 8/12/1989 **Age:** 25

		HOW MUCH HE PITCHED						WHAT HE GAVE UP												THE RESULTS						
Year Team	Lg	G	GS	CG	GF	IP	BFP	H	R	ER	HR	SH	SF	HB	TBB	IBB	SO	WP	Bk	W	L	Pct	Sh	Sv-Op	Hld	ERC	ERA
2010 BG	A	27	27	1	0	148.0	622	140	76	68	14	7	2	3	54	0	128	6	0	9	8	.529	0	0--	-	3.73	4.14
2011 Charltt	A+	22	21	1	0	121.1	510	120	54	50	11	8	2	3	30	1	85	4	0	9	9	.500	0	0--	-	3.42	3.71
2011 Mont	AA	2	2	0	0	11.0	52	14	9	9	4	0	0	2	6	0	11	1	0	1	1	.500	0	0--	-	9.79	7.36
2012 Mont	AA	27	27	0	0	144.0	624	140	73	65	12	8	7	2	69	0	129	4	0	8	7	.533	0	0--	-	4.20	4.06
2013 Erie	AA	15	15	2	0	95.1	383	92	35	33	6	3	2	0	27	0	83	1	1	7	4	.636	0	0--	-	3.33	3.12
2013 Toledo	AAA	13	13	0	0	72.1	311	73	32	28	2	3	6	4	25	0	65	1	0	6	3	.667	0	0--	-	3.63	3.48
2014 Toledo	AAA	26	25	1	0	146.0	639	174	71	66	10	5	6	4	42	1	127	3	0	9	11	.450	0	0--	-	4.62	4.07
2014 Det	AL	7	6	0	1	39.1	164	35	20	19	3	1	1	0	14	2	27	0	0	1	2	.333	0	0-0	-	3.07	4.35

Jeff Locke

Pitches: L **Bats:** L **Pos:** SP-21   LOCK   **Ht:** 6'0" **Wt:** 185 **Born:** 11/20/1987 **Age:** 27

		HOW MUCH HE PITCHED						WHAT HE GAVE UP												THE RESULTS						
Year Team	Lg	G	GS	CG	GF	IP	BFP	H	R	ER	HR	SH	SF	HB	TBB	IBB	SO	WP	Bk	W	L	Pct	Sh	Sv-Op	Hld	ERC	ERA
2014 Bradtn*	A+	1	1	0	0	6.0	24	5	2	2	1	0	0	1	1	0	10	0	0	0	1	.000	0	0--	-	2.66	3.00
2014 Indy*	AAA	9	9	0	0	50.0	220	51	24	23	5	1	1	2	22	0	37	2	0	3	1	.750	0	0--	-	4.51	4.14
2011 Pit	NL	4	4	0	0	16.2	78	21	12	12	3	1	1	1	10	0	5	0	0	0	3	.000	0	0-0	-	7.62	6.48
2012 Pit	NL	8	6	0	1	34.1	148	36	21	21	6	1	0	1	11	0	34	0	0	1	3	.250	0	0-0	-	4.68	5.50
2013 Pit	NL	30	30	0	0	166.1	711	146	69	65	11	8	10	6	84	4	125	8	2	10	7	.588	0	0-0	-	3.72	3.52
2014 Pit	NL	21	21	0	0	131.1	548	127	63	57	16	6	3	4	40	2	89	1	0	7	6	.538	0	0-0	-	3.81	3.91
4 ML YEARS		63	61	0	1	348.2	1485	330	165	155	36	16	14	12	145	6	253	9	2	18	19	.486	0	0-0	-	4.02	4.00

Boone Logan

Pitches: L **Bats:** R **Pos:** RP-35   **Ht:** 6'5" **Wt:** 215 **Born:** 8/13/1984 **Age:** 30

		HOW MUCH HE PITCHED						WHAT HE GAVE UP												THE RESULTS						
Year Team	Lg	G	GS	CG	GF	IP	BFP	H	R	ER	HR	SH	SF	HB	TBB	IBB	SO	WP	Bk	W	L	Pct	Sh	Sv-Op	Hld	ERC	ERA
2014 ColSpr*	AAA	7	0	0	2	6.0	23	3	1	1	1	0	0	0	3	0	6	0	0	0	0	-	0	1--	-	2.36	1.50
2006 CWS	AL	21	0	0	4	17.1	93	21	18	16	2	1	1	3	15	2	15	1	0	0	0	-	0	1-2	2	7.56	8.31
2007 CWS	AL	68	0	0	13	50.2	226	59	30	28	7	2	6	0	20	3	35	2	0	2	1	.667	0	0-2	11	5.18	4.97
2008 CWS	AL	55	0	0	12	42.1	197	57	31	28	7	2	0	1	14	3	42	1	0	2	3	.400	0	0-1	3	6.24	5.95
2009 Atl	NL	20	0	0	7	17.1	82	21	12	10	1	0	0	1	9	3	10	0	0	1	1	.500	0	0-0	1	5.29	5.19
2010 NYY	AL	51	0	0	8	40.0	169	34	13	13	3	0	1	1	20	3	38	1	0	2	0	1.000	0	0-0	13	3.50	2.93
2011 NYY	AL	64	0	0	6	41.2	185	43	20	16	4	2	1	4	13	3	46	1	0	5	3	.625	0	0-2	10	4.04	3.46
2012 NYY	AL	80	0	0	8	55.1	239	48	23	23	6	1	3	2	28	6	68	3	0	7	2	.778	0	1-4	23	3.78	3.74
2013 NYY	AL	61	0	0	9	39.0	159	33	15	14	7	3	3	0	13	4	50	3	0	5	2	.714	0	0-2	11	3.38	3.23
2014 Col	AL	35	0	0	8	25.0	116	31	20	19	6	2	2	1	11	1	32	3	0	2	3	.400	0	0-4	7	6.84	6.84
Postseason		13	0	0	1	7.2	30	7	2	2	1	0	0	1	1	0	9	0	0	0	0	-	0	0-0	2	2.83	2.35
9 ML YEARS		455	0	0	75	328.2	1466	347	182	167	43	13	17	13	143	28	336	15	0	26	15	.634	0	2-17	81	4.74	4.57

Kyle Lohse

Pitches: R Bats: R Pos: SP-31   LOESH   Ht: 6'2" Wt: 210 Born: 10/4/1978 Age: 36

Year	Team	Lg	G	GS	CG	GF	IP	BFP	H	R	ER	HR	SH	SF	HB	TBB	IBB	SO	WP	Bk	W	L	Pct	Sh	Sv-Op	Hld	ERC	ERA
2001	Min	AL	19	16	0	2	90.1	402	102	60	57	16	1	5	8	29	0	64	5	0	4	7	.364	0	0-0	0	5.43	5.68
2002	Min	AL	32	31	1	0	180.2	783	181	92	85	26	3	3	9	70	2	124	6	1	13	8	.619	1	0-1	0	4.55	4.23
2003	Min	AL	33	33	2	0	201.0	850	211	107	103	28	8	5	5	45	1	130	10	1	14	11	.560	1	0-0	0	4.00	4.61
2004	Min	AL	35	34	1	1	194.0	883	240	128	115	28	5	7	7	76	5	111	6	0	9	13	.409	1	0-0	0	5.89	5.34
2005	Min	AL	31	30	0	1	178.2	769	211	85	83	22	3	7	9	44	5	86	4	1	9	13	.409	0	0-0	0	4.91	4.18
2006	2 Tms		34	19	0	6	126.2	566	150	83	82	15	8	5	6	44	4	97	3	1	5	10	.333	0	0-0	0	5.21	5.83
2007	2 Tms	NL	34	32	2	0	192.2	829	207	109	99	22	14	4	12	57	3	122	3	0	9	12	.429	1	0-0	0	4.45	4.62
2008	StL	NL	33	33	0	0	200.0	839	211	88	84	18	6	4	3	49	3	119	5	0	15	6	.714	0	0-0	0	3.77	3.78
2009	StL	NL	23	22	1	0	117.2	512	125	69	62	16	3	5	3	36	2	77	3	1	6	10	.375	1	0-0	0	4.33	4.74
2010	StL	NL	18	18	0	0	92.0	431	129	75	67	9	5	4	3	35	2	54	1	0	4	8	.333	0	0-0	0	6.50	6.55
2011	StL	NL	30	30	1	0	188.1	775	178	80	71	16	8	6	3	42	1	111	1	0	14	8	.636	1	0-0	0	3.05	3.39
2012	StL	NL	33	**33**	0	0	211.0	864	192	74	67	19	11	7	4	38	1	143	1	0	16	3	**.842**	0	0-0	0	2.72	2.86
2013	Mil	NL	32	32	2	0	198.2	806	196	78	74	26	8	2	3	36	1	125	1	0	11	10	.524	1	0-0	0	3.45	3.35
2014	Mil	NL	31	31	2	0	198.1	817	183	87	78	22	9	9	8	45	0	141	1	0	13	9	.591	2	0-0	0	3.21	3.54
06	Min	AL	22	8	0	5	63.2	295	80	50	50	8	1	3	6	25	2	46	1	1	2	5	.286	0	0-0	0	6.10	7.07
06	Cin	NL	12	11	0	1	63.0	271	70	33	32	7	7	2	0	19	2	51	2	0	3	5	.375	0	0-0	0	4.36	4.57
07	Cin	NL	21	21	2	0	131.2	561	143	76	67	16	8	4	6	33	1	80	3	0	6	12	.333	1	0-0	0	4.32	4.58
07	Phi	NL	13	11	0	0	61.0	268	64	33	32	6	6	0	6	24	2	42	0	0	3	0	1.000	0	0-0	0	4.71	4.72
	Postseason		13	8	0	3	46.1	199	49	26	25	8	1	0	1	13	1	39	1	0	2	5	.286	0	0-0	0	4.46	4.86
	14 ML YEARS		418	394	12	10	2370.0	10126	2516	1215	1127	283	92	73	83	646	30	1504	52	4	142	128	.526	9	0-1	0	4.18	4.28

Steve Lombardozzi

Bats: B Throws: R Pos: 2B-20;PH-1   lahm-bar-DOZE-ee   Ht: 6'0" Wt: 200 Born: 9/20/1988 Age: 26

Year	Team	Lg	G	AB	H	2B	3B	HR	(Hm	Rd)	TB	R	RBI	RC	TBB	IBB	SO	HBP	SH	SF	SB	CS	GDP	Avg	OBP	Slg	OPS
2014	Norfolk*	AAA	78	270	73	9	1	0	(-	-)	84	26	30	27	17	2	32	0	2	6	6	4	7	.270	.307	.311	.618
2011	Was	NL	13	31	6	1	0	0	(0	0)	7	3	1	2	1	0	4	0	0	0	0	0	0	.194	.219	.226	.445
2012	Was	NL	126	384	105	16	3	3	(2	1)	136	40	27	46	19	1	46	6	6	1	5	3	1	.273	.317	.354	.671
2013	Was	NL	118	290	75	15	4	1	(1	1)	98	25	22	24	8	1	34	1	5	3	4	3	6	.259	.278	.338	.616
2014	Bal	AL	20	73	21	1	1	0	(0	0)	24	6	2	6	0	0	14	1	0	0	1	0	1	.288	.297	.329	.626
	Postseason		3	3	1	0	0	0	(0	0)	1	0	0	0	0	0	0	0	0	0	0	0	0	.333	.333	.333	.667
	4 ML YEARS		277	778	207	33	5	5	(3	2)	265	74	52	78	28	2	98	8	11	4	10	6	8	.266	.297	.341	.638

James Loney

Bats: L Throws: L Pos: 1B-152;DH-4;PH-3   Ht: 6'3" Wt: 235 Born: 5/7/1984 Age: 31

Year	Team	Lg	G	AB	H	2B	3B	HR	(Hm	Rd)	TB	R	RBI	RC	TBB	IBB	SO	HBP	SH	SF	SB	CS	GDP	Avg	OBP	Slg	OPS
2006	LAD	NL	48	102	29	6	5	4	(1	3)	57	20	18	17	8	1	10	1	0	0	0	0	8	.284	.342	.559	.901
2007	LAD	NL	96	344	114	18	4	15	(5	10)	185	41	67	71	28	5	48	1	0	2	0	1	6	.331	.381	.538	.919
2008	LAD	NL	161	595	172	35	6	13	(5	8)	258	66	90	79	45	6	85	3	1	7	7	4	25	.289	.338	.434	.772
2009	LAD	NL	158	576	162	25	3	13	(1	12)	230	73	90	84	70	10	68	0	1	4	7	3	16	.281	.357	.399	.756
2010	LAD	NL	161	588	157	41	2	10	(6	4)	232	67	88	81	52	9	95	4	0	4	10	5	14	.267	.329	.395	.723
2011	LAD	NL	158	531	153	30	1	12	(7	5)	221	56	65	71	42	7	67	1	3	5	4	0	8	.288	.339	.416	.755
2012	2 Tms		144	434	108	20	0	6	(0	6)	146	37	41	34	28	7	51	0	1	2	0	3	21	.249	.293	.336	.630
2013	TB	AL	158	549	164	33	0	13	(7	6)	236	54	75	75	44	6	77	0	1	4	3	1	16	.299	.348	.430	.778
2014	TB	AL	155	600	174	27	0	9	(4	5)	228	59	69	68	41	2	80	4	0	6	4	0	21	.290	.336	.380	.716
12	LAD	NL	114	334	85	18	0	4	(0	4)	115	32	33	28	23	7	39	0	1	1	0	3	16	.254	.302	.344	.646
12	Bos	AL	30	100	23	2	0	2	(0	2)	31	5	8	6	5	0	12	0	0	1	0	0	5	.230	.264	.310	.574
	Postseason		22	79	28	5	0	3	(1	2)	42	6	16	16	9	1	13	1	0	0	0	0	4	.354	.427	.532	.959
	9 ML YEARS		1239	4319	1233	235	20	95	(36	59)	1793	473	603	580	358	53	581	14	7	34	36	17	135	.285	.340	.415	.755

Evan Longoria

Bats: R Throws: R Pos: 3B-155;DH-8   Ht: 6'2" Wt: 210 Born: 10/7/1985 Age: 29

Year	Team	Lg	G	AB	H	2B	3B	HR	(Hm	Rd)	TB	R	RBI	RC	TBB	IBB	SO	HBP	SH	SF	SB	CS	GDP	Avg	OBP	Slg	OPS
2008	TB	AL	122	448	122	31	2	27	(18	9)	238	67	85	72	46	4	122	6	0	8	7	0	8	.272	.343	.531	.874
2009	TB	AL	157	584	164	44	0	33	(16	17)	307	100	113	102	72	11	140	8	0	7	9	0	**27**	.281	.364	.526	.889
2010	TB	AL	151	574	169	46	5	22	(10	12)	291	96	104	99	72	12	124	5	0	10	15	5	15	.294	.372	.507	.879
2011	TB	AL	133	483	118	26	1	31	(14	17)	239	78	99	91	80	6	93	6	0	5	3	2	11	.244	.355	.495	.850
2012	TB	AL	74	273	79	14	0	17	(8	9)	144	39	55	55	33	6	61	3	0	3	2	3	14	.289	.369	.527	.896
2013	TB	AL	160	614	165	39	3	32	(15	17)	306	91	88	90	70	10	162	3	0	6	1	0	16	.269	.343	.498	.842
2014	TB	AL	**162**	624	158	26	1	22	(12	10)	252	83	91	83	57	11	133	9	1	9	5	0	15	.253	.320	.404	.724
	Postseason		30	115	22	5	0	9	(4	5)	54	16	21	13	11	0	38	0	0	0	1	0	4	.191	.262	.470	.731
	7 ML YEARS		959	3600	975	226	12	184	(93	91)	1777	554	635	592	430	60	835	40	1	48	42	10	106	.271	.351	.494	.845

Javier Lopez

Pitches: L Bats: L Pos: RP-65   Ht: 6'4" Wt: 220 Born: 7/11/1977 Age: 37

Year	Team	Lg	G	GS	CG	GF	IP	BFP	H	R	ER	HR	SH	SF	HB	TBB	IBB	SO	WP	Bk	W	L	Pct	Sh	Sv-Op	Hld	ERC	ERA
2003	Col	NL	75	0	0	11	58.1	242	58	25	24	5	1	0	4	12	2	40	1	3	4	1	.800	0	1-2	15	3.44	3.70
2004	Col	NL	64	0	0	10	40.2	187	45	34	34	1	0	3	2	26	4	20	3	0	1	2	.333	0	0-1	12	5.28	7.52
2005	2 Tms	NL	32	0	0	6	16.1	87	26	20	20	2	1	0	1	11	3	12	0	0	1	1	.500	0	2-4	6	8.82	11.02
2006	Bos	AL	27	0	0	8	16.2	69	13	10	5	1	0	1	2	10	1	11	0	0	1	0	1.000	0	1-1	6	3.96	2.70
2007	Bos	AL	61	0	0	11	40.2	174	36	16	14	2	1	1	4	18	2	26	1	0	2	1	.667	0	0-2	13	3.59	3.10

Year Team	Lg	G	GS	CG	GF	IP	BFP	H	R	ER	HR	SH	SF	HB	TBB	IBB	SO	WP	Bk	W	L	Pct	Sh	Sv-Op	Hld	ERC	ERA
2008 Bos	AL	70	0	0	10	59.1	247	53	18	16	4	1	1	2	27	0	38	1	0	2	0	1.000	0	0-1	10	3.73	2.43
2009 Bos	AL	14	0	0	5	11.2	64	20	13	12	1	1	1	2	9	0	5	1	0	2	0	.000	0	0-0	0	11.00	9.26
2010 2 Tms	NL	77	0	0	18	57.2	235	50	17	15	2	1	2	2	20	3	38	3	0	4	2	.667	0	0-0	11	2.85	2.34
2011 SF	NL	70	0	0	17	53.0	222	42	16	16	0	3	0	3	26	6	40	1	0	5	2	.714	0	1-3	20	2.69	2.72
2012 SF	NL	70	0	0	19	36.0	153	37	13	10	1	1	1	0	14	3	28	2	0	3	0	1.000	0	7-9	18	3.60	2.50
2013 SF	NL	69	0	0	14	39.1	161	30	10	8	1	4	1	0	12	5	37	1	0	4	2	.667	0	1-1	15	1.82	1.83
2014 SF	NL	65	0	0	14	37.2	167	31	14	13	2	3	2	2	19	6	22	1	0	1	1	.500	0	0-2	12	3.00	3.11
05 Col	NL	3	0	0	1	2.0	13	7	5	5	0	0	0	0	0	0	1	0	0	0	0	-	0	0-1	0	18.39	22.50
05 Ari	NL	29	0	0	5	14.1	74	19	15	15	2	1	0	1	11	3	11	0	0	1	1	.500	0	2-3	6	7.63	9.42
10 Pit	NL	50	0	0	14	38.2	166	39	14	12	2	1	2	2	18	3	22	3	0	2	2	.500	0	0-0	6	4.24	2.79
10 SF	NL	27	0	0	4	19.0	69	11	3	3	0	0	0	0	2	0	16	0	0	2	0	1.000	0	0-0	5	0.90	1.42
Postseason		22	0	0	2	13.2	57	12	6	6	0	1	1	0	5	1	11	1	0	1	1	.500	0	0-0	7	2.51	3.95
12 ML YEARS		694	0	0	143	467.1	2008	441	206	187	22	18	10	25	204	35	317	15	3	28	14	.667	0	13-26	138	3.65	3.60

Rafael Lopez

Bats: L Throws: R Pos: C-4;PH-4   Ht: 5'9" Wt: 190 Born: 10/2/1987 Age: 27

Year Team	Lg	G	AB	H	2B	3B	HR	(Hm Rd)	TB	R	RBI	RC	TBB	IBB	SO	HBP	SH	SF	SB	CS	GDP	Avg	OBP	Slg	OPS
2011 Cubs	R	3	11	4	1	0	0	(- -)	5	1	2	2	1	0	1	0	0	0	0	0	0	.364	.417	.455	.871
2011 Boise	A-	54	196	62	8	0	6	(- -)	88	34	37	34	21	1	27	2	0	4	1	2	7	.316	.381	.449	.830
2012 Peoria	A	31	117	31	7	1	0	(- -)	40	14	12	16	17	0	13	0	1	3	1	0	4	.265	.350	.342	.692
2012 Cubs	R	4	15	7	2	1	0	(- -)	11	5	4	4	1	0	4	1	0	0	0	0	1	.467	.529	.733	1.263
2012 Dytona	A+	35	119	32	10	0	2	(- -)	48	18	12	17	13	0	14	0	0	1	1	0	2	.269	.338	.403	.742
2013 Tenn	AA	95	316	78	22	0	8	(- -)	124	44	43	46	49	4	67	1	1	0	0	1	9	.247	.350	.392	.742
2014 Tenn	AA	45	148	44	13	0	4	(- -)	69	21	24	29	29	5	26	0	0	0	1	1	2	.297	.412	.466	.879
2014 Iowa	AAA	61	207	59	4	1	1	(- -)	68	17	27	29	28	1	52	3	1	0	0	0	9	.285	.378	.329	.707
2014 ChC	NL	7	11	2	0	0	0	(0 0)	2	0	1	1	2	0	4	0	0	1	0	0	0	.182	.286	.182	.468

Wilton Lopez

Pitches: R Bats: R Pos: RP-4   Ht: 6'0" Wt: 200 Born: 7/19/1983 Age: 31

Year Team	Lg	G	GS	CG	GF	IP	BFP	H	R	ER	HR	SH	SF	HB	TBB	IBB	SO	WP	Bk	W	L	Pct	Sh	Sv-Op	Hld	ERC	ERA
2014 ColSpr*	AAA	23	1	0	3	43.1	190	58	24	22	4	2	0	1	6	0	35	3	0	1	2	.333	0	0- -		5.02	4.57
2009 Hou	NL	8	2	0	0	19.1	97	32	21	18	4	3	2	1	8	0	9	1	0	0	2	.000	0	0-1	0	9.39	8.38
2010 Hou	NL	68	0	0	14	67.0	262	66	23	22	4	2	2	0	5	1	50	2	2	5	2	.714	0	1-3	14	2.56	2.96
2011 Hou	NL	73	0	0	13	71.0	298	72	26	22	6	4	0	3	18	3	56	1	1	2	6	.250	0	0-6	14	3.60	2.79
2012 Hou	NL	64	0	0	28	66.1	260	61	18	16	4	4	2	2	8	2	54	1	0	6	3	.667	0	10-13	9	2.49	2.17
2013 Col	NL	75	0	0	28	75.1	321	88	35	34	6	1	1	1	18	4	48	0	3	3	4	.429	0	0-5	8	4.27	4.06
2014 Col	NL	4	0	0	1	6.1	36	18	8	8	3	0	1	0	0	0	4	0	0	0	0	-	0	0-0	0	18.93	11.37
6 ML YEARS		292	2	0	84	305.1	1274	337	131	120	27	14	8	7	57	10	221	5	6	16	17	.485	0	11-28	45	3.82	3.54

David Lough

Bats: L Throws: L Pos: LF-85;PR-19;CF-16;RF-6;PH-4   LOW   Ht: 5'11" Wt: 180 Born: 1/20/1986 Age: 29

Year Team	Lg	G	AB	H	2B	3B	HR	(Hm Rd)	TB	R	RBI	RC	TBB	IBB	SO	HBP	SH	SF	SB	CS	GDP	Avg	OBP	Slg	OPS
2012 KC	AL	20	59	14	2	1	0	(0 0)	18	9	2	5	4	0	9	1	0	1	1	0	2	.237	.292	.305	.597
2013 KC	AL	96	315	90	17	4	5	(1 4)	130	35	33	38	10	0	52	3	4	3	5	2	3	.286	.311	.413	.724
2014 Bal	AL	112	174	43	6	3	4	(3 1)	67	31	16	19	15	0	33	1	6	1	8	5	3	.247	.309	.385	.694
3 ML YEARS		228	548	147	25	8	9	(4 5)	215	75	51	62	29	0	94	5	10	5	14	7	8	.268	.308	.392	.701

Aaron Loup

Pitches: L Bats: L Pos: RP-71   LOOP   Ht: 5'11" Wt: 205 Born: 12/19/1987 Age: 27

Year Team	Lg	G	GS	CG	GF	IP	BFP	H	R	ER	HR	SH	SF	HB	TBB	IBB	SO	WP	Bk	W	L	Pct	Sh	Sv-Op	Hld	ERC	ERA
2012 Tor	AL	33	0	0	3	30.2	117	26	10	9	0	2	1	0	2	0	21	1	1	0	2	.000	0	0-1	6	1.59	2.64
2013 Tor	AL	64	0	0	12	69.1	282	66	23	19	5	2	4	7	13	4	53	2	0	4	6	.400	0	2-3	8	3.20	2.47
2014 Tor	AL	71	0	0	15	68.2	283	50	25	24	4	3	3	6	30	5	56	5	0	4	4	.500	0	4-8	13	2.75	3.15
3 ML YEARS		168	0	0	30	168.2	682	142	58	52	9	7	8	13	45	9	130	8	1	8	12	.400	0	6-12	27	2.70	2.77

Mark Lowe

Pitches: R Bats: L Pos: RP-7   Ht: 6'3" Wt: 210 Born: 6/7/1983 Age: 32

Year Team	Lg	G	GS	CG	GF	IP	BFP	H	R	ER	HR	SH	SF	HB	TBB	IBB	SO	WP	Bk	W	L	Pct	Sh	Sv-Op	Hld	ERC	ERA
2014 Clmbs*	AAA	41	0	0	29	41.2	183	46	28	26	4	0	1	1	17	2	47	5	0	4	3	.571	0	17- -		4.74	5.62
2006 Sea	AL	15	0	0	3	18.2	75	12	4	4	1	1	0	2	9	1	20	1	0	1	0	1.000	0	0-0	6	2.61	1.93
2007 Sea	AL	4	0	0	1	2.2	13	2	2	2	1	0	0	0	3	0	3	0	0	0	0	-	0	0-0	2	7.69	6.75
2008 Sea	AL	57	0	0	19	63.2	303	78	44	38	6	3	3	4	34	0	55	2	0	1	5	.167	0	1-5	15	6.10	5.37
2009 Sea	AL	75	0	0	18	80.0	339	71	39	29	7	0	4	0	29	1	69	4	0	2	7	.222	0	3-13	26	3.16	3.26
2010 2 Tms	AL	14	0	0	5	13.1	61	18	9	8	2	0	1	0	6	1	12	1	0	1	3	.250	0	0-0	4	6.82	5.40
2011 Tex	AL	52	0	0	10	45.0	196	46	26	19	6	1	1	0	19	4	42	3	0	2	3	.400	0	1-3	11	4.38	3.80
2012 Tex	AL	36	0	0	12	39.1	162	35	15	15	5	0	3	0	13	0	28	4	2	0	2	.000	0	0-0	3	3.41	3.43
2013 LAA	AL	11	0	0	2	11.2	56	11	12	12	1	2	0	0	11	1	7	2	0	1	0	1.000	0	0-0	1	5.60	9.26
2014 Cle	AL	7	0	0	1	7.0	39	10	7	3	2	1	0	1	6	4	6	1	0	0	1	.000	0	0-0	0	8.50	3.86

			HOW MUCH HE PITCHED								WHAT HE GAVE UP											THE RESULTS							
Year	Team	Lg	G	GS	CG	GF	IP	BFP	H	R	ER	HR	SH	SF	HB	TBB	IBB	SO	WP	Bk	W	L	Pct	Sh	Sv-Op	Hld	ERC	ERA
10	Sea	AL	11	0	0	4	10.1	45	11	5	4	1	0	1	0	5	1	7	1	0	1	3	.250	0	0-0	4	4.70	3.48
10	Tex	AL	3	0	0	1	3.0	16	7	4	4	1	0	0	0	1	0	5	0	0	0	0	-	0	0-0	0	15.67	12.00
	Postseason		4	0	0	1	1.2	13	7	7	7	1	0	0	0	1	0	1	0	0	0	1	.000	0	0-0	0	35.40	37.80
	9 ML YEARS		271	0	0	71	281.1	1244	283	158	130	31	7	13	6	130	12	242	18	2	8	21	.276	0	5-21	52	4.41	4.16

Jed Lowrie

Bats: B Throws: R Pos: SS-130;DH-4;PH-4   LAU-ree   Ht: 6'0" Wt: 190 Born: 4/17/1984 Age: 31

			BATTING																	RUNNING			AVERAGES			
Year	Team	Lg	G	AB	H	2B	3B	HR	(Hm	Rd)	TB	R	RBI	RC	TBB	IBB	SO	HBP	SH	SF	SB	CS	GDP	Avg	OBP	Slg	OPS
2014	Scrmto*	AAA	2	9	2	0	0	0	(-	-)	2	1	0	0	0	0	1	0	0	0	0	0	0	.222	.222	.222	.444
2008	Bos	AL	81	260	67	25	3	2	(0	2)	104	34	46	35	35	0	68	1	2	8	1	0	8	.258	.339	.400	.739
2009	Bos	AL	32	68	10	2	0	2	(1	1)	18	5	11	5	6	0	20	0	0	2	0	0	0	.147	.211	.265	.475
2010	Bos	AL	55	171	49	14	0	9	(3	6)	90	31	24	32	25	0	25	1	0	0	1	1	2	.287	.381	.526	.907
2011	Bos	AL	88	309	78	14	4	6	(3	3)	118	40	36	33	23	2	60	2	1	6	1	1	6	.252	.303	.382	.685
2012	Hou	NL	97	340	83	18	0	16	(9	7)	149	43	42	45	43	0	65	2	0	3	2	0	3	.244	.331	.438	.769
2013	Oak	AL	154	603	175	45	2	15	(7	8)	269	80	75	88	50	3	91	2	3	4	1	0	17	.290	.344	.446	.791
2014	Oak	AL	136	502	125	29	3	6	(4	2)	178	59	50	52	51	5	79	5	2	6	0	0	14	.249	.321	.355	.676
	Postseason		17	51	9	2	0	1	(0	1)	14	6	5	4	7	0	15	1	0	1	0	0	1	.176	.283	.275	.558
	7 ML YEARS		643	2253	587	147	12	56	(27	29)	926	292	284	290	233	10	408	13	8	28	6	2	50	.261	.330	.411	.741

Ed Lucas

Bats: R Throws: R Pos: 2B-20;SS-19;PH-18;1B-6;3B-4;LF-4;RF-3;PR-3   Ht: 6'3" Wt: 215 Born: 5/21/1982 Age: 33

			BATTING																	RUNNING			AVERAGES			
Year	Team	Lg	G	AB	H	2B	3B	HR	(Hm	Rd)	TB	R	RBI	RC	TBB	IBB	SO	HBP	SH	SF	SB	CS	GDP	Avg	OBP	Slg	OPS
2010	Omha	AAA	99	352	108	20	1	13	(-	-)	169	52	50	70	52	3	68	3	5	3	7	1	8	.307	.398	.480	.878
2011	Gwnntt	AAA	81	262	57	14	1	3	(-	-)	82	25	29	26	28	2	74	1	2	2	4	0	4	.218	.294	.313	.606
2011	Missi	AA	42	159	43	6	0	7	(-	-)	70	32	26	25	15	1	38	4	1	2	0	0	2	.270	.344	.440	.785
2012	Salt Lk	AAA	118	412	108	20	2	12	(-	-)	168	61	52	54	28	0	82	6	4	3	5	4	12	.262	.316	.408	.724
2013	NewOr	AAA	46	181	55	12	0	5	(-	-)	82	26	14	29	12	0	37	2	1	0	2	1	2	.304	.354	.453	.807
2014	Jupiter	A+	3	14	6	0	0	0	(-	-)	6	3	2	3	2	0	2	0	0	0	0	0	0	.429	.500	.429	.929
2014	NewOr	AAA	14	46	12	1	0	0	(-	-)	13	5	3	5	7	1	10	1	0	3	0	0	1	.261	.351	.283	.633
2013	Mia	NL	94	351	90	14	1	4	(1	3)	118	43	28	34	26	1	78	2	4	1	1	1	6	.256	.311	.336	.647
2014	Mia	NL	69	179	45	5	0	1	(0	1)	53	19	9	10	8	0	48	0	2	0	1	0	4	.251	.283	.296	.580
	2 ML YEARS		163	530	135	19	1	5	(1	4)	171	62	37	44	34	1	126	2	6	1	2	1	10	.255	.302	.323	.624

Jonathan Lucroy

Bats: R Throws: R Pos: C-136;1B-19;PH-3;DH-1   LOO-croy   Ht: 6'0" Wt: 195 Born: 6/13/1986 Age: 29

			BATTING																	RUNNING			AVERAGES			
Year	Team	Lg	G	AB	H	2B	3B	HR	(Hm	Rd)	TB	R	RBI	RC	TBB	IBB	SO	HBP	SH	SF	SB	CS	GDP	Avg	OBP	Slg	OPS
2010	Mil	NL	75	277	70	9	0	4	(4	0)	91	24	26	23	18	1	44	1	0	1	4	2	9	.253	.300	.329	.628
2011	Mil	NL	136	430	114	16	1	12	(8	4)	168	45	59	50	29	0	99	2	4	3	2	1	7	.265	.313	.391	.703
2012	Mil	NL	96	316	101	17	4	12	(7	5)	162	46	58	61	22	1	44	4	1	3	4	1	12	.320	.368	.513	.881
2013	Mil	NL	147	521	146	25	6	18	(9	9)	237	59	82	78	46	2	69	5	0	8	9	1	16	.280	.340	.455	.795
2014	Mil	NL	153	585	176	53	2	13	(6	7)	272	73	69	90	66	3	71	2	0	2	4	4	13	.301	.373	.465	.837
	Postseason		10	32	8	1	0	1	(1	0)	12	3	5	4	0	0	8	0	0	0	0	0	0	.250	.250	.375	.625
	5 ML YEARS		607	2129	607	120	13	59	(34	25)	930	247	294	302	181	7	327	14	5	17	23	9	57	.285	.343	.437	.779

Ryan Ludwick

Bats: R Throws: L Pos: LF-92;PH-16;DH-5   Ht: 6'2" Wt: 215 Born: 7/13/1978 Age: 36

			BATTING																	RUNNING			AVERAGES			
Year	Team	Lg	G	AB	H	2B	3B	HR	(Hm	Rd)	TB	R	RBI	RC	TBB	IBB	SO	HBP	SH	SF	SB	CS	GDP	Avg	OBP	Slg	OPS
2002	Tex	AL	23	81	19	6	0	1	(1	0)	28	10	9	6	7	0	24	0	0	0	2	1	4	.235	.295	.346	.641
2003	2 Tms	AL	47	162	40	8	1	7	(2	5)	71	17	26	28	12	1	48	0	1	0	2	0	1	.247	.299	.438	.737
2004	Cle	AL	15	50	11	2	0	2	(0	2)	19	3	4	4	2	0	14	2	0	0	0	0	0	.220	.278	.380	.658
2005	Cle	AL	19	41	9	0	0	4	(3	1)	21	8	5	3	7	0	13	0	0	0	0	1	1	.220	.333	.512	.846
2007	StL	NL	120	303	81	22	0	14	(7	7)	145	42	52	45	20	1	72	7	3	0	4	4	1	.267	.339	.479	.818
2008	StL	NL	152	538	161	40	3	37	(18	19)	318	104	113	100	62	3	146	8	1	8	4	4	9	.299	.375	.591	.966
2009	StL	NL	139	486	129	20	1	22	(4	18)	217	63	97	82	41	3	106	7	1	4	4	2	6	.265	.329	.447	.775
2010	2 Tms	NL	136	490	123	27	2	17	(8	9)	205	63	69	76	48	0	121	8	0	5	0	4	13	.251	.325	.418	.743
2011	2 Tms	NL	139	490	116	23	0	13	(6	7)	178	56	75	59	51	4	124	4	2	6	1	1	9	.237	.310	.363	.674
2012	Cin	NL	125	422	116	28	1	26	(16	10)	224	53	80	70	42	3	97	5	1	2	0	1	9	.275	.346	.531	.877
2013	Cin	NL	38	129	31	5	0	2	(1	1)	42	7	12	8	10	0	29	0	0	1	0	0	7	.240	.293	.326	.618
2014	Cin	NL	112	357	87	20	0	9	(4	5)	134	28	45	44	31	1	94	4	1	4	0	2	6	.244	.308	.375	.683
03	Tex	AL	8	26	4	1	0	0	(0	0)	5	3	0	1	4	0	9	0	0	0	0	0	0	.154	.267	.192	.459
03	Cle	AL	39	136	36	7	1	7	(2	5)	66	14	26	27	8	1	39	0	1	0	2	0	1	.265	.306	.485	.791
10	StL	NL	77	281	79	20	2	11	(4	7)	136	44	43	55	24	0	64	4	0	3	0	3	4	.281	.344	.484	.827
10	SD	NL	59	209	44	7	0	6	(4	2)	69	19	26	21	24	0	57	4	0	2	0	1	9	.211	.301	.330	.631
11	SD	NL	101	378	90	18	0	11	(5	6)	141	42	64	44	32	1	87	4	1	5	1	1	8	.238	.301	.373	.674
11	Pit	NL	38	112	26	5	0	2	(1	1)	37	14	11	15	19	3	37	0	1	1	0	0	1	.232	.341	.330	.671
	Postseason		9	34	13	2	0	3	(2	1)	24	5	5	4	5	1	5	0	0	0	0	0	2	.382	.462	.706	1.167
	12 ML YEARS		1065	3549	923	201	8	154	(71	83)	1602	454	587	525	339	16	888	45	10	30	17	20	66	.260	.330	.451	.781

Josh Lueke

Pitches: R Bats: R Pos: RP-25 | LOO-kee | Ht: 6'5" Wt: 245 Born: 12/5/1984 Age: 30

Year Team	Lg	G	GS	CG	GF	IP	BFP	H	R	ER	HR	SH	SF	HB	TBB	IBB	SO	WP	Bk	W	L	Pct	Sh	Sv-Op	Hld	ERC	ERA
2014 Drham*	AAA	32	0	0	22	37.1	154	32	17	14	3	2	1		9	0	40	1	0	0	1	.000	0	12--	-	2.64	3.38
2011 Sea	AL	25	0	0	8	32.2	142	34	22	22	2	2	1	0	13	1	29	5	0	1	1	.500	0	0-0	2	3.96	6.06
2012 TB	AL	3	0	0	2	3.1	21	9	7	7	0	0	2	0	3	0	2	0	0	0	0	-	0	0-0	0	17.54	18.90
2013 TB	AL	19	0	0	6	21.1	99	23	12	12	3	1	2	1	12	1	25	3	0	0	2	.000	0	0-0	2	5.54	5.06
2014 TB	AL	25	0	0	13	30.1	135	38	20	19	7	0	2	1	5	1	19	0	0	1	2	.333	0	0-0	0	5.47	5.64
4 ML YEARS		72	0	0	29	87.2	397	104	61	60	12	3	7	2	33	3	75	8	0	2	5	.286	0	0-0	4	5.31	6.16

Lucas Luetge

Pitches: L Bats: L Pos: RP-12 | LOOT-key | Ht: 6'4" Wt: 205 Born: 3/24/1987 Age: 28

Year Team	Lg	G	GS	CG	GF	IP	BFP	H	R	ER	HR	SH	SF	HB	TBB	IBB	SO	WP	Bk	W	L	Pct	Sh	Sv-Op	Hld	ERC	ERA
2014 Tacom*	AAA	42	0	0	12	62.1	270	58	24	23	6	5	1	4	27	2	70	7	0	3	2	.600	0	3--	-	3.99	3.32
2012 Sea	AL	63	0	0	16	40.2	178	37	20	18	3	1	3	1	24	6	58	5	0	2	2	.500	0	2-3	12	4.01	3.98
2013 Sea	AL	35	0	0	15	37.0	165	42	22	20	2	2	3	2	16	2	27	4	0	1	3	.250	0	0-0	1	4.81	4.86
2014 Sea	AL	12	0	0	4	9.0	38	6	5	5	3	0	0	0	5	0	7	1	0	0	0	-	0	0-0	0	4.31	5.00
3 ML YEARS		110	0	0	35	86.2	381	85	47	43	8	3	6	3	45	8	72	10	0	3	5	.375	0	2-3	13	4.40	4.47

Donald Lutz

Bats: L Throws: R Pos: PH-16;1B-6;LF-4;RF-2;DH-1 | Ht: 6'3" Wt: 250 Born: 2/6/1989 Age: 26

Year Team	Lg	G	AB	H	2B	3B	HR	(Hm	Rd)	TB	R	RBI	RC	TBB	IBB	SO	HBP	SH	SF	SB	CS	GDP	Avg	OBP	Slg	OPS
2010 Billings	R+	55	203	58	10	4	7	(-	-)	97	36	28	36	21	1	45	4	0	5	6	2	4	.286	.356	.478	.834
2011 Dayton	A	123	465	140	23	3	20	(-	-)	229	85	75	81	34	4	125	7	0	0	5	4	8	.301	.358	.492	.850
2012 Bkrsfld	A+	63	253	67	18	3	17	(-	-)	142	42	51	46	19	5	71	4	0	1	7	2	4	.265	.325	.561	.886
2012 Reds	R	4	14	9	2	2	0	(-	-)	15	3	5	7	3	0	4	0	0	0	0	0	0	.643	.706	1.071	1.777
2012 Pnscla	AA	40	149	36	5	1	5	(-	-)	58	17	15	18	13	0	32	3	0	0	1	3	2	.242	.315	.389	.704
2013 Pnscla	AA	65	229	56	12	4	7	(-	-)	97	35	30	32	19	4	56	6	0	1	4	1	4	.245	.318	.424	.741
2014 Pnscla	AA	23	89	32	7	2	6	(-	-)	61	16	16	23	7	1	17	1	0	0	1	0	1	.360	.412	.685	1.098
2014 Lsvlle	AAA	52	195	46	9	2	6	(-	-)	77	26	33	25	17	1	68	4	0	2	4	0	3	.236	.307	.395	.702
2013 Cin	NL	34	58	14	1	0	1	(1	0)	18	5	8	5	1	0	14	0	0	0	2	0	0	.241	.254	.310	.565
2014 Cin	NL	28	51	9	4	0	0	(0	0)	13	2	1	2	3	1	19	0	0	0	0	0	0	.176	.222	.255	.477
2 ML YEARS		62	109	23	5	0	1	(1	0)	31	7	9	7	4	1	33	0	0	0	2	0	0	.211	.239	.284	.523

Jordan Lyles

Pitches: R Bats: R Pos: SP-22 | Ht: 6'4" Wt: 215 Born: 10/19/1990 Age: 24

Year Team	Lg	G	GS	CG	GF	IP	BFP	H	R	ER	HR	SH	SF	HB	TBB	IBB	SO	WP	Bk	W	L	Pct	Sh	Sv-Op	Hld	ERC	ERA
2014 Mdest*	A+	1	1	0	0	3.2	16	3	0	0	0	0	0	0	2	0	4	0	0	0	0	-	0	0--	-	2.87	0.00
2014 ColSpr*	AAA	1	0	0	1	4.2	17	3	0	0	0	0	0	0	2	0	4	0	0	0	1	1.000	0	0--	-	1.98	0.00
2011 Hou	NL	20	15	0	2	94.0	415	107	61	56	14	7	1	5	26	1	67	0	0	2	8	.200	0	0-0	0	4.87	5.36
2012 Hou	NL	25	25	0	0	141.1	628	159	97	80	20	6	4	5	42	4	99	2	0	5	12	.294	1	0-0	0	4.67	5.09
2013 Hou	AL	27	25	0	1	141.2	642	165	98	88	17	0	3	11	49	1	93	5	2	7	9	.438	0	1-1	1	5.20	5.59
2014 Col	NL	22	22	0	0	126.2	546	127	64	61	12	4	3	8	46	1	90	6	0	7	4	.636	0	0-0	0	4.17	4.33
4 ML YEARS		94	87	1	3	503.2	2231	558	320	285	63	17	11	29	163	7	349	13	2	21	33	.389	1	1-1	1	4.73	5.09

Lance Lynn

Pitches: R Bats: R Pos: SP-33 | Ht: 6'5" Wt: 240 Born: 5/12/1987 Age: 28

Year Team	Lg	G	GS	CG	GF	IP	BFP	H	R	ER	HR	SH	SF	HB	TBB	IBB	SO	WP	Bk	W	L	Pct	Sh	Sv-Op	Hld	ERC	ERA
2011 StL	NL	18	2	0	2	34.2	136	25	12	12	3	1	0	1	11	1	40	1	0	1	1	.500	0	1-2	3	2.37	3.12
2012 StL	NL	35	29	0	2	176.0	744	168	76	74	16	4	3	10	64	3	180	3	0	18	7	.720	0	0-0	1	3.87	3.78
2013 StL	NL	33	33	0	0	201.2	856	189	92	89	14	11	8	11	76	0	198	6	0	15	10	.600	0	0-0	0	3.67	3.97
2014 StL	NL	33	33	2	0	203.2	866	185	72	62	13	6	4	7	72	1	181	7	0	15	10	.600	1	0-0	0	3.24	2.74
Postseason		21	5	0	3	39.1	177	42	25	21	6	2	3	1	22	4	37	0	0	5	4	.556	0	0-0	3	5.51	4.81
4 ML YEARS		119	97	2	4	616.0	2602	567	252	237	46	22	15	29	223	5	599	17	0	49	28	.636	1	1-2	4	3.51	3.46

Tyler Lyons

Pitches: L Bats: B Pos: RP-7; SP-4 | Ht: 6'4" Wt: 200 Born: 2/21/1988 Age: 27

Year Team	Lg	G	GS	CG	GF	IP	BFP	H	R	ER	HR	SH	SF	HB	TBB	IBB	SO	WP	Bk	W	L	Pct	Sh	Sv-Op	Hld	ERC	ERA
2011 PlmBh	A+	33	12	1	4	94.0	402	93	51	47	8	3	1	4	29	2	79	4	1	9	4	.692	1	1--	-	3.66	4.50
2012 Sprgfld	AA	12	12	0	0	64.1	274	70	33	28	6	2	3	2	19	0	54	2	0	5	4	.556	0	0--	-	4.22	3.92
2012 Memp	AAA	15	15	3	0	88.1	366	87	42	42	9	4	5	2	18	0	89	0	0	4	9	.308	0	0--	-	3.32	4.28
2013 Memp	AAA	17	16	0	0	100.1	399	85	40	37	6	4	1	6	19	0	86	0	0	7	2	.778	0	0--	-	2.50	3.32
2014 Memp	AAA	14	14	2	0	81.1	346	94	44	40	9	4	3	0	18	1	75	6	1	8	2	.800	1	0--	-	4.33	4.43
2014 Sprgfld	AA	1	1	0	0	2.0	9	3	1	1	0	0	0	0	0	0	3	0	0	0	0	-	0	0--	-	4.47	4.50
2013 StL	NL	12	8	0	0	53.0	223	49	29	28	5	1	0	3	16	0	43	0	0	2	4	.333	0	0-0	0	3.46	4.75
2014 StL	NL	11	4	0	1	36.2	155	33	23	18	4	1	1	2	11	2	36	0	0	0	4	.000	0	0-0	0	3.29	4.42
2 ML YEARS		23	12	0	2	89.2	378	82	52	46	9	2	1	5	27	2	79	0	0	2	8	.200	0	0-0	0	3.39	4.62

Manny Machado

Bats: R Throws: R Pos: 3B-82   muh-CHAH-doe   Ht: 6'2" Wt: 180 Born: 7/6/1992 Age: 22

Year	Team	Lg	G	AB	H	2B	3B	HR	(Hm	Rd)	TB	R	RBI	RC	TBB	IBB	SO	HBP	SH	SF	SB	CS	GDP	Avg	OBP	Slg	OPS
2014	Frdrck*	A+	3	12	8	4	1	0	(-	-)	14	5	2	6	1	0	1	0	0	0	1	0	0	.667	.692	1.167	1.859
2012	Bal	AL	51	191	50	8	3	7	(7	0)	85	24	26	29	9	0	38	0	1	1	2	0	6	.262	.294	.445	.739
2013	Bal	AL	156	667	189	51	3	14	(5	9)	288	88	71	87	29	0	113	2	9	3	6	7	15	.283	.314	.432	.746
2014	Bal	AL	82	327	91	14	0	12	(9	3)	141	38	32	44	20	2	68	3	2	2	2	0	13	.278	.324	.431	.755
	Postseason		6	19	3	1	0	1	(0	1)	7	2	2	1	2	0	6	0	2	0	0	0	1	.158	.238	.368	.607
	3 ML YEARS		289	1185	330	73	6	33	(21	12)	514	150	129	160	58	2	219	5	12	6	10	7	34	.278	.313	.434	.747

Jean Machi

Pitches: R Bats: R Pos: RP-71   GENE ma-CHEE   Ht: 6'0" Wt: 255 Born: 2/1/1982 Age: 33

Year	Team	Lg	G	GS	CG	GF	IP	BFP	H	R	ER	HR	SH	SF	HB	TBB	IBB	SO	WP	Bk	W	L	Pct	Sh	Sv-Op	Hld	ERC	ERA
2012	SF	NL	8	0	0	5	6.2	28	7	5	5	2	0	0	0	1	0	4	0	0	0	0	-	0	0-0	0	4.56	6.75
2013	SF	NL	51	0	0	9	53.0	211	46	15	14	2	1	1	0	12	3	51	2	0	3	1	.750	0	0-2	11	2.30	2.38
2014	SF	NL	71	0	0	13	66.1	249	45	19	19	5	5	1	1	18	3	51	5	1	7	1	.875	0	2-5	17	1.93	2.58
	3 ML YEARS		130	0	0	27	126.0	488	98	39	38	9	6	2	1	31	6	106	7	1	10	2	.833	0	2-7	28	2.22	2.71

Paul Maholm

Pitches: L Bats: L Pos: RP-22; SP-8   mah-HALL-uhm   Ht: 6'2" Wt: 245 Born: 6/25/1982 Age: 33

Year	Team	Lg	G	GS	CG	GF	IP	BFP	H	R	ER	HR	SH	SF	HB	TBB	IBB	SO	WP	Bk	W	L	Pct	Sh	Sv-Op	Hld	ERC	ERA
2005	Pit	NL	6	6	0	0	41.1	168	31	10	10	2	0	0	3	17	0	26	0	0	3	1	.750	0	0-0	0	2.79	2.18
2006	Pit	NL	30	30	0	0	176.0	788	202	98	93	19	7	4	12	81	6	117	3	1	8	10	.444	0	0-0	0	5.58	4.76
2007	Pit	NL	29	29	2	0	177.2	765	204	110	99	22	13	6	6	49	3	105	5	0	10	15	.400	1	0-0	0	4.77	5.02
2008	Pit	NL	31	31	1	0	206.1	853	201	89	85	21	8	8	9	63	2	139	2	1	9	9	.500	1	0-0	0	3.84	3.71
2009	Pit	NL	31	31	0	0	194.2	836	221	102	96	14	7	1	6	60	4	119	11	1	8	9	.471	0	0-0	0	4.45	4.44
2010	Pit	NL	32	32	1	0	185.1	840	228	119	104	15	10	6	9	62	2	102	2	0	9	15	.375	1	0-0	0	5.14	5.10
2011	Pit	NL	26	26	1	0	162.1	687	160	72	66	11	8	10	8	50	6	97	3	0	6	14	.300	1	0-0	0	3.57	3.66
2012	2 Tms	NL	32	31	1	0	189.0	786	178	80	77	20	7	4	11	53	3	140	5	0	13	11	.542	1	0-0	0	3.57	3.67
2013	Atl	NL	26	26	0	0	153.0	670	169	82	75	17	8	2	10	47	3	105	3	0	10	11	.476	0	0-0	0	4.61	4.41
2014	LAD	NL	30	8	0	7	70.2	311	82	44	38	8	3	1	9	28	3	34	2	1	1	5	.167	0	0-0	0	5.31	4.84
12	ChC	NL	21	20	0	0	120.1	503	115	51	50	12	5	4	10	34	2	81	4	0	9	6	.600	0	0-0	0	3.73	3.74
12	Atl	NL	11	11	1	0	68.2	283	63	29	27	8	2	0	1	19	1	59	1	0	4	5	.444	1	0-0	0	3.31	3.54
	10 ML YEARS		273	250	6	7	1556.1	6704	1676	806	744	149	71	42	77	510	32	984	36	4	77	100	.435	4	0-0	0	4.41	4.30

Martin Maldonado

Bats: R Throws: R Pos: C-42;PH-9;1B-2   mar-TEEN   Ht: 6'0" Wt: 230 Born: 8/16/1986 Age: 28

Year	Team	Lg	G	AB	H	2B	3B	HR	(Hm	Rd)	TB	R	RBI	RC	TBB	IBB	SO	HBP	SH	SF	SB	CS	GDP	Avg	OBP	Slg	OPS
2011	Mil	NL	3	1	0	0	0	0	(0	0)	0	0	0	0	0	0	1	0	0	0	0	0	0	.000	.000	.000	.000
2012	Mil	NL	78	233	62	9	0	8	(6	2)	95	22	30	28	17	0	56	2	4	0	1	1	5	.266	.321	.408	.729
2013	Mil	NL	67	183	31	7	1	4	(1	3)	52	13	22	14	13	1	53	3	3	0	0	0	4	.169	.236	.284	.520
2014	Mil	NL	52	111	26	5	0	4	(2	2)	43	14	16	14	11	1	32	3	1	0	0	0	4	.234	.320	.387	.707
	4 ML YEARS		200	528	119	21	1	16	(9	7)	190	49	68	56	41	2	142	8	8	0	1	1	11	.225	.291	.360	.651

Seth Maness

Pitches: R Bats: R Pos: RP-73   MAY-ness   Ht: 6'0" Wt: 190 Born: 10/14/1988 Age: 26

Year	Team	Lg	G	GS	CG	GF	IP	BFP	H	R	ER	HR	SH	SF	HB	TBB	IBB	SO	WP	Bk	W	L	Pct	Sh	Sv-Op	Hld	ERC	ERA
2011	Batvia	A-	10	7	0	0	39.2	151	27	11	4	0	0	1	1	3	0	31	0	0	0	1	.000	0	0- -	-	1.13	0.91
2011	PlmBh	A+	3	0	0	0	8.1	35	7	4	4	0	0	0	1	2	0	8	0	0	1	0	1.000	0	0- -	-	2.37	4.32
2011	QuadC	A	2	0	0	0	5.0	18	4	1	1	0	0	0	0	0	0	3	0	0	1	0	1.000	0	0- -	-	1.34	1.80
2012	PlmBh	A+	7	7	0	0	46.0	177	45	13	11	5	0	0	1	1	0	29	0	0	3	1	.750	0	0- -	-	2.65	2.15
2012	Sprgfld	AA	20	20	1	0	123.2	503	122	50	45	13	3	2	6	9	0	83	2	0	11	3	.786	0	0- -	-	2.94	3.27
2013	Memp	AAA	4	4	0	0	25.0	109	34	12	12	2	1	2	1	3	0	18	0	0	2	2	.500	0	0- -	-	5.10	4.32
2013	StL	NL	66	0	0	4	62.0	249	65	17	16	4	4	0	1	13	7	35	2	0	5	2	.714	0	1-3	15	3.41	2.32
2014	StL	NL	73	0	0	17	80.1	317	77	29	26	7	5	4	2	11	3	55	2	1	6	4	.600	0	3-3	11	2.90	2.91
	Postseason		9	0	0	0	5.0	20	6	2	1	1	0	1	0	0	0	3	0	0	0	0	0-1	1	4.38	1.80
	2 ML YEARS		139	0	0	21	142.1	566	142	46	42	11	9	4	3	24	10	90	4	1	11	6	.647	0	4-6	26	3.12	2.66

Jeff Manship

Pitches: R Bats: R Pos: RP-20   Ht: 6'2" Wt: 210 Born: 1/16/1985 Age: 30

Year	Team	Lg	G	GS	CG	GF	IP	BFP	H	R	ER	HR	SH	SF	HB	TBB	IBB	SO	WP	Bk	W	L	Pct	Sh	Sv-Op	Hld	ERC	ERA
2014	Phillies*	R	2	2	0	0	3.0	11	1	0	0	0	0	0	0	1	0	2	0	0	0	0	-	0	0- -	-	0.69	0.00
2014	LV*	AAA	8	5	1	1	25.1	119	29	14	13	1	1	0	0	18	0	21	1	0	0	1	.000	0	0- -	-	5.74	4.62
2009	Min	AL	11	5	0	1	31.2	146	39	21	20	4	1	3	1	15	0	21	2	0	1	1	.500	0	0-0	0	6.11	5.68
2010	Min	AL	13	1	0	1	29.0	124	34	20	17	3	1	1	0	6	0	21	0	0	2	1	.667	0	0-0	0	4.31	5.28
2011	Min	AL	5	0	0	1	3.1	19	5	3	3	0	0	2	0	4	1	2	0	0	0	0	-	0	0-0	0	8.73	8.10
2012	Min	AL	12	0	0	2	21.2	98	29	19	19	4	1	0	1	7	1	12	0	0	0	0	-	0	0-0	0	6.67	7.89
2013	Col	NL	11	4	0	3	30.2	139	37	25	24	0	4	0	0	12	1	18	0	0	0	5	.000	0	0-0	0	5.87	7.04
2014	Phi	NL	20	0	0	7	23.0	105	24	17	17	1	3	0	0	14	5	16	0	0	1	2	.333	0	0-0	0	4.30	6.65
	6 ML YEARS		72	10	0	15	139.1	631	168	105	100	18	6	9	2	58	8	90	2	0	4	9	.308	0	0-0	1	5.53	6.46

208

Shaun Marcum

Pitches: R **Bats:** R **Pos:** P — **Ht:** 6'0" **Wt:** 195 **Born:** 12/14/1981 **Age:** 33

			HOW MUCH HE PITCHED			WHAT HE GAVE UP													THE RESULTS							
Year Team	Lg	G	GS	CG	GF	IP	BFP	H	R	ER	HR	SH	SF	HB	TBB	IBB	SO	WP	Bk	W	L	Pct	Sh	Sv-Op	Hld	ERC	ERA
2014 Indns*	R	1	1	0	0	2.0	7	1	0	0	0	0	0	0	1	0	3	0	0	0	0	-	0	0--	-	1.62	0.00
2014 Clmbs*	AAA	8	1	0	1	15.1	60	10	5	4	1	0	1	1	6	0	10	1	0	1	0	1.000	0	0--	-	2.36	2.35
2005 Tor	AL	5	0	0	3	8.0	32	6	0	0	0	0	0	0	4	0	4	0	0	0	0	-	0	0-0	0	2.58	0.00
2006 Tor	AL	21	14	0	3	78.1	357	87	44	44	14	1	2	4	38	3	65	1	0	3	4	.429	0	0-0	0	5.80	5.06
2007 Tor	AL	38	25	0	6	159.0	660	149	76	73	27	3	3	5	49	1	122	1	0	12	6	.667	0	1-2	1	4.00	4.13
2008 Tor	AL	25	25	0	0	151.1	630	126	60	57	21	1	3	8	50	2	123	3	0	9	7	.563	0	0-0	0	3.32	3.39
2010 Tor	AL	31	31	1	0	195.1	800	181	84	79	24	1	3	6	43	3	165	3	0	13	8	.619	0	0-0	0	3.24	3.64
2011 Mil	NL	33	33	0	0	200.2	823	175	84	79	22	6	6	0	57	3	158	6	0	13	7	.650	0	0-0	0	2.97	3.54
2012 Mil	NL	21	21	0	0	124.0	527	116	57	51	16	6	2	4	41	2	109	3	2	7	4	.636	0	0-0	0	3.71	3.70
2013 NYM	NL	14	12	0	2	78.1	334	85	48	46	7	6	4	4	21	2	60	2	0	1	10	.091	0	0-0	0	4.17	5.29
Postseason		3	3	0	0	9.2	49	17	16	16	3	1	0	0	5	1	5	0	0	0	3	.000	0	0-0	0	11.38	14.90
8 ML YEARS		188	161	1	14	995.0	4163	925	453	429	131	24	23	31	303	16	806	19	2	58	46	.558	0	1-2	1	3.63	3.88

Michael Mariot

Pitches: R **Bats:** R **Pos:** RP-17 — MARE-ee-utt — **Ht:** 6'0" **Wt:** 190 **Born:** 10/20/1988 **Age:** 26

			HOW MUCH HE PITCHED			WHAT HE GAVE UP													THE RESULTS							
Year Team	Lg	G	GS	CG	GF	IP	BFP	H	R	ER	HR	SH	SF	HB	TBB	IBB	SO	WP	Bk	W	L	Pct	Sh	Sv-Op	Hld	ERC	ERA
2010 Idaho	R+	15	7	0	4	56.0	232	50	29	22	4	1	1	3	16	0	64	5	0	2	2	.500	0	0--	-	3.09	3.54
2011 Wilmg	A+	28	9	0	14	100.1	426	99	47	38	7	2	2	2	21	0	80	9	0	8	4	.667	0	5--	-	3.05	3.41
2012 NWArk	AA	31	14	0	4	113.2	470	111	48	43	12	3	2	4	30	2	81	7	0	6	3	.667	0	1--	-	3.62	3.40
2012 Omha	AAA	2	0	0	1	8.0	31	6	2	2	0	0	0	0	3	0	3	0	0	0	0	-	0	0--	-	2.18	2.25
2013 Omha	AAA	47	1	0	34	60.2	261	59	31	24	4	1	4	2	25	2	66	7	0	4	5	.444	0	11--	-	3.82	3.56
2014 Omha	AAA	14	0	0	6	20.0	87	19	11	11	2	0	0	0	7	0	25	2	0	2	1	.667	0	2--	-	3.48	4.95
2014 KC	AL	17	0	0	8	25.0	118	31	21	18	2	0	2	0	12	1	21	5	1	1	0	1.000	0	0-0	0	5.43	6.48

Jake Marisnick

Bats: R **Throws:** R **Pos:** RF-31;CF-30;LF-2;PH-2;PR-1 — mah-RIZ-nick — **Ht:** 6'4" **Wt:** 225 **Born:** 3/30/1991 **Age:** 24

				BATTING																	RUNNING			AVERAGES			
Year Team	Lg	G	AB	H	2B	3B	HR	(Hm	Rd)	TB	R	RBI	RC	TBB	IBB	SO	HBP	SH	SF		SB	CS	GDP	Avg	OBP	Slg	OPS
2010 B Jays	R	35	122	35	12	0	3	(-	-)	56	17	14	24	13	0	18	5	0	2		14	1	2	.287	.373	.459	.832
2010 Lnsng	A	34	127	28	8	2	1	(-	-)	43	16	12	14	9	0	37	5	2	0		9	2	3	.220	.298	.339	.636
2011 Lnsng	A	118	462	148	27	6	14	(-	-)	229	68	77	95	43	4	91	14	0	4		37	8	9	.320	.392	.496	.888
2012 Dnedin	A+	65	266	70	18	7	6	(-	-)	120	41	35	44	26	0	55	10	2	2		10	5	1	.263	.349	.451	.800
2012 NHam	AA	55	223	52	11	3	2	(-	-)	75	25	15	23	11	0	45	7	2	4		14	4	6	.233	.286	.336	.622
2013 Jupiter	A+	3	15	3	1	0	0	(-	-)	4	2	0	0	0	0	1	0	0	0		0	0	0	.200	.200	.267	.467
2013 Jaxnvl	AA	67	265	78	13	3	12	(-	-)	133	43	46	48	17	0	68	11	2	3		11	6	4	.294	.358	.502	.860
2014 NewOr	AAA	89	343	95	16	4	10	(-	-)	149	50	40	52	17	1	64	9	6	2		24	6	6	.277	.326	.434	.761
2013 Mia	NL	40	109	20	2	1	1	(1	0)	27	6	5	7	6	0	27	1	1	1		3	1	1	.183	.231	.248	.478
2014 2 Tms		65	221	55	8	0	3	(3	0)	72	21	19	19	8	3	67	3	2	3		11	3	2	.249	.281	.326	.607
14 Mia	NL	14	48	8	0	0	0	(0	0)	8	3	0	1	3	1	19	0	0	0		5	0	0	.167	.216	.167	.382
14 Hou	AL	51	173	47	8	0	3	(3	0)	64	18	19	18	5	2	48	3	2	3		6	3	2	.272	.299	.370	.669
2 ML YEARS		105	330	75	10	1	4	(4	0)	99	27	24	26	14	3	94	4	3	4		14	4	3	.227	.264	.300	.564

Nick Markakis

Bats: L **Throws:** L **Pos:** RF-147;DH-6;1B-2 — mar-KAY-kiss — **Ht:** 6'1" **Wt:** 190 **Born:** 11/17/1983 **Age:** 31

				BATTING																	RUNNING			AVERAGES			
Year Team	Lg	G	AB	H	2B	3B	HR	(Hm	Rd)	TB	R	RBI	RC	TBB	IBB	SO	HBP	SH	SF		SB	CS	GDP	Avg	OBP	Slg	OPS
2006 Bal	AL	147	491	143	25	2	16	(9	7)	220	72	62	67	43	3	72	3	3	2		2	0	15	.291	.351	.448	.799
2007 Bal	AL	161	637	191	43	3	23	(15	8)	309	97	112	103	61	5	112	5	1	6		18	6	22	.300	.362	.485	.848
2008 Bal	AL	157	595	182	48	1	20	(11	9)	292	106	87	113	99	7	113	2	0	1		10	7	10	.306	.406	.491	.897
2009 Bal	AL	161	642	188	45	2	18	(8	10)	291	94	101	97	56	0	98	3	0	10		6	2	12	.293	.347	.453	.801
2010 Bal	AL	160	629	187	45	3	12	(8	4)	274	79	60	99	73	9	93	2	0	5		7	3	18	.297	.370	.436	.805
2011 Bal	AL	160	641	182	31	1	15	(8	7)	260	72	73	70	62	6	75	7	0	6		12	3	16	.284	.351	.406	.756
2012 Bal	AL	104	420	125	28	3	13	(9	4)	198	59	54	77	42	3	51	4	0	5		1	1	11	.298	.363	.471	.834
2013 Bal	AL	160	634	172	24	0	10	(6	4)	226	89	59	66	55	3	76	3	0	8		1	2	17	.271	.329	.356	.685
2014 Bal	AL	155	642	177	27	1	14	(8	6)	248	81	50	82	64	4	84	4	0	2		4	2	10	.276	.342	.386	.729
9 ML YEARS		1365	5331	1547	316	16	141	(82	59)	2318	749	658	786	553	40	774	33	4	45		61	25	131	.290	.358	.435	.793

Justin Marks

Pitches: L **Bats:** L **Pos:** RP-1 — **Ht:** 6'3" **Wt:** 205 **Born:** 1/12/1988 **Age:** 27

			HOW MUCH HE PITCHED			WHAT HE GAVE UP													THE RESULTS							
Year Team	Lg	G	GS	CG	GF	IP	BFP	H	R	ER	HR	SH	SF	HB	TBB	IBB	SO	WP	Bk	W	L	Pct	Sh	Sv-Op	Hld	ERC	ERA
2010 Kane	A	20	20	0	0	109.2	473	109	66	60	11	3	2	9	41	0	119	7	0	3	12	.200	0	0--	-	4.31	4.92
2010 Stcktn	A+	5	4	0	0	19.2	84	17	13	10	4	3	1	1	8	0	17	3	0	3	1	.750	0	0--	-	4.23	4.58
2011 Wilmg	A	28	22	2	2	144.2	612	144	66	64	14	6	3	3	49	0	140	5	0	8	8	.500	0	0--	-	3.91	3.98
2012 NWArk	AA	17	17	0	0	85.1	362	79	39	36	8	0	6	2	38	0	73	4	2	3	5	.375	0	0--	-	3.95	3.80
2012 Royals	R	2	1	0	0	5.0	23	4	1	1	0	0	0	0	3	0	8	0	0	0	0	-	0	0--	-	2.41	1.80
2012 Omha	AAA	1	1	0	0	1.2	15	7	9	9	0	0	0	0	3	0	8	0	0	0	0	-	-			33.64	48.60
2013 NWArk	AA	2	2	0	0	11.1	47	7	3	2	1	0	0	0	5	0	12	0	0	2	0	1.000	0	0--	-	2.09	1.59
2013 Omha	AAA	24	20	0	3	129.2	576	138	68	66	7	2	3	4	61	0	117	4	0	6	13	.316	0	0--	-	4.52	4.58
2014 Omha	AAA	13	2	0	0	30.1	147	38	25	19	4	2	0	1	20	1	27	1	0	3	2	.600	0	0--	-	5.92	5.64
2014 Scrmto	AAA	4	0	0	2	3.2	12	0	0	0	0	0	0	0	1	0	2	0	0	0	0	-	0	0--	-	0.09	0.00
2014 RdRck	AAA	5	0	0	2	5.1	26	6	3	3	0	0	1	0	4	1	8	1	0	1	0	1.000	0	0--	-	4.88	5.06
2014 KC	AL	1	0	0	0	2.0	13	4	3	3	0	0	0	0	2	0	0	0	0	0	0	-	0	0-0	0	14.34	13.50

Carlos Marmol

Pitches: R **Bats:** R **Pos:** RP-15 · mar-MOLE · **Ht:** 6'1" **Wt:** 235 **Born:** 10/14/1982 **Age:** 32

Year Team	Lg	G	GS	CG	GF	IP	BFP	H	R	ER	HR	SH	SF	HB	TBB	IBB	SO	WP	Bk	W	L	Pct	Sh	Sv-Op	Hld	ERC	ERA
2014 Lsvlle*	AAA	3	0	0	2	3.2	19	2	3	3	1	0	1	0	6	1	6	2	0	0	1	.000	0	0--	0	7.17	7.36
2006 ChC	NL	19	13	0	1	77.0	356	71	54	52	14	6	2	5	59	2	59	3	1	5	7	.417	0	0-0	0	6.01	6.08
2007 ChC	NL	59	0	0	6	69.1	285	41	11	11	3	1	2	4	35	3	96	5	1	5	1	.833	0	1-2	16	2.11	1.43
2008 ChC	NL	82	0	0	22	87.1	348	40	30	26	10	2	3	6	41	3	114	6	1	2	4	.333	0	7-9	30	1.86	2.68
2009 ChC	NL	79	0	0	29	74.0	335	43	29	28	2	4	1	12	65	3	93	6	1	2	4	.333	0	15-19	27	3.55	3.41
2010 ChC	NL	77	0	0	70	77.2	332	40	23	22	1	0	0	8	52	4	138	2	2	2	3	.400	0	38-43	0	2.18	2.55
2011 ChC	NL	75	0	0	61	74.0	327	54	33	33	5	4	2	9	48	2	99	4	0	2	6	.250	0	34-44	2	3.71	4.01
2012 ChC	NL	61	0	0	47	55.1	247	40	24	21	4	0	0	2	45	0	72	2	0	3	3	.500	0	20-23	2	4.07	3.42
2013 2 Tms	NL	52	0	0	17	49.0	225	40	26	24	7	1	2	4	40	3	59	5	1	2	4	.333	0	2-5	6	5.25	4.41
2014 Mia	NL	15	0	0	6	13.1	66	16	12	12	3	0	0	1	10	2	14	2	0	0	3	.000	0	0-1	1	7.79	8.10
13 ChC	NL	31	0	0	9	27.2	129	26	19	18	6	1	1	3	21	1	32	2	0	2	4	.333	0	2-5	5	6.57	5.86
13 LAD	NL	21	0	0	8	21.1	96	14	7	6	1	0	1	1	19	2	27	3	1	0	0	-	0	0-0	1	3.65	2.53
Postseason		6	0	0	2	9.1	39	7	5	5	2	1	0	0	4	0	14	0	0	1	0	1.000	0	0-0	0	3.50	4.82
9 ML YEARS		519	13	0	259	577.0	2521	385	242	229	49	18	12	51	395	22	744	35	7	23	35	.397	0	117-146	84	3.49	3.57

Nick Maronde

Pitches: L **Bats:** B **Pos:** RP-11 · ma-RON-day · **Ht:** 6'3" **Wt:** 205 **Born:** 9/5/1989 **Age:** 25

Year Team	Lg	G	GS	CG	GF	IP	BFP	H	R	ER	HR	SH	SF	HB	TBB	IBB	SO	WP	Bk	W	L	Pct	Sh	Sv-Op	Hld	ERC	ERA
2014 Salt Lk*	AAA	9	0	0	1	8.2	51	11	9	9	0	0	1	0	15	0	12	2	0	0	0	-	0	0--	-	10.39	9.35
2014 Ark*	AA	7	0	0	2	7.1	42	6	11	11	4	0	0	0	15	0	10	0	0	0	0	-	0	1--	-	14.70	13.50
2014 Angels*	R	2	0	0	0	2.0	9	2	1	1	0	0	0	0	4	0	2	1	0	0	0	-	0	0--	-	3.92	4.50
2014 MhVlly*	A-	3	3	0	0	9.0	32	4	1	1	0	0	0	1	1	0	8	0	0	0	0	-	0	0--	-	0.79	1.00
2014 Akron*	AA	2	2	0	0	8.0	43	19	12	11	2	0	2	0	2	0	9	0	0	0	2	.000	0	0--	-	14.40	12.38
2014 Clmbs*	AA	1	1	0	0	6.0	21	2	0	0	0	0	0	0	1	0	8	0	0	0	0	-	0	0--	-	0.45	0.00
2012 LAA	AL	12	0	0	1	6.0	27	6	1	1	0	0	1	0	3	0	7	0	0	0	0	-	0	0-0	3	3.63	1.50
2013 LAA	AL	10	0	0	2	5.1	28	4	6	4	1	0	0	0	8	1	5	1	0	0	0	-	0	0-0	2	7.27	6.75
2014 LAA	AL	11	0	0	3	6.1	38	12	9	9	0	0	2	1	7	0	7	1	0	0	0	-	0	0-0	1	12.82	12.79
3 ML YEARS		33	0	0	6	17.2	93	22	16	14	1	0	3	1	18	1	19	2	0	0	0	-	0	0-0	6	7.77	7.13

Evan Marshall

Pitches: R **Bats:** R **Pos:** RP-57 · **Ht:** 6'2" **Wt:** 220 **Born:** 4/18/1990 **Age:** 25

Year Team	Lg	G	GS	CG	GF	IP	BFP	H	R	ER	HR	SH	SF	HB	TBB	IBB	SO	WP	Bk	W	L	Pct	Sh	Sv-Op	Hld	ERC	ERA
2011 Yakima	A-	11	0	0	5	12.0	49	10	4	1	0	0	0	0	2	0	13	4	0	0	0	-	0	2--	-	1.70	0.75
2011 Visalia	A+	15	0	0	13	17.0	72	14	6	3	2	0	1	0	5	1	18	1	0	0	1	.000	0	4--	-	2.62	1.59
2011 Mobile	AA	1	0	0	0	2.0	7	2	0	0	0	0	0	0	0	0	0	0	0	0	0	-	0	0--	-	2.31	0.00
2012 Mobile	AA	42	0	0	35	48.2	215	55	24	19	2	2	1	2	16	4	27	2	0	6	3	.667	0	16--	-	4.10	3.51
2013 Reno	AAA	54	0	0	27	58.0	273	75	32	28	2	2	3	5	30	2	59	8	0	3	6	.333	0	3--	-	6.14	4.34
2014 Reno	AAA	14	0	0	5	16.2	62	10	1	1	0	0	0	0	5	0	19	0	0	0	1	.000	0	1--	-	1.37	0.54
2014 Ari	NL	57	0	0	11	49.1	210	50	17	15	3	2	1	2	17	3	54	3	0	4	4	.500	0	0-1	19	3.76	2.74

Sean Marshall

Pitches: L **Bats:** L **Pos:** RP-15 · **Ht:** 6'7" **Wt:** 225 **Born:** 8/30/1982 **Age:** 32

Year Team	Lg	G	GS	CG	GF	IP	BFP	H	R	ER	HR	SH	SF	HB	TBB	IBB	SO	WP	Bk	W	L	Pct	Sh	Sv-Op	Hld	ERC	ERA
2014 Lsvlle*	AAA	2	2	0	0	2.0	9	2	1	1	1	0	0	0	1	0	2	0	0	0	0	-	0	0--	-	7.30	4.50
2006 ChC	NL	24	24	0	0	125.2	563	132	85	78	20	7	1	7	59	3	77	6	0	6	9	.400	0	0-0	0	5.27	5.59
2007 ChC	NL	21	19	0	0	103.1	446	107	52	45	13	7	2	1	35	3	67	4	0	7	8	.467	0	0-0	0	4.18	3.92
2008 ChC	NL	34	7	0	6	65.1	279	60	28	28	9	4	3	4	23	4	58	3	0	3	5	.375	0	1-2	3	3.82	3.86
2009 ChC	NL	55	9	1	10	85.1	373	91	43	41	10	7	1	1	32	4	68	2	0	3	7	.300	0	0-0	7	4.43	4.32
2010 ChC	NL	80	0	0	16	74.2	307	58	25	22	3	2	2	2	25	5	90	1	0	7	5	.583	0	1-3	22	2.26	2.65
2011 ChC	NL	78	0	0	18	75.2	307	66	21	19	1	6	2	0	17	4	79	0	1	6	6	.500	0	5-9	34	2.22	2.26
2012 Cin	NL	73	0	0	22	61.0	256	55	18	17	3	0	0	3	16	2	74	1	1	5	5	.500	0	9-13	22	2.78	2.51
2013 Cin	NL	10	0	0	3	10.1	37	4	3	2	0	0	0	1	2	0	10	2	0	0	1	.000	0	0-0	7	0.76	1.74
2014 Cin	NL	15	0	0	4	14.0	80	23	14	12	1	1	0	2	12	0	14	1	0	0	0	-	0	0-0	1	10.14	7.71
Postseason		6	0	0	0	7.1	28	3	2	2	1	0	0	2	3	1	8	0	0	0	0	-	0	0-0	1	1.36	2.45
9 ML YEARS		396	59	1	79	615.1	2648	596	289	264	60	34	9	23	221	25	537	20	2	37	46	.446	0	16-27	96	3.78	3.86

Alfredo Marte

Bats: R **Throws:** R **Pos:** LF-20;PH-18;RF-7;DH-1 · marr-TAY · **Ht:** 5'11" **Wt:** 195 **Born:** 3/31/1989 **Age:** 26

Year Team	Lg	G	AB	H	2B	3B	HR	(Hm Rd)	TB	R	RBI	RC	TBB	IBB	SO	HBP	SH	SF	SB	CS	GDP	Avg	OBP	Slg	OPS
2010 Visalia	A+	130	516	134	26	3	9	(- -)	193	76	61	63	34	1	107	8	4	3	9	5	14	.260	.314	.374	.688
2011 Mobile	AA	17	43	10	1	0	1	(- -)	14	4	6	4	4	0	10	1	0	1	1	0	0	.233	.306	.326	.632
2011 Visalia	A+	59	234	70	15	3	7	(- -)	112	35	33	39	14	0	43	2	0	5	0	7	.299	.344	.479	.823
2012 Mobile	AA	113	398	117	25	3	20	(- -)	208	68	75	75	34	1	72	11	0	3	6	6	12	.294	.363	.523	.886
2013 Reno	AAA	86	311	87	24	1	7	(- -)	134	37	48	46	22	1	63	6	0	4	2	1	10	.280	.335	.431	.766
2014 Reno	AAA	78	270	86	15	3	11	(- -)	140	46	45	59	39	0	60	4	0	4	6	0	3	.319	.407	.519	.925
2013 Ari	NL	22	43	8	3	0	0	(0 0)	11	4	4	4	4	0	12	1	0	0	0	0	0	.186	.271	.256	.527
2014 Ari	NL	44	106	18	5	1	2	(1 1)	31	8	9	7	6	0	34	1	1	0	1	0	2	.170	.221	.292	.514
2 ML YEARS		66	149	26	8	1	2	(1 1)	42	12	13	11	10	0	46	2	1	0	1	0	2	.174	.236	.282	.518

Andy Marte

Bats: R Throws: R Pos: 3B-4;PH-3   MAR-tay   Ht: 6'1" Wt: 205 Born: 10/21/1983 Age: 31

Year	Team	Lg	G	AB	H	2B	3B	HR	(Hm	Rd)	TB	R	RBI	RC	TBB	IBB	SO	HBP	SH	SF	SB	CS	GDP	Avg	OBP	Slg	OPS
2014	Reno*	AAA	126	471	155	32	3	19	(-	-)	250	81	80	97	48	6	62	1	0	6	1	0	19	.329	.388	.531	.919
2005	Atl	NL	24	57	8	2	1	0	(0	0)	12	3	4	1	7	0	13	0	0	2	0	1	2	.140	.227	.211	.438
2006	Cle	AL	50	164	37	15	1	5	(3	2)	69	20	23	21	13	0	38	1	0	0	0	0	3	.226	.287	.421	.707
2007	Cle	AL	20	57	11	4	0	1	(0	1)	18	3	8	4	2	0	9	1	0	0	0	0	0	.193	.233	.316	.549
2008	Cle	AL	80	235	52	11	1	3	(2	1)	74	21	17	17	14	0	52	1	7	0	1	2	5	.221	.268	.315	.583
2009	Cle	AL	47	155	36	6	1	6	(2	4)	62	20	25	20	14	1	30	1	1	4	0	0	5	.232	.293	.400	.693
2010	Cle	AL	81	170	39	7	2	5	(1	4)	65	18	19	19	17	0	35	0	0	1	0	3	2	.229	.298	.382	.680
2014	Ari	NL	6	16	3	0	0	1	(1	0)	6	1	3	1	0	0	3	0	0	0	0	0	0	.188	.188	.375	.563
	7 ML YEARS		308	854	186	45	6	21	(9	12)	306	86	99	83	67	1	180	4	8	7	1	6	17	.218	.276	.358	.634

Starling Marte

Bats: R Throws: R Pos: LF-114;CF-28;PH-7;PR-1   marr-TAY   Ht: 6'1" Wt: 185 Born: 10/9/1988 Age: 26

Year	Team	Lg	G	AB	H	2B	3B	HR	(Hm	Rd)	TB	R	RBI	RC	TBB	IBB	SO	HBP	SH	SF	SB	CS	GDP	Avg	OBP	Slg	OPS
2014	Indy*	AAA	3	12	1	1	0	0	(-	-)	2	0	0	0	0	0	5	0	0	0	0	0	1	.083	.083	.167	.250
2012	Pit	NL	47	167	43	3	6	5	(3	2)	73	18	17	21	8	0	50	3	2	2	12	5	5	.257	.300	.437	.737
2013	Pit	NL	135	510	143	26	10	12	(5	7)	225	83	35	74	25	2	138	24	6	1	41	15	6	.280	.343	.441	.784
2014	Pit	NL	135	495	144	29	6	13	(5	8)	224	73	56	70	33	0	131	17	0	0	30	11	5	.291	.356	.453	.808
	Postseason		6	24	3	1	0	1	(0	1)	7	2	1	1	1	0	5	1	0	0	1	0	1	.125	.192	.292	.484
	3 ML YEARS		317	1172	330	58	22	30	(13	17)	522	174	108	165	66	2	319	44	8	3	83	31	16	.282	.342	.445	.788

Chris Martin

Pitches: R Bats: R Pos: RP-16   Ht: 6'8" Wt: 215 Born: 6/2/1986 Age: 29

Year	Team	Lg	G	GS	CG	GF	IP	BFP	H	R	ER	HR	SH	SF	HB	TBB	IBB	SO	WP	Bk	W	L	Pct	Sh	Sv-Op	Hld	ERC	ERA
2011	Grnvlle	A	7	1	0	1	29.0	109	16	7	7	1	2	0	3	6	0	28	0	0	4	0	1.000	0	0--	-	1.35	2.17
2011	Salem	A+	13	0	0	9	39.1	151	29	4	4	0	3	1	3	6	0	24	0	0	2	1	.667	0	4--	-	1.62	0.92
2011	Portlnd	AA	3	0	0	1	5.2	29	12	10	10	2	1	0	0	1	0	3	0	0	0	1	.000	0	0--	-	12.86	15.88
2012	Portlnd	AA	23	12	0	3	76.1	328	83	42	38	4	0	2	6	18	0	65	2	0	3	6	.333	0	0--	-	3.90	4.48
2013	Portlnd	AA	12	0	0	10	21.0	74	9	0	0	0	0	0	0	6	0	27	0	0	2	0	1.000	0	3--	-	0.87	0.00
2013	Pwtckt	AAA	30	0	0	16	51.0	212	51	19	18	3	3	0	4	10	2	47	0	0	3	3	.500	0	2--	-	3.28	3.18
2014	ColSpr	AAA	25	0	0	16	26.2	121	33	15	13	2	3	0	2	9	1	36	0	0	1	3	.250	0	5--	-	5.25	4.39
2014	Col	NL	16	0	0	1	15.2	69	22	12	12	2	0	0	0	4	0	14	1	2	0	0	-	0	0-0	3	6.30	6.89

Ethan Martin

Pitches: R Bats: R Pos: RP-2   Ht: 6'2" Wt: 220 Born: 6/6/1989 Age: 26

Year	Team	Lg	G	GS	CG	GF	IP	BFP	H	R	ER	HR	SH	SF	HB	TBB	IBB	SO	WP	Bk	W	L	Pct	Sh	Sv-Op	Hld	ERC	ERA
2010	InldEm	A+	25	22	1	0	113.1	528	120	84	80	10	3	7	7	81	0	105	14	1	9	14	.391	1	0--	-	5.94	6.35
2011	RCuca	A+	16	9	0	1	55.0	267	65	48	45	8	1	1	5	37	0	61	5	1	4	4	.500	0	0--	-	7.03	7.36
2011	Chatt	AA	21	3	0	7	40.1	176	31	21	18	3	1	2	0	29	0	43	5	1	5	3	.625	0	2--	-	3.87	4.02
2012	Chatt	AA	20	20	0	0	118.0	489	89	48	47	5	4	5	3	61	1	112	7	2	8	6	.571	0	0--	-	2.95	3.58
2012	Rdng	AA	7	7	0	0	39.2	164	29	15	14	3	3	2	0	18	0	35	4	0	5	0	1.000	0	0--	-	2.68	3.18
2013	LV	AAA	21	21	1	0	115.2	494	94	56	53	11	5	4	8	67	4	107	9	2	11	5	.688	0	0--	-	4.01	4.12
2014	Clrwtr	A+	3	0	0	0	2.2	14	3	0	0	0	0	0	0	3	0	1	0	0	0	0	-	0	0--	-	6.72	0.00
2014	LV	AAA	29	0	0	5	47.2	206	46	23	22	2	2	2	1	21	1	45	4	0	2	1	.667	0	0--	-	3.68	4.15
2013	Phi	NL	15	8	0	2	40.0	190	42	27	27	9	1	1	1	26	2	47	1	1	2	5	.286	0	0-1	0	6.21	6.08
2014	Phi	NL	2	0	0	1	4.0	17	1	2	2	1	0	0	0	3	0	4	0	0	0	0	-	0	0-0	0	2.21	4.50
	2 ML YEARS		17	8	0	3	44.0	207	43	29	29	10	1	1	1	29	2	51	1	1	2	5	.286	0	0-1	0	5.80	5.93

Leonys Martin

Bats: L Throws: R Pos: CF-152;PH-9;DH-1   lay-OH-niece mar-TEEN   Ht: 6'2" Wt: 190 Born: 3/6/1988 Age: 27

Year	Team	Lg	G	AB	H	2B	3B	HR	(Hm	Rd)	TB	R	RBI	RC	TBB	IBB	SO	HBP	SH	SF	SB	CS	GDP	Avg	OBP	Slg	OPS
2011	Tex	AL	8	8	3	1	0	0	(0	0)	4	2	0	1	0	0	1	0	0	0	0	0	0	.375	.375	.500	.875
2012	Tex	AL	24	46	8	5	2	0	(0	0)	17	6	4	4	4	0	12	0	1	3	0	0	2	.174	.235	.370	.605
2013	Tex	AL	147	457	119	21	6	8	(3	5)	176	66	49	58	28	0	104	8	12	3	36	9	6	.260	.313	.385	.698
2014	Tex	AL	155	533	146	13	7	7	(4	3)	194	68	40	64	39	3	114	2	7	2	31	12	4	.274	.325	.364	.689
	4 ML YEARS		334	1044	276	40	15	15	(7	8)	391	142	95	127	71	3	231	10	20	6	70	21	12	.264	.316	.375	.690

Russell Martin

Bats: R Throws: R Pos: C-107;PH-3;DH-1   Ht: 5'10" Wt: 215 Born: 2/15/1983 Age: 32

Year	Team	Lg	G	AB	H	2B	3B	HR	(Hm	Rd)	TB	R	RBI	RC	TBB	IBB	SO	HBP	SH	SF	SB	CS	GDP	Avg	OBP	Slg	OPS
2006	LAD	NL	121	415	117	26	4	10	(8	2)	181	65	65	58	45	8	57	4	1	3	10	5	17	.282	.355	.436	.792
2007	LAD	NL	151	540	158	32	3	19	(8	11)	253	87	87	84	67	1	89	7	0	6	21	9	16	.293	.374	.469	.843
2008	LAD	NL	155	553	155	25	0	13	(6	7)	219	87	69	89	90	8	83	5	0	2	18	6	16	.280	.385	.396	.781
2009	LAD	NL	143	505	126	19	0	7	(3	4)	166	63	53	62	69	9	80	11	2	1	11	6	18	.250	.352	.329	.680
2010	LAD	NL	97	331	82	13	0	5	(2	3)	110	45	26	40	48	7	61	4	1	3	6	2	7	.248	.347	.332	.679
2011	NYY	AL	125	417	99	17	0	18	(8	10)	170	57	65	56	50	1	81	5	1	3	8	2	19	.237	.324	.408	.732
2012	NYY	AL	133	422	89	18	0	21	(13	8)	170	50	53	50	53	0	95	8	2	0	6	1	13	.211	.311	.403	.713

Year Team	Lg	G	AB	H	2B	3B	HR	(Hm	Rd)	TB	R	RBI	RC	TBB	IBB	SO	HBP	SH	SF	SB	CS	GDP	Avg	OBP	Slg	OPS
2013 Pit	NL	127	438	99	21	0	15	(6	9)	165	51	55	47	58	2	108	8	1	1	9	5	13	.226	.327	.377	.703
2014 Pit	NL	111	379	110	20	0	11	(3	8)	163	45	67	66	59	5	78	15	2	5	4	4	16	.290	.402	.430	.832
Postseason		39	132	28	6	0	4	(2	2)	46	17	16	12	17	0	30	6	0	2	1	0	3	.212	.325	.348	.673
9 ML YEARS		1163	4000	1035	191	7	119	(57	62)	1597	550	540	552	539	41	732	67	10	24	93	40	135	.259	.354	.399	.754

Carlos Martinez

Pitches: R Bats: R Pos: RP-50; SP-7   Ht: 6'0" Wt: 185 Born: 9/21/1991 Age: 23

		HOW MUCH HE PITCHED						WHAT HE GAVE UP												THE RESULTS							
Year Team	Lg	G	GS	CG	GF	IP	BFP	H	R	ER	HR	SH	SF	HB	TBB	IBB	SO	WP	Bk	W	L	Pct	Sh	Sv-Op	Hld	ERC	ERA
2011 QuadC	A	8	8	0	0	38.2	156	27	10	10	1	0	0	4	14	0	50	3	0	3	2	.600	0	0- -	-	2.31	2.33
2011 PlmBh	A+	10	10	0	0	46.0	220	49	31	27	2	1	1	6	30	0	48	7	0	3	3	.500	0	0- -	-	5.47	5.28
2012 PlmBh	A+	7	7	0	0	33.0	141	29	12	11	0	1	1	6	10	0	34	1	0	2	2	.500	0	0- -	-	3.04	3.00
2012 Sprgfld	AA	15	14	0	0	71.1	295	62	27	23	6	3	2	6	22	0	58	1	2	4	3	.571	0	0- -	-	3.27	2.90
2013 Sprgfld	AA	3	3	0	0	11.2	48	11	3	3	1	0	0	1	1	0	9	0	1	1	0	1.000	0	0- -	-	2.75	2.31
2013 Memp	AAA	13	13	0	0	68.0	289	54	22	19	3	2	1	6	27	1	63	6	1	5	3	.625	0	0- -	-	2.85	2.51
2014 Memp	AAA	2	2	0	0	10.1	37	6	0	0	0	0	0	0	1	0	7	0	0	1	0	1.000	0	0- -	-	0.90	0.00
2013 StL	NL	21	1	0	5	28.1	124	31	16	16	1	1	1	3	9	1	24	0	0	2	1	.667	0	1-1	3	4.20	5.08
2014 StL	NL	57	7	0	13	89.1	386	90	41	40	4	7	1	4	36	8	84	8	1	2	4	.333	0	1-6	17	3.79	4.03
Postseason		12	0	0	1	12.2	47	7	5	5	0	0	1	1	3	1	11	1	0	0	1	.000	0	0-0	5	1.18	3.55
2 ML YEARS		78	8	0	18	117.2	510	121	57	56	5	8	2	7	45	9	108	8	1	4	5	.444	0	2-7	20	3.89	4.28

David Martinez

Pitches: R Bats: R Pos: RP-3   da-VEED   Ht: 6'2" Wt: 220 Born: 8/4/1987 Age: 27

		HOW MUCH HE PITCHED						WHAT HE GAVE UP												THE RESULTS							
Year Team	Lg	G	GS	CG	GF	IP	BFP	H	R	ER	HR	SH	SF	HB	TBB	IBB	SO	WP	Bk	W	L	Pct	Sh	Sv-Op	Hld	ERC	ERA
2010 TriCity	A-	17	0	0	0	65.2	271	72	29	22	5	2	1	0	11	0	57	3	1	5	2	.714	0	0- -	-	3.59	3.02
2011 Lxngtn	A	37	5	0	17	66.2	297	77	44	31	7	2	2	3	17	0	44	9	1	5	7	.417	0	2- -	-	4.48	4.19
2012 Lancst	A+	27	26	0	1	160.1	677	181	90	78	19	1	2	5	33	0	114	14	1	9	5	.643	0	0- -	-	4.34	4.38
2013 CpChr	AA	26	18	2	3	129.1	501	109	34	29	10	5	6	3	20	1	86	1	1	14	2	.875	0	1- -	-	2.35	2.02
2013 OKCity	AAA	3	3	0	0	11.0	59	15	12	11	1	1	1	0	11	1	10	1	0	2	2	.000	0	0- -	-	8.38	9.00
2014 OKCity	AAA	22	13	0	4	83.0	364	94	54	52	5	2	4	3	30	2	62	6	0	5	6	.455	0	0- -	-	4.53	5.64
2013 Hou	AL	4	0	0	1	11.1	52	16	11	9	1	4	3	0	3	0	6	1	1	1	0	1.000	0	0-1	0	5.82	7.15
2014 Hou	AL	3	0	0	2	7.0	28	5	4	4	1	0	0	0	2	0	6	0	0	0	0	-	0	0-0	0	2.38	5.14
2 ML YEARS		7	0	0	3	18.1	80	21	15	13	2	4	3	0	5	0	12	1	1	1	0	1.000	0	0-1	0	4.41	6.38

J.D. Martinez

Bats: R Throws: R Pos: LF-83;RF-34;PH-7;DH-5;PR-1   Ht: 6'3" Wt: 220 Born: 8/21/1987 Age: 27

		BATTING																		RUNNING			AVERAGES			
Year Team	Lg	G	AB	H	2B	3B	HR	(Hm	Rd)	TB	R	RBI	RC	TBB	IBB	SO	HBP	SH	SF	SB	CS	GDP	Avg	OBP	Slg	OPS
2014 Toledo*	AAA	17	65	20	3	1	10	(-	-)	55	16	22	19	3	0	17	3	0	0	2	0	2	.308	.366	.846	1.212
2011 Hou	NL	53	208	57	13	0	6	(3	3)	88	29	35	30	13	1	48	2	0	3	0	1	4	.274	.319	.423	.742
2012 Hou	NL	113	395	95	14	3	11	(5	6)	148	34	55	45	40	0	96	1	0	2	0	2	18	.241	.311	.375	.685
2013 Hou	AL	86	296	74	17	0	7	(4	3)	112	24	36	29	10	0	82	0	0	3	2	0	8	.250	.272	.378	.650
2014 Det	AL	123	441	139	30	3	23	(13	10)	244	57	76	75	30	5	126	3	0	6	6	3	8	.315	.358	.553	.912
4 ML YEARS		375	1340	365	74	6	47	(25	22)	592	144	202	179	93	6	352	6	0	14	8	6	38	.272	.319	.442	.761

Michael Martinez

Bats: B Throws: R Pos: PH-12;2B-6;LF-6;PR-3;CF-2;RF-1   Ht: 5'9" Wt: 175 Born: 9/16/1982 Age: 32

		BATTING																		RUNNING			AVERAGES			
Year Team	Lg	G	AB	H	2B	3B	HR	(Hm	Rd)	TB	R	RBI	RC	TBB	IBB	SO	HBP	SH	SF	SB	CS	GDP	Avg	OBP	Slg	OPS
2014 Indy*	AAA	91	315	77	6	6	1	(-	-)	98	34	32	32	29	2	46	1	8	8	7	4	8	.244	.303	.311	.614
2011 Phi	NL	88	209	41	5	2	3	(1	2)	59	25	24	20	18	0	35	0	5	2	3	0	2	.196	.258	.282	.540
2012 Phi	NL	45	115	20	3	0	2	(1	1)	29	10	7	5	5	2	21	0	2	0	0	0	4	.174	.208	.252	.461
2013 Phi	NL	29	40	7	0	0	0	(0	0)	7	5	3	3	0	0	12	0	0	0	1	0	1	.175	.175	.175	.350
2014 Pit	NL	26	39	5	1	0	0	(0	0)	6	2	2	1	4	1	13	0	1	0	0	0	0	.128	.209	.154	.363
Postseason		2	0	0	0	0	0	(0	0)	0	1	0	0	0	0	0	0	0	0	0	0	0	-	-	-	-
4 ML YEARS		188	403	73	9	2	5	(2	3)	101	42	36	29	27	3	81	0	8	2	4	0	7	.181	.231	.251	.482

Nick Martinez

Pitches: R Bats: L Pos: SP-24; RP-5   Ht: 6'1" Wt: 175 Born: 8/5/1990 Age: 24

		HOW MUCH HE PITCHED						WHAT HE GAVE UP												THE RESULTS							
Year Team	Lg	G	GS	CG	GF	IP	BFP	H	R	ER	HR	SH	SF	HB	TBB	IBB	SO	WP	Bk	W	L	Pct	Sh	Sv-Op	Hld	ERC	ERA
2011 Rngrs	R	6	4	0	0	19.2	82	21	6	4	0	1	0	0	2	0	19	2	0	2	1	.667	0	0- -	-	2.59	1.83
2011 Spkane	A-	9	7	0	0	39.0	167	37	18	11	0	1	1	2	16	0	37	2	0	1	2	.333	0	0- -	-	3.35	2.54
2012 Hkry	A	31	20	0	4	117.1	503	121	66	63	8	0	5	4	37	0	109	6	0	8	6	.571	0	1- -	-	3.83	4.83
2013 MrtlBh	A+	22	21	1	0	119.1	499	106	47	38	5	1	3	7	38	0	105	7	3	10	7	.588	0	0- -	-	3.00	2.87
2013 Frisco	AA	5	4	0	1	32.0	112	11	6	4	1	2	0	0	7	0	23	2	0	1	0	1.000	0	0- -	-	0.63	1.13
2014 Frisco	AA	2	2	0	0	9.2	44	8	2	2	0	0	0	1	7	0	9	2	0	0	0	-	0	0- -	-	3.98	1.86
2014 Tex	AL	29	24	0	3	140.1	610	150	79	71	18	1	6	3	55	1	77	7	0	5	12	.294	0	0-0	2	4.76	4.55

Victor Martinez

Bats: B **Throws:** R **Pos:** DH-115;1B-35;C-2;PH-1   **Ht:** 6'2" **Wt:** 210 **Born:** 12/23/1978 **Age:** 36

Year	Team	Lg	G	AB	H	2B	3B	HR	(Hm	Rd)	TB	R	RBI	RC	TBB	IBB	SO	HBP	SH	SF	SB	CS	GDP	Avg	OBP	Slg	OPS
2002	Cle	AL	12	32	9	1	0	1	(1	0)	13	2	5	5	3	0	2	0	0	1	0	0	1	.281	.333	.406	.740
2003	Cle	AL	49	159	46	4	0	1	(0	1)	53	15	16	17	13	0	21	1	0	1	1	1	8	.289	.345	.333	.678
2004	Cle	AL	141	520	147	38	1	23	(8	15)	256	77	108	90	60	11	69	5	0	6	0	1	16	.283	.359	.492	.851
2005	Cle	AL	147	547	167	33	0	20	(10	10)	260	73	80	90	63	9	78	5	0	7	0	1	16	.305	.378	.475	.853
2006	Cle	AL	153	572	181	37	0	16	(4	12)	266	82	93	96	71	8	78	3	0	6	0	0	27	.316	.391	.465	.856
2007	Cle	AL	147	562	169	40	0	25	(12	13)	284	78	114	108	62	12	76	10	0	11	0	0	19	.301	.374	.505	.879
2008	Cle	AL	73	266	74	17	0	2	(2	0)	97	30	35	36	24	4	32	1	0	3	0	0	12	.278	.337	.365	.701
2009	2 Tms	AL	155	588	178	33	1	23	(7	16)	282	88	108	101	75	3	74	3	0	6	1	0	17	.303	.381	.480	.861
2010	Bos	AL	127	493	149	32	1	20	(10	10)	243	64	79	74	40	5	52	0	0	5	1	0	17	.302	.351	.493	.844
2011	Det	AL	145	540	178	40	0	12	(5	7)	254	76	103	103	46	6	51	2	0	7	1	0	20	.330	.380	.470	.850
2013	Det	AL	159	605	182	36	0	14	(7	7)	260	68	83	75	54	10	62	1	0	8	0	2	23	.301	.355	.430	.785
2014	Det	AL	151	561	188	33	0	32	(15	17)	317	87	103	115	70	28	42	4	0	6	3	2	17	.335	.409	.565	.974
09	Cle	AL	99	377	107	21	1	15	(6	9)	175	56	67	64	51	3	51	2	0	5	0	0	11	.284	.368	.464	.832
09	Bos	AL	56	211	71	12	0	8	(1	7)	107	32	41	37	24	0	23	1	0	1	1	0	6	.336	.405	.507	.912
	Postseason		36	137	43	6	1	5	(4	1)	66	19	19	23	11	3	19	3	0	0	0	0	3	.314	.377	.482	.859
	12 ML YEARS		1459	5445	1668	344	3	189	(81	108)	2585	740	927	910	581	96	637	35	0	67	7	7	193	.306	.373	.475	.847

Nick Masset

Pitches: R **Bats:** R **Pos:** RP-51   MASS-et   **Ht:** 6'5" **Wt:** 235 **Born:** 5/17/1982 **Age:** 33

Year	Team	Lg	G	GS	CG	GF	IP	BFP	H	R	ER	HR	SH	SF	HB	TBB	IBB	SO	WP	Bk	W	L	Pct	Sh	Sv-Op	Hld	ERC	ERA
2014	ColSpr*	AAA	9	0	0	4	8.2	30	2	0	0	0	0	0	1	0	9	0	0	1	0	1.000	0	1--	-	0.22	0.00
2006	Tex	AL	8	0	0	7	8.2	36	9	4	4	0	0	2	2	2	0	4	0	0	0	0	-	0	0-0		4.05	4.15
2007	CWS	AL	27	1	0	4	39.1	193	52	33	31	2	1	3	2	26	5	21	4	0	2	3	.400	0	0-1	2	6.63	7.09
2008	2 Tms		42	1	0	12	62.0	271	71	32	27	7	3	1	2	26	4	43	3	1	2	0	1.000	0	1-3	2	5.27	3.92
2009	Cin	NL	74	0	0	15	76.0	292	54	22	20	6	1	1	0	24	0	70	6	0	5	1	.833	0	0-2	20	2.24	2.37
2010	Cin	NL	82	0	0	22	76.2	322	64	31	29	7	3	2	1	33	3	85	8	0	4	4	.500	0	2-5	20	3.23	3.40
2011	Cin	NL	75	0	0	21	70.1	313	76	30	29	5	2	1	1	31	6	62	2	4	3	6	.333	0	1-7	14	4.37	3.71
2014	Col	NL	51	0	0	14	45.0	211	56	31	29	3	1	4	5	24	0	36	2	0	2	0	1.000	0	0-2	1	6.38	5.80
08	CWS	AL	32	1	0	11	44.2	203	55	26	23	4	3	1	2	21	4	32	2	1	1	0	1.000	0	1-1	1	5.78	4.63
08	Cin	AL	10	0	0	1	17.1	68	16	6	4	3	0	0	0	5	0	11	1	0	1	0	1.000	0	0-2	1	3.93	2.08
	Postseason		2	0	0	1	2.0	10	2	1	1	0	0	0	0	2	2	1	0	0	0	0	-	0	0-0	0	3.46	4.50
	7 ML YEARS		359	2	0	95	378.0	1638	382	183	169	30	11	14	13	166	18	321	25	5	18	14	.563	0	4-20	60	4.25	4.02

Justin Masterson

Pitches: R **Bats:** R **Pos:** SP-25; RP-3   **Ht:** 6'6" **Wt:** 250 **Born:** 3/22/1985 **Age:** 30

Year	Team	Lg	G	GS	CG	GF	IP	BFP	H	R	ER	HR	SH	SF	HB	TBB	IBB	SO	WP	Bk	W	L	Pct	Sh	Sv-Op	Hld	ERC	ERA
2014	Clmbs*	AAA	2	2	0	0	11.2	50	9	7	7	0	0	1	0	8	0	10	2	0	0	1	.000	0	0--	-	3.25	5.40
2008	Bos	AL	36	9	0	6	88.1	365	68	31	31	10	1	8	4	40	3	68	1	0	6	5	.545	0	0-1	3	3.51	3.16
2009	2 Tms	AL	42	16	1	4	129.1	568	128	73	65	12	10	7	8	60	3	119	5	0	4	10	.286	0	0-1	6	4.45	4.52
2010	Cle	AL	34	29	1	0	180.0	802	197	107	94	14	5	4	11	73	4	140	12	0	6	13	.316	1	0-0	2	4.68	4.70
2011	Cle	AL	34	33	1	0	216.0	908	211	89	77	11	5	5	11	65	4	158	5	0	12	10	.545	0	0-0	0	3.43	3.21
2012	Cle	AL	34	34	1	0	206.1	906	212	122	113	18	6	11	13	88	1	159	14	0	11	15	.423	0	0-0	0	4.51	4.93
2013	Cle	AL	32	29	3	2	193.0	803	156	75	74	13	5	2	17	76	0	195	8	0	14	10	.583	3	0-0	0	3.17	3.45
2014	2 Tms	AL	28	25	0	1	128.2	592	141	90	84	12	8	1	15	60	2	116	14	0	7	9	.438	0	0-0	0	5.63	5.88
09	Bos	AL	31	6	0	4	72.0	312	72	38	36	7	9	6	6	25	2	67	3	0	3	3	.500	0	0-1	6	4.13	4.50
09	Cle	AL	11	10	1	0	57.1	256	56	35	29	5	1	1	2	35	1	52	2	0	1	7	.125	0	0-0	0	4.85	4.55
14	Cle	AL	19	19	0	0	98.0	452	106	66	60	6	4	1	11	56	2	93	9	0	4	6	.400	0	0-0	0	5.40	5.51
14	StL	NL	9	6	0	1	30.2	140	35	24	24	6	4	0	4	13	0	23	5	0	3	3	.500	0	0-0	0	6.34	7.04
	Postseason		10	0	0	1	11.2	47	11	3	2	0	1	0	2	5	0	11	0	0	1	0	1.000	0	0-1	4	4.23	1.54
	7 ML YEARS		240	175	7	13	1141.2	4944	1113	587	538	90	40	31	83	471	17	955	59	0	60	72	.455	4	0-2	11	4.13	4.24

Darin Mastroianni

Bats: R **Throws:** R **Pos:** RF-10;CF-7;PH-5;PR-5;LF-3   mass-tree-AH-nee   **Ht:** 5'11" **Wt:** 190 **Born:** 8/26/1985 **Age:** 29

Year	Team	Lg	G	AB	H	2B	3B	HR	(Hm	Rd)	TB	R	RBI	RC	TBB	IBB	SO	HBP	SH	SF	SB	CS	GDP	Avg	OBP	Slg	OPS
2014	Roch*	AAA	4	20	9	2	0	0	(-	-)	11	4	2	4	0	0	4	0	0	0	0	1	0	.450	.450	.550	1.000
2014	Buffalo*	AAA	88	344	92	18	1	5	(-	-)	127	52	21	50	40	0	67	4	3	2	20	5	6	.267	.349	.369	.718
2011	Tor	AL	1	2	0	0	0	0	(0	0)	0	0	0	0	0	0	1	0	0	0	0	0	0	.000	.000	.000	.000
2012	Min	AL	77	163	41	3	2	3	(2	1)	57	22	17	24	18	0	45	1	3	1	21	3	4	.252	.328	.350	.678
2013	Min	AL	30	65	12	2	0	0	(0	0)	14	5	5	1	3	0	23	1	3	1	2	1	2	.185	.229	.215	.444
2014	2 Tms	AL	21	43	5	0	0	1	(1	0)	8	7	2	0	1	0	10	0	0	0	1	0	4	.116	.136	.186	.322
14	Min	AL	7	11	0	0	0	0	(0	0)	0	3	0	0	1	0	5	0	0	0	1	0	0	.000	.083	.000	.083
14	Tor	AL	14	32	5	0	0	1	(1	0)	8	4	2	0	0	0	5	0	0	0	0	0	0	.156	.156	.250	.406
	4 ML YEARS		129	273	58	5	2	4	(3	1)	79	34	24	25	22	0	79	2	7	2	24	4	10	.212	.274	.289	.564

Jeff Mathis

Bats: R Throws: R Pos: C-62;PH-2   Ht: 6'0" Wt: 205 Born: 3/31/1983 Age: 32

Year Team	Lg	G	AB	H	2B	3B	HR	(Hm	Rd)	TB	R	RBI	RC	TBB	IBB	SO	HBP	SH	SF	SB	CS	GDP	Avg	OBP	Slg	OPS
2005 LAA	AL	5	3	1	0	0	0	(0	0)	1	1	0	0	0	0	1	0	0	0	0	0	0	.333	.333	.333	.667
2006 LAA	AL	23	55	8	2	0	2	(1	1)	16	9	6	4	7	1	14	0	0	1	0	0	0	.145	.238	.291	.529
2007 LAA	AL	59	171	36	12	0	4	(3	1)	60	24	23	13	15	0	49	2	3	4	0	1	3	.211	.276	.351	.627
2008 LAA	AL	94	283	55	8	0	9	(4	5)	90	35	42	33	30	4	90	3	8	4	2	2	1	.194	.275	.318	.593
2009 LAA	AL	84	237	50	8	0	5	(3	2)	73	26	28	24	22	0	73	4	8	1	2	3	2	.211	.288	.308	.596
2010 LAA	AL	68	205	40	6	1	3	(2	1)	57	19	18	10	6	0	59	1	3	3	3	0	3	.195	.219	.278	.497
2011 LAA	AL	93	247	43	12	0	3	(1	2)	64	18	22	12	15	2	75	2	14	3	1	2	3	.174	.225	.259	.484
2012 Tor	AL	71	211	46	13	0	8	(5	3)	83	25	27	18	9	0	68	0	6	1	1	0	2	.218	.249	.393	.642
2013 Mia	NL	73	232	42	7	1	5	(3	2)	66	14	29	15	21	4	76	1	1	1	0	0	5	.181	.251	.284	.535
2014 Mia	NL	64	175	35	7	0	2	(1	1)	48	12	12	11	15	2	64	0	5	0	0	0	2	.200	.263	.274	.537
Postseason		10	20	9	5	0	0	(0	0)	14	2	2	3	0	0	5	0	1	0	0	0	0	.450	.450	.700	1.150
10 ML YEARS		634	1819	356	75	2	41	(23	18)	558	183	207	140	140	13	569	13	48	18	9	8	21	.196	.256	.307	.563

Daisuke Matsuzaka

Pitches: R Bats: R Pos: RP-25; SP-9   DICE-kay maht-soo-ZAH-kah   Ht: 6'0" Wt: 205 Born: 9/13/1980 Age: 34

Year Team	Lg	G	GS	CG	GF	IP	BFP	H	R	ER	HR	SH	SF	HB	TBB	IBB	SO	WP	Bk	W	L	Pct	Sh	Sv-Op	Hld	ERC	ERA
2014 LsVgs*	AAA	2	2	0	0	12.0	48	7	3	3	0	0	1	0	6	0	12	0	0	0	0	-	0	0--	-	1.71	2.25
2014 StLuci*	A+	1	1	0	0	3.0	11	1	0	0	0	0	0	0	0	0	3	0	0	0	0	-	0	0--	-	0.23	0.00
2014 Bnghtn*	AA	1	1	0	0	6.0	21	3	1	1	0	0	0	0	0	0	3	1	0	1	0	1.000	0	0--	-	0.54	1.50
2014 Bklyn*	A-	1	1	0	0	5.0	19	2	0	0	0	0	0	0	2	0	7	0	0	1	0	1.000	0	0--	-	0.95	0.00
2007 Bos	AL	32	32	1	0	204.2	874	191	100	100	25	3	2	13	80	1	201	5	0	15	12	.556	0	0-0	0	4.10	4.40
2008 Bos	AL	29	29	0	0	167.2	716	128	58	54	12	3	4	7	94	1	154	5	0	18	3	.857	0	0-0	0	3.36	2.90
2009 Bos	AL	12	12	0	0	59.1	283	81	38	38	10	1	1	2	30	1	54	8	0	4	6	.400	0	0-0	0	7.45	5.76
2010 Bos	AL	25	25	0	0	153.2	664	137	84	80	13	3	8	8	74	1	133	4	0	9	6	.600	0	0-0	0	3.89	4.69
2011 Bos	AL	8	7	0	1	37.1	167	32	24	22	4	0	0	1	23	0	26	0	0	3	3	.500	0	0-0	0	4.21	5.30
2012 Bos	AL	11	11	0	0	45.2	215	58	43	42	11	0	3	3	20	0	41	3	0	1	7	.125	0	0-0	0	7.20	8.28
2013 NYM	NL	7	7	0	0	38.2	166	32	21	19	4	4	0	5	16	0	33	0	0	3	3	.500	0	0-0	0	3.70	4.42
2014 NYM	NL	34	9	0	5	83.1	359	62	38	36	6	4	2	6	50	5	78	6	0	3	3	.500	0	1-2	3	3.43	3.89
Postseason		7	7	0	0	35.2	163	39	19	19	4	0	1	1	17	0	33	4	0	3	1	.750	0	0-0	0	5.04	4.79
8 ML YEARS		158	132	1	6	790.1	3444	721	406	391	85	18	20	45	387	9	720	31	0	56	43	.566	0	1-2	3	4.20	4.45

Ryan Mattheus

Pitches: R Bats: R Pos: RP-7   MATH-yooz   Ht: 6'3" Wt: 220 Born: 11/10/1983 Age: 31

Year Team	Lg	G	GS	CG	GF	IP	BFP	H	R	ER	HR	SH	SF	HB	TBB	IBB	SO	WP	Bk	W	L	Pct	Sh	Sv-Op	Hld	ERC	ERA
2014 Syrcse*	AAA	34	0	0	11	40.1	180	47	31	27	5	1	1	0	12	2	32	2	0	1	3	.250	0	2--	-	4.58	6.02
2014 Nats*	R	2	1	0	0	2.1	11	3	2	2	0	0	0	0	0	0	4	0	1	0	0	-	0	0--	-	2.96	7.71
2011 Was	NL	35	0	0	12	32.0	136	26	11	10	1	4	1	2	15	3	13	1	1	2	2	.500	0	0-0	8	2.94	2.81
2012 Was	NL	66	0	0	11	66.1	265	57	22	21	8	2	4	3	19	5	41	3	0	5	3	.625	0	0-0	18	3.19	2.85
2013 Was	NL	37	0	0	13	35.1	166	52	26	25	1	0	3	0	15	0	22	4	1	0	2	.000	0	0-3	6	6.53	6.37
2014 Was	NL	7	0	0	4	8.2	35	7	1	1	0	0	0	1	4	0	4	0	0	0	0	-	0	0-0	0	3.22	1.04
Postseason		3	0	0	0	3.0	12	3	2	2	0	0	0	0	1	0	0	0	0	1	0	1.000	0	0-0	0	3.35	6.00
4 ML YEARS		145	0	0	40	142.1	602	142	60	57	10	6	8	6	53	8	79	8	2	7	7	.500	0	0-3	32	3.91	3.60

Brian Matusz

Pitches: L Bats: L Pos: RP-63   MATT-uss   Ht: 6'4" Wt: 200 Born: 2/11/1987 Age: 28

Year Team	Lg	G	GS	CG	GF	IP	BFP	H	R	ER	HR	SH	SF	HB	TBB	IBB	SO	WP	Bk	W	L	Pct	Sh	Sv-Op	Hld	ERC	ERA
2009 Bal	AL	8	8	0	0	44.2	196	52	24	23	6	2	2	0	14	0	38	0	0	5	2	.714	0	0-0	0	4.91	4.63
2010 Bal	AL	32	32	0	0	175.2	760	173	88	84	19	6	6	7	63	3	143	1	0	10	12	.455	0	0-0	0	3.98	4.30
2011 Bal	AL	12	12	0	0	49.2	245	81	60	59	18	1	2	6	24	1	38	0	0	1	9	.100	0	0-0	0	10.88	10.69
2012 Bal	AL	34	16	0	2	98.1	441	112	61	53	15	2	3	0	41	4	81	0	0	6	10	.375	0	0-0	4	5.25	4.87
2013 Bal	AL	65	0	0	9	51.0	208	43	21	20	3	1	2	2	16	2	50	0	0	2	1	.667	0	0-4	18	2.77	3.53
2014 Bal	AL	63	0	0	11	51.2	226	51	23	20	7	0	2	3	17	4	50	0	0	2	3	.400	0	0-0	14	3.00	3.48
Postseason		6	0	0	2	4.2	17	2	1	1	0	0	0	0	2	1	6	1	0	0	1	.000	0	0-0	2	1.82	1.93
6 ML YEARS		214	68	0	22	470.2	2076	512	277	259	68	12	17	12	175	14	403	1	0	26	37	.413	0	0-7	36	4.82	4.95

Tyler Matzek

Pitches: L Bats: L Pos: SP-19; RP-1   MATT-zick   Ht: 6'3" Wt: 210 Born: 10/19/1990 Age: 24

Year Team	Lg	G	GS	CG	GF	IP	BFP	H	R	ER	HR	SH	SF	HB	TBB	IBB	SO	WP	Bk	W	L	Pct	Sh	Sv-Op	Hld	ERC	ERA
2010 Ashvll	A	18	18	0	0	89.1	376	62	31	29	6	3	4	4	62	0	88	7	3	5	1	.833	0	0--	-	3.59	2.92
2011 Mdest	A+	10	10	0	0	33.0	178	34	37	36	5	1	1	2	46	0	37	5	0	0	3	.000	0	0--	-	9.12	9.82
2011 Ashvll	A	12	12	0	0	64.0	279	45	35	31	3	1	3	2	50	0	74	14	0	5	4	.556	0	0--	-	3.68	4.36
2012 Mdest	A+	28	28	0	0	142.1	649	134	85	73	7	3	1	5	95	0	153	9	0	6	8	.429	0	0--	-	4.52	4.62
2013 Tulsa	AA	26	26	0	0	142.1	627	147	67	60	13	8	5	5	76	0	95	5	2	8	9	.471	0	0--	-	4.99	3.79
2014 ColSpr	AAA	12	12	0	0	66.2	303	70	40	30	8	6	2	0	31	0	61	3	0	5	4	.556	0	0--	-	4.62	4.05
2014 Col	NL	20	19	1	0	117.2	503	120	53	53	9	4	3	3	44	1	91	3	0	6	11	.353	1	0-0	0	4.06	4.05

Joe Mauer

Bats: L Throws: R Pos: 1B-100;DH-19;PH-2   Ht: 6'5" Wt: 230 Born: 4/19/1983 Age: 32

Year	Team	Lg	G	AB	H	2B	3B	HR	(Hm	Rd)	TB	R	RBI	RC	TBB	IBB	SO	HBP	SH	SF	SB	CS	GDP	Avg	OBP	Slg	OPS
2014	CRpds*	A	4	15	6	0	0	0	(-	-)	6	2	1	2	0	0	1	0	0	0	0	0	1	.400	.400	.400	.800
2004	Min	AL	35	107	33	8	1	6	(4	2)	61	18	17	21	11	0	14	1	0	3	1	0	1	.308	.369	.570	.939
2005	Min	AL	131	489	144	26	2	9	(4	5)	201	61	55	78	61	12	64	1	0	3	13	1	9	.294	.372	.411	.783
2006	Min	AL	140	521	181	36	4	13	(3	10)	264	86	84	103	79	21	54	1	0	7	8	3	24	.347	.429	.507	.936
2007	Min	AL	109	406	119	27	3	7	(2	5)	173	62	60	69	57	10	51	3	2	3	7	1	11	.293	.382	.426	.808
2008	Min	AL	146	536	176	31	4	9	(7	2)	242	98	85	103	84	8	50	1	1	11	1	1	21	.328	.413	.451	.864
2009	Min	AL	138	523	191	30	1	28	(16	12)	307	94	96	123	76	14	63	2	0	5	4	1	13	.365	.444	.587	1.031
2010	Min	AL	137	510	167	43	1	9	(1	8)	239	88	75	91	65	14	53	3	0	6	1	4	19	.327	.402	.469	.871
2011	Min	AL	82	296	85	15	0	3	(0	3)	109	38	30	39	32	7	38	3	0	2	0	0	9	.287	.360	.368	.729
2012	Min	AL	147	545	174	31	4	10	(4	6)	243	81	85	108	90	10	88	2	1	3	8	4	23	.319	.416	.446	.861
2013	Min	AL	113	445	144	35	0	11	(5	6)	212	62	47	74	61	7	89	0	0	2	0	1	7	.324	.404	.476	.880
2014	Min	AL	120	455	126	27	2	4	(3	1)	169	60	55	66	60	12	96	1	0	2	3	0	12	.277	.361	.371	.732
	Postseason		9	35	10	1	0	0	(0	0)	11	1	1	2	4	0	7	0	0	0	0	0	0	.286	.359	.314	.673
	11 ML YEARS		1298	4833	1540	309	22	109	(49	60)	2220	748	689	875	676	115	660	18	4	47	46	16	149	.319	.401	.459	.860

Brandon Maurer

Pitches: R Bats: R Pos: RP-31; SP-7   MAUW-er   Ht: 6'5" Wt: 220 Born: 7/3/1990 Age: 24

Year	Team	Lg	G	GS	CG	GF	IP	BFP	H	R	ER	HR	SH	SF	HB	TBB	IBB	SO	WP	Bk	W	L	Pct	Sh	Sv-Op	Hld	ERC	ERA
2010	Ms	R	4	4	0	0	11.0	43	8	4	2	0	0	0	2	2	0	14	1	1	0	1	.000	0	0- -		1.99	1.64
2010	Clinton	A	2	0	0	1	4.1	17	5	2	1	0	0	0	0	0	0	6	0	0	0	1	.000	0	0- -		4.34	2.08
2011	Clinton	A	6	6	0	1	37.0	151	28	16	14	2	0	2	2	14	0	44	3	4	1	3	.250	0	0- -		2.64	3.41
2011	Hi Dsrt	A+	9	7	0	1	42.1	185	47	32	30	8	0	0	3	11	0	37	6	0	2	4	.333	0	0- -		5.04	6.38
2012	Jacksn	AA	24	24	1	0	137.2	575	133	54	49	4	6	3	6	48	0	117	7	2	9	2	.818	0	0- -		3.45	3.20
2013	Tacom	AAA	10	10	0	0	46.2	215	48	29	27	2	1	0	5	26	0	47	3	2	3	4	.429	0	0- -		4.82	5.21
2014	Tacom	AAA	12	1	0	5	19.1	82	18	8	6	2	0	1	0	8	1	24	0	1	0	1	1.000	0	3- -		3.71	2.79
2013	Sea	AL	22	14	0	3	90.0	402	114	66	63	16	1	2	6	27	0	70	9	0	5	8	.385	0	0-0	0	6.20	6.30
2014	Sea	AL	38	7	0	4	69.2	301	74	39	36	6	2	3	0	19	2	55	3	0	1	4	.200	0	0-1	5	3.70	4.65
	2 ML YEARS		60	21	0	7	159.2	703	188	105	99	22	3	5	6	46	2	125	12	0	6	12	.333	0	0-1	5	5.05	5.58

Justin Maxwell

Bats: R Throws: R Pos: RF-7;CF-6;PR-4;PH-3;DH-2;LF-1   Ht: 6'5" Wt: 225 Born: 11/6/1983 Age: 31

Year	Team	Lg	G	AB	H	2B	3B	HR	(Hm	Rd)	TB	R	RBI	RC	TBB	IBB	SO	HBP	SH	SF	SB	CS	GDP	Avg	OBP	Slg	OPS
2014	Omha*	AAA	56	207	59	11	1	8	(-	-)	96	32	29	34	20	0	75	3	0	3	3	2	6	.285	.352	.464	.816
2007	Was	NL	15	26	7	0	0	2	(0	2)	13	5	5	4	1	0	8	0	0	0	1	0	0	.269	.296	.500	.796
2009	Was	NL	40	89	22	4	1	4	(1	3)	40	13	9	15	12	0	32	1	0	0	6	1	1	.247	.343	.449	.793
2010	Was	NL	67	104	15	6	3	0	(1	2)	30	16	12	11	25	2	43	0	0	2	5	1	3	.144	.305	.288	.594
2012	Hou	NL	124	315	72	13	3	18	(10	8)	145	46	53	52	32	0	114	3	0	2	9	4	6	.229	.304	.460	.764
2013	2 Tms	AL	75	234	59	16	3	7	(4	3)	102	35	25	28	23	0	78	4	0	1	6	2	4	.252	.328	.436	.764
2014	KC	AL	20	40	6	1	0	0	(0	0)	7	4	3	2	2	0	20	2	0	1	0	1	0	.150	.222	.175	.397
13	Hou	AL	40	137	33	10	2	2	(0	2)	53	21	8	13	12	0	43	2	0	0	4	1	1	.241	.311	.387	.698
13	KC	AL	35	97	26	6	1	5	(4	1)	49	14	17	15	11	0	35	2	0	1	2	1	3	.268	.351	.505	.857
	6 ML YEARS		341	808	181	40	7	34	(16	18)	337	119	107	112	95	2	295	10	0	6	26	9	14	.224	.311	.417	.728

Trevor May

Pitches: R Bats: R Pos: SP-9; RP-1   Ht: 6'5" Wt: 215 Born: 9/23/1989 Age: 25

Year	Team	Lg	G	GS	CG	GF	IP	BFP	H	R	ER	HR	SH	SF	HB	TBB	IBB	SO	WP	Bk	W	L	Pct	Sh	Sv-Op	Hld	ERC	ERA
2010	Clrwtr	A+	16	14	0	1	70.0	319	53	41	39	7	0	3	5	61	0	90	9	1	5	5	.500	0	0- -		4.87	5.01
2010	Lakwd	A	11	11	0	0	65.0	261	51	22	21	3	0	2	1	20	0	92	5	0	7	3	.700	0	0- -		2.34	2.91
2011	Clrwtr	A+	27	27	3	0	151.1	631	121	65	61	8	5	7	5	67	0	208	8	0	10	8	.556	2	0- -		2.99	3.63
2012	Rdng	AA	28	28	0	0	149.2	660	139	87	81	22	8	4	11	78	0	151	8	1	10	13	.435	0	0- -		4.82	4.87
2013	NwBrit	AA	27	27	2	0	151.2	659	149	79	76	14	2	0	8	67	0	159	8	0	9	9	.500	2	0- -		4.33	4.51
2014	Roch	AAA	18	18	1	0	98.1	400	75	33	31	4	0	3	0	39	0	94	2	0	8	6	.571	1	0- -		2.45	2.84
2014	Min	AL	10	9	0	0	45.2	213	59	41	40	7	0	1	2	22	1	44	3	0	3	6	.333	0	0-0	0	6.80	7.88

John Mayberry

Bats: R Throws: R Pos: PH-33;1B-23;LF-16;CF-11;RF-7;PR-5;DH-2   Ht: 6'6" Wt: 230 Born: 12/21/1983 Age: 31

Year	Team	Lg	G	AB	H	2B	3B	HR	(Hm	Rd)	TB	R	RBI	RC	TBB	IBB	SO	HBP	SH	SF	SB	CS	GDP	Avg	OBP	Slg	OPS
2014	LV*	AAA	9	33	6	2	0	1	(-	-)	11	4	4	3	3	0	11	2	0	0	0	0	0	.182	.289	.333	.623
2009	Phi	NL	39	57	12	3	0	4	(1	3)	27	8	8	5	2	0	23	1	0	0	0	1	0	.211	.250	.474	.724
2010	Phi	NL	11	12	4	0	0	2	(0	2)	10	4	6	4	1	0	4	0	0	0	0	0	0	.333	.385	.833	1.218
2011	Phi	NL	104	267	73	17	1	15	(7	8)	137	37	49	44	26	2	55	2	0	1	8	3	6	.273	.341	.513	.854
2012	Phi	NL	149	441	108	24	0	14	(7	7)	174	53	46	47	34	2	111	2	0	2	1	0	17	.245	.301	.395	.695
2013	Phi	NL	134	353	80	23	1	11	(7	4)	138	47	39	36	27	1	90	3	0	1	5	3	6	.227	.286	.391	.677
2014	2 Tms	AL	78	146	31	10	0	7	(3	4)	62	15	23	19	20	0	35	1	0	1	2	0	4	.212	.310	.425	.734
14	Phi	NL	63	122	26	7	0	6	(2	4)	51	11	21	17	15	0	30	1	0	0	2	0	3	.213	.304	.418	.722
14	Tor	AL	15	24	5	3	0	1	(1	0)	11	4	2	2	5	0	5	0	0	1	0	0	1	.208	.333	.458	.792
	Postseason		2	4	0	0	0	0	(0	0)	0	0	0	0	1	0	0	1	0	0	0	0	0	.000	.000	.000	.000
	6 ML YEARS		515	1276	308	77	2	53	(25	28)	548	164	171	155	110	5	318	9	0	5	14	7	33	.241	.305	.429	.734

Cameron Maybin

Bats: R **Throws:** R **Pos:** CF-86;PH-7;PR-5   **Ht:** 6'3" **Wt:** 205 **Born:** 4/4/1987 **Age:** 28

							BATTING													RUNNING			AVERAGES			
Year	Team	Lg	G	AB	H	2B	3B	HR	(Hm | Rd)	TB	R	RBI	RC	TBB	IBB	SO	HBP	SH	SF	SB	CS	GDP	Avg	OBP	Slg	OPS
2014	ElPaso*	AAA	15	53	14	2	1	1	(- | -)	21	8	6	7	6	0	10	0	0	2	1	0	2	.264	.328	.396	.724
2007	Det	AL	24	49	7	3	0	1	(0 | 1)	13	8	2	2	3	0	21	1	0	0	5	0	0	.143	.208	.265	.473
2008	Fla	NL	8	32	16	2	0	0	(0 | 0)	18	9	2	8	3	0	8	0	1	0	4	0	0	.500	.543	.563	1.105
2009	Fla	NL	54	176	44	12	2	4	(1 | 3)	72	30	13	15	17	1	51	1	4	1	3	3	2	.250	.318	.409	.727
2010	Fla	NL	82	291	68	7	3	8	(5 | 3)	105	46	28	37	24	1	92	5	1	1	9	2	4	.234	.302	.361	.663
2011	SD	NL	137	516	136	24	8	9	(2 | 7)	203	82	40	69	44	2	125	2	4	2	40	8	6	.264	.323	.393	.716
2012	SD	NL	147	507	123	20	5	8	(3 | 5)	177	67	45	52	44	1	110	4	3	3	26	7	12	.243	.306	.349	.656
2013	SD	NL	14	51	8	1	0	1	(0 | 1)	12	7	5	0	4	1	9	1	1	0	4	1	3	.157	.232	.235	.467
2014	SD	NL	95	251	59	13	4	1	(0 | 1)	83	24	15	22	19	2	56	1	0	1	4	3	8	.235	.290	.331	.621
	8 ML YEARS		561	1873	461	82	22	32	(11 | 21)	683	273	150	205	158	8	472	15	14	8	93	24	35	.246	.309	.365	.673

Vin Mazzaro

Pitches: R **Bats:** R **Pos:** RP-5   muh-ZA-roh   **Ht:** 6'2" **Wt:** 220 **Born:** 9/27/1986 **Age:** 28

				HOW MUCH HE PITCHED					WHAT HE GAVE UP											THE RESULTS					
Year	Team	Lg	G	GS	CG	GF	IP	BFP	H	R	ER	HR	SH	SF	HB	TBB	IBB	SO	WP	Bk	W	L	Pct	Sh	Sv-Op	Hld	ERC	ERA
2014	Indy*	AAA	33	1	0	10	50.0	213	47	17	14	2	4	2	1	20	2	34	5	0	5	3	.625	0	4- -	-	3.35	2.52
2009	Oak	AL	17	17	0	0	91.1	423	120	61	54	12	1	3	4	39	3	59	5	0	4	9	.308	0	0-0	-	6.49	5.32
2010	Oak	AL	24	18	0	4	122.1	537	127	70	58	19	4	4	4	50	0	79	5	0	6	8	.429	0	0-0	-	4.86	4.27
2011	KC	AL	7	4	0	2	28.1	131	39	26	26	4	3	3	1	15	1	10	2	0	1	1	.500	0	0-0	-	7.67	8.26
2012	KC	AL	18	6	0	4	44.0	198	55	29	28	3	1	2	3	19	2	26	1	0	4	3	.571	0	0-0	-	5.80	5.73
2013	Pit	NL	57	0	0	17	73.2	304	68	23	23	3	3	1	3	21	3	46	5	1	8	2	.800	0	1-3	6	2.95	2.81
2014	Pit	NL	5	0	0	1	10.1	46	8	4	4	2	1	0	1	5	0	7	0	0	0	0	-	0	0-0	-	3.99	3.48
	Postseason		3	0	0	1	1.2	5	0	0	0	0	0	0	0	0	0	2	0	0	0	0	-	0	0-0	0	0.00	0.00
	6 ML YEARS		128	45	0	28	370.0	1639	417	213	193	43	13	13	16	149	9	227	18	1	23	23	.500	0	1-3	6	5.12	4.69

Zach McAllister

Pitches: R **Bats:** R **Pos:** SP-15; RP-7   **Ht:** 6'6" **Wt:** 240 **Born:** 12/8/1987 **Age:** 27

				HOW MUCH HE PITCHED					WHAT HE GAVE UP											THE RESULTS					
Year	Team	Lg	G	GS	CG	GF	IP	BFP	H	R	ER	HR	SH	SF	HB	TBB	IBB	SO	WP	Bk	W	L	Pct	Sh	Sv-Op	Hld	ERC	ERA
2014	Lk Cty*	A	1	1	0	0	4.1	22	9	3	3	0	0	0	0	1	0	4	0	0	0	0	-	0	0- -	-	9.46	6.23
2014	Clmbs*	AAA	11	11	0	0	69.0	273	57	19	16	3	2	1	1	14	0	59	1	0	7	1	.875	0	0- -	-	2.17	2.09
2011	Cle	AL	4	4	0	0	17.2	84	26	16	12	1	0	0	0	7	1	14	0	0	0	1	.000	0	0-0	-	6.41	6.11
2012	Cle	AL	22	22	0	0	125.1	543	133	78	59	19	2	5	1	38	0	110	0	2	6	8	.429	0	0-0	-	4.37	4.24
2013	Cle	AL	24	24	0	0	134.1	579	134	65	56	13	0	3	6	49	2	101	7	1	9	9	.500	0	0-0	-	4.06	3.75
2014	Cle	AL	22	15	0	2	86.0	377	96	54	50	7	1	5	0	28	1	74	3	0	4	7	.364	0	0-0	1	4.24	5.23
	4 ML YEARS		72	65	0	2	363.1	1583	389	213	177	40	3	13	7	122	4	299	10	3	19	25	.432	0	0-0	1	4.32	4.38

Matt McBride

Bats: R **Throws:** R **Pos:** PH-14;1B-5;RF-3;LF-2   **Ht:** 6'2" **Wt:** 215 **Born:** 5/23/1985 **Age:** 30

							BATTING													RUNNING			AVERAGES			
Year	Team	Lg	G	AB	H	2B	3B	HR	(Hm	Rd)	TB	R	RBI	RC	TBB	IBB	SO	HBP	SH	SF	SB	CS	GDP	Avg	OBP	Slg	OPS
2010	Akron	AA	96	361	102	25	1	17	(-	-)	180	54	64	63	30	3	61	8	0	5	2	2	6	.283	.347	.499	.845
2010	Clmbs	AAA	32	120	32	6	0	4	(-	-)	50	17	11	15	5	0	17	0	2	1	0	0	4	.267	.294	.417	.710
2011	Akron	AA	84	310	92	24	4	14	(-	-)	166	50	53	60	30	1	44	2	1	3	3	0	6	.297	.359	.535	.895
2011	Clmbs	AAA	12	45	7	2	0	1	(-	-)	12	3	3	1	2	0	8	0	0	0	0	0	0	.156	.191	.267	.458
2011	Tulsa	AA	6	17	4	0	0	0	(-	-)	4	4	2	1	0	0	3	1	0	0	0	0	0	.235	.278	.235	.513
2012	ColSpr	AAA	108	439	135	42	6	10	(-	-)	235	73	87	84	19	0	47	1	0	10	0	1	4	.344	.365	.535	.900
2013	ColSpr	AAA	48	180	59	17	1	15	(-	-)	123	31	45	42	11	1	21	0	0	4	0	0	7	.328	.359	.683	1.042
2014	ColSpr	AAA	51	187	57	11	1	7	(-	-)	91	27	35	32	12	0	19	2	0	5	0	1	2	.305	.345	.487	.831
2014	GdJunc	R+	4	13	8	3	0	0	(-	-)	11	6	5	6	3	0	1	0	0	0	1	0	0	.615	.688	.846	1.534
2012	Col	NL	31	78	16	2	0	2	(1	1)	24	8	11	7	1	0	17	1	0	1	0	0	0	.205	.222	.308	.530
2014	Col	NL	21	31	7	2	0	2	(1	1)	15	6	6	4	2	0	12	1	0	0	0	0	0	.226	.294	.484	.778
	2 ML YEARS		52	109	23	4	0	4	(2	2)	39	14	17	11	3	0	29	2	0	1	0	0	4	.211	.243	.358	.601

Brian McCann

Bats: L **Throws:** R **Pos:** C-108;1B-16;DH-14;PH-14;PR-1   **Ht:** 6'3" **Wt:** 230 **Born:** 2/20/1984 **Age:** 31

							BATTING													RUNNING			AVERAGES			
Year	Team	Lg	G	AB	H	2B	3B	HR	(Hm	Rd)	TB	R	RBI	RC	TBB	IBB	SO	HBP	SH	SF	SB	CS	GDP	Avg	OBP	Slg	OPS
2005	Atl	NL	59	180	50	7	0	5	(2	3)	72	20	23	25	18	5	26	1	4	1	1	1	5	.278	.345	.400	.745
2006	Atl	NL	130	442	147	34	0	24	(10	14)	253	61	93	94	41	8	54	3	0	6	2	0	12	.333	.388	.572	.961
2007	Atl	NL	139	504	136	38	0	18	(6	12)	228	51	92	68	35	7	74	5	2	6	0	1	19	.270	.320	.452	.772
2008	Atl	NL	145	509	153	42	1	23	(10	13)	266	68	87	84	57	4	64	4	0	3	5	0	17	.301	.373	.523	.896
2009	Atl	NL	138	488	137	35	1	21	(12	9)	237	63	94	83	49	3	83	5	3	6	4	1	17	.281	.349	.486	.834
2010	Atl	NL	143	479	129	25	0	21	(13	8)	217	63	77	76	74	10	98	9	0	4	5	2	12	.269	.375	.453	.828
2011	Atl	NL	128	466	126	19	0	24	(15	9)	217	51	71	76	57	14	89	2	0	2	3	2	10	.270	.351	.466	.817
2012	Atl	NL	121	439	101	14	0	20	(11	9)	175	44	67	45	44	7	76	1	0	3	0	0	15	.230	.300	.399	.698
2013	Atl	NL	102	356	91	13	0	20	(12	8)	164	43	57	51	39	3	66	5	0	2	0	1	9	.256	.336	.461	.796
2014	NYY	NL	140	495	115	15	1	23	(19	4)	201	57	75	58	32	1	77	7	0	4	0	0	16	.232	.286	.406	.692
	Postseason		12	43	9	1	0	3	(2	1)	19	4	9	5	5	0	16	0	0	1	0	0	0	.209	.286	.442	.728
	10 ML YEARS		1245	4358	1185	242	3	199	(110	89)	2030	521	736	660	446	62	707	42	9	37	23	8	132	.272	.343	.466	.808

James McCann

Bats: R **Throws:** R **Pos:** C-6;PH-3;DH-1   **Ht:** 6'2" **Wt:** 210 **Born:** 6/13/1990 **Age:** 25

								BATTING												RUNNING			AVERAGES			
Year Team	Lg	G	AB	H	2B	3B	HR	(Hm Rd)	TB	R	RBI	RC	TBB	IBB	SO	HBP	SH	SF	SB	CS	GDP	Avg	OBP	Slg	OPS
2011 Tigers	R	5	14	5	1	0	1	(- -)	9	1	6	3	1	0	1	1	0	0	0	0	1	.357	.438	.643	1.080
2011 WMich	A	9	34	2	1	0	0	(- -)	3	0	1	0	2	0	12	1	0	1	0	0	0	.059	.132	.088	.220
2012 Lkland	A+	45	160	46	10	0	0	(- -)	56	24	20	21	10	1	29	5	0	2	3	0	5	.288	.345	.350	.695
2012 Erie	AA	64	220	44	12	0	2	(- -)	62	15	19	12	8	0	44	0	1	1	2	2	11	.200	.227	.282	.509
2013 Erie	AA	119	441	122	30	1	8	(- -)	178	50	54	60	30	1	85	7	1	7	3	3	12	.277	.328	.404	.731
2014 Toledo	AAA	109	417	123	34	0	7	(- -)	178	49	54	64	25	0	90	9	2	7	9	2	11	.295	.343	.427	.770
2014 Det	AL	9	12	3	1	0	0	(0 0)	4	2	0	1	0	0	2	0	0	0	1	0	0	.250	.250	.333	.583

Brandon McCarthy

Pitches: R **Bats:** R **Pos:** SP-32   **Ht:** 6'7" **Wt:** 200 **Born:** 7/7/1983 **Age:** 31

			HOW MUCH HE PITCHED						WHAT HE GAVE UP											THE RESULTS						
Year Team	Lg	G	GS	CG	GF	IP	BFP	H	R	ER	HR	SH	SF	HB	TBB	IBB	SO	WP	Bk	W	L	Pct	Sh	Sv-Op	Hld	ERC	ERA
2005 CWS	AL	12	10	0	0	67.0	277	62	30	30	13	1	1	2	17	0	48	1	1	3	2	.600	0	0-0	0	3.83	4.03
2006 CWS	AL	53	2	0	13	84.2	354	77	44	44	17	3	1	0	33	9	69	5	0	4	7	.364	0	0-1	11	4.10	4.68
2007 Tex	AL	23	22	0	0	101.2	459	111	63	55	9	3	5	3	48	0	59	4	1	5	10	.333	0	0-0	0	4.89	4.87
2008 Tex	AL	5	5	0	0	22.0	93	20	11	10	3	0	2	1	8	0	10	0	0	1	1	.500	0	0-0	0	3.87	4.09
2009 Tex	AL	17	17	1	0	97.1	420	96	55	50	13	0	5	3	36	0	65	0	0	7	4	.636	1	0-0	0	4.22	4.62
2011 Oak	AL	25	25	5	0	170.2	690	168	73	63	11	4	9	0	25	1	123	3	0	9	9	.500	1	0-0	0	2.80	3.32
2012 Oak	AL	18	18	0	0	111.0	469	115	44	40	10	5	4	6	24	2	73	0	0	8	6	.571	0	0-0	0	3.67	3.24
2013 Ari	NL	22	22	2	0	135.0	577	161	71	68	13	6	1	5	21	3	76	1	1	5	11	.313	1	0-0	0	4.29	4.53
2014 2 Tms		32	32	1	0	200.0	836	222	100	90	25	3	4	3	33	4	175	4	0	10	15	.400	1	0-0	0	3.98	4.05
14 Ari	NL	18	18	0	0	109.2	466	131	65	61	15	2	3	2	20	4	93	3	0	3	10	.231	0	0-0	0	4.64	5.01
14 NYY	AL	14	14	1	0	90.1	370	91	35	29	10	1	1	1	13	0	82	1	0	7	5	.583	1	0-0	0	3.23	2.89
9 ML YEARS		207	153	9	13	989.1	4175	1032	490	450	114	25	32	23	245	19	698	18	3	52	65	.444	4	0-1	11	3.89	4.09

Pat McCoy

Pitches: L **Bats:** L **Pos:** RP-14   **Ht:** 6'3" **Wt:** 220 **Born:** 8/3/1988 **Age:** 26

			HOW MUCH HE PITCHED						WHAT HE GAVE UP											THE RESULTS						
Year Team	Lg	G	GS	CG	GF	IP	BFP	H	R	ER	HR	SH	SF	HB	TBB	IBB	SO	WP	Bk	W	L	Pct	Sh	Sv-Op	Hld	ERC	ERA
2010 Ptomc	A+	30	0	0	16	46.0	196	52	20	15	3	0	2	1	12	1	44	0	1	2	1	.667	0	6--	-	4.12	2.93
2011 Hrsbrg	AA	49	0	0	18	52.2	226	53	32	28	7	1	2	2	16	4	53	5	1	1	2	.333	0	4--	-	3.96	4.78
2012 Hrsbrg	AA	50	0	0	10	58.1	254	65	29	24	9	3	0	0	18	2	60	1	1	7	3	.700	0	2--	-	4.66	3.70
2013 Syrcse	AAA	7	0	0	4	6.1	32	12	12	7	2	0	1	0	2	0	3	0	0	0	0	-	0	0--	-	11.51	9.95
2013 Hrsbrg	AA	39	0	0	8	41.2	189	48	24	20	5	0	1	3	12	0	36	2	0	2	1	.667	0	0--	-	4.78	4.32
2014 Erie	AA	9	0	0	1	13.2	60	16	8	6	0	0	1	0	3	0	9	0	0	1	0	1.000	0	1--	-	3.52	3.95
2014 Toledo	AAA	21	0	0	2	31.1	120	25	10	9	3	0	2	1	6	0	25	0	0	2	0	1.000	0	0--	-	2.44	2.59
2014 Det	AL	14	0	0	4	14.0	74	21	6	6	0	0	0	0	13	3	11	0	0	0	0	-	0	0-0	0	8.02	3.86

Andrew McCutchen

Bats: R **Throws:** R **Pos:** CF-146   **Ht:** 5'10" **Wt:** 190 **Born:** 10/10/1986 **Age:** 28

								BATTING												RUNNING			AVERAGES			
Year Team	Lg	G	AB	H	2B	3B	HR	(Hm Rd)	TB	R	RBI	RC	TBB	IBB	SO	HBP	SH	SF	SB	CS	GDP	Avg	OBP	Slg	OPS
2009 Pit	NL	108	433	124	26	9	12	(8 4)	204	74	54	78	54	2	83	2	0	4	22	5	3	.286	.365	.471	.836
2010 Pit	NL	154	570	163	35	5	16	(8 8)	256	94	56	86	70	1	89	5	1	7	33	10	6	.286	.365	.449	.814
2011 Pit	NL	158	572	148	34	5	23	(10 13)	261	87	89	102	89	9	126	9	2	6	23	10	7	.259	.364	.456	.820
2012 Pit	NL	157	593	**194**	29	6	31	(15 16)	328	107	96	**125**	70	13	132	5	0	5	20	12	9	.327	.400	.553	.953
2013 Pit	NL	157	583	185	38	5	21	(9 12)	296	97	84	105	78	12	101	9	0	4	27	10	13	.317	.404	.508	.911
2014 Pit	NL	146	548	172	38	6	25	(10 15)	297	89	83	**109**	84	8	115	10	0	6	18	3	9	.314	**.410**	.542	**.952**
Postseason		6	21	7	1	0	0	(0 0)	8	3	0	3	5	1	3	0	0	0	0	0	0	.333	.462	.381	.842
6 ML YEARS		880	3299	986	200	36	128	(60 68)	1642	548	462	605	445	39	646	40	3	32	143	50	47	.299	.385	.498	.883

Daniel McCutchen

Pitches: R **Bats:** R **Pos:** RP-1   **Ht:** 6'2" **Wt:** 215 **Born:** 9/26/1982 **Age:** 32

			HOW MUCH HE PITCHED						WHAT HE GAVE UP											THE RESULTS						
Year Team	Lg	G	GS	CG	GF	IP	BFP	H	R	ER	HR	SH	SF	HB	TBB	IBB	SO	WP	Bk	W	L	Pct	Sh	Sv-Op	Hld	ERC	ERA
2014 RdRck*	AAA	15	8	1	2	60.0	270	79	47	47	22	1	2	0	13	0	54	2	0	2	5	.286	0	0--	-	7.07	7.05
2014 Charltt*	AAA	7	5	0	1	26.1	125	41	31	31	7	0	2	1	10	0	18	2	0	0	2	.000	0	0--	-	9.26	10.59
2009 Pit	NL	6	6	0	0	36.1	155	38	17	17	6	3	0	1	11	2	19	0	0	1	2	.333	0	0-0	0	4.45	4.21
2010 Pit	NL	28	9	0	4	67.2	316	83	48	46	13	4	4	2	28	0	38	2	0	2	5	.286	0	0-0	0	6.16	6.12
2011 Pit	NL	73	0	0	15	84.2	364	87	38	35	7	4	3	4	33	5	47	7	0	5	3	.625	0	0-0	10	4.23	3.72
2012 Pit	NL	1	0	0	1	0.0	2	1	2	2	1	0	0	0	1	0	0	0	0	0	1	.000	0	0-0	0	-	-
2014 Tex	AL	1	0	0	0	2.1	14	4	3	2	1	0	0	0	2	0	0	0	0	0	0	-	0	0-0	0	12.72	7.71
5 ML YEARS		109	15	0	20	191.0	851	213	108	102	28	11	7	7	75	7	104	9	0	8	11	.421	0	0-0	10	5.13	4.81

John McDonald

Bats: R **Throws:** R **Pos:** 3B-73;SS-16;PR-12;PH-10;2B-2;DH-2   **Ht:** 5'9" **Wt:** 185 **Born:** 9/24/1974 **Age:** 40

								BATTING												RUNNING			AVERAGES			
Year Team	Lg	G	AB	H	2B	3B	HR	(Hm Rd)	TB	R	RBI	RC	TBB	IBB	SO	HBP	SH	SF	SB	CS	GDP	Avg	OBP	Slg	OPS
1999 Cle	AL	18	21	7	0	0	0	(0 0)	7	2	0	1	0	0	3	0	0	0	0	1	2	.333	.333	.333	.667
2000 Cle	AL	9	9	4	0	0	0	(0 0)	4	0	0	2	0	0	1	0	0	0	0	0	0	.444	.444	.444	.889
2001 Cle	AL	17	22	2	1	0	0	(0 0)	3	1	0	0	1	0	7	1	1	0	0	0	0	.091	.167	.136	.303
2002 Cle	AL	93	264	66	11	3	1	(0 1)	86	35	12	24	10	0	50	5	7	2	3	0	4	.250	.288	.326	.614

Year Team	Lg	G	AB	H	2B	3B	HR	(Hm	Rd)	TB	R	RBI	RC	TBB	IBB	SO	HBP	SH	SF	SB	CS	GDP	Avg	OBP	Slg	OPS
2003 Cle	AL	82	214	46	9	1	1	(0	1)	60	21	14	18	11	0	31	2	4	2	3	3	4	.215	.258	.280	.538
2004 Cle	AL	66	93	19	5	1	2	(0	2)	32	17	7	6	4	0	11	0	3	0	0	0	2	.204	.237	.344	.581
2005 2 Tms	AL	68	166	46	6	1	0	(0	0)	54	18	16	19	11	0	24	2	3	2	6	1	6	.277	.326	.325	.651
2006 Tor	AL	104	260	58	7	3	3	(1	2)	80	35	23	20	16	0	41	2	6	2	7	2	8	.223	.271	.308	.579
2007 Tor	AL	123	327	82	20	2	1	(1	0)	109	32	31	35	11	0	48	2	12	1	7	2	4	.251	.279	.333	.612
2008 Tor	AL	84	186	39	8	0	1	(1	0)	50	21	18	11	10	0	25	2	7	2	3	1	3	.210	.255	.269	.524
2009 Tor	AL	73	151	39	7	0	4	(2	2)	58	18	13	16	1	0	18	2	1	1	0	2	1	.258	.271	.384	.655
2010 Tor	AL	63	152	38	9	2	6	(3	3)	69	27	23	20	6	0	26	0	2	3	2	1	5	.250	.273	.454	.727
2011 2 Tms	AL	84	227	52	10	1	2	(2	0)	70	21	22	23	12	0	27	1	3	2	2	4	1	.229	.269	.308	.577
2012 Ari	NL	70	197	49	9	0	6	(4	2)	76	16	22	21	12	5	33	1	2	0	0	1	3	.249	.295	.386	.681
2013 4 Tms	AL	51	69	8	1	0	1	(1	0)	12	8	4	2	6	0	16	1	1	0	0	0	4	.116	.197	.174	.371
2014 LAA	AL	95	76	13	2	0	0	(0	0)	15	4	5	2	7	0	18	2	5	1	1	1	1	.171	.256	.197	.453
05 Tor	AL	37	93	27	3	0	0	(0	0)	30	8	12	13	6	0	12	2	3	2	5	0	3	.290	.340	.323	.662
05 Det	AL	31	73	19	3	1	0	(0	0)	24	10	4	6	5	0	12	0	0	0	1	1	3	.260	.308	.329	.636
11 Tor	AL	65	168	42	8	1	2	(2	0)	58	19	20	21	8	0	18	1	3	2	2	4	1	.250	.285	.345	.630
11 Ari	NL	19	59	10	2	0	0	(0	0)	12	2	2	2	4	0	9	0	0	0	0	0	0	.169	.222	.203	.426
13 Pit	NL	16	31	2	1	0	0	(0	0)	3	0	1	0	3	0	8	1	0	0	0	0	1	.065	.171	.097	.268
13 Cle	AL	8	7	0	0	0	0	(0	0)	0	2	0	0	1	0	1	0	0	0	0	0	0	.000	.125	.000	.125
13 Phi	NL	21	23	4	0	0	1	(1	0)	7	5	3	1	1	0	4	0	1	0	0	0	3	.174	.208	.304	.513
13 Bos	AL	6	8	2	0	0	0	(0	0)	2	1	0	1	1	0	3	0	0	0	0	0	0	.250	.333	.250	.583
Postseason		2	2	0	0	0	0	(0	0)	0	0	0	0	0	0	0	0	0	0	0	0	0	.000	.000	.000	.000
16 ML YEARS		1100	2434	568	105	14	28	(15	13)	785	276	210	220	118	5	379	23	57	18	34	19	48	.233	.273	.323	.596

T.J. McFarland

Pitches: L **Bats:** L **Pos:** RP-36; SP-1   **Ht:** 6'3" **Wt:** 220 **Born:** 6/8/1989 **Age:** 26

		HOW MUCH HE PITCHED						WHAT HE GAVE UP										THE RESULTS						
Year Team	Lg	G	GS	CG	GF	IP	BFP	H	R	ER	HR	SH	SF	HB	TBB	IBB	SO	WP	Bk	W	L	Pct	Sh	Sv-Op	Hld	ERC	ERA
2010 Knstn	A+	24	19	1	3	126.2	537	121	50	44	9	1	0	4	40	0	92	6	1	11	5	.688	0	0- -	-	3.41	3.13
2010 Akron	AA	1	1	0	0	4.0	23	9	6	5	1	0	0	0	2	0	5	0	0	0	0	-	0	0- -	-	14.09	11.25
2011 Knstn	A+	2	2	0	0	12.0	48	9	5	3	2	0	0	0	1	0	12	0	0	0	1	.000	0	0- -	-	1.86	2.25
2011 Akron	AA	25	25	2	0	137.1	590	140	73	59	9	1	4	7	50	0	103	12	3	9	9	.500	0	0- -	-	4.04	3.87
2012 Akron	AA	10	10	1	0	60.1	240	61	18	18	1	0	1	3	12	0	41	1	0	8	2	.800	0	0- -	-	3.17	2.69
2012 Clmbs	AAA	17	17	1	0	102.2	435	112	55	55	9	0	0	1	33	0	55	5	0	8	6	.571	1	0- -	-	4.33	4.82
2014 Norfolk	AAA	5	5	0	0	24.0	105	21	11	10	0	0	0	4	8	0	25	1	1	0	1	.000	0	0- -	-	3.00	3.75
2014 Abrdn	A-	1	0	0	0	1.0	4	0	0	0	0	0	0	1	0	0	2	0	0	1	0	1.000	0	0- -	-	0.95	0.00
2013 Bal	AL	38	1	0	8	74.2	331	83	37	35	7	2	1	0	28	5	58	2	0	4	1	.800	0	0-0	0	4.40	4.22
2014 Bal	AL	37	1	0	14	58.2	255	70	22	18	2	5	0	4	13	2	34	0	0	4	2	.667	0	0-0	5	4.23	2.76
2 ML YEARS		75	2	0	22	133.1	586	153	59	53	9	7	1	4	41	7	92	2	0	8	3	.727	0	0-0	5	4.32	3.58

Jake McGee

Pitches: L **Bats:** L **Pos:** RP-73   **Ht:** 6'3" **Wt:** 235 **Born:** 8/6/1986 **Age:** 28

		HOW MUCH HE PITCHED						WHAT HE GAVE UP										THE RESULTS						
Year Team	Lg	G	GS	CG	GF	IP	BFP	H	R	ER	HR	SH	SF	HB	TBB	IBB	SO	WP	Bk	W	L	Pct	Sh	Sv-Op	Hld	ERC	ERA
2010 TB	AL	8	0	0	3	5.0	20	2	1	1	0	0	0	0	3	0	6	0	0	0	0	-	0	0-0	0	1.32	1.80
2011 TB	AL	37	0	0	9	28.0	124	30	14	14	5	1	0	0	12	1	27	0	0	5	2	.714	0	0-0	4	5.09	4.50
2012 TB	AL	69	0	0	13	55.1	212	33	13	12	3	0	2	1	11	4	73	3	0	5	2	.714	0	0-2	19	1.26	1.95
2013 TB	AL	71	0	0	6	62.2	260	52	28	28	8	1	3	1	22	5	75	4	0	5	3	.625	0	1-5	27	3.07	4.02
2014 TB	AL	73	0	0	31	71.1	274	48	15	15	2	1	1	2	16	1	90	1	0	5	2	.714	0	19-23	14	1.55	1.89
Postseason		5	0	0	1	3.1	17	3	2	2	0	1	0	1	3	1	3	0	0	0	1	.000	0	0-0	2	5.03	5.40
5 ML YEARS		258	0	0	62	222.1	890	165	71	70	18	3	6	4	64	11	271	8	0	20	9	.690	0	20-30	64	2.20	2.83

Casey McGehee

Bats: R **Throws:** R **Pos:** 3B-158;DH-1;PH-1   McGEE   **Ht:** 6'1" **Wt:** 220 **Born:** 10/12/1982 **Age:** 32

		BATTING																		RUNNING			AVERAGES			
Year Team	Lg	G	AB	H	2B	3B	HR	(Hm	Rd)	TB	R	RBI	RC	TBB	IBB	SO	HBP	SH	SF	SB	CS	GDP	Avg	OBP	Slg	OPS
2008 ChC	NL	9	24	4	1	0	0	(0	0)	5	1	5	0	0	0	8	0	0	1	0	0	1	.167	.160	.208	.368
2009 Mil	NL	116	355	107	20	1	16	(6	10)	177	58	66	66	31	2	67	1	0	4	0	2	13	.301	.360	.499	.859
2010 Mil	NL	157	610	174	38	1	23	(13	10)	283	70	104	93	50	5	102	2	0	8	1	1	18	.285	.337	.464	.801
2011 Mil	NL	155	546	122	24	2	13	(8	5)	189	46	67	50	45	4	104	1	0	8	0	3	19	.223	.280	.346	.626
2012 2 Tms	NL	114	318	69	16	1	9	(1	8)	114	36	41	30	29	0	70	2	0	3	1	1	10	.217	.284	.358	.643
2014 Mia	NL	160	616	177	29	1	4	(1	3)	220	56	76	78	67	3	102	1	0	7	4	2	31	.287	.355	.357	.712
12 Pit	NL	92	265	61	13	1	8	(1	7)	100	27	35	26	24	0	60	2	0	2	1	1	7	.230	.297	.377	.674
12 NYY	AL	22	53	8	3	0	1	(0	1)	14	9	6	4	5	0	10	0	0	1	0	0	3	.151	.220	.264	.484
Postseason		6	5	1	0	0	0	(0	0)	1	0	0	1	1	0	2	0	0	0	0	0	0	.200	.333	.200	.533
6 ML YEARS		711	2469	653	128	6	65	(29	36)	988	267	359	316	225	14	453	7	0	31	6	9	92	.264	.324	.400	.724

Dustin McGowan

Pitches: R **Bats:** R **Pos:** RP-45; SP-8   **Ht:** 6'3" **Wt:** 240 **Born:** 3/24/1982 **Age:** 33

		HOW MUCH HE PITCHED						WHAT HE GAVE UP										THE RESULTS						
Year Team	Lg	G	GS	CG	GF	IP	BFP	H	R	ER	HR	SH	SF	HB	TBB	IBB	SO	WP	Bk	W	L	Pct	Sh	Sv-Op	Hld	ERC	ERA
2005 Tor	AL	13	7	0	2	45.1	205	49	34	32	7	0	4	7	17	0	34	7	0	1	3	.250	0	0-0	1	5.47	6.35
2006 Tor	AL	9	3	0	3	27.1	143	35	27	22	2	0	1	2	25	2	22	3	1	1	2	.333	0	0-1	1	7.72	7.24
2007 Tor	AL	27	27	2	0	169.2	705	146	80	77	14	0	6	2	61	3	144	13	0	12	10	.545	1	0-0	0	3.07	4.08
2008 Tor	AL	19	19	1	0	111.1	474	115	60	54	9	2	8	5	38	1	85	5	0	6	7	.462	0	0-0	0	4.13	4.37

Year Team	Lg	HOW MUCH HE PITCHED						WHAT HE GAVE UP													THE RESULTS							
		G	GS	CG	GF	IP	BFP	H	R	ER	HR	SH	SF	HB	TBB	IBB	SO	WP	Bk	W	L	Pct	Sh	Sv-Op	Hld	ERC	ERA
2011 Tor	AL	5	4	0	0	21.0	96	20	15	15	4	0	1	1	13	0	20	3	0	0	2	.000	0	0-0	0	5.50	6.43
2013 Tor	AL	25	0	0	8	25.2	114	19	11	7	2	0	0	2	12	1	26	3	0	0	0	-	0	0-1	6	2.83	2.45
2014 Tor	AL	53	8	0	9	82.0	354	80	41	38	13	0	2	3	33	1	61	2	0	5	3	.625	0	1-5	10	4.50	4.17
7 ML YEARS		158	68	3	22	482.1	2091	464	268	245	51	2	22	22	199	8	392	36	1	25	27	.481	1	1-7	18	4.10	4.57

Collin McHugh

Pitches: R **Bats:** R **Pos:** SP-25   mick-HYOO   **Ht:** 6'2" **Wt:** 195 **Born:** 6/19/1987 **Age:** 28

Year Team	Lg	HOW MUCH HE PITCHED						WHAT HE GAVE UP													THE RESULTS							
		G	GS	CG	GF	IP	BFP	H	R	ER	HR	SH	SF	HB	TBB	IBB	SO	WP	Bk	W	L	Pct	Sh	Sv-Op	Hld	ERC	ERA
2014 OKCity*	AAA	5	3	0	1	19.0	76	15	8	8	0	0	1	0	6	0	13	1	0	0	0	-	0	0- -	-	2.07	3.79
2012 NYM	NL	8	4	0	1	21.1	99	27	21	18	5	2	1	2	8	2	17	0	0	0	4	.000	0	0-0	0	6.83	7.59
2013 2 Tms	NL	7	5	0	2	26.0	125	45	29	29	6	2	2	0	5	0	11	0	0	0	4	.000	0	0-0	0	8.82	10.04
2014 Hou	AL	25	25	0	0	154.2	619	117	53	47	13	6	4	6	41	1	157	6	0	11	9	.550	0	0-0	0	2.34	2.73
13 NYM	NL	3	1	0	2	7.0	34	12	8	8	2	0	1	0	3	0	3	0	0	0	1	.000	0	0-0	0	10.77	10.29
13 Col	NL	4	4	0	0	19.0	91	33	21	21	4	2	1	0	2	0	8	0	0	0	3	.000	0	0-0	0	8.14	9.95
3 ML YEARS		40	34	0	3	202.0	843	189	103	94	24	10	7	8	54	3	185	6	0	11	17	.393	0	0-0	0	3.46	4.19

Michael McKenry

Bats: R **Throws:** R **Pos:** C-50;PH-9   **Ht:** 5'10" **Wt:** 205 **Born:** 3/4/1985 **Age:** 30

Year Team	Lg	BATTING																RUNNING			AVERAGES			
		G	AB	H	2B	3B	HR	(Hm | Rd)	TB	R	RBI	RC	TBB	IBB	SO	HBP	SH	SF	SB	CS	GDP	Avg	OBP	Slg	OPS
2014 ColSpr*	AAA	23	83	26	6	0	3	(- | -)	41	15	12	15	7	0	13	1	1	1	3	0	2	.313	.370	.494	.864
2010 Col	NL	6	8	0	0	0	0	(0 | 0)	0	0	0	0	1	0	5	0	0	0	0	0	0	.000	.111	.000	.111
2011 Pit	NL	58	180	40	12	0	2	(1 | 1)	58	17	11	12	14	2	49	0	5	2	0	1	3	.222	.276	.322	.598
2012 Pit	NL	88	240	56	14	0	12	(3 | 9)	106	25	39	32	29	1	73	3	0	3	0	0	7	.233	.320	.442	.762
2013 Pit	NL	41	115	25	6	0	3	(2 | 1)	40	9	14	11	5	0	24	2	0	0	0	0	2	.217	.262	.348	.610
2014 Col	NL	57	168	53	9	0	8	(4 | 4)	86	23	22	28	22	1	42	1	1	0	0	3	6	.315	.398	.512	.910
5 ML YEARS		250	711	174	41	0	25	(10 | 15)	290	74	86	83	71	4	193	6	6	5	0	4	18	.245	.317	.408	.724

Nate McLouth

mc-CLOWTH

Bats: L **Throws:** R **Pos:** PH-30;LF-28;RF-16;CF-9;PR-3;DH-1   **Ht:** 5'10" **Wt:** 190 **Born:** 10/28/1981 **Age:** 33

Year Team	Lg	BATTING																RUNNING			AVERAGES			
		G	AB	H	2B	3B	HR	(Hm | Rd)	TB	R	RBI	RC	TBB	IBB	SO	HBP	SH	SF	SB	CS	GDP	Avg	OBP	Slg	OPS
2005 Pit	NL	41	109	28	6	0	5	(2 | 3)	49	20	12	9	3	0	20	5	2	1	2	0	3	.257	.305	.450	.755
2006 Pit	NL	106	270	63	16	2	7	(3 | 4)	104	50	16	25	18	0	59	5	3	1	10	1	7	.233	.293	.385	.678
2007 Pit	NL	137	329	85	21	3	13	(5 | 8)	151	62	38	52	39	2	77	9	3	2	22	1	2	.258	.351	.459	.810
2008 Pit	NL	152	597	165	46	4	26	(15 | 11)	297	113	94	105	65	11	93	12	5	6	23	3	5	.276	.356	.497	.853
2009 2 Tms	NL	129	507	130	27	2	20	(9 | 11)	221	86	70	85	68	1	99	9	3	4	19	6	8	.256	.352	.436	.788
2010 Atl	NL	85	242	46	12	1	6	(5 | 1)	78	30	24	23	33	2	57	5	6	2	7	2	3	.190	.298	.322	.620
2011 Atl	NL	81	267	61	12	2	4	(4 | 0)	89	35	16	36	44	4	52	3	7	0	4	2	4	.228	.344	.333	.677
2012 2 Tms		89	266	64	14	1	7	(4 | 3)	101	39	20	30	27	1	61	2	2	1	12	1	2	.241	.314	.380	.694
2013 Bal	AL	146	531	137	31	4	12	(7 | 5)	212	76	36	71	53	1	86	4	4	1	30	7	7	.258	.329	.399	.729
2014 Was	NL	79	139	24	6	0	1	(1 | 0)	33	10	7	8	16	1	35	5	1	1	4	1	0	.173	.280	.237	.517
09 Pit	NL	45	168	43	7	1	9	(5 | 4)	79	27	34	33	21	0	29	4	0	2	7	0	2	.256	.349	.470	.819
09 Atl	NL	84	339	87	20	1	11	(4 | 7)	142	59	36	52	47	1	70	5	3	2	12	6	6	.257	.354	.419	.773
12 Pit	NL	34	57	8	2	0	0	(0 | 0)	10	4	2	1	5	0	18	0	0	0	0	0	0	.140	.210	.175	.385
12 Bal	AL	55	209	56	12	1	7	(4 | 3)	91	35	18	29	22	1	43	2	2	1	12	1	2	.268	.342	.435	.777
Postseason		9	28	9	1	0	1	(0 | 1)	13	3	5	4	1	0	3	0	0	1	3	1	0	.321	.333	.464	.798
10 ML YEARS		1045	3257	803	191	19	101	(55 | 46)	1335	521	333	444	366	23	639	59	36	19	133	24	41	.247	.332	.410	.742

Tommy Medica

Bats: R **Throws:** R **Pos:** 1B-46;PH-41;LF-22;DH-4;PR-1   MEDD-ih-kah   **Ht:** 6'3" **Wt:** 205 **Born:** 4/9/1988 **Age:** 27

Year Team	Lg	BATTING																RUNNING			AVERAGES			
		G	AB	H	2B	3B	HR	(Hm | Rd)	TB	R	RBI	RC	TBB	IBB	SO	HBP	SH	SF	SB	CS	GDP	Avg	OBP	Slg	OPS
2010 Eugene	A-	34	102	18	4	0	0	(- | -)	22	7	9	8	18	0	18	5	2	4	0	2	3	.176	.318	.216	.534
2011 FtWyn	A	44	142	38	19	4	0	(- | -)	66	22	21	24	17	0	33	5	1	0	0	1	2	.268	.366	.465	.831
2011 Padres	R	6	23	9	2	0	1	(- | -)	14	8	6	6	4	0	3	0	0	1	0	0	0	.391	.464	.609	1.073
2011 Lk Els	A+	42	139	42	10	0	6	(- | -)	70	21	17	32	25	1	32	10	0	1	0	1	4	.302	.440	.504	.944
2012 Lk Els	A+	93	355	117	37	5	19	(- | -)	221	65	87	86	41	1	86	7	0	3	1	1	8	.330	.406	.623	1.029
2013 SnAnt	AA	76	280	83	20	3	18	(- | -)	163	48	57	60	28	1	67	8	0	4	4	2	8	.296	.372	.582	.954
2013 Padres	R	5	17	5	2	0	2	(- | -)	13	6	8	4	1	0	7	0	0	0	0	0	0	.294	.333	.765	1.098
2014 ElPaso	AAA	24	89	20	6	2	3	(- | -)	39	8	19	12	9	0	24	3	0	0	0	0	3	.225	.317	.438	.755
2013 SD	NL	19	69	20	2	0	3	(1 | 2)	31	9	10	12	10	0	23	0	0	0	0	0	0	.290	.380	.449	.829
2014 SD	NL	102	240	56	11	2	9	(5 | 4)	98	31	27	28	14	0	75	4	0	1	6	1	5	.233	.286	.408	.694
2 ML YEARS		121	309	76	13	2	12	(6 | 6)	129	40	37	40	24	0	98	4	0	1	6	1	5	.246	.308	.417	.725

Yoervis Medina

Pitches: R **Bats:** R **Pos:** RP-66   yo-EHR-viss meh-DEE-nah   **Ht:** 6'3" **Wt:** 245 **Born:** 7/27/1988 **Age:** 26

Year	Team	Lg	G	GS	CG	GF	IP	BFP	H	R	ER	HR	SH	SF	HB	TBB	IBB	SO	WP	Bk	W	L	Pct	Sh	Sv-Op	Hld	ERC	ERA
2010	Everett	A-	8	8	0	0	40.2	187	49	30	19	4	3	2	2	15	0	48	3	0	3	2	.600	0	0- -	-	5.22	4.20
2010	Tacom	AAA	1	1	0	0	5.2	23	3	0	0	0	0	0	0	4	0	4	0	0	1	0	1.000	0	0- -	-	2.14	0.00
2010	Clinton	A	6	6	0	0	36.0	151	30	10	10	3	0	1	2	12	0	42	3	0	5	0	1.000	0	0- -	-	2.99	2.50
2011	Hi Dsrt	A+	20	19	1	0	101.0	474	139	90	73	19	6	6	5	38	1	73	5	0	1	13	.071	0	0- -	-	7.14	6.50
2011	Ms	R	1	1	0	0	5.0	22	7	4	4	1	0	0	0	1	0	9	1	0	0	0	-	0	0- -	-	6.52	7.20
2011	Jacksn	AA	4	4	0	0	25.0	106	23	13	13	5	2	1	2	9	0	17	2	1	0	1	.000	0	0- -	-	4.53	4.68
2012	Jacksn	AA	46	1	0	13	69.1	303	63	25	25	5	6	0	5	35	3	77	2	1	5	5	.500	0	5- -	-	4.00	3.25
2013	Tacom	AAA	4	0	0	1	6.0	21	2	1	1	0	0	0	0	3	0	7	2	0	0	1	.000	0	0- -	-	1.05	1.50
2013	Sea	AL	63	0	0	19	68.0	291	49	22	22	5	2	1	4	40	7	71	8	0	4	6	.400	0	1-4	19	3.15	2.91
2014	Sea	AL	66	0	0	19	57.0	247	48	18	17	3	0	4	5	28	3	60	8	0	5	3	.625	0	0-1	21	3.47	2.68
	2 ML YEARS		129	0	0	38	125.0	538	97	40	39	8	2	5	9	68	10	131	16	0	9	9	.500	0	1-5	40	3.29	2.81

Kris Medlen

Pitches: R **Bats:** B **Pos:** P   MEDD-linn   **Ht:** 5'10" **Wt:** 190 **Born:** 10/7/1985 **Age:** 29

Year	Team	Lg	G	GS	CG	GF	IP	BFP	H	R	ER	HR	SH	SF	HB	TBB	IBB	SO	WP	Bk	W	L	Pct	Sh	Sv-Op	Hld	ERC	ERA
2009	Atl	NL	37	4	0	10	67.2	294	65	34	32	5	6	2	2	30	2	72	3	1	3	5	.375	0	0-2	1	3.90	4.26
2010	Atl	NL	31	14	0	5	107.2	438	108	48	44	13	7	3	3	21	1	83	1	1	6	2	.750	0	0-0	1	3.60	3.68
2011	Atl	NL	2	0	0	1	2.1	8	1	0	0	0	0	0	0	0	0	2	0	0	0	0	-	0	0-0	0	0.40	0.00
2012	Atl	NL	50	12	2	7	138.0	520	103	26	24	6	1	0	0	23	0	120	3	0	10	1	.909	1	1-2	7	1.69	1.57
2013	Atl	NL	32	31	0	1	197.0	820	194	77	68	18	9	2	8	47	1	157	2	0	15	12	.556	0	0-0	0	3.48	3.11
	Postseason		2	2	0	0	10.1	48	12	10	7	2	1	2	2	1	0	8	0	0	0	2	.000	0	0-0	0	4.88	6.10
	5 ML YEARS		152	61	2	24	512.2	2080	471	185	168	42	23	7	13	121	4	434	9	2	34	20	.630	1	1-4	9	3.02	2.95

Evan Meek

Pitches: R **Bats:** R **Pos:** RP-23   **Ht:** 6'0" **Wt:** 225 **Born:** 5/12/1983 **Age:** 32

Year	Team	Lg	G	GS	CG	GF	IP	BFP	H	R	ER	HR	SH	SF	HB	TBB	IBB	SO	WP	Bk	W	L	Pct	Sh	Sv-Op	Hld	ERC	ERA
2014	Norfolk*	AAA	39	0	0	28	41.2	160	33	13	9	2	1	1	0	4	0	37	1	1	2	0	1.000	0	16- -	-	1.65	1.94
2008	Pit	NL	9	0	0	7	13.0	61	11	11	10	3	1	1	1	12	2	7	3	0	1	0	.000	0	0-0	0	6.46	6.92
2009	Pit	NL	41	0	0	14	47.0	195	34	18	18	2	2	1	0	29	2	42	5	0	1	1	.500	0	0-1	4	3.03	3.45
2010	Pit	NL	70	0	0	16	80.0	324	53	25	19	5	2	1	4	31	4	70	2	0	5	4	.556	0	4-10	15	2.15	2.14
2011	Pit	NL	24	0	0	6	20.2	100	27	11	8	1	1	0	0	12	0	17	2	0	1	1	.500	0	0-0	2	6.12	3.48
2012	Pit	NL	12	0	0	5	12.0	57	14	9	9	1	1	0	1	6	0	8	1	0	0	0	-	0	0-0	1	5.52	6.75
2014	Bal	AL	23	0	0	4	23.1	107	26	16	15	3	4	0	2	11	1	16	1	0	0	4	.000	0	0-1	3	5.50	5.79
	6 ML YEARS		179	0	0	52	196.0	844	165	90	79	15	11	3	8	101	9	160	14	0	7	11	.389	0	4-13	27	3.57	3.63

Jenrry Mejia

Pitches: R **Bats:** R **Pos:** RP-56; SP-7   HENN-ree mah-HEE-ah   **Ht:** 6'0" **Wt:** 205 **Born:** 10/11/1989 **Age:** 25

Year	Team	Lg	G	GS	CG	GF	IP	BFP	H	R	ER	HR	SH	SF	HB	TBB	IBB	SO	WP	Bk	W	L	Pct	Sh	Sv-Op	Hld	ERC	ERA
2010	NYM	NL	33	3	0	8	39.0	183	46	21	20	3	0	1	3	20	2	22	7	0	0	4	.000	0	0-1	2	5.57	4.62
2012	NYM	NL	5	3	0	1	16.0	74	20	10	10	2	1	0	0	9	0	8	1	0	1	2	.333	0	0-0	0	6.55	5.63
2013	NYM	NL	5	5	0	0	27.1	112	28	9	7	2	0	4	0	4	0	27	1	0	1	2	.333	0	0-0	0	3.05	2.30
2014	NYM	NL	63	7	0	49	93.2	417	98	41	38	9	2	0	4	41	8	98	5	0	6	6	.500	0	28-31	2	4.45	3.65
	4 ML YEARS		106	18	0	58	176.0	786	192	81	75	16	3	5	7	74	10	155	14	0	8	14	.364	0	28-32	4	4.65	3.84

Mark Melancon

Pitches: R **Bats:** R **Pos:** RP-72   muh-LANN-sun   **Ht:** 6'2" **Wt:** 215 **Born:** 3/28/1985 **Age:** 30

Year	Team	Lg	G	GS	CG	GF	IP	BFP	H	R	ER	HR	SH	SF	HB	TBB	IBB	SO	WP	Bk	W	L	Pct	Sh	Sv-Op	Hld	ERC	ERA
2009	NYY	AL	13	0	0	4	16.1	74	13	8	7	0	0	0	4	10	0	10	3	0	0	1	.000	0	0-1	0	3.94	3.86
2010	2 Tmo		22	0	0	4	21.1	90	19	10	10	2	0	1	1	0	0	22	2	0	2	0	1.000	0	0- I	8	3.53	4.22
2011	Hou	NL	71	0	0	47	74.1	309	65	28	23	5	2	0	2	26	6	66	1	0	8	4	.667	0	20-25	3	2.98	2.78
2012	Bos	AL	41	0	0	17	45.0	194	45	31	31	8	1	2	3	12	1	41	2	0	0	2	.000	0	1-2	2	4.24	6.20
2013	Pit	NL	72	0	0	24	71.0	279	60	15	11	1	0	1	1	8	0	70	6	0	3	2	.600	0	16-21	26	1.78	1.39
2014	Pit	NL	72	0	0	48	71.0	277	51	15	15	2	1	1	3	11	1	71	3	0	3	5	.375	0	33-37	14	1.54	1.90
10	NYY	AL	2	0	0	2	4.0	19	7	5	4	1	0	1	0	0	0	3	0	0	0	0	-	0	0-0	0	7.95	9.00
10	Hou	NL	20	0	0	2	17.1	71	12	8	6	1	0	0	1	0	0	19	2	0	2	0	1.000	0	0-1	8	2.65	3.12
	Postseason		4	0	0	1	3.2	16	5	4	4	2	0	0	0	1	0	2	0	0	1	0	1.000	0	0-1	0	9.59	9.82
	6 ML YEARS		291	0	0	144	299.0	1223	253	110	97	18	4	5	14	75	8	280	17	0	16	14	.533	0	70-87	53	2.57	2.92

Roman Mendez

Pitches: R **Bats:** R **Pos:** RP-30   **Ht:** 6'2" **Wt:** 190 **Born:** 7/25/1990 **Age:** 24

Year	Team	Lg	G	GS	CG	GF	IP	BFP	H	R	ER	HR	SH	SF	HB	TBB	IBB	SO	WP	Bk	W	L	Pct	Sh	Sv-Op	Hld	ERC	ERA
2010	Grnvlle	A	6	6	0	0	15.0	88	29	24	19	5	0	0	4	10	0	18	1	0	0	2	.000	0	0- -	-	14.82	11.40
2010	Lowell	A-	8	8	0	0	33.0	151	31	21	16	5	1	1	1	19	0	35	4	0	2	3	.400	0	0- -	-	4.79	4.36
2010	Spkane	A-	3	3	0	0	11.2	55	19	11	3	2	1	0	1	3	0	13	0	0	1	1	.500	0	0- -	-	8.01	2.31
2011	Hkry	A	26	20	0	1	117.0	509	117	44	43	7	4	2	6	45	0	130	11	1	9	1	.900	0	1- -	-	3.92	3.31
2012	MrtlBh	A+	18	12	0	3	70.0	304	69	43	40	7	5	2	7	25	0	71	3	0	4	6	.400	0	1- -	-	4.23	5.14
2012	Rngrs	R	3	3	0	0	9.0	36	7	3	3	1	1	1	1	1	0	7	0	0	0	1	.000	0	0- -	-	2.29	3.00

Year Team	Lg	G	GS	CG	GF	IP	BFP	H	R	ER	HR	SH	SF	HB	TBB	IBB	SO	WP	Bk	W	L	Pct	Sh	Sv-Op	Hld	ERC	ERA
2012 Frisco	AA	5	0	0	1	12.1	51	8	3	2	2	0	0	1	4	1	9	0	0	2	0	1.000	0	1--	-	2.43	1.46
2013 Frisco	AA	16	0	0	8	24.2	99	12	6	5	1	3	1	2	11	2	24	2	0	2	0	1.000	0	2--	-	1.52	1.82
2014 RdRck	AAA	25	0	0	12	31.1	144	39	16	14	4	0	1	2	12	0	30	1	0	0	0	.000	0	3--	-	5.91	4.02
2014 Tex	AL	30	0	0	6	33.0	136	20	8	8	2	0	2	2	17	2	22	2	0	0	1	.000	0	0-0	10	2.31	2.18

Melvin Mercedes

Pitches: R **Bats:** R **Pos:** RP-1   **Ht:** 6'3" **Wt:** 250 **Born:** 11/2/1990 **Age:** 24

Year Team	Lg	G	GS	CG	GF	IP	BFP	H	R	ER	HR	SH	SF	HB	TBB	IBB	SO	WP	Bk	W	L	Pct	Sh	Sv-Op	Hld	ERC	ERA
2010 WMich	A	15	0	0	11	19.2	94	16	11	11	0	1	0	3	19	1	12	2	0	1	2	.333	0	3--	-	4.92	5.03
2011 Conn	A-	21	0	0	5	33.2	149	32	17	10	0	1	1	1	16	1	21	4	0	3	1	.750	0	3--	-	3.37	2.67
2011 WMich	A	2	0	0	1	1.2	10	3	2	2	0	0	0	1	1	0	1	0	0	0	0	-	0	0--	-	11.51	10.80
2012 WMich	A	37	0	0	22	64.1	261	54	25	20	3	0	1	2	23	0	43	4	1	0	3	.000	0	9--	-	2.90	2.80
2012 Lkland	A+	1	0	0	1	1.0	5	1	0	0	0	0	0	0	1	0	0	0	0	0	0	-	0	0--	-	5.48	0.00
2013 Lkland	A+	24	0	0	21	28.0	110	23	7	3	1	0	0	1	5	0	17	0	1	3	1	.750	0	11--	-	2.11	0.96
2013 Erie	AA	26	0	0	24	25.0	111	23	10	4	3	1	2	2	9	0	19	2	0	2	1	.667	0	12--	-	3.76	1.44
2014 Toledo	AAA	46	0	0	18	60.1	262	69	35	33	8	1	2	0	16	1	31	3	0	0	3	.000	0	3--	-	4.52	4.92
2014 Det	AL	1	0	0	0	2.0	6	0	0	0	0	0	0	0	0	0	2	0	0	0	0	-	0	0-0	0	0.00	0.00

Jordy Mercer

Bats: R **Throws:** R **Pos:** SS-144;PH-6;RF-1;PR-1   **Ht:** 6'3" **Wt:** 205 **Born:** 8/27/1986 **Age:** 28

Year Team	Lg	G	AB	H	2B	3B	HR	(Hm	Rd)	TB	R	RBI	RC	TBB	IBB	SO	HBP	SH	SF	SB	CS	GDP	Avg	OBP	Slg	OPS
2012 Pit	NL	42	62	13	5	1	1	(1	0)	23	7	5	6	4	0	14	1	0	1	0	1	0	.210	.265	.371	.636
2013 Pit	NL	103	333	95	22	2	8	(1	7)	145	33	27	46	22	6	62	4	5	1	3	2	7	.285	.336	.435	.772
2014 Pit	NL	149	506	129	27	2	12	(3	9)	196	56	55	45	35	12	89	4	5	5	4	1	14	.255	.305	.387	.693
Postseason		5	8	2	0	0	0	(0	0)	2	0	0	0	1	1	2	0	0	0	0	0	0	.250	.333	.250	.583
3 ML YEARS		294	901	237	54	5	21	(5	16)	364	96	87	97	61	18	165	9	10	7	7	4	21	.263	.314	.404	.718

Devin Mesoraco

Bats: R **Throws:** R **Pos:** C-109;PH-9;DH-1   mezz-er-OCK-oh   **Ht:** 6'1" **Wt:** 220 **Born:** 6/19/1988 **Age:** 27

Year Team	Lg	G	AB	H	2B	3B	HR	(Hm	Rd)	TB	R	RBI	RC	TBB	IBB	SO	HBP	SH	SF	SB	CS	GDP	Avg	OBP	Slg	OPS
2014 Pnscla*	AA	3	5	0	0	0	0	(-	-)	0	0	1	0	2	0	1	0	0	1	0	0	0	.000	.250	.000	.250
2014 Lsvlle*	AAA	3	10	3	0	0	1	(-	-)	6	2	2	1	0	0	1	0	0	0	0	0	0	.300	.300	.600	.900
2011 Cin	NL	18	50	9	3	0	2	(2	0)	18	5	6	5	3	1	10	0	0	0	0	0	1	.180	.226	.360	.586
2012 Cin	NL	54	165	35	8	0	5	(4	3)	58	17	14	10	17	4	33	1	0	1	1	1	2	.212	.288	.352	.640
2013 Cin	NL	103	323	77	13	0	9	(5	4)	117	31	42	30	24	4	61	0	0	5	0	2	9	.238	.287	.362	.649
2014 Cin	NL	114	384	105	25	0	25	(14	11)	205	54	80	76	41	4	103	12	0	3	1	3	5	.273	.359	.534	.893
Postseason		1	1	0	0	0	0	(0	0)	0	0	0	0	0	0	0	0	0	0	0	0	0	.000	.000	.000	.000
4 ML YEARS		289	922	226	49	0	41	(25	16)	398	107	142	121	85	13	207	13	0	9	2	6	17	.245	.315	.432	.747

Will Middlebrooks

Bats: R **Throws:** R **Pos:** 3B-62;PH-3;1B-1   **Ht:** 6'3" **Wt:** 220 **Born:** 9/9/1988 **Age:** 26

Year Team	Lg	G	AB	H	2B	3B	HR	(Hm	Rd)	TB	R	RBI	RC	TBB	IBB	SO	HBP	SH	SF	SB	CS	GDP	Avg	OBP	Slg	OPS
2014 Pwtckt*	AAA	29	104	24	1	1	4	(-	-)	39	13	8	11	6	0	30	1	0	1	0	0	2	.231	.277	.375	.652
2012 Bos	AL	75	267	77	14	0	15	(9	6)	136	34	54	46	13	0	70	3	0	3	4	1	8	.288	.325	.509	.835
2013 Bos	AL	94	348	79	18	0	17	(4	13)	148	41	49	29	20	3	98	2	1	3	3	1	13	.227	.271	.425	.696
2014 Bos	AL	63	215	41	10	0	2	(1	1)	57	14	19	15	15	1	70	4	0	0	1	1	7	.191	.256	.265	.522
Postseason		10	25	4	2	0	0	(0	0)	6	2	1	2	3	1	10	0	0	0	0	0	0	.160	.250	.240	.490
3 ML YEARS		232	830	197	42	0	34	(14	20)	341	89	122	90	48	4	238	9	1	6	8	3	28	.237	.284	.411	.695

Miles Mikolas

Pitches: R **Bats:** R **Pos:** SP-10   MIKE-uh-liss   **Ht:** 6'5" **Wt:** 220 **Born:** 8/23/1988 **Age:** 26

Year Team	Lg	G	GS	CG	GF	IP	BFP	H	R	ER	HR	SH	SF	HB	TBB	IBB	SO	WP	Bk	W	L	Pct	Sh	Sv-Op	Hld	ERC	ERA
2014 RdRck*	AAA	16	6	0	7	44.2	190	53	20	16	3	0	0	0	3	0	38	2	1	5	1	.833	0	2--	-	3.49	3.22
2012 SD	NL	25	0	0	9	32.1	144	32	15	13	4	2	0	2	15	0	23	2	0	2	1	.667	0	0-1	1	4.65	3.62
2013 SD	NL	10	0	0	1	1.2	7	0	0	0	0	0	0	1	1	0	1	0	0	0	0	.000	0	0-0	0	1.30	0.00
2014 Tex	AL	10	10	0	0	57.1	255	64	43	41	8	1	2	4	18	2	38	0	1	2	5	.286	0	0-0	0	4.85	6.44
3 ML YEARS		37	10	0	10	91.1	406	96	58	54	12	3	2	7	34	2	62	2	1	4	6	.400	0	0-1	1	4.71	5.32

Wade Miley

Pitches: L **Bats:** L **Pos:** SP-33   MY-lee   **Ht:** 6'0" **Wt:** 220 **Born:** 11/13/1986 **Age:** 28

Year Team	Lg	G	GS	CG	GF	IP	BFP	H	R	ER	HR	SH	SF	HB	TBB	IBB	SO	WP	Bk	W	L	Pct	Sh	Sv-Op	Hld	ERC	ERA
2011 Ari	NL	8	7	0	0	40.0	180	48	20	20	6	3	1	4	18	0	25	1	0	4	2	.667	0	0-0	0	5.90	4.50
2012 Ari	NL	32	29	0	0	194.2	807	193	79	72	14	8	3	2	37	0	144	6	1	16	11	.593	0	0-0	0	3.05	3.33
2013 Ari	NL	33	33	0	0	202.2	847	201	88	80	21	6	2	4	66	4	147	13	0	10	10	.500	0	0-0	0	3.88	3.55
2014 Ari	NL	33	33	0	0	201.1	866	207	103	97	23	8	9	4	75	3	183	9	0	8	12	.400	0	0-0	0	4.31	4.34
4 ML YEARS		106	102	0	0	638.2	2700	649	290	269	64	25	15	10	196	7	499	29	1	38	35	.521	0	0-0	0	3.87	3.79

Andrew Miller

Pitches: L Bats: L Pos: RP-73   Ht: 6'7" Wt: 210 Born: 5/21/1985 Age: 30

Year Team	Lg	G	GS	CG	GF	IP	BFP	H	R	ER	HR	SH	SF	HB	TBB	IBB	SO	WP	Bk	W	L	Pct	Sh	Sv-Op	Hld	ERC	ERA
2006 Det	AL	8	0	0	3	10.1	51	8	9	7	0	0	0	2	10	0	6	1	0	0	1	.000	0	0-0	1	4.79	6.10
2007 Det	AL	13	13	0	0	64.0	309	73	43	40	8	3	1	7	39	0	56	4	1	5	5	.500	0	0-0	0	6.31	5.63
2008 Fla	NL	29	20	0	1	107.1	492	120	78	70	7	10	7	4	56	4	89	4	0	6	10	.375	0	0-0	2	5.04	5.87
2009 Fla	NL	20	14	0	1	80.0	366	85	52	43	7	6	4	2	43	1	59	10	0	3	5	.375	0	0-0	1	4.90	4.84
2010 Fla	NL	9	7	0	1	32.2	171	51	34	31	6	5	2	1	26	2	28	5	0	1	5	.167	0	0-0	0	10.20	8.54
2011 Bos	AL	17	12	0	2	65.0	310	77	43	40	8	6	5	3	41	0	50	2	1	6	3	.667	0	0-0	0	6.48	5.54
2012 Bos	AL	53	0	0	4	40.1	169	28	15	15	3	0	3	2	20	1	51	1	0	3	2	.600	0	0-0	13	2.76	3.35
2013 Bos	AL	37	0	0	11	30.2	135	25	12	9	3	1	0	2	17	0	48	2	0	1	2	.333	0	0-1	6	3.83	2.64
2014 2 Tms	AL	73	0	0	15	62.1	242	33	16	14	3	2	2	5	17	2	103	3	0	5	5	.500	0	1-2	22	1.36	2.02
14 Bos	AL	50	0	0	12	42.1	170	25	13	11	2	2	2	4	13	2	69	2	0	3	5	.375	0	0-0	13	1.62	2.34
14 Bal	AL	23	0	0	3	20.0	72	8	3	3	1	0	0	1	4	0	34	1	0	2	0	1.000	0	1-2	9	0.86	1.35
9 ML YEARS		259	66	0	38	492.2	2245	500	302	269	45	33	24	28	269	10	490	32	2	30	38	.441	0	1-3	45	4.82	4.91

Brad Miller

Bats: L Throws: R Pos: SS-107;2B-13;PH-6;3B-2;PR-2;DH-1   Ht: 6'2" Wt: 200 Born: 10/18/1989 Age: 25

Year Team	Lg	G	AB	H	2B	3B	HR	(Hm	Rd)	TB	R	RBI	RC	TBB	IBB	SO	HBP	SH	SF	SB	CS	GDP	Avg	OBP	Slg	OPS
2011 Clinton	A	14	53	22	4	1	0	(-	-)	28	9	7	12	4	0	9	1	0	1	1	0	1	.415	.458	.528	.986
2012 Hi Dsrt	A+	97	410	139	33	5	11	(-	-)	215	89	56	90	52	2	79	2	4	5	19	6	5	.339	.412	.524	.936
2012 Jacksn	AA	40	147	47	7	2	4	(-	-)	70	21	12	29	22	0	26	0	0	1	4	1	4	.320	.406	.476	.882
2013 Jacksn	AA	42	153	45	7	1	6	(-	-)	72	27	25	27	20	2	30	1	1	0	4	3	1	.294	.379	.471	.850
2013 Tacom	AAA	26	104	37	5	1	6	(-	-)	62	26	28	26	15	0	18	0	0	3	2	1	0	.356	.426	.596	1.022
2013 Sea	AL	76	306	81	11	6	8	(3	5)	128	41	36	41	24	0	52	1	2	2	5	3	2	.265	.318	.418	.737
2014 Sea	AL	123	367	81	15	4	10	(4	6)	134	47	36	41	34	2	95	2	3	2	4	2	2	.221	.288	.365	.653
2 ML YEARS		199	673	162	26	10	18	(7	11)	262	88	72	82	58	2	147	3	5	5	9	5	4	.241	.302	.389	.691

Jim Miller

Pitches: R Bats: R Pos: RP-2   Ht: 6'1" Wt: 200 Born: 4/28/1982 Age: 33

Year Team	Lg	G	GS	CG	GF	IP	BFP	H	R	ER	HR	SH	SF	HB	TBB	IBB	SO	WP	Bk	W	L	Pct	Sh	Sv-Op	Hld	ERC	ERA
2014 S-WB*	AAA	36	0	0	16	57.1	249	56	24	21	3	1	4	2	20	1	60	2	0	6	4	.600	0	2- -	-	3.45	3.30
2008 Bal	AL	8	0	0	5	7.2	39	9	3	1	0	1	1	1	5	2	8	1	0	0	2	.000	0	1-2	0	4.99	1.17
2011 Col	NL	6	0	0	4	7.0	29	3	2	2	0	0	2	0	4	0	5	0	0	0	0	-	0	0-0	0	1.30	2.57
2012 Oak	AL	33	0	0	18	48.2	211	39	15	14	6	0	1	3	27	2	44	1	0	2	1	.667	0	0-0	0	3.91	2.59
2013 NYY	AL	1	0	0	0	1.1	8	3	3	3	1	0	1	0	1	0	0	0	0	0	0	-	0	0-0	0	20.88	20.25
2014 NYY	AL	2	0	0	1	2.2	16	7	6	6	3	0	0	2	2	0	2	0	0	0	0	-	0	0-0	0	30.32	20.25
5 ML YEARS		50	0	0	28	67.1	303	61	29	26	10	1	5	4	39	4	59	2	0	2	3	.400	0	1-2	0	4.69	3.48

Justin Miller

Pitches: R Bats: R Pos: RP-8   Ht: 6'3" Wt: 215 Born: 6/13/1987 Age: 28

Year Team	Lg	G	GS	CG	GF	IP	BFP	H	R	ER	HR	SH	SF	HB	TBB	IBB	SO	WP	Bk	W	L	Pct	Sh	Sv-Op	Hld	ERC	ERA
2010 Bkrsfld	A+	32	0	0	11	47.0	199	35	18	16	3	3	0	4	21	0	52	7	0	4	3	.571	0	0- -	-	2.93	3.06
2011 Frisco	AA	48	0	0	29	69.2	278	46	14	14	2	1	1	4	24	3	77	5	0	9	1	.900	0	13- -	-	1.86	1.81
2013 Frisco	AA	16	0	0	5	16.0	75	16	11	11	1	0	1	4	7	0	21	4	0	1	0	1.000	0	2- -	-	4.80	6.19
2013 RdRck	AAA	11	0	0	4	11.0	58	14	16	12	4	0	1	0	9	0	12	2	0	0	1	.000	0	1- -	-	9.32	9.82
2014 Toledo	AAA	38	0	0	22	44.2	173	30	9	9	2	1	1	4	12	0	39	2	0	2	1	.667	0	5- -	-	1.98	1.81
2014 Det	AL	8	0	0	4	12.1	53	14	9	7	2	1	2	0	2	0	5	0	0	1	0	1.000	0	0-0	0	4.21	5.11

Shelby Miller

Pitches: R Bats: R Pos: SP-31; RP-1   Ht: 6'3" Wt: 215 Born: 10/10/1990 Age: 24

Year Team	Lg	G	GS	CG	GF	IP	BFP	H	R	ER	HR	SH	SF	HB	TBB	IBB	SO	WP	Bk	W	L	Pct	Sh	Sv-Op	Hld	ERC	ERA
2012 StL	NL	6	1	0	0	13.2	54	9	2	2	0	0	0	1	4	0	16	0	0	1	0	1.000	0	0-0	1	1.65	1.32
2013 StL	NL	31	31	1	0	173.1	722	152	65	59	20	7	3	5	57	0	169	2	0	15	9	.625	1	0-0	0	3.34	3.06
2014 StL	NL	32	31	1	0	183.0	764	160	78	76	22	7	4	2	73	4	127	4	0	10	9	.526	1	0-0	0	3.56	3.74
Postseason		3	0	0	0	4.1	19	5	3	3	1	0	0	0	1	0	5	0	0	0	0	-	0	0-0	0	5.07	6.23
3 ML YEARS		69	63	2	1	370.0	1540	321	145	137	42	14	7	8	134	4	312	6	0	26	18	.591	2	0-0	1	3.38	3.33

Brad Mills

Pitches: L Bats: R Pos: SP-3; RP-2   Ht: 6'0" Wt: 185 Born: 3/5/1985 Age: 30

Year Team	Lg	G	GS	CG	GF	IP	BFP	H	R	ER	HR	SH	SF	HB	TBB	IBB	SO	WP	Bk	W	L	Pct	Sh	Sv-Op	Hld	ERC	ERA
2014 Nashv*	AAA	14	12	0	0	75.0	294	51	18	13	5	3	1	4	18	0	77	2	1	4	2	.667	0	0- -	-	1.87	1.56
2014 Buffalo*	AAA	6	6	0	0	32.1	122	26	11	11	2	1	2	0	5	0	26	1	0	2	1	.667	0	0- -	-	2.04	3.06
2009 Tor	AL	2	2	0	0	7.2	42	14	12	12	4	0	1	0	6	0	9	0	0	0	0	-	0	0-0	0	15.52	14.09
2010 Tor	AL	7	3	0	0	22.1	98	20	14	14	2	0	1	1	13	1	18	1	0	1	0	1.000	0	0-0	0	4.26	5.64
2011 Tor	AL	5	4	0	0	18.1	91	23	20	20	4	0	0	2	12	1	18	1	0	1	2	.333	0	0-0	0	7.97	9.82
2012 LAA	AL	1	1	0	0	5.0	18	3	0	0	0	0	0	0	0	0	6	0	0	1	0	1.000	0	0-0	0	0.75	0.00

Year	Team	Lg	G	GS	CG	GF	IP	BFP	H	R	ER	HR	SH	SF	HB	TBB	IBB	SO	WP	Bk	W	L	Pct	Sh	Sv-Op	Hld	ERC	ERA
2014	2 Tms	AL	5	3	0	1	20.2	101	29	22	21	5	0	1	2	11	0	19	1	0	1	1	.500	0	0-0	0	8.84	9.15
14	Oak	AL	3	3	0	0	16.1	73	19	9	8	2	0	0	1	7	0	14	1	0	1	1	.500	0	0-0	0	5.67	4.41
14	Tor	AL	2	0	0	1	4.1	28	10	13	13	3	0	1	1	4	0	5	0	0	0	0	-	0	0-0	0	23.14	27.00
5 ML YEARS			20	13	0	1	74.0	350	89	68	67	15	0	3	5	42	2	70	3	0	4	4	.500	0	0-0	1	7.06	8.15

Tommy Milone

Pitches: L Bats: L Pos: SP-21; RP-1   mah-LONE   Ht: 6'0" Wt: 205 Born: 2/16/1987 Age: 28

Year	Team	Lg	G	GS	CG	GF	IP	BFP	H	R	ER	HR	SH	SF	HB	TBB	IBB	SO	WP	Bk	W	L	Pct	Sh	Sv-Op	Hld	ERC	ERA
2014	Scrmto*	AAA	4	4	0	0	21.0	98	28	16	15	5	1	0	0	9	0	17	1	0	1	1	.500	0	0--	-	7.29	6.43
2014	Roch*	AAA	1	1	0	0	7.0	27	6	1	1	0	0	0	0	2	0	3	1	0	1	0	1.000	0	0--	-	2.42	1.29
2011	Was	NL	5	5	0	0	26.0	110	28	11	11	2	3	2	2	4	2	15	0	0	1	0	1.000	0	0-0	0	3.55	3.81
2012	Oak	AL	31	31	1	0	190.0	791	207	90	79	24	3	3	4	36	2	137	2	0	13	10	.565	0	0-0	0	4.04	3.74
2013	Oak	AL	28	26	1	0	156.1	667	160	83	72	25	0	6	2	39	2	126	1	0	12	9	.571	0	0-0	0	3.98	4.14
2014	2 Tms	AL	22	21	0	1	118.0	519	128	63	55	16	1	2	5	37	2	75	0	0	6	4	.600	0	0-0	0	4.55	4.19
14	Oak	AL	16	16	0	0	96.1	405	91	42	38	12	1	2	4	26	2	61	0	0	6	3	.667	0	0-0	0	3.53	3.55
14	Min	AL	6	5	0	1	21.2	114	37	21	17	4	0	0	1	11	0	14	0	0	0	1	.000	0	0-0	0	9.76	7.06
Postseason			1	1	0	0	6.0	25	5	1	1	0	0	0	1	1	0	6	1	0	0	0	-	0	0-0	0	2.26	1.50
4 ML YEARS			86	83	2	1	490.1	2087	523	247	217	67	7	13	13	116	8	353	3	0	32	23	.582	0	0-0	0	4.12	3.98

Mike Minor

Pitches: L Bats: R Pos: SP-25   Ht: 6'4" Wt: 220 Born: 12/26/1987 Age: 27

Year	Team	Lg	G	GS	CG	GF	IP	BFP	H	R	ER	HR	SH	SF	HB	TBB	IBB	SO	WP	Bk	W	L	Pct	Sh	Sv-Op	Hld	ERC	ERA
2014	Missi*	AA	2	2	0	0	9.0	39	14	8	8	5	0	0	0	0	0	7	0	0	0	2	.000	0	0--	-	9.44	8.00
2014	Gwnntt*	AAA	2	1	0	0	8.1	35	5	5	3	1	0	2	1	3	0	8	0	0	2	0	1.000	0	0--	-	2.29	3.24
2014	Rome*	A	1	1	0	0	5.0	17	1	0	0	0	0	0	0	1	0	4	0	0	0	0	-	0	0--	-	0.27	0.00
2010	Atl	NL	9	8	0	1	40.2	185	53	28	27	6	1	3	1	11	0	43	0	0	3	2	.600	0	0-0	0	5.71	5.98
2011	Atl	NL	15	15	0	0	82.2	361	93	39	38	7	3	1	1	30	5	77	2	0	5	3	.625	0	0-0	0	4.51	4.14
2012	Atl	NL	30	30	0	0	179.1	728	151	88	82	26	8	8	5	56	7	145	3	0	11	10	.524	0	0-0	0	3.28	4.12
2013	Atl	NL	32	32	1	0	204.2	820	177	79	73	22	5	6	1	46	2	181	5	0	13	9	.591	0	0-0	0	2.76	3.21
2014	Atl	NL	25	25	0	0	145.1	637	165	77	77	21	6	2	6	44	2	120	5	0	6	12	.333	0	0-0	0	4.93	4.77
Postseason			1	1	0	0	6.1	26	8	1	1	0	1	0	0	1	0	5	0	0	1	0	1.000	0	0-0	0	4.11	1.42
5 ML YEARS			111	110	1	1	652.2	2731	639	311	297	82	23	20	14	187	16	566	15	0	38	36	.514	0	0-0	0	3.76	4.10

Bryan Mitchell

Pitches: R Bats: L Pos: RP-2; SP-1   Ht: 6'3" Wt: 205 Born: 4/19/1991 Age: 24

Year	Team	Lg	G	GS	CG	GF	IP	BFP	H	R	ER	HR	SH	SF	HB	TBB	IBB	SO	WP	Bk	W	L	Pct	Sh	Sv-Op	Hld	ERC	ERA
2010	Yanks1	R	10	9	0	0	41.2	173	28	24	17	2	1	0	3	22	0	36	5	0	2	1	.667	0	0--	-	2.76	3.67
2010	StIsInd	A-	1	1	0	0	4.0	22	7	4	3	0	0	0	2	1	0	3	1	0	0	1	.000	0	0--	-	9.15	6.75
2011	StIsInd	A-	14	14	0	0	61.2	275	65	34	28	5	1	2	5	31	0	59	10	0	1	3	.250	0	0--	-	5.07	4.09
2012	CtnSC	A	27	26	0	0	120.0	530	107	74	61	7	2	2	8	72	0	121	18	1	9	11	.450	0	0--	-	4.24	4.58
2013	Tampa	A+	24	23	1	0	126.2	570	144	83	72	5	4	8	6	53	0	104	23	0	4	11	.267	0	0--	-	4.66	5.12
2013	Trntn	AA	3	3	0	0	18.2	74	14	5	4	0	0	0	1	5	0	16	4	0	0	0	-	0	0--	-	1.92	1.93
2014	Trntn	AA	14	13	0	0	61.1	272	64	36	33	6	1	3	0	29	1	60	6	0	2	5	.286	0	0--	-	4.55	4.84
2014	S-WB	AAA	9	8	0	0	41.2	178	45	18	17	5	0	2	0	16	0	34	4	0	4	2	.667	0	0--	-	4.73	3.67
2014	NYY	AL	3	1	0	1	11.0	44	10	3	3	0	0	0	2	3	0	7	0	0	0	1	.000	0	0-0	0	3.34	2.45

Jose Molina

Bats: R Throws: R Pos: C-80;PH-2   Ht: 6'0" Wt: 250 Born: 6/3/1975 Age: 40

Year	Team	Lg	G	AB	H	2B	3B	HR	(Hm	Rd)	TB	R	RBI	RC	TBB	IBB	SO	HBP	SH	SF	SB	CS	GDP	Avg	OBP	Slg	OPS
1999	ChC	NL	10	19	5	1	0	0	(0	0)	6	3	1	2	2	1	4	0	0	0	0	0	0	.263	.333	.316	.649
2001	LAA	AL	15	37	10	3	0	2	(0	2)	19	8	4	6	3	0	8	0	2	0	0	0	2	.270	.325	.514	.839
2002	LAA	AL	29	70	19	3	0	0	(0	0)	22	5	5	4	5	0	15	0	4	2	0	2	2	.271	.312	.314	.626
2003	LAA	AL	53	114	21	4	0	0	(0	0)	25	12	6	5	1	0	26	3	4	1	0	0	1	.184	.210	.219	.429
2004	LAA	AL	73	203	53	10	2	3	(1	2)	76	26	25	19	10	0	52	0	5	0	4	1	6	.261	.296	.374	.670
2005	LAA	AL	75	184	42	4	0	6	(2	4)	64	14	25	19	13	0	41	2	4	0	2	0	5	.228	.286	.348	.634
2006	LAA	AL	78	225	54	17	0	4	(0	4)	83	18	22	21	9	0	49	2	7	2	1	0	6	.240	.273	.369	.642
2007	2 Tms	AL	69	191	49	13	0	1	(1	0)	65	18	19	20	5	0	43	0	5	1	2	1	4	.257	.274	.340	.614
2008	NYY	AL	100	268	58	17	0	3	(2	1)	84	32	18	15	12	0	52	6	8	3	0	0	9	.216	.263	.313	.576
2009	NYY	AL	52	138	30	4	0	1	(0	1)	37	15	11	12	14	0	28	1	1	1	0	0	6	.217	.292	.268	.560
2010	Tor	AL	57	167	41	4	0	6	(4	2)	63	13	12	12	9	1	36	5	2	0	1	0	7	.246	.304	.377	.681
2011	Tor	AL	55	171	48	12	1	3	(1	2)	71	19	15	25	15	0	44	1	4	0	2	1	2	.281	.342	.415	.757
2012	TB	AL	102	251	56	9	0	8	(5	3)	89	27	32	23	20	0	60	2	1	0	3	1	9	.223	.286	.355	.640
2013	TB	AL	99	283	66	14	0	2	(1	1)	86	26	18	18	22	1	63	2	3	3	2	1	11	.233	.290	.304	.594
2014	TB	AL	80	225	40	2	0	0	(0	0)	42	4	10	4	14	0	55	2	4	2	3	0	8	.178	.230	.187	.417
07	LAA	AL	40	125	28	8	0	0	(0	0)	36	9	10	9	3	0	30	0	3	0	2	1	3	.224	.242	.288	.530
07	NYY	AL	29	66	21	5	0	1	(1	0)	29	9	9	11	2	0	13	0	2	1	0	0	1	.318	.333	.439	.773
Postseason			19	22	4	0	0	0	(0	0)	4	3	1	2	4	0	5	0	1	0	0	1	0	.182	.308	.182	.490
15 ML YEARS			947	2546	592	117	3	39	(17	22)	832	240	223	205	154	3	576	26	54	15	20	7	78	.233	.282	.327	.608

Yadier Molina

Bats: R Throws: R Pos: C-107;DH-2;1B-1;PH-1   YAH-dee-air   Ht: 5'11" Wt: 220 Born: 7/13/1982 Age: 32

Year	Team	Lg	G	AB	H	2B	3B	HR	(Hm	Rd)	TB	R	RBI	RC	TBB	IBB	SO	HBP	SH	SF	SB	CS	GDP	Avg	OBP	Slg	OPS
2014	Sprgfld*	AA	2	6	5	3	0	0	(-	-)	8	2	2	3	0	0	1	0	0	0	0	0	0	.833	.833	1.333	2.167
2004	StL	NL	51	135	36	6	0	2	(1	1)	48	12	15	15	13	3	20	0	2	1	0	1	4	.267	.329	.356	.684
2005	StL	NL	114	385	97	15	1	8	(6	2)	138	36	49	46	23	3	30	2	8	3	2	3	10	.252	.295	.358	.654
2006	StL	NL	129	417	90	26	0	6	(2	4)	134	29	49	35	26	2	41	8	8	2	1	2	15	.216	.274	.321	.595
2007	StL	NL	111	353	97	15	0	6	(4	2)	130	30	40	38	34	5	43	3	2	4	1	1	18	.275	.340	.368	.708
2008	StL	NL	124	444	135	18	0	7	(2	5)	174	37	56	57	32	4	29	1	3	5	0	2	21	.304	.349	.392	.740
2009	StL	NL	140	481	141	23	1	6	(5	1)	184	45	54	50	50	2	39	6	6	1	9	3	27	.293	.366	.383	.749
2010	StL	NL	136	465	122	19	0	6	(1	5)	159	34	62	55	42	6	51	7	2	5	8	4	19	.262	.329	.342	.671
2011	StL	NL	139	475	145	32	1	14	(5	9)	221	55	65	64	33	4	44	1	5	4	4	5	21	.305	.349	.465	.814
2012	StL	NL	138	505	159	28	0	22	(9	13)	253	65	76	91	45	4	55	5	3	5	12	3	10	.315	.373	.501	.874
2013	StL	NL	136	505	161	44	0	12	(5	7)	241	68	80	84	30	4	55	3	0	3	3	2	14	.319	.359	.477	.836
2014	StL	NL	110	404	114	21	0	7	(3	4)	156	40	38	47	28	4	55	6	1	6	1	1	14	.282	.333	.386	.719
	Postseason		80	286	84	16	0	3	(2	1)	109	23	31	31	25	5	33	1	0	1	1	1	10	.294	.351	.381	.733
	11 ML YEARS		1328	4569	1297	247	3	96	(43	53)	1838	451	584	596	356	41	462	42	40	39	41	27	173	.284	.339	.402	.741

Jesus Montero

Bats: R Throws: R Pos: DH-4;1B-1;PH-1   Ht: 6'3" Wt: 235 Born: 11/28/1989 Age: 25

Year	Team	Lg	G	AB	H	2B	3B	HR	(Hm	Rd)	TB	R	RBI	RC	TBB	IBB	SO	HBP	SH	SF	SB	CS	GDP	Avg	OBP	Slg	OPS
2014	Tacom*	AAA	97	364	104	24	1	16	(-	-)	178	55	74	64	37	4	79	2	0	6	1	0	13	.286	.350	.489	.839
2011	NYY	AL	18	61	20	4	0	4	(3	1)	36	9	12	12	7	2	17	1	0	0	0	0	2	.328	.406	.590	.996
2012	Sea	AL	135	515	134	20	0	15	(6	9)	199	46	62	52	29	4	99	2	0	7	0	2	15	.260	.298	.386	.685
2013	Sea	AL	29	101	21	1	1	3	(1	2)	33	6	9	9	8	0	21	0	0	1	0	1	2	.208	.264	.327	.590
2014	Sea	AL	6	17	4	0	0	1	(1	0)	7	1	2	1	0	0	3	0	0	0	0	0	1	.235	.235	.412	.647
	Postseason		1	2	2	0	0	0	(0	0)	2	1	1	2	0	0	0	0	0	0	0	0	0	1.000	1.000	1.000	2.000
	4 ML YEARS		188	694	179	25	1	23	(11	12)	275	62	85	74	44	6	140	3	0	8	0	3	20	.258	.302	.396	.698

Miguel Montero

Bats: L Throws: R Pos: C-131;PH-4;DH-2   Ht: 5'11" Wt: 210 Born: 7/9/1983 Age: 31

Year	Team	Lg	G	AB	H	2B	3B	HR	(Hm	Rd)	TB	R	RBI	RC	TBB	IBB	SO	HBP	SH	SF	SB	CS	GDP	Avg	OBP	Slg	OPS
2006	Ari	NL	6	16	4	1	0	0	(-	-)	5	0	3	2	1	0	3	0	0	0	0	0	0	.250	.294	.313	.607
2007	Ari	NL	84	214	48	7	0	10	(7	3)	85	30	37	19	20	2	35	3	1	6	0	0	7	.224	.292	.397	.689
2008	Ari	NL	70	184	47	16	1	5	(1	4)	80	24	18	21	19	3	49	2	1	1	0	0	1	.255	.330	.435	.765
2009	Ari	NL	128	425	125	30	0	16	(5	11)	203	61	59	65	38	5	78	3	2	2	1	2	6	.294	.355	.478	.832
2010	Ari	NL	85	297	79	20	2	9	(0	9)	130	36	43	38	29	3	71	2	0	3	0	1	10	.266	.332	.438	.770
2011	Ari	NL	140	493	139	36	1	18	(8	10)	231	65	86	84	47	10	97	8	1	4	1	1	14	.282	.351	.469	.820
2012	Ari	NL	141	486	139	25	2	15	(4	11)	213	65	88	92	73	6	130	12	0	2	0	0	15	.286	.391	.438	.829
2013	Ari	NL	116	413	95	14	0	11	(8	3)	142	44	42	42	51	4	110	5	0	6	0	0	18	.230	.318	.344	.662
2014	Ari	NL	136	489	119	23	0	13	(5	8)	181	40	72	63	56	11	97	9	0	6	0	4	12	.243	.329	.370	.699
	Postseason		9	27	8	2	0	0	(0	0)	10	4	2	3	3	1	6	0	0	0	0	0	0	.296	.367	.370	.737
	9 ML YEARS		906	3017	795	172	6	97	(38	59)	1270	365	448	426	334	44	670	44	5	30	2	8	83	.264	.342	.421	.763

Rafael Montero

Pitches: R Bats: R Pos: SP-8; RP-2   Ht: 6'0" Wt: 185 Born: 10/17/1990 Age: 24

	HOW MUCH HE PITCHED							WHAT HE GAVE UP										THE RESULTS						
Year	Team	Lg	G	GS	CG	GF	IP	BFP	H	R	ER	HR	SH	SF	HB	TBB	IBB	SO	WP	Bk	W	L	Pct	Sh	Sv-Op	Hld	ERC	ERA
2011	Mets	R	7	4	0	0	31.0	136	28	11	5	0	1	5	6	0	32	2	0	1	2	.333	0	1--	-	2.56	1.45
2011	Kngspt	R+	4	4	0	0	17.0	72	17	8	8	2	0	0	6	0	9	1	0	2	1	.667	0	0--	-	4.05	4.24
2011	Bklyn	A-	2	0	0	0	5.0	18	3	2	2	1	0	0	1	0	5	0	0	1	0	1.000	0	0--	-	1.98	3.60
2012	Savann	A	12	12	0	0	71.1	286	61	24	20	4	0	3	1	8	0	54	2	1	6	3	.667	0	0--	-	2.00	2.52
2012	StLuci	A+	8	8	1	0	50.2	193	35	13	12	2	0	1	2	11	0	56	0	1	5	2	.714	0	0--	-	1.70	2.13
2013	Bnghtn	AA	11	11	0	0	66.2	261	51	21	18	2	1	0	0	10	0	72	0	2	7	3	.700	0	0--	-	1.60	2.43
2013	LsVgs	AAA	16	16	0	0	88.2	363	85	35	30	4	1	2	0	25	0	78	1	1	5	4	.556	0	0--	-	3.09	3.05
2014	LsVgs	AAA	16	16	0	0	80.0	338	69	43	32	4	1	3	1	34	0	80	2	1	6	4	.600	0	0--	-	3.12	3.60
2014	Mets	R	1	1	0	0	2.0	9	3	1	1	0	0	0	0	0	0	3	0	0	0	0	-	0	0--	-	4.47	4.50
2014	StLuci	A+	1	1	0	0	4.0	14	2	0	0	0	0	0	0	1	0	4	0	0	0	0	-	0	0--	-	1.01	0.00
2014	NYM	NL	10	8	0	1	44.1	194	44	21	20	8	0	0	0	23	0	42	0	0	1	3	.250	0	0-0	0	5.16	4.06

Adam Moore

Bats: R Throws: R Pos: PH-8;C-1   Ht: 6'3" Wt: 220 Born: 5/8/1984 Age: 31

Year	Team	Lg	G	AB	H	2B	3B	HR	(Hm	Rd)	TB	R	RBI	RC	TBB	IBB	SO	HBP	SH	SF	SB	CS	GDP	Avg	OBP	Slg	OPS
2014	ElPaso*	AAA	91	312	93	20	1	12	(-	-)	151	38	34	55	31	0	78	1	0	3	1	1	8	.298	.360	.484	.844
2014	Padres*	R	2	6	4	3	0	1	(-	-)	10	3	4	4	1	0	0	0	0	0	0	0	0	.667	.714	1.667	2.381
2009	Sea	AL	6	23	5	1	0	1	(1	0)	9	4	2	2	0	0	7	1	0	0	1	0	1	.217	.250	.391	.641
2010	Sea	AL	60	205	40	6	0	4	(1	3)	58	12	15	9	8	1	63	2	1	2	0	1	3	.195	.230	.283	.513
2011	Sea	AL	2	6	1	1	0	0	(0	0)	2	0	0	0	0	0	2	0	0	0	0	0	0	.167	.167	.333	.500
2012	KC	AL	4	11	2	1	0	1	(1	0)	6	1	2	2	1	0	5	0	0	0	0	0	0	.182	.250	.545	.795
2013	KC	AL	5	10	3	1	0	0	(0	0)	4	1	0	1	1	0	2	0	0	0	1	0	0	.300	.364	.400	.764
2014	SD	NL	9	10	2	1	0	0	(0	0)	3	1	1	2	2	1	5	0	0	0	0	0	0	.200	.333	.300	.633
	6 ML YEARS		86	265	53	11	0	6	(3	3)	82	19	20	16	12	2	82	3	1	2	2	1	4	.200	.241	.309	.551

Matt Moore

Pitches: L **Bats:** L **Pos:** SP-2   **Ht:** 6'3" **Wt:** 200 **Born:** 6/18/1989 **Age:** 26

Year	Team	Lg	G	GS	CG	GF	IP	BFP	H	R	ER	HR	SH	SF	HB	TBB	IBB	SO	WP	Bk	W	L	Pct	Sh	Sv-Op	Hld	ERC	ERA
2011	TB	AL	3	1	0	0	9.1	40	9	3	3	1	0	0	0	3	0	15	2	0	1	0	1.000	0	0-0	1	3.54	2.89
2012	TB	AL	31	31	0	0	177.1	759	158	85	75	18	3	4	7	81	5	175	8	1	11	11	.500	0	0-0	0	3.83	3.81
2013	TB	AL	27	27	1	0	150.1	642	119	58	55	14	5	6	4	76	1	143	17	1	17	4	.810	1	0-0	0	3.36	3.29
2014	TB	AL	2	2	0	0	10.0	44	10	3	3	1	0	0	0	5	0	6	0	0	0	0	.000	0	0-0	0	4.48	2.70
	Postseason		4	2	0	0	16.1	69	12	9	8	1	0	0	2	6	1	15	2	0	1	1	.500	0	0-0	0	2.60	4.41
	4 ML YEARS		63	61	1	0	347.0	1485	296	149	136	34	8	10	11	165	6	339	27	2	29	17	.630	1	0-0	1	3.64	3.53

Tyler Moore

Bats: R **Throws:** R **Pos:** 1B-24;PH-16;LF-4;PR-2   **Ht:** 6'2" **Wt:** 220 **Born:** 1/30/1987 **Age:** 28

Year	Team	Lg	G	AB	H	2B	3B	HR	(Hm	Rd)	TB	R	RBI	RC	TBB	IBB	SO	HBP	SH	SF	SB	CS	GDP	Avg	OBP	Slg	OPS
2014	Syrcse*	AAA	84	302	80	21	0	10	(-	-)	131	45	44	50	47	0	77	3	0	2	0	2	3	.265	.367	.434	.801
2012	Was	NL	75	156	41	9	0	10	(3	7)	80	20	29	26	14	0	46	1	0	0	3	0	3	.263	.327	.513	.840
2013	Was	NL	63	167	37	9	0	4	(2	2)	58	16	21	17	8	1	58	1	1	1	0	0	1	.222	.260	.347	.607
2014	Was	NL	42	91	21	2	0	4	(1	3)	35	8	14	10	7	0	29	2	0	0	0	0	2	.231	.300	.385	.685
	Postseason		1	1	1	0	0	0	(0	0)	1	0	2	1	0	0	0	0	0	0	0	0	0	1.000	1.000	1.000	2.000
	3 ML YEARS		180	414	99	20	0	18	(6	12)	173	44	64	53	29	1	133	4	1	1	3	0	6	.239	.295	.418	.713

Franklin Morales

Pitches: L **Bats:** L **Pos:** SP-22; RP-16   **Ht:** 6'1" **Wt:** 210 **Born:** 1/24/1986 **Age:** 29

Year	Team	Lg	G	GS	CG	GF	IP	BFP	H	R	ER	HR	SH	SF	HB	TBB	IBB	SO	WP	Bk	W	L	Pct	Sh	Sv-Op	Hld	ERC	ERA
2007	Col	NL	8	8	0	0	39.1	163	34	15	15	2	4	2	2	14	1	26	0	0	3	2	.600	0	0-0	0	3.04	3.43
2008	Col	NL	5	5	0	0	25.1	120	28	18	18	2	4	2	1	17	2	9	1	3	1	2	.333	0	0-0	0	5.58	6.39
2009	Col	NL	40	2	0	14	40.0	179	38	22	20	4	3	0	1	23	4	41	2	0	3	2	.600	0	7-8	7	4.38	4.50
2010	Col	NL	35	0	0	15	28.2	140	28	22	20	5	1	2	3	24	2	27	3	2	0	4	.000	0	3-6	1	6.53	6.28
2011	2 Tms		50	0	0	13	46.1	193	40	21	19	6	2	1	2	19	1	42	2	1	1	2	.333	0	0-0	10	3.77	3.69
2012	Bos	AL	37	9	0	5	76.1	325	64	38	32	11	0	3	6	30	3	76	3	5	3	4	.429	0	1-1	8	3.68	3.77
2013	Bos	AL	20	1	0	3	25.1	112	24	13	13	2	0	0	3	15	2	21	3	0	2	2	.500	0	0-1	4	4.86	4.62
2014	Col	NL	38	22	0	4	142.1	646	166	90	85	24	7	6	6	65	4	100	5	4	6	9	.400	0	0-0	0	5.97	5.37
11	Col	NL	14	0	0	4	14.0	59	10	6	6	2	1	1	0	8	1	11	1	0	0	1	.000	0	0-0	2	3.36	3.86
11	Bos	AL	36	0	0	9	32.1	134	30	15	13	4	1	0	2	11	0	31	1	1	1	1	.500	0	0-0	8	3.96	3.62
	Postseason		11	2	0	0	14.0	68	18	12	12	1	0	0	2	9	1	7	0	1	0	0	-	0	0-1	1	7.16	7.71
	8 ML YEARS		233	47	0	54	423.2	1878	422	239	222	56	19	17	24	207	19	342	19	15	19	27	.413	0	11-16	30	4.81	4.72

Kendrys Morales

Bats: B **Throws:** R **Pos:** DH-71;1B-27;PH-1   KEN-dreez   **Ht:** 6'1" **Wt:** 225 **Born:** 6/20/1983 **Age:** 32

Year	Team	Lg	G	AB	H	2B	3B	HR	(Hm	Rd)	TB	R	RBI	RC	TBB	IBB	SO	HBP	SH	SF	SB	CS	GDP	Avg	OBP	Slg	OPS
2006	LAA	AL	57	197	46	10	1	5	(1	4)	73	21	22	19	17	1	28	0	0	1	1	1	11	.234	.293	.371	.664
2007	LAA	AL	43	119	35	10	0	4	(2	2)	57	12	15	15	6	2	21	1	0	0	0	1	5	.294	.333	.479	.812
2008	LAA	AL	27	61	13	2	0	3	(0	3)	24	7	8	3	4	0	7	1	0	0	0	1	3	.213	.273	.393	.666
2009	LAA	AL	152	566	173	43	2	34	(21	13)	322	86	108	105	46	10	117	2	0	8	3	7	15	.306	.355	.569	.924
2010	LAA	AL	51	193	56	5	0	11	(7	4)	94	29	39	34	12	3	31	5	0	1	0	1	5	.290	.346	.487	.833
2012	LAA	AL	134	484	132	26	1	22	(10	12)	226	61	73	68	31	4	116	4	0	3	0	1	11	.273	.320	.467	.787
2013	Sea	AL	156	602	167	34	0	23	(12	11)	270	64	80	85	49	6	114	5	0	1	0	0	21	.277	.336	.449	.785
2014	2 Tms	AL	98	367	80	20	0	8	(4	4)	124	28	42	29	27	3	68	3	0	4	0	0	12	.218	.274	.338	.612
14	Min	AL	39	154	36	11	0	1	(0	1)	50	12	18	11	6	1	27	0	0	2	0	0	4	.234	.259	.325	.584
14	Sea	AL	59	213	44	9	0	7	(4	3)	74	16	24	18	21	2	41	3	0	2	0	0	8	.207	.285	.347	.632
	Postseason		16	47	9	1	0	2	(1	1)	16	3	7	3	2	0	8	1	0	1	0	0	1	.191	.235	.340	.576
	8 ML YEARS		718	2589	702	150	4	110	(57	53)	1190	308	387	358	192	26	502	21	0	18	4	12	83	.271	.324	.460	.784

Brent Morel

Bats: R **Throws:** R **Pos:** 3B-13;PH-9;1B-1;PR-1   more-ELL   **Ht:** 6'1" **Wt:** 225 **Born:** 4/21/1987 **Age:** 28

Year	Team	Lg	G	AB	H	2B	3B	HR	(Hm	Rd)	TB	R	RBI	RC	TBB	IBB	SO	HBP	SH	SF	SB	CS	GDP	Avg	OBP	Slg	OPS
2014	Indy*	AAA	92	336	91	19	2	4	(-	-)	126	52	53	45	33	0	67	2	0	5	7	2	12	.271	.335	.375	.710
2010	CWS	AL	21	65	15	3	0	3	(3	0)	27	9	7	4	4	0	17	0	0	1	2	0	2	.231	.271	.415	.687
2011	CWS	AL	126	413	101	18	1	10	(6	4)	151	44	41	36	22	0	57	3	5	1	5	4	8	.245	.287	.366	.653
2012	CWS	AL	35	113	20	2	0	0	(0	0)	22	14	5	4	7	0	39	0	0	0	4	1	3	.177	.225	.195	.420
2013	CWS	AL	12	25	5	0	0	0	(0	0)	5	3	1	3	5	0	7	0	0	0	1	1	1	.200	.333	.200	.533
2014	Pit	NL	23	39	7	2	0	0	(0	0)	9	1	4	1	2	1	9	0	0	0	0	0	1	.179	.220	.231	.450
	5 ML YEARS		217	655	148	25	1	13	(9	4)	214	71	58	48	40	1	129	3	10	2	12	6	15	.226	.273	.327	.600

Mitch Moreland

Bats: L **Throws:** L **Pos:** 1B-22;DH-22;PH-8;LF-2   **Ht:** 6'2" **Wt:** 230 **Born:** 9/6/1985 **Age:** 29

Year	Team	Lg	G	AB	H	2B	3B	HR	(Hm	Rd)	TB	R	RBI	RC	TBB	IBB	SO	HBP	SH	SF	SB	CS	GDP	Avg	OBP	Slg	OPS
2010	Tex	AL	47	145	37	4	0	9	(3	6)	68	20	25	27	25	5	36	1	0	2	3	1	3	.255	.364	.469	.833
2011	Tex	AL	134	464	120	22	1	16	(7	9)	192	60	51	56	39	6	92	4	2	3	2	2	9	.259	.320	.414	.733
2012	Tex	AL	114	327	90	18	0	15	(10	5)	153	41	50	46	23	5	71	1	2	4	1	1	8	.275	.321	.468	.789

Year Team	Lg	G	AB	H	2B	3B	HR	(Hm	Rd)	TB	R	RBI	RC	TBB	IBB	SO	HBP	SH	SF	SB	CS	GDP	Avg	OBP	Slg	OPS
2013 Tex	AL	147	462	107	24	1	23	(10	13)	202	60	60	55	45	1	117	3	0	8	0	0	11	.232	.299	.437	.736
2014 Tex	AL	52	167	41	9	1	2	(1	1)	58	18	23	20	12	0	43	1	2	2	0	0	7	.246	.297	.347	.644
Postseason		25	76	19	4	0	3	(3	0)	32	7	10	12	6	1	18	1	1	0	0	0	3	.250	.313	.421	.734
5 ML YEARS		494	1565	395	77	3	65	(31	34)	673	199	209	204	144	17	359	10	6	19	6	4	38	.252	.316	.430	.746

Nyjer Morgan

Bats: L Throws: L Pos: CF-12;LF-2;PR-1　　　　　　　**Ht: 5'10" Wt: 180 Born: 7/2/1980 Age: 34**

Year Team	Lg	G	AB	H	2B	3B	HR	(Hm	Rd)	TB	R	RBI	RC	TBB	IBB	SO	HBP	SH	SF	SB	CS	GDP	Avg	OBP	Slg	OPS
2014 Clmbs*	AAA	15	60	12	4	0	1	(-	-)	19	4	7	4	3	0	16	0	0	1	1	0	2	.200	.234	.317	.551
2007 Pit	NL	28	107	32	3	4	1	(1	0)	46	15	7	18	9	0	19	1	1	0	7	3	0	.299	.359	.430	.789
2008 Pit	NL	58	160	47	13	0	0	(0	0)	60	26	7	18	10	0	32	3	1	1	9	5	0	.294	.345	.375	.720
2009 2 Tms	NL	120	469	144	15	7	3	(1	2)	182	74	39	69	40	2	74	9	10	5	42	17	9	.307	.369	.388	.757
2010 Was	NL	136	509	129	17	7	0	(0	0)	160	60	24	53	40	1	88	10	15	3	34	17	3	.253	.319	.314	.633
2011 Mil	NL	119	378	115	20	6	4	(0	4)	159	61	37	58	19	0	70	14	15	3	13	4	6	.304	.357	.421	.778
2012 Mil	NL	122	289	69	5	3	3	(3	0)	89	44	16	26	20	0	63	6	7	0	12	5	4	.239	.302	.308	.610
2014 Cle	NL	15	41	14	1	0	1	(0	1)	18	8	6	9	7	0	6	0	3	1	3	0	0	.341	.429	.439	.868
09 Pit	NL	71	278	77	6	5	2	(1	1)	99	39	27	37	29	2	49	5	5	4	18	10	6	.277	.351	.356	.707
09 Was	NL	49	191	67	9	2	1	(0	1)	83	35	12	32	11	0	25	4	5	1	24	7	3	.351	.396	.435	.831
Postseason		10	28	5	2	0	0	(0	0)	7	2	3	2	2	0	11	2	0	0	0	0	1	.179	.281	.250	.531
7 ML YEARS		598	1953	550	74	27	12	(5	7)	714	288	136	251	145	3	352	43	52	13	120	51	21	.282	.343	.366	.708

Mike Morin

Pitches: R Bats: R Pos: RP-60　　　　　MORE-in　　　　　**Ht: 6'4" Wt: 220 Born: 5/3/1991 Age: 24**

		HOW MUCH HE PITCHED						WHAT HE GAVE UP										THE RESULTS						
Year Team	Lg	G	GS	CG	GF	IP	BFP	H	R	ER	HR	SH	SF	HB	TBB	IBB	SO	WP	Bk	W	L	Pct	Sh	Sv-Op	Hld	ERC	ERA
2012 Orem	R+	24	0	0	9	34.2	150	34	23	19	2	2	3	1	14	4	29	6	0	2	2	.500	0	4--	-	3.60	4.93
2013 InldEm	A+	30	0	0	24	39.0	145	30	9	8	2	1	2	1	5	0	43	0	0	3	1	.750	0	13--	-	1.83	1.85
2013 Ark	AA	26	0	0	15	31.0	123	26	7	7	2	2	1	2	5	0	33	3	0	0	2	.000	0	10--	-	2.39	2.03
2014 Ark	AA	5	0	0	5	5.0	17	3	0	0	0	0	0	0	0	0	6	0	0	1	0	1.000	0	3--	-	0.80	0.00
2014 Salt Lk	AAA	4	0	0	2	3.0	16	7	5	4	1	0	0	0	0	0	5	0	0	0	1	.000	0	2--	-	12.91	12.00
2014 InldEm	A+	1	0	0	1	1.0	4	1	0	0	0	0	0	0	0	0	2	0	0	0	0	-	0	1--	-	1.95	0.00
2014 LAA	AL	60	0	0	10	59.0	246	51	22	19	3	2	4	3	19	6	54	3	0	4	4	.500	0	0-2	9	2.76	2.90

Justin Morneau

Bats: L Throws: R Pos: 1B-131;PH-5;DH-1　　　　　MORE-no　　　　　**Ht: 6'4" Wt: 220 Born: 5/15/1981 Age: 34**

Year Team	Lg	G	AB	H	2B	3B	HR	(Hm	Rd)	TB	R	RBI	RC	TBB	IBB	SO	HBP	SH	SF	SB	CS	GDP	Avg	OBP	Slg	OPS
2014 ColSpr*	AAA	1	4	2	0	0	0	(-	-)	2	0	0	0	0	0	0	0	0	0	0	0	0	.500	.500	.500	1.000
2003 Min	AL	40	106	24	4	0	4	(1	3)	40	14	16	11	9	1	30	0	0	0	0	0	4	.226	.287	.377	.664
2004 Min	AL	74	280	76	17	0	19	(9	10)	150	39	58	48	28	8	54	2	0	2	0	0	4	.271	.340	.536	.875
2005 Min	AL	141	490	117	23	4	22	(9	13)	214	62	79	58	44	8	94	4	0	5	0	2	12	.239	.304	.437	.741
2006 Min	AL	157	592	190	37	1	34	(17	17)	331	97	130	118	53	9	93	5	0	11	3	3	10	.321	.375	.559	.934
2007 Min	AL	157	590	160	31	3	31	(15	16)	290	84	111	95	64	11	91	5	0	9	1	1	17	.271	.343	.492	.834
2008 Min	AL	163	623	187	47	4	23	(12	11)	311	97	129	122	76	16	85	3	0	10	0	1	20	.300	.374	.499	.873
2009 Min	AL	135	508	139	31	1	30	(14	16)	262	85	100	91	72	12	86	3	0	7	0	0	12	.274	.363	.516	.878
2010 Min	AL	81	296	102	25	1	18	(4	14)	183	53	56	65	50	7	62	0	0	2	0	0	6	.345	.437	.618	1.055
2011 Min	AL	69	264	60	16	0	4	(0	4)	88	19	30	28	19	1	44	3	0	2	0	0	8	.227	.285	.333	.618
2012 Min	AL	134	505	135	26	2	19	(7	12)	222	63	77	63	49	8	102	6	0	10	1	0	19	.267	.333	.440	.773
2013 2 Tms		152	572	148	36	0	17	(8	9)	235	62	77	71	50	4	110	7	0	6	0	0	13	.259	.323	.411	.734
2014 Col	NL	135	502	160	32	3	17	(11	6)	249	62	82	88	34	4	60	6	0	8	0	3	7	.319	.364	.496	.860
13 Min	AL	127	495	128	32	0	17	(9	8)	211	56	74	64	37	3	98	6	0	5	0	0	10	.259	.315	.426	.741
13 Pit	NL	25	77	20	4	0	0	(0	0)	24	6	3	7	13	1	12	1	0	1	0	0	3	.260	.370	.312	.681
Postseason		13	53	16	4	0	2	(1	1)	26	8	4	4	1	0	5	0	0	0	0	0	0	.302	.315	.491	.805
12 ML YEARS		1438	5328	1498	325	19	238	(108	130)	2575	737	945	858	548	89	911	44	0	72	5	10	132	.281	.349	.483	.832

Bryan Morris

Pitches: R Bats: L Pos: RP-60　　　　　　　**Ht: 6'3" Wt: 225 Born: 3/28/1987 Age: 28**

		HOW MUCH HE PITCHED						WHAT HE GAVE UP										THE RESULTS						
Year Team	Lg	G	GS	CG	GF	IP	BFP	H	R	ER	HR	SH	SF	HB	TBB	IBB	SO	WP	Bk	W	L	Pct	Sh	Sv-Op	Hld	ERC	ERA
2012 Pit	NL	5	0	0	2	5.0	20	2	2	1	0	0	1	0	2	0	6	1	0	0	0	-	0	0-0	0	1.32	1.80
2013 Pit	NL	55	0	0	21	65.0	270	57	25	25	8	0	5	2	28	5	37	6	0	5	7	.417	0	0-0	7	3.78	3.46
2014 2 Tms	NL	60	0	0	10	64.1	272	58	17	13	6	7	3	4	24	6	50	8	1	8	1	.889	0	0-7	17	3.50	1.82
14 Pit	NL	21	0	0	7	23.2	103	25	11	10	4	2	2	2	12	3	14	3	1	4	0	1.000	0	0-3	4	5.75	3.80
14 Mia	NL	39	0	0	3	40.2	169	33	6	3	2	5	1	2	12	3	36	5	0	4	1	.800	0	0-4	13	2.39	0.66
Postseason		1	0	0	1	1.0	4	1	0	0	0	0	0	0	0	0	1	0	0	0	0	-	0	0-0	0	1.95	0.00
3 ML YEARS		120	0	0	33	134.1	562	117	44	39	14	7	9	7	54	11	93	15	1	13	8	.619	0	0-7	24	3.53	2.61

Logan Morrison

Bats: L Throws: L Pos: 1B-79;DH-9;RF-8;PH-5;LF-2   Ht: 6'3" Wt: 245 Born: 8/25/1987 Age: 27

								BATTING											RUNNING			AVERAGES			
Year	Team	Lg	G	AB	H	2B	3B	HR	(Hm | Rd)	TB	R	RBI	RC	TBB	IBB	SO	HBP	SH	SF	SB	CS	GDP	Avg	OBP	Slg	OPS
2014	Tacom*	AAA	18	65	20	2	0	3	(- | -)	31	13	8	13	11	1	8	1	0	0	2	0	3	.308	.416	.477	.893
2010	Fla	NL	62	244	69	20	7	2	(1 | 1)	109	43	18	41	41	0	51	2	0	0	0	1	4	.283	.390	.447	.837
2011	Fla	NL	123	462	114	25	4	23	(12 | 11)	216	54	72	55	54	3	99	5	0	4	2	1	9	.247	.330	.468	.797
2012	Mia	NL	93	296	68	15	1	11	(4 | 7)	118	30	36	27	31	2	58	4	0	3	1	0	9	.230	.308	.399	.707
2013	Mia	NL	85	293	71	13	4	6	(1 | 5)	110	32	36	37	38	5	56	2	0	0	0	0	10	.242	.333	.375	.709
2014	Sea	AL	99	336	88	20	0	11	(7 | 4)	141	41	38	46	24	1	59	3	0	2	5	2	9	.262	.315	.420	.735
	5 ML YEARS		462	1631	410	93	16	53	(25 | 28)	694	200	200	206	188	11	323	16	0	9	8	4	41	.251	.333	.426	.758

Brandon Morrow

Pitches: R Bats: R Pos: RP-7; SP-6   Ht: 6'3" Wt: 210 Born: 7/26/1984 Age: 30

				HOW MUCH HE PITCHED						WHAT HE GAVE UP											THE RESULTS						
Year	Team	Lg	G	GS	CG	GF	IP	BFP	H	R	ER	HR	SH	SF	HB	TBB	IBB	SO	WP	Bk	W	L	Pct	Sh	Sv-Op	Hld	ERC	ERA
2014	Dnedin*	A+	1	0	0	0	1.0	4	0	0	0	0	0	0	0	0	0	1	0	0	0	0	-	0	0- -	-	0.00	0.00
2014	Buffalo*	AAA	2	0	0	0	2.1	9	2	1	1	0	0	0	0	0	0	1	0	0	0	0	-	0	0- -	-	1.44	3.86
2007	Sea	AL	60	0	0	18	63.1	289	56	29	29	3	4	4	1	50	5	66	4	0	3	4	.429	0	0-2	18	4.47	4.12
2008	Sea	AL	45	5	0	24	64.2	265	40	26	24	10	1	0	0	34	1	75	5	0	3	4	.429	0	10-12	3	2.84	3.34
2009	Sea	AL	26	10	0	9	69.2	313	66	38	34	10	1	2	0	44	1	63	3	0	2	4	.333	0	6-8	1	4.99	4.39
2010	Tor	AL	26	26	1	0	146.1	629	136	76	73	11	2	4	9	66	0	178	8	0	10	7	.588	1	0-0	0	3.99	4.49
2011	Tor	AL	30	30	0	0	179.1	777	162	103	94	21	4	9	12	69	1	203	12	1	11	11	.500	0	0-0	0	3.79	4.72
2012	Tor	AL	21	21	3	0	124.2	504	98	45	41	12	1	3	2	41	0	108	3	0	10	7	.588	3	0-0	0	2.73	2.96
2013	Tor	AL	10	10	0	0	54.1	242	63	39	34	12	0	3	1	18	1	42	1	0	2	3	.400	0	0-0	0	5.60	5.63
2014	Tor	AL	13	6	0	2	33.1	148	37	21	21	2	1	0	0	18	0	30	1	1	1	3	.250	0	0-0	1	5.09	5.67
	8 ML YEARS		231	108	4	53	735.2	3167	658	377	350	81	14	25	25	340	9	765	37	2	42	43	.494	4	16-22	23	3.91	4.28

Michael Morse

Bats: R Throws: R Pos: LF-84;1B-43;PH-6;DH-4   Ht: 6'5" Wt: 245 Born: 3/22/1982 Age: 33

								BATTING											RUNNING			AVERAGES			
Year	Team	Lg	G	AB	H	2B	3B	HR	(Hm	Rd)	TB	R	RBI	RC	TBB	IBB	SO	HBP	SH	SF	SB	CS	GDP	Avg	OBP	Slg	OPS
2005	Sea	AL	72	230	64	10	1	3	(3	0)	85	27	23	28	18	0	50	8	0	2	3	1	9	.278	.349	.370	.718
2006	Sea	AL	21	43	16	5	0	0	(0	0)	21	5	11	9	3	0	7	1	0	2	1	0	2	.372	.396	.488	.884
2007	Sea	AL	9	18	8	2	0	0	(0	0)	10	1	3	6	1	0	4	1	0	0	0	0	0	.444	.500	.556	1.056
2008	Sea	AL	5	9	2	1	0	0	(0	0)	3	0	0	1	1	0	4	1	0	0	0	0	0	.222	.364	.333	.697
2009	Was	NL	32	52	13	3	0	3	(3	0)	25	4	10	8	3	0	16	0	0	0	0	0	1	.250	.291	.481	.772
2010	Was	NL	98	266	77	12	2	15	(6	9)	138	36	41	42	22	1	64	4	0	1	0	1	6	.289	.352	.519	.870
2011	Was	NL	146	522	158	36	0	31	(11	20)	287	73	95	96	36	5	126	13	0	4	2	3	9	.303	.360	.550	.910
2012	Was	NL	102	406	118	17	1	18	(7	11)	191	53	62	57	16	0	97	4	0	4	0	1	14	.291	.321	.470	.791
2013	2 Tms		88	312	67	13	0	13	(5	8)	119	34	27	24	21	1	87	3	0	1	0	0	12	.215	.270	.381	.651
2014	SF	NL	131	438	122	32	3	16	(6	10)	208	48	61	55	31	0	121	6	0	4	0	0	19	.279	.336	.475	.811
13	Sea	AL	76	283	64	13	0	13	(5	8)	116	31	27	24	20	1	80	3	0	1	0	0	10	.226	.283	.410	.693
13	Bal	AL	12	29	3	0	0	0	(0	0)	3	3	0	0	1	0	7	0	0	0	0	0	2	.103	.133	.103	.237
	Postseason		5	19	5	0	0	1	(1	0)	8	2	2	2	0	0	4	0	0	0	0	0	1	.263	.263	.421	.684
	10 ML YEARS		704	2296	645	131	7	99	(41	58)	1087	281	333	326	152	7	576	43	0	18	6	6	72	.281	.335	.473	.808

Charlie Morton

Pitches: R Bats: R Pos: SP-26   Ht: 6'5" Wt: 235 Born: 11/12/1983 Age: 31

				HOW MUCH HE PITCHED						WHAT HE GAVE UP											THE RESULTS						
Year	Team	Lg	G	GS	CG	GF	IP	BFP	H	R	ER	HR	SH	SF	HB	TBB	IBB	SO	WP	Bk	W	L	Pct	Sh	Sv-Op	Hld	ERC	ERA
2014	Altna*	AA	1	1	0	0	4.0	17	4	2	2	0	0	0	0	1	0	6	0	0	0	0	-	0	0- -	-	2.77	4.50
2008	Atl	NL	16	15	0	0	74.2	345	80	56	51	9	5	4	2	41	2	48	2	0	4	8	.333	0	0-0	0	5.21	6.15
2009	Pit	NL	18	18	1	0	97.0	416	102	49	49	7	1	5	6	40	0	62	4	0	5	9	.357	1	0-0	0	4.56	4.55
2010	Pit	NL	17	17	0	0	79.2	382	112	79	67	15	6	6	7	26	3	59	5	1	2	12	.143	0	0-0	0	7.10	7.57
2011	Pit	NL	29	29	2	0	171.2	769	186	82	73	6	12	6	13	77	5	110	9	1	10	10	.500	1	0-0	0	4.52	3.83
2012	Pit	NL	9	9	0	0	50.1	223	62	30	26	5	5	2	2	11	1	25	4	0	2	6	.250	0	0-0	0	4.74	4.65
2013	Pit	NL	20	20	0	0	116.0	493	113	51	42	6	6	6	16	36	1	85	5	0	7	4	.636	0	0-0	0	3.84	3.26
2014	Pit	NL	26	26	0	0	157.1	666	143	76	65	9	7	5	19	57	2	126	8	0	6	12	.333	0	0-0	0	3.64	3.72
	Postseason		1	1	0	0	5.2	24	3	2	2	1	1	0	0	4	0	4	0	0	1	0	1.000	0	0-0	0	3.16	3.18
	7 ML YEARS		135	134	3	0	746.2	3294	798	423	373	57	42	26	64	288	14	515	37	2	36	61	.371	2	0-0	0	4.57	4.50

Brandon Moss

Bats: L Throws: R Pos: 1B-67;LF-56;RF-34;DH-12;PH-12   Ht: 6'0" Wt: 210 Born: 9/16/1983 Age: 31

								BATTING											RUNNING			AVERAGES			
Year	Team	Lg	G	AB	H	2B	3B	HR	(Hm	Rd)	TB	R	RBI	RC	TBB	IBB	SO	HBP	SH	SF	SB	CS	GDP	Avg	OBP	Slg	OPS
2007	Bos	AL	15	25	7	2	1	0	(0	0)	11	6	1	3	4	0	6	0	0	0	0	0	1	.280	.379	.440	.819
2008	2 Tms		79	236	58	15	3	8	(4	4)	103	19	34	30	21	1	70	1	0	5	1	2	2	.246	.304	.436	.741
2009	Pit	NL	133	385	91	20	4	7	(4	3)	140	47	41	37	34	3	84	4	0	1	1	5	7	.236	.304	.364	.668
2010	Pit	NL	17	26	4	1	0	0	(0	0)	5	2	2	2	1	0	6	0	0	0	0	0	1	.154	.185	.192	.377
2011	Phi	NL	5	6	0	0	0	0	(0	0)	0	0	0	0	0	0	2	0	0	0	0	0	1	.000	.000	.000	.000
2012	Oak	AL	84	265	77	18	0	21	(9	12)	158	48	52	50	26	2	90	3	0	2	1	1	5	.291	.358	.596	.954
2013	Oak	AL	145	446	114	23	3	30	(10	20)	233	73	87	79	50	3	140	6	0	3	4	2	4	.256	.337	.522	.859
2014	Oak	AL	147	500	117	23	2	25	(12	13)	219	70	81	78	67	7	153	10	0	6	1	0	6	.234	.334	.438	.772
08	Bos	AL	34	78	23	5	1	2	(1	1)	36	7	11	11	6	0	25	0	0	2	1	1	0	.295	.337	.462	.799
08	Pit	NL	45	158	35	10	2	6	(3	3)	67	12	23	19	15	1	45	1	0	3	0	1	2	.222	.284	.424	.712
	Postseason		10	33	4	0	0	1	(0	1)	7	2	1	1	5	0	20	1	0	0	0	0	0	.121	.256	.212	.469
	8 ML YEARS		625	1889	468	102	13	91	(39	52)	869	265	298	279	203	16	551	24	0	14	8	10	27	.248	.326	.460	.786

Jason Motte

Pitches: R Bats: R Pos: RP-29   Ht: 6'0" Wt: 205 Born: 6/22/1982 Age: 33

		HOW MUCH HE PITCHED						WHAT HE GAVE UP												THE RESULTS							
Year	Team	Lg	G	GS	CG	GF	IP	BFP	H	R	ER	HR	SH	SF	HB	TBB	IBB	SO	WP	Bk	W	L	Pct	Sh	Sv-Op	Hld	ERC	ERA
2014	Sprgfld*	AA	5	0	0	0	4.2	16	1	0	0	0	0	0	0	1	0	3	0	0	0	0	-	0	0--	-	0.30	0.00
2014	Memp*	AAA	2	0	0	0	3.0	11	2	0	0	0	0	0	0	0	0	2	0	0	0	0	-	0	0--	-	0.91	0.00
2008	StL	NL	12	0	0	4	11.0	40	5	2	1	0	1	0	0	3	0	16	0	0	0	0	-	0	1-1	4	0.89	0.82
2009	StL	NL	69	0	0	14	56.2	244	57	32	30	10	0	3	2	23	1	54	2	1	4	4	.500	0	0-3	15	4.86	4.76
2010	StL	NL	56	0	0	15	52.1	208	41	13	13	5	1	0	0	18	3	54	1	0	4	2	.667	0	2-3	12	2.68	2.24
2011	StL	NL	78	0	0	27	68.0	268	49	22	17	2	1	3	5	16	2	63	1	0	5	2	.714	0	9-13	18	1.87	2.25
2012	StL	NL	67	0	0	58	72.0	279	49	23	22	9	2	1	2	17	1	86	0	0	4	5	.444	0	42-49	0	2.08	2.75
2014	StL	NL	29	0	0	10	25.0	110	29	14	13	7	0	2	0	9	0	17	1	0	0	1	1.000	0	0-0	1	6.22	4.68
	Postseason		19	0	0	16	21.2	79	12	6	5	2	0	0	0	2	0	10	0	0	1	1	.500	0	8-8	0	1.07	2.08
	6 ML YEARS		311	0	0	126	285.0	1149	230	106	96	33	5	12	9	86	7	290	5	1	18	13	.581	0	54-69	50	2.89	3.03

Mike Moustakas

Bats: L Throws: R Pos: 3B-138;PH-4   moo-STOCK-us   Ht: 6'0" Wt: 195 Born: 9/11/1988 Age: 26

							BATTING														RUNNING			AVERAGES			
Year	Team	Lg	G	AB	H	2B	3B	HR	(Hm	Rd)	TB	R	RBI	RC	TBB	IBB	SO	HBP	SH	SF	SB	CS	GDP	Avg	OBP	Slg	OPS
2014	Omha*	AAA	8	31	11	3	0	1	(-	-)	17	3	5	6	3	0	6	0	0	0	0	0	0	.355	.412	.548	.960
2011	KC	AL	89	338	89	18	1	5	(3	2)	124	26	30	31	22	0	51	1	2	2	2	0	5	.263	.309	.367	.675
2012	KC	AL	149	563	136	34	1	20	(10	10)	232	69	73	64	39	4	124	7	0	5	5	2	4	.242	.296	.412	.708
2013	KC	AL	136	472	110	26	0	12	(5	7)	172	42	42	35	32	1	83	5	1	4	2	4	13	.233	.287	.364	.651
2014	KC	AL	140	457	97	21	1	15	(5	10)	165	45	54	44	35	1	74	3	1	4	1	0	12	.212	.271	.361	.632
	4 ML YEARS		514	1830	432	99	3	52	(23	29)	693	182	199	174	128	6	332	16	4	15	10	6	34	.236	.290	.379	.668

Steven Moya

Bats: L Throws: R Pos: PH-6;RF-5;DH-2;PR-1   MOY-uh   Ht: 6'6" Wt: 230 Born: 8/9/1991 Age: 23

							BATTING														RUNNING			AVERAGES			
Year	Team	Lg	G	AB	H	2B	3B	HR	(Hm	Rd)	TB	R	RBI	RC	TBB	IBB	SO	HBP	SH	SF	SB	CS	GDP	Avg	OBP	Slg	OPS
2010	Tigers	R	40	137	26	5	2	2	(-	-)	41	12	11	8	6	0	64	1	0	0	0	0	0	.190	.229	.299	.528
2011	WMich	A	86	323	66	10	1	13	(-	-)	117	38	39	26	12	1	127	1	0	1	1	1	4	.204	.234	.362	.597
2012	WMich	A	59	243	70	14	3	9	(-	-)	117	28	47	37	11	1	59	1	1	2	5	3	4	.288	.319	.481	.801
2013	Lkland	A+	93	365	93	19	5	12	(-	-)	158	52	55	48	18	0	106	4	0	1	6	0	9	.255	.296	.433	.729
2014	Erie	AA	133	515	142	33	3	35	(-	-)	286	81	105	90	23	2	161	3	0	8	16	4	7	.276	.306	.555	.861
2014	Det	AL	11	8	3	0	0	0	(0	0)	3	2	0	1	0	0	2	0	0	0	0	0	0	.375	.375	.375	.750

Edward Mujica

Pitches: R Bats: R Pos: RP-64   moo-HEE-kah   Ht: 6'3" Wt: 225 Born: 5/10/1984 Age: 31

									WHAT HE GAVE UP												THE RESULTS							
Year	Team	Lg	G	GS	CG	GF	IP	BFP	H	R	ER	HR	SH	SF	HB	TBB	IBB	SO	WP	Bk	W	L	Pct	Sh	Sv-Op	Hld	ERC	ERA
2006	Cle	AL	10	0	0	2	18.1	78	25	6	6	1	0	2	1	0	0	12	0	0	0	1	.000	0	0-0	0	4.50	2.95
2007	Cle	AL	10	0	0	5	13.0	60	19	12	12	3	0	1	0	2	0	7	0	0	0	0	-	0	0-0	0	6.63	8.31
2008	Cle	AL	33	0	0	13	38.2	168	46	29	29	5	0	4	1	10	3	27	1	0	3	2	.600	0	0-2	1	4.82	6.75
2009	SD	NL	67	4	0	15	93.2	393	101	47	41	14	1	3	0	19	4	76	3	1	3	5	.375	0	2-3	11	4.00	3.94
2010	SD	NL	59	0	0	24	69.2	268	59	29	28	14	0	6	0	6	0	72	1	0	2	1	.667	0	0-1	4	2.68	3.62
2011	Fla	NL	67	0	0	11	76.0	297	64	27	25	7	5	1	2	14	5	63	1	0	9	6	.600	0	0-3	17	2.46	2.96
2012	2 Tms		70	0	0	16	65.1	258	56	24	22	7	1	1	1	12	3	47	1	0	0	3	.000	0	2-8	30	2.58	3.03
2013	StL	NL	65	0	0	49	64.2	255	60	20	20	9	3	1	1	5	1	46	0	1	2	1	.667	0	37-41	5	2.75	2.78
2014	Bos	AL	64	0	0	31	60.0	253	69	28	26	6	2	2	0	14	2	43	1	0	2	4	.333	0	8-9	3	4.28	3.90
	12 Mia	NL	41	0	0	14	39.0	161	36	21	19	6	0	1	1	9	2	26	0	0	0	3	.000	0	2-6	12	3.35	4.38
	12 StL	NL	29	0	0	2	26.1	97	20	3	3	1	1	0	0	3	1	21	1	0	0	0	-	0	0-2	18	1.57	1.03
	Postseason		11	0	0	3	9.2	39	10	3	3	1	0	1	0	1	0	4	0	0	1	0	1.000	0	0-0	2	3.16	2.79
	9 ML YEARS		445	4	0	166	499.1	2030	499	222	209	66	13	15	6	82	18	393	8	2	21	23	.477	0	49-67	71	3.39	3.77

Daniel Murphy

Bats: L Throws: R Pos: 2B-126;3B-16;1B-1;PH-1   Ht: 6'1" Wt: 215 Born: 4/1/1985 Age: 30

							BATTING														RUNNING			AVERAGES			
Year	Team	Lg	G	AB	H	2B	3B	HR	(Hm	Rd)	TB	R	RBI	RC	TBB	IBB	SO	HBP	SH	SF	SB	CS	GDP	Avg	OBP	Slg	OPS
2008	NYM	NL	49	131	41	9	3	2	(1	1)	62	24	17	26	18	1	28	1	0	1	0	2	4	.313	.397	.473	.871
2009	NYM	NL	155	508	135	38	4	12	(7	5)	217	60	63	60	38	4	69	1	0	4	4	2	13	.266	.313	.427	.741
2011	NYM	NL	109	391	125	28	2	6	(2	4)	175	49	49	57	24	2	42	3	3	2	5	5	14	.320	.362	.448	.809
2012	NYM	NL	156	571	166	40	3	6	(1	5)	230	62	65	78	36	5	82	1	0	4	10	2	12	.291	.332	.403	.735
2013	NYM	NL	161	658	188	38	4	13	(6	7)	273	92	78	86	32	2	95	2	0	5	23	3	13	.286	.319	.415	.733
2014	NYM	NL	143	596	172	37	2	9	(4	5)	240	79	57	78	39	3	86	2	0	5	13	5	15	.289	.332	.403	.734
	6 ML YEARS		773	2855	827	190	18	48	(21	27)	1197	366	329	385	187	17	402	9	7	23	55	19	71	.290	.333	.419	.752

David Murphy

Bats: L Throws: L Pos: RF-120;PH-13;LF-2;DH-2;PR-1   Ht: 6'3" Wt: 210 Born: 10/18/1981 Age: 33

							BATTING														RUNNING			AVERAGES			
Year	Team	Lg	G	AB	H	2B	3B	HR	(Hm	Rd)	TB	R	RBI	RC	TBB	IBB	SO	HBP	SH	SF	SB	CS	GDP	Avg	OBP	Slg	OPS
2006	Bos	AL	20	22	5	1	0	1	(0	1)	9	4	2	4	4	0	4	0	0	0	0	0	1	.227	.346	.409	.755
2007	2 Tms	AL	46	105	36	12	2	2	(1	1)	58	17	14	23	7	0	20	0	0	0	0	0	1	.343	.384	.552	.936
2008	Tex	AL	108	415	114	28	3	15	(8	7)	193	64	74	62	31	3	70	0	2	6	7	2	7	.275	.321	.465	.786
2009	Tex	AL	128	432	116	24	1	17	(8	9)	193	61	57	60	49	3	106	1	2	9	9	4	5	.269	.338	.447	.785
2010	Tex	AL	138	419	122	26	2	12	(7	5)	188	54	65	68	45	2	71	0	0	3	14	2	6	.291	.358	.449	.806

228

Year	Team	Lg	G	AB	H	2B	3B	HR	(Hm	Rd)	TB	R	RBI	RC	TBB	IBB	SO	HBP	SH	SF	SB	CS	GDP	Avg	OBP	Slg	OPS
2011	Tex	AL	120	404	111	14	2	11	(8	3)	162	46	46	52	33	3	61	0	1	2	11	6	11	.275	.328	.401	.729
2012	Tex	AL	147	457	139	29	3	15	(7	8)	219	65	61	84	54	7	74	4	0	4	10	5	7	.304	.380	.479	.859
2013	Tex	AL	142	436	96	26	1	13	(9	4)	163	51	45	37	37	2	59	1	0	1	1	4	11	.220	.282	.374	.656
2014	Cle	AL	129	416	109	25	1	8	(6	2)	160	40	58	59	36	2	61	2	1	7	2	3	6	.262	.319	.385	.703
07	Bos	AL	3	2	1	0	1	0	(0	0)	3	1	0	1	0	0	1	0	0	0	0	0	0	.500	.500	1.500	2.000
07	Tex	AL	43	103	35	12	1	2	(1	1)	55	16	14	22	7	0	19	0	0	0	1	0	1	.340	.382	.534	.916
	Postseason		27	70	18	4	1	1	(1	0)	27	11	6	12	13	3	14	0	0	0	1	0	0	.257	.373	.386	.759
	9 ML YEARS		978	3106	848	185	15	94	(54	40)	1345	402	422	447	296	22	526	8	6	32	54	26	55	.273	.335	.433	.768

Donnie Murphy

Bats: R Throws: R Pos: 2B-21;DH-7;1B-6;PH-6;3B-5;PR-1 **Ht: 5'10" Wt: 190 Born: 3/10/1983 Age: 32**

Year	Team	Lg	G	AB	H	2B	3B	HR	(Hm	Rd)	TB	R	RBI	RC	TBB	IBB	SO	HBP	SH	SF	SB	CS	GDP	Avg	OBP	Slg	OPS
2014	RdRck*	AAA	6	19	1	0	0	0	(-	-)	1	0	1	0	3	0	7	1	0	1	0	0	1	.053	.208	.053	.261
2014	Lsvlle*	AAA	10	33	5	1	0	1	(-	-)	9	1	3	1	2	0	5	1	0	0	0	0	2	.152	.222	.273	.495
2014	Gwnntt*	AAA	10	42	7	2	0	2	(-	-)	15	6	10	2	0	0	12	1	0	0	0	0	2	.167	.182	.357	.539
2004	KC	AL	7	27	5	3	0	0	(0	0)	8	1	3	2	0	0	7	0	0	0	1	0	1	.185	.185	.296	.481
2005	KC	AL	32	77	12	5	0	1	(0	1)	20	4	8	1	9	0	23	0	1	1	0	1	3	.156	.241	.260	.501
2007	Oak	AL	42	118	26	8	0	6	(2	4)	52	21	21	16	10	0	35	2	1	1	1	0	3	.220	.290	.441	.731
2008	Oak	AL	46	103	19	3	0	3	(2	1)	31	10	13	6	11	0	38	2	0	1	2	1	1	.184	.274	.301	.574
2010	Fla	NL	29	44	14	6	1	3	(2	1)	31	9	16	12	2	0	19	0	1	0	0	0	0	.318	.348	.705	1.052
2011	Fla	NL	36	92	17	4	1	2	(0	2)	29	10	9	5	4	1	21	3	0	1	0	0	0	.185	.240	.315	.555
2012	Mia	NL	52	116	25	6	2	3	(2	1)	44	13	12	12	9	1	35	2	1	1	1	1	4	.216	.281	.379	.661
2013	ChC	NL	46	149	38	8	0	11	(7	4)	79	23	23	22	8	1	48	6	0	0	2	0	1	.255	.319	.530	.849
2014	Tex	AL	45	112	22	3	0	4	(0	4)	37	11	14	11	11	0	38	1	1	3	0	1	2	.196	.268	.330	.598
	9 ML YEARS		335	838	178	46	4	33	(15	18)	331	102	119	87	64	3	264	16	5	8	7	4	15	.212	.279	.395	.674

J.R. Murphy

Bats: R Throws: R Pos: C-30;PH-4;DH-2 **Ht: 5'11" Wt: 195 Born: 5/13/1991 Age: 24**

Year	Team	Lg	G	AB	H	2B	3B	HR	(Hm	Rd)	TB	R	RBI	RC	TBB	IBB	SO	HBP	SH	SF	SB	CS	GDP	Avg	OBP	Slg	OPS
2010	CtnSC	A	87	330	84	15	2	7	(-	-)	124	46	54	42	36	0	64	2	1	5	4	5	8	.255	.327	.376	.703
2011	CtnSC	A	63	256	76	23	0	6	(-	-)	117	31	32	41	19	1	38	0	0	2	2	0	7	.297	.343	.457	.800
2011	Tampa	A+	23	85	22	6	0	1	(-	-)	31	8	14	8	2	0	9	0	0	2	0	0	2	.259	.270	.365	.634
2012	Tampa	A+	67	265	68	14	1	5	(-	-)	99	39	28	33	26	0	41	0	2	1	4	3	12	.257	.322	.374	.696
2012	Trntn	AA	43	147	34	12	1	4	(-	-)	60	23	16	20	16	0	32	2	0	5	0	0	1	.231	.306	.408	.714
2013	Trntn	AA	49	183	49	10	0	6	(-	-)	77	34	25	29	24	0	32	1	1	2	1	0	4	.268	.352	.421	.773
2013	S-WB	AAA	59	230	62	19	0	6	(-	-)	99	26	21	35	23	1	41	3	0	1	0	1	8	.270	.342	.430	.773
2014	S-WB	AAA	51	179	44	9	0	6	(-	-)	71	17	28	21	13	0	42	0	1	3	0	0	7	.246	.292	.397	.689
2013	NYY	AL	16	26	4	1	0	0	(0	0)	5	3	1	0	1	0	9	0	0	0	0	0	0	.154	.185	.192	.377
2014	NYY	AL	32	81	23	4	0	1	(1	0)	30	7	9	10	4	0	22	0	0	0	0	0	0	.284	.318	.370	.688
	2 ML YEARS		48	107	27	5	0	1	(1	0)	35	10	10	10	5	0	31	0	0	0	0	0	0	.252	.286	.327	.613

Wil Myers

Bats: R Throws: R Pos: RF-78;DH-9;PH-3;1B-2;CF-1 **Ht: 6'3" Wt: 205 Born: 12/10/1990 Age: 24**

Year	Team	Lg	G	AB	H	2B	3B	HR	(Hm	Rd)	TB	R	RBI	RC	TBB	IBB	SO	HBP	SH	SF	SB	CS	GDP	Avg	OBP	Slg	OPS
2010	Burlgtn	A	68	242	70	19	1	10	(-	-)	121	42	45	52	48	0	55	2	0	2	10	3	4	.289	.408	.500	.908
2010	Wilmg	A+	58	205	71	18	2	4	(-	-)	105	28	38	48	37	1	39	4	0	1	2	3	5	.346	.453	.512	.966
2011	NWArk	AA	99	354	90	23	1	8	(-	-)	139	50	49	54	52	1	87	4	2	4	9	2	16	.254	.353	.393	.745
2012	NWArk	AA	35	134	46	11	4	13	(-	-)	98	32	30	37	16	0	42	1	0	1	4	1	4	.343	.414	.731	1.146
2012	Omha	AAA	99	388	118	15	5	24	(-	-)	215	66	79	80	45	2	98	3	0	3	2	2	7	.304	.378	.554	.932
2013	Drham	AAA	64	252	72	13	2	14	(-	-)	131	44	57	49	29	1	71	2	0	6	7	1	6	.286	.356	.520	.876
2014	Drham	AAA	7	24	6	1	0	2	(-	-)	13	3	6	6	7	2	7	0	0	0	3	0	0	.250	.419	.542	.961
2013	TB	AL	88	335	98	23	0	13	(5	8)	160	50	53	52	33	6	91	1	0	4	5	2	10	.293	.354	.478	.831
2014	TB	AL	87	325	72	14	0	6	(2	4)	104	37	35	32	34	3	90	0	0	2	6	1	10	.222	.294	.320	.614
	Postseason		5	20	2	0	0	0	(0	0)	2	0	0	0	1	0	7	0	0	0	0	0	0	.100	.143	.100	.243
	2 ML YEARS		175	660	170	37	0	19	(7	12)	264	87	88	84	67	9	181	1	0	6	11	3	20	.258	.324	.400	.724

Xavier Nady

Bats: R Throws: R Pos: PH-15;RF-8;LF-5;1B-1 ZAYV-yer NAY-dee **Ht: 6'2" Wt: 215 Born: 11/14/1978 Age: 36**

Year	Team	Lg	G	AB	H	2B	3B	HR	(Hm	Rd)	TB	R	RBI	RC	TBB	IBB	SO	HBP	SH	SF	SB	CS	GDP	Avg	OBP	Slg	OPS
2014	Tacom*	AAA	22	89	21	3	0	2	(-	-)	30	8	9	9	4	0	17	4	0	1	0	0	6	.236	.296	.337	.633
2000	SD	NL	1	1	1	0	0	0	(0	0)	1	1	0	1	0	0	0	0	0	0	0	0	0	1.000	1.000	1.000	2.000
2003	SD	NL	110	371	99	17	1	9	(5	4)	145	50	39	39	24	0	74	6	2	1	6	2	14	.267	.321	.391	.712
2004	SD	NL	34	77	19	4	0	3	(1	2)	32	7	9	8	5	0	13	1	1	0	0	0	4	.247	.301	.416	.717
2005	SD	NL	124	326	85	15	2	13	(5	8)	143	40	43	37	22	1	67	7	1	0	2	1	5	.261	.321	.439	.760
2006	2 Tms	NL	130	468	131	28	1	17	(10	7)	212	57	63	62	30	7	85	11	2	1	3	3	12	.280	.337	.453	.790
2007	Pit	NL	125	431	120	23	1	20	(7	13)	205	55	72	60	23	2	101	12	0	4	3	1	16	.278	.330	.476	.805
2008	2 Tms		148	555	169	37	1	25	(11	14)	283	76	97	93	39	2	103	9	0	4	2	1	14	.305	.357	.510	.867
2009	NYY	AL	7	28	8	4	0	0	(0	0)	12	4	2	2	1	0	6	0	0	0	0	0	0	.286	.310	.429	.739
2010	ChC	NL	119	317	81	13	0	6	(2	4)	112	33	33	33	17	0	85	8	1	4	0	0	12	.256	.306	.353	.660
2011	Ari	NL	82	206	51	11	0	4	(1	3)	74	26	35	24	10	1	46	3	0	4	0	1	8	.248	.287	.359	.646
2012	2 Tms	NL	59	152	28	6	1	4	(3	1)	48	15	20	14	5	0	37	1	0	0	0	1	4	.184	.253	.316	.569
2014	SD	NL	22	37	5	1	0	3	(2	1)	15	4	4	0	5	0	9	0	0	0	0	0	4	.135	.238	.405	.644
	06 NYM	NL	75	265	70	15	1	14	(10	4)	129	37	40	35	19	4	51	6	1	1	2	1	7	.264	.326	.487	.813

Year Team	Lg	G	AB	H	2B	3B	HR	(Hm	Rd)	TB	R	RBI	RC	TBB	IBB	SO	HBP	SH	SF	SB	CS	GDP	Avg	OBP	Slg	OPS
								BATTING												RUNNING			AVERAGES			
06 Pit	NL	55	203	61	13	0	3	(0	3)	83	20	23	27	11	3	34	5	1	0	1	2	5	.300	.352	.409	.760
08 Pit	NL	89	327	108	26	1	13	(6	7)	175	50	57	59	25	1	55	5	0	3	1	0	9	.330	.383	.535	.919
08 NYY	AL	59	228	61	11	0	12	(5	7)	108	26	40	34	14	1	48	4	0	1	1	1	5	.268	.320	.474	.794
12 Was	NL	40	102	16	3	0	3	(3	0)	28	6	6	0	7	2	24	0	0	0	1	0	3	.157	.211	.275	.486
12 SF	NL	19	50	12	3	1	1	(0	1)	20	6	7	5	6	0	13	1	0	0	0	0	5	.240	.333	.400	.733
Postseason		6	8	1	0	0	0	(0	0)	1	0	2	1	1	0	4	2	0	0	0	0	0	.125	.364	.125	.489
12 ML YEARS		961	2969	797	159	7	104	(47	57)	1282	365	410	362	189	15	626	58	7	18	19	8	95	.268	.323	.432	.755

Mike Napoli

Bats: R Throws: R Pos: 1B-110;DH-7;PH-2   NAPP-uh-lee   Ht: 6'0" Wt: 220 Born: 10/31/1981 Age: 33

Year Team	Lg	G	AB	H	2B	3B	HR	(Hm	Rd)	TB	R	RBI	RC	TBB	IBB	SO	HBP	SH	SF	SB	CS	GDP	Avg	OBP	Slg	OPS
								BATTING												RUNNING			AVERAGES			
2006 LAA	AL	99	268	61	13	0	16	(10	6)	122	47	42	40	51	0	90	5	0	1	2	3	2	.228	.360	.455	.815
2007 LAA	AL	75	219	54	11	1	10	(5	5)	97	40	34	35	33	2	63	5	1	5	5	2	5	.247	.351	.443	.794
2008 LAA	AL	78	227	62	9	1	20	(10	10)	133	39	49	46	35	5	70	5	1	0	7	3	5	.273	.374	.586	.960
2009 LAA	AL	114	382	104	22	1	20	(10	10)	188	60	56	53	40	1	103	7	0	3	3	3	6	.272	.350	.492	.842
2010 LAA	AL	140	453	108	24	1	26	(13	13)	212	60	68	60	42	2	137	11	0	4	4	2	15	.238	.316	.468	.784
2011 Tex	AL	113	369	118	25	0	30	(13	17)	233	72	75	90	58	2	85	3	0	2	4	2	10	.320	.414	.631	1.046
2012 Tex	AL	108	352	80	9	2	24	(11	13)	165	53	56	54	56	5	125	7	0	2	1	0	9	.227	.343	.469	.812
2013 Bos	AL	139	498	129	38	2	23	(11	12)	240	79	92	79	73	3	187	6	0	1	1	1	15	.259	.360	.482	.842
2014 Bos	AL	119	415	103	20	0	17	(6	11)	174	49	55	54	78	3	133	4	0	3	3	2	12	.248	.370	.419	.789
Postseason		47	138	35	6	0	7	(1	6)	62	20	26	24	19	2	46	3	0	2	1	0	2	.254	.352	.449	.801
9 ML YEARS		985	3183	819	171	8	186	(89	97)	1564	499	527	511	466	23	993	53	2	27	30	18	77	.257	.359	.491	.850

Joe Nathan

Pitches: R Bats: R Pos: RP-62   Ht: 6'4" Wt: 230 Born: 11/22/1974 Age: 40

Year Team	Lg	G	GS	CG	GF	IP	BFP	H	R	ER	HR	SH	SF	HB	TBB	IBB	SO	WP	Bk	W	L	Pct	Sh	Sv-Op	Hld	ERC	ERA
		HOW MUCH HE PITCHED						WHAT HE GAVE UP												THE RESULTS							
1999 SF	NL	19	14	0	2	90.1	395	84	45	42	17	2	0	1	46	0	54	2	0	7	4	.636	0	1-1	0	4.78	4.18
2000 SF	NL	20	15	0	0	93.1	426	89	63	54	12	5	5	4	63	4	61	5	0	5	2	.714	0	0-1	0	5.23	5.21
2002 SF	NL	4	0	0	3	3.2	12	1	0	0	0	0	0	0	0	0	2	0	0	0	0	-	0	0-0	0	0.17	0.00
2003 SF	NL	78	0	0	9	79.0	316	51	26	26	7	2	4	3	33	3	83	4	1	12	4	.750	0	0-3	20	2.34	2.96
2004 Min	AL	73	0	0	72	72.1	284	48	14	13	3	2	0	2	23	3	89	5	0	1	2	.333	0	44-47	0	1.78	1.62
2005 Min	AL	69	0	0	58	70.0	276	46	22	21	5	1	2	0	22	1	94	2	0	7	4	.636	0	43-48	0	1.83	2.70
2006 Min	AL	64	0	0	61	68.1	262	38	12	12	3	3	2	1	16	4	95	3	0	7	0	1.000	0	36-38	0	1.18	1.58
2007 Min	AL	68	0	0	60	71.2	282	54	15	15	4	2	2	1	19	2	77	3	0	4	2	.667	0	37-41	0	2.08	1.88
2008 Min	AL	68	0	0	57	67.2	261	43	13	10	5	1	0	2	18	4	74	2	0	1	2	.333	0	39-45	0	1.67	1.33
2009 Min	AL	70	0	0	62	68.2	271	42	16	16	7	1	0	2	22	1	89	4	0	2	2	.500	0	47-52	0	1.89	2.10
2011 Min	AL	48	0	0	33	44.2	191	38	26	24	7	1	2	3	14	2	43	3	0	2	1	.667	0	14-17	8	3.38	4.84
2012 Tex	AL	66	0	0	62	64.1	257	55	23	20	7	1	3	2	13	1	78	5	0	3	5	.375	0	37-40	0	2.73	2.80
2013 Tex	AL	67	0	0	61	64.2	250	36	10	10	2	3	2	1	22	3	73	4	0	6	2	.750	0	43-46	0	1.39	1.39
2014 Det	AL	62	0	0	54	58.0	259	60	32	31	5	1	2	1	29	3	54	4	1	5	4	.556	0	35-42	0	4.53	4.81
Postseason		9	0	0	4	9.0	49	14	9	9	2	0	1	0	8	3	11	1	0	0	2	.000	0	1-3	0	9.91	9.00
14 ML YEARS		776	29	0	585	916.2	3742	685	317	294	84	25	24	23	340	31	966	46	2	62	34	.646	0	376-421	28	2.62	2.89

Daniel Nava

Bats: B Throws: L Pos: RF-69;LF-38;PH-14;1B-11;DH-1   NAH-vah   Ht: 5'11" Wt: 200 Born: 2/22/1983 Age: 32

Year Team	Lg	G	AB	H	2B	3B	HR	(Hm	Rd)	TB	R	RBI	RC	TBB	IBB	SO	HBP	SH	SF	SB	CS	GDP	Avg	OBP	Slg	OPS
								BATTING												RUNNING			AVERAGES			
2014 Pwtckt*	AAA	24	83	21	3	0	3	(-	-)	33	12	14	12	12	1	21	1	0	2	2	1	5	.253	.347	.398	.745
2010 Bos	AL	60	161	39	14	1	1	(1	0)	58	23	26	26	19	1	46	8	0	0	1	1	5	.242	.351	.360	.711
2012 Bos	AL	88	267	65	21	0	6	(1	5)	104	38	33	33	37	1	63	9	2	2	3	0	5	.243	.352	.390	.742
2013 Bos	AL	134	458	139	29	0	12	(5	7)	204	77	66	79	51	2	93	15	4	8	0	2	10	.303	.385	.445	.831
2014 Bos	AL	113	363	98	21	0	4	(0	4)	131	41	37	49	33	1	81	10	0	2	4	2	5	.270	.346	.361	.706
Postseason		9	25	5	1	0	0	(0	0)	6	1	2	2	3	0	9	0	0	0	0	1	1	.200	.286	.240	.526
4 ML YEARS		395	1249	341	85	1	23	(7	16)	497	179	162	187	140	5	283	42	6	12	8	5	25	.273	.362	.398	.760

Dioner Navarro

Bats: B Throws: R Pos: C-112;DH-21;PH-18   dee-AHN-err   Ht: 5'9" Wt: 205 Born: 2/9/1984 Age: 31

Year Team	Lg	G	AB	H	2B	3B	HR	(Hm	Rd)	TB	R	RBI	RC	TBB	IBB	SO	HBP	SH	SF	SB	CS	GDP	Avg	OBP	Slg	OPS
								BATTING												RUNNING			AVERAGES			
2004 NYY	AL	5	7	3	0	0	0	(0	0)	3	2	1	1	0	0	0	0	0	0	0	0	1	.429	.429	.429	.857
2005 LAD	NL	50	176	48	9	0	3	(0	3)	66	21	14	18	20	1	21	2	1	0	0	0	3	.273	.354	.375	.729
2006 2 Tms		81	268	68	9	0	6	(4	2)	95	28	28	27	31	6	51	1	1	1	2	1	7	.254	.332	.354	.687
2007 TB	AL	119	388	88	19	2	9	(5	4)	138	46	44	35	33	3	67	1	7	5	3	1	11	.227	.286	.356	.641
2008 TB	AL	120	427	126	27	0	7	(4	3)	174	43	54	59	34	1	49	3	3	3	0	4	16	.295	.349	.407	.757
2009 TB	AL	115	376	82	15	0	8	(4	4)	121	38	32	22	18	1	51	5	8	3	5	2	14	.218	.261	.322	.583
2010 TB	AL	48	124	24	5	0	1	(1	0)	32	11	7	4	12	0	20	1	5	0	0	1	3	.194	.270	.258	.528
2011 LAD	NL	64	176	34	6	1	5	(3	2)	57	13	17	14	20	4	35	1	3	2	0	0	3	.193	.276	.324	.600
2012 Cin	NL	24	69	20	3	1	2	(0	2)	31	6	12	10	2	1	12	0	1	1	0	0	1	.290	.306	.449	.755
2013 ChC	NL	89	240	72	7	0	13	(9	4)	118	31	34	43	23	1	36	2	0	1	0	1	4	.300	.365	.492	.856
2014 Tor	AL	139	481	132	22	0	12	(8	4)	190	40	69	68	32	1	76	1	0	6	3	0	12	.274	.317	.395	.712
06 LAD	NL	25	75	21	2	0	2	(1	1)	29	5	8	8	11	4	18	0	0	0	1	0	1	.280	.372	.387	.759
06 TB	AL	56	193	47	7	0	4	(3	1)	66	23	20	19	20	2	33	1	1	1	1	1	6	.244	.316	.342	.658
Postseason		18	62	18	4	0	0	(0	0)	22	4	5	6	5	0	13	0	0	0	0	1	2	.290	.343	.355	.698
11 ML YEARS		854	2732	697	122	4	66	(42	24)	1025	279	312	301	225	19	418	17	29	22	13	10	75	.255	.313	.375	.689

Efren Navarro

Bats: L Throws: L Pos: 1B-28;LF-23;PH-11;RF-6;DH-4;PR-1   EFF-ren   Ht: 6'0" Wt: 210 Born: 5/14/1986 Age: 29

Year	Team	Lg	G	AB	H	2B	3B	HR	(Hm	Rd)	TB	R	RBI	RC	TBB	IBB	SO	HBP	SH	SF	SB	CS	GDP	Avg	OBP	Slg	OPS
2014	Salt Lk*	AAA	72	273	89	19	3	4	(-	-)	126	45	50	55	43	1	47	1	0	1	2	1	6	.326	.418	.462	.880
2011	LAA	AL	8	10	2	1	0	0	(0	0)	3	1	0	1	1	0	1	0	1	0	0	0	1	.200	.273	.300	.573
2013	LAA	AL	4	4	1	0	0	0	(0	0)	1	0	1	1	2	0	1	0	0	0	1	0	0	.250	.500	.250	.750
2014	LAA	AL	64	159	39	10	1	1	(1	0)	54	17	14	19	13	2	27	0	2	0	1	3	0	.245	.302	.340	.642
	3 ML YEARS		76	173	42	11	1	1	(1	0)	58	18	15	20	16	2	29	0	3	0	2	3	1	.243	.307	.335	.642

Kristopher Negron

neh-GRONE

Bats: R Throws: R Pos: 3B-25;2B-17;PH-7;SS-2;PR-2;LF-1   Ht: 6'0" Wt: 195 Born: 2/1/1986 Age: 29

Year	Team	Lg	G	AB	H	2B	3B	HR	(Hm	Rd)	TB	R	RBI	RC	TBB	IBB	SO	HBP	SH	SF	SB	CS	GDP	Avg	OBP	Slg	OPS
2010	Carlina	AA	120	470	128	19	6	11	(-	-)	192	79	41	77	51	0	97	16	7	3	34	9	5	.272	.361	.409	.770
2010	Lsvlle	AAA	7	21	4	1	0	0	(-	-)	5	1	0	0	0	0	6	0	0	0	1	0	1	.190	.190	.238	.429
2011	Lsvlle	AAA	123	417	90	16	4	9	(-	-)	141	54	45	41	22	0	102	10	11	5	11	1	9	.216	.269	.338	.607
2012	Lsvlle	AAA	74	284	62	14	2	6	(-	-)	98	34	20	31	22	0	77	6	5	2	17	3	3	.218	.287	.345	.632
2013	Lsvlle	AAA	116	334	75	14	1	5	(-	-)	106	31	30	34	26	0	93	9	6	4	11	3	9	.225	.295	.317	.612
2014	Lsvlle	AAA	75	219	59	15	3	3	(-	-)	89	33	25	31	14	0	54	5	2	0	9	2	6	.269	.328	.406	.734
2012	Cin	NL	4	4	1	0	0	0	(0	0)	1	2	0	1	1	0	2	0	0	0	0	0	0	.250	.400	.250	.650
2014	Cin	NL	49	144	39	10	1	6	(3	3)	69	19	17	23	12	0	40	1	1	0	5	0	2	.271	.331	.479	.810
	2 ML YEARS		53	148	40	10	1	6	(3	3)	70	21	17	24	13	0	42	1	1	0	5	0	2	.270	.333	.473	.806

Chris Nelson

Bats: R Throws: R Pos: 3B-20;PH-7;2B-3;1B-1   Ht: 5'11" Wt: 205 Born: 9/3/1985 Age: 29

Year	Team	Lg	G	AB	H	2B	3B	HR	(Hm	Rd)	TB	R	RBI	RC	TBB	IBB	SO	HBP	SH	SF	SB	CS	GDP	Avg	OBP	Slg	OPS
2014	Lsvlle*	AAA	63	237	65	9	0	4	(-	-)	86	26	38	29	18	2	52	3	0	3	0	2	7	.274	.330	.363	.692
2014	ElPaso*	AAA	24	82	24	6	1	2	(-	-)	38	13	21	17	18	0	16	1	0	1	0	0	5	.293	.422	.463	.885
2010	Col	NL	17	25	7	1	0	0	(0	0)	8	7	0	1	1	0	4	0	1	0	1	0	1	.280	.308	.320	.628
2011	Col	NL	63	180	45	10	1	4	(3	1)	69	20	16	15	7	1	35	1	0	1	3	1	5	.250	.280	.383	.664
2012	Col	NL	111	345	104	21	3	9	(3	6)	158	45	53	56	27	4	84	1	2	2	2	1	9	.301	.352	.458	.810
2013	3 Tms	NL	64	211	48	4	4	3	(0	3)	69	19	24	18	13	0	66	1	0	2	2	1	8	.227	.273	.327	.600
2014	SD	NL	27	73	17	3	0	0	(0	0)	20	5	7	4	7	1	14	0	0	1	1	2	5	.233	.296	.274	.570
13	Col	NL	21	66	16	1	2	0	(0	0)	21	6	4	5	4	0	19	0	0	1	0	0	1	.242	.282	.318	.600
13	NYY	AL	10	36	8	2	0	0	(0	0)	10	3	2	1	1	0	11	0	0	0	0	0	3	.222	.243	.278	.521
13	LAA	AL	33	109	24	1	2	3	(0	3)	38	10	18	12	8	0	36	1	0	1	2	1	4	.220	.277	.349	.626
	5 ML YEARS		282	834	221	39	8	16	(6	10)	324	96	100	94	55	6	203	3	3	6	9	5	28	.265	.311	.388	.699

Jimmy Nelson

Pitches: R Bats: R Pos: SP-12; RP-2   Ht: 6'6" Wt: 245 Born: 6/5/1989 Age: 26

	HOW MUCH HE PITCHED						WHAT HE GAVE UP												THE RESULTS						
Year	Team	Lg	G	GS	CG	GF	IP	BFP	H	R	ER	HR	SH	SF	HB	TBB	IBB	SO	WP	Bk	W	L	Pct	Sh	Sv-Op	Hld	ERC	ERA
2010	Helena	R+	12	0	0	5	26.2	127	30	21	11	2	2	0	0	13	0	33	3	0	2	0	1.000	0	3- -		4.66	3.71
2011	Wisc	A	26	25	1	0	146.0	630	146	81	71	9	3	7	6	65	0	120	13	1	8	9	.471	0	0- -		4.21	4.38
2012	BrvdCt	A+	13	13	1	0	81.1	330	63	24	20	3	7	2	5	25	0	77	5	0	4	4	.500	0	0- -		2.39	2.21
2012	Hntsvl	AA	10	10	0	0	46.0	209	34	25	20	2	1	3	3	37	0	42	4	0	2	4	.333	0	0- -		3.96	3.91
2013	Hntsvl	AA	12	12	1	0	69.0	289	63	34	21	5	0	4	9	15	0	72	4	0	5	4	.556	0	0- -		3.21	2.74
2013	Nashv	AAA	15	15	1	0	83.1	367	74	39	34	2	4	1	4	50	0	91	6	2	5	6	.455	0	0- -		3.88	3.67
2014	Nashv	AAA	17	16	0	1	111.0	431	70	23	18	3	2	1	4	32	0	114	10	1	10	2	.833	0	0- -		1.58	1.46
2013	Mil	NL	4	1	0	1	10.0	37	2	1	1	0	0	1	0	5	0	8	1	0	0	0	-	0	0-0		0.64	0.90
2014	Mil	NL	14	12	0	1	69.1	311	82	42	38	6	1	2	8	19	0	57	4	0	2	9	.182	0	0-0		4.96	4.93
	2 ML YEARS		18	13	0	1	79.1	348	84	43	39	6	1	3	8	24	0	65	5	0	2	9	.182	0	0-0		4.22	4.42

Hector Neris

Pitches: R Bats: R Pos: RP-1   NAIR-ess   Ht: 6'2" Wt: 175 Born: 6/14/1989 Age: 26

	HOW MUCH HE PITCHED						WHAT HE GAVE UP												THE RESULTS						
Year	Team	Lg	G	GS	CG	GF	IP	BFP	H	R	ER	HR	SH	SF	HB	TBB	IBB	SO	WP	Bk	W	L	Pct	Sh	Sv-Op	Hld	ERC	ERA
2011	Lakwd	A-	19	0	0	7	35.0	151	34	21	15	6	1	1	1	9	0	43	3	1	2	1	.667	0	0- -		3.80	3.86
2011	Wmspt	A-	15	0	0	3	24.0	96	17	3	3	1	0	0	1	8	0	29	0	0	1	1	.500	0	0- -		2.13	1.13
2012	Clrwtr	A+	50	0	0	22	78.2	322	64	34	31	7	2	1	4	25	3	94	5	4	4	2	.667	0	6- -		2.85	3.55
2013	Rdng	AA	46	8	0	16	97.0	415	89	51	49	14	1	4	2	39	0	93	4	4	6	4	.600	0	0- -		3.99	4.55
2014	LV	AAA	37	1	0	11	58.0	245	50	29	27	5	1	0	6	19	1	58	3	2	4	3	.571	0	2- -		3.31	4.19
2014	Rdng	AA	11	0	0	3	19.1	76	12	4	4	3	2	0	0	6	0	12	0	0	2	0	1.000	0	0- -		2.99	1.86
2014	Phi	NL	1	0	0	1	1.0	3	0	0	0	0	0	0	0	0	0	1	0	0	1	0	1.000	0	0-0	0	0.00	0.00

Pat Neshek

Pitches: R Bats: B Pos: RP-71   NEE-sheck   Ht: 6'3" Wt: 210 Born: 9/4/1980 Age: 34

	HOW MUCH HE PITCHED						WHAT HE GAVE UP												THE RESULTS						
Year	Team	Lg	G	GS	CG	GF	IP	BFP	H	R	ER	HR	SH	SF	HB	TBB	IBB	SO	WP	Bk	W	L	Pct	Sh	Sv-Op	Hld	ERC	ERA
2006	Min	AL	32	0	0	3	37.0	138	23	9	9	6	0	1	0	6	0	53	0	0	4	2	.667	0	0-2	10	1.68	2.19
2007	Min	AL	74	0	0	20	70.1	278	44	25	23	7	4	5	2	27	5	74	2	0	7	2	.778	0	0-3	15	2.12	2.94
2008	Min	AL	15	0	0	3	13.1	56	12	7	7	2	1	1	0	4	1	15	0	0	1	0	1.000	0	0-2	6	3.29	4.73
2010	Min	AL	11	0	0	3	9.0	43	7	5	5	1	0	0	1	8	0	9	0	0	0	1	.000	0	0-1	1	5.13	5.00

Year	Team	Lg	G	GS	CG	GF	IP	BFP	H	R	ER	HR	SH	SF	HB	TBB	IBB	SO	WP	Bk	W	L	Pct	Sh	Sv-Op	Hld	ERC	ERA
2011	SD	NL	25	0	0	13	24.2	112	19	12	11	4	1	0	1	22	1	20	1	0	1	1	.500	0	0-0	5	5.37	4.01
2012	Oak	AL	24	0	0	5	19.2	77	10	3	3	3	0	2	1	6	1	16	1	0	2	1	.667	0	0-2	4	1.66	1.37
2013	Oak	AL	45	0	0	17	40.1	177	40	17	15	6	0	3	0	15	2	29	1	0	2	1	.667	0	0-0	1	4.06	3.35
2014	Oak	AL	71	0	0	17	67.1	255	44	14	14	4	2	2	2	9	2	68	1	0	7	2	.778	0	6-10	25	1.38	1.87
	Postseason		3	0	0	1	1.2	6	1	1	1	0	0	0	0	0	0	2	0	0	0	1	.000	0	0-0	0	0.75	5.40
	8 ML YEARS		297	0	0	81	281.2	1136	199	92	87	33	8	14	7	97	12	284	6	0	23	11	.676	0	6-20	62	2.46	2.78

Juan Nicasio

Pitches: R **Bats:** R **Pos:** RP-19; SP-14   nih-COSS-ee-oh   **Ht:** 6'3" **Wt:** 210 **Born:** 8/31/1986 **Age:** 28

Year	Team	Lg	G	GS	CG	GF	IP	BFP	H	R	ER	HR	SH	SF	HB	TBB	IBB	SO	WP	Bk	W	L	Pct	Sh	Sv-Op	Hld	ERC	ERA
2014	ColSpr*	AAA	10	4	0	3	35.2	154	41	21	18	4	1	2	1	15	0	36	2	0	3	2	.600	0	1- -	-	5.47	4.54
2011	Col	NL	13	13	0	0	71.2	299	73	35	33	8	1	0	1	18	3	58	1	0	4	4	.500	0	0-0	0	3.69	4.14
2012	Col	NL	11	11	0	0	58.0	257	72	37	34	7	3	1	1	22	1	54	4	0	2	3	.400	0	0-0	0	5.74	5.28
2013	Col	NL	31	31	0	0	157.2	703	168	97	90	17	6	1	5	64	7	119	6	2	9	9	.500	0	0-0	0	4.52	5.14
2014	Col	NL	33	14	0	7	93.2	409	107	59	56	19	5	2	1	31	1	63	3	1	6	6	.500	0	0-0	1	5.43	5.38
	4 ML YEARS		88	69	0	7	381.0	1668	420	228	213	51	15	4	8	135	12	294	14	3	21	22	.488	0	0-0	1	4.76	5.03

Jon Niese

Pitches: L **Bats:** L **Pos:** SP-30   NIECE   **Ht:** 6'3" **Wt:** 220 **Born:** 10/27/1986 **Age:** 28

Year	Team	Lg	G	GS	CG	GF	IP	BFP	H	R	ER	HR	SH	SF	HB	TBB	IBB	SO	WP	Bk	W	L	Pct	Sh	Sv-Op	Hld	ERC	ERA
2008	NYM	NL	3	3	0	0	14.0	69	20	11	11	2	1	0	0	8	0	11	0	0	1	1	.500	0	0-0	0	7.71	7.07
2009	NYM	NL	5	5	0	0	25.2	110	27	12	12	1	2	1	0	9	0	18	1	0	1	1	.500	0	0-0	0	3.76	4.21
2010	NYM	NL	30	30	2	0	173.2	770	192	97	81	20	9	4	9	62	3	148	5	0	9	10	.474	1	0-0	0	4.77	4.20
2011	NYM	NL	27	26	0	0	157.1	694	178	88	77	14	16	2	5	44	4	138	3	0	11	11	.500	0	0-0	0	4.27	4.40
2012	NYM	NL	30	30	0	0	190.1	788	174	77	72	22	8	4	4	49	2	155	6	0	13	9	.591	0	0-0	0	3.21	3.40
2013	NYM	NL	24	24	1	0	143.0	621	158	68	59	10	6	0	4	48	1	105	5	0	8	8	.500	1	0-0	0	4.32	3.71
2014	NYM	NL	30	30	0	0	187.2	786	193	80	71	17	10	5	7	45	0	138	3	0	9	11	.450	0	0-0	0	3.72	3.40
	7 ML YEARS		149	148	3	0	891.2	3838	942	433	383	86	52	16	29	265	10	713	23	0	52	51	.505	2	0-0	0	4.06	3.87

Adrian Nieto

Bats: B **Throws:** R **Pos:** C-46;PR-3;DH-1;PH-1   knee-EH-toe   **Ht:** 6'0" **Wt:** 200 **Born:** 11/12/1989 **Age:** 25

Year	Team	Lg	G	AB	H	2B	3B	HR	(Hm	Rd)	TB	R	RBI	RC	TBB	IBB	SO	HBP	SH	SF	SB	CS	GDP	Avg	OBP	Slg	OPS
2010	Hgrstn	A	60	174	34	4	0	2	(-	-)	44	23	14	14	23	0	44	1	4	1	1	0	4	.195	.291	.253	.544
2011	Auburn	A-	30	106	32	5	4	0	(-	-)	49	20	22	21	17	0	34	1	0	2	2	0	1	.302	.397	.462	.859
2011	Ptomc	A+	2	5	1	0	0	0	(-	-)	1	1	0	0	1	0	2	0	1	0	0	0	0	.200	.333	.200	.533
2011	Hgrstn	A	27	98	25	8	1	3	(-	-)	44	17	12	14	9	0	31	0	0	0	0	0	2	.255	.318	.449	.767
2012	Hgrstn	A	70	257	66	17	0	6	(-	-)	101	32	39	38	35	0	64	2	1	4	4	2	8	.257	.346	.393	.739
2012	Nats	R	8	26	4	1	0	1	(-	-)	8	3	3	2	5	0	7	0	0	0	0	0	1	.154	.290	.308	.598
2013	Ptomc	A+	110	390	111	29	1	11	(-	-)	175	68	53	68	53	1	82	4	1	4	4	2	7	.285	.373	.449	.821
2014	CWS	AL	48	106	25	5	0	2	(1	1)	36	8	7	6	8	0	38	1	3	0	0	1	3	.236	.296	.340	.635

Kirk Nieuwenhuis

Bats: L **Throws:** R **Pos:** PH-31;LF-17;CF-14;RF-6   NEW-enn-hice   **Ht:** 6'3" **Wt:** 225 **Born:** 8/7/1987 **Age:** 27

Year	Team	Lg	G	AB	H	2B	3B	HR	(Hm	Rd)	TB	R	RBI	RC	TBB	IBB	SO	HBP	SH	SF	SB	CS	GDP	Avg	OBP	Slg	OPS
2014	LsVgs*	AAA	57	211	56	13	3	11	(-	-)	108	34	32	34	15	0	56	2	0	1	3	3	7	.265	.319	.512	.831
2012	NYM	NL	91	282	71	12	1	7	(5	2)	106	40	28	28	25	0	98	2	3	2	4	4	2	.252	.315	.376	.691
2013	NYM	NL	47	95	18	3	1	3	(2	1)	32	10	14	8	12	1	32	0	0	1	2	0	1	.189	.278	.337	.615
2014	NYM	NL	61	112	29	14	1	3	(1	2)	54	16	16	16	16	3	39	0	0	2	4	0	1	.259	.346	.482	.828
	3 ML YEARS		199	489	118	29	3	13	(8	5)	192	66	58	52	53	4	169	2	3	5	10	4	4	.241	.315	.393	.708

Wil Nieves

Bats: R **Throws:** R **Pos:** C-34;1B-1;PH-1   **Ht:** 5'11" **Wt:** 190 **Born:** 9/25/1977 **Age:** 37

Year	Team	Lg	G	AB	H	2B	3B	HR	(Hm	Rd)	TB	R	RBI	RC	TBB	IBB	SO	HBP	SH	SF	SB	CS	GDP	Avg	OBP	Slg	OPS
2014	Phillies*	R	6	19	5	2	0	0	(-	-)	7	3	1	2	1	0	1	2	0	0	0	0	1	.263	.364	.368	.732
2014	Clrwtr*	A+	2	4	1	0	0	0	(-	-)	1	0	0	0	0	0	0	0	0	0	0	0	0	.250	.250	.250	.500
2014	Rdng*	AA	3	12	1	0	0	0	(-	-)	1	0	1	0	0	0	2	0	0	0	0	0	0	.083	.083	.083	.167
2002	SD	NL	28	72	13	3	1	0	(0	0)	18	2	3	4	4	4	15	0	0	0	1	0	1	.181	.224	.250	.474
2005	NYY	AL	3	4	0	0	0	0	(0	0)	0	0	0	0	0	0	1	0	0	0	0	0	0	.000	.000	.000	.000
2006	NYY	AL	6	6	0	0	0	0	(0	0)	0	0	0	0	0	0	1	0	0	0	0	0	0	.000	.000	.000	.000
2007	NYY	AL	26	61	10	4	0	0	(0	0)	14	6	8	4	2	0	9	0	3	0	0	0	3	.164	.190	.230	.420
2008	Was	NL	68	176	46	9	1	1	(1	0)	60	15	20	20	13	1	29	0	5	2	0	1	7	.261	.309	.341	.650
2009	Was	NL	72	224	58	6	0	1	(0	1)	67	20	26	21	17	1	45	3	0	5	1	0	7	.259	.313	.299	.612
2010	Was	NL	59	158	32	8	0	3	(1	2)	49	10	16	9	8	2	29	1	4	1	0	0	6	.203	.244	.310	.554
2011	Mil	NL	20	50	7	2	0	0	(0	0)	9	2	0	0	3	1	12	0	1	0	0	0	3	.140	.189	.180	.369
2012	2 Tms	NL	32	83	25	3	0	2	(0	2)	34	7	8	9	4	2	17	0	1	1	0	0	1	.301	.330	.410	.739
2013	Ari	NL	71	195	58	11	0	1	(1	0)	72	16	22	21	8	0	32	0	0	3	0	0	7	.297	.320	.369	.690
2014	Phi	NL	36	122	31	8	0	1	(1	0)	42	9	7	6	1	0	34	2	2	1	1	0	2	.254	.270	.344	.614
	12	Col	NL	16	47	14	2	0	1	(0 | 1)	19	3	5	6	3	1	9	0	0	1	0	0	3	.298	.333	.404	.738
	12	Ari	NL	16	36	11	1	0	1	(0 | 1)	15	4	3	3	1	1	8	0	1	0	0	0	1	.306	.324	.417	.741
	11 ML YEARS		421	1151	280	54	2	9	(4	5)	365	87	110	94	60	11	224	6	16	13	3	2	39	.243	.281	.317	.598

232

Jayson Nix

Bats: R **Throws:** R **Pos:** 3B-19;2B-12;SS-6;PH-5;RF-2;1B-1;PR-1   **Ht:** 5'11" **Wt:** 195 **Born:** 8/26/1982 **Age:** 32

Year	Team	Lg	G	AB	H	2B	3B	HR	(Hm	Rd)	TB	R	RBI	RC	TBB	IBB	SO	HBP	SH	SF	SB	CS	GDP	Avg	OBP	Slg	OPS
2014	Drham*	AAA	55	191	52	15	1	3	(-	-)	78	25	16	27	20	0	36	1	1	3	2	2	3	.272	.340	.408	.748
2008	Col	NL	22	56	7	2	0	0	(0	0)	9	2	2	0	2	2	17	1	0	0	1	0	1	.125	.234	.161	.395
2009	CWS	AL	94	255	57	11	0	12	(4	8)	104	36	32	31	28	1	64	4	1	2	10	2	5	.224	.308	.408	.716
2010	2 Tms	AL	102	331	74	15	0	14	(7	7)	131	32	34	35	20	2	87	7	3	2	1	2	6	.224	.281	.396	.676
2011	Tor	AL	46	136	23	5	1	4	(2	2)	42	15	16	12	12	1	42	2	0	1	4	1	2	.169	.245	.309	.554
2012	NYY	AL	74	177	43	13	0	4	(3	1)	68	24	18	23	14	0	53	2	9	0	6	3	4	.243	.306	.384	.690
2013	NYY	AL	87	267	63	9	1	3	(2	1)	83	32	24	27	24	1	80	5	4	3	13	1	4	.236	.308	.311	.619
2014	3 Tms		41	83	10	0	0	1	(0	1)	13	2	4	0	3	0	28	2	1	1	1	2	2	.120	.169	.157	.325
10	CWS	AL	24	49	8	1	0	1	(0	1)	12	3	5	4	7	2	12	0	1	0	0	0	1	.163	.268	.245	.513
10	Cle	AL	78	282	66	14	0	13	(7	6)	119	29	29	31	13	0	75	7	2	2	1	2	5	.234	.283	.422	.705
14	Phi	NL	18	39	6	0	0	1	(0	1)	9	1	2	0	2	0	18	1	0	0	0	2	1	.154	.214	.231	.445
14	Pit	NL	16	36	4	0	0	0	(0	0)	4	1	1	0	1	0	4	1	1	0	1	0	1	.111	.158	.111	.269
14	KC		7	8	0	0	0	0	(0	0)	0	0	1	0	0	0	6	0	0	1	0	0	0	.000	.000	.000	.000
	Postseason		6	8	2	1	0	0	(0	0)	3	0	0	1	1	0	1	0	0	0	0	0	0	.250	.333	.375	.708
	7 ML YEARS		466	1305	277	55	2	38	(18	20)	450	143	130	128	108	7	371	23	19	9	36	11	24	.212	.282	.345	.627

Hector Noesi

Pitches: R **Bats:** R **Pos:** SP-27; RP-6   NO-ess-ee   **Ht:** 6'3" **Wt:** 205 **Born:** 1/26/1987 **Age:** 28

Year	Team	Lg	G	GS	CG	GF	IP	BFP	H	R	ER	HR	SH	SF	HB	TBB	IBB	SO	WP	Bk	W	L	Pct	Sh	Sv-Op	Hld	ERC	ERA
2011	NYY	AL	30	2	0	14	56.1	247	63	29	28	6	1	2	2	22	4	45	4	0	2	2	.500	0	0-0	4	4.85	4.47
2012	Sea	AL	22	18	0	4	106.2	453	107	71	69	21	3	7	2	39	1	68	1	2	2	12	.143	0	0-0	0	4.77	5.82
2013	Sea	AL	12	1	0	4	27.1	134	42	21	20	3	1	1	1	12	4	21	2	0	0	1	.000	0	0-0	0	7.45	6.59
2014	3 Tms	AL	33	27	1	3	172.1	733	180	98	91	28	4	7	2	56	1	123	9	1	8	12	.400	0	0-0	0	4.55	4.75
14	Sea		2	0	0	2	1.0	6	2	3	3	1	0	1	0	0	0	2	1	0	0	1	.000	0	0-0	0	13.47	27.00
14	Tex		3	0	0	1	5.1	28	11	7	7	0	0	0	0	2	0	4	0	0	0	0	-	0	0-0	0	9.94	11.81
14	CWS		28	27	1	0	166.0	699	167	88	81	27	4	6	2	54	1	117	8	1	8	11	.421	0	0-0	0	4.34	4.39
	4 ML YEARS		97	48	1	25	362.2	1567	392	219	208	58	9	17	7	129	10	257	16	3	12	27	.308	0	0-0	4	4.88	5.16

Ricky Nolasco

Pitches: R **Bats:** R **Pos:** SP-27   **Ht:** 6'2" **Wt:** 225 **Born:** 12/13/1982 **Age:** 32

Year	Team	Lg	G	GS	CG	GF	IP	BFP	H	R	ER	HR	SH	SF	HB	TBB	IBB	SO	WP	Bk	W	L	Pct	Sh	Sv-Op	Hld	ERC	ERA
2014	CRpds*	A	2	2	0	0	9.1	38	10	3	3	1	1	0	0	1	0	8	0	0	0	0	-	0	0--	-	3.40	2.89
2006	Fla	NL	35	22	0	0	140.0	613	157	86	75	20	8	6	10	41	5	99	7	0	11	11	.500	0	0-0	2	4.89	4.82
2007	Fla	NL	5	4	0	0	21.1	99	26	16	13	3	3	5	1	9	2	11	1	0	1	2	.333	0	0-0	0	5.71	5.48
2008	Fla	NL	34	32	1	0	212.1	868	192	88	83	28	6	9	6	42	6	186	1	3	15	8	.652	1	0-0	0	3.03	3.52
2009	Fla	NL	31	31	2	0	185.0	785	188	111	104	23	8	5	2	44	7	195	2	0	13	9	.591	0	0-0	0	3.62	5.06
2010	Fla	NL	26	26	1	0	157.2	665	169	82	79	24	5	5	2	33	1	147	5	0	14	9	.609	0	0-0	0	4.11	4.51
2011	Fla	NL	33	33	2	0	206.0	891	244	117	107	20	11	5	3	44	8	148	6	0	10	12	.455	1	0-0	0	4.34	4.67
2012	Mia	NL	31	31	3	0	191.0	832	214	100	95	18	19	6	8	47	9	125	8	1	12	13	.480	2	0-0	0	4.14	4.48
2013	2 Tms	NL	34	33	0	0	199.1	834	195	90	82	17	10	3	10	46	1	165	5	0	13	11	.542	0	0-0	0	3.38	3.70
2014	Min	AL	27	27	1	0	159.0	695	203	96	95	22	4	5	5	38	1	115	5	0	6	12	.333	0	0-0	0	5.53	5.38
13	Mia	NL	18	18	0	0	112.1	468	112	50	48	11	7	3	4	25	1	90	4	0	5	8	.385	0	0-0	0	3.49	3.85
13	LAD	NL	16	15	0	0	87.0	366	83	40	34	6	3	0	6	21	0	75	1	0	8	3	.727	0	0-0	0	3.25	3.52
	Postseason		1	1	0	0	4.0	16	3	3	3	1	1	0	0	1	0	4	0	0	0	1	.000	0	0-0	0	3.01	6.75
	9 ML YEARS		256	239	10	0	1471.2	6282	1588	786	733	175	74	49	47	344	40	1191	40	4	95	87	.522	4	0-0	2	4.06	4.48

Sean Nolin

Pitches: L **Bats:** L **Pos:** RP-1   **Ht:** 6'4" **Wt:** 230 **Born:** 12/26/1989 **Age:** 25

Year	Team	Lg	G	GS	CG	GF	IP	BFP	H	R	ER	HR	SH	SF	HB	TBB	IBB	SO	WP	Bk	W	L	Pct	Sh	Sv-Op	Hld	ERC	ERA
2010	B Jays	R	1	1	0	0	2.0	7	1	0	0	0	0	0	0	1	0	4	0	0	0	0	-	0	0--	-	1.62	0.00
2010	Auburn	A-	6	6	0	0	19.1	92	25	13	13	0	0	1	2	9	0	22	2	0	0	2	.000	0	0--	-	5.65	6.05
2011	Lnsng	A	25	21	0	3	108.1	447	102	56	42	9	4	5	4	31	0	113	4	1	4	4	.500	0	1--	-	3.40	3.49
2012	Dnedin	A+	17	15	0	0	86.1	344	72	26	21	7	0	1	4	21	0	90	0	0	9	0	1.000	0	0--	-	2.72	2.19
2012	NHam	AA	3	3	0	0	15.0	60	9	3	2	0	0	0	1	6	0	18	0	0	1	0	1.000	0	0--	-	1.68	1.20
2013	NHam	AA	17	17	1	0	92.2	385	89	35	31	6	2	1	2	25	1	103	4	0	8	3	.727	0	0--	-	3.20	3.01
2013	Buffalo	AAA	3	3	0	0	17.2	70	13	3	3	1	3	0	1	10	0	13	0	0	1	1	.500	0	0--	-	3.48	1.53
2014	Buffalo	AAA	17	17	0	0	87.1	370	74	36	34	6	2	1	3	35	0	74	5	0	4	6	.400	0	0--	-	3.14	3.50
2014	B Jays	R	1	1	0	0	2.1	8	1	0	0	0	0	0	0	0	0	5	0	0	0	0	-	0	0--	-	0.40	0.00
2014	Dnedin	A+	2	2	0	0	7.1	32	4	3	3	0	0	0	0	4	0	9	2	0	1	0	.000	0	0--	-	1.54	3.68
2013	Tor	AL	1	1	0	0	1.1	11	7	6	6	1	0	0	0	1	0	0	0	0	0	1	.000	0	0-0	0	52.56	40.50
2014	Tor	AL	1	0	0	1	1.0	4	1	1	1	0	0	0	0	0	0	0	0	0	0	0	-	0	0-0	0	7.45	9.00
	2 ML YEARS		2	1	0	1	2.1	15	8	7	7	1	0	0	0	1	0	0	0	0	0	1	.000	0	0-0	0	32.72	27.00

Bud Norris

Pitches: R **Bats:** R **Pos:** SP-28   **Ht:** 6'0" **Wt:** 220 **Born:** 3/2/1985 **Age:** 30

Year	Team	Lg	G	GS	CG	GF	IP	BFP	H	R	ER	HR	SH	SF	HB	TBB	IBB	SO	WP	Bk	W	L	Pct	Sh	Sv-Op	Hld	ERC	ERA
2014	Bowie*	AA	1	1	0	0	4.1	22	4	3	3	0	0	0	1	5	0	7	0	0	1	0	1.000	0	0--	-	6.83	6.23
2009	Hou	NL	11	10	0	0	55.2	249	59	29	28	9	1	3	3	25	1	54	3	0	6	3	.667	0	0-0	0	5.26	4.53
2010	Hou	NL	27	27	0	0	153.2	683	151	94	84	18	6	4	6	77	3	158	5	2	9	10	.474	0	0-0	0	4.61	4.92
2011	Hou	NL	31	31	0	0	186.0	795	177	93	78	24	9	4	5	70	7	176	3	2	6	11	.353	0	0-0	0	3.96	3.77

HOW MUCH HE PITCHED / WHAT HE GAVE UP / THE RESULTS

Year Team	Lg	G	GS	CG	GF	IP	BFP	H	R	ER	HR	SH	SF	HB	TBB	IBB	SO	WP	Bk	W	L	Pct	Sh	Sv-Op	Hld	ERC	ERA
2012 Hou	NL	29	29	0	0	168.1	733	165	90	87	23	7	2	8	66	2	165	8	0	7	13	.350	0	0-0	0	4.34	4.65
2013 2 Tms	AL	32	30	0	2	176.2	773	196	89	82	17	6	3	5	67	0	147	4	0	10	12	.455	0	0-0	0	4.75	4.18
2014 Bal	AL	28	28	0	0	165.1	687	149	68	67	20	1	4	14	52	2	139	3	0	15	8	.652	0	0-0	0	3.72	3.65
13 Hou	AL	21	21	0	0	126.0	541	135	62	55	11	4	3	4	43	0	90	3	0	6	9	.400	0	0-0	0	4.34	3.93
13 Bal	AL	11	9	0	2	50.2	232	61	27	27	6	2	0	1	24	0	57	1	0	4	3	.571	0	0-0	0	5.81	4.80
6 ML YEARS		158	155	0	2	905.2	3920	897	463	426	111	30	20	41	357	15	839	26	4	53	57	.482	0	0-0	0	4.32	4.23

Daniel Norris

Pitches: L Bats: L Pos: RP-4; SP-1   **Ht: 6'2" Wt: 180 Born: 4/25/1993 Age: 22**

Year Team	Lg	G	GS	CG	GF	IP	BFP	H	R	ER	HR	SH	SF	HB	TBB	IBB	SO	WP	Bk	W	L	Pct	Sh	Sv-Op	Hld	ERC	ERA
2012 Bluefld	R+	11	10	0	0	35.0	166	44	35	31	4	1	4	2	13	0	38	3	0	2	3	.400	0	0- -	-	5.59	7.97
2012 Vancvr	A-	2	2	0	0	7.2	41	14	9	9	0	0	1	0	5	0	5	1	0	0	1	.000	0	0- -	-	9.47	10.57
2013 Lnsng	A	23	22	0	0	85.2	382	84	46	40	6	1	2	4	44	0	99	11	0	1	7	.125	0	0- -	-	4.35	4.20
2013 Dnedin	A+	1	1	0	0	5.0	18	1	0	0	0	0	0	0	2	0	1	0	0	1	0	1.000	0	0- -	-	0.50	0.00
2014 Dnedin	A+	13	13	0	0	66.1	262	50	11	9	0	4	1	0	18	0	76	6	0	6	0	1.000	0	0- -	-	1.76	1.22
2014 NHam	AA	8	8	0	0	35.2	155	32	18	18	5	0	0	2	17	0	49	3	1	3	1	.750	0	0- -	-	4.31	4.54
2014 Buffalo	AAA	5	4	0	0	22.2	85	14	8	8	2	0	0	0	8	0	38	0	0	3	1	.750	0	0- -	-	2.01	3.18
2014 Tor	AL	5	1	0	2	6.2	30	5	4	4	1	0	1	0	5	0	4	0	0	0	0	-	0	0-0	1	4.31	5.40

Derek Norris

Bats: R Throws: R Pos: C-114;PH-18;DH-10   **Ht: 6'0" Wt: 210 Born: 2/14/1989 Age: 26**

Year Team	Lg	G	AB	H	2B	3B	HR	Hm	Rd	TB	R	RBI	RC	TBB	IBB	SO	HBP	SH	SF	SB	CS	GDP	Avg	OBP	Slg	OPS
2012 Oak	AL	60	209	42	8	1	7	(3	4)	73	19	34	27	21	1	66	1	0	1	5	1	6	.201	.276	.349	.625
2013 Oak	AL	98	264	65	16	0	9	(6	3)	108	31	41	30	37	1	71	4	1	2	5	0	5	.246	.345	.409	.754
2014 Oak	AL	127	385	104	19	1	10	(7	3)	155	46	55	66	54	2	86	1	1	1	2	2	12	.270	.361	.403	.763
Postseason		6	13	1	0	0	0	(0	0)	1	0	0	0	0	0	7	0	0	0	0	1	0	.077	.077	.077	.154
3 ML YEARS		285	858	211	43	2	26	(16	10)	336	106	119	133	112	4	223	6	2	4	12	3	23	.246	.336	.392	.727

Ivan Nova

Pitches: R Bats: R Pos: SP-4   ee-VAHN   **Ht: 6'4" Wt: 225 Born: 1/12/1987 Age: 28**

Year Team	Lg	G	GS	CG	GF	IP	BFP	H	R	ER	HR	SH	SF	HB	TBB	IBB	SO	WP	Bk	W	L	Pct	Sh	Sv-Op	Hld	ERC	ERA
2010 NYY	AL	10	7	0	3	42.0	185	44	22	21	4	1	1	1	17	2	26	2	0	1	2	.333	0	0-1	0	4.31	4.50
2011 NYY	AL	28	27	0	1	165.1	704	163	74	68	13	2	6	6	57	3	98	11	0	16	4	.800	0	0-0	0	3.76	3.70
2012 NYY	AL	28	28	0	0	170.1	748	194	100	95	28	3	6	10	56	3	153	6	2	12	8	.600	0	0-0	0	5.32	5.02
2013 NYY	AL	23	20	3	2	139.1	586	135	49	48	9	2	3	14	44	3	116	3	0	9	6	.600	2	0-0	0	3.77	3.10
2014 NYY	AL	4	4	0	0	20.2	96	32	19	19	6	0	2	2	6	0	12	1	0	2	2	.500	0	0-0	0	9.40	8.27
Postseason		2	1	0	0	8.1	34	7	4	4	2	0	0	0	4	0	8	0	0	1	1	.500	0	0-0	0	4.66	4.32
5 ML YEARS		93	86	3	6	537.2	2319	568	264	251	60	8	18	33	180	11	405	23	2	40	22	.645	2	0-1	0	4.48	4.20

Eduardo Nunez

Bats: R Throws: R Pos: 3B-20;SS-20;LF-16;PH-12;PR-9;DH-6;2B-2;RF-2   **Ht: 6'0" Wt: 185 Born: 6/15/1987 Age: 28**

Year Team	Lg	G	AB	H	2B	3B	HR	Hm	Rd	TB	R	RBI	RC	TBB	IBB	SO	HBP	SH	SF	SB	CS	GDP	Avg	OBP	Slg	OPS
2014 Roch*	AAA	11	39	11	1	0	1	(-	-)	15	7	6	4	1	0	8	0	0	1	1	0	2	.282	.293	.385	.677
2014 NwBrit*	AA	4	10	4	0	1	0	(-	-)	6	1	0	3	3	0	2	0	0	0	1	0	0	.400	.538	.600	1.138
2010 NYY	AL	30	50	14	1	0	1	(0	1)	18	12	7	8	3	0	2	0	0	0	5	0	4	.280	.321	.360	.681
2011 NYY	AL	112	309	82	18	2	5	(2	3)	119	38	30	42	22	2	37	0	6	1	22	6	6	.265	.313	.385	.698
2012 NYY	AL	38	89	26	4	1	1	(1	0)	35	14	11	15	6	0	12	1	0	4	11	2	1	.292	.330	.393	.723
2013 NYY	AL	90	304	79	17	4	3	(2	1)	113	38	28	31	20	1	51	3	4	5	10	3	3	.260	.307	.372	.679
2014 Min	AL	72	204	51	7	4	4	(4	0)	78	26	24	21	5	0	31	1	3	0	9	3	7	.250	.271	.382	.654
Postseason		6	11	3	1	1	1	(0	1)	9	4	1	1	0	0	0	0	0	0	2	0	0	.273	.273	.818	1.091
5 ML YEARS		342	956	252	47	11	14	(9	5)	363	128	100	117	56	3	133	5	13	10	57	14	21	.264	.305	.380	.684

Vidal Nuno

Pitches: L Bats: L Pos: SP-28; RP-3   vee-DOLL NOON-yo   **Ht: 5'11" Wt: 195 Born: 7/26/1987 Age: 27**

Year Team	Lg	G	GS	CG	GF	IP	BFP	H	R	ER	HR	SH	SF	HB	TBB	IBB	SO	WP	Bk	W	L	Pct	Sh	Sv-Op	Hld	ERC	ERA
2010 Lk Cty	A	21	16	0	1	94.1	394	104	54	52	13	1	5	7	14	0	94	1	2	6	8	.429	0	0- -	-	4.27	4.96
2011 StIsInd	A-	8	0	0	2	25.0	91	14	3	2	0	1	0	0	3	0	29	1	0	5	0	1.000	0	1- -	-	0.87	0.72
2011 CtnSC	A	7	7	0	0	40.0	151	37	9	8	4	0	0	0	2	0	37	1	1	2	1	.667	0	0- -	-	2.47	1.80
2012 Tampa	A+	11	0	0	1	24.1	102	22	11	8	2	0	0	1	6	0	26	0	0	1	1	.500	0	0- -	-	2.95	2.96
2012 Trntn	AA	20	20	0	0	114.0	465	109	40	31	10	0	4	2	27	0	100	1	1	9	5	.643	0	0- -	-	3.25	2.45
2013 S-WB	AAA	5	5	0	0	25.0	91	14	4	4	2	0	0	0	2	0	30	0	0	2	0	1.000	0	1- -	-	1.03	1.44
2013 NYY	AL	5	3	0	2	20.0	82	16	5	5	2	0	0	1	6	0	9	0	0	1	2	.333	0	0-0	0	2.81	2.25
2014 2 Tms	AL	31	28	0	1	161.2	679	157	89	82	25	3	7	6	46	1	129	5	0	2	12	.143	0	0-0	0	3.98	4.56
14 NYY	AL	17	14	0	1	78.0	339	86	52	47	15	0	6	4	26	1	60	4	0	2	5	.286	0	0-0	0	5.18	5.42
14 Ari	NL	14	14	0	0	83.2	340	71	37	35	10	3	1	2	20	0	69	1	0	0	7	.000	0	0-0	0	2.96	3.76
2 ML YEARS		36	31	0	3	181.2	761	173	94	87	27	3	7	7	52	1	138	5	0	3	14	.176	0	0-0	0	3.85	4.31

Brett Oberholtzer

Pitches: L Bats: L Pos: SP-24 OH-ber-holt-zer Ht: 6'1" Wt: 225 Born: 7/1/1989 Age: 25

Year Team	Lg	G	GS	CG	GF	IP	BFP	H	R	ER	HR	SH	SF	HB	TBB	IBB	SO	WP	Bk	W	L	Pct	Sh	Sv-Op	Hld	ERC	ERA
2010 Rome	A	4	4	0	0	23.0	91	22	5	5	1	1	0	1	5	0	19	2	0	0	2	.000	0	0--	-	3.10	1.96
2010 MrtlBh	A+	22	18	0	3	112.2	474	123	59	52	7	6	4	4	18	0	107	6	0	6	6	.500	0	2--	-	3.52	4.15
2011 Missi	AA	21	21	1	0	127.2	533	119	65	53	6	5	8	1	42	4	93	5	0	9	9	.500	0	0--	-	3.07	3.74
2011 CpChr	AA	6	6	0	0	27.1	117	28	16	16	3	1	0	1	10	0	28	2	0	2	3	.400	0	0--	-	4.35	5.27
2012 CpChr	AA	13	13	0	0	77.0	332	82	41	36	11	5	1	1	21	1	68	4	0	5	3	.625	0	0--	-	4.21	4.21
2012 OKCity	AAA	15	15	0	0	89.2	388	105	48	45	13	3	4	2	19	3	69	3	0	5	7	.417	0	0--	-	4.63	4.52
2013 OKCity	AAA	16	16	0	0	80.1	338	77	48	39	9	2	3	2	25	0	72	4	0	6	6	.500	0	0--	-	3.68	4.37
2014 OKCity	AAA	5	5	0	0	31.0	129	35	17	16	9	1	0	1	3	0	31	2	0	1	2	.333	0	0--	-	5.00	4.65
2013 Hou	AL	13	10	2	1	71.2	293	66	26	22	7	0	1	1	13	0	45	0	0	4	5	.444	1	0-0	0	2.82	2.76
2014 Hou	AL	24	24	0	0	143.2	623	170	73	70	12	5	10	3	28	0	94	2	3	5	13	.278	0	0-0	0	4.22	4.39
2 ML YEARS		37	34	2	1	215.1	916	236	99	92	19	5	11	4	41	0	139	2	3	9	18	.333	1	0-0	0	3.74	3.85

Darren O'Day

Pitches: R Bats: R Pos: RP-68 Ht: 6'4" Wt: 220 Born: 10/22/1982 Age: 32

Year Team	Lg	G	GS	CG	GF	IP	BFP	H	R	ER	HR	SH	SF	HB	TBB	IBB	SO	WP	Bk	W	L	Pct	Sh	Sv-Op	Hld	ERC	ERA
2008 LAA	AL	30	0	0	17	43.1	194	49	24	22	2	2	1	4	14	6	29	1	0	0	1	.000	0	0-0	1	4.20	4.57
2009 2 Tms		68	0	0	15	58.2	233	41	14	12	3	1	3	5	18	1	56	1	0	2	1	.667	0	2-2	20	2.20	1.84
2010 Tex	AL	72	0	0	14	62.0	240	43	15	14	5	1	3	5	12	2	45	0	0	6	2	.750	0	0-2	22	1.93	2.03
2011 Tex	AL	16	0	0	7	16.2	74	17	10	10	7	1	1	2	5	0	18	0	0	0	1	.000	0	0-0	3	6.45	5.40
2012 Bal	AL	69	0	0	10	67.0	263	49	17	17	6	3	1	3	14	2	69	0	0	7	1	.875	0	0-2	15	2.06	2.28
2013 Bal	AL	68	0	0	18	62.0	247	47	16	15	7	1	1	5	15	1	59	1	0	5	3	.625	0	2-6	20	2.60	2.18
2014 Bal	AL	68	0	0	18	68.2	271	42	14	13	6	1	2	8	19	4	73	0	0	5	2	.714	0	4-8	25	1.92	1.70
09 NYM	NL	4	0	0	1	3.0	17	5	2	0	0	0	1	1	1	0	2	0	0	0	0	-	0	0-0	0	7.72	0.00
09 Tex		64	0	0	14	55.2	216	36	12	12	3	1	2	4	17	1	54	1	0	2	1	.667	0	2-2	20	1.95	1.94
Postseason		16	0	0	1	11.2	46	7	4	4	2	1	0	1	2	0	13	0	0	0	1	.000	0	0-0	4	1.85	3.09
7 ML YEARS		391	0	0	99	378.1	1522	288	110	103	36	10	12	32	97	16	349	3	0	25	11	.694	0	8-20	106	2.52	2.45

Rougned Odor

Bats: L Throws: R Pos: 2B-110;PH-5;DH-1 ROOG-ned oh-DORE Ht: 5'11" Wt: 170 Born: 2/3/1994 Age: 21

Year Team	Lg	G	AB	H	2B	3B	HR	(Hm	Rd)	TB	R	RBI	RC	TBB	IBB	SO	HBP	SH	SF	SB	CS	GDP	Avg	OBP	Slg	OPS
2011 Spkane	A-	58	233	61	9	3	2	(-	-)	82	33	29	28	13	0	37	9	1	2	10	4	5	.262	.323	.352	.675
2012 Hkry	A	109	432	112	23	4	10	(-	-)	173	60	47	56	25	0	65	10	2	4	19	10	4	.259	.313	.400	.714
2013 MrtlBh	A+	100	377	115	33	4	5	(-	-)	171	65	59	66	26	1	67	15	2	5	27	8	7	.305	.369	.454	.822
2013 Frisco	AA	30	134	41	8	2	6	(-	-)	71	20	19	25	9	1	24	1	0	0	5	2	3	.306	.354	.530	.884
2014 Frisco	AA	32	129	36	2	1	6	(-	-)	58	21	17	18	7	0	22	0	1	1	6	3	4	.279	.314	.450	.763
2014 Tex	AL	114	386	100	14	7	9	(4	5)	155	39	48	46	17	1	71	5	6	3	4	7	7	.259	.297	.402	.698

Jake Odorizzi

Pitches: R Bats: R Pos: SP-31 oh-duh-RIZZ-ee Ht: 6'2" Wt: 185 Born: 3/27/1990 Age: 25

Year Team	Lg	G	GS	CG	GF	IP	BFP	H	R	ER	HR	SH	SF	HB	TBB	IBB	SO	WP	Bk	W	L	Pct	Sh	Sv-Op	Hld	ERC	ERA
2012 KC	AL	2	2	0	0	7.1	34	8	4	4	1	0	0	0	4	0	4	0	0	0	1	.000	0	0-0	0	5.34	4.91
2013 TB	AL	7	4	0	2	29.2	122	28	13	13	3	0	1	2	8	0	22	1	0	0	1	.000	0	1-1	0	3.62	3.94
2014 TB	AL	31	31	0	0	168.0	719	156	79	77	20	3	8	5	59	0	174	3	0	11	13	.458	0	0-0	0	3.68	4.13
3 ML YEARS		40	37	0	2	205.0	875	192	96	94	24	3	9	7	71	0	200	4	0	11	15	.423	0	1-1	0	3.73	4.13

Eric O'Flaherty

Pitches: L Bats: L Pos: RP-21 Ht: 6'2" Wt: 220 Born: 2/5/1985 Age: 30

Year Team	Lg	G	GS	CG	GF	IP	BFP	H	R	ER	HR	SH	SF	HB	TBB	IBB	SO	WP	Bk	W	L	Pct	Sh	Sv-Op	Hld	ERC	ERA
2014 Stcktn*	A+	1	0	0	0	1.0	3	0	0	0	0	0	0	0	0	0	3	0	0	1	0	1.000	0	0--	-	0.00	0.00
2014 Scrmto*	AAA	7	1	0	0	8.1	33	6	4	4	1	0	1	0	3	0	5	3	0	0	1	.000	0	0--	-	2.63	4.32
2006 Sea	AL	15	0	0	5	11.0	57	18	9	5	2	1	0	0	6	3	6	2	0	0	0	-	0	0-0	1	8.63	4.09
2007 Sea	AL	56	0	0	9	52.1	221	45	26	26	1	0	2	5	20	1	36	4	1	7	1	.875	0	0-1	4	3.04	4.47
2008 Sea	AL	7	0	0	0	6.2	42	16	15	15	2	0	1	2	4	2	4	0	0	0	1	.000	0	0-0	2	17.12	20.25
2009 Atl	NL	78	0	0	8	56.1	236	52	23	19	2	1	1	6	18	4	39	2	0	2	1	.667	0	0-2	15	3.26	3.04
2010 Atl	NL	56	0	0	7	44.0	181	37	14	12	2	1	0	1	18	2	36	3	0	3	2	.600	0	0-1	9	2.97	2.45
2011 Atl	NL	78	0	0	5	73.2	301	59	9	8	2	7	2	3	21	8	67	1	0	2	4	.333	0	0-4	32	2.13	0.98
2012 Atl	NL	64	0	0	7	57.1	230	47	14	11	3	3	1	2	19	2	46	1	0	3	0	1.000	0	0-3	28	2.71	1.73
2013 Atl	NL	19	0	0	2	18.0	70	12	5	5	2	0	1	0	5	1	11	0	0	1	0	1.000	0	0-1	12	1.93	2.50
2014 Oak	AL	21	0	0	6	20.0	80	15	5	5	3	1	0	2	4	0	15	3	0	1	0	1.000	0	1-2	3	2.68	2.25
Postseason		1	0	0	0	1.0	4	2	0	0	0	0	0	0	0	0	0	0	0	0	0	-	0	0-0	0	9.49	0.00
9 ML YEARS		394	0	0	50	339.1	1418	301	120	106	19	14	8	21	115	23	260	16	1	21	9	.700	0	1-14	106	3.08	2.81

Alexi Ogando

Pitches: R Bats: R Pos: RP-27

oh-GONE-doh

Ht: 6'4" Wt: 200 Born: 10/5/1983 Age: 31

Year Team	Lg	G	GS	CG	GF	IP	BFP	H	R	ER	HR	SH	SF	HB	TBB	IBB	SO	WP	Bk	W	L	Pct	Sh	Sv-Op	Hld	ERC	ERA
2010 Tex	AL	44	0	0	12	41.2	171	31	6	6	2	3	2	1	16	2	39	3	0	4	1	.800	0	0-2	7	2.34	1.30
2011 Tex	AL	31	29	1	2	169.0	693	149	73	66	16	2	3	7	43	0	126	5	0	13	8	.619	1	0-0	1	3.01	3.51
2012 Tex	AL	58	1	0	11	66.0	263	49	26	24	9	0	3	2	17	1	66	5	0	2	0	1.000	0	3-6	12	2.50	3.27
2013 Tex	AL	23	18	0	0	104.1	428	87	38	36	11	2	3	5	41	1	72	6	1	7	4	.636	0	0-0	3	3.44	3.11
2014 Tex	AL	27	0	0	10	25.0	122	33	19	19	1	1	0	1	15	1	22	4	0	2	3	.400	0	1-2	7	6.34	6.84
Postseason		18	0	0	2	19.0	81	16	6	5	3	0	0	0	10	2	23	1	0	2	0	1.000	0	0-3	4	3.95	2.37
5 ML YEARS		183	48	1	35	406.0	1677	349	162	151	39	8	11	16	132	5	325	23	1	28	16	.636	1	4-10	26	3.15	3.35

Lester Oliveros

Pitches: R Bats: R Pos: RP-7

ah-lah-VAIR-ohs

Ht: 6'0" Wt: 235 Born: 5/28/1988 Age: 27

Year Team	Lg	G	GS	CG	GF	IP	BFP	H	R	ER	HR	SH	SF	HB	TBB	IBB	SO	WP	Bk	W	L	Pct	Sh	Sv-Op	Hld	ERC	ERA
2014 NwBrit*	AA	26	0	0	24	30.1	125	17	6	3	0	2	1	3	14	1	36	2	0	3	1	.750	0	12--	-	1.70	0.89
2014 Roch*	AAA	24	0	0	7	35.1	147	27	10	9	0	2	1	1	13	1	52	1	0	1	2	.333	0	6- --	-	2.10	2.29
2011 2 Tms	AL	19	0	0	6	21.1	91	21	11	11	0	0	2	0	11	2	13	1	0	0	0	-	0	0-0	1	3.67	4.64
2012 Min	AL	1	0	0	0	1.2	7	1	1	1	0	0	0	0	1	0	1	0	0	0	0	-	0	0-0	0	2.03	5.40
2014 Min	AL	7	0	0	2	6.1	27	6	5	5	2	0	1	0	3	0	5	2	0	0	1	.000	0	0-0	0	5.72	7.11
11 Det	AL	9	0	0	3	8.0	35	8	5	5	0	0	0	0	4	1	4	1	0	0	0	-	0	0-0	1	3.53	5.63
11 Min	AL	10	0	0	3	13.1	56	13	6	6	0	0	2	0	7	1	9	0	0	0	0	-	0	0-0	0	3.75	4.05
3 ML YEARS		27	0	0	8	29.1	125	28	17	17	2	0	3	0	15	2	19	3	0	0	1	.000	0	0-0	1	4.02	5.22

Miguel Olivo

Bats: R Throws: R Pos: C-8

oh-LEEV-oh

Ht: 6'0" Wt: 230 Born: 7/15/1978 Age: 36

Year Team	Lg	G	AB	H	2B	3B	HR	(Hm	Rd)	TB	R	RBI	RC	TBB	IBB	SO	HBP	SH	SF	SB	CS	GDP	Avg	OBP	Slg	OPS
2014 Albq*	AAA	20	76	28	6	0	4	(-	-)	46	10	20	17	3	0	25	2	0	0	0	0	3	.368	.407	.605	1.013
2002 CWS	AL	6	19	4	1	0	1	(0	1)	8	2	5	4	2	0	5	0	0	0	0	0	1	.211	.286	.421	.707
2003 CWS	AL	114	317	75	19	1	6	(4	2)	114	37	27	32	19	0	80	4	4	2	6	4	3	.237	.287	.360	.646
2004 2 Tms	AL	96	301	70	15	4	13	(8	5)	132	46	40	33	20	2	84	3	4	1	7	6	4	.233	.286	.439	.725
2005 2 Tms		91	267	58	11	1	9	(5	4)	98	30	24	23	8	2	80	3	1	2	7	2	7	.217	.246	.367	.613
2006 Fla	NL	127	430	113	22	3	16	(7	9)	189	52	58	49	9	4	103	7	3	3	2	3	9	.263	.287	.440	.727
2007 Fla	NL	122	452	107	20	4	16	(11	5)	183	43	60	43	14	2	123	2	0	1	3	2	13	.237	.262	.405	.667
2008 KC	AL	84	306	78	22	0	12	(3	9)	136	29	41	35	7	2	82	3	0	1	7	0	6	.255	.278	.444	.722
2009 KC	AL	114	390	97	15	5	23	(10	13)	191	51	65	47	19	0	126	5	1	1	5	2	10	.249	.292	.490	.781
2010 Col	NL	112	394	106	17	6	14	(10	4)	177	55	58	49	27	5	117	1	2	3	7	4	6	.269	.315	.449	.765
2011 Sea	AL	130	477	107	19	1	19	(10	9)	185	54	62	44	20	2	140	1	1	8	6	5	7	.224	.253	.388	.641
2012 Sea	AL	87	315	70	14	0	12	(5	7)	120	27	29	21	7	0	85	0	1	0	3	6	8	.222	.239	.381	.620
2013 Mia	NL	33	74	15	2	0	4	(1	3)	29	5	9	6	5	0	23	0	0	1	0	0	0	.203	.250	.392	.642
2014 LAD	NL	8	23	5	0	1	0	(0	0)	7	4	2	1	1	0	12	0	0	1	0	0	1	.217	.240	.304	.544
04 CWS	AL	46	141	38	7	2	7	(4	3)	70	21	26	21	10	1	29	0	4	1	5	4	2	.270	.316	.496	.812
04 Sea	AL	50	160	32	8	2	6	(4	2)	62	25	14	12	10	1	55	3	0	0	2	2	2	.200	.260	.388	.648
05 Sea	AL	54	152	23	4	0	5	(4	1)	42	14	18	6	4	0	49	0	0	1	1	1	3	.151	.172	.276	.448
05 SD	NL	37	115	35	7	1	4	(1	3)	56	16	16	17	4	2	31	3	1	1	6	1	4	.304	.341	.487	.828
Postseason		1	1	0	0	0	0	(0	0)	0	0	0	0	0	0	0	0	0	0	0	0	0	.000	.000	.000	.000
13 ML YEARS		1124	3765	905	177	26	145	(74	71)	1569	435	490	387	158	19	1060	29	17	24	53	34	77	.240	.275	.417	.691

Mike Olt

Bats: R Throws: R Pos: 3B-52;PH-27;1B-12;DH-3

AULT

Ht: 6'2" Wt: 210 Born: 8/27/1988 Age: 26

Year Team	Lg	G	AB	H	2B	3B	HR	(Hm	Rd)	TB	R	RBI	RC	TBB	IBB	SO	HBP	SH	SF	SB	CS	GDP	Avg	OBP	Slg	OPS
2010 Spkane	A-	69	263	77	16	1	9	(-	-)	122	57	43	-	40	0	77	4	-	3	6	0	3	.293	.390	.464	.854
2011 MrtlBh	A+	69	240	64	15	0	14	(-	-)	121	39	42	49	48	1	70	1	0	3	0	1	7	.267	.387	.504	.891
2011 Rngrs	AA	4	14	3	0	0	1	(-	-)	6	2	4	1	1	0	5	0	0	0	0	0	0	.214	.267	.429	.695
2012 Frisco	AA	95	354	102	17	1	28	(-	-)	205	65	82	82	61	5	101	4	0	1	4	0	13	.288	.398	.579	.977
2013 RdRck	AAA	65	230	49	15	0	11	(-	-)	97	37	32	32	35	2	89	1	0	2	0	0	2	.213	.317	.422	.739
2013 Frisco	AA	3	12	4	2	0	1	(-	-)	9	1	2	2	0	0	6	0	0	0	0	0	0	.333	.333	.750	1.083
2013 Iowa	AAA	39	131	22	3	1	3	(-	-)	36	11	8	10	20	0	37	0	0	1	0	0	6	.168	.276	.275	.551
2014 Iowa	AAA	28	106	32	9	0	7	(-	-)	62	16	24	21	8	0	33	0	0	1	1	0	0	.302	.348	.585	.933
2012 Tex	AL	16	33	5	1	0	0	(0	0)	6	2	5	2	5	0	13	0	0	2	1	1	1	.152	.250	.182	.432
2014 ChC	NL	89	225	36	8	0	12	(4	8)	80	23	33	19	25	0	100	3	0	5	0	1	3	.160	.248	.356	.604
2 ML YEARS		105	258	41	9	0	12	(4	8)	86	25	38	21	30	0	113	3	0	7	1	2	4	.159	.248	.333	.582

Shawn O'Malley

Bats: B Throws: R Pos: LF-5;PH-3;PR-3;2B-1;RF-1;DH-1

Ht: 5'11" Wt: 165 Born: 12/28/1987 Age: 27

Year Team	Lg	G	AB	H	2B	3B	HR	(Hm	Rd)	TB	R	RBI	RC	TBB	IBB	SO	HBP	SH	SF	SB	CS	GDP	Avg	OBP	Slg	OPS
2010 Mont	AA	44	144	26	1	3	0	(-	-)	33	18	7	11	16	0	32	6	3	0	9	1	0	.181	.289	.229	.518
2010 Rays	R	2	8	3	0	0	0	(-	-)	3	1	1	1	0	0	0	1	0	1	2	0	0	.375	.400	.375	.775
2010 Charltt	A+	8	25	8	2	2	0	(-	-)	14	8	3	7	4	0	2	3	2	0	4	0	0	.320	.469	.560	1.029
2011 Mont	AA	79	308	85	8	5	1	(-	-)	106	55	23	43	42	2	58	4	7	1	24	13	2	.276	.369	.344	.713
2012 Drham	AAA	67	216	53	4	2	2	(-	-)	67	32	18	24	17	0	49	3	7	4	11	1	1	.245	.304	.310	.614
2012 Mont	AA	35	121	28	3	3	0	(-	-)	37	22	5	14	17	0	24	2	3	1	7	3	1	.231	.333	.306	.639
2013 Mont	AA	91	321	84	12	6	3	(-	-)	117	53	32	46	32	0	60	6	11	3	24	3	3	.262	.337	.364	.702

Year Team	Lg	G	AB	H	2B	3B	HR	(Hm Rd)	TB	R	RBI	RC	TBB	IBB	SO	HBP	SH	SF	SB	CS	GDP	Avg	OBP	Slg	OPS
2014 Ark	AA	11	32	6	0	1	0	(- -)	8	3	5	3	6	0	8	0	1	1	1	0	0	.188	.308	.250	.558
2014 Salt Lk	AAA	89	318	105	19	9	3	(- -)	151	60	38	65	39	0	44	7	9	3	13	4	4	.330	.411	.475	.886
2014 Angels	R	3	10	3	0	1	1	(- -)	8	3	4	2	1	0	4	0	1	0	1	0	0	.300	.364	.800	1.164
2014 LAA	AL	11	16	3	0	0	0	(0 0)	3	3	1	1	0	0	8	0	0	0	2	0	0	.188	.188	.188	.375

Logan Ondrusek

Pitches: R **Bats:** R **Pos:** RP-40

ahn-DREW-seck

Ht: 6'8" **Wt:** 230 **Born:** 2/13/1985 **Age:** 30

Year Team	Lg	G	GS	CG	GF	IP	BFP	H	R	ER	HR	SH	SF	HB	TBB	IBB	SO	WP	Bk	W	L	Pct	Sh	Sv-Op	Hld	ERC	ERA
2014 Lsvlle*	AAA	1	1	0	0	1.0	4	2	0	0	0	0	0	0	0	0	0	0	0	0	0	-	0	0- -	-	9.49	0.00
2010 Cin	NL	60	0	0	11	58.2	240	49	25	24	7	1	1	0	20	1	39	2	0	5	0	1.000	0	0-2	6	3.08	3.68
2011 Cin	NL	66	0	0	14	61.1	268	55	25	22	6	3	4	2	28	7	41	6	0	5	5	.500	0	0-3	14	3.58	3.23
2012 Cin	NL	63	0	0	20	54.2	243	51	23	21	8	1	1	3	31	4	39	5	0	5	2	.714	0	2-4	13	4.81	3.46
2013 Cin	NL	52	0	0	18	55.0	233	53	26	25	8	4	0	1	16	1	53	5	1	3	1	.750	0	0-1	5	3.75	4.09
2014 Cin	NL	40	0	0	10	41.0	189	50	26	25	5	2	1	1	16	1	42	3	0	3	3	.500	0	0-3	4	5.43	5.49
Postseason		3	0	0	0	3.0	13	1	1	1	1	0	0	1	1	0	1	0	0	0	0	-	0	0-0	1	2.68	3.00
5 ML YEARS		281	0	0	73	270.2	1173	258	125	117	34	11	7	7	111	14	214	21	1	21	11	.656	0	2-13	42	4.02	3.89

Jose Ortega

Pitches: R **Bats:** R **Pos:** RP-1

or-TAY-guh

Ht: 5'11" **Wt:** 185 **Born:** 10/12/1988 **Age:** 26

Year Team	Lg	G	GS	CG	GF	IP	BFP	H	R	ER	HR	SH	SF	HB	TBB	IBB	SO	WP	Bk	W	L	Pct	Sh	Sv-Op	Hld	ERC	ERA
2014 Toledo*	AAA	43	1	0	14	58.0	258	50	25	23	4	0	0	3	36	1	48	7	0	2	2	.500	0	1- -	-	4.09	3.57
2012 Det	AL	2	0	0	0	2.2	13	3	1	1	0	0	0	1	1	0	4	0	0	0	0	-	0	0-1	0	6.04	3.38
2013 Det	AL	11	0	0	5	11.2	52	10	5	5	2	1	0	1	6	1	10	0	0	0	2	.000	0	0-1	2	4.34	3.86
2014 Det	AL	1	0	0	0	1.1	9	0	4	4	0	1	0	1	4	0	1	0	0	0	1	.000	0	0-0	0	9.94	27.00
3 ML YEARS		14	0	0	5	15.2	74	13	10	10	3	2	0	2	11	1	15	0	0	0	3	.000	0	0-2	2	5.21	5.74

David Ortiz

Bats: L **Throws:** L **Pos:** DH-131;PH-6;1B-5

Ht: 6'4" **Wt:** 230 **Born:** 11/18/1975 **Age:** 39

Year Team	Lg	G	AB	H	2B	3B	HR	(Hm Rd)	TB	R	RBI	RC	TBB	IBB	SO	HBP	SH	SF	SB	CS	GDP	Avg	OBP	Slg	OPS
1997 Min	AL	15	49	16	3	0	1	(0 1)	22	10	6	7	2	0	19	0	0	0	0	0	1	.327	.353	.449	.802
1998 Min	AL	86	278	77	20	0	9	(2 7)	124	47	46	46	39	3	72	5	0	4	1	0	8	.277	.371	.446	.817
1999 Min	AL	10	20	0	0	0	0	(0 0)	0	1	0	0	5	0	12	0	0	0	0	0	2	.000	.200	.000	.200
2000 Min	AL	130	415	117	36	1	10	(7 3)	185	59	63	66	57	2	81	0	0	6	1	0	13	.282	.364	.446	.810
2001 Min	AL	89	303	71	17	1	18	(6 12)	144	46	48	46	40	8	68	1	1	2	1	0	6	.234	.324	.475	.799
2002 Min	AL	125	412	112	32	1	20	(5 15)	206	52	75	62	43	0	87	3	0	8	1	2	5	.272	.339	.500	.839
2003 Bos	AL	128	448	129	39	2	31	(17 14)	265	79	101	80	58	8	83	1	0	2	0	0	12	.288	.369	.592	.961
2004 Bos	AL	150	582	175	47	3	41	(17 **24**)	351	94	139	**127**	75	8	133	4	0	8	0	0	12	.301	.380	.603	.983
2005 Bos	AL	159	601	180	40	1	47	(20 **27**)	363	119	148	137	102	9	124	1	0	9	1	0	13	.300	.397	.604	1.001
2006 Bos	AL	151	558	160	29	2	**54**	(22 **32**)	355	115	**137**	129	**119**	23	117	4	0	5	1	0	12	.287	.413	.636	1.049
2007 Bos	AL	149	549	182	52	1	35	(16 19)	341	116	117	138	**111**	12	103	4	0	3	3	1	16	.332	**.445**	.621	1.066
2008 Bos	AL	109	416	110	30	1	23	(12 11)	211	74	89	82	70	12	74	1	1	3	1	0	11	.264	.369	.507	.877
2009 Bos	AL	150	541	129	35	1	28	(18 10)	250	77	99	79	74	5	134	5	0	7	0	2	9	.238	.332	.462	.794
2010 Bos	AL	145	518	140	36	1	32	(15 17)	274	86	102	94	82	14	145	2	0	4	0	1	12	.270	.370	.529	.899
2011 Bos	AL	146	525	162	40	1	29	(13 16)	291	84	96	97	78	12	83	1	0	1	1	1	24	.309	.398	.554	.953
2012 Bos	AL	90	324	103	26	0	23	(13 10)	198	65	60	75	56	13	51	0	0	3	0	1	6	.318	.415	.611	1.026
2013 Bos	AL	137	518	160	38	2	30	(12 18)	292	84	103	102	76	**27**	88	1	0	5	4	0	21	.309	.395	.564	.959
2014 Bos	AL	142	518	136	27	0	35	(11 24)	268	59	104	91	75	22	95	3	0	6	0	0	18	.263	.355	.517	.873
Postseason		82	295	87	21	2	17	(12 5)	163	51	60	69	57	11	71	2	0	3	0	1	4	.295	.409	.553	.962
18 ML YEARS		2111	7575	2159	547	18	466	(206 260)	4140	1267	1533	1458	1162	178	1569	36	2	76	15	8	198	.285	.379	.547	.926

Sean O'Sullivan

Pitches: R **Bats:** R **Pos:** SP-2; RP-1

Ht: 6'1" **Wt:** 240 **Born:** 9/1/1987 **Age:** 27

Year Team	Lg	G	GS	CG	GF	IP	BFP	H	R	ER	HR	SH	SF	HB	TBB	IBB	SO	WP	Bk	W	L	Pct	Sh	Sv-Op	Hld	ERC	ERA
2014 LV*	AAA	25	25	1	0	148.2	633	154	82	71	17	2	9	3	50	0	94	3	0	6	10	.375	0	0- -	-	4.26	4.30
2009 LAA	AL	12	10	0	1	51.2	227	60	34	34	12	2	4	1	16	1	29	1	0	4	2	.667	0	0-0	0	5.66	5.92
2010 2 Tms	AL	19	14	0	3	83.2	368	90	53	51	15	0	3	1	31	2	43	4	2	4	6	.400	0	0-0	0	4.93	5.49
2011 KC	AL	12	10	0	1	58.1	273	78	52	47	10	3	4	2	26	1	19	3	0	2	6	.250	0	0-1	0	7.03	7.25
2013 SD	NL	7	3	0	2	25.0	118	31	12	11	0	1	2	1	14	1	12	0	0	0	2	.000	0	0-0	0	5.40	3.96
2014 Phi	NL	3	2	0	1	12.2	52	15	9	9	3	1	0	0	2	0	7	0	0	0	1	.000	0	0-0	0	5.29	6.39
10 LAA	AL	5	1	0	2	13.0	49	7	3	3	1	0	0	0	4	2	6	0	0	1	0	1.000	0	0-0	0	1.33	2.08
10 KC	AL	14	13	0	1	70.2	319	83	50	48	14	0	3	1	27	0	37	4	2	3	6	.333	0	0-0	0	5.76	6.11
5 ML YEARS		53	39	0	8	231.1	1038	274	160	152	40	7	13	5	89	5	110	8	2	10	17	.370	0	0-1	0	5.70	5.91

Dan Otero

Pitches: R **Bats:** R **Pos:** RP-72

oh-TEHR-oh

Ht: 6'3" **Wt:** 215 **Born:** 2/19/1985 **Age:** 30

Year Team	Lg	G	GS	CG	GF	IP	BFP	H	R	ER	HR	SH	SF	HB	TBB	IBB	SO	WP	Bk	W	L	Pct	Sh	Sv-Op	Hld	ERC	ERA
2012 SF	NL	12	0	0	4	12.1	57	19	11	8	0	0	0	2	2	1	8	1	0	0	0	-	0	0-0	0	6.18	5.84

Year Team	Lg	G	GS	CG	GF	IP	BFP	H	R	ER	HR	SH	SF	HB	TBB	IBB	SO	WP	Bk	W	L	Pct	Sh	Sv-Op	Hld	ERC	ERA
						HOW MUCH HE PITCHED					**WHAT HE GAVE UP**											**THE RESULTS**					
2013 Oak	AL	33	0	0	8	39.0	159	42	12	6	0	1	0	0	6	1	27	0	0	2	0	1.000	0	0-1	8	2.90	1.38
2014 Oak	AL	72	0	0	14	86.2	348	80	24	22	4	4	3	2	15	7	45	1	0	8	2	.800	0	1-4	12	2.47	2.28
Postseason		4	0	0	0	5.2	21	4	0	0	0	0	0	0	1	0	2	0	0	0	0	-	0	0-0	1	1.43	0.00
3 ML YEARS		117	0	0	26	138.0	564	141	42	36	4	5	3	4	23	9	80	2	0	10	2	.833	0	1-5	20	2.89	2.35

Adam Ottavino

Pitches: R **Bats:** B **Pos:** RP-75   ott-tah-VEE-no   **Ht:** 6'5" **Wt:** 230 **Born:** 11/22/1985 **Age:** 29

Year Team	Lg	G	GS	CG	GF	IP	BFP	H	R	ER	HR	SH	SF	HB	TBB	IBB	SO	WP	Bk	W	L	Pct	Sh	Sv-Op	Hld	ERC	ERA
						HOW MUCH HE PITCHED					**WHAT HE GAVE UP**											**THE RESULTS**					
2010 StL	NL	5	3	0	0	22.1	110	37	21	21	5	1	0	0	9	1	12	1	0	0	2	.000	0	0-0	0	9.22	8.46
2012 Col	NL	53	0	0	6	79.0	339	76	42	40	9	3	1	1	34	7	81	8	0	5	1	.833	0	0-2	6	4.01	4.56
2013 Col	NL	51	0	0	6	78.1	335	73	27	23	5	6	4	2	31	5	78	9	1	1	3	.250	0	0-0	8	3.42	2.64
2014 Col	NL	75	0	0	16	65.0	272	67	26	26	6	2	3	4	16	1	70	4	0	1	4	.200	0	1-6	21	3.87	3.60
4 ML YEARS		184	3	0	27	244.2	1056	253	116	110	25	12	8	7	90	14	241	22	1	7	10	.412	0	1-8	35	4.20	4.05

Josh Outman

Pitches: L **Bats:** L **Pos:** RP-40   OUT-min   **Ht:** 6'1" **Wt:** 205 **Born:** 9/14/1984 **Age:** 30

Year Team	Lg	G	GS	CG	GF	IP	BFP	H	R	ER	HR	SH	SF	HB	TBB	IBB	SO	WP	Bk	W	L	Pct	Sh	Sv-Op	Hld	ERC	ERA
						HOW MUCH HE PITCHED					**WHAT HE GAVE UP**											**THE RESULTS**					
2014 Clmbs*	AAA	23	1	0	2	22.1	93	21	12	11	2	2	2	2	8	0	20	0	0	3	1	.750	0	0- -	-	4.00	4.43
2008 Oak	AL	6	4	0	0	25.2	116	34	14	13	1	0	2	2	8	1	19	1	0	1	2	.333	0	0-0	0	5.49	4.56
2009 Oak	AL	14	12	0	1	67.1	276	53	30	26	9	1	0	0	25	0	53	1	0	4	1	.800	0	0-0	0	3.04	3.48
2011 Oak	AL	13	9	0	2	58.1	254	62	27	24	4	4	3	0	23	0	35	3	0	3	5	.375	0	0-0	1	4.19	3.70
2012 Col	NL	27	7	0	3	40.2	185	47	37	37	7	2	1	0	20	0	40	5	0	1	3	.250	0	0-0	3	5.92	8.19
2013 Col	NL	61	0	0	8	54.0	238	56	27	26	3	1	2	3	23	2	53	2	0	3	0	1.000	0	0-1	13	4.22	4.33
2014 2 Tms	AL	40	0	0	6	28.1	122	24	10	9	4	1	0	0	16	2	26	1	0	4	0	1.000	0	0-1	2	4.07	2.86
14 Cle	AL	31	0	0	6	24.2	110	22	10	9	4	0	0	0	16	2	24	1	0	4	0	1.000	0	0-1	1	4.76	3.28
14 NYY	AL	9	0	0	0	3.2	12	2	0	0	0	1	0	0	0	0	2	0	0	0	0	-	0	0-0	1	0.69	0.00
6 ML YEARS		161	32	0	20	274.1	1191	276	145	135	28	9	8	5	115	5	226	13	0	16	11	.593	0	0-2	19	4.25	4.43

Lyle Overbay

Bats: L **Throws:** L **Pos:** 1B-83;PH-45   **Ht:** 6'2" **Wt:** 235 **Born:** 1/28/1977 **Age:** 38

Year Team	Lg	G	AB	H	2B	3B	HR	(Hm	Rd)	TB	R	RBI	RC	TBB	IBB	SO	HBP	SH	SF	SB	CS	GDP	Avg	OBP	Slg	OPS
							BATTING													**RUNNING**			**AVERAGES**			
2001 Ari	NL	2	2	1	0	0	0	(0	0)	1	0	0	0	0	0	1	0	0	0	0	0	0	.500	.500	.500	1.000
2002 Ari	NL	10	10	1	0	0	0	(0	0)	1	0	1	0	0	0	5	0	0	0	0	0	0	.100	.100	.100	.200
2003 Ari	NL	86	254	70	20	0	4	(2	2)	102	23	28	34	35	7	67	2	0	2	1	0	8	.276	.365	.402	.767
2004 Mil	NL	159	579	174	53	1	16	(6	10)	277	83	87	94	81	9	128	2	0	6	2	1	11	.301	.385	.478	.863
2005 Mil	NL	158	537	148	34	1	19	(10	9)	241	80	72	84	78	8	98	2	1	4	1	0	17	.276	.367	.449	.816
2006 Tor	AL	157	581	181	46	1	22	(17	5)	295	82	92	89	55	7	96	2	0	2	5	3	19	.312	.372	.508	.880
2007 Tor	AL	122	425	102	30	2	10	(6	4)	166	49	44	45	47	4	78	1	0	3	2	0	12	.240	.315	.391	.706
2008 Tor	AL	158	544	147	32	2	15	(7	8)	228	74	69	73	74	3	116	3	1	5	1	2	24	.270	.358	.419	.777
2009 Tor	AL	132	423	112	35	1	16	(6	10)	197	57	64	64	74	6	95	0	0	3	0	0	8	.265	.372	.466	.838
2010 Tor	AL	154	534	130	37	2	20	(13	7)	231	75	67	75	67	7	131	3	0	3	1	0	9	.243	.329	.433	.762
2011 2 Tms	NL	121	394	92	21	1	9	(4	5)	142	43	47	41	42	2	88	2	1	1	2	1	13	.234	.310	.360	.670
2012 2 Tms	NL	65	116	30	10	0	2	(2	0)	46	12	10	11	13	2	34	0	0	1	0	0	4	.259	.331	.397	.727
2013 NYY	NL	142	445	107	24	1	14	(7	7)	175	43	59	47	36	0	111	0	0	4	2	0	16	.240	.295	.393	.688
2014 Mil	NL	121	258	60	14	0	4	(3	1)	86	24	35	34	36	2	60	1	0	1	2	0	8	.233	.328	.333	.661
11 Pit	NL	103	352	80	17	1	8	(3	5)	123	40	37	33	36	1	77	1	1	1	1	1	12	.227	.300	.349	.649
11 Ari	NL	18	42	12	4	0	1	(1	0)	19	3	10	8	6	1	11	1	0	0	1	0	1	.286	.388	.452	.840
12 Ari	NL	45	96	28	9	0	2	(2	0)	43	11	10	11	12	2	26	0	0	1	0	0	3	.292	.367	.448	.815
12 Atl	NL	20	20	2	1	0	0	(0	0)	3	1	0	0	1	0	8	0	0	0	0	0	1	.100	.143	.150	.293
Postseason		2	4	0	0	0	0	(0	0)	0	0	0	0	0	0	2	0	0	0	0	0	0	.000	.000	.000	.000
14 ML YEARS		1587	5102	1355	356	12	151	(83	68)	2188	645	675	691	638	57	1108	18	3	35	19	7	149	.266	.347	.429	.776

Juan Oviedo

Pitches: R **Bats:** R **Pos:** RP-32   oh-vee-AY-doh   **Ht:** 6'2" **Wt:** 195 **Born:** 3/15/1982 **Age:** 33

Year Team	Lg	G	GS	CG	GF	IP	BFP	H	R	ER	HR	SH	SF	HB	TBB	IBB	SO	WP	Bk	W	L	Pct	Sh	Sv-Op	Hld	ERC	ERA
						HOW MUCH HE PITCHED					**WHAT HE GAVE UP**											**THE RESULTS**					
2014 Drham*	AAA	7	0	0	0	7.0	27	5	3	3	1	0	1	0	1	0	10	0	0	1	0	1.000	0	0- -	-	1.89	3.86
2005 KC	AL	41	0	0	10	53.2	246	73	45	45	9	1	2	3	18	2	32	1	0	3	2	.600	0	0-1	2	6.76	7.55
2006 KC	AL	7	0	0	5	13.1	58	15	7	7	2	0	1	2	5	0	7	0	0	0	0	-	0	0-0	0	5.98	4.73
2007 KC	AL	13	6	0	0	43.2	182	44	21	19	8	0	2	0	10	0	37	1	0	2	4	.333	0	0-0	1	3.98	3.92
2008 KC	AL	45	0	0	12	48.1	205	45	19	16	2	3	2	4	15	2	26	3	0	4	1	.800	0	0-3	7	3.20	2.98
2009 Fla	NL	75	0	0	41	68.2	293	59	33	31	13	4	2	4	27	5	60	1	1	4	6	.400	0	26-33	14	3.96	4.06
2010 Fla	NL	68	0	0	50	65.0	270	62	27	25	5	1	0	0	21	2	71	1	0	4	3	.571	0	30-38	5	3.36	3.46
2011 Fla	NL	68	0	0	51	64.1	268	57	30	29	8	1	2	1	21	2	55	1	0	1	4	.200	0	36-42	3	3.33	4.06
2014 TB	AL	32	0	0	13	31.2	140	27	14	13	3	0	1	3	16	1	26	5	0	3	3	.500	0	1-2	2	3.88	3.69
8 ML YEARS		349	6	0	184	388.2	1662	382	196	185	50	10	12	17	133	14	314	13	2	21	23	.477	0	93-119	31	4.07	4.28

Rudy Owens

Pitches: L **Bats:** L **Pos:** SP-1   **Ht:** 6'3" **Wt:** 240 **Born:** 12/18/1987 **Age:** 27

		HOW MUCH HE PITCHED						WHAT HE GAVE UP												THE RESULTS							
Year	Team	Lg	G	GS	CG	GF	IP	BFP	H	R	ER	HR	SH	SF	HB	TBB	IBB	SO	WP	Bk	W	L	Pct	Sh	Sv-Op	Hld	ERC	ERA
2010	Altna	AA	26	26	0	0	150.0	585	124	46	41	11	7	2	5	23	0	132	3	1	12	6	.667	0	0- -		2.26	2.46
2011	Indy	AAA	21	21	0	0	112.1	494	129	65	63	10	3	6	6	32	2	71	1	0	9	7	.563	0	0- -		4.55	5.05
2012	Indy	AAA	19	19	1	0	117.1	485	112	42	41	12	7	4	6	25	0	85	7	1	8	5	.615	0	0- -		3.32	3.14
2012	OKCity	AAA	8	8	0	0	45.2	197	43	23	22	7	1	4	4	14	1	23	2	0	2	3	.400	0	0- -		4.00	4.34
2013	OKCity	AAA	4	3	0	1	17.0	77	20	8	7	0	0	1	0	9	1	13	3	0	0	3	.000	0	0- -		4.79	3.71
2014	OKCity	AAA	25	21	0	1	135.0	570	136	69	65	10	3	7	8	33	0	104	5	0	8	5	.615	0	1- -		3.57	4.33
2014	Hou	AL	1	1	0	0	5.2	29	9	5	5	1	0	1	1	2	0	1	0	0	0	1	.000	0	0-0	0	8.76	7.94

Chris Owings

Bats: R **Throws:** R **Pos:** SS-61;2B-18;PH-13   **Ht:** 5'10" **Wt:** 190 **Born:** 8/12/1991 **Age:** 23

									BATTING											RUNNING			AVERAGES			
Year	Team	Lg	G	AB	H	2B	3B	HR	(Hm	Rd)	TB	R	RBI	RC	TBB	IBB	SO	HBP	SH	SF	SB	CS	GDP	Avg	OBP	Slg	OPS
2010	Sbend	A	62	255	76	19	2	5	(-	-)	114	39	28	36	9	0	50	2	2	3	1	3	7	.298	.323	.447	.770
2011	Visalia	A+	121	521	128	29	6	11	(-	-)	202	67	50	56	15	0	130	7	8	4	10	4	5	.246	.274	.388	.662
2012	Visalia	A+	59	241	78	16	2	11	(-	-)	131	51	24	46	13	0	63	2	0	1	8	3	3	.324	.362	.544	.905
2012	Mobile	AA	69	297	78	10	3	6	(-	-)	112	35	28	32	11	0	69	1	1	0	4	3	5	.263	.291	.377	.668
2013	Reno	AAA	125	546	180	31	8	12	(-	-)	263	104	81	94	22	2	99	3	4	0	20	7	14	.330	.359	.482	.841
2014	DBcks	R	3	7	4	0	0	0	(-	-)	4	1	2	4	3	0	0	0	0	0	5	0	0	.571	.700	.571	1.271
2014	Reno	AAA	10	40	10	1	0	0	(-	-)	11	6	1	3	0	0	9	0	0	0	3	0	0	.250	.250	.275	.525
2013	Ari	NL	20	55	16	5	0	0	(0	0)	21	5	5	7	6	1	10	0	0	0	2	0	0	.291	.361	.382	.742
2014	Ari	NL	91	310	81	15	6	6	(1	5)	126	34	26	38	16	0	67	2	2	2	8	1	4	.261	.300	.406	.706
	2 ML YEARS		111	365	97	20	6	6	(1	5)	147	39	31	45	22	1	77	2	2	2	10	1	4	.266	.309	.403	.712

Marcell Ozuna

Bats: R **Throws:** R **Pos:** CF-140;LF-11;PH-5;RF-4   oh-ZUNE-uh   **Ht:** 6'1" **Wt:** 230 **Born:** 11/12/1990 **Age:** 24

									BATTING											RUNNING			AVERAGES			
Year	Team	Lg	G	AB	H	2B	3B	HR	(Hm	Rd)	TB	R	RBI	RC	TBB	IBB	SO	HBP	SH	SF	SB	CS	GDP	Avg	OBP	Slg	OPS
2010	Grnsbr	A	6	25	4	0	0	1	(-	-)	7	3	2	1	2	0	10	0	0	0	0	0	0	.160	.222	.280	.502
2010	Jmstwn	A-	68	270	72	11	2	21	(-	-)	150	53	60	47	17	2	94	3	0	3	3	1	7	.267	.314	.556	.870
2011	Grnsbr	A	131	496	132	28	5	23	(-	-)	239	87	71	83	46	2	121	2	6	2	17	2	7	.266	.330	.482	.812
2012	Jupiter	A+	129	489	130	27	2	24	(-	-)	233	89	95	78	44	0	116	3	0	3	8	3	10	.266	.328	.476	.805
2013	Jupiter	A+	4	15	4	1	0	0	(-	-)	5	1	1	1	0	0	4	0	0	0	0	0	0	.267	.267	.333	.600
2013	Jaxnvl	AA	10	42	14	3	1	5	(-	-)	34	6	15	12	3	1	9	1	0	1	1	0	0	.333	.383	.810	1.193
2013	Mia	NL	70	275	73	17	4	3	(0	3)	107	31	32	35	13	0	57	2	1	0	5	1	6	.265	.303	.389	.693
2014	Mia	NL	153	565	152	26	5	23	(12	11)	257	72	85	74	41	1	164	1	0	5	3	1	12	.269	.317	.455	.772
	2 ML YEARS		223	840	225	43	9	26	(12	14)	364	103	117	109	54	1	221	3	1	5	8	2	18	.268	.313	.433	.746

Jordan Pacheco

Bats: R **Throws:** R **Pos:** PH-32;C-19;1B-15;3B-3;2B-2   puh-CHECK-oh   **Ht:** 6'1" **Wt:** 205 **Born:** 1/30/1986 **Age:** 29

									BATTING											RUNNING			AVERAGES			
Year	Team	Lg	G	AB	H	2B	3B	HR	(Hm	Rd)	TB	R	RBI	RC	TBB	IBB	SO	HBP	SH	SF	SB	CS	GDP	Avg	OBP	Slg	OPS
2014	DBcks*	R	4	12	3	0	0	0	(-	-)	3	1	3	1	2	0	1	0	0	1	2	0	0	.250	.333	.250	.583
2014	Reno*	AAA	4	14	4	1	0	0	(-	-)	5	3	3	1	1	0	1	0	0	0	0	0	2	.286	.333	.357	.690
2011	Col	NL	21	84	24	1	0	2	(2	0)	31	5	14	12	3	0	9	1	0	0	0	0	2	.286	.318	.369	.687
2012	Col	NL	132	475	147	32	3	5	(4	1)	200	51	54	64	22	2	61	3	1	4	7	2	13	.309	.341	.421	.762
2013	Col	NL	95	247	59	15	0	1	(1	0)	77	23	22	21	10	0	38	3	1	1	0	0	4	.239	.276	.312	.588
2014	2 Tms	NL	69	153	39	10	1	0	(0	0)	51	10	16	17	9	0	27	1	1	1	0	0	6	.255	.299	.333	.632
14	Col	NL	22	72	17	6	1	0	(0	0)	25	4	8	8	6	0	15	1	0	1	0	0	3	.236	.300	.347	.647
14	Ari	NL	47	81	22	4	0	0	(0	0)	26	6	8	9	3	0	12	0	1	0	0	0	3	.272	.298	.321	.619
	4 ML YEARS		317	959	269	58	4	8	(7	1)	359	89	106	114	44	2	135	8	3	6	7	2	25	.281	.316	.374	.690

Angel Pagan

Bats: B **Throws:** R **Pos:** CF-91;PH-5   ANE-gell pah-GONN   **Ht:** 6'2" **Wt:** 200 **Born:** 7/2/1981 **Age:** 33

									BATTING											RUNNING			AVERAGES			
Year	Team	Lg	G	AB	H	2B	3B	HR	(Hm	Rd)	TB	R	RBI	RC	TBB	IBB	SO	HBP	SH	SF	SB	CS	GDP	Avg	OBP	Slg	OPS
2014	Giants*	R	2	5	3	2	0	0	(-	-)	5	2	0	2	1	0	0	0	0	0	0	0	0	.600	.667	1.000	1.667
2014	Fresno*	AAA	2	8	1	0	0	0	(-	-)	1	0	1	0	0	0	0	0	0	1	0	0	0	.125	.125	.125	.250
2006	ChC	NL	77	170	42	6	2	5	(4	1)	67	28	18	21	15	0	28	0	1	1	4	2	3	.247	.306	.394	.701
2007	ChC	NL	71	148	39	10	2	4	(3	1)	65	21	21	23	10	0	32	0	1	2	4	1	0	.264	.306	.439	.745
2008	NYM	NL	31	91	25	7	1	0	(0	0)	34	12	13	15	11	0	18	0	1	2	4	0	0	.275	.346	.374	.720
2009	NYM	NL	88	343	105	22	11	6	(5	1)	167	54	32	53	25	2	56	0	5	3	14	7	3	.306	.350	.487	.837
2010	NYM	NL	151	579	168	31	7	11	(6	5)	246	80	69	90	44	5	97	1	6	3	37	9	9	.290	.340	.425	.765
2011	NYM	NL	123	478	125	24	4	7	(4	3)	178	68	56	64	44	4	62	1	4	5	32	7	4	.262	.322	.372	.694
2012	SF	NL	154	605	174	38	15	8	(1	7)	266	95	56	91	48	5	97	0	2	4	29	7	6	.288	.338	.440	.778
2013	SF	NL	71	280	79	16	3	5	(3	2)	116	44	30	41	23	0	36	0	0	2	9	4	1	.282	.334	.414	.749
2014	SF	NL	96	383	115	21	2	3	(1	2)	149	56	27	50	25	1	53	1	1	3	16	6	5	.300	.342	.389	.731
	Postseason		16	69	13	3	1	2	(1	1)	24	10	6	3	4	0	12	0	0	1	1	1	0	.188	.230	.348	.578
	9 ML YEARS		862	3077	872	175	47	49	(27	22)	1288	458	322	448	245	17	479	3	21	25	149	43	31	.283	.334	.419	.753

Matt Pagnozzi

Bats: R Throws: R Pos: C-1   Ht: 6'2" Wt: 215 Born: 11/10/1982 Age: 32

Year	Team	Lg	G	AB	H	2B	3B	HR	(Hm	Rd)	TB	R	RBI	RC	TBB	IBB	SO	HBP	SH	SF	SB	CS	GDP	Avg	OBP	Slg	OPS
2014	Nashv*	AAA	71	228	49	5	0	11	(-	-)	87	29	29	27	20	2	63	7	4	0	1	0	6	.215	.298	.382	.680
2009	StL	NL	6	3	0	0	0	0	(0	0)	0	1	0	0	1	0	1	0	1	0	0	0	0	.000	.250	.000	.250
2010	StL	NL	15	39	14	2	0	1	(1	0)	19	4	10	7	2	0	8	1	2	0	0	0	1	.359	.405	.487	.892
2011	2 Tms	NL	12	29	8	0	0	0	(0	0)	8	2	3	4	1	0	10	1	3	0	0	0	1	.276	.323	.276	.598
2013	Hou	AL	9	21	3	0	0	0	(0	0)	3	1	0	0	1	0	3	0	0	0	0	0	0	.143	.182	.143	.325
2014	Mil	NL	1	0	0	0	0	0	(0	0)	0	0	0	0	0	0	0	0	0	0	0	0	0	-	-	-	-
11	Col	NL	7	21	6	0	0	0	(0	0)	6	2	2	3	1	0	8	1	2	0	0	0	0	.286	.348	.286	.634
11	Pit	NL	5	8	2	0	0	0	(0	0)	2	0	1	1	0	0	2	0	1	0	0	0	1	.250	.250	.250	.500
	5 ML YEARS		43	92	25	2	0	1	(1	0)	30	8	13	11	5	0	21	2	6	0	0	0	2	.272	.323	.326	.649

Joe Panik

Bats: L Throws: R Pos: 2B-70;PH-7   PANIC   Ht: 6'1" Wt: 190 Born: 10/30/1990 Age: 24

Year	Team	Lg	G	AB	H	2B	3B	HR	(Hm	Rd)	TB	R	RBI	RC	TBB	IBB	SO	HBP	SH	SF	SB	CS	GDP	Avg	OBP	Slg	OPS
2011	SlmKzr	A-	69	270	92	10	3	6	(-	-)	126	49	54	52	28	0	25	2	0	4	13	5	8	.341	.401	.467	.868
2012	SnJos	A+	130	535	159	27	4	7	(-	-)	215	93	76	85	58	1	54	5	2	5	10	4	13	.297	.368	.402	.770
2013	Rchmd	AA	137	522	134	27	4	4	(-	-)	181	64	57	66	58	1	68	5	8	6	10	5	16	.257	.333	.347	.680
2014	Fresno	AAA	74	293	94	14	4	5	(-	-)	131	50	45	51	27	2	33	3	1	2	3	2	9	.321	.382	.447	.829
2014	SF	NL	73	269	82	10	2	1	(0	1)	99	31	18	33	16	0	33	0	1	1	0	0	4	.305	.343	.368	.711

Jonathan Papelbon

Pitches: R Bats: R Pos: RP-66   PAHP-ill-bonn   Ht: 6'4" Wt: 215 Born: 11/23/1980 Age: 34

			HOW MUCH HE PITCHED						WHAT HE GAVE UP											THE RESULTS							
Year	Team	Lg	G	GS	CG	GF	IP	BFP	H	R	ER	HR	SH	SF	HB	TBB	IBB	SO	WP	Bk	W	L	Pct	Sh	Sv-Op	Hld	ERC	ERA
2005	Bos	AL	17	3	0	4	34.0	148	33	11	10	4	1	0	3	17	2	34	1	0	3	1	.750	0	0-1	4	4.82	2.65
2006	Bos	AL	59	0	0	49	68.1	257	40	8	7	3	1	2	1	13	2	75	2	0	4	2	.667	0	35-41	1	1.22	0.92
2007	Bos	AL	59	0	0	53	58.1	224	30	12	12	5	0	0	4	15	0	84	0	0	1	3	.250	0	37-40	2	1.43	1.85
2008	Bos	AL	67	0	0	62	69.1	273	58	24	18	4	4	1	0	8	0	77	2	0	5	4	.556	0	41-46	0	1.92	2.34
2009	Bos	AL	66	0	0	59	68.0	285	54	15	14	5	1	2	4	24	1	76	0	0	1	1	.500	0	38-41	0	2.78	1.85
2010	Bos	AL	65	0	0	53	67.0	287	57	34	29	7	5	0	2	28	4	76	4	0	5	7	.417	0	37-45	3	3.32	3.90
2011	Bos	AL	63	0	0	54	64.1	255	50	22	21	3	0	1	3	10	1	87	1	0	4	1	.800	0	31-34	1	1.86	2.94
2012	Phi	NL	70	0	0	64	70.0	284	56	22	19	8	3	0	4	18	1	92	0	0	5	6	.455	0	38-42	0	2.75	2.44
2013	Phi	NL	61	0	0	54	61.2	254	59	23	20	6	0	3	1	11	1	57	2	0	5	1	.833	0	29-36	0	2.98	2.92
2014	Phi	NL	66	0	0	52	66.1	259	45	15	15	2	3	0	5	15	1	63	1	0	2	3	.400	0	39-43	0	1.68	2.04
	Postseason		18	0	0	12	27.0	100	14	3	3	0	0	1	0	8	3	23	0	0	2	1	.667	0	7-9	0	1.01	1.00
	10 ML YEARS		593	3	0	504	627.1	2526	482	186	165	47	18	9	27	159	13	721	13	0	35	29	.547	0	325-369	7	2.29	2.37

Jimmy Paredes

Bats: B Throws: R Pos: 3B-16;PH-5;PR-4;2B-3;DH-3   pah-REY-dez   Ht: 6'3" Wt: 200 Born: 11/25/1988 Age: 26

			BATTING																					AVERAGES			
Year	Team	Lg	G	AB	H	2B	3B	HR	(Hm	Rd)	TB	R	RBI	RC	TBB	IBB	SO	HBP	SH	SF	SB	CS	GDP	Avg	OBP	Slg	OPS
2014	Omha*	AAA	65	269	82	18	4	5	(-	-)	123	37	36	43	11	1	78	0	0	0	17	1	3	.305	.332	.457	.789
2014	Norfolk*	AAA	32	132	34	7	1	3	(-	-)	52	11	23	16	6	0	31	0	0	2	4	0	2	.258	.286	.394	.680
2011	Hou	NL	46	168	48	8	2	2	(0	2)	66	16	18	23	9	0	47	0	1	1	5	4	3	.286	.320	.393	.713
2012	Hou	NL	24	74	14	1	1	0	(0	0)	17	7	3	3	6	0	21	0	0	2	2	1	0	.189	.244	.230	.474
2013	Hou	AL	48	125	24	4	0	1	(1	0)	31	8	10	8	6	0	44	1	1	2	4	4	1	.192	.231	.248	.479
2014	2 Tms	AL	27	63	18	4	0	2	(2	0)	28	12	8	6	2	0	16	0	0	0	4	0	1	.286	.308	.444	.752
14	KC	AL	9	10	2	0	0	0	(0	0)	2	3	0	0	0	0	3	0	0	0	2	0	0	.200	.200	.200	.400
14	Bal	AL	18	53	16	4	0	2	(2	0)	26	9	8	6	2	0	13	0	0	0	2	0	1	.302	.327	.491	.818
	4 ML YEARS		145	430	104	17	3	5	(3	2)	142	43	39	40	23	0	128	1	2	5	15	9	5	.242	.279	.330	.609

Blake Parker

Pitches: R Bats: R Pos: RP-18   Ht: 6'3" Wt: 225 Born: 6/19/1985 Age: 30

			HOW MUCH HE PITCHED						WHAT HE GAVE UP											THE RESULTS							
Year	Team	Lg	G	GS	CG	GF	IP	BFP	H	R	ER	HR	SH	SF	HB	TBB	IBB	SO	WP	Bk	W	L	Pct	Sh	Sv-Op	Hld	ERC	ERA
2014	Iowa*	AAA	35	0	0	32	35.2	145	28	8	7	3	0	1	0	13	0	52	0	0	0	1	.000	0	25- -	0	2.71	1.77
2012	ChC	NL	7	0	0	0	6.0	32	10	7	4	3	0	0	0	5	1	6	0	0	0	0		0	0-0	0	14.02	6.00
2013	ChC	NL	49	0	0	18	46.1	195	39	17	14	4	0	1	2	15	1	55	2	0	1	2	.333	0	1-1	7	2.91	2.72
2014	ChC	NL	18	0	0	10	21.0	91	24	13	12	3	0	1	0	4	0	24	1	0	1	1	.500	0	0-0	1	4.24	5.14
	3 ML YEARS		74	0	0	28	73.1	318	73	37	30	10	0	2	2	24	2	85	3	0	2	3	.400	0	1-1	8	4.00	3.68

Jarrod Parker

Pitches: R Bats: R Pos: P   Ht: 6'1" Wt: 195 Born: 11/24/1988 Age: 26

			HOW MUCH HE PITCHED						WHAT HE GAVE UP											THE RESULTS							
Year	Team	Lg	G	GS	CG	GF	IP	BFP	H	R	ER	HR	SH	SF	HB	TBB	IBB	SO	WP	Bk	W	L	Pct	Sh	Sv-Op	Hld	ERC	ERA
2011	Ari	NL	1	1	0	0	5.2	22	4	0	0	0	2	0	0	1	0	1	0	0	0	0		0	0-0	0	1.36	0.00
2012	Oak	AL	29	29	0	0	181.1	751	166	71	70	11	7	8	3	63	3	140	10	0	13	8	.619	0	0-0	0	3.24	3.47
2013	Oak	AL	32	32	1	0	197.0	818	178	92	87	25	8	4	7	63	2	134	7	0	12	8	.600	0	0-0	0	3.57	3.97
	Postseason		4	3	0	0	18.0	77	21	11	10	1	2	0	1	4	0	12	2	0	1	2	.333	0	0-0	0	4.29	5.00
	3 ML YEARS		62	62	1	0	384.0	1591	348	163	157	36	17	12	10	127	5	275	17	0	25	16	.610	0	0-0	0	3.37	3.68

Kyle Parker

Bats: R Throws: R Pos: PH-12;RF-4;1B-2   Ht: 6'0" Wt: 205 Born: 9/30/1989 Age: 25

Year	Team	Lg	G	AB	H	2B	3B	HR	(Hm	Rd)	TB	R	RBI	RC	TBB	IBB	SO	HBP	SH	SF	SB	CS	GDP	Avg	OBP	Slg	OPS
2011	Ashvll	A	117	445	127	23	1	21	(-	-)	215	75	95	82	48	0	133	14	1	8	2	0	20	.285	.367	.483	.850
2012	Mdest	A+	102	390	120	18	6	23	(-	-)	219	86	73	90	66	1	88	6	0	1	1	2	14	.308	.415	.562	.976
2013	Tulsa	AA	123	480	138	23	3	23	(-	-)	236	70	74	81	40	1	99	4	0	4	6	6	14	.288	.345	.492	.836
2014	ColSpr	AAA	128	502	145	31	3	15	(-	-)	227	73	72	77	33	1	102	4	0	3	4	3	14	.289	.336	.452	.788
2014	Col	NL	18	26	5	1	0	0	(0	0)	6	1	1	1	0	0	14	0	0	0	0	0	0	.192	.192	.231	.423

Chris Parmelee

PAR-muh-lee

Bats: L Throws: L Pos: 1B-33;RF-33;LF-22;PH-15;CF-3;PR-2   Ht: 6'1" Wt: 220 Born: 2/24/1988 Age: 27

Year	Team	Lg	G	AB	H	2B	3B	HR	(Hm	Rd)	TB	R	RBI	RC	TBB	IBB	SO	HBP	SH	SF	SB	CS	GDP	Avg	OBP	Slg	OPS
2014	Roch*	AAA	32	118	36	7	0	7	(-	-)	64	13	23	24	14	0	24	1	0	2	0	0	2	.305	.378	.542	.920
2011	Min	AL	21	76	27	6	0	4	(2	2)	45	8	14	19	12	0	13	0	0	0	0	0	0	.355	.443	.592	1.035
2012	Min	AL	64	192	44	10	2	5	(1	4)	73	18	20	18	13	1	52	4	0	1	0	0	4	.229	.290	.380	.671
2013	Min	AL	101	294	67	13	0	8	(2	6)	104	21	24	27	33	0	81	3	0	3	1	1	6	.228	.309	.354	.663
2014	Min	AL	87	250	64	11	0	7	(3	4)	96	27	28	19	17	0	64	2	0	1	0	3	7	.256	.307	.384	.691
	4 ML YEARS		273	812	202	40	2	24	(8	16)	318	74	86	83	75	1	210	9	0	5	1	4	20	.249	.317	.392	.709

Bobby Parnell

Pitches: R Bats: R Pos: RP-1   Ht: 6'3" Wt: 205 Born: 9/8/1984 Age: 30

Year	Team	Lg	G	GS	CG	GF	IP	BFP	H	R	ER	HR	SH	SF	HB	TBB	IBB	SO	WP	Bk	W	L	Pct	Sh	Sv-Op	Hld	ERC	ERA
2008	NYM	NL	6	0	0	3	5.0	19	3	3	3	0	0	0	0	2	0	3	1	0	0	0	-	0	0-0	0	1.59	5.40
2009	NYM	NL	68	8	0	14	88.1	413	101	56	52	8	3	1	4	46	2	74	6	1	4	8	.333	0	1-5	16	5.37	5.30
2010	NYM	NL	41	0	0	10	35.0	149	41	13	11	1	2	0	0	8	2	33	0	0	0	1	.000	0	0-2	9	3.80	2.83
2011	NYM	NL	60	0	0	23	59.1	268	60	29	24	4	6	0	2	27	4	64	8	1	4	6	.400	0	6-12	11	4.01	3.64
2012	NYM	NL	74	0	0	23	68.2	288	65	24	19	4	4	2	1	20	2	61	1	0	5	4	.556	0	7-12	18	3.08	2.49
2013	NYM	NL	49	0	0	41	50.0	198	38	17	12	1	2	3	1	12	3	44	1	0	5	5	.500	0	22-26	1	1.78	2.16
2014	NYM	NL	1	0	0	0	1.0	6	2	1	1	0	0	0	0	1	0	1	0	0	0	0	-	0	0-1	0	12.01	9.00
	7 ML YEARS		299	8	0	114	307.1	1341	310	143	122	18	17	6	8	116	13	280	17	2	18	24	.429	0	36-58	54	3.73	3.57

Gerardo Parra

Bats: L Throws: L Pos: RF-109;LF-27;CF-12;PH-12   jer-AHR-doh PAH-ruh   Ht: 5'11" Wt: 200 Born: 5/6/1987 Age: 28

Year	Team	Lg	G	AB	H	2B	3B	HR	(Hm	Rd)	TB	R	RBI	RC	TBB	IBB	SO	HBP	SH	SF	SB	CS	GDP	Avg	OBP	Slg	OPS
2009	Ari	NL	120	455	132	21	8	5	(4	1)	184	59	60	58	25	1	89	1	4	6	5	7	18	.290	.324	.404	.729
2010	Ari	NL	133	364	95	19	6	3	(1	2)	135	31	30	38	23	10	76	2	3	1	1	0	8	.261	.308	.371	.679
2011	Ari	NL	141	445	130	20	8	8	(3	5)	190	55	46	71	43	16	82	3	0	2	15	1	8	.292	.357	.427	.784
2012	Ari	NL	133	385	105	21	2	7	(5	2)	151	58	36	50	33	4	77	4	6	2	15	9	4	.273	.335	.392	.727
2013	Ari	NL	156	601	161	43	4	10	(6	4)	242	79	48	69	48	3	100	3	7	4	10	10	12	.268	.323	.403	.726
2014	2 Tms	NL	150	529	138	22	4	9	(3	6)	195	64	40	46	32	5	100	5	6	2	9	7	10	.261	.308	.369	.677
14	Ari	NL	104	406	105	18	3	6	(2	4)	147	51	30	37	24	3	72	4	4	2	5	5	6	.259	.305	.362	.667
14	Mil	NL	46	123	33	4	1	3	(1	2)	48	13	10	9	8	2	28	1	2	0	4	2	4	.268	.318	.390	.708
	Postseason		5	18	1	1	0	0	(0	0)	2	1	0	0	1	0	7	0	0	0	0	0	0	.056	.105	.111	.216
	6 ML YEARS		833	2779	761	146	32	42	(22	20)	1097	346	260	332	204	39	524	18	26	17	55	34	60	.274	.326	.395	.720

Manny Parra

Pitches: L Bats: L Pos: RP-53   PAR-uh   Ht: 6'3" Wt: 215 Born: 10/30/1982 Age: 32

Year	Team	Lg	G	GS	CG	GF	IP	BFP	H	R	ER	HR	SH	SF	HB	TBB	IBB	SO	WP	Bk	W	L	Pct	Sh	Sv-Op	Hld	ERC	ERA
2007	Mil	NL	9	2	0	3	26.1	116	25	13	11	1	1	3	2	12	0	26	1	0	1	0	1.000	0	0-0	1	3.83	3.76
2008	Mil	NL	32	29	0	0	166.0	741	181	91	81	18	10	2	2	75	1	147	17	2	10	8	.556	0	0-0	0	4.89	4.39
2009	Mil	NL	27	27	0	0	140.0	671	179	108	99	19	5	3	1	77	5	116	4	1	11	11	.500	0	0-0	0	6.51	6.36
2010	Mil	NL	42	16	0	9	122.0	560	135	76	68	18	6	7	3	63	3	129	14	1	3	10	.231	0	0-0	0	5.53	5.02
2012	Mil	NL	62	0	0	8	58.2	273	62	39	33	3	0	1	3	35	2	61	6	0	2	3	.400	0	0-2	9	4.88	5.06
2013	Cin	NL	57	0	0	8	46.0	188	40	18	17	5	3	1	1	15	0	56	4	0	2	3	.400	0	0-1	16	3.28	3.33
2014	Cin	NL	53	0	0	8	36.2	164	39	20	19	4	4	0	1	18	1	34	2	0	0	3	.000	0	1-2	16	4.94	4.66
	Postseason		3	0	0	3	3.0	12	3	0	0	0	0	0	0	1	0	4	0	0	0	0	-	0	0-0	0	3.35	0.00
	7 ML YEARS		282	74	0	36	595.2	2713	661	365	328	68	29	17	13	295	12	569	48	4	28	39	.418	0	1-5	42	5.22	4.96

Andy Parrino

Bats: B Throws: R Pos: SS-14;2B-4;LF-2;3B-1;PR-1   puh-REE-no   Ht: 6'0" Wt: 190 Born: 10/31/1985 Age: 29

Year	Team	Lg	G	AB	H	2B	3B	HR	(Hm	Rd)	TB	R	RBI	RC	TBB	IBB	SO	HBP	SH	SF	SB	CS	GDP	Avg	OBP	Slg	OPS
2014	RdRck*	AAA	13	53	10	3	0	0	(-	-)	13	4	5	3	3	0	12	3	0	0	0	0	0	.189	.271	.245	.516
2014	Scrmto*	AAA	90	374	107	19	2	7	(-	-)	151	57	52	58	44	1	97	2	1	1	7	1	11	.286	.363	.404	.767
2011	SD	NL	24	44	8	1	0	0	(0	0)	9	3	4	4	9	1	17	1	0	1	1	0	1	.182	.327	.205	.532
2012	SD	NL	55	116	24	5	0	1	(1	0)	32	9	6	9	17	7	35	2	2	1	1	0	2	.207	.316	.276	.592
2013	Oak	AL	14	34	4	2	0	0	(0	0)	6	2	1	0	2	0	12	0	0	0	0	0	1	.118	.167	.176	.343
2014	Oak	AL	21	46	7	3	0	1	(1	0)	13	4	3	0	3	0	14	1	0	0	0	0	1	.152	.216	.283	.498
	4 ML YEARS		114	240	43	11	0	2	(2	0)	60	18	14	13	31	8	78	4	2	3	2	0	5	.179	.281	.250	.531

Curtis Partch

Pitches: R Bats: R Pos: RP-6   PARCH   Ht: 6'5" Wt: 240 Born: 2/13/1987 Age: 28

			HOW MUCH HE PITCHED						WHAT HE GAVE UP										THE RESULTS							
Year	Team	Lg	G	GS	CG	GF	IP	BFP	H	R	ER	HR	SH	SF	HB	TBB	IBB	SO	WP	Bk	W	L	Pct	Sh	Sv-Op	Hld	ERC	ERA
2010	Lynbrg	A+	28	24	0	1	132.0	599	165	93	73	11	6	5	7	45	2	96	14	2	7	11	.389	0	0--	-	5.35	4.98
2010	Carlina	AA	1	1	0	0	3.0	18	7	7	7	2	0	0	1	2	0	1	0	0	0	1	.000	0	0--	-	23.41	21.00
2011	Bkrsfld	A+	21	21	2	0	121.2	561	161	92	71	14	5	8	12	28	0	93	7	1	6	11	.353	0	0--	-	5.71	5.25
2011	Carlina	AA	7	7	0	0	39.0	183	55	32	30	3	2	2	3	13	1	33	1	0	2	2	.500	0	0--	-	6.35	6.92
2012	Pnscla	AA	45	4	0	17	70.1	314	75	38	37	7	2	0	4	33	3	64	7	1	7	4	.636	0	6--	-	4.91	4.73
2012	Bkrsfld	A+	7	0	0	3	12.0	46	7	2	2	1	0	1	0	3	1	15	0	0	0	0	-	0	2--	-	1.39	1.50
2013	Pnscla	AA	8	0	0	5	8.1	32	6	2	2	0	0	0	0	2	0	14	0	0	0	0	-	0	4--	-	1.58	2.16
2013	Lsvlle	AAA	24	0	0	7	28.1	124	27	13	13	2	1	1	2	12	2	31	1	1	1	2	.333	0	2--	-	3.83	4.13
2014	Lsvlle	AAA	41	2	0	14	47.1	214	46	28	28	3	3	4	4	25	2	54	6	1	4	1	.800	0	6--	-	4.36	4.75
2013	Cin	NL	14	0	0	4	23.1	106	17	16	16	8	3	1	4	17	1	16	0	0	0	1	.000	0	0-0	0	6.32	6.17
2014	Cin	NL	6	0	0	4	7.0	30	2	0	0	0	0	0	0	7	0	6	0	0	1	0	1.000	0	0-0	0	1.81	0.00
	2 ML YEARS		20	0	0	8	30.1	136	19	16	16	8	3	1	4	24	1	22	0	0	1	1	.500	0	0-0	0	5.17	4.75

Tyler Pastornicky

Bats: R Throws: R Pos: PH-14;2B-10;PR-4   pas-tor-NICK-ee   Ht: 5'11" Wt: 180 Born: 12/13/1989 Age: 25

			BATTING																RUNNING			AVERAGES			
Year	Team	Lg	G	AB	H	2B	3B	HR	(Hm | Rd)	TB	R	RBI	RC	TBB	IBB	SO	HBP	SH	SF	SB	CS	GDP	Avg	OBP	Slg	OPS
2014	Gwnntt*	AAA	47	176	51	5	1	1	(- | -)	61	13	17	21	11	0	23	0	1	1	7	2	5	.290	.330	.347	.676
2012	Atl	NL	76	169	41	6	1	2	(1 | 1)	55	21	13	15	10	1	32	1	7	1	2	0	5	.243	.287	.325	.613
2013	Atl	NL	20	30	9	1	0	0	(0 | 0)	10	5	0	3	1	0	5	0	2	0	0	0	0	.300	.323	.333	.656
2014	Atl	NL	28	40	8	0	1	0	(0 | 0)	10	4	2	3	6	0	11	0	1	0	0	1	0	.200	.304	.250	.554
	Postseason		1	0	0	0	0	0	(0 | 0)	0	0	0	0	0	0	0	0	0	0	0	0	0	-	-	-	-
	3 ML YEARS		124	239	58	7	2	2	(1 | 1)	75	30	15	21	17	1	48	1	10	1	2	1	5	.243	.295	.314	.608

Joe Paterson

Pitches: L Bats: R Pos: RP-3   Ht: 6'0" Wt: 190 Born: 5/19/1986 Age: 29

			HOW MUCH HE PITCHED						WHAT HE GAVE UP										THE RESULTS							
Year	Team	Lg	G	GS	CG	GF	IP	BFP	H	R	ER	HR	SH	SF	HB	TBB	IBB	SO	WP	Bk	W	L	Pct	Sh	Sv-Op	Hld	ERC	ERA
2014	Reno*	AAA	56	0	0	16	42.2	187	45	16	14	1	2	0	2	19	1	33	1	1	0	2	.000	0	0--	-	4.20	2.95
2011	Ari	NL	62	0	0	17	34.0	150	28	11	11	1	4	2	4	15	0	28	1	0	0	3	.000	0	1-1	10	3.12	2.91
2012	Ari	NL	6	0	0	2	2.2	26	15	11	11	2	0	0	0	3	0	0	0	0	0	0	-	0	0-0	1	53.93	37.13
2013	Ari	NL	2	0	0	2	2.1	11	2	1	1	0	0	3	0	0	0	2	0	0	0	0	-	0	0-0	0	6.30	3.86
2014	Ari	NL	3	0	0	1	1.1	10	4	5	5	0	0	1	1	1	0	0	0	0	0	0	-	0	0-0	0	22.07	33.75
	Postseason		1	0	0	0	0.1	1	0	0	0	0	0	0	0	0	0	1	0	0	0	0	-	0	0-0	0	0.00	0.00
	4 ML YEARS		73	0	0	20	40.1	197	49	28	28	3	4	3	8	19	0	30	1	0	0	3	.000	0	1-1	11	6.08	6.25

Red Patterson

Pitches: R Bats: R Pos: SP-1   Ht: 6'3" Wt: 220 Born: 5/11/1987 Age: 28

			HOW MUCH HE PITCHED						WHAT HE GAVE UP										THE RESULTS							
Year	Team	Lg	G	GS	CG	GF	IP	BFP	H	R	ER	HR	SH	SF	HB	TBB	IBB	SO	WP	Bk	W	L	Pct	Sh	Sv-Op	Hld	ERC	ERA
2010	Ogden	R+	14	14	0	0	67.2	292	70	37	25	6	1	3	6	17	0	66	6	0	6	1	.857	0	0--	-	3.92	3.33
2011	Gt Lks	A	14	14	1	0	81.1	327	70	33	31	5	2	1	4	20	1	79	1	0	5	4	.556	0	0--	-	2.73	3.43
2011	RCuca	A+	14	14	1	0	92.0	369	78	42	40	10	5	4	1	25	0	93	1	1	7	1	.875	1	0--	-	2.92	3.91
2012	Chatt	AA	47	0	0	6	70.1	314	70	29	24	2	4	2	2	32	4	71	3	1	7	1	.875	0	0--	-	3.67	3.07
2013	Albq	AAA	39	12	0	4	107.0	456	99	45	36	14	6	2	2	49	0	109	4	0	7	4	.636	0	1--	-	4.24	3.03
2014	Albq	AAA	29	20	0	3	121.1	536	140	79	78	21	2	6	7	43	2	103	5	0	5	8	.385	0	1--	-	5.61	5.79
2014	LAD	NL	1	1	0	0	4.2	19	2	1	1	0	0	1	0	3	0	1	0	0	0	0	-	0	0-0	0	1.49	1.93

Spencer Patton

Pitches: R Bats: R Pos: RP-9   Ht: 6'1" Wt: 185 Born: 2/20/1988 Age: 27

			HOW MUCH HE PITCHED						WHAT HE GAVE UP										THE RESULTS							
Year	Team	Lg	G	GS	CG	GF	IP	BFP	H	R	ER	HR	SH	SF	HB	TBB	IBB	SO	WP	Bk	W	L	Pct	Sh	Sv-Op	Hld	ERC	ERA
2011	Idaho	R+	19	2	0	6	39.2	179	42	20	15	0	0	1	2	15	0	56	9	0	3	1	.750	0	2--	-	3.66	3.40
2012	Idaho	R+	16	8	0	6	57.0	259	67	43	40	4	4	2	5	21	0	84	6	0	0	7	.000	0	2--	-	5.06	6.32
2013	Wilmg	A+	25	2	0	9	64.1	257	49	19	14	5	1	2	3	20	0	76	5	0	5	2	.714	0	2--	-	2.57	1.96
2013	NWArk	AA	12	0	0	1	18.0	66	9	4	3	1	2	0	3	6	1	27	0	0	0	0	-	0	1--	-	1.66	1.50
2014	Omha	AAA	34	0	0	27	46.1	188	26	21	21	9	2	1	2	22	2	60	2	1	4	3	.571	0	14--	-	2.71	4.08
2014	RdRck	AAA	15	0	0	13	16.0	67	16	6	6	1	1	1	0	3	1	25	3	0	1	1	.500	0	4--	-	2.86	3.38
2014	Tex	AL	9	0	0	2	9.1	35	6	1	1	0	0	0	0	2	0	8	0	0	1	0	1.000	0	0-0	2	1.29	0.96

Troy Patton

Pitches: L Bats: B Pos: RP-17   Ht: 6'1" Wt: 180 Born: 9/3/1985 Age: 29

			HOW MUCH HE PITCHED						WHAT HE GAVE UP										THE RESULTS							
Year	Team	Lg	G	GS	CG	GF	IP	BFP	H	R	ER	HR	SH	SF	HB	TBB	IBB	SO	WP	Bk	W	L	Pct	Sh	Sv-Op	Hld	ERC	ERA
2014	Norfolk*	AAA	4	0	0	1	4.2	21	4	2	2	1	0	0	0	3	1	2	0	0	0	0	-	0	0--	-	4.60	3.86
2014	Padres*	R	3	2	0	0	3.0	10	1	0	0	0	0	0	0	0	0	4	0	0	0	0	-	0	0--	-	0.25	0.00
2014	SnAnt*	AA	2	1	0	0	2.0	8	2	0	0	0	0	0	0	0	0	4	0	0	0	0	-	0	0--	-	1.95	0.00
2007	Hou	NL	3	2	0	1	12.2	54	10	6	5	3	1	0	2	4	0	8	0	0	0	2	.000	0	0-0	0	4.04	3.55
2010	Bal	AL	1	0	0	0	0.2	4	1	0	0	0	0	0	0	1	0	1	0	0	0	0	-	0	0-0	0	10.76	0.00
2011	Bal	AL	20	0	0	4	30.0	119	25	10	10	2	1	1	0	5	1	22	0	0	2	1	.667	0	0-0	2	2.09	3.00
2012	Bal	AL	54	0	0	12	55.2	224	45	15	15	5	0	1	2	12	2	49	1	0	1	0	1.000	0	0-1	9	2.39	2.43
2013	Bal	AL	56	0	0	8	56.0	235	57	25	23	8	2	3	1	16	1	42	0	0	1	0	1.000	0	0-1	8	4.29	3.70

Year	Team	Lg	G	GS	CG	GF	IP	BFP	H	R	ER	HR	SH	SF	HB	TBB	IBB	SO	WP	Bk	W	L	Pct	Sh	Sv-Op	Hld	ERC	ERA
HOW MUCH HE PITCHED									**WHAT HE GAVE UP**												**THE RESULTS**							
2014 2 Tms			17	0	0	7	14.0	63	16	8	8	2	0	0	0	5	1	13	0	0	0	1	.000	0	0-0	1	4.80	5.14
14 Bal	AL		9	0	0	3	6.2	31	9	6	6	1	0	0	0	4	1	5	0	0	0	1	.000	0	0-0	1	7.47	8.10
14 SD	NL		8	0	0	4	7.1	32	7	2	2	1	0	0	0	1	0	8	0	0	0	0	-	0	0-0	0	2.76	2.45
Postseason			3	0	0	0	2.0	11	3	1	1	1	0	0	0	2	0	3	0	0	0	0	-	0	0-0	0	13.58	4.50
6 ML YEARS			151	2	0	32	169.0	699	154	64	61	20	4	5	7	43	5	135	1	0	5	4	.556	0	0-2	20	3.26	3.25

Xavier Paul

Bats: L Throws: R Pos: PH-10;LF-5;PR-1   ZAY-vyer   Ht: 5'9" Wt: 205 Born: 2/25/1985 Age: 30

Year	Team	Lg	G	AB	H	2B	3B	HR	(Hm	Rd)	TB	R	RBI	RC	TBB	IBB	SO	HBP	SH	SF	SB	CS	GDP	Avg	OBP	Slg	OPS
									BATTING												**RUNNING**			**AVERAGES**			
2014 Norfolk*	AAA		81	295	75	12	2	12	(-	-)	127	45	56	42	27	0	83	2	0	5	1	1	9	.254	.316	.431	.747
2014 Reno*	AAA		1	4	0	0	0	0	(-	-)	0	0	1	0	0	0	0	0	0	1	0	0	0	.000	.000	.000	.000
2009 LAD	NL		11	14	3	1	0	1	(0	1)	7	3	1	0	2	0	4	0	0	0	0	1	1	.214	.313	.500	.813
2010 LAD	NL		44	121	28	8	1	0	(0	0)	38	16	11	8	8	0	24	0	3	1	3	1	3	.231	.277	.314	.591
2011 2 Tms	NL		128	243	62	6	5	2	(1	1)	84	30	20	24	13	1	62	0	5	1	16	6	2	.255	.292	.346	.638
2012 Cin	NL		55	86	27	5	1	2	(1	1)	40	8	7	12	9	1	18	0	1	0	4	2	2	.314	.379	.465	.844
2013 Cin	NL		97	209	51	12	0	7	(4	3)	84	24	32	27	27	3	53	3	0	0	1	6	6	.244	.339	.402	.741
2014 Ari	NL		14	20	2	0	0	0	(0	0)	2	2	0	1	1	1	8	0	0	0	0	0	0	.100	.143	.100	.243
11 LAD	NL		7	11	3	0	0	0	(0	0)	3	0	0	1	0	0	5	0	0	0	0	0	0	.273	.273	.273	.545
11 Pit	NL		121	232	59	6	5	2	(1	1)	81	30	20	23	13	1	57	0	5	1	16	6	2	.254	.293	.349	.642
Postseason			3	3	1	0	0	0	(0	0)	1	1	0	0	0	0	1	0	0	0	0	0	0	.333	.333	.333	.667
6 ML YEARS			349	693	173	32	7	12	(6	6)	255	83	71	71	60	6	169	3	9	2	23	11	14	.250	.311	.368	.679

Felipe Paulino

Pitches: R Bats: R Pos: SP-4   paul-EE-no   Ht: 6'3" Wt: 270 Born: 10/5/1983 Age: 31

Year	Team	Lg	G	GS	CG	GF	IP	BFP	H	R	ER	HR	SH	SF	HB	TBB	IBB	SO	WP	Bk	W	L	Pct	Sh	Sv-Op	Hld	ERC	ERA
							HOW MUCH HE PITCHED					**WHAT HE GAVE UP**											**THE RESULTS**					
2014 Charltt*	AAA		5	5	0	0	19.2	102	29	24	21	5	0	2	1	16	0	16	1	0	0	3	.000	0	0- --		10.61	9.61
2007 Hou	NL		5	3	0	0	19.0	85	22	15	15	5	2	0	0	7	1	11	1	0	2	1	.667	0	0-0	1	5.93	7.11
2009 Hou	NL		23	17	0	0	97.2	448	126	73	68	20	8	1	4	37	2	93	5	0	3	11	.214	0	0-1	0	6.70	6.27
2010 Hou	NL		19	14	0	0	91.2	411	95	63	52	4	6	3	3	46	4	83	6	1	1	9	.100	0	0-1	1	4.29	5.11
2011 2 Tms			39	20	0	8	139.1	599	146	74	69	13	5	7	8	55	2	133	7	1	4	10	.286	0	0-1	2	4.60	4.46
2012 KC	AL		7	7	0	0	37.2	156	31	8	7	3	1	1	0	15	0	39	1	0	3	1	.750	0	0-0	0	2.99	1.67
2014 CWS	AL		4	4	0	0	18.1	103	35	24	23	6	0	0	1	12	1	14	2	0	0	2	.000	0	0-0	0	13.27	11.29
11 Col			18	0	0	8	14.2	68	23	12	12	3	0	1	0	7	0	14	1	0	0	4	.000	0	0-1	2	9.44	7.36
11 KC	AL		21	20	0	0	124.2	531	123	62	57	10	5	6	8	48	2	119	6	1	4	6	.400	0	0-0	0	4.11	4.11
6 ML YEARS			97	65	0	8	403.2	1802	455	257	234	51	22	12	16	172	10	373	22	2	13	34	.277	0	0-3	4	5.27	5.22

Ben Paulsen

Bats: L Throws: R Pos: 1B-15;PH-14;RF-3   Ht: 6'4" Wt: 205 Born: 10/27/1987 Age: 27

Year	Team	Lg	G	AB	H	2B	3B	HR	(Hm	Rd)	TB	R	RBI	RC	TBB	IBB	SO	HBP	SH	SF	SB	CS	GDP	Avg	OBP	Slg	OPS
									BATTING												**RUNNING**			**AVERAGES**			
2010 Mdest	A+		130	498	155	29	8	12	(-	-)	236	65	83	83	33	3	113	3	0	7	5	4	10	.311	.353	.474	.827
2011 Tulsa	AA		136	547	132	29	4	19	(-	-)	226	69	78	68	40	6	132	4	2	4	2	3	8	.241	.296	.413	.709
2012 Tulsa	AA		120	436	110	18	3	13	(-	-)	173	58	53	54	37	3	113	2	0	3	1	4	9	.252	.312	.397	.709
2013 ColSpr	AAA		123	459	134	32	10	18	(-	-)	240	64	79	82	37	2	128	2	0	4	2	2	7	.292	.345	.523	.867
2014 ColSpr	AAA		117	435	128	32	6	20	(-	-)	232	76	76	87	58	4	119	2	0	2	4	5	10	.294	.378	.533	.912
2014 Col	NL		31	63	20	4	0	4	(1	3)	36	8	10	11	2	1	19	1	0	0	0	0	1	.317	.348	.571	.920

James Paxton

Pitches: L Bats: L Pos: SP-13   Ht: 6'4" Wt: 220 Born: 11/6/1988 Age: 26

Year	Team	Lg	G	GS	CG	GF	IP	BFP	H	R	ER	HR	SH	SF	HB	TBB	IBB	SO	WP	Bk	W	L	Pct	Sh	Sv-Op	Hld	ERC	ERA
							HOW MUCH HE PITCHED					**WHAT HE GAVE UP**											**THE RESULTS**					
2011 Clinton	A		10	10	0	0	56.0	235	45	21	17	1	3	1	1	30	0	80	6	0	3	3	.500	0	0- --		3.08	2.73
2011 Jacksn	AA		7	7	0	0	39.0	153	28	10	8	2	0	0	1	13	0	51	3	1	3	0	1.000	0	0- --		2.23	1.85
2012 Jacksn	AA		21	21	0	0	106.1	453	96	43	36	5	1	4	1	54	0	110	13	1	9	4	.692	0	0- --		3.68	3.05
2013 Tacom	AAA		28	26	2	0	145.2	640	158	84	72	10	3	5	3	58	0	131	14	0	8	11	.421	1	0- --		4.41	4.45
2014 Tacom	AAA		3	3	0	0	10.1	50	13	7	5	2	0	0	0	6	0	14	0	0	1	0	1.000	0	0- --		6.97	4.35
2014 Everett	A-		1	1	0	0	2.2	10	2	2	2	1	0	0	0	1	0	2	1	0	0	1	.000	0	0- --		4.74	6.75
2013 Sea	AL		4	4	0	0	24.0	94	15	5	4	2	0	0	0	7	2	21	0	0	3	0	1.000	0	0-0	0	1.61	1.50
2014 Sea	AL		13	13	0	0	74.0	303	60	29	25	3	3	1	1	29	2	59	7	0	6	4	.600	0	0-0	0	2.69	3.04
2 ML YEARS			17	17	0	0	98.0	397	75	34	29	5	3	1	1	36	4	80	7	0	9	4	.692	0	0-0	0	2.41	2.66

Brad Peacock

Pitches: R Bats: R Pos: SP-24; RP-4   Ht: 6'1" Wt: 210 Born: 2/2/1988 Age: 27

Year	Team	Lg	G	GS	CG	GF	IP	BFP	H	R	ER	HR	SH	SF	HB	TBB	IBB	SO	WP	Bk	W	L	Pct	Sh	Sv-Op	Hld	ERC	ERA
							HOW MUCH HE PITCHED					**WHAT HE GAVE UP**											**THE RESULTS**					
2014 OKCity*	AAA		1	1	0	0	5.2	25	7	3	3	1	0	0	0	1	0	5	0	0	1	0	1.000	0	0- --		4.94	4.76
2011 Was	NL		3	2	0	0	12.0	48	7	1	1	0	0	0	0	6	0	4	1	0	2	0	1.000	0	0-1	0	1.71	0.75
2013 Hou	AL		18	14	0	1	83.1	365	78	51	48	15	1	1	3	37	0	77	4	0	5	6	.455	0	0-0	2	4.54	5.18
2014 Hou	AL		28	24	0	3	131.2	589	136	80	69	20	0	6	4	70	4	119	6	0	4	9	.308	0	0-0	1	5.29	4.72
3 ML YEARS			49	40	0	4	227.0	1002	221	132	118	35	1	7	7	113	4	200	11	0	11	15	.423	0	0-1	3	4.80	4.68

Steve Pearce

Bats: R **Throws:** R **Pos:** 1B-51;LF-35;PH-13;RF-8;DH-8   **Ht:** 5'11" **Wt:** 210 **Born:** 4/13/1983 **Age:** 32

Year	Team	Lg	G	AB	H	2B	3B	HR	(Hm	Rd)	TB	R	RBI	RC	TBB	IBB	SO	HBP	SH	SF	SB	CS	GDP	Avg	OBP	Slg	OPS
2007	Pit	NL	23	68	20	5	1	0	(0	0)	27	13	6	9	5	0	12	0	0	0	2	1	2	.294	.342	.397	.740
2008	Pit	NL	37	109	27	7	0	4	(0	4)	46	6	15	13	5	0	22	3	0	2	2	0	1	.248	.294	.422	.716
2009	Pit	NL	60	165	34	13	1	4	(3	1)	61	19	16	17	21	0	43	0	0	0	1	0	2	.206	.296	.370	.665
2010	Pit	NL	15	29	8	2	1	0	(0	0)	12	4	5	5	7	0	6	0	0	2	0	0	0	.276	.395	.414	.809
2011	Pit	NL	50	94	19	2	0	1	(1	0)	24	8	10	5	7	0	21	1	1	2	0	0	6	.202	.260	.255	.515
2012	3 Tms		61	159	38	8	1	4	(2	2)	60	16	26	24	20	1	41	3	2	4	1	2	4	.239	.328	.377	.705
2013	Bal	AL	44	119	31	7	0	4	(3	1)	50	14	13	20	15	2	25	4	0	0	1	0	0	.261	.362	.420	.782
2014	Bal	AL	102	338	99	26	0	21	(12	9)	188	51	49	66	40	1	76	4	0	1	5	0	4	.293	.373	.556	.930
12	Bal	AL	28	71	18	4	0	3	(2	1)	31	8	14	12	8	0	17	0	2	2	0	1	1	.254	.321	.437	.758
12	Hou	AL	21	63	16	4	1	0	(0	0)	22	8	2	8	9	1	16	3	0	2	1	1	3	.254	.347	.349	.696
12	NYY	AL	12	25	4	0	0	1	(0	1)	7	6	4	3	5	0	8	0	0	0	0	0	0	.160	.300	.280	.580
8 ML YEARS			392	1081	276	70	4	38	(21	17)	468	131	140	159	120	4	246	15	3	11	12	3	19	.255	.335	.433	.768

Jake Peavy

Pitches: R **Bats:** R **Pos:** SP-32   **Ht:** 6'1" **Wt:** 195 **Born:** 5/31/1981 **Age:** 34

			HOW MUCH HE PITCHED						WHAT HE GAVE UP												THE RESULTS							
Year	Team	Lg	G	GS	CG	GF	IP	BFP	H	R	ER	HR	SH	SF	HB	TBB	IBB	SO	WP	Bk	W	L	Pct	Sh	Sv-Op	Hld	ERC	ERA
2002	SD	NL	17	17	0	0	97.2	430	106	54	49	11	5	2	3	33	4	90	4	1	6	7	.462	0	0-0	0	4.41	4.52
2003	SD	NL	32	32	0	0	194.2	827	173	94	89	33	7	5	6	82	3	156	2	0	12	11	.522	0	0-0	0	4.13	4.11
2004	SD	NL	27	27	0	0	166.1	694	146	49	42	13	5	6	11	53	4	173	1	1	15	6	.714	0	0-0	0	3.18	2.27
2005	SD	NL	30	30	3	0	203.0	812	162	70	65	18	4	5	7	50	3	216	3	1	13	7	.650	3	0-0	0	2.49	2.88
2006	SD	NL	32	32	2	0	202.1	846	187	93	92	23	5	1	6	62	11	215	4	0	11	14	.440	0	0-0	0	3.42	4.09
2007	SD	NL	34	34	0	0	223.1	898	169	67	63	13	5	7	6	68	5	240	4	0	19	6	.760	0	0-0	0	2.27	2.54
2008	SD	NL	27	27	1	0	173.2	709	146	57	55	17	7	1	5	59	1	166	6	0	10	11	.476	0	0-0	0	3.12	2.85
2009	2 Tms		16	16	1	0	101.2	410	80	41	39	8	3	2	1	34	0	110	2	2	9	6	.600	0	0-0	0	2.63	3.45
2010	CWS	AL	17	17	1	0	107.0	450	98	55	55	13	1	5	5	34	2	93	2	1	7	6	.538	1	0-0	0	3.59	4.63
2011	CWS	AL	19	18	1	0	111.2	470	117	61	61	10	1	5	3	24	4	95	4	0	7	7	.500	1	0-0	0	3.59	4.92
2012	CWS	AL	32	32	4	0	219.0	882	191	88	82	27	1	6	10	49	1	194	3	2	11	12	.478	1	0-0	0	3.07	3.37
2013	2 Tms	AL	23	23	2	0	144.2	590	130	70	67	20	2	3	2	36	0	121	0	2	12	5	.706	0	0-0	0	3.25	4.17
2014	2 Tms	AL	32	32	0	0	202.2	852	196	91	84	23	8	11	9	63	2	158	5	2	7	13	.350	0	0-0	0	3.83	3.73
09	SD	NL	13	13	1	0	81.2	335	69	38	36	7	2	2	1	28	0	92	2	1	6	6	.500	0	0-0	0	3.00	3.97
09	CWS	AL	3	3	0	0	20.0	75	11	3	3	1	1	0	0	6	0	18	0	1	3	0	1.000	0	0-0	0	1.38	1.35
13	CWS	AL	13	13	1	0	80.0	324	74	41	38	14	1	2	1	17	0	76	0	1	8	4	.667	0	0-0	0	3.49	4.28
13	Bos	AL	10	10	1	0	64.2	266	56	29	29	6	1	1	1	19	0	45	0	1	4	1	.800	0	0-0	0	2.96	4.04
14	Bos	AL	20	20	0	0	124.0	538	131	67	65	20	4	5	3	46	1	100	2	1	1	9	.100	0	0-0	0	4.83	4.72
14	SF	NL	12	12	0	0	78.2	314	65	24	19	3	4	6	6	17	1	58	3	1	6	4	.600	0	0-0	0	2.40	2.17
Postseason			5	5	0	0	22.1	105	35	23	23	3	2	1	0	8	3	13	1	0	0	3	.000	0	0-0	0	7.56	9.27
13 ML YEARS			338	337	15	0	2147.2	8870	1901	890	843	229	54	59	74	647	40	2027	40	12	139	111	.556	6	0-0	0	3.24	3.53

Joc Pederson

Bats: L **Throws:** L **Pos:** PH-8;CF-7;RF-5;LF-2;PR-2   JOCK   **Ht:** 6'1" **Wt:** 185 **Born:** 4/21/1992 **Age:** 23

Year	Team	Lg	G	AB	H	2B	3B	HR	(Hm	Rd)	TB	R	RBI	RC	TBB	IBB	SO	HBP	SH	SF	SB	CS	GDP	Avg	OBP	Slg	OPS
2010	Ddgrs	R	3	7	0	0	0	0	(-	-)	0	1	0	0	4	0	5	1	0	0	0	0	0	.000	.417	.000	.417
2011	Gt Lks	A	16	50	8	0	0	0	(-	-)	8	4	1	3	7	0	9	2	1	0	2	0	3	.160	.288	.160	.448
2011	Ogden	R+	68	266	94	20	2	11	(-	-)	151	54	64	66	36	3	54	3	0	5	24	5	2	.353	.429	.568	.997
2012	RCuca	A+	110	434	136	26	4	18	(-	-)	224	96	70	89	51	1	81	10	2	2	26	14	4	.313	.396	.516	.913
2013	Chatt	AA	123	439	122	24	3	22	(-	-)	218	81	58	89	70	5	114	5	2	3	31	8	4	.278	.381	.497	.878
2014	Albq	AAA	121	445	135	17	4	33	(-	-)	259	106	78	113	100	3	149	5	1	2	30	13	7	.303	.435	.582	1.017
2014	LAD	NL	18	28	4	0	0	0	(0	0)	4	1	0	1	9	0	11	0	1	0	0	0	1	.143	.351	.143	.494

Dustin Pedroia

Bats: R **Throws:** R **Pos:** 2B-135;PH-1;PR-1   peh-DROY-uh   **Ht:** 5'8" **Wt:** 165 **Born:** 8/17/1983 **Age:** 31

Year	Team	Lg	G	AB	H	2B	3B	HR	(Hm	Rd)	TB	R	RBI	RC	TBB	IBB	SO	HBP	SH	SF	SB	CS	GDP	Avg	OBP	Slg	OPS
2006	Bos	AL	31	89	17	4	0	2	(1	1)	27	5	7	3	7	0	7	1	1	0	1	0	1	.191	.258	.303	.561
2007	Bos	AL	139	520	165	39	1	8	(5	3)	230	86	50	79	47	1	42	7	5	2	7	1	8	.317	.380	.442	.823
2008	Bos	AL	157	653	213	54	2	17	(7	10)	322	118	83	107	50	1	52	7	7	9	20	1	17	.326	.376	.493	.869
2009	Bos	AL	154	626	185	48	1	15	(10	5)	280	115	72	104	74	3	45	5	3	6	20	8	19	.296	.371	.447	.819
2010	Bos	AL	75	302	87	24	1	12	(4	8)	149	53	41	52	37	1	38	4	2	6	9	1	7	.288	.367	.493	.860
2011	Bos	AL	159	635	195	37	3	21	(13	8)	301	102	91	114	86	6	85	1	2	7	26	8	12	.307	.387	.474	.861
2012	Bos	AL	141	563	163	39	3	15	(9	6)	253	81	65	84	48	3	60	5	1	6	20	6	9	.290	.347	.449	.797
2013	Bos	AL	160	641	193	42	2	9	(7	2)	266	91	84	99	73	4	75	3	0	7	17	5	24	.301	.372	.415	.787
2014	Bos	AL	135	551	153	33	0	7	(2	5)	207	72	53	65	51	1	75	1	0	6	6	6	14	.278	.337	.376	.712
Postseason			44	178	44	13	0	5	(2	3)	72	30	25	22	19	0	25	2	1	2	3	1	4	.247	.323	.404	.728
9 ML YEARS			1151	4580	1371	320	13	106	(58	48)	2035	723	546	707	473	20	479	34	21	49	125	37	111	.299	.366	.444	.810

Carlos Peguero

Bats: L **Throws:** L **Pos:** RF-4   peh-GEHR-oh   **Ht:** 6'5" **Wt:** 250 **Born:** 2/22/1987 **Age:** 28

Year	Team	Lg	G	AB	H	2B	3B	HR	(Hm	Rd)	TB	R	RBI	RC	TBB	IBB	SO	HBP	SH	SF	SB	CS	GDP	Avg	OBP	Slg	OPS
2014	Omha*	AAA	104	368	98	17	1	30	(-	-)	207	64	76	73	45	4	138	3	0	2	11	4	9	.266	.349	.563	.912
2011	Sea	AL	46	143	28	3	2	6	(4	2)	53	14	19	12	8	2	54	3	0	1	0	1	0	.196	.252	.371	.622
2012	Sea	AL	17	56	10	2	1	2	(1	1)	20	2	7	5	1	0	28	0	0	0	0	0	0	.179	.193	.357	.550
2013	Sea	AL	2	6	2	0	0	1	(1	0)	5	1	1	1	1	1	2	0	0	0	1	0	0	.333	.429	.833	1.262
2014	KC	AL	4	9	2	1	0	0	(0	0)	3	1	1	1	1	0	5	0	0	0	0	0	0	.222	.300	.333	.633
	4 ML YEARS		69	214	42	6	3	9	(6	3)	81	18	28	19	11	3	89	3	0	1	1	1	0	.196	.245	.379	.623

Mike Pelfrey

Pitches: R **Bats:** R **Pos:** SP-5   PELL-free   **Ht:** 6'7" **Wt:** 250 **Born:** 1/14/1984 **Age:** 31

Year	Team	Lg	G	GS	CG	GF	IP	BFP	H	R	ER	HR	SH	SF	HB	TBB	IBB	SO	WP	Bk	W	L	Pct	Sh	Sv-Op	Hld	ERC	ERA
2014	Roch*	AAA	2	2	0	0	10.0	40	9	1	1	0	0	0	1	3	0	3	0	0	1	0	1.000	0	0- -	-	3.04	0.90
2006	NYM	NL	4	4	0	0	21.1	99	25	14	13	1	1	1	3	12	0	13	2	0	2	1	.667	0	0-0	0	6.05	5.48
2007	NYM	NL	15	13	0	0	72.2	342	85	47	45	6	6	3	9	39	1	45	3	0	3	8	.273	0	0-0	0	5.99	5.57
2008	NYM	NL	32	32	2	0	200.2	851	209	86	83	12	11	5	13	64	1	110	2	0	13	11	.542	0	0-0	0	4.04	3.72
2009	NYM	NL	31	31	0	0	184.1	824	213	112	103	18	8	5	7	66	8	107	1	6	10	12	.455	0	0-0	0	4.83	5.03
2010	NYM	NL	34	33	0	1	204.0	870	213	88	83	12	17	4	6	68	5	113	1	1	15	9	.625	0	1-1	0	3.89	3.66
2011	NYM	NL	34	33	2	0	193.2	860	220	111	102	21	10	8	7	65	7	105	2	2	7	13	.350	0	0-0	0	4.70	4.74
2012	NYM	NL	3	3	0	0	19.2	85	24	5	5	0	1	0	0	4	0	13	1	0	0	0	-	0	0-0	0	3.82	2.29
2013	Min	AL	29	29	0	0	152.2	680	184	92	88	13	1	7	6	53	0	101	1	0	5	13	.278	0	0-0	0	5.13	5.19
2014	Min	AL	5	5	0	0	23.2	119	29	23	21	5	2	2	2	18	0	10	1	0	0	3	.000	0	0-0	0	8.18	7.99
	9 ML YEARS		187	183	4	1	1072.2	4730	1202	578	543	88	57	35	53	389	22	617	14	9	55	70	.440	0	1-1	0	4.67	4.56

Brayan Pena

Bats: B **Throws:** R **Pos:** 1B-53;C-46;PH-21;DH-1   BRIAN   **Ht:** 5'9" **Wt:** 230 **Born:** 1/7/1982 **Age:** 33

Year	Team	Lg	G	AB	H	2B	3B	HR	(Hm	Rd)	TB	R	RBI	RC	TBB	IBB	SO	HBP	SH	SF	SB	CS	GDP	Avg	OBP	Slg	OPS
2005	Atl	NL	18	39	7	2	0	0	(0	0)	9	2	4	4	1	1	7	0	0	0	0	0	1	.179	.200	.231	.431
2006	Atl	NL	23	41	11	2	0	1	(0	1)	16	9	5	4	2	0	5	0	0	0	0	0	2	.268	.302	.390	.693
2007	Atl	NL	16	33	7	0	0	1	(1	0)	10	2	3	0	0	0	3	0	0	0	0	1	2	.212	.212	.303	.515
2008	Atl	NL	14	14	4	1	0	0	(0	0)	5	3	0	0	1	0	2	0	0	0	0	0	0	.286	.333	.357	.690
2009	KC	AL	64	165	45	10	0	6	(3	3)	73	17	18	18	12	2	18	0	4	2	0	0	5	.273	.318	.442	.761
2010	KC	AL	60	158	40	10	0	1	(0	1)	53	11	19	16	12	0	27	1	1	2	2	0	8	.253	.306	.335	.642
2011	KC	AL	72	222	55	11	0	3	(0	3)	75	17	24	23	12	0	24	2	0	4	0	1	6	.248	.288	.338	.625
2012	KC	AL	68	212	50	10	1	2	(1	1)	68	16	25	19	9	0	24	0	1	4	0	1	7	.236	.262	.321	.583
2013	Det	AL	71	229	68	11	0	4	(1	3)	91	19	22	19	6	0	26	2	2	4	0	2	7	.297	.315	.397	.713
2014	Cin	NL	115	348	88	18	1	5	(3	2)	123	23	26	31	20	2	42	0	1	3	2	3	8	.253	.291	.353	.645
	Postseason		1	3	1	0	0	0	(0	0)	1	0	1	0	0	0	0	0	0	0	0	0	1	.333	.333	.333	.667
	10 ML YEARS		521	1461	375	75	2	23	(9	14)	523	119	146	130	75	5	178	5	9	19	4	7	46	.257	.292	.358	.650

Carlos Pena

Bats: L **Throws:** L **Pos:** 1B-16;PH-2   **Ht:** 6'2" **Wt:** 225 **Born:** 5/17/1978 **Age:** 37

Year	Team	Lg	G	AB	H	2B	3B	HR	(Hm	Rd)	TB	R	RBI	RC	TBB	IBB	SO	HBP	SH	SF	SB	CS	GDP	Avg	OBP	Slg	OPS
2014	RdRck*	AAA	20	74	22	3	0	4	(-	-)	37	12	8	12	5	1	15	1	0	0	0	0	2	.297	.350	.500	.850
2001	Tex	AL	22	62	16	4	1	3	(2	1)	31	6	12	11	10	0	17	0	0	0	0	0	1	.258	.361	.500	.861
2002	2 Tms	AL	115	397	96	17	4	19	(10	9)	178	43	52	56	41	0	111	3	0	2	2	2	7	.242	.316	.448	.764
2003	Det	AL	131	452	112	21	6	18	(8	10)	199	51	50	61	53	1	123	6	1	4	4	5	6	.248	.332	.440	.772
2004	Det	AL	142	481	116	22	4	27	(10	17)	227	89	82	73	70	2	146	3	2	5	7	1	11	.241	.338	.472	.810
2005	Det	AL	79	260	61	9	0	18	(14	4)	124	37	44	40	31	2	95	4	0	0	1	3	.235	.325	.477	.802
2006	Bos	AL	18	33	9	2	0	1	(1	0)	14	3	3	3	4	0	10	0	0	0	0	0	.273	.351	.424	.776
2007	TB	AL	148	490	138	29	1	46	(23	23)	307	99	121	114	103	10	142	10	1	8	1	0	7	.282	.411	.627	1.037
2008	TB	AL	139	490	121	24	2	31	(14	17)	242	76	102	92	96	7	166	12	0	9	1	1	6	.247	.377	.494	.871
2009	TB	AL	135	471	107	25	2	**39**	(19	20)	253	91	100	88	87	11	163	9	0	3	3	3	2	.227	.356	.537	.893
2010	TB	AL	144	484	95	18	0	28	(18	10)	197	64	84	73	87	4	158	7	0	4	5	1	2	.196	.325	.407	.732
2011	ChC	NL	153	493	111	27	3	28	(12	16)	228	72	80	79	101	7	161	4	1	7	2	2	6	.225	.357	.462	.819
2012	TB	AL	160	497	98	17	2	19	(11	8)	176	72	61	60	87	2	182	13	0	3	2	3	10	.197	.330	.354	.684
2013	2 Tms	AL	89	280	58	13	1	8	(4	4)	97	38	25	32	43	1	92	4	1	0	1	0	5	.207	.321	.346	.668
2014	Tex	AL	18	59	8	3	0	1	(1	0)	14	4	2	4	4	0	11	0	0	0	1	0	1	.136	.190	.237	.428
	02 Oak	AL	40	124	27	4	0	7	(5	2)	52	12	16	17	15	0	38	1	0	1	0	0	2	.218	.305	.419	.724
	02 Det	AL	75	273	69	13	4	12	(5	7)	126	31	36	39	26	0	73	2	0	1	2	2	5	.253	.321	.462	.783
	13 Hou	AL	85	277	58	13	1	8	(4	4)	97	38	25	32	43	5	89	4	1	0	1	3	5	.209	.324	.350	.674
	13 KC	AL	4	3	0	0	0	0	(0	0)	0	0	0	0	0	0	3	0	0	0	0	0	0	.000	.000	.000	.000
	Postseason		19	67	18	3	1	4	(0	4)	35	13	14	14	13	2	24	0	0	0	3	2	1	.269	.388	.522	.910
	14 ML YEARS		1493	4949	1146	231	26	286	(147	139)	2287	745	818	782	817	51	1577	75	6	45	29	22	71	.232	.346	.462	.808

Francisco Pena

Bats: R **Throws:** R **Pos:** C-1   **Ht:** 6'2" **Wt:** 230 **Born:** 10/12/1989 **Age:** 25

Year	Team	Lg	G	AB	H	2B	3B	HR	(Hm	Rd)	TB	R	RBI	RC	TBB	IBB	SO	HBP	SH	SF	SB	CS	GDP	Avg	OBP	Slg	OPS
2010	Mets	R	10	32	10	1	0	0	(-	-)	11	4	2	5	6	0	6	1	0	0	0	0	0	.313	.436	.344	.780
2010	StLuci	A+	10	37	10	2	0	0	(-	-)	12	3	7	3	2	0	12	0	0	1	0	0	1	.270	.300	.324	.624
2011	StLuci	A+	95	319	71	13	0	5	(-	-)	99	28	37	27	20	0	50	3	0	1	3	1	8	.223	.275	.310	.585
2012	StLuci	A+	41	142	36	10	1	4	(-	-)	60	19	22	19	11	0	29	0	1	1	0	0	1	.254	.305	.423	.728

Year Team	Lg	G	AB	H	2B	3B	HR	(Hm	Rd)	TB	R	RBI	RC	TBB	IBB	SO	HBP	SH	SF	SB	CS	GDP	Avg	OBP	Slg	OPS
								BATTING												**RUNNING**			**AVERAGES**			
2012 Bnghtn	AA	40	126	25	7	0	3	(-	-)	41	14	17	13	16	1	25	2	1	0	1	0	2	.198	.299	.325	.624
2013 Bnghtn	AA	21	69	17	6	0	0	(-	-)	23	4	4	7	7	1	4	1	1	1	0	1	6	.246	.321	.333	.654
2013 LsVgs	AAA	68	218	56	15	1	9	(-	-)	100	22	39	30	10	1	40	3	1	4	1	0	5	.257	.294	.459	.752
2014 Omha	AAA	96	342	82	13	0	27	(-	-)	176	53	61	50	16	1	65	5	2	5	0	3	12	.240	.280	.515	.795
2014 KC	AL	1	0	0	0	0	0	(0	0)	0	0	0	0	0	0	0	0	0	0	0	0	0	-	-	-	-

Ramiro Pena

Bats: B **Throws:** R **Pos:** 2B-38;3B-17;PH-17;SS-15;PR-2   **Ht:** 5'11" **Wt:** 200 **Born:** 7/18/1985 **Age:** 29

Year Team	Lg	G	AB	H	2B	3B	HR	(Hm	Rd)	TB	R	RBI	RC	TBB	IBB	SO	HBP	SH	SF	SB	CS	GDP	Avg	OBP	Slg	OPS
								BATTING												**RUNNING**			**AVERAGES**			
2009 NYY	AL	69	115	33	6	1	1	(1	0)	44	17	10	15	5	0	20	1	0	1	4	1	2	.287	.317	.383	.699
2010 NYY	AL	85	154	35	1	1	0	(1	0)	38	18	18	10	6	0	27	1	4	2	7	1	4	.227	.258	.247	.504
2011 NYY	AL	23	40	4	0	0	1	(1	0)	7	5	4	0	2	0	11	1	2	1	0	0	1	.100	.159	.175	.334
2012 NYY	AL	3	4	1	0	0	0	(0	0)	1	0	0	0	0	0	0	0	0	0	0	0	0	.250	.250	.250	.500
2013 Atl	NL	50	97	27	5	1	3	(2	1)	43	14	12	12	8	0	18	0	1	1	0	2	1	.278	.330	.443	.773
2014 Atl	NL	81	147	36	6	0	3	(2	1)	51	9	9	14	13	3	38	0	4	1	1	0	0	.245	.304	.347	.651
6 ML YEARS		311	557	136	18	3	8	(6	2)	184	63	53	51	34	3	114	2	12	5	12	4	8	.244	.288	.330	.618

Hunter Pence

Bats: R **Throws:** R **Pos:** RF-161;CF-1;PH-1   **Ht:** 6'4" **Wt:** 220 **Born:** 4/13/1983 **Age:** 32

Year Team	Lg	G	AB	H	2B	3B	HR	(Hm	Rd)	TB	R	RBI	RC	TBB	IBB	SO	HBP	SH	SF	SB	CS	GDP	Avg	OBP	Slg	OPS
								BATTING												**RUNNING**			**AVERAGES**			
2007 Hou	NL	108	456	147	30	9	17	(7	10)	246	57	69	77	26	0	95	1	0	1	11	5	10	.322	.360	.539	.899
2008 Hou	NL	157	595	160	34	4	25	(14	11)	277	78	83	82	40	2	124	4	0	3	11	10	14	.269	.318	.466	.783
2009 Hou	NL	159	585	165	26	5	25	(14	11)	276	76	72	80	58	1	109	1	0	3	14	11	25	.282	.346	.472	.818
2010 Hou	NL	156	614	173	29	3	25	(14	11)	283	93	91	89	41	2	105	0	0	3	18	9	11	.282	.325	.461	.786
2011 2 Tms	NL	154	606	190	38	5	22	(5	17)	304	84	97	102	56	3	124	1	0	5	8	2	15	.314	.370	.502	.871
2012 2 Tms	NL	160	617	156	26	4	24	(9	15)	262	87	104	81	56	2	145	7	1	7	5	2	15	.253	.319	.425	.743
2013 SF	NL	162	629	178	35	5	27	(10	17)	304	91	99	91	52	3	115	3	0	3	22	3	17	.283	.339	.483	.822
2014 SF	NL	162	650	180	29	10	20	(5	15)	289	106	74	96	52	3	130	3	0	3	13	6	13	.277	.332	.445	.777
11 Hou	NL	100	399	123	26	3	11	(4	7)	188	49	62	63	30	1	86	1	0	2	7	1	7	.308	.356	.471	.828
11 Phi	NL	54	207	67	12	2	11	(1	10)	116	35	35	39	26	2	38	0	0	3	1	1	8	.324	.394	.560	.954
12 Phi	NL	101	398	108	15	2	17	(7	10)	178	59	59	50	37	1	85	3	0	2	4	2	14	.271	.336	.447	.784
12 SF	NL	59	219	48	11	2	7	(2	5)	84	28	45	31	19	1	60	4	1	5	1	0	1	.219	.287	.384	.671
Postseason		21	81	17	2	0	1	(0	1)	22	10	8	3	4	1	19	0	0	1	2	1	2	.210	.244	.272	.516
8 ML YEARS		1218	4752	1349	247	45	185	(78	107)	2241	672	689	698	381	16	947	20	1	28	102	48	120	.284	.338	.472	.809

Cliff Pennington

Bats: B **Throws:** R **Pos:** SS-23;PH-19;2B-18;3B-8;PR-1   **Ht:** 5'10" **Wt:** 195 **Born:** 6/15/1984 **Age:** 31

Year Team	Lg	G	AB	H	2B	3B	HR	(Hm	Rd)	TB	R	RBI	RC	TBB	IBB	SO	HBP	SH	SF	SB	CS	GDP	Avg	OBP	Slg	OPS
								BATTING												**RUNNING**			**AVERAGES**			
2014 DBcks*	R	5	19	8	1	0	0	(-	-)	9	2	5	4	3	0	4	0	0	0	0	0	0	.421	.500	.474	.974
2014 Reno*	AAA	4	13	5	0	0	0	(-	-)	5	3	0	3	3	0	1	1	0	0	1	0	0	.385	.529	.385	.914
2008 Oak	AL	36	99	24	5	0	0	(0	0)	29	14	9	12	13	0	18	2	2	1	4	1	1	.242	.339	.293	.632
2009 Oak	AL	60	208	58	11	3	4	(3	1)	87	27	21	29	19	0	46	1	1	1	7	5	5	.279	.342	.418	.760
2010 Oak	AL	156	508	127	26	8	6	(2	4)	187	64	46	66	50	0	96	3	12	3	29	5	7	.250	.319	.368	.687
2011 Oak	AL	148	515	136	26	2	8	(3	5)	190	57	58	73	42	1	104	1	8	4	14	9	5	.264	.319	.369	.687
2012 Oak	AL	125	418	90	18	2	6	(0	6)	130	50	28	37	35	0	90	2	5	2	15	6	1	.215	.278	.311	.589
2013 Ari	NL	96	269	65	13	1	1	(1	0)	83	25	18	23	26	5	54	1	2	1	2	0	7	.242	.310	.309	.618
2014 Ari	NL	68	177	45	5	3	2	(1	1)	62	21	10	19	20	0	36	3	1	0	6	1	1	.254	.340	.350	.690
Postseason		5	14	4	0	0	0	(0	0)	4	1	1	2	3	0	4	0	0	0	0	0	0	.286	.412	.286	.697
7 ML YEARS		689	2194	545	104	19	27	(10	17)	768	258	190	259	205	6	444	13	31	11	77	27	27	.248	.315	.350	.665

Brad Penny

Pitches: R **Bats:** R **Pos:** SP-4; RP-4   **Ht:** 6'4" **Wt:** 230 **Born:** 5/24/1978 **Age:** 37

Year Team	Lg	G	GS	CG	GF	IP	BFP	H	R	ER	HR	SH	SF	HB	TBB	IBB	SO	WP	Bk	W	L	Pct	Sh	Sv-Op	Hld	ERC	ERA
		HOW MUCH HE PITCHED						**WHAT HE GAVE UP**												**THE RESULTS**							
2014 Jupiter*	A+	2	2	0	0	10.2	42	10	6	6	0	1	0	2	0	0	4	1	0	0	2	.000	0	0- -	-	2.03	5.06
2014 NewOr*	AAA	5	5	0	0	27.2	113	26	12	7	0	0	0	1	9	0	26	3	0	2	2	.500	0	0- -	-	3.03	2.28
2000 Fla	NL	23	22	0	0	119.2	529	120	70	64	13	6	2	5	60	4	80	4	1	8	7	.533	0	0-0	0	4.70	4.81
2001 Fla	NL	31	31	1	0	205.0	833	183	92	84	15	8	2	7	54	3	154	2	0	10	10	.500	1	0-0	0	2.96	3.69
2002 Fla	NL	24	24	1	0	129.1	574	148	76	67	18	6	4	1	50	7	93	4	0	8	7	.533	1	0-0	0	5.08	4.66
2003 Fla	NL	32	32	0	0	196.1	811	195	96	90	21	7	5	3	56	6	138	3	4	14	10	.583	0	0-0	0	3.73	4.13
2004 2 Tms	NL	24	24	0	0	143.0	590	130	55	50	12	3	3	3	45	6	111	5	0	9	10	.474	0	0-0	0	3.20	3.15
2005 LAD	NL	29	29	1	0	175.1	738	185	78	76	17	7	1	3	41	2	122	3	0	7	9	.438	0	0-0	0	3.77	3.90
2006 LAD	NL	34	33	0	0	189.0	813	206	94	91	19	8	3	9	54	4	148	6	0	16	9	.640	0	0-0	1	4.32	4.33
2007 LAD	NL	33	33	0	0	208.0	865	199	75	70	9	13	9	5	73	2	135	6	0	16	4	**.800**	0	0-0	0	3.41	3.03
2008 LAD	NL	19	17	0	1	94.2	426	112	68	66	13	10	2	3	42	0	51	1	1	6	9	.400	0	0-0	0	5.82	6.27
2009 2 Tms	NL	30	30	1	0	173.1	751	191	102	94	22	0	7	5	51	0	109	6	0	11	9	.550	0	0-0	0	4.54	4.88
2010 StL	NL	9	9	0	0	55.2	232	63	25	20	4	2	3	3	9	1	35	1	0	3	4	.429	0	0-0	0	3.95	3.23
2011 Det	AL	31	31	0	0	181.2	803	222	117	107	24	5	6	4	62	1	74	9	0	11	11	.500	0	0-0	0	5.53	5.30
2012 SF	NL	22	0	0	8	28.0	133	42	22	19	4	1	0	1	9	2	10	2	0	1	0	1.000	0	0-0	0	7.13	6.11
2014 Mia	NL	8	4	0	1	26.0	120	34	20	19	3	2	0	1	13	0	13	2	0	2	1	.667	0	0-0	0	6.80	6.58
04 Fla	NL	21	21	0	0	131.1	545	124	50	46	10	3	3	3	39	6	105	5	0	8	8	.500	0	0-0	0	3.26	3.15
04 LAD	NL	3	3	0	0	11.2	45	6	5	4	2	0	0	0	6	0	6	0	0	1	2	.333	0	0-0	0	2.51	3.09

			HOW MUCH HE PITCHED						WHAT HE GAVE UP												THE RESULTS							
Year	Team	Lg	G	GS	CG	GF	IP	BFP	H	R	ER	HR	SH	SF	HB	TBB	IBB	SO	WP	Bk	W	L	Pct	Sh	Sv-Op	Hld	ERC	ERA
09	Bos	AL	24	24	0	0	131.2	590	160	89	82	17	0	7	5	42	0	89	4	0	7	8	.467	0	0-0	0	5.35	5.61
09	SF	NL	6	6	1	0	41.2	161	31	13	12	5	0	0	0	9	0	20	2	0	4	1	.800	0	0-0	0	2.22	2.59
	Postseason		9	4	0	0	24.2	120	38	22	21	5	2	1	0	13	2	15	1	0	3	2	.600	0	0-1	0	8.87	7.66
	14 ML YEARS		349	319	4	10	1925.0	8218	2030	990	917	194	78	47	53	619	38	1273	54	6	121	101	.545	2	0-0	3	4.20	4.29

David Peralta

Bats: L **Throws:** L **Pos:** RF-40;LF-36;CF-14;PH-4;PR-1   **Ht:** 6'2" **Wt:** 215 **Born:** 8/14/1987 **Age:** 27

			BATTING																		RUNNING			AVERAGES			
Year	Team	Lg	G	AB	H	2B	3B	HR	(Hm	Rd)	TB	R	RBI	RC	TBB	IBB	SO	HBP	SH	SF	SB	CS	GDP	Avg	OBP	Slg	OPS
2011	RioGrnd	IND	85	339	133	30	5	17	(-	-)	224	76	81	89	19	0	44	7	2	6	7	2	-	.392	.429	.661	1.089
2012	Wichita	IND	98	377	125	30	5	3	(-	-)	174	65	70	72	36	1	36	5	0	5	25	8	-	.332	.392	.462	.854
2013	Amarill	IND	42	182	64	14	4	8	(-	-)	110	42	38	40	8	2	22	2	0	2	4	1	-	.352	.381	.604	.986
2013	Visalia	A+	51	208	72	15	0	8	(-	-)	111	29	42	40	9	0	28	0	0	2	1	0	8	.346	.370	.534	.904
2014	Mobile	AA	53	202	60	17	1	6	(-	-)	97	33	46	35	18	2	21	2	0	1	2	0	5	.297	.359	.480	.839
2014	Ari	NL	88	329	94	12	9	8	(5	3)	148	40	36	38	16	0	60	1	1	1	6	3	9	.286	.320	.450	.770

Jhonny Peralta

Bats: R **Throws:** R **Pos:** SS-152;PH-5;DH-1   pah-RALL-tah   **Ht:** 6'2" **Wt:** 215 **Born:** 5/28/1982 **Age:** 33

			BATTING																		RUNNING			AVERAGES			
Year	Team	Lg	G	AB	H	2B	3B	HR	(Hm	Rd)	TB	R	RBI	RC	TBB	IBB	SO	HBP	SH	SF	SB	CS	GDP	Avg	OBP	Slg	OPS
2003	Cle	AL	77	242	55	10	1	4	(3	1)	79	24	21	24	20	0	65	4	2	2	1	3	5	.227	.295	.326	.621
2004	Cle	AL	8	25	6	1	0	0	(0	0)	7	2	2	2	3	0	6	0	0	0	0	1	0	.240	.321	.280	.601
2005	Cle	AL	141	504	147	35	4	24	(14	10)	262	82	78	87	58	3	128	3	1	4	0	2	12	.292	.366	.520	.885
2006	Cle	AL	149	569	146	28	3	13	(7	6)	219	84	68	66	56	0	152	1	3	3	0	1	19	.257	.323	.385	.708
2007	Cle	AL	152	574	155	27	1	21	(16	5)	247	87	72	85	61	2	146	4	1	7	4	4	12	.270	.341	.430	.771
2008	Cle	AL	154	605	167	42	4	23	(11	12)	286	104	89	84	48	2	126	4	2	5	3	1	26	.276	.331	.473	.804
2009	Cle	AL	151	582	148	35	1	11	(2	9)	218	57	83	63	51	0	134	4	2	6	0	2	20	.254	.316	.375	.690
2010	2 Tms	AL	148	551	137	30	2	15	(4	11)	216	60	81	71	53	2	103	1	0	10	1	0	11	.249	.311	.392	.703
2011	Det	AL	146	525	157	25	3	21	(13	8)	251	68	86	77	40	2	95	2	0	9	0	2	17	.299	.345	.478	.824
2012	Det	AL	150	531	127	32	3	13	(6	7)	204	58	63	53	49	3	105	2	1	2	1	2	20	.239	.305	.384	.689
2013	Det	AL	107	409	124	30	0	11	(7	4)	187	50	55	62	35	2	98	1	1	2	3	3	9	.303	.358	.457	.815
2014	StL	NL	157	560	147	38	0	21	(8	13)	248	61	75	74	58	2	112	6	0	4	3	2	19	.263	.336	.443	.779
10	Cle	AL	91	334	82	23	2	7	(3	4)	130	37	43	41	32	1	69	1	0	6	1	0	7	.246	.308	.389	.698
10	Det	AL	57	217	55	7	0	8	(1	7)	86	23	38	30	21	1	34	0	0	4	0	0	4	.253	.314	.396	.710
	Postseason		45	166	47	13	0	8	(5	3)	84	15	24	24	10	0	33	1	1	1	2	0	6	.283	.326	.506	.832
	12 ML YEARS		1540	5677	1516	333	22	177	(91	86)	2424	737	773	748	532	18	1270	32	13	54	16	23	170	.267	.330	.427	.757

Joel Peralta

Pitches: R **Bats:** R **Pos:** RP-69   joe-ELL pah-RALL-tah   **Ht:** 5'11" **Wt:** 210 **Born:** 3/23/1976 **Age:** 39

			HOW MUCH HE PITCHED						WHAT HE GAVE UP												THE RESULTS							
Year	Team	Lg	G	GS	CG	GF	IP	BFP	H	R	ER	HR	SH	SF	HB	TBB	IBB	SO	WP	Bk	W	L	Pct	Sh	Sv-Op	Hld	ERC	ERA
2014	Charltt*	A+	1	1	0	0	1.0	4	1	0	0	0	0	0	0	1	0	0	0	0	0	0	-	0	0-	-	1.95	0.00
2005	LAA	AL	28	0	0	10	34.2	145	28	15	15	6	2	1	0	14	2	30	2	0	1	0	1.000	0	0-0	0	3.40	3.89
2006	KC	AL	64	0	0	21	73.2	304	74	37	36	10	1	3	2	17	2	57	5	0	1	3	.250	0	1-3	17	3.80	4.40
2007	KC	AL	62	0	0	18	87.2	366	93	39	37	9	2	4	2	19	5	66	2	0	1	3	.250	0	1-5	7	3.75	3.80
2008	KC	AL	40	0	0	12	52.2	224	56	37	35	15	1	3	2	14	0	38	1	0	1	2	.333	0	0-1	1	5.38	5.98
2009	Col	NL	27	0	0	6	24.2	113	27	17	17	3	0	1	3	12	2	22	0	0	0	3	.000	0	0-1	6	5.51	6.20
2010	Was	NL	39	0	0	10	49.0	189	30	12	11	5	2	1	1	9	4	49	0	0	1	0	1.000	0	0-2	9	1.43	2.02
2011	TB	AL	71	0	0	18	67.2	256	44	23	22	7	2	2	0	18	3	61	3	0	3	4	.429	0	6-8	19	1.84	2.93
2012	TB	AL	76	0	0	9	67.0	264	49	28	27	9	0	1	1	17	2	84	5	0	2	6	.250	0	2-5	37	2.36	3.63
2013	TB	AL	80	0	0	12	71.1	291	47	31	27	7	2	0	0	34	1	74	1	0	3	8	.273	0	1-4	41	2.53	3.41
2014	TB	AL	69	0	0	12	63.1	265	60	31	31	9	2	1	1	15	1	74	2	0	3	4	.429	0	1-7	18	3.41	4.41
	Postseason		6	0	0	2	5.2	23	4	0	0	0	0	0	0	3	0	4	1	0	0	0	-	0	0-1	1	2.41	0.00
	10 ML YEARS		556	0	0	128	591.2	2417	508	270	258	80	14	17	12	169	22	555	21	0	16	33	.327	0	12-36	155	3.13	3.92

Wily Peralta

Pitches: R **Bats:** R **Pos:** SP-32   **Ht:** 6'1" **Wt:** 245 **Born:** 5/8/1989 **Age:** 26

			HOW MUCH HE PITCHED						WHAT HE GAVE UP												THE RESULTS							
Year	Team	Lg	G	GS	CG	GF	IP	BFP	H	R	ER	HR	SH	SF	HB	TBB	IBB	SO	WP	Bk	W	L	Pct	Sh	Sv-Op	Hld	ERC	ERA
2012	Mil	NL	6	5	0	1	29.0	113	24	8	8	3	0	0	1	11	0	23	1	0	2	1	.667	0	0-0	0	2.61	2.48
2013	Mil	NL	32	32	2	0	183.1	802	187	107	89	19	11	3	7	73	3	129	12	0	11	15	.423	1	0-0	0	4.32	4.37
2014	Mil	NL	32	32	0	0	198.2	838	198	88	78	23	9	3	7	61	0	154	7	0	17	11	.607	0	0-0	0	3.98	3.53
	3 ML YEARS		70	69	2	1	411.0	1753	409	203	175	42	23	6	14	145	3	306	20	0	30	27	.526	1	0-0	0	4.03	3.83

Audry Perez

Bats: R **Throws:** R **Pos:** PH-1   AWE-dree   **Ht:** 5'9" **Wt:** 230 **Born:** 12/23/1988 **Age:** 26

			BATTING																		RUNNING			AVERAGES			
Year	Team	Lg	G	AB	H	2B	3B	HR	(Hm	Rd)	TB	R	RBI	RC	TBB	IBB	SO	HBP	SH	SF	SB	CS	GDP	Avg	OBP	Slg	OPS
2010	Batvia	A-	45	165	52	11	0	4	(-	-)	75	25	47	27	11	0	33	5	0	4	2	3	3	.315	.368	.455	.822
2011	PlmBh	A+	22	86	25	4	0	3	(-	-)	38	7	10	11	2	0	13	0	0	0	0	0	2	.291	.307	.442	.749
2011	Sprgfld	AA	59	230	60	15	0	8	(-	-)	99	28	37	28	5	0	29	2	3	3	0	0	6	.261	.279	.430	.710
2012	Sprgfld	AA	81	312	82	12	1	4	(-	-)	108	28	42	30	6	0	58	3	1	3	0	0	15	.263	.281	.346	.627
2013	Sprgfld	AA	57	215	45	12	0	6	(-	-)	75	16	26	16	3	1	39	4	0	0	0	1	13	.209	.234	.349	.583
2013	Memp	AAA	25	90	19	3	0	0	(-	-)	22	7	7	4	2	0	10	0	1	0	0	0	5	.211	.228	.244	.473

							BATTING													RUNNING			AVERAGES			
Year Team	Lg	G	AB	H	2B	3B	HR	(Hm Rd)	TB	R	RBI	RC	TBB	IBB	SO	HBP	SH	SF		SB	CS	GDP	Avg	OBP	Slg	OPS
2014 Memp	AAA	62	236	69	12	0	6	(- -)	99	27	33	29	4	0	34	0	3	5		0	1	9	.292	.298	.419	.717
2013 StL	NL	2	1	0	0	0	0	(0 0)	0	0	0	0	0	0	1	0	0	0		0	0	0	.000	.000	.000	.000
2014 StL	NL	1	0	0	0	0	0	(0 0)	0	0	0	0	1	0	0	0	0	0		0	0	0	-	1.000	-	-
2 ML YEARS		3	1	0	0	0	0	(0 0)	0	0	0	0	1	0	1	0	0	0		0	0	0	.000	.500	.000	.500

Chris Perez

Pitches: R Bats: R Pos: RP-49   Ht: 6'4" Wt: 230 Born: 7/1/1985 Age: 29

		HOW MUCH HE PITCHED						WHAT HE GAVE UP													THE RESULTS						
Year Team	Lg	G	GS	CG	GF	IP	BFP	H	R	ER	HR	SH	SF	HB	TBB	IBB	SO	WP	Bk	W	L	Pct	Sh	Sv-Op	Hld	ERC	ERA
2014 RCuca*	A+	4	2	0	0	5.0	20	6	5	5	0	0	0	0	1	0	2	0	0	0	1	.000	0	0- -	-	4.01	9.00
2008 StL	NL	41	0	0	23	41.2	177	34	18	16	5	1	3	1	22	0	42	2	0	3	3	.500	0	7-11	6	3.83	3.46
2009 2 Tms		61	0	0	16	57.0	239	41	28	27	8	0	2	6	27	0	68	8	0	1	2	.333	0	2-5	7	3.54	4.26
2010 Cle	AL	63	0	0	37	63.0	260	40	15	12	4	6	1	5	28	3	61	4	0	2	2	.500	0	23-27	9	2.30	1.71
2011 Cle	AL	64	0	0	57	59.2	248	46	24	22	5	4	1	3	26	4	39	1	0	4	7	.364	0	36-40	0	2.98	3.32
2012 Cle	AL	61	0	0	53	57.2	242	49	25	23	6	0	3	2	16	1	59	0	0	0	4	.000	0	39-43	0	2.85	3.59
2013 Cle	AL	54	0	0	41	54.0	243	56	27	26	11	5	0	4	21	2	54	1	0	5	3	.625	0	25-30	1	5.12	4.33
2014 LAD	NL	49	0	0	15	46.1	200	38	23	22	6	1	2	5	25	0	39	4	0	1	3	.250	0	1-2	6	4.32	4.27
09 StL	NL	29	0	0	8	23.2	106	17	12	11	3	0	1	3	15	0	30	4	0	1	1	.500	0	1-2	3	4.01	4.18
09 Cle	AL	32	0	0	8	33.1	133	24	16	16	5	0	1	3	12	0	38	4	0	0	1	.000	0	1-3	4	3.19	4.32
7 ML YEARS		393	0	0	242	379.1	1609	304	160	148	45	17	12	26	165	10	362	20	0	16	24	.400	0	133-158	29	3.46	3.51

Eury Perez

Bats: R Throws: R Pos: CF-2;RF-2   YERR-ee   Ht: 6'0" Wt: 190 Born: 5/30/1990 Age: 25

							BATTING													RUNNING			AVERAGES			
Year Team	Lg	G	AB	H	2B	3B	HR	(Hm Rd)	TB	R	RBI	RC	TBB	IBB	SO	HBP	SH	SF		SB	CS	GDP	Avg	OBP	Slg	OPS
2014 Syrcse*	AAA	57	212	66	13	2	1	(- -)	86	30	11	36	13	0	35	8	4	1		20	3	3	.311	.372	.406	.777
2014 Nats*	R	1	2	0	0	0	0	(- -)	0	0	0	0	0	0	1	0	0	0		0	0	0	.000	.000	.000	.000
2014 Ptomc*	A+	9	28	9	1	0	1	(- -)	13	6	4	5	3	0	4	0	2	0		6	1	0	.321	.387	.464	.851
2012 Was	NL	13	5	1	0	0	0	(0 0)	1	3	0	0	0	0	0	0	0	0		3	0	0	.200	.200	.200	.400
2013 Was	NL	9	8	1	0	0	0	(0 0)	1	1	0	0	0	0	3	0	0	0		1	0	0	.125	.125	.125	.250
2014 NYY	AL	4	10	2	0	0	0	(0 0)	2	2	0	1	0	0	3	0	0	0		1	0	0	.200	.200	.200	.400
3 ML YEARS		26	23	4	0	0	0	(0 0)	4	6	0	1	0	0	6	0	0	0		5	0	0	.174	.174	.174	.348

Hernan Perez

Bats: R Throws: R Pos: 2B-5;3B-2;SS-1;PH-1   HURR-nen   Ht: 6'1" Wt: 185 Born: 3/26/1991 Age: 24

							BATTING													RUNNING			AVERAGES			
Year Team	Lg	G	AB	H	2B	3B	HR	(Hm Rd)	TB	R	RBI	RC	TBB	IBB	SO	HBP	SH	SF		SB	CS	GDP	Avg	OBP	Slg	OPS
2014 Toledo*	AAA	133	547	157	32	7	6	(- -)	221	69	53	77	36	1	65	2	7	4		21	6	16	.287	.331	.404	.735
2012 Det	AL	2	2	1	0	0	0	(0 0)	1	1	0	0	0	0	0	0	0	0		0	0	0	.500	.500	.500	1.000
2013 Det	AL	34	66	13	0	1	0	(0 0)	15	13	5	4	2	0	15	0	2	1		1	0	2	.197	.217	.227	.445
2014 Det	AL	8	5	1	0	0	0	(0 0)	1	1	0	0	1	0	1	0	0	0		0	0	0	.200	.333	.200	.533
Postseason		2	0	0	0	0	0	(0 0)	0	1	0	0	0	0	0	0	0	0		0	0	0	-	-	-	-
3 ML YEARS		44	73	15	0	1	0	(0 0)	17	15	5	4	3	0	16	0	2	1		1	0	2	.205	.234	.233	.467

Juan Perez

Bats: R Throws: R Pos: LF-40;CF-17;PR-11;RF-5;PH-2   Ht: 5'11" Wt: 185 Born: 11/13/1986 Age: 28

							BATTING													RUNNING			AVERAGES			
Year Team	Lg	G	AB	H	2B	3B	HR	(Hm Rd)	TB	R	RBI	RC	TBB	IBB	SO	HBP	SH	SF		SB	CS	GDP	Avg	OBP	Slg	OPS
2010 SnJos	A+	131	551	164	37	10	13	(- -)	260	83	63	86	31	2	116	5	3	6		17	15	9	.298	.337	.472	.809
2011 Rchmd	AA	131	457	117	25	10	4	(- -)	174	58	40	56	28	0	95	4	5	3		22	6	10	.256	.303	.381	.684
2012 Rchmd	AA	126	483	146	26	4	11	(- -)	213	65	53	70	22	0	85	6	2	5		18	15	6	.302	.341	.441	.782
2013 Fresno	AAA	101	382	111	27	5	10	(- -)	178	52	50	59	15	0	75	5	4	3		18	6	5	.291	.323	.466	.789
2014 Fresno	AAA	48	177	56	13	0	7	(- -)	90	33	25	33	14	0	32	3	0	2		7	4	4	.316	.372	.508	.881
2013 SF	NL	34	89	23	5	0	1	(1 0)	31	8	8	10	6	0	21	0	1	1		2	0	3	.258	.302	.348	.650
2014 SF	NL	61	100	17	7	0	1	(0 1)	27	13	3	2	5	0	25	2	2	0		0	1	3	.170	.224	.270	.494
2 ML YEARS		95	189	40	12	0	2	(1 1)	58	21	11	12	11	0	46	2	3	1		2	1	6	.212	.261	.307	.568

Martin Perez

Pitches: L Bats: L Pos: SP-8   mar-TEEN   Ht: 6'0" Wt: 190 Born: 4/4/1991 Age: 24

		HOW MUCH HE PITCHED						WHAT HE GAVE UP													THE RESULTS						
Year Team	Lg	G	GS	CG	GF	IP	BFP	H	R	ER	HR	SH	SF	HB	TBB	IBB	SO	WP	Bk	W	L	Pct	Sh	Sv-Op	Hld	ERC	ERA
2012 Tex	AL	12	6	0	2	38.0	177	47	26	23	3	1	1	2	15	1	25	5	2	1	4	.200	0	0-0	0	5.33	5.45
2013 Tex	AL	20	20	1	0	124.1	529	129	55	50	15	2	3	3	37	0	84	9	2	10	6	.625	0	0-0	0	4.14	3.62
2014 Tex	AL	8	8	2	0	51.1	207	50	25	25	3	1	0	1	19	1	35	1	0	4	3	.571	2	0-0	0	3.82	4.38
3 ML YEARS		40	34	3	2	213.2	913	226	106	98	21	4	4	6	71	2	144	15	4	15	13	.536	2	0-0	0	4.27	4.13

Oliver Perez

Pitches: L **Bats:** L **Pos:** RP-68   **Ht:** 6'3" **Wt:** 220 **Born:** 8/15/1981 **Age:** 33

			HOW MUCH HE PITCHED						WHAT HE GAVE UP									THE RESULTS							
Year Team	Lg	G	GS	CG	GF	IP	BFP	H	R	ER	HR	SH	SF	HB	TBB	IBB	SO	WP	Bk	W	L	Pct	Sh	Sv-Op	Hld	ERC	ERA
2002 SD	NL	16	15	0	0	90.0	387	71	37	35	13	5	3	5	48	1	94	3	0	4	5	.444	0	0-0	0	3.93	3.50
2003 2 Tms	NL	24	24	0	0	126.2	579	129	80	77	22	5	2	4	77	3	141	7	1	4	10	.286	0	0-0	0	5.66	5.47
2004 Pit	NL	30	30	2	0	196.0	805	145	71	65	22	9	5	9	81	2	239	2	1	12	10	.545	1	0-0	0	2.99	2.98
2005 Pit	NL	20	20	0	0	103.0	471	102	68	67	23	5	4	6	70	1	97	3	0	7	5	.583	0	0-0	0	6.44	5.85
2006 2 Tms	NL	22	22	1	0	112.2	529	129	90	82	20	5	10	6	68	0	102	5	1	3	13	.188	1	0-0	0	6.62	6.55
2007 NYM	NL	29	29	0	0	177.0	765	153	90	70	22	4	7	7	79	1	174	6	0	15	10	.600	0	0-0	0	3.76	3.56
2008 NYM	NL	34	34	0	0	194.0	847	167	100	91	24	9	7	11	105	4	180	9	1	10	7	.588	0	0-0	0	4.21	4.22
2009 NYM	NL	14	14	0	0	66.0	324	69	51	50	12	5	4	4	58	2	62	2	0	3	4	.429	0	0-0	0	7.16	6.82
2010 NYM	NL	17	7	0	4	46.1	234	54	37	35	9	1	3	4	42	3	37	4	0	0	5	.000	0	0-0	0	8.27	6.80
2012 Sea	AL	33	0	0	6	29.2	123	27	7	7	1	1	1	0	10	2	24	2	0	1	3	.250	0	0-2	5	2.82	2.12
2013 Sea	AL	61	0	0	22	53.0	229	50	23	22	6	1	0	1	26	3	74	1	0	3	3	.500	0	2-3	8	4.23	3.74
2014 Ari	NL	68	0	0	11	58.2	256	50	25	19	5	4	0	7	24	2	76	3	3	3	4	.429	0	0-1	15	3.53	2.91
03 SD	NL	19	19	0	0	103.2	473	103	65	62	20	4	2	3	65	2	117	6	1	4	7	.364	0	0-0	0	5.74	5.38
03 Pit	NL	5	5	0	0	23.0	106	26	15	15	2	1	0	1	12	1	24	1	0	0	3	.000	0	0-0	0	5.29	5.87
06 Pit	NL	15	15	0	0	76.0	364	88	64	56	13	5	8	3	51	0	61	4	1	2	10	.167	0	0-0	0	6.85	6.63
06 NYM	NL	7	7	1	0	36.2	165	41	26	26	7	0	2	3	17	0	41	1	0	1	3	.250	1	0-0	0	6.16	6.38
Postseason		2	2	0	0	11.2	50	13	6	6	3	2	0	1	3	1	7	0	0	1	0	1.000	0	0-0	0	5.61	4.63
12 ML YEARS		368	195	3	43	1253.0	5549	1146	679	620	179	54	46	64	688	24	1300	47	7	65	79	.451	2	2-6	28	4.66	4.45

Roberto Perez

Bats: R **Throws:** R **Pos:** C-29   **Ht:** 5'11" **Wt:** 225 **Born:** 12/23/1988 **Age:** 26

							BATTING												RUNNING			AVERAGES			
Year Team	Lg	G	AB	H	2B	3B	HR	(Hm	Rd)	TB	R	RBI	RC	TBB	IBB	SO	HBP	SH	SF	SB	CS	GDP	Avg	OBP	Slg	OPS
2010 Lk Cty	A	118	378	82	22	3	6	(-	-)	128	54	38	53	80	0	88	5	2	1	1	2	13	.217	.360	.339	.699
2011 Knstn	A+	94	284	64	16	1	2	(-	-)	88	30	30	38	62	2	79	1	3	1	1	0	7	.225	.365	.310	.675
2012 Akron	AA	95	283	60	16	2	1	(-	-)	83	31	31	33	49	0	67	6	7	4	0	1	11	.212	.336	.293	.630
2013 Akron	AA	32	93	23	5	0	2	(-	-)	34	10	10	19	32	0	25	3	0	1	1	1	4	.247	.453	.366	.819
2013 Clmbs	AAA	67	187	33	12	0	0	(-	-)	45	16	24	12	22	0	59	3	6	4	0	1	6	.176	.269	.241	.509
2014 Clmbs	AAA	53	174	53	11	1	8	(-	-)	90	29	43	37	29	1	51	1	4	1	1	0	5	.305	.405	.517	.922
2014 Cle	AL	29	85	23	5	0	1	(1	0)	31	10	4	8	5	0	26	0	5	0	0	0	2	.271	.311	.365	.676

Salvador Perez

Bats: R **Throws:** R **Pos:** C-146;DH-4;PH-2   **Ht:** 6'3" **Wt:** 240 **Born:** 5/10/1990 **Age:** 25

							BATTING												RUNNING			AVERAGES			
Year Team	Lg	G	AB	H	2B	3B	HR	(Hm	Rd)	TB	R	RBI	RC	TBB	IBB	SO	HBP	SH	SF	SB	CS	GDP	Avg	OBP	Slg	OPS
2011 KC	AL	39	148	49	8	2	3	(1	2)	70	20	21	26	7	0	20	1	0	2	0	0	5	.331	.361	.473	.834
2012 KC	AL	76	289	87	16	0	11	(3	8)	136	38	39	36	12	3	27	1	0	3	0	0	14	.301	.328	.471	.798
2013 KC	AL	138	496	145	25	3	13	(6	7)	215	48	79	77	21	2	63	4	0	5	0	0	13	.292	.323	.433	.757
2014 KC	AL	150	578	150	28	2	17	(8	9)	233	57	70	55	22	2	85	3	0	3	1	0	22	.260	.289	.403	.692
4 ML YEARS		403	1511	431	77	7	44	(18	26)	654	163	209	194	62	7	195	9	0	13	1	0	54	.285	.315	.433	.748

Glen Perkins

Pitches: L **Bats:** L **Pos:** RP-63   **Ht:** 6'0" **Wt:** 205 **Born:** 3/2/1983 **Age:** 32

				HOW MUCH HE PITCHED						WHAT HE GAVE UP									THE RESULTS							
Year Team	Lg	G	GS	CG	GF	IP	BFP	H	R	ER	HR	SH	SF	HB	TBB	IBB	SO	WP	Bk	W	L	Pct	Sh	Sv-Op	Hld	ERC	ERA
2006 Min	AL	4	0	0	1	5.2	20	3	1	1	0	0	0	0	0	0	6	0	0	0	0	-	0	0-0	1	0.60	1.59
2007 Min	AL	19	0	0	3	28.2	115	23	10	10	2	1	1	2	12	0	20	2	0	0	0	-	0	0-0	3	3.32	3.14
2008 Min	AL	26	26	0	0	151.0	661	183	81	74	25	7	4	3	39	0	74	2	1	12	4	.750	0	0-0	0	5.30	4.41
2009 Min	AL	18	17	0	1	96.1	423	120	64	63	13	1	3	1	23	0	45	2	1	6	7	.462	0	0-0	0	5.14	5.89
2010 Min	AL	13	1	0	5	21.2	98	29	16	14	3	1	2	4	5	1	14	0	0	1	1	.500	0	0-0	0	6.56	5.82
2011 Min	AL	65	0	0	17	61.2	253	55	19	17	2	5	1	1	21	5	65	3	0	4	4	.500	0	2-5	17	2.81	2.48
2012 Min	AL	70	0	0	43	70.1	281	57	25	20	8	3	2	3	16	3	78	3	0	3	1	.750	0	16-20	11	2.63	2.56
2013 Min	AL	61	0	0	53	62.2	240	43	16	16	5	2	1	3	15	0	77	0	0	2	0	1.000	0	36-40	0	2.01	2.30
2014 Min	AL	63	0	0	56	61.2	260	62	29	25	7	2	5	2	11	2	66	3	0	4	3	.571	0	34-41	0	3.33	3.65
Postseason		1	0	0	0	0.1	3	2	0	0	0	0	0	0	0	0	0	0	0	0	0	-	0	0-0	0	39.65	0.00
9 ML YEARS		339	44	0	179	559.2	2351	575	261	240	65	22	19	19	142	11	445	15	2	32	20	.615	0	88-106	32	3.90	3.86

Vinnie Pestano

Pitches: R **Bats:** R **Pos:** RP-25   peh-STAH-no   **Ht:** 6'0" **Wt:** 200 **Born:** 2/20/1985 **Age:** 30

				HOW MUCH HE PITCHED						WHAT HE GAVE UP									THE RESULTS							
Year Team	Lg	G	GS	CG	GF	IP	BFP	H	R	ER	HR	SH	SF	HB	TBB	IBB	SO	WP	Bk	W	L	Pct	Sh	Sv-Op	Hld	ERC	ERA
2014 Clmbs*	AAA	32	0	0	16	30.1	126	23	8	6	0	2	1	1	12	0	37	1	0	2	4	.333	0	6- -	-	2.23	1.78
2014 Salt Lk*	AAA	6	0	0	2	8.0	37	7	3	2	1	0	0	1	4	1	12	1	0	1	1	.500	0	0- -	-	4.00	2.25
2010 Cle	AL	5	0	0	5	5.0	23	4	2	2	0	0	0	0	5	0	8	0	0	0	0	-	0	1-1	0	4.56	3.60
2011 Cle	AL	68	0	0	20	62.0	250	41	16	16	5	0	0	3	24	3	84	0	0	1	2	.333	0	2-6	23	2.26	2.32
2012 Cle	AL	70	0	0	13	70.0	286	53	20	20	7	0	2	4	24	1	76	1	0	3	3	.500	0	2-5	36	2.77	2.57
2013 Cle	AL	37	0	0	21	35.1	159	37	18	16	6	0	2	1	21	1	37	2	0	1	2	.333	0	6-9	6	5.84	4.08
2014 2 Tms	AL	25	0	0	5	18.2	78	18	8	6	3	0	1	0	5	0	26	2	0	0	1	.000	0	0-0	1	3.74	2.89
14 Cle	AL	13	0	0	2	9.0	40	13	7	5	2	0	0	0	1	0	13	1	0	0	0	-	0	0-0	0	6.43	5.00
14 LAA	AL	12	0	0	3	9.2	38	5	1	1	1	0	1	0	4	0	13	1	0	0	0	-	0	0-0	1	1.70	0.93
5 ML YEARS		205	0	0	64	191.0	796	153	64	60	21	0	5	8	79	5	231	5	0	5	8	.385	0	11-21	66	3.25	2.83

Jace Peterson

Bats: L Throws: R Pos: 2B-14;3B-10;PH-3;PR-3 JAYCE Ht: 6'0" Wt: 210 Born: 5/9/1990 Age: 25

Year	Team	Lg	G	AB	H	2B	3B	HR	(Hm	Rd)	TB	R	RBI	RC	TBB	IBB	SO	HBP	SH	SF	SB	CS	GDP	Avg	OBP	Slg	OPS
2011	Eugene	A-	73	276	67	9	5	2	(-	-)	92	48	27	42	50	1	53	2	2	3	39	10	4	.243	.360	.333	.693
2012	FtWyn	A	117	444	127	23	9	2	(-	-)	174	78	48	76	62	0	63	5	8	2	51	13	4	.286	.378	.392	.770
2013	Lk Els	A+	113	423	128	17	13	7	(-	-)	192	78	66	82	54	0	58	5	7	7	42	10	6	.303	.382	.454	.836
2014	ElPaso	AAA	68	248	76	21	6	2	(-	-)	115	44	39	49	42	0	50	1	6	2	12	6	3	.306	.406	.464	.870
2014	SnAnt	AA	18	74	23	3	0	1	(-	-)	29	10	7	11	9	0	9	0	0	1	4	3	1	.311	.386	.392	.777
2014	SD	NL	27	53	6	0	0	0	(0	0)	6	3	0	0	2	1	18	1	2	0	2	0	1	.113	.161	.113	.274

Gregorio Petit

Bats: R Throws: R Pos: SS-19;3B-12;2B-4;PR-3;DH-2;PH-2 peh-TEET Ht: 5'10" Wt: 195 Born: 12/10/1984 Age: 30

Year	Team	Lg	G	AB	H	2B	3B	HR	(Hm	Rd)	TB	R	RBI	RC	TBB	IBB	SO	HBP	SH	SF	SB	CS	GDP	Avg	OBP	Slg	OPS
2014	OKCity*	AAA	85	317	94	19	1	10	(-	-)	145	46	43	49	20	2	52	3	3	4	1	3	8	.297	.340	.457	.798
2008	Oak	AL	14	23	8	2	0	0	(0	0)	10	4	0	2	2	0	9	0	0	0	0	0	0	.348	.400	.435	.835
2009	Oak	AL	11	31	7	1	0	0	(0	0)	8	2	1	1	0	0	6	0	0	0	0	0	0	.226	.226	.258	.484
2014	Hou	AL	37	97	27	8	0	2	(1	1)	41	14	9	10	1	0	25	2	0	0	0	1	1	.278	.300	.423	.723
	3 ML YEARS		62	151	42	11	0	2	(1	1)	59	20	10	13	3	0	40	2	0	0	0	1	3	.278	.301	.391	.692

Yusmeiro Petit

Pitches: R Bats: R Pos: RP-27; SP-12 USE-mere-oh pa-TEET Ht: 6'1" Wt: 250 Born: 11/22/1984 Age: 30

			HOW MUCH HE PITCHED					WHAT HE GAVE UP										THE RESULTS						
Year	Team	Lg	G	GS	CG	GF	IP	BFP	H	R	ER	HR	SH	SF	HB	TBB	IBB	SO	WP	Bk	W	L	Pct	Sh	Sv-Op	Hld	ERC	ERA
2006	Fla	NL	15	1	0	5	26.1	129	46	28	28	7	1	1	0	9	1	20	0	0	1	1	.500	0	0-0	0	10.07	9.57
2007	Ari	NL	14	10	0	2	57.0	243	58	30	29	12	1	1	0	18	1	40	0	1	3	4	.429	0	0-0	0	4.56	4.58
2008	Ari	NL	19	8	0	6	56.1	229	45	29	27	12	4	2	1	14	2	42	3	1	3	5	.375	0	0-0	0	3.08	4.31
2009	Ari	NL	23	17	0	2	89.2	407	102	62	58	19	3	0	0	34	1	74	3	0	3	10	.231	0	0-0	0	5.44	5.82
2012	SF	NL	1	1	0	0	4.2	22	7	2	2	0	1	0	0	4	0	1	1	0	0	0	-	0	0-0	0	9.14	3.86
2013	SF	NL	8	7	1	0	48.0	196	46	19	19	4	2	0	0	11	1	47	0	0	4	1	.800	1	0-0	0	3.08	3.56
2014	SF	NL	39	12	1	14	117.0	461	97	51	48	12	0	3	1	22	5	133	0	0	5	5	.500	0	0-0	0	2.40	3.69
	7 ML YEARS		119	56	2	29	399.0	1687	401	221	211	66	12	7	2	112	11	357	7	2	19	26	.422	1	0-0	0	4.03	4.76

Jake Petricka

Pitches: R Bats: R Pos: RP-67 pet-RICH-kah Ht: 6'5" Wt: 205 Born: 6/5/1988 Age: 27

			HOW MUCH HE PITCHED					WHAT HE GAVE UP										THE RESULTS						
Year	Team	Lg	G	GS	CG	GF	IP	BFP	H	R	ER	HR	SH	SF	HB	TBB	IBB	SO	WP	Bk	W	L	Pct	Sh	Sv-Op	Hld	ERC	ERA
2010	Brs	R+	8	8	0	0	34.2	136	25	12	11	1	0	0	2	7	0	38	4	1	2	4	.333	0	0--	-	1.74	2.86
2010	Knapol	A	9	0	0	1	9.2	55	13	11	4	0	1	0	1	8	0	10	4	0	1	0	1.000	0	0--	-	6.72	3.72
2011	Knapol	A	8	8	0	0	41.2	169	39	14	13	0	0	3	0	13	0	48	4	0	3	1	.750	0	0--	-	2.82	2.81
2011	Brs	R+	2	1	0	0	4.0	14	4	0	0	0	0	0	0	0	0	5	0	0	0	0	-	0	0--	-	2.31	0.00
2011	WinSa	A+	13	13	0	0	67.2	303	71	39	33	3	4	1	3	26	0	46	5	0	4	7	.364	0	0--	-	3.96	4.39
2012	WinSa	A+	19	19	0	0	82.2	378	93	58	49	2	2	0	3	46	0	84	9	1	5	5	.500	0	0--	-	5.01	5.33
2012	Brham	AA	10	10	0	0	57.2	257	63	35	35	7	2	3	0	35	0	27	5	0	3	3	.500	0	0--	-	5.81	5.46
2013	Brham	AA	21	1	0	3	39.1	161	36	11	9	1	1	0	1	18	0	41	4	0	3	0	1.000	0	0--	-	3.61	2.06
2013	Charltt	AAA	10	0	0	4	15.1	62	9	2	2	0	0	1	0	7	0	17	1	0	2	0	1.000	0	1--	-	1.59	1.17
2013	CWS	AL	16	0	0	3	19.1	85	20	7	7	1	1	1	1	10	1	10	4	0	1	1	.500	0	0-1	0	4.18	3.26
2014	CWS	AL	67	0	0	33	73.0	307	67	24	24	3	3	4	2	33	4	55	2	0	1	6	.143	0	14-18	10	3.52	2.96
	2 ML YEARS		83	0	0	36	92.1	392	87	31	31	3	4	5	3	43	5	65	6	0	2	7	.222	0	14-19	10	3.66	3.02

Jonathan Pettibone

Pitches: R Bats: L Pos: SP-2 Ht: 6'6" Wt: 225 Born: 7/19/1990 Age: 24

			HOW MUCH HE PITCHED					WHAT HE GAVE UP										THE RESULTS						
Year	Team	Lg	G	GS	CG	GF	IP	BFP	H	R	ER	HR	SH	SF	HB	TBB	IBB	SO	WP	Bk	W	L	Pct	Sh	Sv-Op	Hld	ERC	ERA
2010	Lakwd	A	24	23	1	0	131.1	543	114	63	51	10	8	5	8	41	0	84	9	0	8	6	.571	0	0--	-	3.13	3.49
2011	Clwtr	A+	27	27	0	0	101.0	054	149	02	50	5	7	7	0	04	1	115	7	2	10	11	.476	0	0	-	2.68	2.06
2012	Rdng	AA	19	19	1	0	117.1	488	115	52	43	9	7	2	5	27	0	81	4	0	9	7	.563	0	0--	-	3.33	3.30
2012	LV	AAA	7	7	1	0	42.1	176	31	12	12	0	2	0	0	22	0	32	2	0	4	1	.800	1	0--	-	2.45	2.55
2013	LV	AAA	4	4	0	0	17.1	81	26	15	13	1	2	2	2	5	0	10	1	0	0	2	.000	0	0--	-	6.93	6.75
2013	Rdng	AA	1	1	0	0	5.0	20	5	3	3	0	1	0	0	1	0	4	0	0	0	0	-	0	0--	-	2.76	5.40
2014	LV	AAA	5	5	0	0	26.1	106	22	11	10	0	1	1	0	6	0	13	2	0	2	0	1.000	0	0--	-	1.96	3.42
2013	Phi	NL	18	18	0	0	100.1	437	109	50	45	9	8	2	5	38	3	66	1	0	5	4	.556	0	0-0	0	4.62	4.04
2014	Phi	NL	2	2	0	0	9.0	47	17	10	9	2	1	0	0	3	1	6	0	0	0	1	.000	0	0-0	0	10.08	9.00
	2 ML YEARS		20	20	0	0	109.1	484	126	60	54	11	9	2	5	41	4	72	1	0	5	5	.500	0	0-0	0	5.03	4.45

Thomas Pham

Bats: R Throws: R Pos: LF-2;PH-2;PR-2;RF-1 FAM Ht: 6'1" Wt: 175 Born: 3/8/1988 Age: 27

Year	Team	Lg	G	AB	H	2B	3B	HR	(Hm	Rd)	TB	R	RBI	RC	TBB	IBB	SO	HBP	SH	SF	SB	CS	GDP	Avg	OBP	Slg	OPS
2010	PlmBh	A+	68	237	62	14	4	3	(-	-)	93	42	27	40	42	0	59	3	1	2	13	4	8	.262	.377	.392	.769
2010	Sprgfld	AA	38	121	41	13	1	3	(-	-)	65	19	18	27	18	0	28	1	0	0	4	2	1	.339	.429	.537	.966
2011	Sprgfld	AA	40	142	42	11	3	5	(-	-)	74	31	16	27	18	0	39	1	2	2	3	3	6	.296	.374	.521	.895
2012	Sprgfld	AA	12	39	6	2	0	1	(-	-)	11	3	3	2	4	0	19	0	0	0	0	0	1	.154	.233	.282	.515

Year	Team	Lg	G	AB	H	2B	3B	HR	(Hm	Rd)	TB	R	RBI	RC	TBB	IBB	SO	HBP	SH	SF	SB	CS	GDP	Avg	OBP	Slg	OPS
2013	Sprgfld	AA	45	163	49	6	6	6	(-	-)	85	27	28	33	20	0	42	4	0	1	6	3	4	.301	.388	.521	.910
2013	Memp	AAA	30	106	28	6	1	1	(-	-)	39	6	13	12	7	0	25	0	0	0	2	1	4	.264	.310	.368	.678
2014	Memp	AAA	104	346	112	16	6	10	(-	-)	170	63	44	70	38	1	81	4	0	2	20	2	8	.324	.395	.491	.886
2014	StL	NL	6	2	0	0	0	0	(0	0)	0	0	0	0	0	0	2	0	0	0	0	0	0	.000	.000	.000	.000

Josh Phegley

Bats: R **Throws:** R **Pos:** C-11   FEG-lee   **Ht:** 5'10" **Wt:** 225 **Born:** 2/12/1988 **Age:** 27

Year	Team	Lg	G	AB	H	2B	3B	HR	(Hm	Rd)	TB	R	RBI	RC	TBB	IBB	SO	HBP	SH	SF	SB	CS	GDP	Avg	OBP	Slg	OPS
2010	WinSa	A+	25	89	26	3	0	3	(-	-)	38	16	12	13	7	0	22	0	1	2	0	0	3	.292	.337	.427	.764
2010	Brs	R+	5	15	3	1	0	0	(-	-)	4	1	1	1	2	0	4	1	0	0	0	0	1	.200	.333	.267	.600
2010	Brham	AA	18	72	21	4	0	2	(-	-)	31	7	13	10	2	1	22	1	3	1	0	0	4	.292	.316	.431	.746
2011	Brham	AA	94	364	88	21	2	7	(-	-)	134	43	50	40	23	1	61	4	0	3	1	2	8	.242	.292	.368	.660
2011	Charltt	AAA	22	79	19	4	0	2	(-	-)	29	9	6	10	8	0	18	2	1	0	0	0	3	.241	.326	.367	.693
2012	Charltt	AAA	102	394	105	22	1	6	(-	-)	147	40	48	47	20	1	60	4	0	3	3	0	10	.266	.306	.373	.680
2013	Charltt	AAA	61	231	73	18	1	15	(-	-)	138	39	41	50	15	0	38	7	0	5	1	1	5	.316	.368	.597	.966
2014	Charltt	AAA	107	419	115	30	4	23	(-	-)	222	69	75	75	31	1	72	8	2	7	0	1	9	.274	.331	.530	.861
2013	CWS	AL	65	204	42	7	0	4	(2	2)	61	14	22	12	5	0	41	0	0	2	2	0	6	.206	.223	.299	.522
2014	CWS	AL	11	37	8	2	0	3	(3	0)	19	4	7	2	0	0	11	0	0	1	0	0	0	.216	.211	.514	.724
	2 ML YEARS		76	241	50	9	0	7	(5	2)	80	18	29	14	5	0	52	0	2	3	2	0	6	.207	.221	.332	.553

Cord Phelps

Bats: B **Throws:** R **Pos:** PH-3   **Ht:** 6'1" **Wt:** 210 **Born:** 1/23/1987 **Age:** 28

Year	Team	Lg	G	AB	H	2B	3B	HR	(Hm	Rd)	TB	R	RBI	RC	TBB	IBB	SO	HBP	SH	SF	SB	CS	GDP	Avg	OBP	Slg	OPS
2014	Norfolk*	AAA	99	343	89	13	5	7	(-	-)	133	61	51	51	52	0	60	4	1	3	2	5	16	.259	.361	.388	.748
2011	Cle	AL	35	71	11	2	1	1	(1	0)	18	10	6	3	8	0	17	0	1	0	1	0	2	.155	.241	.254	.494
2012	Cle	AL	14	33	7	0	0	1	(0	1)	10	2	5	5	1	0	10	0	0	0	0	0	0	.212	.235	.303	.538
2013	Cle	AL	4	9	0	0	0	0	(0	0)	0	0	0	0	0	0	2	0	0	0	0	0	0	.000	.000	.000	.000
2014	Bal	AL	3	3	0	0	0	0	(0	0)	0	0	0	0	0	0	0	0	0	0	0	0	1	.000	.000	.000	.000
	4 ML YEARS		56	116	18	2	1	2	(1	1)	28	12	11	8	9	0	29	0	1	0	1	0	3	.155	.216	.241	.457

David Phelps

Pitches: R **Bats:** R **Pos:** SP-17; RP-15   **Ht:** 6'2" **Wt:** 200 **Born:** 10/9/1986 **Age:** 28

			HOW MUCH HE PITCHED						WHAT HE GAVE UP										THE RESULTS						
Year	Team	Lg	G	GS	CG	GF	IP	BFP	H	R	ER	HR	SH	SF	HB	TBB	IBB	SO	WP	Bk	W	L	Pct	Sh	Sv-Op	Hld	ERC	ERA
2012	NYY	AL	33	11	0	5	99.2	414	81	38	37	14	4	3	6	38	2	96	2	2	4	4	.500	0	0-0	3	3.48	3.34
2013	NYY	AL	22	12	0	3	86.2	376	88	50	48	8	1	2	5	35	1	79	2	0	6	5	.545	0	0-1	1	4.38	4.98
2014	NYY	AL	32	17	1	5	113.0	497	115	62	55	13	4	3	7	46	2	92	2	1	5	5	.500	0	1-1	5	4.52	4.38
	Postseason		3	0	0	1	3.1	19	7	4	3	0	0	0	0	1	0	2	0	0	0	2	.000	0	0-0	0	8.97	8.10
	3 ML YEARS		87	40	1	13	299.1	1287	284	150	140	35	9	8	18	119	5	267	6	3	15	14	.517	0	1-2	8	4.13	4.21

Brandon Phillips

Bats: R **Throws:** R **Pos:** 2B-121   **Ht:** 6'0" **Wt:** 200 **Born:** 6/28/1981 **Age:** 34

Year	Team	Lg	G	AB	H	2B	3B	HR	(Hm	Rd)	TB	R	RBI	RC	TBB	IBB	SO	HBP	SH	SF	SB	CS	GDP	Avg	OBP	Slg	OPS
2014	Lsvlle*	AAA	2	5	0	0	0	0	(-	-)	0	0	0	0	1	0	0	0	0	0	0	0	0	.000	.167	.000	.167
2014	Dayton*	A	1	3	2	1	0	0	(-	-)	3	0	0	1	0	0	1	1	0	0	0	0	0	.667	.750	1.000	1.750
2002	Cle	AL	11	31	8	3	1	0	(0	0)	13	5	4	5	3	0	6	1	1	0	0	0	0	.258	.343	.419	.762
2003	Cle	AL	112	370	77	18	1	6	(3	3)	115	36	33	22	14	0	77	3	5	1	4	5	12	.208	.242	.311	.553
2004	Cle	AL	6	22	4	2	0	0	(0	0)	6	1	1	0	2	0	5	0	0	0	0	2	1	.182	.250	.273	.523
2005	Cle	AL	6	9	0	0	0	0	(0	0)	0	1	0	0	0	0	4	0	0	0	0	0	0	.000	.000	.000	.000
2006	Cin	NL	149	536	148	28	1	17	(9	8)	229	65	75	74	35	3	88	6	4	6	25	2	19	.276	.324	.427	.751
2007	Cin	NL	158	650	187	26	6	30	(17	13)	315	107	94	88	33	4	109	12	2	5	32	8	26	.288	.331	.485	.816
2008	Cin	NL	141	559	146	24	7	21	(13	8)	247	80	78	74	39	6	93	5	0	4	23	10	13	.261	.312	.442	.754
2009	Cin	NL	153	584	161	30	5	20	(10	10)	261	78	98	80	44	3	75	6	2	8	25	9	21	.276	.329	.447	.776
2010	Cin	NL	155	626	172	33	5	18	(10	8)	269	100	59	77	46	1	83	8	6	1	16	12	14	.275	.332	.430	.762
2011	Cin	NL	150	610	183	38	2	18	(14	4)	279	94	82	92	44	3	85	9	5	6	14	9	15	.300	.353	.457	.810
2012	Cin	NL	147	580	163	30	1	18	(15	3)	249	86	77	78	28	2	79	8	3	4	15	2	19	.281	.321	.429	.750
2013	Cin	NL	151	606	158	24	2	18	(7	11)	240	80	103	82	39	6	98	8	4	9	5	3	19	.261	.310	.396	.706
2014	Cin	NL	121	462	123	25	0	8	(3	5)	172	44	51	53	23	1	74	6	2	6	2	3	13	.266	.306	.372	.678
	Postseason		9	40	13	4	0	2	(0	2)	23	3	8	10	0	0	5	0	0	1	1	0	0	.325	.317	.575	.892
	13 ML YEARS		1460	5645	1530	281	31	174	(101	73)	2395	777	755	725	350	29	876	72	34	52	161	65	172	.271	.319	.424	.743

A.J. Pierzynski

Bats: L **Throws:** R **Pos:** C-87;PH-15;DH-5   perr-ZINN-ski   **Ht:** 6'3" **Wt:** 235 **Born:** 12/30/1976 **Age:** 38

Year	Team	Lg	G	AB	H	2B	3B	HR	(Hm	Rd)	TB	R	RBI	RC	TBB	IBB	SO	HBP	SH	SF	SB	CS	GDP	Avg	OBP	Slg	OPS
1998	Min	AL	7	10	3	0	0	0	(0	0)	3	1	1	2	1	0	2	1	0	1	0	0	0	.300	.385	.300	.685
1999	Min	AL	9	22	6	2	0	0	(0	0)	8	3	3	3	1	0	4	1	0	0	0	0	0	.273	.333	.364	.697
2000	Min	AL	33	88	27	5	1	2	(1	1)	40	12	11	14	5	0	14	2	0	1	1	0	1	.307	.354	.455	.809
2001	Min	AL	114	381	110	33	2	7	(3	4)	168	51	55	50	16	4	57	4	1	3	1	7	7	.289	.322	.441	.763
2002	Min	AL	130	440	132	31	6	6	(2	4)	193	54	49	60	13	1	61	0	1	2	1	2	14	.300	.334	.439	.773
2003	Min	AL	137	487	152	35	3	11	(6	5)	226	63	74	74	24	12	55	15	2	5	3	1	13	.312	.360	.464	.824
2004	SF	NL	131	471	128	28	2	11	(3	8)	193	45	77	58	19	4	27	15	2	3	0	1	27	.272	.319	.410	.729

BATTING																				RUNNING			AVERAGES			
Year Team	Lg	G	AB	H	2B	3B	HR	(Hm Rd)	TB	R	RBI	RC	TBB	IBB	SO	HBP	SH	SF	SB	CS	GDP	Avg	OBP	Slg	OPS		
2005 CWS	AL	128	460	118	21	0	18	(12 6)	193	61	56	55	23	5	68	12	1	1	0	2	13	.257	.308	.420	.728		
2006 CWS	AL	140	509	150	24	0	16	(9 7)	222	65	64	68	22	6	72	8	3	1	1	0	10	.295	.333	.436	.769		
2007 CWS	AL	136	472	124	24	0	14	(8 6)	190	54	50	49	25	5	66	8	1	3	1	1	21	.263	.309	.403	.712		
2008 CWS	AL	134	534	150	31	1	13	(7 6)	222	66	60	64	19	5	71	8	3	6	1	0	14	.281	.312	.416	.728		
2009 CWS	AL	138	504	151	22	1	13	(8 5)	214	57	49	59	24	6	52	1	3	3	1	1	18	.300	.331	.425	.755		
2010 CWS	AL	128	474	128	29	0	9	(7 2)	184	43	56	51	15	2	39	6	6	2	3	4	17	.270	.300	.388	.688		
2011 CWS	AL	129	464	133	29	1	8	(5 3)	188	38	48	53	23	6	33	5	2	6	0	0	19	.287	.323	.405	.728		
2012 CWS	AL	135	479	133	18	4	27	(18 9)	240	68	77	79	28	5	78	8	1	4	0	0	8	.278	.326	.501	.827		
2013 Tex	AL	134	503	137	24	1	17	(10 7)	214	48	70	61	11	2	76	9	0	6	1	1	14	.272	.297	.425	.722		
2014 2 Tms		102	338	85	12	1	5	(1 4)	114	25	37	31	14	2	54	5	1	4	0	1	13	.251	.288	.337	.625		
14 Bos	AL	72	256	65	10	1	4	(1 3)	89	19	31	23	9	2	40	4	1	4	0	0	11	.254	.286	.348	.633		
14 StL	NL	30	82	20	2	0	1	(0 1)	25	6	6	8	5	0	14	1	0	0	0	1	2	.244	.295	.305	.600		
Postseason		30	100	30	5	1	5	(3 2)	52	16	17	19	10	1	13	2	1	1	2	3	2	.300	.372	.520	.892		
17 ML YEARS		1865	6636	1867	368	23	177	(100 77)	2812	754	837	837	283	65	829	119	28	52	14	21	209	.281	.320	.424	.744		

Kevin Pillar

Bats: R Throws: R Pos: LF-30;CF-16;PH-8;RF-7;DH-3;PR-3 pih-LAHR **Ht: 6'0" Wt: 205 Born: 1/4/1989 Age: 26**

BATTING																				RUNNING			AVERAGES			
Year Team	Lg	G	AB	H	2B	3B	HR	(Hm Rd)	TB	R	RBI	RC	TBB	IBB	SO	HBP	SH	SF	SB	CS	GDP	Avg	OBP	Slg	OPS		
2011 Bluefld	R+	60	236	82	17	3	7	(- -)	126	44	37	46	10	0	36	3	4	3	8	4	4	.347	.377	.534	.911		
2012 Lnsng	A	86	335	108	20	4	5	(- -)	151	49	57	65	35	1	53	3	1	1	35	6	10	.322	.390	.451	.841		
2012 Dnedin	A+	42	164	53	8	2	1	(- -)	68	16	34	26	5	0	17	2	1	6	16	3	0	.323	.339	.415	.754		
2013 NHam	AA	71	304	95	20	2	5	(- -)	134	44	30	48	19	0	31	4	0	0	15	8	6	.313	.361	.441	.802		
2013 Buffalo	AAA	52	201	60	19	4	4	(- -)	99	30	27	33	12	0	39	2	1	2	8	5	4	.299	.341	.493	.868		
2014 Buffalo	AAA	100	405	131	39	3	10	(- -)	206	57	59	76	21	3	48	4	0	4	27	6	8	.323	.359	.509	.868		
2013 Tor	AL	36	102	21	4	0	3	(1 2)	34	11	13	9	4	0	29	2	2	0	0	1	0	.206	.250	.333	.583		
2014 Tor	AL	53	116	31	9	0	2	(2 0)	46	19	7	8	4	0	28	1	0	1	1	2	3	.267	.295	.397	.692		
2 ML YEARS		89	218	52	13	0	5	(3 2)	80	30	20	17	8	0	57	3	2	1	1	3	3	.239	.274	.367	.641		

Stolmy Pimentel

Pitches: R Bats: R Pos: RP-20 STOLE-mee PIM-en-tell **Ht: 6'3" Wt: 230 Born: 2/1/1990 Age: 25**

HOW MUCH HE PITCHED						WHAT HE GAVE UP												THE RESULTS								
Year Team	Lg	G	GS	CG	GF	IP	BFP	H	R	ER	HR	SH	SF	HB	TBB	IBB	SO	WP	Bk	W	L	Pct	Sh	Sv-Op	Hld	ERC	ERA
2010 Salem	A+	26	26	0	0	128.2	535	120	65	58	11	1	3	5	42	1	102	11	2	9	11	.450	0	0- -	-	3.52	4.06
2011 Portlnd	AA	15	15	0	0	50.1	250	75	57	51	8	1	5	8	23	0	30	6	1	0	9	.000	0	0- -	-	8.59	9.12
2011 Salem	A	11	10	0	0	51.2	221	50	29	26	8	2	2	8	16	0	35	5	0	6	4	.600	0	0- -	-	4.62	4.53
2012 Portlnd	AA	22	22	1	0	115.2	495	115	66	59	9	1	2	4	42	0	86	8	0	6	7	.462	0	0- -	-	3.82	4.59
2013 Altna	AA	13	13	1	0	77.1	340	74	36	31	8	2	4	5	35	0	61	4	0	4	3	.571	0	0- -	-	4.30	3.61
2013 Indy	AAA	14	14	1	0	92.0	371	76	38	32	6	3	6	2	21	1	62	5	0	2	6	.250	0	0- -	-	2.36	3.13
2014 Bradtn	A+	1	0	0	0	2.0	6	0	0	0	0	0	0	0	1	0	2	0	0	0	0	-	0	0- -	-	0.32	0.00
2014 Altna	AA	5	3	0	0	6.1	29	6	3	1	0	1	0	0	5	0	6	0	0	0	0	-	0	0- -	-	4.56	1.42
2014 Indy	AAA	1	0	0	1	2.0	6	0	0	0	0	0	0	0	0	0	1	0	0	0	0	-	0	1- -	-	0.00	0.00
2013 Pit	NL	5	0	0	1	9.1	38	6	4	2	0	0	1	0	2	0	9	2	0	0	0	-	0	0-0	1	1.19	1.93
2014 Pit	NL	20	0	0	11	32.2	148	34	19	19	5	0	2	0	16	2	38	2	0	2	1	.667	0	0-0	0	5.17	5.23
2 ML YEARS		25	0	0	12	42.0	186	40	23	21	5	0	2	0	18	2	47	4	0	2	1	.667	0	0-0	1	4.07	4.50

Michael Pineda

Pitches: R Bats: R Pos: SP-13 pah-NAY-dah **Ht: 6'7" Wt: 265 Born: 1/18/1989 Age: 26**

HOW MUCH HE PITCHED						WHAT HE GAVE UP												THE RESULTS								
Year Team	Lg	G	GS	CG	GF	IP	BFP	H	R	ER	HR	SH	SF	HB	TBB	IBB	SO	WP	Bk	W	L	Pct	Sh	Sv-Op	Hld	ERC	ERA
2010 WTenn	AA	13	13	0	0	77.0	316	67	23	19	1	1	0	4	17	1	78	2	0	8	1	.889	0	0- -	-	2.32	2.22
2010 Tacom	AAA	12	12	0	0	62.1	260	54	33	33	9	2	0	3	17	0	76	0	0	3	3	.500	0	0- -	-	3.28	4.76
2013 Tampa	A+	2	2	0	0	8.1	36	7	3	1	0	0	0	0	2	0	7	0	0	0	0	-	0	0- -	-	1.85	1.08
2013 Trntn	AA	2	2	0	0	9.0	40	6	4	4	2	0	0	1	6	0	8	0	0	1	0	1.000	0	0- -	-	4.48	4.00
2013 S-WB	AAA	6	6	0	0	23.1	96	18	10	10	2	0	0	2	6	0	26	1	0	1	1	.500	0	0- -	-	2.52	3.86
2014 S-WB	AAA	2	2	0	0	7.2	33	9	1	1	0	0	0	0	1	0	11	0	0	0	1	.000	0	0- -	-	3.22	1.17
2011 Sea	AL	28	28	0	0	171.0	606	133	76	71	18	4	3	6	55	1	173	0	0	9	10	.474	0	0 0	0	2.73	3.74
2014 NYY	AL	13	13	0	0	76.1	290	56	18	16	5	2	1	0	7	0	59	3	1	5	5	.500	0	0-0	0	1.51	1.89
2 ML YEARS		41	41	0	0	247.1	896	189	94	87	23	6	4	6	62	1	232	3	1	14	15	.483	0	0-0	0	2.31	3.17

Yohan Pino

Pitches: R Bats: R Pos: SP-11 PEEN-oh **Ht: 6'2" Wt: 190 Born: 12/26/1983 Age: 31**

HOW MUCH HE PITCHED						WHAT HE GAVE UP												THE RESULTS								
Year Team	Lg	G	GS	CG	GF	IP	BFP	H	R	ER	HR	SH	SF	HB	TBB	IBB	SO	WP	Bk	W	L	Pct	Sh	Sv-Op	Hld	ERC	ERA
2010 Clmbs	AAA	26	26	1	0	145.2	661	175	101	93	25	4	6	9	47	0	114	3	0	10	9	.526	0	0- -	-	5.66	5.75
2011 Akron	AA	2	0	0	2	1.1	5	2	0	0	0	0	0	0	0	0	2	0	0	0	0	-	0	0- -	-	5.47	0.00
2011 LsVgs	AAA	1	0	0	0	1.2	9	2	2	2	0	0	0	0	2	0	0	0	0	0	0	-	0	0- -	-	7.49	10.80
2011 NHam	AA	36	10	1	8	95.2	385	90	47	44	15	1	0	3	14	0	104	3	0	4	8	.333	0	0- -	-	3.28	4.14
2012 NHam	AA	25	22	2	1	134.0	552	122	58	53	17	1	3	7	29	1	111	4	0	10	8	.556	0	0- -	-	3.23	3.56
2012 LsVgs	AAA	3	3	0	0	9.1	59	29	23	23	1	0	0	0	8	0	8	0	0	0	2	.000	0	0- -	-	18.54	22.18
2013 Pnscla	AA	4	1	0	0	11.0	35	3	0	0	0	0	0	0	0	0	11	0	0	0	0	-	0	0- -	-	0.18	0.00
2013 Lsvlle	AAA	31	16	1	11	121.1	502	116	52	44	7	2	8	1	30	2	107	2	1	5	7	.417	1	6- -	-	2.88	3.26
2014 Roch	AAA	16	9	2	2	73.0	290	47	21	20	9	1	1	3	24	0	72	3	1	10	2	.833	2	- -	-	2.26	2.67
2014 Min	AL	11	11	0	2	60.1	258	66	37	34	8	2	4	1	14	0	50	2	0	2	5	.286	0	0-0	0	4.20	5.07

Josmil Pinto

Bats: R **Throws:** R **Pos:** C-25;DH-21;PH-10　　HOSE-meel PEEN-toe　　**Ht:** 5'11" **Wt:** 210 **Born:** 3/31/1989 **Age:** 26

								BATTING											RUNNING			AVERAGES			
Year Team	Lg	G	AB	H	2B	3B	HR	(Hm Rd)	TB	R	RBI	RC	TBB	IBB	SO	HBP	SH	SF	SB	CS	GDP	Avg	OBP	Slg	OPS
2010 Beloit	A	100	347	78	21	1	10	(- -)	131	60	54	40	32	3	67	5	2	6	2	3	7	.225	.295	.378	.672
2011 Beloit	A	9	32	8	3	0	1	(- -)	14	4	9	4	2	0	10	0	0	2	0	0	1	.250	.278	.438	.715
2011 FtMyrs	A+	64	221	58	11	1	5	(- -)	86	21	32	27	12	1	36	2	0	1	1	0	7	.262	.305	.389	.694
2012 FtMyrs	A+	93	349	103	22	2	12	(- -)	165	45	51	61	39	0	63	0	0	5	0	0	11	.295	.361	.473	.834
2012 NwBrit	AA	12	47	14	4	1	2	(- -)	26	8	9	9	4	0	10	1	0	0	0	0	3	.298	.365	.553	.919
2013 NwBrit	AA	107	386	119	23	1	14	(- -)	186	59	68	78	64	1	71	3	0	0	0	2	8	.308	.411	.482	.892
2013 Roch	AAA	19	70	22	9	0	1	(- -)	34	6	6	11	2	0	12	1	0	2	0	0	6	.314	.333	.486	.819
2014 Roch	AAA	60	208	58	17	1	6	(- -)	95	24	35	37	31	3	37	2	0	1	0	1	9	.279	.376	.457	.833
2013 Min	AL	21	76	26	5	0	4	(3 1)	43	10	12	15	6	0	22	1	0	0	0	0	3	.342	.398	.566	.963
2014 Min	AL	57	169	37	8	0	7	(4 3)	66	25	18	13	24	0	50	1	0	3	0	1	7	.219	.315	.391	.705
2 ML YEARS		78	245	63	13	0	11	(7 4)	109	35	30	28	30	0	72	2	0	3	0	1	10	.257	.339	.445	.784

Jose Pirela

Bats: R **Throws:** R **Pos:** 2B-4;DH-3;PH-1　　**Ht:** 5'10" **Wt:** 191 **Born:** 11/21/1989 **Age:** 25

								BATTING											RUNNING			AVERAGES			
Year Team	Lg	G	AB	H	2B	3B	HR	(Hm Rd)	TB	R	RBI	RC	TBB	IBB	SO	HBP	SH	SF	SB	CS	GDP	Avg	OBP	Slg	OPS
2010 Tampa	A+	130	497	125	15	13	5	(- -)	181	68	61	68	57	1	87	4	8	7	30	7	11	.252	.329	.364	.693
2011 Trntn	AA	128	468	112	21	4	8	(- -)	165	50	45	50	25	1	88	13	8	7	9	7	7	.239	.292	.353	.645
2012 Trntn	AA	82	317	93	19	3	8	(- -)	142	55	33	53	26	1	48	6	7	2	9	3	4	.293	.356	.448	.804
2013 Trntn	AA	124	459	125	27	5	10	(- -)	192	73	62	76	56	0	61	9	1	5	18	3	11	.272	.359	.418	.777
2013 S-WB	AAA	5	23	7	0	0	0	(- -)	7	3	1	2	1	0	2	0	0	0	1	0	0	.304	.333	.304	.638
2014 S-WB	AAA	130	535	163	21	11	10	(- -)	236	87	60	84	37	2	74	3	2	4	15	7	7	.305	.351	.441	.792
2014 NYY	AL	7	24	8	1	2	0	(0 0)	13	6	3	4	1	0	4	0	0	0	0	0	1	.333	.360	.542	.902

Trevor Plouffe

Bats: R **Throws:** R **Pos:** 3B-127;DH-8;PH-1　　PLOOF　　**Ht:** 6'2" **Wt:** 205 **Born:** 6/15/1986 **Age:** 29

								BATTING											RUNNING			AVERAGES			
Year Team	Lg	G	AB	H	2B	3B	HR	(Hm Rd)	TB	R	RBI	RC	TBB	IBB	SO	HBP	SH	SF	SB	CS	GDP	Avg	OBP	Slg	OPS
2010 Min	AL	22	41	6	1	0	2	(1 1)	13	7	6	2	0	0	14	0	2	1	0	0	0	.146	.143	.317	.460
2011 Min	AL	81	286	68	18	1	8	(3 5)	112	47	31	31	25	0	71	4	2	3	3	3	6	.238	.305	.392	.697
2012 Min	AL	119	422	99	19	1	24	(15 9)	192	56	55	48	37	0	92	4	0	2	1	3	9	.235	.301	.455	.756
2013 Min	AL	129	477	121	22	1	14	(8 6)	187	44	52	49	34	1	112	6	1	4	2	1	11	.254	.309	.392	.701
2014 Min	AL	136	520	134	40	2	14	(8 6)	220	69	80	74	53	2	109	4	0	5	2	1	12	.258	.328	.423	.751
5 ML YEARS		487	1746	428	100	5	62	(35 27)	724	223	224	204	149	3	398	18	5	15	8	8	38	.245	.309	.415	.723

Gregory Polanco

Bats: L **Throws:** L **Pos:** RF-83;PH-9;PR-6　　puh-LAHN-ko　　**Ht:** 6'4" **Wt:** 220 **Born:** 9/14/1991 **Age:** 23

								BATTING											RUNNING			AVERAGES			
Year Team	Lg	G	AB	H	2B	3B	HR	(Hm Rd)	TB	R	RBI	RC	TBB	IBB	SO	HBP	SH	SF	SB	CS	GDP	Avg	OBP	Slg	OPS
2010 Pirates	R	53	188	38	5	1	3	(- -)	54	21	23	15	9	0	41	2	0	1	19	2	3	.202	.245	.287	.532
2011 Pirates	R	48	169	40	4	4	3	(- -)	61	34	34	26	24	0	33	3	2	5	18	0	0	.237	.333	.361	.694
2011 StCol	A-	3	10	1	0	0	0	(- -)	1	0	1	0	0	0	2	0	0	0	0	0	1	.100	.100	.100	.200
2012 WV	A	116	437	142	26	6	16	(- -)	228	84	85	89	44	1	64	2	1	1	40	15	8	.325	.388	.522	.910
2013 Bradtn	A+	57	218	68	17	0	6	(- -)	103	29	30	41	16	0	37	3	2	2	24	4	4	.312	.364	.472	.836
2013 Altna	AA	68	243	64	13	2	6	(- -)	99	36	41	38	36	1	36	1	1	5	13	7	3	.263	.354	.407	.762
2013 Indy	AAA	2	9	2	0	0	0	(- -)	2	1	0	0	0	0	0	0	0	0	1	0	0	.222	.222	.222	.444
2014 Indy	AAA	69	274	90	17	5	7	(- -)	138	51	51	54	28	2	49	1	0	2	16	6	3	.328	.390	.504	.894
2014 Pit	NL	89	277	65	9	0	7	(5 2)	95	50	33	32	30	1	59	0	2	2	14	5	1	.235	.307	.343	.650

Jorge Polanco

Bats: B **Throws:** R **Pos:** SS-4;PH-3　　puh-LAHN-ko　　**Ht:** 5'11" **Wt:** 165 **Born:** 7/5/1993 **Age:** 21

								BATTING											RUNNING			AVERAGES			
Year Team	Lg	G	AB	H	2B	3B	HR	(Hm Rd)	TB	R	RBI	RC	TBB	IBB	SO	HBP	SH	SF	SB	CS	GDP	Avg	OBP	Slg	OPS
2010 Twins	R	34	103	23	5	0	1	(- -)	31	12	12	9	12	0	9	0	2	2	2	4	2	.223	.299	.301	.600
2011 Twins	R	51	172	43	8	3	1	(- -)	60	21	16	20	15	0	24	3	2	1	6	4	4	.250	.319	.349	.668
2012 Elizab	R+	51	173	55	15	2	5	(- -)	89	35	27	35	20	0	26	3	3	5	6	3	2	.318	.388	.514	.903
2013 CRpds	A	115	465	143	32	10	5	(- -)	210	76	78	78	42	2	59	3	3	10	4	4	4	.308	.362	.452	.813
2014 FtMyrs	A+	94	378	110	17	6	6	(- -)	157	61	45	60	46	1	60	1	1	6	10	8	8	.291	.364	.415	.780
2014 NwBrit	AA	37	146	41	6	0	1	(- -)	50	13	16	16	9	0	28	0	2	0	7	3	0	.281	.323	.342	.665
2014 Min	AL	5	6	2	1	1	0	(0 0)	5	2	3	4	2	0	2	0	0	0	0	0	0	.333	.500	.833	1.333

A.J. Pollock

Bats: R **Throws:** R **Pos:** CF-68;PH-7;LF-2;PR-2　　**Ht:** 6'1" **Wt:** 195 **Born:** 12/5/1987 **Age:** 27

								BATTING											RUNNING			AVERAGES			
Year Team	Lg	G	AB	H	2B	3B	HR	(Hm Rd)	TB	R	RBI	RC	TBB	IBB	SO	HBP	SH	SF	SB	CS	GDP	Avg	OBP	Slg	OPS
2014 DBcks*	R	2	3	1	1	0	0	(- -)	2	0	0	0	0	0	1	1	0	0	0	0	0	.333	.500	.667	1.167
2014 Reno*	AAA	13	49	8	1	1	0	(- -)	11	4	9	1	2	0	4	0	0	1	0	0	2	.163	.192	.224	.417
2012 Ari	NL	31	81	20	4	1	2	(2 0)	32	8	8	9	9	1	11	0	1	2	1	2	2	.247	.315	.395	.710
2013 Ari	NL	137	443	119	28	5	8	(3 5)	181	64	38	58	33	1	82	2	3	1	12	3	5	.269	.322	.409	.730
2014 Ari	NL	75	265	80	19	6	7	(7 0)	132	41	24	43	19	0	46	2	1	0	14	3	4	.302	.353	.498	.851
3 ML YEARS		243	789	219	51	12	17	(12 5)	345	113	70	110	61	2	139	4	5	3	27	8	11	.278	.331	.437	.769

Drew Pomeranz

Pitches: L Bats: R Pos: SP-10; RP-10   POMM-er-anze   Ht: 6'5" Wt: 240 Born: 11/22/1988 Age: 26

Year	Team	Lg	G	GS	CG	GF	IP	BFP	H	R	ER	HR	SH	SF	HB	TBB	IBB	SO	WP	Bk	W	L	Pct	Sh	Sv-Op	Hld	ERC	ERA
2014	Scrmto*	AAA	8	8	0	0	46.1	194	45	19	19	6	3	1	0	17	1	54	2	0	3	1	.750	0	0- -	-	4.03	3.69
2011	Col	NL	4	4	0	0	18.1	77	19	11	11	0	1	0	1	5	0	13	1	0	2	1	.667	0	0-0	0	3.36	5.40
2012	Col	NL	22	22	0	0	96.2	434	97	57	53	14	8	4	4	46	2	83	8	1	2	9	.182	0	0-0	0	4.78	4.93
2013	Col	NL	8	4	0	0	21.2	105	25	15	15	4	1	1	1	19	1	19	0	0	0	4	.000	0	0-0	0	8.04	6.23
2014	Oak	AL	20	10	0	4	69.0	278	51	22	18	7	1	0	1	26	0	64	0	0	5	4	.556	0	0-0	0	2.70	2.35
4 ML YEARS			54	40	0	4	205.2	894	192	105	97	25	11	5	7	96	3	179	9	1	9	18	.333	0	0-0	0	4.23	4.24

Dalton Pompey

Bats: B Throws: R Pos: LF-9;CF-5;PR-4;DH-3;PH-3   pom-PAY   Ht: 6'2" Wt: 195 Born: 12/11/1992 Age: 22

Year	Team	Lg	G	AB	H	2B	3B	HR	(Hm	Rd)	TB	R	RBI	RC	TBB	IBB	SO	HBP	SH	SF	SB	CS	GDP	Avg	OBP	Slg	OPS
2010	B Jays	R	11	47	9	0	0	2	(-	-)	15	4	5	4	3	0	10	1	0	0	4	1	1	.191	.255	.319	.574
2011	B Jays	R	42	158	41	7	2	4	(-	-)	64	34	12	28	24	0	35	1	1	0	19	0	2	.259	.361	.405	.766
2011	Bluefld	R+	18	68	13	3	0	1	(-	-)	19	15	5	8	14	0	23	3	1	0	4	1	0	.191	.353	.279	.632
2012	Vancvr	A-	11	34	10	3	1	0	(-	-)	15	11	4	8	9	0	7	0	1	0	3	0	0	.294	.442	.441	.883
2012	Bluefld	R+	4	14	5	1	1	0	(-	-)	8	2	1	2	0	0	2	0	0	0	1	0	0	.357	.357	.571	.929
2012	Lnsng	A	5	22	5	0	1	0	(-	-)	7	1	3	1	1	0	5	0	1	0	1	1	0	.227	.261	.318	.579
2013	Lnsng	A	115	437	114	22	9	6	(-	-)	172	68	40	70	63	1	106	5	3	3	38	10	4	.261	.358	.394	.752
2014	Dnedin	A+	70	276	88	12	6	6	(-	-)	130	49	34	57	35	0	56	2	2	2	29	2	3	.319	.397	.471	.868
2014	NHam	AA	31	112	33	5	3	3	(-	-)	53	20	12	20	14	0	18	1	0	0	8	5	2	.295	.378	.473	.851
2014	Buffalo	AAA	12	53	19	5	0	0	(-	-)	24	15	5	10	3	0	10	0	0	0	6	0	0	.358	.393	.453	.846
2014	Tor	AL	17	39	9	1	2	1	(1	0)	17	5	4	3	4	0	12	0	0	0	1	0	0	.231	.302	.436	.738

Rick Porcello

Pitches: R Bats: R Pos: SP-31; RP-1   pore-SELL-oh   Ht: 6'5" Wt: 200 Born: 12/27/1988 Age: 26

Year	Team	Lg	G	GS	CG	GF	IP	BFP	H	R	ER	HR	SH	SF	HB	TBB	IBB	SO	WP	Bk	W	L	Pct	Sh	Sv-Op	Hld	ERC	ERA
2009	Det	AL	31	31	0	0	170.2	720	176	81	75	23	4	2	3	52	0	89	6	1	14	9	.609	0	0-0	0	4.24	3.96
2010	Det	AL	27	27	0	0	162.2	700	188	96	89	18	1	2	7	38	2	84	11	3	10	12	.455	0	0-0	0	4.56	4.92
2011	Det	AL	31	31	0	0	182.0	784	210	103	96	18	5	5	8	46	1	104	12	0	14	9	.609	0	0-0	0	4.57	4.75
2012	Det	AL	31	31	0	0	176.1	783	226	101	90	16	2	3	6	44	3	107	6	0	10	12	.455	0	0-0	0	5.16	4.59
2013	Det	AL	32	29	1	1	177.0	736	185	87	85	18	4	3	3	42	4	142	6	1	13	8	.619	0	0-0	0	3.79	4.32
2014	Det	AL	32	31	3	1	204.2	840	211	89	78	18	3	4	4	41	4	129	0	0	15	13	.536	3	0-0	0	3.50	3.43
Postseason			8	2	0	4	16.1	71	18	10	8	0	0	1	2	2	2	13	1	0	0	2	.000	0	0-0	0	3.06	4.41
6 ML YEARS			184	180	4	2	1073.1	4563	1196	557	513	111	19	19	31	263	14	655	41	5	76	63	.547	3	0-0	0	4.27	4.30

Aaron Poreda

Pitches: L Bats: L Pos: RP-26   puh-RAY-duh   Ht: 6'6" Wt: 240 Born: 10/1/1986 Age: 28

Year	Team	Lg	G	GS	CG	GF	IP	BFP	H	R	ER	HR	SH	SF	HB	TBB	IBB	SO	WP	Bk	W	L	Pct	Sh	Sv-Op	Hld	ERC	ERA
2010	SnAnt	AA	19	0	0	3	25.0	120	18	11	7	1	2	3	4	26	0	25	0	0	1	0	1.000	0	0- -	-	5.11	2.52
2010	Portlnd	AAA	20	1	0	7	29.0	136	13	18	16	0	3	0	4	38	0	22	3	0	1	1	.500	0	0- -	-	4.21	4.97
2011	Tucsn	AAA	41	1	0	7	69.2	336	65	47	42	3	6	4	3	63	0	79	5	0	4	3	.571	0	0- -	-	5.33	5.43
2012	Altna	AA	3	3	0	0	16.0	69	12	6	4	0	0	0	1	11	0	11	0	0	2	0	1.000	0	0- -	-	3.38	2.25
2014	RdRck	AAA	16	0	0	8	16.1	80	21	11	11	0	1	0	2	7	3	28	3	0	1	0	1.000	0	3- -	-	4.98	6.06
2009	2 Tms		14	0	0	6	13.1	61	10	4	4	0	1	0	1	13	1	12	2	0	1	0	1.000	0	0-0	0	4.34	2.70
2014	Tex	AL	26	0	0	2	21.1	97	30	14	14	2	0	0	1	7	1	21	1	0	2	1	.667	0	0-1	4	6.43	5.91
09	CWS	AL	10	0	0	5	11.0	49	9	3	3	0	1	0	1	8	1	12	2	0	1	0	1.000	0	0-0	0	3.81	2.45
09	SD	NL	4	0	0	1	2.1	12	1	1	1	0	0	0	0	5	0	0	0	0	0	0	-	0	0-0	0	6.99	3.86
2 ML YEARS			40	0	0	8	34.2	158	40	18	18	2	1	0	2	20	2	33	3	0	3	1	.750	0	0-1	4	5.63	4.67

Buster Posey

Bats: R Throws: R Pos: C-111;1B-35;PH-6;DH-2   Ht: 6'1" Wt: 215 Born: 3/27/1987 Age: 28

Year	Team	Lg	G	AB	H	2B	3B	HR	(Hm	Rd)	TB	R	RBI	RC	TBB	IBB	SO	HBP	SH	SF	SB	CS	GDP	Avg	OBP	Slg	OPS
2009	SF	NL	7	17	2	0	0	0	(0	0)	2	1	0	0	0	0	4	0	0	0	0	0	0	.118	.118	.118	.235
2010	SF	NL	108	406	124	23	2	18	(6	12)	205	58	67	70	30	5	55	4	0	3	0	2	12	.305	.357	.505	.862
2011	SF	NL	45	162	46	5	0	4	(1	3)	63	17	21	26	18	3	30	4	0	1	3	0	4	.284	.368	.389	.756
2012	SF	NL	148	530	178	39	1	24	(7	17)	291	78	103	111	69	7	96	2	0	9	1	1	19	.336	.408	.549	.957
2013	SF	NL	148	520	153	34	1	15	(8	7)	234	61	72	77	60	8	70	8	0	7	2	1	15	.294	.371	.450	.821
2014	SF	NL	147	547	170	28	2	22	(11	11)	268	72	89	94	47	5	69	3	0	8	0	1	16	.311	.364	.490	.854
Postseason			31	119	29	3	0	4	(1	3)	44	11	14	11	14	2	33	0	0	0	1	0	1	.244	.323	.370	.693
6 ML YEARS			603	2182	673	129	6	83	(33	50)	1063	287	352	378	224	28	324	21	0	28	6	5	66	.308	.374	.487	.861

Martin Prado

mar-TEEN PRAH-doe

Bats: R **Throws:** R **Pos:** 3B-110;2B-21;RF-8;PH-6;LF-4   **Ht:** 6'1" **Wt:** 190 **Born:** 10/27/1983 **Age:** 31

							BATTING													RUNNING			AVERAGES			
Year	Team	Lg	G	AB	H	2B	3B	HR	(Hm | Rd)	TB	R	RBI	RC	TBB	IBB	SO	HBP	SH	SF	SB	CS	GDP	Avg	OBP	Slg	OPS
2006	Atl	NL	24	42	11	1	1	1	(1 | 0)	17	3	9	9	5	0	7	0	2	0	0	0	2	.262	.340	.405	.745
2007	Atl	NL	28	59	17	3	0	0	(0 | 0)	20	5	2	6	3	0	6	0	0	0	0	0	0	.288	.323	.339	.662
2008	Atl	NL	78	228	73	18	4	2	(1 | 1)	105	36	33	39	21	0	29	1	2	2	3	1	3	.320	.377	.461	.838
2009	Atl	NL	128	450	138	38	0	11	(4 | 7)	209	64	49	57	36	1	59	2	11	4	1	3	17	.307	.358	.464	.822
2010	Atl	NL	140	599	184	40	3	15	(4 | 11)	275	100	66	86	40	2	86	3	3	6	5	3	13	.307	.350	.459	.809
2011	Atl	NL	129	551	143	26	2	13	(9 | 4)	212	66	57	57	34	1	52	1	1	3	4	8	16	.260	.302	.385	.687
2012	Atl	NL	156	617	186	42	6	10	(6 | 4)	270	81	70	96	58	2	69	2	4	9	17	4	19	.301	.359	.438	.796
2013	Ari	NL	155	609	172	36	2	14	(7 | 7)	254	70	82	72	47	2	53	2	0	6	3	5	29	.282	.333	.417	.750
2014	2 Tms		143	536	151	26	4	12	(7 | 5)	221	62	58	66	26	0	80	7	0	4	3	1	20	.282	.321	.412	.733
14	Ari	NL	106	403	109	17	4	5	(3 | 2)	149	44	42	43	23	0	57	6	0	4	2	1	17	.270	.317	.370	.686
14	NYY	AL	37	133	42	9	0	7	(4 | 3)	72	18	16	23	3	0	23	1	0	0	1	0	3	.316	.336	.541	.877
	Postseason		1	5	1	0	0	0	(0 | 0)	1	0	0	0	0	0	1	0	0	0	0	0	0	.200	.200	.200	.400
	9 ML YEARS		981	3691	1075	230	22	78	(39 | 39)	1583	487	426	488	270	8	441	18	23	34	36	25	119	.291	.340	.429	.769

Alex Presley

Bats: L **Throws:** L **Pos:** LF-43;CF-21;RF-20;PH-10;DH-5;PR-1   **Ht:** 5'10" **Wt:** 190 **Born:** 7/25/1985 **Age:** 29

							BATTING													RUNNING			AVERAGES			
Year	Team	Lg	G	AB	H	2B	3B	HR	(Hm	Rd)	TB	R	RBI	RC	TBB	IBB	SO	HBP	SH	SF	SB	CS	GDP	Avg	OBP	Slg	OPS
2014	TriCity*	A-	2	5	1	0	1	0	(-	-)	3	1	0	1	1	0	1	0	0	0	0	0	0	.200	.333	.600	.933
2010	Pit	NL	29	23	6	1	0	0	(0	0)	7	2	0	1	1	0	8	0	1	0	1	1	0	.261	.292	.304	.596
2011	Pit	NL	52	215	64	12	6	4	(1	3)	100	27	20	35	13	1	40	1	1	1	9	3	1	.298	.339	.465	.804
2012	Pit	NL	104	346	82	14	7	10	(2	8)	140	46	25	31	18	0	72	2	4	0	9	7	5	.237	.279	.405	.683
2013	2 Tms		57	185	51	5	2	3	(2	1)	69	17	15	17	9	0	39	1	0	0	1	4	3	.276	.313	.373	.686
2014	Hou	AL	89	254	62	6	1	6	(4	2)	88	22	19	29	13	0	44	1	1	2	5	1	3	.244	.281	.346	.628
13	Pit	NL	29	72	19	1	1	2	(2	0)	28	8	4	5	1	0	18	0	0	0	0	1	1	.264	.274	.389	.663
13	Min	AL	28	113	32	4	1	1	(0	1)	41	9	11	12	8	0	21	1	0	0	1	3	2	.283	.336	.363	.699
	5 ML YEARS		321	1023	265	38	16	23	(9	14)	404	114	79	113	54	1	203	5	7	3	25	16	12	.259	.299	.395	.694

Ryan Pressly

Pitches: R **Bats:** R **Pos:** RP-25   **Ht:** 6'3" **Wt:** 205 **Born:** 12/15/1988 **Age:** 26

			HOW MUCH HE PITCHED						WHAT HE GAVE UP										THE RESULTS						
Year	Team	Lg	G	GS	CG	GF	IP	BFP	H	R	ER	HR	SH	SF	HB	TBB	IBB	SO	WP	Bk	W	L	Pct	Sh	Sv-Op	Hld	ERC	ERA
2010	Grnvlle	A	26	24	0	2	113.2	481	110	55	47	9	3	1	5	43	0	96	5	0	5	7	.417	0	0- -	-	3.91	3.72
2011	Salem	A+	26	26	0	0	130.0	573	125	84	65	9	3	5	13	53	0	72	11	0	6	11	.353	0	0- -	-	4.02	4.50
2012	Salem	A+	20	12	0	4	76.0	334	86	58	53	9	3	1	4	26	0	61	10	0	5	3	.625	0	0- -	-	4.99	6.28
2012	Portlnd	AA	14	0	0	7	27.2	113	23	9	9	2	3	1	0	10	2	21	2	0	2	2	.500	0	0- -	-	2.77	2.93
2014	Roch	AAA	35	0	0	19	60.1	256	55	25	20	1	3	0	1	21	1	63	6	0	1	4	.200	0	6- -	-	2.83	2.98
2013	Min	AL	49	0	0	18	76.2	315	71	37	33	5	2	3	0	27	1	49	7	0	3	3	.500	0	0-0	1	3.31	3.87
2014	Min	AL	25	0	0	5	28.1	122	30	10	9	3	2	3	1	8	2	14	1	0	2	0	1.000	0	0-1	2	3.98	2.86
	2 ML YEARS		74	0	0	23	105.0	437	101	47	42	8	4	6	1	35	3	63	8	0	5	3	.625	0	0-1	3	3.49	3.60

Bryan Price

Pitches: R **Bats:** R **Pos:** RP-3   **Ht:** 6'4" **Wt:** 210 **Born:** 11/13/1986 **Age:** 28

			HOW MUCH HE PITCHED						WHAT HE GAVE UP										THE RESULTS						
Year	Team	Lg	G	GS	CG	GF	IP	BFP	H	R	ER	HR	SH	SF	HB	TBB	IBB	SO	WP	Bk	W	L	Pct	Sh	Sv-Op	Hld	ERC	ERA
2010	Akron	AA	40	0	0	8	69.1	305	75	32	25	7	2	3	3	22	2	69	7	1	6	3	.667	0	1- -	-	4.28	3.25
2011	Akron	AA	28	1	0	8	51.2	219	50	20	16	5	3	5	2	15	0	33	2	0	2	3	.400	0	0- -	-	3.57	2.79
2012	Akron	AA	27	0	0	12	50.2	204	44	20	17	6	3	2	3	12	0	46	5	0	2	3	.400	0	4- -	-	3.15	3.02
2012	Clmbs	AAA	13	0	0	5	19.0	96	27	14	14	2	0	0	0	12	0	17	3	0	0	1	.000	0	0- -	-	7.48	6.63
2013	Clmbs	AAA	35	1	0	12	59.0	241	51	20	16	5	2	0	4	12	0	75	4	0	1	3	.250	0	2- -	-	2.75	2.44
2013	Akron	AA	12	0	0	5	16.0	58	6	1	1	0	0	0	0	4	0	17	2	0	1	0	1.000	0	2- -	-	0.65	0.56
2014	Akron	AA	8	0	0	2	10.0	39	7	3	2	2	0	0	0	2	0	16	0	0	1	0	1.000	0	1- -	-	2.31	1.80
2014	Clmbs	AAA	20	0	0	8	26.1	107	19	8	8	3	0	2	0	10	0	28	0	0	0	1	.000	0	4- -	-	2.60	2.73
2014	Cle	AL	3	0	0	2	2.2	19	8	6	6	3	0	0	2	1	0	1	0	0	0	0	-	0	0-0	0	34.50	20.25

David Price

Pitches: L **Bats:** L **Pos:** SP-34   **Ht:** 6'6" **Wt:** 220 **Born:** 8/26/1985 **Age:** 29

			HOW MUCH HE PITCHED						WHAT HE GAVE UP										THE RESULTS						
Year	Team	Lg	G	GS	CG	GF	IP	BFP	H	R	ER	HR	SH	SF	HB	TBB	IBB	SO	WP	Bk	W	L	Pct	Sh	Sv-Op	Hld	ERC	ERA
2008	TB	AL	5	1	0	0	14.0	57	9	4	3	1	0	1	4	0	12	0	0	0	0	-	0	0-0	1	1.86	1.93
2009	TB	AL	23	23	0	0	128.1	557	119	72	63	17	3	2	4	54	0	102	2	0	10	7	.588	0	0-0	0	4.05	4.42
2010	TB	AL	32	31	2	0	208.2	861	170	71	63	15	4	3	5	79	1	188	5	3	19	6	.760	1	0-0	0	2.91	2.72
2011	TB	AL	34	34	0	0	224.1	918	192	93	87	22	4	7	9	63	5	218	2	0	12	13	.480	0	0-0	0	2.97	3.49
2012	TB	AL	31	31	2	0	211.0	836	173	63	60	16	2	3	5	59	2	205	8	1	20	5	.800	1	0-0	0	2.67	2.56
2013	TB	AL	27	27	4	0	186.2	740	178	78	69	16	1	2	3	27	0	151	6	0	10	8	.556	0	0-0	0	2.89	3.33
2014	2 Tms		34	34	3	0	248.1	1009	230	100	90	25	4	3	5	38	1	271	2	0	15	12	.556	0	0-0	0	2.79	3.26
14	TB	AL	23	23	2	0	170.2	689	156	68	59	20	3	3	5	23	1	189	2	0	11	8	.579	0	0-0	0	2.79	3.11
14	Det	AL	11	11	1	0	77.2	320	74	32	31	5	1	0	0	15	0	82	0	0	4	4	.500	0	0-0	0	2.77	3.59
	Postseason		9	4	0	5	32.0	137	35	20	18	6	0	1	0	7	0	30	1	0	1	4	.200	0	1-1	0	4.41	5.06
	7 ML YEARS		186	181	11	0	1221.1	4978	1071	481	435	112	18	21	32	324	9	1147	25	4	86	51	.628	2	0-0	1	2.96	3.21

Jason Pridie

Bats: L Throws: R Pos: LF-1;RF-1   PRY-dee   Ht: 6'1" Wt: 205 Born: 10/9/1983 Age: 31

Year	Team	Lg	G	AB	H	2B	3B	HR	(Hm	Rd)	TB	R	RBI	RC	TBB	IBB	SO	HBP	SH	SF	SB	CS	GDP	Avg	OBP	Slg	OPS
2014	ColSpr*	AAA	108	418	116	17	6	12	(-	-)	181	61	51	67	40	2	74	1	2	2	28	6	4	.278	.341	.433	.774
2008	Min	AL	10	4	0	0	0	0	(0	0)	0	3	0	0	1	0	1	0	1	0	0	0	0	.000	.200	.000	.200
2009	Min	AL	1	0	0	0	0	0	(0	0)	0	0	0	0	0	0	0	0	0	0	0	0	0	-	-	-	-
2011	NYM	NL	101	208	48	11	3	4	(3	1)	77	28	20	22	24	2	64	0	3	1	7	1	2	.231	.309	.370	.679
2012	Phi	NL	9	10	3	1	0	1	(1	0)	7	1	3	2	0	0	0	0	0	0	0	0	0	.300	.300	.700	1.000
2013	Bal	AL	4	10	2	0	0	0	(0	0)	2	0	1	1	0	0	2	0	0	0	0	0	0	.200	.200	.200	.400
2014	Col	NL	2	4	0	0	0	0	(0	0)	0	1	0	0	0	0	2	0	0	0	0	0	0	.000	.000	.000	.000
	6 ML YEARS		127	236	53	12	3	5	(4	1)	86	33	24	25	25	2	69	0	4	1	7	1	2	.225	.298	.364	.662

Jurickson Profar

Bats: B Throws: R Pos: 2B   JURR-ick-sun PRO-farr   Ht: 6'0" Wt: 165 Born: 2/20/1993 Age: 22

Year	Team	Lg	G	AB	H	2B	3B	HR	(Hm	Rd)	TB	R	RBI	RC	TBB	IBB	SO	HBP	SH	SF	SB	CS	GDP	Avg	OBP	Slg	OPS
2010	Spkane	A-	63	252	63	19	0	4	(-	-)	94	42	23	33	28	0	46	0	6	2	8	3	8	.250	.323	.373	.696
2011	Hkry	A	115	430	123	37	8	12	(-	-)	212	86	65	88	65	2	63	11	6	4	23	9	7	.286	.390	.493	.883
2012	Frisco	AA	126	480	135	26	7	14	(-	-)	217	76	62	86	66	5	79	5	2	9	16	4	11	.281	.368	.452	.820
2013	RdRck	AAA	37	144	40	7	2	4	(-	-)	63	27	19	25	21	0	24	0	1	0	6	1	3	.278	.370	.438	.807
2012	Tex	AL	9	17	3	2	0	1	(0	1)	8	2	2	1	0	0	4	0	0	0	0	0	1	.176	.176	.471	.647
2013	Tex	AL	85	286	67	11	0	6	(3	3)	96	30	26	30	26	0	63	5	6	1	2	4	1	.234	.308	.336	.644
	Postseason		1	1	1	0	0	0	(0	0)	1	0	0	0	0	0	0	0	0	0	0	0	0	1.000	1.000	1.000	2.000
	2 ML YEARS		94	303	70	13	0	7	(3	4)	104	32	28	31	26	0	67	5	6	1	2	4	2	.231	.301	.343	.645

Stephen Pryor

Pitches: R Bats: R Pos: RP-1   Ht: 6'4" Wt: 250 Born: 7/23/1989 Age: 25

Year	Team	Lg	G	GS	CG	GF	IP	BFP	H	R	ER	HR	SH	SF	HB	TBB	IBB	SO	WP	Bk	W	L	Pct.	Sh	Sv-Op	Hld	ERC	ERA
2014	Jacksn*	AA	4	0	0	1	3.2	18	5	6	6	2	0	0	0	3	0	3	0	0	0	1	.000	0	0- -	-	12.70	14.73
2014	Tacom*	AAA	24	0	0	8	31.0	135	26	16	16	4	0	2	0	18	0	27	2	0	2	1	.667	0	1- -	-	4.07	4.65
2014	Roch*	AAA	14	0	0	4	20.1	81	6	2	2	2	1	0	0	16	0	22	5	0	1	0	1.000	0	2- -	-	1.91	0.89
2012	Sea	AL	26	0	0	8	23.0	104	22	13	10	5	2	2	0	13	2	27	3	0	3	1	.750	0	0-0	5	5.10	3.91
2013	Sea	AL	7	0	0	2	7.1	26	3	0	0	0	0	0	0	1	0	7	0	0	0	0	-	0	0-1	3	0.55	0.00
2014	Sea	AL	1	0	0	0	1.2	8	1	1	0	0	0	1	0	2	0	1	1	0	0	0	-	0	0-0	0	3.97	0.00
	3 ML YEARS		34	0	0	10	32.0	138	26	14	10	5	2	3	0	16	2	35	4	0	3	1	.750	0	0-1	8	3.64	2.81

Yasiel Puig

Bats: R Throws: R Pos: RF-91;CF-53;PH-5;DH-1   yah-SEE-el PWEEG   Ht: 6'3" Wt: 235 Born: 12/7/1990 Age: 24

Year	Team	Lg	G	AB	H	2B	3B	HR	(Hm	Rd)	TB	R	RBI	RC	TBB	IBB	SO	HBP	SH	SF	SB	CS	GDP	Avg	OBP	Slg	OPS
2012	Ddgrs	R	9	30	12	0	3	4	(-	-)	30	10	11	12	6	1	7	0	0	0	1	1	0	.400	.500	1.000	1.500
2012	RCuca	A+	14	52	17	2	0	1	(-	-)	22	10	4	9	6	0	8	1	0	0	7	4	0	.327	.407	.423	.830
2013	Chatt	AA	40	147	46	12	3	8	(-	-)	88	26	37	33	15	3	29	3	0	2	13	5	0	.313	.383	.599	.982
2013	LAD	NL	104	382	122	21	2	19	(9	10)	204	66	42	62	36	6	97	11	0	3	11	8	6	.319	.391	.534	.925
2014	LAD	NL	148	558	165	37	9	16	(8	8)	268	92	69	95	67	3	124	12	2	1	11	7	7	.296	.382	.480	.863
	Postseason		10	39	13	1	1	0	(0	0)	16	6	4	5	1	0	14	1	0	0	0	1	2	.333	.366	.410	.776
	2 ML YEARS		252	940	287	58	11	35	(17	18)	472	158	111	157	103	9	221	23	2	4	22	15	13	.305	.386	.502	.888

Albert Pujols

Bats: R Throws: R Pos: 1B-116;DH-43;3B-1   POO-holes   Ht: 6'3" Wt: 230 Born: 1/16/1980 Age: 35

Year	Team	Lg	G	AB	H	2B	3B	HR	(Hm	Rd)	TB	R	RBI	RC	TBB	IBB	SO	HBP	SH	SF	SB	CS	GDP	Avg	OBP	Slg	OPS
2001	StL	NL	161	590	194	47	4	37	(18	19)	360	112	130	132	69	6	93	9	1	7	1	3	21	.329	.403	.610	1.013
2002	StL	NL	157	590	185	40	2	34	(14	20)	331	118	127	121	72	13	69	9	0	4	2	4	20	.314	.394	.561	.955
2003	StL	NL	157	591	212	51	1	43	(21	22)	394	137	124	160	79	12	65	10	0	5	5	1	16	.359	.400	.667	1.106
2004	StL	NL	154	592	196	51	2	46	(18	28)	389	133	123	143	84	12	52	7	0	9	5	5	21	.331	.415	.657	1.072
2005	StL	NL	161	591	195	38	2	41	(23	18)	360	129	117	139	97	27	65	9	0	3	16	2	19	.330	.430	.609	1.039
2006	StL	NL	143	535	177	33	1	49	(24	25)	359	119	137	146	92	28	50	4	0	3	7	2	20	.331	.431	.671	1.102
2007	StL	NL	158	565	185	38	1	32	(12	20)	321	99	103	118	99	22	58	7	0	8	2	6	27	.327	.429	.568	.997
2008	StL	NL	148	524	187	44	0	37	(19	18)	342	100	116	130	104	34	54	5	0	8	7	3	16	.357	.462	.653	1.114
2009	StL	NL	160	568	186	45	1	47	(22	25)	374	124	135	145	115	44	64	9	0	8	16	4	23	.327	.443	.658	1.101
2010	StL	NL	159	587	183	39	1	42	(17	25)	350	115	118	131	103	38	76	4	0	6	14	4	23	.312	.414	.596	1.011
2011	StL	NL	147	579	173	29	0	37	(16	21)	313	105	99	100	61	15	58	4	0	7	9	1	29	.299	.366	.541	.906
2012	LAA	AL	154	607	173	50	0	30	(14	16)	313	85	105	100	52	16	76	5	0	6	8	1	19	.285	.343	.516	.859
2013	LAA	AL	99	391	101	19	0	17	(8	9)	171	49	64	54	40	8	55	5	0	7	1	1	18	.258	.330	.437	.767
2014	LAA	AL	159	633	172	37	1	28	(13	15)	295	89	105	86	48	11	71	5	0	9	5	1	28	.272	.324	.466	.790
	Postseason		74	267	88	18	1	18	(7	11)	162	54	52	67	48	20	39	5	0	1	1	2	6	.330	.439	.607	1.046
	14 ML YEARS		2117	7943	2519	561	16	520	(239	281)	4672	1514	1603	1705	1115	286	906	92	1	90	98	38	297	.317	.403	.588	.991

Nick Punto

POON-toh

Bats: B **Throws:** R **Pos:** 2B-52;SS-17;PH-15;PR-4;3B-2;RF-1   **Ht:** 5'9" **Wt:** 195 **Born:** 11/8/1977 **Age:** 37

										BATTING												RUNNING			AVERAGES			
Year	Team	Lg	G	AB	H	2B	3B	HR	(Hm	Rd)	TB	R	RBI	RC	TBB	IBB	SO	HBP	SH	SF	SB	CS	GDP	Avg	OBP	Slg	OPS
2001	Phi	NL	4	5	2	0	0	0	(0	0)	2	0	0	1	0	0	0	0	0	0	0	0	0	.400	.400	.400	.800
2002	Phi	NL	9	6	1	0	0	0	(0	0)	1	0	0	0	0	0	3	0	1	0	0	0	0	.167	.167	.167	.333
2003	Phi	NL	64	92	20	2	0	1	(0	1)	25	14	4	7	7	1	22	0	0	0	2	1	0	.217	.273	.272	.544
2004	Min	AL	38	91	23	0	0	2	(2	0)	29	17	12	15	12	0	19	0	0	0	6	0	2	.253	.340	.319	.658
2005	Min	AL	112	394	94	18	4	4	(3	1)	132	45	26	35	36	0	86	0	7	2	13	8	9	.239	.301	.335	.636
2006	Min	AL	135	459	133	21	7	1	(0	1)	171	73	45	59	47	0	68	1	10	7	17	5	8	.290	.352	.373	.725
2007	Min	AL	150	472	99	18	4	1	(0	1)	128	53	25	37	55	1	90	0	6	3	16	6	7	.210	.291	.271	.562
2008	Min	AL	99	338	96	19	4	2	(1	1)	129	43	28	42	32	1	57	0	5	2	15	6	10	.284	.344	.382	.726
2009	Min	AL	125	359	82	15	1	1	(0	1)	102	56	38	46	61	1	70	1	13	6	16	3	7	.228	.337	.284	.621
2010	Min	AL	88	252	60	11	1	1	(0	1)	76	24	20	25	28	2	50	1	4	3	6	2	3	.238	.313	.302	.615
2011	StL	NL	63	133	37	8	4	1	(0	1)	56	21	20	25	25	3	21	0	6	2	1	1	3	.278	.388	.421	.809
2012	2 Tms		87	160	35	7	0	1	(0	1)	45	20	10	15	25	0	42	0	4	2	6	0	5	.219	.321	.281	.602
2013	LAD	NL	116	294	75	15	0	2	(2	0)	96	34	21	30	33	0	67	0	6	2	3	3	4	.255	.328	.327	.655
2014	Oak	AL	73	198	41	7	2	2	(1	1)	58	21	14	18	25	0	56	0	1	0	3	1	5	.207	.296	.293	.589
12	Bos	AL	65	125	25	6	0	1	(0	1)	34	14	10	10	19	0	33	0	2	2	5	0	5	.200	.301	.272	.573
12	LAD	AL	22	35	10	1	0	0	(0	0)	11	6	0	5	6	0	9	0	2	0	1	0	0	.286	.390	.314	.705
	Postseason		27	62	14	2	0	0	(0	0)	16	0	4	4	10	2	23	0	2	1	0	0	0	.226	.329	.258	.587
	14 ML YEARS		1163	3253	798	141	27	19	(9	10)	1050	421	263	355	386	9	651	3	63	29	104	36	63	.245	.323	.323	.646

Luke Putkonen

putt-COE-nen

Pitches: R **Bats:** R **Pos:** RP-2   **Ht:** 6'6" **Wt:** 215 **Born:** 5/10/1986 **Age:** 29

			HOW MUCH HE PITCHED					WHAT HE GAVE UP											THE RESULTS						
Year	Team	Lg	G	GS	CG	GF	IP	BFP	H	R	ER	HR	SH	SF	HB	TBB	IBB	SO	WP	Bk	W	L	Pct	Sh	Sv-Op	Hld	ERC	ERA
2014 WMich*	A	3	0	0	0	2.2	14	4	4	4	1	0	0	0	2	0	0	0	0	0	1	.000	0	0- -	-	11.06	13.50
2014 Toledo*	AAA	2	0	0	0	4.0	19	7	5	5	1	0	0	0	1	0	0	0	0	0	0	-	0	0- -	-	9.69	11.25
2012 Det	AL	12	0	0	6	16.0	72	19	7	7	0	1	0	0	8	1	10	2	0	0	2	.000	0	1-2	6	4.74	3.94
2013 Det	AL	30	0	0	12	29.2	127	30	11	10	4	2	1	0	9	0	28	5	0	1	3	.250	0	0-0	1	3.94	3.03
2014 Det	AL	2	0	0	0	2.2	18	6	8	8	2	0	0	1	2	0	1	0	0	0	0	-	0	0-0	0	21.83	27.00
3 ML YEARS		44	0	0	18	48.1	217	55	26	25	6	3	1	1	19	1	39	7	0	1	5	.167	0	1-2	1	5.02	4.66

Zach Putnam

Pitches: R **Bats:** R **Pos:** RP-49   **Ht:** 6'2" **Wt:** 225 **Born:** 7/3/1987 **Age:** 27

			HOW MUCH HE PITCHED					WHAT HE GAVE UP											THE RESULTS						
Year	Team	Lg	G	GS	CG	GF	IP	BFP	H	R	ER	HR	SH	SF	HB	TBB	IBB	SO	WP	Bk	W	L	Pct	Sh	Sv-Op	Hld	ERC	ERA
2014 Charltt*	AAA	5	0	0	3	7.0	26	4	0	0	0	0	0	0	1	0	12	0	0	1	0	1.000	0	0- -	-	0.93	0.00
2011 Cle	AL	8	0	0	3	7.1	34	10	5	5	1	0	0	2	1	0	9	1	0	1	1	.500	0	0-1	0	5.82	6.14
2012 Col	NL	2	0	0	0	2.0	9	3	0	0	0	1	0	0	1	0	0	0	0	0	0	-	0	0-0	0	7.26	0.00
2013 ChC	NL	5	0	0	1	3.1	19	9	7	7	1	0	1	0	0	0	4	0	0	0	0	-	0	0-0	0	15.42	18.90
2014 CWS	AL	49	0	0	13	54.2	213	39	14	12	2	1	1	1	20	1	46	5	0	5	3	.625	0	6-7	16	2.21	1.98
4 ML YEARS		64	0	0	17	67.1	275	61	26	24	4	2	2	3	21	1	59	6	0	6	4	.600	0	6-8	16	3.19	3.21

J.J. Putz

PUTS

Pitches: R **Bats:** R **Pos:** RP-18   **Ht:** 6'5" **Wt:** 250 **Born:** 2/22/1977 **Age:** 38

			HOW MUCH HE PITCHED					WHAT HE GAVE UP											THE RESULTS						
Year	Team	Lg	G	GS	CG	GF	IP	BFP	H	R	ER	HR	SH	SF	HB	TBB	IBB	SO	WP	Bk	W	L	Pct	Sh	Sv-Op	Hld	ERC	ERA
2014 Reno*	AAA	2	0	0	0	1.2	8	1	0	0	0	0	0	0	2	0	2	0	0	0	0	-	0	0- -	-	3.97	0.00
2003 Sea	AL	3	0	0	0	3.2	18	4	2	2	0	0	0	0	3	0	3	0	0	0	0	-	0	0-0	0	5.31	4.91
2004 Sea	AL	54	0	0	30	63.0	275	66	35	33	10	3	2	5	24	4	47	1	0	0	3	.000	0	9-13	3	4.97	4.71
2005 Sea	AL	64	0	0	20	60.0	259	58	27	24	8	3	3	2	23	2	45	2	0	6	5	.545	0	1-4	21	4.11	3.60
2006 Sea	AL	72	0	0	57	78.1	303	59	20	20	4	1	2	1	13	1	104	1	0	4	1	.800	0	36-43	5	1.78	2.30
2007 Sea	AL	68	0	0	65	71.2	260	37	11	11	6	2	1	2	13	0	82	3	0	6	1	.857	0	40-42	0	1.21	1.38
2008 Sea	AL	47	0	0	35	46.1	211	46	20	20	4	0	1	2	28	2	56	2	0	6	5	.545	0	15-23	0	4.82	3.88
2009 NYM	NL	29	0	0	6	29.1	135	29	18	17	1	1	2	0	19	4	19	1	0	1	4	.200	0	2-4	10	4.16	5.22
2010 CWS	AL	60	0	0	16	54.0	219	41	18	17	4	1	1	1	15	2	65	4	0	7	5	.583	0	3-7	14	2.19	2.83
2011 Ari	NL	60	0	0	52	58.0	229	41	15	14	4	1	1	1	12	0	61	2	0	2	2	.500	0	45-49	0	1.80	2.17
2012 Ari	NL	57	0	0	52	54.1	218	45	18	17	4	2	1	2	11	1	65	3	0	1	5	.167	0	32-37	0	2.38	2.82
2013 Ari	NL	40	0	0	16	34.1	140	26	9	9	4	0	0	1	17	1	38	0	0	3	1	.750	0	6-11	6	3.29	2.36
2014 Ari	NL	18	0	0	8	13.2	62	17	10	10	1	0	1	1	6	1	14	2	0	1	1	.500	0	0-0	0	5.76	6.59
	Postseason		3	0	0	3	2.1	11	3	1	1	0	0	0	0	1	0	0	0	0	1	0	1.000	0	0-0	0	4.93	3.86
	12 ML YEARS		572	0	0	357	566.2	2329	469	203	194	50	15	17	19	184	18	599	24	0	37	33	.529	0	189-233	59	2.88	3.08

Kevin Quackenbush

Pitches: R **Bats:** R **Pos:** RP-56   **Ht:** 6'4" **Wt:** 220 **Born:** 11/28/1988 **Age:** 26

			HOW MUCH HE PITCHED					WHAT HE GAVE UP											THE RESULTS						
Year	Team	Lg	G	GS	CG	GF	IP	BFP	H	R	ER	HR	SH	SF	HB	TBB	IBB	SO	WP	Bk	W	L	Pct	Sh	Sv-Op	Hld	ERC	ERA
2011 Eugene	A-	17	0	0	15	20.2	76	13	1	1	0	1	0	0	6	0	33	1	0	1	0	1.000	0	9- -	-	1.46	0.44
2011 FtWyn	A	18	0	0	17	21.1	82	12	2	2	0	0	0	0	6	0	38	0	0	1	1	.500	0	9- -	-	1.16	0.84
2012 Lk Els	A+	52	0	0	46	57.2	229	42	9	6	1	2	0	0	22	0	70	3	0	3	2	.600	0	27- -	-	2.13	0.94
2013 SnAnt	AA	29	0	0	23	31.0	121	16	4	1	1	1	1	3	10	1	46	0	1	2	0	1.000	0	13- -	-	1.41	0.29
2013 Tucsn	AAA	28	0	0	11	34.0	151	33	14	11	0	1	0	1	19	1	38	0	0	8	2	.800	0	4- -	-	3.99	2.91
2014 ElPaso	AAA	13	0	0	9	14.1	55	9	2	2	0	1	0	0	4	0	12	0	0	0	0	-	0	6- -	-	1.37	1.26
2014 SD	NL	56	0	0	18	54.1	222	42	15	15	2	1	3	2	18	4	56	1	1	3	3	.500	0	6-7	10	2.25	2.48

Chad Qualls

Pitches: R Bats: R Pos: RP-58   Ht: 6'4" Wt: 240 Born: 8/17/1978 Age: 36

			HOW MUCH HE PITCHED						WHAT HE GAVE UP												THE RESULTS							
Year	Team	Lg	G	GS	CG	GF	IP	BFP	H	R	ER	HR	SH	SF	HB	TBB	IBB	SO	WP	Bk	W	L	Pct	Sh	Sv-Op	Hld	ERC	ERA
2004	Hou	NL	25	0	0	4	33.0	141	34	13	13	3	0	1	4	8	1	24	0	0	4	0	1.000	0	1-2	9	4.02	3.55
2005	Hou	NL	77	0	0	19	79.2	329	73	33	29	7	4	3	6	23	2	60	1	0	6	4	.600	0	0-0	22	3.42	3.28
2006	Hou	NL	81	0	0	13	88.2	356	76	38	37	10	4	4	6	28	6	56	0	0	7	3	.700	0	0-6	23	3.36	3.76
2007	Hou	NL	79	0	0	16	82.2	345	84	29	28	10	6	2	3	25	5	78	2	0	6	5	.545	0	5-10	21	4.07	3.05
2008	Ari	NL	77	0	0	21	73.2	300	61	29	23	4	4	3	3	18	2	71	6	0	4	8	.333	0	9-17	22	2.40	2.81
2009	Ari	NL	51	0	0	44	52.0	217	53	23	21	5	1	0	2	7	2	45	2	0	2	2	.500	0	24-29	0	3.17	3.63
2010	2 Tms		70	0	0	29	59.0	281	85	56	48	7	4	4	2	21	4	49	4	0	3	4	.429	0	12-19	11	6.63	7.32
2011	SD	NL	77	0	0	20	74.1	306	73	30	29	7	7	1	0	20	5	43	4	0	6	8	.429	0	0-5	22	3.38	3.51
2012	3 Tms		60	0	0	15	52.1	231	63	34	31	7	2	2	0	14	4	27	3	0	2	1	.667	0	0-5	14	4.78	5.33
2013	Mia	NL	66	0	0	12	62.0	252	57	18	18	4	4	0	2	19	7	49	1	0	5	2	.714	0	0-2	15	3.09	2.61
2014	Hou	AL	58	0	0	41	51.1	213	54	22	19	5	2	0	2	5	2	43	1	0	1	5	.167	0	19-25	2	3.22	3.33
10	Ari	NL	43	0	0	28	38.0	190	61	41	35	5	4	2	1	15	4	34	3	0	1	4	.200	0	12-16	3	7.80	8.29
10	TB	AL	27	0	0	1	21.0	91	24	15	13	2	0	2	1	6	0	15	1	0	2	0	1.000	0	0-3	8	4.64	5.57
12	Phi	NL	35	0	0	6	31.1	140	39	18	16	7	1	0	0	9	3	19	2	0	1	1	.500	0	0-5	12	5.74	4.60
12	NYY	AL	8	0	0	4	7.1	33	10	5	5	0	0	1	0	3	1	2	1	0	1	0	1.000	0	0-0	0	5.38	6.14
12	Pit	NL	17	0	0	5	13.2	58	14	11	10	0	1	1	0	2	0	6	0	0	0	0	-	0	0-0	2	2.48	6.59
	Postseason		17	0	0	0	22.2	94	24	13	13	3	1	0	0	7	3	17	0	0	1	1	.500	0	0-2	4	4.20	5.16
	11 ML YEARS		721	0	0	234	708.2	2971	713	325	296	69	38	20	30	188	40	545	24	0	46	42	.523	0	70-120	161	3.68	3.76

Carlos Quentin

Bats: R Throws: R Pos: LF-32;PH-14;DH-5   Ht: 6'1" Wt: 235 Born: 8/28/1982 Age: 32

									BATTING											RUNNING			AVERAGES			
Year	Team	Lg	G	AB	H	2B	3B	HR	(Hm	Rd)	TB	R	RBI	RC	TBB	IBB	SO	HBP	SH	SF	SB	CS	GDP	Avg	OBP	Slg	OPS
2014	Lk Els*	A+	4	10	1	0	0	0	(-	-)	1	1	0	0	3	0	2	0	0	0	0	0	0	.100	.308	.100	.408
2014	ElPaso*	AAA	3	8	2	0	0	1	(-	-)	5	1	1	1	0	0	0	0	0	0	0	0	1	.250	.250	.625	.875
2006	Ari	NL	57	166	42	13	3	9	(3	6)	88	23	32	29	15	2	34	8	1	1	1	0	6	.253	.342	.530	.872
2007	Ari	NL	81	229	49	16	0	5	(5	0)	80	29	31	27	18	1	54	11	1	4	2	2	5	.214	.298	.349	.647
2008	CWS	AL	130	480	138	26	1	36	(21	15)	274	96	100	104	66	0	80	20	0	3	7	3	16	.288	.394	.571	.965
2009	CWS	AL	99	351	83	14	0	21	(12	9)	160	47	56	47	31	2	52	15	0	2	3	0	11	.236	.323	.456	.779
2010	CWS	AL	131	453	110	25	2	26	(19	7)	217	73	87	78	50	3	83	20	0	4	2	2	16	.243	.342	.479	.821
2011	CWS	AL	118	421	107	31	0	24	(7	17)	210	53	77	72	34	0	84	23	0	5	1	1	7	.254	.340	.499	.838
2012	SD	NL	86	284	74	21	0	16	(7	9)	143	44	46	45	36	2	41	17	0	1	6	0	7	.261	.374	.504	.877
2013	SD	NL	82	276	76	21	0	13	(4	9)	136	42	44	47	31	0	55	9	0	4	0	0	7	.275	.363	.493	.855
2014	SD	NL	50	130	23	6	0	4	(2	2)	41	9	18	11	17	0	33	4	0	5	0	0	5	.177	.284	.315	.599
	9 ML YEARS		834	2790	702	173	6	154	(80	74)	1349	416	491	460	298	10	516	127	2	30	16	9	79	.252	.347	.484	.831

Jose Quintana

Pitches: L Bats: R Pos: SP-32   KIN-tahn-ah   Ht: 6'1" Wt: 220 Born: 1/24/1989 Age: 26

					HOW MUCH HE PITCHED							WHAT HE GAVE UP								THE RESULTS						
Year	Team	Lg	G	GS	CG	GF	IP	BFP	H	R	ER	HR	SH	SF	HB	TBB	IBB	SO	WP	Bk	W	L	Pct	Sh	Sv-Op	Hld	ERC	ERA
2012	CWS	AL	25	22	0	2	136.1	568	142	62	57	14	5	1	3	42	4	81	10	2	6	6	.500	0	0-0	0	4.13	3.76
2013	CWS	AL	33	33	0	0	200.0	832	188	83	78	23	3	6	5	56	2	164	2	1	9	7	.563	0	0-0	0	3.47	3.51
2014	CWS	AL	32	32	0	0	200.1	830	197	87	74	10	4	6	2	52	3	178	7	0	9	11	.450	0	0-0	0	3.15	3.32
	3 ML YEARS		90	87	0	2	536.2	2230	527	232	209	47	12	13	10	150	9	423	19	3	24	24	.500	0	0-0	0	3.51	3.50

Omar Quintanilla

Bats: L Throws: R Pos: SS-11;2B-2;PH-2   keen-tah-NEE-yah   Ht: 5'9" Wt: 185 Born: 10/24/1981 Age: 33

									BATTING											RUNNING			AVERAGES			
Year	Team	Lg	G	AB	H	2B	3B	HR	(Hm	Rd)	TB	R	RBI	RC	TBB	IBB	SO	HBP	SH	SF	SB	CS	GDP	Avg	OBP	Slg	OPS
2014	LsVgs*	AAA	46	155	36	10	2	3	(-	-)	59	19	27	16	7	1	21	2	4	2	1	1	3	.232	.271	.381	.652
2005	Col	NL	39	128	28	1	1	0	(0	0)	31	16	7	9	9	0	15	0	6	0	2	1	3	.219	.270	.242	.512
2006	Col	NL	11	34	6	1	1	0	(0	0)	9	3	3	2	3	1	9	0	1	0	1	1	1	.176	.243	.265	.508
2007	Col	NL	27	70	16	4	0	0	(0	0)	20	6	5	6	5	0	15	0	0	0	0	0	3	.229	.280	.286	.566
2008	Col	NL	81	210	50	17	0	2	(1	1)	73	28	15	18	15	3	46	0	8	1	0	0	3	.238	.288	.348	.635
2009	Col	NL	58	58	10	2	0	0	(0	0)	12	7	2	4	8	0	27	0	3	0	0	0	0	.172	.270	.207	.400
2011	Tex	AL	11	22	1	0	1	0	(0	0)	3	3	2	0	0	0	9	0	1	0	0	0	0	.045	.045	.136	.182
2012	2 Tms		65	169	41	8	0	4	(3	1)	61	25	16	14	16	1	42	2	1	2	0	1	3	.243	.312	.361	.673
2013	NYM	NL	95	315	70	9	2	2	(1	1)	89	28	21	27	38	7	70	1	3	2	2	0	10	.222	.306	.283	.589
2014	NYM	NL	15	29	6	1	0	0	(0	0)	7	2	3	3	2	0	5	0	0	0	0	1	1	.207	.258	.241	.499
12	NYM	NL	29	70	18	5	0	1	(0	1)	26	13	4	6	8	1	17	2	0	0	0	0	2	.257	.350	.371	.721
12	Bal	AL	36	99	23	3	0	3	(3	0)	35	12	12	8	8	0	25	0	1	2	0	1	1	.232	.284	.354	.638
	9 ML YEARS		402	1035	228	43	5	8	(5	3)	305	118	74	83	96	12	238	3	23	5	5	3	24	.220	.287	.295	.582

Humberto Quintero

Bats: R Throws: R Pos: C-3   oom-BARE-toe keen-TARE-oh   Ht: 5'9" Wt: 215 Born: 8/2/1979 Age: 35

									BATTING											RUNNING			AVERAGES			
Year	Team	Lg	G	AB	H	2B	3B	HR	(Hm	Rd)	TB	R	RBI	RC	TBB	IBB	SO	HBP	SH	SF	SB	CS	GDP	Avg	OBP	Slg	OPS
2014	Tacom*	AAA	74	259	75	17	3	4	(-	-)	110	29	27	34	7	0	49	2	6	2	2	3	12	.290	.311	.425	.736
2003	SD	NL	12	23	5	0	0	0	(0	0)	5	1	2	2	1	1	6	0	0	0	0	0	0	.217	.250	.217	.467
2004	SD	NL	23	72	18	3	0	2	(1	1)	27	7	10	6	5	0	16	0	0	1	0	2	5	.250	.295	.375	.670
2005	Hou	NL	18	54	10	1	0	1	(1	0)	14	6	8	2	1	1	10	0	2	0	0	0	3	.185	.200	.259	.459
2006	Hou	NL	11	21	7	2	0	0	(0	0)	9	2	2	1	1	0	3	0	0	0	0	0	1	.333	.364	.429	.792
2007	Hou	NL	29	53	12	2	0	0	(0	0)	14	2	1	3	2	1	13	2	0	0	0	0	2	.226	.281	.264	.545
2008	Hou	NL	59	168	38	6	0	2	(1	1)	50	16	12	10	6	0	34	4	5	0	0	0	5	.226	.270	.298	.567

Year	Team	Lg	G	AB	H	2B	3B	HR	(Hm	Rd)	TB	R	RBI	RC	TBB	IBB	SO	HBP	SH	SF	SB	CS	GDP	Avg	OBP	Slg	OPS
2009	Hou	NL	60	157	37	8	1	4	(3	1)	59	11	14	13	7	1	41	4	0	0	0	0	8	.236	.286	.376	.662
2010	Hou	NL	88	265	62	10	0	4	(2	2)	84	13	20	20	8	2	59	2	1	0	0	0	5	.234	.262	.317	.579
2011	Hou	NL	79	262	63	12	1	2	(2	0)	83	22	25	14	6	1	53	1	1	2	1	0	10	.240	.258	.317	.575
2012	KC	AL	43	138	32	12	0	1	(1	0)	47	7	19	10	4	0	28	1	0	1	0	1	1	.232	.257	.341	.598
2013	2 Tms		46	131	31	5	0	4	(2	2)	48	8	13	10	6	1	30	1	2	0	0	0	6	.237	.275	.366	.642
2014	Sea	AL	3	2	0	0	0	0	(0	0)	0	0	1	0	0	0	1	0	0	0	0	0	0	.000	.000	.000	.000
13	Phi	NL	24	64	16	4	0	2	(1	1)	26	3	9	7	3	1	15	1	0	0	0	0	3	.250	.294	.406	.700
13	Sea	AL	22	67	15	1	0	2	(1	1)	22	5	4	3	3	0	15	0	2	0	0	0	3	.224	.257	.328	.586
12 ML YEARS			471	1346	315	61	2	20	(13	7)	440	95	127	91	47	9	294	15	11	4	1	3	47	.234	.267	.327	.594

Guillermo Quiroz

Bats: R **Throws:** R **Pos:** C-2   key-ROSE   **Ht:** 6'1" **Wt:** 230 **Born:** 11/29/1981 **Age:** 33

Year	Team	Lg	G	AB	H	2B	3B	HR	(Hm	Rd)	TB	R	RBI	RC	TBB	IBB	SO	HBP	SH	SF	SB	CS	GDP	Avg	OBP	Slg	OPS
2014	Fresno*	AAA	69	240	64	13	1	3	(-	-)	88	22	23	26	8	0	56	2	1	1	0	0	5	.267	.295	.367	.661
2004	Tor	AL	17	52	11	2	0	0	(0	0)	13	2	6	4	2	0	8	2	0	1	1	0	1	.212	.263	.250	.513
2005	Tor	AL	12	36	7	2	0	0	(0	0)	9	3	4	3	2	0	13	1	0	0	0	0	0	.194	.256	.250	.506
2006	Sea	AL	1	2	0	0	0	0	(0	0)	0	0	0	0	0	0	2	0	0	0	0	0	0	.000	.000	.000	.000
2007	Tex	AL	9	10	4	1	0	0	(0	0)	5	1	2	3	1	0	2	0	0	0	0	0	0	.400	.455	.500	.955
2008	Bal	AL	56	134	25	5	0	2	(1	1)	36	12	14	10	12	0	34	1	1	0	0	0	3	.187	.259	.269	.527
2009	Bal	AL	4	14	4	0	0	0	(0	0)	4	0	2	1	0	0	3	0	1	0	0	0	0	.286	.286	.286	.571
2010	Sea	AL	2	7	2	1	0	0	(0	0)	3	1	0	0	0	0	1	0	0	0	0	0	0	.286	.286	.429	.714
2012	Bos	NL	2	2	0	0	0	0	(0	0)	0	0	0	0	0	0	1	0	0	0	0	0	0	.000	.000	.000	.000
2013	SF	NL	43	86	16	7	0	1	(1	0)	26	5	6	3	5	1	21	1	2	1	0	0	4	.186	.237	.302	.539
2014	SF	NL	2	3	0	0	0	0	(0	0)	0	0	0	0	0	0	0	0	0	0	0	0	0	.000	.000	.000	.000
10 ML YEARS			148	346	69	18	0	3	(2	1)	96	24	34	24	22	1	85	5	4	2	1	0	8	.199	.256	.277	.533

Ryan Raburn

RAY-burn

Bats: R **Throws:** R **Pos:** RF-25;DH-25;LF-20;PH-19;1B-1;PR-1   **Ht:** 6'0" **Wt:** 185 **Born:** 4/17/1981 **Age:** 34

Year	Team	Lg	G	AB	H	2B	3B	HR	(Hm	Rd)	TB	R	RBI	RC	TBB	IBB	SO	HBP	SH	SF	SB	CS	GDP	Avg	OBP	Slg	OPS
2014	Clmbs*	AAA	4	17	1	0	0	0	(-	-)	1	2	0	0	1	0	2	0	0	0	0	0	0	.059	.111	.059	.170
2014	Akron*	AA	3	11	5	0	0	0	(-	-)	5	2	4	2	1	0	3	0	0	0	0	0	1	.455	.500	.455	.955
2004	Det	AL	12	29	4	1	0	0	(0	0)	5	4	1	1	2	0	15	0	0	0	1	0	0	.138	.194	.172	.366
2007	Det	AL	49	138	42	12	2	4	(2	2)	70	28	27	21	8	1	33	0	1	1	3	0	7	.304	.340	.507	.847
2008	Det	AL	92	182	43	10	1	4	(2	2)	67	26	20	20	16	1	49	0	1	0	3	1	2	.236	.298	.368	.666
2009	Det	AL	113	261	76	11	2	16	(9	7)	139	44	45	42	26	2	60	2	1	1	5	4	6	.291	.359	.533	.891
2010	Det	AL	113	371	104	25	1	15	(5	10)	176	54	62	54	27	0	92	8	1	3	2	2	8	.280	.340	.474	.814
2011	Det	AL	121	387	99	22	2	14	(7	7)	167	53	49	48	21	2	114	3	4	3	1	1	4	.256	.297	.432	.729
2012	Det	AL	66	205	35	14	0	1	(0	1)	52	14	12	8	13	0	53	2	1	1	1	1	1	.171	.226	.254	.480
2013	Cle	AL	87	243	66	18	0	16	(8	8)	132	40	55	47	29	0	67	4	0	1	0	0	4	.272	.357	.543	.901
2014	Cle	AL	74	195	39	7	0	4	(0	4)	58	18	22	11	13	1	51	1	0	3	0	0	2	.200	.250	.297	.547
Postseason			10	31	9	2	0	2	(1	1)	17	4	5	4	5	0	9	0	0	0	0	0	3	.290	.389	.548	.937
9 ML YEARS			727	2011	508	120	8	74	(33	41)	866	281	293	252	155	7	534	20	9	13	16	9	46	.253	.311	.431	.741

Alexei Ramirez

ah-lexx-AY

Bats: R **Throws:** R **Pos:** SS-158;PH-1   **Ht:** 6'2" **Wt:** 180 **Born:** 9/22/1981 **Age:** 33

Year	Team	Lg	G	AB	H	2B	3B	HR	(Hm	Rd)	TB	R	RBI	RC	TBB	IBB	SO	HBP	SH	SF	SB	CS	GDP	Avg	OBP	Slg	OPS
2008	CWS	AL	136	480	139	22	2	21	(13	8)	228	65	77	78	18	3	61	3	4	4	13	9	14	.290	.317	.475	.792
2009	CWS	AL	148	542	150	14	1	15	(9	6)	211	71	68	74	49	3	66	1	6	8	14	5	15	.277	.333	.389	.723
2010	CWS	AL	156	585	165	29	2	18	(11	7)	252	83	70	72	27	2	82	2	7	5	13	8	12	.282	.313	.431	.744
2011	CWS	AL	158	614	165	31	2	15	(7	8)	245	81	70	74	51	1	84	6	8	5	7	5	19	.269	.328	.399	.727
2012	CWS	AL	158	593	157	24	4	9	(6	3)	216	59	73	70	16	2	77	4	4	4	20	7	15	.265	.287	.364	.651
2013	CWS	AL	158	637	181	39	2	6	(5	1)	242	68	48	67	26	2	68	3	4	4	30	9	17	.284	.313	.380	.693
2014	CWS	AL	158	622	170	35	2	15	(8	7)	254	82	74	79	24	0	81	6	1	4	21	4	21	.273	.305	.408	.713
Postseason			4	12	3	0	0	0	(0	0)	3	1	2	1	1	0	1	0	0	2	0	0	0	.250	.267	.250	.517
7 ML YEARS			1072	4073	1127	194	15	99	(59	40)	1648	509	480	514	211	13	519	25	34	34	118	47	113	.277	.314	.405	.718

Aramis Ramirez

ah-RAH-miss

Bats: R **Throws:** R **Pos:** 3B-126;DH-5;PH-2   **Ht:** 6'1" **Wt:** 205 **Born:** 6/25/1978 **Age:** 37

Year	Team	Lg	G	AB	H	2B	3B	HR	(Hm	Rd)	TB	R	RBI	RC	TBB	IBB	SO	HBP	SH	SF	SB	CS	GDP	Avg	OBP	Slg	OPS
2014	Wisc*	A	2	6	2	0	0	0	(-	-)	2	0	0	0	0	0	1	0	0	0	0	0	0	.333	.333	.333	.667
1998	Pit	NL	72	251	59	9	1	6	(3	3)	88	23	24	26	18	0	72	4	1	1	0	1	3	.235	.296	.351	.646
1999	Pit	NL	18	56	10	2	1	0	(0	0)	14	2	7	4	6	0	9	0	1	1	0	0	0	.179	.254	.250	.504
2000	Pit	NL	73	254	65	15	2	6	(4	2)	102	19	35	28	10	0	36	5	1	4	0	0	9	.256	.293	.402	.695
2001	Pit	NL	158	603	181	40	0	34	(16	18)	323	83	112	108	40	4	100	8	0	4	5	4	9	.300	.350	.536	.885
2002	Pit	NL	142	522	122	26	0	18	(7	11)	202	51	71	49	29	3	95	8	0	11	2	0	17	.234	.279	.387	.666
2003	2 Tms	NL	159	607	165	32	2	27	(10	17)	282	75	106	88	42	3	99	10	0	11	2	2	21	.272	.324	.465	.788
2004	ChC	NL	145	547	174	32	1	36	(22	14)	316	99	103	100	49	6	62	3	0	7	0	2	25	.318	.373	.578	.951
2005	ChC	NL	123	463	140	30	0	31	(11	20)	263	72	92	79	35	4	60	6	0	2	0	1	15	.302	.358	.568	.926
2006	ChC	NL	157	594	173	38	4	38	(14	24)	333	93	119	109	50	4	63	9	0	7	2	1	15	.291	.352	.561	.912
2007	ChC	NL	132	506	157	35	4	26	(17	9)	278	72	101	95	43	8	66	4	0	5	0	0	13	.310	.366	.549	.915
2008	ChC	NL	149	554	160	44	1	27	(17	10)	287	97	111	108	74	7	94	11	0	6	2	2	13	.289	.380	.518	.898

Year Team	Lg	G	AB	H	2B	3B	HR	(Hm	Rd)	TB	R	RBI	RC	TBB	IBB	SO	HBP	SH	SF	SB	CS	GDP	Avg	OBP	Slg	OPS
2009 ChC	NL	82	306	97	14	1	15	(7	8)	158	46	65	66	28	3	43	8	0	0	2	1	8	.317	.389	.516	.905
2010 ChC	NL	124	465	112	21	1	25	(14	11)	210	61	83	64	34	3	90	3	0	5	0	0	10	.241	.294	.452	.745
2011 ChC	NL	149	565	173	35	1	26	(14	12)	288	80	93	96	43	5	69	10	0	8	1	1	12	.306	.361	.510	.871
2012 Mil	NL	149	570	171	50	3	27	(15	12)	308	92	105	97	44	3	82	12	0	4	9	2	14	.300	.360	.540	.901
2013 Mil	NL	92	304	86	18	0	12	(5	7)	140	43	49	44	36	0	55	8	0	3	0	1	8	.283	.370	.461	.831
2014 Mil	NL	133	494	141	23	1	15	(7	8)	211	47	66	66	21	2	75	13	0	3	3	0	18	.285	.330	.427	.757
03 Pit	NL	96	375	105	25	1	12	(6	6)	168	44	67	49	25	3	68	7	0	8	1	1	17	.280	.334	.448	.778
03 ChC	NL	63	232	60	7	1	15	(4	11)	114	31	39	39	17	0	31	3	0	3	1	1	4	.259	.314	.491	.805
Postseason		18	67	13	2	1	4	(1	3)	29	7	10	8	9	0	15	1	0	0	0	0	5	.194	.299	.433	.732
17 ML YEARS		2057	7661	2186	464	23	369	(183	186)	3803	1055	1342	1227	602	55	1170	122	3	82	28	18	210	.285	.344	.496	.840

Erasmo Ramirez

Pitches: R Bats: R Pos: SP-14; RP-3 ehh-RAZ-mo Ht: 5'11" Wt: 200 Born: 5/2/1990 Age: 25

	HOW MUCH HE PITCHED						WHAT HE GAVE UP												THE RESULTS						
Year Team	Lg	G	GS	CG	GF	IP	BFP	H	R	ER	HR	SH	SF	HB	TBB	IBB	SO	WP	Bk	W	L	Pct	Sh	Sv-Op	Hld	ERC	ERA
2014 Hi Dsrt*	A+	1	1	0	0	6.0	28	8	6	5	2	0	0	0	2	0	7	0	0	0	1	.000	0	0- -	-	7.44	7.50
2014 Tacom*	AAA	15	14	0	0	86.1	361	92	43	35	8	1	1	4	13	0	67	9	0	6	5	.545	0	0- -	-	3.59	3.65
2012 Sea	AL	16	8	0	0	59.0	238	47	26	22	6	1	5	3	12	1	48	0	0	1	3	.250	0	0-0	0	2.42	3.36
2013 Sea	AL	14	13	0	0	72.1	321	79	44	40	12	0	3	3	26	0	57	0	0	5	3	.625	0	0-0	0	5.04	4.98
2014 Sea	AL	17	14	0	0	75.1	338	82	44	44	13	1	1	6	34	2	60	3	0	1	6	.143	0	0-0	0	5.68	5.26
3 ML YEARS		47	35	0	2	206.2	897	208	114	106	31	2	9	12	72	3	165	3	0	7	12	.368	0	0-0	0	4.45	4.62

Hanley Ramirez

Bats: R Throws: R Pos: SS-115;PH-7;DH-5 Ht: 6'2" Wt: 225 Born: 12/23/1983 Age: 31

		BATTING																		RUNNING			AVERAGES			
Year Team	Lg	G	AB	H	2B	3B	HR	(Hm	Rd)	TB	R	RBI	RC	TBB	IBB	SO	HBP	SH	SF	SB	CS	GDP	Avg	OBP	Slg	OPS
2005 Bos	AL	2	2	0	0	0	0	(0	0)	0	0	0	0	0	0	2	0	0	0	0	0	0	.000	.000	.000	.000
2006 Fla	NL	158	633	185	46	11	17	(9	8)	304	119	59	101	56	0	128	4	5	2	51	15	7	.292	.353	.480	.833
2007 Fla	NL	154	639	212	48	6	29	(15	14)	359	125	81	115	52	3	95	7	4	4	51	14	10	.332	.386	.562	.948
2008 Fla	NL	153	589	177	34	4	33	(17	16)	318	125	67	116	92	9	122	8	0	4	35	12	5	.301	.400	.540	.940
2009 Fla	NL	151	576	197	42	1	24	(17	7)	313	101	106	122	61	14	101	9	1	5	27	8	9	.342	.410	.543	.954
2010 Fla	NL	142	543	163	28	2	21	(12	9)	258	92	76	90	64	12	93	7	0	5	32	10	14	.300	.378	.475	.853
2011 Fla	NL	92	338	82	16	0	10	(5	5)	128	55	45	46	44	3	66	2	1	0	20	10	6	.243	.333	.379	.712
2012 2 Tms	NL	157	604	155	29	4	24	(11	13)	264	79	92	81	54	4	132	6	0	3	21	7	17	.257	.322	.437	.759
2013 LAD	NL	86	304	105	25	2	20	(8	12)	194	62	57	69	27	3	52	3	0	2	10	2	5	.345	.402	.638	1.040
2014 LAD	NL	128	449	127	35	0	13	(8	5)	201	64	71	69	56	2	84	6	0	1	14	5	10	.283	.369	.448	.817
12 Mia	NL	93	353	87	18	2	14	(7	7)	151	49	48	42	37	1	72	3	0	2	14	4	11	.246	.322	.428	.749
12 LAD	NL	64	251	68	11	2	10	(4	6)	113	30	44	39	17	3	60	3	0	1	7	3	6	.271	.324	.450	.774
Postseason		9	31	10	4	1	1	(0	1)	19	5	7	6	5	3	7	1	0	0	1	0	1	.323	.432	.613	1.045
10 ML YEARS		1223	4677	1403	303	30	191	(102	89)	2339	822	654	809	506	50	875	52	11	26	261	83	83	.300	.373	.500	.873

Jose Ramirez

Pitches: R Bats: R Pos: RP-8 Ht: 6'3" Wt: 190 Born: 1/21/1990 Age: 25

	HOW MUCH HE PITCHED						WHAT HE GAVE UP												THE RESULTS						
Year Team	Lg	G	GS	CG	GF	IP	BFP	H	R	ER	HR	SH	SF	HB	TBB	IBB	SO	WP	Bk	W	L	Pct	Sh	Sv-Op	Hld	ERC	ERA
2010 CtnSC	A	22	21	0	0	115.0	501	106	56	46	3	2	5	9	42	0	105	20	0	6	5	.545	0	0- -	-	3.22	3.60
2011 Tampa	A+	6	6	0	0	24.1	120	35	25	22	3	2	2	1	11	0	25	0	0	0	5	.000	0	0- -	-	7.14	8.14
2011 CtnSC	A	15	15	0	0	79.0	347	84	51	43	9	2	4	4	32	0	74	6	1	5	7	.417	0	0- -	-	4.80	4.90
2012 Tampa	A+	21	18	0	1	98.2	424	92	43	35	7	3	1	5	30	1	94	4	0	7	6	.538	0	0- -	-	3.24	3.19
2013 Trntn	AA	9	8	0	1	42.1	165	28	15	13	7	0	1	3	15	0	50	7	0	1	3	.250	0	1- -	-	2.90	2.76
2013 S-WB	AAA	8	8	0	0	31.1	137	29	20	17	3	0	0	4	21	0	28	2	0	1	3	.250	0	1- -	-	5.52	4.88
2014 S-WB	AAA	9	0	0	2	12.1	60	13	4	2	0	0	0	1	10	1	16	1	0	3	0	1.000	0	1- -	-	5.31	1.46
2014 NYY	AL	8	0	0	5	10.0	49	11	6	6	2	0	0	2	7	0	10	0	0	0	2	.000	0	0-0	0	7.60	5.40

Jose Ramirez

Bats: B Throws: R Pos: SS-66;2B-11;PH-4 Ht: 5'9" Wt: 165 Born: 9/17/1992 Age: 22

		BATTING																		RUNNING			AVERAGES			
Year Team	Lg	G	AB	H	2B	3B	HR	(Hm	Rd)	TB	R	RBI	RC	TBB	IBB	SO	HBP	SH	SF	SB	CS	GDP	Avg	OBP	Slg	OPS
2011 Indns	R	48	194	63	13	4	1	(-	-)	87	30	20	30	7	0	17	2	3	2	12	6	3	.325	.351	.448	.800
2012 MhVlly	A-	3	11	4	2	0	0	(-	-)	6	2	0	2	1	0	0	0	1	0	2	1	0	.364	.417	.545	.962
2012 Lk Cty	A	67	277	98	13	4	3	(-	-)	128	54	27	53	24	1	26	1	8	3	15	6	4	.354	.403	.462	.865
2013 Akron	AA	113	482	131	16	6	3	(-	-)	168	78	38	59	39	1	41	1	7	4	38	16	6	.272	.325	.349	.674
2014 Clmbs	AAA	60	245	74	15	2	5	(-	-)	108	37	29	40	25	2	30	0	2	5	19	11	3	.302	.360	.441	.801
2013 Cle	AL	15	12	4	0	1	0	(0	0)	6	5	0	2	2	0	2	0	0	0	0	0	0	.333	.429	.500	.929
2014 Cle	AL	68	237	62	10	2	2	(1	1)	82	27	17	25	13	0	35	1	13	2	10	1	3	.262	.300	.346	.646
2 ML YEARS		83	249	66	10	3	2	(1	1)	88	32	17	27	15	0	37	1	13	2	10	1	3	.265	.307	.353	.661

Neil Ramirez

Pitches: R Bats: R Pos: RP-50 Ht: 6'4" Wt: 190 Born: 5/25/1989 Age: 26

	HOW MUCH HE PITCHED						WHAT HE GAVE UP												THE RESULTS						
Year Team	Lg	G	GS	CG	GF	IP	BFP	H	R	ER	HR	SH	SF	HB	TBB	IBB	SO	WP	Bk	W	L	Pct	Sh	Sv-Op	Hld	ERC	ERA
2010 Hkry	A	28	26	1	0	140.1	601	150	79	69	14	6	7	17	37	0	142	8	1	10	8	.556	0	0- -	-	4.49	4.43
2011 MrtlBh	A+	1	1	0	0	4.2	17	1	0	0	0	0	0	0	1	0	9	1	0	0	0	-	0	0- -	-	0.29	0.00
2011 RdRck	AAA	18	18	0	0	74.1	318	63	34	30	6	1	1	6	35	0	86	7	0	4	3	.571	0	0- -	-	3.72	3.63
2011 Frisco	AA	6	6	0	0	19.0	77	13	4	4	1	0	1	1	8	0	24	1	1	1	0	1.000	0	0- -	-	2.42	1.89

Year Team	Lg	G	GS	CG	GF	IP	BFP	H	R	ER	HR	SH	SF	HB	TBB	IBB	SO	WP	Bk	W	L	Pct	Sh	Sv-Op	Hld	ERC	ERA
2012 RdRck	AAA	15	15	0	0	74.0	331	78	65	63	12	4	2	6	31	0	63	6	0	6	8	.429	0	0--	-	5.24	7.66
2012 Frisco	AA	13	12	0	0	49.1	208	47	26	23	6	0	5	5	16	0	45	5	1	2	5	.286	0	0--	-	4.15	4.20
2013 Frisco	AA	21	21	0	0	103.0	416	77	46	44	8	4	3	5	42	0	127	10	2	9	3	.750	0	0--	-	2.87	3.84
2013 Tenn	AA	1	1	0	0	4.2	16	1	0	0	0	0	0	0	2	0	5	0	0	0	0	-	0	0--	-	0.61	0.00
2014 Iowa	AAA	6	0	0	1	7.0	33	7	6	6	2	0	0	0	5	0	11	0	0	0	0	-	0	0--	-	6.69	7.71
2014 Cubs	R	2	0	0	0	1.1	9	2	2	1	0	0	0	0	2	0	2	0	0	0	0	-	0	0--	-	9.50	6.75
2014 ChC	NL	50	0	0	10	43.2	177	29	11	7	2	0	0	2	17	0	53	3	1	3	3	.500	0	3-5	16	2.12	1.44

Ramon Ramirez

Pitches: R Bats: R Pos: RP-1   Ht: 5'11" Wt: 200 Born: 8/31/1981 Age: 33

Year Team	Lg	G	GS	CG	GF	IP	BFP	H	R	ER	HR	SH	SF	HB	TBB	IBB	SO	WP	Bk	W	L	Pct	Sh	Sv-Op	Hld	ERC	ERA
2014 Tacom*	AAA	4	0	0	1	4.1	26	6	5	5	0	1	0	2	3	0	5	0	0	0	0	-	0	0--	-	7.79	10.38
2014 Norfolk*	AAA	18	0	0	4	23.2	98	22	10	6	0	0	1	0	8	1	30	1	0	1	1	.500	0	0--	-	2.76	2.28
2006 Col	NL	61	0	0	14	67.2	285	58	28	26	5	2	3	1	27	3	61	2	0	4	3	.571	0	0-2	10	3.09	3.46
2007 Col	NL	22	0	0	5	17.1	78	21	16	16	2	2	2	1	6	2	15	2	0	2	2	.500	0	0-0	3	5.24	8.31
2008 KC	AL	71	0	0	15	71.2	295	57	23	21	2	4	3	0	31	6	70	6	1	3	2	.600	0	1-5	21	2.53	2.64
2009 Bos	AL	70	0	0	16	69.2	301	61	26	22	7	3	0	4	32	4	52	2	2	7	4	.636	0	0-4	12	3.73	2.84
2010 2 Tms		69	0	0	23	69.1	284	52	24	23	7	2	4	0	27	3	46	5	2	1	3	.250	0	3-3	6	2.64	2.99
2011 SF	NL	66	0	0	22	68.2	282	54	24	20	3	2	1	3	26	5	66	6	1	3	3	.500	0	4-5	11	2.57	2.62
2012 NYM	NL	58	0	0	18	63.2	277	58	33	30	4	3	3	0	35	4	52	4	0	3	4	.429	0	1-3	5	3.80	4.24
2013 SF	NL	6	0	0	1	5.2	29	9	8	7	2	1	2	0	5	0	1	1	0	0	0	-	0	0-0	1	13.04	11.12
2014 Bal	AL	1	0	0	1	1.0	4	0	0	0	0	0	0	0	1	0	2	0	0	0	0	-	0	0-0	0	0.95	0.00
10 Bos	AL	44	0	0	17	42.1	178	39	21	21	6	2	4	0	16	2	31	4	1	0	3	.000	0	2-2	2	3.78	4.46
10 SF	NL	25	0	0	6	27.0	106	13	3	2	1	0	0	0	11	1	15	1	1	1	0	1.000	0	1-1	4	1.28	0.67
Postseason		6	0	0	2	4.0	24	6	8	8	2	1	0	1	3	1	2	0	0	0	1	.000	0	0-0	0	11.88	18.00
9 ML YEARS		424	0	0	115	434.2	1835	370	182	165	32	19	18	9	190	27	364	28	6	23	21	.523	0	9-22	65	3.21	3.42

A.J. Ramos

Pitches: R Bats: R Pos: RP-68   Ht: 5'10" Wt: 205 Born: 9/20/1986 Age: 28

Year Team	Lg	G	GS	CG	GF	IP	BFP	H	R	ER	HR	SH	SF	HB	TBB	IBB	SO	WP	Bk	W	L	Pct	Sh	Sv-Op	Hld	ERC	ERA
2014 Jaxnvl*	AA	1	1	0	0	1.0	6	2	1	1	0	0	1	0	1	0	1	0	0	0	0	-	0	0--	-	6.14	9.00
2012 Mia	NL	11	0	0	4	9.1	40	8	4	4	2	0	0	1	4	0	13	0	0	0	0	-	0	0-1	1	4.65	3.86
2013 Mia	NL	68	0	0	18	80.0	338	58	32	28	4	1	3	2	43	3	86	1	0	3	4	.429	0	0-4	11	2.80	3.15
2014 Mia	NL	68	0	0	12	64.0	270	36	16	15	1	3	1	3	43	7	73	7	0	7	1	1.000	0	0-3	20	2.19	2.11
3 ML YEARS		147	0	0	34	153.1	648	102	52	47	7	4	4	6	90	10	172	8	0	10	4	.714	0	0-8	32	2.65	2.76

Cesar Ramos

Pitches: L Bats: L Pos: RP-36; SP-7   Ht: 6'2" Wt: 200 Born: 6/22/1984 Age: 31

Year Team	Lg	G	GS	CG	GF	IP	BFP	H	R	ER	HR	SH	SF	HB	TBB	IBB	SO	WP	Bk	W	L	Pct	Sh	Sv-Op	Hld	ERC	ERA
2009 SD	NL	5	2	0	0	14.2	62	19	5	5	0	0	0	0	4	0	10	0	0	0	1	.000	0	0-0	0	4.78	3.07
2010 SD	NL	14	0	0	4	8.1	47	18	11	11	1	0	0	0	4	0	9	1	1	0	1	.000	0	0-0	2	11.97	11.88
2011 TB	AL	59	0	0	9	43.2	192	36	22	19	4	1	2	3	25	8	31	1	0	0	1	.000	0	0-2	3	3.64	3.92
2012 TB	AL	17	1	0	9	30.0	120	19	7	7	2	0	0	2	10	0	29	0	0	1	0	1.000	0	0-0	3	1.98	2.10
2013 TB	AL	48	0	0	25	67.1	288	66	31	31	6	2	4	2	22	6	53	3	0	2	2	.500	0	1-1	1	3.55	4.14
2014 TB	AL	43	7	0	14	82.2	360	73	39	34	8	3	3	1	39	7	66	4	0	2	6	.250	0	0-2	3	3.53	3.70
6 ML YEARS		186	10	0	61	246.2	1069	231	115	107	21	6	9	8	104	21	198	9	1	5	11	.313	0	1-3	8	3.66	3.90

Wilson Ramos

Bats: R Throws: R Pos: C-87;DH-1   Ht: 6'0" Wt: 235 Born: 8/10/1987 Age: 27

Year Team	Lg	G	AB	H	2B	3B	HR	(Hm	Rd)	TB	R	RBI	RC	TBB	IBB	SO	HBP	SH	SF	SB	CS	GDP	Avg	OBP	Slg	OPS
2014 Hgrstn*	A	1	3	2	0	0	1	(-	-)	5	1	3	2	1	0	0	0	0	0	0	0	0	.667	.750	1.667	2.417
2014 Hrsbrg*	AA	3	11	2	0	0	1	(-	-)	5	1	4	0	0	0	1	0	0	0	0	0	2	.182	.182	.455	.636
2014 Ptomc*	A+	2	9	5	1	0	1	(-	-)	9	1	5	3	0	0	0	0	0	0	0	0	1	.556	.556	1.000	1.556
2010 2 Tms		22	79	22	7	0	1	(1	0)	32	5	5	10	2	0	12	1	0	0	0	0	2	.278	.305	.405	.710
2011 Was	NL	113	389	104	22	1	15	(8	7)	173	48	52	43	38	8	76	2	4	2	0	2	19	.267	.334	.445	.779
2012 Was	NL	25	83	22	2	0	3	(1	2)	33	11	10	12	12	2	19	0	0	1	0	0	1	.265	.364	.398	.752
2013 Was	NL	78	287	78	9	0	16	(6	10)	135	29	59	40	15	1	42	0	0	1	0	1	12	.272	.307	.470	.777
2014 Was	NL	88	341	91	12	0	11	(3	8)	136	32	47	35	17	2	57	0	0	3	0	0	17	.267	.299	.399	.698
10 Min	AL	7	27	8	3	0	0	(0	0)	11	1	2	3	0	0	3	1	0	0	0	0	1	.296	.321	.407	.729
10	NL	15	52	14	4	0	1	(1	0)	21	3	4	7	2	0	9	0	0	0	0	0	1	.269	.296	.404	.700
5 ML YEARS		326	1179	317	52	1	46	(19	27)	509	125	173	140	84	13	206	3	4	7	0	3	51	.269	.317	.432	.749

Anthony Ranaudo

Pitches: R Bats: R Pos: SP-7   ran-AW-doh   Ht: 6'7" Wt: 230 Born: 9/9/1989 Age: 25

Year Team	Lg	G	GS	CG	GF	IP	BFP	H	R	ER	HR	SH	SF	HB	TBB	IBB	SO	WP	Bk	W	L	Pct	Sh	Sv-Op	Hld	ERC	ERA
2011 Grnville	A	10	10	0	0	46.0	188	35	20	17	4	1	1	4	16	0	50	1	0	4	1	.800	0	0--	-	2.88	3.33
2011 Salem	A+	16	16	0	0	81.0	348	80	43	39	6	1	3	9	30	0	67	6	0	5	5	.500	0	0--	-	4.22	4.33
2012 Portlnd	AA	9	9	0	0	37.2	180	41	29	28	4	1	4	3	27	0	27	4	0	1	3	.250	0	0--	-	6.26	6.69

Year	Team	Lg	G	GS	CG	GF	IP	BFP	H	R	ER	HR	SH	SF	HB	TBB	IBB	SO	WP	Bk	W	L	Pct	Sh	Sv-Op	Hld	ERC	ERA
2013	Portlnd	AA	19	19	0	0	109.2	442	80	39	36	9	2	4	3	40	0	106	1	1	8	4	.667	0	0--	-	2.53	2.95
2013	Pwtckt	AAA	6	5	0	1	30.1	126	32	11	10	1	1	0	0	7	0	21	0	0	3	1	.750	0	0--	-	3.31	2.97
2014	Pwtckt	AAA	24	24	1	0	138.0	568	112	45	40	9	1	6	4	54	0	111	2	0	14	4	.778	1	0--	-	2.94	2.61
2014	Bos	AL	7	7	0	0	39.1	170	39	21	21	10	0	4	0	16	0	15	2	0	4	3	.571	0	0-0	0	5.14	4.81

Colby Rasmus

Bats: L Throws: L Pos: CF-87;PH-14;DH-9 **Ht:** 6'2" **Wt:** 195 **Born:** 8/11/1986 **Age:** 28

Year	Team	Lg	G	AB	H	2B	3B	HR	(Hm	Rd)	TB	R	RBI	RC	TBB	IBB	SO	HBP	SH	SF	SB	CS	GDP	Avg	OBP	Slg	OPS
2014	Buffalo*	AAA	6	23	3	0	0	0	(-	-)	3	0	2	0	1	0	9	0	0	0	0	0	0	.130	.167	.130	.297
2009	StL	NL	147	474	119	22	2	16	(7	9)	193	72	52	60	36	3	95	3	5	2	3	1	5	.251	.307	.407	.714
2010	StL	NL	144	464	128	28	3	23	(11	12)	231	85	66	76	63	9	148	1	2	4	12	8	5	.276	.361	.498	.859
2011	2 Tms		129	471	106	24	6	14	(4	10)	184	75	53	50	50	2	116	0	2	3	5	2	10	.225	.298	.391	.688
2012	Tor	AL	151	565	126	21	5	23	(8	15)	226	75	75	74	47	5	149	7	2	4	4	3	7	.223	.289	.400	.689
2013	Tor	AL	118	417	115	26	1	22	(14	8)	209	57	66	76	37	0	135	3	0	1	0	1	4	.276	.338	.501	.840
2014	Tor	AL	104	346	78	21	1	18	(7	11)	155	45	40	38	29	2	124	1	0	0	4	0	1	.225	.287	.448	.735
11	StL	NL	94	338	83	14	6	11	(4	7)	142	61	40	43	45	2	77	0	1	2	5	2	8	.246	.332	.420	.753
11	Tor	AL	35	133	23	10	0	3	(0	3)	42	14	13	7	5	0	39	0	1	1	0	0	2	.173	.201	.316	.517
	Postseason		3	9	4	3	0	0	(0	0)	7	1	1	1	2	0	1	0	0	0	0	0	1	.444	.545	.778	1.323
	6 ML YEARS		793	2737	672	142	18	116	(51	65)	1198	409	352	374	262	21	767	15	11	14	28	15	32	.246	.313	.438	.751

Cory Rasmus

Pitches: R Bats: R Pos: RP-24; SP-6 **Ht:** 6'0" **Wt:** 200 **Born:** 11/6/1987 **Age:** 27

Year	Team	Lg	G	GS	CG	GF	IP	BFP	H	R	ER	HR	SH	SF	HB	TBB	IBB	SO	WP	Bk	W	L	Pct	Sh	Sv-Op	Hld	ERC	ERA
2010	Rome	A	20	12	0	3	83.0	353	77	39	29	6	2	2	2	29	0	72	6	0	6	6	.500	0	1--	-	3.36	3.14
2010	MrtlBh	A+	8	8	0	0	41.1	183	38	19	15	3	3	2	6	18	0	30	1	0	0	3	.000	0	0--	-	4.10	3.27
2011	Lynbrg	A+	7	7	0	0	26.2	123	28	28	21	5	1	0	4	12	0	40	5	0	1	5	.167	0	0--	-	5.77	7.09
2011	Braves	R	1	0	0	0	0.2	5	2	2	2	0	0	0	0	1	0	2	0	0	0	0	-	0	0--	-	22.07	27.00
2012	Missi	AA	50	0	0	27	58.2	247	45	24	24	3	3	5	2	32	2	62	3	0	3	5	.375	0	7--	-	3.15	3.68
2013	Gwnntt	AAA	37	0	0	30	36.2	148	20	8	7	2	0	0	1	22	0	48	1	0	3	1	.750	0	14--	-	2.30	1.72
2013	Salt Lk	AAA	9	0	0	6	9.2	40	6	3	3	0	0	0	0	5	0	8	1	1	1	1	.500	0	3--	-	1.87	2.79
2014	Salt Lk	AAA	22	0	0	14	28.0	123	23	14	13	2	1	3	0	16	3	24	1	0	2	1	.667	0	2--	-	3.30	4.18
2013	2 Tms		19	0	0	6	21.2	103	24	15	13	6	0	1	0	13	2	20	0	1	1	1	.500	0	0-1	2	6.55	5.40
2014	LAA	AL	30	6	0	7	56.0	225	42	17	16	5	0	2	0	17	1	57	0	0	3	2	.600	0	0-0	0	2.31	2.57
13	Atl	NL	3	0	0	2	6.2	31	8	6	6	4	0	0	0	3	0	6	0	0	0	0	-	0	0-0	0	9.21	8.10
13	LAA	AL	16	0	0	4	15.0	72	16	9	7	2	0	1	0	10	2	14	0	1	1	1	.500	0	0-1	2	5.34	4.20
	2 ML YEARS		49	6	0	13	77.2	328	66	32	29	11	0	3	0	30	3	77	0	1	4	3	.571	0	0-1	2	3.36	3.36

Rob Rasmussen

Pitches: L Bats: R Pos: RP-10 **Ht:** 5'10" **Wt:** 170 **Born:** 4/2/1989 **Age:** 26

Year	Team	Lg	G	GS	CG	GF	IP	BFP	H	R	ER	HR	SH	SF	HB	TBB	IBB	SO	WP	Bk	W	L	Pct	Sh	Sv-Op	Hld	ERC	ERA
2010	Grnsbr	A-	5	0	0	1	6.2	27	6	2	1	0	0	0	0	2	0	4	1	0	0	0	-	0	0--	-	2.57	1.35
2011	Jupiter	A+	28	27	1	0	148.1	645	140	75	60	10	7	7	9	71	7	118	9	0	12	10	.545	1	0--	-	4.03	3.64
2012	Jupiter	A+	16	16	0	0	87.2	376	83	52	38	6	4	2	1	36	0	75	11	0	4	7	.364	0	0--	-	3.64	3.90
2012	CpChr	AA	11	10	0	0	54.1	232	58	30	29	6	1	2	1	18	0	44	2	0	4	4	.500	0	0--	-	4.39	4.80
2013	Chatt	AA	16	14	0	1	81.1	327	60	26	23	5	0	1	3	28	0	76	6	0	3	4	.429	0	0--	-	2.41	2.55
2013	Albq	AAA	12	10	0	0	54.1	257	64	42	39	10	3	3	3	32	0	37	2	0	0	7	.000	0	0--	-	6.81	6.46
2014	Buffalo	AAA	35	0	0	8	43.0	177	32	15	13	0	1	0	1	17	0	44	6	0	1	1	.500	0	1--	-	2.15	2.72
2014	Tor	AL	10	0	0	4	11.1	50	8	4	4	1	0	0	2	7	0	13	2	0	0	0	-	0	0-0	2	3.87	3.18

Robbie Ray

Pitches: L Bats: L Pos: SP-6; RP-3 **Ht:** 6'2" **Wt:** 195 **Born:** 10/1/1991 **Age:** 23

Year	Team	Lg	G	GS	CG	GF	IP	BFP	H	R	ER	HR	SH	SF	HB	TBB	IBB	SO	WP	Bk	W	L	Pct	Sh	Sv-Op	Hld	ERC	ERA
2010	Vrmnt	A-	1	0	0	0	1.0	3	0	0	0	0	0	0	0	0	0	2	0	0	0	0	-	0	0--	-	0.00	0.00
2011	Hgrstn	A	20	20	0	0	89.0	375	71	36	31	3	3	1	12	38	0	95	8	0	2	3	.400	0	0--	-	3.18	3.13
2012	Ptomc	A+	22	21	0	1	105.2	485	122	85	77	14	3	4	11	49	0	86	13	1	4	12	.250	0	0--	-	5.96	6.56
2013	Ptomc	A+	16	16	0	0	84.0	341	60	30	29	9	3	1	4	41	0	100	7	0	6	3	.667	0	0--	-	3.21	3.11
2013	Hrsbrg	AA	11	11	1	0	58.0	255	56	28	24	4	1	0	6	21	0	60	1	0	5	2	.714	1	0--	-	3.86	3.72
2014	Toledo	AAA	20	19	0	0	100.1	435	106	51	47	6	3	3	3	44	0	75	6	1	7	6	.538	0	0--	-	4.47	4.22
2014	Det	AL	9	6	0	1	28.2	136	43	26	26	5	1	1	0	11	0	19	2	1	1	4	.200	0	0-0	1	7.72	8.16

J.T. Realmuto

Bats: R Throws: R Pos: C-9;PH-2;PR-1 ray-al-MOO-toh **Ht:** 6'1" **Wt:** 215 **Born:** 3/18/1991 **Age:** 24

Year	Team	Lg	G	AB	H	2B	3B	HR	(Hm	Rd)	TB	R	RBI	RC	TBB	IBB	SO	HBP	SH	SF	SB	CS	GDP	Avg	OBP	Slg	OPS
2010	Mrlns	R	12	40	7	0	0	0	(-	-)	7	2	4	2	7	0	11	0	0	0	0	1	2	.175	.298	.175	.473
2011	Grnsbr	A	96	348	100	16	3	12	(-	-)	158	46	49	56	26	0	78	6	1	0	13	6	9	.287	.347	.454	.801
2012	Jupiter	A+	123	446	114	16	0	8	(-	-)	154	63	46	53	37	1	64	7	3	6	13	5	17	.256	.319	.345	.664
2013	Jaxnvl	AA	106	368	88	21	3	5	(-	-)	130	41	49	45	36	0	68	5	0	7	9	1	7	.239	.310	.353	.663
2014	Jaxnvl	AA	97	375	111	24	6	8	(-	-)	171	66	62	66	41	2	59	3	0	4	18	5	11	.296	.366	.456	.822
2014	Mia	NL	11	29	7	1	1	0	(0	0)	10	4	9	4	1	0	8	0	0	0	0	0	2	.241	.267	.345	.611

Anthony Recker

Bats: R Throws: R Pos: C-52;PH-5;PR-1   Ht: 6'2" Wt: 240 Born: 8/29/1983 Age: 31

							BATTING													RUNNING			AVERAGES			
Year	Team	Lg	G	AB	H	2B	3B	HR	(Hm | Rd)	TB	R	RBI	RC	TBB	IBB	SO	HBP	SH	SF	SB	CS	GDP	Avg	OBP	Slg	OPS
2011	Oak	AL	5	17	3	1	0	0	(0 | 0)	4	3	0	0	4	0	7	0	0	0	0	0	0	.176	.333	.235	.569
2012	2 Tms		22	49	7	2	0	1	(0 | 1)	12	4	4	0	6	0	15	2	1	0	0	0	1	.143	.263	.245	.508
2013	NYM	NL	50	135	29	7	0	6	(4 | 2)	54	17	19	13	13	1	49	0	1	2	0	1	1	.215	.280	.400	.680
2014	NYM	NL	58	174	35	9	0	7	(3 | 4)	65	18	27	17	10	0	64	1	2	2	1	1	2	.201	.246	.374	.620
12	Oak	AL	13	31	4	1	0	0	(0 | 0)	5	3	0	0	4	0	13	1	1	0	0	0	0	.129	.250	.161	.411
12	ChC	NL	9	18	3	1	0	1	(0 | 1)	7	1	4	0	2	0	2	1	0	0	0	0	1	.167	.286	.389	.675
4 ML YEARS			135	375	74	19	0	14	(7 | 7)	135	42	50	30	33	1	135	3	4	4	1	2	4	.197	.265	.360	.625

Josh Reddick

Bats: L Throws: R Pos: RF-107;PH-5;PR-2;CF-1   Ht: 6'2" Wt: 180 Born: 2/19/1987 Age: 28

							BATTING													RUNNING			AVERAGES			
Year	Team	Lg	G	AB	H	2B	3B	HR	(Hm | Rd)	TB	R	RBI	RC	TBB	IBB	SO	HBP	SH	SF	SB	CS	GDP	Avg	OBP	Slg	OPS
2014	Scrmto*	AAA	4	16	7	3	0	0	(- | -)	10	1	0	4	1	0	1	0	0	0	1	1	0	.438	.471	.625	1.096
2014	Stcktn*	A+	5	21	9	2	0	3	(- | -)	20	6	8	7	1	0	6	0	0	0	0	0	0	.429	.455	.952	1.407
2009	Bos	AL	27	59	10	4	0	2	(0 | 2)	20	5	4	4	2	0	17	1	0	0	0	0	0	.169	.210	.339	.549
2010	Bos	AL	29	62	12	3	1	1	(1 | 0)	20	5	5	1	1	0	15	0	0	0	1	0	1	.194	.206	.323	.529
2011	Bos	AL	87	254	71	18	3	7	(2 | 5)	116	41	28	33	19	1	50	1	0	4	1	2	1	.280	.327	.457	.784
2012	Oak	AL	156	611	148	29	5	32	(18 | 14)	283	85	85	73	55	8	151	2	1	4	11	1	15	.242	.305	.463	.768
2013	Oak	AL	114	385	87	19	2	12	(2 | 10)	146	54	56	53	46	1	86	2	1	7	9	2	4	.226	.307	.379	.686
2014	Oak	AL	109	363	96	16	7	12	(5 | 7)	162	53	54	54	28	0	63	1	0	3	1	1	3	.264	.316	.446	.763
Postseason			10	34	6	1	0	2	(0 | 2)	13	3	2	1	3	1	15	0	0	0	0	0	1	.176	.243	.382	.626
6 ML YEARS			522	1734	424	89	18	66	(28 | 38)	747	243	232	218	151	10	382	7	2	18	23	6	24	.245	.305	.431	.736

Todd Redmond

Pitches: R Bats: R Pos: RP-42   Ht: 6'3" Wt: 200 Born: 5/17/1985 Age: 30

			HOW MUCH HE PITCHED						WHAT HE GAVE UP										THE RESULTS					
Year	Team	Lg	G	GS	CG	GF	IP	BFP	H	R	ER	HR	SH	SF	HB	TBB	IBB	SO	WP	Bk	W	L	Pct	Sh	Sv-Op	Hld	ERC	ERA
2012	Cin	NL	1	1	0	0	3.1	22	7	4	4	1	0	0	0	5	0	2	0	0	0	1	.000	0	0-0	0	18.68	10.80
2013	Tor	AL	17	14	0	2	77.0	324	70	38	37	13	1	1	6	23	2	76	1	0	4	3	.571	0	0-0	0	3.91	4.32
2014	Tor	AL	42	0	0	14	75.0	314	73	33	27	5	2	5	2	27	6	60	2	0	1	4	.200	0	1-1	3	3.60	3.24
3 ML YEARS			60	15	0	16	155.1	660	150	75	68	19	3	6	8	55	8	138	3	0	5	8	.385	0	1-1	4	4.02	3.94

Addison Reed

Pitches: R Bats: L Pos: RP-62   Ht: 6'4" Wt: 220 Born: 12/27/1988 Age: 26

			HOW MUCH HE PITCHED						WHAT HE GAVE UP										THE RESULTS					
Year	Team	Lg	G	GS	CG	GF	IP	BFP	H	R	ER	HR	SH	SF	HB	TBB	IBB	SO	WP	Bk	W	L	Pct	Sh	Sv-Op	Hld	ERC	ERA
2011	CWS	AL	6	0	0	2	7.1	33	10	3	3	1	0	0	0	1	0	12	0	0	0	0	-	0	0-0	0	5.24	3.68
2012	CWS	AL	62	0	0	44	55.0	238	57	30	29	6	0	4	2	18	3	54	0	1	3	2	.600	0	29-33	4	4.09	4.75
2013	CWS	AL	68	0	0	59	71.1	295	56	31	30	6	3	6	2	23	2	72	2	0	5	4	.556	0	40-48	0	2.56	3.79
2014	Ari	NL	62	0	0	55	59.1	252	57	31	28	11	1	1	1	15	2	69	3	0	1	7	.125	0	32-38	0	3.76	4.25
4 ML YEARS			198	0	0	160	193.0	818	180	95	90	24	4	11	5	57	7	207	5	1	9	13	.409	0	101-119	4	3.45	4.20

Evan Reed

Pitches: R Bats: R Pos: RP-32   Ht: 6'4" Wt: 255 Born: 12/31/1985 Age: 29

			HOW MUCH HE PITCHED						WHAT HE GAVE UP										THE RESULTS					
Year	Team	Lg	G	GS	CG	GF	IP	BFP	H	R	ER	HR	SH	SF	HB	TBB	IBB	SO	WP	Bk	W	L	Pct	Sh	Sv-Op	Hld	ERC	ERA
2010	Frisco	AA	30	0	0	15	39.0	160	35	7	7	0	0	0	0	13	0	34	3	0	1	1	.500	0	5--	5	2.65	1.62
2010	OKCity	AAA	1	0	0	0	2.0	7	1	1	1	1	0	0	0	0	0	2	0	0	1	0	1.000	0	0--	0	1.73	4.50
2010	Jaxnvl	AA	1	0	0	0	1.2	6	1	0	0	0	0	0	0	1	0	1	0	0	0	0	-	0	0--	-	2.46	0.00
2011	Mrlns	R	8	3	0	0	8.2	38	15	4	3	0	0	0	0	0	0	11	1	0	0	0	-	0	0--	-	6.31	3.12
2011	Jupiter	A+	11	0	0	1	15.2	63	9	7	7	0	0	1	1	10	1	13	2	0	0	1	.000	0	0--	-	2.29	4.02
2012	Jaxnvl	AA	27	0	0	23	34.2	137	24	10	9	1	1	2	0	11	0	43	1	0	3	1	.750	0	12--	-	1.79	2.34
2012	NewOr	AAA	23	0	0	7	32.2	156	43	27	26	2	0	2	0	16	2	27	3	0	2	3	.400	0	1--	-	5.77	7.16
2013	Toledo	AAA	32	0	0	11	49.2	195	38	17	14	1	2	1	0	20	0	49	4	1	1	4	.200	0	1--	-	2.46	2.54
2014	Toledo	AAA	17	1	0	5	23.1	96	26	11	11	0	0	1	0	5	0	26	0	1	0	1	.000	0	0--	-	3.41	4.24
2013	Det	AL	16	0	0	10	23.1	105	28	16	11	2	1	2	1	8	0	17	1	1	1	0	1.000	0	0-0	4	5.04	4.24
2014	Det	AL	32	0	0	9	32.1	145	39	19	15	2	0	1	3	12	1	26	1	1	0	1	.000	0	0-0	4	5.27	4.18
2 ML YEARS			48	0	0	19	55.2	250	67	35	26	4	1	3	4	20	1	43	2	2	0	2	.000	0	0-0	4	5.18	4.20

Nolan Reimold

Bats: R Throws: R Pos: PH-11;RF-10;DH-10;LF-4;PR-1   RYE-mold   Ht: 6'4" Wt: 205 Born: 10/12/1983 Age: 31

							BATTING													RUNNING			AVERAGES			
Year	Team	Lg	G	AB	H	2B	3B	HR	(Hm | Rd)	TB	R	RBI	RC	TBB	IBB	SO	HBP	SH	SF	SB	CS	GDP	Avg	OBP	Slg	OPS
2014	Bowie*	AA	17	54	17	3	0	2	(- | -)	26	10	9	11	12	0	13	0	0	3	1	1	0	.315	.420	.481	.902
2009	Bal	AL	104	358	100	18	2	15	(8 | 7)	167	49	45	47	47	1	77	3	0	3	8	2	8	.279	.365	.466	.831
2010	Bal	AL	39	116	24	5	0	3	(0 | 3)	38	9	14	6	12	0	26	1	0	2	0	0	6	.207	.282	.328	.610
2011	Bal	AL	87	267	66	10	3	13	(8 | 5)	121	40	45	48	28	1	57	6	0	4	7	2	4	.247	.328	.453	.781
2012	Bal	AL	16	67	21	6	0	5	(0 | 5)	42	10	10	15	2	0	14	0	0	0	1	0	3	.313	.333	.627	.960
2013	Bal	AL	40	128	25	3	0	5	(3 | 2)	43	17	12	7	10	2	41	0	0	2	0	1	4	.195	.250	.336	.586

Year	Team	Lg	G	AB	H	2B	3B	HR	(Hm	Rd)	TB	R	RBI	RC	TBB	IBB	SO	HBP	SH	SF	SB	CS	GDP	Avg	OBP	Slg	OPS
2014	2 Tms		29	69	16	5	0	3	(1	2)	30	5	13	9	6	0	32	0	0	3	1	0	0	.232	.282	.435	.717
14	Tor	AL	22	52	11	4	0	2	(0	2)	21	3	9	6	6	0	22	0	0	2	1	0	0	.212	.283	.404	.687
14	Ari	NL	7	17	5	1	0	1	(1	0)	9	2	4	3	0	0	10	0	0	1	0	0	0	.294	.278	.529	.807
6 ML YEARS			315	1005	252	47	5	44	(20	24)	441	130	139	142	105	4	247	10	0	14	17	5	25	.251	.324	.439	.762

Anthony Rendon

Bats: R **Throws:** R **Pos:** 3B-134;2B-28;PH-1 ren-DOAN **Ht:** 6'1" **Wt:** 200 **Born:** 6/6/1990 **Age:** 25

Year	Team	Lg	G	AB	H	2B	3B	HR	(Hm	Rd)	TB	R	RBI	RC	TBB	IBB	SO	HBP	SH	SF	SB	CS	GDP	Avg	OBP	Slg	OPS
2012	Ptomc	A+	9	27	9	2	3	0	(-	-)	17	5	0	7	5	0	4	0	0	0	0	0	0	.333	.438	.630	1.067
2012	Nats	R	5	11	4	1	0	2	(-	-)	11	2	6	4	3	0	3	0	0	0	0	0	0	.364	.500	1.000	1.500
2012	Auburn	A-	8	27	7	2	0	1	(-	-)	12	7	3	4	4	0	6	1	0	0	0	0	0	.259	.375	.444	.819
2012	Hrsbrg	AA	21	68	11	3	1	3	(-	-)	25	14	3	8	11	0	16	3	0	0	0	0	3	.162	.305	.368	.673
2013	Hrsbrg	AA	33	116	37	11	2	6	(-	-)	70	17	24	33	30	0	25	3	0	3	1	0	1	.319	.461	.603	1.064
2013	Syrcse	AAA	3	11	2	1	0	0	(-	-)	3	2	0	1	2	0	3	1	0	0	0	0	0	.182	.357	.273	.630
2013	Was	NL	98	351	93	23	1	7	(3	4)	139	40	35	43	31	3	69	5	2	5	1	1	7	.265	.329	.396	.725
2014	Was	NL	153	613	176	39	6	21	(10	11)	290	111	83	97	58	2	104	5	2	5	17	3	11	.287	.351	.473	.824
2 ML YEARS			251	964	269	62	7	28	(13	15)	429	151	118	140	89	5	173	10	4	10	18	4	18	.279	.343	.445	.788

Ben Revere

Bats: L **Throws:** R **Pos:** CF-141;PH-16;PR-1 **Ht:** 5'9" **Wt:** 165 **Born:** 5/3/1988 **Age:** 27

Year	Team	Lg	G	AB	H	2B	3B	HR	(Hm	Rd)	TB	R	RBI	RC	TBB	IBB	SO	HBP	SH	SF	SB	CS	GDP	Avg	OBP	Slg	OPS
2010	Min	AL	13	28	5	0	0	0	(0	0)	5	1	2	0	2	0	5	0	0	0	0	1	1	.179	.233	.179	.412
2011	Min	AL	117	450	120	9	5	0	(0	0)	139	56	30	51	26	1	41	2	3	0	34	9	7	.267	.310	.309	.619
2012	Min	AL	124	511	150	13	6	0	(0	0)	175	70	32	62	29	0	54	3	6	4	40	9	8	.294	.333	.342	.675
2013	Phi	NL	88	315	96	9	3	0	(0	0)	111	37	17	39	16	1	36	0	5	0	22	8	10	.305	.338	.352	.691
2014	Phi	NL	151	601	184	13	7	2	(1	1)	217	71	28	71	13	1	49	4	7	1	49	8	11	.306	.325	.361	.686
5 ML YEARS			493	1905	555	44	21	2	(1	1)	647	235	109	223	86	3	185	9	21	5	145	35	37	.291	.324	.340	.664

Jose Reyes

Bats: B **Throws:** R **Pos:** SS-142;PR-1 **Ht:** 6'0" **Wt:** 195 **Born:** 6/11/1983 **Age:** 32

Year	Team	Lg	G	AB	H	2B	3B	HR	(Hm	Rd)	TB	R	RBI	RC	TBB	IBB	SO	HBP	SH	SF	SB	CS	GDP	Avg	OBP	Slg	OPS
2014	Dnedin*	A+	2	6	0	0	0	0	(-	-)	0	3	1	0	2	0	0	0	0	0	0	0	0	.000	.250	.000	.250
2003	NYM	NL	69	274	84	12	4	5	(1	4)	119	47	32	46	13	0	36	0	2	3	13	3	1	.307	.334	.434	.769
2004	NYM	NL	53	220	56	16	2	2	(1	1)	82	33	14	25	5	0	31	0	4	0	19	2	1	.255	.271	.373	.644
2005	NYM	NL	161	696	190	24	17	7	(2	5)	269	99	58	84	27	0	78	2	4	4	60	15	7	.273	.300	.386	.687
2006	NYM	NL	153	647	194	30	17	19	(9	10)	315	122	81	121	53	6	81	1	2	0	64	17	6	.300	.354	.487	.841
2007	NYM	NL	160	681	191	36	12	12	(7	5)	287	119	57	99	77	13	78	1	5	5	78	21	6	.280	.354	.421	.775
2008	NYM	NL	159	688	204	37	19	16	(9	7)	327	113	68	117	66	8	82	1	5	3	56	15	9	.297	.358	.475	.833
2009	NYM	NL	36	147	41	7	2	2	(1	1)	58	18	15	20	18	1	19	0	0	1	11	2	2	.279	.355	.395	.750
2010	NYM	NL	133	563	159	29	10	11	(8	3)	241	83	54	76	31	4	63	2	4	3	30	10	8	.282	.321	.428	.749
2011	NYM	NL	126	537	181	31	16	7	(4	3)	265	101	44	90	43	9	41	0	2	4	39	7	5	.337	.384	.493	.877
2012	Mia	NL	160	642	184	37	12	11	(4	7)	278	86	57	92	63	9	56	0	5	6	40	11	10	.287	.347	.433	.780
2013	Tor	AL	93	382	113	20	0	10	(7	3)	163	58	37	61	34	2	47	1	0	2	15	6	6	.296	.353	.427	.780
2014	Tor	AL	143	610	175	33	4	9	(5	4)	243	94	51	77	38	1	73	1	2	4	30	2	4	.287	.328	.398	.726
Postseason			10	44	11	1	1	1	(1	0)	17	7	5	6	3	1	5	0	0	0	3	1	0	.250	.298	.386	.684
12 ML YEARS			1446	6087	1772	312	115	111	(58	53)	2647	973	568	908	468	53	685	9	35	31	455	111	65	.291	.341	.435	.776

Mark Reynolds

Bats: R **Throws:** R **Pos:** 1B-91;3B-42;PH-16;RF-3 **Ht:** 6'2" **Wt:** 220 **Born:** 8/3/1983 **Age:** 31

Year	Team	Lg	G	AB	H	2B	3B	HR	(Hm	Rd)	TB	R	RBI	RC	TBB	IBB	SO	HBP	SH	SF	SB	CS	GDP	Avg	OBP	Slg	OPS
2007	Ari	NL	111	366	102	20	4	17	(7	10)	181	62	62	62	37	4	129	5	1	5	0	1	5	.279	.349	.495	.843
2008	Ari	NL	152	539	129	28	3	28	(13	15)	247	87	97	82	64	0	204	3	1	0	11	2	10	.239	.320	.458	.779
2009	Ari	NL	155	578	150	30	1	44	(19	25)	314	98	102	94	76	3	223	5	0	3	24	9	8	.260	.349	.543	.892
2010	Bal	AL	145	499	99	17	2	32	(21	11)	216	79	85	77	83	7	211	9	0	5	7	4	8	.198	.320	.433	.753
2011	Bal	AL	155	534	118	27	1	37	(17	20)	258	84	86	77	75	2	196	7	0	4	6	4	11	.221	.323	.483	.806
2012	Bal	AL	135	457	101	26	0	23	(11	12)	196	65	69	68	73	2	159	6	0	2	1	3	19	.221	.335	.429	.763
2013	2 Tms	AL	135	445	98	14	0	21	(9	12)	175	55	67	55	51	1	154	5	0	3	3	1	7	.220	.306	.393	.699
2014	Mil	NL	130	378	74	9	0	22	(9	13)	149	47	45	41	47	3	122	3	1	4	5	1	8	.196	.287	.394	.681
13	Cle	AL	99	335	72	8	0	15	(8	7)	125	40	48	39	43	1	123	3	0	3	3	0	7	.215	.307	.373	.680
13	NYY	AL	36	110	26	6	0	6	(1	5)	50	15	19	16	8	0	31	2	0	0	0	1	0	.236	.300	.455	.755
Postseason			13	48	7	0	0	2	(1	1)	13	3	3	2	3	0	19	3	0	1	1	0	1	.146	.241	.271	.512
8 ML YEARS			1118	3796	871	171	11	224	(106	118)	1736	577	613	556	506	22	1398	43	3	32	57	25	78	.229	.324	.457	.782

Scott Rice

Pitches: L **Bats:** L **Pos:** RP-32 **Ht:** 6'6" **Wt:** 225 **Born:** 9/21/1981 **Age:** 33

			HOW MUCH HE PITCHED					WHAT HE GAVE UP										THE RESULTS							
Year	Team	Lg	G	GS	CG	GF	IP	BFP	H	R	ER	HR	SH	SF	HB	TBB	IBB	SO	WP	Bk	W	L	Pct	Sh	Sv-Op	Hld	ERC	ERA
2010	Tulsa	AA	35	0	0	12	46.2	182	23	8	5	0	3	0	2	18	1	33	7	1	2	0	1.000	0	4- -	-	1.24	0.96
2010	ColSpr	AAA	23	0	0	5	22.2	108	27	17	17	0	1	1	2	15	0	15	2	0	0	1	.000	0	3- -	-	5.86	6.75
2011	Chatt	AA	34	0	0	7	50.2	208	42	17	11	3	1	1	1	17	0	42	3	2	4	4	.500	0	1- -	-	2.74	1.95
2012	Albq	AAA	54	0	0	27	59.1	260	58	33	29	3	5	2	4	22	1	47	9	0	2	3	.400	0	9- -	-	3.66	4.40

Year	Team	Lg	G	GS	CG	GF	IP	BFP	H	R	ER	HR	SH	SF	HB	TBB	IBB	SO	WP	Bk	W	L	Pct	Sh	Sv-Op	Hld	ERC	ERA
2014	LsVgs	AAA	6	0	0	0	5.1	22	4	2	2	1	0	0	0	4	0	6	4	0	0	0	-	0	0--	-	5.06	3.38
2013	NYM	NL	73	0	0	7	51.0	213	42	22	21	1	3	2	2	27	4	41	3	1	4	5	.444	0	0-2	17	3.17	3.71
2014	NYM	NL	32	0	0	2	13.2	66	15	9	9	1	1	0	1	12	1	13	5	0	1	2	.333	0	0-2	7	6.68	5.93
2 ML YEARS			105	0	0	9	64.2	279	57	31	30	2	4	2	3	39	5	54	8	1	5	7	.417	0	0-4	24	3.85	4.18

Clayton Richard

Pitches: L Bats: L Pos: P Ht: 6'5" Wt: 245 Born: 9/12/1983 Age: 31

Year	Team	Lg	G	GS	CG	GF	IP	BFP	H	R	ER	HR	SH	SF	HB	TBB	IBB	SO	WP	Bk	W	L	Pct	Sh	Sv-Op	Hld	ERC	ERA
2014	Mobile*	AA	3	3	0	0	15.0	69	23	13	11	2	1	0	0	4	0	7	0	0	0	2	.000	0	0--	-	7.14	6.60
2014	Reno*	AAA	1	1	0	0	6.1	28	11	3	3	1	0	0	0	1	0	1	0	0	1	0	1.000	0	0--	-	8.75	4.26
2008	CWS	AL	13	8	0	3	47.2	215	61	37	32	5	0	1	0	13	2	29	1	1	2	5	.286	0	0-0	0	5.06	6.04
2009	2 Tms		38	26	1	3	153.0	663	154	81	75	17	8	5	3	71	0	114	7	3	9	5	.643	0	0-0	0	4.60	4.41
2010	SD	NL	33	33	1	0	201.2	861	206	89	84	16	6	2	4	78	6	153	4	2	14	9	.609	1	0-0	0	4.09	3.75
2011	SD	NL	18	18	0	0	99.2	427	104	52	43	8	4	1	2	38	2	53	3	1	5	9	.357	0	0-0	0	4.22	3.88
2012	SD	NL	33	33	1	0	218.2	910	228	110	97	31	3	6	6	42	4	107	4	2	14	14	.500	1	0-0	0	3.87	3.99
2013	SD	NL	12	11	0	1	52.2	239	65	44	44	13	6	1	0	21	1	24	0	0	2	5	.286	0	0-0	0	6.55	7.01
09	CWS	AL	26	14	1	3	89.0	387	94	50	46	10	3	4	3	37	0	66	5	2	4	3	.571	0	0-0	0	4.76	4.65
09	SD	NL	12	12	0	0	64.0	276	60	31	29	7	5	1	0	34	0	48	2	1	5	2	.714	0	0-0	0	4.38	4.08
Postseason			2	0	0	0	6.1	25	5	1	1	0	0	0	0	3	0	6	0	0	0	0	-	0	0-0	0	2.74	1.42
6 ML YEARS			147	129	3	7	773.1	3315	818	413	372	90	27	16	15	263	15	480	19	9	46	47	.495	2	0-0	0	4.37	4.33

Garrett Richards

Pitches: R Bats: R Pos: SP-26 Ht: 6'3" Wt: 210 Born: 5/27/1988 Age: 27

Year	Team	Lg	G	GS	CG	GF	IP	BFP	H	R	ER	HR	SH	SF	HB	TBB	IBB	SO	WP	Bk	W	L	Pct	Sh	Sv-Op	Hld	ERC	ERA
2011	LAA	AL	7	3	0	2	14.0	62	16	11	9	4	0	0	0	7	0	9	2	0	0	2	.000	0	0-0	0	6.97	5.79
2012	LAA	AL	30	9	0	4	71.0	318	77	46	37	7	2	4	3	34	1	47	2	0	4	3	.571	0	1-3	5	5.04	4.69
2013	LAA	AL	47	17	1	6	145.0	620	151	73	67	12	9	3	1	44	4	101	11	0	7	8	.467	0	1-2	5	3.78	4.16
2014	LAA	AL	26	26	1	0	168.2	678	124	51	49	5	0	3	7	51	1	164	22	1	13	4	.765	1	0-0	0	2.06	2.61
4 ML YEARS			110	55	2	12	398.2	1678	368	181	162	28	11	10	11	136	6	321	37	1	24	17	.585	1	2-5	10	3.31	3.66

Antoan Richardson

Bats: B Throws: R Pos: PR-6;RF-5;CF-1;PH-1 ant-ON Ht: 5'8" Wt: 165 Born: 10/8/1983 Age: 31

Year	Team	Lg	G	AB	H	2B	3B	HR	(Hm	Rd)	TB	R	RBI	RC	TBB	IBB	SO	HBP	SH	SF	SB	CS	GDP	Avg	OBP	Slg	OPS
2010	Missi	AA	74	272	76	8	1	0	(-	-)	86	60	20	44	41	0	47	12	3	3	24	3	4	.279	.393	.316	.709
2010	Gwnntt	AAA	7	25	7	0	0	0	(-	-)	7	1	2	4	5	0	9	1	0	1	3	0	1	.280	.406	.280	.686
2011	Missi	AA	91	272	77	9	0	1	(-	-)	89	64	21	49	60	1	66	11	9	1	17	5	1	.283	.430	.327	.757
2011	Gwnntt	AAA	2	3	1	0	0	0	(-	-)	1	1	0	0	1	0	1	0	0	0	0	0	0	.333	.500	.333	.833
2012	Bowie	AA	90	290	81	4	4	1	(-	-)	96	68	15	51	61	0	60	7	8	1	26	5	5	.279	.415	.331	.746
2012	Norfolk	AAA	9	25	4	0	0	0	(-	-)	4	4	0	2	7	0	6	0	2	0	1	0	0	.160	.344	.160	.504
2013	NwBrit	AA	33	119	40	6	1	0	(-	-)	48	26	14	25	22	0	25	5	7	1	14	5	2	.336	.456	.403	.859
2013	Roch	AAA	82	302	80	14	7	0	(-	-)	108	57	29	51	52	0	70	5	9	1	25	2	2	.265	.381	.358	.738
2014	S-WB	AAA	93	258	70	7	4	3	(-	-)	94	41	22	45	33	0	56	14	7	3	26	1	2	.271	.380	.364	.744
2011	Atl	NL	9	4	2	0	0	0	(0	0)	2	2	0	1	0	0	0	0	0	0	1	0	0	.500	.500	.500	1.000
2014	NYY	AL	13	16	5	0	0	0	(0	0)	5	2	1	3	1	0	3	0	0	0	5	0	0	.313	.353	.313	.665
2 ML YEARS			22	20	7	0	0	0	(0	0)	7	4	1	4	1	0	3	0	0	0	6	0	0	.350	.381	.350	.731

C.J. Riefenhauser

Pitches: L Bats: L Pos: RP-7 REEF-en-how-zer Ht: 6'0" Wt: 180 Born: 1/30/1990 Age: 25

Year	Team	Lg	G	GS	CG	GF	IP	BFP	H	R	ER	HR	SH	SF	HB	TBB	IBB	SO	WP	Bk	W	L	Pct	Sh	Sv-Op	Hld	ERC	ERA
2010	Princtn	R+	11	0	0	6	19.0	76	14	6	6	1	1	0	0	6	0	16	1	0	1	0	1.000	0	1--	-	2.11	2.84
2010	BG	A	2	2	0	0	9.0	36	7	1	1	0	0	0	0	1	0	4	0	0	1	0	1.000	0	0--	-	1.40	1.00
2011	BG	A	18	18	1	0	101.1	397	77	32	26	7	5	2	2	25	0	99	2	1	6	5	.545	1	0--	-	2.19	2.31
2011	Charltt	A+	8	7	0	0	37.0	157	35	21	17	3	3	3	1	11	0	24	2	0	1	3	.250	0	0--	-	3.31	4.14
2012	Charltt	A+	23	14	0	4	96.1	415	98	55	51	11	2	4	6	32	1	103	2	1	7	8	.467	0	1--	-	4.25	4.76
2012	Mont	AA	9	1	0	0	18.1	80	15	7	7	4	0	2	3	8	0	15	0	0	1	1	.500	0	0--	-	4.65	3.44
2013	Mont	AA	34	0	0	20	53.0	197	28	10	3	3	2	0	1	11	0	48	0	0	4	0	1.000	0	11--	-	1.17	0.51
2013	Drham	AAA	17	0	0	4	20.2	82	14	9	7	2	0	0	0	8	0	22	1	0	2	1	.667	0	0--	-	2.36	3.05
2014	Drham	AAA	39	0	0	12	57.2	240	41	13	9	3	2	1	3	24	0	53	4	0	3	3	.500	0	1--	-	2.46	1.40
2014	TB	AL	7	0	0	1	5.1	24	6	5	5	0	0	0	0	3	1	2	0	0	0	0	-	0	0-0	0	4.39	8.44

Andre Rienzo

Pitches: R Bats: R Pos: SP-11; RP-7 ree-ENN-zo Ht: 6'3" Wt: 190 Born: 7/5/1988 Age: 26

Year	Team	Lg	G	GS	CG	GF	IP	BFP	H	R	ER	HR	SH	SF	HB	TBB	IBB	SO	WP	Bk	W	L	Pct	Sh	Sv-Op	Hld	ERC	ERA
2010	Knapol	A	20	18	2	0	101.0	432	95	45	41	5	3	2	2	32	0	125	6	4	8	4	.667	2	0--	-	3.10	3.65
2011	WinSa	A+	25	22	1	0	116.0	512	108	50	44	4	2	4	3	66	0	118	16	0	6	5	.545	1	0--	-	3.97	3.41
2012	WinSa	A+	4	4	0	0	25.0	96	17	3	3	0	0	1	0	7	0	31	3	1	3	0	1.000	0	0--	-	1.55	1.08
2012	Birm	AA	13	13	1	0	71.2	307	56	31	26	2	3	2	1	33	0	72	3	0	4	3	.571	0	0--	-	2.62	3.27
2012	Charltt	AAA	1	1	0	0	6.2	26	5	1	0	0	1	1	0	2	0	10	1	0	0	0	-	0	0--	-	1.88	0.00
2013	Charltt	AAA	20	20	3	0	113.0	488	105	62	51	7	2	4	4	46	0	113	4	1	8	6	.571	1	0--	-	3.55	4.06

Year	Team	Lg	G	GS	CG	GF	IP	BFP	H	R	ER	HR	SH	SF	HB	TBB	IBB	SO	WP	Bk	W	L	Pct	Sh	Sv-Op	Hld	ERC	ERA
2014	Charltt	AAA	10	9	0	1	46.2	210	44	23	21	4	3	0	1	24	0	43	7	0	1	4	.200	0	0- -	-	4.06	4.05
2013	CWS	AL	10	10	0	0	56.0	250	55	34	30	11	2	1	2	28	0	38	4	0	2	3	.400	0	0-0	0	5.18	4.82
2014	CWS	AL	18	11	0	3	64.2	312	82	54	49	12	2	2	5	33	0	51	6	1	4	5	.444	0	0-0	0	7.05	6.82
	2 ML YEARS		28	21	0	3	120.2	562	137	88	79	23	4	3	7	61	0	89	10	1	6	8	.429	0	0-0	0	6.17	5.89

Alex Rios

Bats: R **Throws:** R **Pos:** RF-114;DH-16;PH-1   **Ht:** 6'5" **Wt:** 210 **Born:** 2/18/1981 **Age:** 34

						BATTING																	RUNNING			AVERAGES			
Year	Team	Lg	G	AB	H	2B	3B	HR	(Hm Rd)	TB	R	RBI	RC	TBB	IBB	SO	HBP	SH	SF	SB	CS	GDP	Avg	OBP	Slg	OPS
2004	Tor	AL	111	426	122	24	7	1	(0 1)	163	55	28	49	31	0	84	2	1	0	15	3	14	.286	.338	.383	.720
2005	Tor	AL	146	481	126	23	6	10	(5 5)	191	71	59	56	28	1	101	5	0	5	14	9	14	.262	.306	.397	.703
2006	Tor	AL	128	450	136	33	6	17	(12 5)	232	68	82	83	35	1	89	3	0	10	15	6	10	.302	.349	.516	.865
2007	Tor	AL	161	643	191	43	7	24	(13 11)	320	114	85	105	55	3	103	6	0	7	17	4	9	.297	.354	.498	.852
2008	Tor	AL	155	635	185	47	8	15	(9 6)	293	91	79	92	44	2	112	2	0	5	32	8	20	.291	.337	.461	.798
2009	2 Tms	AL	149	582	144	31	2	17	(15 2)	230	63	71	64	37	1	107	6	1	7	24	5	21	.247	.296	.395	.691
2010	CWS	AL	147	567	161	29	3	21	(10 11)	259	89	88	84	38	4	93	7	0	5	34	14	21	.284	.334	.457	.791
2011	CWS	AL	145	537	122	22	2	13	(7 6)	187	64	44	35	27	4	68	2	0	4	11	6	20	.227	.265	.348	.613
2012	CWS	AL	157	605	184	37	8	25	(16 9)	312	93	91	103	26	3	92	4	0	5	23	6	18	.304	.334	.516	.850
2013	2 Tms	AL	156	616	171	33	4	18	(7 11)	266	83	81	78	41	2	108	2	0	2	42	7	17	.278	.324	.432	.756
2014	Tex	AL	131	492	138	30	8	4	(1 3)	196	54	54	53	23	3	93	1	0	5	17	9	19	.280	.311	.398	.709
09	Tor	AL	108	436	115	25	2	14	(12 2)	186	52	62	60	31	1	78	6	0	6	19	3	14	.264	.317	.427	.744
09	CWS	AL	41	146	29	6	0	3	(3 0)	44	11	9	4	6	0	29	0	1	1	5	2	7	.199	.229	.301	.530
13	CWS	AL	109	430	119	22	2	12	(6 6)	181	57	55	51	32	2	78	1	0	1	26	6	12	.277	.328	.421	.749
13	Tex	AL	47	186	52	11	2	6	(1 5)	85	26	26	27	9	0	30	1	0	1	16	1	5	.280	.315	.457	.772
	11 ML YEARS		1586	6034	1680	352	61	165	(95 70)	2649	845	762	802	385	24	1050	40	2	55	244	77	183	.278	.323	.439	.762

Rene Rivera

Bats: R **Throws:** R **Pos:** C-89;PH-15;1B-3   ruh-NAY   **Ht:** 5'10" **Wt:** 215 **Born:** 7/31/1983 **Age:** 31

						BATTING																	RUNNING			AVERAGES			
Year	Team	Lg	G	AB	H	2B	3B	HR	(Hm Rd)	TB	R	RBI	RC	TBB	IBB	SO	HBP	SH	SF	SB	CS	GDP	Avg	OBP	Slg	OPS
2004	Sea	AL	2	3	0	0	0	0	(0 0)	0	0	0	0	0	0	1	0	0	0	0	0	0	.000	.000	.000	.000
2005	Sea	AL	16	48	19	3	0	1	(0 1)	25	3	6	8	1	0	11	0	1	0	0	0	0	.396	.408	.521	.929
2006	Sea	AL	35	99	15	4	0	2	(1 1)	25	8	4	4	3	0	29	1	3	0	1	0	2	.152	.184	.253	.437
2011	Min	AL	45	104	15	3	0	1	(0 1)	21	9	5	3	8	0	32	1	0	1	0	0	2	.144	.211	.202	.412
2013	SD	NL	23	67	17	3	1	0	(0 0)	22	4	7	6	2	1	16	0	0	2	0	0	1	.254	.268	.328	.596
2014	SD	NL	103	294	74	18	1	11	(1 10)	127	27	44	41	27	3	76	3	3	2	0	0	6	.252	.319	.432	.751
	6 ML YEARS		224	615	140	31	2	15	(2 13)	220	51	66	62	41	4	165	5	7	5	1	0	11	.228	.279	.358	.637

Carlos Rivero

Bats: R **Throws:** R **Pos:** 3B-3;PH-2;DH-1   **Ht:** 6'3" **Wt:** 200 **Born:** 5/20/1988 **Age:** 27

						BATTING																	RUNNING			AVERAGES			
Year	Team	Lg	G	AB	H	2B	3B	HR	(Hm Rd)	TB	R	RBI	RC	TBB	IBB	SO	HBP	SH	SF	SB	CS	GDP	Avg	OBP	Slg	OPS
2010	Akron	AA	110	406	94	16	2	6	(- -)	132	39	43	37	28	0	81	1	2	7	0	3	15	.232	.278	.325	.603
2011	Rdng	AA	129	491	135	36	0	15	(- -)	216	70	66	73	38	0	106	5	0	4	5	3	12	.275	.331	.440	.771
2011	LV	AAA	7	27	5	2	1	1	(- -)	12	1	5	3	1	0	6	1	0	1	0	0	1	.185	.233	.444	.678
2012	Syrcse	AAA	126	455	138	28	1	10	(- -)	198	57	64	70	33	2	87	1	3	6	6	5	15	.303	.347	.435	.783
2013	Syrcse	AAA	63	210	49	7	0	1	(- -)	59	15	16	19	22	1	40	2	1	4	2	2	4	.233	.307	.281	.588
2013	Hrsbrg	AA	51	186	47	12	0	4	(- -)	71	18	22	20	9	0	54	1	1	2	0	1	12	.253	.288	.382	.670
2014	Portlnd	AA	31	117	25	6	0	2	(- -)	37	14	17	11	8	0	24	4	0	1	0	0	7	.214	.285	.316	.601
2014	Pwtckt	AAA	74	273	78	14	2	5	(- -)	111	32	36	39	23	0	66	2	0	4	0	2	5	.286	.341	.407	.748
2014	Bos	AL	4	7	4	2	0	1	(1 0)	9	1	3	5	1	0	0	0	0	0	0	0	0	.571	.625	1.286	1.911

Anthony Rizzo

Bats: L **Throws:** L **Pos:** 1B-140   **Ht:** 6'3" **Wt:** 240 **Born:** 8/8/1989 **Age:** 25

						BATTING																	RUNNING			AVERAGES			
Year	Team	Lg	G	AB	H	2B	3B	HR	(Hm Rd)	TB	R	RBI	RC	TBB	IBB	SO	HBP	SH	SF	SB	CS	GDP	Avg	OBP	Slg	OPS
2011	SD	NL	49	128	18	8	1	1	(1 0)	31	9	9	7	21	1	46	4	0	0	2	1	2	.141	.281	.242	.523
2012	ChC	NL	87	337	96	15	0	15	(7 8)	156	44	48	57	27	1	62	3	0	1	3	2	7	.285	.342	.463	.805
2013	ChC	NL	160	606	141	40	2	23	(13 10)	254	71	80	74	76	7	127	6	0	2	6	5	12	.233	.323	.419	.742
2014	ChC	NL	140	524	150	28	1	32	(14 18)	276	89	78	99	73	7	116	15	0	4	5	4	8	.286	.386	.527	.913
	4 ML YEARS		436	1595	405	91	4	71	(35 36)	717	213	215	237	197	16	351	28	0	7	16	12	29	.254	.345	.450	.794

Donn Roach

Pitches: R **Bats:** R **Pos:** RP-15; SP-1   **Ht:** 6'0" **Wt:** 195 **Born:** 12/14/1989 **Age:** 25

						HOW MUCH HE PITCHED						WHAT HE GAVE UP									THE RESULTS						
Year	Team	Lg	G	GS	CG	GF	IP	BFP	H	R	ER	HR	SH	SF	HB	TBB	IBB	SO	WP	Bk	W	L	Pct	Sh	Sv-Op	Hld	ERC	ERA
2010	Orem	R+	16	10	0	2	53.2	243	64	39	36	6	2	0	7	16	1	59	7	1	4	1	.800	0	0- -	-	5.35	6.04
2011	CRpds	A	45	0	0	7	70.1	305	73	33	27	1	4	4	3	20	1	68	11	0	5	5	.500	0	2- -	-	3.32	3.45
2012	InldEm	A+	6	6	0	0	41.2	163	36	11	10	1	1	0	1	3	0	29	1	0	5	0	1.000	0	0- -	-	1.82	2.16
2012	Lk Els	A+	8	7	0	0	46.2	192	41	15	9	1	1	0	1	11	0	44	3	0	5	1	.833	0	0- -	-	2.63	1.74
2013	SnAnt	AA	4	3	0	0	17.0	68	9	4	3	0	0	1	1	8	0	5	3	0	1	1	.500	0	0- -	-	1.59	1.59
2013	SnAnt	AA	28	28	0	0	142.2	600	138	73	56	7	5	2	5	40	0	77	11	0	8	12	.400	0	0- -	-	3.22	3.53
2014	ElPaso	AAA	19	13	0	1	77.1	366	98	56	45	2	5	2	7	40	0	44	4	1	4	6	.400	0	0- -	-	5.93	5.24
2014	SD	NL	16	1	0	5	30.1	140	36	17	16	2	3	1	4	15	1	17	4	0	1	0	1.000	0	0-0	0	5.87	4.75

Tanner Roark

Pitches: R Bats: R Pos: SP-31　　　　ROW-ark　　　　Ht: 6'2" Wt: 230 Born: 10/5/1986 Age: 28

		HOW MUCH HE PITCHED						WHAT HE GAVE UP							THE RESULTS						
Year Team	Lg	G GS CG GF	IP	BFP	H R ER	HR SH SF HB	TBB IBB	SO	WP Bk	W L	Pct	Sh	Sv-Op	Hld	ERC	ERA
2010 Frisco	AA	22 17 0 0	105.0	448	113 57 49	8 2 2 2	33 0	75	4 0	10 5	.667	0	0- -	-	4.12	4.20
2010 Hrsbrg	AA	6 6 0 0	36.0	148	35 13 10	5 0 1 0	9 0	33	0 1	1 1	.500	0	0- -	-	3.63	2.50
2011 Hrsbrg	AA	21 21 0 0	117.0	502	125 64 61	10 5 3 4	39 3	92	6 0	9 9	.500	0	0- -	-	4.24	4.69
2012 Syrcse	AAA	28 26 1 0	147.2	645	161 89 72	14 8 7 11	47 3	130	5 0	6 17	.261	0	0- -	-	4.51	4.39
2013 Syrcse	AAA	33 11 0 9	105.2	419	85 43 37	6 2 2 3	20 0	84	2 0	9 3	.750	0	2- -	-	2.13	3.15
2013 Was	NL	14 5 0 1	53.2	204	38 11 9	1 3 2 0	11 0	40	0 0	7 1	.875	0	0-0	1	1.54	1.51
2014 Was	NL	31 31 1 0	198.2	798	178 64 63	16 5 2 6	39 1	138	0 0	15 10	.600	0	0-0	0	2.76	2.85
2 ML YEARS		45 36 1 1	252.1	1002	216 75 72	17 8 4 6	50 1	178	0 0	22 11	.667	1	0-0	1	2.48	2.57

Brian Roberts

Bats: B Throws: R Pos: 2B-91;PH-5　　　　Ht: 5'9" Wt: 175 Born: 10/9/1977 Age: 37

								BATTING												RUNNING		AVERAGES			
Year Team	Lg	G	AB	H	2B	3B	HR	(Hm Rd)	TB	R	RBI	RC	TBB IBB	SO	HBP	SH	SF	SB CS	GDP	Avg	OBP	Slg	OPS
2001 Bal	AL	75	273	69	12	3	2	(0 2)	93	42	17	27	13 0	36	0	3	3	12 3	3	.253	.284	.341	.624
2002 Bal	AL	38	128	29	6	0	1	(1 0)	38	18	11	12	15 0	21	1	3	2	9 2	3	.227	.308	.297	.605
2003 Bal	AL	112	460	124	22	4	5	(3 2)	169	65	41	62	46 1	58	1	4	1	23 6	9	.270	.337	.367	.704
2004 Bal	AL	159	641	175	50	2	4	(0 4)	241	107	53	91	71 1	95	1	15	6	29 12	3	.273	.344	.376	.720
2005 Bal	AL	143	561	176	45	7	18	(9 9)	289	92	73	106	67 5	83	3	5	4	27 10	6	.314	.387	.515	.903
2006 Bal	AL	138	563	161	34	3	10	(6 4)	231	85	55	74	55 4	66	0	6	5	36 7	16	.286	.347	.410	.757
2007 Bal	AL	156	621	180	42	5	12	(6 6)	268	103	57	105	89 6	99	0	2	4	50 7	8	.290	.377	.432	.808
2008 Bal	AL	155	611	181	51	8	9	(6 3)	275	107	57	101	82 3	104	2	3	6	40 10	8	.296	.378	.450	.828
2009 Bal	AL	159	632	179	56	1	16	(4 12)	285	110	79	106	74 3	112	2	1	8	30 7	7	.283	.356	.451	.807
2010 Bal	AL	59	230	64	14	0	4	(2 2)	90	28	15	31	26 1	40	2	1	2	12 2	2	.278	.354	.391	.745
2011 Bal	AL	39	163	36	7	1	3	(1 2)	54	18	19	18	12 0	21	0	2	1	6 1	4	.221	.273	.331	.604
2012 Bal	AL	17	66	12	0	0	0	(0 0)	12	2	5	3	5 0	12	0	1	2	1 1	0	.182	.233	.182	.415
2013 Bal	AL	77	265	66	12	1	8	(6 2)	104	33	39	36	26 1	44	0	1	4	3 1	4	.249	.312	.392	.704
2014 NYY	AL	91	317	75	16	4	5	(1 4)	114	40	21	31	28 1	53	1	1	1	7 4	9	.237	.300	.360	.659
14 ML YEARS		1418	5531	1527	367	39	97	(45 52)	2263	850	542	803	609 26	844	13	48	49	285 73	82	.276	.347	.409	.756

Ryan Roberts

Bats: R Throws: R Pos: 3B-8;PH-1　　　　Ht: 5'11" Wt: 185 Born: 9/19/1980 Age: 34

								BATTING												RUNNING		AVERAGES			
Year Team	Lg	G	AB	H	2B	3B	HR	(Hm Rd)	TB	R	RBI	RC	TBB IBB	SO	HBP	SH	SF	SB CS	GDP	Avg	OBP	Slg	OPS
2014 Pwtckt*	AAA	72	274	76	22	1	7	(- -)	121	40	32	41	23 1	53	2	1	2	3 4	4	.277	.337	.442	.778
2006 Tor	AL	9	13	1	0	0	0	(0 1)	4	1	1	0	1 0	4	0	0	0	0 0	0	.077	.143	.308	.451
2007 Tor	AL	8	13	1	0	0	0	(0 0)	1	2	0	0	2 0	7	1	0	0	0 0	0	.077	.250	.077	.327
2008 Tex	AL	1	1	0	0	0	0	(0 0)	0	0	0	0	0 0	1	0	0	0	0 0	0	.000	.000	.000	.000
2009 Ari	NL	110	305	85	17	2	7	(3 4)	127	41	25	41	40 1	55	3	2	1	7 3	2	.279	.367	.416	.783
2010 Ari	NL	36	66	13	4	0	2	(1 1)	23	8	9	7	3 1	17	0	1	1	0 0	0	.197	.229	.348	.577
2011 Ari	NL	143	482	120	25	2	19	(9 10)	206	86	65	75	66 2	98	2	3	2	18 9	6	.249	.341	.427	.768
2012 2 Tms		143	439	103	19	0	12	(5 7)	158	51	52	46	40 1	92	1	3	6	10 6	13	.235	.296	.360	.656
2013 TB	AL	60	162	40	6	0	5	(3 2)	61	15	17	17	11 0	39	0	0	2	3 0	2	.247	.295	.377	.671
2014 Bos	AL	8	19	2	0	0	0	(0 0)	2	1	0	0	3 0	7	0	0	0	0 0	2	.105	.227	.105	.333
12 Ari	NL	83	252	63	9	0	6	(4 2)	90	28	34	25	22 1	45	0	2	4	6 3	10	.250	.306	.357	.663
12 TB	AL	60	187	40	10	0	6	(1 5)	68	23	18	21	18 0	47	1	1	2	4 3	3	.214	.284	.364	.647
Postseason		5	20	7	1	0	2	(1 1)	14	2	6	2	0 0	4	0	0	0	0 1	0	.350	.350	.700	1.050
9 ML YEARS		518	1500	365	71	4	46	(21 25)	582	205	169	186	166 5	320	7	9	10	35 20	27	.243	.320	.388	.708

Daniel Robertson

Bats: R Throws: R Pos: LF-30;CF-21;RF-18;PH-8;PR-8;DH-2;2B-1　　　　Ht: 5'8" Wt: 170 Born: 9/30/1985 Age: 29

								BATTING												RUNNING		AVERAGES			
Year Team	Lg	G	AB	H	2B	3B	HR	(Hm Rd)	TB	R	RBI	RC	TBB IBB	SO	HBP	SH	SF	SB CS	GDP	Avg	OBP	Slg	OPS
2010 Lk Els	A+	135	533	160	27	9	6	(- -)	223	95	61	91	59 2	52	7	6	4	30 9	11	.300	.375	.418	.793
2011 SnAnt	AA	124	438	124	23	5	5	(- -)	172	97	44	70	55 2	51	7	5	3	20 6	8	.283	.370	.393	.762
2012 Tucsn	AAA	129	490	148	28	4	2	(- -)	190	71	38	75	48 0	58	6	8	1	18 8	13	.302	.371	.388	.758
2013 Tucsn	AAA	136	484	138	24	9	2	(- -)	186	91	53	78	60 1	63	10	5	6	23 6	10	.285	.371	.384	.756
2014 ElPaso	AAA	5	22	8	2	0	2	(- -)	16	6	5	5	1 0	3	0	0	1	0 0	1	.364	.391	.727	1.119
2014 RdRck	AAA	8	28	7	1	1	1	(- -)	13	6	3	5	5 1	4	0	0	0	2 0	1	.250	.364	.464	.828
2014 Tex	AL	70	177	48	9	1	0	(0 0)	59	23	21	23	17 0	28	0	2	1	6 4	3	.271	.333	.333	.667

David Robertson

Pitches: R Bats: R Pos: RP-63　　　　Ht: 5'11" Wt: 195 Born: 4/9/1985 Age: 30

		HOW MUCH HE PITCHED						WHAT HE GAVE UP							THE RESULTS						
Year Team	Lg	G GS CG GF	IP	BFP	H R ER	HR SH SF HB	TBB IBB	SO	WP Bk	W L	Pct	Sh	Sv-Op	Hld	ERC	ERA
2008 NYY	AL	25 0 0 8	30.1	131	29 18 18	3 0 3 0	15 2	36	6 0	4 0	1.000	0	0-0	0	4.12	5.34
2009 NYY	AL	45 0 0 20	43.2	191	36 19 16	4 0 0 1	23 1	63	6 0	2 1	.667	0	1-1	5	3.51	3.30
2010 NYY	AL	64 0 0 10	61.1	273	59 26 26	5 5 3 3	33 6	71	7 2	4 5	.444	0	1-3	14	4.29	3.82
2011 NYY	AL	70 0 0 14	66.2	272	40 9 8	1 1 0 1	35 6	100	6 1	4 0	1.000	0	1-4	34	1.85	1.08
2012 NYY	AL	65 0 0 17	60.2	248	52 19 18	5 0 1 1	19 0	81	1 1	2 7	.222	0	2-5	30	2.95	2.67
2013 NYY	AL	70 0 0 16	66.1	262	51 15 15	5 3 0 2	18 1	77	1 0	5 1	.833	0	3-5	33	2.37	2.04
2014 NYY	AL	63 0 0 55	64.1	259	45 23 22	7 1 0 1	23 2	96	0 0	4 5	.444	0	39-44	0	2.41	3.08
Postseason		19 0 0 7	17.0	73	15 7 7	2 1 0 1	5 3	17	1 0	3 0	1.000	0	0-0	2	2.99	3.71
7 ML YEARS		402 0 0 127	393.1	1636	312 129 123	30 10 7 9	166 18	524	27 4	25 19	.568	0	47-62	116	2.91	2.81

Clint Robinson

Bats: L **Throws:** L **Pos:** PH-7;1B-3   **Ht:** 6'5" **Wt:** 225 **Born:** 2/16/1985 **Age:** 30

Year	Team	Lg	G	AB	H	2B	3B	HR	(Hm	Rd)	TB	R	RBI	RC	TBB	IBB	SO	HBP	SH	SF	SB	CS	GDP	Avg	OBP	Slg	OPS
2010	NWArk	AA	129	477	160	41	5	29	(-	-)	298	90	98	117	58	4	86	6	2	5	4	3	7	.335	.410	.625	1.035
2011	Omha	AAA	134	503	164	35	0	23	(-	-)	268	86	100	106	58	5	88	6	1	4	2	1	18	.326	.399	.533	.932
2012	Omha	AAA	131	487	142	37	1	13	(-	-)	220	70	67	91	79	4	65	3	0	1	1	0	17	.292	.393	.452	.845
2013	NHam	AA	76	289	78	14	2	11	(-	-)	129	41	43	48	40	1	50	3	0	0	1	2	7	.270	.364	.446	.811
2013	Buffalo	AAA	35	108	23	9	0	2	(-	-)	38	13	12	14	19	0	33	0	0	3	0	0	1	.213	.323	.352	.675
2014	Albq	AAA	119	429	134	31	5	18	(-	-)	229	77	80	92	64	2	84	2	0	4	0	0	11	.312	.401	.534	.935
2012	KC	AL	4	4	0	0	0	0	(0	0)	0	0	0	0	0	0	2	0	0	0	0	0	0	.000	.000	.000	.000
2014	LAD	NL	9	9	3	0	0	0	(0	0)	3	3	2	2	1	0	1	0	0	0	0	0	0	.333	.400	.333	.733
	2 ML YEARS		13	13	3	0	0	0	(0	0)	3	3	2	2	1	0	3	0	0	0	0	0	0	.231	.286	.231	.516

Shane Robinson

Bats: R **Throws:** R **Pos:** PH-30;RF-15;LF-5;PR-2;CF-1   **Ht:** 5'9" **Wt:** 165 **Born:** 10/30/1984 **Age:** 30

Year	Team	Lg	G	AB	H	2B	3B	HR	(Hm	Rd)	TB	R	RBI	RC	TBB	IBB	SO	HBP	SH	SF	SB	CS	GDP	Avg	OBP	Slg	OPS
2014	Memp*	AAA	53	191	58	12	0	2	(-	-)	76	33	16	30	22	1	25	2	0	1	4	2	7	.304	.380	.398	.778
2009	StL	NL	11	25	6	1	0	0	(0	0)	7	1	1	1	0	0	2	0	0	1	1	0	1	.240	.231	.280	.511
2011	StL	NL	9	7	0	0	0	0	(0	0)	0	0	0	0	1	0	2	0	0	0	0	0	1	.000	.125	.000	.125
2012	StL	NL	102	166	42	8	0	3	(1	2)	59	20	16	15	14	2	32	0	0	1	1	0	5	.253	.309	.355	.665
2013	StL	NL	99	144	36	2	1	2	(1	1)	46	22	16	18	23	0	17	0	0	4	5	1	2	.250	.345	.319	.664
2014	StL	NL	47	60	9	1	1	0	(0	0)	12	3	4	0	6	0	10	0	0	0	0	1	3	.150	.227	.200	.427
	Postseason		18	24	5	1	0	1	(0	1)	9	4	4	0	1	0	4	0	0	0	0	0	1	.208	.240	.375	.615
	5 ML YEARS		268	402	93	12	2	5	(2	3)	124	46	37	34	44	2	63	0	0	6	7	2	12	.231	.303	.308	.612

Fernando Rodney

Pitches: R **Bats:** R **Pos:** RP-69   **Ht:** 5'11" **Wt:** 220 **Born:** 3/18/1977 **Age:** 38

Year	Team	Lg	G	GS	CG	GF	IP	BFP	H	R	ER	HR	SH	SF	HB	TBB	IBB	SO	WP	Bk	W	L	Pct	Sh	Sv-Op	Hld	ERC	ERA
2002	Det	AL	20	0	0	10	18.0	89	25	15	12	2	2	1	0	10	2	10	0	1	1	3	.250	0	0-4	0	6.77	6.00
2003	Det	AL	27	0	0	11	29.2	143	35	20	20	2	3	3	1	17	1	33	0	0	1	3	.250	0	3-6	3	5.46	6.07
2005	Det	AL	39	0	0	26	44.0	185	39	14	14	5	2	0	2	17	3	42	2	0	2	3	.400	0	9-15	3	3.59	2.86
2006	Det	AL	63	0	0	30	71.2	304	51	36	28	6	2	0	8	34	4	65	3	0	7	4	.636	0	7-11	18	3.01	3.52
2007	Det	AL	48	0	0	12	50.2	223	46	27	24	5	4	2	3	21	0	54	4	0	2	6	.250	0	1-3	12	3.74	4.26
2008	Det	AL	38	0	0	25	40.1	188	34	22	22	3	1	2	3	30	5	49	3	0	0	6	.000	0	13-19	5	4.29	4.91
2009	Det	AL	73	0	0	65	75.2	330	70	38	37	8	4	2	2	41	4	61	5	0	2	5	.286	0	37-38	0	4.31	4.40
2010	LAA	AL	72	0	0	30	68.0	308	70	33	32	4	1	0	5	35	1	53	4	0	4	3	.571	0	14-21	21	4.63	4.24
2011	LAA	AL	39	0	0	15	32.0	150	26	18	16	1	3	0	3	28	0	26	2	0	3	5	.375	0	3-7	10	4.66	4.50
2012	TB	AL	76	0	0	65	74.2	282	43	9	5	2	4	2	3	15	1	76	4	0	2	2	.500	0	48-50	1	1.22	0.60
2013	TB	AL	68	0	0	55	66.2	290	53	27	25	3	1	1	1	36	3	82	4	1	5	4	.556	0	37-45	0	3.02	3.38
2014	Sea	AL	69	0	0	64	66.1	286	61	24	21	3	4	1	3	28	3	76	4	0	1	6	.143	0	**48-51**	0	3.42	2.85
	Postseason		10	0	0	2	10.0	45	7	6	4	0	3	0	1	8	1	13	1	0	1	0	1.000	0	0-2	2	3.38	3.60
	12 ML YEARS		632	0	0	408	637.2	2778	553	283	256	44	31	14	34	312	27	627	35	2	30	50	.375	0	220-270	72	3.57	3.61

Alex Rodriguez

Bats: R **Throws:** R **Pos:** 3B   **Ht:** 6'3" **Wt:** 225 **Born:** 7/27/1975 **Age:** 39

Year	Team	Lg	G	AB	H	2B	3B	HR	(Hm	Rd)	TB	R	RBI	RC	TBB	IBB	SO	HBP	SH	SF	SB	CS	GDP	Avg	OBP	Slg	OPS
1994	Sea	AL	17	54	11	0	0	0	(0	0)	11	4	2	3	3	0	20	0	1	0	3	0	0	.204	.241	.204	.445
1995	Sea	AL	48	142	33	6	2	5	(1	4)	58	15	19	15	6	0	42	0	1	0	4	2	0	.232	.264	.408	.672
1996	Sea	AL	146	601	215	54	1	36	(18	18)	379	141	123	144	59	1	104	4	6	7	15	4	15	.358	.414	.631	1.045
1997	Sea	AL	141	587	176	40	3	23	(16	7)	291	100	84	100	41	1	99	5	4	1	29	6	14	.300	.350	.496	.846
1998	Sea	AL	161	686	213	35	5	42	(18	24)	384	123	124	135	45	0	121	10	3	4	46	13	12	.310	.360	.560	.919
1999	Sea	AL	129	502	143	25	0	42	(20	22)	294	110	111	102	56	2	109	5	1	8	21	7	12	.285	.357	.586	.943
2000	Sea	AL	148	554	175	34	2	41	(13	28)	336	134	132	138	100	5	121	7	0	11	15	4	10	.316	.420	.606	1.026
2001	Tex	AL	162	632	201	34	1	52	(26	26)	393	133	135	148	75	6	131	16	0	9	18	3	17	.318	.399	.622	1.021
2002	Tex	AL	162	624	187	27	2	57	(34	23)	389	125	142	152	87	12	122	10	0	4	9	4	14	.300	.392	.623	1.015
2003	Tex	AL	161	607	181	30	6	47	(26	21)	364	124	118	131	87	10	126	15	0	6	17	3	16	.298	.396	.600	.995
2004	NYY	AL	155	601	172	24	2	36	(17	19)	308	112	106	112	80	6	131	10	0	7	28	4	18	.286	.375	.512	.888
2005	NYY	AL	162	605	194	29	1	48	(26	22)	369	124	130	137	91	8	139	16	0	3	21	6	8	.321	.421	**.610**	1.031
2006	NYY	AL	154	572	166	26	1	35	(20	15)	299	113	121	112	90	8	139	8	0	4	15	4	22	.290	.392	.523	.914
2007	NYY	AL	158	583	183	31	0	54	(26	28)	376	143	156	159	95	11	120	21	0	9	24	4	15	.314	.422	**.645**	1.067
2008	NYY	AL	138	510	154	33	0	35	(21	14)	292	104	103	97	65	9	117	14	0	5	18	3	16	.302	.392	**.573**	.965
2009	NYY	AL	124	444	127	17	1	30	(18	12)	236	78	100	89	80	7	97	8	0	2	14	2	13	.286	.402	.532	.933
2010	NYY	AL	137	522	141	29	2	30	(15	15)	264	74	125	93	59	1	98	3	0	11	4	3	7	.270	.341	.506	.847
2011	NYY	AL	99	373	103	21	0	16	(9	7)	172	67	62	61	47	1	80	5	0	3	4	1	13	.276	.362	.461	.823
2012	NYY	AL	122	463	126	17	1	18	(8	10)	199	74	57	66	51	3	116	10	0	5	13	1	13	.272	.353	.430	.783
2013	NYY	AL	44	156	38	7	0	7	(2	5)	66	21	19	19	23	1	43	2	0	0	4	2	5	.244	.348	.423	.771
	Postseason		75	274	72	16	0	13	(5	8)	127	43	41	43	39	4	75	9	1	3	8	3	6	.263	.369	.464	.833
	20 ML YEARS		2568	9818	2939	519	30	654	(334	320)	5480	1919	1969	2013	1240	92	2075	169	16	101	322	76	240	.299	.384	.558	.942

Fernando Rodriguez

Pitches: R Bats: R Pos: RP-7   Ht: 6'3" Wt: 235 Born: 6/18/1984 Age: 31

		HOW MUCH HE PITCHED					WHAT HE GAVE UP										THE RESULTS						
Year	Team	Lg	G	GS	CG	GF	IP	BFP	H	R	ER	HR	SH	SF	HB	TBB	IBB	SO	WP	Bk	W	L	Pct	Sh	Sv-Op	Hld	ERC	ERA
2014	Scrmto*	AAA	38	0	0	8	45.2	190	40	12	10	2	1	0	3	16	1	53	3	0	3	0	1.000	0	0--	-	3.09	1.97
2009	LAA	AL	1	0	0	0	0.2	6	1	3	2	1	0	0	0	2	0	1	1	0	0	0	-	0	0-0	0	31.03	27.00
2011	Hou	NL	47	0	0	11	52.1	231	51	24	23	6	5	0	3	30	5	57	2	0	2	3	.400	0	0-0	6	4.90	3.96
2012	Hou	NL	71	0	0	9	70.1	309	68	45	42	10	2	2	1	34	7	78	10	0	2	10	.167	0	0-4	13	4.39	5.37
2014	Oak	AL	7	0	0	3	9.0	33	4	1	1	0	0	0	0	2	0	4	0	0	1	0	1.000	0	0-0	1	0.76	1.00
	4 ML YEARS		126	0	0	23	132.1	579	124	73	68	17	7	2	4	68	12	140	13	0	5	13	.278	0	0-4	20	4.36	4.62

Francisco Rodriguez

Pitches: R Bats: R Pos: RP-69   Ht: 6'0" Wt: 195 Born: 1/7/1982 Age: 33

		HOW MUCH HE PITCHED					WHAT HE GAVE UP										THE RESULTS						
Year	Team	Lg	G	GS	CG	GF	IP	BFP	H	R	ER	HR	SH	SF	HB	TBB	IBB	SO	WP	Bk	W	L	Pct	Sh	Sv-Op	Hld	ERC	ERA
2002	LAA	AL	5	0	0	4	5.2	21	3	0	0	0	0	0	1	2	1	13	0	0	0	0	-	0	0-0	0	1.52	0.00
2003	LAA	AL	59	0	0	23	86.0	334	50	30	29	12	2	4	2	35	5	95	7	0	8	3	.727	0	2-6	7	2.25	3.03
2004	LAA	AL	69	0	0	29	84.0	335	51	21	17	2	2	1	1	33	1	123	5	0	4	1	.800	0	12-19	27	1.64	1.82
2005	LAA	AL	66	0	0	58	67.1	279	45	20	20	7	1	1	0	32	3	91	8	0	2	5	.286	0	**45-50**	0	2.52	2.67
2006	LAA	AL	69	0	0	58	73.0	296	52	16	14	6	3	0	1	28	5	98	10	0	2	3	.400	0	**47-51**	0	2.35	1.73
2007	LAA	AL	64	0	0	56	67.1	285	50	22	21	3	1	4	1	34	0	90	7	1	5	2	.714	0	40-46	0	2.74	2.81
2008	LAA	AL	**76**	0	0	69	68.1	288	54	21	17	4	1	1	2	34	4	77	6	0	2	3	.400	0	**62-69**	0	3.06	2.24
2009	NYM	NL	70	0	0	66	68.0	295	51	34	28	7	4	1	1	38	6	73	1	0	3	6	.333	0	35-42	0	3.18	3.71
2010	NYM	NL	53	0	0	46	57.1	236	45	14	14	3	1	1	2	21	4	67	3	1	4	2	.667	0	25-30	0	2.53	2.20
2011	2 Tms	NL	73	0	0	36	71.2	307	67	22	21	4	2	1	2	26	4	79	4	0	6	2	.750	0	23-29	17	3.25	2.64
2012	Mil	NL	78	0	0	13	72.0	305	65	37	35	8	1	3	0	31	1	72	6	0	2	7	.222	0	3-10	32	3.73	4.38
2013	2 Tms	NL	48	0	0	23	46.2	193	42	14	14	7	3	0	1	14	4	54	2	0	3	2	.600	0	10-10	5	3.44	2.70
2014	Mil	NL	69	0	0	66	68.0	268	49	23	23	14	2	0	1	18	1	73	0	0	5	5	.500	0	44-49	0	2.77	3.04
11	NYM	NL	42	0	0	34	42.2	187	44	15	15	3	2	1	2	16	4	46	2	0	2	2	.500	0	23-26	0	3.94	3.16
11	Mil	NL	31	0	0	2	29.0	120	23	7	6	1	0	0	0	10	0	33	2	0	4	0	1.000	0	0-3	17	2.32	1.86
13	Mil	NL	25	0	0	18	24.2	97	17	3	3	2	2	0	0	9	3	26	0	0	1	1	.500	0	10-10	1	2.10	1.09
13	Bal	NL	23	0	0	5	22.0	96	25	11	11	5	1	0	1	5	1	28	2	0	2	1	.667	0	0-0	4	5.11	4.50
	Postseason		26	0	0	8	36.2	158	32	15	12	5	1	3	1	18	2	49	5	0	5	4	.556	0	3-5	6	3.99	2.95
	13 ML YEARS		799	0	0	547	835.1	3442	624	274	253	77	23	17	15	346	39	1005	59	2	46	41	.529	0	348-411	88	2.72	2.73

Guilder Rodriguez

Bats: B Throws: R Pos: 3B-3;2B-2;DH-2;PR-2;SS-1;PH-1   WHEEL-dair   Ht: 6'1" Wt: 190 Born: 7/24/1983 Age: 31

		BATTING																		RUNNING			AVERAGES			
Year	Team	Lg	G	AB	H	2B	3B	HR	(Hm	Rd)	TB	R	RBI	RC	TBB	IBB	SO	HBP	SH	SF	SB	CS	GDP	Avg	OBP	Slg	OPS
2010	Frisco	AA	96	323	86	4	3	0	(-	-)	96	44	23	37	31	0	42	4	14	3	15	5	6	.266	.335	.297	.632
2010	OKCity	AAA	21	67	17	3	0	0	(-	-)	20	17	8	8	9	0	7	0	0	0	4	1	3	.254	.342	.299	.641
2011	Frisco	AA	80	284	78	9	2	0	(-	-)	91	39	37	36	30	2	40	1	6	3	14	4	8	.275	.343	.320	.663
2011	RdRck	AAA	41	137	37	2	0	0	(-	-)	39	20	13	17	21	0	14	0	3	1	3	0	4	.270	.365	.285	.649
2012	Frisco	AA	66	207	43	2	0	0	(-	-)	45	24	13	15	25	1	27	0	6	0	13	4	6	.208	.294	.217	.510
2012	RdRck	AAA	19	58	15	0	0	0	(-	-)	15	5	8	5	8	0	7	0	2	2	1	2	4	.259	.338	.259	.597
2013	Frisco	AA	87	301	71	8	0	1	(-	-)	82	44	13	30	37	0	34	2	6	2	15	7	7	.236	.322	.272	.594
2013	RdRck	AAA	12	47	15	1	0	0	(-	-)	16	10	3	7	6	0	8	0	1	0	2	0	1	.319	.346	.340	.737
2014	Frisco	AA	81	305	82	7	1	0	(-	-)	91	36	20	35	37	0	45	0	6	1	10	7	6	.269	.347	.298	.645
2014	RdRck	AAA	9	30	5	1	0	0	(-	-)	6	4	1	1	4	0	5	0	1	0	0	0	1	.167	.265	.200	.465
2014	Tex	AL	7	12	2	0	0	0	(0	0)	2	2	1	1	1	0	5	0	1	0	0	0	0	.167	.231	.167	.397

Henry Rodriguez

Pitches: R Bats: R Pos: RP-2   Ht: 6'1" Wt: 225 Born: 2/25/1987 Age: 28

		HOW MUCH HE PITCHED					WHAT HE GAVE UP										THE RESULTS						
Year	Team	Lg	G	GS	CG	GF	IP	BFP	H	R	ER	HR	SH	SF	HB	TBB	IBB	SO	WP	Bk	W	L	Pct	Sh	Sv-Op	Hld	ERC	ERA
2014	NewOr*	AAA	17	0	0	5	25.1	122	10	13	12	1	2	0	0	38	0	41	14	1	0	1	.000	0	1--	-	4.32	4.26
2014	WSX*	R	5	0	0	0	5.1	27	3	4	4	0	0	0	1	5	0	14	14	2	0	0	-	0	0-0	-	3.21	6.75
2014	Charltt*	AAA	3	0	0	2	1.2	17	5	4	4	0	0	0	0	8	0	3	4	0	0	1	.000	0	0--	-	41.00	21.60
2009	Oak	AL	3	0	0	1	4.0	20	4	2	1	0	0	0	0	2	0	4	3	0	0	0	-	0	0-0	0	4.28	2.25
2010	Oak	AL	29	0	0	8	27.2	121	25	16	14	2	2	1	1	13	0	33	7	0	1	0	1.000	0	0-1	3	3.70	4.55
2011	Was	NL	59	0	0	21	65.2	295	54	30	26	1	1	1	2	45	1	70	**14**	1	3	3	.500	0	2-5	10	3.59	3.56
2012	Was	NL	35	0	0	20	29.1	131	19	20	19	4	2	1	1	22	0	31	10	1	1	3	.250	0	9-12	2	3.76	5.83
2013	2 Tms	NL	22	0	0	10	22.0	109	20	12	10	2	0	1	2	20	1	12	2	1	0	1	.000	0	0-0	1	5.59	4.09
2014	Mia	NL	2	0	0	0	1.2	11	2	2	2	0	0	0	0	5	0	1	0	0	0	0	-	0	0-0	0	16.74	10.80
13	Was	NL	17	0	0	8	18.0	86	14	8	8	1	0	0	1	16	0	11	2	1	0	1	.000	0	0-0	1	4.44	4.00
13	ChC	NL	5	0	0	2	4.0	23	6	4	2	1	0	1	1	4	1	1	0	0	0	0	-	0	0-0	0	11.69	4.50
	6 ML YEARS		150	0	0	60	150.1	687	124	82	72	9	5	4	7	107	2	151	36	3	5	7	.417	0	11-18	16	4.07	4.31

Paco Rodriguez

Pitches: L Bats: L Pos: RP-19   Ht: 6'3" Wt: 220 Born: 4/16/1991 Age: 24

		HOW MUCH HE PITCHED					WHAT HE GAVE UP										THE RESULTS						
Year	Team	Lg	G	GS	CG	GF	IP	BFP	H	R	ER	HR	SH	SF	HB	TBB	IBB	SO	WP	Bk	W	L	Pct	Sh	Sv-Op	Hld	ERC	ERA
2014	Albq*	AAA	32	0	0	8	28.2	126	26	16	15	4	0	1	0	17	2	35	2	0	2	3	.400	0	1--	-	4.50	4.71
2012	LAD	NL	11	0	0	2	6.2	26	3	1	1	0	0	0	0	4	1	6	0	0	0	1	.000	0	0-0	20	1.37	1.35
2013	LAD	NL	76	0	0	11	54.1	208	30	15	14	5	3	1	2	19	4	63	3	0	3	4	.429	0	2-5	20	1.68	2.32
2014	LAD	NL	19	0	0	1	14.0	53	12	6	6	1	1	0	0	4	0	14	0	0	1	0	1.000	0	0-1	4	2.95	3.86
	Postseason		2	0	0	0	0.2	8	4	2	2	1	0	0	0	2	1	1	0	0	0	0	-	0	0-0	0	75.08	27.00
	3 ML YEARS		106	0	0	14	75.0	287	45	22	21	6	4	1	2	27	5	83	3	0	4	5	.444	0	2-6	24	1.86	2.52

Sean Rodriguez

Bats: R **Throws:** R **Pos:** PH-26;2B-23;DH-22;1B-18;LF-17;3B-9;PR-7;RF-2;SS-1   **Ht:** 6'0" **Wt:** 200 **Born:** 4/26/1985 **Age:** 30

								BATTING												RUNNING			AVERAGES			
Year	Team	Lg	G	AB	H	2B	3B	HR	(Hm | Rd)	TB	R	RBI	RC	TBB	IBB	SO	HBP	SH	SF	SB	CS	GDP	Avg	OBP	Slg	OPS
2008	LAA	AL	59	167	34	8	1	3	(2 | 1)	53	18	10	12	14	0	55	3	2	1	3	1	3	.204	.276	.317	.593
2009	LAA	AL	12	25	5	0	0	2	(0 | 2)	11	4	4	2	3	0	7	0	0	1	0	0	2	.200	.276	.440	.716
2010	TB	AL	118	343	86	19	2	9	(5 | 4)	136	53	40	38	21	1	97	8	5	1	13	3	10	.251	.308	.397	.705
2011	TB	AL	131	373	83	20	3	8	(4 | 4)	133	45	36	41	38	2	87	18	5	2	11	7	8	.223	.323	.357	.679
2012	TB	AL	112	301	64	14	1	6	(3 | 3)	98	36	32	32	27	1	75	3	8	3	5	0	7	.213	.281	.326	.607
2013	TB	AL	96	195	48	10	1	5	(3 | 2)	75	21	23	21	17	0	59	5	3	2	1	3	3	.246	.320	.385	.704
2014	TB	AL	96	237	50	13	3	12	(7 | 5)	105	30	41	29	10	0	66	6	3	3	2	1	3	.211	.258	.443	.701
	Postseason		12	28	5	1	0	1	(0 | 1)	9	6	2	1	2	0	5	0	0	0	0	0	0	.179	.233	.321	.555
	7 ML YEARS		624	1641	370	84	11	45	(24 | 21)	611	207	186	175	130	4	446	43	26	13	35	15	36	.225	.297	.372	.670

Wandy Rodriguez

Pitches: L **Bats:** B **Pos:** SP-6   WAHN-dee   **Ht:** 5'10" **Wt:** 195 **Born:** 1/18/1979 **Age:** 36

			HOW MUCH HE PITCHED						WHAT HE GAVE UP											THE RESULTS						
Year	Team	Lg	G	GS	CG	GF	IP	BFP	H	R	ER	HR	SH	SF	HB	TBB	IBB	SO	WP	Bk	W	L	Pct	Sh	Sv-Op	Hld	ERC	ERA
2014 Altna*	AA	2	2	0	0	8.2	44	11	11	10	3	0	0	0	6	0	7	0	0	0	1	.000	0	0- -	-	8.66	10.38
2005 Hou	NL	25	22	0	0	128.2	560	135	82	79	19	3	3	8	53	2	80	3	3	10	10	.500	0	0-0	0	5.08	5.53
2006 Hou	NL	30	24	0	0	135.2	611	154	96	85	17	7	4	6	63	7	98	6	0	9	10	.474	0	0-0	0	5.45	5.64
2007 Hou	NL	31	31	1	0	182.2	782	179	102	93	22	6	4	5	62	2	158	3	0	9	13	.409	1	0-0	0	3.94	4.58
2008 Hou	NL	25	25	0	0	137.1	587	136	65	54	14	2	5	5	44	3	131	2	3	9	7	.563	0	0-0	0	3.82	3.54
2009 Hou	NL	33	33	1	0	205.2	849	192	77	69	21	8	4	5	63	5	193	2	1	14	12	.538	1	0-0	0	3.47	3.02
2010 Hou	NL	32	32	0	0	195.0	822	183	95	78	16	6	5	9	68	3	178	8	0	11	12	.478	0	0-0	0	3.60	3.60
2011 Hou	NL	30	30	0	0	191.0	808	182	81	74	25	7	3	5	69	7	166	5	0	11	11	.500	0	0-0	0	3.95	3.49
2012 2 Tms	NL	34	33	0	1	205.2	875	205	99	86	21	6	5	3	56	4	139	5	0	12	13	.480	0	0-0	0	3.55	3.76
2013 Pit	NL	12	12	0	0	62.2	260	58	26	25	10	1	1	4	12	1	46	1	1	6	4	.600	0	0-0	0	3.43	3.59
2014 Pit	NL	6	6	0	0	26.2	125	37	25	20	10	2	1	0	8	1	20	0	1	0	2	.000	0	0-0	0	7.91	6.75
12 Hou	NL	21	21	0	0	130.2	558	134	66	55	13	5	3	2	32	2	89	5	0	7	9	.438	0	0-0	0	3.57	3.79
12 Pit	NL	13	12	0	1	75.0	317	71	33	31	8	1	2	1	24	2	50	0	0	5	4	.556	0	0-0	0	3.50	3.72
	Postseason		3	0	0	1	4.2	22	5	2	2	2	1	0	0	5	1	4	0	0	0	1	.000	0	0-0	0	10.58	3.86
	10 ML YEARS		258	248	2	2	1471.0	6279	1461	748	663	175	48	35	50	498	35	1209	35	9	91	94	.492	2	0-0	0	4.03	4.06

Wilking Rodriguez

Pitches: R **Bats:** R **Pos:** RP-2   WILL-king   **Ht:** 6'1" **Wt:** 180 **Born:** 3/2/1990 **Age:** 25

				HOW MUCH HE PITCHED						WHAT HE GAVE UP										THE RESULTS					
Year	Team	Lg	G	GS	CG	GF	IP	BFP	H	R	ER	HR	SH	SF	HB	TBB	IBB	SO	WP	Bk	W	L	Pct	Sh	Sv-Op	Hld	ERC	ERA
2010 BG	A	22	19	0	0	106.1	453	109	66	50	11	3	2	6	28	0	93	10	0	4	10	.286	0	0- -	-	3.92	4.23
2011 HudVal	A-	2	2	0	0	8.1	35	10	6	6	0	0	0	0	2	0	9	1	1	1	1	.500	0	0- -	-	3.99	6.48
2011 BG	A	9	9	0	0	36.2	160	38	21	19	3	0	0	3	14	1	34	2	0	0	3	.000	0	0- -	-	4.40	4.66
2012 Charltt	A+	7	7	0	0	34.0	142	26	22	21	3	0	2	3	15	0	29	5	1	0	4	.000	0	0- -	-	3.25	5.56
2013 Rays	R	8	6	0	1	9.0	32	6	0	0	0	0	0	0	3	0	9	1	0	0	0	-	0	0- -	-	1.80	0.00
2014 NWArk	AA	11	0	0	3	11.0	48	11	3	2	2	1	0	0	4	1	12	0	0	1	0	1.000	0	0- -	-	4.26	1.64
2014 Omha	AAA	13	0	0	4	15.2	67	13	5	5	0	1	0	0	8	2	15	1	0	1	1	.500	0	0- -	-	2.66	2.87
2014 KC	AL	2	0	0	1	2.0	7	1	0	0	0	0	0	0	1	0	1	0	0	0	0	-	0	0-0	0	1.62	0.00

Yorman Rodriguez

Bats: R **Throws:** R **Pos:** RF-4;LF-2;CF-2;PR-2;PH-1   YOUR-man   **Ht:** 6'3" **Wt:** 195 **Born:** 8/15/1992 **Age:** 22

								BATTING												RUNNING			AVERAGES			
Year	Team	Lg	G	AB	H	2B	3B	HR	(Hm	Rd)	TB	R	RBI	RC	TBB	IBB	SO	HBP	SH	SF	SB	CS	GDP	Avg	OBP	Slg	OPS
2010 Billings	R+	43	171	58	8	3	2	(-	-)	78	25	39	30	8	1	30	0	1	4	12	2	1	.339	.361	.456	.817
2011 Dayton	A	79	280	71	10	4	7	(-	-)	110	38	40	37	25	0	84	2	2	1	20	8	7	.254	.318	.393	.711
2012 Bkrsfld	A+	23	90	14	4	0	0	(-	-)	18	7	7	2	3	0	39	0	0	1	4	0	1	.156	.181	.200	.381
2012 Dayton	A	65	258	70	17	3	6	(-	-)	111	35	44	34	12	0	61	2	2	2	7	5	3	.271	.307	.430	.737
2013 Bkrsfld	A+	83	251	63	20	4	9	(-	-)	118	41	35	38	22	0	77	3	1	0	6	3	4	.251	.319	.470	.789
2013 Pnscla	AA	66	262	70	15	2	4	(-	-)	101	30	31	35	25	0	76	0	0	2	4	0	6	.267	.329	.385	.714
2014 Pnscla	AA	119	450	118	20	5	9	(-	-)	175	69	40	61	47	1	117	1	1	3	12	5	12	.262	.331	.389	.720
2014 Cin	NL	11	27	6	0	0	0	(0	0)	6	3	2	1	1	0	12	1	0	0	0	1	0	.222	.270	.222	.490

Chaz Roe

Pitches: R **Bats:** R **Pos:** RP-3   ROW   **Ht:** 6'5" **Wt:** 190 **Born:** 10/9/1986 **Age:** 28

				HOW MUCH HE PITCHED						WHAT HE GAVE UP										THE RESULTS					
Year	Team	Lg	G	GS	CG	GF	IP	BFP	H	R	ER	HR	SH	SF	HB	TBB	IBB	SO	WP	Bk	W	L	Pct	Sh	Sv-Op	Hld	ERC	ERA
2010 ColSpr	AAA	27	27	2	0	158.0	725	210	115	105	18	8	10	7	53	2	115	9	0	9	13	.409	0	0- -	-	6.04	5.98
2011 Tacom	AAA	33	10	0	9	99.2	467	133	85	73	16	2	6	4	38	0	83	11	1	0	7	.000	0	2- -	-	6.59	6.59
2013 Mobile	AA	3	0	0	3	2.1	10	2	1	0	0	0	0	0	0	0	3	0	0	1	0	1.000	0	1- -	-	1.29	0.00
2013 Reno	AAA	22	0	0	21	22.0	87	15	3	3	0	0	1	3	4	0	20	5	0	0	0	-	0	7- -	-	1.60	1.23
2014 NewOr	AAA	47	0	0	27	64.0	262	53	30	26	5	2	2	6	21	1	72	3	0	3	3	.500	0	14- -	-	3.13	3.66
2013 Ari	NL	21	0	0	4	22.1	95	18	10	10	3	2	1	0	13	3	24	1	0	1	0	1.000	0	0-2	1	3.78	4.03
2014 NYY	AL	3	0	0	2	2.0	13	3	3	2	0	0	1	0	3	0	4	1	0	0	0	-	0	0-0	0	9.89	9.00
	2 ML YEARS		24	0	0	6	24.1	108	21	13	12	3	2	2	0	16	3	28	2	0	1	0	1.000	0	0-2	1	4.26	4.44

Esmil Rogers

Pitches: R Bats: R Pos: RP-33; SP-1   ESS-mill   Ht: 6'3" Wt: 200 Born: 8/14/1985 Age: 29

			HOW MUCH HE PITCHED				WHAT HE GAVE UP												THE RESULTS							
Year	Team	Lg	G	GS	CG	GF	IP	BFP	H	R	ER	HR	SH	SF	HB	TBB	IBB	SO	WP	Bk	W	L	Pct	Sh	Sv-Op	Hld	ERC	ERA
2014	Buffalo*	AAA	12	7	0	1	48.2	199	42	17	17	2	0	2	2	18	0	41	4	0	2	2	.500	0	0- -		3.07	3.14
2009	Col	NL	1	1	0	0	4.0	16	3	2	2	0	0	1	0	2	0	3	0	0	0	0	-	0	0-0	0	2.58	4.50
2010	Col	NL	28	8	0	5	72.0	333	94	59	49	5	3	3	5	26	2	66	5	2	2	3	.400	0	0-1	1	5.70	6.13
2011	Col	NL	18	13	0	1	83.0	404	110	65	65	14	4	3	6	47	5	63	5	1	6	6	.500	0	0-0	0	7.49	7.05
2012	2 Tms		67	0	0	19	78.2	348	83	42	41	7	2	2	5	30	4	83	10	0	3	3	.500	0	0-2	8	4.37	4.69
2013	Tor	AL	44	20	0	5	137.2	598	152	76	73	21	0	4	6	44	2	96	7	2	5	9	.357	0	0-1	4	4.92	4.77
2014	Tor	AL	34	1	0	13	45.2	202	50	30	29	8	2	0	2	17	0	44	1	1	2	0	1.000	0	0-1	4	5.23	5.72
12	Col	NL	23	0	0	6	25.2	131	36	23	23	2	0	0	2	18	2	29	5	0	0	2	.000	0	0-2		7.71	8.06
12	Cle	AL	44	0	0	13	53.0	217	47	19	18	5	2	2	3	12	2	54	5	0	3	1	.750	0	0-0	6	2.93	3.06
14	Tor	AL	16	0	0	9	20.2	96	28	17	16	5	0	0	1	7	0	21	1	0	0	0	-	0	0-0	1	7.27	6.97
14	NYY	AL	18	1	0	4	25.0	106	22	13	13	3	2	0	1	10	0	23	0	1	2	0	1.000	0	0-1	3	3.71	4.68
6 ML YEARS			192	43	0	43	421.0	1901	492	274	259	55	11	13	24	166	13	355	28	6	18	21	.462	0	0-5	17	5.45	5.54

Jason Rogers

Bats: R Throws: R Pos: 1B-4;PH-4   Ht: 6'2" Wt: 245 Born: 3/13/1988 Age: 27

			BATTING																		RUNNING			AVERAGES			
Year	Team	Lg	G	AB	H	2B	3B	HR	(Hm	Rd)	TB	R	RBI	RC	TBB	IBB	SO	HBP	SH	SF	SB	CS	GDP	Avg	OBP	Slg	OPS
2010	Brewrs	R	42	160	45	7	1	3	(-	-)	63	31	32	-	20	0	32	3	-	2	5	2	3	.281	.368	.394	.761
2011	Wisc	A	64	240	66	15	2	6	(-	-)	103	29	37	37	22	2	48	2	2	4	6	1	1	.275	.336	.429	.765
2011	Helena	R+	7	27	8	1	0	1	(-	-)	12	3	3	3	2	0	5	0	0	0	0	1	1	.296	.345	.444	.789
2012	Wisc	A	66	239	72	24	1	6	(-	-)	116	39	43	48	37	0	46	1	0	2	5	0	8	.301	.394	.485	.880
2012	BrvdCt	A+	67	233	70	11	0	5	(-	-)	96	33	23	44	42	3	42	4	0	0	7	1	5	.300	.416	.412	.828
2013	Hntsvl	AA	133	481	130	25	2	22	(-	-)	225	69	87	82	59	1	86	1	0	8	7	2	11	.270	.346	.468	.814
2014	Hntsvl	AA	77	287	81	18	2	7	(-	-)	124	42	43	46	31	1	56	3	0	3	5	1	10	.282	.355	.432	.787
2014	Nashv	AAA	57	206	65	11	4	11	(-	-)	117	36	39	44	22	0	38	1	0	3	0	0	10	.316	.379	.568	.947
2014	Mil	NL	8	9	1	1	0	0	(0	0)	2	0	0	0	1	0	1	0	0	0	0	0	0	.111	.200	.222	.422

Miguel Rojas

Bats: R Throws: R Pos: SS-66;3B-19;PH-5;PR-4;2B-3;LF-1   Ht: 6'0" Wt: 150 Born: 2/24/1989 Age: 26

			BATTING																		RUNNING			AVERAGES			
Year	Team	Lg	G	AB	H	2B	3B	HR	(Hm	Rd)	TB	R	RBI	RC	TBB	IBB	SO	HBP	SH	SF	SB	CS	GDP	Avg	OBP	Slg	OPS
2010	Lynbrg	A+	74	244	56	3	2	1	(-	-)	66	28	14	18	11	0	38	3	8	0	12	4	8	.230	.271	.270	.542
2010	Reds	R	1	4	3	0	0	0	(-	-)	3	1	1	1	0	0	0	0	0	0	1	0	0	.750	.750	.750	1.500
2010	Carlina	AA	7	27	6	0	0	0	(-	-)	6	1	4	1	2	0	4	0	0	0	1	1	1	.222	.276	.222	.498
2011	Carlina	AA	68	239	62	6	0	0	(-	-)	68	26	24	21	16	0	39	0	7	3	11	7	5	.259	.302	.285	.587
2011	Reds	R	6	17	8	3	0	0	(-	-)	11	6	6	7	6	0	1	2	0	0	4	1	0	.471	.640	.647	1.287
2012	Pnscla	AA	58	143	30	1	0	0	(-	-)	31	14	10	9	16	0	17	1	0	0	2	3	7	.210	.294	.217	.511
2012	Lsvlle	AAA	44	129	24	3	0	1	(-	-)	30	9	7	6	7	1	16	0	7	1	0	0	0	.186	.226	.233	.459
2013	Chatt	AA	130	420	98	12	2	5	(-	-)	129	45	32	43	40	0	49	3	13	2	10	4	13	.233	.303	.307	.610
2014	Albq	AAA	51	159	48	9	0	4	(-	-)	69	27	13	25	10	3	21	3	0	1	7	3	4	.302	.353	.434	.787
2014	LAD	NL	85	149	27	3	0	1	(0	1)	33	16	9	6	10	1	28	2	1	0	0	0	5	.181	.242	.221	.464

Jimmy Rollins

Bats: B Throws: R Pos: SS-131;PH-6;DH-2   Ht: 5'8" Wt: 180 Born: 11/27/1978 Age: 36

			BATTING																		RUNNING			AVERAGES			
Year	Team	Lg	G	AB	H	2B	3B	HR	(Hm	Rd)	TB	R	RBI	RC	TBB	IBB	SO	HBP	SH	SF	SB	CS	GDP	Avg	OBP	Slg	OPS
2000	Phi	NL	14	53	17	1	1	0	(0	0)	20	5	5	8	2	0	7	0	0	0	3	0	0	.321	.345	.377	.723
2001	Phi	NL	158	656	180	29	12	14	(8	6)	275	97	54	96	48	2	108	2	9	5	46	8	5	.274	.323	.419	.743
2002	Phi	NL	154	637	156	33	10	11	(3	8)	242	82	60	72	54	3	103	4	6	9	31	13	14	.245	.306	.380	.686
2003	Phi	NL	156	628	165	42	6	8	(5	3)	243	85	62	76	54	4	113	0	5	2	20	12	9	.263	.320	.387	.707
2004	Phi	NL	154	657	190	43	12	14	(8	6)	299	119	73	108	57	3	73	3	6	2	30	9	4	.289	.348	.455	.803
2005	Phi	NL	158	677	196	38	11	12	(5	7)	292	115	54	100	47	8	71	4	2	2	41	6	9	.290	.338	.431	.770
2006	Phi	NL	158	689	191	45	9	25	(15	10)	329	127	83	114	57	2	80	5	0	7	36	4	12	.277	.334	.478	.811
2007	Phi	NL	162	716	212	38	20	30	(18	12)	380	139	94	124	49	5	85	7	0	6	41	6	11	.296	.344	.531	.875
2008	Phi	NL	137	556	154	38	9	11	(6	5)	243	76	59	95	58	7	55	5	3	3	47	3	11	.277	.349	.437	.786
2009	Phi	NL	155	672	168	43	5	21	(10	11)	284	100	77	88	44	1	70	2	2	5	31	8	7	.250	.296	.423	.719
2010	Phi	NL	88	350	85	16	3	8	(4	4)	131	48	41	54	40	2	32	1	0	3	17	1	4	.243	.320	.374	.694
2011	Phi	NL	142	567	150	22	2	16	(7	9)	226	87	63	82	58	5	59	3	0	3	30	8	9	.268	.338	.399	.736
2012	Phi	NL	156	632	158	33	5	23	(11	12)	270	102	68	88	62	2	96	0	2	3	30	5	9	.250	.316	.427	.743
2013	Phi	NL	160	600	151	36	2	6	(4	2)	209	65	39	70	59	6	93	1	3	3	22	6	12	.252	.318	.348	.667
2014	Phi	NL	138	538	131	22	4	17	(10	7)	212	78	55	69	64	2	100	1	3	3	28	6	6	.243	.323	.394	.717
Postseason			46	188	47	12	1	3	(1	2)	70	27	15	16	16	0	34	2	1	1	11	4	5	.250	.314	.372	.686
15 ML YEARS			2090	8628	2306	479	111	216	(110	106)	3655	1325	887	1244	753	52	1145	38	41	51	453	95	122	.267	.327	.424	.751

Jamie Romak

Bats: R Throws: R Pos: PH-9;RF-3;1B-1;3B-1;PR-1   RO-mack   Ht: 6'2" Wt: 220 Born: 9/30/1985 Age: 29

			BATTING																		RUNNING			AVERAGES			
Year	Team	Lg	G	AB	H	2B	3B	HR	(Hm	Rd)	TB	R	RBI	RC	TBB	IBB	SO	HBP	SH	SF	SB	CS	GDP	Avg	OBP	Slg	OPS
2010	Wilmg	A+	82	299	91	23	1	7	(-	-)	137	41	48	55	34	1	60	8	0	2	4	2	12	.304	.388	.458	.846
2010	NWArk	AA	45	133	37	6	0	6	(-	-)	61	23	16	24	19	0	30	5	3	0	0	3	1	.278	.389	.459	.847
2011	NWArk	AA	124	439	110	21	1	23	(-	-)	202	66	71	73	55	2	88	8	1	2	6	1	13	.251	.343	.460	.803
2012	Omha	AAA	11	34	5	2	0	0	(-	-)	7	5	2	1	2	0	8	1	0	0	0	0	0	.147	.216	.206	.422
2012	Memp	AAA	31	112	31	8	1	0	(-	-)	41	9	12	14	8	0	24	1	1	2	0	0	10	.277	.325	.366	.691

Year	Team	Lg	G	AB	H	2B	3B	HR	(Hm	Rd)	TB	R	RBI	RC	TBB	IBB	SO	HBP	SH	SF	SB	CS	GDP	Avg	OBP	Slg	OPS
																					BATTING		**RUNNING**		**AVERAGES**		
2012	Sprgfld	AA	64	243	66	11	2	10	(-	-)	111	42	42	42	31	1	53	4	0	3	6	2	6	.272	.359	.457	.816
2013	Memp	AAA	134	458	111	32	1	22	(-	-)	211	69	74	71	49	1	115	6	2	6	6	1	12	.242	.322	.461	.782
2014	Albq	AAA	108	418	117	30	3	24	(-	-)	225	65	85	76	34	0	107	4	0	6	4	1	9	.280	.335	.538	.874
2014	LAD	NL	15	21	1	1	0	0	(0	0)	2	2	3	0	2	0	8	0	0	0	0	0	1	.048	.130	.095	.226

Stefen Romero

Bats: R Throws: R Pos: RF-42;DH-12;LF-11;PH-11;PR-8   STEFF-ehn   **Ht: 6'2" Wt: 220 Born: 10/17/1988 Age: 26**

Year	Team	Lg	G	AB	H	2B	3B	HR	(Hm	Rd)	TB	R	RBI	RC	TBB	IBB	SO	HBP	SH	SF	SB	CS	GDP	Avg	OBP	Slg	OPS
2011	Clinton	A	116	429	120	22	4	16	(-	-)	198	62	65	69	32	2	69	11	1	5	16	9	7	.280	.342	.462	.803
2012	Hi Dsrt	A+	60	258	92	19	3	11	(-	-)	150	47	51	56	13	3	35	3	0	2	6	2	7	.357	.391	.581	.973
2012	Jacksn	AA	56	216	75	15	4	12	(-	-)	134	38	50	50	14	0	37	5	0	5	6	3	6	.347	.392	.620	1.012
2013	Hi Dsrt	A+	5	18	5	1	0	0	(-	-)	6	1	2	2	2	0	1	1	0	0	0	0	2	.278	.381	.333	.714
2013	Tacom	AAA	93	375	104	23	4	11	(-	-)	168	51	74	57	28	0	87	4	0	4	8	4	4	.277	.331	.448	.779
2014	Tacom	AAA	36	151	54	7	2	12	(-	-)	101	26	36	35	8	0	28	1	0	3	1	3	6	.358	.387	.669	1.055
2014	Sea	AL	72	177	34	6	2	3	(1	2)	53	19	11	7	4	0	48	6	2	1	0	4	5	.192	.234	.299	.533

Andrew Romine

Bats: B Throws: R Pos: SS-83;2B-12;PR-6;PH-2;DH-1   ROW-mine   **Ht: 6'1" Wt: 200 Born: 12/24/1985 Age: 29**

Year	Team	Lg	G	AB	H	2B	3B	HR	(Hm	Rd)	TB	R	RBI	RC	TBB	IBB	SO	HBP	SH	SF	SB	CS	GDP	Avg	OBP	Slg	OPS
2010	LAA	AL	5	11	1	0	0	0	(0	0)	1	0	0	0	0	0	4	0	1	0	0	0	0	.091	.091	.091	.182
2011	LAA	AL	10	16	2	0	0	0	(0	0)	2	2	0	0	1	0	6	0	1	0	1	0	0	.125	.176	.125	.301
2012	LAA	AL	12	17	7	0	0	0	(0	0)	7	2	1	5	3	0	3	0	1	0	1	0	0	.412	.500	.412	.912
2013	LAA	AL	47	108	28	3	0	0	(0	0)	31	9	10	12	7	0	24	1	6	1	1	0	2	.259	.308	.287	.595
2014	Det	AL	94	251	57	6	0	2	(1	1)	69	30	12	17	18	0	60	0	4	0	12	2	5	.227	.279	.275	.554
	5 ML YEARS		168	403	95	9	0	2	(1	1)	110	43	23	34	29	0	97	1	13	1	15	2	7	.236	.288	.273	.561

Austin Romine

Bats: R Throws: R Pos: C-3;PH-2;1B-1;DH-1;PR-1   ROW-mine   **Ht: 6'0" Wt: 215 Born: 11/22/1988 Age: 26**

Year	Team	Lg	G	AB	H	2B	3B	HR	(Hm	Rd)	TB	R	RBI	RC	TBB	IBB	SO	HBP	SH	SF	SB	CS	GDP	Avg	OBP	Slg	OPS
2014	S-WB*	AAA	81	285	69	17	0	6	(-	-)	104	33	33	32	24	1	54	0	3	1	1	0	15	.242	.300	.365	.665
2011	NYY	AL	9	19	3	0	0	0	(0	0)	3	2	0	0	1	0	5	0	0	0	0	0	0	.158	.200	.158	.358
2013	NYY	AL	60	135	28	9	0	1	(0	1)	40	15	10	8	8	0	37	1	3	1	1	0	7	.207	.255	.296	.551
2014	NYY	AL	7	13	3	1	0	0	(0	0)	4	2	1	2	0	0	4	0	0	0	0	0	0	.231	.231	.308	.538
	3 ML YEARS		76	167	34	10	0	1	(0	1)	47	19	11	10	9	0	46	1	3	1	1	0	7	.204	.247	.281	.529

Sergio Romo

Pitches: R Bats: R Pos: RP-64   **Ht: 5'10" Wt: 185 Born: 3/4/1983 Age: 32**

	HOW MUCH HE PITCHED						WHAT HE GAVE UP												THE RESULTS						
Year	Team	Lg	G	GS	CG	GF	IP	BFP	H	R	ER	HR	SH	SF	HB	TBB	IBB	SO	WP	Bk	W	L	Pct	Sh	Sv-Op	Hld	ERC	ERA
2008	SF	NL	29	0	0	8	34.0	130	16	13	8	3	2	1	3	8	1	33	0	0	3	1	.750	0	0-0	5	1.27	2.12
2009	SF	NL	45	0	0	9	34.0	143	30	15	15	1	2	0	1	11	0	41	2	0	5	2	.714	0	2-2	10	2.76	3.97
2010	SF	NL	68	0	0	13	62.0	247	46	16	15	6	2	2	4	14	2	70	0	0	5	3	.625	0	0-4	21	2.26	2.18
2011	SF	NL	65	0	0	16	48.0	175	29	8	8	2	2	0	4	5	1	70	0	0	3	1	.750	0	1-2	23	1.08	1.50
2012	SF	NL	69	0	0	27	55.1	215	37	11	11	5	2	0	3	10	1	63	2	0	4	2	.667	0	14-15	23	1.72	1.79
2013	SF	NL	65	0	0	52	60.1	250	53	20	17	5	1	1	1	12	3	58	1	0	5	8	.385	0	38-43	2	2.47	2.54
2014	SF	NL	64	0	0	35	58.0	230	43	24	24	9	2	0	4	12	2	59	2	0	6	4	.600	0	23-28	11	2.54	3.72
	Postseason		16	0	0	11	14.1	54	10	4	4	1	0	0	0	2	0	13	1	0	2	0	1.000	0	4-6	0	1.54	2.51
	7 ML YEARS		405	0	0	160	351.2	1390	254	107	98	31	13	4	16	72	10	394	7	0	31	21	.596	0	78-94	93	1.98	2.51

Bruce Rondon

Pitches: R Bats: R Pos: P   ron-DOAN   **Ht: 6'3" Wt: 275 Born: 12/9/1990 Age: 24**

	HOW MUCH HE PITCHED						WHAT HE GAVE UP												THE RESULTS						
Year	Team	Lg	G	GS	CG	GF	IP	BFP	H	R	ER	HR	SH	SF	HB	TBB	IBB	SO	WP	Bk	W	L	Pct	Sh	Sv-Op	Hld	ERC	ERA
2010	Tigers	R	24	0	0	22	25.2	105	11	2	2	1	3	0	5	14	0	26	1	1	0	0	-	0	15--	-	1.98	0.70
2010	Lkland	A+	4	0	0	2	6.2	23	2	1	1	1	0	0	2	0	0	7	0	0	0	0	-	0	2--	-	1.02	1.35
2011	WMich	A	41	0	0	33	40.0	179	22	11	9	0	4	2	5	34	1	61	11	1	2	2	.500	0	19--	-	2.96	2.03
2012	Lkland	A+	22	0	0	21	23.1	92	12	5	5	1	1	1	1	10	1	34	1	0	1	0	1.000	0	15--	-	1.55	1.93
2012	Erie	AA	21	0	0	19	21.2	90	15	4	2	1	0	0	4	9	0	23	2	1	1	0	1.000	0	12--	-	2.86	0.83
2012	Toledo	AAA	9	0	0	8	8.0	37	5	3	2	1	0	0	0	7	1	9	0	0	1	0	1.000	0	2--	-	3.60	2.25
2013	Toledo	AAA	30	0	0	26	29.2	118	14	6	5	1	1	1	2	13	0	40	2	0	1	1	.500	0	14--	-	1.48	1.52
2013	Det	AL	30	0	0	12	28.2	122	28	11	11	2	1	2	0	11	0	30	7	1	1	2	.333	0	1-3	5	3.69	3.45

Hector Rondon

Pitches: R Bats: R Pos: RP-64   ron-DOAN   **Ht: 6'3" Wt: 180 Born: 2/26/1988 Age: 27**

	HOW MUCH HE PITCHED						WHAT HE GAVE UP												THE RESULTS						
Year	Team	Lg	G	GS	CG	GF	IP	BFP	H	R	ER	HR	SH	SF	HB	TBB	IBB	SO	WP	Bk	W	L	Pct	Sh	Sv-Op	Hld	ERC	ERA
2010	Clmbs	AAA	7	7	0	0	31.2	152	48	32	30	12	0	0	2	10	0	33	0	0	1	3	.250	0	0--	-	9.50	8.53
2011	MhVlly	A-	2	2	0	0	3.0	12	3	1	1	0	0	0	0	0	0	2	0	0	0	0	-	0	0--	-	1.95	3.00
2012	Indns	R	2	2	0	0	3.0	10	0	0	0	0	0	0	0	1	0	6	0	0	0	0	-	0	0--	-	0.13	0.00

Year	Team	Lg	G	GS	CG	GF	IP	BFP	H	R	ER	HR	SH	SF	HB	TBB	IBB	SO	WP	Bk	W	L	Pct	Sh	Sv-Op	Hld	ERC	ERA
2012	Akron	AA	2	0	0	0	4.0	16	4	1	1	0	1	0	0	1	0	3	1	0	0	0	-	0	0- -	-	2.98	2.25
2013	ChC	NL	45	0	0	14	54.2	242	52	29	29	6	4	3	3	25	5	44	4	0	2	1	.667	0	0-1	2	4.10	4.77
2014	ChC	NL	64	0	0	44	63.1	255	52	21	17	2	0	1	0	15	0	63	0	0	4	4	.500	0	29-33	1	2.10	2.42
	2 ML YEARS		109	0	0	58	118.0	497	104	50	46	8	4	4	3	40	5	107	4	0	6	5	.545	0	29-34	3	2.98	3.51

Jorge Rondon

Pitches: R **Bats:** R **Pos:** RP-1   **Ht:** 6'1" **Wt:** 215 **Born:** 2/16/1988 **Age:** 27

Year	Team	Lg	G	GS	CG	GF	IP	BFP	H	R	ER	HR	SH	SF	HB	TBB	IBB	SO	WP	Bk	W	L	Pct	Sh	Sv-Op	Hld	ERC	ERA
2010	QuadC	A	29	19	0	1	108.2	508	121	82	64	6	5	3	13	65	1	76	7	0	4	8	.333	0	0- -	-	5.70	5.30
2011	PlmBh	A+	21	0	0	17	26.2	118	29	13	12	1	6	3	0	13	2	27	5	0	1	5	.167	0	6- -	-	4.36	4.05
2011	Sprgfld	AA	37	0	0	24	37.1	188	43	45	38	4	3	1	5	33	2	30	8	0	1	8	.111	0	7- -	-	7.54	9.16
2012	Sprgfld	AA	33	0	0	13	34.0	145	29	14	13	1	0	3	4	16	0	30	5	4	2	1	.667	0	4- -	-	3.56	3.44
2012	Memp	AAA	13	0	0	6	15.0	64	12	6	6	1	0	0	0	8	0	20	0	1	1	0	1.000	0	1- -	-	3.25	3.60
2013	Memp	AAA	51	0	0	11	67.2	308	72	31	23	6	0	6	2	37	3	42	7	1	3	5	.375	0	1- -	-	4.96	3.06
2014	Memp	AAA	51	0	0	22	62.1	264	59	23	21	3	2	3	3	20	1	51	5	1	5	4	.556	0	10- -	-	3.28	3.03
2014	StL	NL	1	0	0	0	1.0	4	0	0	0	0	0	0	0	1	0	0	0	0	0	0	-	0	0-0	0	0.95	0.00

Adam Rosales

Bats: R **Throws:** R **Pos:** 1B-32;3B-7;2B-5;DH-5;PH-4;SS-3;PR-3   **Ht:** 6'1" **Wt:** 195 **Born:** 5/20/1983 **Age:** 32

							BATTING												RUNNING			AVERAGES			
Year	Team	Lg	G	AB	H	2B	3B	HR	(Hm | Rd)	TB	R	RBI	RC	TBB	IBB	SO	HBP	SH	SF	SB	CS	GDP	Avg	OBP	Slg	OPS
2014	RdRck	AAA	72	272	75	16	3	7	(- | -)	118	42	43	43	28	0	61	4	0	3	3	0	3	.276	.349	.434	.782
2008	Cin	NL	18	29	6	1	0	0	(0 | 0)	7	0	2	2	1	0	4	0	0	0	1	0	0	.207	.233	.241	.475
2009	Cin	NL	87	230	49	10	1	4	(2 | 2)	73	23	19	22	26	0	46	5	2	3	1	2	2	.213	.303	.317	.620
2010	Oak	AL	80	255	69	8	2	7	(1 | 6)	102	31	31	31	19	0	65	1	2	2	2	2	1	.271	.321	.400	.721
2011	Oak	AL	24	61	6	0	0	2	(0 | 2)	12	5	8	0	4	0	13	1	0	2	0	0	4	.098	.162	.197	.358
2012	Oak	AL	42	99	22	5	0	2	(1 | 1)	33	12	8	6	11	1	24	0	0	1	0	0	4	.222	.297	.333	.631
2013	2 Tms		68	147	28	5	0	5	(2 | 3)	48	15	12	6	10	1	34	4	4	1	0	0	4	.190	.259	.327	.586
2014	Tex	AL	56	164	43	7	0	4	(2 | 2)	62	20	19	23	13	0	42	3	0	0	4	2	5	.262	.328	.378	.706
13	Oak	AL	51	136	26	5	0	4	(2 | 2)	43	11	8	5	10	1	31	4	4	0	0	0	4	.191	.267	.316	.583
13	Tex	AL	17	11	2	0	0	1	(0 | 1)	5	4	4	1	0	0	3	0	0	1	0	0	0	.182	.167	.455	.621
	7 ML YEARS		375	985	223	36	3	24	(8 | 16)	337	106	99	90	84	2	228	14	8	9	8	6	20	.226	.294	.342	.636

Wilin Rosario

Bats: R **Throws:** R **Pos:** C-96;PH-9;1B-4   wih-LEAN roh-SORRY-oh   **Ht:** 5'11" **Wt:** 220 **Born:** 2/23/1989 **Age:** 26

							BATTING												RUNNING			AVERAGES			
Year	Team	Lg	G	AB	H	2B	3B	HR	(Hm | Rd)	TB	R	RBI	RC	TBB	IBB	SO	HBP	SH	SF	SB	CS	GDP	Avg	OBP	Slg	OPS
2014	ColSpr*	AAA	2	6	2	1	0	0	(- | -)	3	0	0	0	0	0	1	0	0	0	0	0	1	.333	.333	.500	.833
2011	Col	NL	16	54	11	3	1	3	(1 | 2)	25	6	8	4	2	0	20	0	0	0	0	0	1	.204	.228	.463	.691
2012	Col	NL	117	396	107	19	0	28	(18 | 10)	210	67	71	56	25	2	99	1	0	4	4	5	10	.270	.312	.530	.843
2013	Col	NL	121	449	131	22	1	21	(10 | 11)	218	63	79	62	15	0	109	1	0	1	4	1	7	.292	.315	.486	.801
2014	Col	NL	106	382	102	25	0	13	(7 | 6)	166	46	54	40	23	5	70	0	0	5	1	0	17	.267	.305	.435	.739
	4 ML YEARS		360	1281	351	69	2	65	(36 | 29)	619	182	212	162	65	7	298	2	0	11	9	6	35	.274	.308	.483	.791

B.J. Rosenberg

Pitches: R **Bats:** R **Pos:** RP-13   **Ht:** 6'3" **Wt:** 220 **Born:** 9/17/1985 **Age:** 29

Year	Team	Lg	G	GS	CG	GF	IP	BFP	H	R	ER	HR	SH	SF	HB	TBB	IBB	SO	WP	Bk	W	L	Pct	Sh	Sv-Op	Hld	ERC	ERA
2014	LV*	AAA	18	0	0	6	19.0	92	24	14	14	2	2	0	1	12	1	17	0	0	2	1	.667	0	1- -	-	6.76	6.63
2014	Phillies*	R	2	2	0	0	3.0	10	1	0	0	0	0	0	0	0	0	5	1	0	0	0	-	0	0- -	-	0.25	0.00
2012	Phi	NL	22	1	0	3	25.0	106	18	17	17	4	2	0	2	14	0	24	0	0	1	2	.333	0	0-0	2	3.92	6.12
2013	Phi	NL	22	0	0	5	19.2	86	20	10	10	0	1	0	0	9	1	19	2	0	2	0	1.000	0	1-1	2	3.58	4.58
2014	Phi	NL	13	0	0	6	12.0	59	20	10	9	5	0	0	0	7	0	9	0	0	1	0	1.000	0	0-0	0	12.65	6.75
	3 ML YEARS		57	1	0	14	56.2	251	58	37	36	9	3	0	2	30	1	52	2	0	4	2	.667	0	1-1	4	5.37	5.72

Trevor Rosenthal

Pitches: R **Bats:** R **Pos:** RP-72   **Ht:** 6'2" **Wt:** 220 **Born:** 5/29/1990 **Age:** 25

Year	Team	Lg	G	GS	CG	GF	IP	BFP	H	R	ER	HR	SH	SF	HB	TBB	IBB	SO	WP	Bk	W	L	Pct	Sh	Sv-Op	Hld	ERC	ERA
2012	StL	NL	19	0	0	7	22.2	89	14	7	7	2	1	0	1	7	0	25	1	0	0	2	.000	0	0-0	3	1.89	2.78
2013	StL	NL	74	0	0	15	75.1	311	63	25	22	4	3	0	6	20	0	108	3	0	2	4	.333	0	3-8	29	2.68	2.63
2014	StL	NL	72	0	0	59	70.1	308	57	25	25	2	2	4	4	42	5	87	1	1	2	6	.250	0	45-51	2	3.36	3.20
	Postseason		17	0	0	10	20.1	70	6	0	0	0	0	0	0	5	2	33	0	1	1	0	1.000	0	4-5	0	0.44	0.00
	3 ML YEARS		165	0	0	81	168.1	708	134	57	54	8	6	4	11	69	5	220	5	1	4	12	.250	0	48-59	34	2.85	2.89

Seth Rosin

Pitches: R **Bats:** R **Pos:** RP-3 ro-ZEEN **Ht:** 6'6" **Wt:** 265 **Born:** 11/2/1988 **Age:** 26

Year	Team	Lg	G	GS	CG	GF	IP	BFP	H	R	ER	HR	SH	SF	HB	TBB	IBB	SO	WP	Bk	W	L	Pct	Sh	Sv-Op	Hld	ERC	ERA
2010	SlmKzr	A-	6	1	0	2	11.0	43	9	6	6	0	0	0	0	1	0	9	1	0	1	1	.500	0	0- -	-	1.51	4.91
2011	Augsta	A	39	10	0	10	89.0	365	81	44	33	3	5	0	2	30	0	93	2	0	2	3	.400	0	2- -	-	3.06	3.34
2012	SnJos	A+	34	5	0	16	56.1	236	49	29	27	6	1	1	1	18	1	68	2	1	2	1	.667	0	10- -	-	3.10	4.31
2012	Clrwtr	A+	3	3	0	0	12.0	46	7	5	4	0	2	1	0	4	0	7	0	0	1	0	1.000	0	0- -	-	1.35	3.00
2013	Rdng	AA	26	23	1	1	126.2	531	120	69	61	13	4	6	3	35	1	96	3	1	9	6	.600	0	0- -	-	3.38	4.33
2014	LV	AAA	17	1	0	6	23.0	105	31	17	16	3	1	2	0	9	2	20	2	0	1	3	.250	0	2- -	-	6.28	6.26
2014	Rdng	AA	26	0	0	12	35.1	144	33	9	9	3	0	3	0	10	0	24	1	1	2	2	.500	0	1- -	-	3.23	2.29
2014	Tex	AL	3	0	0	2	4.0	19	6	3	3	0	0	0	0	1	0	3	0	0	1	0	1.000	0	0-0	0	5.46	6.75

Cody Ross

Bats: R **Throws:** L **Pos:** LF-37;PH-30;RF-20 **Ht:** 5'10" **Wt:** 195 **Born:** 12/23/1980 **Age:** 34

Year	Team	Lg	G	AB	H	2B	3B	HR	(Hm	Rd)	TB	R	RBI	RC	TBB	IBB	SO	HBP	SH	SF	SB	CS	GDP	Avg	OBP	Slg	OPS
2014	Reno*	AAA	9	31	9	1	0	0	(-	-)	10	2	7	3	1	0	5	0	0	0	0	0	2	.290	.313	.323	.635
2003	Det	AL	6	19	4	1	0	1	(1	0)	8	1	5	4	1	0	3	1	1	0	0	0	0	.211	.286	.421	.707
2005	LAD	NL	14	25	4	1	0	0	(0	0)	5	1	1	0	1	0	10	0	0	0	0	0	0	.160	.192	.200	.392
2006	3 Tms	NL	101	269	61	12	2	13	(6	7)	116	34	46	36	22	0	65	4	1	2	1	1	8	.227	.293	.431	.724
2007	Fla	NL	66	173	58	19	0	12	(8	4)	113	35	39	42	20	3	38	3	0	1	2	0	2	.335	.411	.653	1.064
2008	Fla	NL	145	461	120	29	5	22	(7	15)	225	59	73	68	33	2	116	7	0	5	6	1	5	.260	.316	.488	.804
2009	Fla	NL	151	559	151	37	1	24	(13	11)	262	73	90	75	34	1	122	9	0	2	5	2	18	.270	.321	.469	.790
2010	2 Tms	NL	153	525	141	28	3	14	(5	9)	217	71	65	68	37	4	121	5	0	2	9	2	9	.269	.322	.413	.735
2011	SF	NL	121	405	97	25	0	14	(6	8)	164	54	52	53	49	4	96	4	0	3	5	2	10	.240	.325	.405	.730
2012	Bos	AL	130	476	127	34	1	22	(13	9)	229	70	81	76	42	3	129	3	1	6	2	3	11	.267	.326	.481	.807
2013	Ari	NL	94	317	88	17	1	8	(4	4)	131	33	38	37	25	1	50	3	1	5	3	2	10	.278	.331	.413	.745
2014	Ari	NL	83	202	51	8	0	2	(1	1)	65	15	15	16	15	0	44	1	0	1	0	0	3	.252	.306	.322	.628
06	LAD	NL	8	14	7	1	1	2	(0	2)	16	4	9	6	0	0	2	0	0	0	1	0	0	.500	.500	1.143	1.643
06	Cin	NL	2	5	1	0	0	0	(0	0)	1	0	0	1	0	0	2	0	0	0	0	0	0	.200	.200	.200	.400
06	Fla	NL	91	250	53	11	1	11	(6	5)	99	30	37	29	22	0	61	4	1	2	0	1	8	.212	.284	.396	.680
10	Fla	NL	120	452	120	24	3	11	(5	6)	183	60	58	58	30	4	100	4	0	1	9	1	7	.265	.316	.405	.721
10	SF	NL	33	73	21	4	0	3	(0	3)	34	11	7	10	7	0	21	1	0	1	0	1	2	.288	.354	.466	.819
	Postseason		15	51	15	5	0	5	(0	5)	35	11	10	12	7	0	11	1	0	0	0	0	1	.294	.390	.686	1.076
	11 ML YEARS		1064	3431	902	211	13	132	(64	68)	1535	446	505	475	279	18	794	40	4	27	33	13	77	.263	.323	.447	.771

David Ross

Bats: R **Throws:** R **Pos:** C-50 **Ht:** 6'2" **Wt:** 230 **Born:** 3/19/1977 **Age:** 38

Year	Team	Lg	G	AB	H	2B	3B	HR	(Hm	Rd)	TB	R	RBI	RC	TBB	IBB	SO	HBP	SH	SF	SB	CS	GDP	Avg	OBP	Slg	OPS
2002	LAD	NL	8	10	2	1	0	1	(0	1)	6	2	2	2	2	0	4	1	0	0	0	0	0	.200	.385	.600	.985
2003	LAD	NL	40	124	32	7	0	10	(5	5)	69	19	18	18	13	0	42	2	0	1	0	0	4	.258	.336	.556	.892
2004	LAD	NL	70	165	28	3	1	5	(2	3)	48	13	15	11	15	1	62	5	0	5	0	0	3	.170	.253	.291	.544
2005	2 Tms	NL	51	125	30	8	1	3	(2	1)	49	11	15	13	6	0	28	2	2	3	0	0	3	.240	.279	.392	.671
2006	Cin	NL	90	247	63	15	1	21	(13	8)	143	37	52	43	37	7	75	3	4	5	0	0	4	.255	.353	.579	.932
2007	Cin	NL	112	311	63	10	0	17	(12	5)	124	32	39	27	30	4	92	0	5	2	0	0	9	.203	.271	.399	.670
2008	2 Tms		60	142	32	9	0	3	(1	2)	50	18	13	19	32	4	39	1	6	1	0	1	3	.225	.369	.352	.721
2009	Atl	NL	54	128	35	9	0	7	(2	5)	65	18	20	20	21	0	39	1	1	0	0	0	1	.273	.380	.508	.888
2010	Atl	NL	59	121	35	13	2	2	(2	0)	58	15	28	22	20	0	28	1	2	1	0	1	5	.289	.392	.479	.871
2011	Atl	NL	52	152	40	7	0	6	(2	4)	65	14	23	22	16	0	51	0	2	0	0	1	4	.263	.333	.428	.761
2012	Atl	NL	62	176	45	7	0	9	(4	5)	79	18	23	21	18	0	60	0	0	2	1	0	5	.256	.321	.449	.770
2013	Bos	AL	36	102	22	5	0	4	(3	1)	39	11	10	7	11	0	42	1	2	0	1	0	3	.216	.298	.382	.681
2014	Bos	AL	50	152	28	7	0	7	(4	3)	56	16	15	13	16	1	58	0	2	1	0	1	1	.184	.260	.368	.629
05	Pit	NL	40	108	24	8	0	3	(2	1)	41	9	15	9	6	0	24	1	1	3	0	0	3	.222	.263	.380	.642
05	SD	NL	11	17	6	0	1	0	(0	0)	8	2	0	4	0	0	4	1	1	0	0	0	0	.353	.389	.471	.859
08	Cin	NL	52	134	31	9	0	3	(1	2)	49	17	13	19	32	4	36	1	5	1	0	1	3	.231	.381	.366	.747
08	Bos	AL	8	8	1	0	0	0	(0	0)	1	1	0	0	0	0	3	0	1	0	0	0	0	.125	.125	.125	.250
	Postseason		14	32	9	3	0	1	(1	0)	15	3	4	4	2	0	11	0	1	0	0	0	0	.281	.324	.469	.792
	13 ML YEARS		744	1955	455	101	5	95	(52	43)	851	224	273	238	237	17	620	17	26	21	2	4	45	.233	.318	.436	.753

Robbie Ross

Pitches: L **Bats:** L **Pos:** RP-15; SP-12 **Ht:** 5'11" **Wt:** 215 **Born:** 6/24/1989 **Age:** 26

Year	Team	Lg	G	GS	CG	GF	IP	BFP	H	R	ER	HR	SH	SF	HB	TBB	IBB	SO	WP	Bk	W	L	Pct	Sh	Sv-Op	Hld	ERC	ERA
2014	RdRck*	AAA	12	9	2	0	60.1	254	66	29	29	7	3	1	3	16	0	43	4	0	5	4	.556	0	0- -	-	4.50	4.33
2012	Tex	AL	58	0	0	9	65.0	265	55	21	16	3	1	2	2	23	3	47	1	1	6	0	1.000	0	0-0	9	2.83	2.22
2013	Tex	AL	65	0	0	16	62.1	267	63	21	21	4	0	0	5	19	2	58	2	0	4	2	.667	0	0-1	15	3.79	3.03
2014	Tex	AL	27	12	0	4	78.1	365	103	65	54	9	2	2	7	30	2	51	6	0	3	6	.333	0	0-0	2	6.34	6.20
	3 ML YEARS		150	12	0	29	205.2	897	221	107	91	16	3	4	14	72	7	156	9	1	13	8	.619	0	0-1	26	4.39	3.98

Tyson Ross

Pitches: R Bats: R Pos: SP-31   Ht: 6'5" Wt: 225 Born: 4/22/1987 Age: 28

				HOW MUCH HE PITCHED				WHAT HE GAVE UP									THE RESULTS					
Year	Team	Lg	G	GS	CG	GF	IP	BFP	H	R	ER	HR	SH	SF	HB	TBB	IBB	SO	WP	Bk	W	L	Pct	Sh	Sv-Op	Hld	ERC	ERA
2010	Oak	AL	26	2	0	9	39.1	169	39	24	24	4	1	4	0	20	0	32	5	0	1	4	.200	0	1-2	2	4.60	5.49
2011	Oak	AL	9	6	0	1	36.0	145	33	12	11	1	1	0	0	13	1	24	2	0	3	3	.500	0	0-0	0	3.09	2.75
2012	Oak	AL	18	13	0	3	73.1	342	96	56	53	7	3	3	5	37	3	46	2	1	2	11	.154	0	0-0	0	6.68	6.50
2013	SD	NL	35	16	0	8	125.0	504	100	51	44	8	3	5	7	44	4	119	7	0	3	8	.273	0	0-0	0	2.84	3.17
2014	SD	NL	31	31	2	0	195.2	811	165	75	61	13	10	4	9	72	2	195	12	0	13	14	.481	1	0-0	0	3.07	2.81
	5 ML YEARS		119	68	2	21	469.1	1971	433	218	193	33	18	16	21	186	10	416	28	1	22	40	.355	1	1-2	2	3.64	3.70

Zac Rosscup

Pitches: L Bats: R Pos: RP-18   ROSS-cup   Ht: 6'2" Wt: 205 Born: 6/9/1988 Age: 27

				HOW MUCH HE PITCHED				WHAT HE GAVE UP									THE RESULTS					
Year	Team	Lg	G	GS	CG	GF	IP	BFP	H	R	ER	HR	SH	SF	HB	TBB	IBB	SO	WP	Bk	W	L	Pct	Sh	Sv-Op	Hld	ERC	ERA
2010	Rays	R	3	1	0	0	8.2	36	5	3	1	0	1	0	1	2	1	6	0	0	0	0	-	0	0- -	-	1.16	1.04
2010	HudVal	A-	9	7	0	1	35.2	142	27	16	12	0	1	2	0	7	0	35	2	0	3	1	.750	0	1- -	-	1.54	3.03
2011	Dytona	A+	11	9	0	0	49.2	211	43	17	14	4	2	1	2	19	0	50	0	0	4	2	.667	0	0- -	-	3.26	2.54
2012	Cubs	R	1	0	0	0	1.2	5	0	0	0	0	0	0	0	0	0	4	0	0	0	0	-	0	0- -	-	0.00	0.00
2012	Peoria	A	3	0	0	0	7.1	24	3	0	0	0	0	0	0	0	0	12	0	0	2	0	1.000	0	0- -	-	0.39	0.00
2012	Tenn	AA	11	1	0	0	22.1	99	14	12	12	1	0	1	1	19	0	29	3	0	1	0	1.000	0	0- -	-	3.49	4.84
2013	Tenn	AA	37	0	0	11	43.1	177	31	12	12	2	0	0	0	19	0	66	3	0	2	1	.667	0	3- -	-	2.38	2.49
2013	Iowa	AAA	9	0	0	2	7.2	36	5	5	0	0	1	1	0	6	0	17	0	0	1	0	1.000	0	0- -	-	2.65	0.00
2014	Iowa	AAA	29	0	0	9	30.0	121	18	7	7	0	2	0	0	15	2	38	2	0	2	0	1.000	0	4- -	-	1.68	2.10
2013	ChC	NL	10	0	0	3	6.2	30	3	1	1	1	0	0	0	7	1	7	0	0	0	0	-	0	0-0	0	3.56	1.35
2014	ChC	NL	18	0	0	5	13.1	66	14	14	14	2	0	0	0	12	1	21	0	0	1	0	1.000	0	0-0	1	6.54	9.45
	2 ML YEARS		28	0	0	8	20.0	96	17	15	15	3	0	0	0	19	2	28	0	0	1	0	1.000	0	0-0	1	5.49	6.75

Michael Roth

Pitches: L Bats: L Pos: RP-7   Ht: 6'1" Wt: 210 Born: 2/15/1990 Age: 25

				HOW MUCH HE PITCHED				WHAT HE GAVE UP									THE RESULTS					
Year	Team	Lg	G	GS	CG	GF	IP	BFP	H	R	ER	HR	SH	SF	HB	TBB	IBB	SO	WP	Bk	W	L	Pct	Sh	Sv-Op	Hld	ERC	ERA
2012	Orem	R+	11	9	0	0	22.0	99	23	13	12	2	0	1	3	11	0	21	2	0	2	0	.000	0	0- -	-	5.31	4.91
2013	Ark	AA	17	15	0	0	79.1	342	77	42	37	8	3	0	9	36	1	51	6	1	6	3	.667	0	0- -	-	4.71	4.20
2014	Ark	AA	22	22	0	0	140.2	578	121	48	41	9	8	5	3	53	1	79	3	0	11	7	.611	0	0- -	-	3.12	2.62
2013	LAA	AL	15	1	0	5	20.0	89	24	16	16	0	1	0	1	6	0	17	2	0	1	1	.500	0	0-0	0	4.26	7.20
2014	LAA	AL	7	0	0	2	12.1	60	16	12	12	2	0	1	3	9	2	9	0	0	1	0	1.000	0	0-0	0	9.10	8.76
	2 ML YEARS		22	1	0	7	32.1	149	40	28	28	2	1	1	4	15	2	26	2	0	2	1	.667	0	0-0	0	5.95	7.79

Ben Rowen

Pitches: R Bats: R Pos: RP-8   Ht: 6'4" Wt: 190 Born: 11/15/1988 Age: 26

				HOW MUCH HE PITCHED				WHAT HE GAVE UP									THE RESULTS					
Year	Team	Lg	G	GS	CG	GF	IP	BFP	H	R	ER	HR	SH	SF	HB	TBB	IBB	SO	WP	Bk	W	L	Pct	Sh	Sv-Op	Hld	ERC	ERA
2010	Spkane	A-	21	0	0	9	33.0	131	18	4	4	0	0	0	1	14	0	30	1	0	2	0	1.000	0	1- -	-	1.47	1.09
2011	Hkry	A	33	0	0	8	59.0	245	55	26	13	1	0	2	1	18	0	43	1	1	5	4	.556	0	2- -	-	2.87	1.98
2012	MrtlBh	A+	38	0	0	31	57.1	213	41	10	10	2	0	2	4	3	0	52	1	1	5	0	1.000	0	19- -	-	1.45	1.57
2013	Frisco	AA	31	0	0	24	33.2	127	23	3	2	1	0	0	0	11	0	28	0	0	3	0	1.000	0	10- -	-	1.89	0.53
2013	RdRck	AAA	20	0	0	12	32.0	121	18	5	3	0	0	0	0	6	1	30	0	0	3	1	.750	0	3- -	-	0.96	0.84
2014	RdRck	AAA	34	0	0	21	47.0	203	47	22	18	2	1	1	6	9	0	31	0	0	3	0	1.000	0	5- -	-	3.29	3.45
2014	Tex	AL	8	0	0	4	8.2	39	10	4	4	0	1	2	0	4	3	7	0	0	0	0	-	0	0-0	0	3.81	4.15

Ryan Rowland-Smith

Pitches: L Bats: L Pos: RP-6   Ht: 6'3" Wt: 250 Born: 1/26/1983 Age: 32

				HOW MUCH HE PITCHED				WHAT HE GAVE UP									THE RESULTS					
Year	Team	Lg	G	GS	CG	GF	IP	BFP	H	R	ER	HR	SH	SF	HB	TBB	IBB	SO	WP	Bk	W	L	Pct	Sh	Sv-Op	Hld	ERC	ERA
2014	Buffalo*	AAA	12	0	0	6	14.0	53	10	8	8	4	0	1	0	3	0	11	0	0	1	0	1.000	0	0- -	-	3.01	5.14
2014	Lsvlle*	AAA	12	1	0	3	15.0	65	19	9	7	0	0	1	0	4	1	9	1	0	0	0	-	0	0- -	-	4.30	4.20
2007	Sea	AL	26	0	0	6	38.2	168	39	19	17	4	1	4	2	15	1	42	0	0	1	0	1.000	0	0-0	3	4.27	3.96
2008	Sea	AL	47	12	0	9	118.1	506	114	49	45	13	2	3	2	48	0	77	2	1	5	3	.625	0	2-3	1	4.05	3.42
2009	Sea	AL	15	15	0	0	96.1	401	87	43	40	9	1	5	4	27	0	52	2	1	5	4	.556	0	0-0	0	3.19	3.74
2010	Sea	AL	27	20	0	2	109.1	510	141	94	82	25	4	6	7	44	2	49	7	0	1	10	.091	0	0-0	0	7.06	6.75
2014	Ari	NL	6	0	0	3	7.1	33	7	5	4	0	1	2	0	4	1	9	1	0	0	0	-	0	0-0	0	3.33	4.91
	5 ML YEARS		121	47	0	20	370.0	1618	388	210	188	51	9	20	15	138	4	229	12	2	12	17	.414	0	2-3	4	4.66	4.57

Ryan Rua

Bats: R Throws: R Pos: LF-17;1B-9;DH-2;3B-1   ROO-ah   Ht: 6'2" Wt: 205 Born: 3/11/1990 Age: 25

				BATTING																RUNNING			AVERAGES			
Year	Team	Lg	G	AB	H	2B	3B	HR	(Hm	Rd)	TB	R	RBI	RC	TBB	IBB	SO	HBP	SH	SF	SB	CS	GDP	Avg	OBP	Slg	OPS
2011	Spkane	A-	7	26	5	0	0	1	(-	-)	8	2	3	1	1	0	6	1	0	0	0	0	0	.192	.250	.308	.558
2011	Rngrs	R	45	162	52	12	5	3	(-	-)	83	41	34	35	20	0	34	1	1	2	10	0	5	.321	.395	.512	.907
2012	Spkane	A-	74	280	82	16	1	7	(-	-)	121	40	43	47	29	0	64	6	2	3	4	1	8	.293	.368	.432	.800
2013	Hkry	A	104	367	92	24	1	29	(-	-)	205	70	82	76	49	2	91	12	0	2	13	2	4	.251	.356	.559	.914
2013	Frisco	AA	23	86	20	2	1	3	(-	-)	33	19	9	10	7	0	24	2	0	0	1	0	2	.233	.305	.384	.689
2014	Frisco	AA	71	257	77	13	1	10	(-	-)	122	34	38	46	30	2	55	1	0	5	5	3	5	.300	.375	.475	.850
2014	RdRck	AAA	58	214	67	13	2	8	(-	-)	108	31	36	41	21	0	42	4	0	2	1	2	3	.313	.382	.505	.886
2014	Tex	AL	28	105	31	7	0	2	(1	1)	44	11	14	13	2	0	18	2	0	0	1	0	6	.295	.321	.419	.740

275

Drew Rucinski

Pitches: R Bats: R Pos: RP-3   ruh-SIN-ski   Ht: 6'2" Wt: 190 Born: 12/30/1988 Age: 26

			HOW MUCH HE PITCHED					WHAT HE GAVE UP												THE RESULTS							
Year	Team	Lg	G	GS	CG	GF	IP	BFP	H	R	ER	HR	SH	SF	HB	TBB	IBB	SO	WP	Bk	W	L	Pct	Sh	Sv-Op	Hld	ERC	ERA
2011	MhVlly	A-	15	0	0	2	25.1	109	27	9	8	3	4	0	5	5	0	30	0	0	2	0	1.000	0	0--	-	4.64	2.84
2011	Indns	R	5	0	0	2	8.1	37	8	4	4	0	1	2	0	2	0	10	2	0	1	0	1.000	0	0--	-	2.38	4.32
2011	Lk Cty	A	2	0	0	1	3.1	15	1	0	0	0	0	0	1	3	0	7	0	0	1	0	1.000	0	0--	-	2.46	0.00
2013	InldEm	A+	5	5	0	0	29.0	115	29	11	6	0	0	1	1	4	0	21	0	0	2	2	.500	0	0--	-	2.67	1.86
2014	Ark	AA	26	26	2	0	148.2	610	142	61	52	7	4	6	6	41	0	140	10	0	10	6	.625	1	0--	-	3.23	3.15
2014	LAA	AL	3	0	0	2	7.1	34	9	4	4	0	0	0	1	2	0	8	0	0	0	0	-	0	0-0	0	4.52	4.91

Darin Ruf

Bats: R Throws: R Pos: PH-23;1B-20;LF-15;3B-1   ROUGH   Ht: 6'3" Wt: 240 Born: 7/28/1986 Age: 28

						BATTING															RUNNING			AVERAGES			
Year	Team	Lg	G	AB	H	2B	3B	HR	(Hm	Rd)	TB	R	RBI	RC	TBB	IBB	SO	HBP	SH	SF	SB	CS	GDP	Avg	OBP	Slg	OPS
2014	Clrwtr*	A+	3	12	3	0	0	0	(-	-)	3	0	2	0	1	0	3	0	0	0	0	0	0	.250	.308	.250	.558
2014	LV*	AAA	23	83	22	6	0	1	(-	-)	31	6	10	10	6	0	16	0	0	2	1	0	3	.265	.308	.373	.681
2014	Phillies*	R	6	23	3	1	0	0	(-	-)	4	3	2	10	3	0	4	1	0	0	0	0	0	.130	.259	.174	.433
2012	Phi	NL	12	33	11	2	1	3	(1	2)	24	4	10	5	2	1	12	0	0	0	0	0	1	.333	.351	.727	1.079
2013	Phi	NL	73	251	62	11	0	14	(11	3)	115	36	30	33	33	1	91	7	0	2	0	0	4	.247	.348	.458	.806
2014	Phi	NL	52	102	24	8	0	3	(3	0)	41	13	8	9	8	0	32	4	1	2	0	0	2	.235	.310	.402	.712
	3 ML YEARS		137	386	97	21	1	20	(15	5)	180	53	48	47	43	2	135	11	1	6	0	0	7	.251	.339	.466	.805

Justin Ruggiano

Bats: R Throws: R Pos: RF-34;PH-29;CF-18;LF-10   rouge-ee-AH-no   Ht: 6'1" Wt: 210 Born: 4/12/1982 Age: 33

						BATTING															RUNNING			AVERAGES			
Year	Team	Lg	G	AB	H	2B	3B	HR	(Hm	Rd)	TB	R	RBI	RC	TBB	IBB	SO	HBP	SH	SF	SB	CS	GDP	Avg	OBP	Slg	OPS
2014	Iowa*	AAA	6	21	3	1	0	0	(-	-)	4	3	0	1	3	0	6	1	0	0	0	0	0	.143	.280	.190	.470
2007	TB	AL	7	14	3	0	0	0	(0	0)	3	2	3	1	1	0	5	0	0	0	0	0	0	.214	.267	.214	.481
2008	TB	AL	45	76	15	4	0	2	(2	0)	25	9	7	4	4	0	27	1	0	0	2	0	0	.197	.247	.329	.576
2011	TB	AL	46	105	26	4	0	4	(3	1)	42	11	13	16	4	0	26	0	1	1	1	1	2	.248	.273	.400	.673
2012	Mia	NL	91	288	90	23	1	13	(4	9)	154	38	36	46	29	0	84	0	1	1	14	8	6	.313	.374	.535	.909
2013	Mia	NL	128	424	94	18	1	18	(3	15)	168	49	50	42	41	1	114	5	1	0	15	8	9	.222	.298	.396	.694
2014	ChC	NL	81	224	63	13	1	6	(2	4)	96	29	28	32	18	0	70	3	1	4	2	4	2	.281	.337	.429	.766
	6 ML YEARS		398	1131	291	62	3	43	(14	29)	488	138	137	141	97	1	326	9	4	6	34	21	21	.257	.319	.431	.751

Carlos Ruiz

Bats: R Throws: R Pos: C-109;PH-3;PR-1   Ht: 5'10" Wt: 205 Born: 1/22/1979 Age: 36

						BATTING															RUNNING			AVERAGES			
Year	Team	Lg	G	AB	H	2B	3B	HR	(Hm	Rd)	TB	R	RBI	RC	TBB	IBB	SO	HBP	SH	SF	SB	CS	GDP	Avg	OBP	Slg	OPS
2014	Clrwtr*	A+	5	17	3	1	0	0	(-	-)	4	4	2	1	1	0	3	1	0	0	1	0	0	.176	.263	.235	.498
2006	Phi	NL	27	69	18	1	1	3	(2	1)	30	5	10	10	5	2	8	1	2	1	0	0	0	.261	.316	.435	.751
2007	Phi	NL	115	374	97	29	2	6	(4	2)	148	42	54	49	42	10	49	5	5	3	6	1	17	.259	.340	.396	.735
2008	Phi	NL	117	320	70	14	0	4	(2	2)	96	47	31	28	44	6	38	4	4	1	1	2	14	.219	.320	.300	.620
2009	Phi	NL	107	322	82	26	1	9	(5	4)	137	32	43	49	47	8	39	4	4	2	3	2	8	.255	.355	.425	.780
2010	Phi	NL	121	371	112	28	1	8	(3	5)	166	43	53	62	55	13	54	6	0	1	0	1	8	.302	.400	.447	.847
2011	Phi	NL	132	410	116	23	0	6	(1	5)	157	49	40	59	48	10	48	10	3	1	1	0	7	.283	.371	.383	.754
2012	Phi	NL	114	372	121	32	0	16	(8	8)	201	56	68	75	29	6	50	16	0	4	4	0	6	.325	.394	.540	.935
2013	Phi	NL	92	310	83	16	0	5	(4	1)	114	30	37	34	18	3	39	7	4	2	1	0	11	.268	.320	.368	.688
2014	Phi	NL	110	381	96	25	1	6	(2	4)	141	43	31	50	46	1	60	12	1	5	4	2	11	.252	.347	.370	.717
	Postseason		46	142	36	8	1	4	(3	1)	58	19	15	24	24	3	16	5	1	0	3	0	2	.254	.380	.408	.789
	9 ML YEARS		935	2929	795	194	6	63	(31	32)	1190	347	367	416	334	59	385	65	23	20	20	8	85	.271	.357	.406	.763

Cameron Rupp

Bats: R Throws: R Pos: C-18   Ht: 6'2" Wt: 250 Born: 9/28/1988 Age: 26

						BATTING															RUNNING			AVERAGES			
Year	Team	Lg	G	AB	H	2B	3B	HR	(Hm	Rd)	TB	R	RBI	RC	TBB	IBB	SO	HBP	SH	SF	SB	CS	GDP	Avg	OBP	Slg	OPS
2010	Wmspt	A-	55	193	42	16	0	5	(-	-)	73	20	28	25	25	0	51	4	0	1	0	0	2	.218	.318	.378	.697
2011	Lakwd	A	99	324	88	19	1	4	(-	-)	121	33	44	45	31	0	96	8	1	4	0	0	5	.272	.346	.373	.720
2012	Clrwtr	A+	104	344	92	22	1	10	(-	-)	146	32	49	53	40	0	77	2	2	2	0	0	9	.267	.345	.424	.770
2013	Rdng	AA	41	143	35	6	0	8	(-	-)	65	18	21	22	14	1	36	4	0	0	0	0	7	.245	.329	.455	.784
2013	LV	AAA	53	182	49	10	0	6	(-	-)	77	18	24	24	10	0	55	1	0	1	1	1	5	.269	.309	.423	.732
2014	LV	AAA	59	194	32	8	0	6	(-	-)	58	19	19	15	21	0	76	3	0	1	0	0	3	.165	.256	.299	.555
2013	Phi	NL	4	13	4	1	0	0	(0	0)	5	1	2	2	1	0	4	0	0	0	0	0	0	.308	.357	.385	.742
2014	Phi	NL	18	60	11	4	0	0	(0	0)	15	4	6	3	4	0	20	0	0	0	0	0	5	.183	.234	.250	.484
	2 ML YEARS		22	73	15	5	0	0	(0	0)	20	5	8	5	5	0	24	0	0	0	0	0	5	.205	.256	.274	.530

Chris Rusin

Pitches: L Bats: L Pos: RP-4   RUSS-inn   Ht: 6'2" Wt: 195 Born: 10/22/1986 Age: 28

				HOW MUCH HE PITCHED					WHAT HE GAVE UP												THE RESULTS							
Year	Team	Lg	G	GS	CG	GF	IP	BFP	H	R	ER	HR	SH	SF	HB	TBB	IBB	SO	WP	Bk	W	L	Pct	Sh	Sv-Op	Hld	ERC	ERA
2014	Iowa*	AAA	23	23	1	0	146.1	620	163	79	70	15	13	4	7	38	5	97	3	0	8	13	.381	1	0--	-	4.41	4.31
2012	ChC	NL	7	7	0	0	29.2	135	38	22	21	4	0	3	0	11	0	21	0	0	2	3	.400	0	0-0	0	6.46	6.37
2013	ChC	NL	13	13	0	0	66.1	282	66	30	29	8	1	1	3	24	3	36	1	0	2	6	.250	0	0-0	0	4.21	3.93
2014	ChC	NL	4	0	0	2	12.2	58	16	10	10	1	1	0	0	5	1	8	1	0	0	0	-	0	0-0	0	5.24	7.11
	3 ML YEARS		24	20	0	2	108.2	475	120	62	60	13	2	1	6	40	4	65	2	0	4	9	.308	0	0-0	0	4.92	4.97

276

James Russell

Pitches: L **Bats:** L **Pos:** RP-65; SP-1   **Ht:** 6'4" **Wt:** 200 **Born:** 1/8/1986 **Age:** 29

			HOW MUCH HE PITCHED					WHAT HE GAVE UP										THE RESULTS						
Year	Team	Lg	G	GS	CG	GF	IP	BFP	H	R	ER	HR	SH	SF	HB	TBB	IBB	SO	WP	Bk	W	L	Pct	Sh	Sv-Op	Hld	ERC	ERA
2010	ChC	NL	57	0	0	11	49.0	219	55	37	27	11	3	4	4	11	0	42	2	0	1	1	.500	0	0-2	6	5.12	4.96
2011	ChC	NL	64	5	0	10	67.2	292	76	37	31	12	4	6	2	14	4	43	1	0	1	6	.143	0	0-2	6	4.51	4.12
2012	ChC	NL	77	0	0	19	69.1	292	67	28	25	5	2	3	1	23	7	55	1	1	7	1	.875	0	2-5	13	3.35	3.25
2013	ChC	NL	74	0	0	7	52.2	214	46	21	21	7	1	1	1	18	6	37	1	0	1	6	.143	0	0-8	19	3.37	3.59
2014	2 Tms	NL	66	1	0	15	57.2	238	45	20	19	3	7	1	1	20	3	42	1	0	0	2	.000	0	1-3	6	2.37	2.97
14	ChC	NL	44	0	0	7	33.1	142	24	14	13	3	5	1	1	16	2	26	1	0	0	2	.000	0	1-3	5	2.76	3.51
14	Atl	NL	22	1	0	8	24.1	96	21	6	6	0	2	0	0	4	1	16	0	0	0	0	-	0	0-0	1	1.86	2.22
5 ML YEARS			338	6	0	62	296.1	1255	289	143	123	38	17	15	9	86	20	219	6	1	10	16	.385	0	3-20	50	3.69	3.74

Josh Rutledge

Bats: R **Throws:** R **Pos:** SS-69;PH-21;2B-17;3B-5;PR-1   **Ht:** 6'1" **Wt:** 190 **Born:** 4/21/1989 **Age:** 26

			BATTING																RUNNING			AVERAGES			
Year	Team	Lg	G	AB	H	2B	3B	HR	(Hm | Rd)	TB	R	RBI	RC	TBB	IBB	SO	HBP	SH	SF	SB	CS	GDP	Avg	OBP	Slg	OPS
2014	ColSpr*	AAA	15	54	18	3	0	1	(- | -)	24	7	5	9	7	1	12	1	1	1	3	3	1	.333	.413	.444	.857
2012	Col	NL	73	277	76	20	5	8	(5 | 3)	130	37	37	37	9	0	54	4	0	1	7	0	8	.274	.306	.469	.775
2013	Col	NL	88	285	67	6	1	7	(5 | 2)	96	45	19	28	22	1	62	2	4	1	12	0	2	.235	.294	.337	.630
2014	Col	NL	105	309	83	16	7	4	(1 | 3)	125	44	33	42	20	0	83	6	5	2	2	3	6	.269	.323	.405	.728
3 ML YEARS			266	871	226	42	13	19	(11 | 8)	351	126	89	107	51	1	199	12	9	4	21	3	16	.259	.308	.403	.711

Brendan Ryan

Bats: R **Throws:** R **Pos:** SS-25;2B-19;1B-5;PR-4;3B-2;PH-2   **Ht:** 6'2" **Wt:** 195 **Born:** 3/26/1982 **Age:** 33

			BATTING																RUNNING			AVERAGES			
Year	Team	Lg	G	AB	H	2B	3B	HR	(Hm | Rd)	TB	R	RBI	RC	TBB	IBB	SO	HBP	SH	SF	SB	CS	GDP	Avg	OBP	Slg	OPS
2014	Tampa*	A+	4	14	4	0	0	0	(- | -)	4	1	2	2	3	0	3	0	0	0	0	0	0	.286	.412	.286	.697
2014	Trntn*	AA	3	11	4	0	0	0	(- | -)	4	3	0	2	2	0	1	0	0	0	0	0	1	.364	.462	.364	.825
2007	StL	NL	67	180	52	9	0	4	(2 | 2)	73	30	12	21	15	0	19	1	3	0	7	0	3	.289	.347	.406	.752
2008	StL	NL	80	197	48	9	0	0	(0 | 0)	57	30	10	12	16	0	31	2	3	0	7	2	4	.244	.307	.289	.596
2009	StL	NL	129	390	114	19	7	3	(1 | 2)	156	55	37	48	24	3	56	6	6	3	14	7	9	.292	.340	.400	.740
2010	StL	NL	139	439	98	19	3	2	(0 | 2)	129	50	36	37	33	5	60	2	9	3	11	4	6	.223	.279	.294	.573
2011	Sea	AL	123	436	108	19	3	3	(0 | 3)	142	51	39	46	34	0	87	10	9	5	13	3	7	.248	.313	.326	.639
2012	Sea	AL	141	407	79	19	3	3	(2 | 1)	113	42	31	35	44	0	98	5	8	6	11	5	4	.194	.277	.278	.555
2013	2 Tms	AL	104	319	63	12	0	4	(1 | 3)	87	30	22	17	23	1	73	2	4	1	4	2	11	.197	.255	.273	.528
2014	NYY	AL	49	114	19	4	0	0	(0 | 0)	23	5	8	2	4	0	30	3	1	2	0	2	2	.167	.211	.202	.413
13	Sea	AL	87	260	50	10	0	3	(1 | 2)	69	23	21	14	21	1	60	1	4	1	4	2	11	.192	.254	.265	.520
13	NYY	AL	17	59	13	2	0	1	(0 | 1)	18	7	1	3	2	0	13	1	0	0	0	0	0	.220	.258	.305	.563
Postseason			3	12	1	1	0	0	(0 | 0)	2	0	0	0	0	0	2	0	0	0	0	0	0	.083	.083	.167	.250
8 ML YEARS			832	2482	581	110	16	19	(6 | 13)	780	293	195	218	193	9	454	31	43	20	67	25	46	.234	.295	.314	.610

Kyle Ryan

Pitches: L **Bats:** L **Pos:** RP-5; SP-1   **Ht:** 6'5" **Wt:** 180 **Born:** 9/25/1991 **Age:** 23

			HOW MUCH HE PITCHED					WHAT HE GAVE UP										THE RESULTS						
Year	Team	Lg	G	GS	CG	GF	IP	BFP	H	R	ER	HR	SH	SF	HB	TBB	IBB	SO	WP	Bk	W	L	Pct	Sh	Sv-Op	Hld	ERC	ERA
2010	Tigers	R	12	12	0	0	54.0	236	58	30	25	2	0	0	6	13	0	46	3	0	2	4	.333	0	0--	-	3.81	4.17
2011	WMich	A	24	24	0	0	137.0	562	145	56	48	3	4	7	9	30	1	99	5	1	6	10	.375	0	0--	-	3.54	3.15
2012	WMich	A	28	28	1	0	158.2	669	176	85	66	7	7	9	6	29	0	105	6	1	7	8	.467	0	0--	-	3.79	3.74
2013	Lkland	A+	24	24	0	0	142.0	584	132	58	50	12	3	3	8	37	0	90	1	1	12	7	.632	0	0--	-	3.32	3.17
2014	Erie	AA	21	21	1	0	126.2	531	140	67	64	15	2	5	1	32	1	78	4	1	7	10	.412	1	0--	-	4.32	4.55
2014	Toledo	AAA	5	5	0	0	33.0	120	21	8	6	0	1	0	0	5	0	20	0	2	3	0	1.000	0	0-0	0	1.16	1.64
2014	Det	AL	6	1	0	1	10.1	41	10	3	3	0	0	0	0	2	0	4	0	1	2	0	1.000	0	0-0	0	2.57	2.61

Hyun-Jin Ryu

he-YUN-jin ree-YOO   **Ht:** 6'2" **Wt:** 255 **Born:** 3/25/1987 **Age:** 28

Pitches: L **Bats:** R **Pos:** SP-26

			HOW MUCH HE PITCHED					WHAT HE GAVE UP										THE RESULTS						
Year	Team	Lg	G	GS	CG	GF	IP	BFP	H	R	ER	HR	SH	SF	HB	TBB	IBB	SO	WP	Bk	W	L	Pct	Sh	Sv-Op	Hld	ERC	ERA
2013	LAD	NL	30	30	2	0	192.0	783	182	67	64	15	7	3	1	49	4	154	5	0	14	8	.636	1	0-0	0	3.13	3.00
2014	LAD	NL	26	26	0	0	152.0	631	152	60	57	8	6	2	3	29	2	139	2	0	14	7	.667	0	0-0	0	3.00	3.38
Postseason			2	2	0	0	10.0	40	9	4	4	0	0	0	0	2	0	5	0	0	1	0	1.000	0	0-0	0	2.21	3.60
2 ML YEARS			56	56	2	0	344.0	1414	334	127	121	23	13	5	4	78	6	293	7	0	28	15	.651	1	0-0	0	3.07	3.17

Marc Rzepczynski

zepp-CHINN-ski   **Ht:** 6'2" **Wt:** 220 **Born:** 8/29/1985 **Age:** 29

Pitches: L **Bats:** L **Pos:** RP-73

			HOW MUCH HE PITCHED					WHAT HE GAVE UP										THE RESULTS						
Year	Team	Lg	G	GS	CG	GF	IP	BFP	H	R	ER	HR	SH	SF	HB	TBB	IBB	SO	WP	Bk	W	L	Pct	Sh	Sv-Op	Hld	ERC	ERA
2009	Tor	AL	11	11	0	0	61.1	261	51	27	25	7	2	1	1	30	0	60	4	1	2	4	.333	0	0-0	0	3.65	3.67
2010	Tor	AL	14	12	0	0	63.2	287	72	37	35	8	1	2	5	30	1	57	4	1	4	4	.500	0	0-0	2	5.71	4.95
2011	2 Tms		71	0	0	7	62.0	256	50	27	23	3	2	0	4	26	1	61	6	0	2	6	.250	0	0-4	18	3.04	3.34
2012	StL	NL	70	0	0	14	46.2	196	46	22	22	7	0	0	0	17	2	33	3	0	1	3	.250	0	0-5	18	4.21	4.24
2013	2 Tms		38	0	0	10	30.2	129	27	13	11	2	1	1	4	10	3	29	0	0	0	0	-	0	0-6	13	3.28	3.23
2014	Cle	AL	73	0	0	8	46.0	196	42	19	14	1	1	2	3	19	3	46	2	0	0	3	.000	0	1-2	13	3.27	2.74
11	Tor	AL	43	0	0	6	39.1	158	28	16	13	2	1	0	3	15	0	33	5	0	2	3	.400	0	0-3	10	2.52	2.97
11	StL	NL	28	0	0	1	22.2	98	22	11	10	1	1	0	1	11	1	28	1	0	0	3	.000	0	0-1	8	4.01	3.97

Year Team	Lg	G	GS	CG	GF	IP	BFP	H	R	ER	HR	SH	SF	HB	TBB	IBB	SO	WP	Bk	W	L	Pct	Sh	Sv-Op	Hld	ERC	ERA
13 StL	NL	11	0	0	4	10.1	50	16	9	9	1	0	1	1	4	1	9	0	0	0	0	-	0	0-0	0	7.69	7.84
13 Cle	AL	27	0	0	6	20.1	79	11	4	2	1	1	0	3	6	2	20	0	0	0	0	-	0	0-0	6	1.57	0.89
Postseason		18	0	0	1	10.2	44	10	5	5	0	0	0	1	2	0	13	1	0	1	0	1.000	0	0-1	7	2.64	4.22
6 ML YEARS		277	23	0	39	310.1	1325	288	145	130	28	7	6	17	132	10	286	19	2	9	20	.310	0	1-11	57	3.92	3.77

CC Sabathia

Pitches: L Bats: L Pos: SP-8 Ht: 6'7" Wt: 285 Born: 7/21/1980 Age: 34

Year Team	Lg	G	GS	CG	GF	IP	BFP	H	R	ER	HR	SH	SF	HB	TBB	IBB	SO	WP	Bk	W	L	Pct	Sh	Sv-Op	Hld	ERC	ERA
2014 Tampa*	A+	1	1	0	0	2.1	12	3	2	2	0	0	0	0	1	0	2	0	0	0	0	-	0	0--	-	4.47	7.71
2014 Trntn*	AA	1	1	0	0	3.2	18	5	5	3	0	0	1	1	1	0	2	0	0	0	1	.000	0	0--	-	5.84	7.36
2001 Cle	AL	33	33	0	0	180.1	763	149	93	88	19	3	5	7	95	1	171	7	3	17	5	.773	0	0-0	0	3.86	4.39
2002 Cle	AL	33	33	2	0	210.0	891	198	109	102	17	5	10	1	88	2	149	6	3	13	11	.542	0	0-0	0	3.74	4.37
2003 Cle	AL	30	30	2	0	197.2	832	190	85	79	19	10	4	6	66	3	141	4	2	13	9	.591	1	0-0	0	3.70	3.60
2004 Cle	AL	30	30	1	0	188.0	787	176	90	86	20	3	6	7	72	3	139	1	1	11	10	.524	1	0-0	0	3.91	4.12
2005 Cle	AL	31	31	1	0	196.2	823	185	92	88	19	6	3	7	62	1	161	7	0	15	10	.600	0	0-0	0	3.55	4.03
2006 Cle	AL	28	28	6	0	192.2	802	182	83	69	17	8	5	7	44	3	172	3	0	12	11	.522	2	0-0	0	3.13	3.22
2007 Cle	AL	34	34	4	0	241.0	975	238	94	86	20	6	6	8	37	1	209	1	0	19	7	.731	1	0-0	0	3.12	3.21
2008 2 Tms		35	35	10	0	253.0	1023	223	85	76	19	9	6	7	59	1	251	2	2	17	10	.630	5	0-0	0	2.78	2.70
2009 NYY	AL	34	34	2	0	230.0	938	197	96	86	18	4	9	9	67	7	197	5	0	19	8	.704	1	0-0	0	2.89	3.37
2010 NYY	AL	34	34	2	0	237.2	970	209	92	84	20	5	8	7	74	6	197	8	1	21	7	.750	0	0-0	0	3.11	3.18
2011 NYY	AL	33	33	3	0	237.1	985	230	87	79	17	8	7	7	61	4	230	2	1	19	8	.704	1	0-0	0	3.27	3.00
2012 NYY	AL	28	28	2	0	200.0	833	184	89	75	22	4	3	8	44	2	197	4	1	15	6	.714	0	0-0	0	3.10	3.38
2013 NYY	AL	32	32	2	0	211.0	908	224	122	112	28	8	8	4	65	5	175	7	1	14	13	.519	0	0-0	0	4.32	4.78
2014 NYY	AL	8	8	0	0	46.0	209	58	31	27	10	1	1	4	10	0	48	2	0	3	4	.429	0	0-0	0	5.98	5.28
08 Cle	AL	18	18	3	0	122.1	507	117	54	52	13	3	3	3	34	1	123	1	2	6	8	.429	2	0-0	0	3.52	3.83
08 Mil	NL	17	17	7	0	130.2	516	106	31	24	6	6	3	4	25	0	128	1	0	11	2	.846	3	0-0	0	2.13	1.65
Postseason		19	18	1	0	107.1	478	116	57	54	14	5	0	5	51	8	101	4	1	9	5	.643	0	0-0	0	5.19	4.53
14 ML YEARS		423	423	37	0	2821.1	11739	2643	1248	1137	265	80	81	89	844	39	2437	59	15	208	119	.636	12	0-0	0	3.42	3.63

Casey Sadler

Pitches: R Bats: R Pos: RP-6 Ht: 6'4" Wt: 215 Born: 7/13/1990 Age: 24

Year Team	Lg	G	GS	CG	GF	IP	BFP	H	R	ER	HR	SH	SF	HB	TBB	IBB	SO	WP	Bk	W	L	Pct	Sh	Sv-Op	Hld	ERC	ERA
2010 StCol	A-	12	1	0	2	24.0	106	30	10	8	1	3	0	0	6	0	21	3	0	3	0	1.000	0	0--	-	4.45	3.00
2011 WV	A	35	0	0	19	66.2	268	51	20	18	5	3	1	7	17	0	57	6	0	5	5	.500	0	4--	-	2.56	2.43
2012 Bradtn	A+	32	17	0	6	130.1	544	125	63	54	7	4	4	11	35	0	93	4	1	4	6	.400	0	2--	-	3.40	3.73
2013 Altna	AA	23	23	1	0	130.1	535	116	54	48	11	3	2	9	42	1	67	2	0	11	7	.611	0	0--	-	3.42	3.31
2013 Indy	AAA	1	1	0	0	6.0	27	7	3	3	1	1	0	0	1	0	5	0	0	0	0	-	0	0--	-	4.25	4.50
2014 Indy	AAA	21	21	1	0	124.2	506	124	49	42	11	3	4	4	24	1	77	2	1	11	4	.733	0	0--	-	3.35	3.03
2014 Pit	NL	6	0	0	2	10.1	49	12	9	9	0	0	2	1	5	0	7	1	0	0	1	.000	0	0-0	0	4.80	7.84

Fernando Salas

Pitches: R Bats: R Pos: RP-57 SAH-lahss Ht: 6'2" Wt: 210 Born: 5/30/1985 Age: 30

Year Team	Lg	G	GS	CG	GF	IP	BFP	H	R	ER	HR	SH	SF	HB	TBB	IBB	SO	WP	Bk	W	L	Pct	Sh	Sv-Op	Hld	ERC	ERA
2014 InldEm*	A+	1	0	0	0	1.0	3	0	0	0	0	0	0	0	0	0	1	0	0	0	0	-	0	0--	-	0.00	0.00
2014 Salt Lk*	AAA	3	0	0	2	2.2	10	2	0	0	0	0	0	0	0	0	0	0	0	0	0	-	0	1--	-	1.13	0.00
2010 StL	NL	27	0	0	11	30.2	133	28	13	12	4	1	1	0	15	2	29	2	0	0	0	-	0	0-1	1	4.03	3.52
2011 StL	NL	68	0	0	46	75.0	295	50	20	19	7	3	0	2	21	3	75	2	0	5	6	.455	0	24-30	6	1.94	2.28
2012 StL	NL	65	0	0	23	58.2	256	56	28	28	5	5	0	1	27	5	60	4	0	1	4	.200	0	0-3	7	3.85	4.30
2013 StL	NL	27	0	0	14	28.0	118	27	15	14	3	1	4	1	6	1	22	2	0	0	3	.000	0	0-2	2	3.22	4.50
2014 LAA	AL	57	0	0	11	58.2	239	50	22	22	5	4	1	1	14	4	61	1	1	5	0	1.000	0	0-1	8	2.54	3.38
Postseason		16	0	0	2	19.0	78	15	9	7	1	0	0	0	4	1	17	1	1	0	0	-	0	0-0	4	1.85	3.32
5 ML YEARS		244	0	0	105	251.0	1041	211	98	95	24	14	6	5	83	15	247	11	1	11	13	.458	0	24-37	24	2.89	3.41

Danny Salazar

Pitches: R Bats: L Pos: SP-20 SAL-uh-zarr Ht: 6'0" Wt: 190 Born: 1/11/1990 Age: 25

Year Team	Lg	G	GS	CG	GF	IP	BFP	H	R	ER	HR	SH	SF	HB	TBB	IBB	SO	WP	Bk	W	L	Pct	Sh	Sv-Op	Hld	ERC	ERA
2010 Lk Cty	A	7	7	0	0	32.1	140	34	16	16	7	1	0	1	13	0	23	3	0	1	1	.500	0	0--	-	5.44	4.45
2011 Indns	R	5	5	0	0	6.2	30	6	3	2	1	0	1	1	2	0	11	1	0	0	0	-	0	0--	-	3.82	2.70
2011 Lk Cty	A	3	3	0	0	8.0	35	8	4	3	0	0	0	2	2	0	7	2	0	0	2	.000	0	0--	-	3.75	3.38
2012 Carlina	A+	16	16	0	0	53.2	215	46	17	16	3	1	1	0	19	0	53	4	1	1	2	.333	0	0--	-	2.96	2.68
2012 Akron	AA	6	6	0	0	34.0	132	25	8	7	1	1	0	0	8	0	23	1	0	4	0	1.000	0	0--	-	1.75	1.85
2013 Akron	AA	7	7	0	0	33.2	133	27	10	10	1	0	0	0	10	0	51	0	1	2	3	.400	0	0--	-	2.28	2.67
2013 Clmbs	AAA	14	13	0	1	59.1	230	44	21	18	4	0	1	2	14	0	78	0	0	4	2	.667	0	1--	-	2.13	2.73
2014 Clmbs	AAA	11	11	2	0	60.2	270	58	28	25	7	1	1	1	28	2	76	6	1	4	6	.400	0	0--	-	4.08	3.71
2013 Cle	AL	10	10	0	0	52.0	211	44	18	18	7	1	0	0	15	0	65	3	0	2	3	.400	0	0-0	0	3.05	3.12
2014 Cle	AL	20	20	1	0	110.0	474	117	57	52	13	1	5	3	35	4	120	3	0	6	8	.429	1	0-0	0	4.30	4.25
Postseason		1	1	0	0	4.0	18	4	3	3	1	0	0	0	2	1	4	0	0	0	1	.000	0	0-0	0	5.04	6.75
2 ML YEARS		30	30	1	0	162.0	685	161	75	70	20	2	5	3	50	4	185	6	0	8	11	.421	1	0-0	0	3.89	3.89

Chris Sale

Pitches: L **Bats**: L **Pos**: SP-26   SAIL   **Ht**: 6'6" **Wt**: 180 **Born**: 3/30/1989 **Age**: 26

Year	Team	Lg	G	GS	CG	GF	IP	BFP	H	R	ER	HR	SH	SF	HB	TBB	IBB	SO	WP	Bk	W	L	Pct	Sh	Sv-Op	Hld	ERC	ERA
2014	Charltt*	AAA	1	1	0	0	4.0	15	1	0	0	0	0	0	0	2	0	11	1	0	0	0	-	0	0- -	-	0.75	0.00
2010	CWS	AL	21	0	0	8	23.1	92	15	5	5	2	1	0	0	10	0	32	1	0	2	1	.667	0	4-4	2	2.30	1.93
2011	CWS	AL	58	0	0	17	71.0	288	52	22	22	6	3	0	2	27	3	79	2	0	2	2	.500	0	8-10	16	2.55	2.79
2012	CWS	AL	30	29	1	0	192.0	772	167	66	65	19	1	3	6	51	5	192	6	0	17	8	.680	0	0-1	0	3.00	3.05
2013	CWS	AL	30	30	4	0	214.1	866	184	81	73	23	2	4	14	46	2	226	8	1	11	14	.440	1	0-0	0	2.92	3.07
2014	CWS	AL	26	26	2	0	174.0	685	129	48	42	13	2	3	11	39	2	208	3	0	12	4	.750	0	0-0	0	2.18	2.17
	5 ML YEARS		165	85	7	25	674.2	2703	547	222	207	63	9	10	33	173	12	737	20	1	44	29	.603	1	12-15	18	2.69	2.76

Jarrod Saltalamacchia

Bats: B **Throws**: R **Pos**: C-107;PH-10;DH-1   salt-ah-luh-MOCK-ee-ah   **Ht**: 6'3" **Wt**: 235 **Born**: 5/2/1985 **Age**: 30

Year	Team	Lg	G	AB	H	2B	3B	HR	(Hm	Rd)	TB	R	RBI	RC	TBB	IBB	SO	HBP	SH	SF	SB	CS	GDP	Avg	OBP	Slg	OPS
2014	Jupiter*	A+	2	7	2	0	0	0	(-	-)	2	0	0	0	1	0	1	0	0	0	0	0	1	.286	.375	.286	.661
2007	2 Tms		93	308	82	13	1	11	(6	5)	130	39	33	32	19	1	75	1	0	1	0	0	8	.266	.310	.422	.732
2008	Tex	AL	61	198	50	13	0	3	(2	1)	72	27	26	29	31	1	74	0	0	1	0	2	1	.253	.352	.364	.716
2009	Tex	AL	84	283	66	12	0	9	(6	3)	105	34	34	30	22	1	97	1	3	1	0	2	3	.233	.290	.371	.661
2010	2 Tms	AL	12	24	4	3	0	0	(0	0)	7	2	2	3	6	0	5	0	0	0	0	0	0	.167	.333	.292	.625
2011	Bos	AL	103	358	84	23	3	16	(6	10)	161	52	56	43	24	1	119	3	0	1	1	0	7	.235	.288	.450	.737
2012	Bos	AL	121	405	90	17	1	25	(12	13)	184	55	59	49	38	0	139	1	0	4	0	1	5	.222	.288	.454	.742
2013	Bos	AL	121	425	116	40	0	14	(9	5)	198	68	65	60	43	3	139	0	0	2	4	1	7	.273	.338	.466	.804
2014	Mia	NL	114	373	82	20	0	11	(5	6)	135	43	44	34	55	4	143	2	0	5	0	1	11	.220	.320	.362	.681
07	Atl	NL	47	141	40	6	0	4	(4	0)	58	11	12	13	10	1	28	1	0	1	0	0	4	.284	.333	.411	.745
07	Tex	AL	46	167	42	7	1	7	(2	5)	72	28	21	19	9	0	47	0	0	0	0	0	4	.251	.290	.431	.721
10	Tex	AL	2	5	1	0	0	0	(0	0)	1	0	1	1	0	0	1	0	0	0	0	0	0	.200	.200	.200	.400
10	Bos	AL	10	19	3	3	0	0	(0	0)	6	2	1	2	6	0	4	0	0	0	0	0	0	.158	.360	.316	.676
	Postseason		10	32	6	1	0	0	(0	0)	7	1	5	2	3	0	19	0	0	0	0	0	0	.188	.257	.219	.476
	8 ML YEARS		709	2374	574	141	5	89	(46	43)	992	320	319	280	238	11	791	8	3	15	5	7	42	.242	.311	.418	.729

Jeff Samardzija

Pitches: R **Bats**: R **Pos**: SP-33   suh-MAHR-jah   **Ht**: 6'5" **Wt**: 225 **Born**: 1/23/1985 **Age**: 30

Year	Team	Lg	G	GS	CG	GF	IP	BFP	H	R	ER	HR	SH	SF	HB	TBB	IBB	SO	WP	Bk	W	L	Pct	Sh	Sv-Op	Hld	ERC	ERA
2008	ChC	NL	26	0	0	6	27.2	124	24	12	7	0	1	1	1	15	2	25	2	0	1	0	1.000	0	1-4	3	3.08	2.28
2009	ChC	NL	20	2	0	7	34.2	161	46	29	29	7	4	1	1	15	1	21	2	0	1	3	.250	0	0-0	0	7.13	7.53
2010	ChC	NL	7	3	0	0	19.1	100	21	22	18	4	0	0	2	20	1	9	1	0	2	2	.500	0	0-0	0	8.45	8.38
2011	ChC	NL	75	0	0	18	88.0	380	64	35	29	5	3	2	5	50	3	87	8	0	8	4	.667	0	0-2	13	3.05	2.97
2012	ChC	NL	28	28	1	0	174.2	723	157	79	74	20	5	4	4	56	2	180	10	0	9	13	.409	0	0-0	0	3.41	3.81
2013	ChC	NL	33	33	2	0	213.2	914	210	109	103	25	4	2	8	78	3	214	11	0	8	13	.381	1	0-0	0	4.11	4.34
2014	2 Tms		33	33	2	0	219.2	879	191	86	73	20	3	7	10	43	3	202	10	0	7	13	.350	1	0-0	0	2.74	2.99
14	ChC	NL	17	17	0	0	108.0	449	99	44	34	7	3	4	6	31	3	103	6	0	2	7	.222	0	0-0	0	3.14	2.83
14	Oak	AL	16	16	2	0	111.2	430	92	42	39	13	0	3	4	12	0	99	4	0	5	6	.455	0	0-0	0	2.34	3.14
	Postseason		1	0	0	0	1.0	4	2	1	1	0	0	0	0	0	0	0	0	0	0	0	-	0	0-0	0	9.49	9.00
	7 ML YEARS		222	99	5	31	777.2	3281	713	372	333	81	20	17	31	277	15	738	44	0	36	48	.429	1	1-6	16	3.61	3.85

Aaron Sanchez

Pitches: R **Bats**: R **Pos**: RP-24   **Ht**: 6'4" **Wt**: 200 **Born**: 7/1/1992 **Age**: 22

Year	Team	Lg	G	GS	CG	GF	IP	BFP	H	R	ER	HR	SH	SF	HB	TBB	IBB	SO	WP	Bk	W	L	Pct	Sh	Sv-Op	Hld	ERC	ERA
2010	B Jays	R	8	8	0	0	19.0	88	19	10	3	1	1	1	4	12	0	28	3	0	0	2	.000	0	0- -	-	5.59	1.42
2010	Auburn	A-	2	2	0	0	6.0	29	4	5	3	0	1	1	0	5	0	9	1	0	1	0	1.000	0	0- -	-	2.82	4.50
2011	Bluefld	R	11	6	0	3	42.2	190	45	27	26	4	3	1	1	18	0	43	2	0	3	2	.600	0	1- -	-	4.46	5.48
2011	Vancvr	A-	3	3	0	0	11.2	51	8	6	6	0	1	0	1	8	0	13	1	0	0	1	.000	0	0- -	-	3.03	4.63
2012	Lnsng	A	25	18	0	0	90.1	377	64	33	25	3	3	3	7	51	0	97	6	2	8	5	.615	0	0- -	-	3.03	2.49
2013	Dnedin	A+	22	20	0	1	86.1	360	63	40	32	4	0	3	5	40	0	75	4	1	4	5	.444	0	0- -	-	2.73	3.34
2014	NHam	AA	14	14	0	0	66.0	285	52	34	28	2	2	2	7	40	1	57	2	1	3	4	.429	0	0- -	-	3.64	3.82
2014	Buffalo	AAA	8	6	0	0	34.1	150	36	20	16	4	2	2	1	17	1	27	2	1	0	3	.000	0	0- -	-	5.06	4.19
2014	Tor	AL	24	0	0	6	33.0	121	14	5	4	1	2	0	1	9	0	27	1	0	2	2	.500	0	3-3	7	0.96	1.09

Anibal Sanchez

Pitches: R **Bats**: R **Pos**: SP-21; RP-1   ah-NEE-bahl   **Ht**: 6'0" **Wt**: 205 **Born**: 2/27/1984 **Age**: 31

Year	Team	Lg	G	GS	CG	GF	IP	BFP	H	R	ER	HR	SH	SF	HB	TBB	IBB	SO	WP	Bk	W	L	Pct	Sh	Sv-Op	Hld	ERC	ERA
2006	Fla	NL	18	17	2	0	114.1	469	90	39	36	9	3	1	4	46	1	72	4	1	10	3	.769	1	0-0	0	2.96	2.83
2007	Fla	NL	6	6	0	0	30.0	151	43	17	16	3	2	2	1	19	1	14	3	0	2	1	.667	0	0-0	0	7.90	4.80
2008	Fla	NL	10	10	0	0	51.2	241	54	35	32	7	4	2	6	27	2	50	1	0	2	5	.286	0	0-0	0	5.40	5.57
2009	Fla	NL	16	16	0	0	86.0	383	84	39	37	10	2	2	1	46	5	71	0	1	4	8	.333	0	0-0	0	4.51	3.87
2010	Fla	NL	32	32	1	0	195.0	841	192	89	77	10	13	3	7	70	5	157	7	0	13	12	.520	1	0-0	0	3.56	3.55
2011	Fla	NL	32	32	3	0	196.1	830	187	85	80	20	12	1	5	64	8	202	4	5	8	9	.471	2	0-0	0	3.57	3.67
2012	2 Tms		31	31	1	0	195.2	820	200	95	84	20	5	7	5	48	3	167	7	1	9	13	.409	1	0-0	0	3.70	3.86
2013	Det	AL	29	29	1	0	182.0	746	156	56	52	9	4	4	2	54	1	202	7	0	14	8	.636	1	0-0	0	2.63	**2.57**
2014	Det	AL	22	21	0	0	126.0	514	108	55	48	4	4	4	3	30	1	102	5	0	8	5	.615	0	0-0	0	2.35	3.43

			HOW MUCH HE PITCHED						WHAT HE GAVE UP												THE RESULTS								
Year	Team	Lg	G	GS	CG	GF	IP	BFP	H	R	ER	HR	SH	SF	HB	TBB	IBB	SO	WP	Bk	W	L	Pct	Sh	Sv-Op	Hld	ERC	ERA
12	Mia	NL	19	19	0	0	121.0	504	119	59	53	12	4	5	2	33	2	110	4	1	5	7	.417	0	0-0	0	3.55	3.94
12	Det	AL	12	12	1	0	74.2	316	81	36	31	8	1	2	3	15	1	57	3	0	4	6	.400	1	0-0	0	3.95	3.74
	Postseason		6	6	0	0	36.2	155	31	14	12	5	0	1	0	14	1	41	4	0	2	4	.333	0	0-0	0	3.30	2.95
	9 ML YEARS		196	194	8	0	1177.0	4995	1114	510	462	92	48	26	35	404	27	1037	38	8	70	64	.522	6	0-0	0	3.48	3.53

Carlos Sanchez

Bats: B **Throws:** R **Pos:** 2B-27;SS-1;PH-1 **Ht:** 5'11" **Wt:** 195 **Born:** 6/29/1992 **Age:** 23

								BATTING													RUNNING			AVERAGES			
Year	Team	Lg	G	AB	H	2B	3B	HR	(Hm	Rd)	TB	R	RBI	RC	TBB	IBB	SO	HBP	SH	SF	SB	CS	GDP	Avg	OBP	Slg	OPS
2011	Brs	R+	5	16	4	1	0	0	(-	-)	5	4	3	3	5	0	2	3	0	0	1	2	0	.250	.500	.313	.813
2011	Knapol	A	63	264	76	10	1	1	(-	-)	91	44	27	31	15	0	49	7	7	1	7	8	5	.288	.341	.345	.686
2012	WinSa	A+	92	365	115	14	6	1	(-	-)	144	58	42	57	31	0	64	7	7	6	19	10	8	.315	.374	.395	.769
2012	Brham	AA	30	119	44	9	1	0	(-	-)	55	17	13	23	10	0	22	2	1	1	7	5	2	.370	.424	.462	.886
2012	Charltt	AAA	11	39	10	2	0	0	(-	-)	12	4	1	2	0	0	6	0	0	0	0	0	1	.256	.256	.308	.564
2013	Charltt	AAA	112	432	104	20	2	0	(-	-)	128	50	28	40	29	1	76	4	11	3	16	7	9	.241	.293	.296	.589
2014	Charltt	AAA	110	437	128	19	6	7	(-	-)	180	60	57	67	36	0	84	5	10	6	16	4	15	.293	.349	.412	.761
2014	CWS	AL	28	100	25	5	0	0	(0	0)	30	6	5	5	3	0	25	0	0	1	1	1	1	.250	.269	.300	.569

Gaby Sanchez

Bats: R **Throws:** R **Pos:** 1B-96;PH-60;DH-3;RF-1 GABB-ee **Ht:** 6'1" **Wt:** 235 **Born:** 9/2/1983 **Age:** 31

								BATTING													RUNNING			AVERAGES			
Year	Team	Lg	G	AB	H	2B	3B	HR	(Hm	Rd)	TB	R	RBI	RC	TBB	IBB	SO	HBP	SH	SF	SB	CS	GDP	Avg	OBP	Slg	OPS
2008	Fla	NL	5	8	3	2	0	0	(0	0)	5	0	1	2	0	0	2	0	0	0	0	0	0	.375	.375	.625	1.000
2009	Fla	NL	21	21	5	0	0	2	(2	0)	11	2	3	3	2	0	3	0	0	0	0	0	1	.238	.304	.524	.828
2010	Fla	NL	151	572	156	37	3	19	(7	12)	256	72	85	88	57	2	101	5	3	6	5	0	14	.273	.341	.448	.788
2011	Fla	NL	159	572	152	35	0	19	(11	8)	244	72	78	77	74	4	97	6	2	7	3	1	18	.266	.352	.427	.779
2012	2 Tms	NL	105	299	65	16	0	7	(1	6)	102	30	30	21	25	2	56	1	0	1	1	0	13	.217	.279	.341	.620
2013	Pit	NL	136	264	67	18	0	7	(1	6)	106	29	36	38	44	1	51	4	0	7	1	0	3	.254	.361	.402	.762
2014	Pit	NL	123	262	60	18	1	7	(1	6)	101	31	33	23	23	0	58	2	0	3	2	0	6	.229	.293	.385	.679
12	Mia	NL	55	183	37	10	0	3	(1	2)	56	12	17	10	12	1	36	0	0	1	0	0	7	.202	.250	.306	.556
12	Pit	NL	50	116	28	6	0	4	(0	4)	46	18	13	11	13	1	20	1	0	0	1	0	6	.241	.323	.397	.720
	Postseason		2	2	0	0	0	0	(0	0)	0	0	0	0	0	0	0	0	0	0	0	0	1	.000	.000	.000	.000
	7 ML YEARS		700	1998	508	126	4	61	(23	38)	825	236	266	252	225	9	368	18	5	24	12	1	55	.254	.332	.413	.744

Hector Sanchez

Bats: B **Throws:** R **Pos:** C-45;PH-27;1B-1 **Ht:** 6'0" **Wt:** 235 **Born:** 11/17/1989 **Age:** 25

								BATTING													RUNNING			AVERAGES			
Year	Team	Lg	G	AB	H	2B	3B	HR	(Hm	Rd)	TB	R	RBI	RC	TBB	IBB	SO	HBP	SH	SF	SB	CS	GDP	Avg	OBP	Slg	OPS
2014	Fresno*	AAA	7	19	3	0	0	1	(-	-)	6	1	3	1	1	0	3	0	0	0	0	0	0	.158	.200	.316	.516
2011	SF	NL	13	31	8	2	0	0	(0	0)	10	0	1	2	3	0	6	0	0	0	0	0	1	.258	.324	.323	.646
2012	SF	NL	74	218	61	15	0	3	(1	2)	85	22	34	22	5	0	52	1	0	3	0	0	8	.280	.295	.390	.685
2013	SF	NL	63	129	32	4	0	3	(0	3)	45	8	19	14	7	0	29	3	0	1	0	0	1	.248	.300	.349	.649
2014	SF	NL	66	163	32	8	0	3	(1	2)	49	8	28	12	8	1	55	2	0	4	0	1	2	.196	.237	.301	.538
	Postseason		4	11	1	0	0	0	(0	0)	1	1	0	1	2	0	7	0	0	0	0	0	0	.091	.231	.091	.322
	4 ML YEARS		216	541	133	29	0	9	(2	7)	189	38	82	50	23	1	142	6	0	8	0	1	12	.246	.280	.349	.630

Tony Sanchez

Bats: R **Throws:** R **Pos:** C-20;PH-5;DH-1 **Ht:** 5'11" **Wt:** 225 **Born:** 5/20/1988 **Age:** 27

								BATTING													RUNNING			AVERAGES			
Year	Team	Lg	G	AB	H	2B	3B	HR	(Hm	Rd)	TB	R	RBI	RC	TBB	IBB	SO	HBP	SH	SF	SB	CS	GDP	Avg	OBP	Slg	OPS
2010	Bradtn	A+	59	207	65	17	0	4	(-	-)	94	31	35	42	28	1	41	11	0	4	2	1	4	.314	.416	.454	.870
2011	Altna	AA	118	402	97	14	1	5	(-	-)	128	46	44	48	47	2	76	14	4	2	5	5	13	.241	.340	.318	.658
2012	Altna	AA	40	141	39	14	1	0	(-	-)	55	22	17	21	18	0	33	3	0	0	1	1	3	.277	.370	.390	.760
2012	Indy	AAA	63	206	48	12	0	8	(-	-)	84	21	26	28	23	0	46	3	2	2	0	0	3	.233	.316	.408	.724
2013	Indy	AAA	76	260	75	26	0	10	(-	-)	131	35	42	49	28	2	60	6	0	2	0	0	10	.288	.360	.504	.072
2013	Altna	AA	4	17	3	1	0	0	(-	-)	4	2	0	0	0	0	3	0	0	0	0	0	0	.176	.176	.235	.412
2014	Indy	AAA	81	268	63	17	0	11	(-	-)	113	30	45	40	38	0	76	4	1	2	0	0	9	.235	.337	.422	.758
2013	Pit	NL	22	60	14	4	0	2	(1	1)	24	9	5	4	3	0	14	2	0	1	0	0	2	.233	.288	.400	.688
2014	Pit	NL	26	75	20	1	0	2	(0	2)	27	3	13	9	3	0	28	1	0	1	0	0	0	.267	.300	.360	.660
	2 ML YEARS		48	135	34	5	0	4	(1	3)	51	12	18	13	6	0	42	3	0	2	0	0	2	.252	.295	.378	.672

Pablo Sandoval

Bats: B **Throws:** R **Pos:** 3B-151;DH-3;PH-3 **Ht:** 5'11" **Wt:** 245 **Born:** 8/11/1986 **Age:** 28

								BATTING													RUNNING			AVERAGES			
Year	Team	Lg	G	AB	H	2B	3B	HR	(Hm	Rd)	TB	R	RBI	RC	TBB	IBB	SO	HBP	SH	SF	SB	CS	GDP	Avg	OBP	Slg	OPS
2008	SF	NL	41	145	50	10	1	3	(1	2)	71	24	24	24	4	1	14	1	0	4	0	0	6	.345	.357	.490	.847
2009	SF	NL	153	572	189	44	5	25	(13	12)	318	79	90	113	52	13	83	4	0	5	5	5	10	.330	.387	.556	.943
2010	SF	NL	152	563	151	34	3	13	(9	4)	230	61	63	55	47	12	81	1	0	5	3	2	26	.268	.323	.409	.732
2011	SF	NL	117	426	134	26	3	23	(7	16)	235	55	70	72	32	9	63	0	1	7	2	4	12	.315	.357	.552	.909
2012	SF	NL	108	396	112	25	2	12	(5	7)	177	59	63	60	38	4	59	1	0	7	1	1	13	.283	.342	.447	.789
2013	SF	NL	141	525	146	27	2	14	(6	8)	219	52	79	78	47	5	79	6	0	6	0	0	19	.278	.341	.417	.758
2014	SF	NL	157	588	164	26	3	16	(9	7)	244	68	73	78	39	6	85	4	0	7	0	0	16	.279	.324	.415	.739
	Postseason		22	83	27	6	0	6	(3	3)	51	9	15	16	5	2	11	0	0	1	0	0	5	.325	.360	.614	.974
	7 ML YEARS		869	3215	946	192	19	106	(52	54)	1494	398	462	480	259	50	464	17	1	41	11	12	102	.294	.346	.465	.811

Jerry Sands

Bats: R Throws: R Pos: PH-8;DH-7   Ht: 6'4" Wt: 220 Born: 9/28/1987 Age: 27

Year	Team	Lg	G	AB	H	2B	3B	HR	Hm	Rd	TB	R	RBI	RC	TBB	IBB	SO	HBP	SH	SF	SB	CS	GDP	Avg	OBP	Slg	OPS
2014	Drham*	AAA	54	190	51	12	0	9	-	-	90	32	36	33	26	0	53	0	0	3	1	0	5	.268	.352	.474	.825
2011	LAD	NL	61	198	50	15	0	4	2	2	77	20	26	25	26	0	51	1	2	1	3	3	5	.253	.338	.389	.727
2012	LAD	NL	9	23	4	2	0	0	0	0	6	2	1	1	1	0	9	0	0	0	0	0	0	.174	.208	.261	.469
2014	TB	AL	12	21	4	0	0	1	1	0	7	1	4	1	0	0	6	1	0	0	0	0	2	.190	.227	.333	.561
	3 ML YEARS		82	242	58	17	0	5	3	2	90	23	31	27	26	0	66	2	2	1	3	3	7	.240	.317	.372	.689

Carlos Santana

Bats: B Throws: R Pos: 1B-94;3B-26;DH-22;C-11;PH-1   Ht: 5'11" Wt: 210 Born: 4/8/1986 Age: 29

Year	Team	Lg	G	AB	H	2B	3B	HR	Hm	Rd	TB	R	RBI	RC	TBB	IBB	SO	HBP	SH	SF	SB	CS	GDP	Avg	OBP	Slg	OPS
2010	Cle	AL	46	150	39	13	0	6	2	4	70	23	22	25	37	2	29	1	0	4	3	0	3	.260	.401	.467	.868
2011	Cle	AL	155	552	132	35	2	27	14	13	252	84	79	81	97	7	133	2	0	7	5	3	15	.239	.351	.457	.808
2012	Cle	AL	143	507	128	27	2	18	7	11	213	72	76	77	91	4	101	3	0	8	3	5	21	.252	.365	.420	.785
2013	Cle	AL	154	541	145	39	1	20	12	8	246	75	74	93	93	6	110	4	0	4	3	1	7	.268	.377	.455	.832
2014	Cle	AL	152	541	125	25	0	27	13	14	231	68	85	88	113	5	124	3	0	3	5	2	13	.231	.365	.427	.792
	Postseason		1	4	2	1	0	0	0	0	3	0	0	0	0	0	1	0	0	0	0	0	0	.500	.500	.750	1.250
	5 ML YEARS		650	2291	569	139	5	98	48	50	1012	322	336	364	431	24	497	13	0	26	19	11	59	.248	.367	.442	.809

Danny Santana

Bats: B Throws: R Pos: CF-69;SS-34;DH-3;PH-3;PR-1   Ht: 5'11" Wt: 175 Born: 11/7/1990 Age: 24

Year	Team	Lg	G	AB	H	2B	3B	HR	Hm	Rd	TB	R	RBI	RC	TBB	IBB	SO	HBP	SH	SF	SB	CS	GDP	Avg	OBP	Slg	OPS
2010	Beloit	A	40	130	31	4	3	0	-	-	41	14	11	12	7	0	40	3	2	2	10	4	2	.238	.289	.315	.604
2010	Elizab	R+	30	140	37	8	1	4	-	-	59	23	16	16	3	0	30	1	0	0	5	4	0	.264	.285	.421	.706
2011	Beloit	A	104	365	90	15	5	7	-	-	136	55	41	41	25	0	98	4	10	5	24	15	6	.247	.298	.373	.671
2012	FtMyrs	A+	121	507	145	21	9	8	-	-	208	70	60	69	29	2	77	5	3	3	17	11	4	.286	.329	.410	.739
2013	NwBrit	AA	131	539	160	22	10	2	-	-	208	66	45	72	24	1	94	8	11	5	30	13	8	.297	.333	.386	.719
2014	Roch	AAA	24	97	26	7	2	0	-	-	37	15	7	12	6	0	28	0	2	0	4	1	1	.268	.311	.381	.692
2014	FtMyrs	A+	3	11	0	0	0	0	-	-	0	0	0	0	1	0	3	0	0	0	1	0	0	.000	.083	.000	.083
2014	Min	AL	101	405	129	27	7	7	3	4	191	70	40	72	19	0	98	3	2	1	20	4	3	.319	.353	.472	.824

Domingo Santana

Bats: R Throws: R Pos: LF-3;RF-2;PH-1   Ht: 6'5" Wt: 225 Born: 8/5/1992 Age: 22

Year	Team	Lg	G	AB	H	2B	3B	HR	Hm	Rd	TB	R	RBI	RC	TBB	IBB	SO	HBP	SH	SF	SB	CS	GDP	Avg	OBP	Slg	OPS
2010	Lakwd	A	49	165	30	10	0	3	-	-	49	27	16	17	29	0	76	6	0	2	5	6	2	.182	.322	.297	.619
2010	Wmspt	A-	54	186	44	9	0	5	-	-	68	28	20	23	23	1	73	5	0	0	4	4	6	.237	.336	.366	.702
2011	Lakwd	A	96	350	94	29	4	7	-	-	152	45	32	54	26	3	120	15	0	0	4	1	3	.269	.345	.434	.780
2011	Lxngtn	A	17	68	26	4	0	5	-	-	45	13	21	18	6	0	15	2	0	0	1	0	2	.382	.447	.662	1.109
2012	Lancst	A+	119	457	138	26	6	23	-	-	245	87	97	95	55	0	148	9	0	4	7	1	10	.302	.385	.536	.921
2013	CpChr	AA	112	416	105	23	2	25	-	-	207	72	64	73	46	1	139	13	0	1	12	5	7	.252	.345	.498	.842
2014	OKCity	AAA	120	443	131	27	2	16	-	-	210	63	81	83	64	1	149	2	0	4	6	4	3	.296	.384	.474	.858
2014	Hou	AL	6	17	0	0	0	0	0	0	0	1	0	0	1	0	14	0	0	0	0	0	0	.000	.056	.000	.056

Ervin Santana

Pitches: R Bats: R Pos: SP-31   Ht: 6'2" Wt: 185 Born: 12/12/1982 Age: 32

Year	Team	Lg	G	GS	CG	GF	IP	BFP	H	R	ER	HR	SH	SF	HB	TBB	IBB	SO	WP	Bk	W	L	Pct	Sh	Sv-Op	Hld	ERC	ERA
2014	Gwnntt*	AAA	1	1	0	0	5.1	28	8	6	5	1	0	0	0	4	0	3	1	0	1	0	1.000	0	0- -	-	9.29	8.44
2005	LAA	AL	23	23	1	0	133.2	583	139	73	69	17	1	4	8	47	2	99	4	0	12	8	.600	1	0-0	0	4.51	4.65
2006	LAA	AL	33	33	0	0	204.0	846	181	106	97	21	4	10	11	70	2	141	10	2	16	8	.667	0	0-0	0	3.51	4.28
2007	LAA	AL	28	26	0	1	150.0	675	174	103	96	26	3	2	8	58	3	126	7	0	7	14	.333	0	0-0	0	5.69	5.76
2008	LAA	AL	32	32	2	0	219.0	897	189	88	85	23	3	5	8	47	2	214	5	1	16	7	.696	1	0-0	0	3.00	3.49
2009	LAA	AL	24	23	1	0	139.2	614	159	83	78	24	2	1	10	47	4	107	4	0	8	8	.500	2	0-0	1	5.47	5.03
2010	LAA	AL	33	33	4	0	222.2	954	221	104	97	27	8	8	12	73	2	169	11	1	17	10	.630	1	0-0	0	4.10	3.92
2011	LAA	AL	33	33	4	0	228.2	949	207	95	86	26	4	7	8	72	4	178	10	1	11	12	.478	1	0-0	0	3.45	3.38
2012	LAA	AL	30	30	1	0	178.0	764	165	109	102	**39**	2	2	9	61	2	133	4	0	9	13	.409	1	0-0	0	4.38	5.16
2013	KC	AL	32	32	0	0	211.0	859	190	85	76	26	2	3	6	51	3	161	6	0	9	10	.474	0	0-0	0	3.19	3.24
2014	Atl	NL	31	31	0	0	196.0	817	193	90	86	16	12	**12**	4	63	4	179	9	0	14	10	.583	0	0-0	0	3.68	3.95
	Postseason		8	2	0	3	22.2	101	21	17	14	4	1	1	3	9	1	14	0	0	2	2	.500	0	0-0	0	4.55	5.56
	10 ML YEARS		299	296	14	1	1882.2	7958	1827	937	872	245	41	54	84	589	28	1507	70	5	119	100	.543	7	0-0	1	3.95	4.17

Hector Santiago

Pitches: L Bats: R Pos: SP-24; RP-6   Ht: 6'0" Wt: 210 Born: 12/16/1987 Age: 27

Year	Team	Lg	G	GS	CG	GF	IP	BFP	H	R	ER	HR	SH	SF	HB	TBB	IBB	SO	WP	Bk	W	L	Pct	Sh	Sv-Op	Hld	ERC	ERA
2014	Salt Lk*	AAA	3	3	0	0	14.0	71	23	12	10	0	1	0	1	7	0	9	0	0	1	1	.500	0	0- -	-	7.91	6.43
2011	CWS	AL	2	0	0	1	5.1	18	1	0	0	0	0	0	0	1	2	1	0	0	0	0	-	0	0-0	0	0.16	0.00
2012	CWS	AL	42	4	0	19	70.1	306	54	26	26	10	2	1	7	40	1	79	5	2	4	1	.800	0	4-6	4	4.11	3.33
2013	CWS	AL	34	23	0	4	149.0	656	137	69	59	17	3	3	15	72	2	137	2	0	4	9	.308	0	0-0	0	4.43	3.56
2014	LAA	AL	30	24	0	2	127.1	544	120	63	53	15	1	3	3	53	1	108	5	1	6	9	.400	0	0-0	1	4.02	3.75
	4 ML YEARS		108	51	0	26	352.0	1524	312	158	138	42	6	7	25	166	7	326	13	3	14	19	.424	0	4-6	5	4.12	3.53

Ramon Santiago

Bats: B **Throws:** R **Pos:** 3B-28;2B-20;SS-20;PH-13;PR-2;LF-1   **Ht:** 5'11" **Wt:** 175 **Born:** 8/31/1979 **Age:** 35

								BATTING														RUNNING			AVERAGES			
Year	Team	Lg	G	AB	H	2B	3B	HR	(Hm	Rd)	TB	R	RBI	RC	TBB	IBB	SO	HBP	SH	SF	SB	CS	GDP	Avg	OBP	Slg	OPS
2002	Det	AL	65	222	54	5	5	4	(3	1)	81	33	20	23	13	0	48	8	4	2	8	5	2	.243	.306	.365	.671
2003	Det	AL	141	444	100	18	1	2	(1	1)	126	41	29	38	33	0	66	10	18	2	10	4	9	.225	.292	.284	.576
2004	Sea	AL	19	39	7	1	0	0	(0	0)	8	8	2	1	3	0	3	1	2	0	0	0	1	.179	.256	.205	.461
2005	Sea	AL	8	8	1	0	0	0	(0	0)	1	2	0	1	1	0	2	3	1	0	0	0	0	.125	.417	.125	.542
2006	Det	AL	43	80	18	1	1	0	(0	0)	21	9	3	3	4	0	14	1	4	0	2	0	1	.225	.244	.263	.506
2007	Det	AL	32	67	19	5	1	0	(0	0)	26	10	7	11	1	0	10	3	3	0	3	0	0	.284	.324	.388	.712
2008	Det	AL	58	124	35	6	2	4	(4	0)	57	30	18	26	22	0	17	5	5	0	1	0	1	.282	.411	.460	.870
2009	Det	AL	93	262	70	6	2	7	(4	3)	101	29	35	33	17	1	57	4	10	3	1	2	3	.267	.318	.385	.704
2010	Det	AL	112	320	84	9	1	3	(3	0)	104	38	22	37	30	0	56	7	8	2	2	2	6	.263	.337	.325	.662
2011	Det	AL	101	258	67	11	3	5	(3	2)	99	29	30	25	17	0	38	4	11	4	0	0	5	.260	.311	.384	.695
2012	Det	AL	93	228	47	7	1	2	(1	1)	62	19	17	17	20	1	39	5	5	1	1	0	7	.206	.283	.272	.555
2013	Det	AL	80	205	46	8	1	1	(1	0)	59	27	14	14	21	0	32	1	6	1	0	1	3	.224	.298	.288	.586
2014	Cin	NL	75	179	44	8	0	2	(1	1)	58	20	17	28	24	0	38	3	7	1	2	1	1	.246	.343	.324	.667
	Postseason		22	51	12	2	0	0	(0	0)	14	1	2	3	1	0	9	0	3	0	0	0	0	.235	.250	.275	.525
	13 ML YEARS		920	2436	592	85	18	30	(21	9)	803	295	214	257	203	2	420	55	84	16	30	15	39	.243	.314	.330	.643

Sergio Santos

Pitches: R **Bats:** R **Pos:** RP-26   **Ht:** 6'3" **Wt:** 215 **Born:** 7/4/1983 **Age:** 31

			HOW MUCH HE PITCHED						WHAT HE GAVE UP												THE RESULTS						
Year	Team	Lg	G	GS	CG	GF	IP	BFP	H	R	ER	HR	SH	SF	HB	TBB	IBB	SO	WP	Bk	W	L	Pct	Sh	Sv-Op	Hld	ERC	ERA
2014	NHam*	AA	2	1	0	0	2.0	11	4	4	4	1	0	0	0	1	0	3	0	0	0	0	-	0	0--	-	14.72	18.00
2014	Buffalo*	AAA	11	0	0	6	10.2	43	3	1	0	0	0	0	1	6	0	16	0	0	1	0	1.000	0	2--	-	1.07	0.00
2010	CWS	AL	56	0	0	13	51.2	235	53	18	17	2	2	1	3	26	3	56	8	0	2	2	.500	0	1-3	14	4.22	2.96
2011	CWS	AL	63	0	0	50	63.1	260	41	25	25	6	1	1	3	29	5	92	5	0	4	5	.444	0	30-36	2	2.46	3.55
2012	Tor	AL	6	0	0	4	5.0	24	6	5	5	1	0	1	0	4	0	4	1	0	0	1	.000	0	2-4	0	7.98	9.00
2013	Tor	AL	29	0	0	6	25.2	90	11	5	5	1	0	2	0	4	2	28	1	0	1	1	.500	0	1-3	8	0.69	1.75
2014	Tor	AL	26	0	0	14	21.0	106	28	22	20	5	0	2	0	18	2	29	4	0	0	3	.000	0	5-8	0	9.19	8.57
	5 ML YEARS		180	0	0	87	166.2	715	139	75	72	15	3	7	6	81	12	209	19	0	7	12	.368	0	39-54	24	3.43	3.89

Luis Sardinas

sar-DEEN-yas

Bats: B **Throws:** R **Pos:** 2B-19;SS-13;3B-7;DH-5;PH-4;PR-2   **Ht:** 6'1" **Wt:** 150 **Born:** 5/16/1993 **Age:** 22

								BATTING														RUNNING			AVERAGES			
Year	Team	Lg	G	AB	H	2B	3B	HR	(Hm	Rd)	TB	R	RBI	RC	TBB	IBB	SO	HBP	SH	SF	SB	CS	GDP	Avg	OBP	Slg	OPS
2010	Rngrs	R	26	103	32	4	0	0	(-	-)	36	22	8	15	7	0	15	2	6	1	8	2	2	.311	.363	.350	.712
2011	Rngrs	R	14	52	16	2	1	0	(-	-)	20	11	7	8	4	0	10	2	0	2	2	1	0	.308	.367	.385	.751
2012	Hkry	A	96	374	109	14	2	2	(-	-)	133	65	30	52	29	0	52	4	2	3	32	9	5	.291	.346	.356	.702
2013	MrtlBh	A+	97	383	114	15	3	1	(-	-)	138	69	31	55	32	1	54	7	5	5	27	8	5	.298	.358	.360	.719
2013	Frisco	AA	29	135	35	4	0	1	(-	-)	42	12	15	12	4	0	21	1	1	0	5	2	4	.259	.286	.311	.597
2014	Frisco	AA	21	87	22	5	1	0	(-	-)	29	12	9	7	3	0	12	0	0	0	1	1	1	.253	.278	.333	.611
2014	RdRck	AAA	60	262	76	15	2	1	(-	-)	98	39	28	31	8	0	39	0	2	1	9	4	6	.290	.310	.374	.684
2014	Tex	AL	43	115	30	6	0	0	(0	0)	36	12	8	9	5	0	21	2	3	0	5	1	5	.261	.303	.313	.616

Josh Satin

Bats: R **Throws:** R **Pos:** PH-18;1B-8;3B-1   SAT-inn   **Ht:** 6'2" **Wt:** 215 **Born:** 12/23/1984 **Age:** 30

								BATTING														RUNNING			AVERAGES			
Year	Team	Lg	G	AB	H	2B	3B	HR	(Hm	Rd)	TB	R	RBI	RC	TBB	IBB	SO	HBP	SH	SF	SB	CS	GDP	Avg	OBP	Slg	OPS
2014	LsVgs*	AAA	100	374	108	27	1	9	(-	-)	164	50	49	66	61	0	79	1	0	4	1	3	14	.289	.386	.439	.825
2011	NYM	NL	25	25	5	1	0	0	(0	0)	6	3	2	1	1	0	11	1	0	0	0	0	1	.200	.259	.240	.499
2012	NYM	NL	1	1	0	0	0	0	(0	0)	0	0	0	0	0	0	1	0	0	0	0	0	0	.000	.000	.000	.000
2013	NYM	NL	75	190	53	15	0	3	(3	0)	77	23	17	27	30	2	56	0	0	1	1	1	4	.279	.376	.405	.781
2014	NYM	NL	25	35	3	2	0	0	(0	0)	5	2	3	2	6	0	14	2	0	0	0	0	2	.086	.256	.143	.399
	4 ML YEARS		116	251	61	18	0	3	(3	0)	88	28	22	30	37	2	82	3	0	1	1	1	7	.243	.346	.351	.696

Joe Saunders

Pitches: L **Bats:** L **Pos:** SP-8; RP-6   **Ht:** 6'3" **Wt:** 215 **Born:** 6/16/1981 **Age:** 34

			HOW MUCH HE PITCHED						WHAT HE GAVE UP												THE RESULTS						
Year	Team	Lg	G	GS	CG	GF	IP	BFP	H	R	ER	HR	SH	SF	HB	TBB	IBB	SO	WP	Bk	W	L	Pct	Sh	Sv-Op	Hld	ERC	ERA
2014	Frisco*	AA	2	2	0	0	9.1	41	11	7	6	3	3	0	1	2	0	6	0	0	0	1	.000	0	0--	-	6.45	5.79
2014	RdRck*	AAA	2	2	0	0	12.0	52	15	3	3	1	0	0	0	5	0	8	1	0	0	1	.000	0	0--	-	5.79	2.25
2014	Omha*	AAA	4	4	0	0	18.2	87	27	17	14	4	1	3	0	5	0	6	0	0	1	2	.333	0	0--	-	7.20	6.75
2014	Norfolk*	AAA	10	0	0	3	12.0	51	11	2	2	0	0	1	0	6	2	8	0	0	0	0	.000	0	0--	-	3.07	1.50
2005	LAA	AL	2	2	0	0	9.1	41	10	8	8	3	0	0	0	4	0	4	1	0	0	0	-	0	0-0	0	6.27	7.71
2006	LAA	AL	13	13	0	0	70.2	302	71	42	37	6	1	2	1	29	1	51	2	1	7	3	.700	0	0-0	0	4.13	4.71
2007	LAA	AL	18	18	0	0	107.1	473	129	56	53	11	0	5	1	34	1	69	3	0	8	5	.615	0	0-0	0	4.96	4.44
2008	LAA	AL	31	31	1	0	198.0	807	187	82	75	21	5	2	6	53	2	103	3	0	17	7	.708	1	0-0	0	3.49	3.41
2009	LAA	AL	31	31	1	0	186.0	805	202	102	95	29	6	4	6	64	2	101	5	1	16	7	.696	1	0-0	0	4.91	4.60
2010	2 Tms		33	33	3	0	203.1	880	232	120	101	25	6	8	5	64	1	114	6	0	9	17	.346	1	0-0	0	4.86	4.47
2011	Ari	NL	33	33	1	0	212.0	874	210	94	87	29	9	5	3	67	4	108	3	0	12	13	.480	1	0-0	0	4.10	3.69
2012	2 Tms		28	28	1	0	174.2	745	195	88	79	21	7	3	2	39	2	112	3	0	9	13	.409	1	0-0	0	4.54	4.07
2013	Sea	AL	32	32	2	0	183.0	820	232	117	107	25	4	3	4	61	5	107	5	0	11	16	.407	0	0-0	0	5.74	5.26
2014	2 Tms	AL	14	8	0	3	43.0	215	65	37	32	9	3	2	0	24	1	23	0	0	0	5	.000	0	0--	-	9.06	6.70
	10 LAA	AL	20	20	2	0	120.2	522	135	70	62	14	5	5	1	45	1	64	3	0	6	10	.375	1	0-0	0	4.88	4.62

Year	Team	Lg	G	GS	CG	GF	IP	BFP	H	R	ER	HR	SH	SF	HB	TBB	IBB	SO	WP	Bk	W	L	Pct	Sh	Sv-Op	Hld	ERC	ERA
							HOW MUCH HE PITCHED						**WHAT HE GAVE UP**											**THE RESULTS**					
10	Ari	NL	13	13	1	0	82.2	358	97	50	39	11	1	3	4	19	0	50	3	0	3	7	.300	0	0-0	0	4.84	4.25
12	Ari	NL	21	21	1	0	130.0	561	146	68	61	17	5	2	2	31	1	89	2	0	6	10	.375	1	0-0	0	4.36	4.22
12	Bal	AL	7	7	0	0	44.2	184	49	20	18	4	2	1	0	8	1	23	1	0	3	3	.500	0	0-0	0	3.71	3.63
14	Tex	AL	8	8	0	0	39.2	198	62	32	27	8	0	3	1	20	0	22	0	0	0	5	.000	0	0-0	0	9.00	6.13
14	Bal	AL	6	0	0	3	3.1	17	3	5	5	1	0	0	1	4	1	1	0	0	0	-		0	0-0	0	9.65	13.50
	Postseason		6	6	0	0	29.1	130	32	14	14	1	2	0	1	17	0	17	0	0	1	1	.500	0	0-0	0	5.14	4.30
	10 ML YEARS		235	229	9	3	1387.1	5962	1533	746	674	179	40	35	30	439	19	792	31	2	89	86	.509	3	0-0	0	4.67	4.37

Michael Saunders

Bats: L Throws: R Pos: RF-68;CF-12;PH-5;PR-4;DH-2;LF-1   Ht: 6'4" Wt: 225 Born: 11/19/1986 Age: 28

Year	Team	Lg	G	AB	H	2B	3B	HR	(Hm	Rd)	TB	R	RBI	RC	TBB	IBB	SO	HBP	SH	SF	SB	CS	GDP	Avg	OBP	Slg	OPS
								BATTING													**RUNNING**			**AVERAGES**			
2014	Tacom*	AAA	15	55	18	3	1	1	(-	-)	26	11	9	13	16	0	15	0	0	0	0	0	0	.327	.479	.473	.952
2009	Sea	AL	46	122	27	1	3	0	(0	0)	34	13	4	8	6	0	40	0	1	0	4	1	1	.221	.258	.279	.537
2010	Sea	AL	100	289	61	11	2	10	(5	5)	106	29	33	31	35	0	84	0	2	1	6	3	1	.211	.295	.367	.662
2011	Sea	AL	58	161	24	5	0	2	(1	1)	35	16	8	2	12	1	56	0	5	1	6	2	1	.149	.207	.217	.424
2012	Sea	AL	139	507	125	31	3	19	(8	11)	219	71	57	67	43	0	132	1	1	1	21	4	6	.247	.306	.432	.738
2013	Sea	AL	132	406	96	23	3	12	(5	7)	161	59	46	49	54	4	118	1	1	6	13	5	6	.236	.323	.397	.720
2014	Sea	AL	78	231	63	11	3	8	(4	4)	104	38	34	37	26	1	59	0	2	4	4	5	2	.273	.341	.450	.791
	6 ML YEARS		553	1716	396	82	14	51	(23	28)	659	226	182	194	176	6	489	2	12	13	54	20	17	.231	.301	.384	.685

Joe Savery

Pitches: L Bats: L Pos: RP-3   SAVE-uh-ree   Ht: 6'3" Wt: 235 Born: 11/4/1985 Age: 29

Year	Team	Lg	G	GS	CG	GF	IP	BFP	H	R	ER	HR	SH	SF	HB	TBB	IBB	SO	WP	Bk	W	L	Pct	Sh	Sv-Op	Hld	ERC	ERA
							HOW MUCH HE PITCHED						**WHAT HE GAVE UP**											**THE RESULTS**					
2014	Scrmto*	AAA	43	0	0	7	44.1	183	37	15	14	4	2	1	1	17	1	45	2	0	7	1	.875	0	2--	-	3.14	2.84
2011	Phi	NL	4	0	0	1	2.2	9	1	0	0	0	1	0	0	0	0	2	0	0	0	-		0	0-0	0	0.31	0.00
2012	Phi	NL	19	0	0	8	25.0	108	26	17	15	4	2	2	1	8	1	16	0	1	1	2	.333	0	0-0	1	4.49	5.40
2013	Phi	NL	18	0	0	8	20.0	86	15	11	7	1	1	1	0	11	0	14	0	0	2	0	1.000	0	0-0	1	2.89	3.15
2014	Oak	AL	3	0	0	2	4.0	15	3	0	0	0	0	0	0	1	0	0	0	0	0	-		0	0-0	0	1.79	0.00
	4 ML YEARS		44	0	0	19	51.2	218	45	28	22	5	4	3	1	20	1	32	0	1	3	2	.600	0	0-0	3	3.33	3.83

Rob Scahill

Pitches: R Bats: L Pos: RP-12   SKAY-hill   Ht: 6'2" Wt: 220 Born: 2/15/1987 Age: 28

Year	Team	Lg	G	GS	CG	GF	IP	BFP	H	R	ER	HR	SH	SF	HB	TBB	IBB	SO	WP	Bk	W	L	Pct	Sh	Sv-Op	Hld	ERC	ERA
							HOW MUCH HE PITCHED						**WHAT HE GAVE UP**											**THE RESULTS**					
2014	ColSpr*	AAA	41	0	0	16	58.1	254	59	32	28	6	2	3	5	18	0	53	3	0	2	3	.400	0	2--	-	4.09	4.32
2012	Col	NL	6	0	0	3	8.2	33	7	1	1	0	0	0	0	3	0	4	0	0	0	0	-	0	0-0	0	2.43	1.04
2013	Col	NL	23	0	0	6	33.1	149	40	19	19	5	3	0	4	9	1	20	1	0	1	0	1.000	0	0-0	1	5.55	5.13
2014	Col	NL	12	0	0	3	15.0	72	17	8	8	3	0	2	1	9	2	11	0	0	1	0	1.000	0	0-1	0	6.37	4.80
	3 ML YEARS		41	0	0	12	57.0	254	64	28	28	8	3	2	5	21	3	35	1	0	2	0	1.000	0	0-1	1	5.25	4.42

Jordan Schafer

Bats: L Throws: L Pos: LF-49;PH-28;CF-20;PR-12;RF-6;DH-1   Ht: 6'1" Wt: 205 Born: 9/4/1986 Age: 28

Year	Team	Lg	G	AB	H	2B	3B	HR	(Hm	Rd)	TB	R	RBI	RC	TBB	IBB	SO	HBP	SH	SF	SB	CS	GDP	Avg	OBP	Slg	OPS
								BATTING													**RUNNING**			**AVERAGES**			
2009	Atl	NL	50	167	34	8	0	2	(0	2)	48	18	8	11	27	3	63	0	0	1	2	1	2	.204	.313	.287	.600
2011	2 Tms	NL	82	302	73	10	3	2	(0	2)	95	46	13	34	28	0	70	2	4	1	22	4	4	.242	.309	.315	.624
2012	Hou	NL	106	313	66	10	2	4	(4	0)	92	40	23	32	36	3	106	3	6	1	27	9	3	.211	.297	.294	.591
2013	Atl	NL	94	231	57	8	3	3	(0	3)	80	32	21	31	29	2	73	0	5	0	22	6	1	.247	.331	.346	.677
2014	2 Tms	NL	104	210	50	9	1	1	(0	1)	64	26	15	20	22	1	48	0	8	0	30	7	1	.238	.310	.305	.615
11	Atl	NL	52	196	47	6	3	1	(0	1)	62	32	7	22	18	0	42	1	4	0	15	4	3	.240	.307	.316	.623
11	Hou	NL	30	106	26	4	0	1	(0	1)	33	14	6	12	10	0	28	1	0	1	7	0	1	.245	.314	.311	.625
14	Atl	NL	63	80	13	4	0	0	(0	0)	17	9	2	3	10	1	20	0	3	0	15	2	1	.163	.256	.213	.468
14	Min	AL	41	130	37	5	1	1	(0	1)	47	17	13	17	12	0	28	0	5	0	15	5	0	.285	.345	.362	.707
	Postseason		1	1	0	0	0	0	(0	0)	0	0	0	0	0	0	1	0	0	0	0	0	0	.000	.000	.000	.000
	5 ML YEARS		436	1223	280	45	9	12	(4	8)	379	162	80	128	142	9	360	5	23	3	103	27	11	.229	.311	.310	.621

Logan Schafer

Bats: L Throws: L Pos: PH-18;LF-17;RF-17;CF-14;PR-5   Ht: 6'1" Wt: 195 Born: 9/8/1986 Age: 28

Year	Team	Lg	G	AB	H	2B	3B	HR	(Hm	Rd)	TB	R	RBI	RC	TBB	IBB	SO	HBP	SH	SF	SB	CS	GDP	Avg	OBP	Slg	OPS
								BATTING													**RUNNING**			**AVERAGES**			
2014	BrvdCt*	A+	2	4	1	1	0	0	(-	-)	2	1	1	28	1	0	0	0	0	0	0	0	0	.250	.400	.500	.900
2014	Nashv*	AAA	41	161	44	13	4	3	(-	-)	74	27	18	27	21	0	33	0	2	1	4	1	1	.273	.355	.460	.815
2011	Mil	NL	8	3	1	0	0	0	(0	0)	1	1	0	0	1	0	1	0	1	0	0	0	0	.333	.500	.333	.833
2012	Mil	NL	16	23	7	1	2	0	(0	0)	12	3	5	4	1	0	3	0	0	1	0	1	0	.304	.304	.522	.842
2013	Mil	NL	134	298	63	15	3	4	(2	2)	96	29	33	31	25	1	60	3	11	0	7	1	5	.211	.279	.322	.601
2014	Mil	NL	65	116	21	9	1	0	(0	0)	32	13	8	11	15	3	27	1	3	1	2	1	0	.181	.278	.276	.554
	4 ML YEARS		223	440	92	25	6	4	(2	2)	141	46	46	46	42	4	91	4	15	2	9	3	5	.209	.283	.320	.603

Tanner Scheppers

Pitches: R Bats: R Pos: SP-4; RP-4   Ht: 6'4" Wt: 200 Born: 1/17/1987 Age: 28

		HOW MUCH HE PITCHED						WHAT HE GAVE UP										THE RESULTS						
Year Team	Lg	G	GS	CG	GF	IP	BFP	H	R	ER	HR	SH	SF	HB	TBB	IBB	SO	WP	Bk	W	L	Pct	Sh	Sv-Op	Hld	ERC	ERA
2014 Frisco*	AA	2	1	0	0	2.0	9	2	1	0	0	0	0	0	1	0	1	1	0	0	0	-	0	0- -	-	3.63	0.00
2014 RdRck*	AAA	3	1	0	0	3.2	19	7	5	5	3	0	0	0	1	0	3	0	0	0	0	-	0	0- -	-	15.67	12.27
2012 Tex	AL	39	0	0	13	32.1	152	47	18	16	6	3	1	2	9	3	30	4	0	1	1	.500	0	1-1	4	7.05	4.45
2013 Tex	AL	76	0	0	11	76.2	302	58	21	16	6	0	0	7	24	4	59	4	0	6	2	.750	0	1-3	27	2.71	1.88
2014 Tex	AL	8	4	0	0	23.0	111	31	24	23	6	0	1	3	10	0	17	2	0	1	0	1.000	0	0-0	1	8.21	9.00
3 ML YEARS		123	4	0	24	132.0	565	136	63	55	18	3	2	12	43	7	106	10	0	7	4	.636	0	2-4	32	4.57	3.75

Max Scherzer

Pitches: R Bats: R Pos: SP-33   SHERR-zer   Ht: 6'3" Wt: 220 Born: 7/27/1984 Age: 30

		HOW MUCH HE PITCHED						WHAT HE GAVE UP										THE RESULTS						
Year Team	Lg	G	GS	CG	GF	IP	BFP	H	R	ER	HR	SH	SF	HB	TBB	IBB	SO	WP	Bk	W	L	Pct	Sh	Sv-Op	Hld	ERC	ERA
2008 Ari	NL	16	7	0	2	56.0	237	48	24	19	5	4	2	5	21	1	66	2	0	0	4	.000	0	0-0	0	3.45	3.05
2009 Ari	NL	30	30	0	0	170.1	741	166	94	89	20	5	6	10	63	1	174	5	1	9	11	.450	0	0-0	0	4.12	4.12
2010 Det	AL	31	31	0	0	195.2	800	174	84	76	20	5	5	7	70	1	184	8	0	12	11	.522	0	0-0	0	3.56	3.50
2011 Det	AL	33	33	0	0	195.0	833	207	101	96	29	3	7	7	56	1	174	12	0	15	9	.625	0	0-0	0	4.48	4.43
2012 Det	AL	32	32	0	0	187.2	787	179	82	78	23	5	1	5	60	2	231	2	1	16	7	.696	0	0-0	0	3.77	3.74
2013 Det	AL	32	32	0	0	214.1	836	152	73	69	18	2	8	4	56	0	240	6	1	21	3	.875	0	0-0	0	2.07	2.90
2014 Det	AL	33	33	1	0	220.1	904	196	80	77	18	4	8	6	63	1	252	10	1	18	5	.783	1	0-0	0	3.04	3.15
Postseason		11	9	0	0	55.1	229	39	22	21	3	1	0	3	24	1	74	3	0	4	2	.667	0	0-0	1	2.51	3.42
7 ML YEARS		207	198	1	2	1239.1	5138	1122	538	493	133	28	37	44	389	7	1321	45	4	91	50	.645	1	0-0	0	3.43	3.58

Nate Schierholtz

SHEER-holtz

Bats: L Throws: R Pos: RF-87;PH-34;LF-4;CF-2;DH-1;PR-1   Ht: 6'2" Wt: 215 Born: 2/15/1984 Age: 31

		BATTING																		RUNNING			AVERAGES			
Year Team	Lg	G	AB	H	2B	3B	HR	(Hm	Rd)	TB	R	RBI	RC	TBB	IBB	SO	HBP	SH	SF	SB	CS	GDP	Avg	OBP	Slg	OPS
2014 Syrcse*	AAA	4	19	3	0	0	1	(-	-)	6	1	4	0	0	0	6	0	0	0	0	0	0	.158	.158	.316	.474
2007 SF	NL	39	112	34	5	3	0	(0	0)	45	9	10	14	2	0	19	1	0	2	3	1	0	.304	.316	.402	.718
2008 SF	NL	19	75	24	8	1	1	(1	0)	37	12	5	12	3	0	8	3	0	0	0	1	1	.320	.370	.493	.864
2009 SF	NL	116	285	76	19	2	5	(1	4)	114	33	29	35	16	3	58	1	0	6	3	1	5	.267	.302	.400	.702
2010 SF	NL	137	227	55	13	3	3	(0	3)	83	34	17	26	20	5	38	3	1	1	4	5	3	.242	.311	.366	.676
2011 SF	NL	115	335	93	22	1	9	(4	5)	144	42	41	46	21	3	61	4	0	2	7	4	5	.278	.326	.430	.756
2012 2 Tms	NL	114	241	62	8	5	6	(0	6)	98	20	21	31	23	2	46	1	1	3	3	2	1	.257	.321	.407	.728
2013 ChC	NL	137	462	116	32	3	21	(11	10)	217	56	68	65	29	3	94	6	1	5	6	3	6	.251	.301	.470	.770
2014 2 Tms	NL	122	353	69	11	4	7	(1	6)	109	32	37	22	20	0	84	4	0	6	4	5	6	.195	.243	.309	.552
12 SF	NL	77	175	44	4	5	5	(0	5)	73	15	16	23	18	2	36	1	0	2	3	2	1	.251	.321	.417	.739
12 Phi	NL	37	66	18	4	0	1	(0	1)	25	5	5	8	5	0	10	0	1	1	0	0	0	.273	.319	.379	.698
14 ChC	NL	99	313	60	10	3	6	(1	5)	94	29	33	19	18	0	76	4	0	6	4	4	6	.192	.240	.300	.541
14 Was	NL	23	40	9	1	1	1	(0	1)	15	3	4	3	2	0	8	0	0	0	0	1	0	.225	.262	.375	.637
Postseason		11	12	2	0	0	0	(0	0)	2	2	1	1	1	0	5	0	0	0	0	0	0	.167	.231	.167	.397
8 ML YEARS		799	2090	529	118	22	52	(18	34)	847	238	228	251	134	16	408	23	3	25	30	22	27	.253	.302	.405	.707

Brian Schlitter

Pitches: R Bats: R Pos: RP-61   Ht: 6'5" Wt: 235 Born: 12/21/1985 Age: 29

		HOW MUCH HE PITCHED						WHAT HE GAVE UP										THE RESULTS						
Year Team	Lg	G	GS	CG	GF	IP	BFP	H	R	ER	HR	SH	SF	HB	TBB	IBB	SO	WP	Bk	W	L	Pct	Sh	Sv-Op	Hld	ERC	ERA
2010 Iowa	AAA	37	0	0	23	45.2	200	44	18	16	3	1	1	1	21	0	42	2	0	2	1	.667	0	13- -	-	3.91	3.15
2012 Dytona	A+	21	0	0	10	27.0	109	27	9	6	1	1	1	1	2	0	19	0	1	0	1	.000	0	2- -	-	2.59	2.00
2012 Tenn	AA	29	0	0	14	42.0	178	43	19	14	2	3	1	0	11	0	44	1	0	3	4	.429	0	6- -	-	3.28	3.00
2013 Tenn	AA	16	0	0	12	21.2	98	24	8	2	0	0	0	1	6	1	13	0	0	0	2	.000	0	2- -	-	3.40	0.83
2013 Iowa	AAA	38	0	0	34	41.2	172	38	15	15	4	1	1	1	9	2	45	2	1	1	4	.200	0	20- -	-	2.86	3.24
2014 Iowa	AAA	7	0	0	4	8.0	37	10	4	3	0	0	0	0	3	0	4	0	0	0	0	-	0	3- -	-	4.52	3.38
2014 Cubs	R	1	0	0	1	1.0	3	0	0	0	0	0	0	0	0	0	0	0	0	0	0	-	0	0- -	-	0.00	0.00
2010 ChC	NL	7	0	0	3	8.0	48	18	11	11	2	0	0	1	5	1	7	0	0	0	1	.000	0	0-0	0	15.07	12.38
2014 ChC	NL	61	0	0	5	56.1	242	58	29	26	2	5	1	2	19	4	31	0	0	2	3	.400	0	0-4	12	3.57	4.15
2 ML YEARS		68	0	0	8	64.1	290	76	40	37	4	5	1	3	24	5	38	0	0	2	4	.333	0	0-4	12	4.76	5.18

Gus Schlosser

Pitches: R Bats: R Pos: RP-15   Ht: 6'4" Wt: 225 Born: 10/20/1988 Age: 26

		HOW MUCH HE PITCHED						WHAT HE GAVE UP										THE RESULTS						
Year Team	Lg	G	GS	CG	GF	IP	BFP	H	R	ER	HR	SH	SF	HB	TBB	IBB	SO	WP	Bk	W	L	Pct	Sh	Sv-Op	Hld	ERC	ERA
2011 Danvle	R	2	0	0	1	5.0	17	1	0	0	0	0	0	0	1	0	8	0	0	0	0	-	0	0- -	-	0.27	0.00
2011 Rome	A	19	0	0	16	29.2	114	22	6	6	0	1	1	1	4	1	34	4	0	2	0	1.000	0	8- -	-	1.44	1.82
2012 Lynbrg	A+	27	27	1	0	165.1	669	156	73	62	9	4	8	6	33	2	139	3	0	13	7	.650	1	0- -	-	2.88	3.38
2013 Missi	AA	25	25	0	0	135.1	556	118	42	36	5	3	0	5	44	0	101	3	0	7	6	.538	0	0- -	-	2.86	2.39
2014 Gwnntt	AAA	25	15	0	1	99.1	431	93	49	46	7	3	0	7	48	0	70	8	0	7	6	.538	0	0- -	-	4.16	4.17
2014 Atl	NL	15	0	0	8	17.2	81	23	16	15	2	2	2	1	6	1	8	3	0	0	1	.000	0	0-1	0	5.84	7.64

Jonathan Schoop

Bats: R Throws: R Pos: 2B-123;3B-17;PH-3;PR-1   SCOPE   Ht: 6'2" Wt: 210 Born: 10/16/1991 Age: 23

								BATTING												RUNNING			AVERAGES			
Year Team	Lg	G	AB	H	2B	3B	HR	(Hm Rd)	TB	R	RBI	RC	TBB	IBB	SO	HBP	SH	SF	SB	CS	GDP	Avg	OBP	Slg	OPS
2010 Orioles	R	17	60	15	4	0	3	(- -)	28	11	16	9	7	1	7	1	0	2	0	0	0	.250	.329	.467	.795
2010 Bluefld	R+	39	133	42	11	1	2	(- -)	61	16	16	22	12	0	14	0	3	0	1	1	6	.316	.372	.459	.831
2010 Frdrck	A+	6	21	5	3	0	0	(- -)	8	5	3	2	1	0	4	0	0	0	0	0	2	.238	.273	.381	.654
2011 Dlmrva	A	51	212	67	12	3	8	(- -)	109	45	34	41	20	0	32	2	1	3	6	4	13	.316	.376	.514	.890
2011 Frdrck	A+	77	299	81	12	2	5	(- -)	112	37	37	38	22	1	44	4	4	0	6	3	4	.271	.329	.375	.704
2012 Bowie	AA	124	485	119	24	1	14	(- -)	187	68	56	65	50	1	103	9	6	5	5	3	12	.245	.324	.386	.710
2013 Norfolk	AAA	70	270	69	11	0	9	(- -)	107	30	34	32	13	1	55	5	0	1	1	2	7	.256	.301	.396	.697
2013 Orioles	R	8	25	9	2	0	3	(- -)	20	9	9	8	6	0	6	0	0	1	0	0	2	.360	.469	.800	1.269
2013 Abrdn	A-	3	14	8	1	0	2	(- -)	15	3	9	6	1	0	1	0	0	0	0	0	1	.571	.600	1.071	1.671
2013 Bal	AL	5	14	4	0	0	1	(1 0)	7	5	1	1	1	0	2	0	0	0	0	0	0	.286	.333	.500	.833
2014 Bal	AL	137	455	95	18	0	16	(5 11)	161	48	45	32	13	0	122	8	5	0	2	0	12	.209	.244	.354	.598
2 ML YEARS		142	469	99	18	0	17	(6 11)	168	53	46	33	14	0	124	8	5	0	2	0	14	.211	.246	.358	.605

Bo Schultz

Pitches: R Bats: R Pos: RP-4   Ht: 6'3" Wt: 220 Born: 9/25/1985 Age: 29

			HOW MUCH HE PITCHED					WHAT HE GAVE UP											THE RESULTS						
Year Team	Lg	G	GS	CG	GF	IP	BFP	H	R	ER	HR	SH	SF	HB	TBB	IBB	SO	WP	Bk	W	L	Pct	Sh	Sv-Op	Hld	ERC	ERA
2010 Kane	A	41	0	0	15	75.1	321	57	31	24	2	2	1	10	34	3	65	3	2	6	1	.857	0	0- -	-	2.88	2.87
2011 Stcktn	A+	7	0	0	2	6.2	37	11	14	11	0	0	1	1	5	0	4	1	0	0	0	-	0	1- -	-	9.15	14.85
2012 Visalia	A+	29	0	0	28	34.0	152	41	21	17	3	2	1	0	10	3	36	2	0	4	2	.667	0	11- -	-	4.51	4.50
2012 Mobile	AA	17	0	0	7	21.1	92	20	8	5	0	2	0	1	7	1	13	1	0	2	3	.400	0	0- -	-	2.81	2.11
2013 Reno	AAA	17	0	0	7	19.2	93	29	12	12	4	1	0	1	7	1	23	4	0	0	2	.000	0	0- -	-	7.83	5.49
2013 Mobile	AA	20	16	0	3	85.0	346	62	29	27	3	5	2	7	29	0	52	10	0	5	4	.556	0	1- -	-	2.34	2.86
2014 Reno	AAA	28	23	1	0	135.1	619	174	109	93	17	5	4	4	46	2	82	4	1	10	8	.556	0	0- -	-	5.76	6.18
2014 Ari	NL	4	0	0	3	8.0	36	13	7	7	1	0	1	0	1	1	5	0	0	0	1	.000	0	0-0	0	6.86	7.88

Skip Schumaker

SHOO-mock-er

Bats: L Throws: R Pos: LF-33;2B-19;PH-18;RF-13;CF-8;PR-1   Ht: 5'10" Wt: 195 Born: 2/3/1980 Age: 35

								BATTING												RUNNING			AVERAGES			
Year Team	Lg	G	AB	H	2B	3B	HR	(Hm Rd)	TB	R	RBI	RC	TBB	IBB	SO	HBP	SH	SF	SB	CS	GDP	Avg	OBP	Slg	OPS
2014 Lsvlle*	AAA	4	12	5	4	0	0	(- -)	9	1	3	3	1	0	3	0	0	0	0	0	0	.417	.462	.750	1.212
2005 StL	NL	27	24	6	1	0	0	(0 0)	7	9	1	2	2	0	2	0	0	0	1	0	0	.250	.308	.292	.599
2006 StL	NL	28	54	10	1	0	1	(0 1)	14	3	2	2	5	1	6	0	1	0	2	1	1	.185	.254	.259	.513
2007 StL	NL	88	177	59	12	2	2	(1 1)	81	19	19	30	8	0	20	0	1	2	1	1	5	.333	.358	.458	.816
2008 StL	NL	153	540	163	22	5	4	(4 4)	219	87	46	74	47	2	60	2	4	1	8	2	19	.302	.359	.406	.765
2009 StL	NL	153	532	161	34	1	4	(2 2)	209	85	35	74	52	2	69	0	1	1	2	2	4	.303	.364	.393	.757
2010 StL	NL	137	476	126	18	1	5	(1 4)	161	66	42	61	43	2	64	4	2	4	5	3	7	.265	.328	.338	.667
2011 StL	NL	117	367	104	19	0	2	(1 1)	129	34	38	43	27	3	50	2	1	3	0	2	10	.283	.333	.351	.685
2012 StL	NL	107	272	75	14	4	1	(1 0)	100	37	28	34	27	2	50	0	3	2	1	1	6	.276	.339	.368	.707
2013 LAD	NL	125	319	84	16	0	2	(1 1)	106	31	30	34	28	0	54	5	3	0	2	2	11	.263	.332	.332	.665
2014 Cin	NL	83	247	58	12	0	2	(1 1)	76	22	22	22	18	0	50	1	3	2	2	1	3	.235	.287	.308	.595
Postseason		30	55	13	3	0	0	(0 0)	16	3	8	6	3	2	10	1	0	1	0	0	3	.236	.283	.291	.574
10 ML YEARS		1018	3008	846	149	13	27	(12 15)	1102	393	263	376	257	12	425	14	19	15	24	15	66	.281	.339	.366	.705

Luke Scott

Bats: L Throws: R Pos: DH   Ht: 6'0" Wt: 220 Born: 6/25/1978 Age: 37

								BATTING												RUNNING			AVERAGES			
Year Team	Lg	G	AB	H	2B	3B	HR	(Hm Rd)	TB	R	RBI	RC	TBB	IBB	SO	HBP	SH	SF	SB	CS	GDP	Avg	OBP	Slg	OPS
2005 Hou	NL	34	80	15	4	2	0	(0 0)	23	6	4	6	9	1	23	0	0	0	1	1	0	.188	.270	.288	.557
2006 Hou	NL	65	214	72	19	6	10	(8 2)	133	31	37	48	30	4	43	4	0	1	2	1	2	.336	.426	.621	1.047
2007 Hou	NL	132	369	94	28	5	18	(8 10)	186	49	64	55	53	4	95	2	0	1	3	1	8	.255	.351	.504	.855
2008 Bal	AL	148	475	122	29	2	23	(11 12)	224	67	65	68	53	10	102	5	0	3	2	2	7	.257	.336	.472	.807
2009 Bal	AL	128	449	116	26	1	25	(18 7)	219	61	77	69	55	5	104	1	0	1	0	0	4	.258	.340	.488	.828
2010 Bal	AL	131	447	127	29	1	27	(19 8)	239	70	72	71	59	4	98	4	0	7	2	0	9	.284	.368	.535	.902
2011 Bal	AL	64	209	46	11	0	9	(5 4)	84	24	22	24	24	1	54	1	0	2	1	1	2	.220	.301	.402	.703
2012 TB	AL	96	314	72	22	1	14	(6 8)	138	35	55	40	21	3	80	5	0	4	5	0	9	.229	.285	.439	.724
2013 TB	AL	91	253	61	13	2	9	(6 3)	105	27	40	37	30	1	63	4	0	4	1	1	5	.241	.326	.415	.741
Postseason		2	2	0	0	0	0	(0 0)	0	1	0	0	1	0	1	0	0	0	0	0	0	.000	.333	.000	.333
9 ML YEARS		889	2810	725	181	20	135	(81 54)	1351	370	436	418	334	33	662	26	0	23	17	7	46	.258	.340	.481	.821

Evan Scribner

SKRIBB-nurr

Pitches: R Bats: R Pos: RP-13   Ht: 6'3" Wt: 190 Born: 7/19/1985 Age: 29

			HOW MUCH HE PITCHED					WHAT HE GAVE UP											THE RESULTS						
Year Team	Lg	G	GS	CG	GF	IP	BFP	H	R	ER	HR	SH	SF	HB	TBB	IBB	SO	WP	Bk	W	L	Pct	Sh	Sv-Op	Hld	ERC	ERA
2014 Scrmto*	AAA	40	0	0	28	47.0	188	39	16	16	4	2	0	1	9	0	72	0	2	4	1	.800	0	16- -	-	2.38	3.06
2011 SD	NL	10	0	0	5	14.0	64	18	11	11	1	0	0	4	4	0	10	0	0	0	0	-	0	0-0	0	4.92	7.07
2012 Oak	AL	30	0	0	13	35.1	148	30	11	10	2	0	0	12	12	0	30	1	0	2	0	1.000	0	1-1	1	2.70	2.55
2013 Oak	AL	18	0	0	12	26.2	114	26	13	13	3	0	0	7	7	0	19	2	0	0	0	-	0	0-0	0	3.38	4.39
2014 Oak	AL	13	0	0	6	11.2	47	11	6	6	4	0	0	1	0	0	11	0	0	1	0	1.000	0	0-0	0	3.89	4.63
Postseason		1	0	0	1	2.0	6	0	0	0	0	0	0	0	0	0	3	0	0	0	0	-	0	0-0	0	0.00	0.00
4 ML YEARS		71	0	0	36	87.2	373	85	41	40	10	0	0	1	23	0	70	3	0	3	0	1.000	0	1-1	1	3.42	4.11

Xavier Scruggs

Bats: R **Throws:** R **Pos:** 1B-5;PH-5   ZAY-vyer   **Ht:** 6'1" **Wt:** 220 **Born:** 9/23/1987 **Age:** 27

Year	Team	Lg	G	AB	H	2B	3B	HR	(Hm	Rd)	TB	R	RBI	RC	TBB	IBB	SO	HBP	SH	SF	SB	CS	GDP	Avg	OBP	Slg	OPS
2010	PlmBh	A+	87	316	85	18	1	13	(-	-)	144	42	53	52	30	2	107	8	0	3	3	0	5	.269	.345	.456	.800
2010	Sprgfld	AA	33	110	27	6	0	8	(-	-)	57	16	21	18	10	0	36	2	0	0	0	0	6	.245	.320	.518	.838
2011	PlmBh	A+	117	411	107	27	3	21	(-	-)	203	57	63	72	40	1	125	13	1	6	4	1	11	.260	.340	.494	.834
2012	Sprgfld	AA	130	452	106	26	1	22	(-	-)	200	64	91	70	58	0	150	9	0	3	8	4	15	.235	.331	.442	.774
2013	Sprgfld	AA	133	448	111	18	1	29	(-	-)	218	67	81	86	82	2	177	12	1	3	11	7	5	.248	.376	.487	.863
2014	Memp	AAA	135	472	135	29	3	21	(-	-)	233	82	87	86	53	0	114	11	0	2	3	5	19	.286	.370	.494	.864
2014	StL	NL	9	15	3	1	0	0	(0	0)	4	0	2	2	2	0	7	1	0	0	0	0	0	.200	.333	.267	.600

Marco Scutaro

Bats: R **Throws:** R **Pos:** 2B-3;PH-2   SKOO-tah-row   **Ht:** 5'10" **Wt:** 185 **Born:** 10/30/1975 **Age:** 39

Year	Team	Lg	G	AB	H	2B	3B	HR	(Hm	Rd)	TB	R	RBI	RC	TBB	IBB	SO	HBP	SH	SF	SB	CS	GDP	Avg	OBP	Slg	OPS
2014	Giants*	R	7	13	3	1	0	0	(-	-)	4	2	1	1	2	0	0	0	0	0	0	0	0	.231	.333	.308	.641
2014	Fresno*	AAA	3	10	1	0	0	0	(-	-)	1	2	1	0	0	0	6	1	0	0	0	0	0	.100	.182	.100	.282
2002	NYM	NL	27	36	8	0	1	1	(1	0)	13	2	6	2	0	0	11	0	1	1	0	1	1	.222	.216	.361	.577
2003	NYM	NL	48	75	16	4	0	2	(0	2)	26	10	6	10	13	2	14	1	1	1	2	0	1	.213	.333	.347	.680
2004	Oak	AL	137	455	124	32	1	7	(6	1)	179	50	43	48	16	1	58	0	5	1	0	0	9	.273	.297	.393	.690
2005	Oak	AL	118	381	94	22	3	9	(5	4)	149	48	37	45	36	1	48	0	4	2	5	2	6	.247	.310	.391	.701
2006	Oak	AL	117	365	97	21	6	5	(1	4)	145	52	41	47	50	0	66	0	3	5	5	1	16	.266	.350	.397	.747
2007	Oak	AL	104	338	88	13	0	7	(2	5)	122	49	41	42	35	1	40	2	2	2	2	1	13	.260	.332	.361	.693
2008	Tor	AL	145	517	138	23	1	7	(5	2)	184	76	60	72	57	0	65	5	6	7	7	2	8	.267	.341	.356	.697
2009	Tor	AL	144	574	162	35	1	12	(7	5)	235	100	60	97	90	0	75	4	5	7	14	5	12	.282	.379	.409	.789
2010	Bos	AL	150	632	174	38	0	11	(6	5)	245	92	56	81	53	1	71	3	4	3	5	4	13	.275	.333	.388	.721
2011	Bos	AL	113	395	118	26	1	7	(3	4)	167	59	54	56	38	1	36	1	7	4	4	2	12	.299	.358	.423	.781
2012	2 Tms	NL	156	620	190	32	4	7	(4	3)	251	87	74	86	40	0	49	4	10	9	9	4	12	.306	.348	.405	.753
2013	SF	NL	127	488	145	23	3	2	(1	1)	180	57	31	61	45	0	34	2	9	3	2	0	13	.297	.357	.369	.726
2014	SF	NL	5	11	1	0	0	0	(0	0)	1	1	0	0	1	0	3	0	1	0	0	0	0	.091	.167	.091	.258
12	Col	NL	95	377	102	16	3	4	(3	1)	136	47	30	40	27	0	35	4	4	3	7	3	5	.271	.324	.361	.684
12	SF	NL	61	243	88	16	1	3	(1	2)	115	40	44	46	13	0	14	0	6	6	2	1	7	.362	.385	.473	.859
	Postseason		23	91	26	8	0	0			34	12	14	17	5	0	7	0	1	0	0	0	1	.286	.323	.374	.697
	13 ML YEARS		1391	4887	1355	269	21	77	(41	36)	1897	683	509	647	474	7	570	22	58	45	55	22	117	.277	.341	.388	.729

Kyle Seager

Bats: L **Throws:** R **Pos:** 3B-157;DH-1;PH-1   SEE-gurr   **Ht:** 6'0" **Wt:** 210 **Born:** 11/3/1987 **Age:** 27

Year	Team	Lg	G	AB	H	2B	3B	HR	(Hm	Rd)	TB	R	RBI	RC	TBB	IBB	SO	HBP	SH	SF	SB	CS	GDP	Avg	OBP	Slg	OPS
2011	Sea	AL	53	182	47	13	0	3	(0	3)	69	22	13	16	13	0	36	2	2	2	3	1	4	.258	.312	.379	.691
2012	Sea	AL	155	594	154	35	1	20	(5	15)	251	62	86	88	46	1	110	5	2	4	13	5	9	.259	.316	.423	.738
2013	Sea	AL	160	615	160	32	2	22	(8	14)	262	79	69	90	68	1	122	7	0	5	9	3	6	.260	.338	.426	.764
2014	Sea	AL	159	590	158	27	4	25	(16	9)	268	71	96	96	52	3	118	8	1	3	7	5	12	.268	.334	.454	.788
	4 ML YEARS		527	1981	519	107	7	70	(29	41)	850	234	264	290	179	5	386	22	5	14	32	14	33	.262	.328	.429	.757

Jean Segura

Bats: R **Throws:** R **Pos:** SS-144;PH-2;PR-1   GENE seg-ER-uh   **Ht:** 5'10" **Wt:** 205 **Born:** 3/17/1990 **Age:** 25

Year	Team	Lg	G	AB	H	2B	3B	HR	(Hm	Rd)	TB	R	RBI	RC	TBB	IBB	SO	HBP	SH	SF	SB	CS	GDP	Avg	OBP	Slg	OPS
2012	2 Tms		45	151	39	4	3	0	(0	0)	49	19	14	16	13	3	23	0	1	1	7	1	1	.258	.315	.325	.640
2013	Mil	NL	146	588	173	20	10	12	(7	5)	249	74	49	72	25	1	84	6	2	2	44	13	11	.294	.329	.423	.752
2014	Mil	NL	146	513	126	14	6	5	(3	2)	167	61	31	45	28	5	70	4	10	2	20	9	13	.246	.289	.326	.614
12	LAA	AL	1	3	0	0	0	0	(0	0)	0	0	0	0	0	0	2	0	0	0	0	0	0	.000	.000	.000	.000
12	Mil	NL	44	148	39	4	3	0	(0	0)	49	19	14	16	13	3	21	0	1	1	7	1	1	.264	.321	.331	.652
	3 ML YEARS		337	1252	338	38	19	17	(10	7)	465	154	94	133	66	9	177	10	13	5	71	23	31	.270	.311	.371	.682

Justin Sellers

Bats: R **Throws:** R **Pos:** 2B-7;SS-6;3B-4;PR-1   **Ht:** 5'10" **Wt:** 160 **Born:** 2/1/1986 **Age:** 29

Year	Team	Lg	G	AB	H	2B	3B	HR	(Hm	Rd)	TB	R	RBI	RC	TBB	IBB	SO	HBP	SH	SF	SB	CS	GDP	Avg	OBP	Slg	OPS
2014	Clmbs*	AAA	102	355	90	18	1	3	(-	-)	119	31	40	39	25	0	48	5	4	6	3	1	5	.254	.307	.335	.642
2011	LAD	NL	36	123	25	9	0	1	(1	0)	37	20	13	15	12	0	21	2	1	1	0	0	1	.203	.283	.301	.583
2012	LAD	NL	19	44	9	3	1	1	(1	0)	17	6	2	2	5	1	14	0	1	0	0	0	0	.205	.286	.386	.672
2013	LAD	NL	27	69	13	1	0	1	(1	0)	17	6	2	4	5	0	20	2	1	0	0	0	3	.188	.263	.246	.510
2014	Cle	AL	17	16	3	0	0	0	(0	0)	3	1	0	1	3	0	4	0	2	0	0	1	0	.188	.316	.188	.503
	4 ML YEARS		99	252	50	13	1	3	(3	0)	74	33	17	22	25	1	59	4	5	1	1	4	.198	.280	.294	.574

Marcus Semien

Bats: R **Throws:** R **Pos:** 3B-33;2B-26;PH-4;SS-3;DH-2   SIM-ee-inn   **Ht:** 6'1" **Wt:** 195 **Born:** 9/17/1990 **Age:** 24

Year	Team	Lg	G	AB	H	2B	3B	HR	(Hm	Rd)	TB	R	RBI	RC	TBB	IBB	SO	HBP	SH	SF	SB	CS	GDP	Avg	OBP	Slg	OPS
2011	Knapol	A	60	229	58	15	2	3	(-	-)	86	35	26	28	22	0	53	2	6	3	3	4	4	.253	.320	.376	.696
2012	WinSa	A+	107	418	114	31	5	14	(-	-)	197	80	59	74	55	1	97	5	6	3	11	5	7	.273	.362	.471	.833
2013	Brham	AA	105	393	114	22	5	15	(-	-)	191	90	49	87	84	3	66	4	2	0	20	5	7	.290	.420	.486	.906
2013	Charltt	AAA	32	125	33	11	1	4	(-	-)	58	20	17	21	14	0	24	1	0	2	4	0	6	.264	.338	.464	.802

						BATTING																RUNNING			AVERAGES			
Year Team	Lg	G	AB	H	2B	3B	HR	(Hm	Rd)	TB	R	RBI	RC	TBB	IBB	SO	HBP	SH	SF	SB	CS	GDP	Avg	OBP	Slg	OPS
2014 Charltt	AAA	83	303	81	20	3	15	(-	-)	152	57	52	61	53	2	59	5	0	5	7	2	4	.267	.380	.502	.881
2013 CWS	AL	21	69	18	4	0	2	(2	0)	28	7	7	7	1	0	22	0	0	1	2	2	1	.261	.268	.406	.673
2014 CWS	AL	64	231	54	10	2	6	(4	2)	86	30	28	31	21	0	70	1	2	0	3	0	6	.234	.300	.372	.673
2 ML YEARS		85	300	72	14	2	8	(6	2)	114	37	35	38	22	0	92	1	2	1	5	2	7	.240	.293	.380	.673

Bryan Shaw

Pitches: R **Bats:** B **Pos:** RP-80 **Ht:** 6'1" **Wt:** 210 **Born:** 11/8/1987 **Age:** 27

		HOW MUCH HE PITCHED						WHAT HE GAVE UP												THE RESULTS							
Year Team	Lg	G	GS	CG	GF	IP	BFP	H	R	ER	HR	SH	SF	HB	TBB	IBB	SO	WP	Bk	W	L	Pct	Sh	Sv-Op	Hld	ERC	ERA
2011 Ari	NL	33	0	0	8	28.1	122	30	9	8	2	0	0	4	8	1	24	1	0	1	0	1.000	0	0-0	9	4.31	2.54
2012 Ari	NL	64	0	0	19	59.1	252	60	29	23	4	4	2	2	24	3	41	4	1	1	6	.143	0	2-4	10	4.08	3.49
2013 Cle	AL	70	0	0	11	75.0	316	60	31	27	4	4	2	4	28	2	73	5	0	7	3	.700	0	1-5	12	2.71	3.24
2014 Cle	AL	**80**	0	0	16	76.1	313	61	26	22	6	5	2	2	22	4	64	4	1	5	5	.500	0	2-9	24	2.45	2.59
Postseason		5	0	0	1	5.2	18	1	0	0	0	0	1	0	1	0	5	0	0	0	0	-	0	0-0	1	0.22	0.00
4 ML YEARS		247	0	0	54	239.0	1003	211	95	80	16	13	6	12	82	10	202	14	2	14	14	.500	0	5-18	55	3.12	3.01

James Shields

Pitches: R **Bats:** R **Pos:** SP-34 **Ht:** 6'3" **Wt:** 215 **Born:** 12/20/1981 **Age:** 33

		HOW MUCH HE PITCHED						WHAT HE GAVE UP												THE RESULTS							
Year Team	Lg	G	GS	CG	GF	IP	BFP	H	R	ER	HR	SH	SF	HB	TBB	IBB	SO	WP	Bk	W	L	Pct	Sh	Sv-Op	Hld	ERC	ERA
2006 TB	AL	21	21	1	0	124.2	540	141	69	67	18	4	3	5	38	5	104	9	0	6	8	.429	0	0-0	0	4.92	4.84
2007 TB	AL	31	31	1	0	215.0	874	202	98	92	28	4	5	10	36	0	184	9	0	12	8	.600	0	0-0	0	3.24	3.85
2008 TB	AL	33	33	3	0	215.0	877	208	94	85	24	6	0	12	40	0	160	6	0	14	8	.636	**2**	0-0	0	3.41	3.56
2009 TB	AL	33	33	0	0	219.2	930	239	113	101	29	6	3	1	52	1	167	3	1	11	12	.478	0	0-0	0	4.16	4.14
2010 TB	AL	34	33	0	0	203.1	899	**246**	**128**	**117**	**34**	5	2	5	51	2	187	13	2	13	15	.464	0	0-0	0	5.21	5.18
2011 TB	AL	33	33	**11**	0	249.1	975	195	83	78	26	5	3	5	65	1	225	4	0	16	12	.571	**4**	0-0	0	2.58	2.82
2012 TB	AL	33	33	3	0	227.2	944	208	103	89	25	3	2	11	58	2	223	7	1	15	10	.600	2	0-0	0	3.28	3.52
2013 KC	AL	34	**34**	2	0	**228.2**	**946**	215	82	80	20	6	7	8	68	0	196	11	**2**	13	9	.591	0	0-0	0	3.45	3.15
2014 KC	AL	34	**34**	1	0	227.0	939	224	95	81	23	3	7	11	44	0	180	12	2	14	8	.636	1	0-0	0	3.41	3.21
Postseason		6	6	0	0	34.1	152	40	20	19	4	1	1	5	8	0	25	3	0	2	4	.333	0	0-0	0	5.08	4.98
9 ML YEARS		286	285	22	0	1910.1	7924	1878	865	790	227	42	32	68	452	11	1626	74	8	114	90	.559	9	0-0	0	3.63	3.72

Matt Shoemaker

Pitches: R **Bats:** R **Pos:** SP-20; RP-7 SHOO-may-kerr **Ht:** 6'2" **Wt:** 225 **Born:** 9/27/1986 **Age:** 28

		HOW MUCH HE PITCHED						WHAT HE GAVE UP												THE RESULTS							
Year Team	Lg	G	GS	CG	GF	IP	BFP	H	R	ER	HR	SH	SF	HB	TBB	IBB	SO	WP	Bk	W	L	Pct	Sh	Sv-Op	Hld	ERC	ERA
2010 RCuca	A+	20	20	2	0	122.1	531	138	75	67	14	0	0	4	39	1	119	10	1	7	8	.467	0	0- -	-	4.75	4.93
2010 Salt Lk	AAA	3	2	0	0	15.1	69	20	10	10	0	0	0	0	8	0	9	0	0	2	1	.667	0	0- -	-	5.83	5.87
2011 Salt Lk	AAA	4	4	0	0	21.0	100	28	19	19	3	0	1	1	12	0	12	2	0	0	2	.000	0	0- -	-	7.50	8.14
2011 Ark	AA	23	23	5	0	156.1	629	132	47	43	17	5	1	8	35	0	129	6	3	12	5	.706	2	0- -	-	2.85	2.48
2012 Salt Lk	AAA	29	29	1	0	176.2	782	230	123	113	25	3	9	5	45	0	124	4	1	11	10	.524	0	0- -	-	5.75	5.76
2013 Salt Lk	AAA	29	29	0	0	184.1	782	212	99	95	27	1	11	8	29	0	160	5	0	11	13	.458	0	0- -	-	4.47	4.64
2014 Salt Lk	AAA	5	5	0	0	25.2	115	34	18	18	2	0	0	2	9	0	26	1	0	1	0	1.000	0	0- -	-	6.17	6.31
2013 LAA	AL	1	1	0	0	5.0	19	2	0	0	0	0	0	0	2	0	5	1	0	0	0	-	0	0-0	0	0.95	0.00
2014 LAA	AL	27	20	0	5	136.0	543	122	49	46	14	3	5	4	24	0	124	5	0	16	4	**.800**	0	0-0	0	2.84	3.04
2 ML YEARS		28	21	0	5	141.0	562	124	49	46	14	3	5	4	26	0	129	6	0	16	4	.800	0	0-0	0	2.75	2.94

Chasen Shreve

Pitches: L **Bats:** L **Pos:** RP-15 CHASE-en SHREEVE **Ht:** 6'3" **Wt:** 190 **Born:** 7/12/1990 **Age:** 24

		HOW MUCH HE PITCHED						WHAT HE GAVE UP												THE RESULTS							
Year Team	Lg	G	GS	CG	GF	IP	BFP	H	R	ER	HR	SH	SF	HB	TBB	IBB	SO	WP	Bk	W	L	Pct	Sh	Sv-Op	Hld	ERC	ERA
2010 Danvle	R	8	0	0	3	16.0	65	16	5	4	1	0	0	2	3	0	20	0	0	2	0	1.000	0	1- -	-	3.64	2.25
2011 Rome	A	34	0	0	12	70.0	308	77	33	30	3	6	1	2	26	4	68	15	0	5	6	.455	0	4- -	-	4.12	3.86
2012 Lynbrg	A+	32	0	0	13	46.0	190	44	16	11	2	4	1	0	17	1	41	3	0	4	4	.500	0	1- -	-	3.40	2.15
2012 Missi	AA	11	0	0	3	18.1	86	17	8	8	1	0	0	0	16	1	16	0	0	2	1	.667	0	0- -	-	5.06	3.93
2013 Missi	AA	36	0	0	15	42.2	192	43	25	21	1	8	4	0	22	4	28	1	0	3	1	.750	0	0- -	-	3.76	4.43
2013 Lynbrg	A+	14	0	0	5	19.2	84	15	7	6	1	0	0	0	8	0	15	2	0	0	1	.000	0	2- -	-	2.41	2.75
2014 Missi	AA	36	0	0	21	54.1	207	42	16	15	2	0	0	1	9	1	76	1	0	3	2	.600	0	7- -	-	1.81	2.48
2014 Gwnntt	AAA	10	0	0	5	9.2	38	9	4	4	2	1	1	0	3	0	11	0	0	2	1	.667	0	2- -	-	4.33	3.72
2014 Atl	NL	15	0	0	4	12.1	50	10	1	1	0	1	0	0	3	0	15	1	0	0	0	-	0	0-0	2	1.88	0.73

J.B. Shuck

Bats: L **Throws:** L **Pos:** LF-25;RF-8;PH-7;PR-5;DH-4 **Ht:** 5'11" **Wt:** 195 **Born:** 6/18/1987 **Age:** 28

						BATTING																RUNNING			AVERAGES			
Year Team	Lg	G	AB	H	2B	3B	HR	(Hm	Rd)	TB	R	RBI	RC	TBB	IBB	SO	HBP	SH	SF	SB	CS	GDP	Avg	OBP	Slg	OPS
2014 Salt Lk*	AAA	102	406	130	18	9	5	(-	-)	181	64	57	72	43	2	30	3	4	9	9	6	11	.320	.382	.446	.828
2011 Hou	NL	37	81	22	2	1	0	(0	0)	26	9	3	9	11	1	7	0	0	0	2	0	3	.272	.359	.321	.680
2013 LAA	AL	129	437	128	20	3	2	(1	1)	160	60	39	54	27	0	54	1	6	7	8	4	10	.293	.331	.366	.697
2014 2 Tms	AL	38	110	16	1	0	2	(1	1)	23	12	9	3	3	1	12	0	1	0	2	0	1	.145	.168	.209	.377
14 LAA	AL	22	84	14	1	0	2	(1	1)	21	10	9	3	3	1	11	0	1	0	2	0	0	.167	.195	.250	.445
14 Cle	AL	16	26	2	0	0	0	(0	0)	2	2	0	0	0	0	1	0	0	0	0	0	1	.077	.077	.077	.154
3 ML YEARS		204	628	166	23	4	4	(2	2)	209	81	51	66	41	2	73	1	7	7	12	4	14	.264	.307	.333	.640

Kevin Siegrist

Pitches: L Bats: L Pos: RP-37   SEE-grist   Ht: 6'5" Wt: 215 Born: 7/20/1989 Age: 25

Year	Team	Lg	G	GS	CG	GF	IP	BFP	H	R	ER	HR	SH	SF	HB	TBB	IBB	SO	WP	Bk	W	L	Pct	Sh	Sv-Op	Hld	ERC	ERA
2010	Batvia	A-	7	4	0	0	21.0	105	24	17	17	1	1	0	3	16	0	14	2	0	0	1	.000	0	0--	-	6.44	7.29
2010	JhsCty	R+	7	5	0	0	32.2	128	28	12	7	3	0	0	4	6	0	31	1	0	4	3	.571	0	0--	-	3.06	1.93
2011	QuadC	A	9	8	0	1	54.2	213	38	12	7	1	1	0	0	15	0	34	4	0	8	1	.889	0	0--	-	1.64	1.15
2011	PlmBh	A+	11	11	0	0	52.2	228	44	23	20	3	3	3	2	30	0	45	4	0	3	3	.000	0	0--	-	3.68	3.42
2012	PlmBh	A+	10	10	0	0	55.1	222	33	18	14	3	0	3	6	22	0	41	1	1	6	0	1.000	0	0--	-	2.12	2.28
2012	Sprgfld	AA	8	5	0	0	32.1	135	26	14	13	4	2	0	5	9	0	27	2	0	1	2	.333	0	0--	-	3.29	3.62
2013	Sprgfld	AA	13	0	0	3	20.0	74	8	5	5	2	0	0	1	7	0	35	1	0	1	1	.500	0	1--	-	1.34	2.25
2013	Memp	AAA	5	0	0	1	7.2	30	3	2	1	0	0	0	0	3	0	9	1	0	1	0	1.000	0	0--	-	0.89	1.17
2014	Sprgfld	AA	5	0	0	0	4.2	21	4	0	0	0	0	0	0	3	0	3	0	0	0	0	-	0	0--	-	3.39	0.00
2014	Memp	AAA	6	0	0	1	6.2	26	3	1	1	0	0	0	0	3	0	11	0	0	0	0	-	0	1--	-	1.18	1.35
2013	StL	NL	45	0	0	15	39.2	152	17	2	2	1	0	0	1	18	1	50	0	0	3	1	.750	0	0-0	11	1.27	0.45
2014	StL	NL	37	0	0	5	30.1	140	32	23	23	5	1	1	2	16	0	37	1	0	1	4	.200	0	0-2	16	5.59	6.82
	Postseason		9	0	0	1	6.0	25	6	3	2	1	0	1	0	0	0	3	2	0	0	0	-	0	0-0	1	2.73	3.00
	2 ML YEARS		82	0	0	20	70.0	292	49	25	25	6	1	1	3	34	1	87	1	0	4	5	.444	0	0-2	27	2.83	3.21

Moises Sierra

Bats: R Throws: R Pos: RF-70;PR-19;LF-9;PH-8;DH-6;CF-4   Ht: 6'1" Wt: 220 Born: 9/24/1988 Age: 26

			BATTING																			RUNNING			AVERAGES			
Year	Team	Lg	G	AB	H	2B	3B	HR	(Hm	Rd)	TB	R	RBI	RC	TBB	IBB	SO	HBP	SH	SF	SB	CS	GDP	Avg	OBP	Slg	OPS
2014	Charltt*	AAA	4	16	4	0	0	0	(-	-)	4	2	0	1	2	0	3	0	0	0	2	0	1	.250	.333	.250	.583
2012	Tor	AL	49	147	33	4	0	6	(3	3)	55	14	15	10	8	0	44	2	0	0	1	0	3	.224	.274	.374	.648
2013	Tor	AL	35	107	31	13	1	1	(0	1)	49	11	13	22	14	1	29	0	0	1	1	0	0	.290	.369	.458	.827
2014	2 Tms		96	161	37	8	2	2	(1	1)	55	22	9	11	8	0	43	0	0	1	3	1	1	.230	.265	.342	.606
14	Tor	AL	13	34	2	0	0	0	(0	0)	2	2	2	0	1	0	9	0	0	0	0	0	1	.059	.086	.059	.145
14	CWS	AL	83	127	35	8	2	2	(1	1)	53	20	7	11	7	0	34	0	0	1	3	1	0	.276	.311	.417	.728
	3 ML YEARS		180	415	101	25	3	9	(4	5)	159	47	37	43	30	1	116	2	0	2	5	1	4	.243	.296	.383	.679

Andrelton Simmons

Bats: R Throws: R Pos: SS-146;PR-1   ANN-drel-ton   Ht: 6'2" Wt: 195 Born: 9/4/1989 Age: 25

			BATTING																			RUNNING			AVERAGES			
Year	Team	Lg	G	AB	H	2B	3B	HR	(Hm	Rd)	TB	R	RBI	RC	TBB	IBB	SO	HBP	SH	SF	SB	CS	GDP	Avg	OBP	Slg	OPS
2012	Atl	NL	49	166	48	8	2	3	(3	0)	69	17	19	23	12	1	21	1	0	3	1	0	5	.289	.335	.416	.751
2013	Atl	NL	157	606	150	27	6	17	(5	12)	240	76	59	60	40	1	55	3	5	4	6	5	16	.248	.296	.396	.692
2014	Atl	NL	146	540	132	18	4	7	(3	4)	179	44	46	41	32	4	60	0	2	2	4	5	25	.244	.286	.331	.617
	Postseason		5	16	4	1	0	0	(0	0)	5	0	2	1	2	0	3	0	1	0	0	0	1	.250	.333	.313	.646
	3 ML YEARS		352	1312	330	53	12	27	(11	16)	488	137	124	124	84	6	136	4	7	9	11	10	46	.252	.297	.372	.669

Shae Simmons

Pitches: R Bats: R Pos: RP-26   SHAY   Ht: 5'11" Wt: 175 Born: 9/3/1990 Age: 24

Year	Team	Lg	G	GS	CG	GF	IP	BFP	H	R	ER	HR	SH	SF	HB	TBB	IBB	SO	WP	Bk	W	L	Pct	Sh	Sv-Op	Hld	ERC	ERA
2012	Braves	R	7	1	0	0	14.1	54	5	1	0	0	0	0	0	8	0	15	2	0	2	0	1.000	0	0--	-	1.14	0.00
2012	Danvle	R	9	0	0	7	10.1	51	11	7	4	0	0	0	0	8	1	21	3	0	0	2	.000	0	2--	-	4.70	3.48
2013	Rome	A	39	0	0	34	42.1	176	26	12	7	0	1	1	4	15	0	66	5	0	1	1	.500	0	24--	-	1.62	1.49
2013	Missi	AA	11	0	0	2	11.0	44	5	3	3	0	1	0	0	7	0	16	1	0	0	0	-	0	0--	-	1.59	2.45
2014	Missi	AA	20	0	0	19	23.0	89	15	2	2	0	0	0	1	6	0	30	0	0	0	0	-	0	14--	-	1.50	0.78
2014	Gwnntt	AAA	2	2	0	0	1.0	7	3	4	4	0	0	0	0	2	0	1	0	0	0	1	.000	0	0--	-	28.18	36.00
2014	Atl	NL	26	0	0	6	21.2	89	15	8	7	1	1	1	0	11	1	23	1	0	1	2	.333	0	1-1	9	2.45	2.91

Alfredo Simon

Pitches: R Bats: R Pos: SP-32   si-MOHN   Ht: 6'6" Wt: 265 Born: 5/8/1981 Age: 34

Year	Team	Lg	G	GS	CG	GF	IP	BFP	H	R	ER	HR	SH	SF	HB	TBB	IBB	SO	WP	Bk	W	L	Pct	Sh	Sv-Op	Hld	ERC	ERA
2008	Bal	AL	4	1	0	0	13.0	59	16	10	9	4	0	1	2	2	0	8	2	0	0	0	-	0	0-0	0	6.45	6.23
2009	Bal	AL	2	2	0	0	6.1	28	8	7	7	5	0	0	0	2	0	3	0	0	0	1	.000	0	0-0	0	10.74	9.95
2010	Bal	AL	49	0	0	35	49.1	222	54	30	27	10	1	2	2	22	2	37	1	0	4	2	.667	0	17-21	1	5.66	4.93
2011	Bal	AL	23	16	0	1	115.2	499	128	69	63	15	1	4	4	40	6	83	2	2	4	9	.308	0	0-0	0	4.83	4.90
2012	Cin	NL	36	0	0	13	61.0	269	65	22	18	2	2	3	6	22	1	52	9	0	3	2	.600	0	1-1	1	4.16	2.66
2013	Cin	NL	63	0	0	20	87.2	359	68	31	28	8	5	2	8	26	2	63	4	0	6	4	.600	0	1-3	6	2.75	2.87
2014	Cin	NL	32	32	0	0	196.1	818	181	80	75	22	7	4	12	56	7	127	3	0	15	10	.600	0	0-0	0	3.49	3.44
	Postseason		2	0	0	1	2.1	11	3	0	0	0	1	0	0	1	0	1	0	0	0	0	-	0	0-0	0	4.93	0.00
	7 ML YEARS		209	51	0	69	529.1	2254	520	249	227	66	16	16	34	170	18	373	21	2	32	28	.533	0	19-25	8	4.06	3.86

Jon Singleton

Bats: L Throws: L Pos: 1B-91;PH-6   Ht: 6'2" Wt: 255 Born: 9/18/1991 Age: 23

			BATTING																			RUNNING			AVERAGES			
Year	Team	Lg	G	AB	H	2B	3B	HR	(Hm	Rd)	TB	R	RBI	RC	TBB	IBB	SO	HBP	SH	SF	SB	CS	GDP	Avg	OBP	Slg	OPS
2010	Lakwd	A	104	376	109	25	2	14	(-	-)	180	64	77	74	62	4	74	6	0	6	9	7	10	.290	.393	.479	.872
2011	Clrwtr	A+	93	320	91	14	0	9	(-	-)	132	48	47	55	56	2	83	1	0	5	3	3	11	.284	.387	.413	.800
2011	Lancst	A+	35	129	43	9	1	4	(-	-)	66	20	16	26	14	1	40	3	0	2	0	0	3	.333	.405	.512	.917
2012	CpChr	AA	131	461	131	27	4	21	(-	-)	229	94	79	95	88	5	131	1	0	5	7	2	6	.284	.396	.497	.893
2013	QuadC	A	6	21	6	2	0	3	(-	-)	17	6	5	6	4	0	5	0	0	0	0	0	0	.286	.400	.810	1.210

Year Team	Lg	G	AB	H	2B	3B	HR	(Hm	Rd)	TB	R	RBI	RC	TBB	IBB	SO	HBP	SH	SF	SB	CS	GDP	Avg	OBP	Slg	OPS
2013 CpChr	AA	11	38	10	2	1	2	(-	-)	20	5	8	8	9	0	16	0	0	1	0	0	0	.263	.396	.526	.922
2013 OKCity	AAA	73	245	54	13	0	6	(-	-)	85	31	31	33	46	1	89	0	0	3	1	0	4	.220	.340	.347	.687
2014 OKCity	AAA	54	195	52	10	1	14	(-	-)	106	37	43	43	42	6	52	1	0	1	1	1	4	.267	.397	.544	.941
2014 Hou	AL	95	310	52	13	0	13	(7	6)	104	42	44	28	50	1	134	1	0	1	2	3	4	.168	.285	.335	.620

Tony Sipp

Pitches: L Bats: L Pos: RP-56   Ht: 6'0" Wt: 190 Born: 7/12/1983 Age: 31

	HOW MUCH HE PITCHED						WHAT HE GAVE UP											THE RESULTS							
Year Team	Lg	G	GS	CG	GF	IP	BFP	H	R	ER	HR	SH	SF	HB	TBB	IBB	SO	WP	Bk	W	L	Pct	Sh	Sv-Op	Hld	ERC	ERA
2014 ElPaso*	AAA	11	0	0	2	14.2	61	14	7	7	1	0	0	1	2	0	21	0	0	1	1	.500	0	0- --	-	2.82	4.30
2009 Cle	AL	46	0	0	8	40.0	168	27	16	13	5	3	0	1	25	2	48	3	0	2	0	1.000	0	0-0	9	3.29	2.93
2010 Cle	AL	70	0	0	16	63.0	266	48	30	29	12	3	2	2	39	3	69	4	0	2	2	.500	0	1-3	15	4.42	4.14
2011 Cle	AL	69	0	0	17	62.1	251	45	22	21	10	1	2	0	24	3	57	2	1	6	3	.667	0	0-1	24	2.87	3.03
2012 Cle	AL	63	0	0	7	55.0	233	47	29	27	9	2	1	1	23	1	51	3	0	1	2	.333	0	1-2	12	3.80	4.42
2013 Ari	NL	56	0	0	11	37.2	175	35	22	20	6	3	1	3	22	2	42	3	1	3	2	.600	0	0-2	5	4.90	4.78
2014 Hou	AL	56	0	0	13	50.2	198	28	19	19	5	2	0	0	17	2	63	3	0	4	3	.571	0	4-6	11	1.57	3.38
6 ML YEARS		360	0	0	72	308.2	1291	230	138	129	47	14	7	6	150	13	330	18	2	18	12	.600	0	6-14	74	3.38	3.76

Grady Sizemore

Bats: L Throws: L Pos: LF-52;RF-26;CF-25;PH-20;PR-3   Ht: 6'2" Wt: 200 Born: 8/2/1982 Age: 32

								BATTING												RUNNING			AVERAGES			
Year Team	Lg	G	AB	H	2B	3B	HR	(Hm	Rd)	TB	R	RBI	RC	TBB	IBB	SO	HBP	SH	SF	SB	CS	GDP	Avg	OBP	Slg	OPS
2014 LV*	AAA	11	46	13	1	0	1	(-	-)	17	5	2	6	5	0	7	0	0	0	0	0	0	.283	.353	.370	.723
2004 Cle	AL	43	138	34	6	2	4	(2	2)	56	15	24	21	14	0	34	5	0	2	2	0	0	.246	.333	.406	.739
2005 Cle	AL	158	640	185	37	11	22	(10	12)	310	111	81	101	52	1	132	7	5	2	22	10	17	.289	.348	.484	.832
2006 Cle	AL	162	655	190	53	11	28	(14	14)	349	134	76	121	78	8	153	13	1	4	22	6	2	.290	.375	.533	.907
2007 Cle	AL	162	628	174	34	5	24	(11	13)	290	118	78	123	101	9	155	17	0	2	33	10	3	.277	.390	.462	.852
2008 Cle	AL	157	634	170	39	5	33	(21	12)	318	101	90	121	98	14	130	11	0	2	38	5	5	.268	.374	.502	.876
2009 Cle	AL	106	436	108	20	6	18	(5	13)	194	73	64	68	60	1	92	4	2	1	13	8	4	.248	.343	.445	.788
2010 Cle	AL	33	128	27	6	2	0	(0	0)	37	15	13	11	9	0	35	2	0	1	4	2	1	.211	.271	.289	.560
2011 Cle	AL	71	268	60	21	1	10	(6	4)	113	34	32	28	18	1	85	6	0	3	0	2	4	.224	.285	.422	.706
2014 2 Tms		112	347	81	19	4	5	(1	4)	123	35	27	39	33	0	76	0	0	1	6	1	10	.233	.299	.354	.654
14 Bos	AL	52	185	40	10	2	2	(0	2)	60	14	15	18	19	0	41	0	0	1	5	0	6	.216	.288	.324	.612
14 Phi	NL	60	162	41	9	2	3	(1	2)	63	21	12	21	14	0	35	0	0	0	1	1	4	.253	.313	.389	.701
Postseason		11	43	12	2	1	2	(0	2)	22	9	3	5	8	3	9	1	0	1	2	1	2	.279	.396	.512	.908
9 ML YEARS		1004	3874	1029	235	47	144	(70	74)	1790	636	485	633	463	34	892	65	8	18	140	44	46	.266	.352	.462	.814

Scott Sizemore

Bats: R Throws: R Pos: 3B-5;1B-2   Ht: 6'0" Wt: 185 Born: 1/4/1985 Age: 30

								BATTING												RUNNING			AVERAGES			
Year Team	Lg	G	AB	H	2B	3B	HR	(Hm	Rd)	TB	R	RBI	RC	TBB	IBB	SO	HBP	SH	SF	SB	CS	GDP	Avg	OBP	Slg	OPS
2014 S-WB*	AAA	81	289	77	17	5	7	(-	-)	125	31	41	42	26	1	87	2	0	2	0	0	6	.266	.329	.433	.762
2010 Det	AL	48	143	32	7	0	3	(1	2)	48	19	14	13	15	0	40	0	4	1	0	0	4	.224	.296	.336	.631
2011 2 Tms	AL	110	368	90	22	1	11	(4	7)	147	50	56	60	53	0	112	2	5	1	5	3	8	.245	.342	.399	.741
2013 Oak	AL	2	6	1	1	0	0	(0	0)	2	0	0	0	0	0	2	0	0	0	0	0	0	.167	.167	.333	.500
2014 NYY	AL	6	16	5	2	0	0	(0	0)	7	3	4	3	0	0	8	0	0	0	0	0	0	.313	.313	.438	.750
11 Det	AL	17	63	14	1	0	0	(0	0)	15	8	4	8	10	0	19	0	1	0	1	1	2	.222	.329	.238	.567
11 Oak	AL	93	305	76	21	1	11	(4	7)	132	42	52	52	43	0	93	2	4	1	4	2	8	.249	.345	.433	.778
4 ML YEARS		166	533	128	32	1	14	(5	9)	204	72	74	76	68	0	162	2	9	2	5	3	12	.240	.327	.383	.710

Tyler Skaggs

Pitches: L Bats: L Pos: SP-18   Ht: 6'4" Wt: 215 Born: 7/13/1991 Age: 23

	HOW MUCH HE PITCHED						WHAT HE GAVE UP											THE RESULTS							
Year Team	Lg	G	GS	CG	GF	IP	BFP	H	R	ER	HR	SH	SF	HB	TBB	IBB	SO	WP	Bk	W	L	Pct	Sh	Sv-Op	Hld	ERC	ERA
2014 Salt Lk*	AAA	1	1	0	0	3.0	19	5	7	2	0	0	0	0	5	0	2	1	0	0	1	.000	0	0- --	-	12.68	6.00
2012 Ari	NL	6	6	0	0	29.1	133	30	20	19	6	1	0	2	13	0	21	1	0	1	3	.250	0	0-0	0	5.31	5.83
2013 Ari	NL	7	7	0	0	38.2	170	38	23	22	7	0	2	2	15	2	36	2	0	2	3	.400	0	0-0	0	4.56	5.12
2014 LAA	AL	18	18	0	0	113.0	464	107	59	54	9	2	5	4	30	1	86	7	0	5	5	.500	0	0-0	0	3.31	4.30
3 ML YEARS		31	31	0	0	181.0	767	175	102	95	22	3	7	8	58	3	143	10	0	8	11	.421	0	0-0	0	3.88	4.72

Kevin Slowey

Pitches: R Bats: R Pos: RP-15; SP-2   Ht: 6'3" Wt: 205 Born: 5/4/1984 Age: 31

	HOW MUCH HE PITCHED						WHAT HE GAVE UP											THE RESULTS							
Year Team	Lg	G	GS	CG	GF	IP	BFP	H	R	ER	HR	SH	SF	HB	TBB	IBB	SO	WP	Bk	W	L	Pct	Sh	Sv-Op	Hld	ERC	ERA
2007 Min	AL	13	11	0	0	66.2	297	82	39	35	16	0	1	0	11	0	47	3	0	4	1	.800	0	0-0	0	5.22	4.73
2008 Min	AL	27	27	3	0	160.1	653	161	74	71	22	1	5	4	24	1	123	1	0	12	11	.522	2	0-0	0	3.48	3.99
2009 Min	AL	16	16	0	0	90.2	394	113	50	49	15	3	5	5	15	1	75	0	0	10	3	.769	0	0-0	0	5.25	4.86
2010 Min	AL	30	28	0	0	155.2	662	172	80	77	21	2	11	4	29	0	116	3	0	13	6	.684	0	0-0	0	4.13	4.45
2011 Min	AL	14	8	0	1	59.0	258	78	44	44	10	3	4	3	5	0	34	0	0	0	8	.000	0	0-0	0	5.31	6.67
2013 Mia	NL	20	14	0	2	92.0	395	106	44	42	12	3	6	4	18	0	76	1	0	3	6	.333	0	0-0	0	4.51	4.11
2014 Mia	NL	17	2	0	4	37.1	169	53	23	22	3	4	4	2	9	1	24	0	0	1	1	.500	0	0-0	0	6.02	5.30
7 ML YEARS		137	106	3	7	662.0	2828	765	354	340	99	16	36	22	111	3	495	11	0	43	36	.544	2	0-0	0	4.49	4.62

Carson Smith

Pitches: R Bats: R Pos: RP-9   Ht: 6'6" Wt: 215 Born: 10/19/1989 Age: 25

						HOW MUCH HE PITCHED			WHAT HE GAVE UP									THE RESULTS							
Year	Team	Lg	G	GS	CG	GF	IP	BFP	H	R	ER	HR	SH	SF	HB	TBB	IBB	SO	WP	Bk	W	L	Pct	Sh	Sv-Op	Hld	ERC	ERA
2012	Hi Dsrt	A+	49	0	0	32	62.0	271	54	22	20	2	5	2	5	28	2	77	11	1	5	1	.833	0	15--	-	3.29	2.90
2013	Jacksn	AA	44	0	0	37	50.0	203	33	12	10	1	1	0	5	17	3	71	7	0	1	3	.250	0	15--	-	1.88	1.80
2014	Tacom	AAA	39	0	0	30	43.0	182	44	19	14	1	1	1	1	13	0	45	2	0	1	3	.250	0	10--	-	3.40	2.93
2014	Sea	AL	9	0	0	1	8.1	29	2	0	0	0	0	0	0	3	0	10	0	0	1	0	1.000	0	0-0	3	0.55	0.00

Chad Smith

Pitches: R Bats: R Pos: RP-10   Ht: 6'3" Wt: 215 Born: 10/2/1989 Age: 25

						HOW MUCH HE PITCHED			WHAT HE GAVE UP									THE RESULTS							
Year	Team	Lg	G	GS	CG	GF	IP	BFP	H	R	ER	HR	SH	SF	HB	TBB	IBB	SO	WP	Bk	W	L	Pct	Sh	Sv-Op	Hld	ERC	ERA
2012	Tigers	R	4	3	0	0	14.2	63	14	2	1	0	0	0	1	6	0	23	0	0	1	0	1.000	0	0--	-	3.44	0.61
2012	Conn	A-	2	0	0	2	6.1	23	3	1	1	0	0	0	0	2	0	8	1	0	0	0	-	0	2--	-	1.04	1.42
2012	WMich	A	8	5	0	1	24.2	99	23	12	12	2	0	1	0	6	0	17	3	0	0	2	.000	0	0--	-	3.07	4.38
2013	WMich	A	43	2	0	8	72.0	286	58	19	17	3	2	2	0	22	2	73	3	0	5	4	.556	0	1--	-	2.35	2.13
2014	Erie	AA	12	0	0	2	20.0	78	15	3	3	0	0	0	0	6	0	18	2	0	1	0	1.000	0	1--	-	1.88	1.35
2014	Toledo	AAA	22	0	0	6	27.0	119	38	15	15	2	2	2	0	5	0	22	1	1	4	3	.571	0	0--	-	5.48	5.00
2014	Det	AL	10	0	0	5	11.2	50	15	7	7	1	0	0	0	3	0	9	0	0	0	0	-	0	0-0	0	5.24	5.40

Joe Smith

Pitches: R Bats: R Pos: RP-76   Ht: 6'2" Wt: 205 Born: 3/22/1984 Age: 31

						HOW MUCH HE PITCHED			WHAT HE GAVE UP									THE RESULTS							
Year	Team	Lg	G	GS	CG	GF	IP	BFP	H	R	ER	HR	SH	SF	HB	TBB	IBB	SO	WP	Bk	W	L	Pct	Sh	Sv-Op	Hld	ERC	ERA
2007	NYM	NL	54	0	0	14	44.1	205	48	18	17	3	2	0	7	21	4	45	2	0	3	2	.600	0	0-0	10	5.04	3.45
2008	NYM	NL	82	0	0	12	63.1	271	51	28	25	4	4	0	4	31	4	52	1	0	6	3	.667	0	0-3	18	3.23	3.55
2009	Cle	AL	37	0	0	5	34.0	142	30	16	13	4	1	1	0	13	0	30	2	0	0	0	-	0	0-1	10	3.49	3.44
2010	Cle	AL	53	0	0	7	40.0	170	30	18	17	4	1	0	1	24	2	32	0	1	2	2	.500	0	0-1	17	3.53	3.83
2011	Cle	AL	71	0	0	13	67.0	267	52	16	15	1	2	2	2	21	1	45	2	0	3	3	.500	0	0-3	16	2.19	2.01
2012	Cle	AL	72	0	0	12	67.0	278	53	27	22	4	1	1	2	25	4	53	1	1	7	4	.636	0	0-3	21	2.60	2.96
2013	Cle	AL	70	0	0	20	63.0	259	54	17	16	5	3	0	3	23	2	54	3	0	6	2	.750	0	3-8	25	3.23	2.29
2014	LAA	AL	76	0	0	26	74.2	285	45	16	15	4	3	0	6	15	3	68	4	0	7	2	.778	0	15-19	18	1.47	1.81
	Postseason		1	0	0	1	0.2	4	1	0	0	0	0	0	0	0	0	1	0	0	0	0	-	0	0-0	1	3.21	0.00
	8 ML YEARS		515	0	0	109	453.1	1877	363	156	140	29	17	4	25	173	20	379	15	2	34	18	.654	0	18-38	135	2.86	2.78

Seth Smith

Bats: L Throws: L Pos: LF-102;RF-43;PH-16;DH-1   Ht: 6'3" Wt: 210 Born: 9/30/1982 Age: 32

						BATTING															RUNNING			AVERAGES			
Year	Team	Lg	G	AB	H	2B	3B	HR	(Hm	Rd)	TB	R	RBI	RC	TBB	IBB	SO	HBP	SH	SF	SB	CS	GDP	Avg	OBP	Slg	OPS
2007	Col	NL	7	8	5	0	1	0	(0	0)	7	4	0	3	0	0	1	0	0	0	0	0	0	.625	.625	.875	1.500
2008	Col	NL	67	108	28	7	0	4	(2	2)	47	13	15	18	15	0	23	0	0	0	1	0	0	.259	.350	.435	.785
2009	Col	NL	133	335	98	20	4	15	(8	7)	171	61	55	63	46	3	67	2	1	3	4	1	5	.293	.378	.510	.889
2010	Col	NL	133	358	88	19	5	17	(12	5)	168	55	52	51	35	1	67	2	0	3	2	1	5	.246	.314	.469	.783
2011	Col	NL	147	476	135	32	9	15	(9	6)	230	67	59	73	46	7	93	4	0	7	10	2	9	.284	.347	.483	.830
2012	Oak	AL	125	383	92	23	2	14	(6	8)	161	55	52	52	50	7	98	5	0	3	2	2	4	.240	.333	.420	.754
2013	Oak	AL	117	368	93	27	0	8	(3	5)	144	49	40	46	39	4	94	3	0	0	0	0	10	.253	.329	.391	.721
2014	SD	AL	136	443	118	31	5	12	(8	4)	195	55	48	68	69	3	87	4	0	4	1	1	9	.266	.367	.440	.807
	Postseason		18	42	11	2	0	2	(1	1)	19	6	7	7	5	2	13	1	0	0	0	0	0	.262	.354	.452	.807
	8 ML YEARS		865	2479	657	159	26	85	(48	37)	1123	359	321	374	300	25	530	20	1	20	20	7	42	.265	.347	.453	.800

Will Smith

Pitches: L Bats: R Pos: RP-78   Ht: 6'5" Wt: 250 Born: 7/10/1989 Age: 25

						HOW MUCH HE PITCHED			WHAT HE GAVE UP									THE RESULTS							
Year	Team	Lg	G	GS	CG	GF	IP	BFP	H	R	ER	HR	SH	SF	HB	TBB	IBB	SO	WP	Bk	W	L	Pct	Sh	Sv-Op	Hld	ERC	ERA
2012	KC	AL	16	16	0	0	89.2	396	111	54	53	12	2	5	1	33	1	59	4	0	6	9	.400	0	0-0	0	5.75	5.32
2013	KC	AL	19	1	0	4	33.1	131	24	16	12	6	0	4	1	7	0	40	0	0	2	1	.667	0	0-3	6	2.47	3.24
2014	Mil	NL	78	0	0	6	65.2	286	62	31	27	6	1	1	3	31	6	86	7	0	1	3	.250	0	1-6	30	4.02	3.70
	3 ML YEARS		113	17	0	10	188.2	813	197	101	92	24	3	10	5	71	7	188	11	0	9	13	.409	0	1-9	36	4.52	4.39

Justin Smoak

Bats: B Throws: L Pos: 1B-79;PH-3   SMOKE   Ht: 6'4" Wt: 230 Born: 12/5/1986 Age: 28

						BATTING															RUNNING			AVERAGES			
Year	Team	Lg	G	AB	H	2B	3B	HR	(Hm	Rd)	TB	R	RBI	RC	TBB	IBB	SO	HBP	SH	SF	SB	CS	GDP	Avg	OBP	Slg	OPS
2014	Tacom*	AAA	56	205	69	13	0	7	(-	-)	103	29	40	45	33	4	41	3	0	8	0	2	5	.337	.422	.502	.924
2010	2 Tms	AL	100	348	76	14	0	13	(4	9)	129	40	48	42	46	4	91	0	0	3	1	0	9	.218	.307	.371	.678
2011	Sea	AL	123	427	100	24	0	15	(10	5)	169	38	55	55	55	4	105	3	0	4	0	0	10	.234	.323	.396	.719
2012	Sea	AL	132	483	105	14	0	19	(4	15)	176	49	51	50	49	2	111	1	0	2	1	0	12	.217	.290	.364	.654
2013	Sea	AL	131	454	108	19	0	20	(9	11)	187	53	50	60	64	1	119	2	0	1	0	0	11	.238	.334	.412	.746
2014	Sea	AL	80	248	50	13	0	7	(4	3)	84	28	30	23	24	0	66	2	0	1	0	1	6	.202	.275	.339	.614
10	Tex	AL	70	235	49	10	0	8	(4	4)	83	29	34	30	38	4	57	0	0	2	1	0	6	.209	.316	.353	.670
10	Sea	AL	30	113	27	4	0	5	(0	5)	46	11	14	12	8	0	34	0	0	1	0	0	3	.239	.287	.407	.694
	5 ML YEARS		566	1960	439	84	0	74	(31	43)	745	208	234	230	238	11	492	8	0	12	2	1	50	.224	.309	.380	.689

290

Jake Smolinski

Bats: R Throws: R Pos: LF-12;RF-9;DH-3;PH-1   smoh-LYNN-skee   Ht: 5'11" Wt: 215 Born: 2/9/1989 Age: 26

									BATTING												RUNNING			AVERAGES			
Year	Team	Lg	G	AB	H	2B	3B	HR	(Hm	Rd)	TB	R	RBI	RC	TBB	IBB	SO	HBP	SH	SF	SB	CS	GDP	Avg	OBP	Slg	OPS
2010	Jupiter	A+	109	405	107	27	3	5	(-	-)	155	45	51	51	31	0	62	3	0	4	8	5	12	.264	.318	.383	.701
2011	Jaxnvl	AA	116	396	97	26	0	7	(-	-)	144	42	36	54	59	5	57	1	3	3	6	5	8	.245	.342	.364	.706
2012	Jaxnvl	AA	112	408	105	24	3	7	(-	-)	156	71	42	69	78	1	74	10	2	2	9	4	8	.257	.388	.382	.770
2013	Jaxnvl	AA	24	56	11	1	0	0	(-	-)	12	8	4	6	13	1	10	1	0	0	1	0	0	.196	.357	.214	.571
2013	NewOr	AAA	95	314	81	14	2	9	(-	-)	126	36	31	47	37	3	61	5	0	1	8	1	8	.258	.345	.401	.746
2013	Mrlns	R	2	6	3	0	0	0	(-	-)	3	1	0	1	1	0	0	0	0	0	0	0	0	.500	.571	.500	1.071
2014	Frisco	AA	72	266	71	15	3	10	(-	-)	122	43	35	45	32	0	54	4	0	5	6	2	4	.267	.349	.459	.807
2014	RdRck	AAA	8	30	8	6	0	0	(-	-)	14	7	6	5	4	0	5	0	0	0	0	0	0	.267	.353	.467	.820
2014	Tex	AL	24	86	30	5	0	3	(1	2)	44	12	12	15	3	0	24	3	0	0	0	0	1	.349	.391	.512	.903

Drew Smyly

Pitches: L Bats: L Pos: SP-25; RP-3   SMILE-ee   Ht: 6'3" Wt: 190 Born: 6/13/1989 Age: 26

				HOW MUCH HE PITCHED				WHAT HE GAVE UP											THE RESULTS					
Year	Team	Lg	G	GS	CG	GF	IP	BFP	H	R	ER	HR	SH	SF	HB	TBB	IBB	SO	WP	Bk	W	L	Pct	Sh	Sv-Op	Hld	ERC	ERA
2012	Det	AL	23	18	0	0	99.1	416	93	49	44	12	2	3	2	33	1	94	3	0	4	3	.571	0	0-0	1	3.68	3.99
2013	Det	AL	63	0	0	9	76.0	303	62	20	20	4	0	1	1	17	1	81	5	0	6	0	1.000	0	2-6	21	2.21	2.37
2014	2 Tms	AL	28	25	1	0	153.0	618	136	57	55	18	1	3	1	42	2	133	8	0	9	10	.474	1	0-0	1	3.17	3.24
14	Det	AL	21	18	0	0	105.1	445	111	48	46	14	0	3	1	31	1	89	4	0	6	9	.400	1	0-0	1	4.26	3.93
14	TB	AL	7	7	1	0	47.2	173	25	9	9	4	1	0	0	11	1	44	4	0	3	1	.750	1	0-0	0	1.28	1.70
	Postseason		10	0	0	1	7.0	30	3	3	2	0	0	0	0	6	1	7	0	0	1	0	1.000	0	0-0	2	1.81	2.57
	3 ML YEARS		114	43	1	9	328.1	1337	291	126	119	34	3	7	4	92	4	308	16	0	19	13	.594	1	2-6	23	3.09	3.26

Travis Snider

Bats: L Throws: L Pos: RF-64;PH-60;LF-36;DH-1   Ht: 6'0" Wt: 235 Born: 2/2/1988 Age: 27

									BATTING												RUNNING			AVERAGES			
Year	Team	Lg	G	AB	H	2B	3B	HR	(Hm	Rd)	TB	R	RBI	RC	TBB	IBB	SO	HBP	SH	SF	SB	CS	GDP	Avg	OBP	Slg	OPS
2008	Tor	AL	24	73	22	6	0	2	(1	1)	34	9	13	13	5	0	23	0	0	2	0	0	0	.301	.338	.466	.803
2009	Tor	AL	77	241	58	14	1	9	(5	4)	101	34	29	30	29	1	78	3	2	1	1	1	5	.241	.328	.419	.748
2010	Tor	AL	82	298	76	20	0	14	(9	5)	138	36	32	40	21	2	79	0	0	0	6	3	3	.255	.304	.463	.767
2011	Tor	AL	49	187	42	14	0	3	(2	1)	65	23	30	21	11	1	56	1	1	2	9	3	5	.225	.269	.348	.616
2012	2 Tms		60	164	41	7	1	4	(3	1)	62	23	17	21	17	0	48	1	0	3	2	0	2	.250	.319	.378	.697
2013	Pit	NL	111	261	56	12	2	5	(4	1)	87	28	25	23	24	3	75	0	0	4	2	3	1	.215	.281	.333	.614
2014	Pit	NL	140	322	85	15	1	13	(4	9)	141	37	38	42	34	2	67	2	1	0	1	1	10	.264	.338	.438	.776
12	Tor	AL	10	36	9	2	0	3	(2	1)	20	6	8	7	3	0	14	0	0	1	0	0	0	.250	.300	.556	.856
12	Pit	NL	50	128	32	5	1	1	(1	0)	42	17	9	14	14	0	34	1	0	2	2	0	2	.250	.324	.328	.652
	Postseason		1	1	0	0	0	0	(0	0)	0	0	0	0	0	0	1	0	0	0	0	0	0	.000	.000	.000	.000
	7 ML YEARS		543	1546	380	88	5	50	(28	22)	628	190	184	190	141	9	426	7	4	8	21	11	26	.246	.310	.406	.716

Scott Snodgress

Pitches: L Bats: L Pos: RP-4   SNOD-gress   Ht: 6'6" Wt: 225 Born: 9/20/1989 Age: 25

				HOW MUCH HE PITCHED				WHAT HE GAVE UP											THE RESULTS					
Year	Team	Lg	G	GS	CG	GF	IP	BFP	H	R	ER	HR	SH	SF	HB	TBB	IBB	SO	WP	Bk	W	L	Pct	Sh	Sv-Op	Hld	ERC	ERA
2011	Gr Falls	R+	16	12	0	0	59.1	254	61	32	22	5	1	2	1	17	0	68	7	1	3	3	.500	0	0--	-	3.71	3.34
2012	Knapol	A	19	19	0	0	99.0	431	86	49	40	4	2	4	7	49	0	84	6	0	3	3	.500	0	0--	-	3.55	3.64
2012	WinSa	A+	8	8	0	0	42.0	165	26	10	7	2	1	0	1	15	0	44	1	0	4	0	1.000	0	0--	-	1.78	1.50
2013	Brham	AA	26	26	2	0	143.2	623	146	90	75	9	7	11	4	59	0	90	4	2	11	11	.500	0	0--	-	4.07	4.70
2014	Brham	AA	21	21	0	0	122.2	528	119	60	53	9	2	2	7	52	0	79	7	0	6	7	.462	0	0--	-	4.09	3.89
2014	Charltt	AAA	8	0	0	1	16.1	69	17	9	9	4	1	0	0	4	0	16	0	0	1	0	1.000	0	0--	-	4.64	4.96
2014	CWS	AL	4	0	0	1	2.1	19	8	7	4	1	0	0	0	3	1	1	1	0	0	0	-	0	0-0	0	27.35	15.43

Brad Snyder

Bats: L Throws: L Pos: 1B-10;PH-1   Ht: 6'3" Wt: 220 Born: 5/25/1982 Age: 33

									BATTING												RUNNING			AVERAGES			
Year	Team	Lg	G	AB	H	2B	3B	HR	(Hm	Rd)	TB	R	RBI	RC	TBB	IBB	SO	HBP	SH	SF	SB	CS	GDP	Avg	OBP	Slg	OPS
2014	RdRck*	AAA	61	232	66	11	1	18	(-	-)	133	46	51	47	25	0	82	0	0	3	3	0	3	.284	.350	.573	.923
2010	ChC	NL	12	27	5	1	0	0	(0	0)	6	1	5	2	1	0	12	0	0	0	0	0	0	.185	.214	.222	.437
2011	ChC	NL	8	9	1	0	0	0	(0	0)	1	1	0	0	0	0	6	0	0	0	0	0	0	.111	.111	.111	.222
2014	Tex	AL	10	30	5	1	0	2	(0	2)	12	3	3	1	4	0	10	0	0	0	0	0	1	.167	.265	.400	.665
	3 ML YEARS		30	66	11	2	0	2	(0	2)	19	5	8	3	5	0	28	0	0	0	0	0	1	.167	.225	.288	.513

Eric Sogard

Bats: L Throws: R Pos: 2B-102;SS-14;PR-9;PH-3;DH-1   SO-guard   Ht: 5'10" Wt: 190 Born: 5/22/1986 Age: 29

									BATTING												RUNNING			AVERAGES			
Year	Team	Lg	G	AB	H	2B	3B	HR	(Hm	Rd)	TB	R	RBI	RC	TBB	IBB	SO	HBP	SH	SF	SB	CS	GDP	Avg	OBP	Slg	OPS
2010	Oak	AL	4	7	3	0	0	0	(0	0)	3	0	0	1	2	0	1	0	0	0	0	1	0	.429	.556	.429	.984
2011	Oak	AL	27	70	14	3	0	2	(0	2)	23	7	4	3	4	0	13	0	0	0	0	0	2	.200	.243	.329	.572
2012	Oak	AL	37	102	17	3	1	2	(0	2)	28	8	7	7	5	0	17	0	1	0	2	0	1	.167	.206	.275	.480
2013	Oak	AL	130	368	98	24	3	2	(0	2)	134	45	35	43	27	2	51	5	6	4	10	5	4	.266	.322	.364	.686
2014	Oak	AL	117	291	65	10	0	1	(1	0)	78	38	22	27	31	0	37	1	4	2	11	4	6	.223	.298	.268	.567
	Postseason		4	9	0	0	0	0	(0	0)	0	0	0	0	1	0	1	0	1	0	0	0	0	.000	.100	.000	.100
	5 ML YEARS		315	838	197	40	4	7	(1	6)	266	98	68	81	69	2	119	6	11	6	23	10	13	.235	.296	.317	.613

Donovan Solano

Bats: R Throws: R Pos: 2B-73;PH-36;SS-4;3B-2   sol-ON-oh   Ht: 5'9" Wt: 205 Born: 12/17/1987 Age: 27

							BATTING													RUNNING			AVERAGES			
Year	Team	Lg	G	AB	H	2B	3B	HR	(Hm | Rd)	TB	R	RBI	RC	TBB	IBB	SO	HBP	SH	SF	SB	CS	GDP	Avg	OBP	Slg	OPS
2014	NewOr*	AAA	6	21	2	1	0	0	(- | -)	3	2	3	0	0	0	5	0	0	1	0	0	1	.095	.091	.143	.234
2012	Mia	NL	93	285	84	11	3	2	(0 | 2)	107	29	28	35	21	1	58	2	3	5	7	0	5	.295	.342	.375	.717
2013	Mia	NL	102	361	90	13	1	3	(0 | 3)	114	33	34	38	23	3	57	7	2	2	3	1	11	.249	.305	.316	.621
2014	Mia	NL	111	310	78	11	1	3	(1 | 2)	100	26	28	35	19	0	61	3	7	1	1	2	5	.252	.300	.323	.623
	3 ML YEARS		306	956	252	35	5	8	(1 | 7)	321	88	90	108	63	4	176	12	12	8	11	3	21	.264	.315	.336	.650

Yangervis Solarte

YAWN-gurr-veess soh-LAHR-tay

Bats: B Throws: R Pos: 3B-111;2B-27;SS-8;LF-7;PH-5   Ht: 5'11" Wt: 195 Born: 7/7/1987 Age: 27

							BATTING													RUNNING			AVERAGES			
Year	Team	Lg	G	AB	H	2B	3B	HR	(Hm | Rd)	TB	R	RBI	RC	TBB	IBB	SO	HBP	SH	SF	SB	CS	GDP	Avg	OBP	Slg	OPS
2010	FtMyrs	A+	45	172	55	9	1	2	(- | -)	72	19	15	-	13	1	13	1	2	0	3	0	8	.320	.328	.419	.790
2010	NwBrit	AA	32	127	35	9	0	3	(- | -)	53	14	19	15	3	0	18	0	1	1	1	1	8	.276	.290	.417	.707
2010	Twins	R	7	23	4	0	0	0	(- | -)	4	3	0	-	1	0	4	0	0	0	0	0	0	.174	.208	.174	.382
2011	NwBrit	AA	121	459	151	36	3	7	(- | -)	214	64	49	78	24	2	38	5	7	2	5	4	18	.329	.367	.466	.834
2012	RdRck	AAA	130	518	150	28	0	11	(- | -)	211	69	54	76	41	1	44	3	0	6	3	1	29	.290	.342	.407	.749
2013	RdRck	AAA	133	526	145	31	0	12	(- | -)	212	66	75	72	39	3	69	2	2	8	3	0	22	.276	.323	.403	.727
2014	S-WB	AAA	5	20	12	3	1	0	(- | -)	17	3	5	7	1	0	2	0	0	0	0	0	0	.600	.619	.850	1.469
2014	2 Tms		131	469	122	19	1	10	(5 | 5)	173	56	48	59	53	1	58	4	3	6	0	1	13	.260	.336	.369	.705
14	NYY	AL	75	252	64	14	0	6	(3 | 3)	96	26	31	33	30	0	34	3	1	3	0	0	8	.254	.337	.381	.718
14	SD	NL	56	217	58	5	1	4	(2 | 2)	77	30	17	26	23	1	24	1	2	3	0	1	5	.267	.336	.355	.691

Jorge Soler

HOR-hay so-LAIR

Bats: R Throws: R Pos: RF-24   Ht: 6'4" Wt: 215 Born: 2/25/1992 Age: 23

							BATTING													RUNNING			AVERAGES			
Year	Team	Lg	G	AB	H	2B	3B	HR	(Hm | Rd)	TB	R	RBI	RC	TBB	IBB	SO	HBP	SH	SF	SB	CS	GDP	Avg	OBP	Slg	OPS
2012	Cubs	R	14	54	13	2	0	2	(- | -)	21	14	10	8	6	0	13	1	0	0	8	0	0	.241	.328	.389	.717
2012	Peoria	A	20	80	27	5	0	3	(- | -)	41	14	15	16	6	2	6	2	0	0	4	1	3	.338	.398	.513	.910
2013	Dytona	A+	55	210	59	13	1	8	(- | -)	98	38	35	35	21	1	38	1	0	4	5	1	3	.281	.343	.467	.810
2014	Tenn	AA	22	65	27	9	1	6	(- | -)	56	13	22	24	12	0	15	0	0	2	0	0	1	.415	.494	.862	1.355
2014	Cubs	R	8	25	10	3	0	1	(- | -)	16	7	6	7	4	0	7	1	0	0	0	0	1	.400	.500	.640	1.140
2014	Iowa	AAA	32	110	31	11	1	8	(- | -)	68	22	29	24	17	2	26	0	0	0	0	1	4	.282	.378	.618	.996
2014	ChC	NL	24	89	26	8	1	5	(1 | 4)	51	11	20	15	6	0	24	0	0	2	1	0	3	.292	.330	.573	.903

Ali Solis

al-LEE so-LEASE

Bats: R Throws: R Pos: C-8;PR-1   Ht: 6'0" Wt: 175 Born: 9/29/1987 Age: 27

							BATTING													RUNNING			AVERAGES			
Year	Team	Lg	G	AB	H	2B	3B	HR	(Hm | Rd)	TB	R	RBI	RC	TBB	IBB	SO	HBP	SH	SF	SB	CS	GDP	Avg	OBP	Slg	OPS
2010	Lk Els	A+	12	37	10	1	0	4	(- | -)	23	6	8	-	2	0	10	0	-	0	0	0	1	.270	.308	.622	.929
2010	SnAnt	AA	11	18	2	0	0	0	(- | -)	2	0	1	0	0	0	5	1	0	0	0	0	1	.111	.158	.111	.269
2011	SnAnt	AA	73	255	67	14	1	6	(- | -)	101	30	26	31	12	2	65	5	1	1	0	0	9	.263	.308	.396	.704
2011	Tucsn	AAA	11	38	8	2	0	0	(- | -)	10	3	3	1	1	0	14	0	0	0	0	0	2	.211	.231	.263	.494
2012	SnAnt	AA	87	329	93	25	1	6	(- | -)	138	26	40	42	11	0	77	1	1	1	1	1	11	.283	.307	.419	.726
2013	Altna	AA	20	61	10	3	0	0	(- | -)	13	7	1	2	3	0	17	1	1	0	2	0	1	.164	.215	.213	.428
2013	Indy	AAA	9	23	5	0	0	0	(- | -)	5	2	2	1	2	0	4	0	0	1	0	0	1	.217	.269	.217	.487
2014	Drham	AAA	73	251	51	7	2	3	(- | -)	71	20	25	14	6	0	75	4	2	3	0	1	4	.203	.231	.283	.514
2012	SD	NL	5	4	0	0	0	0	(0 | 0)	0	0	0	0	0	0	2	0	0	0	0	0	0	.000	.000	.000	.000
2014	TB	AL	8	6	0	0	0	0	(0 | 0)	0	0	1	0	0	0	4	0	1	0	0	0	0	.000	.000	.000	.000
	2 ML YEARS		13	10	0	0	0	0	(0 | 0)	0	0	1	0	0	0	6	0	1	0	0	0	0	.000	.000	.000	.000

Joakim Soria

wah-KEEM SORE-ee-uh

Pitches: R Bats: R Pos: RP-48   Ht: 6'3" Wt: 200 Born: 5/18/1984 Age: 31

			HOW MUCH HE PITCHED						WHAT HE GAVE UP										THE RESULTS						
Year	Team	Lg	G	GS	CG	GF	IP	BFP	H	R	ER	HR	SH	SF	HB	TBB	IBB	SO	WP	Bk	W	L	Pct	Sh	Sv-Op	Hld	ERC	ERA
2007	KC	AL	62	0	0	38	69.0	270	46	20	19	3	1	1	1	19	3	75	2	0	2	3	.400	0	17-21	9	1.63	2.48
2008	KC	AL	63	0	0	57	67.1	260	39	13	12	5	2	2	6	19	1	66	1	1	2	3	.400	0	42-45	0	1.72	1.60
2009	KC	AL	47	0	0	41	53.0	222	44	14	13	5	1	2	2	16	1	69	3	0	3	2	.600	0	30-33	0	2.80	2.21
2010	KC	AL	66	0	0	56	65.2	270	53	13	13	4	3	4	2	16	1	71	3	1	1	2	.333	0	43-46	0	2.27	1.78
2011	KC	AL	60	0	0	47	60.1	256	60	29	27	7	3	2	2	17	0	60	1	0	5	5	.500	0	28-35	0	3.80	4.03
2013	Tex	AL	26	0	0	9	23.2	101	18	10	10	2	1	0	1	14	2	28	2	0	1	0	1.000	0	0-6	6	3.45	3.80
2014	2 Tms	AL	48	0	0	37	44.1	182	38	19	16	2	1	2	2	6	2	48	1	0	2	4	.333	0	18-20	1	2.04	3.25
14	Tex	AL	35	0	0	32	33.1	133	25	12	10	0	1	1	1	4	1	42	0	0	1	3	.250	0	17-19	0	1.38	2.70
14	Det	AL	13	0	0	5	11.0	49	13	7	6	2	0	1	1	2	1	6	1	0	1	1	.500	0	1-1	1	4.92	4.91
	7 ML YEARS		372	0	0	285	383.1	1561	298	118	110	28	12	15	16	107	10	417	13	2	16	19	.457	0	178-200	16	2.38	2.58

292

Alfonso Soriano

Bats: R Throws: R Pos: RF-26;DH-25;LF-11;PH-9   Ht: 6'1" Wt: 195 Born: 1/7/1976 Age: 39

Year	Team	Lg	G	AB	H	2B	3B	HR	(Hm	Rd)	TB	R	RBI	RC	TBB	IBB	SO	HBP	SH	SF	SB	CS	GDP	Avg	OBP	Slg	OPS
1999	NYY	AL	9	8	1	0	0	1	(1	0)	4	2	1	0	0	0	3	0	0	0	0	1	0	.125	.125	.500	.625
2000	NYY	AL	22	50	9	3	0	2	(0	2)	18	5	3	4	1	0	15	0	2	0	2	0	0	.180	.196	.360	.556
2001	NYY	AL	158	574	154	34	3	18	(8	10)	248	77	73	77	29	0	125	3	3	5	43	14	7	.268	.304	.432	.736
2002	NYY	AL	156	696	209	51	2	39	(17	22)	381	128	102	121	23	1	157	14	1	7	41	13	8	.300	.332	.547	.880
2003	NYY	AL	156	682	198	36	5	38	(15	23)	358	114	91	110	38	7	130	12	0	2	35	8	8	.290	.338	.525	.863
2004	Tex	AL	145	608	170	32	4	28	(12	16)	294	77	91	90	33	4	121	10	0	7	18	5	7	.280	.324	.484	.807
2005	Tex	AL	156	637	171	43	2	36	(25	11)	326	102	104	93	33	3	125	7	0	5	30	2	6	.268	.309	.512	.821
2006	Was	NL	159	647	179	41	2	46	(24	22)	362	119	95	114	67	16	160	9	2	3	41	17	3	.277	.351	.560	.911
2007	ChC	NL	135	579	173	42	5	33	(13	20)	324	97	70	91	31	4	130	4	0	3	19	6	9	.299	.337	.560	.897
2008	ChC	NL	109	453	127	27	0	29	(17	12)	241	76	75	77	43	11	103	3	0	4	19	3	9	.280	.344	.532	.876
2009	ChC	NL	117	477	115	25	1	20	(7	13)	202	64	55	61	40	6	118	3	0	2	9	2	7	.241	.303	.423	.726
2010	ChC	NL	147	496	128	40	3	24	(11	13)	246	67	79	75	45	3	123	3	1	3	5	1	12	.258	.322	.496	.818
2011	ChC	NL	137	475	116	27	1	26	(12	14)	223	50	88	59	27	4	113	4	0	2	2	1	15	.244	.289	.469	.759
2012	ChC	NL	151	561	147	33	2	32	(15	17)	280	68	108	89	44	5	153	7	0	3	6	2	18	.262	.322	.499	.821
2013	2 Tms		151	581	148	32	1	34	(22	12)	284	84	101	90	36	3	156	5	0	4	18	9	11	.255	.302	.489	.791
2014	NYY	AL	67	226	50	15	0	6	(5	1)	83	22	23	14	6	1	71	2	0	4	1	0	3	.221	.244	.367	.611
13	ChC	NL	93	362	92	24	1	17	(11	6)	169	47	51	45	15	2	89	3	0	3	10	5	9	.254	.287	.467	.754
13	NYY	AL	58	219	56	8	0	17	(11	6)	115	37	50	45	21	1	67	2	0	1	8	4	2	.256	.325	.525	.850
Postseason			44	174	37	3	0	4	(3	1)	52	14	18	14	9	0	53	3	0	0	10	3	3	.213	.263	.299	.562
16 ML YEARS			1975	7750	2095	481	31	412	(204	208)	3874	1152	1159	1165	496	68	1803	86	9	54	289	84	123	.270	.319	.500	.819

Rafael Soriano

Pitches: R Bats: R Pos: RP-64   Ht: 6'4" Wt: 230 Born: 12/19/1979 Age: 35

Year	Team	Lg	G	GS	CG	GF	IP	BFP	H	R	ER	HR	SH	SF	HB	TBB	IBB	SO	WP	Bk	W	L	Pct	Sh	Sv-Op	Hld	ERC	ERA
2002	Sea	AL	10	8	0	1	47.1	202	45	25	24	8	1	0	0	16	1	32	2	0	0	3	.000	0	1-1	0	3.93	4.56
2003	Sea	AL	40	0	0	12	53.0	201	30	9	9	2	0	1	3	12	1	68	0	0	3	0	1.000	0	1-2	5	1.32	1.53
2004	Sea	AL	6	0	0	0	3.1	23	9	6	5	0	0	0	0	3	0	3	0	0	0	3	.000	0	0-1	0	15.97	13.50
2005	Sea	AL	7	0	0	4	7.1	30	6	2	2	0	0	1	1	1	0	9	0	0	0	0	-	0	0-0	1	2.00	2.45
2006	Sea	AL	53	0	0	14	60.0	241	44	15	15	6	1	1	2	21	0	65	2	0	1	2	.333	0	2-6	18	2.64	2.25
2007	Atl	NL	71	0	0	28	72.0	276	47	26	24	12	0	0	2	15	2	70	0	0	3	3	.500	0	9-12	19	2.05	3.00
2008	Atl	NL	14	0	0	5	14.0	57	7	5	4	1	0	0	1	9	2	16	1	0	0	1	.000	0	3-4	0	2.27	2.57
2009	Atl	NL	77	0	0	52	75.2	307	53	25	25	6	4	2	1	27	4	102	0	0	1	6	.143	0	27-31	6	2.18	2.97
2010	TB	AL	64	0	0	56	62.1	237	36	14	12	4	0	1	1	14	2	57	0	0	3	2	.600	0	45-48	0	1.33	1.73
2011	NYY	AL	42	0	0	8	39.1	164	33	18	18	4	1	0	1	18	2	36	0	0	2	3	.400	0	2-5	23	3.51	4.12
2012	NYY	AL	69	0	0	54	67.2	279	55	17	17	6	0	1	1	24	4	69	3	0	2	1	.667	0	42-46	4	2.79	2.26
2013	Was	NL	68	0	0	58	66.2	277	65	24	23	7	1	0	0	17	2	51	3	0	3	3	.500	0	43-49	0	3.36	3.11
2014	Was	NL	64	0	0	48	62.0	252	51	23	22	4	0	2	2	19	0	59	2	0	4	1	.800	0	32-39	0	2.70	3.19
Postseason			9	0	0	3	12.0	40	7	4	4	3	1	0	0	0	0	7	0	0	0	1	.000	0	1-1	1	1.49	3.00
13 ML YEARS			585	8	0	340	630.2	2546	481	209	200	60	8	9	15	196	20	637	13	0	22	28	.440	0	207-244	76	2.51	2.85

Geovany Soto

Bats: R Throws: R Pos: C-24   Ht: 6'1" Wt: 235 Born: 1/20/1983 Age: 32

Year	Team	Lg	G	AB	H	2B	3B	HR	(Hm	Rd)	TB	R	RBI	RC	TBB	IBB	SO	HBP	SH	SF	SB	CS	GDP	Avg	OBP	Slg	OPS
2014	RdRck*	AAA	10	32	6	2	0	1	(-	-)	11	2	2	2	1	0	10	0	0	0	0	0	1	.188	.212	.344	.556
2014	Frisco*	AA	6	19	7	2	0	0	(-	-)	9	4	1	4	3	0	6	0	0	0	0	0	0	.368	.455	.474	.928
2005	ChC	NL	1	1	0	0	0	0	(0	0)	0	0	0	0	0	0	0	0	0	0	0	0	0	.000	.000	.000	.000
2006	ChC	NL	11	25	5	1	0	0	(0	0)	6	1	2	0	0	0	5	1	0	0	0	0	0	.200	.231	.240	.471
2007	ChC	NL	18	54	21	6	0	3	(2	1)	36	12	8	13	5	0	14	0	0	1	0	0	1	.389	.433	.667	1.100
2008	ChC	NL	141	494	141	35	2	23	(11	12)	249	66	86	81	62	6	121	2	0	5	0	1	11	.285	.364	.504	.868
2009	ChC	NL	102	331	72	19	1	11	(6	5)	126	27	47	34	50	3	77	3	0	5	1	0	19	.218	.321	.381	.702
2010	ChC	NL	105	322	90	19	0	17	(12	5)	160	47	53	59	62	4	83	0	0	3	0	1	5	.280	.393	.497	.890
2011	ChC	NL	125	421	96	26	0	17	(7	10)	173	46	54	43	45	3	124	6	0	2	0	0	12	.228	.310	.411	.721
2012	2 Tms		99	324	64	12	1	11	(3	8)	111	45	39	30	30	1	76	3	2	2	1	0	12	.198	.270	.343	.613
2013	Tex	AL	54	163	40	9	0	9	(7	2)	76	20	22	23	20	0	60	0	1	0	1	2	2	.245	.328	.466	.794
2014	2 Tms	AL	24	80	20	6	0	1	(1	0)	29	8	11	6	6	0	19	0	1	0	0	0	3	.250	.302	.363	.665
12	ChC	NL	52	176	35	6	1	6	(2	4)	61	26	14	15	19	1	35	2	0	0	0	0	6	.199	.284	.347	.631
12	Tex	AL	47	148	29	6	0	5	(1	4)	50	19	25	15	11	0	41	1	2	2	1	0	6	.196	.253	.338	.591
14	Tex	AL	10	38	9	2	0	1	(1	0)	14	5	3	1	0	0	11	0	0	0	0	0	3	.237	.237	.368	.605
14	Oak	AL	14	42	11	4	0	0	(0	0)	15	3	8	5	6	0	8	0	1	0	0	0	0	.262	.354	.357	.711
Postseason			6	19	3	1	0	1	(0	1)	7	1	2	1	3	0	5	0	0	0	0	0	0	.158	.273	.368	.641
10 ML YEARS			680	2215	549	133	4	92	(49	43)	966	272	322	289	280	17	579	15	4	18	3	4	68	.248	.334	.436	.770

Neftali Soto

Bats: R Throws: R Pos: PH-11;1B-7;3B-2;DH-1   neff-TAH-lee   Ht: 6'1" Wt: 215 Born: 2/28/1989 Age: 26

Year	Team	Lg	G	AB	H	2B	3B	HR	(Hm	Rd)	TB	R	RBI	RC	TBB	IBB	SO	HBP	SH	SF	SB	CS	GDP	Avg	OBP	Slg	OPS
2010	Lynbrg	A+	134	522	140	33	2	21	(-	-)	240	73	73	78	32	3	105	8	0	3	0	0	10	.268	.319	.460	.778
2011	Carlina	AA	102	379	103	19	3	30	(-	-)	218	70	76	71	25	0	96	8	0	2	0	1	8	.272	.329	.575	.904
2011	Lsvlle	AAA	4	17	7	0	0	1	(-	-)	10	1	4	4	1	0	2	0	0	0	0	0	0	.412	.444	.588	1.033
2012	Lsvlle	AAA	122	465	114	30	0	14	(-	-)	186	55	59	60	41	3	116	5	0	1	2	1	18	.245	.313	.400	.713
2013	Lsvlle	AAA	118	461	125	21	0	15	(-	-)	191	54	61	61	26	1	103	4	0	4	3	1	20	.271	.313	.414	.727

Year	Team	Lg	G	AB	H	2B	3B	HR	(Hm Rd)	TB	R	RBI	RC	TBB	IBB	SO	HBP	SH	SF	SB	CS	GDP	Avg	OBP	Slg	OPS
									BATTING										RUNNING			AVERAGES			
2014	Lsvlle	AAA	75	278	84	23	0	2	(- -)	113	26	34	41	21	3	41	1	0	3	0	0	13	.302	.350	.406	.756
2013	Cin	NL	13	12	0	0	0	0	(0 0)	0	0	0	0	0	0	6	1	0	0	0	0	1	.000	.077	.000	.077
2014	Cin	NL	21	30	3	1	0	0	(0 0)	4	1	1	0	0	0	8	0	0	1	1	0	2	.100	.097	.133	.230
2 ML YEARS			34	42	3	1	0	0	(0 0)	4	1	1	0	0	0	14	1	0	1	1	0	3	.071	.091	.095	.186

Steven Souza

Bats: R Throws: R Pos: RF-8;PH-8;LF-4;PR-2;CF-1   SOO-zuh   **Ht: 6'4" Wt: 225 Born: 4/24/1989 Age: 26**

Year	Team	Lg	G	AB	H	2B	3B	HR	(Hm Rd)	TB	R	RBI	RC	TBB	IBB	SO	HBP	SH	SF	SB	CS	GDP	Avg	OBP	Slg	OPS
									BATTING										RUNNING			AVERAGES			
2010	Hgrstn	A	81	303	70	16	6	11	(- -)	131	49	56	44	27	0	85	8	1	5	18	4	7	.231	.306	.432	.738
2011	Ptomc	A+	122	390	89	17	2	11	(- -)	143	58	56	60	75	3	131	8	0	5	25	9	5	.228	.360	.367	.726
2012	Hgrstn	A	70	262	76	20	2	17	(- -)	151	48	72	51	22	3	49	3	1	5	7	7	4	.290	.346	.576	.922
2012	Ptomc	A+	27	91	29	2	1	6	(- -)	51	16	13	22	13	0	25	3	0	0	7	1	2	.319	.421	.560	.981
2013	Hrsbrg	AA	77	273	82	23	1	15	(- -)	152	54	44	62	41	1	76	5	0	4	20	6	9	.300	.396	.557	.953
2013	Nats	R	4	10	2	1	0	0	(- -)	3	3	2	2	3	0	4	1	0	1	2	0	0	.200	.400	.300	.700
2014	Syrcse	AAA	96	346	120	25	2	18	(- -)	203	62	75	88	52	3	75	3	0	6	26	7	1	.347	.430	.587	1.017
2014	Hgrstn	A	1	2	1	0	0	0	(- -)	1	0	1	0	0	0	1	0	0	0	1	0	0	.500	.500	.500	1.000
2014	Ptomc	A+	3	9	1	0	0	0	(- -)	1	0	1	0	0	0	4	1	0	0	1	0	0	.111	.200	.111	.311
2014	Was	NL	21	23	3	0	0	2	(1 1)	9	2	2	1	3	0	7	0	0	0	0	0	1	.130	.231	.391	.622

Denard Span

Bats: L Throws: L Pos: CF-147   **Ht: 6'0" Wt: 210 Born: 2/27/1984 Age: 31**

Year	Team	Lg	G	AB	H	2B	3B	HR	(Hm Rd)	TB	R	RBI	RC	TBB	IBB	SO	HBP	SH	SF	SB	CS	GDP	Avg	OBP	Slg	OPS
									BATTING										RUNNING			AVERAGES			
2014	Hgrstn*	A	2	4	2	0	0	0	(- -)	2	3	2	2	3	0	0	0	0	0	1	0	0	.500	.714	.500	1.214
2008	Min	AL	93	347	102	16	7	6	(2 4)	150	70	47	68	50	3	60	4	8	2	18	7	3	.294	.387	.432	.819
2009	Min	AL	145	578	180	16	10	8	(5 3)	240	97	68	100	70	3	89	10	12	6	23	10	7	.311	.392	.415	.807
2010	Min	AL	153	629	166	24	10	3	(0 3)	219	85	58	85	60	0	74	4	10	2	26	4	12	.264	.331	.348	.679
2011	Min	AL	70	284	75	11	5	2	(1 1)	102	37	16	32	27	0	36	0	0	0	6	1	3	.264	.328	.359	.687
2012	Min	AL	128	516	146	38	4	4	(2 2)	204	71	41	69	47	0	62	0	4	1	17	6	10	.283	.342	.395	.738
2013	Was	NL	153	610	170	28	11	4	(2 2)	232	75	47	74	42	0	77	2	7	1	20	6	11	.279	.327	.380	.707
2014	Was	NL	147	610	184	39	8	5	(1 4)	254	94	37	94	50	1	65	0	3	3	31	7	6	.302	.355	.416	.771
Postseason			6	28	10	1	0	0	(0 0)	11	1	1	2	0	0	2	0	0	0	1	0	1	.357	.357	.393	.750
7 ML YEARS			889	3574	1023	172	55	32	(13 19)	1401	529	314	522	346	7	463	22	44	15	141	41	52	.286	.352	.392	.744

Cory Spangenberg

Bats: L Throws: R Pos: 3B-9;PH-6;LF-4;2B-3   SPAN-jen-burg   **Ht: 6'0" Wt: 195 Born: 3/16/1991 Age: 24**

Year	Team	Lg	G	AB	H	2B	3B	HR	(Hm Rd)	TB	R	RBI	RC	TBB	IBB	SO	HBP	SH	SF	SB	CS	GDP	Avg	OBP	Slg	OPS
									BATTING										RUNNING			AVERAGES			
2011	Eugene	A-	25	86	33	10	0	1	(- -)	46	20	20	28	31	1	15	2	0	2	10	4	1	.384	.545	.535	1.080
2011	FtWyn	A	47	189	54	7	1	2	(- -)	69	35	24	26	14	0	42	3	3	0	15	4	0	.286	.345	.365	.710
2012	Lk Els	A+	98	384	104	12	8	1	(- -)	135	53	40	48	26	1	72	6	6	4	27	9	4	.271	.324	.352	.675
2013	Lk Els	A+	54	226	67	13	6	4	(- -)	104	33	31	40	23	1	51	1	3	0	17	3	1	.296	.364	.460	.824
2013	SnAnt	AA	76	287	83	10	3	2	(- -)	105	35	20	36	17	0	61	2	11	2	19	11	2	.289	.331	.366	.697
2014	SnAnt	AA	66	281	93	17	8	2	(- -)	132	38	22	46	15	1	63	0	8	0	14	9	2	.331	.365	.470	.835
2014	Padres	R	2	6	1	0	1	0	(- -)	3	3	2	1	2	0	0	0	0	0	0	0	0	.167	.375	.500	.875
2014	Eugene	A-	6	25	5	0	1	0	(- -)	7	3	2	1	0	0	6	0	0	0	2	0	1	.200	.200	.280	.480
2014	SD	NL	20	62	18	2	1	2	(1 1)	28	7	9	9	2	0	14	0	1	0	4	2	1	.290	.313	.452	.764

George Springer

Bats: R Throws: R Pos: RF-71;CF-8;DH-1   **Ht: 6'3" Wt: 205 Born: 9/19/1989 Age: 25**

Year	Team	Lg	G	AB	H	2B	3B	HR	(Hm Rd)	TB	R	RBI	RC	TBB	IBB	SO	HBP	SH	SF	SB	CS	GDP	Avg	OBP	Slg	OPS
									BATTING										RUNNING			AVERAGES			
2011	TriCity	A-	8	28	5	3	0	1	(- -)	11	8	3	4	2	0	2	3	0	0	4	0	2	.179	.303	.393	.696
2012	Lancst	A+	106	433	137	18	10	22	(- -)	241	101	82	98	56	4	131	6	0	5	28	6	6	.316	.300	.557	.955
2012	CpChr	AA	22	70	10	3	0	2	(- -)	25	8	5	7	6	0	25	1	1	0	4	2	1	.219	.288	.342	.630
2013	CpChr	AA	73	273	81	20	0	19	(- -)	158	56	55	64	42	1	96	5	2	1	23	5	1	.297	.399	.579	.978
2013	OKCity	AAA	62	219	68	7	4	18	(- -)	137	50	53	60	41	0	65	4	0	2	22	3	2	.311	.425	.626	1.050
2014	OKCity	AAA	13	51	18	4	1	3	(- -)	33	17	9	15	9	0	15	1	0	0	4	0	0	.353	.459	.647	1.106
2014	QuadC	A	3	4	1	1	0	0	(- -)	2	1	0	1	3	0	1	0	0	0	2	0	0	.250	.571	.500	1.071
2014	Hou	AL	78	295	68	8	1	20	(5 15)	138	45	51	45	39	4	114	9	0	2	5	2	4	.231	.336	.468	.804

Zeke Spruill

Pitches: R Bats: R Pos: RP-5; SP-1   ZEEK SPROO-ill   **Ht: 6'5" Wt: 190 Born: 9/11/1989 Age: 25**

Year	Team	Lg	G	GS	CG	GF	IP	BFP	H	R	ER	HR	SH	SF	HB	TBB	IBB	SO	WP	Bk	W	L	Pct	Sh	Sv-Op	Hld	ERC	ERA
			HOW MUCH HE PITCHED						WHAT HE GAVE UP												THE RESULTS						
2010	MrtlBh	A+	14	13	1	0	65.0	295	83	44	40	4	3	7	4	13	2	41	1	0	3	5	.375	0	0--	-	4.64	5.54
2010	Braves	R	2	2	0	0	3.0	14	4	1	1	0	0	1	0	1	0	1	0	0	0	0	-	0	0--	-	4.83	3.00
2011	Lynbrg	A+	20	20	5	0	129.2	520	108	56	46	7	7	7	8	23	0	92	5	1	7	9	.438	1	0--	-	2.32	3.19
2011	Missi	AA	7	7	1	0	45.0	195	45	18	16	3	1	3	5	17	0	16	1	0	3	2	.600	0	0--	-	4.24	3.20
2012	Missi	AA	27	27	1	0	161.2	674	158	81	66	8	6	9	6	46	2	106	5	1	9	11	.450	0	0--	-	3.33	3.67
2013	Mobile	AA	5	5	0	0	31.2	128	24	7	5	0	2	1	0	12	1	20	1	0	0	3	.000	0	0--	-	2.20	1.42
2013	Reno	AAA	16	16	1	0	92.0	402	98	48	43	8	9	3	3	33	0	48	0	2	6	5	.545	1	0--	-	4.30	4.21
2014	Reno	AAA	28	11	0	5	79.0	351	89	58	53	10	4	2	2	21	2	71	4	0	3	7	.300	0	1--	-	4.63	6.04

Year	Team	Lg	G	GS	CG	GF	IP	BFP	H	R	ER	HR	SH	SF	HB	TBB	IBB	SO	WP	Bk	W	L	Pct	Sh	Sv-Op	Hld	ERC	ERA
2014	DBcks	R	3	2	0	0	6.0	26	8	5	5	0	0	0	0	1	0	6	0	0	0	2	.000	0	0- -		4.37	7.50
2013	Ari	NL	6	2	0	1	11.1	55	17	11	7	3	1	0	1	5	0	9	0	0	0	2	.000	0	0-0	0	9.30	5.56
2014	Ari	NL	6	1	0	1	22.2	99	27	11	9	0	2	2	1	4	0	14	0	0	1	1	.500	0	0-0	1	3.67	3.57
2 ML YEARS			12	3	0	2	34.0	154	44	22	16	3	3	2	2	9	0	23	0	0	1	3	.250	0	0-0	1	5.36	4.24

Craig Stammen

Pitches: R Bats: R Pos: RP-49   STAMM-enn   Ht: 6'4" Wt: 225 Born: 3/9/1984 Age: 31

			HOW MUCH HE PITCHED						WHAT HE GAVE UP												THE RESULTS							
Year	Team	Lg	G	GS	CG	GF	IP	BFP	H	R	ER	HR	SH	SF	HB	TBB	IBB	SO	WP	Bk	W	L	Pct	Sh	Sv-Op	Hld	ERC	ERA
2009	Was	NL	19	19	1	0	105.2	448	112	67	60	14	4	3	3	24	1	48	7	0	4	7	.364	0	0-0	0	4.03	5.11
2010	Was	NL	35	19	0	3	128.0	562	151	78	73	13	5	6	1	41	4	85	3	0	4	4	.500	0	0-0	1	4.79	5.13
2011	Was	NL	7	0	0	2	10.1	38	3	1	1	0	0	0	0	4	0	12	1	0	1	1	.500	0	0-0	1	0.67	0.87
2012	Was	NL	59	0	0	15	88.1	370	70	27	23	7	5	1	2	36	4	87	3	0	6	1	.857	0	1-2	10	2.84	2.34
2013	Was	NL	55	0	0	14	81.2	339	78	30	25	4	8	4	2	27	3	79	2	1	7	6	.538	0	0-1	7	3.32	2.76
2014	Was	NL	49	0	0	15	72.2	304	78	34	31	5	3	1	3	14	2	56	1	1	4	5	.444	0	0-0	7	3.61	3.84
Postseason			4	0	0	0	3.0	21	5	3	3	1	1	1	3	2	0	3	0	0	0	0	-	0	0-0	1	14.91	9.00
6 ML YEARS			224	38	1	49	486.2	2061	492	237	213	43	25	15	11	146	14	367	17	2	26	24	.520	0	1-3	26	3.72	3.94

Giancarlo Stanton

Bats: R Throws: R Pos: RF-143;DH-2;PH-1   john-CAHR-loh   Ht: 6'6" Wt: 240 Born: 11/8/1989 Age: 25

			BATTING																RUNNING			AVERAGES			
Year	Team	Lg	G	AB	H	2B	3B	HR	(Hm | Rd)	TB	R	RBI	RC	TBB	IBB	SO	HBP	SH	SF	SB	CS	GDP	Avg	OBP	Slg	OPS
2010	Fla	NL	100	359	93	21	1	22	(7 | 15)	182	45	59	56	34	6	123	2	0	1	5	2	7	.259	.326	.507	.833
2011	Fla	NL	150	516	135	30	5	34	(16 | 18)	277	79	87	81	70	6	166	9	0	6	5	5	11	.262	.356	.537	.893
2012	Mia	NL	123	449	130	30	1	37	(16 | 21)	273	75	86	79	46	9	143	5	0	1	6	2	5	.290	.361	.608	.969
2013	Mia	NL	116	425	106	26	0	24	(15 | 9)	204	62	62	66	74	5	140	4	0	1	1	0	10	.249	.365	.480	.845
2014	Mia	NL	145	539	155	31	1	37	(24 | 13)	299	89	105	109	94	24	170	3	0	2	13	1	16	.288	.395	.555	.950
5 ML YEARS			634	2288	619	138	8	154	(78 | 76)	1235	350	399	391	318	50	742	23	0	11	30	10	49	.271	.364	.540	.903

Max Stassi

Bats: R Throws: R Pos: C-6;PH-1   STASS-ee   Ht: 5'10" Wt: 205 Born: 3/15/1991 Age: 24

			BATTING																RUNNING			AVERAGES			
Year	Team	Lg	G	AB	H	2B	3B	HR	(Hm | Rd)	TB	R	RBI	RC	TBB	IBB	SO	HBP	SH	SF	SB	CS	GDP	Avg	OBP	Slg	OPS
2010	Kane	A	110	411	94	21	1	13	(- | -)	156	54	51	50	45	1	141	5	1	3	3	3	12	.229	.310	.380	.690
2011	Stckton	A+	31	121	28	6	0	2	(- | -)	40	22	19	14	16	0	22	2	0	1	1	1	4	.231	.331	.331	.662
2012	Stckton	A+	84	314	84	18	0	15	(- | -)	147	48	45	51	27	0	83	8	0	11	3	1	5	.268	.331	.468	.799
2013	CpChr	AA	76	289	80	20	1	17	(- | -)	153	40	60	52	19	1	68	8	2	5	1	1	11	.277	.333	.529	.863
2014	OKCity	AAA	101	392	97	20	2	9	(- | -)	148	49	45	45	22	1	103	6	3	2	1	0	14	.247	.296	.378	.674
2013	Hou	AL	3	7	2	0	0	0	(0 | 0)	2	0	1	0	0	0	2	1	0	0	0	0	1	.286	.375	.286	.661
2014	Hou	AL	7	20	7	2	0	0	(0 | 0)	9	2	4	4	0	0	6	0	0	0	0	0	0	.350	.350	.450	.800
2 ML YEARS			10	27	9	2	0	0	(0 | 0)	11	2	5	4	0	0	8	1	0	0	0	0	1	.333	.357	.407	.765

Tim Stauffer

Pitches: R Bats: R Pos: RP-41; SP-3   STOFF-er   Ht: 6'1" Wt: 210 Born: 6/2/1982 Age: 33

			HOW MUCH HE PITCHED						WHAT HE GAVE UP												THE RESULTS							
Year	Team	Lg	G	GS	CG	GF	IP	BFP	H	R	ER	HR	SH	SF	HB	TBB	IBB	SO	WP	Bk	W	L	Pct	Sh	Sv-Op	Hld	ERC	ERA
2005	SD	NL	15	14	0	0	81.0	355	92	50	48	10	2	0	2	29	0	49	0	0	3	6	.333	0	0-0	0	5.00	5.33
2006	SD	NL	1	1	0	0	6.0	21	3	2	1	0	0	0	0	1	0	2	0	0	1	0	1.000	0	0-0	0	0.84	1.50
2007	SD	NL	2	2	0	0	7.2	45	15	18	18	5	0	0	1	6	0	6	0	0	0	1	.000	0	0-0	0	18.32	21.13
2009	SD	NL	14	14	0	0	73.0	316	71	31	29	8	2	1	5	34	1	53	1	0	4	7	.364	0	0-0	0	4.60	3.58
2010	SD	NL	32	7	0	12	82.2	326	65	18	17	3	3	0	2	24	5	61	0	0	6	5	.545	0	0-0	0	2.23	1.85
2011	SD	NL	31	31	0	0	185.2	777	180	81	77	20	14	3	8	53	5	128	4	1	9	12	.429	0	0-0	0	3.67	3.73
2012	SD	NL	1	1	0	0	5.0	24	7	4	3	1	0	0	0	3	0	5	0	0	0	0	-	0	0-0	0	8.40	5.40
2013	SD	NL	43	0	0	8	69.2	284	59	29	29	7	3	2	4	20	1	64	0	0	3	1	.750	0	0-1	7	3.06	3.75
2014	SD	NL	44	3	0	22	64.1	273	67	25	25	4	2	1	2	23	4	67	1	1	6	2	.750	0	0-0	0	3.98	3.50
9 ML YEARS			183	73	0	42	575.0	2421	559	258	247	58	26	7	24	193	16	435	6	2	32	34	.485	0	0-1	7	3.85	3.87

Chris Stewart

Bats: R Throws: R Pos: C-46;PH-4   Ht: 6'4" Wt: 210 Born: 2/19/1982 Age: 33

			BATTING																RUNNING			AVERAGES			
Year	Team	Lg	G	AB	H	2B	3B	HR	(Hm | Rd)	TB	R	RBI	RC	TBB	IBB	SO	HBP	SH	SF	SB	CS	GDP	Avg	OBP	Slg	OPS
2014	Bradtn*	A+	3	7	2	0	0	0	(- | -)	2	1	0	0	1	0	1	0	0	0	0	0	0	.286	.375	.286	.661
2014	Indy*	AAA	4	15	6	1	0	0	(- | -)	7	1	0	3	1	0	1	1	0	0	0	0	2	.400	.471	.467	.937
2006	CWS	AL	6	8	0	0	0	0	(0 | 0)	0	0	0	0	0	0	2	0	0	0	0	0	0	.000	.000	.000	.000
2007	Tex	AL	17	37	9	2	0	0	(0 | 0)	11	4	3	3	3	0	6	0	3	0	0	0	2	.243	.300	.297	.597
2008	NYY	AL	1	3	0	0	0	0	(0 | 0)	0	0	0	0	0	0	1	0	0	0	0	0	0	.000	.000	.000	.000
2010	SD	NL	2	0	0	0	0	0	(0 | 0)	0	0	0	0	0	0	0	0	0	0	0	0	0	-	-	-	-
2011	SF	NL	67	162	33	8	0	3	(1 | 2)	50	20	10	10	16	4	18	2	3	0	0	0	2	.204	.283	.309	.592
2012	NYY	AL	55	141	34	8	0	1	(1 | 0)	45	15	13	10	10	0	21	1	3	2	0	1	1	.241	.292	.319	.611
2013	NYY	AL	109	294	62	6	0	4	(3 | 1)	80	28	25	24	30	0	49	6	6	4	4	0	8	.211	.293	.272	.566
2014	Pit	NL	49	136	40	5	0	0	(0 | 0)	45	9	10	15	12	2	27	3	2	1	0	1	2	.294	.362	.331	.693
Postseason			1	0	0	0	0	0	(0 | 0)	0	0	0	0	0	0	0	0	0	0	0	0	0	-	-	-	-
8 ML YEARS			306	781	178	29	0	8	(5 | 3)	231	76	61	62	71	6	124	12	17	7	6	1	15	.228	.300	.296	.595

Ian Stewart

Bats: L Throws: R Pos: 3B-16;1B-6;PH-4;DH-1;PR-1   Ht: 6'3" Wt: 215 Born: 4/5/1985 Age: 30

								BATTING												RUNNING			AVERAGES			
Year	Team	Lg	G	AB	H	2B	3B	HR	(Hm | Rd)	TB	R	RBI	RC	TBB	IBB	SO	HBP	SH	SF	SB	CS	GDP	Avg	OBP	Slg	OPS
2014 Salt Lk*	AAA	36	121	24	3	0	5	(-	-)	42	21	13	14	18	0	42	2	0	1	1	0	1	.198	.310	.347	.657
2007 Col	NL	35	43	9	4	0	1	(1	0)	16	3	9	5	1	0	17	2	0	0	0	0	0	.209	.261	.372	.633
2008 Col	NL	81	266	69	18	2	10	(5	5)	121	33	41	44	30	4	94	7	0	1	1	1	3	.259	.349	.455	.804
2009 Col	NL	147	425	97	19	3	25	(10	15)	197	74	70	59	56	3	138	5	0	5	7	4	7	.228	.322	.464	.785
2010 Col	NL	121	386	99	14	2	18	(6	12)	171	54	61	51	45	8	110	5	0	5	5	2	8	.256	.338	.443	.781
2011 Col	NL	48	122	19	6	1	0	(0	0)	27	14	6	4	14	2	37	0	0	0	3	2	1	.156	.243	.221	.464
2012 ChC	NL	55	179	36	5	2	5	(2	3)	60	16	17	16	21	4	46	2	0	0	0	3	5	.201	.292	.335	.627
2014 LAA	AL	24	68	12	2	3	2	(1	1)	26	8	7	4	3	0	31	1	0	0	1	0	1	.176	.222	.382	.605
Postseason		2	1	0	0	0	0	(0	0)	0	0	0	0	1	0	1	0	0	0	0	0	0	.000	.500	.000	.500
7 ML YEARS		511	1489	341	68	13	61	(28	33)	618	202	211	183	170	21	473	22	0	11	17	12	25	.229	.315	.415	.730

Josh Stinson

Pitches: R Bats: R Pos: RP-8   Ht: 6'4" Wt: 210 Born: 3/14/1988 Age: 27

			HOW MUCH HE PITCHED						WHAT HE GAVE UP										THE RESULTS						
Year	Team	Lg	G	GS	CG	GF	IP	BFP	H	R	ER	HR	SH	SF	HB	TBB	IBB	SO	WP	Bk	W	L	Pct	Sh	Sv-Op	Hld	ERC	ERA
2014 Norfolk*	AAA	22	13	1	3	85.1	373	78	54	52	14	4	3	6	38	0	80	10	0	5	5	.500	0	1- -	-	4.48	5.48
2011 NYM	NL	14	0	0	3	13.0	57	14	10	10	1	1	0	0	7	0	8	0	0	0	2	.000	0	1-2	4	5.05	6.92
2012 Mil	NL	6	1	0	2	9.1	38	7	1	1	1	0	0	0	5	0	3	0	0	0	0	-	0	0-0	0	3.42	0.96
2013 Bal	AL	11	1	0	2	17.0	63	10	7	6	4	0	0	1	3	0	12	0	0	0	0	-	0	0-1	2	2.17	3.18
2014 Bal	AL	8	0	0	4	13.0	61	16	9	9	2	0	0	2	6	0	6	1	0	0	0	-	0	0-0	0	6.86	6.23
4 ML YEARS		39	2	0	11	52.1	219	47	27	26	8	1	0	3	21	0	29	1	0	0	2	.000	0	1-3	6	4.21	4.47

Matt Stites

Pitches: R Bats: L Pos: RP-37   Ht: 5'11" Wt: 195 Born: 5/28/1990 Age: 25

			HOW MUCH HE PITCHED						WHAT HE GAVE UP										THE RESULTS						
Year	Team	Lg	G	GS	CG	GF	IP	BFP	H	R	ER	HR	SH	SF	HB	TBB	IBB	SO	WP	Bk	W	L	Pct	Sh	Sv-Op	Hld	ERC	ERA
2011 Eugene	A-	24	0	0	9	32.2	121	14	7	7	1	0	0	1	8	0	36	3	2	4	0	1.000	0	5- -	-	0.91	1.93
2011 Padres	R	2	0	0	2	2.0	6	0	0	0	0	0	0	0	0	0	3	0	0	0	0	-	0	0-0	-	0.00	0.00
2012 FtWyn	A	42	0	0	37	48.2	175	25	7	4	4	1	1	1	3	0	60	2	1	2	0	1.000	0	13- -	-	0.92	0.74
2013 SnAnt	AA	46	0	0	22	52.0	202	37	16	12	6	1	1	4	8	1	51	1	0	2	2	.500	0	14- -	-	1.82	2.08
2014 Mobile	AA	12	0	0	6	12.0	46	10	5	5	0	2	0	0	3	0	8	0	0	0	1	.000	0	3- -	-	2.16	3.75
2014 Reno	AAA	17	0	0	17	16.0	64	13	6	4	1	0	1	0	6	0	15	0	0	0	0	-	0	12- -	-	2.83	2.25
2014 Ari	NL	37	0	0	11	33.0	148	33	23	21	6	3	1	1	16	1	26	2	0	0	0	-	0	0-0	2	5.01	5.73

Drew Storen

Pitches: R Bats: B Pos: RP-65   STORE-inn   Ht: 6'1" Wt: 195 Born: 8/11/1987 Age: 27

			HOW MUCH HE PITCHED						WHAT HE GAVE UP										THE RESULTS						
Year	Team	Lg	G	GS	CG	GF	IP	BFP	H	R	ER	HR	SH	SF	HB	TBB	IBB	SO	WP	Bk	W	L	Pct	Sh	Sv-Op	Hld	ERC	ERA
2010 Was	NL	54	0	0	22	55.1	232	48	24	22	3	6	2	3	22	3	52	3	0	4	4	.500	0	5-7	10	3.19	3.58
2011 Was	NL	73	0	0	52	75.1	303	57	24	23	8	1	1	2	20	4	74	2	0	6	3	.667	0	43-48	3	2.35	2.75
2012 Was	NL	37	0	0	17	30.1	116	22	8	8	0	0	2	1	8	0	24	1	0	3	1	.750	0	4-5	10	1.79	2.37
2013 Was	NL	68	0	0	20	61.2	267	65	34	31	7	3	1	1	19	2	58	2	0	4	2	.667	0	3-8	24	4.08	4.52
2014 Was	NL	65	0	0	18	56.1	224	44	8	7	2	3	2	3	11	3	46	4	0	2	1	.667	0	11-14	20	1.93	1.12
Postseason		4	0	0	4	4.0	18	3	4	4	0	0	0	0	3	0	6	0	0	1	1	.500	0	1-2	0	3.21	9.00
5 ML YEARS		297	0	0	129	279.0	1142	236	98	91	20	13	8	10	80	12	254	12	0	19	11	.633	0	66-82	67	2.72	2.94

Dan Straily

Pitches: R Bats: R Pos: SP-8; RP-6   STRAY-lee   Ht: 6'2" Wt: 215 Born: 12/1/1988 Age: 26

			HOW MUCH HE PITCHED						WHAT HE GAVE UP										THE RESULTS						
Year	Team	Lg	G	GS	CG	GF	IP	BFP	H	R	ER	HR	SH	SF	HB	TBB	IBB	SO	WP	Bk	W	L	Pct	Sh	Sv-Op	Hld	ERC	ERA
2014 Scrmto*	AAA	10	10	0	0	63.0	257	54	33	33	9	2	2	2	26	0	67	3	0	4	3	.571	0	0- -	-	3.91	4.71
2014 Iowa*	AAA	10	10	0	0	55.0	245	59	34	25	7	3	3	3	20	1	56	2	0	3	5	.375	0	0- -	-	4.66	4.09
2012 Oak	AL	7	7	0	0	39.1	172	36	19	17	11	1	1	2	16	1	32	0	0	2	1	.667	0	0-0	0	4.94	3.89
2013 Oak	AL	27	27	0	0	152.1	640	132	74	67	16	4	5	7	57	0	124	7	0	10	8	.556	0	0-0	0	3.46	3.96
2014 2 Tms		14	8	0	0	52.0	231	53	41	39	10	0	1	2	24	1	47	2	0	1	3	.250	0	0-0	0	5.22	6.75
14 Oak	AL	7	7	0	0	38.1	159	33	21	21	9	0	1	1	15	1	34	2	0	1	2	.333	0	0-0	0	4.31	4.93
14 ChC	NL	7	1	0	0	13.2	72	20	20	18	1	0	0	1	9	0	13	0	0	0	1	.000	0	0-0	0	7.78	11.85
Postseason		1	1	0	0	6.0	22	4	3	3	1	0	0	1	0	0	8	0	0	0	0	-	0	0-0	0	1.99	4.50
3 ML YEARS		48	42	0	0	243.2	1043	221	134	123	37	5	7	11	97	2	203	9	0	13	12	.520	0	0-0	0	4.06	4.54

Stephen Strasburg

Pitches: R Bats: R Pos: SP-34   STRAHS-berg   Ht: 6'4" Wt: 230 Born: 7/20/1988 Age: 26

			HOW MUCH HE PITCHED						WHAT HE GAVE UP										THE RESULTS						
Year	Team	Lg	G	GS	CG	GF	IP	BFP	H	R	ER	HR	SH	SF	HB	TBB	IBB	SO	WP	Bk	W	L	Pct	Sh	Sv-Op	Hld	ERC	ERA
2010 Was	NL	12	12	0	0	68.0	274	56	25	22	5	2	2	0	17	0	92	2	0	5	3	.625	0	0-0	0	2.41	2.91
2011 Was	NL	5	5	0	0	24.0	88	15	5	4	1	1	0	2	2	0	24	0	0	1	1	.500	0	0-0	0	0.97	1.50
2012 Was	NL	28	28	0	0	159.1	653	136	62	56	15	6	4	4	48	1	197	5	0	15	6	.714	0	0-0	0	2.97	3.16
2013 Was	NL	30	30	1	0	183.0	731	136	71	61	16	5	1	12	56	1	191	7	3	8	9	.471	1	0-0	0	2.58	3.00
2014 Was	NL	34	34	0	0	215.0	868	198	86	75	23	9	4	5	43	4	242	7	0	14	11	.560	0	0-0	0	3.02	3.14
5 ML YEARS		109	109	1	0	649.1	2614	541	249	218	59	23	12	21	166	6	746	21	3	43	30	.589	1	0-0	0	2.72	3.02

Huston Street

Pitches: R Bats: R Pos: RP-61   Ht: 6'0" Wt: 195 Born: 8/2/1983 Age: 31

			HOW MUCH HE PITCHED						WHAT HE GAVE UP										THE RESULTS							
Year	Team	Lg	G	GS	CG	GF	IP	BFP	H	R	ER	HR	SH	SF	HB	TBB	IBB	SO	WP	Bk	W	L	Pct	Sh	Sv-Op	Hld	ERC	ERA
2005	Oak	AL	67	0	0	47	78.1	306	53	17	15	3	3	2	2	26	4	72	1	0	5	1	.833	0	23-27	0	1.87	1.72
2006	Oak	AL	69	0	0	55	70.2	290	64	28	26	4	3	3	2	13	3	67	4	0	4	4	.500	0	37-48	1	2.49	3.31
2007	Oak	AL	48	0	0	35	50.0	199	35	20	16	5	2	1	0	12	3	63	0	0	5	2	.714	0	16-21	5	1.84	2.88
2008	Oak	AL	63	0	0	37	70.0	287	58	29	29	6	3	3	1	27	6	69	2	0	7	5	.583	0	18-25	6	2.98	3.73
2009	Col	NL	64	0	0	52	61.2	240	43	22	21	7	3	2	0	13	4	70	0	0	4	1	.800	0	35-37	2	1.83	3.06
2010	Col	NL	44	0	0	39	47.1	187	39	21	19	5	0	1	2	11	4	45	2	1	4	4	.500	0	20-25	0	2.66	3.61
2011	Col	NL	62	0	0	47	58.1	239	62	28	25	10	3	1	1	9	1	55	0	0	1	4	.200	0	29-33	4	4.03	3.86
2012	SD	NL	40	0	0	36	39.0	144	17	8	8	2	1	1	0	11	1	47	1	0	2	1	.667	0	23-24	0	0.99	1.85
2013	SD	NL	58	0	0	52	56.2	222	44	17	17	12	0	1	0	14	1	46	4	0	2	5	.286	0	33-35	0	3.00	2.70
2014	2 Tms		61	0	0	51	59.1	229	42	9	9	4	1	0	0	14	3	57	0	0	2	2	.500	0	41-44	0	1.77	1.37
14	SD	NL	33	0	0	28	33.0	121	18	4	4	3	0	0	0	7	0	34	0	0	1	0	1.000	0	24-25	0	1.33	1.09
14	LAA	AL	28	0	0	23	26.1	108	24	5	5	1	1	0	0	7	3	23	0	0	1	2	.333	0	17-19	0	2.53	1.71
	Postseason		8	0	0	7	9.0	43	14	9	9	2	1	1	0	4	0	5	0	0	0	3	.000	0	3-4	0	8.97	9.00
10 ML YEARS			576	0	0	451	591.1	2343	457	199	185	58	19	15	8	150	30	591	14	1	36	29	.554	0	275-319	18	2.33	2.82

Hunter Strickland

Pitches: R Bats: R Pos: RP-9   Ht: 6'5" Wt: 200 Born: 9/24/1988 Age: 26

			HOW MUCH HE PITCHED						WHAT HE GAVE UP										THE RESULTS							
Year	Team	Lg	G	GS	CG	GF	IP	BFP	H	R	ER	HR	SH	SF	HB	TBB	IBB	SO	WP	Bk	W	L	Pct	Sh	Sv-Op	Hld	ERC	ERA
2010	WV	A	8	8	0	0	43.0	187	58	30	28	6	3	3	5	8	0	15	1	0	0	4	.000	0	0- -	-	6.33	5.86
2010	Bradtn	A+	4	2	0	0	14.0	64	16	11	7	1	1	1	1	6	0	10	0	0	2	1	.667	0	0- -	-	5.04	4.50
2012	Bradtn	A+	10	9	0	1	45.1	188	47	16	15	5	0	1	6	8	0	25	1	0	2	2	.500	0	0- -	-	4.11	2.98
2012	Altna	AA	23	0	0	9	41.1	179	49	23	21	5	1	3	3	14	0	32	1	0	2	2	.500	0	1- -	-	5.58	4.57
2013	SnJos	A+	20	0	0	18	21.0	76	10	2	2	1	1	0	1	5	1	23	0	0	1	0	1.000	0	9- -	-	1.11	0.86
2014	SnJos	A+	3	0	0	0	3.0	11	2	1	1	0	0	0	0	0	0	7	0	0	0	0	-	0	0- -	-	0.91	3.00
2014	Rchmd	AA	38	0	0	27	35.2	135	25	10	8	3	1	2	0	4	0	48	1	0	1	1	.500	0	11- -	-	1.52	2.02
2014	SF	NL	9	0	0	5	7.0	25	5	0	0	0	0	0	0	0	0	9	0	0	1	0	1.000	0	1-1	1	1.08	0.00

Marcus Stroman

Pitches: R Bats: R Pos: SP-20; RP-6   Ht: 5'9" Wt: 185 Born: 5/1/1991 Age: 24

			HOW MUCH HE PITCHED						WHAT HE GAVE UP										THE RESULTS							
Year	Team	Lg	G	GS	CG	GF	IP	BFP	H	R	ER	HR	SH	SF	HB	TBB	IBB	SO	WP	Bk	W	L	Pct	Sh	Sv-Op	Hld	ERC	ERA
2012	Vancvr	A-	7	0	0	2	11.1	45	8	5	4	0	0	0	0	3	0	15	0	0	1	0	1.000	0	0- -	-	1.55	3.18
2012	NHam	AA	8	0	0	0	8.0	38	8	3	3	1	0	1	0	6	0	8	1	0	2	0	1.000	0	0- -	-	5.55	3.38
2013	NHam	AA	20	20	0	0	111.2	459	99	48	41	13	3	2	3	27	0	129	4	0	9	5	.643	0	0- -	-	3.04	3.30
2014	Buffalo	AAA	7	7	1	0	35.2	146	32	14	12	1	1	0	2	9	0	45	0	0	2	4	.333	0	0- -	-	2.74	3.03
2014	Tor	AL	26	20	1	1	130.2	534	125	56	53	7	0	2	3	28	1	111	9	1	11	6	.647	1	1-1	0	2.93	3.65

Pedro Strop

Pitches: R Bats: R Pos: RP-65   STROPE   Ht: 6'1" Wt: 220 Born: 6/13/1985 Age: 30

			HOW MUCH HE PITCHED						WHAT HE GAVE UP										THE RESULTS							
Year	Team	Lg	G	GS	CG	GF	IP	BFP	H	R	ER	HR	SH	SF	HB	TBB	IBB	SO	WP	Bk	W	L	Pct	Sh	Sv-Op	Hld	ERC	ERA
2009	Tex	AL	7	0	0	3	7.0	30	6	6	6	0	0	0	0	4	0	9	0	0	0	0	-	0	0-0	0	3.27	7.71
2010	Tex	AL	15	0	0	5	10.2	60	17	12	12	2	1	0	1	11	0	11	5	1	0	0	-	0	0-0	1	11.92	10.13
2011	2 Tms	AL	23	0	0	6	22.0	90	15	5	5	0	2	1	1	10	0	21	2	2	2	1	.667	0	0-2	4	2.15	2.05
2012	Bal	AL	70	0	0	17	66.1	283	52	18	18	2	1	1	4	37	2	58	5	0	5	2	.714	0	3-10	24	3.22	2.44
2013	2 Tms	AL	66	0	0	22	57.1	254	45	30	29	5	7	0	6	26	2	66	8	1	2	5	.286	0	1-4	17	3.31	4.55
2014	ChC	NL	65	0	0	13	61.0	244	40	19	15	2	0	1	4	25	3	71	6	1	2	4	.333	0	2-6	21	2.12	2.21
11	Tex	AL	11	0	0	4	9.2	44	7	4	4	0	1	1	1	7	0	9	2	2	0	1	.000	0	0-1	0	3.34	3.72
11	Bal	AL	12	0	0	2	12.1	46	8	1	1	0	1	0	0	3	0	12	0	0	2	0	1.000	0	0-1	4	1.39	0.73
13	Bal	AL	29	0	0	15	22.1	111	23	19	18	4	4	0	2	15	2	24	5	1	0	3	.000	0	0-3	3	5.81	7.25
13	ChC	NL	37	0	0	7	35.0	143	22	11	11	1	3	0	4	11	0	42	3	0	2	2	.500	0	1-1	14	1.80	2.83
	Postseason		2	0	0	0	2.1	9	1	0	0	0	0	0	0	1	0	2	0	0	1	0	1.000	0	0-0	0	1.08	0.00
6 ML YEARS			246	0	0	66	224.1	961	175	90	85	11	11	3	16	113	7	236	26	5	11	12	.478	0	6-22	67	3.13	3.41

Drew Stubbs

Bats: R Throws: R Pos: CF-113;PH-27;PR-3   Ht: 6'4" Wt: 205 Born: 10/4/1984 Age: 30

							BATTING													RUNNING			AVERAGES			
Year	Team	Lg	G	AB	H	2B	3B	HR	(Hm	Rd)	TB	R	RBI	RC	TBB	IBB	SO	HBP	SH	SF	SB	CS	GDP	Avg	OBP	Slg	OPS
2009	Cin	NL	42	180	48	5	1	8	(7	1)	79	27	17	22	15	0	49	0	1	0	10	4	1	.267	.323	.439	.762
2010	Cin	NL	150	514	131	19	6	22	(13	9)	228	91	77	74	55	2	168	5	3	6	30	6	6	.255	.329	.444	.773
2011	Cin	NL	158	604	147	22	3	15	(9	6)	220	92	44	66	63	1	205	7	6	1	40	10	2	.243	.321	.364	.686
2012	Cin	NL	136	493	105	13	2	14	(6	8)	164	75	40	45	42	0	166	2	6	1	30	7	2	.213	.277	.333	.610
2013	Cle	AL	146	430	100	21	2	10	(4	6)	155	59	45	50	44	1	141	2	2	3	17	2	3	.233	.305	.360	.665
2014	Col	NL	132	388	112	22	4	15	(12	3)	187	67	43	58	30	1	136	1	2	3	20	3	4	.289	.339	.482	.821
	Postseason		8	28	5	1	1	0	(0	0)	8	4	1	1	2	0	7	0	0	0	0	0	0	.179	.233	.286	.519
6 ML YEARS			764	2609	643	102	18	84	(51	33)	1033	411	266	315	249	5	865	17	20	14	147	32	18	.246	.315	.396	.711

Eric Stults

Pitches: L Bats: L Pos: SP-32   Ht: 6'2" Wt: 220 Born: 12/9/1979 Age: 35

			HOW MUCH HE PITCHED						WHAT HE GAVE UP									THE RESULTS							
Year	Team	Lg	G	GS	CG	GF	IP	BFP	H	R	ER	HR	SH	SF	HB	TBB	IBB	SO	WP	Bk	W	L	Pct	Sh	Sv-Op	Hld	ERC	ERA
2006	LAD	NL	6	2	0	2	17.2	73	17	12	11	4	2	0	0	7	0	5	0	0	1	0	1.000	0	0-0	0	4.91	5.60
2007	LAD	NL	12	5	0	3	38.2	179	50	26	25	5	1	1	1	17	2	30	2	0	1	4	.200	0	0-0	1	6.25	5.82
2008	LAD	NL	7	7	1	0	38.2	167	38	18	15	6	2	0	1	13	2	30	0	0	2	3	.400	1	0-0	0	4.07	3.49
2009	LAD	NL	10	10	1	0	50.0	223	51	27	27	3	3	0	4	26	2	33	2	0	4	3	.571	1	0-0	0	4.67	4.86
2011	Col	NL	6	0	0	2	12.0	53	11	8	8	4	0	0	1	4	1	7	0	0	0	0	-	0	0-0	0	4.94	6.00
2012	2 Tms		20	15	0	2	99.0	413	92	38	32	7	9	5	2	27	0	55	1	1	8	3	.727	0	0-0	0	3.06	2.91
2013	SD	NL	33	33	2	0	203.2	857	219	97	89	18	10	6	2	40	2	131	2	1	11	13	.458	0	0-0	0	3.63	3.93
2014	SD	NL	32	32	0	0	176.0	763	197	93	84	26	13	6	4	45	3	111	3	0	8	17	.320	0	0-0	0	4.54	4.30
12	CWS	AL	2	1	0	1	6.2	30	6	2	2	0	0	0	1	4	0	4	0	0	0	0	-	0	0-0	0	4.14	2.70
12	SD	NL	18	14	0	1	92.1	383	86	36	30	7	9	5	1	23	0	51	1	1	8	3	.727	0	0-0	0	2.98	2.92
8 ML YEARS			126	104	4	6	635.2	2728	675	319	291	73	40	18	15	179	12	402	10	2	35	43	.449	2	0-0	1	4.10	4.12

Eugenio Suarez

Bats: R Throws: R Pos: SS-81;PH-5;3B-2;DH-1;PR-1   SWA-rez   Ht: 5'11" Wt: 180 Born: 7/18/1991 Age: 23

						BATTING															RUNNING			AVERAGES			
Year	Team	Lg	G	AB	H	2B	3B	HR	(Hm	Rd)	TB	R	RBI	RC	TBB	IBB	SO	HBP	SH	SF	SB	CS	GDP	Avg	OBP	Slg	OPS
2011	Tigers	R	12	44	15	7	0	2	(-	-)	28	11	9	11	3	0	4	2	1	0	2	0	1	.341	.408	.636	1.045
2011	Conn	A-	58	204	51	11	5	5	(-	-)	87	37	24	29	18	0	43	4	3	0	9	5	4	.250	.323	.426	.749
2012	WMich	A	135	511	147	34	5	6	(-	-)	209	82	67	87	65	2	116	15	5	7	21	9	6	.288	.380	.409	.789
2013	Lkland	A+	25	103	32	6	2	1	(-	-)	45	17	12	19	14	0	25	4	0	1	2	3	3	.311	.410	.437	.847
2013	Erie	AA	111	442	112	24	4	9	(-	-)	171	53	45	57	46	0	98	6	2	0	9	11	8	.253	.332	.387	.719
2014	Erie	AA	42	155	44	14	1	6	(-	-)	78	26	29	27	15	0	38	0	0	0	7	2	4	.284	.347	.503	.850
2014	Toledo	AAA	12	43	13	4	0	2	(-	-)	23	6	7	10	6	0	9	2	0	1	2	0	2	.302	.404	.535	.939
2014	Det	AL	85	244	59	9	1	4	(2	2)	82	33	23	30	22	1	67	5	5	1	3	2	3	.242	.316	.336	.652

Jesus Sucre

Bats: R Throws: R Pos: C-21   SUE-cray   Ht: 6'0" Wt: 225 Born: 4/30/1988 Age: 27

						BATTING															RUNNING			AVERAGES			
Year	Team	Lg	G	AB	H	2B	3B	HR	(Hm	Rd)	TB	R	RBI	RC	TBB	IBB	SO	HBP	SH	SF	SB	CS	GDP	Avg	OBP	Slg	OPS
2010	MrtlBh	A+	48	191	42	9	0	5	(-	-)	66	14	22	16	7	0	26	1	1	0	1	0	8	.220	.251	.346	.597
2010	Missi	AA	38	145	43	11	1	2	(-	-)	62	20	12	17	1	1	17	0	1	0	0	2	5	.297	.301	.428	.729
2011	Missi	AA	40	137	30	5	0	0	(-	-)	35	13	10	8	6	0	12	1	1	1	0	1	7	.219	.255	.255	.511
2011	Jacksn	AA	32	84	18	3	0	1	(-	-)	24	4	9	5	5	0	7	0	2	0	1	1	5	.214	.258	.286	.544
2012	Jacksn	AA	90	321	87	11	0	1	(-	-)	101	27	30	34	20	2	39	3	4	1	1	1	9	.271	.319	.315	.633
2013	Tacom	AAA	23	87	26	3	0	0	(-	-)	29	10	8	10	7	0	10	0	1	0	1	1	2	.299	.351	.333	.684
2013	Ms	R	6	19	6	1	0	0	(-	-)	7	1	3	2	1	0	2	0	0	0	0	0	0	.316	.350	.368	.718
2014	Tacom	AAA	48	175	48	7	1	2	(-	-)	63	13	16	18	4	0	29	1	0	1	0	1	5	.274	.294	.360	.653
2013	Sea	AL	8	26	5	0	0	0	(0	0)	5	1	3	1	2	0	1	0	0	0	0	0	2	.192	.241	.192	.434
2014	Sea	AL	21	61	13	2	0	0	(0	0)	15	4	5	6	0	0	17	0	3	0	0	0	0	.213	.213	.246	.459
2 ML YEARS			29	87	18	2	0	0	(0	0)	20	5	8	7	2	0	18	0	3	1	0	0	2	.207	.222	.230	.452

Eric Surkamp

Pitches: L Bats: L Pos: RP-35   SIR-camp   Ht: 6'5" Wt: 220 Born: 7/16/1987 Age: 27

						HOW MUCH HE PITCHED						WHAT HE GAVE UP									THE RESULTS							
Year	Team	Lg	G	GS	CG	GF	IP	BFP	H	R	ER	HR	SH	SF	HB	TBB	IBB	SO	WP	Bk	W	L	Pct	Sh	Sv-Op	Hld	ERC	ERA
2014	Charltt*	AAA	18	11	0	6	78.2	348	95	46	41	8	6	3	7	20	0	86	3	1	4	5	.444	0	0- -	-	5.09	4.69
2011	SF	NL	6	6	0	0	26.2	126	32	18	17	1	2	2	2	17	1	13	0	0	2	2	.500	0	0-0	0	6.03	5.74
2013	SF	NL	1	1	0	0	2.2	18	9	7	7	2	0	0	2	0	0	0	0	0	0	1	.000	0	0-0	0	32.56	23.63
2014	CWS	AL	35	0	0	2	24.1	107	22	14	13	3	3	0	1	13	3	20	0	0	2	0	1.000	0	0-0	7	4.18	4.81
3 ML YEARS			42	7	0	2	53.2	251	63	39	37	6	5	2	5	30	4	33	0	0	4	3	.571	0	0-0	7	6.14	6.20

Andrew Susac

Bats: R Throws: R Pos: C-29;PH-6   SOO-sack   Ht: 6'1" Wt: 215 Born: 3/22/1990 Age: 25

						BATTING															RUNNING			AVERAGES			
Year	Team	Lg	G	AB	H	2B	3B	HR	(Hm	Rd)	TB	R	RBI	RC	TBB	IBB	SO	HBP	SH	SF	SB	CS	GDP	Avg	OBP	Slg	OPS
2012	SnJos	A+	102	361	88	16	3	9	(-	-)	137	58	52	55	55	0	100	6	2	2	1	1	8	.244	.351	.380	.731
2013	Rchmd	AA	84	262	67	17	0	12	(-	-)	120	32	46	46	42	0	69	8	3	1	1	0	7	.256	.362	.458	.820
2014	Fresno	AAA	63	213	57	9	0	10	(-	-)	96	34	32	38	34	1	50	5	0	1	0	0	4	.268	.379	.451	.830
2014	SF	NL	35	88	24	8	0	3	(1	2)	41	13	19	16	7	0	28	0	0	0	0	0	0	.273	.326	.466	.792

Ichiro Suzuki

EE-chee-row soo-ZOO-kee

Bats: L Throws: R Pos: RF-119;PH-15;LF-9;PR-9;CF-5;DH-2   Ht: 5'11" Wt: 170 Born: 10/22/1973 Age: 41

						BATTING															RUNNING			AVERAGES			
Year	Team	Lg	G	AB	H	2B	3B	HR	(Hm	Rd)	TB	R	RBI	RC	TBB	IBB	SO	HBP	SH	SF	SB	CS	GDP	Avg	OBP	Slg	OPS
2001	Sea	AL	157	692	242	34	8	8	(5	3)	316	127	69	124	30	10	53	8	4	4	56	14	3	.350	.381	.457	.838
2002	Sea	AL	157	647	208	27	8	8	(4	4)	275	111	51	110	68	27	62	5	3	5	31	15	8	.321	.388	.425	.813
2003	Sea	AL	159	679	212	29	8	13	(8	5)	296	111	62	107	36	7	69	6	3	1	34	8	3	.312	.352	.436	.788
2004	Sea	AL	161	704	262	24	5	8	(4	4)	320	101	60	125	49	19	63	4	2	3	36	11	6	.372	.414	.455	.869
2005	Sea	AL	162	679	206	21	12	15	(8	7)	296	111	68	109	48	23	66	4	2	5	33	8	5	.303	.350	.436	.786
2006	Sea	AL	161	695	224	20	9	9	(6	3)	289	110	49	107	49	16	71	5	1	2	45	2	6	.322	.370	.416	.786
2007	Sea	AL	161	678	238	22	7	6	(3	3)	292	111	68	128	49	13	77	3	4	2	37	8	7	.351	.396	.431	.827

Year	Team	Lg	G	AB	H	2B	3B	HR	(Hm	Rd)	TB	R	RBI	RC	TBB	IBB	SO	HBP	SH	SF	SB	CS	GDP	Avg	OBP	Slg	OPS
2008	Sea	AL	162	686	213	20	7	6	(3	3)	265	103	42	100	51	12	65	5	3	4	43	4	8	.310	.361	.408	.747
2009	Sea	AL	146	639	225	31	4	11	(6	5)	297	88	46	111	32	15	71	4	2	1	26	9	1	.352	.386	.465	.851
2010	Sea	AL	162	680	214	30	3	6	(1	5)	268	74	43	96	45	13	86	3	3	1	42	9	3	.315	.359	.394	.754
2011	Sea	AL	161	677	184	22	3	5	(4	1)	227	80	47	80	39	13	69	0	1	4	40	7	11	.272	.310	.335	.645
2012	2 Tms	AL	162	629	178	28	6	9	(6	3)	245	77	55	63	22	5	61	2	5	5	29	7	12	.283	.307	.390	.696
2013	NYY	AL	150	520	136	15	3	7	(5	2)	178	57	35	56	26	4	63	1	6	2	20	4	6	.262	.297	.342	.639
2014	NYY	AL	143	359	102	13	2	1	(1	0)	122	42	22	39	21	1	68	1	2	2	15	3	3	.284	.324	.340	.664
12	Sea	AL	95	402	105	15	4	5	(1	3)	142	49	28	33	17	4	40	0	0	4	15	2	10	.261	.288	.353	.642
12	NYY	AL	67	227	73	13	1	5	(5	0)	103	28	27	30	5	1	21	2	5	1	14	5	2	.322	.340	.454	.794
Postseason			19	78	27	4	0	1	(1	0)	34	10	8	11	7	2	9	0	1	0	4	3	0	.346	.400	.436	.836
14 ML YEARS			2204	8964	2844	336	85	112	(64	48)	3686	1303	717	1355	565	178	944	51	41	42	487	109	78	.317	.360	.411	.771

Kurt Suzuki

Bats: R **Throws:** R **Pos:** C-119;PH-11;DH-5;PR-1 **Ht:** 5'11" **Wt:** 205 **Born:** 10/4/1983 **Age:** 31

Year	Team	Lg	G	AB	H	2B	3B	HR	(Hm	Rd)	TB	R	RBI	RC	TBB	IBB	SO	HBP	SH	SF	SB	CS	GDP	Avg	OBP	Slg	OPS
2007	Oak	AL	68	213	53	13	0	7	(4	3)	87	27	39	33	24	0	39	3	3	5	0	0	4	.249	.327	.408	.735
2008	Oak	AL	148	530	148	25	1	7	(5	2)	196	54	42	66	44	2	69	11	2	1	2	3	20	.279	.346	.370	.716
2009	Oak	AL	147	570	156	37	1	15	(8	7)	240	74	88	77	28	0	59	8	1	7	8	2	14	.274	.313	.421	.734
2010	Oak	AL	131	495	120	18	2	13	(8	5)	181	55	71	54	33	3	69	12	0	4	3	2	22	.242	.303	.366	.669
2011	Oak	AL	134	460	109	26	0	14	(8	6)	177	54	44	42	38	1	64	7	3	7	2	2	14	.237	.301	.385	.686
2012	2 Tms	AL	118	408	96	20	0	6	(3	3)	134	36	43	39	20	2	73	5	4	5	2	0	5	.235	.276	.328	.605
2013	2 Tms	AL	94	285	66	13	1	5	(2	3)	96	25	32	34	22	6	35	3	2	4	2	0	2	.232	.290	.337	.627
2014	Min	AL	131	452	130	34	0	3	(1	2)	173	37	61	65	34	0	46	9	1	7	0	1	9	.288	.345	.383	.727
12	Oak	AL	75	262	57	15	0	1	(1	0)	75	19	18	16	9	0	53	3	2	2	1	0	3	.218	.250	.286	.536
12	Was	NL	43	146	39	5	0	5	(2	3)	59	17	25	23	11	3	20	2	2	3	1	0	2	.267	.321	.404	.725
13	Was	NL	79	252	56	11	1	3	(0	3)	78	19	25	26	20	6	32	3	2	4	2	0	2	.222	.283	.310	.593
13	Oak	AL	15	33	10	2	0	2	(2	0)	18	6	7	8	2	0	3	0	0	0	0	0	0	.303	.343	.545	.888
Postseason			5	17	4	0	0	0	(0	0)	4	0	2	2	2	0	4	0	0	0	0	0	0	.235	.316	.235	.551
8 ML YEARS			971	3413	878	186	5	70	(39	31)	1284	362	420	410	243	15	434	58	16	40	19	10	90	.257	.314	.376	.690

Anthony Swarzak

Pitches: R **Bats:** R **Pos:** RP-46; SP-4 SWORE-zack **Ht:** 6'4" **Wt:** 210 **Born:** 9/10/1985 **Age:** 29

Year	Team	Lg	G	GS	CG	GF	IP	BFP	H	R	ER	HR	SH	SF	HB	TBB	IBB	SO	WP	Bk	W	L	Pct	Sh	Sv-Op	Hld	ERC	ERA
2009	Min	AL	12	12	0	0	59.0	268	76	43	41	12	1	1	2	20	0	34	0	0	3	7	.300	0	0-0	0	6.50	6.25
2011	Min	AL	27	11	0	2	102.0	441	111	53	49	9	2	3	6	26	1	55	3	1	4	7	.364	0	0-0	0	4.11	4.32
2012	Min	AL	44	5	0	9	96.2	413	106	57	54	15	3	6	0	31	8	62	3	0	3	6	.333	0	0-1	1	4.63	5.03
2013	Min	AL	48	0	0	8	96.0	387	89	33	31	7	2	5	1	22	1	69	1	0	3	2	.600	0	0-2	3	2.94	2.91
2014	Min	AL	50	4	0	11	86.0	378	100	48	44	5	1	2	0	28	5	47	0	2	3	2	.600	0	0-1	3	4.29	4.60
5 ML YEARS			181	32	0	30	439.2	1887	482	234	219	48	9	17	9	127	15	267	7	3	16	24	.400	0	0-4	7	4.29	4.48

Ryan Sweeney

Bats: L **Throws:** L **Pos:** CF-24;RF-22;PH-22;LF-12;DH-2;PR-1 **Ht:** 6'4" **Wt:** 225 **Born:** 2/20/1985 **Age:** 30

Year	Team	Lg	G	AB	H	2B	3B	HR	(Hm	Rd)	TB	R	RBI	RC	TBB	IBB	SO	HBP	SH	SF	SB	CS	GDP	Avg	OBP	Slg	OPS
2014	Kane*	A	2	5	0	0	0	0	(-	-)	0	0	0	0	1	0	1	0	0	0	0	0	0	.000	.167	.000	.167
2006	CWS	AL	18	35	8	0	0	0	(0	0)	8	1	5	1	0	0	7	0	0	0	0	0	1	.229	.229	.229	.457
2007	CWS	AL	15	45	9	3	0	1	(1	0)	15	5	5	2	4	0	5	0	0	0	0	1	2	.200	.265	.333	.599
2008	Oak	AL	115	384	110	18	2	5	(1	4)	147	53	45	56	38	3	67	3	2	6	9	1	9	.286	.350	.383	.733
2009	Oak	AL	134	484	142	31	3	6	(2	4)	197	68	53	63	40	1	67	3	2	5	6	5	14	.293	.348	.407	.755
2010	Oak	AL	82	303	89	20	2	1	(1	0)	116	41	36	38	24	2	41	0	1	3	1	1	14	.294	.342	.383	.725
2011	Oak	AL	108	264	70	11	3	1	(1	0)	90	34	25	35	33	3	48	0	1	1	1	1	7	.265	.346	.341	.687
2012	Bos	AL	63	204	53	19	2	0	(0	0)	76	22	16	20	12	0	43	1	1	1	0	0	1	.260	.303	.373	.675
2013	ChC	NL	70	192	51	13	2	6	(3	3)	86	19	19	23	17	0	31	0	2	1	1	0	3	.266	.324	.448	.772
2014	ChC	NL	77	207	52	9	0	3	(2	1)	70	22	20	23	15	2	33	1	2	1	0	0	4	.251	.304	.338	.642
9 ML YEARS			682	2118	584	124	14	23	(11	12)	805	265	224	261	183	11	342	8	11	18	18	9	55	.276	.333	.380	.713

Nick Swisher

Bats: B **Throws:** L **Pos:** 1B-52;DH-34;PH-5;RF-4;LF-2 **Ht:** 6'0" **Wt:** 200 **Born:** 11/25/1980 **Age:** 34

Year	Team	Lg	G	AB	H	2B	3B	HR	(Hm	Rd)	TB	R	RBI	RC	TBB	IBB	SO	HBP	SH	SF	SB	CS	GDP	Avg	OBP	Slg	OPS
2014	Akron*	AA	2	6	3	2	0	0	(-	-)	5	0	2	2	0	0	1	0	0	0	0	0	0	.500	.500	.833	1.333
2004	Oak	AL	20	60	15	4	0	2	(1	1)	25	11	8	8	8	0	11	2	0	1	0	0	0	.250	.352	.417	.769
2005	Oak	AL	131	462	109	32	1	21	(11	10)	206	66	74	62	55	3	110	4	0	1	0	1	9	.236	.322	.446	.768
2006	Oak	AL	157	556	141	24	2	35	(17	18)	274	106	95	95	97	7	152	11	2	13	1	3	13	.254	.372	.493	.864
2007	Oak	AL	150	539	141	36	1	22	(8	14)	245	84	78	89	100	12	131	10	1	9	2	2	13	.262	.381	.455	.836
2008	CWS	AL	153	497	109	21	1	24	(19	5)	204	86	69	69	82	6	135	4	1	4	3	3	14	.219	.332	.410	.743
2009	NYY	AL	150	498	124	35	1	29	(8	21)	248	84	82	84	97	2	126	3	3	6	0	0	13	.249	.371	.498	.869
2010	NYY	AL	150	566	163	33	3	29	(15	14)	289	91	89	100	58	0	139	6	3	2	1	2	15	.288	.359	.511	.870
2011	NYY	AL	150	526	137	30	0	23	(12	11)	236	81	85	90	95	6	125	5	1	8	2	2	18	.260	.374	.449	.822
2012	NYY	AL	148	537	146	36	0	24	(11	13)	254	75	93	98	77	2	141	4	1	5	2	3	9	.272	.364	.473	.837
2013	Cle	AL	145	549	135	27	2	22	(11	11)	232	74	63	75	77	3	138	4	0	4	1	0	11	.246	.341	.423	.763
2014	Cle	AL	97	360	75	20	0	8	(6	2)	119	33	42	34	36	0	111	0	1	4	0	0	7	.208	.278	.331	.608
Postseason			47	158	26	9	0	4	(3	1)	47	16	8	10	24	0	48	1	1	1	0	0	4	.165	.277	.297	.575
11 ML YEARS			1451	5150	1295	298	11	239	(119	120)	2332	791	778	804	782	41	1319	53	13	50	13	15	122	.251	.353	.453	.806

Matt Szczur

Bats: R Throws: R Pos: RF-13;PH-11;CF-9;LF-6;PR-2;DH-1   SEE-zur   Ht: 6'1" Wt: 195 Born: 7/20/1989 Age: 25

							BATTING													RUNNING			AVERAGES			
Year	Team	Lg	G	AB	H	2B	3B	HR	(Hm | Rd)	TB	R	RBI	RC	TBB	IBB	SO	HBP	SH	SF	SB	CS	GDP	Avg	OBP	Slg	OPS
2010	Cubs	R	1	2	1	0	0	0	(- | -)	1	1	0	1	1	0	0	1	0	0	1	0	0	.500	.750	.500	1.250
2010	Boise	A-	18	73	29	9	0	0	(- | -)	38	17	8	16	6	0	11	1	0	2	1	0	1	.397	.439	.521	.960
2010	Peoria	A	6	26	5	1	1	0	(- | -)	8	6	2	2	3	0	5	1	0	0	0	0	1	.192	.300	.308	.608
2011	Peoria	A	66	274	86	15	1	5	(- | -)	118	55	27	45	21	0	28	2	0	1	17	5	4	.314	.366	.431	.796
2011	Dytona	A+	43	173	45	7	2	5	(- | -)	71	20	19	21	5	0	20	1	2	1	7	0	2	.260	.283	.410	.694
2012	Dytona	A+	78	295	87	19	4	2	(- | -)	120	68	34	55	47	1	50	4	2	4	38	12	2	.295	.394	.407	.801
2012	Tenn	AA	35	143	30	7	4	2	(- | -)	51	24	6	15	14	0	29	1	0	0	4	2	0	.210	.285	.357	.641
2013	Tenn	AA	128	512	144	27	4	3	(- | -)	188	78	44	70	50	0	75	6	3	3	22	12	11	.281	.350	.367	.717
2014	Iowa	AAA	116	414	108	16	1	1	(- | -)	129	52	24	46	30	1	78	3	9	1	30	7	9	.261	.315	.312	.626
2014	ChC	NL	33	62	14	2	0	2	(1 | 1)	22	6	5	7	4	0	11	0	0	0	0	0	1	.226	.273	.355	.628

Jose Tabata

TAH-bah-tah

Bats: R Throws: R Pos: PH-40;RF-37;LF-18;PR-2;CF-1;DH-1   Ht: 5'11" Wt: 210 Born: 8/12/1988 Age: 26

							BATTING													RUNNING			AVERAGES			
Year	Team	Lg	G	AB	H	2B	3B	HR	(Hm | Rd)	TB	R	RBI	RC	TBB	IBB	SO	HBP	SH	SF	SB	CS	GDP	Avg	OBP	Slg	OPS
2014	Indy*	AAA	39	146	41	10	0	0	(- | -)	51	18	12	18	10	0	14	4	0	3	1	2	5	.281	.337	.349	.687
2010	Pit	NL	102	405	121	21	4	4	(3 | 1)	162	61	35	59	28	0	57	2	5	1	19	7	7	.299	.346	.400	.746
2011	Pit	NL	91	334	89	18	1	4	(3 | 1)	121	53	21	41	40	1	61	4	1	3	16	7	8	.266	.349	.362	.711
2012	Pit	NL	103	333	81	20	3	3	(1 | 2)	116	43	16	31	29	0	58	6	6	0	8	12	7	.243	.315	.348	.664
2013	Pit	NL	106	308	87	17	5	6	(4 | 2)	132	35	33	45	23	0	45	5	5	0	3	1	6	.282	.342	.429	.771
2014	Pit	NL	80	174	49	5	2	0	(0 | 0)	58	14	17	17	7	0	26	2	1	2	1	2	12	.282	.314	.333	.647
	Postseason		4	4	0	0	0	0	(0 | 0)	0	0	0	0	0	0	1	0	0	0	0	0	0	.000	.000	.000	.000
	5 ML YEARS		482	1554	427	81	15	17	(11 | 6)	589	206	122	193	127	1	247	19	18	6	47	29	40	.275	.336	.379	.715

Masahiro Tanaka

Pitches: R Bats: R Pos: SP-20   mah-sah-HEE-roh tuh-NAH-kah   Ht: 6'2" Wt: 205 Born: 11/1/1988 Age: 26

			HOW MUCH HE PITCHED						WHAT HE GAVE UP										THE RESULTS						
Year	Team	Lg	G	GS	CG	GF	IP	BFP	H	R	ER	HR	SH	SF	HB	TBB	IBB	SO	WP	Bk	W	L	Pct	Sh	Sv-Op	Hld	ERC	ERA
2010	Tohoku	Jap	20	20	8	0	155.0	643	159	47	43	9	-	-	5	32	1	119	1	0	11	6	.647	1	0- -	-	3.33	2.50
2011	Tohoku	Jap	27	27	14	0	226.1	866	171	35	32	8	-	-	5	27	0	241	7	0	19	5	.792	6	0- -	-	1.60	1.27
2012	Tohoku	Jap	22	22	8	0	173.0	696	160	45	36	4	-	-	2	19	0	169	4	0	10	4	.714	3	0- -	-	2.15	1.87
2013	Tohoku	Jap	28	27	8	1	212.0	822	168	35	30	6	-	-	3	32	0	183	9	0	24	0	1.000	2	1- -	-	1.77	1.27
2014	NYY	AL	20	20	3	0	136.1	542	123	47	42	15	2	3	4	21	0	141	4	0	13	5	.722	1	0-0	0	2.83	2.77

Oscar Taveras

Bats: L Throws: L Pos: RF-62;PH-18;CF-3   Ht: 6'2" Wt: 200 Born: 6/19/1992 Age: 23

							BATTING													RUNNING			AVERAGES			
Year	Team	Lg	G	AB	H	2B	3B	HR	(Hm	Rd)	TB	R	RBI	RC	TBB	IBB	SO	HBP	SH	SF	SB	CS	GDP	Avg	OBP	Slg	OPS
2010	Cards	R	7	30	5	1	0	0	(-	-)	6	1	2	0	1	0	5	0	0	0	1	0	0	.167	.194	.200	.394
2010	JhsCty	R+	53	211	68	13	3	8	(-	-)	111	39	43	39	12	0	41	3	0	3	8	5	5	.322	.362	.526	.889
2011	QuadC	A	78	308	119	27	5	8	(-	-)	180	52	62	74	32	1	52	3	0	4	1	4	5	.386	.444	.584	1.028
2012	Sprgfld	AA	124	477	153	37	7	23	(-	-)	273	83	94	103	42	10	56	7	0	5	10	1	17	.321	.380	.572	.953
2013	Memp	AAA	46	173	53	12	0	5	(-	-)	80	25	32	28	9	1	22	1	1	2	5	1	6	.306	.341	.462	.803
2013	Cards	NL	1	1	1	1	0	0	(-	-)	2	0	0	1	0	0	0	0	0	0	0	0	0	1.000	1.000	2.000	3.000
2014	Memp	AAA	62	239	76	18	1	8	(-	-)	120	36	49	44	19	5	31	2	0	2	1	1	7	.318	.370	.502	.872
2014	StL	NL	80	234	56	8	0	3	(1	2)	73	18	22	22	12	0	37	1	0	1	0	1	10	.239	.278	.312	.590

Chris Taylor

Bats: R Throws: R Pos: SS-47;PH-3   Ht: 6'1" Wt: 190 Born: 8/29/1990 Age: 24

							BATTING													RUNNING			AVERAGES			
Year	Team	Lg	G	AB	H	2B	3B	HR	(Hm	Rd)	TB	R	RBI	RC	TBB	IBB	SO	HBP	SH	SF	SB	CS	GDP	Avg	OBP	Slg	OPS
2012	Everett	A-	57	137	45	12	1	2	(-	-)	65	26	18	30	21	0	18	5	0	2	13	5	1	.328	.430	.474	.905
2012	Clinton	A	12	46	14	0	0	0	(-	-)	14	5	4	6	2	0	4	3	2	0	4	1	1	.304	.373	.304	.677
2013	Hi Dsrt	A+	67	269	90	16	7	7	(-	-)	141	62	44	64	44	0	62	2	0	4	20	2	4	.335	.426	.524	.950
2013	Jacksn	AA	67	256	75	12	4	1	(-	-)	98	46	16	44	40	1	55	2	1	1	18	3	4	.293	.391	.383	.774
2014	Tacom	AAA	75	302	99	22	7	5	(-	-)	150	63	37	61	35	1	74	3	1	5	14	6	7	.328	.397	.497	.894
2014	Sea	AL	47	136	39	8	0	0	(0	0)	47	16	9	18	11	0	39	2	1	1	5	2	3	.287	.347	.346	.692

Michael Taylor

Bats: R Throws: R Pos: LF-8;PH-4;DH-2   Ht: 6'5" Wt: 255 Born: 12/19/1985 Age: 29

							BATTING													RUNNING			AVERAGES			
Year	Team	Lg	G	AB	H	2B	3B	HR	(Hm	Rd)	TB	R	RBI	RC	TBB	IBB	SO	HBP	SH	SF	SB	CS	GDP	Avg	OBP	Slg	OPS
2014	Scrmto*	AAA	59	218	53	14	1	5	(-	-)	84	34	31	33	33	1	50	6	0	1	7	2	9	.243	.357	.385	.742
2014	Charltt*	AAA	64	219	67	18	2	6	(-	-)	107	41	38	43	29	1	50	2	0	4	1	0	3	.306	.386	.489	.874
2011	Oak	AL	11	30	6	0	0	1	(1	0)	9	4	1	4	5	0	11	0	0	0	0	0	0	.200	.314	.300	.614
2012	Oak	AL	6	21	3	1	0	0	(0	0)	4	2	0	0	0	0	10	0	0	0	0	0	0	.143	.143	.190	.333
2013	Oak	AL	9	23	1	0	0	0	(0	0)	1	0	0	0	2	0	5	0	0	0	0	0	1	.043	.120	.043	.163
2014	CWS	AL	11	28	7	1	0	0	(0	0)	8	3	5	0	5	0	9	0	0	0	0	0	0	.250	.364	.286	.649
	4 ML YEARS		37	102	17	2	0	1	(1	0)	22	9	6	1	12	0	35	0	0	0	0	0	2	.167	.254	.216	.470

Michael Taylor

Bats: R Throws: R Pos: CF-10;RF-5;PH-5   Ht: 6'3" Wt: 210 Born: 3/26/1991 Age: 24

								BATTING												RUNNING			AVERAGES			
Year	Team	Lg	G	AB	H	2B	3B	HR	(Hm | Rd)	TB	R	RBI	RC	TBB	IBB	SO	HBP	SH	SF	SB	CS	GDP	Avg	OBP	Slg	OPS
2010	Nats	R	38	128	25	4	3	1	(- | -)	38	14	12	10	14	0	31	1	1	5	1	2	2	.195	.270	.297	.567
2010	Hgrstn	A	5	13	3	1	0	0	(- | -)	4	0	1	1	1	0	2	1	0	0	0	0	0	.231	.333	.308	.641
2011	Hgrstn	A	126	442	112	26	7	13	(- | -)	191	64	68	61	32	0	120	6	4	4	23	12	7	.253	.310	.432	.742
2012	Ptomc	A+	109	384	93	33	2	3	(- | -)	139	51	37	47	40	0	113	3	3	1	19	9	6	.242	.318	.362	.680
2013	Ptomc	A+	133	509	134	41	6	10	(- | -)	217	79	87	85	55	1	131	8	2	7	51	7	10	.263	.340	.426	.767
2014	Hrsbrg	AA	98	384	120	17	2	22	(- | -)	207	74	61	84	50	2	130	4	2	1	34	8	3	.313	.396	.539	.935
2014	Syrcse	AAA	12	44	10	3	1	1	(- | -)	18	7	3	6	7	0	14	0	1	0	3	1	0	.227	.333	.409	.742
2014	Was	NL	17	39	8	3	0	1	(0 | 1)	14	5	5	3	3	0	17	1	0	0	0	2	1	.205	.279	.359	.638

Junichi Tazawa

Pitches: R Bats: R Pos: RP-71   joo-NEE-chee tuh-ZAH-wah   Ht: 5'11" Wt: 200 Born: 6/6/1986 Age: 29

			HOW MUCH HE PITCHED					WHAT HE GAVE UP												THE RESULTS						
Year	Team	Lg	G	GS	CG	GF	IP	BFP	H	R	ER	HR	SH	SF	HB	TBB	IBB	SO	WP	Bk	W	L	Pct	Sh	Sv-Op	Hld	ERC	ERA
2009	Bos	AL	6	4	0	1	25.1	130	43	23	21	4	0	3	3	9	0	13	0	0	2	3	.400	0	0-0	0	9.14	7.46
2011	Bos	AL	3	0	0	2	3.0	13	3	2	2	1	0	0	0	1	0	4	0	0	0	0	-	0	0-0	0	5.31	6.00
2012	Bos	AL	37	0	0	13	44.0	172	37	7	7	1	1	1	2	5	0	45	0	0	1	1	.500	0	1-1	5	1.94	1.43
2013	Bos	AL	71	0	0	10	68.1	284	70	25	24	9	2	5	1	12	1	72	3	1	5	4	.556	0	0-8	25	3.55	3.16
2014	Bos	AL	71	0	0	12	63.0	261	58	23	20	5	1	1	0	17	1	64	5	0	4	3	.571	0	0-5	16	2.97	2.86
	Postseason		13	0	0	0	7.1	26	6	1	1	0	0	0	0	1	0	6	1	0	1	0	1.000	0	0-0	6	1.84	1.23
	5 ML YEARS		188	4	0	38	203.2	860	211	80	74	20	4	10	6	44	2	198	8	1	12	11	.522	0	1-14	46	3.62	3.27

Taylor Teagarden

Bats: R Throws: R Pos: C-9   Ht: 6'0" Wt: 210 Born: 12/21/1983 Age: 31

								BATTING												RUNNING			AVERAGES			
Year	Team	Lg	G	AB	H	2B	3B	HR	(Hm	Rd)	TB	R	RBI	RC	TBB	IBB	SO	HBP	SH	SF	SB	CS	GDP	Avg	OBP	Slg	OPS
2014	LsVgs*	AAA	55	178	54	7	0	14	(-	-)	103	32	39	41	30	2	59	1	0	2	0	0	4	.303	.403	.579	.981
2014	Mets*	R	4	10	2	2	0	0	(-	-)	4	0	0	1	1	0	6	1	0	0	0	0	0	.200	.333	.400	.733
2014	StLuci*	A+	2	6	2	0	0	0	(-	-)	2	1	0	0	0	0	2	0	0	0	0	0	0	.333	.333	.333	.667
2008	Tex	AL	16	47	15	5	0	6	(3	3)	38	10	17	15	5	0	19	1	0	0	0	0	0	.319	.396	.809	1.205
2009	Tex	AL	60	198	43	13	0	6	(2	4)	74	26	24	16	14	0	76	1	3	2	0	0	6	.217	.270	.374	.644
2010	Tex	AL	28	71	11	1	0	4	(1	3)	24	10	6	5	8	0	34	2	4	0	0	0	0	.155	.259	.338	.597
2011	Tex	AL	14	34	8	2	0	0	(0	0)	10	3	2	2	2	0	13	0	0	0	0	0	0	.235	.278	.294	.572
2012	Bal	AL	22	57	9	3	0	2	(2	0)	18	4	9	6	5	0	23	0	2	0	0	0	1	.158	.226	.316	.542
2013	Bal	AL	23	60	10	2	0	2	(0	2)	18	3	5	2	1	0	18	0	1	0	0	1	0	.167	.180	.300	.480
2014	NYM	NL	9	28	4	0	0	1	(1	0)	7	1	5	2	2	0	7	0	0	0	0	0	0	.143	.200	.250	.450
	7 ML YEARS		172	495	100	26	0	21	(9	12)	189	57	68	48	37	0	190	4	10	2	0	1	8	.202	.262	.382	.644

Julio Teheran

Pitches: R Bats: R Pos: SP-33   tay-RONN   Ht: 6'2" Wt: 200 Born: 1/27/1991 Age: 24

			HOW MUCH HE PITCHED					WHAT HE GAVE UP												THE RESULTS						
Year	Team	Lg	G	GS	CG	GF	IP	BFP	H	R	ER	HR	SH	SF	HB	TBB	IBB	SO	WP	Bk	W	L	Pct	Sh	Sv-Op	Hld	ERC	ERA
2011	Atl	NL	5	3	0	0	19.2	87	21	11	11	4	2	1	0	8	0	10	1	0	1	1	.500	0	0-0	0	5.19	5.03
2012	Atl	NL	2	1	0	0	6.1	24	5	4	4	0	0	0	0	1	0	5	0	0	0	0	-	0	0-0	0	1.64	5.68
2013	Atl	NL	30	30	0	0	185.2	774	173	69	66	22	8	5	13	45	4	170	2	0	14	8	.636	0	0-0	0	3.45	3.20
2014	Atl	NL	33	33	4	0	221.0	884	188	82	71	22	13	4	4	51	4	186	1	1	14	13	.519	2	0-0	0	2.71	2.89
	Postseason		1	1	0	0	2.2	17	8	6	6	1	0	1	0	1	0	5	1	0	0	1	.000	0	0-0	0	20.77	20.25
	4 ML YEARS		70	67	4	0	432.2	1769	387	166	152	48	23	10	17	105	8	371	4	1	29	22	.569	2	0-0	0	3.11	3.16

Mark Teixeira

Bats: B Throws: R Pos: 1B-117;DH-4;PH-3   tuh-SHARE-uh   Ht: 6'3" Wt: 215 Born: 4/11/1980 Age: 35

								BATTING												RUNNING			AVERAGES			
Year	Team	Lg	G	AB	H	2B	3B	HR	(Hm	Rd)	TB	R	RBI	RC	TBB	IBB	SO	HBP	SH	SF	SB	CS	GDP	Avg	OBP	Slg	OPS
2003	Tex	AL	146	529	137	29	5	26	(19	7)	254	66	84	78	44	5	120	14	0	2	1	2	14	.259	.331	.480	.811
2004	Tex	AL	145	545	153	34	2	38	(18	20)	305	101	112	120	68	12	117	10	0	2	4	1	6	.281	.370	.560	.929
2005	Tex	AL	162	644	194	41	3	43	(30	13)	370	112	144	148	72	5	124	11	0	3	4	0	18	.301	.379	.575	.954
2006	Tex	AL	162	628	177	45	1	33	(12	21)	323	99	110	114	89	12	128	4	0	6	2	0	17	.282	.371	.514	.886
2007	2 Tms		132	494	151	33	2	30	(14	16)	278	86	105	116	72	13	112	7	0	2	0	0	9	.306	.400	.563	.963
2008	2 Tms		157	574	177	41	0	33	(19	14)	317	102	121	118	97	13	93	7	0	7	2	0	17	.308	.410	.552	.962
2009	NYY	AL	156	609	178	43	3	39	(24	15)	344	103	122	112	81	9	114	12	0	5	2	0	5	.292	.383	.565	.948
2010	NYY	AL	158	601	154	36	0	33	(19	14)	289	113	108	110	93	6	122	13	0	5	0	1	15	.256	.365	.481	.846
2011	NYY	AL	156	589	146	26	1	39	(22	17)	291	90	111	106	76	3	110	11	0	8	4	1	12	.248	.341	.494	.835
2012	NYY	AL	123	451	113	27	1	24	(12	12)	214	66	84	69	54	1	83	7	0	12	2	1	11	.251	.332	.475	.807
2013	NYY	AL	15	53	8	1	0	3	(2	1)	18	5	12	6	8	2	19	1	0	1	0	0	5	.151	.270	.340	.609
2014	NYY	AL	123	440	95	14	0	22	(10	12)	175	56	62	54	58	3	109	6	0	4	1	1	13	.216	.313	.398	.711
07	Tex	AL	78	286	85	24	1	13	(5	8)	150	48	49	58	45	10	66	3	0	1	0	0	5	.297	.397	.524	.921
07	Atl	NL	54	208	66	9	1	17	(9	8)	128	38	56	58	27	3	46	4	0	1	0	0	4	.317	.404	.615	1.020
08	Atl	NL	103	381	108	27	0	20	(11	9)	195	69	78	69	65	9	70	3	0	2	0	0	13	.283	.390	.512	.902
08	LAA	AL	54	193	69	14	0	13	(8	5)	122	33	43	50	32	4	23	4	0	5	2	0	4	.358	.449	.632	1.081
	Postseason		40	153	34	6	0	3	(2	1)	49	21	14	15	24	2	34	4	0	3	1	0	3	.222	.339	.320	.659
	12 ML YEARS		1635	6157	1683	370	18	363	(201	162)	3178	999	1175	1149	812	84	1251	103	0	57	22	7	144	.273	.364	.516	.881

Ruben Tejada

Bats: R Throws: R Pos: SS-114;PH-9;PR-1   Ht: 5'11" Wt: 200 Born: 10/27/1989 Age: 25

								BATTING												RUNNING			AVERAGES			
Year	Team	Lg	G	AB	H	2B	3B	HR	(Hm	Rd)	TB	R	RBI	RC	TBB	IBB	SO	HBP	SH	SF	SB	CS	GDP	Avg	OBP	Slg	OPS
2010	NYM	NL	78	216	46	12	0	1	(0	1)	61	28	15	16	22	3	38	6	8	3	2	2	2	.213	.305	.282	.588
2011	NYM	NL	96	328	93	15	1	0	(0	0)	110	31	36	41	35	3	50	6	4	3	5	1	6	.284	.360	.335	.696
2012	NYM	NL	114	464	134	26	0	1	(0	1)	163	53	25	49	27	0	73	5	3	2	4	4	9	.289	.333	.351	.685
2013	NYM	NL	57	208	42	12	0	0	(0	0)	54	20	10	15	15	0	24	1	3	0	2	1	3	.202	.259	.260	.519
2014	NYM	NL	119	355	84	11	0	5	(1	4)	110	30	34	42	50	11	73	8	4	2	1	2	8	.237	.342	.310	.652
	5 ML YEARS		464	1571	399	76	1	7	(1	6)	498	162	120	163	149	17	258	28	20	10	14	10	28	.254	.328	.317	.645

Tomas Telis

Bats: B Throws: R Pos: C-17;DH-1   TOE-maas tay-LEASE   Ht: 5'8" Wt: 200 Born: 6/18/1991 Age: 24

								BATTING												RUNNING			AVERAGES			
Year	Team	Lg	G	AB	H	2B	3B	HR	(Hm	Rd)	TB	R	RBI	RC	TBB	IBB	SO	HBP	SH	SF	SB	CS	GDP	Avg	OBP	Slg	OPS
2010	Rngrs	R	37	144	47	7	1	2	(-	-)	62	22	35	22	6	0	16	1	4	3	4	1	2	.326	.351	.431	.781
2011	Hkry	A	115	461	137	28	0	1	(-	-)	198	67	69	66	18	0	35	6	5	4	12	6	17	.297	.329	.430	.759
2012	MrtlBh	A+	117	450	111	24	1	4	(-	-)	149	45	43	44	17	2	53	7	7	3	9	2	18	.247	.283	.331	.614
2013	Frisco	AA	91	348	92	19	0	4	(-	-)	123	32	43	37	10	1	46	4	3	4	8	2	13	.264	.290	.353	.643
2014	Frisco	AA	70	267	81	16	2	2	(-	-)	107	31	33	39	17	1	29	1	3	7	7	1	14	.303	.349	.401	.740
2014	RdRck	AAA	36	139	48	7	2	3	(-	-)	68	18	17	24	6	1	12	1	1	0	1	1	4	.345	.377	.489	.866
2014	Tex	AL	18	68	17	2	0	0	(0	0)	19	7	8	7	1	0	10	1	1	0	0	0	2	.250	.271	.279	.551

Nick Tepesch

Pitches: R Bats: R Pos: SP-22; RP-1   TEP-ish   Ht: 6'4" Wt: 225 Born: 10/12/1988 Age: 26

			HOW MUCH HE PITCHED						WHAT HE GAVE UP									THE RESULTS							
Year	Team	Lg	G	GS	CG	GF	IP	BFP	H	R	ER	HR	SH	SF	HB	TBB	IBB	SO	WP	Bk	W	L	Pct	Sh	Sv-Op	Hld	ERC	ERA
2011	Hkry	A	29	23	2	1	138.1	583	147	70	62	14	6	4	13	33	0	118	1	0	7	5	.583	0	0- -	-	4.27	4.03
2012	MrtlBh	A+	12	12	1	0	71.2	299	68	27	23	3	3	2	7	18	0	59	3	0	5	3	.625	1	0- -	-	3.24	2.89
2012	Frisco	AA	16	14	0	0	90.1	382	97	47	43	10	3	3	3	26	0	68	3	2	6	3	.667	0	0- -	-	4.34	4.28
2013	RdRck	AAA	1	1	0	0	5.0	20	5	1	0	0	0	0	0	0	0	5	0	0	1	0	1.000	0	0- -	-	1.95	0.00
2013	Frisco	AA	2	2	0	0	6.0	27	7	1	1	0	0	0	0	2	0	3	0	0	0	0	-	0	0- -	-	3.91	1.50
2014	RdRck	AAA	7	7	1	0	45.2	178	36	8	8	1	1	1	2	9	0	41	2	0	6	1	.857	1	0- -	-	1.98	1.58
2013	Tex	AL	19	17	0	1	93.0	407	100	53	50	12	1	4	7	27	3	76	0	0	4	6	.400	0	0-0	0	4.49	4.84
2014	Tex	AL	23	22	0	1	126.0	537	128	66	61	15	3	4	7	44	2	56	1	0	5	11	.313	0	0-0	0	4.37	4.36
	2 ML YEARS		42	39	0	2	219.0	944	228	119	111	27	4	8	14	71	5	132	1	0	9	17	.346	0	0-0	0	4.42	4.56

Joey Terdoslavich

Bats: B Throws: R Pos: PH-6;1B-2;RF-2   ter-DOSS-low-vitch   Ht: 6'2" Wt: 200 Born: 9/9/1988 Age: 26

								BATTING												RUNNING			AVERAGES			
Year	Team	Lg	G	AB	H	2B	3B	HR	(Hm	Rd)	TB	R	RBI	RC	TBB	IBB	SO	HBP	SH	SF	SB	CS	GDP	Avg	OBP	Slg	OPS
2010	Danvle	R+	49	189	56	10	2	2	(-	-)	76	27	24	27	15	0	27	1	0	0	3	3	2	.296	.351	.402	.753
2010	Rome	A	21	79	25	9	0	0	(-	-)	34	7	10	12	5	0	18	1	0	0	0	0	4	.316	.365	.430	.795
2011	Lynbrg	A+	131	483	138	52	2	20	(-	-)	254	72	82	88	41	4	107	4	0	8	2	0	7	.286	.341	.526	.867
2012	Gwnntt	AAA	53	194	35	4	0	4	(-	-)	51	19	20	13	19	0	50	0	1	1	3	0	3	.180	.252	.263	.515
2012	Missi	AA	78	298	94	24	5	5	(-	-)	143	43	51	55	27	0	62	3	0	5	4	0	8	.315	.372	.480	.852
2013	Gwnntt	AAA	85	321	102	24	1	18	(-	-)	182	48	58	62	23	1	65	1	0	6	3	6	7	.318	.359	.567	.926
2014	Gwnntt	AAA	136	507	130	18	1	15	(-	-)	195	62	61	69	61	5	106	1	0	0	1	3	15	.256	.337	.385	.722
2013	Atl	NL	55	79	17	4	0	0	(0	0)	21	11	4	6	12	1	24	0	0	1	1	0	2	.215	.315	.266	.581
2014	Atl	NL	9	10	3	2	0	0	(0	0)	5	1	2	1	0	0	3	1	0	0	0	0	0	.300	.364	.500	.864
	2 ML YEARS		64	89	20	6	0	0	(0	0)	26	12	6	7	12	1	27	1	0	1	1	0	2	.225	.320	.292	.613

Joe Thatcher

Pitches: L Bats: L Pos: RP-53   Ht: 6'2" Wt: 230 Born: 10/4/1981 Age: 33

				HOW MUCH HE PITCHED						WHAT HE GAVE UP									THE RESULTS							
Year	Team	Lg	G	GS	CG	GF	IP	BFP	H	R	ER	HR	SH	SF	HB	TBB	IBB	SO	WP	Bk	W	L	Pct	Sh	Sv-Op	Hld	ERC	ERA
2007	SD	NL	22	0	0	5	21.0	85	13	6	3	1	0	0	1	6	2	16	0	0	2	2	.500	0	0-0	2	1.49	1.29
2008	SD	NL	25	0	0	7	25.2	128	42	25	24	4	2	3	0	13	2	17	0	0	0	4	.000	0	0-3	5	8.91	8.42
2009	SD	NL	52	0	0	7	45.0	188	37	14	14	2	1	2	4	18	7	55	2	1	1	0	1.000	0	0-1	9	2.87	2.80
2010	SD	NL	65	0	0	12	35.0	137	23	5	5	1	3	2	1	7	2	45	0	0	1	0	1.000	0	0-0	11	1.37	1.29
2011	SD	NL	18	0	0	5	10.0	44	8	5	5	1	0	0	0	7	1	9	0	0	0	0	-	0	0-0	2	3.96	4.50
2012	SD	NL	55	0	0	13	31.2	141	30	13	12	2	2	2	3	14	3	39	0	1	1	4	.200	0	1-1	14	3.82	3.41
2013	2 Tms	NL	72	0	0	16	59.1	164	40	14	14	4	1	2	1	10	0	36	3	0	2	2	.600	0	0-4	15	3.75	3.20
2014	2 Tms	NL	53	0	0	9	30.1	135	36	16	13	3	1	2	4	4	1	27	1	0	2	1	.667	0	0-1	6	4.42	3.86
13	SD	NL	50	0	0	13	30.0	121	28	7	7	3	0	1	1	4	0	29	2	0	3	1	.750	0	0-2	11	2.83	2.10
13	Ari	NL	22	0	0	3	9.1	43	12	7	7	1	1	1	0	6	0	7	1	0	0	1	.000	0	0-2	4	7.19	6.75
14	Ari	NL	37	0	0	7	24.0	100	23	10	7	3	1	1	2	3	1	25	1	0	1	0	1.000	0	0-1	4	3.14	2.63
14	LAA	AL	16	0	0	2	6.1	35	13	6	6	0	0	1	2	1	0	2	0	0	1	1	.500	0	0-0	2	9.96	8.53
	8 ML YEARS		362	0	0	74	238.0	1022	229	98	90	18	10	13	14	79	18	244	6	2	10	13	.435	0	1-10	64	3.51	3.40

Dale Thayer

Pitches: R Bats: R Pos: RP-70   Ht: 6'0" Wt: 210 Born: 12/17/1980 Age: 34

			HOW MUCH HE PITCHED						WHAT HE GAVE UP										THE RESULTS						
Year	Team	Lg	G	GS	CG	GF	IP	BFP	H	R	ER	HR	SH	SF	HB	TBB	IBB	SO	WP	Bk	W	L	Pct	Sh	Sv-Op	Hld	ERC	ERA
2009	TB	AL	11	0	0	3	13.2	59	18	9	7	3	0	0	0	1	0	8	1	0	0	0	-	0	1-1	5	5.38	4.61
2010	TB	AL	1	0	0	0	2.0	13	7	6	6	1	0	0	0	0	0	2	0	0	0	0	-	0	0-0	0	24.30	27.00
2011	NYM	NL	11	0	0	7	10.1	42	12	4	4	0	1	2	0	0	0	5	0	0	0	3	.000	0	0-0	0	2.78	3.48
2012	SD	NL	64	0	0	21	57.2	235	53	24	22	4	4	4	1	12	4	47	2	0	2	2	.500	0	7-10	22	2.68	3.43
2013	SD	NL	69	0	0	13	65.0	270	59	25	24	8	3	1	2	22	2	64	2	0	3	5	.375	0	1-4	18	3.60	3.32
2014	SD	NL	70	0	0	25	65.1	265	53	19	17	9	1	0	2	16	3	62	1	0	4	5	.444	0	0-1	13	2.75	2.34
	6 ML YEARS		226	0	0	69	214.0	884	202	87	80	25	9	7	5	51	9	188	6	0	9	15	.375	0	9-16	53	3.28	3.36

Caleb Thielbar

Pitches: L Bats: R Pos: RP-54   THEEL-bar   Ht: 6'0" Wt: 195 Born: 1/31/1987 Age: 28

			HOW MUCH HE PITCHED						WHAT HE GAVE UP										THE RESULTS						
Year	Team	Lg	G	GS	CG	GF	IP	BFP	H	R	ER	HR	SH	SF	HB	TBB	IBB	SO	WP	Bk	W	L	Pct	Sh	Sv-Op	Hld	ERC	ERA
2010	Wisc	A	30	0	0	9	53.0	241	65	41	33	6	5	1	0	14	3	43	0	0	0	2	.000	0	3- -	-	4.64	5.60
2010	Helena	R+	9	0	0	4	14.2	56	16	7	6	2	0	0	0	0	0	9	1	0	0	0	-	0	0- -	-	3.43	3.68
2011	FtMyrs	A+	3	1	0	1	7.1	29	1	0	0	0	0	0	0	5	0	5	1	0	1	0	1.000	0	0- -	-	0.75	0.00
2012	FtMyrs	A+	7	0	0	6	12.1	45	4	1	0	0	1	0	2	2	0	16	0	0	1	1	.500	0	1- -	-	0.65	0.00
2012	NwBrit	AA	16	0	0	11	25.0	95	18	5	5	1	1	0	0	3	1	26	0	0	2	0	1.000	0	4- -	-	1.41	1.80
2012	Roch	AAA	25	1	0	5	40.1	178	42	19	16	5	1	2	1	16	2	32	3	0	3	1	.750	0	1- -	-	4.43	3.57
2013	Roch	AAA	17	0	0	4	26.1	114	27	13	11	1	0	1	1	8	0	34	2	0	1	1	.500	0	1- -	-	3.50	3.76
2013	Min	AL	49	0	0	16	46.0	171	24	11	9	4	0	1	0	14	4	39	1	0	3	2	.600	0	0-0	15	1.38	1.76
2014	Min	AL	54	0	0	7	47.2	206	51	19	18	3	1	6	1	16	1	35	0	0	2	1	.667	0	0-1	7	4.01	3.40
	2 ML YEARS		103	0	0	23	93.2	377	75	30	27	7	1	7	1	30	5	74	1	0	5	3	.625	0	0-1	8	2.56	2.59

Josh Thole

Bats: L Throws: R Pos: C-53;PH-7;DH-1   TOE-lee   Ht: 6'1" Wt: 205 Born: 10/28/1986 Age: 28

			BATTING																		RUNNING			AVERAGES			
Year	Team	Lg	G	AB	H	2B	3B	HR	(Hm	Rd)	TB	R	RBI	RC	TBB	IBB	SO	HBP	SH	SF	SB	CS	GDP	Avg	OBP	Slg	OPS
2009	NYM	NL	17	53	17	2	1	0	(0	0)	21	2	9	9	4	0	5	0	0	2	1	0	1	.321	.356	.396	.752
2010	NYM	NL	73	202	56	7	1	3	(2	1)	74	17	17	28	24	1	25	1	0	0	1	0	8	.277	.357	.366	.723
2011	NYM	NL	114	340	91	17	0	3	(1	2)	117	22	40	39	38	6	47	4	1	3	0	2	8	.268	.345	.344	.690
2012	NYM	NL	104	321	75	15	0	1	(0	1)	93	24	21	24	27	6	50	1	4	1	0	0	12	.234	.294	.290	.584
2013	Tor	AL	45	120	21	3	1	1	(0	1)	29	11	8	7	12	0	25	1	2	0	0	0	3	.175	.256	.242	.497
2014	Tor	AL	57	133	33	4	0	0	(0	0)	37	11	7	11	14	0	25	0	3	0	0	3	4	.248	.320	.278	.598
	6 ML YEARS		410	1169	293	48	3	8	(3	5)	371	87	102	118	119	13	177	7	10	6	2	5	36	.251	.322	.317	.639

Ian Thomas

Pitches: L Bats: R Pos: RP-16   Ht: 6'4" Wt: 215 Born: 4/20/1987 Age: 28

			HOW MUCH HE PITCHED						WHAT HE GAVE UP										THE RESULTS						
Year	Team	Lg	G	GS	CG	GF	IP	BFP	H	R	ER	HR	SH	SF	HB	TBB	IBB	SO	WP	Bk	W	L	Pct	Sh	Sv-Op	Hld	ERC	ERA
2012	Rome	A	26	0	0	12	45.2	193	45	19	16	4	1	0	0	15	0	58	1	1	5	0	1.000	0	6- -	-	3.63	3.15
2013	Missi	AA	39	13	0	8	104.1	419	72	34	32	7	4	2	1	37	2	123	1	1	7	8	.467	0	1- -	-	2.11	2.76
2014	Gwnntt	AAA	6	1	0	2	13.2	56	12	6	6	1	0	2	0	5	0	16	2	0	1	0	1.000	0	1- -	-	3.17	3.95
2014	Braves	R	3	3	0	0	6.0	23	7	3	3	1	0	0	0	0	0	7	0	0	0	0	-	0	0- -	-	4.12	4.50
2014	Missi	AA	4	0	0	0	3.1	15	4	2	2	1	0	0	0	2	0	4	0	0	0	0	-	0	0- -	-	8.11	5.40
2014	Atl	NL	16	0	0	4	10.2	48	10	5	5	0	1	1	0	6	1	13	1	0	1	2	.333	0	0-0	3	3.37	4.22

Aaron Thompson

Pitches: L Bats: L Pos: RP-7   Ht: 6'3" Wt: 195 Born: 2/28/1987 Age: 28

			HOW MUCH HE PITCHED						WHAT HE GAVE UP										THE RESULTS						
Year	Team	Lg	G	GS	CG	GF	IP	BFP	H	R	ER	HR	SH	SF	HB	TBB	IBB	SO	WP	Bk	W	L	Pct	Sh	Sv-Op	Hld	ERC	ERA
2010	Hrsbrg	AA	26	26	0	0	136.2	616	164	96	88	16	3	7	5	53	0	95	5	2	4	13	.235	0	0- -	-	5.49	5.80
2010	Syrcse	AAA	1	1	0	0	5.0	23	5	1	1	0	0	0	0	3	0	4	0	0	1	0	1.000	0	0- -	-	3.99	1.80
2011	Altna	AA	28	12	0	4	83.2	363	100	55	48	6	10	4	2	20	1	51	9	3	4	7	.364	0	0- -	-	4.43	5.16
2011	Indy	AAA	5	4	0	0	19.0	88	23	6	6	0	0	1	0	9	0	10	0	0	1	0	1.000	0	0- -	-	4.73	2.84
2012	NwBrit	AA	22	13	0	1	86.0	384	115	54	50	9	2	8	8	22	0	45	4	0	3	8	.273	0	0- -	-	6.05	5.23
2013	NwBrit	AA	11	0	0	8	14.2	57	11	1	1	0	0	0	0	3	0	11	0	1	0	1	.000	0	3- -	-	1.58	0.61
2013	Roch	AAA	31	1	0	10	44.0	190	49	20	17	3	2	2	1	13	0	42	3	0	3	2	.600	0	6- -	-	4.18	3.48
2014	Roch	AAA	46	0	0	23	52.0	226	49	27	23	5	2	2	1	25	1	51	4	0	3	3	.500	0	3- -	-	4.09	3.98
2011	Pit	NL	4	1	0	0	7.2	41	13	6	6	2	1	0	0	6	0	1	0	0	0	0	-	0	0-0	0	11.83	7.04
2014	Min	AL	7	0	0	2	7.1	31	8	2	2	0	0	1	0	2	1	6	0	0	0	0	-	0	0-0	1	3.20	2.45
	2 ML YEARS		11	1	0	2	15.0	72	21	8	8	2	1	1	0	8	1	7	0	0	0	0	-	0	0-0	1	7.24	4.80

Taylor Thompson

Pitches: R Bats: R Pos: RP-5   Ht: 6'5" Wt: 225 Born: 6/18/1987 Age: 28

			HOW MUCH HE PITCHED						WHAT HE GAVE UP										THE RESULTS						
Year	Team	Lg	G	GS	CG	GF	IP	BFP	H	R	ER	HR	SH	SF	HB	TBB	IBB	SO	WP	Bk	W	L	Pct	Sh	Sv-Op	Hld	ERC	ERA
2010	Gr Falls	R+	1	0	0	0	2.0	6	0	0	0	0	0	0	0	0	0	2	0	0	0	0	-	0	0- -	-	0.00	0.00
2010	Knapol	A	18	0	0	12	28.2	118	24	9	7	0	0	0	1	10	2	32	3	0	0	1	.000	0	6- -	-	2.41	2.20
2010	WinSa	A+	3	0	0	0	5.0	22	5	1	1	0	0	0	0	4	0	5	1	0	1	0	1.000	0	0- -	-	5.20	1.80
2011	WinSa	A+	41	0	0	37	53.2	232	42	20	15	1	4	2	3	26	3	51	2	0	7	2	.778	0	15- -	-	2.72	2.52
2012	WinSa	A+	33	0	0	27	44.1	173	26	13	12	2	2	1	3	13	0	57	1	0	2	1	.667	0	12- -	-	1.59	2.44
2012	Brs	R+	1	0	0	0	1.0	4	1	0	0	0	0	0	0	0	0	2	0	0	0	0	-	0	0- -	-	1.95	0.00

Year	Team	Lg	G	GS	CG	GF	IP	BFP	H	R	ER	HR	SH	SF	HB	TBB	IBB	SO	WP	Bk	W	L	Pct	Sh	Sv-Op	Hld	ERC	ERA
2013	Brham	AA	32	0	0	28	50.1	200	34	15	12	0	1	1	1	13	0	46	2	0	4	2	.667	0	12--	-	1.47	2.15
2013	Charltt	AAA	12	0	0	8	16.0	81	24	18	14	2	0	1	3	3	0	16	1	0	1	2	.333	0	1--	-	6.74	7.88
2014	Charltt	AAA	39	0	0	23	59.0	253	48	15	14	3	0	1	0	29	0	68	4	0	3	0	1.000	0	7--	-	3.02	2.14
2014	CWS	AL	5	0	0	1	5.1	28	9	6	6	1	0	0	1	4	0	4	0	0	0	0	-	0	0-0	0	12.35	10.13

Tyler Thornburg

Pitches: R Bats: R Pos: RP-27

Ht: 5'11" Wt: 190 Born: 9/29/1988 Age: 26

Year	Team	Lg	G	GS	CG	GF	IP	BFP	H	R	ER	HR	SH	SF	HB	TBB	IBB	SO	WP	Bk	W	L	Pct	Sh	Sv-Op	Hld	ERC	ERA
2012	Mil	NL	8	3	0	3	22.0	95	24	11	11	8	1	0	1	7	0	20	1	0	0	0	-	0	0-0	0	6.44	4.50
2013	Mil	NL	18	7	0	4	66.2	270	53	17	15	1	4	1	3	26	2	48	2	1	3	1	.750	0	0-0	0	2.59	2.03
2014	Mil	NL	27	0	0	4	29.2	131	24	14	14	1	1	1	0	21	0	28	4	0	3	1	.750	0	0-0	5	3.71	4.25
	3 ML YEARS		53	10	0	11	118.1	496	101	42	40	10	6	2	4	54	2	96	7	1	6	2	.750	0	0-0	5	3.55	3.04

Matt Thornton

Pitches: L Bats: L Pos: RP-64

Ht: 6'6" Wt: 235 Born: 9/15/1976 Age: 38

Year	Team	Lg	G	GS	CG	GF	IP	BFP	H	R	ER	HR	SH	SF	HB	TBB	IBB	SO	WP	Bk	W	L	Pct	Sh	Sv-Op	Hld	ERC	ERA
2004	Sea	AL	19	1	0	8	32.2	148	30	15	15	2	2	1	0	25	1	30	2	0	1	2	.333	0	0-0	0	4.75	4.13
2005	Sea	AL	55	0	0	15	57.0	262	54	33	33	13	1	1	0	42	2	57	7	0	0	4	.000	0	0-1	5	6.06	5.21
2006	CWS	AL	63	0	0	54	54.0	227	46	20	20	5	1	3	1	21	4	49	1	0	5	3	.625	0	2-5	18	3.12	3.33
2007	CWS	AL	68	0	0	13	56.1	249	59	31	30	4	0	2	2	26	6	55	3	0	4	4	.500	0	2-7	17	4.35	4.79
2008	CWS	AL	74	0	0	12	67.1	268	48	20	20	5	1	1	2	19	2	77	3	0	5	3	.625	0	1-6	20	2.07	2.67
2009	CWS	AL	70	0	0	17	72.1	291	58	22	22	5	2	1	1	20	2	87	4	0	6	3	.667	0	4-9	24	2.40	2.74
2010	CWS	AL	61	0	0	13	60.2	239	41	18	18	3	0	2	2	20	5	81	1	0	5	4	.556	0	8-10	21	1.89	2.67
2011	CWS	AL	62	0	0	20	59.2	262	60	34	22	3	3	3	0	21	5	63	2	0	2	5	.286	0	3-7	20	3.32	3.32
2012	CWS	AL	74	0	0	18	65.0	266	63	27	25	4	1	1	0	17	4	53	2	0	4	10	.286	0	3-7	26	3.29	3.46
2013	2 Tms	AL	60	0	0	6	43.1	187	47	20	18	4	4	1	2	15	1	30	2	0	0	4	.000	0	0-1	19	4.50	3.74
2014	2 Tms	AL	64	0	0	8	36.0	152	33	9	7	0	2	2	5	8	2	28	0	0	1	3	.250	0	0-4	18	2.69	1.75
13	CWS	AL	40	0	0	3	28.0	116	25	14	12	4	2	0	2	10	1	21	1	0	0	3	.000	0	0-1	18	3.94	3.86
13	Bos	AL	20	0	0	3	15.1	71	22	6	6	0	2	1	0	5	0	9	1	0	0	1	.000	0	0-0	1	5.55	3.52
14	NYY	AL	46	0	0	6	24.2	107	23	9	7	0	2	2	4	6	2	20	0	0	0	3	.000	0	0-4	12	2.83	2.55
14	Was	NL	18	0	0	2	11.1	45	10	0	0	0	0	0	1	2	0	8	0	0	1	0	1.000	0	0-0	6	2.39	0.00
	Postseason		3	0	0	1	3.1	14	2	0	0	0	0	0	0	2	1	2	0	0	-	0	-	0	0-0	1	1.62	0.00
	11 ML YEARS		670	1	0	150	604.1	2551	539	249	230	48	17	17	18	234	34	610	27	0	33	45	.423	0	23-57	188	3.33	3.43

Chris Tillman

Pitches: R Bats: R Pos: SP-34

Ht: 6'5" Wt: 210 Born: 4/15/1988 Age: 27

Year	Team	Lg	G	GS	CG	GF	IP	BFP	H	R	ER	HR	SH	SF	HB	TBB	IBB	SO	WP	Bk	W	L	Pct	Sh	Sv-Op	Hld	ERC	ERA
2009	Bal	AL	12	12	0	0	65.0	285	77	40	39	15	0	0	2	24	1	39	4	0	2	5	.286	0	0-0	0	6.28	5.40
2010	Bal	AL	11	11	0	0	53.2	236	51	37	35	9	1	3	1	31	1	31	2	0	2	5	.286	0	0-0	0	5.12	5.87
2011	Bal	AL	13	13	0	0	62.0	287	77	41	38	5	1	1	4	25	0	46	1	1	3	5	.375	0	0-0	0	5.58	5.52
2012	Bal	AL	15	15	0	0	86.0	347	66	38	28	12	1	2	1	24	0	66	5	0	9	3	.750	0	0-0	0	2.65	2.93
2013	Bal	AL	33	33	1	0	206.1	845	184	87	85	33	4	6	3	68	2	179	6	1	16	7	.696	0	0-0	0	3.72	3.71
2014	Bal	AL	34	34	1	0	207.1	871	189	83	77	21	4	5	4	66	1	150	8	0	13	6	.684	1	0-0	0	3.33	3.34
	6 ML YEARS		118	118	2	0	680.1	2871	644	326	302	95	8	17	15	238	5	511	26	2	45	31	.592	1	0-0	0	3.95	4.00

Shawn Tolleson

Pitches: R Bats: R Pos: RP-64

TAHL-eh-son

Ht: 6'2" Wt: 210 Born: 1/19/1988 Age: 27

Year	Team	Lg	G	GS	CG	GF	IP	BFP	H	R	ER	HR	SH	SF	HB	TBB	IBB	SO	WP	Bk	W	L	Pct	Sh	Sv-Op	Hld	ERC	ERA
2012	LAD	NL	40	0	0	12	37.2	160	30	19	18	4	2	1	1	20	1	39	0	0	3	1	.750	0	0-0	2	3.59	4.30
2013	LAD	NL	1	0	0	0	0.0	2	0	0	0	0	0	0	0	2	0	0	0	0	0	0	-	0	0-0	0		
2014	Tex	AL	64	0	0	11	71.2	296	56	23	22	10	2	3	1	28	5	69	4	0	3	1	.750	0	0-0	7	3.06	2.76
	3 ML YEARS		105	0	0	23	100.1	450	00	42	40	14	4	4	2	50	6	108	4	0	6	2	.750	0	0-0	9	3.31	3.29

Steve Tolleson

Bats: R Throws: R Pos: 2B-55;3B-43;PH-39;PR-10;RF-6;SS-2;LF-1;DH-1

Ht: 5'11" Wt: 185 Born: 11/1/1983 Age: 31

Year	Team	Lg	G	AB	H	2B	3B	HR	(Hm	Rd)	TB	R	RBI	RC	TBB	IBB	SO	HBP	SH	SF	SB	CS	GDP	Avg	OBP	Slg	OPS
2014	Buffalo*	AAA	19	72	17	2	1	1	(-	-)	24	12	9	10	12	0	13	0	0	0	6	1	3	.236	.345	.333	.679
2010	Oak	AL	25	49	14	3	0	1	(1	0)	20	5	4	7	4	0	9	0	0	0	0	0	0	.286	.340	.408	.748
2012	Bal	AL	29	71	13	3	0	2	(2	0)	22	4	6	7	4	0	17	0	1	0	1	0	2	.183	.227	.310	.537
2014	Tor	AL	109	170	43	7	2	3	(2	1)	63	21	16	16	12	0	49	2	4	1	3	1	3	.253	.308	.371	.679
	3 ML YEARS		163	290	70	13	2	6	(5	1)	105	30	26	30	20	0	75	2	5	1	4	1	5	.241	.294	.362	.656

Josh Tomlin

Pitches: R Bats: R Pos: SP-16; RP-9   **Ht:** 6'1" **Wt:** 190 **Born:** 10/19/1984 **Age:** 30

			HOW MUCH HE PITCHED							WHAT HE GAVE UP												THE RESULTS							
Year	Team	Lg	G	GS	CG	GF	IP	BFP	H	R	ER	HR	SH	SF	HB	TBB	IBB	SO	WP	Bk	W	L	Pct	Sh	Sv-Op	Hld	ERC	ERA
2014	Clmbs*	AAA	6	6	1	0	40.0	148	26	10	10	5	1	1	0	33	0	0			2	1	.667	1	0--	-	2.00	2.25
2010	Cle	AL	12	12	1	0	73.0	301	72	38	37	10	3	3	3	19	3	43	1	0	6	4	.600	0	0-0	0	3.89	4.56
2011	Cle	AL	26	26	0	0	165.1	662	157	80	78	24	1	3	3	21	2	89	3	0	12	7	.632	0	0-0	0	3.11	4.25
2012	Cle	AL	21	16	0	0	103.1	452	126	74	73	18	2	3	3	25	3	56	4	0	5	8	.385	0	0-0	0	5.34	6.36
2013	Cle	AL	1	0	0	0	2.0	9	2	0	0	0	0	0	0	0	0	0	0	0	0	0	-	0	0-0	0	1.68	0.00
2014	Cle	AL	25	16	1	6	104.0	446	120	66	55	18	1	3	1	14	3	94	6	0	6	9	.400	1	0-0	0	4.28	4.76
	5 ML YEARS		85	70	2	6	447.2	1870	477	258	243	70	7	12	10	79	11	282	14	0	29	28	.509	1	0-0	0	3.99	4.89

Michael Tonkin

Pitches: R Bats: R Pos: RP-25   TAHN-kin   **Ht:** 6'7" **Wt:** 220 **Born:** 11/19/1989 **Age:** 25

			HOW MUCH HE PITCHED							WHAT HE GAVE UP												THE RESULTS							
Year	Team	Lg	G	GS	CG	GF	IP	BFP	H	R	ER	HR	SH	SF	HB	TBB	IBB	SO	WP	Bk	W	L	Pct	Sh	Sv-Op	Hld	ERC	ERA
2010	Beloit	A	13	12	0	0	65.0	292	76	43	31	7	1	0	8	18	0	40	7	0	3	6	.333	0	0--	-	5.08	4.29
2010	Elizab	R+	10	0	0	3	25.0	101	18	6	3	1	1	0	4	4	1	26	1	0	1	0	1.000	0	1--	-	1.89	1.08
2011	Beloit	A	48	3	0	17	76.2	338	82	41	33	3	3	0	8	24	1	69	6	0	4	3	.571	0	2--	-	4.04	3.87
2012	Beloit	A	22	0	0	7	39.0	154	29	8	6	1	1	2	1	9	1	53	5	0	3	0	1.000	0	6--	-	1.77	1.38
2012	FtMyrs	A+	22	0	0	18	30.1	127	24	12	10	2	1	0	2	11	0	44	1	0	1	1	.500	0	6--	-	2.81	2.97
2013	NwBrit	AA	22	0	0	20	24.1	108	21	10	6	0	0	0	3	8	0	30	2	0	1	2	.333	0	7--	-	2.69	2.22
2013	Roch	AAA	30	0	0	21	32.2	139	33	18	16	3	0	1	1	8	1	36	0	0	1	2	.333	0	14--	-	3.49	4.41
2014	Roch	AAA	39	0	0	28	45.0	190	41	18	14	2	6	3	2	12	3	46	1	0	3	4	.429	0	10--	-	2.73	2.80
2013	Min	AL	9	0	0	6	11.1	47	9	6	1	0	0	0	0	3	0	10	1	0	0	0	-	0	0-0	0	1.82	0.79
2014	Min	AL	25	0	0	8	19.0	87	23	13	10	2	2	1	2	6	0	16	1	0	0	0	-	0	0-0	4	5.36	4.74
	2 ML YEARS		34	0	0	14	30.1	134	32	19	11	2	2	1	2	9	0	26	2	0	0	0	-	0	0-0	4	3.89	3.26

Alex Torres

Pitches: L Bats: L Pos: RP-70   **Ht:** 5'10" **Wt:** 175 **Born:** 12/8/1987 **Age:** 27

			HOW MUCH HE PITCHED							WHAT HE GAVE UP												THE RESULTS							
Year	Team	Lg	G	GS	CG	GF	IP	BFP	H	R	ER	HR	SH	SF	HB	TBB	IBB	SO	WP	Bk	W	L	Pct	Sh	Sv-Op	Hld	ERC	ERA
2011	TB	AL	4	0	0	2	8.0	39	8	4	3	0	0	0	1	7	2	9	0	0	1	1	.500	0	0-0	0	5.11	3.38
2013	TB	AL	39	0	0	5	58.0	226	32	12	11	1	1	1	3	20	1	62	1	0	4	2	.667	0	0-1	5	1.43	1.71
2014	SD	NL	70	0	0	12	54.0	241	46	25	20	2	2	2	3	33	1	51	6	0	2	1	.667	0	0-1	7	3.74	3.33
	Postseason		3	0	0	0	4.0	15	2	0	0	0	0	0	0	0	0	5	0	0	0	0	-	0	0-0	0	0.94	0.00
	3 ML YEARS		113	0	0	19	120.0	506	86	41	34	3	3	3	7	60	4	122	7	0	7	4	.636	0	0-2	12	2.58	2.55

Carlos Torres

Pitches: R Bats: R Pos: RP-72; SP-1   **Ht:** 6'1" **Wt:** 180 **Born:** 10/22/1982 **Age:** 32

			HOW MUCH HE PITCHED							WHAT HE GAVE UP												THE RESULTS							
Year	Team	Lg	G	GS	CG	GF	IP	BFP	H	R	ER	HR	SH	SF	HB	TBB	IBB	SO	WP	Bk	W	L	Pct	Sh	Sv-Op	Hld	ERC	ERA
2009	CWS	AL	8	5	0	2	28.1	130	30	20	19	5	3	3	2	17	2	22	0	0	1	2	.333	0	0-0	0	6.05	6.04
2010	CWS	AL	5	1	0	1	13.2	71	23	13	13	2	0	1	0	9	1	13	0	0	0	1	.000	0	0-0	0	9.84	8.56
2012	Col	NL	31	0	0	9	53.0	231	49	31	31	2	6	4	4	26	1	42	6	0	5	3	.625	0	0-0	1	3.85	5.26
2013	NYM	NL	33	9	0	6	86.1	352	79	34	33	15	4	1	4	17	1	75	4	1	4	6	.400	0	0-0	3	3.47	3.44
2014	NYM	NL	73	1	0	20	97.0	405	89	35	33	11	2	1	2	38	4	96	6	0	8	6	.571	0	2-5	12	3.77	3.06
	5 ML YEARS		150	16	0	38	278.1	1189	270	133	129	35	15	10	12	107	9	248	16	1	18	18	.500	0	2-5	16	4.19	4.17

Wilfredo Tovar

Bats: R Throws: R Pos: SS-1;PH-1   will-FRAY-doe TOE-varr   **Ht:** 5'10" **Wt:** 180 **Born:** 8/11/1991 **Age:** 23

			BATTING																			RUNNING			AVERAGES			
Year	Team	Lg	G	AB	H	2B	3B	HR	(Hm	Rd)	TB	R	RBI	RC	TBB	IBB	SO	HBP	SH	SF	SB	CS	GDP	Avg	OBP	Slg	OPS
2010	StLuci	A+	30	118	29	5	1	0	(-	-)	36	14	6	9	3	1	22	2	1	0	4	3	2	.246	.276	.305	.582
2010	Savann	A	44	160	45	10	0	0	(-	-)	55	12	17	17	8	0	12	3	2	0	4	5	1	.281	.327	.344	.671
2010	Bklyn	A-	18	68	18	2	1	0	(-	-)	22	11	6	7	2	0	9	3	3	1	4	3	0	.265	.311	.324	.634
2011	Savann	A	131	491	123	21	3	2	(-	-)	156	70	41	54	44	1	53	8	3	7	15	9	11	.251	.318	.318	.636
2012	StLuci	A+	65	218	62	17	1	1	(-	-)	84	31	23	34	29	0	17	4	4	1	12	7	8	.284	.377	.385	.762
2012	Bnghtn	AA	57	193	49	11	2	0	(-	-)	64	20	27	21	11	0	22	6	3	4	2	1	6	.254	.308	.332	.640
2013	Roch	AA	133	441	116	14	4	4	(-	-)	150	70	36	51	33	0	49	7	3	2	12	7	11	.263	.323	.340	.663
2014	Bnghtn	AA	78	255	72	8	1	2	(-	-)	88	31	29	32	21	3	22	5	1	3	8	6	11	.282	.345	.345	.690
2014	Mets	R	2	6	2	1	0	0	(-	-)	3	0	2	0	1	0	1	0	0	0	0	1	0	.333	.429	.500	.929
2014	StLuci	A+	5	17	6	2	1	0	(-	-)	10	2	4	5	4	1	2	0	0	0	2	0	1	.353	.522	.588	1.110
2013	NYM	NL	7	15	3	0	0	0	(0	0)	3	1	2	2	1	1	3	1	2	0	1	0	2	.200	.294	.200	.494
2014	NYM	NL	2	3	0	0	0	0	(0	0)	0	0	0	0	0	0	0	0	0	0	0	0	0	.000	.000	.000	.000
	2 ML YEARS		9	18	3	0	0	0	(0	0)	3	1	2	2	1	1	3	1	2	0	1	0	2	.167	.250	.167	.417

Blake Treinen

Pitches: R Bats: R Pos: RP-8; SP-7   TRY-nen   **Ht:** 6'5" **Wt:** 215 **Born:** 6/30/1988 **Age:** 27

			HOW MUCH HE PITCHED							WHAT HE GAVE UP												THE RESULTS							
Year	Team	Lg	G	GS	CG	GF	IP	BFP	H	R	ER	HR	SH	SF	HB	TBB	IBB	SO	WP	Bk	W	L	Pct	Sh	Sv-Op	Hld	ERC	ERA
2011	As	R	3	0	0	2	3.0	7	3	0	0	0	0	0	0	1	0	7	0	0	0	0	-	0	0--	-	3.05	0.00
2011	Burlgtn	A	18	0	0	12	27.0	110	20	13	11	1	3	0	1	7	0	29	2	0	1	1	.500	0	2--	-	1.92	3.67
2012	Stcktn	A+	24	15	1	1	103.0	448	116	60	50	11	0	3	4	23	0	92	5	0	7	7	.500	0	0--	-	4.22	4.37

Year	Team	Lg	G	GS	CG	GF	IP	BFP	H	R	ER	HR	SH	SF	HB	TBB	IBB	SO	WP	Bk	W	L	Pct	Sh	Sv-Op	Hld	ERC	ERA
2013	Hrsbrg	AA	21	20	0	0	118.2	506	125	54	48	9	0	4	4	33	2	86	8	1	6	7	.462	0	0--	-	3.84	3.64
2013	Auburn	A-	2	2	0	0	6.0	18	1	0	0	0	0	0	0	0	0	7	0	0	0	0		0	0--	-	0.07	0.00
2014	Syrcse	AAA	16	16	0	0	80.2	339	78	34	30	4	4	3	4	20	0	64	2	0	8	2	.800	0	0--	-	3.14	3.35
2014	Was	NL	15	7	0	6	50.2	214	57	17	14	1	0	0	2	13	1	30	1	0	2	3	.400	0	0-0	0	3.86	2.49

Carlos Triunfel

Bats: R **Throws:** R **Pos:** SS-10;PH-2;PR-2   TRUE-en-fell   **Ht:** 5'11" **Wt:** 195 **Born:** 2/27/1990 **Age:** 25

Year	Team	Lg	G	AB	H	2B	3B	HR	(Hm	Rd)	TB	R	RBI	RC	TBB	IBB	SO	HBP	SH	SF	SB	CS	GDP	Avg	OBP	Slg	OPS
2014	Albq*	AAA	89	300	67	12	4	4	(-	-)	99	28	40	25	12	2	55	2	4	3	2	1	15	.223	.256	.330	.586
2012	Sea	AL	10	22	5	2	0	0	(0	0)	7	2	3	3	1	0	4	0	1	0	0	0	0	.227	.261	.318	.579
2013	Sea	AL	17	44	6	1	0	0	(0	0)	7	1	2	0	0	0	11	1	1	1	0	0	1	.136	.152	.159	.311
2014	LAD	NL	12	15	2	0	0	1	(1	0)	5	3	1	0	1	0	5	0	0	0	0	0	0	.133	.188	.333	.521
	3 ML YEARS		39	81	13	3	0	1	(1	0)	19	6	6	3	2	0	20	1	2	1	0	0	1	.160	.188	.235	.423

Nicholas Tropeano

Pitches: R **Bats:** R **Pos:** SP-4   TROH-pee-ah-no   **Ht:** 6'4" **Wt:** 205 **Born:** 8/27/1990 **Age:** 24

Year	Team	Lg	G	GS	CG	GF	IP	BFP	H	R	ER	HR	SH	SF	HB	TBB	IBB	SO	WP	Bk	W	L	Pct	Sh	Sv-Op	Hld	ERC	ERA
2011	TriCity	A-	12	12	0	0	53.1	222	42	18	14	1	1	1	1	21	0	63	6	1	3	2	.600	0	0--	-	2.44	2.36
2012	Lxngtn	A	15	14	0	0	87.1	357	77	29	27	3	5	1	2	26	0	97	2	0	6	4	.600	0	0--	-	2.74	2.78
2012	Lancst	A+	12	12	0	0	70.2	299	72	37	26	8	1	2	3	21	0	69	10	0	6	3	.667	0	0--	-	4.08	3.31
2013	CpChr	AA	28	20	1	6	133.2	562	140	65	61	15	5	5	3	39	0	130	5	0	7	10	.412	0	5--	-	4.16	4.11
2014	OKCity	AAA	23	20	0	1	124.2	486	90	44	42	11	1	2	4	33	1	120	5	0	9	5	.643	0	0--	-	2.22	3.03
2014	Hou	AL	4	4	0	0	21.2	91	19	12	11	0	1	1	1	9	1	13	1	0	1	3	.250	0	0-0	0	2.92	4.57

Mike Trout

Bats: R **Throws:** R **Pos:** CF-149;DH-8   **Ht:** 6'2" **Wt:** 230 **Born:** 8/7/1991 **Age:** 23

Year	Team	Lg	G	AB	H	2B	3B	HR	(Hm	Rd)	TB	R	RBI	RC	TBB	IBB	SO	HBP	SH	SF	SB	CS	GDP	Avg	OBP	Slg	OPS
2011	LAA	AL	40	123	27	6	0	5	(1	4)	48	20	16	14	9	0	30	2	0	1	4	0	2	.220	.281	.390	.672
2012	LAA	AL	139	559	182	27	8	30	(16	14)	315	129	83	127	67	4	139	6	0	7	49	5	7	.326	.399	.564	.963
2013	LAA	AL	157	589	190	39	9	27	(13	14)	328	109	97	144	110	10	136	9	0	8	33	7	8	.323	.432	.557	.988
2014	LAA	AL	157	602	173	39	9	36	(19	17)	338	115	111	131	83	6	184	10	0	10	16	2	6	.287	.377	.561	.939
	4 ML YEARS		493	1873	572	111	26	98	(49	49)	1029	373	307	413	269	20	489	27	0	26	102	14	23	.305	.395	.549	.945

Mark Trumbo

Bats: R **Throws:** R **Pos:** 1B-43;LF-41;DH-2;PH-2   **Ht:** 6'4" **Wt:** 235 **Born:** 1/16/1986 **Age:** 29

Year	Team	Lg	G	AB	H	2B	3B	HR	(Hm	Rd)	TB	R	RBI	RC	TBB	IBB	SO	HBP	SH	SF	SB	CS	GDP	Avg	OBP	Slg	OPS
2014	DBcks*	R	4	13	6	1	0	2	(-	-)	13	5	6	5	1	1	3	0	0	0	0	0	0	.462	.500	1.000	1.500
2014	Reno*	AAA	3	11	5	0	0	3	(-	-)	14	6	6	5	1	0	2	0	0	1	0	0	1	.455	.500	1.273	1.773
2010	LAA	AL	8	15	1	0	0	0	(0	0)	1	2	2	0	1	0	8	0	0	0	0	0	0	.067	.125	.067	.192
2011	LAA	AL	149	539	137	31	1	29	(14	15)	257	65	87	69	25	6	120	5	0	4	9	4	17	.254	.291	.477	.768
2012	LAA	AL	144	544	146	19	3	32	(12	20)	267	66	95	80	36	3	153	4	0	2	4	5	12	.268	.317	.491	.808
2013	LAA	AL	159	620	145	30	2	34	(19	15)	281	85	100	74	54	6	184	0	0	4	5	2	18	.234	.294	.453	.747
2014	Ari	NL	88	328	77	15	1	14	(7	7)	136	37	61	44	28	3	89	1	0	5	2	3	8	.235	.293	.415	.707
	5 ML YEARS		548	2046	506	95	7	109	(52	57)	942	255	345	267	144	18	554	10	0	15	20	14	55	.247	.298	.460	.758

Matt Tuiasosopo

Bats: R **Throws:** R **Pos:** LF   too-ee-ah-suh-SOH-poe   **Ht:** 6'2" **Wt:** 225 **Born:** 5/10/1986 **Age:** 29

Year	Team	Lg	G	AB	H	2B	3B	HR	(Hm	Rd)	TB	R	RBI	RC	TBB	IBB	SO	HBP	SH	SF	SB	CS	GDP	Avg	OBP	Slg	OPS
2014	Buffalo*	AAA	59	214	44	8	0	2	(-	*)	58	17	18	17	26	0	64	1	0	2	1	1	5	.206	.289	.271	.560
2014	Charltt*	AAA	63	195	54	10	0	11	(-	-)	97	42	32	43	46	0	56	4	0	0	0	0	5	.277	.424	.497	.922
2008	Sea	AL	14	44	7	2	1	0	(0	0)	11	1	2	1	2	0	16	1	0	0	0	0	0	.159	.213	.250	.463
2009	Sea	AL	7	22	5	1	0	1	(0	1)	9	2	2	2	2	0	5	0	0	1	0	0	0	.227	.280	.409	.689
2010	Sea	AL	50	127	22	5	0	4	(0	4)	39	12	11	8	9	0	49	1	1	0	0	0	3	.173	.234	.307	.541
2013	Det	AL	81	164	40	7	0	7	(5	2)	68	26	30	26	25	0	57	2	0	0	0	0	3	.244	.351	.415	.765
	4 ML YEARS		152	357	74	15	1	12	(5	7)	127	41	45	37	38	0	127	4	1	1	0	0	6	.207	.290	.356	.646

Samuel Tuivailala

Pitches: R **Bats:** R **Pos:** RP-2   TOO-ee-vah-la-la   **Ht:** 6'3" **Wt:** 195 **Born:** 10/19/1992 **Age:** 22

Year	Team	Lg	G	GS	CG	GF	IP	BFP	H	R	ER	HR	SH	SF	HB	TBB	IBB	SO	WP	Bk	W	L	Pct	Sh	Sv-Op	Hld	ERC	ERA
2012	JhsCty	R+	11	0	0	1	13.0	64	12	6	6	1	0	0	0	13	0	23	1	0	0	0		0	0--	-	5.69	4.15
2013	Peoria	A	28	0	0	7	35.1	159	31	22	21	0	1	1	4	20	1	50	4	0	0	3	.000	0	1--	-	3.63	5.35
2014	PlmBh	A+	29	0	0	13	37.2	162	29	16	15	1	0	2	2	18	0	64	4	0	0	1	.000	0	3--	-	2.77	3.58
2014	Sprgfld	AA	17	0	0	3	21.0	88	18	8	6	0	1	0	1	9	1	30	2	0	2	1	.667	0	1--	-	2.87	2.57
2014	Memp	AAA	1	0	0	0	1.1	6	1	0	0	0	0	0	1	0	0	3	1	0	0	0		0	1--	-	3.21	0.00
2014	StL	NL	2	0	0	1	1.0	10	5	4	4	2	0	0	0	2	1	0	0	0	0	0		0	0-0	0	72.46	36.00

Troy Tulowitzki

Bats: R Throws: R Pos: SS-89;PH-3 too-luh-WIT-skee Ht: 6'3" Wt: 215 Born: 10/10/1984 Age: 30

Year Team	Lg	G	AB	H	2B	3B	HR	(Hm	Rd)	TB	R	RBI	RC	TBB	IBB	SO	HBP	SH	SF	SB	CS	GDP	Avg	OBP	Slg	OPS
2006 Col	NL	25	96	23	2	0	1	(0	1)	28	15	6	10	10	3	25	1	1	0	3	0	1	.240	.318	.292	.609
2007 Col	NL	155	609	177	33	5	24	(15	9)	292	104	99	95	57	3	130	9	5	2	7	6	14	.291	.359	.479	.838
2008 Col	NL	101	377	99	24	2	8	(4	4)	151	48	46	42	38	5	56	2	2	2	1	6	16	.263	.332	.401	.732
2009 Col	NL	151	543	161	25	9	32	(17	15)	300	101	92	96	73	4	112	3	0	9	20	11	20	.297	.377	.552	.930
2010 Col	NL	122	470	148	32	3	27	(15	12)	267	89	95	88	48	4	78	5	1	5	11	2	17	.315	.381	.568	.949
2011 Col	NL	143	537	162	36	2	30	(17	13)	292	81	105	101	59	12	79	4	1	5	9	3	16	.302	.372	.544	.916
2012 Col	NL	47	181	52	8	2	8	(3	5)	88	33	27	27	19	1	19	2	0	1	2	2	7	.287	.360	.486	.846
2013 Col	NL	126	446	139	27	0	25	(14	11)	241	72	82	80	57	5	85	4	0	5	1	0	9	.312	.391	.540	.931
2014 Col	NL	91	315	107	18	1	21	(14	7)	190	71	52	70	50	4	57	5	0	5	1	1	4	.340	.432	.603	1.035
Postseason		15	57	12	5	0	1	(0	1)	20	3	6	3	4	0	17	1	0	1	0	1	3	.211	.270	.351	.621
9 ML YEARS		961	3574	1068	205	24	176	(99	77)	1849	614	604	609	411	41	641	35	10	34	55	31	104	.299	.373	.517	.891

Jacob Turner

Pitches: R Bats: R Pos: SP-18; RP-10 Ht: 6'5" Wt: 215 Born: 5/21/1991 Age: 24

Year Team	Lg	G	GS	CG	GF	IP	BFP	H	R	ER	HR	SH	SF	HB	TBB	IBB	SO	WP	Bk	W	L	Pct	Sh	Sv-Op	Hld	ERC	ERA
2014 Jupiter*	A+	2	2	0	0	11.0	40	7	3	3	1	0	0	0	1	0	10	0	0	1	1	.500	0	0- -	-	1.33	2.45
2011 Det	AL	3	3	0	0	12.2	60	17	13	12	3	0	1	1	4	0	8	0	0	0	1	.000	0	0-0	0	7.03	8.53
2012 2 Tms		10	10	0	0	55.0	231	50	32	27	9	1	2	0	16	3	36	5	0	2	5	.286	0	0-0	0	3.42	4.42
2013 Mia	NL	20	20	1	0	118.0	514	116	55	49	11	8	5	4	54	5	77	11	0	3	8	.273	0	0-0	0	4.25	3.74
2014 2 Tms	NL	28	18	0	4	113.0	501	148	81	77	12	6	4	1	33	2	71	6	1	6	11	.353	0	0-0	1	5.59	6.13
12 Det	AL	3	3	0	0	12.1	61	17	11	11	4	0	1	0	7	1	7	1	0	1	1	.500	0	0-0	0	8.66	8.03
12 Mia	NL	7	7	0	0	42.2	170	33	21	16	5	1	1	0	9	2	29	4	0	1	4	.200	0	0-0	0	2.20	3.38
14 Mia	NL	20	12	0	4	78.1	352	106	54	52	8	2	3	1	23	1	54	3	1	4	7	.364	0	0-0	0	5.84	5.97
14 ChC	NL	8	6	0	0	34.2	149	42	27	25	4	4	1	0	10	1	17	3	0	2	4	.333	0	0-0	1	5.03	6.49
4 ML YEARS		61	51	1	4	298.2	1306	331	181	165	35	15	12	6	107	10	192	22	1	11	25	.306	0	0-0	1	4.69	4.97

Justin Turner

Bats: R Throws: R Pos: 3B-59;PH-32;SS-15;2B-14;1B-2;PR-2 Ht: 6'0" Wt: 210 Born: 11/23/1984 Age: 30

Year Team	Lg	G	AB	H	2B	3B	HR	(Hm	Rd)	TB	R	RBI	RC	TBB	IBB	SO	HBP	SH	SF	SB	CS	GDP	Avg	OBP	Slg	OPS
2014 RCuca*	A+	2	5	1	0	0	0	(-	-)	1	1	0	0	2	0	0	0	0	0	0	0	1	.200	.429	.200	.629
2009 Bal	AL	12	18	3	0	0	0	(0	0)	3	2	3	1	4	0	3	0	0	0	0	0	0	.167	.318	.167	.485
2010 2 Tms		9	17	1	1	0	0	(0	0)	2	1	0	0	1	0	3	0	0	0	0	0	0	.059	.111	.118	.229
2011 NYM	NL	117	435	113	30	0	4	(3	1)	155	49	51	59	39	2	59	10	2	1	7	2	9	.260	.334	.356	.690
2012 NYM	NL	94	171	46	13	1	2	(2	0)	67	20	19	19	9	0	24	4	0	1	1	1	9	.269	.319	.392	.711
2013 NYM	NL	86	200	56	13	1	2	(0	2)	77	12	16	17	11	1	34	1	1	1	0	1	6	.280	.319	.385	.704
2014 LAD	NL	109	288	98	21	1	7	(5	2)	142	46	43	55	28	1	58	4	0	2	6	1	6	.340	.404	.493	.897
10 Bal	AL	5	9	0	0	0	0	(0	0)	0	0	0	0	0	0	3	0	0	0	0	0	0	.000	.000	.000	.000
10 NYM	NL	4	8	1	1	0	0	(0	0)	2	1	0	0	1	0	0	0	0	0	0	0	0	.125	.222	.250	.472
6 ML YEARS		427	1129	317	78	3	15	(10	5)	446	130	132	151	92	4	181	19	3	5	14	5	31	.281	.344	.395	.739

Koji Uehara

Pitches: R Bats: R Pos: RP-64 KOH-jee ooh-ih-HAR-uh Ht: 6'2" Wt: 195 Born: 4/3/1975 Age: 40

Year Team	Lg	G	GS	CG	GF	IP	BFP	H	R	ER	HR	SH	SF	HB	TBB	IBB	SO	WP	Bk	W	L	Pct	Sh	Sv-Op	Hld	ERC	ERA
2009 Bal	AL	12	12	0	0	66.2	279	71	33	30	7	1	3	0	12	1	48	0	0	2	4	.333	0	0-0	0	3.56	4.05
2010 Bal	AL	43	0	0	22	44.0	174	37	15	14	5	1	0	0	5	0	55	1	0	1	2	.333	0	13-15	6	2.22	2.86
2011 2 Tms	AL	65	0	0	22	65.0	243	38	17	17	11	1	1	0	9	1	85	0	0	2	3	.400	0	0-1	22	1.48	2.35
2012 Tex	AL	37	0	0	13	36.0	130	20	7	7	4	1	0	0	3	0	43	1	0	0	-	-		1-1	7	1.12	1.75
2013 Bos	AL	73	0	0	40	74.1	265	33	10	9	5	1	1	1	9	2	101	1	0	4	1	.800	0	21-24	13	0.79	1.09
2014 Bos	AL	64	0	0	50	64.1	249	51	18	18	10	3	1	1	8	0	80	1	0	6	5	.545	0	26-31	1	2.35	2.52
11 Bal	AL	43	0	0	19	47.0	174	25	9	9	6	1	1	0	8	1	62	0	0	1	1	.500	0	0-1	13	1.17	1.72
11 Tex	AL	22	0	0	3	18.0	69	13	8	8	5	0	0	0	1	0	23	0	0	1	2	.333	0	0-0	9	2.21	4.00
Postseason		17	0	0	13	16.0	60	12	6	6	4	0	0	0	2	0	20	0	0	1	1	.500	0	7-7	0	2.63	3.38
6 ML YEARS		294	12	0	147	350.1	1340	250	100	95	42	8	7	2	46	4	412	4	0	15	15	.500	0	61-72	49	1.76	2.44

Dan Uggla

Bats: R Throws: R Pos: 2B-39;PH-13;PR-1 UGG-luh Ht: 5'11" Wt: 210 Born: 3/11/1980 Age: 35

Year Team	Lg	G	AB	H	2B	3B	HR	(Hm	Rd)	TB	R	RBI	RC	TBB	IBB	SO	HBP	SH	SF	SB	CS	GDP	Avg	OBP	Slg	OPS
2014 Fresno*	AAA	2	7	2	1	0	0	(-	-)	3	1	1	1	2	0	2	0	0	0	0	0	0	.286	.444	.429	.873
2006 Fla	NL	154	611	172	26	7	27	(10	17)	293	105	90	97	48	1	123	9	7	8	6	6	5	.282	.339	.480	.818
2007 Fla	NL	159	632	155	49	3	31	(18	13)	303	113	88	81	68	0	167	13	4	11	2	1	10	.245	.326	.479	.805
2008 Fla	NL	146	531	138	37	1	32	(15	17)	273	97	92	93	77	6	171	8	0	3	5	5	10	.260	.360	.514	.874
2009 Fla	NL	158	564	137	27	4	31	(21	10)	259	84	90	81	92	4	150	7	1	4	2	1	10	.243	.354	.459	.813
2010 Fla	NL	159	589	169	31	0	33	(14	19)	299	100	105	101	78	2	149	2	0	5	4	1	10	.287	.369	.508	.877
2011 Atl	NL	161	600	140	22	1	36	(18	18)	272	88	82	78	62	2	171	5	0	3	1	3	9	.233	.311	.453	.764
2012 Atl	NL	154	523	115	29	2	19	(7	12)	201	86	78	83	94	5	168	10	0	3	4	3	8	.220	.348	.384	.732
2013 Atl	NL	136	448	80	10	3	22	(8	14)	162	60	55	48	77	2	171	9	0	3	2	0	7	.179	.309	.362	.671
2014 2 Tms	NL	52	141	21	3	0	2	(0	2)	30	14	10	6	11	0	46	4	0	1	0	0	3	.149	.229	.213	.442

(continued)

Year Team	Lg	G	AB	H	2B	3B	HR	(Hm	Rd)	TB	R	RBI	RC	TBB	IBB	SO	HBP	SH	SF	SB	CS	GDP	Avg	OBP	Slg	OPS
14 Atl	NL	48	130	21	3	0	2	(0	2)	30	13	10	6	10	0	40	4	0	1	0	0	3	.162	.241	.231	.472
14 SF	NL	4	11	0	0	0	0	(0	0)	0	1	0	0	1	0	6	0	0	0	0	0	0	.000	.083	.000	.083
Postseason		1	4	0	0	0	0	(0	0)	0	1	0	0	1	0	0	0	0	0	0	0	0	.000	.200	.000	.200
9 ML YEARS		1279	4639	1127	234	16	233	(111	122)	2092	747	690	668	607	22	1301	69	12	41	26	20	72	.243	.337	.451	.788

B.J. Upton

Bats: R **Throws:** R **Pos:** CF-139;PR-2;PH-1 **Ht:** 6'3" **Wt:** 185 **Born:** 8/21/1984 **Age:** 30

Year Team	Lg	G	AB	H	2B	3B	HR	(Hm	Rd)	TB	R	RBI	RC	TBB	IBB	SO	HBP	SH	SF	SB	CS	GDP	Avg	OBP	Slg	OPS
2004 TB	AL	45	159	41	8	2	4	(2	2)	65	19	12	22	15	0	46	1	1	1	4	1	1	.258	.324	.409	.733
2006 TB	AL	50	175	43	5	0	1	(1	0)	51	20	10	17	13	0	40	1	0	0	11	3	1	.246	.302	.291	.593
2007 TB	AL	129	474	142	25	1	24	(13	11)	241	86	82	93	65	4	154	4	1	4	22	8	14	.300	.386	.508	.894
2008 TB	AL	145	531	145	37	2	9	(4	5)	213	85	67	87	97	4	134	2	3	7	44	**16**	13	.273	.383	.401	.784
2009 TB	AL	144	560	135	33	4	11	(7	4)	209	79	55	68	57	0	152	3	3	3	42	14	7	.241	.313	.373	.686
2010 TB	AL	154	536	127	38	4	18	(7	11)	227	89	62	74	67	1	164	2	1	4	42	9	13	.237	.322	.424	.745
2011 TB	AL	153	560	136	27	4	23	(9	14)	240	82	81	79	71	4	161	4	2	3	36	12	16	.243	.331	.429	.759
2012 TB	AL	146	573	141	29	3	28	(17	11)	260	79	78	71	45	0	169	1	4	8	31	6	13	.246	.298	.454	.752
2013 Atl	NL	126	391	72	14	0	9	(7	2)	113	30	26	21	44	2	151	3	1	6	12	5	7	.184	.268	.289	.557
2014 Atl	NL	141	519	108	19	5	12	(6	6)	173	67	35	47	57	5	173	1	3	2	20	7	6	.208	.287	.333	.620
Postseason		28	104	27	6	1	7	(2	5)	56	20	18	17	9	1	32	0	0	1	9	2	4	.260	.316	.538	.854
10 ML YEARS		1233	4478	1090	235	25	139	(73	66)	1792	636	508	579	531	20	1344	22	19	38	264	81	91	.243	.324	.400	.724

Justin Upton

Bats: R **Throws:** R **Pos:** LF-150;PH-2;DH-1 **Ht:** 6'2" **Wt:** 205 **Born:** 8/25/1987 **Age:** 27

Year Team	Lg	G	AB	H	2B	3B	HR	(Hm	Rd)	TB	R	RBI	RC	TBB	IBB	SO	HBP	SH	SF	SB	CS	GDP	Avg	OBP	Slg	OPS
2007 Ari	NL	43	140	31	8	3	2	(2	0)	51	17	11	13	11	4	37	1	0	0	2	0	3	.221	.283	.364	.647
2008 Ari	NL	108	356	89	19	6	15	(12	3)	165	52	42	47	54	6	121	4	0	3	1	4	3	.250	.353	.463	.816
2009 Ari	NL	138	526	158	30	7	26	(14	12)	280	84	86	94	55	3	137	2	1	4	20	5	10	.300	.366	.532	.899
2010 Ari	NL	133	495	135	27	3	17	(8	9)	219	73	69	73	64	5	152	4	1	7	18	8	20	.273	.356	.442	.799
2011 Ari	NL	159	592	171	39	5	31	(20	11)	313	105	88	103	59	9	126	**19**	0	4	21	9	8	.289	.369	.529	.898
2012 Ari	NL	150	554	155	24	4	17	(11	6)	238	107	67	82	63	5	121	5	0	6	18	8	7	.280	.355	.430	.785
2013 Atl	NL	149	558	147	27	2	27	(13	14)	259	94	70	84	75	4	161	5	1	4	8	1	12	.263	.354	.464	.818
2014 Atl	NL	154	566	153	34	2	29	(18	11)	278	77	102	84	60	1	171	6	0	8	8	4	10	.270	.342	.491	.833
Postseason		15	48	11	2	1	2	(0	2)	21	7	4	7	10	0	13	2	0	0	1	0	0	.229	.383	.438	.821
8 ML YEARS		1034	3787	1039	208	32	164	(98	66)	1803	609	535	580	441	37	1026	46	3	36	96	39	73	.274	.354	.476	.830

Juan Uribe

Bats: R **Throws:** R **Pos:** 3B-102;PH-1 yer-EE-bay **Ht:** 6'0" **Wt:** 235 **Born:** 3/22/1979 **Age:** 36

Year Team	Lg	G	AB	H	2B	3B	HR	(Hm	Rd)	TB	R	RBI	RC	TBB	IBB	SO	HBP	SH	SF	SB	CS	GDP	Avg	OBP	Slg	OPS
2014 RCuca*	A+	5	19	6	2	0	0	(-	-)	8	4	3	2	0	0	2	0	0	0	0	0	2	.316	.316	.421	.737
2001 Col	NL	72	273	82	15	11	8	(3	5)	143	32	53	44	8	1	55	2	0	0	3	0	6	.300	.325	.524	.849
2002 Col	NL	155	566	136	25	7	6	(4	2)	193	69	49	53	34	1	120	5	7	6	9	2	17	.240	.286	.341	.627
2003 Col	NL	87	316	80	19	3	10	(6	4)	135	45	33	45	17	0	60	3	6	1	7	2	3	.253	.297	.427	.724
2004 CWS	AL	134	502	142	31	6	23	(16	7)	254	82	74	81	32	1	96	3	11	5	9	11	10	.283	.327	.506	.833
2005 CWS	AL	146	481	121	23	3	16	(10	6)	198	58	71	59	34	0	77	4	11	10	4	6	7	.252	.301	.412	.712
2006 CWS	AL	132	463	109	28	2	21	(13	8)	204	53	71	52	13	1	82	3	9	7	1	1	10	.235	.257	.441	.698
2007 CWS	AL	150	513	120	18	2	20	(15	5)	202	55	68	52	34	2	112	4	7	5	1	9	6	.234	.284	.394	.678
2008 CWS	AL	110	324	80	22	1	7	(5	2)	125	38	40	43	22	0	64	1	5	1	1	3	5	.247	.296	.386	.682
2009 SF	NL	122	398	115	26	4	16	(9	7)	197	50	55	55	25	2	82	1	3	5	3	1	7	.289	.329	.495	.824
2010 SF	NL	148	521	129	24	2	24	(13	11)	229	64	85	68	45	6	92	4	0	5	1	2	20	.248	.310	.440	.749
2011 LAD	NL	77	270	55	12	0	4	(3	1)	79	21	28	13	17	2	60	6	0	2	2	0	12	.204	.264	.293	.557
2012 LAD	NL	66	162	31	9	0	2	(1	1)	46	15	17	13	13	0	37	2	1	1	0	1	6	.191	.258	.284	.542
2013 LAD	NL	132	388	108	22	2	12	(6	6)	170	47	50	51	30	3	81	2	3	3	5	0	12	.278	.331	.438	.769
2014 LAD	NL	103	386	120	23	0	9	(5	4)	170	36	54	48	15	2	77	1	0	2	0	1	15	.311	.337	.440	.777
Postseason		40	140	30	6	0	5	(4	1)	51	15	23	15	7	0	38	1	3	1	2	0	6	.214	.255	.304	.019
14 ML YEARS		1634	5563	1428	297	43	178	(109	69)	2345	665	748	677	339	21	1095	41	63	53	46	39	136	.257	.302	.422	.723

Chase Utley

Bats: L **Throws:** R **Pos:** 2B-147;PH-7;1B-1;DH-1 UTT-lee **Ht:** 6'1" **Wt:** 200 **Born:** 12/17/1978 **Age:** 36

Year Team	Lg	G	AB	H	2B	3B	HR	(Hm	Rd)	TB	R	RBI	RC	TBB	IBB	SO	HBP	SH	SF	SB	CS	GDP	Avg	OBP	Slg	OPS
2003 Phi	NL	43	134	32	10	1	2	(1	1)	50	13	21	19	11	0	22	6	0	1	2	0	3	.239	.322	.373	.696
2004 Phi	NL	94	267	71	11	2	13	(8	5)	125	36	57	37	15	1	40	2	1	2	4	1	6	.266	.308	.468	.776
2005 Phi	NL	147	543	158	39	6	28	(12	16)	293	93	105	102	69	5	109	9	0	7	16	3	10	.291	.376	.540	.915
2006 Phi	NL	160	658	203	40	4	32	(16	16)	347	**131**	102	122	63	1	132	14	0	4	15	4	9	.309	.379	.527	.906
2007 Phi	NL	132	530	176	48	5	22	(14	8)	300	104	103	111	50	1	89	**25**	1	7	9	1	7	.332	.410	.566	.976
2008 Phi	NL	159	607	177	41	4	33	(20	13)	325	113	104	104	64	14	104	**27**	1	8	14	2	9	.292	.380	.535	.915
2009 Phi	NL	156	571	161	28	4	31	(16	15)	290	112	93	115	88	3	110	**24**	0	4	23	0	5	.282	.397	.508	.905
2010 Phi	NL	115	425	117	20	2	16	(10	6)	189	75	65	83	63	3	63	18	0	5	13	2	4	.275	.387	.445	.832
2011 Phi	NL	103	398	103	21	6	11	(8	3)	169	54	44	57	39	4	47	14	1	2	14	0	3	.259	.344	.425	.769
2012 Phi	NL	83	301	77	15	2	11	(8	3)	129	48	45	49	43	7	43	12	0	6	11	1	4	.256	.365	.429	.793
2013 Phi	NL	131	476	135	25	6	18	(8	10)	226	73	69	78	45	4	79	5	0	5	8	3	12	.284	.348	.475	.823
2014 Phi	NL	155	589	159	36	6	11	(8	3)	240	74	78	86	53	12	85	13	0	9	10	1	8	.270	.339	.407	.746
Postseason		46	164	43	7	1	10	(5	5)	82	38	25	34	34	3	38	5	0	1	10	2	3	.262	.402	.500	.902
12 ML YEARS		1478	5499	1569	334	48	228	(127	101)	2683	926	886	972	603	55	923	169	4	60	139	18	80	.285	.370	.488	.858

Chris Valaika

Bats: R **Throws:** R **Pos:** 1B-15;2B-12;PH-11;3B-8;SS-2   vuh-LAKE-uh   **Ht:** 5'11" **Wt:** 205 **Born:** 8/14/1985 **Age:** 29

								BATTING												RUNNING			AVERAGES			
Year	Team	Lg	G	AB	H	2B	3B	HR	(Hm | Rd)	TB	R	RBI	RC	TBB	IBB	SO	HBP	SH	SF	SB	CS	GDP	Avg	OBP	Slg	OPS
2014	Iowa*	AAA	102	352	98	21	0	10	(- | -)	149	43	50	54	31	2	76	7	2	5	2	1	8	.278	.344	.423	.768
2010	Cin	NL	19	38	10	1	0	1	(1 | 0)	14	3	2	2	1	0	9	0	1	0	0	0	2	.263	.282	.368	.650
2011	Cin	NL	14	25	7	1	1	0	(0 | 0)	10	3	0	3	2	0	3	0	0	0	0	0	0	.280	.333	.400	.733
2013	Mia	NL	22	64	14	5	0	1	(0 | 1)	22	4	9	5	3	0	16	1	1	1	0	0	2	.219	.261	.344	.605
2014	ChC	NL	44	121	28	4	0	3	(2 | 1)	41	10	13	12	7	1	35	2	0	1	1	0	5	.231	.282	.339	.621
	4 ML YEARS		99	248	59	11	1	5	(3 | 2)	87	20	24	22	13	1	63	3	2	2	1	0	9	.238	.282	.351	.633

Luis Valbuena

Bats: L **Throws:** R **Pos:** 3B-124;2B-21;PH-18;DH-2   val-BWAY-nah   **Ht:** 5'10" **Wt:** 200 **Born:** 11/30/1985 **Age:** 29

								BATTING												RUNNING			AVERAGES			
Year	Team	Lg	G	AB	H	2B	3B	HR	(Hm | Rd)	TB	R	RBI	RC	TBB	IBB	SO	HBP	SH	SF	SB	CS	GDP	Avg	OBP	Slg	OPS
2008	Sea	AL	18	49	12	5	0	0	(0 | 0)	17	6	1	5	4	0	11	1	0	0	0	0	0	.245	.315	.347	.662
2009	Cle	AL	103	368	92	25	3	10	(2 | 8)	153	52	31	35	26	0	83	0	2	2	2	3	8	.250	.298	.416	.714
2010	Cle	AL	91	275	53	12	0	2	(1 | 1)	71	22	24	21	28	1	61	3	2	2	1	2	5	.193	.273	.258	.531
2011	Cle	AL	17	43	9	0	0	1	(0 | 1)	12	4	1	2	1	0	9	0	0	0	1	0	0	.209	.227	.279	.506
2012	ChC	NL	90	265	58	20	0	4	(2 | 2)	90	26	28	27	36	1	55	0	0	2	0	2	6	.219	.310	.340	.650
2013	ChC	NL	108	331	72	15	1	12	(4 | 8)	125	34	37	43	53	4	63	4	1	2	1	4	4	.218	.331	.378	.708
2014	ChC	NL	149	478	119	33	4	16	(7 | 9)	208	68	51	65	65	4	113	2	1	1	1	2	8	.249	.341	.435	.776
	7 ML YEARS		576	1809	415	110	8	45	(16 | 29)	676	212	173	198	213	10	395	10	6	9	6	13	31	.229	.313	.374	.686

Raul Valdes

Pitches: L **Bats:** L **Pos:** RP-8   **Ht:** 5'11" **Wt:** 190 **Born:** 11/27/1977 **Age:** 37

			HOW MUCH HE PITCHED						WHAT HE GAVE UP											THE RESULTS								
Year	Team	Lg	G	GS	CG	GF	IP	BFP	H	R	ER	HR	SH	SF	HB	TBB	IBB	SO	WP	Bk	W	L	Pct	Sh	Sv-Op	Hld	ERC	ERA
2014	OKCity*	AAA	8	0	0	3	10.1	43	9	4	4	1	0	1	0	0	0	13	1	0	1	0	1.000	0	0- -	-	2.08	3.48
2014	Buffalo*	AAA	23	12	0	5	81.0	349	84	40	36	9	0	4	1	24	2	78	1	1	5	5	.500	0	0- -	-	3.91	4.00
2010	NYM	NL	38	1	0	8	58.2	262	59	33	32	7	2	2	4	27	1	56	2	0	3	3	.500	0	1-3	1	4.70	4.91
2011	2 Tms		13	0	0	3	12.0	55	14	4	4	1	0	0	1	6	2	15	0	0	0	1	.000	0	0-0	0	5.42	3.00
2012	Phi	NL	27	1	0	7	31.0	113	18	10	10	3	1	0	0	5	1	35	0	0	3	2	.600	0	0-1	2	1.32	2.90
2013	Phi	NL	17	1	0	7	35.0	152	42	29	29	7	1	1	2	8	0	37	1	0	1	1	.500	0	0-0	0	5.56	7.46
2014	Hou	AL	8	0	0	2	3.2	19	5	5	5	2	0	0	0	3	0	4	0	0	0	0	-	0	1-2	1	12.00	12.27
11	StL	NL	7	0	0	3	5.1	27	6	2	2	0	0	0	1	4	2	7	0	0	0	1	.000	0	0-0	0	5.20	3.38
11	NYY	AL	6	0	0	0	6.2	28	8	2	2	1	0	0	0	2	0	8	0	0	0	0	-	0	0-0	0	5.47	2.70
	5 ML YEARS		103	3	0	27	140.1	601	138	81	80	20	4	3	7	49	4	147	3	0	7	7	.500	0	2-6	4	4.25	5.13

Jordany Valdespin

jor-DAN-ee VAL-dah-spin

Bats: L **Throws:** R **Pos:** PH-24;2B-17;RF-10;PR-3;CF-2;DH-1   **Ht:** 6'0" **Wt:** 190 **Born:** 12/23/1987 **Age:** 27

								BATTING												RUNNING			AVERAGES			
Year	Team	Lg	G	AB	H	2B	3B	HR	(Hm	Rd)	TB	R	RBI	RC	TBB	IBB	SO	HBP	SH	SF	SB	CS	GDP	Avg	OBP	Slg	OPS
2014	NewOr*	AAA	61	222	60	9	2	8	(-	-)	97	39	29	38	36	2	29	2	3	2	16	10	2	.270	.374	.437	.811
2012	NYM	NL	94	191	46	9	1	8	(5	3)	81	28	26	20	10	0	44	2	3	0	10	3	2	.241	.286	.424	.710
2013	NYM	NL	66	133	25	3	1	4	(2	2)	42	16	16	10	8	0	28	3	0	0	4	3	1	.188	.250	.316	.566
2014	Mia	NL	52	98	21	2	1	3	(1	2)	34	8	10	11	9	0	16	0	6	0	1	0	1	.214	.280	.347	.627
	3 ML YEARS		212	422	92	14	3	15	(8	7)	157	52	52	41	27	0	88	5	9	0	15	6	4	.218	.273	.372	.645

Danny Valencia

vuh-LENN-see-yah

Bats: R **Throws:** R **Pos:** 3B-66;1B-20;PH-13;2B-6;DH-3;PR-1   **Ht:** 6'2" **Wt:** 220 **Born:** 9/19/1984 **Age:** 30

								BATTING												RUNNING			AVERAGES			
Year	Team	Lg	G	AB	H	2B	3B	HR	(Hm	Rd)	TB	R	RBI	RC	TBB	IBB	SO	HBP	SH	SF	SB	CS	GDP	Avg	OBP	Slg	OPS
2014	Omha*	AAA	3	11	3	0	0	1	(-	-)	6	2	1	2	3	0	1	0	0	0	1	0	0	.273	.429	.545	.974
2010	Min	AL	85	299	93	18	1	7	(4	3)	134	30	40	50	20	0	46	0	0	3	2	0	11	.311	.351	.448	.799
2011	Min	AL	154	564	139	28	2	15	(9	6)	216	63	72	57	40	2	102	0	0	4	2	6	15	.246	.294	.383	.677
2012	2 Tms	AL	44	154	29	6	1	3	(3	0)	46	14	21	7	3	0	38	0	0	4	0	1	6	.188	.199	.299	.497
2013	Bal	AL	52	161	49	14	1	8	(4	4)	89	20	23	25	8	0	33	0	0	1	0	2	5	.304	.335	.553	.888
2014	2 Tms	AL	86	264	68	16	1	4	(1	3)	98	20	30	25	14	0	62	2	0	4	1	1	8	.258	.296	.371	.667
12	Min	AL	34	126	25	6	1	2	(2	0)	39	13	17	7	3	0	32	0	0	3	0	1	5	.198	.212	.310	.522
12	Bos	AL	10	28	4	0	0	1	(1	0)	7	1	4	0	0	0	6	0	0	1	0	0	1	.143	.138	.250	.388
14	KC	AL	36	110	31	5	0	2	(0	2)	42	8	11	8	7	0	27	1	0	1	0	0	4	.282	.328	.382	.710
14	Tor	AL	50	154	37	11	1	2	(1	1)	56	12	19	17	7	0	35	1	0	3	1	1	4	.240	.273	.364	.636
	Postseason		3	9	2	1	0	0	(0	0)	3	1	2	1	1	0	3	0	0	1	0	0	0	.222	.273	.333	.606
	5 ML YEARS		421	1442	378	82	6	37	(21	16)	583	147	186	164	85	2	281	2	0	16	5	10	45	.262	.301	.404	.705

Jose Valverde

Pitches: R Bats: R Pos: RP-21

val-VARE-day

Ht: 6'4" Wt: 265 Born: 3/24/1978 Age: 37

Year Team	Lg	G	GS	CG	GF	IP	BFP	H	R	ER	HR	SH	SF	HB	TBB	IBB	SO	WP	Bk	W	L	Pct	Sh	Sv-Op	Hld	ERC	ERA
2003 Ari	NL	54	0	0	33	50.1	204	24	16	12	4	0	1	2	26	2	71	2	0	2	1	.667	0	10-11	8	1.77	2.15
2004 Ari	NL	29	0	0	20	29.2	131	23	17	14	7	3	2	1	17	4	38	4	0	1	2	.333	0	8-10	5	4.25	4.25
2005 Ari	NL	61	0	0	34	66.1	268	51	19	18	5	3	1	2	20	1	75	3	0	3	4	.429	0	15-17	7	2.43	2.44
2006 Ari	NL	44	0	0	35	49.1	223	50	32	32	6	1	3	2	22	3	69	2	0	2	3	.400	0	18-22	1	4.42	5.84
2007 Ari	NL	65	0	0	59	64.1	265	46	21	19	7	0	1	3	26	1	78	1	0	1	4	.200	0	47-54	0	2.77	2.66
2008 Hou	NL	74	0	0	71	72.0	303	62	28	27	10	0	2	2	23	6	83	3	2	6	3	.667	0	44-51	0	3.18	3.38
2009 Hou	NL	52	0	0	45	54.0	219	40	15	14	5	1	2	2	21	1	56	1	0	4	2	.667	0	25-29	1	2.76	2.33
2010 Det	AL	60	0	0	55	63.0	259	41	24	21	5	0	1	3	32	1	63	3	0	2	4	.333	0	26-29	0	2.67	3.00
2011 Det	AL	75	0	0	70	72.1	301	52	21	18	5	2	0	5	34	4	69	3	1	2	4	.333	0	49-49	0	2.71	2.24
2012 Det	AL	71	0	0	67	69.0	294	59	34	29	3	2	3	4	27	5	48	1	0	3	4	.429	0	35-40	0	2.95	3.78
2013 Det	AL	20	0	0	18	19.1	84	18	12	12	6	0	0	2	6	0	19	0	0	0	1	.000	0	9-12	0	5.09	5.59
2014 NYM	NL	21	0	0	13	20.2	95	24	16	13	4	0	0	0	10	3	23	1	0	1	1	.500	0	2-4	0	5.75	5.66
Postseason		14	0	0	9	14.2	76	20	16	16	4	0	1	1	11	2	20	0	0	0	3	.000	0	5-6	0	9.18	9.82
12 ML YEARS		626	0	0	520	630.1	2646	490	255	229	67	12	16	26	264	31	692	24	3	27	33	.450	0	288-328	22	3.04	3.27

Scott Van Slyke

Bats: R Throws: R Pos: LF-32;PH-25;1B-21;CF-21;RF-13;PR-1

Ht: 6'5" Wt: 220 Born: 7/24/1986 Age: 28

Year Team	Lg	G	AB	H	2B	3B	HR	(Hm	Rd)	TB	R	RBI	RC	TBB	IBB	SO	HBP	SH	SF	SB	CS	GDP	Avg	OBP	Slg	OPS
2012 LAD	NL	27	54	9	2	0	2	(1	1)	17	4	7	4	2	0	14	0	1	0	1	0	2	.167	.196	.315	.511
2013 LAD	NL	53	129	31	8	0	7	(4	3)	60	13	19	15	20	0	37	1	0	2	1	1	7	.240	.342	.465	.807
2014 LAD	NL	98	212	63	13	1	11	(2	9)	111	32	29	34	28	0	71	4	0	2	4	2	3	.297	.386	.524	.910
Postseason		2	0	0	0	0	0	(0	0)	0	0	0	0	0	0	0	0	0	0	0	0	0	-	-	-	-
3 ML YEARS		178	395	103	23	1	20	(7	13)	188	49	55	53	50	0	122	5	1	4	6	3	12	.261	.348	.476	.824

Jason Vargas

Pitches: L Bats: L Pos: SP-30

Ht: 6'0" Wt: 215 Born: 2/2/1983 Age: 32

Year Team	Lg	G	GS	CG	GF	IP	BFP	H	R	ER	HR	SH	SF	HB	TBB	IBB	SO	WP	Bk	W	L	Pct	Sh	Sv-Op	Hld	ERC	ERA
2005 Fla	NL	17	13	1	0	73.2	325	71	34	33	4	4	1	4	31	4	59	0	0	5	5	.500	0	0-0	0	3.68	4.03
2006 Fla	NL	12	5	0	3	43.0	213	50	39	35	9	4	4	4	30	3	25	2	0	1	2	.333	0	0-0	0	7.30	7.33
2007 NYM	NL	2	2	0	0	10.1	51	17	14	14	4	0	0	0	2	1	4	1	1	0	1	.000	0	0-0	0	8.95	12.19
2009 Sea	AL	23	14	0	4	91.2	385	98	53	50	16	3	6	3	24	1	54	1	0	3	6	.333	0	0-0	0	4.64	4.91
2010 Sea	AL	31	31	0	0	192.2	811	187	86	81	18	4	7	1	54	3	116	1	4	9	12	.429	0	0-0	0	3.37	3.78
2011 Sea	AL	32	32	4	0	201.0	857	205	105	95	22	3	4	4	59	4	131	3	1	10	13	.435	3	0-0	0	3.86	4.25
2012 Sea	AL	33	33	2	0	217.1	887	201	94	93	35	3	6	3	55	1	141	5	0	14	11	.560	0	0-0	0	3.57	3.85
2013 LAA	AL	24	24	3	0	150.0	644	162	68	67	17	3	3	5	46	2	109	0	1	9	8	.529	2	0-0	0	4.40	4.02
2014 KC	AL	30	30	1	0	187.0	790	197	82	77	19	3	1	6	41	4	128	1	1	11	10	.524	1	0-0	0	3.76	3.71
9 ML YEARS		204	184	11	7	1166.2	4963	1188	575	545	144	27	32	30	342	23	767	14	8	62	68	.477	6	0-0	0	3.98	4.20

Kennys Vargas

Bats: B Throws: R Pos: DH-40;1B-13

KEN-is

Ht: 6'5" Wt: 275 Born: 8/1/1990 Age: 24

Year Team	Lg	G	AB	H	2B	3B	HR	(Hm	Rd)	TB	R	RBI	RC	TBB	IBB	SO	HBP	SH	SF	SB	CS	GDP	Avg	OBP	Slg	OPS
2010 Twins	R	39	142	46	15	1	3	(-	-)	72	24	26	28	13	0	40	3	0	2	1	0	0	.324	.388	.507	.895
2011 Elizab	R+	44	174	56	11	0	6	(-	-)	85	27	33	32	15	0	50	1	0	1	0	0	1	.322	.377	.489	.865
2012 Beloit	A	41	154	49	10	1	11	(-	-)	94	22	36	39	28	3	41	1	0	3	0	0	4	.318	.419	.610	1.030
2013 FtMyrs	A+	125	457	122	33	1	19	(-	-)	214	68	93	77	50	3	105	7	0	6	0	0	20	.267	.344	.468	.813
2014 NwBrit	AA	97	356	100	17	0	17	(-	-)	168	50	63	62	43	3	68	3	0	3	0	2	10	.281	.360	.472	.832
2014 Min	AL	53	215	59	10	1	9	(8	1)	98	26	38	27	12	2	63	3	0	4	0	0	5	.274	.316	.456	.772

Anthony Varvaro

Pitches: R Bats: R Pos: RP-61

var-VAR-oh

Ht: 6'0" Wt: 190 Born: 10/31/1984 Age: 30

Year Team	Lg	G	GS	CG	GF	IP	BFP	H	R	ER	HR	SH	SF	HB	TBB	IBB	SO	WP	Bk	W	L	Pct	Sh	Sv-Op	Hld	ERC	ERA
2010 Sea	AL	4	0	0	2	4.0	24	6	5	5	2	0	0	0	6	0	5	1	0	0	1	.000	0	0-0	0	16.26	11.25
2011 Atl	NL	18	0	0	9	24.0	96	15	7	7	3	2	1	0	11	4	23	1	0	0	2	.000	0	0-1	1	2.28	2.63
2012 Atl	NL	12	0	0	5	16.2	76	16	11	10	2	1	0	2	9	1	21	3	0	1	1	.500	0	0-0	0	4.88	5.40
2013 Atl	NL	62	0	0	30	73.1	306	68	25	23	3	2	0	1	25	3	43	7	0	3	1	.750	0	1-3	6	3.07	2.82
2014 Atl	NL	61	0	0	17	54.2	218	46	18	16	5	0	3	0	13	1	50	5	0	3	3	.500	0	0-1	13	2.57	2.63
5 ML YEARS		157	0	0	63	172.2	720	151	66	61	15	5	4	3	64	9	142	17	0	7	8	.467	0	1-5	20	3.19	3.18

Christian Vazquez

Bats: R Throws: R Pos: C-54;DH-1;PH-1

VAZ-kehz

Ht: 5'9" Wt: 195 Born: 8/21/1990 Age: 24

Year Team	Lg	G	AB	H	2B	3B	HR	(Hm	Rd)	TB	R	RBI	RC	TBB	IBB	SO	HBP	SH	SF	SB	CS	GDP	Avg	OBP	Slg	OPS
2010 Grnvlle	A	79	270	71	11	0	3	(-	-)	91	34	32	32	23	1	62	4	0	2	3	1	8	.263	.328	.337	.665
2011 Grnvlle	A	105	392	111	27	3	18	(-	-)	198	71	84	72	43	2	84	5	0	4	1	1	10	.283	.358	.505	.863
2012 Salem	A+	81	293	78	17	0	7	(-	-)	116	43	41	44	40	0	70	4	3	2	2	2	7	.266	.360	.396	.756
2012 Portlnd	AA	20	73	15	4	0	0	(-	-)	19	11	5	5	8	0	9	0	0	1	0	0	1	.205	.280	.260	.541

Year Team	Lg	G	AB	H	2B	3B	HR	(Hm Rd)	TB	R	RBI	RC	TBB	IBB	SO	HBP	SH	SF	SB	CS	GDP	Avg	OBP	Slg	OPS
2013 Portlnd	AA	96	342	99	19	1	5	(- -)	135	48	48	55	47	0	44	3	3	4	7	5	9	.289	.376	.395	.771
2013 Pwtckt	AAA	1	3	0	0	0	0	(- -)	0	0	0	0	1	0	0	0	0	0	0	0	0	.000	.250	.000	.250
2014 Pwtckt	AAA	66	244	68	17	0	3	(- -)	94	35	20	32	21	2	52	1	2	2	0	1	14	.279	.336	.385	.721
2014 Bos	AL	55	175	42	9	0	1	(1 0)	54	15	20	19	19	1	33	0	3	4	0	0	4	.240	.308	.309	.617

Donnie Veal

Pitches: L Bats: L Pos: RP-7 VEEL **Ht: 6'4" Wt: 235 Born: 9/18/1984 Age: 30**

Year Team	Lg	G	GS	CG	GF	IP	BFP	H	R	ER	HR	SH	SF	HB	TBB	IBB	SO	WP	Bk	W	L	Pct	Sh	Sv-Op	Hld	ERC	ERA
2014 Charltt*	AAA	37	0	0	20	50.0	237	57	36	33	4	4	2	7	27	2	49	9	0	4	5	.444	0	4- -	-	5.75	5.94
2009 Pit	NL	19	0	0	10	16.1	87	18	13	13	2	0	1	2	20	0	16	2	0	1	0	1.000	0	0-0	1	8.89	7.16
2012 CWS	AL	24	0	0	5	13.0	49	5	2	2	0	0	0	0	4	0	19	0	0	0	0	-	0	1-1	4	0.75	1.38
2013 CWS	AL	50	0	0	5	29.1	126	26	16	15	3	0	0	0	16	1	29	4	0	2	3	.400	0	0-1	13	4.02	4.60
2014 CWS	AL	7	0	0	3	6.0	32	6	5	5	0	0	1	1	7	1	6	1	0	0	0	-	0	0-0	2	6.41	7.50
4 ML YEARS		100	0	0	23	64.2	294	55	36	35	5	0	2	3	47	2	70	7	0	3	3	.500	0	1-2	20	4.44	4.87

Will Venable

Bats: L Throws: L Pos: CF-76;RF-75;PH-26;LF-6;PR-5 VENN-uh-bull **Ht: 6'3" Wt: 205 Born: 10/29/1982 Age: 32**

Year Team	Lg	G	AB	H	2B	3B	HR	(Hm Rd)	TB	R	RBI	RC	TBB	IBB	SO	HBP	SH	SF	SB	CS	GDP	Avg	OBP	Slg	OPS
2008 SD	NL	28	110	29	4	2	2	(0 2)	43	16	10	15	13	1	21	0	0	1	1	1	1	.264	.339	.391	.730
2009 SD	NL	95	293	75	14	2	12	(5 7)	129	38	38	34	25	2	89	4	2	6	6	1	6	.256	.323	.440	.763
2010 SD	NL	131	392	96	11	7	13	(6 7)	160	60	51	57	45	8	128	3	0	5	29	7	3	.245	.324	.408	.732
2011 SD	NL	121	370	91	14	7	9	(6 3)	146	49	44	52	31	4	92	5	1	4	26	3	2	.246	.310	.395	.704
2012 SD	NL	148	417	110	26	8	9	(2 7)	179	62	45	66	41	2	94	5	5	2	24	6	2	.264	.335	.429	.765
2013 SD	NL	151	481	129	22	8	22	(15 7)	233	64	53	56	29	4	118	2	2	1	22	6	6	.268	.312	.484	.796
2014 SD	NL	146	406	91	13	2	8	(5 3)	132	47	33	41	33	2	107	4	3	2	11	6	6	.224	.288	.325	.613
7 ML YEARS		820	2469	621	104	36	75	(39 36)	1022	336	274	321	217	23	649	23	13	15	119	30	26	.252	.316	.414	.730

Yordano Ventura

Pitches: R Bats: R Pos: SP-30; RP-1 your-DON-oh ven-TOUR-uh **Ht: 6'0" Wt: 180 Born: 6/3/1991 Age: 24**

Year Team	Lg	G	GS	CG	GF	IP	BFP	H	R	ER	HR	SH	SF	HB	TBB	IBB	SO	WP	Bk	W	L	Pct	Sh	Sv-Op	Hld	ERC	ERA
2010 Royals	R	14	6	0	0	52.2	228	49	28	19	3	0	0	3	17	0	58	3	0	4	2	.667	0	0- -	-	3.23	3.25
2011 Kane	A	19	19	0	0	84.1	351	82	43	40	8	1	3	5	24	0	88	13	1	4	6	.400	0	0- -	-	3.74	4.27
2012 Wilmg	A+	16	16	0	0	76.1	326	66	32	28	7	3	2	5	28	0	98	3	1	3	5	.375	0	0- -	-	3.35	3.30
2012 NWArk	AA	6	6	0	0	29.1	123	23	16	15	1	0	2	4	13	0	25	3	0	1	2	.333	0	0- -	-	3.20	4.60
2012 Royals	R	1	1	0	0	3.2	15	3	1	1	0	0	0	0	1	0	7	1	0	0	0	-	0	0- -	-	2.00	2.45
2013 NWArk	AA	11	11	0	0	57.2	230	39	17	15	3	0	0	4	20	0	74	2	2	3	2	.600	0	0- -	-	2.19	2.34
2013 Omha	AAA	15	14	0	0	77.0	334	80	35	32	4	1	2	3	33	1	81	5	1	5	4	.556	0	0- -	-	4.26	3.74
2013 KC	AL	3	3	0	0	15.1	64	13	6	6	3	0	0	0	6	0	11	1	0	0	1	.000	0	0-0	0	3.83	3.52
2014 KC	AL	31	30	0	0	183.0	782	168	70	65	14	3	4	5	69	1	159	11	1	14	10	.583	0	0-0	0	3.44	3.20
2 ML YEARS		34	33	0	0	198.1	846	181	76	71	17	3	4	5	75	1	170	12	1	14	11	.560	0	0-0	0	3.47	3.22

Jose Veras

Pitches: R Bats: R Pos: RP-46 **Ht: 6'6" Wt: 240 Born: 10/20/1980 Age: 34**

Year Team	Lg	G	GS	CG	GF	IP	BFP	H	R	ER	HR	SH	SF	HB	TBB	IBB	SO	WP	Bk	W	L	Pct	Sh	Sv-Op	Hld	ERC	ERA
2014 Tenn*	AA	4	1	0	0	4.2	17	1	0	0	0	0	0	0	2	0	3	0	0	2	0	1.000	0	0- -	-	0.57	0.00
2014 OKCity*	AAA	2	0	0	1	2.0	8	1	0	0	0	0	0	0	1	0	4	0	0	0	0	-	0	0- -	-	1.41	0.00
2006 NYY	AL	12	0	0	4	11.0	43	8	5	5	2	0	0	0	5	0	6	1	1	0	0	-	0	1-1	1	3.55	4.09
2007 NYY	AL	9	0	0	3	9.1	41	6	6	6	0	0	0	0	7	1	7	1	0	0	0	-	0	2-2	1	2.52	5.79
2008 NYY	AL	60	0	0	15	57.2	253	52	23	23	7	2	1	3	29	6	63	4	0	5	3	.625	0	0-2	10	4.09	3.59
2009 2 Tms	AL	47	0	0	19	50.1	225	42	33	29	8	4	0	6	28	0	40	0	1	4	3	.571	0	0-0	6	4.60	5.19
2010 Fla	NL	48	0	0	11	48.0	201	32	20	20	5	1	0	1	29	0	54	2	0	3	3	.500	0	0-2	19	3.19	3.75
2011 Pit	NL	79	0	0	19	71.0	305	54	32	30	6	2	3	4	34	3	79	5	1	2	4	.333	0	1-8	27	3.06	3.80
2012 Mil	NL	72	0	0	17	67.0	300	61	29	27	5	1	2	2	40	1	79	1	0	5	4	.556	0	1-2	10	4.20	3.63
2013 2 Tms	AL	67	0	0	45	62.2	254	45	23	21	6	2	0	4	22	1	60	2	0	0	5	.000	0	21-25	9	2.61	3.02
2014 2 Tms	AL	46	0	0	11	46.0	203	37	25	23	6	2	1	3	27	1	50	6	0	4	1	.800	0	1-6	6	4.10	4.50
09 NYY	AL	25	0	0	10	25.2	118	23	17	17	5	2	0	4	14	0	18	0	0	3	1	.750	0	0-0	3	5.29	5.96
09 Cle	AL	22	0	0	9	24.2	107	19	16	12	3	2	0	2	14	0	22	0	1	1	2	.333	0	0-0	3	3.92	4.38
13 Hou	AL	42	0	0	38	43.0	169	29	15	14	4	1	0	3	14	0	44	2	0	0	4	.000	0	19-22	6	2.38	2.93
13 Det	AL	25	0	0	7	19.2	85	16	8	7	2	1	0	1	8	1	16	0	0	0	1	.000	0	2-3	9	3.11	3.20
14 ChC	NL	12	0	0	4	13.1	64	12	12	12	2	2	1	3	11	0	13	3	0	0	1	.000	0	0-2	0	6.61	8.10
14 Hou	AL	34	0	0	7	32.2	139	25	13	11	4	0	0	0	16	1	37	3	0	4	0	1.000	0	1-4	6	3.19	3.03
Postseason		8	0	0	1	5.2	24	6	2	2	1	0	0	0	1	1	10	0	0	0	0	-	0	0-1	1	3.68	3.18
9 ML YEARS		440	0	0	144	423.0	1825	337	196	184	45	14	7	23	221	13	438	22	3	23	23	.500	0	27-48	89	3.61	3.91

Drew VerHagen

Pitches: R Bats: R Pos: SP-1   verr-HAY-gen   Ht: 6'6" Wt: 230 Born: 10/22/1990 Age: 24

Year	Team	Lg	G	GS	CG	GF	IP	BFP	H	R	ER	HR	SH	SF	HB	TBB	IBB	SO	WP	Bk	W	L	Pct	Sh	Sv-Op	Hld	ERC	ERA
2012	Tigers	R	2	0	0	0	4.0	16	5	2	1	0	0	0	0	0	0	2	0	0	0	0	-	0	0- -	-	3.37	2.25
2012	Lkland	A+	8	6	0	0	27.0	116	20	13	11	0	0	2	3	14	0	17	8	0	0	3	.000	0	0- -	-	2.83	3.67
2013	Lkland	A+	12	11	0	1	67.1	276	49	27	21	1	3	4	5	27	1	35	4	0	5	3	.625	0	0- -	-	2.36	2.81
2013	Erie	AA	12	12	1	0	60.0	248	53	24	20	3	5	1	4	17	0	40	5	0	2	5	.286	1	0- -	-	2.94	3.00
2014	Toledo	AAA	19	19	0	0	110.1	465	117	47	45	5	5	2	8	25	1	63	5	0	6	7	.462	0	0- -	-	3.67	3.67
2014	Det	AL	1	1	0	0	5.0	20	5	3	3	0	0	0	0	3	0	4	0	0	0	1	.000	0	0-0	0	4.67	5.40

Justin Verlander

Pitches: R Bats: R Pos: SP-32   Ht: 6'5" Wt: 225 Born: 2/20/1983 Age: 32

Year	Team	Lg	G	GS	CG	GF	IP	BFP	H	R	ER	HR	SH	SF	HB	TBB	IBB	SO	WP	Bk	W	L	Pct	Sh	Sv-Op	Hld	ERC	ERA
2005	Det	AL	2	2	0	0	11.1	54	15	9	9	1	0	0	1	5	0	7	1	0	0	2	.000	0	0-0	0	6.41	7.15
2006	Det	AL	30	30	1	0	186.0	776	187	78	75	21	2	4	6	60	1	124	5	1	17	9	.654	1	0-0	0	4.12	3.63
2007	Det	AL	32	32	1	0	201.2	866	181	88	82	20	3	1	19	67	3	183	17	2	18	6	.750	1	0-0	0	3.53	3.66
2008	Det	AL	33	33	1	0	201.0	880	195	119	108	18	4	6	14	87	8	163	6	3	11	17	.393	0	0-0	0	4.17	4.84
2009	Det	AL	35	35	3	0	240.0	982	219	99	92	20	6	4	6	63	5	269	8	4	19	9	.679	1	0-0	0	3.06	3.45
2010	Det	AL	33	33	4	0	224.1	925	190	89	84	14	6	8	6	71	0	219	11	2	18	9	.667	0	0-0	0	2.79	3.37
2011	Det	AL	34	34	4	0	251.0	969	174	73	67	24	2	3	3	57	0	250	7	2	24	5	.828	2	0-0	0	1.92	2.40
2012	Det	AL	33	33	6	0	238.1	956	192	81	70	19	4	3	5	60	2	239	2	1	17	8	.680	1	0-0	0	2.45	2.64
2013	Det	AL	34	34	0	0	218.1	925	212	94	84	19	2	6	4	75	1	217	3	1	13	12	.520	0	0-0	0	3.68	3.46
2014	Det	AL	32	32	0	0	206.0	893	223	114	104	18	6	5	5	65	1	159	5	1	15	12	.556	0	0-0	0	4.19	4.54
	Postseason		15	15	1	0	93.1	379	71	37	34	12	1	1	1	29	0	108	6	1	7	5	.583	1	0-0	0	2.66	3.28
	10 ML YEARS		298	298	20	0	1978.0	8226	1788	844	775	174	35	40	69	610	21	1830	65	17	152	89	.631	6	0-0	0	3.25	3.53

Dayan Viciedo

DYE-yahn vee-see-AY-doe

Bats: R Throws: R Pos: RF-84;LF-55;DH-10;PH-6;1B-4;PR-1   Ht: 5'11" Wt: 240 Born: 3/10/1989 Age: 26

Year	Team	Lg	G	AB	H	2B	3B	HR	(Hm	Rd)	TB	R	RBI	RC	TBB	IBB	SO	HBP	SH	SF	SB	CS	GDP	Avg	OBP	Slg	OPS
2010	CWS	AL	38	104	32	7	0	5	(4	1)	54	17	13	15	2	0	25	0	0	0	1	0	5	.308	.321	.519	.840
2011	CWS	AL	29	102	26	3	0	1	(0	1)	32	11	6	12	9	0	23	2	0	0	1	0	4	.255	.327	.314	.641
2012	CWS	AL	147	505	129	18	1	25	(13	12)	224	64	78	65	28	0	120	6	0	4	0	2	19	.255	.300	.444	.744
2013	CWS	AL	124	441	117	23	3	14	(5	9)	188	43	56	56	24	0	98	3	0	5	0	0	11	.265	.304	.426	.731
2014	CWS	AL	145	523	121	22	3	21	(10	11)	212	65	58	53	32	3	122	5	0	3	0	1	19	.231	.281	.405	.686
	5 ML YEARS		483	1675	425	73	7	66	(32	34)	710	200	211	201	95	3	388	16	0	12	2	3	58	.254	.298	.424	.722

Shane Victorino

Bats: R Throws: R Pos: RF-30   Ht: 5'9" Wt: 190 Born: 11/30/1980 Age: 34

Year	Team	Lg	G	AB	H	2B	3B	HR	(Hm	Rd)	TB	R	RBI	RC	TBB	IBB	SO	HBP	SH	SF	SB	CS	GDP	Avg	OBP	Slg	OPS
2014	Pwtckt*	AAA	9	29	4	1	0	0	(-	-)	5	3	0	0	0	0	6	0	0	0	0	0	1	.138	.138	.172	.310
2014	Lowell*	A-	4	9	0	0	0	0	(-	-)	0	0	0	0	2	0	2	0	0	0	0	0	0	.000	.182	.000	.182
2003	SD	NL	36	73	11	2	0	0	(0	0)	13	8	4	1	7	0	17	1	1	1	7	2	5	.151	.232	.178	.410
2005	Phi	NL	21	17	5	0	0	2	(1	1)	11	5	8	4	0	0	3	0	0	2	0	0	0	.294	.263	.647	.910
2006	Phi	NL	153	415	119	19	8	6	(3	3)	172	70	46	58	24	0	54	14	8	1	4	3	5	.287	.346	.414	.760
2007	Phi	NL	131	456	128	23	3	12	(6	6)	193	78	46	65	37	1	62	10	5	2	37	4	10	.281	.347	.423	.770
2008	Phi	NL	146	570	167	30	8	14	(6	8)	255	102	58	86	45	2	69	7	5	0	36	11	4	.293	.352	.447	.799
2009	Phi	NL	156	620	181	39	13	10	(4	6)	276	102	62	99	60	1	71	6	4	4	25	8	5	.292	.358	.445	.803
2010	Phi	NL	147	587	152	26	10	18	(13	5)	252	84	69	89	53	5	79	7	0	1	34	6	7	.259	.327	.429	.756
2011	Phi	NL	132	519	145	27	16	17	(6	11)	255	95	61	86	55	1	63	6	6	0	19	3	4	.279	.355	.491	.847
2012	2 Tms	NL	154	595	152	29	7	11	(4	7)	228	72	55	76	53	1	80	6	9	3	39	6	5	.255	.321	.383	.704
2013	Bos	AL	122	477	140	26	2	15	(7	8)	215	82	61	77	25	0	75	18	10	2	21	3	5	.294	.351	.451	.801
2014	Bos	AL	30	123	33	6	1	2	(1	1)	47	14	12	13	6	0	21	1	1	2	2	0	3	.268	.303	.382	.685
	12 Phi	NL	101	387	101	17	5	9	(3	6)	155	46	40	50	35	1	49	2	5	2	24	4	4	.261	.324	.401	.724
	12 LAD	NL	53	208	51	12	2	2	(1	1)	73	26	15	26	18	0	31	4	4	1	15	2	1	.245	.316	.351	.667
	Postseason		60	226	58	11	2	7	(4	3)	94	31	42	42	17	4	29	11	4	1	10	1	3	.257	.337	.416	.753
	11 ML YEARS		1228	4452	1233	227	68	107	(51	56)	1917	712	482	654	365	11	594	76	49	18	224	46	57	.277	.341	.431	.771

Carlos Villanueva

Pitches: R Bats: R Pos: RP-37; SP-5   vee-ah-nue-AY-vah   Ht: 6'2" Wt: 215 Born: 11/28/1983 Age: 31

Year	Team	Lg	G	GS	CG	GF	IP	BFP	H	R	ER	HR	SH	SF	HB	TBB	IBB	SO	WP	Bk	W	L	Pct	Sh	Sv-Op	Hld	ERC	ERA
2006	Mil	NL	10	6	0	2	53.2	215	43	22	22	8	1	0	4	11	1	39	0	0	2	2	.500	0	0-0	0	2.85	3.69
2007	Mil	NL	59	6	0	8	114.1	489	101	52	50	16	4	1	3	53	3	99	3	0	8	5	.615	0	1-3	16	4.03	3.94
2008	Mil	NL	47	9	0	8	108.1	464	112	53	49	18	9	1	3	30	1	93	4	0	4	7	.364	0	1-1	11	4.29	4.07
2009	Mil	NL	64	6	0	23	96.0	422	102	58	57	13	4	0	2	35	8	83	4	0	4	10	.286	0	3-8	9	4.44	5.34
2010	Mil	NL	50	0	0	5	52.2	231	48	27	27	7	0	3	4	22	1	67	5	0	2	0	1.000	0	1-4	14	4.08	4.61
2011	Tor	AL	33	13	0	3	107.0	454	103	49	48	11	1	6	4	32	3	68	4	0	6	4	.600	0	0-1	0	3.57	4.04
2012	Tor	AL	38	16	0	4	125.1	521	113	59	58	23	2	4	3	46	4	122	6	1	7	7	.500	0	0-0	2	4.08	4.16
2013	ChC	NL	47	15	0	5	128.2	524	117	58	58	14	7	3	3	40	4	103	0	0	7	8	.467	0	0-1	2	3.43	4.06
2014	ChC	NL	42	5	0	15	77.2	343	89	42	40	6	3	2	3	19	4	72	3	0	5	7	.417	0	2-2	3	4.10	4.64
	Postseason		2	0	0	0	3.2	11	0	0	0	0	0	0	0	0	0	3	0	0	0	0	-	0	0-0	1	0.00	0.00
	9 ML YEARS		390	76	0	79	863.2	3663	828	420	409	116	31	20	29	288	29	746	29	1	45	50	.474	0	8-20	57	3.90	4.26

Jonathan Villar

Bats: B Throws: R Pos: SS-82;PR-6;DH-4 — vee-YARR — Ht: 6'1" Wt: 205 Born: 5/2/1991 Age: 24

Year	Team	Lg	G	AB	H	2B	3B	HR	(Hm	Rd)	TB	R	RBI	RC	TBB	IBB	SO	HBP	SH	SF	SB	CS	GDP	Avg	OBP	Slg	OPS
2010	Lakwd	A	100	371	101	18	4	2	(-	-)	133	61	36	49	26	1	103	8	13	2	38	13	5	.272	.332	.358	.690
2010	Lancst	A+	32	129	29	6	2	3	(-	-)	48	18	19	15	12	0	50	1	0	1	7	2	2	.225	.294	.372	.666
2011	Lancst	A+	47	174	45	7	4	4	(-	-)	72	26	26	29	25	0	56	2	3	3	20	6	0	.259	.353	.414	.767
2011	CpChr	AA	83	324	75	16	2	10	(-	-)	125	52	26	40	29	0	100	4	8	2	14	6	2	.231	.301	.386	.687
2012	CpChr	AA	86	326	85	7	2	11	(-	-)	129	54	50	50	35	1	87	4	8	4	39	8	2	.261	.336	.396	.732
2013	OKCity	AAA	91	339	94	16	8	8	(-	-)	150	47	41	56	32	0	93	2	11	2	31	7	7	.277	.341	.442	.784
2014	OKCity	AAA	51	190	49	2	3	3	(-	-)	66	34	27	29	31	0	61	1	2	1	24	6	1	.258	.363	.347	.711
2013	Hou	AL	58	210	51	9	2	1	(0	1)	67	26	8	22	24	1	71	0	7	0	18	8	5	.243	.321	.319	.640
2014	Hou	AL	87	263	55	13	2	7	(3	4)	93	31	27	24	19	1	80	2	4	1	17	4	4	.209	.267	.354	.620
	2 ML YEARS		145	473	106	22	4	8	(3	5)	160	57	35	46	43	2	151	2	11	1	35	12	9	.224	.291	.338	.629

Pedro Villarreal

Pitches: R Bats: R Pos: RP-12 — VEE-uh-ree-al — Ht: 6'1" Wt: 230 Born: 12/9/1987 Age: 27

Year	Team	Lg	G	GS	CG	GF	IP	BFP	H	R	ER	HR	SH	SF	HB	TBB	IBB	SO	WP	Bk	W	L	Pct	Sh	Sv-Op	Hld	ERC	ERA
2014	Lsvlle*	AAA	42	2	0	11	56.1	238	57	20	20	5	2	1	3	13	1	50	3	0	6	2	.750	0	2- -	-	3.57	3.20
2012	Cin	NL	1	0	0	1	1.0	3	0	0	0	0	0	0	0	0	0	1	0	0	0	0	-	0	0-0	0	0.00	0.00
2013	Cin	NL	2	1	0	0	5.2	32	13	8	8	4	0	0	0	3	0	4	0	0	0	1	.000	0	0-0	0	20.07	12.71
2014	Cin	NL	12	0	0	1	14.2	62	11	7	7	1	0	1	1	7	1	12	1	0	0	2	.000	0	0-0	0	2.95	4.30
	3 ML YEARS		15	1	0	2	21.1	97	24	15	15	5	0	1	1	10	1	17	1	0	0	3	.000	0	0-0	0	6.23	6.33

Nick Vincent

Pitches: R Bats: R Pos: RP-63 — Ht: 5'11" Wt: 180 Born: 7/12/1986 Age: 28

Year	Team	Lg	G	GS	CG	GF	IP	BFP	H	R	ER	HR	SH	SF	HB	TBB	IBB	SO	WP	Bk	W	L	Pct	Sh	Sv-Op	Hld	ERC	ERA
2014	Lk Els*	A+	2	0	0	0	2.0	7	2	0	0	0	0	0	0	0	0	1	0	0	0	0	-	0	0- -	-	2.31	0.00
2012	SD	NL	27	0	0	3	26.1	105	19	5	5	2	1	0	1	7	0	28	1	0	2	0	1.000	0	0-1	5	2.13	1.71
2013	SD	NL	45	0	0	7	46.1	180	33	11	11	1	4	0	2	11	3	49	0	0	6	3	.667	0	1-1	10	1.67	2.14
2014	SD	NL	63	0	0	7	55.0	215	44	22	22	5	3	0	2	11	1	62	1	0	1	2	.333	0	0-2	20	2.39	3.60
	3 ML YEARS		135	0	0	17	127.2	500	96	38	38	8	8	0	5	29	4	139	2	0	9	5	.643	0	1-4	35	2.07	2.68

Arodys Vizcaino

Pitches: R Bats: R Pos: RP-5 — ah-ROH-dis vees-kai-EE-no — Ht: 6'0" Wt: 190 Born: 11/13/1990 Age: 24

Year	Team	Lg	G	GS	CG	GF	IP	BFP	H	R	ER	HR	SH	SF	HB	TBB	IBB	SO	WP	Bk	W	L	Pct	Sh	Sv-Op	Hld	ERC	ERA
2010	Rome	A	14	14	0	0	71.2	292	63	25	19	1	2	3	3	9	0	68	6	2	9	4	.692	0	0- -	-	2.01	2.39
2010	MrtlBh	A+	3	3	0	0	13.2	61	16	9	7	1	2	1	1	3	0	11	1	1	0	0	-	0	0- -	-	4.31	4.61
2011	Lynbrg	A+	9	9	0	0	40.1	161	31	14	11	3	0	1	0	10	0	37	4	1	2	2	.500	0	0- -	-	2.14	2.45
2011	Missi	AA	11	8	0	0	49.2	210	44	21	21	3	1	0	3	18	1	55	4	1	2	3	.400	0	0- -	-	3.24	3.81
2011	Gwnntt	AAA	6	0	0	0	7.0	28	7	3	1	1	1	0	0	0	0	8	0	0	1	0	1.000	0	0- -	-	2.74	1.29
2014	Dytona	A+	9	0	0	5	9.0	35	6	1	1	0	0	0	0	4	0	10	1	0	0	0	-	0	1- -	-	1.99	1.00
2014	Tenn	AA	14	0	0	8	13.2	51	7	4	4	1	0	0	1	3	0	16	1	0	1	1	.500	0	1- -	-	1.33	2.63
2014	Iowa	AAA	17	0	0	4	18.1	91	25	11	11	1	1	0	2	11	1	16	1	0	0	0	-	0	0- -	-	7.04	5.40
2011	Atl	NL	17	0	0	2	17.1	77	16	9	9	1	0	0	1	9	1	17	5	0	1	1	.500	0	0-2	5	3.89	4.67
2014	ChC	NL	5	0	0	5	5.0	22	5	3	3	1	0	0	0	3	0	4	0	0	0	0	-	0	0-0	0	5.79	5.40
	2 ML YEARS		22	0	0	7	22.1	99	21	12	12	2	0	0	1	12	1	21	5	0	1	1	.500	0	0-2	5	4.29	4.84

Ryan Vogelsong

Pitches: R Bats: R Pos: SP-32 — VOH-gull-song — Ht: 6'4" Wt: 215 Born: 7/22/1977 Age: 37

Year	Team	Lg	G	GS	CG	GF	IP	BFP	H	R	ER	HR	SH	SF	HB	TBB	IBB	SO	WP	Bk	W	L	Pct	Sh	Sv-Op	Hld	ERC	ERA
2000	SF	NL	4	0	0	3	6.0	24	4	0	0	0	0	0	0	2	0	6	0	0	0	0	-	0	0-0	0	1.57	0.00
2001	2 Tms	NL	15	2	0	8	34.2	164	39	31	26	6	0	1	2	20	1	24	2	0	0	5	.000	0	0-0	1	6.20	6.75
2003	Pit	NL	6	5	0	0	22.0	108	30	19	16	1	3	1	2	9	3	15	1	0	2	2	.500	0	0-0	0	5.72	6.55
2004	Pit	NL	31	26	0	4	133.0	610	148	97	96	22	8	6	10	67	7	92	3	0	6	13	.316	0	0-0	0	5.89	6.50
2005	Pit	NL	44	0	0	19	81.1	369	82	43	40	5	1	4	8	40	1	52	7	0	2	2	.500	0	0-1	1	4.51	4.43
2006	Pit	NL	20	0	0	7	38.0	178	44	27	27	2	5	4	7	16	2	27	4	1	0	0	-	0	0-0	0	5.31	6.39
2011	SF	NL	30	28	1	1	179.2	752	164	62	54	15	10	3	5	61	6	139	1	1	13	7	.650	1	0-0	0	3.32	2.71
2012	SF	NL	31	31	0	0	189.2	788	171	76	71	17	7	4	8	62	7	158	3	0	14	9	.609	0	0-0	0	3.33	3.37
2013	SF	NL	19	19	0	0	103.2	467	124	73	66	15	4	4	6	38	2	67	3	0	4	6	.400	0	0-0	0	5.64	5.73
2014	SF	NL	32	32	1	0	184.2	780	178	86	82	18	10	3	9	58	2	151	2	0	8	13	.381	0	0-0	0	3.71	4.00
01	SF	NL	13	0	0	8	28.2	130	29	21	18	5	0	1	2	14	0	17	2	0	0	3	.000	0	0-0	1	5.26	5.65
01	Pit	NL	2	2	0	0	6.0	34	10	10	8	1	0	0	0	6	1	7	0	0	0	2	.000	0	0-0	0	11.03	12.00
	Postseason		4	4	0	0	24.2	99	16	3	3	0	0	0	1	10	0	21	0	0	3	0	1.000	0	0-0	0	1.83	1.09
	10 ML YEARS		232	143	2	42	972.2	4240	984	514	478	101	48	30	57	373	31	731	26	2	49	57	.462	1	0-1	2	4.28	4.42

Stephen Vogt

Bats: L **Throws:** R **Pos:** 1B-47;RF-17;C-15;PH-13;DH-5;LF-1   VOTE   **Ht:** 6'0" **Wt:** 215 **Born:** 11/1/1984 **Age:** 30

							BATTING											RUNNING			AVERAGES			
Year	Team	Lg	G	AB	H	2B	3B	HR	(Hm | Rd)	TB	R	RBI	RC	TBB	IBB	SO	HBP	SH	SF	SB	CS	GDP	Avg	OBP	Slg	OPS
2014 Scrmto*		AAA	21	88	32	8	2	3	(- | -)	53	18	19	21	8	0	8	0	0	1	1	0	0	.364	.412	.602	1.015
2012 TB		AL	18	25	0	0	0	0	(0 | 0)	0	0	0	0	2	0	2	0	0	0	0	0	0	.000	.074	.000	.074
2013 Oak		AL	47	135	34	6	1	4	(3 | 1)	54	18	16	15	9	1	28	0	2	2	0	1	2	.252	.295	.400	.695
2014 Oak		AL	84	269	75	10	2	9	(4 | 5)	116	26	35	38	16	2	39	1	0	1	1	0	2	.279	.321	.431	.752
Postseason			5	16	3	0	1	0	(0 | 0)	5	2	1	1	1	0	7	0	0	0	0	0	0	.188	.235	.313	.548
3 ML YEARS			149	429	109	16	3	13	(7 | 6)	170	44	51	53	27	3	69	1	2	3	1	1	4	.254	.298	.396	.694

Edinson Volquez

Pitches: R **Bats:** R **Pos:** SP-31; RP-1   VOLE-kezz   **Ht:** 6'0" **Wt:** 220 **Born:** 7/3/1983 **Age:** 31

			HOW MUCH HE PITCHED					WHAT HE GAVE UP											THE RESULTS							
Year	Team	Lg	G	GS	CG	GF	IP	BFP	H	R	ER	HR	SH	SF	HB	TBB	IBB	SO	WP	Bk	W	L	Pct	Sh	Sv-Op	Hld	ERC	ERA
2005 Tex		AL	6	3	0	0	12.2	75	25	22	20	3	0	1	2	10	0	11	0	0	0	4	.000	0	0-0	0	14.15	14.21
2006 Tex		AL	8	8	0	0	33.1	164	52	28	27	7	0	1	1	17	0	15	0	0	1	6	.143	0	0-0	0	9.27	7.29
2007 Tex		AL	6	6	0	0	34.0	149	34	18	17	4	0	2	2	15	0	29	0	0	2	1	.667	0	0-0	0	4.63	4.50
2008 Cin		NL	33	32	0	1	196.0	838	167	82	70	14	6	5	14	93	5	206	10	1	17	6	.739	0	0-0	0	3.61	3.21
2009 Cin		NL	9	9	0	0	49.2	218	34	25	24	6	2	1	5	32	0	47	2	1	4	2	.667	0	0-0	0	3.77	4.35
2010 Cin		NL	12	12	0	0	62.2	275	59	30	30	6	3	1	3	35	0	67	5	0	4	3	.571	0	0-0	0	4.60	4.31
2011 Cin		NL	20	20	0	0	108.2	489	106	72	69	19	5	6	4	65	3	104	5	2	5	7	.417	0	0-0	0	5.42	5.71
2012 SD		NL	32	32	1	0	182.2	802	160	88	84	14	5	4	9	105	6	174	9	1	11	11	.500	1	0-0	0	4.04	4.14
2013 2 Tms		NL	33	32	0	0	170.1	777	193	114	108	19	9	4	3	77	2	142	16	0	9	12	.429	0	0-0	0	5.11	5.71
2014 Pit		NL	32	31	1	0	192.2	809	166	75	65	17	13	6	14	71	6	140	15	0	13	7	.650	0	0-0	0	3.37	3.04
13 SD		NL	27	27	0	0	142.1	659	168	100	95	14	7	3	3	69	2	116	11	0	9	10	.474	0	0-0	0	5.45	6.01
13 LAD		NL	6	5	0	0	28.0	118	25	14	13	5	2	1	0	8	0	26	5	0	0	2	.000	0	0-0	0	3.45	4.18
Postseason			1	1	0	0	1.2	11	4	4	4	0	0	1	0	2	0	0	0	0	0	1	.000	0	0-0	0	15.90	21.60
10 ML YEARS			191	185	2	1	1042.2	4596	996	554	514	109	43	31	57	520	22	935	62	5	66	59	.528	1	0-0	0	4.43	4.44

Joey Votto

Bats: L **Throws:** R **Pos:** 1B-61;PH-1   VAH-toe   **Ht:** 6'2" **Wt:** 220 **Born:** 9/10/1983 **Age:** 31

							BATTING											RUNNING			AVERAGES			
Year	Team	Lg	G	AB	H	2B	3B	HR	(Hm | Rd)	TB	R	RBI	RC	TBB	IBB	SO	HBP	SH	SF	SB	CS	GDP	Avg	OBP	Slg	OPS
2014 Lsvlle*		AAA	2	6	2	0	0	0	(- | -)	2	1	0	0	0	0	2	0	0	0	0	0	1	.333	.333	.333	.667
2007 Cin		NL	24	84	27	7	0	4	(4 | 0)	46	11	17	17	5	1	15	0	0	0	1	0	0	.321	.360	.548	.908
2008 Cin		NL	151	526	156	32	3	24	(14 | 10)	266	69	84	91	59	9	102	2	0	2	7	5	7	.297	.368	.506	.874
2009 Cin		NL	131	469	151	38	1	25	(14 | 11)	266	82	84	99	70	10	106	4	0	1	4	1	8	.322	.414	.567	.981
2010 Cin		NL	150	547	177	36	2	37	(18 | 19)	328	106	113	132	91	8	125	7	0	3	16	5	11	.324	.424	.600	1.024
2011 Cin		NL	161	599	185	40	3	29	(13 | 16)	318	101	103	131	110	15	129	4	0	6	8	6	20	.309	.416	.531	.947
2012 Cin		NL	111	374	126	44	0	14	(10 | 4)	212	59	56	97	94	18	85	5	0	2	5	3	8	.337	.474	.567	1.041
2013 Cin		NL	162	581	177	30	3	24	(11 | 13)	285	101	73	121	135	19	138	4	0	6	6	3	15	.305	.435	.491	.926
2014 Cin		NL	62	220	56	16	0	6	(6 | 0)	90	32	23	36	47	2	49	3	0	2	1	1	5	.255	.390	.409	.799
Postseason			9	32	8	0	0	0	(0 | 0)	8	3	1	3	4	0	9	0	0	1	0	0	1	.250	.324	.250	.574
8 ML YEARS			952	3400	1055	243	12	163	(90 | 73)	1811	561	553	724	611	82	749	29	0	22	48	24	74	.310	.417	.533	.950

Michael Wacha

Pitches: R **Bats:** R **Pos:** SP-19   WOCK-uh   **Ht:** 6'6" **Wt:** 210 **Born:** 7/1/1991 **Age:** 23

			HOW MUCH HE PITCHED					WHAT HE GAVE UP											THE RESULTS							
Year	Team	Lg	G	GS	CG	GF	IP	BFP	H	R	ER	HR	SH	SF	HB	TBB	IBB	SO	WP	Bk	W	L	Pct	Sh	Sv-Op	Hld	ERC	ERA
2012 Cards		R	3	2	0	0	5.0	19	4	1	1	1	1	0	0	0	0	7	0	0	0	0	-	0	0--	-	2.06	1.80
2012 PlmBh		A+	4	0	0	2	8.0	26	1	0	0	0	0	0	0	1	0	16	1	0	0	0	-	0	0--	-	0.11	0.00
2012 Sprgfld		AA	4	0	0	0	8.0	30	3	1	1	0	0	0	0	3	0	17	1	0	0	0	-	0	0--	-	0.85	1.13
2013 Memp		AAA	15	15	0	0	85.0	333	65	26	25	9	3	2	0	19	0	73	5	0	5	3	.625	0	0--	-	2.25	2.65
2014 Sprgfld		AA	1	1	0	0	2.0	8	1	0	0	0	0	0	0	1	0	1	0	0	0	0	-	0	0--	-	1.41	0.00
2013 StL		NL	15	9	0	2	64.2	260	52	20	20	5	1	3	0	19	0	65	3	0	4	1	.800	0	0-1	0	2.52	2.78
2014 StL		NL	19	19	0	0	107.0	447	95	41	38	6	1	2	5	33	0	94	2	0	5	6	.455	0	0-0	0	3.00	3.20
Postseason			5	5	0	0	30.2	119	16	9	9	3	0	0	1	12	3	33	0	0	4	1	.800	0	0-0	0	1.65	2.64
2 ML YEARS			34	28	0	2	171.2	707	147	61	58	11	2	5	5	52	0	159	5	0	9	7	.563	0	0-1	0	2.81	3.04

Tsuyoshi Wada

Pitches: L **Bats:** L **Pos:** SP-13   sue-YO-she WAH-duh   **Ht:** 5'11" **Wt:** 180 **Born:** 2/21/1981 **Age:** 34

			HOW MUCH HE PITCHED					WHAT HE GAVE UP											THE RESULTS							
Year	Team	Lg	G	GS	CG	GF	IP	BFP	H	R	ER	HR	SH	SF	HB	TBB	IBB	SO	WP	Bk	W	L	Pct	Sh	Sv-Op	Hld	ERC	ERA
2010 Jp-Fkka		Jap	26	26	1	0	169.1	696	145	59	59	11	-	-	1	55	-	169	2	0	17	8	.680	0	0--	-	2.82	3.14
2011 Jp-Fkka		Jap	26	-	4	0	184.2	726	145	33	31	7	-	4	40	-	168	5	0	16	5	.762	2	0--	-	2.02	1.51
2012 Norfolk		AAA	1	1	0	0	2.2	18	6	6	6	1	0	0	0	4	0	1	0	0	0	1	.000	0	0--	-	20.79	20.25
2013 Norfolk		AAA	19	19	0	0	102.2	442	112	50	46	9	3	2	4	35	0	80	1	0	5	6	.455	0	0--	-	4.50	4.03
2014 Iowa		AAA	19	18	0	0	113.2	464	104	36	35	13	2	1	2	28	2	120	3	0	10	6	.625	0	0--	-	3.18	2.77
2014 ChC		NL	13	13	0	0	69.1	289	67	28	25	7	2	1	3	19	1	57	0	0	4	4	.500	0	0-0	0	3.59	3.25

Neil Wagner

Pitches: R Bats: R Pos: RP-10   Ht: 6'0" Wt: 215 Born: 1/1/1984 Age: 31

			HOW MUCH HE PITCHED						WHAT HE GAVE UP									THE RESULTS							
Year Team	Lg	G	GS	CG	GF	IP	BFP	H	R	ER	HR	SH	SF	HB	TBB	IBB	SO	WP	Bk	W	L	Pct	Sh	Sv-Op	Hld	ERC	ERA
2014 Buffalo*	AAA	9	0	0	6	9.0	36	6	4	4	0	0	0	0	3	1	11	1	0	0	1	.000	0	4- -	-	1.47	4.00
2014 B Jays*	R	1	0	0	0	0.0	1	1	1	1	1	0	0	0	0	0	0	0	0	0	0	-	0	0- -	-		
2011 Oak	AL	6	0	0	5	5.0	24	6	7	4	1	0	0	1	3	0	4	0	0	0	0	-	0	0-0	0	7.98	7.20
2013 Tor	AL	36	0	0	8	38.0	161	39	17	16	5	2	1	1	13	1	33	3	1	2	4	.333	0	0-1	10	4.36	3.79
2014 Tor	AL	10	0	0	0	10.0	49	12	9	9	1	0	1	1	4	0	6	0	0	0	0	-	0	0-0	5	5.26	8.10
3 ML YEARS		52	0	0	13	53.0	234	57	33	29	7	2	2	3	20	1	43	3	1	2	4	.333	0	0-1	15	4.84	4.92

Adam Wainwright

Pitches: R Bats: R Pos: SP-32   Ht: 6'7" Wt: 235 Born: 8/30/1981 Age: 33

			HOW MUCH HE PITCHED						WHAT HE GAVE UP									THE RESULTS							
Year Team	Lg	G	GS	CG	GF	IP	BFP	H	R	ER	HR	SH	SF	HB	TBB	IBB	SO	WP	Bk	W	L	Pct	Sh	Sv-Op	Hld	ERC	ERA
2005 StL	NL	2	0	0	1	2.0	9	2	3	3	1	0	0	0	1	0	0	0	0	0	0	-	0	0-0	0	7.30	13.50
2006 StL	NL	61	0	0	10	75.0	309	64	26	26	6	4	1	4	22	2	72	3	0	2	1	.667	0	3-5	17	2.92	3.12
2007 StL	NL	32	32	1	0	202.0	882	212	93	83	13	9	5	9	70	4	136	6	0	14	12	.538	0	0-0	0	4.01	3.70
2008 StL	NL	20	20	1	0	132.0	544	122	51	47	12	6	4	3	34	1	91	3	0	11	3	.786	0	0-0	0	3.14	3.20
2009 StL	NL	34	34	1	0	233.0	970	216	75	68	17	10	5	3	66	1	212	7	0	19	8	.704	0	0-0	0	3.08	2.63
2010 StL	NL	33	33	5	0	230.1	910	186	68	62	15	13	6	4	56	2	213	2	0	20	11	.645	2	0-0	0	2.36	2.42
2012 StL	NL	32	32	3	0	198.2	831	196	96	87	15	9	6	6	52	3	184	5	2	14	13	.519	2	0-0	0	3.41	3.94
2013 StL	NL	34	34	5	0	241.2	956	223	83	79	15	13	2	6	35	2	219	5	0	19	9	.679	2	0-0	0	2.60	2.94
2014 StL	NL	32	32	5	0	227.0	898	184	64	60	10	8	3	7	50	5	179	4	1	20	9	.690	3	0-0	0	2.20	2.38
Postseason		18	9	1	9	67.2	267	58	21	19	6	0	1	1	9	0	76	2	0	4	3	.571	0	4-5	0	2.32	2.53
9 ML YEARS		280	217	21	11	1541.2	6309	1405	559	515	104	72	32	42	386	20	1306	35	3	119	66	.643	9	3-5	17	2.92	3.01

Jordan Walden

Pitches: R Bats: R Pos: RP-58   Ht: 6'5" Wt: 250 Born: 11/16/1987 Age: 27

			HOW MUCH HE PITCHED						WHAT HE GAVE UP									THE RESULTS							
Year Team	Lg	G	GS	CG	GF	IP	BFP	H	R	ER	HR	SH	SF	HB	TBB	IBB	SO	WP	Bk	W	L	Pct	Sh	Sv-Op	Hld	ERC	ERA
2014 Gwnntt*	AAA	2	2	0	0	1.2	8	1	2	2	1	0	0	0	1	0	5	1	0	0	1	.000	0	0- -	-	5.00	10.80
2010 LAA	AL	16	0	0	5	15.1	65	13	4	4	1	0	0	0	7	0	23	1	1	0	1	.000	0	1-1	6	3.21	2.35
2011 LAA	AL	62	0	0	42	60.1	253	49	22	20	3	4	2	1	26	3	67	6	0	5	5	.500	0	32-42	5	2.82	2.98
2012 LAA	AL	45	0	0	20	39.0	172	35	15	15	3	0	1	0	18	1	48	7	0	3	2	.600	0	1-2	8	3.42	3.46
2013 Atl	NL	50	0	0	9	47.0	193	39	19	18	4	1	0	1	14	4	54	6	0	4	3	.571	0	1-3	14	2.63	3.45
2014 Atl	NL	58	0	0	8	50.0	205	33	17	16	2	0	1	0	27	1	62	9	0	0	2	.000	0	3-5	20	2.41	2.88
Postseason		2	0	0	0	2.2	13	3	4	4	0	0	0	1	1	0	3	0	0	0	0	-	0	0-0	0	5.24	13.50
5 ML YEARS		231	0	0	84	211.2	888	169	77	73	13	5	4	2	92	9	254	29	1	12	13	.480	0	38-53	50	2.82	3.10

Christian Walker

Bats: R Throws: R Pos: 1B-6   Ht: 6'0" Wt: 220 Born: 3/28/1991 Age: 24

						BATTING														RUNNING			AVERAGES			
Year Team	Lg	G	AB	H	2B	3B	HR	(Hm	Rd)	TB	R	RBI	RC	TBB	IBB	SO	HBP	SH	SF	SB	CS	GDP	Avg	OBP	Slg	OPS
2012 Abrdn	A-	22	81	23	5	0	2	(-	-)	34	12	9	13	10	0	14	2	0	0	2	1	1	.284	.376	.420	.796
2013 Dlmrva	A	31	116	41	5	0	3	(-	-)	55	19	20	22	11	0	16	3	0	1	0	3	5	.353	.420	.474	.894
2013 Frdrck	A+	55	215	62	17	0	8	(-	-)	103	25	35	36	17	0	41	3	0	4	2	0	4	.288	.343	.479	.822
2013 Bowie	AA	17	62	15	5	0	0	(-	-)	20	7	1	6	6	0	10	1	0	0	0	0	1	.242	.319	.323	.641
2014 Bowie	AA	95	366	110	15	2	20	(-	-)	189	58	77	70	38	3	83	3	0	4	2	1	6	.301	.367	.516	.884
2014 Norfolk	AAA	44	166	43	10	0	6	(-	-)	71	15	19	25	18	1	49	2	0	2	0	0	4	.259	.335	.428	.763
2014 Bal	AL	6	18	3	1	0	1	(1	0)	7	1	1	0	1	0	9	0	0	0	0	0	0	.167	.211	.389	.599

Neil Walker

Bats: B Throws: R Pos: 2B-135;PH-3   Ht: 6'3" Wt: 210 Born: 9/10/1985 Age: 29

						BATTING														RUNNING			AVERAGES			
Year Team	Lg	G	AB	H	2B	3B	HR	(Hm	Rd)	TB	R	RBI	RC	TBB	IBB	SO	HBP	SH	SF	SB	CS	GDP	Avg	OBP	Slg	OPS
2014 Bradtn*	A+	4	1	0	0	0	0	(-	-)	1	1	0	0	1	0	1	0	0	0	0	0	0	.250	.400	.250	.650
2009 Pit	NL	17	36	7	1	0	0	(0	0)	8	5	0	2	4	0	11	0	0	0	1	0	1	.194	.275	.222	.497
2010 Pit	NL	110	426	126	29	3	12	(5	7)	197	57	66	66	34	1	83	3	2	4	2	3	4	.296	.349	.462	.811
2011 Pit	NL	159	596	163	36	4	12	(4	8)	243	76	83	77	54	5	112	4	0	8	9	6	15	.273	.334	.408	.742
2012 Pit	NL	129	472	132	27	0	14	(7	7)	201	62	69	72	47	1	104	2	1	8	7	5	11	.280	.342	.426	.768
2013 Pit	NL	133	478	120	24	4	16	(8	8)	200	62	53	62	50	4	85	15	5	3	1	2	14	.251	.339	.418	.757
2014 Pit	NL	137	512	139	25	3	23	(10	13)	239	74	76	72	45	2	88	11	1	2	2	2	12	.271	.342	.467	.809
Postseason		6	24	2	1	0	0	(0	0)	3	1	1	1	2	0	5	0	0	0	0	0	0	.083	.154	.125	.279
6 ML YEARS		685	2520	687	142	14	77	(34	43)	1088	336	347	351	234	13	483	35	9	25	22	18	57	.273	.340	.432	.771

Taijuan Walker

Pitches: R Bats: R Pos: SP-5; RP-3   Ht: 6'4" Wt: 230 Born: 8/13/1992 Age: 22
TIE-wahn

			HOW MUCH HE PITCHED						WHAT HE GAVE UP									THE RESULTS							
Year Team	Lg	G	GS	CG	GF	IP	BFP	H	R	ER	HR	SH	SF	HB	TBB	IBB	SO	WP	Bk	W	L	Pct	Sh	Sv-Op	Hld	ERC	ERA
2010 Ms	R	4	0	0	0	7.0	27	2	3	1	0	0	0	1	3	0	9	3	0	1	1	.500	0	0- -	-	0.96	1.29
2011 Clinton	A	18	18	1	0	96.2	384	69	33	31	4	0	1	3	39	0	113	6	2	6	5	.545	0	0- -	-	2.41	2.89
2012 Jacksn	AA	25	25	0	0	126.2	550	124	70	66	12	4	3	12	50	0	118	5	0	7	10	.412	0	0- -	-	4.31	4.69
2013 Jacksn	AA	14	14	0	0	84.0	339	58	31	23	6	3	2	6	30	1	96	4	0	4	7	.364	0	0- -	-	2.38	2.46
2013 Tacom	AAA	11	11	0	0	57.1	246	54	25	23	5	0	0	2	27	0	64	2	0	5	3	.625	0	0- -	-	4.14	3.61
2014 Hi Dsrt	A+	1	1	0	0	4.1	18	4	2	1	0	0	0	0	1	0	7	0	0	0	0	-	0	0- -	-	2.34	2.08

Year	Team	Lg	G	GS	CG	GF	IP	BFP	H	R	ER	HR	SH	SF	HB	TBB	IBB	SO	WP	Bk	W	L	Pct	Sh	Sv-Op	Hld	ERC	ERA
2014	Jacksn	AA	1	1	0	0	5.0	19	3	0	0	0	0	0	0	1	0	10	1	0	1	0	1.000	0	0--	-	1.11	0.00
2014	Tacom	AAA	14	14	1	0	73.0	315	68	40	39	13	2	1	7	25	0	74	1	0	6	4	.600	1	0--	-	4.36	4.81
2013	Sea	AL	3	3	0	0	15.0	60	11	7	6	0	0	2	0	4	0	12	0	0	1	0	1.000	0	0-0	0	1.63	3.60
2014	Sea	AL	8	5	1	2	38.0	160	31	12	11	2	0	0	3	18	1	34	2	1	2	3	.400	0	0-0	0	3.34	2.61
	2 ML YEARS		11	8	1	2	53.0	220	42	19	17	2	0	2	3	22	1	46	2	1	3	3	.500	0	0-0	0	2.81	2.89

Josh Wall

Pitches: R **Bats:** R **Pos:** RP-2 **Ht:** 6'6" **Wt:** 215 **Born:** 1/21/1987 **Age:** 28

Year	Team	Lg	G	GS	CG	GF	IP	BFP	H	R	ER	HR	SH	SF	HB	TBB	IBB	SO	WP	Bk	W	L	Pct	Sh	Sv-Op	Hld	ERC	ERA
2014	Salt Lk*	AAA	8	0	0	3	10.2	47	11	7	5	0	0	0	0	5	0	11	1	0	0	0	-	0	1--	-	3.77	4.22
2014	Indy*	AAA	28	0	0	13	34.0	151	35	15	11	2	3	0	1	14	2	35	6	0	0	3	.000	0	3--	-	3.93	2.91
2012	LAD	NL	7	0	0	6	5.2	21	3	3	3	1	0	0	1	1	0	4	2	0	1	0	1.000	0	0-0	0	2.05	4.76
2013	LAD	NL	6	0	0	4	7.0	44	17	14	14	2	2	1	0	6	3	7	0	0	0	1	.000	0	0-0	0	16.61	18.00
2014	LAA	AL	2	0	0	1	1.0	11	5	6	6	0	0	1	0	3	0	0	0	0	0	0	-	0	0-0	0	46.99	54.00
	3 ML YEARS		15	0	0	11	13.2	76	25	23	23	3	2	2	1	10	3	11	2	0	1	1	.500	0	0-0	0	11.83	15.15

Brett Wallace

Bats: L **Throws:** R **Pos:** 1B **Ht:** 6'2" **Wt:** 235 **Born:** 8/26/1986 **Age:** 28

Year	Team	Lg	G	AB	H	2B	3B	HR	(Hm	Rd)	TB	R	RBI	RC	TBB	IBB	SO	HBP	SH	SF	SB	CS	GDP	Avg	OBP	Slg	OPS
2014	Norfolk*	AAA	90	339	90	12	0	10	(-	-)	132	50	35	45	29	4	98	4	0	2	0	1	7	.265	.329	.389	.718
2014	Buffalo*	AAA	38	133	43	5	0	7	(-	-)	69	12	23	27	15	1	33	3	0	0	0	0	3	.323	.404	.519	.923
2010	Hou	NL	51	144	32	6	1	2	(-	-)	46	14	13	10	8	3	50	7	0	0	0	0	3	.222	.296	.319	.615
2011	Hou	NL	115	336	87	22	0	5	(2	3)	124	37	29	31	36	4	91	3	1	2	1	1	12	.259	.334	.369	.703
2012	Hou	NL	66	229	58	10	1	9	(1	8)	97	24	24	27	18	1	73	6	0	1	0	0	2	.253	.323	.424	.746
2013	Hou	AL	79	262	58	14	1	13	(7	6)	113	35	36	34	18	0	104	5	0	0	1	1	5	.221	.284	.431	.716
	4 ML YEARS		311	971	235	52	3	29	(11	18)	380	110	102	102	80	8	318	21	1	3	2	2	22	.242	.313	.391	.704

Zach Walters

Bats: B **Throws:** R **Pos:** PH-26;DH-20;LF-6;2B-5;3B-3;SS-3;RF-2;PR-2 **Ht:** 6'2" **Wt:** 210 **Born:** 9/5/1989 **Age:** 25

Year	Team	Lg	G	AB	H	2B	3B	HR	(Hm	Rd)	TB	R	RBI	RC	TBB	IBB	SO	HBP	SH	SF	SB	CS	GDP	Avg	OBP	Slg	OPS
2010	Yakima	A-	69	275	83	18	4	4	(-	-)	121	44	43	42	16	1	59	1	1	4	14	4	3	.302	.338	.440	.778
2011	Sbend	A	97	361	109	27	6	9	(-	-)	175	69	56	66	42	1	96	3	3	3	12	10	4	.302	.377	.485	.861
2011	Ptomc	A+	30	116	34	7	1	0	(-	-)	43	15	11	15	8	0	33	0	1	1	7	1	0	.293	.336	.371	.707
2012	Ptomc	A+	54	193	52	8	1	5	(-	-)	77	24	24	24	10	1	43	1	0	3	6	3	2	.269	.304	.399	.703
2012	Hrsbrg	AA	43	164	48	11	4	6	(-	-)	85	23	19	27	8	1	38	0	0	0	1	0	5	.293	.326	.518	.844
2012	Syrcse	AAA	29	98	21	4	0	1	(-	-)	28	9	6	7	6	0	28	0	1	0	0	0	2	.214	.260	.286	.545
2013	Syrcse	AAA	134	487	123	32	5	29	(-	-)	252	69	77	73	20	2	134	5	3	6	4	3	7	.253	.286	.517	.803
2014	Syrcse	AAA	60	237	71	18	5	15	(-	-)	144	38	48	49	20	0	62	2	1	1	0	2	6	.300	.358	.608	.965
2014	Clmbs	AAA	7	31	12	4	0	2	(-	-)	22	4	8	7	0	0	5	0	0	0	0	0	0	.387	.387	.710	1.097
2013	Was	NL	8	8	3	0	1	0	(0	0)	5	2	1	2	1	0	0	0	0	0	0	0	1	.375	.444	.625	1.069
2014	2 Tms		62	127	23	3	0	10	(4	6)	56	16	17	10	9	0	48	1	0	0	0	0	0	.181	.241	.441	.682
	14 Was	NL	32	39	8	1	0	3	(0	3)	18	7	5	4	4	0	16	0	0	0	0	0	0	.205	.279	.462	.741
	14 Cle	AL	30	88	15	2	0	7	(4	3)	38	9	12	6	5	0	32	1	0	0	0	0	0	.170	.223	.432	.655
	2 ML YEARS		70	135	26	3	1	10	(4	6)	61	18	18	12	10	0	48	1	0	0	0	0	1	.193	.253	.452	.705

Wei-Chung Wang

way-CHUNG WONG

Pitches: L **Bats:** L **Pos:** RP-14 **Ht:** 6'1" **Wt:** 180 **Born:** 4/25/1992 **Age:** 23

Year	Team	Lg	G	GS	CG	GF	IP	BFP	H	R	ER	HR	SH	SF	HB	TBB	IBB	SO	WP	Bk	W	L	Pct	Sh	Sv-Op	Hld	ERC	ERA
2013	Pirates	R	12	11	0	1	47.1	185	37	18	17	2	1	2	1	4	0	42	3	0	1	3	.250	0	0--	-	1.59	3.23
2014	Brewrs	R	2	2	0	0	3.2	13	1	0	0	0	0	0	0	0	0	3	0	0	0	0	-	0	0--	-	0.16	0.00
2014	Wisc	A	3	3	0	0	13.2	56	13	6	5	0	0	0	4	4	0	10	1	0	0	2	.000	0	0--	-	2.70	3.20
2014	BrvdCt	A+	2	1	0	0	9.2	34	7	2	2	0	1	1	0	0	0	9	0	0	1	0	1.000	0	0--	-	1.12	1.86
2014	Mil	NL	14	0	0	10	17.1	92	30	23	21	6	0	0	1	8	1	13	1	0	0	0	-	0	0-0	0	11.03	10.90

Adam Warren

Pitches: R **Bats:** R **Pos:** RP-69 **Ht:** 6'1" **Wt:** 200 **Born:** 8/25/1987 **Age:** 27

Year	Team	Lg	G	GS	CG	GF	IP	BFP	H	R	ER	HR	SH	SF	HB	TBB	IBB	SO	WP	Bk	W	L	Pct	Sh	Sv-Op	Hld	ERC	ERA
2012	NYY	AL	1	1	0	0	2.1	17	8	6	6	2	0	0	0	2	0	1	0	0	0	0	-	0	0-0	0	33.34	23.14
2013	NYY	AL	34	2	0	17	77.0	331	80	29	29	10	0	0	2	30	2	64	3	0	3	2	.600	0	1-1	9	4.60	3.39
2014	NYY	AL	69	0	0	11	78.2	324	63	27	26	4	5	4	3	24	1	76	4	0	3	6	.333	0	3-6	23	2.45	2.97
	3 ML YEARS		104	3	0	28	158.0	672	151	62	61	16	5	4	5	56	3	141	7	0	6	8	.429	0	4-7	24	3.76	3.47

Logan Watkins

Bats: L **Throws:** R **Pos:** 2B-16;PH-13;RF-2;DH-1   **Ht:** 5'11" **Wt:** 195 **Born:** 8/29/1989 **Age:** 25

Year	Team	Lg	G	AB	H	2B	3B	HR	(Hm	Rd)	TB	R	RBI	RC	TBB	IBB	SO	HBP	SH	SF	SB	CS	GDP	Avg	OBP	Slg	OPS
2010	Peoria	A	118	440	115	15	8	1	(-	-)	149	69	30	58	58	0	97	3	18	1	19	10	5	.261	.351	.339	.689
2011	Dytona	A+	125	441	124	15	12	5	(-	-)	178	70	45	44	44	0	97	7	5	5	21	5	0	.281	.352	.404	.756
2012	Tenn	AA	133	488	137	20	11	9	(-	-)	206	93	52	88	76	0	97	7	14	3	28	7	7	.281	.383	.422	.805
2013	Iowa	AAA	107	412	100	18	7	8	(-	-)	156	51	26	54	52	1	98	4	3	1	10	9	3	.243	.333	.379	.711
2014	Iowa	AAA	103	324	83	21	1	4	(-	-)	118	59	38	44	33	1	77	2	7	2	23	4	5	.256	.327	.364	.691
2013	ChC	NL	27	38	8	1	0	0	(0	0)	9	2	0	3	3	0	14	0	1	0	0	0	0	.211	.268	.237	.505
2014	ChC	NL	31	65	16	3	0	1	(0	1)	22	10	6	6	1	1	16	1	1	0	1	0	0	.246	.269	.338	.607
	2 ML YEARS		58	103	24	4	0	1	(0	1)	31	12	6	9	4	1	30	1	2	0	1	0	0	.233	.269	.301	.569

Tony Watson

Pitches: L **Bats:** L **Pos:** RP-78   **Ht:** 6'4" **Wt:** 225 **Born:** 5/30/1985 **Age:** 30

Year	Team	Lg	G	GS	CG	GF	IP	BFP	H	R	ER	HR	SH	SF	HB	TBB	IBB	SO	WP	Bk	W	L	Pct	Sh	Sv-Op	Hld	ERC	ERA
2011	Pit	NL	43	0	0	6	41.0	174	34	18	18	6	2	1	1	20	4	37	0	0	2	2	.500	0	0-1	10	3.75	3.95
2012	Pit	NL	68	0	0	10	53.1	215	37	21	20	5	2	2	1	23	1	53	1	0	5	2	.714	0	0-2	16	2.62	3.38
2013	Pit	NL	67	0	0	14	71.2	280	51	19	19	5	3	1	6	12	1	54	2	0	3	1	.750	0	2-4	22	1.88	2.39
2014	Pit	NL	78	0	0	3	77.1	305	64	16	14	5	5	3	6	15	0	81	0	0	10	2	.833	0	2-9	34	2.54	1.63
	Postseason		4	0	0	0	4.0	17	4	1	1	1	0	0	0	1	0	1	0	0	0	0	-	0	0-0	1	4.38	2.25
	4 ML YEARS		256	0	0	33	243.1	974	186	74	71	21	12	7	14	70	6	225	3	0	20	7	.741	0	4-16	82	2.54	2.63

Jered Weaver

Pitches: R **Bats:** R **Pos:** SP-34   **Ht:** 6'7" **Wt:** 210 **Born:** 10/4/1982 **Age:** 32

Year	Team	Lg	G	GS	CG	GF	IP	BFP	H	R	ER	HR	SH	SF	HB	TBB	IBB	SO	WP	Bk	W	L	Pct	Sh	Sv-Op	Hld	ERC	ERA
2006	LAA	AL	19	19	0	0	123.0	490	94	36	35	15	2	2	3	33	1	105	2	0	11	2	.846	0	0-0	0	2.57	2.56
2007	LAA	AL	28	28	0	0	161.0	695	178	77	70	17	5	5	2	45	3	115	4	0	13	7	.650	0	0-0	0	4.24	3.91
2008	LAA	AL	30	30	0	0	176.2	745	173	88	85	20	1	4	6	54	4	152	3	0	11	10	.524	0	0-0	0	3.80	4.33
2009	LAA	AL	33	33	4	0	211.0	882	196	91	88	26	6	8	4	66	3	174	3	0	16	8	.667	2	0-0	0	3.56	3.75
2010	LAA	AL	34	34	0	0	224.1	905	187	83	75	23	2	5	0	54	0	233	7	1	13	12	.520	0	0-0	0	2.59	3.01
2011	LAA	AL	33	33	4	0	235.2	926	182	65	63	20	5	5	3	56	0	198	8	0	18	8	.692	2	0-0	0	2.27	2.41
2012	LAA	AL	30	30	3	0	188.2	739	147	63	59	20	0	4	4	45	0	142	2	0	20	5	.800	2	0-0	0	2.48	2.81
2013	LAA	AL	24	24	0	0	154.1	634	139	58	56	17	1	3	7	37	0	117	2	0	11	8	.579	0	0-0	0	3.17	3.27
2014	LAA	AL	34	34	1	0	213.1	888	193	87	85	27	5	4	6	65	1	169	3	0	18	9	.667	0	0-0	0	3.46	3.59
	Postseason		6	3	0	2	20.2	83	12	6	6	5	0	0	0	10	0	22	0	0	2	1	.667	0	0-0	1	3.04	2.61
	9 ML YEARS		265	265	12	0	1688.0	6904	1489	648	616	185	27	40	35	455	12	1405	34	1	131	69	.655	6	0-0	0	3.08	3.28

Daniel Webb

Pitches: R **Bats:** R **Pos:** RP-57   **Ht:** 6'3" **Wt:** 215 **Born:** 8/18/1989 **Age:** 25

Year	Team	Lg	G	GS	CG	GF	IP	BFP	H	R	ER	HR	SH	SF	HB	TBB	IBB	SO	WP	Bk	W	L	Pct	Sh	Sv-Op	Hld	ERC	ERA
2010	Auburn	A-	13	13	0	0	56.2	270	69	43	33	4	4	0	9	26	0	39	2	1	0	6	.000	0	0- -	-	5.95	5.24
2010	Lnsng	A	2	2	0	0	11.2	50	8	7	3	0	1	1	1	6	0	4	2	0	1	1	.500	0	0- -	-	2.42	2.31
2011	Lnsng	A	18	12	0	3	66.0	299	80	53	41	7	2	3	6	24	0	51	3	1	4	5	.444	0	2- -	-	5.62	5.59
2011	B Jays	R	1	0	0	1	1.1	6	2	0	0	0	0	0	0	0	0	0	1	0	0	0	-	0	0- -	-	4.47	0.00
2012	Knapol	A	31	4	0	12	62.0	287	73	51	40	2	5	3	3	27	0	50	7	0	1	8	.111	0	3- -	-	4.82	5.81
2013	WinSa	A+	8	0	0	4	15.0	60	10	2	0	0	0	0	0	5	0	19	1	1	1	0	1.000	0	2- -	-	1.57	0.00
2013	Brham	AA	13	0	0	10	20.1	78	11	4	4	0	1	0	1	5	0	21	1	0	0	0	-	0	4- -	-	1.13	1.77
2013	Charltt	AAA	21	0	0	14	27.1	125	24	15	9	1	2	0	0	17	0	38	5	0	1	1	.500	0	4- -	-	3.63	2.96
2013	CWS	AL	9	0	0	4	11.1	46	9	4	4	0	0	1	0	4	0	10	1	0	0	0	-	0	0-0	1	2.20	3.18
2014	CWS	AL	57	0	0	26	67.2	296	59	31	30	6	1	3	2	42	5	58	13	0	6	5	.545	0	0-2	4	4.18	3.99
	2 ML YEARS		66	0	0	30	79.0	342	68	35	34	6	1	4	2	46	5	68	14	0	6	5	.545	0	0-2	5	3.87	3.87

Ryan Webb

Pitches: R **Bats:** R **Pos:** RP-51   **Ht:** 6'6" **Wt:** 245 **Born:** 2/5/1986 **Age:** 29

Year	Team	Lg	G	GS	CG	GF	IP	BFP	H	R	ER	HR	SH	SF	HB	TBB	IBB	SO	WP	Bk	W	L	Pct	Sh	Sv-Op	Hld	ERC	ERA
2014	Norfolk*	AAA	11	0	0	3	11.1	50	13	8	6	1	0	0	0	2	0	10	1	0	0	2	.000	0	0- -	-	3.75	4.76
2009	SD	NL	28	0	0	9	25.2	117	27	14	11	3	2	1	1	11	1	19	4	0	2	1	.667	0	0-0	6	4.54	3.86
2010	SD	NL	54	0	0	15	59.0	253	64	21	19	1	1	1	1	19	5	44	2	1	3	1	.750	0	0-2	9	3.61	2.90
2011	Fla	NL	53	0	0	10	50.2	214	48	20	18	2	3	1	2	20	5	31	1	1	2	4	.333	0	0-4	8	3.39	3.20
2012	Mia	NL	65	0	0	21	60.1	270	72	30	27	2	0	2	4	20	8	44	0	0	4	3	.571	0	0-0	10	4.44	4.03
2013	Mia	NL	66	0	0	19	80.1	332	70	30	26	5	11	5	2	27	5	54	4	0	2	6	.250	0	0-3	14	2.91	2.91
2014	Bal	AL	51	0	0	13	49.1	207	50	21	21	2	1	0	1	12	2	37	1	1	3	3	.500	0	0-0	11	3.15	3.83
	6 ML YEARS		317	0	0	87	325.1	1393	331	136	122	15	18	10	11	109	26	229	12	3	16	18	.471	0	0-9	48	3.55	3.38

Allen Webster

Pitches: R Bats: R Pos: SP-11 Ht: 6'2" Wt: 190 Born: 2/10/1990 Age: 25

			HOW MUCH HE PITCHED				WHAT HE GAVE UP													THE RESULTS						
Year Team	Lg	G	GS	CG	GF	IP	BFP	H	R	ER	HR	SH	SF	HB	TBB	IBB	SO	WP	Bk	W	L	Pct	Sh	Sv-Op	Hld	ERC	ERA
2010 Gt Lks	A	26	23	0	1	131.1	568	119	55	42	6	4	4	10	53	1	114	5	1	12	9	.571	0	0- -	-	3.44	2.88
2011 RCuca	A+	9	9	0	0	54.0	228	46	18	14	2	0	1	4	21	0	62	1	1	5	2	.714	0	0- -	-	3.09	2.33
2011 Chatt	AA	18	17	1	0	91.0	407	101	53	51	7	9	1	8	36	2	73	5	0	6	3	.667	1	0- -	-	4.85	5.04
2012 Chatt	AA	27	22	0	2	121.2	546	120	63	48	1	9	1	17	57	2	117	10	1	6	8	.429	0	0- -	-	4.09	3.55
2012 Portlnd	AA	2	2	0	0	9.0	46	13	8	8	1	0	0	2	4	0	12	1	0	1	0	1.000	0	0- -	-	7.83	8.00
2013 Pwtckt	AAA	21	21	0	0	105.0	436	71	45	42	9	1	2	16	43	0	116	9	1	8	4	.667	0	0- -	-	2.87	3.60
2014 Pwtckt	AAA	21	20	1	1	122.0	509	106	45	41	9	1	2	5	44	0	100	6	1	4	4	.500	0	1- -	-	3.21	3.02
2013 Bos	AL	8	7	0	1	30.1	145	37	30	29	7	0	5	2	18	0	23	1	0	1	2	.333	0	0-0	0	7.56	8.60
2014 Bos	AL	11	11	0	0	59.0	259	58	35	33	3	0	4	7	28	0	36	2	0	5	3	.625	0	0-0	0	4.46	5.03
2 ML YEARS		19	18	0	1	89.1	404	95	65	62	10	0	9	9	46	0	59	3	0	6	5	.545	0	0-0	0	5.48	6.25

Jemile Weeks

Bats: B Throws: R Pos: 2B-7;PR-4;SS-3;DH-2;PH-2   jah-MYLE   Ht: 5'9" Wt: 165 Born: 1/26/1987 Age: 28

								BATTING												RUNNING			AVERAGES			
Year Team	Lg	G	AB	H	2B	3B	HR	(Hm	Rd)	TB	R	RBI	RC	TBB	IBB	SO	HBP	SH	SF	SB	CS	GDP	Avg	OBP	Slg	OPS
2014 Norfolk*	AAA	63	207	58	12	4	1	(-	-)	81	29	19	36	37	0	30	3	7	3	8	4	3	.280	.392	.391	.783
2014 Abrdn*	A-	3	11	4	1	0	0	(-	-)	5	1	0	2	2	0	1	0	0	0	1	0	0	.364	.462	.455	.916
2014 Orioles*	R	5	16	9	3	1	0	(-	-)	14	5	3	7	3	0	3	0	0	0	1	0	0	.563	.632	.875	1.507
2011 Oak	AL	97	406	123	26	8	2	(1	1)	171	50	36	64	21	1	62	4	2	4	22	11	3	.303	.340	.421	.761
2012 Oak	AL	118	444	98	15	8	2	(1	1)	135	54	20	42	50	0	70	5	9	3	16	5	5	.221	.305	.304	.609
2013 Oak	AL	8	9	1	0	0	0	(0	0)	1	3	0	0	0	0	5	0	0	0	0	0	0	.111	.111	.111	.222
2014 2 Tms	AL	17	37	11	3	1	0	(0	0)	16	8	3	6	4	0	2	1	2	1	2	0	1	.297	.372	.432	.805
14 Bal	AL	3	11	3	0	1	0	(0	0)	5	2	0	1	0	0	0	0	2	0	0	0	1	.273	.273	.455	.727
14 Bos	AL	14	26	8	3	0	0	(0	0)	11	6	3	5	4	0	2	1	0	1	2	0	0	.308	.406	.423	.829
4 ML YEARS		240	896	233	44	17	4	(2	2)	323	115	59	112	75	1	139	10	13	8	40	16	9	.260	.322	.360	.682

Rickie Weeks

Bats: R Throws: R Pos: PH-67;2B-62;DH-2   Ht: 5'10" Wt: 220 Born: 9/13/1982 Age: 32

								BATTING												RUNNING			AVERAGES			
Year Team	Lg	G	AB	H	2B	3B	HR	(Hm	Rd)	TB	R	RBI	RC	TBB	IBB	SO	HBP	SH	SF	SB	CS	GDP	Avg	OBP	Slg	OPS
2003 Mil	NL	7	12	2	1	0	0	(0	0)	3	1	0	0	1	0	6	1	0	0	0	0	0	.167	.286	.250	.536
2005 Mil	NL	96	360	86	13	2	13	(8	5)	142	56	42	49	40	2	96	11	2	1	15	2	11	.239	.333	.394	.727
2006 Mil	NL	95	359	100	15	3	8	(6	2)	145	73	34	53	30	1	92	19	2	3	19	5	6	.279	.363	.404	.766
2007 Mil	NL	118	409	96	21	6	16	(5	11)	177	87	36	65	78	5	116	14	3	2	25	2	3	.235	.374	.433	.807
2008 Mil	NL	129	475	111	22	7	14	(3	11)	189	89	46	67	66	0	115	14	1	4	19	5	5	.234	.342	.398	.740
2009 Mil	NL	37	147	40	5	2	9	(7	2)	76	28	24	27	12	0	39	3	0	0	2	2	1	.272	.340	.517	.857
2010 Mil	NL	160	651	175	32	4	29	(16	13)	302	112	83	110	76	0	184	25	0	2	11	4	5	.269	.366	.464	.830
2011 Mil	NL	118	453	122	26	2	20	(10	10)	212	77	49	68	50	3	107	8	1	3	9	2	6	.269	.350	.468	.818
2012 Mil	NL	157	588	135	29	4	21	(10	11)	235	85	63	77	74	2	169	13	0	2	16	3	9	.230	.328	.400	.728
2013 Mil	NL	104	350	73	20	1	10	(6	4)	125	40	24	28	40	0	105	9	0	0	7	3	13	.209	.306	.357	.663
2014 Mil	NL	121	252	69	19	1	8	(4	4)	114	36	29	38	25	0	73	8	0	1	3	4	7	.274	.357	.452	.809
Postseason		14	45	6	1	1	2	(2	0)	15	5	4	2	2	0	8	2	0	0	0	0	0	.133	.204	.333	.537
11 ML YEARS		1142	4056	1009	203	32	148	(75	73)	1720	684	430	582	492	13	1102	125	9	18	126	32	66	.249	.347	.424	.771

Jayson Werth

Bats: R Throws: R Pos: RF-139;DH-5;PH-5   Ht: 6'5" Wt: 240 Born: 5/20/1979 Age: 36

								BATTING												RUNNING			AVERAGES			
Year Team	Lg	G	AB	H	2B	3B	HR	(Hm	Rd)	TB	R	RBI	RC	TBB	IBB	SO	HBP	SH	SF	SB	CS	GDP	Avg	OBP	Slg	OPS
2002 Tor	AL	15	46	12	2	1	0	(0	0)	16	4	6	5	6	0	11	0	0	1	1	0	4	.261	.340	.348	.687
2003 Tor	AL	26	48	10	4	0	2	(0	2)	20	7	10	6	3	0	22	0	0	0	1	0	0	.208	.255	.417	.672
2004 LAD	NL	89	290	76	11	3	16	(11	5)	141	56	47	47	30	0	85	4	1	4	4	1	1	.262	.338	.486	.825
2005 LAD	NL	102	337	79	22	2	7	(1	6)	126	46	43	44	48	2	114	6	1	3	11	2	10	.234	.338	.374	.711
2007 Phi	NL	94	255	76	11	3	8	(1	7)	117	43	49	57	44	1	73	2	2	1	7	1	0	.298	.404	.459	.863
2008 Phi	NL	134	418	114	16	3	24	(11	13)	208	73	67	74	57	1	119	4	0	3	20	1	2	.273	.363	.498	.861
2009 Phi	NL	159	571	153	26	1	36	(21	15)	289	98	99	107	91	8	156	8	0	6	20	3	11	.268	.373	.506	.879
2010 Phi	NL	156	554	164	46	2	27	(18	9)	295	106	85	91	82	6	147	7	0	9	13	3	11	.296	.388	.532	.921
2011 Was	NL	150	561	130	26	1	20	(10	10)	218	69	58	74	74	5	160	10	0	4	19	3	10	.232	.330	.389	.718
2012 Was	NL	81	300	90	21	3	5	(4	1)	132	42	31	48	42	2	57	1	0	1	8	2	3	.300	.387	.440	.827
2013 Was	NL	129	462	147	24	0	25	(13	12)	246	84	82	94	60	3	101	5	0	5	10	1	9	.318	.398	.532	.931
2014 Was	NL	147	534	156	37	1	16	(5	11)	243	85	82	104	83	3	113	9	0	3	9	1	9	.292	.394	.455	.849
Postseason		49	174	46	10	2	14	(10	4)	102	33	27	30	30	4	58	1	0	1	5	0	3	.264	.374	.586	.960
12 ML YEARS		1282	4376	1207	246	20	186	(95	91)	2051	713	659	751	620	31	1158	56	4	37	123	18	70	.276	.370	.469	.839

Matt West

Pitches: R Bats: R Pos: RP-3   Ht: 6'1" Wt: 200 Born: 11/21/1988 Age: 26

			HOW MUCH HE PITCHED				WHAT HE GAVE UP													THE RESULTS						
Year Team	Lg	G	GS	CG	GF	IP	BFP	H	R	ER	HR	SH	SF	HB	TBB	IBB	SO	WP	Bk	W	L	Pct	Sh	Sv-Op	Hld	ERC	ERA
2011 Spkane	A-	23	0	0	21	26.0	100	23	9	9	3	1	0	3	1	0	35	2	0	1	2	.333	0	9- -	-	2.74	3.12
2011 MrtlBh	A+	1	0	0	0	1.0	4	1	0	0	0	0	0	0	0	0	0	0	0	0	0	-	0	0- -	-	1.95	0.00
2012 MrtlBh	A+	17	0	0	6	20.1	94	18	16	15	1	1	0	2	16	0	14	2	1	0	3	.000	0	0- -	-	4.97	6.64
2013 Rngrs	R	1	1	0	0	0.0	4	2	2	2	0	0	0	0	2	0	0	2	0	0	1	.000	0	0- -	-		
2014 Frisco	AA	8	0	0	4	13.1	48	7	1	1	1	0	0	1	2	0	10	3	0	2	0	1.000	0	3- -	-	1.26	0.68
2014 RdRck	AAA	33	1	0	7	43.1	199	53	25	20	4	0	1	5	16	1	54	4	0	3	3	.500	0	1- -	-	5.63	4.15
2014 Tex	AL	3	0	0	1	4.0	18	6	3	3	0	0	0	0	1	0	3	0	0	0	0	-	0	0-0	0	5.79	6.75

Ryan Wheeler

Bats: L Throws: R Pos: PH-17;3B-12;1B-5   Ht: 6'3" Wt: 235 Born: 7/10/1988 Age: 26

							BATTING														RUNNING			AVERAGES			
Year	Team	Lg	G	AB	H	2B	3B	HR	(Hm	Rd)	TB	R	RBI	RC	TBB	IBB	SO	HBP	SH	SF	SB	CS	GDP	Avg	OBP	Slg	OPS
2014	ColSpr*	AAA	59	210	51	9	0	4	(-	-)	72	18	20	21	15	0	43	1	1	3	0	2	8	.243	.293	.343	.635
2014	Salt Lk*	AAA	25	92	30	1	0	2	(-	-)	37	13	15	14	8	1	19	0	0	2	0	0	2	.326	.373	.402	.775
2012	Ari	NL	50	109	26	6	1	1	(0	1)	37	11	10	7	9	0	22	0	0	1	1	0	4	.239	.294	.339	.634
2013	Col	NL	28	41	9	2	0	0	(0	0)	11	1	7	4	1	0	10	0	0	0	0	0	1	.220	.238	.268	.506
2014	Col	NL	31	56	13	2	0	2	(1	1)	21	6	13	7	5	0	12	0	0	3	0	0	1	.232	.281	.375	.656
	3 ML YEARS		109	206	48	10	1	3	(1	2)	69	18	30	18	15	0	44	0	0	4	1	0	6	.233	.280	.335	.615

Zack Wheeler

Pitches: R Bats: L Pos: SP-32   Ht: 6'4" Wt: 195 Born: 5/30/1990 Age: 25

			HOW MUCH HE PITCHED					WHAT HE GAVE UP											THE RESULTS						
Year	Team	Lg	G	GS	CG	GF	IP	BFP	H	R	ER	HR	SH	SF	HB	TBB	IBB	SO	WP	Bk	W	L	Pct	Sh	Sv-Op	Hld	ERC	ERA
2010	Augsta	A	21	13	0	2	58.2	262	47	27	26	0	1	0	7	38	0	70	13	2	3	3	.500	0	0- -	-	3.63	3.99
2011	SnJos	A+	16	16	0	0	88.0	385	74	44	39	7	2	2	4	47	1	98	6	0	7	5	.583	0	0- -	-	3.68	3.99
2011	StLuci	A+	6	6	0	0	27.0	110	26	6	6	0	0	0	2	5	0	31	3	0	2	2	.500	0	0- -	-	2.74	2.00
2012	Bnghtn	AA	19	19	1	0	116.0	474	92	46	42	2	2	8	11	43	0	117	6	1	10	6	.625	1	0- -	-	2.74	3.26
2012	Buffalo	AAA	6	6	1	0	33.0	134	23	13	12	2	3	2	1	16	0	31	2	0	2	2	.500	1	0- -	-	2.70	3.27
2013	LsVgs	AAA	13	13	0	0	68.2	291	61	35	30	9	1	2	2	27	0	73	1	0	4	2	.667	0	0- -	-	3.75	3.93
2013	NYM	NL	17	17	0	0	100.0	431	90	42	38	10	3	7	4	46	2	84	6	0	7	5	.583	0	0-0	0	3.88	3.42
2014	NYM	NL	32	32	1	0	185.1	794	167	84	73	14	5	3	11	79	3	187	9	0	11	11	.500	1	0-0	0	3.68	3.54
	2 ML YEARS		49	49	1	0	285.1	1225	257	126	111	24	8	10	15	125	5	271	15	0	18	16	.529	1	0-0	0	3.75	3.50

Zelous Wheeler

Bats: R Throws: R Pos: 3B-18;RF-6;PH-6;LF-2;DH-2   ZELL-iss   Ht: 5'10" Wt: 220 Born: 1/16/1987 Age: 28

							BATTING														RUNNING			AVERAGES			
Year	Team	Lg	G	AB	H	2B	3B	HR	(Hm	Rd)	TB	R	RBI	RC	TBB	IBB	SO	HBP	SH	SF	SB	CS	GDP	Avg	OBP	Slg	OPS
2010	Hntsvl	AA	135	480	132	22	2	11	(-	-)	191	76	65	80	70	3	77	15	1	3	8	4	14	.275	.382	.398	.780
2011	Nashv	AAA	17	51	14	3	1	1	(-	-)	22	7	6	9	9	1	8	0	1	0	0	0	2	.275	.383	.431	.815
2011	Hntsvl	AA	65	228	62	20	0	8	(-	-)	106	34	32	43	30	0	49	9	0	1	7	0	7	.272	.377	.465	.842
2012	Norfolk	AAA	14	52	12	2	0	1	(-	-)	17	6	3	5	5	1	8	1	1	0	0	1	3	.231	.310	.327	.637
2012	Bowie	AA	97	334	92	18	2	13	(-	-)	153	48	44	59	38	0	63	10	3	4	5	1	15	.275	.363	.458	.821
2013	Bowie	AA	24	87	26	5	0	1	(-	-)	34	11	11	15	15	0	15	0	0	0	3	0	1	.299	.402	.391	.793
2013	Norfolk	AAA	90	321	86	17	1	10	(-	-)	135	38	45	48	30	1	55	6	0	2	2	1	18	.268	.340	.421	.760
2014	S-WB	AAA	82	304	90	25	0	9	(-	-)	142	49	40	53	28	0	61	6	0	0	1	0	8	.296	.367	.467	.834
2014	NYY	AL	29	57	11	0	0	2	(0	2)	17	6	5	3	2	0	12	1	1	1	0	0	1	.193	.230	.298	.528

Kevin Whelan

Pitches: R Bats: R Pos: RP-1   WAY-lynn   Ht: 5'11" Wt: 205 Born: 1/8/1984 Age: 31

			HOW MUCH HE PITCHED					WHAT HE GAVE UP											THE RESULTS						
Year	Team	Lg	G	GS	CG	GF	IP	BFP	H	R	ER	HR	SH	SF	HB	TBB	IBB	SO	WP	Bk	W	L	Pct	Sh	Sv-Op	Hld	ERC	ERA
2010	S-WB	AAA	17	0	0	5	20.0	91	19	15	14	2	1	1	1	10	0	22	3	0	2	1	.667	0	1- -	-	4.23	6.30
2010	Trntn	AA	24	0	0	11	20.9	128	20	19	19	1	1	2	1	21	0	40	5	0	3	3	.500	0	3- -	-	3.18	5.83
2011	S-WB	AAA	45	0	0	38	52.1	206	38	16	16	5	1	4	0	14	0	54	9	0	2	3	.400	0	23- -	-	2.23	2.75
2012	S-WB	AAA	24	0	0	23	25.1	114	23	10	10	2	1	2	0	16	0	36	3	0	3	0	1.000	0	12- -	-	4.25	3.55
2013	Lsvlle	AAA	47	0	0	20	50.2	226	43	31	28	8	1	2	0	33	0	73	4	0	3	3	.500	0	6- -	-	4.58	4.97
2014	Toledo	AAA	41	0	0	36	43.1	180	30	13	13	0	1	0	0	21	1	54	5	0	2	3	.400	0	20- -	-	2.07	2.70
2011	NYY	AL	2	0	0	1	1.2	10	0	1	1	0	0	0	0	5	0	1	0	0	0	0	-	0	0-0	0	7.00	5.40
2014	Det	AL	1	0	0	0	1.1	9	3	2	2	2	0	0	0	2	0	1	1	0	0	0	-	0	0-0	0	34.53	13.50
	2 ML YEARS		3	0	0	1	3.0	19	3	3	3	2	0	0	0	7	0	2	1	0	0	0	-	0	0-0	0	18.64	9.00

Eli Whiteside

Bats: R Throws: R Pos: C-8   Ht: 6'2" Wt: 220 Born: 10/22/1979 Age: 35

							BATTING														RUNNING			AVERAGES			
Year	Team	Lg	G	AB	H	2B	3B	HR	(Hm	Rd)	TB	R	RBI	RC	TBB	IBB	SO	HBP	SH	SF	SB	CS	GDP	Avg	OBP	Slg	OPS
2014	Iowa*	AAA	63	206	44	13	0	6	(-	-)	75	14	21	23	18	1	50	5	0	1	0	0	6	.214	.291	.364	.655
2005	Bal	AL	9	12	3	0	0	0	(0	0)	3	1	1	0	0	0	2	0	0	0	0	0	1	.250	.250	.250	.500
2009	SF	NL	49	127	29	6	1	2	(1	1)	43	15	13	11	4	1	30	3	0	4	0	0	4	.228	.269	.339	.607
2010	SF	NL	56	126	30	6	1	4	(3	1)	50	19	10	9	8	0	35	3	3	0	1	2	4	.238	.299	.397	.696
2011	SF	NL	82	213	42	8	2	4	(3	1)	66	14	17	11	18	3	59	2	1	2	2	1	9	.197	.264	.310	.574
2012	SF	NL	12	11	1	0	0	0	(0	0)	2	3	2	1	1	0	4	1	0	1	0	0	0	.091	.214	.182	.396
2014	ChC	NL	8	25	3	1	0	0	(0	0)	4	0	2	0	0	0	8	0	0	1	1	0	0	.120	.115	.160	.275
	6 ML YEARS		216	514	108	22	4	10	(7	3)	168	52	45	32	31	4	138	9	4	4	4	3	18	.210	.265	.327	.592

Chase Whitley

Pitches: R Bats: R Pos: SP-12; RP-12   Ht: 6'3" Wt: 215 Born: 6/14/1989 Age: 26

			HOW MUCH HE PITCHED					WHAT HE GAVE UP											THE RESULTS						
Year	Team	Lg	G	GS	CG	GF	IP	BFP	H	R	ER	HR	SH	SF	HB	TBB	IBB	SO	WP	Bk	W	L	Pct	Sh	Sv-Op	Hld	ERC	ERA
2010	StIsInd	A-	28	0	0	26	34.1	132	18	8	5	0	1	0	1	15	1	44	2	0	4	2	.667	0	15- -	-	1.44	1.31
2010	Tampa	A+	2	0	0	0	3.0	11	1	1	1	1	0	0	1	0	0	6	0	0	0	0	-	0	0- -	-	1.69	3.00
2011	Tampa	A+	23	0	0	14	48.1	190	41	13	9	2	1	0	3	10	0	40	4	0	0	1	.000	0	6- -	-	2.51	1.68
2011	Trntn	AA	19	1	0	6	42.2	188	46	21	16	6	2	3	0	19	0	37	1	1	3	4	.429	0	1- -	-	5.03	3.38
2012	Trntn	AA	2	0	0	2	4.0	15	1	0	0	0	0	0	0	2	0	7	1	0	0	0	-	0	1- -	-	0.75	0.00

Year	Team	Lg	G	GS	CG	GF	IP	BFP	H	R	ER	HR	SH	SF	HB	TBB	IBB	SO	WP	Bk	W	L	Pct	Sh	Sv-Op	Hld	ERC	ERA
							HOW MUCH HE PITCHED					WHAT HE GAVE UP												THE RESULTS				
2012	S-WB	AAA	41	2	0	9	80.1	318	61	30	29	7	1	4	2	25	1	66	5	1	9	5	.643	0	1- -	-	2.53	3.25
2013	S-WB	AAA	29	5	0	6	67.2	277	61	24	23	1	3	4	0	21	0	62	7	0	3	2	.600	0	3- -	-	3.13	3.06
2014	S-WB	AAA	10	6	0	0	31.1	122	22	7	7	0	1	1	0	8	0	37	0	0	3	2	.600	0	0- -	-	1.54	2.01
2014	NYY	AL	24	12	0	3	75.2	330	94	44	44	10	1	2	4	18	0	60	2	0	4	3	.571	0	0-0	0	5.37	5.23

Joe Wieland

Pitches: R Bats: R Pos: SP-2; RP-2 WEE-land **Ht: 6'3" Wt: 210 Born: 1/21/1990 Age: 25**

Year	Team	Lg	G	GS	CG	GF	IP	BFP	H	R	ER	HR	SH	SF	HB	TBB	IBB	SO	WP	Bk	W	L	Pct	Sh	Sv-Op	Hld	ERC	ERA
							HOW MUCH HE PITCHED					WHAT HE GAVE UP												THE RESULTS				
2010	Hkry	A	15	15	2	0	89.0	357	84	36	33	4	2	2	3	15	0	71	1	0	7	4	.636	1	0- -	-	2.72	3.34
2010	Bkrsfld	A+	11	10	0	0	59.0	258	67	36	34	6	4	5	2	10	0	62	4	1	4	3	.571	0	0- -	-	3.93	5.19
2011	MrtlBh	A+	14	13	1	0	85.2	333	78	23	20	7	2	0	2	4	0	96	7	0	6	3	.667	1	0- -	-	2.29	2.10
2011	Frisco	AA	7	7	1	0	44.0	175	35	9	6	2	1	1	0	11	0	36	1	0	4	0	1.000	1	0- -	-	2.14	1.23
2011	SnAnt	AA	5	5	0	0	26.0	108	23	10	8	0	2	2	2	6	0	18	1	0	3	1	.750	0	0- -	-	2.44	2.77
2012	Tucsn	AAA	2	2	0	0	7.2	34	10	3	3	0	0	0	0	2	0	11	0	0	0	1	.000	0	0- -	-	4.53	3.52
2014	Padres	R	3	3	0	0	6.0	22	3	2	2	0	0	0	0	1	0	10	1	0	0	1	.000	0	0- -	-	0.80	3.00
2014	SnAnt	AA	2	2	0	0	9.0	34	8	3	2	1	0	0	0	1	0	6	1	0	0	1	.000	0	0- -	-	2.60	2.00
2014	ElPaso	AAA	4	4	0	0	23.2	96	22	9	9	1	1	2	0	4	0	20	0	0	2	1	.667	0	0- -	-	2.45	3.42
2012	SD	NL	5	5	0	0	27.2	119	26	16	14	5	1	2	1	9	2	24	1	0	0	4	.000	0	0-0	0	3.94	4.55
2014	SD	NL	4	2	0	0	11.1	54	16	9	9	3	0	1	0	5	0	8	0	1	1	0	1.000	0	0-0	0	8.09	7.15
	2 ML YEARS		9	7	0	0	39.0	173	42	25	23	8	1	3	1	14	2	32	1	1	1	4	.200	0	0-0	0	5.05	5.31

Matt Wieters

Bats: B Throws: R Pos: C-22;DH-4 WEE-ters **Ht: 6'5" Wt: 240 Born: 5/21/1986 Age: 29**

Year	Team	Lg	G	AB	H	2B	3B	HR	(Hm	Rd)	TB	R	RBI	RC	TBB	IBB	SO	HBP	SH	SF	SB	CS	GDP	Avg	OBP	Slg	OPS
								BATTING													RUNNING			AVERAGES			
2009	Bal	AL	96	354	102	15	1	9	(5	4)	146	35	43	43	28	2	86	1	0	2	0	0	11	.288	.340	.412	.753
2010	Bal	AL	130	446	111	22	1	11	(3	8)	168	37	55	47	47	7	94	2	0	7	1	0	13	.249	.319	.377	.695
2011	Bal	AL	139	500	131	28	0	22	(13	9)	225	72	68	76	48	3	84	2	0	1	1	0	16	.262	.328	.450	.778
2012	Bal	AL	144	526	131	27	1	23	(11	12)	229	67	83	73	60	4	112	4	0	3	3	0	17	.249	.329	.435	.764
2013	Bal	AL	148	523	123	29	0	22	(13	9)	218	59	79	65	43	5	104	0	1	12	2	0	7	.235	.287	.417	.704
2014	Bal	AL	26	104	32	5	0	5	(2	3)	52	13	18	17	6	0	19	0	0	2	0	1	1	.308	.339	.500	.839
	Postseason		6	24	3	1	0	0	(0	0)	4	2	0	0	2	0	4	0	0	0	0	0	0	.125	.192	.167	.359
	6 ML YEARS		683	2453	630	126	3	92	(47	45)	1038	283	346	321	232	21	499	9	1	27	6	2	65	.257	.320	.423	.743

Tom Wilhelmsen

Pitches: R Bats: R Pos: RP-55; SP-2 will-HELM-senn **Ht: 6'6" Wt: 220 Born: 12/16/1983 Age: 31**

Year	Team	Lg	G	GS	CG	GF	IP	BFP	H	R	ER	HR	SH	SF	HB	TBB	IBB	SO	WP	Bk	W	L	Pct	Sh	Sv-Op	Hld	ERC	ERA
							HOW MUCH HE PITCHED					WHAT HE GAVE UP												THE RESULTS				
2011	Sea	AL	25	0	0	10	32.2	136	25	13	12	2	0	2	2	13	0	30	6	1	2	0	1.000	0	0-0	3	2.78	3.31
2012	Sea	AL	73	0	0	48	79.1	326	59	24	22	5	1	2	2	29	3	87	3	0	4	3	.571	0	29-34	7	2.38	2.50
2013	Sea	AL	59	0	0	40	59.0	251	45	28	27	2	3	3	1	33	5	45	6	0	0	3	.000	0	24-29	2	2.87	4.12
2014	Sea	AL	57	2	0	18	79.1	317	47	23	20	6	1	3	2	36	6	72	4	0	3	2	.600	0	1-3	8	2.03	2.27
	4 ML YEARS		214	2	0	116	250.1	1030	176	87	81	15	5	10	7	111	14	234	19	1	9	8	.529	0	54-66	20	2.43	2.91

Andy Wilkins

Bats: L Throws: R Pos: 1B-13;DH-3;PH-1 **Ht: 6'1" Wt: 220 Born: 9/13/1988 Age: 26**

Year	Team	Lg	G	AB	H	2B	3B	HR	(Hm	Rd)	TB	R	RBI	RC	TBB	IBB	SO	HBP	SH	SF	SB	CS	GDP	Avg	OBP	Slg	OPS
								BATTING													RUNNING			AVERAGES			
2010	Gr Falls	R+	53	218	67	14	1	6	(-	-)	101	37	40	42	33	2	31	1	1	3	7	2	3	.307	.396	.463	.859
2011	WinSa	A+	134	434	137	33	0	23	(-	-)	239	72	89	85	56	0	91	0	3	4	2	2	11	.278	.349	.485	.834
2012	Brham	AA	116	435	104	28	1	17	(-	-)	185	68	69	65	63	2	94	1	0	3	6	4	5	.239	.335	.425	.760
2013	Brham	AA	67	243	70	16	0	10	(-	-)	116	37	49	47	38	2	58	2	0	2	3	0	5	.288	.386	.477	.863
2013	Charltt	AAA	58	215	57	13	0	7	(-	-)	91	25	30	29	14	1	52	2	0	3	2	1	1	.265	.312	.423	.735
2014	Charltt	AAA	127	491	144	38	1	30	(-	-)	274	79	85	91	34	5	91	1	0	3	0	1	8	.293	.338	.558	.896
2014	CWS	AL	17	43	6	2	0	0	(0	0)	8	2	2	0	2	0	22	0	0	0	0	0	1	.140	.178	.186	.364

Jackson Williams

Bats: R Throws: R Pos: C-7 **Ht: 5'11" Wt: 200 Born: 5/14/1986 Age: 29**

Year	Team	Lg	G	AB	H	2B	3B	HR	(Hm	Rd)	TB	R	RBI	RC	TBB	IBB	SO	HBP	SH	SF	SB	CS	GDP	Avg	OBP	Slg	OPS
								BATTING													RUNNING			AVERAGES			
2010	Rchmd	AA	60	193	37	9	1	2	(-	-)	54	17	16	19	29	1	54	7	6	1	0	1	6	.192	.317	.280	.597
2010	Fresno	AAA	42	124	28	7	0	3	(-	-)	44	16	15	16	15	1	33	5	0	2	1	1	6	.226	.329	.355	.684
2011	Fresno	AAA	56	125	23	3	0	1	(-	-)	29	13	12	8	17	1	36	2	1	2	0	2	3	.184	.288	.232	.520
2011	Rchmd	AA	18	53	11	2	0	3	(-	-)	22	8	9	6	5	0	9	1	0	0	0	0	0	.208	.288	.415	.703
2012	Fresno	AAA	86	295	73	15	1	11	(-	-)	123	34	40	35	13	2	62	2	1	3	0	0	12	.247	.281	.417	.698
2013	Fresno	AAA	85	261	60	14	2	5	(-	-)	93	30	30	28	21	0	48	2	2	3	0	0	3	.230	.289	.356	.646
2014	ColSpr	AAA	72	242	62	15	0	4	(-	-)	89	26	34	34	37	1	57	1	3	3	3	3	6	.256	.353	.368	.721
2014	Col	NL	7	14	3	0	0	1	(1	0)	6	1	3	3	2	0	4	0	0	0	0	0	1	.214	.313	.429	.741

Jerome Williams

Pitches: R **Bats:** R **Pos:** RP-26; SP-11   **Ht:** 6'3" **Wt:** 240 **Born:** 12/4/1981 **Age:** 33

			HOW MUCH HE PITCHED							WHAT HE GAVE UP										THE RESULTS							
Year	Team	Lg	G	GS	CG	GF	IP	BFP	H	R	ER	HR	SH	SF	HB	TBB	IBB	SO	WP	Bk	W	L	Pct	Sh	Sv-Op	Hld	ERC	ERA
2014	RdRck*	AAA	2	2	0	0	10.1	50	16	8	7	3	1	0	2	1	0	3	0	0	0	1	.000	0	0--	-	8.34	6.10
2003	SF	NL	21	21	2	0	131.0	545	116	54	48	10	6	3	7	49	3	88	2	1	7	5	.583	1	0-0	0	3.42	3.30
2004	SF	NL	22	22	0	0	129.1	559	123	69	61	14	4	9	17	44	1	80	2	1	10	7	.588	0	0-0	0	4.14	4.24
2005	2 Tms		22	20	0	0	122.2	532	119	62	58	14	11	8	10	49	1	70	2	0	6	10	.375	0	0-0	1	4.34	4.26
2006	ChC	NL	5	2	0	1	12.1	61	15	12	10	2	0	3	1	11	1	5	0	0	0	2	.000	0	0-0	0	8.42	7.30
2007	Was	NL	6	6	0	1	30.0	140	34	26	24	6	1	1	0	18	0	15	2	1	0	5	.000	0	0-0	0	6.43	7.20
2011	LAA	AL	10	6	0	1	44.0	184	45	20	18	6	0	1	1	15	0	28	0	0	4	0	1.000	0	0-0	0	4.45	3.68
2012	LAA	AL	32	15	1	7	137.2	572	139	73	70	17	0	4	5	35	1	98	1	0	6	8	.429	1	1-1	0	3.91	4.58
2013	LAA	AL	37	25	0	8	169.1	728	181	93	86	23	1	3	4	55	2	107	5	0	9	10	.474	0	0-0	0	4.53	4.57
2014	3 Tms		37	11	0	14	115.0	497	125	64	61	12	3	2	6	36	2	82	2	0	6	7	.462	0	0-3	2	4.47	4.77
05	SF	NL	4	3	0	0	16.2	73	21	12	12	2	1	0	1	4	1	11	0	0	0	2	.000	0	0-0	0	5.32	6.48
05	ChC	NL	18	17	0	0	106.0	459	98	50	46	12	10	8	9	45	0	59	2	0	6	8	.429	0	0-0	1	4.19	3.91
14	Hou	AL	26	0	0	14	47.2	219	59	33	32	7	3	1	3	16	1	38	2	0	1	4	.200	0	0-3	2	5.70	6.04
14	Tex	AL	2	2	0	0	10.0	48	18	11	11	0	0	0	0	3	0	6	0	0	1	1	.500	0	0-0	0	8.02	9.90
14	Phi	NL	9	9	0	0	57.1	230	48	20	18	5	0	1	3	17	1	38	0	0	4	2	.667	0	0-0	0	2.99	2.83
	Postseason		1	1	0	0	2.0	13	5	3	3	0	1	0	0	1	0	1	0	0	0	0	-	0	0-0	0	12.20	13.50
	9 ML YEARS		192	128	3	31	891.1	3818	897	473	436	104	26	34	51	312	11	573	16	3	48	54	.471	2	1-4	3	4.28	4.40

Josh Willingham

Bats: R **Throws:** R **Pos:** LF-53;DH-33;PH-7;RF-1   **Ht:** 6'2" **Wt:** 230 **Born:** 2/17/1979 **Age:** 36

			BATTING																	RUNNING			AVERAGES			
Year	Team	Lg	G	AB	H	2B	3B	HR	(Hm	Rd)	TB	R	RBI	RC	TBB	IBB	SO	HBP	SH	SF	SB	CS	GDP	Avg	OBP	Slg	OPS
2014	Roch*	AAA	8	27	5	2	0	1	(-	-)	10	3	3	2	1	0	8	1	0	0	0	0	2	.185	.241	.370	.612
2004	Fla	NL	12	25	5	0	0	1	(0	1)	8	2	1	1	4	0	8	0	0	0	0	0	1	.200	.310	.320	.630
2005	Fla	NL	16	23	7	1	0	0	(0	0)	8	3	4	3	2	0	5	2	1	0	0	0	1	.304	.407	.348	.755
2006	Fla	NL	142	502	139	28	2	26	(11	15)	249	62	74	74	54	2	109	11	0	6	2	0	13	.277	.356	.496	.852
2007	Fla	NL	144	521	138	32	4	21	(10	11)	241	75	89	94	66	1	122	16	0	1	8	1	11	.265	.364	.463	.827
2008	Fla	NL	102	351	89	21	5	15	(6	9)	165	54	51	56	48	2	82	14	1	2	3	2	7	.254	.364	.470	.834
2009	Was	NL	133	427	111	29	0	24	(7	17)	212	70	61	61	61	2	104	12	0	2	4	3	11	.260	.367	.496	.863
2010	Was	NL	114	370	99	19	2	16	(11	5)	170	54	56	65	67	3	85	9	0	4	8	0	8	.268	.389	.459	.848
2011	Oak	AL	136	488	120	26	0	29	(15	14)	233	69	98	86	56	3	150	11	0	8	4	1	6	.246	.332	.477	.810
2012	Min	AL	145	519	135	30	1	35	(21	14)	272	85	110	99	76	4	141	14	0	6	3	2	15	.260	.366	.524	.890
2013	Min	AL	111	389	81	20	0	14	(7	7)	143	42	48	51	66	2	128	14	0	8	1	0	8	.208	.342	.368	.709
2014	2 Tms		92	297	64	10	1	14	(5	9)	118	48	40	42	53	3	102	9	0	5	2	0	6	.215	.346	.397	.743
14	Min	AL	68	224	47	5	1	12	(5	7)	90	34	34	37	42	3	78	7	0	5	1	0	2	.210	.345	.402	.747
14	KC	AL	24	73	17	5	0	2	(0	2)	28	14	6	5	11	0	24	2	0	0	1	0	4	.233	.349	.384	.732
	11 ML YEARS		1147	3912	988	216	15	195	(93	102)	1819	564	632	632	553	22	1036	112	2	36	35	9	87	.253	.358	.465	.823

Alex Wilson

Pitches: R **Bats:** R **Pos:** RP-18   **Ht:** 6'0" **Wt:** 215 **Born:** 11/3/1986 **Age:** 28

			HOW MUCH HE PITCHED							WHAT HE GAVE UP										THE RESULTS							
Year	Team	Lg	G	GS	CG	GF	IP	BFP	H	R	ER	HR	SH	SF	HB	TBB	IBB	SO	WP	Bk	W	L	Pct	Sh	Sv-Op	Hld	ERC	ERA
2010	Salem	A+	11	11	0	0	55.2	224	43	24	21	4	1	2	2	15	0	50	1	0	2	1	.667	0	0--	-	2.36	3.40
2010	Portlnd	AA	16	16	0	0	78.1	354	95	59	58	15	1	2	2	34	0	56	3	0	4	5	.444	0	0--	-	6.37	6.66
2011	Portlnd	AA	21	21	0	0	112.0	458	103	42	38	8	0	1	1	37	0	99	6	1	9	4	.692	0	0--	-	3.30	3.05
2011	Pwtckt	AAA	4	4	0	0	21.0	89	19	8	8	2	0	1	0	7	0	24	1	0	1	0	1.000	0	0--	-	3.20	3.43
2012	Pwtckt	AAA	40	3	0	10	72.2	321	76	40	30	3	0	7	0	33	1	78	4	3	5	3	.625	0	1--	-	4.07	3.72
2013	Pwtckt	AAA	14	0	0	2	17.0	71	17	7	7	2	0	1	0	5	2	16	2	0	3	1	.750	0	3--	-	3.63	3.71
2014	Pwtckt	AAA	35	0	0	18	41.1	181	38	21	20	2	1	2	2	23	1	40	0	0	6	1	.857	0	5--	-	4.05	4.35
2013	Bos	AL	26	0	0	9	27.2	127	34	16	15	0	0	1	1	14	1	22	1	0	1	1	.500	0	0-0	1	5.19	4.88
2014	Bos	AL	18	0	0	3	28.1	109	20	8	6	3	0	1	2	5	0	19	1	0	1	0	1.000	0	0-1	0	2.08	1.91
	2 ML YEARS		44	0	0	12	56.0	236	54	24	21	3	0	2	3	19	1	41	2	0	2	1	.667	0	0-1	1	3.55	3.38

Bobby Wilson

Bats: R **Throws:** R **Pos:** C-2   **Ht:** 6'0" **Wt:** 220 **Born:** 4/8/1983 **Age:** 32

			BATTING																	RUNNING			AVERAGES			
Year	Team	Lg	G	AB	H	2B	3B	HR	(Hm	Rd)	TB	R	RBI	RC	TBB	IBB	SO	HBP	SH	SF	SB	CS	GDP	Avg	OBP	Slg	OPS
2014	Reno*	AAA	76	270	72	11	0	3	(-	-)	92	29	38	31	23	1	45	1	3	2	0	2	7	.267	.324	.341	.665
2008	LAA	AL	7	6	1	0	0	0	(0	0)	1	0	1	0	1	0	3	0	0	0	0	0	0	.167	.286	.167	.452
2009	LAA	AL	12	5	1	1	0	0	(0	0)	2	0	0	0	0	0	1	0	1	0	0	0	1	.200	.200	.400	.600
2010	LAA	AL	40	96	22	6	0	4	(3	1)	40	12	15	12	8	0	23	0	2	0	0	0	3	.229	.288	.417	.705
2011	LAA	AL	57	111	21	8	0	1	(1	0)	32	5	8	7	10	1	16	0	4	2	0	2	5	.189	.252	.288	.540
2012	LAA	AL	75	171	36	5	0	3	(2	1)	50	19	13	13	15	0	33	1	13	1	0	0	7	.211	.277	.292	.569
2014	Ari	NL	2	4	1	0	0	0	(0	0)	1	0	0	0	0	0	0	0	0	0	0	0	0	.250	.250	.250	.500
	6 ML YEARS		193	393	82	20	0	8	(5	3)	126	36	37	32	34	1	76	1	20	3	0	2	13	.209	.271	.321	.592

Brian Wilson

Pitches: R **Bats:** R **Pos:** RP-61   **Ht:** 6'1" **Wt:** 205 **Born:** 3/16/1982 **Age:** 33

			HOW MUCH HE PITCHED							WHAT HE GAVE UP										THE RESULTS							
Year	Team	Lg	G	GS	CG	GF	IP	BFP	H	R	ER	HR	SH	SF	HB	TBB	IBB	SO	WP	Bk	W	L	Pct	Sh	Sv-Op	Hld	ERC	ERA
2014	RCuca*	A+	2	2	0	0	2.0	7	1	0	0	0	0	0	0	0	0	2	0	0	0	0	-	0	0--	-	0.54	0.00
2006	SF	NL	31	0	0	9	30.0	141	32	19	18	1	1	4	1	21	2	23	0	0	2	3	.400	0	1-2	4	5.11	5.40
2007	SF	NL	24	0	0	9	23.2	93	16	6	6	1	0	0	1	7	0	18	0	0	1	2	.333	0	6-7	9	1.87	2.28
2008	SF	NL	63	0	0	54	62.1	274	62	32	32	7	2	5	3	28	4	67	2	0	3	2	.600	0	41-47	0	4.41	4.62

Year Team	Lg	G	GS	CG	GF	IP	BFP	H	R	ER	HR	SH	SF	HB	TBB	IBB	SO	WP	Bk	W	L	Pct	Sh	Sv-Op	Hld	ERC	ERA
2009 SF	NL	68	0	0	60	72.1	303	60	27	22	3	4	2	1	27	4	83	4	0	5	6	.455	0	38-45	1	2.61	2.74
2010 SF	NL	70	0	0	59	74.2	311	62	16	15	3	1	0	1	26	5	93	0	0	3	3	.500	0	**48-53**	0	2.51	1.81
2011 SF	NL	57	0	0	45	55.0	243	50	20	19	2	1	1	2	31	0	54	2	0	6	4	.600	0	36-41	0	3.87	3.11
2012 SF	NL	2	0	0	2	2.0	12	4	2	2	0	0	0	0	2	0	2	1	0	0	0	-	0	1-1	0	12.01	9.00
2013 LAD	NL	18	0	0	8	13.2	49	8	1	1	0	0	0	0	4	0	13	0	0	2	1	.667	0	0-0	1	1.35	0.66
2014 LAD	NL	61	0	0	6	48.1	223	49	26	25	5	1	0	4	29	3	54	1	0	2	4	.333	0	1-5	22	5.17	4.66
Postseason		16	0	0	10	17.2	68	9	1	0	0	1	1	1	6	0	24	0	0	2	0	1.000	0	6-7	2	1.26	0.00
9 ML YEARS		394	0	0	252	382.0	1649	343	149	140	22	10	12	13	175	18	407	10	0	24	25	.490	0	172-201	39	3.48	3.30

C.J. Wilson

Pitches: L Bats: L Pos: SP-31

Ht: 6'1" Wt: 210 Born: 11/18/1980 Age: 34

Year Team	Lg	G	GS	CG	GF	IP	BFP	H	R	ER	HR	SH	SF	HB	TBB	IBB	SO	WP	Bk	W	L	Pct	Sh	Sv-Op	Hld	ERC	ERA
2014 Ark*	AA	1	1	0	0	5.1	21	4	2	2	1	0	0	0	2	0	7	0	0	1	0	1.000	0	0- -		3.31	3.38
2005 Tex	AL	24	6	0	5	48.0	220	63	39	37	5	1	2	2	18	1	30	4	1	1	7	.125	0	1-1	4	6.03	6.94
2006 Tex	AL	44	0	0	12	44.1	191	39	23	20	7	1	0	5	18	1	43	0	0	2	4	.333	0	1-2	7	4.25	4.06
2007 Tex	AL	66	0	0	22	68.1	285	50	25	23	4	2	4	6	33	1	63	5	0	2	1	.667	0	12-14	15	3.01	3.03
2008 Tex	AL	50	0	0	41	46.1	214	49	35	31	8	1	1	2	27	2	41	3	0	2	2	.500	0	24-28	1	5.77	6.02
2009 Tex	AL	74	0	0	30	73.2	323	66	29	23	3	3	0	6	32	3	84	3	0	5	6	.455	0	14-18	19	3.40	2.81
2010 Tex	AL	33	33	3	0	204.0	850	161	83	76	10	1	3	10	93	0	170	7	1	15	8	.652	0	0-0	0	3.03	3.35
2011 Tex	AL	34	**34**	3	0	223.1	915	191	89	73	16	3	5	10	74	0	206	6	0	16	7	.696	1	0-0	0	3.07	2.94
2012 LAA	AL	34	**34**	0	0	202.1	865	181	102	86	19	4	6	6	91	2	173	4	1	13	10	.565	0	0-0	0	3.75	3.83
2013 LAA	AL	33	33	0	0	212.1	913	200	93	80	15	4	2	8	85	3	188	14	**2**	17	7	.708	0	0-0	0	3.66	3.39
2014 LAA	AL	31	31	1	0	175.2	761	169	95	88	17	3	7	11	**85**	5	151	9	0	13	10	.565	1	0-0	0	4.46	4.51
Postseason		10	9	0	0	52.1	231	46	32	28	10	3	1	4	29	6	43	3	0	1	5	.167	0	0-0	0	4.79	4.82
10 ML YEARS		423	171	7	110	1298.1	5537	1169	613	537	104	23	30	66	556	18	1149	55	5	86	62	.581	2	52-63	46	3.70	3.72

Josh Wilson

Bats: R Throws: R Pos: 2B-19;3B-4;SS-3;PR-1

Ht: 6'0" Wt: 175 Born: 3/26/1981 Age: 34

Year Team	Lg	G	AB	H	2B	3B	HR	(Hm	Rd)	TB	R	RBI	RC	TBB	IBB	SO	HBP	SH	SF	SB	CS	GDP	Avg	OBP	Slg	OPS
2014 RdRck*	AAA	92	305	75	11	1	5	(-	-)	103	37	33	31	16	1	87	7	0	4	1	2	7	.246	.295	.338	.633
2005 Fla	NL	11	10	1	1	0	0	(0	0)	2	2	0	0	0	0	4	1	0	0	0	0	0	.100	.182	.200	.382
2007 2 Tms		105	282	67	15	3	2	(0	2)	94	28	24	24	17	0	57	5	3	3	6	2	5	.238	.290	.333	.623
2009 3 Tms		72	192	42	11	1	3	(1	2)	64	19	13	14	12	1	44	4	3	0	1	2	4	.219	.279	.333	.612
2010 Sea	AL	108	361	82	14	2	2	(1	1)	106	22	25	31	14	0	74	12	0	1	5	0	6	.227	.278	.294	.572
2011 2 Tms	NL	60	85	19	5	0	2	(0	2)	30	13	5	7	4	0	22	0	3	0	1	0	0	.224	.258	.353	.611
2013 Ari	NL	30	60	12	1	1	1	(1	0)	18	9	4	2	5	0	17	0	0	0	0	0	6	.200	.262	.300	.562
2014 Tex	AL	24	67	16	4	0	0	(0	0)	20	7	8	6	2	0	14	1	2	0	1	0	3	.239	.271	.299	.570
07 Was	NL	15	19	1	0	0	0	(0	0)	1	3	0	0	5	0	6	1	0	0	0	0	0	.053	.280	.053	.333
07 TB	AL	90	263	66	15	3	2	(0	2)	93	25	24	24	12	0	51	4	3	3	6	2	5	.251	.291	.354	.644
09 Ari	NL	11	26	6	1	0	0	(0	0)	7	1	2	4	3	0	3	1	0	0	0	0	2	.231	.333	.269	.603
09 SD	NL	16	38	4	2	0	0	(0	0)	6	2	1	1	3	1	9	1	1	0	0	0	0	.105	.190	.158	.348
09 Sea	AL	45	128	32	8	1	3	(1	2)	51	16	10	9	6	0	32	2	2	0	1	2	2	.250	.294	.398	.693
11 Ari	NL	6	10	2	1	0	0	(0	0)	3	3	1	1	0	0	1	0	0	0	0	0	0	.200	.200	.300	.500
11 Mil	NL	54	75	17	4	0	2	(0	2)	27	10	4	6	4	0	21	0	3	0	1	0	0	.227	.266	.360	.626
7 ML YEARS		410	1057	239	51	7	10	(3	7)	334	100	79	84	54	1	232	23	11	4	14	4	24	.226	.278	.316	.594

Justin Wilson

Pitches: L Bats: L Pos: RP-70

Ht: 6'2" Wt: 205 Born: 8/18/1987 Age: 27

Year Team	Lg	G	GS	CG	GF	IP	BFP	H	R	ER	HR	SH	SF	HB	TBB	IBB	SO	WP	Bk	W	L	Pct	Sh	Sv-Op	Hld	ERC	ERA
2012 Pit	NL	8	0	0	3	4.2	26	10	1	1	0	1	0	0	3	0	7	1	0	0	0	-	0	0-0	0	11.83	1.93
2013 Pit	NL	58	0	0	8	73.2	295	50	17	17	4	3	1	3	28	1	59	5	0	6	1	.857	0	0-3	14	2.20	2.08
2014 Pit	NL	70	0	0	15	60.0	256	49	30	28	4	0	0	3	30	5	61	4	0	3	4	.429	0	0-3	16	3.29	4.20
Postseason		2	0	0	0	2.2	11	2	1	1	0	0	0	0	1	0	3	0	0	0	0	-	0	0-0	0	2.01	3.38
3 ML YEARS		136	0	0	26	138.1	577	109	48	46	8	4	1	6	61	0	127	10	0	9	5	.643	0	0-6	30	2.92	2.99

Chris Withrow

Pitches: R Bats: R Pos: RP-20

with-ROE

Ht: 6'4" Wt: 215 Born: 4/1/1989 Age: 26

Year Team	Lg	G	GS	CG	GF	IP	BFP	H	R	ER	HR	SH	SF	HB	TBB	IBB	SO	WP	Bk	W	L	Pct	Sh	Sv-Op	Hld	ERC	ERA
2010 Chatt	AA	27	27	1	0	129.2	604	146	92	86	13	4	8	11	69	1	120	6	0	4	9	.308	1	0- -	-	5.65	5.97
2011 Chatt	AA	25	25	1	0	128.2	553	111	68	60	8	4	4	5	75	1	130	10	1	6	6	.500	0	0- -	-	3.98	4.20
2012 Chatt	AA	22	7	0	4	60.0	265	52	34	31	3	4	0	2	36	1	64	3	0	3	3	.500	0	2- -	-	3.83	4.65
2013 Albq	AAA	25	0	0	11	26.1	115	25	10	5	0	1	0	0	13	0	33	2	0	4	0	1.000	0	0- -	-	3.42	1.71
2013 LAD	NL	26	0	0	4	34.2	134	20	10	10	5	0	0	0	13	0	43	2	0	3	0	1.000	0	1-2	4	2.11	2.60
2014 LAD	NL	20	0	0	0	21.1	90	10	8	7	1	0	1	1	18	0	28	4	0	0	0	-	0	0-1	6	2.74	2.95
Postseason		4	0	0	0	5.0	23	3	3	3	0	1	0	0	6	0	3	1	1	0	1	.000	0	0-0	0	4.17	5.40
2 ML YEARS		46	0	0	4	56.0	224	30	18	17	6	0	1	1	31	0	71	6	0	3	0	1.000	0	1-3	10	2.38	2.73

Randy Wolf

Pitches: L Bats: L Pos: SP-4; RP-2   Ht: 6'0" Wt: 205 Born: 8/22/1976 Age: 38

		HOW MUCH HE PITCHED						WHAT HE GAVE UP											THE RESULTS							
Year Team	Lg	G	GS	CG	GF	IP	BFP	H	R	ER	HR	SH	SF	HB	TBB	IBB	SO	WP	Bk	W	L	Pct	Sh	Sv-Op	Hld	ERC	ERA
2014 Reno*	AAA	6	6	0	0	34.0	152	40	18	17	1	0	0	0	18	0	35	2	0	5	1	.833	0	0--	-	5.22	4.50
2014 Norfolk*	AAA	6	1	0	2	15.0	68	18	9	7	1	1	2	0	5	0	12	1	0	0	0	-	0	0--	-	4.58	4.20
2014 Salt Lk*	AAA	7	7	0	0	37.2	166	45	20	20	5	4	2	1	12	0	31	1	0	1	1	.500	0	0--	-	5.26	4.78
1999 Phi	NL	22	21	0	0	121.2	552	126	78	75	20	5	1	5	67	0	116	4	0	6	9	.400	0	0-0	0	5.54	5.55
2000 Phi	NL	32	32	1	0	206.1	889	210	107	100	25	10	8	8	83	2	160	1	0	11	9	.550	0	0-0	0	4.54	4.36
2001 Phi	NL	28	25	4	1	163.0	684	150	74	67	15	11	7	10	51	4	152	1	0	10	11	.476	2	0-0	0	3.46	3.70
2002 Phi	NL	31	31	3	0	210.2	855	172	77	75	23	7	6	7	63	5	172	4	0	11	9	.550	2	0-0	0	2.88	3.20
2003 Phi	NL	33	33	2	0	200.0	850	176	101	94	27	8	4	6	78	4	177	6	0	16	10	.615	2	0-0	0	3.67	4.23
2004 Phi	NL	23	23	1	0	136.2	585	145	73	65	20	6	3	5	36	4	89	2	0	5	8	.385	1	0-0	0	4.29	4.28
2005 Phi	NL	13	13	0	0	80.0	346	87	40	39	14	4	1	6	26	2	61	1	0	4	6	.400	0	0-0	0	5.17	4.39
2006 Phi	NL	12	12	0	0	56.2	261	63	37	35	13	2	3	2	33	2	44	2	0	4	0	1.000	0	0-0	0	6.63	5.56
2007 LAD	NL	18	18	0	0	102.2	458	110	55	54	10	5	5	6	39	2	94	4	0	9	6	.600	0	0-0	0	4.52	4.73
2008 2 Tms	NL	33	33	1	0	190.1	823	191	100	91	21	10	4	12	71	4	162	3	0	12	12	.500	1	0-0	0	4.30	4.30
2009 LAD	NL	34	34	0	0	214.1	862	178	81	77	24	12	2	6	58	1	160	4	0	11	7	.611	0	0-0	0	2.89	3.23
2010 Mil	NL	34	34	1	0	215.2	936	213	107	100	29	9	6	9	87	6	142	2	0	13	12	.520	1	0-0	0	4.39	4.17
2011 Mil	NL	33	33	0	0	212.1	903	214	95	87	23	13	6	13	66	1	134	4	1	13	10	.565	0	0-0	0	4.10	3.69
2012 2 Tms	NL	30	26	0	0	157.2	699	196	103	99	23	10	4	7	52	1	104	2	2	5	10	.333	0	0-0	0	5.85	5.65
2014 Mia	NL	6	4	0	1	25.2	113	33	17	15	4	1	0	0	6	0	19	1	0	1	3	.250	0	1-1	0	5.49	5.26
08 SD	NL	21	21	0	0	119.2	522	123	69	63	14	6	2	8	47	0	105	2	0	6	10	.375	0	0-0	0	4.63	4.74
08 Hou	NL	12	12	1	0	70.2	301	68	31	28	7	4	2	4	24	4	57	1	0	6	2	.750	1	0-0	0	3.77	3.57
12 Mil	NL	25	24	0	0	142.1	633	179	94	90	21	8	4	6	45	1	96	2	2	3	10	.231	0	0-0	0	5.86	5.69
12 Bal	NL	5	2	0	1	15.1	66	17	9	9	2	2	0	1	7	0	8	0	0	2	0	1.000	0	0-0	0	5.74	5.28
Postseason		4	4	0	0	19.0	92	24	14	14	5	1	0	1	11	2	12	0	0	1	1	.500	0	0-0	0	7.71	6.63
15 ML YEARS		382	372	13	3	2293.2	9816	2264	1145	1073	291	113	60	102	816	38	1786	41	3	133	120	.526	9	1-1	0	4.19	4.21

Kolten Wong

Bats: L Throws: R Pos: 2B-107;PH-10;PR-1   COLT-enn   Ht: 5'9" Wt: 185 Born: 10/10/1990 Age: 24

		BATTING																		RUNNING			AVERAGES			
Year Team	Lg	G	AB	H	2B	3B	HR	(Hm Rd)	TB	R	RBI	RC	TBB	IBB	SO	HBP	SH	SF	SB	CS	GDP	Avg	OBP	Slg	OPS
2011 QuadC	A	47	194	65	15	2	5	(- -)	99	39	25	40	21	1	24	3	0	4	9	5	4	.335	.401	.510	.911
2012 Sprgfld	AA	126	523	150	23	6	9	(- -)	212	79	52	77	44	2	74	7	2	3	21	11	6	.287	.348	.405	.754
2013 Memp	AAA	107	412	125	21	8	10	(- -)	192	68	45	76	41	3	60	4	2	1	20	1	9	.303	.369	.466	.835
2014 Memp	AAA	18	75	27	4	0	3	(- -)	40	16	13	16	5	0	9	0	0	0	6	0	1	.360	.400	.533	.933
2013 StL	NL	32	59	9	1	0	0	(0 0)	10	6	0	0	3	0	12	0	0	0	3	0	2	.153	.194	.169	.363
2014 StL	NL	113	402	100	14	3	12	(10 2)	156	52	42	41	21	3	71	4	5	1	20	4	12	.249	.292	.388	.680
Postseason		7	6	1	0	0	0	(0 0)	1	0	0	1	0	0	1	0	0	0	1	0	0	.167	.167	.167	.333
2 ML YEARS		145	461	109	15	3	12	(10 2)	166	58	42	41	24	3	83	4	5	1	23	4	14	.236	.280	.360	.640

Alex Wood

Pitches: L Bats: R Pos: SP-24; RP-11   Ht: 6'4" Wt: 215 Born: 1/12/1991 Age: 24

		HOW MUCH HE PITCHED						WHAT HE GAVE UP											THE RESULTS							
Year Team	Lg	G	GS	CG	GF	IP	BFP	H	R	ER	HR	SH	SF	HB	TBB	IBB	SO	WP	Bk	W	L	Pct	Sh	Sv-Op	Hld	ERC	ERA
2012 Rome	A	13	13	0	0	52.2	206	39	18	13	1	1	0	2	14	0	52	1	0	4	3	.571	0	0--	-	1.95	2.22
2013 Missi	AA	10	10	0	0	57.0	227	41	10	8	1	0	1	1	15	0	57	1	0	4	2	.667	0	0--	-	1.71	1.26
2013 Gwnntt	AAA	1	1	0	0	5.0	20	3	1	1	0	0	1	2	2	0	5	3	0	1	0	1.000	0	0--	-	2.96	1.80
2014 Gwnntt	AAA	2	2	0	0	8.2	34	7	1	1	0	0	0	0	4	0	8	1	0	0	0	-	0	0--	-	2.82	1.04
2013 Atl	NL	31	11	0	9	77.2	327	76	29	27	3	6	4	1	27	1	77	4	2	3	3	.500	0	0-0	1	3.40	3.13
2014 Atl	NL	35	24	1	2	171.2	694	151	58	53	16	7	3	6	45	1	170	5	0	11	11	.500	0	0-0	2	3.04	2.78
Postseason		2	0	0	0	3.1	14	3	4	0	1	0	0	0	0	0	3	1	0	0	0	-	0	0-0	0	2.79	0.00
2 ML YEARS		66	35	1	11	249.1	1021	227	87	80	19	13	7	7	72	2	247	9	2	14	14	.500	0	0-0	3	3.15	2.89

Blake Wood

Pitches: R Bats: R Pos: RP-7   Ht: 6'5" Wt: 240 Born: 8/8/1985 Age: 29

		HOW MUCH HE PITCHED						WHAT HE GAVE UP											THE RESULTS							
Year Team	Lg	G	GS	CG	GF	IP	BFP	H	R	ER	HR	SH	SF	HB	TBB	IBB	SO	WP	Bk	W	L	Pct	Sh	Sv-Op	Hld	ERC	ERA
2014 Clmbs*	AAA	9	0	0	1	8.0	43	7	3	1	0	1	0	0	11	0	7	1	0	0	0	-	0	0--	-	6.02	1.13
2014 Omha*	AAA	14	0	0	3	18.1	85	18	14	13	2	1	0	0	16	0	21	7	0	0	0	-	0	0--	-	6.11	6.38
2014 Wilmg*	A+	5	0	0	3	9.2	34	4	1	1	1	0	0	0	2	0	10	0	1	2	1	.667	0	0--	-	0.99	0.93
2014 NWArk*	AA	6	0	0	3	6.2	30	11	6	6	1	0	0	0	2	0	13	0	0	1	0	1.000	0	0--	-	8.71	8.10
2010 KC	AL	51	0	0	13	49.2	220	54	29	28	6	2	6	1	22	5	31	3	0	1	3	.250	0	0-4	15	4.83	5.07
2011 KC	AL	55	0	0	20	69.2	303	66	30	29	5	5	3	3	32	7	62	2	0	5	3	.625	0	1-3	5	3.82	3.75
2013 Cle	AL	2	0	0	1	1.1	8	1	0	0	0	0	0	0	3	0	1	0	0	0	0	-	0	0-0	0	8.88	0.00
2014 Cle	AL	7	0	0	3	6.1	30	4	5	5	0	0	0	1	7	2	7	0	0	0	1	.000	0	0-0	0	3.89	7.11
4 ML YEARS		115	0	0	37	127.0	561	125	64	62	11	7	9	5	64	14	101	5	0	6	7	.462	0	1-7	20	4.27	4.39

Travis Wood

Pitches: L Bats: R Pos: SP-31   Ht: 5'11" Wt: 175 Born: 2/6/1987 Age: 28

		HOW MUCH HE PITCHED						WHAT HE GAVE UP											THE RESULTS							
Year Team	Lg	G	GS	CG	GF	IP	BFP	H	R	ER	HR	SH	SF	HB	TBB	IBB	SO	WP	Bk	W	L	Pct	Sh	Sv-Op	Hld	ERC	ERA
2010 Cin	NL	17	17	0	0	102.2	419	85	45	40	9	3	3	4	26	1	86	0	1	5	4	.556	0	0-0	0	2.64	3.51
2011 Cin	NL	22	18	0	2	106.0	463	118	57	57	10	9	7	4	40	5	76	2	0	6	6	.500	0	0-0	0	4.73	4.84
2012 ChC	NL	26	26	0	0	156.0	649	133	80	74	25	9	4	8	54	3	119	2	1	6	13	.316	0	0-0	0	3.65	4.27

Year	Team	Lg	G	GS	CG	GF	IP	BFP	H	R	ER	HR	SH	SF	HB	TBB	IBB	SO	WP	Bk	W	L	Pct	Sh	Sv-Op	Hld	ERC	ERA
2013	ChC	NL	32	32	0	0	200.0	821	163	73	69	18	7	4	8	66	2	144	6	0	9	12	.429	0	0-0	0	2.90	3.11
2014	ChC	NL	31	31	0	0	173.2	781	190	110	97	20	8	4	7	76	1	146	2	0	8	13	.381	0	0-0	0	5.00	5.03
	Postseason		1	0	0	0	3.1	12	1	0	0	0	0	0	0	1	1	3	0	0	0	0	-	0	0-0	0	0.38	0.00
	5 ML YEARS		128	124	0	2	738.1	3133	689	365	337	82	36	22	31	262	12	571	12	2	34	48	.415	0	0-0	0	3.75	4.11

Rob Wooten

Pitches: R Bats: R Pos: RP-40   WOOT-enn   Ht: 6'1" Wt: 195 Born: 7/21/1985 Age: 29

Year	Team	Lg	G	GS	CG	GF	IP	BFP	H	R	ER	HR	SH	SF	HB	TBB	IBB	SO	WP	Bk	W	L	Pct	Sh	Sv-Op	Hld	ERC	ERA
2011	BrvdCt	A+	12	0	0	6	21.1	83	15	6	6	0	0	1	0	3	0	18	0	0	2	0	1.000	0	1- -	-	1.26	2.53
2011	Hntsvl	AA	36	0	0	27	42.2	188	41	20	16	3	5	0	5	15	2	41	3	1	3	3	.500	0	7- -	-	3.77	3.38
2012	Hntsvl	AA	17	0	0	14	20.2	88	18	4	4	1	1	0	1	7	1	21	2	0	3	0	1.000	0	8- -	-	2.85	1.74
2012	Nashv	AAA	40	0	0	23	52.2	221	49	23	23	4	3	2	2	16	2	49	1	1	0	2	.000	0	7- -	-	3.25	3.93
2013	Nashv	AAA	40	0	0	36	52.0	208	40	17	17	4	3	0	2	12	1	45	5	0	0	1	.000	0	20- -	-	2.21	2.94
2014	Nashv	AAA	21	0	0	18	21.2	97	24	16	14	1	0	1	1	5	1	21	0	0	0	2	.000	0	14- -	-	3.56	5.82
2013	Mil	NL	27	0	0	6	27.2	115	27	12	12	1	1	0	1	8	2	18	0	0	3	1	.750	0	0-1	8	3.16	3.90
2014	Mil	NL	40	0	0	15	34.1	147	42	18	18	1	0	1	1	8	0	29	0	0	1	4	.200	0	0-0	11	4.39	4.72
	2 ML YEARS		67	0	0	21	62.0	262	69	30	30	2	1	1	2	16	2	47	0	0	4	5	.444	0	0-1	19	3.82	4.35

Brandon Workman

Pitches: R Bats: R Pos: SP-15; RP-4   Ht: 6'5" Wt: 225 Born: 8/13/1988 Age: 26

Year	Team	Lg	G	GS	CG	GF	IP	BFP	H	R	ER	HR	SH	SF	HB	TBB	IBB	SO	WP	Bk	W	L	Pct	Sh	Sv-Op	Hld	ERC	ERA
2011	Grnvlle	A	26	26	0	0	131.0	540	128	67	54	10	5	4	5	33	0	115	6	1	6	7	.462	0	0- -	-	3.42	3.71
2012	Salem	A+	20	20	0	0	113.2	454	104	47	43	10	4	3	1	20	0	107	6	1	7	7	.500	0	0- -	-	2.76	3.40
2012	Portlnd	AA	5	5	0	0	25.0	101	23	12	11	2	1	2	0	5	0	23	0	0	3	1	.750	0	0- -	-	2.77	3.96
2013	Portlnd	AA	11	10	0	0	65.2	259	51	29	25	6	2	2	1	17	0	74	3	0	5	1	.833	0	0- -	-	2.42	3.43
2013	Pwtckt	AAA	6	6	0	0	35.1	152	39	13	11	6	2	0	2	13	0	34	1	0	3	1	.750	0	0- -	-	5.47	2.80
2014	Pwtckt	AAA	11	11	0	0	61.1	253	61	28	28	10	1	3	0	17	1	55	1	0	7	1	.875	0	0- -	-	4.03	4.11
2013	Bos	AL	20	3	0	5	41.2	180	44	23	23	5	2	1	0	15	1	47	1	0	6	3	.667	0	0-1	1	4.34	4.97
2014	Bos	AL	19	15	0	2	87.0	378	88	57	50	11	3	3	1	36	0	70	2	0	1	10	.091	0	0-0	1	4.43	5.17
	Postseason		7	0	0	0	8.2	35	7	1	0	0	1	0	0	3	1	4	0	0	0	1	.000	0	0-0	0	2.09	0.00
	2 ML YEARS		39	18	0	7	128.2	558	132	80	73	16	5	4	1	51	1	117	3	0	7	13	.350	0	0-1	2	4.40	5.11

Vance Worley

Pitches: R Bats: R Pos: SP-17; RP-1   Ht: 6'2" Wt: 230 Born: 9/25/1987 Age: 27

Year	Team	Lg	G	GS	CG	GF	IP	BFP	H	R	ER	HR	SH	SF	HB	TBB	IBB	SO	WP	Bk	W	L	Pct	Sh	Sv-Op	Hld	ERC	ERA
2014	Indy*	AAA	7	7	0	0	46.0	185	47	23	22	3	1	0	2	4	0	43	2	0	3	2	.600	0	0- -	-	2.98	4.30
2010	Phi	NL	5	2	0	2	13.0	51	8	2	2	1	2	0	4	4	0	12	1	0	1	1	.500	0	0-0	0	1.66	1.38
2011	Phi	NL	25	21	1	0	131.2	553	116	47	44	10	9	5	3	46	2	119	2	1	11	3	.786	0	0-0	2	3.12	3.01
2012	Phi	NL	23	23	0	0	133.0	590	154	69	62	12	11	3	6	47	4	107	1	0	6	9	.400	0	0-0	0	4.87	4.20
2013	Min	AL	10	10	0	0	48.2	234	82	43	39	9	0	1	3	15	1	25	1	0	1	5	.167	0	0-0	0	9.17	7.21
2014	Pit	NL	18	17	1	0	110.2	458	112	43	35	9	6	4	3	22	1	79	4	0	8	4	.667	0	0-0	0	3.35	2.85
	Postseason		2	0	0	0	1.1	8	3	1	1	0	0	0	0	1	0	0	0	0	0	0	-	0	0-0	1	12.64	6.75
	5 ML YEARS		81	73	2	2	437.0	1886	472	204	182	41	28	13	15	134	8	342	9	1	27	22	.551	1	0-0	2	4.23	3.75

Danny Worth

Bats: R Throws: R Pos: SS-13; 2B-3; PR-3; 1B-1   Ht: 6'1" Wt: 185 Born: 9/30/1985 Age: 29

Year	Team	Lg	G	AB	H	2B	3B	HR	(Hm	Rd)	TB	R	RBI	RC	TBB	IBB	SO	HBP	SH	SF	SB	CS	GDP	Avg	OBP	Slg	OPS
2014	Toledo*	AAA	66	223	47	15	1	1	(-	-)	67	19	18	22	27	0	87	0	1	0	9	0	4	.211	.296	.300	.596
2010	Det	AL	39	106	27	5	0	2	(2	0)	38	10	8	11	6	0	13	0	3	0	1	2	0	.255	.295	.358	.653
2011	Det	AL	30	37	10	2	0	0	(0	0)	12	6	3	3	2	0	9	0	0	0	0	0	0	.270	.308	.324	.632
2012	Det	AL	43	74	16	3	0	0	(0	0)	19	9	3	7	13	0	23	0	2	1	0	0	1	.216	.330	.257	.586
2013	Det	AL	3	2	0	0	0	0	(0	0)	0	0	0	0	0	0	1	0	0	0	0	0	1	.000	.000	.000	.000
2014	Det	AL	20	42	7	1	0	0	(0	0)	8	5	5	2	2	0	12	1	0	1	0	1	1	.167	.217	.190	.408
	Postseason		4	1	0	0	0	0	(0	0)	0	0	0	0	0	0	1	0	0	0	0	0	0	.000	.000	.000	.000
	5 ML YEARS		135	261	60	11	0	2	(2	0)	77	30	19	23	23	0	58	1	5	2	1	3	3	.230	.293	.295	.588

David Wright

Bats: R Throws: R Pos: 3B-133; PH-1   Ht: 6'0" Wt: 205 Born: 12/20/1982 Age: 32

Year	Team	Lg	G	AB	H	2B	3B	HR	(Hm	Rd)	TB	R	RBI	RC	TBB	IBB	SO	HBP	SH	SF	SB	CS	GDP	Avg	OBP	Slg	OPS
2004	NYM	NL	69	263	77	17	1	14	(8	6)	138	41	40	42	14	0	40	3	0	3	6	0	7	.293	.332	.525	.857
2005	NYM	NL	160	575	176	42	1	27	(12	15)	301	99	102	105	72	2	113	7	0	3	17	7	16	.306	.388	.523	.912
2006	NYM	NL	154	582	181	40	5	26	(13	13)	309	96	116	119	66	13	113	5	0	8	20	5	15	.311	.381	.531	.912
2007	NYM	NL	160	604	196	42	1	30	(16	14)	330	113	107	127	94	6	115	6	0	7	34	5	14	.325	.416	.546	.963
2008	NYM	NL	160	626	189	42	2	33	(21	12)	334	115	124	116	94	5	118	4	0	11	15	5	15	.302	.390	.534	.924
2009	NYM	NL	144	535	164	39	3	10	(5	5)	239	88	72	86	74	8	140	3	0	6	27	9	16	.307	.390	.447	.837
2010	NYM	NL	157	587	166	36	3	29	(12	17)	295	87	103	97	69	9	161	2	0	5	19	11	12	.283	.354	.503	.856
2011	NYM	NL	102	389	99	23	1	14	(5	9)	166	60	61	58	52	4	97	3	0	3	13	2	5	.254	.345	.427	.771
2012	NYM	NL	156	581	178	41	2	21	(12	9)	286	91	93	105	81	16	112	3	0	5	15	10	15	.306	.391	.492	.883

	BATTING																			RUNNING			AVERAGES			
Year Team	Lg	G	AB	H	2B	3B	HR	(Hm Rd)	TB	R	RBI	RC	TBB	IBB	SO	HBP	SH	SF	SB	CS	GDP	Avg	OBP	Slg	OPS
2013 NYM	NL	112	430	132	23	6	18	(6 12)	221	63	58	78	55	5	79	5	0	2	17	3	11	.307	.390	.514	.904
2014 NYM	NL	134	535	144	30	1	8	(6 2)	200	54	63	60	42	5	113	4	0	5	8	5	22	.269	.324	.374	.698
Postseason		10	37	8	3	0	1	(0 1)	14	3	6	5	5	1	8	0	0	0	0	0	0	.216	.310	.378	.688
11 ML YEARS		1508	5707	1702	375	26	230	(116 114)	2819	907	939	993	713	73	1201	45	0	65	191	62	148	.298	.377	.494	.871

Jamey Wright

Pitches: R **Bats:** R **Pos:** RP-60; SP-1

Ht: 6'6" **Wt:** 240 **Born:** 12/24/1974 **Age:** 40

	HOW MUCH HE PITCHED						WHAT HE GAVE UP											THE RESULTS						
Year Team	Lg	G	GS	CG	GF	IP	BFP	H	R	ER	HR	SH	SF	HB	TBB	IBB	SO	WP	Bk	W	L	Pct	Sh	Sv-Op	Hld	ERC	ERA
1996 Col	NL	16	15	0	0	91.1	406	105	60	50	8	4	2	7	41	1	45	1	2	4	4	.500	0	0-0	1	5.50	4.93
1997 Col	NL	26	26	1	0	149.2	698	198	113	104	19	8	3	11	71	3	59	6	2	8	12	.400	0	0-0	0	6.96	6.25
1998 Col	NL	34	34	1	0	206.1	919	235	143	130	24	8	6	11	95	3	86	6	3	9	14	.391	0	0-0	0	5.57	5.67
1999 Col	NL	16	16	0	0	94.1	423	110	52	51	10	3	4	4	54	3	49	3	0	4	3	.571	0	0-0	0	6.19	4.87
2000 Mil	NL	26	25	0	1	164.2	718	157	81	75	12	4	6	18	88	5	96	9	2	7	9	.438	0	0-0	0	4.67	4.10
2001 Mil	NL	33	33	1	0	194.2	868	201	115	106	26	7	5	20	98	10	129	6	1	11	12	.478	1	0-0	0	5.36	4.90
2002 2 Tms	NL	23	22	1	0	129.1	585	130	80	76	17	9	6	11	75	9	77	9	0	7	13	.350	1	0-0	0	5.35	5.29
2003 KC	AL	4	4	2	0	25.1	106	23	14	12	1	0	0	1	11	0	19	0	0	1	2	.333	1	0-0	0	3.53	4.26
2004 Col	NL	14	14	0	0	78.2	361	82	39	36	8	1	1	6	45	3	41	3	0	2	3	.400	0	0-0	0	5.26	4.12
2005 Col	NL	34	27	0	1	171.1	782	201	119	104	22	4	3	15	81	4	101	2	2	8	16	.333	0	0-0	1	6.02	5.46
2006 SF	NL	34	21	0	2	156.0	676	167	95	90	16	5	4	10	64	4	79	6	0	6	10	.375	0	0-0	1	4.89	5.19
2007 Tex	AL	20	9	0	3	77.0	330	72	35	31	6	3	2	5	41	2	39	4	0	4	5	.444	0	0-0	1	4.44	3.62
2008 Tex	AL	75	0	0	17	84.1	379	93	57	48	5	3	4	8	35	3	60	5	0	8	7	.533	0	0-6	17	4.74	5.12
2009 KC	AL	65	0	0	14	79.0	350	73	51	38	8	4	0	7	44	5	60	7	0	3	5	.375	0	0-3	12	4.56	4.33
2010 2 Tms	AL	46	0	0	17	58.1	249	55	33	27	3	3	3	3	25	1	28	4	1	1	3	.250	0	0-1	9	3.75	4.17
2011 Sea	AL	60	0	0	19	68.1	286	61	26	24	6	2	1	5	30	3	48	4	0	2	3	.400	0	1-5	16	3.89	3.16
2012 LAD	NL	66	0	0	22	67.2	306	72	35	28	2	3	2	4	30	7	54	2	0	5	3	.625	0	0-0	6	4.07	3.72
2013 TB	AL	66	1	0	15	70.0	288	61	25	24	4	3	3	5	23	3	65	5	0	2	2	.500	0	0-1	6	3.09	3.09
2014 LAD	NL	61	1	0	22	70.1	308	72	35	34	3	6	5	4	27	4	54	5	0	5	4	.556	0	1-2	5	3.84	4.35
02 Mil	NL	19	19	1	0	114.1	515	115	72	68	15	9	6	11	63	8	69	8	0	5	13	.278	1	0-0	0	5.28	5.35
02 StL	NL	4	3	0	0	15.0	70	15	8	8	2	0	0	0	12	1	8	1	0	2	0	1.000	0	0-0	0	5.87	4.80
10 Cle	AL	18	0	0	9	21.1	98	25	18	13	1	1	1	2	9	0	9	1	0	1	2	.333	0	0-0	1	5.10	5.48
10 Sea	AL	28	0	0	8	37.0	151	30	15	14	2	2	2	1	16	1	19	3	1	0	1	.000	0	0-1	8	3.03	3.41
Postseason		2	0	0	1	2.0	11	4	4	4	0	0	0	0	3	0	1	0	0	0	0	-	0	0-0	0	17.05	18.00
19 ML YEARS		719	248	6	133	2036.2	9038	2168	1208	1088	200	80	60	155	978	73	1189	87	13	97	130	.427	3	2-18	74	5.09	4.81

Steven Wright

Pitches: R **Bats:** R **Pos:** RP-5; SP-1

Ht: 6'1" **Wt:** 220 **Born:** 8/30/1984 **Age:** 30

	HOW MUCH HE PITCHED						WHAT HE GAVE UP											THE RESULTS						
Year Team	Lg	G	GS	CG	GF	IP	BFP	H	R	ER	HR	SH	SF	HB	TBB	IBB	SO	WP	Bk	W	L	Pct	Sh	Sv-Op	Hld	ERC	ERA
2010 Clmbs	AAA	9	0	0	4	10.2	49	13	9	9	2	0	0	0	5	0	10	0	0	0	1	.000	0	0--	-	6.32	7.59
2010 Akron	AA	39	0	2	18	64.2	282	73	33	31	4	2	1	3	21	1	48	2	1	2	2	.500	0	5--	-	4.43	4.31
2011 Lk Cty	A	9	9	0	0	46.0	205	48	30	16	3	0	2	3	24	0	33	5	0	1	2	.333	0	0--	-	4.88	3.13
2011 Clmbs	AAA	1	0	0	0	2.2	12	5	2	2	0	0	0	0	0	0	2	1	0	0	0	-	0	0--	-	7.29	6.75
2011 Akron	AA	8	7	0	0	46.2	212	47	32	31	8	1	2	5	28	0	35	14	0	2	4	.333	0	0--	-	6.03	5.98
2011 Knstn	A+	7	4	0	0	38.1	172	47	28	19	7	0	1	1	16	0	27	7	0	1	2	.333	0	0--	-	6.35	4.46
2012 Akron	AA	20	20	1	0	115.2	488	86	44	34	8	3	2	5	62	0	101	11	0	9	6	.600	1	0--	-	3.18	2.65
2012 PortInd	A	1	1	0	0	6.0	24	5	1	1	0	0	0	1	2	0	2	0	0	1	0	1.000	0	0--	-	3.07	1.50
2012 Pwtckt	AAA	4	4	0	0	20.0	88	19	10	7	1	1	0	2	5	0	16	1	0	1	0	1.000	0	0--	-	3.11	3.15
2013 Pwtckt	AAA	24	24	3	0	135.1	586	130	64	52	10	0	6	4	65	0	99	15	0	8	7	.533	3	0--	-	4.14	3.46
2014 PortInd	A	1	1	0	0	5.0	19	5	3	2	1	0	0	0	1	0	4	0	0	1	0	1.000	0	0--	-	4.32	3.60
2014 Pwtckt	AAA	15	15	1	0	95.0	386	86	43	36	9	1	4	1	22	0	68	5	0	5	5	.500	0	0--	-	2.94	3.41
2013 Bos	AL	4	1	0	2	13.1	59	12	8	8	0	0	0	1	9	0	10	2	0	2	0	1.000	0	0-0	0	4.22	5.40
2014 Bos	AL	6	1	0	3	21.0	86	21	8	6	2	0	0	0	4	0	22	1	0	0	1	.000	0	0-0	0	3.25	2.57
2 ML YEARS		10	2	0	5	34.1	145	33	16	14	2	0	0	1	13	0	32	3	0	2	1	.667	0	0-0	0	3.65	3.67

Wesley Wright

Pitches: L **Bats:** R **Pos:** RP-58

Ht: 5'11" **Wt:** 185 **Born:** 1/28/1985 **Age:** 30

	HOW MUCH HE PITCHED						WHAT HE GAVE UP											THE RESULTS						
Year Team	Lg	G	GS	CG	GF	IP	BFP	H	R	ER	HR	SH	SF	HB	TBB	IBB	SO	WP	Bk	W	L	Pct	Sh	Sv-Op	Hld	ERC	ERA
2008 Hou	NL	71	0	0	15	55.2	250	45	34	31	8	1	1	4	34	4	57	2	1	4	3	.571	0	1-1	13	4.21	5.01
2009 Hou	NL	49	0	0	5	44.2	204	53	27	27	9	0	2	0	25	3	47	2	0	3	4	.429	0	0-2	6	6.64	5.44
2010 Hou	NL	14	4	0	3	33.0	148	37	27	21	6	2	1	3	13	0	29	0	0	1	2	.333	0	0-0	0	5.78	5.73
2011 Hou	NL	21	0	0	5	12.0	44	6	2	2	1	0	0	0	5	0	11	1	0	0	0	-	0	0-1	1	1.68	1.50
2012 Hou	NL	77	0	0	13	52.1	223	45	20	19	4	1	0	6	17	0	54	1	0	2	2	.500	0	1-2	19	3.26	3.27
2013 2 Tms	AL	71	0	0	17	53.2	232	54	24	22	7	1	2	3	19	2	55	2	0	0	4	.000	0	0-4	9	4.31	3.69
2014 ChC	NL	58	0	0	15	48.1	209	48	19	17	2	2	3	2	19	2	37	2	0	3	0	.000	0	0-2	5	3.69	3.17
13 Hou	AL	55	0	0	13	41.1	184	45	20	18	5	1	2	3	16	2	40	2	0	0	4	.000	0	0-4	8	4.89	3.92
13 TB	AL	16	0	0	4	12.1	48	9	4	4	2	0	0	0	3	0	15	0	0	0	0	-	0	0-0	1	2.47	2.92
Postseason		2	0	0	1	0.2	4	1	0	0	0	0	0	0	1	1	1	0	0	0	0	-	0	0-0	0	6.98	0.00
7 ML YEARS		361	4	0	73	299.2	1310	288	153	139	37	7	9	18	132	11	290	10	1	10	18	.357	0	2-12	59	4.36	4.17

Kirby Yates

Pitches: R Bats: L Pos: RP-37   Ht: 5'10" Wt: 195 Born: 3/25/1987 Age: 28

		HOW MUCH HE PITCHED						WHAT HE GAVE UP												THE RESULTS						
Year Team	Lg	G	GS	CG	GF	IP	BFP	H	R	ER	HR	SH	SF	HB	TBB	IBB	SO	WP	Bk	W	L	Pct	Sh	Sv-Op	Hld	ERC	ERA
2010 BG	A	27	12	0	14	90.0	379	73	41	33	9	2	6	5	41	3	97	5	1	3	6	.333	0	5--	-	3.45	3.30
2010 Charltt	A+	1	1	0	0	5.1	21	7	3	3	0	0	0	0	2	0	3	0	0	0	0	-	0	0--	-	5.90	5.06
2011 Rays	R	4	4	0	0	6.2	29	6	3	2	0	0	0	1	2	0	3	0	0	0	1	.000	0	0--	-	2.95	2.70
2011 Charltt	A+	16	0	0	11	33.1	137	14	6	6	0	1	0	5	22	0	45	1	2	2	0	1.000	0	2--	-	1.93	1.62
2012 Mont	AA	50	0	0	39	68.0	285	48	21	20	4	4	1	1	39	2	94	8	0	4	2	.667	0	16--	-	2.90	2.65
2013 Drham	AAA	51	0	0	38	61.2	249	38	14	13	2	2	2	5	23	2	93	6	0	3	2	.600	0	20--	-	1.83	1.90
2014 Drham	AAA	21	0	0	21	25.0	97	10	1	1	0	1	0	1	9	0	35	0	1	1	0	1.000	0	16--	-	0.93	0.36
2014 TB	AL	37	0	0	12	36.0	156	33	16	15	4	0	1	3	15	3	42	2	0	0	2	.000	0	1-2	0	3.94	3.75

Christian Yelich

Bats: L Throws: R Pos: LF-138;CF-12;PH-1   YELL-itch   Ht: 6'3" Wt: 200 Born: 12/5/1991 Age: 23

		BATTING																	RUNNING			AVERAGES			
Year Team	Lg	G	AB	H	2B	3B	HR	(Hm Rd)	TB	R	RBI	RC	TBB	IBB	SO	HBP	SH	SF	SB	CS	GDP	Avg	OBP	Slg	OPS
2010 Mrlns	R	6	24	9	1	1	0	(- -)	12	3	3	5	2	0	7	0	0	0	1	0	3	.375	.423	.500	.923
2010 Grnsbr	A	6	23	8	2	0	0	(- -)	10	2	2	3	1	0	6	0	0	0	0	0	1	.348	.375	.435	.810
2011 Grnsbr	A	122	461	144	32	1	15	(- -)	223	73	77	92	55	1	102	3	0	2	32	5	10	.312	.388	.484	.871
2012 Jupiter	A+	106	397	131	29	5	12	(- -)	206	76	48	83	49	2	85	0	1	0	20	6	10	.330	.404	.519	.922
2012 Mrlns	R	1	4	1	0	0	0	(- -)	1	0	0	0	0	0	0	0	0	0	0	0	0	.250	.250	.250	.500
2013 Jupiter	A+	7	26	6	0	0	2	(- -)	12	3	4	4	4	0	8	0	0	0	0	0	1	.231	.333	.462	.795
2013 Jaxnvl	AA	49	193	54	13	6	7	(- -)	100	33	29	36	26	1	52	1	0	2	5	5	2	.280	.365	.518	.883
2013 Mrlns	R	5	17	5	0	1	0	(- -)	7	2	0	2	1	0	5	0	0	0	0	0	0	.294	.333	.412	.745
2014 Jupiter	A+	2	6	2	0	0	0	(- -)	2	2	1	1	1	0	1	0	0	0	1	0	0	.333	.429	.333	.762
2014 NewOr	AAA	2	9	1	0	0	1	(- -)	4	1	4	0	0	0	5	0	0	0	0	0	0	.111	.111	.444	.556
2013 Mia	NL	62	240	69	12	1	4	(0 4)	95	34	16	35	31	1	66	1	0	1	10	0	4	.288	.370	.396	.766
2014 Mia	NL	144	582	165	30	6	9	(2 7)	234	94	54	87	70	3	137	3	3	2	21	7	9	.284	.362	.402	.764
2 ML YEARS		206	822	234	42	7	13	(2 11)	329	128	70	122	101	4	203	4	3	3	31	7	13	.285	.365	.400	.765

Rafael Ynoa

Bats: B Throws: R Pos: 3B-13;PH-3;SS-2;2B-1   ee-NO-uh   Ht: 6'0" Wt: 185 Born: 8/7/1987 Age: 27

		BATTING																	RUNNING			AVERAGES			
Year Team	Lg	G	AB	H	2B	3B	HR	(Hm Rd)	TB	R	RBI	RC	TBB	IBB	SO	HBP	SH	SF	SB	CS	GDP	Avg	OBP	Slg	OPS
2010 Gt Lks	A	124	441	126	19	1	9	(- -)	174	67	51	64	37	0	55	1	14	3	40	14	8	.286	.340	.395	.735
2011 RCuca	A+	126	466	128	21	3	5	(- -)	170	61	54	59	42	0	69	2	9	7	13	11	14	.275	.333	.365	.697
2012 Chatt	AA	113	421	117	23	4	0	(- -)	148	58	37	61	58	0	70	1	9	4	23	9	11	.278	.364	.352	.715
2013 Chatt	AA	128	484	129	30	1	6	(- -)	179	56	33	63	51	2	69	1	7	0	16	11	7	.267	.338	.370	.708
2014 ColSpr	AAA	115	427	127	31	3	5	(- -)	179	66	32	64	38	2	78	2	4	2	7	7	10	.297	.356	.419	.775
2014 Col	NL	19	67	23	6	1	0	(0 0)	31	5	13	13	4	0	9	0	0	0	0	0	1	.343	.380	.463	.843

Chris Young

Pitches: R Bats: R Pos: SP-29; RP-1   Ht: 6'10" Wt: 255 Born: 5/25/1979 Age: 36

		HOW MUCH HE PITCHED						WHAT HE GAVE UP												THE RESULTS						
Year Team	Lg	G	GS	CG	GF	IP	BFP	H	R	ER	HR	SH	SF	HB	TBB	IBB	SO	WP	Bk	W	L	Pct	Sh	Sv-Op	Hld	ERC	ERA
2004 Tex	AL	7	7	0	0	36.1	158	36	21	19	7	1	0	2	10	0	27	1	0	3	2	.600	0	0-0	0	4.26	4.71
2005 Tex	AL	31	31	0	0	164.2	700	162	84	78	19	2	4	7	45	2	137	3	0	12	7	.632	0	0-0	0	3.71	4.26
2006 SD	NL	31	31	0	0	179.1	735	134	72	69	28	8	3	6	69	4	164	6	1	11	5	.688	0	0-0	0	3.12	3.46
2007 SD	NL	30	30	0	0	173.0	705	118	66	60	10	3	6	7	72	0	167	7	4	9	8	.529	0	0-0	0	2.35	3.12
2008 SD	NL	18	18	1	0	102.1	434	84	46	45	13	4	1	1	48	4	93	3	1	7	6	.538	0	0-0	0	3.50	3.96
2009 SD	NL	14	14	0	0	76.0	336	70	47	44	12	4	5	2	40	3	50	1	0	4	6	.400	0	0-0	0	4.55	5.21
2010 SD	NL	4	4	0	0	20.0	82	10	2	2	1	1	0	0	11	0	15	1	0	2	0	1.000	0	0-0	0	1.72	0.90
2011 NYM	NL	4	4	0	0	24.0	95	12	5	5	3	1	0	1	11	0	22	0	0	1	0	1.000	0	0-0	0	2.04	1.88
2012 NYM	NL	20	20	0	0	115.0	493	119	58	53	16	9	4	2	36	5	80	3	0	4	9	.308	0	0-0	0	4.19	4.15
2014 Sea	AL	30	29	0	0	165.0	688	143	70	67	26	4	8	3	60	3	108	5	1	12	9	.571	0	0-0	0	3.63	3.65
Postseason		1	1	0	0	6.2	25	4	0	0	0	0	0	0	2	1	9	0	0	1	0	1.000	0	0-0	0	1.22	0.00
10 ML YEARS		189	188	1	0	1055.2	4426	888	471	442	135	37	32	31	402	21	863	30	7	65	62	.550	0	0-0	0	3.39	3.77

Chris Young

Bats: R Throws: R Pos: LF-73;CF-27;PH-18;RF-7;DH-2;PR-1   Ht: 6'2" Wt: 200 Born: 9/5/1983 Age: 31

		BATTING																	RUNNING			AVERAGES			
Year Team	Lg	G	AB	H	2B	3B	HR	(Hm Rd)	TB	R	RBI	RC	TBB	IBB	SO	HBP	SH	SF	SB	CS	GDP	Avg	OBP	Slg	OPS
2014 LsVgs*	AAA	3	12	8	2	0	2	(- -)	16	7	5	7	2	2	2	0	0	0	1	0	0	.667	.714	1.333	2.048
2014 S-WB*	AAA	4	15	3	0	0	1	(- -)	6	1	2	1	1	0	6	0	0	0	0	0	1	.200	.250	.400	.650
2006 Ari	NL	30	70	17	4	0	2	(1 1)	27	10	10	11	6	0	12	1	0	0	2	1	0	.243	.308	.386	.693
2007 Ari	NL	148	569	135	29	3	32	(14 18)	266	85	68	68	43	1	141	6	1	5	27	6	5	.237	.295	.467	.763
2008 Ari	NL	160	625	155	42	7	22	(9 13)	277	85	85	84	62	2	165	1	6	5	14	5	10	.248	.315	.443	.758
2009 Ari	NL	134	433	92	28	4	15	(9 7)	173	54	42	47	59	2	133	4	3	2	11	4	3	.212	.311	.400	.711
2010 Ari	NL	156	584	150	33	7	27	(20 7)	264	94	91	86	74	0	145	2	1	3	28	7	10	.257	.341	.452	.793
2011 Ari	NL	156	567	134	38	3	20	(14 6)	238	89	71	84	80	4	139	4	1	7	22	9	3	.236	.331	.420	.751
2012 Ari	NL	101	325	75	24	0	14	(5 9)	141	36	41	46	36	0	79	2	0	8	8	3	4	.231	.311	.434	.745
2013 Oak	AL	107	335	67	18	3	12	(4 8)	127	46	40	32	36	3	93	2	0	2	10	3	7	.200	.280	.379	.659
2014 2 Tms	NL	111	325	72	20	0	11	(8 3)	125	40	38	37	32	2	70	5	1	3	8	3	3	.222	.299	.385	.683
14 NYM	NL	88	254	52	12	0	8	(6 2)	88	31	28	25	25	2	54	4	1	3	7	3	3	.205	.283	.346	.630
14 NYY	AL	23	71	20	8	0	3	(2 1)	37	9	10	12	7	0	16	1	0	0	1	0	0	.282	.354	.521	.876
Postseason		12	43	14	2	0	5	(3 2)	31	9	9	12	9	0	18	1	0	0	3	2	0	.326	.453	.721	1.174
9 ML YEARS		1103	3833	897	236	20	155	(82 73)	1638	539	486	495	428	14	977	27	13	28	130	41	45	.234	.313	.427	.741

Delmon Young

Bats: R **Throws:** R **Pos:** DH-39;LF-27;PH-23;RF-2   **Ht:** 6'3" **Wt:** 240 **Born:** 9/14/1985 **Age:** 29

									BATTING											RUNNING			AVERAGES			
Year	Team	Lg	G	AB	H	2B	3B	HR	(Hm	Rd)	TB	R	RBI	RC	TBB	IBB	SO	HBP	SH	SF	SB	CS	GDP	Avg	OBP	Slg	OPS
2006	TB	AL	30	126	40	9	1	3	(1	2)	60	16	10	15	1	0	24	3	0	1	2	2	0	.317	.336	.476	.812
2007	TB	AL	162	645	186	38	4	13	(9	4)	263	65	93	90	26	2	127	3	0	7	10	3	23	.288	.316	.408	.723
2008	Min	AL	152	575	167	28	4	10	(7	3)	233	80	69	74	35	7	105	7	1	5	14	5	19	.284	.336	.405	.741
2009	Min	AL	108	395	112	16	2	12	(7	5)	168	50	60	46	12	1	92	4	0	5	2	5	17	.284	.308	.425	.733
2010	Min	AL	153	570	170	46	1	21	(6	15)	281	77	112	94	28	5	81	6	0	9	5	4	16	.298	.333	.493	.826
2011	2 Tms	AL	124	473	127	21	1	12	(8	4)	186	54	64	57	23	2	85	2	0	5	1	0	19	.268	.302	.393	.695
2012	Det	AL	151	574	153	27	1	18	(9	9)	236	54	74	62	20	1	112	7	0	7	0	2	20	.267	.296	.411	.707
2013	2 Tms	AL	103	334	87	16	0	11	(3	8)	136	30	38	36	20	0	78	4	0	3	0	0	8	.260	.307	.407	.715
2014	Bal	AL	83	242	73	11	1	7	(4	3)	107	27	30	34	10	0	51	3	0	0	2	0	6	.302	.337	.442	.779
11	Min	AL	84	305	81	16	0	4	(1	3)	109	26	32	32	18	2	55	0	0	2	1	0	12	.266	.305	.357	.662
11	Det	AL	40	168	46	5	1	8	(7	1)	77	28	32	25	5	0	30	2	0	3	0	0	7	.274	.298	.458	.756
13	Phi	NL	80	272	71	13	0	8	(3	5)	108	22	31	30	14	0	69	3	0	2	0	0	7	.261	.302	.397	.699
13	TB	AL	23	62	16	3	0	3	(0	3)	28	8	7	6	6	0	9	1	0	1	0	0	1	.258	.329	.452	.780
	Postseason		33	117	31	3	1	9	(5	4)	63	14	18	12	8	2	25	2	0	1	1	1	2	.265	.320	.538	.859
	9 ML YEARS		1066	3934	1115	212	11	107	(54	53)	1670	453	550	508	175	18	755	39	1	42	36	21	128	.283	.317	.425	.742

Eric Young

Bats: B **Throws:** R **Pos:** LF-73;PH-21;PR-8;2B-2;CF-1;DH-1   **Ht:** 5'10" **Wt:** 195 **Born:** 5/25/1985 **Age:** 30

									BATTING											RUNNING			AVERAGES			
Year	Team	Lg	G	AB	H	2B	3B	HR	(Hm	Rd)	TB	R	RBI	RC	TBB	IBB	SO	HBP	SH	SF	SB	CS	GDP	Avg	OBP	Slg	OPS
2014	StLuci*	A+	1	4	1	0	0	0	(-	-)	1	2	0	0	1	0	0	0	0	0	0	0	0	.250	.400	.250	.650
2014	Bnghtn*	AA	3	9	0	0	0	0	(-	-)	0	2	0	0	2	0	3	0	0	0	1	0	0	.000	.182	.000	.182
2009	Col	NL	30	57	14	1	0	1	(1	0)	18	7	1	2	4	0	12	0	0	0	4	4	1	.246	.295	.316	.611
2010	Col	NL	51	172	42	5	1	0	(0	0)	49	26	8	16	17	0	32	0	0	0	17	6	2	.244	.312	.285	.597
2011	Col	NL	77	198	49	4	3	0	(0	0)	59	34	10	27	26	0	38	3	1	1	27	4	1	.247	.342	.298	.640
2012	Col	NL	98	174	55	7	2	4	(2	2)	78	36	15	29	13	0	31	4	5	0	14	2	1	.316	.377	.448	.825
2013	2 Tms	NL	148	539	134	27	7	2	(1	1)	181	70	32	58	46	1	100	2	10	1	46	11	6	.249	.310	.336	.645
2014	NYM	NL	100	280	64	10	5	1	(1	0)	87	48	17	30	24	1	60	5	5	2	30	6	2	.229	.299	.311	.610
13	Col	NL	57	165	40	9	3	1	(0	1)	58	22	6	14	11	0	33	0	4	0	8	4	1	.242	.290	.352	.641
13	NYM	NL	91	374	94	18	4	1	(1	0)	123	48	26	44	35	1	67	2	6	1	38	7	5	.251	.318	.329	.647
	Postseason		2	1	0	0	0	0	(-	-)	0	0	0	0	0	0	0	0	0	0	0	0	0	.000	.000	.000	.000
	6 ML YEARS		504	1420	358	54	18	8	(4	4)	472	221	83	162	130	2	273	14	21	4	138	33	13	.252	.320	.332	.653

Josh Zeid

Pitches: R **Bats:** R **Pos:** RP-23   ZIDE   **Ht:** 6'4" **Wt:** 235 **Born:** 3/24/1987 **Age:** 28

				HOW MUCH HE PITCHED					WHAT HE GAVE UP												THE RESULTS					
Year	Team	Lg	G	GS	CG	GF	IP	BFP	H	R	ER	HR	SH	SF	HB	TBB	IBB	SO	WP	Bk	W	L	Pct	Sh	Sv-Op	Hld	ERC	ERA
2010	Lakwd	A	43	12	0	15	107.1	440	95	41	35	7	7	2	4	27	2	111	7	1	8	4	.667	0	8- -		2.79	2.93
2011	Rdng	AA	21	11	0	6	63.2	275	63	43	40	9	3	4	3	27	0	56	6	0	2	3	.400	0	2- -		4.66	5.65
2011	CpChr	AA	14	1	0	5	16.0	78	23	21	18	5	2	0	1	6	1	15	2	0	0	1	.000	0	0- -		8.37	10.13
2012	CpChr	AA	47	0	0	20	56.1	247	57	35	35	6	0	6	4	20	3	66	9	1	2	0	1.000	0	1- -		4.16	5.59
2013	OKCity	AAA	43	0	0	24	43.2	189	36	17	17	3	1	5	0	27	1	53	6	0	4	1	.800	0	13- -		3.71	3.50
2014	OKCity	AAA	17	0	0	11	18.2	78	14	8	5	2	2	1	0	9	2	21	1	0	2	2	.500	0	7- -		2.92	2.41
2013	Hou	AL	25	0	0	6	27.2	118	26	12	12	3	1	0	1	12	1	24	2	0	0	1	.000	0	1-2		4.07	3.90
2014	Hou	AL	23	0	0	6	20.2	98	30	18	16	6	1	2	1	7	1	18	1	0	0	0	-	0	0-0	3	8.24	6.97
	2 ML YEARS		48	0	0	12	48.1	216	56	30	28	9	2	2	2	19	2	42	3	0	0	1	.000	0	1-2	9	5.76	5.21

Brad Ziegler

Pitches: R **Bats:** R **Pos:** RP-68   ZIGG-lerr   **Ht:** 6'4" **Wt:** 210 **Born:** 10/10/1979 **Age:** 35

				HOW MUCH HE PITCHED					WHAT HE GAVE UP												THE RESULTS					
Year	Team	Lg	G	GS	CG	GF	IP	BFP	H	R	ER	HR	SH	SF	HB	TBB	IBB	SO	WP	Bk	W	L	Pct	Sh	Sv-Op	Hld	ERC	ERA
2008	Oak	AL	47	0	0	21	59.2	229	47	8	7	2	4	3	1	22	3	30	0	0	3	0	1.000	0	11-13	7	2.60	1.06
2009	Oak	AL	69	0	0	23	73.1	313	82	27	25	2	1	3	1	28	4	54	0	0	2	4	.333	0	7-10	14	3.63	3.07
2010	Oak	AL	64	0	0	12	60.2	257	54	24	22	4	1	1	3	28	9	41	0	1	3	7	.300	0	0-4	18	3.48	3.26
2011	2 Tms		66	0	0	16	58.1	239	53	21	14	0	1	2	1	19	3	44	1	0	3	2	.600	0	1-2	10	2.68	2.16
2012	Ari	NL	77	0	0	15	68.2	263	54	21	19	2	2	2	1	21	2	42	1	0	6	1	.857	0	0-2	17	2.33	2.49
2013	Ari	NL	78	0	0	33	73.0	297	61	20	20	3	2	2	3	22	6	44	0	0	8	1	.889	0	13-15	11	2.51	2.22
2014	Ari	NL	68	0	0	11	67.0	281	60	29	26	5	2	4	3	24	6	54	0	0	5	3	.625	0	1-9	29	3.22	3.49
11	Oak	AL	43	0	0	12	37.2	160	38	14	10	0	1	1	1	13	3	29	1	0	3	2	.600	0	1-2	6	3.21	2.39
11	Ari	NL	23	0	0	4	20.2	79	15	7	4	0	0	1	0	6	0	15	0	0	0	0	-	0	0-0	4	1.77	1.74
	Postseason		2	0	0	0	0.1	7	4	4	4	0	0	0	0	2	1	0	0	1	0	0	-	0	0-0	0	115.8	108.0
	7 ML YEARS		469	0	0	131	460.2	1879	411	150	131	18	13	17	13	164	33	309	2	1	30	18	.625	0	33-55	108	3.01	2.56

Ryan Zimmerman

Bats: R **Throws:** R **Pos:** LF-30;3B-23;1B-5;PH-4;DH-2   **Ht:** 6'3" **Wt:** 220 **Born:** 9/28/1984 **Age:** 30

									BATTING											RUNNING			AVERAGES			
Year	Team	Lg	G	AB	H	2B	3B	HR	(Hm	Rd)	TB	R	RBI	RC	TBB	IBB	SO	HBP	SH	SF	SB	CS	GDP	Avg	OBP	Slg	OPS
2014	Ptomc*	A+	4	14	5	1	0	0	(-	-)	6	0	3	6	0	0	1	0	0	1	0	1	0	.357	.333	.429	.762
2005	Was	NL	20	58	23	10	0	0	(0	0)	33	6	6	9	3	0	12	0	0	1	0	0	0	.397	.419	.569	.988
2006	Was	NL	157	614	176	47	3	20	(10	10)	289	84	110	101	61	7	120	2	1	4	11	8	15	.287	.351	.471	.822
2007	Was	NL	162	653	174	43	5	24	(11	13)	299	99	91	83	61	3	125	3	0	5	4	1	26	.266	.330	.458	.788
2008	Was	NL	106	428	121	24	1	14	(7	7)	189	51	51	48	31	4	71	3	0	4	1	1	12	.283	.333	.442	.774
2009	Was	NL	157	610	178	37	3	33	(17	16)	320	110	106	96	72	9	119	2	0	9	2	0	22	.292	.364	.525	.888
2010	Was	NL	142	525	161	32	0	25	(9	16)	268	85	85	97	69	6	98	4	0	5	4	1	16	.307	.388	.510	.899

Year Team	Lg	G	AB	H	2B	3B	HR	(Hm	Rd)	TB	R	RBI	RC	TBB	IBB	SO	HBP	SH	SF	SB	CS	GDP	Avg	OBP	Slg	OPS
2011 Was	NL	101	395	114	21	2	12	(7	5)	175	52	49	58	41	4	73	1	0	3	3	1	14	.289	.355	.443	.798
2012 Was	NL	145	578	163	36	1	25	(16	9)	276	93	95	84	57	8	116	2	0	4	5	2	20	.282	.346	.478	.824
2013 Was	NL	147	568	156	26	2	26	(7	19)	264	84	79	83	60	2	133	2	0	3	6	0	16	.275	.344	.465	.809
2014 Was	NL	61	214	60	19	1	5	(1	4)	96	26	38	32	22	0	37	0	0	4	0	0	6	.280	.342	.449	.790
Postseason		5	21	8	1	0	2	(1	1)	15	3	4	5	0	0	6	0	0	1	0	0	0	.381	.364	.714	1.078
10 ML YEARS		1198	4643	1326	295	18	184	(85	99)	2209	690	710	691	477	40	904	19	1	42	36	14	148	.286	.352	.476	.827

Jordan Zimmermann

Pitches: R Bats: R Pos: SP-32   Ht: 6'2" Wt: 220 Born: 5/23/1986 Age: 29

Year Team	Lg	G	GS	CG	GF	IP	BFP	H	R	ER	HR	SH	SF	HB	TBB	IBB	SO	WP	Bk	W	L	Pct	Sh	Sv-Op	Hld	ERC	ERA
2009 Was	NL	16	16	0	0	91.1	391	95	51	47	10	5	3	4	29	0	92	0	0	3	5	.375	0	0-0	0	4.25	4.63
2010 Was	NL	7	7	0	0	31.0	135	31	20	17	8	1	1	2	10	1	27	0	0	1	2	.333	0	0-0	0	5.02	4.94
2011 Was	NL	26	26	1	0	161.1	662	154	62	57	12	8	2	7	31	2	124	3	1	8	11	.421	0	0-0	0	3.02	3.18
2012 Was	NL	32	32	0	0	195.2	805	186	69	64	18	8	4	8	43	2	153	3	0	12	8	.600	0	0-0	0	3.22	2.94
2013 Was	NL	32	32	4	0	213.1	865	192	81	77	19	9	4	7	40	0	161	3	0	19	9	.679	2	0-0	0	2.79	3.25
2014 Was	NL	32	32	3	0	199.2	800	185	67	59	13	5	3	6	29	0	182	4	0	14	5	.737	2	0-0	0	2.64	2.66
Postseason		2	1	0	0	4.0	18	7	5	5	1	0	0	0	0	0	5	0	0	0	1	.000	0	0-0	0	8.42	11.25
6 ML YEARS		145	145	8	0	892.1	3658	843	350	321	80	36	17	34	182	5	739	13	1	57	40	.588	4	0-0	0	3.11	3.24

Ben Zobrist

ZOH-brist

Bats: B Throws: R Pos: 2B-79;LF-38;SS-31;RF-19;DH-8;CF-7;PH-2   Ht: 6'3" Wt: 210 Born: 5/26/1981 Age: 34

Year Team	Lg	G	AB	H	2B	3B	HR	(Hm	Rd)	TB	R	RBI	RC	TBB	IBB	SO	HBP	SH	SF	SB	CS	GDP	Avg	OBP	Slg	OPS
2014 Charltt*	A+	1	4	1	0	0	0	(-	-)	1	0	0	0	1	0	0	0	0	0	0	0	0	.250	.400	.250	.650
2006 TB	AL	52	183	41	6	2	2	(2	0)	57	10	18	13	10	1	26	0	2	3	2	3	2	.224	.260	.311	.572
2007 TB	AL	31	97	15	2	0	1	(0	1)	20	8	9	0	3	0	21	1	2	2	2	0	1	.155	.184	.206	.391
2008 TB	AL	62	198	50	10	2	12	(4	8)	100	32	30	31	25	1	37	2	0	2	3	0	4	.253	.339	.505	.844
2009 TB	AL	152	501	149	28	7	27	(18	9)	272	91	91	109	91	4	104	2	1	4	17	6	7	.297	.405	.543	.948
2010 TB	AL	151	541	129	28	1	10	(3	7)	191	77	75	84	92	1	107	3	7	12	24	3	10	.238	.346	.353	.699
2011 TB	AL	156	588	158	46	6	20	(9	11)	276	99	91	100	77	1	128	2	2	5	19	6	9	.269	.353	.469	.822
2012 TB	AL	157	560	151	39	7	20	(8	12)	264	88	74	102	97	7	103	3	2	6	14	9	13	.270	.377	.471	.848
2013 TB	AL	157	612	168	36	3	12	(7	5)	246	77	71	85	72	4	91	7	1	6	11	3	18	.275	.354	.402	.756
2014 TB	AL	146	570	155	34	3	10	(4	6)	225	83	52	75	75	4	84	1	2	6	10	5	8	.272	.354	.395	.749
Postseason		21	66	14	2	0	2	(1	1)	22	7	3	2	6	0	14	1	0	0	0	0	1	.212	.288	.333	.621
9 ML YEARS		1064	3850	1016	229	32	114	(55	59)	1651	565	511	599	542	23	701	21	19	46	102	35	72	.264	.354	.429	.783

Mike Zunino

zoo-NEE-no

Bats: R Throws: R Pos: C-130;DH-1;PR-1   Ht: 6'2" Wt: 220 Born: 3/25/1991 Age: 24

Year Team	Lg	G	AB	H	2B	3B	HR	(Hm	Rd)	TB	R	RBI	RC	TBB	IBB	SO	HBP	SH	SF	SB	CS	GDP	Avg	OBP	Slg	OPS
2012 Everett	A-	29	110	41	10	0	10	(-	-)	81	29	35	35	18	1	26	4	0	1	1	0	2	.373	.474	.736	1.210
2012 Jacksn	AA	15	51	17	4	0	3	(-	-)	30	6	8	11	5	1	7	0	0	1	0	0	0	.333	.386	.588	.974
2013 Tacom	AAA	52	203	46	12	3	11	(-	-)	97	38	43	30	17	1	66	5	0	4	0	0	3	.227	.297	.478	.775
2013 Sea	AL	52	173	37	5	0	5	(3	2)	57	22	14	13	16	0	49	3	0	1	1	0	5	.214	.290	.329	.620
2014 Sea	AL	131	438	87	20	2	22	(10	12)	177	51	60	39	17	1	158	17	0	4	0	3	13	.199	.254	.404	.658
2 ML YEARS		183	611	124	25	2	27	(13	14)	234	73	74	52	33	1	207	20	0	5	1	3	18	.203	.265	.383	.648

2014 Fielding Statistics

Among the most jaw-dropping plays of the 2014 season were some of the throws that Yoenis Cespedes made to gun down runners at the plate from his position in left field. If you are of the opinion that Cespedes has the best throwing arm in the game, then the numbers bear that out. Cespedes led all outfielders in assists (16) and in Outfield Arm Runs Saved (14). However, Cespedes' ability to get to fly-balls hit his way was not nearly as impressive. He actually ended up costing the Athletics and Red Sox a combined six runs with his lack of range.

If you were curious who had the best range out in left field in 2014, that would be Christian Yelich with 19 Plus/Minus Runs Saved. He was the bizarro Cespedes. Despite his outstanding range, he ended up costing the Marlins five runs with his less than threatening throwing arm.

For the total package, though, you would want Alex Gordon manning left field for your team. Gordon's got the range (16 Plus/Minus Runs Saved) and the arm (9 Outfield Arm Runs Saved), ranking second behind Yelich and Cespedes in each, respectively, among left fielders. Combined with his Good Fielding Play/Defensive Misplay Runs Saved, Gordon set a new record for Defensive Runs Saved by a left fielder since the genesis of the metric in 2003 with 27.

In this section, you can find Plus/Minus (PM) and Defensive Runs Saved (Runs Saved for short) numbers for every player at every position they played, as well as traditional statistics such as putouts, assists, errors, and fielding percentage. Players are split between "Regulars" (players that played at least 750 innings in the field or 600 innings at catcher) and "All Others". The Regulars are grouped by position and listed in order of most-to-least Runs Saved. Each component of Runs Saved is also shown. A more detailed description of Runs Saved can be found in the glossary.

Fielding data for pitchers can be found in the "Pitchers Hitting, Fielding, and Holding Runners" section.

First Basemen - Regulars

Player	Tm	G	GS	Inn	PO	A	E	DP	Pct.	PM	+/-	GFP/ DME	Bunts/ GDP	Total
Gonzalez,Adrian	LAD	157	152	1325.1	1318	118	6	118	.996	+8	6	2	3	11
Adams,Matt	StL	133	132	1163.0	1115	80	9	111	.993	+10	7	0	1	8
Davis,Chris	Bal	115	104	942.2	909	52	4	97	.996	+9	6	2	0	8
Morneau,Justin	Col	131	126	1105.2	1170	86	4	122	.997	+5	4	3	1	8
Napoli,Mike	Bos	110	109	959.1	904	71	8	92	.992	+10	7	0	0	7
Rizzo,Anthony	ChC	140	140	1259.0	1184	118	9	104	.993	+7	6	1	-1	6
Pujols,Albert	LAA	116	116	1017.0	879	81	3	78	.997	+7	5	1	0	6
Duda,Lucas	NYM	146	136	1225.0	1108	82	7	125	.994	+4	3	2	0	5
Mauer,Joe	Min	100	99	851.0	830	82	3	85	.997	+5	4	1	-1	4
Hosmer,Eric	KC	130	126	1121.2	1043	88	10	85	.991	-1	-1	4	0	3
Teixeira,Mark	NYY	117	116	1021.1	915	66	6	73	.994	+1	1	1	0	2
Goldschmidt,Paul	Ari	109	108	966.1	934	80	7	83	.993	+4	3	-1	-1	1
LaRoche,Adam	Was	136	135	1200.0	1100	93	7	101	.994	-3	-2	1	1	0
Cabrera,Miguel	Det	126	125	1083.1	978	98	5	100	.995	-2	-2	0	1	-1
Loney,James	TB	152	148	1334.0	1111	58	9	78	.992	-6	-5	3	1	-1
Davis,Ike	TOT	124	99	861.0	953	60	9	83	.991	-3	-2	-2	0	-4
Santana,Carlos	Cle	94	93	851.0	842	64	5	71	.995	-7	-5	0	1	-4
Jones,Garrett	Mia	129	122	1080.1	990	107	13	103	.988	-3	-2	-3	0	-5
Singleton,Jon	Hou	91	86	770.2	776	53	11	75	.987	-8	-5	-1	1	-5
Freeman,Freddie	Atl	162	162	1449.0	1271	116	5	130	.996	-13	-9	3	-1	-7
Howard,Ryan	Phi	141	141	1256.1	1224	80	9	103	.993	-7	-5	-5	0	-10
Abreu,Jose	CWS	109	109	957.1	970	69	6	105	.994	-9	-6	-4	0	-10

Second Basemen - Regulars

Player	Tm	G	GS	Inn	PO	A	E	DP	Pct.	Range	PM	+/-	GFP/ DME	GDP	Total
Kinsler,Ian	Det	160	160	1414.0	289	468	9	101	.988	4.82	+30	23	-2	-1	20
Pedroia,Dustin	Bos	135	133	1187.1	247	405	2	96	.997	4.94	+24	19	0	-2	17
LeMahieu,DJ	Col	144	135	1179.2	257	413	6	99	.991	5.11	+20	15	0	1	16
Schoop,Jonathan	Bal	123	112	1010.2	206	338	7	89	.987	4.84	+6	5	0	5	10
Wong,Kolten	StL	107	100	887.0	196	273	12	70	.975	4.76	+9	7	0	2	9
Kendrick,Howie	LAA	154	154	1386.0	267	406	11	83	.984	4.37	+6	4	1	2	7
Phillips,Brandon	Cin	121	121	1054.1	216	307	2	68	.996	4.46	+7	5	1	0	6
Roberts,Brian	NYY	91	85	774.2	135	239	10	34	.974	4.35	+9	7	-2	-2	3
Utley,Chase	Phi	147	147	1321.2	292	423	11	87	.985	4.87	+8	6	-1	-2	3
Beckham,Gordon	TOT	105	103	914.2	205	319	10	75	.981	5.16	-3	-2	3	2	3
Infante,Omar	KC	134	134	1170.0	187	304	11	67	.978	3.78	+4	3	-1	-1	1
Cano,Robinson	Sea	150	149	1304.0	261	427	9	103	.987	4.75	-4	-3	1	2	0
Dozier,Brian	Min	156	155	1361.0	261	475	15	98	.980	4.87	-6	-4	4	0	0
Walker,Neil	Pit	135	132	1175.2	253	374	5	89	.992	4.80	-6	-5	1	2	-2
Gordon,Dee	LAD	144	139	1240.1	256	375	12	84	.981	4.58	-5	-3	-2	0	-5
Gennett,Scooter	Mil	119	110	966.0	202	268	9	62	.981	4.38	-3	-3	0	-2	-5
Hill,Aaron	Ari	116	116	1020.2	215	347	7	69	.988	4.96	-12	-9	2	0	-7
Altuve,Jose	Hou	156	156	1362.1	268	459	10	105	.986	4.80	-13	-10	1	2	-7
Gyorko,Jedd	SD	109	106	951.1	185	281	11	61	.977	4.41	-8	-6	0	-3	-9
Murphy,Daniel	NYM	126	126	1140.1	209	347	15	88	.974	4.39	-8	-6	-1	-3	-10
Kipnis,Jason	Cle	123	121	1075.0	181	347	6	63	.989	4.42	-8	-6	-3	-2	-11
Odor,Rougned	Tex	110	106	933.0	194	275	9	70	.981	4.52	-16	-12	0	1	-11

Third Basemen - Regulars

Player	Tm	G	GS	Inn	PO	A	E	DP	Pct.	Range	PM	+/-	GFP/ DME	Bunts/ GDP	Total
Donaldson,Josh	Oak	150	146	1320.2	131	328	23	43	.952	3.13	+20	15	5	0	20
Uribe,Juan	LAD	102	98	874.1	60	215	6	25	.979	2.83	+22	17	-2	2	17
Arenado,Nolan	Col	111	111	967.0	69	281	15	31	.959	3.26	+18	13	2	1	16
Headley,Chase	TOT	127	124	1082.2	77	234	8	25	.975	2.59	+19	14	-1	0	13
Wright,David	NYM	133	133	1190.0	83	231	15	21	.954	2.37	+17	13	0	0	13
Rendon,Anthony	Was	134	126	1148.2	106	235	15	30	.958	2.67	+3	3	1	8	12
Seager,Kyle	Sea	157	157	1402.0	86	327	8	36	.981	2.65	+13	10	-1	1	10
Beltre,Adrian	Tex	136	136	1171.1	144	206	12	25	.967	2.69	+8	6	1	2	9
Prado,Martin	TOT	110	106	942.2	74	203	13	20	.955	2.64	+14	11	-2	-1	8
Frazier,Todd	Cin	124	118	1046.2	85	204	9	16	.970	2.49	+8	6	0	1	7
Plouffe,Trevor	Min	127	127	1110.2	109	226	14	25	.960	2.71	+6	5	1	0	6
Sandoval,Pablo	SF	151	150	1265.2	89	282	11	27	.971	2.64	+6	5	0	-1	4
Moustakas,Mike	KC	138	126	1148.2	97	241	19	14	.947	2.65	+4	3	-3	-2	-2
Solarte,Yangervis	TOT	111	97	877.2	61	155	12	19	.947	2.21	-1	0	-1	-1	-2

Player	Tm	G	GS	Inn	PO	A	E	DP	Pct.	Range	PM	+/-	GFP/ DME	Bunts/ GDP	Total
Carpenter,Matt	StL	156	155	1371.0	90	288	16	23	.959	2.48	-3	-2	-2	2	-2
McGehee,Casey	Mia	158	158	1409.2	78	241	7	34	.979	2.04	-6	-4	2	0	-2
Asche,Cody	Phi	112	105	924.2	59	206	16	18	.943	2.58	-2	-2	-1	0	-3
Dominguez,Matt	Hou	153	147	1302.2	109	278	11	22	.972	2.67	-7	-6	2	0	-4
Alvarez,Pedro	Pit	99	95	823.1	69	233	25	25	.924	3.30	+3	2	-2	-5	-5
Ramirez,Aramis	Mil	126	126	1077.0	74	184	10	12	.963	2.16	-3	-2	-1	-2	-5
Longoria,Evan	TB	155	154	1381.2	121	262	13	27	.967	2.49	-7	-5	0	0	-5
Freese,David	LAA	122	119	959.1	67	162	8	19	.966	2.15	-11	-9	2	-2	-9
Valbuena,Luis	ChC	124	105	971.0	78	202	9	17	.969	2.60	-11	-8	0	-2	-10
Gillaspie,Conor	CWS	127	120	1063.2	79	216	12	26	.961	2.50	-20	-16	3	1	-12
Johnson,Chris	Atl	150	149	1317.2	56	209	6	18	.978	1.81	-13	-10	-3	0	-13
Chisenhall,Lonnie	Cle	114	108	973.2	60	182	18	9	.931	2.24	-16	-12	1	-3	-14
Castellanos,Nick	Det	145	141	1229.0	75	212	15	22	.950	2.10	-39	-29	1	-2	-30

Shortstops - Regulars

Player	Tm	G	GS	Inn	PO	A	E	DP	Pct.	Range	PM	+/-	GFP/ DME	GDP	Total
Simmons,Andrelton	Atl	146	144	1277.0	217	411	14	99	.978	4.43	+28	21	4	3	28
Cozart,Zack	Cin	147	143	1274.1	204	400	10	73	.984	4.27	+27	20	0	-1	19
Peralta,Jhonny	StL	152	151	1325.1	191	418	12	98	.981	4.14	+17	13	2	2	17
Hardy,J.J.	Bal	141	141	1257.0	187	394	13	99	.978	4.16	+4	3	3	4	10
Mercer,Jordy	Pit	144	137	1222.1	159	439	11	80	.982	4.40	+13	9	-1	1	9
Crawford,Brandon	SF	149	142	1273.0	185	429	21	85	.967	4.34	+7	5	0	3	8
Rollins,Jimmy	Phi	131	129	1170.2	158	398	7	64	.988	4.27	+5	4	2	-2	4
Cabrera,Everth	SD	90	90	804.0	126	254	13	47	.967	4.25	+10	7	0	-4	3
Tejada,Ruben	NYM	114	105	939.1	147	339	8	79	.984	4.66	+7	6	-1	-2	3
Segura,Jean	Mil	144	139	1236.2	180	447	16	83	.975	4.56	+9	7	-2	-3	2
Desmond,Ian	Was	154	154	1377.2	203	416	24	82	.963	4.04	+3	2	-2	1	1
Miller,Brad	Sea	107	105	924.0	146	267	18	48	.958	4.02	-3	-2	1	-2	-3
Hechavarria,Adeiny	Mia	146	146	1294.2	200	438	14	87	.979	4.44	-5	-4	3	-2	-3
Aybar,Erick	LAA	155	154	1365.0	194	359	10	76	.982	3.65	-8	-6	2	1	-3
Escobar,Alcides	KC	162	162	1433.2	213	440	16	91	.976	4.10	-5	-4	1	-1	-4
Ramirez,Alexei	CWS	158	157	1376.2	195	486	15	119	.978	4.45	-14	-10	3	3	-4
Escobar,Eduardo	Min	98	86	771.2	130	224	5	49	.986	4.13	-4	-3	-1	-2	-6
Cabrera,Asdrubal	TOT	93	92	823.2	115	255	14	57	.964	4.04	-6	-5	-1	-1	-7
Castro,Starlin	ChC	133	133	1188.0	148	386	15	74	.973	4.05	-7	-6	-3	2	-7
Ramirez,Hanley	LAD	115	115	919.2	148	246	16	53	.961	3.86	-13	-10	0	1	-9
Bogaerts,Xander	Bos	99	98	880.0	138	256	10	54	.975	4.03	-8	-6	-1	-3	-10
Lowrie,Jed	Oak	130	129	1146.1	146	344	13	71	.974	3.85	-8	-6	-2	-2	-10
Jeter,Derek	NYY	130	129	1138.1	144	256	11	48	.973	3.16	-12	-9	-1	-2	-12
Andrus,Elvis	Tex	153	152	1309.1	237	371	18	94	.971	4.18	-16	-12	-2	1	-13
Reyes,Jose	Tor	142	141	1243.2	160	371	19	75	.965	3.84	-21	-16	-1	1	-16
Escobar,Yunel	TB	136	134	1183.1	168	267	16	50	.965	3.31	-22	-17	-4	-3	-24

Left Fielders - Regulars

Player	Tm	G	GS	Inn	PO	A	E	DP	Pct.	Range	PM	+/-	GFP/ DME	Throws	Total
Gordon,Alex	KC	156	155	1372.2	341	8	2	0	.994	2.29	+29	16	2	9	27
Yelich,Christian	Mia	138	133	1182.0	255	6	1	1	.996	1.99	+34	19	-1	-5	13
Cespedes,Yoenis	TOT	125	122	1090.2	216	16	5	0	.979	1.91	-9	-6	4	14	12
Marte,Starling	Pit	114	107	943.2	151	4	5	0	.969	1.48	+13	7	2	1	10
Ackley,Dustin	Sea	133	127	1130.0	246	4	2	2	.992	1.99	+6	4	1	2	7
Davis,Khris	Mil	134	131	1156.1	252	2	3	0	.988	1.98	+16	9	-1	-3	5
Gardner,Brett	NYY	126	120	1067.1	227	3	2	0	.991	1.94	+5	3	1	-1	3
Upton,Justin	Atl	150	150	1319.2	271	5	8	0	.972	1.88	+12	7	-4	-3	0
Holliday,Matt	StL	150	150	1280.2	240	5	7	1	.972	1.72	+9	5	-1	-4	0
Brantley,Michael	Cle	107	106	931.1	165	10	0	2	1.000	1.69	-8	-5	2	3	0
De Aza,Alejandro	TOT	132	116	1035.1	228	5	3	1	.987	2.03	+5	2	-2	-1	-1
Dickerson,Corey	Col	99	89	803.0	156	2	4	0	.975	1.77	+4	2	-1	-3	-2
Cabrera,Melky	Tor	133	130	1134.2	230	13	2	3	.992	1.93	-23	-13	2	6	-5
Ludwick,Ryan	Cin	92	91	751.2	135	1	0	0	1.000	1.63	-12	-7	2	-1	-6
Brown,Domonic	Phi	127	117	1041.1	182	4	2	2	.989	1.61	-15	-9	-2	3	-8
Coghlan,Chris	ChC	101	91	812.2	164	6	4	2	.977	1.88	-21	-12	0	-2	-14

Center Fielders - Regulars

Player	Tm	G	GS	Inn	PO	A	E	DP	Pct.	Range	PM	+/-	GFP/ DME	Throws	Total
Lagares,Juan	NYM	112	105	945.0	293	6	5	0	.984	2.85	+40	22	0	6	28
Martin,Leonys	Tex	152	140	1247.1	415	11	8	3	.982	3.07	+1	0	3	12	15
Bradley Jr.,Jackie	Bos	113	105	949.0	293	13	1	8	.997	2.90	+18	10	0	4	14
Hamilton,Billy	Cin	144	136	1199.1	342	10	2	3	.994	2.64	+15	8	2	4	14
Eaton,Adam	CWS	121	121	1043.2	312	9	4	1	.988	2.77	+20	11	3	-2	12
Ozuna,Marcell	Mia	140	136	1206.0	325	8	5	0	.985	2.49	+14	8	0	2	10
Jennings,Desmond	TB	118	115	1033.1	307	2	0	0	1.000	2.69	+7	4	2	-2	4
Gomez,Carlos	Mil	145	144	1269.2	355	7	5	2	.986	2.57	+8	4	-1	-1	2
Jones,Adam	Bal	155	153	1368.1	374	7	6	3	.984	2.51	-8	-4	2	4	2
Jackson,Austin	TOT	154	151	1326.0	378	4	6	2	.985	2.59	+9	4	0	-4	0
Stubbs,Drew	Col	113	92	835.0	215	7	7	1	.969	2.39	+3	2	-3	1	0
Span,Denard	Was	147	144	1302.2	377	7	4	3	.990	2.65	-4	-2	0	-1	-3
Ellsbury,Jacoby	NYY	141	138	1237.0	380	3	1	1	.997	2.79	-8	-4	0	-1	-5
Pagan,Angel	SF	91	91	775.1	209	3	1	1	.995	2.46	-8	-5	0	0	-5
Bourn,Michael	Cle	105	104	925.2	235	5	2	1	.992	2.33	-14	-8	1	1	-6
Upton,B.J.	Atl	139	135	1218.1	329	9	7	3	.980	2.50	-14	-8	-2	3	-7
Trout,Mike	LAA	149	149	1314.0	383	4	3	1	.992	2.65	-10	-5	2	-6	-9
McCutchen,Andrew	Pit	146	146	1286.0	301	1	6	0	.981	2.11	+1	0	-4	-7	-11
Crisp,Coco	Oak	111	101	900.2	194	0	3	0	.985	1.94	-20	-11	-1	-5	-17
Revere,Ben	Phi	141	132	1199.0	323	2	4	0	.988	2.44	-19	-10	2	-6	-18
Fowler,Dexter	Hou	111	110	959.0	238	4	5	1	.980	2.27	-29	-16	0	-4	-20

Right Fielders - Regulars

Player	Tm	G	GS	Inn	PO	A	E	DP	Pct.	Range	PM	+/-	GFP/ DME	Throws	Total
Heyward,Jason	Atl	149	148	1317.0	365	9	1	2	.997	2.56	+50	29	2	1	32
Reddick,Josh	Oak	107	99	873.1	193	5	5	2	.975	2.04	+19	11	0	2	13
Stanton,Giancarlo	Mia	143	142	1262.1	319	7	6	1	.982	2.32	+13	8	-1	0	7
Byrd,Marlon	Phi	149	147	1337.1	329	6	6	1	.982	2.25	+6	3	-1	4	6
Parra,Gerardo	TOT	109	101	921.0	192	9	4	3	.980	1.96	+3	1	-1	2	2
Puig,Yasiel	LAD	91	89	790.2	150	7	1	2	.994	1.79	-3	-1	-1	4	2
Calhoun,Kole	LAA	123	112	1036.1	230	9	1	1	.996	2.08	-5	-3	4	1	2
Suzuki,Ichiro	NYY	119	86	811.2	173	4	1	0	.994	1.96	+7	4	-1	-2	1
Markakis,Nick	Bal	147	147	1314.1	295	11	0	1	1.000	2.10	-11	-6	-4	3	1
Granderson,Curtis	NYM	142	130	1177.1	264	6	1	0	.996	2.06	+14	8	0	-8	0
Pence,Hunter	SF	161	161	1425.0	308	9	5	0	.984	2.00	-6	-3	1	0	-2
Rios,Alex	Tex	114	113	962.1	250	6	6	2	.977	2.39	+5	3	-2	-4	-3
Werth,Jayson	Was	139	137	1220.2	247	8	5	1	.981	1.88	-8	-5	0	1	-4
Bautista,Jose	Tor	131	125	1080.2	263	12	4	2	.986	2.29	-20	-11	2	5	-4
Braun,Ryan	Mil	134	133	1165.0	263	5	2	2	.993	2.07	-7	-4	-1	-2	-7
Bruce,Jay	Cin	131	128	1136.1	231	8	5	2	.980	1.89	-16	-9	3	-1	-7
Aoki,Nori	KC	119	118	937.1	209	5	2	1	.991	2.05	-12	-7	-1	0	-8
Arcia,Oswaldo	Min	100	97	846.2	191	8	5	0	.975	2.12	-20	-12	0	2	-10
Murphy,David	Cle	120	109	989.0	204	6	3	1	.986	1.91	-17	-10	-3	-3	-16
Hunter,Torii	Det	128	128	1114.0	218	5	5	1	.978	1.80	-28	-16	0	-2	-18

Catchers - Regulars

Player	Tm	G	GS	Inn	PO	A	E	DP	PB	Pct.	SBA	CS	PCS	CS%	CERA	GFP/ DME	SB	Other	Total
Martin,Russell	Pit	107	106	940.2	785	90	5	7	3	.994	87	28	9	.32	3.29	3	6	3	12
Lucroy,Jonathan	Mil	136	133	1182.1	1013	65	4	5	5	.996	107	24	5	.22	3.62	11	-1	1	11
Rivera,Rene	SD	89	85	734.0	680	66	8	7	7	.989	87	29	4	.33	3.10	3	6	0	9
Molina,Yadier	StL	107	106	931.2	810	56	2	10	3	.998	43	20	1	.47	3.19	-2	5	5	8
Joseph,Caleb	Bal	78	77	672.2	539	42	4	4	7	.993	55	21	2	.38	3.01	-2	5	5	8
Perez,Salvador	KC	146	143	1248.2	1037	72	9	5	5	.992	80	23	2	.29	3.24	-2	4	6	8
Ruiz,Carlos	Phi	109	104	960.0	852	68	5	9	4	.995	95	21	7	.22	3.68	3	2	3	8
Castillo,Wellington	ChC	106	103	916.1	784	93	6	6	7	.993	83	26	2	.31	4.21	5	6	-6	5
Avila,Alex	Det	122	116	1017.2	883	52	5	9	3	.995	97	26	10	.27	3.95	4	2	-1	5
Chirinos,Robinson	Tex	91	88	784.0	585	45	4	7	5	.994	69	25	4	.36	4.59	0	5	-1	4
Flowers,Tyler	CWS	124	120	1052.0	863	70	8	6	9	.991	84	22	4	.26	3.97	-2	1	4	3
Gomes,Yan	Cle	121	121	1052.0	1052	93	14	9	6	.988	93	27	4	.29	3.70	5	2	-5	2
Castro,Jason	Hou	114	110	971.0	767	55	4	4	11	.995	102	21	2	.21	4.16	7	-2	-3	2
Mesoraco,Devin	Cin	109	104	936.2	832	55	3	5	9	.997	67	16	2	.24	3.62	2	-3	3	2
McCann,Brian	NYY	108	101	889.0	859	62	2	4	10	.998	71	22	7	.31	3.76	0	2	0	2
Hanigan,Ryan	TB	79	66	603.2	540	32	1	5	1	.998	36	6	2	.17	3.50	1	-1	2	2
Navarro,Dioner	Tor	112	102	907.1	782	35	3	3	7	.996	69	11	4	.16	3.86	2	-1	0	1

Player	Tm	G	GS	Inn	PO	A	E	DP	PB	Pct.	SBA	CS	PCS	CS%	CERA	GFP/ DME	SB	Other	Total
Conger,Hank	LAA	79	70	637.1	599	37	7	2	1	.989	71	14	4	.20	3.35	-1	-2	4	1
Ellis,A.J.	LAD	92	89	773.2	737	68	4	4	2	.995	61	13	3	.21	3.23	3	-2	0	1
Ramos,Wilson	Was	87	87	775.0	626	54	5	2	4	.993	46	16	2	.35	3.10	-3	4	-1	0
Norris,Derek	Oak	114	93	870.1	745	43	6	3	8	.992	68	8	4	.12	3.13	0	-4	1	-3
Gattis,Evan	Atl	93	89	799.0	723	49	5	2	5	.994	66	13	0	.20	3.30	-4	-2	2	-4
Grandal,Yasmani	SD	76	67	607.2	526	31	4	4	12	.993	55	6	1	.11	3.35	-1	-4	1	-4
Posey,Buster	SF	111	109	929.1	787	51	5	8	5	.994	76	17	8	.22	3.39	-1	-2	-1	-4
Suzuki,Kurt	Min	119	115	1017.2	737	39	4	1	3	.995	75	11	10	.15	4.52	0	-5	0	-5
Zunino,Mike	Sea	130	125	1121.0	1009	85	5	5	8	.995	96	25	3	.26	3.18	-4	1	-4	-7
Montero,Miguel	Ari	131	130	1152.0	1037	65	13	12	5	.988	84	20	6	.24	4.34	-3	-4	0	-7
Molina,Jose	TB	80	70	628.1	659	30	2	2	4	.997	50	12	2	.24	3.77	-6	0	-2	-8
Saltalamacchia,J	Mia	107	103	922.2	741	45	15	6	6	.981	87	15	2	.17	3.59	-5	-3	0	-8
Rosario,Wilin	Col	96	94	824.0	585	54	7	5	12	.989	43	6	1	.14	5.20	-4	0	-4	-8
Iannetta,Chris	LAA	104	92	835.1	744	36	2	5	4	.997	61	12	9	.20	3.74	-5	0	-5	-10
Pierzynski,A.J.	TOT	87	80	721.0	619	34	5	3	5	.992	59	9	2	.15	4.13	-2	-5	-4	-11
d'Arnaud,Travis	NYM	105	103	909.0	829	38	9	2	12	.990	67	9	5	.13	3.68	-4	-4	-7	-15

All Other Fielders

Player	Tm	Pos	G	GS	Inn	PO	A	E	DP	Pct.	Rng	+/-	RS
Abreu, B	NYM	LF	5	5	37	6	0	0	0	1.000	1.46	-1	-1
	NYM	RF	26	21	169	31	0	2	0	.939	1.65	-7	-7
Abreu, T	SF	2B	1	0	5	2	1	0	0	1.000	5.79	0	0
	SF	3B	1	0	2	0	0	0	0	-	.00	0	0
Adames, C	Col	2B	2	1	10	2	6	0	2	1.000	7.20	0	0
	Col	SS	5	1	22	6	10	0	2	1.000	6.45	+1	1
Adams, L	KC	LF	2	0	3	3	0	0	0	1.000	9.00	0	0
	KC	CF	2	0	4	0	0	0	0	-	.00	0	0
Adduci, J	Tex	1B	3	2	13	13	1	0	0	1.000	-	+1	1
	Tex	LF	20	18	165	50	1	0	0	1.000	2.78	+9	6
	Tex	RF	8	4	41	10	0	0	0	1.000	2.20	0	0
Adrianza, E	SF	2B	25	15	151	27	52	2	10	.975	4.71	+3	1
	SF	3B	3	0	5	0	2	0	0	1.000	3.60	0	0
	SF	SS	7	5	42	5	16	0	2	1.000	4.50	-1	-2
Aguilar, J	Cle	1B	12	9	72	71	4	2	4	.974	-	0	0
	Cle	3B	1	0	2	0	0	0	0	-	.00	-1	-1
Ahmed, N	Ari	2B	2	1	11	2	5	0	2	1.000	5.73	0	0
	Ari	SS	18	17	156	25	40	2	11	.970	3.74	+2	2
Alcantara, A	ChC	2B	25	21	209	31	63	1	9	.989	4.05	+5	4
	ChC	CF	48	44	421	111	3	5	0	.958	2.44	+8	3
Almonte, A	TOT	LF	16	10	84	18	0	1	0	.947	1.93	0	0
	TOT	CF	41	39	346	107	6	6	1	.950	2.94	+9	7
Almonte, Z	NYY	LF	6	6	55	13	1	0	0	1.000	2.29	-3	-2
	NYY	RF	4	2	23	6	0	0	0	1.000	2.38	+2	1
Alonso, Y	SD	1B	77	72	629	568	43	2	44	.997	-	+6	9
	SD	3B	3	0	3	0	1	0	0	1.000	2.70	0	0
Altherr, A	Phi	LF	1	1	9	3	0	0	0	1.000	3.00	+1	1
Alvarez, P	Pit	1B	5	5	37	31	1	0	4	1.000	-	0	0
Amarista, A	SD	2B	21	18	152	27	39	0	7	1.000	3.90	0	0
	SD	3B	22	16	161	9	39	2	3	.960	2.68	+5	3
	SD	SS	73	71	626	103	194	6	33	.980	4.27	+10	7
	SD	LF	6	1	16	3	0	0	0	1.000	1.72	+1	0
	SD	CF	21	13	129	36	1	1	1	.974	2.59	+3	2
Anna, D	NYY	2B	3	2	17	1	5	0	0	1.000	3.18	0	0
	NYY	SS	9	5	49	4	14	1	1	.947	3.31	+2	2
Aoki, N	KC	LF	5	1	21	3	0	0	0	1.000	1.29	0	0
Arencibia, J	Tex	1B	22	21	179	144	13	2	17	.987	-	-3	-3
Arias, J	SF	1B	16	8	85	90	5	0	4	1.000	-	0	0
	SF	2B	15	10	81	14	23	0	7	1.000	4.11	-3	-3
	SF	3B	44	12	168	11	36	1	6	.979	2.51	+2	2
	SF	SS	11	10	83	17	21	2	9	.950	4.12	0	1
Arruebarrena, E	LAD	SS	21	9	116	14	26	3	6	.930	3.10	-1	-1
Avila, A	Det	1B	1	0	1	0	0	0	0	-	-	0	0
Aviles, M	Cle	2B	33	28	266	52	86	1	19	.993	4.66	+5	4
	Cle	3B	36	28	257	21	49	7	1	.909	2.45	+1	-1
	Cle	SS	15	12	110	21	37	0	7	1.000	4.75	-2	-1
	Cle	LF	27	17	184	25	1	0	1	1.000	1.27	-3	-3
	Cle	CF	3	1	6	1	0	0	0	1.000	1.59	+1	0
	Cle	RF	3	2	14	2	0	0	0	1.000	1.29	-3	-2
Baez, J	ChC	2B	25	25	210	60	51	5	18	.957	4.76	-2	-2
	ChC	SS	30	27	255	45	89	5	22	.964	4.73	-4	-2
Baker, J	Mia	1B	43	28	258	263	15	2	23	.993	-	-5	-3
	Mia	2B	21	13	133	21	45	1	9	.985	4.47	0	-1
	Mia	3B	2	0	4	0	0	0	0	-	.00	0	0
Barmes, C	Pit	1B	2	0	5	5	0	0	0	1.000	-	0	0
	Pit	2B	14	4	65	10	21	0	1	1.000	4.29	+1	0
	Pit	3B	2	1	9	1	2	0	0	1.000	3.00	0	0
	Pit	SS	27	21	192	22	56	2	10	.975	3.65	+4	3
Barnes, B	Col	LF	18	13	115	19	0	1	0	.950	1.48	0	1
	Col	CF	5	1	16	3	0	0	0	1.000	1.72	-1	0
	Col	RF	55	41	385	92	3	1	1	.990	2.22	+11	5
Barney, D	TOT	2B	79	60	565	96	155	4	29	.984	4.00	+12	10
	TOT	SS	2	1	16	1	5	0	0	1.000	4.09	0	0
Bartlett, J	Min	LF	2	0	7	0	0	0	0	-	.00	-4	-2
Barton, D	Oak	1B	30	15	162	166	12	3	16	.983	-	+4	4
Bautista, J	Tor	1B	12	11	97	75	6	0	6	1.000	-	-1	-1
	Tor	CF	12	5	54	19	0	0	0	1.000	3.17	-3	-2
Baxter, M	LAD	LF	1	1	9	3	0	0	0	1.000	3.00	0	0
Beckham, G	TOT	3B	13	7	78	10	18	2	3	.933	3.23	-4	-3
	TOT	SS	6	2	27	4	11	1	4	.938	5.06	+1	0
Belt, B	SF	1B	59	56	488	499	55	4	48	.993	-	+4	3
	SF	RF	1	0	1	0	0	0	0	-	.00	0	0
Beltran, C	NYY	1B	1	0	5	3	0	0	0	1.000	-	0	0
	NYY	RF	32	31	260	51	2	3	1	.946	1.84	-5	-6
Bernadina, R	TOT	1B	1	1	7	10	0	0	0	1.000	-	0	0
	TOT	LF	17	2	38	6	0	0	0	1.000	1.42	+3	2
	TOT	CF	7	5	45	10	0	0	0	1.000	2.01	-1	0
	TOT	RF	10	4	48	7	0	0	0	1.000	1.30	-1	-1
Bernier, D	Min	2B	2	1	10	2	3	0	1	1.000	4.50	0	0
	Min	SS	3	1	10	1	4	0	0	1.000	4.50	0	0
Berry, Q	Bal	LF	3	0	6	1	0	0	0	1.000	1.50	0	0
	Bal	CF	1	0	1	1	0	0	0	1.000	9.00	0	0
	Bal	RF	1	0	2	0	0	0	0	-	.00	0	0
Betts, M	Bos	2B	14	14	122	25	38	3	7	.955	4.65	+1	-1
	Bos	CF	28	28	250	64	2	0	2	1.000	2.38	-1	0
	Bos	RF	12	8	77	20	1	1	0	.955	2.45	+3	3
Bianchi, J	Mil	2B	4	1	14	2	6	0	1	1.000	5.02	0	0
	Mil	3B	9	5	57	11	13	2	3	.923	3.79	0	0
	Mil	SS	10	9	90	10	29	1	3	.975	3.90	+1	1
Blackmon, C	Col	LF	22	11	114	33	2	5	1	.875	2.76	+3	1
	Col	CF	69	60	513	153	1	2	0	.987	2.70	+3	1
	Col	RF	73	64	574	131	6	0	1	1.000	2.10	0	-1
Blanco, A	Phi	2B	5	2	22	1	8	0	1	1.000	3.68	-1	0
	Phi	3B	10	5	48	1	18	1	0	.950	3.54	+1	1
	Phi	SS	6	4	35	4	10	0	4	1.000	3.57	0	0
Blanco, G	SF	LF	64	36	361	78	1	1	0	.988	1.97	+10	4
	SF	CF	72	56	526	140	5	0	0	1.000	2.48	-17	-7
	SF	RF	1	0	4	1	0	0	0	1.000	2.25	0	0
Blanks, K	TOT	1B	20	14	129	117	12	1	15	.992	-	0	0
	TOT	LF	1	0	1	0	0	0	0	-	.00	0	0
	TOT	RF	3	3	30	5	0	0	0	1.000	-	0	0
Bloomquist, W	Sea	1B	7	5	48	52	5	0	6	1.000	-	-1	-1
	Sea	2B	10	6	62	6	13	0	2	1.000	2.77	-1	-1
	Sea	3B	5	5	44	1	12	0	1	1.000	2.66	+1	1
	Sea	SS	16	12	115	13	21	0	4	1.000	2.66	-1	-1
	Sea	LF	3	3	23	5	0	0	0	1.000	1.96	+1	0
	Sea	RF	1	0	1	0	0	0	0	1.000	9.00	-1	-1
Boesch, B	LAA	LF	3	2	15	0	0	0	0	-	.00	0	0
	LAA	CF	1	0	1	0	0	0	0	-	.00	0	0
	LAA	RF	9	4	46	14	0	1	0	.933	2.74	-1	0
Bogaerts, X	Bos	3B	44	44	385	37	64	10	2	.910	2.36	-11	-7
Bonifacio, E	TOT	2B	31	25	227	49	60	3	19	.973	4.32	-1	-3
	TOT	3B	7	3	38	1	9	0	1	1.000	2.37	+1	1
	TOT	SS	4	3	27	5	8	1	2	.929	4.39	0	0
	TOT	LF	4	1	13	3	0	0	0	1.000	2.08	+1	0
	TOT	CF	65	53	481	123	1	2	1	.984	2.32	+5	3
	TOT	RF	6	5	44	11	1	0	0	1.000	2.45	+3	3
Bour, J	Mia	1B	15	12	106	116	10	0	13	1.000	-	-1	0
Bourgeois, J	Cin	LF	8	6	56	10	1	1	0	.917	1.77	+1	2
	Cin	CF	2	1	7	2	0	0	0	1.000	2.57	+1	1
	Cin	RF	1	0	2	0	0	0	0	-	.00	0	0
Bourjos, P	StL	CF	104	65	649	194	0	2	0	.990	2.69	+16	7
Bradley Jr., J	Bos	LF	1	0	6	0	0	0	0	-	.00	0	0
	Bos	RF	12	6	62	11	0	0	0	1.000	1.60	+1	0
Brantley, M	Cle	CF	46	40	373	106	2	1	0	.991	2.61	-3	-3
Braun, R	Mil	CF	1	0	3	0	0	0	0	-	.00	0	0
Brentz, B	Bos	LF	6	5	46	12	0	0	0	1.000	2.35	-2	-1
	Bos	RF	2	1	10	2	0	0	0	1.000	1.80	+1	0
Brignac, R	Phi	2B	3	1	7	1	3	0	0	1.000	5.14	+1	1
	Phi	3B	20	15	155	9	22	0	2	1.000	1.80	-8	-6
	Phi	SS	3	0	4	1	1	0	0	1.000	4.50	0	0
Brown, A	NYM	LF	8	5	46	9	0	0	0	1.000	1.58	-2	-1
	NYM	RF	4	2	24	6	0	0	0	1.000	2.25	+1	1
Brown, C	Bos	RF	1	0	1	1	0	0	0	1.000	9.00	+1	1
Brown, G	SF	CF	6	1	21	7	0	0	0	1.000	3.00	0	0
Bruce, J	Cin	1B	3	3	26	14	0	2	0	.875	-	-1	-1
Buck, J	TOT	1B	1	0	3	3	2	0	0	1.000	-	0	0
Burns, B	Oak	CF	1	1	8	2	0	1	0	.667	2.25	0	0
Butera, D	LAD	1B	1	1	3	4	0	0	0	.800	-	-1	-1
Butler, B	KC	1B	37	35	310	272	24	2	26	.993	-	-4	-3
Butler, J	StL	RF	1	0	5	1	0	0	0	1.000	1.93	0	0
Cabrera, A	TOT	2B	48	48	432	73	132	1	29	.995	4.27	-15	-10
Cabrera, M	Tor	CF	1	1	9	1	0	0	0	1.000	1.00	-2	-1
	Tor	RF	4	4	30	9	0	0	0	1.000	2.70	0	-1

All Other Fielders

Player	Tm	Pos	G	GS	Inn	PO	A	E	DP	Pct.	Rng	+/-	RS
Cabrera, M	Det	3B	10	8	69	6	13	1	2	.950	2.47	-1	-1
Cain, L	KC	CF	93	93	723	234	4	1	0	.996	2.96	+26	14
	KC	RF	77	29	388	104	4	1	0	.991	2.50	+16	10
Calhoun, K	LAA	1B	2	0	6	4	0	0	0	1.000	-	0	0
Callaspo, A	Oak	1B	23	17	142	128	17	2	14	.986	-	0	1
	Oak	2B	46	41	347	76	104	4	25	.978	4.66	-3	-3
	Oak	3B	19	16	139	8	33	2	4	.953	2.65	-1	0
Campana, T	TOT	LF	6	2	29	8	0	0	0	1.000	2.48	0	0
	TOT	CF	23	12	131	41	0	0	0	1.000	2.82	-1	0
Campbell, E	NYM	1B	18	14	127	125	5	1	15	.992	-	+2	0
	NYM	2B	1	1	9	3	3	0	2	1.000	6.00	0	0
	NYM	3B	19	13	130	5	28	1	3	.971	2.29	0	0
	NYM	SS	2	0	6	1	1	0	0	1.000	3.00	0	0
	NYM	LF	20	6	80	18	2	0	1	1.000	2.24	-3	0
	NYM	RF	3	2	21	6	0	0	0	1.000	2.57	+1	1
Carp, M	TOT	1B	32	22	209	182	15	2	17	.990	-	-2	-1
	TOT	3B	1	0	1	0	0	0	0	-	.00	0	0
	TOT	LF	13	9	68	8	0	0	0	1.000	1.06	-1	0
	TOT	RF	1	0	3	1	0	0	0	1.000	3.00	+1	0
Carpenter, M	StL	RF	2	0	2	1	0	0	0	1.000	5.40	0	0
Carrera, E	Det	LF	1	0	2	4	0	0	0	1.000	18.00	-1	0
	Det	CF	38	13	158	47	1	0	0	1.000	2.73	-3	-1
Carter, C	Hou	1B	14	14	119	123	12	3	13	.978	-	+1	2
	Hou	LF	6	6	58	12	0	0	0	1.000	1.87	-3	-2
Cashner, A	SD	LF	1	0	0	0	0	0	0	-	.00	0	0
Casilla, A	Bal	2B	0	0	1	0	0	0	0	-	.00	0	0
	Bal	3B	1	1	7	0	1	1	0	.500	1.29	-2	-1
Castillo, R	Bos	CF	10	10	89	31	1	0	0	1.000	3.24	-1	2
Cecchini, G	Bos	3B	9	7	71	7	13	1	2	.952	2.54	-1	-1
Cedeno, R	Phi	3B	1	1	9	2	1	0	0	1.000	3.00	0	0
	Phi	SS	2	1	8	2	4	0	1	1.000	6.75	0	0
Cervelli, F	NYY	1B	5	5	40	33	1	0	2	1.000	-	0	-1
Cespedes, Y	TOT	CF	9	3	35	9	0	1	0	.900	2.31	-2	-1
Chavez, E	Sea	LF	11	9	88	17	0	0	0	1.000	1.74	-4	0
	Sea	CF	9	5	46	7	0	0	0	1.000	1.36	-2	-1
	Sea	RF	46	35	318	55	1	0	0	1.000	1.58	-5	-3
Chavez, E	Ari	3B	11	8	82	5	10	0	2	1.000	1.65	-1	0
Chisenhall, L	Cle	1B	11	5	57	52	5	1	5	1.000	-	-1	-2
Choice, M	Tex	LF	41	35	314	75	4	3	0	.963	2.26	-7	-6
	Tex	CF	7	4	40	9	0	0	0	1.000	2.03	-5	-4
	Tex	RF	17	16	141	35	1	1	0	.973	2.30	0	0
Choo, S	Tex	LF	64	63	520	100	3	3	0	.972	1.78	-10	-9
	Tex	RF	12	12	107	29	1	0	0	.968	2.52	-6	-4
Ciriaco, P	KC	2B	13	8	83	17	27	0	7	1.000	4.79	0	-1
	KC	3B	3	3	28	4	1	0	0	1.000	1.61	0	0
	KC	SS	2	0	5	0	0	0	0	-	.00	0	0
Clark, M	Mil	1B	9	7	54	51	3	1	5	.982	-	-1	0
Clevenger, S	Bal	1B	3	2	15	13	0	1	1	.929	-	0	0
Coghlan, C	ChC	RF	4	1	17	7	0	0	0	1.000	3.78	-2	-1
Colabello, C	Min	1B	23	22	199	162	18	2	18	.989	-	-3	-2
	Min	LF	19	17	123	22	2	1	1	.960	1.76	-11	-7
Collins, T	Det	LF	5	2	22	11	0	0	0	1.000	4.50	+2	1
	Det	CF	1	0	1	0	0	0	0	-	.00	0	0
	Det	RF	5	2	19	3	0	0	0	1.000	1.42	-1	0
Colon, C	KC	2B	11	7	70	15	26	0	4	1.000	5.27	+1	0
	KC	3B	5	4	32	2	6	2	1	.800	2.25	-1	1
	KC	SS	2	0	4	0	2	0	0	1.000	4.50	0	0
Colvin, T	SF	LF	43	29	292	49	2	1	1	.981	1.57	-1	-1
	SF	CF	3	2	18	3	0	0	0	1.000	1.50	0	0
Conrad, B	SD	2B	10	9	69	17	15	0	5	1.000	4.17	-2	-2
Constanza, J	Atl	LF	2	0	4	2	0	0	0	1.000	4.50	-1	0
	Atl	RF	1	0	1	0	0	0	0	-	.00	0	0
Cowgill, C	LAA	LF	44	26	272	67	1	1	1	.986	2.25	+4	3
	LAA	CF	11	5	62	14	1	0	0	1.000	2.18	-2	-1
	LAA	RF	49	40	348	94	2	2	1	.980	2.48	+12	7
Craig, A	TOT	1B	41	37	334	325	29	0	25	1.000	-	+1	0
	TOT	LF	11	3	38	12	0	0	0	1.000	2.84	0	0
	TOT	RF	82	78	653	129	3	0	0	1.000	1.82	+5	3
Crawford, C	LAD	LF	94	80	736	132	1	3	0	.978	1.63	+5	1
Cron, C	LAA	1B	36	29	251	221	12	1	24	.996	-	-5	-5
Cruz, N	Bal	LF	60	60	502	113	2	0	0	1.000	2.06	+3	1
	Bal	RF	11	10	79	19	0	0	0	1.000	2.16	+3	2

Player	Tm	Pos	G	GS	Inn	PO	A	E	DP	Pct.	Rng	+/-	RS
Cruz, T	StL	1B	2	0	4	4	0	0	0	1.000	-	0	0
	StL	3B	1	0	3	0	1	0	1	1.000	3.00	0	0
Cuddyer, M	Col	1B	14	11	92	92	7	1	6	.990	-	-3	-1
	Col	3B	3	2	18	1	4	0	0	1.000	2.45	-2	-2
	Col	RF	35	35	279	56	5	0	1	1.000	1.97	-5	-2
Culberson, C	Col	1B	4	3	28	31	3	0	0	1.000	-	0	0
	Col	2B	20	14	129	35	44	1	13	.988	5.51	+1	-1
	Col	3B	32	18	182	11	56	2	5	.971	3.31	+2	-1
	Col	SS	23	13	136	28	47	1	14	.987	4.98	+4	3
Danks, J	CWS	LF	12	10	83	19	1	0	0	1.000	2.18	-3	-3
	CWS	CF	28	19	191	69	0	1	0	.986	3.25	+2	0
	CWS	RF	8	2	33	5	0	0	0	1.000	1.36	0	0
d'Arnaud, C	Pit	SS	1	0	1	0	0	0	0	-	.00	0	0
Davis, C	Bal	3B	21	19	149	9	22	4	3	.886	1.87	0	0
Davis, R	Det	LF	99	72	684	160	6	4	1	.976	2.18	-8	-8
	Det	CF	48	46	374	117	0	1	0	.992	2.82	+1	-3
De Aza, A	TOT	LF	16	12	115	44	1	0	0	1.000	3.52	-3	-1
	TOT	RF	1	1	6	0	0	0	0	-	.00	0	0
Decker, J	Pit	LF	2	0	3	0	0	0	0	-	.00	0	0
DeJesus, D	TB	LF	13	10	88	20	0	0	0	1.000	2.05	+2	1
	TB	RF	3	3	21	5	0	0	0	1.000	2.14	-3	-2
den Dekker, M	NYM	LF	28	27	223	40	1	1	0	.976	1.66	0	0
	NYM	CF	18	14	137	29	3	0	0	1.000	2.11	-2	4
	NYM	RF	1	0	1	0	0	0	0	-	.00	0	0
Denorfia, C	TOT	LF	33	9	125	26	0	0	0	1.000	1.87	0	0
	TOT	CF	14	6	51	14	0	1	0	.933	2.49	-3	-2
	TOT	RF	76	59	515	139	3	1	0	.993	2.48	0	2
Descalso, D	StL	1B	4	3	27	24	2	0	1	1.000	-	0	0
	StL	2B	21	11	106	21	47	1	14	.986	5.76	+1	3
	StL	3B	14	7	71	1	7	0	0	1.000	1.02	-1	-1
	StL	SS	19	9	98	18	29	3	6	.940	4.30	-5	-5
Diaz, J	Tor	2B	5	1	16	3	5	0	2	1.000	4.50	0	0
	Tor	SS	14	10	93	12	23	0	6	1.000	3.38	+2	0
	Tor	LF	1	0	3	2	0	0	0	1.000	6.00	0	0
	Tor	CF	1	0	1	0	0	0	0	-	.00	0	0
	Tor	RF	1	0	1	0	0	0	0	-	.00	0	0
Dickerson, C	Cle	LF	19	14	129	24	2	1	0	.963	1.81	-6	-1
	Cle	CF	5	3	34	11	1	0	0	1.000	3.18	-1	0
	Cle	RF	11	8	72	15	0	1	0	.938	1.88	+1	1
Dickerson, C	Col	CF	9	9	67	15	0	0	0	1.000	2.01	+1	0
Dietrich, D	Mia	2B	44	43	359	58	134	10	24	.950	4.82	-8	-8
	Mia	3B	1	0	8	0	1	0	0	1.000	.00	0	-1
Dobbs, G	TOT	1B	3	3	30	31	3	0	3	1.000	-	-1	-1
Dominguez, C	SF	3B	1	0	3	0	0	0	0	-	.00	-1	-1
	SF	LF	5	4	33	12	0	0	0	1.000	3.27	0	0
Doumit, R	Atl	LF	9	8	67	17	0	0	0	1.000	2.28	+1	1
	Atl	RF	9	7	59	18	0	0	0	1.000	2.75	+1	-1
Drew, S	TOT	2B	34	31	274	57	75	4	15	.971	4.34	+3	0
	TOT	SS	51	46	413	79	125	3	39	.986	4.44	+3	4
Duda, L	NYM	LF	1	1	3	1	0	0	0	1.000	3.00	0	0
Duffy, M	SF	2B	9	5	50	9	16	1	3	.962	4.50	0	0
	SF	3B	2	0	3	0	2	0	0	1.000	6.00	+1	0
	SF	SS	7	5	51	15	13	1	5	.966	4.94	-2	-1
Dunn, A	TOT	1B	23	22	198	207	7	1	24	.995	-	-5	-5
	TOT	LF	4	3	22	8	0	0	0	1.000	3.27	0	0
	TOT	RF	3	2	16	4	0	1	0	.800	2.25	-5	-3
Duvall, A	SF	1B	21	17	148	149	8	1	13	.994	-	+1	2
	SF	3B	1	0	2	0	0	0	0	-	.00	0	0
Dyson, J	KC	LF	3	2	13	4	0	0	0	1.000	2.77	0	0
	KC	CF	106	64	678	224	4	4	0	.983	3.03	+23	14
Ellis, M	StL	1B	3	1	14	15	2	0	5	1.000	-	+1	0
	StL	2B	50	45	392	70	123	0	21	1.000	4.43	+6	7
	StL	3B	3	0	4	0	2	1	1	.667	4.50	-1	-1
Elmore, J	Cin	2B	2	1	9	5	2	0	0	1.000	7.00	0	0
	Cin	SS	3	2	17	2	5	0	1	1.000	3.71	-1	-1
Encarnacion, E	Tor	1B	80	78	694	625	33	8	51	.988	-	-5	-5
	Tor	2B	2	2	15	2	0	0	0	1.000	1.20	-2	-1
Escobar, E	Min	2B	9	6	61	12	16	1	5	.966	4.13	-4	-3
	Min	3B	25	23	200	12	39	3	7	.944	2.30	-3	-1
	Min	LF	2	1	11	3	0	0	0	1.000	2.53	-2	0
	Min	CF	1	1	8	2	2	0	0	1.000	4.50	0	1
Escobar, Y	TB	LF	1	0	0	0	0	0	0	-	.00	0	0

All Other Fielders

Player	Tm	Pos	G	GS	Inn	PO	A	E	DP	Pct.	Rng	+/-	RS
Espinosa, D	Was	2B	89	77	710	157	231	4	58	.990	4.92	-3	-1
	Was	SS	12	8	83	16	28	1	7	.978	4.77	+1	1
Ethier, A	LAD	1B	1	0	3	5	0	0	0	1.000	-	0	0
	LAD	LF	16	11	102	13	0	0	0	1.000	1.14	+2	1
	LAD	CF	68	56	507	120	0	1	0	.992	2.13	-7	-5
	LAD	RF	15	11	105	20	1	0	0	1.000	1.80	-6	-3
Evans, N	Ari	1B	3	1	12	9	2	0	1	1.000	-	0	0
	Ari	3B	1	1	7	1	2	0	1	1.000	3.86	0	0
	Ari	LF	1	0	1	0	0	0	0	-	.00	0	0
Falu, I	TOT	2B	11	5	58	14	11	0	4	1.000	3.90	+3	2
	TOT	3B	3	0	5	0	1	0	1	1.000	1.80	0	0
	TOT	SS	2	1	10	1	3	1	0	.800	3.60	0	0
Fielder, P	Tex	1B	39	39	345	333	14	4	36	.989	-	+1	-2
Figgins, C	LAD	2B	5	4	38	3	13	0	3	1.000	3.82	+1	1
	LAD	3B	10	8	70	4	19	1	0	.958	2.97	+2	2
	LAD	SS	2	0	6	1	0	0	0	1.000	1.50	0	0
	LAD	LF	1	0	1	1	0	0	0	1.000	13.50	0	0
Figueroa, C	TB	2B	16	10	94	19	24	1	4	.977	4.10	-1	-1
Flaherty, R	Bal	1B	3	1	16	12	0	0	1	1.000	-	0	0
	Bal	2B	30	29	259	47	91	2	17	.986	4.80	+4	3
	Bal	3B	43	27	255	13	60	5	7	.936	2.57	+4	4
	Bal	SS	29	21	204	32	51	3	10	.965	3.66	-5	-5
	Bal	LF	1	0	1	0	0	0	0	-	.00	0	0
	Bal	RF	1	0	1	0	0	0	0	-	.00	0	0
Flores, W	NYM	2B	19	17	154	40	46	1	13	.989	5.03	-1	-1
	NYM	3B	1	0	1	0	0	0	0	-	.00	0	0
	NYM	SS	51	50	443	54	135	4	33	.979	3.84	-2	-3
Florimon, P	Min	SS	31	26	225	28	84	2	18	.982	4.49	+3	3
Forsythe, L	TB	1B	1	0	1	0	0	0	0	1.000	-	0	0
	TB	2B	74	58	553	82	149	2	22	.991	3.76	+1	2
	TB	3B	6	1	22	4	6	0	0	1.000	4.09	+2	1
	TB	SS	2	1	10	0	3	0	1	1.000	2.70	+1	0
	TB	LF	3	2	16	2	0	0	0	1.000	1.13	0	0
Francisco, J	Tor	1B	20	15	127	129	6	2	12	.985	-	+2	1
	Tor	3B	74	57	483	37	88	9	11	.933	2.33	-8	-7
Franco, M	Phi	1B	5	2	23	20	2	0	2	1.000	-	0	0
	Phi	3B	12	12	106	11	28	1	3	.975	3.31	+1	1
Francoeur, J	SD	RF	7	6	51	13	0	1	0	.929	2.29	+1	1
Frandsen, K	Was	1B	9	6	58	51	1	0	5	1.000	-	+1	0
	Was	2B	13	9	84	21	31	0	6	1.000	5.57	+1	2
	Was	3B	16	12	122	14	22	2	0	.947	2.66	-4	-1
	Was	LF	21	15	141	27	2	1	0	.967	1.85	-6	-2
Franklin, N	TOT	2B	12	11	96	19	29	2	8	.960	4.50	0	0
	TOT	3B	1	0	1	0	0	0	0	-	.00	0	0
	TOT	SS	10	8	73	4	23	1	5	.964	3.33	+2	2
	TOT	RF	2	1	11	2	0	0	0	1.000	1.64	-1	-1
Frazier, T	Cin	1B	43	37	335	298	27	5	21	.985	-	-1	1
Freiman, N	Oak	1B	33	24	217	211	7	3	24	.986	-	+2	1
Fuld, S	TOT	LF	36	23	224	64	1	0	0	1.000	2.61	+3	0
	TOT	CF	62	58	518	188	5	1	2	.995	3.36	+7	7
	TOT	RF	17	14	122	30	1	1	0	.969	2.29	-2	-4
Furcal, R	Mia	2B	8	8	71	13	19	0	8	1.000	4.06	0	0
Galvis, F	Phi	2B	7	4	40	9	9	0	2	1.000	4.02	0	0
	Phi	3B	11	5	55	1	14	0	1	1.000	2.47	0	0
	Phi	SS	25	23	200	32	79	1	16	.991	5.00	-4	-4
Garcia, A	CWS	RF	46	46	401	84	4	2	0	.978	1.98	-15	-10
Garcia, G	StL	2B	4	2	24	5	7	0	2	1.000	4.50	-1	-1
	StL	SS	1	0	4	3	0	0	0	1.000	9.00	-1	0
Garcia, L	CWS	2B	14	11	101	18	32	3	14	.943	4.46	-2	-1
	CWS	3B	15	11	98	10	25	1	1	.972	3.21	+2	3
	CWS	SS	9	3	43	2	9	1	2	.917	2.28	0	0
	CWS	LF	2	1	13	1	0	0	0	1.000	.69	0	0
	CWS	CF	14	8	77	16	1	1	0	.944	1.98	-3	-1
	CWS	RF	3	0	7	1	0	0	0	1.000	1.23	0	0
Gardner, B	NYY	CF	25	20	177	50	2	0	0	1.000	2.64	+8	4
	NYY	RF	1	1	8	3	0	0	0	1.000	3.38	-2	-2
Gennett, S	Mil	RF	1	0	1	0	0	0	0	-	.00	0	0
Gentry, C	Oak	LF	17	10	92	24	2	1	0	.963	2.53	+3	3
	Oak	CF	50	35	325	90	5	0	2	1.000	2.63	+8	5
	Oak	RF	29	13	143	39	1	0	0	1.000	2.52	+4	2
Getz, C	Tor	2B	10	6	64	8	22	0	1	1.000	4.24	+1	0
Giavotella, J	KC	2B	12	10	92	15	31	1	5	.979	4.50	0	0

Player	Tm	Pos	G	GS	Inn	PO	A	E	DP	Pct.	Rng	+/-	RS
Gillespie, C	TOT	LF	16	15	119	34	0	0	0	1.000	2.57	-2	-2
	TOT	CF	1	0	1	0	0	0	0	-	.00	0	0
	TOT	RF	10	6	63	13	0	2	0	.867	1.86	+1	1
Gimenez, C	TOT	1B	10	6	55	39	1	0	5	1.000	-	-1	0
	TOT	3B	1	0	0	0	0	0	0	-	.00	0	0
Gindl, C	Mil	RF	6	6	48	11	0	0	0	1.000	2.05	0	0
Glenn, B	Tor	RF	4	4	36	8	0	0	0	1.000	2.00	-2	-1
Goebbert, J	SD	1B	25	19	170	166	13	2	6	.989	-	+2	0
	SD	LF	8	4	40	10	0	0	0	1.000	2.27	+1	0
Goins, R	Tor	2B	57	46	396	79	124	1	24	.995	4.61	+1	3
	Tor	SS	15	9	86	12	25	0	5	1.000	3.87	+3	2
Gomes, J	TOT	LF	84	59	553	99	1	4	0	.962	1.63	-15	-10
	TOT	RF	11	8	79	23	1	0	0	1.000	2.75	+1	1
Gomez, H	Mil	2B	1	0	1	0	1	0	0	1.000	9.00	0	0
	Mil	3B	6	1	20	1	3	0	0	1.000	1.80	+1	1
	Mil	SS	7	3	33	3	14	1	3	.944	4.64	0	0
Gonzalez, A	Det	3B	1	0	1	0	0	0	0	-	.00	0	0
	Det	SS	9	8	72	7	21	3	5	.903	3.48	-5	-4
Gonzalez, C	Col	LF	48	48	386	67	1	1	1	.986	1.58	-3	-6
	Col	RF	17	16	139	30	2	0	0	1.000	2.07	+2	1
Gonzalez, M	Hou	1B	1	0	1	2	0	0	0	1.000	-	0	0
	Hou	2B	11	5	59	12	21	0	4	1.000	5.03	-1	-1
	Hou	3B	10	6	57	2	12	2	1	.875	2.21	-3	-3
	Hou	SS	71	64	577	76	200	6	36	.979	4.31	+2	4
	Hou	LF	4	1	14	3	0	0	0	1.000	1.88	-3	-2
	Hou	RF	1	0	0	0	0	0	0	-	.00	0	0
Gore, T	KC	LF	2	0	4	1	0	0	0	1.000	2.25	0	0
Gose, A	Tor	LF	11	6	57	14	1	0	0	1.000	2.38	+3	3
	Tor	CF	65	56	486	142	1	1	0	.993	2.65	+6	1
	Tor	RF	14	12	114	31	0	0	0	1.000	2.45	-1	-2
Gosselin, P	Atl	2B	26	17	158	32	40	2	10	.973	4.11	+3	3
	Atl	3B	9	8	71	4	15	1	3	.950	2.42	0	0
	Atl	SS	8	5	48	8	13	0	4	1.000	3.91	+2	2
	Atl	LF	1	0	1	0	0	0	0	-	.00	-1	-1
Grandal, Y	SD	1B	37	33	291	235	22	3	18	.988	-	-6	-4
Granderson, C	NYM	LF	10	8	62	18	1	1	1	.950	2.77	-3	-1
	NYM	CF	15	11	89	23	1	0	0	1.000	2.42	-2	-2
Green, G	LAA	1B	1	0	4	4	0	0	1	1.000	-	0	0
	LAA	2B	10	4	51	7	23	0	6	1.000	5.33	+1	1
	LAA	3B	5	2	18	2	3	0	0	1.000	2.50	-2	-1
	LAA	SS	1	0	9	0	5	0	0	1.000	5.00	+1	1
	LAA	LF	17	16	126	18	0	0	0	1.000	1.29	-2	-1
Gregorius, D	Ari	2B	11	7	80	13	26	1	3	.975	4.41	+3	2
	Ari	3B	2	1	10	2	1	0	0	1.000	2.70	0	0
	Ari	SS	67	66	581	99	189	5	39	.983	4.46	+2	0
Grichuk, R	StL	LF	5	3	31	7	0	0	0	1.000	2.03	+1	1
	StL	CF	5	3	29	17	0	1	0	.944	5.28	+4	2
	StL	RF	28	16	158	30	2	1	0	.970	1.82	+6	1
Grossman, R	Hou	LF	67	64	558	114	1	2	0	.983	1.85	+2	0
	Hou	CF	6	4	40	7	0	0	0	1.000	1.58	-5	-3
	Hou	RF	32	30	267	56	5	1	1	.984	2.06	+3	6
Guerrero, A	LAD	LF	3	0	14	2	0	0	0	1.000	1.29	-1	-1
Guyer, B	TB	LF	62	51	471	101	0	0	0	1.000	1.93	+4	4
	TB	CF	11	5	64	20	0	0	0	1.000	2.81	-3	-3
	TB	RF	1	0	3	1	0	0	0	1.000	3.00	0	0
Guzman, J	Hou	1B	52	32	311	300	24	2	29	.994	-	+3	1
	Hou	3B	1	0	2	0	0	0	0	-	.00	0	0
	Hou	SS	8	4	41	5	0	0	0	1.000	1.10	-1	-1
Gwynn, T	Phi	LF	16	2	40	9	0	0	0	1.000	2.04	-2	0
	Phi	CF	25	15	141	38	2	0	1	1.000	2.56	-4	-1
	Phi	RF	3	1	9	0	0	0	0	-	.00	-3	-2
Hairston, S	Was	LF	15	11	87	25	0	2	0	.926	2.59	+2	0
	Was	RF	1	0	3	0	0	0	0	-	.00	0	0
Hamilton, J	LAA	LF	68	67	599	148	2	5	0	.968	2.26	-3	-2
	LAA	CF	7	7	70	21	1	0	1	1.000	2.83	+2	1
Hannahan, J	Cin	1B	13	8	75	58	6	1	7	.985	-	0	0
Harper, B	Was	LF	90	82	738	147	9	3	0	.981	1.90	-6	-1
	Was	CF	7	5	41	10	0	1	0	.909	2.20	0	-1
	Was	RF	10	7	63	9	0	0	0	1.000	1.29	0	1
Harrison, J	Pit	2B	17	13	105	26	42	1	9	.986	5.83	+3	2
	Pit	3B	72	55	519	42	138	3	15	.984	3.12	+9	8
	Pit	SS	8	4	41	8	13	1	5	.955	4.61	0	0

All Other Fielders

Player	Tm	Pos	G	GS	Inn	PO	A	E	DP	Pct.	Rng	+/-	RS
	Pit	LF	26	21	181	25	1	0	0	1.000	1.30	-3	0
	Pit	RF	26	23	182	50	3	1	1	.981	2.63	0	3
Hart, C	Sea	1B	2	2	16	15	0	0	1	1.000	-	0	0
	Sea	LF	1	1	9	1	0	1	0	.500	1.00	0	0
	Sea	RF	7	6	46	12	0	0	0	1.000	2.36	-2	-1
Hassan, A	Bos	RF	2	2	17	1	0	0	0	1.000	.53	+1	0
Headley, C	TOT	1B	7	6	54	51	2	1	6	.981	-	0	0
Heisey, C	Cin	LF	53	31	315	76	0	0	0	1.000	2.17	+13	6
	Cin	CF	16	11	115	37	0	0	0	1.000	2.90	-1	0
	Cin	RF	14	13	114	18	0	0	0	1.000	1.43	+4	2
Hernandez, C	Phi	2B	11	8	75	22	15	0	3	1.000	4.42	-1	-1
	Phi	3B	14	12	107	5	19	3	1	.889	2.01	-4	-3
	Phi	SS	4	2	21	6	4	0	1	1.000	4.29	-2	-2
Hernandez, E	TOT	2B	4	3	29	4	8	0	2	1.000	3.72	+1	0
	TOT	3B	3	1	15	0	5	0	0	1.000	3.07	+2	1
	TOT	SS	5	3	28	3	10	0	3	1.000	4.18	+1	1
	TOT	LF	8	8	69	10	2	0	1	1.000	1.57	+1	2
	TOT	CF	18	16	144	50	0	2	0	.962	3.13	+4	2
	TOT	RF	3	1	12	1	1	0	1	1.000	1.50	0	1
Herrera, D	NYM	2B	17	17	147	29	49	3	16	.963	4.78	-1	1
Herrera, E	Mil	2B	7	2	27	4	6	0	1	1.000	3.33	0	0
	Mil	3B	11	1	25	1	8	0	0	1.000	3.20	+2	2
	Mil	SS	14	10	88	17	34	4	7	.927	5.22	-2	-2
	Mil	LF	7	3	32	5	0	0	0	1.000	1.41	-1	0
	Mil	CF	7	4	50	19	0	0	0	1.000	3.42	+4	0
	Mil	RF	15	7	79	14	0	0	0	1.000	1.59	-3	-2
Herrera, J	Bos	1B	1	0	1	1	0	0	0	1.000	-	0	0
	Bos	2B	9	3	36	3	13	0	1	1.000	4.00	0	0
	Bos	3B	14	8	79	4	14	1	0	.947	2.05	0	-1
	Bos	SS	16	13	120	14	38	0	13	1.000	3.90	-2	0
Herrmann, C	Min	LF	12	9	78	13	0	0	0	1.000	1.50	-2	-3
	Min	RF	13	6	80	19	0	1	0	.950	2.14	-2	0
Hicks, A	Min	LF	6	3	22	6	0	0	0	1.000	2.45	0	0
	Min	CF	57	53	479	163	4	2	2	.988	3.14	-11	-3
	Min	RF	8	3	37	4	0	0	0	1.000	1.32	+1	0
Hicks, B	SF	1B	1	0	1	1	0	0	0	1.000	-	0	0
	SF	2B	61	59	530	107	180	5	47	.983	4.87	+1	5
	SF	LF	1	0	0	0	0	0	0	-	.00	-1	0
Hill, A	Ari	3B	7	7	62	2	13	0	1	1.000	2.19	-4	-3
Hoes, L	Hou	LF	36	27	251	50	3	1	0	.981	1.90	+6	8
	Hou	RF	12	8	78	20	1	1	0	.955	2.43	0	-1
Holt, B	Bos	1B	9	8	62	69	1	1	15	.986	-	0	-2
	Bos	2B	11	7	74	12	23	0	4	1.000	4.26	0	0
	Bos	3B	39	37	327	30	73	6	5	.945	2.83	-5	-4
	Bos	SS	12	11	101	14	41	0	6	1.000	4.90	-3	-3
	Bos	LF	8	7	60	7	0	0	0	1.000	1.05	0	-1
	Bos	CF	10	7	58	14	0	0	0	1.000	2.18	+1	-1
	Bos	RF	35	28	265	59	1	0	0	1.000	2.04	+18	10
Holt, T	Cle	LF	1	0	2	1	0	0	0	1.000	4.50	0	0
	Cle	CF	9	3	37	10	0	0	0	1.000	2.43	+3	2
	Cle	RF	28	14	150	32	0	0	0	1.000	1.92	+4	2
Ibanez, R	TOT	1B	8	4	43	35	5	0	4	1.000	-	-1	-1
	TOT	LF	22	17	140	40	0	1	0	.976	2.57	+1	-1
	TOT	RF	5	5	33	8	0	0	0	1.000	2.18	+1	1
Inciarte, E	Ari	LF	37	26	252	67	2	2	0	.972	2.47	+9	8
	Ari	CF	76	71	649	198	8	2	0	.990	2.86	+24	15
	Ari	RF	1	1	8	1	0	1	0	.500	1.13	0	0
Ishikawa, T	TOT	1B	42	21	207	220	15	1	23	.996	-	-1	0
	TOT	LF	8	3	29	10	0	0	0	1.000	3.10	+2	1
Izturis, M	Tor	2B	10	9	77	10	22	0	8	1.000	3.72	0	1
Jackson, B	Ari	CF	1	0	1	2	0	0	0	1.000	18.00	0	0
	Ari	RF	4	1	15	5	0	0	0	1.000	3.07	+1	0
Jay, J	StL	LF	27	7	95	26	0	1	0	.963	2.46	+5	3
	StL	CF	98	91	749	193	2	1	0	.995	2.34	+3	5
	StL	RF	33	11	143	28	0	0	0	1.000	1.76	+3	-2
Jimenez, L	LAA	3B	16	10	101	9	18	0	5	1.000	2.41	-3	-3
Johnson, C	Atl	1B	1	0	2	1	0	0	0	1.000	-	0	0
Johnson, D	Tor	1B	8	6	57	44	4	1	2	.980	-	-1	-1
Johnson, E	Cle	2B	2	2	17	3	7	2	2	.833	5.29	+1	-1
	Cle	3B	1	0	4	0	0	0	0	-	.00	0	0
	Cle	RF	3	3	24	6	0	0	0	1.000	2.25	0	0
Johnson, K	TOT	1B	32	27	246	213	29	4	9	.984	-	+3	0
	TOT	2B	5	3	25	3	4	1	1	.875	2.49	0	0
	TOT	3B	60	41	369	23	67	6	5	.938	2.20	+4	2
	TOT	LF	4	1	9	1	0	0	0	1.000	1.00	+1	0
	TOT	RF	1	1	10	2	0	0	0	1.000	1.80	+1	0
Johnson, R	Mia	LF	23	19	175	32	3	0	1	1.000	1.80	-1	-1
	Mia	CF	1	0	4	2	0	0	0	1.000	4.50	0	0
	Mia	RF	11	6	57	8	1	1	0	.900	1.42	-2	-1
Jones, G	Mia	RF	9	7	60	8	0	0	0	1.000	1.20	-2	-2
Jones, J	Sea	LF	1	1	14	1	0	1	0	.500	.64	-1	-2
	Sea	CF	85	69	649	153	1	1	0	.994	2.14	-11	-9
	Sea	RF	9	2	35	4	0	0	0	1.000	1.02	-1	0
Joseph, C	Bal	1B	4	0	4	10	0	0	0	1.000	-	0	0
Joyce, M	TB	1B	81	70	611	132	5	2	1	.986	2.02	0	1
	TB	RF	15	13	118	24	0	1	0	.960	1.83	-1	-1
Kalish, R	ChC	LF	18	11	105	19	0	1	0	.950	1.63	-3	-4
	ChC	CF	11	8	67	19	0	0	0	1.000	2.54	-1	1
	ChC	RF	11	8	65	17	0	0	0	1.000	2.34	-5	-4
Kawasaki, M	Tor	2B	64	49	445	78	139	5	28	.977	4.39	-4	-3
	Tor	3B	19	18	132	6	37	2	1	.956	2.93	+1	1
	Tor	SS	4	2	15	2	2	0	0	1.000	2.40	0	0
Kelly, D	Det	1B	30	4	84	72	7	1	10	.988	-	-1	0
	Det	2B	1	0	1	0	0	0	0	-	.00	0	0
	Det	3B	41	13	144	8	31	1	3	.975	2.44	-1	-1
	Det	LF	8	5	57	17	0	0	0	1.000	2.68	+5	3
	Det	CF	6	6	52	21	0	0	0	1.000	3.66	+2	1
	Det	RF	11	8	73	12	0	0	0	1.000	1.47	-4	-4
Kemp, M	LAD	LF	44	44	369	60	1	1	0	.984	1.49	-13	-8
	LAD	CF	41	34	326	75	1	4	0	.950	2.10	-20	-12
	LAD	RF	59	59	500	92	5	2	2	.980	1.74	-4	-3
Kiermaier, K	TB	LF	1	0	0	0	0	0	0	-	-	0	0
	TB	CF	42	32	298	100	2	1	1	.990	3.08	-2	1
	TB	RF	68	57	526	137	3	5	1	.966	2.39	+26	14
Kieschnick, R	Ari	LF	5	5	45	7	0	1	0	.875	1.40	-3	-2
	Ari	RF	12	9	39	4	0	0	0	1.000	1.86	0	0
Kobernus, J	Was	2B	3	2	21	1	9	0	4	1.000	4.29	+1	1
Konerko, P	CWS	1B	23	21	183	168	9	0	25	1.000	-	0	0
Kouzmanoff, K	Tex	3B	13	12	108	2	18	2	1	.909	1.67	0	0
Kozma, P	StL	2B	6	4	39	10	11	0	2	1.000	4.85	-2	-2
	StL	SS	8	2	24	9	14	0	5	1.000	8.63	+1	1
Krauss, M	Hou	1B	33	30	238	257	30	4	24	.986	-	-1	-1
	Hou	LF	19	17	139	32	1	0	1	1.000	2.14	+3	1
	Hou	RF	5	2	26	5	0	0	0	1.000	1.73	0	0
Kubel, J	Min	LF	36	35	318	70	0	0	0	1.000	1.98	-13	-9
	Min	RF	4	4	36	6	0	0	0	1.000	1.51	-1	0
La Stella, T	Atl	2B	88	86	722	146	216	6	54	.984	4.51	-8	-4
Lake, J	ChC	LF	53	42	375	91	2	4	1	.959	2.23	+12	3
	ChC	CF	36	28	257	54	0	3	0	.947	1.89	-11	-8
	ChC	RF	1	0	2	0	0	0	0	-	.00	0	0
Lamb, J	Ari	3B	34	33	289	14	61	1	5	.987	2.33	0	0
Lambo, A	Pit	1B	1	1	5	3	0	0	0	1.000	-	0	0
	Pit	RF	6	5	43	12	0	0	0	1.000	2.51	+2	1
Lavarnway, R	Bos	1B	6	2	24	23	3	0	0	1.000	-	+1	0
Lawrie, B	Tor	2B	32	26	193	53	69	2	19	.984	5.69	0	1
	Tor	3B	63	44	403	42	82	2	10	.984	2.77	+1	0
LeMahieu, D	Col	1B	1	0	1	0	0	0	0	-	-	0	0
	Col	3B	7	4	38	2	5	0	0	1.000	1.64	+1	0
	Col	SS	1	0	1	2	0	0	0	-	.00	0	0
Lind, A	Tor	1B	47	43	368	357	23	3	41	.992	-	-6	-3
Liriano, R	SD	2B	34	29	256	57	2	4	0	.937	2.07	+6	-2
Lombardozzi, S	Bal	2B	20	17	161	29	52	1	14	.988	4.54	-6	-5
Lough, D	Bal	LF	85	38	398	102	4	1	0	.991	2.39	+12	7
	Bal	CF	16	9	87	30	0	0	0	1.000	3.10	+7	4
	Bal	RF	6	0	15	3	0	0	0	1.000	1.80	-2	0
Lucas, E	Mia	1B	6	0	14	8	0	0	0	1.000	-	0	0
	Mia	2B	20	16	148	29	56	1	10	.988	5.18	-1	-1
	Mia	3B	4	2	21	0	6	1	0	.857	2.53	-1	0
	Mia	SS	19	13	131	19	45	1	11	.985	4.41	+2	1
	Mia	LF	1	0	8	2	0	0	0	1.000	2.25	0	0
	Mia	RF	3	3	21	5	0	1	0	.833	2.14	+4	2
Lucroy, J	Mil	1B	19	16	129	113	9	1	9	.992	-	0	0
Lutz, D	Cin	1B	6	5	40	36	3	1	3	.975	-	-3	-2
	Cin	LF	4	4	34	6	1	0	1	1.000	1.85	0	1

All Other Fielders

Player	Tm	Pos	G	GS	Inn	PO	A	E	DP	Pct.	Rng	+/-	RS
	Cin	RF	2	1	9	5	0	0	0	1.000	5.00	+1	1
Machado, M	Bal	3B	82	82	737	61	168	9	17	.962	2.80	+6	6
Maldonado, M	Mil	1B	2	1	12	6	2	1	0	.889	-	0	-1
Marisnick, J	TOT	LF	5	0	18	5	0	0	0	1.000	2.50	-1	-1
	TOT	CF	30	26	255	96	3	0	1	1.000	3.50	+12	10
	TOT	RF	31	29	261	68	3	2	1	.973	2.45	+7	5
Markakis, N	Bal	1B	2	2	19	23	1	0	1	1.000	-	-1	-1
Marte, A	Ari	LF	20	19	170	35	1	1	1	.973	1.91	+6	1
	Ari	RF	5	3	37	5	0	1	0	.833	1.23	-2	0
Marte, A	Ari	3B	4	3	29	1	7	0	1	1.000	2.48	-1	-1
Marte, S	Pit	CF	28	16	161	27	0	1	0	.964	1.51	-1	-1
Martinez, J	Det	LF	83	83	689	149	1	4	0	.974	1.96	-5	-1
	Det	RF	34	24	243	49	0	0	0	1.000	1.82	0	0
Martinez, M	Pit	2B	6	6	49	12	10	1	1	.957	4.04	+2	1
	Pit	LF	6	0	12	2	0	0	0	1.000	1.50	0	0
	Pit	CF	2	0	4	0	0	0	0	-	.00	0	0
	Pit	RF	1	1	7	3	0	0	0	1.000	3.86	0	0
Martinez, V	Det	1B	35	33	284	251	16	3	24	.989	-	-7	-4
Mastroianni, D	TOT	LF	3	2	19	3	0	0	0	1.000	1.42	0	0
	TOT	CF	7	4	36	7	1	0	0	1.000	2.00	-1	0
	TOT	RF	10	2	39	12	1	0	0	1.000	2.97	+1	2
Maxwell, J	KC	LF	1	0	2	0	0	0	0	-	.00	0	0
	KC	CF	6	5	45	10	1	0	0	1.000	2.20	-7	-5
	KC	RF	7	7	61	6	0	0	0	1.000	.89	-5	-3
Mayberry, J	TOT	1B	23	10	106	106	7	1	5	.991	-	0	-1
	TOT	LF	16	11	105	19	1	0	0	1.000	1.71	-4	-1
	TOT	CF	11	9	81	21	0	0	0	1.000	2.33	0	-1
	TOT	RF	7	4	33	5	0	0	0	1.000	1.36	0	-1
Maybin, C	SD	CF	86	73	631	161	1	2	1	.988	2.31	+14	4
McBride, M	Col	1B	5	3	28	28	1	0	6	1.000	-	+1	1
	Col	LF	2	0	4	0	0	0	0	-	.00	0	0
	Col	RF	3	2	17	3	1	0	1	1.000	2.16	+1	2
McCann, B	NYY	1B	16	11	103	100	9	1	7	.991	-	-1	-2
McDonald, J	LAA	2B	2	1	11	4	3	0	1	1.000	5.73	0	0
	LAA	3B	73	10	199	16	48	2	5	.970	2.90	+1	1
	LAA	SS	16	5	82	19	19	2	4	.950	4.17	-1	-2
McLouth, N	Was	LF	28	18	173	33	0	0	0	1.000	1.72	+1	0
	Was	CF	9	8	67	16	0	1	0	.941	2.15	+3	2
	Was	RF	16	7	78	15	0	1	0	.938	1.72	-5	-3
Medica, T	SD	1B	46	36	316	292	26	1	29	.997	-	+5	4
	SD	LF	22	19	136	27	0	0	0	1.000	1.78	-3	-3
Mercer, J	Pit	RF	1	0	2	0	0	0	0	-	.00	0	0
Middlebrooks, W	Bos	1B	1	0	3	2	0	0	1	1.000	-	0	0
	Bos	3B	62	57	522	38	99	4	9	.972	2.36	-8	-5
Miller, B	Sea	2B	13	2	45	5	15	1	3	.952	3.97	-2	-2
	Sea	3B	2	0	5	0	0	0	0	-	.00	0	0
Molina, Y	StL	1B	1	1	9	10	1	0	0	1.000	-	0	0
Montero, J	Sea	1B	1	1	6	8	0	0	0	1.000	-	0	0
Moore, T	Was	1B	24	17	165	171	16	3	16	.984	-	+1	2
	Was	LF	4	3	25	8	0	0	0	1.000	2.92	0	1
Morales, K	TOT	1B	27	26	210	219	9	1	23	.996	-	-2	-1
Morel, B	Pit	1B	1	0	1	0	0	0	0	-	-	0	0
	Pit	3B	13	8	74	2	17	0	0	1.000	2.30	+1	1
Moreland, M	Tex	1B	22	22	194	158	14	2	15	.989	-	+1	0
	Tex	LF	2	2	16	4	0	1	0	.800	2.25	+1	1
Morgan, N	Cle	LF	2	1	10	2	0	0	0	1.000	1.80	-1	-1
	Cle	CF	12	11	93	21	0	0	0	1.000	2.03	-8	-4
Morrison, L	Sea	1B	79	74	661	639	46	3	48	.996	-	+2	0
	Sea	LF	2	2	14	2	0	0	0	1.000	1.29	+1	1
	Sea	RF	8	7	57	16	1	0	0	1.000	2.70	+2	1
Morse, M	SF	1B	43	39	336	307	24	3	41	.991	-	+1	0
	SF	LF	84	82	579	107	2	2	0	.982	1.69	-14	-9
Moss, B	Oak	1B	67	54	487	487	21	5	48	.990	-	+1	2
	Oak	LF	56	42	377	75	2	2	0	.975	1.84	0	0
	Oak	RF	34	27	245	48	4	0	1	1.000	1.91	+1	6
Moya, S	Det	RF	5	0	5	0	0	0	0	-	.00	0	0
Murphy, D	NYM	1B	1	0	1	0	0	0	0	-	-	0	0
	NYM	3B	16	16	141	6	26	0	4	1.000	2.04	-1	-1
Murphy, D	Cle	LF	2	2	13	1	0	0	0	1.000	.69	-1	-1
Murphy, D	Tex	1B	6	6	44	28	4	0	4	1.000	-	-2	-1
	Tex	2B	21	18	158	36	49	0	17	1.000	4.83	-2	-2
	Tex	3B	5	1	16	3	2	0	0	1.000	2.81	0	0

Player	Tm	Pos	G	GS	Inn	PO	A	E	DP	Pct.	Rng	+/-	RS
Myers, W	TB	1B	2	0	4	1	0	0	0	1.000	-	0	0
	TB	CF	1	0	2	0	0	0	0	-	.00	0	0
	TB	RF	78	76	674	161	5	4	1	.976	2.22	-9	-7
Nady, X	SD	1B	1	0	1	0	0	0	0	-	-	0	0
	SD	LF	5	3	26	2	0	0	0	1.000	.69	-1	0
	SD	RF	8	3	33	9	0	0	0	1.000	2.45	+1	0
Nava, D	Bos	1B	11	6	63	51	6	1	5	.983	-	+2	0
	Bos	LF	38	31	273	57	1	1	0	.983	1.91	0	3
	Bos	RF	69	57	502	121	8	2	1	.985	2.31	+17	14
Navarro, E	LAA	1B	28	12	153	124	8	1	10	.992	-	0	0
	LAA	LF	23	19	165	41	1	1	0	.977	2.29	+1	0
	LAA	RF	6	4	37	11	1	0	0	1.000	2.92	+2	2
Negron, K	Cin	2B	17	13	125	22	46	0	8	1.000	4.91	+3	2
	Cin	3B	25	22	193	18	41	1	4	.983	2.75	+3	4
	Cin	SS	2	1	9	5	6	0	1	1.000	10.61	0	0
	Cin	LF	1	0	1	0	0	0	0	-	.00	0	0
Nelson, C	SD	1B	1	0	2	1	1	0	1	1.000	-	0	0
	SD	2B	3	3	27	3	9	1	0	.923	4.00	0	0
	SD	3B	20	14	127	10	26	1	2	.973	2.55	+3	2
Nieuwenhuis, K	NYM	LF	17	9	90	15	2	1	0	.944	1.71	0	2
	NYM	CF	14	10	96	26	3	0	0	1.000	2.71	+3	2
	NYM	RF	6	3	31	6	0	0	0	1.000	1.72	+1	0
Nieves, W	Phi	1B	1	0	0	0	0	0	0	-	-	0	0
Nix, J	TOT	1B	1	0	3	3	0	0	0	1.000	-	-1	0
	TOT	2B	12	7	64	14	23	3	6	.925	5.23	-2	-1
	TOT	3B	19	12	110	10	30	0	1	1.000	3.28	+4	2
	TOT	SS	6	3	37	6	10	1	3	.941	3.86	+1	1
	TOT	RF	2	0	3	2	0	0	0	1.000	6.00	0	0
Nunez, E	Min	2B	2	0	3	1	0	0	0	1.000	3.00	0	0
	Min	3B	20	12	124	15	15	3	0	.909	2.17	-2	-2
	Min	SS	20	17	155	19	46	2	7	.970	3.77	+1	1
	Min	LF	16	10	90	23	1	2	0	.923	2.40	-2	1
	Min	RF	2	1	11	5	1	0	1	1.000	4.91	0	0
Olt, M	ChC	1B	12	9	85	93	4	0	10	1.000	-	-1	-1
	ChC	3B	52	48	395	20	72	7	4	.929	2.09	-1	-1
O'Malley, S	LAA	2B	1	0	4	0	1	0	0	1.000	2.25	0	0
	LAA	LF	5	2	28	5	0	0	0	1.000	1.63	0	0
	LAA	RF	1	0	1	0	0	0	0	-	.00	0	0
Ortiz, D	Bos	1B	5	5	43	37	2	0	9	1.000	-	0	-1
Overbay, L	Mil	1B	83	64	590	553	34	5	41	.992	-	-3	-1
Owings, C	Ari	2B	18	18	153	31	48	0	11	1.000	4.66	+1	1
	Ari	SS	61	59	527	77	165	11	36	.957	4.13	+8	5
Ozuna, M	Mia	LF	11	10	93	29	2	0	1	1.000	3.01	-2	1
	Mia	RF	4	0	10	2	0	0	0	1.000	1.80	0	0
Pacheco, J	TOT	1B	15	11	101	84	7	0	5	1.000	-	-2	-2
	TOT	2B	2	1	9	1	0	0	0	1.000	1.00	0	0
	TOT	3B	3	3	25	0	1	1	0	.500	.36	-2	-1
Panik, J	SF	2B	70	66	579	131	184	8	53	.975	4.90	-5	-1
Paredes, J	TOT	2B	3	0	7	0	1	0	0	1.000	1.29	-1	-1
	TOT	3B	16	14	117	8	22	3	3	.909	2.31	-2	-2
Parker, K	Col	1B	2	2	17	15	1	0	2	1.000	-	0	0
	Col	RF	4	1	18	4	1	0	0	1.000	2.45	-2	-1
Parmelee, C	Min	1B	33	16	178	167	18	1	15	.995	-	+2	0
	Min	LF	22	14	127	33	3	0	2	1.000	2.55	-6	-4
	Min	CF	3	1	11	6	0	0	0	1.000	4.91	-1	-1
	Min	RF	33	28	249	63	1	1	1	.985	2.31	-4	-5
Parra, G	TOT	LF	27	18	175	39	0	1	0	.975	2.01	+6	3
	TOT	CF	12	7	65	21	0	2	0	.913	2.91	-10	-6
Parrino, A	Oak	2B	4	3	31	7	11	0	7	1.000	5.17	0	1
	Oak	3B	1	0	2	1	0	0	0	1.000	4.50	0	0
	Oak	SS	14	11	90	12	23	1	4	.972	3.50	+4	3
	Oak	LF	2	1	10	0	0	0	0	-	.00	0	0
Pastornicky, T	Atl	2B	10	10	73	11	18	1	5	.967	3.58	-4	-3
Paul, X	Ari	LF	5	3	28	3	0	0	0	1.000	.95	0	0
Paulsen, B	Col	1B	15	10	99	110	8	0	7	1.000	-	+3	0
	Col	RF	3	3	17	5	0	0	0	1.000	2.65	0	0
Pearce, S	Bal	1B	51	47	416	399	37	1	34	.998	-	+9	9
	Bal	LF	35	27	231	61	4	0	1	1.000	2.53	+8	7
	Bal	RF	8	4	40	14	1	0	0	1.000	3.38	+2	1
Pederson, J	LAD	LF	2	0	5	2	0	0	0	1.000	3.60	0	0
	LAD	CF	7	3	46	11	0	0	0	1.000	2.15	0	1
	LAD	RF	5	0	18	3	0	0	0	1.000	1.50	-1	-1

All Other Fielders

Player	Tm	Pos	G	GS	Inn	PO	A	E	DP	Pct.	Rng	+/-	RS
Peguero, C	KC	RF	4	2	23	3	0	0	0	1.000	1.17	0	0
Pena, B	Cin	1B	53	45	397	365	23	1	35	.997	-	+1	0
Pena, C	Tex	1B	16	16	138	105	9	1	12	.991	-	0	0
Pena, R	Atl	2B	38	14	172	36	46	2	11	.976	4.29	-2	-3
	Atl	3B	17	5	67	4	9	0	1	1.000	1.76	+1	1
	Atl	SS	15	10	108	25	30	5	10	.917	4.57	+2	0
Pence, H	SF	CF	1	0	1	0	0	0	0	-	.00	0	0
Pennington, C	Ari	2B	18	15	137	34	48	0	12	1.000	5.37	+3	3
	Ari	3B	8	8	70	5	19	0	2	1.000	3.07	+2	0
	Ari	SS	23	20	180	24	54	2	13	.975	3.89	-1	-1
Peralta, D	Ari	LF	36	27	260	36	1	3	0	.925	1.28	+2	-2
	Ari	CF	14	13	109	21	0	0	0	1.000	1.73	0	-1
	Ari	RF	40	40	357	75	5	1	2	.988	2.02	+3	7
Perez, E	NYY	CF	2	2	17	6	0	2	0	.750	3.18	0	0
	NYY	RF	2	0	7	2	0	1	0	.667	2.57	0	0
Perez, H	Det	2B	5	0	5	1	2	0	1	1.000	5.40	0	0
	Det	3B	2	0	2	0	0	0	0	-	.00	0	0
	Det	SS	1	1	7	2	0	0	0	1.000	2.57	0	0
Perez, J	SF	LF	40	8	153	29	1	0	0	1.000	1.76	+2	1
	SF	CF	17	12	108	32	1	0	1	1.000	2.75	-5	-4
	SF	RF	5	1	19	4	0	1	0	.800	1.89	0	0
Peterson, J	SD	2B	14	10	90	21	32	2	4	.964	5.28	+1	1
	SD	3B	10	8	67	2	19	2	0	.913	2.84	-2	-1
Petit, G	Hou	2B	4	1	14	2	4	0	1	1.000	3.77	0	0
	Hou	3B	9	1	49	9	16	0	2	1.000	2.92	-1	-1
	Hou	SS	19	17	155	22	50	2	14	.973	4.17	+2	3
Pham, T	StL	LF	2	0	3	2	0	0	0	1.000	6.00	0	0
	StL	RF	1	0	1	0	0	0	0	-	.00	0	0
Pillar, K	Tor	LF	30	14	135	30	0	0	0	1.000	2.00	0	-1
	Tor	CF	16	13	112	33	1	0	0	1.000	2.73	+5	3
	Tor	RF	7	3	35	8	1	0	0	1.000	2.31	+1	3
Pirela, J	NYY	2B	4	3	27	4	7	1	2	.917	3.67	+1	0
Polanco, G	Pit	RF	83	63	619	144	5	2	2	.987	2.17	-11	-3
Polanco, J	Min	SS	4	1	12	3	6	0	3	1.000	6.75	0	1
Pollock, A	Ari	LF	2	1	9	0	0	0	0	-	.00	0	0
	Ari	CF	68	65	576	151	8	1	2	.994	2.48	+11	10
Pompey, D	Tor	LF	9	7	63	9	0	0	0	1.000	1.29	-2	-1
	Tor	CF	5	3	27	8	0	0	0	1.000	2.67	+1	0
Posey, B	SF	1B	35	30	261	246	22	1	20	.996	-	+2	2
Prado, M	TOT	2B	21	20	175	29	64	3	10	.969	4.77	+3	2
	TOT	LF	4	3	31	6	0	0	0	1.000	1.74	0	0
	TOT	RF	8	7	60	9	0	0	0	1.000	1.35	-1	-1
Presley, A	Hou	LF	43	29	263	50	1	0	0	1.000	1.74	+1	0
	Hou	CF	21	14	136	36	0	0	0	1.000	2.38	+6	2
	Hou	RF	20	20	173	29	2	0	0	1.000	1.62	-2	-1
Pridie, J	Col	LF	1	1	8	3	0	0	0	1.000	3.38	+1	1
	Col	RF	1	0	2	0	0	0	0	-	.00	0	0
Puig, Y	LAD	CF	53	52	442	104	8	2	1	.982	2.28	-8	0
Pujols, A	LAA	3B	1	0	6	0	1	0	0	1.000	1.50	0	0
Punto, N	Oak	2B	52	38	364	89	130	6	41	.973	5.42	+1	1
	Oak	3B	2	0	2	0	1	0	0	1.000	5.40	0	0
	Oak	SS	17	10	119	19	36	1	9	.982	4.17	0	0
	Oak	RF	1	0	0	0	0	0	0	-	.00	0	0
Quentin, C	SD	LF	32	31	229	42	1	0	1	1.000	1.69	-3	-3
Quintanilla, O	NYM	2B	2	0	4	0	0	0	0	-	.00	-1	0
	NYM	SS	11	7	71	16	20	1	7	.973	4.54	0	0
Raburn, R	Cle	1B	1	0	1	0	2	0	0	1.000	-	0	0
	Cle	LF	20	14	124	22	1	1	0	.958	1.66	-5	-2
	Cle	RF	25	19	157	23	2	1	1	.962	1.43	-4	-1
Ramirez, J	Cle	2B	11	7	73	14	24	0	6	1.000	4.68	+2	2
	Cle	SS	56	54	499	76	155	4	34	.983	4.17	+4	4
Rasmus, C	Tor	CF	87	80	719	234	3	1	0	.996	2.97	-11	-7
Reddick, J	Oak	CF	1	1	9	2	0	0	0	1.000	2.00	0	0
Reimold, N	TOT	LF	4	4	31	7	0	0	0	1.000	2.03	0	0
	TOT	RF	10	5	47	17	1	1	0	.947	3.45	-2	0
Rendon, A	Was	2B	28	25	215	51	52	0	8	1.000	4.30	+5	4
Reynolds, M	Mil	1B	91	72	658	626	60	3	57	.996	-	+3	2
	Mil	3B	42	29	273	13	67	3	6	.964	2.63	+6	4
	Mil	RF	3	1	12	1	0	0	0	1.000	.75	0	0
Richardson, A	NYY	CF	1	0	3	0	0	0	0	-	.00	0	0
	NYY	RF	5	5	39	8	0	0	0	1.000	1.85	+1	1
Rivera, R	SD	1B	3	0	9	11	0	1	0	.917	-	0	0
Rivero, C	Bos	3B	3	1	14	1	4	1	0	.833	3.21	-4	-3
Roberts, R	Bos	3B	8	7	55	3	10	1	1	.929	2.13	+1	1
Robertson, D	Tex	2B	1	0	4	2	1	0	0	1.000	6.75	0	1
	Tex	LF	30	15	166	34	3	0	0	1.000	2.01	-2	2
	Tex	CF	21	18	139	41	4	2	0	.957	2.91	-7	-4
	Tex	RF	18	8	92	23	0	0	0	1.000	2.25	+3	0
Robinson, C	LAD	1B	3	1	9	7	0	0	1	1.000	-	0	0
Robinson, S	StL	LF	5	0	9	3	0	0	0	1.000	3.00	+1	0
	StL	CF	1	0	0	0	0	0	0	-	.00	0	0
	StL	RF	15	7	74	17	1	0	0	1.000	2.19	0	1
Rodriguez, G	Tex	2B	2	2	18	6	6	0	1	1.000	6.00	+1	1
	Tex	3B	3	1	13	3	2	1	0	.833	3.46	+1	1
	Tex	SS	1	0	1	0	0	0	0	-	.00	0	0
Rodriguez, S	TB	1B	18	14	125	101	8	0	9	1.000	-	+2	1
	TB	2B	23	14	136	32	35	2	5	.971	4.42	+2	0
	TB	3B	9	7	60	6	11	1	1	.944	2.55	-2	0
	TB	SS	1	1	9	0	1	0	0	1.000	1.00	0	0
	TB	LF	17	12	103	16	0	0	0	1.000	1.40	-6	-5
	TB	RF	2	0	3	0	0	0	0	-	.00	-1	0
Rodriguez, Y	Cin	LF	2	2	18	2	1	0	0	1.000	1.00	+1	0
	Cin	CF	2	2	17	4	0	0	0	1.000	2.12	-2	-1
	Cin	RF	4	3	25	6	0	0	0	1.000	2.16	+1	1
Rogers, J	Mil	1B	4	2	14	12	0	1	1	.923	-	0	0
Rojas, M	LAD	2B	3	2	17	2	11	0	2	1.000	6.88	0	0
	LAD	3B	19	10	106	8	28	3	2	.923	3.07	+5	4
	LAD	SS	66	25	284	41	101	4	25	.973	4.51	+10	11
	LAD	LF	1	0	2	0	0	0	0	-	.00	0	0
Romak, J	LAD	1B	1	1	9	14	1	0	3	1.000	-	0	0
	LAD	3B	1	0	0	0	0	0	0	-	.00	0	0
	LAD	RF	3	2	14	3	0	0	0	1.000	1.93	0	0
Romero, S	Sea	LF	11	1	24	3	0	0	0	1.000	1.13	-1	-1
	Sea	RF	42	35	294	64	1	1	0	.985	1.99	+2	-1
Romine, A	Det	2B	12	1	24	7	5	0	2	1.000	4.50	+1	1
	Det	SS	83	71	652	112	206	8	46	.975	4.39	-5	-3
Romine, A	NYY	1B	1	0	3	0	0	0	0	1.000	-	0	0
Rosales, A	Tex	1B	32	27	252	215	22	1	32	.996	-	+4	5
	Tex	2B	5	5	39	7	10	1	3	.944	3.92	+1	1
	Tex	3B	7	5	47	6	8	0	0	1.000	2.68	+2	1
	Tex	SS	3	2	24	2	6	0	1	1.000	3.00	0	0
Rosario, W	Col	1B	4	3	25	25	0	0	7	1.000	-	-1	-1
Ross, C	Ari	LF	37	34	271	34	3	2	0	.949	1.23	-6	-4
	Ari	RF	20	17	133	27	2	1	1	.967	1.97	-1	-1
Rua, R	Tex	1B	9	9	77	54	7	0	7	1.000	-	0	0
	Tex	3B	1	0	1	0	0	0	0	-	.00	0	0
	Tex	LF	17	17	151	33	0	0	0	1.000	1.97	-2	-2
Ruf, D	Phi	1B	20	12	113	106	6	0	9	1.000	-	+1	1
	Phi	3B	1	0	1	0	0	0	0	1.000	9.00	0	0
	Phi	LF	15	13	104	20	0	0	0	1.000	1.73	0	0
Ruggiano, J	ChC	LF	10	6	63	21	1	1	0	.957	3.14	-2	-2
	ChC	CF	18	16	141	42	0	0	0	1.000	2.69	-1	-1
	ChC	RF	34	30	258	52	0	0	0	1.000	1.81	-9	-5
Rutledge, J	Col	2B	17	12	107	25	27	2	6	.963	4.39	-6	-4
	Col	3B	5	5	38	1	8	2	1	.818	2.13	-2	-1
	Col	SS	69	58	515	64	159	9	34	.961	3.89	-9	-9
Ryan, B	NYY	1B	1	0	1	0	0	0	0	1.000	-	0	0
	NYY	2B	19	12	113	25	50	1	11	.987	5.97	+5	5
	NYY	3B	2	2	16	2	7	0	1	1.000	5.06	-1	-1
	NYY	SS	25	19	176	18	44	3	7	.954	3.17	-5	-2
Sanchez, C	CWS	2B	27	26	233	49	72	1	18	.992	4.68	-4	-1
	CWS	SS	1	1	8	1	5	0	0	1.000	6.75	+1	-1
Sanchez, G	Pit	1B	96	52	516	553	39	3	45	.995	-	-3	-3
	Pit	RF	1	0	3	0	0	0	0	-	.00	0	0
Sanchez, H	SF	1B	3	1	27	4	1	0	0	1.000	-	0	0
Santana, C	Cle	3B	26	26	226	25	35	6	3	.909	2.39	-8	-5
Santana, D	Min	SS	34	31	262	53	65	2	15	.983	4.06	-2	-1
	Min	CF	69	62	536	167	5	4	0	.977	2.89	-3	0
Santana, D	Hou	LF	3	3	27	4	1	0	0	1.000	1.67	0	0
	Hou	RF	2	2	16	2	0	0	0	1.000	1.13	-2	-1
Santiago, R	Cin	2B	20	12	128	25	47	1	8	.986	5.08	+1	0
	Cin	3B	28	21	194	22	33	4	2	.932	2.55	0	-2
	Cin	SS	20	16	145	16	50	0	8	1.000	4.09	0	0
	Cin	LF	1	0	1	0	0	0	0	-	.00	0	0

All Other Fielders

Player	Tm	Pos	G	GS	Inn	PO	A	E	DP	Pct.	Rng	+/-	RS
Sardinas, L	Tex	2B	19	15	141	26	33	0	10	1.000	3.76	-3	-2
	Tex	3B	7	4	40	4	7	1	1	.917	2.48	-1	-1
	Tex	SS	13	8	79	14	29	3	6	.935	4.90	+2	1
Satin, J	NYM	1B	8	7	57	50	3	0	4	1.000	-	-1	0
	NYM	3B	1	0	2	0	1	0	0	1.000	4.50	0	0
Saunders, M	Sea	LF	1	0	1	0	0	0	0	-	.00	0	0
	Sea	CF	12	9	75	23	0	0	0	1.000	2.76	-4	-2
	Sea	RF	68	53	481	104	1	0	0	1.000	1.97	+9	7
Schafer, J	TOT	LF	49	32	313	67	2	1	0	.986	1.99	+1	-1
	TOT	CF	20	18	159	52	0	1	0	.981	2.95	-6	-3
	TOT	RF	6	2	30	6	0	0	0	1.000	1.80	+1	0
Schafer, L	Mil	LF	17	10	94	19	1	0	0	1.000	1.91	0	0
	Mil	CF	14	9	84	16	1	0	1	1.000	1.82	-2	-1
	Mil	RF	17	10	107	19	2	1	1	.955	1.76	+6	5
Schierholtz, N	TOT	LF	4	0	12	2	0	0	0	1.000	1.50	0	0
	TOT	CF	2	1	10	0	0	0	0	-	.00	0	0
	TOT	RF	87	80	733	158	9	0	3	1.000	2.05	+12	8
Schoop, J	Bal	3B	17	14	134	13	24	4	0	.902	2.49	+1	1
Schumaker, S	Cin	2B	19	15	130	28	39	3	7	.957	4.63	-3	-2
	Cin	LF	33	26	236	38	0	0	0	1.000	1.45	-3	-3
	Cin	CF	8	7	63	10	0	0	0	1.000	1.43	-1	1
	Cin	RF	13	13	120	23	3	1	1	.963	1.96	-5	-3
Scruggs, X	StL	1B	5	3	33	29	3	1	4	.970	-	0	0
Scutaro, M	SF	2B	3	3	22	4	5	0	0	1.000	3.68	-1	-1
Sellers, J	Cle	2B	7	1	14	0	2	0	0	1.000	1.29	-1	-1
	Cle	3B	4	0	6	0	0	0	0	-	.00	0	0
	Cle	SS	6	4	39	9	14	0	4	1.000	5.31	-1	-1
Semien, M	CWS	2B	26	25	224	51	78	4	23	.970	5.19	-3	-1
	CWS	3B	33	31	279	14	72	10	9	.896	2.77	-3	-3
	CWS	SS	3	1	13	0	3	0	1	1.000	2.08	0	0
Shuck, J	TOT	LF	25	20	190	42	4	0	0	1.000	2.09	+4	5
	TOT	RF	8	4	37	13	0	0	0	1.000	3.16	+3	1
Sierra, M	TOT	LF	9	1	27	7	1	0	1	1.000	2.67	+1	1
	TOT	CF	4	2	19	6	0	0	0	1.000	2.84	-2	-1
	TOT	RF	70	36	372	79	3	3	0	.965	1.98	0	2
Sipp, T	Hou	LF	1	0	0	0	0	0	0	-	.00	0	0
	Hou	RF	1	0	0	0	0	0	0	-		0	0
Sizemore, G	TOT	LF	52	41	371	82	2	1	0	.988	2.04	+2	2
	TOT	CF	25	18	168	48	1	0	1	1.000	2.63	-7	-4
	TOT	RF	26	25	219	32	0	1	0	.970	1.32	+3	0
Sizemore, S	NYY	1B	2	1	7	8	0	0	1	1.000	-	0	0
	NYY	3B	5	4	33	6	6	0	1	1.000	3.27	0	0
Smith, S	SD	LF	102	81	740	157	2	1	0	.994	1.93	+9	2
	SD	RF	43	37	294	62	3	0	1	1.000	1.99	+5	5
Smoak, J	Sea	1B	79	66	608	587	31	2	60	.997	-	-4	-4
Smolinski, J	Tex	LF	12	11	92	17	0	0	0	1.000	1.66	+2	1
	Tex	RF	9	9	80	24	0	0	0	1.000	2.70	+1	0
Snider, T	Pit	LF	36	23	227	44	2	0	2	1.000	1.83	+8	8
	Pit	RF	64	47	386	64	5	1	0	.986	1.61	-11	-4
Snyder, B	Tex	LF	10	8	77	63	4	1	0	.985	-	+1	1
Sogard, E	Oak	2B	102	80	721	154	247	5	49	.988	5.01	+9	5
	Oak	SS	14	12	108	10	33	5	5	.896	3.57	-2	-2
Solano, D	Mia	2B	73	63	576	139	212	1	47	.997	5.48	+1	-1
	Mia	3B	2	1	5	2	2	0	1	1.000	7.20	0	0
	Mia	SS	4	3	32	7	4	0	4	1.000	5.85	+2	1
Solarte, Y	TOT	2B	27	21	173	35	43	2	9	.975	4.06	-2	-2
	TOT	SS	8	2	24	2	6	0	0	1.000	3.04	-1	-1
	TOT	LF	7	4	40	6	0	1	0	.857	1.35	-3	-3
Soler, J	ChC	RF	24	24	205	44	2	2	1	.958	2.02	+2	1
Soriano, A	NYY	LF	11	8	74	14	0	0	0	1.000	1.70	-3	0
	NYY	RF	26	23	190	25	2	2	0	.931	1.28	-9	-4
Soto, N	Cin	1B	7	2	28	20	1	0	0	1.000	-	+1	1
	Cin	3B	2	1	12	1	1	0	0	1.000	1.50	0	0
Souza, S	Was	LF	4	2	20	4	0	1	0	.800	1.80	+1	0
	Was	CF	1	0	3	0	0	0	0	-	.00	0	0
	Was	RF	8	2	23	6	0	0	0	1.000	2.35	0	0
Spangenberg, C	SD	2B	3	3	23	3	5	1	0	.889	3.13	0	0
	SD	3B	9	8	69	4	14	3	0	.857	2.35	-1	-1
	SD	LF	4	3	25	3	0	1	0	.750	1.07	-1	0
Springer, G	Hou	CF	8	7	61	24	0	0	0	1.000	3.54	-4	-2
	Hou	RF	71	70	618	139	6	7	2	.954	2.11	+4	1
Stewart, I	LAA	1B	6	2	25	24	1	0	1	1.000	-	0	0
	LAA	3B	16	14	122	10	15	1	0	.962	1.84	-6	-6
Suarez, E	Det	3B	2	0	9	1	1	0	0	1.000	2.00	+1	1
	Det	SS	81	71	622	113	189	10	49	.968	4.37	-9	-5
Suzuki, I	NYY	LF	9	6	56	9	0	0	0	1.000	1.45	0	0
	NYY	CF	5	2	19	7	0	0	0	1.000	3.32	0	0
Sweeney, R	ChC	LF	12	8	73	12	2	0	0	1.000	1.73	-1	-1
	ChC	CF	24	22	196	46	0	1	0	.979	2.12	+3	1
	ChC	RF	22	18	158	36	5	0	1	1.000	2.34	-1	-1
Swisher, N	Cle	1B	52	52	459	400	39	9	42	.980	-	-6	-4
	Cle	LF	2	2	16	3	0	0	0	1.000	1.69	-3	-2
	Cle	RF	4	4	28	4	0	0	0	1.000	1.29	0	0
Szczur, M	ChC	LF	6	4	35	11	0	0	0	1.000	2.83	0	-1
	ChC	CF	9	4	48	14	0	0	0	1.000	2.63	-5	-3
	ChC	RF	13	4	56	23	1	0	1	1.000	3.88	+3	1
Tabata, J	Pit	LF	18	11	90	19	0	0	0	1.000	1.89	+5	3
	Pit	CF	1	0	5	0	0	0	0	-	.00	0	0
	Pit	RF	37	23	212	35	3	0	0	1.000	1.62	-4	-1
Taveras, O	StL	CF	3	3	21	10	0	0	0	1.000	4.29	0	0
	StL	RF	62	58	479	97	3	1	1	.990	1.88	-8	-5
Taylor, C	Sea	SS	47	40	365	50	127	7	23	.962	4.36	+4	4
Taylor, M	CWS	LF	8	7	64	13	2	0	0	1.000	2.10	-5	-1
Taylor, M	Was	CF	10	4	47	15	0	0	0	1.000	2.87	-2	-1
	Was	RF	5	4	38	16	0	0	0	1.000	3.79	+1	1
Terdoslavich, J	Atl	1B	2	0	4	2	0	0	0	1.000	-	0	0
	Atl	RF	2	1	12	3	0	0	0	1.000	2.25	0	0
Tolleson, S	Tor	2B	55	25	252	56	75	5	14	.963	4.67	+2	1
	Tor	3B	43	11	144	11	28	0	1	1.000	2.44	+2	2
	Tor	SS	2	0	5	1	1	0	0	1.000	3.60	0	0
	Tor	LF	1	0	3	2	0	0	0	1.000	6.00	0	0
	Tor	RF	6	1	22	7	0	1	0	.875	2.86	0	0
Tovar, W	NYM	SS	1	0	4	0	1	0	0	1.000	2.45	0	0
Triunfel, C	LAD	SS	10	4	42	7	9	2	2	.889	3.40	0	-1
Trumbo, M	Ari	1B	43	43	377	363	18	3	42	.992	-	-1	-1
	Ari	LF	41	41	359	65	3	0	0	1.000	1.76	-16	-8
Tulowitzki, T	Col	SS	89	88	740	119	269	4	59	.990	4.72	+7	7
Turner, J	LAD	1B	2	2	19	13	2	0	2	1.000	-	+1	1
	LAD	2B	14	12	109	23	39	3	8	.954	5.13	-2	-1
	LAD	3B	59	45	406	93	99	5	10	.961	2.70	+7	6
	LAD	SS	15	8	86	11	36	4	4	.922	4.92	-1	0
Uggla, D	TOT	2B	39	37	333	67	109	11	21	.941	4.76	-2	-2
Utley, C	Phi	1B	1	0	2	2	0	0	0	1.000	-	0	0
Valaika, C	ChC	1B	15	13	119	99	12	2	13	.982	-	+2	1
	ChC	2B	12	8	77	17	27	0	4	1.000	5.14	0	0
	ChC	3B	8	6	59	8	16	0	2	1.000	3.66	+2	1
	ChC	SS	2	2	15	5	5	0	3	1.000	6.00	0	0
Valbuena, L	ChC	2B	21	17	150	24	41	0	4	1.000	3.89	0	-1
Valdespin, J	Mia	2B	17	16	145	28	45	3	8	.961	4.52	-1	-2
	Mia	CF	2	2	15	7	0	0	0	1.000	4.20	+1	1
	Mia	RF	10	3	35	8	0	0	0	1.000	2.04	+1	1
Valencia, D	TOT	1B	20	6	66	71	5	1	3	.987	-	+1	1
	TOT	2B	3	3	32	5	6	0	0	1.000	3.09	0	1
	TOT	3B	66	57	489	35	113	4	10	.974	2.72	-1	-2
Van Slyke, S	LAD	1B	21	6	96	70	7	2	8	.975	-	+3	1
	LAD	LF	32	26	221	44	0	2	0	.957	1.79	+8	4
	LAD	CF	21	17	143	30	0	0	0	1.000	2.07	0	-2
	LAD	RF	13	1	29	6	1	0	0	1.000	2.20	+1	1
Vargas, K	Min	1B	13	13	107	88	9	3	3	.970	-	-1	-1
Venable, W	SD	LF	6	0	6	4	0	0	0	1.000	6.00	+4	2
	SD	CF	76	56	506	144	2	0	0	1.000	2.63	0	-2
	SD	RF	75	46	443	104	1	0	0	1.000	2.13	+17	8
Viciedo, D	CWS	1B	4	2	22	25	0	0	1	1.000	-	0	0
	CWS	LF	55	45	381	78	2	4	0	.952	1.89	-11	-8
	CWS	RF	84	80	649	137	3	4	0	.972	1.94	-12	-9
Victorino, S	Bos	RF	30	30	264	56	1	0	0	1.000	1.95	+2	1
Villar, J	Hou	SS	82	78	679	104	229	18	45	.949	4.42	-1	-2
Vogt, S	Oak	1B	47	40	347	341	21	2	28	.995	-	+2	-1
	Oak	LF	1	0	0	0	0	0	0	-	.00	-1	0
	Oak	RF	17	13	110	21	0	0	0	1.000	1.71	-2	1
Votto, J	Cin	1B	61	61	539	499	63	7	39	.988	-	+6	5
Walker, C	Bal	1B	6	6	49	45	2	1	5	.979	-	+1	-1
Walters, Z	TOT	2B	5	4	31	7	10	0	3	1.000	4.94	0	0
	TOT	3B	3	1	16	0	2	0	0	1.000	1.13	0	0

All Other Fielders

Player	Tm	Pos	G	GS	Inn	PO	A	E	DP	Pct.	Rng	+/-	RS
	TOT	SS	3	0	7	1	3	0	0	1.000	5.14	+1	1
	TOT	LF	6	4	41	10	0	0	0	1.000	2.21	0	0
	TOT	RF	2	1	11	3	0	1	0	.750	2.45	-1	0
Watkins, L	ChC	2B	16	13	115	30	29	6	9	.908	4.62	-6	-5
	ChC	RF	2	2	14	4	0	0	0	1.000	2.51	0	0
Weeks, J	TOT	2B	7	6	50	7	15	0	1	1.000	3.93	-1	-1
	TOT	SS	3	2	26	3	8	0	2	1.000	3.81	+1	0
Weeks, R	Mil	2B	62	49	449	92	126	7	31	.969	4.37	-19	-17
Wheeler, R	Col	1B	5	3	23	21	2	0	3	1.000	-	0	0
	Col	3B	12	10	76	7	18	0	1	1.000	2.96	-4	-4
Wheeler, Z	NYY	3B	18	10	104	12	19	1	3	.969	2.69	+1	1
	NYY	LF	2	2	13	3	0	1	0	.750	2.08	0	0
	NYY	RF	6	5	36	4	2	0	0	1.000	1.50	-2	0
Wilkins, A	CWS	1B	13	8	80	75	4	0	7	1.000	-	-1	-1
Willingham, J	TOT	LF	53	52	439	103	3	0	2	1.000	2.17	-9	-3
	TOT	RF	1	1	8	3	0	0	0	1.000	3.38	+1	0
Wilson, J	Tex	2B	19	16	133	24	55	0	11	1.000	5.36	+3	3
	Tex	3B	4	3	30	0	11	1	4	.917	3.30	-2	0
	Tex	SS	3	0	13	4	3	0	3	1.000	4.85	+1	1
Worth, D	Det	1B	1	0	1	0	0	1	0	.000	-	-1	-1
	Det	2B	3	1	10	2	0	0	0	1.000	1.80	0	0
	Det	SS	13	11	101	27	31	0	14	1.000	5.19	0	3
Yelich, C	Mia	CF	12	9	77	16	0	1	0	.941	1.88	-3	-3
Ynoa, R	Col	2B	1	0	5	1	3	0	0	1.000	7.71	0	-1
	Col	3B	13	12	111	15	34	0	3	1.000	3.96	+1	0
	Col	SS	2	2	17	2	11	0	3	1.000	6.88	0	0
Young, C	TOT	LF	73	53	497	108	6	1	3	.991	2.06	+9	5
	TOT	CF	27	22	193	52	0	0	0	1.000	2.42	-4	-4
	TOT	RF	7	5	49	8	0	1	0	.889	1.46	-3	-2
Young, D	Bal	LF	27	17	149	29	3	0	0	1.000	1.93	-10	-6
	Bal	RF	2	1	10	3	1	0	1	1.000	3.60	+1	2
Young, E	NYM	2B	2	1	9	3	2	0	0	1.000	4.82	-1	-1
	NYM	LF	73	65	577	128	6	1	1	.993	2.09	+6	5
	NYM	CF	1	0	3	0	0	0	0	-	.00	0	0
Zimmerman, R	Was	1B	5	1	18	23	0	1	2	.958	-	-1	-1
	Was	3B	23	23	184	18	37	3	4	.948	2.69	0	-1
	Was	LF	30	30	266	48	2	0	0	1.000	1.69	-2	-2
Zobrist, B	TB	2B	79	74	625	105	185	6	32	.980	4.18	+7	1
	TB	SS	31	23	236	16	57	2	12	.973	2.78	+1	0
	TB	LF	38	17	175	51	1	0	0	1.000	2.68	+10	6
	TB	CF	7	7	45	12	0	0	0	1.000	2.40	-2	-1
	TB	RF	19	16	139	38	1	0	0	1.000	2.53	-1	0

All Other Catchers

Player	Tm	G	GS	Inn	PO	A	E	DP	PB	Pct.	SBA	CS	PCS	CS%	CERA	GFP/DME	SB	Other	Total
Arencibia,J.P.	Tex	22	21	182.1	160	7	2	1	3	.988	11	2	1	.18	5.38	-2	-1	0	-3
Baker,John	ChC	55	51	463.0	437	30	2	2	5	.996	57	7	2	.12	3.40	0	-3	2	-1
Barnhart,Tucker	Cin	20	14	132.0	110	14	0	2	3	1.000	12	8	0	.67	5.39	2	3	-1	4
Bethancourt,Christian	Atl	31	29	260.1	216	15	3	1	6	.987	13	3	2	.23	3.70	1	0	-2	-1
Buck,John	TOT	24	19	174.0	143	9	1	2	1	.993	14	3	0	.21	3.88	-2	0	0	-2
Butera,Drew	LAD	57	48	445.1	434	30	0	2	9	1.000	32	9	2	.28	3.38	2	2	-1	3
Butler,Daniel	Bos	7	5	49.0	41	2	1	0	2	.977	3	0	0	.00	5.33	0	0	0	0
Casali,Curt	TB	29	22	207.1	212	11	1	0	3	.996	15	2	2	.13	2.52	-1	0	1	0
Centeno,Juan	NYM	9	8	70.0	63	4	2	0	1	.971	6	1	0	.17	3.86	-1	0	0	-1
Cervelli,Francisco	NYY	42	39	348.0	335	20	1	0	2	.997	23	5	1	.22	3.88	1	-1	-1	-1
Clevenger,Steve	Bal	25	18	174.0	130	10	0	2	0	1.000	19	2	1	.11	4.81	0	-2	-1	-3
Corporan,Carlos	Hou	54	48	431.2	359	25	3	4	1	.992	31	6	1	.19	4.07	0	-1	0	-1
Cruz,Tony	StL	47	35	325.0	275	15	1	1	4	.997	23	5	1	.22	4.07	-1	-2	-1	-4
Doumit,Ryan	Atl	2	2	18.0	19	1	1	1	0	.952	7	0	0	.00	3.50	1	-1	0	0
Federowicz,Tim	LAD	22	19	190.0	150	19	3	1	1	.983	22	9	1	.41	3.74	-1	2	0	1
Fryer,Eric	Min	24	22	190.1	152	6	1	1	1	.994	17	1	0	.06	4.73	0	-1	0	-1
Gimenez,Chris	TOT	28	26	225.0	204	12	2	1	1	.991	12	1	1	.08	4.28	-3	-1	0	-4
Gosewisch,Tuffy	Ari	35	31	282.1	241	18	1	1	1	.996	18	7	1	.39	3.89	0	1	-1	0
Hayes,Brett	KC	27	14	143.0	94	5	0	2	1	1.000	8	1	1	.13	6.10	-1	-1	-1	-3
Herrmann,Chris	Min	1	0	1.0	1	0	0	0	0	1.000	0	0	0	-	0.00	0	0	0	0
Hill,Koyie	Phi	10	6	57.0	42	3	0	0	0	1.000	8	1	0	.13	6.47	0	0	0	0
Holaday,Bryan	Det	58	42	395.1	333	23	7	2	4	.981	46	13	1	.28	4.17	0	0	-2	-2
Hundley,Nick	TOT	63	54	508.0	436	30	2	6	4	.996	36	5	0	.14	3.49	1	-3	-2	-4
Jaso,John	Oak	54	47	391.0	338	10	1	0	1	.997	36	4	0	.11	3.31	-3	-3	1	-5
Kottaras,George	TOT	15	8	82.0	79	3	0	1	1	1.000	10	1	0	.10	3.62	-1	-1	0	-2
Kratz,Erik	TOT	36	23	225.0	188	10	0	2	1	1.000	24	6	0	.25	4.28	1	1	0	2
Laird,Gerald	Atl	48	42	377.2	339	28	2	4	7	.995	40	10	1	.25	3.34	0	1	0	1
Leon,Sandy	Was	20	17	157.0	154	9	1	1	1	.994	7	4	1	.57	3.27	0	2	0	2
Lobaton,Jose	Was	64	58	538.2	498	45	2	3	1	.996	38	11	2	.29	2.86	2	1	1	4
Lopez,Rafael	ChC	4	1	20.0	23	1	0	0	0	1.000	2	0	1	.00	4.95	0	0	0	0
Maldonado,Martin	Mil	42	29	274.1	250	22	6	2	2	.978	18	5	1	.28	3.77	1	1	1	3
Martinez,Victor	Det	2	2	17.0	23	2	2	0	1	.926	4	1	0	.25	4.76	0	0	0	0
Mathis,Jeff	Mia	62	52	473.2	389	39	1	4	3	.998	45	12	4	.27	3.99	2	1	2	5
McCann,James	Det	6	2	24.0	22	1	0	0	0	1.000	4	0	0	.00	3.38	0	-1	0	-1
McKenry,Michael	Col	50	45	406.0	312	24	6	1	5	.982	39	5	3	.13	4.19	4	-2	2	4
Moore,Adam	SD	1	1	9.0	8	0	0	0	0	1.000	0	0	0	-	3.00	0	0	0	0
Murphy,JR	NYY	30	21	201.0	169	10	1	1	3	.994	12	2	0	.17	3.40	0	-1	1	0
Nieto,Adrian	CWS	46	32	299.2	201	14	1	0	6	.995	28	3	1	.11	5.38	-2	-2	-1	-5
Nieves,Wil	Phi	34	34	293.0	246	26	1	4	3	.996	31	8	2	.26	3.50	2	1	2	5
Olivo,Miguel	LAD	8	6	55.2	47	4	1	1	0	.981	3	1	0	.33	4.85	-1	0	0	-1
Pacheco,Jordan	TOT	19	19	162.1	132	7	1	0	3	.993	11	1	0	.09	4.49	-1	-1	0	-2
Pagnozzi,Matt	Mil	1	0	1.0	2	0	0	0	0	1.000	0	0	0	-	27.00	0	0	0	0
Pena,Brayan	Cin	46	44	377.1	361	20	2	3	1	.995	26	10	2	.38	2.86	-3	0	2	-1
Pena,Francisco	KC	1	0	1.0	0	1	0	0	0	1.000	1	1	0	1.00	0.00	0	1	0	1
Perez,Roberto	Cle	29	25	232.1	217	24	3	2	1	.988	21	7	1	.33	2.60	3	2	1	6
Phegley,Josh	CWS	11	10	89.1	75	13	1	1	2	.989	8	2	0	.25	4.53	2	0	0	2
Pinto,Josmil	Min	25	25	226.0	173	8	5	0	4	.973	20	0	0	.00	4.74	-1	-3	0	-4
Quintero,Humberto	Sea	3	0	7.0	4	0	0	0	0	1.000	0	0	0	-	1.29	0	0	0	0
Quiroz,Guillermo	SF	2	0	6.2	6	1	0	0	0	1.000	0	0	0	-	12.15	0	0	0	0
Realmuto,J.T.	Mia	9	7	61.1	51	3	1	1	0	.982	5	1	0	.20	5.28	0	0	0	0
Recker,Anthony	NYM	52	43	412.2	378	28	5	2	3	.988	26	9	1	.35	3.10	-1	2	3	4
Romine,Austin	NYY	3	1	15.0	14	2	0	2	0	1.000	1	1	0	1.00	4.80	0	0	0	0
Ross,David	Bos	50	47	418.1	381	27	7	3	3	.983	40	8	1	.20	4.04	-1	-1	-3	-5
Rupp,Cameron	Phi	18	18	158.1	130	18	2	2	1	.987	17	6	1	.35	4.15	1	1	-1	1
Sanchez,Hector	SF	45	33	317.2	261	28	3	1	4	.990	40	9	5	.23	3.68	0	0	1	1
Sanchez,Tony	Pit	20	19	164.2	135	10	5	0	1	.967	20	2	1	.10	3.99	1	-1	0	0
Santana,Carlos	Cle	11	10	93.0	94	10	0	1	2	1.000	12	4	0	.33	4.16	0	1	0	1
Solis,Ali	TB	8	4	24.1	27	0	0	0	1	1.000	1	0	0	.00	8.51	0	0	0	0
Soto,Geovany	TOT	24	24	204.2	194	16	3	3	0	.986	21	8	2	.38	3.78	-1	1	0	0
Stassi,Max	Hou	6	4	36.0	22	5	1	0	2	.964	5	2	0	.40	4.50	1	0	0	1
Stewart,Chris	Pit	46	37	351.0	308	29	3	0	5	.991	37	7	2	.19	3.79	0	1	-1	0
Sucre,Jesus	Sea	21	18	160.0	151	10	1	0	2	.994	13	3	1	.23	2.59	2	1	0	3
Susac,Andrew	SF	29	20	195.1	160	20	0	1	2	1.000	23	6	2	.26	3.46	0	1	0	1
Teagarden,Taylor	NYM	9	8	72.0	54	6	0	0	0	1.000	5	0	0	.00	3.00	0	-1	0	-1
Telis,Tomas	Tex	17	17	149.0	105	6	1	0	0	.991	17	1	0	.06	3.62	-1	-1	0	-2
Thole,Josh	Tor	53	41	356.2	295	11	1	3	9	.997	23	1	3	.04	3.94	-2	-3	0	-5
Vazquez,Christian	Bos	54	50	458.1	338	32	5	4	8	.987	29	15	0	.52	3.71	-1	5	2	6
Vogt,Stephen	Oak	15	8	85.1	71	4	0	0	1	1.000	2	2	1	1.00	3.48	-1	1	0	0
Whiteside,Eli	ChC	8	7	64.0	49	3	0	1	1	1.000	5	0	0	.00	3.23	0	-1	0	-1
Wieters,Matt	Bal	22	22	194.2	169	5	1	0	0	.994	12	1	0	.08	3.88	-1	-1	0	-2
Williams,Jackson	Col	7	4	38.2	37	2	0	0	0	1.000	4	0	0	.00	6.05	0	0	0	0
Wilson,Bobby	Ari	2	1	10.0	10	1	0	0	0	1.000	0	0	0	-	5.40	0	0	0	0

Baserunning

After finishing his first two full seasons as the best baserunner in baseball, Mike Trout fell back a bit in 2014. His 29 Net Gain is hardly a bad total—in fact, it is tied with Jarrod Dyson for 19th-best in baseball—but it is a far cry from the 51 and 49 Net Gain he enjoyed in his first two full seasons. Compared to 2013, Trout was much less aggressive this season. He advanced from first to third on singles 54 percent of the time, down from 61 percent in 2013, and from second to home on singles 65 percent of the time, down from 75 percent. Trout also stole just 16 bases on 18 attempts after attempting 94 steals in his previous two seasons. If 2014 is any indication, Trout is moving a bit toward the power side of the spectrum. That is hardly damaging to his overall value, but it is a bit sad to potentially see the end of Trout as a transcendent five-tool player.

Trout is something of a harbinger of a shakeup among the best of the baserunners, which have traditionally been fairly consistent from year to year. For most of the new names with high Net Gains, the key was an increase in playing time. Ben Revere suffered a broken foot that ended his season in mid-July in 2013. With a full healthy season in 2014, Revere was exceptional. He was one of only four baserunners with 40 or more stolen bases this season, and he was caught stealing on only 8 of his 57 attempts (14 percent). Dee Gordon and Billy Hamilton, two of the other three players with 40-plus steals, were thrown out 23 percent and 29 percent of the time, respectively. Jose Altuve was similarly efficient to Revere with his stolen base attempts, stealing successfully in 56 of his 65 attempts, but his low 22 percent advancement rate from first to third on singles and five baserunning outs limited his overall baserunning value.

Having speed is not an automatic ticket to baserunning success. Look no further than Carlos Gomez, who beat the league average in his advancements from first to third, second to home, and first to home and stole 34 bases but who sabotaged himself with 12 baserunning outs and 3 times doubled off. That resulted in -11 Net Gain, well below average. Yasiel Puig was one worse with -12 Net Gain, really hurting himself with his over-aggressiveness on the basepaths. He was tied with Gomez with 12 baserunning outs, and he also was caught stealing on 7 of his 19 attempts this season. Over the last two seasons, Puig and Gerardo Parra are the only two baserunners who have attempted 35 or more steals and been thrown out at least 40 percent of the time.

As frustrating as it is to see quick runners like Gomez and Puig make so many mistakes, neither player does nearly the damage of some of the slowest runners in baseball. For example, both Billy Butler and Alex Avila finished the season with -31 Net Gain. Butler advanced from first to third on just 1 of 31 opportunities (3 percent) this season. League average in those situations is 29 percent. Avila was about as bad with 2 advancements from first to third in 23 opportunities (9 percent), and he never went first to home on a double in his six chances. Avila took the Tigers from a positive baserunning team to a negative one, and Butler took the Royals from the fourth-best baserunning team to the 10th-best one.

2014 Baserunning

Player	1st to 3rd Moved	1st to 3rd Chances	2nd to Home Moved	2nd to Home Chances	1st to Home Moved	1st to Home Chances	Bases Taken	Out Adv	Doubled Off	BR Outs	GDP	GDP Opps	BR Gain	SB Gain	Net Gain
Abreu,Bobby	0	3	2	3	3	6	1	1	0	1	3	23	-4	+1	-3
Abreu,Jose	5	34	9	16	1	4	12	1	1	2	14	125	-6	+1	-5
Ackley,Dustin	8	24	8	13	2	5	11	0	0	0	10	89	+8	0	+8
Adams,Matt	4	23	9	18	2	6	18	2	1	3	9	123	+4	-1	+3
Alcantara,Arismendy	4	12	5	7	2	2	12	0	0	0	3	47	+15	-2	+13
Almonte,Abraham	2	10	2	5	0	0	3	2	1	3	5	34	-11	-2	-13
Alonso,Yonder	3	14	4	9	4	6	9	2	1	3	8	44	-6	+4	-2
Altuve,Jose	6	27	18	30	3	3	25	4	1	5	20	120	-3	+38	+35
Alvarez,Pedro	3	17	5	11	2	6	10	1	0	1	12	95	-2	+2	0
Amarista,Alexi	7	22	5	11	4	5	16	4	0	4	6	78	+4	+10	+14
Andrus,Elvis	17	27	18	21	9	11	22	4	3	7	21	124	+7	-3	+4
Aoki,Nori	12	36	11	15	2	6	23	4	0	4	5	77	+13	+1	+14
Arcia,Oswaldo	8	19	5	7	2	3	8	3	1	4	6	78	0	-3	-3
Arenado,Nolan	7	24	7	11	1	5	7	1	0	1	13	93	-3	0	-3
Arias,Joaquin	2	10	8	13	1	1	4	1	0	1	1	28	+1	+1	+2
Asche,Cody	5	15	9	20	3	3	9	1	1	2	7	80	+1	-2	-1
Avila,Alex	2	23	4	18	0	6	8	4	2	6	6	77	-25	-6	-31
Aviles,Mike	5	17	8	11	5	5	1	1	2	3	10	85	-7	+4	-3
Aybar,Erick	14	33	14	19	5	9	24	4	3	7	10	120	+9	-2	+7
Baker,Jeff	2	14	5	8	1	3	4	0	0	0	8	40	-4	+1	-3
Baker,John	1	11	2	6	0	1	2	0	1	1	3	36	-6	0	-6
Barmes,Clint	0	4	6	8	1	2	7	1	0	1	2	16	+3	-1	+2
Barnes,Brandon	4	14	5	12	4	6	10	1	2	3	11	69	-5	-3	-8
Barney,Darwin	1	10	3	5	2	4	6	0	2	2	1	45	0	+1	+1
Bautista,Jose	15	34	8	20	6	14	25	4	1	5	18	151	+4	+2	+6
Beckham,Gordon	9	23	13	18	2	4	13	3	0	4	17	88	-5	+3	-2
Belt,Brandon	4	14	4	7	0	4	10	3	0	3	4	44	-2	+1	-1
Beltran,Carlos	4	24	5	15	4	7	7	4	0	4	11	95	-15	+1	-14
Beltre,Adrian	4	44	10	19	9	13	12	2	0	2	15	114	-9	-1	-10
Betts,Mookie	7	19	6	9	2	2	12	1	2	3	2	29	+6	+1	+7
Blackmon,Charlie	11	41	10	18	2	4	12	2	1	4	3	72	-1	+8	+7
Blanco,Gregor	5	28	13	19	2	4	14	7	0	7	4	87	-6	+6	0
Bogaerts,Xander	12	34	11	17	3	8	23	3	0	3	11	118	+14	-4	+10
Bonifacio,Emilio	7	14	9	13	3	9	9	1	3	4	2	46	0	+10	+10
Bourjos,Peter	8	14	3	3	1	1	11	1	0	1	5	57	+13	+3	+16
Bourn,Michael	6	24	8	18	6	9	14	1	1	2	5	63	+5	-2	+3
Bradley Jr.,Jackie	14	27	8	16	2	4	9	2	1	3	10	86	+2	+8	+10
Brantley,Michael	12	41	9	18	8	16	25	2	0	2	16	120	+10	+21	+31
Braun,Ryan	11	32	11	18	1	3	17	7	3	10	17	101	-21	+1	-20
Brown,Domonic	5	20	8	11	3	6	12	4	1	5	9	91	-5	+5	0
Bruce,Jay	4	23	9	21	6	8	13	3	0	3	8	115	+2	+6	+8
Butera,Drew	2	6	5	5	0	1	1	1	1	2	1	29	-2	0	-2
Butler,Billy	1	31	1	10	3	7	13	4	2	6	21	119	-31	0	-31
Byrd,Marlon	2	31	9	15	3	11	21	5	2	7	6	110	-7	-1	-8
Cabrera,Asdrubal	13	33	19	24	3	7	20	6	0	6	15	114	+3	+6	+9
Cabrera,Everth	4	9	6	9	1	3	11	0	0	0	5	39	+9	+2	+11
Cabrera,Melky	12	31	11	17	6	16	22	5	2	8	19	120	-10	+2	-8
Cabrera,Miguel	9	41	18	24	5	11	20	4	1	6	21	117	-11	-1	-12
Cain,Lorenzo	8	18	12	18	2	4	10	0	2	2	9	84	+4	+18	+22
Calhoun,Kole	9	17	9	17	8	14	28	4	0	4	5	81	+21	-1	+20
Callaspo,Alberto	6	29	9	12	1	3	8	2	5	7	18	101	-24	-2	-26
Campbell,Eric	2	8	2	4	2	3	6	0	1	1	5	38	0	+3	+3
Cano,Robinson	14	35	12	24	5	7	30	3	0	3	19	123	+13	+4	+17
Carpenter,Matt	9	46	14	30	4	9	13	5	2	7	3	80	-16	-1	-17
Carter,Chris	2	25	7	15	1	2	12	0	1	1	12	112	-1	+1	0
Castellanos,Nick	5	26	7	16	1	6	9	3	2	5	7	119	-11	-2	-13
Castillo,Welington	1	18	3	7	0	2	4	2	0	2	7	86	-9	0	-9
Castro,Jason	3	23	5	12	2	5	13	0	0	0	11	123	+6	+1	+7
Castro,Starlin	1	26	11	17	1	6	12	1	1	2	18	113	-11	-4	-15
Cervelli,Francisco	1	14	4	7	0	1	6	1	1	2	5	28	-7	+1	-6
Cespedes,Yoenis	7	30	9	15	8	9	16	1	1	2	13	128	+9	+3	+12
Chavez,Endy	3	21	2	8	0	1	8	2	0	2	2	36	-4	+1	-3
Chirinos,Robinson	5	21	5	13	1	4	9	1	1	2	4	44	-3	-2	-5
Chisenhall,Lonnie	17	38	3	9	2	8	17	2	1	3	8	101	+9	+1	+10
Choice,Michael	2	12	2	4	1	2	6	0	1	1	11	48	-6	+1	-5

345

2014 Baserunning

Player	1st to 3rd Moved	Chances	2nd to Home Moved	Chances	1st to Home Moved	Chances	Bases Taken	Out Adv	Doubled Off	BR Outs	GDP	GDP Opps	BR Gain	SB Gain	Net Gain
Choo,Shin-Soo	8	32	14	17	7	9	10	3	0	3	9	67	+1	-5	-4
Coghlan,Chris	9	20	6	10	5	6	11	1	1	2	5	60	+9	-1	+8
Colabello,Chris	1	6	4	4	1	3	5	1	0	1	2	41	+4	-4	0
Conger,Hank	4	13	2	4	1	2	9	2	0	2	6	47	0	-4	-4
Corporan,Carlos	1	10	2	3	0	3	2	0	0	0	3	36	-1	0	-1
Cowgill,Collin	5	13	7	10	4	6	11	2	2	4	4	56	+2	+4	+6
Cozart,Zack	4	16	9	14	1	3	15	2	1	3	13	110	+1	+7	+8
Craig,Allen	9	23	3	10	0	8	11	3	1	4	14	87	-13	0	-13
Crawford,Brandon	5	16	10	14	2	7	19	2	0	2	4	100	+17	-1	+16
Crawford,Carl	6	23	13	15	2	4	8	0	1	1	5	65	+8	+11	+19
Crisp,Coco	6	27	15	19	4	8	15	1	2	3	3	73	+9	+9	+18
Cron,C.J.	2	8	5	8	1	3	3	2	0	3	10	46	-13	0	-13
Cruz,Nelson	9	32	9	19	0	3	10	2	4	6	17	125	-20	-6	-26
Cruz,Tony	0	3	2	5	1	1	4	0	0	0	6	33	-1	-6	-7
Cuddyer,Michael	3	12	4	9	2	2	4	0	0	0	5	40	+1	+3	+4
Culberson,Charlie	6	10	1	7	1	1	2	1	1	2	6	44	-6	-2	-8
d'Arnaud,Travis	2	18	7	7	1	4	8	0	2	2	15	70	-9	+1	-8
Davis,Chris	4	26	6	16	3	7	9	4	2	6	2	95	-11	0	-11
Davis,Ike	4	17	9	14	2	7	8	1	1	2	8	84	-1	-8	-9
Davis,Khris	4	18	15	19	2	6	12	3	0	3	13	109	0	+2	+2
Davis,Rajai	13	23	11	17	6	6	19	1	1	2	7	99	+23	+14	+37
De Aza,Alejandro	6	24	12	22	5	11	11	3	1	5	7	93	-7	-3	-10
DeJesus,David	1	12	4	6	0	1	15	1	1	2	7	49	+3	-6	-3
den Dekker,Matt	6	9	4	6	2	2	8	0	0	0	1	35	+14	-1	+13
Denorfia,Chris	4	12	7	9	1	5	18	0	0	0	6	52	+16	+3	+19
Descalso,Daniel	4	9	4	6	1	1	6	0	0	0	2	24	+8	-5	+3
Desmond,Ian	13	31	5	14	0	2	26	0	1	1	17	134	+16	+14	+30
Dickerson,Corey	6	16	9	12	6	9	14	5	3	8	6	76	-6	-6	-12
Dietrich,Derek	4	10	5	7	2	3	7	0	0	0	1	38	+11	+1	+12
Dominguez,Matt	6	26	4	12	0	4	6	3	0	3	23	114	-23	-2	-25
Donaldson,Josh	10	36	15	23	3	11	25	7	1	8	16	153	-5	+8	+3
Dozier,Brian	24	44	22	27	9	15	25	2	3	5	8	127	+30	+7	+37
Drew,Stephen	0	15	1	3	0	3	3	2	1	3	1	55	-9	-1	-10
Duda,Lucas	4	30	7	16	3	12	13	1	1	2	9	101	-5	-1	-6
Dunn,Adam	2	26	5	18	0	2	14	1	2	3	5	96	-5	-1	-6
Dyson,Jarrod	9	21	8	10	1	1	12	2	1	3	5	55	+7	+22	+29
Eaton,Adam	12	31	13	18	3	11	22	4	1	5	4	67	+9	-3	+6
Ellis,A.J.	1	22	5	16	3	6	10	5	1	6	15	74	-27	0	-27
Ellis,Mark	2	3	5	7	1	2	5	0	0	0	0	37	+10	+2	+12
Ellsbury,Jacoby	8	22	12	22	3	3	14	4	1	5	9	127	+1	+29	+30
Encarnacion,Edwin	7	22	5	7	3	10	11	1	1	2	18	129	-3	+2	-1
Escobar,Alcides	9	26	25	34	2	3	15	4	2	6	12	100	-2	+19	+17
Escobar,Eduardo	6	27	9	19	1	2	15	3	1	4	6	94	0	-1	-1
Escobar,Yunel	8	29	9	14	0	3	19	3	2	5	15	104	-5	-1	-6
Espinosa,Danny	4	12	1	5	0	1	11	0	1	1	5	66	+6	+6	+12
Ethier,Andre	3	25	5	12	1	1	3	1	1	2	5	67	-9	-2	-11
Fielder,Prince	2	13	2	4	1	4	10	2	1	3	5	29	-5	0	-5
Flaherty,Ryan	4	15	5	9	2	2	8	2	0	2	3	59	+4	+1	+5
Flores,Wilmer	3	12	5	6	0	2	4	2	0	3	6	49	-7	+1	-6
Flowers,Tyler	5	24	2	6	1	8	9	1	1	3	10	71	-11	-2	-13
Forsythe,Logan	7	22	4	7	1	6	13	3	0	3	9	70	-1	+2	+1
Fowler,Dexter	16	24	10	17	4	9	14	3	1	4	6	82	+10	+3	+13
Francisco,Juan	2	12	3	5	1	3	7	0	2	2	6	71	-1	-4	-5
Frandsen,Kevin	8	19	3	4	2	3	9	3	0	3	7	44	0	0	0
Frazier,Todd	13	26	9	16	8	16	20	4	2	6	9	104	+6	+4	+10
Freeman,Freddie	11	38	13	22	5	14	21	5	0	5	18	150	-3	-5	-8
Freese,David	10	32	9	18	3	5	6	2	2	4	10	94	-10	-5	-15
Fuld,Sam	6	17	9	14	1	4	13	4	0	4	2	64	+4	+13	+17
Garcia,Avisail	4	7	0	3	0	1	5	1	1	2	5	40	-3	-2	-1
Garcia,Leury	2	5	1	2	2	4	6	0	0	0	6	29	+3	+9	+12
Gardner,Brett	7	30	13	20	3	6	25	3	2	5	3	86	+12	+11	+23
Gattis,Evan	3	22	5	10	1	4	4	1	2	3	9	71	-14	0	-14
Gennett,Scooter	3	11	13	18	4	11	11	1	1	2	11	79	+1	0	+1
Gentry,Craig	8	16	5	12	6	7	6	0	0	0	2	52	+12	+16	+28
Gillaspie,Conor	10	23	9	16	1	3	14	1	1	2	5	79	+10	-8	+2

346

2014 Baserunning

Player	1st to 3rd Moved	1st to 3rd Chances	2nd to Home Moved	2nd to Home Chances	1st to Home Moved	1st to Home Chances	Bases Taken	Out Adv	Doubled Off	BR Outs	GDP	GDP Opps	BR Gain	SB Gain	Net Gain
Goins,Ryan	2	11	3	5	0	1	5	0	1	1	4	36	-1	-2	-3
Goldschmidt,Paul	10	28	19	27	7	10	19	1	2	3	10	103	+14	+3	+17
Gomes,Jonny	4	17	9	9	2	2	5	0	0	0	6	70	+8	0	+8
Gomes,Yan	5	31	6	11	2	6	17	0	1	1	13	97	+3	0	+3
Gomez,Carlos	12	30	11	16	8	12	14	9	3	12	11	85	-21	+10	-11
Gonzalez,Adrian	7	31	12	18	1	14	10	3	2	5	13	124	-15	-1	-16
Gonzalez,Carlos	1	6	4	8	3	4	5	2	1	3	7	69	-5	+3	-2
Gonzalez,Marwin	7	18	5	8	2	4	12	1	0	1	6	55	+9	-6	+3
Gordon,Alex	14	38	16	23	7	10	16	1	1	2	11	117	+15	+6	+21
Gordon,Dee	10	25	24	28	1	2	19	2	3	6	3	92	+13	+26	+39
Gose,Anthony	9	22	3	5	2	5	9	0	0	0	9	59	+7	+5	+12
Gosselin,Phil	0	7	2	3	4	6	0	0	0	0	1	27	0	-2	-2
Grandal,Yasmani	5	20	2	7	0	5	6	2	1	3	7	79	-10	+3	-7
Granderson,Curtis	9	33	6	12	7	12	14	2	0	2	1	92	+13	+4	+17
Gregorius,Didi	12	19	7	11	1	2	8	0	0	0	1	48	+17	+3	+20
Grossman,Robbie	9	31	4	10	3	8	9	2	0	2	7	55	-4	+3	-1
Guyer,Brandon	5	12	8	9	5	5	14	1	0	1	3	75	+21	+4	+25
Guzman,Jesus	0	5	0	3	0	4	7	0	0	0	4	41	+1	+3	+4
Gyorko,Jedd	2	16	7	10	2	5	13	2	0	2	8	75	+3	-1	+2
Hamilton,Billy	11	24	13	15	1	1	19	2	0	2	1	60	+23	+10	+33
Hamilton,Josh	7	22	13	19	4	7	9	5	3	8	2	68	-9	-3	-12
Hanigan,Ryan	0	11	2	4	0	4	8	1	0	1	6	49	-3	+1	-2
Hardy,J.J.	3	30	8	19	4	10	9	2	0	2	12	102	-11	0	-11
Harper,Bryce	7	25	5	9	3	4	10	3	5	8	6	79	-14	-2	-16
Harrison,Josh	6	19	17	27	7	12	19	4	0	4	6	71	+8	+4	+12
Hart,Corey	3	10	2	2	0	4	5	2	0	3	1	44	-3	+2	-1
Headley,Chase	3	28	9	17	3	5	17	4	2	6	17	99	-17	+1	-16
Hechavarria,Adeiny	7	23	12	15	4	6	16	2	3	5	21	116	-7	-3	-10
Heisey,Chris	7	12	1	2	1	5	9	3	0	3	3	54	+3	+5	+8
Herrera,Elian	1	4	1	2	1	2	6	0	2	2	2	24	-1	+2	+1
Heyward,Jason	11	34	15	21	5	12	15	2	0	2	2	78	+14	+12	+26
Hicks,Aaron	8	17	3	5	0	3	9	0	0	0	2	44	+12	-2	+10
Hicks,Brandon	5	12	7	7	1	1	6	0	1	1	5	40	+6	-2	+4
Hill,Aaron	6	23	10	15	4	6	12	2	0	3	16	106	-3	-2	-5
Holaday,Bryan	3	9	3	8	1	4	6	1	0	1	4	31	-1	-1	-2
Holliday,Matt	13	35	12	19	10	17	18	7	0	7	20	157	-5	+2	-3
Holt,Brock	6	24	15	19	5	7	24	2	1	3	7	79	+18	+8	+26
Hosmer,Eric	5	33	10	19	3	5	9	7	1	8	12	107	-24	0	-24
Howard,Ryan	1	28	3	12	2	17	15	0	0	0	10	122	-3	0	-3
Hundley,Nick	1	4	0	0	1	2	1	1	0	1	3	37	-2	+1	-1
Hunter,Torii	15	32	5	12	5	8	16	0	2	2	18	107	+4	-2	+2
Iannetta,Chris	2	19	5	11	4	9	8	1	1	2	3	61	-2	+3	+1
Ibanez,Raul	3	12	3	5	0	4	5	2	0	2	2	48	-2	-1	-3
Inciarte,Ender	5	27	6	11	2	6	15	6	2	8	3	54	-13	+13	0
Infante,Omar	8	30	13	15	5	7	9	3	0	3	7	100	+5	+3	+8
Jackson,Austin	9	22	17	20	7	12	14	2	1	3	15	108	+6	+8	+14
Jaso,John	3	13	4	6	4	6	18	2	0	2	5	61	+12	+2	+14
Jay,Jon	12	38	14	19	4	4	15	5	4	9	17	100	-16	0	-16
Jennings,Desmond	10	20	13	17	5	9	22	0	1	1	10	83	+22	+3	+25
Jeter,Derek	10	33	10	15	0	5	20	2	1	3	15	100	+2	+6	+8
Johnson,Chris	8	33	9	17	3	4	7	2	1	3	23	115	-18	+6	-12
Johnson,Kelly	4	10	5	11	2	4	9	0	1	1	3	58	+7	-2	+5
Johnson,Reed	2	10	2	4	2	2	5	0	1	1	4	51	+2	-2	0
Jones,Adam	12	31	13	16	3	7	24	1	0	1	11	141	+27	+5	+32
Jones,Garrett	3	30	7	20	4	9	18	1	0	1	10	105	+2	-2	0
Jones,James	7	14	6	8	1	4	16	2	0	3	4	66	+11	+25	+36
Joseph,Caleb	4	10	1	6	1	3	1	2	0	2	6	41	-10	-2	-12
Joyce,Matt	7	35	17	22	3	4	9	1	1	2	11	115	+3	-8	-5
Kawasaki,Munenori	8	21	5	11	1	3	6	0	0	0	3	50	+6	+1	+7
Kelly,Don	0	7	4	8	1	3	7	1	0	1	6	41	-2	+4	+2
Kemp,Matt	13	33	9	20	3	8	16	6	2	8	21	112	-21	-2	-23
Kendrick,Howie	12	34	13	23	7	13	21	3	4	7	15	122	-5	+4	-1
Kiermaier,Kevin	13	20	5	8	1	2	14	3	2	5	3	77	+9	-3	+6
Kinsler,Ian	12	27	21	28	7	8	24	3	3	6	20	114	+6	+7	+13
Kipnis,Jason	7	22	17	23	4	6	16	1	2	3	15	106	+5	+16	+21

2014 Baserunning

Player	1st to 3rd Moved	Chances	2nd to Home Moved	Chances	1st to Home Moved	Chances	Bases Taken	Out Adv	Doubled Off	BR Outs	GDP	GDP Opps	BR Gain	SB Gain	Net Gain
Konerko,Paul	0	5	1	1	1	4	0	0	0	0	7	50	-5	0	-5
Krauss,Marc	1	3	2	5	1	3	4	2	0	2	7	40	-7	0	-7
Kubel,Jason	0	7	2	4	1	3	8	0	1	1	1	34	+4	+1	+5
La Stella,Tommy	3	22	1	7	1	4	10	3	1	4	8	51	-14	0	-14
Lagares,Juan	13	29	10	13	3	7	14	2	2	4	6	84	+8	+5	+13
Laird,Gerald	0	5	4	6	0	0	2	0	0	0	6	33	-3	0	-3
Lake,Junior	0	5	6	6	4	5	2	2	1	3	3	46	-4	+1	-3
LaRoche,Adam	5	30	6	16	2	13	17	3	1	5	13	118	-13	+3	-10
Lawrie,Brett	7	13	5	7	0	3	5	1	0	1	0	49	+8	0	+8
LeMahieu,DJ	4	21	15	21	3	8	9	2	4	6	13	88	-17	-10	-27
Lind,Adam	5	13	5	9	3	4	11	0	1	1	8	55	+5	0	+5
Lobaton,Jose	0	5	5	7	2	2	3	2	0	2	5	43	-4	0	-4
Loney,James	8	32	7	24	1	7	22	4	1	6	21	121	-19	+4	-15
Longoria,Evan	12	43	13	21	5	13	20	5	2	7	15	147	-6	+5	-1
Lough,David	3	8	7	8	3	4	2	0	2	2	3	36	-1	-2	-3
Lowrie,Jed	5	28	14	21	4	11	16	4	0	4	14	115	-4	0	-4
Lucas,Ed	3	15	4	7	0	1	6	0	0	0	4	38	+3	+1	+4
Lucroy,Jonathan	8	27	16	22	3	10	14	2	1	3	13	112	0	-4	-4
Ludwick,Ryan	4	19	1	11	0	2	6	1	1	2	6	64	-10	-4	-14
Machado,Manny	4	20	4	7	1	2	13	1	2	3	13	81	-4	+2	-2
Marisnick,Jake	2	8	3	3	1	3	7	3	0	3	2	38	-1	+5	+4
Markakis,Nick	4	52	9	24	2	12	18	1	0	1	10	101	-9	0	-9
Marte,Starling	16	33	16	20	3	7	17	6	2	8	5	105	+5	+8	+13
Martin,Leonys	8	23	11	16	6	7	31	1	0	1	4	84	+35	+7	+42
Martin,Russell	9	34	4	7	6	9	9	2	1	3	16	84	-10	-4	-14
Martinez,J.D.	11	28	7	16	0	4	11	6	1	7	8	113	-11	0	-11
Martinez,Victor	2	45	13	22	1	20	12	3	1	4	17	121	-28	-1	-29
Mathis,Jeff	0	4	3	5	1	2	3	0	1	1	2	33	-1	0	-1
Mauer,Joe	13	38	12	15	7	10	13	0	1	1	12	106	+13	+3	+16
Mayberry,John	2	9	0	5	0	0	7	0	0	0	2	31	+4	0	+4
Maybin,Cameron	5	13	5	5	1	4	5	1	1	2	8	50	-3	-2	-5
McCann,Brian	1	23	3	15	2	6	8	0	0	0	16	110	-11	0	-11
McCutchen,Andrew	12	39	13	22	3	8	11	4	1	5	9	121	-5	+12	+7
McGehee,Casey	12	43	11	21	1	13	20	5	1	6	31	131	-27	0	-27
McKenry,Michael	3	13	3	6	2	5	4	1	0	1	6	32	-5	-6	-11
McLouth,Nate	3	8	3	4	1	1	6	0	0	0	0	27	+10	+2	+12
Medica,Tommy	4	14	3	8	1	3	8	0	1	1	5	53	+2	+4	+6
Mercer,Jordy	2	18	7	17	3	5	12	0	0	0	14	84	+4	+3	+7
Mesoraco,Devin	3	26	5	10	2	7	8	0	1	2	5	73	-5	-5	-10
Middlebrooks,Will	1	8	3	4	1	4	3	1	1	2	7	45	-8	-1	-9
Miller,Brad	4	18	11	14	2	3	8	1	4	6	2	54	-7	0	-7
Molina,Jose	0	8	0	1	0	2	2	0	1	1	8	50	-9	+3	-6
Molina,Yadier	3	30	8	11	1	3	12	1	0	1	14	88	-3	-1	-4
Montero,Miguel	5	29	8	17	1	5	9	2	1	3	12	106	-11	-8	-19
Morales,Kendrys	2	15	1	6	0	7	8	3	1	4	12	77	-18	0	-18
Moreland,Mitch	1	17	5	8	0	2	1	0	1	1	7	36	-11	0	-11
Morneau,Justin	6	27	7	16	4	9	10	3	0	3	7	99	-4	-6	-10
Morrison,Logan	5	12	3	11	1	3	10	2	2	4	9	67	-9	+1	-8
Morse,Michael	4	16	9	18	1	9	12	1	0	1	19	103	-8	0	-8
Moss,Brandon	10	32	3	12	6	13	10	0	1	1	6	114	+6	+1	+7
Moustakas,Mike	4	29	9	13	2	3	7	1	2	3	12	102	-8	+1	-7
Murphy,Daniel	13	34	13	17	6	11	20	2	0	2	15	127	+15	+3	+18
Murphy,David	7	17	6	12	2	5	13	2	1	3	6	91	+5	-4	+1
Myers,Wil	6	16	10	17	3	3	10	2	1	3	10	68	-1	+4	+3
Napoli,Mike	15	39	5	10	1	8	12	3	1	4	12	84	-7	-1	-8
Nava,Daniel	12	27	8	9	2	3	13	1	1	2	5	83	+15	0	+15
Navarro,Dioner	2	28	4	11	0	4	13	3	0	3	12	101	-11	+3	-8
Navarro,Efren	4	13	5	6	1	1	4	0	1	1	0	33	+6	-5	+1
Negron,Kristopher	2	4	4	5	1	1	7	0	0	0	2	24	+9	+5	+14
Norris,Derek	6	23	3	8	6	8	14	1	1	2	12	77	+1	-2	-1
Nunez,Eduardo	2	10	5	8	1	2	9	1	0	1	7	51	+2	+3	+5
Odor,Rougned	6	16	7	8	1	3	7	1	1	2	7	59	+1	-10	-9
Olt,Mike	2	8	2	5	0	2	5	0	0	0	3	43	+3	-2	+1
Ortiz,David	0	19	5	10	1	10	11	3	0	3	18	147	-14	0	-14
Overbay,Lyle	5	16	2	4	2	4	1	0	0	0	8	49	-4	+2	-2

348

2014 Baserunning

Player	1st to 3rd Moved	1st to 3rd Chances	2nd to Home Moved	2nd to Home Chances	1st to Home Moved	1st to Home Chances	Bases Taken	Out Adv	Doubled Off	BR Outs	GDP	GDP Opps	BR Gain	SB Gain	Net Gain
Owings,Chris	4	13	3	5	0	1	7	2	0	2	4	60	+1	+6	+7
Ozuna,Marcell	12	35	7	14	5	9	24	2	1	4	12	111	+9	+1	+10
Pacheco,Jordan	0	5	1	1	0	1	9	0	3	3	6	28	-6	0	-6
Pagan,Angel	8	26	13	18	2	5	14	1	1	2	5	47	+9	+4	+11
Panik,Joe	10	29	7	8	4	6	7	1	0	1	4	54	+9	0	+9
Parmelee,Chris	3	13	2	6	1	7	10	3	1	4	7	46	-10	-6	-16
Parra,Gerardo	6	26	15	20	7	11	15	4	0	4	10	98	+3	-5	-2
Pearce,Steve	9	23	13	17	1	4	7	1	1	2	4	62	+5	+5	+10
Pedroia,Dustin	13	37	15	20	4	11	19	5	1	6	14	125	0	-6	-6
Pena,Brayan	2	17	3	9	2	4	7	7	0	7	8	62	-23	-4	-27
Pena,Ramiro	2	7	2	2	0	0	2	0	0	0	0	37	+6	+1	+7
Pence,Hunter	20	47	7	12	11	14	28	1	1	2	13	133	+29	+1	+30
Pennington,Cliff	4	8	3	4	1	3	6	0	0	0	1	36	+9	+4	+13
Peralta,David	6	16	7	10	3	4	13	0	0	0	9	74	+13	0	+13
Peralta,Jhonny	8	33	10	20	3	6	14	3	4	7	19	139	-1	-20
Perez,Salvador	7	28	6	15	2	6	15	2	0	2	22	132	-7	+1	-6
Phillips,Brandon	10	22	5	8	1	3	10	4	3	7	13	86	-15	-4	-19
Pierzynski,A.J.	6	15	3	8	2	6	5	3	1	4	13	79	-15	-2	-17
Pinto,Josmil	1	9	5	6	3	5	5	1	0	1	7	36	-2	-2	-4
Plouffe,Trevor	13	27	11	19	0	3	21	5	1	6	12	122	+3	0	+3
Polanco,Gregory	6	18	8	13	5	5	10	1	2	3	1	47	+7	+4	+11
Pollock,A.J.	4	13	4	8	0	3	9	0	0	0	4	54	+6	+8	+14
Posey,Buster	7	29	10	16	3	8	18	2	0	2	16	122	+3	-2	+1
Prado,Martin	14	28	7	10	2	9	14	2	2	4	20	97	-7	+1	-6
Presley,Alex	2	12	3	6	0	1	5	1	0	1	3	44	0	+3	+3
Puig,Yasiel	13	36	11	18	7	10	22	9	2	12	7	113	-9	-3	-12
Pujols,Albert	10	35	12	21	1	8	13	6	2	8	28	146	-31	+3	-28
Punto,Nick	4	8	1	4	2	2	5	1	0	1	5	54	+3	+1	+4
Raburn,Ryan	2	8	4	4	0	2	4	1	0	1	8	47	-3	0	-3
Ramirez,Alexei	11	36	20	26	6	9	15	3	2	5	21	138	-4	+13	+9
Ramirez,Aramis	4	21	5	9	0	7	10	2	1	3	18	91	-16	+3	-13
Ramirez,Hanley	9	29	14	17	3	7	12	3	1	5	10	85	-4	+4	0
Ramirez,Jose	3	11	7	10	0	3	11	0	1	1	3	47	+8	+8	+16
Ramos,Wilson	2	11	2	5	3	6	5	2	0	2	17	76	-14	0	-14
Rasmus,Colby	2	8	1	7	2	4	11	0	0	0	1	78	+13	+4	+17
Reddick,Josh	8	25	8	9	2	4	15	0	3	3	3	77	+12	-1	+11
Rendon,Anthony	14	38	23	30	7	9	26	2	1	3	11	117	+25	+11	+36
Revere,Ben	8	22	16	24	3	7	31	0	2	2	11	82	+21	+33	+54
Reyes,Jose	15	36	15	26	7	11	21	8	3	11	4	91	-5	+26	+21
Reynolds,Mark	3	18	4	9	4	7	7	1	1	2	8	77	-4	+3	-1
Rios,Alex	8	21	10	18	2	9	21	0	0	0	19	120	+10	-1	+9
Rivera,Rene	1	8	4	8	0	1	7	1	0	1	6	48	-2	0	-2
Rizzo,Anthony	9	40	12	19	2	9	18	3	2	5	8	102	-3	-2	-5
Roberts,Brian	8	19	6	13	2	5	11	1	1	2	9	70	+2	-1	+1
Robertson,Daniel	1	4	4	5	3	5	13	1	0	1	3	41	+11	-2	+9
Rodriguez,Sean	5	12	4	6	1	1	8	2	0	2	3	47	+5	0	+5
Rojas,Miguel	4	9	5	7	1	1	4	0	1	1	5	28	+1	0	+1
Rollins,Jimmy	9	30	11	15	2	10	22	1	1	2	6	104	+17	+16	+33
Romero,Stefen	5	8	2	5	3	5	3	1	0	1	5	34	0	-8	-8
Romine,Andrew	7	17	7	9	3	5	4	2	0	2	5	50	+1	+8	+9
Rosales,Adam	1	9	4	6	2	3	1	0	1	1	5	41	-4	0	-4
Rosario,Wilin	5	18	4	10	3	7	15	2	0	3	17	81	-7	+1	-6
Ross,Cody	4	14	4	6	0	0	5	1	0	1	3	37	+2	0	+2
Ruggiano,Justin	1	10	5	8	2	6	8	3	1	4	2	44	-5	-6	-11
Ruiz,Carlos	6	20	6	12	2	11	12	1	1	2	11	78	-4	0	-4
Rutledge,Josh	11	22	3	7	0	2	13	1	0	1	6	57	+10	-4	+6
Saltalamacchia,Jarrod	2	21	6	16	2	4	9	3	0	3	11	85	-12	-2	-14
Sanchez,Gaby	2	16	3	8	1	2	5	1	1	2	6	56	-7	+2	-5
Sandoval,Pablo	3	43	9	19	3	11	19	2	0	2	16	125	-8	0	-8
Santana,Carlos	11	35	16	20	0	7	10	4	1	5	13	119	-8	+1	-7
Santana,Danny	6	21	12	14	1	6	20	0	0	0	3	50	+21	+12	+33
Santiago,Ramon	3	8	4	9	1	1	6	2	0	2	1	46	+2	0	+2
Sardinas,Luis	1	7	2	3	4	5	4	2	0	2	5	26	-4	+3	-1
Saunders,Michael	9	17	6	9	2	3	6	0	0	0	2	42	+12	-6	+6
Schafer,Jordan	4	10	4	6	1	2	10	2	0	2	1	41	+7	+16	+23

2014 Baserunning

Player	1st to 3rd Moved	Chances	2nd to Home Moved	Chances	1st to Home Moved	Chances	Bases Taken	Out Adv	Doubled Off	BR Outs	GDP	GDP Opps	BR Gain	SB Gain	Net Gain
Schierholtz,Nate	3	13	6	10	4	6	6	2	0	2	6	83	+1	-6	-5
Schoop,Jonathan	6	15	4	9	2	3	11	0	0	0	12	82	+6	+2	+8
Schumaker,Skip	2	13	4	7	1	4	9	0	0	0	3	34	+5	0	+5
Seager,Kyle	10	28	7	13	2	5	14	9	0	9	12	104	-17	-3	-20
Segura,Jean	8	14	11	14	3	4	16	1	3	4	13	87	+4	+2	+6
Semien,Marcus	1	6	6	7	6	7	6	2	0	2	6	44	+1	+3	+4
Sierra,Moises	3	9	3	3	0	3	2	0	1	1	1	24	-1	+1	0
Simmons,Andrelton	10	30	14	20	3	5	6	2	0	2	25	117	-12	-6	-18
Singleton,Jon	4	20	6	13	0	0	9	1	0	1	4	71	+4	-4	0
Sizemore,Grady	2	14	5	9	1	4	12	2	0	2	10	89	0	+4	+4
Smith,Seth	8	31	9	17	9	10	9	3	1	5	9	85	-7	-1	-8
Smoak,Justin	2	9	3	5	2	2	8	0	0	0	8	49	+4	-2	+2
Snider,Travis	2	14	4	6	4	7	11	2	1	3	10	61	-5	-1	-6
Sogard,Eric	3	17	8	9	2	5	14	1	0	1	6	69	+10	+3	+13
Solano,Donovan	8	21	6	12	3	6	4	2	0	2	5	74	0	-3	-3
Solarte,Yangervis	14	34	8	14	1	4	15	2	0	2	13	83	+4	-2	+2
Soriano,Alfonso	0	3	6	7	2	3	6	0	0	0	3	42	+8	+1	+9
Span,Denard	11	28	13	21	8	13	23	3	1	4	6	72	+13	+17	+30
Springer,George	7	16	5	10	1	1	9	2	0	2	4	85	+8	+1	+9
Stanton,Giancarlo	8	33	15	19	4	7	28	5	2	7	16	154	+6	+11	+17
Stewart,Chris	1	8	2	3	0	0	8	1	0	1	2	27	+4	-2	+2
Stubbs,Drew	8	20	6	13	3	6	10	1	0	1	4	77	+9	+14	+23
Suarez,Eugenio	2	19	6	10	1	5	9	1	1	2	3	66	0	-1	-1
Suzuki,Ichiro	5	28	7	10	3	4	12	2	2	4	3	64	0	+9	+9
Suzuki,Kurt	5	23	4	12	5	10	11	4	1	5	9	96	-11	-2	-13
Sweeney,Ryan	1	9	5	7	3	4	5	0	1	1	4	40	+1	0	+1
Swisher,Nick	1	14	3	7	2	7	7	2	0	2	7	74	-6	0	-6
Tabata,Jose	7	11	3	5	1	2	2	2	0	2	12	49	-8	-3	-11
Taveras,Oscar	5	17	2	5	2	4	5	2	1	3	10	56	-10	-2	-12
Taylor,Chris	1	8	4	5	3	3	3	0	0	0	3	28	+3	+1	+4
Teixeira,Mark	4	29	3	7	1	10	10	3	0	3	13	98	-14	-1	-15
Tejada,Ruben	2	11	3	8	1	5	13	3	0	3	8	72	-4	-3	-7
Tolleson,Steve	0	9	3	6	2	2	5	2	0	2	3	30	-4	+1	-3
Trout,Mike	21	39	17	26	5	8	19	4	1	6	6	141	+17	+12	+29
Trumbo,Mark	2	17	5	12	0	4	11	1	1	2	8	60	-6	-4	-10
Tulowitzki,Troy	7	34	7	17	2	11	19	2	1	3	4	70	+2	-1	+1
Turner,Justin	3	24	12	18	1	4	12	3	1	5	6	74	-7	+4	-3
Upton,B.J.	14	29	8	13	2	5	13	1	0	1	6	85	+15	+6	+21
Upton,Justin	11	36	14	21	1	3	9	1	1	2	10	119	+3	0	+3
Uribe,Juan	6	14	4	12	0	1	7	1	0	1	15	83	-7	-2	-9
Utley,Chase	17	39	18	25	1	4	14	2	5	7	8	156	+5	+8	+13
Valbuena,Luis	4	24	9	18	1	4	22	3	0	3	8	104	+7	-3	+4
Valencia,Danny	0	8	2	8	1	3	9	2	1	3	8	59	-9	-1	-10
Van Slyke,Scott	3	11	4	8	1	1	5	2	0	2	3	44	-2	0	-2
Vargas,Kennys	2	12	2	4	1	2	4	0	1	1	5	58	-1	0	-1
Vazquez,Christian	2	10	4	8	2	3	7	1	0	1	4	34	+1	0	+1
Venable,Will	6	21	9	13	1	3	17	2	2	4	6	68	+4	-1	+3
Viciedo,Dayan	6	29	11	14	2	8	17	2	2	4	19	110	-7	-2	-9
Villar,Jonathan	5	13	4	6	0	0	6	0	1	1	4	46	+4	+9	+13
Vogt,Stephen	10	17	2	2	0	1	7	1	0	1	2	53	+11	+1	+12
Votto,Joey	5	17	2	7	1	4	8	4	1	5	5	43	-12	-1	-13
Walker,Neil	11	35	13	17	3	6	14	1	1	2	12	102	+7	-2	+5
Weeks,Rickie	6	11	7	13	4	5	10	3	1	4	7	45	-3	-5	-8
Werth,Jayson	20	43	16	21	3	6	25	3	0	3	9	144	+29	+7	+36
Willingham,Josh	7	19	8	12	4	8	8	1	0	1	6	65	+6	+2	+8
Wong,Kolten	5	14	10	14	4	6	9	0	0	0	12	102	+9	+12	+21
Wright,David	6	25	9	18	1	4	14	4	1	5	22	126	-17	-2	-19
Yelich,Christian	16	40	21	32	4	6	18	1	1	2	9	71	+13	+7	+20
Young,Chris	6	17	8	12	4	4	4	1	2	3	3	73	+5	+2	+7
Young,Delmon	2	16	3	6	2	3	10	0	0	0	6	45	+4	+2	+6
Young,Eric	5	9	9	11	1	2	12	2	1	3	2	33	+7	+18	+25
Zimmerman,Ryan	2	12	5	8	0	1	9	1	0	1	6	47	+2	0	+2
Zobrist,Ben	17	37	17	22	4	10	25	3	1	4	8	110	+21	0	+21
Zunino,Mike	5	18	7	9	1	4	8	1	0	1	13	99	+1	-6	-5

Career Baserunning
Players with 1000 Career Games
(Data goes back to 2002)

Player	1st to 3rd Moved	Chances	2nd to Home Moved	Chances	1st to Home Moved	Chances	Bases Taken	Out Adv	Doubled Off	BR Outs	GDP	GDP Opps	BR Gain	SB Gain	Net Gain
Abreu,Bobby	101	352	160	258	54	113	194	31	9	41	120	1502	+78	+113	+191
Aybar,Erick	89	185	106	139	27	48	134	28	18	47	75	771	+42	+32	+74
Barmes,Clint	54	154	69	100	27	42	98	8	9	17	54	643	+72	-15	+57
Bautista,Jose	86	247	85	137	43	81	121	24	18	42	112	961	-14	+6	-8
Beltran,Carlos	137	399	149	238	60	111	209	20	14	35	125	1464	+133	+157	+290
Beltre,Adrian	115	391	131	224	50	112	194	37	3	40	201	1608	+1	+23	+24
Bloomquist,Willie	66	185	68	106	28	49	93	15	7	22	47	538	+43	+32	+75
Bourn,Michael	71	226	108	167	46	61	152	14	10	24	26	540	+121	+145	+266
Braun,Ryan	69	228	94	136	42	64	134	22	10	32	96	977	+51	+59	+110
Buck,John	32	155	64	119	13	33	71	12	7	20	86	695	-37	-18	-55
Butler,Billy	30	251	50	135	17	88	117	27	6	33	168	921	-174	-1	-175
Byrd,Marlon	66	282	115	179	46	93	159	25	8	34	104	1017	+26	-6	+20
Cabrera,Melky	83	253	86	139	39	81	152	27	9	38	104	906	+21	+24	+45
Cabrera,Miguel	115	503	158	278	47	128	209	34	12	48	234	1575	-92	-1	-93
Cano,Robinson	94	315	148	233	38	77	178	33	19	52	190	1371	-38	-14	-52
Chavez,Endy	37	144	71	111	21	41	83	14	4	18	58	553	+10	+26	+36
Chavez,Eric	69	221	77	119	34	68	87	13	7	21	108	1017	+15	+16	+31
Crawford,Carl	74	290	170	237	58	108	249	34	20	57	73	1247	+129	+258	+387
Crisp,Coco	90	274	144	206	55	93	186	18	11	30	82	926	+124	+149	+273
Cuddyer,Michael	128	311	109	179	48	84	155	43	12	57	169	1137	-43	+28	-15
DeJesus,David	133	345	112	179	42	77	186	26	14	40	98	848	+79	-57	+22
Drew,Stephen	52	199	70	128	21	62	110	30	9	40	38	715	-8	+9	+1
Dunn,Adam	68	395	109	222	38	115	174	21	8	30	96	1548	+32	+13	+45
Ellis,Mark	94	301	127	217	51	93	169	18	6	25	89	1061	+102	+24	+126
Encarnacion,Edwin	68	226	72	115	30	77	105	20	8	28	110	950	-9	+29	+20
Escobar,Yunel	88	282	98	137	30	65	105	25	16	41	138	794	-71	-15	-86
Ethier,Andre	58	308	116	169	33	67	101	17	9	27	92	1021	+1	-23	-22
Fielder,Prince	43	351	59	147	30	99	145	27	10	37	126	1090	-105	-4	-109
Figgins,Chone	150	287	129	191	47	74	203	33	27	60	74	902	+115	+103	+218
Francoeur,Jeff	78	223	86	139	30	79	119	27	14	43	112	986	-26	-18	-44
Furcal,Rafael	138	362	156	241	37	74	204	21	15	36	77	760	+112	+104	+216
Giambi,Jason	54	264	59	105	15	77	85	25	6	32	83	1065	-51	-1	-52
Gomes,Jonny	51	165	75	115	21	41	99	14	11	26	46	747	+53	+3	+56
Gonzalez,Adrian	55	326	82	196	41	123	140	32	14	47	158	1296	-139	0	-139
Gonzalez,Alex	48	152	73	123	23	44	82	25	4	29	103	897	-27	-10	-37
Gordon,Alex	62	231	112	161	33	63	131	12	7	19	72	773	+78	+19	+97
Granderson,Curtis	83	277	104	180	54	90	151	12	15	27	40	970	+123	+58	+181
Hardy,J.J.	66	239	72	130	24	72	109	16	9	26	124	946	-29	-8	-37
Hart,Corey	45	146	78	114	25	47	104	18	4	23	85	729	+27	+5	+32
Hill,Aaron	73	262	92	146	32	64	136	17	7	25	117	1056	+38	+1	+39
Holliday,Matt	137	399	172	252	61	108	186	38	14	52	188	1442	+18	+33	+51
Howard,Ryan	33	272	71	160	31	113	114	26	9	35	98	1138	-79	+4	-75
Hunter,Torii	163	354	146	229	51	98	219	52	19	72	213	1490	-17	+14	-3
Ibanez,Raul	94	369	127	235	55	98	165	29	12	42	151	1428	-13	-9	-22
Infante,Omar	82	237	97	158	31	61	108	21	16	38	81	921	+4	+16	+20
Jeter,Derek	154	499	161	255	56	133	251	30	12	43	208	1417	+29	+109	+138
Johnson,Kelly	56	210	65	127	33	59	130	12	8	20	56	771	+68	+11	+79
Johnson,Reed	59	221	85	131	38	70	123	20	6	27	77	643	+17	-17	0
Jones,Adam	67	207	77	110	46	69	120	13	8	22	102	877	+56	+19	+75
Kemp,Matt	90	232	106	153	35	57	117	31	22	54	104	943	-24	+52	+28
Kendrick,Howie	91	223	91	149	38	67	127	25	16	43	127	830	-28	+23	-5
Kinsler,Ian	115	256	144	203	42	76	192	17	17	34	114	900	+117	+95	+212
Konerko,Paul	61	416	81	193	16	106	131	26	10	36	213	1390	-204	0	-204
Kubel,Jason	32	180	58	112	19	64	77	20	8	28	89	759	-68	-2	-70
LaRoche,Adam	52	280	74	151	22	79	128	24	10	35	118	1148	-55	-9	-64
Loney,James	65	235	72	129	26	60	129	20	9	31	135	901	-35	+2	-33
Ludwick,Ryan	59	198	52	106	20	40	89	18	6	24	65	796	+11	-23	-12
Markakis,Nick	85	371	124	197	38	97	148	21	4	26	131	1088	+3	+11	+14
Martin,Russell	67	258	95	151	35	61	116	23	13	36	135	885	-51	+13	-38
Martinez,Victor	55	365	96	193	23	117	156	30	7	37	193	1303	-140	-7	-147

351

Career Baserunning
Players with 1000 Career Games
(Data goes back to 2002)

Player	1st to 3rd Moved	1st to 3rd Chances	2nd to Home Moved	2nd to Home Chances	1st to Home Moved	1st to Home Chances	Bases Taken	Out Adv	Doubled Off	BR Outs	GDP	GDP Opps	BR Gain	SB Gain	Net Gain
Mauer,Joe	110	340	128	186	47	105	181	12	9	23	149	1138	+83	+14	+97
McCann,Brian	39	231	34	117	13	79	73	25	8	34	132	1053	-155	+7	-148
McDonald,John	34	116	49	77	9	26	61	18	3	21	46	459	-12	-2	-14
McLouth,Nate	54	163	89	130	21	46	109	6	7	13	41	590	+95	+85	+180
Molina,Yadier	51	267	58	139	18	55	102	24	7	32	173	985	-143	-13	-156
Morneau,Justin	51	272	87	164	25	87	140	35	5	40	132	1257	-56	-15	-71
Olivo,Miguel	46	144	53	90	16	28	94	24	7	32	77	792	-5	-15	-20
Ortiz,David	56	380	89	220	26	126	167	43	14	58	168	1733	-157	-4	-161
Overbay,Lyle	63	298	70	145	32	88	118	19	9	29	149	1070	-82	+5	-77
Pedroia,Dustin	73	259	109	165	41	111	148	31	12	45	111	966	-25	+51	+26
Pena,Carlos	104	309	68	132	31	88	161	29	9	38	70	1110	+61	-15	+46
Pence,Hunter	87	277	91	138	55	73	156	16	10	26	120	987	+74	+6	+80
Peralta,Jhonny	60	308	101	196	30	89	150	34	14	48	170	1283	-113	-30	-143
Phillips,Brandon	113	271	110	163	40	64	193	40	15	57	172	1153	+1	+31	+32
Pierzynski,A.J.	62	310	84	188	20	71	146	46	6	54	201	1345	-174	-16	-190
Pujols,Albert	160	466	185	257	54	134	228	61	16	79	276	1958	-77	+27	-50
Punto,Nick	77	228	80	131	27	48	126	12	10	22	63	724	+75	+32	+107
Ramirez,Alexei	68	204	97	140	38	56	126	15	12	27	113	879	+39	+24	+63
Ramirez,Aramis	69	337	88	200	28	114	142	38	11	49	189	1432	-162	-3	-165
Ramirez,Hanley	85	250	130	195	40	70	153	40	12	53	83	894	+12	+95	+107
Reyes,Jose	115	317	161	238	44	68	237	51	19	70	65	860	+76	+233	+309
Reynolds,Mark	45	176	56	99	19	63	101	14	7	21	78	807	+9	+7	+16
Rios,Alex	81	264	144	214	38	79	181	18	14	32	183	1342	+38	+90	+128
Roberts,Brian	98	314	133	218	36	86	178	25	20	45	79	911	+36	+133	+169
Rodriguez,Alex	114	352	147	223	47	117	182	33	15	48	160	1521	+21	+97	+118
Rollins,Jimmy	149	436	199	289	49	103	283	33	10	43	117	1188	+170	+230	+400
Ross,Cody	52	172	65	104	10	41	96	17	5	23	77	747	+11	+7	+18
Schumaker,Skip	50	215	67	116	18	41	116	15	5	21	66	516	+11	-6	+5
Scutaro,Marco	97	315	106	173	46	110	162	23	12	35	117	1289	+22	+11	+33
Sizemore,Grady	67	225	107	148	29	48	149	11	14	25	46	722	+116	+52	+168
Soriano,Alfonso	108	281	145	220	30	70	187	26	16	42	116	1282	+82	+106	+188
Suzuki,Ichiro	152	575	205	327	64	130	301	31	17	49	75	1313	+164	+241	+405
Swisher,Nick	102	323	83	154	40	94	146	25	16	41	122	1235	+5	-17	-12
Teixeira,Mark	77	354	118	195	42	115	167	39	8	47	144	1574	-19	+8	-11
Uggla,Dan	92	280	93	138	56	98	132	30	10	40	72	949	+52	-14	+38
Upton,B.J.	94	224	96	147	26	53	159	23	10	34	91	917	+81	+102	+183
Upton,Justin	78	218	92	132	44	73	99	14	12	26	73	851	+55	+18	+73
Uribe,Juan	81	234	87	143	18	49	128	13	12	27	130	1100	+17	-35	-18
Utley,Chase	146	313	141	191	52	86	173	22	16	38	80	1289	+181	+103	+284
Victorino,Shane	96	255	103	150	41	75	159	9	16	28	57	822	+124	+132	+256
Weeks,Rickie	82	235	115	160	37	68	145	32	23	55	66	698	+4	+62	+66
Werth,Jayson	91	284	97	146	31	65	132	19	4	24	70	947	+85	+87	+172
Willingham,Josh	84	267	70	127	31	78	84	17	11	28	87	967	-7	+17	+10
Wright,David	105	332	119	182	51	113	175	32	15	50	148	1362	+10	+67	+77
Young,Chris	43	163	77	110	37	54	98	18	10	28	45	786	+54	+48	+102
Young,Delmon	48	204	82	133	24	55	121	24	9	35	128	844	-51	-6	-57
Zimmerman,Ryan	75	247	102	156	42	86	139	18	6	24	148	1110	+29	+8	+37
Zobrist,Ben	81	222	75	131	35	72	152	14	9	23	72	830	+91	+32	+123

2002-2014 MLB Averages

1st to 3rd	2nd to Home	1st to Home
28%	59%	44%

352

2014 Team Baserunning

Team	1st to 3rd Moved	Chances	2nd to Home Moved	Chances	1st to Home Moved	Chances	Bases Taken	Out Adv	Doubled Off	BR Outs	GDP	GDP Opps	BR Gain	SB Gain	Net Gain
Washington Nationals	104	302	100	174	31	66	187	25	11	37	115	1169	+58	+55	+113
Minnesota Twins	105	316	117	181	41	96	193	28	11	39	97	1177	+82	+27	+109
Oakland Athletics	93	328	111	176	50	94	176	22	14	36	116	1201	+50	+43	+93
Philadelphia Phillies	68	279	102	177	26	82	173	22	15	37	95	1102	+17	+57	+74
Cleveland Indians	92	301	107	173	37	87	164	23	11	34	126	1115	+21	+50	+71
Arizona D-Backs	86	291	105	169	31	66	158	19	9	29	115	1111	+43	+20	+63
San Francisco Giants	90	327	116	185	38	82	171	23	6	29	112	1131	+55	+2	+57
New York Mets	75	266	94	149	33	82	148	22	8	31	112	1125	+23	+33	+56
Houston Astros	77	282	83	161	21	55	148	22	4	26	122	1115	+7	+48	+55
Kansas City Royals	84	327	128	201	32	60	157	33	12	45	131	1119	-29	+81	+52
Tampa Bay Rays	100	323	120	187	29	72	204	29	14	44	135	1210	+35	+9	+44
Toronto Blue Jays	95	297	79	156	37	87	171	26	13	40	128	1196	+2	+36	+38
New York Yankees	62	289	87	175	28	72	159	25	12	37	111	1083	-30	+60	+30
Texas Rangers	82	306	118	180	49	85	185	20	9	29	148	1060	+37	-13	+24
Seattle Mariners	96	279	91	152	30	66	155	29	8	40	113	1013	+8	+12	+20
Miami Marlins	88	321	110	190	35	75	171	24	10	35	143	1186	+1	+16	+17
San Diego Padres	73	260	81	141	28	57	154	25	11	38	118	1002	-12	+23	+11
Cincinnati Reds	75	248	77	149	26	63	151	33	9	43	88	1002	-8	+18	+10
Atlanta Braves	83	302	99	162	31	69	108	17	9	26	121	1060	-20	+29	+9
Boston Red Sox	105	326	103	160	32	85	176	33	15	48	137	1223	-4	+13	+9
Los Angeles Angels	114	318	121	197	48	95	174	36	19	57	111	1171	+4	+3	+7
Pittsburgh Pirates	84	308	111	185	42	82	153	28	10	39	126	1164	-8	+10	+2
Chicago Cubs	55	244	95	154	30	72	139	21	12	33	93	1069	+9	-15	-6
Chicago White Sox	76	288	105	169	30	81	153	24	14	41	126	1094	-29	+13	-16
Detroit Tigers	94	335	123	212	39	97	162	31	15	47	137	1177	-45	+24	-21
Baltimore Orioles	71	311	90	171	29	72	130	19	11	30	111	1102	-27	+4	-23
Milwaukee Brewers	69	227	108	164	33	77	133	30	16	46	137	1025	-60	+16	-44
Los Angeles Dodgers	86	321	135	218	27	69	141	38	18	60	119	1127	-88	+38	-50
St Louis Cardinals	83	311	102	181	38	72	153	29	16	45	140	1200	-44	-7	-51
Colorado Rockies	90	310	95	186	37	85	148	27	16	45	121	1095	-49	-11	-60
MLB Totals	2555	8943	3113	5235	1018	2303	4795	783	358	1166	3604	33611			

Relief Pitching

This section documents the performance of the most used relievers of each major league team. To qualify, a reliever must have had at least 10 relief appearances in 2014. In addition to his performance, which is detailed in a variety of metrics, we classify each reliever with a specific role. Most modern bullpens are made up of one closer (CL), one or two set-up men (SU), left-handed pitchers who are used primarily against left-handed hitters (LT), a long man (LM), and some number of utility relievers (UR).

The data contained in this section includes:

Usage: Games in Relief (Rel G), the number of times the pitcher entered the game before the seventh inning (Early Entry), pitching on consecutive days (Cons Days), long outings (LO), and Leverage Index (Lev Ind). We use the Leverage Index calculated by Tom Tango and published on FanGraphs.com. An average Leverage Index is 1.0. If a pitcher pitches frequently in late innings with the game on the line, his leverage index will be high. If he generally pitches in the 6th inning of 7-2 ballgames, his leverage index will be very low.

Inherited Runners: The total (#), the number that scored (Scrd), and the percentage that scored (Pct).

Saves: The conversions and opportunities for three different classifications of Saves: "Easy", "Regular", and "Tough". The definitions of each of these save types can be found in the Baseball Glossary at the end of the book.

Relief Results: Clean Outings (Clean), Blown Save Wins (BS Win), Saves and Save Opportunities (Sv-Opp), Holds, Save/Hold Percentage (Sv/Hld Pct), Opponent OPS (Opp OPS), and reliever ERA (Rel ERA). The definitions of many of these categories can be found in the Baseball Glossary at the end of the book.

Arizona Diamondbacks

Pitcher	Pos	T	Rel G	Early Entry	Cons Days	Long	Lev Ind	#	Scrd	Pct	Easy	Reg	Tough	Clean	Win	BS	Holds	Sv/Hld Pct	Opp OPS	Rel ERA
			Usage					Inherited Runners			Saves			Relief Results		BS		Sv/Hld	Opp	Rel
Reed, Addison	CL	R	62	0	14	4	1.7	8	5	.63	21 - 21	11 - 16	0 - 1	39	0	6	0	.84	.740	4.25
Ziegler, Brad	SU	R	68	2	19	4	1.8	18	6	.33	1 - 1	0 - 5	0 - 3	49	1	8	29	.79	.681	3.49
Marshall, Evan	SU	R	57	6	10	3	1.5	29	5	.17	0 - 0	0 - 0	0 - 1	42	0	1	19	.95	.709	2.74
Perez, Oliver	LT	L	68	15	12	4	1.0	32	10	.31	0 - 0	0 - 0	0 - 1	47	1	1	15	.94	.679	2.91
Thatcher, Joe	LT	L	37	7	9	1	1.0	37	8	.22	0 - 0	0 - 0	0 - 1	24	0	1	4	.80	.670	2.63
De La Rosa, Eury	LT	L	25	9	4	7	0.5	13	10	.77	0 - 0	0 - 0	0 - 1	16	0	1	0	.00	.689	2.95
Delgado, Randall	LM	R	43	20	7	21	0.7	20	9	.45	0 - 0	0 - 0	0 - 0	23	0	0	2	1.00	.631	4.40
Stites, Matt	UR	R	37	4	7	6	0.8	18	2	.11	0 - 0	0 - 0	0 - 0	24	0	0	2	1.00	.825	5.73
Harris, Will	UR	R	29	6	5	3	0.9	10	4	.40	0 - 1	0 - 0	0 - 0	20	0	1	3	.75	.740	4.34
Putz, J.J.	UR	R	18	2	2	1	0.4	10	2	.20	0 - 0	0 - 0	0 - 0	12	0	0	0		.869	6.59
Cahill, Trevor	UR	R	15	4	4	8	0.8	6	2	.33	1 - 2	0 - 0	0 - 0	9	0	1	0	.50	.681	3.04

Atlanta Braves

Pitcher	Pos	T	Rel G	Early Entry	Cons Days	Long	Lev Ind	#	Scrd	Pct	Easy	Reg	Tough	Clean	Win	BS	Holds	Sv/Hld Pct	Opp OPS	Rel ERA
			Usage					Inherited Runners			Saves			Relief Results		BS		Sv/Hld	Opp	Rel
Kimbrel, Craig	CL	R	63	0	19	3	2.3	14	2	.14	25 - 26	20 - 23	2 - 2	52	0	4	0	.92	.430	1.61
Carpenter, David	SU	R	65	1	22	3	1.3	27	4	.15	2 - 3	1 - 2	0 - 1	42	1	3	19	.88	.663	3.54
Walden, Jordan	SU	R	58	0	17	2	1.5	22	8	.36	2 - 2	0 - 1	1 - 2	43	0	2	20	.92	.541	2.88
Simmons, Shae	SU	R	26	2	9	2	1.7	21	5	.24	1 - 1	0 - 0	0 - 0	18	0	0	9	1.00	.598	2.91
Avilan, Luis	LT	L	62	8	16	2	1.1	48	11	.23	0 - 0	0 - 1	0 - 1	41	0	2	8	.80	.764	4.57
Russell, James	LT	L	21	3	6	2	0.4	7	1	.14	0 - 0	0 - 0	0 - 0	16	0	0	1	1.00	.548	2.66
Thomas, Ian	LT	L	16	1	3	1	1.1	9	0	.00	0 - 0	0 - 0	0 - 0	13	0	0	3	1.00	.615	4.22
Shreve, Chasen	LT	L	15	1	4	0	0.4	5	0	.00	0 - 0	0 - 0	0 - 0	14	0	0	2	1.00	.526	0.73
Varvaro, Anthony	UR	R	61	7	14	2	1.0	31	9	.29	0 - 0	0 - 1	0 - 0	45	0	1	13	.93	.632	2.63
Hale, David	UR	R	39	11	5	12	0.7	27	8	.30	0 - 0	0 - 0	0 - 0	23	0	0	4	1.00	.766	3.81
Jaime, Juan	UR	R	16	4	4	3	0.6	7	2	.29	0 - 0	0 - 0	0 - 0	9	0	0	0		.800	5.84
Schlosser, Gus	UR	R	15	1	2	4	0.8	10	5	.50	0 - 0	0 - 1	0 - 0	6	0	1	0	.00	.894	7.64
Wood, Alex	UR	L	11	4	0	4	1.0	4	0	.00	0 - 0	0 - 0	0 - 0	7	0	0	2	1.00	.807	4.70

Baltimore Orioles

Pitcher	Pos	T	Rel G	Early Entry	Cons Days	Long	Lev Ind	#	Scrd	Pct	Easy	Reg	Tough	Clean	Win	BS	Holds	Sv/Hld Pct	Opp OPS	Rel ERA
			Usage					Inherited Runners			Saves			Relief Results		BS		Sv/Hld	Opp	Rel
Britton, Zach	CL	L	71	4	19	7	1.7	10	1	.10	19 - 21	18 - 20	0 - 0	61	0	4	7	.92	.500	1.65
O'Day, Darren	SU	R	68	1	14	2	1.5	30	6	.20	2 - 2	2 - 5	0 - 1	53	1	4	25	.88	.550	1.70
Hunter, Tommy	SU	R	60	4	13	3	1.6	32	5	.16	0 - 0	2 - 0	0 - 2	42	1	6	12	.79	.643	2.97
Miller, Andrew	SU	L	23	0	2	0	1.4	16	5	.31	1 - 1	0 - 0	0 - 1	18	1	1	9	.91	.375	1.35
Matusz, Brian	LT	L	63	11	12	8	1.0	49	10	.20	0 - 0	0 - 0	0 - 3	43	1	3	14	.82	.750	3.48
Brach, Brad	LM	R	46	17	6	15	0.7	25	7	.28	0 - 0	0 - 0	0 - 0	29	0	0	8	1.00	.640	3.18
McFarland, T.J.	LM	L	36	16	9	10	0.7	20	11	.55	0 - 0	0 - 0	0 - 0	22	0	0	5	1.00	.733	2.68
Webb, Ryan	UR	R	51	13	9	2	1.1	22	5	.23	0 - 0	0 - 0	0 - 0	35	0	0	11	1.00	.637	3.83
Meek, Evan	UR	R	23	6	3	3	1.2	15	5	.33	0 - 0	0 - 0	0 - 1	13	0	1	3	.75	.812	5.79
Guilmet, Preston	UR	R	10	1	1	0	0.7	2	1	.50	0 - 0	0 - 0	0 - 0	6	0	0	1	1.00	.633	5.23

Boston Red Sox

Pitcher	Pos	T	Usage					Inherited Runners			Saves			Relief Results						
			Rel G	Early Entry	Cons Days	Long	Lev Ind	#	Scrd	Pct	Easy	Reg	Tough	Clean	BS Win	BS	Holds	Sv/Hld Pct	Opp OPS	Rel ERA
Uehara, Koji	CL	R	64	0	16	5	1.8	10	5	.50	13 - 15	12 - 14	1 - 2	50	2	5	1	.84	.629	2.52
Tazawa, Junichi	SU	R	71	1	20	4	1.5	32	12	.38	0 - 1	0 - 1	0 - 3	52	0	5	16	.76	.660	2.86
Layne, Tom	SU	L	30	5	10	0	1.3	22	7	.32	0 - 0	0 - 1	0 - 0	22	0	1	9	.90	.591	0.95
Breslow, Craig	LT	L	60	14	12	6	0.7	16	2	.13	0 - 0	1 - 2	0 - 0	40	0	1	2	.75	.887	5.96
Miller, Andrew	LT	L	50	1	13	2	1.4	26	2	.08	0 - 0	0 - 0	0 - 0	39	0	0	13	1.00	.492	2.34
Capuano, Chris	LT	L	28	9	3	8	0.9	24	8	.33	0 - 0	0 - 0	0 - 1	16	0	1	4	.80	.770	4.55
Badenhop, Burke	UR	R	70	18	16	10	1.0	57	16	.28	0 - 0	1 - 1	0 - 3	48	0	3	13	.82	.672	2.29
Mujica, Edward	UR	R	64	5	15	3	1.0	14	4	.29	4 - 4	3 - 4	1 - 1	42	0	1	3	.92	.790	3.90
Wilson, Alex	UR	R	18	7	1	6	0.5	6	4	.67	0 - 0	0 - 0	0 - 1	10	0	1	0	.00	.624	1.91

Chicago Cubs

Pitcher	Pos	T	Usage					Inherited Runners			Saves			Relief Results						
			Rel G	Early Entry	Cons Days	Long	Lev Ind	#	Scrd	Pct	Easy	Reg	Tough	Clean	BS Win	BS	Holds	Sv/Hld Pct	Opp OPS	Rel ERA
Rondon, Hector	CL	R	64	1	16	7	1.6	7	0	.00	20 - 22	9 - 11	0 - 0	52	2	4	1	.88	.526	2.42
Strop, Pedro	SU	R	65	1	13	1	1.6	12	2	.17	1 - 1	1 - 5	0 - 0	52	1	4	21	.85	.535	2.21
Ramirez, Neil	SU	R	50	1	5	4	1.2	9	2	.22	3 - 4	0 - 0	0 - 1	43	0	2	16	.90	.550	1.44
Wright, Wesley	LT	L	58	12	14	10	1.0	39	7	.18	0 - 0	0 - 1	0 - 1	43	0	2	9	.82	.667	3.17
Rosscup, Zac	LT	L	18	4	4	2	0.5	13	3	.23	0 - 0	0 - 0	0 - 0	11	0	0	1	1.00	.875	9.45
Russell, James	LM	L	44	7	9	4	1.0	23	9	.39	0 - 0	1 - 1	0 - 2	30	0	2	5	.75	.627	3.51
Villanueva, Carlos	LM	R	37	16	3	16	0.9	22	12	.55	0 - 0	2 - 2	0 - 0	22	0	0	3	1.00	.648	2.64
Grimm, Justin	UR	R	73	16	19	9	0.9	30	5	.17	0 - 1	0 - 0	0 - 0	54	1	1	11	.92	.632	3.78
Schlitter, Brian	UR	R	61	22	16	7	1.2	40	15	.38	0 - 1	0 - 1	0 - 2	39	0	4	12	.75	.682	4.15
Parker, Blake	UR	R	18	3	1	5	0.7	3	0	.00	0 - 0	0 - 0	0 - 0	11	0	0	1	1.00	.784	5.14
Fujikawa, Kyuji	UR	R	15	2	3	1	0.2	11	6	.55	0 - 0	0 - 0	0 - 0	9	0	0	0		.843	4.85
Veras, Jose	UR	R	12	3	1	6	1.6	1	0	.00	0 - 1	0 - 1	0 - 0	6	0	2	0	.00	.845	8.10

Chicago White Sox

Pitcher	Pos	T	Usage					Inherited Runners			Saves			Relief Results						
			Rel G	Early Entry	Cons Days	Long	Lev Ind	#	Scrd	Pct	Easy	Reg	Tough	Clean	BS Win	BS	Holds	Sv/Hld Pct	Opp OPS	Rel ERA
Petricka, Jake	CL	R	67	7	16	11	1.5	40	16	.40	7 - 8	5 - 5	2 - 5	42	0	4	10	.86	.671	2.96
Belisario, Ronald	SU	R	62	9	14	7	1.6	35	14	.40	5 - 6	3 - 6	0 - 0	32	1	4	12	.83	.728	5.56
Putnam, Zach	SU	R	49	8	10	8	1.5	29	3	.10	1 - 1	3 - 4	2 - 2	35	0	1	16	.96	.551	1.98
Guerra, Javy	SU	R	42	6	5	8	1.3	29	15	.52	0 - 1	1 - 3	0 - 2	27	0	5	7	.62	.696	2.91
Downs, Scott	LT	L	38	4	15	4	0.8	28	4	.14	0 - 0	1 - 1	0 - 0	22	0	0	6	1.00	.727	6.08
Surkamp, Eric	LT	L	35	3	13	1	0.9	28	3	.11	0 - 0	0 - 0	0 - 0	23	0	0	7	1.00	.713	4.81
Webb, Daniel	UR	R	57	8	10	17	0.8	42	12	.29	0 - 0	0 - 2	0 - 0	32	0	2	4	.67	.736	3.99
Lindstrom, Matt	UR	R	35	3	6	3	1.3	11	8	.73	5 - 5	1 - 3	0 - 2	19	1	4	0	.60	.893	5.03
Cleto, Maikel	UR	R	28	5	4	6	0.8	14	6	.43	0 - 0	0 - 0	0 - 0	15	0	0	4	1.00	.711	4.60

Cincinnati Reds

Pitcher	Pos	T	Rel G	Early Entry	Cons Days	Long	Lev Ind	#	Scrd	Pct	Easy	Reg	Tough	Clean	Win	BS	Holds	Sv/Hld Pct	Opp OPS	Rel ERA
Chapman, Aroldis	CL	L	54	0	18	6	1.7	8	0	.00	22 - 22	13 - 15	1 - 1	48	0	2	0	.95	.406	2.00
Parra, Manny	SU	L	53	4	13	3	1.2	30	6	.20	0 - 0	1 - 2	0 - 0	40	0	1	16	.94	.781	4.66
Broxton, Jonathan	SU	R	51	0	13	1	1.6	14	4	.29	5 - 5	2 - 8	0 - 0	41	1	6	21	.82	.565	1.86
Marshall, Sean	LT	L	15	3	1	5	0.3	11	5	.45	0 - 0	0 - 0	0 - 0	7	0	0	1	1.00	.961	7.71
LeCure, Sam	UR	R	62	9	11	7	1.2	34	8	.24	0 - 0	0 - 1	0 - 0	42	0	1	17	.94	.787	3.81
Hoover, J.J.	UR	R	54	13	7	19	0.9	24	8	.33	0 - 0	0 - 2	0 - 2	28	0	4	1	.20	.785	4.88
Ondrusek, Logan	UR	R	40	12	5	6	1.0	25	9	.36	0 - 0	0 - 2	0 - 1	22	1	3	4	.57	.802	5.49
Diaz, Jumbo	UR	R	36	1	9	5	1.3	19	3	.16	0 - 0	0 - 1	0 - 0	25	0	1	8	.89	.668	3.38
Contreras, Carlos	UR	R	17	3	0	6	0.3	6	2	.33	0 - 0	0 - 1	0 - 0	8	0	1	0	.00	.765	6.52
Villarreal, Pedro	UR	R	12	5	1	4	0.5	11	0	.00	0 - 0	0 - 0	0 - 0	8	0	0	0		.627	4.30
Christiani, Nick	UR	R	10	5	3	2	0.7	6	1	.17	0 - 0	0 - 0	0 - 0	6	0	0	0		.776	5.54

Cleveland Indians

Pitcher	Pos	T	Rel G	Early Entry	Cons Days	Long	Lev Ind	#	Scrd	Pct	Easy	Reg	Tough	Clean	Win	BS	Holds	Sv/Hld Pct	Opp OPS	Rel ERA
Allen, Cody	CL	R	76	0	23	3	2.0	35	5	.14	11 - 11	9 - 13	4 - 4	60	1	4	9	.89	.601	2.07
Shaw, Bryan	SU	R	80	4	27	6	1.5	35	10	.29	1 - 1	1 - 6	0 - 2	58	1	7	24	.79	.602	2.59
Atchison, Scott	SU	R	70	21	22	1	1.3	41	6	.15	2 - 2	0 - 2	0 - 3	48	0	5	14	.76	.606	2.75
Rzepczynski, Marc	LT	L	73	17	19	1	1.1	57	11	.19	0 - 0	1 - 1	0 - 1	53	0	1	13	.93	.656	2.74
Crockett, Kyle	LT	L	44	16	10	2	0.9	37	9	.24	0 - 0	0 - 0	0 - 0	33	0	0	5	1.00	.657	1.80
Hagadone, Nick	LT	L	35	10	7	2	0.9	33	5	.15	0 - 0	0 - 0	0 - 0	27	0	0	3	1.00	.636	2.70
Axford, John	LM	R	49	6	11	9	1.3	22	6	.27	6 - 7	4 - 5	0 - 1	33	0	3	2	.80	.702	3.92
Outman, Josh	LM	L	31	14	9	4	0.5	18	4	.22	0 - 0	0 - 1	0 - 0	23	0	1	1	.50	.792	3.28
Lee, C.C.	UR	R	37	16	12	3	0.8	27	2	.07	0 - 0	0 - 0	0 - 1	25	0	1	4	.80	.791	4.50
Carrasco, Carlos	UR	R	26	7	2	10	0.5	10	5	.50	0 - 0	1 - 1	0 - 0	16	0	0	0	1.00	.561	2.30
Pestano, Vinnie	UR	R	13	6	3	1	0.6	9	1	.11	0 - 0	0 - 0	0 - 0	8	0	0	0		.940	5.00

Colorado Rockies

Pitcher	Pos	T	Rel G	Early Entry	Cons Days	Long	Lev Ind	#	Scrd	Pct	Easy	Reg	Tough	Clean	Win	BS	Holds	Sv/Hld Pct	Opp OPS	Rel ERA
Hawkins, LaTroy	CL	R	57	0	9	5	1.8	1	0	.00	13 - 15	10 - 11	0 - 0	41	1	3	1	.89	.653	3.31
Ottavino, Adam	SU	R	75	1	22	5	1.5	44	14	.32	1 - 1	0 - 2	0 - 3	48	0	5	21	.81	.735	3.60
Logan, Boone	SU	L	35	0	8	0	1.8	13	5	.38	0 - 0	0 - 3	0 - 1	22	1	4	7	.64	.907	6.84
Brothers, Rex	LT	L	74	6	17	4	1.4	32	14	.44	0 - 1	0 - 2	0 - 3	48	0	6	15	.71	.825	5.59
Friedrich, Christian	LT	L	13	1	4	0	1.3	5	1	.20	0 - 0	0 - 0	0 - 0	10	0	0	3	1.00	.342	1.64
Kahnle, Tommy	LM	R	54	29	8	15	0.8	25	7	.28	0 - 1	0 - 0	0 - 1	28	0	2	8	.80	.628	4.19
Belisle, Matt	UR	R	65	12	14	8	0.9	27	11	.41	0 - 0	0 - 2	0 - 0	43	0	2	6	.75	.759	4.96
Masset, Nick	UR	R	51	8	13	7	0.7	23	13	.57	0 - 0	0 - 0	0 - 2	29	0	2	2	.50	.868	5.80
Brown, Brooks	UR	R	28	5	9	4	0.6	15	5	.33	0 - 0	0 - 0	0 - 0	19	0	0	5	1.00	.563	2.77
Bettis, Chad	UR	R	21	6	4	8	0.7	12	6	.50	0 - 0	0 - 0	0 - 1	9	0	1	1	.50	1.020	9.12
Nicasio, Juan	UR	R	19	2	4	2	0.6	7	3	.43	0 - 0	0 - 0	0 - 0	13	0	0	1	1.00	.675	3.48
Martin, Chris	UR	R	16	7	4	0	0.7	5	0	.00	0 - 0	0 - 0	0 - 0	10	0	0	3	1.00	.915	6.89
Morales, Franklin	UR	L	16	7	2	4	0.8	9	3	.33	0 - 0	0 - 0	0 - 0	8	0	0	0		.899	4.94
Scahill, Rob	UR	R	12	6	0	4	0.8	13	6	.46	0 - 0	0 - 0	0 - 1	6	0	1	0	.00	.875	4.80

Detroit Tigers

Pitcher	Pos	T	Usage					Inherited Runners			Saves			Relief Results						
			Rel G	Early Entry	Cons Days	Long	Lev Ind	#	Scrd	Pct	Easy	Reg	Tough	Clean	BS Win	BS	Holds	Sv/Hld Pct	Opp OPS	Rel ERA
Nathan, Joe	CL	R	62	0	15	9	2.2	5	3	.60	23 - 25	12 - 16	0 - 1	42	2	7	0	.83	.721	4.81
Chamberlain, Joba	SU	R	69	0	21	5	1.6	14	5	.36	2 - 3	0 - 3	0 - 0	51	0	4	29	.89	.647	3.57
Krol, Ian	SU	L	45	7	10	6	1.0	38	16	.42	0 - 0	1 - 1	0 - 3	28	0	3	10	.79	.906	4.96
Coke, Phil	LT	L	62	11	14	9	0.7	52	19	.37	0 - 0	1 - 1	0 - 1	35	0	1	5	.86	.790	3.88
Hardy, Blaine	LT	L	38	12	9	5	0.9	29	8	.28	0 - 0	0 - 0	0 - 1	24	0	1	4	.80	.611	2.54
McCoy, Pat	LT	L	14	3	3	4	0.8	4	2	.50	0 - 0	0 - 0	0 - 0	10	0	0	0		.902	3.86
Alburquerque, Al	UR	R	72	13	17	6	1.0	47	13	.28	0 - 0	0 - 0	1 - 1	51	0	0	17	1.00	.639	2.51
Reed, Evan	UR	R	32	10	5	6	0.5	16	3	.19	0 - 0	0 - 0	0 - 0	19	0	0	4	1.00	.776	4.18
Johnson, Jim	UR	R	16	4	2	4	0.6	11	2	.18	0 - 0	0 - 0	0 - 0	9	0	0	0		.685	6.92
Soria, Joakim	UR	R	13	0	2	1	1.2	6	2	.33	1 - 1	0 - 0	0 - 0	9	0	0	1	1.00	.838	4.91
Smith, Chad	UR	R	10	3	1	2	0.2	5	0	.00	0 - 0	0 - 0	0 - 0	6	0	0	0		.871	5.40

Houston Astros

Pitcher	Pos	T	Usage					Inherited Runners			Saves			Relief Results						
			Rel G	Early Entry	Cons Days	Long	Lev Ind	#	Scrd	Pct	Easy	Reg	Tough	Clean	BS Win	BS	Holds	Sv/Hld Pct	Opp OPS	Rel ERA
Qualls, Chad	CL	R	58	0	13	0	1.5	15	6	.40	11 - 13	6 - 8	2 - 4	43	0	6	2	.78	.667	3.33
Sipp, Tony	SU	L	56	2	14	5	1.3	32	6	.19	2 - 2	1 - 3	1 - 1	46	0	2	11	.88	.517	3.38
Fields, Josh	SU	R	54	6	8	7	1.2	22	8	.36	2 - 2	1 - 3	1 - 3	36	1	4	8	.75	.637	4.45
Farnsworth, Kyle	SU	R	16	1	5	0	0.8	9	4	.44	0 - 0	0 - 0	0 - 1	9	0	1	5	.83	.848	6.17
Downs, Darin	LT	L	45	18	10	3	0.8	28	7	.25	0 - 0	0 - 0	0 - 0	28	0	0	10	1.00	.695	5.45
Chapman, Kevin	LT	L	21	6	5	3	1.3	16	2	.13	0 - 0	0 - 1	0 - 0	13	1	1	5	.83	.778	4.64
Williams, Jerome	LM	R	26	10	2	14	0.7	11	3	.27	0 - 0	0 - 2	0 - 1	10	1	3	2	.40	.836	6.04
Veras, Jose	UR	R	34	2	4	4	1.0	23	10	.43	1 - 2	0 - 2	0 - 0	23	0	3	6	.70	.645	3.03
Zeid, Josh	UR	R	23	7	7	4	0.7	21	9	.43	0 - 0	0 - 0	0 - 0	10	0	0	3	1.00	1.012	6.97
Bass, Anthony	UR	R	21	5	4	5	1.2	18	6	.33	1 - 2	1 - 2	0 - 0	10	0	2	4	.75	.840	6.33
Foltynewicz, Mike	UR	R	16	2	1	3	0.2	7	2	.29	0 - 0	0 - 0	0 - 0	10	0	0	1	1.00	.864	5.30
Buchanan, Jake	UR	R	15	6	1	6	0.9	11	4	.36	0 - 0	0 - 0	0 - 0	8	0	0	0		.706	3.46
Clemens, Paul	UR	R	13	6	0	7	0.3	8	0	.00	0 - 0	0 - 0	0 - 0	5	0	0	1	1.00	.862	5.84

Kansas City Royals

Pitcher	Pos	T	Usage					Inherited Runners			Saves			Relief Results						
			Rel G	Early Entry	Cons Days	Long	Lev Ind	#	Scrd	Pct	Easy	Reg	Tough	Clean	BS Win	BS	Holds	Sv/Hld Pct	Opp OPS	Rel ERA
Holland, Greg	CL	R	65	0	21	5	1.8	5	1	.20	32 - 32	14 - 16	0 - 0	54	0	2	0	.96	.472	1.44
Davis, Wade	SU	R	71	0	18	7	1.6	11	5	.45	2 - 3	0 - 0	1 - 3	62	1	3	33	.92	.408	1.00
Herrera, Kelvin	SU	R	70	9	17	6	1.1	43	9	.21	0 - 1	0 - 0	0 - 0	58	0	1	20	.95	.561	1.41
Bueno, Francisley	LT	L	30	5	6	6	0.5	20	7	.35	0 - 0	0 - 0	0 - 1	16	0	1	5	.83	.741	4.18
Collins, Tim	LT	L	22	2	6	4	0.9	8	4	.50	0 - 0	0 - 0	0 - 1	14	0	1	1	.50	.712	3.86
Downs, Scott	LT	L	17	7	5	1	0.6	9	2	.22	0 - 0	0 - 0	0 - 1	12	0	1	1	.50	.721	3.14
Crow, Aaron	UR	R	67	13	14	4	0.9	28	10	.36	1 - 1	2 - 2	0 - 3	48	0	3	11	.82	.743	4.12
Coleman, Louis	UR	R	31	11	2	5	0.5	14	8	.57	1 - 1	0 - 0	0 - 0	15	0	0	1	1.00	.862	5.56
Frasor, Jason	UR	R	23	6	2	0	0.7	16	4	.25	0 - 0	0 - 0	0 - 0	18	0	0	0		.569	1.53
Mariot, Michael	UR	R	17	6	2	8	0.3	10	1	.10	0 - 0	0 - 0	0 - 0	8	0	0	0		.787	6.48
Coleman, Casey	UR	R	10	6	0	3	0.5	6	0	.00	0 - 0	0 - 0	0 - 0	6	0	0	0		.788	5.25

Los Angeles Angels

Pitcher	Pos	T	Rel G	Early Entry	Cons Days	Long	Lev Ind	#	Scrd	Pct	Easy	Reg	Tough	Clean	BS Win	BS	Holds	Sv/Hld Pct	Opp OPS	Rel ERA
Frieri, Ernesto	CL	R	34	0	10	3	1.3	5	3	.60	7 - 8	4 - 5	0 - 1	23	0	3	3	.82	.844	6.39
Street, Huston	CL	R	28	0	11	2	2.2	0	0	.00	7 - 8	10 - 11	0 - 0	25	1	2	0	.89	.580	1.71
Smith, Joe	SU	R	76	0	27	4	1.5	22	13	.59	14 - 14	1 - 3	0 - 2	61	1	4	18	.89	.491	1.81
Jepsen, Kevin	SU	R	74	8	21	5	1.2	40	14	.35	1 - 1	1 - 2	0 - 1	56	0	2	22	.92	.547	2.63
Grilli, Jason	SU	R	40	9	10	2	1.2	12	4	.33	1 - 1	0 - 0	0 - 1	29	0	1	11	.92	.616	3.48
Thatcher, Joe	LT	L	16	7	6	0	1.1	14	6	.43	0 - 0	0 - 0	0 - 0	11	0	0	2	1.00	1.004	8.53
Maronde, Nick	LT	L	11	1	2	1	0.5	10	5	.50	0 - 0	0 - 0	0 - 0	6	0	0	1	1.00	1.205	12.79
Herrera, Yoslan	LM	R	20	9	4	3	0.7	12	5	.42	0 - 0	0 - 0	0 - 0	14	0	0	0		.829	2.70
Bedrosian, Cam	LM	R	17	7	2	8	1.1	4	2	.50	0 - 0	0 - 1	0 - 0	8	0	1	1	.50	.801	6.52
Morin, Mike	UR	R	60	26	15	6	1.0	43	9	.21	0 - 0	0 - 1	0 - 1	41	0	2	9	.82	.629	2.90
Salas, Fernando	UR	R	57	10	14	8	1.1	12	9	.75	0 - 0	0 - 0	0 - 1	40	0	1	8	.89	.637	3.38
Kohn, Michael	UR	R	25	6	7	3	0.8	9	0	.00	0 - 0	0 - 0	0 - 0	20	0	0	3	1.00	.545	3.04
Rasmus, Cory	UR	R	24	6	4	9	0.8	18	5	.28	0 - 0	0 - 0	0 - 0	15	0	0	0		.612	2.68
Pestano, Vinnie	UR	R	12	6	3	1	0.5	16	3	.19	0 - 0	0 - 0	0 - 0	9	0	0	1	1.00	.479	0.93

Los Angeles Dodgers

Pitcher	Pos	T	Rel G	Early Entry	Cons Days	Long	Lev Ind	#	Scrd	Pct	Easy	Reg	Tough	Clean	BS Win	BS	Holds	Sv/Hld Pct	Opp OPS	Rel ERA
Jansen, Kenley	CL	R	68	0	22	5	2.0	13	5	.38	29 - 30	14 - 18	1 - 1	51	0	5	0	.90	.610	2.76
Howell, J.P.	SU	L	68	3	22	1	1.3	35	2	.06	0 - 0	0 - 0	0 - 0	58	0	0	27	1.00	.547	2.39
Wilson, Brian	SU	R	61	1	12	5	1.3	11	3	.27	0 - 0	1 - 5	0 - 0	47	0	4	22	.85	.771	4.66
Withrow, Chris	SU	R	20	5	1	4	1.4	6	0	.00	0 - 0	0 - 1	0 - 0	16	0	1	6	.86	.551	2.95
Maholm, Paul	LT	L	22	4	4	7	0.2	6	1	.17	0 - 0	0 - 0	0 - 0	11	0	0	0		.765	5.00
Rodriguez, Paco	LM	L	19	9	6	1	0.7	11	0	.00	0 - 0	0 - 1	0 - 0	15	0	1	4	.80	.662	3.86
League, Brandon	UR	R	63	9	13	4	1.2	29	12	.41	0 - 0	0 - 0	0 - 1	45	0	1	11	.92	.683	2.57
Wright, Jamey	UR	R	60	18	10	12	1.0	30	10	.33	0 - 1	1 - 1	0 - 0	37	0	1	5	.86	.679	4.35
Perez, Chris	UR	R	49	9	9	10	0.9	27	7	.26	0 - 0	1 - 2	0 - 0	34	0	1	6	.88	.755	4.27
Baez, Pedro	UR	R	20	4	1	2	0.7	6	1	.17	0 - 0	0 - 0	0 - 0	14	0	0	5	1.00	.537	2.63
Frias, Carlos	UR	R	13	4	1	6	0.6	2	0	.00	0 - 0	0 - 0	0 - 0	6	0	0	1	1.00	.587	4.91

Miami Marlins

Pitcher	Pos	T	Rel G	Early Entry	Cons Days	Long	Lev Ind	#	Scrd	Pct	Easy	Reg	Tough	Clean	BS Win	BS	Holds	Sv/Hld Pct	Opp OPS	Rel ERA
Cishek, Steve	CL	R	67	0	17	7	2.1	7	0	.00	19 - 20	18 - 21	2 - 2	51	0	4	0	.91	.643	3.17
Dunn, Mike	SU	L	75	0	19	6	1.6	44	9	.20	0 - 1	1 - 2	0 - 1	54	0	3	22	.88	.635	3.16
Ramos, A.J.	SU	R	68	2	13	12	1.5	30	7	.23	0 - 0	0 - 2	0 - 1	54	1	3	20	.87	.543	2.11
Morris, Bryan	SU	R	39	3	10	5	1.7	16	10	.63	0 - 0	0 - 2	0 - 2	30	0	4	13	.76	.595	0.66
Jennings, Dan	LT	L	47	16	14	8	0.7	29	12	.41	0 - 0	0 - 1	0 - 1	31	0	2	3	.60	.738	1.34
Slowey, Kevin	LM	R	15	9	0	9	0.4	9	3	.33	0 - 0	0 - 0	0 - 0	6	0	0	0		.956	4.76
Hatcher, Chris	UR	R	52	13	13	10	0.9	32	10	.31	0 - 0	0 - 1	0 - 1	34	0	2	6	.75	.666	3.38
Dyson, Sam	UR	R	31	9	5	10	0.6	18	8	.44	0 - 0	0 - 0	0 - 1	18	0	1	0	.00	.653	2.14
Capps, Carter	UR	R	17	4	1	4	0.5	4	1	.25	0 - 0	0 - 0	0 - 0	10	0	0	1	1.00	.610	3.98
Hand, Brad	UR	L	16	8	2	6	0.4	7	1	.14	0 - 0	0 - 1	0 - 0	10	0	0	0	1.00	.739	4.57
Marmol, Carlos	UR	R	15	1	4	1	1.2	3	0	.00	0 - 0	0 - 0	0 - 0	11	0	1	1	.50	.900	8.10
Gregg, Kevin	UR	R	12	0	4	0	1.0	0	0	.00	0 - 1	0 - 1	0 - 0	7	0	2	4	.67	.974	10.00

Milwaukee Brewers

Pitcher	Pos	T	Usage					Inherited Runners			Saves			Relief Results						
			Rel G	Early Entry	Cons Days	Long	Lev Ind	#	Scrd	Pct	Easy	Reg	Tough	Clean	BS Win	BS	Holds	Sv/Hld Pct	Opp OPS	Rel ERA
Rodriguez, Francisco	CL	R	69	0	25	3	1.5	5	0	.00	31 - 33	12 - 15	1 - 1	53	2	5	0	.90	.648	3.04
Smith, Will	SU	L	78	4	21	3	1.5	35	8	.23	1 - 1	0 - 3	0 - 2	59	1	5	30	.86	.737	3.70
Duke, Zach	LT	L	74	10	19	4	1.1	41	8	.20	0 - 0	0 - 0	0 - 4	57	1	4	12	.75	.578	2.45
Gorzelanny, Tom	LT	L	23	8	2	2	0.4	5	5	1.00	0 - 0	0 - 0	0 - 0	18	0	0	0		.654	0.86
Wang, Wei-Chung	LT	L	14	1	1	5	0.2	3	1	.33	0 - 0	0 - 0	0 - 0	7	0	0	0		1.123	10.90
Estrada, Marco	LM	R	21	15	2	13	0.3	10	3	.30	0 - 0	0 - 0	0 - 0	13	0	0	0		.611	2.89
Kintzler, Brandon	UR	R	64	7	14	4	1.2	37	11	.30	0 - 0	0 - 2	0 - 1	45	0	3	8	.73	.781	3.24
Wooten, Rob	UR	R	40	5	8	4	0.8	21	4	.19	0 - 0	0 - 0	0 - 0	27	0	0	11	1.00	.756	4.72
Jeffress, Jeremy	UR	R	29	2	4	1	1.1	10	3	.30	0 - 0	0 - 0	0 - 1	21	0	1	6	.86	.624	1.88
Thornburg, Tyler	UR	R	27	3	7	7	0.8	6	3	.50	0 - 0	0 - 0	0 - 0	18	0	0	5	1.00	.670	4.25
Henderson, Jim	UR	R	14	1	5	0	1.2	3	0	.00	0 - 0	0 - 0	0 - 0	10	0	0	2	1.00	.945	7.15
Broxton, Jonathan	UR	R	11	0	4	0	1.7	4	1	.25	0 - 1	0 - 1	0 - 0	9	0	2	2	.50	.587	4.35

Minnesota Twins

Pitcher	Pos	T	Usage					Inherited Runners			Saves			Relief Results						
			Rel G	Early Entry	Cons Days	Long	Lev Ind	#	Scrd	Pct	Easy	Reg	Tough	Clean	BS Win	BS	Holds	Sv/Hld Pct	Opp OPS	Rel ERA
Perkins, Glen	CL	L	63	0	17	2	1.9	1	0	.00	25 - 29	8 - 11	1 - 1	45	2	7	0	.83	.720	3.65
Fien, Casey	SU	R	73	1	17	1	1.3	22	6	.27	0 - 1	1 - 4	0 - 0	53	1	4	26	.87	.705	3.98
Duensing, Brian	LT	L	62	9	6	5	1.1	41	13	.32	0 - 0	0 - 0	0 - 4	43	0	4	7	.64	.725	3.31
Thielbar, Caleb	LT	L	54	17	8	6	0.7	38	9	.24	0 - 0	0 - 0	0 - 1	34	0	1	7	.88	.738	3.40
Swarzak, Anthony	LM	R	46	24	4	17	0.7	35	16	.46	0 - 0	0 - 1	0 - 0	24	0	1	3	.75	.723	4.10
Deduno, Samuel	LM	R	22	14	1	13	0.6	10	7	.70	0 - 0	0 - 0	0 - 0	8	0	0	1	1.00	.696	3.21
Burton, Jared	UR	R	68	2	13	6	1.2	22	4	.18	0 - 0	3 - 4	0 - 0	45	0	1	14	.94	.681	4.36
Guerrier, Matt	UR	R	27	3	6	2	0.6	14	5	.36	0 - 0	0 - 0	0 - 1	15	0	1	3	.75	.706	3.86
Tonkin, Michael	UR	R	25	6	6	3	0.8	22	6	.27	0 - 0	0 - 0	0 - 0	14	0	0	4	1.00	.822	4.74
Pressly, Ryan	UR	R	25	7	4	4	0.6	19	4	.21	0 - 0	0 - 0	0 - 1	16	0	1	2	.67	.779	2.86

New York Mets

Pitcher	Pos	T	Usage					Inherited Runners			Saves			Relief Results						
			Rel G	Early Entry	Cons Days	Long	Lev Ind	#	Scrd	Pct	Easy	Reg	Tough	Clean	BS Win	BS	Holds	Sv/Hld Pct	Opp OPS	Rel ERA
Mejia, Jenrry	CL	R	56	0	12	5	2.0	9	4	.44	18 - 18	10 - 12	0 - 1	40	0	3	2	.91	.701	2.72
Familia, Jeurys	SU	R	76	6	18	8	1.4	37	9	.24	0 - 2	4 - 7	1 - 1	53	0	5	23	.85	.587	2.21
Edgin, Josh	LT	L	47	6	16	0	0.9	44	11	.25	0 - 0	0 - 0	0 - 1	38	0	1	5	.83	.539	1.32
Rice, Scott	LT	L	32	1	14	1	1.5	25	2	.08	0 - 0	0 - 1	0 - 1	23	0	2	7	.78	.835	5.93
Eveland, Dana	LT	L	30	7	5	4	0.7	23	6	.26	0 - 0	0 - 1	1 - 1	21	0	1	2	.75	.629	2.62
Matsuzaka, Daisuke	LM	R	25	7	3	13	0.8	9	0	.00	1 - 2	0 - 0	0 - 0	15	0	1	3	.80	.692	3.44
Torres, Carlos	UR	R	72	17	20	21	1.0	33	6	.18	0 - 0	2 - 4	0 - 1	46	0	3	12	.82	.731	3.23
Black, Vic	UR	R	41	6	9	5	1.3	26	1	.04	0 - 0	0 - 0	0 - 0	30	0	0	12	1.00	.617	2.60
Carlyle, Buddy	UR	R	27	8	3	6	0.8	8	2	.25	0 - 0	0 - 0	0 - 0	19	0	0	2	1.00	.547	1.45
Germen, Gonzalez	UR	R	25	5	3	8	0.5	6	3	.50	0 - 0	0 - 1	0 - 0	15	0	1	0	.00	.837	4.75
Valverde, Jose	UR	R	21	0	3	2	1.1	7	0	.00	1 - 2	1 - 2	0 - 0	14	0	2	0	.50	.852	5.66
Farnsworth, Kyle	UR	R	19	0	5	0	1.8	6	1	.17	3 - 3	0 - 1	0 - 0	13	0	1	3	.86	.791	3.18

New York Yankees

Pitcher	Pos	T	Usage Rel G	Early Entry	Cons Days	Long	Lev Ind	Inherited Runners #	Scrd	Pct	Saves Easy	Reg	Tough	Relief Results Clean	BS Win	BS	Holds	Sv/Hld Pct	Opp OPS	Rel ERA
Robertson, David	CL	R	63	0	18	8	2.1	13	2	.15	19 - 20	17 - 20	3 - 4	49	1	5	0	.89	.588	3.08
Betances, Dellin	SU	R	70	16	15	15	1.3	44	11	.25	0 - 0	1 - 5	0 - 0	50	1	4	22	.85	.442	1.40
Warren, Adam	SU	R	69	12	10	16	1.4	38	13	.34	0 - 0	3 - 4	0 - 2	48	0	3	23	.90	.615	2.97
Kelley, Shawn	SU	R	59	7	16	6	1.6	36	6	.17	3 - 4	1 - 1	0 - 2	40	1	3	12	.84	.663	4.53
Thornton, Matt	SU	L	46	7	11	1	1.4	43	14	.33	0 - 0	0 - 1	0 - 3	32	0	4	12	.75	.615	2.55
Hill, Rich	LT	L	14	3	3	0	0.6	15	1	.07	0 - 0	0 - 0	0 - 0	13	0	0	1	1.00	.686	1.69
Huff, David	LM	L	30	11	6	9	0.6	16	1	.06	0 - 0	0 - 0	0 - 0	20	0	0	3	1.00	.624	1.85
Claiborne, Preston	UR	R	18	4	3	6	0.7	12	8	.67	0 - 0	0 - 0	0 - 1	8	0	1	0	.00	.771	3.00
Rogers, Esmil	UR	R	17	5	2	4	0.9	13	4	.31	0 - 0	0 - 0	0 - 1	11	0	1	3	.75	.739	5.40
Phelps, David	UR	R	15	3	0	6	0.9	12	4	.33	0 - 0	1 - 1	0 - 0	7	0	0	5	1.00	.802	4.96
Daley, Matt	UR	R	13	4	3	3	0.6	13	5	.38	0 - 0	0 - 0	0 - 0	7	0	0	1	1.00	.825	5.02
Whitley, Chase	UR	R	12	5	1	5	0.7	8	1	.13	0 - 0	0 - 0	0 - 0	4	0	0	0		.875	6.88
Aceves, Alfredo	UR	R	10	2	3	5	0.6	3	1	.33	0 - 0	0 - 0	0 - 0	3	0	0	1	1.00	.892	6.52

Oakland Athletics

Pitcher	Pos	T	Usage Rel G	Early Entry	Cons Days	Long	Lev Ind	Inherited Runners #	Scrd	Pct	Saves Easy	Reg	Tough	Relief Results Clean	BS Win	BS	Holds	Sv/Hld Pct	Opp OPS	Rel ERA
Doolittle, Sean	CL	L	61	1	16	3	1.5	12	2	.17	14 - 16	6 - 8	2 - 2	51	0	4	5	.87	.459	2.73
Gregerson, Luke	SU	R	72	1	23	3	1.6	23	10	.43	2 - 2	1 - 6	0 - 3	55	0	8	22	.76	.604	2.12
Abad, Fernando	LT	L	69	7	18	0	1.0	38	5	.13	0 - 0	0 - 0	0 - 2	57	0	2	9	.82	.499	1.57
O'Flaherty, Eric	LT	L	21	8	0	1	0.7	5	0	.00	1 - 1	0 - 1	0 - 0	17	0	1	3	.80	.608	2.25
Johnson, Jim	LM	R	38	7	5	6	1.2	11	5	.45	2 - 2	0 - 1	0 - 0	21	0	1	2	.80	.911	7.14
Otero, Dan	UR	R	72	18	21	12	1.3	55	19	.35	1 - 1	0 - 1	0 - 0	49	1	3	12	.81	.609	2.28
Cook, Ryan	UR	R	54	13	12	1	1.0	29	12	.41	0 - 0	0 - 0	1 - 3	38	0	2	7	.80	.585	3.42
Scribner, Evan	UR	R	13	0	2	0	0.1	2	0	.00	0 - 0	0 - 0	0 - 0	9	0	0	0		.777	4.63
Chavez, Jesse	UR	R	11	5	0	6	0.2	7	3	.43	0 - 0	0 - 0	0 - 0	3	0	0	0		.740	3.54
Pomeranz, Drew	UR	L	10	5	3	5	0.5	3	0	.00	0 - 0	0 - 0	0 - 0	7	0	0	0		.573	1.62

Philadelphia Phillies

Pitcher	Pos	T	Usage Rel G	Early Entry	Cons Days	Long	Lev Ind	Inherited Runners #	Scrd	Pct	Saves Easy	Reg	Tough	Relief Results Clean	BS Win	BS	Holds	Sv/Hld Pct	Opp OPS	Rel ERA
Papelbon, Jonathan	CL	R	66	0	19	8	2.2	0	0	.00	18 - 20	21 - 23	0 - 0	58	0	4	0	.91	.500	2.04
Diekman, Jake	SU	L	73	11	16	16	1.4	31	12	.39	0 - 1	0 - 3	0 - 0	47	1	4	18	.82	.692	3.80
Giles, Ken	SU	R	44	0	12	3	1.2	14	2	.14	1 - 1	0 - 0	0 - 0	37	0	0	13	1.00	.450	1.18
Adams, Mike	SU	R	22	1	4	1	1.6	12	0	.00	0 - 0	0 - 2	0 - 0	17	1	2	6	.75	.660	2.89
Dastardo, Antonio	LI	L	67	7	18	7	1.3	21	4	.19	0 - 0	0 - 1	0 - 1	52	0	2	12	.86	.614	3.94
Hollands, Mario	LT	L	50	18	10	7	0.7	20	10	.50	0 - 0	0 - 1	0 - 0	31	0	1	3	.75	.693	4.40
Jimenez, Cesar	LT	L	16	4	3	3	0.4	13	4	.31	0 - 0	0 - 0	0 - 0	12	0	0	0		.639	1.69
De Fratus, Justin	UR	R	54	10	18	8	1.1	32	11	.34	0 - 1	0 - 0	0 - 1	40	0	2	5	.71	.632	2.39
Manship, Jeff	UR	R	20	3	2	5	1.0	1	0	.00	0 - 0	0 - 0	0 - 0	12	0	0	0		.804	6.65
Garcia, Luis	UR	R	13	3	3	5	0.4	5	1	.20	0 - 0	0 - 0	0 - 0	9	0	0	0		.815	6.43
Rosenberg, B.J.	UR	R	13	3	4	4	0.5	6	3	.50	0 - 0	0 - 0	0 - 0	5	0	0	0		1.208	6.75

Pittsburgh Pirates

Pitcher	Pos	T	Rel G	Early Entry	Cons Days	Long	Lev Ind	#	Scrd	Pct	Easy	Reg	Tough	Clean	BS Win	BS	Holds	Sv/Hld Pct	Opp OPS	Rel ERA
Melancon, Mark	CL	R	72	0	16	1	1.9	6	2	.33	24 - 24	9 - 12	0 - 1	57	0	4	14	.92	.473	1.90
Grilli, Jason	CL	R	22	0	4	3	2.0	2	2	1.00	5 - 5	6 - 10	0 - 0	14	0	4	1	.75	.832	4.87
Watson, Tony	SU	L	78	1	21	6	1.8	20	9	.45	0 - 3	2 - 4	0 - 2	63	3	7	34	.84	.613	1.63
Morris, Bryan	SU	R	21	5	2	4	1.2	10	7	.70	0 - 0	0 - 2	0 - 1	11	2	3	4	.57	.833	3.80
Wilson, Justin	LT	L	70	14	16	7	1.2	27	6	.22	0 - 0	0 - 1	0 - 2	50	0	3	16	.84	.643	4.20
Gomez, Jeanmar	LM	R	44	12	5	15	0.8	25	14	.56	0 - 0	1 - 1	0 - 0	23	0	0	2	1.00	.810	3.19
Hughes, Jared	UR	R	63	21	19	6	1.1	37	7	.19	0 - 0	0 - 0	0 - 2	45	0	2	13	.87	.609	1.96
Pimentel, Stolmy	UR	R	20	6	0	7	0.6	9	3	.33	0 - 0	0 - 0	0 - 0	8	0	0	0		.785	5.23
Frieri, Ernesto	UR	R	14	1	4	1	0.5	9	2	.22	0 - 0	0 - 0	0 - 0	10	0	0	0		.992	10.13
Axford, John	UR	R	13	0	3	0	0.6	4	2	.50	0 - 0	0 - 0	0 - 0	8	0	0	0		.648	4.09

San Diego Padres

Pitcher	Pos	T	Rel G	Early Entry	Cons Days	Long	Lev Ind	#	Scrd	Pct	Easy	Reg	Tough	Clean	BS Win	BS	Holds	Sv/Hld Pct	Opp OPS	Rel ERA
Street, Huston	CL	R	33	0	9	2	2.0	0	0	.00	13 - 13	11 - 12	0 - 0	30	0	1	0	.96	.470	1.09
Vincent, Nick	SU	R	63	10	17	1	1.1	42	6	.14	0 - 1	0 - 1	0 - 0	49	0	2	20	.91	.626	3.60
Quackenbush, Kevin	SU	R	56	5	14	8	1.3	24	3	.13	3 - 3	3 - 4	0 - 0	44	0	1	10	.94	.568	2.48
Benoit, Joaquin	SU	R	53	0	13	2	1.6	7	3	.43	6 - 6	5 - 6	0 - 0	45	0	1	16	.96	.459	1.49
Torres, Alex	LT	L	70	13	21	8	0.5	44	5	.11	0 - 0	0 - 0	0 - 1	50	0	1	7	.88	.645	3.33
Garces, Frank	LT	L	15	6	5	1	0.6	14	3	.21	0 - 0	0 - 0	0 - 1	12	0	1	3	.75	.670	2.00
Boyer, Blaine	LM	R	32	11	1	8	0.6	14	4	.29	0 - 0	0 - 0	0 - 0	22	0	0	5	1.00	.628	3.57
Roach, Donn	LM	R	15	6	1	8	0.3	8	2	.25	0 - 0	0 - 0	0 - 0	7	0	0	0		.780	3.95
Thayer, Dale	UR	R	70	6	16	5	1.0	16	4	.25	0 - 0	0 - 1	0 - 0	53	0	1	13	.93	.627	2.34
Stauffer, Tim	UR	R	41	13	4	8	0.8	16	6	.38	0 - 0	0 - 0	0 - 0	27	0	0	0		.698	2.56
Alvarez, R.J.	UR	R	10	3	2	1	0.6	7	2	.29	0 - 0	0 - 0	0 - 0	8	0	0	1	1.00	.388	1.13

San Francisco Giants

Pitcher	Pos	T	Rel G	Early Entry	Cons Days	Long	Lev Ind	#	Scrd	Pct	Easy	Reg	Tough	Clean	BS Win	BS	Holds	Sv/Hld Pct	Opp OPS	Rel ERA
Romo, Sergio	CL	R	64	0	16	1	1.9	12	1	.08	14 - 16	9 - 12	0 - 0	50	1	5	11	.87	.622	3.72
Casilla, Santiago	CL	R	54	0	11	5	1.7	18	3	.17	15 - 15	4 - 8	0 - 0	39	1	4	10	.88	.493	1.70
Machi, Jean	SU	R	71	7	22	4	1.1	40	12	.30	1 - 1	1 - 3	0 - 1	55	0	3	17	.86	.602	2.58
Affeldt, Jeremy	SU	L	62	7	20	3	1.1	27	8	.30	0 - 1	0 - 1	0 - 1	52	0	3	18	.86	.593	2.28
Lopez, Javier	LT	L	65	14	18	1	0.9	41	13	.32	0 - 0	0 - 0	0 - 2	48	0	2	12	.86	.629	3.11
Petit, Yusmeiro	LM	R	27	11	2	12	0.4	4	0	.00	0 - 0	0 - 0	0 - 0	21	0	0	0		.472	1.84
Huff, David	LM	L	16	8	3	5	0.6	6	1	.17	0 - 0	0 - 0	0 - 0	7	0	0	1	1.00	.793	6.30
Gutierrez, Juan	UR	R	61	19	8	9	0.6	36	10	.28	0 - 0	0 - 1	0 - 0	42	0	1	10	.91	.731	3.96
Kontos, George	UR	R	24	8	2	4	0.5	14	8	.57	0 - 0	0 - 0	0 - 0	15	0	0	1	1.00	.587	2.78

Seattle Mariners

Pitcher	Pos T	Usage					Inherited Runners			Saves			Relief Results				Sv/Hld Pct	Opp OPS	Rel ERA
		Rel G	Early Entry	Cons Days	Long	Lev Ind	#	Scrd	Pct	Easy	Reg	Tough	Clean	BS Win	BS	Holds			
Rodney, Fernando	CL R	69	0	18	12	1.9	12	1	.08	34 - 34	13 - 15	1 - 2	49	0	3	0	.94	.646	2.85
Furbush, Charlie	SU L	67	5	17	0	1.1	39	5	.13	0 - 0	1 - 1	0 - 0	50	0	0	20	1.00	.649	3.61
Medina, Yoervis	SU R	66	3	14	4	1.2	24	10	.42	0 - 0	0 - 1	0 - 0	50	0	1	21	.95	.642	2.68
Beimel, Joe	LT L	56	15	9	1	0.7	28	7	.25	0 - 0	0 - 0	0 - 0	45	0	0	9	1.00	.656	2.20
Luetge, Lucas	LT L	12	5	2	0	0.2	8	2	.25	0 - 0	0 - 0	0 - 0	6	0	0	0		.744	5.00
Leone, Dominic	LM R	57	30	7	13	0.9	36	16	.44	0 - 0	0 - 1	0 - 1	36	0	2	7	.78	.624	2.17
Farquhar, Danny	UR R	66	9	7	13	1.0	30	6	.20	0 - 1	1 - 2	0 - 0	50	0	2	13	.88	.607	2.66
Wilhelmsen, Tom	UR R	55	14	8	16	0.8	21	4	.19	0 - 0	1 - 1	0 - 2	38	0	2	8	.82	.536	2.03
Maurer, Brandon	UR R	31	9	2	6	0.8	9	4	.44	0 - 0	0 - 1	0 - 0	23	0	1	5	.83	.535	2.17

St Louis Cardinals

Pitcher	Pos T	Usage					Inherited Runners			Saves			Relief Results				Sv/Hld Pct	Opp OPS	Rel ERA
		Rel G	Early Entry	Cons Days	Long	Lev Ind	#	Scrd	Pct	Easy	Reg	Tough	Clean	BS Win	BS	Holds			
Rosenthal, Trevor	CL R	72	0	24	8	2.5	15	6	.40	28 - 28	14 - 19	3 - 4	50	0	6	2	.89	.641	3.20
Neshek, Pat	SU R	71	3	18	2	1.5	31	10	.32	6 - 7	0 - 1	0 - 2	57	0	4	25	.89	.480	1.87
Martinez, Carlos	SU R	50	6	12	8	1.6	26	3	.12	0 - 1	1 - 5	0 - 0	34	0	5	17	.78	.667	3.79
Siegrist, Kevin	SU L	37	4	6	2	1.4	13	2	.15	0 - 0	0 - 2	0 - 0	22	0	2	16	.89	.818	6.82
Choate, Randy	LT L	61	10	19	1	0.9	39	4	.10	0 - 0	0 - 0	0 - 0	49	0	0	10	1.00	.590	4.50
Freeman, Sam	LT L	44	4	11	5	1.0	8	1	.13	0 - 0	0 - 0	0 - 0	34	0	0	11	1.00	.638	2.61
Greenwood, Nick	LM L	18	9	1	7	0.4	9	0	.00	0 - 0	0 - 0	0 - 0	9	0	0	1	1.00	.738	5.18
Maness, Seth	UR R	73	26	22	10	1.0	65	17	.26	0 - 0	1 - 1	2 - 2	52	0	0	11	1.00	.668	2.91
Motte, Jason	UR R	29	5	5	2	0.4	14	7	.50	0 - 0	0 - 0	0 - 0	17	0	0	1	1.00	.891	4.68

Tampa Bay Rays

Pitcher	Pos T	Usage					Inherited Runners			Saves			Relief Results				Sv/Hld Pct	Opp OPS	Rel ERA
		Rel G	Early Entry	Cons Days	Long	Lev Ind	#	Scrd	Pct	Easy	Reg	Tough	Clean	BS Win	BS	Holds			
McGee, Jake	CL L	73	7	23	8	1.7	30	3	.10	13 - 14	4 - 6	2 - 3	61	2	4	14	.89	.486	1.89
Balfour, Grant	CL R	65	2	16	9	1.7	12	0	.00	3 - 4	8 - 10	1 - 1	50	0	3	11	.88	.688	4.91
Peralta, Joel	SU R	69	1	14	5	1.3	24	2	.08	1 - 5	0 - 2	0 - 0	50	1	6	18	.76	.708	4.41
Boxberger, Brad	SU R	63	19	14	12	1.3	38	7	.18	1 - 1	1 - 3	0 - 1	47	1	3	18	.87	.538	2.37
Beliveau, Jeff	LT L	30	11	5	0	1.0	20	7	.35	0 - 0	1 - 1	0 - 0	21	0	0	6	1.00	.552	2.63
Ramos, Cesar	LM L	36	14	6	13	0.6	14	4	.29	0 - 0	0 - 0	0 - 0	24	0	0	2	1.00	.612	2.92
Gomes, Brandon	LM R	29	14	4	9	0.8	25	10	.40	0 - 0	0 - 0	0 - 0	19	0	0	4	1.00	.664	3.71
Yates, Kirby	UR R	37	9	9	7	0.4	22	6	.27	0 - 0	0 - 0	1 - 2	24	0	1	0	.50	.699	3.75
Oviedo, Juan	UR R	32	8	4	6	0.8	17	4	.24	1 - 1	0 - 0	0 - 1	21	0	1	2	.75	.729	3.69
Lueke, Josh	UR R	25	3	7	5	0.4	14	8	.57	0 - 0	0 - 0	0 - 0	11	0	0	0		.830	5.64
Bell, Heath	UR R	13	5	5	7	0.9	2	1	.50	0 - 0	0 - 0	0 - 0	6	0	0	0		.860	7.27
Geltz, Steve	UR R	11	5	3	0	0.7	8	6	.75	0 - 0	0 - 0	0 - 1	6	0	1	0	.00	.851	3.24

Texas Rangers

Pitcher	Pos	T	Usage					Inherited Runners			Saves			Relief Results						
			Rel G	Early Entry	Cons Days	Long	Lev Ind	#	Scrd	Pct	Easy	Reg	Tough	Clean	BS Win	BS	Holds	Sv/Hld Pct	Opp OPS	Rel ERA
Soria, Joakim	CL	R	35	0	7	2	1.6	1	0	.00	10 - 10	7 - 9	0 - 0	29	0	2	0	.89	.521	2.70
Feliz, Neftali	CL	R	30	4	4	3	1.5	10	4	.40	7 - 8	6 - 6	0 - 0	21	0	1	0	.93	.586	1.99
Cotts, Neal	SU	L	73	0	22	3	1.3	45	8	.18	1 - 1	1 - 4	0 - 4	51	1	7	19	.75	.713	4.32
Frasor, Jason	SU	R	38	6	6	1	1.1	25	9	.36	0 - 0	0 - 1	0 - 1	26	0	2	10	.83	.695	3.34
Mendez, Roman	SU	R	30	6	4	5	1.0	19	7	.37	0 - 0	0 - 0	0 - 0	23	0	0	10	1.00	.556	2.18
Ogando, Alexi	SU	R	27	5	4	9	1.1	15	4	.27	0 - 1	1 - 1	0 - 0	17	0	1	7	.89	.795	6.84
Ross, Robbie	LT	L	15	6	1	3	0.4	13	6	.46	0 - 0	0 - 0	0 - 0	6	0	0	2	1.00	.935	7.85
Claudio, Alex	LT	L	15	1	4	1	0.2	12	5	.42	0 - 0	0 - 0	0 - 0	9	0	0	0		.693	2.92
Kirkman, Michael	LT	L	12	4	3	0	1.4	11	2	.18	0 - 0	0 - 0	0 - 0	10	0	0	2	1.00	.732	1.59
Figueroa, Pedro	LT	L	10	4	1	1	0.6	2	1	.50	0 - 0	0 - 0	0 - 0	8	0	0	0		.746	4.00
Poreda, Aaron	LM	L	26	12	2	1	0.9	13	2	.15	0 - 0	0 - 1	0 - 0	15	1	1	4	.80	.909	5.91
Tolleson, Shawn	UR	R	65	26	11	10	0.9	34	15	.44	0 - 0	0 - 0	0 - 0	41	0	0	7	1.00	.659	2.76
Klein, Phil	UR	R	17	6	0	3	0.8	7	0	.00	0 - 0	0 - 0	0 - 0	12	0	0	0		.679	2.84
Baker, Scott	UR	R	17	6	2	6	0.3	7	1	.14	0 - 0	0 - 0	0 - 0	10	0	0	0		.709	5.13

Toronto Blue Jays

Pitcher	Pos	T	Usage					Inherited Runners			Saves			Relief Results						
			Rel G	Early Entry	Cons Days	Long	Lev Ind	#	Scrd	Pct	Easy	Reg	Tough	Clean	BS Win	BS	Holds	Sv/Hld Pct	Opp OPS	Rel ERA
Janssen, Casey	CL	R	50	0	12	2	1.6	5	0	.00	18 - 21	7 - 9	0 - 0	38	1	5	0	.83	.697	3.94
Loup, Aaron	SU	L	71	17	14	11	1.3	66	15	.23	1 - 2	3 - 4	0 - 2	51	0	4	13	.81	.647	3.15
Cecil, Brett	SU	L	66	5	9	3	1.4	46	11	.24	2 - 2	3 - 3	0 - 2	51	0	2	24	.94	.627	2.70
McGowan, Dustin	SU	R	45	7	9	4	1.2	36	7	.19	0 - 2	1 - 1	0 - 2	31	0	4	10	.73	.689	3.35
Delabar, Steve	SU	R	30	4	5	2	1.1	20	3	.15	0 - 0	0 - 0	0 - 0	18	0	0	12	1.00	.729	4.91
Sanchez, Aaron	SU	R	24	4	4	5	1.3	7	1	.14	1 - 1	1 - 1	1 - 1	19	0	0	7	1.00	.367	1.09
Rasmussen, Rob	LT	L	10	2	1	3	0.5	0	0	.00	0 - 0	0 - 0	0 - 0	8	0	0	2	1.00	.633	3.18
Redmond, Todd	LM	R	42	17	6	19	0.5	21	10	.48	0 - 0	1 - 1	0 - 0	23	0	0	0	1.00	.726	3.24
Santos, Sergio	UR	R	26	2	3	3	1.4	15	7	.47	3 - 4	1 - 1	1 - 3	14	0	3	0	.63	1.062	8.57
Jenkins, Chad	UR	R	21	6	5	7	1.0	16	4	.25	0 - 0	0 - 0	0 - 0	15	0	0	2	1.00	.674	2.56
Rogers, Esmil	UR	R	16	4	1	7	0.2	7	4	.57	0 - 0	0 - 0	0 - 0	9	0	0	1	1.00	.932	6.97
Wagner, Neil	UR	R	10	3	2	3	0.7	6	3	.50	0 - 0	0 - 0	0 - 0	5	0	0	5	1.00	.882	8.10

Washington Nationals

Pitcher	Pos	T	Usage					Inherited Runners			Saves			Relief Results						
			Rel G	Early Entry	Cons Days	Long	Lev Ind	#	Scrd	Pct	Easy	Reg	Tough	Clean	BS Win	BS	Holds	Sv/Hld Pct	Opp OPS	Rel ERA
Soriano, Rafael	CL	R	64	0	12	5	1.7	2	2	1.00	24 - 28	8 - 11	0 - 0	49	1	7	0	.82	.639	3.19
Clippard, Tyler	SU	R	75	0	15	2	1.6	6	0	.00	1 - 3	0 - 4	0 - 0	62	0	6	40	.87	.541	2.18
Storen, Drew	SU	R	65	0	10	1	1.5	24	10	.42	6 - 6	5 - 7	0 - 1	52	0	3	20	.91	.540	1.12
Thornton, Matt	SU	L	18	1	3	0	1.2	12	4	.33	0 - 0	0 - 0	0 - 0	15	0	0	6	1.00	.551	0.00
Blevins, Jerry	LT	L	64	8	10	7	0.8	35	4	.11	0 - 0	0 - 0	0 - 0	43	0	0	9	1.00	.623	4.87
Stammen, Craig	LM	R	49	17	2	18	0.9	27	5	.19	0 - 0	0 - 0	0 - 0	32	0	0	7	1.00	.708	3.84
Detwiler, Ross	LM	L	47	14	2	17	0.6	11	3	.27	0 - 0	1 - 2	0 - 0	27	0	1	3	.80	.734	4.00
Barrett, Aaron	UR	R	50	7	9	4	0.8	40	13	.33	0 - 0	0 - 0	0 - 0	34	0	0	8	1.00	.605	2.66

Pitchers Hitting, Fielding, & Holding Runners, and Hitters Pitching

In a category that is often dominated by Zack Greinke and Travis Wood, Madison Bumgarner asserted himself as the best hitting pitcher in 2014. He set the pace at the position with a .258 batting average among pitchers with at least 20 plate appearances, and he did that over 78 plate appearances. He also hit an incredible four home runs, the same number as qualified position players Joe Mauer, Austin Jackson, Alex Rios, and Derek Jeter. Travis Wood (3) and Mike Leake (2) were the only other pitchers with more than one home run in 2014, and Wood has actually hit three home runs in each of the last two seasons.

The second piece of the section shows the 2014 fielding statistics and success in holding runners for pitchers. A pitcher's Defensive Runs Saved (DRS) is the sum of his Plus/Minus Runs Saved, which evaluates his range, Stolen Base Runs Saved, which measures his ability to control the running game, Bunt Runs Saved, which evaluates his defense of bunts, and Good Fielding Play/Defensive Misplay Runs Saved, which accounts for the good defensive plays he makes as well as the mistakes he makes that are not captured by other components. Dallas Keuchel led all pitchers with 10 Runs Saved, and he posted one of just 16 seasons in which a pitcher allowed only one stolen base with 200 or more innings pitched since 2002 (no one has allowed zero).

The final part of this section shows statistics on Hitters Pitching. Danny Worth and Drew Butera were the only two position players who threw more than an inning in 2014, and both players even managed to strike out a pair of batters. Of course, neither Worth nor Butera made it unscathed through their short stints, allowing a combined six hits and three runs in 3.2 innings of work. Every active position player who has pitched is listed in the Hitters Pitching page, and their statistics there include any numbers they accrued this year, as well.

Pitchers Hitting, Fielding and Holding Runners

Pitcher	T	2014 Hitting						Career Hitting										2014 Fielding and Holding Runners											
		Avg	AB	H	HR	RBI	SH	Avg	AB	H	2B	3B	HR	RBI	BB	SO	SH	Inn	PO	A	E	DP	Pct	SBA	CS	PCS	PPO	CS%	RS
Abad,Fernando, Oak	L	-	0	0	0	0	0	.125	8	1	0	0	0	0	0	4	0	57.1	0	8	0	0	1.000	6	4	0	0	.67	4
Aceves,Alfredo, NYY	R	-	0	0	0	0	0	.000	2	0	0	0	0	0	0	1	0	19.1	2	1	0	0	1.000	0	0	0	0	-	0
Achter,A.J., Min	R	-	0	0	0	0	0	-	0	0	0	0	0	0	0	0	0	11.0	0	1	0	0	1.000	2	1	0	0	.50	-1
Adams,Austin, Cle	R	-	0	0	0	0	0	-	0	0	0	0	0	0	0	0	0	7.0	1	2	0	0	1.000	0	0	0	0	-	0
Adams,Mike, Phi	R	-	0	0	0	0	0	.000	2	0	0	0	0	0	0	0	0	18.2	0	5	0	1	1.000	4	0	0	0	.00	0
Adcock,Nate, Tex	R	-	0	0	0	0	0	.000	1	0	0	0	0	0	0	1	0	10.0	0	0	0	0	-	0	0	0	0	-	0
Affeldt,Jeremy, SF	L	-	0	0	0	0	0	.200	15	3	0	0	0	2	2	4	0	55.1	0	20	0	2	1.000	6	0	0	0	.00	4
Albers,Matt, Hou	R	-	0	0	0	0	0	.059	34	2	0	0	0	0	0	21	3	10.0	0	0	0	0	-	3	2	0	0	.67	0
Alburquerque,Al, Det	R	-	0	0	0	0	0	-	0	0	0	0	0	0	0	0	0	57.1	4	5	0	1	1.000	11	3	0	0	.27	-2
Allen,Cody, Cle	R	-	0	0	0	0	0	-	0	0	0	0	0	0	0	0	0	69.2	2	2	0	0	1.000	5	1	0	0	.20	0
Alvarez,Dario, NYM	L	-	0	0	0	0	0	-	0	0	0	0	0	0	0	0	0	1.1	0	0	0	0	-	0	0	0	0	-	0
Alvarez,Henderson, Mia	R	.193	57	11	0	2	8	.227	88	20	3	0	1	8	1	33	12	187.0	18	36	2	5	.964	12	4	1	0	.33	6
Alvarez,Jose, LAA	L	-	0	0	0	0	0	.000	1	0	0	0	0	0	1	0	0	0.2	0	0	0	0	-	0	0	0	0	-	0
Alvarez,R.J., SD	R	-	0	0	0	0	0	-	0	0	0	0	0	0	0	0	0	8.0	0	2	0	1	1.000	1	0	0	0	.00	1
Ambriz,Hector, SD	R	-	0	0	0	0	0	-	0	0	0	0	0	0	0	0	0	2.0	0	0	0	0	-	0	0	0	0	-	0
Anderson,Brett, Col	L	.143	14	2	0	1	1	.111	18	2	2	0	0	1	0	9	1	43.1	0	5	0	0	1.000	2	1	1	0	.50	-1
Anderson,Chase, Ari	R	.029	34	1	0	0	6	.029	34	1	0	0	0	0	0	14	6	114.1	9	16	1	1	.962	4	2	1	0	.50	2
Archer,Chris, TB	R	.000	4	0	0	0	0	.000	8	0	0	0	0	0	0	4	0	194.2	10	17	4	2	.871	19	5	1	0	.26	-4
Arrieta,Jake, ChC	R	.179	39	7	0	3	6	.156	64	10	2	1	0	6	4	30	11	156.2	17	20	2	1	.949	29	5	1	0	.17	-3
Arroyo,Bronson, Ari	R	.222	27	6	0	0	4	.128	603	77	16	0	6	29	14	266	82	86.0	12	12	1	2	.960	10	5	0	0	.50	0
Atchison,Scott, Cle	R	-	0	0	0	0	0	.000	2	0	0	0	0	0	0	1	0	72.0	5	13	1	1	.947	6	2	0	0	.33	1
Aumont,Phillippe, Phi	R	.000	1	0	0	0	0	.000	1	0	0	0	0	0	0	1	0	5.2	0	0	0	0	-	1	0	0	0	.00	0
Avilan,Luis, Atl	L	-	0	0	0	0	1	.333	3	1	0	0	0	0	0	0	2	43.1	5	10	0	2	1.000	6	1	0	0	.17	2
Axelrod,Dylan, Cin	R	.000	4	0	0	0	0	.167	6	1	0	0	0	0	0	5	0	18.1	1	3	0	0	1.000	2	0	0	0	.00	0
Axford,John, Cle-Pit	R	-	0	0	0	0	0	.000	1	0	0	0	0	0	0	1	0	54.2	2	6	0	0	1.000	7	1	0	0	.14	0
Badenhop,Burke, Bos	R	-	0	0	0	0	0	.094	32	3	1	0	0	2	1	19	5	70.2	9	10	2	6	.905	6	1	0	0	.17	1
Baez,Pedro, LAD	R	-	0	0	0	0	0	-	0	0	0	0	0	0	0	0	0	24.0	1	1	0	0	1.000	0	0	0	0	-	0
Bailey,Homer, Cin	R	.146	41	6	0	3	8	.160	300	48	6	0	0	17	9	118	41	145.2	13	17	0	2	1.000	8	4	1	1	.50	2
Baker,Scott, Tex	R	.000	1	0	0	0	0	.103	29	3	1	0	0	0	0	12	5	80.2	6	1	0	1	1.000	7	2	0	0	.29	2
Balfour,Grant, TB	R	-	0	0	0	0	0	.000	2	0	0	0	0	0	0	2	0	62.1	1	5	0	0	1.000	5	0	0	1	.00	0
Barnes,Matt, Bos	R	-	0	0	0	0	0	-	0	0	0	0	0	0	0	0	0	9.0	1	0	0	0	1.000	1	0	0	0	.00	-1
Barrett,Aaron, Was	R	-	0	0	0	0	0	-	0	0	0	0	0	0	0	0	0	40.2	2	4	1	0	.857	5	2	0	0	.40	0
Bass,Anthony, Hou	R	-	0	0	0	0	0	.105	38	4	0	1	0	6	0	17	1	27.0	2	6	1	0	.889	1	0	0	0	.00	0
Bassitt,Chris, CWS	R	-	0	0	0	0	0	-	0	0	0	0	0	0	0	0	0	29.2	1	4	0	0	1.000	4	1	0	0	.25	0
Bastardo,Antonio, Phi	L	-	0	0	0	0	0	.000	6	0	0	0	0	0	1	3	1	64.0	1	1	1	0	.667	3	0	0	0	.00	-2
Bauer,Trevor, Cle	R	.000	2	0	0	0	0	.000	7	0	0	0	0	0	0	4	1	153.0	9	12	1	4	.955	26	7	1	1	.27	-1
Beato,Pedro, Atl	R	-	0	0	0	0	0	-	0	0	0	0	0	0	0	0	0	4.1	0	0	0	0	-	1	0	0	0	.00	0
Beavan,Blake, Sea	R	-	0	0	0	0	0	.000	2	0	0	0	0	0	0	1	1	4.0	0	1	0	0	1.000	1	1	0	0	1.00	0
Beckett,Josh, LAD	R	.179	39	7	0	2	3	.142	289	41	12	0	3	18	12	110	33	115.2	8	8	2	1	.889	18	6	0	0	.33	-1
Bedard,Erik, TB	L	-	0	0	0	0	0	.150	60	9	1	0	0	1	2	22	8	75.2	2	5	0	0	1.000	1	0	0	0	.00	0
Bedrosian,Cam, LAA	R	-	0	0	0	0	0	-	0	0	0	0	0	0	0	0	0	19.1	2	4	0	0	1.000	2	1	0	0	.50	0
Beeler,Dallas, ChC	R	.250	4	1	0	0	0	.250	4	1	0	0	0	0	0	2	0	11.0	0	3	0	0	1.000	1	1	0	1	1.00	1
Beimel,Joe, Sea	L	-	0	0	0	0	0	.222	45	10	1	0	0	1	2	19	6	45.0	2	11	1	1	.929	4	1	0	2	.25	2
Belisario,Ronald, CWS	R	-	0	0	0	0	0	.000	5	0	0	0	0	0	0	3	0	66.1	2	9	0	0	1.000	5	0	0	0	.00	-1
Belisle,Matt, Col	R	.000	1	0	0	0	0	.082	85	7	3	0	0	3	3	47	18	64.2	6	12	1	1	.947	5	1	0	0	.20	1
Beliveau,Jeff, TB	L	-	0	0	0	0	0	-	0	0	0	0	0	0	0	0	0	24.0	1	1	0	0	1.000	3	0	0	0	.00	0
Bell,Heath, TB	R	-	0	0	0	0	0	.000	6	0	0	0	0	0	0	2	1	17.1	1	2	0	0	1.000	3	1	0	0	.33	-2
Bell,Trevor, Cin	R	-	0	0	0	0	0	.000	1	0	0	0	0	0	0	1	0	0.2	0	0	0	0	-	0	0	0	0	-	0
Benoit,Joaquin, SD	R	-	0	0	0	0	0	.000	9	0	0	0	0	0	0	4	0	54.1	0	5	0	0	1.000	2	1	0	0	.50	-1
Bergman,Christian, Col	R	.053	19	1	0	0	1	.053	19	1	0	0	0	0	0	6	1	54.2	5	6	0	0	1.000	3	1	0	1	.33	1
Betances,Dellin, NYY	R	-	0	0	0	0	0	-	0	0	0	0	0	0	0	0	0	90.0	6	6	2	0	.857	15	3	1	0	.20	-2
Bettis,Chad, Col	R	.000	3	0	0	0	0	.000	14	0	0	0	0	0	0	5	3	24.2	0	10	1	0	.909	1	0	0	0	.00	1
Billings,Bruce, NYY	R	-	0	0	0	0	0	-	0	0	0	0	0	0	0	0	0	4.0	0	0	0	0	-	0	0	0	0	-	0
Black,Vic, NYM	R	-	0	0	0	0	0	-	0	0	0	0	0	0	0	0	0	34.2	2	3	1	1	.833	5	1	1	0	.20	-1
Blevins,Jerry, Was	L	-	0	0	0	0	0	.000	1	0	0	0	0	0	0	1	0	57.1	1	6	0	0	1.000	6	2	0	0	.33	1
Bochy,Brett, SF	R	-	0	0	0	0	0	-	0	0	0	0	0	0	0	0	0	3.1	0	0	0	0	-	0	0	0	0	-	0
Bolsinger,Mike, Ari	R	.105	19	2	0	1	1	.105	19	2	0	0	0	1	0	7	1	52.1	5	11	0	0	1.000	4	3	0	0	.75	2
Bonilla,Lisalverto, Tex	R	-	0	0	0	0	0	-	0	0	0	0	0	0	0	0	0	20.2	3	1	0	0	1.000	4	0	0	0	.00	-1
Boxberger,Brad, TB	R	.000	1	0	0	0	0	.000	3	0	0	0	0	0	0	1	1	64.2	1	5	0	0	1.000	6	2	0	1	.33	-2
Boyer,Blaine, SD	R	-	0	0	0	0	0	.000	8	0	0	0	0	0	0	6	1	40.1	0	6	0	0	1.000	5	2	0	0	.40	0
Brach,Brad, Bal	R	.000	1	0	0	0	0	.000	1	0	0	0	0	0	0	0	0	62.1	2	6	3	1	.727	8	3	1	0	.38	-1
Breslow,Craig, Bos	L	-	0	0	0	0	0	.000	4	0	0	0	0	0	0	2	0	54.1	3	4	0	0	1.000	1	0	0	0	.00	0
Britton,Drake, Bos	L	-	0	0	0	0	0	-	0	0	0	0	0	0	0	0	0	6.2	0	1	0	0	1.000	0	0	0	0	-	0
Britton,Zach, Bal	L	-	0	0	0	0	0	.625	8	5	1	0	1	2	0	1	0	76.1	5	15	0	1	1.000	2	0	0	0	.00	2
Brooks,Aaron, KC	R	-	0	0	0	0	0	-	0	0	0	0	0	0	0	0	0	2.2	0	1	0	0	1.000	1	0	0	0	.00	0
Brothers,Rex, Col	L	-	0	0	0	0	0	.000	4	0	0	0	0	0	0	4	1	56.1	1	8	0	0	1.000	1	0	0	0	.00	-1
Brown,Brooks, Col	R	.000	1	0	0	0	0	.000	1	0	0	0	0	0	0	1	0	26.0	6	5	0	0	1.000	3	0	0	0	.00	1
Broxton,Jonathan, Cin-Mil	R	-	0	0	0	0	0	.000	5	0	0	0	0	0	2	2	1	58.2	2	12	0	1	1.000	3	0	0	0	.00	0
Buchanan,David, Phi	R	.100	30	3	0	2	5	.100	30	3	1	0	0	2	4	10	5	117.2	11	14	3	0	.893	5	1	0	1	.20	0
Buchanan,Jake, Hou	R	.000	1	0	0	0	0	.000	1	0	0	0	0	0	0	0	0	35.1	2	6	1	0	.889	2	1	0	0	.50	0

Pitchers Hitting, Fielding and Holding Runners

Pitcher	T	2014 Hitting						Career Hitting										2014 Fielding and Holding Runners											
		Avg	AB	H	HR	RBI	SH	Avg	AB	H	2B	3B	HR	RBI	BB	SO	SH	Inn	PO	A	E	DP	Pct	SBA	CS	PCS	PPO	CS%	RS
Buchholz,Clay, Bos	R	.500	2	1	0	0	0	.400	5	2	0	0	0	0	0	1	1	170.1	20	16	1	1	.973	11	5	0	0	.45	-1
Buchter,Ryan, Atl	L	-	0	0	0	0	0	-	0	0	0	0	0	0	0	0	0	1.0	0	0	0	0	-	0	0	0	0	-	0
Buckner,Billy, SD	R	.000	1	0	0	0	0	.222	27	6	2	0	0	6	1	8	2	5.2	0	0	0	0	-	0	0	0	0	-	0
Buehrle,Mark, Tor	L	-	0	0	0	0	0	.068	118	8	2	0	1	3	1	55	12	202.0	12	29	1	2	.976	4	3	3	1	.75	2
Bueno,Francisley, KC	L	-	0	0	0	0	0	-	0	0	0	0	0	0	0	0	0	32.1	4	2	0	1	1.000	0	0	0	0	-	-1
Bumgarner,Madison, SF	L	.258	66	17	4	15	8	.166	290	48	8	0	6	31	15	114	35	217.1	8	26	2	2	.944	17	10	9	0	.59	1
Burnett,A.J., Phi	R	.133	60	8	0	1	2	.113	451	51	8	3	3	14	20	221	50	213.2	9	25	1	1	.971	42	9	1	2	.21	-5
Burnett,Sean, LAA	R	-	0	0	0	0	0	.069	29	2	1	0	0	0	4	9	2	0.2	0	0	0	0	-	0	0	0	0	-	0
Burton,Jared, Min	R	-	0	0	0	0	0	.000	2	0	0	0	0	0	0	2	0	64.0	4	6	0	0	1.000	10	0	0	1	.00	-3
Butler,Eddie, Col	R	.000	6	0	0	0	0	.000	6	0	0	0	0	0	0	3	0	16.0	0	4	0	0	1.000	5	0	0	0	.00	-1
Butler,Keith, StL	R	-	0	0	0	0	0	-	0	0	0	0	0	0	0	0	0	2.0	0	0	0	0	-	0	0	0	0	-	0
Cabral,Cesar, NYY	L	-	0	0	0	0	0	-	0	0	0	0	0	0	0	0	0	1.0	0	0	0	0	-	0	0	0	0	-	0
Cahill,Trevor, Ari	R	.083	24	2	0	0	4	.100	150	15	2	1	0	9	2	52	15	110.2	5	12	1	1	.944	21	4	1	0	.19	-3
Cain,Matt, SF	R	.148	27	4	0	0	0	.125	536	67	10	1	6	26	21	262	67	90.1	12	12	2	1	.923	13	5	1	0	.38	0
Caminero,Arquimedes, Mia	R	-	0	0	0	0	0	-	0	0	0	0	0	0	0	0	0	6.2	2	0	0	0	1.000	2	1	0	0	.50	0
Camp,Shawn, Phi	R	-	0	0	0	0	0	1.000	1	1	0	0	0	0	0	0	1	3.1	0	0	0	0	-	0	0	0	0	-	0
Campos,Leonel, SD	R	-	0	0	0	0	0	-	0	0	0	0	0	0	0	0	0	7.0	0	1	0	0	1.000	1	0	0	0	.00	0
Capps,Carter, Mia	R	-	0	0	0	0	0	-	0	0	0	0	0	0	0	0	0	20.1	0	0	0	0	-	6	0	0	0	.00	-1
Capuano,Chris, Bos-NYY	L	-	0	0	0	0	0	.124	370	46	10	0	1	20	9	176	38	97.1	3	9	1	0	.923	2	1	1	0	.50	2
Carlyle,Buddy, NYM	R	1.000	1	1	0	0	0	.175	57	10	0	0	0	4	3	17	7	31.0	2	2	0	0	1.000	2	1	0	0	.50	0
Carpenter,David, Atl	R	-	0	0	0	0	0	.200	5	1	0	0	0	0	0	1	1	61.0	5	5	1	0	.909	2	1	0	0	.50	-1
Carpenter,David, LAA	R	-	0	0	0	0	0	-	0	0	0	0	0	0	0	0	0	3.0	1	1	0	0	1.000	1	0	0	0	.00	0
Carrasco,Carlos, Cle	R	.000	2	0	0	0	0	.000	7	0	0	0	0	0	0	5	2	134.0	10	14	2	2	.923	13	4	0	1	.31	1
Carroll,Scott, CWS	R	-	0	0	0	0	0	-	0	0	0	0	0	0	0	0	0	129.1	8	11	0	1	1.000	11	4	0	0	.36	0
Cashner,Andrew, SD	R	.171	35	6	0	2	6	.204	98	20	2	1	1	5	3	44	14	123.1	4	19	1	1	.958	11	3	0	0	.27	4
Casilla,Santiago, SF	R	.000	1	0	0	0	0	.250	4	1	0	0	0	1	1	1	0	58.1	3	9	1	2	.923	1	0	0	0	.00	3
Cecil,Brett, Tor	L	-	0	0	0	0	0	.000	6	0	0	0	0	0	0	6	0	53.1	0	5	0	0	1.000	11	0	0	0	.00	0
Cedeno,Xavier, Was	L	-	0	0	0	0	0	.000	1	0	0	0	0	0	0	1	0	7.0	0	1	0	0	1.000	0	0	0	0	-	0
Chacin,Jhoulys, Col	R	.333	15	5	0	0	1	.182	203	37	5	0	1	15	7	43	13	63.1	2	10	1	1	.923	3	1	0	0	.33	1
Chafin,Andrew, Ari	L	.500	2	1	0	1	0	.500	2	1	0	0	0	1	0	1	0	14.0	0	2	0	0	1.000	0	0	0	0	-	1
Chamberlain,Joba, Det	R	.000	1	0	0	0	0	.000	6	0	0	0	0	0	1	2	2	63.0	8	3	0	0	1.000	9	2	0	0	.22	-2
Chapman,Aroldis, Cin	L	-	0	0	0	0	0	.000	1	0	0	0	0	0	0	1	0	54.0	1	3	0	0	1.000	10	4	0	0	.40	0
Chapman,Kevin, Hou	L	-	0	0	0	0	0	-	0	0	0	0	0	0	0	0	0	21.1	1	3	0	0	1.000	0	0	0	0	-	0
Chatwood,Tyler, Col	R	.100	10	1	0	0	0	.275	69	19	2	0	0	8	3	16	11	24.0	0	1	1	0	.500	1	1	0	0	1.00	0
Chavez,Jesse, Oak	R	.000	3	0	0	0	0	.000	8	0	0	0	0	0	0	4	3	146.0	14	30	4	3	1.000	7	3	1	0	.43	-2
Chen,Bruce, KC	L	-	0	0	0	0	0	.152	125	19	1	0	3	3	3	58	19	48.1	4	4	1	0	.889	7	1	1	0	.14	0
Chen,Wei-Yin, Bal	L	.000	1	0	0	0	0	.000	6	0	0	0	0	0	0	3	1	185.2	7	24	0	1	1.000	6	1	1	0	.17	2
Choate,Randy, StL	L	-	0	0	0	0	0	.000	5	0	0	0	0	0	0	3	0	36.0	1	7	1	0	.889	4	1	0	0	.25	-1
Christiani,Nick, Cin	R	.000	1	0	0	0	0	.000	1	0	0	0	0	0	0	0	0	13.0	1	0	1	0	.500	2	0	0	0	.00	0
Cingrani,Tony, Cin	L	.143	21	3	0	0	1	.200	50	10	1	0	0	1	0	15	8	63.1	0	3	1	0	.750	3	1	1	1	.33	0
Cishek,Steve, Mia	R	-	0	0	0	0	0	.000	1	0	0	0	0	0	0	0	0	65.1	2	5	2	0	.778	9	4	1	0	.44	-2
Cisnero,Jose, Hou	R	-	0	0	0	0	0	.000	1	0	0	0	0	0	0	1	0	4.2	0	0	0	0	-	1	0	0	0	.00	0
Claiborne,Preston, NYY	R	-	0	0	0	0	1	-	0	0	0	0	0	0	0	0	1	21.0	0	3	0	0	1.000	4	2	0	0	.50	0
Claudio,Alex, Tex	L	-	0	0	0	0	0	-	0	0	0	0	0	0	0	0	0	12.1	1	1	0	0	1.000	1	0	0	0	.00	-1
Clemens,Paul, Hou	R	-	0	0	0	0	0	-	0	0	0	0	0	0	0	0	0	24.2	3	6	0	0	1.000	2	1	0	0	.50	1
Cleto,Maikel, CWS	R	-	0	0	0	0	0	.000	3	0	0	0	0	0	0	3	0	29.1	1	4	0	0	1.000	4	1	0	0	.25	0
Clippard,Tyler, Was	R	-	0	0	0	0	0	.214	14	3	1	0	0	0	6	3	0	70.1	1	7	0	1	1.000	6	2	0	0	.33	1
Cobb,Alex, TB	R	.125	8	1	0	1	0	.091	11	1	1	0	0	1	0	2	0	166.1	7	22	4	3	.879	14	2	0	2	.14	1
Coke,Phil, Det	L	-	0	0	0	0	0	.000	3	0	0	0	0	0	0	3	0	58.0	1	5	0	0	1.000	7	2	1	0	.29	-2
Cole,Gerrit, Pit	R	.174	46	8	1	2	4	.188	80	15	0	0	1	7	3	31	5	138.0	7	24	2	1	.939	26	5	0	1	.19	0
Coleman,Casey, KC	R	-	0	0	0	0	0	.146	48	7	2	1	0	2	1	18	6	12.0	2	1	0	1	1.000	1	1	0	0	1.00	0
Coleman,Louis, KC	R	-	0	0	0	0	0	.000	1	0	0	0	0	0	0	1	0	34.0	1	6	0	0	1.000	2	2	0	0	1.00	1
Collins,Tim, KC	L	-	0	0	0	0	0	.000	1	0	0	0	0	0	0	1	0	21.0	1	5	0	0	1.000	2	0	0	0	.00	1
Collmenter,Josh, Ari	R	.111	54	6	0	2	1	.116	121	14	2	0	0	5	6	41	11	179.1	13	23	0	1	1.000	15	6	0	0	.40	-1
Colome,Alex, TB	R	-	0	0	0	0	0	.000	2	0	0	0	0	0	0	1	0	23.2	0	2	0	0	1.000	1	0	0	0	.00	-2
Colon,Bartolo, NYM	R	.032	62	2	0	0	7	.076	158	12	1	0	0	5	0	89	13	202.1	11	27	5	2	.884	5	2	1	0	.40	2
Contreras,Carlos, Cin	R	.000	1	0	0	0	0	.000	1	0	0	0	0	0	0	1	0	19.1	2	0	0	0	1.000	4	0	0	0	.00	0
Cook,Ryan, Oak	R	-	0	0	0	0	0	-	0	0	0	0	0	0	0	0	0	50.0	3	8	0	1	1.000	5	2	2	0	.40	2
Corcino,Daniel, Cin	R	.333	3	1	0	0	2	.333	3	1	0	0	0	0	0	0	2	18.2	4	3	0	0	1.000	1	1	0	0	1.00	1
Cordier,Erik, SF	R	-	0	0	0	0	0	-	0	0	0	0	0	0	0	0	0	6.0	0	0	0	0	-	1	1	0	0	1.00	0
Correia,Kevin, Min-LAD	R	.273	11	3	0	1	0	.119	294	35	6	0	0	13	11	124	44	154.0	12	19	4	1	.886	9	2	0	0	.22	-1
Cosart,Jarred, Hou-Mia	R	.190	21	4	0	0	3	.190	21	4	0	0	0	0	0	7	3	180.1	20	29	0	7	1.000	10	4	0	0	.40	0
Cotts,Neal, Tex	L	-	0	0	0	0	0	.500	2	1	1	0	0	0	0	0	0	66.2	3	7	0	0	1.000	4	1	1	0	.25	1
Coulombe,Daniel, LAD	L	-	0	0	0	0	0	-	0	0	0	0	0	0	0	0	0	4.1	0	0	0	0	-	0	0	0	0	-	0
Crockett,Kyle, Cle	L	-	0	0	0	0	0	-	0	0	0	0	0	0	0	0	0	30.0	2	1	0	0	1.000	1	0	0	0	.00	-2
Crow,Aaron, KC	R	-	0	0	0	0	0	-	0	0	0	0	0	0	0	0	0	59.0	6	6	0	0	1.000	5	1	0	1	.20	0
Cueto,Johnny, Cin	R	.132	68	9	0	3	12	.101	347	35	1	0	0	10	10	114	64	243.2	21	39	3	0	.952	12	6	2	2	.50	6
Cumpton,Brandon, Pit	R	.118	17	2	0	1	2	.077	26	2	0	0	0	1	2	11	4	70.0	4	8	0	1	1.000	8	2	1	0	.25	1
Daley,Matt, NYY	R	-	0	0	0	0	0	-	0	0	0	0	0	0	0	0	0	14.1	1	3	0	0	1.000	0	0	0	0	-	1
Danks,John, CWS	L	.333	3	1	0	0	0	.083	24	2	0	0	0	0	1	8	3	193.2	4	24	1	0	.966	15	3	1	1	.20	-1

369

Pitchers Hitting, Fielding and Holding Runners

Pitcher	T	2014 Hitting						Career Hitting										2014 Fielding and Holding Runners											
		Avg	AB	H	HR	RBI	SH	Avg	AB	H	2B	3B	HR	RBI	BB	SO	SH	Inn	PO	A	E	DP	Pct	SBA	CS	PCS	PPO	CS%	RS
Darnell,Logan, Min	L	-	0	0	0	0	0	-	0	0	0	0	0	0	0	0	0	24.0	1	2	1	0	.750	0	0	0	0	-	0
Darvish,Yu, Tex	R	.200	5	1	0	0	0	.182	11	2	1	0	0	0	5	0	0	144.1	6	16	0	1	1.000	10	0	0	0	.00	2
Davis,Wade, KC	R	-	0	0	0	0	0	.250	8	2	0	0	0	0	4	3	72.0	4	3	1	0	.875	5	1	0	0	.20	-1
De Fratus,Justin, Phi	R	.000	1	0	0	0	0	.000	1	0	0	0	0	0	0	1	0	52.2	1	2	2	0	.600	6	0	0	0	.00	-2
De La Rosa,Dane, LAA	R	-	0	0	0	0	0	-	0	0	0	0	0	0	0	0	0	2.1	0	4	0	0	1.000	0	0	0	0	-	0
De La Rosa,Eury, Ari	L	.000	2	0	0	0	1	.000	3	0	0	0	0	0	0	2	1	36.2	0	6	0	1	1.000	0	0	0	0	-	0
De La Rosa,Jorge, Col	L	.150	60	9	0	1	6	.130	292	38	4	0	0	18	4	128	26	184.1	4	25	2	1	.935	17	3	2	0	.18	-1
De La Rosa,Rubby, Bos	R	.000	2	0	0	0	0	.188	16	3	0	0	0	0	1	1	0	101.2	12	11	1	1	.958	7	3	0	0	.43	1
De Leon,Jorge, Hou	R	-	0	0	0	0	0	-	0	0	0	0	0	0	0	0	0	7.1	0	1	0	0	1.000	2	1	0	0	.50	0
Deduno,Samuel, Min-Hou	R	.200	5	1	0	0	0	.167	6	1	1	0	0	0	0	5	1	100.2	14	13	3	2	.900	14	1	0	0	.07	-4
deGrom,Jacob, NYM	R	.217	46	10	0	2	6	.217	46	10	2	0	0	2	1	13	6	140.1	6	20	0	4	1.000	12	4	0	0	.33	-1
Delabar,Steve, Tor	R	-	0	0	0	0	0	-	0	0	0	0	0	0	0	0	0	25.2	0	4	0	0	1.000	3	1	0	0	.33	0
Delgado,Randall, Ari	R	.111	9	1	0	0	2	.184	76	14	0	0	0	2	1	32	10	77.2	4	11	1	0	.938	5	0	0	0	.00	-2
Dennick,Ryan, Cin	R	-	0	0	0	0	0	-	0	0	0	0	0	0	0	0	0	4.2	0	1	0	0	1.000	0	0	0	0	-	0
DeSclafani,Anthony, Mia	R	.100	10	1	0	2	0	.100	10	1	0	0	0	2	1	3	0	33.0	1	2	0	0	1.000	6	0	0	0	.00	-2
Despaigne,Odrisamer, SD	R	.000	24	0	0	0	3	.000	24	0	0	0	0	0	1	10	3	96.1	7	17	3	0	.889	15	4	1	0	.27	0
Detwiler,Ross, Was	L	.000	2	0	0	0	1	.061	114	7	0	0	0	3	3	58	9	63.0	4	10	0	1	1.000	5	2	1	0	.40	-3
Diaz,Jairo, LAA	R	-	0	0	0	0	0	-	0	0	0	0	0	0	0	0	0	5.2	0	0	0	0	-	1	0	0	0	.00	0
Diaz,Jumbo, Cin	R	-	0	0	0	0	0	-	0	0	0	0	0	0	0	0	0	34.2	1	1	0	0	1.000	1	0	0	0	.00	0
Dickey,R.A., Tor	R	.000	9	0	0	0	0	.178	202	36	3	0	0	11	4	35	26	215.2	17	23	2	4	.952	5	2	1	1	.40	5
Diekman,Jake, Phi	L	-	0	0	0	0	0	-	0	0	0	0	0	0	0	0	0	71.0	3	9	0	0	1.000	8	3	1	0	.38	-3
Dominguez,Jose, LAD	R	.000	1	0	0	0	0	.000	2	0	0	0	0	0	0	2	0	6.1	1	1	0	0	1.000	1	0	0	0	-	0
Doolittle,Sean, Oak	L	.000	1	0	0	0	0	.000	1	0	0	0	0	0	0	0	0	62.2	1	4	0	0	1.000	7	1	0	0	.14	-1
Doubront,Felix, Bos-ChC	L	.143	7	1	0	0	0	.091	11	1	0	0	0	1	6	2	79.2	5	9	1	1	.933	11	1	1	0	.09	-1
Downs,Darin, Hou	L	-	0	0	0	0	0	-	0	0	0	0	0	0	0	0	0	34.2	2	5	0	0	1.000	5	1	1	0	.20	0
Downs,Scott, CWS-KC	L	-	0	0	0	0	0	.067	45	3	0	0	0	1	3	17	10	38.0	2	4	1	0	.857	4	2	0	1	.50	0
Drabek,Kyle, Tor	R	-	0	0	0	0	0	.000	2	0	0	0	0	0	0	1	0	3.0	0	0	0	0	-	0	0	0	0	-	0
Duensing,Brian, Min	L	-	0	0	0	0	0	.000	6	0	0	0	0	0	0	4	0	54.1	1	8	0	1	1.000	4	2	2	0	.50	1
Duffy,Danny, KC	L	.000	6	0	0	0	1	.000	9	0	0	0	0	0	0	5	1	149.1	4	12	5	0	.762	8	3	1	5	.38	-1
Duke,Zach, Mil	L	.000	1	0	0	0	1	.180	317	57	7	0	2	23	12	117	43	58.2	2	10	0	1	1.000	2	1	0	0	.50	2
Dunn,Mike, Mia	L	-	0	0	0	0	0	.000	4	0	0	0	0	0	0	1	0	57.0	2	6	1	0	.889	3	0	0	0	.00	-1
Dunning,Jake, SF	R	-	0	0	0	0	0	-	0	0	0	0	0	0	0	0	0	0.2	0	0	0	0	-	0	0	0	0	-	0
Dyson,Sam, Mia	R	.000	1	0	0	0	0	.000	2	0	0	0	0	0	0	0	0	42.0	7	4	2	0	.846	7	1	0	0	.14	0
Edgin,Josh, NYM	L	.000	1	0	0	0	0	.000	1	0	0	0	0	0	0	1	0	27.1	1	1	1	0	.667	1	0	0	0	.00	-1
Edwards,Jon, Tex	R	-	0	0	0	0	0	-	0	0	0	0	0	0	0	0	0	8.1	0	1	0	0	1.000	2	0	0	0	.00	0
Elbert,Scott, LAD	L	-	0	0	0	0	0	.167	6	1	0	0	1	0	2	0	4.1	1	0	0	0	1.000	0	0	0	0	-	-1
Elias,Roenis, Sea	L	.000	4	0	0	0	0	.000	4	0	0	0	0	0	0	1	0	163.2	2	22	0	2	1.000	5	2	1	0	.40	2
Eovaldi,Nathan, Mia	R	.089	56	5	0	0	7	.085	130	11	0	0	0	1	4	82	13	199.2	21	30	1	2	.981	5	4	2	0	.80	4
Erlin,Robbie, SD	L	.111	18	2	0	1	0	.088	34	3	0	0	0	2	2	11	2	61.1	3	5	0	0	1.000	2	0	0	0	.00	-1
Escobar,Edwin, Bos	L	-	0	0	0	0	0	-	0	0	0	0	0	0	0	0	0	2.0	0	0	0	0	-	0	0	0	0	-	0
Estrada,Marco, Mil	R	.094	32	3	0	2	5	.143	119	17	4	0	0	7	7	55	20	150.2	6	21	0	0	1.000	22	7	0	1	.32	3
Eveland,Dana, NYM	L	-	0	0	0	0	0	.045	22	1	0	0	0	0	2	13	5	27.1	1	2	0	0	1.000	2	0	0	0	.00	0
Familia,Jeurys, NYM	R	.667	3	2	0	1	0	.500	4	2	0	0	0	1	0	1	0	77.1	5	10	3	0	.833	7	0	0	0	.00	-3
Farmer,Buck, Det	R	-	0	0	0	0	0	-	0	0	0	0	0	0	0	0	0	9.1	0	0	0	0	-	0	0	0	0	-	0
Farnsworth,Kyle, NYM-Hou	R	-	0	0	0	0	0	.074	54	4	1	0	0	3	2	18	8	28.2	0	2	0	1	1.000	3	1	0	0	.33	1
Farquhar,Danny, Sea	R	-	0	0	0	0	0	-	0	0	0	0	0	0	0	0	0	71.0	6	11	0	1	1.000	4	3	0	1	.75	1
Feierabend,Ryan, Tex	L	-	0	0	0	0	0	-	0	0	0	0	0	0	0	0	0	7.1	2	1	1	0	.750	0	0	0	1	-	-1
Feldman,Scott, Hou	R	.000	2	0	0	0	0	.158	57	9	3	0	1	9	0	22	5	180.1	18	18	0	1	1.000	42	7	0	0	.17	-7
Feliz,Neftali, Tex	R	-	0	0	0	0	0	.000	2	0	0	0	0	0	0	0	0	31.2	4	2	0	1	1.000	2	1	0	0	.50	0
Fernandez,Jose, Mia	R	.125	16	2	0	1	2	.197	66	13	1	1	1	6	0	26	9	51.2	4	3	0	0	1.000	3	2	0	0	.67	2
Fields,Josh, Hou	R	-	0	0	0	0	0	-	0	0	0	0	0	0	0	0	0	54.2	2	0	0	0	1.000	7	0	0	0	.00	-3
Fien,Casey, Min	R	-	0	0	0	0	0	-	0	0	0	0	0	0	0	0	0	63.1	0	9	0	1	1.000	1	0	0	0	.00	0
Fiers,Mike, Mil	R	.053	19	1	0	0	7	.073	55	4	0	0	0	2	0	32	14	71.2	5	9	1	1	.933	7	2	0	1	.29	1
Fife,Stephen, LAD	R	.000	3	0	0	0	0	.111	27	3	1	0	0	0	1	15	1	6.0	2	2	0	0	1.000	0	0	0	0	-	0
Figaro,Alfredo, Mil	R	.000	1	0	0	0	0	.200	15	3	0	0	0	2	0	7	0	8.2	1	1	0	0	1.000	0	0	0	0	.00	0
Figueroa,Pedro, Tex	L	-	0	0	0	0	0	-	0	0	0	0	0	0	0	0	0	9.0	1	1	0	0	1.000	0	0	0	0	-	0
Finnegan,Brandon, KC	L	-	0	0	0	0	0	-	0	0	0	0	0	0	0	0	0	7.0	0	1	0	0	1.000	0	0	0	0	-	0
Fister,Doug, Was	R	.077	52	4	0	0	9	.119	67	8	2	0	0	2	1	26	12	164.0	15	21	1	0	.973	1	1	1	0	1.00	2
Flande,Yohan, Col	L	.083	12	1	0	1	4	.083	12	1	0	0	0	1	1	6	4	59.0	6	8	0	0	1.000	3	0	0	0	-	-2
Floyd,Gavin, Atl	R	.111	18	2	0	0	0	.068	74	5	0	0	0	0	2	43	4	54.1	3	9	1	1	.923	3	0	0	0	.00	-1
Flynn,Brian, Mia	L	.000	2	0	0	0	0	.286	7	2	0	0	0	0	0	2	1	7.0	1	0	0	0	1.000	1	0	0	0	.00	1
Foltynewicz,Mike, Hou	R	-	0	0	0	0	0	-	0	0	0	0	0	0	0	0	0	18.2	2	0	0	0	1.000	1	0	0	0	.00	-1
Fornataro,Eric, StL	R	-	0	0	0	0	0	-	0	0	0	0	0	0	0	0	0	9.2	1	1	1	0	.667	0	0	0	0	-	-2
Francis,Jeff, Cin-Oak-NYY	L	.000	2	0	0	0	0	.116	303	35	7	0	0	16	25	102	53	20.0	1	0	0	0	1.000	0	0	0	0	-	-1
Francisco,Frank, CWS	R	-	0	0	0	0	0	-	0	0	0	0	0	0	0	0	0	3.2	0	0	0	0	-	4	0	0	0	.00	-1
Frasor,Jason, Tex-KC	R	-	0	0	0	0	0	-	0	0	0	0	0	0	0	0	0	47.1	1	3	0	2	1.000	9	2	0	0	.22	-1
Freeman,Sam, StL	L	-	0	0	0	0	0	-	0	0	0	0	0	0	0	0	0	38.0	4	9	0	0	1.000	2	1	0	0	.50	3
Frias,Carlos, LAD	R	.000	7	0	0	0	0	.000	7	0	0	0	0	0	0	4	0	32.1	2	3	0	0	1.000	1	1	0	0	1.00	-1
Friedrich,Christian, Col	L	.200	5	1	0	0	0	.100	30	3	1	0	0	3	17	1	24.1	3	3	1	0	.857	0	0	0	0	-	0
Frieri,Ernesto, LAA-Pit	R	-	0	0	0	0	0	.000	1	0	0	0	0	0	0	1	0	41.2	1	3	0	0	1.000	5	0	0	0	-	-1

Pitchers Hitting, Fielding and Holding Runners

Pitcher	T	2014 Hitting						Career Hitting										2014 Fielding and Holding Runners											
		Avg	AB	H	HR	RBI	SH	Avg	AB	H	2B	3B	HR	RBI	BB	SO	SH	Inn	PO	A	E	DP	Pct	SBA	CS	PCS	PPO	CS%	RS
Fujikawa,Kyuji, ChC	R	-	0	0	0	0	0	-	0	0	0	0	0	0	0	0	0	13.0	0	1	0	0	1.000	0	0	0	0	-	-1
Furbush,Charlie, Sea	L	-	0	0	0	0	0	-	0	0	0	0	0	0	0	0	0	42.1	0	3	0	0	1.000	2	0	0	0	.00	-3
Gallardo,Yovani, Mil	R	.111	54	6	0	1	5	.195	416	81	20	0	12	42	12	147	35	192.1	14	26	0	2	1.000	13	4	2	2	.31	-1
Garces,Frank, SD	L	-	0	0	0	0	0	-	0	0	0	0	0	0	0	0	0	9.0	0	1	0	0	1.000	0	0	0	0	-	0
Garcia,Jaime, StL	L	.250	12	3	0	0	3	.153	190	29	2	1	2	11	7	59	16	43.2	1	7	0	1	1.000	0	0	0	0	-	2
Garcia,Luis, Phi	R	-	0	0	0	0	0	.000	2	0	0	0	0	0	0	1	0	14.0	2	2	0	0	1.000	0	0	0	0	-	0
Garcia,Yimi, LAD	R	.000	1	0	0	0	0	.000	1	0	0	0	0	0	0	0	0	10.0	3	1	0	0	1.000	1	0	0	0	.00	0
Garza,Matt, Mil	R	.061	49	3	0	0	7	.087	172	15	3	0	0	3	3	104	20	163.1	11	15	3	0	.897	9	3	2	0	.33	-1
Gausman,Kevin, Bal	R	.000	3	0	0	0	0	.000	4	0	0	0	0	0	0	3	0	113.1	5	11	0	2	1.000	8	3	0	1	.38	0
Gee,Dillon, NYM	R	.026	38	1	0	1	3	.109	183	20	3	1	0	11	9	84	24	137.1	14	24	0	1	1.000	10	3	0	0	.30	2
Geltz,Steve, TB	R	-	0	0	0	0	0	-	0	0	0	0	0	0	0	0	0	8.1	0	0	1	0	.000	1	1	0	0	1.00	0
Germano,Justin, Tex	R	-	0	0	0	0	0	.149	67	10	2	0	0	3	4	31	17	5.1	0	0	0	0	-	0	0	0	0	-	0
Germen,Gonzalez, NYM	R	.000	1	0	0	0	0	.000	2	0	0	0	0	0	0	2	0	30.1	2	2	0	1	1.000	1	0	0	0	.00	0
Gibson,Kyle, Min	R	.250	4	1	0	0	0	.250	4	1	0	0	0	0	0	2	0	179.1	30	27	0	3	1.000	11	4	0	2	.36	4
Giles,Ken, Phi	R	-	0	0	0	0	0	-	0	0	0	0	0	0	0	0	0	45.2	1	3	0	1	1.000	3	3	0	1	1.00	0
Goeddel,Erik, NYM	R	-	0	0	0	0	0	-	0	0	0	0	0	0	0	0	0	6.2	0	0	0	0	-	0	0	0	0	-	0
Gomes,Brandon, TB	R	-	0	0	0	0	0	.000	1	0	0	0	0	1	1	1	0	34.0	0	3	0	0	1.000	1	0	0	1	.00	0
Gomez,Jeanmar, Pit	R	1.000	1	1	0	0	1	.167	18	3	0	0	0	0	0	10	1	62.0	5	8	1	0	.929	10	4	0	0	.40	0
Gonzales,Marco, StL	L	.300	10	3	0	0	2	.300	10	3	2	0	0	0	0	2	0	34.2	1	3	0	1	1.000	2	2	1	0	1.00	1
Gonzalez,Gio, Was	L	.087	46	4	1	2	6	.087	173	15	3	0	3	7	2	71	25	158.2	6	19	1	1	.962	14	6	3	0	.43	-1
Gonzalez,Miguel, Bal	R	.000	5	0	0	0	0	.000	8	0	0	0	0	0	0	3	1	159.0	7	13	1	0	.952	14	2	0	1	.14	-3
Gonzalez,Miguel, Phi	R	-	0	0	0	0	0	-	0	0	0	0	0	0	0	0	0	5.1	0	1	0	0	1.000	1	0	0	0	.00	0
Gorzelanny,Tom, Mil	L	.000	1	0	0	0	0	.092	217	20	0	0	0	13	9	102	24	21.0	2	3	1	0	.833	2	0	0	0	.00	0
Graveman,Kendall, Tor	R	-	0	0	0	0	0	-	0	0	0	0	0	0	0	0	0	4.2	1	1	0	0	1.000	0	0	0	0	-	0
Gray,Sonny, Oak	R	.000	2	0	0	0	2	.000	2	0	0	0	0	0	0	1	2	219.0	18	41	3	3	.952	10	3	0	1	.30	3
Greene,Shane, NYY	R	-	0	0	0	0	0	-	0	0	0	0	0	0	0	0	0	78.2	5	4	4	0	.692	8	3	0	0	.38	-3
Greenwood,Nick, StL	L	.000	5	0	0	0	1	.000	5	0	0	0	0	0	0	1	1	36.0	6	11	0	1	1.000	1	0	0	0	.00	3
Gregerson,Luke, Oak	R	-	0	0	0	0	0	.000	6	0	0	0	0	0	0	1	1	72.1	4	8	0	0	1.000	10	0	0	0	.00	-1
Gregg,Kevin, Mia	R	-	0	0	0	0	0	.000	6	0	0	0	0	0	0	5	0	9.0	0	3	0	0	-	3	0	0	0	.00	-1
Greinke,Zack, LAD	R	.200	60	12	1	3	4	.219	224	49	14	0	4	11	15	44	23	202.1	28	30	1	8	.983	8	2	0	0	.25	5
Grilli,Jason, Pit-LAA	R	-	0	0	0	0	0	.200	15	3	0	0	1	3	0	3	3	54.0	2	7	0	2	1.000	2	0	0	1	.00	1
Grimm,Justin, ChC	R	.000	2	0	0	0	0	.000	3	0	0	0	0	0	0	2	0	69.0	4	6	0	0	1.000	6	0	0	0	.00	-1
Grube,Jarrett, LAA	R	-	0	0	0	0	0	-	0	0	0	0	0	0	0	0	0	0.2	0	0	0	0	-	0	0	0	0	-	0
Guerra,Javy, CWS	R	-	0	0	0	0	0	-	0	0	0	0	0	0	0	1	0	46.1	6	3	1	0	.900	2	0	0	0	.00	-2
Guerrier,Matt, Min	R	-	0	0	0	0	0	.000	3	0	0	0	0	0	1	1	2	28.0	3	3	0	0	1.000	2	0	0	0	.00	0
Guilmet,Preston, Bal	R	-	0	0	0	0	0	-	0	0	0	0	0	0	0	0	0	10.2	0	0	0	0	-	1	0	0	0	.00	0
Guthrie,Jeremy, KC	R	.000	5	0	0	0	1	.089	56	5	2	0	0	1	1	27	5	202.2	12	24	6	1	.857	14	4	1	1	.29	-1
Gutierrez,Juan, SF	R	.000	1	0	0	0	0	.000	7	0	0	0	0	0	0	5	1	63.2	5	4	0	0	1.000	8	1	0	0	.13	-3
Hagadone,Nick, Cle	L	-	0	0	0	0	0	-	0	0	0	0	0	0	0	0	0	23.1	0	3	0	0	1.000	3	1	1	0	.33	0
Hagens,Bradin, Ari	R	-	0	0	0	0	0	-	0	0	0	0	0	0	0	0	0	2.2	0	1	0	0	1.000	0	0	0	0	-	0
Hahn,Jesse, SD	R	.091	22	2	0	1	2	.091	22	2	0	0	0	1	0	12	2	73.1	0	15	0	0	1.000	4	1	0	1	.25	0
Hale,David, Atl	R	.059	17	1	0	1	1	.048	21	1	0	0	0	1	0	11	1	87.1	7	14	0	2	1.000	16	3	0	0	.19	-1
Hamels,Cole, Phi	L	.210	62	13	0	0	7	.174	568	99	14	2	1	28	17	240	58	204.2	6	26	0	1	1.000	28	9	5	1	.32	2
Hammel,Jason, ChC-Oak	R	.135	37	5	0	3	5	.123	203	25	4	0	1	10	5	88	31	176.1	17	12	2	1	.935	15	3	0	2	.20	-1
Hand,Brad, Mia	L	.037	27	1	0	1	4	.061	49	3	0	0	2	0	16	7	111.0	8	24	0	1	1.000	8	2	0	0	.25	4
Happ,J.A., Tor	L	.000	4	0	0	0	0	.090	156	14	2	0	1	6	8	66	24	158.0	0	19	1	0	.950	10	3	1	0	.30	4
Harang,Aaron, Atl	R	.082	61	5	0	1	9	.092	622	57	7	0	1	21	4	276	60	204.1	8	27	0	1	1.000	24	5	0	2	.21	-1
Hardy,Blaine, Det	L	-	0	0	0	0	0	-	0	0	0	0	0	0	0	0	0	39.0	5	9	0	1	1.000	0	0	0	1	-	2
Haren,Dan, LAD	R	.185	54	10	0	5	3	.211	365	77	25	0	2	34	12	105	31	186.0	14	23	1	2	.974	20	5	0	0	.25	0
Harrell,Lucas, Hou	R	-	0	0	0	0	0	.152	66	10	0	0	0	1	3	37	13	12.1	1	1	0	0	1.000	1	0	0	0	.00	0
Harris,Will, Ari	R	-	0	0	0	0	0	-	0	0	0	0	0	0	0	0	0	29.0	0	2	0	0	1.000	1	1	0	0	1.00	0
Harrison,Matt, Tex	L	-	0	0	0	0	0	.000	16	0	0	0	0	0	1	11	2	17.1	0	1	0	0	1.000	0	0	0	0	-	-1
Hatcher,Chris, Mia	R	.000	1	0	0	0	0	.000	8	0	0	0	0	2	6	0	56.0	6	4	0	1	1.000	1	1	0	1	1.00	0
Hawkins,LaTroy, Col	R	.000	1	0	0	0	0	.000	7	0	0	0	0	0	6	1	54.1	5	5	1	0	.909	2	0	0	0	.00	-1
Heaney,Andrew, Mia	L	.125	8	1	0	0	1	.125	8	1	0	0	0	0	2	1	29.1	7	3	0	1	1.000	3	0	0	0	.00	0
Hellickson,Jeremy, TB	R	-	0	0	0	0	0	.167	6	1	0	0	0	0	3	1	63.2	3	7	1	2	.909	6	1	0	0	.17	-1
Hembree,Heath, Bos	R	-	0	0	0	0	0	-	0	0	0	0	0	0	0	0	0	10.0	1	0	0	0	1.000	3	2	0	0	.67	0
Henderson,Jim, Mil	R	-	0	0	0	0	0	-	0	0	0	0	0	0	0	0	0	11.1	1	3	0	1	1.000	2	0	0	0	.00	0
Hendricks,Kyle, ChC	R	.125	24	3	0	1	3	.125	24	3	0	0	0	1	3	11	3	80.1	4	16	0	3	1.000	7	3	0	0	.43	1
Hendriks,Liam, Tor-KC	R	-	0	0	0	0	0	.000	2	0	0	0	0	0	0	1	0	32.2	3	0	0	0	1.000	3	0	0	0	.00	0
Hernandez,Felix, Sea	R	.000	2	0	0	0	1	.118	34	4	1	0	1	7	2	16	5	236.0	11	25	1	2	.973	25	5	1	0	.20	-2
Hernandez,Pedro, Col	L	.000	2	0	0	0	0	.000	2	0	0	0	0	0	0	2	0	5.2	0	1	0	0	1.000	0	0	0	0	-	0
Hernandez,Roberto, Phi-LAD	R	.082	49	4	0	2	9	.060	67	4	0	0	0	2	0	35	11	164.2	11	23	0	2	1.000	27	4	2	0	.15	-1
Herrera,Kelvin, KC	R	-	0	0	0	0	0	-	0	0	0	0	0	0	0	0	0	70.0	5	8	0	0	1.000	8	2	0	0	.25	0
Herrera,Yoslan, LAA	R	-	0	0	0	0	0	.143	7	1	0	0	0	0	0	0	0	16.2	5	0	0	0	1.000	4	0	0	1	-	1
Heston,Chris, SF	R	.000	1	0	0	0	0	.000	1	0	0	0	0	0	0	1	0	5.1	0	0	0	0	-	0	0	0	0	-	0
Hill,Rich, LAA-NYY	L	-	0	0	0	0	0	.123	114	14	3	0	0	6	2	51	6	5.1	0	0	0	0	-	0	0	0	0	.00	0
Hill,Taylor, Was	R	.333	3	1	0	0	0	.333	3	1	0	0	0	0	0	0	0	9.0	0	3	0	0	1.000	0	0	0	0	-	-1
Holdzkom,John, Pit	R	-	0	0	0	0	0	-	0	0	0	0	0	0	0	0	0	9.0	0	0	0	0	-	1	1	0	0	1.00	0
Holland,Derek, Tex	L	-	0	0	0	0	0	.000	12	0	0	0	0	0	2	6	2	37.0	1	2	1	0	.750	3	2	0	0	.67	-2

Pitchers Hitting, Fielding and Holding Runners

Pitcher	T	2014 Hitting						Career Hitting										2014 Fielding and Holding Runners											
		Avg	AB	H	HR	RBI	SH	Avg	AB	H	2B	3B	HR	RBI	BB	SO	SH	Inn	PO	A	E	DP	Pct	SBA	CS	PCS	PPO	CS%	RS
Holland,Greg, KC	R	-	0	0	0	0	0		0	0	0	0	0	0	0	0	0	62.1	4	5	0	0	1.000	5	2	0	0	.40	-1
Hollands,Mario, Phi	L	-	0	0	0	0	0		0	0	0	0	0	0	0	0	0	47.0	5	3	0	1	1.000	6	2	0	0	.33	-2
Holmberg,David, Cin	L	.000	5	0	0	0	2	.000	6	0	0	0	0	0	0	3	2	30.0	2	5	0	1	1.000	2	1	0	0	.50	-1
Hoover,J.J., Cin	R	-	0	0	0	0	0		0	0	0	0	0	0	1	0	0	62.2	5	2	0	0	1.000	1	1	0	0	1.00	-2
House,T.J., Cle	L	.000	2	0	0	0	0	.000	2	0	0	0	0	0	0	2	0	102.0	4	14	2	1	.900	8	2	2	0	.25	-1
Howell,J.P., LAD	L	-	0	0	0	0	0	.182	11	2	0	0	0	1	0	5	0	49.0	5	15	0	1	1.000	7	3	2	1	.43	2
Hudson,Daniel, Ari	R	-	0	0	0	0	0	.229	105	24	5	0	1	21	5	34	14	2.2	0	0	0	0	-	0	0	0	0	-	0
Hudson,Tim, SF	R	.038	53	2	0	1	6	.158	575	91	17	1	3	41	25	179	64	189.1	13	21	2	1	.944	18	3	1	0	.17	-2
Huff,David, SF-NYY	L	.333	3	1	0	0	0	.143	7	1	0	0	0	0	0	4	2	59.0	5	10	1	0	.938	6	2	2	0	.33	0
Hughes,Jared, Pit	R	.000	2	0	0	0	0	.000	5	0	0	0	0	0	0	4	0	64.1	5	18	1	2	.958	10	6	2	1	.60	3
Hughes,Phil, Min	R	.000	6	0	0	0	0	.000	12	0	0	0	0	0	0	6	2	209.2	10	8	1	2	.947	15	1	0	0	.07	-8
Hunter,Tommy, Bal	R	-	0	0	0	0	0	.000	3	0	0	0	0	0	0	2	0	60.2	5	7	2	1	.857	5	1	0	0	.20	0
Hutchison,Drew, Tor	R	.500	4	2	0	0	0	.333	6	2	0	0	0	0	0	2	0	184.2	7	13	1	2	.952	25	3	0	0	.12	-1
Irwin,Phil, Tex	R	-	0	0	0	0	0	.000	1	0	0	0	0	0	0	1	0	4.0	0	0	0	0	-	1	0	0	0	.00	0
Iwakuma,Hisashi, Sea	R	.000	4	0	0	0	1	.000	7	0	0	0	0	0	0	5	1	179.0	17	24	1	1	.976	8	8	0	0	1.00	2
Jackson,Edwin, ChC	R	.175	40	7	0	0	4	.170	247	42	3	0	2	11	11	100	22	140.2	12	20	1	1	.970	19	5	0	4	.26	4
Jaime,Juan, Atl	R	-	0	0	0	0	0		0	0	0	0	0	0	0	0	0	12.1	0	1	0	0	1.000	1	0	0	0	.00	0
Jansen,Kenley, LAD	R	.000	1	0	0	0	0	.333	3	1	0	0	0	0	1	1	0	65.1	6	2	1	1	.889	8	2	0	0	.25	-1
Janssen,Casey, Tor	R	-	0	0	0	0	0	.000	3	0	0	0	0	0	0	2	1	45.2	3	5	1	1	.889	3	0	0	0	.00	-1
Jeffress,Jeremy, Tor-Mil	R	-	0	0	0	0	0		0	0	0	0	0	0	0	0	0	32.0	0	5	1	1	.833	1	0	0	0	-	1
Jenkins,Chad, Tor	R	-	0	0	0	0	0	.000	2	0	0	0	0	0	0	2	0	31.2	1	9	0	2	1.000	2	1	0	0	.50	2
Jennings,Dan, Mia	L	-	0	0	0	0	0	.000	1	0	0	0	0	0	0	0	0	40.1	1	8	1	0	.900	5	1	0	0	.20	-2
Jepsen,Kevin, LAA	R	-	0	0	0	0	0		0	0	0	0	0	0	0	0	0	65.0	3	11	1	1	.933	5	1	0	0	.20	3
Jimenez,Cesar, Phi	L	.000	1	0	0	0	0	.000	1	0	0	0	0	0	0	1	0	16.0	1	1	0	0	.500	2	2	0	0	1.00	0
Jimenez,Ubaldo, Bal	R	.000	1	0	0	0	0	.113	274	31	0	0	0	9	17	94	33	125.1	11	9	0	3	1.000	25	6	0	0	.24	0
Johnson,Erik, CWS	R	.000	3	0	0	0	0	.000	3	0	0	0	0	0	0	0	0	23.2	3	2	0	0	1.000	7	3	0	0	.43	1
Johnson,Jim, Oak-Det	R	.000	1	0	0	0	0	.000	1	0	0	0	0	0	0	1	0	53.1	4	6	1	0	.909	12	0	0	0	.00	-3
Johnson,Kris, Min	L	.000	1	0	0	0	0	.000	3	0	0	0	0	0	0	2	1	13.1	0	4	0	0	1.000	2	1	1	0	.50	0
Jokisch,Eric, ChC	L	.000	3	0	0	0	2	.000	3	0	0	0	0	0	0	0	2	14.1	1	3	0	0	1.000	3	1	1	0	.33	0
Jones,Nate, CWS	R	-	0	0	0	0	0		0	0	0	0	0	0	0	0	0	0.0	0	0	0	0	-	0	0	0	0	-	0
Jordan,Taylor, Was	R	.125	8	1	0	0	0	.136	22	3	0	0	0	0	0	7	4	25.2	3	3	0	0	1.000	1	1	0	0	1.00	0
Joseph,Donnie, KC	L	-	0	0	0	0	0		0	0	0	0	0	0	0	0	0	0.2	0	0	0	0	-	0	0	0	0	-	0
Jurrjens,Jair, Col	R	.000	1	0	0	0	1	.112	223	25	3	1	0	7	18	75	29	9.1	0	0	1	0	.000	3	0	0	0	.00	-1
Kahnle,Tommy, Col	R	.000	3	0	0	0	0	.000	3	0	0	0	0	0	0	1	1	68.2	8	5	2	1	.867	11	1	0	0	.09	-2
Karns,Nate, TB	R	-	0	0	0	0	0	.000	3	0	0	0	0	0	0	1	2	12.0	0	0	0	0	-	1	0	0	0	.00	0
Kazmir,Scott, Oak	L	.000	4	0	0	0	0	.091	22	2	0	0	0	1	0	8	1	190.1	2	18	3	1	.870	20	2	1	0	.10	-1
Kelley,Shawn, NYY	R	-	0	0	0	0	0		0	0	0	0	0	0	0	0	0	51.2	6	4	0	1	1.000	1	0	0	0	.00	1
Kelly,Joe, StL-Bos	R	.250	16	4	0	0	1	.171	82	14	4	0	0	4	0	23	8	96.1	5	6	0	0	1.000	8	1	0	0	.13	-2
Kendrick,Kyle, Phi	R	.136	66	9	0	1	4	.133	330	44	7	1	0	7	15	141	41	199.0	18	29	2	1	.959	12	7	1	0	.58	5
Kennedy,Ian, SD	R	.115	52	6	1	5	6	.133	271	36	8	1	1	18	32	129	36	201.0	12	18	0	1	1.000	23	8	1	1	.35	0
Kershaw,Clayton, LAD	L	.175	63	11	0	3	6	.157	401	63	4	1	1	22	18	125	75	198.1	8	31	2	3	.951	9	4	2	2	.44	7
Keuchel,Dallas, Hou	L	.000	3	0	0	0	0	.080	25	2	0	0	0	1	2	14	5	200.0	18	47	1	3	.985	4	3	1	0	.75	10
Kickham,Mike, SF	L	-	0	0	0	0	0	.167	6	1	1	0	0	0	1	0	0	2.0	0	1	0	0	1.000	1	0	0	0	.00	0
Kimbrel,Craig, Atl	R	-	0	0	0	0	0		0	0	0	0	0	0	0	0	0	61.2	4	6	0	0	1.000	6	1	0	0	.17	0
Kintzler,Brandon, Mil	R	-	0	0	0	0	0	.000	1	0	0	0	0	0	0	0	1	58.1	9	13	0	1	1.000	9	3	0	0	.33	3
Kirkman,Michael, Tex	L	-	0	0	0	0	0		0	0	0	0	0	0	0	0	0	5.2	0	0	0	0	-	3	0	0	0	.00	-1
Klein,Phil, Tex	R	-	0	0	0	0	0		0	0	0	0	0	0	0	0	0	19.0	1	1	1	0	.667	4	0	0	0	.00	-1
Kluber,Corey, Cle	R	.200	5	1	0	0	0	.143	7	1	0	0	0	0	1	3	1	235.2	14	17	0	1	1.000	17	9	0	0	.53	0
Knebel,Corey, Det	R	-	0	0	0	0	0		0	0	0	0	0	0	0	0	0	8.2	1	2	0	0	1.000	2	1	0	0	.50	1
Koehler,Tom, Mia	R	.060	50	3	0	0	8	.067	90	6	0	0	0	1	45	10	191.1	22	14	0	2	1.000	19	6	0	0	.32	-1
Kohn,Michael, LAA	R	-	0	0	0	0	0		0	0	0	0	0	0	0	0	0	23.2	1	0	0	0	1.000	3	0	0	0	.00	0
Kontos,George, SF	R	.000	1	0	0	0	1	.000	3	0	0	0	0	0	0	1	2	32.1	1	3	0	0	1.000	7	3	1	0	.43	0
Korecky,Bobby, Tor	R	-	0	0	0	0	0	1.000	1	1	0	0	0	0	0	0	0	3.1	0	0	0	0	-	0	0	0	0	-	-1
Krol,Ian, Det	L	.000	1	0	0	0	0	.000	1	0	0	0	0	0	0	0	0	32.2	4	4	0	1	1.000	1	1	1	0	1.00	0
Kuroda,Hiroki, NYY	R	.000	3	0	0	0	0	.100	209	21	1	0	0	3	13	72	32	199.0	18	16	1	0	.971	6	2	0	1	.33	-1
Lackey,John, Bos-StL	R	.133	15	2	0	0	4	.103	58	6	2	0	0	2	0	19	7	198.0	12	15	3	0	.900	20	3	0	0	.15	-5
LaFromboise,Bobby, Pit	L	-	0	0	0	0	0		0	0	0	0	0	0	0	0	0	3.2	0	0	0	0	-	0	0	0	0	-	0
Lane,Jason, SD	L	.333	3	1	0	0	0	.241	1211	292	64	7	61	189	123	258	4	10.1	0	2	0	0	1.000	0	0	0	0	-	0
Lannan,John, NYM	L	-	0	0	0	0	0	.105	247	26	5	0	1	11	16	111	21	4.0	0	1	0	0	1.000	0	0	0	0	-	0
Latos,Mat, Cin	R	.100	30	3	0	1	1	.119	295	35	6	0	3	13	6	138	33	102.1	10	12	0	1	1.000	9	2	0	0	.22	0
Layne,Tom, Bos	L	-	0	0	0	0	0		0	0	0	0	0	0	0	0	0	19.0	3	2	0	1	1.000	0	0	0	0	-	0
League,Brandon, LAD	R	.000	2	0	0	0	0	.000	2	0	0	0	0	0	1	1	0	63.0	4	9	3	2	.813	7	3	0	0	.43	-3
Leake,Mike, Cin	R	.176	68	12	2	5	5	.234	295	69	13	1	4	15	9	111	32	214.1	26	30	4	1	.933	16	4	0	2	.25	3
LeBlanc,Wade, LAA-NYY	L	-	0	0	0	0	0	.252	111	28	1	0	0	2	3	25	15	29.2	1	3	0	0	1.000	0	0	0	0	-	3
LeCure,Sam, Cin	R	-	0	0	0	0	0	.095	21	2	0	0	0	1	8	2	56.2	3	2	0	0	1.000	4	0	0	0	.25	0
Lee,C.C., Cle	R	-	0	0	0	0	0		0	0	0	0	0	0	0	0	0	28.0	3	4	1	0	.875	4	2	0	0	.38	0
Lee,Cliff, Phi	L	.250	24	6	0	1	1	.175	291	51	7	1	2	19	5	110	24	81.1	4	8	0	0	1.000	6	2	1	0	.33	-1
Leesman,Charlie, CWS	L	-	0	0	0	0	0		0	0	0	0	0	0	0	0	0	2.2	0	0	0	0	-	1	1	0	0	1.00	0
Leone,Dominic, Sea	R	-	0	0	0	0	0		0	0	0	0	0	0	0	0	0	66.1	3	5	0	0	1.000	11	5	0	0	.45	0
Leroux,Chris, NYY	R	-	0	0	0	0	0	.000	2	0	0	0	0	0	0	0	0	2.0	0	0	0	0	-	1	0	0	0	.00	0

Pitchers Hitting, Fielding and Holding Runners

Pitcher	T	2014 Hitting						Career Hitting										2014 Fielding and Holding Runners											
		Avg	AB	H	HR	RBI	SH	Avg	AB	H	2B	3B	HR	RBI	BB	SO	SH	Inn	PO	A	E	DP	Pct	SBA	CS	PCS	PPO	CS%	RS
Lester,Jon, Bos-Oak	L	.000	5	0	0	0	0	.000	36	0	0	0	0	1	1	22	5	219.2	8	16	2	1	.923	21	5	1	0	.24	-3
Lewis,Colby, Tex	R	.400	5	2	0	1	0	.280	25	7	1	0	0	5	0	9	1	170.1	3	10	1	0	.929	26	8	0	0	.31	-4
Lincecum,Tim, SF	R	.068	44	3	0	1	5	.110	453	50	3	2	0	19	32	234	68	155.2	11	12	1	1	.958	28	6	2	0	.21	-2
Lincoln,Brad, Phi	R	-	0	0	0	0	0	.237	38	9	1	0	0	4	1	14	4	2.1	0	0	0	0	-	0	0	0	0	-	0
Lindblom,Josh, Oak	R	-	0	0	0	0	0	.000	1	0	0	0	0	0	0	1	0	4.2	0	0	0	0	-	0	0	0	0	-	0
Lindstrom,Matt, CWS	R	-	0	0	0	0	0	.000	1	0	0	0	0	0	0	1	0	34.0	1	4	1	1	.833	4	0	0	0	.00	-4
Liriano,Francisco, Pit	L	.111	45	5	0	0	5	.092	109	10	0	0	0	3	8	41	12	162.1	2	24	3	1	.897	24	5	1	0	.21	0
Lobstein,Kyle, Det	L	-	0	0	0	0	0	-	0	0	0	0	0	0	0	0	0	39.1	2	3	0	0	1.000	3	1	0	0	.33	-2
Locke,Jeff, Pit	L	.111	45	5	0	0	3	.102	108	11	0	0	0	0	4	60	8	131.1	4	14	0	1	1.000	13	6	5	0	.46	2
Logan,Boone, Col	L	-	0	0	0	0	0	-	0	0	0	0	0	0	0	0	1	25.0	1	2	1	0	.750	0	0	0	0	-	-1
Lohse,Kyle, Mil	R	.115	61	7	0	5	9	.147	470	69	8	0	0	30	9	153	72	198.1	10	24	1	2	.971	15	5	1	0	.33	2
Lopez,Javier, SF	L	-	0	0	0	0	0	.091	11	1	0	0	0	1	0	5	1	37.2	10	7	1	0	.944	1	0	0	0	.00	-2
Lopez,Wilton, Col	R	-	0	0	0	0	0	.000	6	0	0	0	0	0	0	3	0	6.1	0	1	0	0	1.000	0	0	0	0	-	0
Loup,Aaron, Tor	L	-	0	0	0	0	0	.000	1	0	0	0	0	0	0	0	0	68.2	3	17	1	2	.952	9	1	1	0	.11	2
Lowe,Mark, Cle	R	-	0	0	0	0	0	.000	1	0	0	0	0	0	0	1	0	7.0	0	1	0	0	.000	2	1	0	0	.50	-1
Lueke,Josh, TB	R	-	0	0	0	0	0	-	0	0	0	0	0	0	0	0	0	30.1	3	1	0	0	1.000	0	0	0	0	-	-1
Luetge,Lucas, Sea	L	-	0	0	0	0	0	-	0	0	0	0	0	0	0	0	0	9.0	0	1	0	0	1.000	0	0	0	0	-	0
Lyles,Jordan, Col	R	.188	48	9	1	3	1	.154	117	18	4	0	2	7	6	53	11	126.2	11	19	1	2	.968	6	0	0	0	.00	2
Lynn,Lance, StL	R	.067	60	4	0	1	4	.065	168	11	1	0	0	4	11	101	25	203.2	8	28	1	0	.973	4	3	0	0	.75	3
Lyons,Tyler, StL	L	.000	7	0	0	0	0	.105	19	2	0	0	0	0	2	9	1	36.2	1	7	2	0	.800	2	1	1	0	.50	1
Machi,Jean, SF	R	.000	1	0	0	0	1	.000	2	0	0	0	0	0	0	1	1	66.1	2	18	2	4	.909	6	3	1	1	.50	3
Maholm,Paul, LAD	L	.000	9	0	0	0	5	.109	478	52	4	0	2	18	24	252	35	70.2	4	13	1	0	.944	3	0	0	1	.00	1
Maness,Seth, StL	R	.400	5	2	0	0	0	.300	10	3	0	0	0	0	0	3	0	80.1	9	21	2	4	.938	4	3	0	0	.75	5
Manship,Jeff, Phi	R	.000	2	0	0	0	0	.000	10	0	0	0	0	0	0	3	0	23.0	2	3	0	2	1.000	2	1	0	0	.50	-1
Mariot,Michael, KC	R	-	0	0	0	0	0	-	0	0	0	0	0	0	0	0	0	25.0	3	2	0	1	1.000	0	0	0	0	-	0
Marks,Justin, KC	L	-	0	0	0	0	0	-	0	0	0	0	0	0	0	0	0	2.0	0	0	0	0	-	0	0	0	0	-	0
Marmol,Carlos, Mia	R	-	0	0	0	0	0	.194	31	6	1	0	1	1	0	11	3	13.1	2	1	0	0	1.000	8	0	0	0	.00	-1
Maronde,Nick, LAA	L	-	0	0	0	0	0	-	0	0	0	0	0	0	0	0	0	6.1	0	1	0	0	1.000	2	1	1	0	.50	0
Marshall,Evan, Ari	R	-	0	0	0	0	0	-	0	0	0	0	0	0	0	0	0	49.1	2	8	1	2	.909	4	1	0	0	.25	1
Marshall,Sean, Cin	L	-	0	0	0	0	0	.158	101	16	1	0	1	5	2	48	8	14.0	1	6	0	1	1.000	0	0	0	0	-	1
Martin,Chris, Col	R	-	0	0	0	0	0	-	0	0	0	0	0	0	0	0	0	15.2	1	2	0	0	1.000	0	0	0	0	-	0
Martin,Ethan, Phi	R	-	0	0	0	0	0	.000	9	0	0	0	0	0	0	6	1	4.0	0	0	0	0	-	0	0	0	0	-	0
Martinez,Carlos, StL	R	.250	12	3	0	2	1	.214	14	3	0	0	0	2	0	5	1	89.1	11	23	1	2	.971	8	3	0	0	.38	3
Martinez,David, Hou	R	-	0	0	0	0	0	-	0	0	0	0	0	0	0	0	0	7.0	1	0	0	0	1.000	0	0	0	0	-	0
Martinez,Nick, Tex	R	.000	3	0	0	0	0	.000	3	0	0	0	0	0	0	2	0	140.1	11	11	0	1	1.000	8	4	1	0	.50	1
Masset,Nick, Col	R	-	0	0	0	0	0	.000	5	0	0	0	0	0	0	5	1	45.0	5	3	3	0	.727	6	0	0	1	.00	-1
Masterson,Justin, Cle-StL	R	.182	11	2	0	1	2	.167	30	5	0	0	0	1	0	12	3	128.2	8	22	1	5	.968	7	2	0	0	.29	2
Matsuzaka,Daisuke, NYM	R	.182	11	2	0	1	5	.189	37	7	0	0	0	3	1	16	7	83.1	3	8	0	1	1.000	14	2	1	1	.14	0
Mattheus,Ryan, Was	R	-	0	0	0	0	0	.000	1	0	0	0	0	0	0	1	0	8.2	0	1	0	0	1.000	0	0	0	0	-	0
Matusz,Brian, Bal	L	-	0	0	0	0	0	.125	8	1	0	0	0	0	0	2	0	51.2	1	6	0	0	1.000	1	1	0	0	1.00	0
Matzek,Tyler, Col	L	.184	38	7	0	0	3	.184	38	7	1	0	0	0	2	13	3	117.2	10	15	2	1	.926	8	3	1	0	.38	-2
Maurer,Brandon, Sea	R	.000	1	0	0	0	1	.000	1	0	0	0	0	0	0	1	0	69.2	2	5	0	0	1.000	3	0	0	0	.00	-1
May,Trevor, Min	R	-	0	0	0	0	0	-	0	0	0	0	0	0	0	0	0	45.2	1	1	0	0	1.000	1	0	0	0	.00	0
Mazzaro,Vin, Pit	R	.000	1	0	0	0	0	.176	17	3	0	0	0	1	0	10	5	10.1	1	0	0	0	1.000	2	0	0	0	.00	0
McAllister,Zach, Cle	R	.500	2	1	0	0	0	.167	6	1	0	0	0	0	0	2	0	86.0	5	3	2	0	.800	12	3	0	0	.25	-4
McCarthy,Brandon, Ari-NYY	R	.138	29	4	0	3	3	.067	75	5	0	0	3	3	3	30	6	200.0	11	20	0	1	1.000	22	5	1	0	.23	0
McCoy,Pat, Det	L	-	0	0	0	0	0	-	0	0	0	0	0	0	0	0	0	14.0	0	0	0	0	-	0	0	0	0	-	0
McCutchen,Daniel, Tex	R	-	0	0	0	0	0	.067	30	2	0	0	0	1	1	8	3	2.1	0	0	0	0	-	0	0	0	0	-	0
McFarland,T.J., Bal	L	-	0	0	0	0	1	-	0	0	0	0	0	0	0	0	0	58.2	3	10	1	0	.929	0	0	0	0	-	-2
McGee,Jake, TB	L	-	0	0	0	0	0	-	0	0	0	0	0	0	0	0	0	71.1	1	6	1	0	.875	3	1	1	0	.33	0
McGowan,Dustin, Tor	R	.000	4	0	0	0	0	.143	14	2	0	0	0	0	0	7	1	82.0	3	11	0	2	1.000	8	2	1	0	.25	1
McHugh,Collin, Hou	R	.000	2	0	0	0	1	.083	12	1	0	0	0	0	0	4	1	154.2	12	21	2	0	.943	11	5	0	0	.45	1
Medina,Yoervis, Sea	R	-	0	0	0	0	0	-	0	0	0	0	0	0	0	0	0	57.0	1	6	1	0	.875	5	0	0	0	.00	-1
Meek,Evan, Bal	R	-	0	0	0	0	0	1.000	1	1	0	0	0	0	0	0	0	23.1	2	6	0	0	1.000	3	0	0	0	.00	0
Mejia,Jenrry, NYM	R	.000	17	0	0	0	1	.029	34	1	0	0	0	1	0	16	3	93.2	4	9	0	1	1.000	8	0	0	0	.00	-4
Melancon,Mark, Pit	R	-	0	0	0	0	0	-	0	0	0	0	0	0	1	0	0	71.0	5	12	1	0	.944	2	1	0	0	.50	1
Mendez,Roman, Tex	R	-	0	0	0	0	0	-	0	0	0	0	0	0	0	0	0	33.0	4	2	0	0	1.000	2	0	0	0	.00	-1
Mercedes,Melvin, Det	R	-	0	0	0	0	0	-	0	0	0	0	0	0	0	0	0	2.0	0	1	0	0	1.000	0	0	0	0	-	0
Mikolas,Miles, Tex	R	.000	1	0	0	0	1	.000	4	0	0	0	0	0	0	1	1	57.1	5	5	2	1	.833	2	0	0	0	.00	-2
Miley,Wade, Ari	L	.158	57	9	0	1	9	.149	195	29	5	0	1	12	8	52	26	201.1	7	27	3	2	.919	10	6	2	3	.60	2
Miller,Andrew, Bos-Bal	L	-	0	0	0	0	0	.056	72	4	0	0	0	3	0	36	4	62.1	0	8	1	0	.889	3	1	0	0	.33	0
Miller,Jim, NYY	R	-	0	0	0	0	0	-	0	0	0	0	0	0	0	0	0	2.2	0	0	0	0	-	1	0	0	0	.00	0
Miller,Justin, Det	R	-	0	0	0	0	0	-	0	0	0	0	0	0	0	0	0	12.1	0	1	0	0	1.000	2	0	0	0	.00	0
Miller,Shelby, StL	R	.188	48	9	0	4	13	.144	104	15	7	0	1	6	3	54	21	183.0	15	11	1	0	.963	20	6	1	0	.30	0
Mills,Brad, Oak-Tor	L	.000	3	0	0	0	0	.000	4	0	0	0	0	0	0	2	0	20.2	1	6	0	0	1.000	2	1	0	0	.50	0
Milone,Tommy, Oak-Min	L	.000	4	0	0	0	0	.174	23	4	0	0	1	6	0	4	4	118.0	5	18	1	2	.958	9	2	2	0	.22	1
Minor,Mike, Atl	R	.156	45	7	1	4	2	.121	198	24	5	0	2	10	9	89	15	145.1	4	15	0	1	1.000	10	1	0	1	.10	-4
Mitchell,Bryan, NYY	R	-	0	0	0	0	0	-	0	0	0	0	0	0	0	0	0	11.0	0	2	0	0	1.000	1	1	0	0	1.00	0
Montero,Rafael, NYM	R	.000	11	0	0	0	2	.000	11	0	0	0	0	0	0	5	2	44.1	2	6	0	1	1.000	6	1	0	0	.17	2
Moore,Matt, TB	L	-	0	0	0	0	0	.000	6	0	0	0	0	1	0	2	1	10.0	0	1	0	0	-	0	0	0	0	-	0

Pitchers Hitting, Fielding and Holding Runners

Pitcher	T	2014 Hitting						Career Hitting										2014 Fielding and Holding Runners											
		Avg	AB	H	HR	RBI	SH	Avg	AB	H	2B	3B	HR	RBI	BB	SO	SH	Inn	PO	A	E	DP	Pct	SBA	CS	PCS	PPO	CS%	RS
Morales,Franklin, Col	L	.100	30	3	0	0	6	.177	62	11	0	0	0	2	4	27	8	142.1	7	19	5	1	.839	10	1	0	0	.10	-1
Morin,Mike, LAA	R	-	0	0	0	0	0	-	0	0	0	0	0	0	0	0	0	59.0	5	6	1	0	.917	4	1	0	0	.25	0
Morris,Bryan, Pit-Mia	R	.000	1	0	0	0	0	.167	6	1	0	0	0	0	0	3	0	64.1	2	8	1	0	.909	1	0	2	0	.00	1
Morrow,Brandon, Tor	R	.000	2	0	0	0	0	.000	14	0	0	0	0	0	0	6	0	33.1	3	3	0	0	1.000	2	0	0	0	.00	-1
Morton,Charlie, Pit	R	.050	40	2	0	1	8	.080	213	17	4	0	0	5	2	111	30	157.1	9	23	1	2	.970	18	4	1	3	.22	4
Motte,Jason, StL	R	-	0	0	0	0	0	.000	4	0	0	0	0	0	0	4	0	25.0	1	3	0	0	1.000	1	0	0	1	.00	0
Mujica,Edward, Bos	R	-	0	0	0	0	0	.182	11	2	0	0	0	0	0	4	2	60.0	3	6	1	0	.900	6	2	0	0	.33	0
Nathan,Joe, Det	R	-	0	0	0	0	0	.159	63	10	3	0	2	4	3	17	10	58.0	6	6	0	0	1.000	11	1	1	0	.09	0
Nelson,Jimmy, Mil	R	.143	21	3	0	0	1	.130	23	3	1	0	0	0	0	9	1	69.1	2	6	1	1	.889	7	0	0	0	.00	-4
Neris,Hector, Phi	R	-	0	0	0	0	0	-	0	0	0	0	0	0	0	0	0	1.0	0	0	0	0	-	0	0	0	0	-	0
Neshek,Pat, StL	R	-	0	0	0	0	0	-	0	0	0	0	0	0	0	0	0	67.1	2	8	0	0	1.000	3	1	0	0	.33	1
Nicasio,Juan, Col	R	.083	24	2	0	4	2	.120	100	12	2	0	0	8	6	62	14	93.2	6	11	1	0	.944	8	2	0	0	.25	-1
Niese,Jon, NYM	L	.091	55	5	0	4	4	.151	265	40	5	1	0	14	28	132	26	187.2	2	33	4	2	.897	15	6	2	0	.40	3
Noesi,Hector, Sea-Tex-CWS	R	.000	4	0	0	0	0	.250	8	2	0	0	0	0	0	3	0	172.1	5	21	1	4	.963	9	2	0	0	.22	2
Nolasco,Ricky, Min	R	.000	2	0	0	0	0	.137	371	51	12	0	1	26	21	173	62	159.0	8	13	0	0	1.000	21	5	2	0	.24	-2
Nolin,Sean, Tor	L	-	0	0	0	0	0	-	0	0	0	0	0	0	0	0	0	1.0	0	0	0	0	-	0	0	0	0	-	0
Norris,Bud, Bal	R	.333	3	1	0	1	1	.150	173	26	5	0	0	11	4	58	31	165.1	9	15	1	0	.960	24	9	0	0	.38	-1
Norris,Daniel, Tor	L	-	0	0	0	0	0	-	0	0	0	0	0	0	0	0	0	6.2	0	2	0	0	1.000	1	0	0	0	.00	0
Nova,Ivan, NYY	R	-	0	0	0	0	0	.071	14	1	0	0	0	0	0	13	3	20.2	1	1	0	0	1.000	1	0	1	0	1.00	-1
Nuno,Vidal, NYY-Ari	L	.056	18	1	0	0	6	.056	18	1	0	0	0	0	0	8	6	161.2	4	19	0	1	1.000	7	3	2	0	.43	3
Oberholtzer,Brett, Hou	L	-	0	0	0	0	0	-	0	0	0	0	0	0	0	0	0	143.2	6	16	1	2	.957	12	2	0	1	.17	-2
O'Day,Darren, Bal	R	-	0	0	0	0	0	.000	1	0	0	0	0	0	0	1	0	68.2	4	11	1	0	.938	5	1	1	0	.20	1
Odorizzi,Jake, TB	R	.000	4	0	0	1	1	.000	4	0	0	0	0	1	1	3	1	168.0	6	12	0	1	1.000	10	6	1	1	.60	0
O'Flaherty,Eric, Oak	L	-	0	0	0	0	0	.000	2	0	0	0	0	0	0	2	0	20.0	0	1	0	0	1.000	4	1	0	0	.25	-1
Ogando,Alexi, Tex	R	-	0	0	0	0	0	.500	6	3	0	0	0	0	0	3	0	25.0	0	1	0	0	1.000	3	0	0	0	.00	-1
Oliveros,Lester, Min	R	-	0	0	0	0	0	-	0	0	0	0	0	0	0	0	0	6.1	0	0	0	0	-	0	0	0	0	-	0
Ondrusek,Logan, Cin	R	.000	3	0	0	0	0	.000	7	0	0	0	0	0	0	7	0	41.0	5	2	0	0	1.000	1	1	0	0	1.00	-1
Ortega,Jose, Det	R	-	0	0	0	0	0	-	0	0	0	0	0	0	0	0	0	1.1	0	0	0	0	-	2	1	0	0	.50	0
O'Sullivan,Sean, Phi	R	.000	4	0	0	0	0	.154	13	2	1	0	0	0	0	7	0	12.2	0	2	0	1	1.000	1	0	0	0	.00	0
Otero,Dan, Oak	R	-	0	0	0	0	0	.000	1	0	0	0	0	0	0	1	0	86.2	11	18	0	2	1.000	6	3	1	0	.50	3
Ottavino,Adam, Col	R	-	0	0	0	0	0	.083	24	2	0	0	0	0	1	17	3	65.0	2	6	0	0	1.000	4	1	0	0	.25	0
Outman,Josh, Cle-NYY	L	-	0	0	0	0	0	.042	24	1	0	0	0	1	1	12	0	28.1	2	5	0	1	1.000	1	0	0	0	.00	2
Oviedo,Juan, TB	R	-	0	0	0	0	0	.000	1	0	0	0	0	0	0	0	0	31.2	1	3	1	0	.800	5	0	0	1	.00	4
Owens,Rudy, Hou	L	-	0	0	0	0	0	-	0	0	0	0	0	0	0	0	0	5.2	0	1	0	0	1.000	0	0	0	0	-	0
Papelbon,Jonathan, Phi	R	-	0	0	0	0	0	-	0	0	0	0	0	0	0	0	0	66.1	3	3	0	0	1.000	6	2	0	0	.33	-2
Parker,Blake, ChC	R	-	0	0	0	0	0	-	0	0	0	0	0	0	0	0	0	21.0	0	2	0	0	1.000	4	2	0	0	.50	0
Parnell,Bobby, NYM	R	-	0	0	0	0	0	.111	9	1	0	0	0	0	3	5	5	1.0	0	0	0	0	-	0	0	0	0	-	0
Parra,Manny, Cin	L	-	0	0	0	0	0	.188	144	27	11	1	0	13	6	58	10	36.2	5	6	0	1	1.000	3	2	0	0	.67	1
Partch,Curtis, Cin	R	-	0	0	0	0	0	.000	1	0	0	0	0	0	0	0	0	7.0	0	0	0	0	-	1	0	0	0	.00	0
Paterson,Joe, Ari	L	-	0	0	0	0	0	-	0	0	0	0	0	0	0	0	0	1.1	0	0	0	0	-	0	0	0	0	-	0
Patterson,Red, LAD	R	-	0	0	0	0	0	-	0	0	0	0	0	0	0	0	0	4.2	1	1	0	0	1.000	0	0	0	0	-	0
Patton,Spencer, Tex	R	-	0	0	0	0	0	-	0	0	0	0	0	0	0	0	0	9.1	1	2	0	1	1.000	0	0	0	0	-	0
Patton,Troy, Bal-SD	L	-	0	0	0	0	0	.250	4	1	0	0	0	0	0	1	0	14.0	0	0	0	0	-	0	0	0	0	-	-2
Paulino,Felipe, CWS	R	.000	1	0	0	0	0	.140	57	8	1	0	0	1	1	29	9	18.1	1	0	0	0	1.000	3	0	0	0	.00	-1
Paxton,James, Sea	L	.000	1	0	0	0	1	.000	2	0	0	0	0	0	1	2	1	74.0	1	7	3	1	.727	9	2	0	0	.22	-5
Peacock,Brad, Hou	R	.000	5	0	0	0	0	.000	9	0	0	0	0	0	0	7	1	131.2	7	7	2	1	.875	11	1	0	0	.09	-2
Peavy,Jake, Bos-SF	R	.000	23	0	0	0	1	.164	456	75	15	1	2	27	19	136	46	202.2	23	25	2	3	.960	14	6	0	1	.43	2
Pelfrey,Mike, Min	R	-	0	0	0	0	0	.098	265	26	5	0	0	13	13	71	24	23.2	0	3	0	0	1.000	5	0	0	0	.00	-1
Penny,Brad, Mia	R	.333	6	2	0	0	2	.157	529	83	17	2	3	34	3	173	43	26.0	2	6	0	0	1.000	5	0	0	0	.00	-1
Peralta,Joel, TB	R	-	0	0	0	0	0	.250	4	1	1	0	0	0	0	2	0	63.1	2	5	0	0	1.000	5	0	0	0	.00	0
Peralta,Wily, Mil	R	.053	57	3	0	3	8	.093	118	11	3	0	0	3	3	49	17	198.2	20	23	0	2	1.000	24	5	0	1	.21	-1
Perez,Chris, LAD	R	.000	1	0	0	0	0	.000	2	0	0	0	0	0	0	2	0	46.1	0	5	0	0	1.000	8	1	0	0	.13	0
Perez,Martin, Tex	L	.000	1	0	0	1	0	.000	6	0	0	0	0	0	0	5	1	51.1	1	5	0	1	1.000	4	4	0	1	1.00	0
Perez,Oliver, Ari	L	-	0	0	0	0	0	.158	341	54	1	0	0	15	14	116	39	58.2	1	5	1	0	.857	2	0	0	0	.00	-2
Perkins,Glen, Min	L	-	0	0	0	0	0	.000	4	0	0	0	0	0	0	4	3	61.2	2	8	0	0	1.000	4	2	1	0	.50	3
Pestano,Vinnie, Cle-LAA	R	-	0	0	0	0	0	-	0	0	0	0	0	0	0	0	0	18.2	1	1	0	0	1.000	1	1	0	0	1.00	-1
Petit,Yusmeiro, SF	R	.040	25	1	0	1	1	.049	103	5	0	0	0	3	3	44	5	117.0	7	5	2	0	.857	19	4	0	0	.21	-5
Petricka,Jake, CWS	R	-	0	0	0	0	0	-	0	0	0	0	0	0	0	0	0	73.0	6	7	0	1	1.000	6	4	1	0	.67	1
Pettibone,Jonathan, Phi	R	.000	2	0	0	0	0	.097	31	3	1	0	0	3	3	15	0	9.0	0	1	0	0	1.000	0	0	0	0	-	0
Phelps,David, NYY	R	.000	4	0	0	0	1	.000	6	0	0	0	0	0	0	3	1	113.0	10	18	0	2	1.000	13	6	2	1	.46	3
Pimentel,Stolmy, Pit	R	.000	5	0	0	0	0	.000	5	0	0	0	0	0	0	3	0	32.2	1	0	0	0	1.000	5	1	0	0	.20	0
Pineda,Michael, NYY	R	-	0	0	0	0	0	.200	5	1	0	0	0	2	0	0	0	76.1	2	9	1	0	.917	9	4	1	0	.44	-1
Pino,Yohan, Min	R	-	0	0	0	0	0	-	0	0	0	0	0	0	0	0	0	60.1	6	6	0	0	1.000	4	1	0	1	.25	-1
Pomeranz,Drew, Oak	L	-	0	0	0	0	0	.206	34	7	2	0	1	1	1	19	7	69.0	1	8	0	0	1.000	6	0	0	0	.00	0
Porcello,Rick, Det	R	.000	4	0	0	0	1	.190	21	4	0	0	0	2	0	8	3	204.2	18	17	4	2	.897	14	7	0	0	.50	0
Poreda,Aaron, Tex	L	-	0	0	0	0	0	-	0	0	0	0	0	0	0	0	0	21.1	0	1	0	0	1.000	6	3	0	0	.50	-2
Pressly,Ryan, Min	R	-	0	0	0	0	0	-	0	0	0	0	0	0	0	0	0	28.1	1	5	0	0	1.000	5	1	1	0	.20	-1
Price,Bryan, Cle	R	-	0	0	0	0	0	-	0	0	0	0	0	0	0	0	0	2.2	0	0	0	0	-	0	0	0	0	-	0
Price,David, TB-Det	L	.000	4	0	0	0	0	.071	28	2	0	0	0	2	13	0	0	248.1	4	18	1	1	.957	16	4	1	1	.25	-1
Pryor,Stephen, Sea	R	-	0	0	0	0	0	-	0	0	0	0	0	0	0	0	0	1.2	0	0	0	0	-	0	0	0	0	-	0

Pitchers Hitting, Fielding and Holding Runners

Pitcher	T	2014 Hitting						Career Hitting										2014 Fielding and Holding Runners											
		Avg	AB	H	HR	RBI	SH	Avg	AB	H	2B	3B	HR	RBI	BB	SO	SH	Inn	PO	A	E	DP	Pct	SBA	CS	PCS	PPO	CS%	RS
Putkonen,Luke, Det	R	-	0	0	0	0	0	-	0	0	0	0	0	0	0	0	0	2.2	1	0	0	0	1.000	1	0	0	0	.00	0
Putnam,Zach, CWS	R	-	0	0	0	0	0	-	0	0	0	0	0	0	0	0	0	54.2	3	4	0	0	1.000	9	2	0	0	.22	-1
Putz,J.J., Ari	R	-	0	0	0	0	0	-	0	0	0	0	0	0	0	0	0	13.2	0	2	0	1	1.000	2	0	0	0	.00	-1
Quackenbush,Kevin, SD	R	-	0	0	0	0	0	-	0	0	0	0	0	0	0	0	0	54.1	3	5	0	0	1.000	3	1	0	0	.33	0
Qualls,Chad, Hou	R	-	0	0	0	0	0	.000	6	0	0	0	0	0	0	5	0	51.1	4	8	0	0	1.000	11	2	1	0	.18	-1
Quintana,Jose, CWS	L	.000	9	0	0	0	1	.000	14	0	0	0	0	0	1	8	2	200.1	4	25	0	6	1.000	14	5	2	0	.36	4
Ramirez,Erasmo, Sea	R	.000	2	0	0	0	1	.000	6	0	0	0	0	0	0	2	1	75.1	2	8	0	0	1.000	8	2	1	0	.25	-1
Ramirez,Jose, NYY	R	-	0	0	0	0	0	-	0	0	0	0	0	0	0	0	0	10.0	0	1	0	0	-	1	0	0	0	.00	0
Ramirez,Neil, ChC	R	-	0	0	0	0	0	-	0	0	0	0	0	0	0	0	0	43.2	3	1	0	0	1.000	6	0	0	0	.00	-1
Ramirez,Ramon, Bal	R	-	0	0	0	0	0	.333	6	2	0	0	0	0	0	3	1	1.0	1	0	0	0	1.000	0	0	0	0	-	0
Ramos,A.J., Mia	R	-	0	0	0	0	0	-	0	0	0	0	0	0	0	0	0	64.0	2	6	0	0	1.000	10	3	0	0	.30	-2
Ramos,Cesar, TB	L	.000	1	0	0	0	0	.000	6	0	0	0	0	0	0	4	0	82.2	4	8	2	0	.857	3	0	0	0	.00	-1
Ranaudo,Anthony, Bos	R	.000	5	0	0	0	0	.000	5	0	0	0	0	0	0	3	0	39.1	2	3	0	0	1.000	4	1	0	0	.25	-1
Rasmus,Cory, LAA	R	-	0	0	0	0	0	-	0	0	0	0	0	0	0	0	0	56.0	3	8	1	1	.917	5	2	1	0	.40	0
Rasmussen,Rob, Tor	L	-	0	0	0	0	0	-	0	0	0	0	0	0	0	0	0	11.1	0	1	0	0	1.000	0	0	0	0	-	0
Ray,Robbie, Det	L	.500	2	1	0	0	0	.500	2	1	0	0	0	0	0	0	0	28.2	2	6	0	1	1.000	6	3	2	0	.50	2
Redmond,Todd, Tor	R	.000	1	0	0	0	1	.000	5	0	0	0	0	0	1	2	1	75.0	2	2	2	0	.667	13	6	0	0	.46	-2
Reed,Addison, Ari	R	-	0	0	0	0	0	-	0	0	0	0	0	0	0	0	0	59.1	2	1	1	0	.750	7	0	0	0	.00	-3
Reed,Evan, Det	R	-	0	0	0	0	0	-	0	0	0	0	0	0	0	0	0	32.1	3	2	1	0	.833	7	2	0	0	.29	0
Rice,Scott, NYM	L	-	0	0	0	0	0	-	0	0	0	0	0	0	0	0	0	13.2	1	4	0	0	1.000	1	1	1	0	1.00	-1
Richards,Garrett, LAA	R	.000	11	0	0	0	0	.000	13	0	0	0	0	0	0	5	0	168.2	10	13	3	0	.885	13	3	0	0	.23	-1
Riefenhauser,C.J., TB	L	-	0	0	0	0	0	-	0	0	0	0	0	0	0	0	0	5.1	0	1	0	0	1.000	0	0	0	0	-	0
Rienzo,Andre, CWS	R	-	0	0	0	0	0	-	0	0	0	0	0	0	0	0	0	64.2	7	7	3	0	.824	3	0	0	0	.00	-2
Roach,Donn, SD	R	.250	4	1	0	0	0	.250	4	1	1	0	0	0	0	1	0	30.1	2	6	0	1	1.000	6	2	0	0	.33	0
Roark,Tanner, Was	R	.121	58	7	0	0	11	.153	72	11	1	0	0	1	1	26	12	198.2	9	25	2	5	.944	13	5	0	1	.38	4
Robertson,David, NYY	R	-	0	0	0	0	0	-	0	0	0	0	0	0	0	0	0	64.1	5	4	0	0	1.000	9	1	0	0	.11	-1
Rodney,Fernando, Sea	R	-	0	0	0	0	0	.000	1	0	0	0	0	0	0	0	0	66.1	3	6	1	0	.900	7	1	1	0	.14	-2
Rodriguez,Fernando, Oak	R	-	0	0	0	0	0	.000	4	0	0	0	0	0	0	3	0	68.0	0	0	0	0	-	0	0	0	0	-	0
Rodriguez,Francisco, Mil	R	-	0	0	0	0	0	.500	2	1	0	0	0	0	0	1	0	68.0	4	5	0	0	1.000	8	1	0	0	.13	1
Rodriguez,Henry, Mia	R	-	0	0	0	0	0	.000	2	0	0	0	0	0	0	2	0	1.2	0	0	0	0	-	3	1	0	0	.33	0
Rodriguez,Paco, LAD	L	-	0	0	0	0	0	.000	1	0	0	0	0	0	0	1	0	14.0	0	4	0	0	1.000	2	1	1	1	.50	2
Rodriguez,Wandy, Pit	L	.250	8	2	0	0	0	.133	445	59	10	0	0	21	10	130	53	26.2	1	8	1	2	.900	2	0	0	0	.00	0
Rodriguez,Wilking, KC	R	-	0	0	0	0	0	-	0	0	0	0	0	0	0	0	0	2.0	0	1	0	0	-	0	0	0	1	-	0
Roe,Chaz, NYY	R	-	0	0	0	0	0	.000	1	0	0	0	0	0	0	1	0	2.0	1	0	0	0	1.000	0	0	0	0	-	0
Rogers,Esmil, Tor-NYY	R	.000	1	0	0	0	0	.208	53	11	3	0	0	1	0	21	10	45.2	0	3	0	0	1.000	3	0	0	0	.00	-2
Romo,Sergio, SF	R	-	0	0	0	0	0	.000	4	0	0	0	0	0	0	3	0	58.0	3	7	1	0	.909	3	1	0	0	.33	1
Rondon,Hector, ChC	R	-	0	0	0	0	0	-	0	0	0	0	0	0	0	0	0	63.1	9	10	0	1	1.000	7	1	0	0	.14	1
Rondon,Jorge, StL	R	-	0	0	0	0	0	-	0	0	0	0	0	0	0	0	0	1.0	0	0	0	0	-	0	0	0	0	-	0
Rosenberg,B.J., Phi	R	-	0	0	0	0	0	.333	3	1	0	0	0	1	0	1	1	12.0	0	0	0	0	-	1	1	0	0	1.00	0
Rosenthal,Trevor, StL	R	.000	1	0	0	0	0	.000	2	0	0	0	0	0	0	2	0	70.1	3	8	1	1	.917	2	0	0	0	.00	-1
Rosin,Seth, Tex	R	-	0	0	0	0	0	-	0	0	0	0	0	0	0	0	0	4.0	0	0	0	0	-	0	0	0	0	-	0
Ross,Robbie, Tex	L	.000	1	0	0	0	0	.000	3	0	0	0	0	0	0	1	1	0	78.1	2	8	2	0	.833	4	2	0	0	.50	1
Ross,Tyson, SD	R	.179	56	10	0	3	2	.174	92	16	1	0	0	3	3	42	5	195.2	16	37	3	3	.946	41	10	1	1	.24	-2
Rosscup,Zac, ChC	L	-	0	0	0	0	0	-	0	0	0	0	0	0	0	0	0	13.1	0	0	0	0	-	0	0	0	0	-	0
Roth,Michael, LAA	L	-	0	0	0	0	0	-	0	0	0	0	0	0	0	0	0	12.1	1	5	1	2	.857	3	1	0	0	.33	0
Rowen,Ben, Tex	R	-	0	0	0	0	0	-	0	0	0	0	0	0	0	0	0	8.2	3	0	0	0	1.000	3	0	0	0	.00	0
Rowland-Smith,Ryan, Ari	L	.000	1	0	0	0	0	.000	5	0	0	0	0	0	0	4	0	7.1	0	1	0	0	.000	0	0	0	0	-	-1
Rucinski,Drew, LAA	R	-	0	0	0	0	0	-	0	0	0	0	0	0	0	0	0	7.1	1	1	0	0	1.000	0	0	0	0	-	0
Rusin,Chris, ChC	L	.000	3	0	0	0	0	.118	34	4	0	1	0	2	0	9	2	12.2	2	2	0	0	1.000	1	0	0	0	.00	-1
Russell,James, ChC-Atl	L	.000	2	0	0	0	0	.067	15	1	0	0	0	0	0	5	0	57.2	2	6	0	0	1.000	6	1	0	0	.17	0
Ryan,Kyle, Det	L	-	0	0	0	0	0	-	0	0	0	0	0	0	0	0	0	10.1	2	1	0	0	1.000	0	0	0	0	-	0
Ryu,Hyun-Jin, LAD	L	.149	47	7	0	2	8	.181	105	19	5	1	0	7	3	40	14	152.0	7	25	1	0	.970	3	1	0	0	.33	3
Rzepczynski,Marc, Cle	L	-	0	0	0	0	0	.000	1	0	0	0	0	0	0	0	0	46.0	3	5	1	0	.889	3	1	0	0	.33	-3
Sabathia,CC, NYY	L	.000	2	0	0	0	0	.225	111	25	3	0	3	15	1	30	3	46.0	1	5	0	0	1.000	1	0	0	0	.00	-3
Sadler,Casey, Pit	R	-	0	0	0	0	0	-	0	0	0	0	0	0	0	0	0	10.1	3	1	0	0	1.000	0	0	0	0	-	0
Salas,Fernando, LAA	R	-	0	0	0	0	0	.000	4	0	0	0	0	0	0	2	0	58.2	6	7	0	1	1.000	4	0	0	0	.00	0
Salazar,Danny, Cle	R	.000	3	0	0	0	0	.000	5	0	0	0	0	0	0	5	0	110.0	3	6	0	1	1.000	5	2	0	1	.40	1
Sale,Chris, CWS	L	.000	3	0	0	0	0	.000	5	0	0	0	0	0	0	4	1	174.0	4	13	0	0	1.000	8	4	1	0	.50	1
Samardzija,Jeff, ChC-Oak	R	.176	34	6	0	3	2	.125	160	20	5	0	2	10	6	64	21	219.2	18	23	3	2	.930	27	8	1	1	.30	-1
Sanchez,Aaron, Tor	R	-	0	0	0	0	0	-	0	0	0	0	0	0	0	0	0	33.0	0	11	1	0	.917	5	1	0	1	.20	0
Sanchez,Anibal, Det	R	.200	5	1	0	1	0	.091	241	22	1	1	0	7	16	112	31	126.0	11	18	0	2	1.000	16	3	0	1	.19	-1
Santana,Ervin, Atl	R	.111	63	7	0	1	8	.125	88	11	2	0	3	2	4	43	9	196.0	17	20	1	1	.974	13	6	0	1	.46	2
Santiago,Hector, LAA	L	.250	4	1	0	0	0	.125	8	1	0	0	0	0	0	2	0	127.1	3	17	2	0	.909	17	7	6	0	.41	3
Santos,Sergio, Tor	R	-	0	0	0	0	0	.000	1	0	0	0	0	0	0	0	0	21.0	2	1	0	0	1.000	6	0	0	0	.00	-1
Saunders,Joe, Tex-Bal	L	-	0	0	0	0	0	.133	128	17	1	0	0	6	6	34	15	43.0	2	6	1	1	.889	2	1	0	0	.50	0
Savery,Joe, Oak	L	-	0	0	0	0	0	.000	2	0	0	0	0	0	0	1	1	4.0	0	0	0	0	-	0	0	0	0	-	0
Scahill,Rob, Col	R	-	0	0	0	0	0	.000	2	0	0	0	0	0	0	1	0	15.0	3	2	0	0	1.000	2	0	0	0	.00	0
Scheppers,Tanner, Tex	R	-	0	0	0	0	0	-	0	0	0	0	0	0	0	0	0	23.0	0	3	1	0	.750	1	0	0	0	.00	0
Scherzer,Max, Det	R	.000	2	0	0	0	2	.165	79	13	3	0	0	4	4	23	10	220.1	9	17	1	2	.963	23	10	0	0	.43	-4
Schlitter,Brian, ChC	R	1.000	1	1	0	0	0	1.000	1	1	0	0	0	0	0	0	0	56.1	4	15	0	1	1.000	2	2	0	1	1.00	1

Pitchers Hitting, Fielding and Holding Runners

Pitcher	T	2014 Hitting						Career Hitting										2014 Fielding and Holding Runners											
		Avg	AB	H	HR	RBI	SH	Avg	AB	H	2B	3B	HR	RBI	BB	SO	SH	Inn	PO	A	E	DP	Pct	SBA	CS	PCS	PPO	CS%	RS
Schlosser,Gus, Atl	R	1.000	1	1	0	0	0	1.000	1	1	0	0	0	0	0	0	0	17.2	1	3	1	0	.800	3	0	0	0	.00	1
Schultz,Bo, Ari	R	.000	1	0	0	0	0	.000	1	0	0	0	0	0	0	0	0	8.0	1	2	0	0	1.000	0	0	0	0	-	0
Scribner,Evan, Oak	R	-	0	0	0	0	0	-	0	0	0	0	0	0	0	0	0	11.2	0	1	0	0	1.000	0	0	0	0	-	0
Shaw,Bryan, Cle	R	-	0	0	0	0	0	-	0	0	0	0	0	0	0	0	0	76.1	1	10	0	0	1.000	13	2	0	0	.15	-1
Shields,James, KC	R	.286	7	2	0	1	0	.213	47	10	1	0	0	4	2	13	1	227.0	18	30	4	0	.923	11	5	0	4	.45	1
Shoemaker,Matt, LAA	R	.000	1	0	0	0	1	.000	1	0	0	0	0	0	0	1	1	136.0	7	12	3	1	.864	10	3	0	2	.30	2
Shreve,Chasen, Atl	L	-	0	0	0	0	0	-	0	0	0	0	0	0	0	0	0	12.1	0	3	0	0	1.000	2	1	1	0	.50	0
Siegrist,Kevin, StL	L	-	0	0	0	0	0	.000	1	0	0	0	0	0	0	1	0	30.1	0	6	0	0	1.000	7	1	0	0	.14	-1
Simmons,Shae, Atl	R	-	0	0	0	0	0	-	0	0	0	0	0	0	0	0	0	21.2	0	1	0	0	1.000	0	0	0	0	-	0
Simon,Alfredo, Cin	R	.119	59	7	0	2	7	.114	70	8	3	0	0	2	1	27	7	196.1	15	26	2	0	.953	23	8	0	1	.35	4
Sipp,Tony, Hou	L	-	0	0	0	0	0	-	0	0	0	0	0	0	0	0	0	50.2	4	4	0	0	1.000	4	2	0	0	.50	0
Skaggs,Tyler, LAA	L	.000	3	0	0	0	0	.100	20	2	0	0	0	1	0	11	5	113.0	2	17	1	0	.950	16	7	4	0	.44	-3
Slowey,Kevin, Mia	R	.000	5	0	0	0	0	.077	39	3	1	0	0	2	2	17	7	37.1	5	5	0	0	1.000	3	1	0	0	.33	-1
Smith,Carson, Sea	R	-	0	0	0	0	0	-	0	0	0	0	0	0	0	0	0	8.1	0	1	0	0	1.000	1	1	0	0	1.00	0
Smith,Chad, Det	R	-	0	0	0	0	0	-	0	0	0	0	0	0	0	0	0	11.2	0	2	0	1	1.000	0	0	0	0	-	0
Smith,Joe, LAA	R	-	0	0	0	0	0	.000	2	0	0	0	0	0	0	2	0	74.2	3	12	0	1	1.000	4	0	0	0	.00	1
Smith,Will, Mil	L	-	0	0	0	0	0	-	0	0	0	0	0	0	0	0	0	65.2	0	7	1	0	.875	4	2	1	0	.50	0
Smyly,Drew, Det-TB	L	.000	1	0	0	0	0	.000	2	0	0	0	0	0	0	1	0	153.0	5	20	1	1	.962	24	9	7	0	.38	0
Snodgress,Scott, CWS	L	-	0	0	0	0	0	-	0	0	0	0	0	0	0	0	0	2.1	0	0	0	0	-	0	0	0	0	-	0
Soria,Joakim, Tex-Det	R	-	0	0	0	0	0	-	0	0	0	0	0	0	0	0	0	44.1	1	6	1	0	.875	1	1	1	0	1.00	0
Soriano,Rafael, Was	R	-	0	0	0	0	0	.000	4	0	0	0	0	0	0	1	0	62.0	2	4	0	0	1.000	5	2	0	0	.40	0
Spruill,Zeke, Ari	R	.200	5	1	0	0	0	.167	6	1	1	0	0	0	0	2	0	22.2	0	2	1	0	.667	1	0	0	0	.00	-1
Stammen,Craig, Was	R	.286	7	2	0	0	1	.202	89	18	7	0	0	10	4	35	10	72.2	3	6	1	2	.900	6	1	0	0	.17	-1
Stauffer,Tim, SD	R	.143	7	1	0	0	1	.150	140	21	3	0	0	12	4	63	17	64.1	7	5	0	2	1.000	3	2	0	0	.67	-1
Stinson,Josh, Bal	R	-	0	0	0	0	0	.000	1	0	0	0	0	0	1	1	0	13.0	2	0	0	0	1.000	1	0	0	0	.00	0
Stites,Matt, Ari	R	-	0	0	0	0	0	-	0	0	0	0	0	0	0	0	0	33.0	1	5	0	0	1.000	0	0	0	0	-	1
Storen,Drew, Was	R	-	0	0	0	0	0	.500	2	1	0	0	0	0	0	1	0	56.1	2	8	0	0	1.000	5	1	0	0	.20	0
Straily,Dan, Oak-ChC	R	.000	1	0	0	0	0	.000	3	0	0	0	0	0	2	3	0	52.0	0	4	0	0	1.000	5	1	0	0	.20	-1
Strasburg,Stephen, Was	R	.100	60	6	0	3	9	.148	182	27	7	0	1	13	12	72	25	215.0	13	25	4	2	.905	19	6	0	0	.32	3
Street,Huston, SD-LAA	R	-	0	0	0	0	0	.000	2	0	0	0	0	0	0	0	0	59.1	5	5	0	1	1.000	7	0	0	0	.00	-1
Strickland,Hunter, SF	R	-	0	0	0	0	0	-	0	0	0	0	0	0	0	0	0	7.0	1	0	0	0	1.000	1	1	0	0	1.00	0
Stroman,Marcus, Tor	R	-	0	0	0	0	0	-	0	0	0	0	0	0	0	0	0	130.2	7	19	0	0	1.000	5	1	0	1	.20	1
Strop,Pedro, ChC	R	-	0	0	0	0	0	-	0	0	0	0	0	0	0	0	0	61.0	3	3	0	1	1.000	2	1	0	0	.50	-1
Stults,Eric, SD	L	.083	48	4	0	1	4	.172	186	32	7	0	1	12	6	69	20	176.0	10	28	2	2	.950	18	3	1	0	.17	2
Surkamp,Eric, CWS	L	-	0	0	0	0	0	.111	9	1	0	0	0	1	1	5	0	24.1	1	6	0	1	1.000	3	0	0	0	.00	2
Swarzak,Anthony, Min	R	-	0	0	0	0	0	.000	5	0	0	0	0	0	0	4	0	86.0	8	7	0	0	1.000	2	0	0	0	.00	0
Tanaka,Masahiro, NYY	R	.111	9	1	0	0	0	.111	9	1	0	0	0	0	0	5	0	136.1	12	14	0	1	1.000	7	1	1	0	.14	4
Tazawa,Junichi, Bos	R	-	0	0	0	0	0	-	0	0	0	0	0	0	0	0	0	63.0	1	6	3	0	.700	0	0	0	1	-	2
Teheran,Julio, Atl	R	.106	66	7	0	6	8	.155	129	20	4	0	0	8	4	38	14	221.0	16	32	0	2	1.000	19	5	1	5	.26	5
Tepesch,Nick, Tex	R	.500	2	1	0	0	0	.200	5	1	0	0	0	0	0	1	0	126.0	6	18	0	1	1.000	10	6	3	1	.60	-1
Thatcher,Joe, Ari-LAA	L	-	0	0	0	0	0	.000	1	0	0	0	0	0	0	1	0	30.1	1	0	0	0	1.000	3	1	0	0	.33	-2
Thayer,Dale, SD	R	.000	1	0	0	0	0	.000	3	0	0	0	0	0	0	1	0	65.1	2	6	0	0	1.000	11	2	0	0	.18	-3
Thielbar,Caleb, Min	L	-	0	0	0	0	0	-	0	0	0	0	0	0	0	0	0	47.2	2	7	1	0	.900	6	1	1	0	.17	2
Thomas,Ian, Atl	L	-	0	0	0	0	0	-	0	0	0	0	0	0	0	0	0	10.2	3	1	0	0	1.000	1	0	0	1	.00	-1
Thompson,Aaron, Min	L	-	0	0	0	0	0	-	0	0	0	0	0	0	1	0	0	7.1	1	0	0	0	1.000	0	0	0	0	-	0
Thompson,Taylor, CWS	R	-	0	0	0	0	0	-	0	0	0	0	0	0	0	0	0	5.1	0	2	0	0	1.000	1	0	0	0	.00	0
Thornburg,Tyler, Mil	R	.000	1	0	0	0	0	.045	22	1	1	0	0	0	0	10	2	29.2	3	3	0	0	1.000	3	1	0	0	.33	0
Thornton,Matt, NYY-Was	L	-	0	0	0	0	0	.000	1	0	0	0	0	0	0	1	0	36.0	4	6	0	0	1.000	7	2	1	0	.29	0
Tillman,Chris, Bal	R	.000	4	0	0	0	1	.000	10	0	0	0	0	0	3	3	3	207.1	10	19	2	0	.935	4	3	0	1	.75	2
Tolleson,Shawn, Tex	R	-	0	0	0	0	0	-	0	0	0	0	0	0	0	0	0	71.2	5	6	0	0	1.000	6	3	0	0	.33	-2
Tomlin,Josh, Cle	R	-	0	0	0	0	0	.571	7	4	0	0	0	1	0	3	0	104.0	10	10	2	2	.909	3	2	0	0	.67	1
Tonkin,Michael, Min	R	-	0	0	0	0	0	-	0	0	0	0	0	0	0	0	0	19.0	1	4	0	0	1.000	4	0	0	1	.00	0
Torres,Alex, SD	L	.000	1	0	0	0	0	.000	1	0	0	0	0	0	0	1	0	54.0	3	8	2	1	.846	5	1	1	0	.20	1
Torres,Carlos, NYM	R	.000	5	0	0	0	2	.091	33	3	0	0	0	2	2	19	6	97.0	4	8	1	3	.923	5	0	0	0	.00	-2
Treinen,Blake, Was	R	.083	12	1	0	0	2	.083	12	1	0	0	0	0	1	8	2	50.2	6	12	1	0	.947	2	1	0	0	.50	-3
Tropeano,Nicholas, Hou	R	.000	1	0	0	0	0	.000	1	0	0	0	0	0	1	0	0	21.2	3	2	0	1	1.000	2	1	0	0	.50	0
Tuivailala,Samuel, StL	R	-	0	0	0	0	0	-	0	0	0	0	0	0	0	0	0	1.0	0	0	0	0	-	0	0	0	0	-	0
Turner,Jacob, Mia-ChC	R	.174	23	4	0	0	5	.097	72	7	2	1	0	0	1	36	10	113.0	14	14	0	1	1.000	20	3	1	1	.15	-4
Uehara,Koji, Bos	R	-	0	0	0	0	0	.000	2	0	0	0	0	0	1	1	0	64.1	3	7	0	0	1.000	2	1	0	1	.50	0
Valdes,Raul, Hou	L	-	0	0	0	0	0	.385	13	5	2	0	0	1	0	3	5	3.2	0	0	0	0	-	0	0	0	0	-	0
Valverde,Jose, NYM	R	-	0	0	0	0	0	.500	2	1	1	0	0	0	0	1	0	20.2	0	2	0	0	.000	5	0	0	0	.00	-2
Vargas,Jason, KC	L	-	0	0	0	0	0	.262	61	16	4	0	0	4	3	16	2	187.0	7	22	2	3	.935	17	3	0	0	.18	2
Varvaro,Anthony, Atl	R	-	0	0	0	0	0	.000	1	0	0	0	0	0	0	1	0	54.2	1	4	0	0	1.000	1	0	0	0	.00	-2
Veal,Donnie, CWS	L	-	0	0	0	0	0	-	0	0	0	0	0	0	0	0	0	6.0	0	0	0	0	-	1	0	0	0	.00	0
Ventura,Yordano, KC	R	.250	4	1	0	0	1	.250	4	1	0	0	0	0	0	3	1	183.0	26	20	2	0	.958	2	1	0	0	.50	0
Veras,Jose, ChC-Hou	R	-	0	0	0	0	0	-	0	0	0	0	0	0	1	0	0	46.0	4	1	0	0	1.000	6	0	0	0	.00	-1
VerHagen,Drew, Det	R	-	0	0	0	0	0	-	0	0	0	0	0	0	0	0	0	5.0	0	0	0	0	-	2	2	0	0	1.00	0
Verlander,Justin, Det	R	.333	6	2	0	0	1	.063	32	2	0	0	0	0	0	15	10	206.0	10	23	6	2	.846	17	4	0	0	.24	0
Villanueva,Carlos, ChC	R	.000	10	0	0	0	3	.102	108	11	0	0	0	4	3	52	15	77.2	3	12	0	0	1.000	13	1	0	0	.08	-3
Villarreal,Pedro, Cin	R	.500	2	1	0	0	0	.333	3	1	0	0	0	0	0	1	0	14.2	0	0	0	0	-	1	1	0	0	1.00	0

Pitchers Hitting, Fielding and Holding Runners

Pitcher	T	2014 Hitting						Career Hitting										2014 Fielding and Holding Runners											
		Avg	AB	H	HR	RBI	SH	Avg	AB	H	2B	3B	HR	RBI	BB	SO	SH	Inn	PO	A	E	DP	Pct	SBA	CS	PCS	PPO	CS%	RS
Vincent,Nick, SD	R	.000	1	0	0	0	0	.000	2	0	0	0	0	0	0	2	0	55.0	2	9	1	1	.917	1	0	0	0	.00	0
Vizcaino,Arodys, ChC	R	-	0	0	0	0	0	-	0	0	0	0	0	0	0	0	0	5.0	0	0	0	0	-	0	0	0	0	-	-1
Vogelsong,Ryan, SF	R	.115	61	7	0	2	2	.145	256	37	8	0	0	9	14	107	31	184.2	11	19	2	1	.938	18	6	0	1	.33	2
Volquez,Edinson, Pit	R	.038	53	2	0	2	8	.085	271	23	2	0	1	8	7	138	43	192.2	9	26	3	2	.921	16	7	1	0	.44	1
Wacha,Michael, StL	R	.034	29	1	0	2	3	.080	50	4	0	0	0	5	0	28	4	107.0	12	13	0	1	1.000	2	2	1	0	1.00	2
Wada,Tsuyoshi, ChC	L	.050	20	1	0	0	3	.050	20	1	0	0	0	0	1	10	3	69.1	4	8	0	0	1.000	1	1	1	0	1.00	3
Wagner,Neil, Tor	R	-	0	0	0	0	0	-	0	0	0	0	0	0	0	0	0	10.0	0	2	0	0	1.000	1	0	0	0	.00	0
Wainwright,Adam, StL	R	.181	72	13	0	6	7	.202	510	103	25	1	6	39	19	164	41	227.0	20	30	1	2	.980	8	2	0	0	.25	5
Walden,Jordan, Atl	R	-	0	0	0	0	0	-	0	0	0	0	0	0	0	0	0	50.0	4	3	0	0	1.000	9	1	0	0	.11	-1
Walker,Taijuan, Sea	R	-	0	0	0	0	0	-	0	0	0	0	0	0	0	0	0	38.0	3	7	0	1	1.000	3	0	0	0	.00	2
Wall,Josh, LAA	R	-	0	0	0	0	0	-	0	0	0	0	0	0	0	0	0	1.0	0	0	0	0	-	0	0	0	0	-	0
Wang,Wei-Chung, Mil	L	-	0	0	0	0	0	-	0	0	0	0	0	0	0	0	0	17.1	1	1	0	0	1.000	1	0	0	0	.00	-1
Warren,Adam, NYY	R	-	0	0	0	0	0	-	0	0	0	0	0	0	0	0	0	78.2	2	6	2	0	.800	3	2	0	0	.67	0
Watson,Tony, Pit	L	.333	3	1	0	0	0	.167	6	1	0	0	0	0	0	5	2	77.1	7	11	1	0	.947	6	2	0	0	.33	0
Weaver,Jered, LAA	R	.000	2	0	0	0	0	.118	34	4	0	0	0	1	2	14	0	213.1	12	25	2	0	.949	30	5	0	3	.17	0
Webb,Daniel, CWS	R	-	0	0	0	0	0	-	0	0	0	0	0	0	0	0	0	67.2	3	7	3	0	.769	8	1	0	0	.13	-2
Webb,Ryan, Bal	R	-	0	0	0	0	0	.200	5	1	0	0	0	0	0	4	0	49.1	2	6	0	0	1.000	7	1	0	0	.14	0
Webster,Allen, Bos	R	-	0	0	0	0	0	-	0	0	0	0	0	0	0	0	0	59.0	8	5	0	0	1.000	4	2	0	0	.50	0
West,Matt, Tex	R	-	0	0	0	0	0	-	0	0	0	0	0	0	0	0	0	4.0	0	0	0	0	-	0	0	0	0	-	0
Wheeler,Zack, NYM	R	.080	50	4	0	3	12	.100	80	8	2	0	0	5	2	37	15	185.1	10	22	2	2	.941	10	3	0	1	.30	-1
Whelan,Kevin, Det	R	-	0	0	0	0	0	-	0	0	0	0	0	0	0	0	0	1.1	0	0	0	0	-	0	0	0	0	-	0
Whitley,Chase, NYY	R	.200	5	1	0	0	0	.200	5	1	0	0	0	0	0	0	0	75.2	7	6	0	0	1.000	11	6	0	0	.55	0
Wieland,Joe, SD	R	.000	3	0	0	0	0	.182	11	2	1	0	0	2	0	4	0	11.1	0	1	1	0	.500	0	0	0	0	-	0
Wilhelmsen,Tom, Sea	R	-	0	0	0	0	0	-	0	0	0	0	0	0	0	0	0	79.1	8	8	1	0	.941	4	0	0	0	.00	-2
Williams,J. Hou-Tex-Phi	R	.167	12	2	0	3	4	.119	134	16	3	0	0	4	1	59	23	115.0	7	12	0	2	1.000	7	2	0	1	.29	-1
Wilson,Alex, Bos	R	-	0	0	0	0	0	-	0	0	0	0	0	0	0	0	0	28.1	3	3	0	0	1.000	1	1	0	0	1.00	1
Wilson,Brian, LAD	R	-	0	0	0	0	0	.000	9	0	0	0	0	0	0	2	1	48.1	1	1	1	0	.667	10	3	0	0	.30	-3
Wilson,C.J., LAA	L	.000	2	0	0	0	0	.087	23	2	0	1	0	0	3	9	4	175.2	9	22	3	1	.912	20	7	0	1	.35	1
Wilson,Justin, Pit	L	.000	1	0	0	0	0	.000	6	0	0	0	0	0	0	6	1	60.0	1	3	1	0	.800	8	1	1	0	.13	-3
Withrow,Chris, LAD	R	-	0	0	0	0	0	.000	1	0	0	0	0	0	0	1	1	21.1	1	1	1	1	.667	6	2	0	0	.33	0
Wolf,Randy, Mia	L	.143	7	1	0	0	0	.184	694	128	33	0	5	58	32	231	79	25.2	3	5	0	1	1.000	2	1	1	0	.50	1
Wood,Alex, Atl	L	.073	41	3	0	2	5	.048	62	3	0	0	2	2	2	43	6	171.2	3	25	2	2	.933	11	4	1	4	.36	0
Wood,Blake, Cle	R	-	0	0	0	0	0	.000	1	0	0	0	0	0	0	0	0	6.1	1	1	0	0	1.000	3	1	0	0	.33	1
Wood,Travis, ChC	L	.232	56	13	3	10	7	.192	239	46	8	1	9	28	4	87	20	173.2	6	18	0	3	1.000	13	3	0	0	.23	4
Wooten,Rob, Mil	R	-	0	0	0	0	0	.000	1	0	0	0	0	0	0	3	0	34.1	5	1	1	0	.857	2	1	0	0	.50	-1
Workman,Brandon, Bos	R	.000	3	0	0	0	1	.000	3	0	0	0	0	0	0	3	1	87.0	8	5	1	0	.929	20	7	0	0	.35	-2
Worley,Vance, Pit	R	.063	32	2	0	0	5	.127	118	15	3	0	0	7	2	47	14	110.2	4	12	1	0	.941	3	3	0	0	1.00	-1
Wright,Jamey, LAD	R	.000	5	0	0	0	1	.144	443	64	15	1	1	17	12	179	52	70.1	5	12	0	0	1.000	4	0	0	0	.00	-1
Wright,Steven, Bos	R	-	0	0	0	0	0	-	0	0	0	0	0	0	0	0	0	21.0	2	4	0	1	1.000	1	0	0	1	.00	0
Wright,Wesley, ChC	L	-	0	0	0	0	0	.063	16	1	0	0	0	0	0	8	1	48.1	2	12	0	0	1.000	4	2	0	0	.50	3
Yates,Kirby, TB	R	-	0	0	0	0	0	-	0	0	0	0	0	0	0	0	0	36.0	1	4	0	0	1.000	3	1	0	0	.33	0
Young,Chris, Sea	R	.000	1	0	0	0	0	.144	202	29	6	1	1	14	10	81	27	165.0	7	10	1	0	.944	17	4	0	0	.24	-2
Zeid,Josh, Hou	R	.000	1	0	0	0	0	.000	1	0	0	0	0	0	0	1	0	20.2	1	7	0	0	1.000	1	0	0	1	.00	1
Ziegler,Brad, Ari	R	.000	1	0	0	0	0	.143	7	1	0	0	0	0	0	3	0	67.0	6	16	2	2	.917	1	0	0	0	.00	2
Zimmermann,Jordan, Was	R	.182	55	10	0	1	9	.171	257	44	5	0	1	12	10	79	37	199.2	13	19	1	0	.970	7	4	0	0	.57	2

Hitters Pitching

Player	2014 Pitching										Career Pitching										
	G	W	L	Sv	IP	H	R	ER	BB	SO	ERA	G	W	L	Sv	IP	H	R	ER	BB	SO	ERA
Anna,Dean, NYY	1	-	-	-	1.0	3	2	2	-	-	18.00	1	0	0	0	1.0	3	2	2	0	0	18.00
Arencibia,J.P., Tex	1	-	-	-	1.0	1	-	-	-	-	0.00	1	0	0	0	1.0	1	0	0	0	0	0.00
Baker,John, ChC	1	1	-	-	1.0	-	-	-	1	-	0.00	1	1	0	0	1.0	0	0	0	1	0	0.00
Butera,Drew, LAD	2	-	-	-	1.2	2	2	2	-	2	10.80	3	0	0	0	2.2	2	2	2	1	3	6.75
Carp,Mike, Bos-Tex	1	-	-	-	1.0	-	1	1	5	-	9.00	1	0	0	0	1.0	0	1	1	5	0	9.00
Cuddyer,Michael, Col	-	-	-	-	-	-	-	-	-	-		1	0	0	0	1.0	2	0	0	1	0	0.00
Davis,Chris, Bal	-	-	-	-	-	-	-	-	-	-		1	1	0	0	2.0	2	0	0	1	2	0.00
Descalso,Daniel, StL	1	-	-	-	0.1	-	-	-	-	-	0.00	1	0	0	0	0.1	0	0	0	0	0	0.00
Dunn,Adam, CWS-Oak	1	-	-	-	1.0	2	1	1	1	-	9.00	1	0	0	0	1.0	2	1	1	1	0	9.00
Elmore,Jake, Cin	-	-	-	-	-	-	-	-	-	-		1	0	0	0	0.1	0	0	0	0	0	0.00
Garcia,Leury, CWS	1	-	1	-	1.0	1	2	2	2	-	18.00	1	0	1	0	1.0	1	2	2	2	0	18.00
Gentry,Craig, Oak	-	-	-	-	-	-	-	-	-	-		1	0	0	0	1.0	3	2	2	1	0	18.00
Gimenez,Chris, Tex-Cle	1	-	-	-	1.0	-	-	-	-	1	0.00	1	0	0	0	1.0	0	0	0	0	1	0.00
Harrison,Josh, Pit	-	-	-	-	-	-	-	-	-	-		1	0	0	0	0.1	0	0	0	0	0	0.00
Kelly,Don, Det	-	-	-	-	-	-	-	-	-	-		1	0	0	0	0.1	0	0	0	0	0	0.00
Maldonado,Martin, Mil	1	-	-	-	1.0	1	-	-	-	-	0.00	1	0	0	0	1.0	1	0	0	0	0	0.00
Marte,Andy, Ari	-	-	-	-	-	-	-	-	-	-		1	0	0	0	1.0	0	0	0	0	1	0.00
Mathis,Jeff, Mia	-	-	-	-	-	-	-	-	-	-		2	0	0	0	2.0	4	2	2	1	0	9.00
McDonald,John, LAA	-	-	-	-	-	-	-	-	-	-		1	0	0	0	0.1	2	0	0	0	1	0.00
Moreland,Mitch, Tex	1	-	-	-	1.0	-	-	-	-	-	0.00	1	0	0	0	1.0	0	0	0	0	0	0.00
Murphy,David, Cle	-	-	-	-	-	-	-	-	-	-		1	0	0	0	1.0	1	0	0	0	1	0.00
Overbay,Lyle, Mil	1	-	-	-	0.1	-	-	-	-	-	0.00	1	0	0	0	0.1	0	0	0	0	0	0.00
Raburn,Ryan, Cle	-	-	-	-	-	-	-	-	-	-		1	0	0	0	1.0	0	0	0	0	1	0.00
Recker,Anthony, NYM	-	-	-	-	-	-	-	-	-	-		1	0	0	0	1.0	1	2	2	1	0	18.00
Romine,Andrew, Det	1	-	-	-	1.0	4	3	3	-	1	27.00	1	0	0	0	1.0	4	3	3	0	1	27.00
Ross,Cody, Ari	-	-	-	-	-	-	-	-	-	-		1	0	0	0	1.0	1	0	0	0	0	0.00
Schumaker,Skip, Cin	1	-	-	-	1.0	-	-	-	1	-	0.00	4	0	0	0	4.0	4	2	2	5	3	4.50
Snider,Travis, Pit	1	-	-	-	1.0	1	2	2	2	1	18.00	1	0	0	0	1.0	1	2	2	2	1	18.00
Swisher,Nick, Cle	-	-	-	-	-	-	-	-	-	-		1	0	0	0	1.0	1	0	0	1	1	0.00
Tolleson,Steve, Tor	2	-	-	-	1.0	1	-	-	-	1	0.00	2	0	0	0	1.0	1	0	0	0	1	0.00
Wilson,Josh, Tex	-	-	-	-	-	-	-	-	-	-		3	0	1	0	3.0	4	3	3	3	0	9.00
Worth,Danny, Det	2	-	-	-	2.0	4	1	1	-	2	4.50	2	0	0	0	2.0	4	1	1	0	2	4.50

378

Hitter Analysis

The Hitter Analysis section provides a set of detailed information on hitters who had at least 100 plate appearances in 2014. It is information that has not always been widely available because of the logistical challenges in their data collection. The data in this section covers:

PA - Plate Appearances
Pit - Pitches Seen
T - Pitches Taken
Sw - Pitches Swung At
St - Pitches Taken for a Strike
B - Pitches Taken for a Ball
S/M - Swings and Misses
F - Foul Balls Hit
InP - Pitches Hit In Play
P/PA - Pitches Per Plate Appearance
GB - Groundballs Hit
LD - Line Drives Hit
FB - Flyballs Hit

Additionally, we have a pair of categories that combine several of those fields in order to group players into two sets of groupings:

1. Very Patient, Patient, Neutral, Aggressive, or Very Aggressive
2. Groundball Hitters, Medium Hitters, or Flyball (Air) Hitters

For many of the established baseball stars, these categories confirm their reputations. For example, Joey Votto finished with the 10th most pitches per plate appearance, 4.33, in his injury-shortened 2014 season. For him and fellow patient hitters like Mike Napoli (4.47 P/PA), Mike Trout (4.45 P/PA), Brett Gardner (4.44

P/PA), Matt Carpenter (4.37 P/PA), and Carlos Santana (4.30 P/PA), we could probably add a second "Very" to make them Very, Very Patient hitters.

Many of baseball's younger players, however, haven't established the same reputations outside of scouts and the most savvy prospect mavens. A few of those players are in the company of Votto and the other Very Patient Hitters. Jon Singleton, the new Astros first baseman, actually tops the list with 4.49 pitches per plate appearance. Twins catcher Josmil Pinto (4.46 P/PA) and Red Sox centerfielder/everywhere fielder Mookie Betts (4.36) are not too far behind.

Of course, patience at the plate is not the only path to stardom. Jose Altuve just finished a spectacular season in which he led baseball with a .341 batting average, and he did that with the fewest pitches per plate appearance, 3.11, in baseball. When you rack up hits like Altuve did, you don't need many walks to frequently reach first base. Exciting young players like Nolan Arenado (3.45 P/PA) and Rougned Odor (3.52) have similarly impatient approaches, though they have not been as extreme or as successful as the Astros' second baseman.

Hitter Analysis

Hitter	PA	PS	T	Sw	St	B	S/M	F	In P	P/PA	Group	GB	LD	FB	Hits
Bobby Abreu*	155	647	403	244	143	260	45	85	114	4.17	Very Patient	56	25	33	Ground
Jose Abreu	622	2351	1101	1250	255	846	341	480	429	3.78	Aggressive	195	100	134	Ground
Dustin Ackley*	542	2054	1166	888	436	730	140	331	417	3.78	Aggressive	187	76	150	Medium
Matt Adams*	563	2050	976	1074	309	667	219	435	420	3.64	Very Aggressive	145	102	173	Air
Jim Adduci*	114	453	226	227	70	156	52	98	77	3.97	Patient	38	10	25	Air
Ehire Adrianza#	106	393	179	214	50	129	41	95	78	3.71	Aggressive	27	19	30	Air
Arismendy Alcantara#	300	1174	652	522	242	410	159	175	188	3.91	Patient	94	22	68	Ground
Abraham Almonte#	220	798	438	360	148	290	91	122	147	3.63	Very Aggressive	69	29	39	Ground
Yonder Alonso*	288	1026	540	486	161	379	71	181	234	3.56	Very Aggressive	100	44	90	Air
Jose Altuve	707	2200	1081	1119	368	713	105	401	613	3.11	Very Aggressive	290	139	181	Ground
Pedro Alvarez*	445	1718	908	810	248	660	244	281	285	3.86	Neutral	129	45	111	Medium
Alexi Amarista*	466	1743	922	821	338	584	116	338	367	3.74	Aggressive	173	80	100	Ground
Elvis Andrus	685	2736	1710	1026	639	1071	145	341	539	3.99	Patient	306	107	109	Ground
Nori Aoki*	549	2087	1145	942	365	780	92	399	451	3.80	Neutral	265	90	73	Ground
Oswaldo Arcia*	410	1647	794	853	215	579	296	311	246	4.02	Patient	90	53	103	Air
Nolan Arenado	467	1611	766	845	229	537	136	329	380	3.45	Very Aggressive	142	78	158	Air
J.P. Arencibia	222	834	381	453	104	277	124	186	143	3.76	Aggressive	48	23	72	Air
Joaquin Arias	204	722	344	378	119	225	50	155	173	3.54	Very Aggressive	90	31	51	Ground
Cody Asche*	434	1577	845	732	289	556	178	255	299	3.63	Very Aggressive	121	70	105	Air
Alex Avila*	457	1862	1098	764	331	767	256	266	242	4.07	Very Patient	107	60	73	Ground
Mike Aviles	374	1358	683	675	252	431	97	267	311	3.63	Very Aggressive	131	62	104	Medium
Erick Aybar#	642	2136	1068	1068	356	712	131	398	539	3.33	Very Aggressive	256	118	145	Ground
Javier Baez	229	939	500	439	162	338	185	136	118	4.10	Very Patient	48	16	53	Air
Jeff Baker	225	842	447	395	157	290	77	158	160	3.74	Aggressive	77	39	44	Ground
John Baker*	208	816	441	375	130	311	85	161	129	3.92	Patient	59	32	34	Ground
Clint Barmes	116	446	248	198	89	159	40	73	85	3.84	Neutral	32	18	35	Air
Brandon Barnes	313	1130	469	661	127	342	212	251	198	3.61	Very Aggressive	87	40	60	Ground
Darwin Barney	262	983	527	456	205	322	68	181	207	3.75	Aggressive	88	41	76	Medium
Jose Bautista	673	2743	1660	1083	510	1150	203	416	464	4.08	Very Patient	187	83	193	Air
Gordon Beckham	483	1830	942	888	294	648	158	357	373	3.79	Neutral	167	58	145	Medium
Brandon Belt*	235	936	452	484	112	340	135	198	151	3.98	Patient	57	27	66	Air
Carlos Beltran#	449	1682	936	746	297	639	124	294	328	3.75	Aggressive	145	54	129	Air
Adrian Beltre	614	2331	1227	1104	374	853	175	449	480	3.80	Neutral	203	106	171	Medium
Christian Bethancourt	117	391	169	222	49	120	68	67	87	3.34	Very Aggressive	47	13	27	Ground
Mookie Betts	213	928	593	335	240	353	45	131	159	4.36	Very Patient	64	33	61	Air
Charlie Blackmon*	648	2460	1174	1286	361	813	202	577	507	3.80	Neutral	205	107	183	Air
Gregor Blanco*	444	1737	949	788	288	661	148	317	323	3.91	Patient	124	66	119	Air
Willie Bloomquist	139	497	240	257	84	156	50	104	103	3.58	Very Aggressive	51	23	26	Ground
Xander Bogaerts	594	2449	1347	1102	504	843	250	443	409	4.12	Very Patient	155	84	168	Air
Emilio Bonifacio#	426	1692	896	796	319	577	146	335	315	3.97	Patient	155	63	75	Ground
Peter Bourjos	294	1117	598	519	189	409	129	198	192	3.80	Neutral	94	35	47	Ground
Michael Bourn*	487	1898	1056	842	358	698	190	317	335	3.90	Neutral	162	78	82	Ground
Jackie Bradley Jr.*	423	1646	875	771	306	569	202	303	266	3.89	Neutral	121	47	93	Medium
Michael Brantley*	676	2415	1413	1002	461	952	94	348	560	3.57	Very Aggressive	257	143	157	Ground
Ryan Braun	580	2080	1043	1037	330	713	225	392	420	3.59	Very Aggressive	197	83	138	Ground
Domonic Brown*	512	1928	972	956	283	689	190	380	386	3.77	Aggressive	192	67	126	Ground
Jay Bruce*	545	2142	1136	1006	328	808	293	363	350	3.93	Patient	157	72	118	Medium
Drew Butera	192	749	414	335	150	264	65	138	132	3.90	Neutral	44	32	55	Air
Billy Butler	603	2143	1126	1017	385	741	187	369	461	3.55	Very Aggressive	228	102	131	Ground
Marlon Byrd	637	2394	1038	1356	272	766	414	533	409	3.76	Aggressive	151	93	165	Air
Asdrubal Cabrera#	616	2274	1116	1158	304	812	228	478	452	3.69	Aggressive	169	84	186	Air
Everth Cabrera#	391	1597	871	726	295	576	143	299	284	4.08	Very Patient	180	56	33	Ground
Melky Cabrera#	621	2295	1260	1035	427	833	129	398	508	3.70	Aggressive	249	107	149	Ground
Miguel Cabrera	685	2531	1267	1264	344	923	275	484	505	3.69	Aggressive	202	125	178	Air
Lorenzo Cain	502	1853	936	917	315	621	214	338	365	3.69	Aggressive	186	83	95	Ground
Kole Calhoun*	537	2000	1067	933	360	707	193	347	393	3.72	Aggressive	171	93	127	Medium
Alberto Callaspo#	451	1790	1084	706	377	707	74	272	360	3.97	Patient	152	75	133	Air
Eric Campbell	211	889	482	407	152	330	100	169	138	4.21	Very Patient	76	24	38	Ground
Robinson Cano*	665	2321	1208	1113	320	888	150	433	530	3.49	Very Aggressive	279	120	131	Ground
Mike Carp*	149	557	311	246	103	208	52	97	97	3.74	Aggressive	45	20	32	Ground
Matt Carpenter*	709	3101	2076	1025	834	1242	113	417	495	4.37	Very Patient	200	116	172	Medium
Chris Carter	572	2336	1213	1123	336	877	400	394	329	4.08	Very Patient	89	71	169	Air
Nick Castellanos	579	2239	1098	1141	301	797	317	424	400	3.87	Neutral	140	114	146	Air
Welington Castillo	417	1633	908	725	324	584	167	276	282	3.92	Patient	114	53	113	Air
Jason Castro*	512	2035	1051	984	316	735	264	402	318	3.97	Patient	142	62	113	Medium
Starlin Castro	569	2122	1141	981	373	768	197	354	430	3.73	Aggressive	195	96	139	Ground
Francisco Cervelli	162	633	373	260	123	250	67	88	105	3.91	Patient	46	27	32	Ground
Yoenis Cespedes	645	2412	1194	1218	405	789	256	483	479	3.74	Aggressive	161	88	230	Air
Endy Chavez*	258	956	525	431	211	314	66	152	213	3.71	Aggressive	98	38	62	Ground
Robinson Chirinos	338	1256	653	603	233	420	124	236	243	3.72	Aggressive	98	49	87	Air
Lonnie Chisenhall*	533	2045	986	1059	329	657	184	488	386	3.84	Neutral	144	90	146	Air
Michael Choice	280	1078	628	450	244	384	102	161	187	3.85	Neutral	93	25	69	Ground
Shin-Soo Choo*	529	2155	1284	871	438	846	208	335	328	4.07	Very Patient	163	76	97	Ground
Chris Coghlan*	432	1684	924	760	291	633	146	305	309	3.90	Neutral	131	78	96	Medium
Chris Colabello	220	860	466	394	151	315	123	132	139	3.91	Patient	73	19	47	Ground

Hitter Analysis

Hitter	PA	PS	T	Sw	St	B	S/M	F	In P	P/PA	Group	GB	LD	FB	Hits
Tyler Colvin*	149	565	294	271	89	205	85	91	95	3.79	Neutral	45	15	35	Medium
Hank Conger#	260	1015	557	458	162	395	101	178	179	3.90	Patient	63	29	80	Air
Carlos Corporan#	190	723	347	376	91	256	92	148	136	3.81	Neutral	52	28	53	Air
Collin Cowgill	293	1116	643	473	239	404	121	164	188	3.81	Neutral	88	28	64	Ground
Zack Cozart	543	1967	1018	949	372	646	132	385	432	3.62	Very Aggressive	189	75	160	Medium
Allen Craig	505	1932	1053	879	362	691	167	362	350	3.83	Neutral	189	74	87	Ground
Brandon Crawford*	564	2150	1134	1016	328	806	272	370	374	3.81	Neutral	139	74	154	Air
Carl Crawford*	370	1303	586	717	161	425	126	298	292	3.52	Very Aggressive	133	82	75	Ground
Coco Crisp#	536	2148	1306	842	442	864	108	330	404	4.01	Patient	156	81	159	Air
C.J. Cron	253	969	483	486	171	312	114	191	181	3.83	Neutral	63	46	72	Air
Nelson Cruz	678	2530	1286	1244	359	927	330	436	478	3.73	Aggressive	200	82	196	Air
Tony Cruz	150	584	304	280	106	198	47	124	109	3.89	Neutral	60	20	27	Ground
Michael Cuddyer	205	757	375	382	121	254	71	150	161	3.69	Aggressive	78	39	44	Ground
Charlie Culberson	233	844	401	443	138	263	123	166	154	3.62	Very Aggressive	78	21	50	Ground
Jordan Danks*	132	518	272	246	67	205	93	81	72	3.92	Patient	31	14	26	Medium
Travis d'Arnaud	421	1550	813	737	250	563	127	287	323	3.68	Aggressive	134	63	124	Air
Chris Davis*	525	2190	1178	1012	311	867	351	378	283	4.17	Very Patient	97	69	115	Air
Ike Davis*	427	1766	1097	669	352	745	123	260	286	4.14	Very Patient	113	66	107	Air
Khris Davis	549	2069	1028	1041	279	749	295	361	385	3.77	Aggressive	149	82	152	Air
Rajai Davis	494	1742	850	892	278	572	157	344	391	3.53	Very Aggressive	192	73	118	Ground
Alejandro De Aza*	528	2079	1086	993	361	725	224	405	364	3.94	Patient	146	93	110	Medium
David DeJesus*	273	1143	667	476	215	452	67	214	195	4.19	Very Patient	85	42	67	Medium
Matt den Dekker*	174	669	408	261	128	280	61	82	118	3.84	Neutral	55	31	30	Ground
Chris Denorfia	358	1419	833	586	334	499	128	195	263	3.96	Patient	147	52	60	Ground
Daniel Descalso*	184	676	377	299	118	259	56	114	129	3.67	Aggressive	55	22	50	Air
Ian Desmond	648	2480	1255	1225	393	862	356	456	413	3.83	Neutral	206	73	132	Ground
Chris Dickerson*	112	458	250	208	69	181	66	80	62	4.09	Very Patient	26	13	21	Medium
Corey Dickerson*	478	1905	924	981	300	624	225	417	339	3.99	Patient	124	90	123	Air
Derek Dietrich*	183	713	421	292	145	276	65	105	122	3.90	Neutral	51	23	46	Air
Matt Dominguez	607	2272	1173	1099	417	756	236	415	448	3.74	Aggressive	196	79	171	Air
Josh Donaldson	695	2714	1554	1160	459	1095	274	404	482	3.91	Patient	219	65	198	Air
Ryan Doumit#	166	657	354	303	118	236	95	99	109	3.96	Patient	46	19	44	Air
Brian Dozier	707	2956	1799	1157	669	1130	195	482	480	4.18	Very Patient	176	94	203	Air
Stephen Drew*	300	1259	722	537	226	496	118	221	198	4.20	Very Patient	61	34	100	Air
Lucas Duda*	596	2459	1469	990	471	998	255	352	383	4.13	Very Patient	117	78	187	Air
Adam Dunn*	511	2196	1330	866	394	936	283	309	274	4.30	Very Patient	92	64	118	Air
Jarrod Dyson*	290	1116	635	481	222	413	69	196	216	3.85	Neutral	123	27	46	Ground
Adam Eaton*	538	2095	1165	930	460	705	115	408	407	3.89	Neutral	237	80	80	Ground
A.J. Ellis	347	1457	925	532	329	596	85	214	233	4.20	Very Patient	102	39	89	Ground
Mark Ellis	202	853	479	374	169	310	50	178	146	4.22	Very Patient	67	29	44	Ground
Jacoby Ellsbury*	635	2354	1284	1070	388	896	149	431	489	3.71	Aggressive	203	120	163	Medium
Edwin Encarnacion	542	2241	1287	954	407	880	177	381	396	4.13	Very Patient	144	65	187	Air
Alcides Escobar	620	2207	1054	1153	345	709	195	450	508	3.56	Very Aggressive	213	118	157	Air
Eduardo Escobar#	465	1743	838	905	300	538	181	378	346	3.75	Aggressive	140	82	119	Medium
Yunel Escobar	529	1899	1037	862	309	728	134	306	422	3.59	Very Aggressive	204	83	127	Ground
Danny Espinosa#	364	1324	643	681	176	467	237	232	212	3.64	Very Aggressive	85	42	65	Medium
Andre Ethier*	380	1452	774	678	241	533	138	271	269	3.82	Neutral	139	58	71	Ground
Prince Fielder*	178	614	356	258	102	254	50	81	127	3.45	Very Aggressive	64	24	39	Ground
Ryan Flaherty*	312	1167	607	560	180	427	141	202	217	3.74	Aggressive	99	39	71	Ground
Wilmer Flores	274	1028	524	504	197	327	65	209	230	3.75	Aggressive	91	46	92	Air
Tyler Flowers	442	1728	855	873	272	583	299	324	250	3.91	Patient	119	59	71	Ground
Logan Forsythe	336	1356	790	566	297	493	95	235	236	4.04	Very Patient	95	45	93	Air
Dexter Fowler#	505	2085	1187	898	323	864	214	356	328	4.13	Very Patient	141	69	113	Air
Juan Francisco*	320	1253	670	583	209	461	195	214	174	3.92	Patient	67	28	79	Air
Kevin Frandsen	236	778	371	407	125	246	69	141	197	3.30	Very Aggressive	91	41	60	Ground
Todd Frazier	660	2555	1332	1223	383	949	318	443	462	3.87	Neutral	190	100	171	Air
Freddie Freeman*	708	2826	1430	1396	285	1145	348	583	465	3.99	Patient	170	144	151	Air
David Freese	511	1984	1085	899	381	704	209	347	343	3.88	Neutral	167	88	88	Ground
Sam Fuld*	402	1675	1011	664	396	615	93	275	296	4.17	Very Patient	142	57	85	Ground
Freddy Galvis#	128	514	282	232	101	181	49	93	90	4.02	Patient	36	7	44	Air
Avisail Garcia	190	702	322	380	79	243	129	121	130	3.69	Aggressive	73	20	37	Ground
Leury Garcia#	155	540	247	293	86	161	70	121	102	3.48	Very Aggressive	58	13	23	Ground
Brett Gardner*	636	2821	1776	1045	678	1098	154	451	440	4.44	Very Patient	176	91	155	Air
Evan Gattis	401	1424	673	751	197	476	207	270	274	3.55	Very Aggressive	106	46	122	Air
Scooter Gennett*	474	1624	761	863	226	535	132	346	385	3.43	Very Aggressive	155	94	127	Medium
Craig Gentry	258	959	560	399	208	352	69	138	190	3.72	Aggressive	88	38	53	Ground
Conor Gillaspie*	506	1846	944	902	266	678	144	369	389	3.65	Very Aggressive	153	84	151	Air
Chris Gimenez	128	522	302	225	108	194	44	94	87	4.12	Very Patient	40	20	27	Ground
Jake Goebbert*	115	445	260	185	90	170	50	66	69	3.87	Neutral	25	20	24	Air
Ryan Goins*	193	723	375	348	152	223	65	137	146	3.75	Aggressive	76	25	36	Ground
Paul Goldschmidt	479	1976	1211	765	392	819	189	273	299	4.13	Very Patient	134	67	98	Medium
Jonny Gomes	321	1348	831	517	314	517	122	203	192	4.20	Very Patient	50	46	96	Air
Yan Gomes	518	1997	1003	994	340	663	244	379	371	3.86	Neutral	136	89	146	Air
Carlos Gomez	644	2301	988	1313	196	792	345	531	437	3.57	Very Aggressive	158	91	172	Air
Adrian Gonzalez*	660	2502	1230	1272	317	913	258	524	490	3.79	Neutral	188	116	185	Air

382

Hitter Analysis

Hitter	PA	PS	T	Sw	St	B	S/M	F	In P	P/PA	Group	GB	LD	FB	Hits
Carlos Gonzalez*	281	1053	486	567	114	372	169	207	191	3.75	Aggressive	89	29	71	Medium
Marwin Gonzalez#	310	1143	605	538	232	373	98	209	231	3.69	Aggressive	115	41	67	Ground
Alex Gordon*	643	2655	1511	1144	464	1047	249	454	441	4.13	Very Patient	188	85	168	Air
Dee Gordon*	650	2459	1319	1140	554	765	156	476	508	3.78	Neutral	275	98	88	Ground
Anthony Gose*	274	1041	545	496	185	360	143	183	170	3.80	Neutral	92	29	28	Ground
Tuffy Gosewisch	132	494	246	248	97	149	39	104	105	3.74	Aggressive	55	18	31	Ground
Phil Gosselin	136	514	298	216	121	177	44	70	102	3.78	Aggressive	56	16	24	Ground
Yasmani Grandal#	443	1889	1136	753	372	764	194	291	268	4.26	Very Patient	114	52	102	Air
Curtis Granderson*	654	2702	1565	1137	469	1096	276	433	428	4.13	Very Patient	145	80	199	Air
Grant Green	103	368	178	190	76	102	33	76	81	3.57	Very Aggressive	38	17	26	Ground
Didi Gregorius*	299	1192	627	565	207	420	121	222	222	3.99	Patient	82	43	94	Air
Randal Grichuk	116	454	222	232	68	154	69	83	80	3.91	Patient	31	12	36	Air
Robbie Grossman#	422	1776	1093	683	371	722	141	282	260	4.21	Very Patient	105	61	88	Medium
Brandon Guyer	294	1113	548	565	166	382	123	227	215	3.79	Neutral	97	39	58	Ground
Jesus Guzman	184	758	455	303	162	293	73	117	113	4.12	Very Patient	49	31	33	Ground
Tony Gwynn*	127	486	296	190	106	190	31	71	88	3.83	Neutral	38	15	24	Ground
Jedd Gyorko	443	1691	924	767	286	638	198	266	303	3.82	Neutral	132	66	105	Medium
Billy Hamilton#	611	2319	1242	1077	453	789	193	425	459	3.80	Neutral	169	86	152	Air
Josh Hamilton*	381	1392	655	737	149	506	270	231	236	3.65	Very Aggressive	87	58	91	Air
Ryan Hanigan	263	1066	645	421	236	409	55	176	190	4.05	Very Patient	71	41	76	Air
J.J. Hardy	569	2222	1339	883	565	774	167	284	432	3.91	Patient	185	82	161	Medium
Bryce Harper*	395	1539	753	786	191	562	223	311	252	3.90	Neutral	106	53	84	Medium
Josh Harrison	550	1968	932	1036	315	617	203	390	443	3.58	Very Aggressive	163	105	169	Air
Corey Hart	255	958	484	474	154	330	136	164	174	3.76	Aggressive	70	29	75	Air
Chase Headley#	531	2144	1229	915	392	837	192	374	349	4.04	Very Patient	141	95	111	Medium
Adeiny Hechavarria	574	1917	840	1077	253	587	176	440	460	3.34	Very Aggressive	237	98	105	Ground
Chris Heisey	299	1078	496	582	153	343	150	214	218	3.61	Very Aggressive	74	37	100	Air
Cesar Hernandez#	125	495	259	236	90	169	58	95	83	3.96	Patient	41	20	16	Ground
Enrique Hernandez	134	540	302	238	106	196	38	100	100	4.03	Patient	38	21	41	Air
Elian Herrera#	140	515	248	267	76	172	60	106	101	3.68	Aggressive	42	20	32	Medium
Jonathan Herrera#	104	374	210	164	92	118	29	65	70	3.60	Very Aggressive	35	13	15	Ground
Jason Heyward*	649	2548	1450	1098	446	1004	200	420	478	3.93	Patient	217	90	170	Medium
Aaron Hicks#	225	952	591	361	178	413	71	157	133	4.23	Very Patient	70	26	33	Ground
Brandon Hicks	242	985	523	462	121	402	178	153	131	4.07	Very Patient	39	21	67	Air
Aaron Hill	541	2090	1148	942	386	762	155	371	416	3.86	Neutral	143	102	171	Air
L.J. Hoes	136	557	313	244	105	208	62	87	95	4.10	Very Patient	51	18	25	Ground
Bryan Holaday	171	617	287	330	92	195	72	133	125	3.61	Very Aggressive	57	23	36	Ground
Matt Holliday	667	2450	1260	1190	300	960	219	495	476	3.67	Aggressive	217	79	180	Medium
Brock Holt*	492	2023	1214	809	514	700	116	334	359	4.11	Very Patient	177	93	82	Ground
Eric Hosmer*	547	2112	1093	1019	341	752	177	426	416	3.86	Neutral	212	70	132	Ground
Ryan Howard*	648	2637	1363	1274	331	1032	418	472	384	4.07	Very Patient	156	85	143	Air
Nick Hundley	233	859	412	447	123	289	117	170	160	3.69	Aggressive	59	36	63	Air
Torii Hunter	586	2001	929	1072	277	652	234	371	467	3.41	Very Aggressive	221	99	144	Ground
Chris Iannetta	373	1494	842	652	227	615	175	257	220	4.01	Patient	84	45	91	Air
Raul Ibanez*	280	1121	605	516	177	428	136	192	188	4.00	Patient	85	35	66	Medium
Ender Inciarte*	447	1561	780	781	267	513	105	307	369	3.49	Very Aggressive	180	83	86	Ground
Omar Infante	575	2039	1183	856	447	736	126	258	472	3.55	Very Aggressive	177	106	183	Air
Travis Ishikawa*	119	479	252	227	84	168	61	91	75	4.03	Patient	18	23	34	Air
Austin Jackson	656	2697	1565	1132	563	1002	219	450	463	4.11	Very Patient	193	118	151	Air
John Jaso*	344	1313	718	595	222	496	112	234	249	3.82	Neutral	91	64	94	Air
Jon Jay*	468	1650	845	805	252	593	137	326	342	3.53	Very Aggressive	174	95	67	Ground
Desmond Jennings	542	2160	1246	914	442	804	184	349	381	3.99	Patient	175	63	122	Ground
Derek Jeter	634	2214	1088	1126	334	754	156	464	506	3.49	Very Aggressive	303	90	99	Ground
Chris Johnson	611	2230	999	1231	304	695	355	449	427	3.65	Very Aggressive	204	114	107	Ground
Kelly Johnson*	297	1145	627	518	196	431	115	208	195	3.87	Neutral	95	41	58	Ground
Reed Johnson	201	699	307	392	122	185	92	145	155	3.46	Very Aggressive	65	30	57	Air
Adam Jones	682	2483	1103	1380	292	811	363	499	518	3.64	Very Aggressive	242	90	183	Medium
Garrett Jones*	547	2199	1156	1043	345	811	214	445	384	4.02	Patient	143	75	162	Air
James Jones*	328	1223	630	593	253	377	127	217	249	3.73	Aggressive	124	55	50	Ground
Caleb Joseph	275	1095	577	518	205	372	113	219	186	3.98	Patient	58	39	81	Air
Matt Joyce*	493	2015	1136	879	305	831	234	329	316	4.09	Very Patient	135	60	119	Air
Ryan Kalish*	130	491	253	238	84	169	51	93	94	3.78	Aggressive	55	17	18	Ground
Munenori Kawasaki*	274	1134	713	421	291	422	60	161	200	4.14	Very Patient	103	55	28	Ground
Don Kelly*	185	759	431	328	141	290	54	139	135	4.10	Very Patient	53	33	47	Air
Matt Kemp	599	2298	1221	1077	360	861	326	349	402	3.84	Neutral	173	104	125	Medium
Howie Kendrick	674	2510	1310	1200	446	864	237	451	512	3.72	Aggressive	305	96	107	Ground
Kevin Kiermaier*	364	1295	673	622	203	470	131	224	267	3.56	Very Aggressive	132	42	77	Ground
Ian Kinsler	726	2568	1349	1219	498	851	126	480	613	3.54	Very Aggressive	228	119	261	Air
Jason Kipnis*	555	2238	1295	943	458	837	175	365	403	4.03	Patient	184	90	124	Ground
Paul Konerko	224	845	453	392	167	286	89	144	159	3.77	Aggressive	65	36	58	Air
Erik Kratz	115	434	206	228	73	133	58	81	89	3.77	Aggressive	36	16	36	Air
Marc Krauss*	208	889	547	342	188	359	77	133	132	4.27	Very Patient	50	25	57	Air
Jason Kubel*	176	787	470	317	152	318	90	130	97	4.47	Very Patient	37	28	32	Air
Tommy La Stella*	360	1489	851	638	285	566	98	257	283	4.14	Very Patient	134	64	81	Ground
Juan Lagares	452	1697	869	828	330	539	148	342	338	3.75	Aggressive	148	71	105	Ground

Hitter Analysis

Hitter	PA	PS	T	Sw	St	B	S/M	F	In P	P/PA	Group	GB	LD	FB	Hits
Gerald Laird	167	585	301	284	102	199	49	116	119	3.50	Very Aggressive	46	26	44	Air
Junior Lake	326	1232	524	708	143	381	278	229	201	3.78	Aggressive	81	29	80	Air
Jake Lamb*	133	512	263	249	79	184	64	95	90	3.85	Neutral	47	15	28	Ground
Adam LaRoche*	586	2365	1418	947	433	985	188	365	394	4.04	Very Patient	144	87	162	Air
Brett Lawrie	282	1042	532	510	181	351	93	205	212	3.70	Aggressive	99	29	83	Medium
DJ LeMahieu	538	1985	1015	970	343	672	146	418	406	3.69	Aggressive	222	81	92	Ground
Adam Lind*	318	1269	719	550	237	482	100	208	242	3.99	Patient	113	50	79	Air
Rymer Liriano	121	445	247	198	85	162	61	66	71	3.68	Aggressive	34	17	19	Ground
Jose Lobaton#	230	876	444	432	130	314	110	169	153	3.81	Neutral	75	36	42	Ground
James Loney*	651	2408	1285	1123	423	862	138	459	526	3.70	Aggressive	223	140	163	Medium
Evan Longoria	700	2522	1338	1184	432	906	272	411	501	3.60	Very Aggressive	195	102	203	Air
David Lough*	197	683	345	338	113	232	58	132	148	3.47	Very Aggressive	45	31	56	Air
Jed Lowrie#	566	2103	1089	1014	295	794	138	445	431	3.72	Aggressive	134	104	189	Air
Ed Lucas	189	740	393	347	150	243	77	137	133	3.92	Patient	72	31	28	Ground
Jonathan Lucroy	655	2551	1488	1063	531	957	133	414	516	3.89	Neutral	217	115	184	Medium
Ryan Ludwick	400	1521	751	770	212	539	209	290	268	3.80	Neutral	98	70	99	Air
Manny Machado	354	1290	636	654	193	443	144	247	263	3.64	Very Aggressive	126	53	80	Ground
Martin Maldonado	126	487	278	209	101	177	47	82	80	3.87	Neutral	26	13	33	Air
Jake Marisnick	237	921	458	463	160	298	122	182	159	3.89	Neutral	60	34	60	Air
Nick Markakis*	710	2818	1679	1139	628	1051	113	466	560	3.97	Patient	257	110	193	Medium
Alfredo Marte	114	458	223	235	73	150	76	86	73	4.02	Patient	28	17	27	Air
Starling Marte	545	2072	1004	1068	306	698	276	428	364	3.80	Neutral	165	82	102	Ground
Leonys Martin*	583	2144	1034	1110	333	701	237	445	428	3.68	Aggressive	197	86	109	Air
Russell Martin	460	1936	1145	791	348	797	163	320	308	4.21	Very Patient	150	59	97	Ground
J.D. Martinez	480	1873	845	1028	213	632	290	417	321	3.90	Patient	130	73	118	Air
Victor Martinez#	641	2586	1474	1112	472	1002	93	494	525	4.03	Patient	213	112	200	Air
Jeff Mathis	195	717	372	345	126	246	108	121	116	3.68	Aggressive	46	24	40	Air
Joe Mauer*	518	2170	1344	826	507	837	136	329	361	4.19	Very Patient	183	98	79	Ground
John Mayberry	168	693	390	303	128	262	66	125	112	4.13	Very Patient	40	20	52	Air
Cameron Maybin	272	1020	575	445	197	378	105	144	196	3.75	Aggressive	111	33	50	Ground
Brian McCann*	538	2061	1156	905	399	757	131	352	422	3.83	Neutral	137	93	189	Air
Andrew McCutchen	648	2640	1468	1172	400	1068	260	473	439	4.07	Very Patient	175	82	182	Air
Casey McGehee	691	2543	1474	1069	502	972	167	381	521	3.68	Aggressive	263	95	163	Ground
Michael McKenry	192	762	417	345	138	279	79	139	127	3.97	Patient	45	37	44	Air
Nate McLouth*	162	631	401	230	150	251	36	88	106	3.90	Neutral	53	10	39	Ground
Tommy Medica	259	1038	561	477	201	360	130	181	166	4.01	Patient	75	31	60	Medium
Jordy Mercer	555	2053	1111	942	401	710	178	337	427	3.70	Aggressive	199	84	135	Ground
Devin Mesoraco	440	1727	916	811	262	654	239	288	284	3.93	Patient	97	65	122	Air
Will Middlebrooks	234	933	549	384	210	339	100	139	145	3.99	Patient	59	36	49	Medium
Brad Miller*	411	1420	740	680	252	488	150	250	278	3.45	Very Aggressive	114	52	104	Air
Jose Molina	247	923	430	493	139	291	105	212	176	3.72	Aggressive	95	21	54	Ground
Yadier Molina	445	1688	862	826	228	634	116	354	356	3.79	Neutral	179	81	94	Ground
Miguel Montero*	560	2161	1119	1042	279	840	215	429	398	3.86	Neutral	182	82	131	Air
Tyler Moore	100	382	215	167	76	139	49	56	62	3.82	Neutral	27	13	22	Medium
Kendrys Morales#	401	1485	781	704	255	526	155	246	303	3.70	Aggressive	148	54	101	Ground
Mitch Moreland*	184	740	393	347	129	264	87	132	128	4.02	Patient	56	28	41	Medium
Justin Morneau*	550	1920	875	1045	217	658	160	435	450	3.49	Very Aggressive	198	104	148	Medium
Logan Morrison*	365	1276	662	614	213	449	104	231	279	3.50	Very Aggressive	110	66	101	Air
Michael Morse	482	1784	844	940	221	623	238	381	321	3.70	Aggressive	145	70	106	Medium
Brandon Moss*	580	2357	1253	1104	341	912	306	448	350	4.06	Very Patient	105	73	169	Air
Mike Moustakas*	500	2069	1071	998	306	765	159	451	388	4.14	Very Patient	149	78	159	Air
Daniel Murphy*	642	2346	1223	1123	391	832	140	468	468	3.65	Very Aggressive	218	145	151	Ground
David Murphy*	462	1728	949	779	324	625	130	286	363	3.74	Aggressive	167	67	128	Medium
Donnie Murphy	128	515	257	258	65	192	83	97	78	4.02	Patient	36	10	30	Medium
Wil Myers	361	1376	783	593	256	527	149	207	237	3.81	Neutral	114	37	86	Medium
Mike Napoli	500	2235	1346	889	436	910	230	365	205	4.47	Very Patient	129	54	102	Medium
Daniel Nava#	408	1691	1037	654	406	631	92	278	284	4.14	Very Patient	128	57	99	Medium
Dioner Navarro#	520	1975	1060	915	372	688	148	356	411	3.80	Neutral	164	99	148	Air
Efren Navarro*	174	705	412	293	150	262	45	114	134	4.05	Very Patient	62	34	36	Ground
Kristopher Negron	158	579	277	302	87	190	83	114	105	3.66	Aggressive	52	18	32	Ground
Adrian Nieto#	118	458	264	194	90	174	55	68	71	3.88	Neutral	33	18	17	Ground
Kirk Nieuwenhuis*	130	571	325	246	89	236	80	91	75	4.39	Very Patient	30	23	21	Medium
Wil Nieves	128	424	179	245	64	115	75	79	91	3.31	Very Aggressive	39	22	28	Medium
Derek Norris	442	1757	1059	698	344	715	137	260	301	3.98	Patient	138	56	106	Medium
Eduardo Nunez	213	752	362	390	123	239	55	159	176	3.53	Very Aggressive	96	28	47	Ground
Rougned Odor*	417	1467	736	731	252	484	119	288	324	3.52	Very Aggressive	154	47	113	Ground
Mike Olt	258	1079	641	438	229	412	155	153	130	4.18	Very Patient	50	16	64	Air
David Ortiz*	602	2409	1340	1069	348	992	202	438	429	4.00	Patient	157	76	196	Air
Lyle Overbay*	296	1146	645	501	186	459	128	174	199	3.87	Neutral	103	38	58	Ground
Chris Owings	332	1220	614	606	228	386	120	239	247	3.67	Aggressive	108	58	76	Ground
Marcell Ozuna	612	2388	1275	1113	430	845	334	373	406	3.90	Patient	197	71	137	Ground
Jordan Pacheco	165	617	349	268	136	213	43	97	128	3.74	Aggressive	54	34	39	Medium
Angel Pagan#	413	1481	823	658	275	548	82	242	334	3.59	Very Aggressive	150	89	93	Ground
Joe Panik*	287	1099	617	482	207	410	69	175	238	3.83	Neutral	119	54	64	Ground
Chris Parmelee*	270	1147	596	551	184	412	115	249	187	4.25	Very Patient	67	39	80	Air

384

Hitter Analysis

Hitter	PA	PS	T	Sw	St	B	S/M	F	In P	P/PA	Group	GB	LD	FB	Hits
Gerardo Parra*	574	2055	1033	1022	315	718	176	409	437	3.58	Very Aggressive	230	95	102	Ground
Steve Pearce	383	1527	815	712	234	581	172	277	263	3.99	Patient	92	51	120	Air
Dustin Pedroia	609	2498	1414	1084	512	902	127	475	482	4.10	Very Patient	233	115	134	Ground
Brayan Pena#	372	1362	709	653	228	481	85	258	310	3.66	Very Aggressive	136	72	101	Medium
Ramiro Pena#	165	592	277	315	88	189	71	131	113	3.59	Very Aggressive	46	25	38	Medium
Hunter Pence	708	2811	1498	1313	455	1043	320	470	523	3.97	Very Aggressive	273	73	177	Ground
Cliff Pennington#	201	811	460	351	146	314	54	155	142	4.03	Very Patient	58	29	52	Air
David Peralta*	348	1227	625	602	200	425	132	200	270	3.53	Very Aggressive	129	57	83	Ground
Jhonny Peralta	628	2476	1274	1202	324	950	272	478	452	3.94	Patient	178	104	170	Air
Juan Perez	109	370	191	179	73	118	35	67	77	3.39	Very Aggressive	32	11	32	Air
Salvador Perez	606	2029	916	1113	315	601	169	448	496	3.35	Very Aggressive	194	106	196	Air
Gregorio Petit	100	359	179	180	63	116	40	68	72	3.59	Very Aggressive	32	16	24	Medium
Brandon Phillips	499	1851	868	983	284	584	207	380	396	3.71	Aggressive	174	88	132	Medium
A.J. Pierzynski*	362	1233	524	709	134	390	122	298	289	3.41	Very Aggressive	133	61	93	Ground
Kevin Pillar	122	421	192	229	82	110	52	88	89	3.45	Very Aggressive	45	14	29	Ground
Josmil Pinto	197	879	514	365	170	344	74	169	122	4.46	Very Patient	57	15	50	Medium
Trevor Plouffe	582	2288	1322	966	436	886	195	355	416	3.93	Patient	158	89	168	Air
Gregory Polanco*	312	1276	734	542	247	487	119	200	222	4.09	Very Patient	109	42	69	Ground
A.J. Pollock	287	1068	600	468	246	354	76	172	220	3.72	Aggressive	114	31	74	Ground
Buster Posey	605	2326	1291	1035	416	875	151	398	486	3.84	Neutral	203	118	164	Medium
Martin Prado	573	2218	1334	884	559	775	105	319	460	3.87	Neutral	223	101	135	Ground
Alex Presley*	271	1037	556	481	204	352	88	180	213	3.83	Neutral	99	39	74	Medium
Yasiel Puig	640	2306	1220	1086	286	934	283	366	437	3.60	Very Aggressive	223	64	144	Medium
Albert Pujols	695	2555	1347	1208	427	920	177	460	571	3.68	Aggressive	261	108	202	Medium
Nick Punto#	224	938	547	391	195	352	71	177	143	4.19	Very Patient	63	31	47	Medium
Carlos Quentin	155	569	263	306	50	213	82	123	101	3.67	Aggressive	45	13	43	Air
Ryan Raburn	212	832	453	379	144	309	97	135	147	3.92	Patient	61	34	52	Medium
Alexei Ramirez	657	2234	1100	1134	386	714	188	400	546	3.40	Very Aggressive	257	107	179	Ground
Aramis Ramirez	531	1805	801	1004	192	609	206	376	422	3.40	Very Aggressive	163	95	164	Air
Hanley Ramirez	512	1943	1035	908	269	766	170	372	366	3.79	Neutral	165	77	124	Medium
Jose Ramirez#	266	1016	520	496	174	346	74	205	217	3.82	Neutral	95	49	57	Ground
Wilson Ramos	361	1152	491	661	115	376	139	235	287	3.19	Very Aggressive	159	62	66	Air
Colby Rasmus*	376	1512	795	717	260	535	221	274	222	4.02	Patient	75	51	93	Air
Anthony Recker	189	736	418	318	155	263	93	111	114	3.89	Neutral	31	20	61	Air
Josh Reddick*	396	1428	722	706	205	517	126	276	303	3.61	Very Aggressive	98	53	150	Air
Anthony Rendon	683	2710	1607	1103	571	1036	154	433	516	3.97	Patient	204	104	202	Air
Ben Revere*	626	2257	1313	944	569	744	73	311	560	3.61	Very Aggressive	352	114	78	Ground
Jose Reyes#	655	2308	1178	1130	391	787	150	437	543	3.52	Very Aggressive	221	120	191	Medium
Mark Reynolds	433	1757	906	851	246	660	272	318	261	4.06	Very Patient	99	36	125	Air
Alex Rios	521	2045	1127	918	392	735	157	357	404	3.93	Patient	173	95	136	Medium
Rene Rivera	329	1278	611	667	164	447	172	272	223	3.88	Neutral	77	46	96	Air
Anthony Rizzo*	616	2478	1397	1081	440	957	226	443	412	4.02	Patient	147	90	170	Air
Brian Roberts#	348	1402	711	691	217	494	94	331	266	4.03	Patient	92	66	105	Air
Daniel Robertson	197	793	479	314	189	290	35	127	152	4.03	Patient	80	24	43	Ground
Sean Rodriguez	259	962	466	496	140	326	135	184	177	3.71	Aggressive	66	29	76	Air
Miguel Rojas	162	611	324	287	113	211	37	128	122	3.77	Aggressive	80	9	28	Ground
Jimmy Rollins#	609	2528	1462	1066	490	972	160	462	444	4.15	Very Patient	177	85	178	Air
Stefen Romero	190	720	351	369	111	240	101	136	132	3.79	Neutral	54	22	53	Air
Andrew Romine#	273	1049	546	503	173	373	110	198	195	3.84	Neutral	110	34	43	Ground
Adam Rosales	181	721	395	326	137	258	64	139	122	3.98	Patient	40	30	51	Air
Wilin Rosario	410	1321	627	694	177	450	166	211	317	3.22	Very Aggressive	159	60	98	Ground
Cody Ross	219	858	484	374	165	319	67	148	159	3.92	Patient	73	38	48	Ground
David Ross	171	710	365	345	113	252	127	121	97	4.15	Very Patient	36	20	38	Air
Ryan Rua	109	414	224	190	82	142	44	59	87	3.80	Neutral	45	20	22	Ground
Darin Ruf	117	469	256	213	71	185	68	72	73	4.01	Patient	32	14	26	Medium
Justin Ruggiano	250	993	507	486	127	380	157	170	159	3.97	Patient	65	31	60	Air
Carlos Ruiz	445	1803	1102	701	386	716	106	268	327	4.05	Very Patient	134	76	115	Medium
Josh Rutledge	342	1322	691	631	245	446	134	264	233	3.87	Neutral	104	46	77	Medium
Brendan Ryan	124	479	202	277	55	147	65	125	87	3.86	Neutral	36	13	36	Air
Jarrod Saltalamacchia#	435	1804	956	848	260	696	300	313	235	4.15	Very Patient	88	52	95	Air
Carlos Sanchez#	104	384	192	192	77	115	42	74	76	3.69	Aggressive	32	20	24	Medium
Gaby Sanchez	290	1155	655	500	222	433	102	191	207	3.98	Patient	78	38	90	Air
Hector Sanchez#	177	665	254	411	59	195	116	183	112	3.76	Very Aggressive	38	23	51	Air
Pablo Sandoval#	638	2254	952	1302	196	756	215	577	510	3.53	Very Aggressive	217	105	187	Medium
Carlos Santana#	660	2841	1782	1059	524	1258	212	427	420	4.30	Very Patient	167	81	168	Air
Danny Santana#	430	1643	795	848	311	484	188	350	310	3.82	Neutral	134	76	82	Ground
Ramon Santiago#	214	813	508	305	192	316	41	115	149	3.80	Neutral	57	34	46	Medium
Luis Sardinas#	125	482	252	230	101	151	41	92	97	3.86	Neutral	59	20	15	Ground
Michael Saunders*	263	1028	595	433	177	418	94	161	178	3.92	Patient	70	37	61	Air
Jordan Schafer*	240	834	382	452	103	279	110	172	170	3.48	Very Aggressive	75	34	32	Ground
Logan Schafer*	136	537	286	251	86	200	52	106	93	3.95	Patient	40	16	34	Medium
Nate Schierholtz*	383	1477	690	787	196	494	170	342	275	3.86	Neutral	110	54	109	Air
Jonathan Schoop	481	1742	804	938	270	534	249	351	338	3.62	Very Aggressive	163	46	122	Ground
Skip Schumaker*	271	1054	568	486	209	359	93	191	202	3.89	Neutral	111	40	47	Ground
Kyle Seager*	654	2563	1504	1059	504	1000	193	390	476	3.92	Patient	173	105	194	Air

385

Hitter Analysis

Hitter	PA	PS	T	Sw	St	B	S/M	F	In P	P/PA	Group	GB	LD	FB	Hits
Jean Segura	557	1944	1001	943	371	630	132	356	455	3.49	Very Aggressive	254	79	98	Ground
Marcus Semien	255	1078	628	450	224	404	101	186	163	4.23	Very Patient	64	33	62	Air
J.B. Shuck*	114	354	181	173	76	105	18	56	99	3.11	Very Aggressive	55	8	33	Ground
Moises Sierra	170	682	320	362	94	226	105	138	119	4.01	Patient	58	23	37	Ground
Andrelton Simmons	576	1928	983	945	314	669	128	333	484	3.35	Very Aggressive	249	78	148	Air
Jon Singleton*	362	1627	931	696	273	658	255	264	177	4.49	Very Patient	70	25	82	Air
Grady Sizemore*	381	1565	850	715	291	559	128	315	272	4.11	Very Patient	114	55	103	Air
Seth Smith*	521	2124	1278	846	417	861	167	318	360	4.08	Very Patient	170	76	114	Ground
Justin Smoak#	276	1110	630	480	201	429	119	177	184	4.02	Patient	78	34	72	Air
Travis Snider*	359	1436	807	629	245	562	123	250	256	4.00	Patient	125	49	79	Ground
Eric Sogard*	329	1149	668	481	245	423	50	171	260	3.49	Very Aggressive	101	58	84	Medium
Donovan Solano	340	1285	686	599	270	416	89	253	257	3.78	Aggressive	125	58	63	Ground
Yangervis Solarte#	535	1993	1134	859	387	747	99	340	420	3.72	Aggressive	189	81	146	Medium
Alfonso Soriano	238	892	407	485	131	276	154	172	159	3.75	Aggressive	56	32	71	Air
Denard Span*	668	2454	1403	1051	520	883	89	411	551	3.67	Aggressive	247	128	160	Ground
George Springer	345	1387	725	662	192	533	266	213	183	4.02	Patient	83	28	72	Air
Giancarlo Stanton	638	2597	1500	1097	409	1091	340	386	371	4.08	Very Patient	153	73	145	Air
Chris Stewart	154	576	353	223	139	214	36	75	112	3.74	Aggressive	43	32	33	Medium
Drew Stubbs	424	1704	1012	692	356	656	204	231	257	4.02	Patient	112	53	87	Medium
Eugenio Suarez	277	1091	648	443	252	396	107	154	182	3.94	Patient	62	38	76	Air
Ichiro Suzuki*	385	1516	811	705	290	521	114	296	295	3.94	Patient	168	65	57	Ground
Kurt Suzuki	503	1998	1144	854	407	737	89	351	414	3.97	Patient	183	90	139	Medium
Ryan Sweeney*	226	930	548	382	201	347	45	160	177	4.12	Very Patient	82	48	45	Ground
Nick Swisher#	401	1666	928	738	291	637	187	297	254	4.15	Very Patient	95	61	96	Air
Jose Tabata	186	657	333	324	105	228	54	119	151	3.53	Very Aggressive	84	32	31	Ground
Oscar Taveras*	248	954	511	443	168	343	55	190	198	3.85	Neutral	102	39	57	Ground
Chris Taylor	151	570	310	260	103	207	72	89	99	3.77	Aggressive	39	20	36	Air
Mark Teixeira#	508	2087	1213	874	399	814	187	352	335	4.11	Very Patient	139	71	125	Air
Ruben Tejada	419	1578	859	719	256	603	123	308	288	3.77	Aggressive	115	69	100	Air
Josh Thole*	150	621	341	280	118	223	43	126	111	4.14	Very Patient	67	19	21	Ground
Steve Tolleson	189	731	399	332	141	258	83	123	126	3.87	Neutral	47	23	50	Air
Mike Trout	705	3136	1949	1187	662	1287	248	511	428	4.45	Very Patient	145	81	202	Air
Mark Trumbo	362	1378	702	676	213	489	194	238	244	3.81	Neutral	109	37	98	Air
Troy Tulowitzki	375	1430	839	591	276	563	102	226	263	3.81	Neutral	99	61	102	Air
Justin Turner	322	1338	726	612	242	484	96	284	232	4.16	Very Patient	113	54	65	Ground
Dan Uggla	157	618	334	284	95	239	80	108	96	3.94	Patient	37	16	43	Air
B.J. Upton	582	2220	1151	1069	322	829	353	365	351	3.81	Neutral	148	62	133	Air
Justin Upton	641	2575	1327	1248	374	953	346	498	403	4.02	Patient	160	81	162	Air
Juan Uribe	404	1425	617	808	162	455	180	317	311	3.53	Very Aggressive	146	59	106	Ground
Chase Utley*	664	2549	1491	1058	512	979	141	404	513	3.84	Neutral	201	126	185	Air
Chris Valaika	131	492	236	256	80	156	51	118	87	3.76	Aggressive	44	18	25	Ground
Luis Valbuena*	547	2281	1262	1019	383	879	225	427	367	4.17	Very Patient	114	74	174	Air
Jordany Valdespin*	113	437	261	176	96	165	25	63	88	3.87	Neutral	38	8	30	Medium
Danny Valencia	284	1082	599	483	226	373	117	160	206	3.81	Neutral	92	50	64	Ground
Scott Van Slyke	246	983	560	423	169	391	113	167	143	4.00	Patient	50	29	64	Air
Kennys Vargas#	234	881	420	461	114	306	126	179	156	3.76	Aggressive	74	29	53	Ground
Christian Vazquez	201	807	471	336	173	298	54	133	149	4.01	Patient	83	24	38	Ground
Will Venable*	448	1720	901	819	279	622	213	302	304	3.84	Neutral	139	55	97	Ground
Dayan Viciedo	563	2053	1011	1042	271	740	263	375	404	3.65	Very Aggressive	185	70	149	Medium
Shane Victorino	133	527	293	234	123	170	40	89	105	3.96	Patient	44	25	33	Medium
Jonathan Villar#	289	1070	563	507	184	379	153	166	188	3.70	Aggressive	90	33	52	Ground
Stephen Vogt*	287	1186	699	487	261	438	59	197	231	4.13	Very Patient	76	45	109	Air
Joey Votto*	272	1179	714	465	210	504	88	204	173	4.33	Very Patient	70	46	56	Medium
Neil Walker#	571	2176	1138	1038	332	806	175	436	427	3.81	Neutral	163	96	165	Air
Zach Walters#	137	539	229	310	50	179	94	137	79	3.93	Patient	31	17	31	Air
Rickie Weeks	286	1071	587	484	185	402	139	166	180	3.74	Aggressive	102	33	45	Ground
Jayson Werth	629	2667	1689	978	610	1079	177	377	424	4.24	Very Patient	169	85	170	Air
Matt Wieters#	112	404	202	202	58	144	32	83	87	3.61	Very Aggressive	24	26	37	Air
Josh Willingham	364	1534	966	568	325	641	166	202	200	4.21	Very Patient	72	30	98	Air
Kolten Wong*	433	1630	846	784	284	562	139	308	337	3.76	Aggressive	153	61	109	Ground
David Wright	586	2214	1198	1016	362	836	188	401	427	3.78	Aggressive	170	100	157	Air
Christian Yelich*	660	2812	1703	1109	570	1133	211	448	450	4.26	Very Patient	267	93	78	Ground
Chris Young	366	1457	790	667	244	546	131	277	259	3.98	Patient	74	50	132	Air
Delmon Young	255	931	413	518	99	314	131	196	191	3.65	Very Aggressive	96	41	54	Ground
Eric Young#	316	1190	643	547	227	416	112	208	227	3.77	Aggressive	135	40	39	Ground
Ryan Zimmerman	240	924	562	362	212	350	68	113	181	3.85	Neutral	79	38	64	Medium
Ben Zobrist#	654	2563	1579	984	565	1014	132	358	494	3.92	Patient	238	90	160	Ground
Mike Zunino	476	1773	812	961	234	578	337	340	284	3.72	Aggressive	96	47	140	Air

For some players Swings and Misses, Fouls, and Balls in Play do not add up to overall Swings. This is because of the rare occasions when a swing results in a Catcher Interference.

Switch Hitters
* Bats Left

Pitcher Analysis

Similar to the Hitter Analysis section, Pitcher Analysis categorizes a pitcher's tendencies. For pitchers, the data includes their number of batters faced and pitches thrown; strikes and balls thrown; groundballs, line drives, and flyballs allowed; percentage of strikes and swinging strike rate; and their frequency in a variety of counts.

The 2014 season provided more evidence of the importance of throwing strikes. There were 13 starters who faced at least 500 batters and threw strikes 61 percent of the time or less. Here is how they fared:

Pitcher	Str%	ERA
C.J. Wilson	58%	4.51
Nick Martinez	60%	4.55
Ubaldo Jimenez	60%	4.81
Francisco Liriano	60%	3.38
A.J. Burnett	61%	4.59
Justin Masterson	61%	5.88
Zack Wheeler	61%	3.54
Kyle Gibson	61%	4.47
Jordan Lyles	61%	4.33
Jacob Turner	61%	6.13
Edwin Jackson	61%	6.33
Jorge De La Rosa	61%	4.10
Roberto Hernandez	61%	4.10

Collectively, those 13 starters combined for a 4.58 ERA. The league average for starters was 3.82 in 2014.

On the other end of the spectrum, there were 13 starters who faced at least 500 batters and threw strikes 68 percent of the time or more. They include some of the biggest stars in the game, such as Clayton Kershaw and Madison Bumgarner, but even the ones that are not household names enjoyed success with their strike-throwing approaches:

Pitcher	Str%	ERA
Phil Hughes	73%	3.52
David Price	70%	3.26
Jordan Zimmermann	70%	2.66
Clayton Kershaw	69%	1.77
John Lackey	69%	3.82
Brandon McCarthy	69%	4.05
Hisashi Iwakuma	69%	3.52
Carlos Carrasco	68%	2.67
Andrew Cashner	68%	2.55
Madison Bumgarner	68%	2.98
Bartolo Colon	68%	4.09
Doug Fister	68%	2.41
Corey Kluber	68%	2.44

Collectively, those 13 starters had an ERA of 3.09, 73 points better than league average and 149 points better than the 13 starters with the lowest strike percentages. It's clear that throwing strikes, whether they be in the zone or out, swinging or looking, is key to a pitcher's success.

Pitcher Analysis
Pitchers with 50+ Batters Faced in 2014

Pitcher	BF	Pitches	K	BB	GB	LD	FB	Str%	S/Str	Counts 1-0	0-1	Full	2 Strike	3 Ball
Fernando Abad	216	821	51	15	59	25	60	66%	16%	84	112	24	115	35
Alfredo Aceves	85	323	16	4	15	13	36	68%	16%	29	44	9	48	14
Mike Adams	79	313	21	8	27	6	15	64%	12%	29	44	8	45	14
Jeremy Affeldt	225	838	41	14	110	28	27	62%	17%	96	104	27	108	37
Al Alburquerque	236	960	63	21	67	29	53	64%	22%	116	102	34	146	45
Cody Allen	279	1139	91	26	57	24	76	64%	22%	104	154	47	168	61
Henderson Alvarez	772	2611	111	33	325	132	147	67%	11%	290	379	69	303	105
Brett Anderson	180	664	29	13	83	23	30	64%	14%	69	92	16	80	32
Chase Anderson	486	1892	105	40	132	81	118	64%	16%	179	259	53	261	84
Chris Archer	822	3160	173	72	262	126	175	63%	15%	350	390	107	410	165
Jake Arrieta	614	2416	167	41	194	88	112	64%	17%	249	321	77	341	112
Bronson Arroyo	357	1253	47	19	150	55	75	66%	11%	115	186	37	158	57
Scott Atchison	280	1037	49	14	127	40	49	64%	15%	112	140	29	135	40
Luis Avilan	193	712	25	21	80	26	32	59%	14%	95	71	23	75	44
Dylan Axelrod	72	310	20	4	15	14	18	65%	20%	22	43	14	45	19
John Axford	243	1040	63	36	74	19	45	58%	18%	105	125	47	133	75
Burke Badenhop	289	1064	40	19	136	44	43	64%	6%	110	130	35	135	46
Pedro Baez	92	351	18	5	25	10	33	68%	15%	36	38	11	48	17
Homer Bailey	604	2278	124	45	212	86	121	65%	18%	232	302	78	306	111
Scott Baker	332	1193	55	14	66	64	131	67%	14%	131	158	32	151	47
Grant Balfour	270	1127	57	41	74	36	59	59%	14%	124	125	50	149	76
Aaron Barrett	174	675	49	20	47	26	29	61%	21%	80	80	18	84	37
Anthony Bass	119	431	7	7	53	20	30	61%	11%	45	55	14	45	24
Chris Bassitt	137	527	21	13	38	26	32	64%	10%	54	65	19	73	29
Antonio Bastardo	271	1139	81	34	45	25	79	60%	21%	116	133	44	159	69
Trevor Bauer	663	2591	143	60	157	104	184	63%	15%	287	313	93	356	140
Josh Beckett	475	1909	107	39	136	62	122	62%	17%	184	252	75	268	109
Erik Bedard	342	1397	64	29	81	49	111	63%	13%	132	178	64	191	82
Cam Bedrosian	93	408	20	12	25	13	23	63%	17%	36	51	20	59	23
Joe Beimel	184	624	25	14	69	28	42	65%	13%	63	83	17	80	30
Ronald Belisario	292	1084	47	18	128	38	50	64%	11%	128	136	33	135	47
Matt Belisle	282	1052	43	19	97	52	62	68%	12%	89	158	32	148	44
Jeff Beliveau	100	389	28	7	25	15	22	68%	14%	28	64	7	58	13
Heath Bell	88	352	12	8	42	9	12	59%	11%	36	45	13	39	20
Joaquin Benoit	205	810	64	14	43	18	62	64%	29%	76	96	35	115	47
Christian Bergman	249	886	31	10	67	52	86	67%	10%	77	140	28	112	41
Dellin Betances	341	1365	135	24	81	35	58	65%	20%	114	196	49	211	68
Chad Bettis	127	499	13	10	45	24	29	61%	10%	64	51	20	50	32
Vic Black	148	561	32	19	42	18	32	60%	19%	76	58	18	73	31
Jerry Blevins	240	976	66	23	57	36	54	65%	18%	78	142	38	140	50
Mike Bolsinger	238	845	48	17	88	36	44	67%	13%	79	127	25	117	37
Lisalverto Bonilla	83	319	17	12	22	11	20	55%	22%	37	41	10	36	20
Brad Boxberger	247	1056	104	20	47	19	48	68%	22%	83	151	38	177	48
Blaine Boyer	160	625	29	8	51	25	44	68%	15%	51	89	18	84	26
Brad Brach	254	1045	54	25	60	31	74	63%	21%	108	124	39	140	56
Craig Breslow	260	977	37	28	69	44	75	62%	11%	125	105	32	120	52
Zach Britton	285	1053	62	23	146	25	23	64%	21%	127	129	25	140	43
Rex Brothers	273	1098	55	39	66	51	53	58%	19%	112	132	40	138	79
Brooks Brown	104	405	21	5	45	11	21	61%	23%	47	45	19	54	23
Jonathan Broxton	231	904	49	19	73	16	70	65%	17%	89	115	27	118	39
David Buchanan	503	1817	71	32	192	73	114	62%	13%	217	218	53	213	92
Jake Buchanan	154	561	20	12	70	29	18	64%	15%	64	73	16	73	26
Clay Buchholz	737	2741	132	54	250	102	184	63%	14%	291	357	84	351	131
Mark Buehrle	857	3082	119	46	295	152	228	64%	10%	352	405	93	366	131
Francisley Bueno	142	482	20	7	50	21	41	64%	15%	57	64	9	52	18
Madison Bumgarner	873	3372	219	43	262	117	211	68%	17%	294	487	101	496	125
A.J. Burnett	935	3472	190	96	315	127	177	61%	15%	402	422	116	434	209
Jared Burton	272	1013	46	25	75	40	80	65%	19%	114	126	27	133	46
Eddie Butler	76	259	3	7	33	16	15	59%	8%	39	29	7	27	15
Trevor Cahill	499	1928	105	55	159	80	89	59%	18%	214	226	63	234	113
Matt Cain	374	1440	70	32	120	51	95	63%	15%	142	192	46	175	72
Carter Capps	86	365	25	5	19	11	23	65%	21%	35	43	11	56	15
Chris Capuano	429	1640	84	34	118	78	103	63%	14%	167	219	56	214	89
Buddy Carlyle	119	467	28	5	31	18	35	67%	14%	36	70	10	64	16
David Carpenter	259	999	67	16	64	41	65	69%	18%	78	155	27	150	35
Carlos Carrasco	529	1956	140	29	187	69	98	68%	20%	196	278	51	295	77
Scott Carroll	573	2115	64	45	237	90	117	62%	10%	227	285	69	244	109

389

Pitcher Analysis
Pitchers with 50+ Batters Faced in 2014

Pitcher	BF	Pitches	K	BB	GB	LD	FB	Str%	S/Str	Counts 1-0	0-1	Full	2 Strike	3 Ball
Andrew Cashner	506	1797	93	29	180	76	117	68%	12%	185	253	48	241	77
Santiago Casilla	218	861	45	15	85	22	44	63%	17%	92	106	31	115	43
Brett Cecil	234	895	76	27	70	32	28	62%	27%	108	105	26	125	50
Jhoulys Chacin	272	1027	42	28	84	43	69	63%	14%	100	140	37	134	60
Andrew Chafin	60	258	10	8	21	7	11	58%	13%	25	31	12	33	20
Joba Chamberlain	263	1039	59	24	92	40	41	63%	18%	112	127	42	149	60
Aroldis Chapman	202	935	106	24	30	15	24	64%	33%	85	107	42	153	51
Kevin Chapman	97	375	19	11	31	9	23	63%	12%	33	55	12	52	21
Tyler Chatwood	101	354	20	8	32	20	18	57%	17%	49	38	12	39	18
Jesse Chavez	621	2400	136	49	180	97	152	66%	14%	227	325	68	339	104
Bruce Chen	223	868	36	16	52	38	75	65%	11%	83	108	29	103	40
Wei-Yin Chen	772	2977	136	35	240	126	220	66%	13%	298	385	99	394	132
Randy Choate	148	589	32	13	58	16	21	62%	18%	61	75	28	79	36
Nick Christiani	57	184	8	6	20	7	14	63%	9%	21	24	5	21	10
Tony Cingrani	280	1112	61	35	63	39	79	60%	14%	129	125	39	139	72
Steve Cishek	275	1142	84	21	70	43	51	64%	15%	90	159	35	163	53
Preston Claiborne	96	367	16	10	28	12	30	61%	19%	42	41	12	44	20
Alex Claudio	54	209	14	4	21	9	6	65%	19%	29	21	5	30	8
Paul Clemens	118	416	16	13	35	18	32	61%	10%	51	52	14	45	22
Maikel Cleto	138	565	32	23	35	11	34	58%	20%	70	60	26	74	41
Tyler Clippard	278	1148	82	23	62	23	83	66%	23%	103	149	41	157	54
Alex Cobb	681	2611	149	47	264	77	129	64%	18%	271	344	95	353	124
Phil Coke	257	941	41	20	105	40	44	64%	17%	115	107	30	117	51
Gerrit Cole	571	2197	138	40	181	70	117	65%	16%	214	286	73	306	99
Casey Coleman	55	231	5	6	28	9	7	60%	7%	24	26	10	28	18
Louis Coleman	154	613	24	18	47	24	40	61%	19%	59	78	20	75	30
Tim Collins	90	377	15	11	24	8	26	61%	11%	36	45	13	52	23
Josh Collmenter	719	2719	115	39	212	116	218	65%	13%	290	342	73	349	110
Alex Colome	97	385	13	10	28	16	30	61%	14%	32	55	16	45	24
Bartolo Colon	846	3011	151	30	253	141	249	68%	9%	288	462	74	406	108
Carlos Contreras	94	390	19	17	19	12	26	55%	15%	54	32	18	45	30
Ryan Cook	202	749	50	22	57	26	43	64%	18%	90	94	16	103	38
Daniel Corcino	80	317	15	10	16	12	25	58%	16%	41	34	13	37	20
Kevin Correia	687	2522	79	40	240	106	210	62%	10%	283	305	84	281	125
Jarred Cosart	766	2947	115	73	308	110	150	62%	11%	321	374	94	366	156
Neal Cotts	286	1081	63	23	67	48	78	65%	16%	97	148	33	148	50
Kyle Crockett	122	494	28	8	45	15	21	67%	13%	45	68	14	72	20
Aaron Crow	244	934	34	24	79	35	69	61%	12%	115	106	35	120	53
Johnny Cueto	961	3659	242	65	285	119	213	65%	16%	356	478	131	497	172
Brandon Cumpton	309	1113	46	18	102	65	64	65%	11%	116	154	30	142	48
Matt Daley	63	226	10	6	10	8	27	65%	11%	22	32	6	32	10
John Danks	855	3298	129	74	266	122	241	64%	13%	330	436	111	419	164
Logan Darnell	112	394	22	8	38	22	20	64%	16%	50	43	10	50	16
Yu Darvish	605	2312	182	49	134	84	151	64%	18%	230	299	66	324	110
Wade Davis	279	1210	109	23	68	32	43	65%	23%	109	154	47	185	60
Justin De Fratus	219	831	49	12	60	33	60	67%	19%	75	116	24	115	34
Eury De La Rosa	158	605	32	14	46	20	41	62%	15%	73	73	17	78	31
Jorge De La Rosa	768	3067	139	67	275	95	163	61%	17%	348	345	145	372	196
Rubby De La Rosa	441	1751	74	35	148	72	104	63%	14%	211	192	72	232	97
Samuel Deduno	443	1723	83	46	161	61	79	61%	15%	184	219	58	212	101
Jacob deGrom	565	2236	144	43	166	85	115	66%	19%	210	295	76	319	103
Steve Delabar	114	480	21	19	22	17	30	61%	17%	53	49	19	60	34
Randall Delgado	339	1459	86	35	74	44	92	61%	24%	147	162	66	194	87
Anthony DeSclafani	146	548	26	5	38	26	43	68%	14%	49	79	13	75	21
Odrisamer Despaigne	404	1549	65	32	151	55	84	62%	13%	162	194	56	199	82
Ross Detwiler	274	1036	39	21	95	42	68	64%	11%	112	127	31	124	49
Jumbo Diaz	142	585	37	14	36	28	27	63%	21%	61	62	26	82	36
R.A. Dickey	914	3513	173	74	270	131	242	65%	17%	337	482	118	482	174
Jake Diekman	313	1316	100	35	74	45	52	61%	23%	141	160	54	184	82
Sean Doolittle	236	928	89	8	31	24	80	73%	23%	67	145	20	158	25
Felix Doubront	364	1360	51	33	103	61	107	61%	12%	155	175	49	163	79
Darin Downs	148	532	27	19	43	16	39	61%	22%	60	66	15	63	27
Scott Downs	165	693	25	20	74	15	30	60%	15%	71	76	28	89	44
Brian Duensing	229	873	33	20	79	33	61	62%	14%	94	110	34	91	49
Danny Duffy	606	2429	113	53	154	78	198	64%	12%	248	298	76	304	129
Zach Duke	238	979	74	17	82	31	29	62%	21%	88	130	47	139	60
Mike Dunn	245	988	67	22	48	28	67	65%	22%	87	123	36	144	50
Sam Dyson	181	683	33	15	81	24	23	65%	17%	72	88	19	91	34

Pitcher Analysis
Pitchers with 50+ Batters Faced in 2014

Pitcher	BF	Pitches	K	BB	GB	LD	FB	Str%	S/Str	1-0	0-1	Full	2 Strike	3 Ball
Josh Edgin	104	409	28	6	35	10	24	63%	22%	43	47	17	61	22
Roenis Elias	693	2661	143	64	211	96	158	62%	16%	278	330	106	337	152
Nathan Eovaldi	854	3198	142	43	290	144	213	66%	14%	317	432	99	421	139
Robbie Erlin	264	1007	46	15	81	54	63	65%	14%	93	133	33	135	47
Marco Estrada	624	2534	127	44	145	79	220	65%	17%	244	329	102	363	133
Dana Eveland	115	475	27	6	42	15	21	63%	17%	51	57	14	68	23
Jeurys Familia	322	1221	73	32	120	31	58	62%	21%	150	144	40	158	66
Kyle Farnsworth	128	479	18	15	35	30	29	61%	18%	54	56	16	58	28
Danny Farquhar	290	1139	81	22	76	49	57	65%	18%	120	145	41	165	54
Scott Feldman	765	2964	107	50	276	132	180	63%	11%	299	391	94	377	127
Neftali Feliz	122	482	21	11	24	19	45	65%	16%	42	68	18	69	26
Jose Fernandez	205	787	70	13	59	20	42	68%	22%	72	108	18	124	27
Josh Fields	231	950	70	17	44	29	68	65%	19%	95	121	35	137	48
Casey Fien	260	987	51	10	63	37	96	70%	16%	84	148	23	138	25
Mike Fiers	274	1122	76	17	59	35	83	65%	15%	116	134	37	163	50
Doug Fister	662	2468	98	24	255	88	178	68%	9%	231	355	69	322	101
Yohan Flande	241	897	34	16	107	37	40	65%	11%	91	120	19	108	38
Gavin Floyd	229	831	45	13	79	32	49	65%	19%	82	110	20	103	34
Mike Foltynewicz	84	326	14	7	18	13	32	61%	16%	40	36	9	44	16
Jeff Francis	82	312	15	3	26	14	22	63%	11%	32	39	9	41	15
Jason Frasor	196	832	46	18	61	31	38	61%	14%	77	103	39	112	52
Sam Freeman	169	667	35	19	59	21	25	62%	19%	79	69	23	96	34
Carlos Frias	137	487	29	7	52	15	33	69%	15%	49	74	12	65	19
Christian Friedrich	110	399	27	10	27	17	25	63%	22%	48	48	15	52	21
Ernesto Frieri	184	777	48	14	39	24	57	65%	16%	70	105	31	117	41
Kyuji Fujikawa	64	234	17	6	17	9	13	62%	22%	24	30	5	32	11
Charlie Furbush	177	672	51	9	39	28	43	69%	21%	65	97	14	98	22
Yovani Gallardo	817	3216	146	54	304	121	174	62%	12%	353	379	108	392	161
Jaime Garcia	177	631	39	7	70	25	32	65%	19%	70	85	11	77	24
Luis Garcia	69	285	12	13	30	5	8	59%	21%	35	26	15	39	22
Matt Garza	680	2538	126	50	207	99	172	66%	14%	242	345	85	335	116
Kevin Gausman	476	1951	88	38	142	80	121	62%	15%	206	226	70	242	106
Dillon Gee	570	2120	94	43	183	76	156	64%	12%	227	271	64	270	107
Gonzalez Germen	133	506	31	14	31	17	38	62%	23%	58	55	24	71	33
Kyle Gibson	757	2800	107	57	315	110	154	61%	15%	325	348	97	318	150
Ken Giles	166	694	64	11	39	13	36	67%	25%	62	91	17	107	27
Brandon Gomes	138	545	24	11	33	23	47	65%	17%	54	69	17	74	25
Jeanmar Gomez	270	975	38	23	95	51	57	62%	14%	95	134	32	110	49
Marco Gonzales	156	623	31	21	37	23	42	62%	17%	61	79	22	86	36
Gio Gonzalez	653	2623	162	56	186	77	152	63%	18%	274	316	107	351	148
Miguel Gonzalez	671	2552	111	51	185	104	207	64%	13%	259	336	82	326	124
Tom Gorzelanny	95	374	23	8	27	13	22	64%	16%	37	49	10	50	16
Sonny Gray	899	3295	183	74	348	115	159	63%	15%	375	431	112	426	170
Shane Greene	345	1353	81	29	112	48	63	63%	17%	141	171	45	181	71
Nick Greenwood	145	489	17	5	71	22	28	67%	11%	54	70	11	64	18
Luke Gregerson	284	1006	59	15	106	31	66	66%	21%	112	141	27	136	40
Zack Greinke	821	3210	207	43	271	127	159	65%	18%	307	419	115	439	147
Jason Grilli	235	937	57	21	47	38	62	64%	18%	93	113	36	130	47
Justin Grimm	292	1134	70	27	94	30	66	61%	17%	112	140	35	139	64
Javy Guerra	198	772	38	20	53	28	50	63%	13%	94	84	24	99	38
Matt Guerrier	124	440	12	10	40	20	40	60%	17%	63	48	8	37	21
Jeremy Guthrie	864	3235	124	49	290	131	244	65%	12%	315	463	98	403	135
Juan Gutierrez	268	960	44	16	74	40	87	65%	14%	102	132	22	114	42
Nick Hagadone	91	351	27	6	19	13	25	64%	19%	40	44	7	46	16
Jesse Hahn	306	1180	70	32	97	43	53	63%	17%	123	155	28	152	58
David Hale	383	1411	44	39	163	54	74	60%	16%	182	149	47	161	87
Cole Hamels	829	3136	198	59	254	123	170	66%	19%	318	417	98	447	146
Jason Hammel	715	2796	158	44	198	109	192	64%	16%	305	347	92	383	126
Brad Hand	474	1790	67	39	176	62	112	62%	12%	197	232	52	208	93
J.A. Happ	673	2710	133	51	196	96	191	64%	12%	254	358	85	363	121
Aaron Harang	876	3394	161	71	244	141	234	64%	13%	359	439	120	450	167
Blaine Hardy	167	643	31	20	59	22	32	62%	13%	76	75	18	82	37
Dan Haren	776	3096	145	36	240	113	226	64%	12%	299	408	107	406	148
Lucas Harrell	66	284	9	9	24	13	11	54%	10%	38	23	11	28	21
Will Harris	120	479	35	9	25	18	29	63%	18%	54	58	17	63	25
Matt Harrison	84	343	10	12	29	15	16	57%	12%	38	33	22	40	27
Chris Hatcher	232	922	60	12	75	31	52	66%	16%	80	130	31	135	45
LaTroy Hawkins	226	828	32	13	84	40	56	68%	10%	75	120	21	105	28

Pitcher Analysis
Pitchers with 50+ Batters Faced in 2014

Pitcher	BF	Pitches	K	BB	GB	LD	FB	Str%	S/Str	1-0	0-1	Full	2 Strike	3 Ball
Andrew Heaney	126	479	20	7	42	18	33	64%	15%	50	65	15	62	23
Jeremy Hellickson	281	1178	54	21	74	46	83	64%	16%	104	157	40	164	55
Jim Henderson	50	188	17	4	9	7	11	63%	25%	21	23	6	26	10
Kyle Hendricks	321	1156	47	15	118	48	81	65%	13%	116	168	28	144	45
Liam Hendriks	143	551	23	7	42	27	40	65%	13%	43	87	15	65	22
Felix Hernandez	912	3434	248	46	340	106	159	66%	19%	323	492	110	490	153
Roberto Hernandez	722	2737	105	73	259	106	156	61%	14%	317	318	91	335	149
Kelvin Herrera	285	1125	59	26	95	52	46	64%	20%	129	128	36	157	52
Yoslan Herrera	77	313	13	9	26	13	16	64%	13%	25	46	5	38	15
Derek Holland	145	572	25	5	46	19	46	65%	16%	49	78	16	67	22
Greg Holland	240	1002	90	20	62	22	45	64%	24%	104	117	36	152	51
Mario Hollands	204	772	35	21	73	28	40	60%	14%	83	101	21	90	39
David Holmberg	137	516	18	16	35	16	42	57%	15%	60	62	15	54	29
J.J. Hoover	275	1145	75	31	47	31	87	62%	18%	105	143	44	150	66
T.J. House	429	1576	80	22	193	68	56	65%	15%	169	209	45	212	68
J.P. Howell	199	808	48	25	69	21	30	55%	19%	90	93	37	93	62
Tim Hudson	789	2784	120	34	330	130	161	66%	14%	289	394	84	351	113
David Huff	258	973	39	23	90	43	58	65%	12%	99	121	28	118	45
Jared Hughes	256	884	36	19	122	35	32	63%	17%	99	110	30	98	48
Phil Hughes	855	3046	186	16	234	149	258	73%	13%	234	509	53	455	70
Tommy Hunter	241	866	45	12	92	43	46	67%	12%	84	122	25	105	39
Drew Hutchison	786	3051	184	60	190	98	238	64%	18%	316	380	108	401	153
Hisashi Iwakuma	709	2542	154	21	266	112	152	69%	14%	239	381	53	335	73
Edwin Jackson	633	2492	123	63	171	112	151	61%	18%	282	285	83	316	137
Juan Jaime	62	277	18	9	12	10	10	60%	21%	27	33	12	37	16
Kenley Jansen	268	1061	101	19	51	40	54	70%	25%	88	157	23	169	35
Casey Janssen	192	701	28	7	52	33	66	67%	12%	60	106	21	95	26
Jeremy Jeffress	135	508	29	10	53	23	14	65%	12%	53	68	21	67	27
Chad Jenkins	136	440	18	6	63	16	31	70%	9%	42	66	8	55	12
Dan Jennings	182	714	38	17	60	24	39	60%	20%	86	74	27	95	40
Kevin Jepsen	260	1059	75	23	76	31	52	63%	20%	90	134	49	154	59
Cesar Jimenez	65	260	8	7	20	6	23	61%	15%	23	33	8	34	12
Ubaldo Jimenez	553	2306	116	77	144	77	128	60%	12%	247	264	111	302	165
Erik Johnson	109	459	18	15	32	18	24	56%	16%	57	44	18	53	27
Jim Johnson	263	982	42	35	100	35	37	61%	13%	95	131	29	113	59
Kris Johnson	64	254	12	9	18	14	9	61%	19%	30	28	8	30	15
Eric Jokisch	66	249	10	4	26	12	13	63%	13%	29	25	7	31	13
Taylor Jordan	124	429	17	8	50	17	27	64%	14%	44	63	15	51	21
Jair Jurrjens	50	195	9	3	13	10	13	62%	11%	18	26	7	23	10
Tommy Kahnle	285	1099	63	31	88	32	67	62%	19%	143	101	36	148	65
Scott Kazmir	777	2983	164	50	241	104	205	66%	15%	295	399	87	406	135
Shawn Kelley	220	889	67	20	43	29	56	64%	24%	85	110	33	131	44
Joe Kelly	415	1580	66	42	162	63	70	60%	12%	178	194	62	198	96
Kyle Kendrick	865	3102	121	57	292	136	227	63%	12%	317	437	87	371	144
Ian Kennedy	846	3402	207	70	217	123	206	65%	16%	307	445	115	481	174
Clayton Kershaw	749	2722	239	31	243	89	137	69%	21%	234	401	68	415	89
Dallas Keuchel	808	3020	146	48	376	102	114	64%	14%	281	422	115	391	153
Craig Kimbrel	244	1047	95	26	48	27	41	65%	27%	102	130	40	167	56
Brandon Kintzler	239	867	31	16	106	34	46	64%	10%	97	110	22	103	38
Phil Klein	79	317	23	10	18	5	21	59%	23%	37	36	13	43	23
Corey Kluber	951	3500	269	51	296	132	180	68%	10%	341	490	93	514	137
Tom Koehler	803	2941	153	71	239	99	216	63%	14%	327	377	90	367	145
Michael Kohn	101	439	26	20	13	15	25	57%	18%	51	41	19	56	32
George Kontos	125	469	27	11	34	16	37	65%	15%	54	59	13	60	19
Ian Krol	154	611	28	13	44	32	34	62%	13%	73	72	27	79	39
Hiroki Kuroda	820	3097	146	35	292	131	200	64%	16%	326	400	90	389	122
John Lackey	833	3078	164	47	268	131	205	69%	15%	268	458	92	428	124
Mat Latos	420	1533	74	26	116	69	123	65%	13%	172	206	43	187	64
Tom Layne	76	304	14	8	25	15	13	61%	12%	33	37	12	41	18
Brandon League	273	956	38	27	133	29	35	59%	14%	136	107	33	111	51
Mike Leake	902	3215	164	50	354	134	175	64%	12%	358	421	91	408	139
Wade LeBlanc	121	448	21	7	36	21	32	63%	14%	49	54	15	58	23
Sam LeCure	251	973	48	24	75	38	58	60%	14%	115	107	36	127	53
C.C. Lee	127	500	26	12	35	19	30	65%	13%	52	66	16	71	27
Cliff Lee	352	1273	72	12	125	56	77	68%	12%	122	195	30	189	43
Dominic Leone	272	1080	70	25	93	35	42	63%	21%	119	133	26	150	46
Jon Lester	885	3493	220	48	253	123	221	65%	16%	344	447	116	484	157
Colby Lewis	762	2802	133	48	185	128	248	66%	12%	261	418	76	351	122

Pitcher Analysis
Pitchers with 50+ Batters Faced in 2014

Pitcher	BF	Pitches	K	BB	GB	LD	FB	Str%	S/Str	1-0	0-1	Full	2 Strike	3 Ball
										Counts				
Tim Lincecum	673	2665	134	63	219	107	137	62%	16%	306	303	91	341	149
Matt Lindstrom	158	555	18	12	63	25	35	64%	12%	70	63	17	64	29
Francisco Liriano	691	2714	175	81	227	78	112	60%	24%	306	316	96	365	166
Kyle Lobstein	164	630	27	14	55	21	46	62%	14%	77	68	19	78	36
Jeff Locke	548	1962	89	40	203	80	119	64%	15%	230	248	56	246	94
Boone Logan	116	433	32	11	34	17	17	62%	26%	48	56	12	56	27
Kyle Lohse	817	3002	141	45	244	117	247	66%	13%	292	416	78	397	118
Javier Lopez	167	599	22	19	79	15	26	61%	14%	58	82	18	68	37
Aaron Loup	283	1084	56	30	99	37	47	61%	16%	122	123	44	139	66
Josh Lueke	135	487	19	5	47	23	40	69%	14%	49	70	9	65	14
Jordan Lyles	546	2100	90	46	203	89	101	61%	13%	235	246	70	245	118
Lance Lynn	866	3450	181	72	262	116	213	63%	15%	345	437	131	447	188
Tyler Lyons	155	535	36	11	45	17	42	67%	17%	59	78	12	69	24
Jean Machi	249	927	51	18	90	34	49	64%	20%	99	127	21	120	41
Paul Maholm	311	1173	34	28	130	47	62	60%	10%	139	136	46	128	68
Seth Maness	317	1094	55	11	136	46	61	68%	13%	104	161	28	131	35
Jeff Manship	105	372	16	14	31	16	25	59%	18%	44	48	13	43	23
Michael Mariot	118	480	21	12	32	19	34	58%	15%	51	56	22	55	36
Carlos Marmol	66	269	14	10	17	7	14	61%	18%	23	39	10	35	15
Evan Marshall	210	823	54	17	82	23	30	65%	23%	80	102	21	115	32
Sean Marshall	80	298	14	12	27	16	8	62%	20%	33	37	10	36	17
Chris Martin	69	253	14	4	31	10	10	68%	13%	21	38	7	39	8
Carlos Martinez	386	1379	84	36	128	54	68	64%	22%	164	176	33	180	65
Nick Martinez	610	2406	77	55	155	93	223	60%	11%	288	273	99	275	146
Nick Masset	211	759	36	24	75	30	40	60%	15%	84	91	27	89	43
Justin Masterson	592	2249	116	69	221	77	82	61%	16%	260	276	77	275	131
Daisuke Matsuzaka	359	1446	78	50	88	43	85	60%	15%	157	164	59	181	93
Brian Matusz	226	914	53	17	53	23	76	64%	16%	94	111	27	114	44
Tyler Matzek	503	1764	91	44	177	71	108	63%	14%	209	221	47	203	98
Brandon Maurer	301	1134	55	19	88	40	95	65%	15%	110	153	35	151	52
Trevor May	213	839	44	22	51	33	59	63%	16%	80	113	26	106	49
Zach McAllister	377	1462	74	28	114	56	101	66%	12%	144	184	53	195	73
Brandon McCarthy	836	3044	175	33	326	141	153	69%	14%	274	449	83	426	112
Pat McCoy	74	254	11	13	31	8	10	59%	13%	37	24	8	29	17
T.J. McFarland	255	865	34	13	120	37	37	66%	13%	102	113	23	101	35
Jake McGee	274	1151	90	16	62	31	70	66%	21%	97	152	37	172	51
Dustin McGowan	354	1403	61	33	98	39	118	61%	18%	144	163	65	179	84
Collin McHugh	619	2486	157	41	171	98	137	64%	18%	256	309	86	355	119
Yoervis Medina	247	909	60	28	81	33	38	60%	17%	111	105	32	117	53
Evan Meek	107	409	16	11	36	16	21	63%	14%	48	46	13	55	19
Jenrry Mejia	417	1550	98	41	136	55	81	65%	18%	171	202	50	216	78
Mark Melancon	277	975	71	11	108	37	43	69%	21%	84	159	21	139	31
Roman Mendez	136	552	22	17	41	11	43	61%	15%	65	60	18	72	31
Miles Mikolas	255	931	38	18	78	44	72	66%	12%	96	125	29	124	41
Wade Miley	866	3217	183	75	301	123	165	63%	16%	318	419	106	424	163
Andrew Miller	242	992	103	17	53	25	35	65%	24%	98	127	25	150	38
Justin Miller	53	193	5	2	17	8	20	66%	8%	24	21	4	24	5
Shelby Miller	764	2858	127	73	216	103	222	64%	12%	303	362	89	369	138
Brad Mills	101	413	19	11	28	14	27	60%	14%	47	46	14	51	25
Tommy Milone	519	1925	75	37	156	84	156	62%	12%	194	250	60	240	97
Mike Minor	637	2424	120	44	184	106	163	64%	12%	250	310	96	324	118
Rafael Montero	194	837	42	23	42	27	55	59%	15%	78	96	52	107	66
Franklin Morales	646	2429	100	65	198	114	151	62%	14%	283	293	81	295	138
Mike Morin	246	918	54	19	72	28	64	65%	19%	92	128	25	127	45
Bryan Morris	272	939	50	24	111	36	40	63%	23%	98	127	21	116	40
Brandon Morrow	148	618	30	18	50	19	30	60%	16%	71	63	22	75	33
Charlie Morton	666	2504	126	57	249	96	102	63%	13%	258	323	77	320	122
Jason Motte	110	410	17	9	31	18	35	65%	16%	41	55	11	53	17
Edward Mujica	253	951	43	14	83	41	69	69%	15%	80	138	23	136	31
Joe Nathan	259	1062	54	29	72	39	62	61%	16%	104	125	50	136	68
Jimmy Nelson	311	1109	57	19	108	44	71	64%	15%	112	151	33	133	57
Pat Neshek	255	985	68	9	59	19	92	72%	18%	83	149	18	156	24
Juan Nicasio	409	1616	63	31	140	61	104	63%	13%	168	207	55	212	86
Jon Niese	786	2792	138	45	277	131	173	65%	12%	289	384	83	343	129
Hector Noesi	733	2753	123	56	206	116	220	64%	15%	277	367	97	355	134
Ricky Nolasco	695	2641	115	38	221	118	190	63%	15%	293	321	84	319	130
Bud Norris	687	2746	139	52	202	99	178	64%	13%	273	343	94	360	142
Ivan Nova	96	328	12	6	37	15	23	66%	8%	34	43	12	39	14

Pitcher Analysis
Pitchers with 50+ Batters Faced in 2014

Pitcher	BF	Pitches	K	BB	GB	LD	FB	Str%	S/Str	Counts 1-0	0-1	Full	2 Strike	3 Ball
Vidal Nuno	679	2588	129	46	187	93	211	66%	13%	227	385	79	351	107
Brett Oberholtzer	623	2251	94	28	181	99	207	66%	12%	245	301	58	299	86
Darren O'Day	271	1067	73	19	74	29	63	67%	21%	111	140	31	148	46
Jake Odorizzi	719	3028	174	59	141	101	230	64%	16%	277	389	118	403	159
Eric O'Flaherty	80	321	15	4	31	10	16	63%	15%	32	39	15	46	19
Alexi Ogando	122	494	22	15	29	16	38	62%	15%	51	58	23	68	28
Logan Ondrusek	189	681	42	16	57	22	49	62%	19%	82	87	15	82	34
Sean O'Sullivan	52	192	7	2	16	9	16	67%	11%	22	24	7	21	10
Dan Otero	349	1216	45	15	159	67	56	68%	15%	107	191	26	150	42
Adam Ottavino	272	1086	70	16	84	35	61	66%	18%	103	147	38	154	51
Josh Outman	122	510	26	16	41	9	26	59%	20%	54	57	25	66	36
Juan Oviedo	140	528	26	16	31	10	52	61%	17%	57	68	16	71	30
Jonathan Papelbon	259	1020	63	15	72	27	73	67%	19%	93	137	35	148	44
Blake Parker	91	359	24	4	20	14	29	65%	18%	40	44	12	46	17
Manny Parra	164	629	34	18	53	23	27	64%	21%	60	88	25	85	35
Troy Patton	63	235	13	5	22	5	16	64%	15%	29	28	8	29	12
Felipe Paulino	103	417	14	12	31	19	26	58%	11%	48	41	21	53	33
James Paxton	303	1182	59	29	114	47	47	61%	14%	138	143	40	144	66
Brad Peacock	589	2373	119	70	145	83	165	62%	14%	254	288	76	302	131
Jake Peavy	852	3225	158	63	232	118	253	65%	15%	303	448	117	421	156
Mike Pelfrey	119	457	10	18	38	16	33	55%	9%	60	50	13	45	31
Brad Penny	120	448	13	13	46	19	25	62%	7%	49	58	12	49	23
Joel Peralta	265	1091	74	15	56	34	80	68%	18%	96	154	41	169	52
Wily Peralta	838	3192	154	61	322	113	166	62%	14%	349	405	133	390	176
Chris Perez	200	832	39	25	49	25	56	61%	15%	96	90	36	118	49
Martin Perez	207	777	35	19	79	34	37	61%	12%	84	94	29	97	42
Oliver Perez	256	1000	76	24	64	31	49	66%	20%	98	140	37	158	51
Glen Perkins	260	946	66	11	63	41	74	70%	17%	90	132	26	133	37
Vinnie Pestano	78	325	26	5	16	6	25	65%	22%	34	37	11	49	17
Yusmeiro Petit	461	1678	133	22	108	64	132	68%	19%	143	263	38	245	54
Jake Petricka	307	1191	55	33	135	37	41	63%	13%	120	157	30	158	59
David Phelps	497	1925	92	46	142	83	120	61%	9%	187	250	72	233	107
Stolmy Pimentel	148	593	38	16	25	20	45	64%	22%	54	78	20	82	30
Michael Pineda	290	1140	59	7	86	41	93	71%	16%	97	181	28	165	34
Yohan Pino	258	1012	50	14	54	44	91	66%	12%	103	129	29	127	46
Drew Pomeranz	278	1138	64	26	85	34	67	62%	14%	134	118	40	154	68
Rick Porcello	840	3055	129	41	321	144	190	66%	12%	299	440	65	392	109
Aaron Poreda	97	369	21	7	29	17	19	66%	16%	34	47	11	53	16
Ryan Pressly	122	387	14	8	45	26	25	65%	14%	50	53	7	44	14
David Price	1009	3730	271	38	280	140	259	70%	16%	303	576	106	561	137
Zach Putnam	213	862	46	20	77	22	46	63%	23%	83	111	37	122	50
J.J. Putz	62	259	14	6	22	6	12	63%	18%	19	38	11	37	15
Kevin Quackenbush	222	919	56	18	53	38	52	64%	15%	80	125	31	125	50
Chad Qualls	213	697	43	5	91	28	40	71%	15%	72	113	13	94	18
Jose Quintana	830	3346	178	52	264	130	196	64%	14%	281	460	127	439	161
Erasmo Ramirez	338	1293	60	34	89	45	102	63%	18%	133	160	46	174	63
Neil Ramirez	177	746	53	17	27	25	52	61%	23%	75	81	35	108	44
A.J. Ramos	270	1097	73	43	62	28	57	61%	23%	115	133	39	153	64
Cesar Ramos	360	1311	66	39	109	47	92	62%	12%	150	160	47	153	73
Anthony Ranaudo	170	635	15	16	46	19	70	61%	9%	71	76	20	68	36
Cory Rasmus	225	881	57	17	58	28	66	67%	10%	94	111	21	123	34
Rob Rasmussen	50	183	13	7	12	5	11	64%	22%	17	27	5	30	9
Robbie Ray	136	547	19	11	37	25	43	62%	10%	62	67	18	68	29
Todd Redmond	314	1205	60	27	73	42	108	64%	13%	118	162	36	156	55
Addison Reed	252	967	69	15	48	39	79	69%	20%	86	146	22	151	33
Evan Reed	145	583	26	12	58	21	25	61%	18%	63	65	20	78	29
Scott Rice	66	272	13	12	26	5	8	57%	25%	36	25	11	38	19
Garrett Richards	678	2627	164	51	231	96	127	63%	18%	303	306	78	361	122
Andre Rienzo	312	1266	51	33	99	49	72	60%	15%	151	134	52	159	71
Donn Roach	140	499	17	15	65	17	19	62%	12%	53	64	14	59	25
Tanner Roark	798	2999	138	39	249	124	228	65%	13%	278	420	93	383	125
David Robertson	259	1088	96	23	61	32	45	63%	21%	101	140	46	161	63
Fernando Rodney	286	1138	76	28	85	42	48	64%	17%	115	153	40	155	61
Francisco Rodriguez	268	1045	73	18	76	37	60	64%	19%	109	133	39	142	52
Paco Rodriguez	53	235	14	4	16	10	7	62%	21%	28	21	11	37	13
Wandy Rodriguez	125	457	20	8	39	14	39	64%	13%	48	64	13	54	21
Esmil Rogers	202	849	44	17	51	27	58	63%	15%	81	100	37	119	52

Pitcher Analysis
Pitchers with 50+ Batters Faced in 2014

Pitcher	BF	Pitches	K	BB	GB	LD	FB	Str%	S/Str	Counts 1-0	0-1	Full	2 Strike	3 Ball
Sergio Romo	230	866	59	12	56	27	69	68%	22%	71	125	26	135	32
Hector Rondon	255	999	63	15	87	41	49	67%	17%	90	135	34	138	46
B.J. Rosenberg	59	256	9	7	13	11	19	59%	14%	27	22	15	34	22
Trevor Rosenthal	308	1263	87	42	65	43	63	63%	21%	134	145	46	179	71
Robbie Ross	365	1355	51	30	145	52	74	65%	12%	118	202	44	161	64
Tyson Ross	811	3119	195	72	297	109	115	62%	21%	342	387	103	418	166
Zac Rosscup	66	295	21	12	9	8	15	58%	25%	34	30	12	44	21
Michael Roth	60	247	9	9	22	7	9	55%	12%	35	22	11	29	17
Chris Rusin	58	195	8	5	21	8	15	63%	13%	24	28	8	22	11
James Russell	238	925	42	20	65	40	62	65%	12%	84	127	35	124	49
Hyun-Jin Ryu	631	2443	139	29	213	101	135	65%	14%	242	324	87	333	112
Marc Rzepczynski	196	748	46	19	74	23	27	61%	26%	93	78	27	94	41
CC Sabathia	209	798	48	10	70	32	43	68%	16%	62	124	20	121	26
Fernando Salas	239	943	61	14	46	47	66	66%	20%	87	131	29	140	41
Danny Salazar	474	1869	120	35	106	72	130	64%	18%	193	232	55	251	85
Chris Sale	685	2753	208	39	172	78	173	67%	20%	225	393	87	405	122
Jeff Samardzija	879	3339	202	43	309	119	188	66%	17%	301	482	101	474	126
Aaron Sanchez	121	465	27	9	54	12	16	61%	11%	56	52	13	58	24
Anibal Sanchez	514	2097	102	30	169	72	129	65%	15%	204	268	82	280	103
Ervin Santana	817	2987	179	63	237	137	181	64%	20%	307	405	103	401	145
Hector Santiago	544	2273	108	53	115	73	187	62%	12%	242	262	85	304	124
Sergio Santos	106	412	29	18	24	15	20	59%	26%	50	45	14	56	24
Joe Saunders	215	847	23	24	75	38	53	57%	9%	90	99	31	93	52
Rob Scahill	72	248	11	9	22	11	17	60%	20%	28	30	10	31	15
Tanner Scheppers	111	416	17	10	45	11	25	60%	12%	48	51	15	46	21
Max Scherzer	904	3638	252	63	211	125	239	66%	19%	333	477	120	541	156
Brian Schlitter	242	906	31	19	109	38	35	62%	9%	105	114	30	97	51
Gus Schlosser	81	304	8	6	19	21	24	64%	11%	31	42	9	38	13
Bryan Shaw	313	1247	64	22	98	39	77	65%	17%	129	160	45	168	67
James Shields	939	3632	180	44	313	143	236	65%	15%	346	486	125	482	166
Matt Shoemaker	543	2101	124	24	157	75	149	64%	18%	202	285	81	278	100
Chasen Shreve	50	204	15	3	15	5	11	67%	18%	18	25	6	32	7
Kevin Siegrist	140	579	37	16	25	17	41	63%	16%	49	74	24	81	36
Shae Simmons	89	369	23	11	28	13	12	62%	20%	33	45	13	51	21
Alfredo Simon	818	3014	127	56	293	128	187	65%	14%	310	403	95	376	138
Tony Sipp	198	818	63	17	35	24	53	65%	22%	76	105	31	121	40
Tyler Skaggs	464	1703	86	30	169	64	104	66%	13%	169	241	50	228	78
Kevin Slowey	169	591	24	9	53	29	48	72%	13%	49	91	19	87	23
Chad Smith	50	196	9	3	14	10	14	65%	12%	14	26	9	26	10
Joe Smith	285	1105	68	15	114	29	50	67%	13%	94	158	32	156	45
Will Smith	286	1124	86	31	72	37	54	61%	22%	134	131	37	150	66
Drew Smyly	618	2592	133	42	159	87	189	65%	16%	235	354	89	370	112
Joakim Soria	182	692	48	6	54	27	44	67%	15%	68	95	24	99	32
Rafael Soriano	252	1008	59	19	54	33	84	66%	20%	109	118	41	140	52
Zeke Spruill	99	325	14	4	40	17	20	68%	11%	33	48	11	38	15
Craig Stammen	304	1135	56	14	109	53	65	65%	18%	119	151	34	150	48
Tim Stauffer	273	1095	67	23	75	50	54	65%	17%	106	139	37	161	53
Josh Stinson	61	236	6	6	24	8	15	59%	14%	25	27	6	23	14
Matt Stites	148	557	26	16	42	17	41	61%	18%	57	70	20	70	35
Drew Storen	224	807	46	11	83	23	52	68%	16%	82	115	18	113	28
Dan Straily	231	881	47	24	55	25	76	60%	20%	122	91	27	109	46
Stephen Strasburg	868	3295	242	43	257	127	176	67%	18%	302	470	80	480	121
Huston Street	229	927	57	14	57	32	68	66%	20%	82	128	34	133	45
Marcus Stroman	534	2082	111	28	210	72	108	65%	14%	222	266	62	271	88
Pedro Strop	244	909	71	25	77	34	29	63%	25%	108	121	26	123	44
Eric Stults	763	2833	111	45	253	123	208	64%	13%	284	390	99	358	145
Eric Surkamp	107	418	20	13	28	14	27	59%	15%	52	46	12	51	23
Anthony Swarzak	378	1405	47	28	134	59	108	64%	11%	152	180	42	182	66
Masahiro Tanaka	542	2009	141	21	172	90	107	67%	20%	205	267	60	284	82
Junichi Tazawa	261	988	64	17	65	49	64	65%	18%	105	122	34	137	41
Julio Teheran	884	3271	186	51	217	133	273	66%	17%	350	441	87	442	134
Nick Tepesch	537	2029	56	44	177	101	147	62%	10%	234	244	66	228	114
Joe Thatcher	135	534	27	4	33	22	41	70%	16%	44	70	17	74	20
Dale Thayer	265	1055	62	16	70	37	72	67%	15%	96	138	39	151	53
Caleb Thielbar	206	813	35	16	47	39	62	63%	12%	89	94	33	100	44
Tyler Thornburg	131	511	28	21	29	15	36	59%	18%	60	55	18	63	35
Matt Thornton	152	637	28	8	61	14	34	65%	13%	70	71	20	83	28

Pitcher Analysis
Pitchers with 50+ Batters Faced in 2014

Pitcher	BF	Pitches	K	BB	GB	LD	FB	Str%	S/Str	Counts				
										1-0	0-1	Full	2 Strike	3 Ball
Chris Tillman	871	3411	150	66	260	129	252	63%	12%	368	411	104	431	166
Shawn Tolleson	296	1166	69	28	79	35	82	61%	16%	132	134	30	146	57
Josh Tomlin	446	1715	94	14	124	89	118	67%	15%	144	248	56	236	71
Michael Tonkin	87	332	16	6	26	15	19	65%	13%	34	41	9	44	15
Alex Torres	241	991	51	33	70	34	45	58%	22%	107	103	47	134	75
Carlos Torres	405	1576	96	38	123	46	94	63%	19%	158	206	51	206	77
Blake Treinen	214	734	30	13	99	36	32	66%	13%	92	100	17	95	26
Nicholas Tropeano	91	367	13	9	27	9	31	61%	15%	42	44	18	50	24
Jacob Turner	501	1819	71	33	189	80	116	61%	14%	214	219	57	200	96
Koji Uehara	249	950	80	8	50	35	70	71%	28%	90	133	25	148	31
Jose Valverde	95	374	23	10	20	13	27	62%	17%	42	40	11	51	23
Jason Vargas	790	3003	128	41	230	138	232	64%	15%	294	423	93	387	140
Anthony Varvaro	218	899	50	13	76	27	50	67%	15%	80	114	32	125	42
Yordano Ventura	782	2985	159	69	257	115	168	63%	17%	304	399	113	399	146
Jose Veras	203	847	50	27	53	26	41	58%	15%	94	94	38	105	60
Justin Verlander	893	3409	159	65	258	129	264	64%	15%	341	443	109	445	171
Carlos Villanueva	343	1305	72	19	100	49	93	64%	18%	139	165	36	169	57
Pedro Villarreal	62	217	12	7	15	11	16	62%	16%	30	28	5	29	10
Nick Vincent	215	860	62	11	44	29	59	67%	18%	84	108	29	124	38
Ryan Vogelsong	780	3058	151	58	211	133	205	63%	13%	295	391	135	399	173
Edinson Volquez	809	2977	140	71	285	95	186	64%	14%	322	390	92	399	140
Michael Wacha	447	1694	94	33	126	67	110	66%	16%	160	231	44	252	63
Tsuyoshi Wada	289	1146	57	19	74	47	85	64%	14%	117	143	39	155	51
Adam Wainwright	898	3258	179	50	296	153	190	66%	14%	347	423	105	434	143
Jordan Walden	205	867	62	27	52	22	41	60%	25%	86	98	44	120	55
Taijuan Walker	160	625	34	18	48	28	27	63%	16%	61	81	16	80	33
Wei-Chung Wang	92	357	13	8	27	14	29	61%	13%	38	47	14	44	24
Adam Warren	324	1332	76	24	98	51	67	63%	18%	138	163	43	185	62
Tony Watson	305	1199	81	15	93	40	62	67%	20%	107	172	34	172	43
Jered Weaver	888	3352	169	65	207	121	302	63%	15%	392	416	108	425	156
Daniel Webb	296	1177	58	42	99	34	59	57%	19%	144	126	49	139	92
Ryan Webb	207	723	37	12	75	35	44	66%	13%	75	105	21	91	31
Allen Webster	259	956	36	28	86	40	61	60%	19%	102	119	37	115	57
Zack Wheeler	794	3308	187	79	273	95	138	61%	17%	359	367	139	438	204
Chase Whitley	330	1265	60	18	111	51	83	64%	18%	127	170	40	162	60
Joe Wieland	54	215	8	5	15	9	17	59%	14%	20	27	9	24	13
Tom Wilhelmsen	317	1221	72	36	106	39	60	63%	20%	130	155	45	170	70
Jerome Williams	497	1832	82	36	165	85	120	65%	13%	183	258	62	241	88
Alex Wilson	109	412	19	5	36	15	31	68%	11%	42	58	10	57	13
Brian Wilson	223	1020	54	29	51	32	51	58%	15%	94	115	50	141	75
C.J. Wilson	761	3108	151	85	243	115	150	58%	13%	314	383	147	381	218
Justin Wilson	256	1032	61	30	82	23	55	63%	16%	101	132	35	138	55
Chris Withrow	90	385	28	18	20	7	16	57%	24%	46	37	24	55	33
Randy Wolf	113	430	19	6	32	21	31	63%	12%	46	56	15	48	24
Alex Wood	694	2683	170	45	212	90	160	65%	16%	262	351	93	364	132
Travis Wood	781	3045	146	76	185	125	228	63%	11%	333	374	96	391	152
Rob Wooten	147	593	29	8	57	21	29	65%	16%	53	88	24	86	28
Brandon Workman	378	1429	70	36	110	59	98	64%	12%	159	182	46	186	70
Vance Worley	458	1578	79	22	170	70	104	68%	9%	171	215	41	209	59
Jamey Wright	308	1096	54	27	121	44	50	64%	14%	120	151	32	141	53
Steven Wright	86	346	22	4	34	12	12	61%	10%	38	41	17	47	18
Wesley Wright	209	772	37	19	76	35	35	60%	15%	95	93	21	93	41
Kirby Yates	156	690	42	15	31	22	43	64%	15%	63	85	28	97	40
Chris Young	688	2718	108	60	113	96	297	64%	12%	283	341	85	357	136
Josh Zeid	98	378	18	7	27	18	22	62%	19%	38	45	9	47	17
Brad Ziegler	281	979	54	24	125	34	37	62%	18%	113	124	28	118	44
Jordan Zimmermann	800	2924	182	29	228	136	204	70%	16%	236	451	78	416	99

Pitchers' Repertoires

This section includes a breakdown of how often every pitcher who appeared in a Major League game in 2014 threw each type of pitch in his repertoire. Who used their fastball the most this year? Among non-position players, hard-throwing Rays reliever Jake McGee led the way, using his heater 96 percent of the time. Hitters knew what was coming, but most of the time they still couldn't hit it. How often did Adam Wainwright unleash his knee-buckling curveball? To opposing batters' dismay, Uncle Charlie made up a full 28 percent of his offerings. You'll even find information on Detroit's knuckleballing utility infielder/jack-of-all-trades Danny Worth and the rest of the position players who were forced onto the bump this season. If it was thrown this season, it's in the Pitchers' Repertoires section.

Player	Fastball Velocity	Pitch Repertoire						
		Fastball	Cutter	Curve	Slider	Change	Splitter	Other
Abad,Fernando	92.0	65%	<1%	27%	-	7%	-	
Aceves,Alfredo	92.6	46%	15%	28%	-	9%	2%	
Achter,A.J.	90.2	62%	-	-	17%	21%	-	
Adams,Austin	96.5	69%	-	-	25%	6%	-	
Adams,Mike	90.3	47%	32%	16%	-	5%	-	
Adcock,Nate	93.6	64%	-	-	34%	2%	-	
Affeldt,Jeremy	91.6	67%	-	24%	-	-	9%	
Albers,Matt	92.6	64%	-	<1%	23%	12%	-	
Alburquerque,Al	93.6	36%	-	-	64%	-	-	
Allen,Cody	95.3	62%	-	38%	-	-	-	
Alvarez,Dario	89.9	48%	-	-	52%	-	-	
Alvarez,Henderson	93.5	64%	-	1%	12%	23%	-	
Alvarez,Jose	89.0	40%	-	40%	20%	-	-	
Alvarez,R.J.	94.9	73%	-	-	22%	5%	-	
Ambriz,Hector	93.4	55%	-	6%	39%	-	-	
Anderson,Brett	89.8	50%	-	10%	34%	6%	-	
Anderson,Chase	91.0	61%	-	19%	-	20%	-	
Anna,Dean	61.2	100%	-	-	-	-	-	
Archer,Chris	94.6	66%	-	-	29%	5%	-	
Arencibia,J.P.	71.7	100%	-	-	-	-	-	
Arrieta,Jake	93.5	47%	28%	18%	<1%	6%	-	
Arroyo,Bronson	85.4	47%	-	13%	22%	18%	-	
Atchison,Scott	92.1	31%	53%	16%	-	<1%		
Aumont,Phillippe	94.4	51%	-	15%	33%	-	-	
Avilan,Luis	92.8	82%	-	10%	<1%	9%	-	
Axelrod,Dylan	88.9	50%	-	5%	34%	10%	-	
Axford,John	94.7	68%	-	16%	17%	-	-	
Badenhop,Burke	89.3	72%	-	-	11%	17%	-	
Baez,Pedro	95.3	81%	-	-	12%	7%	-	
Bailey,Homer	94.2	58%	-	8%	22%	-	12%	
Baker,John	77.0	91%	-	-	9%	-	-	
Baker,Scott	89.3	64%	-	-	30%	7%	-	
Balfour,Grant	91.6	59%	-	5%	32%	4%	-	
Barnes,Matt	93.9	63%	-	19%	-	18%	-	
Barrett,Aaron	93.5	64%	-	-	35%	2%	-	
Bass,Anthony	93.8	60%	-	<1%	32%	7%	-	
Bassitt,Chris	91.8	48%	-	18%	26%	7%	-	
Bastardo,Antonio	91.5	63%	-	-	36%	1%	-	
Bauer,Trevor	94.0	50%	13%	12%	11%	9%	-	Screwball 5%
Beato,Pedro	91.5	60%	18%	6%	-	16%	-	
Beavan,Blake	86.5	70%	5%	3%	22%	-	-	
Beckett,Josh	91.9	36%	17%	31%	-	17%	-	
Bedard,Erik	87.9	40%	23%	23%	-	14%	<1%	
Bedrosian,Cam	94.5	74%	-	-	18%	7%	-	
Beeler,Dallas	89.8	46%	33%	14%	-	-	7%	
Beimel,Joe	86.4	71%	-	5%	12%	12%	-	
Belisario,Ronald	93.9	77%	1%	-	18%	-	4%	
Belisle,Matt	91.3	65%	-	8%	25%	2%	-	
Beliveau,Jeff	89.5	56%	20%	20%	-	3%	-	
Bell,Heath	91.4	53%	-	29%	-	-	18%	
Bell,Trevor	92.2	83%	-	-	6%	11%	-	
Benoit,Joaquin	94.7	50%	-	-	18%	32%	-	
Bergman,Christian	89.0	54%	-	7%	25%	14%	-	
Betances,Dellin	96.6	53%	-	-	47%	-	-	
Bettis,Chad	93.2	67%	14%	3%	-	16%	-	

Player	Fastball Velocity	Pitch Repertoire						
		Fastball	Cutter	Curve	Slider	Change	Splitter	Other
Billings,Bruce	87.3	63%	-	4%	20%	13%	-	
Black,Vic	95.6	73%	-	27%	-	<1%	-	
Blevins,Jerry	91.1	51%	19%	18%	-	12%	-	
Bochy,Brett	88.1	72%	14%	-	14%	-	-	
Bolsinger,Mike	87.9	66%	-	33%	-	<1%	-	
Bonilla,Lisalverto	91.9	60%	-	-	15%	25%	-	
Boxberger,Brad	93.1	65%	-	<1%	2%	33%	-	
Boyer,Blaine	93.1	70%	-	9%	21%	<1%	-	
Brach,Brad	93.4	68%	-	-	18%	14%	-	
Breslow,Craig	88.4	61%	19%	5%	-	15%	-	
Britton,Drake	92.4	58%	-	-	39%	3%	-	
Britton,Zach	95.1	91%	-	-	9%	-	-	
Brooks,Aaron	91.9	62%	-	1%	17%	20%	-	
Brothers,Rex	92.8	64%	-	-	31%	5%	-	
Brown,Brooks	94.3	52%	-	2%	24%	22%	-	
Broxton,Jonathan	93.2	78%	-	<1%	21%	-	-	
Buchanan,David	90.3	40%	30%	9%	-	21%	-	
Buchanan,Jake	88.5	56%	-	19%	16%	9%	-	
Buchholz,Clay	91.6	45%	25%	16%	-	11%	3%	
Buchter,Ryan	92.0	50%	17%	33%	-	-	-	
Buckner,Billy	87.7	59%	-	28%	-	13%	-	
Buehrle,Mark	83.9	49%	16%	13%	-	22%	-	
Bueno,Francisley	89.4	60%	-	-	23%	10%	6%	
Bumgarner,Madison	92.1	44%	-	14%	35%	8%	-	
Burnett,A.J.	91.7	59%	-	33%	-	8%	-	
Burnett,Sean	86.5	79%	-	-	21%	-	-	
Burton,Jared	91.5	49%	-	-	14%	37%	-	
Butera,Drew	86.5	58%	-	-	-	42%	-	
Butler,Eddie	93.1	64%	-	1%	13%	22%	-	
Butler,Keith	87.5	57%	-	30%	-	13%	-	
Cabral,Cesar	89.2	37%	-	-	61%	2%	-	
Cahill,Trevor	90.0	63%	-	15%	3%	19%	-	
Cain,Matt	91.6	51%	-	13%	19%	17%	-	
Caminero,Arquimedes	95.5	67%	4%	-	5%	-	24%	
Camp,Shawn	86.2	59%	-	-	33%	8%	-	
Campos,Leonel	94.3	59%	-	-	35%	6%	-	
Capps,Carter	97.4	75%	-	-	23%	2%	-	
Capuano,Chris	89.3	44%	-	8%	21%	28%	-	
Carlyle,Buddy	90.5	83%	13%	2%	-	1%	-	
Carp,Mike	80.2	53%	-	-	-	-	-	Knuckleball 47%
Carpenter,David	95.6	72%	-	-	26%	2%	-	
Carpenter,David	89.3	66%	-	-	34%	-	-	
Carrasco,Carlos	95.3	56%	-	9%	21%	13%	-	
Carroll,Scott	89.7	58%	8%	13%	3%	17%	-	
Cashner,Andrew	94.3	71%	-	2%	17%	10%	-	
Casilla,Santiago	94.3	63%	-	20%	14%	3%	-	
Cecil,Brett	92.8	34%	16%	44%	-	6%	-	
Cedeno,Xavier	91.4	27%	39%	6%	26%	2%	-	
Chacin,Jhoulys	88.0	56%	-	9%	22%	12%	-	
Chafin,Andrew	90.7	68%	-	-	18%	13%	-	
Chamberlain,Joba	93.5	44%	-	21%	34%	<1%	-	
Chapman,Aroldis	100.3	69%	-	-	24%	7%	-	
Chapman,Kevin	92.2	58%	-	-	39%	3%	-	
Chatwood,Tyler	92.6	82%	-	5%	12%	<1%	-	
Chavez,Jesse	91.3	31%	38%	14%	-	17%	-	

Player	Fastball Velocity	Fastball	Cutter	Curve	Slider	Change	Splitter Other
Chen,Bruce	84.2	39%	-	13%	31%	17%	-
Chen,Wei-Yin	91.8	66%	-	7%	16%	12%	-
Choate,Randy	84.5	69%	-	-	31%	-	-
Christiani,Nick	92.4	77%	15%	-	8%	<1%	-
Cingrani,Tony	91.3	74%	-	<1%	12%	13%	-
Cishek,Steve	91.7	51%	-	-	48%	<1%	-
Cisnero,Jose	93.7	72%	-	18%	4%	6%	-
Claiborne,Preston	91.0	54%	-	-	24%	22%	-
Claudio,Alex	84.3	51%	-	-	29%	20%	-
Clemens,Paul	92.3	62%	-	18%	-	20%	-
Cleto,Maikel	97.1	66%	-	-	24%	7%	4%
Clippard,Tyler	91.8	48%	-	7%	-	34%	10%
Cobb,Alex	91.7	42%	-	20%	-	38%	-
Coke,Phil	93.7	64%	3%	-	19%	14%	-
Cole,Gerrit	95.5	67%	-	16%	12%	5%	-
Coleman,Casey	94.0	70%	-	6%	23%	<1%	-
Coleman,Louis	88.6	62%	-	-	38%	<1%	-
Collins,Tim	92.3	59%	-	19%	-	22%	-
Collmenter,Josh	86.0	70%	-	7%	-	23%	-
Colome,Alex	94.2	59%	-	4%	23%	14%	-
Colon,Bartolo	88.7	83%	-	-	12%	6%	-
Contreras,Carlos	93.3	77%	-	13%	-	10%	-
Cook,Ryan	94.2	65%	-	-	26%	9%	-
Corcino,Daniel	88.9	60%	-	-	31%	10%	-
Cordier,Erik	99.3	72%	-	-	28%	-	-
Correia,Kevin	89.9	37%	31%	17%	-	14%	-
Cosart,Jarred	93.6	70%	-	26%	-	4%	-
Cotts,Neal	91.0	52%	35%	-	12%	1%	-
Coulombe,Daniel	91.2	41%	-	23%	25%	11%	-
Crockett,Kyle	89.3	66%	-	-	28%	6%	-
Crow,Aaron	92.0	65%	-	-	32%	4%	-
Cueto,Johnny	93.1	47%	23%	4%	10%	15%	-
Cumpton,Brandon	92.7	73%	-	-	20%	7%	-
Daley,Matt	85.8	67%	-	27%	-	5%	-
Danks,John	88.6	44%	19%	9%	-	28%	-
Darnell,Logan	89.8	55%	-	7%	21%	18%	-
Darvish,Yu	92.4	54%	11%	9%	21%	4%	2%
Davis,Wade	95.7	61%	20%	19%	-	-	-
De Fratus,Justin	91.6	51%	-	-	44%	5%	-
De La Rosa,Dane	89.6	76%	-	13%	-	11%	-
De La Rosa,Eury	88.6	41%	-	13%	34%	12%	-
De La Rosa,Jorge	92.3	41%	23%	4%	7%	26%	-
De La Rosa,Rubby	94.0	59%	-	3%	11%	27%	-
De Leon,Jorge	95.3	58%	-	-	25%	17%	-
Deduno,Samuel	89.5	66%	-	22%	6%	6%	-
deGrom,Jacob	93.5	61%	-	10%	17%	12%	-
Delabar,Steve	93.3	65%	-	-	12%	-	23%
Delgado,Randall	93.2	63%	-	7%	10%	20%	-
Dennick,Ryan	90.2	54%	-	-	32%	14%	-
Descalso,Daniel	85.0	100%	-	-	-	-	-
DeSclafani,Anthony	92.5	70%	-	-	26%	5%	-
Despaigne,Odrisamer	90.5	49%	21%	19%	-	11%	-
Detwiler,Ross	93.0	86%	-	10%	-	4%	-
Diaz,Jairo	97.2	81%	-	-	19%	-	-
Diaz,Jumbo	97.3	63%	-	-	30%	7%	-

Player	Fastball Velocity	Fastball	Cutter	Curve	Slider	Change	Splitter	Other
Dickey,R.A.	81.9	12%	-	-	-	2%	-	Knuckleball 85%
Diekman,Jake	96.9	71%	-	-	29%	<1%	-	
Dominguez,Jose	96.9	71%	-	-	25%	4%	-	
Doolittle,Sean	94.0	88%	-	-	11%	1%	-	
Doubront,Felix	89.5	58%	15%	10%	-	17%	-	
Downs,Darin	89.8	53%	-	6%	33%	8%	-	
Downs,Scott	86.9	64%	-	21%	15%	<1%	-	
Drabek,Kyle	91.1	49%	38%	13%	-	-	-	
Duensing,Brian	91.1	59%	-	6%	27%	9%	-	
Duffy,Danny	93.2	68%	-	22%	-	9%	-	
Duke,Zach	89.7	49%	19%	13%	16%	3%	-	
Dunn,Adam	80.7	86%	-	5%	9%	-	-	
Dunn,Mike	94.8	57%	-	1%	42%	-	-	
Dunning,Jake	87.7	54%	-	-	46%	-	-	
Dyson,Sam	95.6	80%	-	-	14%	6%	-	
Edgin,Josh	92.4	50%	26%	-	20%	4%	-	
Edwards,Jon	94.8	68%	-	-	32%	-	-	
Elbert,Scott	88.8	54%	-	-	46%	-	-	
Elias,Roenis	92.0	52%	-	23%	-	24%	-	
Eovaldi,Nathan	95.7	63%	-	9%	25%	3%	-	
Erlin,Robbie	89.7	61%	-	17%	6%	16%	-	
Escobar,Edwin	93.3	69%	-	19%	-	11%	-	
Estrada,Marco	89.0	57%	-	13%	-	30%	-	
Eveland,Dana	90.6	38%	-	-	58%	4%	-	
Familia,Jeurys	96.4	75%	-	-	25%	<1%	-	
Farmer,Buck	93.1	58%	-	-	16%	26%	-	
Farnsworth,Kyle	92.5	75%	1%	-	22%	2%	-	
Farquhar,Danny	93.3	21%	57%	16%	-	7%	-	
Feierabend,Ryan	89.0	58%	-	13%	18%	11%	-	
Feldman,Scott	88.9	33%	35%	27%	-	-	5%	
Feliz,Neftali	93.1	72%	-	-	17%	11%	-	
Fernandez,Jose	95.1	52%	-	16%	21%	11%	-	
Fields,Josh	94.4	66%	-	20%	-	14%	-	
Fien,Casey	92.9	53%	39%	-	7%	-	-	
Fiers,Mike	89.6	63%	11%	17%	-	9%	-	
Fife,Stephen	89.3	29%	-	30%	9%	33%	-	
Figaro,Alfredo	95.0	69%	-	12%	18%	<1%	-	
Figueroa,Pedro	94.0	66%	-	-	27%	7%	-	
Finnegan,Brandon	92.5	72%	-	-	12%	16%	-	
Fister,Doug	87.9	64%	-	9%	15%	13%	-	
Flande,Yohan	90.2	62%	-	-	16%	22%	-	
Floyd,Gavin	91.9	57%	18%	18%	-	7%	-	
Flynn,Brian	90.4	63%	-	16%	12%	9%	-	
Foltynewicz,Mike	96.7	73%	-	10%	6%	11%	-	
Fornataro,Eric	92.8	81%	-	18%	-	1%	-	
Francis,Jeff	87.2	51%	-	21%	17%	11%	-	
Francisco,Frank	92.2	67%	-	5%	-	-	28%	
Frasor,Jason	91.9	65%	-	-	18%	-	17%	
Freeman,Sam	93.5	63%	-	-	10%	27%	-	
Frias,Carlos	94.4	59%	27%	6%	-	8%	-	
Friedrich,Christian	91.5	56%	-	8%	30%	6%	-	
Frieri,Ernesto	94.0	78%	-	-	17%	4%	-	
Fujikawa,Kyuji	90.8	55%	20%	4%	-	-	20%	
Furbush,Charlie	91.8	56%	-	4%	39%	<1%	-	
Gallardo,Yovani	91.4	56%	-	19%	25%	<1%	-	

Player	Fastball Velocity	Fastball	Cutter	Curve	Slider	Change	Splitter	Other
Garces,Frank	91.9	57%	-	-	36%	8%	-	
Garcia,Jaime	90.6	59%	18%	6%	-	16%	-	
Garcia,Leury	84.3	76%	-	-	-	24%	-	
Garcia,Luis	95.0	62%	-	-	38%	-	-	
Garcia,Yimi	91.7	66%	-	-	31%	3%	-	
Garza,Matt	92.5	68%	-	10%	22%	<1%	-	
Gausman,Kevin	94.8	71%	-	-	7%	4%	19%	
Gee,Dillon	89.2	60%	-	13%	11%	16%	-	
Geltz,Steve	92.8	70%	-	-	17%	13%	-	
Germano,Justin	85.5	65%	-	18%	3%	14%	-	
Germen,Gonzalez	92.7	65%	-	-	14%	21%	-	
Gibson,Kyle	91.3	63%	-	3%	22%	13%	-	
Giles,Ken	97.2	60%	-	-	40%	-	-	
Gimenez,Chris	84.5	83%	-	-	-	17%	-	
Goeddel,Erik	93.5	71%	-	18%	-	-		11%
Gomes,Brandon	91.4	33%	35%	-	11%	-		22%
Gomez,Jeanmar	90.7	58%	-	-	15%	27%	-	
Gonzales,Marco	89.6	57%	-	10%	6%	27%	-	
Gonzalez,Gio	92.0	65%	-	17%	-	18%	-	
Gonzalez,Miguel (PHI)	95.0	63%	-	22%	-	15%	-	
Gonzalez,Miguel (BAL)	91.0	58%	-	13%	16%	-		14%
Gorzelanny,Tom	89.2	60%	-	-	24%	17%	-	
Graveman,Kendall	92.9	72%	16%	-	8%	-		3%
Gray,Sonny	93.0	56%	-	27%	9%	9%	-	
Greene,Shane	93.1	52%	26%	-	18%	4%	-	
Greenwood,Nick	88.4	61%	-	3%	13%	23%	-	
Gregerson,Luke	88.4	46%	-	<1%	47%	6%	-	
Gregg,Kevin	90.6	62%	21%	-	10%	-		7%
Greinke,Zack	91.9	54%	-	10%	19%	16%	-	
Grilli,Jason	93.1	60%	-	-	34%	6%	-	
Grimm,Justin	94.0	67%	-	18%	14%	-	-	
Grube,Jarrett	87.7	43%	-	-	57%	-	-	
Guerra,Javy	93.9	58%	-	16%	22%	4%	-	
Guerrier,Matt	89.7	64%	-	5%	25%	6%	-	
Guilmet,Preston	89.5	49%	-	-	10%	-		41%
Guthrie,Jeremy	91.7	53%	-	9%	18%	20%	-	
Gutierrez,Juan	93.5	59%	-	17%	18%	6%	-	
Hagadone,Nick	94.6	76%	-	-	24%	-	-	
Hagens,Bradin	88.9	25%	53%	16%	-	6%	-	
Hahn,Jesse	90.9	61%	-	29%	2%	7%	-	
Hale,David	90.9	66%	-	-	19%	15%	-	
Hamels,Cole	92.3	52%	16%	9%	-	22%	-	
Hammel,Jason	92.3	59%	-	5%	32%	4%	-	
Hand,Brad	92.4	65%	-	22%	<1%	13%	-	
Happ,J.A.	92.7	72%	-	12%	6%	10%	-	
Harang,Aaron	89.3	54%	12%	11%	17%	6%	-	
Hardy,Blaine	89.1	41%	-	21%	19%	19%	-	
Haren,Dan	87.7	35%	39%	10%	-	-		16%
Harrell,Lucas	91.1	65%	14%	9%	-	13%	-	
Harris,Will	91.7	71%	-	25%	-	3%	-	
Harrison,Matt	89.4	79%	-	6%	2%	13%	-	
Hatcher,Chris	95.1	61%	-	-	17%	22%	-	
Hawkins,LaTroy	93.2	75%	-	8%	16%	1%	-	
Heaney,Andrew	90.4	66%	-	-	23%	11%	-	
Hellickson,Jeremy	90.2	53%	-	19%	-	28%	-	

Player	Fastball Velocity	Pitch Repertoire						
		Fastball	Cutter	Curve	Slider	Change	Splitter	Other
Hembree,Heath	91.9	78%	-	-	19%	3%	-	
Henderson,Jim	93.9	81%	-	-	19%	-	-	
Hendricks,Kyle	87.9	61%	12%	8%	-	18%	-	
Hendriks,Liam	91.3	64%	-	6%	18%	12%	-	
Hernandez,Felix	92.4	43%	-	16%	8%	32%	-	
Hernandez,Pedro	86.0	56%	34%	-	-	10%	-	
Hernandez,Roberto	90.3	64%	-	-	11%	25%	-	
Herrera,Kelvin	98.1	74%	-	6%	-	19%	-	
Herrera,Yoslan	93.2	53%	-	20%	-	-	27%	
Heston,Chris	89.7	59%	-	17%	17%	6%	-	
Hill,Rich	90.3	45%	3%	53%	-	-	-	
Hill,Taylor	90.2	63%	-	11%	19%	7%	-	
Holdzkom,John	95.5	94%	-	-	-	6%	-	
Holland,Derek	92.3	58%	-	13%	26%	3%	-	
Holland,Greg	95.8	55%	-	-	43%	-		2%
Hollands,Mario	93.0	68%	8%	-	19%	5%	-	
Holmberg,David	87.9	60%	-	2%	9%	29%	-	
Hoover,J.J.	93.0	66%	-	20%	11%	3%	-	
House,T.J.	90.7	56%	-	4%	23%	17%	-	
Howell,J.P.	86.2	68%	-	31%	-	<1%	-	
Hudson,Daniel	95.0	67%	-	-	4%	29%	-	
Hudson,Tim	89.0	54%	-	8%	23%	-	15%	
Huff,David	91.6	53%	33%	2%	-	11%	-	
Hughes,Jared	92.4	85%	-	-	14%	1%	-	
Hughes,Phil	92.1	65%	21%	14%	-	<1%	-	
Hunter,Tommy	96.1	68%	7%	25%	-	<1%	-	
Hutchison,Drew	92.2	65%	-	-	23%	12%	-	
Irwin,Phil	88.2	70%	-	19%	-	11%	-	
Iwakuma,Hisashi	88.9	48%	-	3%	20%	-	28%	
Jackson,Edwin	92.7	60%	<1%	8%	27%	5%	-	
Jaime,Juan	96.2	81%	-	11%	-	8%	-	
Jansen,Kenley	93.7	94%	-	-	6%	-	-	
Janssen,Casey	89.3	45%	30%	16%	5%	4%	-	
Jeffress,Jeremy	96.4	76%	-	22%	-	2%	-	
Jenkins,Chad	90.9	80%	-	-	16%	4%	-	
Jennings,Dan	92.5	57%	-	-	43%	-	-	
Jepsen,Kevin	95.5	62%	-	21%	-	17%	-	
Jimenez,Cesar	88.4	55%	-	-	27%	17%	-	
Jimenez,Ubaldo	90.5	59%	-	3%	21%	3%	13%	
Johnson,Erik	89.6	47%	-	6%	41%	6%	-	
Johnson,Jim	93.6	74%	-	16%	-	10%	-	
Johnson,Kris	91.6	66%	-	2%	17%	15%	-	
Jokisch,Eric	89.3	58%	-	6%	8%	27%	-	
Jones,Nate	95.8	62%	-	-	24%	14%	-	
Jordan,Taylor	89.1	61%	-	-	14%	24%	-	
Joseph,Donnie	89.3	43%	-	-	57%	-	-	
Jurrjens,Jair	89.6	62%	-	-	17%	21%	-	
Kahnle,Tommy	94.6	70%	-	-	12%	18%	-	
Karns,Nate	93.2	66%	-	29%	-	5%	-	
Kazmir,Scott	91.0	54%	9%	6%	12%	20%	-	
Kelley,Shawn	92.2	42%	-	-	58%	-	-	
Kelly,Joe	94.7	66%	-	17%	6%	11%	-	
Kendrick,Kyle	89.7	45%	27%	9%	-	19%	-	
Kennedy,Ian	91.8	62%	8%	16%	-	14%	-	
Kershaw,Clayton	93.0	55%	-	14%	29%	<1%	-	

Player	Fastball Velocity	Pitch Repertoire						
		Fastball	Cutter	Curve	Slider	Change	Splitter	Other
Keuchel,Dallas	89.7	57%	7%	-	21%	15%	-	
Kickham,Mike	90.5	60%	-	-	40%	-	-	
Kimbrel,Craig	97.1	73%	-	27%	-	-	-	
Kintzler,Brandon	92.1	81%	-	-	13%	6%	-	
Kirkman,Michael	88.8	51%	-	-	48%	-		1%
Klein,Phil	91.6	51%	43%	-	5%	<1%	-	
Kluber,Corey	93.2	52%	28%	16%	-	4%	-	
Knebel,Corey	94.3	61%	-	36%	-	3%	-	
Koehler,Tom	92.9	60%	-	21%	15%	3%	-	
Kohn,Michael	94.3	72%	-	-	18%	10%	-	
Kontos,George	91.3	38%	31%	-	27%	4%	-	
Korecky,Bobby	90.0	10%	84%	-	5%	-	-	
Krol,Ian	91.8	67%	-	24%	-	10%	-	
Kuroda,Hiroki	91.1	45%	2%	4%	21%	-		27%
Lackey,John	91.7	64%	-	10%	24%	3%	-	
LaFromboise,Bobby	89.7	68%	-	-	23%	9%	-	
Lane,Jason	86.1	53%	-	1%	9%	36%	-	
Lannan,John	87.8	66%	-	16%	11%	7%	-	
Latos,Mat	90.7	66%	-	8%	14%	12%	-	
Layne,Tom	90.0	48%	43%	9%	-	-	-	
League,Brandon	93.8	78%	-	-	5%	-		17%
Leake,Mike	90.7	50%	21%	11%	11%	6%	-	
LeBlanc,Wade	87.8	45%	15%	14%	-	25%	-	
LeCure,Sam	87.4	57%	-	30%	4%	10%	-	
Lee,C.C.	92.3	62%	-	-	38%	-		<1%
Lee,Cliff	89.6	57%	14%	6%	2%	20%	-	
Leesman,Charlie	86.5	78%	-	-	18%	4%	-	
Leone,Dominic	94.5	56%	21%	-	18%	5%	-	
Leroux,Chris	90.1	52%	-	-	37%	12%	-	
Lester,Jon	91.8	50%	31%	16%	-	3%	-	
Lewis,Colby	88.7	62%	-	8%	22%	8%	-	
Lincecum,Tim	89.6	47%	-	8%	22%	24%	-	
Lincoln,Brad	92.0	49%	-	39%	-	-		12%
Lindblom,Josh	89.8	63%	-	11%	6%	20%	-	
Lindstrom,Matt	93.1	52%	29%	-	18%	-		1%
Liriano,Francisco	92.6	43%	-	-	32%	25%	-	
Lobstein,Kyle	88.4	58%	21%	5%	-	15%	-	
Locke,Jeff	90.5	62%	-	14%	-	24%	-	
Logan,Boone	92.3	60%	-	-	40%	-	-	
Lohse,Kyle	89.4	46%	-	12%	30%	13%	-	
Lopez,Javier	85.6	71%	17%	-	6%	7%	-	
Lopez,Wilton	90.3	63%	-	-	17%	20%	-	
Loup,Aaron	92.3	69%	-	-	12%	19%	-	
Lowe,Mark	92.2	35%	-	-	65%	-	-	
Lueke,Josh	93.0	58%	-	-	20%	-		22%
Luetge,Lucas	90.6	50%	-	8%	39%	3%	-	
Lyles,Jordan	91.3	65%	-	8%	19%	8%	-	
Lynn,Lance	92.4	79%	-	8%	10%	2%	-	
Lyons,Tyler	89.7	61%	-	5%	25%	9%	-	
Machi,Jean	92.7	36%	-	-	15%	-		49%
Maholm,Paul	87.2	52%	-	16%	21%	11%	-	
Maldonado,Martin	80.2	100%	-	-	-	-	-	
Maness,Seth	89.6	72%	-	2%	9%	17%	-	
Manship,Jeff	91.6	55%	-	5%	28%	13%	-	
Mariot,Michael	91.6	62%	-	4%	21%	13%	-	

Player	Fastball Velocity	Pitch Repertoire						
		Fastball	Cutter	Curve	Slider	Change	Splitter	Other
Marks,Justin	90.0	62%	-	4%	24%	11%	-	
Marmol,Carlos	93.7	48%	-	-	52%	-	-	
Maronde,Nick	91.0	69%	-	-	23%	9%	-	
Marshall,Evan	93.9	62%	-	16%	-	21%	-	
Marshall,Sean	87.5	28%	-	36%	37%	-	-	
Martin,Chris	94.3	64%	19%	-	17%	-	-	
Martin,Ethan	92.1	65%	-	6%	23%	6%	-	
Martinez,Carlos	96.7	64%	-	-	27%	9%	-	
Martinez,David	90.8	58%	-	-	19%	10%	14%	
Martinez,Nick	91.2	67%	-	7%	15%	11%	-	
Masset,Nick	92.8	53%	16%	23%	-	-		7%
Masterson,Justin	88.9	82%	-	-	18%	<1%	-	
Matsuzaka,Daisuke	90.3	44%	23%	12%	17%	<1%		4%
Mattheus,Ryan	92.9	74%	-	-	17%	-		9%
Matusz,Brian	90.6	56%	-	7%	26%	11%	-	
Matzek,Tyler	92.7	55%	-	5%	29%	11%	-	
Maurer,Brandon	94.4	53%	29%	5%	-	13%	-	
May,Trevor	91.9	60%	-	13%	11%	16%	-	
Mazzaro,Vin	91.4	68%	-	-	30%	3%	-	
McAllister,Zach	92.9	74%	-	10%	9%	7%		<1%
McCarthy,Brandon	92.9	62%	14%	24%	-	<1%	-	
McCoy,Pat	91.2	67%	-	-	26%	8%	-	
McCutchen,Daniel	89.3	49%	-	-	22%	-		29%
McFarland,T.J.	90.7	73%	-	-	18%	9%	-	
McGee,Jake	96.3	96%	-	4%	-	-	-	
McGowan,Dustin	94.0	70%	-	<1%	18%	11%	-	
McHugh,Collin	91.6	40%	-	23%	32%	5%	-	
Medina,Yoervis	94.8	68%	-	-	32%	<1%	-	
Meek,Evan	91.5	32%	52%	11%	-	-		6%
Mejia,Jenrry	92.5	57%	-	15%	19%	9%	-	
Melancon,Mark	92.8	27%	48%	24%	-	<1%	-	
Mendez,Roman	94.6	67%	-	-	19%	6%		8%
Mercedes,Melvin	93.5	65%	-	-	13%	22%	-	
Mikolas,Miles	92.7	62%	-	12%	17%	9%	-	
Miley,Wade	91.2	61%	-	2%	26%	11%	-	
Miller,Andrew	93.9	58%	-	-	42%	-	-	
Miller,Jim	92.6	76%	-	5%	16%	3%	-	
Miller,Justin	91.8	62%	-	-	38%	-	-	
Miller,Shelby	93.5	72%	6%	19%	-	2%	-	
Mills,Brad	87.3	55%	5%	18%	-	22%	-	
Milone,Tommy	86.6	49%	15%	12%	-	24%	-	
Minor,Mike	90.3	61%	-	16%	15%	8%	-	
Mitchell,Bryan	94.0	41%	32%	27%	-	-	-	
Montero,Rafael	92.2	72%	-	-	15%	13%	-	
Moore,Matt	91.5	58%	11%	13%	-	18%	-	
Morales,Franklin	91.3	56%	-	11%	27%	7%	-	
Moreland,Mitch	92.1	93%	-	-	-	7%	-	
Morin,Mike	91.6	50%	-	-	27%	23%	-	
Morris,Bryan	95.4	53%	39%	-	8%	-	-	
Morrow,Brandon	94.0	59%	4%	3%	19%	15%	-	
Morton,Charlie	91.1	68%	-	25%	-	7%	-	
Motte,Jason	93.9	59%	39%	-	-	2%	-	
Mujica,Edward	90.9	44%	-	-	23%	-		33%
Nathan,Joe	91.6	55%	-	15%	29%	1%	-	
Nelson,Jimmy	93.6	73%	-	-	25%	2%	-	

Player	Fastball Velocity	Pitch Repertoire						
		Fastball	Cutter	Curve	Slider	Change	Splitter	Other
Neris,Hector	93.0	56%	-	-	-	-	44%	
Neshek,Pat	90.3	53%	-	-	34%	13%	-	
Nicasio,Juan	92.7	70%	-	-	25%	5%	-	
Niese,Jon	88.5	50%	24%	17%	-	9%	-	
Noesi,Hector	93.0	51%	-	9%	13%	26%	-	
Nolasco,Ricky	90.1	49%	-	14%	27%	-	10%	
Nolin,Sean	92.9	89%	-	6%	-	6%	-	
Norris,Bud	93.4	60%	4%	<1%	26%	9%	-	
Norris,Daniel	91.2	61%	-	10%	11%	18%	-	
Nova,Ivan	91.9	66%	-	30%	-	4%	-	
Nuno,Vidal	88.8	48%	-	16%	26%	10%	-	
O'Day,Darren	87.3	55%	-	-	44%	<1%	-	
O'Flaherty,Eric	89.9	74%	-	-	26%	<1%	-	
O'Sullivan,Sean	90.9	56%	-	5%	21%	18%	-	
Oberholtzer,Brett	89.5	54%	<1%	20%	-	25%	-	
Odorizzi,Jake	90.3	57%	-	5%	13%	24%	-	
Ogando,Alexi	93.9	68%	-	-	22%	10%	-	
Oliveros,Lester	93.8	78%	-	-	19%	3%	-	
Ondrusek,Logan	93.4	61%	15%	13%	-	-	12%	
Ortega,Jose	92.5	77%	-	-	17%	6%	-	
Otero,Dan	90.2	72%	-	3%	12%	14%	-	
Ottavino,Adam	94.3	52%	-	-	47%	<1%	-	
Outman,Josh	89.8	55%	-	3%	34%	8%	-	
Overbay,Lyle	80.2	83%	-	17%	-	-	-	
Oviedo,Juan	91.7	49%	-	-	3%	47%	-	
Owens,Rudy	87.7	63%	-	18%	-	20%	-	
Papelbon,Jonathan	91.3	68%	-	-	15%	-	17%	
Parker,Blake	90.5	69%	-	24%	-	-	8%	
Parnell,Bobby	92.3	84%	-	4%	-	12%	-	
Parra,Manny	93.0	45%	-	-	42%	-	13%	
Partch,Curtis	95.8	71%	-	-	21%	8%	-	
Paterson,Joe	83.0	65%	-	-	35%	-	-	
Patterson,Red	87.4	59%	-	11%	7%	23%	-	
Patton,Spencer	91.9	82%	-	-	17%	1%	-	
Patton,Troy	89.7	43%	-	25%	21%	11%	-	
Paulino,Felipe	92.9	52%	-	8%	22%	18%	-	
Paxton,James	94.8	67%	6%	18%	-	9%	-	
Peacock,Brad	92.1	59%	-	19%	15%	8%	-	
Peavy,Jake	90.0	52%	18%	12%	8%	10%	-	
Pelfrey,Mike	90.8	80%	-	4%	8%	-	9%	
Penny,Brad	91.7	70%	<1%	17%	-	3%	10%	
Peralta,Joel	89.6	39%	<1%	26%	-	-	34%	
Peralta,Wily	95.8	66%	-	-	29%	5%	-	
Perez,Chris	94.3	72%	-	-	25%	4%	-	
Perez,Martin	90.3	64%	-	9%	10%	17%	-	
Perez,Oliver	91.3	63%	-	-	37%	-	-	
Perkins,Glen	93.4	74%	-	-	26%	-	-	
Pestano,Vinnie	89.9	80%	-	-	20%	-	-	
Petit,Yusmeiro	88.9	50%	-	24%	17%	9%	-	
Petricka,Jake	94.2	70%	-	-	12%	18%	-	
Pettibone,Jonathan	90.8	58%	12%	-	12%	19%	-	
Phelps,David	90.2	47%	30%	15%	-	8%	-	
Pimentel,Stolmy	93.3	51%	-	-	10%	-	38%	
Pineda,Michael	92.5	55%	-	-	34%	11%	-	
Pino,Yohan	88.3	58%	-	7%	23%	12%	-	

Player	Fastball Velocity	Pitch Repertoire						
		Fastball	Cutter	Curve	Slider	Change	Splitter	Other
Pomeranz,Drew	91.1	72%	-	27%	-	<1%	-	
Porcello,Rick	90.4	59%	-	16%	12%	14%	-	
Poreda,Aaron	95.4	68%	-	-	29%	3%	-	
Pressly,Ryan	93.3	46%	-	20%	34%	-	-	
Price,Bryan	93.7	68%	-	-	23%	9%	-	
Price,David	93.2	57%	14%	9%	-	20%	-	
Pryor,Stephen	91.7	66%	-	3%	29%	3%	-	
Putkonen,Luke	91.4	64%	-	24%	-	-	12%	
Putnam,Zach	90.1	18%	-	-	26%	-	56%	
Putz,J.J.	89.6	61%	-	-	2%	-	37%	
Quackenbush,Kevin	91.3	73%	-	17%	-	-	10%	
Qualls,Chad	92.6	62%	-	-	38%	-	<1%	
Quintana,Jose	91.6	57%	6%	25%	-	13%	-	
Ramirez,Erasmo	91.1	52%	-	10%	11%	26%	-	
Ramirez,Jose	94.6	67%	-	-	15%	18%	-	
Ramirez,Neil	94.3	72%	-	11%	17%	-	-	
Ramirez,Ramon	90.3	47%	-	-	13%	40%	-	
Ramos,A.J.	91.3	56%	-	1%	26%	17%	-	
Ramos,Cesar	90.0	56%	-	8%	25%	10%	-	
Ranaudo,Anthony	91.6	66%	-	21%	3%	11%	-	
Rasmus,Cory	92.8	43%	-	15%	22%	20%	-	
Rasmussen,Rob	93.4	68%	-	19%	6%	7%	-	
Ray,Robbie	91.3	62%	-	5%	7%	26%	-	
Redmond,Todd	90.4	70%	-	-	25%	5%	-	
Reed,Addison	92.4	75%	-	-	24%	<1%	-	
Reed,Evan	96.0	67%	-	-	30%	3%	-	
Rice,Scott	89.4	67%	-	-	22%	-	11%	
Richards,Garrett	96.3	64%	-	6%	30%	<1%	-	
Riefenhauser,C.J.	89.7	52%	-	-	33%	16%	-	
Rienzo,Andre	91.2	32%	41%	22%	-	4%	<1%	
Roach,Donn	89.0	67%	-	21%	-	-	12%	
Roark,Tanner	91.1	67%	-	8%	15%	10%	-	
Robertson,David	91.8	63%	-	36%	-	<1%	-	
Rodney,Fernando	94.9	68%	-	-	-	32%	-	
Rodriguez,Fernando	93.7	57%	20%	17%	-	7%	-	
Rodriguez,Francisco	90.6	55%	-	16%	-	29%	-	
Rodriguez,Henry	96.9	77%	-	-	21%	2%	-	
Rodriguez,Paco	87.8	32%	35%	-	30%	2%	-	
Rodriguez,Wandy	88.4	55%	-	32%	-	13%	-	
Rodriguez,Wilking	94.8	82%	-	6%	-	12%	-	
Roe,Chaz	91.5	61%	-	-	39%	-	-	
Rogers,Esmil	93.7	55%	5%	8%	30%	<1%	2%	
Romine,Andrew	85.8	89%	-	4%	-	4%	-	Knuckleball 4%
Romo,Sergio	88.0	36%	-	-	52%	12%	-	
Rondon,Hector	95.7	74%	9%	-	17%	<1%	-	
Rondon,Jorge	95.7	80%	-	-	20%	-	-	
Rosenberg,B.J.	92.6	62%	<1%	8%	25%	4%	-	
Rosenthal,Trevor	96.8	78%	1%	4%	-	17%	-	
Rosin,Seth	90.2	65%	-	-	15%	20%	-	
Ross,Robbie	90.5	75%	-	7%	13%	5%	-	
Ross,Tyson	93.2	55%	-	-	41%	4%	-	
Rosscup,Zac	92.0	77%	-	-	23%	-	-	
Roth,Michael	84.9	52%	-	4%	12%	32%	-	
Rowen,Ben	79.2	79%	-	-	21%	-	-	
Rowland-Smith,Ryan	87.9	64%	-	22%	12%	2%	-	

Player	Fastball Velocity	Pitch Repertoire						
		Fastball	Cutter	Curve	Slider	Change	Splitter	Other
Rucinski,Drew	92.8	48%	-	-	26%	10%	15%	
Rusin,Chris	88.3	52%	31%	5%	7%	5%	-	
Russell,James	89.0	43%	12%	8%	21%	17%	-	
Ryan,Kyle	89.4	65%	18%	-	11%	6%	-	
Ryu,Hyun-Jin	90.9	52%	-	13%	16%	19%	-	
Rzepczynski,Marc	91.5	56%	-	-	43%	<1%	-	
Sabathia,CC	88.8	57%	2%	-	23%	18%	-	
Sadler,Casey	92.3	81%	-	-	18%	1%	-	
Salas,Fernando	91.2	60%	-	-	16%	24%	-	
Salazar,Danny	94.6	76%	-	<1%	11%	13%	-	
Sale,Chris	93.8	53%	-	-	18%	29%	-	
Samardzija,Jeff	94.4	55%	12%	-	21%	-	12%	
Sanchez,Aaron	97.1	88%	-	11%	-	<1%	-	
Sanchez,Anibal	92.1	47%	-	8%	23%	21%	-	
Santana,Ervin	92.3	52%	-	<1%	33%	14%	-	
Santiago,Hector	90.9	61%	8%	-	9%	21%	-	Screwball 1%
Santos,Sergio	93.9	51%	-	-	38%	10%	-	
Saunders,Joe	90.7	64%	-	8%	15%	13%	-	
Savery,Joe	91.0	81%	-	-	7%	12%	-	
Scahill,Rob	93.8	56%	-	8%	28%	7%	-	
Scheppers,Tanner	94.1	75%	-	-	19%	5%	-	
Scherzer,Max	92.8	55%	-	10%	14%	21%	-	
Schlitter,Brian	92.7	87%	-	-	13%	<1%	-	
Schlosser,Gus	89.5	71%	-	-	22%	7%	-	
Schultz,Bo	95.3	66%	-	-	22%	13%	-	
Schumaker,Skip	88.5	65%	-	6%	-	29%	-	
Scribner,Evan	91.2	65%	-	24%	11%	-	-	
Shaw,Bryan	91.0	<1%	71%	<1%	27%	1%	-	
Shields,James	92.4	41%	24%	12%	-	22%	-	
Shoemaker,Matt	90.5	51%	-	9%	18%	-	21%	
Shreve,Chasen	91.5	63%	-	-	26%	-	11%	
Siegrist,Kevin	94.2	87%	-	-	8%	5%	-	
Simmons,Shae	94.9	68%	-	-	24%	-	8%	
Simon,Alfredo	94.0	58%	13%	11%	-	-	17%	
Sipp,Tony	92.4	59%	-	-	27%	15%	-	
Skaggs,Tyler	92.1	65%	-	24%	-	10%	-	
Slowey,Kevin	89.2	66%	-	4%	23%	7%	-	
Smith,Carson	93.7	47%	-	-	46%	7%	-	
Smith,Chad	93.2	84%	-	-	16%	-	-	
Smith,Joe	88.7	71%	-	-	29%	-	-	
Smith,Will	93.0	56%	-	10%	33%	<1%	-	
Smyly,Drew	89.9	52%	16%	28%	-	4%	-	
Snider,Travis	83.6	74%	-	-	-	20%	-	
Snodgress,Scott	91.0	48%	-	6%	43%	3%	-	
Soria,Joakim	90.2	66%	-	11%	13%	10%	-	
Soriano,Rafael	91.5	37%	34%	-	29%	<1%	-	
Spruill,Zeke	91.9	65%	-	19%	13%	2%	-	
Stammen,Craig	91.6	59%	-	12%	28%	<1%	-	
Stauffer,Tim	90.6	54%	21%	8%	-	16%	-	
Stinson,Josh	92.0	62%	-	16%	13%	9%	-	
Stites,Matt	95.8	69%	-	-	25%	5%	-	
Storen,Drew	93.3	53%	-	-	29%	18%	-	
Straily,Dan	88.7	59%	-	5%	23%	14%	-	
Strasburg,Stephen	94.8	61%	-	17%	1%	20%	-	
Street,Huston	89.3	47%	-	-	35%	18%	-	

Player	Fastball Velocity	Pitch Repertoire						
		Fastball	Cutter	Curve	Slider	Change	Splitter	Other
Strickland,Hunter	98.1	69%	-	-	25%	5%	-	
Stroman,Marcus	93.5	55%	16%	16%	6%	7%	-	
Strop,Pedro	95.0	60%	-	-	38%	<1%	1%	
Stults,Eric	87.9	50%	-	9%	17%	24%	-	
Surkamp,Eric	88.8	43%	20%	26%	-	12%	-	
Swarzak,Anthony	92.2	69%	-	-	28%	4%	-	
Tanaka,Masahiro	91.2	41%	6%	6%	22%	<1%	25%	
Tazawa,Junichi	93.9	56%	-	11%	8%	-	25%	
Teheran,Julio	90.4	61%	-	11%	20%	9%	-	
Tepesch,Nick	89.9	57%	27%	12%	-	4%	-	
Thatcher,Joe	86.0	77%	-	-	23%	-	-	
Thayer,Dale	92.2	78%	-	-	18%	4%	-	
Thielbar,Caleb	88.8	64%	-	5%	27%	4%	-	
Thomas,Ian	90.7	59%	-	15%	8%	18%	-	
Thompson,Aaron	89.1	49%	-	1%	49%	1%	-	
Thompson,Taylor	90.8	65%	-	-	16%	-	19%	
Thornburg,Tyler	93.6	60%	-	25%	-	15%	-	
Thornton,Matt	95.1	86%	<1%	-	7%	7%	-	
Tillman,Chris	90.7	64%	5%	18%	-	13%	-	
Tolleson,Shawn	92.4	63%	14%	-	11%	12%	-	
Tolleson,Steve	75.2	92%	-	8%	-	-	-	
Tomlin,Josh	89.0	47%	31%	15%	-	7%	-	
Tonkin,Michael	93.4	80%	-	-	19%	1%	-	
Torres,Alex	92.5	62%	-	<1%	6%	32%	-	
Torres,Carlos	91.9	35%	49%	14%	-	2%	-	
Treinen,Blake	94.8	79%	-	-	14%	6%	-	
Tropeano,Nicholas	90.4	58%	-	20%	-	20%	2%	
Tuivailala,Samuel	96.9	71%	-	29%	-	-	-	
Turner,Jacob	92.5	64%	-	10%	17%	9%	-	
Uehara,Koji	88.2	50%	2%	<1%	-	-	48%	
Valdes,Raul	86.4	68%	-	-	30%	3%	-	
Valverde,Jose	93.0	77%	-	-	-	-	23%	
Vargas,Jason	87.3	57%	-	12%	-	31%	-	
Varvaro,Anthony	92.5	59%	-	25%	-	16%	-	
Veal,Donnie	92.5	65%	-	28%	-	8%	-	
Ventura,Yordano	97.0	65%	5%	14%	-	15%	-	
Veras,Jose	92.8	59%	-	27%	-	-	13%	
VerHagen,Drew	90.6	68%	-	16%	-	-	16%	
Verlander,Justin	92.3	56%	-	16%	15%	13%	-	
Villanueva,Carlos	89.1	47%	-	16%	19%	18%	-	
Villarreal,Pedro	92.8	50%	29%	-	20%	2%	-	
Vincent,Nick	89.8	41%	55%	-	-	3%	-	
Vizcaino,Arodys	95.2	74%	-	22%	-	4%	-	
Vogelsong,Ryan	90.5	47%	21%	19%	-	14%	-	
Volquez,Edinson	93.2	55%	-	26%	-	19%	-	
Wacha,Michael	93.2	58%	10%	13%	-	19%	-	
Wada,Tsuyoshi	88.9	59%	-	4%	20%	17%	-	
Wagner,Neil	94.9	77%	-	-	16%	6%	-	
Wainwright,Adam	90.2	41%	30%	28%	-	2%	-	
Walden,Jordan	95.9	64%	-	-	25%	11%	-	
Walker,Taijuan	94.7	60%	9%	14%	-	18%	-	
Wall,Josh	91.0	51%	-	-	49%	-	-	
Wang,Wei-Chung	90.9	68%	-	14%	<1%	17%	-	
Warren,Adam	94.2	42%	-	9%	33%	16%	-	
Watson,Tony	94.4	68%	-	-	10%	21%	-	

Player	Fastball Velocity	Pitch Repertoire						
		Fastball	Cutter	Curve	Slider	Change	Splitter	Other
Weaver,Jered	86.3	52%	-	19%	10%	19%	-	
Webb,Daniel	95.4	68%	-	-	17%	15%	-	
Webb,Ryan	92.0	60%	-	-	31%	9%	-	
Webster,Allen	92.0	60%	-	1%	17%	22%	-	
West,Matt	95.0	75%	-	13%	-	12%	-	
Wheeler,Zack	95.0	62%	-	16%	15%	7%	-	
Whelan,Kevin	92.7	55%	-	-	18%	-	26%	
Whitley,Chase	90.7	45%	-	-	31%	24%	-	
Wieland,Joe	91.8	67%	-	20%	-	13%	-	
Wilhelmsen,Tom	95.4	59%	16%	15%	-	10%	-	
Williams,Jerome	91.4	47%	27%	13%	-	14%	-	
Wilson,Alex	92.5	49%	34%	-	11%	6%	-	
Wilson,Brian	92.1	34%	57%	7%	2%	<1%	-	
Wilson,C.J.	90.8	53%	8%	17%	10%	13%	-	Knuckleball <1%
Wilson,Justin	95.2	73%	21%	6%	-	<1%	-	
Withrow,Chris	95.0	54%	-	9%	36%	1%	-	
Wolf,Randy	87.7	56%	-	19%	12%	13%	-	
Wood,Alex	89.8	59%	-	23%	-	18%	-	
Wood,Blake	95.6	81%	-	-	13%	6%	-	
Wood,Travis	88.3	53%	29%	4%	7%	8%	-	
Wooten,Rob	89.8	29%	51%	-	14%	-		7%
Workman,Brandon	90.4	55%	19%	22%	-	4%	-	
Worley,Vance	89.5	68%	22%	8%	-	1%	-	
Worth,Danny	88.0	3%	-	-	-	-	-	Knuckleball 97%
Wright,Jamey	90.6	25%	42%	20%	3%	10%	-	
Wright,Steven	83.5	15%	-	1%	-	-	-	Knuckleball 84%
Wright,Wesley	90.2	53%	-	23%	15%	10%	-	
Yates,Kirby	92.4	54%	-	3%	38%	5%	-	
Young,Chris	85.3	66%	-	<1%	27%	6%	-	
Zeid,Josh	93.8	57%	-	-	28%	14%	-	
Ziegler,Brad	84.6	63%	-	-	18%	19%	-	
Zimmermann,Jordan	93.8	70%	-	8%	19%	3%	-	

Pinch Hitting

This section contains a record of the pinch hit performance of active major league baseball players. For a player's seasonal totals to be included, he needed at least 10 plate appearances or 10 total bases as a pinch hitter in 2014. For his career totals to be included, he needs at least 100 career plate appearances as a pinch hitter.

The hardest-working pinch hitter in 2014 was Ryan Doumit of the Braves. Doumit recorded 70 at-bats as a pinch hitter this season and was one of only six players with even 50 pinch hit at-bats—Brandon Barnes, Reed Johnson, Gaby Sanchez, Travis Snider, and Rickie Weeks were the others. Prior to this season, Doumit had been successful as a pinch hitter in his career. He hit .262/.344/.393 in 107 pinch hit at-bats before 2014. His fall to .200/.250/.343 in the role this year mirrored an overall decrease in production.

He only saw 30 pinch hit at-bats, but John Mayberry was still the most productive pinch hitter this season. He launched four home runs and four doubles in those limited opportunities, which powered his 1.371 on-base plus slugging (OPS). He was the only batter with at least 25 pinch hit at-bats with an OPS above 1.000. Chris Heisey (.957) and Ike Davis (.976) each came close in 44 and 32 at-bats, respectively.

Pinch Hitting
Pinch Hitters with 10+ PAs or 10+ Total Bases in 2014

Batter	B	AB	H	2B	3B	HR	RBI	TBB	IBB	SO	GDP	Avg	OBP	Slg	OPS
Bobby Abreu	L	39	5	1	0	0	0	4	0	5	1	.128	.209	.154	.363
Matt Adams	L	9	3	0	0	0	1	1	1	3	0	.333	.400	.333	.733
Jim Adduci	L	12	2	0	0	0	2	0	0	4	0	.167	.167	.167	.333
Ehire Adrianza	B	17	3	1	0	0	1	1	0	5	0	.176	.222	.235	.458
Pedro Alvarez	L	15	1	1	0	0	2	1	0	5	1	.067	.125	.133	.258
Alexi Amarista	L	11	2	0	0	1	3	0	0	4	0	.182	.182	.455	.636
Joaquin Arias	R	34	7	2	0	0	2	1	0	4	0	.206	.222	.265	.487
Cody Asche	L	10	1	1	0	0	2	1	0	5	0	.100	.182	.200	.382
Mike Aviles	R	12	1	0	0	0	0	0	0	3	0	.083	.083	.083	.167
Jeff Baker	R	38	12	1	1	1	9	2	1	11	3	.316	.350	.474	.824
John Baker	L	12	2	0	0	0	2	0	0	5	0	.167	.167	.167	.333
Brandon Barnes	R	61	17	4	3	2	5	3	0	23	2	.279	.313	.541	.853
Darwin Barney	R	14	1	0	0	0	0	1	0	4	0	.071	.278	.071	.349
Roger Bernadina	L	23	2	1	0	0	1	0	0	9	0	.087	.160	.130	.290
Charlie Blackmon	L	14	3	0	0	0	3	2	0	3	0	.214	.353	.214	.567
Gregor Blanco	L	25	7	0	0	0	5	2	0	8	0	.280	.333	.280	.613
Emilio Bonifacio	B	12	3	0	0	0	0	1	1	4	0	.250	.308	.250	.558
Justin Bour	L	17	1	0	0	0	2	4	0	5	0	.059	.238	.059	.297
Peter Bourjos	R	13	3	1	1	0	0	3	0	4	0	.231	.375	.462	.837
Reid Brignac	L	14	2	1	0	0	2	1	0	10	0	.143	.200	.214	.414
Domonic Brown	L	21	4	1	0	0	1	2	0	7	1	.190	.292	.238	.530
Kole Calhoun	L	9	1	0	0	0	0	1	0	2	0	.111	.200	.111	.311
Alberto Callaspo	B	12	3	0	0	0	3	5	0	1	0	.250	.471	.250	.721
Tony Campana	L	10	1	0	1	0	0	0	0	3	0	.100	.182	.300	.482
Eric Campbell	R	28	8	3	0	0	4	7	0	6	1	.286	.421	.393	.814
Mike Carp	L	18	3	0	0	0	2	3	0	7	0	.167	.318	.167	.485
Endy Chavez	L	13	6	1	0	0	1	0	0	1	0	.462	.462	.538	1.000
Eric Chavez	L	24	3	0	0	1	1	7	0	8	2	.125	.323	.250	.573
Lonnie Chisenhall	L	13	6	3	0	1	4	1	1	2	0	.462	.500	.923	1.423
Michael Choice	R	12	4	0	0	1	2	0	0	6	0	.333	.308	.583	.891
Steve Clevenger	L	8	2	1	0	0	2	3	1	1	0	.250	.455	.375	.830
Chris Coghlan	L	22	4	0	0	0	2	3	0	5	0	.182	.280	.182	.462
Tyler Colvin	L	14	1	0	1	0	1	1	0	5	1	.071	.133	.214	.348
Carl Crawford	L	15	3	0	0	0	0	2	0	3	0	.200	.294	.200	.494
Coco Crisp	B	7	2	0	0	0	0	4	0	2	0	.286	.545	.286	.831
C.J. Cron	R	12	1	0	0	0	0	0	0	2	1	.083	.083	.083	.167
Charlie Culberson	R	18	3	1	0	1	5	0	0	5	2	.167	.200	.389	.589
Ike Davis	L	32	9	2	0	3	12	4	1	8	0	.281	.351	.625	.976
Khris Davis	R	11	0	0	0	0	0	0	0	3	0	.000	.000	.000	.000
David DeJesus	L	11	0	0	0	0	0	5	0	6	1	.000	.353	.000	.353
Chris Denorfia	R	32	3	0	0	0	2	3	0	8	1	.094	.171	.094	.265
Daniel Descalso	L	46	9	5	0	0	5	6	0	12	1	.196	.302	.304	.606
Corey Dickerson	L	18	6	1	0	0	1	3	2	5	0	.333	.429	.389	.817
Greg Dobbs	L	28	3	0	0	0	0	1	0	7	0	.107	.138	.107	.245
Ryan Doumit	B	70	14	4	0	2	7	4	0	26	1	.200	.250	.343	.593
Lucas Duda	L	10	2	0	0	1	3	0	0	2	0	.200	.200	.500	.700
Matt Duffy	R	15	6	1	0	0	6	0	0	3	0	.400	.400	.467	.867
Adam Dunn	L	9	2	0	0	0	1	3	1	4	0	.222	.417	.222	.639
Mark Ellis	R	18	3	0	0	0	0	1	0	4	0	.167	.250	.167	.417
Danny Espinosa	B	10	1	0	0	0	0	3	1	5	0	.100	.357	.100	.457
Andre Ethier	L	31	9	2	0	0	8	8	0	9	1	.290	.450	.355	.805
Nick Evans	R	12	5	2	0	1	6	1	0	6	0	.417	.462	.833	1.295
Chone Figgins	B	17	4	1	0	0	0	5	0	5	0	.235	.435	.294	.729
Logan Forsythe	R	24	5	2	0	0	2	1	0	9	1	.208	.269	.292	.561
Juan Francisco	L	14	2	0	0	1	2	2	0	9	0	.143	.250	.357	.607
Kevin Frandsen	R	47	11	1	0	1	2	2	0	5	0	.234	.280	.319	.599
Evan Gattis	R	13	2	1	0	0	3	1	1	4	1	.154	.214	.231	.445
Scooter Gennett	L	19	4	0	0	1	4	3	3	7	1	.211	.318	.368	.687
Craig Gentry	R	15	2	0	0	0	0	1	0	4	0	.133	.188	.133	.321
Jake Goebbert	L	22	6	0	0	0	3	4	1	7	0	.273	.385	.273	.657
Jonny Gomes	R	26	6	0	0	2	7	8	2	10	1	.231	.389	.462	.850
Anthony Gose	L	8	3	1	0	0	0	2	0	1	0	.375	.500	.500	1.000
Yasmani Grandal	B	20	4	1	0	2	3	4	0	10	1	.200	.333	.550	.883
Grant Green	R	11	4	2	0	0	2	0	0	0	0	.364	.364	.545	.909
Randal Grichuk	R	18	6	1	0	1	2	0	0	7	1	.333	.333	.556	.889
Brandon Guyer	R	25	5	1	0	0	0	1	0	7	0	.200	.259	.240	.499

Pinch Hitting
Pinch Hitters with 10+ PAs or 10+ Total Bases in 2014

Batter	B	AB	H	2B	3B	HR	RBI	TBB	IBB	SO	GDP	Avg	OBP	Slg	OPS
Jesus Guzman	R	16	1	0	0	0	1	3	0	7	0	.063	.211	.063	.273
Tony Gwynn	L	30	2	1	0	0	2	5	0	7	0	.067	.200	.100	.300
Scott Hairston	R	38	5	2	0	1	6	2	0	14	1	.132	.200	.263	.463
Jack Hannahan	L	14	2	0	0	0	0	0	0	7	1	.143	.143	.143	.286
Josh Harrison	R	20	3	0	0	1	2	1	0	6	0	.150	.190	.300	.490
Chris Heisey	R	44	12	3	1	4	11	2	0	10	1	.273	.298	.659	.957
Cesar Hernandez	B	32	7	0	0	0	1	4	1	12	1	.219	.297	.219	.516
Elian Herrera	B	15	2	1	0	0	0	0	0	7	0	.133	.133	.200	.333
Nick Hundley	R	24	5	1	0	0	1	0	0	6	0	.208	.208	.250	.458
Chris Iannetta	R	10	2	1	0	0	2	1	1	5	0	.200	.231	.300	.531
Raul Ibanez	L	24	5	2	0	0	4	2	0	5	0	.208	.269	.292	.561
Travis Ishikawa	L	25	7	0	0	1	6	2	0	11	1	.280	.333	.400	.733
John Jaso	L	16	6	2	0	2	3	3	0	4	0	.375	.474	.875	1.349
Jon Jay	L	18	6	2	0	0	4	1	0	3	0	.333	.350	.444	.794
Kelly Johnson	L	11	0	0	0	0	0	3	0	5	0	.000	.214	.000	.214
Reed Johnson	R	67	16	3	0	1	12	0	0	13	3	.239	.280	.328	.608
Garrett Jones	L	11	1	0	0	0	0	2	1	5	1	.091	.231	.091	.322
Matt Joyce	L	20	4	0	0	0	4	2	0	7	0	.200	.261	.200	.461
Ryan Kalish	L	23	7	2	1	0	0	1	0	1	1	.304	.333	.478	.812
Munenori Kawasaki	L	9	3	0	0	0	0	2	0	0	0	.333	.455	.333	.788
Don Kelly	L	10	2	0	0	0	1	1	0	4	0	.200	.273	.200	.473
Matt Kemp	R	8	0	0	0	0	0	2	1	6	1	.000	.200	.000	.200
Kevin Kiermaier	L	9	4	0	0	0	1	0	0	4	0	.444	.444	.444	.889
Roger Kieschnick	L	14	3	1	0	0	0	0	0	6	0	.214	.214	.286	.500
Paul Konerko	R	27	8	1	0	0	3	2	0	5	1	.296	.355	.333	.688
Erik Kratz	R	11	2	0	0	2	3	1	1	4	0	.182	.250	.727	.977
Marc Krauss	L	11	2	0	0	0	2	2	0	5	0	.182	.308	.182	.490
Junior Lake	R	27	4	0	0	0	0	4	0	15	0	.148	.258	.148	.406
Andrew Lambo	L	15	5	1	0	0	0	0	0	4	0	.333	.333	.400	.733
Adam Lind	L	14	5	1	0	0	3	2	1	1	1	.357	.438	.429	.866
Ed Lucas	R	18	2	0	0	0	0	0	0	5	1	.111	.111	.111	.222
Ryan Ludwick	R	14	3	1	0	0	3	0	0	2	0	.214	.250	.286	.536
Donald Lutz	L	15	3	2	0	0	0	1	0	7	0	.200	.250	.333	.583
Alfredo Marte	R	17	4	1	0	1	4	0	0	8	0	.235	.235	.471	.706
Michael Martinez	B	11	1	0	0	0	1	1	0	3	0	.091	.167	.091	.258
John Mayberry	R	30	12	4	0	4	12	2	0	7	1	.400	.438	.933	1.371
Matt McBride	R	13	3	2	0	0	1	0	0	4	0	.231	.286	.385	.670
Brian McCann	L	13	3	0	0	1	4	0	0	2	0	.231	.286	.462	.747
John McDonald	R	6	2	0	0	0	1	1	0	0	1	.333	.429	.333	.762
Nate McLouth	L	23	2	0	0	0	1	5	0	7	0	.087	.267	.087	.354
Tommy Medica	R	40	8	3	0	1	3	0	0	16	0	.200	.200	.350	.550
Tyler Moore	R	14	1	1	0	0	2	2	0	8	0	.071	.188	.143	.330
Brandon Moss	L	9	2	1	0	0	2	1	0	3	0	.222	.417	.333	.750
David Murphy	L	10	4	0	0	0	3	2	0	1	0	.400	.462	.400	.862
Xavier Nady	R	12	1	0	0	1	1	3	0	4	2	.083	.267	.333	.600
Daniel Nava	B	12	2	1	0	0	3	2	0	5	0	.167	.286	.250	.536
Dioner Navarro	B	17	5	0	0	1	5	1	0	6	0	.294	.333	.471	.804
Efren Navarro	L	6	2	1	1	0	3	4	0	0	0	.333	.600	.833	1.433
Kirk Nieuwenhuis	L	28	8	5	0	0	2	2	1	12	0	.286	.333	.464	.798
Derek Norris	R	15	4	1	0	1	5	3	0	2	2	.267	.389	.533	.922
Eduardo Nunez	R	12	2	0	1	0	0	0	0	1	2	.167	.167	.333	.500
Mike Olt	R	19	2	0	0	0	0	7	0	10	0	.105	.346	.105	.451
Lyle Overbay	L	34	11	2	0	1	8	6	0	8	0	.324	.425	.471	.896
Chris Owings	R	12	3	1	0	0	0	1	0	4	0	.250	.308	.333	.641
Jordan Pacheco	R	29	10	1	0	0	3	3	0	4	0	.345	.406	.379	.786
Kyle Parker	R	12	2	0	0	0	0	0	0	6	0	.167	.167	.167	.333
Chris Parmelee	L	13	5	1	0	0	7	0	0	5	0	.385	.385	.462	.846
Gerardo Parra	L	11	1	0	0	0	1	1	0	1	1	.091	.167	.091	.258
Tyler Pastornicky	R	13	3	0	0	0	0	1	0	5	0	.231	.286	.231	.516
Xavier Paul	L	10	0	0	0	0	0	0	0	5	0	.000	.000	.000	.000
Ben Paulsen	L	14	4	1	0	1	2	0	0	6	0	.286	.286	.571	.857
Steve Pearce	R	13	4	0	0	1	4	0	0	5	0	.308	.308	.538	.846
Brayan Pena	B	19	7	1	0	1	3	2	0	2	1	.368	.429	.579	1.008
Ramiro Pena	B	15	5	1	0	0	0	2	1	7	0	.333	.412	.400	.812
Cliff Pennington	B	17	4	0	0	1	1	1	0	3	0	.235	.316	.412	.728
A.J. Pierzynski	L	15	5	0	0	0	0	0	0	2	1	.333	.333	.333	.667
Josmil Pinto	R	9	1	0	0	0	2	0	0	3	2	.111	.100	.111	.211
Alex Presley	L	10	1	0	0	0	0	0	0	3	0	.100	.100	.100	.200
Nick Punto	B	14	0	0	0	0	0	1	0	5	0	.000	.067	.000	.067
Carlos Quentin	R	11	4	1	0	2	7	2	0	6	0	.364	.500	1.000	1.500

413

Pinch Hitting

Pinch Hitters with 10+ PAs or 10+ Total Bases in 2014

Batter	B	AB	H	2B	3B	HR	RBI	TBB	IBB	SO	GDP	Avg	OBP	Slg	OPS
Ryan Raburn	R	17	3	2	0	0	4	2	0	3	1	.176	.263	.294	.557
Colby Rasmus	L	12	4	0	0	3	4	2	0	5	0	.333	.429	1.083	1.512
Nolan Reimold	R	8	2	0	0	1	5	1	0	5	0	.250	.273	.625	.898
Ben Revere	L	16	4	0	0	0	0	0	0	2	0	.250	.250	.250	.500
Mark Reynolds	R	13	3	0	0	1	2	2	0	4	1	.231	.375	.462	.837
Rene Rivera	R	11	1	0	0	0	0	2	0	3	0	.091	.286	.091	.377
Shane Robinson	R	26	4	0	1	0	2	4	0	3	1	.154	.267	.231	.497
Sean Rodriguez	R	23	5	0	0	1	5	3	0	9	0	.217	.308	.348	.656
Stefen Romero	R	8	2	0	0	1	3	1	0	0	3	.250	.400	.625	1.025
Cody Ross	R	28	10	2	0	0	2	2	0	7	0	.357	.400	.429	.829
Darin Ruf	R	20	2	0	0	0	1	1	0	5	0	.100	.217	.100	.317
Justin Ruggiano	R	27	8	4	1	0	0	2	0	10	0	.296	.345	.519	.863
Josh Rutledge	R	17	4	3	0	0	3	3	0	9	0	.235	.381	.412	.793
Jarrod Saltalamacchia	B	8	1	0	0	1	2	2	0	3	0	.125	.300	.500	.800
Gaby Sanchez	R	52	13	6	0	2	13	6	0	12	1	.250	.333	.481	.814
Hector Sanchez	B	23	5	1	0	1	5	3	0	8	0	.217	.296	.391	.688
Ramon Santiago	B	11	2	1	0	0	0	0	0	7	0	.182	.182	.273	.455
Josh Satin	R	14	0	0	0	0	0	2	0	7	0	.000	.176	.000	.176
Jordan Schafer	L	25	4	1	0	0	0	2	0	4	1	.160	.222	.200	.422
Logan Schafer	L	13	2	0	0	0	1	2	1	3	0	.154	.250	.154	.404
Nate Schierholtz	L	33	3	0	0	1	2	1	0	9	2	.091	.118	.182	.299
Skip Schumaker	L	16	3	0	0	0	1	2	0	4	0	.188	.278	.188	.465
Grady Sizemore	L	15	3	0	0	1	2	4	0	5	0	.200	.368	.400	.768
Seth Smith	L	15	4	1	0	1	2	1	0	3	1	.267	.313	.533	.846
Travis Snider	L	52	13	2	0	2	8	7	1	11	1	.250	.350	.404	.754
Donovan Solano	R	32	5	0	0	0	2	0	0	6	0	.156	.182	.156	.338
Neftali Soto	R	10	2	1	0	0	1	0	0	4	0	.200	.182	.300	.482
Drew Stubbs	R	23	9	2	0	1	6	4	0	6	0	.391	.481	.609	1.090
Ichiro Suzuki	L	13	6	0	0	0	2	2	0	2	0	.462	.533	.462	.995
Kurt Suzuki	R	8	3	2	0	0	2	3	0	0	0	.375	.545	.625	1.170
Ryan Sweeney	L	19	3	1	0	0	1	2	0	1	0	.158	.238	.211	.449
Matt Szczur	R	11	1	1	0	0	0	0	0	2	0	.091	.091	.182	.273
Jose Tabata	R	36	9	2	0	0	5	1	0	7	2	.250	.282	.306	.588
Oscar Taveras	L	17	6	0	0	0	5	0	0	3	0	.353	.353	.353	.706
Steve Tolleson	R	32	4	0	1	1	3	4	0	14	0	.125	.243	.281	.524
Justin Turner	R	30	12	3	0	0	10	1	0	7	1	.400	.406	.500	.906
Dan Uggla	R	10	0	0	0	0	0	1	0	3	1	.000	.231	.000	.231
Chris Valaika	R	10	3	1	0	0	4	0	0	2	1	.300	.273	.400	.673
Luis Valbuena	L	16	1	1	0	0	3	2	0	7	1	.063	.167	.125	.292
Jordany Valdespin	L	18	3	0	0	1	2	5	0	3	0	.167	.348	.333	.681
Danny Valencia	R	12	1	0	0	1	3	1	0	4	0	.083	.154	.333	.487
Scott Van Slyke	R	23	6	2	0	1	5	2	0	11	0	.261	.320	.478	.798
Will Venable	L	23	8	0	0	1	4	2	0	4	0	.348	.400	.478	.878
Stephen Vogt	L	12	2	1	0	0	2	1	1	2	0	.167	.231	.250	.481
Zach Walters	B	21	3	0	0	2	2	5	0	7	0	.143	.308	.429	.736
Logan Watkins	L	12	5	1	0	0	0	0	0	4	0	.417	.417	.500	.917
Rickie Weeks	R	56	14	0	0	1	6	9	0	22	1	.250	.373	.304	.677
Ryan Wheeler	L	12	2	0	0	0	4	1	0	3	0	.167	.200	.167	.367
Kolten Wong	L	10	3	0	0	1	3	0	0	3	0	.300	.300	.600	.900
Chris Young	R	16	2	0	0	1	3	2	0	6	0	.125	.222	.313	.535
Delmon Young	R	20	10	1	1	1	6	2	0	4	1	.500	.565	.800	1.365
Eric Young	B	18	4	1	0	0	0	3	0	6	0	.222	.333	.278	.611

Career Pinch Hitting
Active Pinch Hitters with 100+ PAs in their careers

Batter	B	AB	H	2B	3B	HR	RBI	TBB	IBB	SO	GDP	Avg	OBP	Slg	OPS
Bobby Abreu	L	126	23	1	1	1	11	23	5	35	1	.183	.309	.230	.539
Jeff Baker	R	222	48	9	2	6	29	20	4	82	9	.216	.283	.356	.639
Roger Bernadina	L	100	21	6	0	0	4	8	0	32	1	.210	.288	.270	.558
Willie Bloomquist	R	99	23	1	1	1	12	6	1	18	3	.232	.278	.293	.571
Alberto Callaspo	B	95	21	2	0	2	14	13	0	16	3	.221	.312	.305	.617
Ronny Cedeno	R	89	23	6	0	3	8	9	0	23	1	.258	.340	.427	.767
Endy Chavez	L	146	42	8	3	2	15	7	1	16	5	.288	.320	.425	.745
Eric Chavez	L	125	25	5	0	3	17	13	2	33	3	.200	.271	.312	.583
Brooks Conrad	B	163	29	9	0	7	26	15	1	66	2	.178	.247	.362	.609
Chris Denorfia	R	135	30	7	0	3	18	14	0	29	5	.222	.289	.341	.630
Daniel Descalso	L	114	21	8	0	0	11	8	0	29	1	.184	.250	.254	.504
Greg Dobbs	L	403	98	21	2	10	75	34	8	86	7	.243	.300	.380	.679
Ryan Doumit	B	177	42	9	0	5	28	16	3	55	6	.237	.308	.373	.681
Andre Ethier	L	94	26	4	0	3	25	20	2	28	6	.277	.409	.415	.824
Juan Francisco	L	118	21	3	0	4	14	13	0	50	3	.178	.265	.305	.570
Kevin Frandsen	R	149	38	4	1	2	19	7	1	21	2	.255	.306	.336	.642
Jason Giambi	L	178	41	3	0	11	36	33	5	63	3	.230	.362	.433	.795
Jonny Gomes	R	160	28	6	0	9	31	30	4	66	2	.175	.320	.381	.701
Jesus Guzman	R	128	31	7	0	6	30	15	1	36	4	.242	.324	.438	.762
Tony Gwynn	L	161	42	8	3	0	14	18	1	33	2	.261	.339	.348	.687
Scott Hairston	R	254	47	9	0	13	34	27	1	95	5	.185	.267	.374	.641
Chris Heisey	R	138	39	8	2	10	35	11	0	38	2	.283	.335	.587	.922
Raul Ibanez	L	161	32	9	0	5	27	18	2	32	5	.199	.276	.348	.624
Travis Ishikawa	L	144	40	8	1	2	20	11	1	37	2	.278	.333	.389	.722
Kelly Johnson	L	87	17	3	1	1	10	20	2	24	1	.195	.346	.287	.633
Reed Johnson	R	279	77	14	0	6	40	11	1	64	9	.276	.332	.391	.723
Garrett Jones	L	88	16	4	0	0	11	9	2	23	3	.182	.260	.227	.487
Matt Joyce	L	90	18	6	1	1	16	16	2	29	1	.200	.318	.322	.640
Jason Kubel	L	105	21	4	0	4	14	14	1	39	4	.200	.294	.352	.646
Ryan Ludwick	R	112	30	8	0	5	18	11	2	29	1	.268	.341	.473	.814
John Mayberry	R	112	34	6	0	7	21	9	1	29	3	.304	.355	.545	.900
Nate McLouth	L	143	25	6	1	1	12	15	1	37	0	.175	.264	.252	.516
Brandon Moss	L	96	20	5	1	2	13	9	0	32	2	.208	.294	.344	.637
Xavier Nady	R	129	31	4	0	7	19	20	1	33	8	.240	.357	.434	.791
David Ortiz	L	90	16	3	1	5	19	22	3	23	2	.178	.336	.400	.736
Lyle Overbay	L	140	33	7	0	4	27	17	2	46	3	.236	.314	.371	.686
Xavier Paul	L	138	28	7	1	5	13	6	1	47	6	.203	.241	.377	.618
Brayan Pena	B	108	27	5	0	2	14	9	0	22	4	.250	.300	.352	.652
A.J. Pierzynski	L	124	32	5	0	4	20	12	5	20	7	.258	.329	.395	.724
Nick Punto	B	98	17	4	0	0	2	17	0	32	0	.173	.296	.214	.510
Ryan Raburn	R	92	15	4	0	4	15	12	1	29	2	.163	.271	.337	.608
Ryan Roberts	R	104	27	3	0	0	9	7	0	27	1	.260	.316	.288	.604
Shane Robinson	R	102	21	4	1	0	6	14	0	18	2	.206	.299	.265	.564
Cody Ross	R	97	29	7	0	5	16	13	0	27	0	.299	.389	.526	.915
Gaby Sanchez	R	121	26	10	0	5	25	22	2	29	4	.215	.342	.421	.764
Nate Schierholtz	L	180	49	9	1	4	24	13	1	39	4	.272	.316	.400	.716
Skip Schumaker	L	173	40	9	1	1	14	10	1	31	4	.231	.280	.301	.580
Seth Smith	L	183	57	13	5	7	42	30	2	48	3	.311	.406	.552	.957
Travis Snider	L	122	28	6	0	5	17	10	1	34	2	.230	.293	.402	.695
Justin Turner	R	127	34	9	0	0	24	9	0	24	7	.268	.314	.339	.653
Jordany Valdespin	L	89	15	1	0	7	17	14	0	27	0	.169	.295	.416	.711
Will Venable	L	110	21	3	2	1	11	12	1	33	0	.191	.268	.282	.550
Rickie Weeks	R	83	19	1	1	2	7	15	1	32	3	.229	.360	.337	.697
Eric Young	B	130	29	3	1	1	4	18	0	33	2	.223	.327	.285	.611

Manufactured Runs, Productive Outs, & Unproductive Outs

With the power decline that has hit baseball over the recent half-decade, the ability to move baserunners over and score them without relying exclusively on three-run bombs has once again become paramount. And that rededication to small ball has extended beyond the National League. Specifically, the Royals finished comfortably in first in baseball with 204 Manufactured Runs and were second to the Cardinals with 291 Productive Outs.

The Royals were the ultimate speed-over-power team this season. Their 153 stolen bases were 15 more than the second place team. That effort was spearheaded by Jarrod Dyson (36), Alcides Escobar (31), and Lorenzo Cain (28). They were three of only 21 players with at least 25 stolen bases this season. Even Billy Butler, who is likely the slowest player in baseball, got in on the act with a critical stolen base in Game 3 of the ALDS! Meanwhile, the Royals hit just 95 home runs this season, the fewest in baseball. Many of their traditional sluggers like Butler, Eric Hosmer, and Mike Moustakas had disappointing seasons in terms of their power, but they were all among the league leaders in Productive Outs, and Omar Infante led them all with 39 Productive Outs, tied for fifth most in baseball. Escobar and Nori Aoki were the primary beneficiaries of their work, combining for 65 Manufactured Runs.

The Royals' success in the little things may have been exactly what the team needed to finally reach the playoffs. In contrast, the Angels have been a perennially successful team, and their consistency in manufacturing runs provides a window into their team philosophy. They finished just behind the Royals with 192 Manufactured Runs in 2014. In the last 13 seasons, the Angels have finished outside of the top four in Manufactured Runs only once. Team totals of Manufactured Runs, Productive Outs, and Unproductive Outs, as well as the totals allowed by each team, can be found on the following pages.

Giancarlo Stanton had an MVP-caliber season for the Marlins, highlighted by his NL-leading 37 home runs. However, Stanton also set the pace with 101 Unproductive Outs. Several other noted sluggers finished high in Unproductive Outs, such as Albert Pujols (98), Matt Holliday (94), and Freddie Freeman (91). In contrast, Adrian Gonzalez finished the season with 45 Productive Outs, the most in baseball. He was also first with the exact same total in 2013. Miguel Cabrera was not too far behind with 40 Productive Outs, which is another feather in the cap of the two-time MVP winner. The rest of the individual leaders in Manufactured Run Contributions, Productive Outs, and Unproductive Outs can be found on the following pages.

Players with the most Manufactured Runs, Productive Outs, & Unproductive Outs

Manufactured Runs		Productive Outs		Unproductive Outs	
Gordon, Dee, LAD	36	Gonzalez, Adrian, LAD	45	Stanton, Giancarlo, Mia	101
Reyes, Jose, Tor	36	Andrus, Elvis, Tex	44	Utley, Chase, Phi	99
Gomez, Carlos, Mil	35	Aybar, Erick, LAA	43	Pujols, Albert, LAA	98
Revere, Ben, Phi	34	Cabrera, Miguel, Det	40	Donaldson, Josh, Oak	96
Escobar, Alcides, KC	33	Infante, Omar, KC	39	Holliday, Matt, StL	94
Andrus, Elvis, Tex	32	Utley, Chase, Phi	39	Freeman, Freddie, Atl	91
Dozier, Brian, Min	32	Hunter, Torii, Det	37	Dozier, Brian, Min	90
Aoki, Nori, KC	32	Jeter, Derek, NYY	36	Cespedes, Yoenis, Oak-Bos	89
Aybar, Erick, LAA	31	Parra, Gerardo, Ari-Mil	35	Ramirez, Alexei, CWS	89
Hamilton, Billy, Cin	30	Kendrick, Howie, LAA	35	Longoria, Evan, TB	87
Kinsler, Ian, Det	30	Rollins, Jimmy, Phi	34	Rendon, Anthony, Was	86
Eaton, Adam, CWS	29	Pujols, Albert, LAA	34	Jones, Adam, Bal	86
Yelich, Christian, Mia	29	Posey, Buster, SF	33	Pence, Hunter, SF	85
Span, Denard, Was	28	Ellsbury, Jacoby, NYY	33	Bogaerts, Xander, Bos	84
Kendrick, Howie, LAA	28	Cano, Robinson, Sea	33	Peralta, Jhonny, StL	84
Pence, Hunter, SF	27	Ortiz, David, Bos	32	Bautista, Jose, Tor	83
Segura, Jean, Mil	27	Morneau, Justin, Col	32	McCutchen, Andrew, Pit	83
LeMahieu, DJ, Col	26	Mercer, Jordy, Pit	32	Perez, Salvador, KC	83
Altuve, Jose, Hou	25	Moustakas, Mike, KC	31	Sandoval, Pablo, SF	83
Davis, Rajai, Det	25	Gardner, Brett, NYY	31	Trout, Mike, LAA	82
Puig, Yasiel, LAD	25	LaRoche, Adam, Was	31	Puig, Yasiel, LAD	82
Gordon, Alex, KC	24	Hosmer, Eric, KC	30	Rollins, Jimmy, Phi	82
Young, Eric, NYM	24	LeMahieu, DJ, Col	30	Murphy, Daniel, NYM	82
Martin, Leonys, Tex	24	Crawford, Brandon, SF	30	Werth, Jayson, Was	82
Jackson, Austin, Det-Sea	23	Smith, Seth, SD	30	Cozart, Zack, Cin	80
Cespedes, Yoenis, Oak-Bos	23	Butler, Billy, KC	29	Howard, Ryan, Phi	79
Frazier, Todd, Cin	22	Zobrist, Ben, TB	29	Rios, Alex, Tex	78
Gardner, Brett, NYY	22	Kinsler, Ian, Det	29	Carter, Chris, Hou	78
Harrison, Josh, Pit	22	Amarista, Alexi, SD	29	Adams, Matt, StL	77
Ramirez, Alexei, CWS	22	Dozier, Brian, Min	29	Frazier, Todd, Cin	77
Upton, B.J., Atl	21	Martin, Leonys, Tex	29	Castro, Jason, Hou	76
Trout, Mike, LAA	21	Wong, Kolten, StL	29	Hill, Aaron, Ari	75
Marte, Starling, Pit	21	Wright, David, NYM	29	Plouffe, Trevor, Min	75
Brantley, Michael, Cle	21	Cabrera, Melky, Tor	29	Desmond, Ian, Was	75
Calhoun, Kole, LAA	21	Howard, Ryan, Phi	29	Cruz, Nelson, Bal	74
Cano, Robinson, Sea	20	Joyce, Matt, TB	28	LaRoche, Adam, Was	73
Werth, Jayson, Was	20	Phillips, Brandon, Cin	28	Martinez, J.D., Det	73
Hechavarria, Adeiny, Mia	20	Bautista, Jose, Tor	28	Altuve, Jose, Hou	73
Longoria, Evan, TB	20	Murphy, Daniel, NYM	28	Ortiz, David, Bos	73
Kipnis, Jason, Cle	20	Adams, Matt, StL	28	Upton, Justin, Atl	72
Zobrist, Ben, TB	20	Hechavarria, Adeiny, Mia	28	Cabrera, Asdrubal, Cle-Was	72
Desmond, Ian, Was	19	Martinez, Victor, Det	28	Wright, David, NYM	72
Dyson, Jarrod, KC	19	Beltre, Adrian, Tex	28	Lowrie, Jed, Oak	72
McCutchen, Andrew, Pit	19	Werth, Jayson, Was	28	Escobar, Yunel, TB	71
Stubbs, Drew, Col	19	Lucroy, Jonathan, Mil	28	Encarnacion, Edwin, Tor	71
Cain, Lorenzo, KC	19	Perez, Salvador, KC	28	Moss, Brandon, Oak	71
Bogaerts, Xander, Bos	19	Upton, Justin, Atl	28	Mercer, Jordy, Pit	71
Rendon, Anthony, Was	19	Revere, Ben, Phi	27	Pedroia, Dustin, Bos	71
Venable, Will, SD	19	Donaldson, Josh, Oak	27	Abreu, Jose, CWS	71
Bautista, Jose, Tor	19	Aviles, Mike, Cle	27	Johnson, Chris, Atl	71
Blanco, Gregor, SF	19	Rendon, Anthony, Was	27	Castellanos, Nick, Det	71
		Aoki, Nori, KC	27		
		Peralta, Jhonny, StL	27		
		Prado, Martin, Ari-NYY	27		

Manufactured Runs, Productive Outs, & Unproductive Outs Produced by Team

Team	Manufactured Runs	Productive Outs	Unproductive Outs
Arizona Diamondbacks	157	283	686
Atlanta Braves	134	245	667
Baltimore Orioles	123	205	680
Boston Red Sox	141	230	738
Chicago White Sox	134	224	696
Chicago Cubs	126	246	710
Cincinnati Reds	135	283	640
Cleveland Indians	151	258	680
Colorado Rockies	153	283	650
Detroit Tigers	168	284	651
Houston Astros	133	202	717
Kansas City Royals	204	291	689
Los Angeles Dodgers	173	286	703
Los Angeles Angels	192	282	692
Miami Marlins	148	265	701
Milwaukee Brewers	165	267	621
Minnesota Twins	172	239	746
New York Yankees	147	261	646
New York Mets	129	278	689
Oakland Athletics	146	213	736
Philadelphia Phillies	142	278	694
Pittsburgh Pirates	145	264	700
San Diego Padres	140	255	633
San Francisco Giants	153	248	707
Seattle Mariners	145	227	628
St Louis Cardinals	135	295	701
Tampa Bay Rays	148	248	719
Texas Rangers	177	284	647
Toronto Blue Jays	152	258	707
Washington Nationals	149	285	716

Manufactured Runs, Productive Outs, & Unproductive Outs Allowed by Team

Team	Manufactured Runs	Productive Outs	Unproductive Outs
Arizona Diamondbacks	155	291	629
Atlanta Braves	156	269	748
Baltimore Orioles	112	252	684
Boston Red Sox	153	263	704
Chicago White Sox	189	269	685
Chicago Cubs	180	290	693
Cincinnati Reds	111	240	669
Cleveland Indians	159	245	733
Colorado Rockies	197	314	700
Detroit Tigers	170	240	704
Houston Astros	171	282	665
Kansas City Royals	136	251	715
Los Angeles Dodgers	153	238	687
Los Angeles Angels	162	248	671
Miami Marlins	165	316	678
Milwaukee Brewers	133	254	656
Minnesota Twins	149	268	718
New York Yankees	144	240	706
New York Mets	139	236	704
Oakland Athletics	157	242	650
Philadelphia Phillies	161	321	690
Pittsburgh Pirates	178	286	648
San Diego Padres	127	241	720
San Francisco Giants	142	273	635
Seattle Mariners	137	226	659
St Louis Cardinals	124	262	690
Tampa Bay Rays	137	220	704
Texas Rangers	158	231	703
Toronto Blue Jays	142	243	704
Washington Nationals	120	216	638

Managers Record

The early offseason has been kind to managers overall, but Ron Gardenhire was fired after his 13th season with the Twins. Only Mike Scioscia, who just finished his 15th season with the Angels, had a longer tenure with his current team. Gardenhire had a reputation as an old-school manager, but he had adapted in recent seasons. That showed up especially in his diminished reliance on sacrifice bunts. In 2008 and 2009, he led the AL with 73 and 62 sacrifice bunt attempts, but over the last three seasons, his attempts called declined from 49 in 2012 to 37 in 2013 to 31 in 2014. Whether or not his managerial style was an issue, Gardenhire would have been hard-pressed to survive the Twins' recent lack of success. The team lost at least 92 games for the fourth consecutive season in 2014.

In addition, the Astros fired Bo Porter, and Ron Washington resigned from the Rangers late in the season. Porter had not enjoyed much success with the rebuilding Astros in his two seasons (.364 winning percentage), but his firing was likely more the result of internal disagreements with the front office. Meanwhile, the Rangers underperformed this season under Washington. They were a preseason favorite in the AL West, but they fell apart after a series of injuries to key players. Washington resigned from the team 87 losses into their eventual 95-loss season.

It is not all doom and gloom for managers. After another excellent season with the Orioles, Buck Showalter continues to pad his managerial resume. The Orioles are the fourth team Showalter has managed in his career, and this season, they became his longest stop along the way. The reason for his recent longevity is the team's success. Showalter has a 377-328 record with a team few expected to compete in the frequently top-heavy AL East, but he's reached the playoffs in two of the last three seasons. Showalter is up to third among active managers with 1,259 wins, trailing only Scioscia (1,331) and Bruce Bochy of the Giants (1,618).

The tools we have to evaluate managers are divided into several categories:

Lineups: Number of Different Lineups Used (LUp), the percentage of players who had the platoon advantage at the start of the game (PL%).

Substitution: Pinch Hitters Used (PH), Pinch Runners Used (PR), Defensive Substitutes Used (DS).

Pitchers Usage: Quick Hooks (Quick), Slow Hooks (Slow), Long Outings by Starting Pitchers (LO), Relievers Used on Consecutive Days (RCD), Long Saves (LS), Relievers Used (Rel).

For Quick Hooks, we calculate a "Damage Score" for each pitcher and each game, which is his pitches thrown plus 10 times his runs allowed. The bottom 25 percent of the games in each league are Quick Hooks. If the manager takes his pitcher out after 92 pitches and one run allowed (102), that will be a Quick Hook. The top 25 percent are Slow Hooks. If a pitcher throws 114 pitches and gives up four runs (154), that will be a Slow Hook. If a pitcher throws more than 110 pitches in a start, that's a Long Outing. Yes, this is redundant of Slow Hooks; thanks for noticing.

Tactics: Stolen Base Attempts (SBA), Sacrifice Bunt Attempts (SacA), Runners Moving with the Pitch (RM), Pitchouts ordered (PO).

Intentional Walks: Intentional Walks issued (#), Intentional Walks resulting in a Good Outcome (Good), Intentional Walks resulting Not in a Good Outcome (NG), Intentional Walks Blowing up on the Manager (Bomb). A good result is (1) the next hitter grounds into a double play, or (2) the team in the field gets out of the inning without additional runs scoring. A "Bomb" means that multiple runs score in the inning after the intentional walk. If the hitter after the IBB grounds into a double play, then we count that intentional walk as a success even if multiple runs score after that.

Results: Wins (W), Losses (L), and Winning Percentage (Pct.).

Manny Acta

Year	Team	Lg	G	LUp	PL%	PH	PR	DS	Quick	Slow	LO	RCD	LS	Rel	SBA	SacA	RM	PO	#	Good	NG	Bomb	W	L	Pct
				LINEUPS		SUBSTITUTION			PITCHER USAGE						TACTICS				INTENTIONAL BB				RESULTS		
2007	Nationals	NL	162	101	.65	295	32	78	53	28	5	183	1	588	92	86	70	28	44	28	16	8	73	89	.451
2008	Nationals	NL	161	133	.62	293	31	39	38	46	6	119	4	517	124	95	63	24	44	27	17	8	59	102	.366
2009	Nationals	NL	87	66	.62	145	11	20	14	25	1	91	1	282	54	43	62	5	26	13	13	6	26	61	.299
2010	Indians	AL	162	142	.63	79	20	39	44	49	18	81	6	470	124	41	142	20	36	17	19	10	69	93	.426
2011	Indians	AL	162	134	.71	76	44	43	47	49	20	107	0	483	131	40	144	29	34	20	14	10	80	82	.494
2012	Indians	AL	156	116	.76	68	20	72	38	54	14	94	1	464	149	21	135	23	27	12	15	9	65	91	.417
162-Game Average				126	.67	174	29	53	43	46	12	123	2	510	123	59	112	23	38	21	17	9	68	94	.420

Sandy Alomar, Jr.

Year	Team	Lg	G	LUp	PL%	PH	PR	DS	Quick	Slow	LO	RCD	LS	Rel	SBA	SacA	RM	PO	#	Good	NG	Bomb	W	L	Pct
				LINEUPS		SUBSTITUTION			PITCHER USAGE						TACTICS				INTENTIONAL BB				RESULTS		
2012	Indians	AL	6	6	.61	12	2	1	1	1	0	9	0	30	5	3	3	0	0	0	0	0	3	3	.500
162-Game Average				162	.61	324	54	27	27	27	0	243	0	810	135	81	81	0	0	0	0	0	81	81	.500

Brad Ausmus

Year	Team	Lg	G	LUp	PL%	PH	PR	DS	Quick	Slow	LO	RCD	LS	Rel	SBA	SacA	RM	PO	#	Good	NG	Bomb	W	L	Pct
				LINEUPS		SUBSTITUTION			PITCHER USAGE						TACTICS				INTENTIONAL BB				RESULTS		
2014	Tigers	AL	162	103	.51	79	43	44	28	55	43	99	1	473	147	32	144	13	34	17	17	5	90	72	.556
162-Game Average				103	.51	79	43	44	28	55	43	99	1	473	147	32	144	13	34	17	17	5	90	72	.556

Dusty Baker

Year	Team	Lg	G	LUp	PL%	PH	PR	DS	Quick	Slow	LO	RCD	LS	Rel	SBA	SacA	RM	PO	#	Good	NG	Bomb	W	L	Pct
				LINEUPS		SUBSTITUTION			PITCHER USAGE						TACTICS				INTENTIONAL BB				RESULTS		
1994	Giants	NL	115	76	.53	177	16	9	29	25	2	86	12	288	154	88		78	40	24	16	8	55	60	.478
1995	Giants	NL	144	97	.41	230	36	13	32	50	8	90	8	381	184	101		77	51	32	19	14	67	77	.465
1996	Giants	NL	162	129	.51	250	17	15	24	58	15	94	8	425	166	103		96	60	37	23	15	68	94	.420
1997	Giants	NL	162	114	.71	212	17	22	46	25	17	132	4	481	170	85		93	57	36	21	12	90	72	.556
1998	Giants	NL	163	130	.62	224	20	12	43	38	8	113	5	433	153	111		41	68	42	26	9	89	74	.546
1999	Giants	NL	162	119	.62	233	16	16	30	51	27	111		450	165	113		40	41	25	16	10	86	76	.531
2000	Giants	NL	162	82	.56	233	26	22	38	50	25	91	3	384	118	86		37	26	17	9	2	97	65	.599
2001	Giants	NL	162	122	.48	261	22	19	40	48	10	114	4	439	99	95		45	49	33	16	6	90	72	.556
2002	Giants	NL	162	118	.43	223	32	38	29	56	53	106	8	417	95	89	42	41	44	28	16	10	95	66	.590
2003	Cubs	NL	162	114	.49	272	25	43	24	58	65	111	3	420	104	93	31	24	36	23	13	4	88	74	.543
2004	Cubs	NL	162	113	.44	254	16	19	37	41	42	129	8	460	94	108	71	62	33	22	11	7	89	73	.549
2005	Cubs	NL	162	121	.59	240	21	29	40	46	36	103	2	457	104	88	107	70	48	27	21	7	79	83	.488
2006	Cubs	NL	162	133	.56	271	9	26	45	39	22	165	2	542	100	108	139	46	44	28	16	11	66	96	.407
2008	Reds	NL	162	119	.58	285	28	27	26	63	39	124	2	507	132	100	101	37	40	28	12	4	74	88	.457
2009	Reds	NL	162	130	.45	252	15	35	30	62	35	115	1	478	136	120	118	23	36	29	7	4	78	84	.481
2010	Reds	NL	162	120	.46	258	19	49	36	41	22	140	0	502	136	91	157	13	32	22	10	9	91	71	.562
2011	Reds	NL	162	142	.42	240	29	42	34	51	20	115	0	501	147	102	226	33	47	26	21	5	79	83	.488
2012	Reds	NL	162	121	.43	201	19	39	33	39	30	78	4	425	114	108	148	19	33	22	11	3	97	65	.599
2013	Reds	NL	162	95	.54	236	20	27	39	40	14	90	3	461	102	110	157	21	28	23	5	3	90	72	.556
162-Game Average				118	.52	245	22	27	35	47	26	113	4	454	137	102	118	48	44	28	16	8	84	78	.519

Bud Black

Year	Team	Lg	G	LUp	PL%	PH	PR	DS	Quick	Slow	LO	RCD	LS	Rel	SBA	SacA	RM	PO	#	Good	NG	Bomb	W	L	Pct
				LINEUPS		SUBSTITUTION			PITCHER USAGE						TACTICS				INTENTIONAL BB				RESULTS		
2007	Padres	NL	163	115	.62	279	18	13	63	28	13	122	0	485	79	85	73	56	48	28	20	11	89	74	.546
2008	Padres	NL	162	113	.63	286	25	20	55	36	17	109	0	491	53	75	78	31	61	30	31	17	63	99	.389
2009	Padres	NL	162	137	.64	264	8	34	50	37	8	118	5	527	111	99	84	55	58	42	16	6	75	87	.463
2010	Padres	NL	162	135	.61	285	16	45	55	33	10	132	7	499	174	99	135	31	51	35	16	8	90	72	.556
2011	Padres	NL	162	140	.58	288	20	43	40	36	10	110	2	490	214	69	184	41	56	31	25	13	71	91	.438
2012	Padres	NL	162	132	.74	280	26	35	45	49	11	126	5	529	201	89	162	21	48	34	14	7	76	86	.469
2013	Padres	NL	162	145	.66	271	24	37	35	46	4	102	1	488	152	78	122	12	31	20	11	8	76	86	.469
2014	Padres	NL	162	157	.74	313	23	29	49	33	13	104	1	481	125	74	116	15	32	24	8	4	77	85	.475
162-Game Average				134	.65	283	20	32	49	37	11	115	3	498	139	83	119	33	48	30	18	9	77	85	.475

Bruce Bochy

Year	Team	Lg	G	LUp	PL%	PH	PR	DS	Quick	Slow	LO	RCD	LS	Rel	SBA	SacA	RM	PO	#	Good	NG	Bomb	W	L	Pct
				LINEUPS		SUBSTITUTION			PITCHER USAGE						TACTICS				INTENTIONAL BB				RESULTS		
1995	Padres	NL	144	96	.59	262	30	23	44	41	17	38	3	337	170	68		38	37	19	18	11	70	74	.486
1996	Padres	NL	162	114	.52	289	29	15	51	33	10	67	12	411	164	73		65	47	29	18	12	91	71	.562
1997	Padres	NL	162	111	.60	291	26	9	45	45	3	81	11	426	200	84		58	37	20	17	11	76	86	.469
1998	Padres	NL	162	108	.65	280	62	44	44	45	9	81	12	369	116	84		27	45	31	14	10	98	64	.605
1999	Padres	NL	162	137	.60	298	51	21	44	36	4	68	5	403	241	60		29	48	29	19	13	74	88	.457

Year	Team	Lg	G	LINEUPS		SUBSTITUTION			PITCHER USAGE						TACTICS				INTENTIONAL BB				RESULTS		
				LUp	PL%	PH	PR	DS	Quick	Slow	LO	RCD	LS	Rel	SBA	SacA	RM	PO	#	Good	NG	Bomb	W	L	Pct
2000	Padres	NL	162	134	.52	285	44	14	41	47	14	105	5	443	184	52		27	50	21	29	11	76	86	.469
2001	Padres	NL	162	116	.60	255	54	27	32	47	6	85	10	422	173	43		23	54	31	23	13	79	83	.488
2002	Padres	NL	162	123	.66	259	44	56	39	40	17	106	4	459	115	63	74	14	61	38	23	14	66	96	.407
2003	Padres	NL	162	134	.58	339	20	29	34	43	16	100	3	473	115	63	41	6	52	33	19	12	64	98	.395
2004	Padres	NL	162	96	.54	261	28	47	47	32	15	76	3	437	77	75	96	14	39	24	15	10	87	75	.537
2005	Padres	NL	162	128	.58	285	31	49	46	36	23	87	1	456	143	89	111	16	45	33	12	8	82	80	.506
2006	Padres	NL	162	111	.60	264	64	48	43	42	24	111	2	475	154	77	110	21	63	43	20	10	88	74	.543
2007	Giants	NL	162	128	.72	264	50	45	26	50	36	132	2	496	152	86	119	10	41	29	12	3	71	91	.438
2008	Giants	NL	162	134	.68	276	32	39	24	59	42	97	6	478	154	77	155	5	59	40	19	8	72	90	.444
2009	Giants	NL	162	134	.65	231	21	52	42	40	32	84	8	457	106	93	118	5	49	32	17	10	88	74	.543
2010	Giants	NL	162	126	.55	224	45	70	29	37	40	118	12	477	87	102	144	12	58	41	17	8	92	70	.568
2011	Giants	NL	162	138	.62	245	49	42	38	38	44	108	3	480	136	79	175	11	46	36	10	6	86	76	.531
2012	Giants	NL	162	112	.75	220	32	55	22	50	31	136	9	526	157	87	176	15	42	30	12	5	94	68	.580
2013	Giants	NL	162	109	.70	263	19	45	33	52	23	143	4	524	93	78	164	7	64	46	18	6	76	86	.469
2014	Giants	NL	162	131	.66	236	29	64	45	41	19	102	1	475	83	53	147	12	35	25	10	9	88	74	.543
	162-Game Average			122	.62	268	38	40	39	43	21	97	6	454	142	75	125	21	49	32	17	10	81	81	.500

Tim Bogar

Year	Team	Lg	G	LINEUPS		SUBSTITUTION			PITCHER USAGE						TACTICS				INTENTIONAL BB				RESULTS		
				LUp	PL%	PH	PR	DS	Quick	Slow	LO	RCD	LS	Rel	SBA	SacA	RM	PO	#	Good	NG	Bomb	W	L	Pct
2014	Rangers	AL	22	21	.56	1	5	0	10	3	3	11	0	76	29	6	23	1	9	5	4	3	14	8	.636
	162-Game Average			155	.56	7	37	0	74	22	22	81	0	560	214	44	169	7	66	37	29	22	103	59	.636

Terry Collins

Year	Team	Lg	G	LINEUPS		SUBSTITUTION			PITCHER USAGE						TACTICS				INTENTIONAL BB				RESULTS		
				LUp	PL%	PH	PR	DS	Quick	Slow	LO	RCD	LS	Rel	SBA	SacA	RM	PO	#	Good	NG	Bomb	W	L	Pct
1994	Astros	NL	115	74	.54	185	20	13	6	6	0	37	4	268	168	90		37	28	17	11	5	66	49	.574
1995	Astros	NL	144	106	.49	302	38	11	15	7	8	100	8	394	236	97		44	39	27	12	8	76	68	.528
1996	Astros	NL	162	111	.41	257	30	38	13	12	9	70	10	371	243	94		35	42	30	12	6	82	80	.506
1997	Angels	AL	162	117	.70	86	34	22	10	16	15	67	8	400	198	55		60	25	13	12	4	84	78	.519
1998	Angels	AL	162	119	.57	100	64	33	15	11	28	86	11	415	138	69		38	16	6	10	4	85	77	.525
1999	Angels	AL	133	113	.56	93	26	16	10	16	10	68	2	315	93	39		7	10	1	9	3	51	82	.383
2011	Mets	NL	162	121	.68	312	18	28	32	42	23	126	5	514	165	88	151	9	48	35	13	9	77	85	.475
2012	Mets	NL	162	141	.69	329	16	38	39	36	19	113	0	505	117	75	149	8	29	18	11	3	74	88	.457
2013	Mets	NL	162	132	.61	266	12	33	33	42	15	131	4	535	149	67	128	3	38	30	8	3	74	88	.457
2014	Mets	NL	162	135	.55	247	17	26	28	46	23	111	6	489	135	73	119	2	38	23	15	4	79	83	.488
	162-Game Average			124	.58	231	29	27	21	25	16	96	6	447	174	79	137	26	33	21	12	5	79	83	.488

Don Cooper

Year	Team	Lg	G	LINEUPS		SUBSTITUTION			PITCHER USAGE						TACTICS				INTENTIONAL BB				RESULTS		
				LUp	PL%	PH	PR	DS	Quick	Slow	LO	RCD	LS	Rel	SBA	SacA	RM	PO	#	Good	NG	Bomb	W	L	Pct
2011	White Sox	AL	2	2	.39	0	1	0	1	0	0	2	1	6	1	1	1	0	1	0	1	1	1	1	.500
	162-Game Average			162	.39	0	81	0	81	0	0	162	81	486	81	81	81	0	81	0	81	81	81	81	.500

Tony DeFrancesco

Year	Team	Lg	G	LINEUPS		SUBSTITUTION			PITCHER USAGE						TACTICS				INTENTIONAL BB				RESULTS		
				LUp	PL%	PH	PR	DS	Quick	Slow	LO	RCD	LS	Rel	SBA	SacA	RM	PO	#	Good	NG	Bomb	W	L	Pct
2012	Astros	NL	41	41	.64	82	10	12	21	7	2	24	5	150	34	16	45	14	15	9	6	4	16	25	.390
	162-Game Average			162	.64	324	40	47	83	28	8	95	20	593	134	63	178	55	60	30	24	16	63	99	.389

John Farrell

Year	Team	Lg	G	LINEUPS		SUBSTITUTION			PITCHER USAGE						TACTICS				INTENTIONAL BB				RESULTS		
				LUp	PL%	PH	PR	DS	Quick	Slow	LO	RCD	LS	Rel	SBA	SacA	RM	PO	#	Good	NG	Bomb	W	L	Pct
2011	Blue Jays	AL	162	131	.43	64	48	22	40	41	26	62	3	474	183	40	181	22	28	17	11	5	81	81	.500
2012	Blue Jays	AL	162	131	.50	94	30	16	49	44	7	84	3	495	164	46	211	15	20	11	9	7	73	89	.451
2013	Red Sox	AL	162	126	.68	93	41	20	28	46	34	71	4	450	142	32	147	5	10	5	5	3	97	65	.599
2014	Red Sox	AL	162	145	.55	101	24	17	29	53	28	107	1	493	88	26	124	4	19	11	8	2	71	91	.438
	162-Game Average			133	.54	88	36	19	37	46	24	81	3	478	144	36	166	12	19	11	8	4	81	82	.497

Terry Francona

Year	Team	Lg	G	LINEUPS		SUBSTITUTION			PITCHER USAGE						TACTICS				INTENTIONAL BB				RESULTS		
				LUp	PL%	PH	PR	DS	Quick	Slow	LO	RCD	LS	Rel	SBA	SacA	RM	PO	#	Good	NG	Bomb	W	L	Pct
1997	Phillies	NL	162	98	.66	288	19	28	28	54	22	102	9	409	148	91		30	42	23	19	9	68	94	.420
1998	Phillies	NL	162	84	.53	256	20	19	34	57	20	88	7	385	142	85		16	27	10	17	8	75	87	.463
1999	Phillies	NL	162	85	.51	239	13	31	29	41	16	111	7	441	160	81		27	24	14	10	6	77	85	.475

Year	Team	Lg	G	LINEUPS		SUBSTITUTION			PITCHER USAGE						TACTICS				INTENTIONAL BB				RESULTS		
				LUp	PL%	PH	PR	DS	Quick	Slow	LO	RCD	LS	Rel	SBA	SacA	RM	PO	#	Good	NG	Bomb	W	L	Pct
2000	Phillies	NL	162	108	.53	278	17	14	38	43	25	102	5	414	132	89		16	32	22	10	7	65	97	.401
2004	Red Sox	AL	162	141	.65	116	65	58	41	48	32	105	8	437	98	18	91	28	28	22	6	4	98	64	.605
2005	Red Sox	AL	162	104	.67	110	46	37	25	55	30	99	3	442	57	21	79	11	28	18	10	5	95	67	.586
2006	Red Sox	AL	162	116	.59	93	54	49	36	44	13	94	9	454	74	33	98	16	25	11	14	7	86	76	.531
2007	Red Sox	AL	162	109	.60	84	34	23	41	35	32	89	4	451	120	45	90	14	20	14	6	4	96	66	.593
2008	Red Sox	AL	162	131	.59	62	40	40	50	30	20	90	11	466	155	40	87	8	17	10	7	4	95	67	.586
2009	Red Sox	AL	162	113	.58	85	47	28	36	50	30	68	6	463	165	29	68	9	24	15	9	6	95	67	.586
2010	Red Sox	AL	162	143	.62	125	48	34	32	63	49	84	3	443	85	36	125	26	30	17	13	4	89	73	.549
2011	Red Sox	AL	162	123	.67	89	44	11	52	46	27	89	4	444	144	29	163	34	11	6	5	2	90	72	.556
2013	Indians	AL	162	121	.75	78	45	24	47	34	18	122	2	540	153	41	158	5	26	15	11	6	92	70	.568
2014	Indians	AL	162	133	.78	123	16	24	37	37	18	150	7	573	131	58	128	3	51	29	22	13	85	77	.525
	162-Game Average			115	.62	145	36	30	38	46	25	100	6	454	126	50	109	17	28	16	11	6	86	76	.531

Ron Gardenhire

Year	Team	Lg	G	LINEUPS		SUBSTITUTION			PITCHER USAGE						TACTICS				INTENTIONAL BB				RESULTS		
				LUp	PL%	PH	PR	DS	Quick	Slow	LO	RCD	LS	Rel	SBA	SacA	RM	PO	#	Good	NG	Bomb	W	L	Pct
2002	Twins	AL	161	111	.69	141	36	42	54	25	10	84	1	435	141	48	44	11	24	16	8	4	94	67	.584
2003	Twins	AL	162	126	.63	144	50	26	49	33	13	85	2	399	138	59	37	14	35	16	19	6	90	72	.556
2004	Twins	AL	162	131	.59	129	45	29	56	21	20	106	4	435	162	66	121	18	27	15	12	7	92	70	.568
2005	Twins	AL	162	135	.58	104	45	26	50	21	5	87	1	396	146	59	138	16	38	28	10	3	83	79	.512
2006	Twins	AL	162	97	.62	93	36	21	60	31	3	82	5	421	143	48	130	11	25	14	11	4	96	66	.593
2007	Twins	AL	162	139	.63	104	42	25	45	30	8	99	4	438	142	45	148	11	33	14	19	9	79	83	.488
2008	Twins	AL	163	103	.64	109	26	12	47	29	5	115	3	485	144	73	143	17	38	25	13	8	88	75	.540
2009	Twins	AL	163	129	.63	83	54	34	43	25	12	115	3	480	117	62	100	21	20	9	11	6	87	76	.534
2010	Twins	AL	162	112	.62	86	55	30	57	28	5	106	1	465	96	47	140	14	19	12	7	4	94	68	.580
2011	Twins	AL	162	150	.58	93	48	21	34	44	17	82	1	457	131	44	170	5	37	21	16	9	63	99	.389
2012	Twins	AL	162	121	.62	64	45	24	42	31	4	82	1	499	172	49	207	10	43	27	16	6	66	96	.407
2013	Twins	AL	162	139	.66	103	42	28	41	43	6	78	1	511	85	37	137	14	31	13	18	7	66	96	.407
2014	Twins	AL	162	132	.64	97	44	23	40	40	2	82	2	491	135	31	149	5	24	11	13	6	70	92	.432
	162-Game Average			125	.62	104	44	26	48	31	8	92	2	455	135	51	128	13	30	17	13	6	82	80	.506

Bob Geren

Year	Team	Lg	G	LINEUPS		SUBSTITUTION			PITCHER USAGE						TACTICS				INTENTIONAL BB				RESULTS		
				LUp	PL%	PH	PR	DS	Quick	Slow	LO	RCD	LS	Rel	SBA	SacA	RM	PO	#	Good	NG	Bomb	W	L	Pct
2007	Athletics	AL	162	140	.57	64	31	24	39	43	14	112	9	446	72	31	91	22	60	38	22	10	76	86	.469
2008	Athletics	AL	162	133	.59	91	57	37	49	32	5	87	4	441	109	44	62	18	45	25	20	10	75	86	.466
2009	Athletics	AL	162	129	.59	77	27	40	54	40	5	108	11	488	181	37	71	6	30	15	15	7	75	87	.463
2010	Athletics	AL	162	126	.63	108	28	26	57	30	19	81	8	423	194	58	138	11	29	16	13	3	81	81	.500
2011	Athletics	AL	63	47	.62	42	9	3	25	11	7	50	2	177	57	18	54	9	15	7	8	4	27	36	.429
	162-Game Average			131	.60	87	35	30	51	36	11	100	9	451	140	43	95	15	41	23	18	8	76	86	.469

John Gibbons

Year	Team	Lg	G	LINEUPS		SUBSTITUTION			PITCHER USAGE						TACTICS				INTENTIONAL BB				RESULTS		
				LUp	PL%	PH	PR	DS	Quick	Slow	LO	RCD	LS	Rel	SBA	SacA	RM	PO	#	Good	NG	Bomb	W	L	Pct
2004	Blue Jays	AL	50	36	.68	42	3	2	16	8	7	22	1	130	34	2	47	21	11	5	6	3	20	30	.400
2005	Blue Jays	AL	162	124	.66	148	11	37	55	18	9	77	12	432	107	28	128	45	29	13	16	9	80	82	.494
2006	Blue Jays	AL	161	120	.53	112	32	40	59	33	17	94	16	482	98	20	127	40	56	32	24	12	87	75	.537
2007	Blue Jays	AL	162	131	.46	139	48	33	45	37	31	75	9	420	79	35	99	37	34	17	17	6	83	79	.512
2008	Blue Jays	AL	74	60	.48	53	15	18	12	20	12	43	0	205	70	23	39	10	26	16	10	6	35	39	.473
2013	Blue Jays	AL	162	136	.63	124	31	24	55	44	14	69	2	487	153	41	160	4	33	17	16	6	74	88	.457
2014	Blue Jays	AL	162	128	.72	202	41	49	45	37	20	73	8	449	99	49	161	6	23	17	6	2	83	79	.512
	162-Game Average			127	.60	142	31	35	50	34	19	79	8	452	111	34	132	28	37	20	16	8	80	82	.494

Kirk Gibson

Year	Team	Lg	G	LINEUPS		SUBSTITUTION			PITCHER USAGE						TACTICS				INTENTIONAL BB				RESULTS		
				LUp	PL%	PH	PR	DS	Quick	Slow	LO	RCD	LS	Rel	SBA	SacA	RM	PO	#	Good	NG	Bomb	W	L	Pct
2010	Diamondbacks	NL	83	57	.64	154	7	11	25	21	8	43	1	247	69	28	62	19	19	13	6	2	34	49	.410
2011	Diamondbacks	NL	162	118	.57	253	9	13	33	51	15	116	2	463	188	74	143	12	16	10	6	3	94	68	.580
2012	Diamondbacks	NL	162	140	.56	231	11	9	35	50	16	104	4	461	144	77	120	8	18	11	7	1	81	81	.500
2013	Diamondbacks	NL	162	138	.59	285	22	15	31	44	9	121	0	527	103	67	108	3	42	31	11	5	81	81	.500
2014	Diamondbacks	NL	159	135	.55	247	19	18	43	41	5	92	1	479	117	67	140	13	42	28	14	10	63	96	.396
	162-Game Average			131	.57	260	15	15	37	46	12	106	2	484	138	70	128	12	30	21	10	5	79	83	.488

Joe Girardi

Year	Team	Lg	G	LINEUPS		SUBSTITUTION			PITCHER USAGE						TACTICS				INTENTIONAL BB				RESULTS		
				LUp	PL%	PH	PR	DS	Quick	Slow	LO	RCD	LS	Rel	SBA	SacA	RM	PO	#	Good	NG	Bomb	W	L	Pct
2006	Marlins	NL	162	117	.50	250	44	**66**	46	40	28	76	3	438	168	97	108	42	58	37	21	7	78	84	.481
2008	Yankees	AL	162	114	.63	97	37	42	**60**	37	12	88	10	475	157	38	**173**	**36**	37	22	15	8	89	73	.549
2009	Yankees	AL	162	106	.73	97	**61**	42	36	45	27	88	**13**	461	139	44	83	33	28	14	14	9	**103**	59	.636
2010	Yankees	AL	162	114	.72	117	44	31	43	39	33	76	3	430	133	47	152	20	37	26	11	6	95	67	.586
2011	Yankees	AL	162	94	.69	72	41	53	51	36	21	88	2	465	193	50	151	26	43	30	13	4	**97**	65	.599
2012	Yankees	AL	162	107	.70	149	33	48	37	53	21	115	7	485	120	47	145	10	32	17	15	6	**95**	67	.586
2013	Yankees	AL	162	141	.59	119	15	29	42	50	23	82	4	428	146	49	131	4	34	20	14	6	85	77	.525
2014	Yankees	AL	162	142	.74	100	27	33	51	28	10	95	7	475	138	44	132	8	23	10	13	9	84	78	.519
	162-Game Average			117	.66	125	38	43	46	41	22	89	6	457	149	52	134	22	37	22	15	7	91	71	.562

Fredi Gonzalez

Year	Team	Lg	G	LINEUPS		SUBSTITUTION			PITCHER USAGE						TACTICS				INTENTIONAL BB				RESULTS		
				LUp	PL%	PH	PR	DS	Quick	Slow	LO	RCD	LS	Rel	SBA	SacA	RM	PO	#	Good	NG	Bomb	W	L	Pct
2007	Marlins	NL	162	96	.50	284	29	34	33	**56**	20	138	5	560	139	91	79	22	60	36	24	**16**	71	91	.438
2008	Marlins	NL	161	106	.51	255	38	49	38	39	8	120	3	511	104	61	75	17	66	42	24	14	84	77	.522
2009	Marlins	NL	162	97	.58	281	28	49	48	26	12	116	0	**530**	110	86	88	20	60	38	22	15	87	75	.537
2010	Marlins	NL	70	31	.41	104	12	16	14	13	11	35	1	193	56	33	64	10	18	11	7	5	34	36	.486
2011	Braves	NL	162	119	.60	260	27	29	53	36	21	**144**	0	510	121	95	139	19	**73**	**49**	24	13	89	73	.549
2012	Braves	NL	162	108	.61	268	18	27	50	34	9	115	4	460	133	67	116	20	40	28	12	11	94	68	.580
2013	Braves	NL	162	115	.50	214	**40**	51	50	42	8	124	2	466	95	79	94	11	35	26	9	4	96	66	.593
2014	Braves	NL	162	103	.45	206	**34**	34	27	41	20	122	3	472	128	70	106	23	36	24	12	8	79	83	.488
	162-Game Average			104	.53	252	30	39	42	39	15	123	2	499	119	78	102	19	52	34	18	12	85	77	.525

Ozzie Guillen

Year	Team	Lg	G	LINEUPS		SUBSTITUTION			PITCHER USAGE						TACTICS				INTENTIONAL BB				RESULTS		
				LUp	PL%	PH	PR	DS	Quick	Slow	LO	RCD	LS	Rel	SBA	SacA	RM	PO	#	Good	NG	Bomb	W	L	Pct
2004	White Sox	AL	162	134	.58	**132**	35	15	28	**65**	48	86	8	399	129	**84**	97	17	36	15	**21**	8	83	79	.512
2005	White Sox	AL	162	112	.51	100	32	21	31	56	35	114	5	412	204	68	148	15	42	27	15	6	**99**	63	.611
2006	White Sox	AL	162	87	.60	**135**	42	38	28	68	35	83	7	398	141	61	85	27	**59**	39	20	9	90	72	.556
2007	White Sox	AL	162	124	.56	100	26	23	26	53	**33**	131	2	463	123	54	92	13	50	24	**26**	15	72	90	.444
2008	White Sox	AL	163	100	.52	75	49	37	42	48	14	100	3	463	101	44	98	8	42	29	13	6	89	74	.546
2009	White Sox	AL	162	124	.52	105	48	19	50	37	16	70	4	415	162	45	114	15	41	23	**18**	10	79	83	.488
2010	White Sox	AL	162	115	.51	85	46	36	41	51	24	61	**8**	407	**234**	60	220	25	41	26	15	10	88	74	.543
2011	White Sox	AL	160	111	.52	73	47	28	34	45	28	63	**8**	404	133	65	172	40	**49**	**35**	14	7	78	82	.488
2012	Marlins	NL	162	116	.60	234	23	29	24	39	27	126	2	483	190	89	137	**23**	61	**38**	23	13	69	93	.426
	162-Game Average			114	.55	116	39	27	34	51	29	93	5	427	158	63	129	20	47	28	18	9	83	79	.512

A.J. Hinch

Year	Team	Lg	G	LINEUPS		SUBSTITUTION			PITCHER USAGE						TACTICS				INTENTIONAL BB				RESULTS		
				LUp	PL%	PH	PR	DS	Quick	Slow	LO	RCD	LS	Rel	SBA	SacA	RM	PO	#	Good	NG	Bomb	W	L	Pct
2009	Diamondbacks	NL	133	115	.63	222	10	13	24	50	24	61	5	392	113	64	41	5	24	12	12	6	58	75	.436
2010	Diamondbacks	NL	79	56	.53	120	7	4	12	40	21	39	1	207	58	19	51	7	19	9	10	9	31	48	.392
	162-Game Average			131	.59	261	13	13	28	69	34	76	5	458	131	63	70	9	33	16	17	11	68	94	.420

Clint Hurdle

Year	Team	Lg	G	LINEUPS		SUBSTITUTION			PITCHER USAGE						TACTICS				INTENTIONAL BB				RESULTS		
				LUp	PL%	PH	PR	DS	Quick	Slow	LO	RCD	LS	Rel	SBA	SacA	RM	PO	#	Good	NG	Bomb	W	L	Pct
2002	Rockies	NL	140	100	.52	274	28	41	33	46	17	104	3	437	139	46	50	13	38	22	16	11	67	73	.479
2003	Rockies	NL	162	108	.47	317	17	32	35	40	5	87	4	500	100	82	26	16	51	31	20	13	74	88	.457
2004	Rockies	NL	162	131	.57	289	18	35	36	**63**	20	74	1	473	77	**128**	67	12	**84**	**54**	**30**	12	68	94	.420
2005	Rockies	NL	162	135	.60	273	21	40	42	**60**	17	89	2	459	97	114	119	22	54	28	26	**15**	67	95	.414
2006	Rockies	NL	162	111	.49	259	17	22	34	**52**	17	107	2	499	135	**156**	114	28	81	45	**36**	**23**	76	86	.469
2007	Rockies	NL	163	96	.51	283	32	29	45	37	13	112	1	529	131	**112**	109	26	61	30	**31**	14	**90**	73	.552
2008	Rockies	NL	162	131	.49	253	20	31	40	43	16	85	2	485	**178**	**111**	116	**43**	49	31	18	6	74	88	.457
2009	Rockies	NL	46	42	.60	73	8	10	11	14	3	31	0	135	45	26	34	3	11	8	3	1	18	28	.391
2011	Pirates	NL	162	134	.60	278	26	63	**58**	27	1	134	3	**549**	160	101	173	20	65	39	**26**	13	72	90	.444
2012	Pirates	NL	162	133	.55	270	26	**60**	50	33	3	74	2	483	125	82	120	17	30	18	12	3	79	83	.488
2013	Pirates	NL	162	127	.51	**289**	24	61	61	25	7	76	3	465	136	83	**172**	20	26	22	4	2	94	68	.580
2014	Pirates	NL	162	123	.50	**322**	28	38	47	40	7	91	0	452	151	85	**187**	**24**	43	26	**17**	7	88	74	.543
	162-Game Average			123	.53	285	24	41	44	43	11	95	2	490	132	101	115	22	53	32	21	11	78	84	.481

Brandon Hyde

Year	Team	Lg	G	LINEUPS		SUBSTITUTION			PITCHER USAGE						TACTICS				INTENTIONAL BB				RESULTS		
				LUp	PL%	PH	PR	DS	Quick	Slow	LO	RCD	LS	Rel	SBA	SacA	RM	PO	#	Good	NG	Bomb	W	L	Pct
2011	Marlins	NL	1	1	.44	0	0	0	0	0	1	1	0	3	0	0	1	0	1	1	0	0	0	1	.000
	162-Game Average			162	.44	0	0	0	0	0	162	162	0	486	0	0	162	0	162	162	0	0	0	162	.000

Davey Johnson

Year	Team	Lg	G	LINEUPS		SUBSTITUTION			PITCHER USAGE						TACTICS				INTENTIONAL BB				RESULTS		
				LUp	PL%	PH	PR	DS	Quick	Slow	LO	RCD	LS	Rel	SBA	SacA	RM	PO	#	Good	NG	Bomb	W	L	Pct
1994	Reds	NL	115	79	.54	195	22	12	32	28	2	56	12	261	170	86	0	41	23	15	8	1	66	48	.579
1995	Reds	NL	144	105	.55	257	18	31	56	18	1	60	16	329	258	88	0	10	32	16	16	10	85	59	.590
1996	Orioles	AL	163	99	.68	85	33	38	48	48	13	67	9	378	117	62	0	6	35	13	22	11	88	74	.543
1997	Orioles	AL	162	109	.56	104	36	43	65	23	5	84	11	400	89	75	0	10	31	16	15	9	98	64	.605
1999	Dodgers	NL	162	109	.53	236	22	9	36	40	8	67	4	399	235	126	0	19	26	17	9	7	77	85	.475
2000	Dodgers	NL	162	89	.59	252	26	11	20	15	10		6	371	137	80	51	11	14	8	6	2	86	76	.531
2011	Nationals	NL	83	59	.45	143	20	23	40	13	1	51	1	271	58	51	85	0	19	10	9	6	40	43	.482
2012	Nationals	NL	162	93	.60	252	30	42	57	30	10	105	1	482	140	67	158	2	32	21	11	7	98	64	.605
2013	Nationals	NL	162	108	.54	233	23	33	46	39	27	99	0	440	116	91	148	1	17	8	9	3	86	76	.531
	162-Game Average			99	.35	226	29	18	47	36	18	66	15	354	173	88	176	18	33	18	15	8	92	70	.568

Tony LaRussa

Year	Team	Lg	G	LINEUPS		SUBSTITUTION			PITCHER USAGE						TACTICS				INTENTIONAL BB				RESULTS		
				LUp	PL%	PH	PR	DS	Quick	Slow	LO	RCD	LS	Rel	SBA	SacA	RM	PO	#	Good	NG	Bomb	W	L	Pct
1994	Athletics	AL	114	97	.62	89	28	14	43	21	5	60	4	308	130	31		32	30	20	10	4	51	63	.447
1995	Athletics	AL	144	120	.54	113	38	24	33	38	19	46	7	358	158	42		42	26	18	8	4	67	77	.465
1996	Cardinals	NL	162	120	.52	246	25	13	32	48	24	90	8	413	207	117		41	43	28	15	7	88	74	.543
1997	Cardinals	NL	162	146	.54	307	17	18	34	42	16	81	2	399	224	77		79	34	26	8	2	73	89	.451
1998	Cardinals	NL	162	146	.52	259	7	18	62	31	13	82	14	429	174	85		34	38	25	13	8	83	79	.512
1999	Cardinals	NL	161	138	.47	264	32	28	50	41	13	96	14	454	182	103		30	38	20	18	11	75	86	.466
2000	Cardinals	NL	162	137	.53	240	35	25	40	31	11	63	18	386	138	107		34	28	21	7	6	95	67	.586
2001	Cardinals	NL	162	117	.47	256	26	13	46	36	7	140	7	485	126	102		25	36	21	15	4	93	69	.574
2002	Cardinals	NL	162	117	.52	340	27	41	58	33	23	110	6	472	128	106	75	13	39	25	14	8	97	65	.599
2003	Cardinals	NL	162	126	.50	352	28	51	38	49	36	113	9	460	114	108	56	9	36	28	8	2	85	77	.525
2004	Cardinals	NL	162	119	.53	275	25	69	30	48	31	120	16	469	158	88	158	9	24	17	7	4	105	57	.648
2005	Cardinals	NL	162	138	.55	270	25	48	40	38	22	88	4	436	119	92	153	9	27	16	11	7	100	62	.617
2006	Cardinals	NL	161	131	.56	272	11	53	50	34	21	95	6	469	91	86	123	13	35	21	14	3	83	78	.516
2007	Cardinals	NL	162	148	.60	317	19	37	46	44	8	102	5	516	89	85	120	23	25	10	15	11	78	84	.481
2008	Cardinals	NL	162	140	.64	275	26	57	52	40	16	101	11	506	105	87	114	18	21	13	8	1	86	76	.531
2009	Cardinals	NL	162	126	.52	289	12	51	55	38	17	102	8	481	106	93	91	17	23	15	8	1	91	71	.562
2010	Cardinals	NL	162	135	.55	292	16	28	52	40	16	80	5	455	120	87	151	22	32	17	15	8	86	76	.531
2011	Cardinals	NL	162	126	.57	262	36	86	47	44	20	94	8	468	96	101	179	17	44	23	21	14	90	72	.556
	162-Game Average			132	.54	268	25	38	46	40	18	95	9	453	140	91	122	27	33	21	12	6	87	75	.537

Tom Lawless

Year	Team	Lg	G	LINEUPS		SUBSTITUTION			PITCHER USAGE						TACTICS				INTENTIONAL BB				RESULTS		
				LUp	PL%	PH	PR	DS	Quick	Slow	LO	RCD	LS	Rel	SBA	SacA	RM	PO	#	Good	NG	Bomb	W	L	Pct
2014	Astros	AL	24	23	.64	18	6	9	8	3	5	7	1	67	39	9	35	3	6	2	4	1	11	13	.458
	162-Game Average			155	.64	122	41	61	54	20	34	47	7	452	263	61	236	20	41	14	27	7	74	88	.457

Jim Leyland

Year	Team	Lg	G	LINEUPS		SUBSTITUTION			PITCHER USAGE						TACTICS				INTENTIONAL BB				RESULTS		
				LUp	PL%	PH	PR	DS	Quick	Slow	LO	RCD	LS	Rel	SBA	SacA	RM	PO	#	Good	NG	Bomb	W	L	Pct
1994	Pirates	NL	114	94	.56	170	16	13	12	9	1	48	4	285	78	48		38	52	29	23	15	53	61	.465
1995	Pirates	NL	144	124	.56	282	8	4	13	12	11	71	4	391	139	69		51	50	30	20	10	58	86	.403
1996	Pirates	NL	162	117	.53	299	18	14	27	8	11	60	11	422	175	101		46	50	23	27	13	73	89	.451
1997	Marlins	NL	162	105	.59	258	36	31	21	12	18	65	2	404	173	91		38	41	25	16	9	92	70	.568
1998	Marlins	NL	162	96	.59	277	13	15	18	24	31	73	8	420	172	91		31	61	36	25	11	54	108	.333
1999	Rockies	NL	162	124	.56	294	11	12	11	29	21	72	5	421	113	88		11	46	24	22	14	72	90	.444
2006	Tigers	AL	162	120	.53	81	34	38	52	32	16	52	3	390	100	57	128	9	35	23	12	9	95	67	.586
2007	Tigers	AL	162	108	.53	77	31	49	40	43	14	70	5	443	133	35	123	20	41	24	17	13	88	74	.543
2008	Tigers	AL	162	131	.56	66	25	50	29	47	20	72	4	420	94	40	114	10	63	37	26	13	74	88	.457
2009	Tigers	AL	163	126	.55	125	52	50	47	47	38	86	3	439	105	60	132	19	42	26	16	6	86	77	.528
2010	Tigers	AL	162	129	.58	130	11	47	36	54	45	70	6	416	99	54	174	31	29	14	15	4	81	81	.500
2011	Tigers	AL	162	127	.63	86	42	87	43	39	39	84	1	421	69	62	172	7	34	17	17	10	95	67	.586
2012	Tigers	AL	162	121	.58	76	33	62	38	41	37	103	4	420	82	46	151	14	35	21	14	7	88	74	.543
2013	Tigers	AL	162	109	.61	105	40	34	25	48	50	77	6	428	55	42	180	6	29	16	13	8	93	69	.574
	162-Game Average			120	.57	171	27	37	31	33	26	74	5	422	117	65	147	24	45	25	19	11	81	81	.500

Joe Maddon

Year	Team	Lg	G	LUp	PL%	PH	PR	DS	Quick	Slow	LO	RCD	LS	Rel	SBA	SacA	RM	PO	#	Good	NG	Bomb	W	L	Pct
				LINEUPS		SUBSTITUTION			PITCHER USAGE						TACTICS				INTENTIONAL BB				RESULTS		
1996	Angels	AL	22	19	.64	21	5	0	7	6	6	10	3	48	11	20		6	4	3	1	1	8	14	.364
1998	Angels	AL	8	4	.57	2	4	0	1	5	3	5	3	12	2	7		0	1	0	1	0	6	2	.750
1999	Angels	AL	29	19	.58	29	4	1	6	0	4	20	0	85	23	12		7	3	1	2	1	19	10	.655
2006	Devil Rays	AL	162	145	.54	81	26	51	41	39	16	79	10	484	186	51	132	48	39	19	20	13	61	101	.377
2007	Devil Rays	AL	162	122	.53	80	19	16	31	56	19	113	1	483	179	40	118	50	31	18	13	4	66	96	.407
2008	Rays	AL	162	115	.69	133	16	39	48	37	14	112	7	448	192	31	113	26	29	15	14	8	97	65	.599
2009	Rays	AL	162	123	.66	140	21	18	28	51	23	139	3	510	255	29	99	15	22	10	12	7	84	78	.519
2010	Rays	AL	162	129	.67	174	31	18	41	34	26	135	2	491	219	45	166	12	34	28	6	3	96	66	.593
2011	Rays	AL	162	130	.67	137	16	31	34	36	47	112	6	438	217	42	187	4	38	23	15	4	91	71	.562
2012	Rays	AL	162	151	.62	156	37	52	43	38	33	123	3	472	178	40	181	7	35	25	10	6	90	72	.556
2013	Rays	AL	163	147	.64	193	27	56	52	38	16	111	6	485	111	26	117	6	38	21	17	11	92	71	.564
2014	Rays	AL	162	130	.58	171	23	15	44	35	26	110	3	494	90	54	143	2	27	20	7	3	77	85	.475
162-Game Average				132	.62	141	24	32	40	40	25	114	5	471	177	42	139	20	32	20	13	7	84	78	.519

Charlie Manuel

Year	Team	Lg	G	LUp	PL%	PH	PR	DS	Quick	Slow	LO	RCD	LS	Rel	SBA	SacA	RM	PO	#	Good	NG	Bomb	W	L	Pct
				LINEUPS		SUBSTITUTION			PITCHER USAGE						TACTICS				INTENTIONAL BB				RESULTS		
2000	Indians	AL	162	102	.64	73	40	26	21	12	20	104	7	462	147	59		30	45	28	17	9	90	72	.556
2001	Indians	AL	162	114	.61	105	30	49	28	17	10	120	3	484	120	67		43	44	30	14	11	91	71	.562
2002	Indians	AL	86	67	.61	57	10	19	14	17	25	47	0	222	57	21	34	3	21	12	9	4	39	47	.453
2005	Phillies	NL	162	80	.64	265	36	19	42	28	13	119	6	442	143	86	76	11	51	35	16	9	88	74	.543
2006	Phillies	NL	162	81	.65	301	42	49	28	43	22	126	2	500	117	79	74	16	63	35	28	12	85	77	.525
2007	Phillies	NL	162	87	.64	264	56	75	40	40	19	128	6	498	157	84	90	30	62	41	21	16	89	73	.549
2008	Phillies	NL	162	77	.65	291	62	60	33	42	24	124	1	468	161	88	92	34	64	46	18	11	92	70	.568
2009	Phillies	NL	162	68	.67	283	20	16	32	55	32	107	3	459	147	74	65	3	31	19	12	3	93	69	.574
2010	Phillies	NL	162	94	.64	276	17	19	37	50	39	114	1	451	129	64	120	3	42	27	15	6	97	65	.599
2011	Phillies	NL	162	105	.69	264	26	22	49	39	48	74	1	394	120	80	141	5	41	31	10	5	102	60	.630
2012	Phillies	NL	162	131	.68	281	22	48	35	56	30	93	5	440	139	91	125	6	33	21	12	5	81	81	.500
2013	Phillies	NL	120	90	.61	196	29	29	20	38	16	73	1	331	88	53	90	1	23	13	10	7	53	67	.442
162-Game Average				97	.65	236	35	38	34	39	26	109	3	457	135	75	98	16	46	30	16	9	89	73	.549

Mike Matheny

Year	Team	Lg	G	LUp	PL%	PH	PR	DS	Quick	Slow	LO	RCD	LS	Rel	SBA	SacA	RM	PO	#	Good	NG	Bomb	W	L	Pct
				LINEUPS		SUBSTITUTION			PITCHER USAGE						TACTICS				INTENTIONAL BB				RESULTS		
2012	Cardinals	NL	162	122	.62	286	37	33	53	37	8	118	5	506	128	95	144	16	28	13	15	7	88	74	.543
2013	Cardinals	NL	162	89	.56	237	30	41	42	49	25	114	4	483	67	73	125	6	26	20	6	6	97	65	.599
2014	Cardinals	NL	162	119	.56	258	21	35	53	32	17	119	5	485	89	81	155	10	35	20	15	7	90	72	.556
162-Game Average				110	.58	260	29	36	49	39	17	117	5	491	95	83	141	11	30	18	12	7	92	70	.568

Don Mattingly

Year	Team	Lg	G	LUp	PL%	PH	PR	DS	Quick	Slow	LO	RCD	LS	Rel	SBA	SacA	RM	PO	#	Good	NG	Bomb	W	L	Pct
				LINEUPS		SUBSTITUTION			PITCHER USAGE						TACTICS				INTENTIONAL BB				RESULTS		
2011	Dodgers	NL	161	140	.57	233	29	44	45	40	30	86	1	461	166	93	181	13	48	27	21	12	82	79	.509
2012	Dodgers	NL	162	127	.59	247	22	43	51	39	20	118	2	506	148	105	153	8	62	38	24	15	86	76	.531
2013	Dodgers	NL	162	145	.55	210	18	47	40	30	18	118	3	504	106	99	131	10	44	28	16	7	92	70	.568
2014	Dodgers	NL	162	124	.51	237	17	62	49	31	15	107	5	496	188	67	168	2	35	20	15	8	94	68	.580
162-Game Average				134	.56	232	22	49	46	35	21	107	3	493	152	91	158	8	47	28	19	11	89	73	.549

Lloyd McClendon

Year	Team	Lg	G	LUp	PL%	PH	PR	DS	Quick	Slow	LO	RCD	LS	Rel	SBA	SacA	RM	PO	#	Good	NG	Bomb	W	L	Pct
				LINEUPS		SUBSTITUTION			PITCHER USAGE						TACTICS				INTENTIONAL BB				RESULTS		
2001	Pirates	NL	162	131	.51	255	17	32	45	38	2	85	5	410	166	83		52	74	44	30	19	62	100	.383
2002	Pirates	NL	161	121	.45	261	38	65	62	30	3	98	2	458	135	93	73	67	93	61	32	22	72	89	.447
2003	Pirates	NL	162	114	.57	315	27	59	46	35	27	114	10	457	123	99	55	73	58	34	24	13	75	87	.463
2004	Pirates	NL	161	114	.50	278	13	58	50	40	26	133	1	464	103	100	91	61	64	37	27	16	72	89	.447
2005	Pirates	NL	136	123	.53	218	8	19	37	34	15	86	5	357	84	62	83	37	60	32	28	16	55	81	.404
2014	Mariners	AL	162	141	.69	93	48	33	61	21	11	87	3	497	138	48	187	30	36	21	15	9	87	75	.537
162-Game Average				128	.54	244	26	46	52	34	14	103	4	454	129	83	101	55	66	39	27	16	73	89	.451

Jack McKeon

Year	Team	Lg	G	LUp	PL%	PH	PR	DS	Quick	Slow	LO	RCD	LS	Rel	SBA	SacA	RM	PO	#	Good	NG	Bomb	W	L	Pct
				LINEUPS		SUBSTITUTION			PITCHER USAGE						TACTICS				INTENTIONAL BB				RESULTS		
1997	Reds	NL	63	50	.46	102	18	7	23	11	5	44	3	154	79	42		18	16	6	10	7	33	30	.524
1998	Reds	NL	162	132	.55	288	30	25	49	25	10	107	20	366	137	98		7	42	29	13	8	77	85	.475
1999	Reds	NL	163	95	.50	251	30	38	58	23	9	93	28	381	218	88		14	46	30	16	5	96	67	.589

Year	Team	Lg	G	LUp	PL%	PH	PR	DS	Quick	Slow	LO	RCD	LS	Rel	SBA	SacA	RM	PO	#	Good	NG	Bomb	W	L	Pct
2000	Reds	NL	163	117	.51	270	31	41	52	27	10	96	24	387	138	82		24	53	36	17	10	85	77	.525
2003	Marlins	NL	124	57	.43	171	26	21	32	35	3̄3̄	63	6	280	150	92	41	17	28	16	12	10	75	49	.605
2004	Marlins	NL	162	90	.48	224	27	34	42	37	20	95	12	404	139	104	96	19	61	40	21	13	83	79	.512
2005	Marlins	NL	162	82	.43	246	24	36	44	35	36	103	7	449	134	106	106	16	57	37	20	10	83	79	.512
2011	Marlins	NL	90	65	.53	146	22	16	29	15	13	63	0	278	87	74	67	10	43	25	18	10	40	50	.444
162-Game Average				102	.49	253	31	32	49	31	20	99	15	402	161	102	93	19	52	33	19	11	85	77	.525

John McLaren

Year	Team	Lg	G	LUp	PL%	PH	PR	DS	Quick	Slow	LO	RCD	LS	Rel	SBA	SacA	RM	PO	#	Good	NG	Bomb	W	L	Pct
2007	Mariners	AL	84	52	.48	55	40	18	17	23	19	49	6	247	56	20	76	18	19	10	9	5	43	41	.512
2008	Mariners	AL	72	48	.50	31	16	4	17	24	9	45	1	197	65	17	63	11	12	6	6	5	25	47	.347
2011	Nationals	NL	3	3	.56	2	0	1	1	0	2	3	0	12	6	2	8	1	2	1	1	0	2	1	.667
162-Game Average				105	.49	90	57	23	36	48	31	99	7	465	129	40	150	31	34	17	16	10	71	91	.438

Bob Melvin

Year	Team	Lg	G	LUp	PL%	PH	PR	DS	Quick	Slow	LO	RCD	LS	Rel	SBA	SacA	RM	PO	#	Good	NG	Bomb	W	L	Pct
2003	Mariners	AL	162	81	.62	81	63	33	27	46	43	56	6	366	145	44	37	5	24	14	10	4	93	69	.574
2004	Mariners	AL	162	151	.59	109	66	26	26	63	43	82	5	414	152	56	123	24	32	18	14	8	63	99	.389
2005	Diamondbacks	NL	162	120	.68	310	26	38	26	56	36	123	11	458	93	93	101	30	43	27	16	9	77	85	.475
2006	Diamondbacks	NL	162	114	.72	278	11	35	37	42	15	86	0	461	106	83	61	30	44	28	16	8	76	86	.469
2007	Diamondbacks	NL	162	146	.57	243	11	61	35	42	31	96	2	469	133	74	70	25	38	30	8	4	90	72	.556
2008	Diamondbacks	NL	162	134	.57	263	27	30	41	39	16	102	0	444	81	87	79	28	41	27	14	9	82	80	.506
2009	Diamondbacks	NL	29	29	.62	47	6	8	7	4	3	17	0	91	29	17	13	3	3	1	2	2	12	17	.414
2011	Athletics	AL	99	87	.71	33	13	17	24	23	18	59	2	283	103	34	87	23	9	5	4	3	47	52	.475
2012	Athletics	AL	162	132	.71	111	17	18	63	29	5	93	2	462	154	41	116	30	34	21	13	6	94	68	.580
2013	Athletics	AL	162	133	.77	166	14	35	48	28	7	84	7	447	102	32	74	8	23	18	5	3	96	66	.593
2014	Athletics	AL	162	137	.77	187	38	44	45	30	11	101	2	441	103	28	91	16	28	20	8	5	88	74	.543
162-Game Average				132	.67	187	30	35	39	41	23	92	4	443	123	60	87	23	33	21	11	6	84	78	.519

Brad Mills

Year	Team	Lg	G	LUp	PL%	PH	PR	DS	Quick	Slow	LO	RCD	LS	Rel	SBA	SacA	RM	PO	#	Good	NG	Bomb	W	L	Pct
2010	Astros	NL	162	128	.51	280	17	51	29	52	41	121	1	507	136	90	122	8	39	30	9	5	76	86	.469
2011	Astros	NL	162	121	.49	284	31	31	25	65	38	125	2	503	151	95	135	11	59	38	21	9	56	106	.346
2012	Astros	NL	121	103	.60	181	22	22	20	49	12	102	0	391	117	54	115	10	25	12	13	6	39	82	.322
162-Game Average				128	.53	271	25	38	27	60	33	127	1	510	147	87	135	11	45	29	16	7	62	100	.383

Bo Porter

Year	Team	Lg	G	LUp	PL%	PH	PR	DS	Quick	Slow	LO	RCD	LS	Rel	SBA	SacA	RM	PO	#	Good	NG	Bomb	W	L	Pct
2013	Astros	AL	162	138	.60	107	40	26	48	43	14	84	6	448	171	51	155	22	32	19	13	8	51	111	.315
2014	Astros	AL	138	120	.66	69	21	15	28	42	16	74	2	371	120	22	127	18	26	13	13	6	59	79	.428
162-Game Average				139	.63	95	33	22	41	46	16	85	4	442	157	39	152	22	31	17	14	8	59	103	.364

Bryan Price

Year	Team	Lg	G	LUp	PL%	PH	PR	DS	Quick	Slow	LO	RCD	LS	Rel	SBA	SacA	RM	PO	#	Good	NG	Bomb	W	L	Pct
2014	Reds	NL	162	130	.54	220	21	33	35	37	26	82	3	428	174	87	135	9	33	21	12	5	76	86	.469
162-Game Average				130	.54	220	21	33	35	37	26	82	3	428	174	87	135	9	33	21	12	5	76	86	.469

Mike Quade

Year	Team	Lg	G	LUp	PL%	PH	PR	DS	Quick	Slow	LO	RCD	LS	Rel	SBA	SacA	RM	PO	#	Good	NG	Bomb	W	L	Pct
2010	Cubs	NL	37	32	.52	44	1	15	10	11	6	20	3	111	18	14	16	4	9	8	1	0	24	13	.649
2011	Cubs	NL	162	125	.50	259	30	66	30	56	35	125	4	495	92	78	113	23	45	32	13	9	71	91	.438
162-Game Average				128	.50	247	25	66	33	55	33	118	6	493	90	75	105	22	44	33	11	7	77	85	.475

Mike Redmond

Year	Team	Lg	G	LUp	PL%	PH	PR	DS	Quick	Slow	LO	RCD	LS	Rel	SBA	SacA	RM	PO	#	Good	NG	Bomb	W	L	Pct
2013	Marlins	NL	162	132	.52	240	8	9	47	30	4	88	1	471	107	81	124	2	58	42	16	7	62	**100**	.383
2014	Marlins	NL	162	102	.50	279	9	14	51	37	8	107	4	487	79	81	100	8	35	23	12	7	77	85	.475
162-Game Average				117	.51	260	9	12	49	34	6	98	3	479	93	81	112	5	47	33	14	7	70	93	.429

Rick Renteria

Year	Team	Lg	G	LUp	PL%	PH	PR	DS	Quick	Slow	LO	RCD	LS	Rel	SBA	SacA	RM	PO	#	Good	NG	Bomb	W	L	Pct
2014	Cubs	NL	162	137	.63	275	9	20	50	42	12	103	1	537	105	77	106	5	37	23	14	8	73	89	.451
162-Game Average				137	.63	275	9	20	50	42	12	103	1	537	105	77	106	5	37	23	14	8	73	89	.451

Jim Riggleman

Year	Team	Lg	G	LUp	PL%	PH	PR	DS	Quick	Slow	LO	RCD	LS	Rel	SBA	SacA	RM	PO	#	Good	NG	Bomb	W	L	Pct
1994	Padres	NL	117	93	.63	184	28	19	11	5	3	53	10	273	116	80		52	62	34	28	11	47	70	.402
1995	Cubs	NL	144	92	.56	196	9	30	15	8	13	119	12	414	142	90		53	68	45	23	12	73	71	.507
1996	Cubs	NL	162	87	.54	326	34	21	17	11	7	114	11	439	158	79		65	55	33	22	10	76	86	.469
1997	Cubs	NL	162	127	.50	280	40	44	13	5	2	113	9	441	176	103		74	51	38	13	6	68	94	.420
1998	Cubs	NL	163	104	.60	273	26	35	16	14	20	133	6	449	109	89		26	48	22	26	15	90	73	.552
1999	Cubs	NL	162	122	.61	312	25	30	16	19	8	105	4	441	104	94		20	48	21	27	15	67	95	.414
2008	Mariners	AL	90	70	.60	75	30	22	21	25	19	50	4	272	57	27	88	10	25	17	8	3	36	54	.400
2009	Nationals	NL	75	60	.51	115	15	33	24	16	4	63	6	250	59	44	36	8	33	17	16	8	33	42	.440
2010	Nationals	NL	162	131	.58	271	33	67	50	32	9	101	5	494	151	101	158	13	57	37	20	10	69	93	.426
2011	Nationals	NL	75	59	.58	105	22	23	24	15	2	54	5	220	80	47	89	3	22	16	6	3	38	37	.507
162-Game Average				117	.57	264	32	40	26	19	11	112	9	456	142	93	150	40	58	35	23	11	74	88	.457

Edwin Rodriguez

Year	Team	Lg	G	LUp	PL%	PH	PR	DS	Quick	Slow	LO	RCD	LS	Rel	SBA	SacA	RM	PO	#	Good	NG	Bomb	W	L	Pct
2010	Marlins	NL	92	60	.42	152	12	20	22	23	13	72	1	288	62	37	69	9	24	17	7	3	46	46	.500
2011	Marlins	NL	71	50	.51	114	10	10	14	17	14	49	0	227	49	47	62	5	28	19	9	4	32	39	.451
162-Game Average				109	.46	264	22	30	36	40	27	120	1	512	110	83	130	14	52	36	16	7	78	84	.481

Ron Roenicke

Year	Team	Lg	G	LUp	PL%	PH	PR	DS	Quick	Slow	LO	RCD	LS	Rel	SBA	SacA	RM	PO	#	Good	NG	Bomb	W	L	Pct
2011	Brewers	NL	162	105	.45	260	31	36	36	43	31	92	1	434	125	**104**	141	14	16	9	7	4	96	66	.593
2012	Brewers	NL	162	110	.45	322	20	25	36	50	23	**149**	1	512	197	91	152	8	20	12	8	2	83	79	.512
2013	Brewers	NL	162	125	.47	275	15	34	39	47	7	96	2	501	**192**	86	157	6	29	22	7	6	74	88	.457
2014	Brewers	NL	162	115	.44	253	19	37	33	48	12	114	1	478	145	**92**	127	11	20	16	4	4	82	80	.506
162-Game Average				114	.45	278	21	33	36	47	18	113	1	481	165	93	144	10	21	15	7	4	84	78	.519

Ryne Sandberg

Year	Team	Lg	G	LUp	PL%	PH	PR	DS	Quick	Slow	LO	RCD	LS	Rel	SBA	SacA	RM	PO	#	Good	NG	Bomb	W	L	Pct
2013	Phillies	NL	42	34	.66	66	4	6	6	12	7	18	0	135	14	15	26	0	10	6	4	4	20	22	.476
2014	Phillies	NL	162	105	.70	259	20	31	37	**62**	**30**	111	0	461	135	72	140	1	**43**	**31**	12	6	73	89	.451
162-Game Average				110	.70	250	19	29	34	59	29	102	0	473	118	69	132	1	42	29	13	8	74	88	.457

Mike Scioscia

Year	Team	Lg	G	LUp	PL%	PH	PR	DS	Quick	Slow	LO	RCD	LS	Rel	SBA	SacA	RM	PO	#	Good	NG	Bomb	W	L	Pct
2000	Angels	AL	162	75	.62	110	41	4	56	42	6	95	9	441	145	63		40	44	28	16	7	82	80	.506
2001	Angels	AL	162	130	.62	118	30	8	29	41	5	81	9	384	168	66		50	47	22	25	12	75	87	.463
2002	Angels	AL	162	102	.64	**162**	57	26	36	33	34	88	8	400	168	62	52	30	24	15	9	5	99	63	.611
2003	Angels	AL	162	130	.64	134	54	40	50	48	11	60	4	375	190	64	79	25	38	26	12	3	77	85	.475
2004	Angels	AL	162	126	.57	94	32	44	37	40	22	61	11	343	189	70	**229**	33	27	18	9	3	92	70	.568
2005	Angels	AL	162	124	.65	92	37	37	47	37	24	88	9	379	218	58	160	43	24	15	9	4	95	67	.586
2006	Angels	AL	162	114	.63	103	45	38	38	49	21	99	9	380	205	37	**166**	22	27	18	9	6	89	73	.549
2007	Angels	AL	162	127	.66	103	26	19	39	40	14	94	4	396	**194**	41	**166**	44	22	12	10	5	94	68	.580
2008	Angels	AL	162	125	.63	74	30	36	37	48	**21**	87	1	383	177	39	151	31	32	22	10	6	**100**	62	.617
2009	Angels	AL	162	123	.69	80	26	37	47	47	33	91	1	434	211	55	**137**	40	35	22	13	6	97	65	.599
2010	Angels	AL	162	133	.59	96	31	23	41	52	48	76	0	410	156	58	**223**	28	33	17	16	8	80	82	.494
2011	Angels	AL	162	129	.64	88	14	24	31	37	**55**	57	1	386	187	**69**	**212**	46	34	25	9	5	86	76	.531

Year	Team	Lg	G	LINEUPS		SUBSTITUTION			PITCHER USAGE						TACTICS				INTENTIONAL BB				RESULTS		
				LUp	PL%	PH	PR	DS	Quick	Slow	LO	RCD	LS	Rel	SBA	SacA	RM	PO	#	Good	NG	Bomb	W	L	Pct
2012	Angels	AL	162	121	.55	73	33	47	37	47	31	96	8	444	167	61	236	33	20	11	9	7	89	73	.549
2013	Angels	AL	162	118	.56	88	26	39	31	44	29	130	8	496	116	48	205	41	36	19	17	11	78	84	.481
2014	Angels	AL	162	125	.58	123	46	59	49	39	22	141	0	543	120	35	189	14	41	31	10	5	98	64	.605
	162-Game Average			120	.62	103	35	32	40	43	25	90	5	413	174	55	170	35	32	20	12	6	89	73	.549

Buck Showalter

Year	Team	Lg	G	LINEUPS		SUBSTITUTION			PITCHER USAGE						TACTICS				INTENTIONAL BB				RESULTS		
				LUp	PL%	PH	PR	DS	Quick	Slow	LO	RCD	LS	Rel	SBA	SacA	RM	PO	#	Good	NG	Bomb	W	L	Pct
1994	Yankees	AL	113	79	.59	95	31	3	24	30	0	38	7	241	95	34		22	24	13	11	4	70	43	.619
1995	Yankees	AL	145	107	.68	124	30	20	29	42	37	57	6	302	80	27		29	21	14	7	1	79	65	.549
1998	Diamondbacks	NL	162	124	.62	252	17	15	34	40	7	43	6	368	111	68		13	32	16	16	9	65	97	.401
1999	Diamondbacks	NL	162	97	.63	220	20	17	37	48	25	74	3	382	176	75		15	48	29	19	8	100	62	.617
2000	Diamondbacks	NL	162	99	.60	250	32	11	46	26	18	74	12	390	141	89		10	53	28	25	16	85	77	.525
2003	Rangers	AL	162	133	.61	88	51	41	35	33	12	93	7	494	90	35	80	12	45	24	21	14	71	91	.438
2004	Rangers	AL	162	120	.64	86	15	24	53	30	12	82	10	468	105	30	88	5	29	19	10	3	89	73	.549
2005	Rangers	AL	162	98	.59	57	22	11	42	39	17	79	8	454	82	11	103	5	31	10	21	16	79	83	.488
2006	Rangers	AL	162	95	.57	39	34	22	41	27	10	85	4	489	77	30	72	8	18	11	7	5	80	82	.494
2010	Orioles	AL	57	42	.74	20	11	13	23	9	10	24	1	144	38	13	31	1	10	9	1	1	34	23	.596
2011	Orioles	AL	162	117	.53	60	39	27	43	40	14	61	2	478	106	32	133	6	42	31	11	5	69	93	.426
2012	Orioles	AL	162	120	.62	78	28	31	37	42	10	88	0	492	87	46	145	6	36	25	11	5	93	69	.574
2013	Orioles	AL	162	100	.65	90	23	21	31	39	19	84	4	473	108	37	104	4	32	11	21	13	85	77	.525
2014	Orioles	AL	162	120	.49	77	29	51	37	34	17	89	2	479	64	50	101	10	25	16	9	4	96	66	.593
	162-Game Average			112	.61	119	30	24	40	37	16	75	6	437	105	45	103	11	34	20	15	8	85	77	.525

Dale Sveum

Year	Team	Lg	G	LINEUPS		SUBSTITUTION			PITCHER USAGE						TACTICS				INTENTIONAL BB				RESULTS		
				LUp	PL%	PH	PR	DS	Quick	Slow	LO	RCD	LS	Rel	SBA	SacA	RM	PO	#	Good	NG	Bomb	W	L	Pct
2008	Brewers	NL	12	3	.48	32	2	1	7	2	1	12	0	46	5	13	6	1	2	1	1	0	7	5	.583
2012	Cubs	NL	162	101	.60	277	23	44	46	48	8	117	1	493	139	61	153	13	36	24	12	8	61	101	.377
2013	Cubs	NL	162	107	.60	277	12	17	42	47	19	112	1	489	95	58	122	8	43	29	14	8	66	96	.407
	162-Game Average			102	.60	283	18	30	46	47	14	116	1	496	115	64	135	11	39	26	13	8	65	97	.401

Jim Tracy

Year	Team	Lg	G	LINEUPS		SUBSTITUTION			PITCHER USAGE						TACTICS				INTENTIONAL BB				RESULTS		
				LUp	PL%	PH	PR	DS	Quick	Slow	LO	RCD	LS	Rel	SBA	SacA	RM	PO	#	Good	NG	Bomb	W	L	Pct
2001	Dodgers	NL	162	111	.50	264	34	20	46	42	8	84	4	409	131	81		10	37	19	18	9	86	76	.531
2002	Dodgers	NL	162	102	.52	317	39	37	49	36	21	118	9	423	133	81	46	18	45	31	14	5	92	70	.568
2003	Dodgers	NL	162	103	.64	269	22	64	52	29	22	148	11	438	116	97	32	10	35	23	12	8	85	77	.525
2004	Dodgers	NL	162	94	.70	295	25	19	49	34	16	128	16	459	143	81	93	7	47	32	15	8	93	69	.574
2005	Dodgers	NL	162	129	.64	303	31	37	44	40	20	126	2	459	93	76	97	17	34	21	13	6	71	91	.438
2006	Pirates	NL	162	121	.43	264	22	22	37	43	12	156	3	505	91	80	75	12	62	39	23	15	67	95	.414
2007	Pirates	NL	162	124	.49	240	12	26	33	40	13	113	0	495	98	80	90	12	55	30	25	11	68	94	.420
2009	Rockies	NL	116	87	.63	186	25	28	28	27	27	83	3	349	116	73	82	9	40	28	12	7	74	42	.638
2010	Rockies	NL	162	135	.65	257	30	41	38	40	34	128	0	513	141	64	135	11	54	34	20	10	83	79	.512
2011	Rockies	NL	162	134	.62	252	21	30	35	47	21	129	1	517	160	94	231	18	47	27	20	11	73	89	.451
2012	Rockies	NL	162	140	.55	264	33	33	74	33	6	111	2	575	140	88	165	18	61	36	25	12	64	98	.395
	162-Game Average			119	.58	272	27	33	45	38	19	124	5	480	127	84	108	13	48	30	18	10	80	82	.494

Alan Trammell

Year	Team	Lg	G	LINEUPS		SUBSTITUTION			PITCHER USAGE						TACTICS				INTENTIONAL BB				RESULTS		
				LUp	PL%	PH	PR	DS	Quick	Slow	LO	RCD	LS	Rel	SBA	SacA	RM	PO	#	Good	NG	Bomb	W	L	Pct
2003	Tigers	AL	162	129	.72	138	29	14	48	39	15	73	14	451	161	92	66	28	35	22	13	7	43	119	.265
2004	Tigers	AL	162	131	.65	105	29	19	47	36	26	79	6	432	136	62	99	9	33	16	17	10	72	90	.444
2005	Tigers	AL	162	119	.49	75	26	16	35	39	13	87	2	425	94	56	129	11	33	21	12	7	71	91	.438
2014	Diamondbacks	NL	3	3	.63	6	2	0	1	0	0	1	0	9	2	1	3	0	1	1	0	0	1	2	.333
	162-Game Average			127	.62	107	28	16	43	38	18	80	7	436	130	70	98	16	34	20	14	8	62	100	.383

Bobby Valentine

Year	Team	Lg	G	LINEUPS		SUBSTITUTION			PITCHER USAGE						TACTICS				INTENTIONAL BB				RESULTS		
				LUp	PL%	PH	PR	DS	Quick	Slow	LO	RCD	LS	Rel	SBA	SacA	RM	PO	#	Good	NG	Bomb	W	L	Pct
1996	Mets	NL	31	28	.67	88	7	3	7	4	1	11	1	75	20	27	0	2	14	8	6	2	12	19	.387
1997	Mets	NL	162	131	.65	313	39	23	52	30	8	70	11	376	171	102	0	27	43	28	15	6	88	74	.543
1998	Mets	NL	162	124	.64	305	42	34	45	36	23	80	7	399	108	157	0	50	59	42	17	10	88	74	.543
1999	Mets	NL	163	76	.57	323	43	26	56	24	14	108	8	439	211	109	0	43	53	35	18	9	97	66	.595
2000	Mets	NL	162	118	.34	299	38	32	37	37	18	90	7	411	112	118	0	0	42	27	15	7	94	68	.580
2001	Mets	NL	162	143	.43	298	33	34	38	40	7	83	6	397	114	88	0	0	60	30	30	16	82	80	.506

Year	Team	Lg	G	LUp	PL%	PH	PR	DS	Quick	Slow	LO	RCD	LS	Rel	SBA	SacA	RM	PO	# Good	NG	Bomb	W	L	Pct
2002	Mets	NL	161	122	.62	323	48	32	15	42	29	87	2	451	129	98	81	41	75	49	26	13	75	86	.466
2012	Red Sox	AL	162	143	.61	107	30	25	34	52	21	91	6	489	128	44	148	18	33	22	11	5	69	93	.426
	162-Game Average			125	.61	243	45	14	38	46	31	79	14	369	158	90	115	25	45	27	18	10	82	80	.506

Robin Ventura

Year	Team	Lg	G	LUp	PL%	PH	PR	DS	Quick	Slow	LO	RCD	LS	Rel	SBA	SacA	RM	PO	# Good	NG	Bomb	W	L	Pct
2012	White Sox	AL	162	75	.48	72	64	23	39	44	34	104	4	466	152	42	174	13	29	17	12	7	85	77	.525
2013	White Sox	AL	162	116	.47	76	47	33	24	52	38	133	0	470	147	24	132	15	24	12	12	4	63	99	.389
2014	White Sox	AL	162	115	.55	85	49	44	26	59	29	96	5	453	121	26	150	28	42	25	17	5	73	89	.451
	162-Game Average			102	.50	78	53	33	30	52	34	111	3	463	140	31	152	19	32	18	14	5	74	88	.457

Ron Washington

Year	Team	Lg	G	LUp	PL%	PH	PR	DS	Quick	Slow	LO	RCD	LS	Rel	SBA	SacA	RM	PO	# Good	NG	Bomb	W	L	Pct
2007	Rangers	AL	162	139	.60	89	30	53	47	46	4	78	9	467	113	76	67	13	38	19	19	11	75	87	.463
2008	Rangers	AL	162	129	.64	118	16	14	31	53	11	85	3	458	106	53	74	20	44	19	25	20	79	83	.488
2009	Rangers	AL	162	123	.55	48	11	11	39	47	28	80	9	436	185	44	80	5	14	9	5	3	87	75	.537
2010	Rangers	AL	162	112	.52	86	39	31	46	42	35	110	4	481	171	68	160	10	24	15	9	0	90	72	.556
2011	Rangers	AL	162	106	.48	66	18	23	43	39	40	76	2	417	188	52	182	3	21	12	9	6	96	66	.593
2012	Rangers	AL	162	79	.47	94	25	37	30	48	33	91	0	428	135	46	155	22	15	10	5	5	93	69	.574
2013	Rangers	AL	163	113	.60	142	23	19	48	41	28	105	3	475	195	53	169	11	35	24	11	6	91	72	.558
2014	Rangers	AL	140	109	.54	96	16	16	35	51	11	65	0	400	135	43	155	6	34	25	9	4	53	87	.379
	162-Game Average			116	.55	94	23	26	41	47	24	88	4	453	156	55	132	11	29	17	12	7	84	78	.519

Eric Wedge

Year	Team	Lg	G	LUp	PL%	PH	PR	DS	Quick	Slow	LO	RCD	LS	Rel	SBA	SacA	RM	PO	# Good	NG	Bomb	W	L	Pct
2003	Indians	AL	162	145	.67	117	43	27	47	34	18	89	5	428	147	67	54	12	37	22	15	8	68	94	.420
2004	Indians	AL	162	114	.72	91	34	20	44	38	22	121	0	479	149	57	129	28	47	26	21	18	80	82	.494
2005	Indians	AL	162	111	.66	88	18	16	45	45	15	90	3	409	98	53	79	9	20	11	9	7	93	69	.574
2006	Indians	AL	162	111	.59	98	13	13	31	52	27	48	1	377	78	40	83	15	35	21	14	11	78	84	.481
2007	Indians	AL	162	117	.60	116	41	25	34	38	20	79	2	395	113	40	108	16	42	24	18	9	96	66	.593
2008	Indians	AL	162	136	.54	112	31	18	40	35	17	78	4	399	106	56	98	5	28	6	22	11	81	81	.500
2009	Indians	AL	162	148	.59	63	28	11	32	41	21	67	3	445	115	52	74	8	31	14	17	9	65	97	.401
2011	Mariners	AL	162	152	.68	52	30	22	39	45	30	50	1	351	165	43	161	7	27	20	7	6	67	95	.414
2012	Mariners	AL	162	141	.69	87	36	21	44	35	14	89	5	451	139	45	116	8	39	20	19	7	75	87	.463
2013	Mariners	AL	162	143	.70	78	36	33	50	36	8	82	2	448	72	43	97	3	48	19	29	12	71	91	.438
	162-Game Average			132	.65	90	31	21	41	40	19	79	3	418	118	50	100	11	35	18	17	10	77	85	.475

Walt Weiss

Year	Team	Lg	G	LUp	PL%	PH	PR	DS	Quick	Slow	LO	RCD	LS	Rel	SBA	SacA	RM	PO	# Good	NG	Bomb	W	L	Pct
2013	Rockies	NL	162	136	.56	260	18	32	50	42	0	96	2	503	144	80	149	15	52	28	24	7	74	88	.457
2014	Rockies	NL	162	134	.51	270	12	26	40	49	2	119	0	547	133	69	140	11	32	16	16	7	66	96	.407
	162-Game Average			135	.54	265	15	29	45	46	1	108	1	525	139	75	145	13	42	22	20	7	70	92	.432

Matt Williams

Year	Team	Lg	G	LUp	PL%	PH	PR	DS	Quick	Slow	LO	RCD	LS	Rel	SBA	SacA	RM	PO	# Good	NG	Bomb	W	L	Pct
2014	Nationals	NL	162	100	.56	248	17	33	62	33	11	67	1	458	124	87	91	3	26	15	11	6	96	66	.593
	162-Game Average			100	.56	248	17	33	62	33	11	67	1	458	124	87	91	3	26	15	11	6	96	66	.593

Ned Yost

Year	Team	Lg	G	LUp	PL%	PH	PR	DS	Quick	Slow	LO	RCD	LS	Rel	SBA	SacA	RM	PO	# Good	NG	Bomb	W	L	Pct
2003	Brewers	NL	162	97	.44	304	22	39	23	59	18	90	6	460	138	85	40	23	43	28	15	9	68	94	.420
2004	Brewers	NL	161	131	.60	283	25	20	39	41	27	63	2	423	178	79	108	8	27	16	11	8	67	94	.416
2005	Brewers	NL	162	99	.46	259	18	35	26	41	42	71	2	395	113	89	97	50	52	23	29	10	81	81	.500
2006	Brewers	NL	162	106	.48	238	12	14	33	44	18	77	4	427	108	80	82	16	34	14	20	12	75	87	.463
2007	Brewers	NL	162	109	.60	259	11	41	37	42	18	117	7	492	128	74	94	19	37	28	9	9	83	79	.512
2008	Brewers	NL	150	74	.48	217	5	16	37	39	23	69	5	399	141	61	105	31	30	17	13	7	83	67	.553
2010	Royals	AL	127	80	.57	56	25	6	22	39	20	65	0	332	127	40	128	18	25	16	9	5	55	72	.433
2011	Royals	AL	162	87	.58	36	28	16	42	42	21	56	7	420	211	65	203	19	42	27	15	5	71	91	.438
2012	Royals	AL	162	118	.57	60	34	15	48	37	10	108	1	500	170	37	149	25	44	29	15	11	72	90	.444

Year	Team	Lg	G	LUp	PL%	PH	PR	DS	Quick	Slow	LO	RCD	LS	Rel	SBA	SacA	RM	PO	#	Good	NG	Bomb	W	L	Pct
2013	Royals	AL	162	127	.60	79	**48**	39	43	44	21	72	2	427	185	48	168	25	21	12	9	5	86	76	.531
2014	Royals	AL	162	101	.52	51	**63**	46	37	51	26	93	1	451	**189**	45	159	3	14	7	7	3	89	73	.549
	162-Game Average			105	.54	172	27	27	36	45	23	82	3	442	158	66	125	22	34	20	14	8	78	84	.481

Categories of this record are Games Managed (G), Number of Different Lineups Used (LUp), the percentage of players who had the platoon advantage at the start of the game (PL%), Pinch Hitters Used (PH), Pinch Runners Used (PR), Defensive Substitutes Used (DS), Quick Hooks (Quick), Slow Hooks (Slow), Long Outings by Starting Pitchers (LO), Relievers Used on Consecutive Days (RCD), Long Saves (LS), Relievers Used (Rel), Stolen Base Attempts (SBA), Sacrifice Bunt Attempts (SacA), Runners Moving with the Pitch (RM), Pitchouts Ordered (PO), Intentional Walks Issued (#), Intentional Walks resulting in a Good Outcome (Good), Intentional Walks resulting Not in a Good Outcome (NG), Intentional Walks Blowing Up on the Manager (Bomb), Wins (W), Losses (L), and Winning Percentage (Pct).

2014 American League Managers

Manager	G	LINEUPS LUp	LINEUPS PL%	SUBSTITUTION PH	SUBSTITUTION PR	SUBSTITUTION DS	PITCHER USAGE Quick	PITCHER USAGE Slow	PITCHER USAGE LO	PITCHER USAGE RCD	PITCHER USAGE LS	PITCHER USAGE Rel	TACTICS SBA	TACTICS SacA	TACTICS RM	TACTICS PO	INTENTIONAL BB #	INTENTIONAL BB Good	INTENTIONAL BB NG	INTENTIONAL BB Bomb	RESULTS W	RESULTS L	RESULTS Pct
Brad Ausmus, Det	162	103	.51	79	43	44	28	55	**43**	99	1	473	147	32	144	13	34	17	17	5	90	72	.556
John Farrell, Bos	162	**145**	.55	101	24	17	29	53	28	107	1	493	88	26	124	4	19	11	8	2	71	91	.438
Terry Francona, Cle	162	133	.78	123	16	24	37	37	18	**150**	7	**573**	131	**58**	128	3	**51**	29	**22**	**13**	85	77	.525
Ron Gardenhire, Min	162	132	.64	97	44	23	40	40	2	82	2	491	135	31	149	5	24	11	13	6	70	**92**	.432
John Gibbons, Tor	162	128	.72	**202**	41	49	45	37	20	73	**8**	449	99	49	161	6	23	17	6	2	83	79	.512
Joe Girardi, NYY	162	142	.74	100	27	33	51	28	10	95	7	475	138	44	132	8	23	10	13	9	84	78	.519
Joe Maddon, TB	162	130	.58	171	23	15	44	35	26	110	3	494	90	54	143	2	27	20	7	3	77	85	.475
Lloyd McClendon, Sea	162	141	.69	93	48	33	**61**	21	11	87	3	497	138	48	**187**	**30**	36	21	15	9	87	75	.537
Bob Melvin, Oak	162	137	.77	187	38	44	45	30	11	101	2	441	103	28	91	16	28	20	8	5	88	74	.543
Mike Scioscia, LAA	162	125	.58	123	46	**59**	49	39	22	141	0	543	120	35	**189**	14	41	**31**	10	5	**98**	64	.605
Buck Showalter, Bal	162	120	.49	77	29	51	37	34	17	89	2	479	64	50	101	10	25	16	9	4	96	66	.593
Robin Ventura, CWS	162	115	.55	85	49	44	26	**59**	29	96	5	453	121	26	150	28	42	25	17	5	73	89	.451
Ned Yost, KC	162	101	.52	51	**63**	46	37	51	26	93	1	451	**189**	45	159	3	14	7	7	3	89	73	.549
162-Game Average		128	.62	112	36	35	40	42	20	99	3	481	124	40	146	11	30	19	12	6	81	81	.500

Manager	G	LINEUPS LUp	LINEUPS PL%	SUBSTITUTION PH	SUBSTITUTION PR	SUBSTITUTION DS	PITCHER USAGE Quick	PITCHER USAGE Slow	PITCHER USAGE LO	PITCHER USAGE RCD	PITCHER USAGE LS	PITCHER USAGE Rel	TACTICS SBA	TACTICS SacA	TACTICS RM	TACTICS PO	INTENTIONAL BB #	INTENTIONAL BB Good	INTENTIONAL BB NG	INTENTIONAL BB Bomb	RESULTS W	RESULTS L	RESULTS Pct
Tim Bogar, Tex	22	21	.56	1	5	0	10	3	3	11	0	76	29	6	23	1	9	5	4	3	14	8	.636
Tom Lawless, Hou	24	23	.64	18	6	9	8	3	5	7	1	67	39	9	35	3	6	2	4	1	11	13	.458
Bo Porter, Hou	138	120	.66	69	21	15	28	42	16	74	2	371	120	22	127	18	26	13	13	6	59	79	.428
Ron Washington, Tex	140	109	.54	96	16	16	35	51	11	65	0	400	135	43	155	6	34	25	9	4	53	87	.379

2014 National League Managers

Manager	G	LINEUPS LUp	LINEUPS PL%	SUBSTITUTION PH	SUBSTITUTION PR	SUBSTITUTION DS	PITCHER USAGE Quick	PITCHER USAGE Slow	PITCHER USAGE LO	PITCHER USAGE RCD	PITCHER USAGE LS	PITCHER USAGE Rel	TACTICS SBA	TACTICS SacA	TACTICS RM	TACTICS PO	INTENTIONAL BB #	INTENTIONAL BB Good	INTENTIONAL BB NG	INTENTIONAL BB Bomb	RESULTS W	RESULTS L	RESULTS Pct
Bud Black, SD	162	**157**	.74	313	23	29	49	33	13	104	1	481	125	74	116	15	32	24	8	4	77	85	.475
Bruce Bochy, SF	162	131	.66	236	29	**64**	45	41	19	102	1	475	83	53	147	12	35	25	10	9	88	74	.543
Terry Collins, NYM	162	135	.55	247	17	26	28	46	23	111	**6**	489	135	73	119	2	38	23	15	4	79	83	.488
Kirk Gibson, Ari	159	135	.55	247	19	18	43	41	5	92	1	479	117	67	140	13	42	28	14	**10**	63	**96**	.396
Fredi Gonzalez, Atl	162	103	.45	206	**34**	34	27	41	20	**122**	3	472	128	70	106	23	36	24	12	8	79	83	.488
Clint Hurdle, Pit	162	123	.50	**322**	28	38	47	40	7	91	0	452	151	85	**187**	24	**43**	26	**17**	7	88	74	.543
Mike Matheny, StL	162	119	.56	258	21	35	53	32	17	119	5	485	89	81	155	10	35	20	15	7	90	72	.556
Don Mattingly, LAD	162	124	.51	237	17	62	49	31	15	107	5	496	**188**	67	168	2	35	20	15	8	94	68	.580
Bryan Price, Cin	162	130	.54	220	21	33	35	37	26	82	3	428	174	87	135	9	33	21	12	5	76	86	.469
Mike Redmond, Mia	162	102	.50	279	9	14	51	37	8	107	4	487	79	81	100	8	33	23	12	7	77	85	.475
Rick Renteria, ChC	162	137	.63	275	9	20	50	42	12	103	1	537	105	77	106	5	37	23	14	8	73	89	.451
Ron Roenicke, Mil	162	115	.44	253	19	37	33	48	12	114	1	478	145	**92**	127	11	20	16	4	4	82	80	.506
Ryne Sandberg, Phi	162	105	.70	259	20	31	37	**62**	**30**	111	0	461	135	72	140	1	**43**	**31**	12	6	73	89	.451
Walt Weiss, Col	162	134	.51	270	12	26	40	49	2	119	0	**547**	133	69	140	11	32	16	16	7	66	**96**	.407
Matt Williams, Was	162	100	.56	248	17	33	**62**	33	11	67	1	458	124	87	91	3	26	15	11	6	**96**	66	.593
162-Game Average		124	.56	258	20	33	43	41	15	104	2	482	128	76	132	10	35	22	13	7	80	82	.494

Manager	G	LINEUPS LUp	LINEUPS PL%	SUBSTITUTION PH	SUBSTITUTION PR	SUBSTITUTION DS	PITCHER USAGE Quick	PITCHER USAGE Slow	PITCHER USAGE LO	PITCHER USAGE RCD	PITCHER USAGE LS	PITCHER USAGE Rel	TACTICS SBA	TACTICS SacA	TACTICS RM	TACTICS PO	INTENTIONAL BB #	INTENTIONAL BB Good	INTENTIONAL BB NG	INTENTIONAL BB Bomb	RESULTS W	RESULTS L	RESULTS Pct
Alan Trammell, Ari	3	3	.63	6	2	0	1	0	0	1	0	9	2	1	3	0	1	1	0	0	1	2	.333

Ballparks and Park Indices

A Park Index tells you whether a given park is favorable to hitters or pitchers compared to other MLB parks. For example, Yankee Stadium, with its short porch in right field, had a home run park index of 148 in 2014, meaning it allowed 48 percent more home runs than an average park. That made it the homer-friendliest park in baseball. Coors Field in Colorado was not too far behind with a 130 home run index, and its runs index of 150 was far and away the highest in baseball.

Park indices are calculated so that they are not affected by the quality of the home team's players. This is achieved through a comparison of what both the ballpark's home team and its opponents accomplished at that ballpark compared to what the same team and its opponents accomplished on the road.

To calculate the park index for home runs in a given ballpark, for example, we take the total home runs of both the home team and its opponents during home games at that ballpark and compare it to the total home runs of that same team and its opponents in road games. We then divide each of those totals by the at-bats in the equivalent situations, so that if there are more at-bats in either situation, the index is not biased. The result is then multiplied by 100 so that it centers there.

The park indices for doubles, triples, walks, strikeouts and home runs by lefties and righties are determined relative to at-bats, similar to how the home runs calculation was outlined. Indices of at-bats, runs, hits, errors and infield fielding errors (E-Infield) are calculated relative to games. The three batting average indices are already relative to at-bats, so they are calculated as is.

A park with an index of exactly 100 is neutral and therefore should have no effect on a particular stat. An index above 100 means the ballpark favors that statistic. For example, the doubles index in Fenway Park of 152 in 2014 is above 100, so it means that 52 percent more doubles are hit in that park than in a neutral park.

There were no new parks or changed dimensions for the 2014 season, but this is the second year of changes to both Safeco Field in Seattle and PETCO Park in San Diego. Starting in 2013, both parks moved in some of their fences to encourage offense in parks that had traditionally skewed very pitcher-friendly. After one season, both of those changes appeared to have the desired effect. Seattle's home run index increased from 62 in 2012 to 97 in 2013, and San Diego's home run index increased from 62 in 2012 to 94 in 2013. This season, Seattle continued its trajectory and actually finished with a 110 home run index, fourth highest in the AL. In contrast, San Diego's home run index declined to 81, barely higher than their 77 home run index from 2010-2012, the three seasons prior to the park change.

Finally, the 2014 season kicked off with a pair of games in Australia. Even though the Diamondbacks were listed as the home team in those contests, they are excluded from their home games in the calculation of their park factors. However, those games are included in the road game calculations for both teams.

Arizona Diamondbacks - Chase Field
LF: 330 CF: 407 RF: 334

	2014 Season							2012-2014						
	Home Games			Away Games				Home Games			Away Games			
	D'Backs	Opp	Total	D'Backs	Opp	Total	Index	D'Backs	Opp	Total	D'Backs	Opp	Total	Index
G	79	79	158	83	83	166		241	241	482	245	245	490	
Avg	.262	.260	.261	.236	.270	.253	103	.261	.261	.261	.250	.261	.255	102
AB	2684	2773	5457	2868	2760	5628	102	8045	8471	16516	8645	8245	16890	99
R	338	373	711	277	369	646	116	1072	1087	2159	962	1038	2000	110
H	702	721	1423	677	746	1423	105	2102	2211	4313	2161	2148	4309	102
2B	139	143	282	120	153	273	107	452	460	912	416	435	851	110
3B	30	22	52	17	12	29	185	74	51	125	37	50	87	147
HR	61	85	146	57	69	126	120	213	256	469	200	229	429	112
BB	206	193	399	192	276	468	88	736	627	1363	720	744	1464	95
SO	551	643	1194	614	635	1249	99	1714	1857	3571	1859	1839	3698	99
Foul Outs	53	48	101	46	37	83	125	159	171	330	160	132	292	116
E	47	53	100	54	49	103	102	132	125	257	134	130	264	99
E-Infield	18	21	39	21	24	45	91	55	58	113	57	57	114	101
LHB-Avg	.258	.275	.267	.237	.268	.252	106	.254	.269	.262	.239	.262	.250	105
LHB-HR	23	36	59	23	22	45	135	81	97	178	73	80	153	117
RHB-Avg	.264	.248	.256	.235	.272	.254	101	.266	.255	.261	.258	.260	.259	101
RHB-HR	38	49	87	34	47	81	111	132	159	291	127	149	276	109

Atlanta Braves - Turner Field
LF: 335 CF: 401 RF: 330

	2014 Season							2012-2014						
	Home Games			Away Games				Home Games			Away Games			
	Braves	Opp	Total	Braves	Opp	Total	Index	Braves	Opp	Total	Braves	Opp	Total	Index
G	81	81	162	81	81	162		243	243	486	243	243	486	
Avg	.242	.245	.243	.240	.257	.248	98	.250	.240	.245	.241	.251	.246	100
AB	2651	2785	5436	2817	2679	5496	99	7930	8318	16248	8404	7987	16391	99
R	280	287	567	293	310	603	94	995	838	1833	966	907	1873	98
H	641	681	1322	675	688	1363	97	1986	2000	3986	2025	2005	4030	99
2B	105	114	219	135	130	265	84	369	373	742	381	381	762	98
3B	9	8	17	13	14	27	64	40	28	68	33	39	72	95
HR	62	67	129	61	54	115	113	222	192	414	231	201	432	97
BB	240	234	474	232	238	470	102	824	637	1461	757	708	1465	101
SO	693	727	1420	676	574	1250	115	2011	2044	4055	2031	1721	3752	109
Foul Outs	49	50	99	49	50	99	101	168	158	326	171	147	318	103
E	46	48	94	39	41	80	118	136	150	286	120	127	247	116
E-Infield	22	20	42	15	15	30	140	59	63	122	50	53	103	118
LHB-Avg	.240	.257	.250	.272	.263	.267	93	.262	.248	.255	.254	.249	.252	101
LHB-HR	15	24	39	21	23	44	91	102	77	179	103	76	179	101
RHB-Avg	.243	.235	.239	.222	.252	.235	102	.242	.235	.238	.231	.252	.242	99
RHB-HR	47	43	90	40	31	71	127	120	115	235	128	125	253	94

Baltimore Orioles - Oriole Park at Camden Yards
LF: 337 CF: 406 RF: 320

	2014 Season							2012-2014						
	Home Games			Away Games				Home Games			Away Games			
	Orioles	Opp	Total	Orioles	Opp	Total	Index	Orioles	Opp	Total	Orioles	Opp	Total	Index
G	81	81	162	81	81	162		243	243	486	243	243	486	
Avg	.258	.239	.248	.254	.249	.252	99	.260	.253	.256	.249	.251	.250	103
AB	2731	2809	5540	2865	2698	5563	100	8186	8524	16710	8590	8202	16792	100
R	341	285	626	364	308	672	93	1110	1028	2138	1052	979	2031	105
H	705	670	1375	729	672	1401	98	2129	2156	4285	2140	2057	4197	102
2B	123	134	257	141	134	275	94	404	401	805	428	421	849	95
3B	7	7	14	9	13	22	64	18	23	41	28	35	63	65
HR	107	68	175	104	83	187	94	349	284	633	288	253	541	118
BB	199	238	437	202	234	436	101	647	724	1371	650	702	1352	102
SO	614	583	1197	671	591	1262	95	1769	1801	3570	1956	1719	3675	98
Foul Outs	58	67	125	68	70	138	91	192	173	365	209	217	426	86
E	41	38	79	46	44	90	88	118	144	262	129	124	253	104
E-Infield	17	15	32	21	17	38	84	51	60	111	52	49	101	110
LHB-Avg	.241	.243	.242	.253	.247	.250	97	.256	.254	.255	.247	.250	.249	103
LHB-HR	34	35	69	25	33	58	121	158	140	298	107	116	223	133
RHB-Avg	.267	.234	.252	.255	.251	.253	99	.263	.252	.257	.251	.251	.251	103
RHB-HR	73	33	106	79	50	129	82	191	144	335	181	137	318	107

Boston Red Sox - Fenway Park
LF: 310 CF: 420 RF: 302

	2014 Season							2012-2014						
	Home Games			Away Games				Home Games			Away Games			
	Red Sox	Opp	Total	Red Sox	Opp	Total	Index	Red Sox	Opp	Total	Red Sox	Opp	Total	Index
G	81	81	162	81	81	162		243	243	486	243	243	486	
Avg	.256	.265	.261	.233	.254	.243	107	.273	.260	.267	.248	.253	.251	106
AB	2717	2872	5589	2834	2746	5580	100	8282	8555	16837	8524	8093	16617	101
R	324	374	698	310	341	651	107	1162	1117	2279	1059	1060	2119	108
H	696	760	1456	659	698	1357	107	2265	2224	4489	2115	2049	4164	108
2B	171	190	361	111	126	237	152	587	500	1087	397	389	786	136
3B	8	16	24	12	16	28	86	35	45	80	30	40	70	113
HR	49	67	116	74	87	161	72	220	234	454	246	266	512	88
BB	295	253	548	240	229	469	117	802	761	1563	742	774	1516	102
SO	627	639	1266	710	574	1284	98	1850	1908	3758	1992	1775	3767	98
Foul Outs	46	61	107	57	71	128	83	133	152	285	166	220	386	73
E	58	52	110	34	40	74	149	152	150	302	121	124	245	123
E-Infield	24	19	43	11	17	28	154	62	56	118	41	45	86	137
LHB-Avg	.260	.268	.264	.235	.253	.244	108	.284	.256	.270	.255	.252	.253	107
LHB-HR	17	31	48	38	46	84	60	96	90	186	125	132	257	72
RHB-Avg	.253	.261	.257	.231	.255	.242	106	.264	.263	.264	.243	.254	.248	106
RHB-HR	32	36	68	36	41	77	85	124	144	268	121	134	255	103

Chicago Cubs - Wrigley Field
LF: 355 CF: 400 RF: 353

	2014 Season							2012-2014						
	Home Games			Away Games				Home Games			Away Games			
	Cubs	Opp	Total	Cubs	Opp	Total	Index	Cubs	Opp	Total	Cubs	Opp	Total	Index
G	81	81	162	81	81	162		243	243	486	243	243	486	
Avg	.242	.242	.242	.236	.261	.249	97	.246	.247	.246	.232	.256	.244	101
AB	2698	2838	5536	2810	2719	5529	100	8046	8425	16471	8371	7981	16352	101
R	308	329	637	306	378	684	93	975	1058	2033	854	1097	1951	104
H	652	687	1339	663	711	1374	97	1977	2082	4059	1942	2047	3989	102
2B	147	145	292	123	151	274	106	438	449	887	394	421	815	108
3B	17	11	28	14	13	27	104	47	45	92	38	59	97	94
HR	69	63	132	88	52	140	94	236	224	460	230	226	456	100
BB	227	247	474	215	257	472	100	694	822	1516	634	795	1429	105
SO	741	703	1444	736	608	1344	107	1933	1924	3857	2009	1699	3708	103
Foul Outs	53	45	98	59	65	124	79	137	125	262	168	166	334	78
E	46	38	84	57	33	90	93	164	144	308	144	143	287	107
E-Infield	17	13	30	21	14	35	86	74	57	131	60	65	125	105
LHB-Avg	.253	.259	.256	.233	.241	.237	108	.252	.246	.249	.229	.243	.235	106
LHB-HR	33	16	49	41	23	64	77	100	72	172	112	84	196	87
RHB-Avg	.230	.231	.231	.239	.274	.258	90	.240	.248	.244	.235	.265	.250	98
RHB-HR	36	47	83	47	29	76	109	136	152	288	118	142	260	110

Chicago White Sox - U.S. Cellular Field
LF: 330 CF: 400 RF: 335

	2014 Season							2012-2014						
	Home Games			Away Games				Home Games			Away Games			
	White Sox	Opp	Total	White Sox	Opp	Total	Index	White Sox	Opp	Total	White Sox	Opp	Total	Index
G	81	81	162	81	81	162		243	243	486	243	243	486	
Avg	.253	.261	.257	.252	.269	.260	99	.257	.254	.255	.248	.260	.254	101
AB	2735	2855	5590	2808	2689	5497	102	8140	8479	16619	8484	8099	16583	100
R	335	392	727	325	366	691	105	1054	1129	2183	952	1028	1980	110
H	692	746	1438	708	722	1430	101	2091	2154	4245	2103	2103	4206	101
2B	134	141	275	145	131	276	98	358	385	743	386	395	781	95
3B	18	15	33	14	16	30	108	38	30	68	42	43	85	80
HR	74	77	151	81	63	144	103	275	283	558	239	225	464	120
BB	224	275	499	193	282	475	103	708	812	1520	581	757	1338	113
SO	692	654	1346	670	498	1168	113	1839	1953	3792	1933	1694	3627	104
Foul Outs	69	63	132	57	47	104	125	196	193	389	179	166	345	113
E	49	57	106	58	48	106	100	147	153	300	151	126	277	108
E-Infield	27	25	52	24	22	46	113	65	62	127	64	50	114	111
LHB-Avg	.247	.256	.252	.258	.271	.265	95	.246	.254	.250	.245	.268	.257	97
LHB-HR	17	37	54	21	28	49	105	100	124	224	99	99	198	113
RHB-Avg	.257	.265	.261	.249	.266	.257	102	.263	.254	.259	.249	.254	.251	103
RHB-HR	57	40	97	60	35	95	103	175	159	334	140	126	266	125

Cincinnati Reds - Great American Ballpark
LF: 328 CF: 404 RF: 325

| | 2014 Season | | | | | | | 2012-2014 | | | | | | |
| | Home Games | | | Away Games | | | | Home Games | | | Away Games | | | |
	Reds	Opp	Total	Reds	Opp	Total	Index	Reds	Opp	Total	Reds	Opp	Total	Index
G	81	81	162	81	81	162		242	242	484	244	244	488	
Avg	.241	.227	.234	.235	.248	.241	97	.249	.236	.242	.244	.245	.244	99
AB	2626	2751	5377	2769	2651	5420	99	7950	8344	16294	8421	8028	16449	100
R	306	286	592	289	326	615	96	996	890	1886	966	899	1865	102
H	632	625	1257	650	657	1307	96	1976	1968	3944	2053	1964	4017	99
2B	118	126	244	136	134	270	91	387	383	770	437	391	828	94
3B	12	8	20	8	10	18	112	37	38	75	33	40	73	104
HR	77	88	165	54	75	129	129	262	286	548	196	199	395	140
BB	225	259	484	190	248	438	111	764	685	1449	717	684	1401	104
SO	606	721	1327	646	569	1215	110	1876	2082	3958	1887	1752	3639	110
Foul Outs	60	65	125	60	53	113	112	160	168	328	166	158	324	102
E	35	53	88	37	56	93	95	110	149	259	127	169	296	88
E-Infield	11	22	33	15	25	40	83	44	54	98	45	82	127	78
LHB-Avg	.219	.236	.228	.243	.260	.251	91	.255	.241	.247	.261	.252	.256	96
LHB-HR	24	36	60	14	26	40	156	99	128	227	73	80	153	152
RHB-Avg	.253	.221	.237	.230	.239	.234	101	.245	.232	.239	.235	.239	.237	101
RHB-HR	53	52	105	40	49	89	116	163	158	321	123	119	242	133

Cleveland Indians - Progressive Field
LF: 325 CF: 405 RF: 325

| | 2014 Season | | | | | | | 2012-2014 | | | | | | |
| | Home Games | | | Away Games | | | | Home Games | | | Away Games | | | |
	Indians	Opp	Total	Indians	Opp	Total	Index	Indians	Opp	Total	Indians	Opp	Total	Index
G	81	81	162	81	81	162		243	243	486	243	243	486	
Avg	.256	.243	.249	.251	.257	.254	98	.253	.248	.250	.253	.263	.258	97
AB	2713	2873	5586	2862	2725	5587	100	8113	8588	16701	8452	8080	16532	101
R	323	321	644	346	332	678	95	1004	1035	2039	1077	1125	2202	93
H	694	698	1392	717	700	1417	98	2052	2131	4183	2135	2129	4264	98
2B	141	150	291	143	140	283	103	423	443	866	417	431	848	101
3B	8	11	19	15	21	36	53	24	26	50	46	60	106	47
HR	72	72	144	70	63	133	108	223	235	458	226	221	447	101
BB	250	225	475	254	239	493	96	790	756	1546	831	805	1636	94
SO	560	757	1317	629	693	1322	100	1743	2076	3819	1816	1839	3655	103
Foul Outs	43	39	82	65	52	117	70	143	140	283	172	158	330	85
E	61	41	102	55	54	109	94	163	138	301	147	137	284	106
E-Infield	30	17	47	20	24	44	107	66	55	121	59	64	123	98
LHB-Avg	.263	.236	.252	.250	.253	.251	100	.258	.250	.255	.254	.260	.256	99
LHB-HR	53	34	87	47	29	76	110	153	126	279	135	113	248	109
RHB-Avg	.239	.249	.245	.252	.260	.257	95	.242	.246	.245	.250	.267	.260	94
RHB-HR	19	38	57	23	34	57	105	70	109	179	91	108	199	92

Colorado Rockies - Coors Field
LF: 347 CF: 415 RF: 350

| | 2014 Season | | | | | | | 2012-2014 | | | | | | |
| | Home Games | | | Away Games | | | | Home Games | | | Away Games | | | |
	Rockies	Opp	Total	Rockies	Opp	Total	Index	Rockies	Opp	Total	Rockies	Opp	Total	Index
G	81	81	162	81	81	162		243	243	486	243	243	486	
Avg	.322	.284	.303	.228	.267	.247	123	.307	.290	.298	.239	.271	.254	117
AB	2868	2903	5771	2744	2637	5381	107	8531	8782	17313	8257	7983	16240	107
R	500	444	944	255	374	629	150	1420	1354	2774	799	1114	1913	145
H	924	825	1749	627	703	1330	132	2618	2547	5165	1970	2163	4133	125
2B	171	173	344	136	147	283	113	501	521	1022	395	468	863	111
3B	33	22	55	8	21	29	177	101	64	165	28	60	88	176
HR	119	90	209	67	83	150	130	307	279	586	204	228	432	127
BB	209	266	475	188	265	453	98	697	776	1473	577	838	1415	98
SO	546	525	1071	735	549	1284	78	1610	1634	3244	2088	1648	3736	81
Foul Outs	39	45	84	65	47	112	70	115	124	239	151	162	313	72
E	46	46	92	60	45	105	88	156	191	347	162	127	289	120
E-Infield	15	21	36	17	13	30	120	48	73	121	57	48	105	115
LHB-Avg	.323	.279	.301	.237	.253	.245	123	.304	.276	.290	.239	.267	.253	114
LHB-HR	46	30	76	31	28	59	121	127	94	221	81	77	158	133
RHB-Avg	.321	.287	.304	.223	.275	.248	122	.308	.299	.304	.238	.274	.255	119
RHB-HR	73	60	133	36	55	91	135	180	185	365	123	151	274	124

Detroit Tigers - Comerica Park
LF: 345   CF: 420   RF: 330

| | 2014 Season | | | | | | | 2012-2014 | | | | | | |
| | Home Games | | | Away Games | | | | Home Games | | | Away Games | | | |
	Tigers	Opp	Total	Tigers	Opp	Total	Index	Tigers	Opp	Total	Tigers	Opp	Total	Index
G	81	81	162	81	81	162		243	243	486	243	243	486	
Avg	.282	.264	.273	.272	.261	.266	102	.287	.256	.271	.266	.255	.261	104
AB	2681	2818	5499	2949	2801	5750	96	8137	8442	16579	8704	8212	16916	98
R	364	368	732	393	337	730	100	1182	1028	2210	1097	971	2068	107
H	756	744	1500	801	731	1532	98	2333	2157	4490	2316	2096	4412	102
2B	142	142	284	183	174	357	83	419	418	837	477	428	905	94
3B	20	24	44	6	18	24	192	60	62	122	28	45	73	171
HR	76	66	142	79	61	140	106	256	198	454	238	208	446	104
BB	227	230	457	216	232	448	107	758	678	1436	727	684	1411	104
SO	501	588	1089	643	656	1299	88	1457	1958	3415	1863	2032	3895	89
Foul Outs	53	65	118	63	55	118	105	184	181	365	153	159	312	119
E	50	51	101	51	54	105	96	140	131	271	136	141	277	98
E-Infield	22	20	42	18	22	40	105	55	46	101	44	61	105	96
LHB-Avg	.244	.238	.240	.270	.259	.262	91	.273	.252	.260	.258	.256	.257	101
LHB-HR	12	29	41	22	32	54	79	86	97	183	76	101	177	107
RHB-Avg	.294	.289	.292	.272	.263	.269	109	.294	.259	.279	.271	.254	.264	106
RHB-HR	64	37	101	57	29	86	123	170	101	271	162	107	269	102

Houston Astros - Minute Maid Park
LF: 315   CF: 435   RF: 326

| | 2014 Season | | | | | | | 2012-2014 | | | | | | |
| | Home Games | | | Away Games | | | | Home Games | | | Away Games | | | |
	Astros	Opp	Total	Astros	Opp	Total	Index	Astros	Opp	Total	Astros	Opp	Total	Index
G	81	81	162	81	81	162		243	243	486	243	243	486	
Avg	.245	.257	.251	.239	.264	.251	100	.239	.261	.251	.239	.274	.256	98
AB	2676	2830	5506	2771	2689	5460	101	8032	8617	16649	8279	8061	16340	102
R	318	362	680	311	361	672	101	927	1174	2101	895	1191	2086	101
H	655	726	1381	662	711	1373	101	1918	2253	4171	1982	2207	4189	100
2B	117	146	263	123	128	251	104	349	440	789	395	424	819	95
3B	11	18	29	8	12	20	144	40	54	94	23	56	79	117
HR	90	73	163	73	66	139	116	250	258	508	207	245	452	110
BB	247	233	480	248	251	499	95	724	816	1540	660	824	1484	102
SO	736	572	1308	706	565	1271	102	2191	1804	3995	2151	1587	3738	105
Foul Outs	47	49	96	67	55	122	78	152	151	303	185	188	373	80
E	56	50	106	50	41	91	116	174	164	338	175	132	307	110
E-Infield	26	14	40	26	16	42	95	80	56	136	70	60	130	105
LHB-Avg	.222	.256	.241	.229	.262	.246	98	.223	.263	.244	.234	.272	.253	96
LHB-HR	37	36	73	28	27	55	130	104	103	207	85	108	193	108
RHB-Avg	.261	.257	.259	.246	.266	.256	101	.249	.260	.255	.243	.275	.259	99
RHB-HR	53	37	90	45	39	84	107	146	155	301	122	137	259	112

Kansas City Royals - Kauffman Stadium
LF: 330   CF: 410   RF: 330

| | 2014 Season | | | | | | | 2012-2014 | | | | | | |
| | Home Games | | | Away Games | | | | Home Games | | | Away Games | | | |
	Royals	Opp	Total	Royals	Opp	Total	Index	Royals	Opp	Total	Royals	Opp	Total	Index
G	81	81	162	81	81	162		243	243	486	243	243	486	
Avg	.255	.264	.259	.270	.237	.254	102	.264	.262	.263	.261	.251	.256	103
AB	2658	2846	5504	2887	2688	5575	99	8112	8536	16648	8618	8032	16650	100
R	300	342	642	351	282	633	101	965	1049	2014	1010	922	1932	104
H	677	750	1427	779	636	1415	101	2144	2237	4381	2247	2019	4266	103
2B	137	138	275	149	116	265	105	411	408	819	424	364	788	104
3B	15	16	31	14	15	29	108	53	57	110	47	40	87	126
HR	43	59	102	52	69	121	85	160	216	376	178	230	408	92
BB	186	214	400	194	226	420	96	603	711	1314	603	740	1343	98
SO	465	591	1056	520	577	1097	98	1378	1784	3162	1687	1769	3456	92
Foul Outs	68	62	130	65	64	129	102	198	195	393	187	193	380	103
E	51	43	94	53	58	111	85	143	131	274	159	149	308	89
E-Infield	15	14	29	24	20	44	66	48	59	107	68	47	115	93
LHB-Avg	.242	.264	.253	.272	.240	.256	99	.258	.267	.263	.258	.256	.257	102
LHB-HR	22	20	42	25	28	53	83	79	91	170	84	100	184	92
RHB-Avg	.264	.263	.264	.268	.234	.252	105	.270	.258	.264	.263	.247	.255	103
RHB-HR	21	39	60	27	41	68	87	81	125	206	94	130	224	92

Los Angeles Angels - Angel Stadium of Anaheim
LF: 330   CF: 400   RF: 330

	2014 Season							2012-2014						
	Home Games			Away Games				Home Games			Away Games			
	Angels	Opp	Total	Angels	Opp	Total	Index	Angels	Opp	Total	Angels	Opp	Total	Index
G	81	81	162	81	81	162		243	243	486	243	243	486	
Avg	.253	.235	.244	.265	.238	.252	97	.265	.242	.253	.266	.255	.261	97
AB	2776	2862	5638	2876	2671	5547	102	8160	8499	16659	8616	8114	16730	100
R	362	310	672	411	320	731	92	1062	990	2052	1211	1076	2287	90
H	701	672	1373	763	635	1398	98	2162	2055	4217	2296	2066	4362	97
2B	135	130	265	169	98	267	98	401	385	786	446	379	825	96
3B	11	5	16	20	9	29	54	43	26	69	49	31	80	87
HR	73	55	128	82	71	153	82	232	214	446	274	265	539	83
BB	243	233	476	249	271	520	90	692	714	1406	772	806	1578	89
SO	620	719	1339	646	623	1269	104	1710	1984	3694	1890	1715	3605	103
Foul Outs	60	62	122	49	65	114	105	169	166	335	154	194	348	97
E	39	60	99	44	60	104	95	147	156	303	146	184	330	92
E-Infield	10	31	41	15	24	39	105	61	62	123	53	73	126	98
LHB-Avg	.242	.239	.240	.250	.237	.243	99	.258	.235	.244	.253	.252	.253	97
LHB-HR	20	22	42	27	34	61	70	56	94	150	66	124	190	80
RHB-Avg	.258	.231	.246	.275	.238	.259	95	.268	.248	.259	.273	.257	.266	97
RHB-HR	53	33	86	55	37	92	90	176	120	296	208	141	349	85

Los Angeles Dodgers - Dodger Stadium
LF: 330   CF: 395   RF: 330

	2014 Season							2012-2014						
	Home Games			Away Games				Home Games			Away Games			
	Dodgers	Opp	Total	Dodgers	Opp	Total	Index	Dodgers	Opp	Total	Dodgers	Opp	Total	Index
G	81	81	162	81	81	162		243	243	486	243	243	486	
Avg	.254	.232	.243	.276	.253	.265	92	.257	.234	.245	.264	.248	.256	96
AB	2693	2826	5519	2867	2693	5560	99	7978	8321	16299	8511	8004	16515	99
R	328	307	635	390	310	700	91	917	863	1780	1087	933	2020	88
H	685	656	1341	791	682	1473	91	2049	1950	3999	2243	1986	4229	95
2B	151	139	290	151	123	274	107	400	376	776	452	378	830	95
3B	14	2	16	24	22	46	35	27	18	45	51	56	107	43
HR	71	81	152	63	61	124	123	195	213	408	193	178	371	111
BB	232	200	432	287	229	516	84	689	674	1363	787	754	1541	90
SO	609	711	1320	637	662	1299	102	1732	2053	3785	1816	1888	3704	104
Foul Outs	30	59	89	52	47	99	91	131	145	276	168	159	327	86
E	63	58	121	44	56	100	121	168	140	308	146	165	311	99
E-Infield	31	16	47	17	18	35	134	77	52	129	61	66	127	102
LHB-Avg	.268	.244	.255	.275	.255	.265	96	.263	.246	.255	.258	.252	.255	100
LHB-HR	25	35	60	17	28	45	136	68	83	151	54	74	128	120
RHB-Avg	.246	.224	.235	.276	.252	.265	89	.252	.227	.239	.267	.245	.256	93
RHB-HR	46	46	92	46	33	79	116	127	130	257	139	104	243	107

Miami Marlins - Marlins Park
LF: 340   CF: 416   RF: 335

	2014 Season							2012-2014						
	Home Games			Away Games				Home Games			Away Games			
	Marlins	Opp	Total	Marlins	Opp	Total	Index	Marlins	Opp	Total	Marlins	Opp	Total	Index
G	81	81	162	81	81	162		243	243	486	243	243	486	
Avg	.260	.257	.258	.246	.272	.259	100	.247	.256	.252	.238	.264	.250	100
AB	2693	2845	5538	2845	2760	5605	99	7973	8468	16441	8451	8124	16575	99
R	349	315	664	296	359	655	101	930	990	1920	837	1054	1891	102
H	700	731	1431	699	750	1449	99	1972	2164	4136	2011	2141	4152	100
2B	138	134	272	116	149	265	104	373	416	789	361	407	768	104
3B	26	24	50	10	16	26	195	69	70	139	37	58	95	148
HR	59	45	104	63	69	132	80	150	151	301	204	217	421	72
BB	254	212	466	247	246	493	96	751	700	1451	666	779	1445	101
SO	626	607	1233	793	583	1376	91	1801	1779	3580	2078	1701	3779	96
Foul Outs	40	39	79	52	40	92	87	163	140	303	175	145	320	95
E	44	51	95	53	42	95	100	144	140	284	144	136	280	101
E-Infield	18	15	33	18	23	41	80	65	48	113	54	60	114	99
LHB-Avg	.256	.243	.248	.235	.283	.263	94	.241	.253	.248	.237	.268	.255	97
LHB-HR	16	19	35	26	27	53	65	35	65	100	62	98	160	62
RHB-Avg	.262	.270	.265	.251	.262	.256	104	.250	.258	.254	.238	.260	.248	102
RHB-HR	43	26	69	37	42	79	90	115	86	201	142	119	261	78

Milwaukee Brewers - Miller Park
LF: 344   CF: 400   RF: 345

| | 2014 Season | | | | | | | 2012-2014 | | | | | | |
| | Home Games | | | Away Games | | | | Home Games | | | Away Games | | | |
	Brewers	Opp	Total	Brewers	Opp	Total	Index	Brewers	Opp	Total	Brewers	Opp	Total	Index
G	81	81	162	81	81	162		243	243	486	243	243	486	
Avg	.257	.241	.249	.243	.258	.251	99	.259	.254	.257	.249	.256	.252	102
AB	2641	2791	5432	2821	2756	5577	97	8037	8498	16535	8456	8127	16583	100
R	329	325	654	321	332	653	100	1093	1072	2165	973	1005	1978	109
H	680	674	1354	686	712	1398	97	2085	2162	4247	2104	2083	4187	101
2B	140	113	253	157	136	293	89	410	367	777	425	387	812	96
3B	10	7	17	18	15	33	53	58	30	88	52	40	92	96
HR	77	92	169	73	75	148	117	278	306	584	231	205	436	134
BB	225	197	422	198	234	432	100	701	701	1402	595	721	1316	107
SO	550	664	1214	647	582	1229	101	1723	2021	3744	1897	1752	3649	103
Foul Outs	51	48	99	68	63	131	78	165	171	336	166	163	329	102
E	42	55	97	57	55	112	87	136	169	305	176	169	345	88
E-Infield	14	24	38	23	21	44	86	55	68	123	70	66	136	90
LHB-Avg	.275	.243	.252	.237	.246	.243	104	.262	.255	.257	.249	.249	.249	103
LHB-HR	13	41	54	6	30	36	147	45	147	192	37	98	135	139
RHB-Avg	.253	.240	.248	.245	.268	.254	97	.259	.254	.256	.249	.262	.254	101
RHB-HR	64	51	115	67	45	112	108	233	159	392	194	107	301	133

Minnesota Twins - Target Field
LF: 339   CF: 411   RF: 328

| | 2014 Season | | | | | | | 2012-2014 | | | | | | |
| | Home Games | | | Away Games | | | | Home Games | | | Away Games | | | |
	Twins	Opp	Total	Twins	Opp	Total	Index	Twins	Opp	Total	Twins	Opp	Total	Index
G	81	81	162	81	81	162		243	243	486	243	243	486	
Avg	.260	.285	.273	.248	.275	.261	105	.261	.277	.269	.243	.279	.261	103
AB	2755	2954	5709	2812	2711	5523	103	8212	8727	16939	8481	8227	16708	101
R	368	419	787	347	358	705	112	1037	1241	2278	993	1156	2149	106
H	716	842	1558	696	746	1442	108	2142	2418	4560	2064	2297	4361	105
2B	159	170	329	157	149	306	104	437	482	919	434	432	866	105
3B	16	22	38	11	16	27	136	44	57	101	28	42	70	142
HR	67	72	139	61	75	136	99	204	244	448	206	269	475	93
BB	288	206	494	256	202	458	104	812	639	1451	770	692	1462	98
SO	620	517	1137	709	514	1223	90	1780	1520	3300	2048	1439	3487	93
Foul Outs	60	62	122	53	70	123	96	151	184	335	154	198	352	94
E	57	47	104	40	49	89	117	149	135	284	136	170	306	93
E-Infield	17	20	37	16	22	38	97	58	54	112	52	73	125	90
LHB-Avg	.266	.277	.272	.251	.278	.264	103	.269	.269	.269	.249	.280	.263	102
LHB-HR	28	22	50	22	29	51	100	84	101	185	106	112	218	86
RHB-Avg	.255	.292	.274	.245	.273	.258	106	.252	.283	.270	.237	.278	.259	104
RHB-HR	39	50	89	39	46	85	96	120	143	263	100	157	257	98

New York Mets - Citi Field
LF: 335   CF: 408   RF: 330

| | 2014 Season | | | | | | | 2012-2014 | | | | | | |
| | Home Games | | | Away Games | | | | Home Games | | | Away Games | | | |
	Mets	Opp	Total	Mets	Opp	Total	Index	Mets	Opp	Total	Mets	Opp	Total	Index
G	81	81	162	81	81	162		243	243	486	243	243	486	
Avg	.224	.247	.236	.252	.248	.250	94	.228	.245	.237	.254	.259	.256	92
AB	2623	2809	5432	2849	2725	5574	97	7967	8461	16428	8514	8145	16659	99
R	286	286	572	343	332	675	85	841	970	1811	1057	1041	2098	86
H	588	693	1281	718	677	1395	92	1819	2069	3888	2162	2111	4273	91
2B	130	143	273	145	118	263	107	366	392	758	458	403	861	89
3B	10	10	20	9	21	30	68	33	30	63	39	56	95	67
HR	59	71	130	66	70	136	98	185	249	434	209	205	414	106
BB	242	266	508	274	243	517	101	756	730	1486	775	725	1500	100
SO	597	671	1268	667	632	1299	100	1928	1967	3895	1970	1785	3755	105
Foul Outs	51	47	98	59	45	104	97	149	189	338	163	178	341	101
E	45	49	94	59	40	99	95	126	136	262	172	134	306	86
E-Infield	21	19	40	26	16	42	95	53	53	106	72	65	137	77
LHB-Avg	.221	.246	.234	.265	.257	.261	89	.227	.242	.234	.253	.268	.260	90
LHB-HR	28	33	61	37	33	70	93	87	106	193	104	94	198	101
RHB-Avg	.227	.247	.237	.240	.241	.241	99	.230	.246	.239	.255	.253	.254	94
RHB-HR	31	38	69	29	37	66	104	98	143	241	105	111	216	111

New York Yankees - Yankee Stadium
LF: 318   CF: 408   RF: 314

| | 2014 Season | | | | | | | 2012-2014 | | | | | | |
| | Home Games | | | Away Games | | | | Home Games | | | Away Games | | | |
	Yankees	Opp	Total	Yankees	Opp	Total	Index	Yankees	Opp	Total	Yankees	Opp	Total	Index
G	81	81	162	81	81	162		243	243	486	243	243	486	
Avg	.247	.251	.249	.244	.249	.246	101	.255	.252	.254	.247	.257	.252	101
AB	2677	2842	5519	2820	2726	5546	100	7960	8483	16443	8510	8190	16700	98
R	304	326	630	329	338	667	94	1047	1004	2051	1040	999	2039	101
H	662	712	1374	687	680	1367	101	2030	2139	4169	2102	2106	4208	99
2B	117	119	236	130	139	269	88	349	429	778	425	435	860	92
3B	9	10	19	17	19	36	53	21	25	46	42	42	84	56
HR	88	97	185	59	67	126	148	301	283	584	235	242	477	124
BB	218	199	417	234	199	433	97	754	632	1386	729	634	1363	103
SO	558	734	1292	575	636	1211	107	1707	2056	3763	1816	1865	3681	104
Foul Outs	58	64	122	58	53	111	110	163	181	344	187	155	342	102
E	47	42	89	45	45	90	99	127	119	246	108	150	258	95
E-Infield	17	17	34	19	17	36	94	48	50	98	54	61	115	85
LHB-Avg	.253	.244	.249	.236	.242	.239	104	.269	.244	.257	.245	.250	.247	104
LHB-HR	69	40	109	44	22	66	161	203	114	317	145	102	247	129
RHB-Avg	.238	.256	.249	.256	.256	.256	97	.237	.259	.250	.250	.263	.257	97
RHB-HR	19	57	76	15	45	60	132	98	169	267	90	140	230	119

Oakland Athletics - O.co Coliseum
LF: 330   CF: 400   RF: 330

| | 2014 Season | | | | | | | 2012-2014 | | | | | | |
| | Home Games | | | Away Games | | | | Home Games | | | Away Games | | | |
	Athletics	Opp	Total	Athletics	Opp	Total	Index	Athletics	Opp	Total	Athletics	Opp	Total	Index
G	81	81	162	81	81	162		241	241	482	245	245	490	
Avg	.255	.231	.243	.234	.235	.234	104	.246	.234	.240	.245	.247	.246	98
AB	2699	2761	5460	2846	2690	5536	99	8039	8394	16433	8554	8126	16680	100
R	376	282	658	353	290	643	102	1066	862	1928	1143	949	2092	94
H	688	638	1326	666	631	1297	102	1980	1963	3943	2092	2005	4097	98
2B	124	120	244	129	90	219	113	392	368	760	429	335	764	101
3B	19	5	24	14	6	20	122	49	24	73	41	20	61	121
HR	74	65	139	72	82	154	92	246	203	449	281	254	535	85
BB	311	197	508	275	209	484	106	889	636	1525	820	660	1480	105
SO	516	615	1131	588	629	1217	94	1717	1786	3503	1952	1777	3729	95
Foul Outs	89	84	173	70	51	121	145	307	287	594	195	190	385	157
E	51	53	104	60	56	116	90	151	135	286	168	145	313	93
E-Infield	22	17	39	19	22	41	95	65	42	107	64	55	119	91
LHB-Avg	.258	.236	.249	.228	.246	.235	106	.242	.239	.240	.252	.256	.254	95
LHB-HR	40	22	62	36	29	65	94	119	90	209	151	111	262	80
RHB-Avg	.251	.227	.237	.242	.227	.233	102	.251	.230	.239	.236	.240	.238	101
RHB-HR	34	43	77	36	53	89	90	127	113	240	130	143	273	90

Philadelphia Phillies - Citizens Bank Park
LF: 329   CF: 401   RF: 329

| | 2014 Season | | | | | | | 2012-2014 | | | | | | |
| | Home Games | | | Away Games | | | | Home Games | | | Away Games | | | |
	Phillies	Opp	Total	Phillies	Opp	Total	Index	Phillies	Opp	Total	Phillies	Opp	Total	Index
G	81	81	162	81	81	162		243	243	486	243	243	486	
Avg	.239	.242	.240	.245	.262	.253	95	.247	.248	.247	.250	.264	.257	96
AB	2769	2878	5647	2834	2668	5502	103	8137	8531	16668	8466	8077	16543	101
R	303	326	629	316	361	677	93	971	1043	2014	942	1073	2015	100
H	661	697	1358	695	699	1394	97	2009	2116	4125	2116	2132	4248	97
2B	116	139	255	135	145	280	89	380	435	815	397	433	830	97
3B	17	10	27	10	22	32	82	49	35	84	38	58	96	87
HR	64	78	142	61	56	117	118	230	263	493	193	201	394	124
BB	223	260	483	220	261	481	98	690	712	1402	624	724	1348	103
SO	660	691	1351	646	564	1210	109	1813	2050	3863	1792	1789	3581	107
Foul Outs	67	62	129	46	40	86	146	165	197	362	170	168	338	106
E	50	51	101	33	54	87	116	156	149	305	125	152	277	110
E-Infield	26	18	44	16	29	45	98	81	60	141	53	68	121	117
LHB-Avg	.246	.226	.238	.253	.255	.254	94	.248	.247	.248	.254	.261	.257	96
LHB-HR	39	22	61	40	25	65	93	118	84	202	104	71	175	118
RHB-Avg	.226	.252	.243	.230	.266	.253	96	.245	.249	.247	.244	.266	.257	96
RHB-HR	25	56	81	21	31	52	150	112	179	291	89	130	219	128

Pittsburgh Pirates - PNC Park
LF: 325   CF: 399   RF: 320

| | 2014 Season | | | | | | | | 2012-2014 | | | | | | | |
| | Home Games | | | Away Games | | | | | Home Games | | | Away Games | | | |
	Pirates	Opp	Total	Pirates	Opp	Total	Index		Pirates	Opp	Total	Pirates	Opp	Total	Index
G	81	81	162	81	81	162			243	243	486	243	243	486	
Avg	.274	.241	.257	.245	.253	.249	103		.252	.236	.244	.246	.253	.250	98
AB	2733	2773	5506	2803	2656	5459	101		8007	8283	16290	8427	8069	16496	99
R	350	299	649	332	332	664	98		956	843	1799	1011	1039	2050	88
H	748	669	1417	688	672	1360	104		2021	1954	3975	2074	2043	4117	97
2B	144	121	265	131	114	245	107		407	337	744	382	371	753	100
3B	18	7	25	12	19	31	80		51	24	75	51	51	102	74
HR	62	56	118	94	72	166	70		198	151	349	289	231	520	68
BB	262	244	506	258	255	513	98		692	689	1381	741	815	1556	90
SO	551	603	1154	693	625	1318	87		1765	1829	3594	2163	1852	4015	91
Foul Outs	56	42	98	53	53	106	92		151	123	274	169	136	305	91
E	57	48	105	52	48	100	105		169	155	324	158	140	298	109
E-Infield	18	19	37	14	19	33	112		64	73	137	59	63	122	112
LHB-Avg	.260	.249	.254	.218	.239	.229	111		.247	.229	.238	.229	.249	.239	100
LHB-HR	36	19	55	34	26	60	91		107	56	163	120	81	201	84
RHB-Avg	.281	.237	.259	.260	.262	.261	99		.255	.240	.248	.256	.256	.256	97
RHB-HR	26	37	63	60	46	106	59		91	95	186	169	150	319	58

San Diego Padres - PETCO Park
LF: 336   CF: 396   RF: 322

| | 2014 Season | | | | | | | | 2013-2014 | | | | | | | |
| | Home Games | | | Away Games | | | | | Home Games | | | Away Games | | | |
	Padres	Opp	Total	Padres	Opp	Total	Index		Padres	Opp	Total	Padres	Opp	Total	Index
G	81	81	162	81	81	162			162	162	324	162	162	324	
Avg	.231	.219	.224	.222	.264	.243	92		.234	.228	.231	.237	.270	.253	91
AB	2587	2736	5323	2707	2655	5362	99		5268	5560	10828	5543	5342	10885	99
R	267	236	503	268	341	609	83		558	543	1101	595	734	1329	83
H	597	598	1195	602	702	1304	92		1235	1266	2501	1313	1441	2754	91
2B	106	123	229	118	135	253	91		221	233	454	249	295	544	84
3B	18	7	25	12	14	26	97		35	24	59	21	35	56	106
HR	54	47	101	55	70	125	81		120	127	247	135	146	281	88
BB	247	231	478	221	231	452	107		489	485	974	446	502	948	103
SO	626	678	1304	668	606	1274	103		1268	1327	2595	1335	1128	2463	106
Foul Outs	46	43	89	43	46	89	101		83	90	173	97	91	188	93
E	43	48	91	58	51	109	83		86	94	180	98	95	193	93
E-Infield	18	16	34	18	21	39	87		35	33	68	29	36	65	105
LHB-Avg	.231	.218	.225	.238	.269	.252	89		.236	.232	.234	.239	.261	.250	94
LHB-HR	32	20	52	27	31	58	88		56	62	118	49	59	108	107
RHB-Avg	.231	.219	.224	.206	.261	.235	95		.233	.224	.228	.235	.276	.256	89
RHB-HR	22	27	49	28	39	67	76		64	65	129	86	87	173	76

San Francisco Giants - AT&T Park
LF: 339   CF: 399   RF: 309

| | 2014 Season | | | | | | | | 2012-2014 | | | | | | | |
| | Home Games | | | Away Games | | | | | Home Games | | | Away Games | | | |
	Giants	Opp	Total	Giants	Opp	Total	Index		Giants	Opp	Total	Giants	Opp	Total	Index
G	81	81	162	81	81	162			244	244	488	242	242	484	
Avg	.258	.232	.245	.251	.251	.251	98		.261	.236	.248	.262	.258	.260	96
AB	2674	2725	5399	2849	2687	5536	98		8085	8330	16415	8548	8066	16614	98
R	325	288	613	340	326	666	92		920	895	1815	1092	1059	2151	84
H	691	631	1322	716	674	1390	95		2110	1969	4079	2238	2077	4315	94
2B	117	133	250	140	133	273	94		398	412	810	426	427	853	96
3B	29	29	58	13	19	32	186		78	62	140	56	48	104	136
HR	53	54	107	79	79	158	69		128	174	302	214	246	460	66
BB	210	195	405	217	194	411	101		712	708	1420	667	691	1358	106
SO	611	648	1259	634	563	1197	108		1622	1938	3560	1798	1766	3564	101
Foul Outs	40	46	86	68	44	112	79		150	161	311	177	156	333	95
E	49	46	95	51	36	87	109		151	124	275	171	139	310	88
E-Infield	20	21	41	21	14	35	117		70	51	121	67	55	122	98
LHB-Avg	.280	.245	.262	.256	.256	.256	102		.270	.232	.253	.253	.257	.255	99
LHB-HR	17	24	41	29	30	59	68		49	64	113	87	83	170	66
RHB-Avg	.241	.221	.231	.247	.247	.247	93		.252	.239	.245	.269	.258	.263	93
RHB-HR	36	30	66	50	49	99	71		79	110	189	127	163	290	67

Seattle Mariners - Safeco Field
LF: 331 CF: 405 RF: 326

	2014 Season							2013-2014						
	Home Games			Away Games				Home Games			Away Games			
	Mariners	Opp	Total	Mariners	Opp	Total	Index	Mariners	Opp	Total	Mariners	Opp	Total	Index
G	81	81	162	81	81	162		162	162	324	162	162	324	
Avg	.238	.219	.228	.249	.242	.245	93	.238	.237	.238	.242	.253	.248	96
AB	2605	2698	5303	2845	2691	5536	96	5349	5618	10967	5659	5429	11088	99
R	281	256	537	353	298	651	82	591	632	1223	667	676	1343	91
H	619	590	1209	709	650	1359	89	1275	1332	2607	1371	1375	2746	95
2B	105	104	209	142	123	265	82	235	271	506	261	271	532	96
3B	11	6	17	21	15	36	49	17	17	34	32	31	63	55
HR	73	67	140	63	70	133	110	161	149	310	163	162	325	96
BB	187	215	402	209	248	457	92	446	447	893	479	494	973	93
SO	612	667	1279	620	650	1270	105	1261	1387	2648	1324	1227	2551	105
Foul Outs	67	67	134	42	51	93	150	139	124	263	96	99	195	136
E	36	42	78	46	47	93	84	77	89	166	93	83	176	94
E-Infield	15	20	35	20	17	37	95	28	41	69	46	34	80	86
LHB-Avg	.253	.227	.241	.260	.249	.256	94	.253	.240	.248	.258	.250	.255	97
LHB-HR	55	26	81	39	32	71	120	113	63	176	107	73	180	99
RHB-Avg	.210	.212	.211	.229	.235	.232	91	.213	.234	.226	.215	.256	.239	95
RHB-HR	18	41	59	24	38	62	99	48	86	134	56	89	145	93

St Louis Cardinals - Busch Stadium
LF: 336 CF: 400 RF: 335

	2014 Season							2012-2014						
	Home Games			Away Games				Home Games			Away Games			
	Cardinals	Opp	Total	Cardinals	Opp	Total	Index	Cardinals	Opp	Total	Cardinals	Opp	Total	Index
G	81	81	162	81	81	162		243	243	486	243	243	486	
Avg	.259	.236	.247	.247	.249	.248	100	.273	.240	.256	.256	.258	.257	99
AB	2649	2813	5462	2777	2640	5417	101	8122	8434	16556	8483	8084	16567	100
R	332	308	640	287	295	582	110	1114	877	1991	1053	970	2023	98
H	686	664	1350	685	657	1342	101	2216	2020	4236	2175	2087	4262	99
2B	152	135	287	123	118	241	118	470	388	858	417	400	817	105
3B	13	15	28	8	11	19	146	43	37	80	35	50	85	94
HR	57	55	112	48	68	116	96	191	169	360	198	200	398	91
BB	251	239	490	220	231	451	108	735	668	1403	750	689	1439	98
SO	499	636	1135	634	585	1219	92	1556	1938	3494	1879	1755	3634	96
Foul Outs	58	67	125	63	53	116	107	171	166	337	152	132	284	119
E	40	37	77	48	46	94	82	125	117	242	145	139	284	85
E-Infield	21	11	32	22	17	39	82	68	41	109	65	56	121	90
LHB-Avg	.270	.239	.255	.269	.250	.260	98	.283	.249	.266	.263	.258	.260	102
LHB-HR	23	20	43	19	25	44	99	76	68	144	67	85	152	96
RHB-Avg	.249	.234	.241	.229	.248	.238	101	.265	.232	.249	.251	.259	.255	98
RHB-HR	34	35	69	29	43	72	93	115	101	216	131	115	246	87

Tampa Bay Rays - Tropicana Field Surface: FieldTurf
LF: 315 CF: 404 RF: 322

	2014 Season							2012-2014						
	Home Games			Away Games				Home Games			Away Games			
	Rays	Opp	Total	Rays	Opp	Total	Index	Rays	Opp	Total	Rays	Opp	Total	Index
G	81	81	162	81	81	162		243	243	486	244	244	488	
Avg	.250	.226	.238	.244	.242	.243	98	.245	.225	.235	.250	.244	.247	95
AB	2697	2810	5507	2819	2708	5527	100	8006	8385	16391	8446	8028	16474	100
R	317	302	619	295	323	618	100	989	869	1858	1020	979	1999	93
H	673	636	1309	688	656	1344	97	1962	1883	3845	2113	1957	4070	95
2B	125	109	234	138	127	265	89	373	345	718	436	364	800	90
3B	6	11	17	18	7	25	68	38	39	77	39	27	66	117
HR	51	66	117	66	79	145	81	214	196	410	243	241	484	85
BB	285	245	530	242	237	479	111	888	686	1574	799	747	1546	102
SO	549	738	1287	575	699	1274	101	1745	2185	3930	1873	1945	3818	103
Foul Outs	65	81	146	51	72	123	119	200	205	405	156	180	336	121
E	32	43	75	56	42	98	77	105	112	217	156	130	286	76
E-Infield	13	17	30	22	18	40	75	43	46	89	60	54	114	78
LHB-Avg	.275	.211	.240	.247	.234	.240	100	.244	.219	.231	.248	.251	.249	93
LHB-HR	18	21	39	24	35	59	67	91	92	183	103	108	211	82
RHB-Avg	.234	.238	.236	.242	.249	.245	96	.246	.229	.238	.252	.239	.246	97
RHB-HR	33	45	78	42	44	86	91	123	104	227	140	133	273	88

Texas Rangers - Rangers Ballpark in Arlington
LF: 332   CF: 400   RF: 325

| | 2014 Season | | | | | | | 2012-2014 | | | | | | |
| | Home Games | | | Away Games | | | | Home Games | | | Away Games | | | |
	Rangers	Opp	Total	Rangers	Opp	Total	Index	Rangers	Opp	Total	Rangers	Opp	Total	Index
G	81	81	162	81	81	162		244	244	488	243	243	486	
Avg	.251	.270	.261	.262	.274	.268	97	.268	.259	.263	.260	.254	.257	103
AB	2661	2865	5526	2799	2690	5489	101	8146	8526	16672	8489	8073	16562	100
R	298	425	723	339	348	687	105	1119	1107	2226	1056	1009	2065	107
H	668	773	1441	732	737	1469	98	2186	2207	4393	2205	2051	4256	103
2B	116	146	262	144	183	327	80	395	422	817	430	441	871	93
3B	17	22	39	11	7	18	215	43	48	91	40	37	77	117
HR	51	82	133	60	78	138	96	244	250	494	243	242	485	101
BB	208	245	453	209	260	469	96	699	723	1422	658	726	1384	102
SO	558	547	1105	604	563	1167	94	1574	1909	3483	1758	1796	3554	97
Foul Outs	41	62	103	53	77	130	79	133	162	295	175	223	398	74
E	59	62	121	47	61	108	112	141	195	336	136	152	288	116
E-Infield	22	22	44	17	23	40	110	60	80	140	56	64	120	116
LHB-Avg	.237	.269	.256	.250	.270	.261	98	.262	.261	.261	.245	.252	.249	105
LHB-HR	18	45	63	20	35	55	109	93	125	218	88	106	194	110
RHB-Avg	.260	.270	.265	.268	.277	.272	97	.272	.257	.265	.268	.256	.262	101
RHB-HR	33	37	70	40	43	83	86	151	125	276	155	136	291	95

Toronto Blue Jays - Rogers Centre Surface: FieldTurf
LF: 328   CF: 400   RF: 328

| | 2014 Season | | | | | | | 2012-2014 | | | | | | |
| | Home Games | | | Away Games | | | | Home Games | | | Away Games | | | |
	Blue Jays	Opp	Total	Blue Jays	Opp	Total	Index	Blue Jays	Opp	Total	Blue Jays	Opp	Total	Index
G	81	81	162	81	81	162		243	243	486	243	243	486	
Avg	.266	.249	.257	.251	.258	.254	101	.258	.254	.256	.247	.261	.254	101
AB	2751	2842	5593	2798	2688	5486	102	8117	8556	16673	8456	8099	16555	101
R	387	332	719	336	354	690	104	1135	1112	2247	1016	1114	2130	105
H	732	707	1439	703	693	1396	103	2092	2177	4269	2087	2113	4200	102
2B	147	175	322	135	156	291	109	431	536	967	371	433	804	119
3B	16	16	32	8	16	24	131	44	26	70	26	46	72	97
HR	98	88	186	79	63	142	128	295	309	604	265	241	506	119
BB	236	240	476	266	250	516	90	757	747	1504	728	817	1545	97
SO	599	649	1248	552	550	1102	111	1757	1908	3665	1768	1641	3409	107
Foul Outs	80	68	148	75	67	142	102	242	183	425	217	189	406	104
E	43	56	99	44	42	86	115	149	174	323	150	140	290	111
E-Infield	14	22	36	20	17	37	97	54	63	117	61	53	114	103
LHB-Avg	.266	.256	.262	.257	.251	.254	103	.257	.257	.257	.254	.257	.255	101
LHB-HR	41	33	74	31	31	62	118	108	129	237	92	122	214	110
RHB-Avg	.266	.244	.253	.245	.262	.255	99	.258	.252	.255	.241	.264	.252	101
RHB-HR	57	55	112	48	32	80	136	187	180	367	173	119	292	125

Washington Nationals - Nationals Park
LF: 336   CF: 403   RF: 335

| | 2014 Season | | | | | | | 2012-2014 | | | | | | |
| | Home Games | | | Away Games | | | | Home Games | | | Away Games | | | |
	Nationals	Opp	Total	Nationals	Opp	Total	Index	Nationals	Opp	Total	Nationals	Opp	Total	Index
G	81	81	162	81	81	162		243	243	486	243	243	486	
Avg	.269	.243	.256	.237	.245	.241	106	.269	.245	.257	.242	.241	.242	106
AB	2736	2839	5575	2806	2695	5501	101	8180	8471	16651	8413	8034	16447	101
R	362	279	641	324	276	600	107	1078	878	1956	995	897	1892	103
H	737	690	1427	666	661	1327	108	2201	2074	4275	2035	1940	3975	108
2B	143	126	269	122	116	238	112	405	428	833	420	369	789	104
3B	8	7	15	19	21	40	37	31	30	61	48	44	92	65
HR	63	45	108	89	65	154	69	234	174	408	273	207	480	84
BB	266	185	451	251	167	418	106	732	620	1352	728	634	1362	98
SO	640	674	1314	664	614	1278	101	1777	1967	3744	2044	1882	3926	94
Foul Outs	51	58	109	46	47	93	116	179	173	352	156	152	308	113
E	54	53	107	46	50	96	111	152	161	313	149	140	289	108
E-Infield	21	19	40	11	17	28	143	58	63	121	49	54	103	117
LHB-Avg	.277	.246	.261	.216	.247	.232	112	.272	.247	.259	.233	.249	.241	107
LHB-HR	27	17	44	31	31	62	69	95	68	163	103	101	204	80
RHB-Avg	.264	.241	.252	.252	.244	.248	102	.267	.243	.255	.248	.236	.242	105
RHB-HR	36	28	64	58	34	92	69	139	106	245	170	106	276	87

2014 American League Ballpark Index Rankings

Home Park	Avg	AB	R	H	2B	3B	HR	BB	SO	FO	E	E-Inf	LHB Avg	LHB HR	RHB Avg	RHB HR
Twins (Target Field)	105	103	112	108	104	136	99	104	90	96	117	97	103	100	106	96
Red Sox (Fenway Park)	107	100	107	107	152	86	72	117	98	83	149	154	108	60	106	85
Rangers (Rangers Ballpark in Arlington)	97	101	105	98	80	215	96	96	94	79	112	110	98	109	97	86
White Sox (U.S. Cellular Field)	99	102	105	101	98	108	103	103	113	125	100	113	95	105	102	103
Blue Jays (Rogers Centre)	101	102	104	103	109	131	128	90	111	102	115	97	103	118	99	136
Athletics (O.co Coliseum)	104	99	102	102	113	122	92	106	94	145	90	95	106	94	102	90
Royals (Kauffman Stadium)	102	99	101	101	105	108	85	96	98	102	85	66	99	83	105	87
Astros (Minute Maid Park)	100	101	101	101	104	144	116	95	102	78	116	95	98	130	101	107
Tigers (Comerica Park)	102	96	100	98	83	192	106	107	88	105	96	105	91	79	109	123
Rays (Tropicana Field)	98	100	100	97	89	68	81	111	101	119	77	75	100	67	96	91
Indians (Progressive Field)	98	100	95	98	103	53	108	96	100	70	94	107	100	110	95	105
Yankees (Yankee Stadium)	101	100	94	101	88	53	148	97	107	110	99	94	104	161	97	132
Orioles (Oriole Park at Camden Yards)	99	100	93	98	94	64	94	101	95	91	88	84	97	121	99	82
Angels (Angel Stadium of Anaheim)	97	102	92	98	98	54	82	90	104	105	95	105	99	70	95	90
Mariners (Safeco Field)	93	96	82	89	82	49	110	92	105	150	84	95	94	120	91	99

2014 National League Ballpark Index Rankings

Home Park	Avg	AB	R	H	2B	3B	HR	BB	SO	FO	E	E-Inf	LHB Avg	LHB HR	RHB Avg	RHB HR
Rockies (Coors Field)	123	107	150	132	113	177	130	98	78	70	88	120	123	121	122	135
Diamondbacks (Chase Field)	103	102	116	105	107	185	120	88	99	125	102	91	106	135	101	111
Cardinals (Busch Stadium)	100	101	110	101	118	146	96	108	92	107	82	82	98	99	101	93
Nationals (Nationals Park)	106	101	107	108	112	37	69	106	101	116	111	143	112	69	102	69
Marlins (Marlins Park)	100	99	101	99	104	195	80	96	91	87	100	80	94	65	104	90
Brewers (Miller Park)	99	97	100	97	89	53	117	100	101	78	87	86	104	147	97	108
Pirates (PNC Park)	103	101	98	104	107	80	70	98	87	92	105	112	111	91	99	59
Reds (Great American Ballpark)	97	99	96	96	91	112	129	111	110	112	95	83	91	156	101	116
Braves (Turner Field)	98	99	94	97	84	64	113	102	115	101	118	140	93	91	102	127
Cubs (Wrigley Field)	97	100	93	97	106	104	94	100	107	79	93	86	108	77	90	109
Phillies (Citizens Bank Park)	95	103	93	97	89	82	118	98	109	146	116	98	94	93	96	150
Giants (AT&T Park)	98	98	92	95	94	186	69	101	108	79	109	117	102	68	93	71
Dodgers (Dodger Stadium)	92	99	91	91	107	35	123	84	102	91	121	134	96	136	89	116
Mets (Citi Field)	94	97	85	92	107	68	98	101	100	97	95	95	89	93	99	104
Padres (PETCO Park)	92	99	83	92	91	97	81	107	103	101	83	87	89	88	95	76

2014 AL Home Runs

Home Park	Index
Yankees	148
Blue Jays	128
Astros	116
Mariners	110
Indians	108
Tigers	106
White Sox	103
Twins	99
Rangers	96
Orioles	94
Athletics	92
Royals	85
Angels	82
Rays	81
Red Sox	72

2014 AL LHB Home Runs

Home Park	Index
Yankees	161
Astros	130
Orioles	121
Mariners	120
Blue Jays	118
Indians	110
Rangers	109
White Sox	105
Twins	100
Athletics	94
Royals	83
Tigers	79
Angels	70
Rays	67
Red Sox	60

2014 AL RHB Home Runs

Home Park	Index
Blue Jays	136
Yankees	132
Tigers	123
Astros	107
Indians	105
White Sox	103
Mariners	99
Twins	96
Rays	91
Angels	90
Athletics	90
Royals	87
Rangers	86
Red Sox	85
Orioles	82

2014 NL Home Runs

Home Park	Index
Rockies	130
Reds	129
Dodgers	123
Diamondbacks	120
Phillies	118
Brewers	117
Braves	113
Mets	98
Cardinals	96
Cubs	94
Padres	81
Marlins	80
Pirates	70
Giants	69
Nationals	69

2014 NL LHB Home Runs

Home Park	Index
Reds	156
Brewers	147
Dodgers	136
Diamondbacks	135
Rockies	121
Cardinals	99
Mets	93
Phillies	93
Braves	91
Pirates	91
Padres	88
Cubs	77
Nationals	69
Giants	68
Marlins	65

2014 NL RHB Home Runs

Home Park	Index
Phillies	150
Rockies	135
Braves	127
Dodgers	116
Reds	116
Diamondbacks	111
Cubs	109
Brewers	108
Mets	104
Cardinals	93
Marlins	90
Padres	76
Giants	71
Nationals	69
Pirates	59

2014 AL Avg	
Home Park	Index
Red Sox	107
Twins	105
Athletics	104
Tigers	102
Royals	102
Blue Jays	101
Yankees	101
Astros	100
White Sox	99
Orioles	99
Indians	98
Rays	98
Rangers	97
Angels	97
Mariners	93

2014 AL LHB Avg	
Home Park	Index
Red Sox	108
Athletics	106
Yankees	104
Blue Jays	103
Twins	103
Indians	100
Rays	100
Royals	99
Angels	99
Astros	98
Rangers	98
Orioles	97
White Sox	95
Mariners	94
Tigers	91

2014 AL RHB Avg	
Home Park	Index
Tigers	109
Red Sox	106
Twins	106
Royals	105
Athletics	102
White Sox	102
Astros	101
Orioles	99
Blue Jays	99
Yankees	97
Rangers	97
Rays	96
Indians	95
Angels	95
Mariners	91

2014 NL Avg	
Home Park	Index
Rockies	123
Nationals	106
Pirates	103
Diamondbacks	103
Marlins	100
Cardinals	100
Brewers	99
Braves	98
Giants	98
Cubs	97
Reds	97
Phillies	95
Mets	94
Padres	92
Dodgers	92

2014 NL LHB Avg	
Home Park	Index
Rockies	123
Nationals	112
Pirates	111
Cubs	108
Diamondbacks	106
Brewers	104
Giants	102
Cardinals	98
Dodgers	96
Marlins	94
Phillies	94
Braves	93
Reds	91
Mets	89
Padres	89

2014 NL RHB Avg	
Home Park	Index
Rockies	122
Marlins	104
Nationals	102
Braves	102
Reds	101
Cardinals	101
Diamondbacks	101
Pirates	99
Mets	99
Brewers	97
Phillies	96
Padres	95
Giants	93
Cubs	90
Dodgers	89

2014 AL Doubles	
Home Park	Index
Red Sox	152
Athletics	113
Blue Jays	109
Royals	105
Twins	104
Astros	104
Indians	103
White Sox	98
Angels	98
Orioles	94
Rays	89
Yankees	88
Tigers	83
Mariners	82
Rangers	80

2014 AL Triples	
Home Park	Index
Rangers	215
Tigers	192
Astros	144
Twins	136
Blue Jays	131
Athletics	122
Royals	108
White Sox	108
Red Sox	86
Rays	68
Orioles	64
Angels	54
Yankees	53
Indians	53
Mariners	49

2014 AL Errors	
Home Park	Index
Red Sox	149
Twins	117
Astros	116
Blue Jays	115
Rangers	112
White Sox	100
Yankees	99
Tigers	96
Angels	95
Indians	94
Athletics	90
Orioles	88
Royals	85
Mariners	84
Rays	77

2014 NL Doubles	
Home Park	Index
Cardinals	118
Rockies	113
Nationals	112
Pirates	107
Dodgers	107
Diamondbacks	107
Mets	107
Cubs	106
Marlins	104
Giants	94
Padres	91
Reds	91
Phillies	89
Brewers	89
Braves	84

2014 NL Triples	
Home Park	Index
Marlins	195
Giants	186
Diamondbacks	185
Rockies	177
Cardinals	146
Reds	112
Cubs	104
Padres	97
Phillies	82
Pirates	80
Mets	68
Braves	64
Brewers	53
Nationals	37
Dodgers	35

2014 NL Errors	
Home Park	Index
Dodgers	121
Braves	118
Phillies	116
Nationals	111
Giants	109
Pirates	105
Diamondbacks	102
Marlins	100
Mets	95
Reds	95
Cubs	93
Rockies	88
Brewers	87
Padres	83
Cardinals	82

2012-2014 American League Ballpark Index Rankings

Home Park	Avg	AB	R	H	2B	3B	HR	BB	SO	FO	E	E-Inf	Avg	HR	Avg	HR
							TOTALS						LHB		RHB	
White Sox (U.S. Cellular Field)	101	100	110	101	95	80	120	113	104	113	108	111	97	113	103	125
Red Sox (Fenway Park)	106	101	108	108	136	113	88	102	98	73	123	137	107	72	106	103
Rangers (Rangers Ballpark in Arlington)	103	100	107	103	93	117	101	102	97	74	116	116	105	110	101	95
Tigers (Comerica Park)	104	98	107	102	94	171	104	104	89	119	98	96	101	107	106	102
Twins (Target Field)	103	101	106	105	105	142	93	98	93	94	93	90	102	86	104	98
Blue Jays (Rogers Centre)	101	101	105	102	119	97	119	97	107	104	111	103	101	110	101	125
Orioles (Oriole Park at Camden Yards)	103	100	105	102	95	65	118	102	98	86	104	110	103	133	103	107
Royals (Kauffman Stadium)	103	100	104	103	104	126	92	98	92	103	89	93	102	92	103	92
Astros (Minute Maid Park)	98	102	101	100	95	117	110	102	105	80	110	105	96	108	99	112
Yankees (Yankee Stadium)	101	98	101	99	92	56	124	103	104	102	95	85	104	129	97	119
Athletics (O.co Coliseum)	98	100	94	98	101	121	85	105	95	157	93	91	95	80	101	90
Rays (Tropicana Field)	95	100	93	95	90	117	85	102	103	121	76	78	93	82	97	88
Indians (Progressive Field)	97	101	93	98	101	47	101	94	103	85	106	98	99	109	94	92
Mariners (Safeco Field)[1]	96	99	91	95	96	55	96	93	105	136	94	86	97	99	95	93
Angels (Angel Stadium of Anaheim)	97	100	90	97	96	87	83	89	103	97	92	98	97	80	97	85

2012-2014 National League Ballpark Index Rankings

Home Park	Avg	AB	R	H	2B	3B	HR	BB	SO	FO	E	E-Inf	Avg	HR	Avg	HR
							TOTALS						LHB		RHB	
Rockies (Coors Field)	117	107	126	125	111	176	127	98	81	72	120	115	114	133	119	124
Diamondbacks (Chase Field)	102	99	110	102	110	147	112	95	99	116	99	101	105	117	101	109
Brewers (Miller Park)	102	100	109	101	96	96	134	107	103	102	88	90	103	139	101	133
Cubs (Wrigley Field)	101	101	104	102	108	94	100	105	103	78	107	105	106	87	98	110
Nationals (Nationals Park)	106	101	103	108	104	65	84	98	94	113	108	117	107	80	105	87
Reds (Great American Ballpark)	99	100	102	99	94	104	140	104	110	102	88	78	96	152	101	133
Marlins (Marlins Park)	100	99	102	100	104	148	72	101	96	95	101	99	97	62	102	78
Phillies (Citizens Bank Park)	96	101	100	97	97	87	124	103	107	106	110	117	96	118	96	128
Cardinals (Busch Stadium)	99	100	98	99	105	94	91	98	96	119	85	90	102	96	98	87
Braves (Turner Field)	100	99	98	99	98	95	97	101	109	103	116	118	101	101	99	94
Dodgers (Dodger Stadium)	96	99	88	95	95	43	111	90	104	86	99	102	100	120	93	107
Pirates (PNC Park)	98	99	88	97	100	74	68	90	91	91	109	112	100	84	97	58
Mets (Citi Field)	92	99	86	91	89	67	106	100	105	101	86	77	90	101	94	111
Giants (AT&T Park)	96	98	84	94	96	136	66	106	101	95	88	98	99	66	93	67
Padres (PETCO Park)[1]	91	99	83	91	84	106	88	103	106	93	93	105	94	107	89	76

2012-2014 AL Home Runs	Index
Home Park	
Yankees	124
White Sox	120
Blue Jays	119
Orioles	118
Astros	110
Tigers	104
Indians	101
Rangers	101
Mariners[1]	96
Twins	93
Royals	92
Red Sox	88
Athletics	85
Rays	85
Angels	83

2012-2014 AL LHB Home Runs	Index
Home Park	
Orioles	133
Yankees	129
White Sox	113
Rangers	110
Blue Jays	110
Indians	109
Astros	108
Tigers	107
Mariners[1]	99
Royals	92
Twins	86
Rays	82
Angels	80
Athletics	80
Red Sox	72

2012-2014 AL RHB Home Runs	Index
Home Park	
Blue Jays	125
White Sox	125
Yankees	119
Astros	112
Orioles	107
Red Sox	103
Tigers	102
Twins	98
Rangers	95
Mariners[1]	93
Royals	92
Indians	92
Athletics	90
Rays	88
Angels	85

2012-2014 NL Home Runs	Index
Home Park	
Reds	140
Brewers	134
Rockies	127
Phillies	124
Diamondbacks	112
Dodgers	111
Mets	106
Cubs	100
Braves	97
Cardinals	91
Padres[1]	88
Nationals	84
Marlins	72
Pirates	68
Giants	66

2012-2014 NL LHB Home Runs	Index
Home Park	
Reds	152
Brewers	139
Rockies	133
Dodgers	120
Phillies	118
Diamondbacks	117
Padres[1]	107
Braves	101
Mets	101
Cardinals	96
Cubs	87
Pirates	84
Nationals	80
Giants	66
Marlins	62

2012-2014 NL RHB Home Runs	Index
Home Park	
Reds	133
Brewers	133
Phillies	128
Rockies	124
Mets	111
Cubs	110
Diamondbacks	109
Dodgers	107
Braves	94
Cardinals	87
Nationals	87
Marlins	78
Padres[1]	76
Giants	67
Pirates	58

1. 2013-2014 Only

2012-2014 AL Avg	
Home Park	Index
Red Sox	106
Tigers	104
Twins	103
Royals	103
Orioles	103
Rangers	103
Blue Jays	101
White Sox	101
Yankees	101
Astros	98
Athletics	98
Indians	97
Angels	97
Mariners[1]	96
Rays	95

2012-2014 AL LHB Avg	
Home Park	Index
Red Sox	107
Rangers	105
Yankees	104
Orioles	103
Royals	102
Twins	102
Tigers	101
Blue Jays	101
Indians	99
White Sox	97
Mariners[1]	97
Angels	97
Astros	96
Athletics	95
Rays	93

2012-2014 AL RHB Avg	
Home Park	Index
Red Sox	106
Tigers	106
Twins	104
Royals	103
White Sox	103
Orioles	103
Blue Jays	101
Rangers	101
Athletics	101
Astros	99
Angels	97
Yankees	97
Rays	97
Mariners[1]	95
Indians	94

2012-2014 NL Avg	
Home Park	Index
Rockies	117
Nationals	106
Diamondbacks	102
Brewers	102
Cubs	101
Marlins	100
Braves	100
Cardinals	99
Reds	99
Pirates	98
Phillies	96
Dodgers	96
Giants	96
Mets	92
Padres[1]	91

2012-2014 NL LHB Avg	
Home Park	Index
Rockies	114
Nationals	107
Cubs	106
Diamondbacks	105
Brewers	103
Cardinals	102
Braves	101
Dodgers	100
Pirates	100
Giants	99
Marlins	97
Reds	96
Phillies	96
Padres[1]	94
Mets	90

2012-2014 NL RHB Avg	
Home Park	Index
Rockies	119
Nationals	105
Marlins	102
Reds	101
Brewers	101
Diamondbacks	101
Braves	99
Cubs	98
Cardinals	98
Pirates	97
Phillies	96
Mets	94
Dodgers	93
Giants	93
Padres[1]	89

2012-2014 AL Doubles	
Home Park	Index
Red Sox	136
Blue Jays	119
Twins	105
Royals	104
Indians	101
Athletics	101
Mariners[1]	96
Angels	96
Orioles	95
White Sox	95
Astros	95
Tigers	94
Rangers	93
Yankees	92
Rays	90

2012-2014 AL Triples	
Home Park	Index
Tigers	171
Twins	142
Royals	126
Athletics	121
Rangers	117
Rays	117
Astros	117
Red Sox	113
Blue Jays	97
Angels	87
White Sox	80
Orioles	65
Yankees	56
Mariners[1]	55
Indians	47

2012-2014 AL Errors	
Home Park	Index
Red Sox	123
Rangers	116
Blue Jays	111
Astros	110
White Sox	108
Indians	106
Orioles	104
Tigers	98
Yankees	95
Mariners[1]	94
Athletics	93
Twins	93
Angels	92
Royals	89
Rays	76

2012-2014 NL Doubles	
Home Park	Index
Rockies	111
Diamondbacks	110
Cubs	108
Cardinals	105
Nationals	104
Marlins	104
Pirates	100
Braves	98
Phillies	97
Giants	96
Brewers	96
Dodgers	95
Reds	94
Mets	89
Padres[1]	84

2012-2014 NL Triples	
Home Park	Index
Rockies	176
Marlins	148
Diamondbacks	147
Giants	136
Padres[1]	106
Reds	104
Brewers	96
Braves	95
Cardinals	94
Cubs	94
Phillies	87
Pirates	74
Mets	67
Nationals	65
Dodgers	43

2012-2014 NL Errors	
Home Park	Index
Rockies	120
Braves	116
Phillies	110
Pirates	109
Nationals	108
Cubs	107
Marlins	101
Dodgers	99
Diamondbacks	99
Padres[1]	93
Brewers	88
Reds	88
Giants	88
Mets	86
Cardinals	85

1. 2013-2014 Only

2014 Lefty/Righty Statistics

The following section includes platoon splits for all hitters with at least 20 plate appearances and pitchers with at least 20 batters faced in 2014. It contains batting average, on base percentage, and slugging percentage along with a count of at-bats, hits, doubles, triples, home runs, RBI, walks, and strikeouts for hitters against both right and left-handed pitchers. Many prominent hitters, including Miguel Cabrera, Jonathan Lucroy, Anthony Rendon, and Bryce Harper, displayed balanced approaches that resulted in similar production against pitchers of either handedness. Meanwhile, sluggers like Josh Donaldson, Matt Holliday, and Robinson Cano feasted on opposite-handed pitchers while being limited somewhat by pitchers with the same handedness. Among switch-hitters, Victor Martinez and Ben Zobrist excelled while batting from the right side against left-handed pitchers, while Angel Pagan and Pablo Sandoval performed better in their left-handed at-bats. Jose Reyes and Chase Headley were comfortable from either side of the plate.

For pitchers, these stats reflect the performance of opposing batters. Some pitchers dominate same-handed hitters but are exposed against opposite-handed batters, while others are equally successful against batters of either hand. For example, against Cardinals lefty Randy Choate, left-handed hitters simply did not have a chance this year, collecting only 7 hits in 75 at-bats for a paltry .093 average. Meanwhile, righties teed off on Choate to the tune of a .385 batting average. However, Kevin Siegrist, another lefty in the Cardinals bullpen, was much more balanced, allowing a .308 batting average to lefties and limiting righties to a .247 average. Once you take into account Siegrist's higher rate of extra-base hits allowed against righties, the gap narrows even further, with a difference of only .016 in OPS for righties and lefties against Siegrist. While Siegrist is basically just as comfortable facing batters of either handedness, Choate's skill set lends itself to a more specialized role.

Batters vs. Left-Handed and Right-Handed Pitchers

Batter	vs	Avg	AB	H	2B	3B	HR	RBI	BB	SO	OBP	Slg
Abreu,Bobby	L	.200	15	3	0	0	0	1	1	2	.250	.200
Bats Left	R	.254	118	30	9	0	1	13	19	19	.353	.356
Abreu,Jose	L	.353	136	48	10	1	10	23	19	34	.437	.662
Bats Right	R	.305	420	128	25	1	26	84	32	97	.364	.555
Ackley,Dustin	L	.212	151	32	6	2	1	18	7	36	.255	.298
Bats Left	R	.259	351	91	21	2	13	47	25	54	.310	.442
Adams,Matt	L	.190	121	23	2	1	3	15	6	36	.231	.298
Bats Left	R	.318	406	129	32	4	12	53	20	78	.349	.505
Adduci,Jim	L	.000	8	0	0	0	0	0	0	4	.000	.000
Bats Left	R	.183	93	17	3	0	1	8	10	23	.257	.247
Adrianza,Ehire	L	.200	25	5	1	0	0		1	8	.259	.240
Bats Both	R	.250	72	18	5	0	0	4	3	14	.286	.319
Aguilar,Jesus	L	.167	18	3	0	0	0	2	4	8	.304	.167
Bats Right	R	.067	15	1	0	0	0		1		.067	.067
Ahmed,Nick	L	.176	34	6	1	0	0	0	2	5	.222	.206
Bats Right	R	.222	36	8	1	0	1	4	1	5	.243	.333
Alcantara,Arismendy	L	.244	78	19	4	0	3	8	10	20	.344	.410
Bats Both	R	.190	200	38	7	2	7	21	7	73	.215	.350
Almonte,Abraham	L	.253	75	19	6	0	1	5	4	14	.296	.373
Bats Both	R	.217	129	28	4	1	2	10	8	46	.263	.310
Almonte,Zoilo	L	.200	5	1	0	0	0		0	2	.200	.200
Bats Both	R	.129	31	4	0	0	1	3	0	12	.129	.226
Alonso,Yonder	L	.216	51	11	5	0	0	4	5	13	.293	.314
Bats Left	R	.245	216	53	14	1	7	23	12	23	.283	.417
Altuve,Jose	L	.414	152	63	11	0	4	14	9	14	.447	.566
Bats Right	R	.319	508	162	36	3	3	45	27	39	.356	.419
Alvarez,Pedro	L	.175	80	14	1	0	2	12	7	25	.241	.263
Bats Left	R	.245	318	78	12	1	16	44	38	88	.330	.440
Amarista,Alexi	L	.200	105	21	1	0	0	6	5	20	.236	.210
Bats Left	R	.252	318	80	12	2	5	34	24	49	.302	.349
Andrus,Elvis	L	.310	150	49	12	0	0	10	17	13	.374	.386
Bats Right	R	.247	461	114	23	1	2	31	29	83	.292	.315
Anna,Dean	L	.000	7	0	0	0	0	1	1	3	.125	.000
Bats Left	R	.200	15	3	1	0	1	2	1	3	.235	.467
Aoki,Nori	L	.363	124	45	7	1	0	12	12	11	.428	.435
Bats Left	R	.259	367	95	15	5	1	31	31	38	.323	.335
Arcia,Oswaldo	L	.198	131	26	4	1	3	15	10	46	.261	.313
Bats Left	R	.249	241	60	12	2	17	42	21	81	.321	.527
Arenado,Nolan	L	.313	112	35	4	2	8	17	11	14	.375	.598
Bats Right	R	.278	320	89	30	0	10	44	14	44	.311	.466
Arencibia,J.P.	L	.239	67	16	5	0	5	15	4	20	.303	.537
Bats Right	R	.147	136	20	4	0	5	20	6	42	.205	.287
Arias,Joaquin	L	.305	105	32	8	0	0	8	6	9	.339	.381
Bats Right	R	.193	88	17	1	0	0	7	2	14	.209	.205
Arruebarrena,Erisbel	L	.222	9	2	0	0	0	1	1	5	.300	.222
Bats Both	R	.188	32	6	1	0	0	3	2	12	.229	.219
Asche,Cody	L	.268	82	22	3	0	3	13	6	26	.318	.415
Bats Left	R	.248	315	78	22	0	7	33	27	76	.306	.384
Avila,Alex	L	.226	106	24	5	0	1	12	7	42	.287	.302
Bats Left	R	.215	284	61	17	0	10	35	54	109	.340	.380
Aviles,Mike	L	.259	139	36	8	0	2	12	6	17	.286	.360
Bats Right	R	.239	205	49	8	1	3	27	7	32	.264	.332
Aybar,Erick	L	.248	161	40	8	2	1	17	8	15	.281	.342
Bats Both	R	.289	429	124	22	2	6	51	28	47	.335	.392
Baez,Javier	L	.143	49	7	1	0	3	5	4	26	.222	.347
Bats Right	R	.177	164	29	5	0	6	15	11	69	.229	.317
Baker,Jeff	L	.319	119	38	7	2	2	18	8	22	.362	.462
Bats Right	R	.191	89	17	3	2	1	10	6	20	.292	.303
Baker,John	L	.161	31	5	2	0	0	6	3	17	.235	.226
Bats Left	R	.199	151	30	5	0	0	9	16	41	.281	.232
Barmes,Clint	L	.238	21	5	1	0	0	0	0	5	.273	.286
Bats Right	R	.247	81	20	4	0	0	7	9	13	.340	.296
Barnes,Brandon	L	.259	112	29	8	0	0	12	8	29	.308	.330
Bats Right	R	.256	180	46	9	4	8	15	7	71	.283	.483
Barney,Darwin	L	.275	69	19	3	1	0	6	8	11	.359	.348
Bats Right	R	.226	168	38	8	1	3	17	9	23	.275	.339
Barnhart,Tucker	L	.083	12	1	0	0	0	0	0	2	.083	.083
Bats Both	R	.214	42	9	0	0	1	1	4	8	.283	.286
Barton,Daric	L	.200	15	3	1	0	0		0	4	.200	.267
Bats Left	R	.143	42	6	0	0	0	5	5	10	.245	.143
Bautista,Jose	L	.345	116	40	3	0	10	19	21	19	.449	.629
Bats Right	R	.270	437	118	24	0	25	84	83	77	.391	.497
Beckham,Gordon	L	.293	116	34	10	0	2	11	9	20	.349	.431
Bats Right	R	.203	330	67	17	0	7	33	13	61	.242	.318
Belt,Brandon	L	.266	64	17	2	0	2	9	5	14	.324	.391
Bats Left	R	.233	150	35	6	0	10	18	13	50	.299	.473
Beltran,Carlos	L	.196	143	28	9	0	3	12	9	32	.242	.322
Bats Both	R	.254	260	66	14	0	12	37	28	48	.331	.446
Beltre,Adrian	L	.351	131	46	10	0	5	23	22	19	.442	.542
Bats Right	R	.316	418	132	23	1	14	54	35	55	.369	.476
Bernadina,Roger	L	.154	13	2	0	0	0	2	0	3	.214	.154
Bats Left	R	.170	53	9	3	0	1	7	10	16	.323	.283
Bethancourt,Christian	L	.409	22	9	1	0	0	2	1	1	.435	.455
Bats Right	R	.209	91	19	2	0	0	7	2	25	.234	.231
Betts,Mookie	L	.328	58	19	4	1	1	4	3	11	.361	.483
Bats Right	R	.275	131	36	8	0	4	14	18	20	.371	.427
Bianchi,Jeff	L	.240	25	6	0	0	0	6	0	7	.231	.240
Bats Right	R	.133	45	6	1	0	0	0	3	10	.188	.156
Blackmon,Charlie	L	.267	150	40	6	1	4	20	2	20	.297	.400
Bats Left	R	.296	443	131	21	2	15	52	29	76	.347	.454
Blanco,Andres	L	.308	26	8	3	0	0	0	0	3	.308	.423
Bats Both	R	.238	21	5	2	0	1	3	2	3	.304	.476
Blanco,Gregor	L	.296	125	37	9	1	0	14	10	24	.346	.384
Bats Left	R	.243	268	65	9	5	5	24	31	53	.328	.369
Blanks,Kyle	L	.300	30	9	0	0	2	4	4	8	.389	.500
Bats Right	R	.320	25	8	1	0	0	3	4	8	.433	.360
Bloomquist,Willie	L	.282	71	20	2	0	1	8	2	15	.297	.352
Bats Right	R	.274	62	17	4	0	0	6	2	17	.297	.339
Boesch,Brennan	L	.333	3	1	0	0	1	1	1	0	.500	1.333
Bats Left	R	.181	72	13	2	0	1	6	1	19	.187	.250
Bogaerts,Xander	L	.263	156	41	11	0	5	16	12	29	.326	.429
Bats Right	R	.230	382	88	17	1	7	30	27	109	.286	.335
Bonifacio,Emilio	L	.365	104	38	8	1	3	13	8	29	.411	.548
Bats Both	R	.221	290	64	9	3	0	11	18	56	.266	.272
Bour,Justin	L	.200	5	1	1	0	0	2	0	2	.200	.400
Bats Left	R	.290	69	20	2	0	1	9	9	17	.372	.362
Bourgeois,Jason	L	.400	5	2	0	1	0	0	1	2	.500	.800
Bats Right	R	.214	28	6	0	0	0	1	0	4	.214	.214
Bourjos,Peter	L	.194	103	20	1	2	3	9	6	37	.252	.330
Bats Left	R	.255	161	41	8	3	1	15	14	41	.320	.360
Bourn,Michael	L	.224	143	32	7	2	0	11	7	36	.268	.301
Bats Left	R	.272	301	82	10	8	3	17	28	78	.335	.389
Bradley Jr.,Jackie	L	.231	134	31	9	1	1	13	9	41	.304	.336
Bats Left	R	.180	250	45	10	1	0	17	22	80	.245	.228
Brantley,Michael	L	.307	205	63	12	1	5	29	19	25	.378	.449
Bats Left	R	.337	406	137	33	1	15	68	33	31	.388	.534
Braun,Ryan	L	.279	140	39	6	3	7	22	7	26	.309	.514
Bats Right	R	.262	390	102	24	3	12	59	34	87	.329	.431
Brentz,Bryce	L	.571	7	4	1	0	0	1	0	1	.571	.714
Bats Right	R	.211	19	4	1	0	0	1	0	8	.211	.263
Brignac,Reid	L	.000	10	0	0	0	0	0	0	3	.000	.000
Bats Left	R	.254	71	18	5	1	1	10	9	30	.338	.394
Brown,Andrew	L	.133	15	2	0	0	0	0	2	4	.278	.133
Bats Right	R	.207	29	6	1	0	2	7	1	11	.226	.448
Brown,Domonic	L	.217	106	23	5	0	1	16	4	21	.243	.292
Bats Left	R	.240	367	88	17	1	9	47	30	70	.297	.365
Bruce,Jay	L	.161	118	19	3	0	6	17	7	41	.217	.339
Bats Left	R	.235	375	88	18	1	12	49	37	108	.301	.384
Buck,John	L	.244	41	10	0	0	1	3	3	11	.295	.317
Bats Right	R	.208	48	10	2	0	0	3	5	15	.283	.250
Butera,Drew	L	.216	37	8	1	0	2	5	5	11	.310	.405
Bats Right	R	.180	133	24	5	1	1	9	12	30	.255	.256
Butler,Billy	L	.321	137	44	7	0	4	17	15	26	.367	.400
Bats Right	R	.255	412	105	25	0	5	49	26	70	.301	.352
Byrd,Marlon	L	.258	163	42	8	0	9	22	9	47	.301	.472
Bats Right	R	.266	428	114	20	2	16	61	27	138	.317	.435
Cabrera,Asdrubal	L	.250	172	43	15	1	3	21	7	32	.288	.401
Bats Both	R	.236	381	90	16	3	11	40	42	76	.316	.381
Cabrera,Everth	L	.253	83	21	5	0	1	5	5	21	.292	.349
Bats Both	R	.226	274	62	8	1	2	15	15	65	.266	.285
Cabrera,Melky	L	.276	152	42	9	1	5	20	13	15	.337	.447
Bats Both	R	.310	416	129	26	2	11	53	30	52	.355	.462
Cabrera,Miguel	L	.301	153	46	16	1	6	24	18	35	.364	.536
Bats Right	R	.317	458	145	36	0	19	85	42	82	.373	.520
Cain,Lorenzo	L	.313	144	42	12	0	3	16	8	31	.357	.470
Bats Right	R	.297	337	100	17	4	2	37	16	77	.331	.389
Calhoun,Kole	L	.252	103	26	6	1	2	14	9	25	.322	.388
Bats Left	R	.277	390	108	25	2	15	44	29	79	.326	.467
Callaspo,Alberto	L	.196	148	29	5	0	1	9	14	20	.268	.250
Bats Both	R	.238	256	61	10	0	3	30	26	30	.303	.313
Campana,Tony	L	.200	10	2	0	0	0	0	0	3	.273	.200
Bats Left	R	.185	65	12	1	1	0	5	0	13	.185	.231

Batters vs. Left-Handed and Right-Handed Pitchers

Batter	vs	Avg	AB	H	2B	3B	HR	RBI	BB	SO	OBP	Slg
Campbell,Eric	L	.250	92	23	4	0	2	12	10	28	.324	.359
Bats Right	R	.276	98	27	5	0	1	4	7	27	.321	.357
Cano,Robinson	L	.294	228	67	16	0	2	30	22	26	.356	.390
Bats Left	R	.327	367	120	21	2	12	52	39	42	.398	.493
Carp,Mike	L	.130	23	3	0	0	0	3	1	5	.231	.130
Bats Left	R	.184	103	19	5	1	0	10	15	26	.301	.252
Carpenter,Matt	L	.262	183	48	10	1	2	20	28	42	.364	.361
Bats Left	R	.277	412	114	23	1	6	39	67	69	.380	.381
Carrera,Ezequiel	L	.357	14	5	1	0	0	0	1	2	.438	.429
Bats Left	R	.236	55	13	3	1	0	2	2	12	.263	.327
Carter,Chris	L	.244	135	33	7	0	10	25	22	52	.350	.519
Bats Right	R	.220	372	82	14	1	27	63	34	130	.291	.481
Casali,Curt	L	.125	16	2	1	0	0	0	4	5	.333	.188
Bats Right	R	.179	56	10	2	0	0	3	4	18	.246	.214
Castellanos,Nick	L	.237	139	33	8	1	3	13	17	37	.319	.374
Bats Right	R	.266	394	105	23	3	8	53	19	103	.301	.401
Castillo,Rusney	L	.250	8	2	0	0	0	0	0	1	.250	.250
Bats Right	R	.357	28	10	1	0	2	6	3	5	.438	.607
Castillo,Welington	L	.301	93	28	4	0	5	9	6	24	.350	.505
Bats Right	R	.216	287	62	15	0	8	37	20	78	.279	.352
Castro,Jason	L	.237	118	28	7	0	2	12	4	40	.272	.347
Bats Left	R	.216	347	75	14	2	12	44	30	111	.290	.372
Castro,Starlin	L	.304	115	35	9	1	1	13	11	24	.362	.426
Bats Right	R	.288	413	119	24	0	13	52	24	76	.333	.441
Cecchini,Garin	L	.000	6	0	0	0	0	0	0	3	.000	.000
Bats Left	R	.320	25	8	3	0	1	4	3	8	.433	.560
Centeno,Juan	L	.000	3	0	0	0	0	0	0	3	.000	.000
Bats Left	R	.222	27	6	0	0	0	2	3	2	.300	.222
Cervelli,Francisco	L	.267	45	12	2	1	1	5	2	15	.313	.422
Bats Right	R	.317	101	32	9	0	1	8	9	26	.395	.436
Cespedes,Yoenis	L	.199	141	28	5	1	7	17	14	36	.269	.397
Bats Right	R	.279	459	128	31	5	15	83	21	92	.311	.466
Chavez,Endy	L	.069	29	2	1	0	0	1	2	3	.129	.103
Bats Left	R	.305	203	62	11	2	2	22	13	27	.344	.409
Chavez,Eric	L	.167	6	1	0	0	0	0	2	2	.375	.167
Bats Left	R	.254	63	16	3	1	3	8	9	17	.342	.476
Chirinos,Robinson	L	.237	93	22	2	0	6	14	9	22	.308	.452
Bats Right	R	.239	213	51	13	0	7	26	8	49	.283	.399
Chisenhall,Lonnie	L	.294	109	32	4	1	1	8	10	24	.353	.376
Bats Left	R	.276	369	102	25	0	12	51	29	75	.340	.442
Choice,Michael	L	.203	79	16	2	1	4	10	12	20	.304	.405
Bats Right	R	.172	174	30	4	0	5	26	9	49	.223	.282
Choo,Shin-Soo	L	.236	140	33	4	0	4	10	15	50	.323	.350
Bats Left	R	.244	315	77	15	1	9	30	43	81	.348	.384
Ciriaco,Pedro	L	.100	10	1	0	0	0	0	0	2	.100	.100
Bats Right	R	.243	37	9	2	0	0	2	0	7	.263	.297
Clark,Matt	L	-	0	0	0	0	0	0	0	0	-	-
Bats Left	R	.185	27	5	0	0	3	7	2	8	.226	.519
Clevenger,Steve	L	.143	7	1	1	0	0	0	0	1	.143	.286
Bats Left	R	.232	82	19	7	1	0	8	8	18	.300	.341
Coghlan,Chris	L	.247	89	22	4	0	2	10	13	19	.350	.360
Bats Left	R	.294	296	87	24	5	7	31	26	62	.353	.480
Colabello,Chris	L	.211	71	15	4	0	1	14	6	24	.273	.310
Bats Right	R	.239	134	32	9	0	5	25	8	42	.287	.418
Collins,Tyler	L	.200	5	1	0	0	0	0	0	0	.200	.200
Bats Left	R	.263	19	5	0	0	1	4	1	4	.300	.421
Colon,Christian	L	.375	16	6	1	0	0	3	2	1	.444	.438
Bats Right	R	.310	29	9	4	1	0	3	1	3	.333	.517
Colvin,Tyler	L	.300	20	6	2	0	0	2	2	8	.364	.400
Bats Left	R	.210	119	25	8	3	2	16	6	37	.252	.378
Conger,Hank	L	.188	16	3	0	0	0	1	7	4	.435	.188
Bats Both	R	.223	215	48	12	0	4	24	15	53	.279	.335
Conrad,Brooks	L	.000	11	0	0	0	0	1	1	6	.077	.000
Bats Both	R	.158	19	3	1	0	1	1	2	8	.238	.368
Corporan,Carlos	L	.222	72	16	2	0	2	5	3	18	.273	.333
Bats Both	R	.245	98	24	4	0	4	14	11	19	.321	.408
Cowgill,Collin	L	.288	125	36	8	1	3	12	10	27	.350	.440
Bats Right	R	.215	135	29	2	0	2	9	16	47	.312	.274
Cozart,Zack	L	.262	107	28	5	1	2	10	9	16	.319	.383
Bats Right	R	.211	399	84	13	4	2	28	16	63	.254	.278
Craig,Allen	L	.233	120	28	10	1	3	17	9	31	.285	.408
Bats Right	R	.208	341	71	10	0	5	29	26	82	.277	.282
Crawford,Brandon	L	.320	153	49	8	4	3	23	20	39	.395	.484
Bats Left	R	.213	338	72	12	6	7	46	39	90	.291	.346
Crawford,Carl	L	.321	56	18	4	0	2	13	4	9	.381	.500
Bats Left	R	.296	287	85	10	3	6	33	12	46	.330	.415

Batter	vs	Avg	AB	H	2B	3B	HR	RBI	BB	SO	OBP	Slg
Crisp,Coco	L	.227	150	34	7	0	4	16	13	22	.287	.353
Bats Both	R	.256	313	80	14	3	5	31	53	44	.358	.367
Cron,C.J.	L	.258	93	24	7	0	4	12	4	19	.289	.462
Bats Right	R	.255	149	38	5	1	7	25	6	42	.288	.443
Cruz,Nelson	L	.314	137	43	9	1	8	22	22	29	.407	.569
Bats Right	R	.258	476	123	23	1	32	86	33	111	.310	.513
Cruz,Tony	L	.158	38	6	1	0	0	3	4	7	.238	.184
Bats Right	R	.216	97	21	4	0	1	14	9	21	.283	.289
Cuddyer,Michael	L	.412	51	21	5	0	5	13	7	8	.483	.804
Bats Right	R	.302	139	42	10	1	5	18	7	22	.333	.496
Culberson,Charlie	L	.172	58	10	3	1	0	6	5	16	.246	.259
Bats Right	R	.204	152	31	4	1	3	18	7	46	.256	.303
Danks,Jordan	L	.150	20	3	0	0	1	2	4	7	.292	.300
Bats Left	R	.237	97	23	2	0	1	8	10	39	.306	.289
d'Arnaud,Travis	L	.242	99	24	8	0	3	10	7	21	.292	.414
Bats Right	R	.241	286	69	14	3	10	31	25	43	.306	.416
Davis,Chris	L	.188	149	28	7	0	9	26	10	51	.261	.416
Bats Left	R	.199	301	60	9	0	17	46	50	122	.318	.399
Davis,Ike	L	.094	32	3	0	0	0	0	3	12	.171	.094
Bats Left	R	.247	328	81	19	0	11	51	60	66	.360	.405
Davis,Khris	L	.258	124	32	9	0	6	22	8	33	.301	.476
Bats Right	R	.239	377	90	28	2	16	47	24	89	.298	.451
Davis,Rajai	L	.356	149	53	14	2	4	18	7	26	.382	.557
Bats Right	R	.247	312	77	13	0	4	33	15	49	.290	.327
De Aza,Alejandro	L	.138	87	12	2	2	0	4	4	26	.194	.207
Bats Left	R	.277	390	108	22	6	8	37	35	93	.340	.426
DeJesus,David	L	.143	7	1	0	0	0	0	1	1	.333	.143
Bats Left	R	.251	231	58	15	2	6	19	29	42	.345	.411
den Dekker,Matt	L	.200	15	3	0	0	0	0	4	4	.400	.200
Bats Left	R	.255	137	35	11	0	0	7	17	30	.338	.336
Denorfia,Chris	L	.220	150	33	5	2	1	8	14	31	.287	.300
Bats Right	R	.239	180	43	7	2	2	13	11	39	.281	.333
Descalso,Daniel	L	.364	33	12	2	0	0	3	6	3	.475	.424
Bats Left	R	.211	128	27	9	0	0	7	14	30	.294	.281
Desmond,Ian	L	.273	150	41	10	0	5	20	13	41	.331	.440
Bats Right	R	.248	443	110	16	3	19	71	33	142	.307	.427
Diaz,Jonathan	L	.118	17	2	0	0	0	0	2	6	.250	.118
Bats Right	R	.190	21	4	1	0	0	4	1	8	.261	.238
Dickerson,Chris	L	.250	12	3	0	0	0	1	2	4	.357	.250
Bats Left	R	.221	86	19	4	0	2	5	10	34	.302	.337
Dickerson,Corey	L	.253	91	23	6	0	3	14	7	26	.306	.418
Bats Left	R	.328	345	113	21	6	21	62	30	75	.379	.606
Dietrich,Derek	L	.143	21	3	1	0	0	1	0	7	.182	.190
Bats Left	R	.241	137	33	5	2	5	16	13	31	.346	.416
Dobbs,Greg	L	.500	2	1	0	0	0	0	0	0	.500	.500
Bats Left	R	.154	39	6	1	0	0	2	1	8	.171	.179
Dominguez,Matt	L	.242	157	38	6	0	6	19	9	33	.282	.395
Bats Right	R	.204	407	83	11	0	10	38	20	92	.246	.305
Donaldson,Josh	L	.275	153	42	10	1	14	32	24	25	.380	.627
Bats Right	R	.248	455	113	21	1	15	66	52	105	.329	.398
Doumit,Ryan	L	.167	30	5	0	0	1	5	0	10	.167	.267
Bats Both	R	.205	127	26	4	0	4	12	7	39	.250	.331
Dozier,Brian	L	.264	182	48	13	0	8	24	19	41	.337	.467
Bats Right	R	.233	416	97	20	1	15	47	70	88	.349	.394
Drew,Stephen	L	.129	62	8	3	0	0	2	5	22	.194	.177
Bats Left	R	.172	209	36	11	1	7	24	22	53	.249	.335
Duda,Lucas	L	.180	111	20	2	0	2	10	11	41	.264	.252
Bats Left	R	.273	403	110	25	0	28	82	58	94	.372	.543
Duffy,Matt	L	.400	30	12	1	0	0	3	1	5	.455	.433
Bats Right	R	.133	30	4	1	0	0	5	0	9	.133	.167
Dunn,Adam	L	.153	59	9	1	0	2	6	10	21	.282	.271
Bats Left	R	.230	370	85	17	0	20	58	61	138	.345	.438
Duvall,Adam	L	.184	38	7	0	0	1	2	3	11	.262	.263
Bats Right	R	.200	35	7	2	0	2	3	0	9	.200	.429
Dyson,Jarrod	L	.250	52	13	0	1	0	5	5	13	.316	.288
Bats Left	R	.274	208	57	4	3	1	19	17	39	.326	.337
Eaton,Adam	L	.299	134	40	5	1	0	12	14	24	.373	.351
Bats Left	R	.301	352	106	21	9	1	23	29	59	.358	.420
Ellis,A.J.	L	.215	65	14	1	0	2	8	18	14	.388	.323
Bats Right	R	.183	218	40	8	0	1	17	35	43	.301	.234
Ellis,Mark	L	.195	82	16	3	0	0	4	6	14	.256	.232
Bats Right	R	.167	96	16	3	0	0	8	8	24	.250	.198
Ellsbury,Jacoby	L	.300	180	54	12	2	5	21	16	36	.355	.472
Bats Left	R	.258	395	102	15	3	11	49	33	57	.316	.395
Encarnacion,Edwin	L	.263	95	25	5	1	5	11	17	14	.375	.495
Bats Right	R	.270	382	103	22	1	29	87	45	68	.349	.560

Batters vs. Left-Handed and Right-Handed Pitchers

Batter	vs	Avg	AB	H	2B	3B	HR	RBI	BB	SO	OBP	Slg
Escobar,Alcides	L	.313	147	46	9	2	2	14	6	25	.342	.442
Bats Right	R	.275	432	119	25	3	1	36	17	58	.309	.354
Escobar,Eduardo	L	.328	131	43	13	0	4	15	5	24	.358	.519
Bats Both	R	.252	302	76	22	2	2	22	19	69	.296	.358
Escobar,Yunel	L	.270	111	30	5	0	1	7	13	14	.347	.342
Bats Right	R	.255	365	93	13	0	6	32	30	46	.317	.340
Espinosa,Danny	L	.301	103	31	8	1	3	10	8	25	.374	.485
Bats Both	R	.183	230	42	6	2	5	17	10	97	.241	.291
Ethier,Andre	L	.222	45	10	2	0	0	4	4	14	.300	.267
Bats Left	R	.253	296	75	15	6	4	38	27	60	.325	.385
Evans,Nick	L	.294	17	5	2	0	2	6	0	8	.294	.765
Bats Right	R	.200	5	1	0	0	0	1	1	2	.333	.200
Falu,Irving	L	.000	12	0	0	0	0	0	0	1	.000	.000
Bats Both	R	.167	18	3	0	0	0	1	4	4	.304	.167
Federowicz,Tim	L	.190	21	4	0	0	0	2	2	4	.280	.190
Bats Right	R	.080	50	4	3	0	1	3	1	14	.098	.200
Fielder,Prince	L	.237	59	14	4	0	2	8	3	7	.281	.407
Bats Left	R	.253	91	23	4	0	1	8	22	17	.404	.330
Figgins,Chone	L	.174	23	4	1	0	0	0	4	7	.296	.217
Bats Both	R	.243	37	9	2	0	0	1	10	8	.417	.297
Figueroa,Cole	L	.000	1	0	0	0	0	0	0	0	.000	.000
Bats Left	R	.238	42	10	2	1	0	6	4	4	.292	.333
Flaherty,Ryan	L	.174	46	8	1	0	3	7	3	17	.224	.391
Bats Left	R	.230	235	54	14	1	4	25	19	51	.300	.349
Flores,Wilmer	L	.119	59	7	3	0	0	3	6	13	.212	.169
Bats Right	R	.290	200	58	10	1	6	26	6	18	.309	.440
Florimon,Pedro	L	.111	27	3	0	0	0	0	3	6	.200	.111
Bats Both	R	.082	49	4	1	1	0	1	5	16	.167	.143
Flowers,Tyler	L	.255	106	27	2	0	6	16	2	40	.288	.443
Bats Right	R	.236	301	71	14	1	9	34	23	119	.300	.379
Forsythe,Logan	L	.241	141	34	7	1	5	16	11	37	.297	.411
Bats Right	R	.206	160	33	5	0	1	10	14	34	.279	.256
Fowler,Dexter	L	.327	107	35	7	1	2	15	17	19	.419	.467
Bats Both	R	.260	327	85	14	3	6	20	49	89	.361	.376
Francisco,Juan	L	.116	43	5	0	0	1	4	3	21	.204	.186
Bats Left	R	.238	244	58	16	2	15	39	24	95	.306	.504
Franco,Maikel	L	.125	32	4	0	0	0	2	1	9	.152	.125
Bats Right	R	.250	24	6	2	0	0	3	0	4	.240	.333
Francoeur,Jeff	L	.143	14	2	0	0	0	0	2	3	.250	.143
Bats Right	R	.000	10	0	0	0	0	1	1	4	.083	.000
Frandsen,Kevin	L	.303	76	23	2	0	0	5	1	8	.312	.329
Bats Right	R	.236	144	34	6	0	1	12	5	18	.293	.299
Franklin,Nick	L	.133	15	2	0	0	0	1	1	7	.235	.133
Bats Both	R	.167	66	11	2	1	1	5	5	25	.219	.273
Frazier,Todd	L	.254	126	32	7	0	4	15	18	32	.345	.405
Bats Right	R	.278	471	131	15	1	25	65	34	107	.334	.473
Freeman,Freddie	L	.260	181	47	8	1	5	23	24	48	.358	.398
Bats Left	R	.300	426	128	35	3	13	55	66	97	.397	.488
Freese,David	L	.320	100	32	11	0	2	19	12	19	.386	.490
Bats Right	R	.243	362	88	14	1	8	36	26	105	.302	.354
Freiman,Nate	L	.224	67	15	4	0	5	13	4	15	.268	.507
Bats Right	R	.200	20	4	1	0	0	2	1	8	.273	.250
Fryer,Eric	L	.206	34	7	2	0	0	4	1	5	.229	.265
Bats Right	R	.220	41	9	2	0	1	1	4	10	.304	.341
Fuld,Sam	L	.265	98	26	6	1	0	15	11	13	.336	.347
Bats Left	R	.229	253	58	10	3	4	21	32	50	.315	.340
Furcal,Rafael	L	.200	5	1	0	0	0	0	0	1	.200	.200
Bats Both	R	.167	30	5	0	1	0	2	2	6	.219	.233
Galvis,Freddy	L	.182	44	8	1	1	1	6	0	8	.178	.318
Bats Both	R	.173	75	13	2	0	3	6	8	22	.253	.320
Garcia,Avisail	L	.333	45	15	3	0	3	12	5	11	.392	.600
Bats Right	R	.213	127	27	5	0	4	17	9	33	.273	.346
Garcia,Leury	L	.161	62	10	3	0	0	2	0	16	.159	.210
Bats Both	R	.169	83	14	0	0	1	4	5	32	.216	.205
Gardner,Brett	L	.262	164	43	4	1	3	12	15	41	.333	.354
Bats Left	R	.253	391	99	21	7	14	46	41	93	.325	.450
Gattis,Evan	L	.343	70	24	4	0	5	14	2	19	.356	.614
Bats Right	R	.244	299	73	13	1	17	38	20	78	.308	.465
Gennett,Scooter	L	.103	39	4	1	0	0	0	1	11	.125	.128
Bats Left	R	.307	401	123	30	3	9	54	21	56	.338	.464
Gentry,Craig	L	.266	124	33	4	1	0	2	9	19	.331	.315
Bats Right	R	.241	108	26	2	0	0	10	8	25	.305	.259
Getz,Chris	L	.000	6	0	0	0	0	0	0	1	.000	.000
Bats Left	R	.211	19	4	1	0	0	0	1	3	.286	.263
Giambi,Jason	L	-	0	0	0	0	0	0	0	0	-	-
Bats Left	R	.133	60	8	2	0	2	5	9	12	.257	.267

Batter	vs	Avg	AB	H	2B	3B	HR	RBI	BB	SO	OBP	Slg
Giavotella,Johnny	L	.125	8	1	0	0	0	0	1	1	.222	.125
Bats Right	R	.241	29	7	1	0	1	5	0	4	.281	.379
Gillaspie,Conor	L	.221	104	23	7	0	1	10	4	22	.248	.317
Bats Left	R	.300	360	108	24	5	6	47	32	56	.360	.444
Gillespie,Cole	L	.275	51	14	2	0	0	4	6	6	.351	.314
Bats Right	R	.174	23	4	0	0	1	1	0	7	.174	.304
Gimenez,Chris	L	.200	35	7	3	0	0	1	3	8	.263	.286
Bats Right	R	.259	81	21	7	0	0	10	9	21	.333	.346
Goebbert,Jake	L	.000	8	0	0	0	0	0	1	3	.200	.000
Bats Left	R	.237	93	22	1	3	1	10	11	29	.324	.344
Goins,Ryan	L	.158	38	6	1	1	0	4	0	11	.158	.237
Bats Left	R	.196	143	28	5	2	1	11	5	31	.221	.280
Goldschmidt,Paul	L	.384	73	28	6	0	3	10	23	18	.526	.589
Bats Right	R	.282	333	94	33	1	16	59	41	92	.362	.532
Gomes,Jonny	L	.276	170	47	4	0	4	24	27	43	.373	.371
Bats Right	R	.165	103	17	4	0	2	13	8	45	.248	.262
Gomes,Yan	L	.331	145	48	7	1	6	21	8	29	.361	.517
Bats Right	R	.256	340	87	18	2	15	53	16	91	.292	.453
Gomez,Carlos	L	.258	124	32	7	1	6	16	13	22	.352	.476
Bats Right	R	.291	450	131	27	3	17	57	34	119	.357	.478
Gomez,Hector	L	.333	6	2	0	0	0	1	1	1	.429	.333
Bats Right	R	.071	14	1	1	0	0	0	0	8	.071	.143
Gonzalez,Adrian	L	.201	159	32	8	0	4	30	13	44	.261	.327
Bats Left	R	.303	432	131	33	0	23	86	43	68	.362	.539
Gonzalez,Alex	L	.200	5	1	0	0	0	0	1	0	.333	.200
Bats Right	R	.160	25	4	0	1	0	2	1	4	.192	.240
Gonzalez,Carlos	L	.241	87	21	6	0	2	12	2	25	.256	.379
Bats Left	R	.237	173	41	9	1	9	26	17	45	.309	.457
Gonzalez,Marwin	L	.333	39	13	3	0	0	3	1	6	.366	.410
Bats Both	R	.268	246	66	12	1	6	20	16	52	.321	.398
Gordon,Alex	L	.256	168	43	8	0	8	26	19	44	.340	.446
Bats Left	R	.271	395	107	26	1	11	48	46	82	.356	.425
Gordon,Dee	L	.295	132	39	7	2	0	5	7	19	.340	.379
Bats Left	R	.287	477	137	17	10	2	29	24	88	.322	.377
Gose,Anthony	L	.180	50	9	2	0	0	1	4	18	.241	.220
Bats Left	R	.238	189	45	6	1	2	12	21	56	.329	.312
Gosewisch,Tuffy	L	.222	54	12	2	0	0	1	2	7	.250	.259
Bats Right	R	.227	75	17	6	0	1	6	1	17	.237	.347
Gosselin,Phil	L	.275	51	14	2	0	0	0	4	10	.339	.314
Bats Right	R	.260	77	20	2	0	1	3	1	17	.278	.325
Grandal,Yasmani	L	.162	74	12	2	0	0	6	17	27	.323	.189
Bats Both	R	.241	303	73	17	1	15	43	41	88	.329	.452
Granderson,Curtis	L	.245	155	38	5	0	7	24	17	49	.330	.413
Bats Left	R	.220	409	90	22	2	13	42	62	92	.324	.379
Green,Grant	L	.356	45	16	3	0	0	5	0	7	.348	.422
Bats Right	R	.204	54	11	2	0	1	6	2	13	.228	.296
Gregorius,Didi	L	.137	51	7	1	1	0	3	6	14	.228	.196
Bats Left	R	.247	219	54	8	4	6	24	16	38	.304	.402
Grichuk,Randal	L	.242	62	15	3	0	3	4	1	16	.254	.435
Bats Right	R	.250	48	12	3	1	0	4	4	15	.308	.354
Grossman,Robbie	L	.216	88	19	2	0	1	10	10	22	.293	.273
Bats Both	R	.239	272	65	12	2	5	27	45	83	.350	.353
Guyer,Brandon	L	.297	111	33	6	1	1	9	6	23	.366	.396
Bats Right	R	.243	148	36	9	0	2	17	10	29	.311	.345
Guzman,Jesus	L	.183	104	19	2	0	1	8	11	32	.261	.231
Bats Right	R	.197	61	12	2	0	1	1	8	20	.290	.279
Gwynn,Tony	L	.000	21	0	0	0	0	0	3	5	.125	.000
Bats Left	R	.190	84	16	2	1	0	3	12	18	.299	.238
Gyorko,Jedd	L	.228	92	21	6	0	1	11	16	20	.343	.326
Bats Right	R	.205	308	63	11	1	9	40	20	80	.260	.334
Hairston,Scott	L	.250	52	13	4	0	0	4	3	15	.293	.327
Bats Right	R	.120	25	3	0	0	1	4	1	11	.172	.240
Hamilton,Billy	L	.264	140	37	8	2	1	13	6	22	.297	.371
Bats Both	R	.246	423	104	17	6	5	35	28	95	.291	.350
Hamilton,Josh	L	.330	91	30	5	0	4	15	5	32	.367	.516
Bats Left	R	.239	247	59	16	0	6	29	27	76	.318	.377
Hanigan,Ryan	L	.143	49	7	3	0	2	6	8	9	.276	.327
Bats Right	R	.239	176	42	6	0	3	28	23	30	.330	.324
Hannahan,Jack	L	.000	1	0	0	0	0	0	0	0	.000	.000
Bats Left	R	.191	47	9	3	0	0	2	2	17	.224	.255
Hardy,J.J.	L	.226	133	30	7	0	3	10	9	20	.275	.346
Bats Right	R	.283	396	112	21	0	6	42	20	84	.321	.381
Harper,Bryce	L	.263	95	25	3	2	3	12	10	30	.333	.432
Bats Left	R	.276	257	71	7	0	10	20	28	74	.348	.420
Harrison,Josh	L	.345	113	39	10	0	2	10	5	12	.370	.487
Bats Right	R	.307	407	125	28	7	11	42	17	69	.340	.491

Batters vs. Left-Handed and Right-Handed Pitchers

Batter	vs	Avg	AB	H	2B	3B	HR	RBI	BB	SO	OBP	Slg
Hart,Corey	L	.196	92	18	2	0	2	12	6	23	.286	.283
Bats Right	R	.207	140	29	7	0	4	9	10	36	.260	.343
Hayes,Brett	L	.053	19	1	0	0	0	0	1	3	.100	.053
Bats Right	R	.182	33	6	1	0	1	2	0	9	.182	.303
Headley,Chase	L	.248	121	30	4	0	4	11	13	32	.341	.380
Bats Both	R	.241	349	84	16	1	9	38	38	90	.323	.370
Hechavarria,Adeiny	L	.321	106	34	4	1	1	7	3	15	.336	.406
Bats Right	R	.265	430	114	16	9	0	27	23	71	.301	.344
Heisey,Chris	L	.205	83	17	7	0	3	6	3	17	.230	.398
Bats Right	R	.229	192	44	8	2	5	16	12	47	.280	.370
Hernandez,Cesar	L	.290	31	9	1	0	0	1	1	8	.303	.323
Bats Both	R	.217	83	18	1	0	1	3	8	25	.286	.265
Hernandez,Enrique	L	.200	30	6	2	0	0	0	5	4	.314	.267
Bats Right	R	.264	91	24	4	3	3	14	7	17	.323	.473
Herrera,Dilson	L	.182	11	2	0	0	0	0	3	4	.357	.182
Bats Right	R	.229	48	11	0	1	3	11	4	13	.288	.458
Herrera,Elian	L	.226	31	7	1	0	0	0	0	11	.226	.258
Bats Both	R	.288	104	30	6	1	0	5	3	25	.306	.365
Herrera,Jonathan	L	.250	36	9	1	0	0	4	1	11	.317	.278
Bats Both	R	.222	54	12	0	2	0	5	6	13	.300	.296
Herrmann,Chris	L	.250	16	4	0	0	0	1	1	2	.294	.250
Bats Left	R	.203	59	12	3	0	0	3	3	15	.242	.254
Heyward,Jason	L	.169	142	24	2	0	2	14	12	35	.252	.225
Bats Left	R	.304	431	131	24	3	9	44	55	63	.384	.436
Hicks,Aaron	L	.279	68	19	7	0	0	7	15	22	.410	.382
Bats Both	R	.178	118	21	1	0	1	11	21	34	.300	.212
Hicks,Brandon	L	.176	68	12	3	1	2	5	17	23	.345	.338
Bats Right	R	.154	136	21	3	0	6	17	15	54	.243	.309
Hill,Aaron	L	.242	124	30	4	1	4	13	9	20	.293	.387
Bats Right	R	.244	377	92	22	2	6	47	19	72	.284	.361
Hill,Koyie	L	.143	7	1	0	0	0	0	0	2	.143	.143
Bats Both	R	.286	14	4	1	0	0	1	1	3	.333	.357
Hoes,L.J.	L	.227	66	15	4	0	3	7	7	16	.293	.424
Bats Right	R	.107	56	6	1	0	0	4	3	15	.150	.125
Holaday,Bryan	L	.151	73	11	1	1	0	3	4	18	.188	.192
Bats Right	R	.301	83	25	4	0	0	12	4	19	.337	.349
Holliday,Matt	L	.301	133	40	11	0	8	26	30	27	.440	.564
Bats Right	R	.263	441	116	26	0	12	64	44	73	.347	.404
Holt,Brock	L	.293	164	48	12	3	1	11	12	43	.343	.421
Bats Left	R	.274	285	78	11	2	3	18	21	55	.324	.358
Holt,Tyler	L	.311	45	14	1	0	0	2	1	14	.326	.333
Bats Right	R	.192	26	5	1	0	0	0	2	11	.276	.231
Hosmer,Eric	L	.264	148	39	11	0	2	16	6	26	.297	.378
Bats Left	R	.273	355	97	24	1	7	42	29	67	.326	.406
Howard,Ryan	L	.230	161	37	5	0	10	32	19	70	.323	.447
Bats Left	R	.221	408	90	13	1	13	63	48	120	.305	.353
Hundley,Nick	L	.242	33	8	1	0	0	2	3	9	.297	.273
Bats Right	R	.243	185	45	6	0	6	20	7	54	.268	.373
Hunter,Torii	L	.308	146	45	7	0	5	20	7	24	.340	.459
Bats Right	R	.278	403	112	26	2	12	63	16	65	.312	.442
Iannetta,Chris	L	.272	114	31	7	0	6	19	20	21	.388	.491
Bats Right	R	.240	192	46	15	0	1	24	34	70	.363	.333
Ibanez,Raul	L	.024	41	1	1	0	0	2	4	9	.109	.049
Bats Left	R	.195	205	40	7	3	5	24	29	50	.295	.332
Inciarte,Ender	L	.273	128	35	4	1	0	4	10	14	.326	.320
Bats Left	R	.279	290	81	14	1	4	23	15	39	.315	.376
Infante,Omar	L	.217	138	30	8	0	2	8	9	19	.265	.319
Bats Right	R	.264	390	103	13	3	4	58	24	49	.305	.344
Ishikawa,Travis	L	.182	11	2	1	0	0	2	1	6	.250	.273
Bats Left	R	.260	96	25	3	1	3	16	8	28	.318	.406
Izturis,Maicer	L	.357	14	5	1	0	0	0	0	2	.357	.429
Bats Both	R	.238	21	5	0	0	0	1	2	2	.304	.238
Jackson,Austin	L	.299	174	52	9	1	1	14	17	40	.356	.379
Bats Right	R	.239	423	101	21	5	3	33	30	104	.289	.333
Jaso,John	L	.167	24	4	1	0	0	5	2	5	.259	.208
Bats Left	R	.272	283	77	17	3	9	35	26	55	.344	.449
Jay,Jon	L	.375	88	33	5	1	0	17	4	21	.404	.455
Bats Left	R	.283	325	92	11	2	3	29	24	57	.364	.357
Jennings,Desmond	L	.265	117	31	9	1	5	10	14	29	.346	.487
Bats Right	R	.238	362	86	21	1	5	26	33	79	.310	.343
Jeter,Derek	L	.244	168	41	4	0	2	16	9	18	.289	.304
Bats Right	R	.262	413	108	15	1	2	34	26	69	.309	.317
Jimenez,Luis	L	.174	23	4	2	0	0	2	0	8	.208	.261
Bats Right	R	.143	14	2	0	0	0	0	0	5	.200	.143
Johnson,Chris	L	.395	114	45	9	0	3	18	8	25	.435	.553
Bats Right	R	.231	468	108	18	0	7	40	15	134	.256	.314

Batter	vs	Avg	AB	H	2B	3B	HR	RBI	BB	SO	OBP	Slg
Johnson,Dan	L	.200	10	2	0	0	1	5	1	2	.250	.500
Bats Left	R	.214	28	6	2	0	0	2	6	8	.361	.286
Johnson,Kelly	L	.184	38	7	3	1	1	5	5	8	.295	.395
Bats Left	R	.220	227	50	11	1	6	22	24	63	.296	.357
Johnson,Reed	L	.303	66	20	4	0	1	6	0	16	.319	.409
Bats Right	R	.198	121	24	11	0	1	19	1	21	.238	.314
Jones,Adam	L	.344	154	53	11	1	9	20	11	30	.399	.604
Bats Right	R	.261	490	128	19	1	20	76	8	103	.282	.427
Jones,Garrett	L	.221	68	15	3	0	0	3	5	19	.274	.265
Bats Left	R	.250	428	107	30	2	15	50	41	97	.314	.435
Jones,James	L	.247	89	22	4	1	0	2	3	20	.272	.315
Bats Left	R	.251	223	56	5	4	0	7	9	47	.280	.309
Joseph,Caleb	L	.202	89	18	2	0	5	10	5	25	.250	.393
Bats Right	R	.210	157	33	7	0	4	18	12	44	.272	.331
Joyce,Matt	L	.147	34	5	1	0	1	7	0	17	.143	.265
Bats Left	R	.263	384	101	22	2	8	45	62	94	.365	.393
Kalish,Ryan	L	.333	9	3	0	0	0	0	1	2	.400	.333
Bats Left	R	.241	112	27	4	4	0	5	7	26	.286	.348
Kawasaki,Munenori	L	.283	46	13	1	0	0	3	4	11	.340	.304
Bats Left	R	.253	194	49	6	1	0	14	18	38	.324	.294
Kelly,Don	L	.120	25	3	0	1	0	1	6	8	.290	.200
Bats Left	R	.268	138	37	5	0	0	6	14	21	.340	.304
Kemp,Matt	L	.264	148	39	7	2	6	26	14	29	.321	.459
Bats Right	R	.295	393	116	31	1	19	63	38	116	.355	.524
Kendrick,Howie	L	.327	156	51	11	0	3	17	13	26	.379	.455
Bats Right	R	.282	461	130	22	5	4	58	35	84	.337	.377
Kiermaier,Kevin	L	.203	74	15	1	1	1	8	1	20	.213	.284
Bats Left	R	.280	257	72	15	7	9	27	22	51	.342	.498
Kieschnick,Roger	L	.000	10	0	0	0	0	0	0	5	.000	.000
Bats Left	R	.258	31	8	1	0	1	2	0	11	.258	.387
Kinsler,Ian	L	.281	171	48	11	1	4	22	7	16	.313	.427
Bats Right	R	.273	513	140	29	3	13	70	22	63	.305	.417
Kipnis,Jason	L	.208	168	35	3	0	1	12	9	37	.256	.244
Bats Left	R	.256	332	85	22	1	5	29	41	63	.337	.373
Konerko,Paul	L	.252	119	30	5	0	4	16	6	28	.286	.395
Bats Right	R	.146	89	13	3	0	1	6	4	23	.214	.213
Kottaras,George	L	.000	5	0	0	0	0	0	0	4	.000	.000
Bats Left	R	.280	25	7	0	0	3	5	6	12	.406	.640
Kouzmanoff,Kevin	L	.462	13	6	3	0	0	2	1	1	.500	.692
Bats Right	R	.324	34	11	3	0	2	8	1	6	.378	.588
Kozma,Pete	L	.250	8	2	1	0	0	0	2	1	.400	.375
Bats Right	R	.333	15	5	2	0	0	0	1	3	.375	.467
Kratz,Erik	L	.208	53	11	2	0	3	9	2	9	.232	.415
Bats Right	R	.228	57	13	2	0	2	4	2	13	.254	.368
Krauss,Marc	L	.400	10	4	0	0	1	2	0	4	.400	.700
Bats Left	R	.182	176	32	6	0	5	19	21	50	.273	.301
Kubel,Jason	L	.194	36	7	1	1	0	5	5	12	.310	.278
Bats Left	R	.233	120	28	5	0	1	8	14	47	.313	.300
La Stella,Tommy	L	.311	61	19	5	1	0	11	8	12	.391	.426
Bats Left	R	.236	258	61	11	0	1	20	28	28	.313	.291
Lagares,Juan	L	.349	86	30	4	1	2	7	4	19	.387	.488
Bats Right	R	.264	330	87	20	2	2	40	16	68	.303	.355
Laird,Gerald	L	.186	43	8	3	0	0	2	3	11	.239	.256
Bats Right	R	.211	109	23	5	0	0	8	11	22	.289	.257
Lake,Junior	L	.213	94	20	4	1	3	10	7	33	.272	.372
Bats Right	R	.210	214	45	6	2	6	15	7	77	.234	.341
Lamb,Jake	L	.136	22	3	0	1	0	1	0	7	.136	.227
Bats Left	R	.250	104	26	4	0	4	10	6	30	.288	.404
Lambo,Andrew	L	-	0	0	0	0	0	0	0	0	-	-
Bats Left	R	.256	39	10	4	0	0	1	0	8	.256	.359
LaRoche,Adam	L	.204	137	28	3	0	5	16	15	43	.284	.336
Bats Left	R	.280	357	100	16	0	21	76	67	65	.390	.501
Lawrie,Brett	L	.197	61	12	4	0	2	7	3	15	.234	.361
Bats Right	R	.263	198	52	5	0	10	31	13	34	.321	.439
LeMahieu,DJ	L	.286	119	34	3	0	1	9	9	21	.333	.336
Bats Right	R	.261	375	98	12	5	4	33	24	76	.308	.352
Leon,Sandy	L	.217	23	5	1	0	0	0	1	6	.250	.261
Bats Both	R	.122	41	5	0	0	1	3	5	14	.217	.195
Lind,Adam	L	.061	33	2	0	0	0	0	4	11	.162	.061
Bats Left	R	.354	257	91	24	2	6	40	24	37	.409	.533
Liriano,Rymer	L	.212	52	11	1	0	1	4	2	20	.255	.288
Bats Right	R	.228	57	13	1	0	0	2	7	19	.318	.246
Lobaton,Jose	L	.230	61	14	0	0	0	4	2	14	.254	.230
Bats Both	R	.235	153	36	9	0	2	8	13	47	.299	.333
Lombardozzi,Steve	L	.071	14	1	0	0	0	0	0	2	.071	.071
Bats Both	R	.339	59	20	1	1	0	2	0	12	.350	.390

Batters vs. Left-Handed and Right-Handed Pitchers

Batter	vs	Avg	AB	H	2B	3B	HR	RBI	BB	SO	OBP	Slg
Loney,James	L	.256	172	44	7	0	1	20	5	32	.287	.314
Bats Left	R	.304	428	130	20	0	8	49	36	48	.355	.407
Longoria,Evan	L	.273	154	42	10	1	5	20	24	28	.376	.448
Bats Right	R	.247	470	116	16	0	17	71	33	105	.301	.389
Lough,David	L	.100	20	2	1	0	0	0	0	3	.100	.150
Bats Left	R	.266	154	41	5	3	4	16	15	30	.333	.416
Lowrie,Jed	L	.228	145	33	8	1	1	11	12	26	.281	.317
Bats Both	R	.258	357	92	21	2	5	39	39	53	.337	.370
Lucas,Ed	L	.329	73	24	3	0	1	5	1	14	.338	.411
Bats Right	R	.198	106	21	2	0	0	4	7	34	.248	.217
Lucroy,Jonathan	L	.304	138	42	17	1	1	16	15	19	.374	.464
Bats Right	R	.300	447	134	36	1	12	53	51	52	.372	.465
Ludwick,Ryan	L	.253	91	23	8	0	4	14	9	25	.324	.473
Bats Right	R	.241	266	64	12	0	5	31	22	69	.303	.342
Lutz,Donald	L	.333	3	1	0	0	0	0	0	1	.333	.333
Bats Left	R	.167	48	8	4	0	0	1	3	18	.216	.250
Machado,Manny	L	.240	96	23	6	0	2	6	4	22	.277	.365
Bats Right	R	.294	231	68	8	0	10	26	16	46	.343	.459
Maldonado,Martin	L	.250	44	11	3	0	2	9	1	17	.267	.455
Bats Right	R	.224	67	15	2	0	2	7	10	15	.350	.343
Marisnick,Jake	L	.327	49	16	2	0	0	2	3	10	.370	.367
Bats Right	R	.227	172	39	6	0	3	17	5	57	.254	.314
Markakis,Nick	L	.280	182	51	6	0	1	8	16	33	.343	.330
Bats Left	R	.274	460	126	21	1	13	42	46	51	.342	.409
Marte,Alfredo	L	.242	33	8	2	1	1	5	2	11	.286	.455
Bats Right	R	.137	73	10	3	0	1	4	4	23	.192	.219
Marte,Starling	L	.303	89	27	6	1	1	10	6	28	.354	.427
Bats Right	R	.288	406	117	23	5	12	46	27	103	.356	.458
Martin,Leonys	L	.250	136	34	0	0	2	9	6	32	.287	.294
Bats Left	R	.282	397	112	13	7	5	31	33	82	.337	.388
Martin,Russell	L	.257	74	19	1	0	0	9	20	21	.423	.270
Bats Right	R	.298	305	91	19	0	11	58	39	57	.396	.469
Martinez,J.D.	L	.307	114	35	9	1	9	27	11	29	.362	.640
Bats Right	R	.318	327	104	21	2	14	49	19	97	.357	.523
Martinez,Michael	L	.071	14	1	0	0	0	0	1	5	.133	.071
Bats Both	R	.160	25	4	1	0	0	2	3	8	.250	.200
Martinez,Victor	L	.371	143	53	10	0	12	29	14	14	.430	.692
Bats Both	R	.323	418	135	23	0	20	74	56	28	.402	.522
Mastroianni,Darin	L	.103	29	3	0	0	1	2	0	4	.103	.207
Bats Right	R	.143	14	2	0	0	0	0	1	6	.200	.143
Mathis,Jeff	L	.273	44	12	2	0	1	5	1	11	.289	.386
Bats Right	R	.176	131	23	5	0	1	7	14	53	.255	.237
Mauer,Joe	L	.268	164	44	3	0	1	21	20	36	.349	.305
Bats Left	R	.282	291	82	24	2	3	34	40	60	.367	.409
Maxwell,Justin	L	.087	23	2	0	0	0	2	1	11	.154	.087
Bats Right	R	.235	17	4	1	0	0	1	1	9	.316	.294
Mayberry,John	L	.243	70	17	8	0	5	15	11	10	.341	.571
Bats Right	R	.184	76	14	2	0	2	8	9	25	.279	.289
Maybin,Cameron	L	.211	90	19	3	2	1	4	5	21	.253	.322
Bats Right	R	.248	161	40	10	2	0	11	14	35	.311	.335
McBride,Matt	L	.313	16	5	2	0	2	5	2	6	.389	.813
Bats Right	R	.133	15	2	0	0	0	1	0	6	.188	.133
McCann,Brian	L	.292	137	40	6	1	8	30	5	24	.324	.526
Bats Left	R	.209	358	75	9	0	15	45	27	53	.272	.360
McCutchen,Andrew	L	.280	100	28	4	1	6	13	17	17	.392	.520
Bats Right	R	.321	448	144	34	5	19	70	67	98	.415	.547
McDonald,John	L	.192	26	5	1	0	0	2	3	4	.300	.231
Bats Right	R	.160	50	8	1	0	0	3	4	14	.232	.180
McGehee,Casey	L	.219	114	25	4	0	1	20	17	17	.316	.281
Bats Right	R	.303	502	152	25	1	3	56	50	85	.364	.375
McKenry,Michael	L	.279	43	12	2	0	3	6	11	11	.426	.535
Bats Right	R	.328	125	41	7	0	5	16	11	31	.387	.504
McLouth,Nate	L	.190	21	4	1	0	0	0	3	6	.292	.238
Bats Left	R	.169	118	20	5	0	1	7	13	29	.277	.237
Medica,Tommy	L	.245	98	24	4	0	6	14	5	25	.288	.469
Bats Right	R	.225	142	32	7	2	3	13	9	50	.284	.366
Mercer,Jordy	L	.314	121	38	8	0	3	20	6	13	.349	.455
Bats Right	R	.236	385	91	19	2	9	35	29	76	.292	.366
Mesoraco,Devin	L	.291	79	23	5	0	4	16	17	17	.418	.506
Bats Right	R	.269	305	82	20	0	21	64	24	86	.342	.541
Middlebrooks,Will	L	.170	53	9	3	0	0	5	4	20	.228	.226
Bats Right	R	.198	162	32	7	0	2	14	11	50	.266	.278
Miller,Brad	L	.170	94	16	1	3	2	8	6	35	.233	.309
Bats Left	R	.238	273	65	14	1	8	28	28	60	.307	.385
Molina,Jose	L	.255	51	13	1	0	0	2	3	11	.309	.275
Bats Right	R	.155	174	27	1	0	0	8	11	44	.207	.161

Batter	vs	Avg	AB	H	2B	3B	HR	RBI	BB	SO	OBP	Slg
Molina,Yadier	L	.278	97	27	4	0	4	14	10	15	.352	.443
Bats Right	R	.283	307	87	17	0	3	24	18	40	.327	.368
Montero,Miguel	L	.198	106	21	6	0	2	16	7	27	.252	.311
Bats Left	R	.256	383	98	17	0	11	56	49	70	.348	.386
Moore,Tyler	L	.207	29	6	0	0	2	4	4	13	.303	.414
Bats Right	R	.242	62	15	2	0	2	10	3	16	.299	.371
Morales,Kendrys	L	.239	134	32	7	0	4	19	8	22	.281	.381
Bats Both	R	.206	233	48	13	0	4	23	19	46	.271	.313
Morel,Brent	L	.130	23	3	1	0	0	3	2	3	.200	.174
Bats Right	R	.250	16	4	1	0	0	1	0	6	.250	.313
Moreland,Mitch	L	.120	25	3	1	0	0	2	3	9	.214	.160
Bats Left	R	.268	142	38	8	1	2	21	9	34	.312	.380
Morgan,Nyjer	L	.000	1	0	0	0	0	0	1	1	.500	.000
Bats Left	R	.350	40	14	1	0	1	6	6	5	.426	.450
Morneau,Justin	L	.254	130	33	7	0	3	18	6	18	.288	.377
Bats Left	R	.341	372	127	25	3	14	64	28	42	.389	.538
Morrison,Logan	L	.333	90	30	7	0	2	10	4	16	.368	.478
Bats Left	R	.236	246	58	13	0	9	28	20	43	.296	.398
Morse,Michael	L	.248	141	35	11	1	8	16	11	47	.316	.511
Bats Right	R	.293	297	87	21	2	8	45	20	74	.346	.458
Moss,Brandon	L	.264	87	23	2	0	4	11	12	32	.366	.425
Bats Left	R	.228	413	94	21	2	21	70	55	121	.328	.441
Moustakas,Mike	L	.172	99	17	5	0	3	8	8	16	.241	.313
Bats Left	R	.223	358	80	16	1	12	46	27	58	.279	.374
Murphy,Daniel	L	.274	146	40	4	2	2	11	10	21	.325	.370
Bats Left	R	.293	450	132	33	0	7	46	29	65	.334	.413
Murphy,David	L	.238	80	19	2	1	1	17	4	14	.279	.325
Bats Left	R	.268	336	90	23	0	7	41	32	47	.328	.399
Murphy,Donnie	L	.233	30	7	1	0	2	7	3	6	.294	.467
Bats Right	R	.183	82	15	2	0	2	7	8	32	.258	.280
Murphy,JR	L	.270	37	10	1	0	1	4	2	7	.308	.378
Bats Right	R	.295	44	13	3	0	0	5	2	15	.326	.364
Myers,Wil	L	.192	99	19	5	0	1	12	9	27	.259	.273
Bats Right	R	.235	226	53	9	0	5	23	25	63	.308	.341
Nady,Xavier	L	.200	15	3	1	0	2	2	4	4	.368	.667
Bats Right	R	.091	22	2	0	0	1	2	1	5	.130	.227
Napoli,Mike	L	.300	110	33	7	0	4	10	29	33	.450	.473
Bats Right	R	.230	305	70	13	0	13	45	49	100	.339	.400
Nava,Daniel	L	.159	63	10	2	0	0	3	4	18	.209	.190
Bats Both	R	.293	300	88	19	0	4	34	29	63	.372	.397
Navarro,Dioner	L	.280	132	37	4	0	4	15	8	16	.324	.402
Bats Both	R	.272	349	95	18	0	8	54	24	60	.315	.393
Navarro,Efren	L	.321	28	9	1	0	0	1	1	6	.345	.357
Bats Left	R	.229	131	30	9	1	1	13	12	21	.294	.336
Negron,Kristopher	L	.318	44	14	4	0	4	10	4	10	.375	.682
Bats Right	R	.250	100	25	6	1	2	7	8	30	.312	.390
Nelson,Chris	L	.161	31	5	1	0	0	4	0	3	.156	.194
Bats Right	R	.286	42	12	2	0	0	3	7	11	.388	.333
Nieto,Adrian	L	.273	22	6	2	0	0	0	3	5	.360	.364
Bats Both	R	.226	84	19	3	0	2	7	5	33	.278	.333
Nieuwenhuis,Kirk	L	.222	9	2	0	0	0	0	1	4	.300	.222
Bats Left	R	.262	103	27	14	1	3	16	15	35	.350	.505
Nieves,Wil	L	.200	30	6	1	0	1	2	0	10	.226	.333
Bats Right	R	.272	92	25	7	0	0	5	1	24	.284	.348
Nix,Jayson	L	.091	44	4	0	0	0	0	3	17	.149	.091
Bats Right	R	.154	39	6	0	0	1	4	0	11	.190	.231
Norris,Derek	L	.311	151	47	9	0	5	29	21	25	.393	.470
Bats Right	R	.244	234	57	10	1	5	26	33	61	.340	.359
Nunez,Eduardo	L	.232	99	23	5	2	1	8	0	15	.232	.354
Bats Right	R	.267	105	28	2	2	3	16	5	16	.306	.410
Odor,Rougned	L	.248	109	27	2	0	2	7	6	26	.305	.321
Bats Left	R	.264	277	73	12	7	7	41	11	45	.294	.433
Olivo,Miguel	L	.000	3	0	0	0	0	0	0	1	.000	.000
Bats Right	R	.250	20	5	0	1	0	2	1	11	.273	.350
Olt,Mike	L	.165	79	13	2	0	6	10	11	28	.264	.418
Bats Right	R	.158	146	23	6	0	6	23	14	72	.240	.322
Ortiz,David	L	.275	171	47	13	0	11	37	18	32	.349	.544
Bats Left	R	.256	347	89	14	0	24	67	57	63	.359	.504
Overbay,Lyle	L	.185	27	5	0	0	0	2	2	11	.241	.185
Bats Left	R	.238	231	55	14	0	4	33	34	49	.337	.351
Owings,Chris	L	.309	68	21	6	2	1	4	2	14	.329	.500
Bats Right	R	.248	242	60	9	4	5	22	14	53	.292	.380
Ozuna,Marcell	L	.245	110	27	3	0	6	20	8	34	.292	.436
Bats Right	R	.275	455	125	23	5	17	65	33	130	.323	.459
Pacheco,Jordan	L	.283	60	17	6	0	0	5	4	13	.328	.383
Bats Right	R	.237	93	22	4	1	0	11	5	14	.280	.301

Batters vs. Left-Handed and Right-Handed Pitchers

Batter	vs	Avg	AB	H	2B	3B	HR	RBI	BB	SO	OBP	Slg
Pagan,Angel	L	.239	138	33	8	0	2	8	9	28	.286	.341
Bats Both	R	.335	245	82	13	2	1	19	16	25	.374	.416
Panik,Joe	L	.373	83	31	3	2	0	6	1	12	.381	.458
Bats Left	R	.274	186	51	7	0	1	12	15	21	.327	.328
Paredes,Jimmy	L	.400	10	4	0	0	1	2	0	2	.400	.700
Bats Both	R	.264	53	14	4	0	1	6	2	14	.291	.396
Parker,Kyle	L	.125	8	1	0	0	0	0	0	5	.125	.125
Bats Right	R	.222	18	4	1	0	0	1	0	9	.222	.278
Parmelee,Chris	L	.325	77	25	4	0	3	10	5	24	.366	.494
Bats Left	R	.225	173	39	7	0	4	18	12	40	.282	.335
Parra,Gerardo	L	.206	97	20	1	0	1	9	12	27	.306	.247
Bats Left	R	.273	432	118	21	4	8	31	20	73	.309	.396
Parrino,Andy	L	.150	20	3	2	0	0	1	1	5	.227	.250
Bats Both	R	.154	26	4	1	0	1	2	2	9	.207	.308
Pastornicky,Tyler	L	.350	20	7	0	1	0	0	4	6	.458	.450
Bats Right	R	.050	20	1	0	0	0	2	2	5	.136	.050
Paul,Xavier	L	.000	4	0	0	0	0	0	0	2	.000	.000
Bats Left	R	.125	16	2	0	0	0	0	1	6	.176	.125
Paulsen,Ben	L	.333	12	4	0	0	3	4	0	3	.333	1.083
Bats Left	R	.314	51	16	4	0	1	6	2	16	.352	.451
Pearce,Steve	L	.327	98	32	10	0	9	18	13	13	.405	.704
Bats Right	R	.279	240	67	16	0	12	31	27	63	.360	.496
Pederson,Joc	L	.000	5	0	0	0	0	0	1	3	.167	.000
Bats Left	R	.174	23	4	0	0	0	0	8	8	.387	.174
Pedroia,Dustin	L	.250	152	38	14	0	3	12	17	24	.325	.401
Bats Right	R	.288	399	115	19	0	4	41	34	51	.341	.366
Pena,Brayan	L	.184	76	14	4	0	0	7	3	12	.213	.237
Bats Both	R	.272	272	74	14	1	5	19	17	30	.313	.386
Pena,Carlos	L	.077	13	1	1	0	0	1	0	4	.077	.154
Bats Left	R	.152	46	7	2	0	1	1	4	7	.220	.261
Pena,Ramiro	L	.286	28	8	0	0	1	2	0	9	.286	.393
Bats Both	R	.235	119	28	6	0	2	7	13	29	.308	.336
Pence,Hunter	L	.284	183	52	8	2	4	19	19	39	.355	.415
Bats Right	R	.274	467	128	21	8	16	55	33	91	.323	.456
Pennington,Cliff	L	.265	49	13	3	1	1	4	7	9	.368	.429
Bats Both	R	.250	128	32	2	2	1	6	13	27	.329	.320
Peralta,David	L	.197	76	15	3	1	0	4	4	21	.247	.263
Bats Left	R	.312	253	79	9	8	8	32	12	39	.342	.506
Peralta,Jhonny	L	.265	113	30	12	0	4	18	25	25	.401	.478
Bats Right	R	.262	447	117	26	0	17	57	33	87	.317	.434
Perez,Juan	L	.163	49	8	2	0	1	2	2	14	.212	.265
Bats Right	R	.176	51	9	5	0	0	1	3	11	.236	.275
Perez,Roberto	L	.167	24	4	0	0	0	0	2	8	.231	.167
Bats Right	R	.311	61	19	5	0	1	4	3	18	.344	.443
Perez,Salvador	L	.226	133	30	2	1	4	16	10	17	.286	.346
Bats Right	R	.270	445	120	26	1	13	54	12	68	.290	.420
Peterson,Jace	L	.250	12	3	0	0	0	0	1	6	.357	.250
Bats Left	R	.073	41	3	0	0	0	0	1	12	.095	.073
Petit,Gregorio	L	.379	29	11	4	0	2	5	1	8	.400	.724
Bats Right	R	.235	68	16	4	0	0	4	0	17	.257	.294
Phegley,Josh	L	.200	10	2	0	0	2	2	0	2	.200	.800
Bats Right	R	.222	27	6	2	0	1	5	0	9	.214	.407
Phillips,Brandon	L	.229	109	25	5	0	1	9	10	19	.292	.303
Bats Right	R	.278	353	98	20	0	7	42	13	55	.310	.394
Pierzynski,A.J.	L	.204	93	19	2	0	1	10	1	13	.232	.258
Bats Left	R	.269	245	66	10	1	4	27	13	41	.309	.367
Pillar,Kevin	L	.304	46	14	4	0	1	4	2	10	.327	.457
Bats Right	R	.243	70	17	5	0	1	3	2	18	.274	.357
Pinto,Josmil	L	.186	59	11	3	0	2	5	12	22	.324	.339
Bats Right	R	.236	110	26	5	0	5	13	12	28	.310	.418
Pirela,Jose	L	.833	6	5	1	1	0	3	0	1	.833	1.333
Bats Right	R	.167	18	3	0	1	0	0	1	3	.211	.278
Plouffe,Trevor	L	.278	151	42	15	1	2	15	17	24	.353	.430
Bats Right	R	.249	369	92	25	1	12	65	36	85	.318	.420
Polanco,Gregory	L	.171	82	14	0	0	2	10	6	20	.222	.244
Bats Left	R	.262	195	51	9	0	5	23	24	39	.342	.385
Pollock,A.J.	L	.280	50	14	2	3	3	10	4	5	.333	.620
Bats Right	R	.307	215	66	17	3	4	14	15	41	.358	.470
Pompey,Dalton	L	.071	14	1	0	0	0	0	2	5	.188	.071
Bats Both	R	.320	25	8	1	2	1	4	2	7	.370	.640
Posey,Buster	L	.304	168	51	10	1	8	32	13	16	.357	.518
Bats Right	R	.314	379	119	18	1	14	57	34	53	.366	.478
Prado,Martin	L	.366	112	41	7	1	5	17	7	11	.398	.580
Bats Right	R	.259	424	110	19	3	7	41	19	69	.300	.368
Presley,Alex	L	.375	24	9	1	0	0	1	0	3	.360	.417
Bats Left	R	.230	230	53	5	1	6	18	13	41	.273	.339

Batter	vs	Avg	AB	H	2B	3B	HR	RBI	BB	SO	OBP	Slg
Puig,Yasiel	L	.258	128	33	5	1	2	8	20	21	.377	.359
Bats Right	R	.307	430	132	32	8	14	61	47	103	.384	.516
Pujols,Albert	L	.263	156	41	9	0	6	20	9	14	.301	.436
Bats Right	R	.275	477	131	28	1	22	85	39	57	.331	.476
Punto,Nick	L	.238	101	24	4	0	1	11	9	25	.300	.307
Bats Both	R	.175	97	17	3	2	1	3	16	31	.292	.278
Quentin,Carlos	L	.180	50	9	2	0	1	7	6	21	.283	.280
Bats Right	R	.175	80	14	4	0	3	11	11	12	.284	.338
Quintanilla,Omar	L	.333	3	1	0	0	0	0	0	0	.333	.333
Bats Left	R	.192	26	5	1	0	0	3	2	5	.250	.231
Raburn,Ryan	L	.195	123	24	5	0	4	14	12	32	.263	.333
Bats Right	R	.208	72	15	2	0	0	8	1	19	.227	.236
Ramirez,Alexei	L	.273	154	42	10	0	5	18	6	21	.309	.435
Bats Right	R	.274	468	128	25	2	10	56	18	60	.304	.400
Ramirez,Aramis	L	.327	101	33	6	0	8	20	9	16	.400	.624
Bats Right	R	.275	393	108	17	1	7	46	12	59	.310	.377
Ramirez,Hanley	L	.282	103	29	8	0	4	11	18	22	.393	.476
Bats Right	R	.283	346	98	27	0	9	60	38	62	.362	.439
Ramirez,Jose	L	.291	79	23	3	1	0	6	4	13	.321	.354
Bats Both	R	.247	158	39	7	1	2	11	9	22	.290	.342
Ramos,Wilson	L	.325	80	26	3	0	3	15	3	13	.345	.475
Bats Right	R	.249	261	65	9	0	8	32	14	44	.285	.375
Rasmus,Colby	L	.195	87	17	5	0	4	9	12	35	.293	.391
Bats Left	R	.236	259	61	16	1	14	31	17	89	.285	.467
Realmuto,J.T.	L	1.000	1	1	0	0	0	1	0	0	1.000	1.000
Bats Right	R	.214	28	6	1	1	0	8	1	8	.241	.321
Recker,Anthony	L	.114	35	4	1	0	0	2	1	15	.139	.143
Bats Right	R	.223	139	31	8	0	7	25	9	49	.272	.432
Reddick,Josh	L	.222	99	22	1	1	0	8	7	21	.280	.253
Bats Left	R	.280	264	74	15	6	12	46	21	42	.330	.519
Reimold,Nolan	L	.265	34	9	3	0	1	10	4	15	.317	.441
Bats Right	R	.200	35	7	2	0	2	3	2	17	.243	.429
Rendon,Anthony	L	.313	160	50	13	1	3	17	13	24	.362	.463
Bats Right	R	.278	453	126	26	5	18	66	45	80	.347	.477
Revere,Ben	L	.341	179	61	3	3	1	8	3	18	.355	.408
Bats Left	R	.291	422	123	10	4	1	20	10	31	.312	.341
Reyes,Jose	L	.281	167	47	12	1	1	19	12	15	.326	.383
Bats Both	R	.289	443	128	21	3	8	32	26	58	.328	.404
Reynolds,Mark	L	.173	98	17	3	0	3	6	13	25	.277	.296
Bats Right	R	.204	280	57	6	0	19	39	34	97	.291	.429
Rios,Alex	L	.325	123	40	13	4	2	24	7	19	.353	.545
Bats Right	R	.266	369	98	17	4	2	30	16	74	.296	.350
Rivera,Rene	L	.280	100	28	7	0	6	20	11	19	.351	.530
Bats Right	R	.237	194	46	11	1	5	24	16	57	.302	.381
Rizzo,Anthony	L	.300	140	42	5	0	8	23	23	28	.421	.507
Bats Left	R	.281	384	108	23	1	24	55	50	88	.373	.534
Roberts,Brian	L	.253	79	20	2	1	1	9	9	12	.330	.342
Bats Both	R	.231	238	55	14	3	4	12	19	41	.290	.366
Robertson,Daniel	L	.330	97	32	9	0	0	15	11	10	.398	.423
Bats Right	R	.200	80	16	0	1	0	6	6	18	.253	.225
Robinson,Shane	L	.152	33	5	1	0	0	2	4	5	.243	.182
Bats Right	R	.148	27	4	0	1	0	2	2	5	.207	.222
Rodriguez,Sean	L	.221	122	27	7	2	5	22	10	32	.295	.434
Bats Right	R	.200	115	23	6	1	7	19	0	34	.214	.452
Rodriguez,Yorman	L	.167	6	1	0	0	0	0	0	3	.167	.167
Bats Right	R	.238	21	5	0	0	0	2	1	9	.304	.238
Rojas,Miguel	L	.061	33	2	2	0	0	3	4	3	.162	.121
Bats Right	R	.216	116	25	1	0	1	6	6	25	.266	.250
Rollins,Jimmy	L	.237	152	36	6	2	3	14	17	28	.318	.362
Bats Both	R	.246	386	95	16	2	14	41	47	72	.326	.407
Romak,Jamie	L	.000	11	0	0	0	0	0	1	6	.083	.000
Bats Right	R	.100	10	1	1	0	0	3	1	2	.182	.200
Romero,Stefen	L	.207	116	24	3	2	1	5	2	31	.238	.293
Bats Right	R	.164	61	10	3	0	2	6	2	17	.227	.311
Romine,Andrew	L	.333	54	18	3	0	0	1	2	9	.357	.389
Bats Both	R	.198	197	39	3	0	2	11	16	51	.258	.244
Rosales,Adam	L	.281	64	18	4	0	2	10	10	20	.387	.438
Bats Right	R	.250	100	25	3	0	2	9	3	22	.286	.340
Rosario,Wilin	L	.317	101	32	9	0	8	18	5	14	.346	.644
Bats Right	R	.249	281	70	16	0	5	36	18	56	.290	.359
Ross,Cody	L	.254	71	18	1	0	1	6	7	11	.329	.310
Bats Right	R	.252	131	33	7	0	1	9	8	33	.293	.328
Ross,David	L	.228	57	13	3	0	4	7	8	21	.318	.491
Bats Right	R	.158	95	15	4	0	3	8	8	37	.223	.295
Rua,Ryan	L	.387	31	12	4	0	0	3	0	3	.406	.516
Bats Right	R	.257	74	19	3	0	2	11	2	15	.286	.378

Batters vs. Left-Handed and Right-Handed Pitchers

Batter	vs	Avg	AB	H	2B	3B	HR	RBI	BB	SO	OBP	Slg
Ruf,Darin	L	.295	61	18	5	0	3	7	7	16	.392	.525
Bats Right	R	.146	41	6	3	0	0	1	1	16	.167	.220
Ruggiano,Justin	L	.305	82	25	6	1	3	13	5	25	.333	.512
Bats Right	R	.268	142	38	7	0	3	15	13	45	.340	.380
Ruiz,Carlos	L	.250	88	22	8	1	2	6	18	17	.400	.432
Bats Right	R	.253	293	74	17	0	4	25	28	43	.329	.352
Rupp,Cameron	L	.000	7	0	0	0	0	0	0	3	.000	.000
Bats Right	R	.208	53	11	4	0	0	6	4	17	.263	.283
Rutledge,Josh	L	.309	81	25	3	2	2	9	8	21	.371	.469
Bats Right	R	.254	228	58	13	5	2	24	12	62	.306	.382
Ryan,Brendan	L	.120	25	3	1	0	0	0	0	7	.120	.160
Bats Right	R	.180	89	16	3	0	0	8	4	23	.235	.213
Saltalamacchia,Jarrod	L	.216	88	19	4	0	2	8	6	33	.271	.330
Bats Both	R	.221	285	63	16	0	9	36	49	110	.333	.372
Sanchez,Carlos	L	.364	33	12	4	0	0	2	1	4	.382	.485
Bats Both	R	.194	67	13	1	0	0	3	2	21	.214	.209
Sanchez,Gaby	L	.256	133	34	14	0	3	21	12	22	.318	.429
Bats Right	R	.202	129	26	4	1	4	12	11	36	.268	.341
Sanchez,Hector	L	.224	49	11	1	0	1	6	0	11	.224	.306
Bats Both	R	.184	114	21	7	0	2	22	8	44	.242	.298
Sanchez,Tony	L	.077	13	1	0	0	0	1	0	11	.071	.077
Bats Right	R	.306	62	19	1	0	2	12	3	17	.348	.419
Sandoval,Pablo	L	.199	191	38	6	1	5	19	11	31	.244	.319
Bats Both	R	.317	397	126	20	2	11	54	28	54	.363	.461
Sands,Jerry	L	.091	11	1	0	0	1	2	0	5	.091	.364
Bats Right	R	.300	10	3	0	0	0	2	0	1	.364	.300
Santana,Carlos	L	.271	177	48	11	0	8	28	36	33	.395	.469
Bats Both	R	.212	364	77	14	0	19	57	77	91	.351	.407
Santana,Danny	L	.301	123	37	8	2	2	11	7	42	.338	.447
Bats Both	R	.326	282	92	19	5	5	29	12	56	.359	.482
Santiago,Ramon	L	.362	47	17	3	0	1	7	5	9	.434	.489
Bats Both	R	.205	132	27	5	0	1	10	19	29	.312	.265
Sardinas,Luis	L	.333	27	9	3	0	0	4	1	2	.379	.444
Bats Both	R	.239	88	21	3	0	0	4	4	19	.280	.273
Satin,Josh	L	.130	23	3	2	0	0	3	5	9	.310	.217
Bats Right	R	.000	12	0	0	0	0	0	1	5	.143	.000
Saunders,Michael	L	.262	61	16	2	1	0	8	9	19	.352	.328
Bats Left	R	.276	170	47	9	2	8	26	17	40	.337	.494
Schafer,Jordan	L	.143	49	7	1	0	0	5	6	16	.236	.163
Bats Left	R	.267	161	43	8	1	1	10	16	32	.333	.348
Schafer,Logan	L	.214	14	3	2	0	0	1	2	5	.313	.357
Bats Left	R	.176	102	18	7	1	0	7	13	22	.274	.265
Schierholtz,Nate	L	.200	65	13	1	1	0	9	3	24	.243	.246
Bats Left	R	.194	288	56	10	3	7	28	17	60	.243	.323
Schoop,Jonathan	L	.200	130	26	4	0	2	6	7	40	.252	.277
Bats Right	R	.212	325	69	14	0	14	39	6	82	.240	.385
Schumaker,Skip	L	.222	45	10	0	0	0	3	4	10	.286	.222
Bats Left	R	.238	202	48	12	0	2	19	14	40	.288	.327
Seager,Kyle	L	.242	219	53	12	2	4	24	11	46	.291	.370
Bats Left	R	.283	371	105	15	2	21	72	41	72	.358	.504
Segura,Jean	L	.182	110	20	3	0	1	5	12	15	.274	.236
Bats Right	R	.263	403	106	11	6	4	26	16	55	.293	.350
Semien,Marcus	L	.271	85	23	4	0	3	10	5	23	.311	.424
Bats Right	R	.212	146	31	6	2	3	18	16	47	.294	.342
Shuck,J.B.	L	.136	22	3	0	0	0	1	1	1	.174	.136
Bats Left	R	.148	88	13	1	0	2	8	2	11	.167	.227
Sierra,Moises	L	.232	69	16	4	2	1	4	3	22	.264	.391
Bats Right	R	.228	92	21	4	0	1	5	5	21	.266	.304
Simmons,Andrelton	L	.250	100	25	3	2	2	13	7	7	.299	.380
Bats Right	R	.243	440	107	15	2	5	33	25	53	.283	.320
Singleton,Jon	L	.247	77	19	5	0	4	16	10	31	.337	.468
Bats Left	R	.142	233	33	8	0	9	28	40	103	.267	.292
Sizemore,Grady	L	.175	97	17	4	1	1	7	6	30	.223	.268
Bats Left	R	.256	250	64	15	3	4	20	27	46	.327	.388
Smith,Seth	L	.240	50	12	4	0	0	8	16	9	.424	.320
Bats Left	R	.270	393	106	27	5	12	40	53	78	.359	.455
Smoak,Justin	L	.222	108	24	7	0	2	13	7	28	.276	.343
Bats Both	R	.186	140	26	6	0	5	17	17	38	.275	.336
Smolinski,Jake	L	.476	21	10	2	0	2	6	1	4	.500	.857
Bats Right	R	.308	65	20	3	0	1	6	2	20	.357	.400
Snider,Travis	L	.381	42	16	4	0	2	5	4	7	.435	.619
Bats Left	R	.246	280	69	11	1	11	33	30	60	.324	.411
Snyder,Brad	L	-	0	0	0	0	0	0	0	0	-	-
Bats Left	R	.167	30	5	1	0	2	3	4	10	.265	.400
Sogard,Eric	L	.195	41	8	0	0	0	7	5	3	.283	.195
Bats Left	R	.228	250	57	10	0	1	15	26	34	.301	.280

Batter	vs	Avg	AB	H	2B	3B	HR	RBI	BB	SO	OBP	Slg
Solano,Donovan	L	.243	74	18	2	0	1	7	2	18	.263	.311
Bats Right	R	.254	236	60	9	1	2	21	17	43	.311	.326
Solarte,Yangervis	L	.291	165	48	11	1	3	20	11	23	.341	.424
Bats Both	R	.243	304	74	8	0	7	28	42	35	.334	.339
Soler,Jorge	L	.286	21	6	1	1	0	4	0	5	.273	.429
Bats Right	R	.294	68	20	7	0	5	16	6	19	.347	.618
Soriano,Alfonso	L	.247	89	22	6	0	3	12	3	30	.269	.416
Bats Right	R	.204	137	28	9	0	3	11	3	41	.228	.336
Soto,Geovany	L	.265	34	9	3	0	0	4	3	10	.324	.353
Bats Right	R	.239	46	11	3	0	1	7	3	9	.286	.370
Soto,Neftali	L	.200	15	3	1	0	0	0	0	4	.200	.267
Bats Right	R	.000	15	0	0	0	0	1	0	4	.000	.000
Souza,Steven	L	.500	6	3	0	0	2	2	1	1	.571	1.500
Bats Right	R	.000	17	0	0	0	0	0	2	6	.105	.000
Span,Denard	L	.269	171	46	8	2	1	16	17	27	.337	.357
Bats Left	R	.314	439	138	31	6	4	21	33	38	.362	.440
Spangenberg,Cory	L	.333	15	5	0	0	0	3	0	4	.333	.333
Bats Left	R	.277	47	13	2	1	2	6	2	10	.306	.489
Springer,George	L	.194	72	14	2	0	4	13	18	26	.385	.389
Bats Right	R	.242	223	54	6	1	16	38	21	88	.317	.493
Stanton,Giancarlo	L	.343	108	37	10	0	7	17	20	19	.445	.630
Bats Right	R	.274	431	118	21	1	30	88	74	151	.382	.536
Stassi,Max	L	.333	3	1	1	0	0	0	0	0	.333	.667
Bats Right	R	.353	17	6	1	0	0	4	0	6	.353	.412
Stewart,Chris	L	.486	35	17	3	0	0	5	3	3	.526	.571
Bats Right	R	.228	101	23	2	0	0	5	9	24	.307	.248
Stewart,Ian	L	.300	10	3	0	1	1	3	0	5	.300	.800
Bats Left	R	.155	58	9	2	2	1	4	3	26	.210	.310
Stubbs,Drew	L	.328	131	43	6	1	7	17	15	44	.395	.550
Bats Right	R	.268	257	69	16	3	8	26	15	92	.309	.447
Suarez,Eugenio	L	.238	84	20	3	1	1	9	9	19	.323	.333
Bats Right	R	.244	160	39	6	0	3	14	13	48	.313	.338
Sucre,Jesus	L	.182	22	4	1	0	0	1	0	6	.182	.227
Bats Right	R	.231	39	9	1	0	0	4	0	11	.231	.256
Susac,Andrew	L	.333	30	10	4	0	1	9	6	10	.444	.567
Bats Right	R	.241	58	14	4	0	2	10	1	18	.254	.414
Suzuki,Ichiro	L	.333	63	21	2	0	1	9	7	12	.394	.413
Bats Left	R	.274	296	81	11	2	0	13	14	56	.308	.324
Suzuki,Kurt	L	.331	130	43	11	0	1	20	7	17	.371	.438
Bats Right	R	.270	322	87	23	0	2	41	27	29	.334	.360
Sweeney,Ryan	L	.292	24	7	1	0	0	3	2	5	.346	.333
Bats Left	R	.246	183	45	8	0	3	17	13	28	.298	.339
Swisher,Nick	L	.168	101	17	4	0	0	6	15	20	.274	.208
Bats Both	R	.224	259	58	16	0	8	36	21	91	.279	.378
Szczur,Matt	L	.346	26	9	2	0	1	1	1	3	.370	.538
Bats Right	R	.139	36	5	0	0	1	4	3	8	.205	.222
Tabata,Jose	L	.348	46	16	2	1	0	6	1	4	.362	.435
Bats Right	R	.258	128	33	3	1	0	11	6	22	.297	.297
Taveras,Oscar	L	.238	42	10	1	0	0	4	3	10	.289	.262
Bats Left	R	.240	192	46	7	0	3	18	9	27	.276	.323
Taylor,Chris	L	.276	58	16	4	0	0	2	7	16	.354	.345
Bats Right	R	.295	78	23	4	0	0	7	4	23	.341	.346
Taylor,Michael	L	.231	13	3	0	0	0	0	2	5	.333	.231
Bats Right	R	.267	15	4	1	0	0	0	3	4	.389	.333
Taylor,Michael	L	.333	6	2	2	0	0	0	1	3	.429	.667
Bats Right	R	.182	33	6	1	0	1	5	2	14	.250	.303
Teagarden,Taylor	L	.000	4	0	0	0	0	0	0	1	.000	.000
Bats Right	R	.167	24	4	0	0	1	5	2	6	.231	.292
Teixeira,Mark	L	.220	123	27	5	0	4	13	19	24	.333	.358
Bats Both	R	.215	317	68	9	0	18	49	39	85	.305	.413
Tejada,Ruben	L	.238	84	20	2	0	0	5	17	23	.369	.262
Bats Right	R	.236	271	64	9	0	5	29	33	50	.333	.325
Telis,Tomas	L	.200	10	2	0	0	0	1	0	3	.200	.200
Bats Both	R	.259	58	15	2	0	0	7	1	7	.283	.293
Thole,Josh	L	.294	34	10	0	0	0	0	1	6	.314	.294
Bats Left	R	.232	99	23	4	0	0	7	13	19	.321	.273
Tolleson,Steve	L	.319	113	36	7	1	3	12	8	28	.366	.478
Bats Right	R	.123	57	7	0	1	0	4	4	21	.194	.158
Trout,Mike	L	.275	149	41	10	0	9	20	26	47	.386	.523
Bats Right	R	.291	453	132	29	9	27	91	57	137	.374	.574
Trumbo,Mark	L	.250	80	20	5	0	4	13	9	27	.333	.463
Bats Right	R	.230	248	57	10	1	10	48	19	62	.279	.399
Tulowitzki,Troy	L	.397	78	31	7	0	9	17	17	9	.515	.833
Bats Right	R	.321	237	76	11	1	12	35	33	48	.402	.527
Turner,Justin	L	.323	93	30	8	1	3	14	8	16	.385	.527
Bats Right	R	.349	195	68	13	0	4	29	20	42	.413	.477

Batters vs. Left-Handed and Right-Handed Pitchers

Batter	vs	Avg	AB	H	2B	3B	HR	RBI	BB	SO	OBP	Slg
Uggla,Dan	L	.108	37	4	0	0	1	4	1	11	.154	.189
Bats Right	R	.163	104	17	3	0	1	6	10	35	.254	.221
Upton,B.J.	L	.200	110	22	3	0	0	2	22	37	.338	.227
Bats Right	R	.210	409	86	16	5	12	33	35	136	.271	.362
Upton,Justin	L	.286	119	34	4	0	11	26	19	42	.384	.597
Bats Right	R	.266	447	119	30	2	18	76	41	129	.331	.463
Uribe,Juan	L	.291	86	25	7	0	1	12	5	14	.326	.407
Bats Right	R	.317	300	95	16	0	8	42	10	63	.340	.450
Utley,Chase	L	.233	180	42	9	2	3	24	22	30	.327	.356
Bats Left	R	.286	409	117	27	4	8	54	31	55	.344	.430
Valaika,Chris	L	.263	38	10	2	0	0	3	1	11	.275	.316
Bats Right	R	.217	83	18	2	0	3	10	6	24	.286	.349
Valbuena,Luis	L	.217	83	18	4	0	1	11	9	24	.309	.301
Bats Left	R	.256	395	101	29	4	15	40	56	89	.347	.463
Valdespin,Jordany	L	.429	7	3	0	0	0	0	1	1	.500	.429
Bats Left	R	.198	91	18	2	1	3	10	8	15	.263	.341
Valencia,Danny	L	.321	112	36	8	1	2	15	9	16	.371	.464
Bats Right	R	.211	152	32	8	0	2	15	5	46	.238	.303
Van Slyke,Scott	L	.315	108	34	10	0	8	17	17	33	.415	.630
Bats Right	R	.279	104	29	3	1	3	12	11	38	.353	.413
Vargas,Kennys	L	.228	92	21	5	0	1	14	7	28	.287	.315
Bats Both	R	.309	123	38	5	1	8	24	5	35	.338	.561
Vazquez,Christian	L	.189	37	7	2	0	0	4	6	8	.295	.243
Bats Right	R	.254	138	35	7	0	1	16	13	25	.312	.326
Venable,Will	L	.200	60	12	2	0	1	8	2	15	.222	.283
Bats Left	R	.228	346	79	11	2	7	25	31	92	.298	.332
Viciedo,Dayan	L	.221	140	31	9	1	5	10	9	30	.272	.407
Bats Right	R	.235	383	90	13	2	16	48	23	92	.284	.405
Victorino,Shane	L	.325	40	13	1	0	1	7	1	6	.333	.425
Bats Right	R	.241	83	20	5	1	1	5	5	15	.289	.361
Villar,Jonathan	L	.230	87	20	7	1	1	6	6	24	.277	.368
Bats Both	R	.199	176	35	6	1	6	21	13	56	.262	.347
Vogt,Stephen	L	.205	39	8	2	1	1	6	3	5	.262	.385
Bats Left	R	.291	230	67	8	1	8	29	13	34	.331	.439
Votto,Joey	L	.293	58	17	4	0	5	16	6	15	.348	.621
Bats Left	R	.241	162	39	12	0	1	7	41	34	.403	.333
Walker,Neil	L	.280	107	30	4	0	2	8	10	19	.353	.374
Bats Both	R	.269	405	109	21	3	21	68	35	69	.339	.491
Walters,Zach	L	.289	38	11	1	0	4	5	2	9	.325	.632
Bats Both	R	.135	89	12	2	0	6	12	7	39	.206	.360
Watkins,Logan	L	.143	7	1	0	0	0	0	0	2	.143	.143
Bats Left	R	.259	58	15	3	0	1	6	1	14	.283	.362
Weeks,Jemile	L	.000	5	0	0	0	0	0	0	0	.000	.000
Bats Both	R	.344	32	11	3	1	0	3	4	2	.421	.500
Weeks,Rickie	L	.256	133	34	10	1	7	14	16	35	.361	.504
Bats Right	R	.294	119	35	9	0	1	15	9	38	.351	.395
Werth,Jayson	L	.331	127	42	7	1	4	19	24	28	.437	.496
Bats Right	R	.280	407	114	30	0	12	63	59	85	.381	.442
Wheeler,Ryan	L	.167	6	1	0	0	0	1	0	2	.143	.167
Bats Left	R	.240	50	12	2	0	2	12	5	10	.298	.400
Wheeler,Zelous	L	.261	23	6	0	0	1	3	1	6	.320	.391
Bats Right	R	.147	34	5	0	0	1	2	1	6	.167	.235
Whiteside,Eli	L	.000	3	0	0	0	0	0	0	1	.000	.000
Bats Right	R	.136	22	3	1	0	0	2	0	7	.130	.182
Wieters,Matt	L	.238	21	5	1	0	2	5	0	7	.227	.571
Bats Both	R	.325	83	27	4	0	3	13	6	12	.367	.482
Wilkins,Andy	L	.333	3	1	0	0	0	0	0	1	.333	.333
Bats Left	R	.125	40	5	2	0	0	2	2	21	.167	.175
Willingham,Josh	L	.258	89	23	3	0	5	9	18	20	.380	.461
Bats Right	R	.197	208	41	7	1	9	31	35	82	.332	.370
Wilson,Josh	L	.393	28	11	2	0	0	5	0	6	.393	.464
Bats Right	R	.128	39	5	2	0	0	3	2	8	.190	.179
Wong,Kolten	L	.315	73	23	2	0	3	6	0	10	.324	.466
Bats Left	R	.234	329	77	12	3	9	36	21	61	.285	.371
Worth,Danny	L	.087	23	2	0	0	0	1	0	7	.120	.087
Bats Right	R	.263	19	5	1	0	0	4	2	5	.333	.316
Wright,David	L	.367	120	44	8	0	3	17	10	21	.412	.508
Bats Right	R	.241	415	100	22	1	5	46	32	92	.299	.335
Yelich,Christian	L	.317	142	45	9	3	1	15	14	34	.376	.444
Bats Left	R	.273	440	120	21	3	8	39	56	103	.358	.389
Ynoa,Rafael	L	.318	22	7	3	0	0	4	1	2	.348	.455
Bats Both	R	.356	45	16	3	1	0	9	3	7	.396	.467
Young,Chris	L	.149	74	11	3	0	2	9	15	20	.290	.270
Bats Right	R	.243	251	61	17	0	9	29	17	50	.301	.418
Young,Delmon	L	.282	85	24	4	1	2	10	2	15	.299	.424
Bats Right	R	.312	157	49	7	0	5	20	8	36	.357	.452
Young,Eric	L	.225	80	18	1	3	0	4	2	19	.253	.313
Bats Both	R	.230	200	46	9	2	1	13	22	41	.316	.310
Zimmerman,Ryan	L	.288	52	15	7	0	0	6	6	3	.356	.423
Bats Right	R	.278	162	45	12	1	5	32	16	34	.337	.457
Zobrist,Ben	L	.340	156	53	12	0	3	14	16	16	.399	.474
Bats Both	R	.246	414	102	22	3	7	38	59	68	.338	.365
Zunino,Mike	L	.252	131	33	8	0	5	14	6	42	.295	.427
Bats Right	R	.176	307	54	12	2	17	46	11	116	.237	.394
AL	L	.257	-	-	-	-	-	-	-	-	.319	.393
	R	.251	-	-	-	-	-	-	-	-	.314	.389
NL	L	.251	-	-	-	-	-	-	-	-	.316	.384
	R	.249	-	-	-	-	-	-	-	-	.310	.382
MLB	L	.254	-	-	-	-	-	-	-	-	.318	.388
	R	.250	-	-	-	-	-	-	-	-	.312	.386

Pitchers vs. Left-Handed and Right-Handed Batters

Pitcher	vs	Avg	AB	H	2B	3B	HR	RBI	BB	SO	OBP	Slg
Abad,Fernando	L	.191	89	17	2	0	1	2	7	35	.280	.247
Throws Left	R	.162	105	17	1	0	3	8	8	16	.217	.257
Aceves,Alfredo	L	.379	29	11	1	0	4	10	2	5	.419	.828
Throws Right	R	.235	51	12	3	0	2	5	2	11	.278	.412
Achter,A.J.	L	.389	18	7	1	0	0	1	2	1	.450	.444
Throws Right	R	.250	28	7	1	1	2	6	1	4	.276	.571
Adams,Austin	L	.273	11	3	1	0	1	3	0	1	.273	.636
Throws Right	R	.333	18	6	2	0	0	3	1	3	.368	.444
Adams,Mike	L	.389	18	7	2	0	1	2	2	4	.450	.667
Throws Right	R	.176	51	9	1	1	0	2	6	17	.263	.235
Adcock,Nate	L	.316	19	6	1	0	1	4	4	3	.458	.526
Throws Right	R	.263	19	5	0	0	1	6	1	6	.333	.421
Affeldt,Jeremy	L	.231	104	24	6	0	1	7	7	19	.304	.317
Throws Left	R	.228	101	23	4	1	0	10	7	22	.275	.287
Albers,Matt	L	.261	23	6	2	0	0	0	2	4	.320	.348
Throws Right	R	.267	15	4	1	0	0	3	1	4	.353	.333
Alburquerque,Al	L	.245	110	27	3	0	5	15	9	32	.311	.409
Throws Right	R	.190	100	19	0	1	2	8	12	31	.281	.270
Allen,Cody	L	.141	128	18	5	0	3	8	10	59	.201	.250
Throws Right	R	.250	120	30	8	0	4	16	16	32	.341	.417
Alvarez,Henderson	L	.274	412	113	22	1	6	27	16	66	.302	.376
Throws Right	R	.276	308	85	13	0	8	29	17	45	.326	.396
Alvarez,R.J.	L	.125	8	1	0	0	0	1	4	3	.417	.125
Throws Right	R	.111	18	2	0	0	0	2	1	6	.190	.111
Anderson,Brett	L	.326	46	15	2	0	0	6	2	6	.354	.370
Throws Left	R	.244	119	29	10	1	1	9	11	23	.305	.370
Anderson,Chase	L	.225	191	43	8	3	7	24	22	39	.306	.408
Throws Right	R	.302	245	74	11	3	9	28	18	66	.350	.482
Archer,Chris	L	.228	412	94	17	2	5	34	46	100	.308	.316
Throws Right	R	.262	317	83	11	0	7	47	26	73	.322	.363
Arrieta,Jake	L	.198	263	50	12	2	2	16	23	84	.269	.285
Throws Right	R	.207	309	64	10	0	3	26	18	83	.252	.269
Arroyo,Bronson	L	.233	176	41	9	0	4	13	12	22	.288	.352
Throws Right	R	.331	154	51	6	1	6	22	7	25	.362	.500
Atchison,Scott	L	.267	90	24	6	0	2	12	8	20	.323	.400
Throws Right	R	.207	174	36	8	2	2	11	6	29	.233	.310
Aumont,Phillippe	L	.615	13	8	1	1	2	7	0	3	.615	1.308
Throws Right	R	.375	16	6	2	0	1	7	5	3	.500	.688
Avilan,Luis	L	.264	87	23	4	0	2	15	10	15	.350	.379
Throws Left	R	.312	77	24	5	1	0	10	11	10	.400	.403
Axelrod,Dylan	L	.111	27	3	0	0	2	3	3	6	.200	.333
Throws Right	R	.268	41	11	2	1	3	3	1	14	.286	.585
Axford,John	L	.187	91	17	4	0	2	10	20	30	.333	.297
Throws Right	R	.243	107	26	5	0	4	18	16	33	.341	.402
Badenhop,Burke	L	.255	98	25	8	1	1	11	10	10	.333	.388
Throws Right	R	.276	163	45	9	0	0	17	9	30	.310	.331
Baez,Pedro	L	.179	39	7	1	0	2	3	2	9	.220	.359
Throws Right	R	.196	46	9	0	0	1	3	3	9	.240	.261
Bailey,Homer	L	.270	230	62	13	1	5	21	26	43	.350	.400
Throws Right	R	.230	313	72	16	0	11	33	19	81	.280	.387
Baker,Scott	L	.259	162	42	9	1	10	26	9	36	.297	.512
Throws Right	R	.265	151	40	15	1	5	23	5	19	.294	.477
Balfour,Grant	L	.200	115	23	7	3	2	15	23	33	.338	.365
Throws Right	R	.234	111	26	2	3	1	12	18	24	.338	.333
Barnes,Matt	L	.333	15	5	2	0	1	2	0	4	.333	.667
Throws Right	R	.286	21	6	3	0	0	2	2	4	.333	.429
Barrett,Aaron	L	.275	51	14	5	0	0	7	9	14	.377	.373
Throws Right	R	.192	99	19	3	0	1	13	11	35	.277	.253
Bass,Anthony	L	.259	58	15	3	0	2	11	3	5	.306	.414
Throws Right	R	.333	51	17	1	0	4	11	4	2	.386	.588
Bassitt,Chris	L	.317	63	20	4	0	0	5	8	12	.411	.381
Throws Right	R	.250	56	14	4	0	0	7	5	9	.317	.321
Bastardo,Antonio	L	.175	80	14	3	2	2	11	15	28	.302	.338
Throws Left	R	.195	149	29	9	1	2	20	19	53	.291	.309
Bauer,Trevor	L	.249	285	71	11	1	9	37	38	77	.339	.389
Throws Right	R	.268	298	80	22	0	7	32	22	66	.331	.413
Beckett,Josh	L	.252	222	56	16	0	13	25	23	58	.321	.500
Throws Right	R	.198	202	40	10	0	4	12	16	49	.271	.307
Bedard,Erik	L	.273	77	21	8	0	3	12	7	20	.333	.494
Throws Left	R	.275	229	63	13	0	7	29	22	44	.339	.424
Bedrosian,Cam	L	.350	40	14	3	0	2	8	10	10	.480	.575
Throws Right	R	.225	40	9	2	0	0	4	2	10	.256	.275
Beeler,Dallas	L	.294	17	5	1	1	0	3	6	2	.478	.471
Throws Right	R	.238	21	5	1	0	0	1	1	4	.273	.286
Beimel,Joe	L	.188	80	15	2	0	2	4	2	17	.217	.288
Throws Left	R	.282	85	24	6	0	2	8	12	8	.367	.424

Pitcher	vs	Avg	AB	H	2B	3B	HR	RBI	BB	SO	OBP	Slg
Belisario,Ronald	L	.315	111	35	3	0	3	20	13	18	.394	.423
Throws Right	R	.281	153	43	7	0	1	23	5	29	.315	.346
Belisle,Matt	L	.289	114	33	3	2	4	15	11	26	.357	.456
Throws Right	R	.295	139	41	10	0	1	29	8	17	.322	.388
Beliveau,Jeff	L	.146	41	6	1	0	1	3	4	13	.239	.244
Throws Left	R	.271	48	13	1	0	0	6	3	15	.321	.292
Bell,Heath	L	.279	43	12	3	0	1	8	6	8	.385	.419
Throws Right	R	.387	31	12	3	0	0	5	2	4	.457	.484
Benoit,Joaquin	L	.157	89	14	5	0	1	3	8	36	.232	.247
Throws Right	R	.144	97	14	2	1	2	9	6	28	.192	.247
Bergman,Christian	L	.280	100	28	8	3	1	6	6	18	.327	.450
Throws Right	R	.346	136	47	11	2	8	25	4	13	.362	.632
Betances,Dellin	L	.163	160	26	4	1	0	8	8	66	.205	.200
Throws Right	R	.135	148	20	5	0	4	15	16	69	.232	.250
Bettis,Chad	L	.345	55	19	2	0	2	10	6	9	.410	.491
Throws Right	R	.411	56	23	9	0	2	17	4	4	.459	.679
Black,Vic	L	.208	53	11	1	1	1	3	11	11	.344	.321
Throws Right	R	.205	73	15	3	0	1	5	8	21	.293	.288
Blevins,Jerry	L	.160	106	17	6	0	0	9	6	40	.202	.217
Throws Left	R	.298	104	31	4	0	3	18	17	26	.398	.423
Bolsinger,Mike	L	.337	98	33	6	3	2	16	9	20	.385	.520
Throws Right	R	.284	116	33	6	3	5	16	8	28	.325	.517
Bonilla,Lisalverto	L	.179	39	7	1	1	1	5	7	6	.304	.333
Throws Right	R	.194	31	6	1	0	1	2	5	11	.324	.323
Boxberger,Brad	L	.107	103	11	1	0	3	8	10	46	.198	.204
Throws Right	R	.198	116	23	4	0	6	13	10	58	.271	.388
Boyer,Blaine	L	.305	59	18	2	1	2	7	3	6	.339	.475
Throws Right	R	.178	90	16	10	0	0	8	5	23	.219	.289
Brach,Brad	L	.250	92	23	6	0	4	17	13	19	.330	.446
Throws Right	R	.192	130	25	5	0	2	4	12	35	.266	.277
Breslow,Craig	L	.291	103	30	5	0	4	11	13	11	.381	.456
Throws Left	R	.341	126	43	8	1	4	20	15	26	.411	.516
Britton,Drake	L	.000	6	0	0	0	0	0	2	3	.250	.000
Throws Left	R	.263	19	5	2	0	0	2	0	1	.263	.368
Britton,Zach	L	.170	88	15	0	0	0	3	5	22	.215	.170
Throws Left	R	.182	170	31	7	0	4	13	18	40	.265	.294
Brooks,Aaron	L	.714	7	5	1	0	0	5	2	0	.800	.857
Throws Right	R	.636	11	7	3	0	1	8	1	2	.643	1.182
Brothers,Rex	L	.309	97	30	3	1	4	19	19	21	.424	.485
Throws Left	R	.271	129	35	5	1	3	17	20	34	.366	.395
Brown,Brooks	L	.209	43	9	0	0	1	4	3	8	.255	.279
Throws Right	R	.208	53	11	1	0	2	8	2	13	.246	.340
Broxton,Jonathan	L	.222	81	18	3	0	0	6	10	22	.304	.259
Throws Right	R	.181	127	23	3	2	4	13	9	27	.241	.331
Buchanan,David	L	.227	198	45	4	1	2	15	19	28	.305	.288
Throws Right	R	.293	256	75	17	1	10	36	13	43	.336	.484
Buchanan,Jake	L	.307	75	23	4	0	2	13	11	6	.395	.440
Throws Right	R	.286	63	18	2	0	2	9	1	14	.308	.413
Buchholz,Clay	L	.284	373	106	22	4	9	49	38	72	.356	.437
Throws Right	R	.259	293	76	14	0	8	41	16	60	.307	.389
Buckner,Billy	L	.333	9	3	1	0	1	2	3	0	.500	.778
Throws Right	R	.231	13	3	0	0	0	1	1	4	.286	.231
Buehrle,Mark	L	.269	212	57	14	1	4	16	13	34	.317	.401
Throws Left	R	.293	583	171	42	0	11	56	33	85	.330	.422
Bueno,Francisley	L	.206	63	13	1	0	1	9	2	12	.235	.270
Throws Left	R	.343	67	23	8	1	2	12	5	8	.378	.582
Bumgarner,Madison	L	.224	174	39	9	0	1	12	5	58	.246	.293
Throws Left	R	.244	636	155	31	2	20	63	38	161	.291	.393
Burnett,A.J.	L	.250	372	93	28	2	10	61	60	87	.368	.417
Throws Right	R	.261	429	112	23	2	10	51	36	103	.319	.394
Burton,Jared	L	.227	97	22	0	0	2	11	12	16	.306	.289
Throws Right	R	.250	144	36	12	0	4	25	13	30	.323	.417
Butler,Eddie	L	.423	26	11	1	2	2	6	2	0	.464	.846
Throws Right	R	.293	41	12	4	0	0	5	5	3	.370	.390
Cahill,Trevor	L	.346	214	74	18	2	5	35	24	30	.411	.519
Throws Right	R	.226	217	49	8	1	4	31	31	75	.329	.327
Cain,Matt	L	.253	162	41	7	0	6	18	18	34	.330	.407
Throws Right	R	.231	173	40	10	1	7	21	14	36	.291	.422
Caminero,Arquimedes	L	.250	8	2	0	0	0	2	1	2	.333	.250
Throws Right	R	.316	19	6	1	0	2	6	3	6	.409	.684
Campos,Leonel	L	.143	14	2	1	0	0	0	1	5	.200	.214
Throws Right	R	.467	15	7	1	0	0	3	3	4	.556	.533
Capps,Carter	L	.324	34	11	1	0	1	7	3	8	.395	.441
Throws Right	R	.182	44	8	1	0	0	2	2	17	.229	.205
Capuano,Chris	L	.321	106	34	5	1	7	25	6	17	.357	.585
Throws Left	R	.242	277	67	17	2	3	24	28	67	.315	.350

Pitchers vs. Left-Handed and Right-Handed Batters

Pitcher	vs	Avg	AB	H	2B	3B	HR	RBI	BB	SO	OBP	Slg
Carlyle,Buddy	L	.250	56	14	2	1	1	3	0	12	.250	.375
Throws Right	R	.158	57	9	2	0	1	3	5	16	.226	.246
Carpenter,David	L	.220	109	24	5	0	3	10	8	32	.286	.349
Throws Right	R	.287	129	37	3	0	2	15	8	35	.331	.357
Carrasco,Carlos	L	.196	230	45	6	0	3	17	19	65	.255	.261
Throws Right	R	.221	262	58	9	1	4	20	10	75	.257	.309
Carroll,Scott	L	.292	305	89	15	5	10	35	35	31	.369	.472
Throws Right	R	.284	204	58	13	0	3	27	10	33	.341	.392
Cashner,Andrew	L	.240	229	55	11	3	5	25	19	48	.295	.380
Throws Right	R	.230	239	55	11	1	2	14	10	45	.263	.310
Casilla,Santiago	L	.200	80	16	3	0	1	6	7	23	.264	.275
Throws Right	R	.161	118	19	2	0	2	6	8	22	.233	.229
Cecil,Brett	L	.247	81	20	2	2	2	12	8	25	.319	.395
Throws Left	R	.213	122	26	3	1	0	7	19	51	.315	.254
Cedeno,Xavier	L	.400	15	6	1	0	1	5	0	2	.400	.667
Throws Left	R	.267	15	4	1	0	0	0	0	3	.267	.333
Chacin,Jhoulys	L	.245	106	26	7	0	3	18	19	14	.354	.396
Throws Right	R	.280	132	37	11	1	5	17	9	28	.329	.492
Chafin,Andrew	L	.231	13	3	1	0	0	4	1	4	.333	.308
Throws Left	R	.278	36	10	1	0	0	2	7	6	.395	.306
Chamberlain,Joba	L	.252	119	30	3	1	1	13	14	28	.331	.319
Throws Right	R	.237	114	27	5	0	2	13	10	31	.310	.333
Chapman,Aroldis	L	.132	38	5	1	0	0	1	3	25	.214	.158
Throws Left	R	.118	136	16	5	0	1	6	21	81	.239	.176
Chapman,Kevin	L	.261	46	12	1	1	0	3	9	13	.382	.326
Throws Left	R	.278	36	10	1	0	3	7	2	6	.308	.556
Chatwood,Tyler	L	.160	50	8	1	0	1	5	5	8	.232	.240
Throws Right	R	.333	39	13	2	0	3	8	3	12	.400	.615
Chavez,Jesse	L	.247	316	78	8	0	8	27	29	68	.315	.348
Throws Right	R	.260	246	64	10	0	9	30	20	68	.317	.411
Chen,Bruce	L	.310	58	18	0	2	1	13	3	9	.339	.431
Throws Left	R	.357	143	51	9	1	6	25	13	27	.409	.559
Chen,Wei-Yin	L	.268	179	48	7	1	3	16	7	32	.302	.369
Throws Left	R	.266	546	145	36	1	20	57	28	104	.301	.445
Choate,Randy	L	.093	75	7	1	0	1	6	8	28	.205	.147
Throws Left	R	.385	52	20	2	0	1	7	5	4	.458	.481
Christiani,Nick	L	.429	14	6	4	0	1	5	4	1	.526	.929
Throws Right	R	.167	36	6	1	0	1	4	2	7	.211	.278
Cingrani,Tony	L	.204	49	10	1	0	1	5	9	17	.328	.286
Throws Left	R	.272	191	52	11	0	11	27	26	44	.359	.503
Cishek,Steve	L	.213	136	29	6	1	2	15	10	54	.270	.316
Throws Right	R	.266	109	29	6	2	1	11	11	30	.328	.385
Cisnero,Jose	L	.400	10	4	1	0	0	3	3	1	.538	.500
Throws Right	R	.400	10	4	0	0	0	4	1	4	.417	.400
Claiborne,Preston	L	.344	32	11	3	1	0	3	3	7	.400	.500
Throws Right	R	.250	52	13	3	0	1	11	7	9	.328	.365
Claudio,Alex	L	.190	21	4	1	0	0	2	1	8	.227	.238
Throws Left	R	.345	29	10	3	0	0	5	3	6	.406	.448
Clemens,Paul	L	.236	55	13	5	0	2	13	7	11	.333	.436
Throws Right	R	.319	47	15	3	0	3	5	6	5	.396	.574
Cleto,Maikel	L	.170	53	9	1	1	2	7	15	12	.362	.340
Throws Right	R	.254	59	15	1	1	1	8	8	20	.362	.356
Clippard,Tyler	L	.237	135	32	4	0	3	14	14	35	.309	.333
Throws Right	R	.130	115	15	3	1	2	7	9	47	.197	.226
Cobb,Alex	L	.207	299	62	12	0	7	27	24	66	.272	.318
Throws Right	R	.252	317	80	13	0	4	24	23	83	.315	.331
Coke,Phil	L	.257	105	27	5	1	2	20	8	26	.310	.381
Throws Left	R	.333	126	42	7	1	3	20	12	15	.394	.476
Cole,Gerrit	L	.249	241	60	9	4	6	18	26	60	.335	.394
Throws Right	R	.247	271	67	15	1	5	30	14	78	.294	.365
Coleman,Casey	L	.333	21	7	1	0	0	4	4	3	.440	.381
Throws Right	R	.321	28	9	2	0	0	2	2	2	.367	.393
Coleman,Louis	L	.233	43	10	3	0	0	4	6	10	.327	.302
Throws Right	R	.319	91	29	5	0	6	19	12	14	.400	.571
Collins,Tim	L	.273	22	6	2	0	0	3	2	7	.346	.364
Throws Left	R	.235	51	12	0	0	2	6	9	8	.361	.353
Collmenter,Josh	L	.282	340	96	16	3	8	32	17	46	.323	.418
Throws Right	R	.207	323	67	17	0	10	37	22	69	.255	.353
Colome,Alex	L	.217	46	10	1	0	0	4	8	6	.327	.239
Throws Right	R	.225	40	9	2	0	1	5	2	7	.262	.350
Colon,Bartolo	L	.260	419	109	21	3	9	47	18	74	.292	.389
Throws Right	R	.287	380	109	20	0	13	41	12	77	.313	.442
Contreras,Carlos	L	.216	37	8	1	0	1	5	10	13	.383	.324
Throws Right	R	.282	39	11	3	0	1	10	7	6	.383	.436
Cook,Ryan	L	.262	65	17	4	2	1	7	13	13	.385	.431
Throws Right	R	.138	109	15	4	0	2	14	9	37	.213	.229

Pitcher	vs	Avg	AB	H	2B	3B	HR	RBI	BB	SO	OBP	Slg
Corcino,Daniel	L	.167	24	4	1	0	1	3	2	4	.231	.333
Throws Right	R	.200	45	9	2	0	1	6	8	11	.333	.311
Cordier,Erik	L	.091	11	1	0	0	0	0	1	4	.286	.091
Throws Right	R	.333	12	4	0	0	0	3	1	5	.429	.333
Correia,Kevin	L	.310	332	103	22	2	9	47	34	35	.368	.470
Throws Right	R	.291	302	88	19	2	11	47	6	44	.316	.477
Cosart,Jarred	L	.251	334	84	11	2	5	28	48	59	.343	.341
Throws Right	R	.258	345	89	17	1	4	40	25	56	.310	.348
Cotts,Neal	L	.270	89	24	6	0	3	14	8	25	.337	.438
Throws Left	R	.250	168	42	10	0	3	18	15	38	.317	.363
Coulombe,Daniel	L	.375	8	3	0	0	0	0	1	2	.444	.375
Throws Left	R	.167	12	2	1	0	1	4	1	2	.231	.500
Crockett,Kyle	L	.206	63	13	4	0	0	4	3	20	.275	.270
Throws Left	R	.283	46	13	2	0	2	8	5	8	.353	.457
Crow,Aaron	L	.271	96	26	5	1	4	18	10	11	.336	.469
Throws Right	R	.215	121	26	2	1	6	17	14	23	.296	.397
Cueto,Johnny	L	.194	408	79	11	1	9	26	36	107	.269	.292
Throws Right	R	.194	465	90	23	1	13	35	29	135	.254	.331
Cumpton,Brandon	L	.304	112	34	8	1	0	12	13	20	.391	.393
Throws Right	R	.289	166	48	9	0	2	25	5	26	.315	.380
Daley,Matt	L	.294	17	5	3	0	2	3	5	3	.478	.824
Throws Right	R	.189	37	7	1	0	2	9	1	7	.205	.378
Danks,John	L	.251	191	48	11	3	3	19	17	22	.322	.387
Throws Left	R	.275	570	157	39	2	22	79	57	107	.344	.467
Darnell,Logan	L	.348	23	8	2	0	0	3	2	4	.400	.435
Throws Left	R	.295	78	23	5	1	5	15	6	18	.345	.577
Darvish,Yu	L	.246	345	85	16	2	11	35	38	116	.321	.400
Throws Right	R	.233	206	48	12	1	2	10	11	66	.275	.330
Davis,Wade	L	.189	127	24	1	2	0	5	17	52	.285	.228
Throws Right	R	.112	125	14	2	0	0	5	6	57	.170	.128
De Fratus,Justin	L	.209	67	14	4	2	0	2	4	19	.250	.328
Throws Right	R	.230	135	31	5	1	4	23	8	30	.288	.370
De La Rosa,Eury	L	.309	55	17	3	0	1	7	5	16	.377	.418
Throws Left	R	.233	86	20	3	0	1	13	9	16	.320	.302
De La Rosa,Jorge	L	.196	158	31	4	1	2	12	14	42	.260	.272
Throws Left	R	.250	519	130	27	5	19	66	53	97	.328	.432
De La Rosa,Rubby	L	.305	213	65	15	4	4	21	21	35	.363	.469
Throws Right	R	.279	183	51	9	0	8	24	14	39	.333	.459
De Leon,Jorge	L	.308	13	4	0	0	0	1	2	2	.400	.308
Throws Right	R	.313	16	5	1	1	2	6	1	2	.333	.875
Deduno,Samuel	L	.255	196	50	8	2	4	20	31	40	.365	.378
Throws Right	R	.254	185	47	10	0	5	29	15	43	.325	.389
deGrom,Jacob	L	.224	214	48	11	2	3	17	23	56	.303	.336
Throws Right	R	.231	299	69	14	0	4	27	20	88	.276	.318
Delabar,Steve	L	.135	37	5	0	0	0	2	10	10	.347	.135
Throws Right	R	.264	53	14	3	1	3	12	9	11	.375	.528
Delgado,Randall	L	.234	141	33	8	1	3	17	18	35	.321	.369
Throws Right	R	.244	156	38	11	1	3	21	17	51	.326	.385
Dennick,Ryan	L	.143	7	1	0	0	1	3	3	1	.400	.571
Throws Left	R	.462	13	6	1	0	1	4	1	2	.467	.769
DeSclafani,Anthony	L	.333	66	22	4	0	3	11	2	14	.362	.530
Throws Right	R	.273	66	18	6	0	1	10	3	12	.301	.409
Despaigne,Odrisamer	L	.258	182	47	7	1	4	14	20	24	.340	.374
Throws Right	R	.216	176	38	6	0	2	22	12	41	.274	.284
Detwiler,Ross	L	.226	84	19	1	0	0	5	3	13	.278	.238
Throws Left	R	.312	157	49	9	0	5	26	18	26	.383	.465
Diaz,Jairo	L	.143	14	2	1	0	0	0	0	6	.143	.214
Throws Right	R	.333	6	2	1	0	0	2	3	2	.500	.500
Diaz,Jumbo	L	.275	51	14	2	1	1	8	8	13	.367	.412
Throws Right	R	.200	75	15	4	0	2	8	6	24	.256	.333
Dickey,R.A.	L	.221	357	79	24	2	6	31	41	72	.309	.350
Throws Right	R	.242	463	112	24	3	20	58	33	101	.304	.436
Diekman,Jake	L	.239	92	22	3	0	1	11	5	38	.273	.304
Throws Left	R	.253	174	44	10	2	3	26	30	62	.363	.385
Dominguez,Jose	L	.167	12	2	1	1	0	1	1	4	.286	.417
Throws Right	R	.357	14	5	0	0	2	7	2	4	.438	.786
Doolittle,Sean	L	.118	76	9	3	0	0	2	0	32	.118	.158
Throws Left	R	.195	149	29	3	0	5	16	8	57	.234	.315
Doubront,Felix	L	.337	101	34	7	0	2	15	9	18	.393	.465
Throws Left	R	.256	223	57	19	0	10	36	24	33	.329	.475
Downs,Darin	L	.203	69	14	4	1	1	11	11	19	.337	.333
Throws Left	R	.255	55	14	4	0	1	6	8	8	.344	.382
Downs,Scott	L	.225	80	18	8	0	1	5	7	16	.287	.363
Throws Left	R	.277	65	18	4	1	1	9	13	9	.397	.415
Duensing,Brian	L	.242	95	23	6	0	0	12	5	16	.282	.305
Throws Left	R	.264	110	29	7	0	6	16	15	17	.352	.491

Pitchers vs. Left-Handed and Right-Handed Batters

Pitcher	vs	Avg	AB	H	2B	3B	HR	RBI	BB	SO	OBP	Slg
Duffy,Danny	L	.137	124	17	3	0	0	4	13	25	.225	.161
Throws Left	R	.230	417	96	18	2	12	41	40	88	.301	.369
Duke,Zach	L	.198	96	19	0	2	2	9	9	37	.267	.302
Throws Left	R	.242	124	30	2	1	1	12	8	37	.288	.298
Dunn,Mike	L	.220	109	24	5	0	2	11	9	28	.277	.321
Throws Left	R	.219	105	23	7	0	2	12	13	39	.328	.343
Dyson,Sam	L	.284	67	19	3	0	1	7	11	8	.407	.373
Throws Right	R	.234	94	22	1	2	0	14	4	25	.265	.287
Edgin,Josh	L	.185	65	12	3	0	2	12	3	18	.217	.323
Throws Left	R	.219	32	7	1	0	0	2	3	10	.286	.250
Edwards,Jon	L	.438	16	7	1	0	0	2	1	3	.471	.500
Throws Right	R	.286	21	6	0	0	0	3	4	6	.423	.286
Elias,Roenis	L	.212	132	28	7	1	3	12	16	37	.307	.348
Throws Left	R	.257	478	123	27	0	13	56	48	106	.334	.395
Eovaldi,Nathan	L	.296	436	129	22	5	10	52	19	74	.330	.438
Throws Right	R	.266	354	94	24	1	4	40	24	68	.315	.373
Erlin,Robbie	L	.279	68	19	4	3	0	11	6	12	.329	.426
Throws Left	R	.299	174	52	11	0	6	19	9	34	.333	.466
Estrada,Marco	L	.226	266	60	12	1	14	36	21	54	.283	.436
Throws Right	R	.254	303	77	19	1	15	41	23	73	.309	.472
Eveland,Dana	L	.241	54	13	3	0	0	3	4	17	.305	.296
Throws Left	R	.216	51	11	2	0	2	6	2	10	.286	.373
Familia,Jeurys	L	.293	133	39	9	1	3	13	17	19	.377	.444
Throws Right	R	.134	149	20	2	1	0	11	15	54	.216	.161
Farmer,Buck	L	.364	22	8	1	1	2	9	2	8	.417	.773
Throws Right	R	.235	17	4	2	1	0	2	3	3	.409	.471
Farnsworth,Kyle	L	.286	42	12	1	1	1	5	7	4	.373	.429
Throws Right	R	.299	67	20	6	1	1	13	8	14	.364	.463
Farquhar,Danny	L	.240	121	29	4	0	2	10	12	35	.319	.322
Throws Right	R	.206	141	29	6	0	3	14	10	46	.266	.312
Feierabend,Ryan	L	.235	17	4	2	0	0	5	0	2	.222	.353
Throws Left	R	.533	15	8	2	0	0	2	2	2	.588	.667
Feldman,Scott	L	.270	381	103	19	4	6	26	30	53	.327	.388
Throws Right	R	.261	314	82	20	0	10	42	20	54	.317	.420
Feliz,Neftali	L	.127	55	7	0	0	3	5	7	8	.222	.291
Throws Right	R	.241	54	13	1	0	2	6	4	13	.293	.370
Fernandez,Jose	L	.247	97	24	4	2	1	5	9	29	.311	.361
Throws Right	R	.126	95	12	1	0	3	12	4	41	.162	.232
Fields,Josh	L	.268	97	26	3	1	1	14	6	27	.314	.351
Throws Right	R	.218	110	24	7	1	1	15	11	43	.286	.327
Fien,Casey	L	.255	110	28	7	0	3	7	7	19	.294	.400
Throws Right	R	.269	134	36	4	3	4	22	3	32	.281	.433
Fiers,Mike	L	.188	117	22	3	0	2	9	10	34	.252	.265
Throws Right	R	.175	137	24	6	0	5	11	7	42	.214	.328
Fife,Stephen	L	.333	12	4	1	0	1	1	0	3	.333	.667
Throws Right	R	.231	13	3	0	0	2	3	1	2	.333	.692
Figaro,Alfredo	L	.238	21	5	1	0	1	2	1	7	.273	.429
Throws Right	R	.375	16	6	0	1	1	2	0	1	.375	.688
Figueroa,Pedro	L	.111	18	2	0	0	0	2	2	2	.227	.111
Throws Left	R	.444	18	8	1	0	1	4	1	1	.500	.667
Finnegan,Brandon	L	.333	9	3	1	0	0	0	0	3	.333	.444
Throws Left	R	.167	18	3	1	0	0	2	1	7	.211	.222
Fister,Doug	L	.263	316	83	14	2	7	25	13	54	.304	.386
Throws Right	R	.228	307	70	4	2	11	22	11	44	.256	.362
Flande,Yohan	L	.164	61	10	2	0	1	14	5	11	.235	.246
Throws Left	R	.294	153	45	14	0	4	16	11	23	.339	.464
Floyd,Gavin	L	.301	103	31	3	1	2	11	10	23	.365	.408
Throws Right	R	.231	104	24	2	0	4	10	3	22	.204	.305
Flynn,Brian	L	.333	6	2	0	0	0	2	0	0	.333	.333
Throws Left	R	.385	26	10	2	1	0	4	3	6	.448	.538
Foltynewicz,Mike	L	.333	39	13	2	1	3	6	4	5	.395	.667
Throws Right	R	.263	38	10	3	0	0	3	3	9	.317	.342
Fornataro,Eric	L	.214	14	3	0	0	0	1	1	2	.250	.214
Throws Right	R	.320	25	8	3	0	0	5	0	1	.346	.440
Francis,Jeff	L	.286	21	6	0	0	1	6	1	6	.318	.429
Throws Left	R	.218	55	12	4	0	2	7	2	9	.254	.400
Francisco,Frank	L	.400	10	4	1	0	2	4	1	3	.455	1.100
Throws Right	R	.333	9	3	0	0	0	1	2	2	.455	.333
Frasor,Jason	L	.250	64	16	3	0	1	11	8	19	.324	.344
Throws Right	R	.224	107	24	7	0	2	16	10	27	.295	.346
Freeman,Sam	L	.298	57	17	1	0	2	6	7	13	.397	.421
Throws Left	R	.195	87	17	2	0	0	2	12	22	.300	.218
Frias,Carlos	L	.317	60	19	2	0	2	12	2	10	.339	.450
Throws Right	R	.200	70	14	3	0	2	6	5	19	.253	.329
Friedrich,Christian	L	.138	29	4	0	1	0	0	1	11	.194	.207
Throws Left	R	.318	66	21	4	1	3	13	9	16	.397	.545

Pitcher	vs	Avg	AB	H	2B	3B	HR	RBI	BB	SO	OBP	Slg
Frieri,Ernesto	L	.260	104	27	3	0	9	21	10	31	.330	.548
Throws Right	R	.313	64	20	6	1	2	11	4	17	.362	.531
Fujikawa,Kyuji	L	.385	26	10	0	0	0	3	3	6	.467	.385
Throws Right	R	.276	29	8	0	0	2	7	3	11	.353	.483
Furbush,Charlie	L	.241	79	19	3	0	1	4	2	27	.277	.316
Throws Left	R	.253	83	21	2	0	3	9	7	24	.315	.386
Gallardo,Yovani	L	.235	315	74	14	1	5	26	31	66	.304	.333
Throws Right	R	.279	433	121	12	1	16	52	23	80	.320	.423
Garces,Frank	L	.250	24	6	2	0	1	5	1	8	.308	.458
Throws Left	R	.182	11	2	1	0	0	0	0	2	.182	.273
Garcia,Jaime	L	.326	43	14	2	0	2	8	1	11	.370	.512
Throws Left	R	.202	124	25	9	1	4	11	6	28	.244	.387
Garcia,Luis	L	.194	31	6	1	0	1	6	5	7	.306	.323
Throws Right	R	.333	24	8	2	0	1	6	8	5	.500	.542
Garcia,Yimi	L	.077	13	1	0	0	0	0	1	3	.143	.077
Throws Right	R	.227	22	5	0	0	2	3	0	6	.227	.500
Garza,Matt	L	.223	273	61	16	1	5	27	24	56	.290	.344
Throws Right	R	.241	340	82	16	1	7	42	26	70	.296	.356
Gausman,Kevin	L	.254	252	64	12	3	4	21	29	52	.327	.373
Throws Right	R	.269	175	47	7	0	3	19	9	36	.302	.360
Gee,Dillon	L	.254	264	67	6	1	10	30	24	38	.321	.398
Throws Right	R	.246	248	61	14	1	8	23	19	56	.304	.407
Geltz,Steve	L	.100	10	1	0	0	1	1	1	5	.182	.400
Throws Right	R	.250	20	5	0	0	2	7	4	9	.423	.550
Germano,Justin	L	.286	7	2	0	0	1	3	1	0	.375	.714
Throws Right	R	.375	16	6	2	1	0	4	2	3	.450	.625
Germen,Gonzalez	L	.321	53	17	4	0	6	11	6	9	.390	.736
Throws Right	R	.203	64	13	3	0	1	4	8	22	.301	.297
Gibson,Kyle	L	.268	365	98	21	4	3	36	35	36	.333	.373
Throws Right	R	.245	326	80	9	0	9	40	22	71	.294	.356
Giles,Ken	L	.152	66	10	2	0	1	4	5	26	.208	.227
Throws Right	R	.174	86	15	5	0	0	3	6	38	.228	.233
Goeddel,Erik	L	.250	8	2	0	0	0	2	1	2	.333	.250
Throws Right	R	.071	14	1	0	0	0	1	3	4	.235	.071
Gomes,Brandon	L	.245	49	12	2	0	1	5	4	14	.302	.347
Throws Right	R	.208	77	16	3	0	4	16	7	10	.271	.403
Gomez,Jeanmar	L	.391	92	36	8	1	3	12	14	13	.467	.598
Throws Right	R	.230	148	34	7	2	3	25	9	25	.281	.365
Gonzales,Marco	L	.143	28	4	1	0	0	4	2	5	.219	.179
Throws Left	R	.267	105	28	7	0	4	11	19	26	.379	.448
Gonzalez,Gio	L	.221	140	31	6	3	1	13	15	43	.299	.329
Throws Left	R	.233	443	103	19	4	9	45	41	119	.299	.354
Gonzalez,Miguel	L	.259	336	87	19	2	13	27	32	56	.329	.443
Throws Right	R	.249	273	68	10	0	12	31	19	55	.306	.418
Gonzalez,Miguel	L	.400	10	4	1	0	0	1	2	2	.500	.500
Throws Right	R	.313	16	5	1	0	1	3	1	3	.353	.563
Gorzelanny,Tom	L	.324	34	11	1	0	0	4	5	10	.439	.353
Throws Left	R	.216	51	11	1	0	1	4	3	13	.259	.294
Gray,Sonny	L	.221	434	96	19	1	10	38	47	101	.300	.339
Throws Right	R	.245	371	91	8	1	5	40	27	82	.301	.313
Greene,Shane	L	.281	160	45	5	1	4	14	18	30	.365	.400
Throws Right	R	.242	149	36	5	0	4	17	11	51	.305	.356
Greenwood,Nick	L	.235	51	12	2	0	1	6	2	8	.264	.333
Throws Left	R	.273	88	24	4	0	4	12	3	9	.304	.455
Gregerson,Luke	L	.221	113	25	5	0	0	3	6	20	.261	.265
Throws Right	R	.219	151	33	9	0	6	26	9	39	.265	.397
Gregg,Kevin	L	.304	23	7	1	1	1	3	2	4	.360	.565
Throws Right	R	.308	13	4	1	0	1	3	3	2	.438	.615
Greinke,Zack	L	.246	366	90	13	1	7	23	19	90	.283	.344
Throws Right	R	.248	404	100	21	2	12	43	24	117	.290	.399
Grilli,Jason	L	.256	82	21	1	2	0	10	13	21	.366	.317
Throws Right	R	.250	120	30	7	0	4	17	8	36	.302	.408
Grimm,Justin	L	.188	85	16	1	0	1	10	12	29	.293	.235
Throws Right	R	.250	172	43	7	2	3	24	15	41	.318	.366
Guerra,Javy	L	.217	92	20	4	0	1	13	13	20	.336	.293
Throws Right	R	.280	75	21	6	0	2	13	7	18	.337	.440
Guerrier,Matt	L	.288	52	15	3	0	0	6	7	7	.373	.346
Throws Right	R	.259	58	15	5	0	1	8	3	5	.297	.397
Guilmet,Preston	L	.111	18	2	0	1	0	0	1	6	.158	.222
Throws Right	R	.273	22	6	0	0	2	7	1	6	.292	.545
Guthrie,Jeremy	L	.297	444	132	18	3	19	60	29	71	.348	.480
Throws Right	R	.241	345	83	12	0	4	32	20	53	.291	.310
Gutierrez,Juan	L	.226	84	19	4	0	5	13	9	13	.292	.452
Throws Right	R	.258	159	41	7	7	2	21	7	31	.296	.428
Hagadone,Nick	L	.217	46	10	1	1	1	4	4	15	.280	.348
Throws Left	R	.211	38	8	1	0	2	5	2	12	.250	.395

Pitchers vs. Left-Handed and Right-Handed Batters

Pitcher	vs	Avg	AB	H	2B	3B	HR	RBI	BB	SO	OBP	Slg
Hahn,Jesse	L	.227	141	32	4	2	4	18	10	31	.288	.369
Throws Right	R	.200	125	25	7	0	0	10	22	39	.327	.256
Hale,David	L	.289	152	44	8	2	1	18	22	17	.381	.388
Throws Right	R	.243	185	45	7	1	4	23	17	27	.311	.357
Hamels,Cole	L	.218	147	32	6	0	3	12	21	34	.316	.320
Throws Left	R	.240	601	144	34	0	11	46	38	164	.290	.351
Hammel,Jason	L	.237	295	70	11	1	12	28	19	64	.288	.403
Throws Right	R	.233	361	84	14	3	11	36	25	94	.291	.380
Hand,Brad	L	.224	125	28	5	1	1	11	12	21	.290	.304
Throws Left	R	.280	300	84	19	2	9	38	27	46	.342	.447
Happ,J.A.	L	.268	123	33	12	1	6	19	15	30	.345	.528
Throws Left	R	.259	491	127	28	5	16	58	36	103	.310	.434
Harang,Aaron	L	.289	370	107	23	1	5	34	35	72	.350	.397
Throws Right	R	.259	417	108	19	2	10	46	36	89	.316	.386
Hardy,Blaine	L	.203	64	13	1	0	1	8	7	14	.288	.266
Throws Left	R	.266	79	21	2	0	0	7	13	17	.366	.291
Haren,Dan	L	.227	361	82	16	0	15	38	21	90	.272	.396
Throws Right	R	.277	364	101	27	2	12	49	15	55	.305	.462
Harrell,Lucas	L	.333	30	10	3	0	0	5	5	5	.417	.433
Throws Right	R	.360	25	9	4	0	2	8	4	4	.433	.760
Harris,Will	L	.255	51	13	2	0	2	6	3	14	.309	.412
Throws Right	R	.250	56	14	7	0	1	12	6	21	.328	.429
Harrison,Matt	L	.231	13	3	1	0	0	1	1	5	.286	.308
Throws Left	R	.298	57	17	3	0	1	6	11	5	.420	.404
Hatcher,Chris	L	.222	99	22	4	2	2	12	8	26	.278	.364
Throws Right	R	.277	119	33	7	0	2	15	4	34	.301	.387
Hawkins,LaTroy	L	.238	101	24	7	2	2	9	10	19	.306	.406
Throws Right	R	.255	110	28	5	0	1	12	3	13	.270	.327
Heaney,Andrew	L	.212	33	7	2	1	0	0	3	7	.278	.333
Throws Left	R	.309	81	25	2	1	6	16	4	13	.364	.580
Hellickson,Jeremy	L	.213	141	30	7	0	3	14	8	33	.258	.326
Throws Right	R	.353	116	41	7	0	5	14	13	21	.423	.543
Hembree,Heath	L	.364	11	4	2	0	0	2	1	1	.417	.545
Throws Right	R	.259	27	7	2	0	1	3	4	5	.355	.444
Henderson,Jim	L	.429	14	6	2	0	1	2	3	7	.529	.786
Throws Right	R	.258	31	8	1	0	2	3	1	10	.281	.484
Hendricks,Kyle	L	.237	139	33	4	0	1	10	12	20	.296	.288
Throws Right	R	.247	158	39	8	0	3	12	3	27	.279	.354
Hendriks,Liam	L	.295	61	18	4	2	1	5	4	12	.338	.475
Throws Right	R	.286	70	20	4	0	2	10	3	11	.333	.429
Hernandez,Felix	L	.201	492	99	13	5	4	20	28	134	.246	.272
Throws Right	R	.197	360	71	17	0	12	38	18	114	.240	.344
Hernandez,Pedro	L	.429	7	3	0	0	0	1	1	1	.556	.429
Throws Left	R	.250	12	3	0	0	0	2	1	1	.286	.250
Hernandez,Roberto	L	.250	284	71	15	0	8	34	48	32	.358	.387
Throws Right	R	.249	341	85	21	3	11	46	25	73	.313	.425
Herrera,Kelvin	L	.244	123	30	7	0	0	6	13	38	.316	.301
Throws Right	R	.186	129	24	6	0	0	11	13	21	.276	.233
Herrera,Yoslan	L	.406	32	13	5	0	0	4	6	4	.500	.563
Throws Right	R	.250	36	9	2	0	0	4	3	9	.308	.306
Heston,Chris	L	.455	11	5	0	0	0	3	1	0	.462	.455
Throws Right	R	.111	9	1	0	0	0	0	2	4	.273	.111
Hill,Rich	L	.250	16	4	0	0	0	0	4	7	.429	.250
Throws Left	R	.500	6	3	0	0	0	1	2	2	.625	.500
Hill,Taylor	L	.389	18	7	1	0	0	1	2	2	.450	.444
Throws Right	R	.429	21	9	2	1	0	7	1	3	.500	.619
Holdzkom,John	L	.133	15	2	0	0	0	0	0	7	.133	.133
Throws Right	R	.133	15	2	0	0	1	2	2	7	.235	.333
Holland,Derek	L	.265	34	9	3	0	0	3	0	6	.265	.353
Throws Left	R	.243	103	25	8	0	0	5	5	19	.275	.320
Holland,Greg	L	.177	124	22	3	0	2	9	11	43	.244	.250
Throws Right	R	.160	94	15	2	0	1	4	9	47	.231	.213
Hollands,Mario	L	.241	79	19	4	1	0	10	8	18	.307	.316
Throws Left	R	.263	99	26	4	0	3	14	13	17	.354	.394
Holmberg,David	L	.280	25	7	0	0	2	4	6	5	.438	.520
Throws Left	R	.233	86	20	3	0	6	12	10	13	.340	.477
Hoover,J.J.	L	.333	105	35	5	2	6	22	4	26	.357	.590
Throws Right	R	.159	132	21	4	1	7	20	27	49	.296	.364
House,T.J.	L	.252	119	30	3	0	2	12	5	26	.280	.328
Throws Left	R	.297	279	83	12	4	8	24	17	54	.353	.455
Howell,J.P.	L	.170	88	15	2	0	1	7	13	23	.284	.227
Throws Left	R	.198	81	16	4	0	1	5	12	25	.301	.284
Hudson,Tim	L	.281	381	107	21	7	7	38	24	51	.327	.428
Throws Right	R	.258	357	92	13	4	8	35	10	69	.283	.384
Huff,David	L	.257	105	27	5	0	0	9	6	17	.304	.305
Throws Left	R	.268	127	34	1	0	5	10	17	22	.354	.394

Pitcher	vs	Avg	AB	H	2B	3B	HR	RBI	BB	SO	OBP	Slg
Hughes,Jared	L	.214	98	21	1	0	2	7	11	12	.306	.286
Throws Right	R	.240	125	30	4	0	2	10	8	24	.302	.320
Hughes,Phil	L	.249	429	107	17	3	7	34	11	101	.267	.352
Throws Right	R	.289	395	114	29	0	9	44	5	85	.303	.430
Hunter,Tommy	L	.245	110	27	7	0	2	10	5	15	.276	.364
Throws Right	R	.243	115	28	7	0	2	12	7	30	.290	.357
Hutchison,Drew	L	.263	384	101	29	1	17	58	42	95	.334	.477
Throws Right	R	.224	321	72	18	1	6	26	18	89	.272	.343
Irwin,Phil	L	.250	8	2	0	0	0	1	1	1	.333	.250
Throws Right	R	.444	9	4	0	0	1	2	1	1	.545	.778
Iwakuma,Hisashi	L	.273	366	100	15	1	11	29	10	72	.293	.410
Throws Right	R	.210	319	67	12	0	9	31	11	82	.240	.332
Jackson,Edwin	L	.341	255	87	24	3	5	45	33	47	.412	.518
Throws Right	R	.268	302	81	20	2	13	47	30	76	.339	.477
Jaime,Juan	L	.333	21	7	1	0	0	5	5	9	.462	.381
Throws Right	R	.241	29	7	0	1	1	3	4	9	.353	.414
Jansen,Kenley	L	.284	116	33	5	0	2	13	9	34	.331	.379
Throws Right	R	.169	130	22	5	1	3	10	10	67	.229	.292
Janssen,Casey	L	.260	77	20	4	0	3	7	4	11	.305	.429
Throws Right	R	.262	103	27	4	0	3	12	3	17	.280	.388
Jeffress,Jeremy	L	.392	51	20	3	0	1	10	5	9	.458	.510
Throws Right	R	.221	68	15	1	0	0	1	5	20	.274	.235
Jenkins,Chad	L	.315	54	17	7	0	1	8	3	6	.362	.500
Throws Right	R	.227	75	17	1	0	1	2	3	12	.256	.280
Jennings,Dan	L	.299	77	23	2	1	1	10	9	17	.364	.390
Throws Left	R	.265	83	22	3	1	2	7	8	21	.326	.398
Jepsen,Kevin	L	.219	114	25	5	0	3	17	10	36	.286	.342
Throws Right	R	.167	120	20	3	0	1	13	13	39	.254	.217
Jimenez,Cesar	L	.167	18	3	0	0	1	4	4	2	.304	.333
Throws Left	R	.282	39	11	1	0	0	3	3	6	.333	.308
Jimenez,Ubaldo	L	.244	258	63	11	1	9	34	53	59	.380	.399
Throws Right	R	.238	210	50	12	0	5	21	24	57	.316	.367
Johnson,Erik	L	.342	38	13	5	1	1	8	11	4	.500	.605
Throws Right	R	.264	53	14	1	0	0	8	4	14	.316	.283
Johnson,Jim	L	.333	111	37	4	1	4	26	22	16	.445	.495
Throws Right	R	.302	106	32	5	0	1	13	13	26	.398	.377
Johnson,Kris	L	.250	20	5	0	0	0	1	1	5	.286	.250
Throws Left	R	.353	34	12	1	1	2	6	8	7	.476	.618
Jokisch,Eric	L	.300	10	3	0	0	0	1	0	2	.300	.300
Throws Left	R	.288	52	15	3	0	3	7	4	8	.339	.519
Jordan,Taylor	L	.186	43	8	2	0	0	1	3	5	.255	.233
Throws Right	R	.388	67	26	8	0	3	16	5	12	.427	.642
Jurrjens,Jair	L	.448	29	13	1	1	2	4	3	6	.500	.759
Throws Right	R	.412	17	7	1	0	2	6	0	3	.444	.824
Kahnle,Tommy	L	.184	125	23	5	0	4	13	10	30	.250	.320
Throws Right	R	.228	123	28	4	1	3	22	21	33	.333	.350
Karns,Nate	L	.111	18	2	0	0	0	0	4	7	.273	.111
Throws Right	R	.200	25	5	1	0	3	5	0	6	.259	.600
Kazmir,Scott	L	.273	176	48	7	0	2	17	13	42	.326	.347
Throws Left	R	.227	541	123	28	1	14	52	37	122	.280	.360
Kelley,Shawn	L	.226	93	21	7	0	0	9	12	35	.311	.301
Throws Right	R	.235	102	24	1	1	5	16	8	32	.297	.412
Kelly,Joe	L	.243	189	46	4	2	3	18	30	33	.356	.333
Throws Right	R	.246	171	42	6	2	5	25	12	33	.304	.392
Kendrick,Kyle	L	.290	334	97	20	2	13	47	29	61	.347	.479
Throws Right	R	.265	441	117	19	3	12	48	28	60	.322	.404
Kennedy,Ian	L	.240	350	84	21	3	8	35	30	95	.303	.386
Throws Right	R	.259	405	105	22	2	8	43	40	112	.324	.383
Kershaw,Clayton	L	.193	135	26	3	1	1	3	5	45	.225	.252
Throws Left	R	.197	574	113	26	4	8	34	26	194	.233	.298
Keuchel,Dallas	L	.243	177	43	1	1	3	10	9	47	.284	.311
Throws Left	R	.255	565	144	37	1	8	50	39	99	.307	.366
Kimbrel,Craig	L	.147	116	17	1	0	1	6	13	55	.244	.181
Throws Right	R	.135	96	13	3	0	1	8	13	40	.239	.198
Kintzler,Brandon	L	.250	80	20	7	0	0	8	7	7	.310	.338
Throws Right	R	.304	138	42	5	0	8	22	9	24	.345	.514
Kirkman,Michael	L	.357	14	5	2	0	0	2	1	2	.471	.500
Throws Left	R	.000	5	0	0	0	0	0	0	1	.000	.000
Klein,Phil	L	.308	26	8	2	1	3	4	6	5	.438	.808
Throws Right	R	.073	41	3	2	0	0	1	4	18	.191	.122
Kluber,Corey	L	.244	467	114	29	4	10	37	36	144	.300	.388
Throws Right	R	.221	420	93	18	1	4	30	15	125	.255	.298
Knebel,Corey	L	.300	20	6	0	1	0	6	1	7	.333	.400
Throws Right	R	.313	16	5	2	0	0	2	2	4	.389	.438
Koehler,Tom	L	.241	374	90	15	4	5	34	33	82	.307	.342
Throws Right	R	.256	340	87	13	2	11	41	38	71	.334	.403

Pitchers vs. Left-Handed and Right-Handed Batters

Pitcher	vs	Avg	AB	H	2B	3B	HR	RBI	BB	SO	OBP	Slg
Kohn,Michael	L	.108	37	4	1	0	1	3	13	12	.358	.216
Throws Right	R	.171	41	7	2	0	0	3	7	14	.292	.220
Kontos,George	L	.143	42	6	0	1	0	0	10	13	.308	.190
Throws Right	R	.250	72	18	6	0	1	13	1	14	.260	.375
Krol,Ian	L	.261	69	18	5	2	1	11	5	15	.329	.435
Throws Left	R	.348	69	24	5	0	5	21	8	13	.410	.638
Kuroda,Hiroki	L	.262	412	108	18	2	12	46	26	69	.304	.403
Throws Right	R	.234	355	83	18	1	8	35	9	77	.264	.358
Lackey,John	L	.258	396	102	22	4	11	41	26	79	.303	.417
Throws Right	R	.274	380	104	19	1	13	48	21	85	.312	.432
Lane,Jason	L	.000	11	0	0	0	0	0	0	1	.000	.000
Throws Left	R	.250	28	7	1	0	1	1	0	5	.250	.393
Lannan,John	L	.364	11	4	0	1	2	4	1	2	.417	1.091
Throws Left	R	.375	8	3	1	0	1	3	1	0	.444	.875
Latos,Mat	L	.237	186	44	8	1	3	16	9	35	.270	.339
Throws Right	R	.244	197	48	5	2	6	21	17	39	.310	.381
Layne,Tom	L	.159	44	7	1	0	0	7	4	11	.229	.182
Throws Left	R	.318	22	7	2	1	0	3	4	3	.429	.500
League,Brandon	L	.313	80	25	3	0	0	14	11	10	.404	.350
Throws Right	R	.260	154	40	8	0	0	16	16	28	.333	.312
Leake,Mike	L	.290	362	105	30	1	10	38	21	54	.340	.461
Throws Right	R	.242	463	112	22	2	13	48	29	110	.292	.382
LeBlanc,Wade	L	.242	33	8	2	0	0	3	2	6	.324	.303
Throws Left	R	.247	77	19	1	0	2	7	5	15	.286	.338
LeCure,Sam	L	.215	93	20	4	1	3	13	13	24	.324	.376
Throws Right	R	.333	126	42	8	0	3	16	11	24	.384	.468
Lee,C.C.	L	.250	28	7	3	0	0	2	2	6	.300	.357
Throws Right	R	.284	81	23	3	1	3	11	10	20	.379	.457
Lee,Cliff	L	.238	63	15	0	0	1	6	0	18	.250	.286
Throws Left	R	.320	266	85	16	3	6	32	12	54	.345	.470
Leone,Dominic	L	.295	95	28	5	1	2	12	9	20	.368	.432
Throws Right	R	.166	145	24	4	2	2	15	16	50	.248	.262
Lester,Jon	L	.258	190	49	12	2	3	14	11	52	.307	.389
Throws Left	R	.230	631	145	31	1	13	52	37	168	.273	.344
Lewis,Colby	L	.320	387	124	27	3	10	51	31	67	.370	.483
Throws Right	R	.283	307	87	18	1	15	47	17	66	.328	.495
Lincecum,Tim	L	.256	277	71	9	7	6	41	38	45	.346	.404
Throws Right	R	.259	320	83	21	4	13	40	25	89	.319	.472
Lindblom,Josh	L	.235	17	4	1	0	0	0	2	2	.350	.294
Throws Right	R	.500	2	1	0	0	1	2	0	0	.500	2.000
Lindstrom,Matt	L	.303	76	23	5	2	2	16	6	9	.357	.500
Throws Right	R	.381	63	24	5	0	1	12	6	9	.429	.508
Liriano,Francisco	L	.270	115	31	5	0	3	11	13	40	.349	.391
Throws Left	R	.206	480	99	19	2	10	47	68	135	.306	.317
Lobstein,Kyle	L	.217	46	10	2	0	1	5	5	11	.294	.326
Throws Left	R	.245	102	25	6	1	2	14	9	16	.304	.382
Locke,Jeff	L	.190	105	20	2	0	2	10	9	12	.254	.267
Throws Left	R	.274	390	107	20	2	14	46	31	77	.333	.444
Logan,Boone	L	.318	44	14	1	0	3	9	6	17	.392	.545
Throws Left	R	.304	56	17	3	0	3	10	5	15	.365	.518
Lohse,Kyle	L	.254	347	88	13	3	13	44	24	58	.304	.421
Throws Right	R	.239	398	95	20	1	9	38	21	83	.282	.362
Lopez,Javier	L	.194	93	18	6	0	1	14	6	18	.248	.290
Throws Left	R	.271	48	13	1	0	1	5	13	4	.429	.354
Lopez,Wilton	L	.385	13	5	0	0	0	0	0	2	.385	.385
Throws Right	R	.591	22	13	2	0	3	11	0	2	.565	1.091
Loup,Aaron	L	.161	87	14	2	3	2	14	6	20	.237	.322
Throws Left	R	.234	154	36	12	0	2	22	21	[illegible]	[illegible]	.331
Lowe,Mark	L	.300	10	3	1	0	0	0	4	4	.500	.400
Throws Right	R	.318	22	7	3	0	2	6	2	2	.360	.727
Lueke,Josh	L	.261	69	18	2	0	3	9	2	7	.282	.420
Throws Right	R	.345	58	20	3	0	4	19	3	12	.375	.603
Luetge,Lucas	L	.133	15	2	0	0	1	3	2	4	.235	.333
Throws Left	R	.222	18	4	0	0	2	3	3	3	.333	.556
Lyles,Jordan	L	.289	242	70	17	2	7	23	31	39	.381	.463
Throws Right	R	.235	243	57	14	2	5	32	15	51	.284	.370
Lynn,Lance	L	.244	336	82	21	2	6	27	39	65	.325	.372
Throws Right	R	.234	441	103	25	1	7	36	33	116	.293	.342
Lyons,Tyler	L	.091	33	3	0	0	0	1	3	12	.189	.091
Throws Left	R	.280	107	30	6	1	4	19	8	24	.333	.467
Machi,Jean	L	.226	84	19	5	1	3	14	5	16	.270	.417
Throws Right	R	.186	140	26	7	1	2	14	13	35	.258	.293
Maholm,Paul	L	.289	83	24	3	0	2	10	7	10	.348	.398
Throws Left	R	.301	193	58	11	2	6	26	21	24	.375	.472
Maness,Seth	L	.314	105	33	7	0	4	22	7	12	.357	.495
Throws Right	R	.232	190	44	5	1	3	21	4	43	.249	.316

Pitcher	vs	Avg	AB	H	2B	3B	HR	RBI	BB	SO	OBP	Slg
Manship,Jeff	L	.219	32	7	1	0	0	5	7	7	.359	.250
Throws Right	R	.304	56	17	4	3	1	9	7	9	.381	.536
Mariot,Michael	L	.321	56	18	5	0	0	6	8	8	.406	.411
Throws Right	R	.271	48	13	2	0	2	11	4	13	.315	.438
Marmol,Carlos	L	.414	29	12	2	0	2	6	4	7	.500	.690
Throws Right	R	.154	26	4	0	0	1	6	6	7	.313	.269
Maronde,Nick	L	.385	13	5	0	1	0	4	3	3	.500	.538
Throws Left	R	.467	15	7	3	1	0	6	4	4	.550	.800
Marshall,Evan	L	.300	70	21	5	0	1	6	8	19	.367	.414
Throws Right	R	.246	118	29	7	0	2	10	9	35	.310	.356
Marshall,Sean	L	.458	24	11	2	0	0	11	6	5	.567	.542
Throws Left	R	.293	41	12	4	0	1	7	6	9	.408	.463
Martin,Chris	L	.333	24	8	1	1	0	0	3	7	.407	.458
Throws Right	R	.341	41	14	4	0	2	10	1	7	.357	.585
Martinez,Carlos	L	.297	145	43	7	4	3	18	22	19	.387	.462
Throws Right	R	.244	193	47	6	1	1	14	14	65	.308	.301
Martinez,David	L	.200	15	3	0	1	1	4	1	1	.250	.533
Throws Right	R	.182	11	2	1	0	0	0	1	5	.250	.273
Martinez,Nick	L	.279	305	85	22	2	11	40	40	42	.360	.472
Throws Right	R	.271	240	65	13	2	7	33	15	35	.317	.429
Masset,Nick	L	.368	68	25	4	1	1	18	10	14	.451	.500
Throws Right	R	.284	109	31	11	0	2	19	14	22	.375	.440
Masterson,Justin	L	.320	269	86	20	4	7	47	37	46	.408	.502
Throws Right	R	.239	230	55	9	3	5	31	32	70	.359	.370
Matsuzaka,Daisuke	L	.209	115	24	8	3	4	17	23	32	.343	.435
Throws Right	R	.209	182	38	11	1	2	16	27	46	.326	.313
Mattheus,Ryan	L	.250	12	3	1	0	0	0	3	2	.400	.333
Throws Right	R	.222	18	4	2	0	0	5	1	2	.300	.333
Matusz,Brian	L	.223	103	23	5	1	2	10	6	29	.277	.350
Throws Left	R	.277	101	28	10	0	5	15	11	24	.351	.525
Matzek,Tyler	L	.147	109	16	4	1	1	5	8	33	.205	.229
Throws Left	R	.306	340	104	25	4	8	38	36	58	.374	.474
Maurer,Brandon	L	.237	118	28	2	1	3	12	8	32	.283	.347
Throws Right	R	.289	159	46	11	1	3	24	11	23	.331	.428
May,Trevor	L	.298	84	25	8	0	3	12	13	21	.392	.500
Throws Right	R	.327	104	34	6	1	4	27	9	23	.388	.519
Mazzaro,Vin	L	.200	15	3	0	0	1	2	3	1	.333	.400
Throws Right	R	.208	24	5	1	0	1	2	2	6	.296	.375
McAllister,Zach	L	.286	161	46	12	2	4	23	12	37	.330	.460
Throws Right	R	.275	182	50	9	1	3	23	16	37	.330	.385
McCarthy,Brandon	L	.292	415	121	23	2	10	48	19	93	.322	.429
Throws Right	R	.267	378	101	20	1	15	44	14	82	.296	.444
McCoy,Pat	L	.208	24	5	1	0	0	2	4	6	.321	.250
Throws Left	R	.432	37	16	5	0	0	4	9	5	.543	.568
McFarland,T.J.	L	.266	94	25	4	0	1	10	8	20	.343	.340
Throws Left	R	.324	139	45	11	0	1	15	5	14	.352	.424
McGee,Jake	L	.236	72	17	5	0	0	2	3	31	.267	.306
Throws Left	R	.170	182	31	3	0	2	16	13	59	.232	.220
McGowan,Dustin	L	.257	144	37	11	1	4	14	18	29	.352	.431
Throws Right	R	.250	172	43	5	1	9	24	15	32	.307	.448
McHugh,Collin	L	.220	336	74	8	4	7	27	26	80	.279	.330
Throws Right	R	.190	226	43	8	0	6	19	15	77	.251	.305
Medina,Yoervis	L	.195	82	16	1	0	0	9	19	26	.356	.207
Throws Right	R	.250	128	32	6	1	3	18	9	34	.308	.383
Meek,Evan	L	.318	44	14	4	0	1	7	5	7	.388	.477
Throws Right	R	.261	46	12	0	0	2	10	6	9	.370	.391
Mejia,Jenrry	L	.239	176	42	6	0	2	16	24	46	.340	.307
Throws Right	R	.289	194	56	5	2	7	26	17	52	.349	.443
Melancon,Mark	L	.164	122	20	3	0	1	5	5	40	.202	.213
Throws Right	R	.223	139	31	2	0	1	12	6	31	.265	.259
Mendez,Roman	L	.175	57	10	1	0	1	8	13	6	.338	.246
Throws Right	R	.172	58	10	2	1	1	4	4	16	.231	.293
Mikolas,Miles	L	.266	128	34	7	1	3	22	11	18	.326	.406
Throws Right	R	.294	102	30	2	0	5	14	7	20	.354	.461
Miley,Wade	L	.265	170	45	5	1	5	21	15	38	.333	.394
Throws Left	R	.270	600	162	31	2	18	72	60	145	.333	.418
Miller,Andrew	L	.163	92	15	3	0	2	10	5	48	.206	.261
Throws Left	R	.145	124	18	4	0	1	7	12	55	.245	.202
Miller,Justin	L	.222	18	4	1	0	1	3	1	2	.263	.444
Throws Right	R	.333	30	10	4	0	1	8	1	3	.333	.567
Miller,Shelby	L	.238	307	73	12	2	10	37	38	56	.321	.388
Throws Right	R	.235	371	87	17	2	12	35	35	71	.301	.388
Mills,Brad	L	.481	27	13	3	1	3	18	3	4	.545	1.000
Throws Left	R	.267	60	16	1	0	2	5	8	15	.353	.383
Milone,Tommy	L	.258	93	24	4	1	3	9	6	10	.310	.419
Throws Left	R	.273	381	104	20	2	13	41	31	65	.333	.438

Pitchers vs. Left-Handed and Right-Handed Batters

Pitcher	vs	Avg	AB	H	2B	3B	HR	RBI	BB	SO	OBP	Slg
Minor,Mike	L	.357	126	45	8	1	2	15	10	28	.403	.484
Throws Left	R	.265	453	120	23	2	19	51	34	92	.323	.450
Mitchell,Bryan	L	.313	16	5	2	1	0	3	3	3	.450	.563
Throws Right	R	.217	23	5	2	0	0	0	0	4	.250	.304
Montero,Rafael	L	.293	92	27	5	2	5	14	11	15	.369	.554
Throws Right	R	.215	79	17	5	0	3	6	12	27	.319	.392
Moore,Matt	L	.333	9	3	0	1	0	1	2	1	.455	.556
Throws Left	R	.233	30	7	2	0	1	2	3	5	.303	.400
Morales,Franklin	L	.253	162	41	2	2	5	24	12	24	.317	.383
Throws Left	R	.313	399	125	28	1	19	56	53	76	.392	.531
Morin,Mike	L	.283	113	32	6	1	1	14	12	21	.357	.381
Throws Right	R	.181	105	19	4	0	2	9	7	33	.235	.276
Morris,Bryan	L	.256	90	23	2	0	2	10	16	15	.382	.344
Throws Right	R	.243	144	35	6	0	4	20	8	35	.284	.368
Morrow,Brandon	L	.303	66	20	6	2	2	8	11	15	.403	.545
Throws Right	R	.270	63	17	4	1	0	7	7	15	.343	.365
Morton,Charlie	L	.243	284	69	11	3	2	34	36	65	.340	.324
Throws Right	R	.252	294	74	11	2	7	35	21	61	.324	.374
Motte,Jason	L	.211	38	8	0	0	3	7	4	7	.286	.447
Throws Right	R	.344	61	21	4	0	4	13	5	10	.382	.607
Mujica,Edward	L	.315	108	34	13	1	4	14	4	20	.339	.565
Throws Right	R	.276	127	35	6	0	2	14	10	23	.324	.370
Nathan,Joe	L	.280	132	37	5	0	3	20	19	23	.368	.386
Throws Right	R	.245	94	23	4	0	2	12	10	31	.321	.351
Nelson,Jimmy	L	.275	142	39	12	0	5	18	12	27	.340	.465
Throws Right	R	.309	139	43	10	1	1	19	7	30	.364	.417
Neshek,Pat	L	.196	92	18	4	0	2	6	5	22	.237	.304
Throws Right	R	.176	148	26	3	0	2	18	4	46	.205	.236
Nicasio,Juan	L	.309	165	51	10	2	7	23	19	22	.378	.521
Throws Right	R	.273	205	56	11	1	12	35	12	41	.315	.512
Niese,Jon	L	.254	173	44	5	3	3	22	7	37	.286	.370
Throws Left	R	.273	546	149	29	4	14	51	38	101	.325	.418
Noesi,Hector	L	.244	377	92	11	2	18	57	32	66	.301	.427
Throws Right	R	.307	287	88	14	2	10	35	24	57	.360	.474
Nolasco,Ricky	L	.334	320	107	20	3	11	44	27	47	.387	.519
Throws Right	R	.297	323	96	22	4	11	44	11	68	.324	.492
Norris,Bud	L	.255	329	84	13	3	12	35	33	70	.331	.422
Throws Right	R	.226	287	65	14	1	8	28	19	69	.293	.366
Norris,Daniel	L	.091	11	1	0	0	1	2	2	4	.231	.364
Throws Left	R	.308	13	4	0	0	0	1	3	0	.412	.308
Nova,Ivan	L	.346	52	18	2	0	0	4	2	8	.379	.385
Throws Right	R	.412	34	14	1	0	6	12	4	4	.474	.971
Nuno,Vidal	L	.193	140	27	5	0	4	13	15	36	.268	.314
Throws Left	R	.273	477	130	28	2	21	65	31	93	.322	.472
Oberholtzer,Brett	L	.292	137	40	2	1	4	12	3	28	.317	.409
Throws Left	R	.295	440	130	32	2	8	52	25	66	.328	.432
O'Day,Darren	L	.189	95	18	3	1	4	10	10	27	.264	.368
Throws Right	R	.164	146	24	6	0	2	6	9	46	.250	.247
Odorizzi,Jake	L	.230	344	79	14	3	10	39	28	109	.288	.375
Throws Right	R	.257	300	77	10	1	10	31	31	65	.329	.397
O'Flaherty,Eric	L	.233	30	7	0	0	0	0	3	9	.303	.233
Throws Left	R	.186	43	8	1	0	3	4	1	6	.239	.419
Ogando,Alexi	L	.300	50	15	1	0	1	9	4	10	.352	.380
Throws Right	R	.327	55	18	4	0	0	8	11	12	.448	.400
Oliveros,Lester	L	.000	7	0	0	0	0	0	1	2	.125	.000
Throws Right	R	.375	16	6	2	0	2	7	2	3	.421	.875
Ondrusek,Logan	L	.306	62	19	1	0	2	10	9	21	.397	.419
Throws Right	R	.290	107	31	9	0	3	14	7	21	.333	.458
O'Sullivan,Sean	L	.364	22	8	1	0	1	1	2	5	.417	.545
Throws Right	R	.259	27	7	0	0	2	6	0	2	.259	.481
Otero,Dan	L	.283	138	39	7	1	1	15	8	20	.329	.370
Throws Right	R	.219	187	41	5	0	3	23	7	25	.245	.294
Ottavino,Adam	L	.347	75	26	5	1	3	15	5	15	.383	.560
Throws Right	R	.238	172	41	10	0	3	19	11	55	.296	.349
Outman,Josh	L	.169	59	10	1	0	3	10	8	16	.269	.339
Throws Left	R	.304	46	14	6	1	1	3	8	10	.407	.543
Oviedo,Juan	L	.242	62	15	5	1	1	11	7	14	.314	.403
Throws Right	R	.207	58	12	5	0	2	6	9	12	.343	.397
Owens,Rudy	L	.417	12	5	0	0	0	2	0	0	.462	.417
Throws Left	R	.308	13	4	2	0	1	3	2	1	.375	.692
Papelbon,Jonathan	L	.182	121	22	5	0	0	7	8	25	.238	.223
Throws Right	R	.200	115	23	2	0	2	7	7	38	.270	.270
Parker,Blake	L	.171	35	6	1	1	1	4	2	13	.216	.343
Throws Right	R	.353	51	18	5	0	2	9	2	11	.370	.569
Parra,Manny	L	.256	82	21	5	0	1	12	8	18	.322	.354
Throws Left	R	.305	59	18	3	0	3	11	10	16	.414	.508

Pitcher	vs	Avg	AB	H	2B	3B	HR	RBI	BB	SO	OBP	Slg
Partch,Curtis	L	.200	10	2	0	0	0	0	5	3	.467	.200
Throws Right	R	.000	13	0	0	0	0	0	2	3	.133	.000
Patton,Spencer	L	.273	11	3	1	0	0	0	1	1	.333	.364
Throws Right	R	.136	22	3	0	0	0	0	1	7	.174	.136
Patton,Troy	L	.214	28	6	0	0	1	4	3	8	.290	.321
Throws Left	R	.333	30	10	4	0	1	4	2	5	.375	.567
Paulino,Felipe	L	.333	48	16	3	1	5	13	6	7	.418	.750
Throws Right	R	.452	42	19	2	0	1	9	6	7	.521	.571
Paxton,James	L	.205	44	9	1	0	0	3	6	14	.300	.227
Throws Left	R	.227	225	51	10	2	3	17	23	45	.300	.329
Peacock,Brad	L	.273	308	84	16	1	11	38	39	68	.355	.438
Throws Right	R	.259	201	52	8	2	9	30	31	51	.359	.453
Peavy,Jake	L	.249	373	93	16	5	16	45	36	73	.318	.448
Throws Right	R	.265	388	103	28	2	7	36	27	85	.317	.402
Pelfrey,Mike	L	.196	56	11	2	0	2	9	10	7	.309	.339
Throws Right	R	.462	39	18	2	0	3	10	8	3	.571	.744
Penny,Brad	L	.279	43	12	4	2	1	5	3	8	.326	.535
Throws Right	R	.361	61	22	4	0	2	14	10	5	.458	.525
Peralta,Joel	L	.247	146	36	7	0	4	11	9	44	.293	.377
Throws Right	R	.240	100	24	7	1	5	14	6	30	.283	.480
Peralta,Wily	L	.305	384	117	20	1	14	53	26	77	.349	.471
Throws Right	R	.217	374	81	9	0	9	27	35	77	.293	.313
Perez,Chris	L	.200	70	14	3	1	3	12	14	17	.352	.400
Throws Right	R	.247	97	24	2	3	3	14	11	22	.333	.423
Perez,Martin	L	.256	43	11	4	0	1	5	1	12	.289	.419
Throws Left	R	.273	143	39	10	1	2	15	18	23	.354	.399
Perez,Oliver	L	.281	96	27	6	0	3	16	6	31	.343	.438
Throws Left	R	.184	125	23	6	1	2	11	18	45	.306	.296
Perkins,Glen	L	.284	67	19	3	1	2	11	3	18	.324	.448
Throws Left	R	.249	173	43	11	2	5	18	8	48	.278	.422
Pestano,Vinnie	L	.440	25	11	2	0	2	5	0	4	.440	.760
Throws Right	R	.149	47	7	0	1	1	4	5	22	.226	.255
Petit,Yusmeiro	L	.257	202	52	10	1	10	27	16	47	.312	.465
Throws Right	R	.193	233	45	14	2	2	19	6	86	.214	.296
Petricka,Jake	L	.310	116	36	10	0	2	18	13	18	.382	.448
Throws Right	R	.208	149	31	3	0	1	18	20	37	.301	.248
Pettibone,Jonathan	L	.375	16	6	1	0	0	2	2	2	.444	.438
Throws Right	R	.407	27	11	1	0	2	7	1	4	.429	.667
Phelps,David	L	.227	220	50	7	3	7	27	28	52	.320	.382
Throws Right	R	.300	217	65	9	2	6	28	18	40	.363	.442
Pimentel,Stolmy	L	.268	56	15	1	1	1	9	11	17	.391	.375
Throws Right	R	.260	73	19	4	0	4	11	5	21	.316	.479
Pineda,Michael	L	.196	148	29	8	2	2	7	4	32	.216	.318
Throws Right	R	.205	132	27	3	0	3	8	3	27	.222	.295
Pino,Yohan	L	.284	134	38	9	0	3	12	10	25	.336	.418
Throws Right	R	.272	103	28	6	0	5	23	4	25	.291	.476
Pomeranz,Drew	L	.232	56	13	1	0	2	3	6	17	.306	.357
Throws Left	R	.196	194	38	3	0	5	13	20	47	.274	.289
Porcello,Rick	L	.268	441	118	25	7	9	43	29	68	.315	.417
Throws Right	R	.268	347	93	10	3	9	36	12	61	.294	.392
Poreda,Aaron	L	.333	33	11	6	0	0	2	3	10	.389	.515
Throws Left	R	.339	56	19	4	0	2	11	4	11	.393	.518
Pressly,Ryan	L	.308	39	12	2	1	1	3	5	7	.400	.487
Throws Right	R	.261	69	18	4	1	2	10	3	7	.280	.435
Price,David	L	.258	244	63	9	1	5	21	8	61	.292	.365
Throws Left	R	.234	715	167	38	3	20	66	30	210	.265	.379
Putnam,Zach	L	.235	102	24	3	1	1	9	10	20	.310	.314
Throws Right	R	.170	88	15	1	0	1	3	10	26	.253	.216
Putz,J.J.	L	.600	20	12	3	0	0	3	2	5	.636	.750
Throws Right	R	.147	34	5	1	1	1	7	4	9	.250	.324
Quackenbush,Kevin	L	.196	107	21	4	0	1	5	6	29	.250	.262
Throws Right	R	.231	91	21	5	0	1	11	12	27	.314	.319
Qualls,Chad	L	.303	99	30	4	1	4	20	4	18	.343	.485
Throws Right	R	.229	105	24	2	0	1	5	1	25	.236	.276
Quintana,Jose	L	.268	209	56	12	0	3	25	15	50	.317	.368
Throws Left	R	.253	557	141	27	4	7	50	37	128	.299	.354
Ramirez,Erasmo	L	.282	170	48	5	0	6	23	24	33	.372	.418
Throws Right	R	.270	126	34	6	1	7	17	10	27	.348	.500
Ramirez,Jose	L	.063	16	1	1	0	0	0	4	6	.250	.125
Throws Right	R	.417	24	10	2	0	2	8	3	4	.517	.750
Ramirez,Neil	L	.200	60	12	4	0	0	3	11	23	.324	.267
Throws Right	R	.173	98	17	3	1	2	10	6	30	.236	.286
Ramos,A.J.	L	.151	86	13	3	0	0	3	23	30	.336	.186
Throws Right	R	.172	134	23	10	0	1	16	20	43	.287	.269
Ramos,Cesar	L	.244	119	29	3	1	3	14	8	26	.289	.361
Throws Left	R	.227	194	44	10	0	5	23	31	40	.333	.356

Pitchers vs. Left-Handed and Right-Handed Batters

Pitcher	vs	Avg	AB	H	2B	3B	HR	RBI	BB	SO	OBP	Slg
Ranaudo,Anthony	L	.280	75	21	0	1	5	11	11	8	.364	.507
Throws Right	R	.240	75	18	4	1	5	10	5	7	.280	.520
Rasmus,Cory	L	.234	94	22	4	0	3	10	6	27	.275	.372
Throws Right	R	.179	112	20	4	0	2	7	11	30	.252	.268
Rasmussen,Rob	L	.133	15	2	1	0	0	0	4	5	.316	.200
Throws Left	R	.231	26	6	0	0	1	3	3	8	.355	.346
Ray,Robbie	L	.351	37	13	3	0	1	5	2	7	.375	.514
Throws Left	R	.349	86	30	10	1	4	18	9	12	.411	.628
Redmond,Todd	L	.287	115	33	10	1	2	16	16	23	.379	.443
Throws Right	R	.245	163	40	11	0	3	23	11	37	.289	.368
Reed,Addison	L	.219	114	25	6	0	2	10	10	35	.286	.325
Throws Right	R	.267	120	32	7	1	9	25	5	34	.296	.567
Reed,Evan	L	.305	59	18	3	1	2	5	6	13	.379	.492
Throws Right	R	.300	70	21	2	0	0	8	6	13	.367	.329
Rice,Scott	L	.262	42	11	3	0	0	5	8	12	.392	.333
Throws Left	R	.400	10	4	0	0	1	1	4	1	.571	.700
Richards,Garrett	L	.194	340	66	14	0	3	24	27	91	.257	.262
Throws Right	R	.209	277	58	8	0	2	20	24	73	.282	.260
Riefenhauser,C.J.	L	.111	9	1	0	0	0	1	2	1	.273	.111
Throws Left	R	.417	12	5	1	0	0	1	1	1	.462	.500
Rienzo,Andre	L	.299	147	44	9	0	8	31	23	30	.397	.524
Throws Right	R	.309	123	38	9	1	4	20	10	21	.375	.496
Roach,Donn	L	.341	41	14	3	0	1	10	6	4	.451	.488
Throws Right	R	.289	76	22	4	0	1	9	9	13	.372	.382
Roark,Tanner	L	.235	378	89	20	1	11	36	28	54	.291	.381
Throws Right	R	.242	368	89	14	0	5	20	11	84	.271	.321
Robertson,David	L	.157	127	20	2	1	1	7	11	54	.225	.213
Throws Right	R	.234	107	25	5	0	6	15	12	42	.317	.449
Rodney,Fernando	L	.289	149	43	8	0	2	15	12	42	.344	.383
Throws Right	R	.178	101	18	2	0	1	8	16	34	.303	.228
Rodriguez,Fernando	L	.091	11	1	1	0	0	1	2	3	.231	.182
Throws Right	R	.150	20	3	0	0	0	1	0	1	.150	.150
Rodriguez,Francisco	L	.176	125	22	3	1	4	8	5	36	.214	.312
Throws Right	R	.221	122	27	1	0	10	15	13	37	.296	.475
Rodriguez,Paco	L	.241	29	7	1	0	1	1	2	11	.290	.379
Throws Left	R	.263	19	5	1	0	0	2	2	3	.333	.316
Rodriguez,Wandy	L	.353	17	6	0	0	1	5	1	3	.368	.529
Throws Left	R	.320	97	31	12	0	9	19	7	17	.365	.722
Rogers,Esmil	L	.325	83	27	3	0	5	14	13	17	.417	.542
Throws Right	R	.235	98	23	5	1	3	17	4	27	.279	.398
Romo,Sergio	L	.256	78	20	5	0	3	9	7	11	.341	.436
Throws Right	R	.172	134	23	2	0	6	13	5	48	.207	.321
Rondon,Hector	L	.255	106	27	3	0	1	9	8	21	.304	.311
Throws Right	R	.188	133	25	2	0	1	10	7	42	.229	.226
Rosenberg,B.J.	L	.357	14	5	0	0	2	4	6	4	.550	.786
Throws Right	R	.395	38	15	2	1	3	7	1	5	.410	.737
Rosenthal,Trevor	L	.181	116	21	5	0	0	10	20	34	.299	.224
Throws Right	R	.257	140	36	8	1	2	17	22	53	.367	.371
Ross,Robbie	L	.283	106	30	6	0	3	24	8	19	.342	.425
Throws Left	R	.336	217	73	12	1	6	34	22	32	.408	.484
Ross,Tyson	L	.230	357	82	12	2	5	34	43	97	.319	.317
Throws Right	R	.231	359	83	12	1	8	37	29	98	.295	.337
Rosscup,Zac	L	.200	25	5	1	0	0	8	5	13	.333	.240
Throws Left	R	.310	29	9	5	0	2	6	7	8	.444	.690
Roth,Michael	L	.286	14	4	0	0	1	4	4	5	.444	.500
Throws Left	R	.364	33	12	2	0	1	6	5	4	.476	.515
Rowen,Ben	L	.556	9	5	1	0	0	2	1	0	.545	.667
Throws Right	R	.217	23	5	1	0	0	2	3	7	.296	.261
Rowland-Smith,Ryan	L	.273	11	3	0	0	0	3	0	4	.250	.273
Throws Left	R	.267	15	4	1	0	0	2	4	5	.400	.333
Rucinski,Drew	L	.154	13	2	0	0	0	0	1	2	.214	.154
Throws Right	R	.389	18	7	2	0	0	4	1	6	.450	.500
Rusin,Chris	L	.208	24	5	1	0	0	5	0	4	.208	.250
Throws Left	R	.393	28	11	4	0	1	7	5	4	.485	.643
Russell,James	L	.284	88	25	4	1	3	14	9	19	.351	.455
Throws Left	R	.165	121	20	2	0	0	7	11	23	.239	.182
Ryan,Kyle	L	.300	10	3	1	0	0	1	0	3	.300	.400
Throws Left	R	.241	29	7	2	0	0	1	2	1	.290	.310
Ryu,Hyun-Jin	L	.283	138	39	7	0	1	9	4	26	.310	.355
Throws Left	R	.249	453	113	28	2	7	46	25	113	.290	.366
Rzepczynski,Marc	L	.180	100	18	2	0	0	7	7	31	.241	.200
Throws Left	R	.338	71	24	7	1	1	11	12	15	.437	.507
Sabathia,CC	L	.160	25	4	0	0	1	6	2	8	.290	.280
Throws Left	R	.321	168	54	14	0	9	24	8	40	.356	.565
Sadler,Casey	L	.200	20	4	2	0	0	4	1	2	.227	.300
Throws Right	R	.381	21	8	3	0	0	5	4	5	.481	.524

Pitcher	vs	Avg	AB	H	2B	3B	HR	RBI	BB	SO	OBP	Slg
Salas,Fernando	L	.188	112	21	2	1	1	8	11	26	.260	.250
Throws Right	R	.271	107	29	8	1	4	20	3	35	.295	.477
Salazar,Danny	L	.246	167	41	9	0	4	16	19	51	.324	.371
Throws Right	R	.289	263	76	17	0	9	34	16	69	.330	.456
Sale,Chris	L	.165	121	20	2	0	0	2	6	47	.211	.182
Throws Left	R	.214	509	109	20	1	13	43	33	161	.274	.334
Samardzija,Jeff	L	.241	381	92	22	1	9	30	23	98	.287	.375
Throws Right	R	.228	434	99	16	4	11	47	20	104	.272	.359
Sanchez,Aaron	L	.150	40	6	0	0	1	3	5	10	.244	.225
Throws Right	R	.116	69	8	1	0	0	2	4	17	.176	.130
Sanchez,Anibal	L	.219	283	62	16	1	2	18	15	64	.258	.304
Throws Right	R	.241	191	46	11	2	2	23	15	38	.300	.351
Santana,Ervin	L	.291	398	116	24	4	8	42	27	83	.331	.432
Throws Right	R	.235	328	77	18	0	8	36	36	96	.314	.363
Santiago,Hector	L	.244	131	32	6	0	1	5	9	28	.293	.313
Throws Left	R	.249	353	88	10	0	14	44	44	80	.335	.397
Santos,Sergio	L	.244	45	11	4	0	1	7	8	18	.345	.400
Throws Right	R	.415	41	17	7	0	4	13	10	11	.529	.878
Saunders,Joe	L	.288	52	15	0	0	0	1	3	6	.327	.288
Throws Left	R	.373	134	50	13	1	9	32	21	17	.456	.687
Scahill,Rob	L	.391	23	9	0	0	2	4	6	4	.517	.652
Throws Right	R	.216	37	8	4	0	1	9	3	7	.279	.405
Scheppers,Tanner	L	.318	66	21	2	0	4	19	6	14	.395	.530
Throws Right	R	.323	31	10	0	0	2	4	4	3	.400	.516
Scherzer,Max	L	.242	495	120	30	0	13	50	42	138	.303	.382
Throws Right	R	.232	328	76	19	2	5	25	21	114	.281	.348
Schlitter,Brian	L	.288	73	21	5	1	2	21	8	10	.354	.466
Throws Right	R	.261	142	37	4	0	0	15	11	21	.323	.289
Schlosser,Gus	L	.333	27	9	2	0	2	7	4	2	.424	.630
Throws Right	R	.326	43	14	5	0	0	11	2	6	.348	.442
Schultz,Bo	L	.353	17	6	0	0	1	7	0	2	.353	.529
Throws Right	R	.412	17	7	3	0	0	3	1	3	.421	.588
Scribner,Evan	L	.158	19	3	0	0	0	0	0	6	.158	.158
Throws Right	R	.296	27	8	1	0	4	6	0	5	.321	.778
Shaw,Bryan	L	.294	109	32	9	0	2	14	8	25	.345	.431
Throws Right	R	.168	173	29	2	1	4	18	14	39	.233	.260
Shields,James	L	.261	460	120	26	3	9	47	29	96	.309	.389
Throws Right	R	.251	414	104	20	4	14	36	15	84	.286	.420
Shoemaker,Matt	L	.257	268	69	15	1	8	22	11	59	.291	.410
Throws Right	R	.222	239	53	10	1	6	22	13	65	.263	.347
Shreve,Chasen	L	.273	22	6	1	0	0	1	2	8	.333	.318
Throws Left	R	.167	24	4	1	0	0	0	1	7	.200	.208
Siegrist,Kevin	L	.308	39	12	1	0	1	8	7	10	.417	.410
Throws Left	R	.247	81	20	5	1	4	11	9	27	.330	.481
Simmons,Shae	L	.122	41	5	2	0	1	7	7	11	.245	.244
Throws Right	R	.286	35	10	3	0	0	4	4	12	.359	.371
Simon,Alfredo	L	.251	370	93	18	1	12	43	33	62	.312	.403
Throws Right	R	.238	369	88	16	0	10	33	23	65	.302	.363
Sipp,Tony	L	.138	87	12	1	1	3	12	10	22	.227	.276
Throws Left	R	.176	91	16	3	1	2	6	7	41	.235	.297
Skaggs,Tyler	L	.290	93	27	3	1	2	13	6	17	.333	.409
Throws Left	R	.242	330	80	17	0	7	35	24	69	.298	.358
Slowey,Kevin	L	.338	68	23	6	0	3	16	7	12	.397	.559
Throws Right	R	.366	82	30	6	2	0	8	2	12	.379	.488
Smith,Carson	L	.000	11	0	0	0	0	0	1	5	.083	.000
Throws Right	R	.133	15	2	0	0	0	0	2	5	.235	.133
Smith,Chad	L	.417	24	10	4	0	1	6	1	4	.440	.708
Throws Right	R	.217	23	5	2	0	0	1	2	5	.280	.304
Smith,Joe	L	.206	136	28	4	1	2	14	11	36	.289	.294
Throws Right	R	.136	125	17	2	1	2	10	4	32	.169	.216
Smith,Will	L	.167	96	16	2	1	2	10	10	47	.245	.271
Throws Left	R	.299	154	46	12	2	4	21	21	39	.391	.481
Smyly,Drew	L	.171	158	27	4	1	4	12	6	46	.201	.285
Throws Left	R	.264	413	109	29	1	14	43	36	87	.322	.441
Soria,Joakim	L	.255	102	26	7	2	1	9	3	26	.283	.392
Throws Right	R	.174	69	12	3	1	1	11	3	22	.213	.290
Soriano,Rafael	L	.218	110	24	6	1	2	8	8	30	.269	.345
Throws Right	R	.227	119	27	8	1	2	13	11	29	.301	.361
Spruill,Zeke	L	.289	45	13	2	0	0	3	3	5	.347	.333
Throws Right	R	.311	45	14	3	0	0	6	1	9	.313	.378
Stammen,Craig	L	.286	126	36	5	2	3	10	10	23	.338	.429
Throws Right	R	.268	157	42	9	0	2	22	4	33	.297	.363
Stauffer,Tim	L	.282	124	35	8	0	0	15	9	28	.333	.347
Throws Right	R	.264	121	32	8	0	4	13	14	39	.346	.430
Stinson,Josh	L	.259	27	7	2	0	1	5	2	1	.310	.444
Throws Right	R	.346	26	9	1	0	1	7	4	5	.469	.500

Pitchers vs. Left-Handed and Right-Handed Batters

Pitcher	vs	Avg	AB	H	2B	3B	HR	RBI	BB	SO	OBP	Slg
Stites,Matt	L	.192	52	10	2	1	2	4	10	11	.333	.385
Throws Right	R	.307	75	23	6	0	4	18	6	15	.354	.547
Storen,Drew	L	.253	91	23	3	0	1	8	3	18	.274	.319
Throws Right	R	.184	114	21	4	0	1	9	8	28	.254	.246
Straily,Dan	L	.226	106	24	7	0	5	13	16	24	.331	.434
Throws Right	R	.296	98	29	10	0	5	22	8	23	.355	.551
Strasburg,Stephen	L	.234	355	83	17	0	11	32	22	93	.278	.375
Throws Right	R	.254	452	115	23	2	12	47	21	149	.293	.394
Street,Huston	L	.185	108	20	3	0	1	2	8	24	.241	.241
Throws Right	R	.208	106	22	2	0	3	7	6	33	.250	.311
Strickland,Hunter	L	.200	10	2	1	0	0	0	0	2	.200	.300
Throws Right	R	.200	15	3	0	0	0	0	0	7	.200	.200
Stroman,Marcus	L	.232	259	60	16	1	5	22	19	58	.287	.359
Throws Right	R	.269	242	65	5	1	2	24	9	53	.298	.322
Strop,Pedro	L	.214	84	18	4	0	1	8	14	24	.323	.298
Throws Right	R	.169	130	22	4	0	1	8	11	47	.255	.223
Stults,Eric	L	.295	190	56	11	1	6	24	7	25	.322	.458
Throws Left	R	.279	505	141	25	0	20	62	38	86	.330	.448
Surkamp,Eric	L	.174	46	8	1	0	3	7	7	11	.296	.391
Throws Left	R	.318	44	14	1	0	0	6	6	9	.400	.341
Swarzak,Anthony	L	.282	163	46	12	1	1	19	16	20	.346	.387
Throws Right	R	.293	184	54	10	2	4	35	12	27	.333	.435
Tanaka,Masahiro	L	.238	281	67	14	0	7	21	10	65	.269	.363
Throws Right	R	.242	231	56	12	1	8	23	11	76	.280	.407
Tazawa,Junichi	L	.241	116	28	5	0	2	10	6	33	.279	.336
Throws Right	R	.238	126	30	10	1	3	22	11	31	.297	.405
Teheran,Julio	L	.239	418	100	18	4	13	45	31	86	.292	.395
Throws Right	R	.223	394	88	12	0	9	31	20	100	.265	.322
Tepesch,Nick	L	.234	273	64	16	3	9	33	31	33	.311	.414
Throws Right	R	.311	206	64	11	2	6	20	13	23	.369	.471
Thatcher,Joe	L	.289	76	22	6	0	2	13	1	18	.317	.447
Throws Left	R	.298	47	14	1	0	1	6	3	9	.353	.383
Thayer,Dale	L	.217	106	23	2	0	5	12	6	21	.259	.377
Throws Right	R	.214	140	30	6	0	4	9	10	41	.276	.343
Thielbar,Caleb	L	.289	97	28	2	3	2	15	7	24	.327	.433
Throws Left	R	.271	85	23	4	1	1	9	9	11	.337	.376
Thomas,Ian	L	.318	22	7	1	0	0	2	3	6	.385	.364
Throws Left	R	.167	18	3	0	0	0	0	3	7	.286	.167
Thompson,Aaron	L	.294	17	5	2	0	0	1	0	4	.294	.412
Throws Left	R	.273	11	3	1	0	0	2	2	2	.357	.364
Thompson,Taylor	L	.455	11	5	0	1	0	2	1	3	.500	.636
Throws Right	R	.333	12	4	0	0	1	2	3	1	.500	.583
Thornburg,Tyler	L	.119	42	5	1	0	0	2	12	13	.315	.143
Throws Right	R	.288	66	19	7	0	1	13	9	15	.368	.439
Thornton,Matt	L	.250	80	20	1	0	0	13	3	16	.307	.263
Throws Left	R	.236	55	13	3	1	0	6	5	12	.306	.327
Tillman,Chris	L	.249	438	109	19	2	9	37	35	82	.307	.363
Throws Right	R	.225	356	80	15	3	12	39	31	68	.287	.385
Tolleson,Shawn	L	.216	111	24	4	0	4	12	10	28	.282	.360
Throws Right	R	.212	151	32	5	1	6	22	18	41	.294	.377
Tomlin,Josh	L	.250	220	55	7	2	11	29	6	49	.268	.450
Throws Right	R	.314	207	65	15	2	7	30	8	45	.341	.507
Tonkin,Michael	L	.333	27	9	3	0	2	6	1	3	.357	.667
Throws Right	R	.292	48	14	2	0	0	9	5	13	.375	.333
Torres,Alex	L	.256	90	23	3	0	1	10	25	23	.415	.322
Throws Left	R	.209	110	23	5	0	1	7	8	28	.275	.282
Torres,Carlos	L	.218	133	29	4	0	4	10	24	40	.342	.338
Throws Right	R	.262	229	60	17	0	7	26	14	56	.306	.428
Treinen,Blake	L	.337	98	33	4	1	1	11	5	12	.369	.429
Throws Right	R	.238	101	24	2	0	0	5	8	18	.306	.257
Tropeano,Nicholas	L	.241	54	13	2	1	0	9	8	7	.333	.315
Throws Right	R	.240	25	6	1	0	0	2	1	6	.296	.280
Turner,Jacob	L	.308	185	57	11	1	4	29	18	17	.369	.443
Throws Right	R	.335	272	91	19	1	8	43	15	54	.367	.500
Uehara,Koji	L	.197	132	26	2	0	8	15	4	38	.219	.394
Throws Right	R	.240	104	25	8	0	2	7	4	42	.275	.375
Valverde,Jose	L	.200	35	7	1	1	1	4	7	12	.333	.371
Throws Right	R	.340	50	17	3	0	3	8	3	11	.377	.580
Vargas,Jason	L	.268	183	49	8	1	2	11	6	31	.306	.355
Throws Left	R	.266	556	148	30	2	17	60	35	97	.311	.419
Varvaro,Anthony	L	.149	74	11	2	1	2	7	5	23	.198	.284
Throws Right	R	.273	128	35	8	0	3	16	8	27	.314	.406
Veal,Donnie	L	.200	10	2	0	1	0	4	3	3	.400	.400
Throws Left	R	.308	13	4	1	0	0	2	4	3	.471	.385
Ventura,Yordano	L	.232	405	94	12	3	9	32	39	87	.299	.343
Throws Right	R	.250	296	74	19	2	5	32	30	72	.326	.378

Pitcher	vs	Avg	AB	H	2B	3B	HR	RBI	BB	SO	OBP	Slg
Veras,Jose	L	.200	60	12	1	0	4	9	15	21	.355	.417
Throws Right	R	.227	110	25	5	1	2	21	12	29	.320	.345
VerHagen,Drew	L	.308	13	4	1	0	0	3	3	4	.438	.385
Throws Right	R	.250	4	1	0	0	0	0	0	0	.250	.250
Verlander,Justin	L	.239	460	110	22	6	10	45	45	101	.308	.378
Throws Right	R	.321	352	113	29	3	8	56	20	58	.361	.489
Villanueva,Carlos	L	.268	123	33	8	1	4	12	7	29	.311	.447
Throws Right	R	.290	193	56	18	0	2	35	12	43	.337	.415
Villarreal,Pedro	L	.176	17	3	1	0	1	2	3	4	.333	.412
Throws Right	R	.222	36	8	2	0	0	3	4	8	.293	.278
Vincent,Nick	L	.274	73	20	6	0	3	13	7	14	.346	.479
Throws Right	R	.190	126	24	6	0	2	14	4	48	.221	.286
Vizcaino,Arodys	L	.000	8	0	0	0	0	1	2	2	.200	.000
Throws Right	R	.455	11	5	1	0	1	2	1	2	.500	.818
Vogelsong,Ryan	L	.287	342	98	27	3	8	36	23	76	.334	.453
Throws Right	R	.223	358	80	19	2	10	39	35	75	.303	.372
Volquez,Edinson	L	.236	301	71	18	1	10	32	38	61	.326	.402
Throws Right	R	.235	404	95	16	0	7	30	33	79	.307	.327
Wacha,Michael	L	.224	196	44	9	0	1	16	19	40	.295	.286
Throws Right	R	.243	210	51	13	1	5	19	14	54	.301	.386
Wada,Tsuyoshi	L	.184	49	9	0	0	0	0	3	12	.245	.184
Throws Left	R	.270	215	58	17	3	7	21	16	45	.325	.474
Wagner,Neil	L	.333	24	8	3	1	0	6	3	4	.393	.542
Throws Right	R	.211	19	4	3	0	1	5	1	2	.286	.526
Wainwright,Adam	L	.244	381	93	19	1	3	24	32	86	.302	.323
Throws Right	R	.203	449	91	20	1	7	33	18	93	.244	.298
Walden,Jordan	L	.188	85	16	4	0	2	9	13	33	.293	.306
Throws Right	R	.185	92	17	1	0	0	8	14	29	.292	.196
Walker,Taijuan	L	.253	83	21	3	1	1	7	16	18	.380	.349
Throws Right	R	.179	56	10	2	0	1	3	2	16	.233	.268
Wang,Wei-Chung	L	.333	27	9	2	0	2	6	1	5	.379	.630
Throws Left	R	.375	56	21	6	1	4	18	7	8	.444	.732
Warren,Adam	L	.178	129	23	7	1	1	15	14	40	.253	.271
Throws Right	R	.252	159	40	10	1	3	19	10	36	.306	.384
Watson,Tony	L	.179	78	14	2	1	1	7	5	20	.261	.269
Throws Left	R	.253	198	50	6	1	4	17	10	61	.292	.354
Weaver,Jered	L	.255	502	128	20	0	19	51	43	109	.315	.408
Throws Right	R	.212	306	65	15	1	8	27	22	60	.273	.346
Webb,Daniel	L	.217	115	25	5	0	1	13	21	18	.336	.287
Throws Right	R	.256	133	34	8	3	5	27	21	40	.361	.474
Webb,Ryan	L	.212	66	14	2	0	1	3	10	13	.325	.288
Throws Right	R	.283	127	36	6	0	1	18	2	24	.295	.354
Webster,Allen	L	.250	116	29	5	1	1	17	18	16	.367	.336
Throws Right	R	.279	104	29	5	2	2	14	10	20	.350	.423
Wheeler,Zack	L	.259	332	86	20	0	8	39	50	81	.353	.392
Throws Right	R	.223	364	81	14	1	6	33	29	106	.300	.316
Whitley,Chase	L	.315	162	51	6	3	6	24	12	31	.366	.500
Throws Right	R	.301	143	43	10	0	4	14	6	29	.338	.455
Wieland,Joe	L	.318	22	7	0	0	2	3	3	5	.400	.591
Throws Right	R	.346	26	9	4	0	1	4	2	3	.379	.615
Wilhelmsen,Tom	L	.165	127	21	2	0	2	10	19	21	.277	.228
Throws Right	R	.176	148	26	6	1	4	10	17	51	.262	.311
Williams,Jerome	L	.290	238	69	15	0	6	29	25	46	.358	.429
Throws Right	R	.264	212	56	12	0	6	28	11	36	.314	.406
Wilson,Alex	L	.250	48	12	6	1	1	4	3	6	.308	.479
Throws Right	R	.151	53	8	1	0	2	4	2	13	.193	.283
Wilson,Brian	L	.297	74	22	7	0	2	6	17	24	.441	.473
Throws Right	R	.235	115	27	5	0	3	19	12	30	.318	.357
Wilson,C.J.	L	.201	164	33	5	0	2	18	21	45	.304	.268
Throws Left	R	.277	491	136	20	0	15	69	64	106	.365	.409
Wilson,Justin	L	.253	79	20	3	0	2	8	7	19	.314	.367
Throws Left	R	.201	144	29	4	2	2	11	23	42	.324	.299
Withrow,Chris	L	.000	27	0	0	0	0	1	3	11	.097	.000
Throws Right	R	.233	43	10	3	0	1	5	15	17	.441	.372
Wolf,Randy	L	.235	17	4	0	0	0	2	3	2	.350	.235
Throws Left	R	.326	89	29	9	1	4	13	3	17	.348	.584
Wood,Alex	L	.247	166	41	8	1	3	8	12	47	.306	.361
Throws Left	R	.236	467	110	17	0	13	40	33	123	.290	.355
Wood,Blake	L	.167	12	2	1	0	0	1	4	4	.375	.250
Throws Right	R	.200	10	2	1	0	0	4	3	3	.429	.300
Wood,Travis	L	.220	177	39	11	0	4	25	11	44	.268	.350
Throws Left	R	.297	509	151	33	0	16	73	65	102	.381	.456
Wooten,Rob	L	.306	49	15	2	1	0	3	3	9	.346	.388
Throws Right	R	.307	88	27	7	0	1	14	5	20	.347	.420
Workman,Brandon	L	.262	191	50	8	0	6	25	26	42	.347	.398
Throws Right	R	.264	144	38	8	1	5	25	10	28	.314	.438

Pitchers vs. Left-Handed and Right-Handed Batters

Pitcher	vs	Avg	AB	H	2B	3B	HR	RBI	BB	SO	OBP	Slg
Worley,Vance	L	.255	200	51	5	0	5	16	16	35	.311	.355
Throws Right	R	.274	223	61	11	2	4	24	6	44	.296	.395
Wright,Jamey	L	.238	122	29	3	1	1	16	14	29	.317	.303
Throws Right	R	.299	144	43	5	0	2	21	13	25	.362	.375
Wright,Steven	L	.250	36	9	0	0	2	4	0	10	.250	.417
Throws Right	R	.261	46	12	1	0	0	3	4	12	.320	.283
Wright,Wesley	L	.273	77	21	0	0	0	8	5	20	.321	.273
Throws Left	R	.255	106	27	7	0	2	13	14	17	.341	.377
Yates,Kirby	L	.250	36	9	1	0	2	6	8	11	.400	.444
Throws Right	R	.238	101	24	5	0	2	13	7	31	.297	.347
Young,Chris	L	.260	346	90	23	2	16	36	37	53	.332	.477
Throws Right	R	.199	266	53	16	0	10	31	23	55	.260	.372
Zeid,Josh	L	.455	33	15	3	0	2	10	3	5	.500	.727
Throws Right	R	.278	54	15	1	1	4	13	4	13	.322	.556
Ziegler,Brad	L	.183	93	17	6	0	2	7	13	15	.284	.312
Throws Right	R	.279	154	43	6	2	3	26	11	39	.331	.403
Zimmermann,Jordan	L	.258	380	98	14	3	7	30	15	78	.289	.366
Throws Right	R	.231	377	87	16	4	6	31	14	104	.264	.342
AL	L	.251	-	-	-	-	-	-	-	-	.318	.384
	R	.253	-	-	-	-	-	-	-	-	.311	.394
NL	L	.252	-	-	-	-	-	-	-	-	.319	.380
	R	.249	-	-	-	-	-	-	-	-	.309	.386
MLB	L	.251	-	-	-	-	-	-	-	-	.318	.382
	R	.251	-	-	-	-	-	-	-	-	.310	.390

2014 Leader Boards

This section contains myriad leaderboards, both traditional ones such as runs scored for hitters and strikeouts per nine innings for pitchers as well as non-traditional ones such as percent of pitches taken and number of pitches thrown of at least 100 mph. The leaderboards can provide insight into players that cannot be easily gleaned from their basic statistics. For example, Mike Trout is renowned for his power and his speed, but Trout also embodied the mantra of early-in-the-order hitters to see a lot of pitches. He actually led baseball by seeing 4.45 pitches per plate appearance this season.

Some of the leaderboards are created with the complex pitch data collected by Baseball Info Solutions, such as the percentage of pitches thrown in the strike zone. Phil Hughes was the standout by that measure in 2014, throwing 54.7 percent of his pitches in the zone (does not include pitches out of the zone that are called strikes or swung at). He was the only pitcher this season to throw more pitches in the zone than out of it. Hughes has always been a strike thrower, but he has lived in the zone increasingly over the last two seasons, and that aggressiveness has clearly worked for him. Hughes enjoyed the best season of his career in 2014 with a 3.52 ERA and 186 strikeouts. Moving to Target Field might have helped, as well.

Bill James also provides his own leaderboards, which include Runs Created, Tough Losses and Power/Speed Numbers. All in all, we've included every leaderboard we could think of that might be interesting.

Here are some definitions to help clarify parts of the leaderboards that may not be familiar to all readers:

BPS stands for "Batting Average plus Slugging Percentage." BPS makes more sense than OPS for some leaderboards that involve pitches.

OutZ is "Pitches Outside the Strike Zone."

Holds Adjusted Save Percentage is calculated by dividing holds plus saves by holds plus save opportunities.

2014 American League Batting Leaders

Batting Average
(minimum 502 PA)

Altuve,Jose, Hou	.341
Martinez,Victor, Det	.335
Brantley,Michael, Cle	.327
Beltre,Adrian, Tex	.324
Abreu,Jose, CWS	.317
Cano,Robinson, Sea	.314
Cabrera,Miguel, Det	.313
Cain,Lorenzo, KC	.301
Cabrera,Melky, Tor	.301
Eaton,Adam, CWS	.300

On Base Percentage
(minimum 502 PA)

Martinez,Victor, Det	.409
Bautista,Jose, Tor	.403
Beltre,Adrian, Tex	.388
Brantley,Michael, Cle	.385
Abreu,Jose, CWS	.383
Cano,Robinson, Sea	.382
Trout,Mike, LAA	.377
Altuve,Jose, Hou	.377
Fowler,Dexter, Hou	.375
Cabrera,Miguel, Det	.371

Slugging Average
(minimum 502 PA)

Abreu,Jose, CWS	.581
Martinez,Victor, Det	.565
Trout,Mike, LAA	.561
Encarnacion,Edwin, Tor	.547
Cruz,Nelson, Bal	.525
Bautista,Jose, Tor	.524
Cabrera,Miguel, Det	.524
Ortiz,David, Bos	.517
Brantley,Michael, Cle	.506
Beltre,Adrian, Tex	.492

Home Runs

Cruz,Nelson, Bal	40
Carter,Chris, Hou	37
Abreu,Jose, CWS	36
Trout,Mike, LAA	36
Bautista,Jose, Tor	35
Ortiz,David, Bos	35
Encarnacion,Edwin, Tor	34
Martinez,Victor, Det	32
Donaldson,Josh, Oak	29
Jones,Adam, Bal	29

Games

Escobar,Alcides, KC	162
Longoria,Evan, TB	162
Kinsler,Ian, Det	161
Cabrera,Miguel, Det	159
Cruz,Nelson, Bal	159
Jones,Adam, Bal	159
Pujols,Albert, LAA	159
Seager,Kyle, Sea	159
3 tied with	158

Plate Appearances

Kinsler,Ian, Det	726
Markakis,Nick, Bal	710
Altuve,Jose, Hou	707
Dozier,Brian, Min	707
Trout,Mike, LAA	705
Longoria,Evan, TB	700
Donaldson,Josh, Oak	695
Pujols,Albert, LAA	695
Andrus,Elvis, Tex	685
Cabrera,Miguel, Det	685

At Bats

Kinsler,Ian, Det	684
Altuve,Jose, Hou	660
Jones,Adam, Bal	644
Markakis,Nick, Bal	642
Pujols,Albert, LAA	633
Longoria,Evan, TB	624
Ramirez,Alexei, CWS	622
Andrus,Elvis, Tex	619
Kendrick,Howie, LAA	617
Cruz,Nelson, Bal	613

Hits

Altuve,Jose, Hou	225
Brantley,Michael, Cle	200
Cabrera,Miguel, Det	191
Kinsler,Ian, Det	188
Martinez,Victor, Det	188
Cano,Robinson, Sea	187
Jones,Adam, Bal	181
Kendrick,Howie, LAA	181
Beltre,Adrian, Tex	178
Markakis,Nick, Bal	177

Singles

Altuve,Jose, Hou	168
Loney,James, TB	138
Kendrick,Howie, LAA	136
Markakis,Nick, Bal	135
Cano,Robinson, Sea	134
Brantley,Michael, Cle	133
Reyes,Jose, Tor	129
Kinsler,Ian, Det	127
3 tied with	125

Doubles

Cabrera,Miguel, Det	52
Altuve,Jose, Hou	47
Brantley,Michael, Cle	45
Kinsler,Ian, Det	40
Plouffe,Trevor, Min	40
Trout,Mike, LAA	39
Cano,Robinson, Sea	37
Pujols,Albert, LAA	37
Cespedes,Yoenis, Oak-Bos	36
6 tied with	35

Triples

Bourn,Michael, Cle	10
Eaton,Adam, CWS	10
Trout,Mike, LAA	9
De Aza,Alejandro, CWS-Bal	8
Gardner,Brett, NYY	8
Kiermaier,Kevin, TB	8
Rios,Alex, Tex	8
4 tied with	7

Total Bases

Trout,Mike, LAA	338
Abreu,Jose, CWS	323
Cruz,Nelson, Bal	322
Cabrera,Miguel, Det	320
Martinez,Victor, Det	317
Brantley,Michael, Cle	309
Jones,Adam, Bal	302
Altuve,Jose, Hou	299
Pujols,Albert, LAA	295
Bautista,Jose, Tor	290

Runs Scored

Trout,Mike, LAA	115
Dozier,Brian, Min	112
Bautista,Jose, Tor	101
Cabrera,Miguel, Det	101
Kinsler,Ian, Det	100
Brantley,Michael, Cle	94
Reyes,Jose, Tor	94
Donaldson,Josh, Oak	93
Calhoun,Kole, LAA	90
2 tied with	89

RBI

Trout,Mike, LAA	111
Cabrera,Miguel, Det	109
Cruz,Nelson, Bal	108
Abreu,Jose, CWS	107
Pujols,Albert, LAA	105
Ortiz,David, Bos	104
Bautista,Jose, Tor	103
Martinez,Victor, Det	103
Cespedes,Yoenis, Oak-Bos	100
2 tied with	98

Walks

Santana,Carlos, Cle	113
Bautista,Jose, Tor	104
Dozier,Brian, Min	89
Trout,Mike, LAA	83
Napoli,Mike, Bos	78
Donaldson,Josh, Oak	76
Ortiz,David, Bos	75
Zobrist,Ben, TB	75
Dunn,Adam, CWS-Oak	71
Martinez,Victor, Det	70

Strikeouts

Trout,Mike, LAA	184
Carter,Chris, Hou	182
Davis,Chris, Bal	173
Dunn,Adam, CWS-Oak	159
Flowers,Tyler, CWS	159
Zunino,Mike, Sea	158
Moss,Brandon, Oak	153
Avila,Alex, Det	151
Castro,Jason, Hou	151
Jackson,Austin, Det-Sea	144

2014 American League Batting Leaders

Intentional Walks

Martinez,Victor, Det	28
Ortiz,David, Bos	22
Cano,Robinson, Sea	20
Abreu,Jose, CWS	15
Beltre,Adrian, Tex	13
Mauer,Joe, Min	12
Bautista,Jose, Tor	11
Fielder,Prince, Tex	11
Longoria,Evan, TB	11
Pujols,Albert, LAA	11

BA Bases Loaded
(minimum 10 PA)

Infante,Omar, KC	.750
Carter,Chris, Hou	.625
Ortiz,David, Bos	.625
Middlebrooks,Will, Bos	.583
Brantley,Michael, Cle	.545
Cespedes,Yoenis, Oak-Bos	.545
Murphy,David, Cle	.500
Jackson,Austin, Det-Sea	.455
Pedroia,Dustin, Bos	.455
Cruz,Nelson, Bal	.444

Sacrifice Hits

Gardner,Brett, NYY	13
Ramirez,Jose, Cle	13
Aviles,Mike, Cle	11
Andrus,Elvis, Tex	9
Chavez,Endy, Sea	9
Jennings,Desmond, TB	9
Aoki,Nori, KC	8
Escobar,Alcides, KC	8
Jeter,Derek, NYY	8
Kawasaki,Munenori, Tor	8

Sacrifice Flies

Cabrera,Miguel, Det	11
Trout,Mike, LAA	10
Jackson,Austin, Det-Sea	9
Joyce,Matt, TB	9
Longoria,Evan, TB	9
Pujols,Albert, LAA	9
Aybar,Erick, LAA	8
Butler,Billy, KC	8
Dozier,Brian, Min	8
12 tied with	7

BA Close & Late
(minimum 50 PA)

Holt,Brock, Bos	.349
Kawasaki,Munenori, Tor	.346
Markakis,Nick, Bal	.346
Suzuki,Kurt, Min	.342
Aybar,Erick, LAA	.333
Bautista,Jose, Tor	.333
Gillaspie,Conor, CWS	.333
Pujols,Albert, LAA	.333
Kinsler,Ian, Det	.330
Cabrera,Miguel, Det	.329

Batting Average w/ RISP
(minimum 100 PA)

Brantley,Michael, Cle	.376
Murphy,David, Cle	.360
Eaton,Adam, CWS	.355
Navarro,Dioner, Tor	.343
Cano,Robinson, Sea	.339
Gordon,Alex, KC	.338
Cabrera,Miguel, Det	.336
Santana,Danny, Min	.333
Norris,Derek, Oak	.330
Martinez,Victor, Det	.326

SLG vs. LHP
(minimum 125 PA)

Martinez,Victor, Det	.692
Abreu,Jose, CWS	.662
Martinez,J.D., Det	.640
Bautista,Jose, Tor	.629
Donaldson,Josh, Oak	.627
Jones,Adam, Bal	.604
Cruz,Nelson, Bal	.569
Altuve,Jose, Hou	.566
Davis,Rajai, Det	.557
Rios,Alex, Tex	.545

SLG vs. RHP
(minimum 377 PA)

Trout,Mike, LAA	.574
Encarnacion,Edwin, Tor	.560
Abreu,Jose, CWS	.555
Brantley,Michael, Cle	.534
Martinez,Victor, Det	.522
Cabrera,Miguel, Det	.520
Cruz,Nelson, Bal	.513
Ortiz,David, Bos	.504
Seager,Kyle, Sea	.504
Bautista,Jose, Tor	.497

Leadoff Hitters OBP
(minimum 150 PA)

Altuve,Jose, Hou	.363
Eaton,Adam, CWS	.362
Choo,Shin-Soo, Tex	.357
Martin,Leonys, Tex	.354
Grossman,Robbie, Hou	.340
Markakis,Nick, Bal	.339
Santana,Danny, Min	.339
Gardner,Brett, NYY	.337
Aoki,Nori, KC	.336
Calhoun,Kole, LAA	.336

Cleanup Hitters SLG
(minimum 150 PA)

Martinez,Victor, Det	.574
Encarnacion,Edwin, Tor	.518
Kendrick,Howie, LAA	.513
Beltre,Adrian, Tex	.505
Seager,Kyle, Sea	.503
Cespedes,Yoenis, Oak-Bos	.484
Jones,Adam, Bal	.475
Lind,Adam, Tor	.471
Cruz,Nelson, Bal	.466
Ortiz,David, Bos	.462

BA vs. LHP
(minimum 125 PA)

Altuve,Jose, Hou	.414
Martinez,Victor, Det	.371
Aoki,Nori, KC	.363
Davis,Rajai, Det	.356
Abreu,Jose, CWS	.353
Beltre,Adrian, Tex	.351
Bautista,Jose, Tor	.345
Jones,Adam, Bal	.344
Zobrist,Ben, TB	.340
Gomes,Yan, Cle	.331

BA vs. RHP
(minimum 377 PA)

Brantley,Michael, Cle	.337
Cano,Robinson, Sea	.327
Martinez,Victor, Det	.323
Altuve,Jose, Hou	.319
Cabrera,Miguel, Det	.317
Beltre,Adrian, Tex	.316
Cabrera,Melky, Tor	.310
Abreu,Jose, CWS	.305
Loney,James, TB	.304
Eaton,Adam, CWS	.301

Home BA
(minimum 251 PA)

Altuve,Jose, Hou	.366
Beltre,Adrian, Tex	.355
Brantley,Michael, Cle	.353
Abreu,Jose, CWS	.336
Martinez,Victor, Det	.324
Aoki,Nori, KC	.322
Cabrera,Miguel, Det	.320
Suzuki,Kurt, Min	.316
Eaton,Adam, CWS	.313
Cano,Robinson, Sea	.308

Away BA
(minimum 251 PA)

Martinez,Victor, Det	.346
Martinez,J.D., Det	.325
Cano,Robinson, Sea	.320
Hosmer,Eric, KC	.318
Altuve,Jose, Hou	.318
Gillaspie,Conor, CWS	.311
Cabrera,Miguel, Det	.306
Brantley,Michael, Cle	.302
Kendrick,Howie, LAA	.300
Abreu,Jose, CWS	.300

OBP vs. LHP
(minimum 125 PA)

Napoli,Mike, Bos	.450
Bautista,Jose, Tor	.449
Altuve,Jose, Hou	.447
Beltre,Adrian, Tex	.442
Abreu,Jose, CWS	.437
Martinez,Victor, Det	.430
Aoki,Nori, KC	.428
Cruz,Nelson, Bal	.407
Zobrist,Ben, TB	.399
Jones,Adam, Bal	.399

OBP vs. RHP
(minimum 377 PA)

Martinez,Victor, Det	.402
Cano,Robinson, Sea	.398
Bautista,Jose, Tor	.391
Brantley,Michael, Cle	.388
Trout,Mike, LAA	.374
Cabrera,Miguel, Det	.373
Beltre,Adrian, Tex	.369
Joyce,Matt, TB	.365
Abreu,Jose, CWS	.364
Fowler,Dexter, Hou	.361

2014 American League Batting Leaders

Stolen Bases

Altuve,Jose, Hou	56
Ellsbury,Jacoby, NYY	39
Davis,Rajai, Det	36
Dyson,Jarrod, KC	36
Escobar,Alcides, KC	31
Martin,Leonys, Tex	31
Reyes,Jose, Tor	30
Cain,Lorenzo, KC	28
Andrus,Elvis, Tex	27
Jones,James, Sea	27

Caught Stealing

Andrus,Elvis, Tex	15
Martin,Leonys, Tex	12
Davis,Rajai, Det	11
De Aza,Alejandro, CWS-Bal	10
Altuve,Jose, Hou	9
Aybar,Erick, LAA	9
Eaton,Adam, CWS	9
Rios,Alex, Tex	9
Aoki,Nori, KC	8
3 tied with	7

Highest SB Success Pct
(minimum 20 SBA)

Jones,James, Sea	96.4
Brantley,Michael, Cle	95.8
Reyes,Jose, Tor	93.8
Gentry,Craig, Oak	90.9
Ellsbury,Jacoby, NYY	88.6
Kipnis,Jason, Cle	88.0
Altuve,Jose, Hou	86.2
Cain,Lorenzo, KC	84.8
Fuld,Sam, Oak-Min	84.0
Ramirez,Alexei, CWS	84.0

Lowest SB Success Pct
(minimum 20 SBA)

Eaton,Adam, CWS	62.5
De Aza,Alejandro, CWS-Bal	63.0
Aybar,Erick, LAA	64.0
Andrus,Elvis, Tex	64.3
Rios,Alex, Tex	65.4
Aoki,Nori, KC	68.0
Jennings,Desmond, TB	71.4
Martin,Leonys, Tex	72.1
3 tied with	75.0

Steals of Third

Dyson,Jarrod, KC	10
Altuve,Jose, Hou	8
Villar,Jonathan, Hou	8
Davis,Rajai, Det	7
Jones,James, Sea	7
Reyes,Jose, Tor	7
5 tied with	6

Grounded Into DP

Pujols,Albert, LAA	28
Dominguez,Matt, Hou	23
Perez,Salvador, KC	22
Andrus,Elvis, Tex	21
Butler,Billy, KC	21
Cabrera,Miguel, Det	21
Loney,James, TB	21
Ramirez,Alexei, CWS	21
Altuve,Jose, Hou	20
Kinsler,Ian, Det	20

Grounded Into DP Pct
(minimum 50 GIDP Ops)

Rasmus,Colby, Tor	1.28
Drew,Stephen, Bos-NYY	1.82
Davis,Chris, Bal	2.11
Hamilton,Josh, LAA	2.94
Fuld,Sam, Oak-Min	3.13
Gardner,Brett, NYY	3.49
Miller,Brad, Sea	3.70
Vogt,Stephen, Oak	3.77
Gentry,Craig, Oak	3.85
2 tied with	3.90

Hit By Pitch

Zunino,Mike, Sea	17
Choo,Shin-Soo, Tex	12
Jones,Adam, Bal	12
Abreu,Jose, CWS	11
Gordon,Alex, KC	11
Guyer,Brandon, TB	11
Moss,Brandon, Oak	10
Nava,Daniel, Bos	10
Trout,Mike, LAA	10
8 tied with	9

Pitches Seen

Trout,Mike, LAA	3136
Dozier,Brian, Min	2956
Santana,Carlos, Cle	2841
Gardner,Brett, NYY	2821
Markakis,Nick, Bal	2818
Bautista,Jose, Tor	2743
Andrus,Elvis, Tex	2736
Donaldson,Josh, Oak	2714
Jackson,Austin, Det-Sea	2697
Gordon,Alex, KC	2655

At Bats Per Home Run
(minimum 502 PA)

Carter,Chris, Hou	13.7
Encarnacion,Edwin, Tor	14.0
Ortiz,David, Bos	14.8
Cruz,Nelson, Bal	15.3
Abreu,Jose, CWS	15.4
Bautista,Jose, Tor	15.8
Trout,Mike, LAA	16.7
Davis,Chris, Bal	17.3
Martinez,Victor, Det	17.5
Dunn,Adam, CWS-Oak	19.5

Highest GB/FB Ratio
(minimum 502 PA)

Aoki,Nori, KC	3.63
Jeter,Derek, NYY	3.06
Eaton,Adam, CWS	2.96
Kendrick,Howie, LAA	2.85
Andrus,Elvis, Tex	2.81
Mauer,Joe, Min	2.32
Cano,Robinson, Sea	2.13
Cain,Lorenzo, KC	1.96
Freese,David, LAA	1.90
Martin,Leonys, Tex	1.81

Lowest GB/FB Ratio
(minimum 502 PA)

Carter,Chris, Hou	0.53
Moss,Brandon, Oak	0.62
Cespedes,Yoenis, Oak-Bos	0.70
Lowrie,Jed, Oak	0.71
Trout,Mike, LAA	0.72
McCann,Brian, NYY	0.72
Encarnacion,Edwin, Tor	0.77
Dunn,Adam, CWS-Oak	0.78
Ortiz,David, Bos	0.80
Davis,Chris, Bal	0.84

Pitches Per Plate App
(minimum 502 PA)

Trout,Mike, LAA	4.45
Gardner,Brett, NYY	4.44
Santana,Carlos, Cle	4.30
Dunn,Adam, CWS-Oak	4.30
Mauer,Joe, Min	4.19
Dozier,Brian, Min	4.18
Davis,Chris, Bal	4.17
Encarnacion,Edwin, Tor	4.13
Gordon,Alex, KC	4.13
Fowler,Dexter, Hou	4.13

Pct Pitches Taken
(minimum 1500 Pitches)

Willingham,Josh, Min-KC	63.0
Gardner,Brett, NYY	63.0
Santana,Carlos, Cle	62.7
Andrus,Elvis, Tex	62.5
Trout,Mike, LAA	62.1
Mauer,Joe, Min	61.9
Zobrist,Ben, TB	61.6
Grossman,Robbie, Hou	61.5
Nava,Daniel, Bos	61.3
Dozier,Brian, Min	60.9

Best BPS on OutZ
(minimum 502 PA)

Martinez,Victor, Det	.767
Beltre,Adrian, Tex	.686
Brantley,Michael, Cle	.636
Altuve,Jose, Hou	.633
Infante,Omar, KC	.629
Encarnacion,Edwin, Tor	.627
Trout,Mike, LAA	.617
Dozier,Brian, Min	.612
Abreu,Jose, CWS	.601
McCann,Brian, NYY	.597

Worst BPS on OutZ
(minimum 502 PA)

Dunn,Adam, CWS-Oak	.238
Jackson,Austin, Det-Sea	.258
Moss,Brandon, Oak	.266
Gardner,Brett, NYY	.275
De Aza,Alejandro, CWS-Bal	.283
Bogaerts,Xander, Bos	.312
Kipnis,Jason, Cle	.323
Viciedo,Dayan, CWS	.323
Castro,Jason, Hou	.330
Butler,Billy, KC	.350

2014 American League Batting Leaders

Best OPS vs Fastballs
(minimum 251 PA)

Martinez,Victor, Det	.966
Cruz,Nelson, Bal	.954
Abreu,Jose, CWS	.945
Bautista,Jose, Tor	.931
Beltre,Adrian, Tex	.912
Ortiz,David, Bos	.906
Cabrera,Miguel, Det	.885
Brantley,Michael, Cle	.878
Seager,Kyle, Sea	.866
Encarnacion,Edwin, Tor	.849

Best OPS vs Curveballs
(minimum 50 PA)

Longoria,Evan, TB	1.135
Kinsler,Ian, Det	1.052
Cabrera,Miguel, Det	.990
Cespedes,Yoenis, Oak-Bos	.982
Ortiz,David, Bos	.953
Aybar,Erick, LAA	.951
Escobar,Alcides, KC	.885
Brantley,Michael, Cle	.863
Moss,Brandon, Oak	.843
Martinez,Victor, Det	.842

Best OPS vs Changeups
(minimum 50 PA)

Trout,Mike, LAA	1.420
Cabrera,Miguel, Det	1.098
Pujols,Albert, LAA	.986
Jones,Adam, Bal	.979
Hamilton,Josh, LAA	.929
Donaldson,Josh, Oak	.925
Ramirez,Alexei, CWS	.923
Navarro,Dioner, Tor	.915
Arcia,Oswaldo, Min	.910
2 tied with	.898

Best OPS vs Sliders
(minimum 32 PA)

Martinez,Victor, Det	1.201
Trout,Mike, LAA	1.158
Lind,Adam, Tor	1.090
Norris,Derek, Oak	1.063
Saunders,Michael, Sea	1.055
Bautista,Jose, Tor	1.050
Chisenhall,Lonnie, Cle	1.044
Grossman,Robbie, Hou	.976
Gardner,Brett, NYY	.973
Willingham,Josh, Min-KC	.973

OPS
(minimum 502 PA)

Martinez,Victor, Det	.974
Abreu,Jose, CWS	.964
Trout,Mike, LAA	.939
Bautista,Jose, Tor	.928
Encarnacion,Edwin, Tor	.901
Cabrera,Miguel, Det	.895
Brantley,Michael, Cle	.890
Beltre,Adrian, Tex	.879
Ortiz,David, Bos	.873
Cruz,Nelson, Bal	.859

OPS First Half
(minimum 260 PA)

Trout,Mike, LAA	1.005
Martinez,Victor, Det	.991
Abreu,Jose, CWS	.972
Encarnacion,Edwin, Tor	.959
Cruz,Nelson, Bal	.923
Beltre,Adrian, Tex	.917
Chisenhall,Lonnie, Cle	.915
Bautista,Jose, Tor	.910
Brantley,Michael, Cle	.901
Cabrera,Miguel, Det	.898

OPS Second Half
(minimum 201 PA)

Martinez,Victor, Det	.954
Bautista,Jose, Tor	.951
Abreu,Jose, CWS	.948
Ortiz,David, Bos	.927
Cabrera,Miguel, Det	.890
Brantley,Michael, Cle	.877
Altuve,Jose, Hou	.860
Carter,Chris, Hou	.860
Santana,Carlos, Cle	.860
Trout,Mike, LAA	.849

OPS by Catchers
(minimum 251 PA)

Norris,Derek, Oak	.775
Iannetta,Chris, LAA	.773
Gomes,Yan, Cle	.731
Suzuki,Kurt, Min	.712
McCann,Brian, NYY	.711
Chirinos,Robinson, Tex	.710
Perez,Salvador, KC	.700
Flowers,Tyler, CWS	.696
Navarro,Dioner, Tor	.695
Avila,Alex, Det	.691

OPS by First Basemen
(minimum 251 PA)

Abreu,Jose, CWS	.982
Encarnacion,Edwin, Tor	.964
Cabrera,Miguel, Det	.918
Santana,Carlos, Cle	.912
Napoli,Mike, Bos	.784
Morrison,Logan, Sea	.766
Pujols,Albert, LAA	.731
Loney,James, TB	.718
Hosmer,Eric, KC	.717
Mauer,Joe, Min	.717

OPS by Second Basemen
(minimum 251 PA)

Cano,Robinson, Sea	.835
Altuve,Jose, Hou	.824
Dozier,Brian, Min	.762
Kendrick,Howie, LAA	.736
Kinsler,Ian, Det	.728
Zobrist,Ben, TB	.717
Pedroia,Dustin, Bos	.714
Odor,Rougned, Tex	.701
Roberts,Brian, NYY	.669
Kipnis,Jason, Cle	.651

OPS by Third Basemen
(minimum 251 PA)

Beltre,Adrian, Tex	.886
Donaldson,Josh, Oak	.810
Seager,Kyle, Sea	.794
Machado,Manny, Bal	.755
Plouffe,Trevor, Min	.744
Gillaspie,Conor, CWS	.737
Longoria,Evan, TB	.724
Chisenhall,Lonnie, Cle	.716
Freese,David, LAA	.706
Castellanos,Nick, Det	.698

OPS by Shortstops
(minimum 251 PA)

Escobar,Eduardo, Min	.733
Reyes,Jose, Tor	.726
Bogaerts,Xander, Bos	.724
Ramirez,Alexei, CWS	.711
Cabrera,Asdrubal, Cle	.710
Aybar,Erick, LAA	.698
Escobar,Alcides, KC	.694
Hardy,J.J., Bal	.682
Suarez,Eugenio, Det	.671
Lowrie,Jed, Oak	.669

OPS by Left Fielders
(minimum 251 PA)

Martinez,J.D., Det	.923
Cruz,Nelson, Bal	.916
Brantley,Michael, Cle	.904
Cabrera,Melky, Tor	.819
Joyce,Matt, TB	.792
Gordon,Alex, KC	.783
Cespedes,Yoenis, Oak-Bos	.775
Choo,Shin-Soo, Tex	.746
Hamilton,Josh, LAA	.740
Davis,Rajai, Det	.718

OPS by Center Fielders
(minimum 251 PA)

Trout,Mike, LAA	.942
Santana,Danny, Min	.843
Jones,Adam, Bal	.771
Fowler,Dexter, Hou	.768
Ellsbury,Jacoby, NYY	.764
Eaton,Adam, CWS	.763
Cain,Lorenzo, KC	.729
Crisp,Coco, Oak	.716
Rasmus,Colby, Tor	.698
Jennings,Desmond, TB	.698

OPS by Right Fielders
(minimum 251 PA)

Bautista,Jose, Tor	.957
Springer,George, Hou	.791
Calhoun,Kole, LAA	.783
Hunter,Torii, Det	.776
Arcia,Oswaldo, Min	.770
Reddick,Josh, Oak	.757
Markakis,Nick, Bal	.732
Rios,Alex, Tex	.712
Aoki,Nori, KC	.708
Viciedo,Dayan, CWS	.701

OPS by Designated Hitters
(minimum 125 PA)

Martinez,Victor, Det	.973
Pujols,Albert, LAA	.943
Abreu,Jose, CWS	.910
Ortiz,David, Bos	.890
Lind,Adam, Tor	.884
Carter,Chris, Hou	.841
Cruz,Nelson, Bal	.822
DeJesus,David, TB	.820
Vargas,Kennys, Min	.820
Encarnacion,Edwin, Tor	.794

2014 American League Batting Leaders

OPS Batting Left vs. LHP
(minimum 125 PA)

Ortiz,David, Bos	.893
Aoki,Nori, KC	.863
McCann,Brian, NYY	.850
Ellsbury,Jacoby, NYY	.828
Brantley,Michael, Cle	.826
Gordon,Alex, KC	.787
Holt,Brock, Bos	.763
Cano,Robinson, Sea	.746
Eaton,Adam, CWS	.724
Gardner,Brett, NYY	.687

OPS Batting Left vs. RHP
(minimum 377 PA)

Martinez,Victor, Det	.923
Brantley,Michael, Cle	.923
Cano,Robinson, Sea	.891
Ortiz,David, Bos	.863
Seager,Kyle, Sea	.862
Cabrera,Melky, Tor	.817
Gillaspie,Conor, CWS	.805
Calhoun,Kole, LAA	.793
Dunn,Adam, CWS-Oak	.783
Chisenhall,Lonnie, Cle	.782

OPS Batting Right vs. LHP
(minimum 125 PA)

Martinez,Victor, Det	1.123
Abreu,Jose, CWS	1.098
Bautista,Jose, Tor	1.079
Altuve,Jose, Hou	1.013
Donaldson,Josh, Oak	1.007
Jones,Adam, Bal	1.003
Martinez,J.D., Det	1.003
Beltre,Adrian, Tex	.984
Cruz,Nelson, Bal	.977
Davis,Rajai, Det	.939

OPS Batting Right vs. RHP
(minimum 377 PA)

Trout,Mike, LAA	.948
Abreu,Jose, CWS	.919
Encarnacion,Edwin, Tor	.909
Cabrera,Miguel, Det	.893
Bautista,Jose, Tor	.888
Beltre,Adrian, Tex	.845
Cruz,Nelson, Bal	.823
Pujols,Albert, LAA	.807
Cespedes,Yoenis, Oak-Bos	.777
Altuve,Jose, Hou	.775

OPS vs. LHP
(minimum 125 PA)

Martinez,Victor, Det	1.123
Abreu,Jose, CWS	1.098
Bautista,Jose, Tor	1.079
Altuve,Jose, Hou	1.013
Donaldson,Josh, Oak	1.007
Jones,Adam, Bal	1.003
Martinez,J.D., Det	1.003
Beltre,Adrian, Tex	.984
Cruz,Nelson, Bal	.977
Davis,Rajai, Det	.939

OPS vs. RHP
(minimum 377 PA)

Trout,Mike, LAA	.948
Brantley,Michael, Cle	.923
Martinez,Victor, Det	.923
Abreu,Jose, CWS	.919
Encarnacion,Edwin, Tor	.909
Cabrera,Miguel, Det	.893
Cano,Robinson, Sea	.891
Bautista,Jose, Tor	.888
Ortiz,David, Bos	.863
Seager,Kyle, Sea	.862

RC Per 27 Outs vs. LHP
(minimum 125 PA)

Beltre,Adrian, Tex	9.8
Abreu,Jose, CWS	9.3
Bautista,Jose, Tor	9.1
Norris,Derek, Oak	8.9
Martinez,Victor, Det	8.9
Altuve,Jose, Hou	8.3
Donaldson,Josh, Oak	7.7
Napoli,Mike, Bos	7.5
Davis,Rajai, Det	7.1
Brantley,Michael, Cle	7.0

RC Per 27 Outs vs. RHP
(minimum 377 PA)

Trout,Mike, LAA	8.3
Martinez,Victor, Det	7.4
Cano,Robinson, Sea	7.3
Seager,Kyle, Sea	7.1
Abreu,Jose, CWS	7.1
Brantley,Michael, Cle	7.1
Bautista,Jose, Tor	6.7
Cabrera,Miguel, Det	6.6
Gillaspie,Conor, CWS	6.5
Encarnacion,Edwin, Tor	6.4

Highest RBI %
(minimum 502 PA)

Trout,Mike, LAA	45.75
Abreu,Jose, CWS	44.84
Martinez,Victor, Det	44.22
Cabrera,Miguel, Det	42.04
Bautista,Jose, Tor	41.45
Ortiz,David, Bos	41.42
Brantley,Michael, Cle	40.74
Encarnacion,Edwin, Tor	40.60
Cano,Robinson, Sea	39.42
Donaldson,Josh, Oak	39.29

Lowest RBI %
(minimum 502 PA)

Andrus,Elvis, Tex	20.71
Kipnis,Jason, Cle	21.49
Bogaerts,Xander, Bos	22.32
Escobar,Yunel, TB	22.40
Martin,Leonys, Tex	22.50
Jennings,Desmond, TB	23.92
Dominguez,Matt, Hou	24.12
Escobar,Alcides, KC	24.33
Lowrie,Jed, Oak	24.74
Fowler,Dexter, Hou	24.75

Highest Strikeout per PA
(minimum 502 PA)

Davis,Chris, Bal	.330
Carter,Chris, Hou	.318
Dunn,Adam, CWS-Oak	.311
Castro,Jason, Hou	.295
Moss,Brandon, Oak	.264
Trout,Mike, LAA	.261
Choo,Shin-Soo, Tex	.248
Freese,David, LAA	.243
Castellanos,Nick, Det	.242
2 tied with	.232

Lowest Strikeout per PA
(minimum 502 PA)

Martinez,Victor, Det	.066
Altuve,Jose, Hou	.075
Brantley,Michael, Cle	.083
Aoki,Nori, KC	.089
Suzuki,Kurt, Min	.091
Aybar,Erick, LAA	.097
Cano,Robinson, Sea	.102
Pujols,Albert, LAA	.102
Cabrera,Melky, Tor	.108
Kinsler,Ian, Det	.109

Home Runs At Home

Carter,Chris, Hou	21
Encarnacion,Edwin, Tor	19
McCann,Brian, NYY	19
Trout,Mike, LAA	19
Bautista,Jose, Tor	18
Seager,Kyle, Sea	16
Abreu,Jose, CWS	15
Cruz,Nelson, Bal	15
Martinez,Victor, Det	15
Jones,Adam, Bal	14

Home Runs Away

Cruz,Nelson, Bal	25
Ortiz,David, Bos	24
Abreu,Jose, CWS	21
Donaldson,Josh, Oak	18
Bautista,Jose, Tor	17
Martinez,Victor, Det	17
Trout,Mike, LAA	17
Carter,Chris, Hou	16
4 tied with	15

2014 American League Batting Leaders

Under Age 26: AB Per HR
(minimum 502 PA)

Trout,Mike, LAA	16.7
Viciedo,Dayan, CWS	24.9
Perez,Salvador, KC	34.0
Dominguez,Matt, Hou	35.3
Chisenhall,Lonnie, Cle	36.8
Bogaerts,Xander, Bos	44.8
Castellanos,Nick, Det	48.5
Hosmer,Eric, KC	55.9
Altuve,Jose, Hou	94.3
Eaton,Adam, CWS	486.0

Under Age 26: OPS
(minimum 502 PA)

Trout,Mike, LAA	.939
Altuve,Jose, Hou	.830
Chisenhall,Lonnie, Cle	.770
Eaton,Adam, CWS	.763
Hosmer,Eric, KC	.716
Castellanos,Nick, Det	.700
Perez,Salvador, KC	.692
Viciedo,Dayan, CWS	.686
Bogaerts,Xander, Bos	.660
Dominguez,Matt, Hou	.586

Under Age 26: RC/27 Outs
(minimum 502 PA)

Trout,Mike, LAA	7.9
Altuve,Jose, Hou	6.1
Eaton,Adam, CWS	5.8
Chisenhall,Lonnie, Cle	5.2
Hosmer,Eric, KC	4.3
Castellanos,Nick, Det	4.1
Viciedo,Dayan, CWS	3.4
Perez,Salvador, KC	3.3
Bogaerts,Xander, Bos	2.7
Dominguez,Matt, Hou	2.4

Swing and Miss %
(minimum 1500 Pitches Seen)

Singleton,Jon, Hou	36.9
Carter,Chris, Hou	36.0
Zunino,Mike, Sea	35.4
Davis,Chris, Bal	35.3
Flowers,Tyler, CWS	35.2
Arcia,Oswaldo, Min	34.9
Avila,Alex, Det	33.9
Dunn,Adam, CWS-Oak	33.1
Rasmus,Colby, Tor	31.3
Willingham,Josh, Min-KC	29.6

Highest First Swing %
(minimum 502 PA)

Jones,Adam, Bal	37.2
Cabrera,Miguel, Det	37.0
Castellanos,Nick, Det	36.9
Altuve,Jose, Hou	36.5
Abreu,Jose, CWS	36.1
Carter,Chris, Hou	34.1
Cano,Robinson, Sea	32.9
Davis,Chris, Bal	32.8
Castro,Jason, Hou	32.1
Longoria,Evan, TB	32.0

Lowest First Swing %
(minimum 502 PA)

Hardy,J.J., Bal	4.2
Pedroia,Dustin, Bos	9.4
Trout,Mike, LAA	10.7
Gardner,Brett, NYY	11.4
Suzuki,Kurt, Min	11.4
Mauer,Joe, Min	11.6
Dozier,Brian, Min	12.8
Rios,Alex, Tex	12.9
Jackson,Austin, Det-Sea	13.8
Kipnis,Jason, Cle	14.9

Home RC Per 27 Outs
(minimum 251 PA)

Brantley,Michael, Cle	8.5
Abreu,Jose, CWS	8.4
Beltre,Adrian, Tex	8.2
Trout,Mike, LAA	8.1
Seager,Kyle, Sea	7.3
Encarnacion,Edwin, Tor	7.2
Altuve,Jose, Hou	7.2
Cabrera,Miguel, Det	6.9
Eaton,Adam, CWS	6.7
Cano,Robinson, Sea	6.5

Road RC Per 27 Outs
(minimum 251 PA)

Martinez,Victor, Det	9.3
Bautista,Jose, Tor	8.0
Trout,Mike, LAA	7.7
Santana,Carlos, Cle	7.3
Moss,Brandon, Oak	7.0
Abreu,Jose, CWS	7.0
Martinez,J.D., Det	6.9
Cano,Robinson, Sea	6.7
Cruz,Nelson, Bal	6.6
Ortiz,David, Bos	6.5

Lead Changing RBI

Trout,Mike, LAA	42
Cabrera,Miguel, Det	41
Pujols,Albert, LAA	41
Brantley,Michael, Cle	40
Abreu,Jose, CWS	38
Bautista,Jose, Tor	37
Cespedes,Yoenis, Oak-Bos	34
Longoria,Evan, TB	33
Donaldson,Josh, Oak	32
Martinez,Victor, Det	31

2014 National League Batting Leaders

Batting Average (minimum 502 PA)		On Base Percentage (minimum 502 PA)		Slugging Average (minimum 502 PA)		Home Runs	
Morneau,Justin, Col	.319	McCutchen,Andrew, Pit	.410	Stanton,Giancarlo, Mia	.555	Stanton,Giancarlo, Mia	37
Harrison,Josh, Pit	.315	Stanton,Giancarlo, Mia	.395	McCutchen,Andrew, Pit	.542	Rizzo,Anthony, ChC	32
McCutchen,Andrew, Pit	.314	Werth,Jayson, Was	.394	Rizzo,Anthony, ChC	.527	Duda,Lucas, NYM	30
Posey,Buster, SF	.311	Rizzo,Anthony, ChC	.386	Kemp,Matt, LAD	.506	Frazier,Todd, Cin	29
Revere,Ben, Phi	.306	Freeman,Freddie, Atl	.386	Morneau,Justin, Col	.496	Upton,Justin, Atl	29
Span,Denard, Was	.302	Puig,Yasiel, LAD	.382	Upton,Justin, Atl	.491	Gonzalez,Adrian, LAD	27
Lucroy,Jonathan, Mil	.301	Carpenter,Matt, StL	.375	Harrison,Josh, Pit	.490	LaRoche,Adam, Was	26
Puig,Yasiel, LAD	.296	Lucroy,Jonathan, Mil	.373	Posey,Buster, SF	.490	4 tied with	25
Werth,Jayson, Was	.292	Holliday,Matt, StL	.370	Gonzalez,Adrian, LAD	.482		
Castro,Starlin, ChC	.292	Ramirez,Hanley, LAD	.369	Duda,Lucas, NYM	.481		

Games		Plate Appearances		At Bats		Hits	
Freeman,Freddie, Atl	162	Carpenter,Matt, StL	709	Pence,Hunter, SF	650	Revere,Ben, Phi	184
Pence,Hunter, SF	162	Freeman,Freddie, Atl	708	McGehee,Casey, Mia	616	Span,Denard, Was	184
McGehee,Casey, Mia	160	Pence,Hunter, SF	708	Rendon,Anthony, Was	613	Pence,Hunter, SF	180
Gonzalez,Adrian, LAD	159	McGehee,Casey, Mia	691	Span,Denard, Was	610	McGehee,Casey, Mia	177
Carpenter,Matt, StL	158	Rendon,Anthony, Was	683	Gordon,Dee, LAD	609	Gordon,Dee, LAD	176
Frazier,Todd, Cin	157	Span,Denard, Was	668	Freeman,Freddie, Atl	607	Lucroy,Jonathan, Mil	176
Peralta,Jhonny, StL	157	Holliday,Matt, StL	667	Revere,Ben, Phi	601	Rendon,Anthony, Was	176
Sandoval,Pablo, SF	157	Utley,Chase, Phi	664	Frazier,Todd, Cin	597	Freeman,Freddie, Atl	175
Holliday,Matt, StL	156	3 tied with	660	Murphy,Daniel, NYM	596	McCutchen,Andrew, Pit	172
2 tied with	155			Carpenter,Matt, StL	595	Murphy,Daniel, NYM	172

Singles		Doubles		Triples		Total Bases	
Revere,Ben, Phi	162	Lucroy,Jonathan, Mil	53	Gordon,Dee, LAD	12	Stanton,Giancarlo, Mia	299
McGehee,Casey, Mia	143	Freeman,Freddie, Atl	43	Crawford,Brandon, SF	10	McCutchen,Andrew, Pit	297
Gordon,Dee, LAD	138	Gonzalez,Adrian, LAD	41	Hechavarria,Adeiny, Mia	10	Rendon,Anthony, Was	290
Span,Denard, Was	132	Goldschmidt,Paul, Ari	39	Pence,Hunter, SF	10	Pence,Hunter, SF	289
Murphy,Daniel, NYM	124	Rendon,Anthony, Was	39	Peralta,David, Ari	9	Gonzalez,Adrian, LAD	285
Blackmon,Charlie, Col	122	Span,Denard, Was	39	Puig,Yasiel, LAD	9	Freeman,Freddie, Atl	280
Pence,Hunter, SF	121	Harrison,Josh, Pit	38	Hamilton,Billy, Cin	8	Upton,Justin, Atl	278
Yelich,Christian, Mia	120	Kemp,Matt, LAD	38	Span,Denard, Was	8	Rizzo,Anthony, ChC	276
Carpenter,Matt, StL	119	McCutchen,Andrew, Pit	38	3 tied with	7	3 tied with	274
Sandoval,Pablo, SF	119	Peralta,Jhonny, StL	38				

Runs Scored		RBI		Walks		Strikeouts	
Rendon,Anthony, Was	111	Gonzalez,Adrian, LAD	116	Carpenter,Matt, StL	95	Howard,Ryan, Phi	190
Pence,Hunter, SF	106	Stanton,Giancarlo, Mia	105	Stanton,Giancarlo, Mia	94	Byrd,Marlon, Phi	185
Carpenter,Matt, StL	99	Upton,Justin, Atl	102	Freeman,Freddie, Atl	90	Desmond,Ian, Was	183
Gomez,Carlos, Mil	95	Howard,Ryan, Phi	95	McCutchen,Andrew, Pit	84	Upton,B.J., Atl	173
Span,Denard, Was	94	Duda,Lucas, NYM	92	Werth,Jayson, Was	83	Upton,Justin, Atl	171
Yelich,Christian, Mia	94	LaRoche,Adam, Was	92	LaRoche,Adam, Was	82	Stanton,Giancarlo, Mia	170
Freeman,Freddie, Atl	93	Desmond,Ian, Was	91	Granderson,Curtis, NYM	79	Ozuna,Marcell, Mia	164
Gordon,Dee, LAD	92	Holliday,Matt, StL	90	Holliday,Matt, StL	74	Johnson,Chris, Atl	159
Puig,Yasiel, LAD	92	Kemp,Matt, LAD	89	Rizzo,Anthony, ChC	73	Bruce,Jay, Cin	149
3 tied with	89	Posey,Buster, SF	89	Yelich,Christian, Mia	70	2 tied with	145

2014 National League Batting Leaders

Intentional Walks

Stanton,Giancarlo, Mia	24
Mercer,Jordy, Pit	12
Utley,Chase, Phi	12
Montero,Miguel, Ari	11
Tejada,Ruben, NYM	11
Crawford,Brandon, SF	10
Goldschmidt,Paul, Ari	10
Gonzalez,Adrian, LAD	9
LaRoche,Adam, Was	9
2 tied with	8

BA Bases Loaded
(minimum 10 PA)

Mesoraco,Devin, Cin	.778
Desmond,Ian, Was	.667
La Stella,Tommy, Atl	.545
Holliday,Matt, StL	.500
Jay,Jon, StL	.500
Ludwick,Ryan, Cin	.500
Morneau,Justin, Col	.500
Ramos,Wilson, Was	.500
3 tied with	.455

Sacrifice Hits

Miller,Shelby, StL	13
Cueto,Johnny, Cin	12
Wheeler,Zack, NYM	12
Roark,Tanner, Was	11
Segura,Jean, Mil	10
9 tied with	9

Sacrifice Flies

Gonzalez,Adrian, LAD	11
Crawford,Brandon, SF	10
Carpenter,Matt, StL	9
Utley,Chase, Phi	9
LaRoche,Adam, Was	8
Morneau,Justin, Col	8
Posey,Buster, SF	8
Upton,Justin, Atl	8
4 tied with	7

BA Close & Late
(minimum 50 PA)

Posey,Buster, SF	.368
McCutchen,Andrew, Pit	.360
Span,Denard, Was	.355
Stubbs,Drew, Col	.343
Harrison,Josh, Pit	.341
Walker,Neil, Pit	.337
Belt,Brandon, SF	.333
Pena,Brayan, Cin	.329
LaRoche,Adam, Was	.324
Heyward,Jason, Atl	.324

Batting Average w/ RISP
(minimum 100 PA)

Holliday,Matt, StL	.361
Martin,Russell, Pit	.360
Pence,Hunter, SF	.351
Posey,Buster, SF	.346
Werth,Jayson, Was	.338
Gonzalez,Adrian, LAD	.333
Gomez,Carlos, Mil	.331
Gennett,Scooter, Mil	.327
Dickerson,Corey, Col	.325
Uribe,Juan, LAD	.324

SLG vs. LHP
(minimum 125 PA)

Stanton,Giancarlo, Mia	.630
Van Slyke,Scott, LAD	.630
Arenado,Nolan, Col	.598
Upton,Justin, Atl	.597
Holliday,Matt, StL	.564
Johnson,Chris, Atl	.553
Stubbs,Drew, Col	.550
Posey,Buster, SF	.518
Braun,Ryan, Mil	.514
Morse,Michael, SF	.511

SLG vs. RHP
(minimum 377 PA)

Dickerson,Corey, Col	.606
McCutchen,Andrew, Pit	.547
Duda,Lucas, NYM	.543
Gonzalez,Adrian, LAD	.539
Morneau,Justin, Col	.538
Stanton,Giancarlo, Mia	.536
Rizzo,Anthony, ChC	.534
Goldschmidt,Paul, Ari	.532
Kemp,Matt, LAD	.524
Puig,Yasiel, LAD	.516

Leadoff Hitters OBP
(minimum 150 PA)

Carpenter,Matt, StL	.375
Yelich,Christian, Mia	.365
Harrison,Josh, Pit	.359
Span,Denard, Was	.356
Gomez,Carlos, Mil	.356
Pagan,Angel, SF	.346
Heyward,Jason, Atl	.343
Coghlan,Chris, ChC	.336
Inciarte,Ender, Ari	.335
Blackmon,Charlie, Col	.335

Cleanup Hitters SLG
(minimum 150 PA)

Kemp,Matt, LAD	.565
Tulowitzki,Troy, Col	.543
Walker,Neil, Pit	.502
Duda,Lucas, NYM	.488
Upton,Justin, Atl	.476
Sandoval,Pablo, SF	.457
Gonzalez,Adrian, LAD	.455
Grandal,Yasmani, SD	.450
LaRoche,Adam, Was	.448
Trumbo,Mark, Ari	.436

BA vs. LHP
(minimum 125 PA)

Johnson,Chris, Atl	.395
Wright,David, NYM	.367
Stanton,Giancarlo, Mia	.343
Revere,Ben, Phi	.341
Werth,Jayson, Was	.331
Stubbs,Drew, Col	.328
Crawford,Brandon, SF	.320
Baker,Jeff, Mia	.319
Yelich,Christian, Mia	.317
Van Slyke,Scott, LAD	.315

BA vs. RHP
(minimum 377 PA)

Morneau,Justin, Col	.341
Dickerson,Corey, Col	.328
McCutchen,Andrew, Pit	.321
Adams,Matt, StL	.318
Sandoval,Pablo, SF	.317
Span,Denard, Was	.314
Posey,Buster, SF	.314
Harrison,Josh, Pit	.307
Puig,Yasiel, LAD	.307
Gennett,Scooter, Mil	.307

Home BA
(minimum 251 PA)

Dickerson,Corey, Col	.363
Span,Denard, Was	.348
Blackmon,Charlie, Col	.331
McCutchen,Andrew, Pit	.328
Morneau,Justin, Col	.327
Harrison,Josh, Pit	.319
LeMahieu,DJ, Col	.316
Rizzo,Anthony, ChC	.315
Adams,Matt, StL	.313
Stanton,Giancarlo, Mia	.310

Away BA
(minimum 251 PA)

Posey,Buster, SF	.348
Murphy,Daniel, NYM	.322
Harrison,Josh, Pit	.312
Revere,Ben, Phi	.311
Morneau,Justin, Col	.309
Ramirez,Aramis, Mil	.309
Castro,Starlin, ChC	.307
Carpenter,Matt, StL	.305
Puig,Yasiel, LAD	.305
Freeman,Freddie, Atl	.304

OBP vs. LHP
(minimum 125 PA)

Stanton,Giancarlo, Mia	.445
Holliday,Matt, StL	.440
Werth,Jayson, Was	.437
Johnson,Chris, Atl	.435
Rizzo,Anthony, ChC	.421
Van Slyke,Scott, LAD	.415
Wright,David, NYM	.412
Peralta,Jhonny, StL	.401
Crawford,Brandon, SF	.395
Stubbs,Drew, Col	.395

OBP vs. RHP
(minimum 377 PA)

McCutchen,Andrew, Pit	.415
Freeman,Freddie, Atl	.397
LaRoche,Adam, Was	.390
Morneau,Justin, Col	.389
Puig,Yasiel, LAD	.384
Heyward,Jason, Atl	.384
Stanton,Giancarlo, Mia	.382
Werth,Jayson, Was	.381
Carpenter,Matt, StL	.380
Dickerson,Corey, Col	.379

2014 National League Batting Leaders

Stolen Bases		Caught Stealing		Highest SB Success Pct		Lowest SB Success Pct	
				(minimum 20 SBA)		(minimum 20 SBA)	
Gordon,Dee, LAD	64	Hamilton,Billy, Cin	23	Stubbs,Drew, Col	87.0	LeMahieu,DJ, Col	50.0
Hamilton,Billy, Cin	56	Gordon,Dee, LAD	19	Inciarte,Ender, Ari	86.4	Segura,Jean, Mil	69.0
Revere,Ben, Phi	49	Gomez,Carlos, Mil	12	Revere,Ben, Phi	86.0	Cabrera,Everth, SD	69.2
Gomez,Carlos, Mil	34	Marte,Starling, Pit	11	McCutchen,Andrew, Pit	85.7	Hamilton,Billy, Cin	70.9
Span,Denard, Was	31	Blackmon,Charlie, Col	10	Rendon,Anthony, Was	85.0	Frazier,Todd, Cin	71.4
Marte,Starling, Pit	30	LeMahieu,DJ, Col	10	Heyward,Jason, Atl	83.3	Harrison,Josh, Pit	72.0
Young,Eric, NYM	30	Segura,Jean, Mil	9	Wong,Kolten, StL	83.3	Pagan,Angel, SF	72.7
Blackmon,Charlie, Col	28	4 tied with	8	Young,Eric, NYM	83.3	Marte,Starling, Pit	73.2
Rollins,Jimmy, Phi	28			Desmond,Ian, Was	82.8	Blackmon,Charlie, Col	73.7
Bonifacio,Emilio, ChC-Atl	26			Rollins,Jimmy, Phi	82.4	Gomez,Carlos, Mil	73.9

Steals of Third		Grounded Into DP		Grounded Into DP Pct		Hit By Pitch	
				(minimum 50 GIDP Ops)			
Hamilton,Billy, Cin	14	McGehee,Casey, Mia	31	Granderson,Curtis, NYM	1.09	Jay,Jon, StL	20
Gomez,Carlos, Mil	9	Simmons,Andrelton, Atl	25	Hamilton,Billy, Cin	1.67	Gomez,Carlos, Mil	19
Gordon,Dee, LAD	9	Johnson,Chris, Atl	23	Heyward,Jason, Atl	2.56	Holliday,Matt, StL	17
Rollins,Jimmy, Phi	9	Wright,David, NYM	22	Gordon,Dee, LAD	3.26	Marte,Starling, Pit	17
Amarista,Alexi, SD	7	Hechavarria,Adeiny, Mia	21	Carpenter,Matt, StL	3.75	Martin,Russell, Pit	15
Blackmon,Charlie, Col	6	Kemp,Matt, LAD	21	Crawford,Brandon, SF	4.00	Rizzo,Anthony, ChC	15
Stubbs,Drew, Col	6	Holliday,Matt, StL	20	Blackmon,Charlie, Col	4.17	Blackmon,Charlie, Col	13
Inciarte,Ender, Ari	5	Morse,Michael, SF	19	Blanco,Gregor, SF	4.60	Ramirez,Aramis, Mil	13
3 tied with	4	Peralta,Jhonny, StL	19	Marte,Starling, Pit	4.76	Utley,Chase, Phi	13
		3 tied with	18	Young,Chris, NYM	4.92	4 tied with	12

Pitches Seen		At Bats Per Home Run		Highest GB/FB Ratio		Lowest GB/FB Ratio	
		(minimum 502 PA)		(minimum 502 PA)		(minimum 502 PA)	
Carpenter,Matt, StL	3101	Stanton,Giancarlo, Mia	14.6	Revere,Ben, Phi	4.51	Duda,Lucas, NYM	0.63
Freeman,Freddie, Atl	2826	Rizzo,Anthony, ChC	16.4	Yelich,Christian, Mia	3.42	Valbuena,Luis, ChC	0.66
Yelich,Christian, Mia	2812	Duda,Lucas, NYM	17.1	Gordon,Dee, LAD	3.13	Granderson,Curtis, NYM	0.73
Pence,Hunter, SF	2811	LaRoche,Adam, Was	19.0	Segura,Jean, Mil	2.59	Hill,Aaron, Ari	0.84
Rendon,Anthony, Was	2710	Upton,Justin, Atl	19.5	LeMahieu,DJ, Col	2.41	Adams,Matt, StL	0.84
Granderson,Curtis, NYM	2702	Frazier,Todd, Cin	20.6	Hechavarria,Adeiny, Mia	2.26	Rizzo,Anthony, ChC	0.86
Werth,Jayson, Was	2667	Kemp,Matt, LAD	21.6	Parra,Gerardo, Ari-Mil	2.25	Jones,Garrett, Mia	0.88
McCutchen,Andrew, Pit	2640	Gonzalez,Adrian, LAD	21.9	Johnson,Chris, Atl	1.91	LaRoche,Adam, Was	0.89
Howard,Ryan, Phi	2637	McCutchen,Andrew, Pit	21.9	Simmons,Andrelton, Atl	1.68	Crawford,Brandon, SF	0.90
Stanton,Giancarlo, Mia	2597	Walker,Neil, Pit	22.3	Marte,Starling, Pit	1.62	Byrd,Marlon, Phi	0.92

Pitches Per Plate App		Pct Pitches Taken		Best BPS on OutZ		Worst BPS on OutZ	
(minimum 502 PA)		(minimum 1500 Pitches)		(minimum 502 PA)		(minimum 502 PA)	
Carpenter,Matt, StL	4.37	Carpenter,Matt, StL	66.9	Span,Denard, Was	.759	Desmond,Ian, Was	.266
Yelich,Christian, Mia	4.26	Werth,Jayson, Was	63.3	Harrison,Josh, Pit	.663	Crawford,Brandon, SF	.282
Werth,Jayson, Was	4.24	Davis,Ike, NYM-Pit	62.1	Posey,Buster, SF	.660	Valbuena,Luis, ChC	.323
Valbuena,Luis, ChC	4.17	Goldschmidt,Paul, Ari	61.3	Rizzo,Anthony, ChC	.637	Gomez,Carlos, Mil	.339
Rollins,Jimmy, Phi	4.15	Prado,Martin, Ari	61.3	Werth,Jayson, Was	.622	LeMahieu,DJ, Col	.345
Granderson,Curtis, NYM	4.13	Ruiz,Carlos, Phi	61.1	Sandoval,Pablo, SF	.619	Peralta,Jhonny, StL	.354
Duda,Lucas, NYM	4.13	Yelich,Christian, Mia	60.6	McCutchen,Andrew, Pit	.615	Mercer,Jordy, Pit	.358
Smith,Seth, SD	4.08	Smith,Seth, SD	60.2	Ramirez,Aramis, Mil	.582	Davis,Khris, Mil	.360
McCutchen,Andrew, Pit	4.07	Grandal,Yasmani, SD	60.1	Gordon,Dee, LAD	.576	Smith,Seth, SD	.361
Stanton,Giancarlo, Mia	4.07	LaRoche,Adam, Was	60.0	Lucroy,Jonathan, Mil	.576	Bruce,Jay, Cin	.373

2014 National League Batting Leaders

Best OPS vs Fastballs
(minimum 251 PA)

McCutchen,Andrew, Pit	.986
Goldschmidt,Paul, Ari	.973
Harrison,Josh, Pit	.941
Kemp,Matt, LAD	.933
Freeman,Freddie, Atl	.919
Martin,Russell, Pit	.901
Castro,Starlin, ChC	.895
Werth,Jayson, Was	.887
Rendon,Anthony, Was	.878
Posey,Buster, SF	.877

Best OPS vs Curveballs
(minimum 50 PA)

Rizzo,Anthony, ChC	1.135
Stanton,Giancarlo, Mia	1.128
Dickerson,Corey, Col	1.044
Segura,Jean, Mil	.983
Freeman,Freddie, Atl	.925
Gomez,Carlos, Mil	.918
Morneau,Justin, Col	.898
Werth,Jayson, Was	.885
Marte,Starling, Pit	.881
Adams,Matt, StL	.872

Best OPS vs Changeups
(minimum 50 PA)

Stanton,Giancarlo, Mia	1.317
McCutchen,Andrew, Pit	1.238
Valbuena,Luis, ChC	1.184
Dickerson,Corey, Col	1.059
Heyward,Jason, Atl	1.017
Desmond,Ian, Was	1.010
Holliday,Matt, StL	.997
Gennett,Scooter, Mil	.932
Asche,Cody, Phi	.898
Kemp,Matt, LAD	.891

Best OPS vs Sliders
(minimum 32 PA)

Crawford,Carl, LAD	1.320
Turner,Justin, LAD	1.036
Young,Chris, NYM	1.032
Van Slyke,Scott, LAD	1.025
Puig,Yasiel, LAD	1.023
Gattis,Evan, Atl	1.016
Span,Denard, Was	1.015
Blanco,Gregor, SF	.996
Barnes,Brandon, Col	.985
3 tied with	.971

OPS
(minimum 502 PA)

McCutchen,Andrew, Pit	.952
Stanton,Giancarlo, Mia	.950
Rizzo,Anthony, ChC	.913
Puig,Yasiel, LAD	.863
Morneau,Justin, Col	.860
Posey,Buster, SF	.854
Kemp,Matt, LAD	.852
Werth,Jayson, Was	.849
Freeman,Freddie, Atl	.847
2 tied with	.837

OPS First Half
(minimum 260 PA)

Tulowitzki,Troy, Col	1.048
McCutchen,Andrew, Pit	.995
Goldschmidt,Paul, Ari	.949
Stanton,Giancarlo, Mia	.933
Puig,Yasiel, LAD	.915
Smith,Seth, SD	.895
Gomez,Carlos, Mil	.880
Lucroy,Jonathan, Mil	.879
Rizzo,Anthony, ChC	.879
Freeman,Freddie, Atl	.878

OPS Second Half
(minimum 201 PA)

Stanton,Giancarlo, Mia	.982
Posey,Buster, SF	.978
Rizzo,Anthony, ChC	.978
Marte,Starling, Pit	.975
Kemp,Matt, LAD	.971
Gonzalez,Adrian, LAD	.929
Werth,Jayson, Was	.922
Arenado,Nolan, Col	.896
Dickerson,Corey, Col	.896
Harrison,Josh, Pit	.887

OPS by Catchers
(minimum 251 PA)

Mesoraco,Devin, Cin	.876
Lucroy,Jonathan, Mil	.851
Posey,Buster, SF	.849
Martin,Russell, Pit	.843
Gattis,Evan, Atl	.843
Rivera,Rene, SD	.776
Rosario,Wilin, Col	.749
Ruiz,Carlos, Phi	.719
d'Arnaud,Travis, NYM	.718
Molina,Yadier, StL	.717

OPS by First Basemen
(minimum 251 PA)

Goldschmidt,Paul, Ari	.938
Rizzo,Anthony, ChC	.913
Morneau,Justin, Col	.860
Freeman,Freddie, Atl	.847
Duda,Lucas, NYM	.831
Gonzalez,Adrian, LAD	.825
LaRoche,Adam, Was	.814
Votto,Joey, Cin	.802
Adams,Matt, StL	.780
Jones,Garrett, Mia	.712

OPS by Second Basemen
(minimum 251 PA)

Walker,Neil, Pit	.811
Murphy,Daniel, NYM	.771
Gennett,Scooter, Mil	.757
Utley,Chase, Phi	.751
Panik,Joe, SF	.709
Gordon,Dee, LAD	.703
Phillips,Brandon, Cin	.678
Wong,Kolten, StL	.675
LeMahieu,DJ, Col	.664
Espinosa,Danny, Was	.659

OPS by Third Basemen
(minimum 251 PA)

Harrison,Josh, Pit	.922
Arenado,Nolan, Col	.828
Rendon,Anthony, Was	.827
Frazier,Todd, Cin	.792
Valbuena,Luis, ChC	.791
Uribe,Juan, LAD	.771
Ramirez,Aramis, Mil	.761
Carpenter,Matt, StL	.748
Sandoval,Pablo, SF	.739
Alvarez,Pedro, Pit	.733

OPS by Shortstops
(minimum 251 PA)

Tulowitzki,Troy, Col	1.044
Ramirez,Hanley, LAD	.810
Peralta,Jhonny, StL	.776
Castro,Starlin, ChC	.774
Desmond,Ian, Was	.743
Rollins,Jimmy, Phi	.716
Crawford,Brandon, SF	.716
Mercer,Jordy, Pit	.692
Rutledge,Josh, Col	.687
Hechavarria,Adeiny, Mia	.664

OPS by Left Fielders
(minimum 251 PA)

Dickerson,Corey, Col	.909
Upton,Justin, Atl	.842
Smith,Seth, SD	.828
Morse,Michael, SF	.820
Coghlan,Chris, ChC	.817
Holliday,Matt, StL	.817
Crawford,Carl, LAD	.780
Marte,Starling, Pit	.780
Davis,Khris, Mil	.772
Yelich,Christian, Mia	.756

OPS by Center Fielders
(minimum 251 PA)

McCutchen,Andrew, Pit	.952
Pollock,A.J., Ari	.843
Gomez,Carlos, Mil	.837
Blackmon,Charlie, Col	.816
Stubbs,Drew, Col	.805
Ozuna,Marcell, Mia	.784
Span,Denard, Was	.771
Jay,Jon, StL	.750
Pagan,Angel, SF	.741
Lagares,Juan, NYM	.705

OPS by Right Fielders
(minimum 251 PA)

Stanton,Giancarlo, Mia	.960
Puig,Yasiel, LAD	.912
Werth,Jayson, Was	.843
Blackmon,Charlie, Col	.792
Braun,Ryan, Mil	.786
Pence,Hunter, SF	.777
Byrd,Marlon, Phi	.759
Heyward,Jason, Atl	.736
Granderson,Curtis, NYM	.714
Parra,Gerardo, Ari-Mil	.684

OPS by Pitchers
(minimum 50 PA)

Bumgarner,Madison, SF	.767
Wood,Travis, ChC	.723
Greinke,Zack, LAD	.612
Lyles,Jordan, Col	.548
Leake,Mike, Cin	.543
Miller,Shelby, StL	.512
deGrom,Jacob, NYM	.506
Hamels,Cole, Phi	.452
Kershaw,Clayton, LAD	.442
Wainwright,Adam, StL	.436

2014 National League Batting Leaders

OPS Batting Left vs. LHP
(minimum 125 PA)

Rizzo,Anthony, ChC	.928
Crawford,Brandon, SF	.879
Yelich,Christian, Mia	.819
Howard,Ryan, Phi	.770
Revere,Ben, Phi	.763
Freeman,Freddie, Atl	.756
Granderson,Curtis, NYM	.742
Blanco,Gregor, SF	.730
Carpenter,Matt, StL	.725
Gordon,Dee, LAD	.719

OPS Batting Left vs. RHP
(minimum 377 PA)

Dickerson,Corey, Col	.985
Morneau,Justin, Col	.927
Duda,Lucas, NYM	.915
Rizzo,Anthony, ChC	.907
Gonzalez,Adrian, LAD	.901
LaRoche,Adam, Was	.891
Freeman,Freddie, Atl	.885
Adams,Matt, StL	.854
Walker,Neil, Pit	.831
Sandoval,Pablo, SF	.824

OPS Batting Right vs. LHP
(minimum 125 PA)

Stanton,Giancarlo, Mia	1.075
Van Slyke,Scott, LAD	1.045
Holliday,Matt, StL	1.004
Johnson,Chris, Atl	.988
Upton,Justin, Atl	.981
Arenado,Nolan, Col	.973
Stubbs,Drew, Col	.944
Werth,Jayson, Was	.933
Wright,David, NYM	.921
Peralta,Jhonny, StL	.879

OPS Batting Right vs. RHP
(minimum 377 PA)

McCutchen,Andrew, Pit	.962
Stanton,Giancarlo, Mia	.918
Puig,Yasiel, LAD	.901
Goldschmidt,Paul, Ari	.894
Kemp,Matt, LAD	.879
Posey,Buster, SF	.844
Lucroy,Jonathan, Mil	.837
Gomez,Carlos, Mil	.835
Harrison,Josh, Pit	.832
Rendon,Anthony, Was	.824

OPS vs. LHP
(minimum 125 PA)

Stanton,Giancarlo, Mia	1.075
Van Slyke,Scott, LAD	1.045
Holliday,Matt, StL	1.004
Johnson,Chris, Atl	.988
Upton,Justin, Atl	.981
Arenado,Nolan, Col	.973
Stubbs,Drew, Col	.944
Werth,Jayson, Was	.933
Rizzo,Anthony, ChC	.928
Wright,David, NYM	.921

OPS vs. RHP
(minimum 377 PA)

Dickerson,Corey, Col	.985
McCutchen,Andrew, Pit	.962
Morneau,Justin, Col	.927
Stanton,Giancarlo, Mia	.918
Duda,Lucas, NYM	.915
Rizzo,Anthony, ChC	.907
Gonzalez,Adrian, LAD	.901
Puig,Yasiel, LAD	.901
Goldschmidt,Paul, Ari	.894
LaRoche,Adam, Was	.891

RC Per 27 Outs vs. LHP
(minimum 125 PA)

Stanton,Giancarlo, Mia	9.2
Holliday,Matt, StL	9.2
Johnson,Chris, Atl	8.5
Upton,Justin, Atl	8.2
Werth,Jayson, Was	8.1
Stubbs,Drew, Col	8.0
Van Slyke,Scott, LAD	7.4
Rizzo,Anthony, ChC	7.1
Lucroy,Jonathan, Mil	7.1
Arenado,Nolan, Col	7.0

RC Per 27 Outs vs. RHP
(minimum 377 PA)

McCutchen,Andrew, Pit	7.9
Morneau,Justin, Col	7.7
Duda,Lucas, NYM	7.4
LaRoche,Adam, Was	7.4
Dickerson,Corey, Col	7.2
Freeman,Freddie, Atl	6.9
Stanton,Giancarlo, Mia	6.9
Gonzalez,Adrian, LAD	6.8
Werth,Jayson, Was	6.8
Puig,Yasiel, LAD	6.8

Highest RBI %
(minimum 502 PA)

Stanton,Giancarlo, Mia	41.22
Morneau,Justin, Col	40.26
Gonzalez,Adrian, LAD	39.93
Duda,Lucas, NYM	38.88
Werth,Jayson, Was	38.70
Posey,Buster, SF	38.56
Braun,Ryan, Mil	38.17
Rizzo,Anthony, ChC	37.81
McCutchen,Andrew, Pit	37.25
Holliday,Matt, StL	37.19

Lowest RBI %
(minimum 502 PA)

Hechavarria,Adeiny, Mia	19.27
Revere,Ben, Phi	19.97
Segura,Jean, Mil	20.65
Gordon,Dee, LAD	21.78
Cozart,Zack, Cin	21.95
Upton,B.J., Atl	22.44
Span,Denard, Was	23.98
LeMahieu,DJ, Col	24.42
Simmons,Andrelton, Atl	25.44
Johnson,Chris, Atl	25.90

Highest Strikeout per PA
(minimum 502 PA)

Upton,B.J., Atl	.297
Howard,Ryan, Phi	.293
Byrd,Marlon, Phi	.290
Desmond,Ian, Was	.282
Bruce,Jay, Cin	.273
Ozuna,Marcell, Mia	.268
Upton,Justin, Atl	.267
Stanton,Giancarlo, Mia	.266
Johnson,Chris, Atl	.260
Kemp,Matt, LAD	.242

Lowest Strikeout per PA
(minimum 502 PA)

Revere,Ben, Phi	.078
Span,Denard, Was	.097
Simmons,Andrelton, Atl	.104
Lucroy,Jonathan, Mil	.108
Morneau,Justin, Col	.109
Posey,Buster, SF	.114
Segura,Jean, Mil	.126
Utley,Chase, Phi	.128
Sandoval,Pablo, SF	.133
Murphy,Daniel, NYM	.134

Home Runs At Home

Stanton,Giancarlo, Mia	24
Frazier,Todd, Cin	20
Upton,Justin, Atl	18
Kemp,Matt, LAD	17
Arenado,Nolan, Col	16
Dickerson,Corey, Col	15
5 tied with	14

Home Runs Away

Rizzo,Anthony, ChC	18
Duda,Lucas, NYM	16
McCutchen,Andrew, Pit	15
Pence,Hunter, SF	15
Gonzalez,Adrian, LAD	14
Granderson,Curtis, NYM	13
Peralta,Jhonny, StL	13
Reynolds,Mark, Mil	13
Stanton,Giancarlo, Mia	13
Walker,Neil, Pit	13

2014 National League Batting Leaders

Under Age 26: AB Per HR
(minimum 502 PA)

Stanton,Giancarlo, Mia	14.6
Rizzo,Anthony, ChC	16.4
Ozuna,Marcell, Mia	24.6
Rendon,Anthony, Was	29.2
Freeman,Freddie, Atl	33.7
Puig,Yasiel, LAD	34.9
Castro,Starlin, ChC	37.7
Marte,Starling, Pit	38.1
Heyward,Jason, Atl	52.1
Yelich,Christian, Mia	64.7

Under Age 26: OPS
(minimum 502 PA)

Stanton,Giancarlo, Mia	.950
Rizzo,Anthony, ChC	.913
Puig,Yasiel, LAD	.863
Freeman,Freddie, Atl	.847
Rendon,Anthony, Was	.824
Marte,Starling, Pit	.808
Castro,Starlin, ChC	.777
Ozuna,Marcell, Mia	.772
Yelich,Christian, Mia	.764
Heyward,Jason, Atl	.735

Under Age 26: RC/27 Outs
(minimum 502 PA)

Player	RC/27
Stanton,Giancarlo, Mia	7.3
Rizzo,Anthony, ChC	6.8
Puig,Yasiel, LAD	6.2
Freeman,Freddie, Atl	6.0
Rendon,Anthony, Was	5.7
Yelich,Christian, Mia	5.4
Heyward,Jason, Atl	5.3
Marte,Starling, Pit	5.1
Castro,Starlin, ChC	4.9
Ozuna,Marcell, Mia	4.6

Swing and Miss %
(minimum 1500 Pitches Seen)

Player	%
Saltalamacchia,J, Mia	35.9
Upton,B.J., Atl	33.6
Howard,Ryan, Phi	33.3
Reynolds,Mark, Mil	32.3
Stanton,Giancarlo, Mia	31.6
Byrd,Marlon, Phi	30.8
Alvarez,Pedro, Pit	30.5
Kemp,Matt, LAD	30.4
Stubbs,Drew, Col	30.4
Ozuna,Marcell, Mia	30.3

Highest First Swing %
(minimum 502 PA)

Player	%
Gomez,Carlos, Mil	50.6
Ramirez,Aramis, Mil	42.7
Sandoval,Pablo, SF	42.0
Freeman,Freddie, Atl	41.2
Upton,B.J., Atl	41.2
Puig,Yasiel, LAD	41.1
Byrd,Marlon, Phi	40.5
Holliday,Matt, StL	40.5
Morneau,Justin, Col	40.1
Hechavarria,Adeiny, Mia	36.6

Lowest First Swing %
(minimum 502 PA)

Player	%
Carpenter,Matt, StL	6.5
Revere,Ben, Phi	8.2
Smith,Seth, SD	13.9
Lucroy,Jonathan, Mil	14.5
Utley,Chase, Phi	14.8
Yelich,Christian, Mia	15.5
Rollins,Jimmy, Phi	16.5
Werth,Jayson, Was	16.5
Rendon,Anthony, Was	17.3
Mercer,Jordy, Pit	17.8

Home RC Per 27 Outs
(minimum 251 PA)

Dickerson,Corey, Col	9.1
Stanton,Giancarlo, Mia	8.7
McCutchen,Andrew, Pit	8.0
Rizzo,Anthony, ChC	7.6
LaRoche,Adam, Was	7.6
Holliday,Matt, StL	7.3
Blackmon,Charlie, Col	7.3
Gomez,Carlos, Mil	7.0
Werth,Jayson, Was	6.6
Morneau,Justin, Col	6.6

Road RC Per 27 Outs
(minimum 251 PA)

Posey,Buster, SF	8.2
Werth,Jayson, Was	7.8
Puig,Yasiel, LAD	7.0
McCutchen,Andrew, Pit	7.0
Harrison,Josh, Pit	6.7
Morneau,Justin, Col	6.6
Duda,Lucas, NYM	6.6
Ramirez,Hanley, LAD	6.4
Gonzalez,Adrian, LAD	6.3
Rizzo,Anthony, ChC	6.1

Lead Changing RBI

Player	RBI
Holliday,Matt, StL	37
Stanton,Giancarlo, Mia	37
Utley,Chase, Phi	37
Gonzalez,Adrian, LAD	36
Howard,Ryan, Phi	34
LaRoche,Adam, Was	34
McGehee,Casey, Mia	34
Rizzo,Anthony, ChC	33
Werth,Jayson, Was	33
4 tied with	31

2014 American League Pitching Leaders

Earned Run Average (minimum 162 IP)		Winning Percentage (minimum 15 Decisions)		Opponent Batting Average (minimum 162 IP)		Baserunners Per 9 IP (minimum 162 IP)	
Hernandez,Felix, Sea	2.14	Shoemaker,Matt, LAA	.800	Hernandez,Felix, Sea	.200	Hernandez,Felix, Sea	8.43
Sale,Chris, CWS	2.17	Scherzer,Max, Det	.783	Richards,Garrett, LAA	.201	Sale,Chris, CWS	9.26
Kluber,Corey, Cle	2.44	Richards,Garrett, LAA	.765	Sale,Chris, CWS	.205	Iwakuma,Hisashi, Sea	9.55
Lester,Jon, Bos-Oak	2.46	Sale,Chris, CWS	.750	Cobb,Alex, TB	.231	Richards,Garrett, LAA	9.71
Richards,Garrett, LAA	2.61	Chen,Wei-Yin, Bal	.727	Gray,Sonny, Oak	.232	Price,David, TB-Det	9.89
Cobb,Alex, TB	2.87	Tanaka,Masahiro, NYY	.722	Dickey,R.A., Tor	.233	Kluber,Corey, Cle	10.08
Keuchel,Dallas, Hou	2.93	Hernandez,Felix, Sea	.714	Kluber,Corey, Cle	.233	Lester,Jon, Bos-Oak	10.12
Gray,Sonny, Oak	3.08	Tillman,Chris, Bal	.684	Young,Chris, Sea	.234	Hughes,Phil, Min	10.39
Scherzer,Max, Det	3.15	Kluber,Corey, Cle	.667	Lester,Jon, Bos-Oak	.236	Kuroda,Hiroki, NYY	10.54
Ventura,Yordano, KC	3.20	Weaver,Jered, LAA	.667	Tillman,Chris, Bal	.238	Kazmir,Scott, Oak	10.64

Games		Games Started		Complete Games		Shutouts	
Shaw,Bryan, Cle	80	Dickey,R.A., Tor	34	Keuchel,Dallas, Hou	5	Porcello,Rick, Det	3
Allen,Cody, Cle	76	Hernandez,Felix, Sea	34	Kluber,Corey, Cle	3	Buchholz,Clay, Bos	2
Smith,Joe, LAA	76	Kluber,Corey, Cle	34	Porcello,Rick, Det	3	Gray,Sonny, Oak	2
Jepsen,Kevin, LAA	74	Price,David, TB-Det	34	Price,David, TB-Det	3	Perez,Martin, Tex	2
Cotts,Neal, Tex	73	Shields,James, KC	34	Tanaka,Masahiro, NYY	3	22 tied with	1
Fien,Casey, Min	73	Tillman,Chris, Bal	34	9 tied with	2		
McGee,Jake, TB	73	Weaver,Jered, LAA	34				
Miller,Andrew, Bos-Bal	73	Gray,Sonny, Oak	33				
Rzepczynski,Marc, Cle	73	Scherzer,Max, Det	33				
3 tied with	72	11 tied with	32				

Wins		Losses		No Decisions		Wild Pitches	
Kluber,Corey, Cle	18	Lewis,Colby, Tex	14	Tillman,Chris, Bal	15	Richards,Garrett, LAA	22
Scherzer,Max, Det	18	Correia,Kevin, Min	13	Archer,Chris, TB	13	Hernandez,Felix, Sea	18
Weaver,Jered, LAA	18	Dickey,R.A., Tor	13	Bauer,Trevor, Cle	13	Gray,Sonny, Oak	15
Chen,Wei-Yin, Bal	16	Hutchison,Drew, Tor	13	Hernandez,Felix, Sea	13	Darvish,Yu, Tex	14
Hughes,Phil, Min	16	Oberholtzer,Brett, Hou	13	Kuroda,Hiroki, NYY	12	Kuroda,Hiroki, NYY	13
Lester,Jon, Bos-Oak	16	Odorizzi,Jake, TB	13	Peacock,Brad, Hou	12	Webb,Daniel, CWS	13
Shoemaker,Matt, LAA	16	Porcello,Rick, Det	13	Quintana,Jose, CWS	12	Shields,James, KC	12
7 tied with	15	9 tied with	12	Shields,James, KC	12	Gibson,Kyle, Min	11
				Milone,Tommy, Oak-Min	11	Ventura,Yordano, KC	11
				Santiago,Hector, LAA	11	Scherzer,Max, Det	10

Strikeouts		Walks Allowed		Intentional Walks Allowed		Hit Batters	
Price,David, TB-Det	271	Wilson,C.J., LAA	85	Belisario,Ronald, CWS	7	Dickey,R.A., Tor	14
Kluber,Corey, Cle	269	Jimenez,Ubaldo, Bal	77	Otero,Dan, Oak	7	Guthrie,Jeremy, KC	14
Scherzer,Max, Det	252	Danks,John, CWS	74	Ramos,Cesar, TB	7	Norris,Bud, Bal	14
Hernandez,Felix, Sea	248	Dickey,R.A., Tor	74	Johnson,Jim, Oak-Det	6	Carroll,Scott, CWS	12
Lester,Jon, Bos-Oak	220	Gray,Sonny, Oak	74	Morin,Mike, LAA	6	7 tied with	11
Sale,Chris, CWS	208	Archer,Chris, TB	72	Redmond,Todd, Tor	6		
Hughes,Phil, Min	186	Peacock,Brad, Hou	70	Wilhelmsen,Tom, Sea	6		
Hutchison,Drew, Tor	184	Ventura,Yordano, KC	69	11 tied with	5		
Gray,Sonny, Oak	183	Tillman,Chris, Bal	66				
Darvish,Yu, Tex	182	2 tied with	65				

2014 American League Pitching Leaders

Runs Allowed

Verlander,Justin, Det	114
Buchholz,Clay, Bos	108
Lewis,Colby, Tex	107
Danks,John, CWS	106
Dickey,R.A., Tor	101
Guthrie,Jeremy, KC	100
Price,David, TB-Det	100
Noesi,Hector, Sea-Tex-CWS	98
Nolasco,Ricky, Min	96
2 tied with	95

Hits Allowed

Price,David, TB-Det	230
Buehrle,Mark, Tor	228
Shields,James, KC	224
Verlander,Justin, Det	223
Hughes,Phil, Min	221
Guthrie,Jeremy, KC	215
Lewis,Colby, Tex	211
Porcello,Rick, Det	211
Kluber,Corey, Cle	207
Danks,John, CWS	205

Doubles Allowed

Buehrle,Mark, Tor	56
Verlander,Justin, Det	51
Danks,John, CWS	50
Scherzer,Max, Det	49
Dickey,R.A., Tor	48
Hutchison,Drew, Tor	47
Kluber,Corey, Cle	47
Price,David, TB-Det	47
Hughes,Phil, Min	46
Shields,James, KC	46

Home Runs Allowed

Noesi,Hector, Sea-Tex-CWS	28
Weaver,Jered, LAA	27
Dickey,R.A., Tor	26
Young,Chris, Sea	26
Danks,John, CWS	25
Gonzalez,Miguel, Bal	25
Lewis,Colby, Tex	25
Price,David, TB-Det	25
4 tied with	23

Run Support Per Nine IP
(minimum 162 IP)

Wilson,C.J., LAA	6.40
Weaver,Jered, LAA	5.86
Verlander,Justin, Det	5.68
Chen,Wei-Yin, Bal	5.67
Lewis,Colby, Tex	5.60
Kazmir,Scott, Oak	5.58
Danks,John, CWS	5.34
Gibson,Kyle, Min	5.32
Scherzer,Max, Det	5.27
Norris,Bud, Bal	5.12

% Pitches In Strike Zone
(minimum 162 IP)

Hughes,Phil, Min	54.7
Chen,Wei-Yin, Bal	48.6
Price,David, TB-Det	47.0
Scherzer,Max, Det	46.1
Dickey,R.A., Tor	46.1
Guthrie,Jeremy, KC	45.9
Ventura,Yordano, KC	45.6
Kazmir,Scott, Oak	45.4
Quintana,Jose, CWS	44.8
Danks,John, CWS	44.7

Pitches Per Start
(minimum 30 GS)

Scherzer,Max, Det	110.2
Price,David, TB-Det	109.7
Lester,Jon, Bos-Oak	109.2
Shields,James, KC	106.8
Verlander,Justin, Det	106.5
Quintana,Jose, CWS	104.6
Dickey,R.A., Tor	103.3
Danks,John, CWS	103.1
Kluber,Corey, Cle	102.9
Guthrie,Jeremy, KC	101.1

Pitches Per Batter
(minimum 162 IP)

Hughes,Phil, Min	3.56
Iwakuma,Hisashi, Sea	3.59
Buehrle,Mark, Tor	3.60
Porcello,Rick, Det	3.64
Gray,Sonny, Oak	3.67
Lewis,Colby, Tex	3.68
Kluber,Corey, Cle	3.68
Price,David, TB-Det	3.70
Gibson,Kyle, Min	3.70
Buchholz,Clay, Bos	3.72

Quality Starts

Hernandez,Felix, Sea	27
Lester,Jon, Bos-Oak	27
Gray,Sonny, Oak	26
Kluber,Corey, Cle	26
Price,David, TB-Det	24
Shields,James, KC	24
Dickey,R.A., Tor	23
Scherzer,Max, Det	22
Ventura,Yordano, KC	22
Weaver,Jered, LAA	22

Batters Faced

Price,David, TB-Det	1009
Kluber,Corey, Cle	951
Shields,James, KC	939
Dickey,R.A., Tor	914
Hernandez,Felix, Sea	912
Scherzer,Max, Det	904
Gray,Sonny, Oak	899
Verlander,Justin, Det	893
Weaver,Jered, LAA	888
Lester,Jon, Bos-Oak	885

Innings Pitched

Price,David, TB-Det	248.1
Hernandez,Felix, Sea	236.0
Kluber,Corey, Cle	235.2
Shields,James, KC	227.0
Scherzer,Max, Det	220.1
Lester,Jon, Bos-Oak	219.2
Gray,Sonny, Oak	219.0
Dickey,R.A., Tor	215.2
Weaver,Jered, LAA	213.1
Hughes,Phil, Min	209.2

Most Pitches in a Game

Keuchel,Dallas, Hou	128
Sale,Chris, CWS	127
Wilson,C.J., LAA	127
Darvish,Yu, Tex	126
Dickey,R.A., Tor	126
Happ,J.A., Tor	125
Wilson,C.J., LAA	125
Happ,J.A., Tor	124
Scherzer,Max, Det	124
Shields,James, KC	124

Stolen Bases Allowed

Feldman,Scott, Hou	35
Weaver,Jered, LAA	25
Hutchison,Drew, Tor	22
Hernandez,Felix, Sea	20
Bauer,Trevor, Cle	19
Jimenez,Ubaldo, Bal	19
Kazmir,Scott, Oak	18
Lewis,Colby, Tex	18
Lester,Jon, Bos-Oak	16
Nolasco,Ricky, Min	16

Caught Stealing Off

Scherzer,Max, Det	10
Kluber,Corey, Cle	9
Norris,Bud, Bal	9
Smyly,Drew, Det-TB	9
Iwakuma,Hisashi, Sea	8
Lewis,Colby, Tex	8
7 tied with	7

Stolen Base Pct Allowed
(minimum 162 IP)

Iwakuma,Hisashi, Sea	0.0
Buehrle,Mark, Tor	25.0
Keuchel,Dallas, Hou	25.0
Tillman,Chris, Bal	25.0
Odorizzi,Jake, TB	40.0
Kluber,Corey, Cle	47.1
Porcello,Rick, Det	50.0
Sale,Chris, CWS	50.0
Ventura,Yordano, KC	50.0
2 tied with	54.5

Pickoffs

Smyly,Drew, Det-TB	7
Duffy,Danny, KC	6
Santiago,Hector, LAA	6
Buehrle,Mark, Tor	4
Shields,James, KC	4
Skaggs,Tyler, LAA	4
Tepesch,Nick, Tex	4
Phelps,David, NYY	3
Weaver,Jered, LAA	3
19 tied with	2

2014 American League Pitching Leaders

Strikeouts Per 9 IP
(minimum 162 IP)

Sale,Chris, CWS	10.76
Scherzer,Max, Det	10.29
Kluber,Corey, Cle	10.27
Price,David, TB-Det	9.82
Hernandez,Felix, Sea	9.46
Odorizzi,Jake, TB	9.32
Lester,Jon, Bos-Oak	9.01
Hutchison,Drew, Tor	8.97
Richards,Garrett, LAA	8.75
Cobb,Alex, TB	8.06

Opp On-Base Percentage
(minimum 162 IP)

Hernandez,Felix, Sea	.243
Sale,Chris, CWS	.262
Iwakuma,Hisashi, Sea	.268
Richards,Garrett, LAA	.268
Price,David, TB-Det	.272
Kluber,Corey, Cle	.279
Lester,Jon, Bos-Oak	.281
Hughes,Phil, Min	.284
Kuroda,Hiroki, NYY	.286
Kazmir,Scott, Oak	.291

Opp Slugging Average
(minimum 162 IP)

Richards,Garrett, LAA	.261
Hernandez,Felix, Sea	.303
Sale,Chris, CWS	.305
Cobb,Alex, TB	.325
Gray,Sonny, Oak	.327
Archer,Chris, TB	.336
Kluber,Corey, Cle	.345
Keuchel,Dallas, Hou	.353
Lester,Jon, Bos-Oak	.354
Kazmir,Scott, Oak	.357

Opponent OPS
(minimum 162 IP)

Richards,Garrett, LAA	.529
Hernandez,Felix, Sea	.546
Sale,Chris, CWS	.567
Cobb,Alex, TB	.619
Kluber,Corey, Cle	.624
Gray,Sonny, Oak	.627
Lester,Jon, Bos-Oak	.635
Iwakuma,Hisashi, Sea	.642
Price,David, TB-Det	.647
Kazmir,Scott, Oak	.648

Home Runs Per Nine IP
(minimum 162 IP)

Richards,Garrett, LAA	0.27
Quintana,Jose, CWS	0.45
Keuchel,Dallas, Hou	0.49
Kluber,Corey, Cle	0.53
Archer,Chris, TB	0.55
Cobb,Alex, TB	0.60
Gibson,Kyle, Min	0.60
Hernandez,Felix, Sea	0.61
Gray,Sonny, Oak	0.62
Lester,Jon, Bos-Oak	0.66

Batting Average vs. LHB
(minimum 125 BF)

Duffy,Danny, KC	.137
Allen,Cody, Cle	.141
Robertson,David, NYY	.157
Betances,Dellin, NYY	.163
Sale,Chris, CWS	.165
Wilhelmsen,Tom, Sea	.165
Smyly,Drew, Det-TB	.171
Holland,Greg, KC	.177
Warren,Adam, NYY	.178
Kelly,Joe, Bos	.183

Batting Average vs. RHB
(minimum 225 BF)

McHugh,Collin, Hou	.190
Hernandez,Felix, Sea	.197
Young,Chris, Sea	.199
Richards,Garrett, LAA	.209
Iwakuma,Hisashi, Sea	.210
Weaver,Jered, LAA	.212
Sale,Chris, CWS	.214
Carrasco,Carlos, Cle	.221
Kluber,Corey, Cle	.221
Shoemaker,Matt, LAA	.222

Opp BA w/ RISP
(minimum 125 BF)

McHugh,Collin, Hou	.153
Norris,Bud, Bal	.173
Darvish,Yu, Tex	.180
Hernandez,Felix, Sea	.182
Cobb,Alex, TB	.191
Young,Chris, Sea	.195
Kazmir,Scott, Oak	.196
Chen,Wei-Yin, Bal	.204
Kluber,Corey, Cle	.207
Jimenez,Ubaldo, Bal	.209

OBP vs. Leadoff Hitter
(minimum 150 BF)

Iwakuma,Hisashi, Sea	.230
Richards,Garrett, LAA	.238
Smyly,Drew, Det-TB	.241
Hernandez,Felix, Sea	.248
Sale,Chris, CWS	.249
Young,Chris, Sea	.250
Ventura,Yordano, KC	.259
Odorizzi,Jake, TB	.263
Price,David, TB-Det	.266
Shields,James, KC	.268

Strikeouts / Walks Ratio
(minimum 162 IP)

Hughes,Phil, Min	11.63
Iwakuma,Hisashi, Sea	7.33
Price,David, TB-Det	7.13
Hernandez,Felix, Sea	5.39
Sale,Chris, CWS	5.33
Kluber,Corey, Cle	5.27
Lester,Jon, Bos-Oak	4.58
Kuroda,Hiroki, NYY	4.17
Shields,James, KC	4.09
Scherzer,Max, Det	4.00

Highest GB/FB Ratio
(minimum 162 IP)

Keuchel,Dallas, Hou	3.30
Gray,Sonny, Oak	2.19
Hernandez,Felix, Sea	2.14
Cobb,Alex, TB	2.05
Gibson,Kyle, Min	2.05
Richards,Garrett, LAA	1.82
Iwakuma,Hisashi, Sea	1.75
Porcello,Rick, Det	1.69
Wilson,C.J., LAA	1.62
Kluber,Corey, Cle	1.57

Lowest GB/FB Ratio
(minimum 162 IP)

Young,Chris, Sea	0.38
Odorizzi,Jake, TB	0.61
Weaver,Jered, LAA	0.69
Lewis,Colby, Tex	0.75
Hutchison,Drew, Tor	0.80
Scherzer,Max, Det	0.88
Hughes,Phil, Min	0.91
Noesi,Hector, Sea-Tex-CWS	0.94
Verlander,Justin, Det	0.98
Vargas,Jason, KC	0.99

Sacrifice Flies Allowed

Guthrie,Jeremy, KC	10
Hutchison,Drew, Tor	10
Oberholtzer,Brett, Hou	10
Archer,Chris, TB	9
Lewis,Colby, Tex	9
Young,Chris, Sea	9
Bauer,Trevor, Cle	8
Odorizzi,Jake, TB	8
Scherzer,Max, Det	8
7 tied with	7

Sacrifice Hits Allowed

Gray,Sonny, Oak	8
Buehrle,Mark, Tor	6
Lester,Jon, Bos-Oak	6
McHugh,Collin, Hou	6
Verlander,Justin, Det	6
9 tied with	5

GIDP Induced

Keuchel,Dallas, Hou	36
Porcello,Rick, Det	30
Buehrle,Mark, Tor	24
Elias,Roenis, Sea	23
Wilson,C.J., LAA	23
Gibson,Kyle, Min	22
Gray,Sonny, Oak	22
4 tied with	21

GIDP Per Nine IP
(minimum 162 IP)

Keuchel,Dallas, Hou	1.62
Porcello,Rick, Det	1.32
Elias,Roenis, Sea	1.26
Wilson,C.J., LAA	1.18
Gibson,Kyle, Min	1.10
Noesi,Hector, Sea-Tex-CWS	1.10
Buehrle,Mark, Tor	1.07
Guthrie,Jeremy, KC	0.93
Gray,Sonny, Oak	0.90
Kazmir,Scott, Oak	0.90

2014 American League Pitching Leaders

Saves

Rodney,Fernando, Sea	48
Holland,Greg, KC	46
Robertson,David, NYY	39
Britton,Zach, Bal	37
Nathan,Joe, Det	35
Perkins,Glen, Min	34
Uehara,Koji, Bos	26
Janssen,Casey, Tor	25
Allen,Cody, Cle	24
Doolittle,Sean, Oak	22

Blown Saves

Gregerson,Luke, Oak	8
Cotts,Neal, Tex	7
Nathan,Joe, Det	7
Perkins,Glen, Min	7
Shaw,Bryan, Cle	7
Hunter,Tommy, Bal	6
Peralta,Joel, TB	6
Qualls,Chad, Hou	6
6 tied with	5

Save Pct
(minimum 20 Save Ops)

Holland,Greg, KC	95.8
Rodney,Fernando, Sea	94.1
Britton,Zach, Bal	90.2
Soria,Joakim, Tex-Det	90.0
Robertson,David, NYY	88.6
Allen,Cody, Cle	85.7
Doolittle,Sean, Oak	84.6
Uehara,Koji, Bos	83.9
Janssen,Casey, Tor	83.3
Nathan,Joe, Det	83.3

Save Opportunities

Rodney,Fernando, Sea	51
Holland,Greg, KC	48
Robertson,David, NYY	44
Nathan,Joe, Det	42
Britton,Zach, Bal	41
Perkins,Glen, Min	41
Uehara,Koji, Bos	31
Janssen,Casey, Tor	30
Allen,Cody, Cle	28
Doolittle,Sean, Oak	26

Easy Saves

Rodney,Fernando, Sea	34
Holland,Greg, KC	32
Perkins,Glen, Min	25
Nathan,Joe, Det	23
Britton,Zach, Bal	19
Robertson,David, NYY	19
Janssen,Casey, Tor	18
Doolittle,Sean, Oak	14
Smith,Joe, LAA	14
2 tied with	13

Regular Saves

Britton,Zach, Bal	18
Robertson,David, NYY	17
Holland,Greg, KC	14
Rodney,Fernando, Sea	13
Nathan,Joe, Det	12
Uehara,Koji, Bos	12
Street,Huston, LAA	10
Allen,Cody, Cle	9
Balfour,Grant, TB	8
Perkins,Glen, Min	8

Tough Saves

Allen,Cody, Cle	4
Robertson,David, NYY	3
Doolittle,Sean, Oak	2
McGee,Jake, TB	2
Petricka,Jake, CWS	2
Putnam,Zach, CWS	2
Qualls,Chad, Hou	2
15 tied with	1

Holds Adjusted Saves %
(minimum 20 Save Ops + Holds)

Furbush,Charlie, Sea	100.0
Holland,Greg, KC	95.8
Miller,Andrew, Bos-Bal	95.8
Putnam,Zach, CWS	95.7
Medina,Yoervis, Sea	95.5
Herrera,Kelvin, KC	95.2
Rodney,Fernando, Sea	94.1
Cecil,Brett, Tor	93.5
Davis,Wade, KC	92.3
Jepsen,Kevin, LAA	92.3

Relief Wins

Davis,Wade, KC	9
Leone,Dominic, Sea	8
Otero,Dan, Oak	8
Brach,Brad, Bal	7
Smith,Joe, LAA	7
Allen,Cody, Cle	6
Atchison,Scott, Cle	6
Crow,Aaron, KC	6
Uehara,Koji, Bos	6
Webb,Daniel, CWS	6

Relief Losses

Cotts,Neal, Tex	9
Belisario,Ronald, CWS	8
Balfour,Grant, TB	6
Fields,Josh, Hou	6
Fien,Casey, Min	6
Kelley,Shawn, NYY	6
Petricka,Jake, CWS	6
Rodney,Fernando, Sea	6
Warren,Adam, NYY	6
10 tied with	5

Relief Games

Shaw,Bryan, Cle	80
Allen,Cody, Cle	76
Smith,Joe, LAA	76
Jepsen,Kevin, LAA	74
Cotts,Neal, Tex	73
Fien,Casey, Min	73
McGee,Jake, TB	73
Miller,Andrew, Bos-Bal	73
Rzepczynski,Marc, Cle	73
3 tied with	72

Holds

Davis,Wade, KC	33
Chamberlain,Joba, Det	29
Fien,Casey, Min	26
O'Day,Darren, Bal	25
Cecil,Brett, Tor	24
Shaw,Bryan, Cle	24
Warren,Adam, NYY	23
4 tied with	22

Relief Innings

Betances,Dellin, NYY	90.0
Otero,Dan, Oak	86.2
Warren,Adam, NYY	78.2
Britton,Zach, Bal	76.1
Shaw,Bryan, Cle	76.1
Wilhelmsen,Tom, Sea	75.1
Redmond,Todd, Tor	75.0
Smith,Joe, LAA	74.2
Petricka,Jake, CWS	73.0
Gregerson,Luke, Oak	72.1

Inherited Runners Scrd %
(minimum 30 IR)

McGee,Jake, TB	10.0
Furbush,Charlie, Sea	12.8
Abad,Fernando, Oak	13.2
Allen,Cody, Cle	14.3
Atchison,Scott, Cle	14.6
Hagadone,Nick, Cle	15.2
Hunter,Tommy, Bal	15.6
Downs,Scott, CWS-KC	16.2
Kelley,Shawn, NYY	16.7
Miller,Andrew, Bos-Bal	16.7

Relief Opp On Base Pct
(minimum 50 IP)

Doolittle,Sean, Oak	.197
Betances,Dellin, NYY	.218
Miller,Andrew, Bos-Bal	.229
Davis,Wade, KC	.229
Sipp,Tony, Hou	.231
Smith,Joe, LAA	.234
Boxberger,Brad, TB	.237
Holland,Greg, KC	.238
McGee,Jake, TB	.242
Uehara,Koji, Bos	.244

Relief Opp Slugging Avg
(minimum 50 IP)

Davis,Wade, KC	.179
Betances,Dellin, NYY	.224
Miller,Andrew, Bos-Bal	.227
Holland,Greg, KC	.234
McGee,Jake, TB	.244
Britton,Zach, Bal	.252
Abad,Fernando, Oak	.253
Smith,Joe, LAA	.257
Doolittle,Sean, Oak	.262
Herrera,Kelvin, KC	.266

2014 American League Pitching Leaders

Relief Opp BA Vs LHB
(minimum 50 AB)

Boxberger,Brad, TB	.107
Doolittle,Sean, Oak	.118
Feliz,Neftali, Tex	.127
Sipp,Tony, Hou	.138
Allen,Cody, Cle	.141
Robertson,David, NYY	.157
Loup,Aaron, Tor	.161
Betances,Dellin, NYY	.163
Miller,Andrew, Bos-Bal	.163
Maurer,Brandon, Sea	.167

Relief Opp BA Vs RHB
(minimum 50 AB)

Davis,Wade, KC	.112
Sanchez,Aaron, Tor	.116
Betances,Dellin, NYY	.135
Smith,Joe, LAA	.136
Cook,Ryan, Oak	.138
Miller,Andrew, Bos-Bal	.145
Wilson,Alex, Bos	.151
Holland,Greg, KC	.160
Abad,Fernando, Oak	.162
O'Day,Darren, Bal	.164

Relief Opp Batting Average
(minimum 50 IP)

Betances,Dellin, NYY	.149
Davis,Wade, KC	.151
Miller,Andrew, Bos-Bal	.153
Boxberger,Brad, TB	.155
Sipp,Tony, Hou	.157
Wilhelmsen,Tom, Sea	.169
Doolittle,Sean, Oak	.169
Holland,Greg, KC	.170
Smith,Joe, LAA	.172
O'Day,Darren, Bal	.174

Relief Earned Run Average
(minimum 50 IP)

Davis,Wade, KC	1.00
Betances,Dellin, NYY	1.40
Herrera,Kelvin, KC	1.41
Holland,Greg, KC	1.44
Abad,Fernando, Oak	1.57
Britton,Zach, Bal	1.65
O'Day,Darren, Bal	1.70
Smith,Joe, LAA	1.81
McGee,Jake, TB	1.89
Putnam,Zach, CWS	1.98

Rel OBP 1st Batter Faced
(minimum 40 BF)

Britton,Zach, Bal	.155
Doolittle,Sean, Oak	.164
Betances,Dellin, NYY	.176
Brach,Brad, Bal	.196
Webb,Ryan, Bal	.196
Beimel,Joe, Sea	.200
Robertson,David, NYY	.206
Atchison,Scott, Cle	.214
Crockett,Kyle, Cle	.214
McGee,Jake, TB	.219

Rel Opp BA w/ Runners On
(minimum 50 IP)

Wilhelmsen,Tom, Sea	.125
Boxberger,Brad, TB	.128
Abad,Fernando, Oak	.129
Miller,Andrew, Bos-Bal	.133
Betances,Dellin, NYY	.146
O'Day,Darren, Bal	.160
Davis,Wade, KC	.170
Robertson,David, NYY	.170
Doolittle,Sean, Oak	.171
Smith,Joe, LAA	.177

Relief Opp BA w/ RISP
(minimum 50 IP)

O'Day,Darren, Bal	.089
Abad,Fernando, Oak	.100
Cecil,Brett, Tor	.120
Wilhelmsen,Tom, Sea	.125
Betances,Dellin, NYY	.128
Davis,Wade, KC	.150
Miller,Andrew, Bos-Bal	.151
Holland,Greg, KC	.154
Atchison,Scott, Cle	.157
Hunter,Tommy, Bal	.160

Fastest Avg Fastball-Relief
(minimum 50 IP)

Herrera,Kelvin, KC	98.1
Betances,Dellin, NYY	96.6
McGee,Jake, TB	96.3
Hunter,Tommy, Bal	96.1
Holland,Greg, KC	95.8
Davis,Wade, KC	95.7
Jepsen,Kevin, LAA	95.5
Webb,Daniel, CWS	95.4
Wilhelmsen,Tom, Sea	95.3
Allen,Cody, Cle	95.3

Fastest Average Fastball
(minimum 162 IP)

Ventura,Yordano, KC	97.0
Richards,Garrett, LAA	96.3
Archer,Chris, TB	94.6
Sale,Chris, CWS	93.8
Norris,Bud, Bal	93.4
Kluber,Corey, Cle	93.2
Price,David, TB-Det	93.2
Gray,Sonny, Oak	93.0
Noesi,Hector, Sea-Tex-CWS	93.0
Scherzer,Max, Det	92.8

Slowest Average Fastball
(minimum 162 IP)

Dickey,R.A., Tor	81.9
Buehrle,Mark, Tor	83.9
Young,Chris, Sea	85.3
Weaver,Jered, LAA	86.3
Vargas,Jason, KC	87.3
Danks,John, CWS	88.6
Lewis,Colby, Tex	88.7
Iwakuma,Hisashi, Sea	88.9
Feldman,Scott, Hou	88.9
Keuchel,Dallas, Hou	89.7

Pitches 100+ Velocity

Herrera,Kelvin, KC	116
Ventura,Yordano, KC	107
Betances,Dellin, NYY	14
Foltynewicz,Mike, Hou	7
McGee,Jake, TB	4
Hunter,Tommy, Bal	3
Diaz,Jairo, LAA	2
Maurer,Brandon, Sea	2
Morrow,Brandon, Tor	2
4 tied with	1

Pitches 95+ Velocity

Ventura,Yordano, KC	1856
Richards,Garrett, LAA	1594
Archer,Chris, TB	1093
McGee,Jake, TB	1000
Samardzija,Jeff, Oak	956
Gausman,Kevin, Bal	831
Herrera,Kelvin, KC	827
Salazar,Danny, Cle	783
Price,David, TB-Det	774
Carrasco,Carlos, Cle	773

Pitches Less Than 80 MPH

Dickey,R.A., Tor	2854
Weaver,Jered, LAA	1405
Smyly,Drew, Det-TB	1392
Lester,Jon, Bos-Oak	1142
Buehrle,Mark, Tor	1113
Capuano,Chris, Bos-NYY	1086
Feldman,Scott, Hou	793
Young,Chris, Sea	763
Milone,Tommy, Oak-Min	754
Kazmir,Scott, Oak	726

Lowest % Fastballs
(minimum 162 IP)

Dickey,R.A., Tor	12.2
Feldman,Scott, Hou	32.9
Shields,James, KC	41.4
Cobb,Alex, TB	41.9
Hernandez,Felix, Sea	43.4
Danks,John, CWS	44.4
Kuroda,Hiroki, NYY	44.6
Buchholz,Clay, Bos	44.9
Iwakuma,Hisashi, Sea	47.9
Buehrle,Mark, Tor	49.0

Highest % Fastballs
(minimum 162 IP)

Young,Chris, Sea	66.4
Archer,Chris, TB	65.9
Chen,Wei-Yin, Bal	65.8
Ventura,Yordano, KC	65.3
Hutchison,Drew, Tor	65.1
Hughes,Phil, Min	64.7
Tillman,Chris, Bal	64.5
Richards,Garrett, LAA	63.8
Gibson,Kyle, Min	62.6
Lewis,Colby, Tex	61.9

Highest % Curveballs
(minimum 162 IP)

Gray,Sonny, Oak	27.1
Feldman,Scott, Hou	27.0
Quintana,Jose, CWS	24.6
Elias,Roenis, Sea	23.2
Cobb,Alex, TB	20.0
Weaver,Jered, LAA	19.3
Tillman,Chris, Bal	17.6
Wilson,C.J., LAA	16.6
Lester,Jon, Bos-Oak	16.4
Hernandez,Felix, Sea	16.2

2014 American League Pitching Leaders

Highest % Changeups
(minimum 162 IP)

Cobb,Alex, TB	38.1
Hernandez,Felix, Sea	32.2
Vargas,Jason, KC	30.5
Sale,Chris, CWS	28.6
Danks,John, CWS	28.2
Noesi,Hector, Sea-Tex-CWS	26.5
Elias,Roenis, Sea	24.4
Odorizzi,Jake, TB	24.3
Buehrle,Mark, Tor	22.5
Shields,James, KC	21.9

Highest % Sliders
(minimum 162 IP)

Richards,Garrett, LAA	30.0
Archer,Chris, TB	28.9
Young,Chris, Sea	27.0
Norris,Bud, Bal	26.1
Hutchison,Drew, Tor	23.0
Lewis,Colby, Tex	22.2
Gibson,Kyle, Min	21.8
Kuroda,Hiroki, NYY	21.4
Keuchel,Dallas, Hou	20.7
Iwakuma,Hisashi, Sea	20.4

Balks

Deduno,Samuel, Min-Hou	4
Elias,Roenis, Sea	4
Oberholtzer,Brett, Hou	3
8 tied with	2

Strikeout/Hit Ratio
(minimum 50 IP)

Miller,Andrew, Bos-Bal	3.12
Boxberger,Brad, TB	3.06
Betances,Dellin, NYY	2.93
Davis,Wade, KC	2.87
Holland,Greg, KC	2.43
Doolittle,Sean, Oak	2.34
Sipp,Tony, Hou	2.25
Robertson,David, NYY	2.13
Allen,Cody, Cle	1.90
McGee,Jake, TB	1.88

Opp OPS vs Fastballs
(minimum 251 BF)

McGee,Jake, TB	.464
Britton,Zach, Bal	.505
Richards,Garrett, LAA	.553
Stroman,Marcus, Tor	.571
Sale,Chris, CWS	.572
Duffy,Danny, KC	.589
Tillman,Chris, Bal	.613
Keuchel,Dallas, Hou	.615
Carrasco,Carlos, Cle	.642
Lester,Jon, Bos-Oak	.644

Opp OPS vs Curveballs
(minimum 100 BF)

Hernandez,Felix, Sea	.359
Kluber,Corey, Cle	.395
Lester,Jon, Bos-Oak	.502
Duffy,Danny, KC	.526
Weaver,Jered, LAA	.530
McHugh,Collin, Hou	.533
Quintana,Jose, CWS	.551
Gray,Sonny, Oak	.557
Smyly,Drew, Det-TB	.585
Cobb,Alex, TB	.587

Opp OPS vs Changeups
(minimum 100 BF)

Hernandez,Felix, Sea	.443
Capuano,Chris, Bos-NYY	.495
Cobb,Alex, TB	.555
Chavez,Jesse, Oak	.561
Sale,Chris, CWS	.562
Porcello,Rick, Det	.616
Kazmir,Scott, Oak	.617
Price,David, TB-Det	.639
Sanchez,Anibal, Det	.640
Vargas,Jason, KC	.657

Opp OPS vs Sliders
(minimum 64 BF)

Miller,Andrew, Bos-Bal	.309
Smith,Joe, LAA	.332
Carrasco,Carlos, Cle	.349
Betances,Dellin, NYY	.364
O'Day,Darren, Bal	.424
Gray,Sonny, Oak	.451
Ramos,Cesar, TB	.457
Richards,Garrett, LAA	.462
Qualls,Chad, Hou	.463
Tanaka,Masahiro, NYY	.465

Earned Runs

Verlander,Justin, Det	104
Danks,John, CWS	102
Buchholz,Clay, Bos	101
Lewis,Colby, Tex	98
Nolasco,Ricky, Min	95
Guthrie,Jeremy, KC	93
Hutchison,Drew, Tor	92
Noesi,Hector, Sea-Tex-CWS	91
Price,David, TB-Det	90
2 tied with	89

Hits Per Nine Innings
(minimum 162 IP)

Hernandez,Felix, Sea	6.48
Richards,Garrett, LAA	6.62
Sale,Chris, CWS	6.67
Cobb,Alex, TB	7.68
Gray,Sonny, Oak	7.68
Young,Chris, Sea	7.80
Kluber,Corey, Cle	7.91
Lester,Jon, Bos-Oak	7.95
Dickey,R.A., Tor	7.97
Scherzer,Max, Det	8.01

2014 National League Pitching Leaders

Earned Run Average
(minimum 162 IP)

Kershaw,Clayton, LAD	1.77
Cueto,Johnny, Cin	2.25
Wainwright,Adam, StL	2.38
Fister,Doug, Was	2.41
Hamels,Cole, Phi	2.46
Alvarez,Henderson, Mia	2.65
Zimmermann,Jordan, Was	2.66
Greinke,Zack, LAD	2.71
Lynn,Lance, StL	2.74
Wood,Alex, Atl	2.78

Winning Percentage
(minimum 15 Decisions)

Kershaw,Clayton, LAD	.875
Zimmermann,Jordan, Was	.737
Fister,Doug, Was	.727
Cueto,Johnny, Cin	.690
Wainwright,Adam, StL	.690
Cole,Gerrit, Pit	.688
Greinke,Zack, LAD	.680
Arrieta,Jake, ChC	.667
Ryu,Hyun-Jin, LAD	.667
Volquez,Edinson, Pit	.650

Opponent Batting Average
(minimum 162 IP)

Cueto,Johnny, Cin	.194
Kershaw,Clayton, LAD	.196
Liriano,Francisco, Pit	.218
Wainwright,Adam, StL	.222
Ross,Tyson, SD	.230
Teheran,Julio, Atl	.232
Garza,Matt, Mil	.233
Hamels,Cole, Phi	.235
Volquez,Edinson, Pit	.235
Miller,Shelby, StL	.236

Baserunners Per 9 IP
(minimum 162 IP)

Kershaw,Clayton, LAD	7.81
Cueto,Johnny, Cin	9.20
Wainwright,Adam, StL	9.56
Teheran,Julio, Atl	9.90
Zimmermann,Jordan, Was	9.92
Bumgarner,Madison, SF	10.06
Fister,Doug, Was	10.10
Roark,Tanner, Was	10.10
Strasburg,Stephen, Was	10.30
Collmenter,Josh, Ari	10.34

Games

Smith,Will, Mil	78
Watson,Tony, Pit	78
Familia,Jeurys, NYM	76
Clippard,Tyler, Was	75
Dunn,Mike, Mia	75
Ottavino,Adam, Col	75
Brothers,Rex, Col	74
Duke,Zach, Mil	74
4 tied with	73

Games Started

Burnett,A.J., Phi	34
Cueto,Johnny, Cin	34
Strasburg,Stephen, Was	34
8 tied with	33

Complete Games

Kershaw,Clayton, LAD	6
Wainwright,Adam, StL	5
Bumgarner,Madison, SF	4
Cueto,Johnny, Cin	4
Teheran,Julio, Atl	4
Alvarez,Henderson, Mia	3
Zimmermann,Jordan, Was	3
4 tied with	2

Shutouts

Alvarez,Henderson, Mia	3
Wainwright,Adam, StL	3
Bumgarner,Madison, SF	2
Cashner,Andrew, SD	2
Cueto,Johnny, Cin	2
Kershaw,Clayton, LAD	2
Lohse,Kyle, Mil	2
Teheran,Julio, Atl	2
Zimmermann,Jordan, Was	2
14 tied with	1

Wins

Kershaw,Clayton, LAD	21
Cueto,Johnny, Cin	20
Wainwright,Adam, StL	20
Bumgarner,Madison, SF	18
Greinke,Zack, LAD	17
Peralta,Wily, Mil	17
Fister,Doug, Was	16
4 tied with	15

Losses

Burnett,A.J., Phi	18
Stults,Eric, SD	17
Jackson,Edwin, ChC	15
Eovaldi,Nathan, Mia	14
Ross,Tyson, SD	14
8 tied with	13

No Decisions

Eovaldi,Nathan, Mia	13
Gallardo,Yovani, Mil	13
Miley,Wade, Ari	13
Zimmermann,Jordan, Was	13
Hamels,Cole, Phi	12
Koehler,Tom, Mia	12
Liriano,Francisco, Pit	12
Miller,Shelby, StL	12
5 tied with	11

Wild Pitches

Lincecum,Tim, SF	15
Volquez,Edinson, Pit	15
Greinke,Zack, LAD	12
Liriano,Francisco, Pit	12
Ross,Tyson, SD	12
Kennedy,Ian, SD	11
10 tied with	9

Strikeouts

Cueto,Johnny, Cin	242
Strasburg,Stephen, Was	242
Kershaw,Clayton, LAD	239
Bumgarner,Madison, SF	219
Greinke,Zack, LAD	207
Kennedy,Ian, SD	207
Hamels,Cole, Phi	198
Ross,Tyson, SD	195
Burnett,A.J., Phi	190
Wheeler,Zack, NYM	187

Walks Allowed

Burnett,A.J., Phi	96
Liriano,Francisco, Pit	81
Wheeler,Zack, NYM	79
Wood,Travis, ChC	76
Miley,Wade, Ari	75
Hernandez,Roberto, Phi-LAD	73
Miller,Shelby, StL	73
Lynn,Lance, StL	72
Ross,Tyson, SD	72
3 tied with	71

Intentional Walks Allowed

Hale,David, Atl	8
Martinez,Carlos, StL	8
Mejia,Jenry, NYM	8
Avilan,Luis, Atl	7
Gomez,Jeanmar, Pit	7
Haren,Dan, LAD	7
Hernandez,Roberto, Phi-LAD	7
Ramos,A.J., Mia	7
Simon,Alfredo, Cin	7
6 tied with	6

Hit Batters

Morton,Charlie, Pit	19
Burnett,A.J., Phi	16
Cueto,Johnny, Cin	15
Volquez,Edinson, Pit	14
Leake,Mike, Cin	13
Simon,Alfredo, Cin	12
Kendrick,Kyle, Phi	11
Wheeler,Zack, NYM	11
5 tied with	9

2014 National League Pitching Leaders

Runs Allowed

Burnett,A.J., Phi	122
Wood,Travis, ChC	110
Kendrick,Kyle, Phi	108
Eovaldi,Nathan, Mia	107
Jackson,Edwin, ChC	105
Miley,Wade, Ari	103
Haren,Dan, LAD	101
Colon,Bartolo, NYM	97
Leake,Mike, Cin	93
Stults,Eric, SD	93

Hits Allowed

Eovaldi,Nathan, Mia	223
Colon,Bartolo, NYM	218
Leake,Mike, Cin	217
Harang,Aaron, Atl	215
Kendrick,Kyle, Phi	214
Miley,Wade, Ari	207
Burnett,A.J., Phi	205
Hudson,Tim, SF	199
3 tied with	198

Doubles Allowed

Leake,Mike, Cin	52
Burnett,A.J., Phi	51
Eovaldi,Nathan, Mia	46
Lynn,Lance, StL	46
Vogelsong,Ryan, SF	46
Jackson,Edwin, ChC	44
Wood,Travis, ChC	44
Haren,Dan, LAD	43
Kennedy,Ian, SD	43
2 tied with	42

Home Runs Allowed

Estrada,Marco, Mil	29
Haren,Dan, LAD	27
Stults,Eric, SD	26
Kendrick,Kyle, Phi	25
Morales,Franklin, Col	24
Leake,Mike, Cin	23
Miley,Wade, Ari	23
Peralta,Wily, Mil	23
Strasburg,Stephen, Was	23
6 tied with	22

Run Support Per Nine IP
(minimum 162 IP)

De La Rosa,Jorge, Col	6.20
Bumgarner,Madison, SF	5.76
Kershaw,Clayton, LAD	5.63
Fister,Doug, Was	5.16
Lohse,Kyle, Mil	5.08
Wood,Travis, ChC	5.08
Colon,Bartolo, NYM	5.03
Greinke,Zack, LAD	5.03
Haren,Dan, LAD	4.84
Peralta,Wily, Mil	4.80

% Pitches In Strike Zone
(minimum 162 IP)

Eovaldi,Nathan, Mia	49.5
Alvarez,Henderson, Mia	47.9
Kershaw,Clayton, LAD	47.8
Miller,Shelby, StL	47.5
Niese,Jon, NYM	47.3
Colon,Bartolo, NYM	47.2
Zimmermann,Jordan, Was	47.1
Roark,Tanner, Was	45.8
Hudson,Tim, SF	45.3
Volquez,Edinson, Pit	45.0

Pitches Per Start
(minimum 30 GS)

Cueto,Johnny, Cin	107.6
Lynn,Lance, StL	104.5
Hamels,Cole, Phi	104.5
Wheeler,Zack, NYM	103.4
Kennedy,Ian, SD	103.1
Harang,Aaron, Atl	102.8
Bumgarner,Madison, SF	102.2
Burnett,A.J., Phi	102.1
Wainwright,Adam, StL	101.8
Ross,Tyson, SD	100.6

Pitches Per Batter
(minimum 162 IP)

Alvarez,Henderson, Mia	3.38
Hudson,Tim, SF	3.53
Niese,Jon, NYM	3.55
Colon,Bartolo, NYM	3.56
Leake,Mike, Cin	3.56
Kendrick,Kyle, Phi	3.59
Wainwright,Adam, StL	3.63
Kershaw,Clayton, LAD	3.63
Zimmermann,Jordan, Was	3.66
Santana,Ervin, Atl	3.66

Quality Starts

Cueto,Johnny, Cin	29
Hamels,Cole, Phi	25
Harang,Aaron, Atl	25
Teheran,Julio, Atl	25
Wainwright,Adam, StL	25
Kershaw,Clayton, LAD	24
Lynn,Lance, StL	24
Strasburg,Stephen, Was	24
Zimmermann,Jordan, Was	24
3 tied with	22

Batters Faced

Cueto,Johnny, Cin	961
Burnett,A.J., Phi	935
Leake,Mike, Cin	902
Wainwright,Adam, StL	898
Teheran,Julio, Atl	884
Harang,Aaron, Atl	876
Bumgarner,Madison, SF	873
Strasburg,Stephen, Was	868
Lynn,Lance, StL	866
Miley,Wade, Ari	866

Innings Pitched

Cueto,Johnny, Cin	243.2
Wainwright,Adam, StL	227.0
Teheran,Julio, Atl	221.0
Bumgarner,Madison, SF	217.1
Strasburg,Stephen, Was	215.0
Leake,Mike, Cin	214.1
Burnett,A.J., Phi	213.2
Hamels,Cole, Phi	204.2
Harang,Aaron, Atl	204.1
Lynn,Lance, StL	203.2

Most Pitches in a Game

Hamels,Cole, Phi	133
Burnett,A.J., Phi	131
Beckett,Josh, LAD	128
Lee,Cliff, Phi	128
Teheran,Julio, Atl	128
Lynn,Lance, StL	126
Samardzija,Jeff, ChC	126
Burnett,A.J., Phi	125
Hamels,Cole, Phi	125
Hamels,Cole, Phi	125

Stolen Bases Allowed

Burnett,A.J., Phi	33
Ross,Tyson, SD	31
Arrieta,Jake, ChC	24
Hernandez,Roberto, Phi-LAD	23
Lincecum,Tim, SF	22
Cole,Gerrit, Pit	21
Hamels,Cole, Phi	19
Harang,Aaron, Atl	19
Liriano,Francisco, Pit	19
Peralta,Wily, Mil	19

Caught Stealing Off

Bumgarner,Madison, SF	10
Ross,Tyson, SD	10
Burnett,A.J., Phi	9
Hamels,Cole, Phi	9
Kennedy,Ian, SD	8
Simon,Alfredo, Cin	8
Estrada,Marco, Mil	7
Kendrick,Kyle, Phi	7
Volquez,Edinson, Pit	7
14 tied with	6

Stolen Base Pct Allowed
(minimum 162 IP)

Fister,Doug, Was	0.0
Eovaldi,Nathan, Mia	20.0
Lynn,Lance, StL	25.0
Miley,Wade, Ari	40.0
Bumgarner,Madison, SF	41.2
Kendrick,Kyle, Phi	41.7
Zimmermann,Jordan, Was	42.9
Cueto,Johnny, Cin	50.0
Santana,Ervin, Atl	53.8
Kershaw,Clayton, LAD	55.6

Pickoffs

Bumgarner,Madison, SF	9
Hamels,Cole, Phi	6
Teheran,Julio, Atl	6
Locke,Jeff, Pit	5
Miley,Wade, Ari	5
Wood,Alex, Atl	5
5 tied with	4

2014 National League Pitching Leaders

Strikeouts Per 9 IP		Opp On-Base Percentage		Opp Slugging Average		Opponent OPS	
(minimum 162 IP)		(minimum 162 IP)		(minimum 162 IP)		(minimum 162 IP)	
Kershaw,Clayton, LAD	10.85	Kershaw,Clayton, LAD	.231	Kershaw,Clayton, LAD	.289	Kershaw,Clayton, LAD	.521
Strasburg,Stephen, Was	10.13	Cueto,Johnny, Cin	.261	Wainwright,Adam, StL	.310	Cueto,Johnny, Cin	.574
Liriano,Francisco, Pit	9.70	Wainwright,Adam, StL	.271	Cueto,Johnny, Cin	.313	Wainwright,Adam, StL	.580
Kennedy,Ian, SD	9.27	Zimmermann,Jordan, Was	.277	Ross,Tyson, SD	.327	Zimmermann,Jordan, Was	.631
Greinke,Zack, LAD	9.21	Teheran,Julio, Atl	.279	Liriano,Francisco, Pit	.331	Roark,Tanner, Was	.632
Wheeler,Zack, NYM	9.08	Fister,Doug, Was	.280	Hamels,Cole, Phi	.345	Ross,Tyson, SD	.634
Bumgarner,Madison, SF	9.07	Roark,Tanner, Was	.281	Garza,Matt, Mil	.351	Teheran,Julio, Atl	.639
Ross,Tyson, SD	8.97	Bumgarner,Madison, SF	.281	Roark,Tanner, Was	.351	Hamels,Cole, Phi	.641
Cueto,Johnny, Cin	8.94	Strasburg,Stephen, Was	.286	Wheeler,Zack, NYM	.352	Garza,Matt, Mil	.644
Wood,Alex, Atl	8.91	Greinke,Zack, LAD	.287	Zimmermann,Jordan, Was	.354	Liriano,Francisco, Pit	.645

Home Runs Per Nine IP		Batting Average vs. LHB		Batting Average vs. RHB		Opp BA w/ RISP	
(minimum 162 IP)		(minimum 125 BF)		(minimum 225 BF)		(minimum 125 BF)	
Wainwright,Adam, StL	0.40	Kimbrel,Craig, Atl	.147	Petit,Yusmeiro, SF	.193	Cueto,Johnny, Cin	.161
Kershaw,Clayton, LAD	0.41	Melancon,Mark, Pit	.164	Cueto,Johnny, Cin	.194	Kershaw,Clayton, LAD	.190
Lynn,Lance, StL	0.57	Rodriguez,Francisco, Mil	.176	Kershaw,Clayton, LAD	.197	Hamels,Cole, Phi	.192
Zimmermann,Jordan, Was	0.59	Rosenthal,Trevor, StL	.181	Beckett,Josh, LAD	.198	Lynn,Lance, StL	.194
Ross,Tyson, SD	0.60	Papelbon,Jonathan, Phi	.182	Wainwright,Adam, StL	.203	Liriano,Francisco, Pit	.195
Hamels,Cole, Phi	0.62	Kahnle,Tommy, Col	.184	Liriano,Francisco, Pit	.206	Lyles,Jordan, Col	.196
Eovaldi,Nathan, Mia	0.63	Fiers,Mike, Mil	.188	Arrieta,Jake, ChC	.207	Bumgarner,Madison, SF	.200
Harang,Aaron, Atl	0.66	Kershaw,Clayton, LAD	.193	Collmenter,Josh, Ari	.207	Leake,Mike, Cin	.201
Garza,Matt, Mil	0.66	Cueto,Johnny, Cin	.194	Peralta,Wily, Mil	.217	Wainwright,Adam, StL	.209
Alvarez,Henderson, Mia	0.67	De La Rosa,Jorge, Col	.196	Hammel,Jason, ChC	.217	Alvarez,Henderson, Mia	.209

OBP vs. Leadoff Hitter		Strikeouts / Walks Ratio		Highest GB/FB Ratio		Lowest GB/FB Ratio	
(minimum 150 BF)		(minimum 162 IP)		(minimum 162 IP)		(minimum 162 IP)	
Zimmermann,Jordan, Was	.229	Kershaw,Clayton, LAD	7.71	Ross,Tyson, SD	2.58	Teheran,Julio, Atl	0.79
Ryu,Hyun-Jin, LAD	.232	Zimmermann,Jordan, Was	6.28	Alvarez,Henderson, Mia	2.21	Wood,Travis, ChC	0.81
Strasburg,Stephen, Was	.251	Strasburg,Stephen, Was	5.63	Hudson,Tim, SF	2.05	Collmenter,Josh, Ari	0.97
Estrada,Marco, Mil	.258	Bumgarner,Madison, SF	5.09	Liriano,Francisco, Pit	2.03	Miller,Shelby, StL	0.97
Colon,Bartolo, NYM	.258	Colon,Bartolo, NYM	5.03	Leake,Mike, Cin	2.02	Lohse,Kyle, Mil	0.99
Arrieta,Jake, ChC	.261	Greinke,Zack, LAD	4.81	Wheeler,Zack, NYM	1.98	Colon,Bartolo, NYM	1.02
Kershaw,Clayton, LAD	.261	Fister,Doug, Was	4.08	Peralta,Wily, Mil	1.94	Vogelsong,Ryan, SF	1.03
Gonzalez,Gio, Was	.265	Haren,Dan, LAD	4.03	Miley,Wade, Ari	1.82	Harang,Aaron, Atl	1.04
Alvarez,Henderson, Mia	.271	Wood,Alex, Atl	3.78	Burnett,A.J., Phi	1.78	Kennedy,Ian, SD	1.05
Roark,Tanner, Was	.272	Cueto,Johnny, Cin	3.72	Kershaw,Clayton, LAD	1.77	Haren,Dan, LAD	1.06

Sacrifice Flies Allowed		Sacrifice Hits Allowed		GIDP Induced		GIDP Per Nine IP	
						(minimum 162 IP)	
Santana,Ervin, Atl	12	Kendrick,Kyle, Phi	17	Alvarez,Henderson, Mia	24	Alvarez,Henderson, Mia	1.16
Burnett,A.J., Phi	11	Stults,Eric, SD	13	Peralta,Wily, Mil	24	Peralta,Wily, Mil	1.09
Lohse,Kyle, Mil	9	Teheran,Julio, Atl	13	Wainwright,Adam, StL	24	De La Rosa,Jorge, Col	1.03
Miley,Wade, Ari	9	Volquez,Edinson, Pit	13	Morton,Charlie, Pit	22	Koehler,Tom, Mia	0.99
Kennedy,Ian, SD	8	Santana,Ervin, Atl	12	De La Rosa,Jorge, Col	21	Wheeler,Zack, NYM	0.97
Diekman,Jake, Phi	7	Burnett,A.J., Phi	11	Koehler,Tom, Mia	21	Ross,Tyson, SD	0.97
Hamels,Cole, Phi	7	Harang,Aaron, Atl	11	Ross,Tyson, SD	21	Wainwright,Adam, StL	0.95
Leake,Mike, Cin	7	5 tied with	10	Greinke,Zack, LAD	20	Wood,Alex, Atl	0.94
Morales,Franklin, Col	7			Leake,Mike, Cin	20	Niese,Jon, NYM	0.91
4 tied with	6			Wheeler,Zack, NYM	20	Greinke,Zack, LAD	0.89

2014 National League Pitching Leaders

Saves			Blown Saves			Save Pct			Save Opportunities		
						(minimum 20 Save Ops)					
Kimbrel,Craig, Atl	47		Broxton,Jonathan, Cin-Mil	8		Street,Huston, SD	96.0		Kimbrel,Craig, Atl	51	
Rosenthal,Trevor, StL	45		Ziegler,Brad, Ari	8		Chapman,Aroldis, Cin	94.7		Rosenthal,Trevor, StL	51	
Jansen,Kenley, LAD	44		Morris,Bryan, Pit-Mia	7		Kimbrel,Craig, Atl	92.2		Jansen,Kenley, LAD	49	
Rodriguez,Francisco, Mil	44		Soriano,Rafael, Was	7		Cishek,Steve, Mia	90.7		Rodriguez,Francisco, Mil	49	
Cishek,Steve, Mia	39		Watson,Tony, Pit	7		Papelbon,Jonathan, Phi	90.7		Cishek,Steve, Mia	43	
Papelbon,Jonathan, Phi	39		Brothers,Rex, Col	6		Mejia,Jenrry, NYM	90.3		Papelbon,Jonathan, Phi	43	
Chapman,Aroldis, Cin	36		Clippard,Tyler, Was	6		Jansen,Kenley, LAD	89.8		Soriano,Rafael, Was	39	
Melancon,Mark, Pit	33		Reed,Addison, Ari	6		Rodriguez,Francisco, Mil	89.8		Chapman,Aroldis, Cin	38	
Reed,Addison, Ari	32		Rosenthal,Trevor, StL	6		Melancon,Mark, Pit	89.2		Reed,Addison, Ari	38	
Soriano,Rafael, Was	32		7 tied with	5		Hawkins,LaTroy, Col	88.5		Melancon,Mark, Pit	37	

Easy Saves			Regular Saves			Tough Saves			Holds Adjusted Saves %		
									(minimum 20 Save Ops + Holds)		
Rodriguez,Francisco, Mil	31		Papelbon,Jonathan, Phi	21		Rosenthal,Trevor, StL	3		Howell,J.P., LAD	100.0	
Jansen,Kenley, LAD	29		Kimbrel,Craig, Atl	20		Cishek,Steve, Mia	2		Benoit,Joaquin, SD	96.4	
Rosenthal,Trevor, StL	28		Cishek,Steve, Mia	18		Kimbrel,Craig, Atl	2		Street,Huston, SD	96.0	
Kimbrel,Craig, Atl	25		Jansen,Kenley, LAD	14		Maness,Seth, StL	2		Marshall,Evan, Ari	95.0	
Melancon,Mark, Pit	24		Rosenthal,Trevor, StL	14		Chapman,Aroldis, Cin	1		Chapman,Aroldis, Cin	94.7	
Soriano,Rafael, Was	24		Chapman,Aroldis, Cin	13		Eveland,Dana, NYM	1		Kimbrel,Craig, Atl	92.2	
Chapman,Aroldis, Cin	22		Rodriguez,Francisco, Mil	12		Familia,Jeurys, NYM	1		Melancon,Mark, Pit	92.2	
Reed,Addison, Ari	21		Reed,Addison, Ari	11		Jansen,Kenley, LAD	1		Walden,Jordan, Atl	92.0	
Rondon,Hector, ChC	20		Street,Huston, SD	11		Rodriguez,Francisco, Mil	1		Storen,Drew, Was	91.2	
Cishek,Steve, Mia	19		2 tied with	10		Walden,Jordan, Atl	1		2 tied with	90.9	

Relief Wins			Relief Losses			Relief Games			Holds		
Dunn,Mike, Mia	10		Hoover,J.J., Cin	10		Smith,Will, Mil	78		Clippard,Tyler, Was	40	
Watson,Tony, Pit	10		Bastardo,Antonio, Phi	7		Watson,Tony, Pit	78		Watson,Tony, Pit	34	
Morris,Bryan, Pit-Mia	8		Belisle,Matt, Col	7		Familia,Jeurys, NYM	76		Smith,Will, Mil	30	
Torres,Carlos, NYM	8		Reed,Addison, Ari	7		Clippard,Tyler, Was	75		Ziegler,Brad, Ari	29	
Clippard,Tyler, Was	7		Brothers,Rex, Col	6		Dunn,Mike, Mia	75		Howell,J.P., LAD	27	
Hughes,Jared, Pit	7		Dunn,Mike, Mia	6		Ottavino,Adam, Col	75		Neshek,Pat, StL	25	
Machi,Jean, SF	7		Mejia,Jenrry, NYM	6		Brothers,Rex, Col	74		Broxton,Jonathan, Cin-Mil	23	
Neshek,Pat, StL	7		Rosenthal,Trevor, StL	6		Duke,Zach, Mil	74		Familia,Jeurys, NYM	23	
Ramos,A.J., Mia	7		Torres,Carlos, NYM	6		3 tied with	73		Dunn,Mike, Mia	22	
3 tied with	6		8 tied with	5					Wilson,Brian, LAD	22	

Relief Innings			Inherited Runners Scrd %			Relief Opp On Base Pct			Relief Opp Slugging Avg		
			(minimum 30 IR)			(minimum 50 IP)			(minimum 50 IP)		
Torres,Carlos, NYM	92.0		Howell,J.P., LAD	5.7		Benoit,Joaquin, SD	.212		Chapman,Aroldis, Cin	.172	
Maness,Seth, StL	80.1		Choate,Randy, StL	10.3		Neshek,Pat, StL	.217		Kimbrel,Craig, Atl	.189	
Familia,Jeurys, NYM	77.1		Torres,Alex, SD	11.4		Chapman,Aroldis, Cin	.234		Ramos,A.J., Mia	.236	
Watson,Tony, Pit	77.1		Blevins,Jerry, Was	11.4		Melancon,Mark, Pit	.236		Melancon,Mark, Pit	.238	
Stammen,Craig, Was	72.2		Vincent,Nick, SD	14.3		Kimbrel,Craig, Atl	.242		Papelbon,Jonathan, Phi	.246	
Diekman,Jake, Phi	71.0		Grimm,Justin, ChC	16.7		Casilla,Santiago, SF	.245		Benoit,Joaquin, SD	.247	
Melancon,Mark, Pit	71.0		Wright,Wesley, ChC	17.9		Papelbon,Jonathan, Phi	.254		Casilla,Santiago, SF	.247	
Clippard,Tyler, Was	70.1		Torres,Carlos, NYM	18.2		Rodriguez,Francisco, Mil	.256		Walden,Jordan, Atl	.249	
Rosenthal,Trevor, StL	70.1		Hughes,Jared, Pit	18.9		Clippard,Tyler, Was	.257		Strop,Pedro, ChC	.252	
Grimm,Justin, ChC	69.0		Duke,Zach, Mil	19.5		Romo,Sergio, SF	.259		Neshek,Pat, StL	.263	

2014 National League Pitching Leaders

Relief Opp BA Vs LHB
(minimum 50 AB)

Choate,Randy, StL	.093
Matsuzaka,Daisuke, NYM	.138
Kimbrel,Craig, Atl	.147
Varvaro,Anthony, Atl	.149
Ramos,A.J., Mia	.151
Giles,Ken, Phi	.152
Benoit,Joaquin, SD	.157
Blevins,Jerry, Was	.160
Melancon,Mark, Pit	.164
Smith,Will, Mil	.167

Relief Opp BA Vs RHB
(minimum 50 AB)

Chapman,Aroldis, Cin	.118
Clippard,Tyler, Was	.130
Street,Huston, SD	.131
Familia,Jeurys, NYM	.134
Kimbrel,Craig, Atl	.135
Benoit,Joaquin, SD	.144
Frias,Carlos, LAD	.151
Carlyle,Buddy, NYM	.158
Hoover,J.J., Cin	.159
Casilla,Santiago, SF	.161

Relief Opp Batting Average
(minimum 50 IP)

Chapman,Aroldis, Cin	.121
Kimbrel,Craig, Atl	.142
Benoit,Joaquin, SD	.151
Ramos,A.J., Mia	.164
Casilla,Santiago, SF	.177
Neshek,Pat, StL	.183
Walden,Jordan, Atl	.186
Strop,Pedro, ChC	.187
Bastardo,Antonio, Phi	.188
Clippard,Tyler, Was	.188

Relief Earned Run Average
(minimum 50 IP)

Storen,Drew, Was	1.12
Benoit,Joaquin, SD	1.49
Kimbrel,Craig, Atl	1.61
Watson,Tony, Pit	1.63
Casilla,Santiago, SF	1.70
Morris,Bryan, Pit-Mia	1.82
Neshek,Pat, StL	1.87
Melancon,Mark, Pit	1.90
Hughes,Jared, Pit	1.96
Chapman,Aroldis, Cin	2.00

Rel OBP 1st Batter Faced
(minimum 40 BF)

Edgin,Josh, NYM	.149
Vincent,Nick, SD	.164
Neshek,Pat, StL	.183
Walden,Jordan, Atl	.190
Duke,Zach, Mil	.216
Gutierrez,Juan, SF	.217
Rodriguez,Francisco, Mil	.217
Quackenbush,Kevin, SD	.218
Blevins,Jerry, Was	.219
Storen,Drew, Was	.219

Rel Opp BA w/ Runners On
(minimum 50 IP)

Chapman,Aroldis, Cin	.125
Benoit,Joaquin, SD	.127
Quackenbush,Kevin, SD	.165
Thayer,Dale, SD	.168
Rodriguez,Francisco, Mil	.171
Strop,Pedro, ChC	.178
Hughes,Jared, Pit	.180
Wilson,Justin, Pit	.182
Casilla,Santiago, SF	.188
Kimbrel,Craig, Atl	.189

Relief Opp BA w/ RISP
(minimum 50 IP)

Chapman,Aroldis, Cin	.111
Benoit,Joaquin, SD	.114
Hughes,Jared, Pit	.127
Rodriguez,Francisco, Mil	.143
Quackenbush,Kevin, SD	.167
Martinez,Carlos, StL	.169
Thayer,Dale, SD	.169
Familia,Jeurys, NYM	.173
Varvaro,Anthony, Atl	.175
Jansen,Kenley, LAD	.176

Fastest Avg Fastball-Relief
(minimum 50 IP)

Chapman,Aroldis, Cin	100.3
Kimbrel,Craig, Atl	97.1
Diekman,Jake, Phi	96.9
Martinez,Carlos, StL	96.9
Rosenthal,Trevor, StL	96.8
Familia,Jeurys, NYM	96.4
Walden,Jordan, Atl	95.9
Rondon,Hector, ChC	95.7
Carpenter,David, Atl	95.6
Morris,Bryan, Pit-Mia	95.4

Fastest Average Fastball
(minimum 162 IP)

Peralta,Wily, Mil	95.8
Eovaldi,Nathan, Mia	95.7
Wheeler,Zack, NYM	95.0
Strasburg,Stephen, Was	94.8
Simon,Alfredo, Cin	94.0
Zimmermann,Jordan, Was	93.8
Alvarez,Henderson, Mia	93.5
Miller,Shelby, StL	93.5
Ross,Tyson, SD	93.2
Volquez,Edinson, Pit	93.2

Slowest Average Fastball
(minimum 162 IP)

Collmenter,Josh, Ari	86.0
Haren,Dan, LAD	87.7
Fister,Doug, Was	87.9
Stults,Eric, SD	87.9
Wood,Travis, ChC	88.3
Niese,Jon, NYM	88.5
Colon,Bartolo, NYM	88.7
Hudson,Tim, SF	89.0
Harang,Aaron, Atl	89.3
Lohse,Kyle, Mil	89.4

Pitches 100+ Velocity

Chapman,Aroldis, Cin	473
Martinez,Carlos, StL	44
Cordier,Erik, SF	32
Giles,Ken, Phi	22
Capps,Carter, Mia	13
Rosenthal,Trevor, StL	13
Diekman,Jake, Phi	9
Kimbrel,Craig, Atl	8
Eovaldi,Nathan, Mia	3
Strickland,Hunter, SF	2

Pitches 95+ Velocity

Peralta,Wily, Mil	1768
Eovaldi,Nathan, Mia	1607
Wheeler,Zack, NYM	1357
Strasburg,Stephen, Was	1210
Cole,Gerrit, Pit	1101
Samardzija,Jeff, ChC	956
Rosenthal,Trevor, StL	917
Diekman,Jake, Phi	880
Familia,Jeurys, NYM	861
Morris,Bryan, Pit-Mia	798

Pitches Less Than 80 MPH

Estrada,Marco, Mil	990
Wainwright,Adam, StL	893
Stults,Eric, SD	733
Collmenter,Josh, Ari	645
Arroyo,Bronson, Ari	619
Beckett,Josh, LAD	584
Lohse,Kyle, Mil	583
Morton,Charlie, Pit	564
Vogelsong,Ryan, SF	560
Cosart,Jarred, Mia	550

Lowest % Fastballs
(minimum 162 IP)

Haren,Dan, LAD	34.9
Wainwright,Adam, StL	40.7
De La Rosa,Jorge, Col	41.0
Liriano,Francisco, Pit	42.9
Bumgarner,Madison, SF	43.5
Kendrick,Kyle, Phi	45.1
Lohse,Kyle, Mil	45.7
Vogelsong,Ryan, SF	46.6
Cueto,Johnny, Cin	47.4
Niese,Jon, NYM	49.6

Highest % Fastballs
(minimum 162 IP)

Colon,Bartolo, NYM	82.6
Lynn,Lance, StL	79.0
Miller,Shelby, StL	72.3
Zimmermann,Jordan, Was	70.3
Collmenter,Josh, Ari	70.2
Garza,Matt, Mil	67.5
Roark,Tanner, Was	66.8
Peralta,Wily, Mil	65.7
Hernandez,Roberto, Phi-LAD	64.3
Fister,Doug, Was	63.7

Highest % Curveballs
(minimum 162 IP)

Burnett,A.J., Phi	33.1
Wainwright,Adam, StL	27.6
Volquez,Edinson, Pit	25.9
Wood,Alex, Atl	22.7
Koehler,Tom, Mia	21.5
Miller,Shelby, StL	19.2
Gallardo,Yovani, Mil	19.1
Vogelsong,Ryan, SF	18.6
Strasburg,Stephen, Was	17.2
Niese,Jon, NYM	16.9

2014 National League Pitching Leaders

Highest % Changeups
(minimum 162 IP)

De La Rosa,Jorge, Col	26.2
Liriano,Francisco, Pit	25.3
Hernandez,Roberto, Phi-LAD	24.5
Stults,Eric, SD	23.9
Alvarez,Henderson, Mia	23.2
Collmenter,Josh, Ari	23.1
Hamels,Cole, Phi	22.4
Strasburg,Stephen, Was	20.5
Volquez,Edinson, Pit	18.7
Kendrick,Kyle, Phi	18.7

Highest % Sliders
(minimum 162 IP)

Ross,Tyson, SD	41.2
Bumgarner,Madison, SF	34.9
Santana,Ervin, Atl	32.9
Liriano,Francisco, Pit	31.8
Lohse,Kyle, Mil	29.7
Kershaw,Clayton, LAD	29.4
Peralta,Wily, Mil	29.3
Miley,Wade, Ari	25.8
Eovaldi,Nathan, Mia	24.7
Gallardo,Yovani, Mil	24.5

Balks

Morales,Franklin, Col	4
Perez,Oliver, Ari	3
Cingrani,Tony, Cin	2
Hatcher,Chris, Mia	2
Kershaw,Clayton, LAD	2
Martin,Chris, Col	2
39 tied with	1

Strikeout/Hit Ratio
(minimum 50 IP)

Chapman,Aroldis, Cin	5.05
Kimbrel,Craig, Atl	3.17
Benoit,Joaquin, SD	2.29
Ramos,A.J., Mia	2.03
Fernandez,Jose, Mia	1.94
Bastardo,Antonio, Phi	1.88
Walden,Jordan, Atl	1.88
Jansen,Kenley, LAD	1.84
Strop,Pedro, ChC	1.78
Clippard,Tyler, Was	1.74

Opp OPS vs Fastballs
(minimum 251 BF)

Cueto,Johnny, Cin	.523
Arrieta,Jake, ChC	.536
Kershaw,Clayton, LAD	.548
Cashner,Andrew, SD	.550
Bumgarner,Madison, SF	.573
deGrom,Jacob, NYM	.578
Collmenter,Josh, Ari	.602
Zimmermann,Jordan, Was	.615
Fister,Doug, Was	.618
2 tied with	.627

Opp OPS vs Curveballs
(minimum 100 BF)

Wainwright,Adam, StL	.480
Beckett,Josh, LAD	.567
Koehler,Tom, Mia	.582
Wood,Alex, Atl	.590
Volquez,Edinson, Pit	.596
Wheeler,Zack, NYM	.603
Morton,Charlie, Pit	.606
Vogelsong,Ryan, SF	.645
Strasburg,Stephen, Was	.672
Harang,Aaron, Atl	.680

Opp OPS vs Changeups
(minimum 100 BF)

Cueto,Johnny, Cin	.389
Gee,Dillon, NYM	.472
Strasburg,Stephen, Was	.475
Liriano,Francisco, Pit	.476
Hamels,Cole, Phi	.500
Clippard,Tyler, Was	.512
Buchanan,David, Phi	.535
Greinke,Zack, LAD	.572
Gonzalez,Gio, Was	.617
De La Rosa,Jorge, Col	.618

Opp OPS vs Sliders
(minimum 64 BF)

Petit,Yusmeiro, SF	.437
Neshek,Pat, StL	.441
Kershaw,Clayton, LAD	.467
Strop,Pedro, ChC	.480
Ramos,A.J., Mia	.504
De Fratus,Justin, Phi	.505
Samardzija,Jeff, ChC	.508
Leake,Mike, Cin	.509
Hammel,Jason, ChC	.512
Smith,Will, Mil	.512

Earned Runs

Burnett,A.J., Phi	109
Kendrick,Kyle, Phi	102
Jackson,Edwin, ChC	99
Eovaldi,Nathan, Mia	97
Miley,Wade, Ari	97
Wood,Travis, ChC	97
Colon,Bartolo, NYM	92
Leake,Mike, Cin	88
Santana,Ervin, Atl	86
Morales,Franklin, Col	85

Hits Per Nine Innings
(minimum 162 IP)

Cueto,Johnny, Cin	6.24
Kershaw,Clayton, LAD	6.31
Liriano,Francisco, Pit	7.21
Wainwright,Adam, StL	7.30
Ross,Tyson, SD	7.59
Teheran,Julio, Atl	7.66
Hamels,Cole, Phi	7.74
Volquez,Edinson, Pit	7.75
De La Rosa,Jorge, Col	7.86
Miller,Shelby, StL	7.87

2014 American League Fielding Leaders

2B Pivot %
(minimum 98 G)

Schoop,Jonathan, Bal	0.797
Beckham,Gordon, CWS-LAA	0.706
Kendrick,Howie, LAA	0.694
Dozier,Brian, Min	0.688
Odor,Rougned, Tex	0.679
Cano,Robinson, Sea	0.670
Pedroia,Dustin, Bos	0.663
Altuve,Jose, Hou	0.658
Kinsler,Ian, Det	0.602
Kipnis,Jason, Cle	0.536

SS Pivot %
(minimum 98 G)

Andrus,Elvis, Tex	0.731
Ramirez,Alexei, CWS	0.690
Escobar,Alcides, KC	0.679
Aybar,Erick, LAA	0.667
Hardy,J.J., Bal	0.643
Lowrie,Jed, Oak	0.603
Reyes,Jose, Tor	0.576
Escobar,Eduardo, Min	0.550
Miller,Brad, Sea	0.521
Bogaerts,Xander, Bos	0.458

Highest Pct CS by Catchers
(minimum 600 INN or 50 SBA)

Joseph,Caleb, Bal	38.2
Chirinos,Robinson, Tex	36.2
McCann,Brian, NYY	31.0
Gomes,Yan, Cle	29.0
Perez,Salvador, KC	28.8
Avila,Alex, Det	26.8
Flowers,Tyler, CWS	26.2
Zunino,Mike, Sea	26.0
Molina,Jose, TB	24.0
Castro,Jason, Hou	20.6

Lowest Pct CS by Catchers
(minimum 600 INN or 50 SBA)

Norris,Derek, Oak	11.8
Suzuki,Kurt, Min	14.7
Navarro,Dioner, Tor	15.9
Hanigan,Ryan, TB	16.7
Iannetta,Chris, LAA	19.7
Conger,Hank, LAA	19.7
Castro,Jason, Hou	20.6
Molina,Jose, TB	24.0
Zunino,Mike, Sea	26.0
Flowers,Tyler, CWS	26.2

2B Double Play %
(minimum 98 G)

Schoop,Jonathan, Bal	0.667
Odor,Rougned, Tex	0.653
Cano,Robinson, Sea	0.590
Beckham,Gordon, CWS-LAA	0.585
Kendrick,Howie, LAA	0.553
Kinsler,Ian, Det	0.550
Altuve,Jose, Hou	0.544
Pedroia,Dustin, Bos	0.540
Kipnis,Jason, Cle	0.532
Dozier,Brian, Min	0.523

3B Double Play %
(minimum 98 G)

Seager,Kyle, Sea	0.524
Donaldson,Josh, Oak	0.506
Freese,David, LAA	0.447
Gillaspie,Conor, CWS	0.424
Beltre,Adrian, Tex	0.420
Longoria,Evan, TB	0.411
Plouffe,Trevor, Min	0.411
Dominguez,Matt, Hou	0.333
Castellanos,Nick, Det	0.300
Moustakas,Mike, KC	0.265

SS Double Play %
(minimum 98 G)

Ramirez,Alexei, CWS	0.685
Andrus,Elvis, Tex	0.669
Hardy,J.J., Bal	0.642
Aybar,Erick, LAA	0.612
Reyes,Jose, Tor	0.573
Escobar,Alcides, KC	0.564
Escobar,Eduardo, Min	0.540
Lowrie,Jed, Oak	0.524
Miller,Brad, Sea	0.518
Bogaerts,Xander, Bos	0.505

Errors

Donaldson,Josh, Oak	23
Bogaerts,Xander, Bos	20
Miller,Brad, Sea	19
Moustakas,Mike, KC	19
Reyes,Jose, Tor	19
Andrus,Elvis, Tex	18
Chisenhall,Lonnie, Cle	18
Villar,Jonathan, Hou	18
Escobar,Alcides, KC	16
Escobar,Yunel, TB	16

Fielding Errors

Moustakas,Mike, KC	11
Semien,Marcus, CWS	11
Singleton,Jon, Hou	11
Villar,Jonathan, Hou	11
Andrus,Elvis, Tex	10
Beckham,Gordon, CWS-LAA	10
Castellanos,Nick, Det	10
Cabrera,Asdrubal, Cle	9
Lowrie,Jed, Oak	9
Swisher,Nick, Cle	9

Throwing Errors

Donaldson,Josh, Oak	17
Gomes,Yan, Cle	13
Bogaerts,Xander, Bos	12
Miller,Brad, Sea	11
Reyes,Jose, Tor	11
Chisenhall,Lonnie, Cle	10
Dozier,Brian, Min	9
Escobar,Yunel, TB	9
6 tied with	8

Range Factor for 2B
(minimum 98 games)

Beckham,Gordon, CWS-LAA	5.16
Sogard,Eric, Oak	5.01
Pedroia,Dustin, Bos	4.94
Dozier,Brian, Min	4.87
Schoop,Jonathan, Bal	4.84
Kinsler,Ian, Det	4.82
Altuve,Jose, Hou	4.80
Cano,Robinson, Sea	4.75
Odor,Rougned, Tex	4.52
Kipnis,Jason, Cle	4.42

Range Factor for 3B
(minimum 98 games)

Donaldson,Josh, Oak	3.13
Plouffe,Trevor, Min	2.71
Beltre,Adrian, Tex	2.69
Dominguez,Matt, Hou	2.67
Moustakas,Mike, KC	2.65
Seager,Kyle, Sea	2.65
Gillaspie,Conor, CWS	2.50
Longoria,Evan, TB	2.49
Chisenhall,Lonnie, Cle	2.24
Freese,David, LAA	2.15

Range Factor for SS
(minimum 98 games)

Ramirez,Alexei, CWS	4.45
Andrus,Elvis, Tex	4.18
Hardy,J.J., Bal	4.16
Escobar,Eduardo, Min	4.13
Escobar,Alcides, KC	4.10
Bogaerts,Xander, Bos	4.03
Miller,Brad, Sea	4.02
Lowrie,Jed, Oak	3.85
Reyes,Jose, Tor	3.84
Aybar,Erick, LAA	3.65

2014 National League Fielding Leaders

2B Pivot %
(minimum 98 G)

Wong,Kolten, StL	0.763
LeMahieu,DJ, Col	0.691
Hill,Aaron, Ari	0.667
Walker,Neil, Pit	0.663
Gordon,Dee, LAD	0.633
Murphy,Daniel, NYM	0.610
Phillips,Brandon, Cin	0.577
Gennett,Scooter, Mil	0.565
Utley,Chase, Phi	0.551
Gyorko,Jedd, SD	0.517

SS Pivot %
(minimum 98 G)

Simmons,Andrelton, Atl	0.740
Castro,Starlin, ChC	0.729
Ramirez,Hanley, LAD	0.667
Hechavarria,Adeiny, Mia	0.633
Crawford,Brandon, SF	0.625
Cozart,Zack, Cin	0.618
Tejada,Ruben, NYM	0.603
Peralta,Jhonny, StL	0.592
Mercer,Jordy, Pit	0.578
Desmond,Ian, Was	0.548

Highest Pct CS by Catchers
(minimum 600 INN or 50 SBA)

Molina,Yadier, StL	46.5
Ramos,Wilson, Was	34.8
Rivera,Rene, SD	33.3
Martin,Russell, Pit	32.2
Castillo,Welington, ChC	31.3
Mesoraco,Devin, Cin	23.9
Montero,Miguel, Ari	23.8
Lucroy,Jonathan, Mil	22.4
Posey,Buster, SF	22.4
Ruiz,Carlos, Phi	22.1

Lowest Pct CS by Catchers
(minimum 600 INN or 50 SBA)

Grandal,Yasmani, SD	10.9
Baker,John, ChC	12.3
d'Arnaud,Travis, NYM	13.4
Rosario,Wilin, Col	14.0
Saltalamacchia,J, Mia	17.2
Gattis,Evan, Atl	19.7
Ellis,A.J., LAD	21.3
Ruiz,Carlos, Phi	22.1
Posey,Buster, SF	22.4
Lucroy,Jonathan, Mil	22.4

2B Double Play %
(minimum 98 G)

Wong,Kolten, StL	0.602
Walker,Neil, Pit	0.540
Phillips,Brandon, Cin	0.520
LeMahieu,DJ, Col	0.514
Gordon,Dee, LAD	0.497
Murphy,Daniel, NYM	0.482
Hill,Aaron, Ari	0.472
Gennett,Scooter, Mil	0.453
Gyorko,Jedd, SD	0.392
Utley,Chase, Phi	0.386

3B Double Play %
(minimum 98 G)

Uribe,Juan, LAD	0.512
Rendon,Anthony, Was	0.483
Arenado,Nolan, Col	0.481
McGehee,Casey, Mia	0.431
Prado,Martin, Ari	0.405
Alvarez,Pedro, Pit	0.377
Carpenter,Matt, StL	0.355
Frazier,Todd, Cin	0.350
Sandoval,Pablo, SF	0.343
Wright,David, NYM	0.316

SS Double Play %
(minimum 98 G)

Simmons,Andrelton, Atl	0.676
Peralta,Jhonny, StL	0.645
Castro,Starlin, ChC	0.644
Desmond,Ian, Was	0.611
Crawford,Brandon, SF	0.597
Mercer,Jordy, Pit	0.589
Tejada,Ruben, NYM	0.584
Ramirez,Hanley, LAD	0.575
Cozart,Zack, Cin	0.563
Hechavarria,Adeiny, Mia	0.548

Errors

Alvarez,Pedro, Pit	25
Desmond,Ian, Was	24
Crawford,Brandon, SF	21
Asche,Cody, Phi	16
Carpenter,Matt, StL	16
Ramirez,Hanley, LAD	16
Segura,Jean, Mil	16
6 tied with	15

Fielding Errors

Carpenter,Matt, StL	14
Asche,Cody, Phi	12
Crawford,Brandon, SF	12
Desmond,Ian, Was	11
Murphy,Daniel, NYM	11
Mercer,Jordy, Pit	10
Wright,David, NYM	10
Howard,Ryan, Phi	9
Rutledge,Josh, Col	9
10 tied with	8

Throwing Errors

Alvarez,Pedro, Pit	24
Saltalamacchia,J, Mia	14
Desmond,Ian, Was	13
Rendon,Anthony, Was	11
Ramirez,Hanley, LAD	10
Crawford,Brandon, SF	9
Hechavarria,Adeiny, Mia	9
Montero,Miguel, Ari	9
5 tied with	8

Range Factor for 2B
(minimum 98 games)

LeMahieu,DJ, Col	5.11
Hill,Aaron, Ari	4.96
Utley,Chase, Phi	4.87
Walker,Neil, Pit	4.80
Wong,Kolten, StL	4.76
Gordon,Dee, LAD	4.58
Phillips,Brandon, Cin	4.46
Gyorko,Jedd, SD	4.41
Murphy,Daniel, NYM	4.39
Gennett,Scooter, Mil	4.38

Range Factor for 3B
(minimum 98 games)

Alvarez,Pedro, Pit	3.30
Arenado,Nolan, Col	3.26
Uribe,Juan, LAD	2.83
Rendon,Anthony, Was	2.67
Sandoval,Pablo, SF	2.64
Valbuena,Luis, ChC	2.60
Asche,Cody, Phi	2.58
Prado,Martin, Ari	2.57
Frazier,Todd, Cin	2.49
Carpenter,Matt, StL	2.48

Range Factor for SS
(minimum 98 games)

Tejada,Ruben, NYM	4.66
Segura,Jean, Mil	4.56
Hechavarria,Adeiny, Mia	4.44
Simmons,Andrelton, Atl	4.43
Mercer,Jordy, Pit	4.40
Crawford,Brandon, SF	4.34
Cozart,Zack, Cin	4.27
Rollins,Jimmy, Phi	4.27
Peralta,Jhonny, StL	4.14
Castro,Starlin, ChC	4.05

2014 Active Career Batting Leaders

Batting Average (minimum 1000 PA)		On Base Percentage (minimum 1000 PA)		Slugging Average (minimum 1000 PA)		Home Runs	
Cabrera,Miguel	.320	Votto,Joey	.417	Pujols,Albert	.588	Rodriguez,Alex	654
Mauer,Joe	.319	Pujols,Albert	.403	Cabrera,Miguel	.564	Pujols,Albert	520
Suzuki,Ichiro	.317	Mauer,Joe	.401	Rodriguez,Alex	.558	Ortiz,David	466
Pujols,Albert	.317	Giambi,Jason	.399	Braun,Ryan	.550	Dunn,Adam	462
Votto,Joey	.310	Cabrera,Miguel	.396	Trout,Mike	.549	Giambi,Jason	440
Cano,Robinson	.310	Trout,Mike	.395	Ortiz,David	.547	Konerko,Paul	439
Jeter,Derek	.310	Abreu,Bobby	.395	Stanton,Giancarlo	.540	Soriano,Alfonso	412
Posey,Buster	.308	Fielder,Prince	.388	Votto,Joey	.533	Beltre,Adrian	395
Holliday,Matt	.308	Puig,Yasiel	.386	Howard,Ryan	.526	Cabrera,Miguel	390
Braun,Ryan	.306	McCutchen,Andrew	.385	Goldschmidt,Paul	.523	Beltran,Carlos	373

Games		At Bats		Hits		Total Bases	
Jeter,Derek	2747	Jeter,Derek	11195	Jeter,Derek	3465	Rodriguez,Alex	5480
Rodriguez,Alex	2568	Rodriguez,Alex	9818	Rodriguez,Alex	2939	Jeter,Derek	4921
Abreu,Bobby	2425	Beltre,Adrian	9145	Suzuki,Ichiro	2844	Pujols,Albert	4672
Beltre,Adrian	2424	Suzuki,Ichiro	8964	Beltre,Adrian	2604	Beltre,Adrian	4379
Konerko,Paul	2349	Rollins,Jimmy	8628	Pujols,Albert	2519	Ortiz,David	4140
Giambi,Jason	2260	Abreu,Bobby	8480	Abreu,Bobby	2470	Konerko,Paul	4083
Hunter,Torii	2233	Konerko,Paul	8393	Konerko,Paul	2340	Beltran,Carlos	4064
Suzuki,Ichiro	2204	Hunter,Torii	8336	Hunter,Torii	2327	Abreu,Bobby	4026
Beltran,Carlos	2173	Beltran,Carlos	8271	Beltran,Carlos	2322	Hunter,Torii	3874
Ibanez,Raul	2161	Pujols,Albert	7943	Rollins,Jimmy	2306	Soriano,Alfonso	3874

Doubles		Triples		Runs Scored		RBI	
Abreu,Bobby	574	Crawford,Carl	120	Jeter,Derek	1923	Rodriguez,Alex	1969
Pujols,Albert	561	Reyes,Jose	115	Rodriguez,Alex	1919	Pujols,Albert	1603
Ortiz,David	547	Rollins,Jimmy	111	Pujols,Albert	1514	Ortiz,David	1533
Jeter,Derek	544	Suzuki,Ichiro	85	Abreu,Bobby	1453	Giambi,Jason	1441
Beltre,Adrian	528	Granderson,Curtis	82	Beltran,Carlos	1392	Konerko,Paul	1412
Rodriguez,Alex	519	Beltran,Carlos	77	Rollins,Jimmy	1325	Beltre,Adrian	1384
Soriano,Alfonso	481	Furcal,Rafael	69	Suzuki,Ichiro	1303	Beltran,Carlos	1376
Rollins,Jimmy	479	Victorino,Shane	68	Ortiz,David	1267	Cabrera,Miguel	1369
Hunter,Torii	476	Jeter,Derek	66	Beltre,Adrian	1256	Abreu,Bobby	1363
Beltran,Carlos	469	DeJesus,David	63	Hunter,Torii	1229	Ramirez,Aramis	1342

Walks		Intentional Walks		Hit By Pitch		Strikeouts	
Abreu,Bobby	1476	Pujols,Albert	286	Giambi,Jason	180	Dunn,Adam	2379
Giambi,Jason	1366	Cabrera,Miguel	190	Jeter,Derek	170	Rodriguez,Alex	2075
Dunn,Adam	1317	Ortiz,David	178	Rodriguez,Alex	169	Abreu,Bobby	1840
Rodriguez,Alex	1240	Suzuki,Ichiro	178	Utley,Chase	169	Jeter,Derek	1840
Ortiz,David	1162	Howard,Ryan	150	Johnson,Reed	133	Soriano,Alfonso	1803
Pujols,Albert	1115	Fielder,Prince	149	Quentin,Carlos	127	Hunter,Torii	1636
Jeter,Derek	1082	Gonzalez,Adrian	135	Weeks,Rickie	125	Howard,Ryan	1591
Beltran,Carlos	971	Dunn,Adam	122	Ramirez,Aramis	122	Pena,Carlos	1577
Konerko,Paul	921	Abreu,Bobby	115	Pierzynski,A.J.	119	Giambi,Jason	1572
Cabrera,Miguel	859	Mauer,Joe	115	Willingham,Josh	112	Ortiz,David	1569

2014 Active Career Batting Leaders

Sacrifice Hits		Sacrifice Flies		Stolen Bases		Seasons Played	
Jeter,Derek	97	Rodriguez,Alex	101	Suzuki,Ichiro	487	Giambi,Jason	20
Andrus,Elvis	87	Beltran,Carlos	94	Crawford,Carl	470	Hawkins,LaTroy	20
Chavez,Endy	86	Giambi,Jason	93	Reyes,Jose	455	Jeter,Derek	20
Dempster,Ryan	85	Pujols,Albert	90	Rollins,Jimmy	453	Rodriguez,Alex	20
Santiago,Ramon	84	Konerko,Paul	86	Abreu,Bobby	400	Ibanez,Raul	19
Arroyo,Bronson	82	Abreu,Bobby	85	Jeter,Derek	358	Wright,Jamey	19
Wolf,Randy	79	Ramirez,Aramis	82	Figgins,Chone	341	Abreu,Bobby	18
Crisp,Coco	76	Beltre,Adrian	78	Rodriguez,Alex	322	Hunter,Torii	18
Kershaw,Clayton	75	Ortiz,David	76	Furcal,Rafael	314	Konerko,Paul	18
Lohse,Kyle	72	Morneau,Justin	72	Beltran,Carlos	311	Ortiz,David	18

At Bats Per Home Run		Grounded Into DP		Highest SB Success Pct		Lowest SB Success Pct	
(minimum 1000 AB)				(minimum 100 SBA)		(minimum 100 SBA)	
Howard,Ryan	14.7	Pujols,Albert	297	Utley,Chase	88.5	DeJesus,David	51.2
Stanton,Giancarlo	14.9	Jeter,Derek	287	Trout,Mike	87.9	Castro,Starlin	63.6
Dunn,Adam	14.9	Konerko,Paul	282	Werth,Jayson	87.2	Fowler,Dexter	67.1
Rodriguez,Alex	15.0	Hunter,Torii	248	Beltran,Carlos	86.4	Hunter,Torii	67.2
Pujols,Albert	15.3	Rodriguez,Alex	240	Dyson,Jarrod	85.7	Hart,Corey	68.0
Carter,Chris	15.8	Cabrera,Miguel	234	McLouth,Nate	84.7	Pence,Hunter	68.0
Ortiz,David	16.3	Beltre,Adrian	231	Ellsbury,Jacoby	84.6	De Aza,Alejandro	68.7
Davis,Chris	16.4	Ramirez,Aramis	210	Kipnis,Jason	83.8	Johnson,Kelly	69.8
Giambi,Jason	16.5	Pierzynski,A.J.	209	Getz,Chris	83.2	Martin,Russell	69.9
Reynolds,Mark	16.9	Ortiz,David	198	Escobar,Alcides	83.1	Morgan,Nyjer	70.2

Strikeouts / Walks Ratio		At Bats Per GIDP		OPS		Secondary Average	
(minimum 1000 AB)		(minimum 1000 AB)		(minimum 1000 PA)		(minimum 1000 PA)	
Pujols,Albert	.813	Bourn,Michael	153.2	Pujols,Albert	.991	Dunn,Adam	.453
Hanigan,Ryan	.900	Stubbs,Drew	144.9	Cabrera,Miguel	.960	Trout,Mike	.442
Mauer,Joe	.976	Gordon,Dee	136.7	Votto,Joey	.950	Giambi,Jason	.431
Pedroia,Dustin	1.013	Granderson,Curtis	125.1	Trout,Mike	.945	Pujols,Albert	.424
Aoki,Nori	1.021	Bonifacio,Emilio	117.0	Rodriguez,Alex	.942	Stanton,Giancarlo	.421
Callaspo,Alberto	1.028	Suzuki,Ichiro	114.9	Ortiz,David	.926	Rodriguez,Alex	.418
Martinez,Victor	1.096	Schafer,Jordan	111.2	Braun,Ryan	.918	Ortiz,David	.417
Jaso,John	1.131	Young,Eric	109.2	Giambi,Jason	.916	Votto,Joey	.416
Johnson,Dan	1.132	Blackmon,Charlie	105.0	Fielder,Prince	.910	Bautista,Jose	.410
Giambi,Jason	1.151	Saunders,Michael	100.9	Holliday,Matt	.908	Abreu,Bobby	.405

Highest Strikeout per PA		Lowest Strikeout per PA		Plate Appearances		At Bats Per RBI	
(minimum 1000 PA)		(minimum 1000 PA)				(minimum 1000 AB)	
Flowers,Tyler	.348	Aoki,Nori	.080	Jeter,Derek	12602	Howard,Ryan	4.6
Francisco,Juan	.344	Callaspo,Alberto	.090	Rodriguez,Alex	11344	Ortiz,David	4.9
Carter,Chris	.336	Revere,Ben	.091	Abreu,Bobby	10081	Pujols,Albert	5.0
Reynolds,Mark	.319	Molina,Yadier	.092	Beltre,Adrian	10001	Rodriguez,Alex	5.0
Davis,Chris	.310	Frandsen,Kevin	.093	Suzuki,Ichiro	9663	Cabrera,Miguel	5.0
Saltalamacchia,J	.300	Pedroia,Dustin	.093	Rollins,Jimmy	9511	Giambi,Jason	5.0
Stubbs,Drew	.297	Simmons,Andrelton	.096	Konerko,Paul	9505	Teixeira,Mark	5.2
Alvarez,Pedro	.296	Pujols,Albert	.098	Beltran,Carlos	9398	Fielder,Prince	5.5
Wallace,Brett	.295	Suzuki,Ichiro	.098	Pujols,Albert	9241	Hamilton,Josh	5.5
2 tied with	.286	Reyes,Jose	.103	Hunter,Torii	9125	Braun,Ryan	5.6

2014 Active Career Pitching Leaders

Earned Run Average (minimum 750 IP)		Winning Percentage (minimum 100 Decisions)		Opponent Batting Average (minimum 750 IP)		Baserunners Per 9 IP (minimum 750 IP)	
Kershaw,Clayton	2.48	Kershaw,Clayton	.667	Rodriguez,Francisco	.205	Kershaw,Clayton	9.67
Rodriguez,Francisco	2.73	Weaver,Jered	.655	Nathan,Joe	.206	Nathan,Joe	10.29
Nathan,Joe	2.89	Scherzer,Max	.645	Kershaw,Clayton	.209	Bumgarner,Madison	10.49
Wainwright,Adam	3.01	Wainwright,Adam	.643	Young,Chris	.226	Hamels,Cole	10.50
Bumgarner,Madison	3.06	Sabathia,CC	.636	Cain,Matt	.227	Price,David	10.52
Hernandez,Felix	3.07	Lester,Jon	.634	Benoit,Joaquin	.228	Weaver,Jered	10.55
Price,David	3.21	Hudson,Tim	.633	Gonzalez,Gio	.232	Rodriguez,Francisco	10.61
Zimmermann,Jordan	3.24	Verlander,Justin	.631	Latos,Mat	.233	Zimmermann,Jordan	10.68
Cueto,Johnny	3.27	Price,David	.628	Price,David	.234	Latos,Mat	10.69
Hamels,Cole	3.27	Lee,Cliff	.611	Lincecum,Tim	.234	Wainwright,Adam	10.70

Games		Games Started		Complete Games		Shutouts	
Hawkins,LaTroy	1000	Buehrle,Mark	461	Sabathia,CC	37	Hudson,Tim	13
Farnsworth,Kyle	893	Hudson,Tim	457	Colon,Bartolo	35	Colon,Bartolo	12
Rodriguez,Francisco	799	Colon,Bartolo	436	Buehrle,Mark	29	Lee,Cliff	12
Nathan,Joe	776	Sabathia,CC	423	Lee,Cliff	29	Sabathia,CC	12
Affeldt,Jeremy	722	Burnett,A.J.	404	Hudson,Tim	26	Burnett,A.J.	10
Qualls,Chad	721	Lohse,Kyle	394	Burnett,A.J.	24	7 tied with	9
Wright,Jamey	719	Wolf,Randy	372	Hernandez,Felix	23		
Lopez,Javier	694	Arroyo,Bronson	369	Shields,James	22		
Thornton,Matt	670	Lackey,John	354	Wainwright,Adam	21		
Frasor,Jason	647	Harang,Aaron	352	Verlander,Justin	20		

Wins		Losses		Innings Pitched		Batters Faced	
Hudson,Tim	214	Buehrle,Mark	152	Buehrle,Mark	3084.2	Buehrle,Mark	12878
Sabathia,CC	208	Burnett,A.J.	150	Hudson,Tim	3003.0	Hudson,Tim	12480
Colon,Bartolo	204	Colon,Bartolo	141	Sabathia,CC	2821.1	Colon,Bartolo	11773
Buehrle,Mark	199	Dempster,Ryan	133	Colon,Bartolo	2786.0	Sabathia,CC	11739
Burnett,A.J.	155	Arroyo,Bronson	131	Burnett,A.J.	2567.1	Burnett,A.J.	10966
Lackey,John	152	Wright,Jamey	130	Dempster,Ryan	2387.0	Dempster,Ryan	10412
Verlander,Justin	152	Harang,Aaron	128	Lohse,Kyle	2370.0	Lohse,Kyle	10126
Arroyo,Bronson	145	Lohse,Kyle	128	Arroyo,Bronson	2364.2	Arroyo,Bronson	10016
Lee,Cliff	143	Hudson,Tim	124	Wolf,Randy	2293.2	Wolf,Randy	9816
2 tied with	142	Haren,Dan	122	Lackey,John	2263.1	Lackey,John	9655

Strikeouts		Walks Allowed		Hit Batters		Wild Pitches	
Sabathia,CC	2437	Dempster,Ryan	1071	Wright,Jamey	155	Burnett,A.J.	155
Burnett,A.J.	2370	Burnett,A.J.	1051	Burnett,A.J.	132	Hernandez,Felix	116
Colon,Bartolo	2101	Wright,Jamey	978	Hudson,Tim	117	Lackey,John	105
Dempster,Ryan	2075	Hudson,Tim	880	Lackey,John	108	Lincecum,Tim	99
Peavy,Jake	2027	Sabathia,CC	844	Arroyo,Bronson	103	Haren,Dan	93
Hudson,Tim	2016	Colon,Bartolo	832	Wolf,Randy	102	Wright,Jamey	87
Hernandez,Felix	1951	Wolf,Randy	816	Dempster,Ryan	91	Jackson,Edwin	83
Beckett,Josh	1901	Buehrle,Mark	701	Sabathia,CC	89	Dempster,Ryan	80
Haren,Dan	1881	Perez,Oliver	688	Santana,Ervin	84	Hudson,Tim	80
Verlander,Justin	1830	Harang,Aaron	661	2 tied with	83	Jimenez,Ubaldo	79

2014 Active Career Pitching Leaders

Saves	
Nathan,Joe	376
Rodriguez,Francisco	348
Papelbon,Jonathan	325
Valverde,Jose	288
Street,Huston	275
Rodney,Fernando	220
Soriano,Rafael	207
Putz,J.J.	189
Kimbrel,Craig	186
Soria,Joakim	178

Save Pct	
(minimum 50 Save Ops)	
Holland,Greg	91.1
Kimbrel,Craig	90.7
Cishek,Steve	90.1
Nathan,Joe	89.3
Soria,Joakim	89.0
Feliz,Neftali	88.8
Chapman,Aroldis	88.3
Papelbon,Jonathan	88.1
Valverde,Jose	87.8
Frieri,Ernesto	87.7

Home Runs Allowed	
Buehrle,Mark	339
Colon,Bartolo	330
Arroyo,Bronson	324
Wolf,Randy	291
Lohse,Kyle	283
Haren,Dan	274
Harang,Aaron	272
Dempster,Ryan	267
Sabathia,CC	265
Chen,Bruce	254

Strikeouts Per 9 IP	
(minimum 750 IP)	
Rodriguez,Francisco	10.83
Scherzer,Max	9.59
Nathan,Joe	9.48
Lincecum,Tim	9.44
Kershaw,Clayton	9.44
Perez,Oliver	9.34
Liriano,Francisco	9.16
Benoit,Joaquin	8.92
Gonzalez,Gio	8.86
Farnsworth,Kyle	8.77

Opp On-Base Percentage	
(minimum 750 IP)	
Kershaw,Clayton	.273
Nathan,Joe	.282
Price,David	.288
Weaver,Jered	.288
Rodriguez,Francisco	.288
Bumgarner,Madison	.289
Hamels,Cole	.289
Latos,Mat	.292
Zimmermann,Jordan	.292
Kuroda,Hiroki	.293

Opp Slugging Average	
(minimum 750 IP)	
Kershaw,Clayton	.308
Rodriguez,Francisco	.331
Nathan,Joe	.331
Hernandez,Felix	.350
Gonzalez,Gio	.354
Wainwright,Adam	.357
Wilson,C.J.	.357
Price,David	.360
Johnson,Josh	.361
Lincecum,Tim	.363

Hits Per Nine Innings	
(minimum 750 IP)	
Rodriguez,Francisco	6.72
Nathan,Joe	6.73
Kershaw,Clayton	6.76
Cain,Matt	7.54
Young,Chris	7.57
Benoit,Joaquin	7.63
Gonzalez,Gio	7.79
Lincecum,Tim	7.83
Latos,Mat	7.84
Price,David	7.89

Home Runs Per Nine IP	
(minimum 750 IP)	
Kershaw,Clayton	0.54
Wainwright,Adam	0.61
Billingsley,Chad	0.67
Johnson,Josh	0.67
Hernandez,Felix	0.70
Sanchez,Anibal	0.70
Hudson,Tim	0.70
Affeldt,Jeremy	0.71
Masterson,Justin	0.71
Wilson,C.J.	0.72

Strikeouts / Walks Ratio	
(minimum 750 IP)	
Haren,Dan	4.07
Zimmermann,Jordan	4.06
Lee,Cliff	3.93
Bumgarner,Madison	3.91
Hamels,Cole	3.77
Greinke,Zack	3.60
Shields,James	3.60
Price,David	3.54
Fister,Doug	3.54
Nolasco,Ricky	3.46

Stolen Base Pct Allowed	
(minimum 750 IP)	
Cueto,Johnny	37.9
Buehrle,Mark	42.8
Fister,Doug	50.0
Kershaw,Clayton	52.6
Duke,Zach	53.3
Greinke,Zack	54.4
Colon,Bartolo	55.0
Capuano,Chris	58.2
Billingsley,Chad	58.7
Arroyo,Bronson	58.7

GIDP Induced	
Buehrle,Mark	334
Hudson,Tim	315
Wright,Jamey	272
Colon,Bartolo	261
Sabathia,CC	248
Burnett,A.J.	223
Penny,Brad	217
Dempster,Ryan	210
Maholm,Paul	206
Lackey,John	204

GIDP Per Nine IP	
(minimum 750 IP)	
Wright,Jamey	1.20
Maholm,Paul	1.19
Lannan,John	1.18
Porcello,Rick	1.15
Saunders,Joe	1.11
Duke,Zach	1.05
Masterson,Justin	1.04
Wilson,C.J.	1.04
Richard,Clayton	1.04
Hernandez,Roberto	1.03

Complete Game %	
(minimum 100 GS)	
Wainwright,Adam	0.10
Lee,Cliff	0.09
Sabathia,CC	0.09
Kershaw,Clayton	0.08
Colon,Bartolo	0.08
Shields,James	0.08
Hernandez,Felix	0.08
Harrison,Matt	0.07
Verlander,Justin	0.07
Buehrle,Mark	0.06

Quality Start Pct	
(minimum 100 GS)	
Kershaw,Clayton	70.8
Wainwright,Adam	70.0
Hernandez,Felix	68.3
Price,David	68.0
Weaver,Jered	67.5
Hamels,Cole	66.8
Johnson,Josh	65.0
Bumgarner,Madison	64.9
Cain,Matt	64.6
Strasburg,Stephen	64.2

Walks Per 9 IP	
(minimum 750 IP)	
Fister,Doug	1.73
Zimmermann,Jordan	1.84
Haren,Dan	1.86
Lee,Cliff	1.94
Kuroda,Hiroki	1.99
Buehrle,Mark	2.05
Baker,Scott	2.07
Nolasco,Ricky	2.10
Shields,James	2.13
Bumgarner,Madison	2.16

Games Finished	
Nathan,Joe	585
Rodriguez,Francisco	547
Valverde,Jose	520
Papelbon,Jonathan	504
Street,Huston	451
Rodney,Fernando	408
Gregg,Kevin	380
Hawkins,LaTroy	357
Putz,J.J.	357
Soriano,Rafael	340

2014 American League Bill James Leaders

Top Game Scores

Pitcher	Date	Opp	IP	H	R	ER	BB	SO	GS
Tomlin,Josh, Cle	6/28	Sea	9.0	1	0	0	0	11	96
Carrasco,Carlos, Cle	9/17	Hou	9.0	2	0	0	1	12	94
Buchholz,Clay, Bos	7/13	Hou	9.0	3	0	0	0	12	93
Lester,Jon, Bos	5/3	Oak	8.0	1	0	0	2	15	93
Kluber,Corey, Cle	7/24	KC	9.0	2	1	0	0	10	91
Darvish,Yu, Tex	5/9	Bos	8.2	2	0	0	2	12	90
Kluber,Corey, Cle	7/30	Sea	9.0	3	0	0	0	8	89
Lackey,John, Bos	6/18	Min	9.0	3	0	0	1	9	89
Stroman,Marcus, Tor	9/8	ChC	9.0	3	0	0	0	8	89
7 tied with									88

Worst Game Scores

Pitcher	Date	Opp	IP	H	R	ER	BB	SO	GS
Lewis,Colby, Tex	7/10	LAA	2.1	13	13	11	0	1	-16
Paulino,Felipe, CWS	4/18	Tex	3.2	13	10	10	3	3	-5
Williams,Jerome, Tex	8/1	Cle	4.0	13	10	10	3	2	-5
Ramirez,Erasmo, Sea	8/27	Tex	3.0	9	10	10	1	1	1
Price,David, Det	8/27	NYY	2.0	12	8	8	1	3	2
Mikolas,Miles, Tex	7/7	Hou	3.1	12	9	9	0	5	5
Paxton,James, Sea	9/22	Tor	2.2	7	9	8	6	1	5
Tillman,Chris, Bal	5/21	Pit	1.0	7	8	8	3	1	5
Whitley,Chase, NYY	6/23	Tor	3.1	11	8	8	3	2	5
Scherzer,Max, Det	6/17	KC	4.0	10	10	10	1	5	6

Runs Created

Trout,Mike, LAA	131
Martinez,Victor, Det	115
Brantley,Michael, Cle	114
Abreu,Jose, CWS	113
Bautista,Jose, Tor	112
Cabrera,Miguel, Det	110
Altuve,Jose, Hou	106
Cano,Robinson, Sea	106
Donaldson,Josh, Oak	105
Beltre,Adrian, Tex	99

Runs Created Per 27 Outs

Trout,Mike, LAA	7.9
Martinez,Victor, Det	7.8
Abreu,Jose, CWS	7.6
Bautista,Jose, Tor	7.1
Brantley,Michael, Cle	7.1
Beltre,Adrian, Tex	6.8
Cano,Robinson, Sea	6.6
Cabrera,Miguel, Det	6.5
Encarnacion,Edwin, Tor	6.3
Altuve,Jose, Hou	6.1

Offensive Winning %

Trout,Mike, LAA	.800
Martinez,Victor, Det	.770
Abreu,Jose, CWS	.768
Brantley,Michael, Cle	.752
Cano,Robinson, Sea	.745
Bautista,Jose, Tor	.737
Beltre,Adrian, Tex	.717
Cabrera,Miguel, Det	.702
Seager,Kyle, Sea	.686
Encarnacion,Edwin, Tor	.684

Secondary Average

(minimum 502 PA)

Trout,Mike, LAA	.439
Bautista,Jose, Tor	.438
Santana,Carlos, Cle	.414
Encarnacion,Edwin, Tor	.413
Ortiz,David, Bos	.400
Carter,Chris, Hou	.385
Dunn,Adam, CWS-Oak	.364
Abreu,Jose, CWS	.362
Martinez,Victor, Det	.360
Dozier,Brian, Min	.358

Isolated Power

(minimum 502 PA)

Encarnacion,Edwin, Tor	.279
Trout,Mike, LAA	.274
Abreu,Jose, CWS	.264
Carter,Chris, Hou	.264
Ortiz,David, Bos	.255
Cruz,Nelson, Bal	.254
Bautista,Jose, Tor	.239
Martinez,Victor, Det	.230
Cabrera,Miguel, Det	.211
Davis,Chris, Bal	.209

Power / Speed Number

(minimum 502 PA)

Ellsbury,Jacoby, NYY	22.7
Trout,Mike, LAA	22.2
Dozier,Brian, Min	22.0
Brantley,Michael, Cle	21.4
Gardner,Brett, NYY	18.8
Ramirez,Alexei, CWS	17.5
Kinsler,Ian, Det	15.9
Gordon,Alex, KC	14.7
Reyes,Jose, Tor	13.8
Donaldson,Josh, Oak	12.5

Speed Scores

Martin,Leonys, Tex	8.54
Ellsbury,Jacoby, NYY	8.24
Trout,Mike, LAA	7.93
Gardner,Brett, NYY	7.91
Bourn,Michael, Cle	7.86
Crisp,Coco, Oak	7.66
Reyes,Jose, Tor	7.65
Rios,Alex, Tex	7.37
Cain,Lorenzo, KC	7.35
Escobar,Alcides, KC	7.29

Cheap Wins

Chen,Wei-Yin, Bal	6
Kuroda,Hiroki, NYY	5
Cosart,Jarred, Hou	4
Kazmir,Scott, Oak	4
Weaver,Jered, LAA	4
Dickey,R.A., Tor	3
Hughes,Phil, Min	3
Noesi,Hector, Sea-Tex-CWS	3
Norris,Bud, Bal	3
Verlander,Justin, Det	3

Tough Losses

Dickey,R.A., Tor	7
Duffy,Danny, KC	7
Lester,Jon, Bos-Oak	7
Price,David, TB-Det	6
Elias,Roenis, Sea	5
Gray,Sonny, Oak	5
11 tied with	4

2014 National League Bill James Leaders

Top Game Scores

Pitcher	Date	Opp	IP	H	R	ER	BB	SO	GS
Kershaw,Clayton, LAD	6/18	Col	9.0	0	0	0	0	15	102
Bumgarner,Madison, SF	8/26	Col	9.0	1	0	0	0	13	98
Arrieta,Jake, ChC	9/16	Cin	9.0	1	0	0	1	13	97
Zimmermann,J. Was	9/28	Mia	9.0	0	0	0	1	10	96
Zimmermann,J. Was	6/8	SD	9.0	2	0	0	0	12	95
Cashner,Andrew, SD	4/11	Det	9.0	1	0	0	2	11	94
Wainwright,Adam, StL	5/20	Ari	9.0	1	0	0	0	9	94
Cueto,Johnny, Cin	4/16	Pit	9.0	3	0	0	0	12	93
Bumgarner,Madison, SF	8/3	NYM	9.0	2	0	0	1	10	92
Lincecum,Tim, SF	6/25	SD	9.0	0	0	0	1	6	92

Worst Game Scores

Pitcher	Date	Opp	IP	H	R	ER	BB	SO	GS
Cumpton,Brandon, Pit	5/31	LAD	3.2	11	11	10	2	2	-3
Nicasio,Juan, Col	6/10	Atl	3.2	11	10	10	2	2	-1
Frias,Carlos, LAD	9/17	Col	0.2	10	8	8	0	0	0
Arroyo,Bronson, Ari	4/15	NYM	3.1	10	9	9	1	1	4
Villanueva,Carlos, ChC	4/12	StL	3.0	10	9	9	0	2	5
Lackey,John, StL	8/9	Bal	5.0	13	9	9	2	3	6
Maholm,Paul, LAD	5/14	Mia	3.2	11	10	5	3	0	6
Miley,Wade, Ari	8/5	KC	4.2	9	10	10	3	4	7
Arrieta,Jake, ChC	8/6	Col	5.0	13	9	9	0	3	8
Harang,Aaron, Atl	6/18	Phi	5.0	13	9	8	3	4	8
Minor,Mike, Atl	6/10	Col	4.0	11	8	8	3	3	8

Runs Created

McCutchen,Andrew, Pit	109
Stanton,Giancarlo, Mia	109
Werth,Jayson, Was	104
Freeman,Freddie, Atl	101
Rizzo,Anthony, ChC	99
Gomez,Carlos, Mil	98
Holliday,Matt, StL	97
Rendon,Anthony, Was	97
Pence,Hunter, SF	96
2 tied with	95

Runs Created Per 27 Outs

McCutchen,Andrew, Pit	7.5
Stanton,Giancarlo, Mia	7.3
Werth,Jayson, Was	7.2
Rizzo,Anthony, ChC	6.8
Morneau,Justin, Col	6.6
Posey,Buster, SF	6.3
Puig,Yasiel, LAD	6.2
Duda,Lucas, NYM	6.1
Harrison,Josh, Pit	6.1
Gomez,Carlos, Mil	6.0

Offensive Winning %

McCutchen,Andrew, Pit	.791
Stanton,Giancarlo, Mia	.766
Werth,Jayson, Was	.761
Rizzo,Anthony, ChC	.751
Puig,Yasiel, LAD	.730
Duda,Lucas, NYM	.729
Posey,Buster, SF	.726
Freeman,Freddie, Atl	.715
Harrison,Josh, Pit	.715
Gomez,Carlos, Mil	.702

Secondary Average

(minimum 502 PA)

Stanton,Giancarlo, Mia	.466
McCutchen,Andrew, Pit	.414
Rizzo,Anthony, ChC	.389
LaRoche,Adam, Was	.368
Duda,Lucas, NYM	.368
Upton,Justin, Atl	.341
Werth,Jayson, Was	.335
Gomez,Carlos, Mil	.334
Smith,Seth, SD	.332
Kemp,Matt, LAD	.331

Isolated Power

(minimum 502 PA)

Stanton,Giancarlo, Mia	.267
Rizzo,Anthony, ChC	.240
McCutchen,Andrew, Pit	.228
Duda,Lucas, NYM	.228
Upton,Justin, Atl	.221
Kemp,Matt, LAD	.220
Davis,Khris, Mil	.214
Gonzalez,Adrian, LAD	.206
LaRoche,Adam, Was	.196
Walker,Neil, Pit	.195

Power / Speed Number

(minimum 502 PA)

Gomez,Carlos, Mil	27.4
Desmond,Ian, Was	24.0
Frazier,Todd, Cin	23.7
Blackmon,Charlie, Col	22.6
Rollins,Jimmy, Phi	21.2
McCutchen,Andrew, Pit	20.9
Stanton,Giancarlo, Mia	19.2
Rendon,Anthony, Was	18.8
Marte,Starling, Pit	18.1
Pence,Hunter, SF	15.8

Speed Scores

Young,Eric, NYM	8.73
Marte,Starling, Pit	8.38
Gomez,Carlos, Mil	8.07
Span,Denard, Was	7.89
Revere,Ben, Phi	7.71
Segura,Jean, Mil	7.63
Blackmon,Charlie, Col	7.60
Venable,Will, SD	7.26
Rollins,Jimmy, Phi	6.99
Lagares,Juan, NYM	6.93

Cheap Wins

Santana,Ervin, Atl	5
Bumgarner,Madison, SF	4
Kendrick,Kyle, Phi	4
8 tied with	3

Tough Losses

Wood,Alex, Atl	8
Hamels,Cole, Phi	7
Lynn,Lance, StL	6
Minor,Mike, Atl	6
Ross,Tyson, SD	6
Strasburg,Stephen, Was	6
Stults,Eric, SD	6
Teheran,Julio, Atl	6
6 tied with	5

Additional Bill James Leaders

AL Batters Win Shares

Trout,Mike, LAA	40
Cano,Robinson, Sea	34
Brantley,Michael, Cle	31
Altuve,Jose, Hou	30
Martinez,Victor, Det	30
Abreu,Jose, CWS	29
Bautista,Jose, Tor	28
Cabrera,Miguel, Det	28
Seager,Kyle, Sea	28
3 tied with	27

NL Batters Win Shares

McCutchen,Andrew, Pit	33
Stanton,Giancarlo, Mia	31
Posey,Buster, SF	30
Freeman,Freddie, Atl	28
Rizzo,Anthony, ChC	28
Carpenter,Matt, StL	27
Gomez,Carlos, Mil	27
Puig,Yasiel, LAD	27
Werth,Jayson, Was	27
7 tied with	26

AL Pitchers Win Shares

Hernandez,Felix, Sea	22
Kluber,Corey, Cle	21
Lester,Jon, Bos-Oak	18
Scherzer,Max, Det	18
Britton,Zach, Bal	17
Sale,Chris, CWS	17
Keuchel,Dallas, Hou	16
Price,David, TB-Det	16
4 tied with	15

NL Pitchers Win Shares

Wainwright,Adam, StL	23
Cueto,Johnny, Cin	22
Kershaw,Clayton, LAD	22
Bumgarner,Madison, SF	16
Kimbrel,Craig, Atl	16
Lynn,Lance, StL	16
Zimmermann,Jordan, Was	16
5 tied with	15

Batters Win Shares

Rodriguez,Alex	475
Pujols,Albert	428
Jeter,Derek	413
Abreu,Bobby	356
Beltran,Carlos	333
Cabrera,Miguel	330
Giambi,Jason	325
Suzuki,Ichiro	305
Beltre,Adrian	300
Rollins,Jimmy	296

Pitchers Win Shares

Hudson,Tim	216
Buehrle,Mark	211
Sabathia,CC	202
Colon,Bartolo	178
Nathan,Joe	163
Hernandez,Felix	161
Lee,Cliff	149
Verlander,Justin	149
Rodriguez,Francisco	145
Peavy,Jake	137

AL Component ERA
(minimum 162 IP)

Hernandez,Felix, Sea	1.81
Richards,Garrett, LAA	2.06
Sale,Chris, CWS	2.18
Kluber,Corey, Cle	2.57
Lester,Jon, Bos-Oak	2.70
Iwakuma,Hisashi, Sea	2.77
Price,David, TB-Det	2.79
Cobb,Alex, TB	2.87
Gray,Sonny, Oak	2.99
Kazmir,Scott, Oak	3.00

NL Component ERA
(minimum 162 IP)

Kershaw,Clayton, LAD	1.53
Cueto,Johnny, Cin	2.18
Wainwright,Adam, StL	2.20
Zimmermann,Jordan, Was	2.64
Teheran,Julio, Atl	2.71
Roark,Tanner, Was	2.76
Bumgarner,Madison, SF	2.83
Hamels,Cole, Phi	2.88
Garza,Matt, Mil	2.92
Fister,Doug, Was	2.98

AL Highest Avg Game Score
(minimum 30 GS)

Hernandez,Felix, Sea	65.12
Kluber,Corey, Cle	62.62
Lester,Jon, Bos-Oak	60.78
Price,David, TB-Det	60.41
Scherzer,Max, Det	59.52
Gray,Sonny, Oak	57.27
Shields,James, KC	55.62
Hughes,Phil, Min	55.53
Kazmir,Scott, Oak	55.16
Ventura,Yordano, KC	54.90

AL Lowest Avg Game Score
(minimum 30 GS)

Danks,John, CWS	47.81
Verlander,Justin, Det	49.44
Gibson,Kyle, Min	49.74
Wilson,C.J., LAA	49.97
Guthrie,Jeremy, KC	50.22
Buehrle,Mark, Tor	51.41
Vargas,Jason, KC	52.00
Hutchison,Drew, Tor	52.31
Odorizzi,Jake, TB	52.55
Chen,Wei-Yin, Bal	52.65

AL Lowest Offensive Win %

Dominguez,Matt, Hou	.241
Bogaerts,Xander, Bos	.278
Kipnis,Jason, Cle	.345
Andrus,Elvis, Tex	.349
Perez,Salvador, KC	.366
Castro,Jason, Hou	.368
Viciedo,Dayan, CWS	.390
Jackson,Austin, Det-Sea	.391
Lowrie,Jed, Oak	.400
Infante,Omar, KC	.405

NL Highest Avg Game Score
(minimum 30 GS)

Cueto,Johnny, Cin	65.29
Wainwright,Adam, StL	62.13
Hamels,Cole, Phi	61.10
Bumgarner,Madison, SF	59.15
Teheran,Julio, Atl	58.85
Greinke,Zack, LAD	58.66
Zimmermann,Jordan, Was	58.56
Strasburg,Stephen, Was	58.06
Ross,Tyson, SD	58.00
Roark,Tanner, Was	57.26

NL Lowest Avg Game Score
(minimum 30 GS)

Wood,Travis, ChC	46.55
Stults,Eric, SD	48.06
Kendrick,Kyle, Phi	48.28
Eovaldi,Nathan, Mia	49.15
Burnett,A.J., Phi	50.38
Miley,Wade, Ari	50.97
Haren,Dan, LAD	51.28
Colon,Bartolo, NYM	52.00
Hudson,Tim, SF	52.00
2 tied with	52.09

NL Lowest Offensive Win %

Cozart,Zack, Cin	.272
Simmons,Andrelton, Atl	.307
LeMahieu,DJ, Col	.318
Parra,Gerardo, Ari-Mil	.347
Segura,Jean, Mil	.350
Hill,Aaron, Ari	.373
Hechavarria,Adeiny, Mia	.374
Upton,B.J., Atl	.382
Mercer,Jordy, Pit	.382
Jones,Garrett, Mia	.444

Home Run Robberies

It was a great year to be a power hitter in 2014. Home run robberies were down. This season, there were only 33 home run robberies, 13 fewer than last season and the fewest since 2008. That decline in robberies mirrored an overall decline in home runs. Hitters combined to hit just 4,186 home runs this season, 366 fewer than the next lowest season since the 1998 expansion. Perhaps it was that power decline, or perhaps it was just luck. Either way, it was only the second time since 2004 that there were fewer than 40 robberies.

Home Run Robberies 2004-2014

Season	HR Robberies
2004	53
2005	47
2006	41
2007	44
2008	31
2009	40
2010	41
2011	41
2012	43
2013	46
2014	33

In 2013, Carlos Gomez led the way with five robberies, which were the most by a player in a season since we began tracking the statistic back in 2004. In all, there were 46 robberies across baseball, which, while not too different from the totals from recent seasons, were the most in nearly a decade.

Gomez dropped to only one home run robbery, victimizing Joey Votto once again on May 1! If you recall, Gomez robbed Votto of a would-be game-winning home run with two outs in the ninth on July 8, 2013. At the time, the Reds were down one run and had a runner on base. It was not quite as dramatic this time around—although I'm sure Votto was similarly exasperated—but it was enough for Gomez to reach 12 home run robberies in his career, which ties him with Torii Hunter for the most by a player since we started tracking them in 2004.

Career Home Run Robbery Leaders (2004-2014)

Player	HR Robberies
Torii Hunter	12
Carlos Gomez	12
Ichiro Suzuki	9
Jason Bay	9
Coco Crisp	8

The Reds enjoyed a modicum of revenge this season in robbing four home runs, themselves. That was one more than the second-place Mets and two more than the six teams with two robberies. Jay Bruce had two of the Reds' robberies, and, interestingly, both were with Johnny Cueto on the mound. Bartolo Colon of the Mets also benefited from a pair of home run robberies, one courtesy of Juan Lagares and the other of Matt den Dekker.

The following page lists all 33 home run robberies from 2014 along with some context for the robbery, such as the inning, score, and number of baserunners.

Home Run Robberies

Date	Matchup	Fielder	Pos	Pitcher	Batter	Inn.	Outs	Men On	Score
04/04/2014	Reds@Mets	Eric Young	7	Jenrry Mejia	Brandon Phillips	1	1		0-0
04/17/2014	Red Sox@White Sox	Adam Eaton	8	Chris Sale	David Ortiz	1	2		0-0
04/22/2014	Cardinals@Mets	Matt Holliday	7	Adam Wainwright	Chris Young	5	0	1	2-0
04/26/2014	Reds@Braves	Ryan Ludwick	7	Mike Leake	Freddie Freeman	3	1		1-2
05/01/2014	Brewers@Reds	Carlos Gomez	8	Marco Estrada	Joey Votto	1	1		0-0
05/03/2014	Diamondbacks@Padres	Cameron Maybin	8	Ian Kennedy	Paul Goldschmidt	5	0		2-0
05/13/2014	White Sox@Athletics	Leury Garcia	8	Frank Francisco	Yoenis Cespedes	6	1	2	0-7
05/15/2014	Rays@Angels	Desmond Jennings	8	Erik Bedard	C.J. Cron	4	2	3	1-0
05/16/2014	Mets@Nationals	Jayson Werth	9	Rafael Soriano	Daniel Murphy	9	2	12	2-5
05/17/2014	Mets@Nationals	Juan Lagares	8	Bartolo Colon	Jayson Werth	6	0		5-2
05/23/2014	Royals@Angels	Lorenzo Cain	8	Louis Coleman	David Freese	7	1	12	1-5
05/26/2014	Yankees@Cardinals	Brett Gardner	7	Alfredo Aceves	Yadier Molina	11	1	1	3-3
05/27/2014	Rangers@Twins	Aaron Hicks	8	Phil Hughes	Donnie Murphy	2	1	23	0-0
05/27/2014	Indians@White Sox	Michael Bourn	8	Cody Allen	Paul Konerko	8	1	1	1-2
06/02/2014	Mets@Phillies	Matt den Dekker	8	Bartolo Colon	Ryan Howard	2	0		1-0
06/11/2014	Athletics@Angels	Coco Crisp	8	Tommy Milone	Josh Hamilton	2	0		0-0
06/27/2014	Red Sox@Yankees	Brock Holt	9	Brandon Workman	Brian Roberts	2	1		0-1
07/01/2014	Cubs@Red Sox	Mookie Betts	9	Nate Schierholtz	Nate Schierholtz	2	2		0-0
07/02/2014	Angels@White Sox	Josh Hamilton	7	Tyler Skaggs	Gordon Beckham	1	1		0-0
07/02/2014	Rangers@Orioles	Leonys Martin	8	Miles Mikolas	Nelson Cruz	2	0		1-0
07/21/2014	Mets@Mariners	Dustin Ackley	7	Dominic Leone	Travis d'Arnaud	6	1		1-4
08/01/2014	Rockies@Tigers	J.D. Martinez	7	Justin Verlander	Nolan Arenado	1	2		0-0
08/02/2014	Blue Jays@Astros	Robbie Grossman	9	Tony Sipp	Juan Francisco	8	2	1	2-4
08/10/2014	Marlins@Reds	Jay Bruce	9	Johnny Cueto	Giancarlo Stanton	8	0		2-7
08/18/2014	Orioles@White Sox	Nick Markakis	9	Bud Norris	Conor Gillaspie	7	2	1	3-2
08/19/2014	Angels@Red Sox	Kole Calhoun	9	Jered Weaver	Brock Holt	2	2	12	0-1
08/25/2014	Rays@Orioles	Adam Jones	8	Chris Tillman	Evan Longoria	6	0	12	1-9
09/04/2014	Diamondbacks@Padres	A.J. Pollock	8	Randall Delgado	Rene Rivera	3	0		4-0
09/08/2014	Astros@Mariners	Michael Saunders	9	Brandon Maurer	Robbie Grossman	7	1		0-1
09/11/2014	Cardinals@Reds	Jay Bruce	9	Johnny Cueto	Matt Adams	7	0		0-0
09/23/2014	White Sox@Tigers	J.D. Martinez	7	David Price	Josh Phegley	5	2		0-0
09/23/2014	Rockies@Padres	Brandon Barnes	7	Adam Ottavino	Rene Rivera	8	0		3-2
09/24/2014	Brewers@Reds	Billy Hamilton	8	Daniel Corcino	Ryan Braun	3	2		0-0

Win Shares

Bill James devised Win Shares as a way to relate a player's individual statistics to the number of wins he contributed to his team. As a single number, Win Shares allows us to easily compare accomplishments of each player to other players and to compare players across positions and across seasons.

Felix Hernandez had 22 Win Shares to lead all American League pitchers in 2014, the most he has had since the 23 he had in 2010, the only time he won a Cy Young Award (though less than the 26 he had in 2009). And over in the National League, Clayton Kershaw had 23 and 22 Win Shares, respectively, in his two Cy Young Award winning seasons of 2011 and 2013. This past season he posted 22 Win Shares again; though, with the time he missed at the beginning of the season, that actually trails the 23 Win Shares accrued by Adam Wainwright.

We credit a team with three Win Shares for each win. If a team wins 100 games, then 300 Win Shares—or 300 thirds of a win—will be divided up among all the players on that team according to their individual contributions. If a team wins 70 games, there will be 210 Win Shares to be distributed to the players on that team, and so on.

The following pages contain the sum of a player's Win Shares prior to 2005, followed by his individual season totals from 2005 through 2014. Career totals are also included for each player.

The quality of the team does not affect an individual player's Win Shares. A great player on a bad team will rate just as well as a great player on a good team.

Win Shares adjusts for offensive environment, so it is a great tool to use for looking at the greatest individual seasons in baseball history, as well as the greatest players of all time.

Win Shares are also a great tool for evaluating award voting and Hall of Fame credentials. Generally, 30 or more Win Shares indicates an MVP-caliber season; 20 Win Shares indicates a season worthy of the Cy Young Award.

For a complete description of how Win Shares are calculated, as well as countless essays using Win Shares to analyze various facets of the game, check out Bill James' book, *Win Shares*.

WIN SHARES BY YEAR

Player	<05	05	06	07	08	09	10	11	12	13	14	Career
Abreu,Jose											29	29
Ackley,Dustin								14	16	11	12	53
Adams,Matt									1	12	15	28
Affeldt,Jeremy	21	1	3	5	6	10	3	6	5	1	6	67
Albers,Matt			0	0	4	2	5	3	6	5	1	26
Allen,Cody									1	8	14	23
Altuve,Jose								2	17	11	30	60
Alvarez,Henderson								4	5	7	14	30
Alvarez,Pedro							14	3	22	18	11	68
Amarista,Alexi								1	6	10	13	30
Andrus,Elvis						17	20	18	23	15	13	106
Aoki,Nori									15	17	17	49
Archer,Chris									0	10	11	21
Arcia,Oswaldo										6	10	16
Arenado,Nolan										9	12	21
Arrieta,Jake							5	5	0	3	12	25
Arroyo,Bronson	18	11	20	11	10	13	14	3	13	9	5	127
Asche,Cody										4	10	14
Atchison,Scott	2	0		2				2	6	1	8	23
Avila,Alex						3	7	27	15	6	14	72
Aybar,Erick			1	2	15	20	9	20	16	14	20	117
Bailey,Homer				2	0	5	5	5	12	11	8	48
Baker,Jeff		1	3	1	7	7	4	3	3	6	6	41
Balfour,Grant	5		0	11	5	6	8	15	10	4		64
Barmes,Clint	4	9	6	0	12	13	10	10	10	2	1	77
Barton,Daric				3	9	6	21	4	3	5	0	51
Bautista,Jose	0	0	9	12	8	6	34	36	13	18	28	164
Beckett,Josh	28	12	11	18	11	16	2	16	7	0	7	128
Belisle,Matt	0	4	3	5	0	1	11	7	8	5	3	47
Bell,Heath	2	0	1	13	6	12	15	11	4	5	0	69
Beltran,Carlos	129	21	34	25	29	14	8	26	18	22	7	333
Beltre,Adrian	115	13	17	16	13	10	26	16	25	22	27	300
Benoit,Joaquin	12	6	4	10	2		9	8	7	14	12	84
Betances,Dellin								0		0	14	14
Betts,Mookie											8	8
Blackmon,Charlie								1	1	7	16	25
Blanco,Gregor					11	0	6		12	13	15	57
Bloomquist,Willie	8	4	5	2	5	7	3	8	9	5	5	61
Bonifacio,Emilio				1	2	7	5	20	6	7	11	59
Bourn,Michael			0	4	7	23	18	22	28	14	11	127
Boxberger,Brad									2	1	8	11
Brantley,Michael						3	5	11	18	21	31	89
Braun,Ryan				22	23	36	25	37	28	9	17	197
Britton,Zach								6	3	1	17	27
Brown,Domonic							0	4	5	19	10	38
Broxton,Jonathan		0	9	10	10	16	6	0	11	1	9	72
Bruce,Jay					7	9	16	22	18	21	10	103
Buchholz,Clay				3	0	6	18	6	9	12	2	56
Buck,John	4	10	8	7	8	6	17	14	9	12	2	97
Buehrle,Mark	69	22	9	17	16	16	12	15	12	10	13	211
Bumgarner,Madison						1	8	12	11	12	16	60
Burnett,A.J.	38	11	9	11	14	12	4	5	11	9	3	127
Burton,Jared					5	6	3	1	6	5	4	32
Butler,Billy				7	8	18	20	17	21	16	12	119
Byrd,Marlon	21	6	2	13	12	20	19	8	1	23	16	141
Cabrera,Asdrubal				7	12	18	9	25	19	12	15	117
Cabrera,Everth						14	3	0	11	19	8	55
Cabrera,Melky		0	13	12	5	14	8	19	25	7	19	122
Cabrera,Miguel	31	27	33	29	20	25	30	38	32	37	28	330
Cain,Lorenzo							6	0	7	12	19	44
Cain,Matt		5	11	12	14	20	15	15	16	5	1	114
Calhoun,Kole									0	8	20	28
Callaspo,Alberto			1	1	6	17	11	17	15	13	5	86
Camp,Shawn	4	0	5	0	3	5	7	4	6	0	0	34
Cano,Robinson		12	17	21	12	18	34	30	34	35	34	247
Carpenter,Matt								0	9	35	27	71
Carrasco,Carlos							0	3	5	0	12	20
Carter,Chris							0	0	8	13	15	36
Cashner,Andrew							2	1	2	10	9	24
Casilla,Alexi			0	1	9	4	6	7	5	2	0	34
Casilla,Santiago	0	0	0	4	3	0	8	8	9	6	12	50
Castellanos,Nick										0	13	13
Castillo,Welington							1	0	4	10	12	27

WIN SHARES BY YEAR

Player	<05	05	06	07	08	09	10	11	12	13	14	Career
Castro,Jason							4		8	18	10	40
Castro,Starlin							12	25	23	7	20	87
Cedeno,Ronny		2	5	1	5	7	9	10	4	5	0	48
Cespedes,Yoenis									24	14	18	56
Chamberlain,Joba				5	11	6	5	3	1	2	5	38
Chapman,Aroldis							2	4	21	12	13	52
Chavez,Eric	118	20	16	6	3	0	0	6	8	9	2	188
Chen,Wei-Yin									12	7	12	31
Chirinos,Robinson								1		0	11	12
Chisenhall,Lonnie								6	4	7	18	35
Choo,Shin-Soo		0	4	1	16	23	27	8	25	31	9	144
Cishek,Steve							1	6	10	14	10	41
Clippard,Tyler				1	1	5	9	13	11	10	10	60
Cobb,Alex								3	6	13	13	35
Coghlan,Chris						21	8	4	1	5	15	54
Collmenter,Josh								10	5	7	12	34
Correia,Kevin	3	2	6	8	0	8	1	4	5	9	3	49
Cosart,Jarred										5	10	15
Cowgill,Collin								2	4	2	8	16
Cozart,Zack								1	11	12	8	32
Crawford,Brandon								5	13	11	22	51
Crawford,Carl	39	22	21	20	11	19	32	8	3	13	12	200
Crisp,Coco	25	20	9	16	11	4	14	15	18	21	15	168
Cron,C.J.											8	8
Cruz,Nelson		0	3	4	7	16	19	16	17	16	22	120
Cuddyer,Michael	14	7	22	16	7	17	15	17	6	19	6	146
Cueto,Johnny					6	7	12	12	21	5	22	85
Danks,John				4	17	16	16	8	1	3	7	72
d'Arnaud,Travis										1	8	9
Darvish,Yu									14	18	10	42
Davis,Chris					8	7	1	4	19	33	12	84
Davis,Ike							16	6	15	7	10	54
Davis,Khris										6	12	18
Davis,Rajai			0	5	5	13	14	6	11	6	14	74
Davis,Wade						2	8	6	7	2	15	40
De Aza,Alejandro				1		1	1	9	18	16	11	57
De La Rosa,Jorge	0	2	2	3	5	12	8	4	0	12	11	59
deGrom,Jacob											11	11
DeJesus,David	9	16	14	15	22	16	11	8	15	12	4	142
Desmond,Ian						2	11	16	18	25	19	91
Dickerson,Corey										4	15	19
Dickey,R.A.	11	0	0		3	3	15	11	19	11	11	84
Dobbs,Greg	1	2	1	7	8	2	1	7	6	3	0	38
Donaldson,Josh							0		8	32	27	67
Doolittle,Sean									5	8	11	24
Doumit,Ryan		6	2	6	20	4	9	9	10	9	0	75
Downs,Scott	3	5	6	8	11	6	8	10	5	4	1	67
Dozier,Brian									4	19	19	42
Drew,Stephen			6	16	21	16	20	10	6	17	4	116
Duda,Lucas							0	11	13	8	25	57
Duffy,Danny								1	2	3	12	18
Duke,Zach		10	10	2	3	12	1	4	2	2	7	53
Dunn,Adam	72	25	18	18	21	24	18	1	13	13	13	236
Dyson,Jarrod							2	2	8	7	9	28
Eaton,Adam									2	5	20	27
Ellis,Mark	32	21	14	20	13	11	19	9	12	16	2	169
Ellsbury,Jacoby				6	16	21	1	34	6	22	22	128
Encarnacion,Edwin		4	14	16	14	6	8	11	31	22	19	145
Escobar,Alcides					0	4	12	8	14	10	20	68
Escobar,Eduardo								0	2	2	13	17
Escobar,Yunel				12	13	24	14	20	9	18	10	120
Ethier,Andre			11	13	23	21	22	18	22	16	10	156
Familia,Jeurys									0	0	9	9
Farnsworth,Kyle	24	14	5	3	3	2	5	12	1	2	1	72
Feldman,Scott		1	3	1	4	14	2	2	4	10	9	50
Fielder,Prince		2	16	27	23	36	23	33	27	18	3	208
Fister,Doug						4	7	18	11	14	14	68
Flaherty,Ryan									2	7	9	18
Flowers,Tyler						0	0	3	3	3	10	19
Floyd,Gavin	2	0	0	2	15	13	12	11	10	0	3	68
Fowler,Dexter					0	15	13	16	15	13	16	88
Francisco,Frank	6	0	3	6	9	5	7	2	1	0		39
Francoeur,Jeff		12	15	20	5	9	8	17	6	1	0	93

WIN SHARES BY YEAR

Player	<05	05	06	07	08	09	10	11	12	13	14	Career
Frasor,Jason	9	6	4	3	2	10	5	5	2	5	5	56
Frazier,Todd									3	13	15	20 →	51
Freeman,Freddie							0	19	18	35	28	100
Freese,David						1	8	13	19	9	12	62
Fuld,Sam					0	4	1	9	3	2	12	31
Gallardo,Yovani				9	2	10	11	13	16	8	9	78
Gardner,Brett					3	9	17	16	2	22	19	88
Garza,Matt			1	4	12	12	10	10	5	10	8	72
Gattis,Evan										11	12	23
Gennett,Scooter										9	14	23
Gentry,Craig						0	0	5	9	11	8	33
Giambi,Jason	236	24	22	6	14	7	6	5	2	3	0	325
Gibson,Kyle										0	8	8
Gillaspie,Conor					0			1	0	9	16	26
Goldschmidt,Paul								6	17	36	20	79
Gomes,Jonny	0	14	6	8	2	10	18	6	13	12	7	96
Gomes,Yan									2	14	18	34
Gomez,Carlos				2	13	6	4	7	12	21	27	92
Gonzalez,Adrian	1	1	16	25	24	34	35	27	24	24	26	237
Gonzalez,Gio					0	2	15	15	17	11	8	68
Gonzalez,Miguel									10	10	10	30
Gordon,Alex				12	15	2	3	24	20	21	26	123
Gordon,Dee								6	3	2	22	33
Gorzelanny,Tom		0	3	11	0	2	7	4	6	4	3	40
Grandal,Yasmani									11	4	12	27
Granderson,Curtis	0	6	20	25	20	20	16	26	21	4	17	175
Gray,Sonny										5	13	18
Gregerson,Luke						5	9	4	9	7	8	42
Gregg,Kevin	8	2	4	10	11	7	9	4	2	8	0	65
Gregorius,Didi									0	10	9	19
Greinke,Zack	9	3	1	9	15	26	11	10	16	17	15	132
Grossman,Robbie										7	10	17
Guerrier,Matt	0	5	5	9	2	11	7	4	1	2	1	47
Guthrie,Jeremy	1	0	0	12	13	7	15	8	7	12	9	84
Guyer,Brandon									0	0	8	8
Gyorko,Jedd										12	11	23
Hairston,Scott	3	0	0	7	9	14	5	3	12	2	0	55
Hamels,Cole			8	15	18	10	16	17	18	13	15	130
Hamilton,Billy										2	15	17
Hamilton,Josh				11	26	11	30	15	26	12	12	143
Hammel,Jason			0	2	3	10	8	5	10	4	9	51
Hanigan,Ryan				1	4	8	13	11	18	5	8	68
Happ,J.A.				0	2	15	6	1	5	3	7	39
Harang,Aaron	12	11	18	17	6	7	1	8	8	1	10	99
Hardy,J.J.		11	3	19	20	6	10	22	20	16	17	144
Haren,Dan	3	13	14	17	19	20	14	18	6	4	5	133
Harper,Bryce									21	19	9	49
Harrison,Josh								5	4	3	25	37
Hawkins,LaTroy	66	5	4	5	6	10	0	6	2	7	9	120
Headley,Chase				0	8	16	15	16	32	17	15	119
Hechavarria,Adeiny									3	5	13	21
Hernandez,Felix		8	8	14	13	26	23	16	15	16	22	161
Hernandez,Roberto			1	22	3	0	12	2	0	3	4	47
Herrera,Kelvin								0	10	5	10	25
Heyward,Jason							23	11	22	14	23	93
Hill,Aaron		9	14	20	5	25	12	13	25	12	10	145
Holland,Greg							0	9	11	18	15	53
Holliday,Matt	9	17	19	27	21	25	25	21	21	25	26	236
Holt,Brock									3	1	12	16
Hosmer,Eric								13	10	18	14	55
Howard,Ryan	1	10	29	26	24	26	20	21	7	9	15	188
Hudson,Tim	106	14	7	17	10	4	20	14	12	6	6	216
Hughes,Phil				4	0	10	11	1	9	2	14	51
Hunter,Tommy					0	8	10	3	4	10	8	43
Hunter,Torii	81	11	17	22	21	20	23	17	24	16	13	265
Iannetta,Chris			1	5	17	10	3	16	8	10	17	87
Ibanez,Raul	54	17	25	23	21	17	19	12	9	14	2	213
Inciarte,Ender											10	10
Infante,Omar	18	7	5	4	9	7	19	18	14	16	9	126
Iwakuma,Hisashi									8	20	11	39
Izturis,Maicer	1	6	13	16	11	17	7	13	5	3	1	93
Jackson,Austin							18	14	22	15	11	80
Jackson,Edwin	2	0	1	2	10	17	9	12	9	1	0	63

WIN SHARES BY YEAR

Player	<05	05	06	07	08	09	10	11	12	13	14	Career
Jansen,Kenley							6	6	15	16	11	54
Jaso,John					0		16	5	21	9	9	60
Jay,Jon							8	13	15	17	16	69
Jennings,Desmond							0	11	13	20	13	57
Jeter,Derek	220	26	32	24	18	28	19	13	23	0	10	413
Jimenez,Ubaldo			0	4	11	19	22	6	3	13	3	81
Johnson,Chris						0	15	8	17	20	11	71
Johnson,Jim			0	0	8	7	3	11	17	11	0	57
Johnson,Kelly		9		19	19	6	21	16	14	12	7	123
Johnson,Reed	20	10	16	3	13	3	3	8	8	3	3	90
Jones,Adam			1	0	9	13	15	16	26	23	25	128
Jones,Garrett				0		10	13	12	23	8	9	75
Joyce,Matt					6	1	10	19	13	11	10	70
Jurrjens,Jair				2	11	17	4	12	0	0	0	46
Kazmir,Scott	1	10	13	13	12	6	0	0		8	10	73
Kemp,Matt			3	10	19	26	15	37	21	6	20	157
Kendrick,Howie			6	9	15	15	19	18	16	13	27	138
Kendrick,Kyle				9	3	2	5	7	8	5	4	43
Kennedy,Ian				2	0	0	11	20	11	2	9	55
Kershaw,Clayton					5	12	15	23	19	22	22	118
Keuchel,Dallas									0	3	16	19
Kiermaier,Kevin										0	9	9
Kimbrel,Craig							4	17	18	17	16	72
Kinsler,Ian			12	17	24	24	13	22	15	20	24	171
Kipnis,Jason								6	24	27	10	67
Kluber,Corey								0	1	9	21	31
Koehler,Tom									0	3	8	11
Konerko,Paul	89	24	21	16	10	18	29	24	15	9	0	255
Kubel,Jason	3		1	12	12	19	12	13	13	5	3	93
Kuroda,Hiroki					10	5	11	12	16	16	11	81
La Stella,Tommy											9	9
Lackey,John	24	16	16	21	13	12	11	1		10	11	135
Lagares,Juan										7	15	22
Laird,Gerald	4	1	5	10	9	14	6	3	5	6	2	65
Lannan,John				2	9	9	4	8	2	1	0	35
LaRoche,Adam	7	11	16	16	16	17	16	1	22	14	20	156
Lawrie,Brett								10	14	9	10	43
League,Brandon	1	0	5	0	4	3	8	11	8	0	4	44
Leake,Mike							7	9	8	12	10	46
Lee,Cliff	10	13	10	1	24	17	16	22	14	19	3	149
LeMahieu,DJ								0	6	8	9	23
Lester,Jon			5	4	18	17	17	14	8	12	18	113
Lincecum,Tim				8	25	22	14	16	0	4	3	92
Lind,Adam			3	7	7	21	9	11	9	15	13	95
Lindstrom,Matt				5	6	2	4	5	4	5	1	32
Lohse,Kyle	31	10	4	9	12	3	0	9	16	12	11	117
Loney,James			3	16	14	18	18	16	5	19	13	122
Longoria,Evan					19	24	28	25	14	24	21	155
Lopez,Javier	6	0	2	4	6	0	6	6	4	5	3	42
Lowrie,Jed					7	1	8	5	11	23	11	79
Lucroy,Jonathan							4	15	15	19	26	79
Ludwick,Ryan	6	0		10	24	19	17	12	16	1	9	114
Lynn,Lance								2	11	7	16	36
Machado,Manny									7	20	12	39
Machi,Jean									0	4	8	12
Maholm,Paul		4	7	5	9	8	4	7	11	3	0	58
Maness,Seth										6	8	14
Markakis,Nick			12	20	23	16	22	19	16	11	20	159
Marmol,Carlos			1	11	12	10	16	8	6	1	0	65
Marshall,Sean			2	6	4	5	10	11	11	2	0	51
Marte,Starling									5	20	17	42
Martin,Leonys								0	1	14	14	29
Martin,Russell			14	22	20	16	9	14	12	16	22	145
Martinez,J.D.								6	7	3	19	35
Martinez,Victor	24	22	18	29	7	21	17	24		11	30	203
Mathis,Jeff		0	0	2	7	4	3	4	5	4	1	30
Matsuzaka,Daisuke				12	16	2	7	1	0	1	3	48
Mauer,Joe	6	22	30	21	30	32	27	10	25	23	14	240
Maybin,Cameron				0	3	2	8	17	13	0	5	48
McCann,Brian		6	22	15	18	20	19	23	12	16	19	170
McCarthy,Brandon		5	5	3	1	5	11	7		3	8	48
McCutchen,Andrew						18	22	28	40	34	33	175
McDonald,John	9	4	3	8	1	3	5	6	4	0	1	44

Player	<05	05	06	07	08	09	10	11	12	13	14	Career
McGee,Jake							0	2	8	5	15	30
McGehee,Casey			0	17	23	9	5				17	71
McHugh,Collin									0	0	13	13
McLouth,Nate		1	2	10	24	19	4	9	6	14	1	90
Melancon,Mark						1	2	10	0	15	15	43
Mercer,Jordy									2	13	10	25
Mesoraco,Devin								1	3	8	26	38
Miller,Andrew			0	2	0	2	0	2	4	2	9	21
Miller,Brad										10	11	21
Miller,Shelby									2	10	10	22
Molina,Jose	11	7	5	4	9	4	4	7	6	4	4	65
Molina,Yadier	5	14	9	12	15	20	17	18	29	29	19	187
Montero,Miguel			0	3	4	13	9	29	26	10	15	109
Morneau,Justin	10	7	26	18	28	18	17	4	10	14	16	168
Morris,Bryan									0	4	8	12
Morrison,Logan							9	11	4	7	11	42
Morrow,Brandon				5	7	4	7	7	10	0	0	40
Morse,Michael		5	2	2	0	2	9	25	13	3	13	74
Moss,Brandon				1	5	5	0	0	13	20	17	61
Moustakas,Mike								4	14	5	9	32
Mujica,Edward			1	0	0	4	4	8	7	10	4	38
Murphy,Daniel					6	10		14	20	22	21	93
Murphy,David			0	5	11	11	15	9	20	5	14	90
Napoli,Mike			10	8	12	10	12	23	12	16	10	113
Nava,Daniel							5		5	18	11	39
Navarro,Dioner	0	4	5	6	17	5	2	3	4	11	17	74
Neshek,Pat			6	8	1		0	1	3	2	13	34
Niese,Jon					0	1	6	4	13	6	8	38
Nolasco,Ricky			5	0	14	6	7	5	8	9	3	57
Norris,Bud						3	3	7	4	8	11	36
Norris,Derek									7	11	16	34
O'Day,Darren					2	9	9	0	10	8	10	48
Odor,Rougned											11	11
O'Flaherty,Eric			0	4	0	4	5	12	8	3	2	38
Olivo,Miguel	16	7	13	7	7	9	11	10	4	1	0	85
Ortiz,David	75	30	27	27	15	11	18	18	15	22	19	277
Otero,Dan									0	5	9	14
Overbay,Lyle	23	17	17	6	14	12	15	6	2	7	7	126
Owings,Chris										2	8	10
Ozuna,Marcell										8	19	27
Pagan,Angel			3	5	3	12	23	15	27	11	14	113
Panik,Joe											10	10
Papelbon,Jonathan		4	19	15	15	15	10	12	14	11	14	129
Pearce,Steve					2	2	2	1	6	4	19	36
Peavy,Jake	25	16	12	21	13	6	6	5	17	7	9	137
Pedroia,Dustin			2	18	26	24	12	27	17	25	17	168
Pelfrey,Mike			0	1	12	4	12	3	2	3	0	37
Pena,Brayan		0	1	0	0	2	4	5	3	2	8	25
Pena,Carlos	34	7	0	28	22	17	16	18	10	4	0	156
Pence,Hunter				18	19	17	21	24	18	25	26	168
Peralta,Jhonny	5	25	15	21	19	10	16	22	12	19	22	186
Peralta,Joel		2	5	6	0	0	5	8	6	7	3	42
Peralta,Wily									3	5	12	20
Perez,Salvador								7	10	23	17	57
Perkins,Glen			1	2	7	2	0	8	10	13	9	52
Petricka,Jake										1	8	9
Phillips,Brandon	5	0	14	17	19	19	18	22	19	22	13	168
Pierzynski,A.J.	71	11	14	8	8	10	12	11	19	17	6	187
Pineda,Michael								10			8	18
Plouffe,Trevor							0	6	8	8	17	39
Polanco,Gregory											8	8
Pollock,A.J.									2	14	10	26
Porcello,Rick						13	5	8	7	9	13	55
Posey,Buster						0	20	9	38	24	30	121
Prado,Martin			2	1	9	12	22	12	23	15	15	111
Price,David					1	6	17	13	19	12	16	84
Puig,Yasiel										17	27	44
Pujols,Albert	139	34	37	32	34	39	32	26	25	10	19	427
Punto,Nick	5	6	12	5	10	11	5	8	3	8	5	78
Putnam,Zach									0	0	9	9
Putz,J.J.	3	5	17	20	5	1	8	13	10	5	0	87
Qualls,Chad	4	7	9	9	11	8	0	5	1	6	7	67
Quentin,Carlos			5	5	23	8	15	16	11	14	2	99

Player	<05	05	06	07	08	09	10	11	12	13	14	Career
Quintana,Jose									9	13	12	34
Raburn,Ryan	0			4	3	9	11	10	1	13	0	51
Ramirez,Alexei					18	15	20	20	14	15	21	123
Ramirez,Aramis	77	18	21	21	25	15	13	25	22	10	15	262
Ramirez,Hanley		0	25	27	32	34	22	10	17	23	18	208
Ramirez,Ramon			7	0	9	8	7	7	2	0	0	40
Ramos,A.J.									0	5	8	13
Ramos,Wilson							3	13	3	8	10	37
Rasmus,Colby						13	17	11	15	20	8	84
Reddick,Josh						0	1	7	16	13	13	50
Rendon,Anthony										12	26	38
Revere,Ben							0	9	11	10	16	46
Reyes,Jose	16	16	28	24	28	5	19	26	23	15	19	219
Reynolds,Mark				14	17	20	16	16	12	11	7	113
Richards,Garrett								0	1	6	13	20
Rios,Alex	7	9	18	22	20	11	18	4	22	15	9	155
Rivera,Rene	0	2	2						2	2	14	22
Rizzo,Anthony								0	12	14	28	54
Roark,Tanner										7	15	22
Roberts,Brian	35	28	13	22	20	20	7	3	1	9	7	165
Roberts,Ryan			0	0	0	8	1	19	9	4	0	41
Robertson,David					2	3	4	11	7	12	12	51
Rodney,Fernando	1	6	8	3	4	10	6	1	19	11	10	79
Rodriguez,Francisco	27	14	17	15	16	10	11	10	5	7	13	145
Rodriguez,Wandy		2	2	7	9	16	11	10	9	3	0	69
Rollins,Jimmy	80	21	25	28	24	19	14	25	21	20	19	296
Romo,Sergio					4	4	8	9	11	9	8	53
Rondon,Hector										2	11	13
Rosenthal,Trevor									2	7	11	20
Ross,Cody	1	0	6	10	16	16	14	14	13	8	2	100
Ross,David	7	3	13	7	5	6	6	7	6	2	2	64
Ross,Tyson							0	3	0	5	13	21
Ruggiano,Justin					0	1		4	11	8	8	32
Ruiz,Carlos			2	13	6	13	19	18	24	9	15	119
Ryan,Brendan				5	2	14	8	13	11	4	1	58
Ryu,Hyun-Jin										13	9	22
Sabathia,CC	49	12	15	24	23	18	20	19	14	8	0	202
Sale,Chris							5	11	19	15	17	67
Saltalamacchia,J				5	6	6	0	7	8	15	5	52
Samardzija,Jeff					3	0	0	7	8	7	11	36
Sanchez,Anibal			10	1	0	5	11	10	10	17	8	72
Sandoval,Pablo					6	27	9	23	18	22	21	126
Santana,Carlos							7	22	21	26	22	98
Santana,Danny											18	18
Santana,Ervin		6	12	3	19	6	14	14	2	14	9	99
Santiago,Ramon	9	0	1	2	6	7	9	5	3	3	8	53
Saunders,Joe		0	4	7	18	11	6	12	8	3	0	69
Saunders,Michael						1	6	2	17	10	10	46
Scherzer,Max					4	9	13	10	14	20	18	88
Schierholtz,Nate				2	3	8	5	13	8	14	2	55
Schumaker,Skip		0	0	7	16	18	14	11	7	8	4	85
Scutaro,Marco	13	11	11	8	15	21	15	11	21	16	0	142
Seager,Kyle								3	24	23	28	78
Segura,Jean									4	21	13	38
Shaw,Bryan								3	4	7	8	22
Shields,James			6	12	15	11	3	20	12	18	15	112
Shoemaker,Matt										1	11	12
Simmons,Andrelton									8	19	13	40
Simon,Alfredo					0	0	4	3	6	7	11	31
Smith,Joe				3	6	2	3	8	6	9	14	51
Smith,Seth				1	3	14	9	13	11	10	20	81
Smyly,Drew									6	10	10	26
Snider,Travis					3	4	8	3	5	5	10	38
Solano,Donovan									8	9	10	27
Solarte,Yangervis											16	16
Soriano,Alfonso	87	16	26	20	16	10	15	11	19	21	0	241
Soriano,Rafael	8	1	7	9	2	12	14	4	13	11	0	91
Soto,Geovany		0	0	3	21	8	15	10	5	8	2	72
Span,Denard					16	21	20	6	15	19	26	123
Springer,George											10	10
Stanton,Giancarlo							13	19	19	15	31	97
Storen,Drew							5	15	5	3	12	40
Strasburg,Stephen							5	2	14	11	13	45

Player	<05	05	06	07	08	09	10	11	12	13	14	Career
WIN SHARES BY YEAR												
Street,Huston		16	14	10	10	15	9	7	9	8	14	112
Stroman,Marcus											9	9
Stubbs,Drew						5	18	13	6	10	11	63
Suarez,Eugenio											9	9
Suzuki,Ichiro	112	22	24	33	19	28	23	15	11	10	8	305
Suzuki,Kurt				7	17	17	10	8	10	6	14	89
Sweeney,Ryan			0	0	12	12	8	7	3	6	5	53
Swisher,Nick	1	12	20	18	12	18	22	19	24	17	5	168
Tanaka,Masahiro											12	12
Teheran,Julio								0	0	12	15	27
Teixeira,Mark	36	33	21	25	28	26	24	22	16	1	10	242
Tejada,Ruben							3	11	14	4	15	47
Thornton,Matt	2	1	7	4	10	12	12	5	7	3	4	67
Tillman,Chris						2	1	1	8	14	13	39
Trout,Mike								3	38	40	40	121
Trumbo,Mark							0	14	19	14	8	55
Tulowitzki,Troy			1	24	9	24	25	25	5	21	16	150
Turner,Justin						0	0	15	4	3	18	40
Uehara,Koji						4	9	8	5	18	13	57
Uggla,Dan			23	16	24	18	24	21	23	10	1	160
Upton,B.J.	4		2	22	23	13	18	20	17	3	9	131
Upton,Justin				1	8	19	14	26	16	21	21	126
Uribe,Juan	44	17	11	13	11	13	16	2	2	15	14	158
Utley,Chase	13	25	27	28	30	32	25	18	13	22	24	257
Valbuena,Luis					1	6	4	0	5	9	17	42
Valverde,Jose	14	13	4	14	14	11	10	15	11	1	0	107
Van Slyke,Scott									1	3	9	13
Vargas,Jason		4	1	0		3	10	8	11	7	10	54
Venable,Will					3	8	15	12	17	14	10	79
Ventura,Yordano										1	13	14
Veras,Jose			1	1	5	2	4	5	6	9	4	37
Verlander,Justin		0	15	16	8	21	17	27	23	14	8	149
Victorino,Shane	0	1	11	11	20	22	23	23	17	19	2	149
Villanueva,Carlos			4	8	6	2	2	7	6	6	2	43
Vogt,Stephen									0	4	8	12
Volquez,Edinson		0	0	2	16	2	3	0	6	0	11	40
Votto,Joey				3	19	24	33	33	27	30	8	177
Wainwright,Adam		0	9	13	11	21	20		9	16	23	122
Walker,Neil						0	16	20	21	20	21	98
Warren,Adam									0	6	8	14
Watson,Tony								3	5	8	11	27
Weaver,Jered			14	12	11	17	19	24	16	10	12	135
Weeks,Rickie	0	9	10	14	16	7	29	18	14	4	9	130
Werth,Jayson	13	9		13	17	26	22	17	13	26	27	183
Wheeler,Zack										5	8	13
Wilhelmsen,Tom								3	13	8	8	32
Willingham,Josh	0	0	14	19	13	11	14	18	22	10	8	129
Wilson,Brian			1	5	9	15	17	9	0	2	0	58
Wilson,C.J.		0	3	9	2	11	15	20	9	13	5	87
Wong,Kolten										1	10	11
Wood,Alex										4	13	17
Wright,David	9	26	30	34	27	20	25	14	30	26	15	256
Wright,Jamey	48	4	4	5	3	4	3	6	3	5	2	87
Yelich,Christian										8	22	30
~~Young,Chris~~	2	10	12	12	5	1	3	3	3		9	60
Young,Chris			2	14	17	8	19	21	9	7	8	105
Young,Delmon			2	17	13	7	22	10	7	7	8	93
Zimmerman,Ryan		2	24	20	9	21	23	15	22	23	8	167
Zimmermann,Jordan						3	1	11	15	15	16	61
Zobrist,Ben			2	1	8	27	21	28	27	26	18	158
Zunino,Mike										2	11	13

Replay Appeal

Bill James

In 2014 Major League Baseball instituted a new rule, under which a manager had a limited right to ask for a videotape review of a play, if he felt that the umpire had gotten the call wrong. Pursuant to this rule there were 1,053 plays that were appealed.

Sticking with that number for just a second. . .that is 35 plays per team, over the course off the season. A team plays 162 games, so that means that in more than three games out of four, almost four out of five, an average team did not use its appeal. I would predict, based on this, that the number of plays which are appealed will increase over time. It seemed to me, just watching the games, that there were a substantial number of games in which a team had a play that could have been appealed early in the game, but they didn't use the appeal because they didn't want to lose it in case they needed it for a bigger play later in the game.

But if the appeal is going unused in almost 80% of games, it would seem to me that teams must be sitting on a resource that they will never in fact use a very high percentage of the time—and it is actually more than 80%, more like 90%, because if your appeal is upheld then you don't lose the right of appeal. Intuitively, that seems like an ineffective use of the strategy.

Anyway, the Cubs led the majors in aggressive use of the appeal, asking for reviews of 56 plays, while the Oakland A's were last with 26. Of the Cubs' 56 objections, 25 went in their favor, while 31 went against them, whereas with the A's, 14 of their objections were upheld against 12 denied. The data shows that when teams were aggressive in using their challenges they got a reversal less often as a percentage of the challenges—as you would expect—but that overall the more aggressive protesters gained more reversals. The squeaky wheels got the grease.

There are different ways to interpret the results. The Nationals were the big winners in the Replay Game. They protested 32 times—a normal number— but won 21 of the 32. Their opponents protested only 22 calls—almost the lowest number in the majors—and lost most of those, so the Nationals wound up 11 plays to the good on the season—21 gained, 10 lost. On the other end of the scale were the Texas Rangers, who wound up losing 9 calls.

But you could also figure the won-lost record of each team on appealed calls; the Yankees were 33-21, the same as the Nationals, whereas the Rangers were 35-53. The Cubs, who were involved in 90 protested calls, were 37-53. The data also shows that when teams were active in the protest business, their opponents also tended to be active; I don't know if that's relevant or not. There could be a cause-and-effect thing there, or it could be just that some teams had bad umpires; I don't know. Or it could mean nothing.

Anyway, of the 1053 protests by managers, 554 were upheld (and reversed), which is a little over half. In addition to those 1053 plays that went to video review, there were another 223 plays that were sent directly to review by the umpires themselves. When THAT happened, for some reason, the call usually was *not* reversed; only 50 of those 223 were reversed, which drags the overall reversal percentage down below 50%.

Add those together, 1053 and 223, and there were 1276 plays on which the umpires asked for semi-divine guidance. Of those 1,276 plays, over 80% were either Tag Plays or Force Plays. Force plays involve a straightforward issue of TIME; was the ball there first, or the runner? That's a fairly simple issue, so the video umpires felt comfortable reversing well over half of those calls, 56.5%. 56.5% means that 30% more were upheld than were denied.

Tag plays are harder; many times you can't really see whether the tag was made or wasn't, so those resulted in a much lower success percentage, 42.6%. 42.6% means that 35% more are denied than are upheld. In the other 20% of calls. . .the 20% that weren't either tag plays or force plays; actually it is less than 20%. The most common of those are home runs; there were 82 protested plays on possible home runs. Only 30% of those resulted in reversals, but of course when one of those *is* reversed, that's a high-impact play.

Only 47 fair or foul calls were protested (or double-checked) all year, a surprisingly low number, and only 13 of those were reversed, suggesting that umpires apparently don't miss that one too often.

A new rule or new practice can be considered "successful" if there is zero percent chance that you're going to get rid of it and go back to the old way. There is zero chance that we're going to get rid of this, and go back to allowing blown calls to stand; that's not even an issue. The questions before us now are whether to expand replay appeal, when to expand it, how to expand it. By that standard, the rule was a complete success.

The most obvious impact of the review rule was not anticipated. The most obvious impact was a dramatic reduction in on-field arguments between managers and umpires.

The implementation of the rule was not perfect. The mechanics and protocols of the system weren't in place far in advance of the season, and the preliminary version used in Spring Training differed from the full system in place for the regular season. By the end of April, managers had started to get a feel for the system. The system as it evolved was, the manager would rush out almost immediately after the play to position himself as if arguing with the umpire, but actually staring back into the dugout for a signal. Someone in a video room back near the clubhouse would study the play and determine as quickly as possible whether there was conclusive evidence of an umpire's error, and, upon reaching a conclusion, would send a runner to the dugout to deliver the message to the bench coach, who would give the manager a thumbs up or thumbs down or whatever. The manager would then either protest the play, or return quietly to the dugout.

There is a lesson in this. Being an old person, I remember baseball before salary arbitration. Before salary arbitration, every spring training was accompanied by news of "holdouts". Holdouts were nasty salary battles between player and team, in which the player refused to report to spring training because he felt his contract offer was unreasonable. These were, in many cases, bitter, ruinous conflicts that poisoned the relationship between the player and team, often beyond repair.

Then arbitration came along, and. . .presto, holdouts disappeared. For a while, people would try to say that arbitration cases had become a cause of hard feelings between players and teams. This was the silliest thing that anyone could possibly say. The cause of hard feelings between players and teams was that players felt they were not being given a fair salary offer. Arbitration very dramatically reduced the conflict between players and owners, especially young players, by creating a mechanism to resolve the dispute.

The same thing happened here; once we created a mechanism to resolve the disputes—even though it may have been a flawed mechanism—the conflicts just immediately disappeared. That's the real mark of success for the rule, the reason no one would even suggest going back to the way it was before.

Instant Replay Summary

Replay Type	Total Replays	Overturned	Percent
Tag Play	544	232	42.6
Force Play	508	287	56.5
Boundary Call (Over Fence)	82	25	30.5
Hit By Pitch	48	22	45.8
Fair or Foul	47	13	27.7
Trap or Catch	27	21	77.8
Record Keeping	10	2	20.0
Missed Base	9	2	22.2
Passed Runner	1	0	0.00
Total	1276	604	47.3

Challenges

Team	Challenges	Overturned	Percent	Opponent			Net
				Challenges	Overturned	Percent	
Nationals	32	21	65.6	22	10	45.5	11
Yankees	28	23	82.1	26	16	61.5	7
Braves	34	23	67.6	31	17	54.8	6
Angels	37	20	54.1	37	15	40.5	5
Rays	48	21	43.8	33	16	48.5	5
Marlins	27	19	70.4	26	14	53.8	5
Giants	35	22	62.9	37	17	45.9	5
Royals	35	22	62.9	42	18	42.9	4
Twins	36	19	52.8	33	15	45.5	4
Cubs	56	25	44.6	34	22	64.7	3
Pirates	35	20	57.1	39	18	46.2	2
Orioles	29	14	48.3	31	13	41.9	1
Red Sox	37	19	51.4	33	18	54.5	1
Indians	33	17	51.5	29	16	55.2	1
Mets	30	13	43.3	20	12	60.0	1
Padres	33	20	51.5	40	17	42.5	0
Athletics	26	14	53.8	33	15	45.5	-1
Diamondbacks	36	18	50.0	36	19	52.8	-1
Cardinals	31	12	38.7	28	13	46.4	-1
Astros	31	19	61.3	39	21	53.8	-2
Phillies	32	14	43.8	28	17	60.7	-3
White Sox	35	16	45.7	37	20	54.1	-4
Tigers	39	23	59.0	40	27	67.5	-4
Mariners	35	20	57.1	40	24	60.0	-4
Dodgers	38	22	57.9	51	26	51.0	-4
Blue Jays	48	16	33.3	49	22	44.9	-6
Brewers	28	17	60.7	42	23	54.8	-6
Reds	27	12	44.4	34	20	58.8	-8
Rockies	38	14	36.8	39	22	56.4	-8
Rangers	44	22	50.0	44	31	70.5	-9
Total	1053	554	52.6				

Hall of Fame Monitor

Bill James

There are certain types of performance that are characteristic of those who will be elected to the Hall of Fame. If you hit .300, that helps you get into the Hall of Fame; if you hit .280, it doesn't. If you hit 30 homers, 40 homers, that puts a few chips on your stack; if you hit 20 homers, 15, that doesn't get you anywhere. If you drive in 100 runs a year, that helps; if you drive in 90, that doesn't help. If you win a Gold Glove, play in an All Star game, win an MVP Award, those things tend to mark you as a Hall of Fame candidate; if you don't do those things, you get left out.

The Hall of Fame elects about two, three players a year, over time, so there should be about two or three players in each year of birth who are on the path toward the Hall of Fame. The question is, who are they? That's what this section is about. Among those players born in 1988—Matt Adams, Mike Moustakas, Dellin Betances, Elvis Andrus, Clayton Kershaw, Craig Kimbrel—which ones are well positioned to eventually join the immortals?

Of course, one year is not the same as the other; there are five players born in 1982 who are better Hall of Fame candidates than anyone born in 1981. The charts that follow attempt to add up all of the things that a player has done that would mark him as a Hall of Famer. If the total points are 100 or more, the player could be said to be a certain Hall of Famer, barring his involvement in some sort of Pete Rose- or Barry Bonds-type activity. There are only five players active in 2014 who meet that standard: Miguel Cabrera, Albert Pujols, Alex Rodriguez, Ichiro Suzuki and Derek Jeter; actually, Alex Rodriguez was not exactly active in 2014, and also it may be a little bit late for him to avoid involvement in any serious scandals. We also listed Chipper Jones on these lists because, while he was not active in 2014, he is still at an age where he reasonably could be.

Obviously, there are many more than five active players who will eventually be in the Hall of Fame; there probably are 40. What we are saying is that there are only five active players who, based on what they have already done, would appear to be locked in to Cooperstown, unless there is a black mark beside their names. Others will reach that status before they retire, and others beyond them will be voted in although it may not be entirely obvious. Generally speaking, if a player's final total is below 70, he probably won't make it, but if it is above 70 he has a realistic shot.

Leading Hall of Fame Candidates Born in 1992

Player	Points
Manny Machado	4
Bryce Harper	4

Leading Hall of Fame Candidates Born in 1991

Player	Points
Mike Trout	32

Leading Hall of Fame Candidates Born in 1990

Player	Points
Starlin Castro	19
Jose Altuve	17

Leading Hall of Fame Candidates Born in 1989

Player	Points
Freddie Freeman	17
Giancarlo Stanton	15
Chris Sale	11
Madison Bumgarner	11
Jason Heyward	10

Leading Hall of Fame Candidates Born in 1988

Player	Points
Clayton Kershaw	37
Craig Kimbrel	36
Aroldis Chapman	22
Elvis Andrus	18
Neftali Feliz	15

Leading Hall of Fame Candidates Born in 1987

Player	Points
Buster Posey	32
Justin Upton	18
Paul Goldschmidt	18
Kenley Jansen	14
Michael Brantley	13
Jay Bruce	12
Alex Avila	10
Kyle Seager	10
Austin Jackson	10

Leading Hall of Fame Candidates Born in 1986

Player	Points
Felix Hernandez	35
Andrew McCutchen	32
Pablo Sandoval	18
Matt Wieters	17
Chris Davis	17
Billy Butler	16
Jonathan Lucroy	15
Johnny Cueto	13
Carlos Santana	11
Jordan Zimmermann	10

Leading Hall of Fame Candidates Born in 1985

Player	Points
Evan Longoria	27
David Price	21
Adam Jones	19
Greg Holland	17
Carlos Gonzalez	17
Matt Carpenter	16
Asdrubal Cabrera	15
Chris Perez	12
Ian Desmond	11
Mark Melancon	11

Leading Hall of Fame Candidates Born in 1984

Player	Points
Prince Fielder	47
Brian McCann	36
Troy Tulowitzki	33
Matt Kemp	30
Tim Lincecum	30
Joakim Soria	26
Ryan Zimmerman	23
Melky Cabrera	22
Jon Lester	20
Alex Gordon	18

Leading Hall of Fame Candidates Born in 1983

Player	Points
Miguel Cabrera	115
Joe Mauer	79
Ryan Braun	55
Justin Verlander	51
Hanley Ramirez	50
Dustin Pedroia	48
Jose Reyes	46
Joey Votto	41
Huston Street	32
Hunter Pence	25

Leading Hall of Fame Candidates Born in 1982

Player	Points
Robinson Cano	74
Francisco Rodriguez	66
Adrian Gonzalez	56
David Wright	55
Yadier Molina	50
Ian Kinsler	36
Brian Wilson	27
Jered Weaver	26
Jhonny Peralta	25
Grady Sizemore	23

Leading Hall of Fame Candidates Born in 1981

Player	Points
Josh Hamilton	36
Justin Morneau	33
Curtis Granderson	33
Carl Crawford	31
Adam Wainwright	29
Ben Zobrist	28
Brandon Phillips	27
Jake Peavy	21
Alex Rios	17
James Shields	17

Leading Hall of Fame Candidates Born in 1978

Player	Points
Jimmy Rollins	66
Chase Utley	63
Victor Martinez	56
Aramis Ramirez	51
Cliff Lee	37
Jose Valverde	35
Vernon Wells	33
Jason Bay	31
Carlos Pena	21
Chone Figgins	19

Leading Hall of Fame Candidates Born in 1975

Player	Points
Alex Rodriguez	188
David Ortiz	69
Scott Rolen	65
Francisco Cordero	47
Torii Hunter	39
Tim Hudson	36
Placido Polanco	34
Chris Carpenter	33
Marco Scutaro	15

Leading Hall of Fame Candidates Born in 1980

Player	Points
Albert Pujols	167
Mark Teixeira	63
Matt Holliday	60
Jonathan Papelbon	60
CC Sabathia	46
Jose Bautista	34
Dan Uggla	30
Shane Victorino	22
Josh Beckett	21
Nick Swisher	19

Leading Hall of Fame Candidates Born in 1977

Player	Points
Carlos Beltran	70
Andruw Jones	63
Roy Halladay	61
Juan Pierre	36
Rafael Furcal	34
Roy Oswalt	31
J.J. Putz	27
Fernando Rodney	27
Brian Roberts	26
Eric Chavez	26

Leading Hall of Fame Candidates Born in 1974

Player	Points
Derek Jeter	164
Miguel Tejada	83
Bobby Abreu	79
Joe Nathan	79
R.A. Dickey	10

Leading Hall of Fame Candidates Born in 1973

Player	Points
Ichiro Suzuki	109
Todd Helton	98
Johnny Damon	56
Bartolo Colon	32

Leading Hall of Fame Candidates Born in 1979

Player	Points
Adrian Beltre	62
Ryan Howard	54
Adam Dunn	50
Johan Santana	45
Mark Buehrle	31
Rafael Soriano	26
Jayson Werth	24
Carlos Ruiz	20
Adam LaRoche	17
Michael Cuddyer	17

Leading Hall of Fame Candidates Born in 1976

Player	Points
Lance Berkman	72
Michael Young	69
Alfonso Soriano	63
Paul Konerko	50
Carlos Lee	50
A.J. Pierzynski	32
Kyle Farnsworth	15

Leading Hall of Fame Candidates Born in 1972

Player	Points
Chipper Jones	108
Andy Pettitte	56
Jason Isringhausen	46
Raul Ibanez	30
LaTroy Hawkins	27

Leading Hall of Fame Candidates Born in **1971**	
Player	**Points**
Jason Giambi	77

Confessions and Projections

Bill James

This is the Fort Sumter of the 2015 Baseball Season. Welcome to our projections; we're going to tell you here who will hit what in 2015. We're going to be wrong quite a bit. The projections for 2015 will follow; our first duty is to review the 2014 projections, and face up to our mistakes. In this section of the 2014 book we had projections for 424 hitters, or 424 hitters who actually played in 2014; we may have also included projections for a few players who didn't get a turn at bat. Those 424 projections can be sorted into five classes:

A. Players who had significantly less playing time in 2014 than we had projected for them,
B. Players who had significantly more playing time in 2014 than we had projected,
C. Players who hit more than we projected that they would hit,
D. Players who hit less than we projected that they would hit, and
E. Players whose projections turned out to be basically right both as to playing time and productivity.

This is how many of each of those types we had:

A	B	C	D	E
122	23	16	98	165

I'll try to point you to the most relevant examples of each type, and I'll include in this summary about 10% of the players from each group.

Players who had significantly less playing time than we projected.

There are basically three kinds of players in this group: Players who got hurt, young players that we projected to get playing time which failed to materialize, and players who lost their jobs because they didn't play well.

There are many more players who get less playing time than projected than who get more playing time than projected, because we don't really know who will step forward and who will fall back. It's like this: Does a team want to go into spring training with five potential starting pitchers, or seven? Of course, you want to go into spring training with as many starting pitchers as you can get, because you just never know. Some people are going to get hurt or underperform; you want to know what Plan B is.

If we only project playing time for the players that we BELIEVE will play next year, we're not telling you what Plan B is. We figure that if a player might have a substantial amount of playing time next year, we should tell you how well we believe he should hit. This frequently leads us to project much more playing time for young players than they will actually have. Like Caleb Gindl, Jake Elmore, Ryan Wheeler and Pedro Florimon.

Hitter	Label	G	AB	R	H	D	T	HR	RBI	BB	SO	SB	Avg	Slg
Gindl,Caleb	Actual	8	19	0	3	0	0	0	0	4	5	0	.158	.158
Gindl,Caleb	Projected	131	477	58	127	29	3	14	57	48	99	5	.266	.428

Hitter	Label	G	AB	R	H	D	T	HR	RBI	BB	SO	SB	Avg	Slg
Elmore,Jake	Actual	5	11	0	2	0	0	0	0	1	4	0	.182	.182
Elmore,Jake	Projected	86	290	41	78	15	2	3	28	34	41	15	.269	.366

Hitter	Label	G	AB	R	H	D	T	HR	RBI	BB	SO	SB	Avg	Slg
Wheeler,Ryan	Actual	31	56	6	13	2	0	2	13	5	12	0	.232	.375
Wheeler,Ryan	Projected	121	370	43	102	23	1	9	60	22	77	3	.276	.416

Hitter	Label	G	AB	R	H	D	T	HR	RBI	BB	SO	SB	Avg	Slg
Florimon,Pedro	Actual	33	76	7	7	1	1	0	1	8	22	6	.092	.132
Florimon,Pedro	Projected	142	440	49	105	21	1	8	46	38	113	15	.239	.345

There are also lots of veteran players every year that we sensibly and routinely project normal playing time for, not going out on a limb or anything, but they get hurt and can't play. Like (in 2014) Prince Fielder, Matt Wieters, Joey Votto and Shane Victorino:

Hitter	Label	G	AB	R	H	D	T	HR	RBI	BB	SO	SB	Avg	Slg
Fielder,Prince	Actual	42	150	19	37	8	0	3	16	25	24	0	.247	.360
Fielder,Prince	Projected	158	589	87	171	35	1	32	108	90	111	1	.290	.516

Hitter	Label	G	AB	R	H	D	T	HR	RBI	BB	SO	SB	Avg	Slg
Wieters,Matt	Actual	26	104	13	32	5	0	5	18	6	19	0	.308	.500
Wieters,Matt	Projected	145	525	64	133	30	1	22	80	53	105	2	.253	.440

Hitter	Label	G	AB	R	H	D	T	HR	RBI	BB	SO	SB	Avg	Slg
Votto,Joey	Actual	62	220	32	56	16	0	6	23	47	49	1	.255	.409
Votto,Joey	Projected	152	558	92	173	40	2	25	89	111	130	7	.310	.523

Hitter	Label	G	AB	R	H	D	T	HR	RBI	BB	SO	SB	Avg	Slg
Victorino,Shane	Actual	30	123	14	33	6	1	2	12	6	21	2	.268	.382
Victorino,Shane	Projected	148	549	83	148	28	5	14	58	44	81	23	.270	.415

There are also, every season, a certain number of older players that. . .the clock just runs out on them. We don't know when the clock will run out on a player; we know that it will, but we don't really know when, so we miss that. Like Rafael Furcal, Dan Uggla, Jason Kubel and Paul Konerko:

Hitter	Label	G	AB	R	H	D	T	HR	RBI	BB	SO	SB	Avg	Slg
Furcal,Rafael	Actual	9	35	4	6	0	1	0	2	2	7	0	.171	.229
Furcal,Rafael	Projected	91	357	52	94	16	2	6	31	35	47	10	.263	.370

Hitter	Label	G	AB	R	H	D	T	HR	RBI	BB	SO	SB	Avg	Slg
Uggla,Dan	Actual	52	141	14	21	3	0	2	10	11	46	0	.149	.213
Uggla,Dan	Projected	143	479	71	102	22	1	23	66	72	163	2	.213	.407

Hitter	Label	G	AB	R	H	D	T	HR	RBI	BB	SO	SB	Avg	Slg
Kubel,Jason	Actual	45	156	12	35	6	1	1	13	19	59	1	.224	.295
Kubel,Jason	Projected	132	440	52	107	24	2	17	69	47	129	1	.243	.423

Hitter	Label	G	AB	R	H	D	T	HR	RBI	BB	SO	SB	Avg	Slg
Konerko,Paul	Actual	81	208	15	43	8	0	5	22	10	51	0	.207	.317
Konerko,Paul	Projected	147	539	62	146	24	0	23	80	62	92	0	.271	.443

OK, there are 122 players in that group and I've given you the full data for 12 of them, so we'll move on.

Players who had significantly more playing time in 2014 than we projected.

There are not so many of these. In 2014 there were 23, including Dee Gordon and Steve Pearce:

Hitter	Label	G	AB	R	H	D	T	HR	RBI	BB	SO	SB	Avg	Slg
Gordon,Dee	Actual	148	609	92	176	24	12	2	34	31	107	64	.289	.378
Gordon,Dee	Projected	55	186	25	49	6	2	0	11	15	33	22	.263	.317

Hitter	Label	G	AB	R	H	D	T	HR	RBI	BB	SO	SB	Avg	Slg
Pearce,Steve	Actual	102	338	51	99	26	0	21	49	40	76	5	.293	.556
Pearce,Steve	Projected	75	184	23	49	13	0	6	27	21	36	2	.266	.435

Two of these 23 players, Pearce and Justin Turner, played more than we expected because they played better than we expected, but as a whole they did not; as a whole these 23 players played much more than we had thought that they might, but no better. They were just players for whom a hole opened up for them, and they stepped into it.

Players who hit more than we projected that they would hit.

This, again, is a small group, 16 players. In part this group is small for the same reasons; in a sense, we are projecting what players are capable of doing, but not all players will do what they are capable of doing. Some players in any season will fall short of what they are capable of doing—whereas very few players in any season will do things that there was no real reason to believe they had in them.

Also, this group was small in 2014 because it was a pitcher's year. When it's a pitcher's year, there are a lot of hitters who underachieve. We were doing this in the early 1990s, and for several years we had a running debate about why so many hitters were hitting **better** than we thought they would hit. We finally accepted, about 1996, that this was just the new reality; teams were scoring 850 runs a season. Now we're on the other end of that:

Hitter	Label	G	AB	R	H	D	T	HR	RBI	BB	SO	SB	Avg	Slg
Brantley,Michael	Actual	156	611	94	200	45	2	20	97	52	56	23	.327	.506
Brantley,Michael	Projected	150	553	72	153	28	3	8	60	49	66	18	.277	.382

Hitter	Label	G	AB	R	H	D	T	HR	RBI	BB	SO	SB	Avg	Slg
Martinez,Victor	Actual	151	561	87	188	33	0	32	103	70	42	3	.335	.565
Martinez,Victor	Projected	150	575	70	173	36	0	15	92	55	64	0	.301	.442

Players who hit less than we projected they would hit.

There were 98 of these; 16 players who hit more than we thought they would hit, 98 who hit less. I'll give you ten of them—or I could just give you the Red Sox starting lineup (rim shot). It is literally true that every player in the Red Sox early-season lineup underachieved relative to his projections except David Ortiz; Ortiz hit 24 points lower than we had projected, but the projection is generally accurate. Everybody else was short.

A lot of these are projections that are not really terrible; we were just a little bit optimistic. Like Anthony Recker, Alejandro De Aza, Carlos Santana and Matt Holliday:

Hitter	Label	G	AB	R	H	D	T	HR	RBI	BB	SO	SB	Avg	Slg
Recker,Anthony	Actual	58	174	18	35	9	0	7	27	10	64	1	.201	.374
Recker,Anthony	Projected	72	217	26	51	11	1	8	27	22	63	1	.235	.406

Hitter	Label	G	AB	R	H	D	T	HR	RBI	BB	SO	SB	Avg	Slg
De Aza,Alejandro	Actual	142	477	56	120	24	8	8	41	39	119	17	.252	.386
De Aza,Alejandro	Projected	142	547	82	155	32	4	13	57	47	113	20	.283	.428

Hitter	Label	G	AB	R	H	D	T	HR	RBI	BB	SO	SB	Avg	Slg
Santana,Carlos	Actual	152	541	68	125	25	0	27	85	113	124	5	.231	.427
Santana,Carlos	Projected	148	541	83	144	38	1	23	87	102	103	4	.266	.468

Hitter	Label	G	AB	R	H	D	T	HR	RBI	BB	SO	SB	Avg	Slg
Holliday,Matt	Actual	156	574	83	156	37	0	20	90	74	100	4	.272	.441
Holliday,Matt	Projected	151	570	98	170	39	1	25	99	72	110	6	.298	.502

Mike Trout is in this category; obviously Trout had a good season and may win the MVP award, but he struck out a lot more than we thought he would, and we over-projected his batting average by 44 points:

Hitter	Label	G	AB	R	H	D	T	HR	RBI	BB	SO	SB	Avg	Slg
Trout,Mike	Actual	157	602	115	173	39	9	36	111	83	184	16	.287	.561
Trout,Mike	Projected	159	598	134	198	36	11	30	96	96	128	39	.331	.579

Other of our over-projections were more serious—like Nick Swisher, Jay Bruce, Chris Davis, Jean Segura and Allen Craig:

Hitter	Label	G	AB	R	H	D	T	HR	RBI	BB	SO	SB	Avg	Slg
Swisher,Nick	Actual	97	360	33	75	20	0	8	42	36	111	0	.208	.331
Swisher,Nick	Projected	144	501	72	125	28	1	22	73	78	132	1	.250	.441

Hitter	Label	G	AB	R	H	D	T	HR	RBI	BB	SO	SB	Avg	Slg
Bruce,Jay	Actual	137	493	71	107	21	1	18	66	44	149	12	.217	.373
Bruce,Jay	Projected	160	607	92	157	36	3	34	102	67	170	7	.259	.496

Hitter	Label	G	AB	R	H	D	T	HR	RBI	BB	SO	SB	Avg	Slg
Davis,Chris	Actual	127	450	65	88	16	0	26	72	60	173	2	.196	.404
Davis,Chris	Projected	160	582	92	161	38	1	41	113	57	193	3	.277	.557

Hitter	Label	G	AB	R	H	D	T	HR	RBI	BB	SO	SB	Avg	Slg
Segura,Jean	Actual	146	513	61	126	14	6	5	31	28	70	20	.246	.326
Segura,Jean	Projected	155	606	82	180	22	9	11	58	33	81	48	.297	.417

Hitter	Label	G	AB	R	H	D	T	HR	RBI	BB	SO	SB	Avg	Slg
Craig,Allen	Actual	126	461	41	99	20	1	8	46	35	113	2	.215	.315
Craig,Allen	Projected	136	505	75	156	33	1	19	94	40	90	2	.309	.491

Sometimes we have too-friendly projections for young players like Segura, sometimes for veterans like Bruce and Swisher, but most often for veterans; young players who don't produce more often wind up in the "players who didn't get playing time" category than in the "playing time correct; just didn't produce" category.

Players whose projections turned out to be basically right both as to playing time and productivity.

There were 165 of these, which means that I get to share 17 of them with you. My favorites among these are players who, by luck, we happen to get a couple of key categories exactly right. Like Edwin Encarnacion:

Hitter	Label	G	AB	R	H	D	T	HR	RBI	BB	SO	SB	Avg	Slg
Encarnacion,E.	Actual	128	477	75	128	27	2	34	98	62	82	2	.268	.547
Encarnacion,E.	Projected	150	544	89	152	32	1	34	98	74	82	7	.274	.520

Adam Jones, we got his batting average and home runs exactly right:

Hitter	Label	G	AB	R	H	D	T	HR	RBI	BB	SO	SB	Avg	Slg
Jones,Adam	Actual	159	644	88	181	30	2	29	96	19	133	7	.281	.469
Jones,Adam	Projected	160	633	94	178	33	3	29	93	32	131	13	.281	.480

Garrett Jones, we got his home runs right and missed by very small margins on RBI and batting average:

Hitter	Label	G	AB	R	H	D	T	HR	RBI	BB	SO	SB	Avg	Slg
Jones,Garrett	Actual	146	496	59	122	33	2	15	53	46	116	0	.246	.411
Jones,Garrett	Projected	127	351	42	87	22	1	15	52	30	85	3	.248	.444

Obviously, that's just luck when that happens; throw 400 darts, one of them will hit the center of the target just by dumb luck. Billy Hamilton, we overall didn't have a great projection, but we did get his home runs and RBI right:

Hitter	Label	G	AB	R	H	D	T	HR	RBI	BB	SO	SB	Avg	Slg
Hamilton,Billy	Actual	152	563	72	141	25	8	6	48	34	117	56	.250	.355
Hamilton,Billy	Projected	145	584	97	156	21	5	6	48	57	116	96	.267	.351

Albert Pujols almost wound up in the category of players who achieved less than we thought he would, because we were 18 points high on his batting average and 62 points high in slugging, but we did happen to get his doubles and RBI right on the nose:

Hitter	Label	G	AB	R	H	D	T	HR	RBI	BB	SO	SB	Avg	Slg
Pujols,Albert	Actual	159	633	89	172	37	1	28	105	48	71	5	.272	.466
Pujols,Albert	Projected	152	572	91	166	37	0	33	105	76	74	5	.290	.528

Of course, these type of perfect matches in certain columns are not what we generally mean by "basically right both as to playing time and productivity." Generally it is a looser, more general match. Like Torii Hunter or Starling Marte:

Hitter	Label	G	AB	R	H	D	T	HR	RBI	BB	SO	SB	Avg	Slg
Hunter,Torii	Actual	142	549	71	157	33	2	17	83	23	89	4	.286	.446
Hunter,Torii	Projected	152	594	81	167	31	1	19	87	43	126	5	.281	.433

Hitter	Label	G	AB	R	H	D	T	HR	RBI	BB	SO	SB	Avg	Slg
Marte,Starling	Actual	135	495	73	144	29	6	13	56	33	131	30	.291	.453
Marte,Starling	Projected	149	556	90	163	31	11	15	55	29	131	41	.293	.469

A lot of players—most players, actually, had worse strikeout/walk ratios than we had projected for them even when we got the other stuff right, because of the way the strike zone was being called in 2014:

Hitter	Label	G	AB	R	H	D	T	HR	RBI	BB	SO	SB	Avg	Slg
Solano,Donovan	Actual	111	310	26	78	11	1	3	28	19	61	1	.252	.323
Solano,Donovan	Projected	102	321	31	83	15	1	3	29	20	50	3	.259	.340

Hitter	Label	G	AB	R	H	D	T	HR	RBI	BB	SO	SB	Avg	Slg
Zunino,Mike	Actual	131	438	51	87	20	2	22	60	17	158	0	.199	.404
Zunino,Mike	Projected	118	336	45	75	16	2	13	43	28	96	1	.223	.399

Hitter	Label	G	AB	R	H	D	T	HR	RBI	BB	SO	SB	Avg	Slg
Castillo,Welington	Actual	110	380	28	90	19	0	13	46	26	102	0	.237	.389
Castillo,Welington	Projected	123	415	46	109	24	0	13	50	37	100	1	.263	.414

Surprisingly, strikeouts and walks are difficult to project; they bounce around more than you would think they would. Projecting strikeouts and walks accurately is more difficult than projecting batting averages accurately. Chris Carter hit 10 more home runs than we had projected for him, although it was generally an accurate projection:

Hitter	Label	G	AB	R	H	D	T	HR	RBI	BB	SO	SB	Avg	Slg
Carter,Chris	Actual	145	507	68	115	21	1	37	88	56	182	5	.227	.491
Carter,Chris	Projected	145	502	73	120	28	1	27	84	68	172	3	.239	.460

Lonnie Chisenhall is an interesting one. Early in the year he had a great hot streak, and I was getting a lot of questions like "Did you ever have any idea that Lonnie Chisenhall was going to be this good?" But by the end of the season, Chisenhall was actually slightly *below* what we had projected for him:

Hitter	Label	G	AB	R	H	D	T	HR	RBI	BB	SO	SB	Avg	Slg
Chisenhall,Lonnie	Actual	142	478	62	134	29	1	13	59	39	99	3	.280	.427
Chisenhall,Lonnie	Projected	132	455	65	121	28	2	18	69	32	85	3	.266	.455

Matt Kemp was up and down and over and out, but on the whole he was who we thought he was:

Hitter	Label	G	AB	R	H	D	T	HR	RBI	BB	SO	SB	Avg	Slg
Kemp,Matt	Actual	150	541	77	155	38	3	25	89	52	145	8	.287	.506
Kemp,Matt	Projected	142	543	87	157	30	3	23	85	50	147	20	.289	.483

When Edwin Encarnacion was out with an injury, some of his playing time was picked up by Juan Francisco, who we also had projected accurately, generally speaking:

Hitter	Label	G	AB	R	H	D	T	HR	RBI	BB	SO	SB	Avg	Slg
Francisco,Juan	Actual	106	287	40	63	16	2	16	43	27	116	0	.220	.456
Francisco,Juan	Projected	100	252	31	64	15	1	13	41	17	80	0	.254	.476

We had fairly accurate projections for both of the Upton brothers:

Hitter	Label	G	AB	R	H	D	T	HR	RBI	BB	SO	SB	Avg	Slg
Upton,Justin	Actual	154	566	77	153	34	2	29	102	60	171	8	.270	.491
Upton,Justin	Projected	155	588	104	162	33	4	27	83	75	153	12	.276	.483

Hitter	Label	G	AB	R	H	D	T	HR	RBI	BB	SO	SB	Avg	Slg
Upton,B.J.	Actual	141	519	67	108	19	5	12	35	57	173	20	.208	.333
Upton,B.J.	Projected	146	530	69	121	29	2	17	60	61	174	24	.228	.387

That's got to be a record for strikeouts by brothers, doesn't it, 344 strikeouts by two brothers? And, in closing, Giancarlo:

Hitter	Label	G	AB	R	H	D	T	HR	RBI	BB	SO	SB	Avg	Slg
Stanton,Giancarlo	Actual	145	539	89	155	31	1	37	105	94	170	13	.288	.555
Stanton,Giancarlo	Projected	139	513	86	142	33	2	38	97	75	152	3	.277	.571

Thanks for reading, and here's how everybody will hit in 2015.

Hitter	Team	Age	G	AB	H	2B	3B	HR	R	RBI	RC	RC27	BB	SO	SB	CS	SB%	Avg	OBP	Slg	OPS
Abreu,Jose	CWS	28	151	599	187	40	2	38	89	121	128	8.04	58	128	3	2	.60	.312	.383	.576	.959
Ackley,Dustin	Sea	27	140	491	126	26	4	11	66	53	62	4.37	48	83	8	4	.67	.257	.324	.393	.717
Adams,Matt	StL	26	140	521	151	34	2	22	65	82	83	5.80	30	108	2	2	.50	.290	.330	.489	.819
Alcantara,Arismendy	ChC	23	154	582	151	38	8	19	82	70	84	4.96	48	154	32	9	.78	.259	.317	.450	.767
Alonso,Yonder	SD	28	87	276	79	18	1	8	29	36	43	5.62	26	39	5	2	.71	.286	.350	.446	.795
Altuve,Jose	Hou	25	156	642	203	41	3	7	82	55	99	5.69	37	63	46	13	.78	.316	.357	.422	.779
Alvarez,Pedro	Pit	28	151	540	130	25	2	29	66	88	78	4.91	60	168	6	3	.67	.241	.319	.456	.774
Amarista,Alexi	SD	26	132	351	90	15	3	5	38	37	38	3.74	22	50	9	3	.75	.256	.302	.359	.661
Andrus,Elvis	Tex	26	157	617	167	28	4	3	86	55	71	4.00	54	95	30	12	.71	.271	.333	.344	.677
Aoki,Nori	KC	33	139	480	136	23	3	4	63	38	61	4.51	43	40	15	8	.65	.283	.353	.369	.722
Arcia,Oswaldo	Min	24	147	531	143	30	4	30	78	96	89	5.93	47	155	3	2	.60	.269	.333	.510	.844
Arenado,Nolan	Col	24	152	593	170	47	3	20	73	79	93	5.70	36	74	2	1	.67	.287	.330	.477	.807
Arencibia,J.P.	Tex	29	95	287	67	14	0	15	33	44	34	4.02	15	79	0	0	.00	.233	.281	.439	.720
Arias,Joaquin	SF	30	88	174	46	7	1	1	18	16	17	3.43	6	21	2	1	.67	.264	.293	.333	.626
Asche,Cody	Phi	25	132	433	119	29	2	14	54	63	64	5.28	37	99	2	1	.67	.275	.332	.448	.780
Avila,Alex	Det	28	125	417	96	25	1	13	48	56	54	4.37	65	144	1	0	1.00	.230	.337	.388	.725
Aviles,Mike	Cle	34	98	266	68	13	1	6	32	30	29	3.73	11	38	8	4	.67	.256	.288	.380	.667
Aybar,Erick	LAA	31	153	590	164	32	4	7	76	59	71	4.25	32	66	16	8	.67	.278	.321	.381	.702
Baez,Javier	ChC	22	152	612	148	33	1	32	79	72	82	4.50	48	214	23	10	.70	.242	.298	.456	.754
Baker,Jeff	Mia	34	87	187	48	11	1	5	22	22	23	4.27	14	50	1	1	.50	.257	.312	.406	.718
Baker,John	ChC	34	65	184	40	8	0	2	16	17	16	2.89	20	47	0	0	.00	.217	.298	.293	.591
Barmes,Clint	Pit	36	89	232	53	11	0	4	22	22	21	3.03	14	48	1	1	.50	.228	.287	.328	.614
Barnes,Brandon	Col	29	87	172	43	10	1	4	22	18	20	3.97	11	49	4	2	.67	.250	.303	.390	.692
Barney,Darwin	LAD	29	106	305	74	15	1	3	34	25	29	3.25	19	40	3	1	.75	.243	.296	.328	.624
Bautista,Jose	Tor	34	144	541	142	27	1	34	94	95	102	6.60	97	105	5	3	.62	.262	.380	.505	.885
Beckham,Gordon	LAA	28	103	305	74	18	0	7	38	32	33	3.70	22	54	3	1	.75	.243	.308	.370	.679
Belt,Brandon	SF	27	155	542	153	35	4	24	78	80	95	6.28	63	134	8	4	.67	.282	.360	.494	.855
Beltran,Carlos	NYY	38	117	438	115	25	1	18	58	64	65	5.20	46	87	4	2	.67	.263	.335	.447	.783
Beltre,Adrian	Tex	36	157	607	183	36	1	25	83	92	104	6.36	47	86	2	1	.67	.301	.356	.488	.843
Bethancourt,Christian	Atl	23	118	379	99	16	1	8	36	43	40	3.66	14	67	8	4	.67	.261	.289	.372	.661
Betts,Mookie	Bos	22	154	560	180	41	5	15	112	76	115	7.65	77	74	40	11	.78	.321	.405	.493	.898
Blackmon,Charlie	Col	28	125	416	118	23	2	11	61	49	58	4.94	25	64	17	7	.71	.284	.333	.428	.761
Blanco,Gregor	SF	31	142	417	105	17	3	4	55	35	48	3.91	52	90	18	7	.72	.252	.338	.336	.673
Bloomquist,Willie	Sea	37	52	149	40	6	1	1	19	11	15	3.51	8	28	3	2	.60	.268	.310	.342	.652
Bogaerts,Xander	Bos	22	156	592	156	33	2	16	76	66	78	4.62	53	135	4	3	.57	.264	.328	.407	.735
Bonifacio,Emilio	Atl	30	103	300	78	12	3	2	39	19	33	3.75	23	67	19	7	.73	.260	.315	.340	.655
Borbon,Julio	Bal	29	68	112	31	4	1	1	14	9	13	4.02	8	16	7	3	.70	.277	.325	.357	.682
Bourjos,Peter	StL	28	94	203	51	8	3	4	29	19	23	3.86	15	50	7	3	.70	.251	.318	.379	.698
Bourn,Michael	Cle	32	145	564	145	23	6	4	76	40	62	3.77	51	145	23	9	.72	.257	.322	.340	.662
Bradley Jr.,Jackie	Bos	25	129	390	88	23	2	6	53	36	39	3.31	37	104	8	4	.67	.226	.298	.341	.639
Brantley,Michael	Cle	28	153	574	169	34	3	13	80	71	89	5.63	52	60	20	6	.77	.294	.357	.432	.789
Braun,Ryan	Mil	31	142	553	162	35	3	26	85	93	99	6.48	51	118	14	6	.70	.293	.359	.508	.867
Brown,Domonic	Phi	27	141	480	127	25	2	17	61	71	67	4.88	43	86	9	4	.69	.265	.326	.431	.758
Bruce,Jay	Cin	28	156	592	147	33	2	29	87	92	86	4.97	62	172	11	5	.69	.248	.323	.458	.780
Bryant,Kris	ChC	23	152	530	141	32	1	33	105	75	96	6.32	66	171	18	6	.75	.266	.347	.517	.864
Butera,Drew	LAD	31	47	136	29	6	0	2	11	11	11	2.67	9	28	0	0	.00	.213	.267	.301	.569
Butler,Billy	KC	29	159	596	173	38	0	17	67	86	94	5.78	62	102	0	0	.00	.290	.361	.440	.801
Byrd,Marlon	Phi	37	152	570	145	31	2	18	67	71	69	4.20	34	164	3	2	.60	.254	.306	.411	.716
Cabrera,Asdrubal	Was	29	145	532	138	33	2	14	72	64	69	4.51	45	105	10	4	.71	.259	.325	.408	.733
Cabrera,Everth	SD	28	110	380	102	17	3	3	51	28	46	4.18	35	79	26	8	.76	.268	.333	.353	.686
Cabrera,Melky	Tor	30	134	544	162	32	3	12	76	67	82	5.52	41	69	7	4	.64	.298	.349	.434	.783
Cabrera,Miguel	Det	32	158	610	196	43	1	34	102	123	137	8.58	79	112	2	1	.67	.321	.403	.562	.965
Cain,Lorenzo	KC	29	135	483	137	26	4	7	62	54	65	4.79	34	100	23	7	.77	.284	.335	.398	.732
Calhoun,Kole	LAA	27	148	574	162	36	5	20	96	78	91	5.69	49	107	8	4	.67	.282	.340	.467	.807
Callaspo,Alberto	Oak	32	122	369	93	17	1	6	40	38	42	3.94	38	42	1	1	.50	.252	.324	.352	.676
Campbell,Eric	NYM	28	62	128	34	8	0	2	15	14	17	4.65	15	26	3	1	.75	.266	.343	.375	.718
Cano,Robinson	Sea	32	160	617	191	42	2	22	88	96	111	6.73	56	81	7	3	.70	.310	.374	.491	.865
Carp,Mike	Tex	29	62	119	30	6	0	4	14	16	15	4.38	12	29	0	0	.00	.252	.336	.403	.739
Carpenter,Matt	StL	29	155	566	167	40	3	10	97	68	93	6.01	83	94	4	3	.57	.295	.391	.429	.820
Carter,Chris	Hou	28	146	509	123	26	1	33	75	90	82	5.49	64	167	5	2	.71	.242	.330	.491	.821
Castellanos,Nick	Det	23	146	521	136	31	3	15	58	62	66	4.43	38	115	3	2	.60	.261	.314	.407	.721
Castillo, Rusney	Bos	27	145	522	136	31	4	22	84	67	77	5.09	44	89	32	7	.82	.261	.316	.462	.778
Castillo,Welington	ChC	28	118	421	109	23	0	14	42	53	55	4.57	35	101	1	1	.50	.259	.323	.413	.737
Castro,Jason	Hou	28	121	408	102	24	1	13	48	49	53	4.49	41	111	1	1	.50	.250	.325	.409	.734
Castro,Starlin	ChC	25	150	582	165	34	5	12	68	63	79	4.87	35	100	9	5	.64	.284	.329	.421	.749
Cecchini,Garin	Bos	24	133	469	123	26	2	8	60	59	62	4.61	58	112	14	4	.78	.262	.345	.377	.722
Cervelli,Francisco	NYY	29	72	229	60	11	1	3	28	26	27	4.13	23	50	2	1	.67	.262	.337	.358	.695
Cespedes,Yoenis	Bos	29	145	572	153	31	4	25	84	95	84	5.16	39	117	8	4	.67	.267	.319	.467	.785
Chavez,Endy	Sea	37	71	148	37	6	0	1	14	10	13	3.02	8	20	2	1	.67	.250	.288	.311	.599
Chirinos,Robinson	Tex	31	94	299	73	16	0	10	34	39	36	4.14	25	61	1	0	1.00	.244	.309	.398	.707
Chisenhall,Lonnie	Cle	26	142	499	135	31	2	17	68	71	72	5.13	39	93	3	1	.75	.271	.328	.443	.771
Choice,Michael	Tex	25	82	241	59	10	1	8	31	36	30	4.26	24	61	2	1	.67	.245	.318	.394	.713
Choo,Shin-Soo	Tex	32	151	551	146	31	2	17	81	64	83	5.26	80	148	10	5	.67	.265	.371	.421	.792
Coghlan,Chris	ChC	30	105	293	77	20	2	5	37	28	39	4.61	32	59	8	4	.67	.263	.339	.396	.735
Colabello,Chris	Min	31	71	188	50	12	0	8	22	33	28	5.28	17	49	0	0	.00	.266	.330	.457	.788
Colon,Christian	KC	26	56	118	31	5	0	2	15	13	13	3.80	9	11	5	2	.71	.263	.315	.356	.671
Conger,Hank	LAA	27	89	242	59	13	0	6	27	29	28	3.98	23	50	0	0	.00	.244	.315	.372	.687
Corporan,Carlos	Hou	31	52	162	39	8	0	5	16	19	18	3.80	10	37	0	0	.00	.241	.297	.383	.680
Cowgill,Collin	LAA	29	78	158	40	8	1	4	22	18	20	4.37	15	36	4	1	.80	.253	.326	.392	.718
Cozart,Zack	Cin	29	149	520	130	28	3	9	64	48	56	3.71	30	82	7	2	.78	.250	.295	.367	.662

535

2015 Hitter Projections

PLAYER			BATTING												BASERUNNING			AVERAGES			
Hitter	Team	Age	G	AB	H	2B	3B	HR	R	RBI	RC	RC27	BB	SO	SB	CS	SB%	Avg	OBP	Slg	OPS
Craig,Allen	Bos	30	130	492	138	30	1	15	64	79	72	5.27	39	99	2	1	.67	.280	.338	.437	.775
Crawford,Brandon	SF	28	154	522	125	25	5	9	56	55	58	3.77	54	125	4	3	.57	.239	.313	.358	.671
Crawford,Carl	LAD	33	118	412	117	21	4	9	62	48	57	4.91	25	70	21	7	.75	.284	.331	.420	.751
Crisp,Coco	Oak	35	136	497	126	23	3	12	75	53	65	4.48	58	73	22	6	.79	.254	.332	.384	.716
Cron,C.J.	LAA	25	143	466	123	30	2	16	53	71	61	4.60	22	93	3	2	.60	.264	.299	.440	.738
Cruz,Nelson	Bal	34	152	574	151	33	1	33	77	98	91	5.55	50	143	6	3	.67	.263	.325	.497	.822
Cruz,Tony	StL	28	50	139	31	7	0	2	13	15	12	2.89	10	26	0	0	.00	.223	.280	.317	.597
Cuddyer,Michael	Col	36	134	504	144	31	2	19	73	75	82	5.87	46	96	7	3	.70	.286	.348	.468	.816
Danks,Jordan	CWS	28	85	194	49	9	1	6	25	21	26	4.60	23	60	4	2	.67	.253	.332	.402	.734
d'Arnaud,Travis	NYM	26	122	451	125	25	2	19	63	63	71	5.65	40	75	1	1	.50	.277	.337	.468	.805
Davidson,Matt	CWS	24	45	142	30	6	0	7	16	17	16	3.71	13	48	0	0	.00	.211	.277	.401	.679
Davis,Chris	Bal	29	154	547	138	31	1	36	84	99	91	5.77	59	194	3	1	.75	.252	.332	.510	.842
Davis,Ike	Pit	28	128	322	78	19	0	14	42	47	48	5.09	52	81	1	1	.50	.242	.349	.432	.781
Davis,Khris	Mil	27	140	512	134	38	1	25	75	79	79	5.39	44	116	6	3	.67	.262	.327	.486	.814
Davis,Rajai	Det	34	114	327	86	18	2	5	44	31	38	3.95	18	61	25	9	.74	.263	.309	.376	.686
De Aza,Alejandro	Bal	31	128	428	114	25	4	9	58	41	56	4.52	36	102	15	8	.65	.266	.330	.407	.737
DeJesus,David	TB	35	98	272	69	15	2	5	35	27	33	4.19	29	51	2	2	.50	.254	.341	.379	.720
den Dekker,Matt	NYM	27	57	123	33	8	1	2	18	13	16	4.52	11	29	4	2	.67	.268	.333	.398	.732
Denorfia,Chris	Sea	34	112	291	74	13	2	5	36	24	33	3.90	23	57	7	3	.70	.254	.311	.364	.675
Descalso,Daniel	StL	28	71	117	28	7	1	1	14	12	12	3.47	11	22	1	1	.50	.239	.315	.342	.657
Desmond,Ian	Was	29	156	604	159	34	3	21	74	78	82	4.71	43	165	21	8	.72	.263	.316	.434	.750
Dickerson,Corey	Col	26	151	514	158	34	8	25	87	78	100	7.16	41	103	9	7	.56	.307	.360	.551	.910
Dietrich,Derek	Mia	25	88	315	80	15	3	15	55	44	45	4.96	25	74	3	1	.75	.254	.323	.463	.786
Dirks,Andy	Det	29	128	429	118	22	2	11	63	47	59	4.87	35	72	10	4	.71	.275	.331	.413	.744
Dominguez,Matt	Hou	25	155	553	129	26	1	18	57	73	59	3.62	35	99	0	0	.00	.233	.283	.382	.664
Donaldson,Josh	Oak	29	151	575	154	33	1	25	85	93	91	5.58	67	111	7	3	.70	.268	.349	.459	.808
Doumit,Ryan	Atl	34	85	203	50	12	0	6	21	25	24	4.08	16	48	1	0	1.00	.246	.311	.394	.705
Dozier,Brian	Min	28	152	575	143	33	3	19	90	67	78	4.61	68	110	17	8	.68	.249	.334	.416	.750
Drew,Stephen	NYY	32	132	470	107	28	4	12	55	52	54	3.85	51	121	4	2	.67	.228	.305	.381	.685
Duda,Lucas	NYM	29	147	494	123	29	1	24	66	76	77	5.38	69	133	2	1	.67	.249	.349	.457	.807
Dyson,Jarrod	KC	30	130	322	82	10	3	1	48	22	35	3.64	29	58	39	10	.80	.255	.316	.314	.630
Eaton,Adam	CWS	26	136	537	158	31	8	4	87	42	77	5.16	49	85	20	9	.69	.294	.358	.404	.762
Ellis,A.J.	LAD	34	106	318	76	14	1	6	33	38	38	4.08	50	59	0	0	.00	.239	.348	.346	.694
Ellis,Mark	StL	38	87	237	57	10	0	3	26	22	22	3.14	18	44	3	2	.60	.241	.310	.321	.631
Ellsbury,Jacoby	NYY	31	141	582	165	31	4	14	88	63	86	5.24	47	92	38	10	.79	.284	.341	.423	.764
Encarnacion,Edwin	Tor	32	147	551	146	30	1	35	86	99	99	6.32	72	90	4	2	.67	.265	.355	.514	.869
Escobar,Alcides	KC	28	160	584	156	27	5	4	68	50	63	3.77	26	85	27	7	.79	.267	.303	.351	.654
Escobar,Eduardo	Min	26	133	422	112	25	3	6	52	38	50	4.17	26	84	4	2	.67	.265	.310	.382	.691
Escobar,Yunel	TB	32	150	544	143	24	1	9	60	53	64	4.13	54	73	2	2	.50	.263	.335	.360	.695
Espinosa,Danny	Was	28	88	247	54	13	1	7	28	24	25	3.33	18	84	6	2	.75	.219	.298	.364	.663
Ethier,Andre	LAD	33	141	459	124	29	2	12	55	62	66	5.09	50	98	2	2	.50	.270	.350	.420	.770
Fielder,Prince	Tex	31	160	578	166	34	1	29	85	103	111	6.99	93	107	1	1	.50	.287	.394	.500	.894
Flaherty,Ryan	Bal	28	85	190	45	9	1	6	22	24	21	3.74	15	42	1	1	.50	.237	.306	.389	.696
Flores,Wilmer	NYM	23	78	290	79	18	1	9	36	42	39	4.81	15	43	1	0	1.00	.272	.310	.434	.745
Flowers,Tyler	CWS	29	122	390	92	18	1	17	46	48	49	4.28	36	137	1	0	1.00	.236	.309	.418	.727
Forsythe,Logan	TB	28	101	282	70	13	2	6	36	28	34	4.13	31	61	5	2	.71	.248	.329	.372	.701
Fowler,Dexter	Hou	29	138	495	136	27	7	10	79	47	77	5.48	76	125	13	6	.68	.275	.375	.418	.793
Francisco,Juan	Tor	28	121	331	83	20	2	18	43	54	49	5.14	26	108	0	0	.00	.251	.309	.486	.796
Franco,Maikel	Phi	22	128	487	127	29	2	16	59	69	61	4.39	22	73	3	1	.75	.261	.293	.427	.720
Frandsen,Kevin	Was	33	68	112	30	6	0	1	11	10	12	3.80	5	12	1	0	1.00	.268	.328	.348	.676
Franklin,Nick	TB	24	152	551	136	28	3	15	64	62	71	4.38	64	142	16	6	.73	.247	.325	.390	.715
Frazier,Todd	Cin	29	153	569	150	31	2	26	78	82	85	5.20	52	122	14	6	.70	.264	.332	.462	.794
Freeman,Freddie	Atl	25	157	589	173	39	2	22	94	97	105	6.53	76	134	3	2	.60	.294	.380	.479	.859
Freese,David	LAA	32	138	461	124	25	1	12	56	64	62	4.77	43	118	1	1	.50	.269	.339	.406	.745
Fuld,Sam	Oak	33	77	133	31	6	1	1	17	11	13	3.22	16	19	6	3	.67	.233	.315	.316	.631
Gallo,Joey	Tex	21	146	538	127	23	0	34	81	81	82	5.16	72	207	5	2	.71	.236	.326	.468	.795
Galvis,Freddy	Phi	25	57	163	38	9	1	3	18	16	16	3.30	9	31	2	1	.67	.233	.273	.356	.629
Garcia,Avisail	CWS	24	153	585	173	23	3	20	80	81	87	5.40	33	134	13	7	.65	.296	.335	.440	.703
Garcia,Leury	CWS	24	09	104	31	4	2	1	16	8	12	2.94	7	36	12	3	.80	.231	.270	.313	.583
Gardner,Brett	NYY	31	147	549	142	25	6	11	91	50	73	4.56	64	130	26	9	.74	.259	.341	.386	.728
Gattis,Evan	Atl	28	111	405	104	23	1	24	48	66	61	5.27	26	93	0	0	.00	.257	.310	.496	.806
Gennett,Scooter	Mil	25	152	540	157	32	4	10	69	54	74	4.96	28	80	9	5	.64	.291	.326	.420	.746
Gentry,Craig	Oak	31	106	245	66	9	1	1	36	21	27	3.82	20	42	18	5	.78	.269	.337	.327	.664
Gillaspie,Conor	CWS	27	137	489	131	25	4	11	54	55	64	4.64	42	76	1	1	.50	.268	.327	.403	.730
Goins,Ryan	Tor	27	63	148	38	8	1	1	14	13	15	3.51	9	28	1	1	.50	.257	.299	.345	.644
Goldschmidt,Paul	Ari	27	154	590	179	47	2	32	107	115	131	8.17	96	140	14	6	.70	.303	.403	.553	.955
Gomes,Jonny	Oak	34	105	260	61	11	0	9	33	37	31	4.03	32	86	1	1	.50	.235	.334	.381	.715
Gomes,Yan	Cle	27	120	426	121	28	2	18	55	66	67	5.71	26	97	1	0	1.00	.284	.331	.486	.817
Gomez,Carlos	Mil	29	152	555	149	29	5	20	88	67	74	4.93	40	141	32	11	.74	.268	.330	.447	.777
Gonzalez,Adrian	LAD	33	160	613	177	39	1	27	84	109	106	6.31	65	117	1	1	.50	.289	.360	.488	.848
Gonzalez,Carlos	Col	29	126	485	138	30	4	24	80	81	85	6.28	43	126	13	5	.72	.285	.345	.511	.857
Gonzalez,Marwin	Hou	26	107	300	75	17	1	5	31	25	32	3.67	17	49	4	2	.67	.250	.295	.363	.658
Gordon,Alex	KC	31	155	583	159	38	2	19	87	74	89	5.39	65	134	11	5	.69	.273	.353	.443	.795
Gordon,Dee	LAD	27	145	598	165	22	9	2	83	36	71	4.08	39	99	62	19	.77	.276	.322	.353	.675
Gose,Anthony	Tor	24	129	418	102	16	4	6	62	35	46	3.64	39	120	34	13	.72	.244	.313	.344	.658
Gosewisch,Tuffy	Ari	31	40	125	28	8	0	2	11	12	11	2.95	7	22	0	0	.00	.224	.265	.336	.601
Gosselin,Phil	Atl	26	46	154	42	8	1	1	18	11	17	3.91	9	26	2	1	.67	.273	.317	.357	.674
Grandal,Yasmani	SD	26	128	434	113	28	1	17	62	65	70	5.65	68	109	3	1	.75	.260	.362	.447	.809
Granderson,Curtis	NYM	34	142	517	123	22	4	24	81	67	74	4.83	68	143	9	4	.69	.238	.332	.435	.767
Gregorius,Didi	Ari	25	110	402	104	18	5	7	55	38	48	4.16	34	61	4	2	.67	.259	.321	.381	.702

536

2015 Hitter Projections

PLAYER			BATTING												BASERUNNING			AVERAGES			
Hitter	Team	Age	G	AB	H	2B	3B	HR	R	RBI	RC	RC27	BB	SO	SB	CS	SB%	Avg	OBP	Slg	OPS
Grichuk,Randal	StL	23	145	545	133	30	5	25	83	72	69	4.29	29	122	9	6	.60	.244	.282	.455	.737
Grossman,Robbie	Hou	25	80	230	61	12	1	4	32	21	31	4.63	32	58	8	5	.62	.265	.360	.378	.738
Guerrero,Alex	LAD	28	153	553	154	29	6	24	59	79	80	5.17	17	111	9	3	.75	.278	.300	.483	.783
Gutierrez,Franklin	Sea	32	89	327	76	17	1	8	38	34	33	3.36	22	85	9	4	.69	.232	.283	.364	.647
Guyer,Brandon	TB	29	79	213	60	15	2	4	35	24	31	5.20	16	38	7	2	.78	.282	.343	.427	.771
Guzman,Jesus	Hou	31	69	120	31	7	0	3	13	16	15	4.33	11	28	2	1	.67	.258	.326	.392	.717
Gyorko,Jedd	SD	26	137	514	132	27	0	21	65	78	70	4.74	45	113	3	2	.60	.257	.320	.432	.752
Hamilton,Billy	Cin	24	153	559	147	24	6	6	83	48	65	3.88	44	108	62	24	.72	.263	.318	.360	.677
Hamilton,Josh	LAA	34	149	569	151	35	2	25	79	91	86	5.31	52	163	5	3	.62	.265	.331	.466	.797
Hanigan,Ryan	TB	34	110	300	72	12	0	4	27	32	32	3.65	40	45	1	0	1.00	.240	.335	.320	.655
Hardy,J.J.	Bal	32	154	605	154	30	1	18	69	69	72	4.15	39	106	0	0	.00	.255	.302	.397	.699
Harper,Bryce	Was	22	147	531	148	25	5	24	87	64	91	6.10	67	124	10	5	.67	.279	.362	.480	.842
Harrison,Josh	Pit	27	152	538	158	38	6	11	78	57	78	5.23	26	73	19	8	.70	.294	.330	.448	.778
Hart,Corey	Sea	33	107	365	93	21	2	16	50	50	51	4.84	29	91	4	2	.67	.255	.322	.455	.776
Headley,Chase	NYY	31	140	489	128	29	1	14	61	60	69	4.92	59	112	8	4	.67	.262	.350	.411	.761
Hechavarria,Adeiny	Mia	26	147	540	142	22	6	3	53	46	55	3.54	29	86	9	6	.60	.263	.302	.343	.644
Heisey,Chris	Cin	30	83	172	43	9	1	6	23	19	21	4.17	10	40	4	2	.67	.250	.306	.419	.725
Hernandez,Enrique	Mia	23	147	528	135	29	3	13	61	50	63	4.12	39	68	7	5	.58	.256	.308	.396	.704
Herrera,Elian	Mil	30	59	117	31	6	1	1	15	10	14	4.14	10	24	5	2	.71	.265	.323	.359	.682
Heyward,Jason	Atl	25	154	572	156	31	4	19	88	71	90	5.53	74	109	17	7	.71	.273	.362	.441	.803
Hicks,Aaron	Min	25	80	219	54	11	2	4	34	24	28	4.33	33	52	6	3	.67	.247	.348	.370	.718
Hicks,Brandon	SF	29	56	123	27	6	0	4	17	14	13	3.48	13	43	1	1	.50	.220	.299	.366	.665
Hill,Aaron	Ari	33	128	458	118	27	1	13	56	57	57	4.32	33	78	5	3	.62	.258	.315	.406	.721
Hoes,L.J.	Hou	25	51	136	37	7	1	2	19	14	18	4.63	15	25	4	2	.67	.272	.344	.382	.727
Holaday,Bryan	Det	27	58	143	34	7	0	1	13	13	12	2.84	9	28	1	1	.50	.238	.288	.308	.595
Holliday,Matt	StL	35	156	589	170	39	1	23	94	98	103	6.36	74	111	5	2	.71	.289	.378	.475	.854
Holt,Brock	Bos	27	147	622	176	33	6	5	83	48	81	4.64	53	106	20	8	.71	.283	.340	.379	.720
Hosmer,Eric	KC	25	149	576	163	34	2	16	75	75	84	5.25	48	100	8	3	.73	.283	.340	.432	.773
Howard,Ryan	Phi	35	151	560	132	25	1	27	69	102	76	4.62	66	194	0	0	.00	.236	.322	.429	.750
Hundley,Nick	Bal	31	91	256	58	12	1	7	24	30	26	3.40	19	71	1	1	.50	.227	.285	.363	.648
Hunter,Torii	Det	39	140	535	151	28	1	17	72	79	75	5.04	35	103	5	3	.62	.282	.333	.434	.767
Iannetta,Chris	LAA	32	121	390	90	21	1	13	49	54	53	4.56	70	115	3	2	.60	.231	.356	.390	.746
Ibanez,Raul	KC	43	85	213	47	11	1	8	23	29	24	3.74	22	51	1	1	.50	.221	.297	.394	.691
Iglesias,Jose	Det	25	147	510	131	17	2	4	58	39	49	3.31	28	79	14	6	.70	.257	.299	.322	.621
Inciarte,Ender	Ari	24	108	345	97	14	2	4	49	43	43	4.42	22	42	20	5	.80	.281	.324	.368	.692
Infante,Omar	KC	33	132	470	129	21	3	7	51	50	56	4.23	27	60	7	3	.70	.274	.315	.377	.692
Jackson,Austin	Sea	28	154	577	159	31	7	8	88	55	78	4.77	55	142	17	7	.71	.276	.341	.395	.736
Jaso,John	Oak	31	102	316	82	18	1	8	42	41	44	4.87	43	53	2	1	.67	.259	.355	.399	.754
Jay,Jon	StL	30	143	421	121	22	2	5	56	44	55	4.70	33	76	7	4	.64	.287	.356	.385	.741
Jennings,Desmond	TB	28	135	487	126	27	4	12	78	46	67	4.75	54	98	20	6	.77	.259	.338	.405	.742
Johnson,Chris	Atl	30	137	468	130	27	1	11	44	58	60	4.59	23	123	3	2	.60	.278	.316	.410	.726
Johnson,Kelly	Bal	33	105	289	67	15	2	10	37	33	36	4.18	34	81	4	2	.67	.232	.319	.401	.720
Johnson,Micah	CWS	24	134	454	120	19	3	5	42	38	49	3.65	32	76	25	15	.62	.264	.313	.352	.665
Jones,Adam	Bal	29	161	646	182	33	2	29	93	94	95	5.28	27	135	9	4	.69	.282	.321	.474	.794
Jones,Garrett	Mia	34	121	339	82	21	1	12	39	45	43	4.33	30	82	1	1	.50	.242	.305	.416	.721
Jones,James	Sea	26	65	143	37	5	2	1	18	10	16	3.85	10	28	11	2	.85	.259	.307	.343	.650
Joseph,Caleb	Bal	29	69	196	47	10	0	6	20	25	22	3.84	14	42	1	0	1.00	.240	.294	.383	.676
Joyce,Matt	TB	30	129	377	93	24	1	13	51	51	53	4.82	53	96	3	2	.60	.247	.344	.419	.763
Kawasaki,Munenori	Tor	34	84	186	45	7	1	0	21	14	17	3.11	19	32	2	1	.67	.242	.322	.290	.612
Kelly,Don	Det	35	79	120	28	4	1	2	15	10	12	3.35	12	20	3	1	.75	.233	.308	.333	.642
Kemp,Matt	LAD	30	152	551	159	33	3	25	86	88	96	6.27	53	149	13	6	.68	.289	.353	.495	.849
Kendrick,Howie	LAA	31	151	587	169	34	3	10	74	70	78	4.78	36	110	11	6	.65	.288	.334	.407	.742
Kiermaier,Kevin	TB	25	154	454	127	22	9	11	68	43	66	5.12	36	84	17	8	.68	.280	.335	.441	.776
Kinsler,Ian	Det	33	156	639	171	37	2	19	101	80	88	4.83	55	79	16	6	.73	.268	.332	.421	.753
Kipnis,Jason	Cle	28	151	570	153	31	3	14	84	71	82	5.04	66	110	26	6	.81	.268	.347	.407	.754
Kratz,Erik	KC	35	84	247	60	16	0	10	29	36	32	4.45	20	49	0	0	.00	.243	.300	.429	.729
Krauss,Marc	Hou	27	55	105	25	6	0	4	14	15	15	4.88	15	27	1	0	1.00	.238	.339	.410	.748
Kubel,Jason	Min	33	59	138	33	7	1	5	15	20	18	4.46	15	43	0	0	.00	.239	.318	.413	.731
La Stella,Tommy	Atl	26	154	528	152	29	2	4	47	63	73	5.02	66	56	5	2	.71	.288	.368	.373	.741
Lagares,Juan	NYM	26	133	477	134	28	4	5	54	49	58	4.31	25	94	14	7	.67	.281	.322	.388	.710
Laird,Gerald	Atl	35	68	169	39	9	0	1	17	15	15	3.00	15	34	1	0	1.00	.231	.301	.302	.603
Lake,Junior	ChC	25	69	156	40	8	1	5	20	15	19	4.15	9	44	6	3	.67	.256	.301	.417	.718
Lamb,Jake	Ari	24	138	496	139	31	5	19	75	58	83	6.03	54	129	3	1	.75	.280	.351	.478	.829
LaRoche,Adam	Was	35	151	532	133	27	1	24	70	84	79	5.14	72	133	2	1	.67	.250	.342	.440	.781
Lawrie,Brett	Tor	25	118	438	120	23	4	16	61	57	64	5.17	33	76	8	4	.67	.274	.332	.454	.786
LeMahieu,DJ	Col	26	148	488	137	22	4	4	56	43	57	4.13	30	79	12	8	.60	.281	.324	.367	.691
Lind,Adam	Tor	31	132	457	129	27	1	17	56	69	71	5.63	41	93	0	0	.00	.282	.343	.457	.800
Lindor,Francisco	Cle	21	151	552	146	19	4	11	77	61	67	4.15	53	101	25	14	.64	.264	.329	.373	.702
Lobaton,Jose	Was	30	86	229	56	12	0	4	24	23	25	3.76	24	56	0	0	.00	.245	.319	.349	.668
Loney,James	TB	31	151	585	166	33	1	11	59	77	79	4.88	46	80	4	2	.67	.284	.338	.400	.738
Longoria,Evan	TB	29	156	588	156	35	1	27	85	98	93	5.57	68	136	4	2	.67	.265	.347	.466	.813
Lough,David	Bal	29	89	194	52	8	2	4	26	20	24	4.30	12	29	7	3	.70	.268	.314	.392	.706
Lowrie,Jed	Oak	31	146	555	147	38	2	12	70	68	75	4.78	58	92	1	0	1.00	.265	.338	.405	.743
Lucas,Ed	Mia	33	75	197	50	9	0	3	23	18	21	3.69	15	42	2	1	.67	.254	.307	.345	.652
Lucroy,Jonathan	Mil	29	150	555	161	36	2	15	68	77	87	5.70	57	74	5	3	.62	.290	.359	.443	.803
Ludwick,Ryan	Cin	36	78	200	48	11	0	7	21	30	24	4.11	19	52	0	0	.00	.240	.315	.400	.715
Machado,Manny	Bal	22	155	630	176	39	3	19	84	74	89	5.06	39	109	7	3	.70	.279	.323	.441	.765
Maldonado,Martin	Mil	28	60	142	33	7	0	4	14	19	15	3.58	12	36	0	0	.00	.232	.301	.366	.667
Marisnick,Jake	Hou	24	146	496	126	22	3	11	59	51	55	3.76	23	111	31	10	.76	.254	.290	.377	.667
Markakis,Nick	Bal	31	152	602	169	34	1	14	80	67	86	5.14	61	81	4	2	.67	.281	.351	.410	.761

2015 Hitter Projections

Hitter	Team	Age	G	AB	H	2B	3B	HR	R	RBI	RC	RC27	BB	SO	SB	CS	SB%	Avg	OBP	Slg	OPS
Marte,Starling	Pit	26	135	503	140	29	8	14	79	54	72	4.98	30	121	29	13	.69	.278	.336	.451	.788
Martin,Leonys	Tex	27	150	494	137	22	6	8	70	49	64	4.51	37	96	28	12	.70	.277	.331	.395	.726
Martin,Russell	Pit	32	130	458	113	21	0	14	57	62	60	4.47	65	98	6	4	.60	.247	.352	.384	.736
Martinez,J.D.	Det	27	131	470	134	29	2	21	56	79	76	5.83	34	114	5	3	.62	.285	.336	.489	.825
Martinez,Victor	Det	36	154	572	176	35	0	22	76	96	103	6.75	60	54	2	1	.67	.308	.376	.484	.861
Mathis,Jeff	Mia	32	62	139	26	6	0	3	12	15	10	2.30	11	48	0	0	.00	.187	.252	.295	.547
Mauer,Joe	Min	32	138	513	154	33	1	9	73	68	84	6.05	73	96	3	2	.60	.300	.388	.421	.809
Mayberry,John	Tor	31	75	147	34	9	0	5	18	18	17	3.88	13	38	2	1	.67	.231	.298	.395	.693
Maybin,Cameron	SD	28	132	489	126	23	5	8	69	45	60	4.23	46	113	17	6	.74	.258	.324	.374	.698
McCann,Brian	NYY	31	131	473	121	22	0	23	55	78	68	5.01	46	79	1	1	.50	.256	.328	.448	.776
McCutchen,Andrew	Pit	28	154	552	165	34	5	22	92	77	107	7.06	78	110	19	7	.73	.299	.392	.498	.891
McGehee,Casey	Mia	32	156	570	150	29	1	9	56	76	68	4.19	55	103	2	2	.50	.263	.329	.365	.694
McKenry,Michael	Col	30	84	244	64	15	0	8	28	31	34	4.88	25	53	2	1	.67	.262	.333	.422	.755
McLouth,Nate	Was	33	75	165	38	8	1	4	23	16	19	3.83	20	34	6	2	.75	.230	.332	.364	.695
Medica,Tommy	SD	27	112	275	73	16	2	13	38	46	42	5.35	22	74	5	2	.71	.265	.327	.480	.807
Mercer,Jordy	Pit	28	134	454	122	28	2	11	54	53	59	4.59	33	75	4	2	.67	.269	.322	.412	.734
Mesoraco,Devin	Cin	27	122	411	105	26	1	21	54	71	63	5.34	42	89	1	1	.50	.255	.332	.477	.809
Middlebrooks,Will	Bos	26	127	459	112	21	1	19	52	70	55	4.10	28	121	4	2	.67	.244	.292	.418	.710
Miller,Brad	Sea	25	113	387	102	17	4	12	57	47	54	4.88	40	80	6	3	.67	.264	.334	.421	.755
Molina,Jose	TB	40	71	150	32	5	0	2	11	10	11	2.40	10	37	1	1	.50	.213	.272	.287	.558
Molina,Yadier	StL	32	137	503	148	30	0	11	53	65	73	5.32	39	61	3	2	.60	.294	.350	.419	.769
Montero,Miguel	Ari	31	133	471	120	26	1	14	52	68	63	4.67	63	106	0	0	.00	.255	.343	.403	.746
Morales,Kendrys	Sea	32	123	460	122	26	0	16	50	65	62	4.77	34	91	0	0	.00	.265	.320	.426	.746
Moran,Colin	Hou	22	127	473	135	23	0	10	46	55	62	4.77	32	95	0	0	.00	.285	.331	.397	.728
Moreland,Mitch	Tex	29	138	447	116	26	1	16	57	63	61	4.78	40	95	1	1	.50	.260	.323	.430	.753
Morneau,Justin	Col	34	138	488	137	31	1	17	60	78	76	5.63	46	78	0	0	.00	.281	.349	.453	.802
Morrison,Logan	Sea	27	108	363	94	22	2	12	46	49	53	5.08	43	59	4	2	.67	.259	.342	.430	.772
Morse,Michael	SF	33	114	370	98	22	1	15	42	52	52	4.97	25	101	0	0	.00	.265	.322	.451	.773
Moss,Brandon	Oak	31	146	480	117	27	1	25	68	78	71	5.06	56	147	2	2	.50	.244	.329	.460	.789
Moustakas,Mike	KC	26	142	466	113	29	1	17	52	62	57	4.19	34	81	2	1	.67	.242	.300	.418	.718
Murphy,Daniel	NYM	30	156	616	178	42	2	10	79	71	84	4.92	40	89	13	6	.68	.289	.334	.412	.747
Murphy,David	Cle	33	121	347	90	20	1	9	40	44	45	4.52	33	55	3	2	.60	.259	.325	.401	.726
Murphy,Donnie	Tex	32	61	133	30	7	0	6	16	19	15	3.75	10	36	1	1	.50	.226	.290	.414	.703
Myers,Wil	TB	24	148	559	150	31	2	22	80	88	86	5.40	62	145	13	5	.72	.268	.341	.449	.790
Napoli,Mike	Bos	33	135	464	114	25	1	23	65	72	73	5.39	74	159	3	2	.60	.246	.355	.453	.808
Nava,Daniel	Bos	32	84	270	75	17	0	5	38	35	38	5.02	32	55	3	2	.60	.278	.373	.396	.769
Navarro,Dioner	Tor	31	120	414	110	19	0	11	40	53	52	4.43	33	65	2	1	.67	.266	.321	.391	.713
Nieto,Adrian	CWS	25	51	113	28	6	0	2	9	8	12	3.67	9	37	0	0	.00	.248	.309	.354	.663
Nieuwenhuis,Kirk	NYM	27	58	104	25	7	1	3	14	12	13	4.23	10	30	2	1	.67	.240	.307	.413	.720
Nieves,Wil	Phi	37	40	128	31	5	0	1	9	11	11	2.95	5	25	1	0	1.00	.242	.276	.305	.581
Norris,Derek	Oak	26	119	388	101	21	1	14	58	58	59	5.31	56	86	5	2	.71	.260	.357	.428	.784
Nunez,Eduardo	Min	28	79	201	54	10	2	3	26	21	24	4.16	11	29	10	3	.77	.269	.310	.383	.693
Odor,Rougned	Tex	21	149	517	141	19	8	16	63	68	67	4.54	26	87	11	8	.58	.273	.311	.433	.745
Olt,Mike	ChC	26	102	253	54	13	0	14	32	41	32	4.16	31	89	1	1	.50	.213	.304	.431	.735
Ortiz,David	Bos	39	144	542	149	35	0	32	80	102	104	6.88	81	106	1	0	1.00	.275	.371	.517	.888
Overbay,Lyle	Mil	38	90	181	42	11	0	4	19	21	21	3.93	22	45	1	0	1.00	.232	.319	.359	.678
Owings,Chris	Ari	23	142	481	133	23	5	9	60	46	60	4.42	20	95	16	5	.76	.277	.307	.401	.708
Ozuna,Marcell	Mia	24	153	563	157	30	6	23	76	90	87	5.54	40	141	4	2	.67	.279	.328	.476	.804
Pacheco,Jordan	Ari	29	63	133	36	8	0	1	13	14	15	4.02	7	17	1	0	1.00	.271	.317	.353	.670
Pagan,Angel	SF	33	147	568	158	31	5	7	80	54	73	4.53	44	85	21	9	.70	.278	.331	.387	.718
Panik,Joe	SF	24	132	473	130	21	3	4	55	44	55	4.14	37	56	4	2	.67	.275	.327	.357	.685
Parker,Kyle	Col	25	147	532	142	30	2	17	65	68	69	4.55	31	114	5	4	.56	.267	.307	.427	.734
Parmelee,Chris	Min	27	87	217	56	13	1	7	24	28	30	4.84	23	47	0	0	.00	.258	.335	.424	.759
Parra,Gerardo	Mil	28	146	524	142	29	5	9	67	48	67	4.49	40	96	10	6	.62	.271	.327	.397	.724
Pearce,Steve	Bal	32	108	353	97	25	1	16	49	53	60	6.05	41	71	5	2	.71	.275	.355	.487	.842
Pederson,Joc	LAD	23	152	546	147	23	2	26	84	71	90	5.69	73	174	29	12	.71	.269	.355	.462	.817
Pedroia,Dustin	Bos	31	151	606	176	41	1	12	89	70	92	5.50	64	75	11	5	.69	.290	.361	.421	.782
Pena,Brayan	Cin	33	72	163	42	9	0	2	13	16	17	3.62	9	20	1	1	.50	.258	.301	.360	.650
Pena,Ramiro	Atl	29	84	195	48	8	1	3	21	16	20	3.51	16	39	2	1	.67	.246	.303	.344	.647
Pence,Hunter	SF	32	160	620	171	32	4	22	88	86	92	5.26	52	126	12	6	.67	.276	.335	.447	.782
Pennington,Cliff	Ari	31	78	203	50	9	1	2	24	16	21	3.50	21	41	6	3	.67	.246	.323	.330	.653
Peralta,David	Ari	27	116	397	115	22	6	10	54	59	59	5.38	25	56	6	3	.67	.290	.333	.451	.784
Peralta,Jhonny	StL	33	148	551	146	34	1	18	65	76	77	4.92	53	118	2	2	.50	.265	.333	.428	.761
Perez,Roberto	Cle	26	49	145	34	9	0	3	17	20	17	3.98	21	40	0	0	.00	.234	.331	.359	.690
Perez,Salvador	KC	25	138	526	149	28	2	16	58	75	72	4.97	22	65	1	0	1.00	.283	.316	.435	.751
Phillips,Brandon	Cin	34	150	586	155	29	2	15	74	75	71	4.24	36	93	7	4	.64	.265	.315	.398	.712
Pierzynski,A.J.	StL	38	120	410	106	19	1	10	38	46	45	3.85	19	62	0	0	.00	.259	.296	.383	.679
Pillar,Kevin	Tor	26	53	168	49	14	1	4	23	20	25	5.33	8	24	8	3	.73	.292	.328	.458	.786
Pinto,Josmil	Min	26	57	210	58	15	1	8	28	31	36	6.16	28	44	0	0	.00	.276	.364	.471	.835
Piscotty,Stephen	StL	24	134	482	130	29	0	9	56	60	60	4.36	37	56	12	6	.67	.270	.322	.386	.708
Plouffe,Trevor	Min	29	137	513	130	32	2	17	65	67	68	4.59	45	101	3	2	.60	.253	.317	.423	.740
Polanco,Gregory	Pit	23	148	535	144	26	3	14	91	80	75	4.84	58	96	31	12	.72	.269	.341	.407	.748
Pollock,A.J.	Ari	27	142	511	142	34	5	9	72	50	70	4.84	36	76	22	7	.76	.278	.327	.417	.743
Pompey,Dalton	Tor	22	127	395	104	21	8	9	76	40	56	4.84	40	74	25	10	.71	.263	.331	.425	.756
Posey,Buster	SF	28	146	542	169	34	1	21	71	89	102	7.11	58	75	1	0	1.00	.312	.382	.494	.877
Prado,Martin	NYY	31	154	602	169	36	2	13	75	67	81	4.83	42	77	5	3	.62	.281	.331	.412	.743
Presley,Alex	Hou	29	75	185	52	8	2	4	24	17	25	4.78	13	31	5	3	.62	.281	.332	.411	.742
Profar,Jurickson	Tex	22	120	406	103	20	3	10	54	44	52	4.39	45	72	10	5	.67	.254	.330	.392	.721
Puig,Yasiel	LAD	24	153	572	181	39	7	23	102	81	116	7.54	67	119	15	9	.62	.316	.399	.530	.929
Pujols,Albert	LAA	35	156	617	174	39	0	31	91	107	108	6.31	68	76	5	2	.71	.282	.358	.496	.854

2015 Hitter Projections

Hitter	Team	Age	G	AB	H	2B	3B	HR	R	RBI	RC	RC27	BB	SO	SB	CS	SB%	Avg	OBP	Slg	OPS
Punto,Nick	Oak	37	87	187	41	8	1	1	21	14	17	3.01	24	48	3	1	.75	.219	.308	.289	.597
Quentin,Carlos	SD	32	110	407	102	25	0	21	59	72	62	5.29	45	82	1	0	1.00	.251	.343	.467	.810
Raburn,Ryan	Cle	34	68	146	34	8	0	5	18	21	17	3.95	12	39	1	0	1.00	.233	.300	.390	.690
Ramirez,Alexei	CWS	33	159	621	167	31	2	13	73	70	73	4.11	30	81	18	8	.69	.269	.307	.388	.695
Ramirez,Aramis	Mil	37	138	517	144	30	1	19	64	82	76	5.28	38	84	2	1	.67	.279	.340	.451	.790
Ramirez,Hanley	LAD	31	151	580	168	37	1	23	93	85	100	6.18	66	111	20	9	.69	.290	.367	.476	.843
Ramirez,Jose	Cle	22	134	464	122	21	4	5	62	38	53	3.88	34	53	31	13	.70	.263	.315	.358	.672
Ramos,Wilson	Was	27	102	392	107	19	0	15	42	58	54	4.93	24	59	0	0	.00	.273	.315	.436	.751
Rasmus,Colby	Tor	28	123	416	98	23	2	19	59	53	55	4.47	41	131	4	2	.67	.236	.307	.438	.745
Realmuto,J.T.	Mia	24	53	111	29	7	1	2	16	16	15	4.70	11	18	5	1	.83	.261	.328	.396	.724
Recker,Anthony	NYM	31	53	152	35	8	0	6	17	19	18	3.97	14	47	1	1	.50	.230	.299	.401	.701
Reddick,Josh	Oak	28	140	466	115	25	4	18	66	64	62	4.55	43	93	5	3	.62	.247	.312	.433	.745
Rendon,Anthony	Was	25	153	571	164	39	5	20	97	78	99	6.26	63	93	13	4	.76	.287	.362	.478	.840
Revere,Ben	Phi	27	145	594	178	14	6	1	72	34	72	4.37	25	49	46	12	.79	.300	.330	.348	.679
Reyes,Jose	Tor	32	152	605	175	33	6	10	91	52	87	5.15	48	69	30	9	.77	.289	.343	.413	.756
Reynolds,Mark	Mil	31	98	253	55	11	0	15	36	39	34	4.42	34	89	3	2	.60	.217	.322	.439	.761
Rios,Alex	Tex	34	142	517	138	29	3	12	64	61	64	4.30	30	94	18	8	.69	.267	.311	.404	.715
Rivera,Rene	SD	31	90	293	75	17	0	8	28	38	36	4.29	22	64	0	0	.00	.256	.310	.396	.706
Rizzo,Anthony	ChC	25	158	598	164	39	1	34	91	99	108	6.41	74	120	6	4	.60	.274	.362	.513	.875
Roberts,Brian	NYY	37	90	274	67	16	1	5	36	25	31	3.84	28	48	6	3	.67	.245	.317	.365	.682
Rodriguez,Alex	NYY	39	126	433	114	20	0	22	68	76	70	5.65	57	107	8	3	.73	.263	.356	.462	.817
Rodriguez,Sean	TB	30	69	121	28	7	1	4	16	16	14	3.87	10	34	2	1	.67	.231	.321	.405	.726
Rojas,Miguel	LAD	26	92	202	45	6	0	2	21	15	16	2.60	15	28	5	3	.62	.223	.280	.282	.562
Rollins,Jimmy	Phi	36	154	602	144	29	3	15	81	56	71	3.97	61	100	24	7	.77	.239	.311	.372	.683
Romero,Stefen	Sea	26	56	117	31	6	1	4	14	17	15	4.48	5	26	1	1	.50	.265	.312	.436	.748
Romine,Andrew	Det	29	79	182	45	5	1	1	22	13	17	3.13	14	36	8	4	.67	.247	.301	.302	.603
Rosario,Wilin	Col	26	126	464	131	25	1	24	67	76	73	5.68	25	90	2	1	.67	.282	.319	.496	.815
Ross,Cody	Ari	34	91	251	65	15	0	7	28	33	31	4.31	20	57	1	1	.50	.259	.321	.402	.724
Rua,Ryan	Tex	25	124	378	108	22	2	12	50	52	57	5.43	30	76	5	3	.62	.286	.340	.450	.790
Ruf,Darin	Phi	28	59	124	34	8	0	5	17	18	20	5.78	13	33	0	0	.00	.274	.362	.460	.821
Ruggiano,Justin	ChC	33	109	325	87	20	1	11	42	44	47	5.05	30	87	8	4	.67	.268	.333	.437	.770
Ruiz,Carlos	Phi	36	112	379	100	25	0	7	42	44	49	4.53	41	57	3	2	.60	.264	.350	.385	.735
Russell,Addison	ChC	21	139	536	153	20	2	21	80	57	78	5.20	33	101	12	7	.63	.285	.327	.448	.775
Rutledge,Josh	Col	26	121	428	120	27	5	10	63	45	60	5.00	27	92	9	4	.69	.280	.330	.437	.767
Ryan,Brendan	NYY	33	64	136	29	6	1	1	14	10	11	2.65	10	30	2	1	.67	.213	.287	.294	.581
Saltalamacchia,Jarrod	Mia	30	126	435	101	27	1	16	58	58	55	4.27	50	155	1	1	.50	.232	.313	.409	.722
Sanchez,Carlos	CWS	23	129	458	117	21	2	3	46	36	45	3.36	27	90	16	7	.70	.255	.297	.330	.627
Sanchez,Gaby	Pit	31	101	203	50	13	0	6	24	24	26	4.39	24	41	2	1	.67	.246	.335	.399	.734
Sanchez,Hector	SF	25	71	158	37	8	0	3	11	24	15	3.22	9	39	0	0	.00	.234	.284	.342	.626
Sandoval,Pablo	SF	28	151	571	164	33	2	18	69	82	87	5.56	46	83	1	0	1.00	.287	.344	.447	.790
Sano,Miguel	Min	22	147	511	115	27	4	32	67	70	77	5.02	67	175	5	3	.62	.225	.315	.481	.796
Santana,Carlos	Cle	29	149	517	129	32	1	24	75	83	88	5.87	104	113	4	2	.67	.250	.378	.455	.833
Santana,Danny	Min	24	145	577	166	35	9	7	84	50	78	4.82	27	124	29	10	.74	.288	.322	.416	.738
Santana,Domingo	Hou	22	153	551	142	30	1	21	73	79	79	4.96	62	191	9	5	.64	.258	.333	.430	.763
Santiago,Ramon	Cin	35	70	138	32	5	1	1	15	12	12	2.92	13	27	1	1	.50	.232	.312	.304	.616
Saunders,Michael	Sea	28	135	430	105	22	3	13	62	49	56	4.41	52	118	10	5	.67	.244	.326	.400	.726
Schafer,Jordan	Min	28	66	113	27	5	1	1	14	9	12	3.47	13	27	11	4	.73	.239	.323	.327	.650
Schierholtz,Nate	Was	31	91	203	48	11	1	6	22	23	22	3.64	12	44	2	2	.50	.236	.289	.389	.678
Schoop,Jonathan	Bal	23	144	478	114	21	0	17	55	51	51	3.63	23	110	3	1	.75	.238	.279	.389	.668
Schumaker,Skip	Cin	35	79	165	43	9	0	1	19	14	17	3.59	14	30	1	1	.50	.261	.326	.333	.659
Scutaro,Marco	SF	39	88	252	70	13	0	3	33	24	31	4.40	23	27	2	1	.67	.278	.343	.365	.708
Seager,Corey	LAD	21	144	577	160	36	8	9	81	59	75	4.64	34	154	4	3	.57	.277	.318	.414	.732
Seager,Kyle	Sea	27	159	607	162	36	2	22	74	86	88	5.10	58	119	8	4	.67	.267	.338	.442	.779
Segura,Jean	Mil	25	145	535	150	17	7	8	70	44	66	4.33	30	69	29	11	.73	.280	.322	.383	.705
Semien,Marcus	CWS	24	136	492	124	28	3	18	78	62	73	5.10	65	108	13	4	.76	.252	.341	.431	.771
Shuck,J.B.	Cle	28	61	141	38	5	1	1	18	16	16	3.96	12	13	4	2	.67	.270	.327	.340	.667
Simmons,Andrelton	Atl	25	155	574	147	24	5	12	63	56	65	3.92	39	56	6	4	.60	.256	.305	.378	.683
Singleton,Jon	Hou	23	148	514	114	26	2	24	78	81	72	4.66	88	174	4	2	.67	.222	.337	.420	.757
Sizemore,Grady	Phi	32	90	279	68	16	2	7	35	30	35	4.27	31	63	5	2	.71	.244	.326	.391	.717
Smith,Seth	SD	32	131	408	109	26	3	13	57	52	63	5.46	52	90	2	1	.67	.267	.354	.441	.795
Smoak,Justin	Sea	28	89	248	58	12	0	8	27	30	30	4.11	32	62	0	0	.00	.234	.326	.379	.705
Smolinski,Jake	Tex	26	124	378	96	23	2	10	52	41	52	4.74	47	73	7	3	.70	.254	.338	.405	.743
Snider,Travis	Pit	27	119	296	77	18	1	11	40	41	42	4.94	30	71	3	2	.60	.260	.330	.439	.769
Sogard,Eric	Oak	29	102	252	64	12	1	2	32	23	27	3.66	25	30	8	4	.67	.254	.324	.333	.657
Solano,Donovan	Mia	27	106	304	77	14	1	3	28	27	30	3.42	18	51	2	1	.67	.253	.302	.336	.637
Solarte,Yangervis	SD	27	123	440	120	25	1	8	51	48	56	4.54	36	49	1	1	.50	.273	.331	.389	.719
Soler,Jorge	ChC	23	146	542	134	36	4	28	79	94	86	5.47	67	128	2	1	.67	.247	.330	.483	.813
Soriano,Alfonso	NYY	39	101	320	76	19	0	15	38	45	39	4.12	20	93	4	2	.67	.238	.291	.438	.728
Soto,Geovany	Oak	32	88	277	66	17	0	10	33	38	36	4.44	32	79	0	0	.00	.238	.319	.408	.727
Souza,Steven	Was	26	108	312	90	19	1	13	58	60	58	6.56	44	71	23	8	.74	.288	.376	.481	.857
Span,Denard	Was	31	151	605	174	33	6	5	86	50	82	4.85	54	73	25	9	.74	.288	.348	.387	.735
Spangenberg,Cory	SD	24	136	520	149	23	8	6	69	46	65	4.36	27	110	30	17	.64	.287	.322	.396	.718
Springer,George	Hou	25	151	572	150	24	3	38	105	106	99	5.99	62	200	27	8	.77	.262	.340	.514	.854
Stanton,Giancarlo	Mia	25	144	541	150	34	2	40	91	104	116	7.65	86	170	9	3	.75	.277	.380	.569	.950
Stassi,Max	Hou	24	82	252	61	14	1	7	27	32	27	3.68	12	64	1	0	1.00	.242	.277	.389	.665
Stewart,Chris	Pit	33	85	225	53	10	0	2	21	19	21	3.16	21	34	1	1	.50	.236	.306	.307	.613
Stubbs,Drew	Col	30	132	403	99	18	2	12	61	40	50	4.19	38	137	20	6	.77	.246	.314	.390	.703
Suarez,Eugenio	Det	23	85	282	70	16	2	6	35	31	34	4.09	27	66	8	4	.67	.248	.321	.383	.703
Suzuki,Ichiro	NYY	41	121	352	94	12	1	3	37	22	36	3.57	19	51	12	4	.75	.267	.308	.332	.641
Suzuki,Kurt	Min	31	130	456	117	26	0	7	44	55	50	3.82	33	55	1	1	.50	.257	.317	.360	.676

2015 Hitter Projections

Hitter	Team	Age	G	AB	H	2B	3B	HR	R	RBI	RC	RC27	BB	SO	SB	CS	SB%	Avg	OBP	Slg	OPS
Sweeney,Ryan	ChC	30	71	194	53	11	1	3	23	21	25	4.61	17	33	1	0	1.00	.273	.335	.387	.722
Swisher,Nick	Cle	34	142	520	123	30	1	19	66	70	69	4.51	71	149	1	1	.50	.237	.332	.408	.739
Tabata,Jose	Pit	26	71	149	42	8	1	1	19	13	18	4.29	11	20	3	2	.60	.282	.344	.369	.713
Taveras,Oscar	StL	23	148	547	155	36	2	15	69	86	78	5.15	35	71	4	2	.67	.283	.328	.439	.766
Taylor,Chris	Sea	24	135	486	128	30	5	4	78	39	61	4.31	51	118	25	10	.71	.263	.335	.370	.705
Teixeira,Mark	NYY	35	119	425	100	22	0	22	60	72	61	4.87	58	101	1	1	.50	.235	.337	.442	.779
Tejada,Ruben	NYM	25	109	358	90	17	1	3	39	29	37	3.56	34	56	2	2	.50	.251	.325	.330	.655
Thole,Josh	Tor	28	75	196	50	10	0	2	17	18	21	3.74	20	30	0	0	.00	.255	.327	.337	.664
Tolleson,Steve	Tor	31	91	221	56	12	1	4	25	22	27	4.18	23	48	7	3	.70	.253	.327	.371	.698
Trout,Mike	LAA	23	157	611	192	38	10	35	131	106	146	8.93	92	153	28	6	.82	.314	.411	.581	.992
Trumbo,Mark	Ari	29	147	580	144	29	2	30	73	101	80	4.74	46	158	4	3	.57	.248	.305	.460	.765
Tuiasosopo,Matt	CWS	29	76	144	33	6	0	4	18	17	17	3.98	20	44	1	0	1.00	.229	.327	.354	.681
Tulowitzki,Troy	Col	30	122	453	140	28	2	25	81	80	95	7.84	58	81	3	2	.60	.309	.392	.545	.937
Turner,Justin	LAD	30	120	324	94	23	1	5	41	37	46	5.16	27	52	4	2	.67	.290	.350	.414	.764
Upton,B.J.	Atl	30	109	324	73	17	1	10	42	34	38	3.86	37	107	13	5	.72	.225	.309	.377	.685
Upton,Justin	Atl	27	156	587	158	35	3	28	95	88	98	5.87	71	166	11	5	.69	.269	.355	.482	.837
Uribe,Juan	LAD	36	118	361	93	19	1	9	36	46	42	4.06	22	77	1	1	.50	.258	.304	.391	.694
Utley,Chase	Phi	36	146	551	146	30	3	16	77	73	77	4.91	57	88	10	3	.77	.265	.349	.417	.766
Valbuena,Luis	ChC	29	132	407	98	25	1	12	52	45	52	4.35	51	92	2	2	.50	.241	.328	.396	.724
Valencia,Danny	Tor	30	85	239	63	15	1	6	26	31	30	4.41	14	45	1	1	.50	.264	.307	.410	.717
Van Slyke,Scott	LAD	28	106	313	89	23	1	14	46	48	57	6.53	41	83	5	3	.62	.284	.371	.498	.869
Vargas,Kennys	Min	24	143	524	145	26	1	24	69	61	83	5.69	49	115	0	0	.00	.277	.342	.468	.810
Vazquez,Christian	Bos	24	110	344	88	21	0	3	40	35	38	3.84	36	60	1	1	.50	.256	.326	.343	.669
Venable,Will	SD	32	148	422	106	18	3	13	55	46	53	4.29	35	111	14	5	.74	.251	.313	.400	.714
Viciedo,Dayan	CWS	26	123	387	101	18	1	17	49	53	52	4.73	24	81	0	0	.00	.261	.311	.444	.755
Victorino,Shane	Bos	34	129	490	130	25	5	12	71	50	64	4.55	37	75	18	6	.75	.265	.326	.410	.736
Villar,Jonathan	Hou	24	91	281	68	11	2	6	38	28	33	3.88	27	82	28	8	.78	.242	.311	.359	.670
Vogt,Stephen	Oak	30	85	236	66	13	1	7	28	33	34	5.17	18	33	1	1	.50	.280	.331	.432	.763
Votto,Joey	Cin	31	158	573	171	40	1	24	92	88	118	7.56	114	134	6	4	.60	.298	.418	.497	.916
Walker,Neil	Pit	29	145	545	146	33	2	19	73	78	79	5.12	50	101	4	2	.67	.268	.337	.440	.778
Wallace,Brett	Tor	28	72	270	69	15	0	10	33	32	36	4.66	22	79	0	0	.00	.256	.319	.422	.741
Walters,Zach	Cle	25	123	449	115	23	4	22	63	70	62	4.81	25	121	1	1	.50	.256	.297	.472	.769
Weeks,Rickie	Mil	32	132	451	108	25	2	16	67	46	59	4.42	54	132	8	4	.67	.239	.335	.410	.745
Werth,Jayson	Was	36	143	533	150	31	1	19	82	78	90	6.06	77	126	9	3	.75	.281	.378	.450	.829
Wieters,Matt	Bal	29	146	524	135	29	1	22	64	80	75	5.00	52	104	1	1	.50	.258	.326	.443	.769
Wong,Kolten	StL	24	133	479	129	21	4	12	70	50	63	4.59	32	71	25	7	.78	.269	.318	.405	.723
Wright,David	NYM	32	136	542	155	34	2	16	74	79	87	5.76	64	117	11	6	.65	.286	.366	.445	.810
Yelich,Christian	Mia	23	152	614	180	34	7	13	102	64	101	5.94	79	139	23	8	.74	.293	.376	.435	.810
Ynoa,Rafael	Col	27	47	144	39	10	1	1	17	11	18	4.37	13	24	3	2	.60	.271	.331	.375	.706
Young,Chris	NYY	31	93	238	55	15	1	9	32	30	31	4.33	27	60	7	3	.70	.231	.317	.416	.733
Young,Delmon	Bal	29	98	292	80	16	1	9	32	40	38	4.64	13	60	1	1	.50	.274	.314	.428	.742
Young,Eric	NYM	30	86	191	48	8	2	1	30	12	21	3.69	18	39	18	5	.78	.251	.325	.330	.655
Zimmerman,Ryan	Was	30	127	493	139	31	1	19	73	75	81	5.93	53	99	3	1	.75	.282	.354	.465	.819
Zobrist,Ben	TB	34	156	596	158	36	3	15	84	72	88	5.16	86	100	11	5	.69	.265	.361	.411	.772
Zunino,Mike	Sea	24	135	451	101	22	2	23	60	65	52	3.86	25	142	0	0	.00	.224	.280	.435	.714

Pitcher Projections: 53, 63% accurate

Bill James

Let us say, for the sake of argument, that our projections for pitchers are 53 to 64% accurate. What exactly does that mean?

Comparing our projections published in this section of last year's book with actual 2014 performance, I marked a projection for innings pitched as "accurate" if the 2014 innings pitched were within 12% of the projection, plus 12 innings; so, for example, if we had projected that a pitcher would pitch 200 innings in 2014 and he actually pitched 164 innings, I would mark that as "accurate", whereas if he pitched 163 innings, I would mark that as "inaccurate". The projection of innings pitched for Jordan Lyles is marked as "accurate" as to innings pitched:

Pitcher	Label	G	GS	IP	H	HR	BB	SO	W	L	Pct	Sv	ERA
Lyles,Jordan	Actual	22	22	127	127	12	46	90	7	4	.636	0	4.33
Lyles,Jordan	Projected	25	25	141	161	16	44	101	5	11	.313	0	4.79

Whereas this projection, for Tim Lincecum, is marked as "inaccurate" as to innings pitched:

Pitcher	Label	G	GS	IP	H	HR	BB	SO	W	L	Pct	Sv	ERA
Lincecum,Tim	Actual	33	26	156	154	19	63	134	12	9	.571	1	4.74
Lincecum,Tim	Projected	31	31	194	170	17	80	203	12	10	.545	0	3.53

Just by dumb luck, we happened to get Lincecum's 2014 won-lost record almost exactly right, although the rest of the projection is not very good. If Lincecum had pitched 159 innings, we would mark that as "accurate", since 159 innings is close enough to 194 to be considered "right", but 156 innings. . .I'm sorry; that's just too far from the mark. The projections for Felix Hernandez and Wei-Yin Chen are accurate as to innings pitched:

Pitcher	Label	G	GS	IP	H	HR	BB	SO	W	L	Pct	Sv	ERA
Hernandez,Felix	Actual	34	34	236	170	16	46	248	15	6	.714	0	2.14
Hernandez,Felix	Projected	33	33	222	204	16	53	209	15	10	.600	0	3.20

Pitcher	Label	G	GS	IP	H	HR	BB	SO	W	L	Pct	Sv	ERA
Chen,Wei-Yin	Actual	31	31	186	193	23	35	136	16	6	.727	0	3.54
Chen,Wei-Yin	Projected	27	27	161	160	22	46	124	8	10	.444	0	3.91

While the projections for Phil Hughes and Ubaldo Jimenez are deemed "inaccurate":

Pitcher	Label	G	GS	IP	H	HR	BB	SO	W	L	Pct	Sv	ERA
Hughes,Phil	Actual	32	32	210	221	16	16	186	16	10	.615	0	3.52
Hughes,Phil	Projected	29	29	170	174	25	47	146	8	11	.421	0	4.13

Pitcher	Label	G	GS	IP	H	HR	BB	SO	W	L	Pct	Sv	ERA
Jimenez,Ubaldo	Actual	25	22	125	113	14	77	116	6	9	.400	0	4.81
Jimenez,Ubaldo	Projected	31	31	185	173	16	86	171	9	11	.450	0	3.94

The projection for Wei-Yin Chen is the opposite of that for Lincecum, in that Lincecum's projection is not really a good match for his performance, but Lincecum has almost exactly the won-lost record we expected, whereas Chen's performance actually is a good match for his projection, but it looks off because the won-lost record is all wrong.

A lot of relievers are projected to pitch 50 innings or less. If a reliever is projected to pitch 50 innings, we consider the projection accurate if he pitches anywhere between 32 and 68 innings. So, for example, we would consider the projections for Tony Sipp and Wesley Wright to be accurate:

Pitcher	Label	G	GS	IP	H	HR	BB	SO	W	L	Pct	Sv	ERA
Sipp,Tony	Actual	56	0	51	28	5	17	63	4	3	.571	4	3.38
Sipp,Tony	Projected	60	0	51	41	8	25	54	3	3	.500	0	3.71

Pitcher	Label	G	GS	IP	H	HR	BB	SO	W	L	Pct	Sv	ERA
Wright,Wesley	Actual	58	0	48	48	2	19	37	0	3	.000	0	3.17
Wright,Wesley	Projected	65	0	48	44	5	17	44	3	3	.500	0	3.75

Well. . .you'd have to consider *those* projections accurate; they're actually right. This reminds me of a Little Johnny joke from the 1950s: The teacher says, "Johnny, how much is 2 + 2", and Johnny says "4", and the teacher, "That's very good, Johnny," and Little Johnny says "Very good, hell, that's perfect." We don't have to be perfect to consider ourselves accurate; for a reliever, we'll settle for a Kelvin Herrera or David Carpenter level of accuracy:

Pitcher	Label	G	GS	IP	H	HR	BB	SO	W	L	Pct	Sv	ERA
Herrera,Kelvin	Actual	70	0	70	54	0	26	59	4	3	.571	0	1.41
Herrera,Kelvin	Projected	62	0	64	51	6	20	70	4	3	.571	0	2.67

Pitcher	Label	G	GS	IP	H	HR	BB	SO	W	L	Pct	Sv	ERA
Carpenter,David	Actual	65	0	61	61	5	16	67	6	4	.600	3	3.54
Carpenter,David	Projected	71	0	74	68	7	24	75	4	4	.500	0	3.53

Whereas we would not consider these two to be accurate innings pitched projections:

Pitcher	Label	G	GS	IP	H	HR	BB	SO	W	L	Pct	Sv	ERA
Furbush,Charlie	Actual	67	0	42	40	4	9	51	1	5	.167	1	3.61
Furbush,Charlie	Projected	69	0	66	59	9	26	67	3	4	.429	0	3.82

Pitcher	Label	G	GS	IP	H	HR	BB	SO	W	L	Pct	Sv	ERA
Kintzler,Brandon	Actual	64	0	58	62	8	16	31	3	3	.500	0	3.24
Kintzler,Brandon	Projected	75	0	82	77	4	21	65	6	3	.667	0	2.96

By these standards, 53% of our projections from last season are considered accurate; 47% are inaccurate. The other half of our accuracy scoring system is based on ERA. We consider an ERA projection to be accurate if the actual ERA is within 10%, plus 5 runs. If a pitcher pitches 50 innings and has a 3.00 projected ERA, a 10% margin would be less than 2 runs, so that's not a realistic level of accuracy; we're not going to be right within one run very often no matter what we do. With this system, these four would be considered accurate ERA projections:

Pitcher	Label	G	GS	IP	H	HR	BB	SO	W	L	Pct	Sv	ERA
Perkins,Glen	Actual	63	0	62	62	7	11	66	4	3	.571	34	3.65
Perkins,Glen	Projected	68	0	70	72	8	17	59	4	4	.500	35	3.86

Pitcher	Label	G	GS	IP	H	HR	BB	SO	W	L	Pct	Sv	ERA
Lopez,Javier	Actual	65	0	38	31	2	19	22	1	1	.500	0	3.11
Lopez,Javier	Projected	68	0	41	38	1	14	30	3	2	.600	0	3.07

Pitcher	Label	G	GS	IP	H	HR	BB	SO	W	L	Pct	Sv	ERA
Vogelsong,Ryan	Actual	32	32	185	178	18	58	151	8	13	.381	0	4.00
Vogelsong,Ryan	Projected	30	30	182	181	18	62	146	9	11	.450	0	3.91

Pitcher	Label	G	GS	IP	H	HR	BB	SO	W	L	Pct	Sv	ERA
Vargas,Jason	Actual	30	30	187	197	19	41	128	11	10	.524	0	3.71
Vargas,Jason	Projected	31	31	191	195	25	56	127	10	11	.476	0	4.01

Whereas these five would not:

Pitcher	Label	G	GS	IP	H	HR	BB	SO	W	L	Pct	Sv	ERA
Gray,Sonny	Actual	33	33	219	187	15	74	183	14	10	.583	0	3.08
Gray,Sonny	Projected	28	28	177	173	9	63	156	10	9	.526	0	3.56

Pitcher	Label	G	GS	IP	H	HR	BB	SO	W	L	Pct	Sv	ERA
Samardzija,Jeff	Actual	33	33	220	191	20	43	202	7	13	.350	0	2.99
Samardzija,Jeff	Projected	32	32	211	198	24	76	194	11	13	.458	0	3.80

Pitcher	Label	G	GS	IP	H	HR	BB	SO	W	L	Pct	Sv	ERA
Greinke,Zack	Actual	32	32	202	190	19	43	207	17	8	.680	0	2.71
Greinke,Zack	Projected	31	31	214	200	18	55	200	15	9	.625	0	3.32

Pitcher	Label	G	GS	IP	H	HR	BB	SO	W	L	Pct	Sv	ERA
Shaw,Bryan	Actual	80	0	76	61	6	22	64	5	5	.500	2	2.59
Shaw,Bryan	Projected	73	0	82	78	5	30	67	5	5	.500	0	3.62

Pitcher	Label	G	GS	IP	H	HR	BB	SO	W	L	Pct	Sv	ERA
Blevins,Jerry	Actual	64	0	57	48	3	23	66	2	3	.400	0	4.87
Blevins,Jerry	Projected	65	0	58	50	6	19	54	4	3	.571	0	3.10

By these standards, 64% of our ERA projections are accurate, whereas 36% are not accurate. We projected only one pitcher to win 20 games—and he did;

Pitcher	Label	G	GS	IP	H	HR	BB	SO	W	L	Pct	Sv	ERA
Kershaw,Clayton	Actual	27	27	198	139	9	31	239	21	3	.875	0	1.77
Kershaw,Clayton	Projected	33	33	230	172	14	55	234	20	5	.800	0	2.50

I think that is the first time that has happened in about ten years, that we projected a pitcher to win twenty games and he actually did; I don't think that has happened since Randy Johnson was in his heyday. I think also that our projections last year were the most accurate ever, although the uptick was not really meaningful.

In last year's projections there were

60 players who had exactly the correct number of losses (not including zeroes),
45 players who had exactly the correct number of wins,
40 players who had exactly the correct number of home runs allowed,
23 players who had exactly the correct number of game appearances,
19 players who had exactly the correct winning percentages,
14 players who had exactly the correct number of games started,
9 players who had exactly the correct number of hits allowed,
8 players who had exactly the correct numbers of walks,
7 players who had exactly the correct number of strikeouts,
5 players who had exactly the correct number of innings pitched, and
1 player who had exactly the right number of Saves.
Huston Street, 41 Saves.

Our understanding of how to project pitchers is certainly a lot greater now than it was when we started doing this, twenty years ago or more. We hope you get something out of it, and no, you cannot sue us if you finish last in your fantasy league.

2015 Pitcher Projections

Pitcher	Team	Age	G	GS	IP	H	HR	BB	SO	HB	W	L	Pct	Sv	BR/9	ERA
Abad,Fernando	Oak	29	61	0	50	49	5	13	43	2	3	3	.500	0	11.5	3.60
Adams,Mike	Phi	36	58	0	55	45	4	21	55	1	3	3	.500	0	11	2.95
Affeldt,Jeremy	SF	36	56	0	50	44	2	17	41	3	3	2	.600	0	11.5	3.06
Albers,Matt	Hou	32	56	0	63	61	5	22	45	2	3	4	.429	0	12.1	3.71
Alburquerque,Al	Det	29	65	0	57	45	5	29	75	3	4	3	.571	0	12.2	3.32
Allen,Cody	Cle	26	73	0	71	57	7	26	86	1	4	4	.500	34	10.6	2.92
Alvarez,Henderson	Mia	25	30	30	185	193	17	37	104	7	10	11	.476	0	11.5	3.70
Anderson,Chase	Ari	27	27	27	152	149	17	48	137	5	8	9	.471	0	12	3.85
Archer,Chris	TB	26	32	32	192	174	16	73	176	10	11	11	.500	0	12	3.56
Arrieta,Jake	ChC	29	31	31	195	178	18	66	174	8	12	10	.545	0	11.6	3.55
Arroyo,Bronson	Ari	38	12	12	74	76	11	14	45	2	4	4	.500	0	11.2	3.89
Atchison,Scott	Cle	39	64	0	66	61	5	13	50	1	4	3	.571	0	10.2	2.73
Avilan,Luis	Atl	25	61	0	50	47	3	25	35	3	2	3	.400	0	13.5	3.96
Axelrod,Dylan	Cin	29	10	8	37	38	4	12	29	1	2	2	.500	0	12.4	4.14
Axford,John	Pit	32	70	0	66	57	7	37	77	2	3	4	.429	0	13.1	3.95
Badenhop,Burke	Bos	32	67	0	64	65	4	15	43	2	4	3	.571	0	11.5	3.38
Bailey,Homer	Cin	29	26	26	165	160	18	47	139	7	9	10	.474	0	11.7	3.71
Baker,Scott	Tex	33	24	10	79	78	11	17	63	2	4	4	.500	0	11.1	3.65
Balfour,Grant	TB	37	66	0	66	48	5	37	69	1	4	3	.571	0	11.7	3.00
Barrett,Aaron	Was	27	66	0	64	50	2	25	79	1	5	2	.714	0	10.7	2.39
Bastardo,Antonio	Phi	29	61	0	60	45	5	31	73	2	3	3	.500	0	11.7	3.15
Bauer,Trevor	Cle	24	29	29	172	163	19	82	170	11	7	12	.368	0	13.4	4.29
Beachy,Brandon	Atl	28	24	24	148	121	15	56	149	3	9	7	.563	0	10.9	3.28
Bedard,Erik	TB	36	8	7	38	37	4	17	36	1	2	3	.400	0	13	4.03
Beimel,Joe	Sea	38	51	0	40	40	5	15	24	1	2	3	.400	0	12.6	4.05
Belisario,Ronald	CWS	32	65	0	64	63	4	21	49	4	3	4	.429	0	12.4	3.66
Belisle,Matt	Col	35	68	0	67	73	5	17	52	2	4	4	.500	0	12.4	3.90
Beliveau,Jeff	TB	28	58	0	50	41	3	21	63	1	3	2	.600	0	11.3	3.06
Bell,Heath	NYY	37	31	0	30	31	4	13	29	1	1	2	.333	0	13.5	4.50
Benoit,Joaquin	SD	37	66	0	64	47	7	18	72	1	4	3	.571	40	9.3	2.39
Bergman,Christian	Col	27	15	15	87	95	13	17	53	2	5	5	.500	0	11.8	4.24
Betances,Dellin	NYY	27	67	0	84	71	7	36	100	6	5	5	.500	4	12.1	3.32
Betancourt,Rafael	Col	40	40	0	35	31	4	12	37	0	2	2	.500	0	11.1	3.34
Billingsley,Chad	LAD	30	18	18	106	101	7	34	92	4	7	5	.583	0	11.8	3.57
Black,Vic	NYM	27	64	0	57	43	3	33	65	3	4	3	.571	0	12.5	3.16
Blevins,Jerry	Was	31	65	0	58	49	5	21	56	3	4	3	.571	0	11.3	3.10
Boxberger,Brad	TB	27	62	0	65	46	6	24	94	3	5	2	.714	2	10.1	2.49
Boyer,Blaine	SD	33	37	0	49	52	5	10	36	2	3	3	.500	0	11.8	3.67
Brach,Brad	Bal	29	57	0	66	57	6	26	71	2	4	3	.571	0	11.6	3.27
Breslow,Craig	Bos	34	58	0	52	50	5	23	41	1	3	3	.500	0	12.8	3.98
Britton,Drake	Bos	26	55	0	55	63	5	30	43	1	2	4	.333	0	15.4	5.24
Britton,Zach	Bal	27	66	0	71	71	6	28	51	2	4	4	.500	38	12.8	3.93
Brothers,Rex	Col	27	68	0	48	43	4	30	58	1	3	3	.500	0	13.9	4.13
Brown,Brooks	Col	30	40	0	38	43	4	13	27	2	2	2	.500	0	13.7	4.74
Broxton,Jonathan	Mil	31	62	0	60	50	4	19	62	3	4	2	.667	40	10.8	2.85
Buchanan,David	Phi	26	24	24	146	159	15	47	93	9	6	11	.353	0	13.3	4.44
Buchanan,Jake	Hou	25	20	20	112	129	9	23	65	3	5	7	.417	0	12.5	4.10
Buchholz,Clay	Bos	30	29	29	196	183	19	62	156	8	12	10	.545	0	11.6	3.58
Buehrle,Mark	Tor	36	32	32	201	218	21	47	116	5	10	12	.455	0	12.1	3.94
Bueno,Francisley	KC	34	33	0	31	31	2	9	23	1	2	2	.500	0	11.9	3.48
Bumgarner,Madison	SF	25	33	33	216	191	19	50	199	6	15	9	.625	0	10.3	3.13
Burnett,A.J.	Phi	38	32	32	203	193	21	83	189	12	9	13	.409	0	12.8	3.99
Burton,Jared	Min	34	65	0	64	58	6	23	53	4	4	3	.571	2	12	3.52
Cahill,Trevor	Ari	27	30	23	137	134	13	67	101	5	6	9	.400	0	13.5	4.27
Cain,Matt	SF	30	29	29	179	152	18	56	146	5	12	8	.600	0	10.7	3.22
Capps,Carter	Mia	24	57	0	61	57	6	22	74	3	3	4	.429	0	12.1	3.54
Capuano,Chris	NYY	36	17	11	68	70	8	20	57	1	3	4	.429	0	12	3.97
Carlyle,Buddy	NYM	37	65	0	69	66	9	20	66	2	4	4	.500	0	11.5	3.65
Carpenter,David	Atl	29	68	0	67	63	6	19	70	4	4	4	.500	0	11.6	3.36
Carrasco,Carlos	Cle	28	30	30	179	177	18	46	159	7	10	10	.500	0	11.6	3.67
Carroll,Scott	CWS	30	15	10	59	68	6	21	33	3	2	4	.333	0	14	4.88
Cashner,Andrew	SD	28	29	29	186	167	14	47	152	4	13	8	.619	0	10.5	3.15
Casilla,Santiago	SF	34	58	0	63	50	4	21	53	3	4	3	.571	38	10.6	2.71
Cecil,Brett	Tor	28	64	0	56	56	6	24	48	2	3	4	.429	0	13.2	4.18
Chacin,Jhoulys	Col	27	23	23	131	124	12	49	97	4	8	7	.533	0	12.2	3.71
Chamberlain,Joba	Det	29	64	0	60	59	6	26	60	3	3	4	.429	0	13.2	4.20
Chapman,Aroldis	Cin	27	66	0	65	39	4	29	106	3	4	3	.571	47	9.8	2.08
Chapman,Kevin	Hou	27	30	0	34	29	2	21	38	1	2	2	.500	0	13.5	3.71
Chatwood,Tyler	Col	25	8	8	46	51	4	15	30	2	2	3	.400	0	13.3	4.30
Chavez,Jesse	Oak	31	35	15	127	127	14	40	113	4	6	8	.429	0	12.1	3.90
Chen,Bruce	KC	38	27	14	88	94	12	25	62	3	4	6	.400	0	12.5	4.40
Chen,Wei-Yin	Bal	29	31	31	196	196	25	44	147	4	10	11	.476	0	11.2	3.72
Choate,Randy	StL	39	57	0	34	28	2	12	30	1	2	1	.667	0	11.4	2.91
Cingrani,Tony	Cin	25	18	15	91	70	12	44	104	2	5	5	.500	0	11.5	3.46
Cishek,Steve	Mia	29	66	0	64	55	3	21	70	3	4	3	.571	44	11.1	2.81
Cleto,Maikel	CWS	26	35	0	38	37	4	26	42	3	1	3	.250	0	15.6	5.21
Clippard,Tyler	Was	30	75	0	73	52	8	25	78	2	6	2	.750	0	9.7	2.47
Cobb,Alex	TB	27	29	29	178	164	13	53	161	8	11	9	.550	0	11.4	3.39
Coke,Phil	Det	32	66	0	60	66	4	23	49	1	3	4	.429	0	13.5	4.35
Cole,Gerrit	Pit	24	30	30	189	171	13	57	171	9	12	9	.571	0	11.3	3.33

2015 Pitcher Projections

Pitcher	Team	Age	G	GS	IP	H	HR	BB	SO	HB	W	L	Pct	Sv	BR/9	ERA
Coleman,Louis	KC	29	31	0	36	29	4	15	39	1	2	2	.500	0	11.2	3.25
Collmenter,Josh	Ari	29	32	27	174	164	18	43	129	3	11	9	.550	0	10.9	3.41
Colome,Alex	TB	26	26	26	159	155	9	68	132	9	8	10	.444	0	13.1	3.85
Colon,Bartolo	NYM	42	29	29	192	202	20	29	130	3	11	11	.500	0	11	3.61
Cook,Ryan	Oak	28	70	0	68	52	3	28	68	4	5	3	.625	0	11.1	2.51
Corbin,Patrick	Ari	25	25	25	158	158	15	41	137	7	9	9	.500	0	11.7	3.70
Correia,Kevin	LAD	34	30	18	123	138	16	31	72	3	6	8	.429	0	12.6	4.39
Cosart,Jarred	Mia	25	31	31	187	175	9	85	133	5	10	11	.476	0	12.8	3.66
Cotts,Neal	Tex	35	67	0	63	55	4	21	70	2	4	3	.571	0	11.1	3.00
Crain,Jesse	Hou	33	55	0	52	44	4	17	55	1	4	2	.667	0	10.7	2.60
Crow,Aaron	KC	28	57	0	50	48	6	21	41	1	2	3	.400	0	12.6	3.96
Cueto,Johnny	Cin	29	32	32	228	195	21	60	192	13	15	10	.600	0	10.6	3.20
Cumpton,Brandon	Pit	26	16	5	56	60	4	18	35	5	3	4	.429	0	13.3	4.02
Danks,John	CWS	30	30	30	183	187	24	64	129	6	8	12	.400	0	12.6	4.28
Darnell,Logan	Min	26	11	6	36	42	5	14	26	2	1	3	.250	0	14.5	5.50
Darvish,Yu	Tex	28	31	31	200	162	20	74	248	7	13	9	.591	0	10.9	3.24
Davis,Wade	KC	29	73	0	74	71	7	28	65	3	4	5	.444	2	12.4	3.77
De Fratus,Justin	Phi	27	55	0	52	47	3	16	51	4	3	3	.500	0	11.6	3.12
De La Rosa,Dane	LAA	32	47	0	44	36	3	24	44	1	3	2	.600	0	12.5	3.27
De La Rosa,Eury	Ari	25	37	0	56	52	4	25	53	3	3	3	.500	0	12.9	3.86
De La Rosa,Jorge	Col	34	32	32	186	178	20	68	149	8	11	10	.524	0	12.3	3.87
De La Rosa,Rubby	Bos	26	61	8	95	93	8	41	82	4	5	6	.455	0	13.1	4.07
Deduno,Samuel	Hou	31	34	6	84	76	6	39	68	7	4	5	.444	0	13.1	3.75
deGrom,Jacob	NYM	27	29	29	185	178	11	56	164	3	11	9	.550	0	11.5	3.41
Delabar,Steve	Tor	31	56	0	62	50	7	39	76	5	3	4	.429	0	13.6	4.06
Delgado,Randall	Ari	25	44	5	81	80	11	31	71	3	4	5	.444	0	12.7	4.22
Dempster,Ryan	FA	38	27	27	165	156	21	70	154	5	8	10	.444	0	12.6	3.87
Detwiler,Ross	Was	29	46	0	58	62	5	17	37	3	3	3	.500	0	12.7	4.03
Diaz,Jumbo	Cin	31	66	0	66	57	6	25	63	3	4	3	.571	0	11.6	3.27
Dickey,R.A.	Tor	40	33	33	210	196	24	68	158	10	12	12	.500	0	11.7	3.73
Diekman,Jake	Phi	28	71	0	70	61	3	38	88	4	4	4	.500	0	13.2	3.47
Doolittle,Sean	Oak	28	62	0	64	45	4	10	77	1	5	2	.714	29	7.9	1.55
Doubront,Felix	ChC	27	16	13	70	72	8	30	61	3	3	5	.375	0	13.5	4.50
Downs,Darin	Hou	30	36	0	31	31	2	14	28	1	1	2	.333	0	13.4	4.06
Downs,Scott	KC	39	62	0	55	50	3	26	42	1	3	3	.500	0	12.6	3.60
Duensing,Brian	Min	32	60	0	49	54	5	17	32	1	2	3	.400	0	13.2	4.41
Duffy,Danny	KC	26	28	28	169	152	16	66	153	7	9	10	.474	0	12	3.67
Duke,Zach	Mil	32	71	0	52	60	5	15	32	1	2	3	.400	0	13.2	4.50
Dunn,Mike	Mia	30	71	0	54	47	4	22	62	1	3	3	.500	0	11.7	3.33
Dyson,Sam	Mia	27	45	0	64	66	2	24	38	6	3	4	.429	0	13.5	3.80
Edgin,Josh	NYM	28	37	0	31	28	3	13	30	1	2	2	.500	0	12.2	3.77
Elias,Roenis	Sea	26	30	30	171	159	17	70	152	9	8	11	.421	0	12.5	3.84
Eovaldi,Nathan	Mia	25	32	32	195	201	13	52	144	5	11	11	.500	0	11.9	3.65
Erlin,Robbie	SD	24	12	10	51	58	6	15	45	1	2	3	.400	0	13.1	4.41
Estrada,Marco	Mil	31	45	9	128	120	18	35	113	2	7	7	.500	0	11	3.52
Familia,Jeurys	NYM	25	73	0	74	71	5	35	69	3	4	5	.444	2	13.3	3.89
Farquhar,Danny	Sea	28	64	0	72	59	4	23	79	4	5	3	.625	0	10.8	2.75
Feldman,Scott	Hou	32	29	29	182	187	19	52	114	8	9	11	.450	0	12.2	3.91
Feliz,Neftali	Tex	27	61	0	61	45	6	21	58	2	4	2	.667	38	10	2.66
Fernandez,Jose	Mia	22	24	24	148	105	9	45	174	3	12	4	.750	0	9.3	2.55
Fields,Josh	Hou	29	63	0	64	53	5	22	73	2	4	3	.571	10	10.8	2.81
Fien,Casey	Min	31	69	0	58	55	8	11	53	0	4	3	.571	2	10.2	3.26
Fiers,Mike	Mil	30	28	28	175	148	19	41	180	6	12	7	.632	0	10	3.09
Fister,Doug	Was	31	28	28	186	190	16	34	128	10	11	9	.550	0	11.3	3.58
Flande,Yohan	Col	29	22	8	65	76	5	23	43	2	3	4	.429	0	14	4.71
Floyd,Gavin	FA	32	23	23	144	144	17	46	113	8	7	9	.438	0	12.4	4.13
Foltynewicz,Mike	Hou	23	12	12	71	66	7	37	67	5	3	5	.375	0	13.7	4.31
Frasor,Jason	KC	37	61	0	48	42	4	19	48	2	3	3	.500	0	11.8	3.38
Freeman,Sam	StL	28	49	0	42	37	3	18	37	2	2	2	.500	0	12.2	3.43
Frieri,Ernesto	FA	29	65	0	65	51	10	27	82	4	4	3	.571	0	11.4	3.50
Furbush,Charlie	Sea	29	64	0	38	33	5	12	40	2	2	2	.500	0	11.1	3.32
Gallardo,Yovani	Mil	29	30	30	181	172	20	57	167	2	10	10	.500	0	11.5	3.63
Garcia,Jaime	StL	28	24	24	139	140	13	32	116	2	8	7	.533	0	11.3	3.56
Garza,Matt	Mil	31	29	29	186	171	20	55	156	6	11	10	.524	0	11.2	3.48
Gausman,Kevin	Bal	24	31	31	195	190	18	63	177	3	11	11	.500	0	11.8	3.69
Gee,Dillon	NYM	29	25	25	160	159	20	45	121	8	8	10	.444	0	11.9	3.88
Gibson,Kyle	Min	27	31	31	187	198	15	62	134	4	9	11	.450	0	12.7	3.99
Gomes,Brandon	TB	30	27	0	35	30	4	12	40	1	2	2	.500	0	11.1	3.09
Gomez,Jeanmar	Pit	27	48	0	60	62	6	22	40	2	3	4	.429	0	12.9	4.20
Gonzalez,Gio	Was	29	32	32	197	167	15	73	196	4	13	9	.591	0	11.1	3.24
Gonzalez,Miguel	Bal	31	26	26	164	151	22	51	119	7	9	9	.500	0	11.5	3.73
Gorzelanny,Tom	Mil	32	57	0	54	53	6	19	46	2	3	3	.500	0	12.3	3.83
Gray,Sonny	Oak	25	33	33	215	200	13	74	184	5	12	11	.522	0	11.7	3.39
Greene,Shane	NYY	26	10	10	61	68	5	22	56	4	2	4	.333	0	13.9	4.57
Greenwood,Nick	StL	27	24	2	44	47	5	11	26	2	2	3	.400	0	12.3	4.09
Gregerson,Luke	Oak	31	67	0	68	54	5	16	64	2	5	3	.625	0	9.5	2.38
Gregg,Kevin	Mia	37	48	0	48	45	5	24	43	2	2	3	.400	0	13.3	4.31
Greinke,Zack	LAD	31	32	32	204	190	17	47	194	4	14	9	.609	0	10.6	3.26
Griffin,A.J.	Oak	27	24	24	138	120	20	35	115	4	8	7	.533	0	10.4	3.39
Grilli,Jason	LAA	38	66	0	58	50	5	20	69	3	4	3	.571	0	11.3	3.10

547

2015 Pitcher Projections

PLAYER			HOW MUCH			WHAT HE WILL GIVE UP					THE RESULTS					
Pitcher	Team	Age	G	GS	IP	H	HR	BB	SO	HB	W	L	Pct	Sv	BR/9	ERA
Grimm,Justin	ChC	26	70	0	68	70	5	25	58	2	3	4	.429	0	12.8	3.97
Guerra,Javy	CWS	29	46	0	52	52	4	23	44	3	2	3	.400	5	13.5	4.15
Guthrie,Jeremy	KC	36	31	31	198	210	27	51	114	10	9	13	.409	0	12.3	4.27
Gutierrez,Juan	SF	31	62	0	63	65	8	18	49	2	3	4	.429	0	12.1	4.00
Hagadone,Nick	Cle	29	66	0	62	53	7	29	68	1	3	4	.429	0	12	3.63
Hale,David	Atl	27	39	8	96	100	8	40	66	5	4	7	.364	0	13.6	4.31
Hamels,Cole	Phi	31	32	32	216	193	21	57	202	6	13	11	.542	0	10.7	3.29
Hammel,Jason	Oak	32	26	26	161	162	19	45	124	7	8	10	.444	0	12	3.91
Hand,Brad	Mia	25	30	19	131	124	15	58	102	1	6	8	.429	0	12.6	3.98
Hanrahan,Joel	Det	33	54	0	50	44	7	33	54	1	2	3	.400	0	14	4.32
Happ,J.A.	Tor	32	30	29	184	184	24	69	160	3	9	12	.429	0	12.5	4.16
Harang,Aaron	Atl	37	28	28	174	182	20	60	136	4	8	12	.400	0	12.7	4.24
Hardy,Blaine	Det	28	47	0	50	47	5	20	42	1	3	3	.500	0	12.2	3.78
Haren,Dan	LAD	34	31	31	181	179	24	35	154	4	11	9	.550	0	10.8	3.63
Harris,Will	Ari	30	62	0	53	47	4	19	59	3	3	3	.500	0	11.7	3.40
Harrison,Matt	Tex	29	23	23	140	146	13	56	88	1	6	9	.400	0	13	4.24
Harvey,Matt	NYM	26	26	26	174	144	11	42	184	7	13	6	.684	0	10	2.84
Hatcher,Chris	Mia	30	60	0	64	61	6	20	63	1	4	4	.500	0	11.5	3.52
Hawkins,LaTroy	Col	42	55	0	53	54	4	11	35	1	4	2	.667	28	11.2	3.23
Hellickson,Jeremy	TB	28	31	31	171	169	21	52	137	6	8	11	.421	0	11.9	3.89
Hembree,Heath	Bos	26	53	0	52	47	5	20	54	2	3	3	.500	0	11.9	3.46
Henderson,Jim	Mil	32	36	0	32	27	4	13	36	1	2	2	.500	0	11.5	3.38
Hendricks,Kyle	ChC	25	28	28	176	168	8	39	135	6	12	8	.600	0	10.9	3.17
Hendriks,Liam	KC	26	13	7	45	48	4	7	33	2	2	3	.400	0	11.4	3.80
Hernandez,David	Ari	30	54	0	54	46	6	21	58	3	3	3	.500	0	11.7	3.33
Hernandez,Felix	Sea	29	32	32	224	193	16	47	216	7	16	9	.640	0	9.9	2.89
Hernandez,Roberto	LAD	34	31	31	198	206	24	75	123	13	9	13	.409	0	13.4	4.50
Herrera,Kelvin	KC	25	69	0	71	58	5	25	72	3	5	3	.625	0	10.9	2.79
Hochevar,Luke	KC	31	54	0	67	67	8	19	51	3	3	4	.429	0	12	3.90
Holland,Derek	Tex	28	30	30	184	182	24	53	155	4	10	11	.476	0	11.7	3.86
Holland,Greg	KC	29	65	0	64	47	3	21	84	0	4	3	.571	43	9.6	2.11
Hoover,J.J.	Cin	27	61	0	64	47	6	29	73	1	4	3	.571	0	10.8	2.81
House,T.J.	Cle	25	29	29	171	194	15	53	134	8	7	12	.368	0	13.4	4.47
Howell,J.P.	LAD	32	60	0	42	32	3	19	40	2	3	2	.600	0	11.4	3.00
Hudson,Daniel	Ari	28	55	0	58	57	6	16	50	2	3	3	.500	0	11.6	3.57
Hudson,Tim	SF	39	29	29	170	162	12	36	108	7	11	8	.579	0	10.9	3.28
Huff,David	NYY	30	41	0	53	59	8	16	36	1	2	4	.333	0	12.9	4.75
Hughes,Jared	Pit	29	62	0	63	62	4	21	45	5	3	4	.429	0	12.6	3.71
Hughes,Phil	Min	29	32	32	213	223	28	30	182	6	12	12	.500	0	10.9	3.72
Hunter,Tommy	Bal	28	62	0	64	67	9	12	40	2	3	4	.429	4	11.4	3.94
Hutchison,Drew	Tor	24	32	32	185	178	21	60	182	10	10	11	.476	0	12.1	3.84
Iwakuma,Hisashi	Sea	34	32	32	205	184	24	32	170	3	14	9	.609	0	9.6	3.07
Jackson,Edwin	ChC	31	28	28	164	176	18	64	130	3	7	11	.389	0	13.3	4.50
Jansen,Kenley	LAD	27	67	0	65	41	5	18	101	2	5	2	.714	47	8.4	1.66
Janssen,Casey	Tor	33	66	0	62	56	5	11	52	2	4	3	.571	38	10	2.76
Jeffress,Jeremy	Mil	27	52	0	54	52	2	24	54	1	3	3	.500	0	12.8	3.67
Jenkins,Chad	Tor	27	19	0	34	39	5	8	19	1	1	2	.333	0	12.7	4.50
Jennings,Dan	Mia	28	65	0	61	61	3	28	55	0	3	4	.429	0	13.1	3.84
Jepsen,Kevin	LAA	30	69	0	62	57	5	22	61	2	4	3	.571	0	11.8	3.34
Jimenez,Ubaldo	Bal	31	30	30	169	156	16	90	155	6	8	11	.421	0	13.4	4.10
Johnson,Erik	CWS	25	24	24	136	142	11	62	100	6	6	9	.400	0	13.9	4.50
Johnson,Jim	Det	32	49	0	46	47	3	21	32	3	2	3	.400	0	13.9	4.30
Johnson,Josh	SD	31	18	18	94	91	7	34	86	3	5	5	.500	0	12.3	3.45
Jokisch,Eric	ChC	25	27	27	174	171	16	46	140	5	10	9	.526	0	11.5	3.57
Jones,Nate	CWS	29	31	0	31	29	2	13	32	1	2	2	.500	0	12.5	3.48
Kahnle,Tommy	Col	25	43	0	50	41	5	28	52	0	3	2	.600	0	12.4	3.60
Karns,Nate	TB	27	22	22	124	119	18	56	131	5	5	9	.357	0	13.1	4.50
Kazmir,Scott	Oak	31	32	32	187	180	20	51	168	7	10	11	.476	0	11.5	3.61
Kelley,Shawn	NYY	31	63	0	53	46	6	21	60	1	3	3	.500	0	11.5	3.40
Kelly,Casey	SD	25	23	23	131	147	12	20	107	8	7	8	.467	0	12	3.92
Kelly,Joe	Bos	27	28	28	172	176	14	70	117	9	8	11	.421	0	13.3	4.19
Kendrick,Kyle	Phi	30	31	31	192	207	23	54	108	9	8	14	.364	0	12.7	4.31
Kennedy,Ian	SD	30	32	32	194	188	23	69	179	9	10	12	.455	0	12.3	3.99
Kershaw,Clayton	LAD	27	33	33	232	172	13	45	245	4	21	5	.808	0	8.6	2.37
Keuchel,Dallas	Hou	27	31	31	214	224	19	58	142	5	11	13	.458	0	12.1	3.87
Kimbrel,Craig	Atl	27	65	0	64	35	3	23	102	2	5	2	.714	56	8.4	1.55
Kintzler,Brandon	Mil	30	66	0	62	60	5	16	45	1	4	3	.571	0	11.2	3.19
Kluber,Corey	Cle	29	32	32	234	237	21	54	233	10	13	13	.500	0	11.6	3.65
Koehler,Tom	Mia	29	30	30	186	183	19	72	145	7	9	12	.429	0	12.7	3.97
Kontos,George	SF	30	57	0	62	55	6	17	58	1	4	3	.571	0	10.6	3.05
Krol,Ian	Det	24	52	0	45	45	6	15	46	2	2	3	.400	0	12.4	4.00
Kuroda,Hiroki	NYY	40	31	31	191	184	20	37	139	5	11	10	.524	0	10.6	3.39
Lackey,John	StL	36	31	31	197	204	23	46	155	8	10	12	.455	0	11.8	3.88
Latos,Mat	Cin	27	28	28	184	162	16	52	162	5	12	9	.571	0	10.7	3.23
Layne,Tom	Bos	30	64	0	46	41	3	18	35	3	2	3	.400	0	12.1	3.13
League,Brandon	LAD	32	62	0	58	58	3	23	41	3	3	3	.500	0	13	3.88
Leake,Mike	Cin	27	32	32	207	214	26	49	143	8	10	13	.435	0	11.8	3.91
LeBlanc,Wade	LAA	30	18	6	48	50	5	15	38	1	3	3	.500	0	12.4	3.94
LeCure,Sam	Cin	31	60	0	55	53	6	23	50	2	3	4	.429	0	12.8	4.09
Lee,C.C.	Cle	28	50	0	37	33	3	14	42	3	2	2	.500	0	12.2	3.41

548

2015 Pitcher Projections

PLAYER			HOW MUCH			WHAT HE WILL GIVE UP					THE RESULTS					
Pitcher	Team	Age	G	GS	IP	H	HR	BB	SO	HB	W	L	Pct	Sv	BR/9	ERA
Lee,Cliff	Phi	36	30	30	213	205	20	31	194	3	13	10	.565	0	10.1	3.17
Lester,Jon	Oak	31	33	33	217	202	20	56	198	7	13	11	.542	0	11	3.36
Lewis,Colby	Tex	35	29	29	172	181	26	49	145	7	8	11	.421	0	12.4	4.34
Lincecum,Tim	SF	31	30	30	182	164	17	74	184	5	10	10	.500	0	12	3.66
Lindstrom,Matt	CWS	35	63	0	57	63	3	21	43	2	2	4	.333	0	13.6	4.42
Liriano,Francisco	Pit	31	30	30	182	163	16	83	182	6	10	10	.500	0	12.5	3.71
Locke,Jeff	Pit	27	25	25	145	141	14	57	114	6	7	9	.438	0	12.7	3.97
Logan,Boone	Col	30	52	0	37	36	5	16	40	2	2	2	.500	0	13.1	4.38
Lohse,Kyle	Mil	36	32	32	203	200	22	42	131	5	12	10	.545	0	11	3.55
Lopez,Javier	SF	37	63	0	40	36	1	17	28	1	2	2	.500	0	12.2	3.38
Loup,Aaron	Tor	27	65	0	62	57	4	21	49	5	4	3	.571	0	12	3.34
Lyles,Jordan	Col	24	25	25	150	167	16	52	108	9	7	10	.412	0	13.7	4.68
Lynn,Lance	StL	28	32	32	195	185	15	70	179	9	11	11	.500	0	12.2	3.65
Lyons,Tyler	StL	27	35	6	71	70	7	17	64	2	4	4	.500	0	11.3	3.55
Machi,Jean	SF	33	66	0	63	57	5	16	51	2	4	3	.571	0	10.7	2.86
Maness,Seth	StL	26	73	0	80	82	8	11	52	3	5	4	.556	6	10.8	3.26
Marshall,Evan	Ari	25	62	0	55	58	2	21	51	3	3	3	.500	0	13.4	3.93
Marshall,Sean	Cin	32	35	0	32	30	2	16	31	1	2	2	.500	0	13.2	3.94
Martinez,Carlos	StL	23	27	27	164	150	9	60	146	12	10	9	.526	0	12.2	3.51
Masset,Nick	Col	33	51	0	48	49	4	22	42	2	3	3	.500	0	13.7	4.31
Masterson,Justin	StL	30	31	31	194	189	15	93	164	15	9	13	.409	0	13.8	4.22
Matsuzaka,Daisuke	NYM	34	25	4	55	50	6	27	49	3	3	4	.429	0	13.1	4.09
Matusz,Brian	Bal	28	64	0	52	54	7	18	43	1	2	3	.400	0	12.6	4.33
Matzek,Tyler	Col	24	28	28	175	185	17	80	132	4	8	11	.421	0	13.8	4.58
Maurer,Brandon	Sea	24	46	3	65	70	6	23	56	3	3	5	.375	0	13.3	4.43
May,Trevor	Min	25	28	28	165	166	20	77	162	8	7	11	.389	0	13.7	4.58
McAllister,Zach	Cle	27	35	12	101	107	10	31	80	3	5	7	.417	0	12.6	4.10
McCarthy,Brandon	NYY	31	30	30	187	202	20	32	135	5	9	11	.450	0	11.5	3.80
McFarland,T.J.	Bal	26	57	0	65	73	4	19	45	3	3	4	.429	0	13.2	4.15
McGee,Jake	TB	28	70	0	70	56	5	18	81	1	5	3	.625	35	9.6	2.44
McGowan,Dustin	Tor	33	52	4	64	61	8	27	53	2	3	4	.429	0	12.7	4.22
McHugh,Collin	Hou	28	30	30	187	172	16	50	167	9	11	10	.524	0	11.1	3.37
Medina,Yoervis	Sea	26	64	0	58	49	5	31	59	4	3	4	.429	0	13	3.88
Medlen,Kris	Atl	29	25	25	155	143	12	36	132	4	10	7	.588	0	10.6	3.19
Mejia,Jenrry	NYM	25	62	0	62	63	5	25	52	2	3	4	.429	29	13.1	4.06
Melancon,Mark	Pit	30	68	0	72	62	4	11	70	3	5	3	.625	40	9.5	2.38
Mikolas,Miles	Tex	26	12	12	75	80	7	18	54	2	4	4	.500	0	12	3.84
Miley,Wade	Ari	28	30	30	184	187	18	63	145	3	10	11	.476	0	12.4	3.91
Miller,Andrew	Bal	30	69	0	61	55	5	22	65	4	3	3	.500	2	12	3.39
Miller,Shelby	StL	24	31	31	184	164	23	69	170	7	10	10	.500	0	11.7	3.72
Milone,Tommy	Min	28	28	28	171	185	21	49	136	4	8	11	.421	0	12.5	4.26
Minor,Mike	Atl	27	30	30	182	175	24	49	163	4	10	11	.476	0	11.3	3.71
Montero,Rafael	NYM	24	25	25	146	127	9	52	139	1	10	7	.588	0	11.1	3.21
Moore,Matt	TB	26	20	20	112	93	10	55	118	4	6	6	.500	0	12.2	3.62
Morales,Franklin	Col	29	39	21	139	140	20	63	113	8	6	9	.400	0	13.7	4.73
Morin,Mike	LAA	24	62	0	60	53	4	16	61	3	4	2	.667	0	10.8	2.85
Morris,Bryan	Mia	28	58	0	62	60	6	23	49	2	3	4	.429	0	12.3	3.92
Morton,Charlie	Pit	31	31	31	192	193	13	67	137	17	10	12	.455	0	13	3.94
Motte,Jason	StL	33	65	0	65	52	8	19	69	2	4	3	.571	0	10.1	2.77
Mujica,Edward	Bos	31	66	0	62	61	8	11	49	1	4	3	.571	4	10.6	3.34
Nathan,Joe	Det	40	60	0	58	47	5	24	63	2	4	3	.571	35	11.3	3.10
Nelson,Jimmy	Mil	26	29	29	169	148	8	61	162	12	11	8	.579	0	11.8	3.30
Neshek,Pat	StL	34	68	0	70	60	7	13	62	2	5	3	.625	3	9.6	2.57
Nicasio,Juan	Col	28	43	7	78	84	10	29	62	2	4	5	.444	0	13.3	4.62
Niese,Jon	NYM	28	30	30	189	197	18	51	149	6	10	11	.476	0	12.1	3.86
Noesi,Hector	CWS	28	30	28	184	202	27	59	134	4	7	13	.350	0	13	4.70
Nolasco,Ricky	Min	32	31	31	188	207	21	45	148	6	9	12	.429	0	12.4	4.12
Norris,Bud	Bal	30	28	28	166	163	20	59	152	8	8	11	.421	0	12.5	4.07
Nova,Ivan	NYY	28	11	11	67	72	7	21	51	4	3	5	.375	0	13	4.43
Nuno,Vidal	Ari	27	29	28	171	167	23	46	140	5	9	10	.474	0	11.5	3.79
Oberholtzer,Brett	Hou	25	26	26	162	173	19	34	121	3	8	10	.444	0	11.7	3.89
O'Day,Darren	Bal	32	68	0	66	50	7	17	63	6	5	3	.625	0	10	2.59
Odorizzi,Jake	TB	25	30	30	166	154	20	58	156	4	9	10	.474	0	11.7	3.74
O'Flaherty,Eric	Oak	30	62	0	54	45	4	15	42	3	4	2	.667	0	10.5	2.67
Ogando,Alexi	Tex	31	19	19	106	94	11	44	85	4	6	6	.500	0	12.1	3.65
Ondrusek,Logan	Cin	30	48	0	49	48	6	18	39	1	2	3	.400	0	12.3	3.86
Otero,Dan	Oak	30	68	0	82	80	3	13	56	3	5	4	.556	0	10.5	2.74
Ottavino,Adam	Col	29	72	0	63	66	6	20	58	3	3	4	.429	0	12.7	4.14
Outman,Josh	NYY	30	53	0	47	48	4	22	41	1	2	3	.400	0	13.6	4.40
Papelbon,Jonathan	Phi	34	67	0	67	54	5	14	75	3	5	3	.625	34	9.5	2.42
Parker,Jarrod	Oak	26	27	27	166	153	15	54	126	6	9	9	.500	0	11.5	3.52
Parnell,Bobby	NYM	30	52	0	50	49	3	14	44	1	3	3	.500	13	11.5	3.42
Parra,Manny	Cin	32	55	0	40	42	4	18	38	1	2	3	.400	0	13.7	4.50
Paulino,Felipe	CWS	31	6	6	31	35	4	20	28	1	1	3	.250	0	16.3	6.10
Paxton,James	Sea	26	28	28	162	155	11	69	149	2	8	10	.444	0	12.6	3.78
Peacock,Brad	Hou	27	27	25	132	126	18	62	127	4	6	9	.400	0	13.1	4.30
Peavy,Jake	SF	34	31	31	207	189	24	59	180	7	12	11	.522	0	11.1	3.52
Pelfrey,Mike	Min	31	27	27	144	165	12	62	83	6	5	11	.313	0	14.6	5.00
Peralta,Joel	TB	39	70	0	67	54	8	21	68	1	4	3	.571	0	10.2	2.82
Peralta,Wily	Mil	26	31	31	192	195	18	68	158	8	9	12	.429	0	12.7	4.03

2015 Pitcher Projections

Pitcher	Team	Age	G	GS	IP	H	HR	BB	SO	HB	W	L	Pct	Sv	BR/9	ERA
Perez,Chris	LAD	29	52	0	50	42	7	23	49	4	3	3	.500	0	12.4	3.96
Perez,Martin	Tex	24	13	13	79	85	7	27	57	2	4	5	.444	0	13	4.22
Perez,Oliver	Ari	33	65	0	54	53	7	24	55	3	2	4	.333	0	13.3	4.33
Perkins,Glen	Min	32	64	0	63	65	7	13	54	2	3	4	.429	36	11.4	3.71
Pestano,Vinnie	LAA	30	55	0	54	45	5	22	63	2	4	2	.667	0	11.5	3.17
Petit,Yusmeiro	SF	30	26	26	154	152	19	29	142	1	9	8	.529	0	10.6	3.51
Petricka,Jake	CWS	27	64	0	64	66	4	32	47	1	3	4	.429	20	13.9	4.22
Phelps,David	NYY	28	28	11	93	91	10	38	82	5	4	6	.400	0	13	4.16
Pineda,Michael	NYY	26	25	25	151	125	14	22	146	5	11	5	.688	0	9.1	2.74
Pino,Yohan	Min	31	25	25	150	155	20	42	127	5	7	9	.438	0	12.1	4.14
Pomeranz,Drew	Oak	26	22	15	91	83	10	37	88	2	5	6	.455	0	12.1	3.76
Porcello,Rick	Det	26	32	32	209	233	20	45	132	6	11	13	.458	0	12.2	4.00
Pressly,Ryan	Min	26	43	0	47	48	3	17	35	1	3	3	.500	0	12.6	3.64
Price,David	Det	29	32	32	223	201	21	36	211	5	16	9	.640	0	9.8	3.03
Putnam,Zach	CWS	27	55	0	58	58	3	20	52	1	3	3	.500	10	12.3	3.57
Putz,J.J.	FA	38	42	0	36	29	3	16	40	1	2	2	.500	0	11.5	3.00
Quackenbush,Kevin	SD	26	60	0	62	49	1	23	69	3	5	2	.714	4	10.9	2.47
Qualls,Chad	Hou	36	64	0	63	66	6	12	48	2	3	4	.429	23	11.4	3.43
Quintana,Jose	CWS	26	32	32	200	196	16	54	160	3	11	11	.500	0	11.4	3.51
Ramirez,Erasmo	Sea	25	14	14	81	84	9	25	62	4	4	5	.444	0	12.6	4.11
Ramirez,Neil	ChC	26	66	0	60	52	7	26	66	4	3	3	.500	0	12.3	3.75
Ramos,A.J.	Mia	28	69	0	65	46	3	38	74	2	4	3	.571	0	11.9	2.77
Ramos,Cesar	TB	31	41	3	71	71	8	29	50	2	3	5	.375	0	12.9	4.18
Ranaudo,Anthony	Bos	25	28	28	161	152	18	68	122	4	8	9	.471	0	12.5	3.91
Rasmus,Cory	LAA	27	32	12	84	67	8	39	85	1	6	4	.600	0	11.5	3.11
Redmond,Todd	Tor	30	36	0	62	64	8	20	52	2	3	4	.429	0	12.5	4.35
Reed,Addison	Ari	26	64	0	61	54	7	17	68	2	4	3	.571	43	10.8	3.10
Richards,Garrett	LAA	27	31	31	202	190	14	64	162	8	13	9	.591	0	11.7	3.48
Rienzo,Andre	CWS	26	13	5	36	36	4	18	31	1	1	3	.250	0	13.8	4.50
Roark,Tanner	Was	28	31	31	195	192	16	41	147	7	12	9	.571	0	11.1	3.46
Robertson,David	NYY	30	65	0	68	52	5	22	91	2	5	3	.625	38	10.1	2.38
Rodney,Fernando	Sea	38	68	0	67	55	3	29	69	3	4	3	.571	47	11.7	2.96
Rodriguez,Francisco	Mil	33	66	0	65	54	8	19	71	1	4	3	.571	40	10.2	2.91
Rodriguez,Paco	LAD	24	62	0	50	36	4	22	59	1	4	2	.667	0	10.6	2.70
Rodriguez,Wandy	Pit	36	24	24	136	133	17	39	111	4	7	8	.467	0	11.6	3.84
Rogers,Esmil	NYY	29	43	2	60	67	7	22	49	3	2	4	.333	0	13.8	4.80
Romo,Sergio	SF	32	65	0	61	46	6	12	66	3	5	2	.714	9	9	2.21
Rondon,Bruce	Det	24	46	0	44	35	2	20	51	3	3	2	.600	0	11.9	3.07
Rondon,Hector	ChC	27	64	0	66	64	6	20	61	2	4	4	.500	40	11.7	3.55
Rosenthal,Trevor	StL	25	68	0	66	51	4	31	78	4	4	3	.571	50	11.7	2.86
Ross,Robbie	Tex	26	26	10	65	70	6	22	49	4	3	4	.429	0	13.3	4.43
Ross,Tyson	SD	28	32	32	204	194	15	76	179	9	11	11	.500	0	12.3	3.71
Russell,James	Atl	29	69	0	59	59	7	20	42	2	3	4	.429	0	12.4	4.12
Ryu,Hyun-Jin	LAD	28	31	31	198	192	13	43	168	2	14	8	.636	0	10.8	3.27
Rzepczynski,Marc	Cle	29	67	0	36	35	3	14	33	2	2	2	.500	0	12.8	3.75
Sabathia,CC	NYY	34	30	30	205	201	22	55	184	7	11	12	.478	0	11.5	3.69
Salas,Fernando	LAA	30	61	0	66	56	6	16	66	2	5	2	.714	0	10.1	2.73
Salazar,Danny	Cle	25	28	28	162	150	17	56	189	3	9	9	.500	0	11.6	3.61
Sale,Chris	CWS	26	30	30	207	169	19	47	230	11	15	8	.652	0	9.9	2.96
Samardzija,Jeff	Oak	30	33	33	211	194	22	54	193	8	12	11	.522	0	10.9	3.41
Sanchez,Anibal	Det	31	29	29	184	174	13	48	168	4	12	8	.600	0	11.1	3.33
Santana,Ervin	Atl	32	31	31	195	187	26	59	157	7	10	12	.455	0	11.7	3.83
Santiago,Hector	LAA	27	26	26	146	134	15	65	132	10	8	8	.500	0	12.9	4.01
Santos,Sergio	Tor	31	55	0	55	46	5	32	67	2	3	3	.500	0	13.1	3.76
Scheppers,Tanner	Tex	28	62	0	62	64	7	21	55	6	3	4	.429	0	13.2	4.35
Scherzer,Max	Det	30	32	32	215	191	22	61	232	6	14	10	.583	0	10.8	3.31
Schlitter,Brian	ChC	29	45	0	42	44	3	13	32	1	2	2	.500	0	12.4	3.86
Shaw,Bryan	Cle	27	74	0	71	66	5	23	59	4	4	4	.500	0	11.8	3.30
Shields,James	KC	33	33	33	220	212	24	51	197	8	12	12	.500	0	11.1	3.56
Shoemaker,Matt	LAA	28	29	29	177	189	22	34	145	7	10	10	.500	0	11.7	3.92
Siegrist,Kevin	StL	25	65	0	62	44	6	29	76	4	4	3	.571	0	11.2	2.76
Simon,Alfredo	Cin	34	31	31	193	187	21	56	134	13	10	12	.455	0	11.9	3.78
Sipp,Tony	Hou	31	62	0	57	44	8	21	62	1	4	3	.571	0	10.4	3.00
Smith,Joe	LAA	31	73	0	73	57	4	19	61	4	6	2	.750	0	9.9	2.34
Smith,Will	Mil	25	71	0	59	64	6	22	53	2	3	4	.429	0	13.4	4.42
Smyly,Drew	TB	26	29	29	180	161	19	49	174	3	11	9	.550	0	10.6	3.30
Soria,Joakim	Det	31	53	0	50	42	4	11	54	2	4	2	.667	5	9.9	2.52
Soriano,Rafael	Was	35	63	0	62	51	5	18	59	1	5	2	.714	8	10.2	2.76
Spruill,Zeke	Ari	25	24	5	46	50	3	14	29	2	2	3	.400	0	12.9	4.11
Stammen,Craig	Was	31	48	0	64	66	6	17	50	1	4	4	.500	0	11.8	3.66
Stauffer,Tim	SD	33	44	0	58	60	5	20	45	2	3	3	.500	0	12.7	3.88
Stites,Matt	Ari	25	48	0	44	41	5	15	38	1	2	2	.500	0	11.7	3.68
Storen,Drew	Was	27	66	0	60	52	4	14	55	2	4	2	.667	38	10.2	2.70
Straily,Dan	ChC	26	25	25	144	127	17	56	141	6	8	8	.500	0	11.8	3.69
Strasburg,Stephen	Was	26	33	33	209	172	19	50	237	7	16	7	.696	0	9.9	2.93
Street,Huston	LAA	31	63	0	62	48	7	15	61	0	4	3	.571	38	9.1	2.47
Stroman,Marcus	Tor	24	29	29	184	172	14	44	183	5	12	8	.600	0	10.8	3.28
Strop,Pedro	ChC	30	66	0	64	53	3	28	68	4	4	3	.571	0	12	3.09
Stults,Eric	SD	35	31	31	168	182	19	40	114	3	8	10	.444	0	12.1	4.02
Surkamp,Eric	CWS	27	47	0	35	34	3	11	33	2	2	2	.500	0	12.1	3.60

2015 Pitcher Projections

Pitcher	Team	Age	G	GS	IP	H	HR	BB	SO	HB	W	L	Pct	Sv	BR/9	ERA
Swarzak,Anthony	Min	29	44	0	65	73	7	19	40	1	3	4	.429	0	12.9	4.43
Tanaka,Masahiro	NYY	26	25	25	163	184	21	28	167	5	15	7	.682	0	12	2.94
Tazawa,Junichi	Bos	29	68	0	63	60	5	15	63	1	4	3	.571	0	10.9	3.14
Teheran,Julio	Atl	24	30	30	206	195	22	50	175	11	12	11	.522	0	11.2	3.54
Tepesch,Nick	Tex	26	17	17	86	91	9	26	57	5	4	6	.400	0	12.8	4.29
Thatcher,Joe	LAA	33	57	0	33	31	2	7	34	2	2	1	.667	0	10.9	3.00
Thayer,Dale	SD	34	66	0	65	62	7	18	57	2	4	3	.571	0	11.4	3.32
Thielbar,Caleb	Min	28	55	0	48	46	4	16	41	1	3	3	.500	0	11.8	3.38
Thornburg,Tyler	Mil	26	51	0	53	50	5	25	50	2	3	3	.500	0	13.1	4.08
Thornton,Matt	Was	38	60	0	36	33	2	10	35	2	2	2	.500	0	11.2	3.00
Tillman,Chris	Bal	27	32	32	201	192	26	65	162	4	10	12	.455	0	11.7	3.81
Tolleson,Shawn	Tex	27	60	0	67	56	8	27	73	1	4	3	.571	0	11.3	3.36
Tomlin,Josh	Cle	30	27	11	78	81	12	13	54	2	4	5	.444	0	11.1	3.81
Tonkin,Michael	Min	25	32	0	34	34	2	10	33	2	2	2	.500	0	12.2	3.44
Torres,Alex	SD	27	66	0	48	44	3	27	52	2	2	3	.400	0	13.7	3.94
Torres,Carlos	NYM	32	73	2	96	90	10	32	86	3	5	5	.500	0	11.7	3.47
Treinen,Blake	Was	27	16	6	48	51	3	13	34	2	3	3	.500	0	12.4	3.75
Tropeano,Nicholas	Hou	24	26	26	154	144	16	47	143	5	9	8	.529	0	11.5	3.56
Turner,Jacob	ChC	24	27	19	114	121	12	39	76	3	5	7	.417	0	12.9	4.26
Uehara,Koji	Bos	40	65	0	65	48	8	8	75	1	5	2	.714	35	7.9	1.80
Vargas,Jason	KC	32	30	30	186	190	23	46	124	4	9	12	.429	0	11.6	3.82
Varvaro,Anthony	Atl	30	63	0	58	50	4	18	53	2	4	3	.571	0	10.9	2.79
Ventura,Yordano	KC	24	32	32	197	181	14	78	188	9	11	11	.500	0	12.2	3.61
Veras,Jose	Hou	34	64	0	61	50	6	31	65	3	3	3	.500	0	12.4	3.54
Verlander,Justin	Det	32	30	30	198	181	17	63	186	5	12	10	.545	0	11.3	3.41
Villanueva,Carlos	ChC	31	45	5	88	86	11	25	76	3	5	5	.500	0	11.7	3.68
Villarreal,Pedro	Cin	27	30	0	36	39	5	10	27	2	2	2	.500	0	12.8	4.50
Vincent,Nick	SD	28	71	0	62	51	5	16	65	3	4	2	.667	0	10.2	2.61
Vogelsong,Ryan	SF	37	31	31	191	187	19	62	155	8	10	11	.476	0	12.1	3.82
Volquez,Edinson	Pit	31	31	31	190	175	18	78	167	9	10	11	.476	0	12.4	3.79
Wacha,Michael	StL	23	29	29	172	143	13	50	161	3	12	7	.632	0	10.3	3.03
Wada,Tsuyoshi	ChC	34	27	27	151	157	18	45	133	5	8	9	.471	0	12.3	4.05
Wainwright,Adam	StL	33	32	32	226	204	14	45	192	6	16	9	.640	0	10.2	2.99
Walden,Jordan	Atl	27	57	0	51	44	3	23	58	1	3	3	.500	0	12	3.35
Walker,Taijuan	Sea	22	27	27	154	141	18	63	155	12	7	10	.412	0	12.6	3.97
Warren,Adam	NYY	27	64	0	78	82	7	26	62	3	3	5	.375	0	12.8	4.15
Watson,Tony	Pit	30	78	0	79	64	7	16	73	5	6	3	.667	0	9.7	2.39
Weaver,Jered	LAA	32	33	33	207	180	23	59	169	5	14	9	.609	0	10.6	3.26
Webb,Daniel	CWS	25	57	0	63	56	4	36	60	2	3	4	.429	0	13.4	3.71
Webb,Ryan	Bal	29	56	0	53	54	3	15	38	2	3	3	.500	0	12.1	3.57
Webster,Allen	Bos	25	28	28	153	152	12	69	132	16	7	10	.412	0	13.9	4.35
Wheeler,Zack	NYM	25	30	30	179	157	14	76	173	10	10	10	.500	0	12.2	3.57
Whitley,Chase	NYY	26	25	6	58	58	6	16	51	2	3	4	.429	0	11.8	3.72
Wilhelmsen,Tom	Sea	31	64	0	63	51	5	30	56	3	4	3	.571	0	12	3.29
Williams,Jerome	Phi	33	34	15	120	130	16	36	80	5	5	9	.357	0	12.8	4.50
Wilson,Alex	Bos	28	52	0	59	62	5	26	51	1	3	4	.429	0	13.6	4.42
Wilson,Brian	LAD	33	60	0	48	43	3	26	52	2	3	3	.500	0	13.3	3.75
Wilson,C.J.	LAA	34	32	32	177	160	14	80	156	8	10	9	.526	0	12.6	3.76
Wilson,Justin	Pit	27	69	0	60	50	5	28	53	3	4	3	.571	0	12.2	3.45
Withrow,Chris	LAD	26	35	0	36	32	3	22	37	1	2	2	.500	0	13.8	4.00
Wood,Alex	Atl	24	31	31	202	179	13	58	201	6	13	9	.591	0	10.8	3.16
Wood,Travis	ChC	28	31	31	185	179	20	72	146	8	9	11	.450	0	12.6	3.99
Wooten,Rob	Mil	29	45	0	40	39	3	10	35	2	2	2	.500	0	11.5	3.38
Workman,Brandon	Bos	26	37	8	75	75	11	27	71	1	4	5	.444	0	12.4	4.20
Worley,Vance	Pit	27	29	29	181	198	17	40	137	6	9	11	.450	0	12.1	3.93
Wright,Jamey	LAD	40	61	0	66	66	4	25	49	4	4	4	.500	0	13	3.82
Wright,Steven	Bos	30	12	2	42	43	4	16	32	2	2	3	.400	0	13.1	4.29
Wright,Wesley	ChC	30	54	0	49	47	5	18	43	3	3	3	.500	0	12.5	3.86
Yates,Kirby	TB	28	64	0	62	45	4	27	81	3	4	3	.571	0	10.9	2.61
Young,Chris	Sea	36	26	26	136	126	20	50	96	2	7	9	.438	0	11.8	3.97
Ziegler,Brad	Ari	35	69	0	66	60	3	22	45	2	4	3	.571	0	11.5	3.00
Zimmermann,Jordan	Was	29	32	32	204	190	17	34	168	7	14	8	.636	0	10.2	3.13

Career Targets

This section estimates probabilities for players reaching important career milestones. Bill James originally developed the method under the name "The Favorite Toy." It predicts the probability a player will accumulate certain career statistics based on his age and performance level. The full details of how the system works are explained in the glossary.

After one of the most impressive starts to a career in baseball history, Mike Trout has made his way onto many of the leaderboards. Still just 23 years old, Trout already has 572 hits, 98 home runs, 373 runs scored, and 307 runs batted in his career. He is exemplary in every category, but his pace of runs scored may be the most outstanding. He has scored the most runs in baseball in two of his three full seasons and finished second in baseball and first in the AL in the other year. If he continues to play at this level for even a few more seasons, he'll force his way into conversations about 3,000 hits, 500 home runs, and the like. According to The Favorite Toy, those discussions might already be warranted.

The player that currently sits atop most of the hitting lists is Miguel Cabrera, who enjoyed another tremendously productive season as a 31 year old in 2014. Cabrera is 10 home runs shy of 400 for his career and has already passed 2,000 hits, so he could join both the 500-homer club and the 3,000-hit club while still in his mid-30s.

We predicted a no-hitter! In last year's Handbook, we gave Clayton Kershaw a 16 percent chance of throwing a no-hitter sometime in his career, and on June 18, he proved us right! Yu Darvish was our top no-hitter candidate last year, and he came within an inning of completing the feat in early May. It was a good year for the no-hitter predictor. Kershaw tops our list this year, going for his second.

3,000 Hits	
% chance to reach milestone	
Jeter,Derek	done
Beltre,Adrian	94%
Cabrera,Miguel	81%
Pujols,Albert	73%
Suzuki,Ichiro	71%
Cano,Robinson	40%
Rodriguez,Alex	33%
Altuve,Jose	26%
Trout,Mike	24%
Rollins,Jimmy	22%
Jones,Adam	20%
Reyes,Jose	20%
Andrus,Elvis	20%
Markakis,Nick	19%
Castro,Starlin	18%
McCutchen,Andrew	17%
Butler,Billy	16%
Freeman,Freddie	15%
Gonzalez,Adrian	12%
Pedroia,Dustin	12%
Upton,Justin	12%
Wright,David	12%
Brantley,Michael	10%
Pence,Hunter	8%
Hosmer,Eric	7%
Holliday,Matt	5%
Kendrick,Howie	5%
Sandoval,Pablo	5%
Loney,James	4%
Escobar,Alcides	4%
Cabrera,Melky	4%
Rios,Alex	3%
Murphy,Daniel	3%
Mauer,Joe	3%
Span,Denard	3%
Jackson,Austin	2%
Heyward,Jason	2%
Kinsler,Ian	2%
Prado,Martin	1%
Seager,Kyle	< 1%
Longoria,Evan	< 1%
Stanton,Giancarlo	< 1%

Career Targets

762 Home Runs
% chance to break record

Cabrera,Miguel	1%

2,298 RBI
% chance to break record

Cabrera,Miguel	23%
Pujols,Albert	3%
Trout,Mike	1%

2,296 Runs Scored
% chance to break record

Trout,Mike	10%
Cabrera,Miguel	< 1%

4,257 Hits
% chance to break record

Cabrera,Miguel	2%

900 Home Runs
% chance to reach milestone

2,000 RBI
% chance to reach milestone

Cabrera,Miguel	58%
Pujols,Albert	42%
Rodriguez, Alex	27%
Trout,Mike	10%
Gonzalez,Adrian	3%

6,857 Total Bases
% chance to break record

Cabrera,Miguel	12%
Trout,Mike	7%

4,000 Hits
% chance to reach milestone

Cabrera,Miguel	9%
Altuve,Jose	3%
Trout,Mike	3%

800 Home Runs
% chance to reach milestone

600 Home Runs
% chance to reach milestone

Rodriguez, Alex	done
Pujols,Albert	73%
Cabrera,Miguel	40%
Dunn,Adam	35%
Stanton,Giancarlo	16%
Trout,Mike	14%
Davis,Chris	7%
Encarnacion,Edwin	3%
Jones,Adam	< 1%

793 Doubles
% chance to break record

Cabrera,Miguel	19%
Cano,Robinson	8%
Pujols,Albert	7%
Trout,Mike	4%
Altuve,Jose	3%

Most Likely No-Hitter
% chance to reach milestone

Kershaw,Clayton	25%
Sale,Chris	23%
Strasburg,Stephen	21%
Kluber,Corey	20%
Scherzer,Max	20%
Darvish,Yu	18%
Hernandez,Felix	18%
Price,David	16%
Bumgarner,Madison	15%
Wheeler,Zack	15%

700 Home Runs
% chance to reach milestone

Cabrera,Miguel	11%
Pujols,Albert	5%
Stanton,Giancarlo	4%
Trout,Mike	3%

500 Home Runs
% chance to reach milestone

Pujols,Albert	done
Rodriguez, Alex	done
Ortiz,David	97%
Dunn,Adam	96%
Cabrera,Miguel	91%
Beltre,Adrian	35%
Stanton,Giancarlo	35%
Trout,Mike	30%
Davis,Chris	24%
Encarnacion,Edwin	23%
Jones,Adam	15%

1,000 Stolen Bases
% chance to reach milestone

The 300-Win Candidates

Bill James

For about 40 years, I have been ridiculing the notion that 300-game winners were on the verge of extinction, and so far, I have been proven right. Every time a pitcher wins his 300th game, a good many sportswriters will write either

a) That this is the last pitcher who will ever win 300 games, or

b) That there is one more guy who looks like he is going to get there, but after that there won't be any more.

I've always insisted that this was nonsense—because it was—but now I have to say that it may not be nonsense any more. .400 hitters are extinct, 30-game winners are extinct, and I now believe it is possible that 300-game winners may be going extinct. Sportswriters were saying that 300-game winners were going extinct when this was obviously untrue, if you looked at the pitchers' ages and their career wins. It isn't obviously untrue now.

Here's a way to think about the problem. If a pitcher is going to win 300 games, he needs to have 15 wins by age 21, 30 wins by age 22, 45 wins by age 23, 60 wins by age 24, etc.; he needs to stay on a 300-win pace of about 15 wins a year. Maybe he doesn't need to be on that schedule, but he has to be close to that schedule; he can't limp in to age 30 at 45 wins. Let's say he needs to be at 80% of that schedule—which history proves he doesn't absolutely need to be, but it's a way of thinking about the problem.

In 1974 there were 25 major league pitchers who had at least 50 career wins and at least 80% of the "schedule" wins; twenty-five. Ten of those 25 had at least 160 career wins; yes, there were people saying that there would be no more 300-game winners, but it was a silly thing to say, because there were 25 candidates. You had to figure that a few of them would get there. In 1984 there were 14 such pitchers; in 1994, 11. In 2004 there were 13. In 2014 there were seven (Kershaw, Bumgarner, Sabathia, Felix, Verlander, Buehrle and Greinke.)

Pitchers who are on schedule or ahead of schedule are precursors to 300-game winners. If the number of precursors goes down, the number of 300-game winners is going down—and the number of pitchers who are on schedule is way down. It's down 72% in the last 40 years; it's down 46% in the last 10 years.

The chart which accompanies this article suggests that one or two pitchers from this generation (1.57) should win 300 games—but it could just as easily turn out to be none. Three years ago the best 300-win candidate was Roy Halladay, but Halladay is gone now. Two years ago the best candidate was Sabathia, but Sabathia is not in a good position anymore. A year ago the best candidate was Verlander, but Verlander did not have a good year. Now the best candidate appears to be Kershaw, but Kershaw is ten years away from 300 wins. Projecting a pitcher ten years ahead is like projecting April's batting averages into September. I do not expect to see another 300-game winner in the next ten years, and I'm not confident that I will see another one in my lifetime.

Pitchers on Course For 300 Wins

Name	2014 Age	R/L	W	L	EWL	Momentum	Chance
Kershaw, Clayton	26	L	98	49	18.0	.901	31%
Hernandez, Felix	28	R	125	92	14.6	.894	26%
Shields, James	32	R	114	90	13.1	.878	16%
Verlander, Justin	31	R	152	89	13.6	.825	12%
Scherzer, Max	29	R	91	50	17.4	.816	9%
Lester, Jon	30	L	116	67	14.8	.821	9%
Price, David	28	L	86	51	15.0	.846	9%
Wainwright, Adam	32	R	119	66	15.8	.798	8%
Buehrle, Mark	35	L	199	152	11.0	.731	6%
Hamels, Cole	30	L	108	83	10.5	.847	5%
Colon, Bartolo	41	R	204	141	13.0	.665	5%
Cueto, Johnny	28	R	85	57	15.8	.794	4%
Weaver, Jered	31	R	131	69	14.7	.752	4%
Dickey, R.A.	39	R	89	82	13.0	.802	3%
Greinke, Zack	30	R	123	90	15.3	.727	2%
Lohse, Kyle	35	R	142	128	11.5	.738	2%
Hudson, Tim	38	R	214	124	9.0	.666	2%
Lackey, John	35	R	152	117	11.5	.685	1%
Santana, Ervin	31	R	119	100	12.0	.755	1%
Burnett, A.J.	37	R	155	150	10.0	.735	1%
Haren, Dan	33	R	142	122	11.4	.708	1%
Harang, Aaron	36	R	122	128	10.4	.653	<1%
Peavy, Jake	33	R	139	111	8.8	.714	<1%

EWL: Established Win Level

Baseball Glossary

% Inherited Scored

The percentage of inherited baserunners a relief pitcher allows to score.

% Pitches Taken

The percentage of pitches that a batter does not swing at out of the total number of pitches thrown to him.

1st Batter Average

The Batting Average that a relief pitcher allows to the first batter he faces when he enters a game.

1st Batter OBP

The On-Base Percentage that a relief pitcher allows to the first batter he faces when he enters a game.

1st to 3rd (Baserunning)

"Moved" is the number of times a runner goes from 1st base to 3rd base on a SINGLE. "Chances" are the number of times a runner is on 1st base and a batter is credited with a SINGLE.

1st to Home (Baserunning)

"Moved" is the number of times a runner goes from 1st base to home on a DOUBLE. "Chances" are the number of times a runner is on 1st base and a batter is credited with a DOUBLE.

2nd to Home (Baserunning)

"Moved" is the number of times a runner goes from 2nd base to home on a SINGLE. "Chances" are the number of times a runner is on 2nd base and a batter is credited with a SINGLE.

Active Career Batting Leaders

A list of batting leaders among active (appearing in the most recent season) players. An active player is eligible when he meets the minimum requirements for the following categories:

> 1,000 At Bats—Batting Average, On-Base Percentage, Slugging Average, At Bats Per HR, At Bats Per GDP, At Bats Per RBI, Strikeout to Walk Ratio
> 100 Stolen Base Attempts—Stolen Base Success Percentage

Active Career Pitching Leaders

A list of pitching leaders among active (appearing in the most recent season) players. An active player is eligible when he meets the minimum requirements for the following categories:

> 750 Innings Pitched—Earned Run Average, Opponent Batting Average, all "Per 9 Innings" categories, Strikeout to Walk Ratio
> 250 Games Started—Complete Game Frequency
> 100 Decisions—Win-Loss Percentage

AVG Allowed ScPos

The Batting Average allowed by a pitcher while pitching with runners in scoring position.

AVG Bases Loaded
The Batting Average of a hitter while batting with the bases loaded.

Base Taken
A player is credited with a Base Taken whenever he moves up a base on a Wild Pitch, Passed Ball, Balk, Sacrifice Fly, or Defensive Indifference.

Batting Average
Hits divided by at bats.

Blown Save
When a relief pitcher enters a game in a Save Situation (see definition for Save Situation) and allows the other team to score the tying or go-ahead run.

Bomb (Intentional Walk)
An Intentional Walk is counted as a "Bomb" if
1. The next batter, after the IBB, does not ground into a double play, and
2. Multiple runs are scored in the inning, after the intentional walk.

BR Gain (Baserunning)
BR Gain (or Loss if a negative number) is the total of all the types of extra baserunning advances minus the (triple) penalty for all the BR Outs compared with what would be expected based on the MLB averages.

BR Outs (Baserunning)
BR Outs include the sum of Outs Advancing, Doubled Offs, and when a runner is tagged out on the bases when another runner moves up on a Wild Pitch, Passed Ball, or scores on a Sacrifice Fly.

BS Win
A Blown Save Win is a "win" credited to a reliever who has blown a save opportunity.

Career Targets
This method, once called the Favorite Toy, is a way to estimate the probability that a player will achieve a specific career goal. In this example, 3,000 hits will be used. The four components of the formula are:

1. Needed Hits. This is the number of Hits (or any statistic) that a player needs to reach a desired goal.

2. Years Remaining. This is the estimated number of years remaining in the player's career. It is determined using the player's age (on June 30th of the previous year; use 2013 when making the calculation after the 2013 season is complete). The formula is (42 - age) divided by two. This means a player who is 20 years old will have 11 remaining seasons, a player who is 25 years old will have 8.5 remaining seasons and a player who is 35 years old will have 3.5 remaining seasons. If the player is a catcher, then multiply his remaining seasons by .7. The only stipulation is that years remaining must always be greater than or equal to 1.5.

3. Established Hit Level. The Established Hit Level is a weighted average of the player's hits over the past three seasons. To calculate the Established Hit Level after the 2013 season is complete, add 2011 Hits, (2012 Hits multiplied by two) and (2013 Hits multiplied by three), then divide by six. If the Established Hit

Level is less than 75% of the most recent performance (2013 Hits in this case), then the Established Hit Level is equal to .75 times the most recent performance.

4. Projected Remaining Hits. This is calculated by multiplying Years Remaining by the Established Hit Level.

The probability of achieving the specified goal is found by dividing Projected Remaining Hits by Needed Hits, then subtracting .5. The maximum that any player has of achieving a goal is .97 raised to the power of (Need Hits / Established Hit Level). This prevents the possibility of a player reaching a goal from being higher than 100 percent, which is impossible.

Catcher's ERA
The ERA for a catcher is equal to the ERA of pitchers pitching while the catcher is playing behind the plate. It is calculated exactly like ERA for pitchers. Take the number of earned runs allowed while the catcher is playing, multiply it by 9 and then divide it by the total number of defensive innings that the catcher was behind the plate.

Cheap Win
A starting pitcher who wins the game with a game score under 50 gets credit for a cheap win. See Game Score.

Clean Outing
A Clean Outing is a game in which the reliever is not charged with a run (earned or otherwise) AND does not allow an inherited runner to score.

Cleanup Slugging Average
The Slugging Average of a batter when he bats in the cleanup spot, or fourth, in the batting order.

Close and Late
A situation in a game that is very similar to a Save Situation. The following requirements are necessary for a Close and Late game:
1. The game is in the seventh inning or later AND
2. The batting team is either leading by one run or tied OR
3. The tying run is on base, at bat, or on deck.

Component ERA (ERC)
A statistic that estimates what a pitcher's ERA should have been, based on his pitching performance. The ERC formula is calculated as follows:

1. Subtract the pitcher's Home Runs Allowed from his Hits Allowed.
2. Multiply Step 1 by 1.255.
3. Multiply his Home Runs Allowed by four.
4. Add Steps 2 and 3 together.
5. Multiply Step 4 by .89.
6. Add his Walks and Hit Batsmen.
7. Multiply Step 6 by .475.
8. Add Steps 5 and 7 together.

This yields the pitcher's total base estimate (PTB), which is:

$$PTB = 0.89 \times (1.255 \times (H - HR) + 4 \times HR) + 0.475 \times (BB + HB)$$

For those pitchers for whom there is intentional walk data, use this formula instead:

$$PTB = 0.89 \times (1.255 \times (H - HR) + 4 \times HR) + 0.56 \times (BB + HB - IBB)$$

9. Add Hits and Walks and Hit Batsmen.
10. Multiply Step 9 by PTB.
11. Divide Step 10 by Batters Facing Pitcher. If BFP data is unavailable, approximate it by multiplying Innings Pitched by 2.9, then adding Step 9.
12. Multiply Step 11 by 9.
13. Divide Step 12 by Innings Pitched.
14. Subtract .56 from Step 13.

This is the pitcher's ERC, which is:

$$\frac{(H + BB + HB) \times PTB}{BFP \times IP} \times 9 - 0.56$$

If the result after Step 13 is less than 2.24, adjust the formula as follows:

$$\frac{(H + BB + HB) \times PTB}{BFP \times IP} \times 9 \times 0.75$$

Consecutive Days
A count of how many times the pitcher was used after having pitched on the previous day or (in a few cases) in an earlier game on the same day.

Defensive Runs Saved
Defensive Runs Saved (Runs Saved, for short) is the innovative metric introduced by John Dewan in *The Fielding Bible—Volume II* and modified in *The Fielding Bible—Volume III*. The Runs Saved value indicates how many runs a player saved or cost his team in the field compared to the average player at his position. A player of zero Runs Saved is about average; a positive number of runs saved indicates above-average defense, below-average fielders post negative Runs Saved totals. There are seven components of Runs Saved:

Plus Minus Runs Saved (all positions except Catcher)
Adjusted Earned Runs Saved (Catchers)
Stolen Base Runs Saved (Catchers, Pitchers)
Bunt Runs Saved (Corner Infielders, Pitchers, Catchers)
Double Play Runs Saved (Infielders)
Outfield Arm Runs Saved (Outfielders)
Good Play/Misplay Runs Saved (All Positions)

Double Play %
Successful Double Plays divided by the number of Double Play opportunities. This statistic includes both the fielder who started the play and the pivot man.

Double Play Opportunity
A fielder is considered to have a double play opportunity when a ground ball is hit with a runner on first base and less than 2 outs and that fielder is involved in the play. This is used to calculate Double Play % and Pivot %.

Doubled Off
A runner is Doubled Off when he is out for failing to get back to his base before he, or the base, is tagged after a ball hit in the air is caught.

Early Entry
A count of the number of times the reliever entered the game in the sixth inning or earlier.

Earned Run Average
The number of earned runs that a pitcher surrenders per nine innings that he pitches. It is calculated by multiplying the total earned runs allowed by nine and dividing by the total number of innings pitched.

Easy Save
This label is used to separate Saves by difficulty level (Easy or Tough). A Save is considered Easy if the relief pitcher enters the game, pitches one inning or less, and the first batter he faces does not at least represent the tying run.

Fielding Percentage
The percentage of plays a player makes in the field without making an error out of the total number of opportunities. It is calculated by adding (Putouts plus Assists) and dividing by (Putouts plus Assists plus Errors).

Games Finished
The relief pitcher who is in the game for each team when the game ends is credited with a Game Finished.

Game Score
To determine the starting pitcher's Game Score:
Start with 50.
Add 1 point for each out recorded by the starting pitcher.
Add 2 points for each inning the pitcher completes after the fourth inning.
Add 1 point for each strikeout.
Subtract 2 points for each hit allowed.
Subtract 4 points for each earned run allowed.
Subtract 2 points for an unearned run.
Subtract 1 point for each walk.

GDP
Grounded into Double Play.

GDP Opportunity
This is a situation where the batter has a chance to ground into a double play. It occurs with at least a runner on first base and less than two outs.

Ground / Fly Ratio (Grd/Fly, GB/FB)
Calculated for both batters and pitchers. For batters, it is the number of groundballs hit divided by the number of flyballs hit. For pitchers, it is exactly the same but uses the number of groundballs and flyballs allowed. Every fair batted ball is included except for bunts and line drives.

Hold
A relief pitcher is given a Hold anytime he enters the game in a Save Situation (see definition for Save Situation), records one out or more, and exits the game without giving up the lead. If the pitcher finishes the game, then he will only earn credit for a Save. He cannot receive credit for both a Hold and a Save.

Holds Adjusted Save Percentage (same as Save/Hold Percentage)
Holds plus Saves divided by Holds plus Saves Opportunities.

Inherited Runner
When a relief pitcher enters the game, any runner who was on base at the time is considered an Inherited Runner.

Isolated Power
Slugging Average minus Batting Average.

K/BB Ratio
Strikeouts divided by Walks.

Leadoff On-Base Percentage
The On-Base Percentage of a batter when he bats leadoff, or first, in the batting order.

Leverage Index
Leverage is the amount of swing in the possible change in win probability, compared to the average swing in all situations. The average swing value, by definition, is indexed to 1.00.

If the score of the game is 12-0 or 14-1 the possible changes in win probability will be very close to negligible. Whether the pitcher gives up a home run or gets a double play ball doesn't really change the outcome of the game. There won't be much swing in either direction for the probability of the win. But in the late innings of a close game, the change in win probability among the various events will have rather wild swings. With a runner on first, two outs, down by one, and in the bottom of the ninth, the game can hinge on one swing of the bat. A home run and an out will both end the game, but with different outcomes for the teams involved. The Leverage Index we use (LI) was developed at the website Tangotiger.net, and compiled at the website Fangraphs.com.

Long Outing
A Long Outing is one in which the starting pitcher throws more than 110 pitches. Prior to 2002, we used 120 pitches as the cutoff in the Manager's Record section.

Long Save
A Long Save is when the pitcher credited with a save pitches more than one inning.

Manufactured Runs
1. A run that scores without a hit, or a run on which the only hit(s) is/are infield hits, is always scored as a Manufactured Run.
2. A run which is driven in by a home run is never scored a Manufactured Run, under any circumstance.
3. A run which is driven in by a double or a triple is scored as a Manufactured Run only if *two* of the four bases result from advancing on one of these four acts: a sacrifice bunt, a stolen base, a hit and run, or a bunt single.
4. Otherwise, a run is considered to be a Manufactured Run if two of the four bases do not result from the runner being forced along by a walk, a hit batsman, or a safe hit reaching the outfield.
5. A forceout or fielder's choice which does not improve the position of the base runners should not be counted as contributing toward a Manufactured Run.   Advancing on a forceout or a fielder's choice DOES count toward a manufactured run, if the play is one which improves the position of the baserunners.
6. A base "gained" on a double play does not count as a contribution to a Manufactured Run. A run scored on a double play is a Manufactured Run only if two of the OTHER bases are not attributable to forced advancement.

Not Good Outcome (Intentional Walk)
A Not Good Outcome (NG) for an Intentional Walk occurs when one run scored in the inning after the intentional walk (and the next batter after the intentional walk did not ground into a double play).

Offensive Winning Percentage (OWP)
A player's Offensive Winning Percentage is the winning percentage of a hypothetical team which has an offense consisting of nine of that player, and pitching and defense which is average for the player's league. It is calculated by taking the square of RC/27 (see the definition for Runs Created per 27 Outs), dividing it by the sum of the square of RC/27 and the square of the average runs scored per game in the league.

On-Base Percentage
(Hits plus Walks plus Hit by Pitcher) divided by (At Bats plus Walks plus Hit by Pitcher plus Sacrifice Flies).

$$\frac{H + BB + HBP}{AB + BB + HBP + SF}$$

Opponent Batting Average
Hits Allowed divided by (Batters Faced minus Walks minus Hit Batsmen minus Sacrifice Hits minus Sacrifice Flies minus Catcher's Interference).

$$\frac{H}{BFP - BB - HBP - SH - SF - CI}$$

Opposition OPS
The OPS of the hitters facing the pitcher.

Out Advancing
A runner is out advancing when he is tagged out attempting to score from 2nd base on a single or from 1st base on a double, or attempting to go from 1st base to 3rd base on a single.

PA*
Used in the denominator for the calculation of On-Base Percentage. It is calculated by subtracting (Sacrifice Hits plus Times Reached Base on Defensive Interference) from Plate Appearances (see definition for Plate Appearances).

Park Index
To calculate the park index for home runs in a given ballpark, we take the total home runs of both the home team and its opponents at the ballpark and compare it to the total home runs of the home team and its opponents in other games. We then divide each of those totals by the at-bats in the equivalent situations, so that if there are more at-bats in either situation the index is not skewed. The result is then multiplied by 100 to yield the familiar form.

The park indices for doubles, triples, walks, strikeouts and home runs by lefties and righties are determined like home runs above—relative to at-bats. Indices of at-bats, runs, hits, errors and infield fielding errors (E-Infield) are calculated relative to games. The three batting average indices are calculated as is, since these are already relative to at-bats.

PCS (Pitchers' Caught Stealing)
The number of runners officially scored as Caught Stealing where the pitcher initiated the play. The normal Caught Stealing is when a runner is out attempting to steal a base but the play was initiated by the catcher. PCS plays are often referred to as pickoffs, but differ when the runner breaks towards the next base as opposed to returning to the base he was currently on. Pickoffs occur when the pitcher throws to a base that a runner is leading from, and the runner is out attempting to return to that base. Pickoffs are not an official statistic.

Pitches per PA
The total number of pitches a hitter sees divided by his total Plate Appearances.

Pivot %
Successful Double Plays turned by pivot man divided by the number of Double Play opportunities with that pivot man involved.

Plate Appearances
At Bats plus Total Walks plus Hit By Pitches plus Sacrifice Hits plus Sacrifice Flies plus Times Reached on Defensive Interference.

Platoon Advantage %
Platoon Advantage % is the percentage of players in the starting lineup who have the platoon advantage (i.e. bats right against a left-handed pitcher or bats left against a right-hander) against the starting pitcher; e.g. if the opposing starting pitcher is right handed and the batting team has six left-handed batters in its lineup, the platoon advantage for that game would be 67%.

Plus/Minus System

The Plus/Minus System is a method for evaluating defensive play on batted balls. It is made possible by a game scoring system in which each batted ball is rated for type (line drive, grounder, etc.), velocity within its type (hard, medium or soft), and location on the field. A player gets credit (a "plus" number) if he makes a play that at least one other player at his position missed during the season and he loses credit (a "minus" number") if he misses a play that at least one player made. The size of the credits are proportional to the percentage of times all players make the play. All plays for each player at his position are summed to get his total plus/minus for the season. A total of zero would be average and any other number would approximate how many plays more or less the player made than the average player at the position for the number of chances the player had to field batted balls.

Power/Speed Number

A single number that reflects a combination of power and speed. To calculate the Power/Speed Number, multiply Home Runs by Stolen Bases by two, and divide by the sum of Home Runs and Stolen Bases.

$$\frac{2 \times HR \times SB}{HR + SB}$$

PPO (Pitcher Pickoff)

The number of baserunners thrown out when a pitcher throws to a base with a leading baserunner, and the runner is tagged out attempting to return to the base. PPO is not an official statistic and does not count toward Caught Stealing totals.

Productive Out

An out made by the batter which moves at least one baserunner up at least one base. See also Unproductive Out.

Quality Start

A game where the starting pitcher pitches for at least six innings and allows no more than three earned runs.

Quality Start Percentage

Quality Starts divided by Games Started (see the definition for Quality Start).

Quick Hooks

Used in the Manager's Record. For Quick Hooks and Slow Hooks a score is calculated for each game that is the sum of the number of Pitches plus 10 times the number of Runs Allowed. The bottom 25% of scores in the league are considered to be Quick Hooks.

Range Factor

The number of Successful Chances (Putouts plus Assists) times nine divided by the number of Defensive Innings Played.

RBI %

The percentage of all potential runs driven in by a certain hitter. Simply put, it's RBIs divided by RBI Opportunities. RBI Opportunities are a weighted total for baserunners available to be driven in by the batter. They are defined like so:

1.00 for each runner on third base with less than 2 outs, plus

.70 for each runner on third base with 2 outs, plus

.70 for each runner on second base, plus

.40 for each runner on first base, plus

.10 for each bases-empty plate appearance.

Regular Saves

Any save which does not meet the definition either of an Easy Save or a Tough Save is a "Regular" Save.

Run Support Per 9 IP

The total number of runs scored by a pitcher's team while he is in the game multiplied by nine and divided by total Innings Pitched.

Runs Created

"Runs Created" is an estimate of the number of a team's runs which are created by each individual hitter. The Cincinnati Reds scored 820 runs last year, let us say. How many of those were created by Joey Votto? How many by Brandon Phillips? How many by Jay Bruce?

There are many different formulas for estimating runs created. . .did you want the one that involves swinging a dead cat in the cemetery under a full moon? Yeah, I don't blame you. . .worm-eaten persimmons are so hard to find in the modern world.

This is the one we use now; it is complicated enough. First, there is an "A" Factor in the formula, a "B" Factor, and a "C" factor. The "A" Factor, which represents the number of times the hitter is on base, is Hits, Plus Walks, Plus Hit Batsmen, Minus Caught Stealing, Minus Grounded Into Double Play. The "B" Factor, which represents the hitter's ability to advance other runners, is 1.125 times the player's Singles, plus 1.69 times his Doubles, plus 3.02 times his Triples, plus 3.73 times his Home Runs, plus .29 times his Walks and Hit Batsmen, not counting intentional walks, plus .492 times Sacrifice Hits, Sacrifice Flies and Stolen Bases, minus .04 times Strikeouts. The "C" Factor, which represents opportunities, is At Bats, Plus Walks, Plus Hit By Pitch, Plus Sacrifice Hits, Plus Sacrifice Flies.

Having made these initial calculations of the A, B and C factors, we then change the "A" factor to "A plus 2.4 times C".

We change the "B" factor to "B plus 3 times C".

We change the "C" factor to "9 times C".

Multiply A times B, divide by the new C ("9 times C"), and subtract .90 times by the original C.

This is our first, temporary estimate of the player's runs created. What we have done here is to ask these questions:

1. How many runs would a team probably score that consisted of eight "ordinary" type of hitters, plus this particular hitter?
2. How many of those runs would be created by the eight ordinary type of hitters?
3. What is the difference and thus, how many runs did our player create?

To estimate this, we have placed our player in the context of eight hitters with a .300 on base percentage (2.4 divided by 8) and a .375 advancement percentage (3 divided by 8). For each trip through the batting order, the eight ordinary-type hitters would produce 9/10 of a run (2.4 times 3, divided by 8). The "9" in the denominator is eight ordinary hitters plus our man. The "-.9" being subtracted at the end is the runs created by the "ordinary" hitters. In essence, we have placed the hitter in a neutral solution, measured the neutral solution without our hitter, measured it with our hitter, and then estimated the contribution of this hitter as being the difference between the two.

We're not quite done. After that, we adjust the player's runs created estimate for his performance in two "run-sensitive" situations. Suppose that a player whose overall batting average is .250, has batted 100 times with runners in scoring position, and has gone 30-for-100. That's five hits better than expected, 30 hits where we would have expected 25. His team will score an extra five runs because he has done that, and so we increase the player's runs created estimate by five runs. If the player has hit poorly with runners in scoring position, we decrease it by the shortfall in the same way.

Suppose that a player has batted 250 times with runners on base, 250 times with the bases empty, and that he has hit 20 home runs overall. We would expect him to have hit 10 with men on base, 10 with the bases empty, right?

Suppose that he didn't. Suppose that he hit 12 with the bases empty, 8 with men on base. His team would score two runs less than expected because he did this, and we would thus penalize him two runs for the shortfall.

This is our second runs created estimate the player's runs created, adjusted for his batting performance in run sensitive situations.

Suppose, however, that we figure the runs created for all of the individuals on a team, and we add them up, and it doesn't match the runs actually scored by the team? What if the formulas say that the team should have scored 800 runs, but they actually scored 820?

Then obviously, the formulas missed. We're trying to measure the runs ACTUALLY created by each hitter as best we can, in the real world, not the theoretical impact of some combination of singles, doubles, triples and walks. If the actual number is different than the estimates, we have to adjust the estimates to fit the facts. In this case—820 runs scored with only 800 runs created— we would multiply each runs created estimate by 820/800, or 1.025. Then we round it off to an integer, and that's the player's estimated runs created.

Let go of that cat, Arthur. Heck, the moon isn't full for three weeks, anyway.

Runs Created per 27 Outs (RC/27)

This statistic estimates the number of runs per game that a team made up of nine of the same player would score. To calculate RC/27, multiply Runs Created by league outs per team game, divide the result by outs made by the player (the sum of at bats plus sacrifice hits plus sacrifice flies plus caught stealing plus grounded into double plays, minus hits). The formula written out is:

$$\frac{\frac{RC \times 3 \times LgIP}{2 \times LgG}}{AB - H + SH + SF + CS + GDP}$$

Runs Saved

See Defensive Runs Saved.

Save Opportunities

The sum of Saves and Blown Saves (see Save Situation).

Save/Hold Percentage (same as Holds Adjusted Saves Percentage)

The sum of Saves and Holds, divided by the sum of Saves, Holds, and Blown Saves.

For several years we figured "Save Percentage", which is simply Saves divided by Save Opportunities, and this stat had some currency in the game. But the Save Percentage severely discriminates against middle relievers, who have no real chance to be credited with the Save, since they will be taken out of the game and replaced by the Closer even if they throw 110 miles an hour and strike out everybody they see. Middle relievers typically have Save Percentages of zero, even if they pitch well. The Save/Hold Percentage is a much more realistic evaluation of a pitcher's success in Save situations.

Save Percentage

A pitcher's Saves divided by the total number of Save Situations he faces (see definition for Save Situation).

Save Situation

A relief pitcher is in a Save Situation when he enters the game with his team in the lead, has the opportunity to finish the game, is not the winning pitcher of record at the time, and meets any one of the three following conditions:

1.The pitcher's team is leading by no more than three runs and the pitcher has the chance to pitch for at least one inning,

OR

2.The pitcher enters the game with the potential tying run on base, at bat, or on deck,

OR

3. The pitcher pitches three or more effective innings regardless of the lead. The determination of a save in this situation is made by the official scorer.

It is not possible to have more than one save credited to a single team in a game.

SB Gain (Baserunning)

Stolen Base attempts must be successful greater than about two thirds of the time to have a positive result on the number of runs scored. SB gain is therefore the number of bases stolen minus two times the number of caught stealing (SB Gain = SB - 2CS). For example, a runner steals 30 bases and is caught stealing 7 times. His SB Gain would be 30 - 2*7 = +16. Another runner steals 10 bases and is caught stealing 6 times. His SB Gain (actually a loss) would be 10 - 2*6 = -2.

SB Success Percentage

Stolen Bases divided by the number of Stolen Base attempts (Stolen Bases plus Caught Stealing).

$$\frac{SB}{SB + CS}$$

Secondary Average

A number meant to reflect everything else except for batting average. A player will have a high Secondary Average if he hits for power, takes walks and steals bases. It is calculated with the following formula:

$$\frac{TB - H + BB + SB}{AB}$$

Similarity Score

A number which reflects the similarity between two different statistical lines, either for a player or for a team. A score of 1,000 means that the statistical lines are identical.

Slow Hooks

Used in the Manager's Record. For Quick Hooks and Slow Hooks a score is calculated for each game that is the sum of the number of Pitches plus 10 times the number of Runs Allowed. The top 25% of scores in the league are considered to be Slow Hooks.

Slugging Average

Total Bases divided by At Bats.

$$\frac{TB}{AB}$$

Speed Score

Speed score is an estimate of a player's running speed, based on six indicators of running speed found in his batting and fielding records. Those six indicators are stolen base success rate, the frequency of stolen base attempts, triples, grounding into double plays, runs scored as a percentage of times on base, and defensive position and range.

The full process of estimating Speed Scores is long and complex, and can be found on Bill James Online or by contacting Baseball Info Solutions.

Total Bases

Hits plus Doubles plus (2 times Triples) plus (3 times Home Runs).

$$H + 2B + (2 \times 3B) + (3 \times HR)$$

Tough Loss

A starting pitcher who loses the game with a game score (see definition for Game Score) over 50 gets credit for a tough loss.

Tough Save

This label is used to separate Saves by difficulty level (Easy or Tough). A Save is considered Tough if the relief pitcher enters the game with the tying run on base.

Unproductive Out

An out made by the batter which is not the third out of an inning, but comes with runners on base which fails to advance any baserunner, or results in a weaker baserunner configuration than before the out. See also Productive Out.

Win Probability

The probability of a team winning the game determined at any time during the game based on the score, inning, outs and base situation.

Winning Percentage

Wins divided by (Wins plus Losses).

Minor League Abbreviation Key

Abbreviation	Team	Level	League	MLB Affiliate	First Year	Last Year
Abrdn	Aberdeen IronBirds	A-	New York-Penn League	Baltimore Orioles	2002	2014
Akron	Akron Aeros	AA	Eastern League	Cleveland Indians	1997	2014
Albq	Albuquerque Isotopes	AAA	Pacific Coast League	Los Angeles Dodgers	2009	2014
Altna	Altoona Curve	AA	Eastern League	Pittsburgh Pirates	1999	2014
Amarill	Amarillo Sox	IND	Independent League	Independent	2014	2014
Angels	AZL Angels	R	Arizona League	Los Angeles Angels	2001	2014
Ark	Arkansas Travelers	AA	Texas League	Los Angeles Angels	2001	2014
As	AZL Athletics	R	Arizona League	Oakland Athletics	1988	2014
Ashvll	Asheville Tourists	A	South Atlantic League	Colorado Rockies	1994	2014
Auburn	Auburn Doubledays	A-	New York-Penn League	Toronto Blue Jays	2001	2010
Auburn	Auburn Doubledays	A-	New York-Penn League	Washington Nationals	2011	2014
Augsta	Augusta GreenJackets	A	South Atlantic League	San Francisco Giants	2005	2014
B Jays	GCL Blue Jays	R	Gulf Coast League	Toronto Blue Jays	2007	2014
Batvia	Batavia Muckdogs	A-	New York-Penn League	St Louis Cardinals	2007	2012
Beloit	Beloit Snappers	A	Midwest League	Oakland Athletics	2013	2014
Beloit	Beloit Snappers	A	Midwest League	Minnesota Twins	2005	2012
BG	Bowling Green Hot Rods	A	Midwest League	Tampa Bay Rays	2010	2014
Billings	Billings Mustangs	R+	Pioneer League	Cincinnati Reds	1974	2014
Bklyn	Brooklyn Cyclones	A-	New York-Penn League	New York Mets	2001	2014
Bkrsfld	Bakersfield Blaze	A+	California League	Cincinnati Reds	2011	2014
Bkrsfld	Bakersfield Blaze	A+	California League	Texas Rangers	2005	2010
Bluefld	Bluefield Blue Jays	R+	Appalachian League	Toronto Blue Jays	2011	2014
Bnghtn	Binghamton Mets	AA	Eastern League	New York Mets	1992	2014
Boise	Boise Hawks	A-	Northwest League	Chicago Cubs	2001	2014
Bowie	Bowie Baysox	AA	Eastern League	Baltimore Orioles	1993	2014
Bradtn	Bradenton Marauders	A+	Florida State League	Pittsburgh Pirates	2010	2014
Braves	GCL Braves	R	Gulf Coast League	Atlanta Braves	1976	2014
Brewrs	AZL Brewers	R	Arizona League	Milwaukee Brewers	2001	2014
Brham	Birmingham Barons	AA	Southern League	Chicago White Sox	1986	2014
Brs	Bristol White Sox	R+	Appalachian League	Chicago White Sox	1995	2013
BrvdCt	Brevard County Manatees	A+	Florida State League	Milwaukee Brewers	2005	2014
Buffalo	Buffalo Bisons	AAA	International League	Toronto Blue Jays	2013	2014
Buffalo	Buffalo Bisons	AAA	International League	New York Mets	2009	2012
Burlgtn	Burlington Bees	A	Midwest League	Kansas City Royals	2001	2010
Burlgtn	Burlington Royals	R+	Appalachian League	Kansas City Royals	2007	2014
Burlgtn	Burlington Bees	A	Midwest League	Oakland Athletics	2011	2012
Cards	GCL Cardinals	R	Gulf Coast League	St Louis Cardinals	2007	2014
Carlina	Carolina Mudcats	AA	Southern League	Cincinnati Reds	2009	2011
Carlina	Carolina Mudcats	A+	Carolina League	Cleveland Indians	2012	2014
Casper	Casper Ghosts	R+	Pioneer League	Colorado Rockies	2008	2011
Charltt	Charlotte Knights	AAA	International League	Chicago White Sox	1999	2014
Charltt	Charlotte Stone Crabs	A+	Florida State League	Tampa Bay Rays	2009	2014
Chatt	Chattanooga Lookouts	AA	Southern League	Los Angeles Dodgers	2009	2014
Chnchi	Chunichi Dragons	Jap	Central League	Japan	1954	2014
Clinton	Clinton LumberKings	A	Midwest League	Seattle Mariners	2009	2014
Clmbs	Columbus Clippers	AAA	International League	Cleveland Indians	2009	2014
Clrwtr	Clearwater Threshers	A+	Florida State League	Philadelphia Phillies	2004	2014
ColSpr	Colorado Springs Sky Sox	AAA	Pacific Coast League	Colorado Rockies	1993	2014
Conn	Connecticut Tigers	A-	New York-Penn League	Detroit Tigers	2010	2014
CpChr	Corpus Christi Hooks	AA	Texas League	Houston Astros	2005	2014
CRpds	Cedar Rapids Kernels	A	Midwest League	Los Angeles Angels	1993	2012
CRpds	Cedar Rapids Kernels	A	Midwest League	Minnesota Twins	2013	2014
CtnSC	Charleston RiverDogs	A	South Atlantic League	New York Yankees	2005	2014
Cubs	AZL Cubs	R	Arizona League	Chicago Cubs	1993	2014
Danvle	Danville Braves	R+	Appalachian League	Atlanta Braves	1993	2014
Dayton	Dayton Dragons	A	Midwest League	Cincinnati Reds	2000	2014
DBcks	AZL Diamondbacks	R	Arizona League	Arizona Diamondbacks	2011	2014
Ddgrs	AZL Dodgers	R	Arizona League	Los Angeles Dodgers	2009	2014
Dlmrva	Delmarva Shorebirds	A	South Atlantic League	Baltimore Orioles	1997	2014
Dnedin	Dunedin Blue Jays	A+	Florida State League	Toronto Blue Jays	1990	2014

Minor League Abbreviation Key

Abbreviation	Team	Level	League	MLB Affiliate	First Year	Last Year
Drham	Durham Bulls	AAA	International League	Tampa Bay Rays	1998	2014
Dytona	Daytona Cubs	A+	Florida State League	Chicago Cubs	1993	2014
Elizab	Elizabethton Twins	R+	Appalachian League	Minnesota Twins	1974	2014
ElPaso	El Paso Chihuahuas	AAA	Pacific Coast League	San Diego Padres	2014	2014
Erie	Erie SeaWolves	AA	Eastern League	Detroit Tigers	2001	2014
Eugene	Eugene Emeralds	A-	Northwest League	San Diego Padres	2001	2014
Everett	Everett AquaSox	A-	Northwest League	Seattle Mariners	1995	2014
Fkka	Fukuoka SoftBank Hawks	Jap	Pacific League	Japan	2005	2014
Frdrck	Frederick Keys	A+	Carolina League	Baltimore Orioles	1990	2014
Fresno	Fresno Grizzlies	AAA	Pacific Coast League	San Francisco Giants	1998	2014
Frisco	Frisco RoughRiders	AA	Texas League	Texas Rangers	2003	2014
FtMyrs	Fort Myers Miracle	A+	Florida State League	Minnesota Twins	1993	2014
FtWyn	Fort Wayne TinCaps	A	Midwest League	San Diego Padres	2009	2014
GdJunc	Grand Junction Rockies	R+	Pioneer League	Colorado Rockies	2012	2014
Giants	AZL Giants	R	Arizona League	San Francisco Giants	2000	2014
Gr Falls	Great Falls Voyagers	R+	Pioneer League	Chicago White Sox	2008	2014
Grnsbr	Greensboro Grasshoppers	A	South Atlantic League	Miami Marlins	2005	2014
Grnvlle	Greeneville Astros	R+	Appalachian League	Houston Astros	2004	2014
Grnvlle	Greenville Drive	A	South Atlantic League	Boston Red Sox	2006	2014
Gt Lks	Great Lakes Loons	A	Midwest League	Los Angeles Dodgers	2007	2014
Gwnntt	Gwinnett Braves	AAA	International League	Atlanta Braves	2009	2014
Helena	Helena Brewers	R+	Pioneer League	Milwaukee Brewers	2003	2014
Hgrstn	Hagerstown Suns	A	South Atlantic League	Washington Nationals	2007	2014
Hi Dsrt	High Desert Mavericks	A+	California League	Seattle Mariners	2007	2014
Hkry	Hickory Crawdads	A	South Atlantic League	Texas Rangers	2009	2014
Hnshn	Hanshin Tigers	Jap	Central League	Japan	1961	2014
Hntsvl	Huntsville Stars	AA	Southern League	Milwaukee Brewers	1999	2014
Hrsbrg	Harrisburg Senators	AA	Eastern League	Washington Nationals	1991	2014
HudVal	Hudson Valley Renegades	A-	New York-Penn League	Tampa Bay Rays	1997	2014
Idaho	Idaho Falls Chukars	R+	Pioneer League	Kansas City Royals	2004	2014
Indns	AZL Indians	R	Arizona League	Cleveland Indians	2009	2014
Indy	Indianapolis Indians	AAA	International League	Pittsburgh Pirates	2005	2014
InldEm	Inland Empire 66ers	A+	California League	Los Angeles Dodgers	2007	2010
InldEm	Inland Empire 66ers	A+	California League	Los Angeles Angels	2011	2014
Iowa	Iowa Cubs	AAA	Pacific Coast League	Chicago Cubs	1982	2014
Jacksn	Jackson Generals	AA	Southern League	Seattle Mariners	2011	2014
Jaxnvl	Jacksonville Suns	AA	Southern League	Miami Marlins	2009	2014
JhsCty	Johnson City Cardinals	R+	Appalachian League	St Louis Cardinals	1975	2014
Jmstwn	Jamestown Jammers	A-	New York-Penn League	Miami Marlins	2002	2012
Jmstwn	Jamestown Jammers	A-	New York-Penn League	Pittsburgh Pirates	2013	2014
Jupiter	Jupiter Hammerheads	A+	Florida State League	Miami Marlins	2002	2014
Kane	Kane County Cougars	A	Midwest League	Oakland Athletics	2003	2010
Kane	Kane County Cougars	A	Midwest League	Kansas City Royals	2011	2012
Kane	Kane County Cougars	A	Midwest League	Chicago Cubs	2013	2014
Knapol	Kannapolis Intimidators	A	South Atlantic League	Chicago White Sox	2001	2014
Kngspt	Kingsport Mets	R+	Appalachian League	New York Mets	1984	2014
Knstn	Kinston Indians	A+	Carolina League	Cleveland Indians	1990	2011
Lakwd	Lakewood BlueClaws	A	South Atlantic League	Philadelphia Phillies	2001	2014
Lancst	Lancaster JetHawks	A+	California League	Houston Astros	2009	2014
Lncstr	Lancaster Barnstormers	IND	Independent League	Independent	2014	2014
Lk Cty	Lake County Captains	A	Midwest League	Cleveland Indians	2010	2014
Lk Els	Lake Elsinore Storm	A+	California League	San Diego Padres	2001	2014
Lkland	Lakeland Flying Tigers	A+	Florida State League	Detroit Tigers	2007	2014
Lnsng	Lansing Lugnuts	A	Midwest League	Toronto Blue Jays	2005	2014
Lowell	Lowell Spinners	A-	New York-Penn League	Boston Red Sox	1996	2014
LsVgs	Las Vegas 51s	AAA	Pacific Coast League	New York Mets	2013	2014
LsVgs	Las Vegas 51s	AAA	Pacific Coast League	Toronto Blue Jays	2009	2012
Lsvlle	Louisville Bats	AAA	International League	Cincinnati Reds	2000	2014
LV	Lehigh Valley IronPigs	AAA	International League	Philadelphia Phillies	2008	2014
Lxngtn	Lexington Legends	A	South Atlantic League	Kansas City Royals	2013	2014

Minor League Abbreviation Key

Abbreviation	Team	Level	League	MLB Affiliate	First Year	Last Year
Lxngtn	Lexington Legends	A	South Atlantic League	Houston Astros	2001	2012
Lynbrg	Lynchburg Hillcats	A+	Carolina League	Cincinnati Reds	2010	2010
Lynbrg	Lynchburg Hillcats	A+	Carolina League	Atlanta Braves	2011	2014
Mdest	Modesto Nuts	A+	California League	Colorado Rockies	2005	2014
Mdlnd	Midland RockHounds	AA	Texas League	Oakland Athletics	1999	2014
Memp	Memphis Redbirds	AAA	Pacific Coast League	St Louis Cardinals	1998	2014
Mets	GCL Mets	R	Gulf Coast League	New York Mets	2013	2014
Mets	GCL Mets	R	Gulf Coast League	New York Mets	2004	2011
MhVlly	Mahoning Valley Scrappers	A-	New York-Penn League	Cleveland Indians	1999	2014
Missi	Mississippi Braves	AA	Southern League	Atlanta Braves	2005	2014
Mobile	Mobile BayBears	AA	Southern League	Arizona Diamondbacks	2007	2014
Mont	Montgomery Biscuits	AA	Southern League	Tampa Bay Rays	2004	2014
Mrlns	GCL Marlins	R	Gulf Coast League	Miami Marlins	1992	2014
MrtlBh	Myrtle Beach Pelicans	A+	Carolina League	Atlanta Braves	1999	2010
MrtlBh	Myrtle Beach Pelicans	A+	Carolina League	Texas Rangers	2011	2014
Ms	AZL Mariners	R	Arizona League	Seattle Mariners	1989	2014
Msoula	Missoula Osprey	R+	Pioneer League	Arizona Diamondbacks	1999	2014
Nashv	Nashville Sounds	AAA	Pacific Coast League	Milwaukee Brewers	2005	2014
Nats	GCL Nationals	R	Gulf Coast League	Washington Nationals	2005	2014
NewOr	New Orleans Zephyrs	AAA	Pacific Coast League	Miami Marlins	2009	2014
NHam	New Hampshire Fisher Cats	AA	Eastern League	Toronto Blue Jays	2004	2014
Norfolk	Norfolk Tides	AAA	International League	Baltimore Orioles	2007	2014
NWArk	NW Arkansas Naturals	AA	Texas League	Kansas City Royals	2008	2014
NwBrit	New Britain Rock Cats	AA	Eastern League	Minnesota Twins	1997	2014
Ogden	Ogden Raptors	R+	Pioneer League	Los Angeles Dodgers	2003	2014
OKCity	Oklahoma City RedHawks	AAA	Pacific Coast League	Texas Rangers	2009	2010
OKCity	Oklahoma City RedHawks	AAA	Pacific Coast League	Houston Astros	2011	2014
Omha	Omaha Royals	AAA	Pacific Coast League	Kansas City Royals	1969	2010
Omha	Omaha Storm Chasers	AAA	Pacific Coast League	Kansas City Royals	2011	2014
Orem	Orem Owlz	R+	Pioneer League	Los Angeles Angels	2005	2014
Orix	Orix Buffaloes	Jap	Pacific League	Japan	2005	2014
Orioles	GCL Orioles	R	Gulf Coast League	Baltimore Orioles	2007	2014
Padres	AZL Padres	R	Arizona League	San Diego Padres	2004	2014
Peoria	Peoria Chiefs	A	Midwest League	Chicago Cubs	2005	2012
Peoria	Peoria Chiefs	A	Midwest League	St. Louis Cardinals	2013	2014
Phillies	GCL Phillies	R	Gulf Coast League	Philadelphia Phillies	1999	2014
Pirates	GCL Pirates	R	Gulf Coast League	Pittsburgh Pirates	1968	2014
PlmBh	Palm Beach Cardinals	A+	Florida State League	St Louis Cardinals	2003	2014
Pnscla	Pensacola Blue Wahoos	AA	Southern League	Cincinnati Reds	2012	2014
Portlnd	Portland Sea Dogs	AA	Eastern League	Boston Red Sox	2003	2014
Portlnd	Portland Beavers	AAA	Pacific Coast League	San Diego Padres	2001	2010
Ptomc	Potomac Nationals	A+	Carolina League	Washington Nationals	2005	2014
Pwtckt	Pawtucket Red Sox	AAA	International League	Boston Red Sox	1977	2014
QuadC	Quad Cities River Bandits	A	Midwest League	Houston Astros	2013	2014
QuadC	Quad Cities River Bandits	A	Midwest League	St Louis Cardinals	2008	2012
Rays	GCL Rays	R	Gulf Coast League	Tampa Bay Rays	2009	2014
Rchmd	Richmond Flying Squirrels	AA	Eastern League	San Francisco Giants	2010	2014
RCuca	Rancho Cucamonga Quakes	A+	California League	Los Angeles Dodgers	2001	2014
Rdng	Reading Phillies	AA	Eastern League	Philadelphia Phillies	1967	2014
RdRck	Round Rock Express	AAA	Pacific Coast League	Texas Rangers	2011	2014
Reds	AZL Reds	R	Arizona League	Cincinnati Reds	2010	2014
RedSx	GCL Red Sox	R	Gulf Coast League	Boston Red Sox	1989	2014
Reno	Reno Aces	AAA	Pacific Coast League	Arizona Diamondbacks	2009	2014
RioGrnd	Rio Grande Valley White Wings	IND	Independent League	Independent	2014	2014
Rngrs	AZL Rangers	R	Arizona League	Texas Rangers	2003	2014
Roch	Rochester Red Wings	AAA	International League	Minnesota Twins	2003	2014
Rome	Rome Braves	A	South Atlantic League	Atlanta Braves	2003	2014
Royals	AZL Royals	R	Arizona League	Kansas City Royals	2004	2014
S-WB	Scranton/Wilkes-Barre	AAA	International League	New York Yankees	2007	2014
Salem	Salem Red Sox	A+	Carolina League	Boston Red Sox	2009	2014

Minor League Abbreviation Key

Abbreviation	Team	Level	League	MLB Affiliate	First Year	Last Year
Salt Lk	Salt Lake Bees	AAA	Pacific Coast League	Los Angeles Angels	2006	2014
Savann	Savannah Sand Gnats	A	South Atlantic League	New York Mets	2007	2014
Sbend	South Bend Silver Hawks	A	Midwest League	Arizona Diamondbacks	1997	2014
Scrmto	Sacramento River Cats	AAA	Pacific Coast League	Oakland Athletics	2000	2014
SlmKzr	Salem-Keizer Volcanoes	A-	Northwest League	San Francisco Giants	1997	2014
SnAnt	San Antonio Missions	AA	Texas League	San Diego Padres	2007	2014
SnJos	San Jose Giants	A+	California League	San Francisco Giants	1990	2014
Spkane	Spokane Indians	A-	Northwest League	Texas Rangers	2003	2014
Sprgfld	Springfield Cardinals	AA	Texas League	St Louis Cardinals	2005	2014
Stcktn	Stockton Ports	A+	California League	Oakland Athletics	2005	2014
StCol	State College Spikes	A-	New York-Penn League	Pittsburgh Pirates	2007	2012
StLuci	St. Lucie Mets	A+	Florida State League	New York Mets	1990	2014
Syrcse	Syracuse Chiefs	AAA	International League	Washington Nationals	2009	2014
Tacom	Tacoma Rainiers	AAA	Pacific Coast League	Seattle Mariners	1995	2014
Tampa	Tampa Yankees	A+	Florida State League	New York Yankees	1994	2014
Tenn	Tennessee Smokies	AA	Southern League	Chicago Cubs	2007	2014
Tigers	GCL Tigers	R	Gulf Coast League	Detroit Tigers	1995	2014
Tohoku	Tohoku Rakuten Golden Eagles	Jap	Pacific League	Japan	2005	2014
Toledo	Toledo Mud Hens	AAA	International League	Detroit Tigers	1987	2014
TriCity	Tri-City Dust Devils	A-	Northwest League	Colorado Rockies	2001	2014
TriCity	Tri-City ValleyCats	A-	New York-Penn League	Houston Astros	2002	2014
Trntn	Trenton Thunder	AA	Eastern League	New York Yankees	2003	2014
Tucsn	Tucson Padres	AAA	Pacific Coast League	San Diego Padres	2011	2013
Tulsa	Tulsa Drillers	AA	Texas League	Colorado Rockies	2003	2014
Twins	GCL Twins	R	Gulf Coast League	Minnesota Twins	1989	2014
Vancvr	Vancouver Canadians	A-	Northwest League	Oakland Athletics	1999	2010
Vancvr	Vancouver Canadians	A-	Northwest League	Toronto Blue Jays	2011	2014
Visalia	Visalia Rawhide	A+	California League	Arizona Diamondbacks	2007	2014
Vrmnt	Vermont Lake Monsters	A-	New York-Penn League	Washington Nationals	2006	2010
Wichita	Wichita Wingnuts	IND	Independent League	Independent	2014	2014
Wilmg	Wilmington Blue Rocks	A+	Carolina League	Kansas City Royals	2007	2014
WinSa	Winston-Salem Dash	A+	Carolina League	Chicago White Sox	2009	2014
Wisc	Wisconsin Timber Rattlers	A	Midwest League	Milwaukee Brewers	2009	2014
WMich	West Michigan Whitecaps	A	Midwest League	Detroit Tigers	1997	2014
Wmspt	Williamsport Crosscutters	A-	New York-Penn League	Philadelphia Phillies	2007	2014
Wrcstr	Worcester Tornadoes	IND	Can-Am League	Independent	2000	2012
WTenn	West Tenn Diamond Jaxx	AA	Southern League	Seattle Mariners	2007	2010
WV	West Virginia Power	A	South Atlantic League	Pittsburgh Pirates	2009	2014
Yakima	Yakima Bears	A-	Northwest League	Arizona Diamondbacks	2001	2012
Yanks1	GCL Yankees 1	R	Gulf Coast League	New York Yankees	1984	2014
Yanks2	GCL Yankees 2	R	Gulf Coast League	New York Yankees	2014	2014

Baseball Info Solutions

Baseball Info Solutions (BIS) opened its doors back in 2002 and has been on the leading edge of the advanced statistical study of baseball ever since. The company's mission is to provide the most accurate, in-depth, timely professional baseball data, including cutting-edge research and analysis, striving to educate major league teams and the public about baseball analytics.

BIS employs a staff of expert baseball analysts and an army of highly trained video scouts who conduct several passes of each game, recording everything from basic box score data to times and locations of balls in play, pitch types and locations, defensive shifts, and much more.

The company's analysts and programmers dissect the data, producing a variety of predictive studies and analytics, including, for example, Defensive Runs Saved. Defensive Runs Saved estimates the number of runs a defender saves or costs his teams because of his ability to convert balls in play into outs, defend bunts, turn double plays, prevent baserunner advancements, and several other factors. A couple of the more recent advancements are Strike Zone Plus/Minus—which measures the number of extra strikes drawn from umpires due to the specific skills and characteristics of catchers, pitchers, batters, and the umpires themselves—and Stolen Base Red Light/Green Light—which predicts baserunner success rates on stolen bases against various pitcher-catcher combinations, even if they have never faced each other.

Baseball Info Solutions was co-founded by John Dewan, who has been a leader in baseball analytics for more than 25 years. From his first partnership with Bill James as the Executive Director of Project Scoresheet to co-founding STATS, Inc. and his 15-year tenure there as CEO, John has continually broken new ground in sports data and analytics. Through products and publications such as *The Bill James Handbook* and *The Fielding Bible*, John, Bill, and BIS have continued that tradition to this day.

For data inquiries, potential job openings, or additional information, please contact BIS at:

Baseball Info Solutions
41 S. 2nd Street
Coplay, PA 18037
610-261-2370
info@baseballinfosolutions.com
www.baseballinfosolutions.com

Acknowledgments

The production of the Bill James Handbook is a marathon compacted into a sprint. In order to get the Handbook onto shelves by November 1, we only have a couple of weeks from when the regular season ends and the ink dries on player statistics to when we have to submit the completed volume to the publisher. That takes a lot of work, and we want to properly thank everyone who made it possible.

As always, that list has to start with Bill James himself. The foundation of the content of the Handbook was built in his original Baseball Abstract back in 1977, and Bill continues to play a huge role in its production. That role includes everything from designing new sections like Shifts and the World's No. 1 Starting Pitcher to writing many of the section introductions and even projecting statistics for hitters and pitchers both famous and anonymous to the casual baseball fan.

John Dewan and his wife Sue Dewan are the majority owners of Baseball Info Solutions. John and Sue have innumerable demands on their time, including the Franciscan Works mission in Ebola-ravaged Liberia. (If you are so inclined, they would greatly appreciate a donation through FranciscanWorks.org.) That did not prevent them from working through their nights and weekends to ensure that Baseball Info Solutions and the Handbook stayed on track.

Ben Jedlovec is now President of BIS, which really means that he tries his best to stay out of everyone else's way during the Handbook, helping where possible.

Vice President of Information Technology Jeff Spoljaric made it through his seventh and final Handbook with BIS. He has taken a leading role on the Handbook and with the company, especially in recent years, and he will be missed.

Patrick Coyle was the office MVP of the Handbook process. As well as handling the production responsibilities of the Handbook for the second consecutive year, Pat has also been serving as the interim Director of the IT department. In addition, Greg Thomas and Ben Stanczak have been serving double duty, balancing their Handbook tasks with their other IT responsibilities.

Jon Vrecsics, Jim Swavely, Dan Casey, Mike Piekarski, Todd Radcliffe, and Andy Johnson are the veterans of our Operations department, which has dramatically expanded over the last year and now includes Eric Nehs, Kevin Morrissey, and

Tim Kwilos. They have all been fantastic in coordinating our expanded data collection in 2014, and they are also the parties most responsible for the unbelievable accuracy of the statistics in the Handbook. They double and triple-check every number on every page. If you find any data that conflicts with another published source, rest assured that they put in the time so that we are confident that our numbers are the correct ones.

Joe Rosales and Scott Spratt have done their best to pick up the slack in the Research and Development Department with Ben's shift in responsibilities. Together with interns Dan Lependorf, Doug Wachter and Dan Foehrenbach, they have been hard at work turning the collected data into analytics.

Jim Capuano, Director of Business Development, leads the effort to bring the innovative research and analysis to both our clients and the public.

Carol Olsen has been a godsend in taking many of the day-to-day responsibilities of running a business off everyone's plates.

With the expansion in our data collection, our small army of video scouts is not so small anymore. They definitely did not disappoint. They included Caleb Abney, Rich Battoglia, Jason Bell, Conner Brackhahn, Joe Brehm, Anthony Calao, Sam Cassell, Nick Cerami, Nick Cichielo, Mike Cordisco, Will Creager, Matthew Doppelt, Dan Edwards, Jayme Edwards, Rebecca Fishbein, Dan Foehrenbach, Steve Garrity, Colin Gotzon, Josh Hofer, Geehoon Hong, Andy Houk, Dylan Jedlovec, Alex Kapacinskas, Jeremy Kaufman, Thomas Kawamura, Ryan Klimek, John Kokales, Keanan Lamb, Nick Lampe, Robbie Lannon, Rod Larson, Stefan Lechmanik, Jimmy Lee, Josh Lipman, Steve Markson, Nick Masse, Mick Mattaliano, James McDonough, Justin McShea, James Mehall, Vincent Messana, Noah Michel, Spencer Moody, Chris Mosch, James Nero, Pranjal Neupane, Tom Pachecho, Jason Paff, Michael Pangrazi, Nathan Phares, Matt Poloni, Ryan Powers, Jon Presser, Alex Reiner, Corey Robinson, Matthew Rosa, Josh Ruffin, Ryan Salsbury, Nick Siefken, Tucker Stobbe, Kelly Sutphin, Randall Taylor, Ryan Thomas, Ryan Trauger, Josh Tuchman, Zeke Turrentine, Dan Weigel, Ezra Wise, and Ashley Wu.

Our partners at ACTA Publications include President and Co-Publisher Greg Pierce, as well as Tom Wright, Emily Heath, Mary Eggert, Abby Pierce, Isz, Patricia Lynch, and Hugh Spector.

Thank you to our friends in the baseball industry who have helped us over the years. They include Greg Ambrosius, Andy Andres, David Appelman, Jim Callis, Dave Cameron, Sean Forman, Matthew Futterman, Peter Gammons, Vince Genarro, Jason Grey, Eric Karabell, Brian Kenny, Peter Kreutzer, Michael Lehrer, Ed Macedo, Gene McCaffrey, Bob Meyerhoff, Mike Murphy, Rob Neyer, Alex Patton, Mike Phillips, David Pinto, Joe Posnanski, Adam Richman, Hal Richman, Peter Schoenke, Ron Shandler, Joe Sheehan, John Sickels, Mark Simon, Dave Studenmund, Tom Tango, Mark Watson, Rick Wilton, and Don Zminda.

Thank you to reader Curt Young, who suggested a breakdown of batting stats by position. Thank you to Steve Ruskowski for your assistance in stat-checking.

There is not enough space to directly thank everyone who made this book possible, but we really appreciate the work of everyone who played a part but we could not specifically mention. And most of all, thanks to our readers who made it this far. We're so glad that you share our love for baseball and desire to understand it in the finest detail.

Notes

Notes

Notes

Notes

Notes

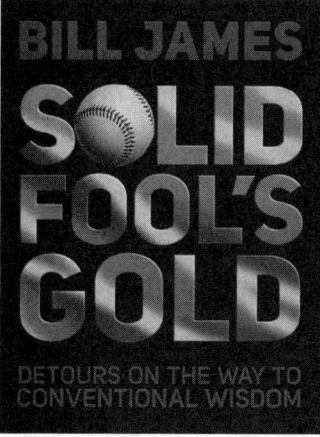